PHILIP'S

C000302373

STREET ̶ ̶S

London

First published 2000 by

Philip's, a division of
Octopus Publishing Group Ltd
2–4 Heron Quays, London E14 4JP

Second edition 2003
Second impression with revisions 2005

ISBN-10 0-540-08461-1 hardback
ISBN-10 0-540-08462-X spiral
ISBN-10 0-540-08463-8 paperback

ISBN-13 978-0-540-08461-6 hardback
ISBN-13 978-0-540-08462-3 spiral
ISBN-13 978-0-540-08463-0 paperback

© Philip's 2005

Ordnance Survey®

This product includes mapping data licensed
from Ordnance Survey® with the permission of
the Controller of Her Majesty's Stationery Office.
© Crown copyright 2005. All rights reserved.
Licence number 100011710

This product contains driver restriction
information derived from Teleatlas
© TeleatlasDRI

Printed and bound in Spain
by Cayfosa-Quebecor.

Contents

II	**Key to map pages**	
IV	Administrative and Postcode boundaries	
VI	**Route planning**	
X	**Key to map symbols**	
1	**Street maps**	
228	**Keys to enlarged map pages and symbols**	
229	**Enlarged street maps**	
271	**Index**	
380	**List of numbered locations**	
391	Hospitals	
392	Shopping, theatres, cinemas	
394	Central London buses	
396	Local rail and London Underground	
398	Places of interest	

Digital Data

The exceptionally high-quality mapping found in this atlas is available as digital data in TIFF format, which is easily convertible to other bitmapped (raster) image formats.

The index is also available in digital form as a standard database table. It contains all the details found in the printed index together with the National Grid reference for the map square in which each entry is named.

For further information and to discuss your requirements, please contact Philip's on
020 7644 6932 or james.mann@philips-maps.co.uk

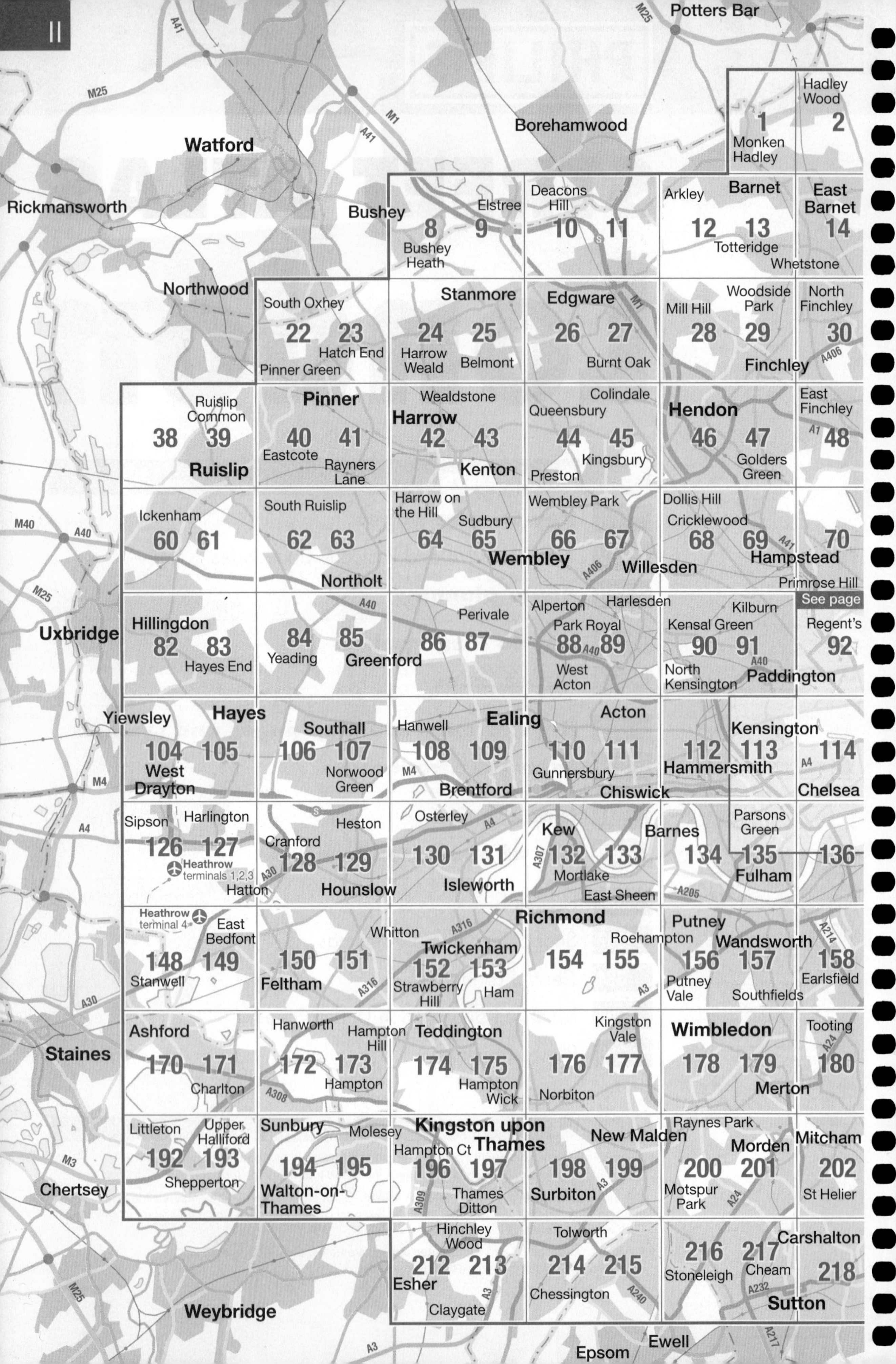
Potters Bar
M25
A41
M25
M1
A41
Borehamwood
Watford
Hadley Wood
1
2
Monken Hadley
Rickmansworth
Bushey
Elstree
Deacons Hill
Arkley
Barnet
East Barnet
8
9
10
11
12
13
14
Bushey Heath
Totteridge
Whetstone
Northwood
South Oxhey
Stanmore
Edgware
Mill Hill
Woodside Park
North Finchley
22
23
24
25
26
27
28
29
30
Hatch End
Pinner Green
Harrow Weald
Belmont
Burnt Oak
Finchley
A406
Ruislip Common
Pinner
Wealdstone
Harrow
Colindale
Queensbury
Hendon
East Finchley
38
39
40
41
42
43
44
45
46
47
A1
48
Eastcote
Rayners Lane
Ruislip
Kenton
Kingsbury
Preston
Golders Green
M40
A40
Ickenham
South Ruislip
Harrow on the Hill
Sudbury
Wembley Park
Dollis Hill
Cricklewood
60
61
62
63
64
65
66
67
68
69
A41
70
Wembley
Willesden
Hampstead
Primrose Hill
Northolt
A406
M25
Uxbridge
A40
Perivale
Alperton
Harlesden
Kilburn
See page
Hillingdon
Park Royal
Kensal Green
Regent's
82
83
84
85
86
87
88
A40
89
90
91
92
Hayes End
Yeading
Greenford
West Acton
North Kensington
A40
Paddington
Yiewsley
Hayes
Southall
Hanwell
Ealing
Acton
Kensington
104
105
106
107
108
109
110
111
112
113
114
West Drayton
Norwood Green
M4
Brentford
Gunnersbury
Chiswick
Hammersmith
A4
Chelsea
M4
A4
Sipson
Harlington
Heston
Osterley
A4
Kew
Barnes
Parsons Green
Cranford
126
127
128
129
130
131
A307
132
133
134
135
136
Heathrow terminals 1,2,3
A30
Hatton
Hounslow
Isleworth
Mortlake
East Sheen
A205
Fulham
Heathrow terminal 4
East Bedfont
Whitton
A316
Richmond
Putney
Roehampton
Wandsworth
A214
Twickenham
148
149
150
151
152
153
154
155
156
157
158
Stanwell
Feltham
A316
Strawberry Hill
Ham
A3
Putney Vale
Southfields
Earlsfield
A30
Ashford
Hanworth
Hampton Hill
Teddington
Kingston Vale
Wimbledon
Tooting
A24
Staines
170
171
172
173
174
175
176
177
178
179
180
Charlton
A308
Hampton
Hampton Wick
Norbiton
Merton
Littleton
Upper Halliford
Sunbury
Molesey
Kingston upon Thames
Hampton Ct
New Malden
Raynes Park
Morden
Mitcham
192
193
194
195
196
197
198
199
200
201
202
M3
Shepperton
Chertsey
Walton-on-Thames
A309
Thames Ditton
Surbiton
A3
Motspur Park
A24
St Helier
Hinchley Wood
Tolworth
Carshalton
212
213
214
215
216
217
218
Esher
Stoneleigh
Cheam
A3
Chessington
A240
A232
Claygate
Sutton
M25
Weybridge
A217
Ewell
Epsom
A3

Key to map pages

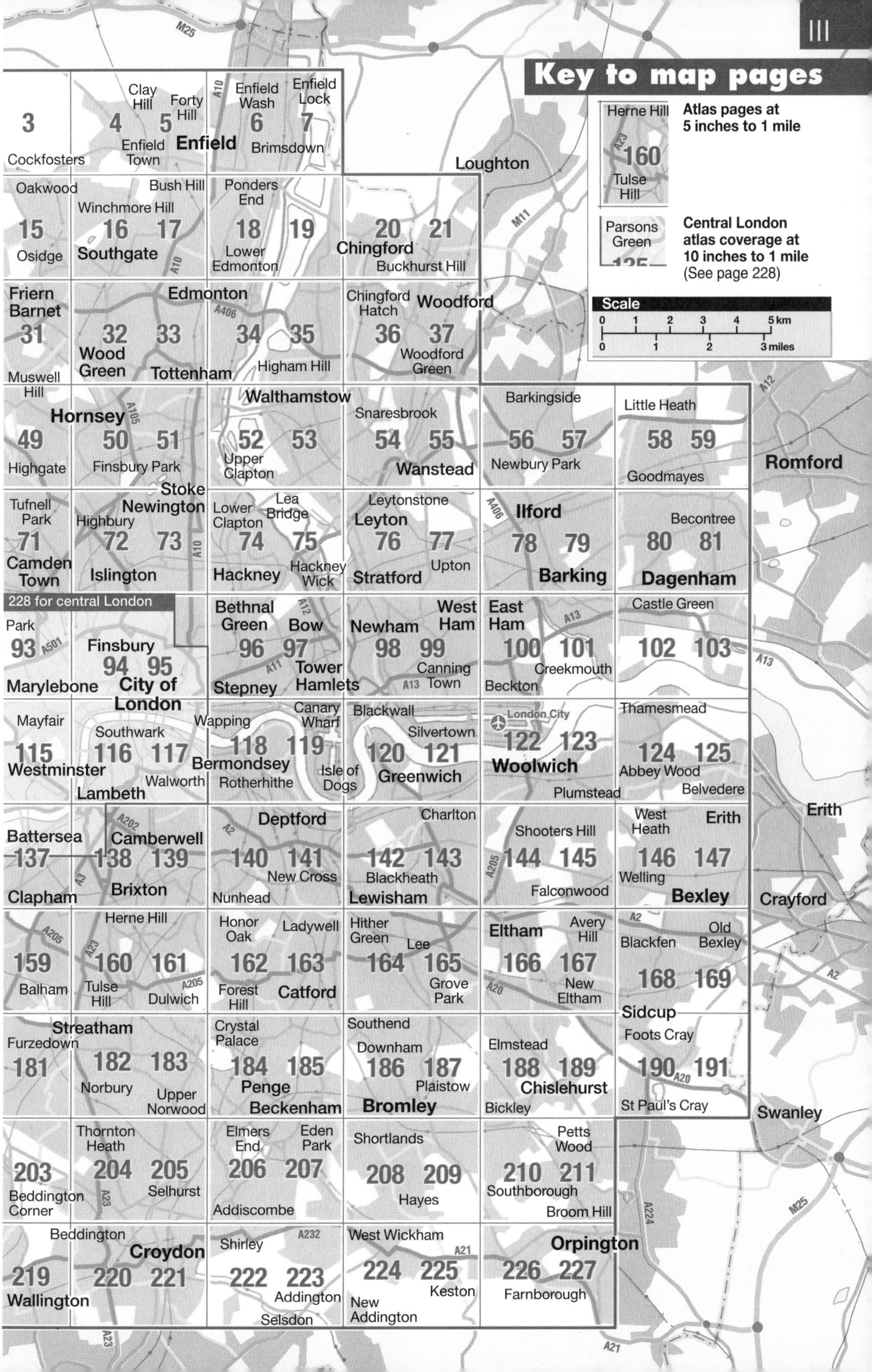
Herne Hill
A23
160
Tulse Hill
Atlas pages at 5 inches to 1 mile
Parsons Green
125
Central London atlas coverage at 10 inches to 1 mile (See page 228)
Scale
0 1 2 3 4 5 km
0 1 2 3 miles
M25
Loughton
M11
Romford
A12
A13
Erith
Crayford
Swanley
A2
M25
A224
A21
3 Cockfosters
Clay Hill
Forty Hill
4 5
Enfield Town
Enfield
A10
Enfield Wash
Enfield Lock
6 7
Brimsdown
Oakwood
15 Osidge
Bush Hill
Winchmore Hill
16 17
Southgate
Ponders End
18 19
Lower Edmonton
20 21
Chingford
Buckhurst Hill
Friern Barnet
31
Muswell Hill
Edmonton
A406
32 33
Wood Green
Tottenham
34 35
Higham Hill
Chingford Hatch
Woodford
36 37
Woodford Green
Hornsey
A105
49 Highgate
50 51
Finsbury Park
Walthamstow
52 53
Upper Clapton
Snaresbrook
54 55
Wanstead
Barkingside
56 57
Newbury Park
Little Heath
58 59
Goodmayes
Tufnell Park
71
Camden Town
Stoke Newington
Highbury
72 73
Islington
Lower Clapton
Lea Bridge
74 75
Hackney
Hackney Wick
Leytonstone
Leyton
76 77
Stratford
Upton
Ilford
78 79
Barking
Becontree
80 81
Dagenham
228 for central London
Park
93 A501
Marylebone
Finsbury
94 95
City of London
Bethnal Green
Bow
96 97
A11
Stepney
Tower Hamlets
Newham
West Ham
98 99
Canning Town
A13
East Ham
100 101
Creekmouth
Beckton
Castle Green
102 103
Mayfair
115
Westminster
Southwark
116 117
Lambeth
Walworth
Wapping
118 119
Bermondsey
Rotherhithe
Canary Wharf
Isle of Dogs
Blackwall
Silvertown
120 121
Greenwich
London City
122 123
Woolwich
Plumstead
Thamesmead
124 125
Abbey Wood
Belvedere
Battersea
137
Clapham
A202
Camberwell
138 139
Brixton
A3
Deptford
A2
140 141
New Cross
Nunhead
Charlton
142 143
Blackheath
Lewisham
Shooters Hill
A205
144 145
Falconwood
West Heath
Erith
146 147
Welling
Bexley
159
Balham
A205
Herne Hill
160 161
Tulse Hill
Dulwich
Honor Oak
Ladywell
162 163
Forest Hill
Catford
Hither Green
Lee
164 165
Grove Park
Eltham
Avery Hill
166 167
A20
New Eltham
Blackfen
Old Bexley
168 169
Sidcup
Streatham
Furzedown
181
182 183
Norbury
Upper Norwood
Crystal Palace
184 185
Penge
Beckenham
Southend
Downham
186 187
Plaistow
Bromley
Elmstead
188 189
Chislehurst
Bickley
Foots Cray
190 191
St Paul's Cray
203
Beddington Corner
Thornton Heath
204 205
Selhurst
Elmers End
Eden Park
206 207
Addiscombe
Shortlands
208 209
Hayes
Petts Wood
210 211
Southborough
Broom Hill
Beddington
219
Wallington
Croydon
220 221
A23
Shirley
A232
222 223
Addington
Selsdon
West Wickham
A21
224 225
Keston
New Addington
Orpington
226 227
Farnborough

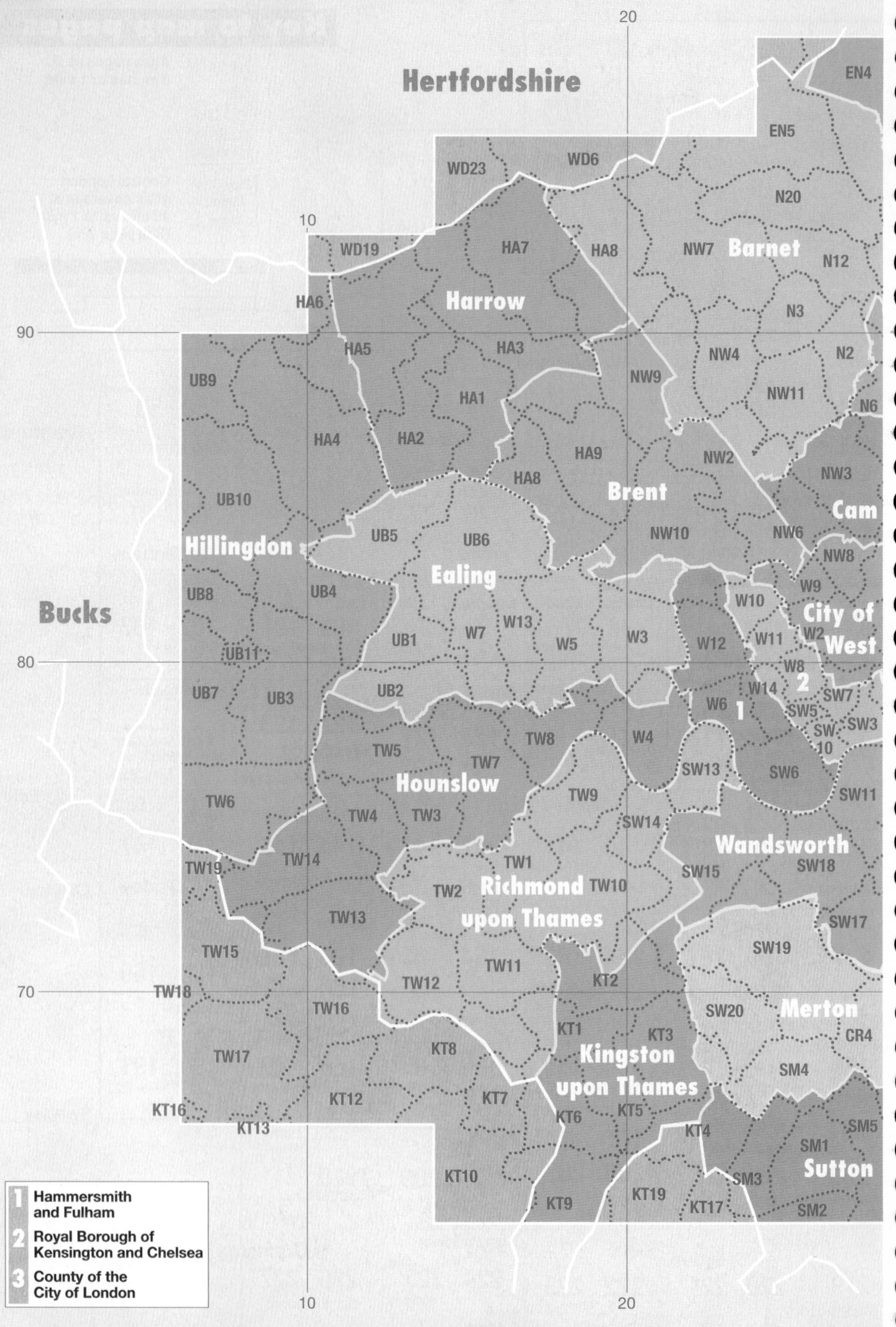
Hertfordshire
Bucks
Harrow
Barnet
Hillingdon
Brent
Ealing
Cam
City of West
Hounslow
Richmond upon Thames
Wandsworth
Merton
Kingston upon Thames
Sutton
EN4
EN5
WD6
WD23
N20
WD19
HA7
HA8
NW7
N12
HA6
N3
HA5
HA3
NW4
N2
UB9
HA1
NW9
NW11
N6
HA4
HA2
HA9
NW2
NW3
UB10
HA8
UB5
UB6
NW10
NW6
NW8
UB8
UB4
W10
W9
W13
W7
UB1
W5
W3
W12
W11
W2
UB11
W8
UB7
UB3
UB2
W14
2
W6
1
SW7
SW5
SW3
SW10
TW5
TW8
W4
TW7
SW13
SW6
TW6
TW9
SW11
TW4
TW3
SW14
TW19
TW14
TW1
SW18
SW15
TW2
TW10
TW13
SW17
TW15
SW19
TW11
TW12
KT2
TW18
TW16
SW20
KT1
KT3
CR4
TW17
KT8
SM4
KT12
KT7
KT16
KT6
KT5
KT13
KT4
SM5
SM1
KT10
SM3
KT9
KT19
KT17
SM2
10
20
90
80
70
1 Hammersmith and Fulham
2 Royal Borough of Kensington and Chelsea
3 County of the City of London

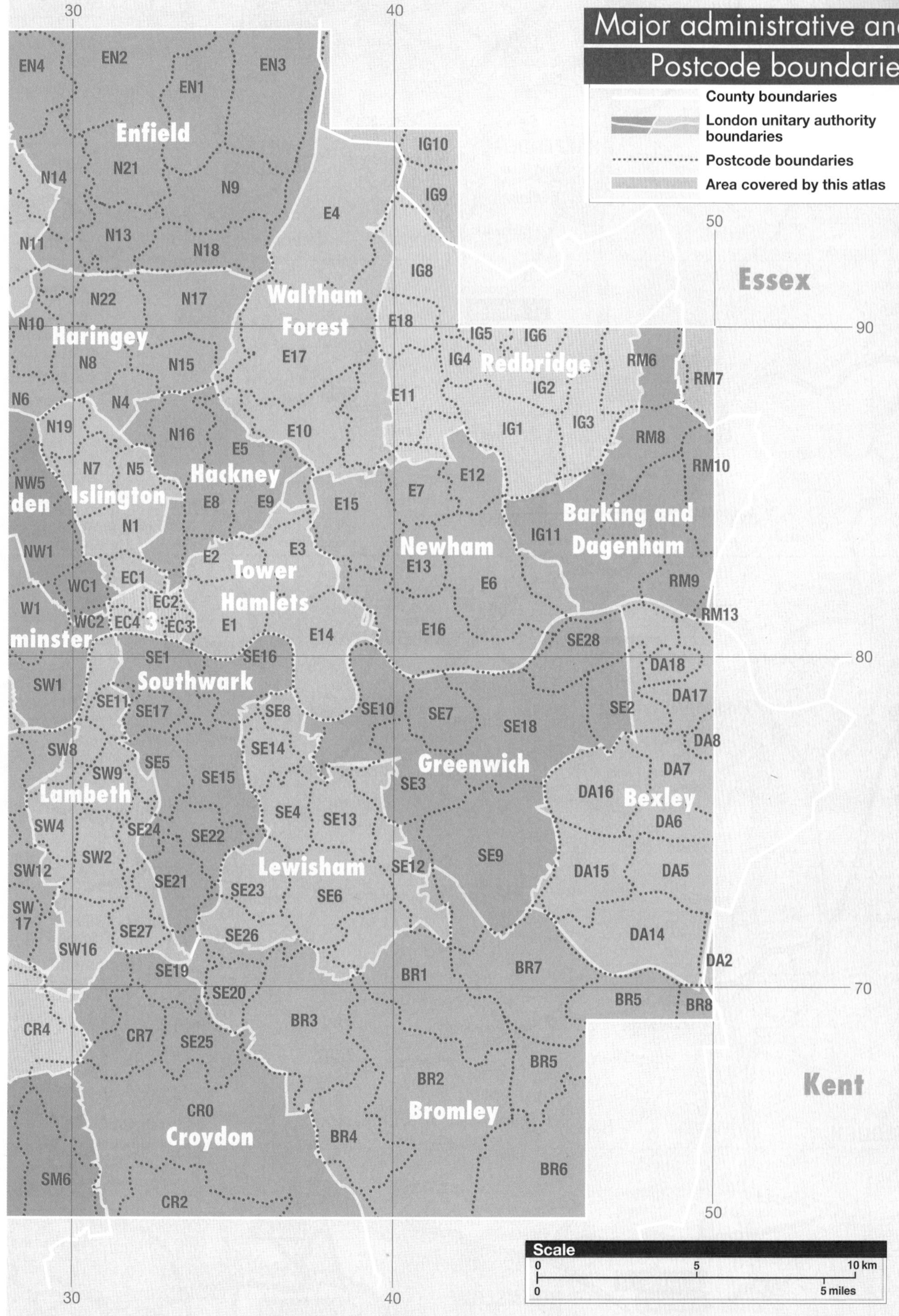

Major administrative and Postcode boundaries

County boundaries
London unitary authority boundaries
.... Postcode boundaries
Area covered by this atlas

Scale

0   5   10 km

0   5 miles

EN4, EN2, EN1, EN3, Enfield, N14, N21, N9, N11, N13, N18, IG10, IG9, E4, N10, N22, N17, Waltham Forest, E18, IG8, Haringey, N8, N15, E17, IG5, IG6, Redbridge, RM6, RM7, N6, N4, N19, N16, E10, E11, IG4, IG2, IG1, IG3, RM8, RM10, NW5, N7, N5, Hackney, E5, E12, E7, Barking and Dagenham, RM13, den, N1, E8, E9, E15, IG11, RM9, NW1, E2, E3, Tower Hamlets, Newham, E13, E6, WC1, EC1, Islington, W1, WC2, EC2, EC4 3, EC3, E1, E14, E16, SE28, RM13, minster, SE1, SE16, DA18, SW1, SE11, Southwark, SE8, SE10, SE7, SE2, DA17, SW8, SE17, SE14, SE18, DA8, SW9, SE5, SE15, SE3, Greenwich, DA16, Bexley, DA7, Lambeth, SW4, SE24, SE22, SE4, SE13, DA6, SW2, SE21, Lewisham, SE12, SE9, DA15, DA5, SW12, SE23, SE6, DA14, SW17, SE27, SW16, SE19, SE26, BR1, BR7, DA2, SE20, BR5, BR8, CR4, CR7, SE25, BR3, BR5, CR0, Croydon, BR4, BR2, Bromley, BR6, SM6, CR2, Essex, Kent

Luton
Kensworth
Caddington
Slip End
Kensworth Common
Studham
Markyate
Jockey End
Flamstead
Trowley Bottom
Little Gaddesden
Great Gaddesden
Water End
Nettleden
Potten End
Piccotts End
Gadebridge
Bourne End
Boxmoor
Hemel Hempstead
Whelpley Hill
Felden
Bovingdon
Bovingdon Green
Leyhill
Primrosehill
Kings Langley
Chipperfield
Flaunden
Latimer
Sarratt
Chenies
Little Chalfont
Chorleywood
Croxley Green
RICKMANSWORTH
Maple Cross
Batchworth Heath
Chalfont Common
Northwood
Harefield
Denham Green
Tatling End
Denham
Fulmer
Iver Heath
Uxbridge
Ickenham
Ruislip
Ruislip Common
Eastcote
Rayners Lane
Pinner
Hatch End
Hillingdon
Cowley
Yiewsley
West Drayton
Yeading
Hayes
Southall
Greenford
George Green
Iver
SLOUGH
Richings Park
Langley
Upton
Harmondsworth
Sipson
Harlington
Cranford
Heston
Datchet
Colnbrook
Longford
Poyle
Horton
HEATHROW AIRPORT
Stanwell
Stanwell Moor
Wraysbury
West Bedfont
East Bedfont
Hythe End
HOUNSLOW
Isleworth
Brentford
Feltham
Twickenham
Peter's Green
Kimpton
Codicote
Blackmore End
Ayot St Lawrence
East Hyde
Kinsbourne Green
Batford
HARPENDEN
Marshall's Heath
Wheathampstead
Hatching Green
Redbourn
Childwick Green
Sandridge
Jersey Farm
Townsend
Marshalswick
St Albans
Fleetville
St Stephens
The Camp
Sopwell
Colney Heath
Chiswell Green
Bedmond
London Colney
Bricket Wood
Colney Street
Abbots Langley
Radlett
Shenleybury
Shenley
Aldenham
Letchmore Heath
Green Street
Watford
BOREHAMWOOD
Elstree
Oxhey
Bushey
Bushey Heath
South Oxhey
Eastbury
Stanmore
Edgware
Harrow Weald
Wealdstone
HARROW
Greenhill
Harrow on the Hill
Kingsbury
Wembley
Sudbury
Northolt
Alperton
Perivale
EALING
Hanwell
Acton
Chiswick
Kew
Kew Br.
Hammersmith
Mortlake
Richmond
Roehampton
Putney
Fulham
Chelsea
Westminster
Paddington
Kensington
Wandsworth
Battersea
Clapham
Balham
Old Knebworth
Knebworth
Datchworth
Datchworth Green
Woolmer Green
Oaklands
Bull's Green
Burnham Green
Welwyn
Harmer Green
Tewin
Ayot St Peter
Digswell Park
WELWYN GARDEN CITY
Panshanger
Woodhall
Hall Grove
Hatfield Hyde
Cole Green
Letty Green
Stanborough
Hatfield Garden Village
The Ryde
Essendon
Hatfield
South Hatfield
Wildhill
Little Berkhamsted
Woodside
Epping Green
Welham Green
Bell Bar
Newgate Street
Water End
Brookmans Park
Northaw
South Mimms
SOUTH MIMMS SERVICES
POTTERS BAR
BARNET
Monken Hadley
Arkley
Totteridge
LONDON GATEWAY SERVICES
East Barnet
Friern Barnet
Mill Hill
Finchley
Hendon
Golders Green
Highgate
Hampstead
Cricklewood
Willesden
Harlesden
Kilburn
Camden
HESTON SERVICES
LONDON HEATHROW
NORTHOLT
DENHAM
NORTH CIRCULAR ROAD
Ver
Lea
Colne

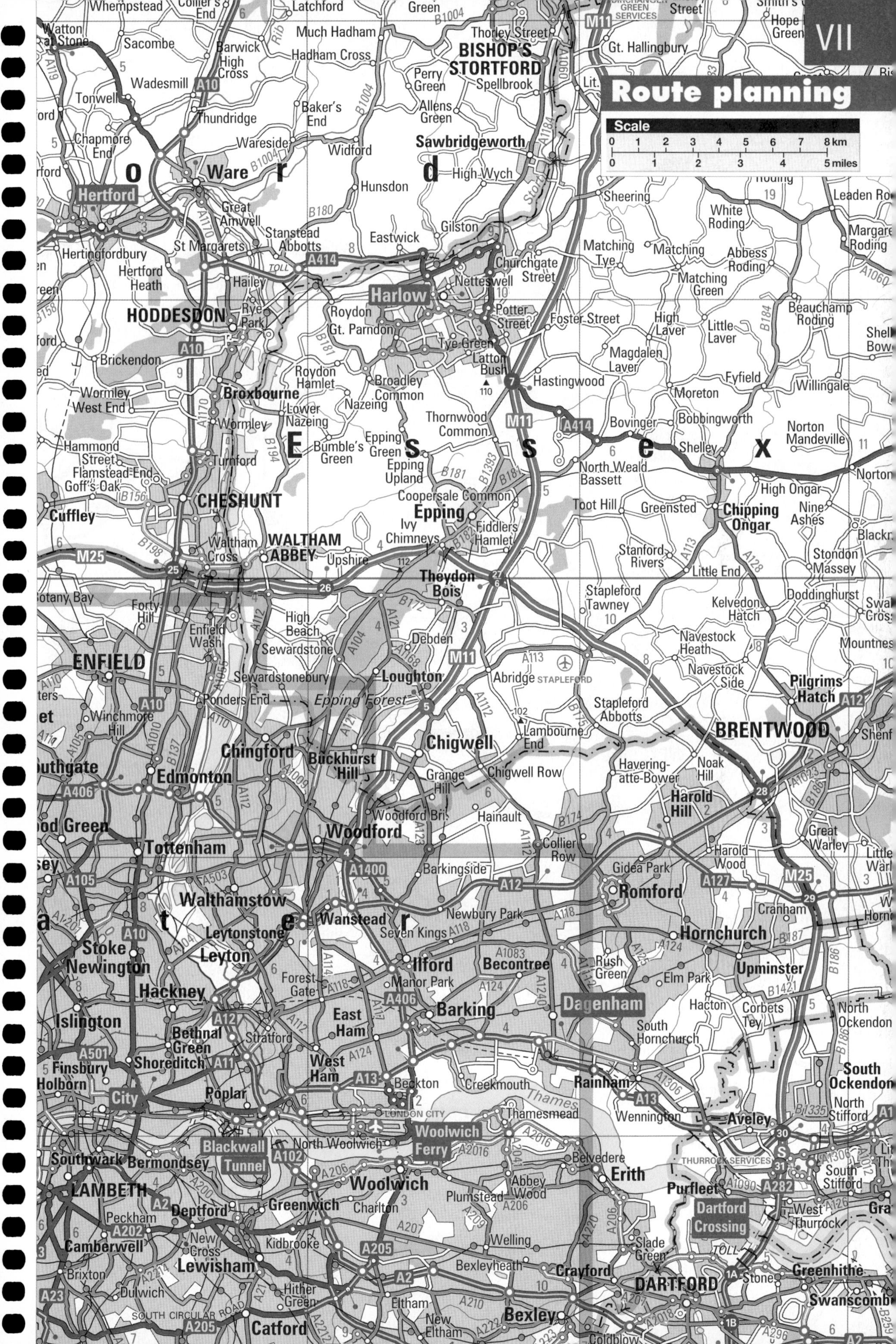

Northwood
Harefield
Hatch End
Harrow Weald
Pinner
Wealdstone
Kingsbury
Hendon
Denham Green
Ruislip Common
HARROW
Greenhill
Eastcote
Rayners Lane
Harrow on the Hill
Golders Green
Highgate
Hornsey
Tatling End
Ruislip
Ickenham
Denham
Wembley
Cricklewood
Hampstead
Willesden
Camden
Uxbridge
Northolt
Sudbury
Alperton
Harlesden
Kilburn
Iver Heath
Perivale
Hillingdon
Cowley
Yeading
Greenford
George Green
Iver
SLOUGH
Yiewsley
Hayes
Southall
EALING
Acton
Paddington
Kensington
West Drayton
Hanwell
Richings Park
Langley
Westminster
Chiswick
Harmondsworth
Harlington
Sipson
Cranford
HESTON SERVICES
Hammersmith
Chelsea
Brentford
Kew
Datchet
Colnbrook
Heston
Kew Br.
Fulham
Battersea
Longford
Poyle
LONDON HEATHROW
Isleworth
Mortlake
Putney
Horton
HEATHROW AIRPORT
HOUNSLOW
Clapham
Richmond
Wraysbury
Stanwell Moor
West Bedfont
Stanwell
East Bedfont
Roehampton
Wandsworth
Balham
Hythe End
Feltham
Twickenham
EGHAM
Staines
Ashford
Hanworth
Teddington
Ham
Kingston Vale
Upper Tooting
Hampton
Wimbledon
Merton
Laleham
Littleton
Raynes Park
Virginia Water
Thorpe
Sunbury-on-Thames
West Molesey
East Molesey
Thames Ditton
Kingston upon Thames
Morden
Mitcham
Shepperton
Surbiton
New Malden
Lyne
CHERTSEY
Walton-on-Thames
Long Ditton
Tolworth
Worcester Park
St Helier
Hackbridge
Addlestone
Esher
Hook
Carshalton
Ottershaw
WEYBRIDGE
Hersham
Chessington
Cheam
Sutton
Wallington
New Haw
Claygate
Ewell
FAIROAKS
Woodham
Byfleet
Whiteley Village
Belmont
Oxshott
EPSOM
Cobham
West Byfleet
Woodmansterne
Stoke D'Abernon
Wisley
Wood Field
BANSTEAD
Cheapside
WOKING
Pyrford
Downside
Great Burgh
Chipstead
Leatherhead Common
Ashtead
Burgh Heath
Old Woking
Ripley
Martyr's Green
Mayford
Send Marsh
Send
Ockham
Fetcham
Leatherhead
Tadworth
Kingswood
Hooley
Burntcommon
Little Bookham
Headley
Walton on the Hill
Lower Kingswood
Sutton Green
Effingham
East Horsley
Great Bookham
West Horsley
Mickleham
Merstham
Slyfield
Burpham
West Clandon
Westhumble
BOX HILL
Redhill
Nutfield
East Clandon
Ranmore Common
Dorking
Buckland
Merrow
Pixham
Betchworth
Earlswood
Newland's Corner
Brockham
Guildford
Reigate
Gomshall
Abinger Hammer
Westcott
Strood Green
Doversgreen
Ridge Green
Albury
Shere
Shalford
Wotton
North Holmwood
Sidlow
Salfords
Chilworth
Blackheath
Brook
Leigh
Sutton
Abinger Common
Wonersh
Farley Green
Nalderswood
South Holmwood
Bramley
Peaslake
Holmbury St Mary
Coldharbour
Parkgate
Norwood Hill
Meath Green
Shamley Green
Hurt Wood
Beare
Hookwood
Horley
G
r
e
a
L
o
n
S
u
r
r
e
M25
M40
M4
M3
M23
A40
A4
A30
A308
A316
A3
A24
A217
A240
A243
A309
A205
A214
A406
A41
A232
A25

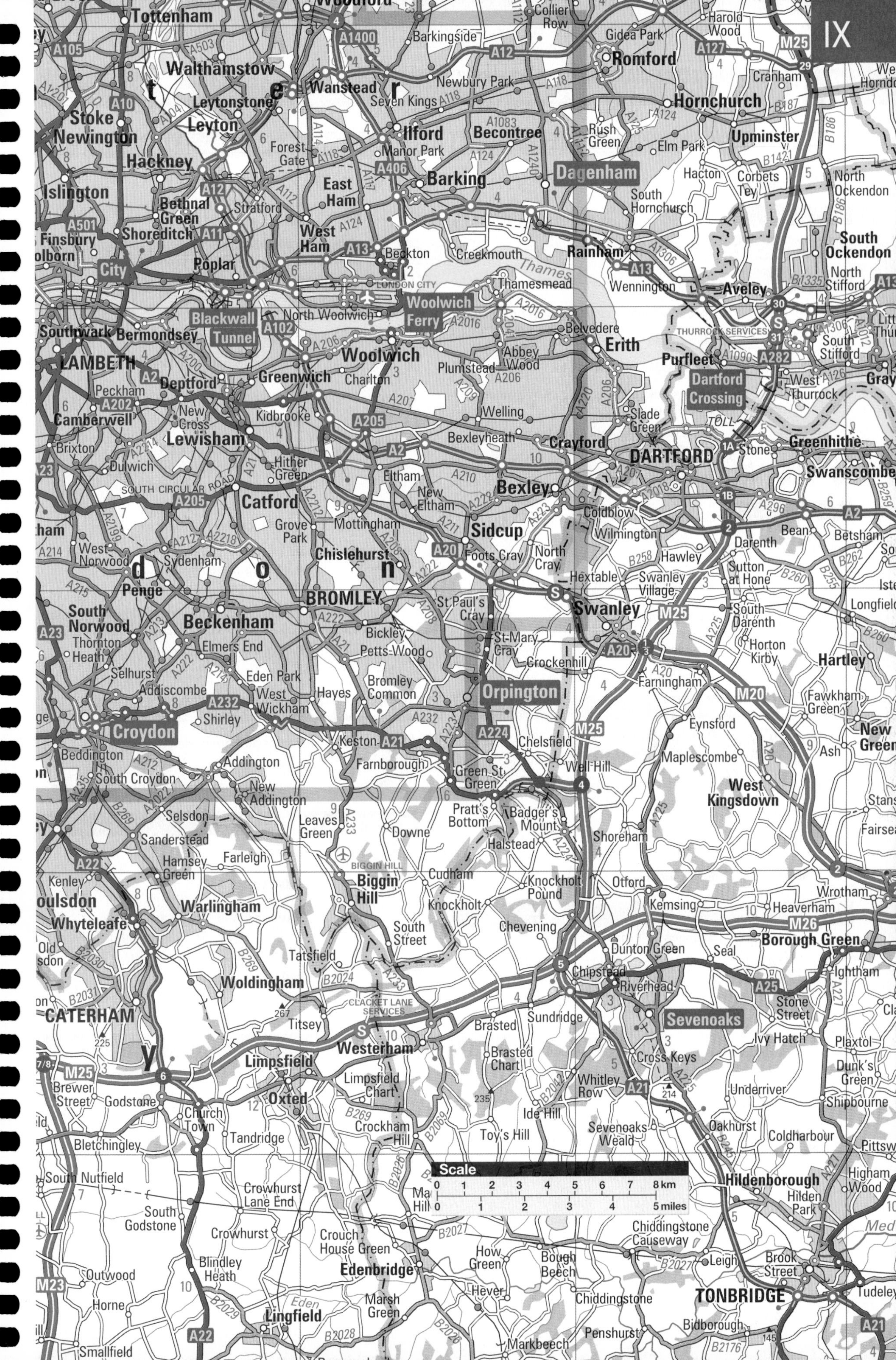
Tottenham
Woodford
Collier Row
Harold Wood
Gidea Park
Romford
Barkingside
Walthamstow
Wanstead
Newbury Park
Seven Kings
Leytonstone
Hornchurch
Cranham
Stoke Newington
Leyton
Ilford
Becontree
Rush Green
Upminster
Elm Park
Forest Gate
Manor Park
Hackney
Dagenham
Hacton
Corbets Tey
North Ockendon
Islington
Barking
East Ham
South Hornchurch
Bethnal Green
Stratford
Shoreditch
West Ham
Finsbury
Holborn
Beckton
Creekmouth
Rainham
South Ockendon
North Stifford
City
Poplar
Thames
Thamesmead
Wennington
Aveley
LONDON CITY
Woolwich Ferry
Blackwall Tunnel
North Woolwich
Southwark
Bermondsey
THURROCK SERVICES
Belvedere
Erith
South Stifford
LAMBETH
Woolwich
Abbey Wood
Purfleet
Dartford Crossing
West Thurrock
Deptford
Greenwich
Charlton
Plumstead
Peckham
Camberwell
New Cross
Kidbrooke
Welling
Slade Green
TOLL
Lewisham
Brixton
Bexleyheath
Crayford
DARTFORD
Stone
Greenhithe
Dulwich
Hither Green
Swanscombe
Eltham
SOUTH CIRCULAR ROAD
Catford
New Eltham
Bexley
Coldblow
West Norwood
Grove Park
Mottingham
Sidcup
Wilmington
Darenth
Bean
Betsham
Sydenham
Chislehurst
Foots Cray
North Cray
Hawley
Sutton at Hone
Penge
Hextable
Swanley Village
BROMLEY
St Paul's Cray
Swanley
South Darenth
Longfield
South Norwood
Beckenham
Bickley
Thornton Heath
Elmers End
St Mary Cray
Horton Kirby
Petts Wood
Crockenhill
Hartley
Selhurst
Eden Park
Farningham
Addiscombe
West Wickham
Hayes
Bromley Common
Orpington
Fawkham Green
Shirley
Eynsford
Croydon
Keston
Chelsfield
New Ash Green
Beddington
Farnborough
Well Hill
Maplescombe
Addington
Green St Green
South Croydon
West Kingsdown
New Addington
Pratt's Bottom
Badger's Mount
Selsdon
Leaves Green
Downe
Halstead
Shoreham
Fairseat
Sanderstead
Hamsey Green
Farleigh
BIGGIN HILL
Kenley
Biggin Hill
Cudham
Knockholt Pound
Otford
Wrotham
Coulsdon
Warlingham
Knockholt
Kemsing
Heaverham
Whyteleafe
South Street
Chevening
Borough Green
Dunton Green
Seal
Tatsfield
Chipstead
Riverhead
Ightham
Woldingham
CLACKET LANE SERVICES
Stone Street
CATERHAM
Titsey
Brasted
Sundridge
Sevenoaks
Westerham
Ivy Hatch
Plaxtol
Brasted Chart
Cross Keys
Limpsfield
Brewer Street
Godstone
Limpsfield Chart
Whitley Row
Underriver
Dunk's Green
Oxted
Shipbourne
Church Town
Ide Hill
Sevenoaks Weald
Tandridge
Crockham Hill
Toy's Hill
Oakhurst
Coldharbour
Bletchingley
Scale
South Nutfield
Crowhurst Lane End
Hildenborough
Higham Wood
Hilden Park
South Godstone
Crowhurst
Crouch House Green
Chiddingstone Causeway
How Green
Bough Beech
Leigh
Brook Street
Outwood
Blindley Heath
Edenbridge
Horne
Hever
Chiddingstone
TONBRIDGE
Tudeley
Eden
Marsh Green
Lingfield
Bidborough
Penshurst
Smallfield
Markbeech
Medway
M25
M26
M20
M23
A21
A22
A2
A20
A13
A12
A127
A406

Key to map symbols

Roads

 Motorway with junction number

Primary route – single, dual carriageway

A road – single, dual carriageway

B road – single, dual carriageway

Through-route – single, dual carriageway

Minor road – single, dual carriageway

Road under construction

Rural track, private road or narrow road in urban area

Path, bridleway, byway open to all traffic, road used as public path

Tunnel, covered road

Congestion Charge Zone boundary
Roads within the zone are outlined in red

Gate or obstruction, car pound

P P&R Parking, park and ride

Crooked Billet Junction name

Pedestrianised or restricted access area

Public transport

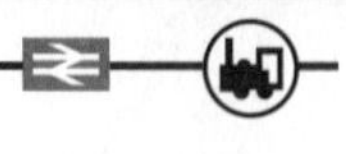

Railway station, private railway station

London Underground station, Docklands Light Railway station

Tramway or miniature railway, Tramlink station

Bus, coach station

Scale

5 inches to 1 mile   1:12672

0   220 yds   440 yds   660 yds   ½ mile

0   250m   500 m   750 m   1km

Emergency services

Ambulance, police, fire station

H + Hospital, accident and emergency entrance

General features

Market, public amenity site

Information centre, post office

VILLA House   Roman, non-Roman antiquity

100   .304   House number, spot height – metres

Christian place of worship

Mosque, synagogue

Other place of worship

Houses, important buildings

Woods, parkland / common

123 Adjoining page number

Leisure facilities

Camp site, caravan site

Golf course, picnic site, view point

Boundaries

NW6 Postcode boundaries

Westminster County and unitary authority boundaries

Water features

Barking Creek   Water name

Tidal water

River or canal – minor, major

Stream

Water

Abbreviations

Acad	Academy	Ent	Enterprise	L Ctr	Leisure Centre	Recn Gd	Recreation Ground
Allot Gdns	Allotments	Ex H	Exhibition Hall	LC	Level Crossing	Resr	Reservoir
Bndstd	Bandstand	Fball	Football	Liby	Library	Ret Pk	Retail Park
Btcl	Botanical	Gdns	Gardens	Mkt	Market	Sch	School
Bwg Gn	Bowling	Glf C	Golf Course	Meml	Memorial	Sh Ctr	Shopping Centre
Cemy	Cemetery	Glf Crs	Golf Course	Mon	Monument	Sp	Sports
Ctr	Centre	Drv Rng	Golf Driving Range	Mus	Museum	Stad	Stadium
C Ctr	Civic Centre	Gn	Green	Nat Res	Nature Reserve	Sw Pool	Swimming Pool
CH	Club House	Gd	Ground	Obsy	Observatory	Tenn Cts	Tennis courts
Ctry Pk	Country Park	Hort	Horticultural	Pav	Pavilion	TH	Town Hall
Coll	College	Ind Est	Industrial Estate	Pk	Park	Trad Est	Trading Estate
Ct	Court	Inst	Institute	Pl Fld	Playing Field	Univ	University
Crem	Crematorium	Int	Interchange	Pal	Royal Palace	YH	Youth Hostel
Crkt	Cricket	Ct	Law Court	PH	Public House		

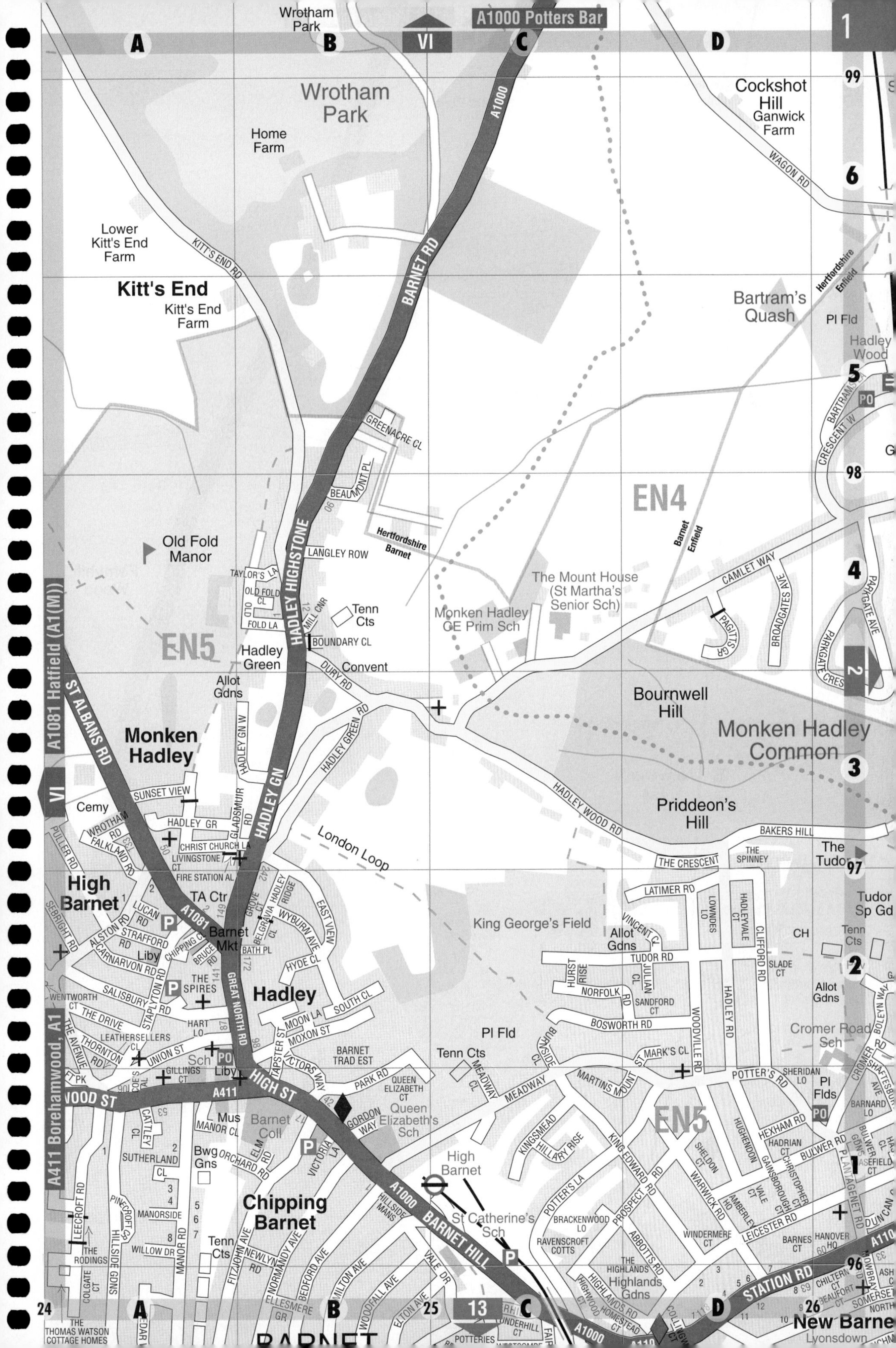

A1000 Potters Bar
Wrotham Park
Home Farm
Cockshot Hill
Ganwick Farm
WAGON RD
Lower Kitt's End Farm
KITT'S END RD
Kitt's End
Kitt's End Farm
BARNET RD
Bartram's Quash
Pl Fld
Hadley Wood
GREENACRE CL
BEAUMONT PL
EN4
Hertfordshire
Barnet
Enfield
Old Fold Manor
HADLEY HIGHSTONE
LANGLEY ROW
TAYLOR'S LA
OLD FOLD CL
FOLD LA
MILL CNR
BOUNDARY CL
Tenn Cts
The Mount House (St Martha's Senior Sch)
Monken Hadley CE Prim Sch
CAMLET WAY
BROADGATES AVE
PAGITTS GR
PARKGATE AVE
EN5
Hadley Green
Convent
DURY RD
A1081 Hatfield (A1(M))
ST ALBANS RD
Allot Gdns
Bournwell Hill
Monken Hadley Common
Monken Hadley
HADLEY GREEN RD
HADLEY GN W
HADLEY GN
Priddeon's Hill
HADLEY WOOD RD
BAKERS HILL
Cemy
SUNSET VIEW
WROTHAM RD
HADLEY GR
GLADSMUIR RD
London Loop
FALKLAND RD
CHRIST CHURCH LA
LIVINGSTONE CT
PULLER RD
THE CRESCENT
THE SPINNEY
The Tudor
High Barnet
FIRE STATION AL
TA Ctr
GROVE CT
HADLEY RIDGE
LATIMER RD
LOWNDES LO
HADLEYVALE CT
CLIFFORD RD
Tudor Sp Gd
SEBRIGHT RD
LUCAN RD
A1081
WYBURN AVE
EAST VIEW
King George's Field
VINCENT CL
Allot Gdns
CH
Tenn Cts
ALSTON RD
STRAFFORD RD
CHIPPING CL
Barnet Mkt
BELGRAVIA CL
HYDE CL
BATH PL
TUDOR RD
SLADE CT
CARNARVON RD
Liby
BRUCE RD
HURST RISE
JULIAN CL
NORFOLK RD
HADLEY RD
WOODVILLE RD
Allot Gdns
BOLEYN WAY
THE SPIRES
Hadley
SOUTH CL
SANDFORD CT
WENTWORTH CT
SALISBURY RD
STAPLYTON RD
GREAT NORTH RD
MOON LA
THE DRIVE
HART LO
MOXON ST
BOSWORTH RD
Cromer Road Sch
LEATHERSELLERS CL
Pl Fld
THORNTON RD
UNION ST
Sch
TAPSTER ST
BARNET TRAD EST
BURNSIDE CL
Tenn Cts
MARK'S CL
THE AVENUE
GILLINGS CT
Liby
VICTORS WAY
PARK RD
MEADWAY CL
QUEEN ELIZABETH CT
MEADWAY
MARTINS MOUNT
POTTER'S RD
SHERIDAN LO
Pl Flds
CROMER RD
SHAFTESBURY AVE
BARNARD LO
HIGH ST
A411
WOOD ST
Queen Elizabeth's Sch
GORDON WAY
Mus
Barnet Coll
MANOR CL
CATTLEY CL
EN5
KINGSMEAD
HILLARY RISE
KING EDWARD RD
SHELDON CT
HUGHENDON
HEXHAM RD
HADRIAN CT
BULWER RD
BULWER GDNS
ASEFIELD CT
SUTHERLAND CL
Bwg Gns
ORCHARD RD
ELM DR
VICTORIA LA
High Barnet
A411 Borehamwood, A1
LEECROFT RD
PINECROFT CR
MANORSIDE
WILLOW DR
MANOR RD
Chipping Barnet
A1000
BARNET HILL
HILLSIDE MANS
St Catherine's Sch
POTTER'S LA
PROSPECT RD
WARWICK RD
AMBERLEY CT
VALE CT
GAINSBOROUGH CT
CHRISTOPHER CT
PLANTAGENET RD
DUNCAN
THE RODINGS
HILLSIDE GDNS
Tenn Cts
FITZJOHN AVE
NEWLYN RD
NORMANDY AVE
BEDFORD AVE
MILTON AVE
VALE DR
BRACKENWOOD LO
RAVENSCROFT COTTS
ABBOTTS RD
THE HIGHLANDS
Highlands Gdns
WINDERMERE CT
LEICESTER RD
BARNES CT
HANOVER HO
COLGATE CT
ELLESMERE GR
WOODFALL AVE
ELTON AVE
HIGHWOOD CT
HIGHLANDS RD
HOMESTEAD CT
STATION RD
CHILTERN CT
BEAUFORT CT
MOWBRAY
SOMERSET
THE THOMAS WATSON COTTAGE HOMES
UNDERHILL CT
POTTERIES
A1000
New Barnet
Lyonsdown
BARNET
A B C D
VI
1 2 3 4 5 6
99 98 97 96
24 25 26
13
2

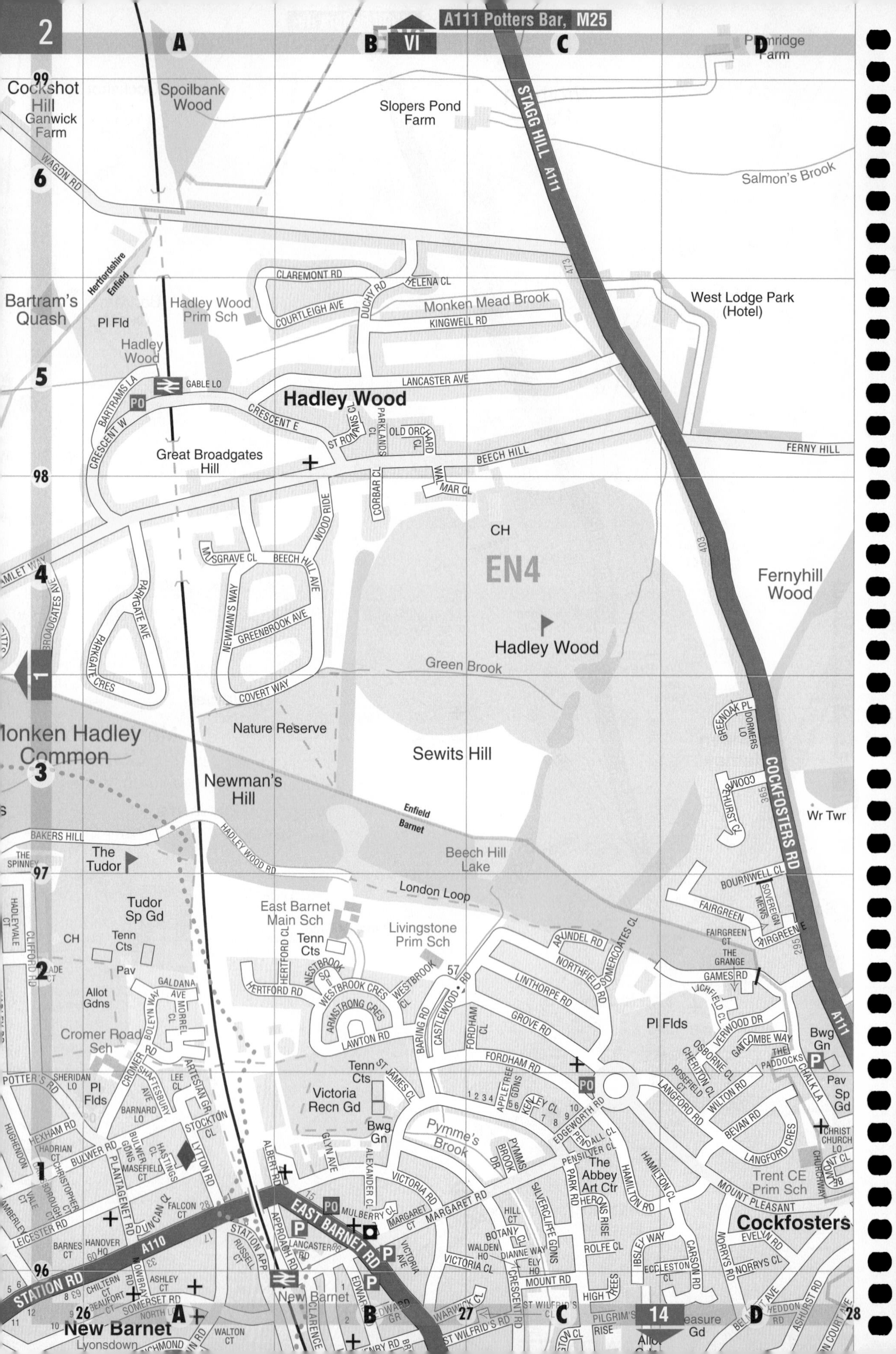
A111 Potters Bar, M25
VI
A
B
C
D
Cockshot Hill
Ganwick Farm
Spoilbank Wood
Slopers Pond Farm
Plumridge Farm
STAGG HILL A111
Salmon's Brook
WAGON RD
Hertfordshire
Enfield
Bartram's Quash
Pl Fld
Hadley Wood Prim Sch
Hadley Wood
CLAREMONT RD
HELENA CL
DUCHY RD
COURTLEIGH AVE
Monken Mead Brook
KINGWELL RD
West Lodge Park (Hotel)
LANCASTER AVE
GABLE LO
BARTRAMS LA
PO
Hadley Wood
CRESCENT E
CRESCENT W
ST RONANS CL
PARKLANDS CL
OLD ORCHARD CL
FERNY HILL
Great Broadgates Hill
BEECH HILL
CORBAR CL
WALMAR CL
WOOD RIDE
CH
EN4
MUSGRAVE CL
BEECH HILL AVE
HAMLET WAY
BROADGATES AVE
PARKGATE AVE
NEWMAN'S WAY
GREENBROOK AVE
Fernyhill Wood
Hadley Wood
PARKGATE CRES
COVERT WAY
Green Brook
Monken Hadley Common
Nature Reserve
Sewits Hill
GREENOAK PL
DORMERS LO
COCKFOSTERS RD
Newman's Hill
COMBEHURST CL
Wr Twr
Enfield
Barnet
BAKERS HILL
HADLEY WOOD RD
THE SPINNEY
The Tudor
Beech Hill Lake
BOURNWELL CL
London Loop
Tudor Sp Gd
East Barnet Main Sch
SOVEREIGN MEWS
FAIRGREEN
HADLEYVALE CT
CLIFFORD RD
CH
Tenn Cts
Livingstone Prim Sch
FAIRGREEN CT
FAIRGREEN E
Tenn Cts
ARUNDEL RD
SOMERCOATES CL
HERTFORD CL
NORTHFIELD RD
THE GRANGE
Pav
WESTBROOK SQ
57
GAMES RD
GALDANA AVE
HERTFORD RD
WESTBROOK CRES
WESTBROOK CL
LINTHORPE RD
Allot Gdns
BOLEYN WAY
MORREL CL
ARMSTRONG CRES
CASTLEWOOD RD
FORDHAM CL
LICHFIELD CL
VERWOOD DR
Pl Flds
BARING RD
GROVE RD
Bwg Gn
A111
Cromer Road Sch
LAWTON RD
GATCOMBE WAY
THE PADDOCKS
OSBORNE CL
CHERITON CL
Tenn Cts
ST JAMES CL
FORDHAM RD
CHALK LA
CROMER RD
ARTESIAN GR
POTTER'S RD
SHERIDAN LO
Pl Flds
SHAFTESBURY AVE
LEE CL
Victoria Recn Gd
APPLETREE GDNS
KENLEY CL
PO
ROSEFIELD CT
WILTON RD
Pav
Sp Gd
BARNARD LO
LANGFORD RD
EDGEWORTH RD
HEXHAM RD
HADRIAN CT
STOCKTON CL
Bwg Gn
Pymme's Brook
PENDALL CL
BEVAN RD
CHRIST CHURCH LO
HUGHENDON
BULWER RD
BULWER GDNS
MASEFIELD CT
HASTINGS CL
LYTTON RD
GLYN AVE
ALEXANDER CL
PYMMS BROOK DR
HAMILTON CL
LANGFORD CRES
GAINSBOROUGH CT
CHRISTOPHER CT
PLANTAGENET RD
ALBERT RD
PENSILVER CL
The Abbey Art Ctr
HAMILTON RD
Trent CE Prim Sch
CHURCHWAY
VALE CT
VICTORIA RD
MOUNT PLEASANT
KIMBERLEY
DUNCAN CL
FALCON CT
EAST BARNET RD
PO
SILVERCLIFFE GDNS
PARK RD
LEICESTER RD
HANOVER HO
STATION APP
APPROACH RD
MULBERRY CL
MARGARET CT
MARGARET RD
HILL CT
HERONS RISE
IBSLEY WAY
Cockfosters
BARNES CT
A110
RUSSELL CT
LANCASTER RD
BOTANY CL
WALDEN HO
DIANNE WAY
ELY HO
VICTORIA CL
ROLFE CL
CARSON RD
NORRYS RD
EVELYN RD
NORRYS CL
96
STATION RD
ASHLEY CT
MOWBRAY RD
CHILTERN CT
BEAUFORT CT
SOMERSET RD
VICTORIA AVE
CRESCENT RD
MOUNT RD
ECCLESTON CL
HIGH TREES
New Barnet
EDWARD GR
WARWICK CL
ST WILFRID'S CL
PILGRIM'S RISE
Pleasure Gd
HEDDON RD
ASHURST RD
NORTH LO
26
A
B
27
C
14
D
28
New Barnet
Lyonsdown
WALTON CT
RICHMOND
CLARENCE
ST WILFRID'S RD
Allot
99
6
5
98
4
3
97
2
1
1

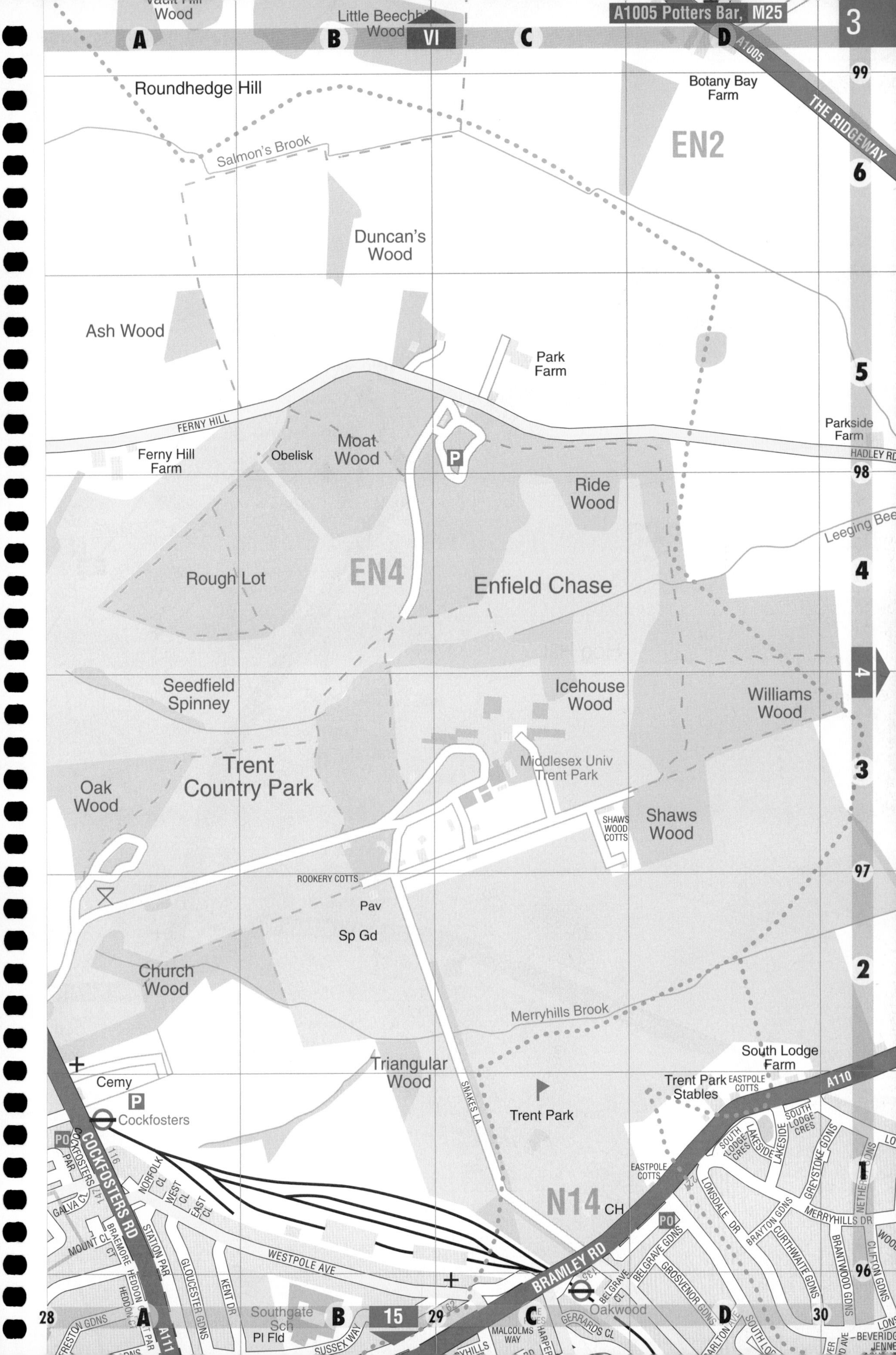
Little Beechhill Wood
VI
A B C D
99
Roundhedge Hill
Botany Bay Farm
THE RIDGEWAY
A1005
EN2
Salmon's Brook
6
Duncan's Wood
Ash Wood
Park Farm
5
FERNY HILL
Ferny Hill Farm
Obelisk
Moat Wood
Parkside Farm
HADLEY RD
98
Ride Wood
Leeging Bee
EN4
Rough Lot
Enfield Chase
4
Seedfield Spinney
Icehouse Wood
Williams Wood
Middlesex Univ Trent Park
Trent Country Park
Oak Wood
3
SHAWS WOOD COTTS
Shaws Wood
ROOKERY COTTS
97
Pav
Sp Gd
Church Wood
2
Merryhills Brook
South Lodge Farm
Triangular Wood
Cemy
Trent Park
Trent Park Stables
EASTPOLE COTTS
A110
SNAKES LA
Cockfosters
COCKFOSTERS RD
COCKFOSTERS PAR
GALVA CL
MOUNT CL
BRAEMORE CT
HEDDON CT
STATION PAR
NORFOLK CL
WEST CL
EAST CL
GLOUCESTER GDNS
KENT DR
WESTPOLE AVE
N14
CH
BRAMLEY RD
SOUTH LODGE CRES
LAKESIDE
GREYSTOKE GDNS
LONSDALE DR
BRAYTON GDNS
CURTHWAITE GDNS
MERRYHILLS DR
BRANTWOOD GDNS
CLIFTON GDNS
NETHER GDNS
1
BELGRAVE GDNS
BELGRAVE CL
GROSVENOR GDNS
96
Oakwood
GERRARDS CL
Southgate Sch
Pl Fld
SUSSEX WAY
MALCOLMS WAY
28
A
B
15
29
C
D
30
A111
BEVERIDGE

A
B
VII
C
D
99
6
5
98
4
3
97
2
1
96
30
31
16
32
King's Oak
Plain
St John's
CE
Prim Sch
STRAYFIELD RD
ROSSENDALE
CL
Nursery
The
Red House
Queenswood
Farm
Rectory
Farm
Turkey Brook
The Kings Oak
(Private)
EN2
THE RIDGEWAY
Cuckolds Hill
Hotel
ROUND HEDGE WAY
KINGFISHER
CT
WILLIAM COVELL CL
SPRING COURT RD
Chase
Farm
Allot Gdns
Cemy
Parkside
Farm
HADLEY RD
OAK AVE
MOUNT VIEW
HIGH OAKS
ARAGON CL
HAREFIELD
CL
COMREDDY CL
LAVENDER GDNS
RENDLESHAM RD
Leeging Beech Gutter
Vicarage
Farm
RIDGE CREST
HUNTERS WAY
ALBUHERA CL
SHOOTERS RD
LAVENDER HILL
FARORNA WLK
HARRIS CL
LEE VIEW
HEDGE HILL
Gordon
Hill
FARMLANDS
JAYCROFT
HARDY WAY
ACORN CL
FAIRVIEW RD
Cts
HANSART WAY
DRAPERS RD
JOHN GOOCH DR
PADSTOW RD
HEDGE HILL
BANKSIDE
BANBURY
HOLTWHITE'S HILL
WOODSIDE
CT
Hog Hill
WOODRIDGE CL
AVALON CL
CHASEWOOD AVE
HEATHER DR
AMESBURY CT 1
CAPSTAN RIDE 2
KINGS CHACE VIEW 3
CROFTON WAY
LANSDOWNE HO
DUNRAVEN DR
SORBUS
CT
MCADAM
DR
PERRY MEAD
ABBOTS CRES
WELLESLEY
PARK
MEWS
Williams
Wood
VALLEY FIELDS CRES
CAVELL DR
AUDLEY RD
BYCULLAH RD
ROWANTREE RD
COPPERWOOD
LO
BYRON CT
SIMON
PETER
CT
North London
Nuffield
THE GROVE
UPLANDS PARK RD
STOCKBRIDGE HO
CANFORD CL
ROBSON CL
ROWANWOOD MEWS
HOLLY
TREE
LO
HERMITAGE CL
ENGLEFIELD
CL
HAVENHURST RISE
VULCAN GATE
CHASE RIDINGS
RIDGEMOUNT GDNS
CULLODEN RD
CEDARWOOD
HO
BYCULLAH AVE
PARK WAY
WINDMILL GDNS
SLADES GDNS
THE GLADE
POSTERN GN
COLONELS WLK
TEMPLE GR
PINEWOOD
CT
THE
OAKS
OAKDENE
HO
ELIZABETH AVE
Allot
Gdns
TRENTWOOD SIDE
GRAFTON RD
ELMER CL
BERKELEY
LO
SLADES HILL
FIONA
CT
HIGH
DENE
GLEBE AVE
A1005
TAUNTON DR
SLADES CL
SLADES RISE
HUNTING GATE CL
115
WINDMILL HILL A110
PO
LINKSIDE GDNS
LINKSIDE CL
LINKS SIDE
OLD PARK VIEW
MILLERS GREEN CL
HIGH
ACRE
OLD PARK RD
CALSHOT WAY
BADGERS CL
WAVERLEY RD
ENFIELD RD
Liby
FOXMEAD CL
BINCOTE RD
WINSMOOR CT 1
THORPE CT 2
WANSBECK CT 3
THE OLD SCHOOL HO 4
BARRYDENE CT 5
WYNDCROFT CL
South Lodge
Farm
A110
COTSWOLD WAY
Merryhills
Prim Sch
World's End
Salmon's Brook
CRESCENT RD
VERMONT CL
CLAREMONT
HTS
MOUNTFORD
HO
CH
THE HASELWOOD DR
COPPICE
OLD PARK RD S
THE GLEN
GLADBECK
COTSWOLD
GN
GLENBROOK N
GLENBROOK S
LAKESIDE
SOUTH LODGE CRES
GREYSTOKE GDNS
NETHERBY GDNS
LOWTHER DR
CULGAITH GDNS
BEWCASTLE GDNS
CORBY CRES
LONSDALE DR N
CHILTERN DENE
Boxer's
Lake
Highlands
Sch
Enfield
LONSDALE DR
N21
BRAYTON GDNS
MERRYHILLS DR
CURTHWAITE GDNS
BRANTWOOD GDNS
CLIFTON GDNS
WOODEND GDNS
SILVERDALE
ROUNDHILL DR
RUSHEY HILL
WORLDS END LA
Grange Park
Prim Sch
LINDAL CRES
CHADWICK AVE
TARNBANK
SIMPSON CL
CORFIELD RD
HANSEN DR
LAIDLAW DR
HANBURY DR
FLEMING
BARNABAS
CT
MACLEOD RD
TRESILIAN AVE
BUCHANAN CL
1 ADAM LO
4 PITMAN HO
5 SYDENHAM AVE
UPLANDS WAY
Allot
Gdns
BEVERIDGE CT 1
JENNER CT 2

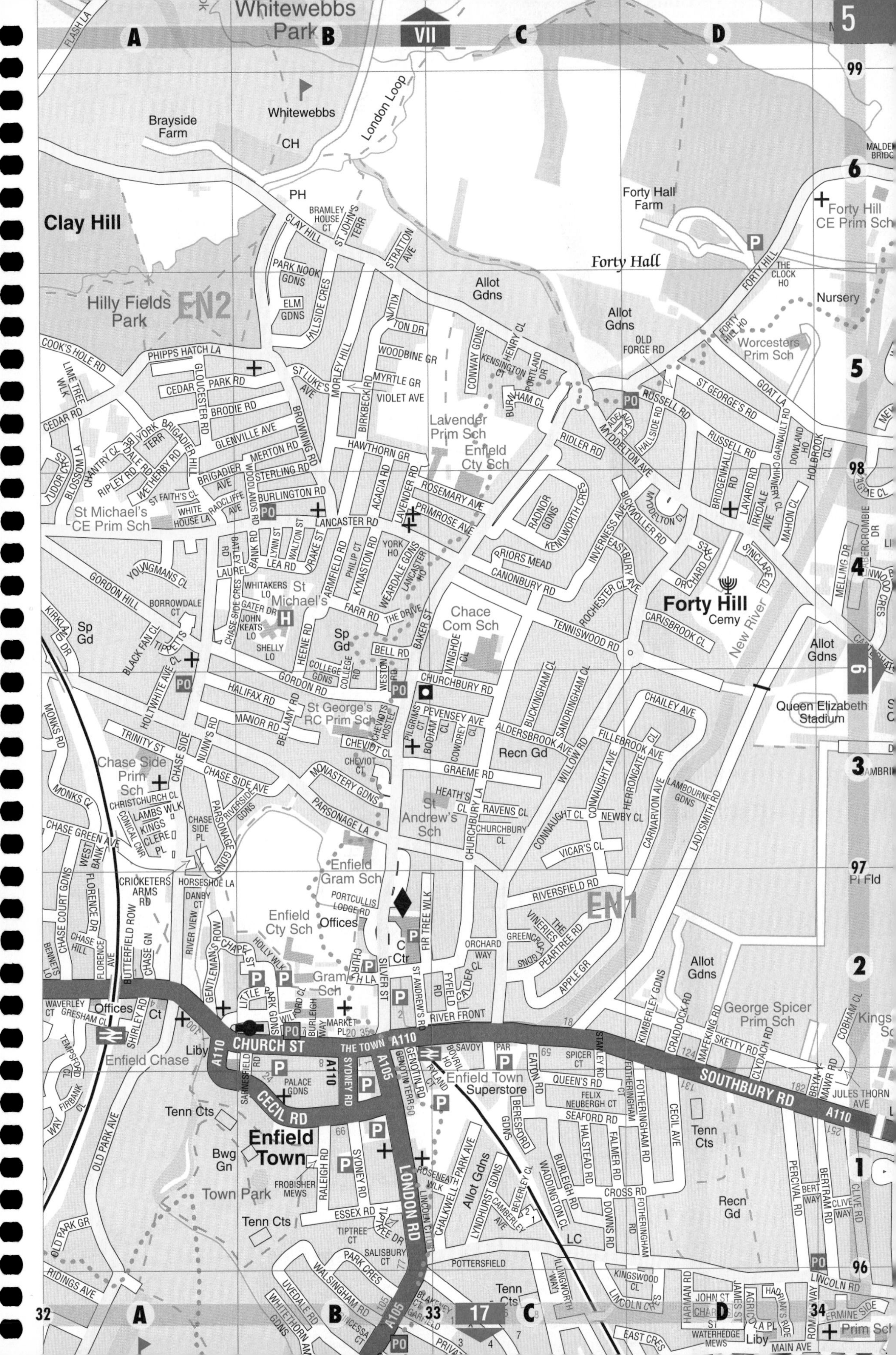
Whitewebbs Park
VII
A
B
C
D
99
Whitewebbs
Brayside Farm
CH
London Loop
PH
Clay Hill
Hilly Fields Park
EN2
Forty Hall Farm
Forty Hall
Forty Hill CE Prim Sch
Allot Gdns
Nursery
Worcesters Prim Sch
THE CLOCK HO
6
5
98
4
3
97
2
1
96
Lavender Prim Sch
Enfield Cty Sch
St Michael's CE Prim Sch
St Michael's
Sp Gd
Chace Com Sch
Forty Hill
Cemy
New River
Queen Elizabeth Stadium
St George's RC Prim Sch
Chase Side Prim Sch
Recn Gd
St Andrew's Sch
Enfield Gram Sch
Enfield Cty Sch
Offices
C Ctr
EN1
Gram Sch
George Spicer Prim Sch
Enfield Chase
Liby
CHURCH ST
THE TOWN
A110
A105
CECIL RD
SOUTHBURY RD
Enfield Town
Enfield Town Superstore
Tenn Cts
Bwg Gn
Town Park
Allot Gdns
LONDON RD
LC
Recn Gd
PI Fld
Kings Sc
POTTERSFIELD
Prim Sch
CLAY HILL
BRAMLEY HOUSE CT
ST JOHN'S TERR
STRATTON AVE
PARK NOOK GDNS
ELM GDNS
HILLSIDE CRES
PHIPPS HATCH LA
COOK'S HOLE RD
CEDAR RD
GLOUCESTER RD
PARK RD
BRODIE RD
GLENVILLE AVE
MERTON RD
STERLING RD
BURLINGTON RD
LANCASTER RD
ST LUKE'S AVE
MORLEY HILL
BIRKBECK RD
BROWNING RD
WOODBINE GR
MYRTLE GR
VIOLET AVE
HAWTHORN GR
ACACIA RD
LAVENDER RD
ROSEMARY AVE
PRIMROSE AVE
CONWAY GDNS
HENRY CL
KENSINGTON CT
PORTLAND DR
OLD FORGE RD
RUSSELL RD
ST GEORGE'S RD
GOAT LA
FORTY HILL
MYDDELTON AVE
RIDLER RD
RADNOR GDNS
KENILWORTH CRES
PRIORS MEAD
CANONBURY RD
INVERNESS AVE
EASTBURY AVE
ROCHESTER CL
CARISBROOK CL
TENNISWOOD RD
GORDON HILL
GORDON RD
HALIFAX RD
MANOR RD
BELLAMY RD
TRINITY ST
CHASE SIDE
CHASE SIDE AVE
NUNN'S RD
CHEVIOT CL
MONASTERY GDNS
PARSONAGE LA
CHURCHBURY RD
CHURCHBURY LA
PEVENSEY AVE
GRAEME RD
RAVENS CL
ALDERSBROOK AVE
BUCKINGHAM CL
SANDRINGHAM CL
WILLOW RD
CHAILEY AVE
FILLEBROOK AVE
CONNAUGHT AVE
HERRONGATE CL
CARNARVON AVE
LADYSMITH RD
NEWBY CL
VICAR'S CL
RIVERSFIELD RD
PEARTREE RD
APPLE GR
MONKS RD
CHASE GREEN AVE
CHASE COURT GDNS
FLORENCE DR
BUTTERFIELD ROW
CHASE GN
GENTLEMAN'S ROW
RIVER VIEW
HORSESHOE LA
SILVER ST
FIR TREE WLK
ST ANDREW'S RD
RIVER FRONT
EATON RD
QUEEN'S RD
SEAFORD RD
HALSTEAD RD
FALMER RD
FOTHERINGHAM RD
CECIL AVE
KIMBERLEY GDNS
CRADDOCK RD
MAFEKING RD
SKETTY RD
CLYDACH RD
PERCIVAL RD
BERTRAM RD
CLIVE RD
OLD PARK AVE
OLD PARK GR
RIDINGS AVE
RALEIGH RD
SYDNEY RD
ESSEX RD
WALSINGHAM RD
UVEDALE RD
PARK CRES
CHALKWELL PARK AVE
LYNDHURST GDNS
WADDINGTON CL
BURLEIGH RD
DOWNS RD
CROSS RD
KINGSWOOD CL
LINCOLN CRES
LINCOLN RD
JOHN ST
JAMES ST
WATERHEDGE MEWS
MAIN AVE
ERMINE SIDE
JULES THORN AVE
A
B
C
D

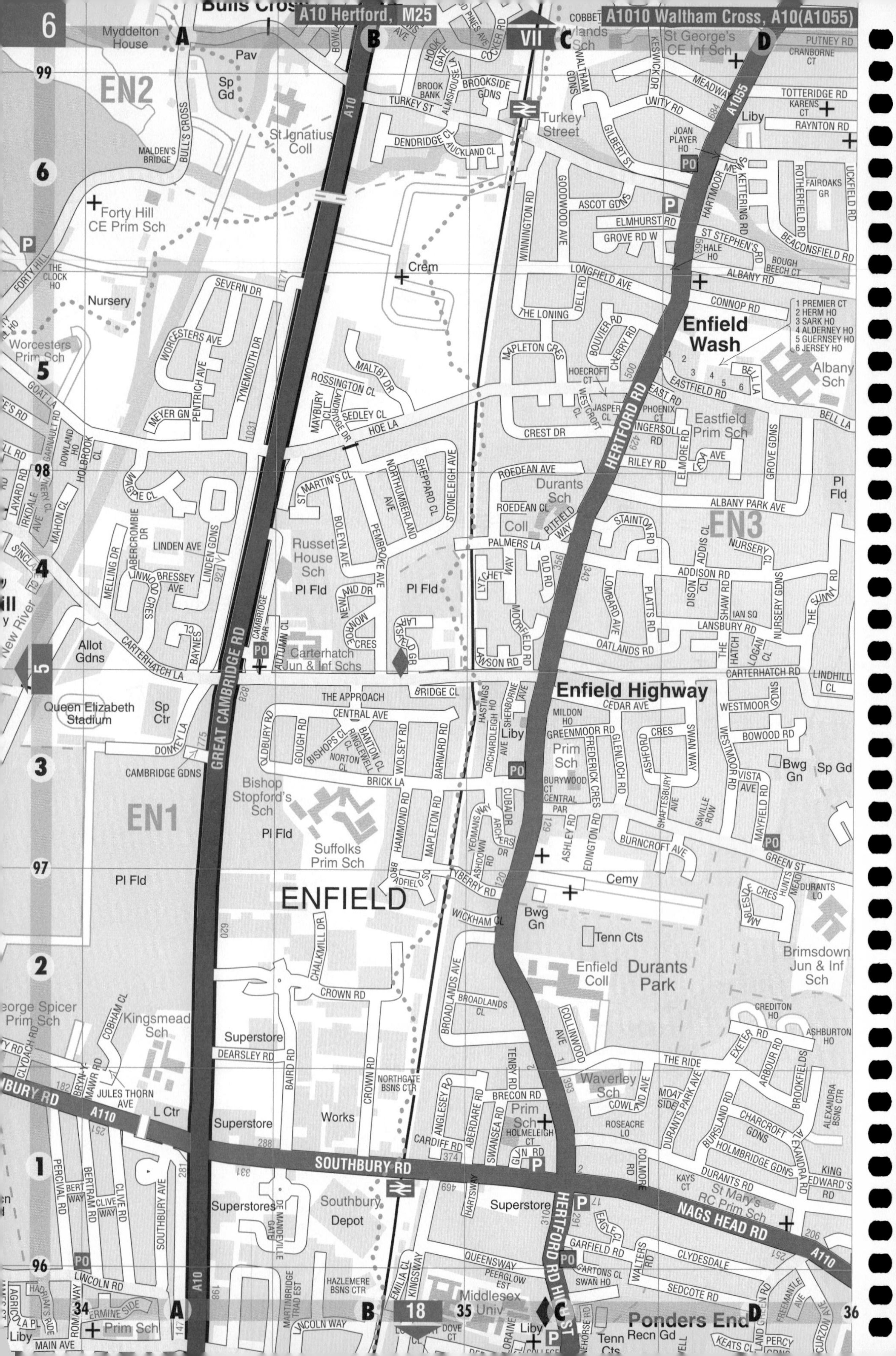

6
Bulls Cross
A10 Hertford, M25
A1010 Waltham Cross, A10(A1055)
VII
A
B
C
D
Myddelton House
Pav
Sp Gd
EN2
St Ignatius Coll
Malden's Bridge
Bull's Cross
Forty Hill CE Prim Sch
Forty Hill
The Clock Ho
Nursery
Worcesters Prim Sch
Goat La
Severn Dr
Worcesters Ave
Tynemouth Dr
Pentrich Ave
Meyer Gn
Garnault Rd
Dowland Ho
Holbrook Cl
Layard Rd
Irkdale Ave
Mahon Cl
Magpie Cl
Linden Ave
Linden Gdns
Abercrombie Dr
Melling Dr
Inwood Cres
Bressey Ave
Baynes Cl
Allot Gdns
Carterhatch La
New River
Queen Elizabeth Stadium
Sp Ctr
Donkey La
Cambridge Gdns
Great Cambridge Rd
Cambridge Par
Autumn Cl
EN1
Pl Fld
Kingsmead Sch
George Spicer Prim Sch
Clydach Rd
Cobham Cl
Bryn-y-Mawr Rd
Jules Thorn Ave
Southbury Rd
A110
L Ctr
Percival Rd
Bertram Rd
Bert Way
Clive Way
Clive Rd
Southbury Ave
Lincoln Rd
Hadrian's Ride
Agricola Pl
Ermine Side
Romney Way
Main Ave
Liby
Prim Sch
A10
Turkey St
Bowling
Pines Ave
Hook Gate
Almshouse La
Brook Bank
Brookside Gdns
Cocker Rd
Dendridge Cl
Auckland Cl
Turkey Street
Crem
Maltby Dr
Rossington Cl
Maybury Cl
Landridge Dr
Sedley Cl
Hoe La
St Martin's Cl
Northumberland Ave
Sheppard Cl
Stoneleigh Ave
Bolyen Ave
Pembroke Ave
Russet House Sch
Newland Dr
Monroe Cres
Larksfield Gr
Carterhatch Jun & Inf Schs
The Approach
Bridge Cl
Central Ave
Oldbury Rd
Gough Rd
Bishops Cl
Banton Cl
Ringlewell Cl
Norton Cl
Wolsey Rd
Barnard Rd
Brick La
Bishop Stopford's Sch
Suffolks Prim Sch
Hammond Rd
Mapleton Rd
Broadfield Sq
ENFIELD
Chalkmill Dr
Crown Rd
Superstore
Dearsley Rd
Baird Rd
Northgate Bsns Ctr
Works
Superstores
De Mandeville Gate
Southbury Depot
Martinbridge Trad Est
Hazlemere Bsns Ctr
Lincoln Way
Emilia Cl
Kingsway
Middlesex Univ
18
34
35
36
Cobbett
Aylands Sch
Waltham Gdns
St George's CE Inf Sch
Keswick Dr
Meadway
Unity Rd
Gilbert St
Joan Player Ho
Putney Rd
Cranborne Ct
Totteridge Rd
Karens Ct
Raynton Rd
A1055
Hartmoor Mews
Kettering Rd
Rotherfield Rd
Fairoaks Gr
Uckfield Rd
Beaconsfield Rd
Winnington Rd
Goodwood Ave
Ascot Gdns
Elmhurst Rd
Grove Rd W
St Stephen's Rd
Hale Ho
Bough Beech Ct
Albany Rd
Longfield Ave
Dell Rd
The Loning
Connop Rd
Enfield Wash
1 Premier Ct
2 Herm Ho
3 Sark Ho
4 Alderney Ho
5 Guernsey Ho
6 Jersey Ho
Albany Sch
Bouvier Rd
Cherry Rd
Mapleton Cres
Hoecroft Ct
Westcroft Cl
Jasper Cl
Phoenix Ct
Eastfield Rd
East Rd
Bell La
Hertford Rd
Ingersoll Rd
Eastfield Prim Sch
Crest Dr
Elmore Rd
Lyda Ave
Riley Rd
Grove Gdns
Roedean Ave
Roedean Cl
Durants Sch
Coll
Pitfield Way
Albany Park Ave
EN3
Pl Fld
Palmers La
Stainton Rd
Nursery Cl
Addis Cl
Addison Rd
Lytchet Way
Old Rd
Lombard Ave
Platts Rd
Dison Cl
Shaw Rd
Nursery Gdns
The Sunny Rd
Ian Sq
Moorfield Rd
Lansbury Rd
Oatlands Rd
The Hatch
Logan Cl
Lawson Rd
Carterhatch Rd
Lindhill Cl
Enfield Highway
Hastings Ave
Sherborne Ave
Cedar Ave
Westmoor Gdns
Mildon Ho
Greenmoor Rd
Glenloch Rd
Frederick Cres
Ashford Cres
Swan Way
Westmoor Rd
Bowood Rd
Orchardleigh Ave
Prim Sch
Burywood Ct
Central Par
Shaftesbury Ave
Saville Row
Vista Ave
Mayfield Rd
Bwg Gn
Sp Gd
Yeomans Way
Cuba Dr
Archers Dr
Ashdown Rd
Ashley Rd
Edington Rd
Burncroft Ave
Green St
Tyberry Rd
Cemy
Durants Lo
Amberside Cl
Hunts Mead
Wickham Cl
Tenn Cts
Enfield Coll
Durants Park
Brimsdown Jun & Inf Sch
Broadlands Ave
Broadlands Cl
Collinwood Ave
Crediton Ho
Exeter Rd
Ashburton Ho
The Ride
Arbour Rd
Brookfields
Tenby Rd
Waverley Sch
Cowland Ave
Moat Side
Durants Park Ave
Bursland Rd
Charcroft Gdns
Alexandra Bsns Ctr
Anglesey Rd
Aberdare Rd
Brecon Rd
Swansea Rd
Holmeleigh Ct
Glyn Rd
Cardiff Rd
Roseacre Lo
Holmbridge Gdns
Alexandra Rd
Colmore Rd
Kays Ct
Durants Rd
King Edward's Rd
Hartsway
Superstore
St Mary's RC Prim Sch
Nags Head Rd
Eagle Cl
Garfield Rd
Walters Rd
Clydesdale
Queensway
Peerglow Est
Cartons Cl
Swan Ho
Sedcote Rd
Hertford Rd High St
Freemantle Ave
Ponders End
Recn Gd
Tenn Cts
Keats Cl
Percy
Curzon Ave
Dove Ct
99
98
97
96
5
4
3
2
1

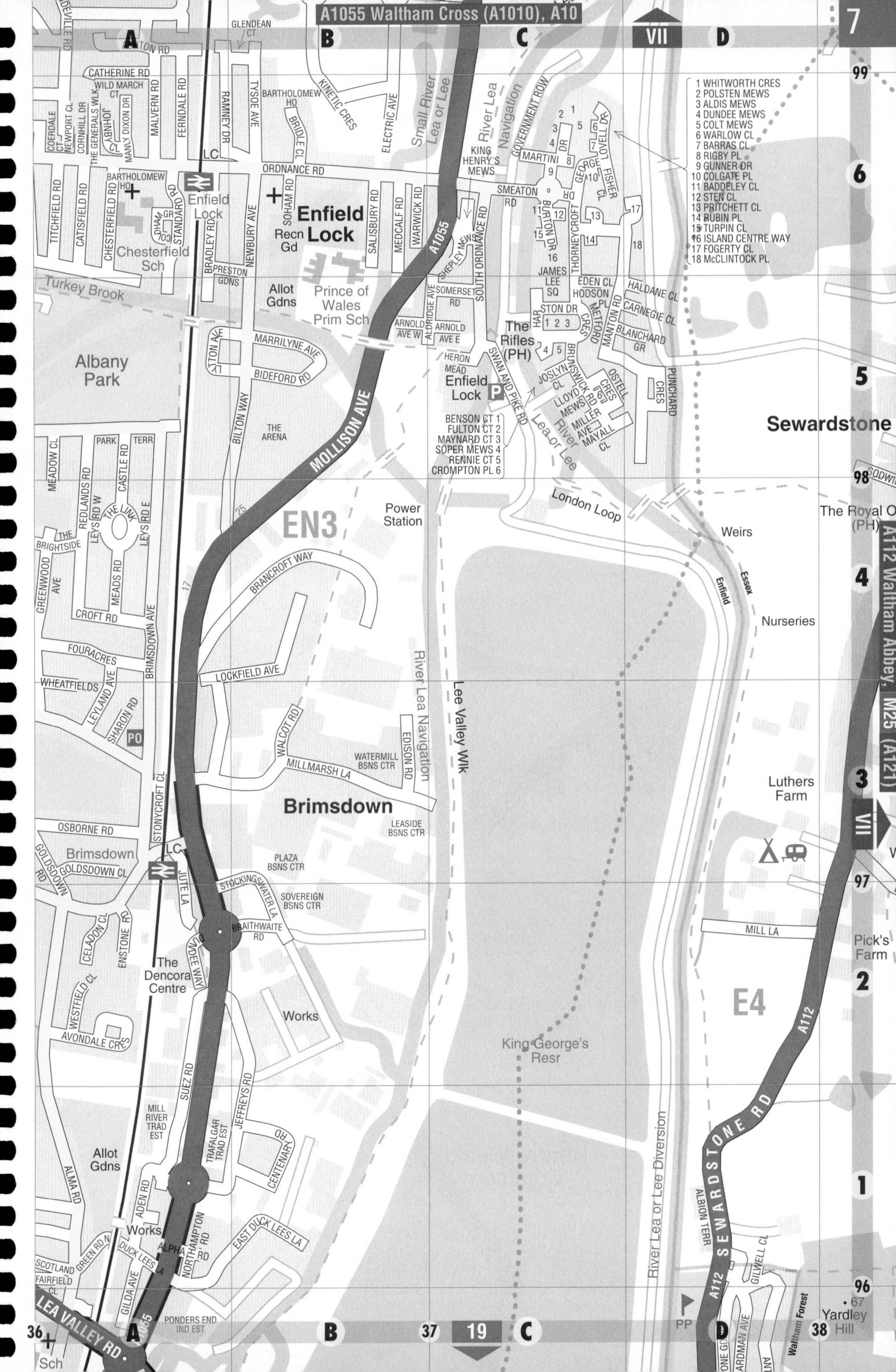

A1055 Waltham Cross (A1010), A10
7
A
B
C
VII
D
99
6
5
98
4
3
97
2
1
96
36
37
19
38
1 WHITWORTH CRES
2 POLSTEN MEWS
3 ALDIS MEWS
4 DUNDEE MEWS
5 COLT MEWS
6 WARLOW CL
7 BARRAS CL
8 RIGBY PL
9 GUNNER DR
10 COLGATE PL
11 BADDELEY CL
12 STEN CL
13 PRITCHETT CL
14 RUBIN PL
15 TURPIN CL
16 ISLAND CENTRE WAY
17 FOGERTY CL
18 McCLINTOCK PL
BENSON CT 1
FULTON CT 2
MAYNARD CT 3
SOPER MEWS 4
RENNIE CT 5
CROMPTON PL 6
Enfield Lock
Recn Gd
Chesterfield Sch
Prince of Wales Prim Sch
Allot Gdns
Albany Park
Turkey Brook
ORDNANCE RD
CATHERINE RD
GLENDEAN CT
BARTHOLOMEW HO
KINETIC CRES
ELECTRIC AVE
Small River Lea or Lee
River Lea Navigation
GOVERNMENT ROW
KING HENRY'S MEWS
SMEATON RD
MARTINI DR
SOUTH ORDNANCE RD
SHEPLEY MEWS
A1055
MOLLISON AVE
SOMERSET RD
ARNOLD AVE W
ARNOLD AVE E
ALDRIDGE AVE
HERON MEAD
SWAN AND PIKE RD
The Rifles (PH)
JAMES LEE SQ
EDEN CL
HODSON PL
HALDANE CL
CARNEGIE CL
BLANCHARD GR
METFORD CRES
MANTON RD
BRUNSWICK RD
JOSLYN CL
LLOYD MEWS
MILLER AVE
MAYALL CL
OSTELL CRES
PUNCHARD CRES
THORNEYCROFT DR
BURTON DR
FISHER CL
LOVELL DR
River Lea or Lee
London Loop
Sewardstone
The Royal O (PH)
Weirs
Enfield
Essex
Nurseries
A112 Waltham Abbey, M25 (A121)
Luthers Farm
MILL LA
Pick's Farm
E4
A112
SEWARDSTONE RD
ALBION TERR
GILWELL CL
Waltham Forest
Yardley Hill
PP
MARRILYNE AVE
BIDEFORD RD
BILTON WAY
THE ARENA
Power Station
EN3
BRANCROFT WAY
LOCKFIELD AVE
WALCOT RD
MILLMARSH LA
WATERMILL BSNS CTR
EDISON RD
River Lea Navigation
Lee Valley Wlk
Brimsdown
LEASIDE BSNS CTR
PLAZA BSNS CTR
SOVEREIGN BSNS CTR
STOCKINGSWATER LA
BRAITHWAITE RD
JUTE LA
The Dencora Centre
Works
King George's Resr
River Lea or Lee Diversion
SUEZ RD
TRAFALGAR TRAD EST
JEFFREYS RD
CENTENARY RD
MILL RIVER TRAD EST
EAST DUCK LEES LA
DUCK LEES LA
ALPHA RD
NORTHAMPTON RD
ADEN RD
PONDERS END IND EST
LEA VALLEY RD
Sch
PARK TERR
MEADOW CL
REDLANDS RD
CASTLE RD
THE LINK
LEYS RD W
LEYS RD E
THE BRIGHTSIDE
GREENWOOD AVE
MEADS RD
CROFT RD
BRIMSDOWN AVE
FOURACRES
WHEATFIELDS
LEYLAND AVE
SHARON RD
PO
STONYCROFT CL
OSBORNE RD
Brimsdown
GOLDSDOWN CL
GOLDSDOWN RD
CELADON CL
ENSTONE RD
WESTFIELD CL
AVONDALE CRES
ALMA RD
SCOTLAND GREEN RD N
FAIRFIELD CL
GILDA AVE
TITCHFIELD RD
CATISFIELD RD
CHESTERFIELD RD
STANDARD RD
BRADLEY RD
PRESTON GDNS
NEWBURY AVE
SOHAM RD
SALISBURY RD
MEDCALF RD
WARWICK RD
MALVERN RD
FERNDALE RD
RAMNEY DR
TYSOE AVE
BRIDLE CL
CORNHILL DR
NEWPORT CL
THE GENERALS WLK
MANLY DIXON DR
WILD MARCH CT
LC

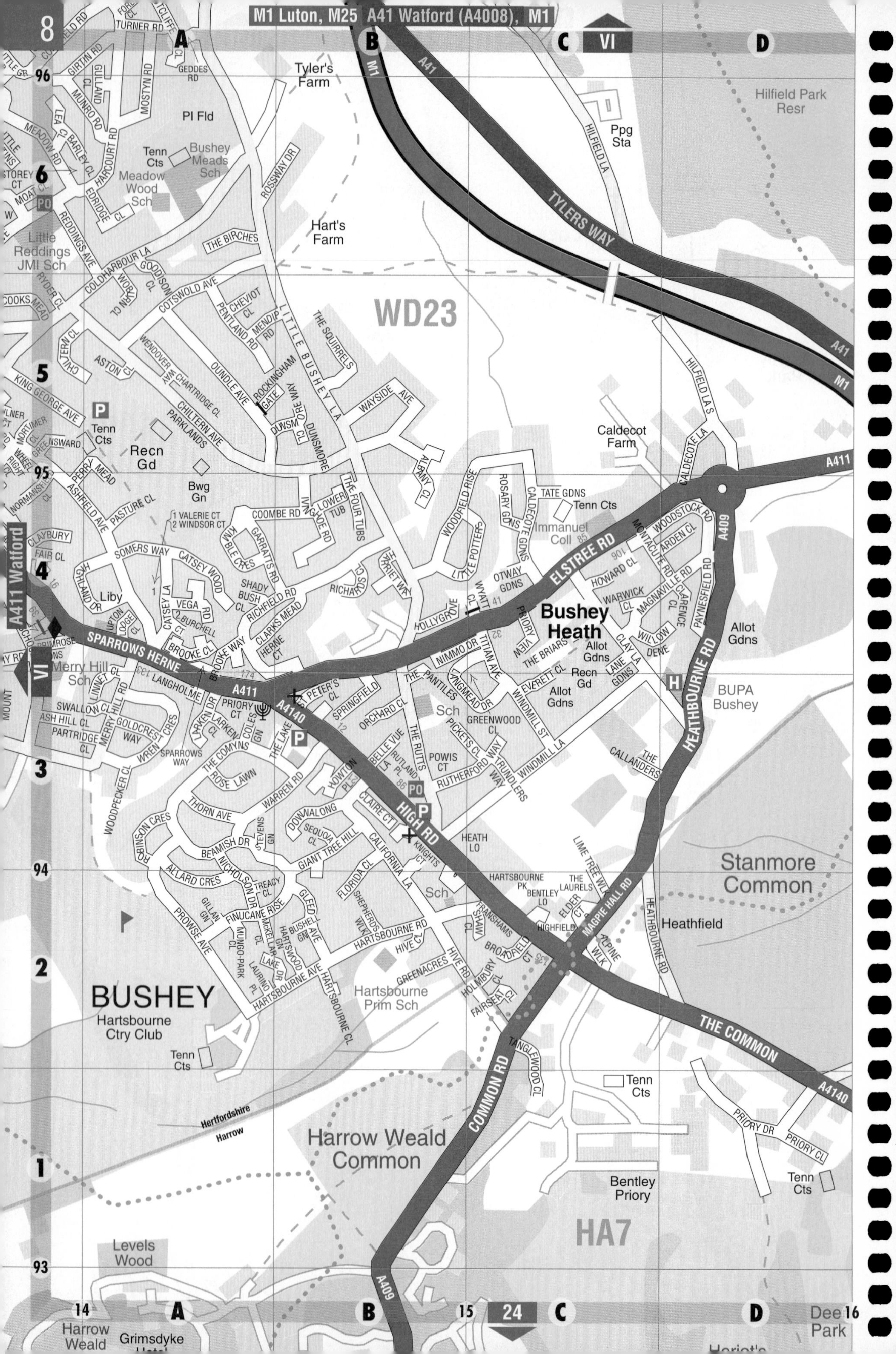
8
M1 Luton, M25 A41 Watford (A4008), M1
VI
A
B
C
D
96
95
94
93
6
5
4
3
2
1
Tyler's Farm
Hart's Farm
Pl Fld
Tenn Cts
Bushey Meads Sch
Meadow Wood Sch
Little Reddings JMI Sch
PO
Ppg Sta
Hilfield Park Resr
HILFIELD LA
TYLERS WAY
A41
M1
WD23
Caldecot Farm
A411
A409
A4140
CALDECOTE LA
Tenn Cts
Immanuel Coll
ELSTREE RD
Bushey Heath
Allot Gdns
Recn Gd
BUPA Bushey
HEATHBOURNE RD
Stanmore Common
Heathfield
MAGPIE HALL RD
THE COMMON
HIGH RD
SPARROWS HERNE
A411 Watford
Merry Hill Sch
Liby
Recn Gd
Bwg Gn
BUSHEY
Hartsbourne Ctry Club
Hartsbourne Prim Sch
Sch
HEATH LO
Tenn Cts
Hertfordshire
Harrow
Harrow Weald Common
COMMON RD
Bentley Priory
HA7
PRIORY DR
PRIORY CL
Levels Wood
Harrow Weald
Grimsdyke
14
15
24
16
Dee Park
COLDHARBOUR LA
COTSWOLD AVE
LITTLE BUSHEY LA
THE SQUIRRELS
WAYSIDE AVE
OUNDLE AVE
CHILTERN AVE
PARKLANDS
KING GEORGE AVE
ASHFIELD AVE
PASTURE CL
SOMERS WAY
CATSEY WOOD
CATSEY LA
BROOKE WAY
RICHFIELD RD
CLARKS MEAD
COOMBE RD
GARRATTS RD
THE FOUR TUBS
HOLLYGROVE
WOODFIELD RISE
ROSARY GDNS
CALDECOTE GDNS
TATE GDNS
OTWAY GDNS
PRIORY VIEW
THE BRIARS
NIMMO DR
TITIAN AVE
WINDMILL ST
WINDMILL LA
EVERETT CL
CLAY LA
LANE GDNS
WILLOW DENE
WARWICK CL
HOWARD CL
MONTAGUE RD
MAGNAVILLE RD
CLARENCE CL
PAYNESFIELD RD
WOODSTOCK RD
ARDEN CL
THE CALLANDERS
THE PANTILES
LONGMEAD DR
GREENWOOD CL
PICKETS CL
POWIS CT
RUTHERFORD WAY
TRUNDLERS WAY
THE RUTTS
RUTLAND PL
BELLE VUE LA
ORCHARD CL
SPRINGFIELD
ST PETER'S CL
HOWTON PL
CLAIRE CT
CALIFORNIA LA
KNIGHTS CT
FLORIDA CL
SHEPHERDS WLK
HARTSBOURNE RD
HARTSBOURNE AVE
HARTSBOURNE CL
HARTSBOURNE PK
GREENACRES
HIVE RD
HIVE CL
HOLMBURY CT
FAIRSEAT CL
BROADFIELD CT
FRANSHAMS
SHAW CL
HIGHFIELD
BENTLEY LO
THE LAURELS
ELDER CT
LIME TREE WLK
ALPINE WLK
TANGLEWOOD CL
HEATHBOURNE RD
WARREN RD
THE LAKE
COLES GN
PRIORY CT
THE COMYNS
ROSE LAWN
THORN AVE
ROBINSON CRES
BEAMISH DR
STEVENS GN
DOWNALONG
SEQUOIA CL
GIANT TREE HILL
ALLARD CRES
NICHOLSON DR
TREACY CL
FINUCANE RISE
GILLAN GN
PROWSE AVE
MUNGO-PARK CL
MCKELLAR CL
LAURINO PL
LAKE DR
HARTSWOOD GN
BUSHELL GN
GLEED AVE
LANGHOLME
LARKEN DR
LARKEN CL
SWALLOW CL
LINNET CL
MERRY HILL RD
ASH HILL CL
PARTRIDGE CL
GOLDCREST WAY
WREN CRES
SPARROWS WAY
WOODPECKER CL
UPTON LODGE CL
PRIMROSE
CLAYBURY
FAIR CL
HIGHLAND DR
VEGA RD
BURCHELL CT
BROOKE CL
SHADY BUSH CL
KIMBLE CRES
IVANHOE RD
LOWER TUB
DUNSMORE
DUNSMORE WAY
DUNSMORE CL
ROCKINGHAM GATE
CHARTRIDGE CL
WENDOVER WAY
PENTLAND RD
CHEVIOT CL
MENDIP RD
ASTON CL
CHILTERN CL
PERRY MEAD
NORMANSFIELD CL
GREENSWARD
MORTIMER CL
1 VALERIE CT
2 WINDSOR CT
ALBANY CL
THE BIRCHES
ROSSWAY DR
WORKMAN CL
GOODISON CL
RYDER CL
COOKS MEAD
REDDINGS AVE
EDRIDGE CL
HARCOURT RD
BARLEY CL
LEA CL
MEADOW RD
MUNRO RD
GULLAND CL
GIRTIN RD
MOSTYN RD
TURNER RD
GEDDES RD
MOAT CL
STOREY CT
WYATT CL
LITTLE POTTERS
MOUNT
H
P

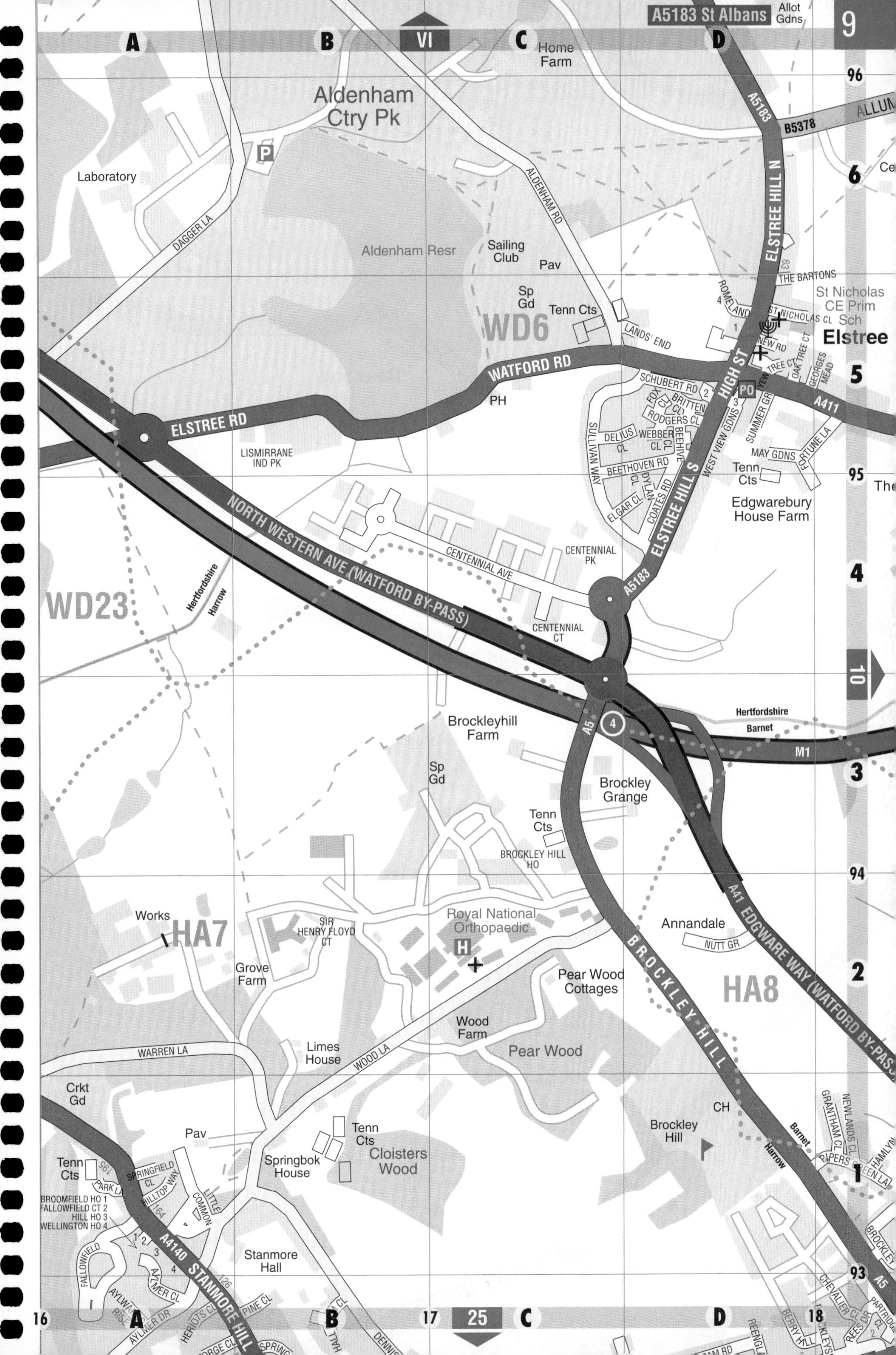

A5183 St Albans
Allot Gdns
A
B
VI
C
D
Home Farm
Aldenham Ctry Pk
Laboratory
DAGGER LA
ALDENHAM RD
Aldenham Resr
Sailing Club
Pav
Sp Gd
Tenn Cts
WD6
LANDS' END
WATFORD RD
PH
ELSTREE RD
LISMIRRANE IND PK
NORTH WESTERN AVE (WATFORD BY-PASS)
CENTENNIAL AVE
CENTENNIAL PK
CENTENNIAL CT
A5183
ELSTREE HILL N
ELSTREE HILL S
B5378
THE BARTONS
ROMELAND
ST NICHOLAS CL
St Nicholas CE Prim Sch
Elstree
NEW RD
HIGH ST
SCHUBERT RD
FOX CL
BRITTEN CL
RODGERS CL
DELIUS CL
WEBBER CL
BEEHIVE
SULLIVAN WAY
BEETHOVEN RD
DYLAN CL
ELGAR CL
COATES RD
WEST VIEW GDNS
SUMMER GR
YEW TREE CT
OAK TREE CT
GEORGES MEAD
PO
A411
MAY GDNS
FORTUNE LA
Tenn Cts
Edgwarebury House Farm
WD23
Hertfordshire
Harrow
Brockleyhill Farm
A5
4
Hertfordshire
Barnet
M1
Sp Gd
Brockley Grange
Tenn Cts
BROCKLEY HILL HO
A41
EDGWARE WAY (WATFORD BY-PASS)
Annandale
NUTT GR
Works
HA7
SIR HENRY FLOYD CT
Royal National Orthopaedic
H
Grove Farm
Pear Wood Cottages
BROCKLEY HILL
HA8
WARREN LA
Limes House
WOOD LA
Wood Farm
Pear Wood
Crkt Gd
CH
Brockley Hill
Barnet
Harrow
Pav
Tenn Cts
Cloisters Wood
Springbok House
Tenn Cts
SPRINGFIELD CL
PARK LA
HILLTOP WAY
LITTLE COMMON
BROOMFIELD HO 1
FALLOWFIELD CT 2
HILL HO 3
WELLINGTON HO 4
FALLOWFIELD
A4140
STANMORE HILL
AYLMER CL
AYLWARDS RISE
AYLMER DR
Stanmore Hall
HERIOTS CL
PINE CL
GRANTHAM CL
NEWLANDS CL
PIPERS GREEN LA
HAMLYN
BROCKLEY
CHEVALIER CL
PARTRIDGE CL
REES DR
BERRY HILL
ALLUM
96
6
5
95
4
10
3
94
2
1
93
16
17
18
25

Elstree
A
B
VI
C
D
96
ALLUM LA
B5378
A5183
ELSTREE HILL
Cemy
HARTFIELD AVE
DEACON'S HILL RD
CAVENDISH CRES
LAKESIDE
BERKELEY CL
ASCOT CL
HARTFIELD CL
HARTFIELD AVE
THE RISE
WENTWORTH AVE
SHIREMEADE
SHERATON CL
LOWTHER CL
NICHOLAS RD
HADLEY CL
ALWYN CL
CLARE CL
BELMOR
SUMMER HILL
LODGE AVE
GRANGE
BISHOPS AVE
TAUBER CL
KNOWL WAY
KNOWL PK
HILL CREST LO
FIR TREE CT
ALLUM LA
WOODSIDE
BLATTNER CL
DEACONS CL
Furzehill Sch
Allot Gdns
Sch
MELROSE AVE
TENNISON AVE
MILTON DR
BYRON AVE
VALE AVE
MASEFIELD AVE
LULLINGTON GARTH
CARRINGTON AVE
ELMWOOD AVE
6
THE BARTONS
St Nicholas CE Prim Sch
Elstree
ST NICHOLAS CL
NEW RD
OAK TREE CT
GEORGES MEAD
5
PO
A411
SUMMER GR
FORTUNE LA
MAY GDNS
Abbotsbury
BARNET LA
DEACONS HTS
Deacons
WD6
Elstree Tunnel
Woodcock Hill
Tenn Cts
A411
Tenn Cts
95
Edgwarebury House Farm
The Leys
Penniwells Farm
4
Tenn Cts
Tenn Cts
Edgwarebury Ctry Club
Hertfordshire
Barnet
NW7
9
Hertfordshire
Barnet
M1
M1
3
Edgwarebury Farm
Bury Farm
Edgware Bury
EDGWAREBURY LA
94
Clay La
Cemy
Pl Fld
Broadfields Inf Sch
Pav
Broadfields Jun Sch
HARTLAND CL
HARTLAND DR
M1 EDGWARE WAY (WATFORD BY-PASS)
2
HA8
HA8
WARRENS SHAWE LA
MEADFIELD
MEADFIELD GN
BUSHFIELD CL
BUSHFIELD CRES
BURRELL CL
PENTLAND AVE
HAMONDE CL
CROMARTY RD
MORAY CL
RANNOCH CL
KINGSLEY CT
TAYSIDE DR
ALDRIDGE AVE
GLENDEVON CL
Sch
PO
GLENGALL RD
PARSONS RD
PARSONS GR
FRANCKLYN GDNS
HARROWES MEADE
BULLESCROFT RD
WOLMER GDNS
CROSSGATE
BEULAH CL
CRANMER RD
ASHFORD CT
WYRE GR
MARLBOROUGH AVE
ROSENS WLK
LYNFORD GDNS
WINDSOR AVE
BROADFIELDS AVE
PARKSIDE DR
BLACKWELL GDNS
WOLMER CL
Sch
HURSTMEAD CT
GRENVILLE CT
BROADHURST AVE
Edgwarebury Park
Tenn Cts
Pav
CH
GRANTHAM CL
NEWLANDS CL
HAMLYN CL
PIPERS GREEN LA
Barnet
Harrow
1
Edgwarebury
HA7
BROCKLEY AVE
A5
93
CHEVALIER CL
REES DR
PARTRIDGE CL
BERRY HILL
A410
SPUR RD
A41
GOLDSMITH CT
COLLINSON CT
POWIS CT
SPALDING CT
GARRICK CT
EATON CT
EDGWARE WAY (WATFORD BY-PASS)
CANONS CNR
1 WARE CT
2 WAKEMAN HO
3 ABINGDON CT
4 CHICHELLE HO
5 HAVILLAND CT
MARTYN CT
STERLING AVE
RANELAGH CL
Pl Fld
18
A
B
19
26
C
D
20

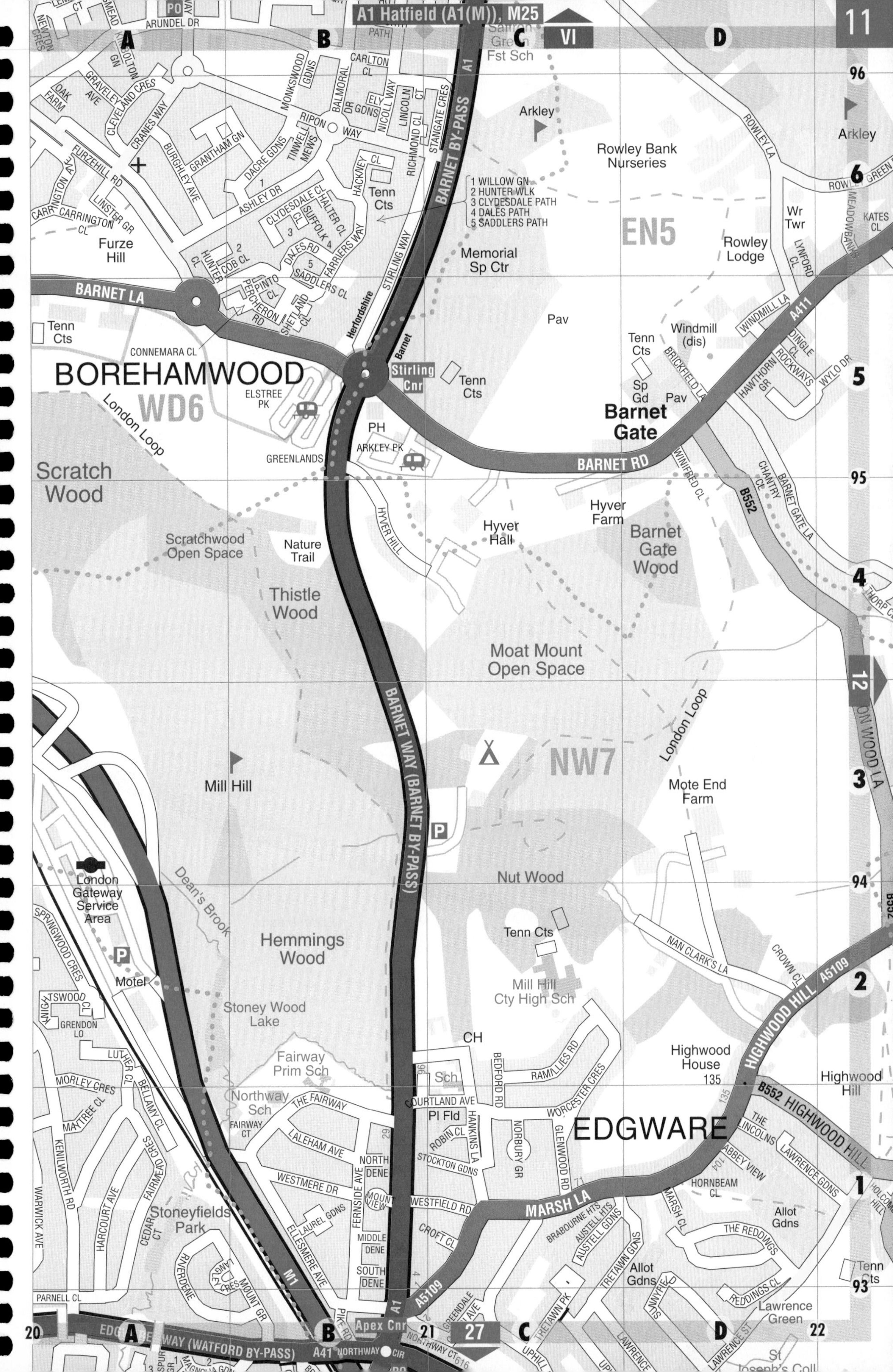

A **B** **C** VI **D**

A1 Hatfield (A1(M)), M25

96

Arkley

Salmon Green Fst Sch

Arkley

Rowley Bank Nurseries

EN5 6

Wr Twr

Rowley Lodge

ROW GREEN

KATES CL

1 WILLOW GN
2 HUNTER WLK
3 CLYDESDALE PATH
4 DALES PATH
5 SADDLERS PATH

Memorial Sp Ctr

Windmill (dis)

5

Pav

Tenn Cts

Sp Gd Pav

BARNET LA

Tenn Cts

BOREHAMWOOD

WD6

ELSTREE PK

GREENLANDS

Stirling Cnr

Tenn Cts

Barnet Gate

BARNET RD

95

London Loop

PH

ARKLEY PK

Scratch Wood

Hyver Hall

Hyver Farm

Barnet Gate Wood

B552

Scratchwood Open Space

Nature Trail

HYVER HILL

Hyver Hall

4

THORP CL

Thistle Wood

Moat Mount Open Space

12

Mill Hill

NW7

Mote End Farm

3

London Loop

94

B552

London Gateway Service Area

Dean's Brook

Nut Wood

Nan Clark's La

Hemmings Wood

Tenn Cts

Motel

Stoney Wood Lake

Mill Hill Cty High Sch

CROWN CL

A5109

2

Fairway Prim Sch

CH

Highwood House 135

Highwood Hill

Northway Sch

FAIRWAY CT

Sch

Pl Fld

HIGHWOOD HILL

B552

HIGHWOOD HILL

EDGWARE

THE LINCOLNS

LAWRENCE GDNS

Stoneyfields Park

THE FAIRWAY

LALEHAM AVE

COURTLAND AVE

ROBIN CL

STOCKTON GDNS

NORBURY GR

GLENWOOD RD

ABBEY VIEW

HORNBEAM CL

LAWRENCE GREEN

1

WESTMERE DR

NORTH DENE

WESTFIELD RD

MARSH LA

MARSH LA

Allot Gdns

THE REDDINGS

MIDDLE DENE

CROFT CL

BRABOURNE HTS

AUSTELL GDNS

Allot Gdns

REDDINGS CL

SOUTH DENE

Lawrence Green

Tenn Cts

93

A **B** Apex Cnr **C** **D** 22

EDGWARE WAY (WATFORD BY-PASS)

A41 Northway

21 27

NW7

St Joseph's Coll

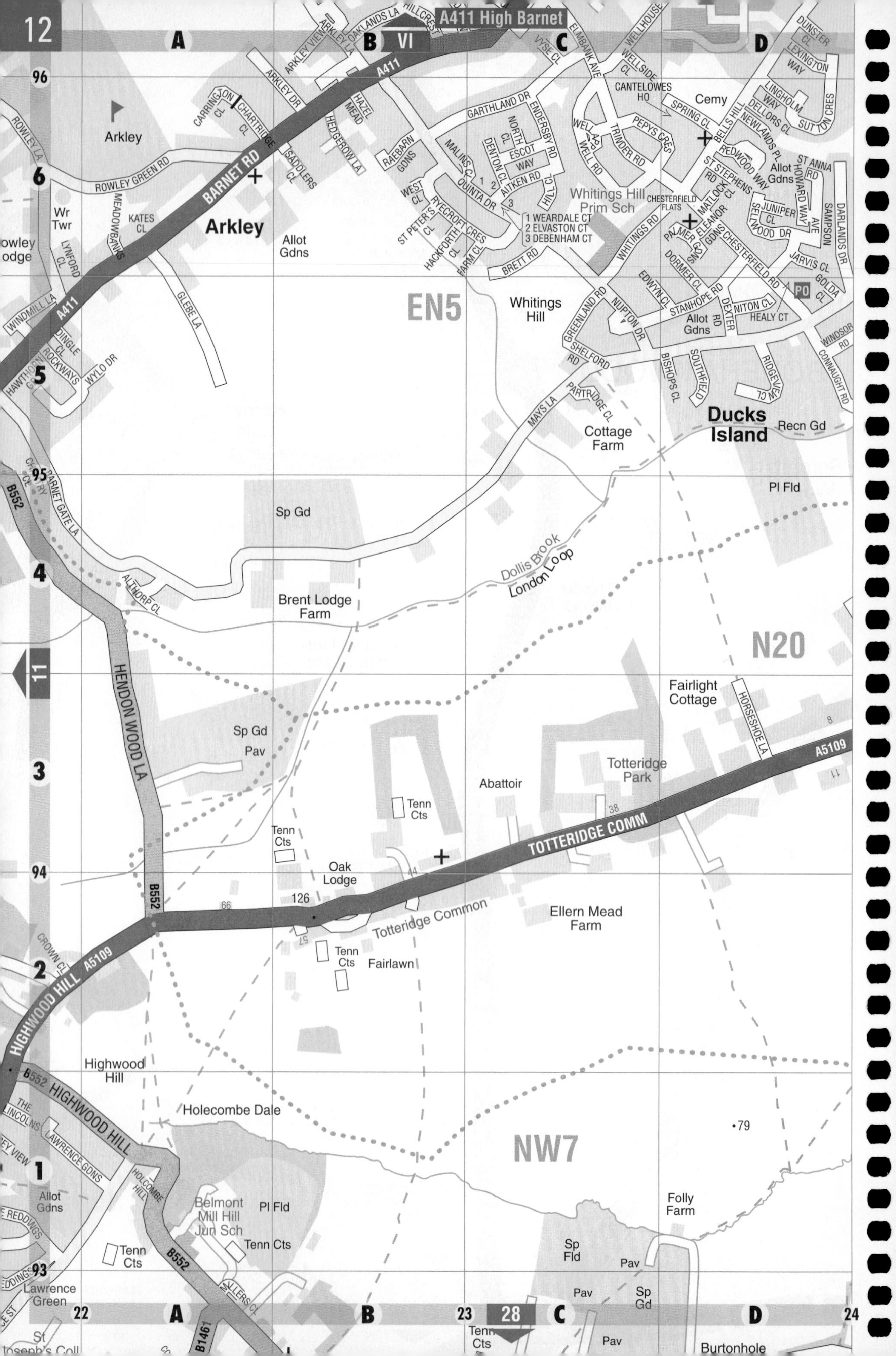
A411 High Barnet
Arkley
Arkley
Barnet Rd
Rowley Green Rd
Allot Gdns
Whitings Hill
Whitings Hill Prim Sch
Cemy
EN5
Ducks Island
Recn Gd
Cottage Farm
Pl Fld
Sp Gd
Brent Lodge Farm
Dollis Brook
London Loop
N20
Fairlight Cottage
Hendon Wood La
Sp Gd
Pav
Totteridge Park
Abattoir
Totteridge Comm
Tenn Cts
Oak Lodge
Totteridge Common
Ellern Mead Farm
Fairlawn
Highwood Hill
Holecombe Dale
NW7
Belmont Mill Hill Jun Sch
Pl Fld
Folly Farm
Lawrence Green
Burtonhole

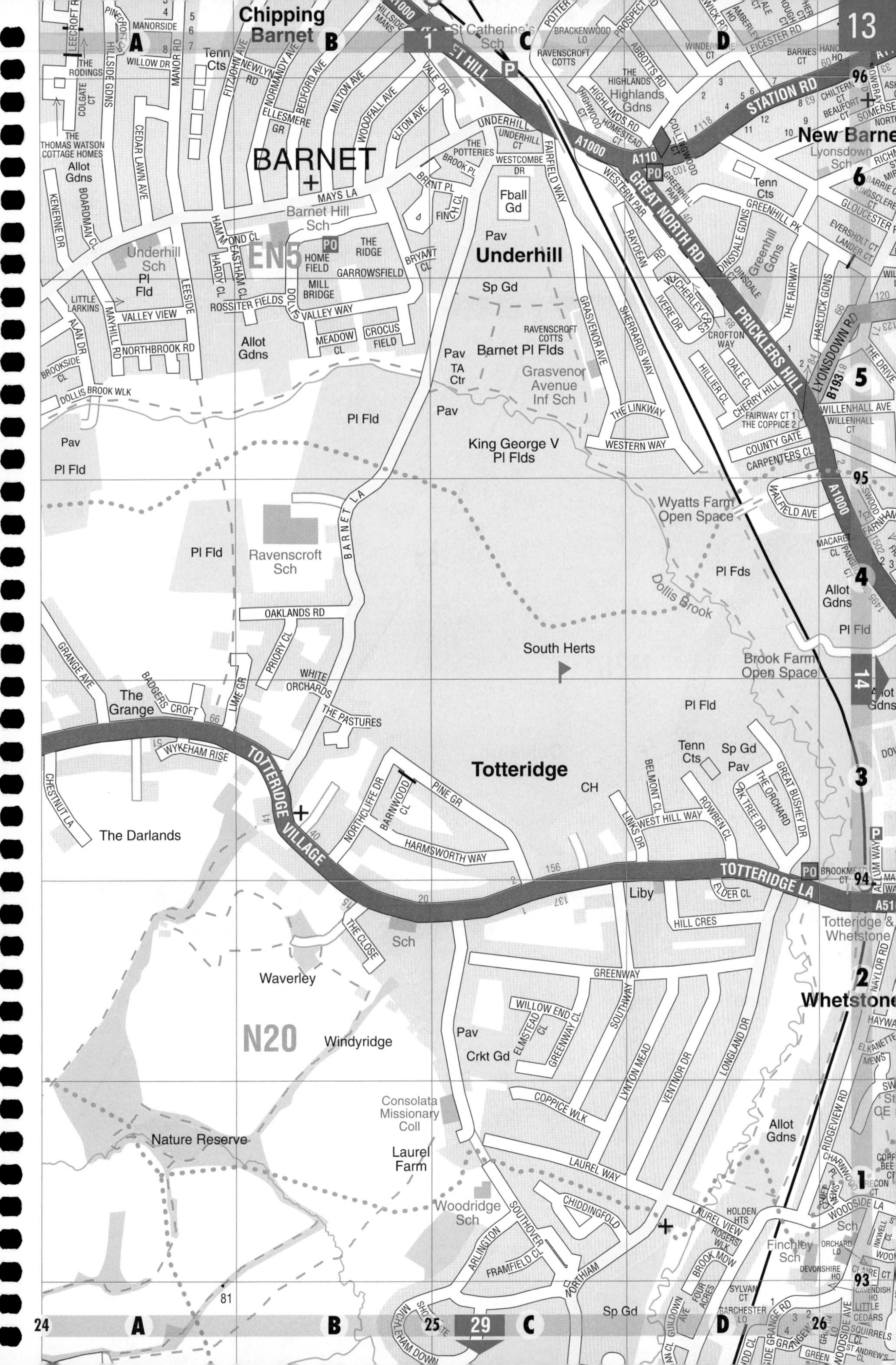
Chipping Barnet
A
B
C
D
1
St Catherine's Sch
BARNET
EN5
Underhill
Barnet Hill Sch
Underhill Sch
Pl Fld
Allot Gdns
MAYS LA
MANORSIDE
WILLOW DR
MANOR RD
FITZJOHN AVE
NEWLYN RD
NORMANDY AVE
BEDFORD AVE
MILTON AVE
WOODFALL AVE
ELTON AVE
VALE DR
ELLESMERE GR
UNDERHILL
WESTCOMBE DR
THE POTTERIES
BROOK PL
BRENT PL
FINCH CL
FAIRFIELD WAY
Fball Gd
Pav
Sp Gd
THE RODINGS
COLGATE CT
HILLSIDE GDNS
CEDAR LAWN AVE
THE THOMAS WATSON COTTAGE HOMES
KENERNE DR
BOARDMAN CL
LEECROFT RD
PINECROFT
Tenn Cts
HOME FIELD
THE RIDGE
GARROWSFIELD
BRYANT CL
MILL BRIDGE
ROSSITER FIELDS
DOLLIS VALLEY WAY
MEADOW CL
CROCUS FIELD
HAMMOND CL
HARDY CL
EASTHAM CL
LEESIDE
LITTLE LARKINS
MAYHILL RD
VALLEY VIEW
NORTHBROOK RD
ALAN DR
BROOKSIDE CL
DOLLIS BROOK WLK
RAVENSCROFT COTTS
Barnet Pl Flds
Grasvenor Avenue Inf Sch
TA Ctr
King George V Pl Flds
GRASVENOR AVE
SHERRARDS WAY
THE LINKWAY
WESTERN WAY
Highlands Gdns
THE HIGHLANDS
HIGHLANDS RD
HIGHWOOD CT
HOMESTEAD CT
ABBOTTS RD
PROSPECT RD
BRACKENWOOD LO
RAVENSCROFT COTTS
POTTERS RD
WINDERMERE CT
LEICESTER RD
STATION RD
A1000
A110
GREAT NORTH RD
PRICKLERS HILL
COLLINGWOOD CT
GREENHILL PAR
WESTERN PAR
RAYDEAN RD
IVERE DR
WYCHERLEY CR
CROFTON WAY
HILLIER CL
DALE CL
CHERRY HILL
FAIRWAY CT
THE COPPICE
COUNTY GATE
CARPENTERS CL
WILLENHALL AVE
WILLENHALL CT
LYONSDOWN RD
HASLUCK GDNS
THE FAIRWAY
DINSDALE GDNS
Greenhill Gdns
GREENHILL PK
GLOUCESTER RD
EVERSHOLT CT
LANDER CT
BARNES CT
CHILTERN CT
BEAUFORT CT
New Barnet
Lyonsdown Sch
THE DRIVE
B193
Wyatts Farm Open Space
WALFIELD AVE
MACARET CL
Pl Fds
Dollis Brook
Allot Gdns
Pl Fld
Brook Farm Open Space
14
Ravenscroft Sch
BARNET LA
OAKLANDS RD
PRIORY CL
WHITE ORCHARDS
THE PASTURES
South Herts
GRANGE AVE
The Grange
BADGERS CROFT
LIME GR
WYKEHAM RISE
TOTTERIDGE VILLAGE
CHESTNUT LA
The Darlands
Totteridge
CH
NORTHCLIFFE DR
BARNWOOD CL
PINE GR
HARMSWORTH WAY
LINKS DR
BELMONT CL
WEST HILL WAY
ROWBEN CL
OAK TREE DR
THE ORCHARD
GREAT BUSHEY DR
Tenn Cts
Sp Gd
Pav
TOTTERIDGE LA
A5109
BROOKMEAD CT
ALLUM WAY
Liby
ELDER CL
HILL CRES
Totteridge & Whetstone
Whetstone
NAYLOR RD
THE CLOSE
Sch
Waverley
N20
Windyridge
GREENWAY
SOUTHWAY
WILLOW END CL
ELMSTEAD CL
GREENWAY CL
Pav
Crkt Gd
COPPICE WLK
LYNTON MEAD
VENTNOR DR
LONGLAND DR
Consolata Missionary Coll
Laurel Farm
Nature Reserve
LAUREL WAY
Allot Gdns
RIDGEVIEW RD
CHIDDINGFOLD
Woodridge Sch
SOUTHOVER
ARLINGTON
FRAMFIELD CL
NORTHIAM
LAUREL VIEW
HOLDEN HTS
ROGERS WLK
BROOK MDW
FOUR ACRES
SYLVAN CT
BARCHESTER LO
Finchley Sch
ORCHARD LO
DEVONSHIRE HO
WOODSIDE LA
WOODSIDE AVE
CAVENDISH HO
LITTLE CEDARS
SQUIRRELS CL
ST ANDREWS CL
GREEN
GUILDOWN AVE
MICHLEHAM DOWN
Sp Gd
24
25
29
26
96
95
94
93
6
5
4
3
2
1

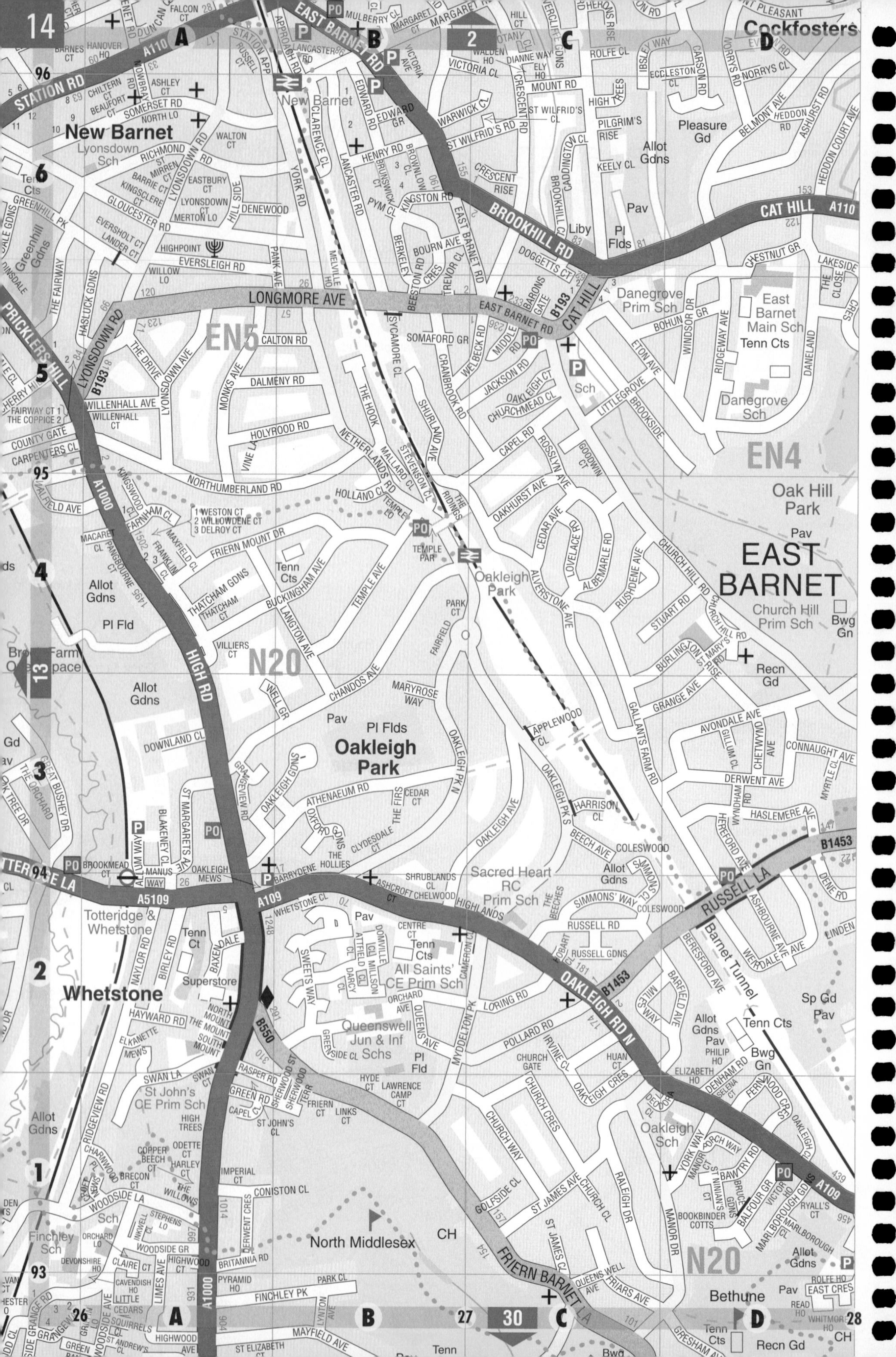

14
A
B
C
D
2
Cockfosters
New Barnet
STATION RD
EAST BARNET RD
A110
FALCON CT
DUNCAN CT
MULBERRY CL
MARGARET CT
MARGARET RD
HILL CT
HERONS RISE
MOUNT PLEASANT
BARNES CT
HANOVER HO
STATION APP
RUSSELL CT
APPROACH RD
LANCASTER RD
VICTORIA AVE
VICTORIA CL
WALDEN HO
DIANNE WAY
ELY HO
ISLEY WAY
ROLFE CL
ECCLESTON CL
CARSON RD
MORRYS RD
NORRYS CL
CHILTERN CT
MOWBRAY RD
ASHLEY CT
BEAUFORT CT
SOMERSET RD
NORTH LO
CLARENCE CL
EDWARD RD
EDWARD GR
MOUNT RD
HIGH TREES
ST WILFRID'S CL
PILGRIM'S RISE
Pleasure Gd
BELMONT AVE
HEDDON CL
HEDDON RD
ASHURST RD
HEDDON COURT AVE
WALTON CT
Lyonsdown Sch
RICHMOND CT
ST MIRREN CT
BARRIE CT
KINGSCLERE CT
EASTBURY CT
LYONSDOWN RD
HENRY RD
BROWNLOW RD
WARWICK CL
ST WILFRID'S RD
CADDINGTON CL
Allot Gdns
KEELY CL
CRESCENT RISE
CRESCENT RD
Tenn Cts
GREENHILL PK
GLOUCESTER RD
LYONSDOWN CT
MERTON LO
DENEWOOD
HILL SIDE
YORK RD
BRUNSWICK
PYM CL
KINGSTON RD
BROOKHILL RD
BROOKHILL CL
Pav
CAT HILL
Greenhill Gdns
EVERSHOLT CT
LANDER CT
HIGHPOINT
EVERSLEIGH RD
WILLOW LO
PARK AVE
MELVILLE HO
BERKELEY
BEESTON RD
BOURN AVE
TREVOR CL
Liby
Pl Flds
DOGGETTS CT
CHESTNUT GR
LAKESIDE
THE CLOSE
PRICKLERS HILL
THE FAIRWAY
HASLUCK GDNS
LONGMORE AVE
SYCAMORE CL
EAST BARNET RD
BARONS GATE
B193
Danegrove Prim Sch
BOHUN GR
WINDSOR DR
RIDGEWAY AVE
East Barnet Main Sch
LYONSDOWN RD
THE DRIVE
LYONSDOWN AVE
EN5
CALTON RD
DALMENY RD
MONKS AVE
SOMAFORD GR
WELBECK RD
MIDDLE
JACKSON RD
CRANBROOK RD
ETON AVE
DANELAND
LITTLEGROVE
BROOKSIDE
Sch
Danegrove Sch
WILLENHALL AVE
WILLENHALL CT
FAIRWAY CT
THE COPPICE
COUNTY GATE
CARPENTERS CL
HOLYROOD RD
VINE LA
THE HOOK
NETHERLANDS RD
MALLARD CL
STEVENSON CL
SHURLAND AVE
OAKLEIGH CT
CHURCHMEAD CL
CAPEL RD
ROSSLYN AVE
GOODWIN CT
EN4
Oak Hill Park
NORTHUMBERLAND RD
HOLLAND CL
TEMPLE LO
THE RIDINGS
OAKHURST AVE
CEDAR AVE
LOVELACE RD
ALBEMARLE RD
RUSHDENE AVE
CHURCH HILL RD
KINGSWOOD
FAIRFIELD AVE
A1000
FARNHAM CL
WESTON CT
WILLOWDENE CT
DELROY CT
MACARET CL
PANGBOURNE
MAXFIELD CL
FRANKLIN CL
FRIERN MOUNT DR
Tenn Cts
TEMPLE PAR
Oakleigh Park
EAST BARNET
THATCHAM GDNS
THATCHAM CT
BUCKINGHAM AVE
TEMPLE AVE
ALVERSTONE AVE
STUART RD
Church Hill Prim Sch
Bwg Gn
Pl Fld
VILLIERS CT
LANGTON AVE
PARK CT
FAIRFIELD
N20
HIGH RD
13
Allot Gdns
WELL GR
CHANDOS AVE
MARYROSE WAY
BURLINGTON RISE
ST MARY'S RISE
Recn Gd
GRANGE AVE
GALLANTS FARM RD
Pl Flds
APPLEWOOD CL
AVONDALE AVE
GILLUM CL
CHETWYND AVE
CONNAUGHT AVE
DOWNLAND CL
Oakleigh Park
OAKLEIGH PK N
OAKLEIGH PK S
GREAT BUSHEY DR
THE ORCHARD
OAK TREE DR
OAKLEIGH GDNS
GRANVIEW RD
ATHENAEUM RD
THE FIRS
CEDAR CT
OXFORD GDNS
CLYDESDALE CT
THE HOLLIES
OAKLEIGH AVE
HARRISON CL
DERWENT AVE
WYNDHAM RD
MYRTLE CL
HASLEMERE AVE
B1453
BLAKENEY CL
ST MARGARETS AVE
ALLUM WAY
BROOKMEAD CT
MANUS WAY
OAKLEIGH MEWS
BARRYDENE
BEECH AVE
COLESWOOD
SIMMONS' CL
HEREFORD AVE
RUSSELL LA
DENE RD
TOTTERIDGE LA
A5109
A109
WHETSTONE CL
SHRUBLANDS CL
ASHCROFT CT
CHELWOOD
HIGHLANDS
Sacred Heart RC Prim Sch
THE BEECHES
SIMMONS' WAY
Allot Gdns
ASHBOURNE AVE
LINDEN
Totteridge & Whetstone
Tenn Ct
BAXENDALE
NAYLOR RD
BIRLEY RD
CENTRE CT
DOMVILLE CL
ATTFIELD CL
MILLSON CL
DARCY CL
SWEETS WAY
Tenn Cts
All Saints' CE Prim Sch
CAMERON CL
RUSSELL RD
HOBART CL
RUSSELL GDNS
Barnet Tunnel
BERESFORD AVE
WEARDALE AVE
Whetstone
Superstore
NORTH MOUNT
THE MOUNT
SOUTH MOUNT
HAYWARD RD
ELKANETTE MEWS
B550
ORCHARD AVE
QUEENS AVE
MYDDELTON PK
LORING RD
OAKLEIGH RD N
MILES WAY
BARFIELD AVE
Sp Gd
Pav
Allot Gdns
Tenn Cts
Queenswell Jun & Inf Schs
GREENSIDE CL
Pl Fld
POLLARD RD
IRVINE CL
CHURCH GATE
HUAN CT
PHILIP HO
ELIZABETH HO
DENHAM RD
SELENA CT
Bwg Gn
SWAN LA
SWAN CT
RASPER RD
SHERWOOD ST
SHERWOOD TERR
HYDE CT
LAWRENCE CAMP CT
OAKLEIGH CRES
FERNWOOD CRES
St John's CE Prim Sch
GREEN RD
CAPEL CT
ST JOHN'S CL
FRIERN CT
LINKS CT
CHURCH CRES
CHURCH WAY
Oakleigh Sch
DEAN CL
Allot Gdns
RIDGEVIEW RD
HIGH TREES
ODETTE CT
COPPER BEECH CT
HARLEY CT
IMPERIAL CT
CHARNWOOD
BRECON CT
THE WILLOWS
CONISTON CL
GOLFSIDE CL
ST JAMES AVE
CHURCH CL
RALEIGH DR
YORK WAY
MANOR CL
ORCHARD WAY
ST NINIAN'S CT
BAWTRY RD
BRUCE GDNS
BALFOUR GR
VICTOR
MARLBOROUGH GDNS
RYALL'S CT
A109
WOODSIDE LA
Sch
STEPHENS LO
INKWELL CL
WOODSIDE GR
DERWENT CRES
North Middlesex
CH
MANOR DR
BOOKBINDER COTTS
MARLBOROUGH
Finchley Sch
ORCHARD HO
DEVONSHIRE HO
CLAIRE CT
HIGHWOOD CT
BRITANNIA RD
ST JAMES CL
QUEENSWELL AVE
FRIARS AVE
N20
Allot Gdns
ROLFE HO
EAST CRES
CAVENDISH HO
LITTLE CEDARS
LIMES AVE
PYRAMID HO
PARK CL
FINCHLEY PK
FRIERN BARNET LA
Bethune
Pav
READ HO
WHITMORE HO
GRANGE RD
WOODSIDE AVE
SQUIRRELS
HIGHWOOD
LYNTON AVE
MAYFIELD AVE
ST ELIZABETH CT
Tenn
30
Tenn Cts
Recn Gd
CH
GRESHAM AVE
GREEN
ST ANDREW'S
26
27
28
93
94
95
96
1
2
3
4
5
6

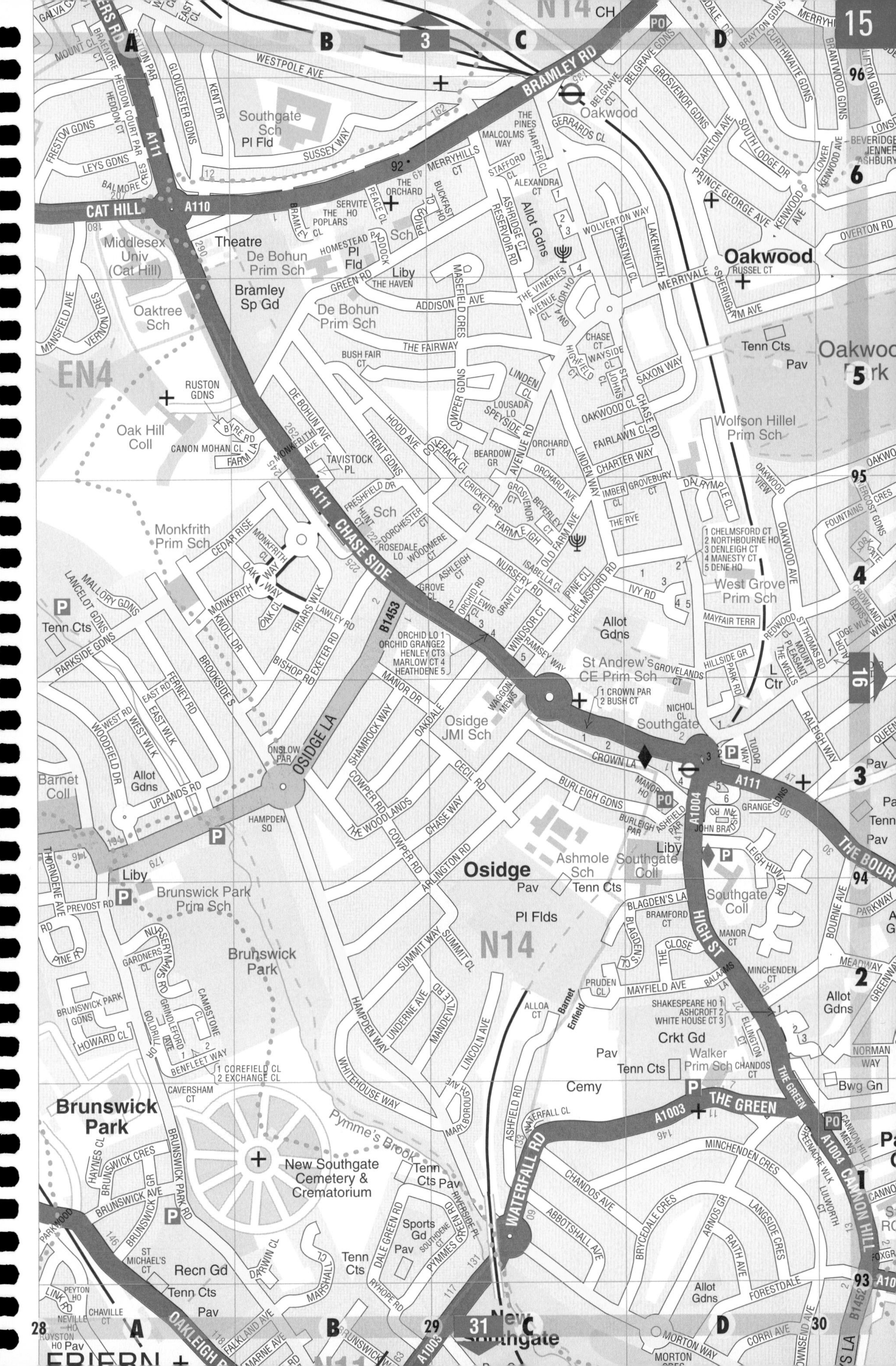

A
B
C
D
3
N14
BRAMLEY RD
WESTPOLE AVE
Southgate Sch
Pl Fld
Oakwood
CAT HILL
A110
A111
Middlesex Univ (Cat Hill)
Theatre
De Bohun Prim Sch
Bramley Sp Gd
Oaktree Sch
EN4
Oak Hill Coll
Oakwood
Oakwood Park
Tenn Cts
Pav
Wolfson Hillel Prim Sch
Monkfrith Prim Sch
CHASE SIDE
OSIDGE LA
B1453
West Grove Prim Sch
St Andrew's CE Prim Sch
Allot Gdns
Osidge JMI Sch
Southgate
Barnet Coll
Osidge
Ashmole Sch
Southgate Coll
Pl Flds
N14
Brunswick Park Prim Sch
Brunswick Park
HIGH ST
A1004
THE GREEN
A1003
Crkt Gd
Walker Prim Sch
Cemy
New Southgate Cemetery & Crematorium
Pymme's Brook
WATERFALL RD
CANNON HILL
Recn Gd
Sports Gd
Brunswick Park
OAKLEIGH
New Southgate
16
31

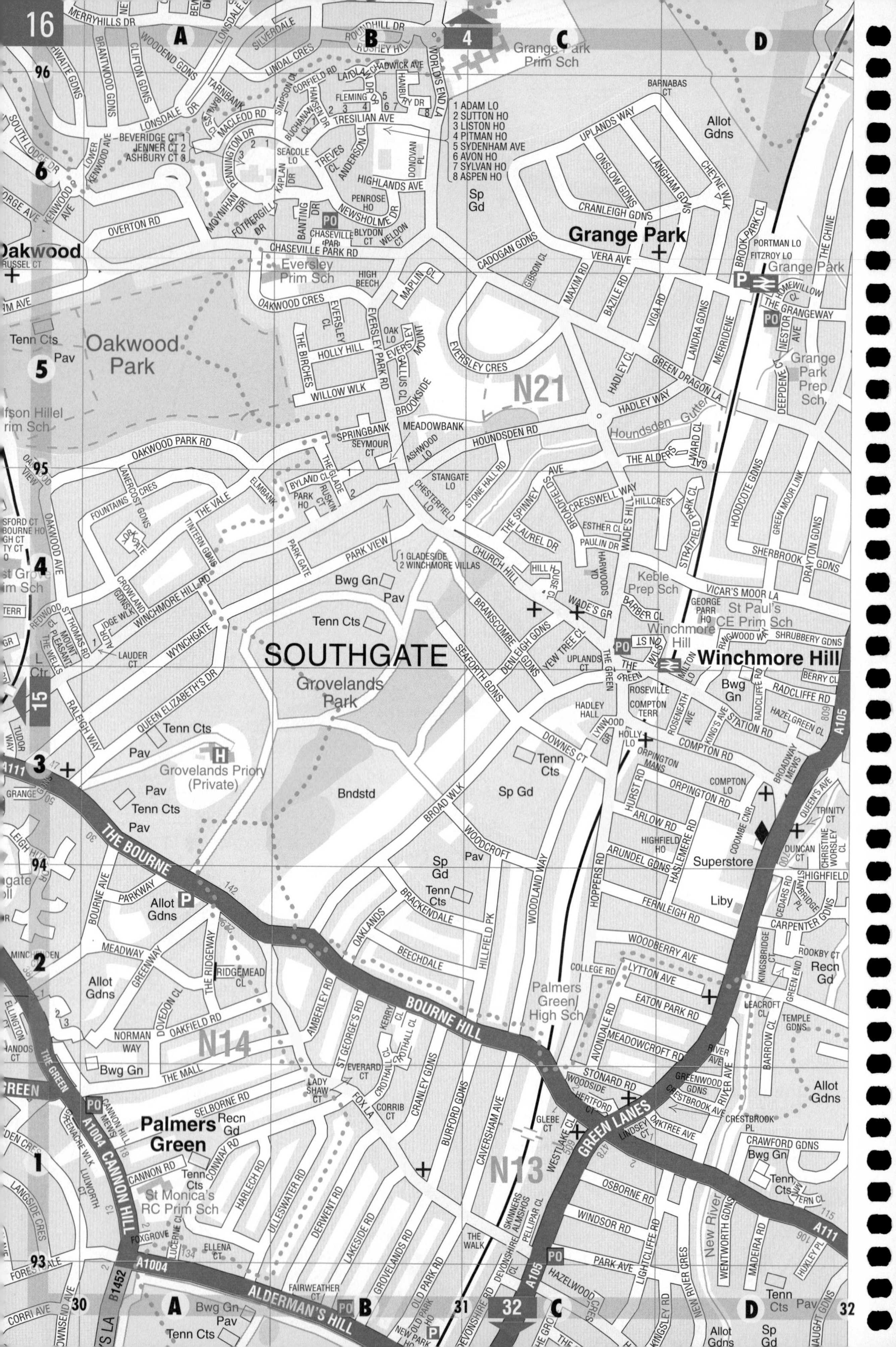

A
B
C
D
4
96
6
5
95
4
3
94
2
93
1
30
31
32
15
32
SOUTHGATE
Oakwood
Grange Park
Winchmore Hill
Palmers Green
N21
N14
N13
Oakwood Park
Grovelands Park
Grovelands Priory (Private)
Grange Park Prim Sch
Eversley Prim Sch
Grange Park Prep Sch
Keble Prep Sch
St Paul's CE Prim Sch
Palmers Green High Sch
St Monica's RC Prim Sch
Superstore
Liby
Allot Gdns
Tenn Cts
Pav
Bwg Gn
Sp Gd
Bndstd
Recn Gd
L Ctr
PO
1 ADAM LO
2 SUTTON HO
3 LISTON HO
4 PITMAN HO
5 SYDENHAM AVE
6 AVON HO
7 SYLVAN HO
8 ASPEN HO
1 GLADESIDE
2 WINCHMORE VILLAS
BEVERIDGE CT 1
JENNER CT 2
ASHBURY CT 3
MERRYHILLS DR
WOODEND GDNS
BRANTWOOD GDNS
CLIFTON GDNS
LONSDALE DR
SILVERDALE
LINDAL CRES
ROUNDHILL DR
RUSHEY HILL
WORLD'S END LA
CHADWICK AVE
CORFIELD RD
TRESILIAN AVE
MACLEOD RD
TARNBANK
PENNINGTON DR
SOUTH LODGE DR
KENWOOD AVE
OVERTON RD
MOYNIHAN DR
FOTHERGILL DR
KAPLAN DR
BANTING DR
SEACOLE LO
TREVES CL
ANDERSON CL
DONOVAN PL
HIGHLANDS AVE
PENROSE HO
NEWSHOLME DR
CHASEVILLE PARK RD
BLYDON CT
WELDON CT
HIGH BEECH
OAKWOOD CRES
EVERSLEY CL
EVERSLEY PARK RD
MAPLIN CL
HOLLY HILL
THE BIRCHES
WILLOW WLK
OAK LO
EVERSLEY MOUNT
GALLUS CL
BROOKSIDE
EVERSLEY CRES
CADOGAN GDNS
UPLANDS WAY
ONSLOW GDNS
LANGHAM GDNS
CHEYNE WLK
CRANLEIGH GDNS
BARNABAS CT
VERA AVE
GIBSON CL
MAXIM RD
BAZILE RD
VIGA RD
LANDRA GDNS
MERRIDENE
HADLEY CL
GREEN DRAGON LA
HADLEY WAY
BROOK PARK CL
PORTMAN LO
FITZROY LO
THE CHINE
HOMEWILLOW CL
THE GRANGEWAY
NESTOR AVE
DEEPDENE CT
Houndsden Gutter
HOUNDSDEN RD
OAKWOOD PARK RD
SPRINGBANK
SEYMOUR CT
MEADOWBANK
ASHWOOD LO
STANGATE LO
STONE HALL RD
THE ALDERS
WARD CL
CRESSWELL WAY
HILLCREST
BROADFIELDS AVE
THE SPINNEY
LAUREL DR
ESTHER CL
PAULIN DR
HARWOODS YD
WADE'S HILL
STRATFIELD PARK CL
HOODCOTE GDNS
GREEN MOOR LINK
DRAYTON GDNS
SHERBROOK GDNS
VICAR'S MOOR LA
LANERCOST GDNS
FOUNTAINS CRES
THE VALE
ELMBANK
BYLAND CL
THE GLADE
RUSKIN CT
PARK HO
CHESTERFIELD LO
CHURCH HILL
HILL HOUSE CL
TINTERN GDNS
PARK GATE
PARK VIEW
CROWLAND GDNS
WINCHMORE HILL RD
WYNCHGATE
REDWOOD CL
ST THOMAS RD
MOUNT PLEASANT
THE WELLS
LAUDER CT
QUEEN ELIZABETH'S DR
RALEIGH WAY
OAKWOOD AVE
BRANSCOMBE GDNS
SEAFORTH GDNS
DENLEIGH GDNS
YEW TREE CL
WADE'S GR
BARBER CL
UPLANDS CT
THE GREEN
ROSEVILLE
COMPTON TERR
HADLEY HALL
LYNWOOD GR
HOLLY LO
GEORGE PARR HO
Winchmore Hill
WILSON ST
MILTON LO
RINGWOOD WAY
SHRUBBERY GDNS
BERRY CL
RADCLIFFE RD
HAZELGREEN CL
STATION RD
KING'S AVE
ROSENEATH AVE
COMPTON RD
DOWNES CT
ORPINGTON MANS
ORPINGTON RD
COMPTON LO
HURST RD
ARLOW RD
HIGHFIELD HO
ARUNDEL GDNS
HASLEMERE RD
HOPPERS RD
COOMBE CNR
BROADWAY MEWS
QUEEN'S AVE
TRINITY CT
DUNCAN CT
CHRISTINE WORSLEY CL
HIGHFIELD
STANBRIDGE PL
CEDARS RD
FERNLEIGH RD
CARPENTER GDNS
WOODBERRY AVE
KINGSBRIDGE CT
GREEN END
ROOKBY CT
COLLEGE RD
LYTTON AVE
EATON PARK RD
LEACROFT CL
TEMPLE GDNS
BARROW CL
AVONDALE RD
MEADOWCROFT RD
RIVER AVE
GREENWOOD GDNS
CRESTBROOK AVE
CRESTBROOK PL
OAKTREE AVE
CRAWFORD GDNS
STONARD RD
WOODSIDE
HERTFORD CT
LINDSEY CT
GLEBE CT
WESTLAKE CL
GREEN LANES
OSBORNE RD
WINDSOR RD
PARK AVE
HAZELWOOD CRES
LIGHTCLIFFE RD
KINGSLEY RD
NEW RIVER CRES
New River
WENTWORTH GDNS
MADEIRA RD
HUXLEY PL
A111
A105
A1004
B1452
BROAD WLK
WOODCROFT
WOODLAND WAY
HILLFIELD PK
BRACKENDALE
BEECHDALE
OAKLANDS
AMBERLEY RD
ST GEORGE'S RD
KERRY CT
CROTHALL CL
EVERARD CT
LADY SHAW CT
FOX LA
CORRIB CT
CRANLEY GDNS
BURFORD GDNS
CAVERSHAM AVE
SKINNERS ALMSHOS
PELLIPAR CL
DEVONSHIRE CL
THE WALK
BOURNE HILL
THE BOURNE
BOURNE AVE
PARKWAY
MEADWAY
GREENWAY
THE RIDGEWAY
RIDGEMEAD CL
DOVEDON CL
OAKFIELD RD
NORMAN WAY
THE MALL
SELBORNE RD
CANNON HILL MEWS
CANNON HILL
CANNON RD
CONWAY RD
HARLECH RD
ULLESWATER RD
DERWENT RD
LAKESIDE RD
GROVELANDS RD
OLD PARK RD
FAIRWEATHER CT
ALDERMAN'S HILL
FOXGROVE
LUCERNE CL
ELLENA CT
GREENACRE WLK
LULWORTH CT
LANGSIDE CRES
FORESDALE
CORRI AVE
TOWNSEND AVE
ELLINGTON
THE GREEN
GREEN
MINCHENDEN
GRANGE GDNS
TUDOR WAY
Tenn Cts

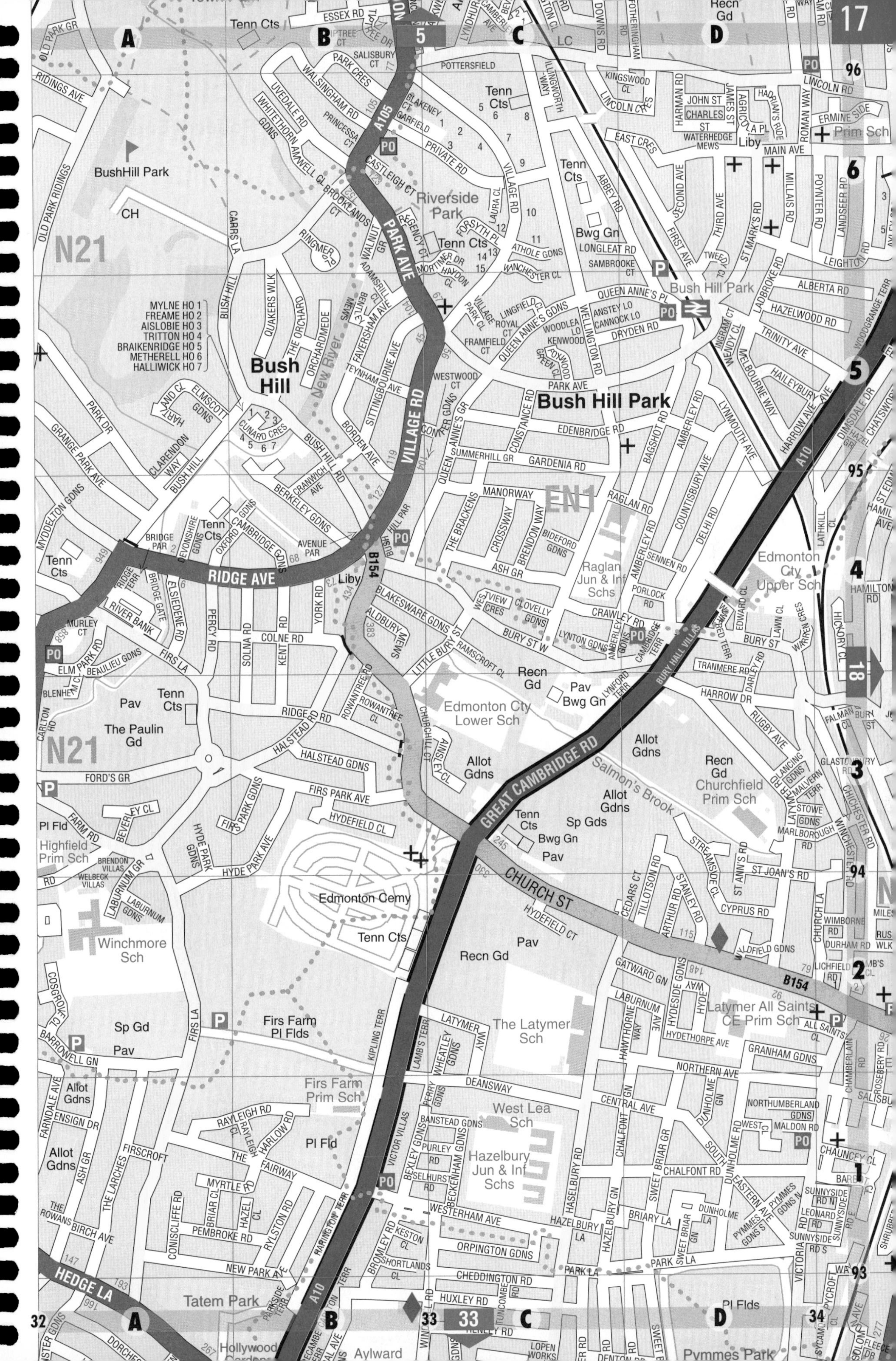
A
B
C
D
5
Tenn Cts
ESSEX RD
OLD PARK GR
RIDINGS AVE
SALISBURY CT
PARK CRES
WALSINGHAM RD
POTTERSFIELD
LC
DOWNS RD
FOTHERINGHAM
Recn Gd
96
KINGSWOOD CL
LINCOLN CRES
LINCOLN RD
HARMAN RD
JOHN ST
CHARLES ST
JAMES ST
AGRICOLA PL
HADRIAN'S RIDE
ROMAN WAY
ERMINE SIDE
Prim Sch
WATERHEDGE MEWS
Liby
MAIN AVE
EAST CRES
UVEDALE RD
WHITETHORN GDNS
PRINCESSA CT
BLAKENEY CT
GARFIELD CT
PRIVATE RD
A105
PO
ANNWELL CL
BROOKLANDS CT
CASTLEIGH CT
Riverside Park
VILLAGE RD
LAURA CL
ILLINGWORTH WAY
ABBEY RD
SECOND AVE
FIRST AVE
THIRD AVE
ST MARK'S RD
MILLAIS RD
POYNTER RD
LANDSEER RD
6
BushHill Park
CH
OLD PARK RIDINGS
N21
CARRS LA
RINGMER PL
WALNUT GR
REGENCY CT
FORSYTH PL
PARK AVE
Tenn Cts
ATHOLE GDNS
Bwg Gn
LONGLEAT RD
SAMBROOKE CT
WINCHESTER CL
MORTIMER DR
HAYDON CL
ADAMSRILL CL
TWEED CT
LEIGHTON RD
ALBERTA RD
LADBROKE RD
Bush Hill Park
P
QUEEN ANNE'S PL
ANSTEY LO
CANNOCK LO
DRYDEN RD
LINGFIELD CL
ROYAL CT
QUEEN ANNE'S GDNS
WOODLEA LO
KENWOOD
WELLINGTON RD
FOXWOOD GREEN CL
FRAMFIELD CT
VILLAGE PARK CL
HAZELWOOD RD
TRINITY AVE
WOODGRANGE TERR
INGRAM CT
WENDY CL
MELBOURNE WAY
HAILEYBURY AVE
HARROW AVE
DIMSDALE DR
CHATSWORTH
MYLNE HO 1
FREAME HO 2
AISLOBIE HO 3
TRITTON HO 4
BRAIKENRIDGE HO 5
METHERELL HO 6
HALLIWICK HO 7
BUSH HILL
QUAKERS WLK
THE ORCHARD
ORCHARDMEDE
MEWS
BENTLEY
FAVERSHAM AVE
TEYNHAM AVE
New River
Bush Hill
SITTINGBOURNE AVE
WESTWOOD CT
PARK AVE
Bush Hill Park
CONSTANCE RD
EDENBRIDGE RD
BAGSHOT RD
AMBERLEY RD
LYNMOUTH AVE
HARTLAND CL
ELMSCOTT GDNS
PARK DR
CUNARD CRES
BORDEN AVE
VILLAGE RD
COWPER GDNS
QUEEN ANNE'S GR
SUMMERHILL GR
GARDENIA RD
COUNTISBURY AVE
A10
95
GRANGE PARK AVE
CLARENDON WAY
BUSH HILL
BUSH HILL RD
CRANWICH AVE
BERKELEY GDNS
MANORWAY
EN1
RAGLAN RD
DELHI RD
LATHKILL CL
HAMILTON AVE
MYDDELTON GDNS
Tenn Cts
BRIDGE PAR
DEVONSHIRE GDNS
OXFORD GDNS
CAMBRIDGE GDNS
AVENUE PAR
BUSH HILL PAR
THE BRACKENS
CROSSWAY
BRENDON WAY
BIDEFORD GDNS
AMBERLEY RD
SENNEN RD
Edmonton Cty Upper Sch
4
HAMILTON RD
949
RIDGE AVE
RIDGE TERR
BRIDGE GATE
ELSIEDENE RD
PERCY RD
YORK RD
B154
Liby
ASH GR
Raglan Jun & Inf Schs
PORLOCK RD
EDWARD CL
LAWN CL
WARREN CRES
HICKORY CL
MURLEY CT
RIVER BANK
SOLNA RD
KENT RD
COLNE RD
BLAKESWARE GDNS
WESTVIEW CRES
CLOVELLY GDNS
CRAWLEY RD
LYNTON GDNS
CAMBRIDGE TERR
BURY ST W
BURY ST
PO
ELM PARK RD
BEAULIEU GDNS
FIRS LA
ALDBURY MEWS
LITTLE BURY ST
RAMSCROFT CL
Recn Gd
Pav
Bwg Gn
LYNFORD TERR
BURY HALL VILLAS
TRANMERE RD
DARLEY RD
18
BLENHEIM CL
Pav
Tenn Cts
The Paulin Gd
CARLTON HO
RIDGE RD
ROWANTREE RD
ROWANTREE CL
CHURCHILL CT
Edmonton Cty Lower Sch
HARROW DR
RUGBY AVE
FALMAN CL
BURY ST
N21
HALSTEAD RD
HALSTEAD GDNS
AINSLEY CL
Allot Gdns
GREAT CAMBRIDGE RD
Allot Gdns
Recn Gd
Churchfield Prim Sch
Salmon's Brook
LANCING GDNS
MALVERN TERR
GLASTONBURY RD
3
P
FORD'S GR
FIRS PARK AVE
FIRS PARK GDNS
HYDEFIELD CL
Allot Gdns
Sp Gds
Tenn Cts
Bwg Gn
Pav
LATYMER RD
STOWE GDNS
MARLBOROUGH RD
CHICHESTER RD
WINCHESTER RD
Pl Fld
FARM RD
BEVERLEY CL
Highfield Prim Sch
BRENDON VILLAS
WELBECK VILLAS
LABURNUM GR
HYDE PARK GDNS
HYDE PARK AVE
Edmonton Cemy
245
CHURCH ST
STREAMSIDE CL
ST ANN'S RD
ST JOAN'S RD
94
LABURNUM GDNS
Winchmore Sch
Tenn Cts
HYDEFIELD CT
CEDARS CT
TILLOTSON RD
ARTHUR RD
STANLEY RD
CYPRUS RD
CHURCH LA
WIMBORNE RD
DURHAM RD
MILES
Pav
Recn Gd
115
WILDFIELD GDNS
LAMB'S CL
GATWARD GN
HYDESIDE GDNS
HYDE WAY
LICHFIELD RD
2
COSGROVE CL
B154
Latymer All Saints CE Prim Sch
P
ALL SAINTS' CL
Sp Gd
Pav
FIRS LA
P
Firs Farm Pl Flds
KIPLING TERR
LAMB'S TERR
WHEATLEY GDNS
LATYMER WAY
The Latymer Sch
HAWTHORNE WAY
LABURNUM AVE
HYDETHORPE AVE
GRANHAM GDNS
CHAMBERLAIN RD
ROSEBERY RD
SALISBURY
BARROWELL GN
Allot Gdns
FARNDALE AVE
ENSIGN DR
Firs Farm Prim Sch
DEANSWAY
West Lea Sch
CENTRAL AVE
NORTHERN AVE
NORTHUMBERLAND GDNS
WEST CL
MALDON RD
Allot Gdns
ASH GR
THE LARCHES
FIRSCROFT
RAYLEIGH RD
RAYLEIGH CL
HARLOW RD
THE FAIRWAY
Pl Fld
PERRY GDNS
BANSTEAD GDNS
PURLEY RD
BEXLEY GDNS
Hazelbury Jun & Inf Schs
HASELBURY RD
CHALFONT
SWEET BRIAR GR
DUNHOLME GN
DUNHOLME RD
CHALFONT RD
SOUTH EASTERN AVE
PO
CHAUNCEY CL
1
MYRTLE RD
CONISCLIFFE RD
BRIAR CL
HAZEL CL
RYLSTON RD
VICTOR VILLAS
PO
SELHURST RD
BECKENHAM GDNS
WESTERHAM AVE
HAZELBURY LA
HAZELBURY GN
BRIARY LA
DUNHOLME LA
PYMMES GDNS N
PYMMES GDNS S
SUNNYSIDE RD N
LEONARD RD
SUNNYSIDE RD E
SUNNYSIDE RD S
BARBOT CL
THE ROWANS
BIRCH AVE
PEMBROKE RD
HARINGTON TERR
BROMLEY RD
KESTON CL
ORPINGTON GDNS
SWEET BRIAR GN
PARK LA
VICTORIA RD
147
HEDGE LA
193
NEW PARK AVE
SHORTLANDS CL
CHEDDINGTON RD
PARK LA
PYCROFT WAY
93
Tatem Park
PARKSIDE TERR
A10
HUXLEY RD
TUNCOMBE RD
Pl Flds
32
A
B
33
33
C
D
34
Hollywood Gardens
Aylward
HENLEY RD
LOPEN WORKS
DENTON RD
Pymmes Park
SYCAMORE
SOLOMON AVE
FLEECE DR

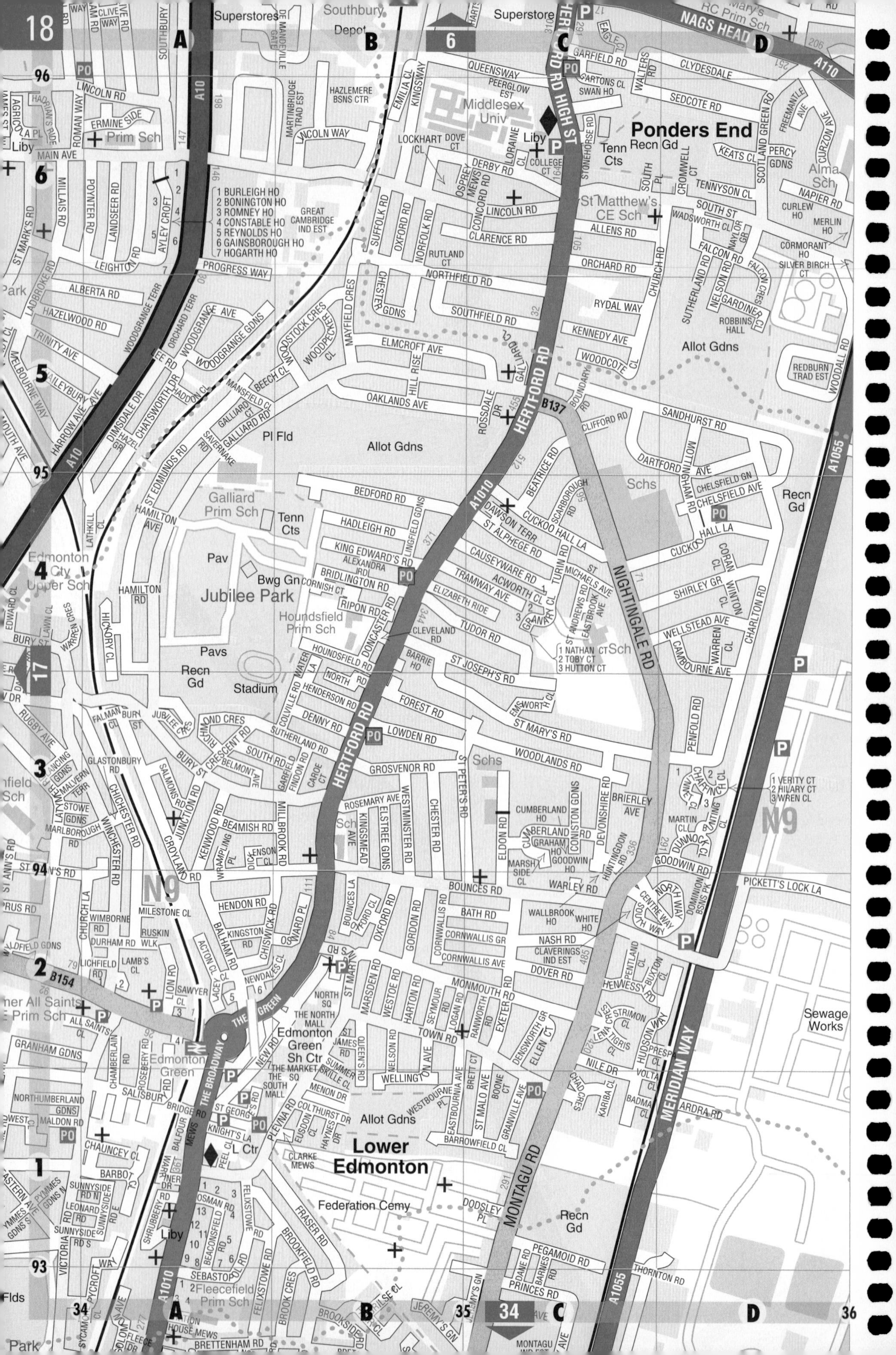

Ponders End
Lower Edmonton
Middlesex Univ
Jubilee Park
Edmonton Green Sh Ctr
Federation Cemy
Sewage Works
Allot Gdns
Recn Gd
Galliard Prim Sch
Houndsfield Prim Sch
St Matthew's CE Sch
Fleecefield Prim Sch
Edmonton City Upper Sch
Edmonton Green
Stadium
Bwg Gn
Tenn Cts
Pav
Pl Fld
Schs
Superstores
Superstore
Southbury Depot
Hazlemere Bsns Ctr
Great Cambridge Ind Est
Martinbridge Trad Est
Redburn Trad Est
Claverings Ind Est
Dominion Bsns Pk
HERTFORD RD
HERTFORD RD HIGH ST
NIGHTINGALE RD
MONTAGU RD
MERIDIAN WAY
NAGS HEAD RD
THE BROADWAY
SOUTHBURY RD
LINCOLN RD
QUEENSWAY
CLYDESDALE
SEDCOTE RD
GARFIELD RD
ORCHARD RD
NORTHFIELD RD
SOUTHFIELD RD
ELMCROFT AVE
OAKLANDS AVE
SANDHURST RD
BEDFORD RD
HADLEIGH RD
KING EDWARD'S RD
CUCKOO HALL LA
ST MARY'S RD
WOODLANDS RD
GROSVENOR RD
BOUNCES RD
PICKETT'S LOCK LA
GOODWIN RD
NILE DR
ARDRA RD
PEGAMOID RD
PRINCES RD
THORNTON RD
PROGRESS WAY
ALBERTA RD
HAZELWOOD RD
ST EDMUNDS RD
LOWDEN RD
FOREST RD
TUDOR RD
ST JOSEPH'S RD
1 BURLEIGH HO
2 BONINGTON HO
3 ROMNEY HO
4 CONSTABLE HO
5 REYNOLDS HO
6 GAINSBOROUGH HO
7 HOGARTH HO
1 NATHAN CT
2 TOBY CT
3 HUTTON CT
1 VERITY CT
2 HILARY CT
3 WREN CL
A10
A1010
A1055
A110
B137
B154
N9
6
17
34
A
B
C
D
96
95
94
93
35
36

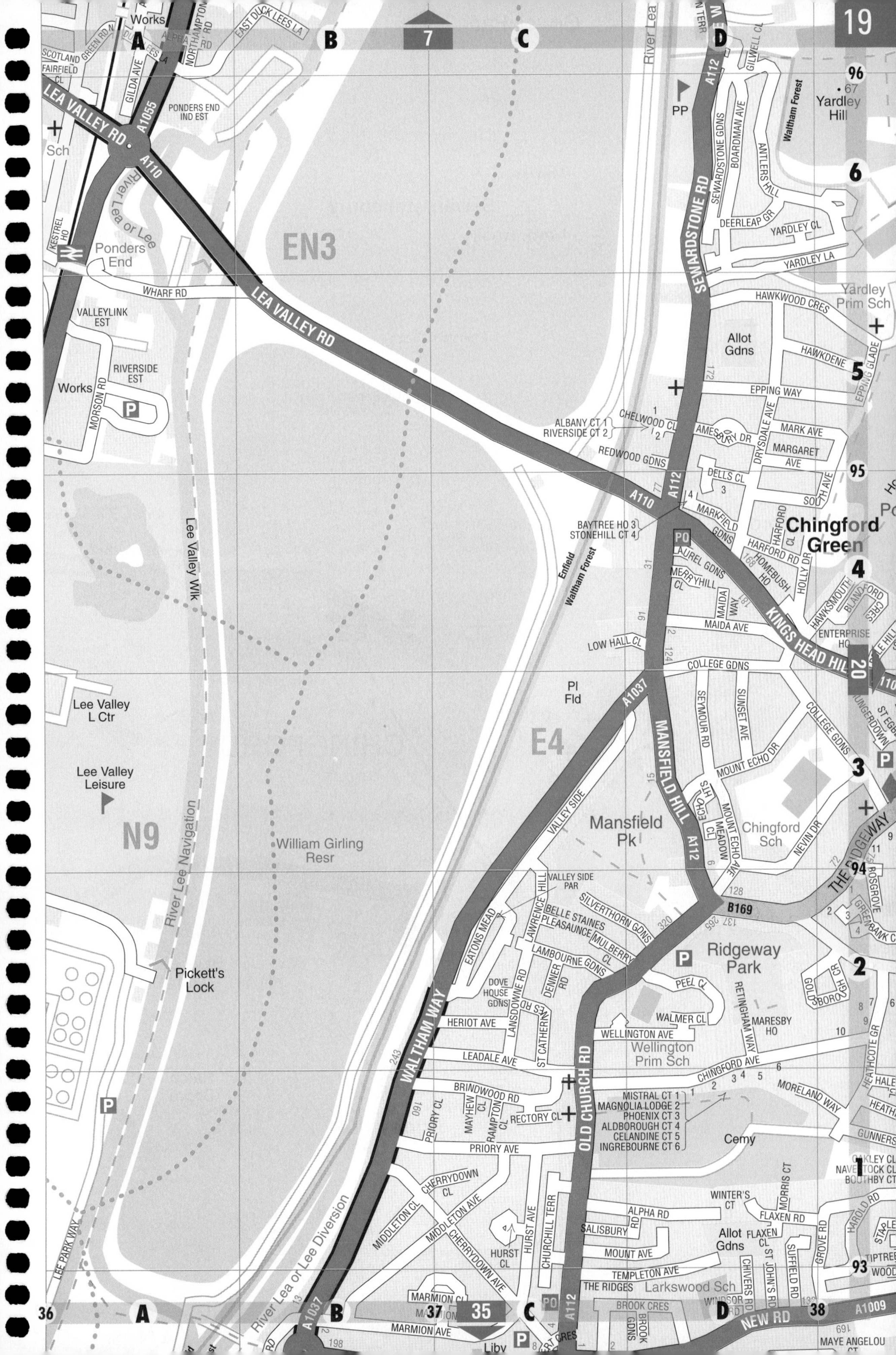

A
B
7
C
D
Works
PONDERS END IND EST
EAST DUCK LEES LA
NORTHAMPTON RD
GILDA AVE
SCOTLAND GREEN RD N
FAIRFIELD CL
LEA VALLEY RD
A1055
A110
Sch
River Lea or Lee
KESTREL HO
Ponders End
WHARF RD
VALLEYLINK EST
RIVERSIDE EST
Works
MORSON RD
EN3
LEA VALLEY RD
River Lea
PP
SEWARDSTONE RD
A112
SEWARDSTONE GDNS
BOARDMAN AVE
GILWELL CL
ANTLERS HILL
DEERLEAP GR
YARDLEY CL
YARDLEY LA
Waltham Forest
96
67
Yardley Hill
6
Yardley Prim Sch
HAWKWOOD CRES
HAWKDENE
Allot Gdns
5
EPPING GLADE
EPPING WAY
ALBANY CT 1
RIVERSIDE CT 2
CHELWOOD CL
AMESBURY DR
DRYSDALE AVE
MARK AVE
MARGARET AVE
REDWOOD GDNS
DELLS CL
SOUTH AVE
95
A110
BAYTREE HO 3
STONEHILL CT 4
MARKFIELD GDNS
Chingford Green
HARFORD CL
HARFORD RD
HOMEBUSH HO
HOLLY DR
PO
LAUREL GDNS
MERRYHILL CL
MAIDA WAY
Enfield
Waltham Forest
4
HAWKSMOUTH
BLANDFORD CRES
KINGS HEAD HILL
MAIDA AVE
ENTERPRISE HO
LOW HALL CL
COLLEGE GDNS
20
Pl Fld
A1037
SEYMOUR RD
SUNSET AVE
COLLEGE GDNS
HUNGERDOWN
MANSFIELD HILL
MOUNT ECHO DR
E4
3
P
Lee Valley L Ctr
Lee Valley Leisure
Lee Valley Wlk
ECHO HTS
ECHO CL
MEADOW CL
MOUNT ECHO AVE
Chingford Sch
NEVIN DR
THE RIDGEWAY
Mansfield Pk
VALLEY SIDE
N9
William Girling Resr
River Lee Navigation
A112
VALLEY SIDE PAR
94
ROSGROVE
SILVERTHORN GDNS
BELLE STAINES PLEASAUNCE
MULBERRY CL
B169
GREENBANK C
EATONS MEAD
LAWRENCE HILL
LAMBOURNE GDNS
Ridgeway Park
P
2
Pickett's Lock
DOVE HOUSE GDNS
LANSDOWNE RD
DENNER RD
PEEL CL
GOLDSBOROUGH CR
WALTHAM WAY
HERIOT AVE
ST CATHERINES RD
WALMER CL
RETINGHAM WAY
MARESBY HO
WELLINGTON AVE
Wellington Prim Sch
HEATHCOTE GR
LEADALE AVE
CHINGFORD AVE
OLD CHURCH RD
BRINDWOOD RD
MISTRAL CT 1
MAGNOLIA LODGE 2
PHOENIX CT 3
ALDBOROUGH CT 4
CELANDINE CT 5
INGREBOURNE CT 6
MORELAND WAY
PRIORY CL
MAYHEW CL
RAMPTON CL
RECTORY CL
P
Cemy
GUNNERS
PRIORY AVE
OAKLEY CL
NAVESTOCK CL
BOOTHBY CT
1
CHERRYDOWN CL
MIDDLETON CL
MIDDLETON AVE
CHERRYDOWN AVE
CHURCHILL TERR
HURST AVE
HURST CL
MORRIS CT
WINTER'S CT
FLAXEN RD
HAROLD RD
ALPHA RD
SALISBURY RD
Allot Gdns
FLAXEN CL
ST JOHN'S RD
SUFFIELD RD
GROVE RD
MOUNT AVE
93
River Lea or Lee Diversion
LEE PARK WAY
TEMPLETON AVE
THE RIDGES
Larkswood Sch
CHIVERS RD
WINDSOR RD
MARMION CL
36
A
A1037
B
37
35
C
PO
A112
BROOK CRES
D
NEW RD
38
A1009
MARMION AVE
P
Liby
BROOK GDNS
MAYE ANGELOU CT

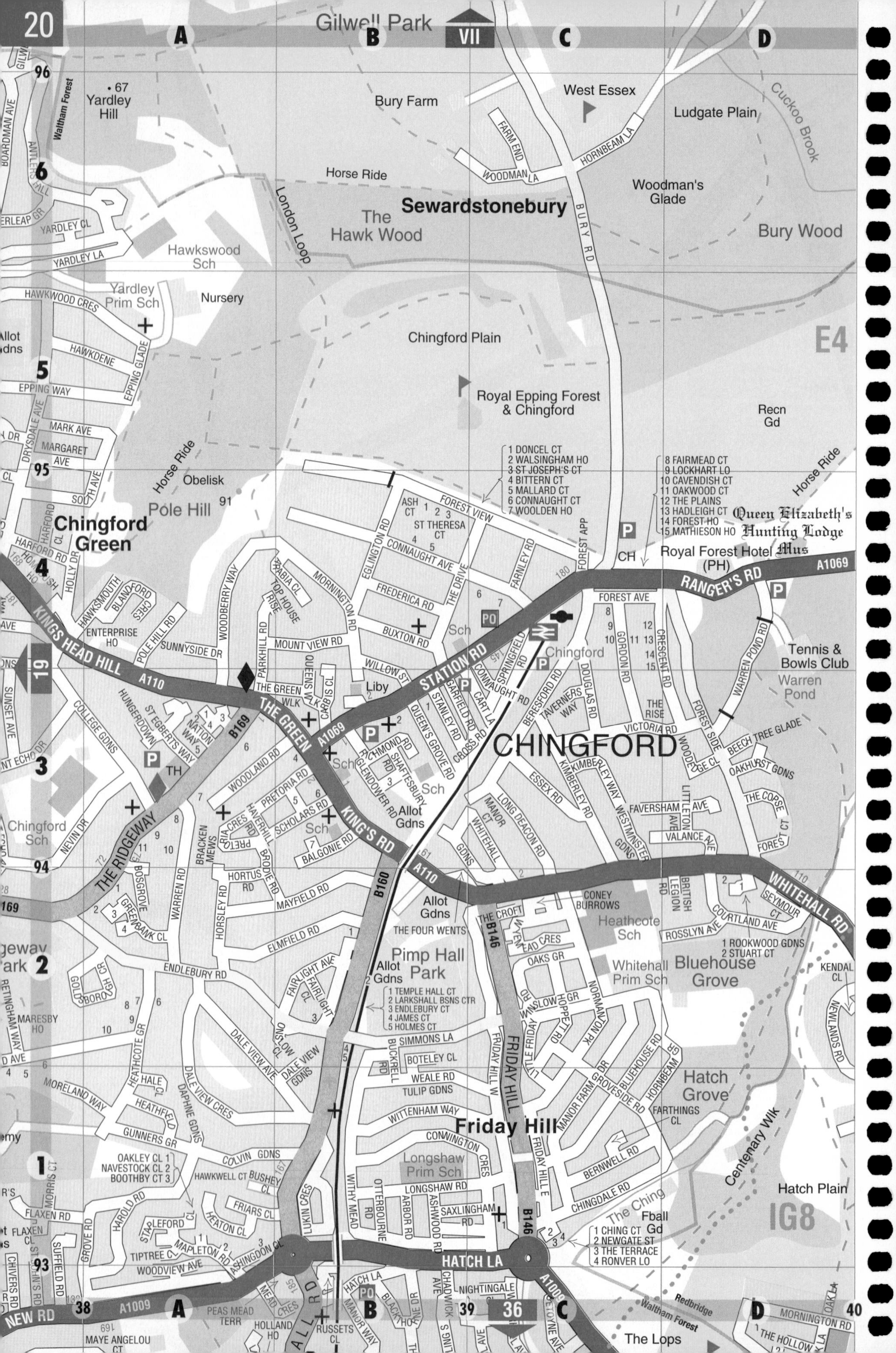
Gilwell Park
VII
A
B
C
D
West Essex
Ludgate Plain
Cuckoo Brook
Bury Farm
67
Yardley Hill
Waltham Forest
BOARDMAN AVE
ANTLERS HILL
FARM END
HORNBEAM LA
WOODMAN LA
Horse Ride
London Loop
Woodman's Glade
Sewardstonebury
The Hawk Wood
BURY RD
Bury Wood
YARDLEY CL
YARDLEY LA
Hawkswood Sch
Yardley Prim Sch
Nursery
HAWKWOOD CRES
HAWKDENE
EPPING GLADE
Chingford Plain
E4
EPPING WAY
Royal Epping Forest & Chingford
Recn Gd
DRYSDALE AVE
MARK AVE
MARGARET AVE
SOUTH AVE
Horse Ride
Obelisk
91
Pole Hill
1 DONCEL CT
2 WALSINGHAM HO
3 ST JOSEPH'S CT
4 BITTERN CT
5 MALLARD CT
6 CONNAUGHT CT
7 WOOLDEN HO
8 FAIRMEAD CT
9 LOCKHART LO
10 CAVENDISH CT
11 OAKWOOD CT
12 THE PLAINS
13 HADLEIGH CT
14 FOREST HO
15 MATHIESON HO
Horse Ride
Queen Elizabeth's Hunting Lodge
Mus
Chingford Green
HARFORD CL
HARFORD RD
HOLLY DR
ASH CT
FOREST VIEW
ST THERESA CT
EGLINGTON RD
CONNAUGHT AVE
FARNLEY RD
FOREST APP
CH
Royal Forest Hotel (PH)
RANGER'S RD
A1069
KINGS HEAD HILL
HAWKSMOUTH
BLANDFORD CRES
ENTERPRISE HO
POLE HILL RD
WOODBERRY WAY
ARABIA CL
TOP HOUSE RISE
MORNINGTON RD
FREDERICA RD
THE DRIVE
FOREST AVE
GORDON RD
CRESCENT RD
SUNNYSIDE DR
PARKHILL RD
MOUNT VIEW RD
BUXTON RD
PO
Sch
STATION RD
SPRINGFIELD RD
Chingford
WARREN POND RD
Tennis & Bowls Club
Warren Pond
A110
19
THE GREEN WLK
QUEENS WLK
CARBIS CL
WILLOW ST
Liby
GARFIELD RD
CONNAUGHT RD
CART LA
BERESFORD RD
TAVERNERS WAY
DOUGLAS RD
THE RISE
VICTORIA RD
FOREST SIDE
BEECH TREE GLADE
SUNSET AVE
COLLEGE GDNS
HUNGERDOWN
ST EGBERTS WAY
NATION WAY
B169
THE GREEN
RICHMOND RD
SHAFTESBURY
QUEEN'S GROVE RD
STANLEY RD
CROSS RD
CHINGFORD
WOODED GE CL
OAKHURST GDNS
TH
WOODLAND RD
PRETORIA RD
GLENDOWER RD
KIMBERLEY RD
KIMBERLEY WAY
ESSEX RD
FAVERSHAM AVE
THE COPSE
FOREST CT
Chingford Sch
NEVIN DR
THE RIDGEWAY
BRACKEN MEWS
HAVERHILL RD
SCHOLARS RD
BALGONIE RD
KING'S RD
Allot Gdns
MANOR CT
WHITEHALL GDNS
LONG DEACON RD
WESTMINSTER GDNS
LITTLETON AVE
VALANCE AVE
94
BOSGROVE
WARREN RD
HORSLEY RD
HORTUS RD
BRODIE RD
MAYFIELD RD
B160
A110
WHITEHALL RD
CONEY BURROWS
BRITISH LEGION RD
SEYMOUR CT
COURTLAND AVE
GREENBANK CL
ELMFIELD RD
Allot Gdns
THE FOUR WENTS
THE CROFT
B146
Heathcote Sch
ROSSLYN AVE
1 ROOKWOOD GDNS
2 STUART CT
KENDAL CL
ENDLEBURY RD
GOLDSBOROUGH CR
FAIRLIGHT AVE
FAIRLIGHT CL
Pimp Hall Park
Allot Gdns
OAKS GR
Whitehall Prim Sch
Bluehouse Grove
1 TEMPLE HALL CT
2 LARKSHALL BSNS CTR
3 ENDLEBURY CT
4 JAMES CT
5 HOLMES CT
WINSLOW GR
HOPPETT RD
NORMANTON PK
NEWLANDS RD
MARESBY HO
HEATHCOTE GR
DALE VIEW AVE
ONSLOW CL
DALE VIEW GDNS
SIMMONS LA
BUCKRELL RD
BOTELEY CL
FRIDAY HILL W
FRIDAY HILL
LITTLE FRIDAY RD
BLUEHOUSE RD
HORNBEAM GR
Hatch Grove
MORELAND WAY
HALE CL
HEATHFIELD
DAPHNE GDNS
DALE VIEW CRES
WEALE RD
TULIP GDNS
WITTENHAM WAY
MANOR FARM DR
GROVESIDE RD
FARTHINGS CL
Friday Hill
Centenary Wlk
GUNNERS GR
COLVIN GDNS
CONNINGTON CRES
Longshaw Prim Sch
FRIDAY HILL E
BERNWELL RD
OAKLEY CL 1
NAVESTOCK CL 2
BOOTHBY CT 3
MORRIS CT
HAWKWELL CT
BUSHEY CL
LUKIN CRES
WITHY MEAD
OTTERBOURNE RD
LONGSHAW RD
ARBOR RD
ASHWOOD RD
SAXLINGHAM RD
CHINGDALE RD
Hatch Plain
FLAXEN RD
HAROLD RD
STAPLEFORD CL
FRIARS CL
HEATON CL
The Ching
Fball Gd
IG8
FLAXEN CL
GROVE RD
MAPLETON RD
TIPTREE C
ASHINGDON CL
1 CHING CT
2 NEWGATE ST
3 THE TERRACE
4 RONVER LO
93
CHIVERS RD
SUFFIELD RD
WOODVIEW AVE
HATCH LA
B146
A1009
NEW RD
38
A1009
PEAS MEAD TERR
MEAD CRES
ALLRD
HATCH LA
PO
MANOR WAY
RUSSETS CL
NIGHTINGALE
CHADWICK AVE
39
36
Redbridge
Waltham Forest
The Lops
MORNINGTON RD
THE HOLLOW
OAK LA
40
HOLLAND HO
MAYE ANGELOU CT

A104 Epping (B1393), M25 (A121)
VII
A121 Loughton, M11 (A1168)
Long Hills
Epping Forest
Centenary Wlk
Palmer's Bridge
Mon
The Warren
Warren Hill
Oaklands Sch
The Willows
IG10
69 Warren Hill
Magpie Hill
Connaught Water
Rangers Rd
Epping New Rd
High Rd
Loughton
Manor Rd
Holmehurst
The Ching
The Warren Wood (PH)
Trinity Terr
Powell's Forest
Oak Hall
Waltham Forest
Epping Forest
Pondfield End
The Fountains
Richmond Pk
The Stables
Guy's Retreat
The Drive
Powell Rd
North End
Ardmore La
Hawsted
Queensbury
St John's CE Prim Sch
IG9
Greenhill
Luctons Ave
Forest Side
Waikato Lo
Ormonde Rise
Roebuck La
Little Pluckett's Way
Stradbroke Gr
The Meadway
Amberley Rd
Gladstone Rd
Russell Rd
Whitehall Plain
Brook Rd
Church Rd
Scotland Rd
Palace Gdns
Dalefield
1 Rayburne Ct
2 The Laurels
3 Moblin Lo
4 Silvers
5 Makinen Ho
Glenmead
St James Gate
The Green
Palmerston Rd
B170
Roding La
Buckhurst Hill
Devon Cl
Westbury La
The Daiglen Sch
Stag La
Queen's Rd
Salisbury Gdns
Tilney Dr 1
Tilney Rd 2
Tilney Ct 3
Hurstcombe 4
The Birkbeck
Princes Rd
Lower Queen's Rd
Mountbatten Ct
Allot Gdns
Holly House
Knighton Gn
High Road Buckhurst Hill
Lord's Bushes
Buckhurst Hill
Reeds Forest
1 Hepworth Ho
2 Whitehall Lo
Bancrofts Sch
IG8
Knighton Wood
Woodford Wells
Monkhams La
Essex
Redbridge
Forest Edge
Broadfield Way
Roding Valley
Station Way
1 Station App
2 Station Par
Woodford
Trinity RC High Sch (Upper)
St Antony's
A110
A104
A121
The Sidings 1
Lukinstone Cl 2
Seymour Cl 3
Sp Gd
37

A
B
C
D
VI
93
92
91
90
6
5
4
3
2
1
10
11
12
40
Young Hangings
Little Furze Prim Sch
Pl Fld
OTLEY WAY
ST ANDREWS RD
South Oxhey
Old Hangings
The Plantation
Pond Wood
Oxhey Wood Schs
WD19
Oxhey Woods
Oxhey wood
A4125 Watford
A4125
SANDY LA
Tenn Cts
Eastbury
Northwood HQ
THE WOODS
B4542
PRESTWICK RD
Greenfields JMI Sch
Allot Gdns
Nanscot Wood
Hertfordshire
Harrow
Hillingdon
Pinnerwood House
Pinnerwood Farm
HA6
SEVEN ACRES
WATFORD RD
NORTHWOOD
Pinner Hill
Pinnerwood Park
HILLSIDE RD
Hillside Schs
Northwood & Pinner Com
POTTER STREET HILL
PINNER HILL
ALBURY DR
MARSWORTH AVE
Pinner Wood Schs
Northwood Comp Sch
NORTHWOOD HILLS CIR
PINNER RD
RICKMANSWORTH RD
UXBRIDGE ROAD (PINNER)
A404
Recn Gd
Pinner Green
Northwood Recn Gd
Northwood
Northwood Hills
JOEL ST
B472
B466
Little Common
Harlyn
HAZELDENE DR
A4125 Rickmansworth (A404)
A404 Rickmansworth, M25
A4125

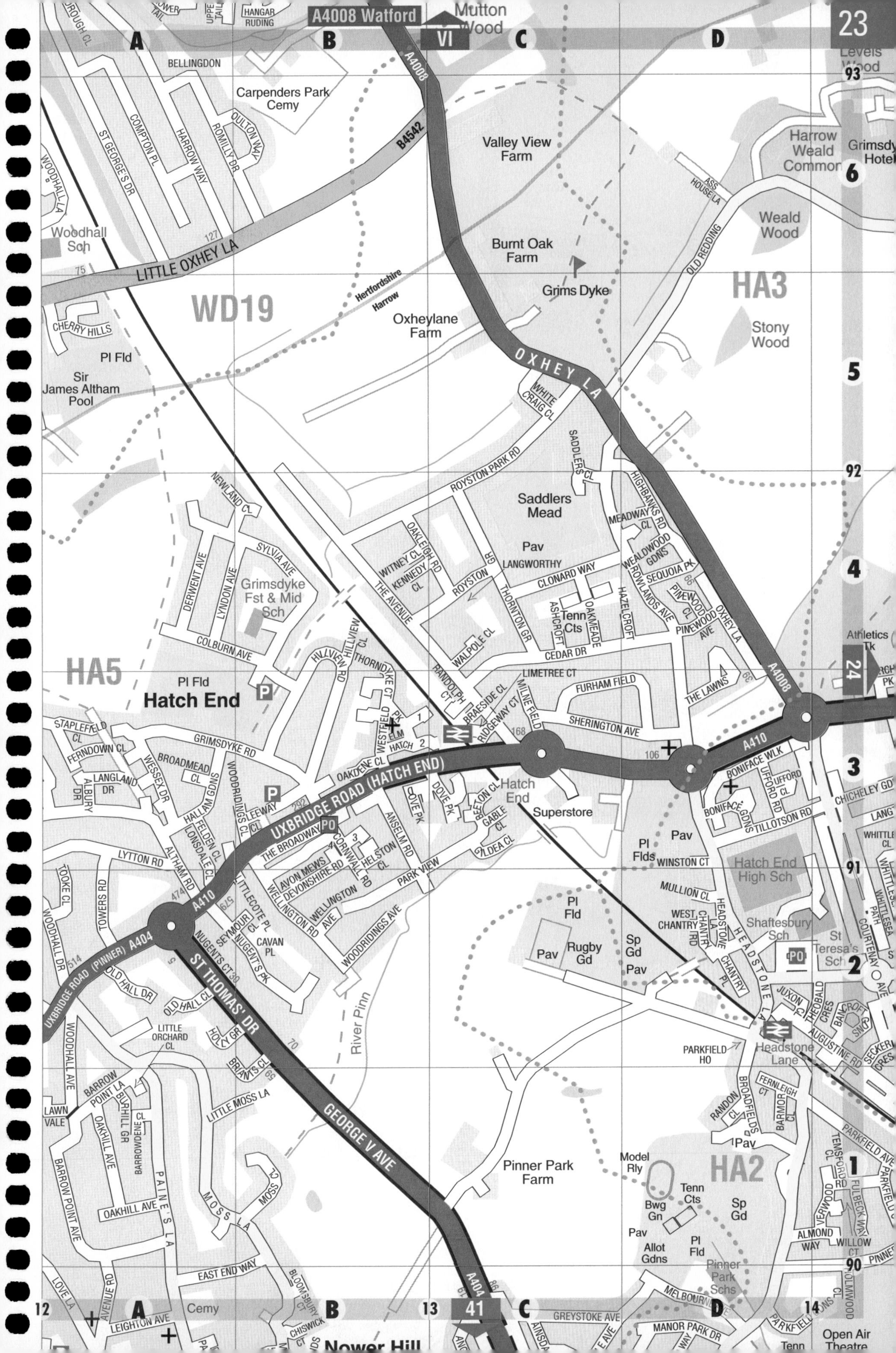
A4008 Watford
VI
A
B
C
D
Mutton Wood
Levels Wood
93
BELLINGDON
HANGAR RUDING
Carpenders Park Cemy
COMPTON PL
ST GEORGE'S DR
HARROW WAY
ROMILLY DR
OULTON WAY
B4542
A4008
Valley View Farm
Harrow Weald Common
Grimsdyke Hotel
6
ASS HOUSE LA
OLD REDDING
Weald Wood
WOODHALL LA
Woodhall Sch
127
LITTLE OXHEY LA
75
Burnt Oak Farm
Grims Dyke
HA3
WD19
Hertfordshire
Harrow
Oxheylane Farm
Stony Wood
CHERRY HILLS
Pl Fld
Sir James Altham Pool
OXHEY LA
WHITE CRAIG CL
5
SADDLERS CL
92
ROYSTON PARK RD
NEWLAND CL
Saddlers Mead
HIGHBANKS RD
MEADWAY CL
SYLVIA AVE
DERWENT AVE
LYNDON AVE
Grimsdyke Fst & Mid Sch
OAKLEIGH RD
WITNEY CL
KENNEDY CL
THE AVENUE
ROYSTON GR
Pav
LANGWORTHY
CLONARD WAY
WEALDWOOD GDNS
ROWLANDS AVE
SEQUOIA PK
PINEWOOD CL
4
THORNTON GR
ASHCROFT
Tenn Cts
OAKMEADE
HAZELCROFT
PINEWOOD AVE
OXHEY LA
HILLVIEW CL
HILLVIEW RD
THORNDYKE CT
WALPOLE CL
COLBURN AVE
CEDAR DR
Athletics Tk
24
HA5
Pl Fld
Hatch End
RANDOLPH CT
LIMETREE CT
BRAESIDE CL
MILNE FIELD
FURHAM FIELD
THE LAWNS
A4008
RIDGEWAY CT
SHERINGTON AVE
168
STAPLEFIELD CL
FERNDOWN CL
GRIMSDYKE RD
WESTFIELD PK
ELM
HATCH
BROADMEAD CL
WESSEX DR
A410
106
BONIFACE WLK
UFFORD CL
UFFORD RD
3
LANGLAND DR
ALBURY DR
HALLAM GDNS
WOODRIDINGS CL
OAKDENE CL
UXBRIDGE ROAD (HATCH END)
DOVE PK
Hatch End
BEETON CL
BONIFACE GDNS
TILLOTSON RD
CHICHELEY GDNS
LEEWAY
292
PO
LOVE PK
GABLE CL
Superstore
FELDEN CL
LONSDALE CL
THE BROADWAY
CORNWALL RD
ANSELM RD
Pav
WHITTLE CL
LYTTON RD
ALTHAM RD
LITTLECOTE PL
AVON MEWS
DEVONSHIRE RD
HELSTON CL
PARK VIEW
ILDEA CL
Pl Flds
WINSTON CT
Hatch End High Sch
91
TOOKE CL
TOWERS RD
474
A410
WELLINGTON RD
WELLINGTON AVE
MULLION CL
WOODHALL DR
SEYMOUR CL
NUGENTS PK
CAVAN PL
WOODRIDINGS AVE
Pl Fld
WEST CHANTRY
CHANTRY RD
HEADSTONE LA
Shaftesbury Sch
St Teresa's Sch
COURTENAY AVE
UXBRIDGE ROAD (PINNER) A404
514
OLD HALL DR
NUGENTS CT
ST THOMAS' DR
Pav
Rugby Gd
Sp Gd
Pav
CHANTRY PL
PO
2
OLD HALL CL
JUXON CL
THEOBALD CRES
BANCROFT
LITTLE ORCHARD CL
HOLLY GR
River Pinn
PARKFIELD HO
Headstone Lane
AUGUSTINE RD
WOODHALL AVE
BARROW POINT LA
BRIANTS CL
70
LAWN VALE
BURHILL GR
BARROWDENE CL
LITTLE MOSS LA
GEORGE V AVE
FERNLEIGH CT
RANDON CL
BROADFIELDS
BARMOR CL
OAKHILL AVE
PAINE'S LA
BARROW POINT AVE
Pav
PARKFIELD AVE
Pinner Park Farm
Model Rly
HA2
TEMSFORD CL
1
MOSS CL
MOSS LA
OAKHILL AVE
Tenn Cts
Bwg Gn
Sp Gd
VERWOOD RD
FULBECK WAY
Pav
Allot Gdns
Pl Fld
ALMOND WAY
WILLOW CT
90
PINNER
EAST END WAY
Pinner Park Schs
LOVE LA
AVENUE RD
BLOOMSBURY CT
A404
MELBOURNE
OLMWOOD
12
A
Cem y
B
13
41
C
GREYSTOKE AVE
D
14
PARKFIELD
LEIGHTON AVE
CHISWICK CT
Nower Hill
MANOR PARK DR
Open Air Theatre
Tenn

Levels Wood
Harrow Weald Common
Grimsdyke Hotel
Weald Wood
OLD REDDING
The Kiln
HA7
Deer Park
Heriot's Wood
Priory House
Harrow Weald Common
Tenn Cts
BROOKSHILL DR
Lower Priory Farm
Stony Wood
Copse Farm
Hillside
Bentley Wood High Sch
HA3
BROOKSHILL
Harrow Coll (Harrow Weald Campus)
Allot Gdns
Harrow Weald Cemy
The Bannister Sp Ctr
Athletics Tk
UXBRIDGE RD (HARROW WEALD)
A410
A409
Whittlesea Sch
Recn Gd
Weald Fst & Mid Schs
Hatch End High Sch
Cedars Fst & Mid Schs
Harrow Weald
HIGH RD
Shaftesbury Sch
St Teresa's Sch
Headstone Lane
Allot Gdns
HARROW
HIGH ST
Belmont Mid Sch
Open Air Theatre

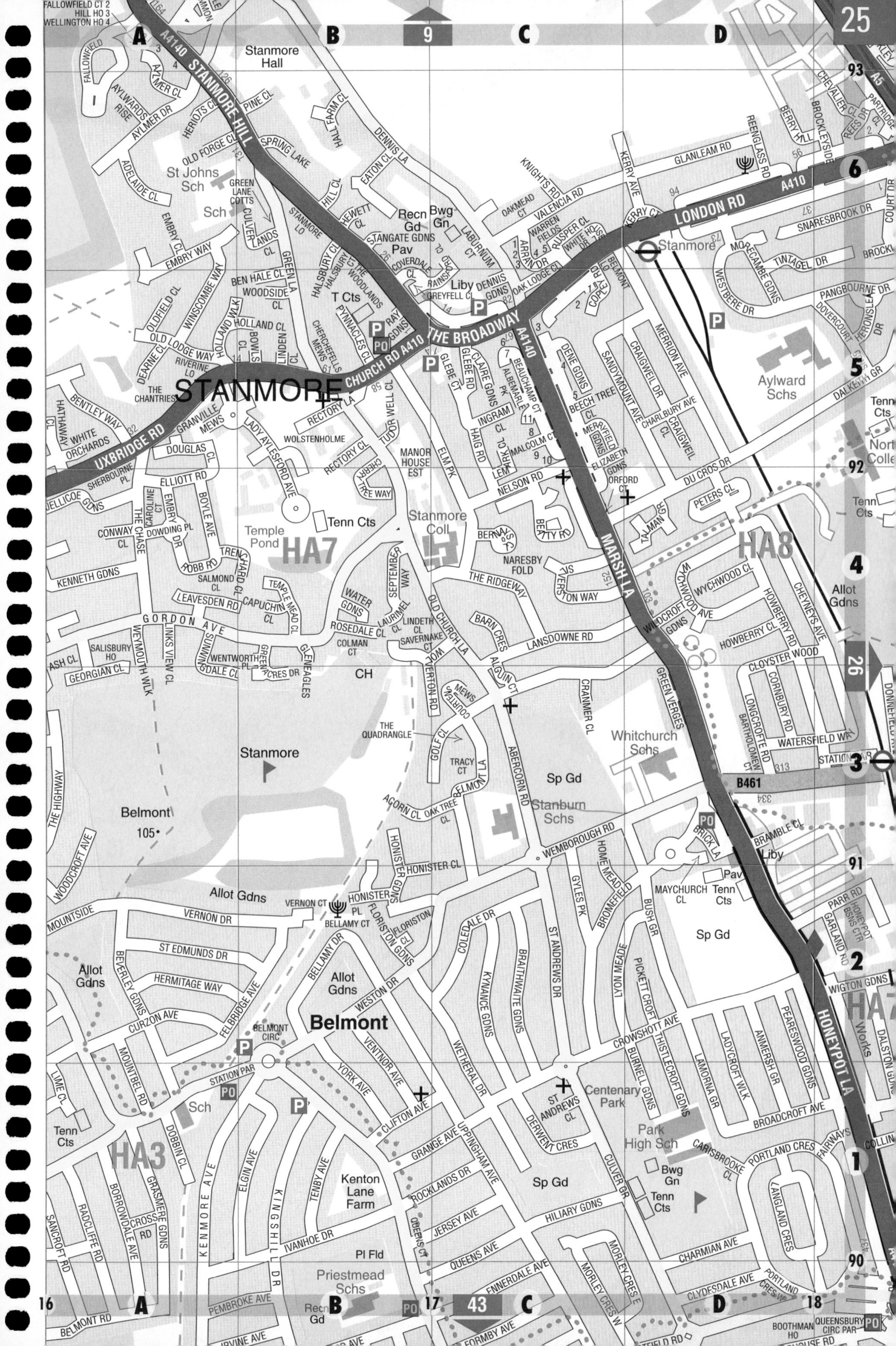

25
FALLOWFIELD CT 2
HILL HO 3
WELLINGTON HO 4
A
B
9
C
D
Stanmore Hall
STANMORE HILL
A4140
FALLOWFIELD
AYLMER CL
AYLWARDS RISE
AYLMER DR
HERIOTS CL
PINE CL
OLD FORGE CL
SPRING LAKE
ADELAIDE CL
St Johns Sch
GREEN LANE COTTS
Sch
EMBRY CL
EMBRY WAY
CULVER LANDS
STANMORE LO
HALL FARM CL
DENNIS LA
EATON CL
HILL CL
HEWETT CL
Recn Gd
Bwg Gn
STANGATE GDNS
Pav
COVERDALE CL
RAINSFORD CL
LABURNUM CT
HALSBURY CL
THE WOODLANDS
GREYFELL CL
Liby
DENNIS GDNS
OAK LODGE CL
T Cts
PYNNACLES CL
CHERCHEFELLS MEWS
BEN HALE CL
WOODSIDE CL
OLDFIELD CL
WINSCOMBE WAY
HOLLAND WLK
HOLLAND CL
BOWLS CL
LINDEN CL
OLD LODGE WAY
RIVERINE LO
DEARNE CL
THE CHANTRIES
STANMORE
CHURCH RD A410
THE BROADWAY
A4140
RAY GDNS
GLEBE CT
GLEBE RD
CLAIRE GDNS
ALBEMARLE PK
BEAUCHAMP CT
INGRAM CL
HAIG RD
ELM PK
KIRK CL
LEMON
MALCOLM CT
NELSON RD
KNIGHTS RD
OAKMEAD CT
VALENCIA RD
WARREN FIELDS
RUSPER CL
WHITE HO DR
ARRAN DR
KERRY AVE
KERRY CT
GLANLEAM RD
REENGLASS RD
LONDON RD
A410
Stanmore
BELMONT
COPLEY RD
DENE GDNS
BEECH TREE CL
MERRYFIELD GDNS
ELIZABETH GDNS
ORFORD CT
MERRION AVE
CRAIGWEIL DR
SANDYMOUNT AVE
CHARLBURY AVE
CRAIGWEIL CL
CRAIGWEIL AVE
DU CROS DR
PETERS CL
TALMAN GR
BERRY HILL
BROCKLEYSIDE
CHEVALIER CL
REES DR
PARTRIDGE
93
A5
6
SNARESBROOK DR
COURT DR
MORECAMBE GDNS
TINTAGEL DR
BROCKL
WESTBERE DR
PANGBOURNE DR
HERONSLEA DR
DOVERCOURT
Aylward Schs
5
DALKEITH GR
Tenn Cts
Nort Colle
92
Tenn Cts
HA8
4
Allot Gdns
UXBRIDGE RD
GRANVILLE MEWS
LADY AYLESFORD AVE
RECTORY LA
RECTORY CL
TUDOR WELL CL
CHERRY TREE WAY
MANOR HOUSE EST
WOLSTENHOLME
HATHAWAY
BENTLEY WAY
WHITE ORCHARDS
DOUGLAS CL
SHERBOURNE PL
ELLIOTT RD
JELLICOE GDNS
CAROLINE CL
EMBRY DR
BOYLE AVE
THE CHASE
CONWAY CL
DOWDING PL
Temple Pond
HA7
Tenn Cts
Stanmore Coll
BERNAYS CL
BEATTY RD
NARESBY FOLD
MARSH LA
TRENCHARD CL
ROBB RD
SALMOND CL
KENNETH GDNS
TEMPLE MEAD CL
CAPUCHIN CL
LEAVESDEN RD
GORDON AVE
WATER GDNS
SEPTEMBER WAY
LAURIMEL CL
LINDETH CL
SAVERNAKE CT
OLD CHURCH LA
THE RIDGEWAY
VISCOUNT
VERSTON WAY
BARN CRES
LANSDOWNE RD
WILDCROFT GDNS
WYCHWOOD AVE
WYCHWOOD CL
HOWBERRY RD
HOWBERRY CL
CHEYNEYS AVE
CLOYSTER WOOD
26
ROSEDALE CL
SALISBURY HO
ASH CL
GEORGIAN CL
WEYMOUTH WLK
LINKS VIEW CL
SUNNINGDALE CL
WENTWORTH PL
GREENACRES DR
GLENEAGLES
COLMAN CT
CH
MERTON RD
COURTENAY MEWS
ALCUIN CT
CRANMER CL
GREEN VERGES
CORNBURY RD
LONGCROFTE RD
BARTHOLOMEW CT
WATERSFIELD WAY
STATION PAR
3
DONNEFIELD
THE QUADRANGLE
GOLF CL
TRACY CT
BELMONT LA
ABERCORN RD
Whitchurch Schs
Sp Gd
Stanmore
Belmont
105
THE HIGHWAY
WOODCROFT AVE
ACORN CL
OAK TREE CL
Stanburn Schs
WEMBOROUGH RD
B461
BRICK LA
BRAMBLE CL
Liby
HONISTER CL
HONISTER GDNS
HOMEMEAD
GYLES PK
BROMEFIELD
MAYCHURCH CL
Pav
Tenn Cts
91
Allot Gdns
MOUNTSIDE
VERNON DR
VERNON CT
BELLAMY CT
HONISTER PL
FLORISTON GDNS
FLORISTON CL
COLEDALE DR
ST ANDREWS DR
BUSH GR
Sp Gd
PARR RD
HONEYPOT BSNS CTR
GARLAND RD
2
ST EDMUNDS DR
HERMITAGE WAY
BEVERLEY GDNS
FELBRIDGE AVE
BELLAMY DR
Allot Gdns
WESTON DR
KYNANCE GDNS
BRAITHWAITE GDNS
LYON MEADE
PICKETT CROFT
WIGTON GDNS
HA7
Allot Gdns
CURZON AVE
Belmont
BELMONT CIRC
VENTNOR AVE
WETHERAL DR
CROWSHOTT AVE
THISTLECROFT GDNS
LAMORNA GR
LADYCROFT WLK
AMMERSH GR
PEARESWOOD GDNS
HONEYPOT LA
Works
DALSTON
LIME CL
MOUNTBEL RD
STATION PAR
Sch
YORK AVE
BURNELL GDNS
Centenary Park
BROADCROFT AVE
Tenn Cts
HA3
DOBBIN CL
CLIFTON AVE
GRANGE AVE
UPPINGHAM AVE
ST ANDREWS CL
DERWENT CRES
Park High Sch
CARISBROOKE CL
PORTLAND CRES
FAIRWAYS
COLLIN
1
ROCKLANDS DR
KENMORE AVE
ELGIN AVE
KINGSHILL DR
TENBY AVE
Kenton Lane Farm
Sp Gd
CULVER GR
Bwg Gn
Tenn Cts
LANGLAND CRES
GRASMERE GDNS
CROSS RD
BORROWDALE AVE
RADCLIFFE RD
SANCROFT RD
JERSEY AVE
HILIARY GDNS
QUEENS CT
IVANHOE DR
QUEENS AVE
Pl Fld
MORLEY CRES E
CHARMIAN AVE
90
Priestmead Schs
ENNERDALE AVE
CLYDESDALE AVE
PORTLAND CRES W
16
A
PEMBROKE AVE
Recn Gd
B
17
43
C
MORLEY CRES W
D
18
BELMONT RD
IRVINE AVE
FORMBY AVE
BOOTHMAN HO
QUEENSBURY CIRC PAR

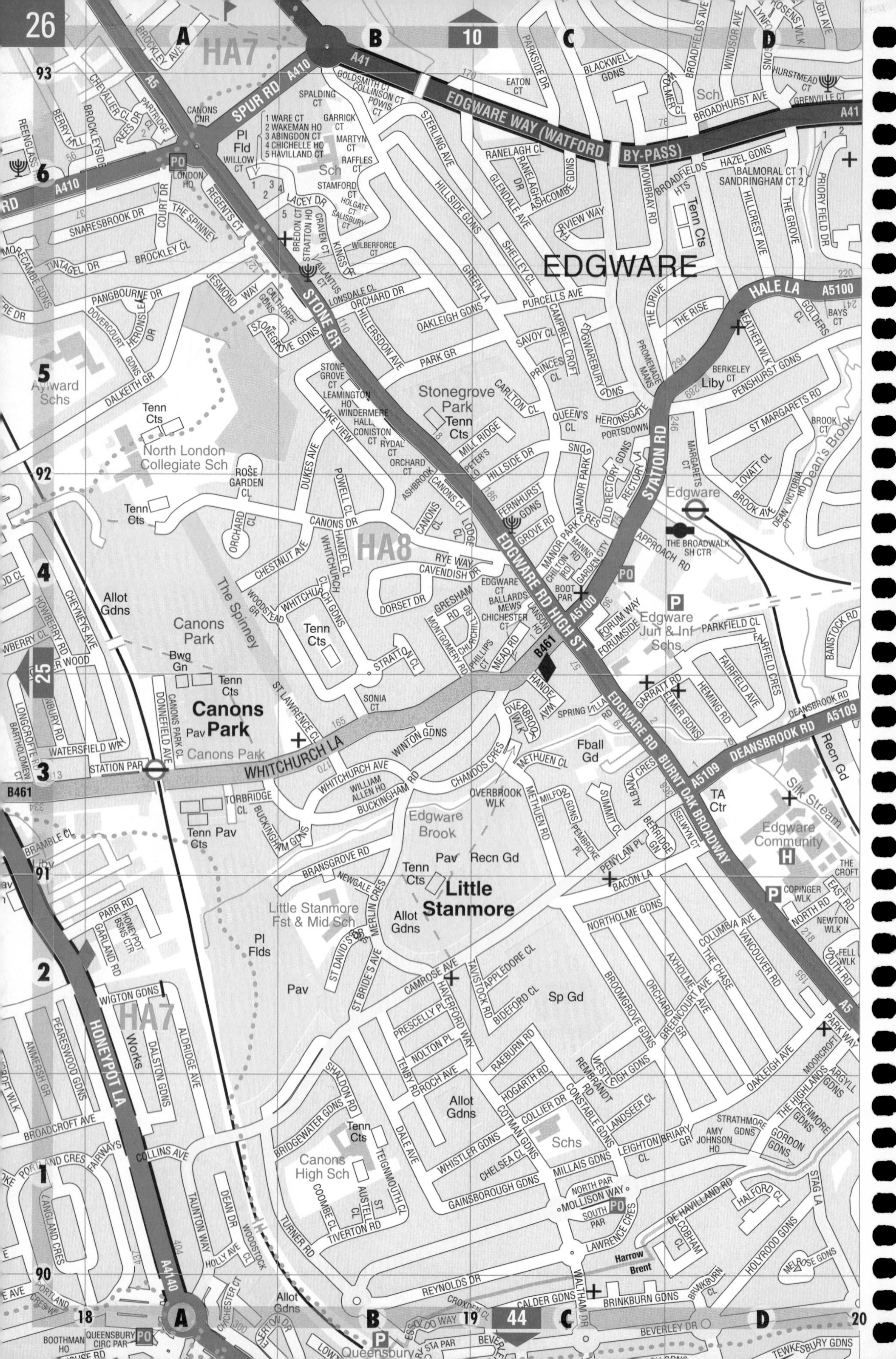
A
B
C
D
10
HA7
EDGWARE
HA8
EDGWARE WAY (WATFORD BY-PASS)
A41
SPUR RD
A410
A5
STONE GR
EDGWARE RD HIGH ST
STATION RD
A5100
HALE LA
A5109
DEANSBROOK RD
EDGWARE RD BURNT OAK BROADWAY
WHITCHURCH LA
B461
HONEYPOT LA
A4140
Stonegrove Park
Canons Park
North London Collegiate Sch
Aylward Schs
The Spinney
Little Stanmore
Edgware Brook
Little Stanmore Fst & Mid Sch
Canons High Sch
Edgware Jun & Inf Schs
Edgware Community
Edgware
THE BROADWALK SH CTR
Silk Stream
Dean's Brook
Harrow
Brent
Queensbury
25
44
93
92
91
90
6
5
4
3
2
1
18
19
20

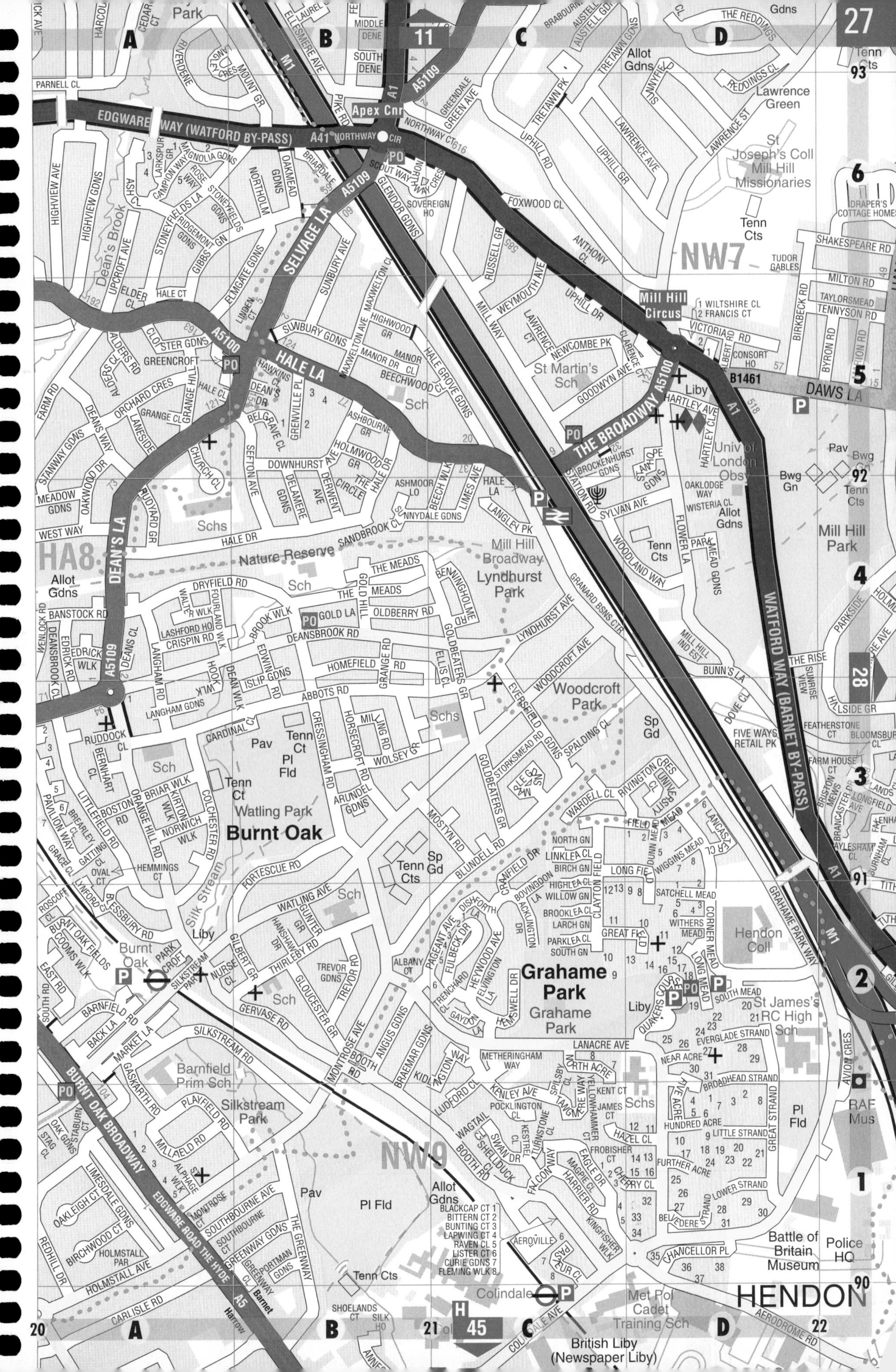
A
B
C
D
11
M1
A1
A5109
EDGWARE WAY (WATFORD BY-PASS)
A41
NORTHWAY CIR
Apex Cnr
PARNELL CL
RIVERDENE
MOUNT GR
ELLESMERE AVE
MIDDLE DENE
SOUTH DENE
PIKE RD
GREEN AVE
NORTHWAY CT
THE REDDINGS
REDDINGS CL
Allot Gdns
TRETAWN GDNS
TRETAWN PK
UPHILL RD
UPHILL GR
LAWRENCE AVE
LAWRENCE ST
Lawrence Green
St Joseph's Coll Mill Hill Missionaries
Tenn Cts
93
6
DRAPER'S COTTAGE HOMES
SHAKESPEARE RD
TUDOR GABLES
MILTON RD
TAYLORSMEAD
TENNYSON RD
BIRKBECK RD
BYRON RD
NW7
HIGHVIEW AVE
HIGHVIEW GDNS
Dean's Brook
UPCROFT AVE
STONEYFIELDS LA
STONEYFIELDS GDNS
RIDGEMONT GDNS
GIBBS GN
NORTHOLM
OAKMEAD GDNS
BRIARDALE
SCOUT WAY
NORTHWAY CRES
GLENDOR GDNS
SOVEREIGN HO
SELVAGE LA
SUNBURY AVE
MAXWELTON AVE
FOXWOOD CL
RUSSELL GR
WEYMOUTH AVE
ANTHONY CL
UPHILL DR
MILL WAY
Mill Hill Circus
1 WILTSHIRE CL
2 FRANCIS CT
VICTORIA RD
ALBERT RD
CONSORT HO
B1461
DAWS LA
5
ELDER CL
HALE CT
ELMGATE GDNS
LINDEN CT
A5100
HALE LA
CLOISTER GDNS
GREENCROFT
SUNBURY GDNS
HIGHWOOD GR
MANOR DR
MANOR CL
BEECHWOOD CL
HALE GROVE GDNS
LAWRENCE CT
NEWCOMBE PK
CLARENCE CT
St Martin's Sch
GOODWYN AVE
THE BROADWAY
Liby
HARTLEY AVE
HARTLEY CL
FARM RD
ALDERS RD
ORCHARD CRES
GRANGE HILL
GRANGE CL
HALE CL
HAWKINS CL
DEAN'S DR
BELGRAVE CL
GRENVILLE PL
ASHBOURNE GR
Sch
STANWAY GDNS
DEANS WAY
LANESIDE
CHURCH CL
SEFTON AVE
DOWNHURST AVE
HOLMWOOD GR
DELAMERE GDNS
DERWENT AVE
THE HALE DR
CIRCLE
ASHMOOR LO
BEECH WLK
LIMES AVE
HALE LA
BROCKENHURST GDNS
STATION RD
STANHOPE GDNS
Univ of London Obsy
OAKLODGE WAY
WISTERIA CL
Allot Gdns
Pav
Bwg Gn
92
Tenn Cts
MEADOW GDNS
OAKWOOD DR
RUDYARD GR
Schs
WEST WAY
HALE DR
SANDBROOK CL
SUNNYDALE GDNS
LANGLEY PK
SYLVAN AVE
WOODLAND WAY
Tenn Cts
FLOWER LA
PARK MEAD GDNS
Mill Hill Park
HA8
DEAN'S LA
Nature Reserve
Mill Hill Broadway
Lyndhurst Park
THE MEADS
4
Allot Gdns
DRYFIELD RD
FOURLAND WLK
WALTER WLK
BROOK WLK
GOLD HILL
BENNINGHOLME RD
BANSTOCK RD
LASHFORD HO
CRISPIN RD
GOLD LA
OLDBERRY RD
GRANARD BSNS CTR
LYNDHURST AVE
WATFORD WAY (BARNET BY-PASS)
PARKSIDE
WENLOCK RD
DEANSBROOK RD
EDRICK RD
EDRICK WLK
DEANS CL
LANGHAM RD
HOOK WLK
EDWIN GDNS
GRANGE RD
HOMEFIELD RD
GOLDBEATERS GR
ELLIS CL
WOODCROFT AVE
MILL HILL IND EST
BUNN'S LA
THE RISE
SUNRISE VIEW
28
ISLIP GDNS
DEAN WLK
ABBOTS RD
Woodcroft Park
LANGHAM GDNS
CARDINAL CL
Tenn Ct
Pav
Pl Fld
CRESSINGHAM RD
HORSECROFT RD
MILLING RD
WOLSEY GR
Schs
EVERSFIELD GDNS
SPALDING CL
Sp Gd
DOVE CL
FIVE WAYS RETAIL PK
HILLSIDE GR
FEATHERSTONE CT
BLOOMSBURY CL
RUDDOCK CL
BERNHART CL
Sch
Tenn Ct
STORKSMEAD RD
FARM HOUSE CT
3
PAVILION WAY
LITTLEFIELD RD
BOSTON RD
ORANGE HILL RD
BRIAR WLK
KIRTON WLK
NORWICH WLK
COLCHESTER RD
Watling Park
Burnt Oak
ARUNDEL GDNS
GOLDBEATERS GR
WARDELL CL
RIVINGTON CRES
UNIVERSITY CL
FIELD MEAD
DUNN MEAD
LANCASTER CL
BRISTON MEWS
BRANCASTER PL
LONGFIELD AVE
AYLESHAM CL
BURNHAM CL
BREARLEY CL
GATTING CL
OVAL CT
HEMMINGS CT
FORTESCUE RD
MOSTYN RD
BLUNDELL RD
Tenn Cts
Sp Gd
CRANFIELD DR
NORTH GN
LINKLEA CL
BIRCH GN
HIGHLEA CL
WILLOW GN
BROOKLEA CL
LARCH GN
PARKLEA CL
SOUTH GN
CLAYTON FIELD
LONG FIELD
WIGGINS MEAD
SATCHELL MEAD
WITHERS MEAD
GREAT FIELD
CORNER MEAD
Hendon Coll
GRAHAME PARK WAY
91
GRACE CL
LYNFORD CL
ROSCOFF CL
BURNT OAK FIELDS
COOMS WLK
BESSBURY RD
Silk Stream
WATLING AVE
GUNTER GR
HANSHAW DR
DISHFORTH LA
BOVINGDON LA
ACKLINGTON DR
Burnt Oak
PARK CROFT
Liby
SILKSTREAM PAR
GILBERT GR
NURSE CL
THIRLEBY RD
TREVOR GDNS
TREVOR RD
ALBANY CT
PAGEANT AVE
FULBECK DR
HEYWOOD AVE
ELVINGTON LA
Grahame Park
Liby
QUAKERS COURSE
LONG MEAD
SOUTH MEAD
St James's RC High Sch
2
EAST RD
SOUTH RD
BARNFIELD RD
BACK LA
MARKET LA
GERVASE RD
Sch
GLOUCESTER GR
MONTROSE AVE
ANGUS GDNS
BRAEMAR GDNS
TRENCHARD CL
GAYDON LA
HEMSWELL DR
LANACRE AVE
NEAR ACRE
EVERGLADE STRAND
BROADHEAD STRAND
AVION CRES
SILKSTREAM RD
GASKARTH RD
Barnfield Prim Sch
BOOTH RD
KIDLINGTON WAY
METHERINGHAM WAY
NORTH ACRE
SPILSBY CL
TANGMERE WAY
YELLOWHAMMER CT
KENT CT
Schs
FIVE ACRE
GREAT STRAND
Pl Fld
RAF Mus
PO
BURNT OAK BROADWAY
PLAYFIELD RD
Silkstream Park
LUDFORD CL
KENLEY AVE
POCKLINGTON CL
JAMES CT
HAZEL CL
HUNDRED ACRE
LITTLE STRAND
STAG CL
STABURN GDNS
MILLFIELD RD
WAGTAIL CL
SHELDUCK CL
SWAN DR
KESTREL CL
TURNSTONE CL
FROBISHER CT
EAGLE DR
FURTHER ACRE
NW9
EDGWARE ROAD THE HYDE
ALPHAGE WLK
BOOTH RD
FALCON WAY
MAGPIE CL
HARRIER RD
CHERRY CL
1
LIMESDALE GDNS
MONTROSE CT
SOUTHBOURNE AVE
Pav
Pl Fld
Allot Gdns
KINGFISHER WLK
LOWER STRAND
OAKLEIGH CT
BIRCHWOOD CT
HOLMSTALL PAR
SOUTHBOURNE CRES
GREENWAY GDNS
THE GREENWAY
BLACKCAP CT 1
BITTERN CT 2
BUNTING CT 3
LAPWING CT 4
RAVEN CL 5
LISTER CT 6
CURIE GDNS 7
FLEMING WLK 8
AEROVILLE
PASTEUR CL
BELVEDERE STRAND
Battle of Britain Museum
Police HQ
REDHILL DR
HOLMSTALL AVE
GREENWAY
PORTMAN GDNS
Tenn Cts
CHANCELLOR PL
90
A5
Barnet
Harrow
CARLISLE RD
Colindale
Met Pol Cadet Training Sch
HENDON
20
SHOELANDS CT
SILK HO
21
45
COLINDALE AVE
AERODROME RD
22
British Liby (Newspaper Liby)

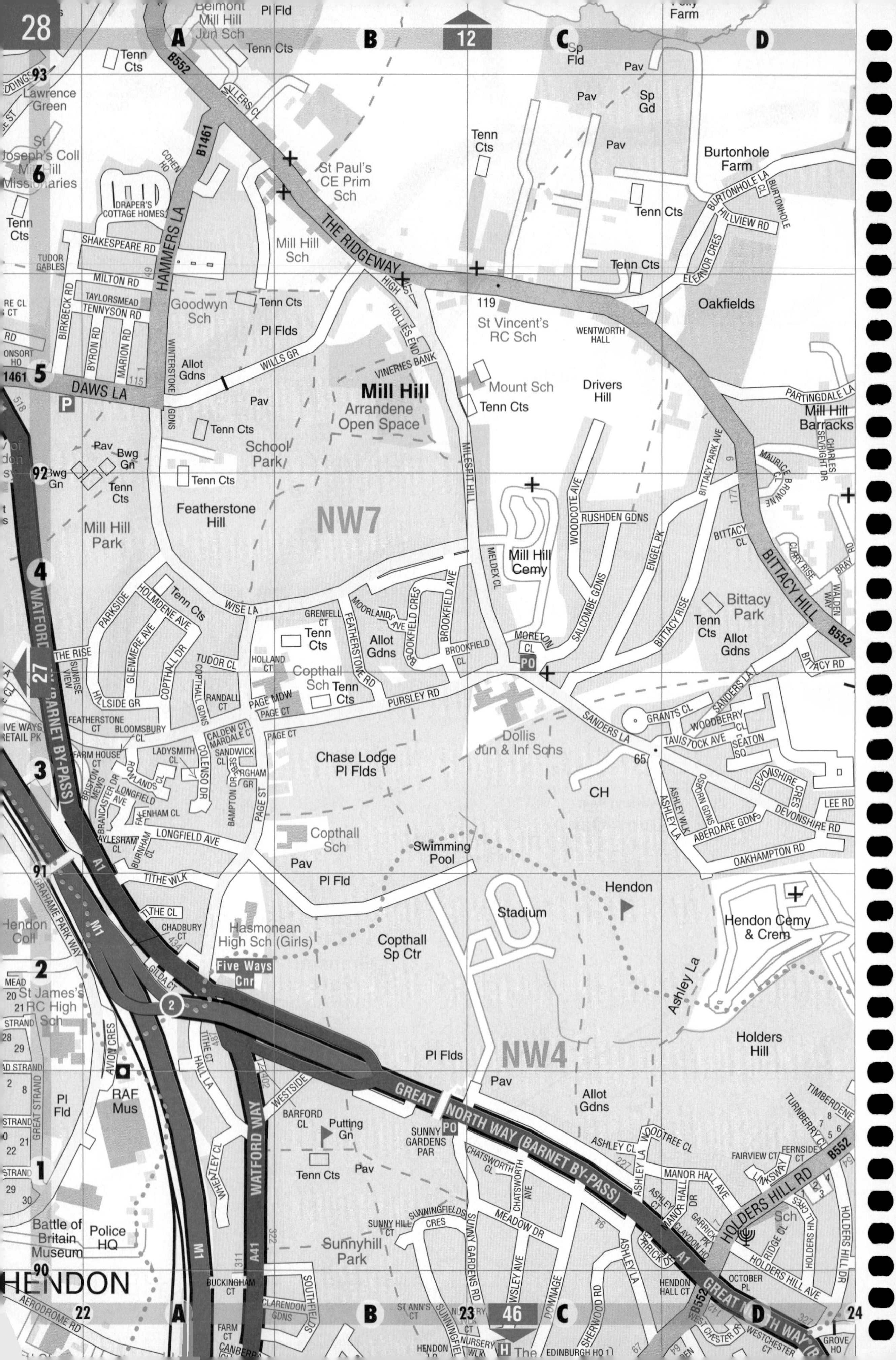
A
B
12
C
D
Belmont Mill Hill Jun Sch
Pl Fld
Polly Farm
Tenn Cts
B552
Lawrence Green
St Joseph's Coll Mill Hill Missionaries
Millers Cl
B1461
Cohen Ho
St Paul's CE Prim Sch
Draper's Cottage Homes
Shakespeare Rd
Hammers La
Mill Hill Sch
The Ridgeway
Tudor Gables
Milton Rd
Taylorsmead
Tennyson Rd
Birkbeck Rd
Byron Rd
Marion Rd
Goodwyn Sch
Pl Flds
Winterstoke Gdns
Allot Gdns
Wills Gr
Daws La
High St
Hollies End
Vineries Bank
Mill Hill
Arrandene Open Space
Pav
School Park
Bwg Gn
Featherstone Hill
Mill Hill Park
NW7
Sp Fld
Sp Gd
Burtonhole Farm
Burtonhole La
Burtonhole Cl
Hillview Rd
Eleanor Cres
Oakfields
119
St Vincent's RC Sch
Wentworth Hall
Mount Sch
Drivers Hill
Partingdale La
Mill Hill Barracks
Bittacy Park Ave
Maurice Browne Cl
Charles Sevright Dr
Millspit Hill
Woodcote Ave
Rushden Gdns
Mill Hill Cemy
Meldex Cl
Salcombe Gdns
Engel Pk
Bittacy Cl
Bittacy Rise
Bittacy Hill
Bittacy Park
Curry Rise
Bray Rd
Walden Way
Allot Gdns
Bittacy Rd
Moreton Cl
PO
Wise La
Parkside
Holmdene Ave
Glenmere Ave
Copthall Dr
The Rise
Sunrise View
Hillside Gr
Tudor Cl
Copthall Gdns
Randall Ct
Holland Ct
Grenfell Ct
Moorlands Ave
Featherstone Rd
Brookfield Cres
Brookfield Ave
Brookfield Ct
Copthall Sch
Page Mdw
Page Ct
Pursley Rd
Watford Way (Barnet By-Pass)
27
Five Ways Retail Pk
Featherstone Ct
Bloomsbury Cl
Farm House Ct
Ladysmith Cl
Caldew Ct
Mardale Ct
Sandwick Cl
Colenso Dr
Bampton Dr
Page St
Chase Lodge Pl Flds
Dollis Jun & Inf Schs
Sanders La
Grants Cl
Woodberry Cl
Tavistock Ave
Seaton Sq
65
CH
Ashley Wlk
Ashley La
Osborn Gdns
Aberdare Gdns
Devonshire Cres
Devonshire Rd
Lee Rd
Oakhampton Rd
Briston Mews
Rowlands Cl
Longfield Ave
Brancaster Dr
Fakenham Cl
Aylesham Cl
Burnham Cl
Swimming Pool
Pl Fld
Tithe Wlk
The Cl
Chadbury Ct
Hasmonean High Sch (Girls)
Copthall Sp Ctr
Stadium
Hendon
Hendon Cemy & Crem
Grahame Park Way
Hendon Coll
A1
M1
Gilda Ct
Five Ways Cnr
St James's RC High Sch
Avion Cres
Tithe Ct
Hall La
Holders Hill
NW4
Pl Flds
Pav
RAF Mus
Westside
Barford Cl
Putting Gn
Great North Way (Barnet By-Pass)
Sunny Gardens Par
Allot Gdns
Ashley Cl
Woodtree Cl
Timberdene
Turnberry Ct
Fernside Ct
Fairview Ct
Linksway
Holders Hill Rd
Wheatley Cl
Watford Way
A41
Tenn Cts
Chatsworth Cl
Chatsworth Ave
Meadow Dr
Manor Hall Ave
Manor Hall Dr
Ashley Ct
Garrick Pk
Claydon Ho
Ridge Cl
Holders Hill Cres
Holders Hill Dr
Holders Hill Ave
October Pl
Battle of Britain Museum
Police HQ
Sunny Hill Ct
Sunningfields Cres
Sunny Gardens Rd
Sunnyhill Park
Hawsley Ave
Downage
Sherwood Rd
Ashley La
Hendon Hall Ct
HENDON
Aerodrome Rd
Buckingham Ct
Clarendon Gdns
Southfields
St Ann's Ct
Nursery Ct
46
Westchester Dr
Westchester Ct
Grove Ho
Farm Ct
Canberra
Hendon
Nursery Wlk
Edinburgh Ho
22
23
24
93
92
91
90
6
5
4
3
2
1

A
B
13
C
D
Finchley Sch
93
Sp Gd
Woodside Park
N12
Tenn Cts
Bwg Gn
Folly Brook
CHANCTONBURY WAY
CISSBURY RING N
CISSBURY RING S
LULLINGTON GARTH
Allot Gdns
Frith Manor Sch
SOUTHOVER
ARLINGTON
FRAMFIELD CL
NORTHIAM
MICHLEHAM DOWN
SHORTGATE
TILLINGHAM WAY
TWINEHAM GN
RIVERSIDE HO
HOLDEN RD
Woodside Park
STATION APP
BROOKDENE
VICARAGE CT
THE GARTH
GARDEN CT
WOODSIDE PARK RD
WOODSIDE GRANGE RD
GRANGEWAY
BUDD CL
SYLVAN CT
BARCHESTER LO
GUILDOWN AVE
FOUR ACRES
LORIAN CL
BROOK MDW
LAUREL VIEW
HOLDEN HTS
DEVONSHIRE HO
CLAIRE CT
LIMES AVE
CAVENDISH HO
LITTLE CEDARS
SQUIRRELS
GREEN BANK
THE OAKS
CLIVEDEN CL
ARDEN GRANGE
AVENUE
ASHBOURNE
HOLDEN AVE
HOPTREE CL
HOLMDENE
DOWNING CT
FINCHLEY LO
THE GABLES
CLARENDON HO
LODGE LA
Northside Prim Sch
WORCESTER CT
AVON CT
AVONDALE AVE
GAINSBOROUGH CT
GAINSBOROUGH RD
NETHERFIELD RD
PERCY RD
Sch
HUGHES CT
NETHER ST
BIRKBECK RD
DALE GR
HUTTON GR
92
VIVIAN CT
QUEENSGATE CT
ALBANY
ALEXANDRA GR
HILLCOURT AVE
MOSSBOROUGH CL
MOSS HALL CT
THYRA GR
GREENLAWNS
MOSS HALL GR
MOSS HALL CRES
Superstore
VINE LO
4
PAMELA CT
THE LANTERNS
Moss Hall Schs
BLISSLAND CT
WOODBERRY
West Finchley
ESSEX PK
FINCHLEY CT
THE FOUNTAINS
BALLARDS LA
30
GRANVILLE RD
SOLAR CT
ETCHINGHAM CT
CHISLEHURST AVE
3
HOLDENHURST
FINCHLEY
Pavs
Tenn Cts
Bwg Gn
SEYMOUR RD
NIGEL CT
ROSSANNE HO
PARK CRES
ETCHINGHAM PARK RD
91
WOODLANDS AVE
QUEEN'S AVE
Victoria Park
PARK VIEW RD
PARK AVE
2
Manorside Sch
LONG LA
SQUIRES LA
MONTPELIER RD
AVONDALE RD
CROMWELL RD
DOUGLAS CT
NURSERY AVE
Allot Gdns
1
MANOR COTTS
RICHMOND RD
Pl Fld
90
BRIARFIELD AVE
CHARLES CT
ROSEMARY AVE
DUDLEY RD
BRIARFIELD AVE
TANGLE TREE CL
Middlesex Cty Crkt Sch
Sp Gd
Pav
MANOR VIEW
A406
A504
EAST END RD
Akiva Sch
St Theresa's RC Prim Sch
26
D
47
C
25
B
A
24
SCAYNES LINK
PYCOMBE CNR
RODMELL SLOPE
OFFHAM SLOPE
WOLSTONBURY
SINGLETON SCARP
FOLKINGTON CNR
SADDLESCOMBE WAY
POYNINGS WAY
STEYNINGS WAY
WALMINGTON FOLD
SUSSEX RING
ARGYLE RD
WESTBURY RD
SPRINGFIELD CL
COURT HOUSE RD
WESTLEIGH CT
THE LAURELS
Tenn Ct
LINKSIDE
CHESTERFIELD RD
WESTBURY GR
NETHERCOURT AVE
FURSBY AVE
WEST AVE
COURT HOUSE GDNS
BRENT WAY
MAPLE CT
SALIX CT
HAMILTON WAY
PENSTEMON CL
FINCHLEY WAY
CEDAR CT
THE DRIVE
HOWCROFT CRES
WESTERN CT
HUNTLY DR
WENTWORTH AVE
WENTWORTH PK
GRUNEISEN RD
BROWNLOW RD
NW7
Nether Court
Finchley
Dollis Brook
BARHAM CT
READING WAY
HOLMES AVE
APPROACH LA
ROSS AVE
GAWTHORNE AVE
HENRY DARLOT DR
LIDBURY RD
KENNY RD
ROBERTS RD
WARREN WAY
WILLIAMSON WAY
Inglis Barracks
KELLY RD
PRICE CL
DREW AVE
TWINN RD
WESTLINTON CL
FRITH LA
BURTONHOLE LA
BITTACY BSNS CTR
Mill Hill East
BITTACY CT
NEW RD
VINEYARD AVE
DOLLISCROFT
B552
B1462
ABERCORN CL
MALLOW MEAD
ABERCORN RD
RYTH CT
BROOK CL
DOLLIS RD
LINKS VIEW
THORNFIELD PAR 1
THORNFIELD CT 2
MILL CT 3
THORNFIELD AVE
Pl Fld
Allot Gdns
BOSE CL
Pav
Sch
HOLDERS HILL PAR
OAKDALE LO
PARAGON CT
FORELAND CT
RYDAL CL
HOLDERS HILL RD
HAWTHORN MEWS
CLAREMONT PK
LYNDHURST GDNS
Tenn Cts
GRASS PK
DOLLIS AVE
GRENVILLE CL
KINGSWOOD PK
QUEENSWOOD PK
HENDON AVE
VILLAGE RD
CYPRUS GDNS
ST MARY'S AVE
PRESTON PK
BLAKE LO
FREELAND PK
1 COLERNE CT
2 CUMBERLAND GDNS
CYPRUS AVE
Windsor Open Space
WINDSOR RD
WINDSOR CL
CRANMER CT
PAUL CT
Coll
WICKLIFFE AVE
GREENACRES
SALISBURY CT
SALISBURY AVE
ARUNDEL LO
NORTH CRES
ARDEN RD
SURREY CT
RAWLINS CT
ELIZABETH HELEN CT
VOYSEY CL
WAVERLEY GR
FITZALAN RD
ROCKLANDS
Allot Gdns
OAKDENE PK
LANSDOWNE RD
GORDON RD
GROSVENOR RD
EVERSLEIGH RD
EVERSLEIGH CT
ELM PARK RD
SELLERS HALL CL
CHESTNUT ROW
NETHER CL
CRESCENT RD
DOLLIS CT
CRESCENT RISE
NETHER ST
DOLLIS PK
BRUNSWICK HO
CLIFTON AVE
CHURCH CRES
VICTORIA AVE
PEWTERERS CT
Ct
Liby
PRIORY CL
RECTORY CL
RATHGAR CL
Schs
A5000
A598
REGENCY HO
COLLEGE
HENDON LA
GRAVEL HILL
LABURNUM LO
ST MICHAEL'S CL
TEMPLE CL
BIBSWORTH RD
BIBSWORTH LO
EMBASSY LO
CYPRUS RD
REGENT'S PARK RD
COLOSSEUM CT
STANHOPE CT
STANHOPE AVE
FLOWER LO
CAVENDISH AVE
DERBY LO
ELLERTON LO
SPENCER CL
THE AVENUE
Church End
TEMPLARS CRES
HOLMWOOD GDNS
WINDERMERE AVE
PAVILION MEWS
SPRING PL
MOUNTFIELD RD
UPPER HOWES
LUKES CT
PARK GDNS
CORNWALL AVE
CORNWALL CL
ADAMS CL
FALKLAND AVE
GROVE AVE
THE GROVE
SHAKESPEARE RD
POPES DR
ALAN LO
ALBERT PL
PREMIER HO
REDBOURNE HO
REDBOURNE AVE
DORSET MEWS
PRINCES AVE
STANTON CL
CLAVERLEY GR
CLAVERLEY VILLAS
MILLERS YD
ST PAUL'S WAY
THE RIDGEWAY
WILLOW WAY
PARKSIDE
DUKES AVE
VINES AVE
OAKFIELD CT
OAKFIELD RD
N3
HERVEY CL
BERKELEY CT
CLAIGMAR GDNS
CADOGAN GDNS
STRATHMORE GDNS
VINEYARD GR
DOLLIS MEWS
Finchley Central
WOOTTON GR
ARCADIA AVE
STATION CL
STATION RD
GLENHILL CL
LICHFIELD GR
SYLVAN AVE
Pav
Tenn Cts
Sp Gd

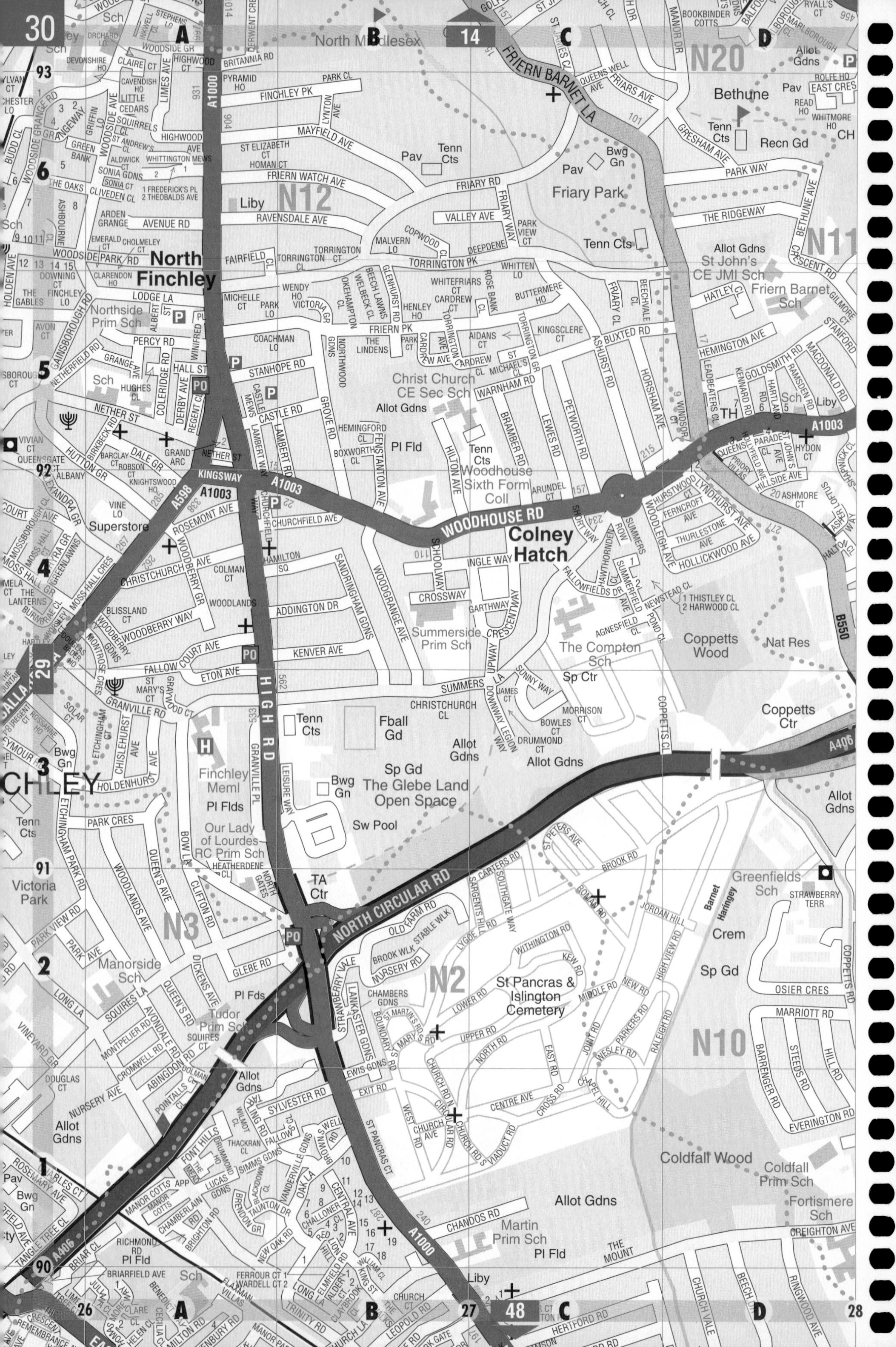

A
B
C
D
14
North Middlesex
N20
N12
N11
N3
N2
N10
North Finchley
Colney Hatch
Friary Park
Bethune
Recn Gd
FRIERN BARNET LA
FRIARY RD
FINCHLEY PK
MAYFIELD AVE
FRIERN WATCH AVE
RAVENSDALE AVE
AVENUE RD
TORRINGTON PK
PARK WAY
THE RIDGEWAY
BETHUNE AVE
GRESHAM AVE
VALLEY AVE
FRIERN PK
BUXTED RD
WOODHOUSE RD
KINGSWAY
A1003
A1000
A598
A406
B550
HIGH RD
NORTH CIRCULAR RD
Christ Church CE Sec Sch
Woodhouse Sixth Form Coll
St John's CE JMI Sch
Friern Barnet Sch
Northside Prim Sch
Summerside Prim Sch
The Compton Sch
Coppetts Wood
Nat Res
Coppetts Ctr
Finchley Meml
Our Lady of Lourdes RC Prim Sch
The Glebe Land Open Space
Sw Pool
Fball Gd
Sp Gd
TA Ctr
Manorside Sch
Tudor Prim Sch
Victoria Park
St Pancras & Islington Cemetery
Greenfields Sch
Crem
Coldfall Wood
Coldfall Prim Sch
Fortismere Sch
Martin Prim Sch
Allot Gdns
Tenn Cts
Superstore
Liby
Pl Fld
CHRISTCHURCH AVE
WOODBERRY WAY
FALLOW COURT AVE
SUMMERS LA
GRANVILLE RD
PARK CRES
ETCHINGHAM PARK RD
WOODLANDS AVE
GLEBE RD
LONG LA
CHANDOS RD
CREIGHTON AVE
OSIER CRES
MARRIOTT RD
EVERINGTON RD
BROOK RD
JORDAN HILL
HIGH VIEW RD
ST PANCRAS CT
THE MOUNT
Barnet
Haringey
29
48
90
91
92
93
26
27
28

31
A
B
C
D
15
FRIERN BARNET
New Southgate
N11
N14
N22
N10
N8
Arnos Park
Arnos Grove
OAKLEIGH RD S
FRIERN BARNET RD
BOWES RD
STATION RD
TELFORD RD (NORTH CIRCULAR RD)
PINKHAM WAY NORTH CIRCULAR RD
BOUNDS GREEN RD
WILMER WAY
POWYS LA
BOWES RD (NORTH
COLNEY HATCH LA
ALBERT RD
DURNSFORD RD
ALEXANDRA PARK RD
MUSWELL HILL BDWY
BROWNLOW RD
Colney Hatch
Hollickwood Park
Hollickwood Prim Sch
St Martin of Porres RC Prim Sch
Middlesex Univ (Bounds Green)
Wood Green Tunnel
Muswell Hill
Alexandra Park Sch
Rhodes Avenue Prim Sch
Bowes Prim Sch
Bloomfield Sch
Coppetts Wood Prim Sch
Our Lady of Muswell RC Prim Sch
Norfolk House Sch
Fortismere Sch (South Wing)
Alexandra Palace
The Lake
Mast
Alexandra Park
Superstore
Friern Bridge Ret Pk
Bounds Green Ind Est
Bounds Green
Allot Gdns
Recn Gd
Tenn Cts
Fball Ctr
Liby
Sch
Pav
6
5
4
3
2
1
93
92
91
90
28
29
49
30
32

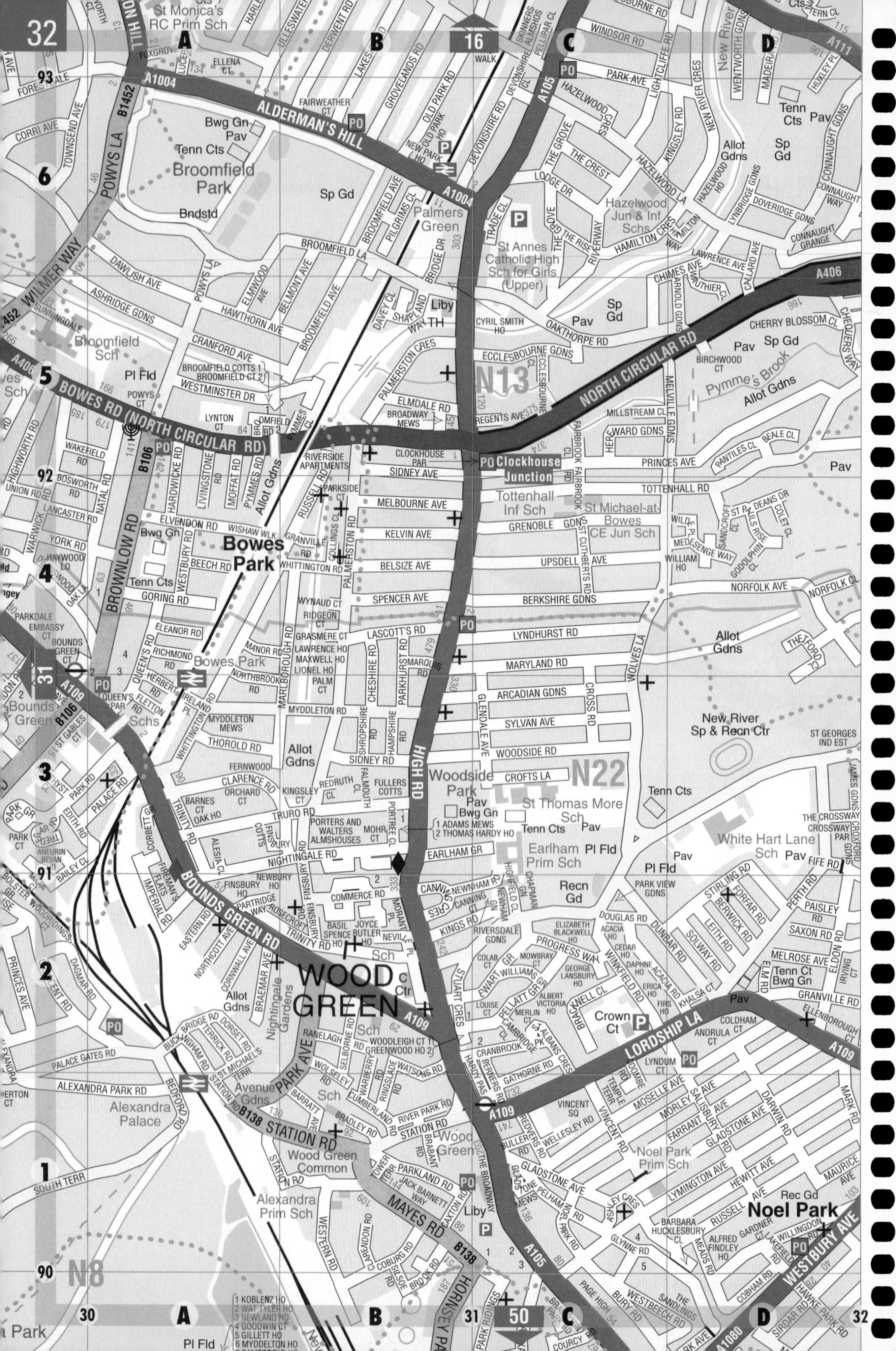
Broomfield Park
Palmers Green
Bowes Park
WOOD GREEN
Noel Park
N13
N22
N8
ALDERMAN'S HILL
NORTH CIRCULAR RD
BOWES RD (NORTH CIRCULAR RD)
HIGH RD
BOUNDS GREEN RD
LORDSHIP LA
STATION RD
MAYES RD
WESTBURY AVE
Alexandra Palace
Wood Green Common
Clockhouse Junction
New River Sp & Recn Ctr
White Hart Lane Sch
St Thomas More Sch
St Annes Catholic High Sch for Girls (Upper)
Hazelwood Jun & Inf Schs
Broomfield Sch
Woodside Park
Alexandra Prim Sch
Noel Park Prim Sch
Earlham Prim Sch
Tottenhall Inf Sch
St Michael-at-Bowes CE Jun Sch
1 KOBLENZ HO
2 WAT TYLER HO
3 NEWLAND HO
4 GOODWIN CT
5 GILLETT HO
6 MYDDELTON HO

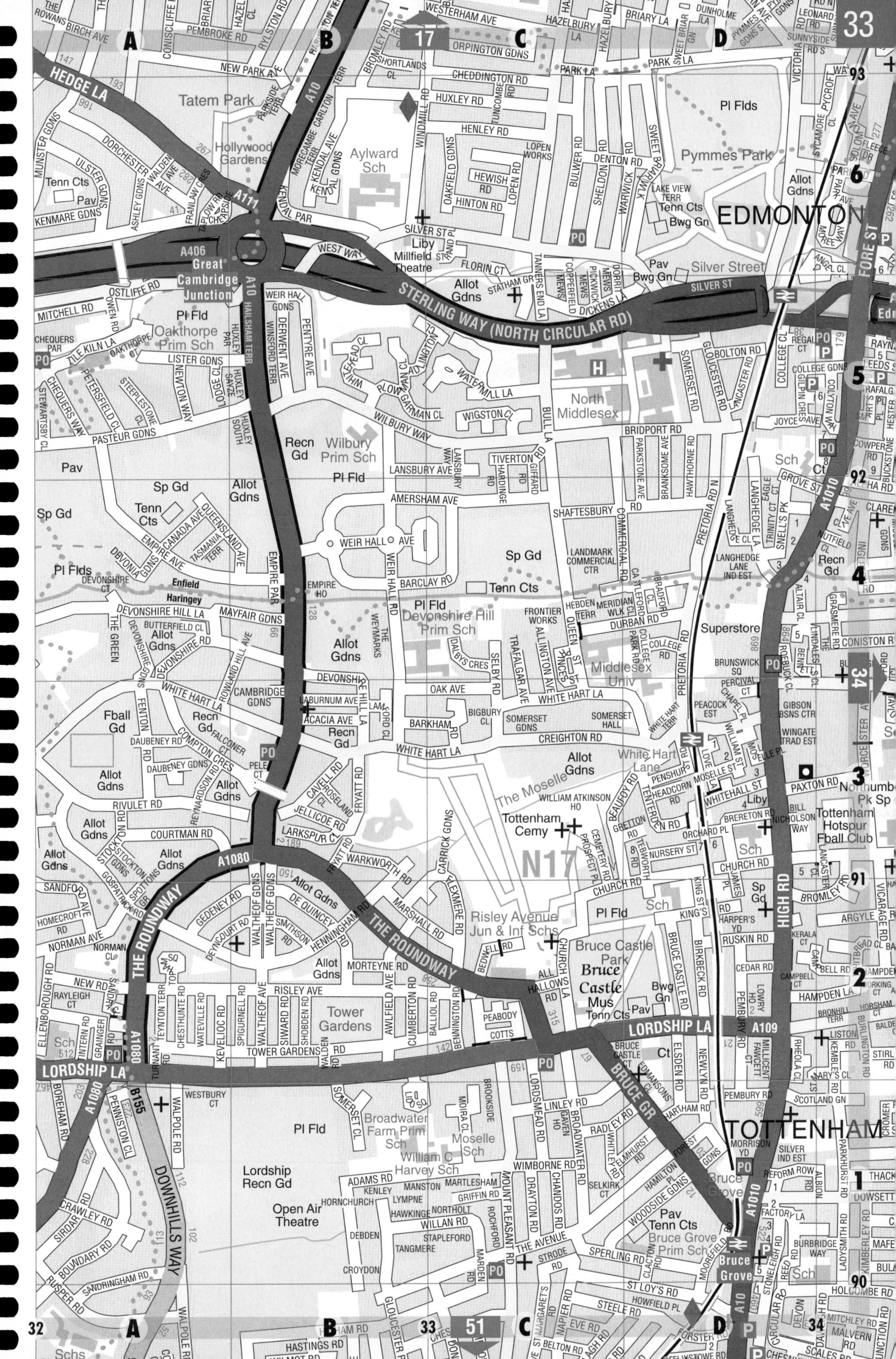
17
A
B
C
D
6
5
4
3
2
1
93
92
91
90
HEDGE LA
Tatem Park
Hollywood Gardens
Aylward Sch
Pl Flds
Pymmes Park
EDMONTON
Great Cambridge Junction
A406
A10
A111
STERLING WAY (NORTH CIRCULAR RD)
SILVER ST
Silver Street
WESTERHAM AVE
PEMBROKE RD
ORPINGTON GDNS
NEW PARK AVE
CHEDDINGTON RD
HUXLEY RD
HENLEY RD
DENTON RD
HEWISH RD
HINTON RD
KENMARE GDNS
Tenn Cts
Pav
Oakthorpe Prim Sch
MITCHELL RD
OSTLIFFE RD
TILE KILN LA
LISTER GDNS
PASTEUR GDNS
WILBURY WAY
Wilbury Prim Sch
Recn Gd
North Middlesex
BRIDPORT RD
LANSBURY AVE
AMERSHAM AVE
SHAFTESBURY RD
WEIR HALL AVE
BARCLAY RD
Sp Gd
Allot Gdns
Tenn Cts
Pl Flds
Enfield
Haringey
DEVONSHIRE HILL LA
MAYFAIR GDNS
Devonshire Hill Prim Sch
DURBAN RD
Superstore
Middlesex Univ
WHITE HART LA
OAK AVE
CREIGHTON RD
White Hart Lane
The Moselle
Tottenham Cemy
N17
Tottenham Hotspur Fball Club
Northumb Pk Sp
PAXTON RD
HIGH RD
A1010
FORE ST
Fball Gd
RIVULET RD
COURTMAN RD
A1080
THE ROUNDWAY
Risley Avenue Jun & Inf Schs
Bruce Castle Park
Bruce Castle Mus
CHURCH RD
RISLEY AVE
Tower Gardens
TOWER GARDENS RD
LORDSHIP LA
A109
BRUCE GR
TOTTENHAM
Pl Fld
Broadwater Farm Prim Sch
Moselle Sch
William C Harvey Sch
Lordship Recn Gd
Open Air Theatre
DOWNHILLS WAY
B155
THE AVENUE
Pav Tenn Cts
Bruce Grove Prim Sch
Bruce Grove
STEELE RD
32
51
34

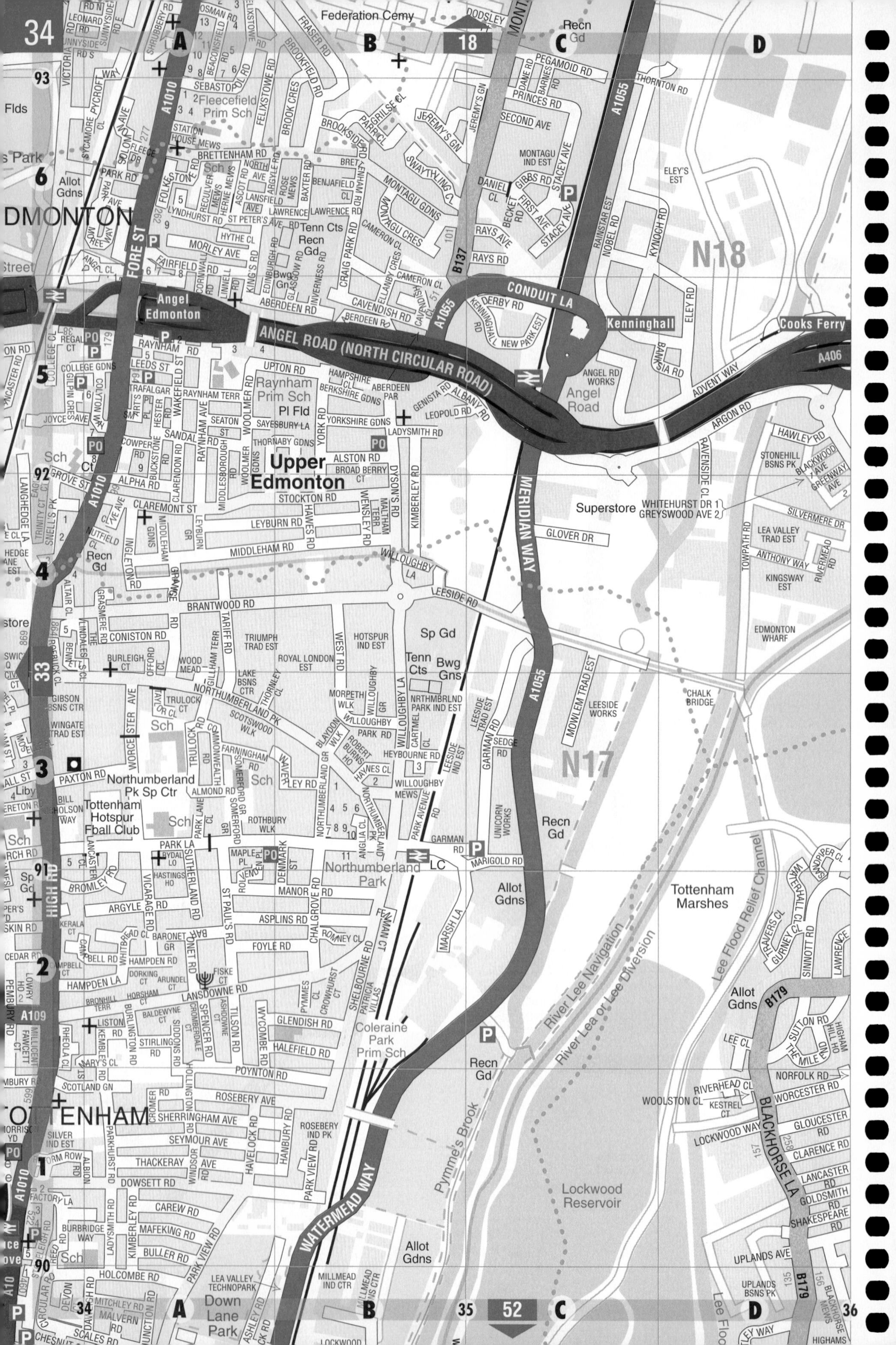

A
B
18
C
D
93
Federation Cemy
DODSLEY
Recn Gd
PEGAMOID RD
THORNTON RD
PRINCES RD
SECOND AVE
MONTAGU IND EST
STACEY AVE
ELEY'S EST
Fleecefield Prim Sch
STATION HOUSE MEWS
BRETTENHAM RD
SEBASTOPOL RD
FELIXSTOWE RD
BROOK CRES
BROOKFIELD RD
FRASER RD
PARR CL
GRILSE CL
BROOKSIDE RD
JEREMY'S GN
SWAYTHLING CL
MONTAGU GDNS
MONTAGU CRES
CAMERON CL
DANIEL CL
GIBBS RD
FIRST AVE
BECKET RD
RAYS AVE
RAYS RD
RAINSTAR EST
NOBEL RD
KYNOCH RD
N18
Flds
Park
6
Allot Gdns
EDMONTON
PARK RD
SOLOMON AVE
SYCAMORE CL
PYCROFT WAY
VICTORIA RD
LEONARD RD
SUNNYSIDE RD
Sch
FOLKESTONE RD
RECULVER MEWS
HERNE MEWS
NORTH AVE
ARGYLE RD
ROSE MEWS
BAXTER RD
BENJAFIELD CL
BRETTENHAM RD
LANSFIELD AVE
LAWRENCE RD
LYNDHURST RD
ST PETER'S AVE
HYTHE CL
MORLEY AVE
FAIRFIELD RD
Tenn Cts
Recn Gd
Bwg Gns
CORNWALL RD
LINNELL RD
KING'S RD
EDINBURGH RD
GLASGOW RD
INVERNESS RD
CRAIG PARK RD
ELLANBY CRES
CAVENDISH RD
ABERDEEN RD
CONDUIT LA
DERBY RD
KENNINGHALL RD
NEW PARK EST
Kenninghall
ELEY RD
BANKSIA RD
Cooks Ferry
FORE ST
A1010
B137
A1055
Street
Angel Edmonton
ANGEL ROAD (NORTH CIRCULAR ROAD)
A406
5
COLLEGE CL
REGAL CT
COLLEGE GDNS
GILPIN CRES
COLYTON WAY
RAYNHAM RD
LEEDS ST
TRAFALGAR PL
RAYNHAM TERR
UPTON RD
Raynham Prim Sch
Pl Fld
HAMPSHIRE RD
ABERDEEN PAR
BERKSHIRE GDNS
GENISTA RD
ALBANY RD
LEOPOLD RD
ANGEL RD WORKS
Angel Road
ADVENT WAY
ARGON RD
JOYCE AVE
HESTER RD
WAKEFIELD ST
RAYNHAM AVE
SEATON ST
WOOLMER RD
SAYESBURY LA
YORKSHIRE GDNS
LADYSMITH RD
THORNABY GDNS
YORK RD
COWPER RD
SANDAL RD
BUCKSTONE RD
CLARENDON RD
MIDDLESBOROUGH RD
WOOLMER GDNS
Upper Edmonton
ALSTON RD
BROAD BERRY CT
DYSON'S RD
KIMBERLEY RD
HAWLEY RD
STONEHILL BSNS PK
BLACKWOOD AVE
GREENWAY AVE
RAVENSIDE CL
92
Sch
Ct
GROVE ST
ALPHA RD
STOCKTON RD
WENSLEY RD
MALTHAM TERR
MERIDIAN WAY
Superstore
WHITEHURST DR 1
GREYSWOOD AVE 2
SILVERMERE DR
LANGHEDGE LA
TRINITY CT
SNELL'S PK
CLAREMONT ST
LEYBURN RD
HAWES RD
GLOVER DR
LEA VALLEY TRAD EST
TOWPATH RD
NUTFIELD RD
MIDDLEHAM RD
INGLETON RD
WILLOUGHBY LA
ANTHONY WAY
RIVERMEAD RD
KINGSWAY EST
4
HEDGE LANE EST
Recn Gd
ALTAIR CL
GRANGE RD
LEESIDE RD
BRANTWOOD RD
EDMONTON WHARF
store
GRASMERE RD
CONISTON RD
TARIFF RD
TRIUMPH TRAD EST
HOTSPUR IND EST
WEST RD
Sp Gd
Tenn Cts
Bwg Gns
33
BURLEIGH CT
OFFORD CL
WOOD MEAD
GILLHAM TERR
LAKE BSNS CTR
ROYAL LONDON EST
THORNLEY CL
GIBSON BSNS CTR
WINGATE TRAD EST
TRULOCK CT
NORTHUMBERLAND PK
MORPETH WLK
WILLOUGHBY GR
NRTHMBRLND PARK IND EST
LEESIDE TRAD EST
MOWLEM TRAD EST
LEESIDE WORKS
CHALK BRIDGE
Sch
WORCESTER AVE
SCOTSWOOD WLK
WILLOUGHBY PARK RD
HEYBOURNE RD
LEESIDE IND EST
GARMAN RD
SEDGE RD
N17
3
PAXTON RD
Northumberland Pk Sp Ctr
TRULOCK RD
COMMONWEALTH RD
FARNINGHAM RD
SOMERFORD GR
WAVERLEY RD
BLAYDON WLK
ROBERT BURNS HO
HAYNES CL
WILLOUGHBY MEWS
CARTMEL CL
Tottenham Hotspur Fball Club
ALMOND RD
Sch
PARK LANE CL
ROTHBURY WLK
NORTHUMBERLAND GR
ANGLIA CL
PARK AVENUE RD
UNICORN WORKS
Recn Gd
Sch
LANCASTER RD
PARK LA
BYDAL LO
HASTINGS HO
MAPLE PL
DENMARK ST
GARMAN RD
MARIGOLD RD
91
BROMLEY RD
Northumberland Park
LC
SUTHERLAND RD
VICARAGE RD
MANOR RD
Allot Gdns
Tottenham Marshes
ARGYLE RD
ST PAUL'S RD
ASPLINS RD
CHALGROVE RD
FENMAN CT
MARSH LA
HIGH RD
KERALA CT
WHITBREAD CL
BARONET GR
BARONET RD
ROMNEY CL
FOYLE RD
SHELBOURNE RD
PATRICIA VILLAS
River Lee Navigation
River Lea or Lee Diversion
Lee Flood Relief Channel
TRAVERS CL
GURNEY CL
SINNOTT RD
LAWRENCE RD
CEDAR RD
CAMPBELL CT
2
HAMPDEN RD
DORKING CT
ARUNDEL CT
FISKE CT
HAMPDEN LA
PYMMES CL
CROWHURST CT
Allot Gdns
B179
PEMBURY RD
LOWRY HO
HORSHAM CT
LANSDOWNE RD
BALDEWYNE CT
SPENCER RD
ASHDOWNE CT
TILSON RD
WYCOMBE RD
GLENDISH RD
A109
LISTON RD
KEMBLE RD
BURLINGTON RD
STIRLING RD
SIDDONS RD
CROMBEDALE
Coleraine Park Prim Sch
HALEFIELD RD
SUTTON RD
HIGHAM HILL HO
THE MILE END
LEE CL
MILLICENT FAWCETT CT
RHEOLA CL
MARY'S CL
HOLLINGTON RD
POYNTON RD
Recn Gd
NORFOLK RD
SCOTLAND GN
ROSEBERY AVE
RIVERHEAD CL
WORCESTER RD
WOOLSTON CL
KESTREL CT
TOTTENHAM
CROMER RD
SHERRINGHAM AVE
ROSEBERY IND PK
Pymme's Brook
BLACKHORSE LA
GLOUCESTER RD
SILVER IND EST
SEYMOUR AVE
HAVELOCK RD
HANBURY RD
LOCKWOOD WAY
CLARENCE RD
1
WORM ROW
ALBION RD
PARKHURST RD
THACKERAY AVE
WINDSOR RD
PARK VIEW RD
WATERMEAD WAY
LANCASTER RD
DOWSETT RD
Lockwood Reservoir
GOLDSMITH RD
FACTORY LA
CAREW RD
SHAKESPEARE RD
BURBRIDGE WAY
MAFEKING RD
LADYSMITH RD
KIMBERLEY RD
Sch
BULLER RD
PARK VIEW RD
Allot Gdns
UPLANDS AVE
90
HOLCOMBE RD
LEA VALLEY TECHNOPARK
MILLMEAD IND CTR
UPLANDS BSNS PK
CIRCULAR RD
DEVON RD
MITCHLEY RD
MALVERN RD
SCALES RD
Down Lane Park
ASHLEY RD
34
A
B
35
52
C
D
36
BLACKHORSE MEWS
HIGHAMS

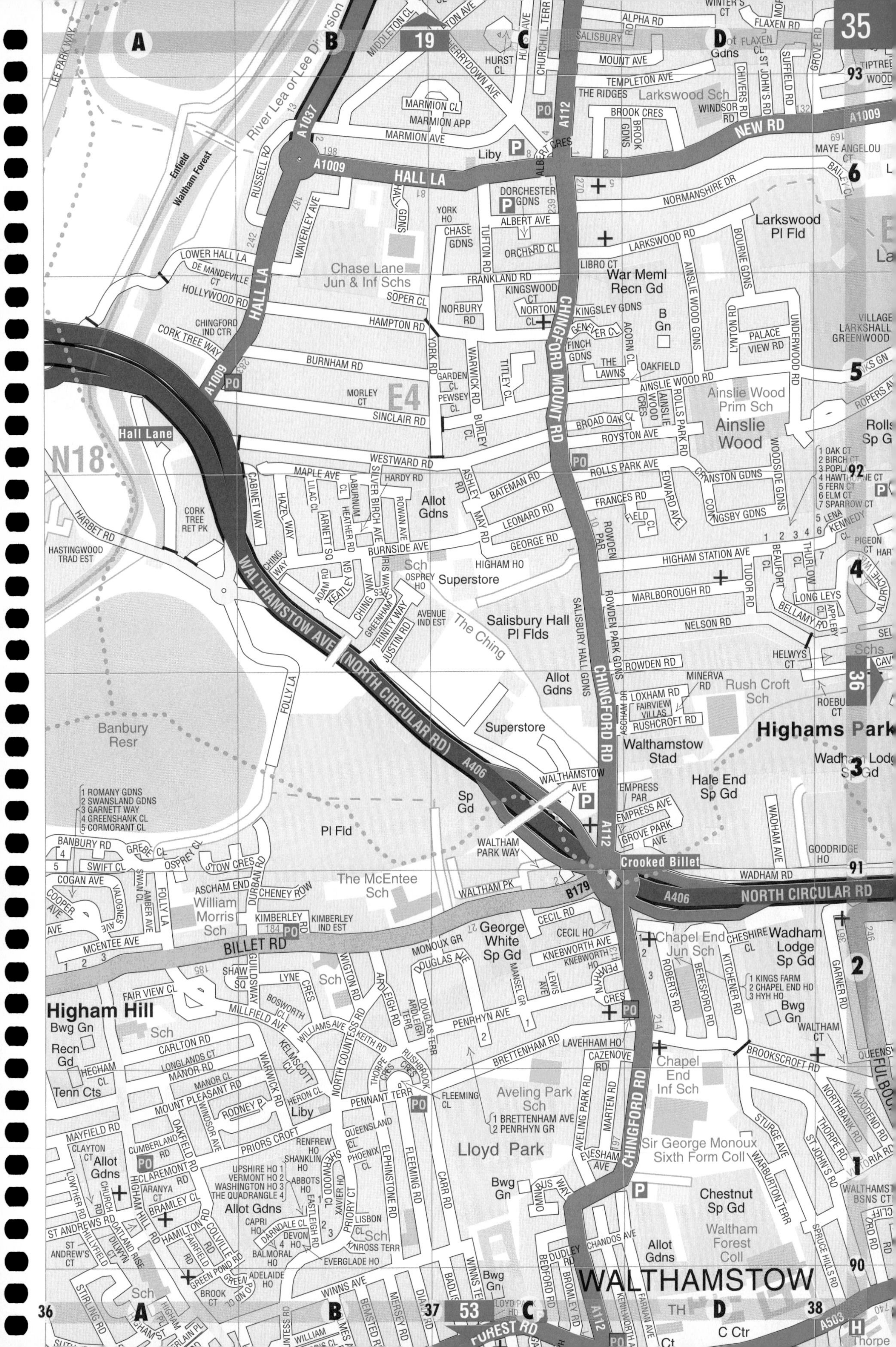

35
A
B
C
D
19
River Lea or Lee Diversion
LEE PARK WAY
MIDDLETON CL
CHURCHILL TERR
ALPHA RD
SALISBURY
FLAXEN RD
Gdns
MOUNT AVE
TEMPLETON AVE
THE RIDGES
Larkswood Sch
WINDSOR RD
BROOK CRES
NEW RD
A1009
A1037
A112
HURST CL
CHERRYDOWN AVE
MARMION CL
MARMION APP
MARMION AVE
RUSSELL RD
HALL LA
Liby
ALBERT CRES
MAYE ANGELOU CT
BAILEY CL
NORMANSHIRE DR
DORCHESTER GDNS
ALBERT AVE
YORK HO
CHASE GDNS
TUFTON RD
ORCHARD CL
LARKSWOOD RD
Larkswood Pl Fld
WAVERLEY AVE
LOWER HALL LA
DE MANDEVILLE CT
HOLLYWOOD RD
Chase Lane Jun & Inf Schs
LIBRO CT
FRANKLAND RD
War Meml Recn Gd
SOPER CL
KINGSWOOD CT
NORTON CL
NORBURY RD
KINGSLEY GDNS
B Gn
CHINGFORD IND CTR
HAMPTON RD
CORK TREE WAY
FINCH GDNS
ACORN CL
AINSLIE WOOD GDNS
BOURNE GDNS
LYNTON RD
UNDERWOOD RD
PALACE VIEW RD
VILLAGE LARKSHALL GREENWOOD
BURNHAM RD
YORK RD
GARDEN CL
PEWSEY CL
WARWICK RD
TITLEY CL
CHINGFORD MOUNT RD
THE LAWNS
OAKFIELD
AINSLIE WOOD RD
Ainslie Wood Prim Sch
MORLEY CT
E4
SINCLAIR RD
BURLEY CL
BROAD OAK CL
ROLLS PARK RD
Ainslie Wood
Hall Lane
ROYSTON AVE
WESTWARD RD
N18
MAPLE AVE
HARDY RD
ROLLS PARK AVE
CRANSTON GDNS
WOODSIDE GDNS
1 OAK CT
2 BIRCH CT
4 HAWTHORNE CT
5 FERN CT
6 ELM CT
7 SPARROW CT
CABINET WAY
HAZEL WAY
LILAC CL
LABURNUM CL
SILVER BIRCH AVE
ROWAN AVE
Allot Gdns
BATEMAN RD
ASHLEY RD
MAY RD
LEONARD RD
FRANCES RD
FIELD CL
EDWARD AVE
CONINGSBY GDNS
CORK TREE RET PK
HEATHER RD
ARNETT SQ
HARBET RD
HASTINGWOOD TRAD EST
BURNSIDE AVE
Sch
GEORGE RD
ROWDEN PAR
HIGHAM STATION AVE
BEAUFORT CL
THURLOW CL
PIGEON CT
CHING WAY
ADAM RD
KEATLEY GN
OSPREY HO
Superstore
HIGHAM HO
MARLBOROUGH RD
TUDOR RD
LONG LEYS
BELLAMY RD
APPLEBY CL
WALTHAMSTOW AVE
GREENHAM CL
TRINITY WAY
JUSTIN RD
AVENUE IND EST
The Ching
Salisbury Hall Pl Flds
NELSON RD
HELWYS CT
Schs
NORTH CIRCULAR RD
SALISBURY HALL GDNS
ROWDEN PARK GDNS
ROWDEN RD
MINERVA RD
Rush Croft Sch
LOXHAM RD
FAIRVIEW VILLAS
RUSHCROFT RD
ASCHAM DR
ROEBUCK CT
Highams Park
FOLLY LA
Banbury Resr
CHINGFORD RD
Walthamstow Stad
A406
WALTHAMSTOW AVE
Hale End Sp Gd
WADHAM AVE
1 ROMANY GDNS
2 SWANSLAND GDNS
3 GARNETT WAY
4 GREENSHANK CL
5 CORMORANT CL
Sp Gd
EMPRESS PAR
EMPRESS AVE
GROVE PARK AVE
BANBURY RD
GREBE CL
OSPREY CL
SWIFT CL
Pl Fld
WALTHAM PARK WAY
STOW CRES
GOODRIDGE HO
Crooked Billet
WADHAM RD
COGAN AVE
VALOGNES AVE
SWAN CL
FOLLY LA
DURBAN RD
ASCHAM END
CHENEY ROW
The McEntee Sch
WALTHAM PK
B179
COOPER AVE
AMBER AVE
William Morris Sch
KIMBERLEY RD
KIMBERLEY IND EST
CECIL RD
George White Sp Gd
CECIL HO
Chapel End Jun Sch
CHESHIRE CL
Wadham Lodge Sp Gd
MCENTEE AVE
BILLET RD
MONOUX GR
KNEBWORTH AVE
KNEBWORTH HO
GARNER RD
SHAW SQ
GUILDSWAY
LYNE CRES
WIGTON RD
ARDLEIGH RD
DOUGLAS AVE
MANSEL GR
LEWIS AVE
ROBERTS RD
BERESFORD RD
KITCHENER RD
1 KINGS FARM
2 CHAPEL END HO
3 HYH HO
Higham Hill
FAIR VIEW CL
BOSWORTH CL
MILLFIELD AVE
ARDLEIGH TERR
PENRHYN AVE
PENRHYN CRES
Bwg Gn
Recn Gd
Sch
CARLTON RD
WILLIAMS AVE
KEITH RD
DOUGLAS TERR
LAVEHHAM HO
WALTHAM CT
BRETTENHAM RD
BROOKSCROFT RD
LONGLANDS CT
MANOR RD
KELMSCOTT CL
RUSHBROOK CRES
CAZENOVE RD
Chapel End Inf Sch
QUEENSWOOD
HECHAM CL
MANOR CL
THORPE CRES
FLEEMING CL
Tenn Cts
MOUNT PLEASANT RD
HERON CL
PENNANT TERR
Aveling Park Sch
NORTHBANK RD
WOODEND RD
RODNEY PL
WARWICK RD
NORTH COUNTESS RD
MARTEN RD
STURGE AVE
THORPE RD
ST JOHN'S RD
OAKFIELD RD
WINDSOR AVE
QUEENSLAND HO
1 BRETTENHAM AVE
2 PENRHYN GR
AVELING PARK RD
MAYFIELD RD
PRIORS CROFT
RENFREW HO
SHANKLIN HO
PHOENIX CL
ELPHINSTONE RD
FLEEMING RD
Lloyd Park
Sir George Monoux Sixth Form Coll
WARBURTON TERR
CLAYTON CT
CUMBERLAND RD
Allot Gdns
CLAREMONT RD
UPSHIRE HO 1
VERMONT HO 2
WASHINGTON HO 3
THE QUADRANGLE 4
ABBOTS HO
EASTLEIGH RD
EVESHAM AVE
WALTHAMSTOW BSNS CTR
ARANYA CT
BRAMLEY CL
HIGHAM HILL RD
CHURCH RD
Allot Gdns
PRIORY CT
XAVIER HO
CARR RD
Bwg Gn
BUS WAY
Chestnut Sp Gd
LOWTHER RD
ST ANDREWS RD
OATLAND RISE
HAMILTON RD
COLVILLE RD
CAPRI HO
DARNDALE CL
DEVON HO
LISBON CL
Sch
KINROSS TERR
Waltham Forest Coll
SPRUCE HILLS RD
ST ANDREW'S CT
HILLYFIELD
DILWYN CT
FAIRFIELD RD
GREEN POND RD
BALMORAL HO
EVERGLADE HO
CHANDOS AVE
Allot Gdns
STIRLING RD
ADELAIDE HO
WINNS AVE
BADLIS RD
WINNS TERR
Bwg Gn
DUDLEY RD
BEDFORD RD
BROMLEY RD
WALTHAMSTOW
BROOK CT
Sch
36
37
53
38
LLOYD PARK HO
FOREST RD
KENILWORTH AVE
FARMAN AVE
TH
C Ctr
A503
Thorpe
MERSEY RD
BEMSTED RD
WILLIAM
HIGHAM PL
HIGHAM ST
93
92
91
90
6
5
4
3
2
1

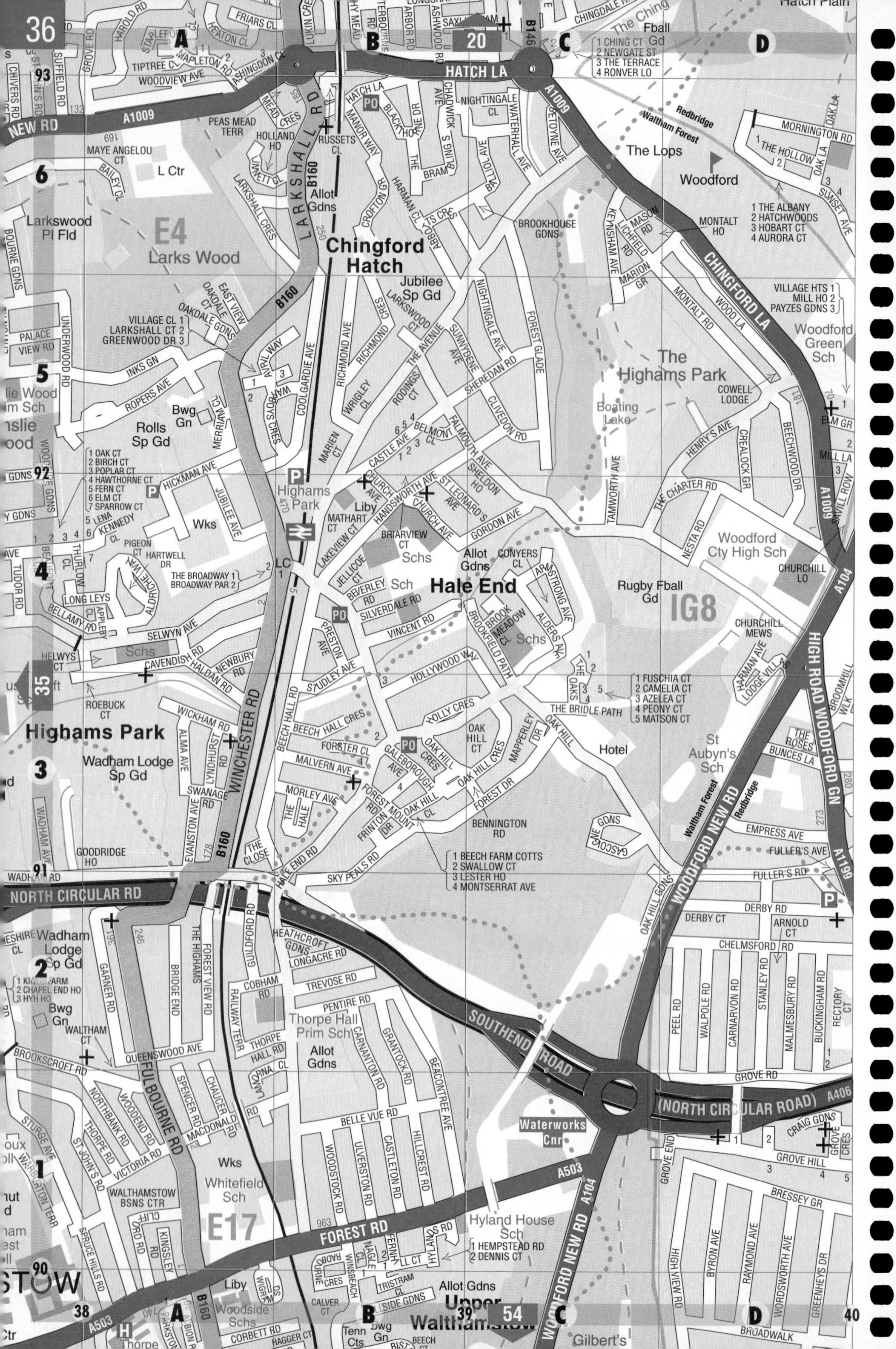
Chingford Hatch
Hale End
Highams Park
Larks Wood
The Highams Park
The Lops
Woodford
Upper Walthamstow
E4
IG8
E17
HATCH LA
NEW RD
LARKSHALL RD
WINCHESTER RD
NORTH CIRCULAR RD
SOUTHEND ROAD
(NORTH CIRCULAR ROAD)
FOREST RD
WOODFORD NEW RD
HIGH ROAD WOODFORD GN
CHINGFORD LA
FULBOURNE RD
Waterworks Cnr

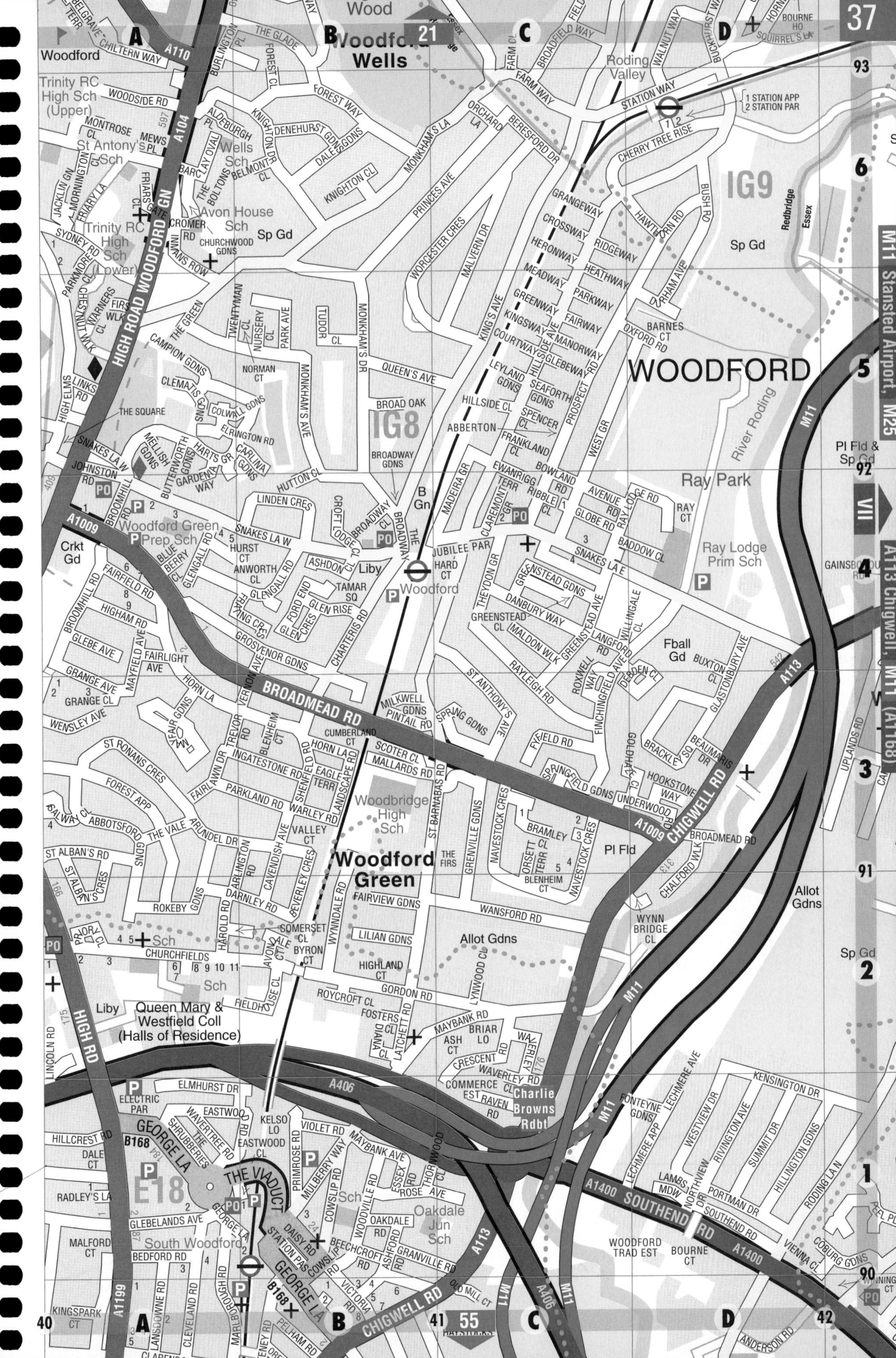

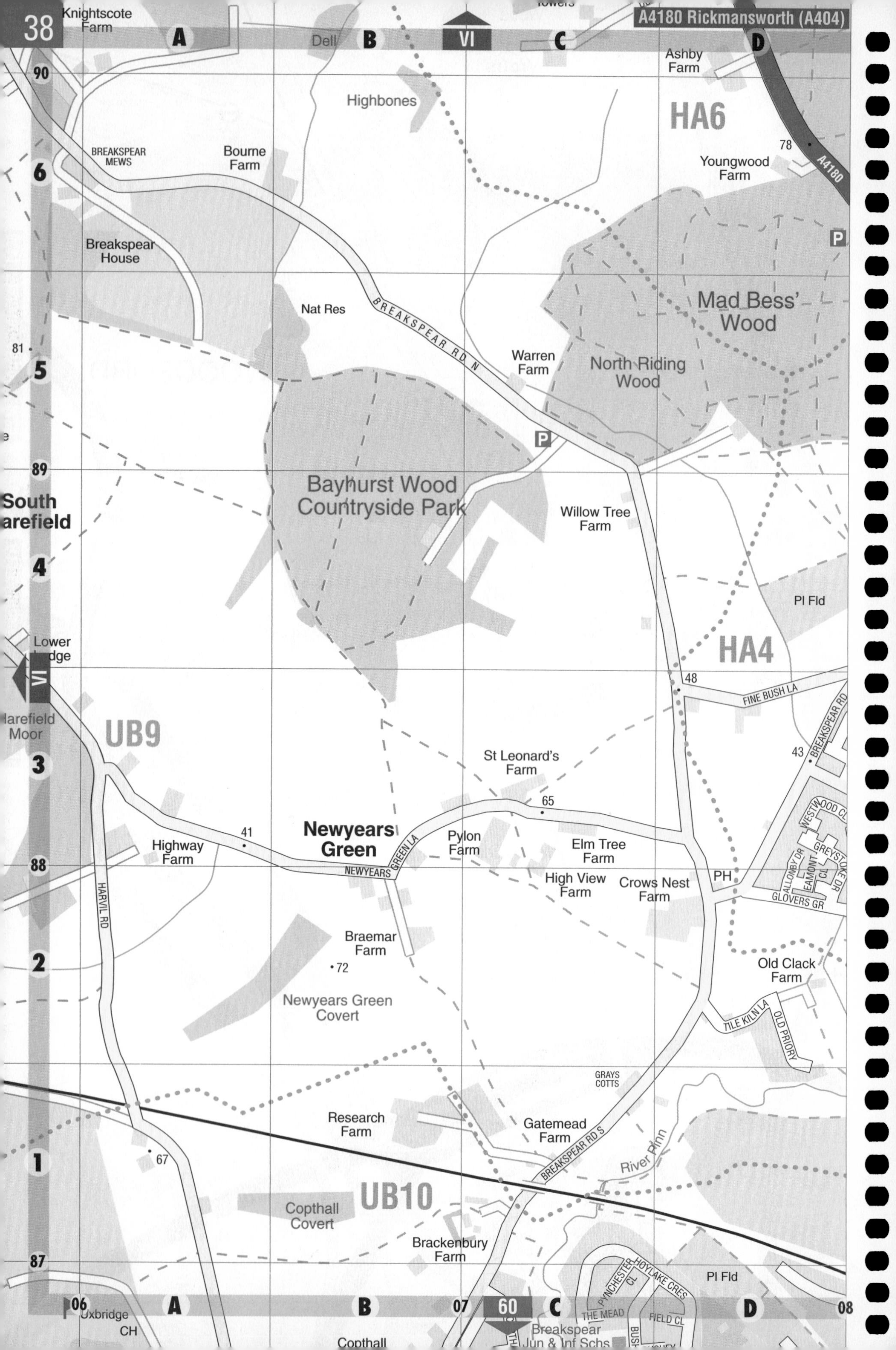

A4180 Rickmansworth (A404)
Knightscote Farm
Dell
Ashby Farm
Highbones
HA6
BREAKSPEAR MEWS
Bourne Farm
Youngwood Farm
A4180
Breakspear House
Mad Bess' Wood
Nat Res
BREAKSPEAR RD N
Warren Farm
North Riding Wood
Bayhurst Wood Countryside Park
South Harefield
Willow Tree Farm
Pl Fld
Lower Lodge
HA4
FINE BUSH LA
Harefield Moor
UB9
St Leonard's Farm
BREAKSPEAR RD
WESTWOOD CL
Newyears Green
Pylon Farm
Elm Tree Farm
GREYSTOKE DR
Highway Farm
NEWYEARS GREEN LA
HARVIL RD
High View Farm
Crows Nest Farm
PH
ALLONBY DR
EAMONT CL
GLOVERS GR
Braemar Farm
Old Clack Farm
Newyears Green Covert
TILE KILN LA
OLD PRIORY
GRAYS COTTS
Research Farm
Gatemead Farm
BREAKSPEAR RD S
River Pinn
UB10
Copthall Covert
Brackenbury Farm
PYNCHESTER CL
HOYLAKE CRES
Pl Fld
Uxbridge CH
THE MEAD
FIELD CL
Breakspear Jun & Inf Schs
Copthall

VI
60

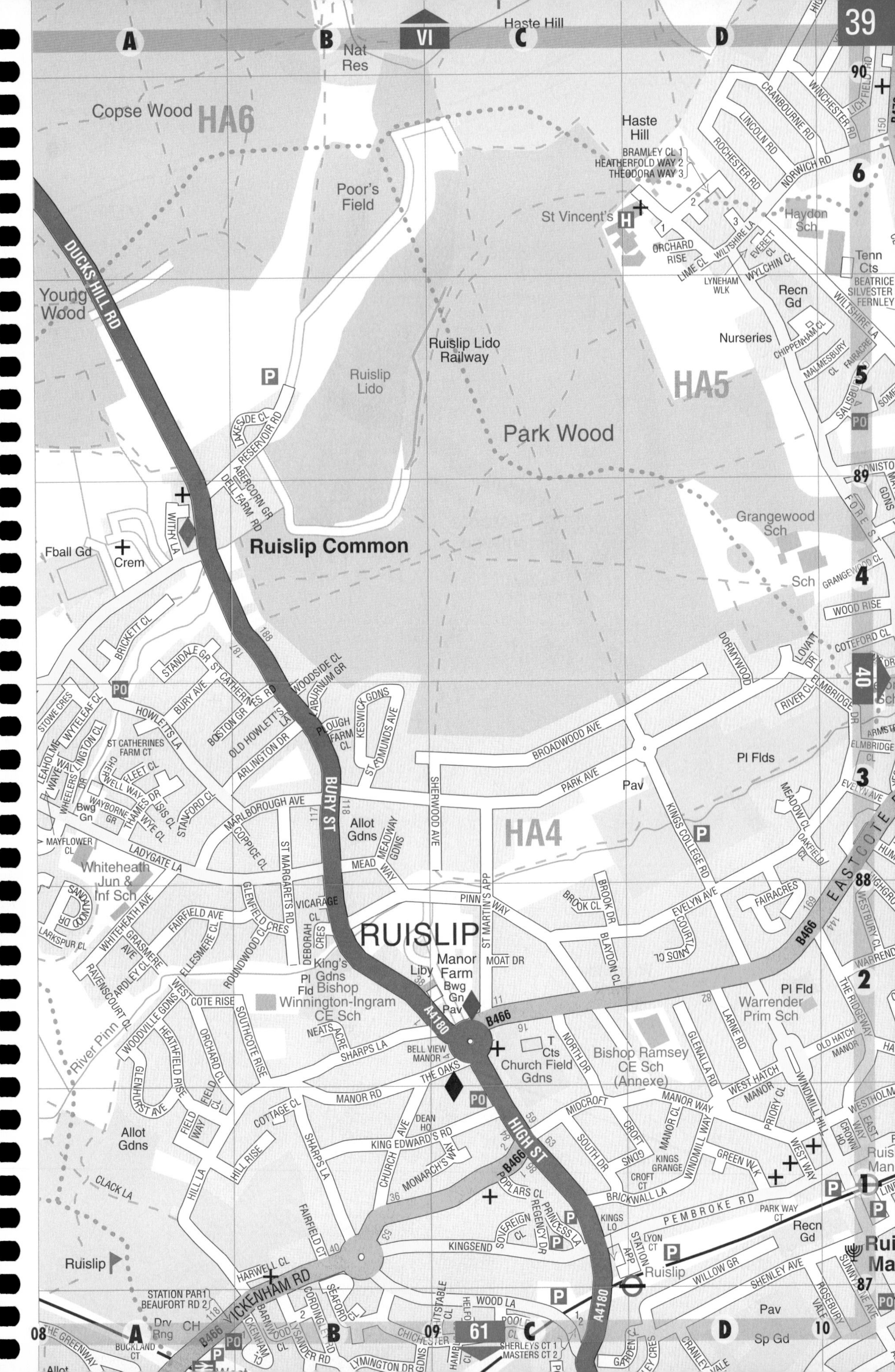

A
B
C
D
VI
Haste Hill
Nat Res
Copse Wood
HA6
Poor's Field
Haste Hill
BRAMLEY CL 1
HEATHERFOLD WAY 2
THEODORA WAY 3
St Vincent's
Young Wood
DUCKS HILL RD
Ruislip Lido
Ruislip Lido Railway
HA5
Park Wood
Ruislip Common
Fball Gd
Crem
Grangewood Sch
Haydon Sch
Recn Gd
Nurseries
Tenn Cts
HA4
RUISLIP
BURY ST
HIGH ST
Pl Flds
Pav
Allot Gdns
Whiteheath Jun & Inf Sch
King's Gdns
Bishop Winnington-Ingram CE Sch
Manor Farm
Liby
Church Field Gdns
Bishop Ramsey CE Sch (Annexe)
Warrender Prim Sch
Pl Fld
River Pinn
Allot Gdns
Ruislip
Recn Gd
Pav
Sp Gd
08
09
10
61
40
90
89
88
87
6
5
4
3
2
1

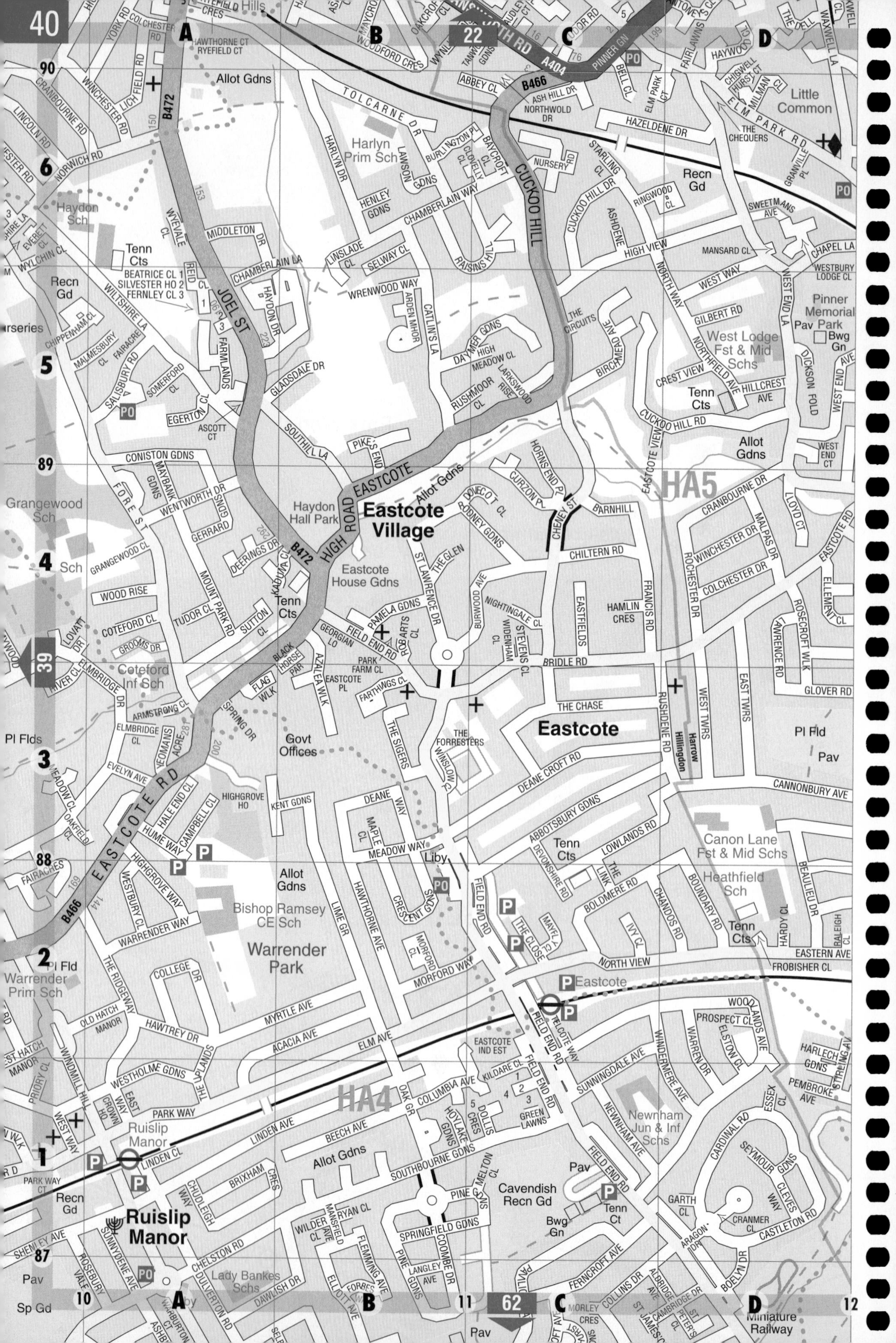

A
B
C
D
22
A404
PINNER GN
B466
B472
Allot Gdns
TOLCARNE DR
Harlyn Prim Sch
HARLYN DR
LAWSON GDNS
HENLEY GDNS
CHAMBERLAIN WAY
BURLINGTON PL
CLOVELLY CL
BAYCROFT CL
NURSERY RD
CUCKOO HILL
ABBEY CL
ASH HILL DR
NORTHWOLD DR
HAZELDENE DR
ELM PARK RD
Little Common
THE CHEQUERS
GRANVILLE PL
CHIGWELL HURST CT
MILMAN CL
HAYWOOD CL
FAIRLAWNS CL
BELL CL
ELM PARK CT
WAXWELL LA
THE DELL
STARLING CL
Recn Gd
RINGWOOD CL
CUCKOO HILL DR
ASHDENE
HIGH VIEW
NORTH WAY
SWEETMANS AVE
MANSARD CL
CHAPEL LA
WESTBURY LODGE CL
WEST WAY
WEST END LA
GILBERT RD
Pinner Memorial Park
Pav
Bwg Gn
West Lodge Fst & Mid Schs
NORTHFIELD AVE
CREST VIEW
HILLCREST AVE
Tenn Cts
DICKSON FOLD
WEST END AVE
CUCKOO HILL RD
Allot Gdns
WEST END CT
EASTCOTE VIEW
HA5
CRANBOURNE DR
LLOYD CT
WINCHESTER DR
MALPAS DR
ROCHESTER DR
COLCHESTER DR
EASTCOTE RD
ELLEMENT CL
ROSECROFT WLK
LAWRENCE RD
GLOVER RD
EAST TWRS
WEST TWRS
RUSHDENE RD
Harrow
Hillingdon
Pl Fld
Pav
CANNONBURY AVE
Canon Lane Fst & Mid Schs
Heathfield Sch
BEAULIEU DR
HARDY CL
RALEIGH CL
EASTERN AVE
FROBISHER CL
Tenn Cts
HAYDON DR
CHAMBERLAIN LA
MIDDLETON DR
WYEVALE CL
REID CL
JOEL ST
FARMLANDS
GLADSDALE DR
SOUTHILL LA
PIKES END
LINSLADE CL
SELWAY CL
WRENWOOD WAY
ARDEN MHOR
CATLIN'S LA
RAISINS HILL
THE CIRCUITS
DAYMER GDNS
HIGH MEADOW CL
RUSHMOOR CL
LARKSWOOD RISE
BIRCHMEAD AVE
HORNS END PL
CURZON PL
CHENEY ST
BARNHILL
CHILTERN RD
EASTFIELDS
HAMLIN CRES
FRANCIS RD
YORK RD
COLCHESTER RD
HAWTHORNE CT
RYEFIELD CT
WINCHESTER RD
LICHFIELD RD
CRANBOURNE RD
LINCOLN RD
NORWICH RD
Haydon Sch
EVERETT CL
WYLCHIN CL
Tenn Cts
BEATRICE CL 1
SILVESTER HO 2
FERNLEY CL 3
Recn Gd
WILTSHIRE LA
CHIPPENHAM CL
MALMESBURY CL
FAIRACRE
SALISBURY RD
SOMERFORD CL
EGERTON CL
ASCOTT CT
CONISTON GDNS
MAYBANK GDNS
WENTWORTH DR
GERRARD GDNS
FORE ST
Grangewood Sch
GRANGEWOOD CL
DEERINGS DR
KADUNA CL
WOOD RISE
MOUNT PARK RD
TUDOR CL
SUTTON CL
COTEFORD CL
GROOMS DR
LOVATT DR
39
RIVER CL
ELMBRIDGE DR
Coteford Inf Sch
ARMSTRONG CL
ELMBRIDGE CL
YEOMANS ACRE
Pl Flds
EVELYN AVE
MEADOW CL
OAKFIELD
HALE END CL
CAMPBELL CL
HUME WAY
HIGHGROVE HO
FAIRACRES
HIGHGROVE WAY
WESTBURY CL
WARRENDER WAY
EASTCOTE RD
HIGH ROAD EASTCOTE
Haydon Hall Park
Eastcote Village
Allot Gdns
DOVECOT CL
RODNEY GDNS
ST LAWRENCE DR
THE GLEN
Eastcote House Gdns
Tenn Cts
PAMELA GDNS
ROBARTS CL
BURWOOD AVE
NIGHTINGALE CL
WIDENHAM CL
STEVENS CL
BRIDLE RD
GEORGIAN LO
FIELD END RD
BLACK HORSE PAR
AZALEA WLK
PARK FARM CL
EASTCOTE PL
FARTHINGS CL
FLAG WLK
SPRING DR
Govt Offices
THE SIGERS
WINSLOW CL
THE FORRESTERS
THE CHASE
Eastcote
DEANE CROFT RD
KENT GDNS
DEANE WAY
MAPLE CL
MEADOW WAY
Liby
ABBOTSBURY GDNS
DEVONSHIRE RD
Tenn Cts
LOWLANDS RD
THE LINK
BOLDMERE RD
CHANDOS RD
BOUNDARY RD
IVY CL
MAYFLY CL
THE CLOSE
NORTH VIEW
Allot Gdns
Bishop Ramsey CE Sch
LIME GR
HAWTHORNE AVE
CRESCENT GDNS
MORFORD CL
MORFORD WAY
Warrender Park
COLLEGE DR
THE RIDGEWAY
Pl Fld
Warrender Prim Sch
OLD HATCH MANOR
HAWTREY DR
MYRTLE AVE
ACACIA AVE
ELM AVE
Eastcote
TELCOTE WAY
EASTCOTE IND EST
WOODLANDS AVE
PROSPECT CL
ELSTON CL
WARREN DR
WINDERMERE AVE
HARLECH GDNS
STIRLING AVE
PEMBROKE AVE
SUNNINGDALE AVE
NEWNHAM AVE
Newnham Jun & Inf Schs
KILDARE CL
GREEN LAWNS
DOLLIS CRES
COLUMBIA AVE
HOYLAKE GDNS
OAK GR
HA4
WINDMILL HILL
WESTHOLME GDNS
THE UPLANDS
EAST WAY
CROWN HO
PARK WAY
LINDEN AVE
BEECH AVE
Allot Gdns
SOUTHBOURNE GDNS
MELTON CL
Pav
Cavendish Recn Gd
Bwg Gn
Tenn Ct
FIELD END RD
ESSEX CL
CARDINAL RD
SEYMOUR GDNS
CLEVES WAY
GARTH CL
CRANMER CL
CASTLETON RD
ARAGON DR
BOELYN DR
PRIORY CL
WEST WAY
Ruislip Manor
LINDEN CL
PARK WAY CT
Recn Gd
Ruislip Manor
BRIXHAM CRES
CHUDLEIGH WAY
PINE GDNS
WILDER CL
RYAN CL
MANSFIELD AVE
FLEMMING AVE
SPRINGFIELD GDNS
COOMBE DR
LANGLEY AVE
FERNCROFT AVE
COLLINS DR
ALDRIDGE AVE
CAMBRIDGE CL
ST PETER'S
SHENLEY AVE
SUNNYDENE AVE
ROSEBURY VALE
CHELSTON RD
DULVERTON RD
Lady Bankes Schs
DAWLISH DR
ELLIOTT AVE
FORBES
Pav
Sp Gd
WARBURTON CT
62
MORLEY CRES
Miniature Railway
90
6
5
89
4
3
88
2
1
87
10
11
12

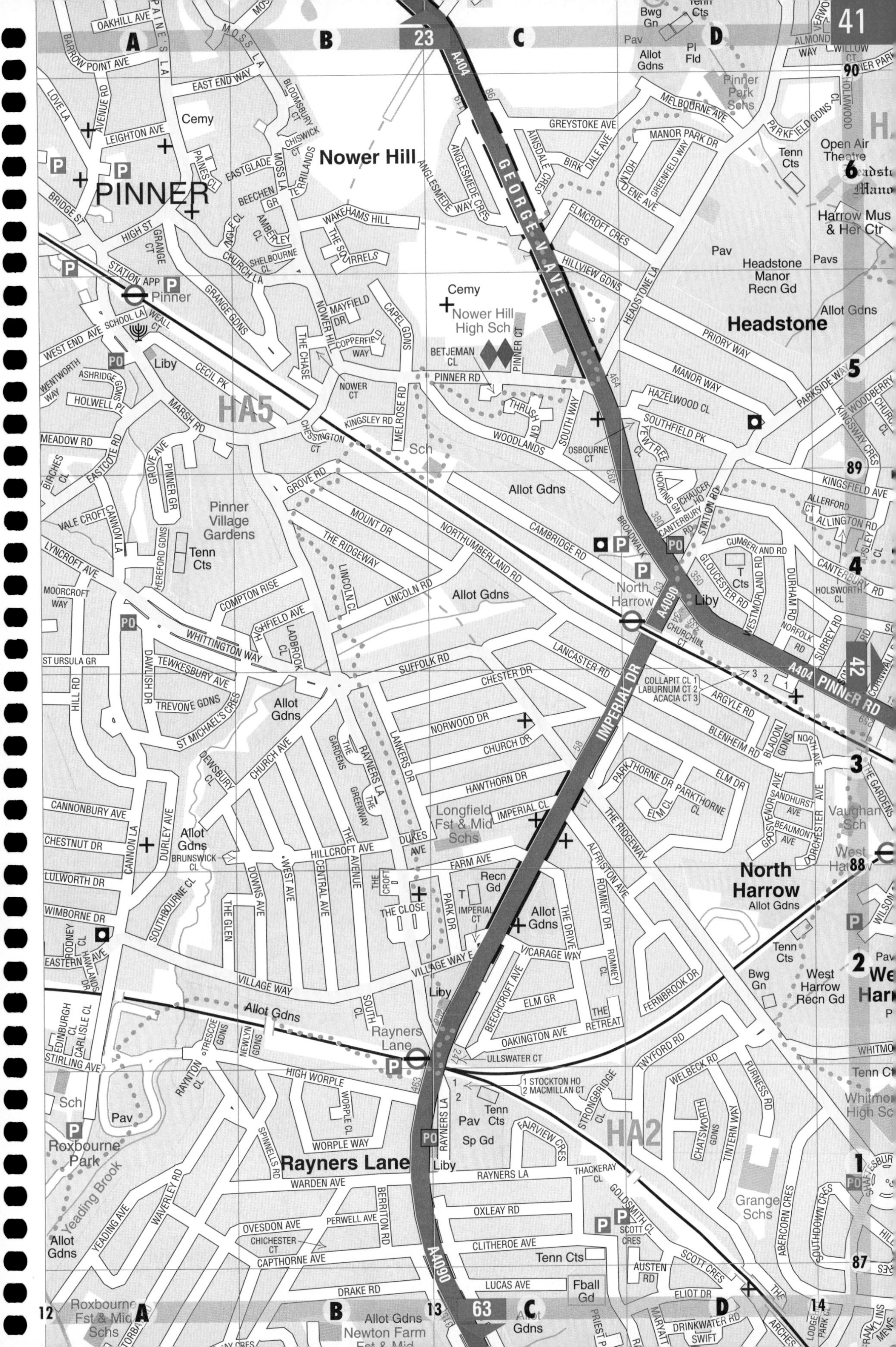

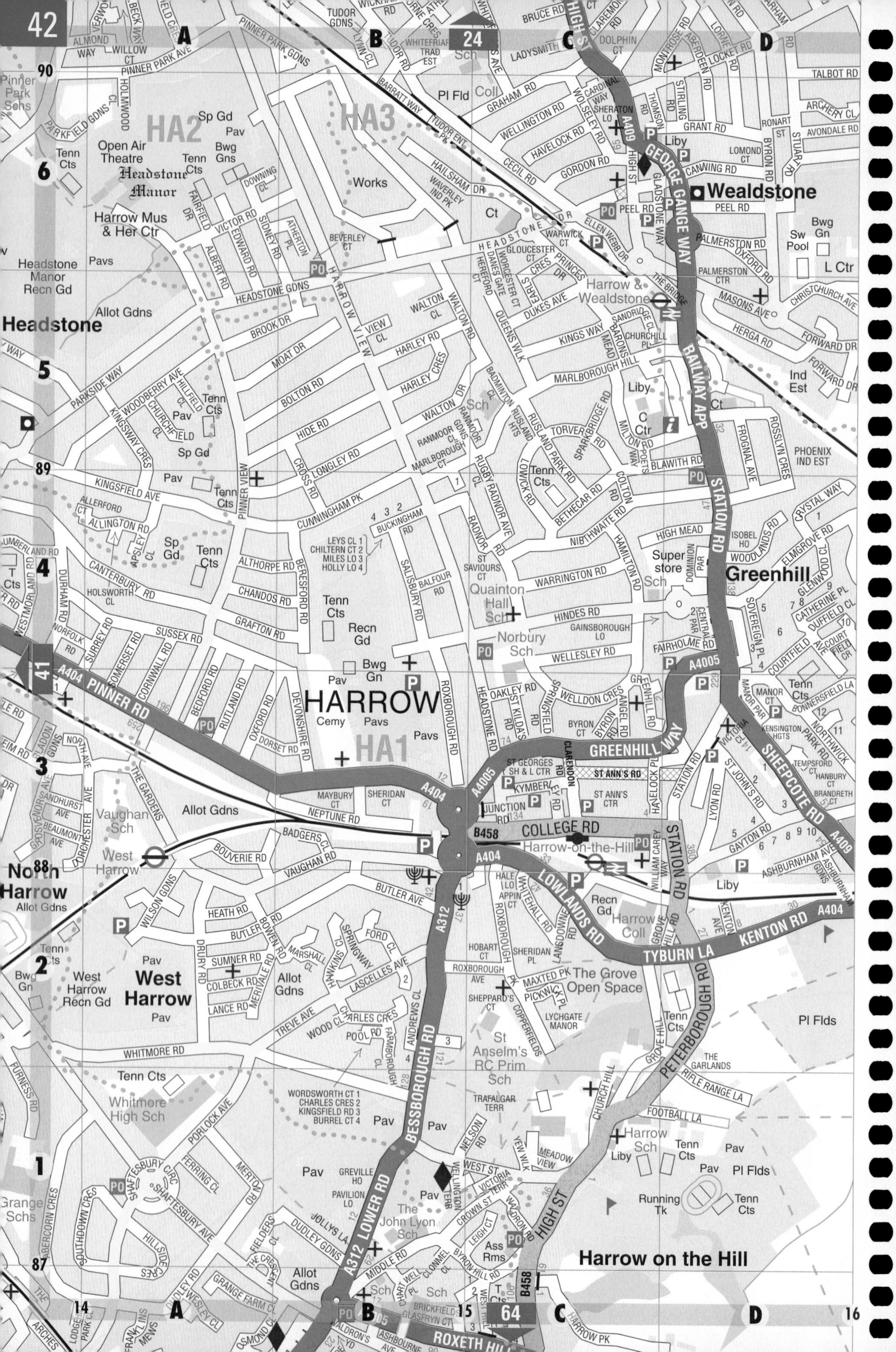
HA2
HA3
HA1
Headstone Manor
Harrow Mus & Her Ctr
Headstone Manor Recn Gd
Headstone
Wealdstone
Harrow & Wealdstone
Greenhill
HARROW
North Harrow
West Harrow
Harrow on the Hill
The Grove Open Space
Harrow Sch
St Anselm's RC Prim Sch
The John Lyon Sch
Whitmore High Sch
Vaughan Sch
Harrow Coll
Quainton Hall Sch
Norbury Sch
PINNER RD
GREENHILL WAY
STATION RD
GEORGE GANGE WAY
RAILWAY APP
SHEEPCOTE RD
LOWLANDS RD
TYBURN LA
KENTON RD
COLLEGE RD
BESSBOROUGH RD
LOWER RD
PETERBOROUGH RD
HIGH ST
ROXETH HILL
A404
A4005
A409
A312
B458
24
41
64
16
14
15

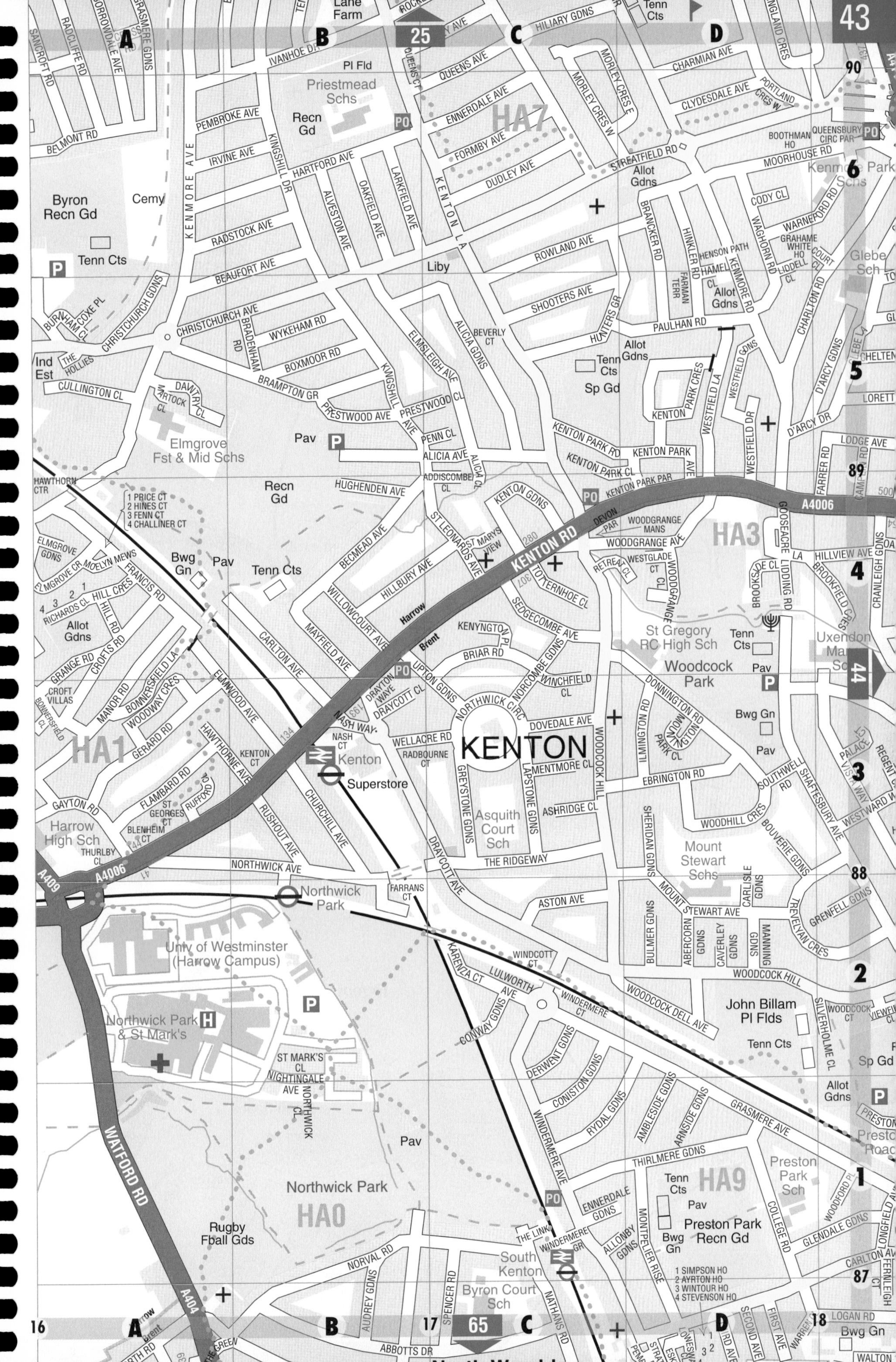

25
HA7
Priestmead Schs
Recn Gd
Byron Recn Gd
Cemy
Tenn Cts
Liby
Allot Gdns
Kenmore Park Schs
Glebe Sch
Elmgrove Fst & Mid Schs
Recn Gd
Pav
Tenn Cts
Sp Gd
KENTON RD
A4006
HA3
St Gregory RC High Sch
Woodcock Park
Uxendon Manor Sch
44
HA1
KENTON
Kenton
Superstore
Asquith Court Sch
Harrow High Sch
Mount Stewart Schs
Northwick Park
Univ of Westminster (Harrow Campus)
Northwick Park & St Mark's
John Billam Pl Flds
WATFORD RD
Northwick Park
HA0
HA9
Rugby Fball Gds
Preston Park Sch
Preston Park Recn Gd
South Kenton
Byron Court Sch
65

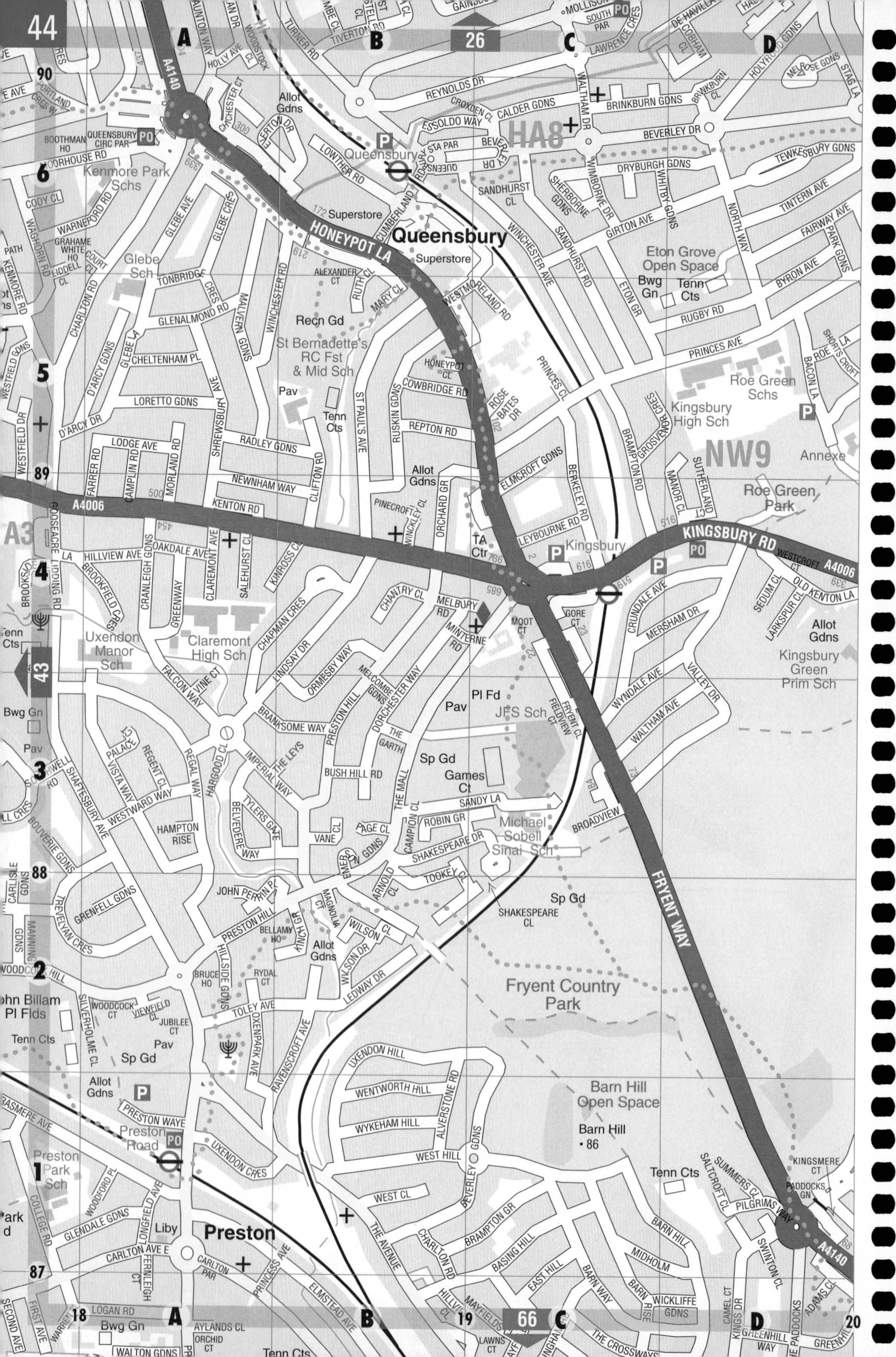
Queensbury
Preston
HA8
NW9
Fryent Country Park
Barn Hill Open Space
Barn Hill • 86
HONEYPOT LA
KINGSBURY RD
FRYENT WAY
A4140
A4006
Kenmore Park Schs
Glebe Sch
St Bernadette's RC Fst & Mid Sch
Claremont High Sch
Uxendon Manor Sch
Kingsbury High Sch
Roe Green Schs
Roe Green Park
Kingsbury Green Prim Sch
Eton Grove Open Space
JFS Sch
Michael Sobell Sinai Sch
Preston Park Sch
Kingsbury
Preston Road
26
43
66

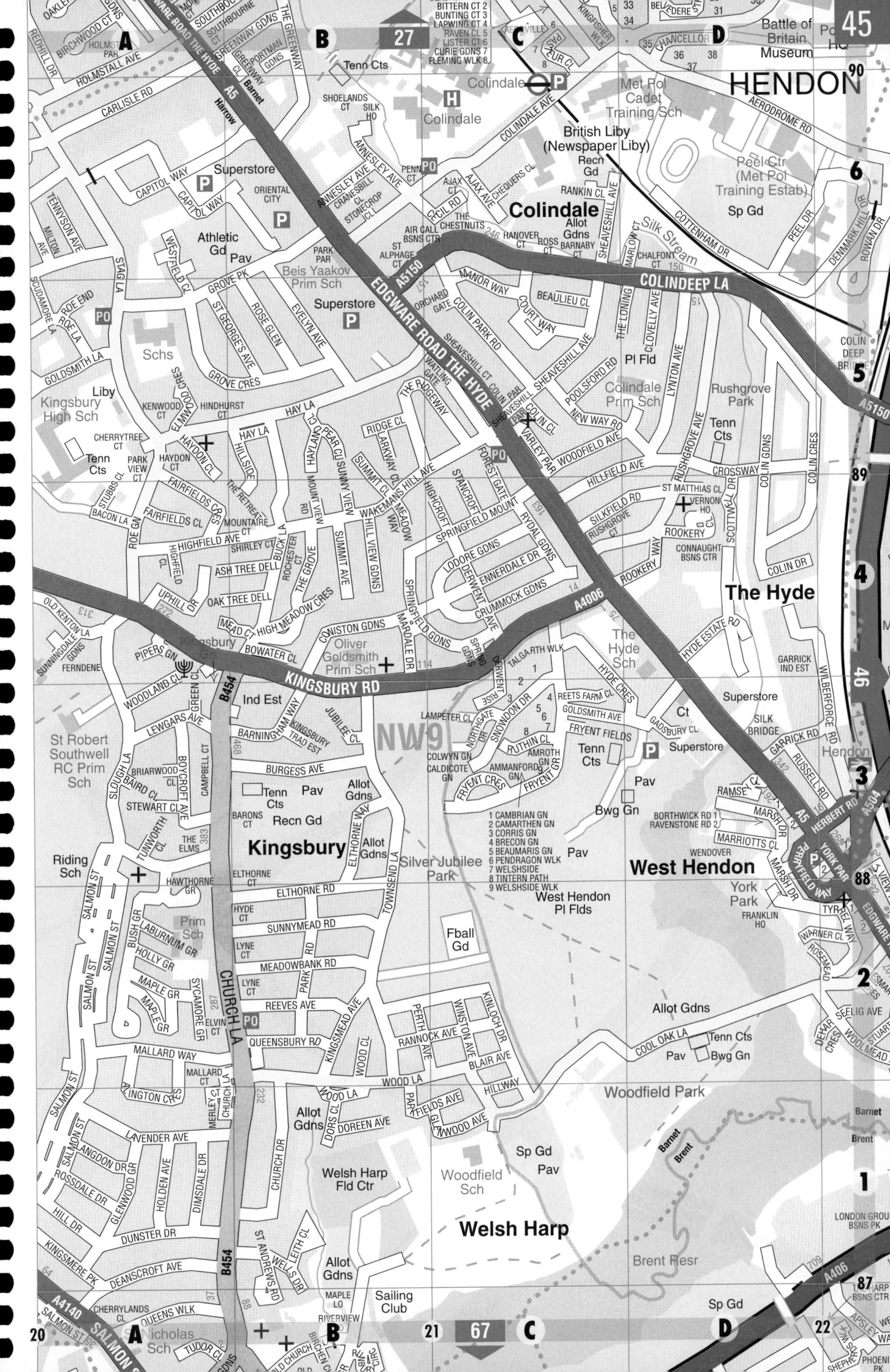
27
67
A
B
C
D
HENDON
Colindale
Kingsbury
West Hendon
The Hyde
Welsh Harp
NW9
EDGWARE ROAD THE HYDE
A5
A5150
COLINDEEP LA
A4006
KINGSBURY RD
B454
CHURCH LA
A4140
A406
A504
Barnet
Harrow
Brent
Battle of Britain Museum
Met Pol Cadet Training Sch
British Liby (Newspaper Liby)
Peel Ctr (Met Pol Training Estab)
Colindale
Superstore
ORIENTAL CITY
Athletic Gd
Pav
Beis Yaakov Prim Sch
Schs
Liby
Kingsbury High Sch
Tenn Cts
Recn Gd
Allot Gdns
Sp Gd
Pl Fld
Colindale Prim Sch
Rushgrove Park
The Hyde Sch
Oliver Goldsmith Prim Sch
Ind Est
St Robert Southwell RC Prim Sch
Riding Sch
Prim Sch
Silver Jubilee Park
West Hendon Pl Flds
Bwg Gn
York Park
Fball Gd
Woodfield Park
Woodfield Sch
Welsh Harp Fld Ctr
Brent Resr
Sailing Club
St Nicholas Sch
GARRICK IND EST
SILK BRIDGE
CONNAUGHT BSNS CTR
LONDON GROUP BSNS PK
AIR CALL BSNS CTR
COLIN DEEP BRIDGE
Silk Stream
AERODROME RD
COTTENHAM DR
COLINDALE AVE
CAPITOL WAY
CARLISLE RD
HOLMSTALL AVE
GROVE PK
HAY LA
HIGHFIELD AVE
WOODFIELD AVE
HILLFIELD AVE
CROSSWAY
SHEAVESHILL AVE
LYNTON AVE
RUSHGROVE AVE
COLIN PARK RD
MANOR WAY
WAKEMANS HILL AVE
SPRINGFIELD MOUNT
BURGESS AVE
ELTHORNE RD
SUNNYMEAD RD
MEADOWBANK RD
REEVES AVE
QUEENSBURY RD
MALLARD WAY
WOOD LA
COOL OAK LA
TOWNSEND LA
SALMON ST
DUNSTER DR
DEANSCROFT AVE
CHURCH DR
FRYENT FIELDS
HYDE ESTATE RD
WILBERFORCE RD
1 CAMBRIAN GN
2 CAMARTHEN GN
3 CORRIS GN
4 BRECON GN
5 BEAUMARIS GN
6 PENDRAGON WLK
7 WELSHSIDE
8 TINTERN PATH
9 WELSHSIDE WLK
BITTERN CT 2
BUNTING CT 3
LAPWING CT 4
RAVEN CL 5
LISTER CT 6
CURIE GDNS 7
FLEMING WLK 8
BORTHWICK RD 1
RAVENSTONE RD 2
20
21
22
1
2
3
4
5
6
87
88
89
90
46

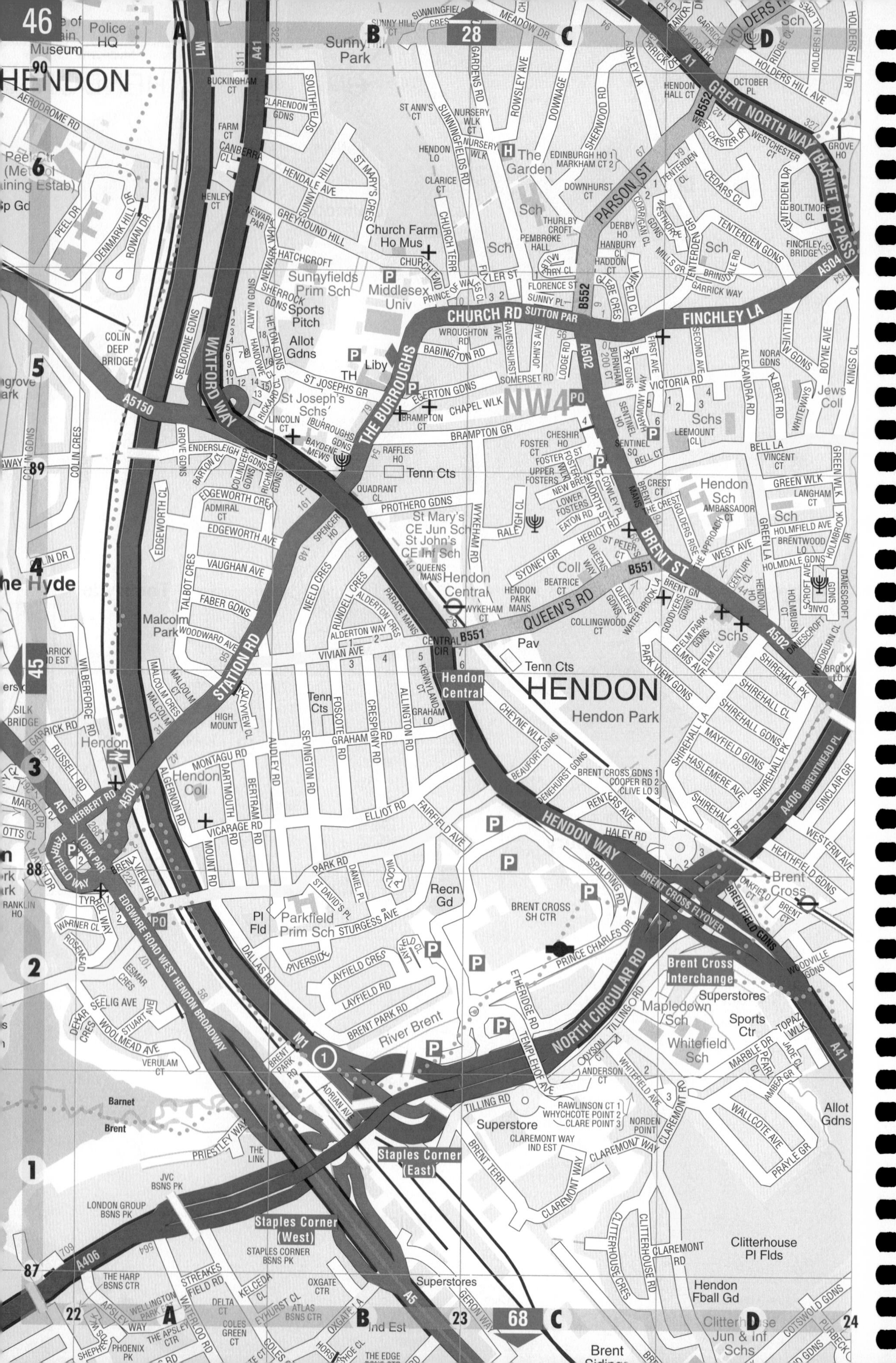

HENDON
Police HQ
Sunny Hill Park
28
Museum
AERODROME RD
Peel Ctr
GREAT NORTH WAY (BARNET BY-PASS)
HOLDERS HILL AVE
WATFORD WAY
M1
A41
A1
A502
A504
A5150
B552
B551
A406
A5
CHURCH RD
SUTTON PAR
FINCHLEY LA
THE BURROUGHS
PARSON ST
Church Farm Ho Mus
Middlesex Univ
Sunnyfields Prim Sch
Sports Pitch
Allot Gdns
Liby
TH
COLIN DEEP BRIDGE
St Joseph's Schs
NW4
Tenn Cts
St Mary's CE Jun Sch
St John's CE Inf Sch
Hendon Central
QUEEN'S RD
BRENT ST
Hendon Sch
Jews Coll
The Hyde
Malcolm Park
STATION RD
Hendon Coll
Hendon Park
HENDON WAY
Pav
BRENT CROSS SH CTR
Recn Gd
Parkfield Prim Sch
Pl Fld
River Brent
NORTH CIRCULAR RD
BRENT CROSS FLYOVER
Brent Cross
Brent Cross Interchange
Superstores
Mapledown Sch
Whitefield Sch
Sports Ctr
Allot Gdns
Staples Corner (East)
Staples Corner (West)
Superstore
EDGWARE ROAD WEST HENDON BROADWAY
Barnet
Brent
Clitterhouse Pl Flds
Hendon Fball Gd
Clitterhouse Jun & Inf Schs
Brent Sidings
45
68
A
B
C
D
22
23
24
87
88
89
90
1
2
3
4
5
6

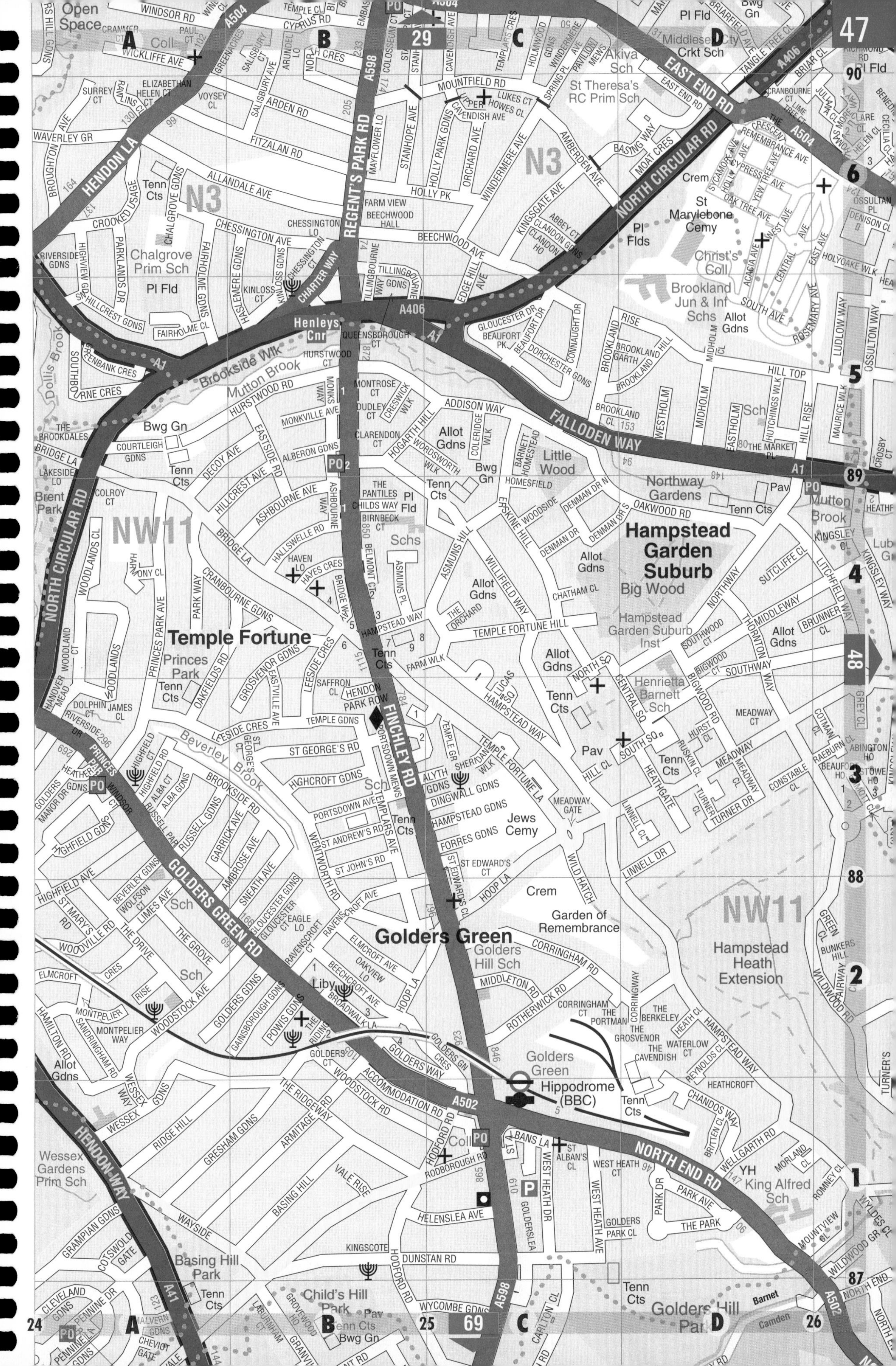

47
48
29
69
24
25
26
A
B
C
D
A
B
C
D
6
5
4
3
2
1
90
89
88
87
Open Space
Coll
WINDSOR RD
CRANMER
WICKLIFFE AVE
CYPRUS RD
TEMPLE CL
Middlesex Cty Crkt Sch
Pl Fld
Bwg Gn
Akiva Sch
EAST END RD
TANGLE TREE CL
A406
A504
A598
PO
ELIZABETH HELEN CT
SURREY CT
VOYSEY CL
ARDEN RD
MOUNTFIELD RD
LUKES CT
HOWES CT
UPPER CAVENDISH AVE
St Theresa's RC Prim Sch
HENDON LA
WAVERLEY GR
FITZALAN RD
N3
REGENT'S PARK RD
NORTH CIRCULAR RD
ALLANDALE AVE
HOLLY PK
CHALGROVE GDNS
Tenn Cts
Crem
St Marylebone Cemy
Christ's Coll
Brookland Jun & Inf Schs
Allot Gdns
CROOKED USAGE
CHESSINGTON AVE
FARM VIEW
BEECHWOOD HALL
BEECHWOOD AVE
KINGSGATE AVE
Pl Flds
Chalgrove Prim Sch
Pl Fld
HILLCREST GDNS
FAIRHOLME CL
CHARTER WAY
TILLINGBOURNE GDNS
Henleys Cnr
QUEENSBOROUGH CT
A1
A406
GLOUCESTER DR
BEAUFORT PK
DORCHESTER GDNS
CONNAUGHT DR
BROOKLAND RISE
BROOKLAND HILL
HILL TOP
Brookside Wlk
Mutton Brook
HURSTWOOD RD
Dollis Brook
SOUTHBOURNE CRES
MONTROSE CT
DUDLEY CT
CRESWICK WLK
ADDISON WAY
FALLODEN WAY
WESTHOLM
MIDHOLM
EASTHOLM
HILL RISE
MAURICE WLK
THE MARKET PL
Bwg Gn
THE BROOKDALES
BRIDGE LA
COURTLEIGH GDNS
MONKVILLE AVE
CLARENDON CT
HOGARTH HILL
WORDSWORTH WLK
COLERIDGE WLK
Little Wood
Bwg Gn
HOMESFIELD
Northway Gardens
Pav
Tenn Cts
Mutton Brook
OAKWOOD RD
Brent Park
COLROY CT
DECOY AVE
HILLCREST AVE
ASHBOURNE AVE
ALBERON GDNS
THE PANTILES
CHILDS WAY
BIRNBECK CT
Pl Fld
NW11
Hampstead Garden Suburb
Big Wood
DENMAN DR
WOODSIDE
ERSKINE HILL
ASMUNS HILL
WILLIFIELD WAY
HALLSWELLE RD
HAVEN LO
HAYES CRES
Schs
ASMUNS PL
BELMONT CT
NORTH CIRCULAR RD
WOODLANDS CL
HARMONY CL
PARK WAY
CRANBOURNE GDNS
SUTCLIFFE CL
NORTHWAY
LITCHFIELD WAY
KINGSLEY WAY
CHATHAM CL
THE ORCHARD
HAMPSTEAD WAY
TEMPLE FORTUNE HILL
Hampstead Garden Suburb Inst
SOUTHWOOD CT
MIDDLEWAY
THORNTON WAY
BRUNNER CL
Temple Fortune
Princes Park
WOODLANDS
PRINCES PARK AVE
OAKFIELDS RD
GROSVENOR GDNS
LEESIDE CRES
FARM WLK
NORTH SQ
CENTRAL SQ
Henrietta Barnett Sch
BIGWOOD RD
SOUTHWAY
HANOVER MEAD
DOLPHIN CT
JAMES CL
SAFFRON CL
HENDON PARK ROW
FINCHLEY RD
LUCAS SQ
MEADWAY CT
COTMAN CL
GREY CL
RIVERSIDE DR
LEESIDE CRES
TEMPLE GDNS
EASTVILLE AVE
ST GEORGE'S RD
Beverley Brook
SOUTH SQ
Pav
HILL CL
Tenn Cts
HEATHGATE
RUSKIN CL
MEADWAY
CONSTABLE CL
RAEBURN CL
ABINGTON HO
BEAUFORT HO
STOWE HO
PRINCES PAR
HIGHFIELD RD
ALBA GDNS
BROOKSIDE RD
HIGHCROFT GDNS
ALYTH GDNS
DINGWALL GDNS
TEMPLE FORTUNE LA
MEADWAY GATE
TURNER DR
HIGHFIELD GDNS
WINDSOR CT
RUSSELL GDNS
GARRICK AVE
AMBROSE AVE
PORTSDOWN AVE
ST ANDREW'S RD
HAMPSTEAD GDNS
Jews Cemy
FORRES GDNS
LINNELL CL
LINNELL DR
ST JOHN'S RD
ST EDWARD'S CT
WENTWORTH RD
TEMPLARS AVE
HIGHFIELD AVE
BEVERLEY GDNS
WOLFSON CT
LIMES AVE
GOLDERS GREEN RD
SNEATH AVE
GLOUCESTER GDNS
EAGLE LO
RAVENSCROFT AVE
HOOP LA
Crem
Garden of Remembrance
WILD HATCH
NW11
Hampstead Heath Extension
ST MARY'S RD
WOODVILLE RD
THE DRIVE
THE GROVE
ELMCROFT AVE
OAKVIEW LO
Golders Green
Golders Hill Sch
CORRINGHAM RD
BUNKERS HILL
FAIRWAY
WILDWOOD RD
ELMCROFT CRES
RISE
Sch
BEECHCROFT AVE
Liby
BROADWALK LA
MIDDLETON RD
ROTHERWICK RD
CORRINGHAM CT
THE PORTMAN
THE BERKELEY
THE GROSVENOR
THE CAVENDISH
WATERLOW CT
HEATH CL
HAMPSTEAD WAY
MONTPELIER RD
MONTPELIER WAY
SANDRINGHAM RD
HAMILTON RD
WOODSTOCK AVE
GOLDERS GDNS
GAINSBOROUGH GDNS
POWIS GDNS
THE RIDING
GOLDERS CT
GOLDERS WAY
GOLDERS GN CRES
Golders Green
Hippodrome (BBC)
REYNOLDS CL
HEATHCROFT
TURNER'S WOOD
Allot Gdns
WESSEX WAY
WESSEX GDNS
THE RIDGEWAY
WOODSTOCK RD
ACCOMMODATION RD
A502
Tenn Cts
CHANDOS WAY
BRITTEN CL
WELLGARTH RD
HENDON WAY
RIDGE HILL
GRESHAM GDNS
ARMITAGE RD
HODFORD RD
Coll
ST ALBANS LA
ST ALBAN'S CL
WEST HEATH CT
NORTH END RD
YH
King Alfred Sch
MORLAND CL
ROMNEY CL
Wessex Gardens Prim Sch
BASING HILL
VALE RISE
RODBOROUGH RD
WEST HEATH DR
GOLDERSLEA
WEST HEATH AVE
PARK DR
PARK AVE
THE PARK
WYLDES CL
WAYSIDE
HELENSLEA AVE
GOLDERS PARK CL
MOUNTVIEW CL
WILDWOOD GR
GRAMPIAN GDNS
COTSWOLD GATE
Basing Hill Park
KINGSCOTE
DUNSTAN RD
NORTH END
Tenn Cts
Child's Hill Park
Pav
Tenn Cts
Bwg Gn
WYCOMBE GDNS
CARLTON CL
Golders Hill Park
Barnet
Camden
A41
CLEVELAND GDNS
PENNINE DR
PENNINE PAR
MALVERN GDNS
CHEVIOT GATE
LABURNUM CT
GROVEWOOD HO
A598

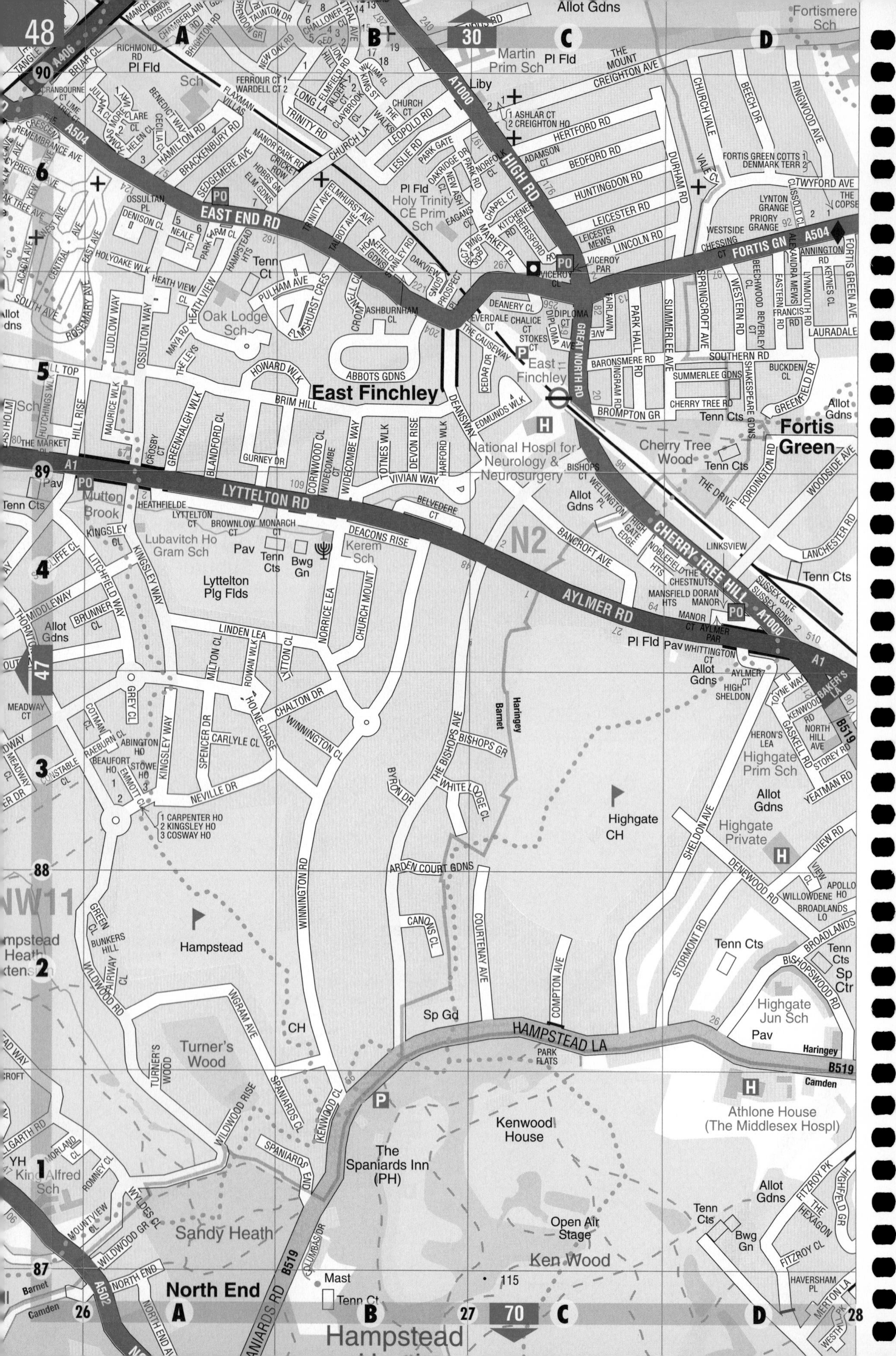
A
B
C
D
30
Allot Gdns
Fortismere Sch
Martin Prim Sch
Pl Fld
THE MOUNT
CREIGHTON AVE
Liby
A1000
HIGH RD
A406
A504
90
RICHMOND RD
BRIAR CL
FERROUR CT
WARDELL CT
FLAXMAN VILLAS
TRINITY RD
LONG LA
CHURCH LA
LEOPOLD RD
LESLIE RD
CHURCH CT
1 ASHLAR CT
2 CREIGHTON HO
HERTFORD RD
BEDFORD RD
HUNTINGDON RD
LEICESTER RD
LINCOLN RD
LEICESTER MEWS
ADAMSON CT
CHURCH VALE
BEECH DR
RINGWOOD AVE
DURHAM RD
VALE CL
FORTIS GREEN COTTS
DENMARK TERR
TWYFORD AVE
LYNTON GRANGE
PRIORY GRANGE
WESTSIDE
CHESSING CT
FORTIS GN
FORTIS GREEN AVE
6
REMEMBRANCE AVE
CYPRESS AVE
HAMILTON RD
BRACKENBURY RD
SEDGEMERE AVE
MANOR PARK RD
EAST END RD
PO
OSSULTAN PL
DENISON CL
NEALE CL
PARK FARM CL
HAMPSTEAD HTS
Holy Trinity CE Prim Sch
TRINITY AVE
ELMHURST AVE
TALBOT AVE
STANLEY RD
OAKVIEW GDNS
PROSPECT PL
EAGANS CL
MARKET PL
KITCHENER RD
BERESFORD RD
VICEROY CT
VICEROY PAR
GREAT NORTH RD
HOLYOAKE WLK
HEATH VIEW
Tenn Ct
PULHAM AVE
ELMSHURST CRES
ASHBURNHAM CL
CROMWELL CL
Oak Lodge Sch
SOUTH AVE
ROSEMARY AVE
LUDLOW WAY
OSSULTON WAY
MAYA RD
THE LEYS
DEANERY CL
EVERDALE CT
CHALICE CT
STOKES CT
DIPLOMA CT
DIPLOMA AVE
THE CAUSEWAY
East Finchley
FAIRLAWN AVE
PARK HALL RD
SUMMERLEE AVE
SPRINGCROFT AVE
WESTERN RD
BEECHWOOD AVE
EASTERN RD
FRANCIS RD
LAURADALE
SOUTHERN RD
5
HOWARD WLK
ABBOTS GDNS
CEDAR DR
BARONSMERE RD
SUMMERLEE GDNS
BUCKDEN CL
GREENFIELD DR
HILL TOP
HUTCHINGS WLK
HILL RISE
MAURICE WLK
BRIM HILL
East Finchley
DEANSWAY
EDMUNDS WLK
INGRAM RD
CHERRY TREE RD
BROMPTON GR
Tenn Cts
Allot Gdns
Fortis Green
THE MARKET PL
CROSBY CT
GREENHALGH WLK
BLANDFORD CL
GURNEY DR
CORNWOOD CL
WIDECOMBE WAY
TOTNES WLK
DEVON RISE
HARFORD WLK
National Hospl for Neurology & Neurosurgery
Cherry Tree Wood
FORDINGTON RD
WOODSIDE AVE
THE DRIVE
89
A1
Pav
Mutton Brook
LYTTELTON RD
VIVIAN WAY
BELVEDERE CT
BISHOPS CT
WELLINGTON PL
Tenn Cts
HEATHFIELDE
LYTTELTON CT
BROWNLOW CT
MONARCH CT
DEACONS RISE
Kerem Sch
KINGSLEY CL
Lubavitch Ho Gram Sch
Tenn Cts
Bwg Gn
N2
BANCROFT AVE
HIGH GATE EDGE
CHERRY TREE HILL
NOBLEFIELD HTS
THE CHESTNUTS
LINKSVIEW
LANCHESTER RD
4
LITCHFIELD WAY
KINGSLEY WAY
Lyttelton Plg Flds
NORRICE LEA
CHURCH MOUNT
AYLMER RD
MANSFIELD HTS
DORAN MANOR
MANOR CT
AYLMER PAR
SUSSEX GATE
SUSSEX GDNS
MIDDLEWAY
BRUNNER CL
Allot Gdns
LINDEN LEA
MILTON CL
ROWAN WALK
LYTTON CL
Pl Fld
Pav
WHITTINGTON CT
AYLMER CT
HIGH SHELDON
TOYNE WAY
KENWOOD RD
BAKER'S LA
B519
47
MEADWAY CT
GREY CL
HOLNE CHASE
CHALTON DR
WINNINGTON CL
Barnet
Haringey
BISHOPS GR
THE BISHOPS AVE
HERON'S LEA
GASKELL RD
NORTH HILL AVE
STOREY RD
YEATMAN RD
3
CONSTABLE CL
COTMAN CL
RAEBURN CL
ABINGTON HO
BEAUFORT HO
STOWE HO
EMMOTT CL
KINGSLEY WAY
SPENCER DR
CARLYLE CL
NEVILLE DR
BYRON DR
WHITE LODGE CL
Highgate Prim Sch
Allot Gdns
1 CARPENTER HO
2 KINGSLEY HO
3 COSWAY HO
Highgate CH
SHELDON AVE
Highgate Private
VIEW RD
88
NW11
WINNINGTON RD
ARDEN COURT GDNS
DENEWOOD RD
WILLOWDENE
APOLLO HO
BROADLANDS LO
Hampstead Heath Extension
GREEN CL
BUNKERS HILL
FAIRWAY CL
Hampstead
CANONS CL
COURTENAY AVE
STORMONT RD
Tenn Cts
BROADLANDS RD
2
WILDWOOD RD
WIGRAM AVE
CH
COMPTON AVE
BISHOPSWOOD RD
Sp Ctr
Highgate Jun Sch
Sp Gd
HAMPSTEAD LA
PARK FLATS
Pav
Haringey
B519
Camden
Turner's Wood
TURNER'S WOOD
SPANIARDS CL
KENWOOD CL
Kenwood House
Athlone House (The Middlesex Hospl)
WILDWOOD RISE
SPANIARDS END
The Spaniards Inn (PH)
1
YH
King Alfred Sch
MORLAND CL
ROMNEY CL
MOUNTVIEW CL
WYLDES CL
WILDWOOD GR
Sandy Heath
Open Air Stage
Allot Gdns
FITZROY PK
THE HEXAGON
FITZROY CL
Tenn Cts
Bwg Gn
Ken Wood
87
A502
NORTH END
North End
SPANIARDS RD
COLUMBAS DR
Mast
Tenn Ct
115
HAVERSHAM PL
MERTON LA
Barnet
Camden
26
27
70
28
Hampstead
NORTH END AVE

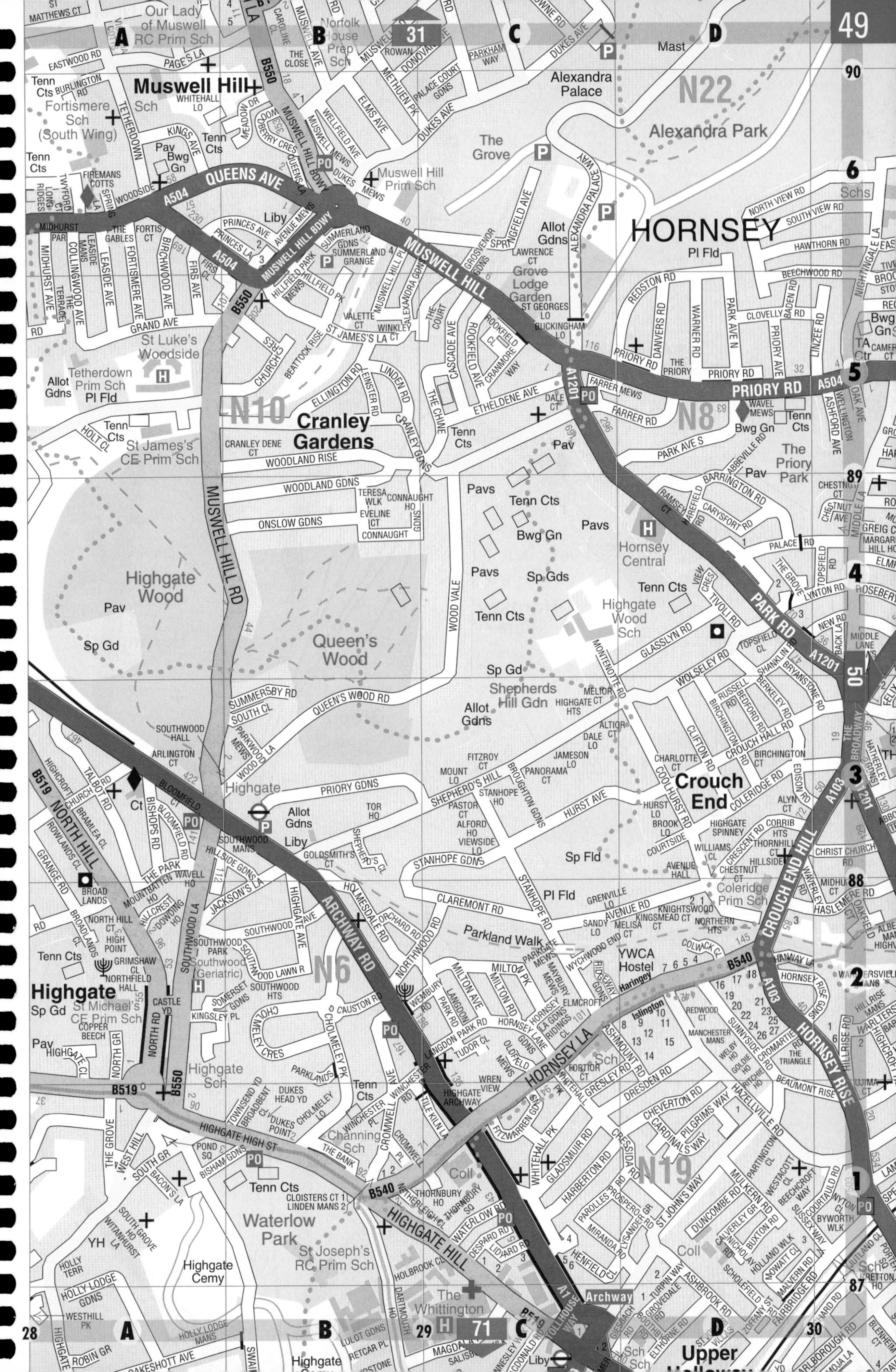
49
A
B
C
D
31
Muswell Hill
Our Lady of Muswell RC Prim Sch
Norfolk House Prep Sch
Fortismere Sch
Fortismere Sch (South Wing)
Alexandra Palace
Mast
N22
Alexandra Park
The Grove
Muswell Hill Prim Sch
QUEENS AVE
A504
MUSWELL HILL BDWY
MUSWELL HILL RD
MUSWELL HILL
B550
HORNSEY
Allot Gdns
Grove Lodge Garden
ALEXANDRA PALACE WAY
PRIORY RD
A1201
A504
N10
N8
St Luke's Woodside
Tetherdown Prim Sch
Cranley Gardens
St James's CE Prim Sch
Highgate Wood
Queen's Wood
WOODLAND RISE
WOODLAND GDNS
ONSLOW GDNS
WOOD VALE
The Priory Park
Hornsey Central
Highgate Wood Sch
PARK RD
Shepherds Hill Gdn
QUEEN'S WOOD RD
SHEPHERD'S HILL
Crouch End
CROUCH HALL RD
CROUCH END HILL
A103
Coleridge Prim Sch
Highgate
ARCHWAY RD
N6
NORTH HILL
B519
Southwood Park (Geriatric)
St Michael's CE Prim Sch
Highgate Sch
HIGHGATE HIGH ST
Channing Sch
YWCA Hostel
Parkland Walk
HORNSEY LA
B540
N19
HORNSEY RISE
Waterlow Park
St Joseph's RC Prim Sch
HIGHGATE HILL
Highgate Cemy
The Whittington
Archway
A1
Upper Holloway
Haringey
Islington
28
29
30
71
50
90
89
88
87
6
5
4
3
2
1

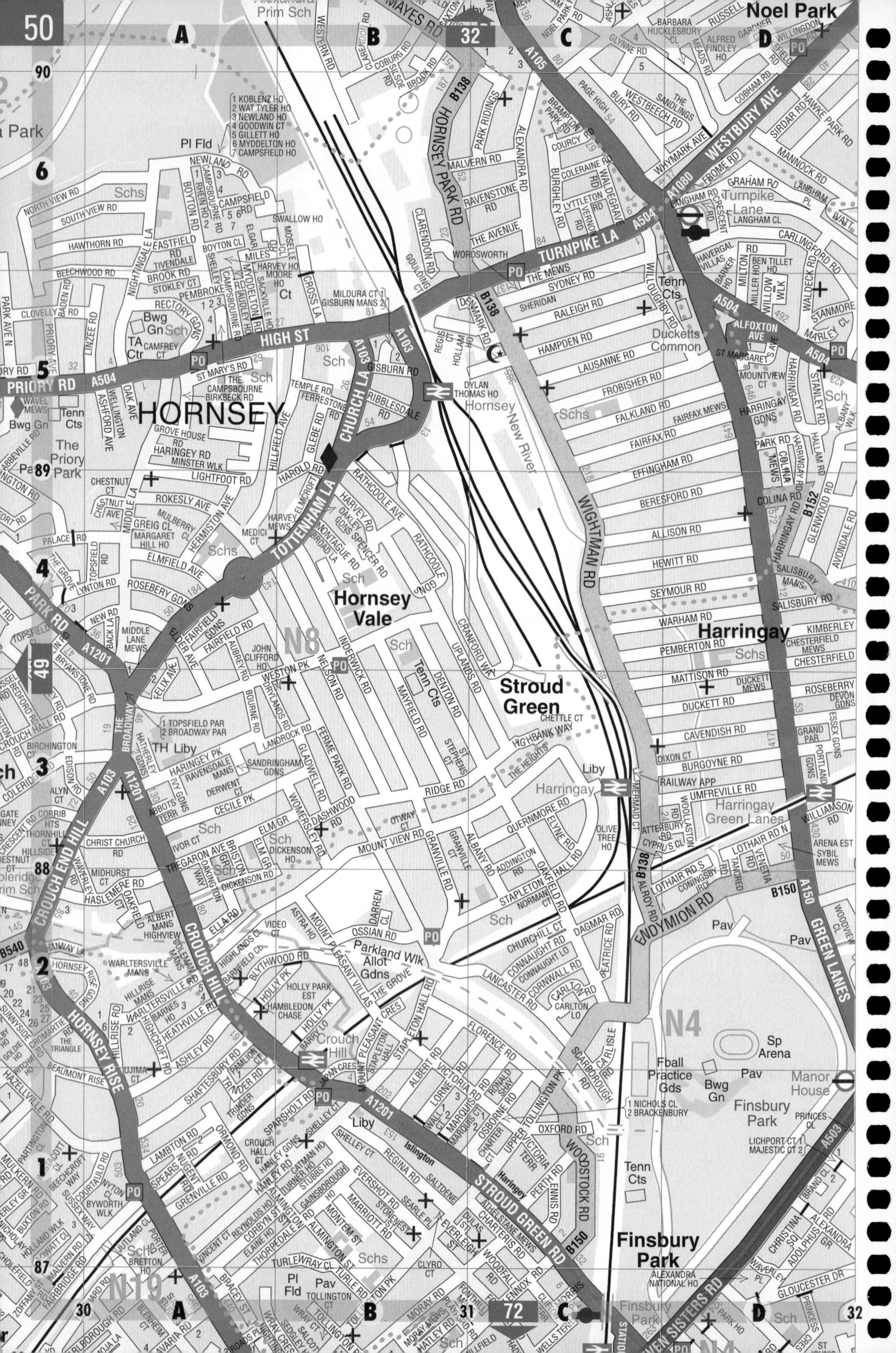
A
B
32
C
D
Noel Park
90
6
5
89
4
3
88
2
1
87
HORNSEY
Hornsey Vale
Stroud Green
Harringay
Finsbury Park
N8
N4
N19
Turnpike Lane
Hornsey
Harringay
Harringay Green Lanes
Crouch Hill
Manor House
Finsbury Park
New River
The Priory Park
Ducketts Common
Parkland Wlk
Sp Arena
Fball Practice Gds
PRIORY RD
HIGH ST
TURNPIKE LA
WESTBURY AVE
GREEN LANES
WIGHTMAN RD
HORNSEY PARK RD
CHURCH LA
TOTTENHAM LA
PARK RD
CROUCH END HILL
CROUCH HILL
HORNSEY RISE
THE BROADWAY
STROUD GREEN RD
ENDYMION RD
SEVEN SISTERS RD
MOUNT VIEW RD
RIDGE RD
A504
A103
A1201
A105
A1080
A503
B138
B150
B152
B540
49
Islington
Haringey
30
31
72
32

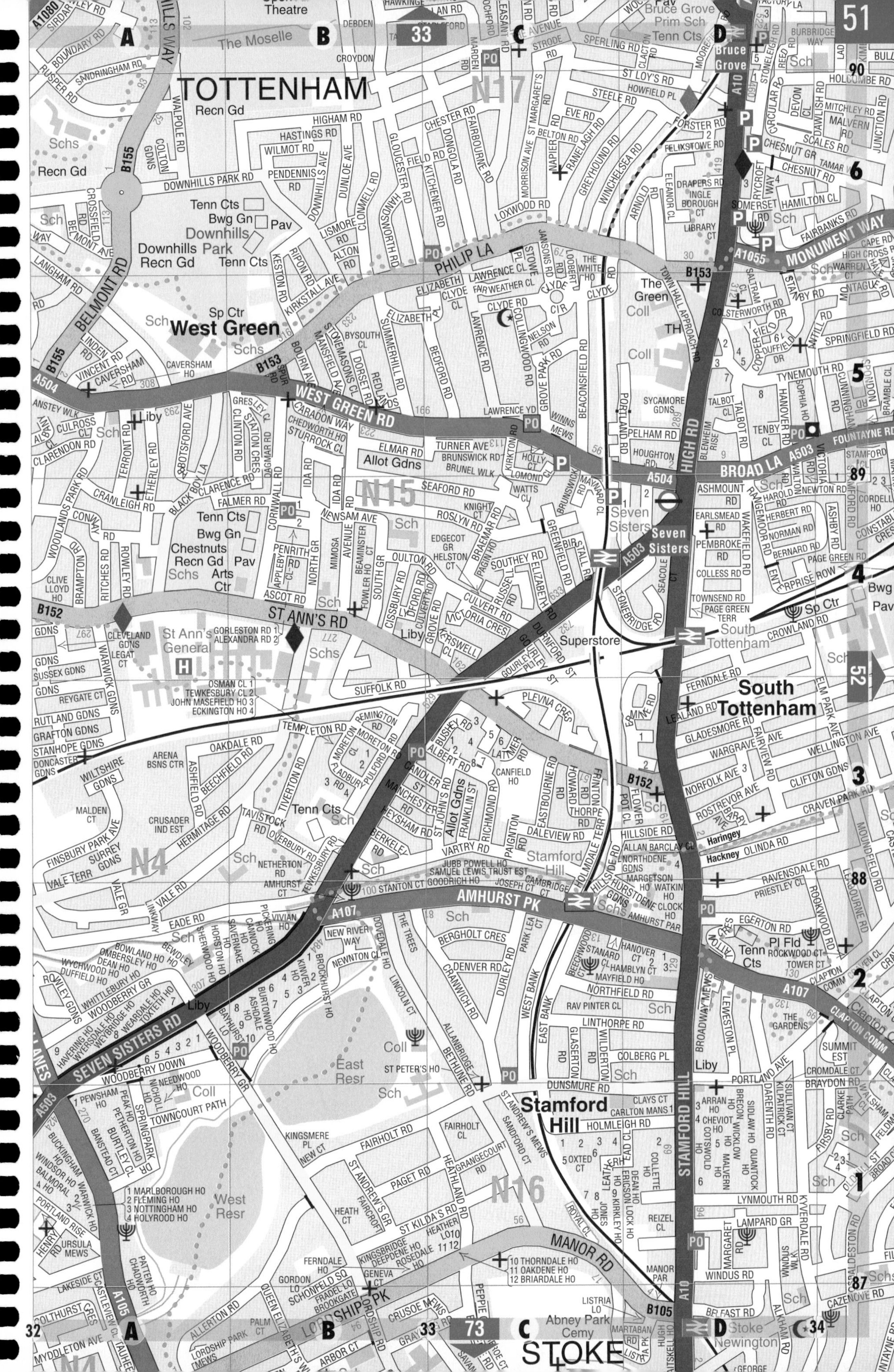
TOTTENHAM
Recn Gd
N17
Bruce Grove Prim Sch
Tenn Cts
Bruce Grove
The Moselle
Theatre
A1080
B155
Schs
Recn Gd
Tenn Cts
Bwg Gn
Pav
Downhills Park
Downhills Recn Gd
DOWNHILLS PARK RD
BELMONT RD
PHILIP LA
West Green
Sp Ctr
Sch
B153
WEST GREEN RD
A504
The Green
Coll
TH
HIGH RD
TOWN HALL APPROACH RD
MONUMENT WAY
A1055
BROAD LA
A503
Seven Sisters
N15
Allot Gdns
Tenn Cts
Bwg Gn
Chestnuts Recn Gd
Pav
Arts Ctr
B152
ST ANN'S RD
St Ann's General
Liby
Superstore
South Tottenham
South Tottenham
N4
Tenn Cts
Allot Gdns
Stamford Hill
AMHURST PK
A107
Haringey
Hackney
SEVEN SISTERS RD
East Resr
West Resr
Coll
Stamford Hill
STAMFORD HILL
A10
N16
MANOR RD
B105
LORDSHIP PK
A105
Abney Park Cemy
STOKE
Stoke Newington
CLAPTON COMM
33
52
73
32
34
A
B
C
D
1
2
3
4
5
6

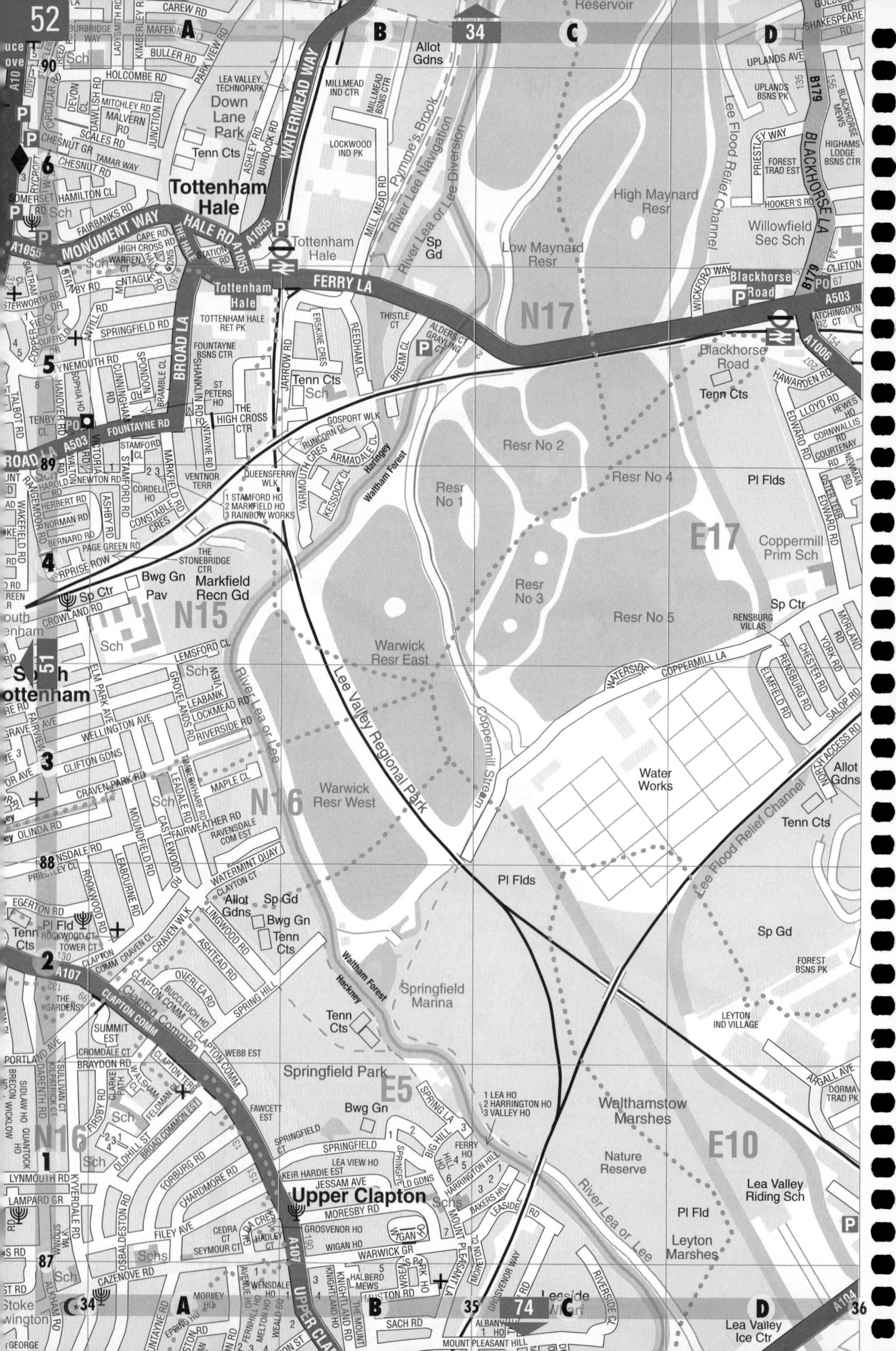

Tottenham Hale
Down Lane Park
Tenn Cts
Lea Valley Technopark
Millmead Ind Ctr
Lockwood Ind Pk
Watermead Way
Monument Way
Hale Rd
Ferry La
Broad La
Fountayne Rd
Reservoir
High Maynard Resr
Low Maynard Resr
Lee Flood Relief Channel
River Lea or Lee Navigation
River Lea or Lee Diversion
Pymme's Brook
Blackhorse La
Blackhorse Road
Willowfield Sec Sch
Uplands Bsns Pk
Forest Trad Est
Highams Lodge Bsns Ctr
N17
N15
N16
E17
E10
E5
Resr No 1
Resr No 2
Resr No 3
Resr No 4
Resr No 5
Markfield Recn Gd
Warwick Resr East
Warwick Resr West
Lee Valley Regional Park
Coppermill Stream
Coppermill La
Coppermill Prim Sch
Water Works
Pl Flds
Sp Gd
South Tottenham
Springfield Marina
Springfield Park
Clapton Common
Walthamstow Marshes
Nature Reserve
Leyton Marshes
Lea Valley Riding Sch
Leyton Ind Village
Forest Bsns Pk
Upper Clapton
River Lea or Lee
Lea Valley Ice Ctr
Leyside Wharf
34
35
36
51
74
A
B
C
D
1
2
3
4
5
6
87
88
89
90

WALTHAMSTOW
E17
E10
A
B
C
D
35
75
36
37
38
90
89
88
87
6
5
4
3
2
1
54
FOREST RD
A503
A112
A104
A1006
B159
B161
HOE ST
HIGH ST
LEA BRIDGE RD
MARKHOUSE RD
BLACKHORSE RD
CHURCH RD
HIGH RD
HIGH ROAD LEYTON
LEYTON GREEN RD
ST JAMES'S ST
SELBORNE RD
The Bell
Walthamstow Central
Walthamstow Queens Road
St James Street
Queens Road Cemy
Allot Gdns
Waltham Forest Coll
Thorpe Coombe Coll
The Holy Family Coll
Vestry Ho (Mus)
South Grove Prim Sch
Kelmscott L Ctr
Kelmscott Sch
St Saviour's CE Prim Sch
Barn Croft Sch
Sybourn Inf Sch Annexe
Church Mead Jun Sch
The Lammas Sch
St Joseph's RC Inf Sch
George Mitchell Com Sch
Dawlish Prim Sch
Liby
Fball Gd
Sp Gd
Tenn Cts
ROXWELL TRAD PK
CROMWELL EST
FAIRWAYS BSNS PK
ADAMS CT 1
LANGBOURNE CT 2
NATHANIEL CT 3
FLANDERS 4
WINNS AVE
FOREST RD
COLERIDGE RD
MILTON RD
CHURCH HILL
ST MARY RD
ORFORD RD
GROSVENOR PARK RD
PRIORY AVE
CEDARS AVE
SHRUBLAND RD
QUEEN'S RD
MARKHOUSE AVE
CHELMSFORD RD
BOUNDARY RD
CAPWORTH ST
BEAUMONT RD
PARK RD
LAMMAS RD
RIGG APP
ARGALL WAY
SOUTH ACCESS RD
OVERTON RD
MARSH LA

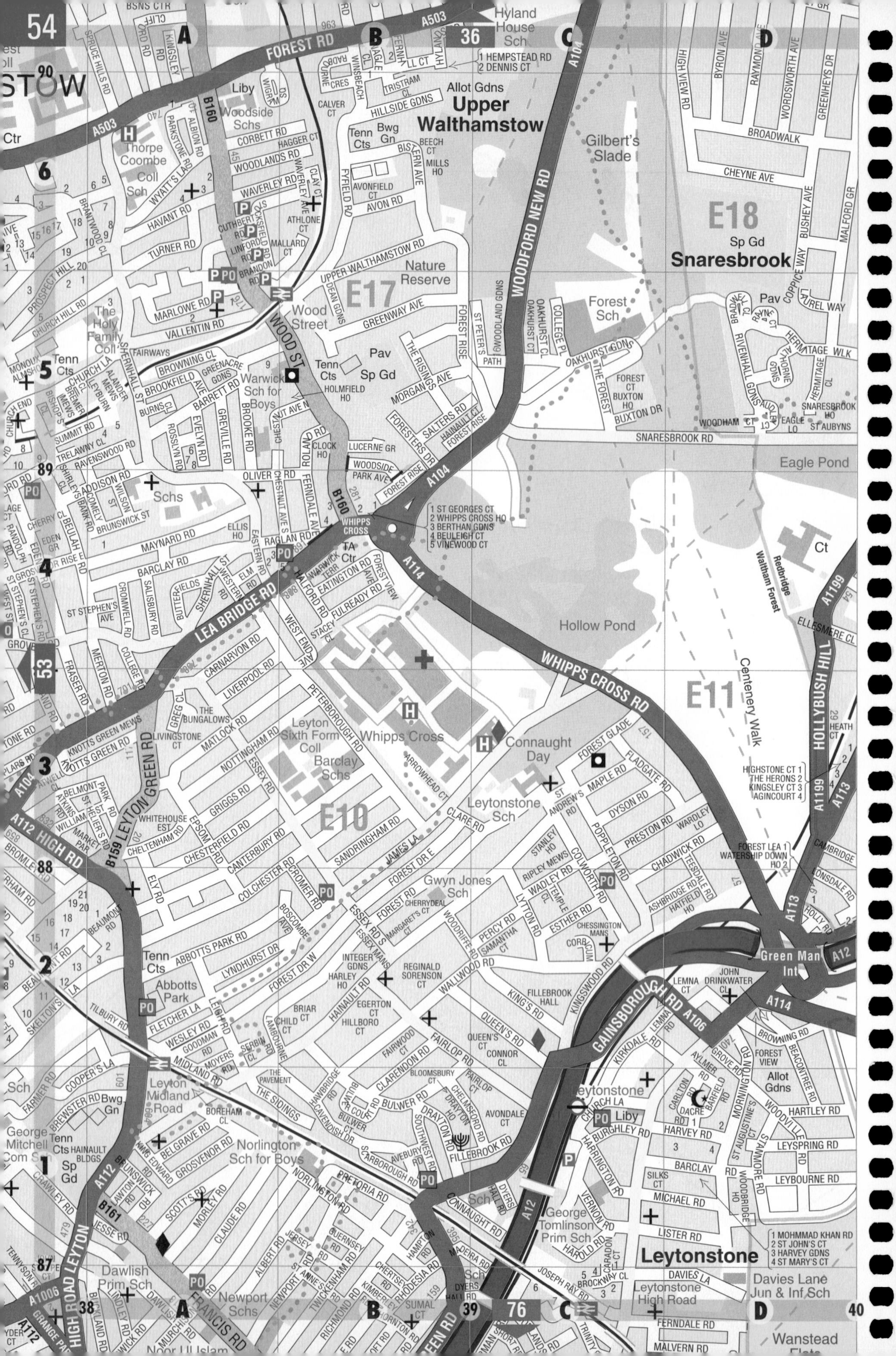
Upper Walthamstow
Snaresbrook
Leytonstone
E17
E18
E11
E10
FOREST RD
WOODFORD NEW RD
WHIPPS CROSS RD
LEA BRIDGE RD
HIGH ROAD LEYTON
HOLLYBUSH HILL
SNARESBROOK RD
GAINSBOROUGH RD
LEYTON GREEN RD
WOOD ST
Wood Street
Hyland House Sch
Allot Gdns
Gilbert's Slade
Nature Reserve
Forest Sch
Eagle Pond
Hollow Pond
Centenery Walk
Whipps Cross
Leyton Sixth Form Coll
Connaught Day
Leytonstone Sch
Gwyn Jones Sch
Abbotts Park
Leyton Midland Road
Norlington Sch for Boys
George Mitchell Com Sch
Dawlish Prim Sch
Newport Schs
George Tomlinson Prim Sch
Davies Lane Jun & Inf Sch
Leytonstone High Road
Green Man Int
Warwick Sch for Boys
The Holy Family Coll
Thorpe Coombe Coll Sch
Woodside Schs
Barclay Schs
Redbridge
Waltham Forest
1 HEMPSTEAD RD
2 DENNIS CT
1 ST GEORGES CT
2 WHIPPS CROSS HO
3 BERTHAN GDNS
4 BEULEIGH CT
5 VINEWOOD CT
HIGHSTONE CT 1
THE HERONS 2
KINGSLEY CT 3
AGINCOURT 4
1 MOHMMAD KHAN RD
2 ST JOHN'S CT
3 HARVEY GDNS
4 ST MARY'S CT
36
53
76
40
A503
A104
A114
A112
A12
A1199
A113
A106
B160
B159
B161

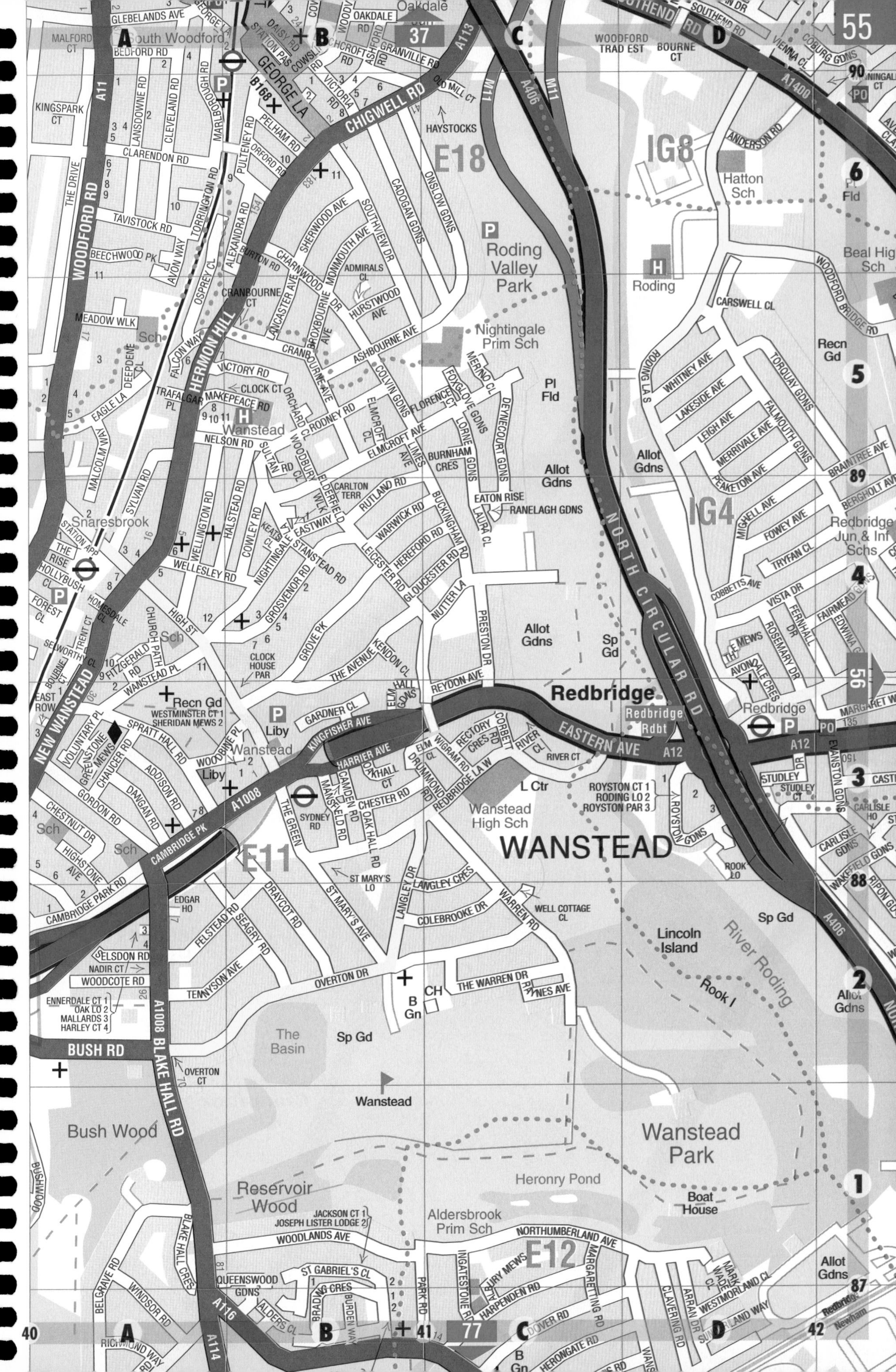
South Woodford
Oakdale
Woodford Trad Est
Bourne Ct
IG8
E18
Roding Valley Park
Nightingale Prim Sch
Hatton Sch
Beal High Sch
Roding
Redbridge Jun & Inf Schs
IG4
Snaresbrook
Wanstead
Redbridge
Redbridge Rdbt
Wanstead High Sch
WANSTEAD
E11
Lincoln Island
River Roding
Rook I
The Basin
Bush Wood
Reservoir Wood
Heronry Pond
Wanstead Park
Boat House
Aldersbrook Prim Sch
E12
NORTH CIRCULAR RD
EASTERN AVE
CHIGWELL RD
HERMON HILL
WOODFORD RD
NEW WANSTEAD
BLAKE HALL RD
BUSH RD
CAMBRIDGE PK
WOODLANDS AVE
NORTHUMBERLAND AVE
HIGH ST
OVERTON DR
37
56
77
40
41
42
87
88
89
90

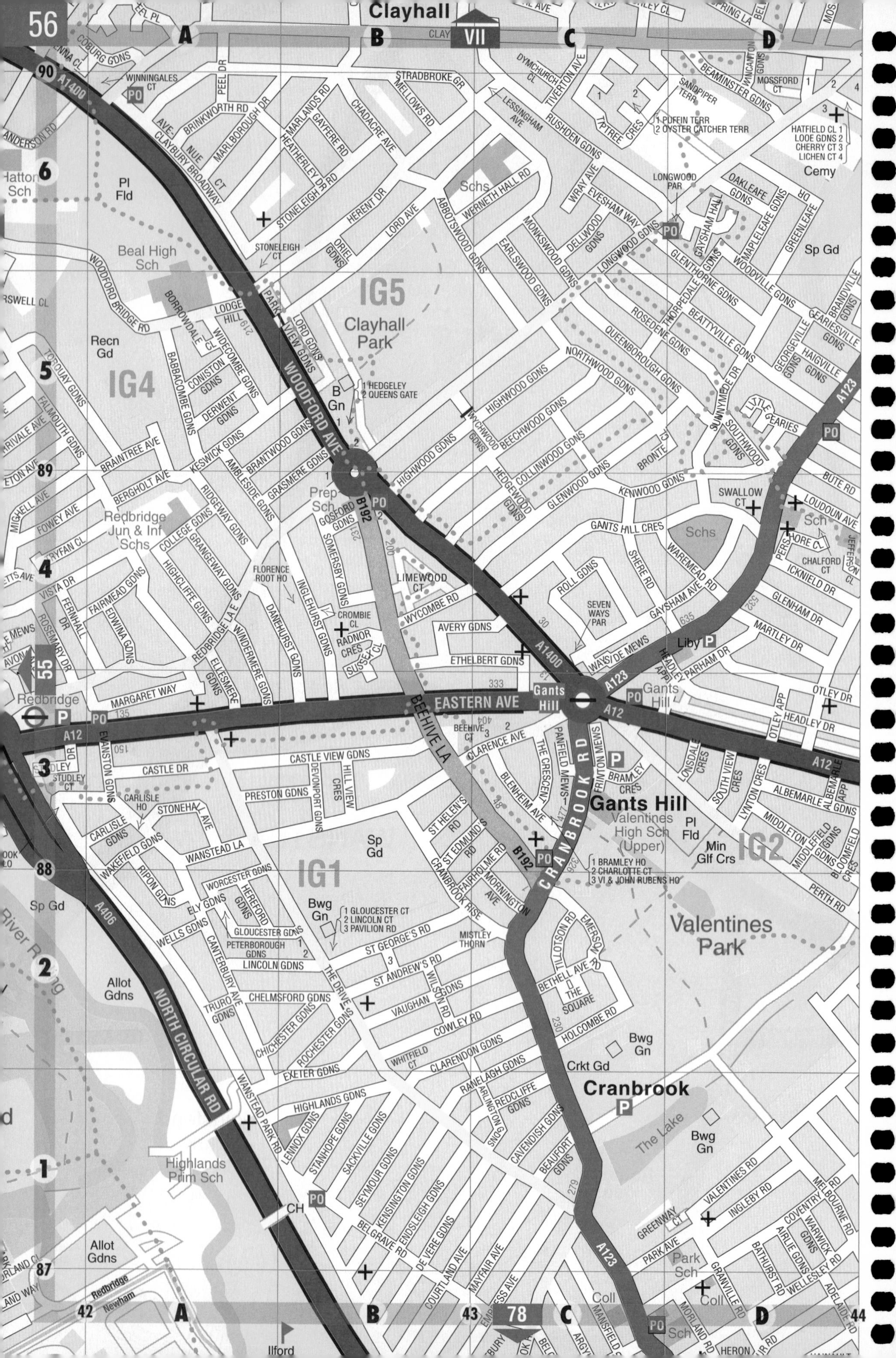

Clayhall
VII
A
B
C
D
IG5
Clayhall Park
IG4
IG1
IG2
Gants Hill
Valentines Park
Cranbrook
The Lake
Redbridge
Beal High Sch
Redbridge Jun & Inf Schs
Valentines High Sch (Upper)
Highlands Prim Sch
WOODFORD AVE
EASTERN AVE
CRANBROOK RD
BEEHIVE LA
NORTH CIRCULAR RD
A1400
A12
A123
A406
B192
55
78
42
43
44
90
89
88
87
6
5
4
3
2
1
1 HEDGELEY
2 QUEENS GATE
1 PUFFIN TERR
2 OYSTER CATCHER TERR
HATFIELD CL 1
LOOE GDNS 2
CHERRY CT 3
LICHEN CT 4
1 BRAMLEY HO
2 CHARLOTTE CT
3 VI & JOHN RUBENS HO
1 GLOUCESTER CT
2 LINCOLN CT
3 PAVILION RD

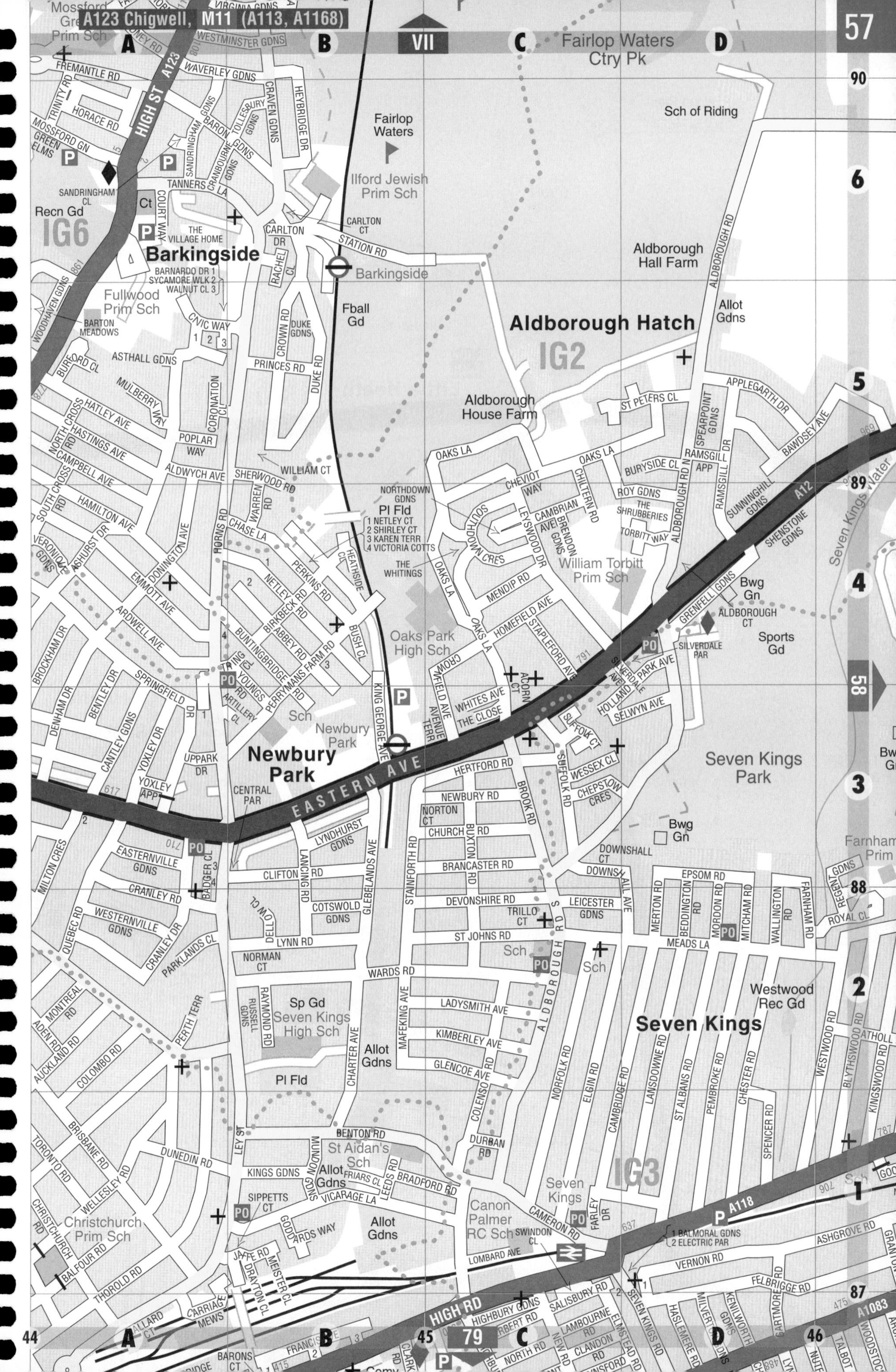
A123 Chigwell, M11 (A113, A1168)
Fairlop Waters Ctry Pk
Fairlop Waters
Ilford Jewish Prim Sch
Sch of Riding
Barkingside
Aldborough Hall Farm
Aldborough Hatch
IG6
IG2
IG3
Fullwood Prim Sch
Aldborough House Farm
Fball Gd
Pl Fld
William Torbitt Prim Sch
Oaks Park High Sch
Newbury Park
Seven Kings Park
Sports Gd
Bwg Gn
Seven Kings Water
Sp Gd
Seven Kings High Sch
Allot Gdns
Westwood Rec Gd
Seven Kings
St Aidan's Sch
Canon Palmer RC Sch
Christchurch Prim Sch
EASTERN AVE
HIGH RD
HIGH ST
A12
A118
A1083
A123
Recn Gd
THE VILLAGE HOME
Farnham Prim

A
B
VII
C
D
Fairlop Plain
PAINTERS RD
IG2
Allot Gdns
HAINAULT RD
Red House Farm
Hainault House
Willow Farm
Little Heath Sch
Hargreaves
ST JAMES GDNS
Little Heath
RM6
EASTERN AVE
A12
B177
King George
Goodmayes
Seven Kings Water
Redbridge Coll
Ethel Davis Sch
Pl Fld
Grove Prim Sch
Chadwell Heath
BARLEY LA
The Chadwell Heath Foundation Sch
Farnham Green Prim Sch
Chadwell Heath
St Chad's Park
Min Glf Crs
Barking & Dagenham
Redbridge
IG3
Barley Lane Sch
Barley La Rec Gd
HIGH RD
A118
TUDOR PAR
Superstore
Goodmayes
Mayfield Sch & Coll
GOODMAYES RD
GOODMAYES RET PK
RM8
A1083
GREEN LA
B191
Fossway Allot Gdns
CHADWELL HEATH IND PK
46
47
48
80
57
90
89
88
87
6
5
4
3
2
1

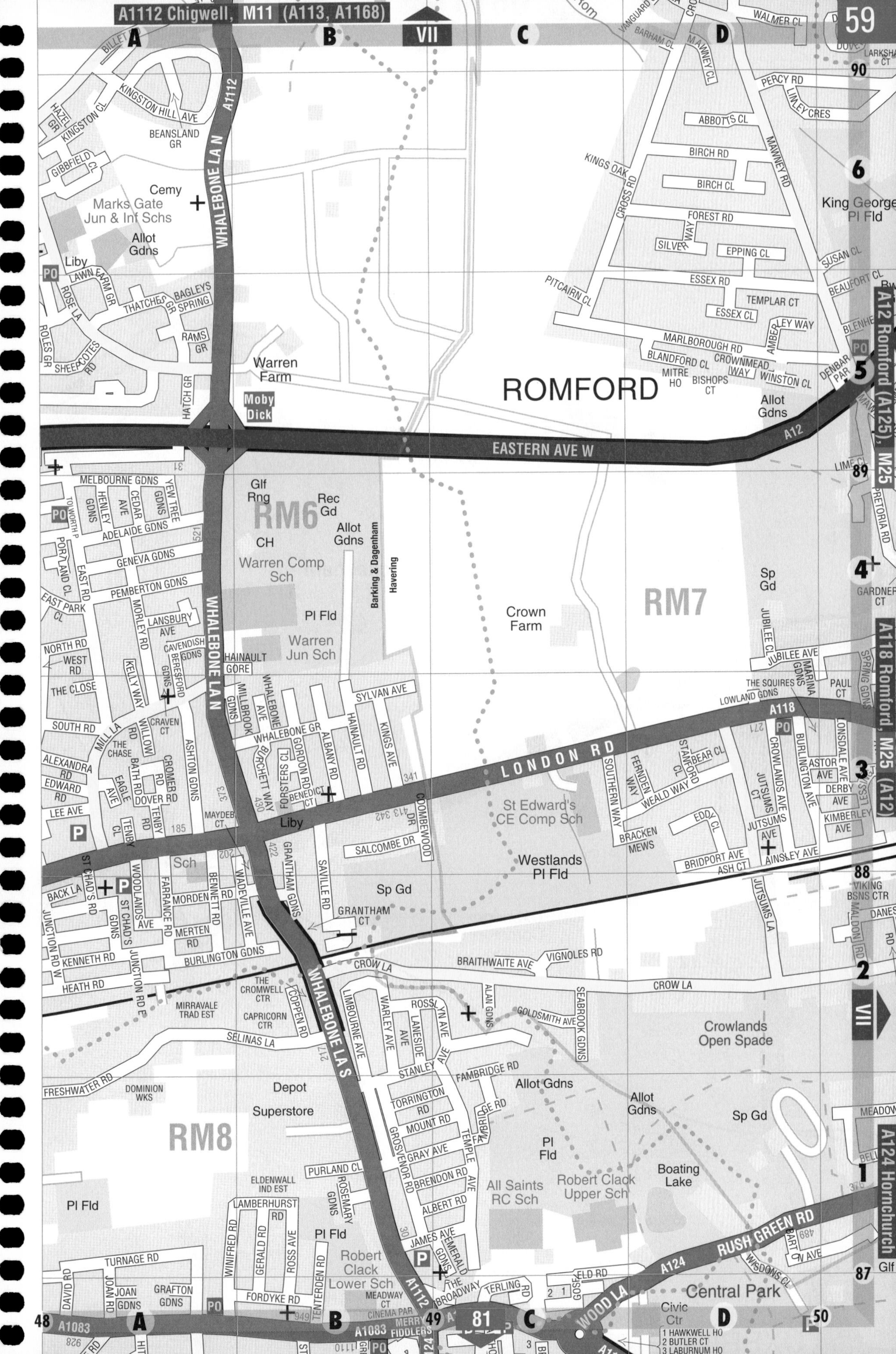
A1112 Chigwell, M11 (A113, A1168)
VII
ROMFORD
RM6
RM7
RM8
WHALEBONE LA N
WHALEBONE LA S
EASTERN AVE W
LONDON RD
CROW LA
RUSH GREEN RD
WOOD LA
Warren Farm
Crown Farm
Westlands Pl Fld
Crowlands Open Space
Central Park
Boating Lake
Robert Clack Upper Sch
Robert Clack Lower Sch
All Saints RC Sch
St Edward's CE Comp Sch
Warren Comp Sch
Warren Jun Sch
Marks Gate Jun & Inf Schs
King George Pl Fld
Barking & Dagenham
Havering
A12 Romford (A125), M25
A118 Romford, M25 (A12)
A124 Hornchurch
A1083
81

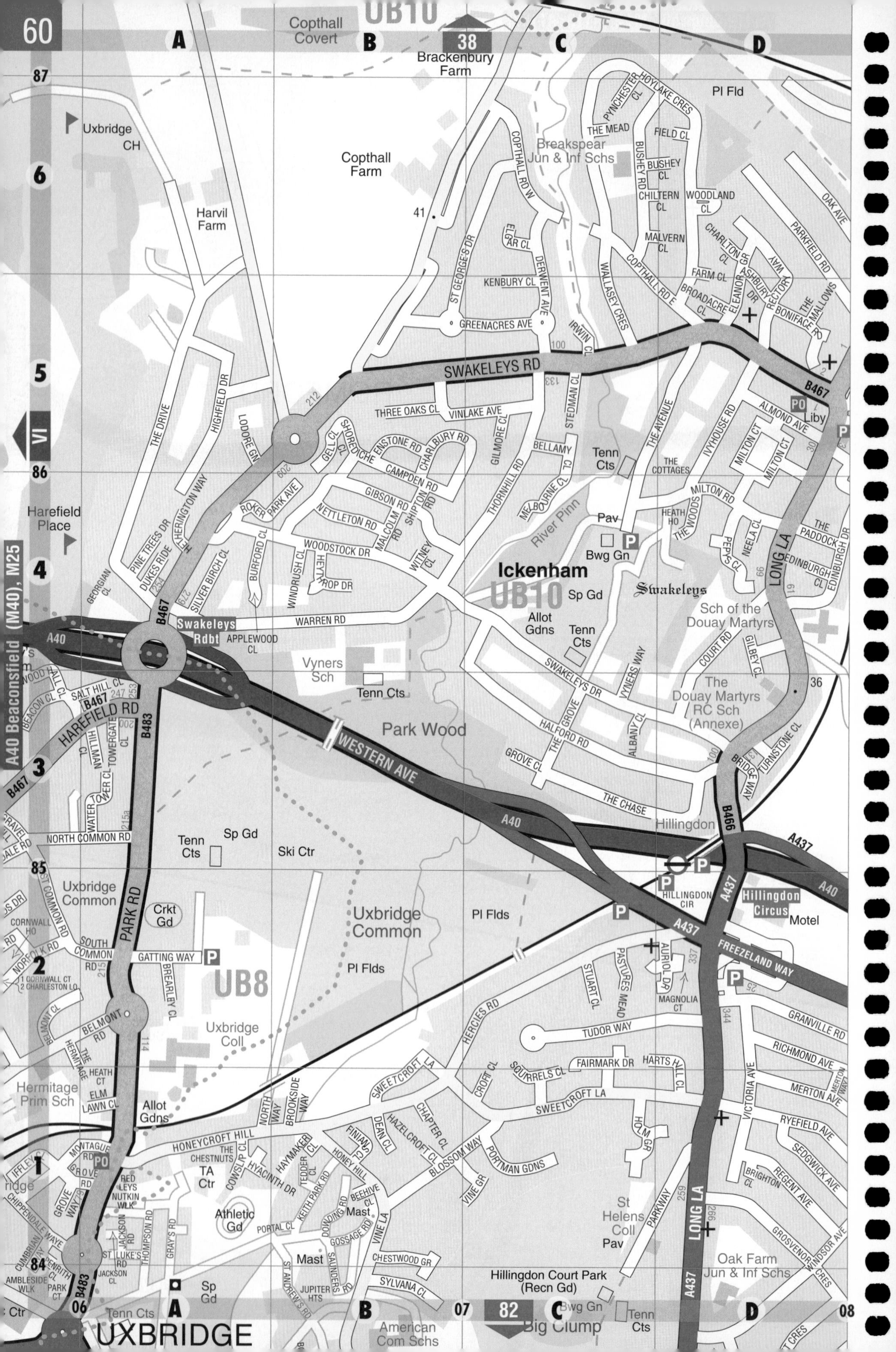

Copthall Covert
UB10
38
Brackenbury Farm
Uxbridge CH
Copthall Farm
Harvil Farm
Breakspear Jun & Inf Schs
Pl Fld
SWAKELEYS RD
Harefield Place
Ickenham
UB10
Swakeleys
Swakeleys Rdbt
Vyners Sch
Park Wood
WESTERN AVE
Sch of the Douay Martyrs
The Douay Martyrs RC Sch (Annexe)
River Pinn
Hillingdon
Hillingdon Circus
Motel
FREEZELAND WAY
LONG LA
Uxbridge Common
PARK RD
UB8
Uxbridge Coll
Hermitage Prim Sch
Ski Ctr
Pl Flds
St Helens Coll
Oak Farm Jun & Inf Schs
Hillingdon Court Park (Recn Gd)
Athletic Gd
TA Ctr
American Com Schs
Big Clump
UXBRIDGE
A40 Beaconsfield (M40), M25
82

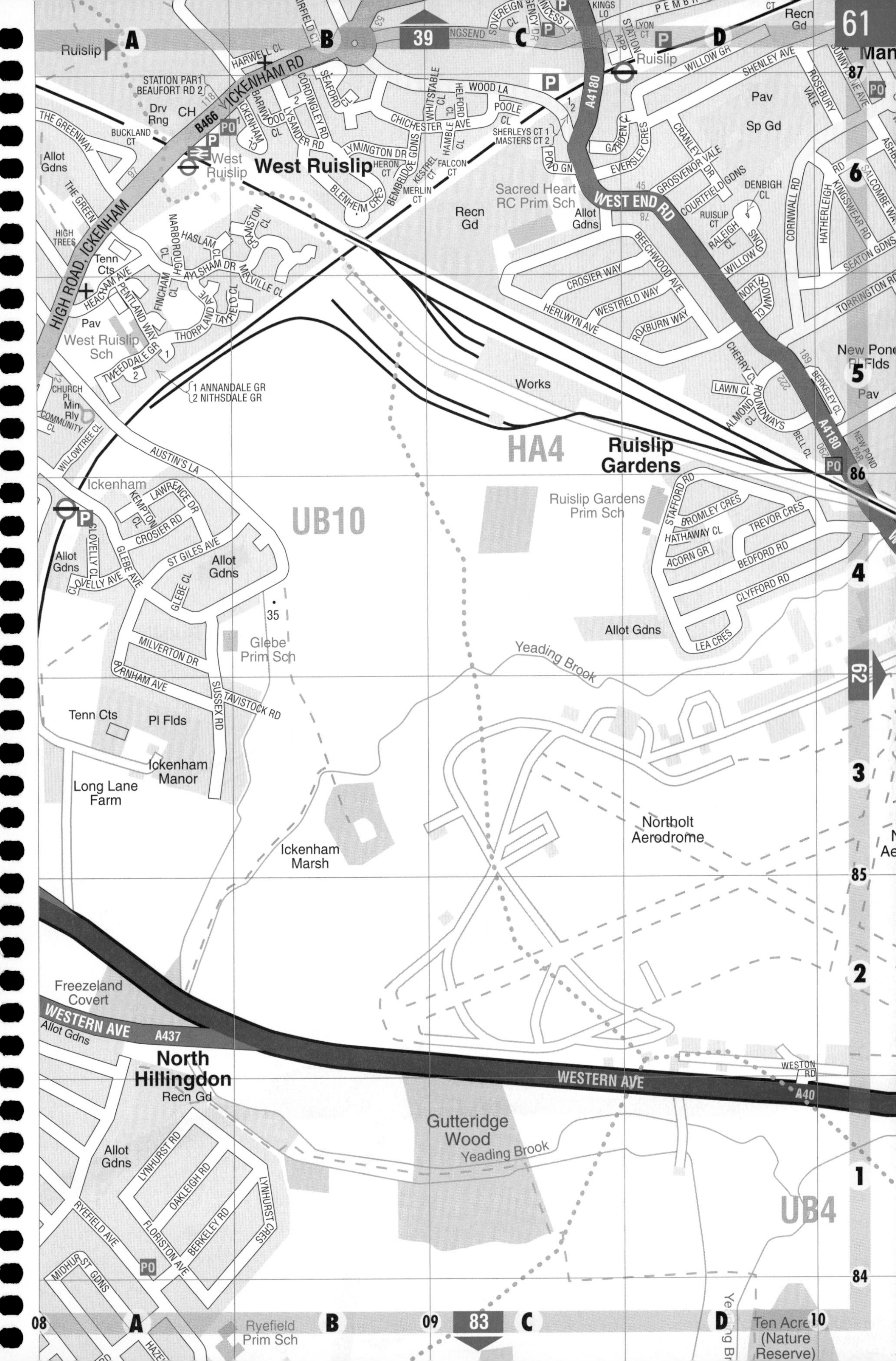
39
A
B
C
D
Ruislip
HARWELL CL
VICKENHAM RD
B466
STATION PAR 1
BEAUFORT RD 2
Drv Rng
CH
THE GREENWAY
BUCKLAND CT
Allot Gdns
West Ruislip
West Ruislip
BARNWOOD CL
ICKENHAM CL
LYSANDER RD
CORDINGLEY RD
SEAFORD CL
CHICHESTER AVE
WHITSTABLE CL
HELFORD CL
HAMBLE CL
WOOD LA
POOLE CL
LYMINGTON DR
BEMBRIDGE GDNS
KESTREL CT
HERON CT
FALCON CT
MERLIN CT
BLENHEIM CRES
SHERLEYS CT 1
MASTERS CT 2
POND GN
SOVEREIGN CL
REGENCY DR
PRINCESS LA
KINGS LO
STATION APP
LYON CT
Recn Gd
A4180
WILLOW GR
SHENLEY AVE
ROSEBURY VALE
SUNNYMEDE AVE
87
Pav
Sp Gd
GARDEN CL
EVERSLEY CRES
CRANLEY DR
GROSVENOR VALE
COURTFIELD GDNS
DENBIGH CL
RUISLIP CT
RALEIGH CL
WILLOW GDNS
CORNWALL RD
HATHERLEIGH RD
KINGSWEAR RD
SALCOMBE WAY
SEATON GDNS
TORRINGTON RD
6
HIGH ROAD, ICKENHAM
THE GREEN
HIGH TREES
Tenn Cts
HEACHAM AVE
PENTLAND WAY
NARBOROUGH CL
HASLAM CL
CRANSTON CL
AYLSHAM DR
MELVILLE CL
FINCHAM CL
THORPLAND AVE
TAYFIELD CL
Pav
West Ruislip Sch
TWEEDDALE GR
1 ANNANDALE GR
2 NITHSDALE GR
Sacred Heart RC Prim Sch
Recn Gd
Allot Gdns
WEST END RD
CROSIER WAY
BEECHWOOD AVE
WESTFIELD WAY
HERLWYN AVE
ROXBURN WAY
NORTH VIEW DOWN CL
CHERRY CL
LAWN CL
ALMOND CL
ROUNDWAYS
BERKELEY CL
BELL CL
New Pond Pl Flds
5
Pav
Works
CHURCH PL
Min Rly
COMMUNITY CL
WILLOWTREE CL
AUSTIN'S LA
HA4
Ruislip Gardens
NEW POND PAR
86
Ickenham
KEMPTON CL
LAWRENCE DR
CROSIER RD
LOVELLY CL
GLEBE AVE
ST GILES AVE
Allot Gdns
GLEBE CL
UB10
Ruislip Gardens Prim Sch
STAFFORD RD
BROMLEY CRES
TREVOR CRES
HATHAWAY CL
ACORN GR
BEDFORD RD
CLYFFORD RD
4
35
MILVERTON DR
Glebe Prim Sch
BURNHAM AVE
SUSSEX RD
TAVISTOCK RD
Allot Gdns
LEA CRES
Yeading Brook
62
Tenn Cts
Pl Flds
Ickenham Manor
Long Lane Farm
3
Northolt Aerodrome
Ickenham Marsh
85
2
Freezeland Covert
WESTERN AVE
A437
Allot Gdns
North Hillingdon
Recn Gd
WESTERN AVE
WESTON RD
A40
Gutteridge Wood
Yeading Brook
1
Allot Gdns
LYNHURST RD
OAKLEIGH RD
LYNHURST CRES
BERKELEY RD
RYEFIELD AVE
FLORISTON AVE
MIDHURST GDNS
UB4
84
08
A
Ryefield Prim Sch
B
09
83
C
D
Ten Acre (Nature Reserve)
10

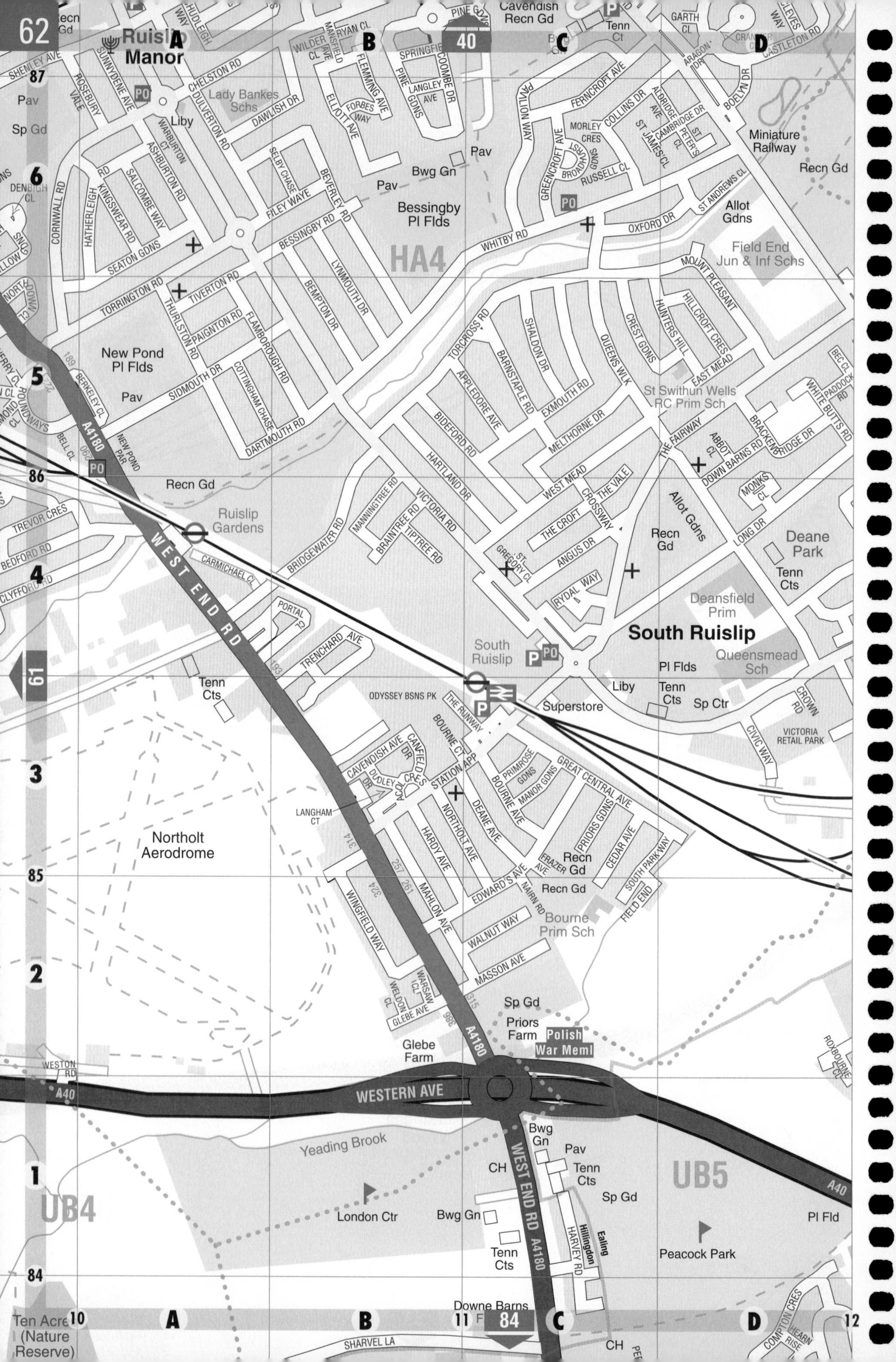
A
B
C
D
40
84
61
87
6
5
86
4
3
85
2
1
84
10
11
12
Ruislip Manor
Lady Bankes Schs
Liby
Pav
Sp Gd
Bessingby Pl Flds
Bwg Gn
HA4
Miniature Railway
Recn Gd
Allot Gdns
Field End Jun & Inf Schs
New Pond Pl Flds
Recn Gd
Ruislip Gardens
St Swithun Wells RC Prim Sch
Deane Park
Tenn Cts
Deansfield Prim
South Ruislip
Queensmead Sch
Pl Flds
Sp Ctr
Superstore
South Ruislip
Odyssey Bsns Pk
Victoria Retail Park
Northolt Aerodrome
Bourne Prim Sch
Sp Gd
Priors Farm
Polish War Meml
Glebe Farm
Western Ave
A40
A4180
West End Rd
Yeading Brook
London Ctr
UB4
UB5
Peacock Park
Pl Fld
Hillingdon
Ealing
Downe Barns
Ten Acre (Nature Reserve)
Sharvel La
Whitby Rd
Torrington Rd
Sidmouth Dr
Bridgewater Rd
Victoria Rd
Long Dr
Station App
Great Central Ave
Masson Ave
Cavendish Recn Gd
Tenn Ct

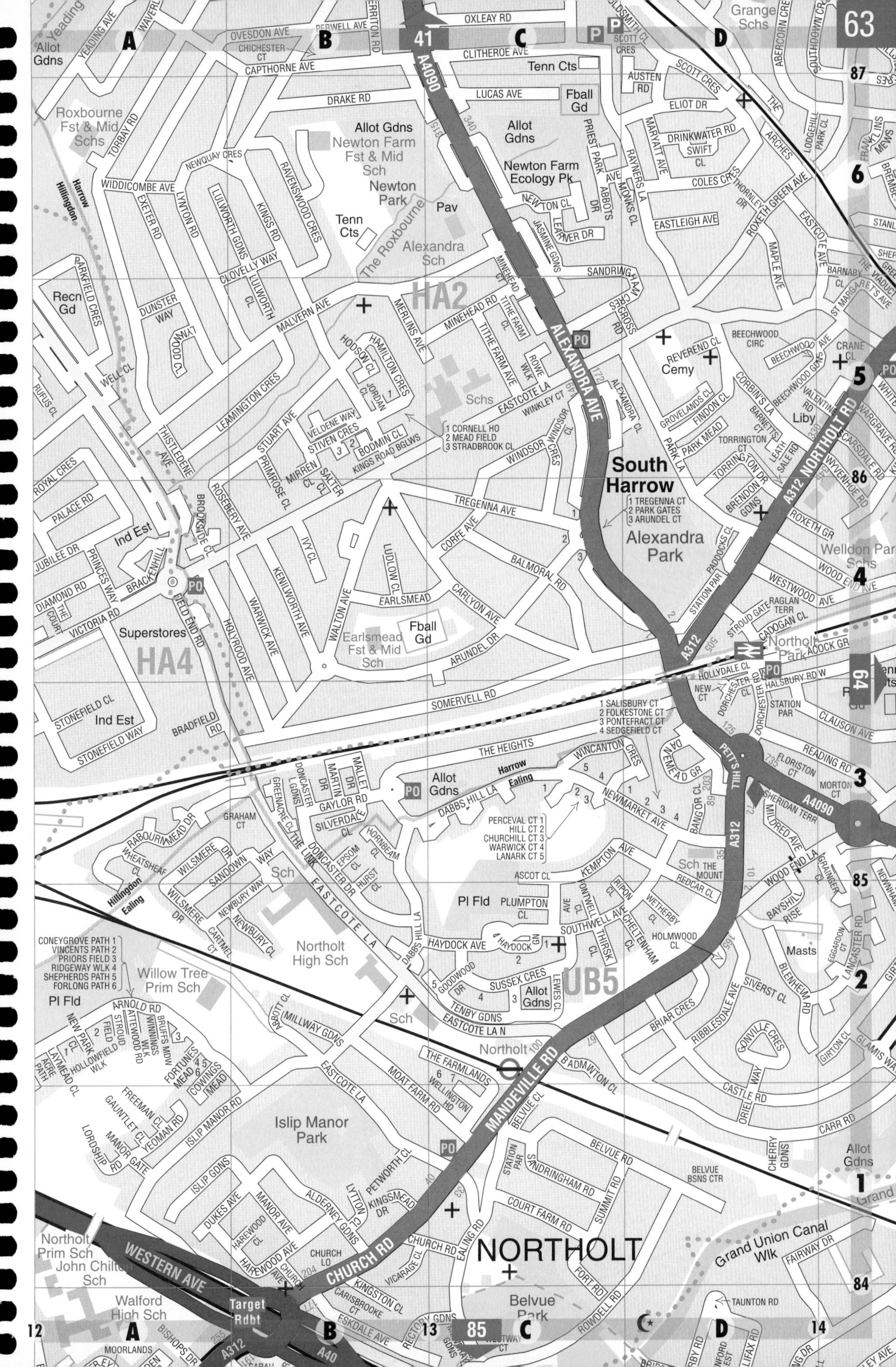

41
A4090
OXLEAY RD
CLITHEROE AVE
Tenn Cts
LUCAS AVE
Fball Gd
DRAKE RD
CAPTHORNE AVE
OVESDON AVE
Allot Gdns
Roxbourne Fst & Mid Schs
Newton Farm Fst & Mid Sch
Newton Farm Ecology Pk
Newton Park
Alexandra Sch
HA2
MALVERN AVE
ALEXANDRA AVE
South Harrow
1 TREGENNA CT
2 PARK GATES
3 ARUNDEL CT
Alexandra Park
Cemy
Liby
NORTHOLT RD
A312
TREGENNA AVE
Earlsmead Fst & Mid Sch
HA4
Superstores
Ind Est
SOMERVELL RD
1 SALISBURY CT
2 FOLKESTONE CT
3 PONTEFRACT CT
4 SEDGEFIELD CT
1 CORNELL HO
2 MEAD FIELD
3 STRADBROOK CL
Northolt Park
PETT'S HILL
PERCEVAL CT 1
HILL CT 2
CHURCHILL CT 3
WARWICK CT 4
LANARK CT 5
Pl Fld
Northolt High Sch
Willow Tree Prim Sch
CONEYGROVE PATH 1
VINCENTS PATH 2
PRIORS FIELD 3
RIDGEWAY WLK 4
SHEPHERDS PATH 5
FORLONG PATH 6
UB5
EASTCOTE LA
MANDEVILLE RD
Northolt
Islip Manor Park
Masts
NORTHOLT
CHURCH RD
WESTERN AVE
Target Rdbt
Belvue Park
Grand Union Canal Wlk
Northolt Prim Sch
John Chilton Sch
Walford High Sch
A40
A B C D
87 6 5 86 4 3 85 2 1 84
12 13 14
64
85

Harrow on the Hill
Roxeth
Superstore
HA2
HA1
UB6
South Harrow
Sudbury Hill Harrow
Sudbury Hill
Northolt Park
Greenford
The John Lyon Sch
Bowden House (Private)
The Clementine Churchill
St George's RC Prim Sch
St Dominic's Coll(RC)
Orley Farm Sch
Welldon Park Schs
Ealing Northern Sp Ctr
Horsenden Prim Sch
Roxeth Recn Gd
Sudbury Hill Pl Flds
The Ballot Box (PH)
Running Tk
Harrow
Ealing
ROXETH HILL
SUDBURY HILL
LONDON RD
HIGH ST
NORTHOLT RD
GREENFORD RD
WHITTON AVE W
SOUTH HILL AVE
WOOD END RD
HARROW PK
MOUNT PARK RD
EASTCOTE AVE
ROXETH GREEN AVE
HALSBURY RD E
CAVENDISH AVE
ROSEBANK AVE
FERNBANK AVE
HORSENDEN LA N
BERKELEY AVE
OLDFIELD LA N
CARR RD
AURIOL DR
STATION APP
ALLINGTON CL
HILL RISE
ROCKWARE AVE
Grand Union Canal Paddington Branch
Grand Union Canal Walk
A312
A4005
A4090
A4127
B458
1 HUTTON CL
2 BRASHER CL
3 HEMERY RD
4 TESSA SANDERSON WAY
5 HAMMOND CL
ATHENA CL 1
BRICKFIELDS 2
WEST HILL HALL 3
THE MOAT LO 4
EDWARD CT 5
CHYNGTON CT 6
THOMAS HEWLETT HO 1
JEM PATERSON CT 2
GREENBANKS 3
LYDIA LO 4
WALTON CROFT 5
A
B
C
D
87
86
85
84
6
5
4
3
2
1
14
15
16
42
63
86

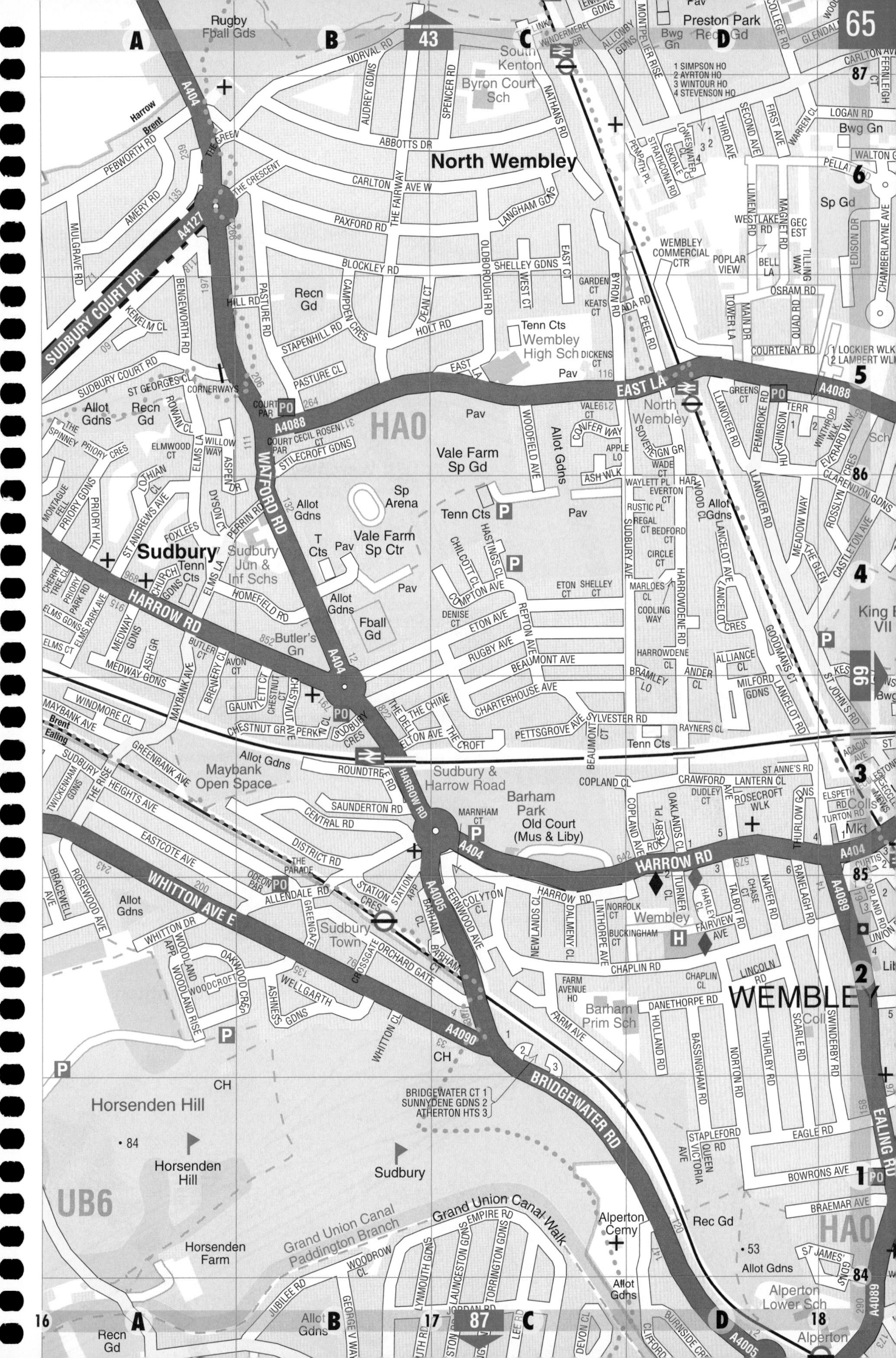

43
North Wembley
South Kenton
Byron Court Sch
Preston Park Rec Gd
Sudbury
Sudbury Court Dr
Watford Rd
Harrow Rd
East La
North Wembley
Vale Farm Sp Gd
Vale Farm Sp Ctr
Wembley High Sch
Sudbury Jun & Inf Schs
Butler's Gn
Sudbury & Harrow Road
Barham Park
Old Court (Mus & Liby)
Maybank Open Space
Sudbury Town
Whitton Ave E
Bridgewater Rd
WEMBLEY
Barham Prim Sch
Horsenden Hill
Horsenden Farm
UB6
HA0
Grand Union Canal Paddington Branch
Grand Union Canal Walk
Alperton Cemy
Alperton Lower Sch
Alperton
Ealing Rd
Wembley Commercial Ctr
BRIDGEWATER CT 1
SUNNYDENE GDNS 2
ATHERTON HTS 3
1 SIMPSON HO
2 AYRTON HO
3 WINTOUR HO
4 STEVENSON HO
1 LOCKIER WLK
2 LAMBERT WLK
87
86
85
84
66

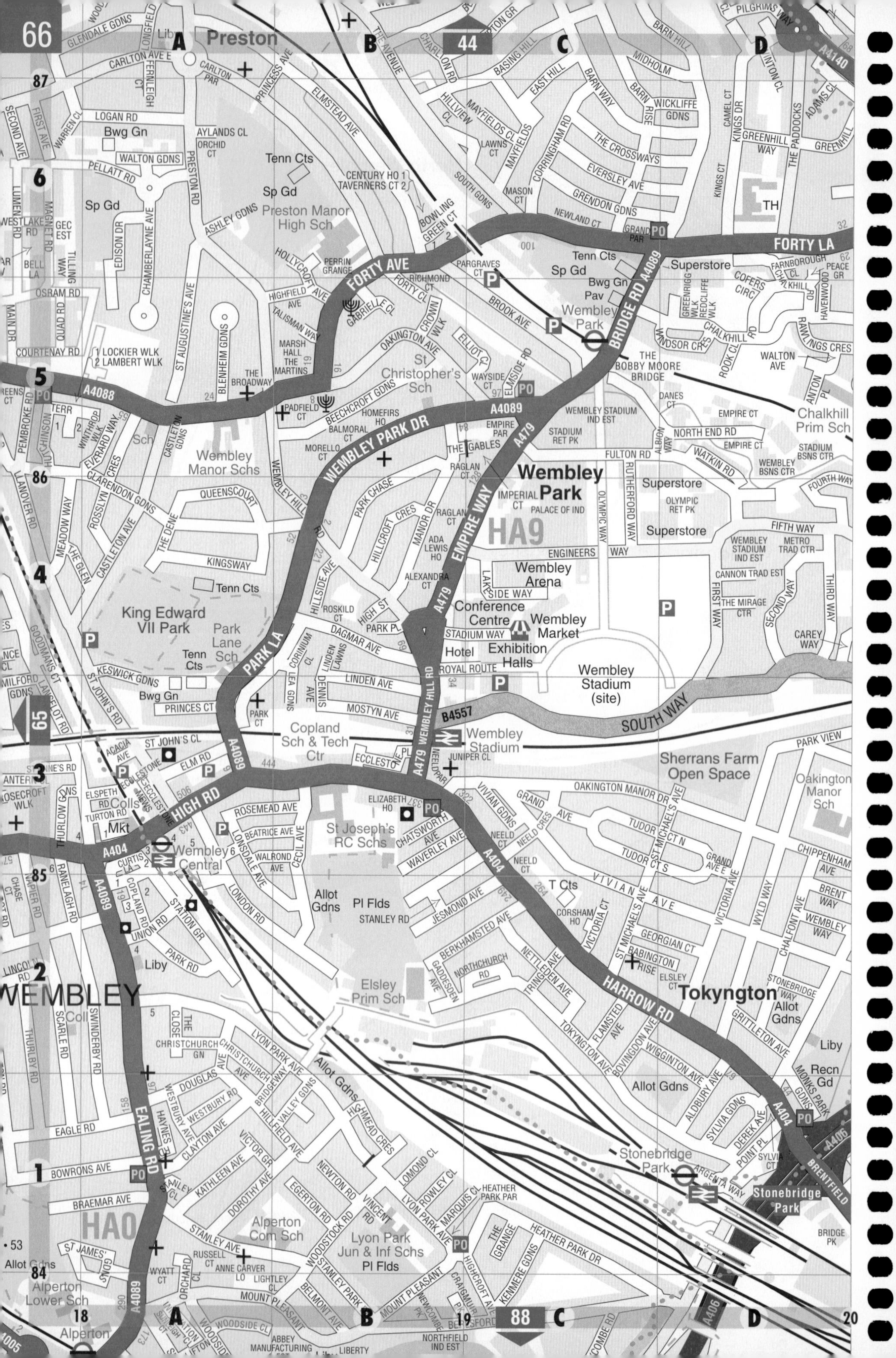
Preston
44
Wembley Park
HA9
Wembley Arena
Conference Centre
Wembley Market
Exhibition Halls
Wembley Stadium (site)
King Edward VII Park
Preston Manor High Sch
Wembley Manor Schs
St Christopher's Sch
Copland Sch & Tech Ctr
St Joseph's RC Schs
Elsley Prim Sch
Sherrans Farm Open Space
Oakington Manor Sch
Chalkhill Prim Sch
Tokyngton
WEMBLEY
HA0
Alperton Com Sch
Lyon Park Jun & Inf Schs
Alperton Lower Sch
Stonebridge Park
FORTY LA
FORTY AVE
WEMBLEY PARK DR
EMPIRE WAY
BRIDGE RD
PARK LA
HIGH RD
HARROW RD
EALING RD
SOUTH WAY
WEMBLEY HILL RD
A4088
A4089
A479
A404
B4557
A406
A4140
65
88

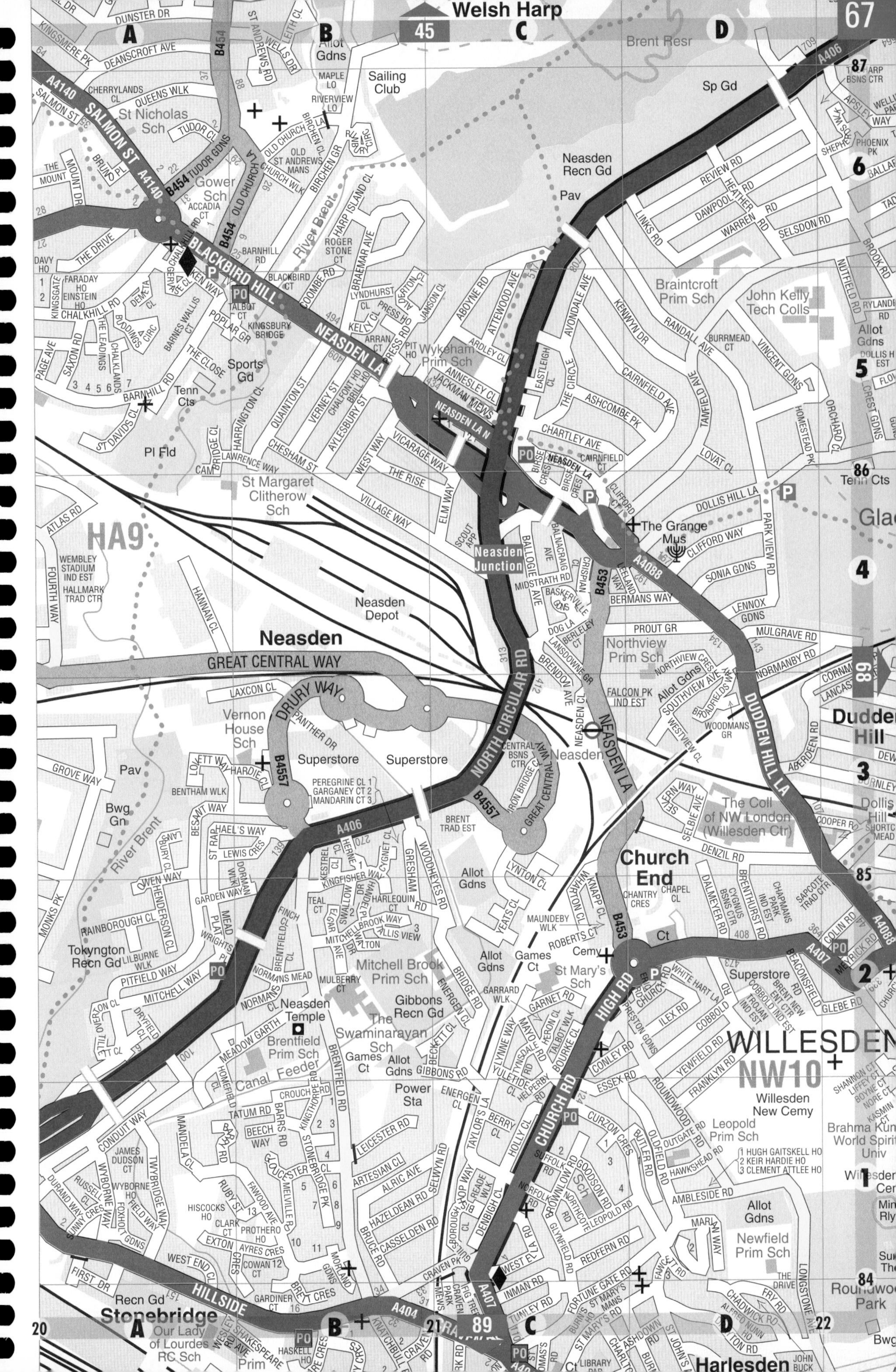

Welsh Harp
45
A
B
C
D
Brent Resr
Sailing Club
Allot Gdns
Sp Gd
Neasden Recn Gd
Pav
St Nicholas Sch
Gower Sch
SALMON ST
A4140
B454
BLACKBIRD HILL
NEASDEN LA
NORTH CIRCULAR RD
A406
Braintcroft Prim Sch
John Kelly Tech Colls
Wykeham Prim Sch
Sports Gd
Tenn Cts
Pl Fld
St Margaret Clitherow Sch
HA9
WEMBLEY STADIUM IND EST
HALLMARK TRAD CTR
Neasden Depot
Neasden Junction
The Grange Mus
A4088
B453
Neasden
GREAT CENTRAL WAY
DRURY WAY
Vernon House Sch
Superstore
Northview Prim Sch
FALCON PK IND EST
DUDDEN HILL LA
Dudden Hill
The Coll of NW London (Willesden Ctr)
Church End
BRENT TRAD EST
B4557
Allot Gdns
Bwg Gn
River Brent
Tokyngton Recn Gd
Mitchell Brook Prim Sch
Neasden Temple
Gibbons Recn Gd
The Swaminarayan Sch
Brentfield Prim Sch
Canal Feeder
Games Ct
Power Sta
St Mary's Sch
HIGH RD
CHURCH RD
A407
WILLESDEN
NW10
Willesden New Cemy
Leopold Prim Sch
Newfield Prim Sch
Roundwood Park
HILLSIDE
A404
Stonebridge
Our Lady of Lourdes RC Sch
Recn Gd
Harlesden
89
20
21
22
84
85
86
87
1
2
3
4
5
6
68

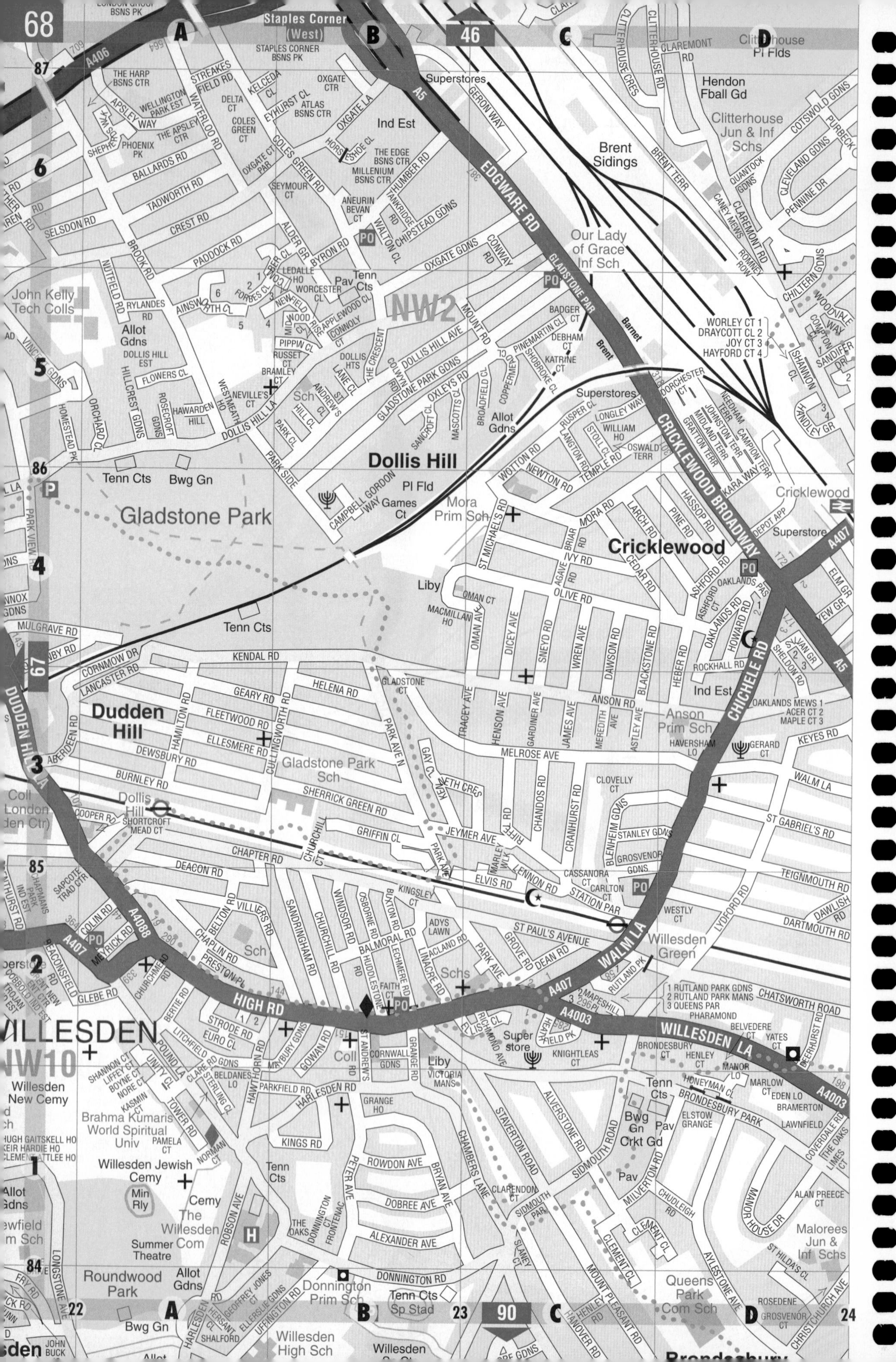
Staples Corner (West)
46
A
B
C
D
A406
STAPLES CORNER BSNS PK
THE HARP BSNS CTR
STREAKES FIELD RD
WELLINGTON PARK EST
APSLEY WAY
THE APSLEY CTR
PHOENIX PK
DELTA CT
COLES GREEN CT
WATERLOO RD
KELCEDA CL
EYHURST CL
ATLAS BSNS CTR
OXGATE CTR
OXGATE LA
Superstores
GERON WAY
A5
Ind Est
THE EDGE BSNS CTR
MILLENIUM BSNS CTR
HUMBER RD
COLES GREEN RD
OXGATE CT PAR
BALLARDS RD
TADWORTH RD
SEYMOUR CT
ANEURIN BEVAN CT
TANKRIDGE RD
WALTON CL
CHIPSTEAD GDNS
PO
CREST RD
SELSDON RD
PADDOCK RD
BROOK RD
ALDER GR
BYRON RD
OXGATE GDNS
CONWAY RD
EDGWARE RD
GLADSTONE PAR
Our Lady of Grace Inf Sch
Brent Sidings
BRENT TERR
CLITTERHOUSE CRES
CLITTERHOUSE RD
CLAREMONT RD
Clitterhouse Pl Flds
Hendon Fball Gd
Clitterhouse Jun & Inf Schs
COTSWOLD GDNS
PURBECK
QUANTOCK GDNS
CLEVELAND GDNS
PENNINE DR
CANEY MEWS
CLAREMONT RD
ROMNEY ROW
CHILTERN GDNS
WOODVALE WAY
COMPTON CT
SANDIFER DR
SHANNON CL
HANDLEY GR
WORLEY CT 1
DRAYCOTT CL 2
JOY CT 3
HAYFORD CT 4
John Kelly Tech Colls
NUTFIELD RD
RYLANDES RD
Allot Gdns
DOLLIS HILL EST
LEDALLE HO
WORCESTER CL
Pav
Tenn Cts
AINSWORTH CL
FORBES CL
NEWFIELD RISE
APPLEWOOD CL
CONNOLLY CT
NW2
BADGER CT
DEBHAM CT
KATRINE CT
PINEMARTIN CL
SHOBROKE CL
MOUNT RD
Barnet
Brent
PIPPIN CL
RUSSET CT
BRAMLEY CT
DOLLIS HTS
LANE CL
THE CRESCENT
COLWYN
DOLLIS HILL AVE
GLADSTONE PARK GDNS
OXLEYS RD
BROADFIELD CL
COPPERMEAD CL
FLOWERS CL
HILLCREST GDNS
ROSECROFT GDNS
HAWARDEN HILL
WESTMEATH HO
NEVILLE'S CT
Sch
HILL CL
ST ANDREW'S CL
PARK CL
SANCROFT CL
MASCOTTS CL
Allot Gdns
Superstores
RUSPER CL
LONGLEY WAY
WILLIAM HO
DORCHESTER CT
NEEDHAM TERR
JOHNSTON TERR
MIDLAND TERR
GRATTON TERR
CAMPION TERR
KARA WAY
OSWALD TERR
CRICKLEWOOD BROADWAY
HOMESTEAD PK
ORCHARD CL
DOLLIS HILL LA
PARK SIDE
Dollis Hill
Pl Fld
Games Ct
CAMPBELL GORDON WAY
Tenn Cts
Bwg Gn
Gladstone Park
WOTTON RD
NEWTON RD
LANGTON RD
STOLL CL
TEMPLE RD
Mora Prim Sch
ST MICHAEL'S RD
MORA RD
BRIAR RD
LARCH RD
PINE RD
HASSOP RD
DEPOT APP
Cricklewood
Superstore
A407
Cricklewood
IVY RD
AGAVE RD
CEDAR RD
ASHFORD RD
OAKLANDS PAS
OLIVE RD
Liby
OMAN CT
MACMILLAN HO
OMAN AVE
DICEY AVE
SNEYD RD
WREN AVE
DAWSON RD
BLACKSTONE RD
HEBER RD
OAKLANDS RD
HOWARD RD
CHICHELE RD
SHELDON RD
SYLVAN GR
ELM GR
VEW GR
ROCKHALL RD
Ind Est
Tenn Cts
MULGRAVE RD
67
CORNMOW DR
LANCASTER RD
KENDAL RD
HELENA RD
GEARY RD
GLADSTONE CT
TRACEY AVE
HENSON AVE
GARDINER AVE
JAMES AVE
MEREDITH AVE
ASTLEY AVE
ANSON RD
Anson Prim Sch
HAVERSHAM LO
GERARD CT
KEYES RD
OAKLANDS MEWS 1
ACER CT 2
MAPLE CT 3
Dudden Hill
DUDDEN HILL LA
ABERDEEN RD
HAMILTON RD
FLEETWOOD RD
ELLESMERE RD
CULLINGWORTH RD
DEWSBURY RD
BURNLEY RD
Gladstone Park Sch
PARK AVE N
GAY CL
KENNETH CRES
MELROSE AVE
WALM LA
CLOVELLY CT
CHANDOS RD
CRANHURST RD
BLENHEIM GDNS
STANLEY GDNS
GROSVENOR GDNS
ST GABRIEL'S RD
Coll London
Dollis Hill
COOPER RD
SHORTCROFT MEAD CT
SHERRICK GREEN RD
GRIFFIN CL
JEYMER AVE
RIFFEL RD
CHURCHILL CT
CHAPTER RD
DEACON RD
PARK AVE
MARLEY WLK
LENNON RD
CASSANORA CT
CARLTON CT
STATION PAR
PO
TEIGNMOUTH RD
ELVIS RD
KINGSLEY CT
SAPCOTE TRAD CTR
CHAPMANS PARK IND EST
COLIN RD
MEYRICK RD
A4088
VILLIERS RD
BELTON RD
CHAPLIN RD
PRESTON PL
SANDRINGHAM RD
CHURCHILL RD
WINDSOR RD
OSBORNE RD
BUXTON RD
ADYS LAWN
ST PAUL'S AVENUE
GROVE RD
DEAN RD
WESTLY CT
LYDFORD RD
DAWLISH RD
DARTMOUTH RD
Willesden Green
A407
BEACONSFIELD RD
Sch
BALMORAL RD
LECHMERE RD
HUDDLESTONE RD
ACLAND RD
LINACRE RD
Schs
PARK AVE
CHURCHMEAD RD
GLEBE RD
BERTIE RD
HIGH RD
FAITH CT
RUTLAND PK
1 RUTLAND PARK GDNS
2 RUTLAND PARK MANS
3 QUEENS PAR
PHARAMOND
CHATSWORTH ROAD
MAPESHILL PL
A4003
WILLESDEN LA
BELVEDERE CT
YATES CT
DEERHURST RD
WILLESDEN
NW10
STRODE RD
EURO CL
MAYBURY GDNS
GOWAN RD
ST ANDREW'S
Coll
CORNWALL GDNS
GRANGE RD
Liby
VICTORIA MANS
ELLIS CL
RICHMOND AVE
HEATHFIELD PK
Super store
KNIGHTLEAS CT
BRONDESBURY CT
HENLEY CT
MANOR LO
HONEYMAN CL
MARLOW CT
EDEN LO
BRAMERTON
BRONDESBURY PARK
LAWNFIELD
A4003
Willesden New Cemy
SHANNON CT
LIFFEY CT
BOYNE CT
NORE CT
KASMIN CT
LITCHFIELD GDNS
POUND LA
UNITY CL
CLARE RD
STERLING CL
BELDANES LO
HAWTHORN RD
PARKFIELD RD
HARLESDEN RD
GRANGE HO
Tenn Cts
Bwg Gn
Crkt Gd
Pav
ELSTOW GRANGE
Brahma Kumaris World Spiritual Univ
HUGH GAITSKELL HO
KEIR HARDIE HO
CLEMENT ATTLEE HO
PAMELA CT
TOWER RD
NORMAN CT
KINGS RD
ALVERSTONE RD
STAVERTON ROAD
SIDMOUTH ROAD
MILVERTON RD
CHUDLEIGH RD
MANOR HOUSE DR
COVERDALE RD
THE OAKS
LIMES CT
Willesden Jewish Cemy
Min Rly
Cemy
Tenn Cts
ROWDON AVE
PETER AVE
BRYAN AVE
CHAMBERS LANE
CLARENDON CT
ALAN PREECE CT
The Willesden
Summer Com Theatre
ROBSON AVE
H
DONNINGTON CT
FRONTENAC
THE OAKS
DOBREE AVE
ALEXANDER AVE
SIDMOUTH PAR
SLANEY CT
CLEMENT CL
CLEMENT CL
AYLESTONE AVE
Malorees Jun & Inf Schs
ST HILDA'S CL
Roundwood Park
Allot Gdns
LONGSTONE AVE
FRY RD
GEOFFREY JONES CT
ELLERSLIE GDNS
UFFINGTON RD
Donnington Prim Sch
DONNINGTON RD
Tenn Cts
Sp Stad
MOUNT PLEASANT RD
Queens Park Com Sch
ROSEDENE
GROSVENOR CT
CHRISTCHURCH AVE
HARLESDEN RD
HERSANT CL
SHALFORD
Bwg Gn
Willesden High Sch
HENLEY RD
HANOVER RD
JOHN BUCK
87
6
5
86
4
3
85
2
1
84
22
23
90
24

Child's Hill
West Hampstead
HAMPSTEAD
NW2
NW3
NW6
Brondesbury
South Hampste
Golders Hill Park
West Heath
Leg of Mutton Pond
FINCHLEY RD
HENDON WAY
CRICKLEWOOD LA
SHOOT-UP HILL
WILLESDEN LA
IVERSON RD
WEST END LA
FORTUNE GREEN RD
Hampstead Cemy
Kilburn Grange Park
West Hampstead Thameslink

North End
Hampstead Heath
Parliament Hill
Ken Wood
Highgate Ponds
East Heath
Vale of Health
NW3
Hampstead Ponds
HAMPSTEAD
Maitland Park
South Hampstead
Primrose Hill
NORTH END WAY
SPANIARDS RD
HEATH ST
HAMPSTEAD HIGH ST
ROSSLYN HILL
HAVERSTOCK HILL
FLEET RD
FITZJOHN'S AVE
FINCHLEY RD
ADELAIDE RD
BELSIZE PARK GARDENS
University College Sch
Royal Free
Swiss Cottage
Belsize Park
Finchley Road & Frognal
The Freud Mus
Central Sch of Speech & Drama
St Paul's CE Prim Sch
Primrose Hill Tunnels
Belsize New Tunnel
Belsize Tunnel
48
69
92
229
230

A
B
C
D
49
Waterlow Park
St Joseph's RC Prim Sch
Highgate Cemy
Highgate Cemy
The Whittington
Archway
Upper Holloway
Upper Holloway
HOLLOWAY RD
JUNCTION RD
ST JOHN'S GR
HIGHGATE WEST HILL
MILLFIELD PL
HOLLY LODGE GDNS
OAKESHOTT AVE
MAKEPEACE AVE
LANGBOURNE AVE
BROMWICH AVE
SWAIN'S LA
HILLWAY
HOLLY VILLAGE
ST ANN'S CL
WEST HILL CT
BROOKFIELD
Brookfield Prim Sch
DARTMOUTH PARK HILL
MAGDALA AVE
ANATOLA RD
GIRDLESTONE WLK
BREDGAR RD
HARGRAVE PK
BICKERTON RD
TREMLETT GR
N19
Whittington Park
Yerbury Prim Sch
FOXHAM RD
BEVERSBROOK RD
MERCERS RD
TYTHERTON RD
WEDMORE ST
TAVISTOCK TERR
Dartmouth Park
Tenn Cts
Bwg Gn
William Ellis Sch
La Saint Union RC Sec Sch
HIGHGATE RD
WOODSOME RD
YORK RISE
DARTMOUTH PARK RD
LAURIER RD
CHETWYND RD
SPENCER RISE
CHURCHILL RD
CATHCART HILL
STATION RD
Univ of North London (Tufnell Park Hall)
Sp Gd
TUFNELL PARK RD
Tufnell Park
ST GEORGE'S AVE
N7
ARCHIBALD RD
ANSON RD
Tufnell Park Prim Sch
CARLETON RD
Holloway Sch
HILLDROP RD
DALMENY AVE
HM Prison
Parliament Hill Sch
Athletics Gd
Sw Pool
Gospel Oak
GORDON HOUSE RD
Acland Burghley Sch
FORTRESS RD
Tufnell Park
Gospel Oak
HIGHGATE RD
LADY SOMERSET RD
BRECKNOCK RD
OSPRINGE RD
COUNTESS RD
NW5
City Farm
Carlton Prim Sch
Liby
LEIGHTON RD
Kentish Town
Kentish Town
REGIS RD
CAMDEN RD
KENTISH TOWN RD
CAVERSHAM RD
GAISFORD ST
Jews Free Sch
CAMDEN PARK RD
The Camden Sch for Girls
PATSHULL RD
LAWFORD RD
Kentish Town West
MALDEN RD
PRINCE OF WALES RD
CASTLE RD
HAWLEY RD
CHALK FARM RD
Roundhouse Theatre
Chalk Farm
CAMDEN TOWN
NW1
Superstore
Camden Mkt
Camden Rd
AGAR GR
YORK WAY
N1
Freightliner Terminal
Fball Gd
28
29
30
231
93
232
72
87
86
85
84
6
5
4
3
2
1

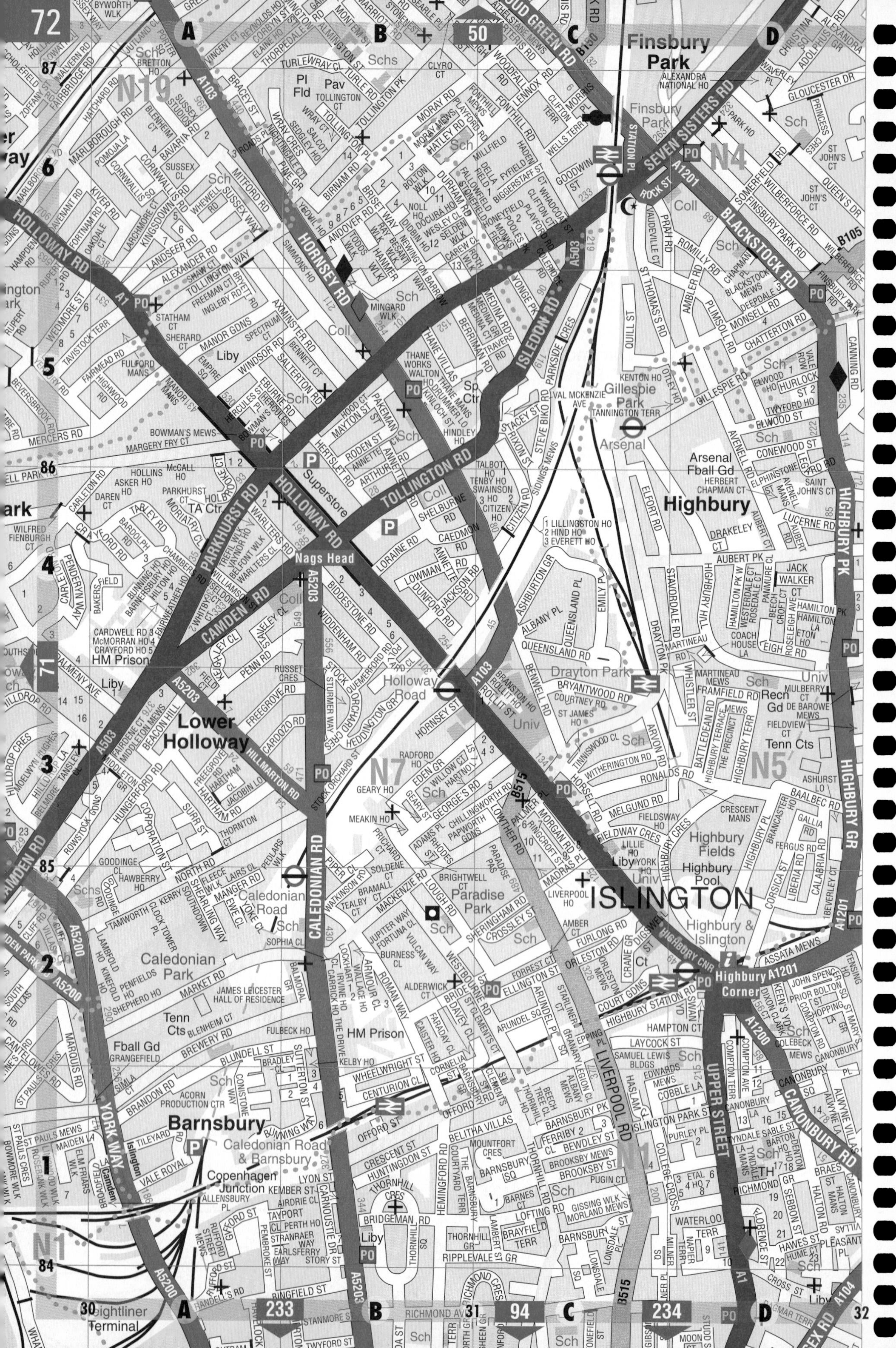
50
Finsbury Park
N19
N4
HOLLOWAY RD
HORNSEY RD
SEVEN SISTERS RD
BLACKSTOCK RD
TOLLINGTON PK
TOLLINGTON WAY
TOLLINGTON RD
ISLEDON RD
PARKHURST RD
CAMDEN RD
Nags Head
Superstore
Gillespie Park
Arsenal
Arsenal Fball Gd
Highbury
HIGHBURY PK
HIGHBURY GR
HM Prison
Lower Holloway
Holloway Road
Drayton Park
HILLMARTON RD
N7
N5
CALEDONIAN RD
Caledonian Road
Caledonian Park
Paradise Park
Highbury Fields
Highbury Pool
ISLINGTON
Highbury & Islington
Highbury Corner
LIVERPOOL RD
UPPER STREET
CANONBURY RD
YORK WAY
Barnsbury
Caledonian Road & Barnsbury
Copenhagen Junction
N1
Freightliner Terminal
71
233
94
234
A
B
C
D
32
87
86
85
84
30
31

A
B
C
D
51
STOKE NEWINGTON
Abney Park Cemy
Clissold Park
Tenn Cts
Bwg Gn
Shacklewell
Canonbury
Kingsland
De Beauvoir Town
Dalston
Dalston Kingsland
Dalston Jct
Stoke Newington
Rectory Road
Essex Road
Ridley
Kingsland Basin
N4
N16
N5
N1
E8
LORDSHIP PK
BROWNSWOOD RD
GREEN LANES
STOKE NEWINGTON CHURCH ST
STOKE NEWINGTON HIGH ST
STOKE NEWINGTON RD
KINGSLAND HIGH ST
KINGSLAND RD
RECTORY RD
MANOR RD
ALBION RD
NEWINGTON GREEN RD
ESSEX RD
ST PAUL'S RD
BALLS POND RD
SOUTHGATE RD
QUEENSBRIDGE RD
EVERING RD
MANSE RD
HIGHBURY NEW PK
HIGHBURY QUADRANT
MILDMAY PK
GROSVENOR AVE
CLISSOLD CRES
CLISSOLD RD
SHACKLEWELL LA
DOWNHAM RD
A105
A10
B104
B105
B111
A1199
A104
B102
B108
A1200
74
86
85
84
87
6
5
4
3
2
1
32
A
235
B
33
95
C
D
34

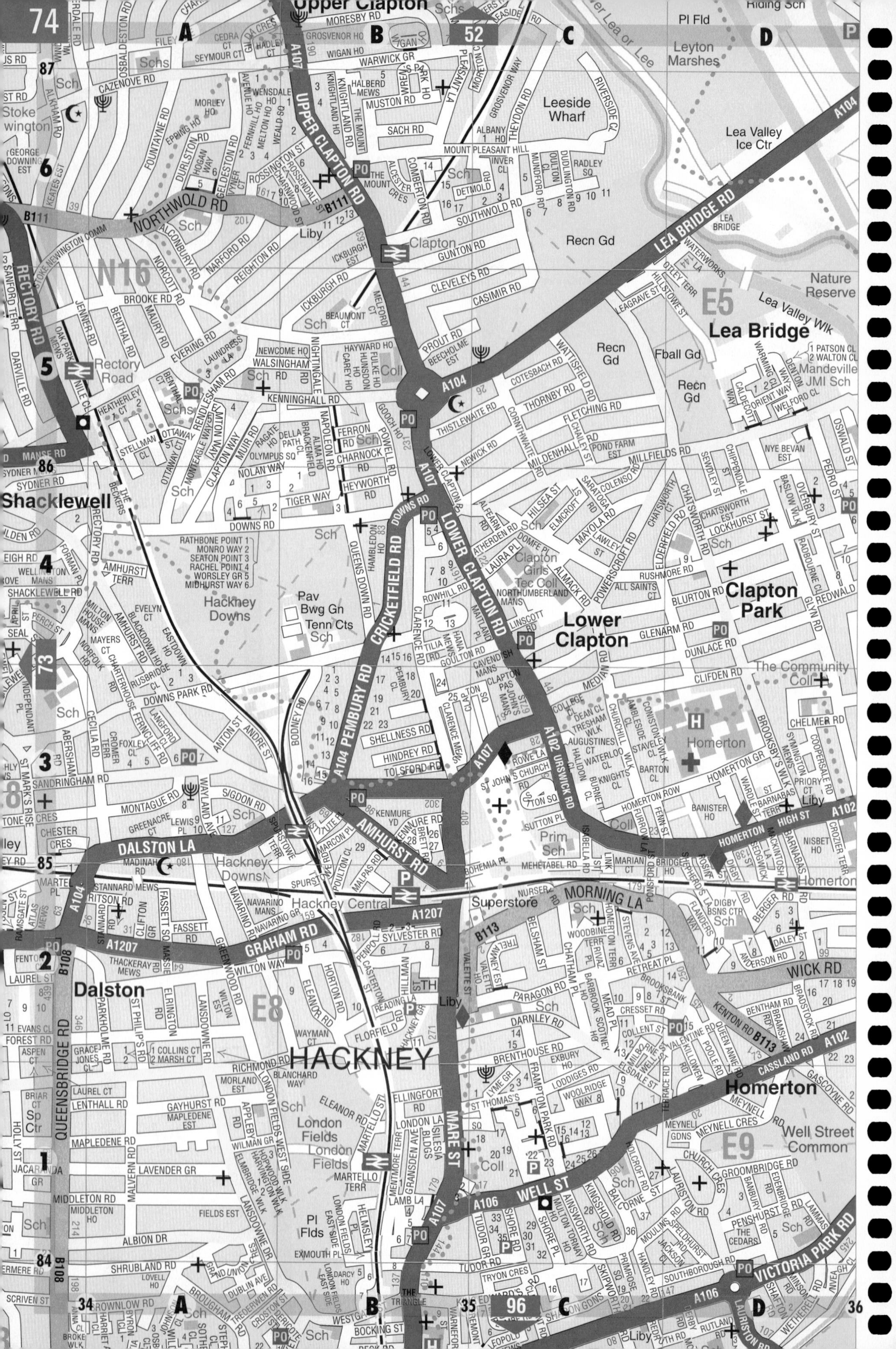

Upper Clapton
Leyton Marshes
Leeside Wharf
Lea Valley Ice Ctr
LEA BRIDGE RD
Nature Reserve
Lea Valley Wlk
Lea Bridge
E5
N16
Stoke Newington
Rectory Road
Clapton
Recn Gd
Fball Gd
Mandeville JMI Sch
NORTHWOLD RD
UPPER CLAPTON RD
LOWER CLAPTON RD
CRICKETFIELD RD
PEMBURY RD
AMHURST RD
DALSTON LA
GRAHAM RD
Shacklewell
Hackney Downs
Clapton Park
Lower Clapton
Homerton
HOMERTON HIGH ST
MORNING LA
WICK RD
Hackney Central
Superstore
Dalston
E8
HACKNEY
MARE ST
London Fields
WELL ST
E9
Well Street Common
VICTORIA PARK RD
QUEENSBRIDGE RD
CASSLAND RD
A
B
C
D
52
96
73
1
2
3
4
5
6
34
35
36
84
85
86
87

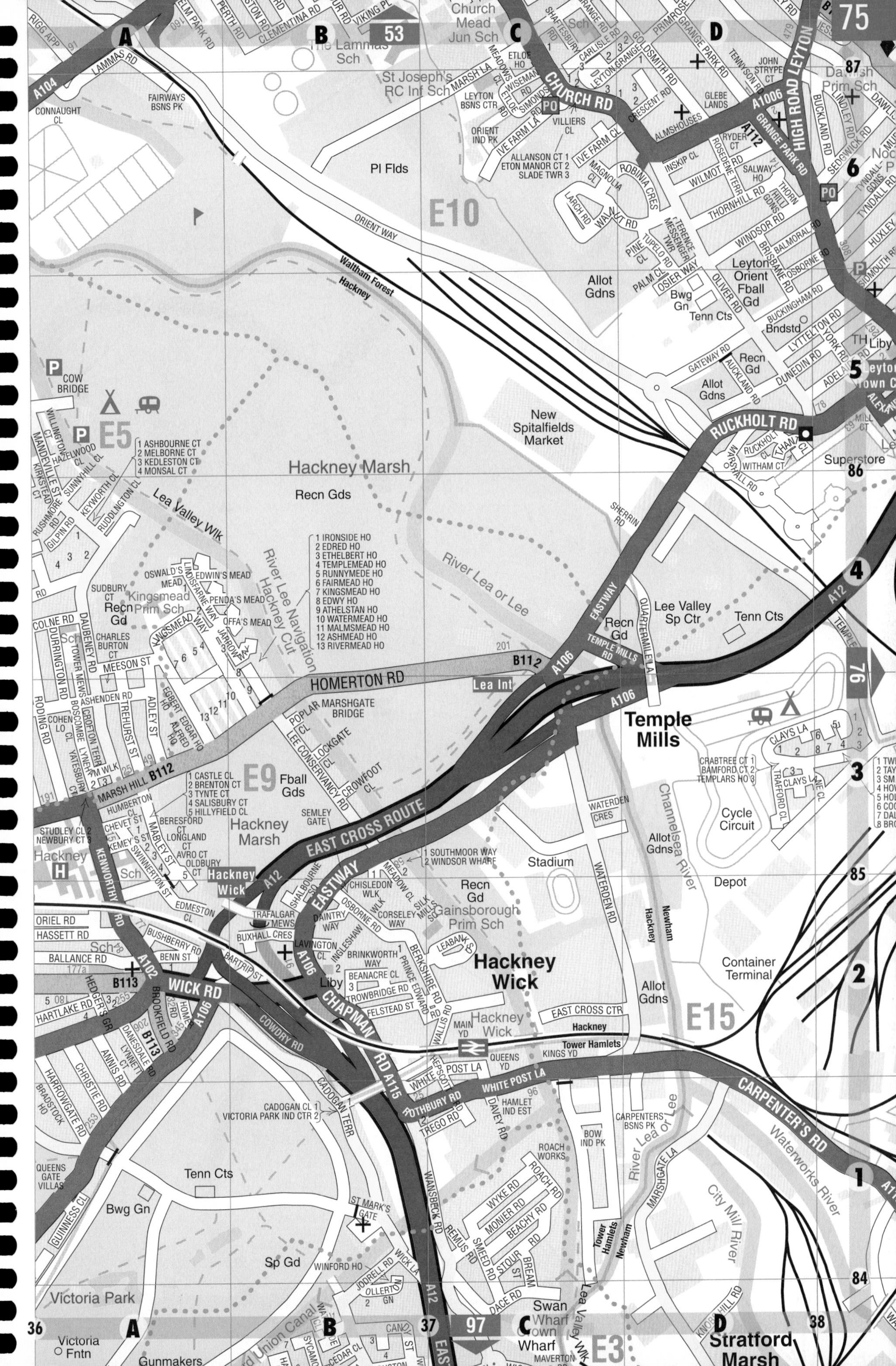

53
E10
Church Mead Jun Sch
The Lammas Sch
St Joseph's RC Inf Sch
Pl Flds
CHURCH RD
HIGH ROAD LEYTON
ORIENT WAY
Waltham Forest
Hackney
Allot Gdns
Leyton Orient Fball Gd
New Spitalfields Market
RUCKHOLT RD
Hackney Marsh
Recn Gds
Lea Valley Wlk
River Lee Navigation
Hackney Cut
River Lea or Lee
E5
COW BRIDGE
Kingsmead Prim Sch
HOMERTON RD
EASTWAY
Lee Valley Sp Ctr
Temple Mills
76
E9
Fball Gds
EAST CROSS ROUTE
MARSH HILL
Hackney Wick
Stadium
Gainsborough Prim Sch
Cycle Circuit
Channelsea River
Depot
Container Terminal
E15
WICK RD
CHAPMAN RD
WHITE POST LA
CARPENTER'S RD
Waterworks River
City Mill River
Tenn Cts
Bwg Gn
Sp Gd
Victoria Park
Victoria Fntn
Gunmakers
97
Swan Wharf
Wharf
E3
Stratford Marsh

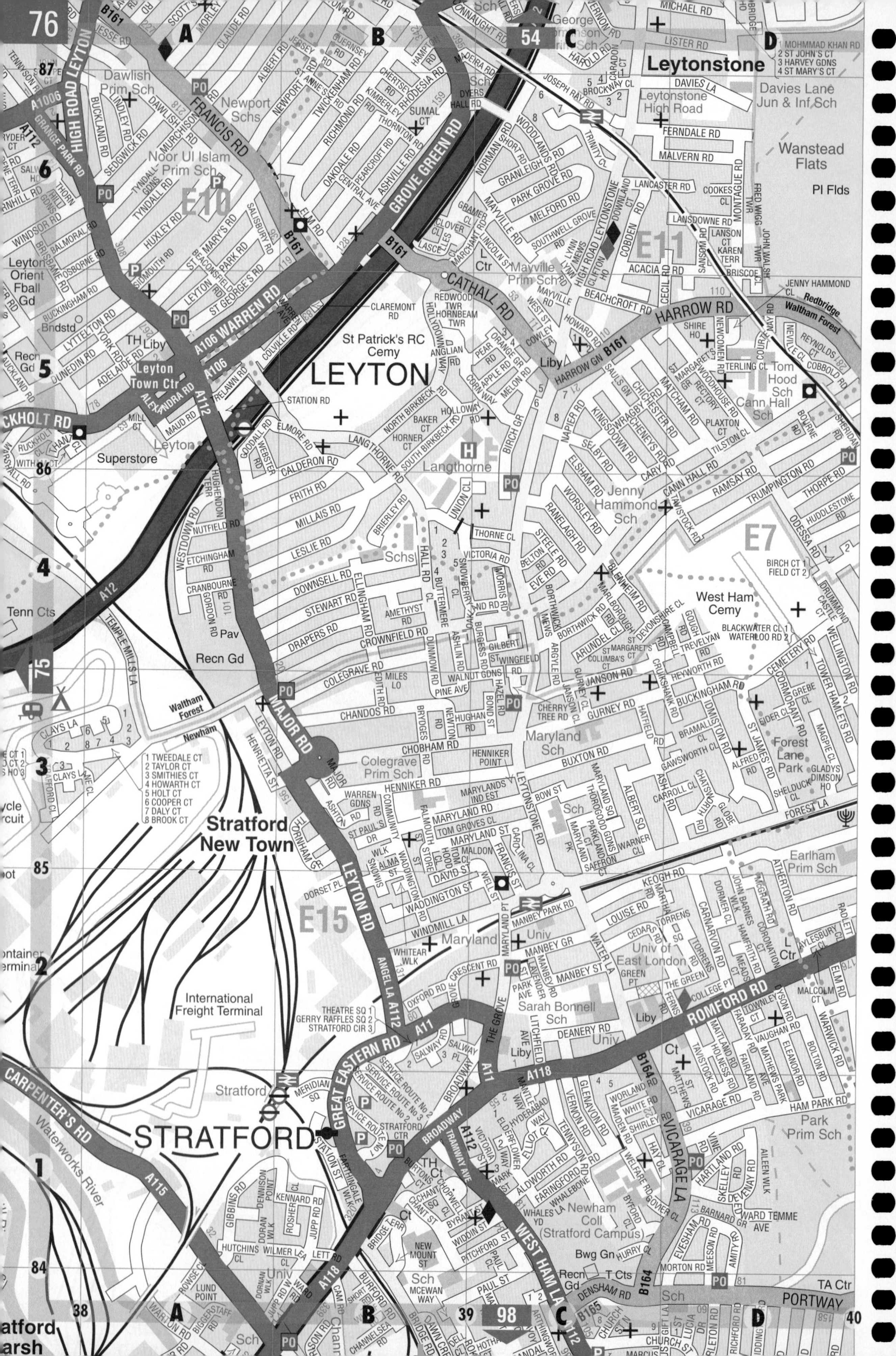
A
B
C
D
54
Leytonstone
1 MOHMMAD KHAN RD
2 ST JOHN'S CT
3 HARVEY GDNS
4 ST MARY'S CT
Davies Lane Jun & Inf Sch
Leytonstone High Road
Wanstead Flats
Pl Flds
Dawlish Prim Sch
Newport Schs
Noor Ul Islam Prim Sch
E10
E11
HIGH ROAD LEYTON
FRANCIS RD
GROVE GREEN RD
Leyton Orient Fball Gd
Mayville Prim Sch
CATHALL RD
HARROW RD
Redbridge
Waltham Forest
St Patrick's RC Cemy
LEYTON
Leyton Town Ctr
A106 WARREN RD
Tom Hood Sch
Cann Hall Sch
Langthorne
Jenny Hammond Sch
E7
West Ham Cemy
Superstore
Tenn Cts
Recn Gd
Waltham Forest
Newham
MAJOR RD
Colegrave Prim Sch
Maryland Sch
Forest Lane Park
1 TWEEDALE CT
2 TAYLOR CT
3 SMITHIES CT
4 HOWARTH CT
5 HOLT CT
6 COOPER CT
7 DALY CT
8 BROOK CT
Stratford New Town
LEYTON RD
E15
Earlham Prim Sch
Univ of East London
International Freight Terminal
THEATRE SQ 1
GERRY RAFFLES SQ 2
STRATFORD CIR 3
GREAT EASTERN RD
ROMFORD RD
Sarah Bonnell Sch
CARPENTER'S RD
Waterworks River
Stratford
STRATFORD
BROADWAY
Newham Coll (Stratford Campus)
Park Prim Sch
VICARAGE LA
WEST HAM LA
PORTWAY
75
98
38
39
40
87
86
85
84
1
2
3
4
5
6

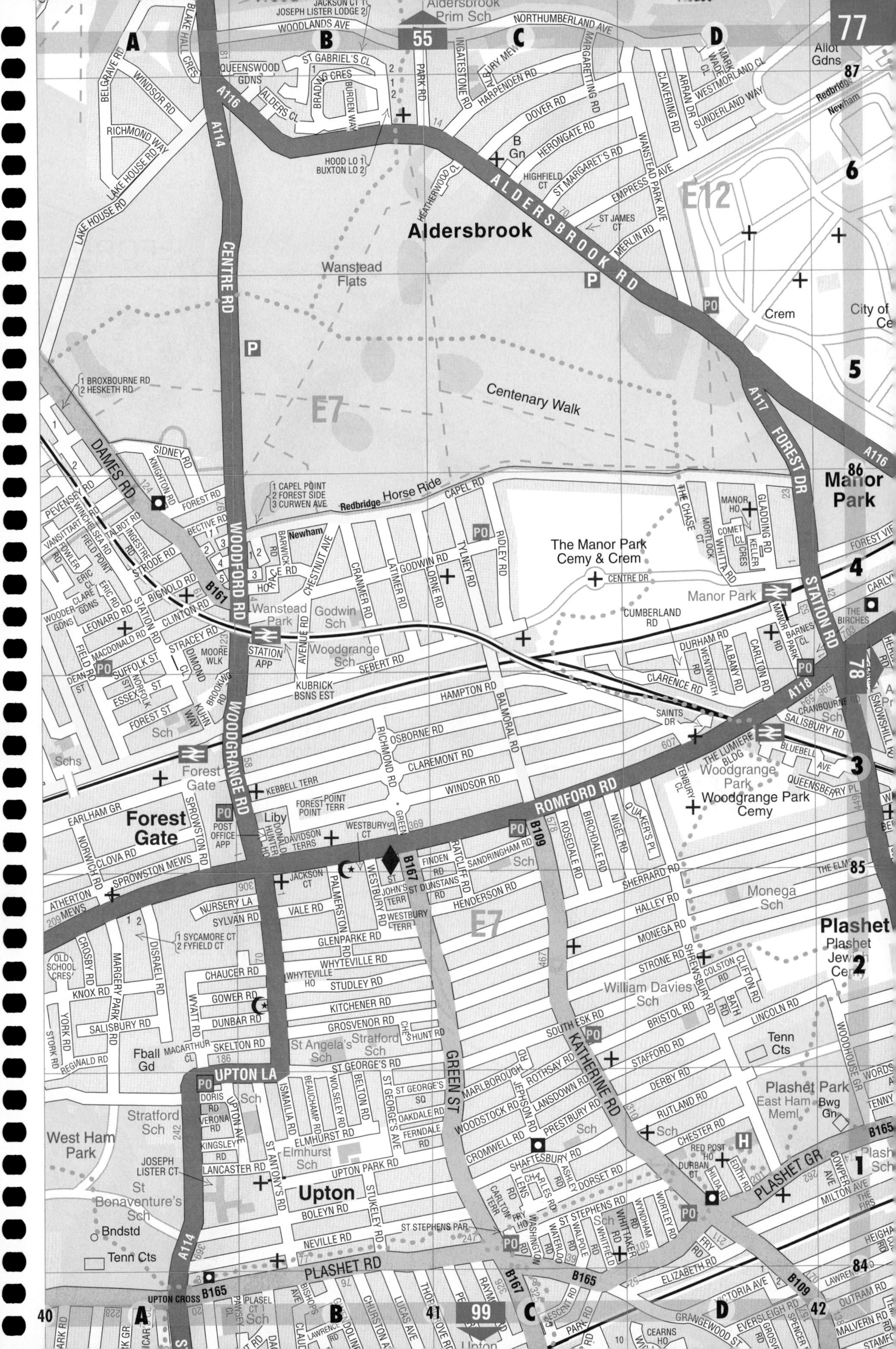

A
B
C
D
55
Aldersbrook Prim Sch
NORTHUMBERLAND AVE
WOODLANDS AVE
ST GABRIEL'S CL
QUEENSWOOD GDNS
Aldersbrook
Wanstead Flats
ALDERSBROOK RD
E12
Crem
City of
Centenary Walk
E7
CENTRE RD
WOODFORD RD
DAMES RD
FOREST DR
Manor Park
The Manor Park Cemy & Crem
Redbridge Horse Ride
Newham
Wanstead Park
Godwin Sch
Woodgrange Sch
ROMFORD RD
Forest Gate
Woodgrange Park
Woodgrange Park Cemy
WOODGRANGE RD
Monega Sch
Plashet
Plashet Jewish Cemy
William Davies Sch
KATHERINE RD
GREEN ST
Tenn Cts
St Angela's Sch
Stratford Sch
UPTON LA
Plashet Park
East Ham Meml
Bwg Gn
West Ham Park
Stratford Sch
St Bonaventure's Sch
Elmhurst Sch
Upton
Bndstd
Fball Gd
PLASHET RD
PLASHET GR
UPTON CROSS
6
5
4
3
2
1
86
85
84
87
78
40
41
42
99

56
ILFORD
IG1
Manor Park
City of London Cemy
Little Ilford
E12
Plashet
Plashet Jewish Cemy
Plashet Park
IG11
E6
Ilford Interchange
NORTH CIRCULAR RD
ROMFORD RD
HIGH ST N
ILFORD LA
LITTLE ILFORD LA
BROWNING RD
EAST AVE
STATION RD
FOREST DR
ILFORD HILL
Alders Brook
River Roding
Barking Flyover
Sports Gd
Allot Gdns
100
77

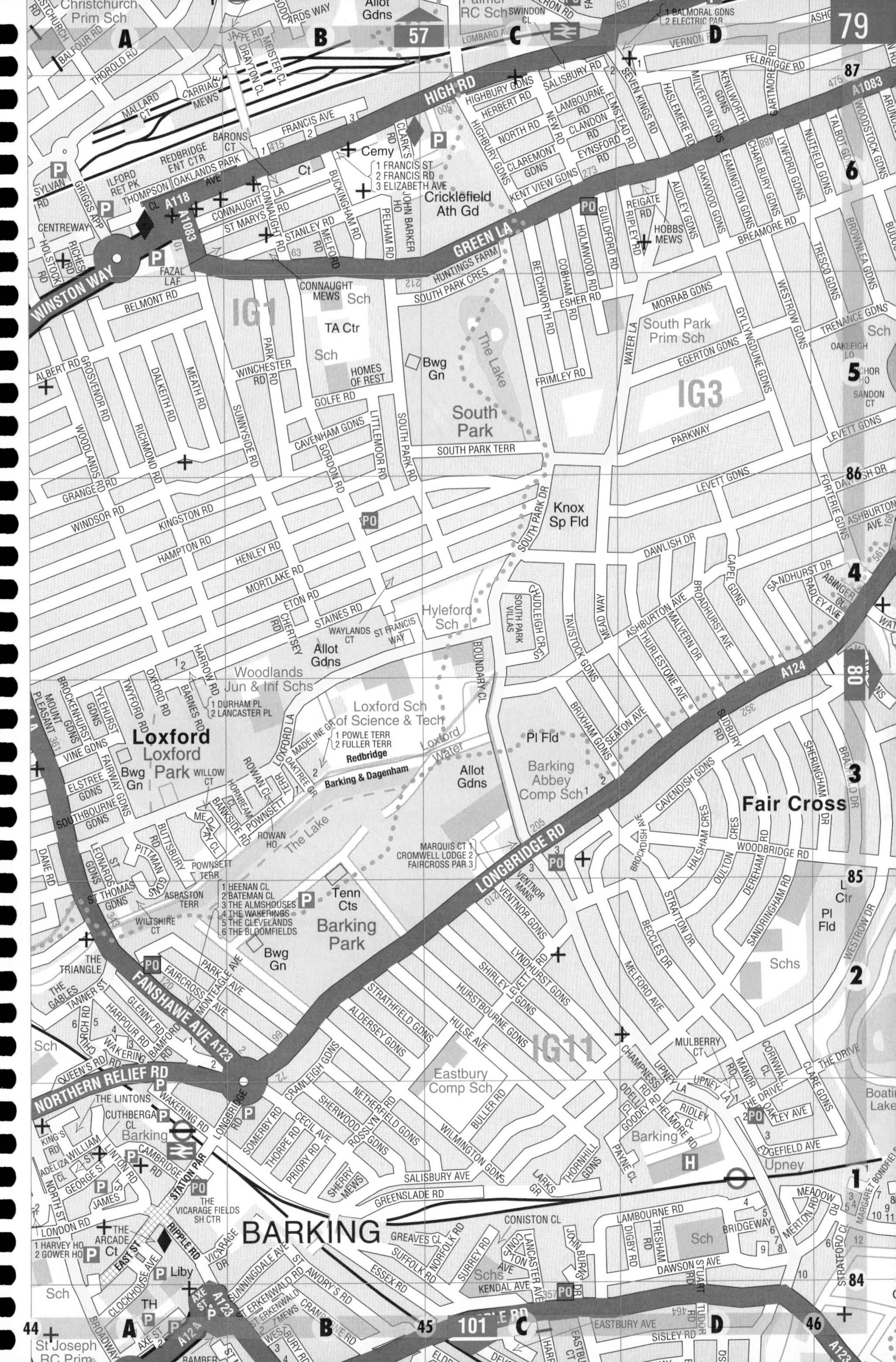

Christchurch Prim Sch
Allot Gdns
57
HIGH RD
GREEN LA
WINSTON WAY
Cricklefield Ath Gd
IG1
IG3
South Park
The Lake
Knox Sp Fld
Hyleford Sch
Woodlands Jun & Inf Schs
Loxford Sch of Science & Tech
Loxford
Loxford Park
Loxford Water
Redbridge
Barking & Dagenham
Barking Abbey Comp Sch
Fair Cross
LONGBRIDGE RD
Barking Park
FANSHAWE AVE A123
NORTHERN RELIEF RD
IG11
Eastbury Comp Sch
BARKING
Upney
South Park Prim Sch
TA Ctr
A124
A1083
A118
80
101
45
46
44
St Joseph RC Prim

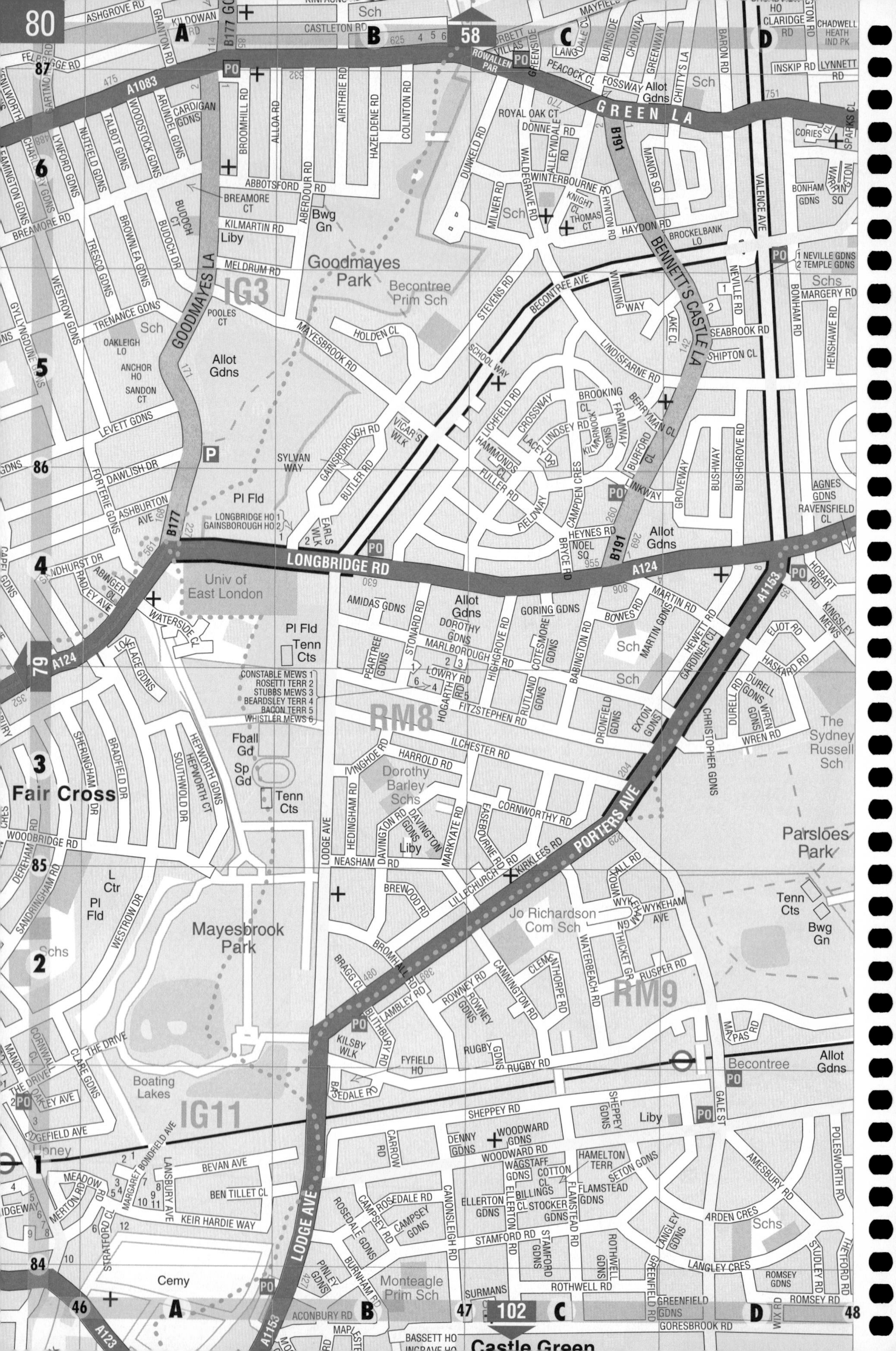
Goodmayes Park
Becontree Prim Sch
IG3
RM8
RM9
IG11
LONGBRIDGE RD
GREEN LA
GOODMAYES LA
BENNETT'S CASTLE LA
PORTERS AVE
LODGE AVE
Univ of East London
Mayesbrook Park
Fair Cross
Dorothy Barley Schs
Jo Richardson Com Sch
Parsloes Park
The Sydney Russell Sch
Monteagle Prim Sch
Becontree
Boating Lakes
Castle Green
CONSTABLE MEWS 1
ROSETTI TERR 2
STUBBS MEWS 3
BEARDSLEY TERR 4
BACON TERR 5
WHISTLER MEWS 6
1 NEVILLE GDNS
2 TEMPLE GDNS
LONGBRIDGE HO 1
GAINSBOROUGH HO 2
58
102
79

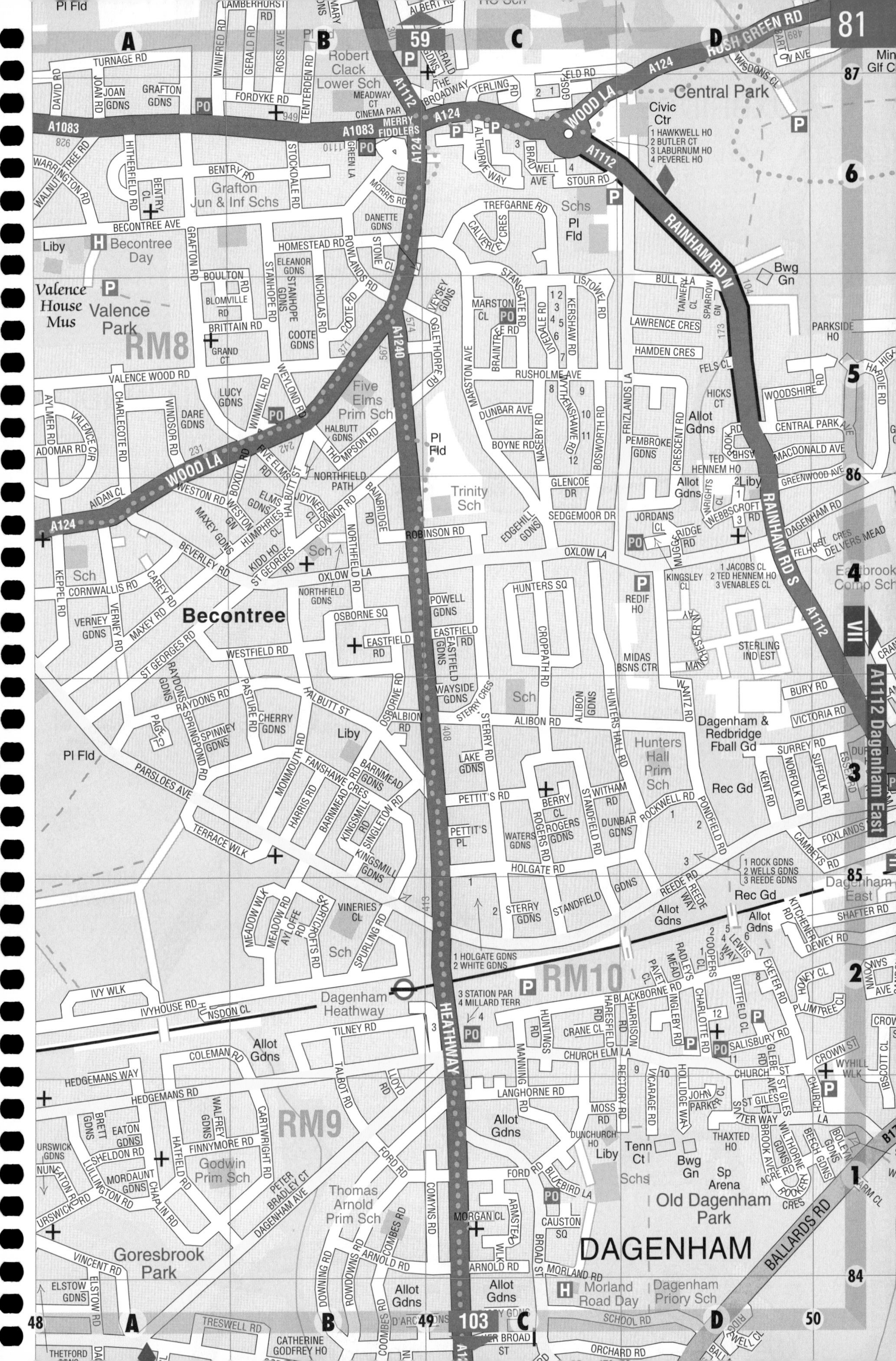
A
B
C
D
59
103
48
49
50
87
86
85
84
6
5
4
3
2
1
VII
RM8
RM9
RM10
Becontree
DAGENHAM
A1083
A1112
A124
A1240
RUSH GREEN RD
WOOD LA
RAINHAM RD N
RAINHAM RD S
HEATHWAY
A1112 Dagenham East
BALLARDS RD
TURNAGE RD
DAVID RD
JOAN RD
JOAN GDNS
GRAFTON GDNS
FORDYKE RD
WINIFRED RD
GERALD RD
ROSS AVE
TENTERDEN RD
LAMBERHURST RD
Robert Clack Lower Sch
MEADWAY CT
CINEMA PAR
MERRY FIDDLERS
THE BROADWAY
TERLING RD
GOSFIELD RD
WISDONS CL
Central Park
Civic Ctr
1 HAWKWELL HO
2 BUTLER CT
3 LABURNUM HO
4 PEVEREL HO
WARRINGTON RD
WALNUT TREE RD
HITHERFIELD RD
BENTRY CL
BENTRY RD
Grafton Jun & Inf Schs
STOCKDALE RD
GREEN LA
MORRIS RD
ALTHORNE WAY
BRADWELL AVE
STOUR RD
BECONTREE AVE
Liby
Becontree Day
Valence House Mus
Valence Park
GRAFTON RD
HOMESTEAD RD
DANETTE GDNS
STONE CL
TREFGARNE RD
CALVERLEY CRES
Schs
Pl Fld
BOULTON RD
BLOMVILLE RD
BRITTAIN RD
GRAND CT
ELEANOR GDNS
STANHOPE RD
STANHOPE GDNS
NICHOLAS RD
COOTE GDNS
COOTE RD
ROWLANDS RD
VEYSEY GDNS
OGLETHORPE RD
MARSTON CL
MARSTON AVE
STANSGATE RD
BRAINTREE RD
UVEDALE RD
KERSHAW RD
LISTOWEL RD
BULL LA
TANNERY CL
SPARROW GN
Bwg Gn
LAWRENCE CRES
HAMDEN CRES
PARKSIDE HO
FELS CL
VALENCE WOOD RD
LUCY GDNS
WINMILL RD
WEYLOND RD
Five Elms Prim Sch
RUSHOLME AVE
WYTHENSHAWE RD
FRIZLANDS LA
HICKS CT
WOODSHIRE RD
HARDIE RD
AYLMER RD
VALENCE CIR
CHARLECOTE RD
WINDSOR RD
DARE GDNS
DUNBAR AVE
BOYNE RD
NASEBY RD
BOSWORTH RD
PEMBROKE GDNS
CRESCENT RD
Allot Gdns
CENTRAL PARK AVE
MACDONALD AVE
TED HENNEM HO
ADOMAR RD
HALBUTT GDNS
THOMPSON RD
FIVE ELMS RD
BOXOLL RD
NORTHFIELD PATH
GLENCOE DR
SEDGEMOOR DR
GREENWOOD AVE
WRIGHTS CL
WEBBSCROFT RD
DAGENHAM RD
AIDAN CL
WESTON RD
WESTON GN
ELMS GDNS
HALBUTT ST
JOYNERS CL
CONNOR RD
BAINBRIDGE RD
Trinity Sch
JORDANS CL
MUGGERIDGE RD
DELVERS MEAD
FELHURST CRES
MAXEY GDNS
HUMPHRIES CL
KIDD HO
ST GEORGES RD
ROBINSON RD
EDGEHILL GDNS
OXLOW LA
KINGSLEY CL
1 JACOBS CL
2 TED HENNEM HO
3 VENABLES CL
Eastbrook Comp Sch
Sch
BEVERLEY RD
CAREY RD
CORNWALLIS RD
KEPPEL RD
VERNEY RD
VERNEY GDNS
MAXEY RD
NORTHFIELD RD
NORTHFIELD GDNS
HUNTERS SQ
REDIF HO
POWELL GDNS
OSBORNE SQ
EASTFIELD RD
EASTFIELD GDNS
CROPPATH RD
MIDAS BSNS CTR
MANCHESTER WAY
STERLING IND EST
WESTFIELD RD
RAYDONS GDNS
RAYDONS RD
PASTURE RD
WAYSIDE GDNS
STERRY CRES
ALBION GDNS
HUNTERS HALL RD
WANTZ RD
BURY RD
VICTORIA RD
CHERRY GDNS
ALBION RD
ALIBON RD
Dagenham & Redbridge Fball Gd
PAGE CL
SPINNEY GDNS
SPRINGPOND RD
MONMOUTH RD
Pl Fld
LAKE GDNS
STERRY RD
Hunters Hall Prim Sch
SURREY RD
NORFOLK RD
SUFFOLK RD
ESSEX RD
KENT RD
PARSLOES AVE
FANSHAWE CRES
BARNMEAD GDNS
BARNMEAD RD
HARRIS RD
KINGSMILL RD
SINGLETON RD
PETTIT'S RD
PETTIT'S PL
BERRY CL
ROGERS RD
ROGERS GDNS
WATERS GDNS
STANDFIELD RD
WITHAM RD
DUNBAR GDNS
ROCKWELL RD
PONDFIELD RD
Rec Gd
FOXLANDS RD
CAMBEYS RD
TERRACE WLK
KINGSMILL GDNS
HOLGATE RD
1 ROCK GDNS
2 WELLS GDNS
3 REEDE GDNS
Dagenham East
MEADOW WLK
MEADOW RD
AYLOFFE RD
SHORTCROFTS RD
VINERIES CL
STERRY GDNS
STANDFIELD GDNS
REEDE RD
REEDE WAY
KITCHENER RD
SHAFTER RD
DEWEY RD
SPURLING RD
1 HOLGATE GDNS
2 WHITE GDNS
COOPERS
LEWIS WAY
RADLEYS MEAD
PAVET CL
HONEY CL
HOWARD AVE
IVY WLK
IVYHOUSE RD
HUNSDON CL
Dagenham Heathway
3 STATION PAR
4 MILLARD TERR
BLACKBORNE RD
HARESFIELD RD
HARRISON RD
INGLEBY RD
CHARLOTTE RD
BUTTFIELD CL
EXETER RD
PLUMTREE CL
TILNEY RD
HUNTINGS RD
CRANE CL
SALISBURY RD
CROWN ST
COLEMAN RD
HEDGEMANS WAY
HEDGEMANS RD
LLOYD RD
TALBOT RD
MANNING RD
CHURCH ELM LA
RECTORY RD
VICARAGE RD
HOLLIDGE WAY
GLEBE RD
CHURCH ST
WYHILL WLK
CHURCH LA
LANGHORNE RD
JOHN PARKER CL
ST GILES CL
SPITTER WAY
ST GILES AVE
BRETT GDNS
EATON GDNS
WALFREY GDNS
CARTWRIGHT RD
FINNYMORE RD
HATFIELD RD
MOSS RD
DUNCHURCH HO
Tenn Ct
Bwg Gn
THAXTED HO
BROOK AVE
WILTHORNE GDNS
BEECH GDNS
BOLEYN GDNS
URSWICK GDNS
SHELDON RD
Godwin Prim Sch
PETER BRADLEY CT
FORD RD
Liby
Sp Arena
ACRE RD
ROCKERY CRES
NUNEATON RD
LULLINGTON RD
MORDAUNT GDNS
CHAPLIN RD
DAGENHAM AVE
Thomas Arnold Prim Sch
COMYNS RD
ARMSTEAD WLK
BLUEBIRD LA
Old Dagenham Park
URSWICK RD
COMBES RD
MORGAN CL
CAUSTON SQ
VINCENT RD
DOWNING RD
RODOWNS RD
ARNOLD RD
BROAD ST
Goresbrook Park
ELSTOW GDNS
ELSTOW RD
MORLAND RD
Morland Road Day
Dagenham Priory Sch
TRESWELL RD
D'ARCY GDNS
SCHOOL RD
CATHERINE GODFREY HO
THETFORD RD
ORCHARD RD
LOWER BROAD ST

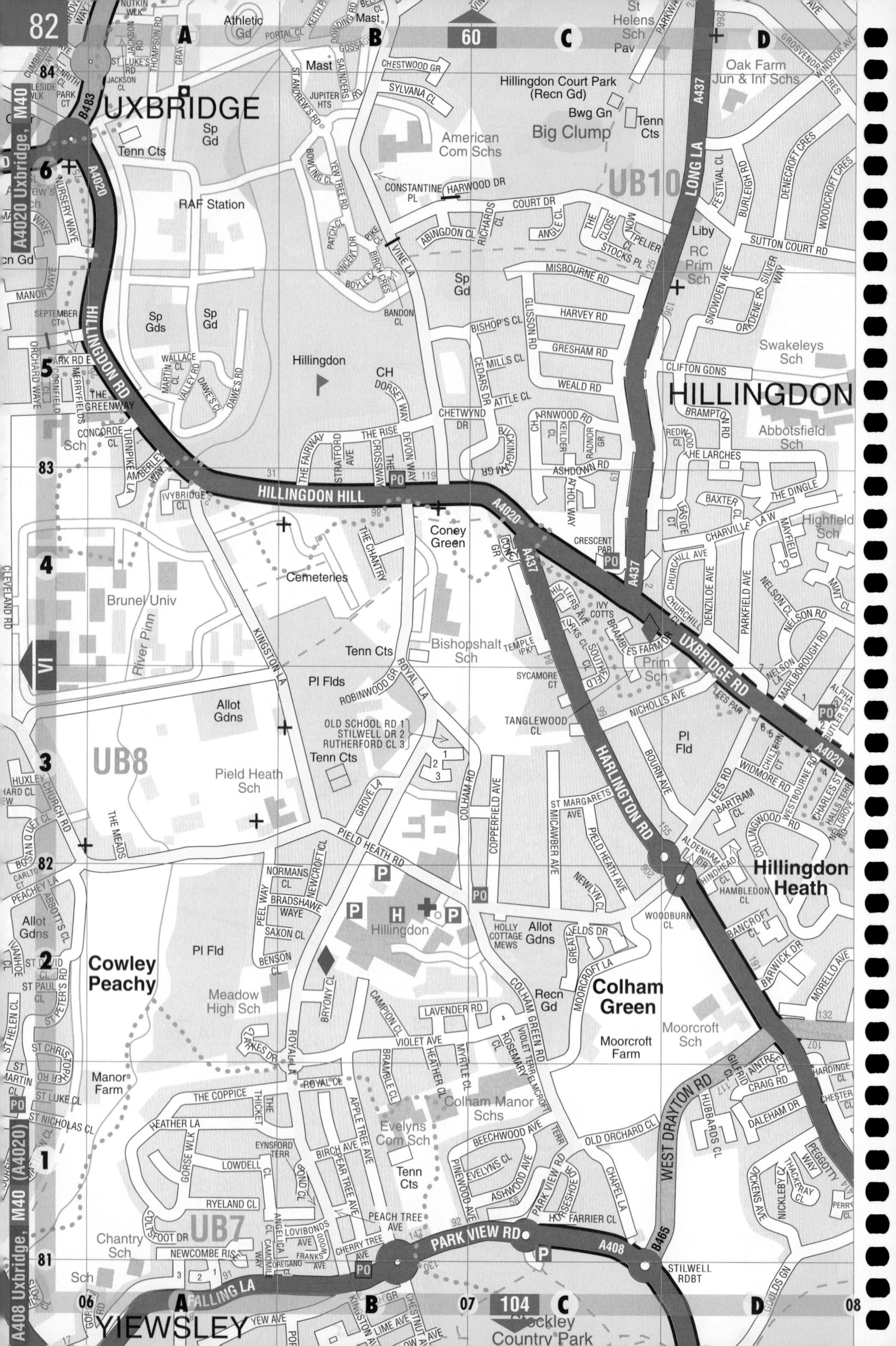
60
A
B
C
D
UXBRIDGE
HILLINGDON
Hillingdon Heath
Colham Green
Cowley Peachy
YIEWSLEY
UB10
UB8
UB7
HILLINGDON RD
HILLINGDON HILL
UXBRIDGE RD
HARLINGTON RD
LONG LA
PARK VIEW RD
FALLING LA
WEST DRAYTON RD
A4020
A437
A408
B465
B483
A4020 Uxbridge, M40
A408 Uxbridge, M40 (A4020)
Athletic Gd
Mast
St Helens Sch
Pav
Oak Farm Jun & Inf Schs
Hillingdon Court Park (Recn Gd)
Bwg Gn
Big Clump
Tenn Cts
American Com Schs
RAF Station
Sp Gd
Sp Gds
Hillingdon
CH
Liby
RC Prim Sch
Swakeleys Sch
Abbotsfield Sch
Highfield Sch
Coney Green
Cemeteries
Brunel Univ
River Pinn
Bishopshalt Sch
Pl Flds
Allot Gdns
Pield Heath Sch
Prim Sch
Pl Fld
Meadow High Sch
Recn Gd
Moorcroft Farm
Moorcroft Sch
Manor Farm
Colham Manor Schs
Evelyns Com Sch
Chantry Sch
Sch
STILWELL RDBT
Stockley Country Park
06
07
08
104
81
82
83
1
2
3
4
5
6
84
VI

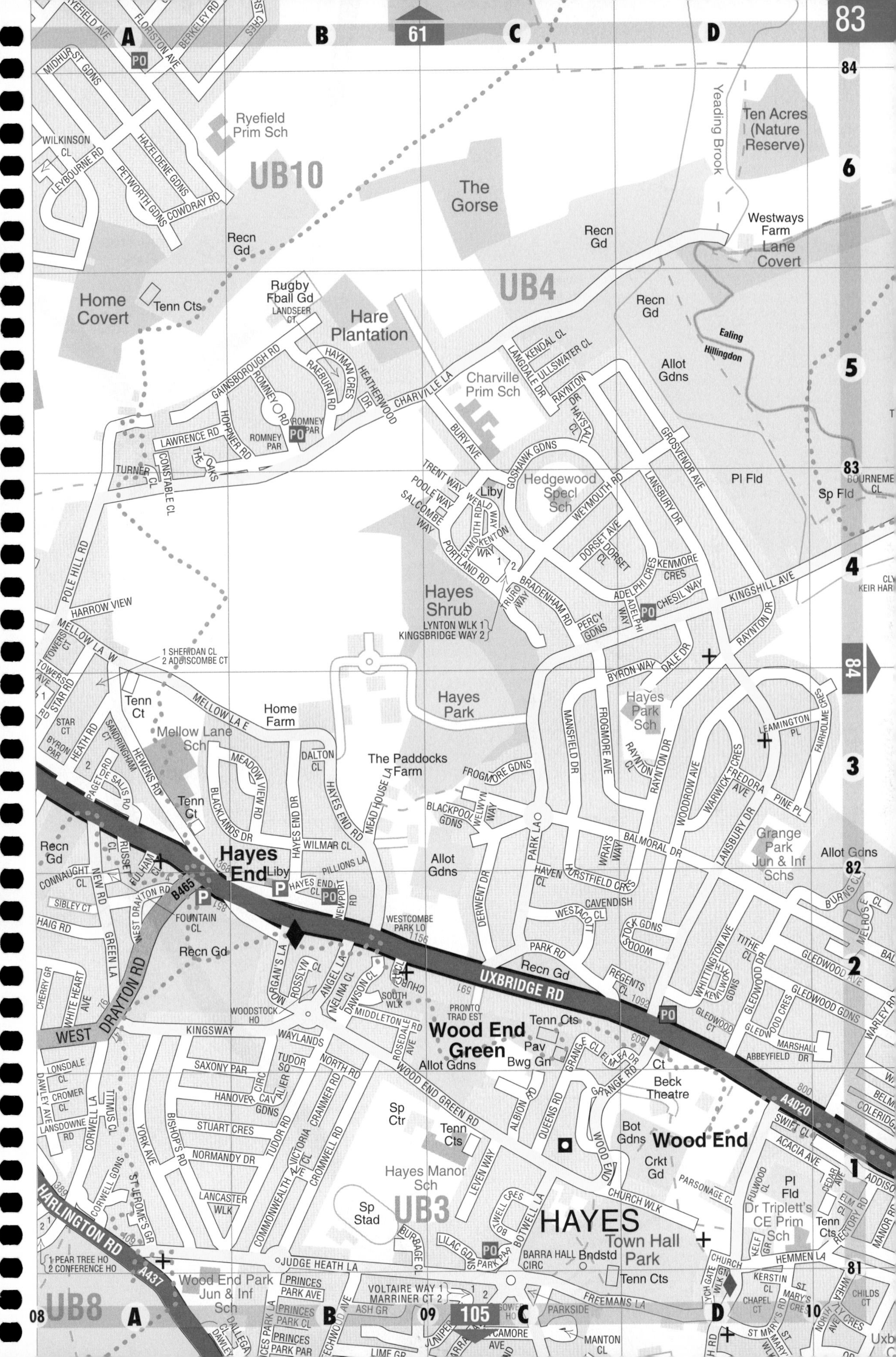
A
B
61
C
D
84
6
5
83
4
3
82
2
1
81
84
UB10
UB4
UB3
UB8
Ryefield Prim Sch
The Gorse
Ten Acres (Nature Reserve)
Yeading Brook
Westways Farm
Lane Covert
Recn Gd
Home Covert
Tenn Cts
Rugby Fball Gd
Hare Plantation
Charville Prim Sch
Allot Gdns
Ealing
Hillingdon
Hedgewood Specl Sch
Liby
Pl Fld
Sp Fld
Hayes Shrub
Hayes Park
Home Farm
Mellow Lane Sch
The Paddocks Farm
Hayes Park Sch
Grange Park Jun & Inf Schs
Hayes End
Wood End Green
Pav
Bwg Gn
Beck Theatre
Bot Gdns
Wood End
Crkt Gd
Sp Ctr
Hayes Manor Sch
Sp Stad
HAYES
Town Hall Park
Bndstd
Dr Triplett's CE Prim Sch
Wood End Park Jun & Inf Sch
UXBRIDGE RD
A4020
WEST DRAYTON RD
B465
HARLINGTON RD
A437
CHARVILLE LA
KINGSHILL AVE
MELLOW LA W
MELLOW LA E
POLE HILL RD
JUDGE HEATH LA
CHURCH WLK
HEMMEN LA
FREEMANS LA
08
09
10
105

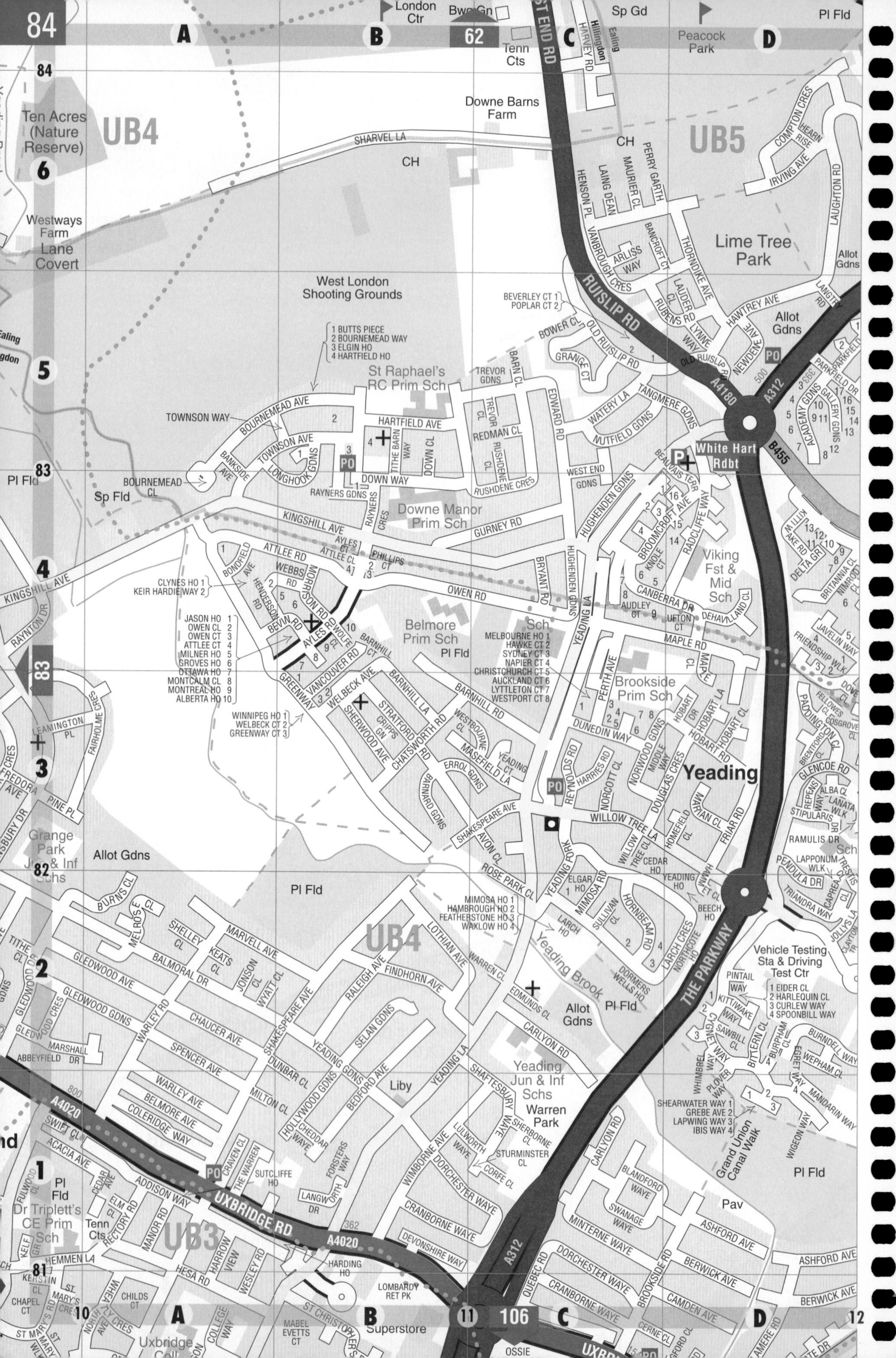

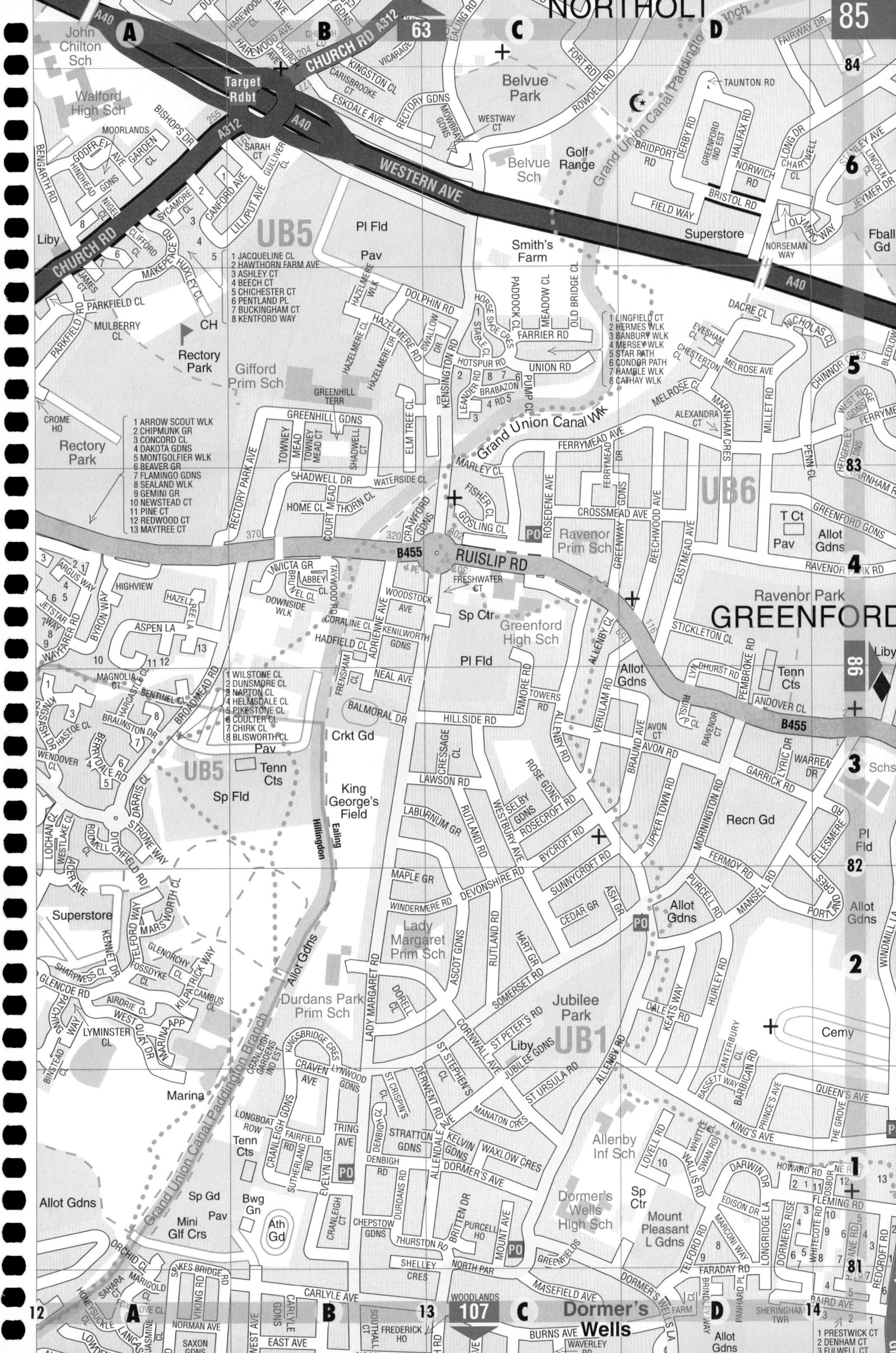

NORTHOLT
85
63
A
B
C
D
84
John Chilton Sch
Walford High Sch
Target Rdbt
A40
A312
CHURCH RD
Belvue Park
Belvue Sch
Golf Range
Grand Union Canal Paddington Branch
WESTERN AVE
TAUNTON RD
DERBY RD
HALIFAX RD
BRIDPORT RD
GREENFORD IND EST
NORWICH RD
LONG DR
CHARTWELL CL
BRISTOL RD
FIELD WAY
Superstore
NORSEMAN WAY
OLYMPIC WAY
STANLEY AVE
LINCOLN RD
JEYMER DR
Fball Gd
6
KINGSTON CL
CARISBROOKE CT
ESKDALE AVE
RECTORY GDNS
MOWBRAY GDNS
WESTWAY CT
VICARAGE
EALING RD
FORT RD
ROWDELL RD
HAREWOOD AVE
HAREWOOD CL
MOORLANDS
GODFREY AVE
HINDHEAD GDNS
GARDEN CL
BISHOPS DR
SARAH CT
GULLIVER CL
CANFORD AVE
LILLIPUT AVE
SYCAMORE CL
CLIFFORD RD
NIGEL CL
BENGARTH RD
Liby
MAKEPEACE RD
HUXLEY CL
JAMES CT
PARKFIELD CL
PARKFIELD RD
MULBERRY CL
CH
Rectory Park
UB5
1 JACQUELINE CL
2 HAWTHORN FARM AVE
3 ASHLEY CT
4 BEECH CT
5 CHICHESTER CT
6 PENTLAND PL
7 BUCKINGHAM CT
8 KENTFORD WAY
Pl Fld
Pav
Smith's Farm
PADDOCK CL
MEADOW CL
OLD BRIDGE CL
FARRIER RD
UNION RD
HOTSPUR RD
HORSE SHOE CRES
STABLE CL
LEANDER RD
BRABAZON RD
PUMP CL
1 LINGFIELD CT
2 HERMES WLK
3 BANBURY WLK
4 MERSEY WLK
5 STAR PATH
6 CONDOR PATH
7 HAMBLE WLK
8 CATHAY WLK
A40
DACRE CL
NICHOLAS CL
EVESHAM CL
CHESTERTON CL
MELROSE AVE
MELROSE CL
MARNHAM CRES
MILLET RD
CHINNOR CRES
BLEDLOW CL
WEST RIDGE GDNS
FERRYMEAD
5
ALEXANDRA CT
HAZELMERE WLK
HAZELMERE CL
HAZELMERE DR
DOLPHIN RD
SWALLOW DR
KENSINGTON RD
Gifford Prim Sch
GREENHILL TERR
CROME HO
1 ARROW SCOUT WLK
2 CHIPMUNK GR
3 CONCORD CL
4 DAKOTA GDNS
5 MONTGOLFIER WLK
6 BEAVER GR
7 FLAMINGO GDNS
8 SEALAND WLK
9 GEMINI GR
10 NEWSTEAD CT
11 PINE CT
12 REDWOOD CT
13 MAYTREE CT
GREENHILL GDNS
TOWNEY MEAD
TOWNEY MEAD CT
SHADWELL CT
ELM TREE CL
Grand Union Canal Wk
FERRYMEAD AVE
FERRYMEAD DR
PENN CL
HENGERLEY GDNS
BARNHAM RD
83
RECTORY PARK AVE
SHADWELL DR
WATERSIDE CL
MARLEY CL
HOME CL
COURT MEAD
THORN CL
FISHER CL
GOSLING CL
ROSEDENE AVE
GREENWAY GDNS
CROSSMEAD AVE
BEECHWOOD AVE
UB6
T Ct
Pav
Allot Gdns
GREENFORD GDNS
CRAWFORD GDNS
PO
Ravenor Prim Sch
B455
RUISLIP RD
EASTMEAD AVE
RAVENOR PARK RD
4
Ravenor Park
GREENFORD
HIGHVIEW
ARGUS WAY
JETSTAR WAY
WAYFARER RD
BYRON WAY
HAZELTREE LA
ASPEN LA
INVICTA GR
BRUNEL CL
ABBEY CL
TAYWOOD RD
DOWNSIDE WLK
WOODSTOCK AVE
FRESHWATER CT
Sp Ctr
Greenford High Sch
ALLENBY CL
STICKLETON CL
PEMBROKE RD
CORALINE CL
KENILWORTH GDNS
HADFIELD CL
ADRIENNE AVE
NEAL AVE
FRENSHAM CL
MAGNOLIA CT
HARCASTLE CL
SENTINEL CL
BROADMEAD RD
1 WILSTONE CL
2 DUNSMORE CL
3 NAPTON CL
4 HELMSDALE CL
5 PIKESTONE CL
6 COULTER CL
7 CHIRK CL
8 BLISWORTH CL
Pl Fld
ENMORE RD
TOWERS RD
Allot Gdns
VERULAM RD
LYNDHURST RD
Tenn Cts
Liby
98
ANDOVER CL
B455
KINGSASH DR
HASTOE CL
BRAUNSTON DR
BERRYDALE RD
WENDOVER CL
BALMORAL DR
HILLSIDE RD
Crkt Gd
ALLENBY RD
BRAUND AVE
AVON CT
AVON RD
RUISLIP CL
RAVENOR CT
LYRIC DR
WARREN DR
GARRICK RD
3
Schs
Pav
UB5
Tenn Cts
Sp Fld
King George's Field
CRESSAGE CL
ROSE GDNS
LAWSON RD
SELBY GDNS
ROSECROFT RD
UPPER TOWN RD
MORNINGTON RD
Recn Gd
ELLESMERE RD
Pl Fld
DARRIS CL
STRONE WAY
LOCHAN CL
WESTLAKE CL
RODWELL CL
DITCHFIELD RD
ACER AVE
Hillingdon
Ealing
LABURNUM GR
RUTLAND RD
WESTBURY AVE
BYCROFT RD
SUNNYCROFT RD
FERMOY RD
82
MAPLE GR
WINDERMERE RD
DEVONSHIRE RD
ASH GR
CEDAR GR
PURCELL RD
MANSELL RD
PORTLAND CRES
Allot Gdns
Superstore
KENNET DR
TELFORD WAY
MARSWORTH CL
GLENORCHY CL
FOSSDYKE CL
KILPATRICK WAY
SHARPNESS CL
GLENCOE RD
AIRDRIE CL
CAMBUS CL
WEST QUAY DR
MARINA APP
PATCHING WAY
LYMINSTER CL
BINSTEAD CL
Lady Margaret Prim Sch
ASCOT GDNS
RUTLAND RD
HART GR
SOMERSET RD
Allot Gdns
PO
HURLEY RD
2
WINDMILL LA
Allot Gdns
Durdans Park Prim Sch
LADY MARGARET RD
DORELL CL
CORNWALL AVE
ST PETER'S RD
Jubilee Park
UB1
DALE'S RD
KEAT'S WAY
Cemy
KINGSBRIDGE CRES
CRANLEIGH GARDENS IND EST
CRAVEN AVE
LYNWOOD GDNS
ST STEPHEN'S CL
Liby
JUBILEE GDNS
ST URSULA RD
ALLENBY RD
CANTERBURY CL
BARBICAN RD
BASSETT WAY
PRINCE'S AVE
QUEEN'S AVE
THE GROVE
KING'S AVE
Marina
ST CRISPIN'S
DERWENT RD
MANATON CRES
LONGBOAT ROW
CRANLEIGH GDNS
FAIRFIELD RD
SUTHERLAND RD
TRING AVE
DENBIGH CL
STRATTON GDNS
ALLENDALE AVE
KELVIN GDNS
WAXLOW CRES
Allenby Inf Sch
LOVELL RD
WHITTLE CL
SWAN RD
WALLIS RD
DARWIN DR
HOWARD RD
1
Tenn Cts
EVELYN GR
PO
DENBIGH RD
DURDANS RD
DORMER'S AVE
Sp Gd
Bwg Gn
Allot Gdns
Pav
Mini Glf Crs
Ath Gd
CRANLEIGH CT
CHEPSTOW GDNS
THURSTON RD
BRITTEN DR
PURCELL HO
MOUNT AVE
Dormer's Wells High Sch
Sp Ctr
Mount Pleasant L Gdns
EDISON DR
MARCONI WAY
LONGRIDGE LA
DORMERS RISE
WHITECOTE RD
FLEMING RD
OSBORNE RD
REDCROFT RD
81
ORCHID CL
SYKES BRIDGE RD
SAHARA CT
MARIGOLD CL
FOXGLOVE CL
HONEYSUCKLE CL
VIKING RD
SHELLEY CRES
NORTH PAR
GREENFIELDS
TELFORD RD
FARADAY RD
MASEFIELD AVE
DORMER'S WELLS LA
CARLYLE AVE
CARLYLE GDNS
WOODLANDS
13
107
FARM
BRINDLEY WAY
PANHARD PL
SHERINGHAM TWR
14
BAIRD AVE
12
NORMAN AVE
SAXON GDNS
WEST AVE
EAST AVE
LANCASTER
JASMINE CT
LOWDEN
SOUTHALL CT
FREDERICK HO
BURNS AVE
WAVERLEY RD
Dormer's Wells
Allot Gdns
1 PRESTWICK CT
2 DENHAM CT
3 FULWELL CT

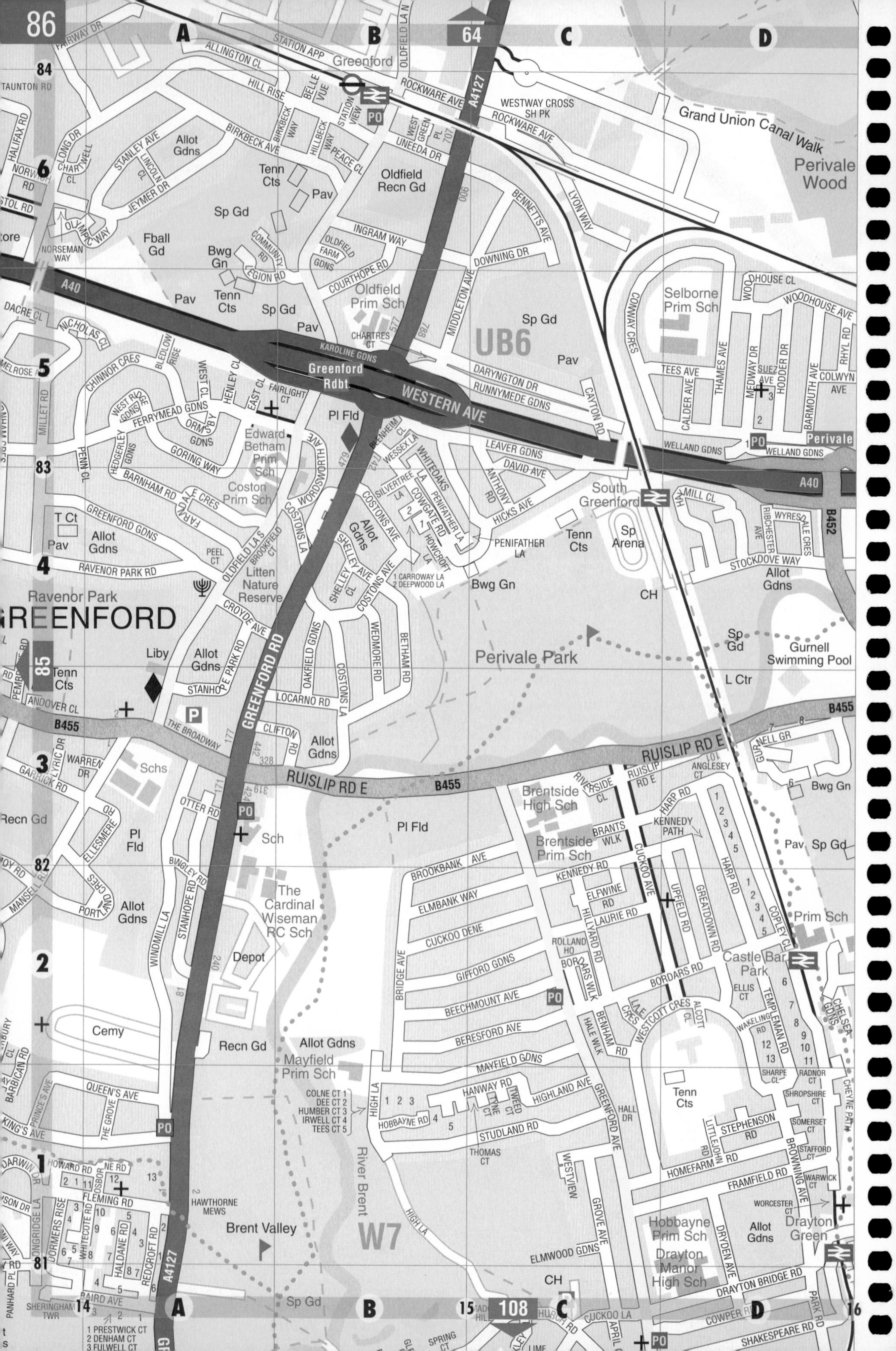
A
B
C
D
64
108
84
83
82
81
6
5
4
3
2
1
14
15
16
85
Greenford
STATION APP
ALLINGTON CL
HILL RISE
BELLE VUE
STATION VIEW
OLDFIELD LA N
ROCKWARE AVE
A4127
WESTWAY CROSS SH PK
Grand Union Canal Walk
Perivale Wood
TAUNTON RD
HALIFAX RD
FAIRWAY DR
BIRKBECK AVE
BIRKBECK WAY
HILLBECK WAY
PEACE CL
UNEEDA DR
WEST GREEN PL
STANLEY AVE
LINCOLN CL
JEYMER DR
LONG DR
CHARTWELL CL
NORWICH RD
Allot Gdns
Tenn Cts
Pav
Sp Gd
Oldfield Recn Gd
BENNETTS AVE
LYON WAY
OLYMPIC WAY
NORSEMAN WAY
Fball Gd
Bwg Gn
COMMUNITY RD
LEGION RD
OLDFIELD FARM GDNS
INGRAM WAY
COURTHOPE RD
DOWNING DR
MIDDLETON AVE
Oldfield Prim Sch
CHARTRES CT
KAROLINE GDNS
WOODHOUSE CL
WOODHOUSE AVE
Selborne Prim Sch
CONWAY CRES
A40
DACRE CL
NICHOLAS CL
MELROSE AVE
CHINNOR CRES
BLEDLOW RISE
WEST CL
HENLEY CL
EAST CL
FAIRLIGHT CT
Greenford Rdbt
WESTERN AVE
UB6
DARYNGTON DR
RUNNYMEDE GDNS
CAYTON RD
TEES AVE
CALDER AVE
THAMES AVE
MEDWAY DR
SUEZ AVE
HODDER DR
BARMOUTH AVE
RHYL RD
COLWYN AVE
WELLAND GDNS
Perivale
PO
MILLET RD
WEST RIDGE GDNS
FERRYMEAD GDNS
ORMSBY GDNS
GORING WAY
HEDGERLEY GDNS
PENN CL
BARNHAM RD
Edward Betham Prim Sch
Coston Prim Sch
FARNDALE CRES
Pl Fld
WORDSWORTH AVE
BLENHEIM CL
WESSEX LA
WHITEOAKS
SILVERTREE LA
COWGATE RD
PENIFATHER LA
HOWCROFT LA
LEAVER GDNS
DAVID AVE
ANTHONY RD
HICKS AVE
South Greenford
Sp Arena
MILL CL
RIBCHESTER AVE
WYRESDALE CRES
B452
T Ct
GREENFORD GDNS
PEEL CT
RAVENOR PARK RD
OLDFIELD LA S
BROOKFIELD CT
COSTONS LA
COSTONS AVE
SHELLEY AVE
SHELLEY CL
1 CARROWAY LA
2 DEEPWOOD LA
PENIFATHER LA
Bwg Gn
STOCKDOVE WAY
CH
Ravenor Park
GREENFORD
Litten Nature Reserve
CROYDE AVE
Perivale Park
OAKFIELD GDNS
WEDMORE RD
BETHAM RD
Gurnell Swimming Pool
L Ctr
Liby
PAINSHAM RD
GREENFORD RD
STANHOPE RD
LOCARNO RD
ANDOVER CL
B455
THE BROADWAY
CLIFTON RD
RUISLIP RD E
GURNELL GR
LYRIC DR
WARREN DR
GARRICK RD
Schs
OTTER RD
Brentside High Sch
RIVERSIDE CL
ANGLESEY CT
HARP RD
KENNEDY PATH
BRANTS WLK
Brentside Prim Sch
Recn Gd
ELLESMERE RD
Sch
BROOKBANK AVE
KENNEDY RD
ELFWINE RD
CUCKOO AVE
UPFIELD RD
GREATDOWN RD
COPLEY CL
MANSELL RD
PORTLAND CRES
BINGLEY RD
The Cardinal Wiseman RC Sch
ELMBANK WAY
LAURIE RD
Prim Sch
CUCKOO DENE
ROLLAND HO
HILLYARD RD
Castle Bar Park
WINDMILL LA
Depot
BRIDGE AVE
GIFFORD GDNS
BORDARS WLK
BORDARS RD
ELLIS CT
TEMPLEMAN RD
BEECHMOUNT AVE
BENHAM RD
LYLE CRES
WESTCOTT CRES
ALCOTT CL
CHELSEA GDNS
Cemy
BERESFORD AVE
WAKELING RD
BARBICAN RD
HALE WALK
Allot Gdns
Mayfield Prim Sch
MAYFIELD GDNS
SHARPE CL
RADNOR CT
CHEYNE PATH
QUEEN'S AVE
PRINCE'S AVE
THE GROVE
KING'S AVE
COLNE CT 1
DEE CT 2
HUMBER CT 3
IRWELL CT 4
TEES CT 5
HIGH LA
HOBBAYNE RD
HANWAY RD
TYNE CT
TWEED CT
HIGHLAND AVE
GREENFORD AVE
HALL DR
SHROPSHIRE CT
STUDLAND RD
THOMAS CT
STEPHENSON RD
SOMERSET CT
LITTLEJOHN RD
STAFFORD CT
River Brent
WESTVIEW
HOMEFARM RD
FRAMFIELD RD
BROWNING AVE
WARWICK CT
WORCESTER CT
DARWIN DR
HOWARD RD
OSBORNE RD
FLEMING RD
HAWTHORNE MEWS
Drayton Green
DORMERS RISE
WHITECOTE RD
HALDANE RD
REDCROFT RD
LONGRIDGE LA
Brent Valley
W7
GROVE AVE
Hobbayne Prim Sch
DRYDEN AVE
Drayton Manor High Sch
ELMWOOD GDNS
DRAYTON BRIDGE RD
PANHARD PL
PAIRD AVE
SHERINGHAM TWR
1 PRESTWICK CT
2 DENHAM CT
3 FULWELL CT
Sp Gd
CUCKOO LA
COWPER RD
SPRING CT
SHAKESPEARE RD
PARK RD

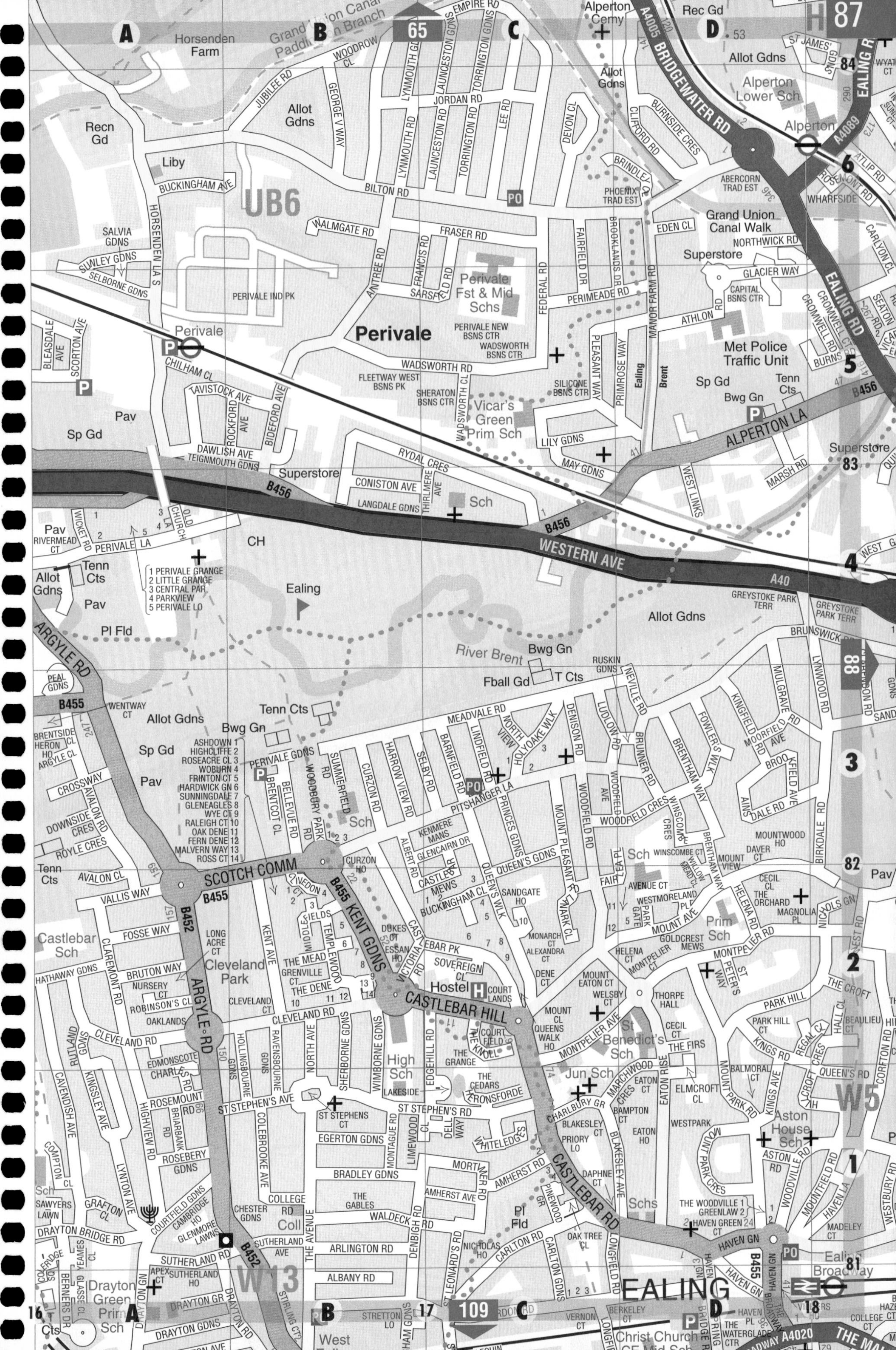
A
B
C
D
65
Horsenden Farm
Grand Union Canal Paddington Branch
Recn Gd
Liby
Allot Gdns
UB6
Perivale
Perivale Fst & Mid Schs
PERIVALE IND PK
PERIVALE NEW BSNS CTR
WADSWORTH BSNS CTR
FLEETWAY WEST BSNS PK
SHERATON BSNS CTR
SILICONE BSNS CTR
Vicar's Green Prim Sch
PHOENIX TRAD EST
ABERCORN TRAD EST
Grand Union Canal Walk
Superstore
CAPITAL BSNS CTR
Met Police Traffic Unit
Alperton
Alperton Lower Sch
Alperton Cemy
Rec Gd
BRIDGEWATER RD
EALING RD
ALPERTON LA
WESTERN AVE
A40
B456
B455
B452
A4005
A4089
A4020
Sp Gd
Pav
Tenn Cts
Bwg Gn
CH
Ealing
River Brent
Fball Gd
T Cts
Allot Gdns
Pl Fld
1 PERIVALE GRANGE
2 LITTLE GRANGE
3 CENTRAL PAR
4 PARKVIEW
5 PERIVALE LO
ASHDOWN 1
HIGHCLIFFE 2
ROSEACRE CL 3
WOBURN 4
FRINTON CT 5
HARDWICK GN 6
SUNNINGDALE 7
GLENEAGLES 8
WYE CT 9
RALEIGH CT 10
OAK DENE 11
FERN DENE 12
MALVERN WAY 13
ROSS CT 14
PITSHANGER LA
SCOTCH COMM
KENT GDNS
CASTLEBAR HILL
CASTLEBAR RD
ARGYLE RD
Castlebar Sch
Cleveland Park
Hostel
High Sch
Coll
St Benedict's Sch
Jun Sch
Prim Sch
Aston House Sch
Schs
W13
W5
EALING
Ealing Broadway
Drayton Green Prim Sch
West Ealing
Christ Church CE Mid Sch
THE MALL
88
109
16
17
18
81
82
83
84
1
2
3
4
5
6

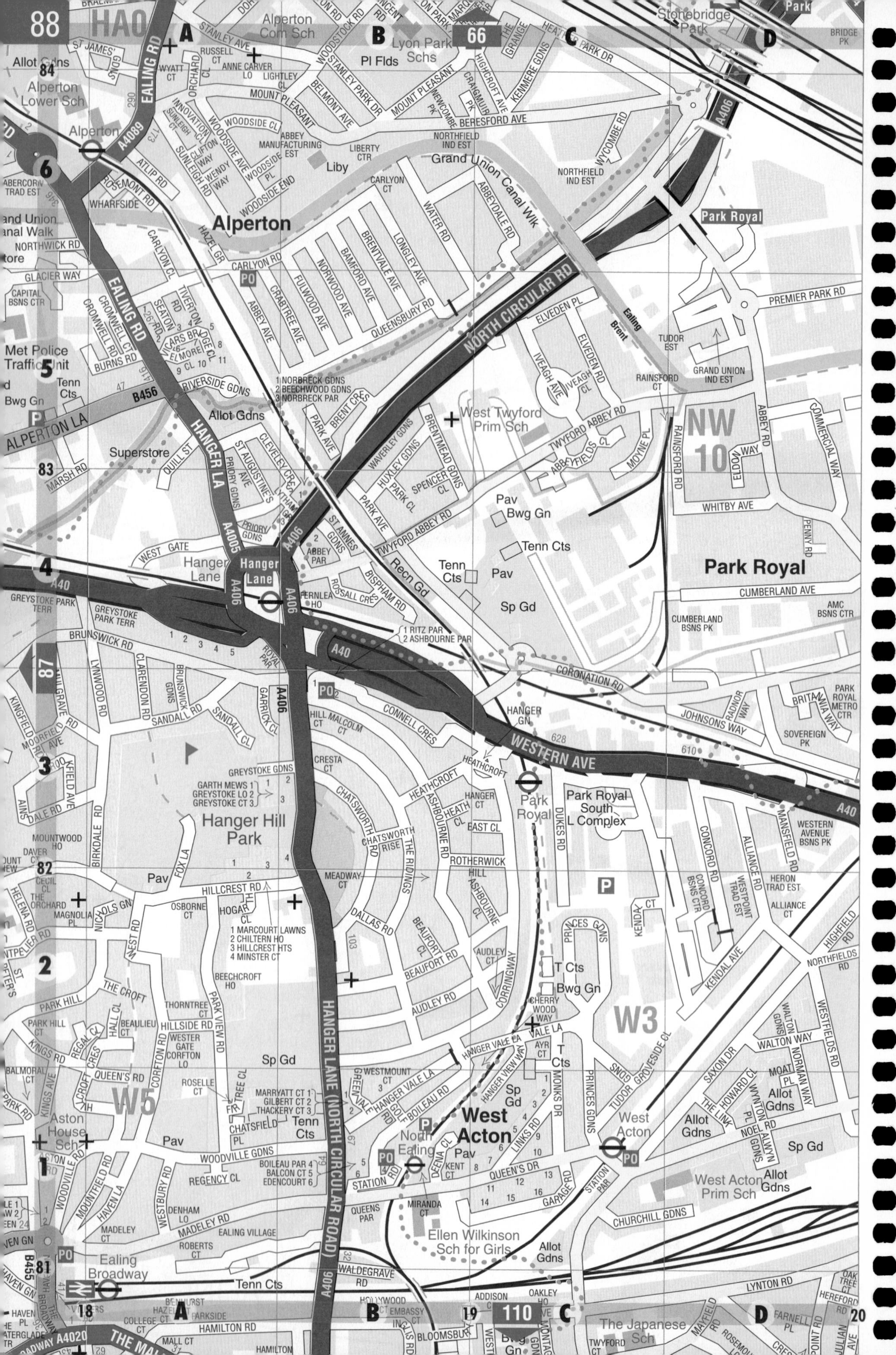
HA0
A
B
C
D
66
Alperton
Alperton Com Sch
Lyon Park Schs
Pl Flds
Stonebridge Park
Park
BRIDGE PK
Alperton Lower Sch
Allot Gdns
84
EALING RD
A4089
STANLEY AVE
RUSSELL CT
ANNE CARVER LO
LIGHTLEY CL
MOUNT PLEASANT
WOODSTOCK RD
STANLEY PARK DR
BELMONT AVE
HIGHCROFT AVE
CRAIGMUIR PK
NEWCOMBE PK
KENMERE GDNS
THE GRANGE
HEATHER PARK DR
BERESFORD AVE
NORTHFIELD IND EST
Grand Union Canal Wlk
WYCOMBE RD
A406
6
ABERCORN TRAD EST
ATLIP RD
ROSEMONT RD
WHARFSIDE
WOODSIDE CL
WOODSIDE AVE
WOODSIDE END
WENDY WAY
CLIFTON WAY
INNOVATION CL
SUNLEIGH CT
SUNLEIGH RD
ABBEY MANUFACTURING EST
Liby
LIBERTY CTR
CARLYON CT
WATER RD
ABBEYDALE RD
Grand Union Canal Walk
NORTHWICK RD
GLACIER WAY
CAPITAL BSNS CTR
HAZEL GR
CARLYON RD
CARLYON CL
PO
ABBEY AVE
CRABTREE AVE
FULWOOD AVE
NORWOOD AVE
BAMFORD AVE
BRENTVALE AVE
LONGLEY AVE
QUEENSBURY RD
NORTH CIRCULAR RD
Park Royal
PREMIER PARK RD
TUDOR EST
GRAND UNION IND EST
RAINSFORD CT
ELVEDEN PL
ELVEDEN RD
IVEAGH AVE
IVEAGH CL
Ealing
Brent
Met Police Traffic Unit
5
Tenn Cts
Bwg Gn
CROMWELL RD
CROMWELL CT
BURNS RD
TIVERTON RD
SEATON RD
VICARS BRIDGE CL
ELMORE CL
RIVERSIDE GDNS
B456
ALPERTON LA
P
1 NORBRECK GDNS
2 BEECHWOOD GDNS
3 NORBRECK PAR
PARK AVE
BRENT CRES
West Twyford Prim Sch
TWYFORD ABBEY RD
ABBEYFIELDS CL
MOYNE PL
NW 10
RAINSFORD RD
ABBEY RD
ELDON WAY
COMMERCIAL WAY
WHITBY AVE
PENNY RD
Allot Gdns
Superstore
83
MARSH RD
QUILL ST
HANGER LA
ST AUGUSTINE'S AVE
PRIORY GDNS
CLEVELEY CRES
LYTHAM CT
WAVERLEY GDNS
HUXLEY GDNS
PARK CL
BRENTMEAD GDNS
SPENCER GDNS
SPENCER CL
Pav
Bwg Gn
Tenn Cts
Park Royal
4
A40
WEST GATE
Hanger Lane
A4005
PRIORY GDNS
ST ANNES GDNS
ABBEY PAR
Recn Gd
Tenn Cts
Pav
Sp Gd
CUMBERLAND AVE
CUMBERLAND BSNS PK
AMC BSNS CTR
GREYSTOKE PARK TERR
GREYSTOKE PARK TERR
FERNLEA HO
ROSSALL CRES
BISPHAM RD
1 RITZ PAR
2 ASHBOURNE PAR
BRUNSWICK RD
ROYAL PAR
87
CLARENDON RD
BRUNSWICK GDNS
LYNWOOD RD
MILGRAVE RD
KINGFIELD RD
MOORFIELD AVE
SANDALL RD
SANDALL CL
GARRICK CL
HILL MALCOLM CT
CONNELL CRES
CORONATION RD
HANGER GN
WESTERN AVE
628
610
JOHNSONS WAY
RADNOR WAY
BRITANNIA WAY
PARK ROYAL METRO CTR
SOVEREIGN PK
3
CRESTA CT
HEATHCROFT
GREYSTOKE GDNS
GARTH MEWS 1
GREYSTOKE LO 2
GREYSTOKE CT 3
Hanger Hill Park
CHATSWORTH RD
CHATSWORTH RISE
THE RIDINGS
ASHBOURNE RD
HANGER CT
HEATH CL
EAST CL
ROTHERWICK HILL
ASHBOURNE CL
Park Royal
Park Royal South L Complex
DUKES RD
CONCORD RD
ALLIANCE RD
CONCORD BSNS CTR
WESTPOINT TRAD EST
MANSFIELD RD
WESTERN AVENUE BSNS PK
HERON TRAD EST
ALLIANCE CT
A40
AINSDALE RD
BIRKDALE RD
MOUNTWOOD HO
DAVER CT
82
CECIL CL
THE ORCHARD
HELENA RD
MAGNOLIA PL
NICHOLS GN
Pav
FOX LA
HILLCREST RD
OSBORNE CT
HOGARTH CL
MEADWAY CT
1 MARCOURT LAWNS
2 CHILTERN HO
3 HILLCREST HTS
4 MINSTER CT
DALLAS RD
BEAUFORT CL
BEAUFORT RD
AUDLEY CT
CORRINGWAY
PRINCES GDNS
T Cts
Bwg Gn
KENDAL CT
KENDAL AVE
HIGHFIELD RD
NORTHFIELDS RD
2
WEST RD
BEECHCROFT HO
THE CROFT
PARK HILL
PARK HILL CT
REGAL CT
HALL CL
BEAULIEU CT
THORNTREE CT
HILLSIDE RD
PARK VIEW RD
AUDLEY RD
CHERRY WOOD WAY
VALE LA
W3
WALTON GDNS
WALTON WAY
WESTFIELDS RD
NORMAN WAY
KINGS RD
WESTER GATE
CORFTON LO
CORFTON RD
Sp Gd
HANGER VALE LA
HANGER VIEW WAY
AYR CT
T Cts
MONKS DR
PRINCES GDNS
TUDOR GDNS
GROVESIDE CL
SAXON DR
HOWARD CL
MOAT PL
BALMORAL CT
QUEEN'S RD
KINGS AVE
W5
ROSELLE CT
FIR TREE CL
WESTMOUNT CT
GREEN VALE
HANGER VALE LA
BOILEAU RD
GOLF CL
Sp Gd
West Acton
THE LINK
WYNTON PL
Allot Gdns
Allot Gdns
MARRYATT CT 1
GILBERT CT 2
THACKERY CT 3
Tenn Cts
CHATSFIELD PL
Pav
Aston House Sch
1
WOODVILLE RD
MOUNTFIELD RD
HAVEN LA
WESTBURY RD
WOODVILLE GDNS
REGENCY CL
BOILEAU PAR 4
BALCON CT 5
EDENCOURT 6
STATION RD
PO
North Ealing
DENA CL
Pav
KENT CT
LINKS RD
QUEEN'S DR
GARAGE RD
STATION PAR
West Acton
PO
NOEL RD
ALLWYN GDNS
Sp Gd
West Acton Prim Sch
Allot Gdns
DENHAM LO
MADELEY CT
MADELEY RD
EALING VILLAGE
ROBERTS CT
QUEENS PAR
MIRANDA CT
Ellen Wilkinson Sch for Girls
Allot Gdns
CHURCHILL GDNS
B455
81
PO
Ealing Broadway
HANGER LANE (NORTH CIRCULAR ROAD)
WALDEGRAVE RD
Tenn Cts
LYNTON RD
ADDISON
OAKLEY HO
OAK TREE CT
HEREFORD RD
18
VILLIERS
BENHURST CT
HAZEL CT
PARKSIDE
COLLEGE CT
HAMILTON RD
MALL CT
HAMILTON
HOLLYWOOD CT
EMBASSY
INGLIS RD
BLOOMSBURY
19
110
The Japanese Sch
TWYFORD
MAYFIELD RD
ROSEMONT
FARNELL PL
20
THE MALL
BROADWAY A4020
HAVEN PL
HAVEN GN

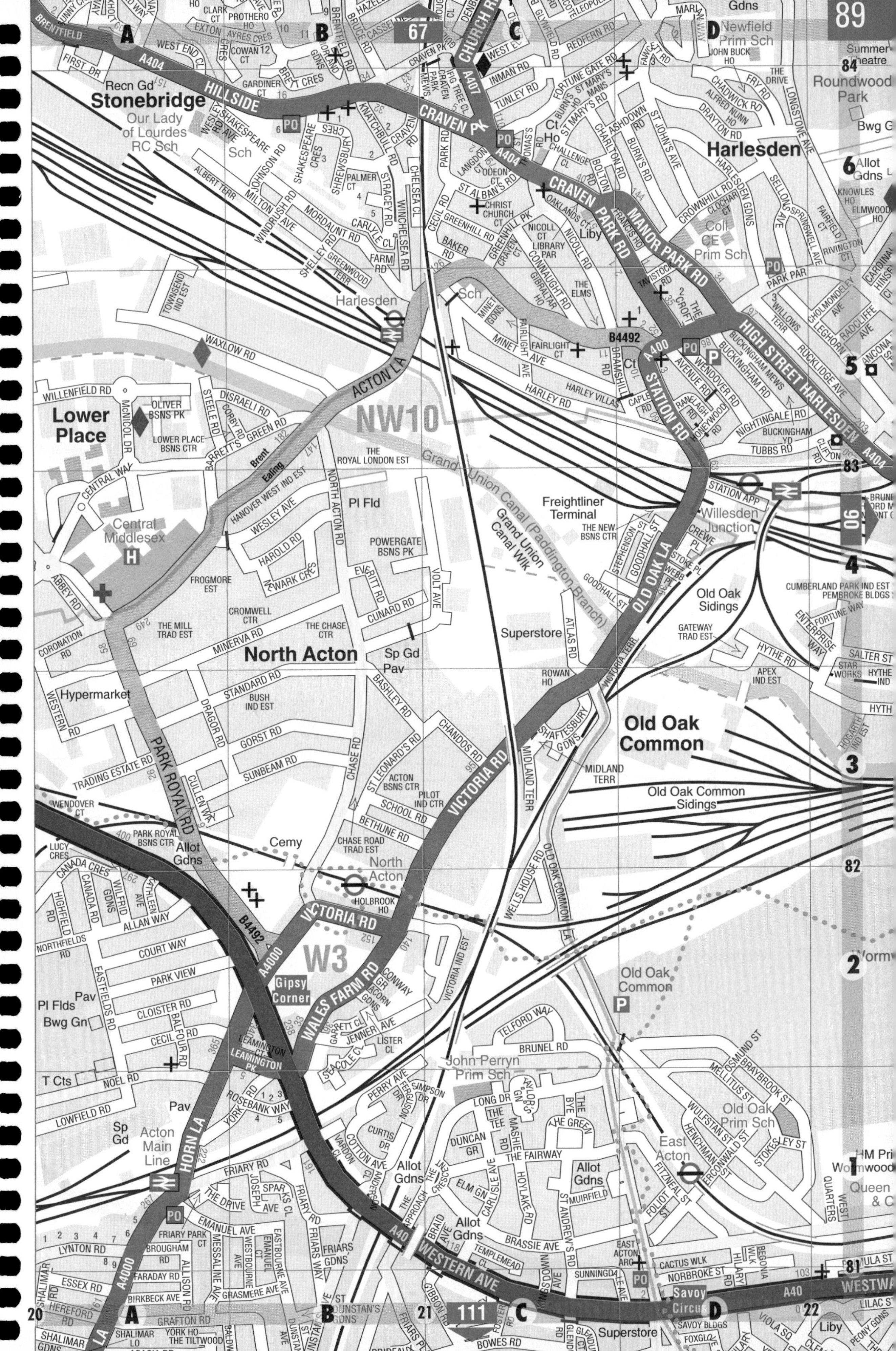

Stonebridge
Our Lady of Lourdes RC Sch
Harlesden
Lower Place
NW10
North Acton
Old Oak Common
W3
Gipsy Corner
Central Middlesex
Freightliner Terminal
Willesden Junction
Old Oak Sidings
Old Oak Common Sidings
Grand Union Canal (Paddington Branch)
HILLSIDE
CRAVEN PK
CRAVEN PARK RD
MANOR PARK RD
HIGH STREET HARLESDEN
ACTON LA
OLD OAK LA
STATION RD
VICTORIA RD
PARK ROYAL RD
WALES FARM RD
HORN LA
WESTERN AVE
Acton Main Line
North Acton
East Acton
John Perryn Prim Sch
Old Oak Prim Sch
Roundwood Park

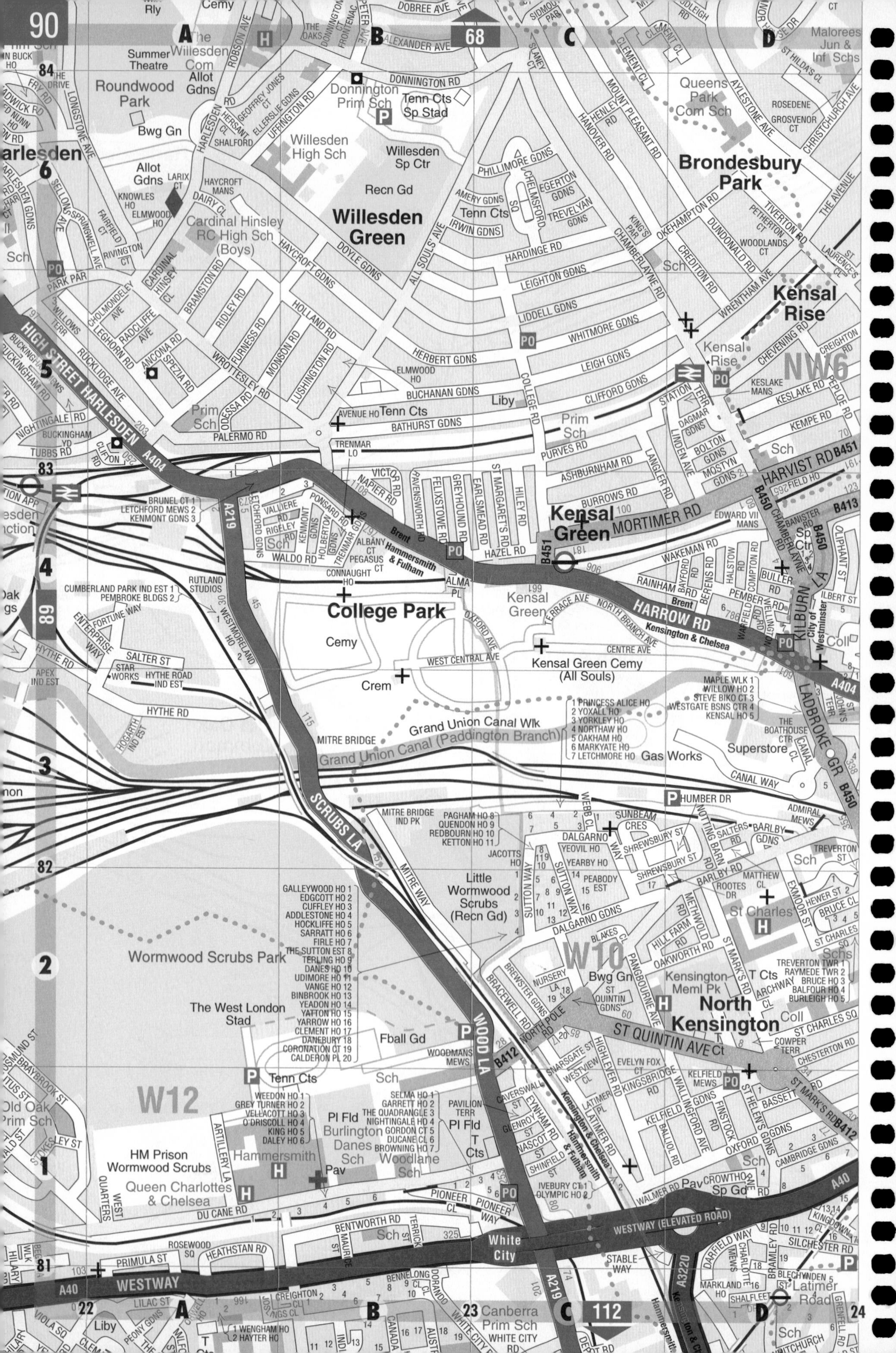
68
Willesden Green
Brondesbury Park
Kensal Rise
NW6
Harlesden
Kensal Green
College Park
Cemy
Crem
Kensal Green Cemy (All Souls)
Grand Union Canal Wlk
Grand Union Canal (Paddington Branch)
Gas Works
Superstore
Wormwood Scrubs Park
Little Wormwood Scrubs (Recn Gd)
The West London Stad
Fball Gd
W10
W12
North Kensington
HM Prison Wormwood Scrubs
Hammersmith
Queen Charlottes & Chelsea
Burlington Danes Sch
Woodlane Sch
White City
Kensington Meml Pk
St Charles
Roundwood Park
Willesden High Sch
Willesden Sp Ctr
Recn Gd
Cardinal Hinsley RC High Sch (Boys)
Donnington Prim Sch
Queens Park Com Sch
Summer Theatre
The Willesden Com
Allot Gdns
Bwg Gn
HIGH STREET HARLESDEN
HARROW RD
SCRUBS LA
WOOD LA
WESTWAY
WESTWAY (ELEVATED ROAD)
ST QUINTIN AVE
LADBROKE GR
KILBURN LA
MORTIMER RD
HARVIST RD
CHAMBERLAYNE RD
COLLEGE RD
DONNINGTON RD
DU CANE RD
A404
A219
A40
A3220
B450
B451
B412
B413
Canberra Prim Sch
Latimer Road
112
22
23
24
81
82
83
84

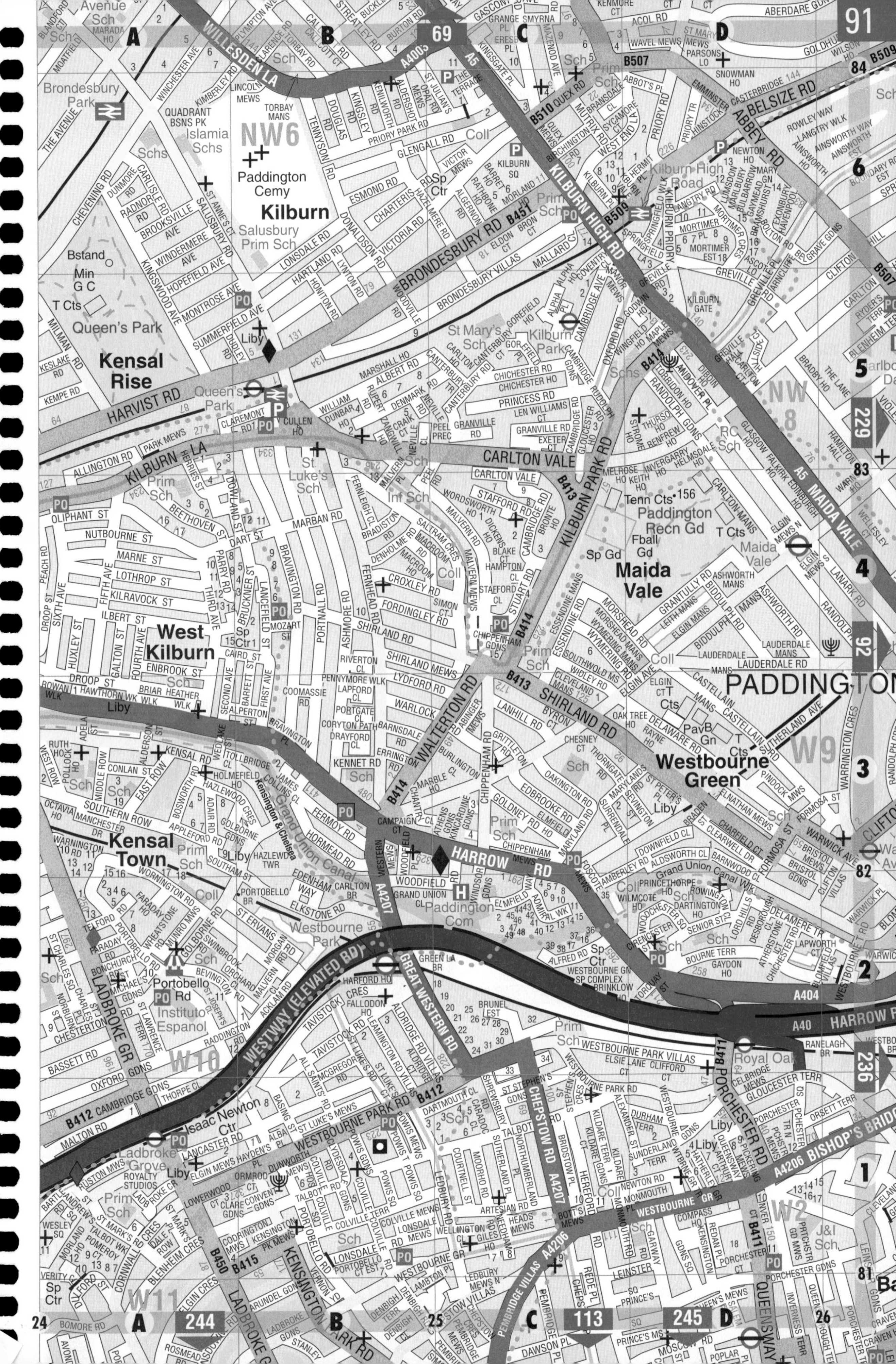

91
A
B
C
D
69
84
Kilburn
Kensal Rise
West Kilburn
Kensal Town
Maida Vale
PADDINGTON
Westbourne Green
NW6
NW8
W9
W10
W11
W2
Brondesbury Park
Queen's Park
Paddington Cemy
Paddington Recn Gd
Paddington Com
Westbourne Park
Royal Oak
Ladbroke Grove
Portobello Rd
Instituto Espanol
Grand Union Canal
Kensington & Chelsea
WILLESDEN LA
KILBURN HIGH RD
BRONDESBURY RD
HARVIST RD
KILBURN LA
CARLTON VALE
KILBURN PARK RD
MAIDA VALE
ABBEY RD
BELSIZE RD
SHIRLAND RD
HARROW RD
WALTERTON RD
GREAT WESTERN RD
WESTWAY (ELEVATED RD)
WESTBOURNE PARK RD
WESTBOURNE GR
CHEPSTOW RD
PORCHESTER RD
QUEENSWAY
LADBROKE GR
KENSINGTON PARK RD
BISHOP'S BRIDGE
A5
A404
A40
A4207
A4206
B412
B413
B414
B450
B507
B509
B510
B411
B415
6
5
4
3
2
1
83
82
81
92
229
236
24
25
26
244
113
245

A
B
C
D
70
230
229
236
91
114
237
84
83
82
81
26
27
28
6
5
4
3
2
1
NW6
NW3
NW8
NW1
W9
W2
Primrose Hill
Primrose Hill Tunnels
Barrow Hill
St John's Barracks
St John's Wood
Marlborough Day
SS John & Elizabeth
(North) Wellington
Wellington (South)
Lord's (MCC & Middlesex Cty Crkt Gd)
Crkt Mus
Maida Vale
Maida Vale Psychiatric
Winfield House
Tenn Ct
Tenn Cts
Pav
Boating Lake
The Holme
London Business Sch
Lisson Green
Lisson Grove
Little Venice
Warwick Avenue
St Mary's Gardens
Antq Mkt
Marylebone
Govt Offices
Charter Nightingale
Edgware Road
Baker Street
PADDINGTON
Paddington Basin
Marylebone Flyover
St Mary's
Med Sch
Rd closed until 2006
Paddington
Bayswater
Marble Arch
Speakers' Corner
Art Gall
FINCHLEY RD
WELLINGTON RD
ABBEY RD
MAIDA VALE
AVENUE RD
PRINCE ALBERT RD
(Regent's Canal)
Grand Union Canal
OUTER CIRCLE
PARK RD
ST JOHN'S WOOD ROAD
GROVE END RD
LISSON GR
CLIFTON GDNS
HARROW RD
WESTWAY (ELEVATED)
HARROW RD (UNDER)
A40 MARYLEBONE FLYOVER
MARYLEBONE RD
EDGWARE RD
PRAED ST
SUSSEX GDNS
BISHOP'S BRIDGE RD
GLOUCESTER PL
BAKER ST
SEYMOUR ST
NORTH CARRIAGE DR
QUEENSWAY
BELSIZE RD
BOUNDARY RD
LOUDOUN ROAD
MARLBOROUGH HILL
HAMILTON TERR
WARWICK AVE
BLOMFIELD ROAD
EASTBOURNE TERR
WESTBOURNE TERR
GLOUCESTER TERR
CONNAUGHT ST
OLD MARYLEBONE RD
CHAPEL ST

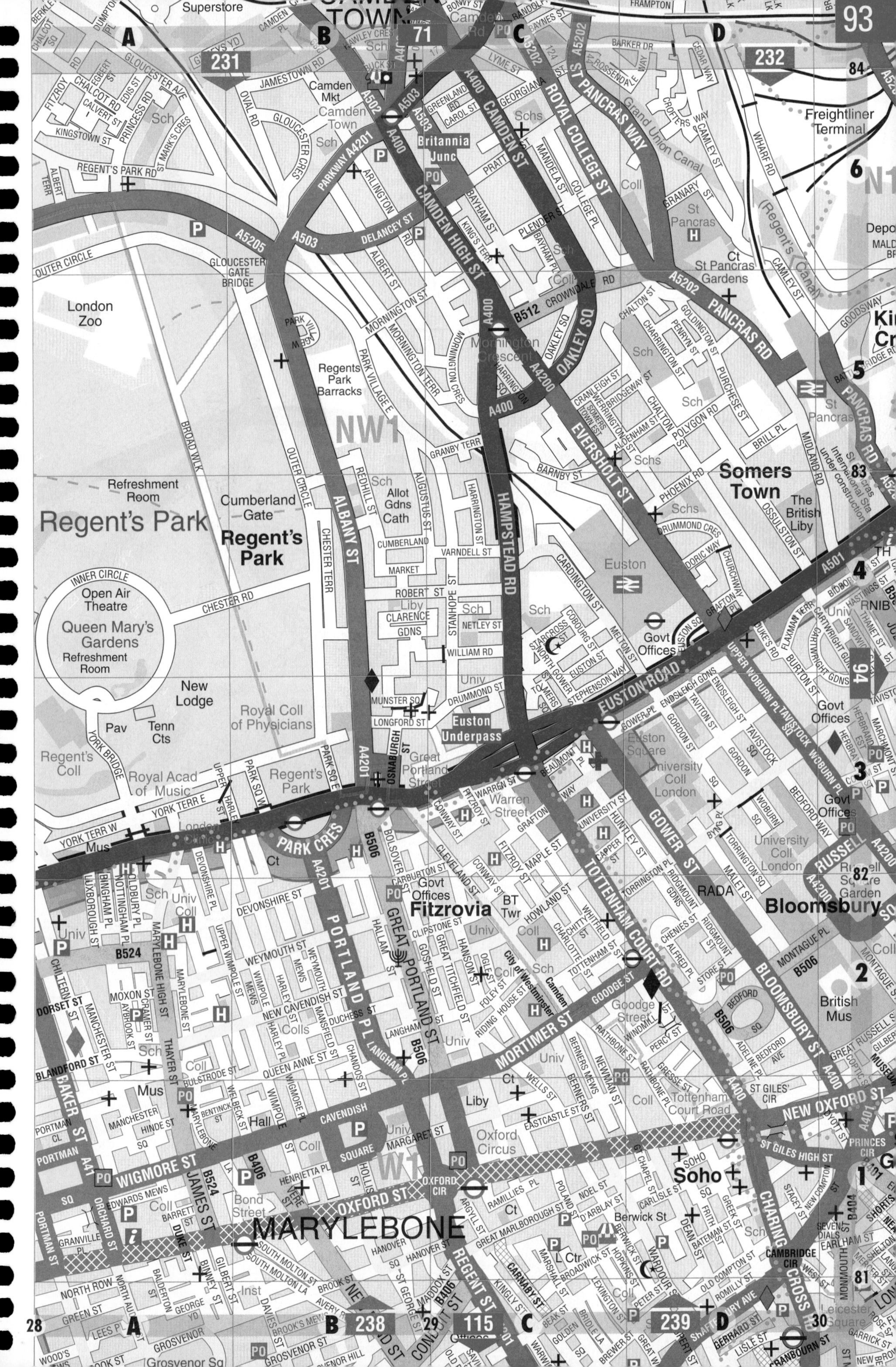
93
A
B
C
D
231
71
232
CAMDEN TOWN
Superstore
Freightliner Terminal
Camden Mkt
Camden Town
Britannia Junc
Grand Union Canal
(Regent's Canal)
St Pancras
St Pancras Gardens
London Zoo
Regents Park Barracks
NW1
Somers Town
The British Liby
Refreshment Room
Cumberland Gate
Regent's Park
Open Air Theatre
Queen Mary's Gardens
New Lodge
Royal Coll of Physicians
Euston
Euston Underpass
Govt Offices
Euston Square
University Coll London
Warren Street
Great Portland Street
Regent's Coll
Royal Acad of Music
Fitzrovia
BT Twr
Goodge Street
Tottenham Court Road
Bloomsbury
British Mus
Russell Square Garden
RADA
Oxford Circus
Bond Street
MARYLEBONE
W1
Soho
Berwick St
Cambridge Cir
Leicester Square
ALBANY ST
HAMPSTEAD RD
CAMDEN HIGH ST
ROYAL COLLEGE ST
ST PANCRAS WAY
PANCRAS RD
EUSTON ROAD
GOWER ST
TOTTENHAM COURT RD
BLOOMSBURY ST
PORTLAND PL
GREAT PORTLAND ST
MORTIMER ST
OXFORD ST
WIGMORE ST
BAKER ST
REGENT ST
CHARING CROSS RD
NEW OXFORD ST
MARYLEBONE HIGH ST
PARK CRES
OUTER CIRCLE
INNER CIRCLE
CHESTER RD
BROAD WLK
28
238
29
115
239
30

A
B
C
D
233
72
234
84
6
5
4
3
2
1
83
82
81
93
30
31
32
240
116
241
N1
WC1
WC2
EC1
ISLINGTON
FINSBURY
Pentonville
King's Cross
St Pancras
Bloomsbury
St Giles
Clerkenwell
Gray's Inn
Holborn
Angel
Camden Pas
Freightliner Terminal
Depot
MALDEN LANE BRIDGE
Regent's Canal
Barnard Park
Bsns Design Ctr
Chapel Mkt
St Pancras International Sta under construction
The British Liby
Coram's Fields
Russell Square Garden
University Coll London
British Mus
Lincoln's Inn Fields
Public Record Office
Royal Courts of Justice
Somerset House
Smithfield Mkt
St Barts
City Thameslink
Farringdon
Leather Lane
Chancery Lane
The City Univ
Eastman Dental
Covent Garden
Leicester Square
Old Covent Garden
Inner Temple Garden
Govt Offices
YORK WAY
CALEDONIAN RD
COPENHAGEN ST
PENTONVILLE RD
KING'S CROSS RD
GRAY'S INN RD
ROSEBERY AVE
FARRINGDON RD
ST JOHN ST
GOSWELL RD
UPPER ST
LIVERPOOL RD
ESSEX RD
CLERKENWELL RD
THEOBALD'S RD
GUILFORD ST
SOUTHAMPTON ROW
HUNTER ST
JUDD ST
HIGH HOLBORN
HOLBORN
HOLBORN VIADUCT
NEW OXFORD ST
KINGSWAY
ALDWYCH
CHANCERY LA
FLEET ST
LUDGATE HILL
NEWGATE
NEW BRIDGE ST
FARRINGDON ST
LONG ACRE
CHARING CROSS RD
BLOOMSBURY ST
RUSSELL SQ
EUSTON RD
PANCRAS RD
VICTORIA EMBANKMENT
STRAND
ST GILES HIGH ST
WHITE LION HILL
PUDDLE DOCK
A5200
A5203
A501
A201
A401
A4200
A1
A401
A5201
A40
A4
B515
B501
B502
B503
B504
B506
B400
B401
B402
B404
B500
B521
A3211

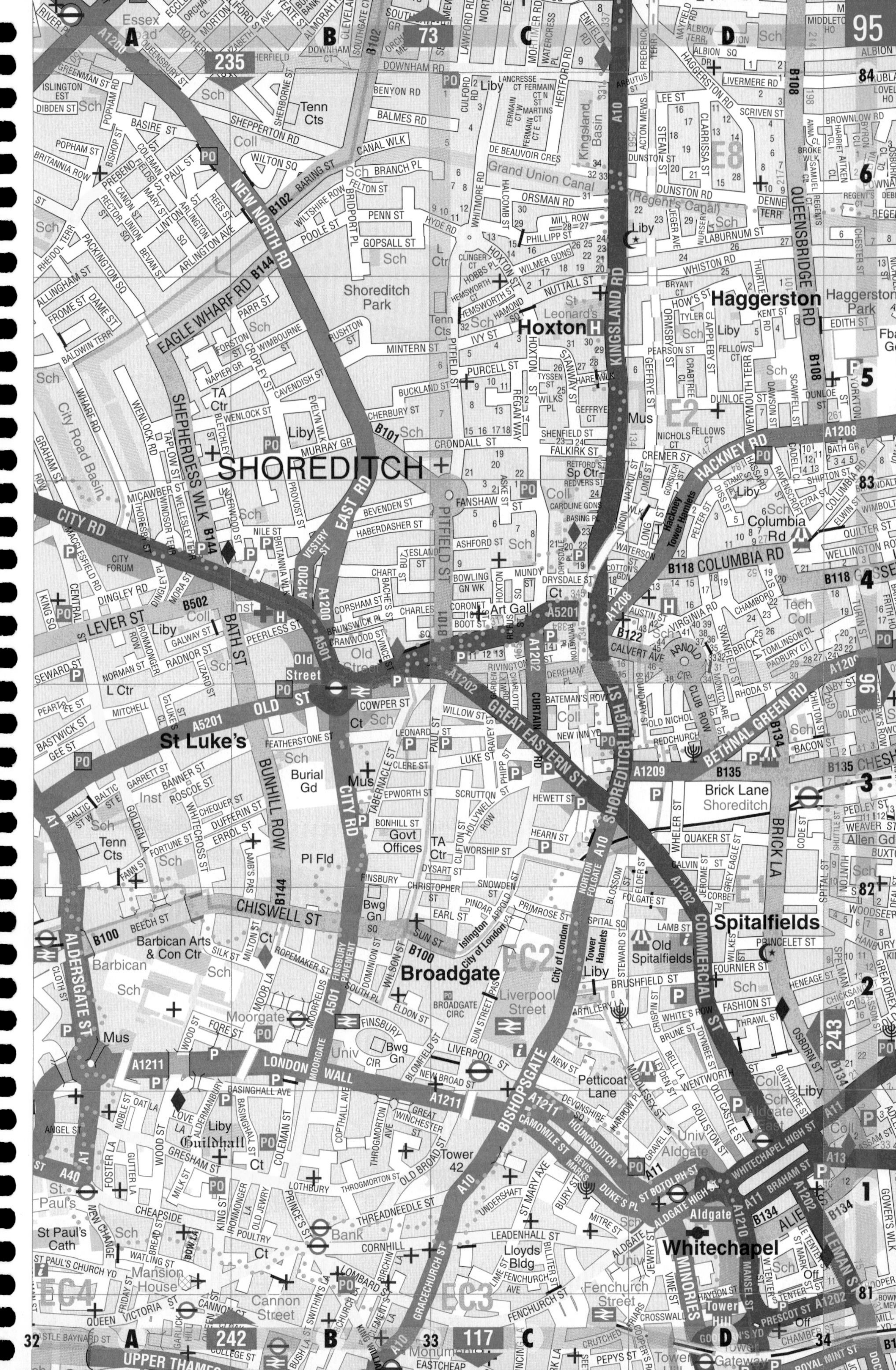
A
B
C
D
73
235
SHOREDITCH
Hoxton
Haggerston
Haggerston Park
St Luke's
Spitalfields
Broadgate
Whitechapel
Shoreditch Park
City Road Basin
Grand Union Canal
(Regent's Canal)
Kingsland Basin
Columbia Rd
Brick Lane Shoreditch
Old Spitalfields
Barbican Arts & Con Ctr
Barbican
Moorgate
Liverpool Street
Old Street
Bunhill Fields
Burial Gd
Govt Offices
Guildhall
Tower 42
Lloyds Bldg
Petticoat Lane
Aldgate
Aldgate East
Bank
Mansion House
Cannon Street
Fenchurch Street
Tower Hill
Tower Gateway
St Paul's Cath
St. Paul's
Monument
E8
E2
E1
EC2
EC3
EC4
NEW NORTH RD
KINGSLAND RD
QUEENSBRIDGE RD
HACKNEY RD
COLUMBIA RD
CITY RD
OLD ST
EAST RD
PITFIELD ST
SHEPHERDESS WLK
BATH ST
BUNHILL ROW
CHISWELL ST
ALDERSGATE ST
LONDON WALL
MOORGATE
BISHOPSGATE
GREAT EASTERN ST
SHOREDITCH HIGH ST
COMMERCIAL ST
BETHNAL GREEN RD
BRICK LA
WHITECHAPEL HIGH ST
MINORIES
LEMAN ST
CHEAPSIDE
CANNON ST
UPPER THAMES ST
A1200
A1202
A1208
A1209
A1211
A5201
A501
A10
A11
A13
A1
A40
B100
B101
B102
B108
B118
B122
B134
B135
B144
B502
32
A
242
B
33
117
C
D
34
243
96
1
2
3
4
5
6

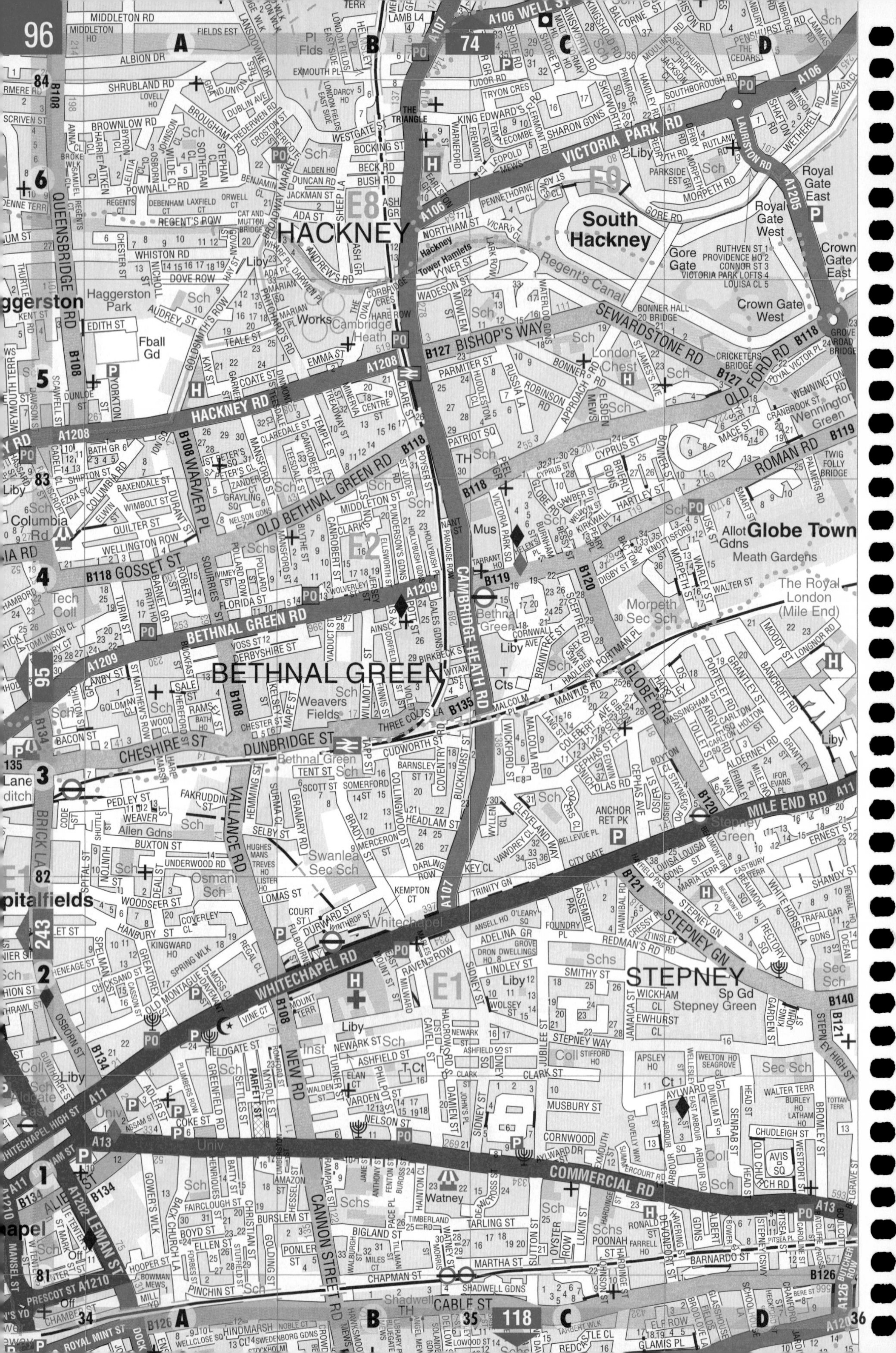
A
B
C
D
74
HACKNEY
E8
E9
South Hackney
Haggerston
Haggerston Park
Regent's Canal
VICTORIA PARK RD
MIDDLETON RD
ALBION DR
QUEENSBRIDGE RD
HACKNEY RD
BISHOP'S WAY
SEWARDSTONE RD
OLD FORD RD
ROMAN RD
Royal Gate East
Royal Gate West
Crown Gate East
Crown Gate West
Gore Gate
Cambridge Heath
Globe Town
Meath Gardens
The Royal London (Mile End)
Morpeth Sec Sch
E2
OLD BETHNAL GREEN RD
GOSSET ST
BETHNAL GREEN RD
BETHNAL GREEN
CAMBRIDGE HEATH RD
Bethnal Green
Weavers Fields
CHESHIRE ST
DUNBRIDGE ST
VALLANCE RD
BRICK LA
Spitalfields
Columbia Rd
Swanlea Sec Sch
Osmani Sch
MILE END RD
Stepney Green
GLOBE RD
WHITECHAPEL RD
Whitechapel
E1
STEPNEY
STEPNEY GN
Stepney Green
STEPNEY WAY
COMMERCIAL RD
NEW RD
CANNON STREET RD
LEMAN ST
WHITECHAPEL HIGH ST
Aldgate East
Watney
CABLE ST
Shadwell
ROYAL MINT ST
THE HIGHWAY
95
243
6
5
4
3
2
1
84
83
82
81
34
35
36
118

97
A
B
C
D
75
119
84
83
82
81
36
37
38
98
6
5
4
3
2
1
Victoria Park
Victoria Fntn
Gunmakers Gate
Bnstand
Hertford Union Canal
Sp Gd
Bwg Gn
Old Ford
Swan Wharf
Crown Wharf
Iceland Wharf
Stratford Marsh
THE MARSHGATE CTR
Pudding Mill Lane
St Clement's Wharf
Vulcan Wharf
River Lea or Lee
Bow Back River
City Mill River
Lea Valley Wlk
Grove Hall Park
Meeson's Wharf
Tredegar Wharf
BOW
Mile End Park
Four Seasons Green
Bow Road
Bow Church
Bromley
Recn Gd
Mile End
Univ of London
The Royal London (St Clements)
Tower Hamlets Cemy
Coll (Annexe)
E3
Allot Gdns
St Andrew's
Devons Road
Hackney Coll
Gas Works
Mile End Park (South)
Regent's Canal
Shandy Park
TOWER HAMLETS
East London Stadium
Halley Prim Sch
Bow Common
Furze Green
Langdon Park
Limehouse Fields
Brickfield Gardens
Limehouse Cut
Bartlett Park
POPLAR
Limehouse Basin
Limehouse
GROVE RD
BOW RD
EAST CROSS ROUTE
FAIRFIELD RD
DEVONS RD
ST PAUL'S WAY
BURDETT RD
BEN JONSON RD
EAST INDIA DOCK RD
BLACKWALL TUNNEL NORTHERN APPROACH
COMMERCIAL ROAD
OLD FORD RD
PARNELL RD
ROMAN RD
BRUCE RD
A11
A12
A13
A1205
A1261
B118
B119
B140
B142

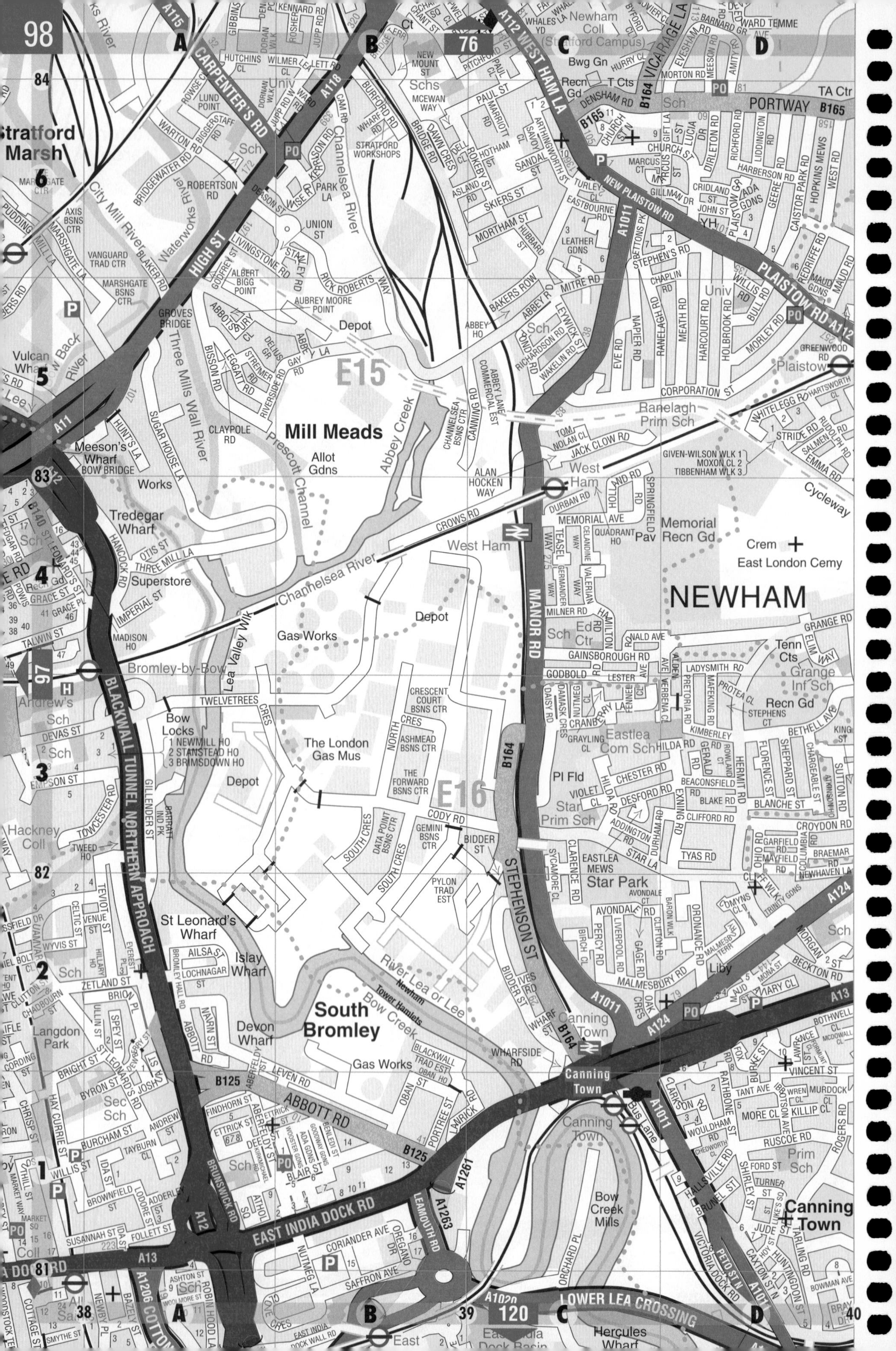
Stratford Marsh
Mill Meads
E15
E16
NEWHAM
South Bromley
West Ham
Canning Town
Plaistow
Bromley-by-Bow
Memorial Recn Gd
East London Cemy
Star Park
Gas Works
The London Gas Mus
Three Mills Wall River
Channelsea River
Abbey Creek
Prescott Channel
River Lea or Lee
Bow Creek
HIGH ST
CARPENTER'S RD
WEST HAM LA
MANOR RD
STEPHENSON ST
BLACKWALL TUNNEL NORTHERN APPROACH
EAST INDIA DOCK RD
LOWER LEA CROSSING
PLAISTOW RD
NEW PLAISTOW RD
PORTWAY
ABBOTT RD
VICARAGE LA
CORPORATION ST
Canning Town
Bow Creek Mills
Hercules Wharf
76
97
120
A
B
C
D
84
83
82
81
6
5
4
3
2
1
38
39
40

77
WEST HAM
Upton Park
Plaistow
Canning Town
Custom House
E7
E13
E6
E16
PLASHET RD
PLASHET GR
STOPFORD RD
GREEN ST
HIGH ST
THE BROADWAY
GREENGATE ST
BARKING RD
PRINCE REGENT LA
NEWHAM WAY
CENTRAL PARK RD
BALAAM ST
CONNAUGHT RD
VICTORIA DOCK RD
UPTON CROSS
Queen's Mkt
Boleyn Gd (West Ham Utd FC)
Newham General
Newham Sixth Form Coll
Newham Ctr for Mental Health
Brampton Manor Sch
Roman Road Prim Sch
Tollgate Prim Sch
Stadium
Prince Regent
Rosetta Prim Sch
Scott Wilkie Prim Sch
King George V Park
Becton District Park
Calverton Prim Sch
St Helen's RC Prim Sch
Curwen Sch
Lister Com Sch
Plaistow Prim Sch
Priory Park
Cleves Prim Sch
EAST HAM IND EST
100
121
40
41
42
A
B
C
D
1
2
3
4
5
6
81
82
83
84

A
B
C
D
78
EAST HAM
Wallend
Beckton
Central Park
Flanders Pl Fld
Langdon Sch
Barking Flyover
NORTH CIRCULAR RD
A406
A124
A117
A13
B167
BARKING RD
HIGH ST N
HIGH ST S
RON LEIGHTON WAY
RANCLIFFE RD
NEWHAM WAY
ROYAL DOCKS RD
WOOLWICH MANOR WAY
ROYAL ALBERT WAY
ROYAL ALBERT RD
River Roding
ABBEY RD
Superstore
Recn Gd
East Ham Jewish Cemy
Brampton Prim Sch
Brampton Park
Gooseley's Pl Flds
BECKTON TRIANGLE RET PK
GATEWAY RET PK
Beckton Alps
Ski Ctr
Allot Gdns
Golf Range
North Beckton Prim Sch
EAST BECKTON DIST CTR
MARY ROSE MALL
Kingsford Com Sch
Beckton District Park
The Will Thorne Pav
New Becton Park
Winsor Prim Sch
Gallions Reach
Cyprus
Beckton Park
E6
99
122
81
82
83
84
42
43
44

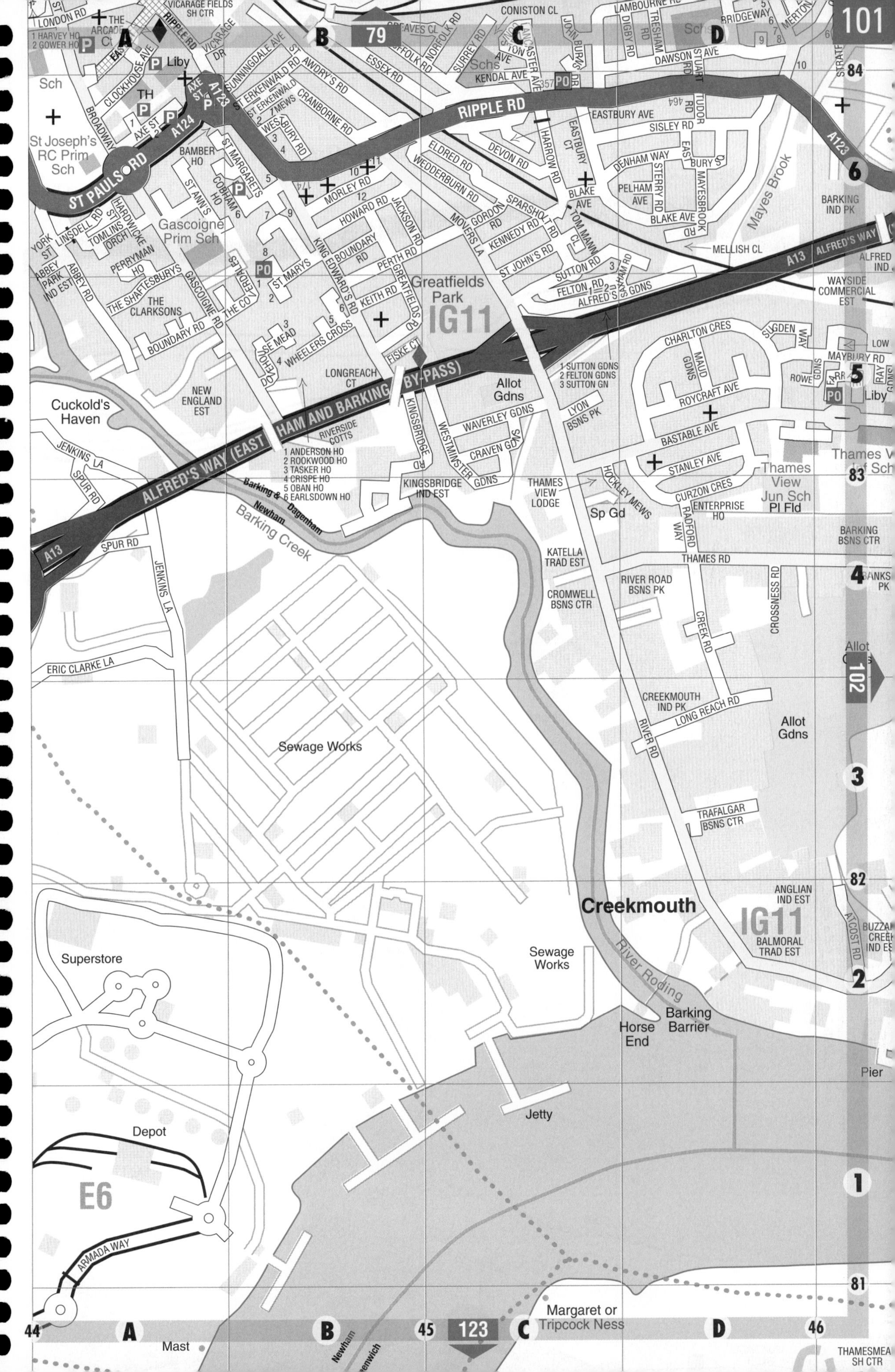
RIPPLE RD
ST PAULS RD
ALFRED'S WAY (EAST HAM AND BARKING BY-PASS)
A13
A123
A124
Greatfields Park
IG11
Gascoigne Prim Sch
St Joseph's RC Prim Sch
Cuckold's Haven
NEW ENGLAND EST
Barking Creek
Sewage Works
Creekmouth
River Roding
Barking Barrier
Horse End
Jetty
Superstore
Depot
E6
ARMADA WAY
Margaret or Tripcock Ness
Mast
JENKINS LA
SPUR RD
ERIC CLARKE LA
RIVER RD
THAMES RD
LONG REACH RD
CREEKMOUTH IND PK
TRAFALGAR BSNS CTR
ANGLIAN IND EST
BALMORAL TRAD EST
Allot Gdns
Thames View Jun Sch
Mayes Brook
BARKING IND PK
WAYSIDE COMMERCIAL EST
Pier
THAMESMEAD SH CTR

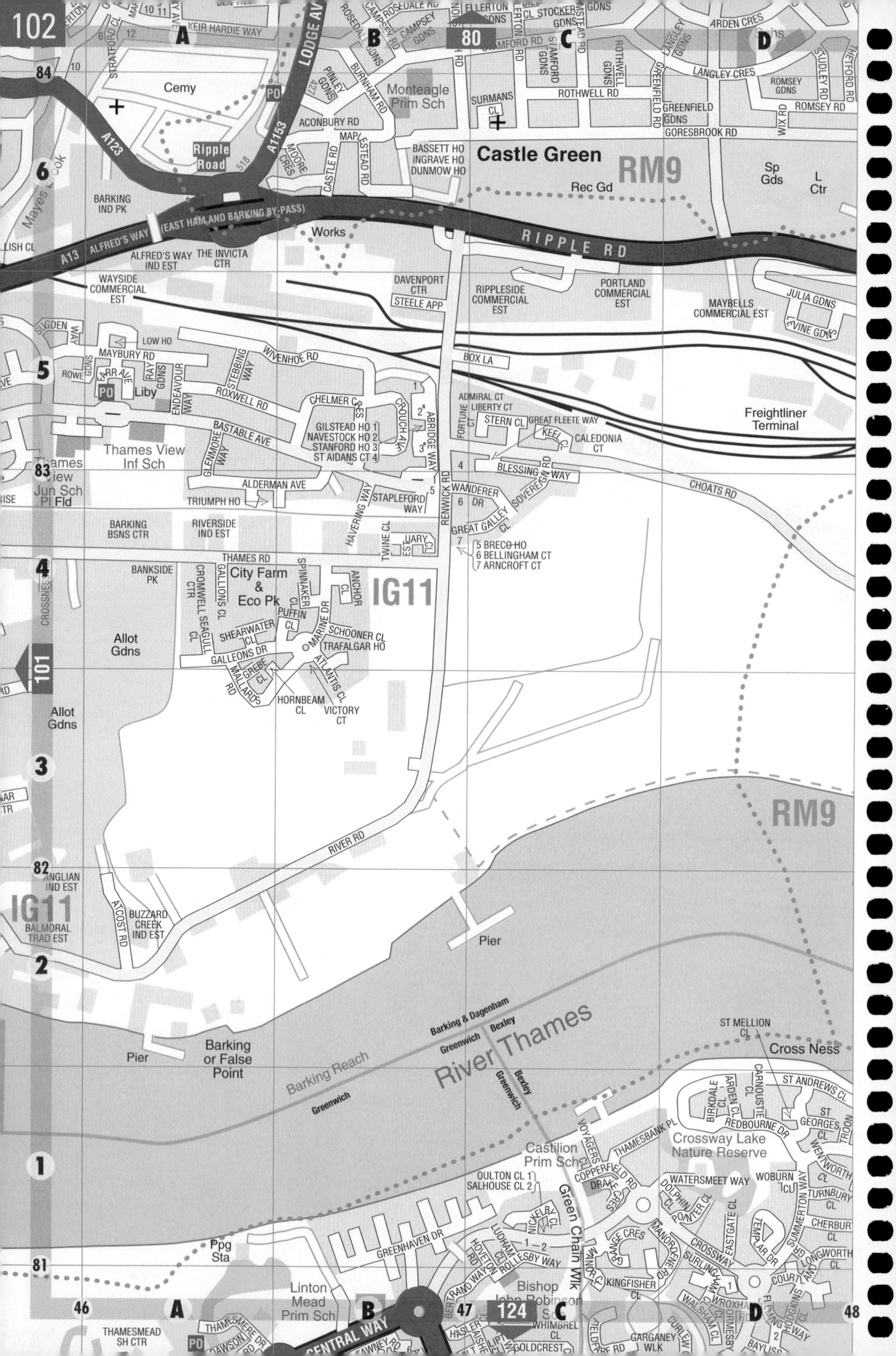

80
Castle Green
RM9
Cemy
Ripple Road
Monteagle Prim Sch
BARKING IND PK
RIPPLE RD
ALFRED'S WAY (EAST HAM AND BARKING BY-PASS)
Works
Rec Gd
Sp Gds
L Ctr
ALFRED'S WAY IND EST
THE INVICTA CTR
WAYSIDE COMMERCIAL EST
DAVENPORT CTR
RIPPLESIDE COMMERCIAL EST
PORTLAND COMMERCIAL EST
MAYBELLS COMMERCIAL EST
Freightliner Terminal
Thames View Inf Sch
Thames View Jun Sch
Pl Fld
BARKING BSNS CTR
RIVERSIDE IND EST
City Farm & Eco Pk
IG11
BANKSIDE PK
Allot Gdns
Allot Gdns
RENWICK RD
RIVER RD
CHOATS RD
Pier
Barking or False Point
Pier
River Thames
Barking Reach
Barking & Dagenham
Bexley
Greenwich
Cross Ness
Crossway Lake Nature Reserve
Castilion Prim Sch
Green Chain Wlk
Ppg Sta
Linton Mead Prim Sch
Bishop John Robinson Sch
THAMESMEAD SH CTR
ANGLIAN IND EST
BALMORAL TRAD EST
BUZZARD CREEK IND EST
RM9
101
124

DAGENHAM
Goresbrook Park
Arnold Prim Sch
81
Allot Gdns
Allot Gdns
Morland Road Day
Dagenham Priory Sch
RM10
RM9
RM13
SE28
RIPPLE RD
NEW RD
A1306 Rainham
Marsh Green Prim Sch
Motor Works
Dagenham Dock
Dagenham Breach
THAMES GATEWAY PK
Horse Shoe Corner
Power Sta
Ind Est
Works
Jetties
Jetty
River Thames
Halfway Reach
Beam River
Crossness Pumping Station
Drv Rng
Heathway
CHEQUERS LA
KENT AVE
CHOATS MANOR WAY
HINDMANS WAY
THUNDERER RD
BREACH LA
MERRIELANDS RET PK
Barking & Dagenham
Bexley
Havering
125

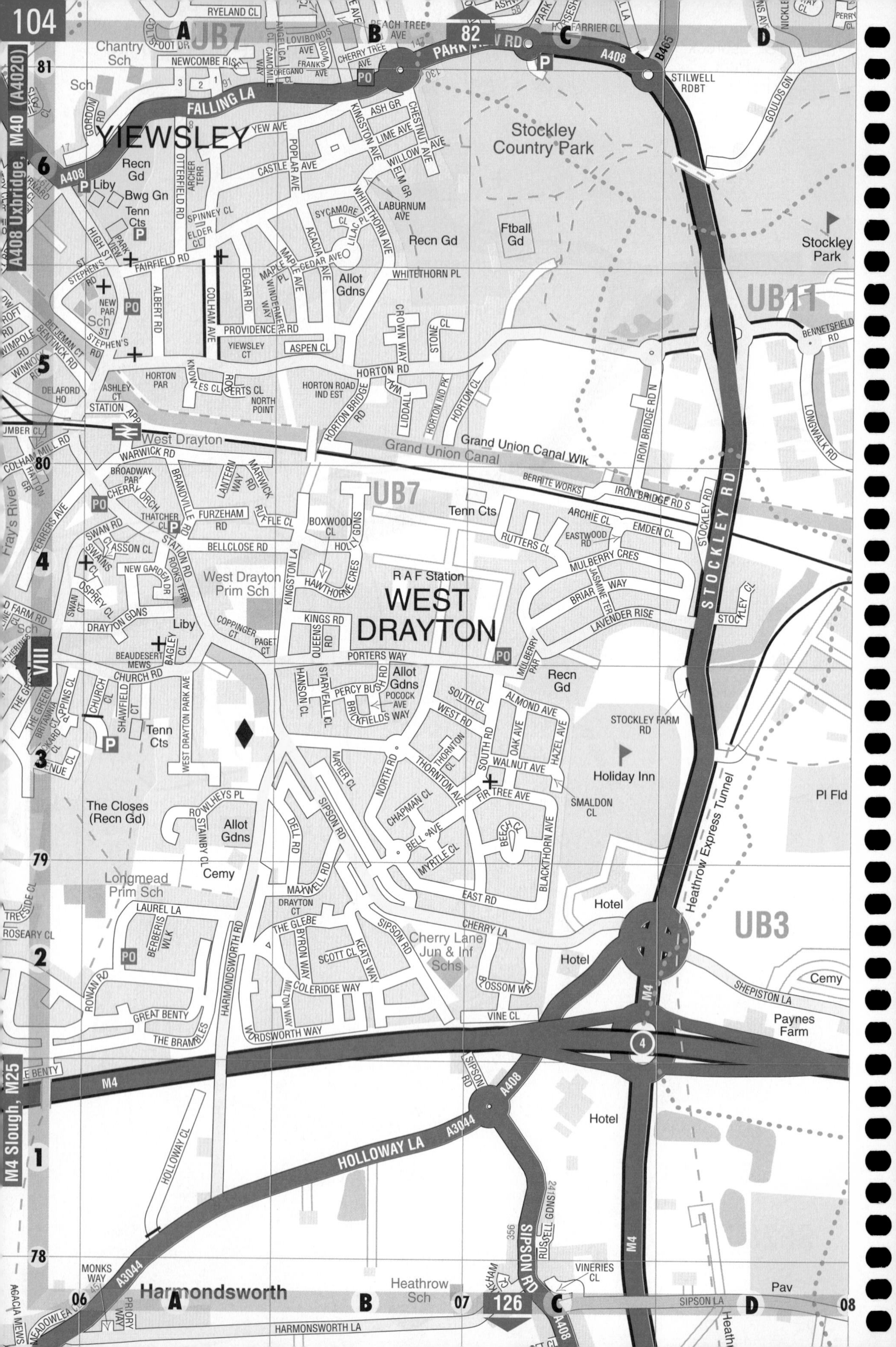

A
B
C
D
82
UB7
YIEWSLEY
FALLING LA
PARK VIEW RD
A408
B465
STILWELL RDBT
Stockley Country Park
GOULDS GN
RYELAND CL
COLTSFOOT DR
Chantry Sch
NEWCOMBE RISE
LOVIBONDS AVE
FRANKS AVE
OREGANO CL
CAMOMILE WAY
ANGELICA
BEACH TREE AVE
CHERRY TREE AVE
FARRIER CL
PO
81
Sch
GORDON RD
YEW AVE
ASH GR
LIME AVE
CHESTNUT AVE
KINGSTON AVE
WILLOW AVE
ELM GR
CASTLE AVE
POPLAR AVE
OTTERFIELD RD
ARCHER TERR
Recn Gd
Liby
Bwg Gn
Tenn Cts
6
SPINNEY CL
ELDER CL
SYCAMORE CL
LILAC PL
ACACIA AVE
WHITETHORN AVE
LABURNUM AVE
Recn Gd
Ftball Gd
Stockley Park
HIGH ST
PARK VIEW
FAIRFIELD RD
STEPHEN'S RD
MAPLE PL
MAPLE AVE
CEDAR AVE
WINDERMERE WAY
EDGAR RD
Allot Gdns
WHITETHORN PL
UB11
NEW PAR
Sch
ALBERT RD
COLHAM AVE
PROVIDENCE RD
CROWN WAY
STONE CL
BENNETSFIELD RD
BETJEMAN CT
BENTINCK RD
WIMPOLE RD
WINNOCK RD
YIEWSLEY CT
ASPEN CL
5
HORTON PAR
KNOWLES CL
ROBERTS CL
NORTH POINT
HORTON ROAD IND EST
HORTON RD
HORTON BRIDGE RD
LIDDALL WAY
HORTON IND PK
HORTON CL
IRON BRIDGE RD N
LONGWALK RD
DELAFORD HO
ASHLEY CT
STATION APP
West Drayton
Grand Union Canal
Grand Union Canal Wlk
COLHAM MILL RD
WARWICK RD
HATTON GR
80
BROADWAY PAR
CHERRY ORCH
BRANDVILLE RD
LANTERN WAY
MARWICK RD
BERRITE WORKS
IRON BRIDGE RD S
STOCKLEY RD
Fray's River
FERRERS AVE
UB7
Tenn Cts
THATCHER CL
FURZEHAM RD
RUKFLE CL
BOXWOOD CL
ARCHIE CL
EMDEN CL
EASTWOOD RD
RUTTERS CL
SWAN RD
CLASSON CL
SWANS
BELLCLOSE RD
HOLLY GDNS
4
NEW GARDEN DR
ROOKS TERR
STATION RD
West Drayton Prim Sch
KINGSTON LA
HAWTHORNE CRES
R A F Station
WEST DRAYTON
MULBERRY CRES
BRIAR WAY
JASMINE TER
LAVENDER RISE
STOCKLEY CL
OSPREY CL
SWAN CT
DRAYTON GDNS
Liby
COPPINGER CT
PAGET CT
KINGS RD
QUEENS RD
PORTERS WAY
MULBERRY PAR
Recn Gd
VIII
BEAUDESERT MEWS
BAGLEY CL
CHURCH RD
HANSON CL
STARVEALL CL
PERCY BUSH RD
Allot Gdns
POCOCK AVE
BRICKFIELDS WAY
SOUTH CL
ALMOND AVE
WEST RD
STOCKLEY FARM RD
THE GREEN
BRITANNIA CL
PIPPINS CL
CHURCH CL
SHAWFIELD CT
WEST DRAYTON PARK AVE
Tenn Cts
NAPIER CL
NORTH RD
THORNTON CL
SOUTH RD
OAK AVE
HAZEL AVE
Holiday Inn
3
THORNTON AVE
WALNUT AVE
FIR TREE AVE
SMALDON CL
Pl Fld
ROWLHEYS PL
The Closes (Recn Gd)
STAINBY CL
Allot Gdns
DELL RD
SIPSON RD
CHAPMAN CL
BELL AVE
MYRTLE CL
BEECH CL
BLACKTHORN AVE
Heathrow Express Tunnel
79
Cemy
Longmead Prim Sch
MAXWELL RD
EAST RD
TREESIDE CL
LAUREL LA
DRAYTON CT
Hotel
ROSEARY CL
BERBERIS WLK
HARMONDSWORTH RD
THE GLEBE
BYRON WAY
SIPSON RD
CHERRY LA
Cherry Lane Jun & Inf Schs
UB3
2
SCOTT CL
KEATS WAY
Hotel
ROWAN RD
COLERIDGE WAY
BLOSSOM WAY
Cemy
SHEPISTON LA
M4
GREAT BENTY
MILTON WAY
VINE CL
Paynes Farm
THE BRAMBLES
WORDSWORTH WAY
4
M4
SIPSON RD
A408
Hotel
1
HOLLOWAY CL
HOLLOWAY LA
A3044
RUSSELL GDNS
SIPSON RD
M4
78
MONKS WAY
A3044
Harmondsworth
Heathrow Sch
VINERIES CL
Pav
06
A
B
07
126
C
SIPSON LA
D
08
PRIORY WAY
MEADOWLEA CL
HARMONSWORTH LA
ACACIA MEWS
M4 Slough, M25
A408 Uxbridge, M40 (A4020)

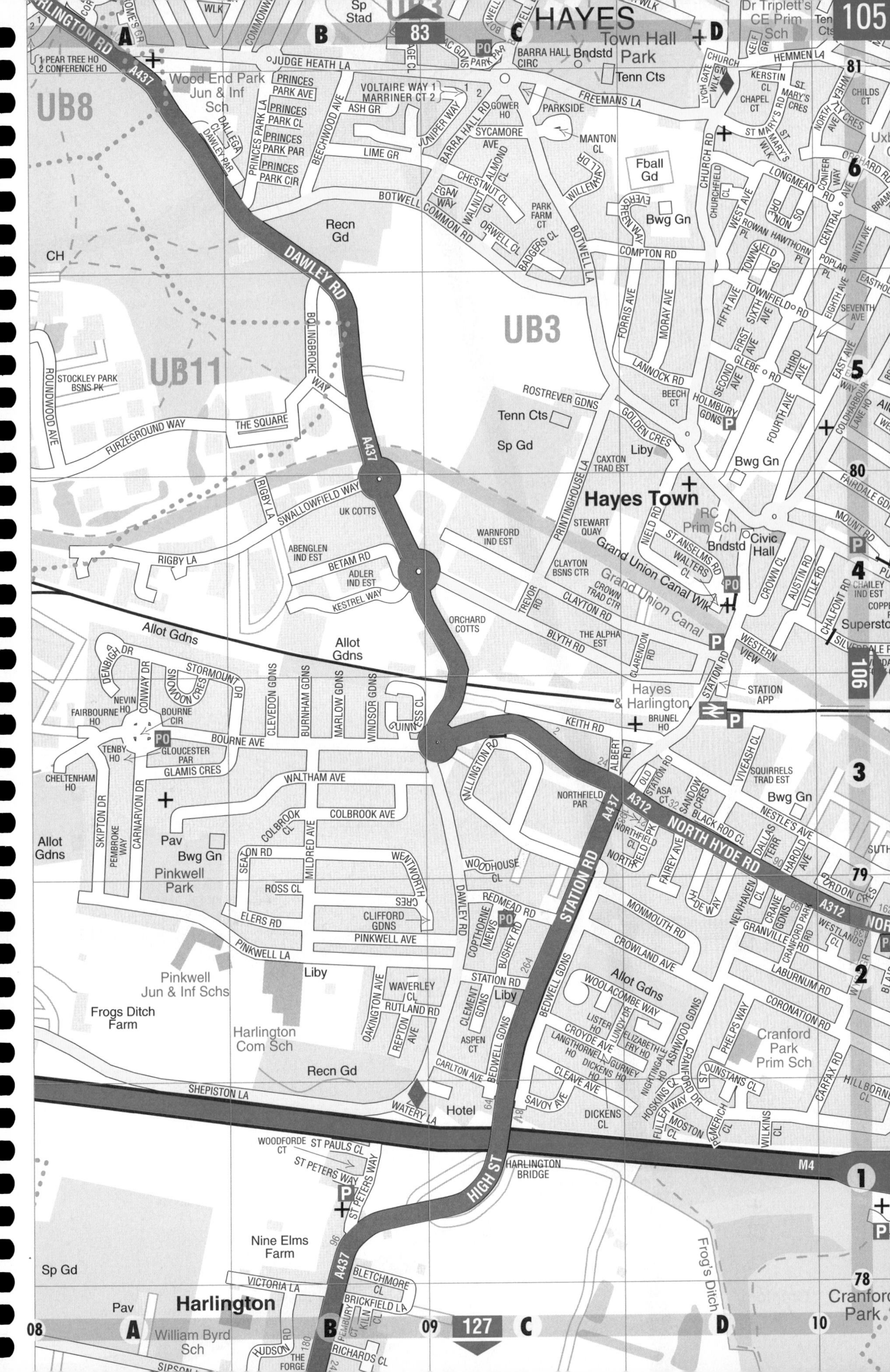
HAYES
83
A
B
C
D
Hayes Town
UB8
UB11
UB3
Harlington
HARLINGTON RD
A437
DAWLEY RD
1 PEAR TREE HO
2 CONFERENCE HO
Wood End Park Jun & Inf Sch
JUDGE HEATH LA
PRINCES PARK AVE
PRINCES PARK CL
PRINCES PARK PAR
PRINCES PARK CIR
PRINCES PARK LA
DALLEGA CL
DAWLEY PAR
VOLTAIRE WAY
MARRINER CT
ASH GR
BEECHWOOD AVE
LIME GR
JUNIPER WAY
BARRA HALL RD
BARRA HALL CIRC
GOWER HO
SYCAMORE AVE
ALMOND CL
CHESTNUT CL
EGAN WAY
WALNUT CL
ORWELL CL
BOTWELL COMMON RD
BOTWELL LA
PARK FARM CT
BADGERS CL
PARKSIDE
MANTON CL
WILLENHALL DR
FREEMANS LA
Bndstd
Town Hall Park
Tenn Cts
Fball Gd
EVERGREEN WAY
Bwg Gn
COMPTON RD
CHURCH RD
CHURCHFIELD CL
LYCH GATE WLK
Dr Triplett's CE Prim Sch
HEMMEN LA
KERSTIN CL
CHAPEL CT
ST MARY'S RD
ST MARY'S CRES
ST MARY'S WLK
CHILDS CT
LONGMEAD
WEST AVE
ROWAN PL
HAWTHORN PL
TOWNFIELD SQ
TOWNFIELD RD
FIFTH AVE
SIXTH AVE
FIRST AVE
SECOND AVE
THIRD AVE
FOURTH AVE
EIGHTH AVE
SEVENTH AVE
NINTH AVE
CENTRAL AVE
POPLAR PL
CONIFER WAY
ORCHARD RD
EAST AVE
EASTHOLM
GLEBE RD
COLDHARBOUR LANE HO
Recn Gd
CH
BOLINGBROKE WAY
STOCKLEY PARK BSNS PK
ROUNDWOOD AVE
FURZEGROUND WAY
THE SQUARE
ROSTREVER GDNS
FORRIS AVE
MORAY AVE
LANNOCK RD
BEECH CT
HOLMBURY GDNS
GOLDEN CRES
Liby
Tenn Cts
Sp Gd
CAXTON TRAD EST
PRINTINGHOUSE LA
STEWART QUAY
RC Prim Sch
Civic Hall
NIELD RD
ST ANSELMS RD
WALTERS CL
CROWN CL
AUSTIN RD
LITTLE RD
CHALFONT RD
CHAILEY IND EST
Superstore
FAIRDALE GDNS
MOUNT RD
RIGBY LA
SWALLOWFIELD WAY
UK COTTS
ABENGLEN IND EST
BETAM RD
ADLER IND EST
KESTREL WAY
WARNFORD IND EST
CLAYTON BSNS CTR
Grand Union Canal Wlk
Grand Union Canal
CROWN TRAD CTR
TREVOR RD
CLAYTON RD
BLYTH RD
THE ALPHA EST
CLARENDON RD
ORCHARD COTTS
Allot Gdns
WESTERN VIEW
STATION RD
STATION APP
Hayes & Harlington
BRUNEL HO
KEITH RD
106
DENBIGH DR
CONWAY DR
SNOWDON CRES
STORMOUNT DR
NEVIN HO
FAIRBOURNE HO
BOURNE CIR
BOURNE AVE
TENBY HO
GLOUCESTER PAR
GLAMIS CRES
CHELTENHAM HO
CLEVEDON GDNS
BURNHAM GDNS
MARLOW GDNS
WINDSOR GDNS
GUINNESS CL
WALTHAM AVE
COLBROOK AVE
COLBROOK CL
MILDRED AVE
SEATON RD
WENTWORTH CRES
ROSS CL
ELERS RD
CLIFFORD GDNS
PINKWELL AVE
PINKWELL LA
SKIPTON DR
PEMBROKE WAY
CARNARVON DR
Pav
Bwg Gn
Pinkwell Park
WILLINGTON RD
ALBERT RD
NORTHFIELD PAR
OLD STATION RD
ASA CT
SANDOW CRES
VIVEASH CL
SQUIRRELS TRAD EST
A312
NORTH HYDE RD
BLACK ROD CL
NESTLE'S AVE
DALLAS TERR
HAROLD AVE
NORTHFIELD CL
NORTHFIELD PK
FAIREY AVE
HYDE WAY
WOODHOUSE CL
REDMEAD RD
COPTHORNE MEWS
BUSHEY RD
DAWLEY RD
STATION RD
MONMOUTH RD
CROWLAND AVE
NEWHAVEN CL
CRANE GDNS
CRANFORD PARK RD
GRANVILLE RD
WESTLANDS CL
GORDON CRES
LABURNUM RD
Pinkwell Jun & Inf Schs
Liby
Frogs Ditch Farm
Harlington Com Sch
OAKINGTON AVE
WAVERLEY CL
RUTLAND RD
REPTON AVE
CLEMENT GDNS
ASPEN CT
BEDWELL GDNS
Allot Gdns
WOOLACOMBE WAY
LISTER HO
LUNDY DR
ELIZABETH FRY HO
CROYDE AVE
LANGTHORNE HO
GURNEY HO
DICKENS HO
CLEAVE AVE
SAVOY AVE
DICKENS CL
ASHWOOD GDNS
NIGHTINGALE HO
HOSKINS CL
CRANFORD DR
FULLER WAY
MOSTON CL
PEMERICH CL
ST DUNSTANS CL
PHELPS WAY
CORONATION RD
Cranford Park Prim Sch
CARFAX RD
HILLBORNE CL
WILKINS CL
Recn Gd
CARLTON AVE
SHEPISTON LA
WATERY LA
Hotel
M4
WOODFORDE CT
ST PAULS CL
ST PETERS WAY
HIGH ST
HARLINGTON BRIDGE
Frog's Ditch
Nine Elms Farm
Sp Gd
BLETCHMORE CL
VICTORIA LA
BRICKFIELD LA
PEMBURY CT
KILN CL
Pav
William Byrd Sch
HUDSON RD
THE FORGE
RICHARDS CL
SIPSON
Cranford Park
127
08
09
10
81
80
79
78
1
2
3
4
5
6

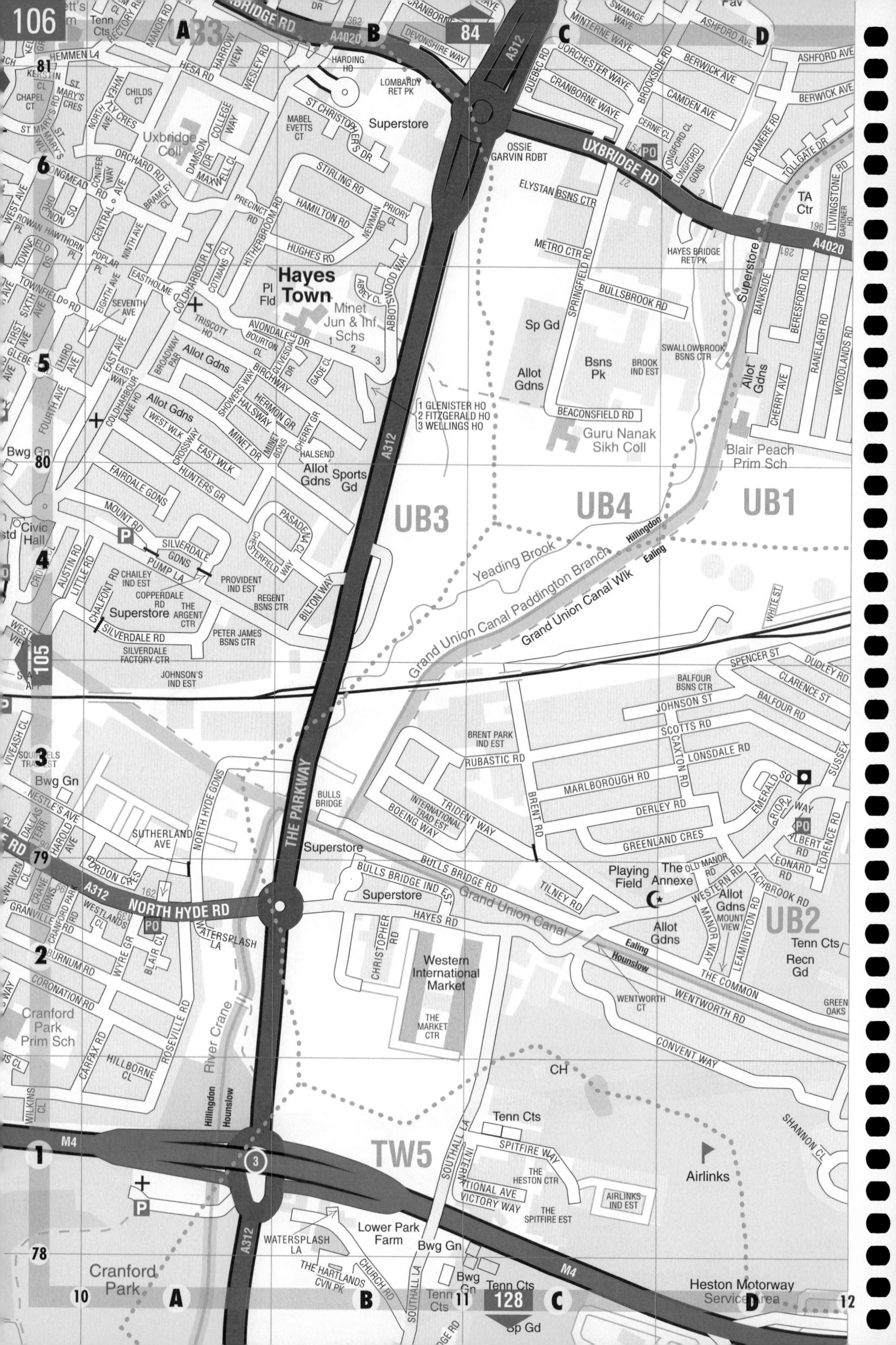
Hayes Town
UB3
UB4
UB1
UB2
TW5
UXBRIDGE RD
A4020
A312
THE PARKWAY
NORTH HYDE RD
M4
Grand Union Canal Paddington Branch
Grand Union Canal Wlk
Grand Union Canal
Yeading Brook
River Crane
Uxbridge Coll
Minet Jun & Inf Schs
Guru Nanak Sikh Coll
Blair Peach Prim Sch
Western International Market
Cranford Park Prim Sch
Cranford Park
Airlinks
Lower Park Farm
Heston Motorway Service Area
OSSIE GARVIN RDBT
84
105
128
A
B
C
D
81
80
79
78
10
11
12
6
5
4
3
2
1

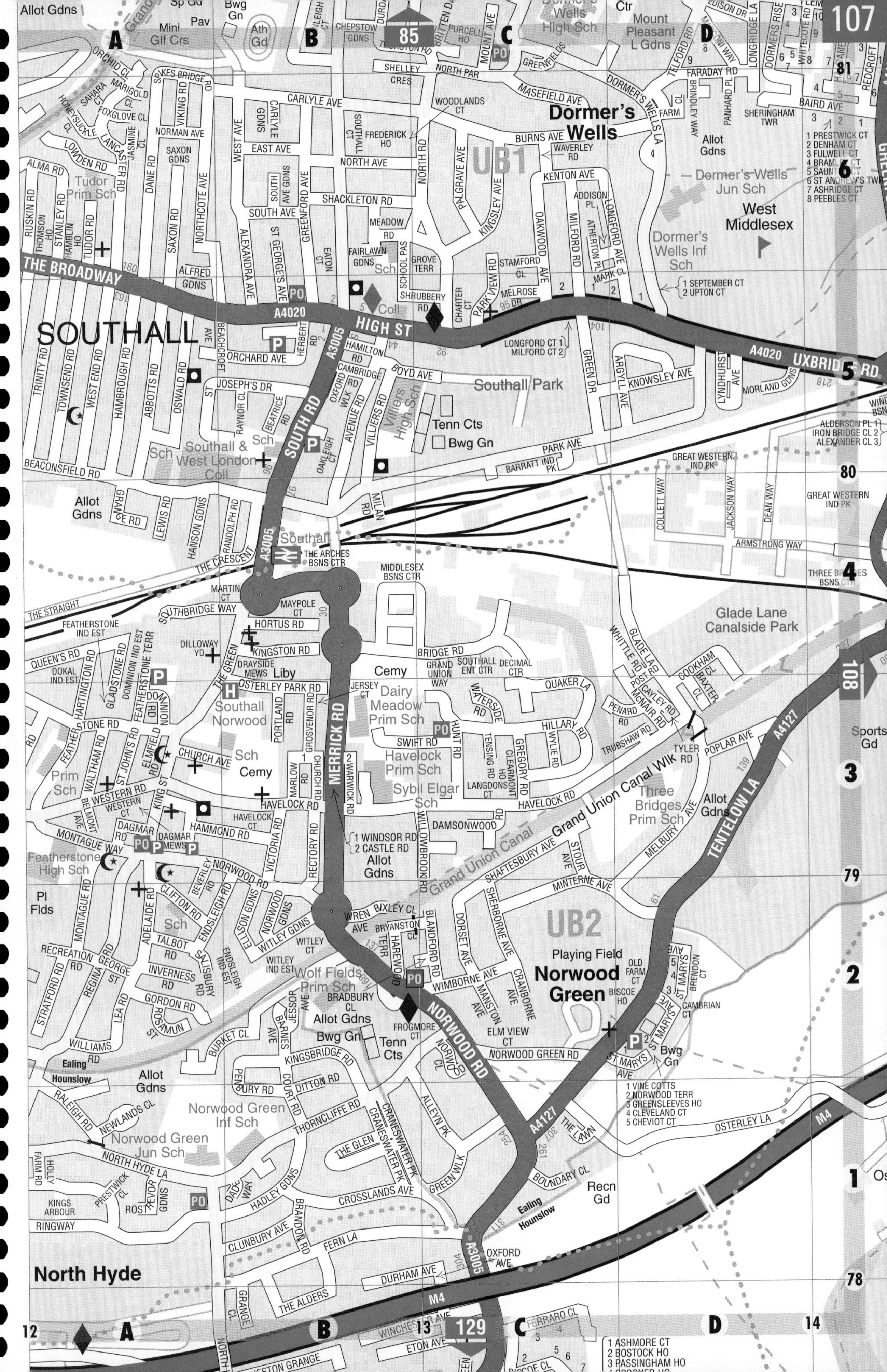
SOUTHALL
Dormer's Wells
UB1
UB2
Norwood Green
North Hyde
THE BROADWAY
HIGH ST
UXBRIDGE RD
SOUTH RD
MERRICK RD
NORWOOD RD
TENTELOW LA
Grand Union Canal
Southall Park
Glade Lane Canalside Park
West Middlesex
M4
85
129
108

Brent Valley
86
UB1
UB2
W7
TW7
Hanwell
UXBRIDGE RD
GREENFORD RD
WINDMILL LA
BOSTON RD
LOWER BOSTON RD
Churchfields Recn Gd
Ealing
Grand Union Canal Wlk
Sports Gd
Sp Ctr
Pl Fld
The Aviary
Elthorne Park
Elthorne Park High Sch
City of Westminster Cemy
Trumper's Wood
Osterley Lock
River Brent
Grand Union Canal
Osterley Park Farm
Osterley Park
Osterley Park House
Hare & Hounds (PH)
Wyke Green
SYON LA
OSTERLEY LA
West Middlesex
Drayton Manor High Sch
Hobbayne Prim Sch
WATERSIDE TRAD CTR
GREAT WESTERN IND PK
THREE BRIDGES BSNS CTR
WINDMILL BRIDGE
1 PRESTWICK CT
2 DENHAM CT
3 FULWELL CT
4 BRAMLEY CT
5 SAUNTON CT
6 ST ANDREW'S TWR
7 ASHRIDGE CT
8 PEEBLES CT
1 WATER LILY CL
2 COMER CRES
3 TULIP CL
1 QUEEN TERR COTTS
2 THORNWELL CT
3 ST MARK'S CT
4 DU BURSTOW TERR
5 CHURCHFIELD RD
6 MALLARD CL
1 SHERIDAN CT
2 KIPLING CT
107
130

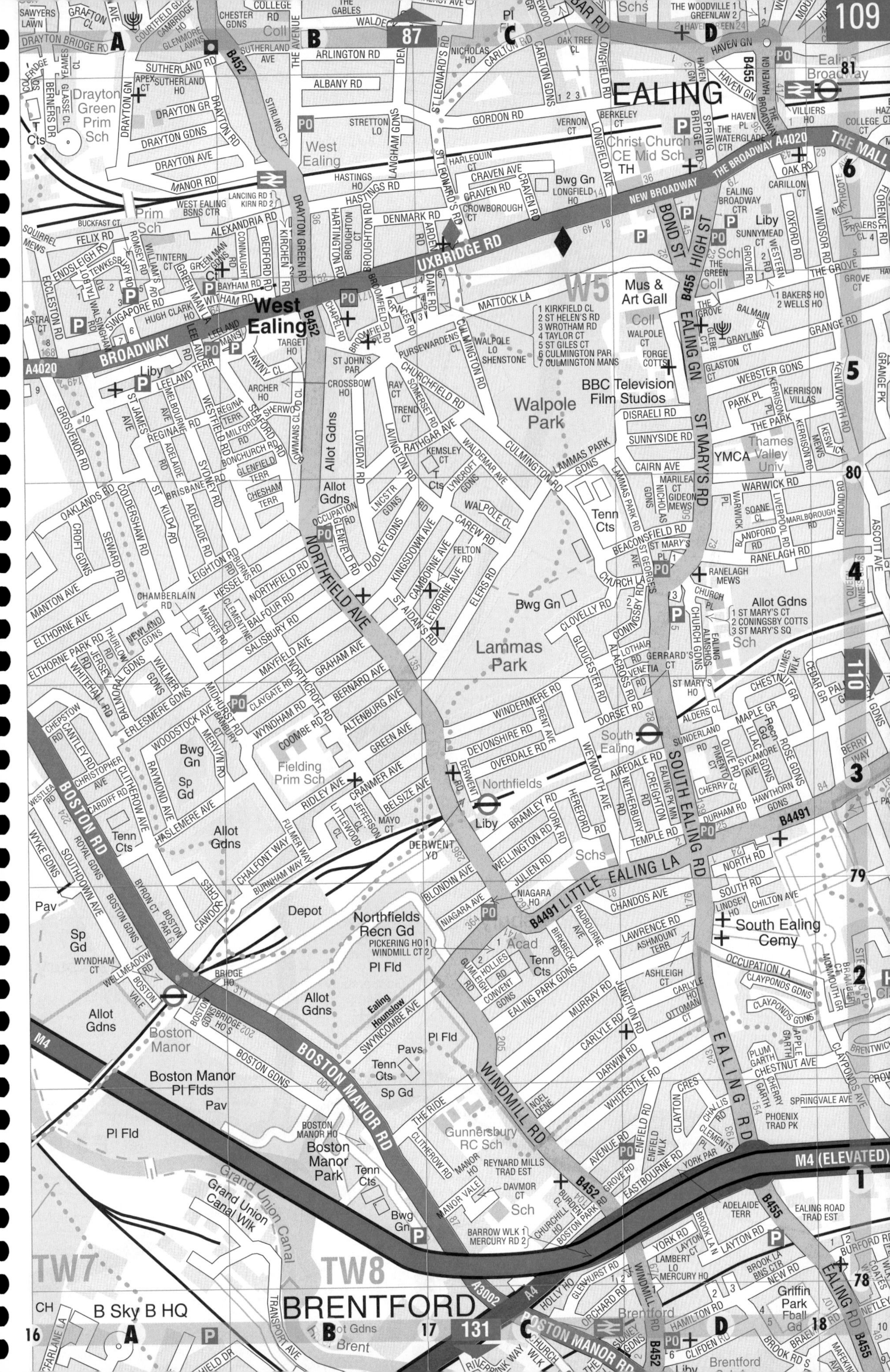
EALING
West Ealing
BRENTFORD
W5
TW7
TW8
87
81
80
79
78
110
131
16
17
18
A
B
C
D
1
2
3
4
5
6
UXBRIDGE RD
THE BROADWAY A4020
NEW BROADWAY
BROADWAY
A4020
THE MALL
B452
B455
B4491
A3002
A4
M4
M4 (ELEVATED)
DRAYTON BRIDGE RD
DRAYTON GREEN RD
DRAYTON GR
DRAYTON GDNS
DRAYTON AVE
DRAYTON RD
MANOR RD
Drayton Green Prim Sch
West Ealing
ARLINGTON RD
ALBANY RD
GORDON RD
HASTINGS RD
DENMARK RD
CRAVEN AVE
CRAVEN RD
ST LEONARD'S RD
LONGFIELD AVE
CARLTON GDNS
CARLTON RD
Christ Church CE Mid Sch
HIGH ST
BOND ST
HAVEN GN
THE HAVEN
Ealing Broadway
Mus & Art Gall
Coll
ALEXANDRIA RD
FELIX RD
ENDSLEIGH RD
SINGAPORE RD
HUGH CLARK HO
ECCLESTON RD
LEELAND TERR
ST JAMES AVE
REGINA RD
MELBOURNE AVE
WESTFIELD RD
ADELAIDE RD
SYDNEY RD
BRISBANE RD
ST KILDA RD
COLDERSHAW RD
GROSVENOR RD
SEWARD RD
OAKLANDS RD
CROFT GDNS
LEIGHTON RD
NORTHFIELD RD
MANITON AVE
ELTHORNE AVE
ELTHORNE PARK RD
BALMORAL GDNS
MATTOCK LA
CULMINGTON RD
CHURCHFIELD RD
RATHGAR AVE
LAVINGTON RD
LOVEDAY RD
Allot Gdns
Walpole Park
BBC Television Film Studios
ST MARY'S RD
EALING GN
GRANGE RD
WEBSTER GDNS
THE PARK
Thames Valley Univ
YMCA
SUNNYSIDE RD
CAIRN AVE
WARWICK RD
RANELAGH RD
Tenn Cts
BEACONSFIELD RD
CHURCH LA
CLOVELLY RD
Bwg Gn
Lammas Park
NORTHFIELD AVE
DUDLEY GDNS
KINGSDOWN AVE
CAMBORNE AVE
ELERS RD
SALISBURY RD
MAYFIELD AVE
GRAHAM AVE
BERNARD AVE
WINDERMERE RD
DEVONSHIRE RD
OVERDALE RD
South Ealing
Northfields
Liby
SOUTH EALING RD
WEYMOUTH AVE
Fielding Prim Sch
BOSTON RD
WOODSTOCK AVE
RAYMOND AVE
HASLEMERE AVE
Sp Gd
Bwg Gn
Depot
Northfields Recn Gd
Pl Fld
LITTLE EALING LA
South Ealing Cemy
CHANDOS AVE
OCCUPATION LA
WINDMILL RD
EALING RD
Boston Manor
Boston Manor Pl Flds
Pav
BOSTON MANOR RD
Boston Manor Park
Gunnersbury RC Sch
Grand Union Canal
Grand Union Canal Wlk
B Sky B HQ
Ealing
Hounslow
Griffin Park Fball Gd

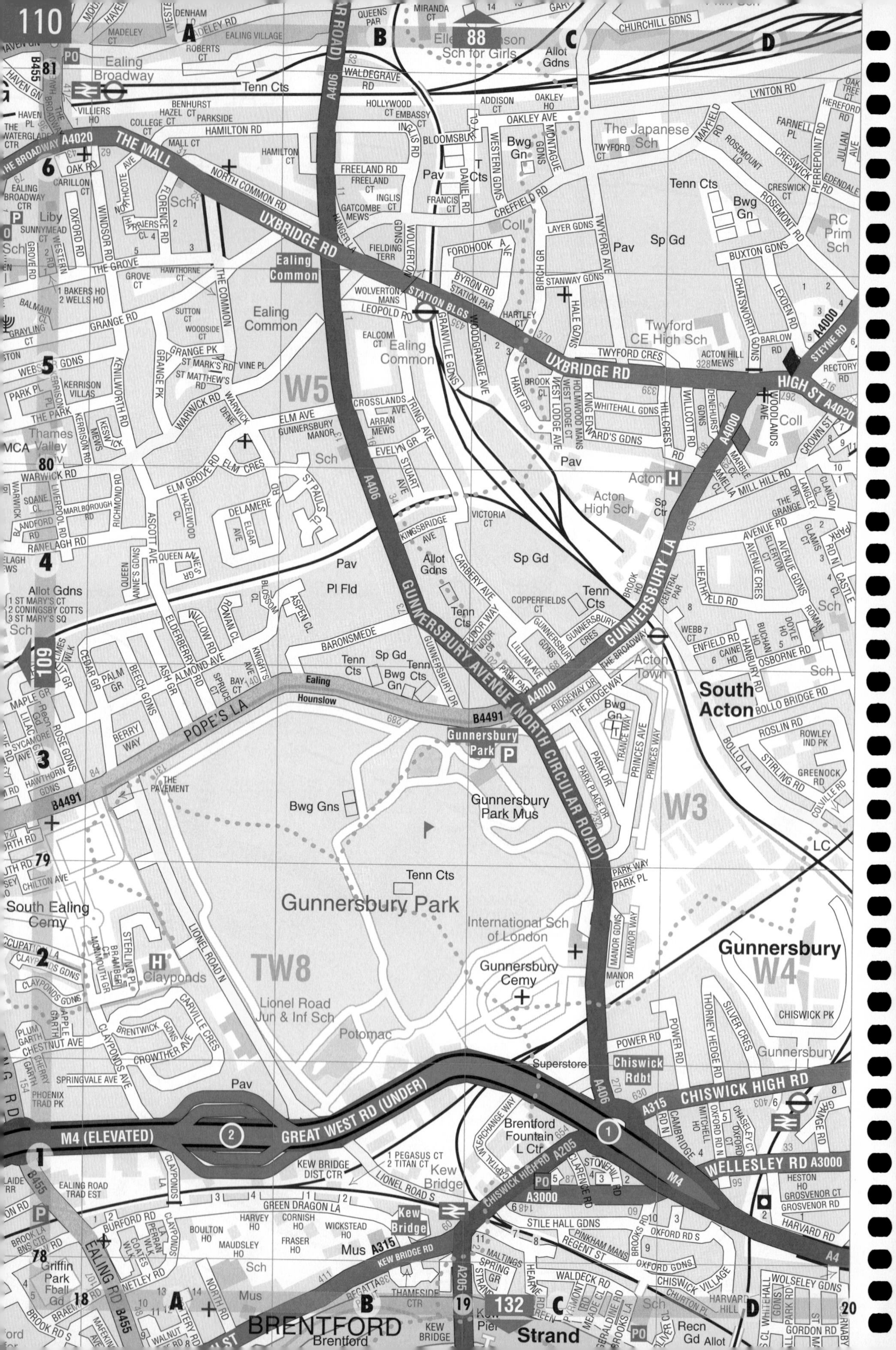

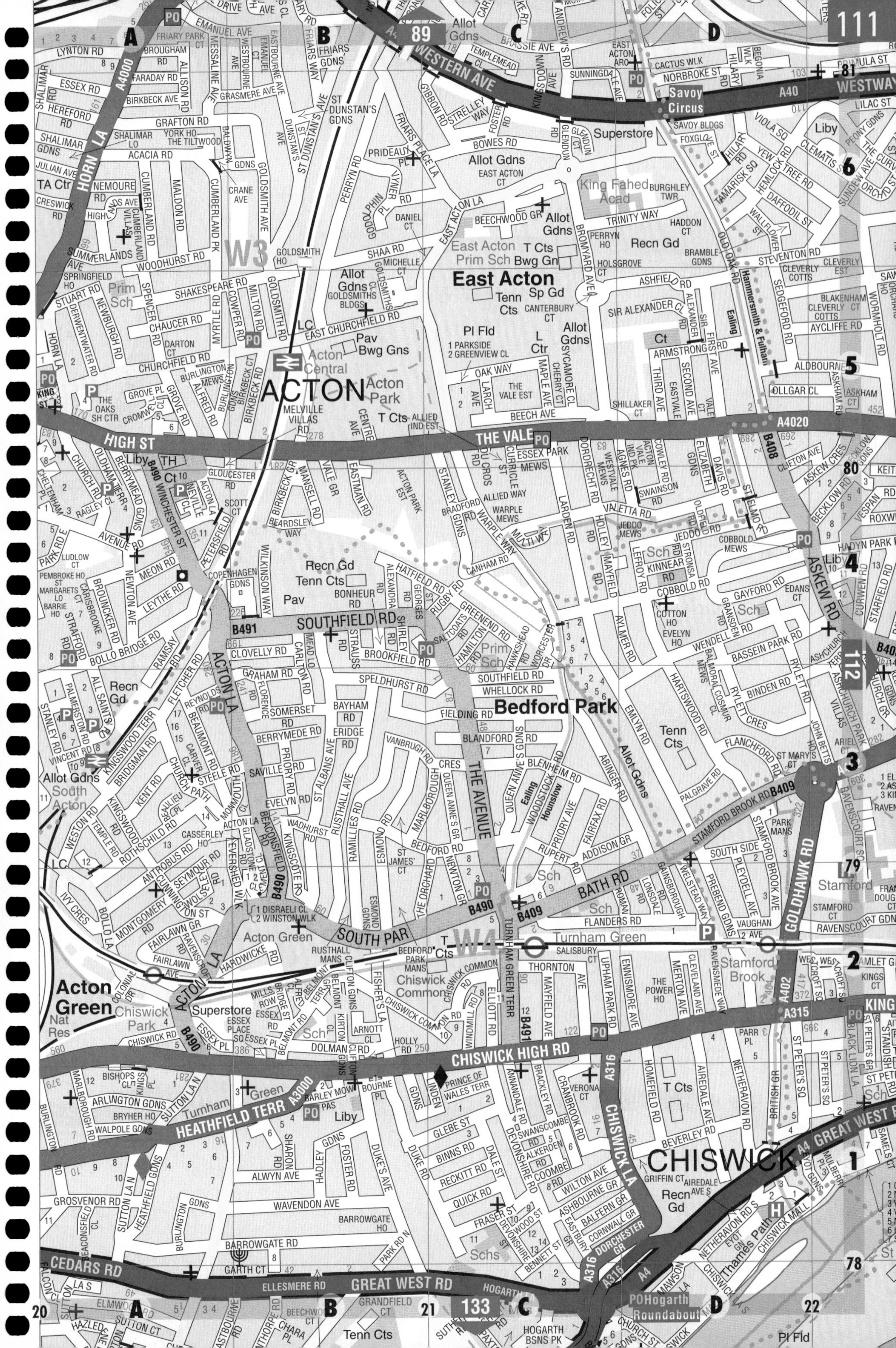
89
WESTERN AVE
WESTWAY
A40
Savoy Circus
81
HORN LA
A4000
W3
East Acton
ACTON
Acton Central
Acton Park
EAST ACTON LA
EAST CHURCHFIELD RD
CHURCHFIELD RD
HIGH ST
THE VALE
A4020
OLD OAK RD
King Fahed Acad
Superstore
SHAKESPEARE RD
WOODHURST RD
STEVENTON RD
ASHFIELD RD
ARMSTRONG RD
ALDBOURNE RD
OLLGAR CL
BEECH AVE
B408
ASKEW RD
B490
WINCHESTER ST
SOUTHFIELD RD
B491
ACTON LA
Bedford Park
THE AVENUE
BATH RD
B409
STAMFORD BROOK RD
GOLDHAWK RD
Turnham Green
SOUTH PAR
W4
Acton Green
Chiswick Common
Chiswick Park
Stamford Brook
CHISWICK HIGH RD
A315
A316
CHISWICK LA
HEATHFIELD TERR
A3000
CHISWICK
A4
GREAT WEST RD
CEDARS RD
Hogarth Roundabout
Thames Path
CHISWICK MALL
Recn Gd
Allot Gdns
Tenn Cts
112
80
79
78
133
20
21
22
A
B
C
D
1
2
3
4
5
6

112
90
111
134
A
B
C
D
22
23
24
81
80
79
78
6
5
4
3
2
1
WESTWAY
WESTWAY (ELEVATED ROAD)
White City
Shepherd's Bush
W12
W11
W14
W6
HAMMERSMITH
Brook Green
River Thames
Thames Path
UXBRIDGE RD
GOLDHAWK RD
GLENTHORNE RD
KING ST
HAMMERSMITH RD
GREAT WEST RD
Hammersmith Flyover
WOOD LA
SHEPHERD'S BUSH RD
FULHAM PALACE RD
ASKEW RD
PADDENSWICK RD
DALLING RD
BEADON RD
TALGARTH RD
WEST CROSS ROUTE
Holland Park Rdbt
BBC Television Ctr
QPR Fball Gd
Ravenscourt Park
Hammersmith Broadway
HAMMERSMITH BRIDGE
Charing Cross
Shepherd's Bush Common
Phoenix High Sch
Wormholt Park
LONSDALE RD
CASTELNAU

A
B
C
D
91
245
244
254
114
135
255
W11
W8
W14
SW5
Notting Hill
Holland Park
KENSINGTON
West Kensington
Earl's Court
West Brompton
Kensington Olympia
Olympia Ex Ctr
Earl's Court Ex Ctr
Kensington Palace
Kensington Palace Green
Bayswater
Queensway
High Street Kensington
Notting Hill Gate
Holland Park Tenn Gd
Holland Park Sch
Avondale Park
Ladbroke Square Gardens
The Queen's Club
Barons Court Cemy
Round Pond
Diana Princess of Wales Memorial Walk
THE BROAD WLK
THE DIAL WLK
Orme Square Gate
Black Lion Gate
Inverness Terrace Gate
Palace Gate
Gall & Mus
Kensington Village
NOTTING HILL GATE
HOLLAND PARK AVE
KENSINGTON HIGH ST
KENSINGTON CHURCH ST
KENSINGTON PARK RD
LADBROKE GR
PEMBRIDGE VILLAS
QUEENSWAY
HOLLAND RD
ADDISON RD
HAMMERSMITH RD
WARWICK RD
WARWICK GDNS
PEMBROKE RD
CROMWELL RD
WEST CROMWELL RD
EARL'S COURT RD
OLD BROMPTON RD
TALGARTH RD
NORTH END RD
CAMPDEN HILL RD
HOLLAND WLK
ADDISON CRES
LANSDOWNE WLK
PORTLAND RD
CLARENDON RD
ABINGDON RD
MARLOES RD
KNARESBOROUGH
FINBOROUGH RD
REDCLIFFE
A402
A4204
A4206
A315
A3220
A4
A3218
B450
B415
B405
B316
B317
B411
B325
24
25
26
78
79
80
81
1
2
3
4
5
6

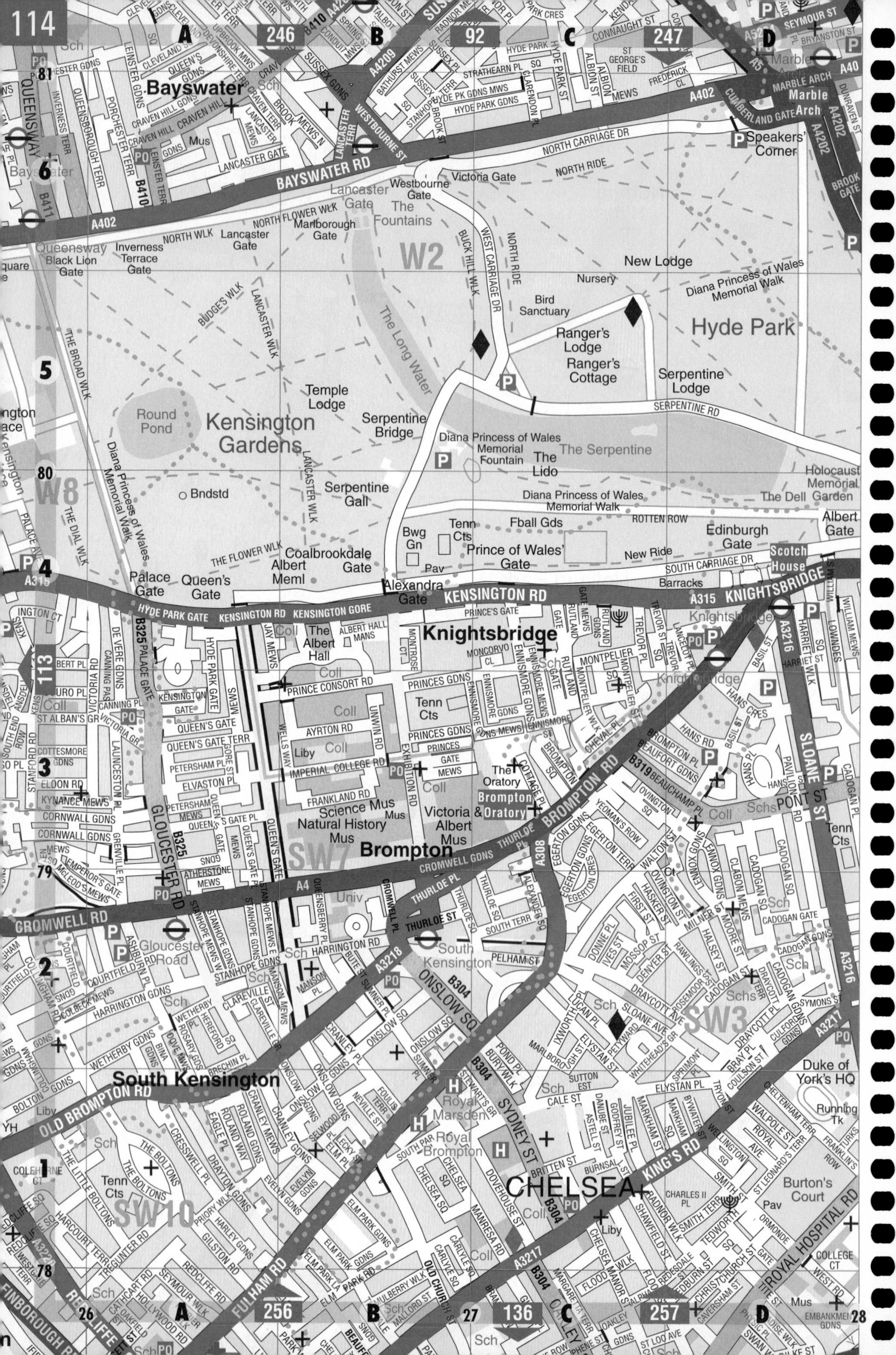
A
B
C
D
246
92
247
Bayswater
Queensway
Bayswater Rd
A402
North Carriage Dr
North Ride
Victoria Gate
Speakers' Corner
Marble Arch
Cumberland Gate
Lancaster Gate
Westbourne Gate
The Fountains
Marlborough Gate
North Flower Wlk
North Wlk
Lancaster Gate
Inverness Terrace Gate
Queensway Black Lion Gate
W2
New Lodge
Nursery
Diana Princess of Wales Memorial Walk
Bird Sanctuary
Ranger's Lodge
Ranger's Cottage
Hyde Park
Serpentine Lodge
Serpentine Rd
The Long Water
West Carriage Dr
Buck Hill Wlk
The Broad Wlk
Round Pond
Kensington Gardens
Temple Lodge
Serpentine Bridge
Diana Princess of Wales Memorial Fountain
The Lido
The Serpentine
Holocaust Memorial Garden
The Dell
Serpentine Gall
Bndstd
Diana Princess of Wales Memorial Walk
W8
The Dial Wlk
Rotten Row
Albert Gate
Edinburgh Gate
Bwg Gn
Tenn Cts
Fball Gds
Prince of Wales' Gate
New Ride
South Carriage Dr
Scotch House
The Flower Wlk
Coalbrookdale Gate
Albert Meml
Pav
Palace Gate
Queen's Gate
Alexandra Gate
Barracks
A315
Kensington Rd
Knightsbridge
Hyde Park Gate
Kensington Gore
Prince's Gate
113
The Albert Hall
Coll
Knightsbridge
Prince Consort Rd
Princes Gdns
Imperial College Rd
Exhibition Rd
The Oratory
Brompton Oratory
Science Mus
Natural History Mus
Victoria & Albert Mus
Brompton
SW7
Brompton Rd
Beauchamp Pl
Pont St
Sloane St
Gloucester Rd
Cromwell Rd
Cromwell Gdns
Thurloe Pl
A4
Queen's Gate
Gloucester Road
South Kensington
Pelham St
Onslow Sq
Fulham Rd
SW3
Sloane Ave
Draycott Ave
Duke of York's HQ
Running Tk
South Kensington
Old Brompton Rd
Royal Marsden
Royal Brompton
Sydney St
Chelsea
King's Rd
Burton's Court
Royal Hospital Rd
The Boltons
SW10
Fulham Rd
Redcliffe Gdns
256
136
257
Embankment Gdns

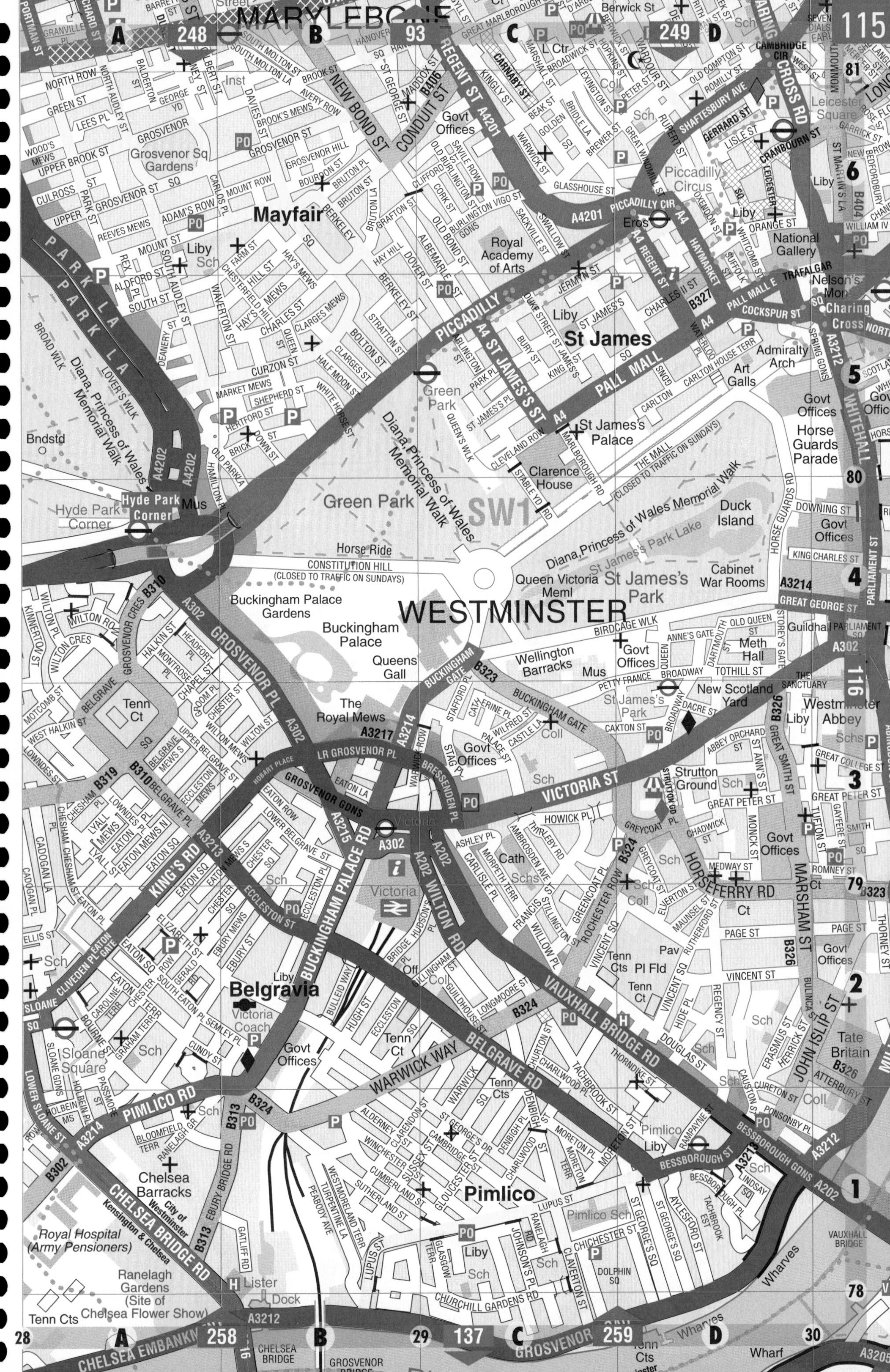

MARYLEBONE
Mayfair
St James
WESTMINSTER
SW1
Belgravia
Pimlico
Green Park
Buckingham Palace
Buckingham Palace Gardens
St James's Park
Piccadilly Circus
National Gallery
Royal Academy of Arts
Westminster Abbey
New Scotland Yard
Tate Britain
Chelsea Barracks
Royal Hospital (Army Pensioners)
Ranelagh Gardens (Site of Chelsea Flower Show)
Sloane Square
Victoria
Hyde Park Corner
Grosvenor Sq Gardens
Trafalgar Sq
Charing Cross
Horse Guards Parade
Duck Island
Cabinet War Rooms
Clarence House
St James's Palace
Wellington Barracks
The Royal Mews
Queens Gall
PICCADILLY
PALL MALL
PARK LA
GROSVENOR PL
VICTORIA ST
VAUXHALL BRIDGE RD
BELGRAVE RD
BUCKINGHAM PALACE RD
WHITEHALL
REGENT ST
NEW BOND ST
CHELSEA BRIDGE RD
PIMLICO RD
KING'S RD

250
94
251
Royal Courts of Justice
Aldwych
Strand
Somerset House
Covent Garden
Old Covent Garden
Leicester Square
Long Acre
Cambridge Circ
Charing Cross Rd
Temple
Victoria Embankment
Inner Temple Garden
Temple Pier
Blackfriars Underpass
Blackfriars Bridge
Puddle Dock
Blackfriars
River Bus Route
Millennium Bridge
King's Reach
River Thames
Waterloo Bridge
National Gallery
Trafalgar Sq
Nelson's Mon
Charing Cross
Northumberland Ave
Cleopatra's Needle
Embankment Pier
Embankment
Festival Pier
National Theatre
Gallery
Royal Festival Hall
Hungerford Bridge (Foot and Rail)
Admiralty Arch
Art Galls
Whitehall
Horse Guards Parade
Horseguards Ave
Govt Offices
Downing St
Richmond Terr
King Charles St
Parliament St
Westminster
Bridge St
Great George St
Westminster Bridge
Westminster Bridge Rd
Jubilee Gdns
London Eye
Old County Hall
South Bank
York Rd
Waterloo
Waterloo Int
Waterloo Rd
Waterloo East
The Cut
Stamford St
Upper Ground
Southwark St
Southwark
Blackfriars Rd
Tate Modern
Hopton St
Lavington St
Borough Rd
St George's Cir
London Rd
Elephant & Castle
Lambeth North
Baylis Rd
Lambeth
New Palace Yard
Houses of Parliament
Old Palace Yard
Westminster Abbey
Scotland Yard
Guildhall
Meth Hall
Albert Embankment
St Thomas'
Lambeth Palace Rd
Archbishop's Park
Lambeth Palace
Lambeth Rd
Lambeth Bridge
Millbank
Abingdon St
Great Peter St
Marsham St
Horseferry Rd
Tate Britain
John Islip St
Atterbury St
Thames Path
Geraldine Mary Harmsworth Park
Imperial War Mus
St George's Rd
Kennington Rd
SE11
Kennington Lane
Black Prince Rd
Vauxhall Walk
Spring Gardens
Vauxhall
Vauxhall Bridge
Vauxhall Cross
Bessborough Gdns
Kennington
Kennington Park Rd
Newington
Newington Butts
SE17
Harleyford Rd
The Oval
Durham St
Wharves
Wharf
Parry St
115
260
138
261
80
81
79
78
30
31
32
A
B
C
D
1
2
3
4
5
6

CITY OF LONDON
BERMONDSEY
The Borough
Walworth
Whitechapel
EC4
EC3
E1
SE1
SE16
SE17
SE15
UPPER THAMES ST
LOWER THAMES ST
SOUTHWARK BRIDGE RD
SOUTHWARK ST
BOROUGH HIGH ST
TOOLEY ST
LONG LA
GREAT DOVER ST
NEW KENT RD
OLD KENT RD
GRANGE RD
SOUTHWARK PARK RD
TOWER BRIDGE RD
ABBEY ST
DRUID ST
BERMONDSEY ST
WALWORTH RD
DUNTON RD
UNION ST
EAST SMITHFIELD
TOWER HILL
Thames Path
River Bus Route
Bankside Pier
Swan Lane Pier
Custom House
London Bridge City Pier
Tower Millennium Pier
St Katharine Pier
Butler's Wharf Pier
City Hall
The Globe Theatre
The Tower
Traitors Gate
Elephant & Castle
Bricklayers Arms
Caledonian Market
Burgess Park
252
95
253
118
263
262
139
32
33
34

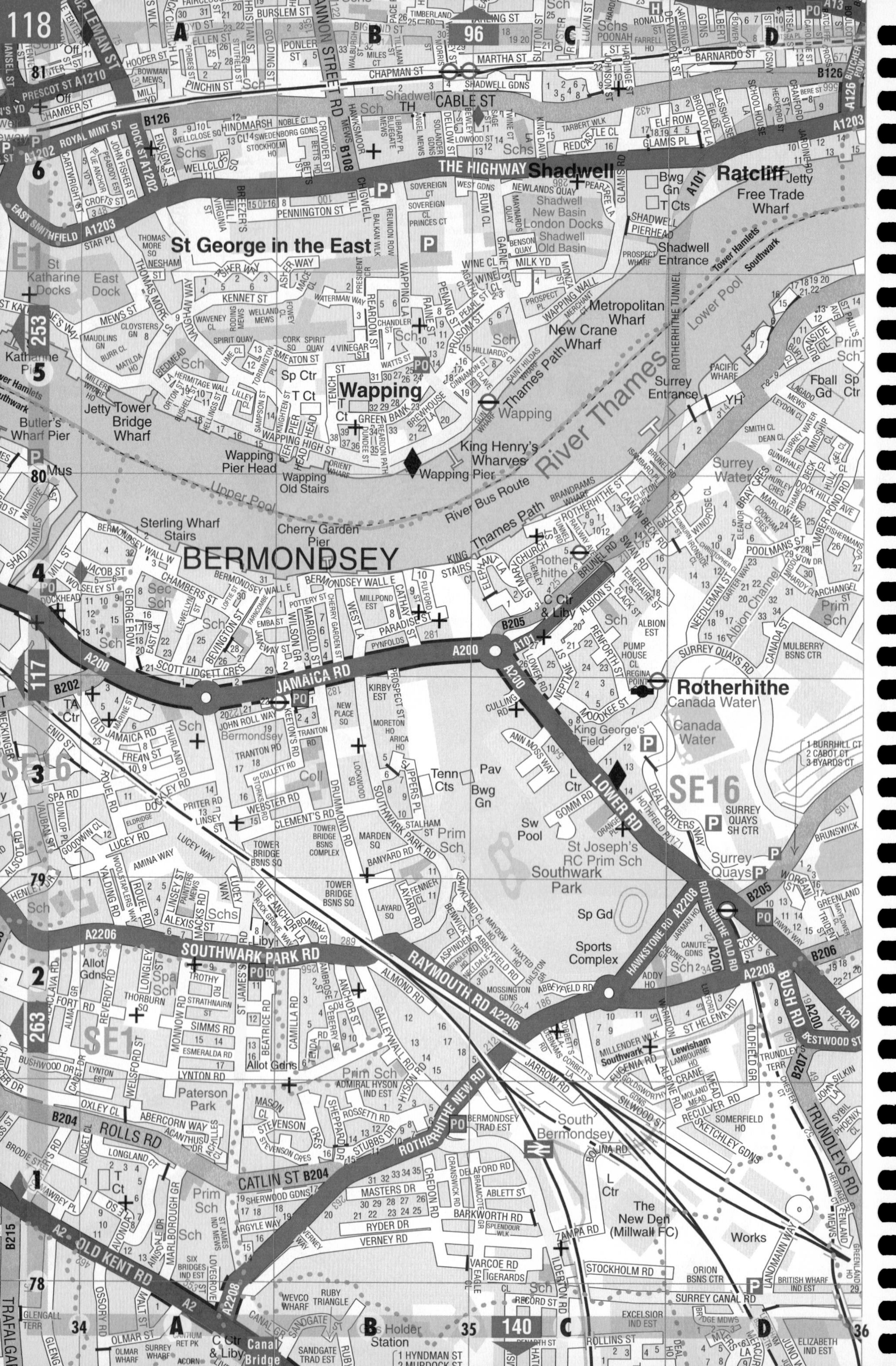
118
96
St George in the East
Shadwell
Ratcliff
Free Trade Wharf
Shadwell New Basin
London Docks
Shadwell Old Basin
Shadwell Entrance
St Katharine Docks
East Dock
Wapping
Metropolitan Wharf
New Crane Wharf
Thames Path
Lower Pool
River Thames
Surrey Entrance
Tower Bridge Wharf
Butler's Wharf Pier
Wapping Pier Head
Wapping Old Stairs
Wapping Pier
King Henry's Wharves
River Bus Route
Upper Pool
Sterling Wharf Stairs
Cherry Garden Pier
BERMONDSEY
Surrey Water
Rotherhithe
Canada Water
King George's Field
Southwark Park
St Joseph's RC Prim Sch
Surrey Quays
Surrey Quays Sh Ctr
Sports Complex
Paterson Park
South Bermondsey
The New Den (Millwall FC)
Gas Holder Station
Canal Bridge
THE HIGHWAY
JAMAICA RD
SOUTHWARK PARK RD
RAYMOUTH RD
LOWER RD
ROTHERHITHE NEW RD
OLD KENT RD
ROLLS RD
CATLIN ST
SE1
SE16
E1
140
117
253
263

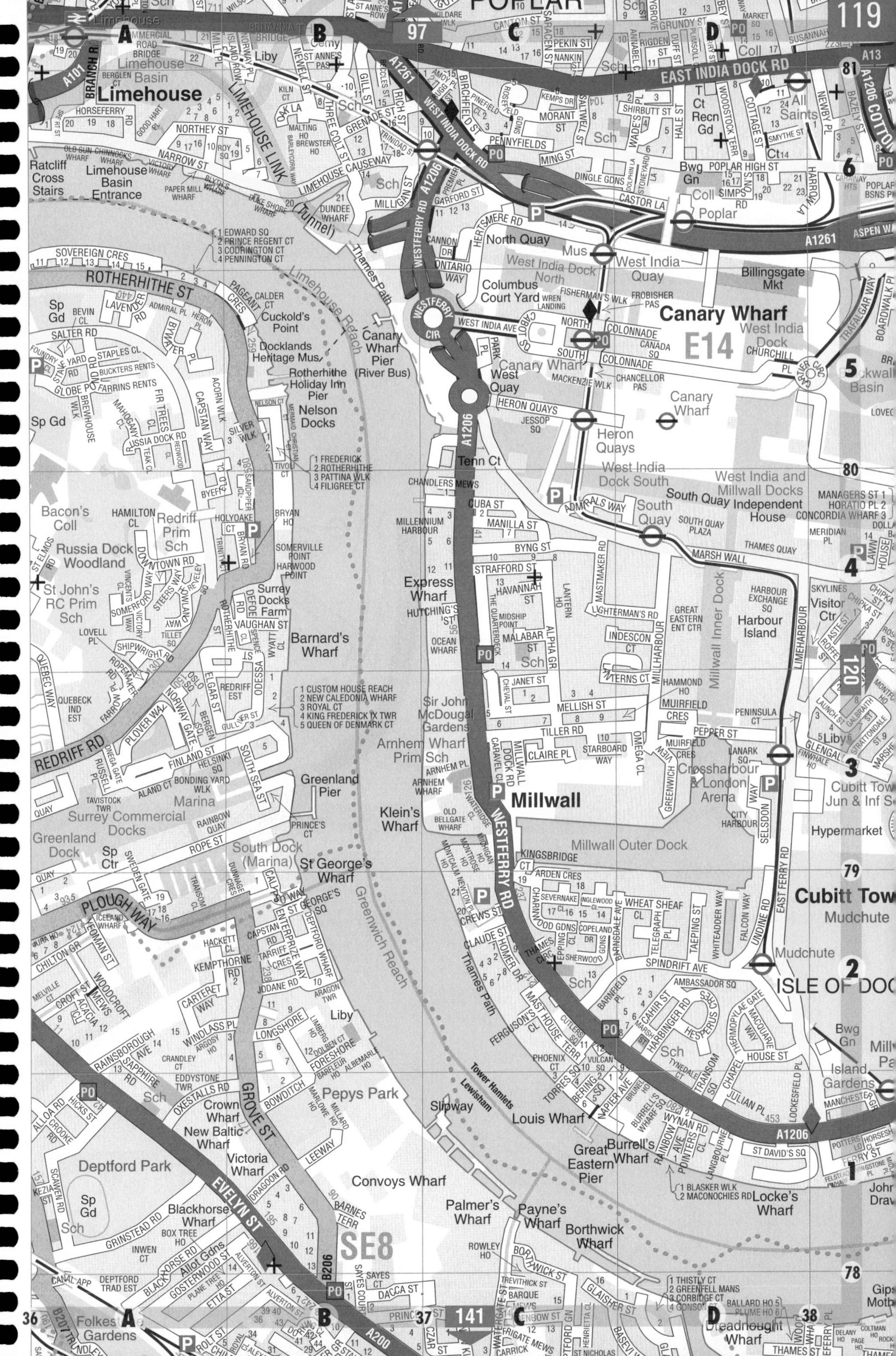

POPLAR
97
Limehouse
Limehouse Basin
Ratcliff Cross Stairs
Limehouse Basin Entrance
LIMEHOUSE LINK
LIMEHOUSE CAUSEWAY
NARROW ST
EAST INDIA DOCK RD
WEST INDIA DOCK RD
POPLAR HIGH ST
A1261
A1206
A13
WESTFERRY RD
North Quay
West India Quay
West India Dock North
Billingsgate Mkt
Columbus Court Yard
Canary Wharf
E14
West India Dock
Heron Quays
West India Dock South
West India and Millwall Docks
South Quay
MARSH WALL
Harbour Island
Millwall Inner Dock
Millwall
Millwall Outer Dock
Crossharbour & London Arena
Cubitt Town
Mudchute
ISLE OF DOGS
Island Gardens
Limehouse Reach
Greenwich Reach
Thames Path
ROTHERHITHE ST
Cuckold's Point
Docklands Heritage Mus
Rotherhithe Holiday Inn Pier
Nelson Docks
Canary Wharf Pier (River Bus)
Russia Dock Woodland
Surrey Docks Farm
Barnard's Wharf
REDRIFF RD
Surrey Commercial Docks
Greenland Dock
Greenland Pier
South Dock (Marina)
St George's Wharf
PLOUGH WAY
GROVE ST
EVELYN ST
Deptford Park
Pepys Park
Convoys Wharf
SE8
Sir John McDougal Gardens
Arnhem Wharf Prim Sch
Klein's Wharf
Express Wharf
Louis Wharf
Burrell's Wharf
Great Eastern Pier
Locke's Wharf
Palmer's Wharf
Payne's Wharf
Borthwick Wharf
Dreadnought Wharf
Tower Hamlets
Lewisham
A B C D
36 37 38
141
120
81 80 79 78
1 2 3 4 5 6

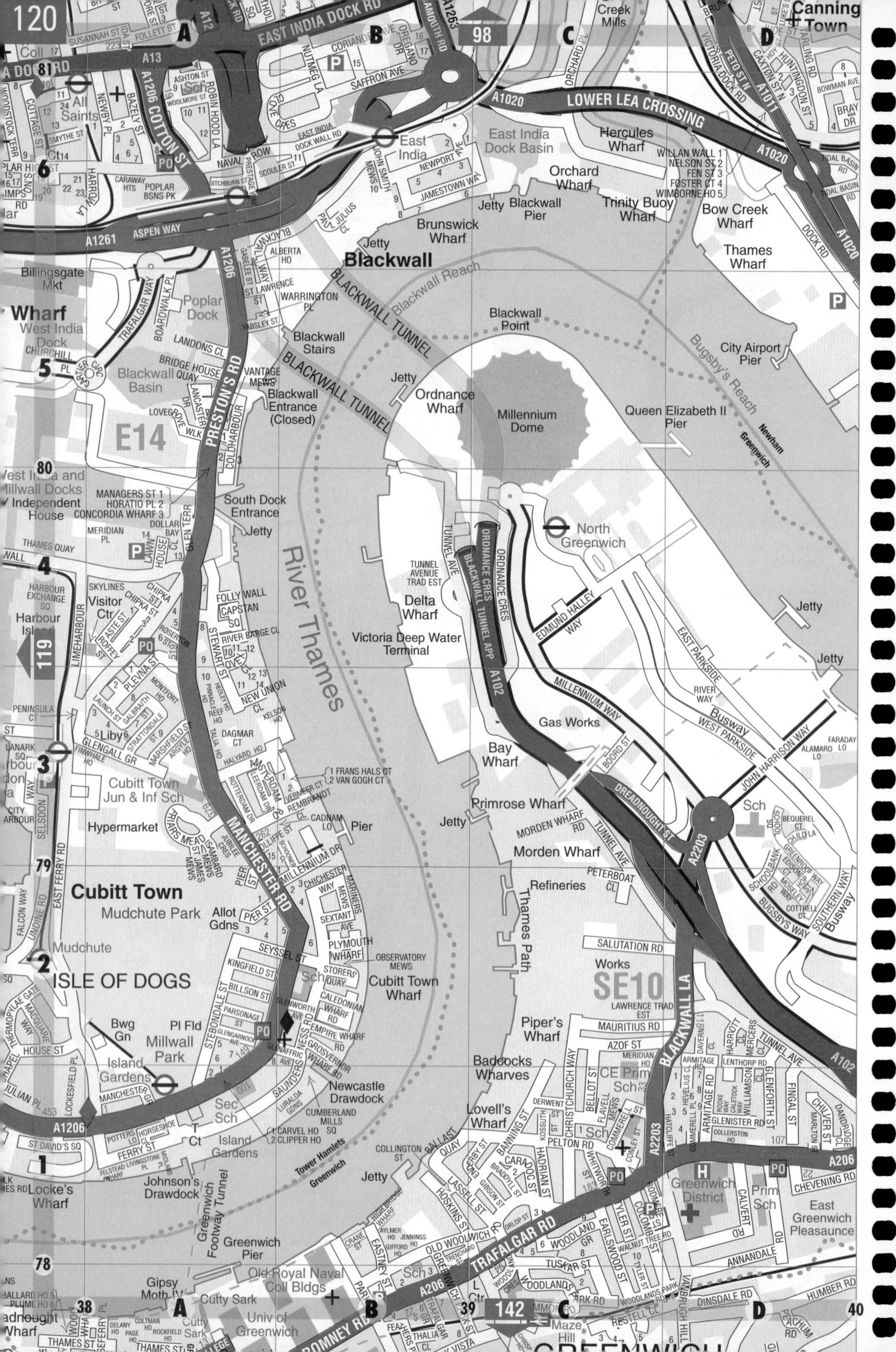

Canning Town
Creek Mills
EAST INDIA DOCK RD
LOWER LEA CROSSING
East India Dock Basin
Hercules Wharf
Orchard Wharf
Trinity Buoy Wharf
Bow Creek Wharf
Thames Wharf
Blackwall Pier
Brunswick Wharf
Blackwall
BLACKWALL TUNNEL
Blackwall Reach
Blackwall Point
Blackwall Stairs
City Airport Pier
Bugsby's Reach
Ordnance Wharf
Millennium Dome
Queen Elizabeth II Pier
Newham
Greenwich
North Greenwich
All Saints
East India
Billingsgate Mkt
Poplar Dock
West India Dock
Blackwall Basin
Blackwall Entrance (Closed)
E14
PRESTON'S RD
South Dock Entrance
River Thames
Tunnel Avenue Trad Est
Delta Wharf
Victoria Deep Water Terminal
EDMUND HALLEY WAY
MILLENNIUM WAY
Gas Works
Busway
JOHN HARRISON WAY
Bay Wharf
Primrose Wharf
Morden Wharf
Refineries
Thames Path
SE10
Works
Piper's Wharf
Badcocks Wharves
Lovell's Wharf
BLACKWALL LA
TUNNEL AVE
Visitor Ctr
Harbour Island
Cubitt Town Jun & Inf Sch
Hypermarket
Cubitt Town
Mudchute Park
Mudchute
ISLE OF DOGS
MANCHESTER RD
Millwall Park
Island Gardens
Cubitt Town Wharf
Newcastle Drawdock
Johnson's Drawdock
Greenwich Footway Tunnel
Greenwich Pier
Tower Hamlets
Greenwich
Locke's Wharf
Gipsy Moth IV
Cutty Sark
Old Royal Naval Coll Bldgs
Univ of Greenwich
TRAFALGAR RD
ROMNEY RD
Greenwich District
East Greenwich Pleasaunce
Maze Hill
GREENWICH
98
119
142

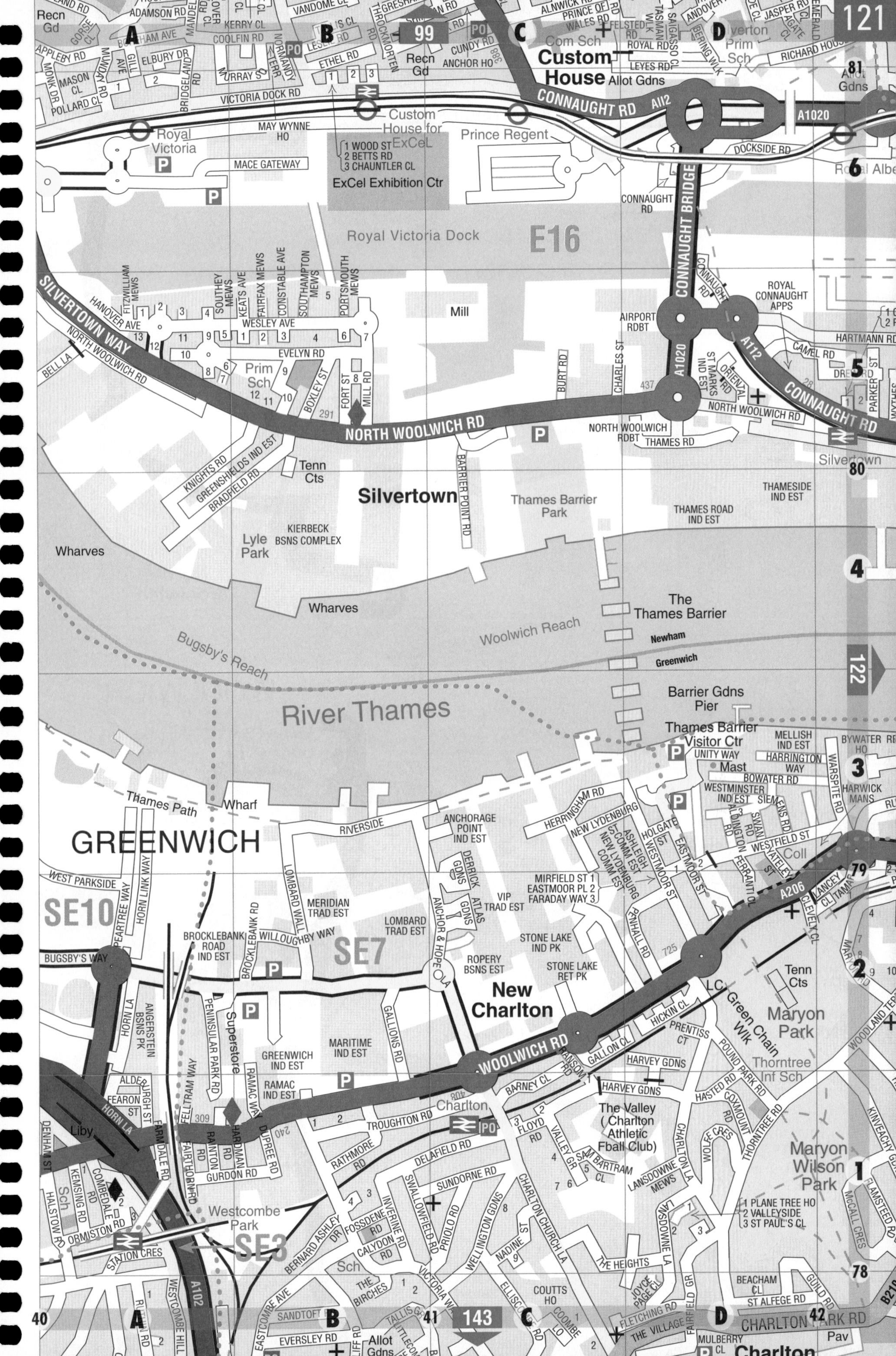
Custom House
Royal Victoria Dock
E16
Royal Victoria
Custom House for ExCeL
Prince Regent
ExCel Exhibition Ctr
1 WOOD ST
2 BETTS RD
3 CHAUNTLER CL
CONNAUGHT RD
CONNAUGHT BRIDGE
VICTORIA DOCK RD
SILVERTOWN WAY
NORTH WOOLWICH RD
Silvertown
Thames Barrier Park
Lyle Park
KIERBECK BSNS COMPLEX
Wharves
Woolwich Reach
Bugsby's Reach
River Thames
Newham
Greenwich
The Thames Barrier
Barrier Gdns Pier
Thames Barrier Visitor Ctr
GREENWICH
SE10
SE7
SE3
Thames Path
New Charlton
WOOLWICH RD
The Valley (Charlton Athletic Fball Club)
Maryon Park
Maryon Wilson Park
1 PLANE TREE HO
2 VALLEYSIDE
3 ST PAUL'S CL
MIRFIELD ST 1
EASTMOOR PL 2
FARADAY WAY 3
Westcombe Park
Charlton
CHARLTON PARK RD
99
122
143

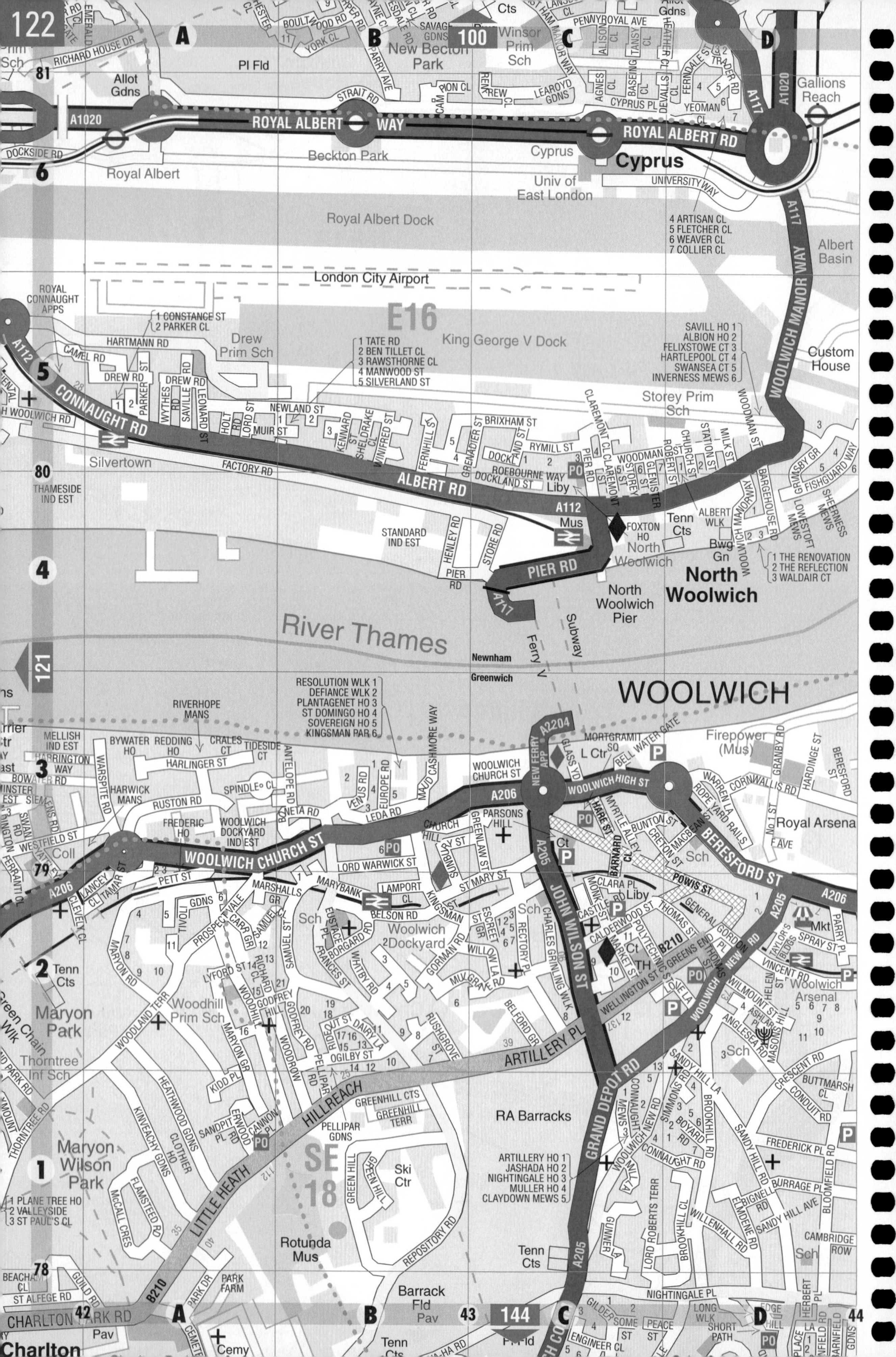
ROYAL ALBERT WAY
ROYAL ALBERT RD
Beckton Park
Royal Albert
Cyprus
Univ of East London
Royal Albert Dock
London City Airport
E16
King George V Dock
CONNAUGHT RD
ALBERT RD
Silvertown
PIER RD
North Woolwich
North Woolwich Pier
River Thames
WOOLWICH
WOOLWICH CHURCH ST
WOOLWICH HIGH ST
BERESFORD ST
JOHN WILSON ST
GRAND DEPOT RD
Woolwich Dockyard
Woolwich Arsenal
Royal Arsenal
RA Barracks
Rotunda Mus
Maryon Park
Maryon Wilson Park
SE 18
Charlton
WOOLWICH MANOR WAY
Custom House
Albert Basin
Gallions Reach
New Beckton Park

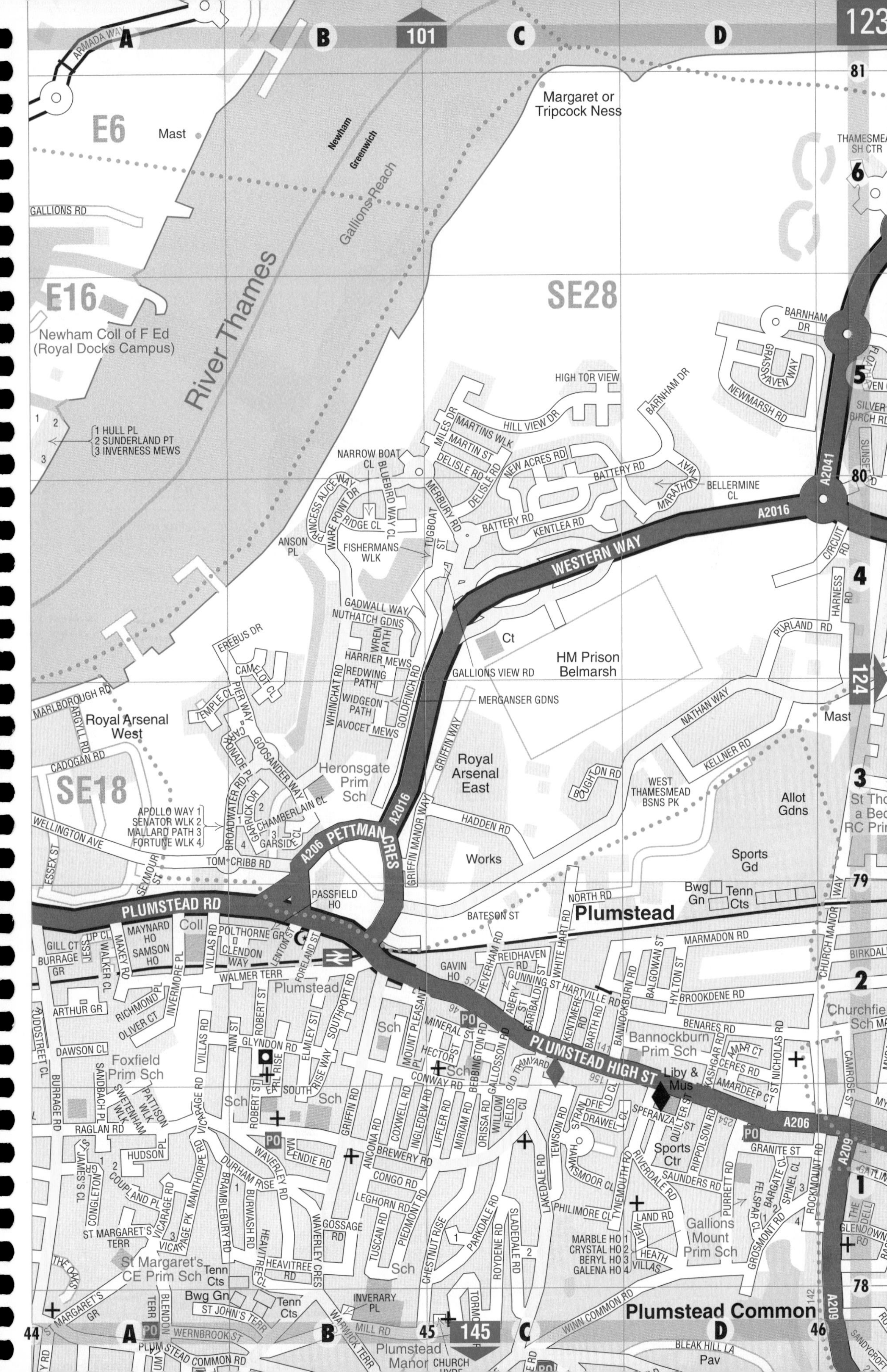
A
B
101
C
D
81
ARMADA WAY
E6
Mast
Margaret or
Tripcock Ness
Newham
Greenwich
Gallions Reach
THAMESMEAD
SH CTR
6
GALLIONS RD
River Thames
E16
SE28
Newham Coll of F Ed
(Royal Docks Campus)
BARNHAM
DR
GRASSHAVEN WAY
NEWMARSH RD
HIGH TOR VIEW
BARNHAM DR
5
SILVER
BIRCH RD
SUNSET RD
1 HULL PL
2 SUNDERLAND PT
3 INVERNESS MEWS
HILL VIEW DR
MARTINS WLK
MARTIN ST
MILES DR
NARROW BOAT
CL
BLUEBIRD WAY
DELISLE RD
NEW ACRES RD
BATTERY RD
MARATHON WAY
BELLERMINE
CL
A2041
80
PRINCESS ALICE WAY
WARE POINT DR
RIDGE CL
MERBURY RD
A2016
BATTERY RD
KENTLEA RD
ANSON
PL
FISHERMANS
WLK
TUGBOAT ST
WESTERN WAY
CIRCUIT RD
4
HARNESS RD
GADWALL WAY
NUTHATCH GDNS
WREN PATH
PURLAND RD
EREBUS DR
CAMELOT CL
HARRIER MEWS
REDWING
PATH
Ct
HM Prison
Belmarsh
124
GALLIONS VIEW RD
MARLBOROUGH RD
TEMPLE CL
PIER WAY
WIDGEON
PATH
GOLDFINCH RD
MERGANSER GDNS
NATHAN WAY
Mast
Royal Arsenal
West
ARGYLL RD
AVOCET MEWS
WHINCHAT RD
GRIFFIN WAY
CADOGAN RD
CARRONADE PL
GOOSANDER WAY
Heronsgate
Prim
Sch
Royal
Arsenal
East
KELLNER RD
SE18
BOUGHTON RD
WEST
THAMESMEAD
BSNS PK
3
Allot
Gdns
St Thom
a Beck
RC Prim
GARRICK DR
CHAMBERLAIN CL
APOLLO WAY 1
SENATOR WLK 2
MALLARD PATH 3
FORTUNE WLK 4
WELLINGTON AVE
BROADWATER RD
GARSIDE CL
A206 PETTMAN CRES
HADDEN RD
GRIFFIN MANOR WAY
ESSEX ST
SEYMOUR ST
TOM CRIBB RD
Works
Sports
Gd
PASSFIELD
HO
NORTH RD
Bwg
Gn
Tenn
Cts
79
PLUMSTEAD RD
Coll
BATESON ST
Plumstead
MAYNARD
HO
SAMSON
HO
POLTHORNE GR
CLENDON
WAY
LENTON ST
FORELAND ST
MARMADON RD
BIRKDALE RD
GILL CT
JESSUP CL
BURRAGE
GR
MAXEY RD
WALKER CL
VILLAS RD
REIDHAVEN
RD
HEVERHAM RD
WHITE HART RD
BALGOWAN ST
HYLTON ST
CHURCH MANOR WAY
WALMER TERR
Plumstead
GAVIN
HO
GUNNING ST
HARTVILLE RD
BROOKDENE RD
2
ARTHUR GR
RICHMOND PL
INVERMORE PL
OLIVER CT
ROBERT ST
SOUTHPORT RD
Sch
MOUNT PLEASANT
PO
MINERAL ST
ABERY ST
GARIBALDI ST
KENTMERE RD
BARTH RD
BANNOCKBURN RD
Bannockburn
Prim Sch
BENARES RD
Churchfield
Sch
DAWSON CL
Foxfield
Prim Sch
ANN ST
VILLAS RD
GLYNDON RD
ELMLEY ST
RISE WAY
HECTOR ST
BEBBINGTON RD
GALLOSSON RD
OLD TRAMYARD
PLUMSTEAD HIGH ST
Liby &
Mus
KASHGAR RD
AMAR CT
CERES RD
AMARDEEP CT
ST NICHOLAS RD
CAMROSE ST
SANDBACH PL
SWETENHAM
WLK
PATTISON
WALK
VICARAGE RD
EARL RISE
SOUTH RISE
Sch
ROBERT ST
GRIFFIN RD
CONWAY RD
COXWELL RD
INGLEDEW RD
LIFFLER RD
MIRIAM RD
ORISSA RD
WILLOW
FIELDS CL
TEWSON RD
STRANDFIELD CL
DRAWELL CL
SPERANZA ST
QUILTER ST
RIPPOLSON RD
A206
BURRAGE RD
RAGLAN RD
HUDSON
PL
PO
MAJENDIE RD
ANCONA RD
BREWERY RD
HAWKSMOOR CL
TYNEMOUTH RD
Sports
Ctr
RIVERDALE RD
GRANITE ST
A209
ST JAMES'S CL
CONGLETON GR
COUPLAND PL
VICARAGE RD
MANTHORPE RD
DURHAM RISE
BRAMBLEBURY RD
BURWASH RD
WAVERLEY RD
CONGO RD
LEGHORN RD
LAKEDALE RD
SAUNDERS RD
PURRETT RD
BARGATE CL
SPINEL CL
FELSPAR CL
GROSMONT RD
ROCKMOUNT RD
1
GATLING RD
THE DELL
GLENDOWN RD
BASTION
PHILIMORE CL
LAND RD
Gallions
Mount
Prim Sch
ST MARGARET'S
TERR
VICARAGE PK
GOSSAGE
RD
HEAVITREE CL
WAVERLEY CRES
TUSCAN RD
PIEDMONT RD
CHESTNUT RISE
PARKDALE RD
ROYDENE RD
SLADEDALE RD
MARBLE HO 1
CRYSTAL HO 2
BERYL HO 3
GALENA HO 4
VIEW
HEATH
VILLAS
THE OAKS
St Margaret's
CE Prim Sch
Tenn
Cts
HEAVITREE
RD
Sch
78
Bwg Gn
ST JOHN'S TERR
Tenn
Cts
INVERARY
PL
TORMOUNT RD
WINN COMMON RD
Plumstead Common
ST MARGARET'S GR
TERR
BLENDON
44
A
PO
WERNBROOK ST
B
WARWICK TERR
MILL RD
45
145
C
D
46
PLUMSTEAD COMMON RD
Plumstead
Manor
CHURCH
BLEAK HILL LA
Pav
SANDYCROFT

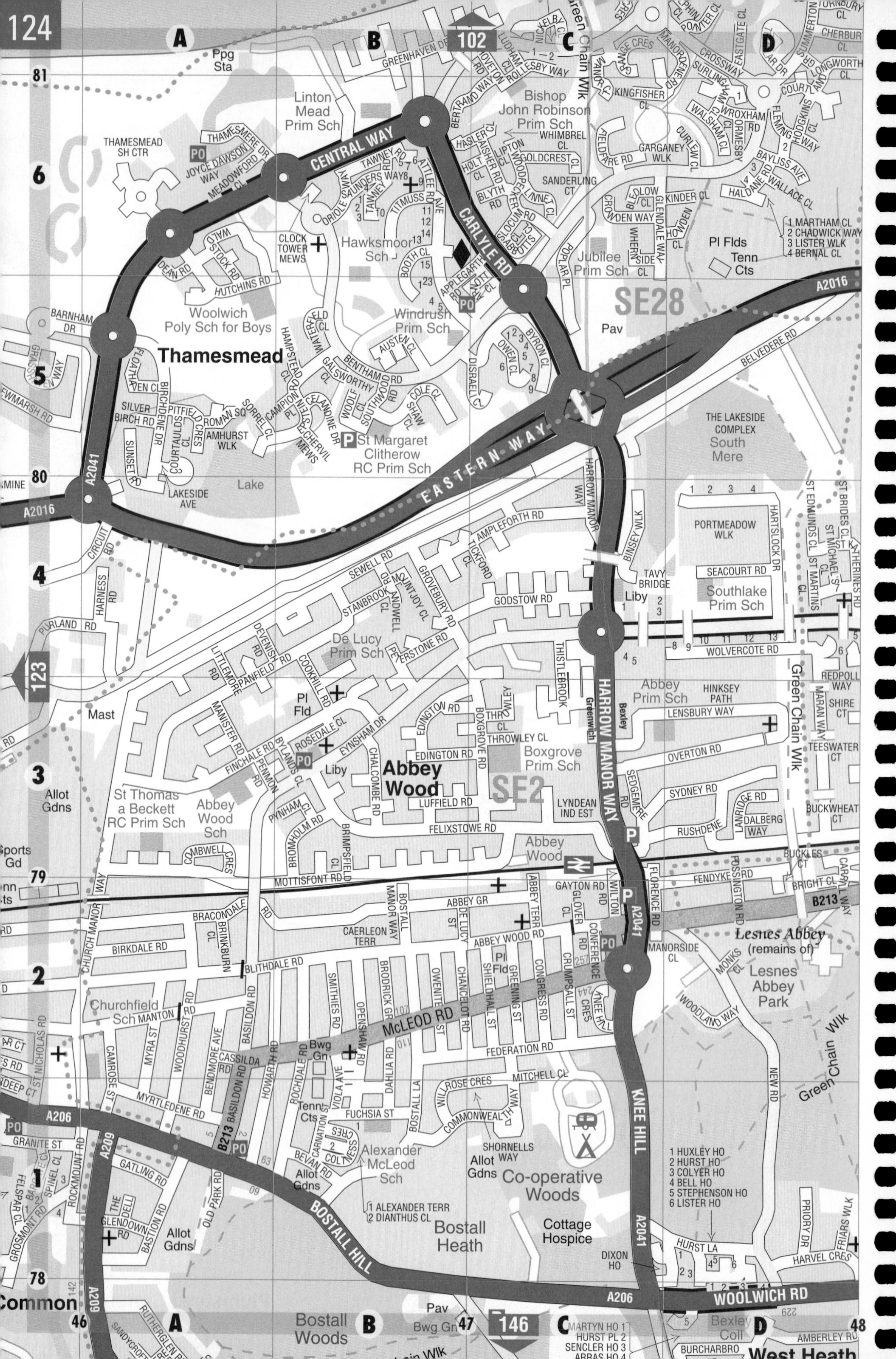

124
A
B
102
C
D
81
Ppg Sta
GREENHAVEN DR
LUDHAM CL
NICKELBY CL
Green Chain Wlk
GRANGE CRES
MANOR DENE RD
EASTGATE CL
SUMMERTON WAY
TURNBURY CL
CHERBURY CL
LONGWORTH CL
CROSSWAY
SURLINGHAM CL
ROLLESBY WAY
LOVETON RD
BERTRAND WAY
Bishop John Robinson Prim Sch
KINGFISHER CL
WROXHAM RD
ORMESBY
WALSHAM CL
COURTLAND GR
FLEMING WAY
HODGKINS WAY
Linton Mead Prim Sch
THAMESMEAD SH CTR
THAMESMERE DR
JOYCE DAWSON WAY
MEADOWFORD CL
PO
CENTRAL WAY
TAWNEY RD
SAUNDERS WAY
ORIOLE WAY
ATTLEE AVE
TITMUSS AVE
HASLER CL
HOLT CL
FISHER RD
LIPTON CL
WHIMBREL CL
GOLDCREST CL
SANDERLING CT
GARGANEY WLK
FIELDFARE RD
CURLEW CL
BAYLISS AVE
HALDANE RD
WALLACE CL
6
BLYTH RD
WOODPECKER RD
LINNET CL
SLOCUM CL
ABBOTTS CL
BLEDLOW CL
CROWDEN WAY
GLENDALE WAY
KINDER CL
HOWDEN CL
WHERNSIDE CL
1 MARTHAM CL
2 CHADWICK WAY
3 LISTER WLK
4 BERNAL CL
CLOCK TOWER MEWS
Hawksmoor Sch
BOOTH CL
CARLYLE RD
APPLEGARTH RD
POPLAR PL
Jubilee Prim Sch
Pl Flds
Tenn Cts
WALDSTOCK RD
DEAN RD
HUTCHINS RD
SE28
A2016
Woolwich Poly Sch for Boys
Windrush Prim Sch
WATERFIELD CL
Pav
BARNHAM DR
GRASSHAVEN WAY
Thamesmead
HAMPSTEAD CL
AUSTEN CL
BYRON CL
OWEN CL
BELVEDERE RD
5
NEWMARSH RD
FLOATHAVEN CL
BIRCHDENE DR
SILVER BIRCH RD
PITFIELD CRES
ROMAN SQ
SORREL CL
CAMPION PL
CELANDINE DR
GALSWORTHY CL
BENTHAM RD
WOOLF CL
SOUTHWOOD RD
COLE CL
SHAW CL
DISRAELI CL
CHERVIL MEWS
AMHURST WLK
COURTAULDS CL
SUNSET RD
St Margaret Clitherow RC Prim Sch
EASTERN WAY
THE LAKESIDE COMPLEX
South Mere
80
MINE
A2041
LAKESIDE AVE
Lake
HARROW MANOR WAY
BINSEY WLK
PORTMEADOW WLK
HARTSLOCK DR
ST EDMUNDS CL
ST BRIDES CL
ST MICHAELS CL
ST KATHERINES RD
ST MARTINS CL
CIRCUIT WAY
AMPLEFORTH RD
TICKFORD CL
SEWELL RD
GROVEBURY RD
MOUNTJOY CL
4
HARNESS RD
STANBROOK RD
ANDWELL CL
GODSTOW RD
TAVY BRIDGE
Liby
SEACOURT RD
Southlake Prim Sch
PURLAND RD
DEVENISH RD
De Lucy Prim Sch
PERSTONE RD
WOLVERCOTE RD
REDPOLL WAY
123
LITTLEMORE RD
PANFIELD RD
COOKHILL RD
THISTLEBROOK
Abbey Prim Sch
HINKSEY PATH
Green Chain Wlk
MARAN WAY
SHIRE CT
Mast
Pl Fld
MANISTER RD
EDINGTON RD
BOXGROVE RD
THROWLEY CL
LENSBURY WAY
Greenwich
Bexley
ROSEDALE CL
EYNSHAM DR
FINCHALE RD
BYLANDS CL
PENMON RD
EDINGTON RD
Boxgrove Prim Sch
OVERTON RD
TEESWATER CT
3
Allot Gdns
St Thomas a Beckett RC Prim Sch
Abbey Wood Sch
Abbey Wood
CHALCOMBE RD
SE2
LUFFIELD RD
LYNDEAN IND EST
SEDGEMERE RD
SYDNEY RD
LANRIDGE RD
DALBERG WAY
BUCKWHEAT CT
PYNHAM CL
BROMHOLM RD
BRIMPSFIELD CL
FELIXSTOWE RD
RUSHDENE
Sports Gd
COMBWELL CRES
Abbey Wood
BUCKLES CT
79
MOTTISFONT RD
GAYTON RD
FLORENCE RD
FOSSINGTON RD
FENDYKE RD
BRIGHT CL
CARRILL WAY
B213
CHURCH MANOR WAY
BRACONDALE RD
BOSTALL MANOR WAY
ABBEY GR
DE LUCY ST
ABBEY TERR
WILTON RD
GLOVER CL
BRINKBURN CL
CAERLEON TERR
ABBEY WOOD RD
CONFERENCE RD
Lesnes Abbey (remains of)
MANORSIDE CL
BIRKDALE RD
BLITHDALE RD
Pl Fld
MONKS CL
Lesnes Abbey Park
2
BASILDON RD
SMITHIES RD
BRODRICK GR
OWENITE ST
CHANCELOT RD
SHIELDHALL ST
GREENING ST
CONGRESS RD
CRUMPSALL ST
KNEE HILL CRES
WOODLAND WAY
Churchfield Sch
MANTON RD
OPENSHAW RD
McLEOD RD
ST NICHOLAS RD
MYRA ST
WOODHURST RD
BENDMORE AVE
CASSILDA RD
HOWARTH RD
ROCHDALE RD
Bwg Gn
DAHLIA RD
FEDERATION RD
Green Chain Wlk
CAMROSE ST
MYRTLEDENE RD
VIOLA AVE
WILLROSE CRES
MITCHELL CL
NEW RD
A206
BASILDON RD
Tenn Cts
FUCHSIA ST
BOSTALL LA
COMMONWEALTH WAY
KNEE HILL
GRANITE ST
A209
CARNATION ST
COLTNESS CRES
SHORNELLS WAY
1 HUXLEY HO
2 HURST HO
3 COLYER HO
4 BELL HO
5 STEPHENSON HO
6 LISTER HO
ROCKMOUNT RD
GATLING RD
Alexander McLeod Sch
BEVAN RD
Allot Gdns
Co-operative Woods
1
SPINEL CL
FELSPAR CL
OLD PARK RD
BOSTALL HILL
PRIORY DR
FRIARS WLK
GROSMONT RD
THE DELL
GLENDOWN RD
BASTION RD
Allot Gdns
1 ALEXANDER TERR
2 DIANTHUS CL
Bostall Heath
Cottage Hospice
A2041
HURST LA
DIXON HO
HARVEL CRES
78
Common
A206
WOOLWICH RD
46
RUTHERGLEN RD
SANDYCROFT
Bostall Woods
Pav
Bwg Gn
47
146
MARTYN HO 1
HURST PL 2
SENCLER HO 3
ABBAS HO 4
Bexley Coll
BURCHARBRO
AMBERLEY RD
West Heath
48

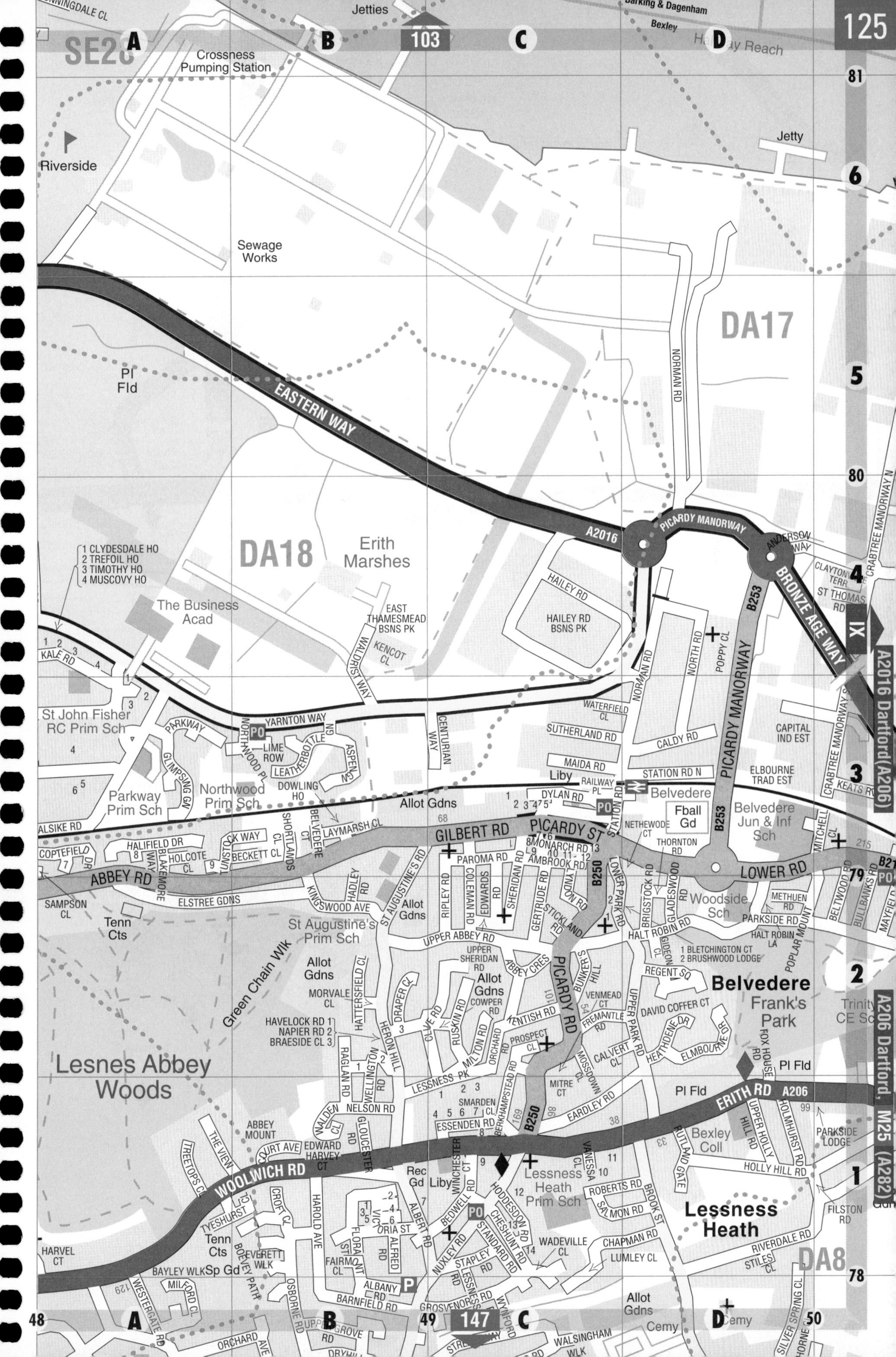

A
B
C
D
103
Jetties
Crossness Pumping Station
Riverside
Sewage Works
Barking & Dagenham
Bexley
Jetty
DA17
DA18
Erith Marshes
EASTERN WAY
A2016
PICARDY MANORWAY
BRONZE AGE WAY
B253
NORMAN RD
Pl Fld
1 CLYDESDALE HO
2 TREFOIL HO
3 TIMOTHY HO
4 MUSCOVY HO
The Business Acad
EAST THAMESMEAD BSNS PK
KENCOT CL
WALDRIST WAY
HAILEY RD
HAILEY RD BSNS PK
NORTH RD
POPPY CL
CAPITAL IND EST
ELBOURNE TRAD EST
CRABTREE MANORWAY N
CRABTREE MANORWAY S
CLAYTON TERR
ST THOMAS RD
ANDERSON WAY
KEATS RD
A2016 Dartford (A206)
A206 Dartford, M25 (A282)
KALE RD
St John Fisher RC Prim Sch
PARKWAY
YARNTON WAY
NORTHWOOD PL
LIME ROW
LEATHERBOTTLE GN
ASPEN GN
CENTURIAN WAY
WATERFIELD CL
SUTHERLAND RD
CALDY RD
MAIDA RD
STATION RD N
Liby
RAILWAY PL
Belvedere
GLIMPSING GN
Parkway Prim Sch
Northwood Prim Sch
DOWLING HO
Allot Gdns
DYLAN RD
Fball Gd
Belvedere Jun & Inf Sch
ALSIKE RD
HALIFIELD DR
TUNSTOCK WAY
SHORTLANDS CL
BELVEDERE CT
LAYMARSH CL
GILBERT RD
PICARDY ST
STATION RD
NETHEWODE CT
THORNTON RD
MITCHELL CL
COPTEFIELD DR
HOLCOTE CL
BECKETT CL
BLAKEMORE WAY
MONARCH RD
AMBROOK RD
PAROMA RD
LOWER RD
ABBEY RD
ELSTREE GDNS
SAMPSON CL
Tenn Cts
KINGSWOOD AVE
HADLEY RD
ST AUGUSTINE'S RD
RIPLEY RD
COLEMAN RD
EDWARDS RD
SHERIDAN RD
GERTRUDE RD
LYNDON RD
B250
LOWER PARK RD
BRIGSTOCK RD
GLADESWOOD RD
Woodside Sch
METHUEN RD
BELTWOOD RD
BULLBANKS RD
MAYFIELD
St Augustine's Prim Sch
UPPER ABBEY RD
STICKLAND RD
HALT ROBIN RD
PARKSIDE RD
HALT ROBIN LA
POPLAR MOUNT
Green Chain Wlk
UPPER SHERIDAN RD
ABBEY CRES
GIDEON CL
1 BLETCHINGTON CT
2 BRUSHWOOD LODGE
REGENT SQ
Belvedere
Frank's Park
Trinity CE Sc
HATTERSFIELD CL
MORVALE CL
DRAPER CL
PICARDY RD
BUNKERS HILL
VENMEAD CT
UPPER PARK RD
DAVID COFFER CT
FREMANTLE RD
COWPER RD
KENTISH RD
HAVELOCK RD 1
NAPIER RD 2
BRAESIDE CL 3
HERON HILL
CLIVE RD
RUSKIN RD
MILTON RD
ORCHARD RD
PROSPECT CL
MOSSDOWN CL
CALVERT CL
HEATHDENE DR
ELMBOURNE DR
FOX HOUSE RD
Pl Fld
Lesnes Abbey Woods
RAGLAN RD
WELLINGTON RD
LESSNESS PK
BERKHAMPSTEAD RD
MITRE CT
EARDLEY RD
ERITH RD
A206
UPPER HOLLY HILL RD
HOLMHURST RD
NELSON RD
SMARDEN CL
ESSENDEN RD
WALDEN CL
GLOUCESTER RD
ABBEY MOUNT
COURT AVE
EDWARD HARVEY CT
TREETOPS CL
THE VIEW
WOOLWICH RD
Rec Gd
Liby
WINCHESTER CT
Lessness Heath Prim Sch
VANESSA CL
RUTLAND GATE
Bexley Coll
PARKSIDE LODGE
HOLLY HILL RD
ROBERTS RD
SALMON RD
BROOK ST
Lessness Heath
TYESHURST CL
CROFT CL
HAROLD AVE
VICTORIA ST
ALBERT RD
BEDWELL RD
HODDESDON RD
CHESHUNT RD
STANDARD RD
FILSTON RD
Tenn Cts
BOEVEY PATH
EVERETT WLK
FLORA ST
ALFRED RD
FAIRMONT CL
NUXLEY RD
STAPLEY RD
WADEVILLE CL
CHAPMAN RD
LUMLEY CL
RIVERDALE RD
STILES CL
HARVEL CT
BAYLEY WLK
Sp Gd
MILFORD CL
ALBANY RD
LESSNESS RD
DA8
WESTERGATE RD
BARNFIELD RD
GROSVENOR RD
WYNFORD
Allot Gdns
Cemy
SILVER SPRING CL
ORCHARD AVE
OSBORNE RD
UPPER GROVE RD
147
WALSINGHAM WLK
81
6
5
80
4
3
79
2
1
78
48
49
50

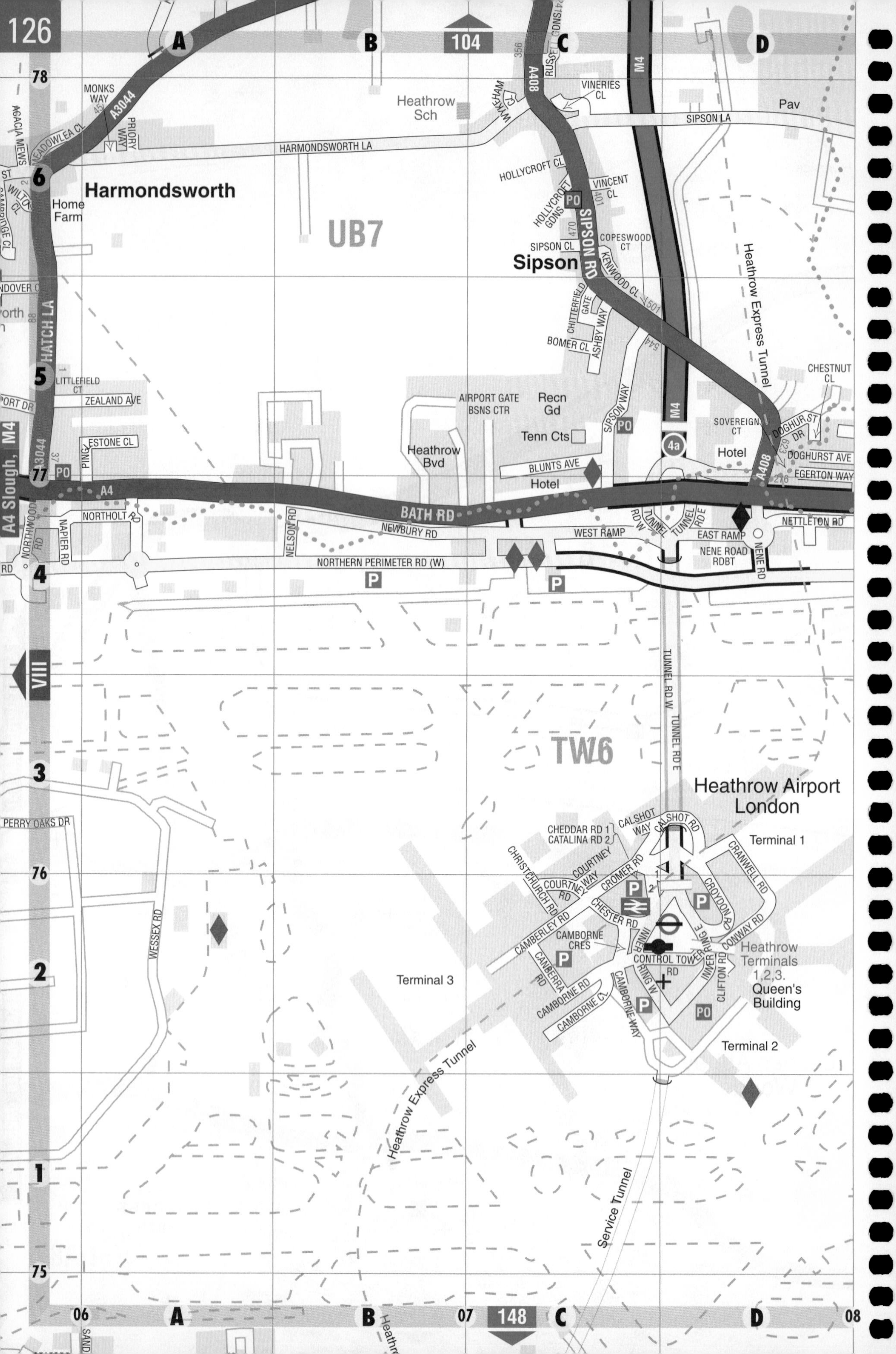

A
B
104
C
D
78
MONKS WAY
A3044
PRIORY WAY
MEADOWLEA CL
ACACIA MEWS
Heathrow Sch
WYKEHAM CL
A408
RUSSELL GDNS
VINERIES CL
M4
Pav
SIPSON LA
HARMONDSWORTH LA
6
Harmondsworth
Home Farm
WILTON CL
HOLLYCROFT CL
VINCENT CL
HOLLYCROFT GDNS
PO
UB7
SIPSON RD
COPESWOOD CT
SIPSON CL
Sipson
KENWOOD CL
Heathrow Express Tunnel
HATCH LA
CHITTERFIELD GATE
ASHBY WAY
BOMER CL
CHESTNUT CL
5
LITTLEFIELD CT
ZEALAND AVE
AIRPORT GATE BSNS CTR
Recn Gd
SIPSON WAY
SOVEREIGN CT
DOGHURST DR
ESTONE CL
Heathrow Bvd
Tenn Cts
4a
Hotel
DOGHURST AVE
A3044
BLUNTS AVE
EGERTON WAY
A4 Slough, M4
77
PO
A4
Hotel
BATH RD
NORTHOLT RD
NAPIER RD
NORTHWOOD RD
NELSON RD
NEWBURY RD
WEST RAMP
TUNNEL RD W
TUNNEL RD E
EAST RAMP
NETTLETON RD
NENE ROAD RDBT
NENE RD
4
NORTHERN PERIMETER RD (W)
P
VIII
TUNNEL RD W
TUNNEL RD E
TW6
3
Heathrow Airport London
PERRY OAKS DR
CHEDDAR RD
CATALINA RD
CALSHOT WAY
CALSHOT RD
Terminal 1
CHRISTCHURCH RD
COURTNEY WAY
COURTNEY RD
CROMER RD
CRANWELL RD
76
CROYDON RD
CHESTER RD
CAMBERLEY RD
CAMBORNE CRES
INNER RING W
INNER RING E
CONWAY RD
Heathrow Terminals 1,2,3.
WESSEX RD
2
CANBERRA RD
CONTROL TOWER RD
Terminal 3
CAMBORNE RD
CAMBORNE CL
CAMBORNE WAY
CLIFTON RD
Queen's Building
Terminal 2
Heathrow Express Tunnel
1
Service Tunnel
75
06
A
B
07
148
C
D
08

Nine Elms Farm
Sports Gd
Pav
William Byrd Sch
Hotel
Harlington
Gravel Pits
Frog's Ditch
Cranford Park
UB3
HIGH ST
VICTORIA LA
BLETCHMORE CL
BRICKFIELD LA
PEMBURY CT
KILN CL
HUDSON RD
THE FORGE
GOTHIC CT
RICHARDS CL
FELLOWES CT
SHORTLANDS
SIPSON LA
FELBRIDGE CT
MANOR LA
PONDSIDE CL
MANSE CL
GILPIN WAY
PROVIDENCE LA
CRANFORD LA
THE CRESCENT
WEST END LA
HIGH STREET HARLINGTON
FIELD CL
RAYWOOD CL
TASKER CL
CROFT CL
HARLINGTON CL
Sp Gd
GRAMPIAN CL
QUANTOCK CL
WARNER CL
PENNINE WAY
Poultry Farm
LITTLE ELMS
The White House
ACORN GR
SAUNTON AVE
PENDELL AVE
STRATHEARN AVE
LANGLEY CRES
ETON RD
WINCHESTER RD
OXFORD AVE
WINDSOR PARK RD
MALVERN RD
CRANESWATER
BROWNING RAVES RD
BOLTON'S LA
NEW RD
BRENDON CL
CHEVIOT CL
HALL LA
HEATH CL
MENDIP CL
MARLBOROUGH CRES
DAVID CL
CAROLINE PL
NOBEL DR
MONDIAL WAY
Hotel
Hotels
Harlington Cnr
TRIUMPH CL
Hotels
Hotel
Hotel
PARK LA
The White Hart (PH)
BATH RD
A437
A4
Visitor Ctr
WORLD BSNS CTR
Customs House
NEWALL RD
NEPTUNE RD
HATTON RD N
NORTHROP RD
NORTHERN PERIMETER RD
CRANFORD LA
P
P
ENFIELD ROAD RDBT
ENFIELD RD
ELGIN CRES
ELY RD
ESHER CRES
EPSOM SQ
EASTERN PERIMETER RD
EASTERN BSNS PK
128
EASTCHURCH ROAD RDBT
EXETER WAY
VANGAURD WAY
EXETER RD
EXETER RD
EASTCHURCH RD
TW6
ELECTRA AVE
EAGLE RD
ELMDON RD
CRANFORD LA
EASTERN PERIMETER RD
A30
HATTON CROSS RDBT
VISCOUNT WAY
Hatton Cross
LITHGOW'S RD
P
TURPIN WAY
DICK
STEAM FARM LA
SOUTHERN PERIMETER
GREAT SOUTH-WEST RD
HATTON RD
RADIUS PK
Hatton
ST THERESA'S RD
ST ANTHONY'S WAY
FAGG'S RD
DOCKWELL CL
GREEN
MYRTLE AVE
WELLINGTON RD
A B C D
78 6 5 77 4 3 76 2 1 75
08 09 10

105
149

Cranford Park
M4
Bwg Gn
Tenn Cts
Heston Motorway Service Area
Cranford Park
UB3
Cranford Comm Coll
Sp Gd
NORTH RD
PARKWAY TRAD EST
HESTON PHOENIX DISTRIBUTION PK
SOUTH RD
Berkeley Prim Sch
The Queen's Head (PH)
Rectory Farm
The Cedars Prim Sch
Avenue Park
Allot Gdns
THE PARKWAY
CRANFORD LA
TW5
The White Hart (PH)
A4
BATH RD
Cranford
Waggoners Rdbt
Liby
Henleys Rdbt
PARKLANDS PAR
ALL SAINTS CT
A30
A3006
A312
Allot Gdns
Cranford Jun Sch
TW6
River Crane
GREAT SOUTH-WEST RD
Recn Gd
CRANEBANK
THE HASLEMERE & HEATHROW EST
HEATHROW CAUSEWAY EST
HEATHROW INTERNATIONAL TRAD EST
WALLBROOK BSNS CTR
Beavers Comm Prim Sch
Hounslow West
Barracks
TW4
SUN LIFE TRAD EST
Resr
TW14
CAUSEWAY
PROLOGIS PK
Beavers Lane Camp
LAWRENCE EST
MAPLE GR BSNS CTR
TAMIAN IND EST
Allot Gdns
CENTRAL PK EST
NORTH FELTHAM TRAD EST
RIVER GDNS BSNS CTR
HASLEMERE IND EST
FREEHOLD IND CTR
FAIRWAY EST
A315
106
127
150

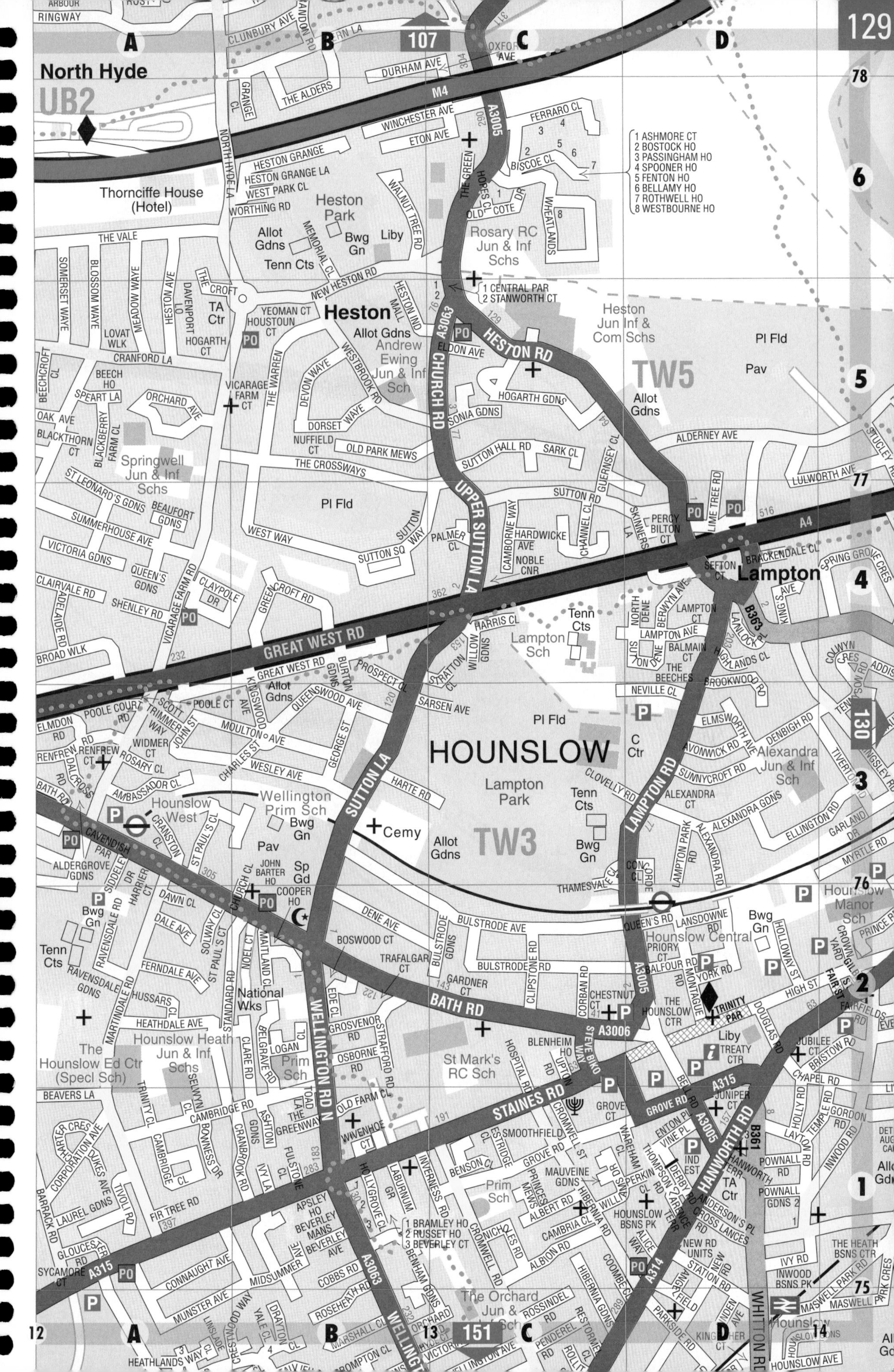
North Hyde
UB2
M4
A3005
107
Thorncliffe House (Hotel)
Heston Park
Allot Gdns
Bwg Gn
Liby
Tenn Cts
Rosary RC Jun & Inf Schs
1 ASHMORE CT
2 BOSTOCK HO
3 PASSINGHAM HO
4 SPOONER HO
5 FENTON HO
6 BELLAMY HO
7 ROTHWELL HO
8 WESTBOURNE HO
1 CENTRAL PAR
2 STANWORTH CT
Heston
Heston Jun Inf & Com Schs
TW5
Pl Fld
Pav
Andrew Ewing Jun & Inf Sch
HESTON RD
CHURCH RD
UPPER SUTTON LA
Springwell Jun & Inf Schs
TA Ctr
A4
GREAT WEST RD
Lampton
Lampton Sch
HOUNSLOW
Lampton Park
TW3
C Ctr
Alexandra Jun & Inf Sch
Hounslow West
Wellington Prim Sch
Cemy
SUTTON LA
LAMPTON RD
Hounslow Central
Hounslow Manor Sch
BATH RD
A3006
National Wks
Hounslow Heath Jun & Inf Schs
The Hounslow Ed Ctr (Specl Sch)
St Mark's RC Sch
The Hounslow Ctr
STAINES RD
A315
WELLINGTON RD N
A3063
HANWORTH RD
B361
A314
1 BRAMLEY HO
2 RUSSET HO
3 BEVERLEY CT
The Orchard Jun & Inf Sch
Hounslow Bsns Pk
The Heath Bsns Ctr
Inwood Bsns Pk
WHITTON RD
Hounslow
130
151
A
B
C
D
78
6
5
77
4
3
76
2
1
75
12
13
14

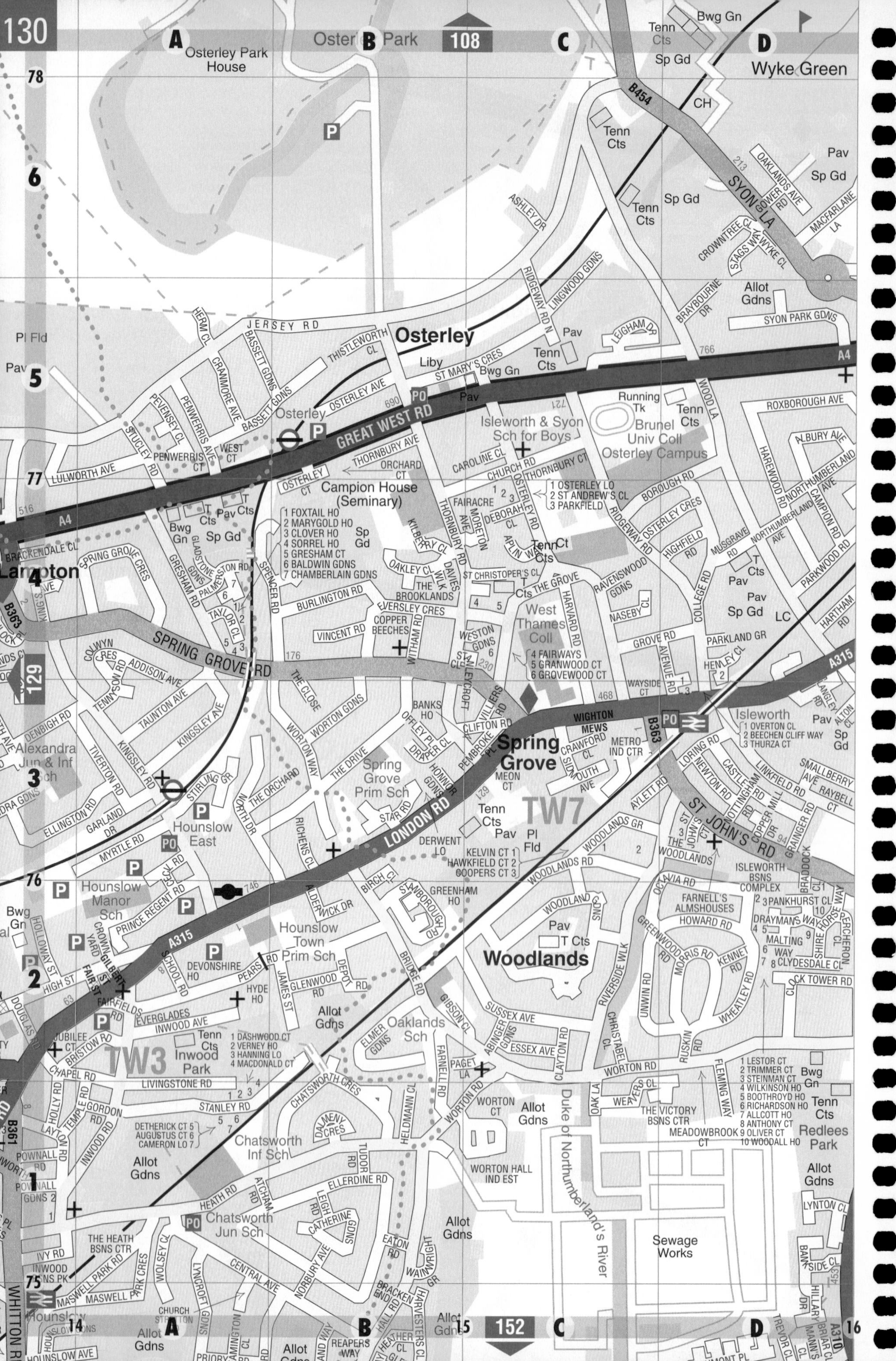
A
B
C
D
Osterley Park
108
Osterley Park House
Wyke Green
Bwg Gn
Tenn Cts
Sp Gd
CH
B454
SYON LA
OAKLANDS AVE
GOWER RD
MACFARLANE LA
CROWNTREE CL
STAGS WAY
WYKE CL
Pav
Allot Gdns
SYON PARK GDNS
BRAYBOURNE DR
ASHLEY DR
RIDGEWAY RD N
LINGWOOD GDNS
LEIGHAM DR
78
6
5
4
3
2
1
77
76
75
Pl Fld
JERSEY RD
HERM CL
BASSETT GDNS
CRANMORE AVE
THISTLEWORTH CL
Osterley
Liby
ST MARY'S CRES
A4
766
WOOD LA
Running Tk
Brunel Univ Coll Osterley Campus
Isleworth & Syon Sch for Boys
ROXBOROUGH AVE
ALBURY AVE
NORTHUMBERLAND AVE
HAREWOOD RD
CAMPION RD
PARKWOOD RD
HARTHAM RD
GREAT WEST RD
OSTERLEY AVE
PEVENSEY CL
PENWERRIS AVE
STUCLEY RD
LULWORTH AVE
WEST CT
THORNBURY AVE
ORCHARD CT
OSTERLEY CT
Campion House (Seminary)
CAROLINE CL
CHURCH RD
THORNBURY CT
OSTERLEY RD
1 OSTERLEY LO
2 ST ANDREW'S CL
3 PARKFIELD
BOROUGH RD
OSTERLEY CRES
HIGHFIELD RD
MUSGRAVE RD
1 FOXTAIL HO
2 MARYGOLD HO
3 CLOVER HO
4 SORREL HO
5 GRESHAM CT
6 BALDWIN GDNS
7 CHAMBERLAIN GDNS
FAIRACRE
MORETON AVE
DEBORAH CL
APLIN WAY
KILBERRY CL
OAKLEY CL
THE BROOKLANDS
DAVIES WLK
ST CHRISTOPER'S CL
THE GROVE
RAVENSWOOD GDNS
COLLEGE RD
LC
BRACKENDALE CL
SPRING GROVE CRES
Lampton
GRESHAM RD
GLADSTONE GDNS
PALMERSTON RD
TAYLOR CL
SPENCER RD
BURLINGTON RD
EVERSLEY CRES
COPPER BEECHES
VINCENT RD
WITHAM RD
West Thames Coll
HARVARD RD
NASEBY CL
GROVE RD
AVENUE RD
PARKLAND GR
HENLEY CL
A315
B363
SPRING GROVE RD
176
COLWYN CRES
ADDISON AVE
TENNYSON RD
TAUNTON AVE
KINGSLEY AVE
DENBIGH RD
Alexandra Jun & Inf Sch
TIVERTON RD
KINGSLEY RD
ELLINGTON RD
GARLAND DR
STIRLING GR
THE CLOSE
WORTON GDNS
WORTON WAY
THE DRIVE
THE ORCHARD
NORTH DR
RICHENS CL
BANKS HO
OFFLEY PL
DRAPER CL
WESTON GDNS
STANLEYCROFT CL
4 FAIRWAYS
5 GRANWOOD CT
6 GROVEWOOD CT
VILLIERS RD
CLIFTON RD
PEMBROKE PL
WIGHTON MEWS
Spring Grove
CRAWFORD CL
SIDMOUTH AVE
MEON CT
METRO IND CTR
WAYSIDE CT
Isleworth
1 OVERTON CL
2 BEECHEN CLIFF WAY
3 THURZA CT
LORING RD
NEWTON RD
CASTLE RD
NOTTINGHAM RD
COPPER MILL DR
LINKFIELD RD
SMALLBERRY AVE
RAYBELL CT
GRAINGER RD
ST JOHN'S RD
Spring Grove Prim Sch
STAR RD
HONNOR GDNS
LONDON RD
Tenn Cts
TW7
Pl Fld
Hounslow East
MYRTLE RD
DERWENT LO
KELVIN CT 1
HAWKFIELD CT 2
COOPERS CT 3
WOODLANDS GR
WOODLANDS RD
AYLETT RD
THE WOODLANDS
ISLEWORTH BSNS COMPLEX
BRADDOCK CL
PANKHURST CL
DRAYMANS WAY
SHIRE HORSE WAY
PERCHERON CL
MALTING WAY
CLYDESDALE CL
CLOCK TOWER RD
Hounslow Manor Sch
CECIL RD
PRINCE REGENT RD
746
ALDERWICK DR
BIRCH CL
STANBOROUGH CL
GREENHAM HO
WOODLAND GDNS
OCTAVIA RD
FARNELL'S ALMSHOUSES
HOWARD RD
GREENWOOD RD
MORRIS RD
KENNET RD
Bwg Gn
HOLLOWAY ST
CROWN YARD
A315
SCHOOL RD
DEVONSHIRE HO
PEARS RD
Hounslow Town Prim Sch
JAMES ST
GLENWOOD RD
DEPOT RD
BRIDGE RD
Woodlands
RIVERSIDE WLK
UNWIN RD
WHEATLEY RD
HIGH ST
GILBERT ST
FAIR ST
HYDE HO
FAIRFIELDS RD
EVERGLADES
INWOOD AVE
Allot Gdns
Oaklands Sch
GIBSON CL
ELMER GDNS
SUSSEX AVE
ABINGER GDNS
ESSEX AVE
CLAYTON RD
CHRISTABEL CL
RUSKIN RD
DOUGLAS RD
JUBILEE CT
BRISTOW RD
TW3
Inwood Park
1 DASHWOOD CT
2 VERNEY HO
3 HANNING LO
4 MACDONALD CT
FARNELL RD
PAGET LA
WORTON RD
FLEMING WAY
1 LESTOR CT
2 TRIMMER CT
3 STEINMAN CT
4 WILKINSON HO
5 BOOTHROYD HO
6 RICHARDSON HO
7 ALLCOTT HO
8 ANTHONY CT
9 OLIVER CT
10 WOODALL HO
CHAPEL RD
LIVINGSTONE RD
STANLEY RD
CHATSWORTH CRES
WORTON CT
OAK LA
WEAVERS CL
THE VICTORY BSNS CTR
MEADOWBROOK CT
Redlees Park
HOLLY RD
TEMPLE RD
GORDON RD
LAYTON RD
INWOOD RD
DETHERICK CT 5
AUGUSTUS CT 6
CAMERON LO 7
DALMENY CRES
HELDMANN CL
Duke of Northumberland's River
B361
POWNALL RD
POWNALL GDNS
Chatsworth Inf Sch
TUDOR RD
WORTON HALL IND EST
ELLERDINE RD
HEATH RD
ATCHAM RD
LEIGH RD
CATHERINE GDNS
Chatsworth Jun Sch
LYNTON CL
EATON RD
WAINWRIGHT GR
Sewage Works
BANKSIDE CL
IVY RD
THE HEATH BSNS CTR
INWOOD BSNS PK
MASWELL PARK RD
MASWELL PARK CRES
WOLSEY CL
LYNGROFT GDNS
CENTRAL AVE
NORBURY AVE
BRACKEN END
HARVESTERS CL
HILLARY DR
WHITTON RD
Hounslow
HOUNSLOW GDNS
HOUNSLOW AVE
CHURCH STATION
LEAMINGTON CL
PRIORY RD
REAPERS WAY
HEATHER CL
TREVOR CL
MANN'S CL
BRIAR CL
A310
14
15
16
152
129

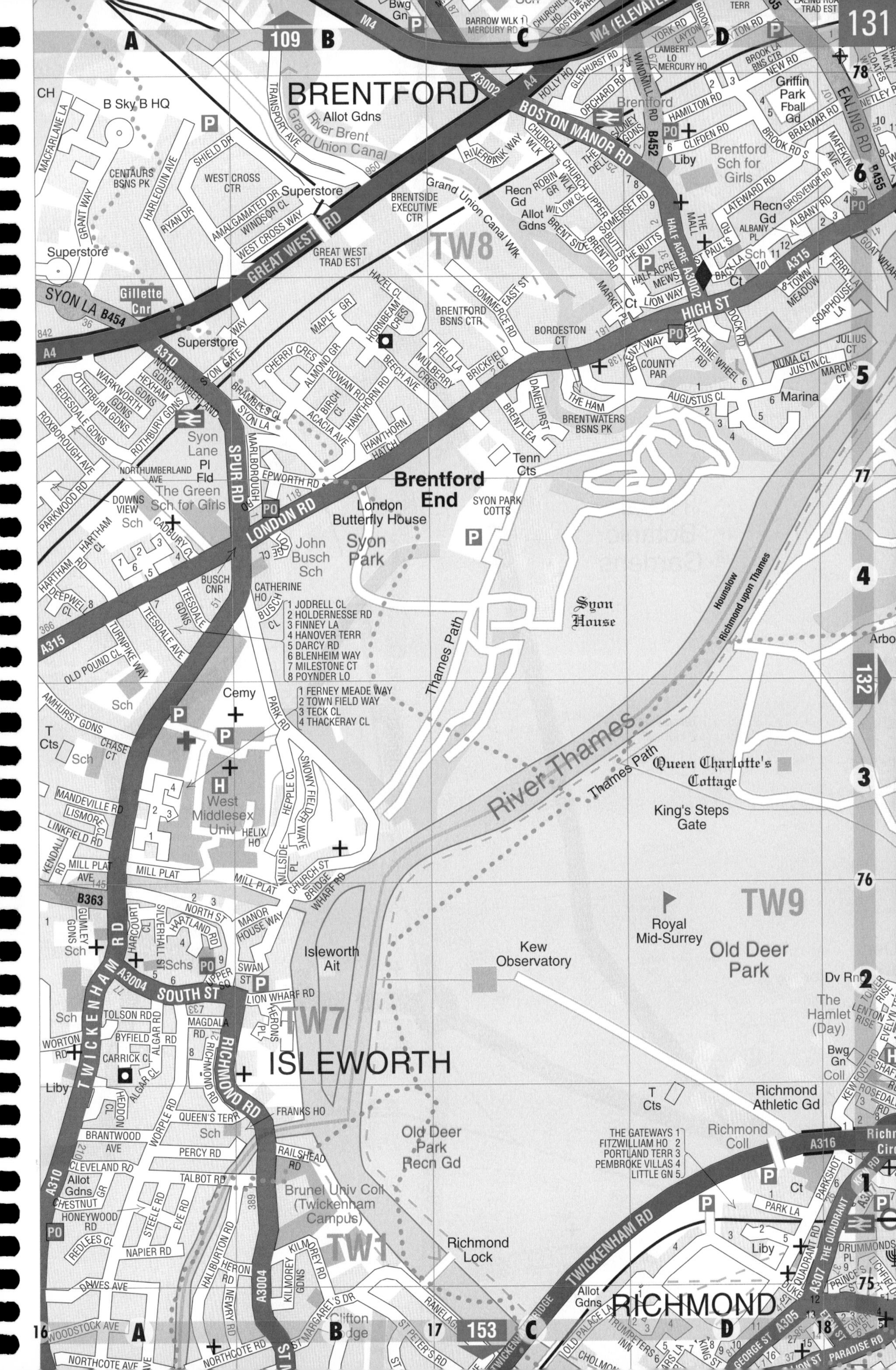

A
109
B
C
D
BRENTFORD
B Sky B HQ
CH
Allot Gdns
River Brent
Grand Union Canal
MACFARLANE LA
CENTAURS BSNS PK
SHIELD DR
HARLEQUIN AVE
WEST CROSS CTR
RYAN DR
AMALGAMATED DR
WINDSOR CL
WEST CROSS WAY
Superstore
GREAT WEST RD
GREAT WEST TRAD EST
GRANT WAY
TRANSPORT AVE
M4
M4 (ELEVATED)
A4
A3002
BOSTON MANOR RD
Brentford
HOLLY HO
GLENHURST RD
ORCHARD RD
CHURCH WLK
RIVERBANK WAY
Grand Union Canal Wlk
BRENTSIDE EXECUTIVE CTR
TW8
Recn Gd
Allot Gdns
ROBIN GR
WILLOW CL
BRENT SIDE
UPPER BUTTS
SOMERSET RD
THE BUTTS
BRENT RD
HALF ACRE
HALF ACRE MEWS
LION WAY
MARKET PL
HIGH ST
B452
WINDMILL RD
CLIFDEN RD
HAMILTON RD
Liby
Brentford Sch for Girls
THE MALL
ST PAUL'S RD
LATEWARD RD
Recn Gd
ALBANY PL
ALBANY RD
GROSVENOR RD
BACK LA
Sch
Ct
A315
TOWN MEADOW
FERRY LA
SOAPHOUSE LA
GOAT WHARF
EALING RD
B455
Griffin Park Fball Gd
BRAEMAR RD
BROOK RD S
MAFEKING AVE
NEW RD
BROOK LA BNS CTR
YORK RD
LAYTON CT
LAMBERT LO
MERCURY HO
BARROW WLK
MERCURY RD
BOSTON PARK
CHURCHILL HO
Bwg Gn
TERR
TRAD EST
78
6
SYON LA
B454
Gillette Cnr
A4
Superstore
SYON GATE WAY
A310
NORTHUMBERLAND GDNS
HEXHAM GDNS
WARKWORTH GDNS
OTTERBURN GDNS
REDESDALE GDNS
ROTHBURY GDNS
ROXBOROUGH AVE
Syon Lane
Pl Fld
NORTHUMBERLAND AVE
The Green Sch for Girls
DOWNS VIEW
PARKWOOD RD
Sch
SPUR RD
MARLBOROUGH
EPWORTH RD
BRAMBLES CL
SYON LA
CHERRY CRES
ALMOND GR
MAPLE GR
HAZEL CL
HORNBEAM CRES
ROWAN RD
BIRCH CL
ACACIA AVE
HAWTHORN RD
BEECH AVE
HAWTHORN HATCH
MULBERRY CRES
FIELD LA
BRICKFIELD CL
COMMERCE RD
EAST ST
BRENTFORD BSNS CTR
BORDESTON CT
BRENT WAY
COUNTY PAR
CATHERINE WHEEL RD
DOCK RD
DANEHURST
BRENT LEA
THE HAM
BRENTWATERS BSNS PK
AUGUSTUS CL
Marina
NUMA CT
JUSTIN CL
JULIUS CT
MARCUS CT
5
Tenn Cts
77
LONDON RD
Brentford End
London Butterfly House
SYON PARK COTTS
Syon Park
John Busch Sch
LOVE LA
HARTHAM CL
HARTHAM RD
DEEPWELL CL
CADBURY CL
BUSCH CNR
TEESDALE GDNS
TEESDALE AVE
TURNPIKE WAY
CATHERINE HO
BUSCH CL
1 JODRELL CL
2 HOLDERNESSE RD
3 FINNEY LA
4 HANOVER TERR
5 DARCY RD
6 BLENHEIM WAY
7 MILESTONE CT
8 POYNDER LO
A315
OLD POUND CL
Thames Path
Syon House
Hounslow
Richmond upon Thames
4
Arbor
132
AMHURST GDNS
Sch
Cemy
PARK RD
1 FERNEY MEADE WAY
2 TOWN FIELD WAY
3 TECK CL
4 THACKERAY CL
T Cts
Sch
CHASE CT
West Middlesex Univ
HELIX HO
MANDEVILLE RD
LISMORE CL
LINKFIELD RD
KENDALL RD
MILL PLAT AVE
MILL PLAT
HEPPLE CL
SNOWY FIELDER WAYE
MILLSIDE PL
CHURCH ST
BRIDGE WHARF RD
River Thames
Thames Path
Queen Charlotte's Cottage
King's Steps Gate
3
76
B363
NORTH ST
HARTLAND RD
SILVERHALL ST
HARCOURT CL
MANOR HOUSE WAY
GUMLEY GDNS
Sch
Schs
SWAN ST
UPPER SQ
Isleworth Ait
A3004
SOUTH ST
LION WHARF RD
HERONS PL
TW9
Royal Mid-Surrey
Kew Observatory
Old Deer Park
2
Dv Rnge
The Hamlet (Day)
TOWER RISE
LENTON RISE
EVELYN TERR
Bwg Gn
Coll
KEW FOOT RD
SHAFTESBURY RD
ROSEDALE RD
TW7
TWICKENHAM RD
TOLSON RD
BYFIELD RD
ALGAR RD
MAGDALA RD
RICHMOND RD
WORTON RD
CARRICK CL
ALGAR CL
ISLEWORTH
Liby
HEDDON CL
WORPLE RD
QUEEN'S TERR
FRANKS HO
T Cts
Richmond Athletic Gd
BRANTWOOD AVE
PERCY RD
Sch
RAILSHEAD RD
Old Deer Park Recn Gd
THE GATEWAYS 1
FITZWILLIAM HO 2
PORTLAND TERR 3
PEMBROKE VILLAS 4
LITTLE GN 5
Richmond Coll
A316
Richmond Circus
A310
CLEVELAND RD
Allot Gdns
CHESTNUT GR
TALBOT RD
STEELE RD
EVE RD
HONEYWOOD RD
Brunel Univ Coll (Twickenham Campus)
PARK LA
Ct
PARKSHOT
KEW RD
1
PO
REDLEES CL
NAPIER RD
HALIBURTON RD
HERON RD
KILMOREY RD
KILMOREY GDNS
TW1
Richmond Lock
TWICKENHAM RD
Liby
QUADRANT RD
THE QUADRANT
A307
DRUMMONDS PL
PRINCES ST
LICHFIELD CT
75
DAWES AVE
NEWRY RD
Allot Gdns
RICHMOND
WOODSTOCK AVE
A
B
Clifton Lodge
17
153
C
D
ST MARGARET'S DR
RANELAGH DR
ST PETER'S RD
OLD PALACE LA
TRUMPETERS INN
KING ST
GEORGE ST
A305
18
PARADISE RD
NORTHCOTE AVE
NORTHCOTE RD
16

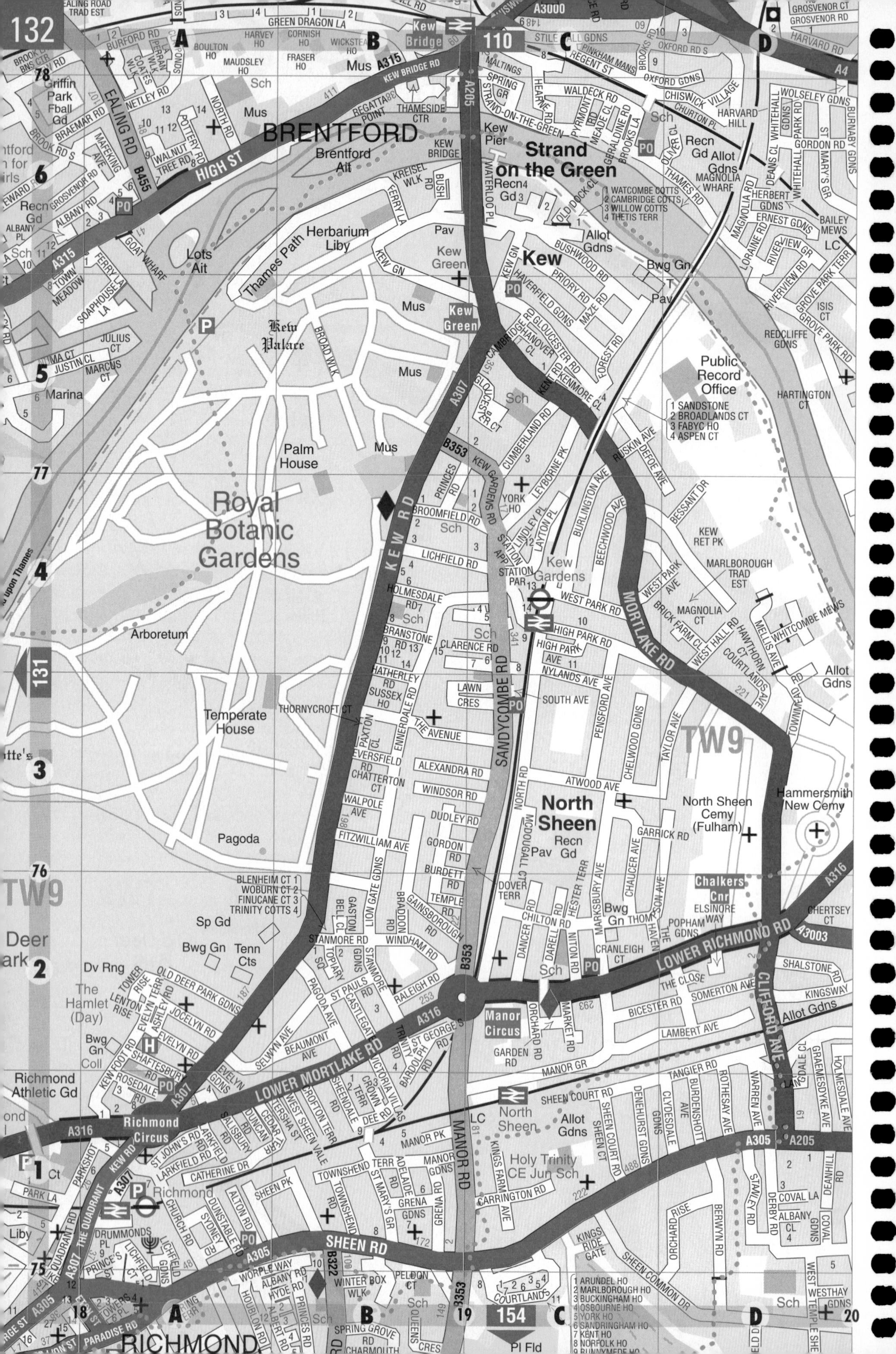
BRENTFORD
Strand on the Green
Kew
Royal Botanic Gardens
North Sheen
Kew Palace
Palm House
Temperate House
Pagoda
Arboretum
Public Record Office
North Sheen Cemy (Fulham)
Hammersmith New Cemy
Richmond Athletic Gd
Manor Circus
Chalkers Cnr
Richmond Circus
Kew Gardens
Kew Bridge
Kew Green
North Sheen
Holy Trinity CE Jun Sch
TW9
HIGH ST
KEW RD
MORTLAKE RD
SANDYCOMBE RD
LOWER MORTLAKE RD
LOWER RICHMOND RD
SHEEN RD
MANOR RD
CLIFFORD AVE
KEW BRIDGE RD
RICHMOND

110
131
154

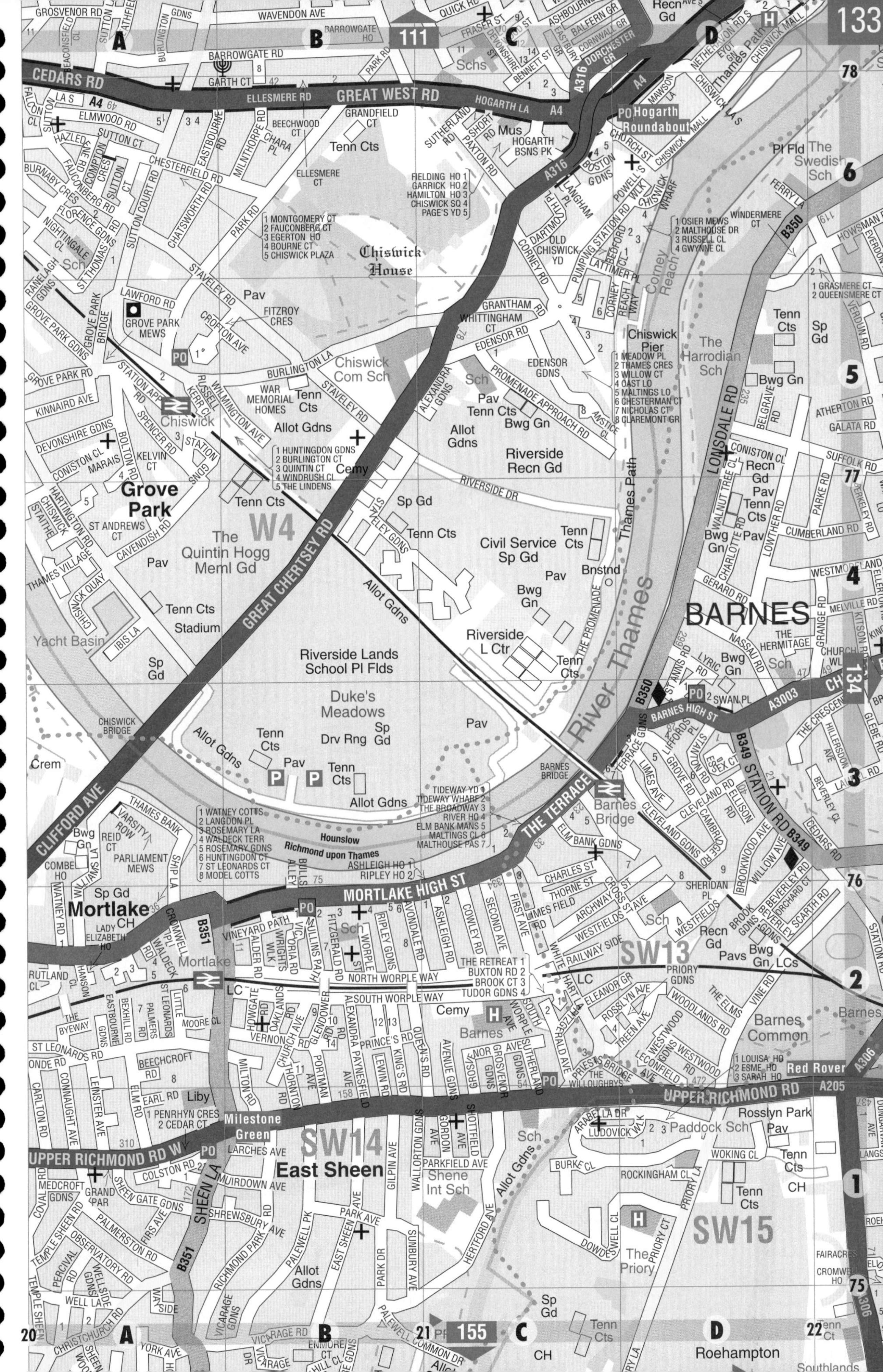
Chiswick House
Grove Park
W4
The Quintin Hogg Meml Gd
Riverside Lands School Pl Flds
Duke's Meadows
Civil Service Sp Gd
Riverside Recn Gd
River Thames
BARNES
Mortlake
SW13
SW14
East Sheen
SW15
Barnes Common
The Priory
Roehampton
GREAT WEST RD
GREAT CHERTSEY RD
MORTLAKE HIGH ST
UPPER RICHMOND RD
UPPER RICHMOND RD W
CLIFFORD AVE
THE TERRACE
BARNES HIGH ST
STATION RD
LONSDALE RD
SHEEN LA
CEDARS RD
Hogarth Roundabout
Chiswick
Barnes Bridge
Mortlake
Milestone Green
Chiswick Pier
The Harrodian Sch
Corney Reach
Thames Path
Yacht Basin
CHISWICK BRIDGE
BARNES BRIDGE
Hounslow
Richmond upon Thames
Shene Int Sch
Paddock Sch
Rosslyn Park
Red Rover
The Swedish Sch
Chiswick Com Sch
Stadium
Crem
111
155
134
78
77
76
75
20
21
22

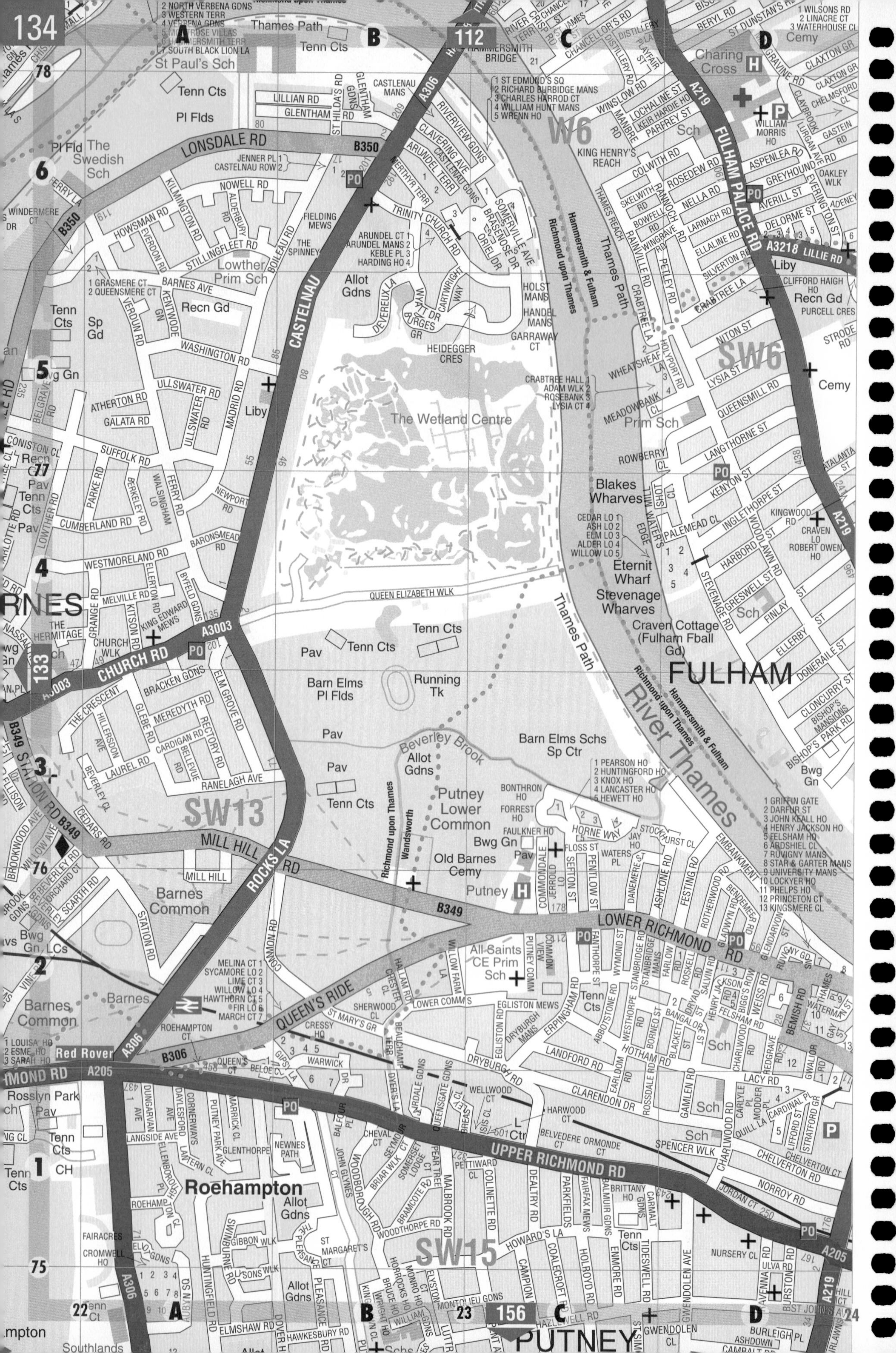
112
Hammersmith Bridge
Thames Path
Tenn Cts
St Paul's Sch
Pl Flds
The Swedish Sch
LONSDALE RD
B350
CASTELNAU
A306
W6
King Henry's Reach
Charing Cross
FULHAM PALACE RD
A219
Lowther Prim Sch
Recn Gd
The Wetland Centre
SW6
Liby
Cemy
Queen Elizabeth Wlk
CHURCH RD
A3003
Tenn Cts
Barn Elms Pl Flds
Running Tk
Blakes Wharves
Eternit Wharf
Stevenage Wharves
Craven Cottage (Fulham Fball Gd)
FULHAM
River Thames
Barn Elms Schs Sp Ctr
Beverley Brook
Allot Gdns
Putney Lower Common
SW13
MILL HILL RD
ROCKS LA
Old Barnes Cemy
Barnes Common
B349
LOWER RICHMOND RD
QUEEN'S RIDE
Barnes
All Saints CE Prim Sch
Red Rover
A205
UPPER RICHMOND RD
Roehampton
Rosslyn Park
SW15
156
PUTNEY
133

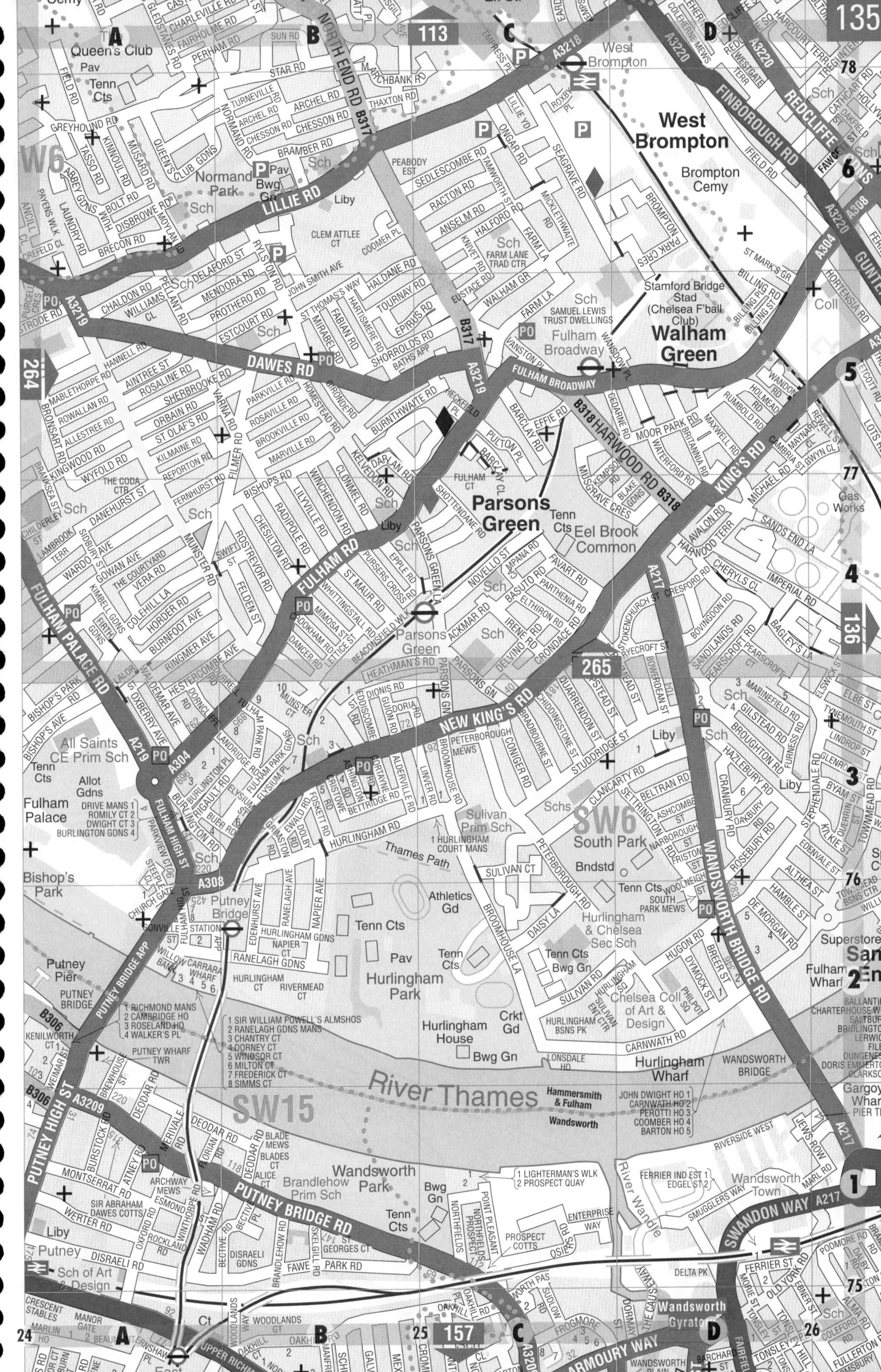
113
West Brompton
Brompton Cemy
Queen's Club
Normand Park
Stamford Bridge Stad (Chelsea F'ball Club)
Walham Green
Fulham Broadway
Parsons Green
Eel Brook Common
Gas Works
All Saints CE Prim Sch
Fulham Palace
Bishop's Park
Putney Bridge
Putney Pier
Hurlingham Park
Hurlingham House
Athletics Gd
South Park
Hurlingham & Chelsea Sec Sch
Chelsea Coll of Art & Design
Hurlingham Wharf
Wandsworth Bridge
River Thames
Hammersmith & Fulham
Wandsworth
Wandsworth Park
Brandlehow Prim Sch
River Wandle
Wandsworth Town
Wandsworth Gyratory
Putney
Sch of Art & Design
Sands End
Fulham Wharf
Gargoyle Wharf
W6
SW6
SW15
LILLIE RD
DAWES RD
FULHAM RD
NORTH END RD
FULHAM BROADWAY
HARWOOD RD
KING'S RD
NEW KING'S RD
FULHAM PALACE RD
FULHAM HIGH ST
PUTNEY BRIDGE APP
PUTNEY HIGH ST
PUTNEY BRIDGE RD
WANDSWORTH BRIDGE RD
SWANDON WAY
FINBOROUGH RD
REDCLIFFE GDNS
HURLINGHAM RD
CARNWATH RD
STUDDRIDGE ST
A3218
A3220
A3219
B317
B318
A304
A308
A219
A217
A3209
B306
264
265
136
157
24
25
26
78
77
76
75
A
B
C
D
1
2
3
4
5
6

SW10
A
B
C
D
114
FULHAM RD
REDCLIFFE GDNS
FINBOROUGH RD
KING'S RD
OLD CHURCH ST
BEAUFORT ST
OAKLEY ST
ROYAL HOSPITAL RD
CHELSEA EMB
Chelsea & Westminster
Cadogan Pier
Chelsea Reach
ALBERT BRIDGE (SUSPENSION)
Kensington & Chelsea
Wandsworth
CHEYNE WLK
GUNTER GR
EDITH GR
CREMORNE RD
BATTERSEA BRIDGE
Bridge Wharf
Ransome's Dock
Terrace Wlk
Thames Path
Fountain Lake
Old Ferry Wharf
Chelsea Wharf
Cremorne Wharf
River Thames
Chelsea Creek
Gas Works
BATTERSEA BRIDGE RD
ALBERT BRIDGE RD
Festival Pleasure Gardens
CENTRAL AVE
SW11
BATTERSEA
WESTBRIDGE RD
VICARAGE CRES
Hammersmith & Fulham
Wandsworth
Chelsea Harbour Pier
135
266
267
PRINCE OF WALES DR
BATTERSEA PARK RD
Regent Wharf
LOMBARD RD
BATTERSEA HIGH ST
YORK RD
Heliport
Battersea Reach
Sands End
Fulham Wharf
Sherwood Wharf
Gargoyle Wharf
WANDSWORTH BRIDGE
Trad Est
York Gdns
FALCON RD
LATCHMERE RD
Falcon Park
Christ Church CE Prim Sch
THE VILLAGE
Clapham Junction
ST JOHN'S HILL
BATTERSEA RISE
ELSPETH RD
LAVENDER SWEEP
CLAPHAM JUNCTION EST
SWANDON WAY
Wandsworth Town
EAST HILL
NORTH SIDE WANDSWORTH COMM
CLAPHAM COMMON
Belleville Prim Sch
158
1
2
3
4
5
6
26
27
28
75
76
77
78

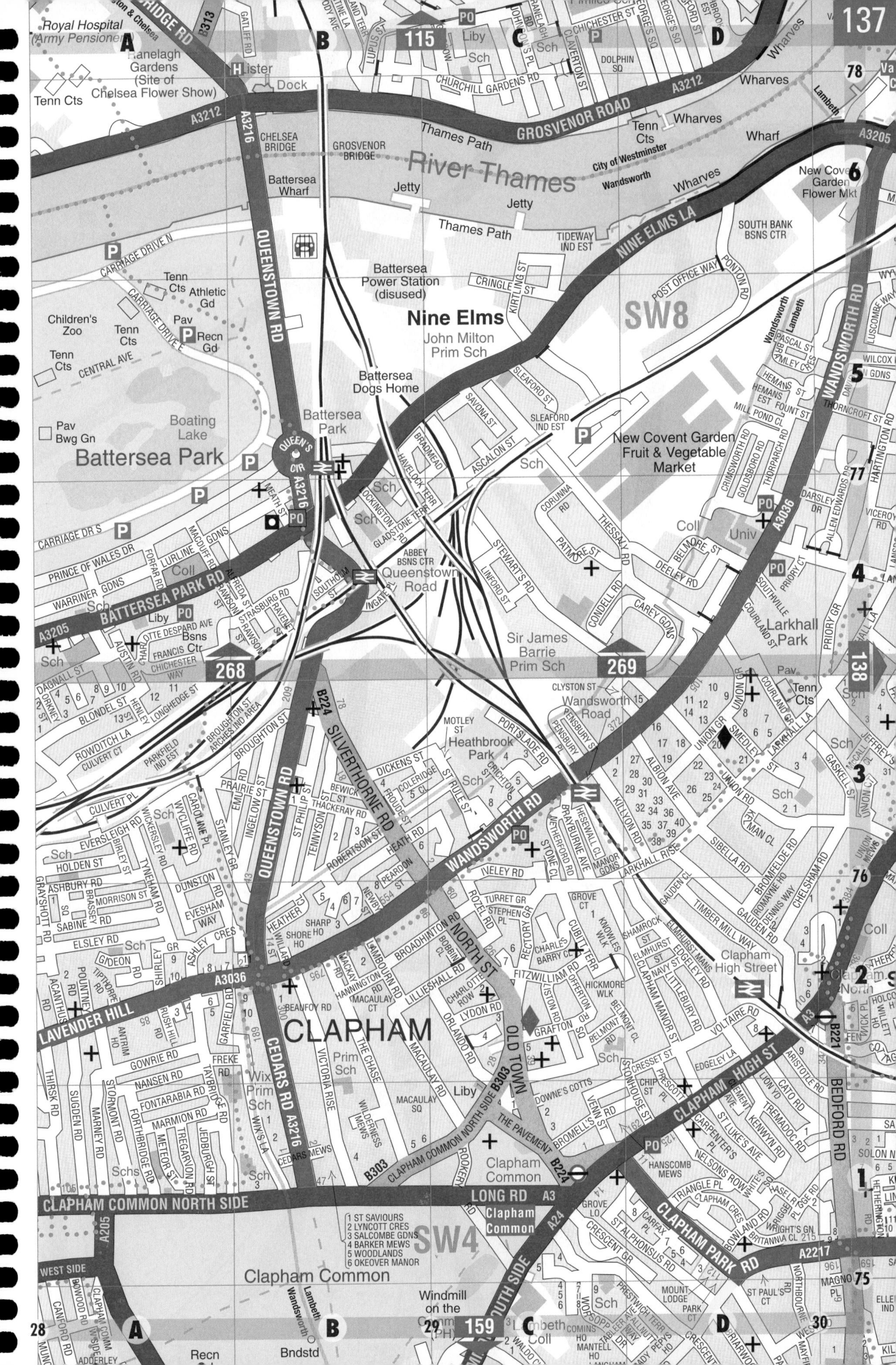
Royal Hospital (Army Pensioners)
Ranelagh Gardens (Site of Chelsea Flower Show)
River Thames
Battersea Power Station (disused)
Nine Elms
SW8
New Covent Garden Fruit & Vegetable Market
Battersea Park
Battersea Dogs Home
Queenstown Road
Wandsworth Road
Larkhall Park
Clapham High Street
CLAPHAM
Clapham Common
SW4
GROSVENOR ROAD
NINE ELMS LA
QUEENSTOWN RD
BATTERSEA PARK RD
WANDSWORTH RD
SILVERTHORNE RD
LAVENDER HILL
CEDARS RD
CLAPHAM HIGH ST
CLAPHAM PARK RD
CLAPHAM COMMON NORTH SIDE
LONG RD
BEDFORD RD
1 ST SAVIOURS
2 LYNCOTT CRES
3 SALCOMBE GDNS
4 BARKER MEWS
5 WOODLANDS
6 OKEOVER MANOR
115
268
269
138
159
28
29
30

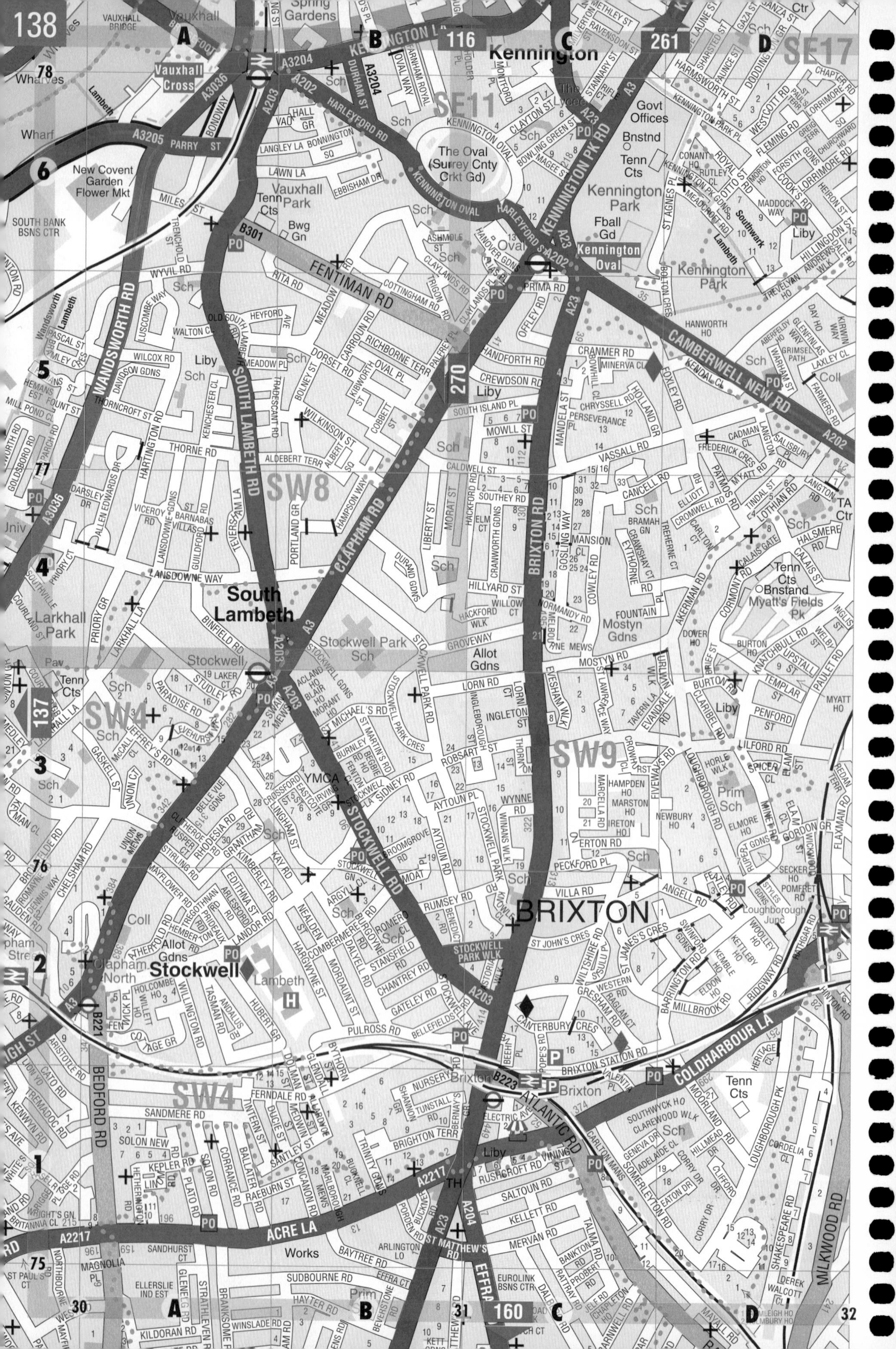

Vauxhall
Kennington
SE11
SE17
Vauxhall Cross
The Oval (Surrey Cnty Crkt Gd)
Vauxhall Park
Kennington Park
Kennington Oval
Govt Offices
New Covent Garden Flower Mkt
SOUTH BANK BSNS CTR
FENTIMAN RD
KENNINGTON PK RD
KENNINGTON OVAL
HARLEYFORD RD
CAMBERWELL NEW RD
WANDSWORTH RD
SOUTH LAMBETH RD
CLAPHAM RD
BRIXTON RD
STOCKWELL RD
SW8
SW9
SW4
South Lambeth
Stockwell
Stockwell Park Sch
Larkhall Park
Myatt's Fields Pk
Mostyn Gdns
Allot Gdns
BRIXTON
Brixton
Clapham North
Lambeth
COLDHARBOUR LA
ACRE LA
ATLANTIC RD
BEDFORD RD
EFFRA RD
MILKWOOD RD
LOUGHBOROUGH PK
Loughborough Junc
Works
ELLERSLIE IND EST
EUROLINK BSNS CTR
A3
A23
A202
A203
A204
A2217
A3036
A3204
A3205
B221
B223
B301
116
261
270
137
160

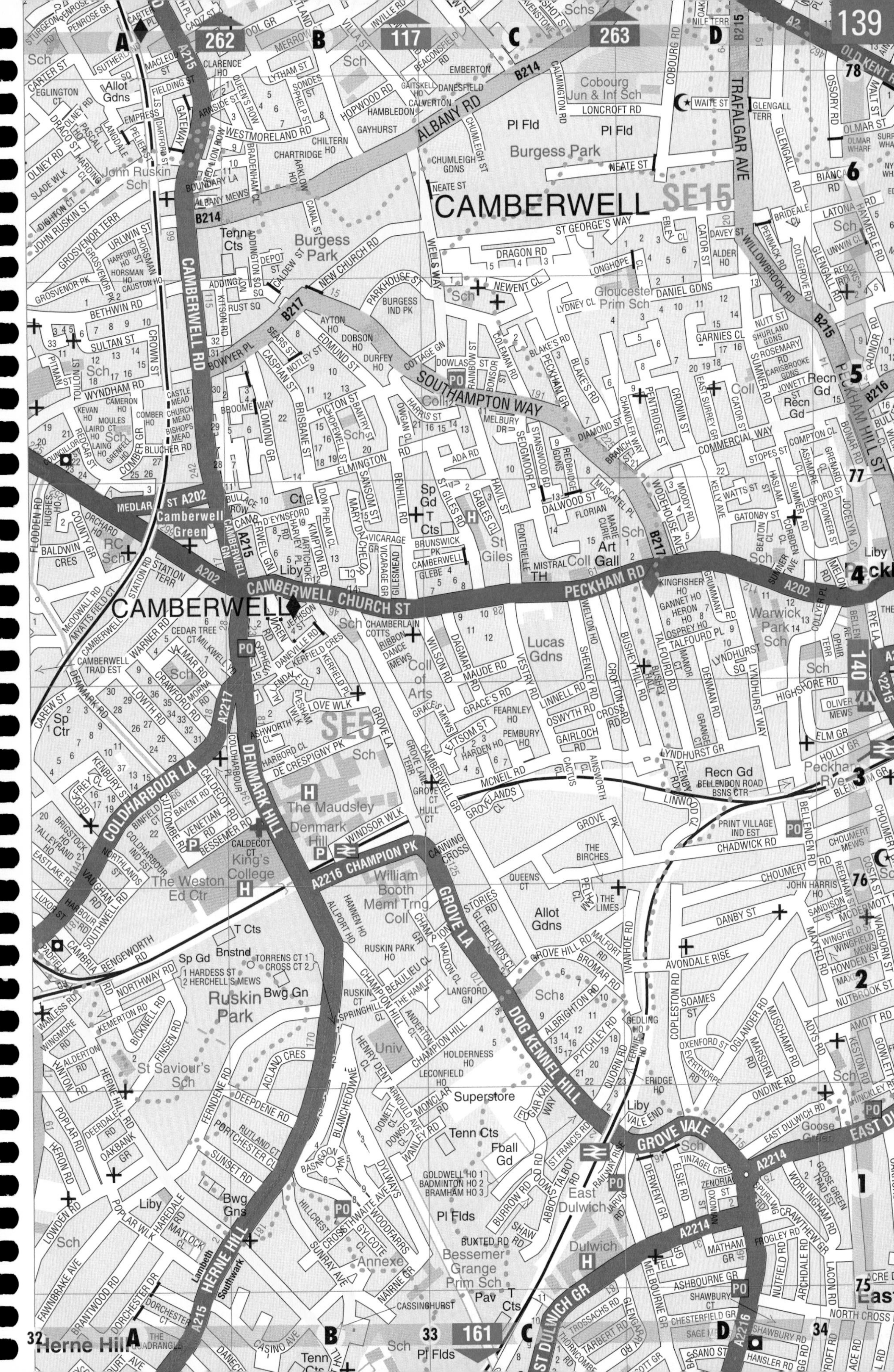
262
117
263
CAMBERWELL
SE15
SE5
Burgess Park
ALBANY RD
B214
CAMBERWELL RD
A215
SOUTHAMPTON WAY
B217
TRAFALGAR AVE
B215
PECKHAM HILL ST
PECKHAM RD
CAMBERWELL CHURCH ST
A202
Camberwell Green
COLDHARBOUR LA
A2217
DENMARK HILL
A2216
CHAMPION PK
GROVE LA
DOG KENNEL HILL
GROVE VALE
A2214
EAST DULWICH
HERNE HILL
Ruskin Park
King's College
The Maudsley
Denmark Hill
Lucas Gdns
Coll of Arts
Cobourg Jun & Inf Sch
Gloucester Prim Sch
Warwick Park Sch
William Booth Meml Trng Coll
The Weston Ed Ctr
St Saviour's Sch
Bessemer Grange Prim Sch
East Dulwich
Dulwich
Peckham Rye
Superstore
Allot Gdns
Recn Gd
BELLENDON ROAD BSNS CTR
PRINT VILLAGE IND EST
Goose Green
140
161
Herne Hill
32
33
34
75
76
77
78
A
B
C
D
1
2
3
4
5
6

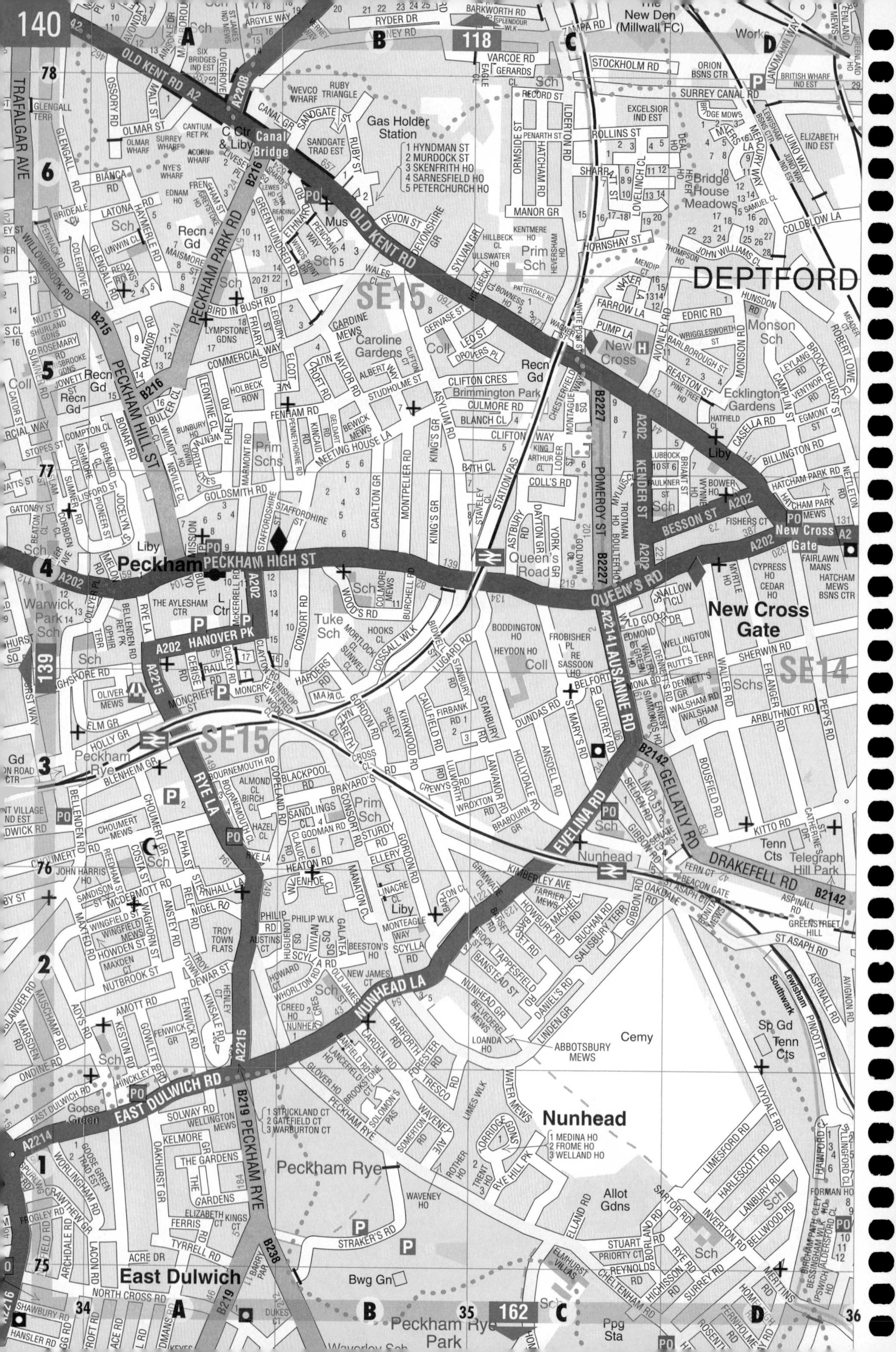

DEPTFORD
Peckham
New Cross Gate
New Cross
Nunhead
East Dulwich
Peckham Rye
Peckham Rye Park
SE15
SE14
OLD KENT RD
PECKHAM HIGH ST
QUEEN'S RD
RYE LA
EAST DULWICH RD
NUNHEAD LA
EVELINA RD
LAUSANNE RD
GELLATLY RD
DRAKEFELL RD
PECKHAM HILL ST
PECKHAM PARK RD
HANOVER PK
KENDER ST
BESSON ST
POMEROY ST
PECKHAM RYE
TRAFALGAR AVE
Gas Holder Station
Caroline Gardens
Brimmington Park
Ecklington Gardens
Bridge House Meadows
Telegraph Hill Park
Queen's Road
Nunhead
Peckham Rye
Cemy
Allot Gdns
The New Den (Millwall FC)
118
139
162

River Thames
SE8
119
Palmer's Wharf
Payne's Wharf
Borthwick Wharf
Blackhorse Wharf
Dreadnought Wharf
Dowell's Wharf
EVELYN ST
CREEK RD
A200
A2209 DEPTFORD CHURCH ST
DEPTFORD HIGH ST
Deptford
Deptford Creek
Greenwich
GREENWICH HIGH RD
GREENWICH SOUTH ST
NORMAN RD
Folkestone Gardens
SANFORD ST
Fordham Park
PAGNELL ST
B207
Superstore
New Cross Gate
New Cross
NEW CROSS RD
DEPTFORD BROADWAY
DEPTFORD BRIDGE
BLACKHEATH RD
A2
A20
AMERSHAM RD
FLORENCE RD
B218
LEWISHAM WAY
SE14
Goldsmiths' Coll Univ of London
SE13
St Johns
BROOKMILL RD
Ravensbourne River
Ravensbourne Park
Elverson Road
LOAMPIT HILL
LOAMPIT VALE
THURSTON RD
MALPAS RD
B2142
ENDWELL RD
Brockley
BROCKLEY RD
SE4
Hilly Fields Park
Prendergast Sch
ADELAIDE AVE
B236
LADYWELL RD
Ladywell
Brockley Cemy
Ladywell Cemy
MOLESWORTH ST
A21
LEWISHAM HIGH ST
142
163
36
37
38
75
76
77
78
A
B
C
D
1
2
3
4
5
6

GREENWICH
National Maritime Mus
Greenwich Park
Old Royal Observatory Greenwich (Mus Annexe)
Old Royal Naval Coll Blds
Univ of Greenwich
Cutty Sark
Gipsy Moth IV
Greenwich Pier
Greenwich Footway Tunnel
The Queen's House
Maze Hill House Gate
One Tree Hill
Maze Hill Gate
St Mary's Gate
National Fan Mus
Flamsteed House
Meridian Building
South Building
Tea House
Bndstd
Croomshill Gate
Vanbrugh Park Gate
The Wilderness (Deer Park)
The John Roan Sch
Ranger's House
Blackheath Gate
Blackheath The Point
Whitfield's Mound
Blackheath Vale
Blackheath
Sixth Form Coll
Blackheath RC Prim Sch
Kid Brook
Lee Green
LEWISHAM
Loampit Vale
Elverson Road
Greenwich
Maze Hill
East Greenwich Pleasaunce
SE10
SE3
SE13
TRAFALGAR RD
ROMNEY RD
CREEK RD
GREENWICH HIGH RD
GREENWICH SOUTH ST
BLACKHEATH HILL
SHOOTERS HILL RD
CHARLTON WAY
HYDE VALE
LEWISHAM RD
LOAMPIT VALE
LEWISHAM HIGH ST
MOLESWORTH ST
BELMONT HILL
LEE TERR
LEE HIGH RD
LEE RD
PRINCE OF WALES RD
PRINCE CHARLES RD
MONTPELIER ROW
ROYAL PAR
BLACKHEATH VILLAGE
GENERAL WOLFE RD
CROOM'S HILL
ROYAL HILL
KING WILLIAM WLK
MAZE HILL
VANBRUGH HILL
WESTCOMBE PARK RD
HARE AND BILLET RD
MOUNTS POND RD
GOFFERS RD
DUKE HUMPHREY RD
TRANQUIL VALE
ELIOT VALE
ELIOT PL
LONG POND RD
DARTMOUTH ROW
DARTMOUTH HILL
LEWISHAM HILL
BLACKHEATH RISE
GRANVILLE PK
ST JOSEPH'S VALE
A206
A200
A2
A2211
A20
A21
A2210
A2212
B209
B210
B212
B220
B236
120
141
164
A
B
C
D
1
2
3
4
5
6
75
76
77
78
38
39
40

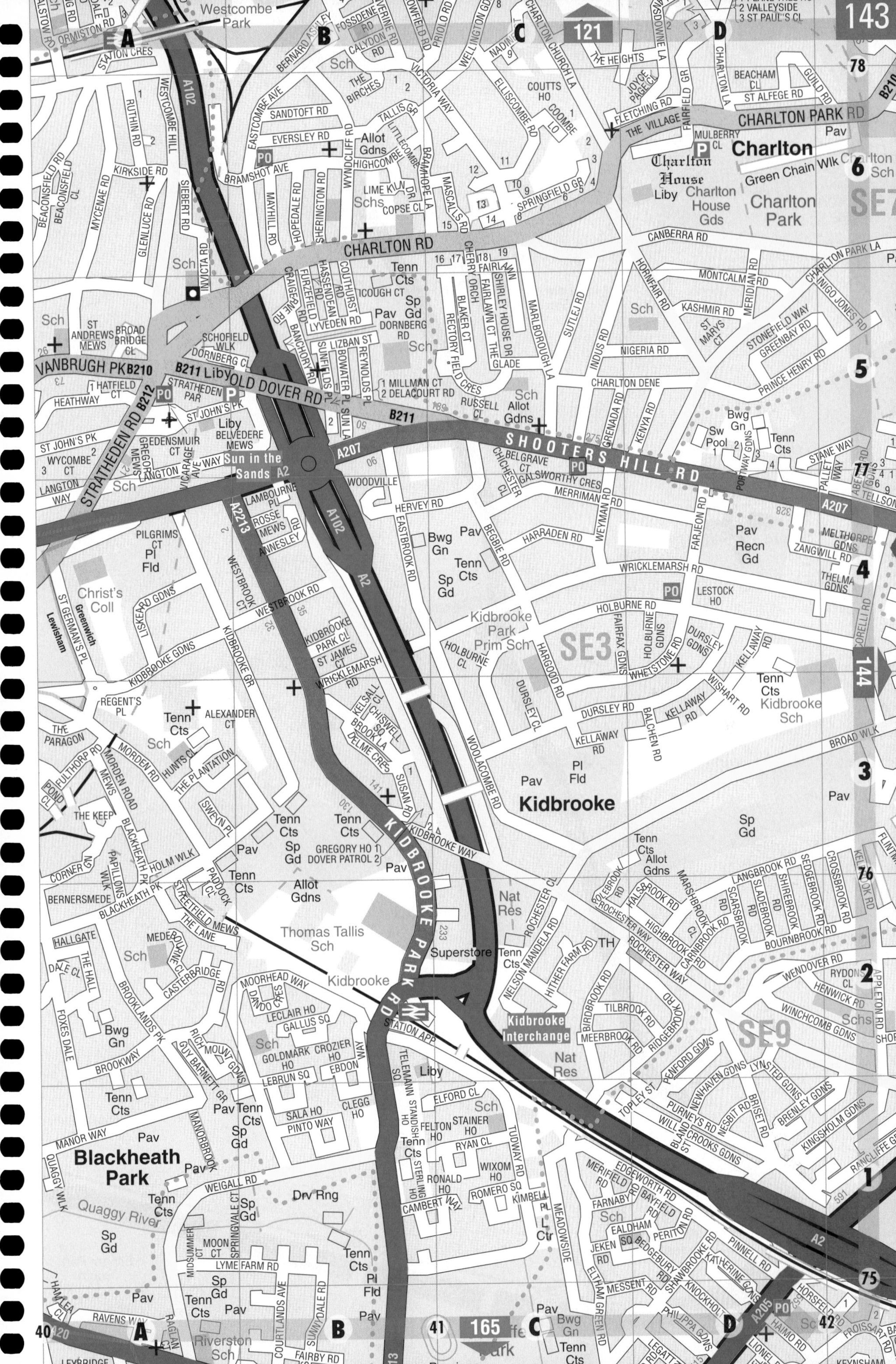

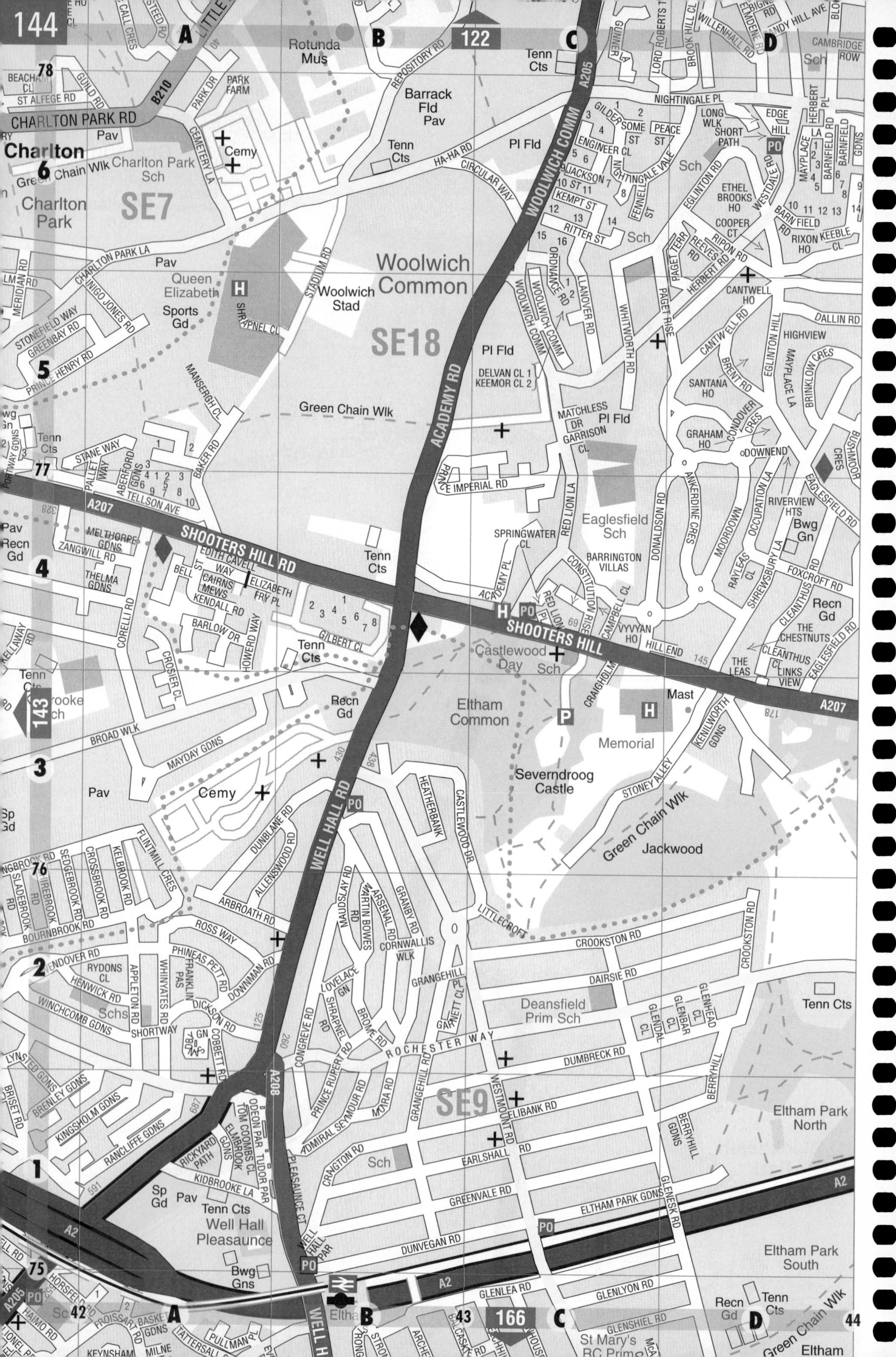
Charlton
SE7
SE18
SE9
Woolwich Common
Charlton Park
Eltham Common
Severndroog Castle
Jackwood
Eltham Park North
Eltham Park South
Well Hall Pleasaunce
SHOOTERS HILL RD
SHOOTERS HILL
WOOLWICH COMM
ACADEMY RD
WELL HALL RD
ROCHESTER WAY
CHARLTON PARK RD
CHARLTON PARK LA
Green Chain Wlk
Rotunda Mus
Barrack Fld Pav
Woolwich Stad
Queen Elizabeth
Eaglesfield Sch
Castlewood Day Sch
Memorial
Deansfield Prim Sch
A207
A205
A208
A2
B210
122
143
166

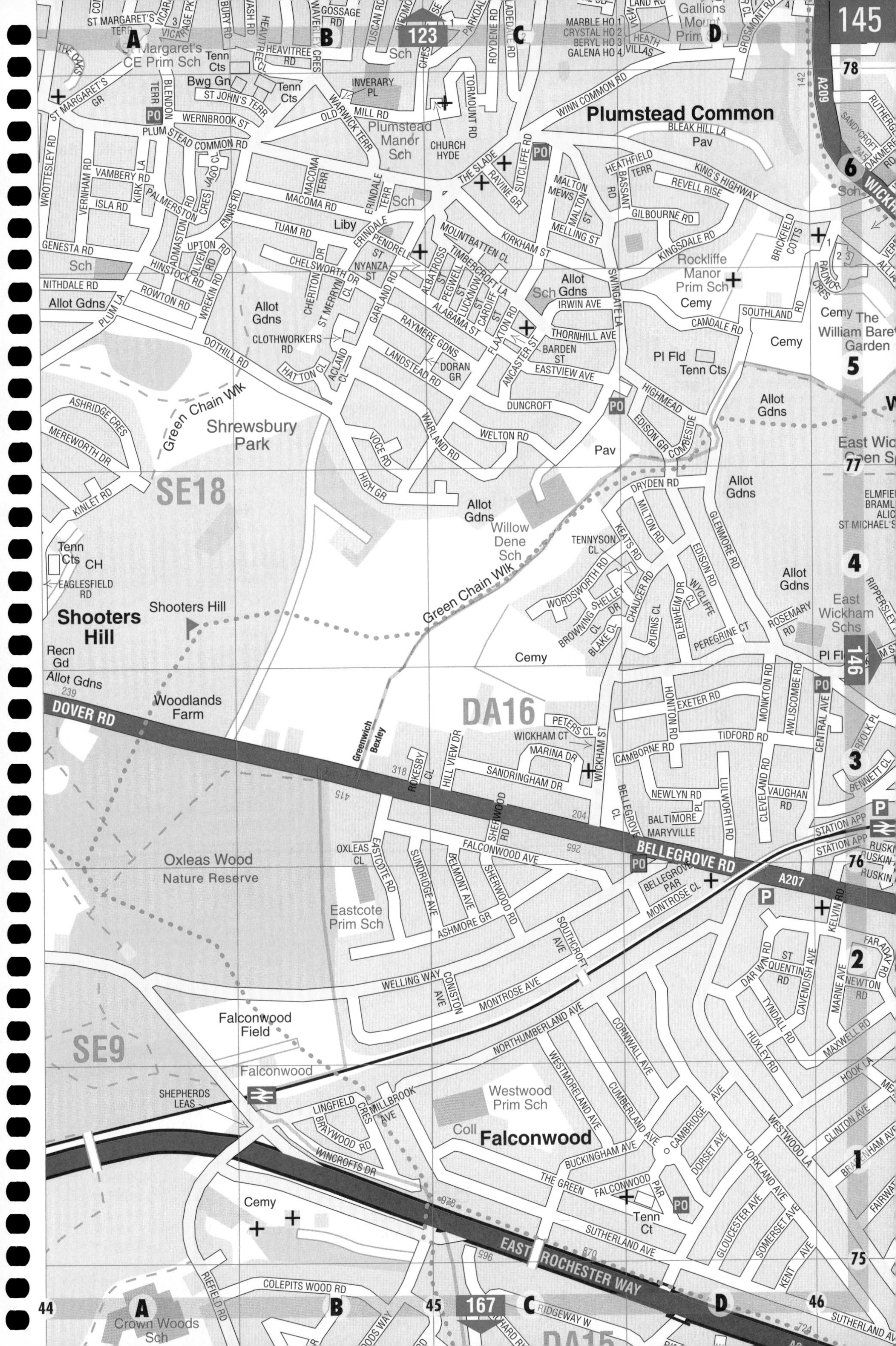
Plumstead Common
Shooters Hill
Shrewsbury Park
SE18
DA16
SE9
DA15
Oxleas Wood
Nature Reserve
Falconwood
Falconwood Field
Woodlands Farm
Green Chain Wlk
DOVER RD
BELLEGROVE RD
A207
A209
EAST ROCHESTER WAY
St Margaret's CE Prim Sch
Plumstead Manor Sch
Rockliffe Manor Prim Sch
Willow Dene Sch
Eastcote Prim Sch
Westwood Prim Sch
Crown Woods Sch
East Wickham Schs
Gallions Mount Prim Sch
The William Barefoot Garden
Allot Gdns
Cemy
Pav
Liby
Tenn Cts
Pl Fld
Recn Gd
WINN COMMON RD
PLUMSTEAD COMMON RD
WERNBROOK ST
KING'S HIGHWAY
KIRKHAM ST
SWINGATE LA
CANDALE RD
SOUTHLAND RD
DOTHILL RD
WICKHAM ST
WELLING WAY
MONTROSE AVE
NORTHUMBERLAND AVE
WESTWOOD LA
SUTHERLAND AVE
BUCKINGHAM AVE
FALCONWOOD AVE
COLEPITS WOOD RD
RIDGEWAY W
123
167
146
44
45
46
A
B
C
D
1
2
3
4
5
6
75
76
77
78

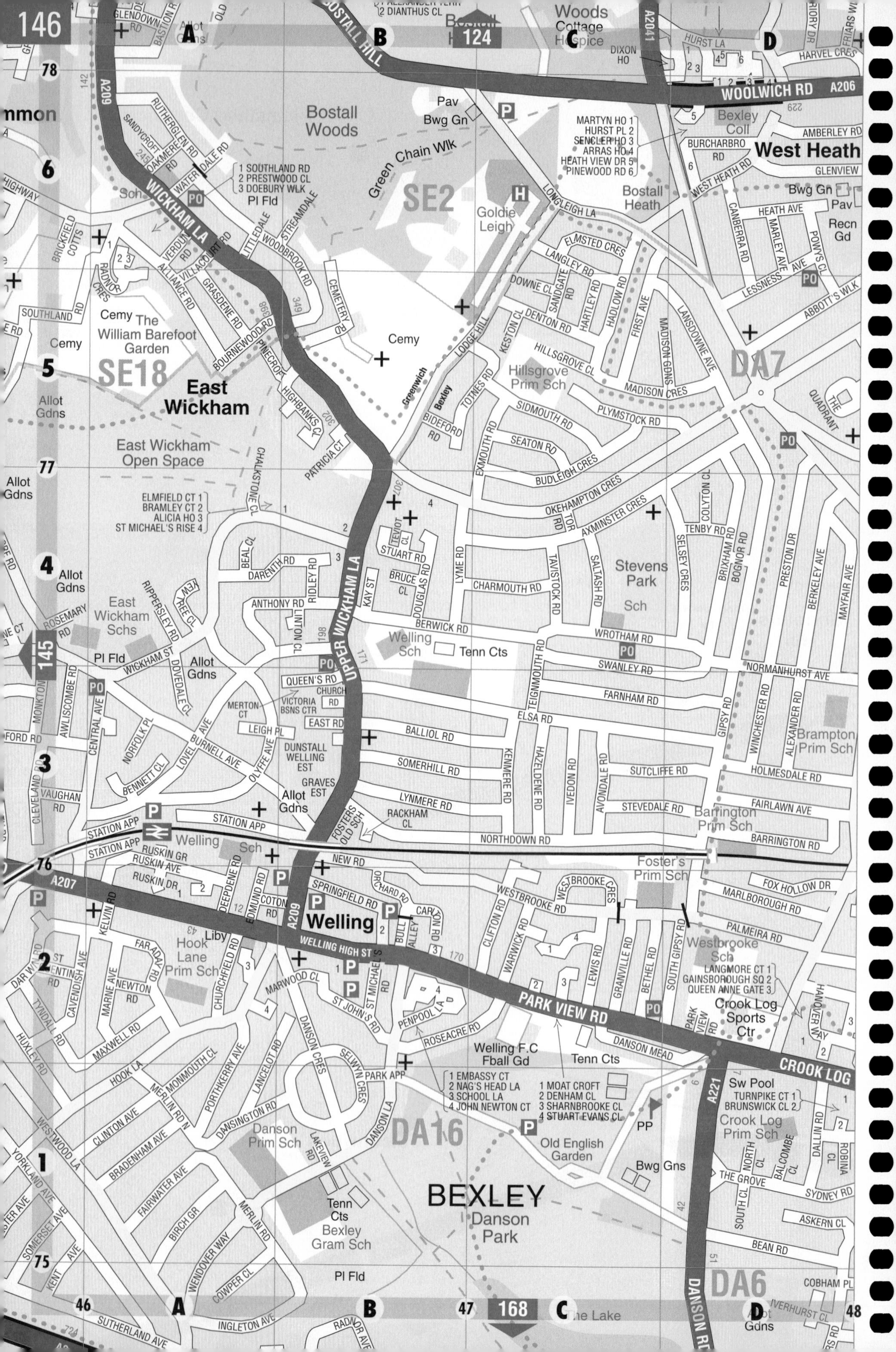

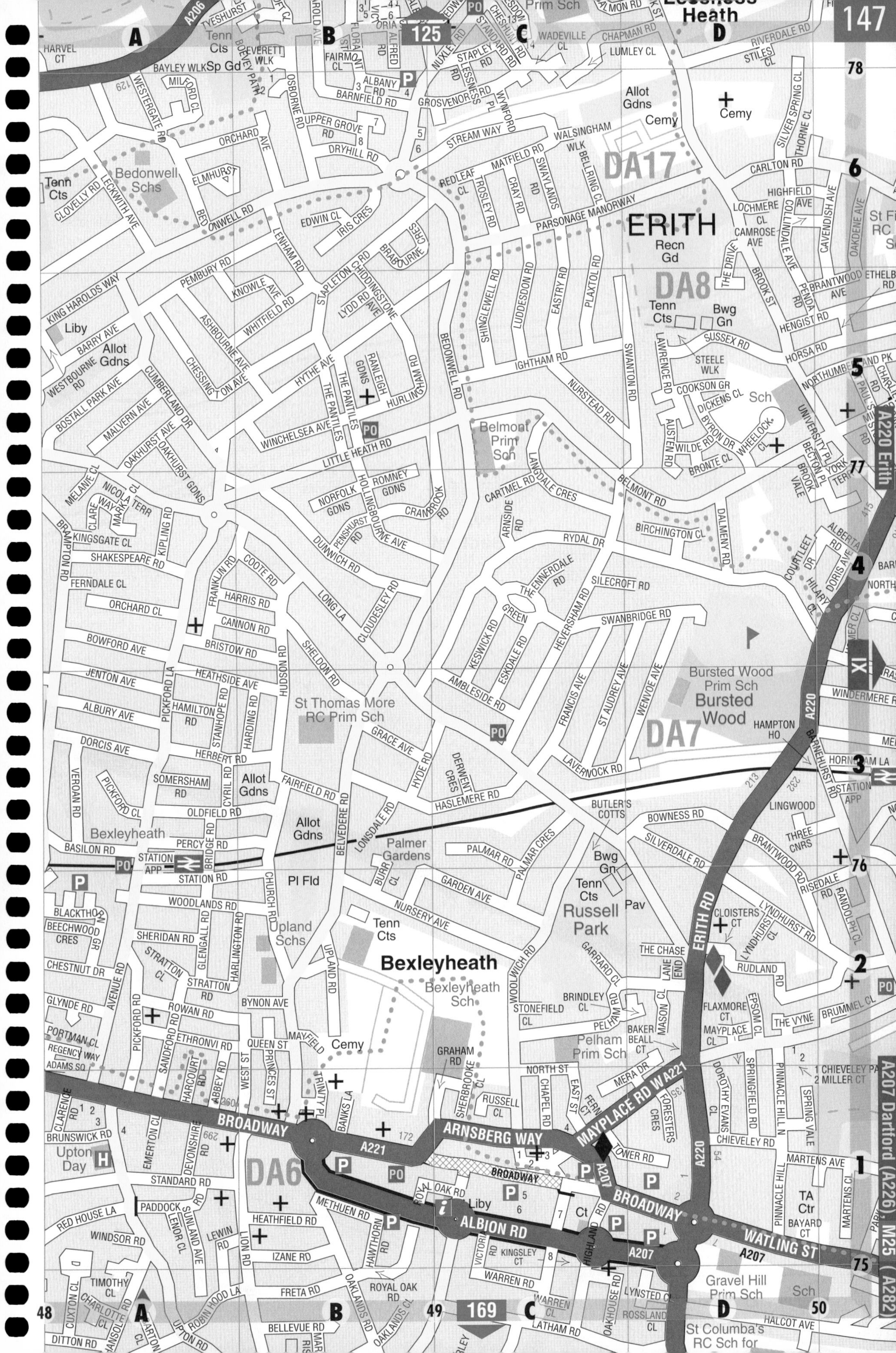

125
169
Heath
ERITH
DA17
DA8
DA7
DA6
Bexleyheath
Russell Park
Bursted Wood
Bursted Wood Prim Sch
Belmont Prim Sch
St Thomas More RC Prim Sch
Upland Schs
Bexleyheath Sch
Pelham Prim Sch
Gravel Hill Prim Sch
Bedonwell Schs
Palmer Gardens
BROADWAY
ARNSBERG WAY
ALBION RD
WATLING ST
ERITH RD
MAYPLACE RD W
A220 Erith
A207 Dartford (A226), M25 (A282)
BELMONT RD
PARSONAGE MANORWAY
LITTLE HEATH RD
WOOLWICH RD
BEDONWELL RD
KING HAROLDS WAY
BOSTALL PARK AVE
LONG LA
HURLINGHAM RD
RYDAL DR
SWANBRIDGE RD
BARNEHURST RD

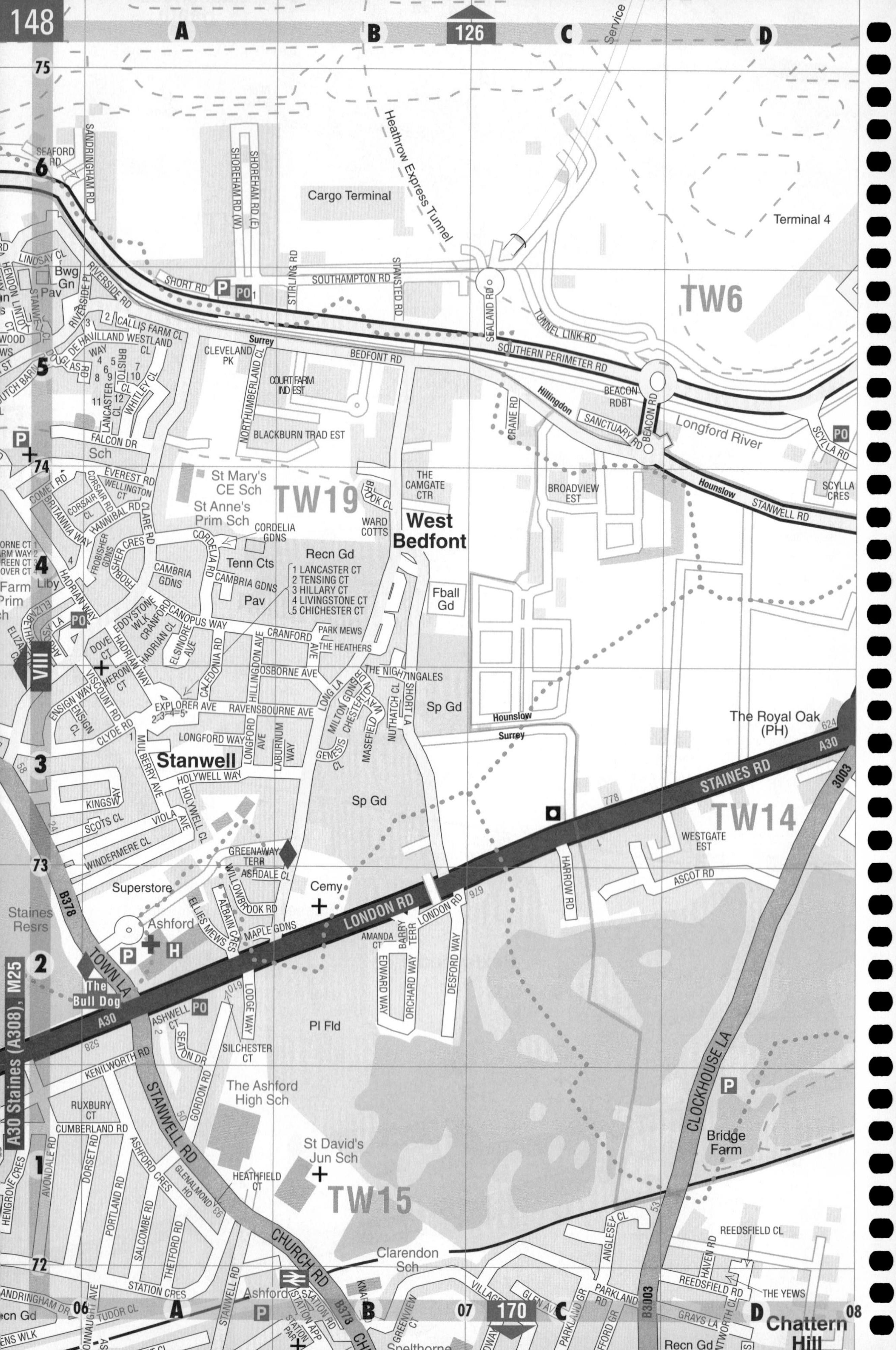
A
B
126
C
D
Heathrow Express Tunnel
Cargo Terminal
Terminal 4
TW6
Service
SHOREHAM RD (W)
SHOREHAM RD (E)
SANDRINGHAM RD
SEAFORD RD
SHORT RD
STIRLING RD
SOUTHAMPTON RD
STANSTED RD
SEALAND RD
TUNNEL LINK RD
SOUTHERN PERIMETER RD
Surrey
BEDFONT RD
CLEVELAND PK
NORTHUMBERLAND CL
COURT FARM IND EST
BLACKBURN TRAD EST
CRANE RD
Hillingdon
SANCTUARY RD
BEACON RDBT
BEACON RD
Longford River
SCYLLA RD
SCYLLA CRES
Hounslow
STANWELL RD
LINDSAY CL
HENDON
Bwg Gn
Pav
RIVERSIDE RD
RIVERSIDE PL
CALLIS FARM CL
DE HAVILLAND WAY
WESTLAND CL
DOUGLAS RD
BRISTOL CL
LANCASTER CL
WHITLEY CL
FALCON DR
Sch
EVEREST RD
WELLINGTON CT
COMET RD
CORSAIR RD
CORSAIR CL
BRITANNIA WAY
HANNIBAL RD
CLARE RD
St Mary's CE Sch
St Anne's Prim Sch
TW19
BROOK CL
THE CAMGATE CTR
WARD COTTS
West Bedfont
BROADVIEW EST
CORDELIA GDNS
CORDELIA RD
FROBISHER GDNS
FROBISHER CRES
Recn Gd
Tenn Cts
CAMBRIA GDNS
1 LANCASTER CT
2 TENSING CT
3 HILLARY CT
4 LIVINGSTONE CT
5 CHICHESTER CT
Pav
Fball Gd
Farm
Prim
Liby
HADRIAN WAY
EDDYSTONE WLK
CRANFORD CL
CANOPUS WAY
HADRIAN CL
ELSINORE AVE
CALEDONIA RD
HILLINGDON AVE
CRANFORD AVE
PARK MEWS
THE HEATHERS
DOVE CT
HERON CT
VISCOUNT RD
OSBORNE AVE
THE NIGHTINGALES
NUTHATCH CL
SHORT LA
LONG LA
MILTON GDNS
CHESTERTON DR
WALDEN
ENSIGN WAY
ENSIGN CL
CLYDE RD
EXPLORER AVE
RAVENSBOURNE AVE
Sp Gd
Hounslow
Surrey
The Royal Oak (PH)
LONGFORD WAY
LONGFORD AVE
LABURNUM WAY
GENESIS CL
MASEFIELD
Stanwell
MULBERRY AVE
HOLYWELL WAY
HOLYWELL CL
KINGSWAY
SCOTS CL
VIOLA AVE
WINDERMERE CL
Sp Gd
STAINES RD
A30
TW14
WESTGATE EST
ASCOT RD
HARROW RD
GREENAWAY TERR
ASHDALE CL
WILLOWBROOK RD
ALBAIN CRES
ELLIES MEWS
MAPLE GDNS
Superstore
Cemy
LONDON RD
LONDON RD
AMANDA CT
BARRY TERR
EDWARD WAY
ORCHARD WAY
DESFORD WAY
Staines Resrs
Ashford
B378
TOWN LA
The Bull Dog
A30
ASHWELL CT
SEATON DR
LODGE WAY
Pl Fld
KENILWORTH RD
SILCHESTER CT
CLOCKHOUSE LA
RUXBURY CT
STANWELL RD
GORDON RD
The Ashford High Sch
CUMBERLAND RD
Bridge Farm
St David's Jun Sch
A30 Staines (A308), M25
HENGROVE CRES
AVONDALE RD
DORSET RD
PORTLAND RD
ASHFORD CRES
SALCOMBE RD
THETFORD RD
GLENALMOND HO
HEATHFIELD CT
TW15
CHURCH RD
Clarendon Sch
ANGLESEY CL
REEDSFIELD CL
HAVEN RD
REEDSFIELD RD
THE YEWS
STATION CRES
STANWELL RD
Ashford
STATION RD
STATION APP
STATION PAR
KNAPP
GREENVIEW CT
VILLAGE
GLEN AVE
PARKLAND GR
PARKLAND RD
B3003
GRAYS LA
WENTWORTH CL
ANDRINGHAM DR
CONNAUGHT AVE
TUDOR CL
Recn Gd
Spelthorne
Chattern Hill
06
07
08
170
72
73
74
75
VIII

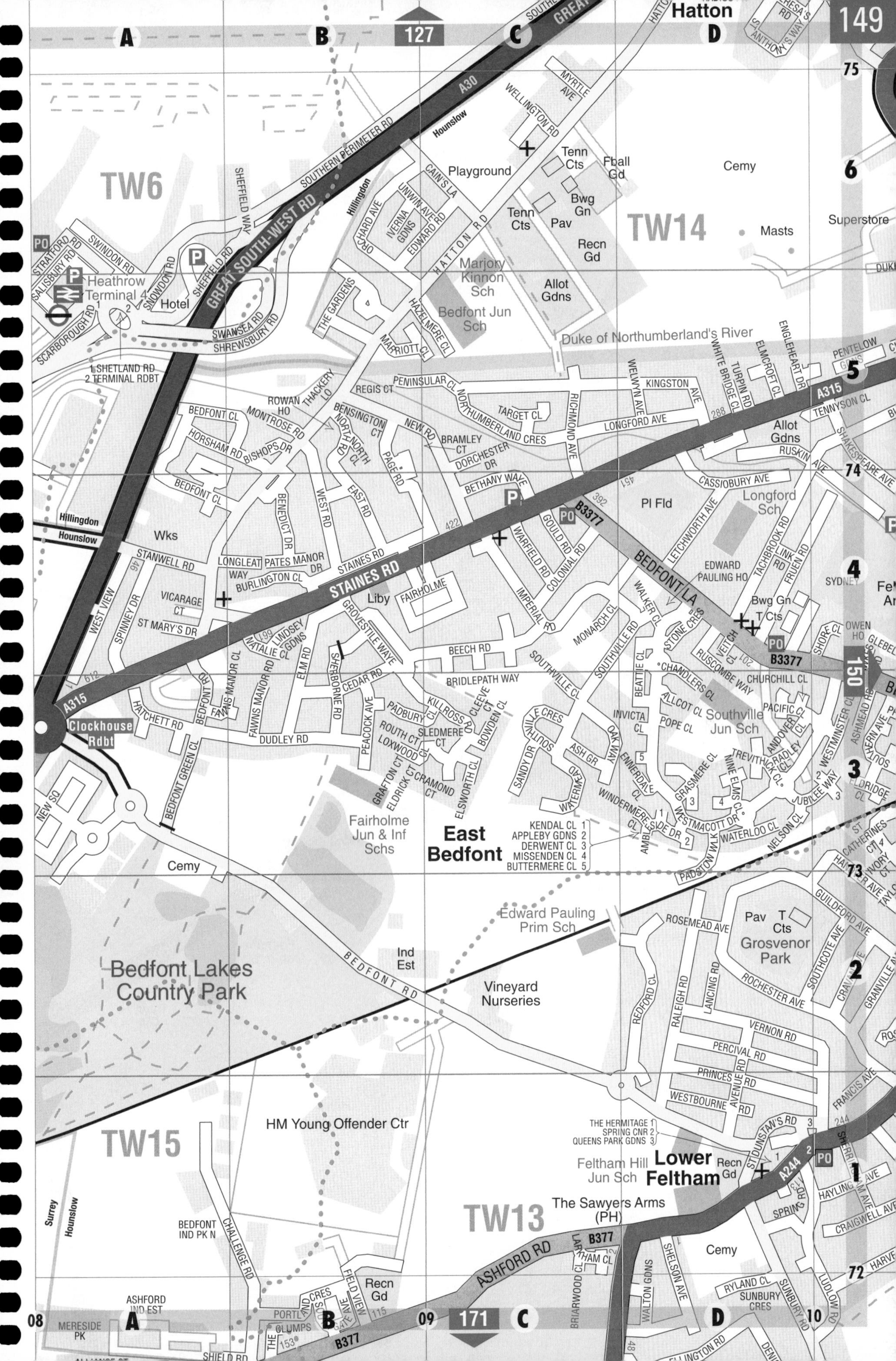

Hatton
127
A
B
C
D
75
6
5
74
4
150
3
73
2
1
72
08
09
10
171
TW6
TW14
TW15
TW13
Heathrow Terminal 4
Hotel
1 SHETLAND RD
2 TERMINAL RDBT
GREAT SOUTH-WEST RD
A30
SOUTHERN PERIMETER RD
Hounslow
Hillingdon
SHEFFIELD WAY
SHEFFIELD RD
SWINDON RD
STRATFORD RD
SALISBURY RD
SNOWDON RD
SCARBOROUGH RD
SWANSEA RD
SHREWSBURY RD
Playground
CAIN'S LA
UNWIN AVE
IVERNA GDNS
EDWARD RD
ORCHARD AVE
HATTON RD
WELLINGTON RD
MYRTLE AVE
Tenn Cts
Fball Gd
Bwg Gn
Pav
Recn Gd
Allot Gdns
Cemy
Masts
Superstore
Marjory Kinnon Sch
Bedfont Jun Sch
THE GARDENS
HAZELMERE CL
MARRIOTT CL
Duke of Northumberland's River
ENGLEHEART DR
ELMCROFT CL
TURPIN RD
WHITE BRIDGE CL
PENTELOW GDNS
TENNYSON CL
A315
KINGSTON AVE
WELWYN AVE
RICHMOND AVE
PENINSULAR CL
REGIS CT
NORTHUMBERLAND CRES
TARGET CL
LONGFORD AVE
ROWAN HO
THACKERY LO
BEDFONT CL
MONTROSE RD
HORSHAM RD
BISHOPS DR
BENSINGTON CT
NORTH RD
NORTH CL
NEW RD
BRAMLEY CT
DORCHESTER DR
PAGE RD
EAST RD
WEST RD
BENEDICT DR
BETHANY WAYE
Allot Gdns
RUSKIN AVE
SHAKESPEARE AVE
CASSIOBURY AVE
Pl Fld
Longford Sch
LETCHWORTH AVE
B3377
BEDFONT LA
GOULD RD
WARFIELD RD
COLONIAL RD
IMPERIAL RD
Wks
Hillingdon
Hounslow
STANWELL RD
LONGLEAT WAY
PATES MANOR DR
BURLINGTON CL
STAINES RD
VICARAGE CT
ST MARY'S DR
WEST VIEW
SPINNEY DR
Liby
FAIRHOLME
GROVESTILE WAYE
LINDSEY GDNS
NATALIE CL
ELM RD
SHERBORNE RD
BEECH RD
MONARCH CL
SOUTHVILLE RD
WALKER CL
STONE CRES
EDWARD PAULING HO
TACHBROOK RD
LINK RD
FRUEN RD
SYDNEY
Bwg Gn
T Cts
VEITCH CL
RUSCOMBE WAY
CHURCHILL CL
SHORE CL
OWEN HO
GLEBELANDS
BRIDLEPATH WAY
SOUTHVILLE CL
BEATTIE CL
CHANDLERS CL
Clockhouse Rdbt
A315
HATCHETT RD
BEDFONT RD
FAWNS MANOR CL
FAWNS MANOR RD
CEDAR RD
PEACOCK AVE
PADBURY CT
KILLROSS RD
CLEEVE CT
BOWDEN CL
SOUTHVILLE CRES
INVICTA CL
ALLCOT CL
POPE CL
Southville Jun Sch
PACIFIC CL
ANDOVER CL
WESTMINSTER CL
ASHMEAD RD
DUDLEY RD
ROUTH CT
SLEDMERE CT
LOXWOOD CL
SANDY DR
ASH GR
OAK WAY
ENNERDALE CL
GRASMERE CL
NINE ELMS CL
TREVITHICK CL
RADLEY CL
JUBILEE WAY
BEDFONT GREEN CL
NEW SQ
GRAFTON CT
ELDRICK CT
CRAMOND CT
ELSWORTH CL
WATERMEAD
WINDERMERE CL
AMBLESIDE DR
WESTMACOTT DR
PADSTOW WLK
WATERLOO CL
NELSON CL
Fairholme Jun & Inf Schs
East Bedfont
KENDAL CL 1
APPLEBY GDNS 2
DERWENT CL 3
MISSENDEN CL 4
BUTTERMERE CL 5
Cemy
ST CATHERINES CT
HANOVER AVE
IVORY CT
Edward Pauling Prim Sch
ROSEMEAD AVE
Pav
T Cts
Grosvenor Park
GUILDFORD AVE
SOUTHCOTE AVE
Bedfont Lakes Country Park
BEDFONT RD
Ind Est
Vineyard Nurseries
REDFORD CL
RALEIGH RD
LANCING RD
ROCHESTER AVE
GRANVILLE AVE
VERNON RD
PERCIVAL RD
PRINCES RD
AVENUE RD
WESTBOURNE RD
FRANCIS AVE
HM Young Offender Ctr
THE HERMITAGE 1
SPRING CNR 2
QUEENS PARK GDNS 3
ST DUNSTAN'S RD
Feltham Hill Jun Sch
Lower Feltham
Recn Gd
A244
SPRING RD
HAYLING AVE
CRAIGWELL AVE
Surrey
Hounslow
BEDFONT IND PK N
CHALLENGE RD
The Sawyers Arms (PH)
ASHFORD RD
B377
LARKHAM CL
BRIARWOOD CL
WALTON GDNS
SHELSON AVE
Cemy
RYLAND CL
SUNBURY CRES
SUNBURY RD
LUDLOW RD
ASHFORD IND EST
MERESIDE PK
PORTLAND CRES
THE CLUMPS
GATE AVE
FIELD VIEW
Recn Gd
SHIELD RD

A
B
C
D
128
172
149
75
74
73
72
6
5
4
3
2
1
10
11
12
North Feltham
FELTHAM
Hanworth
TW14
TW13
STAINES RD
A315
A312
A244
A314
B3377
FAGG'S RD
HARLINGTON RD W
HARLINGTON RD E
HOUNSLOW RD
UXBRIDGE RD
HIGH ST
BEDFONT LA
HANWORTH RD
HATTON GN
HERON WAY
NORTH FELTHAM TRAD EST
SPUR RD
RIVER GDNS BSNS CTR
MAPLE GR BSNS CTR
DULBOROUGH WAY
TAMIAN IND EST
TAMIAN WAY
CLEMENTS CT
CENTRAL PK EST
Allot Gdns
HASLEMERE IND EST
PIER RD
DELLBOW RD
FREEHOLD IND CTR
AMBERLEY WAY
FAIRWAY EST
DOCKWELL'S IND EST
ISLAY GDNS
Garden Ctr
FAIRWAY CL
ARMADALE RD
SPACE WAVE
CHALMERS WAY
CENTRAL WAY
FALCON WAY
WILLOW HO
RIVER GDNS
Superstore
Cemy
Masts
MERCURY CTR
Duke of Northumberland's River
MILL WAY
ROMAN CL
CH
DUKES GREEN AVE
THE GRIFFIN CTR
THE VALE
BABER BRIDGE PAR
BABER BRIDGE
Hounslow Heath
River
ENGLEHEART DR
PENTELOW GDNS
CLIVE RD
MINIMAX CL
BYWARD AVE
BEESTON WAY
LANSBURY AVE
GARDNER PL
BABER DR
CHANDLER CT
TURPIN RD
PO
TENNYSON CL
BURNS AVE
ROSSLYN AVE
BUCKINGHAM AVE
BECKETTS CL
FIELD RD
VIOLA AVE
Allot Gdns
SHAKESPEARE AVE
SHAFTESBURY AVE
GLADSTONE AVE
RUSKIN AVE
Pl Fld
CARLTON AVE
CHICHESTER WAY
DENHAM RD
FAREHAM RD
Longford Sch
THE DELL
WALSHAM RD
HELEN AVE
CLYMPING DENE
SPARROW FARM DR
P
THE DRIVE
Sparrow Farm Schs
TACHBROOK RD
LINK RD
FRUEN RD
1 FRANK TOWELL CT
2 BRASSEY CL
3 EASTLEIGH WAY
4 ORCHARD RD
5 PEACH RD
6 ALMOND CL
7 HAZEL GR
8 HUNTER HO
9 HAWTHORNE RD
10 TILLEY RD
11 PLUM CL
13 MAGNOLIA CT
14 LEMON GR
15 BELVEDERE HO
16 FELBRIDGE CT
T Cts
BRAINTON AVE
CENTRAL PAR
FINCH DR
CYGNET AVE
SYDNEY
Feltham Arena
Bwg Gn
CAMBRIA CT
NURSERY CL
FERN GR
PARK WAY
Pl Fld
DURHAM RD
OWEN HO
SHORE CL
GLEBELANDS RD
HAWKES RD
STATION PAR
STATION ESTATE RD
LOCOMOTIVE DR
HILL CL
PACIFIC CL
ANDOVER CL
WESTMINSTER CL
ASHMEAD RD
PROCTORS CL
TYNAN CL
SANDYCOMBE RD
SYDNEY RD
MANOR PL
NEW RD
Feltham
LC
QUEEN'S RD
GLOUCESTER RD
NORFOLK RD
HEREFORD RD
Tenn Cts
CROMWELL RD
KINGS RD
BEAUCLERK CL
SALISBURY RD
BOUNDARIES RD
TREVITHICK CL
BRADLEY CL
NINE ELMS CL
JUBILEE WAY
SOUTHERN AVE
ELDRIDGE CL
RAILWAY TERR
Ct
CARDINAL RD
FLORENCE RD
ASHFIELD AVE
DE BROOME RD
SLATTERY RD
WYATT CL
WIGLEY RD
NELSON CL
WATERLOO CL
ST CATHERINES CT
IVORY CT
HANOVER AVE
TAYLORS CT
HIGHFIELD RD
BOWSLEY CT
THE CENTRE
NEW CHAPEL SQ
VICTORIA RD
The Victoria Jun Sch
Sch
DANESBURY RD
CAMDEN AVE
ALFRED RD
LAFONE AVE
ELTHORNE CT
WESTBURY
AMESBURY RD
WIGLEY RD
MARLBOROUGH RD
EASTBOURNE
Pav
Grosvenor Park
GUILDFORD AVE
WILTON WLK
MONO LA
THE GREEN
Liby
DEVONSHIRE CT
ASTRID HO
BROWELLS LA
Feltham Comm Sch
SOUTHCOTE AVE
CRAVAN AVE
GRANVILLE AVE
AIR PARK WAY
WILTON PAR
FELTHAM BSNS COMPLEX
ROCHESTER AVE
MANOR LA
MOSS GDNS
CAVENDISH TERR
WOODLAWN
VERNON RD
ROSE GDNS
1 PARKFIELD PAR
2 ROCHESTER PAR
3 THE VINEYARDS
4 CHERVIL CL
Sp Gd
Sp Ctr
FRANCIS AVE
VINEYARD RD
MAPLE IND EST
MAPLE WAY
ELMWOOD AVE
FOREST RD
Hanworth Park House
Hanworth Park
FELTHAM CORPORATE CTR
OLAF PALME HOUSE
SANDALWOOD RD
PINEWOOD RD
CHARLESTON CL
TAWNY CL
PARKFIELD AVE
PARKFIELD RD
POPLAR WAY
PLANE TREE CRES
ASPEN WAY
FELTHAMBROOK IND EST
CHESTNUT WAY
ROKERIES CL
ST DUNSTAN'S RD
SHERRINGHAM AVE
HAYLING AVE
CRAIGWELL AVE
PARKFIELD CRES
APRIL CL
SPRING RD
HARVEST RD
SYCAMORE CL
BADGER CL
TANGLEWOOD WAY
FOXWOOD CL
ELMGATE AVE
CLIFTON AVE
HOUNSLOW RD
BROOKSIDE
PINKCOAT CL
ROEBUCK CL
CAMROSE AVE
FERNSIDE AVE
SUNBURY CRES
SUNBURY RD
LUDLOW RD
DEERHURST CL
HUNTSMAN CL
FELTHAMBROOK WAY
CLIFTON PAR
TUDOR CT
1 BLAKEWOOD CL
2 SHAKESPEARE WAY
THE HOLLANDS
COTTINGTON RD

129
A
B
C
D
A315
A3063
A314
WELLINGTON RD S
WHITTON RD
Hounslow
TW3
TW4
TW2
TW13
The Orchard Jun & Inf Sch
The Heathland Sch
Hounslow Heath Nature Reserve
CONNAUGHT AVE
MIDSUMMER AVE
MUNSTER AVE
COBBS RD
ROSEHEATH RD
MARSHALL CL
BROMPTON CL
BERESFORD GDNS
YEW TREE WLK
AVONDALE GDNS
VICTORIA AVE
WELLINGTON AVE
ROSEVILLE AVE
GRANVILLE AVE
ST AUBYN'S AVE
ST HELIERS AVE
ROSSINDEL RD
PENDEREL RD
ALBION RD
CAMBRIA CL
STATION RD
KINGFISHER CT
ARGYLE RD
THE AVENUE
ST STEPHEN'S RD
MURRAY AVE
CARRINGTON AVE
HAMILTON CRES
PARK AVE
CEDAR AVE
B361
HOUNSLOW AVE
MASWELL PARK RD
INWOOD BSNS PK
SHERIDAN CT 1
PICKWICK CL 2
HEATHLANDS CT 3
BRAMLEY WAY 4
HEATHLANDS WAY
FRAMPTON RD
WRAYSBURY CL
DORNEY WAY
RAGLAN CL
BEAULIEU CL
NURSERY GDNS
GARRISON CL
CARLTON HO
NELSON GDNS
B358
NELSON RD
WYNDHAM CRES
BODICEA MEWS 1
SHELBURNE DR 2
FOUR SQUARE CT 3
SLADE HO 1
JAMIESON HO 2
SIMPSON RD
MEADOW CL
CONWAY RD
STEPHENSON RD
COLLINGWOOD CL
RODNEY RD
ATHERLEY WAY 1
DUNLEARY CL 2
DANIEL CL 3
EDGAR RD
HANWORTH RD
HARVEY RD
REDFERN AVE
GODFREY WAY
Cemy
Recn Gd
WILLS CRES
GRASMERE AVE
RYDAL GDNS
RUNNYMEDE RD
DERWENT RD
CONISTON RD
WHITTON WAY
Tenn Cts
Pav
Nelson Prim Sch
GILPIN CRES
RUNNYMEDE GDNS
NELSON RD
ST EDMUND'S LA
EVELYN CL
CAMELLIA PL
VINCAM CL
ASHDALE WAY
TRANMERE RD
St Edmund's RC Prim Sch
CONSTANCE RD
Nursery
MONTROSE AVE
1 MALLARD CL
2 BRUNEL WLK
3 BRACKEN CL
4 HEATHER WLK
HEATHSIDE
THE BIRCHES
LEA CL
BIRD WLK
MILL FARM BSNS PK
Hounslow
Richmond upon Thames
River Crane
Crem
FARM RD
MILLFIELD RD
GRAFTON CL
MILL FARM CRES
PEMBRIDGE AVE
CHESTER AVE
GLASBROOK AVE
ALBEMARLE AVE
VILLIERS AVE
CHEYNE AVE
SHERINGHAM AVE
LYNDHURST AVE
WAVERLEY AVE
POWDER MILL LA
CHILTERN AVE
ELLERMAN AVE
Tenn Cts
Sp Gd
Heathfield Jun & Inf Schs
STIRLING RD
SPRINGFIELD RD
GOSTLING RD
COBBETT RD
WARBURTON RD
LONGFORD RD
HOSPITAL BRIDGE RD
CRANBROOK DR
BRYANSTON AVE
BLANDFORD AVE
FAIRFIELD AVE
RYECROFT AVE
STRATHEARN AVE
Bishop Perrin CE Prim Sch
Allot Gdns
Whitton Sch
ROSS HO
ROSS RD
152
WOODLAWN CRES
CRANE PARK RD
Liby
A316
Games Ct
Sp Gd
River Crane
Crane Park
Hospital Bridge Rdbt
PEVENSEY RD
BEXHILL CL
MEADOW RD
LITTLE PARK DR
OAKS AVE
SUNNINGDALE AVE
CANTERBURY RD
BRAID CL
TOWFIELD RD
NORMAN AVE
LORDS CL
BARNLEA CL
1 TOWFIELD CT
2 NORMAN HO
3 RIVER CRANE WAY
SAXON HO
SAXON AVE
EDMUND GR
HILL GR
GARDNER HO
EXETER HO
GATFIELD HO
Pl Fld
WATERMILL WAY
SHORE GR
GATFIELD GR
BASDEN GR
EVANS GR
BEACH GR
Crane Park Prim Sch
Recn Gd
NENE GDNS
FOUNTAINS CL
FOUNTAINS AVE
CHURCHFIELDS AVE
SEKHON TERR
GREAT CHERTSEY RD
BEECH WAY
ELM CL
RIVER WAY
WILLOW WAY
BYEWAYS
COURT CL
RIVERMEADS AVE
WARWICK LO
HOSPITAL BRIDGE RD
FULWELL PARK AVE
NANOEL RD
PORTUGAL GDNS
A305
STAINES RD
COURT CLOSE AVE
HOUNSLOW RD
MARKET PAR
NEWGATE CL
HAMPTON FARM IND EST
1 WHITELY CT
2 BUTTS COTTS
WINCHESTER RD
BIDEFORD CL
EXETER RD
YORK WAY
LINCOLN RD
SUNRISE CL
BELL LA
HAMPTON RD W
A312
THE LION CTR
HANWORTH TRAD EST
REX HO
WILLOW COTTS
MOUNT
RIDGE WAY
WINSLOW WAY
LONGFORD CL
WEBB HO
SWIFT RD
DEVONSHIRE
Oriel Prim Sch
LINKS IND EST
OGDEN HO
SWINFIELD CL
CROSBY CL
CRESSWELL RD
Apex Cnr
TWICKENHAM RD
HAMPTON RD E
BROADLANDS
GLEBE WAY
WHITELEYS WAY
BUTTS CRES
SOUTH CL
Allot Gdns
1 EDWIN STRAY HO
2 CRANE HO
3 GLEBE HO
4 CHERTSEY HO
5 WHITELEYS HO
6 BUTTS HO
7 GLEBE COTTS
CH Twickenham
Fulwell Park
Drv Rng
LONGFORD HO
173
Superstore
STOURTON AVE
AIRLAWN CL
AUGUSTUS CT
CRISPEN RD
12
13
14
72
73
74
75
1
2
3
4
5
6

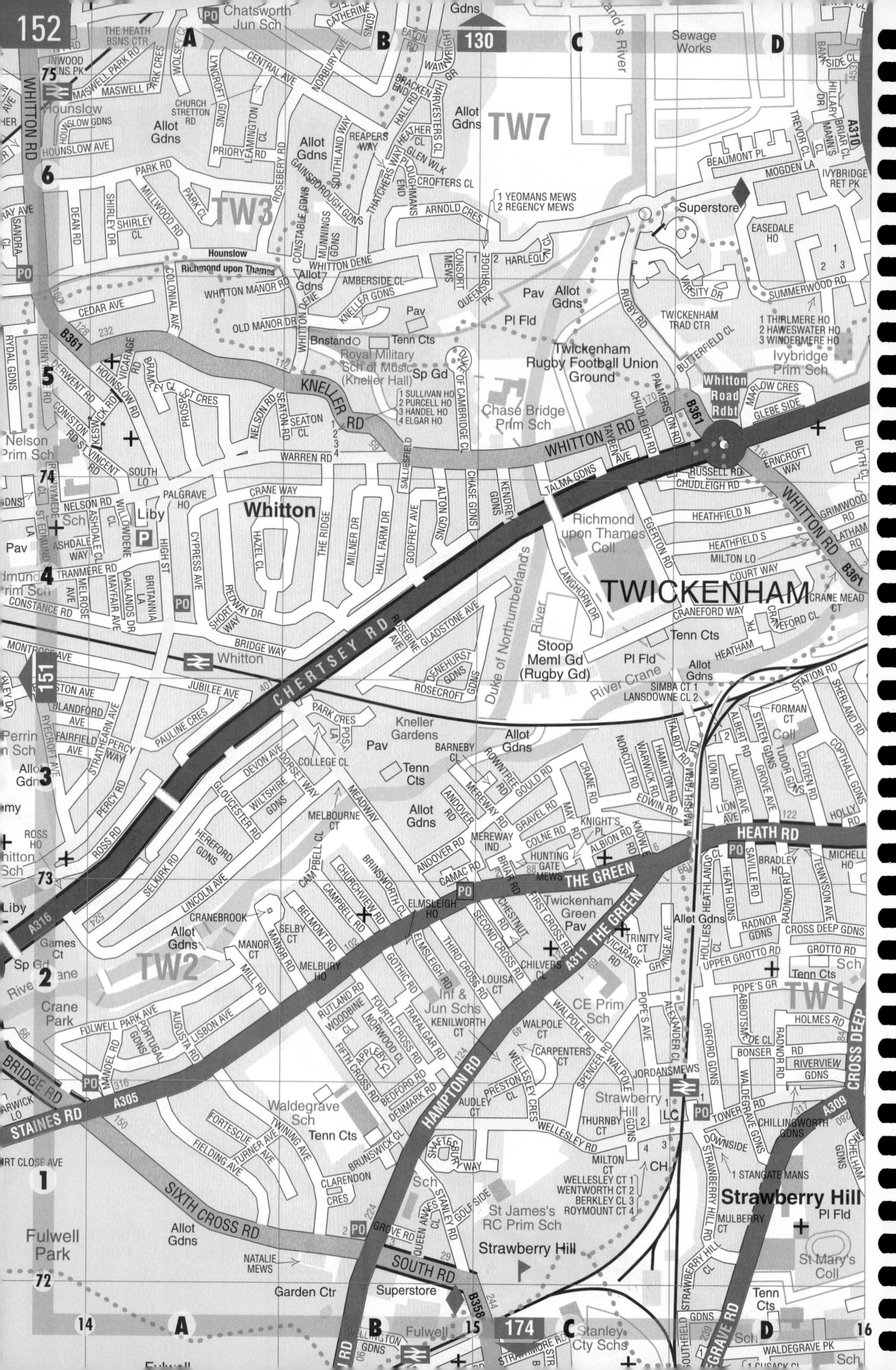

Richmond Lock
131
RICHMOND
TWICKENHAM BRIDGE
TWICKENHAM RD
ST MARGARET'S RD
THE AVENUE
St Margarets Rdbt
CHERTSEY RD
London Road Rdbt
TW7
River Crane
St Margarets
Twickenham
RICHMOND RD
RICHMOND BRIDGE
Cambridge Park
Marble Hill Park
TW1
Marble Hill
Thames Path
Orleans Park Sec Sch
York House
River Thames
Eel Pie Island
Ham House
TW10
Deutsche Schule
The Russell Prim Sch
Strathmore Sch
The Russell Sch
St Catherine's Convent Girls Prep & Senior Schs
Grey Court Sch
Ham
PETERSHAM RD
STRAWBERRY VALE
CROSS DEEP
154
175
Sudbrook
Meadlands Prim Sch

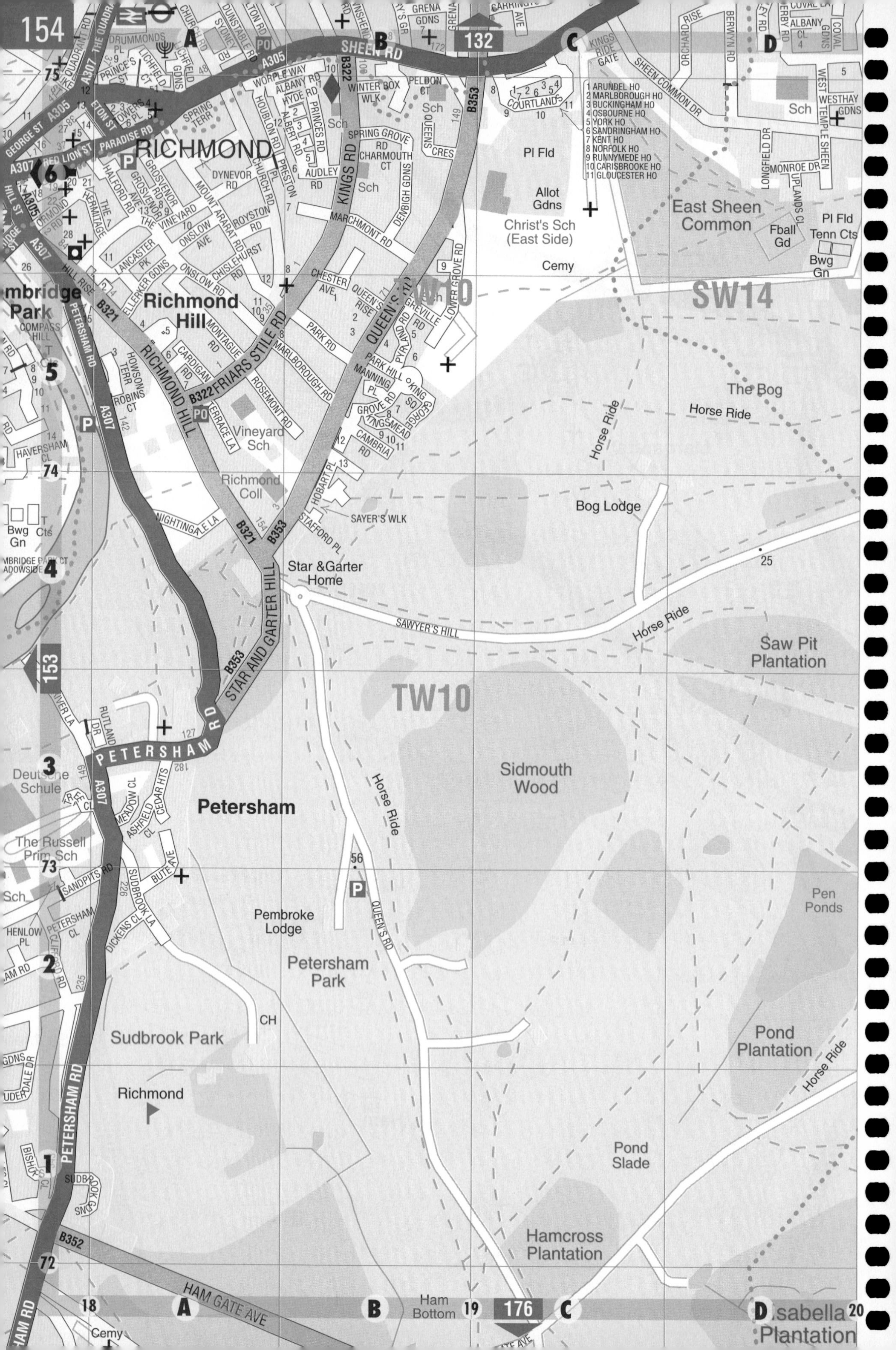

132
SHEEN RD
RICHMOND
Richmond Hill
Petersham
PETERSHAM RD
QUEEN'S RD
KINGS RD
FRIARS STILE RD
RICHMOND HILL
STAR AND GARTER HILL
SAWYER'S HILL
East Sheen Common
SW14
TW10
The Bog
Horse Ride
Bog Lodge
Star &Garter Home
Richmond Coll
Vineyard Sch
Christ's Sch (East Side)
Cemy
Saw Pit Plantation
Sidmouth Wood
Pembroke Lodge
Petersham Park
Sudbrook Park
Pen Ponds
Pond Plantation
Pond Slade
Hamcross Plantation
Ham Bottom
Isabella Plantation
HAM GATE AVE
Deutsche Schule
The Russell Prim Sch
1 ARUNDEL HO
2 MARLBOROUGH HO
3 BUCKINGHAM HO
4 OSBOURNE HO
5 YORK HO
6 SANDRINGHAM HO
7 KENT HO
8 NORFOLK HO
9 RUNNYMEDE HO
10 CARISBROOKE HO
11 GLOUCESTER HO
153
176

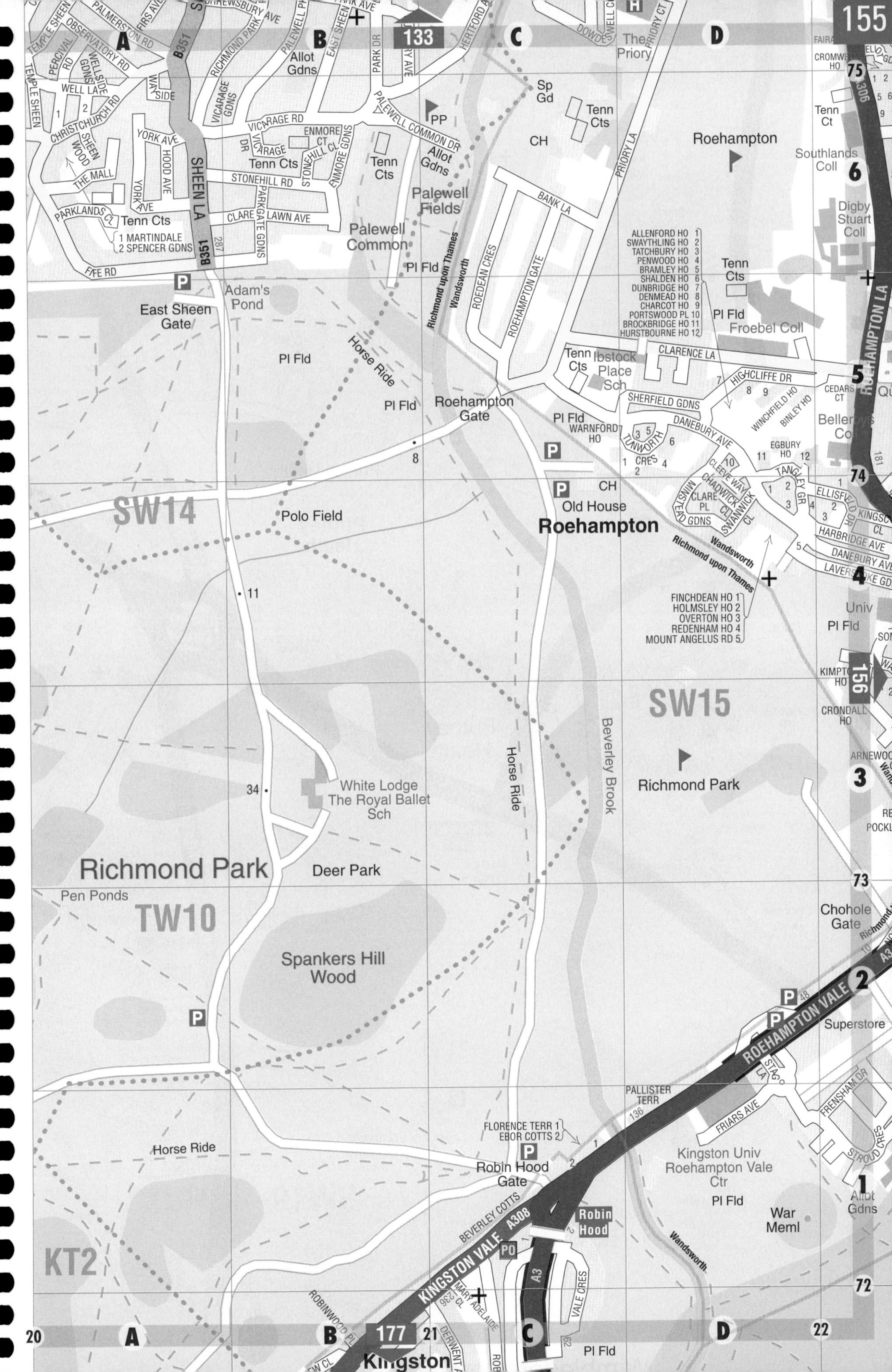

Roehampton
Richmond Park
SW14
SW15
TW10
KT2
Polo Field
White Lodge
The Royal Ballet
Sch
Deer Park
Spankers Hill
Wood
Pen Ponds
Beverley Brook
Horse Ride
East Sheen
Gate
Roehampton
Gate
Robin Hood
Gate
Adam's
Pond
Palewell
Common
Palewell
Fields
Old House
Kingston Univ
Roehampton Vale
Ctr
War
Meml
Superstore
Chohole
Gate
Froebel Coll
Digby
Stuart
Coll
Southlands
Coll
Ibstock
Place
Sch
The
Priory
SHEEN LA
ROEHAMPTON LA
ROEHAMPTON VALE
KINGSTON VALE
Kingston
Richmond upon Thames
Wandsworth
ALLENFORD HO 1
SWAYTHLING HO 2
TATCHBURY HO 3
PENWOOD HO 4
BRAMLEY HO 5
SHALDEN HO 6
DUNBRIDGE HO 7
DENMEAD HO 8
CHARCOT HO 9
PORTSWOOD PL 10
BROCKBRIDGE HO 11
HURSTBOURNE HO 12
FINCHDEAN HO 1
HOLMSLEY HO 2
OVERTON HO 3
REDENHAM HO 4
MOUNT ANGELUS RD 5
FLORENCE TERR 1
EBOR COTTS 2
1 MARTINDALE
2 SPENCER GDNS
133
156
177

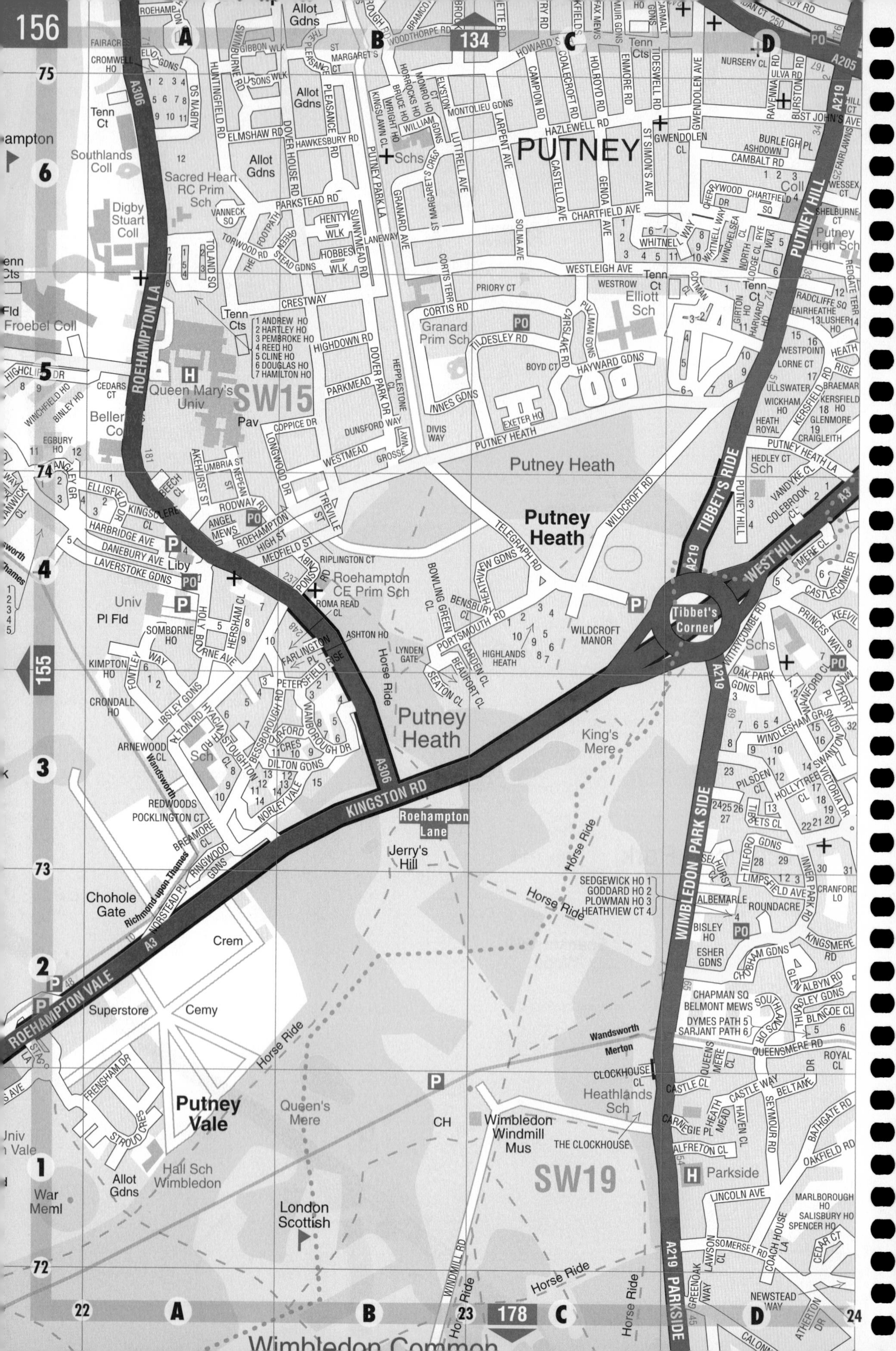

134
155
178
A
B
C
D
PUTNEY
SW15
SW19
Putney Heath
Putney Vale
Tibbet's Corner
Roehampton Lane
Jerry's Hill
King's Mere
Queen's Mere
Wimbledon Windmill Mus
London Scottish
Wimbledon Common
Queen Mary's Univ
Roehampton CE Prim Sch
Granard Prim Sch
Elliott Sch
Putney High Sch
Heathlands Sch
Parkside
Southlands Coll
Digby Stuart Coll
Froebel Coll
Sacred Heart RC Prim Sch
Hall Sch Wimbledon
Superstore
Cemy
Crem
Chohole Gate
War Meml
ROEHAMPTON LA
ROEHAMPTON VALE
KINGSTON RD
PUTNEY HEATH
PUTNEY HILL
TIBBET'S RIDE
WEST HILL
WIMBLEDON PARK SIDE
PARKSIDE
PUTNEY PARK LA
TELEGRAPH RD
WILDCROFT RD
WINDMILL RD
Horse Ride
Wandsworth
Merton
Richmond upon Thames
A3
A306
A219
A205
75
74
73
72
22
23
24

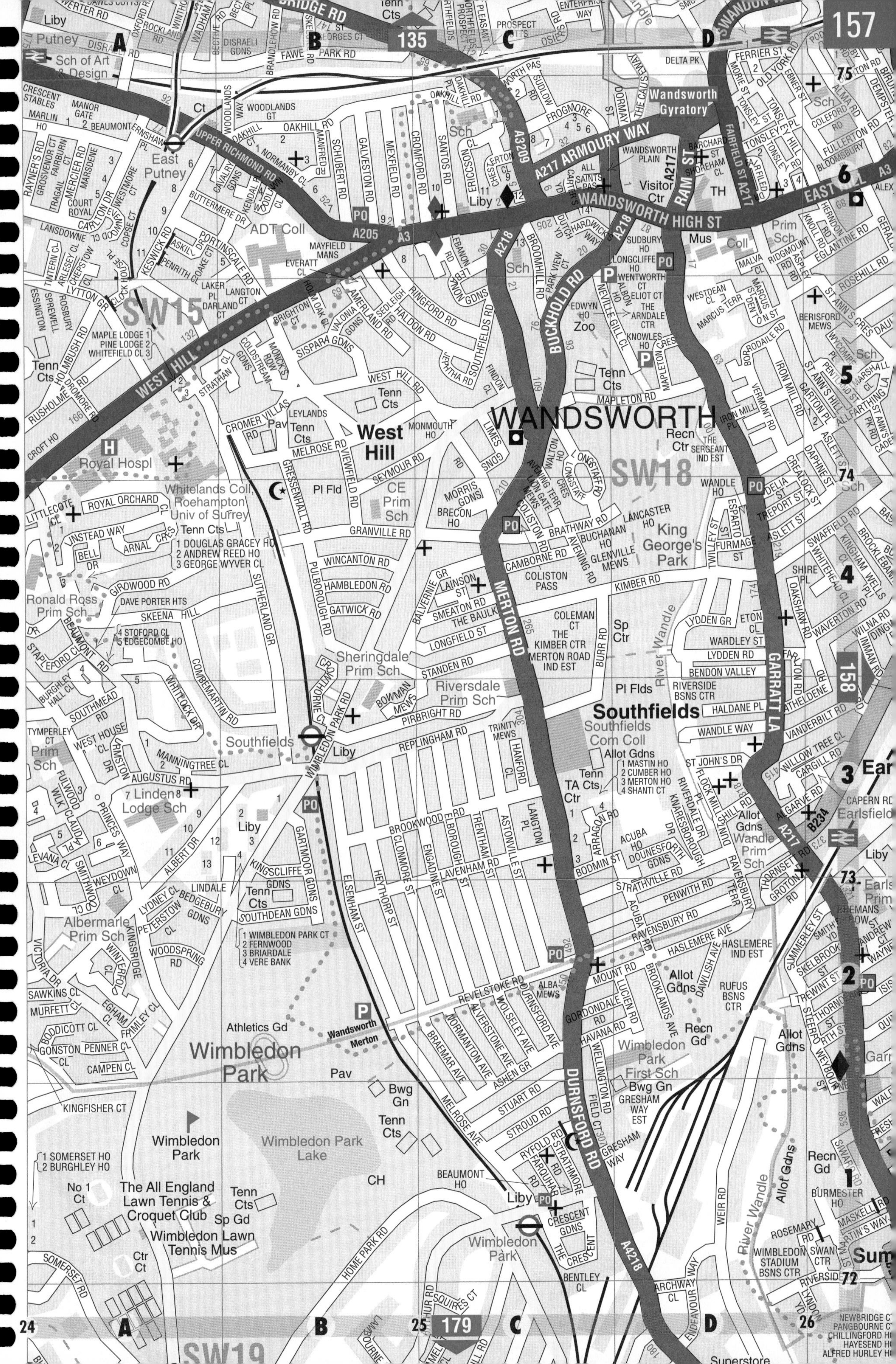
WANDSWORTH
SW18
SW15
SW19
West Hill
Southfields
Wimbledon Park
Wimbledon Park Lake
East Putney
Putney
Wandsworth Gyratory
WANDSWORTH HIGH ST
A217 ARMOURY WAY
UPPER RICHMOND RD
WEST HILL
MERTON RD
DURNSFORD RD
GARRATT LA
BUCKHOLD RD
Royal Hospl
Whitelands Coll, Roehampton Univ of Surrey
King George's Park
River Wandle
Sheringdale Prim Sch
Riversdale Prim Sch
Southfields Com Coll
Albermarle Prim Sch
Linden Lodge Sch
Ronald Ross Prim Sch
The All England Lawn Tennis & Croquet Club
Wimbledon Lawn Tennis Mus
Wimbledon Park First Sch
Athletics Gd
Wandsworth Merton
Earlsfield
WIMBLEDON STADIUM BSNS CTR
135
158
179
A
B
C
D
1
2
3
4
5
6
24
25
26
72
73
74
75

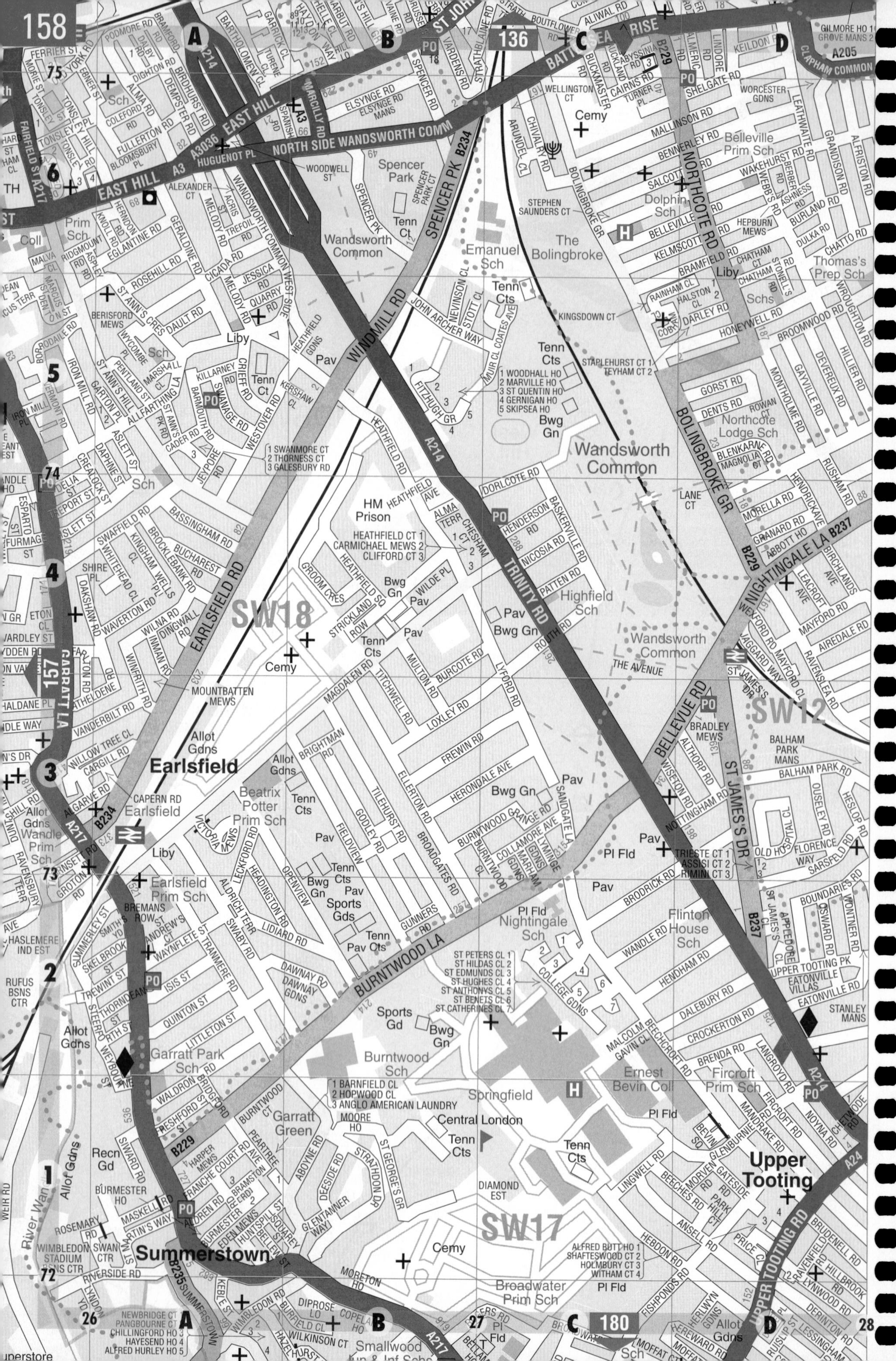
136
157
180
SW18
SW12
SW17
Earlsfield
Summerstown
Upper Tooting
Wandsworth Common
Spencer Park
The Bolingbroke
HM Prison
Emanuel Sch
Springfield
Central London
Ernest Bevin Coll
Burntwood Sch
Garratt Green
Garratt Park Sch
Beatrix Potter Prim Sch
Earlsfield Prim Sch
Wandle Prim Sch
Highfield Sch
Nightingale Sch
Flinton House Sch
Fircroft Prim Sch
Broadwater Prim Sch
Northcote Lodge Sch
Belleville Prim Sch
Dolphin Sch
Thomas's Prep Sch
Smallwood Jun & Inf Schs
Wimbledon Stadium
Diamond Est
Haslemere Ind Est
Rufus Bsns Ctr
River Wandle
EAST HILL
NORTH SIDE WANDSWORTH COMM
BATTERSEA RISE
WANDSWORTH COMMON WEST SIDE
SPENCER PK
WINDMILL RD
TRINITY RD
EARLSFIELD RD
GARRATT LA
BURNTWOOD LA
BOLINGBROKE GR
NORTHCOTE RD
NIGHTINGALE LA
BELLEVUE RD
ST JAMES'S DR
UPPER TOOTING RD
CLAPHAM COMMON
A3
A205
A214
A217
A24
A3036
B229
B234
B235
B237
SUMMERSTOWN
HEATHFIELD RD
MAGDALEN RD
THE AVENUE

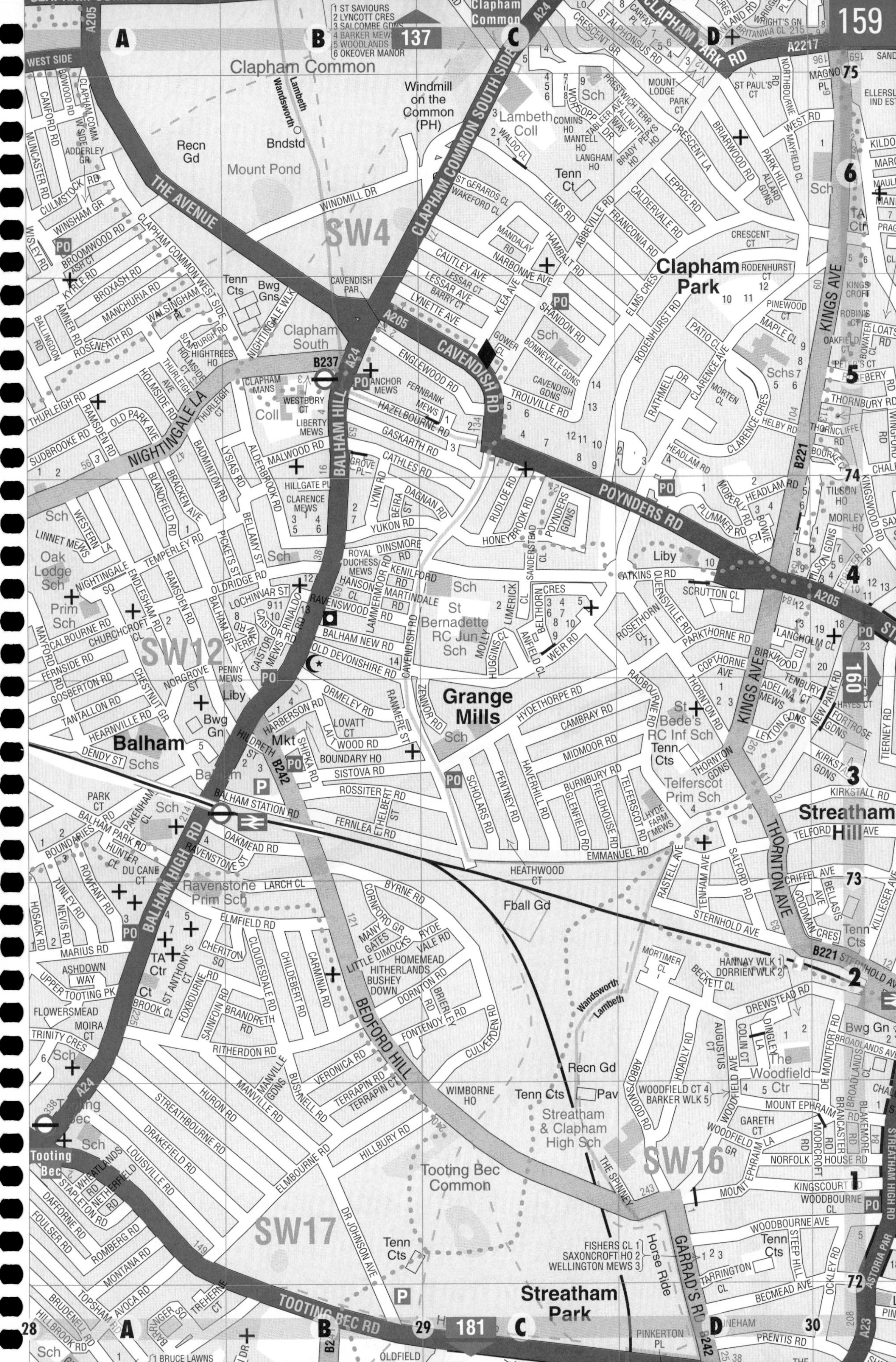

137
1 ST SAVIOURS
2 LYNCOTT CRES
3 SALCOMBE GDNS
4 BARKER MEWS
5 WOODLANDS
6 OKEOVER MANOR
Clapham Common
Clapham Common
WEST SIDE
A205
A24
A2217
CLAPHAM PARK RD
CRESCENT GR
ST ALPHONSUS RD
Lambeth
Wandsworth
Windmill on the Common (PH)
Recn Gd
Bndstd
Mount Pond
WINDMILL DR
THE AVENUE
CLAPHAM COMMON SOUTH SIDE
SW4
Lambeth Coll
Sch
PRESTWICH TERR
WORSOPP
TABLEER AVE
ALLNUTT WAY
BRADY HO
PEPYS HO
COMINS HO
MANTELL HO
LANGHAM HO
WALDO CL
Tenn Ct
MOUNT LODGE
PARK CT
ST PAUL'S CT
NORTHBOURNE
MAGNOLIA PL
ELLERSLIE IND EST
WEST RD
MAYFIELD CL
PARK HILL
ALLARD GDNS
BRIARWOOD RD
CRESCENT LA
LEPPOC RD
CALDERVALE RD
FRANCONIA RD
ABBEVILLE RD
ELMS RD
HAMBALT RD
ST GERARDS CL
WAKEFORD CL
MANDALAY RD
NARBONNE AVE
CAUTLEY AVE
LESSAR CT
LESSAR AVE
BARRY CT
LYNETTE AVE
CAVENDISH PAR
CAVENDISH RD
KLEA AVE
SHANDON RD
GOWER CL
BONNEVILLE GDNS
CAVENDISH GDNS
TROUVILLE RD
Clapham Park
RODENHURST RD
RODENHURST CT
CRESCENT CT
ELMS CRES
PINEWOOD CT
MAPLE CL
PATIO CL
CLARENCE AVE
MORTEN CL
RATHMELL DR
CLARENCE CRES
Schs
HELBY RD
HEADLAM RD
KINGS AVE
B221
KINGS CROFT
ROBINS CT
LOATS RD
OAKFIELD CT
BOWATER CT
PETERS CT
ROSEBERY
THORNBURY RD
THORNCLIFFE RD
BOURKE CL
WINGFORD RD
CHALE RD
TILSON HO
MORLEY HO
TILSON GDNS
KINGSWOOD RD
TA Ctr
KILDOREN
MARGATE
MAULEY
PRAGUE
MUNCASTER RD
CANFORD RD
BOWOOD RD
CLAPHAM COMM W SIDE
ADDERLEY GR
CULMSTOCK RD
WINSHAM GR
BROOMWOOD RD
ASH CT
KYRLE RD
BROXASH RD
MANCHURIA RD
WALSINGHAM PL
AMNER RD
BALLINGDON RD
ROSENEATH RD
CLAPHAM COMMON WEST SIDE
SUMBURGH RD
HOLMSIDE RD
THURLEIGH AVE
HIGHTREES HO
NIGHTINGALE WLK
Tenn Cts
Bwg Gns
Clapham South
B237
CLAPHAM MANS
WESTBURY CT
LIBERTY MEWS
Coll
ANCHOR MEWS
ENGLEWOOD RD
FERNBANK MEWS
HAZELBOURNE RD
GASKARTH RD
CATHLES RD
THURLEIGH RD
RAMSDEN RD
OLD PARK AVE
NIGHTINGALE LA
SUDBROOKE RD
THURLEIGH CT
BADMINTON RD
LYSIAS RD
ALDERBROOK RD
MALWOOD RD
BALHAM HILL
HILLGATE PL
GROVE PL
CLARENCE MEWS
LYNN RD
BEIRA ST
DAGNAN RD
YUKON RD
POYNDERS RD
RUDLOE RD
HONEYBROOK RD
POYNDERS GDNS
SANDERSTEAD CL
Liby
ATKINS RD
SCRUTTON CL
QUEENSVILLE RD
TEMPERLEY RD
BLANDFIELD RD
BRACKEN AVE
BELLAMY ST
PICKETS ST
WESTERN LA
LINNET MEWS
Oak Lodge Sch
NIGHTINGALE SQ
ENDLESHAM RD
OLDRIDGE RD
LOCHINVAR ST
RINALDO RD
CAISTOR RD
RAVENSWOOD RD
ROYAL DUCHESS MEWS
DINSMORE RD
KENILFORD RD
HANSON CL
MARTINDALE RD
LAMMERMOOR RD
St Bernadette RC Jun Sch
LIMERICK CL
BELTHORN CRES
WEIR RD
ANFIELD CL
MOLLY HUGGINS CL
ROSETHORN CL
PARKTHORNE RD
Prim Sch
CALBOURNE RD
CHURCHCROFT CL
SW12
BALHAM GR
BALHAM NEW RD
OLD DEVONSHIRE RD
CAVENDISH RD
MAYFORD RD
FERNSIDE RD
GOSBERTON RD
TANTALLON RD
HEARNVILLE RD
CHESTNUT GR
NORGROVE ST
PENNY MEWS
CAISTOR MEWS
Liby
Bwg Gn
Balham
DENDY ST
Schs
HILDRETH ST
B242
HARBERSON RD
ORMELEY RD
LOVATT CT
WOOD RD
Mkt
SHIPKA RD
BOUNDARY HO
SISTOVA RD
ROSSITER RD
ETHELBERT ST
FERNLEA RD
RAMMERE ST
ZENNOR RD
Grange Mills
HYDETHORPE RD
CAMBRAY RD
MIDMOOR RD
RADBOURNE RD
THORNTON RD
COPTHORNE AVE
BIRKWOOD CL
LANGHOLM CL
St Bede's RC Inf Sch
Tenn Cts
TENBURY CT
ADELINA MEWS
HAYES CT
NEW PARK RD
FORTROSE GDNS
LEYTON GDNS
160
Telferscot Prim Sch
THORNTON GDNS
KIRKSTALL GDNS
KIRKSTALL RD
Streatham Hill
TELFORD AVE
Sch
SCHOLARS RD
PENTNEY RD
HAVERHILL RD
BURNBURY RD
GLENFIELD RD
FIELDHOUSE RD
TELFERSCOT RD
LHYDE FARM MEWS
EMMANUEL RD
PARK CT
BALHAM PARK RD
PAKENHAM CL
BALHAM STATION RD
OAKMEAD RD
RAVENSTONE ST
BOUNDARIES RD
HUNTER CL
DU CANE CT
ROWFANT RD
TUNLEY RD
NEVIS RD
HOSACK RD
Ravenstone Prim Sch
LARCH CL
HEATHWOOD CT
Fball Gd
RASTELL AVE
STENHAM AVE
SALFORD RD
THORNTON AVE
CRIFFEL AVE
BELLASIS AVE
GOODMAN CRES
KILLIESER AVE
STERNHOLD AVE
Tenn Cts
BALHAM HIGH RD
ELMFIELD RD
CHERITON SQ
CLOUDESDALE RD
CHILDEBERT RD
CARMINIA RD
BYRNE RD
CORNFORD GR
MANY GATES
LITTLE DIMOCKS
RYDE VALE RD
HOMEMEAD
HITHERLANDS
BUSHEY DOWN
DORNTON RD
MARIUS RD
ASHDOWN WAY
UPPER TOOTING PK
TA Ctr
ST ANTHONY'S CT
FOXBOURNE RD
Ct
BROOK CL
SAINFOIN RD
BRANDRETH RD
FLOWERSMEAD
MOIRA CT
TRINITY CRES
RITHERDON RD
BEDFORD HILL
BRIERLEY RD
FONTENOY RD
CULVERDEN RD
MORTIMER CL
BECKETT CL
HANNAY WLK 1
DORRIEN WLK 2
B221
STERNHOLD AVE
DREWSTEAD RD
Wandsworth
Lambeth
AUGUSTUS CT
HOADLY RD
COLIN CT
DINGLEY LA
The Woodfield Ctr
DE MONTFORT RD
Bwg Gn
BROADLANDS AVE
MANVILLE GDNS
MANVILLE RD
VERONICA RD
TERRAPIN RD
TERRAPIN CT
BUSHNELL RD
WIMBORNE HO
Recn Gd
Tenn Cts
Pav
ABBOTSWOOD RD
WOODFIELD CT 4
BARKER WLK 5
WOODFIELD AVE
MOUNT EPHRAIM
BRANCASTER RD
BLAKEMORE
A24
Tooting Bec
HURON RD
STREATHBOURNE RD
DRAKEFIELD RD
LOUISVILLE RD
HILLBURY RD
ELMBOURNE RD
Streatham & Clapham High Sch
THE SPINNEY
SW16
GARETH CT
WOODFIELD GR
MOUNT EPHRAIM LA
MOORCROFT RD
NORFOLK HOUSE RD
STREATHAM HIGH RD
Tooting Bec
Sch
WHEATLANDS
STAPLETON RD
NETHERFIELD RD
DAFFORNE RD
FOULSER RD
Tooting Bec Common
KINGSCOURT RD
WOODBOURNE CL
MOUNT EPHRAIM LA
SW17
ROMBERG RD
DR JOHNSON AVE
Tenn Cts
FISHERS CL 1
SAXONCROFT HO 2
WELLINGTON MEWS 3
Horse Ride
GARRAD'S RD
WOODBOURNE AVE
STEEP HILL
Tenn Cts
TARRINGTON CL
OCKLEY RD
BECMEAD AVE
ASTORIA PAR
A23
MONTANA RD
TOPSHAM RD
AVOCA RD
TREHERNE CT
BRUDENELL RD
HILLBROOK RD
Streatham Park
TOOTING BEC RD
PINKERTON PL
PRENTIS RD
OLDFIELD
1 BRUCE LAWNS
181
28
29
30
72
73
74
75
A
B
C
D
1
2
3
4
5
6

160
138
159
182
A
B
C
D
6
5
4
3
2
1
75
74
73
72
30
31
32
ACRE LA
A2217
Works
SUDBOURNE RD
EFFRA RD
EFFRA CT
KELLETT RD
MERVAN RD
ARLINGTON LO
BAYTREE RD
ST MATTHEW'S RD
ST MATTHEWS RD
EUROLINK BSNS CTR
EFFRA ROAD RET PK
FITCH CT
DALBERG RD
RAILTON RD
SANDHURST CT
MAGNOLIA PL
NORTHBOURNE
ELLERSLIE IND EST
GLENELG RD
STRATHLEVEN RD
BRANKSOME RD
HAYTER RD
KILDORAN RD
MARGATE RD
MAULEVERER RD
MANDRELL RD
WINSLADE RD
WINTERWELL RD
HAYCROFT RD
BONHAM RD
TORRENS RD
HORSFORD RD
TRENT RD
Lambeth Coll
KETT GDNS
DRAY GDNS
EFFRA MANS
CROWNSTONE RD
TRELAWN RD
MORVAL RD
BRIXTON WATER LA
A2214
DULWICH RD
CHAUCER RD
SPENSER RD
SHAKESPEARE RD
MILTON RD
MUMFORD RD
REGENT RD
HERNE PL
Herne Hill
B223
B222
Brockwell Lido
PARK VIEW HO
HERNE HILL HO
Pav
Bwg Gn
Tenn Cts
Brockwell Park
SE24
LAMBERT RD
GLANVILLE RD
ST SAVIOUR'S RD
JOSEPHINE AVE
HELIX GDNS
ARODENE RD
HELIX RD
APPACH RD
BLENHEIM GDNS
ARLINGFORD RD
BRAILSFORD RD
TULSE HILL
TULSE HO
TENDRING HO
WEST RD
MAYFIELD CL
PARK HILL
Sch
TA Ctr
PRAGUE PL
CRESCENT CT
RODENHURST CT
CLAUDIA JONES WAY
RAMILLES CL
KINGS CROFT
KINGS AVE
Allot Gdns
PINEWOOD CT
MAPLE CL
ROBIN'S CT
OAKFIELD CT
BOWATER CT
LOATS RD
JOHN ASHBY CL
PETER'S CT
LYHAM RD
Sp Gd
JEBB AVE
WATERWORKS RD
CHERRY LAUREL WLK
RALEIGH GDNS
FAIRMOUNT RD
BEECHDALE RD
CALIDORE CL
VIRGINIA WLK
LEANDER RD
WASHBROOK HO
IRBY HO
HOLT HO
Prim Sch
POVEY HO
BARTELL HO
BROCKWELL PARK ROW
ROSEBERY
THORNBURY RD
THORNCLIFFE CT
HM Prison
WINGFORD RD
RENTON CL
BEWLEY CT
TUDOR CL
ENDYMION RD
ELM PK
MERREDENE ST
SOMERS RD
BRIXTON HILL
CLARENCE CRES
HELBY RD
BOURKE CL
LYHAM CL
DUMBARTON RD
CHALE RD
HYPERION HO
SOMERS PL
BRADING RD
WIMBART RD
OSTADE RD
MEDORA RD
TILSON HO
MORLEY HO
KINGSWOOD RD
DOVERFIELD RD
FELSBERG RD
HEADLAM RD
BOWIE CL
SAXBY RD
DEERDENE GDNS
FAIRVIEW PL
CRASTER RD
CRAIGNAIR RD
PAPWORTH WAY
CROSBY WLK
TILSON GDNS
FORSTER RD
NEW PARK RD
BRIXTON HILL PL
HOLMEWOOD RD
BROCKHAM DR
Inst
CLAVERDALE RD
HAMBRIDGE WAY
Tulse Hill
A205
MORRISH RD
RODMILL LA
REDLANDS WAY
MAPLESTEAD RD
ATHLONE RD
MACKIE RD
HILLWORTH RD
HARDEL WLK
BODLEY MANOR WAY
BROCKWELL PARK GDNS
A215
STREATHAM PL
SULINA RD
LANGHOLM CL
ASPINALL HO
HAYES CT
TENBURY CT
VIBART GDNS
ROMAN RISE
ROMAN FIELD RD
UPPER TULSE HILL
SAXONFIELD CL
EWEN CRES
ATWATER CL
BANNISTER CL
TRINITY RISE
DUTTON HO
CONSTANTINE HO
POULLETT HO
AXFORD HO
BELLO CL
Liby
TERRY HO
SKIFFINGTON CL
Cts
MONTRELL RD
TIERNEY RD
FORTROSE GDNS
LEYTON GDNS
CHALLICE WAY
MARNFIELD CRES
HUGGINS PL
RICKARD CL
GAYWOOD CL
SCOLES CRES
DERONDA RD
DEERBROOK RD
BERWYN RD
TRUST WLK
KIRKSTALL GDNS
KIRKSTALL RD
TIERNEY TERR
PULLMAN CT
GARDEN LA
SW2
ELMETREE CL
CHRISTCHURCH RD
ABBOTS PK
HIGH TREES
MORRISON HO
JARRETT CL
ABBESS CL
ROMOLA RD
NORWOOD RD
ST FAITH'S RD
Streatham Hill
TELFORD AVE
THORNTON AVE
CORNER FIELDE
DAYSBROOK RD
ARBORFIELD CL
BARSTOW CRES
DUCAVEL HO
COBURG CRES
HART HO
ROYCROFT CL
MASKALL CL
A204
COPPIN HO
HARDEL RISE
PERRAN RD
SALFORD RD
CRIFFEL AVE
BARRHILL RD
KILLIESER AVE
WAVERTREE RD
BATY HO
PRESENTATION MEWS
PONTON HO
CHALNER HO
Tulse Hill
STATION RISE
PARK RD
MALEY AVE
BELLASIS AVE
GOODMAN CRES
Tenn Cts
BLAIRDERRY RD
ARDWELL RD
STREATHAM HILL
WYATT PARK RD
NORMANHURST RD
NUTHURST AVE
BUSHELL CL
PALACE RD
REDHILL CT
LANERCOST RD
LANERCOST CL
PROBYN RD
LUPIN CL
PARADE MEWS
FAWLEY CT
ELMCOURT RD
ORFORD CT
DOWNTON AVE
EMSWORTH ST
CRICKLADE AVE
HILLSIDE RD
HILLSIDE GDNS
ULVERSTONE RD
B221
STERNHOLD AVE
BARCOMBE AVE
FAYGATE RD
NORTHSTEAD RD
KINFAUNS RD
WILLIAM BROWN CT
LANCASTER CT
DREWSTEAD RD
DINGLEY LA
COLIN CT
Bwg Gn
BROADLANDS AVE
AMESBURY AVE
HAILSHAM AVE
STREATHAM CL
MAYTREE WLK
KINGSMEAD RD
DESPARD HO
PALACE CT
ST MARTIN'S CT
PENRITH PL
The Woodfield Ctr
DE MONTFORT RD
LYDHURST AVE
KEYMER RD
ADARE WLK
MOUNTEARL GDNS
HITHERFIELD RD
LEIGHAM VALE
HARPENDEN RD
ULLSWATER RD
HAWKLEY GDNS
DALTON ST
MOUNT EPHRAIM LA
CHALCOT MEWS
STREATHAM CT
CROMER CT
ALBANS CL
BRANCASTER RD
BLAKEMORE RD
GARETH CT
MOORCROFT RD
MANOR CT
CHERRY TREE DR
GARDEN FLATS
BELENOYD CT
MOUNT NOD RD
STOCKFIELD RD
CANUTE CT
TRAEMORE CT
TINA CT
PEVENSEY CT
KNOLLY'S RD
KNOLLY'S CL
PORTAL CL
ROYAL CIR
CAMBRIAN RD
YORK HILL
SNOW HO
WAYLETT PL
NORFOLK HOUSE RD
KINGSCOURT RD
WOODBOURNE CL
WOODBOURNE AVE
STREATHAM HIGH RD
THE HIGH PAR
WOODLEIGH GDNS
LEIGHAM AVE
LEIGHAM COURT RD
BARNARD CT
ROSEDENE AVE
ROMEYN RD
THURLOW TOWERS
BROXHOLM RD
LANSDOWNE HILL
CANTERBURY GR
STEEP HILL
CONIFER GDNS
CULVERHOUSE GDNS
LEIGH ORCHARD CL
Dunraven Sch
GLENNIE RD
EGREMONT RD
IVYMOUNT RD
CHARTHAM GR
PYRMONT GR
WALDECK GR
VILLAS RD
BLOOM GR
Pl Fld
ASTORIA PAR
GRACEFIELD GDNS
IVYDAY GR
LEITHCOTE PATH
MILFORD MEWS
CAROLINE CT
GLYN CT
ST PETER'S GDNS
YEOMAN CL
PRIORESS RD
FRIAR MEWS
HAINTHORPE RD
FRANKLIN CL
SAINTS CL
NETTLEFOLD PL
BECMEAD AVE
BUTTERWORTH CT
PENDENNIS RD
NEWCOMBE GDNS
LEITHCOTE GDNS
CAREW HO
CHICHESTER MEWS
DODBROOKE RD
THURLESTONE RD
SELSDON RD
WOLFINGTON RD
COTSWOLD ST
BEADMAN ST
BEADMAN PL
KNIGHT'S HILL SQ
A23
PINFOLD RD
PRENTIS RD
FARM AVE
ANGLES RD
UJIMA HO
ROUGH RD
SAMUEL JOHNSON CL
LEIGHAM CT
ROCKHAMPTON RD
UFFINGTON RD
SE27

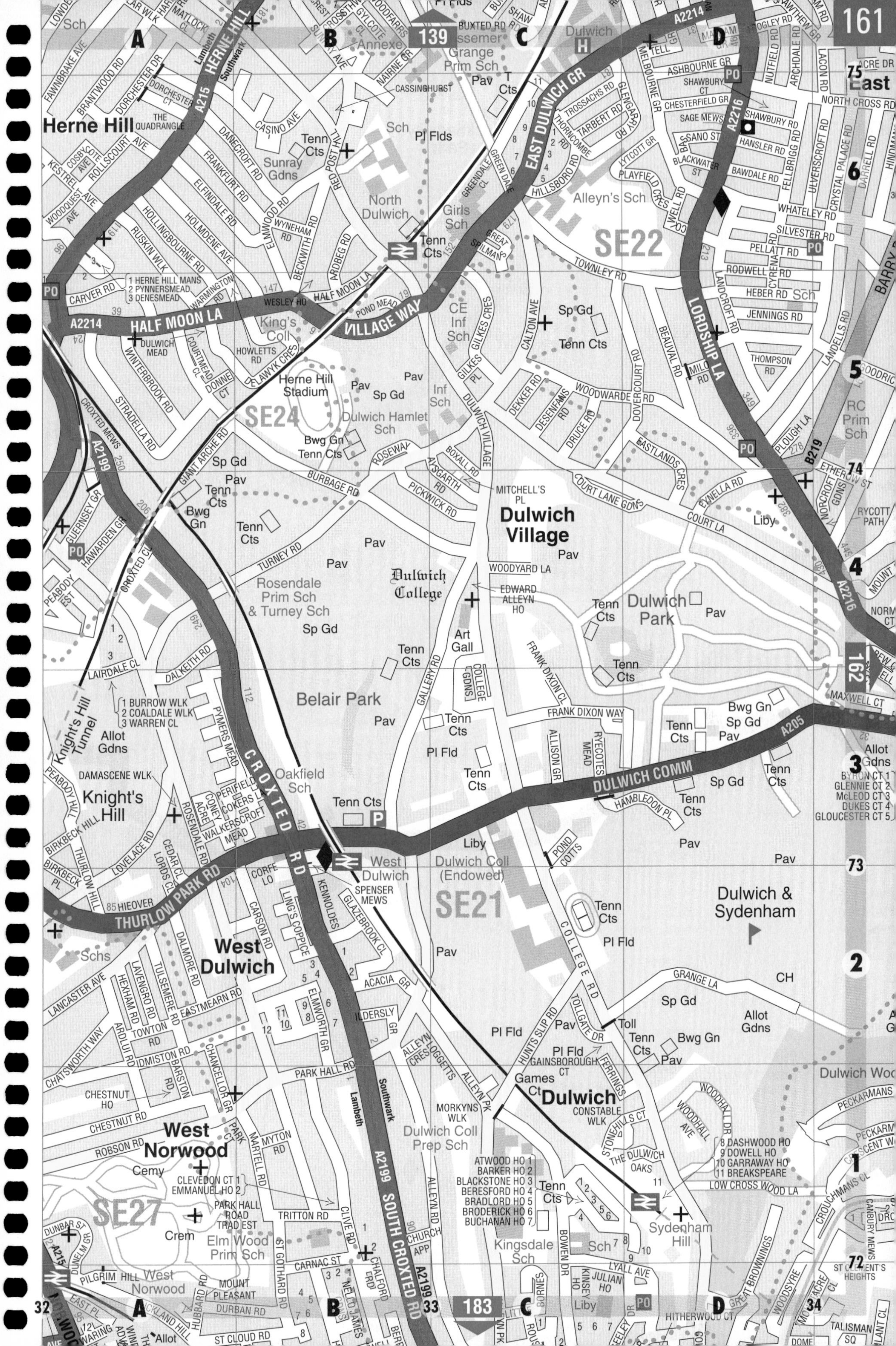
139
A
B
C
D
Herne Hill
Lambeth
Southwark
HERNE HILL
A215
Annexe
Grange Prim Sch
Dulwich
East Dulwich Gr
A2214
SE22
East
Sunray Gdns
North Dulwich
Girls Sch
Alleyn's Sch
HALF MOON LA
VILLAGE WAY
King's Coll
Herne Hill Stadium
SE24
Dulwich Hamlet Sch
CE Inf Sch
Inf Sch
LORDSHIP LA
A2216
Dulwich Village
Dulwich College
Dulwich Park
Art Gall
Rosendale Prim Sch & Turney Sch
Belair Park
Knight's Hill Tunnel
Knight's Hill
Oakfield Sch
CROXTED RD
A2199
DULWICH COMM
A205
West Dulwich
Dulwich Coll (Endowed)
SE21
Dulwich & Sydenham
THURLOW PARK RD
West Dulwich
West Norwood
Cemy
Crem
SE27
Elm Wood Prim Sch
Dulwich
Dulwich Coll Prep Sch
Kingsdale Sch
Sydenham Hill
SOUTH CROXTED RD
Dulwich Wood
183
32
33
34
162
75
74
73
72
1
2
3
4
5
6

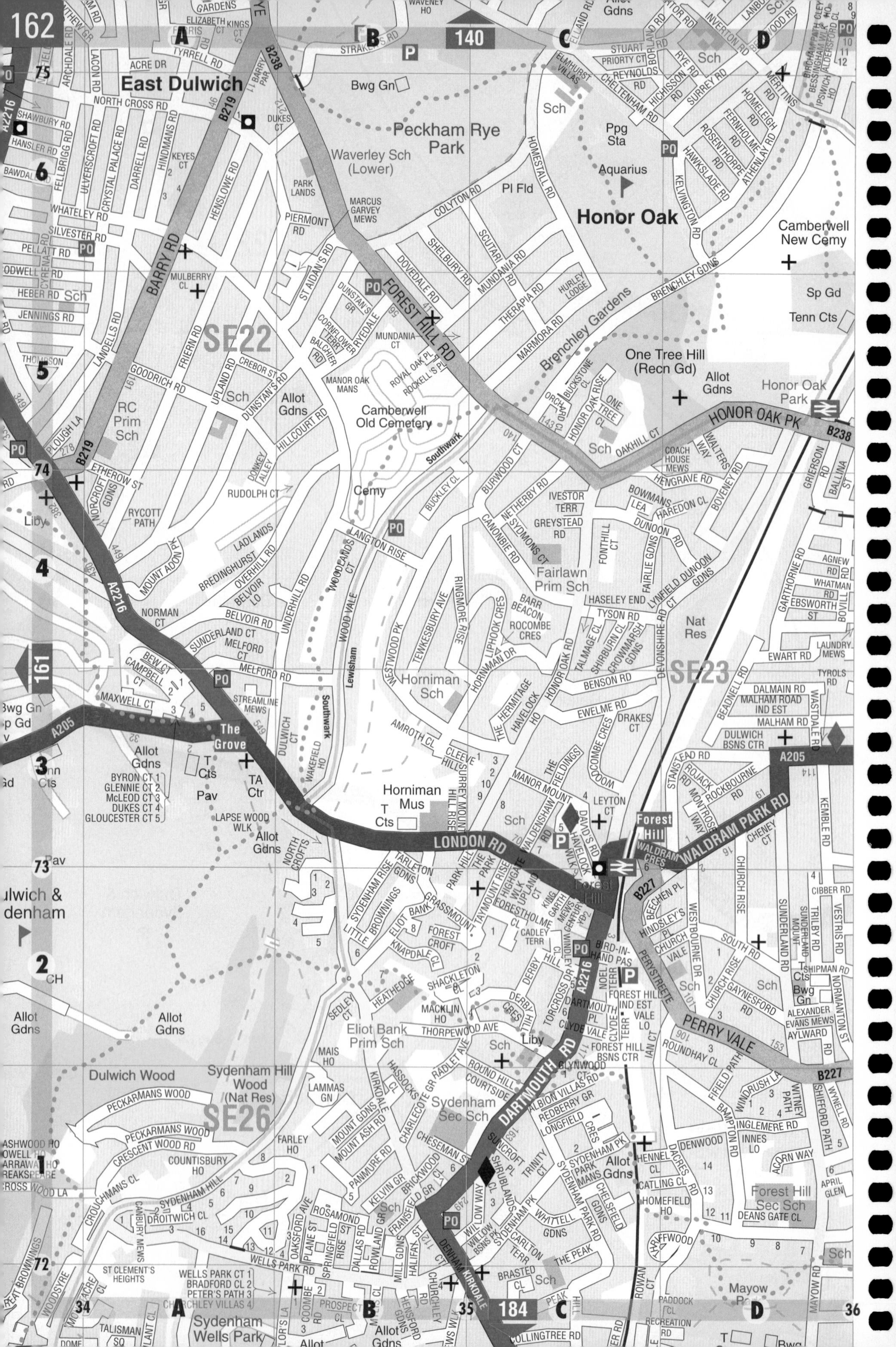
East Dulwich
Peckham Rye Park
Honor Oak
Camberwell New Cemy
SE22
Brenchley Gardens
One Tree Hill (Recn Gd)
Honor Oak Park
Camberwell Old Cemetery
Fairlawn Prim Sch
Horniman Sch
SE23
The Grove
Horniman Mus
Forest Hill
Eliot Bank Prim Sch
Dulwich Wood
Sydenham Hill Wood (Nat Res)
SE26
Sydenham Sec Sch
Forest Hill Sec Sch
Sydenham Wells Park
Mayow Pk
140
161
184
BARRY RD
FOREST HILL RD
LONDON RD
DARTMOUTH RD
WALDRAM PARK RD
PERRY VALE
HONOR OAK PK

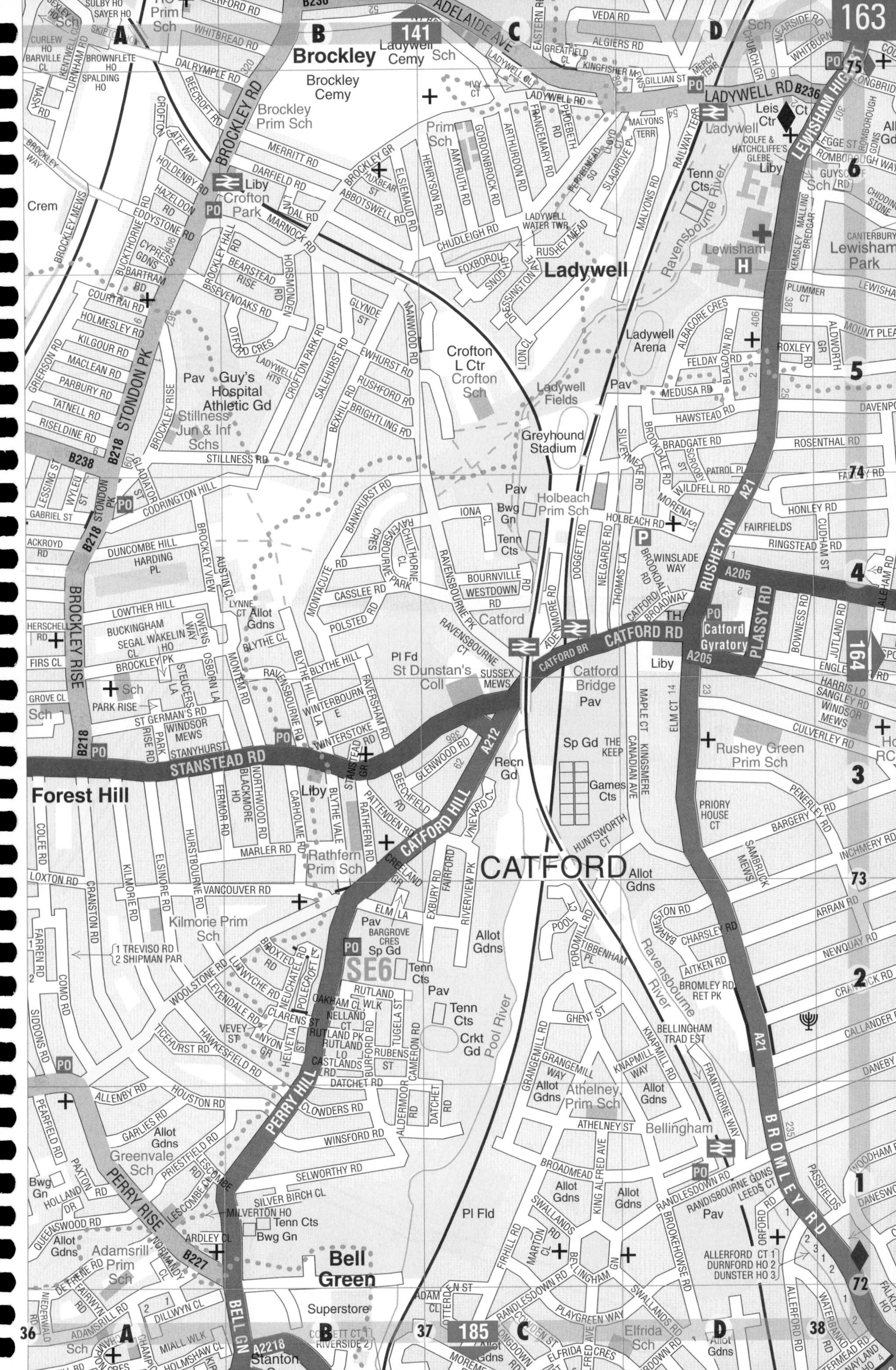
Brockley
Ladywell
Forest Hill
CATFORD
Bell Green
Bellingham
Lewisham Park
Catford Gyratory
STANSTEAD RD
CATFORD RD
CATFORD HILL
PERRY HILL
BROMLEY RD
RUSHEY GN
LADYWELL RD
BROCKLEY RD
STONDON PK
BROCKLEY RISE
PERRY RISE
SE6

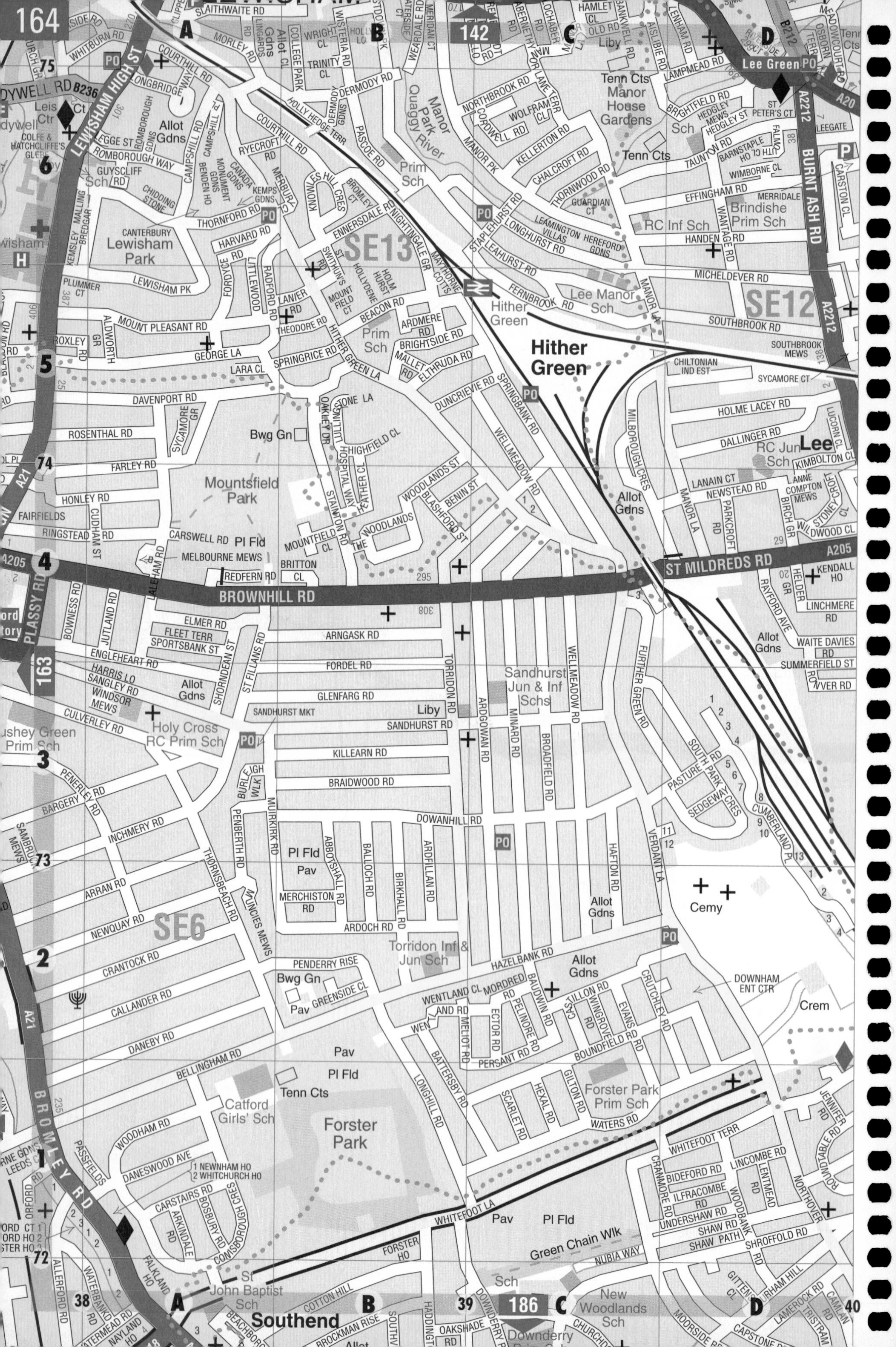
A
B
C
D
142
SLAITHWAITE RD
WHITBURN RD
MORLEY RD
COURTHILL RD
LONGBRIDGE WAY
LEWISHAM HIGH ST
B236
Leis Ctr
COLFE & HATCHCLIFFE'S GLEBE
LEGGE ST
ROMBOROUGH GDNS
ROMBOROUGH WAY
GUYSCLIFF RD
Sch
CAMPSHILL RD
CAMPSHILL PL
BENDEN HO
MONUMENT GDNS
CANADA GDNS
CHIDDING STONE
Allot Gdns
RYECROFT RD
KEMPS GDNS
THORNFORD RD
CANTERBURY
Lewisham Park
LEWISHAM PK
KEMSLEY
MALLING
BREDGAR
PLUMMER CT
HARVARD RD
FORDYCE RD
LITTLEWOOD
RADFORD RD
LANIER RD
THEODORE RD
MOUNT PLEASANT RD
ROXLEY RD
ALDWORTH GR
GEORGE LA
LARA CL
SPRINGRICE RD
Lingards Gdns
Allot Gdns
COLLEGE PARK
WRIGHT CL
WISTERIA RD
HOLLY LO
TRINITY CL
DERMODY RD
DERMODY GDNS
HOLLY HEDGE TERR
COURTHILL RD
PASCOE RD
MERBURY CL
KNOWLES HILL CRES
BROMLEY CT
ENNERSDALE RD
NIGHTINGALE GR
SE13
SMITHIES RD
ST SWITHUN'S RD
HOLLYDENE
HOLM HURST
MOUNT FIELD CT
BEACON RD
Prim Sch
ARDMERE RD
BRIGHTSIDE RD
MALLET RD
ELTHRUDA RD
HITHER GREEN LA
MAYTHORNE COTTS
Manor Park
Quaggy River
Prim Sch
WEARDALE RD
MERIDIAN CT
ABERNETHY RD
LOCHABER RD
HAMLET CL
OLD RD
Liby
Tenn Cts
Manor House Gardens
Tenn Cts
NORTHBROOK RD
CORDWELL RD
WOLFRAM CL
KELLERTON RD
MANOR PK
CHALCROFT RD
THORNWOOD RD
GUARDIAN CT
STAPLEHURST RD
LONGHURST RD
LEAMINGTON VILLAS
HEREFORD GDNS
LEAHURST RD
FERNBROOK RD
Lee Manor Sch
Hither Green
MANOR LA
LENHAM RD
LAMPMEAD RD
BRIGHTFIELD RD
HEDGLEY MEWS
HEDGLEY ST
Sch
TAUNTON RD
BARNSTAPLE HO
FAITH CL HO
Lee Green
B212
A20
A2212
ST PETER'S CT
LEEGATE
BURNT ASH RD
WIMBORNE CL
CARSTON CL
EFFINGHAM RD
MERRIDALE
Brindishe Prim Sch
RC Inf Sch
HANDEN RD
WANTAGE RD
MICHELDEVER RD
SE12
SOUTHBROOK RD
SOUTHBROOK MEWS
Hither Green
CHILTONIAN IND EST
SYCAMORE CT
HOLME LACEY RD
DALLINGER RD
RC Jun Sch
Lee
KIMBOLTON CL
LUCORN CL
LANAIN CT
NEWSTEAD RD
LANNE COMPTON MEWS
STONEYCROFT CL
WILDWOOD CL
BIRCH GR
MANOR LA
PARKCROFT RD
MILBOROUGH CRES
Allot Gdns
DAVENPORT RD
SYCAMORE GR
ROSENTHAL RD
Bwg Gn
STONE LA
OAKLEY DR
HIGHFIELD CL
HOSPITAL WAY
HEATHER CL
FARLEY RD
Mountsfield Park
HONLEY RD
FAIRFIELDS
CUDHAM ST
RINGSTEAD RD
CARSWELL RD
Pl Fld
MELBOURNE MEWS
LALEHAM RD
REDFERN RD
BRITTON CL
MOUNTFIELD CL
STAINTON RD
THE WOODLANDS
WOODLANDS ST
BLASHFORD ST
BENIN ST
DUNCRIEVIE RD
SPRINGBANK RD
WELLMEADOW RD
A21
A205
PLASSY RD
BROWNHILL RD
ST MILDREDS RD
KENDALL HO
HELDER GR
RAYFORD AVE
LINCHMERE RD
Allot Gdns
WAITE DAVIES RD
SUMMERFIELD ST
RONVER RD
163
BOWNESS RD
JUTLAND RD
ELMER RD
FLEET TERR
SPORTSBANK ST
ENGLEHEART RD
HARRIS LO
SANGLEY RD
WINDSOR MEWS
Allot Gdns
SHORNDEAN ST
ST FILLANS RD
ARNGASK RD
FORDEL RD
GLENFARG RD
SANDHURST MKT
SANDHURST RD
Liby
KILLEARN RD
BRAIDWOOD RD
TORRIDON RD
Sandhurst Jun & Inf Schs
ARDGOWAN RD
MINARD RD
BROADFIELD RD
WELLMEADOW RD
FURTHER GREEN RD
SOUTH PARK CRES
PASTURE RD
SEDGEWAY
CUMBERLAND PL
CULVERLEY RD
Holy Cross RC Prim Sch
Rushey Green Prim Sch
BURLEIGH WLK
PENERLEY RD
BARGERY RD
INCHMERY RD
SAMBRUCK MEWS
PENBERTH RD
MUIRKIRK RD
DOWANHILL RD
Pl Fld
Pav
ABBOTSHALL RD
BALLOCH RD
BIRKHALL RD
ARDFILLAN RD
MERCHISTON RD
ARDOCH RD
HAFTON RD
VERDANT LA
Allot Gdns
Cemy
ARRAN RD
THORNSBEACH RD
MUNCIES MEWS
SE6
NEWQUAY RD
CRANTOCK RD
PENDERRY RISE
Torridon Inf & Jun Sch
HAZELBANK RD
Allot Gdns
Bwg Gn
GREENSIDE CL
Pav
DOWNHAM ENT CTR
Crem
CALLANDER RD
WENTLAND CL
WENTLAND RD
MORDRED RD
BAUDWIN RD
CASTILLON RD
WINGROVE RD
EVANS RD
CRUTCHLEY RD
MELLOT RD
ECTOR RD
PELINORE RD
PERSANT RD
BOUNDFIELD RD
DANEBY RD
BELLINGHAM RD
Pav
Pl Fld
Tenn Cts
Catford Girls' Sch
Forster Park
BATTERSBY RD
LONGHILL RD
SCARLET RD
HEXAL RD
GILTON RD
Forster Park Prim Sch
WATERS RD
JENNIFER RD
ROUNDTABLE RD
BROMLEY RD
WOODHAM RD
DANESWOOD AVE
1 NEWNHAM HO
2 WHITCHURCH HO
PASSFIELDS
CARSTAIRS RD
ARKINDALE RD
BOSBURY RD
CONISBOROUGH CRES
WHITEFOOT TERR
CRANMORE RD
BIDEFORD RD
ILFRACOMBE RD
LINCOMBE RD
LENTMEAD RD
WOODBANK RD
NORTHOVER
UNDERSHAW RD
SHAW RD
SHAW PATH
SHROFFOLD RD
WHITEFOOT LA
Pav
Pl Fld
Green Chain Wlk
NUBIA WAY
FORSTER HO
FALKLAND HO
ALLERFORD RD
WATERBANK RD
WINTERMEAD RD
NAYLAND HO
St John Baptist Sch
Southend
COTTON HILL
BROCKMAN RISE
Sch
39
186
DOWNDERRY RD
OAKSHADE RD
Downderry
CHURCHDOWN
New Woodlands Sch
GITTENS CL
DURHAM HILL
MOORSIDE RD
CAPSTONE RD
LAMERROCK RD
TRISTRAM RD
CAMLAN RD
40
75
74
73
72
38
6
5
4
3
2
1

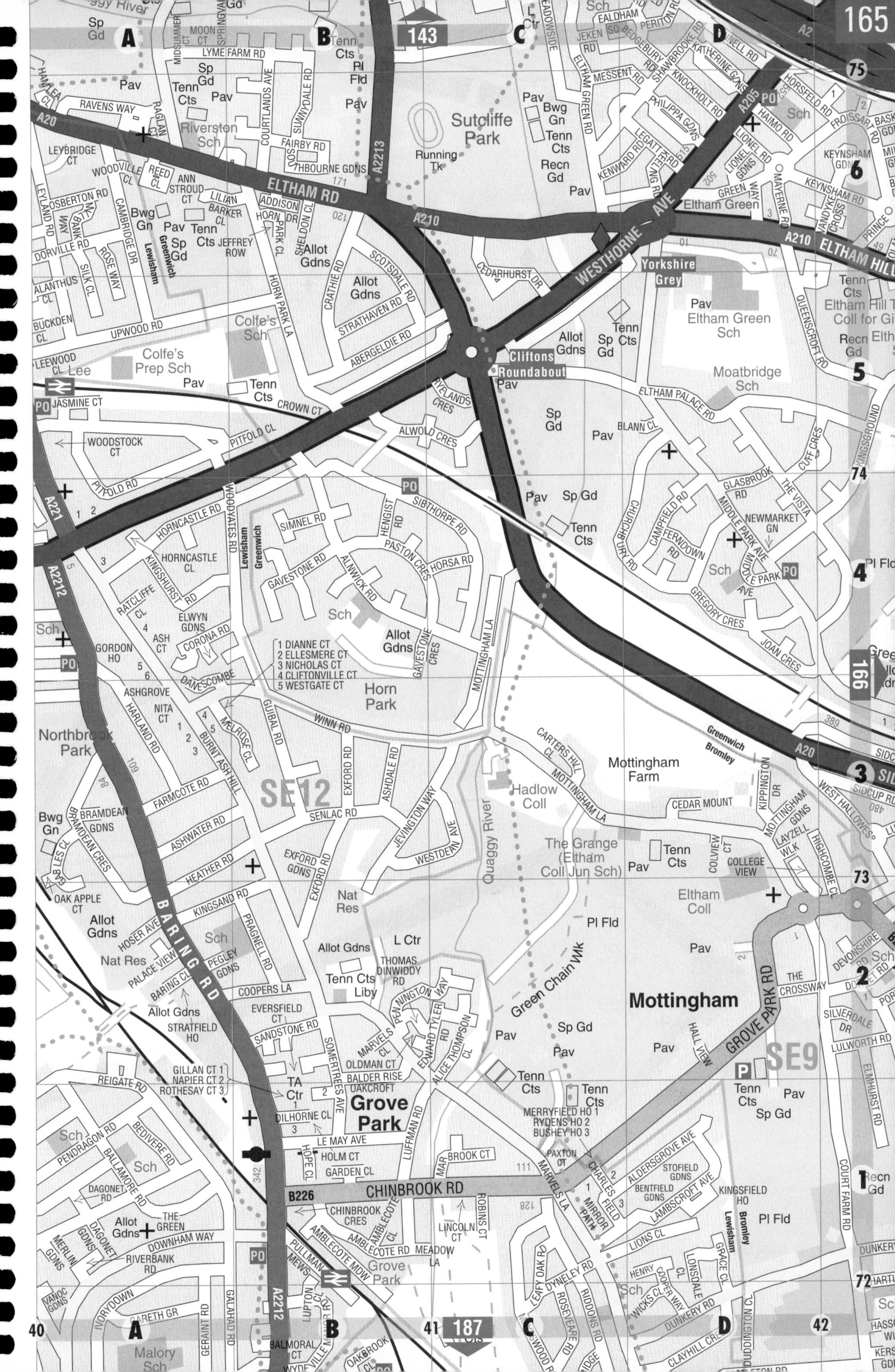

A
B
C
D
143
ELTHAM RD
A20
A2213
A210
ELTHAM HILL
WESTHORNE AVE
A205
Sutcliffe Park
Running Tk
Riverston Sch
RAVENS WAY
RAGLAN CT
LYME FARM RD
MOON CT
MIDSUMMER CT
COURTLANDS AVE
SUNNYDALE RD
FAIRBY RD
THBOURNE GDNS
LEYBRIDGE CT
WOODVILLE CL
REED CL
ANN STROUD CT
LILIAN BARKER CL
ADDISON DR
HORN PARK CL
SHELDON CL
JEFFREY ROW
OSBERTON RD
LEYLAND RD
CAMBRIDGE DR
DORVILLE RD
ROSE WAY
SILK CL
ALANTHUS CL
BUCKDEN CL
UPWOOD RD
LEEWOOD CL
Lee
Colfe's Sch
Colfe's Prep Sch
JASMINE CT
WOODSTOCK CT
PITFOLD CL
PITFOLD RD
CROWN CT
HORN PARK LA
CRATHIE RD
SCOTSDALE RD
STRATHAVEN RD
ABERGELDIE RD
Allot Gdns
CEDARHURST DR
Cliftons Roundabout
RYELANDS CRES
ALWOLD CRES
Yorkshire Grey
Eltham Green
Eltham Green Sch
Moatbridge Sch
Eltham Hill Tech Coll for Girls
QUEENSCROFT RD
ELTHAM PALACE RD
BLANN CL
KINGSGROUND
CUFF CRES
THE VISTA
GLASBROOK RD
NEWMARKET GN
MIDDLE PARK AVE
CAMPFIELD RD
FERNDOWN RD
CHURCHBURY RD
GREGORY CRES
JOAN CRES
EALDHAM
PERITON RD
JEKEN RD
BEDGEBURY RD
SHAWBROOKE RD
KATHERINE GDNS
MESSENT RD
ELTHAM GREEN RD
KNOCKHOLT RD
PHILIPPA GDNS
LEGATT RD
KEELING RD
KENWARD RD
HORSFELD RD
HAIMO RD
LIONEL RD
LIONEL GDNS
GREEN WAY
MAYERNE RD
KEYNSHAM GDNS
KEYNSHAM RD
FROISSART RD
VANDYKE CROSS
PRINCE
SIBTHORPE RD
HENGIST RD
SIMNEL RD
PASTON CRES
HORSA RD
GAVESTONE RD
ALNWICK RD
GAVESTONE CRES
MOTTINGHAM LA
HORNCASTLE RD
HORNCASTLE CL
KINGSHURST RD
WOODYATES RD
RATCLIFFE CL
ELWYN GDNS
CORONA RD
ASH CT
GORDON HO
DANESCOMBE
1 DIANNE CT
2 ELLESMERE CT
3 NICHOLAS CT
4 CLIFTONVILLE CT
5 WESTGATE CT
Horn Park
WINN RD
Lewisham
Greenwich
A221
A2212
ASHGROVE
HARLAND RD
NITA CT
BURNT ASH HILL
MELROSE CL
GUIBAL RD
Northbrook Park
SE12
EXFORD RD
ASHDALE RD
FARMCOTE RD
BRAMDEAN GDNS
BRAMDEAN CRES
ASHWATER RD
SENLAC RD
JEVINGTON WAY
WESTDEAN AVE
HEATHER RD
EXFORD GDNS
OAK APPLE CT
GABLES CL
KINGSAND RD
HOSER AVE
PRAGNELL RD
BARING RD
Nat Res
PALACE VIEW
PEGLEY GDNS
BARING CL
STRATFIELD HO
COOPERS LA
EVERSFIELD CT
SANDSTONE RD
THOMAS DINWIDDY RD
PENNINGTON WAY
EDWARD TYLER RD
ALICE THOMPSON CL
MARVELS CL
OLDMAN CT
BALDER RISE
OAKCROFT
SOMERTREES AVE
GILLAN CT 1
NAPIER CT 2
ROTHESAY CT 3
REIGATE RD
TA Ctr
DILHORNE CL
Grove Park
LE MAY AVE
HOPE CL
HOLM CT
GARDEN CL
LUFFMAN RD
MARBROOK CT
CHINBROOK RD
B226
CHINBROOK CRES
AMBLECOTE CL
AMBLECOTE RD
AMBLECOTE MDW
MEADOW LA
LINCOLN CT
ROBINS CT
PENDRAGON RD
BEDIVERE RD
BALLAMORE RD
DAGONET RD
DAGONET GDNS
MERLIN GDNS
THE GREEN
DOWNHAM WAY
RIVERBANK RD
VANOC GDNS
IVORYDOWN
GARETH GR
GERAINT RD
GALAHAD RD
PULLMAN MEWS
LUPTON CL
Malory Sch
BALMORAL CT
WYDEVILLE MANOR RD
Quaggy River
Hadlow Coll
CARTERS HILL CL
Mottingham Farm
CEDAR MOUNT
KIPPINGTON DR
MOTTINGHAM GDNS
LAYZELL WLK
HIGHCOMBE CL
The Grange (Eltham Coll Jun Sch)
COLVIEW CT
COLLEGE VIEW
Eltham Coll
Green Chain Wk
Mottingham
GROVE PARK RD
HALL VIEW
SE9
THE CROSSWAY
DEVONSHIRE RD
SILVERDALE DR
LULWORTH RD
ELMHURST RD
COURT FARM RD
MERRYFIELD HO 1
RYDENS HO 2
BUSHEY HO 3
PAXTON CT
CHARLES FIELD
MIRROR PATH
MARVELS LA
ALDERSGROVE AVE
STOFIELD GDNS
BENTFIELD GDNS
LAMBSCROFT AVE
KINGSFIELD HO
LIONS CL
HENRY COOPER WAY
WICKS CL
LONSDALE CL
GRACE CL
DUNKERY RD
DUDDINGTON CL
CLAYHILL CRES
LEAFY OAK RD
DYNELEY RD
ROSEVEARE RD
RIDDONS RD
Bromley
WEST HALLOWES
SIDCUP RD
166
187
40
41
42
72
73
74
75
1
2
3
4
5
6

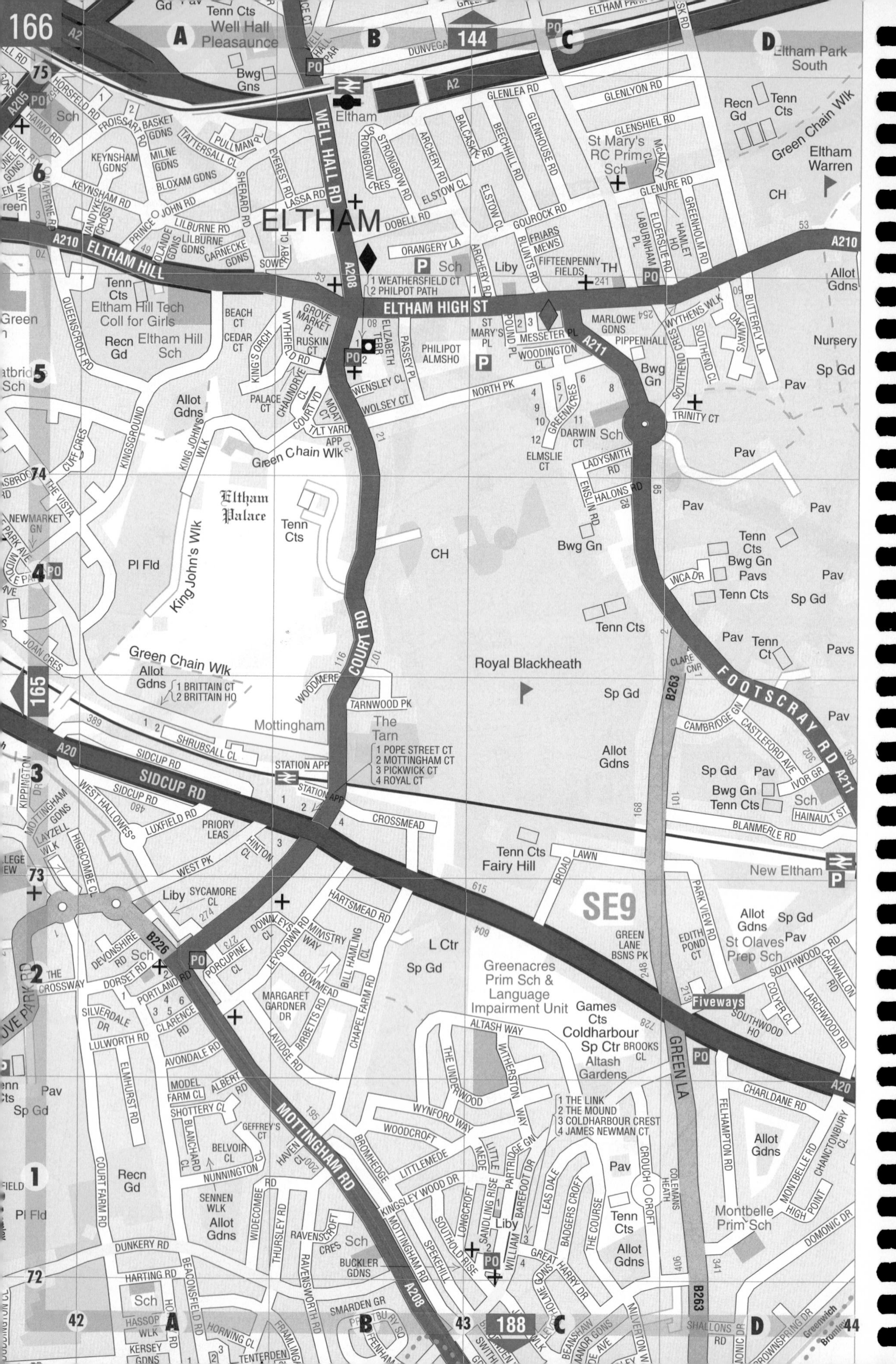

Avery Hill
Avery Hill Park
Univ of Greenwich Avery Hill Campus Mansion Site
Univ of Greenwich Avery Hill Campus Southwood Site
SE9
DA15
New Eltham
Longlands
BR7
Crown Woods Sch
Our Lady of the Rosary RC Prim Sch
Hollyoak Wood Park
Willersley Park
Burnt Oak Jun Sch
Dulverton Prim Sch
King George's Field
Longlands Prim Sch
Sparrow's Farm L Ctr
Valley L Ctr
Green Chain Wlk
Mulligan's
BEXLEY RD
BLACKFEN RD
EAST ROCHESTER WAY
AVERY HILL RD
HALFWAY ST
SIDCUP RD
MAIN RD
SIDCUP BY PASS RD
DORLAND HO 1
WOOTTON HO 2
WAYFIELD LINK 3
TEYNHAM HO 4
OSPRINGE CT 5
TRINITY MEWS 6
LONGLANDS CT 1
THE FIRS 2
SANDALWOOD HO 3
BUCKTHORN HO 4
MOAT CT 5

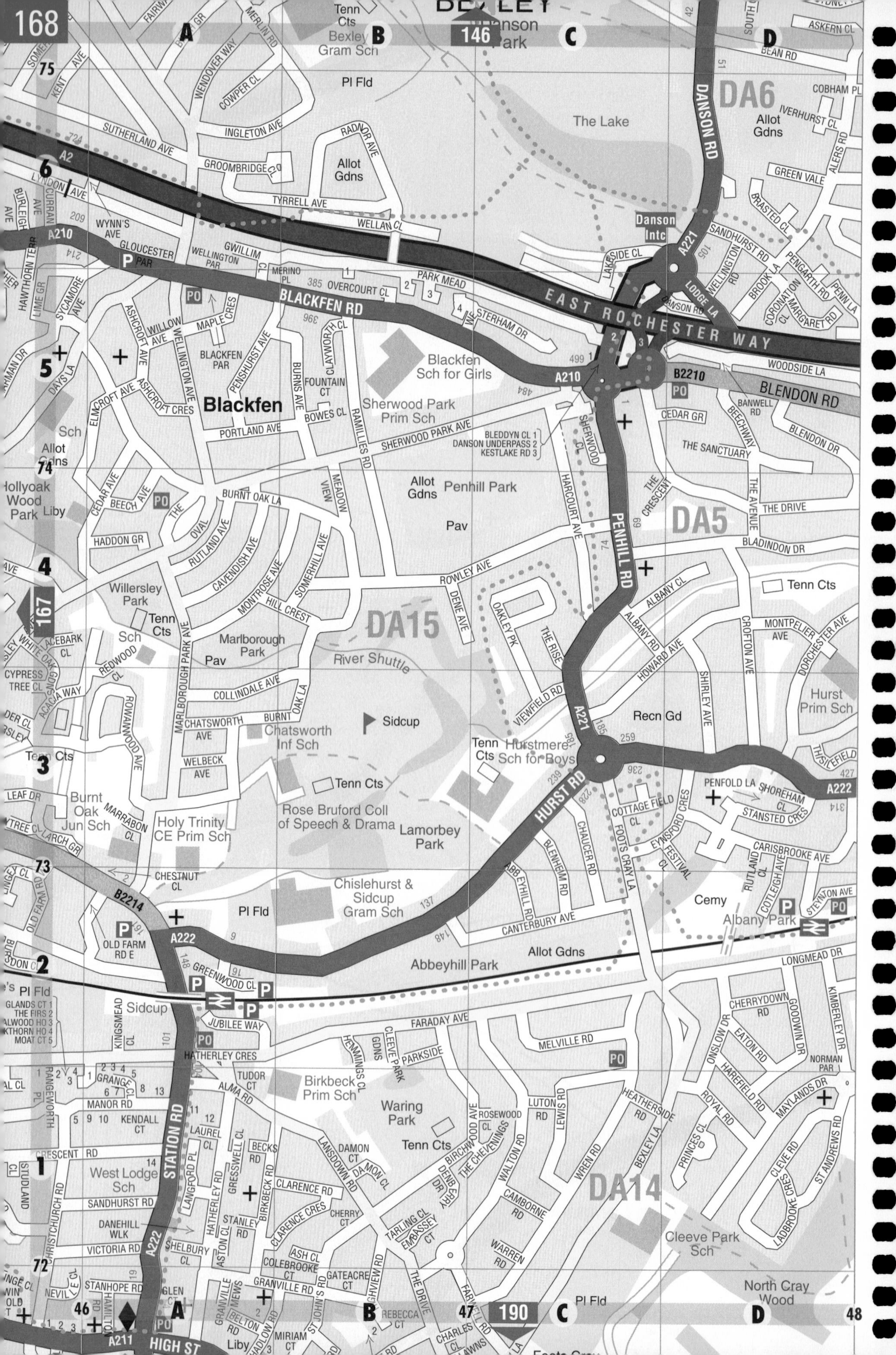
Blackfen
Bexley Gram Sch
Danson Park
The Lake
DA6
DA5
DA15
DA14
Allot Gdns
Danson Intc
EAST ROCHESTER WAY
BLACKFEN RD
BLENDON RD
DANSON RD
PENHILL RD
HURST RD
STATION RD
HIGH ST
Blackfen Sch for Girls
Sherwood Park Prim Sch
Penhill Park
Hollyoak Wood Park
Willersley Park
Marlborough Park
River Shuttle
Sidcup
Chatsworth Inf Sch
Rose Bruford Coll of Speech & Drama
Lamorbey Park
Hurstmere Sch for Boys
Hurst Prim Sch
Recn Gd
Burnt Oak Jun Sch
Holy Trinity CE Prim Sch
Chislehurst & Sidcup Gram Sch
Abbeyhill Park
Albany Park
Cemy
Birkbeck Prim Sch
Waring Park
West Lodge Sch
Cleeve Park Sch
North Cray Wood
146
167
190
48

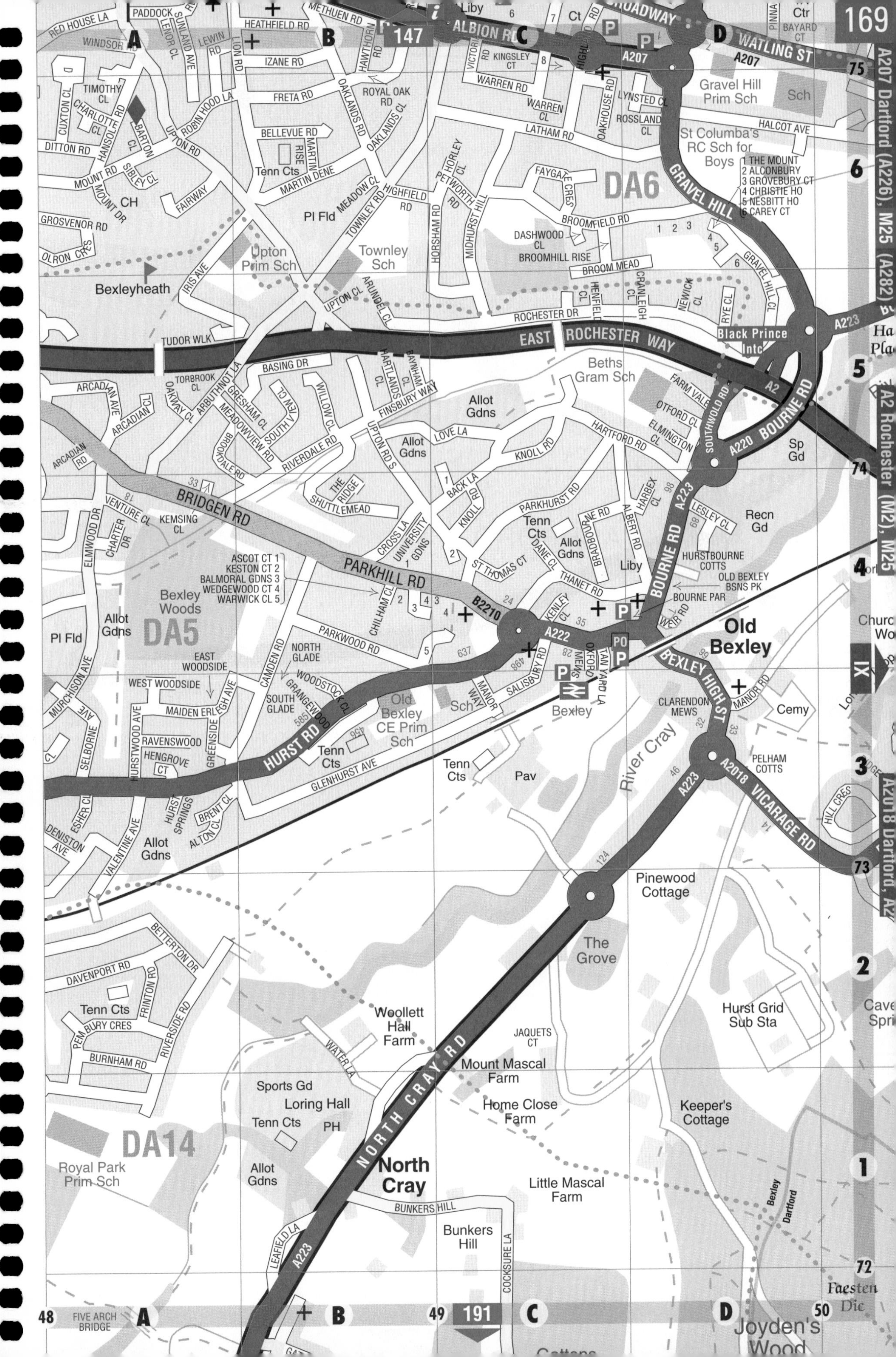
Bexleyheath
Old Bexley
North Cray
DA6
DA5
DA14
EAST ROCHESTER WAY
BRIDGEN RD
PARKHILL RD
HURST RD
NORTH CRAY RD
BOURNE RD
GRAVEL HILL
WATLING ST
VICARAGE RD
BEXLEY HIGH ST
River Cray
Bexley Woods
Upton Prim Sch
Townley Sch
Beths Gram Sch
Gravel Hill Prim Sch
St Columba's RC Sch for Boys
Old Bexley CE Prim Sch
Royal Park Prim Sch
Black Prince Intc
Pinewood Cottage
The Grove
Woollett Hall Farm
Mount Mascal Farm
Home Close Farm
Little Mascal Farm
Keeper's Cottage
Hurst Grid Sub Sta
Bunkers Hill
Loring Hall
Joyden's Wood
A2 Rochester (M2), M25
A207 Dartford (A226), M25 (A282)
A2018 Dartford, A2
147
191

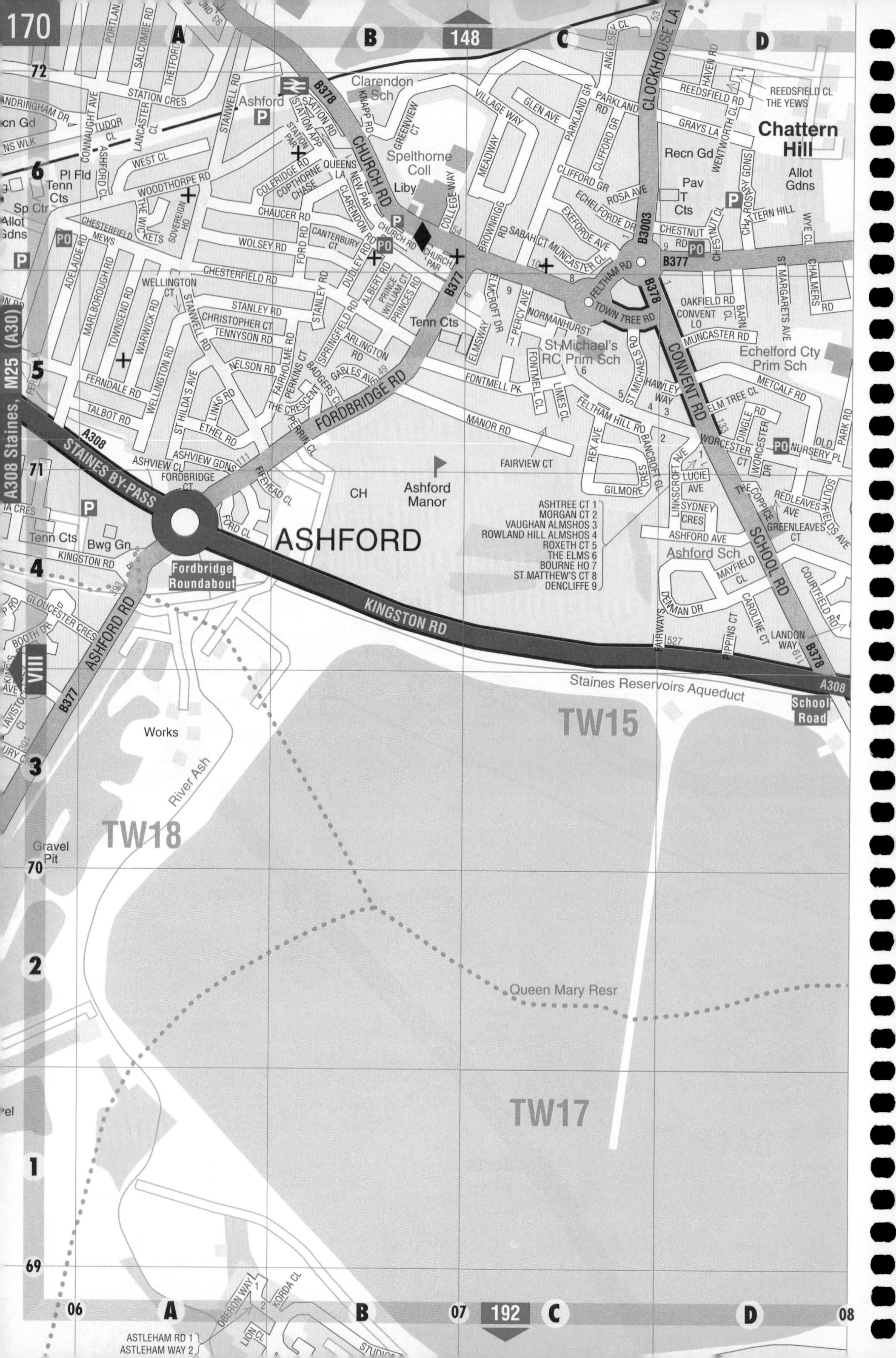

A
B
148
C
D
72
Ashford
Clarendon Sch
Spelthorne Coll
Liby
Chattern Hill
Recn Gd
Pav
T Cts
Allot Gdns
Pl Fld
Tenn Cts
Sp Ctr
STATION CRES
STANWELL RD
B378
CHURCH RD
CLOCKHOUSE LA
PARKLAND RD
VILLAGE WAY
GLEN AVE
REEDSFIELD RD
REEDSFIELD CL
THE YEWS
GRAYS LA
WENTWORTH CL
CHATTERN HILL
CLIFFORD GR
ROSA AVE
ECHELFORDE DR
EXEFORDE AVE
MUNCASTER CL
B3003
CHESTNUT RD
B377
WOODTHORPE RD
WEST CL
CHAUCER RD
WOLSEY RD
CHESTERFIELD RD
CHESTERFIELD MEWS
WELLINGTON CT
STANLEY RD
CHRISTOPHER CT
TENNYSON RD
NELSON RD
FERNDALE RD
TALBOT RD
ETHEL RD
ASHVIEW GDNS
ASHVIEW CL
FORDBRIDGE CT
FORDBRIDGE RD
FEATHAM RD
TOWN TREE RD
FELTHAM RD
CONVENT RD
OAKFIELD RD
CONVENT LO
MUNCASTER RD
Echelford Cty Prim Sch
METCALF RD
ELM TREE CL
Tenn Cts
St Michael's RC Prim Sch
NORMANHURST
FONTMELL PK
FONTMELL CL
MANOR RD
FAIRVIEW CT
FELTHAM HILL RD
HAWLEY WAY
WORCESTER CT
NURSERY PL
Ashford Manor
CH
ASHFORD
ASHTREE CT 1
MORGAN CT 2
VAUGHAN ALMSHOS 3
ROWLAND HILL ALMSHOS 4
ROXETH CT 5
THE ELMS 6
BOURNE HO 7
ST MATTHEW'S CT 8
DENCLIFFE 9
GILMORE CRES
LUCIE AVE
SYDNEY CRES
ASHFORD AVE
Ashford Sch
MAYFIELD CL
SCHOOL RD
REDLEAVES AVE
GREENLEAVES CT
DENMAN DR
CAROLINE CT
PIPPINS CT
COURTFIELD RD
LANDON WAY
A308
STAINES BY-PASS
Fordbridge Roundabout
KINGSTON RD
ASHFORD RD
Tenn Cts
Bwg Gn
Staines Reservoirs Aqueduct
School Road
TW15
Works
River Ash
TW18
Gravel Pit
Queen Mary Resr
TW17
A308 Staines, M25 (A30)
70
69
06
07
192
08
OBERON WAY
KORDA CL
ASTLEHAM RD 1
ASTLEHAM WAY 2

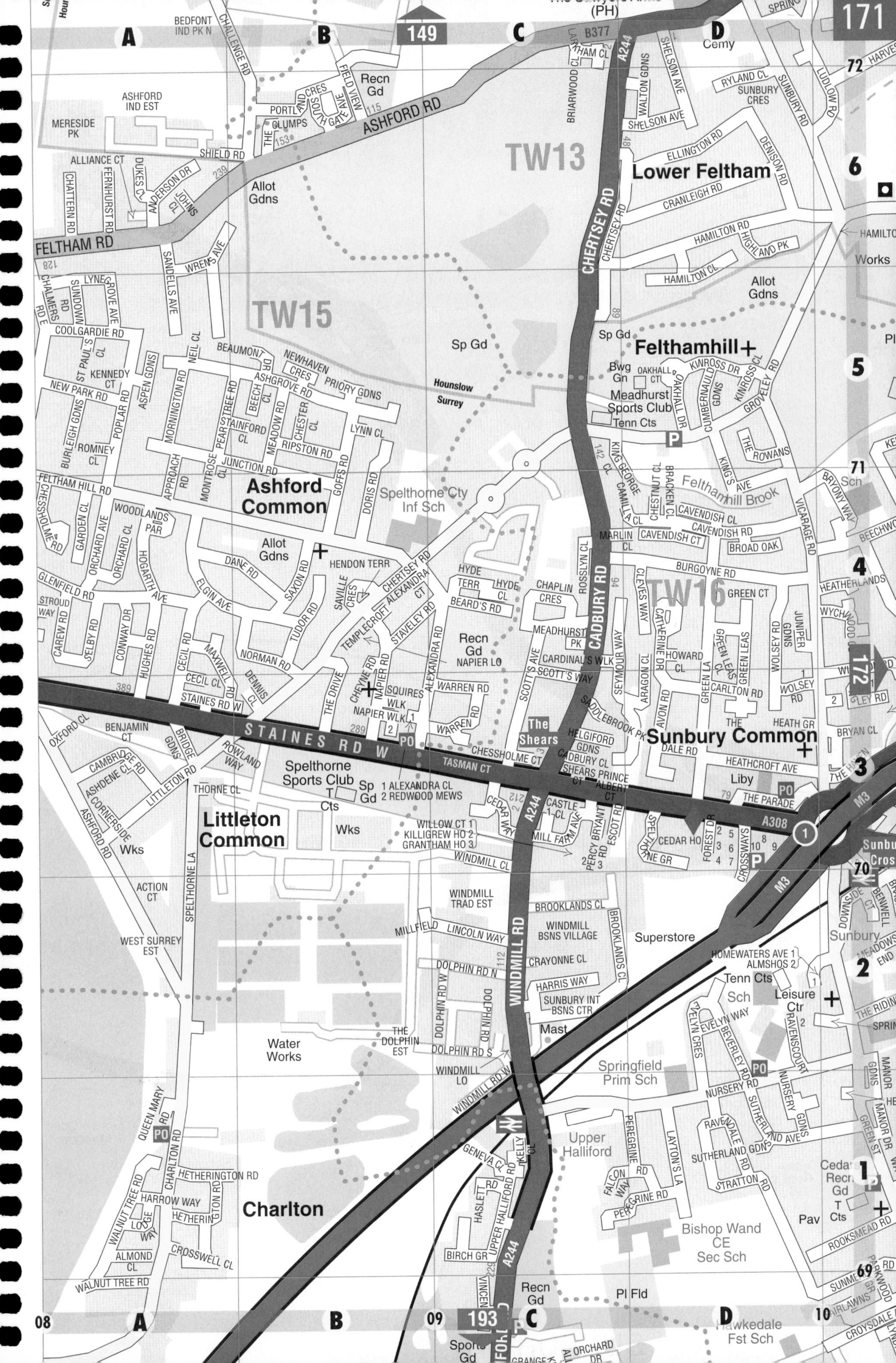

149
A
B
C
D
TW13
TW15
TW16
Lower Feltham
Felthamhill
Ashford Common
Sunbury Common
Littleton Common
Charlton
Upper Halliford
ASHFORD RD
FELTHAM RD
CHERTSEY RD
CADBURY RD
STAINES RD W
WINDMILL RD
A244
A308
M3
B377
Hounslow
Surrey
Spelthorne Cty Inf Sch
Spelthorne Sports Club
Springfield Prim Sch
Bishop Wand CE Sec Sch
Hawkedale Fst Sch
Meadhurst Sports Club
Windmill Trad Est
Windmill Bsns Village
Sunbury Int Bsns Ctr
Water Works
Superstore
Leisure Ctr
The Shears
193
172
08
09
10
72
71
70
69
6
5
4
3
2
1

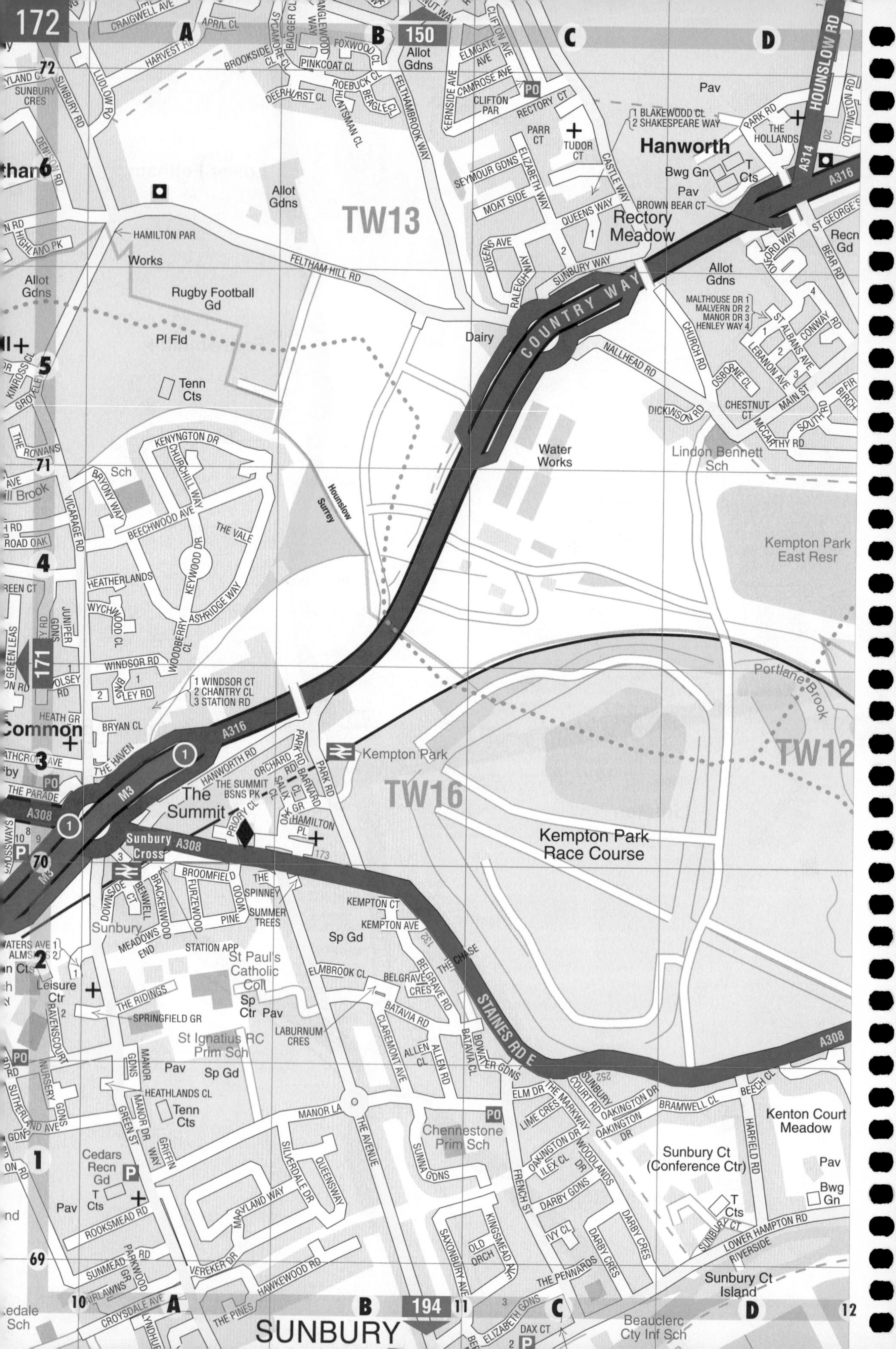

150
194
171
173
TW13
TW16
TW12
Hanworth
SUNBURY
Rectory Meadow
Kempton Park Race Course
Kempton Park East Resr
Kempton Park
Water Works
Sunbury Cross
The Summit
Common
COUNTRY WAY
STAINES RD E
HOUNSLOW RD
FELTHAM HILL RD
A316
A308
A314
M3
Rugby Football Gd
St Paul's Catholic Coll
St Ignatius RC Prim Sch
Chennestone Prim Sch
Lindon Bennett Sch
Sunbury Ct (Conference Ctr)
Sunbury Ct Island
Kenton Court Meadow
Cedars Recn Gd
Beauclerc Cty Inf Sch
Portlane Brook
Hounslow
Surrey

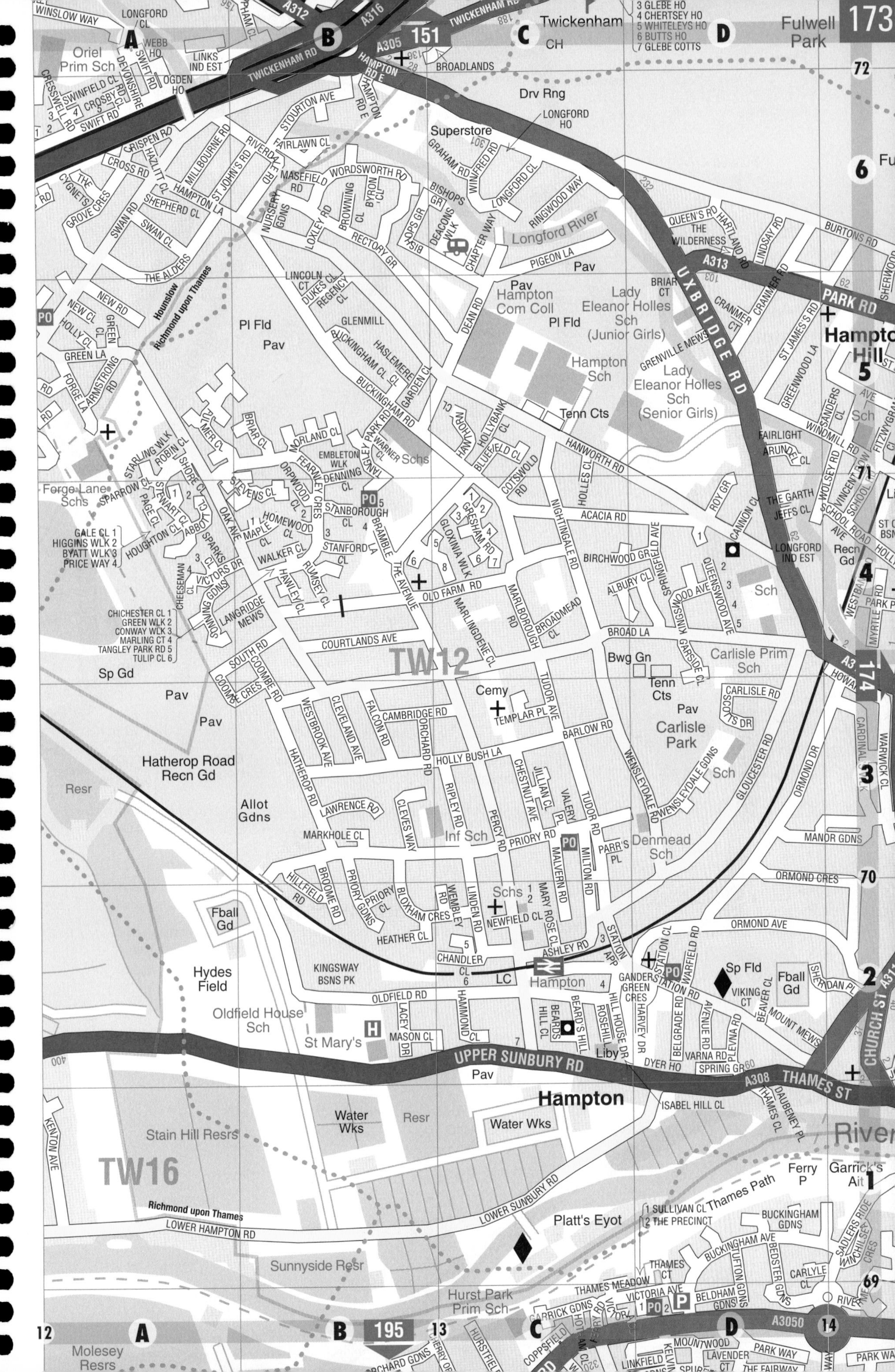

Twickenham
Fulwell Park
Hampton Hill
Hampton
TW12
TW16
Oriel Prim Sch
Hampton Com Coll
Lady Eleanor Holles Sch (Junior Girls)
Lady Eleanor Holles Sch (Senior Girls)
Hampton Sch
Carlisle Prim Sch
Carlisle Park
Denmead Sch
Forge Lane Schs
Hatherop Road Recn Gd
Hydes Field
Oldfield House Sch
St Mary's
Stain Hill Resrs
Sunnyside Resr
Hurst Park Prim Sch
Platt's Eyot
Garrick's Ait
Molesey Resrs
Longford River
UXBRIDGE RD
UPPER SUNBURY RD
LOWER SUNBURY RD
LOWER HAMPTON RD
THAMES ST
PARK RD
TWICKENHAM RD
HAMPTON RD E
CHURCH ST
Thames Path
Richmond upon Thames
Hounslow
151
174
195

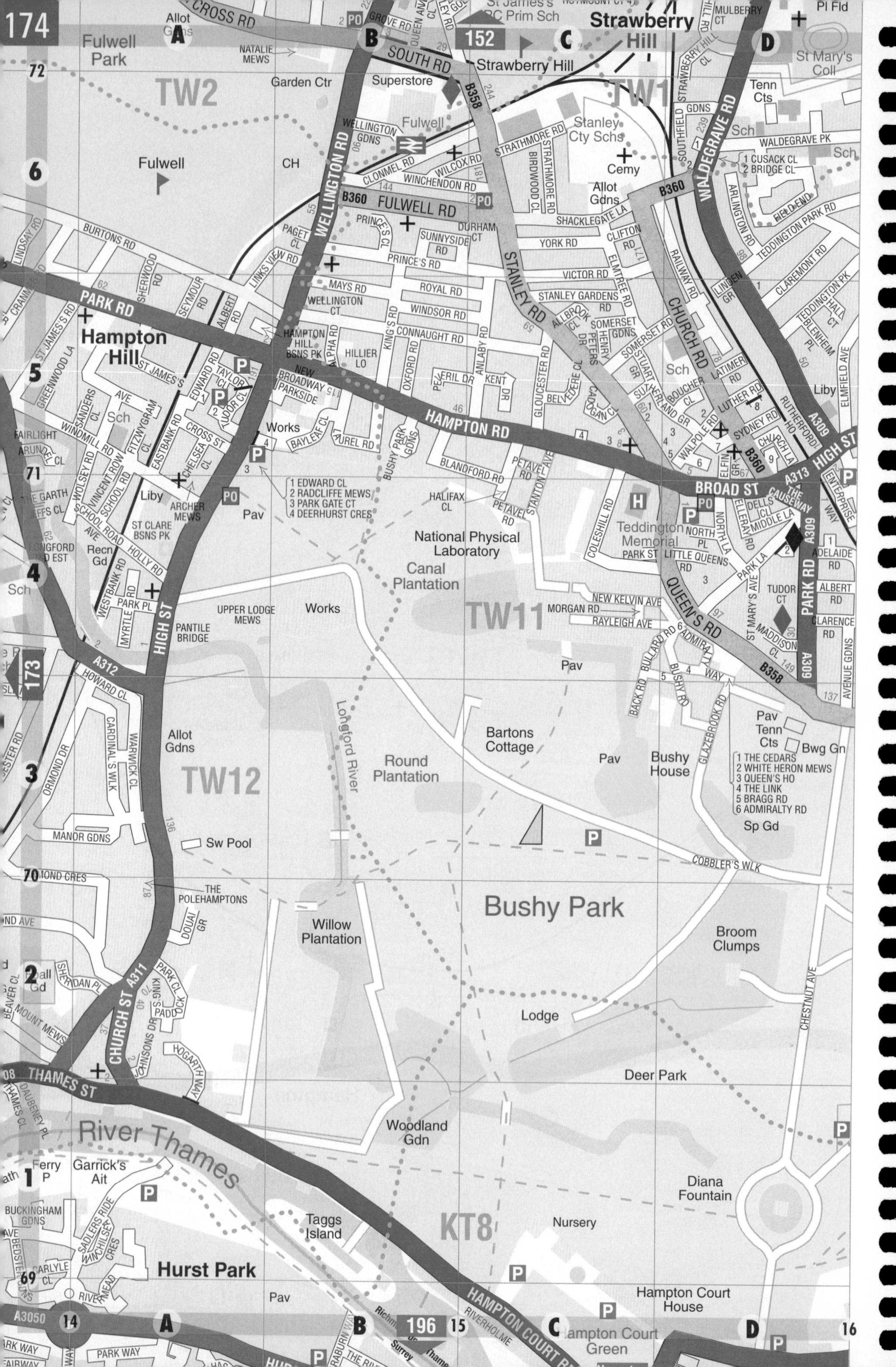
Fulwell Park
Allot Gdns
CROSS RD
NATALIE MEWS
GROVE RD
152
Strawberry Hill
SOUTH RD
Strawberry Hill
Garden Ctr
Superstore
TW2
TW1
B358
Fulwell
WELLINGTON GDNS
Stanley Cty Schs
STRATHMORE RD
BIRDWOOD CL
Fulwell
CH
WELLINGTON RD
CLONMEL RD
WILCOX RD
WINCHENDON RD
Cemy
Allot Gdns
B360
FULWELL RD
PO
WALDEGRAVE RD
WALDEGRAVE PK
1 CUSACK CL
2 BRIDGE CL
SOUTHFIELD GDNS
St Mary's Coll
Tenn Cts
Sch
Pl Fld
MULBERRY CT
STRAWBERRY HILL CL
LINDSAY RD
BURTONS RD
PAGET CL
PRINCE'S CL
SUNNYSIDE RD
DURHAM CT
SHACKLEGATE LA
CLIFTON RD
YORK RD
ARLINGTON RD
FIELD END
TEDDINGTON PARK RD
LINKS VIEW RD
PRINCE'S RD
VICTOR RD
STANLEY RD
MAYS RD
ROYAL RD
ELMTREE RD
RAILWAY RD
CLAREMONT RD
STANLEY GARDENS RD
PARK RD
Hampton Hill
SHERWOOD RD
SEYMOUR RD
ALBERT RD
WELLINGTON CT
WINDSOR RD
ALLBROOK CL
SOMERSET GDNS
SOMERSET RD
CHURCH RD
LINDEN GR
TEDDINGTON PK
HALL CT
BLENHEIM PL
ST JAMES'S RD
GREENWOOD LA
ST JAMES'S AVE
HAMPTON HILL BSNS PK
ALPHA RD
HILLIER LO
KING'S RD
CONNAUGHT RD
ANLABY RD
NEW BROADWAY
PARKSIDE
OXFORD RD
PEARL CL
ERIL DR
KENT DR
GLOUCESTER RD
BELVEDERE CL
HENRY PETERS DR
CADOGAN CL
STUART GR
SUTHERLAND GR
BOUCHER CL
LATIMER RD
LUTHER RD
ELMFIELD AVE
Liby
Sch
A309
HIGH ST
RUTHERFORD CL
SYDNEY RD
CHURCH LA
FAIRLIGHT
SANDERS CL
WINDMILL RD
FITZWYGRAM CL
EDWARD RD
TAYLOR CL
TUDOR CL
CROSS ST
EASTBANK RD
ARUNDEL CL
WOLSEY RD
VINCENT ROW
SCHOOL RD
CHELSEA CL
Works
BAYLEAF CL
LAUREL RD
BUSHY PARK GDNS
HAMPTON RD
BLANDFORD RD
PETAVEL RD
WALPOLE RD
ELFIN GR
B360
BROAD ST
A313
THE CAUSEWAY
ENTERPRISE WAY
1 EDWARD CL
2 RADCLIFFE MEWS
3 PARK GATE CT
4 DEERHURST CRES
HALIFAX CL
GARTH
JEFFS CL
SCHOOL ROAD AVE
Liby
ARCHER MEWS
ST CLARE BSNS PK
PO
Pav
National Physical Laboratory
STANTON RD
COLESHILL RD
Teddington Memorial
NORTH PL
NORTH LA
ELLERAY RD
DELLS CL
MIDDLE LA
PARK ST
LITTLE QUEENS RD
ADELAIDE RD
LONGFORD IND EST
Recn Gd
HOLLY RD
Canal Plantation
PARK LA
TUDOR CT
ALBERT RD
PARK RD
Sch
WESTBANK RD
PARK PL
MYRTLE RD
UPPER LODGE MEWS
Works
TW11
NEW KELVIN AVE
MORGAN RD
RAYLEIGH AVE
QUEEN'S RD
ST MARY'S AVE
MADDISON CL
CLARENCE RD
PANTILE BRIDGE
HIGH ST
A312
173
HOWARD CL
Pav
BULLARD RD
ADMIRALTY WAY
BUSHY RD
BACK RD
GLAZEBROOK RD
B358
A309
AVENUE GDNS
Longford River
Bartons Cottage
Pav
Tenn Cts
Bwg Gn
CARDINAL'S WLK
WARWICK CL
ORMOND DR
Allot Gdns
TW12
Round Plantation
Pav
Bushy House
1 THE CEDARS
2 WHITE HERON MEWS
3 QUEEN'S HO
4 THE LINK
5 BRAGG RD
6 ADMIRALTY RD
Sp Gd
MANOR GDNS
Sw Pool
COBBLER'S WLK
ORMOND CRES
THE POLEHAMPTONS
Bushy Park
ORMOND AVE
DOUAI GR
Willow Plantation
Broom Clumps
Ball Gd
SHERIDAN PL
PARK CL
KING'S PADDOCK
CHURCH ST
A311
JOHNSONS DR
Lodge
CHESTNUT AVE
MOUNT MEWS
HOGARTH WAY
THAMES ST
Deer Park
DAUBENEY PL
THAMES CL
River Thames
Woodland Gdn
Ferry
Garrick's Ait
Diana Fountain
BUCKINGHAM GDNS
SADLERS RIDE
WINCHILSEA CRES
Taggs Island
KT8
Nursery
Hurst Park
CARLYLE CL
RIVERMEAD
Pav
Hampton Court House
A3050
HAMPTON COURT RD
RIVERHOLME
Hampton Court Green
196
PARK WAY
Surrey

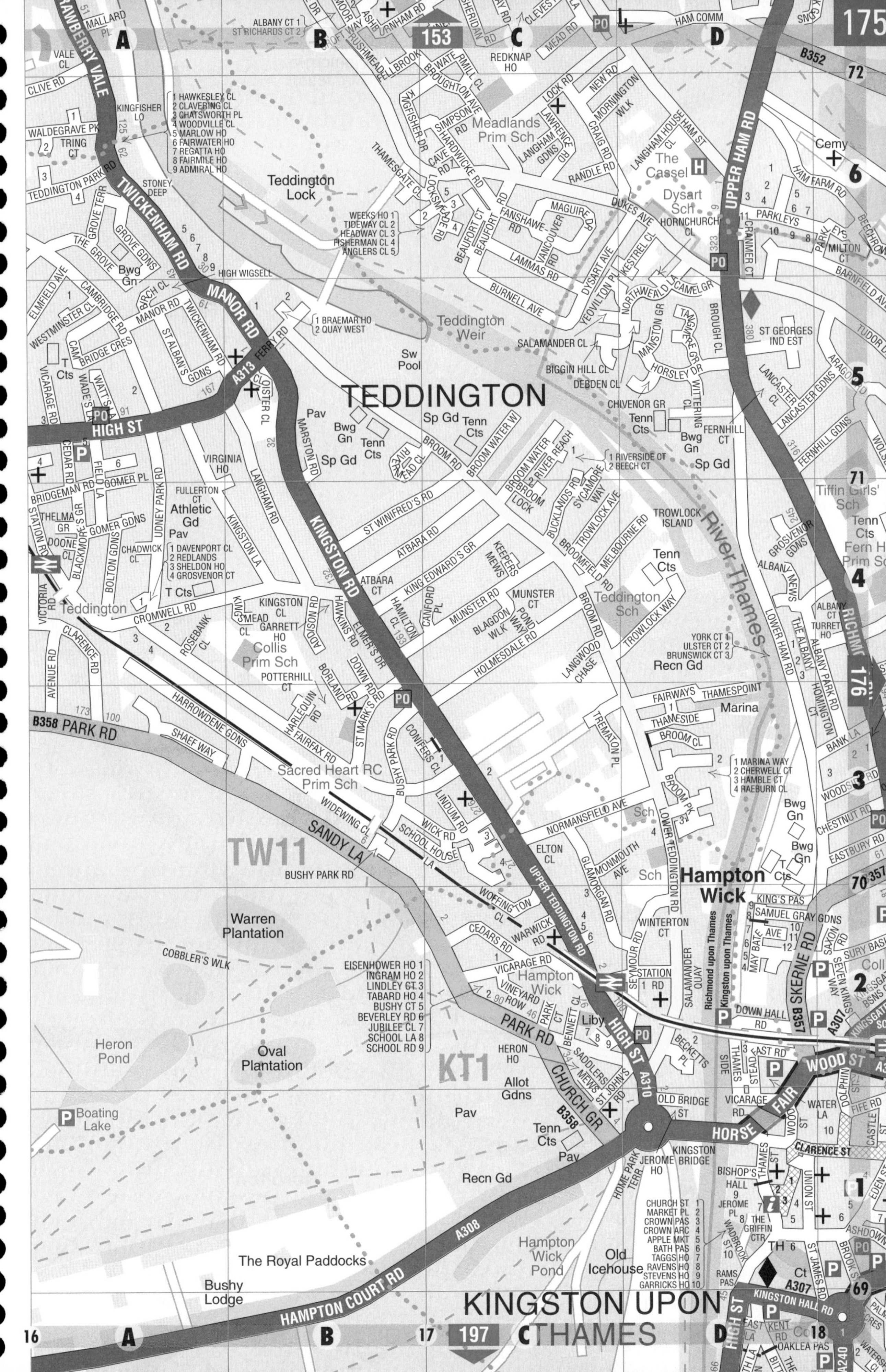
TEDDINGTON
Teddington Lock
Teddington Weir
River Thames
Hampton Wick
TW11
KT1
KINGSTON UPON THAMES
Warren Plantation
Oval Plantation
Heron Pond
Boating Lake
The Royal Paddocks
Bushy Lodge
Hampton Wick Pond
Old Icehouse
Meadlands Prim Sch
The Cassel
Dysart Sch
Collis Prim Sch
Sacred Heart RC Prim Sch
Teddington Sch
Tiffin Girls' Sch
TWICKENHAM RD
MANOR RD
KINGSTON RD
HIGH ST
PARK RD
SANDY LA
HAMPTON COURT RD
UPPER HAM RD
UPPER TEDDINGTON RD
CHURCH GR
HORSE FAIR
WOOD ST
LOWER HAM RD
BROOM RD
FERRY RD
STATION RD
BUSHY PARK RD
LOWER TEDDINGTON RD
153
197
176
16
17
18

A
B
154
C
D
B352
72
HAM GATE AVE
TW10
Hamcross
Plantation
Ham
Bottom
Isabella
Plantation
Ham
Common
HAM GATE AVE
Horse Ride
High
Wood
Park Gate
House
Cemy
6
HAM FARM RD
PARKLEYS
CRANMER CT
MILTON CT
BEECHROW
CHURCH RD
THE SHIRES
BARNFIELD AVE
BARNFIELD GDNS
GARTHSIDE
TUDOR DR
ST GEORGES
IND EST
HM
Remand
Ctr
HAM RIDINGS
Allot
Gdns
Richmond Park
QUEEN'S RD
SOPWITH CL
HATCH PL
Thatchedhouse
Lodge
5
LANCASTER CL
LANCASTER GDNS
ARAGON RD
CRANMER RD
BAINBRIDGE CL
LATCHMERE CL
ANNE BOLEYN'S
WLK
GARTH RD
BEARD RD
COMPETT RD
PARKFIELDS RD
WILMER CL
WILMER CRES
PARK RD
PARK GDNS
WOODCOTE CL
LADDERSTILE RIDE
Liby
PO
FERNHILL GDNS
WOLSEY DR
CARDINAL AVE
HOLLYBUSH RD
LATCHMERE LA
Allot
Gdns
71
Tiffin Girls'
Sch
King
Clump
Canbury
Sch
WARBOYS RD
WARBOYS APP
Tenn
Cts
Fern Hill
Prim Sch
Recn
Gd
Latchmere
Jun & Inf
Schs
ALDERSBROOK DR
CRANLEIGH GDNS
WINGFIELD RD
GROSVENOR GDNS
ALBANY MEWS
4
ASTOR CL
PARKGATE CL
A308
Thames
LOWER HAM RD
DURLSTON RD
ST ALBANS RD
STUDLAND RD
LATCHMERE RD
ST AGATHA'S DR
KELVEDON CL
UPPER PARK RD
KINGSNYMPTON PK
MAGNOLIA CL
HAYGREEN CL
Sp Gd
St Agatha's
RC Prim
Sch
ALBANY CT
TURRET HO
THE ALBANY
ALBANY PARK RD
HOMINGTON CT
RICHMOND RD
ST ALBANS RD
THE KEEP
P
HEATHERDALE CL
DUTCH GDNS
WINDMILL RISE
175
1 WALTON HO
2 BERKELEY CL
3 CANBURY CT
EARLE GDNS
STANTON RD
DINTON RD
BOCKHAMPTON RD
BERTRAM RD
WINCHESTER CL
BANK LA
ARCHER CL
PARK FARM RD
CHESFIELD RD
Sch
WYNDHAM RD
LIVERPOOL RD
CRESCENT RD
CUMBERLAND HO
MORECOMBE CL
MARINA WAY
CHERWELL CT
HAMBLE CT
RAEBURN CL
3
WOODSIDE RD
OSBORNE RD
THORPE RD
BURTON RD
KING'S RD
NEW RD
TUDOR RD
CHERRYWOOD CL
QUEEN'S RD
BEAUMONT CL
BOYD CL
DEER PARK CL
EATON DR
BERYSTEDE
CH
Bwg
Gn
CHESTNUT RD
WINDSOR RD
BEARFIELD RD
CROSS RD
SHORTLANDS RD
PO
ROSEWOOD CT
ALEXANDRA RD
B351
Sch
EASTBURY RD
RICHMOND PARK RD
ELM RD
YORK RD
Schs
PRINCES RD
BLENHEIM GDNS
T
Cts
Pav
70
B357
GIBBON RD
HARDINGS CL
LOWTHER RD
CLIFTON RD
PARK CL
KING'S PAS
SAMUEL GRAY GDNS
SAXON RD
ACRE RD
CANBURY AVE
CRAVEN RD
WILLOUGHBY RD
GLENVILLE RD
BRUNSWICK RD
PO
CRAIGSIDE
FAIRVIEW CT
FORSYTHE CT
BADMINTON
MAY BATE AVE
SKERNE RD
SURY BASIN
EAST RD
DAVID TWIGG CL
WAIGHTS CT
BERESFORD RD
ELTON RD
GALSWORTHY RD
2
SEVEN KINGS WAY
Coll
KINGSGATE BSNS CTR
RIDE
DEACON RD
AUDRIC CL
CARLISLE CL
H
Kingston
WOLSEY CL
COWLEAZE RD
ELM CRES
ELM GR
MANORGATE RD
MANOR CT
WOLVERTON AVE
P
TOWN HALL RD
B357
A307
KINGSGATE RD
SOPWITH WAY
PO
Ct
CANBURY PARK RD
BOSWELL CT
BURNHAM ST
GORDON RD
Kingston
COOMBE RD
ANDHURST CT
DUMBLETON CL
WOOD ST
A308
JOHN AUSTIN CL
TITHE BARN CL
BIRKENHEAD AVE
STATION RD
SYLVESTRUS CL
JEMMETT CL
WESSEX CL
REVELL RD
CROMWELL RD
A308
QUEEN ELIZABETH RD
CHESHAM RD
COBHAM RD
NORBITON AVE
Norbiton
1 BRACKENDALE
2 WOODSTOCK CT
3 PINKERTON CT
4 LAMBOURNE GR
5 MARYLAND CT
WATER LA
FIFE RD
HARDMAN RD
RIVERSTONE CT
NORBITON HALL
A238
HOMERSHAM RD
LOVEKYN CL
Tiffin
Sch
LONDON RD
CHATHAM RD
NEVILLE RD
GLOUCESTER RD
KENLEY RD
CLARENCE ST
A307
CASTLE ST
CLARENCE ST
FAIRFIELD N
A308
CLEVEDON RD
CHESTER HO
ORME RD
1
UNION ST
EDEN ST
WESTON
FAIRFIELD RD
CAVERSHAM RD
MINERVA RD
CHURCH RD
A2043
AYCLIFFE CT
Norbiton
KT1
THAMES ST
THE GRIFFIN CTR
P
Mus
Ctr
Liby
FAIRFIELD RD
Univ
VICTORIA RD
ALBERT RD
CAMBRIDGE GDNS
ERNEST SQ
ERNEST RD
PORCHESTER RD
ROSEBERY SQ
ROSEBERY RD
ASHDOWN RD
WHEATFIELD WAY
Pav
Recn Gd
Sch
HAWKS RD
LINDEN CRES
PORTMAN RD
EXCELSIOR CL
WASHINGTON RD
ST PETERS RD
CAMBRIDGE RD
CHARTER SQ
69
A307
Ct
BROOK ST
LITTLEFIELD HO
ORCHARD RD
SOMERSET RD
WAY
BARRITT RD
WATERS RD
KINGSTON HALL RD
ST JAMES RD
FAIRFIELD S
FALCONRY CT
MILLFIELD
KINGSWORTHY CL
ROWLLS RD
FRANKLIN
VINCENT RD
HAMPDEN RD
WATERS SQ
CHARTER RD
DOUGLAS RD
WILLOW CT
LIME CT
KING HENRY'S RD
NORBITON COMMON RD
FLEETWOOD RD
18
A
B
19
198
C
D
20
KENT RD
OAKLEA PAS
PALMER CRES
GRANGE RD
KNIGHT'S PK
AVENUE RD
MILL ST
GREEN LEAS
MILL PL
ATHENA CL
DUDLEY RD
LIVESEY CL
WINERY LA
BONNER HILL RD
Cemy
A240

A B 155 C D

Robin Hood

War Meml

Wandsworth

72

6

5

71

4

178

3

70

2

1

69

22

20 A 21 199 B C D 22

Horse Ride

P

Kingston Vale

SW15

Pl Fld

Richmond upon Thames

Kingston upon Thames

ROBINWOOD PL

WOODVIEW CL

CEDAR CL

KINGSTON HILL PL

ULLSWATER CL

ULLSWATER CRES

GRASMERE AVE

DERWENT AVE

MAR ADELAIDE CL

BEVERLEY

VALE CRES

A3

WINDERMERE RD

ROBIN HOOD LA

Walkden Hall
(Hall of Residence)

Sch

Combe Hurst

Kingston Univ

BOWNESS CRES

RYDAL GDNS

ROBIN HOOD LA

ROBIN HOOD RD

KESWICK AVE

Pav

Tenn Cts

Horse Ride

Horse Ride

Kingston upon Thames

Merton

SW19

Allot Gdns

Mill Corner

KINGSTON HILL

COOMBE PL

COOMBE RANDOLPH PL

COOMBE WOOD RD

CORSCOMBE CL

PAGET PL

COOMBE RIDINGS

COOMBE PK

Allot Gdns

Pl Fld

ROBIN HOOD WAY KINGSTON BY PASS

KT2

Warren House

THE WATERGARDENS

Coombe Hill

FAIRLAWN CL

COTSWOLD CL

WARREN PK

WARREN RD

HIGH COOMBE PL

WARREN CUTTING

GOLF CLUB DR

SW20

Pl Fld

Tenn Cts

BARN

ELLERTON

Coombe Wood

RENFREW RD

STOKE RD

GEORGE RD

COOMBE NEVILLE

EDGECOMBE CL

COOMBE END

CH

THE LEIGH

GREENWOOD PK

COOMBE HILL RD

BEVERLEY LA

HENLEY DR

NAT Res

Nat Res

PRESTON RD

HOOD RD

MELVILLE AVE

BURDETT RD

Holy Cross Prep RC Sch

THE DRIVE

GATEHOUSE CL

Schs

BALLARD CL

Coombe

123

COOMBE LA W

LORD CHANCELLOR WLK

SOUTHWOOD AVE

B283

FITZGEORGE AVE

WARREN RISE

MOOR PARK GDNS

COOMBE HILL GLADE

DEVEY CL

WARBANK LA

A3

A3

187

BEVERLEY AVE

HOLLAND AVE

COTTENHAM PARK RD

BROOK GDNS

COOMBE RISE

ORCHARD RISE

WEST RD

CROWN

COOMBE HOUSE CHASE

NEVILLE AVE

THE FAIRWAY

OAKCOMBE CL

WONFORD CL

THE CHESTERS

New Victoria

H

Coombe Lane

COOMBE LANE FLYOVER 1
BEVERLEY CT 2

Kingston upon Thames

Merton

BEVERLEY WAY KINGSTON BY PASS

WEST COOMBE AVE

PO

A238

A238

Pl Flds

ALBION RD

CARDINAL CRES

HIGH DR

BEECHCROFT AVE

BRANKSOME AVE

MATLOCK WAY

WOODLANDS WAY

CROMFORD WAY

BUXTON DR

TRAPS LA

THE MOAT

BADGERS WLK

SOAM ES WLK

KT3

Coombe Brook

Malden

ELY CL

A3

ARUNDEL RD

DICKERAGE RD

OLIVER RD

CLARENCE AVE

OAK RD

OVERDALE AVE

DARLEY DR

Coombe Girls Sch

BAKEWELL WAY

LANGLEY GR

CARLTON RD

SELBORNE RD

BURBERRY CL

GOLFSIDE

DELL WLK

LINKSIDE

CH

Tenn Cts

Sp Gd

CH

CAMBRIDGE AVE

ROSEBERRY AVE

Allot Gdns

1 PERTH CL
2 HUNTLEY V

THE TRIANGLE

PO

MUYBRIDGE RD

MIDLETON RD

LONG WLK

ASHCOMBE SQ

THE LABURNUM GR

MYRTLE GR

THE CLOSE

THE CRESCENT

LAWN CL

WOODSIDE RD

POPLAR GR

ROWAN RD

SYCAMORE GR

EDGAR CT

FORSYTH CT

Allot Gdns

Tenn Cts

WARWICK RD

DICKERAGE HILL

LINCOLN

MOUNT PLEASANT RD

Corpus Christi RC Prim Sch

BEECH GR

BEACONSFIELD RD

SALISBURY RD

Bwg Gn

POPLAR

St N

Sch

COOMBE RD

HOPPINGWOOD AVE

ORCHARD AVE

ALRIC AVE

77

811

2

99

117

2

328

1

2

1

2

156
177
200
SW15
SW19
SW20
Wimbledon Common
London Scottish
Gravelly Hill
Caesar's Camp
Royal Wimbledon
Crooked Billet
Cannizaro Park
Copse Hill
Cottenham Park
Raynes Park
Bushey Mead
The Buddhapadipa Temple
The Study Prep Sch
King's Coll Sch
Wimbledon Common Prep Sch
Wimbledon Coll
Norwegian Sch
Ursuline High Sch
Hall Sch
Atkinson Morley
St Matthew's CE Fst Sch
Hollymount Prim Sch
Horse Ride
PARKSIDE
HIGH ST
THE CAUSEWAY
CANNIZARO RD
WEST SIDE COMM
WOODHAYES RD
COTTENHAM PARK RD
COPSE HILL
COOMBE LA
DURHAM RD
WORPLE RD
KINGSTON RD
BUSHEY RD
WEST BARNES LA
BEVERLEY WAY
KINGSTON BY PASS
SUNSET RD
CAMP RD

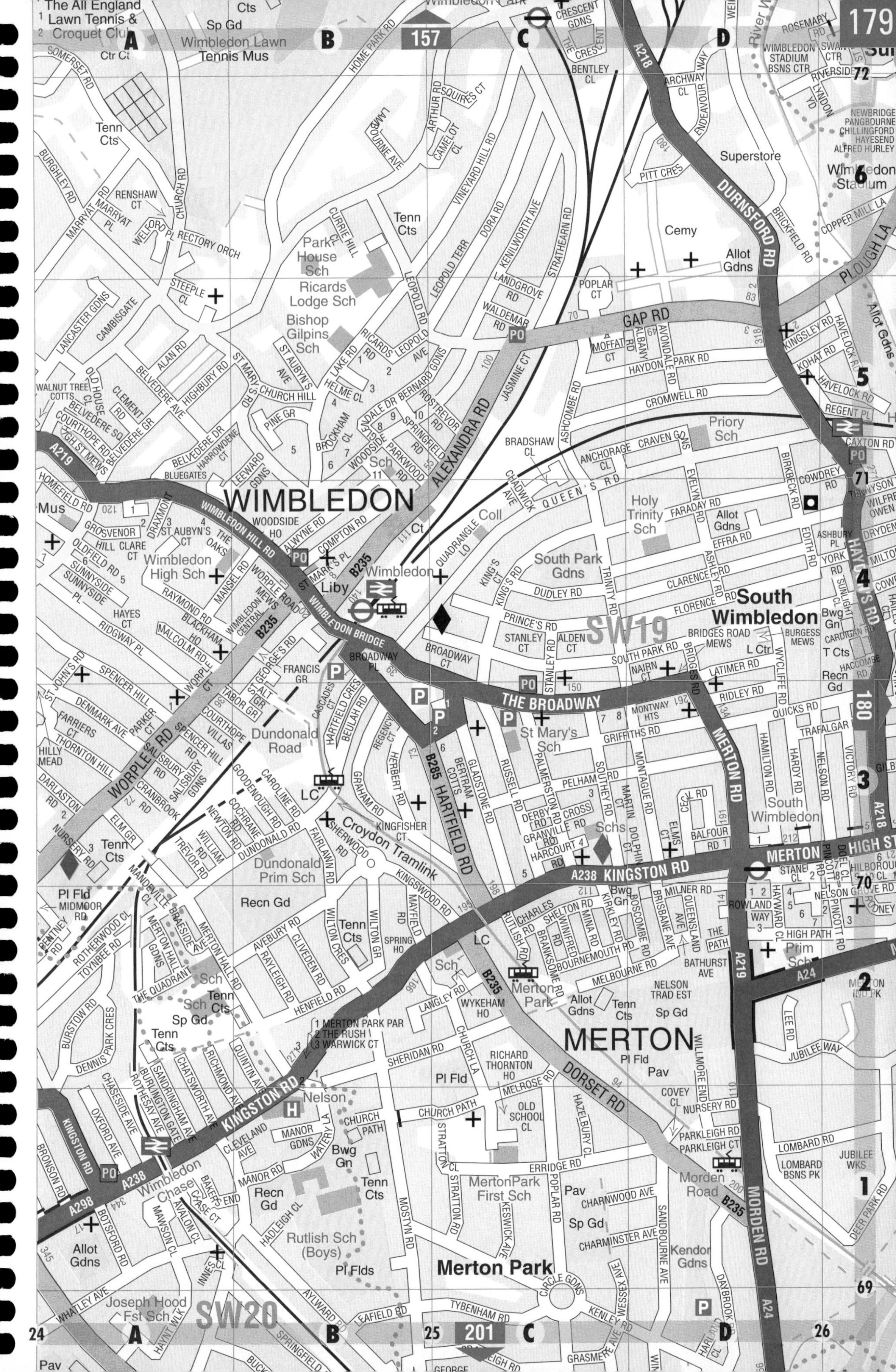

The All England Lawn Tennis & Croquet Club
Wimbledon Lawn Tennis Mus
157
A
B
C
D
WIMBLEDON
SOUTH Wimbledon
SW19
MERTON
Merton Park
SW20
Wimbledon Chase
Wimbledon
Dundonald Road
Merton Park
Morden Road
South Wimbledon
Croydon Tramlink
Wimbledon Stadium
Wimbledon Stadium Bsns Ctr
Superstore
Cemy
Allot Gdns
Priory Sch
Holy Trinity Sch
South Park Gdns
Park House Sch
Ricards Lodge Sch
Bishop Gilpins Sch
Wimbledon High Sch
St Mary's Sch
Dundonald Prim Sch
Rutlish Sch (Boys)
Merton Park First Sch
Joseph Hood Fst Sch
Kendor Gdns
Nelson Trad Est
Lombard Bsns Pk
Jubilee Wks
Merton Ind Pk
Recn Gd
Tenn Cts
Sp Gd
Pl Fld
Coll
Liby
WIMBLEDON HILL RD
WORPLE RD
ALEXANDRA RD
THE BROADWAY
MERTON RD
HARTFIELD RD
KINGSTON RD
DORSET RD
MORDEN RD
DURNSFORD RD
GAP RD
HAYDONS RD
MERTON HIGH ST
PLOUGH LA
QUEEN'S RD
WIMBLEDON BRIDGE
A219
A218
A238
A298
A24
B235
B285
180
201
6
5
4
3
2
1
24
25
26
69
70
71
72

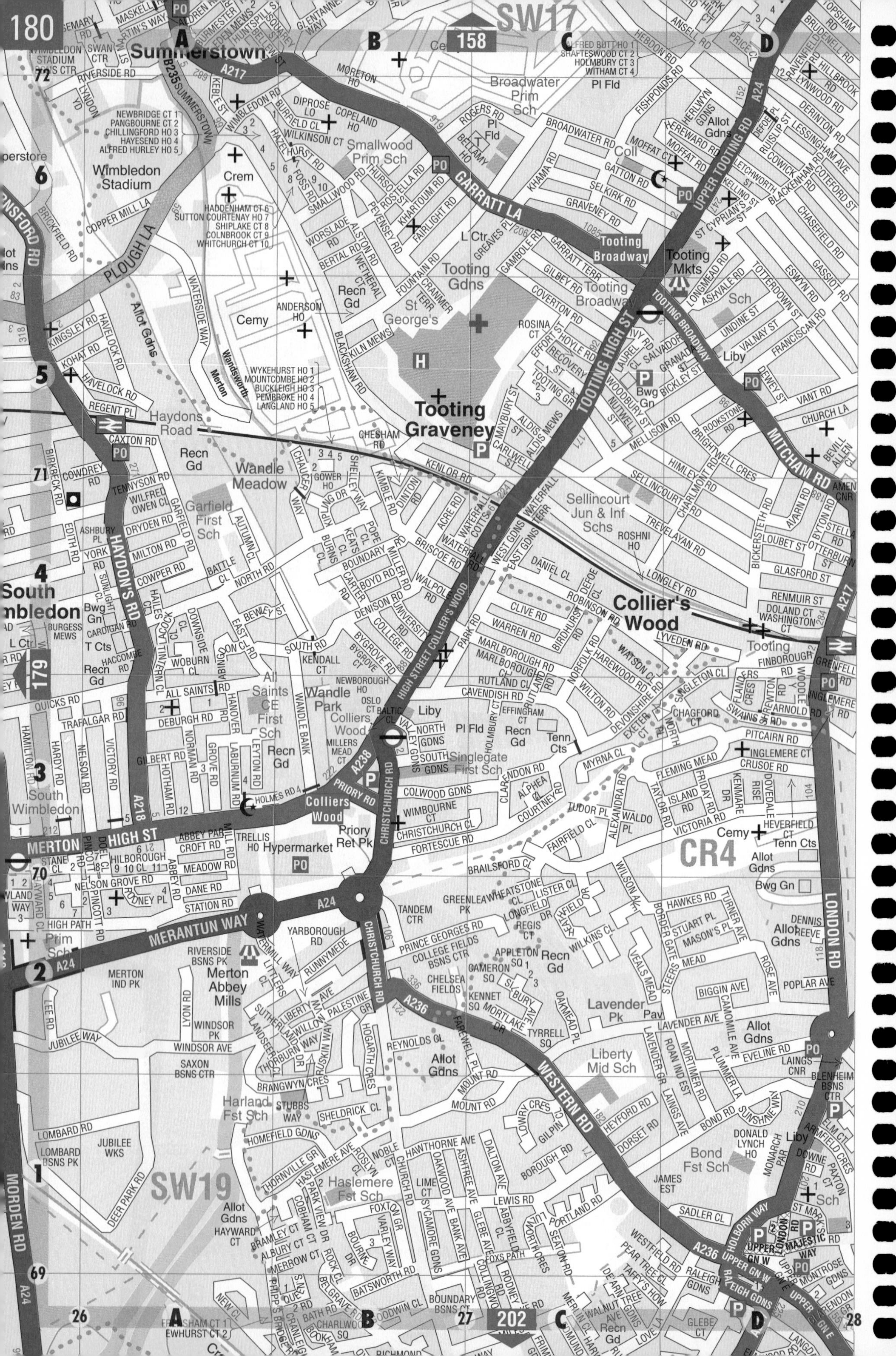

180
SW17
158
A
B
C
D
Summerstown
Wimbledon Stadium
Crem
Smallwood Prim Sch
Broadwater Prim Sch
Pl Fld
GARRATT LA
PLOUGH LA
Cemy
Recn Gd
St George's
Tooting Gdns
L Ctr
Tooting Broadway
Tooting Mkts
UPPER TOOTING RD
TOOTING HIGH ST
TOOTING BROADWAY
Tooting Graveney
Haydons Road
Wandle Meadow
Garfield First Sch
HAYDON'S RD
South Wimbledon
Sellincourt Jun & Inf Schs
MITCHAM RD
Collier's Wood
Tooting
HIGH STREET COLLIER'S WOOD
All Saints CE First Sch
Wandle Park
Colliers Wood
Liby
Singlegate First Sch
Priory Ret Pk
Hypermarket
MERTON HIGH ST
CHRISTCHURCH RD
CR4
Cemy
Allot Gdns
Bwg Gn
Tenn Cts
MERANTUN WAY
Merton Abbey Mills
MERTON IND PK
RIVERSIDE BSNS PK
WINDSOR AVE
SAXON BSNS CTR
Recn Gd
Lavender Pk
Liberty Mid Sch
WESTERN RD
LONDON RD
Harland Fst Sch
Haslemere Fst Sch
Bond Fst Sch
JAMES EST
LOMBARD BSNS PK
JUBILEE WKS
SW19
MORDEN RD
179
202
26
27
28
69
70
71
72
1
2
3
4
5
6

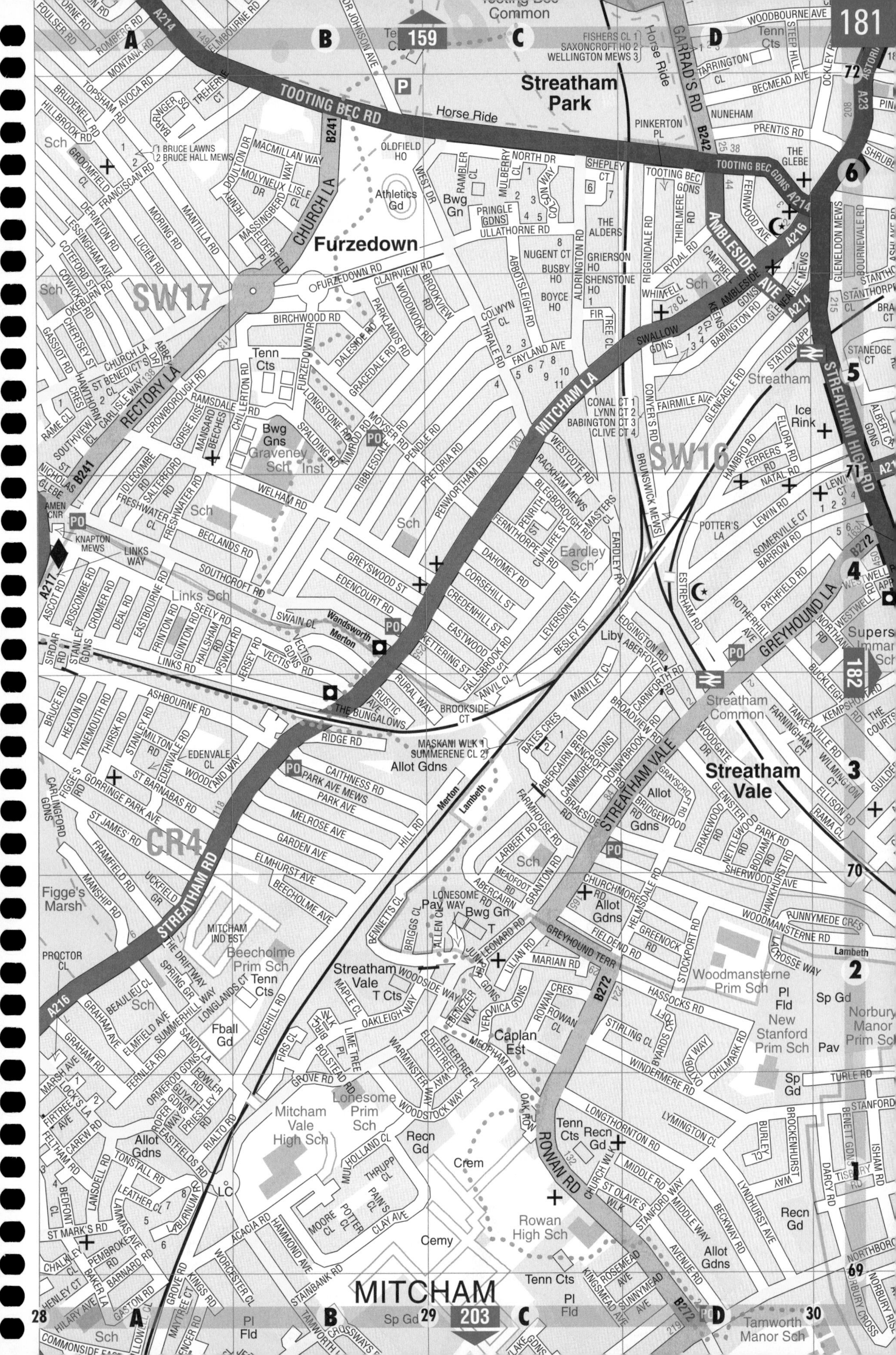
Streatham Park
Furzedown
Tooting Bec Common
TOOTING BEC RD
SW17
SW16
CR4
Streatham
Streatham Common
Streatham Vale
MITCHAM
MITCHAM LA
STREATHAM RD
STREATHAM HIGH RD
STREATHAM VALE
GREYHOUND LA
ROWAN RD
RECTORY LA
CHURCH LA
AMBLESIDE AVE
TOOTING BEC GDNS
GARRAD'S RD
Figge's Marsh
Mitcham Vale High Sch
Rowan High Sch
Woodmansterne Prim Sch
Beecholme Prim Sch
Lonesome Prim Sch
Graveney Sch
Eardley Sch
Links Sch
Tamworth Manor Sch
Caplan Est
Crem
Cemy
Allot Gdns
Athletics Gd
Ice Rink
159
182
203

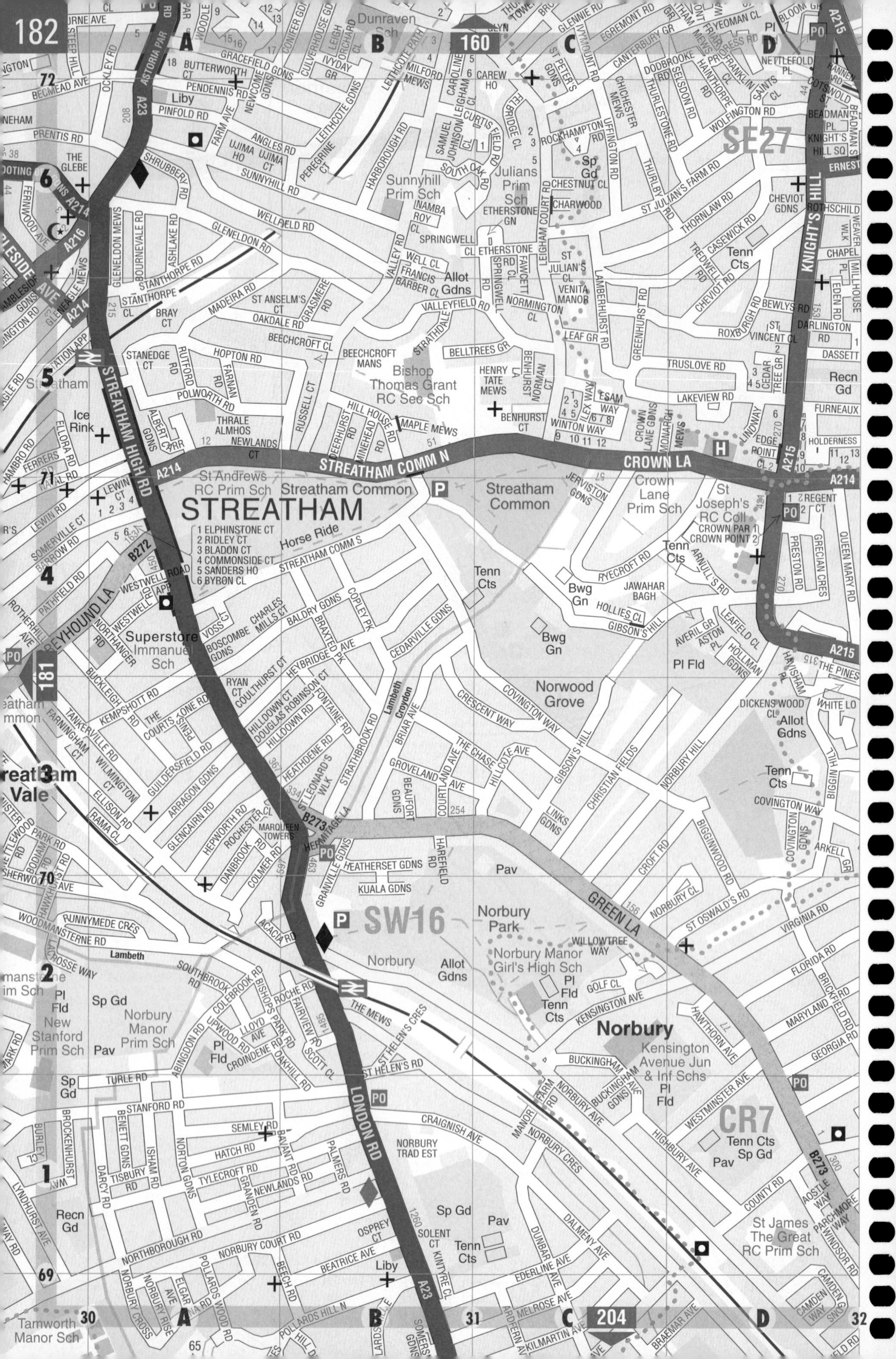
STREATHAM
Streatham Common
SW16
SE27
CR7
Norbury
STREATHAM HIGH RD
STREATHAM COMM N
CROWN LA
GREEN LA
LONDON RD
KNIGHT'S HILL
Norwood Grove
Norbury Park
160
204
181

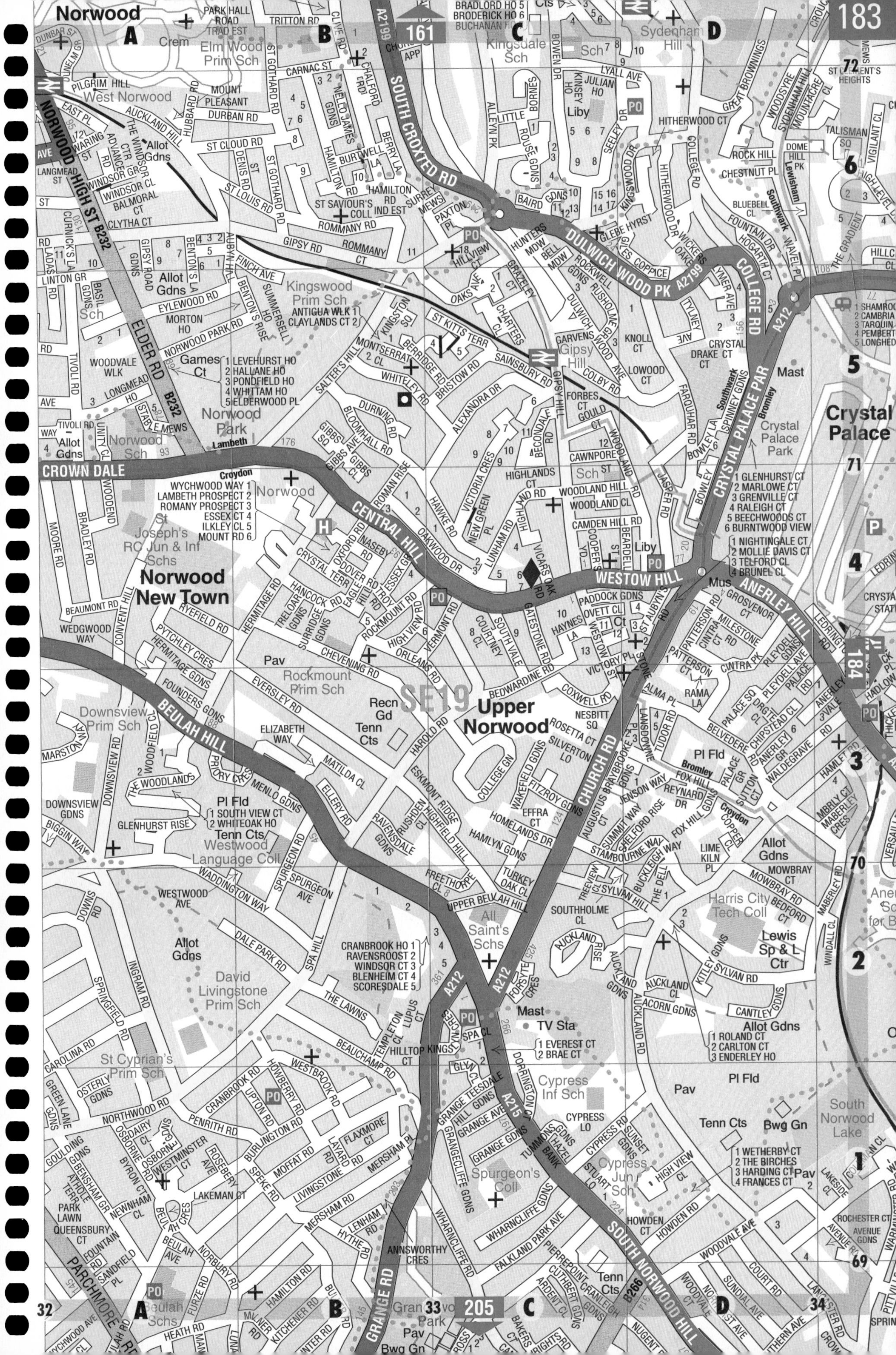

183
161
184
205
32
33
34
Norwood
Crem
Elm Wood Prim Sch
West Norwood
Kingsdale Sch
Sydenham Hill
SOUTH CROXTED RD
DULWICH WOOD PK
COLLEGE RD
CRYSTAL PALACE PAR
Crystal Palace
Crystal Palace Park
Gipsy Hill
Kingswood Prim Sch
NORWOOD HIGH ST B232
ELDER RD
CROWN DALE
CENTRAL HILL
WESTOW HILL
ANERLEY HILL
Norwood Park
Norwood New Town
St Joseph's RC Jun & Inf Schs
Rockmount Prim Sch
SE19
Upper Norwood
BEULAH HILL
CHURCH RD
Downsview Prim Sch
Westwood Language Coll
David Livingstone Prim Sch
St Cyprian's Prim Sch
All Saint's Schs
TV Sta
Mast
Cypress Inf Sch
Spurgeon's Coll
Cypress Jun Sch
Harris City Tech Coll
Lewis Sp & L Ctr
South Norwood Lake
SOUTH NORWOOD HILL
GRANGE RD
PARCHMORE RD
Beulah Schs
Grangewood Park

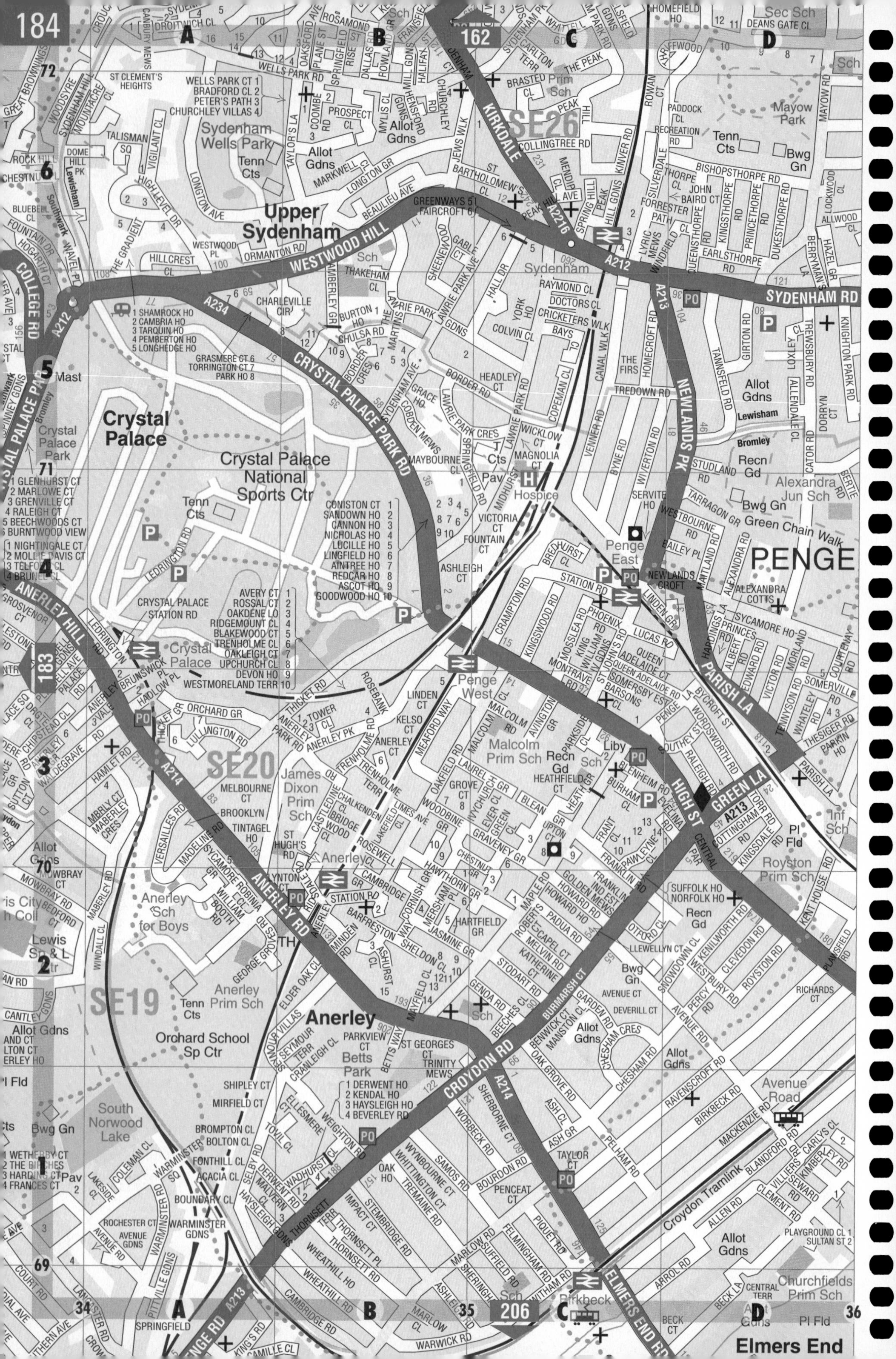

184
162
183
206
A
B
C
D
72
6
5
4
3
2
1
71
70
69
34
35
36
SE26
SE20
SE19
Upper Sydenham
Sydenham Wells Park
Crystal Palace
Crystal Palace Park
Crystal Palace National Sports Ctr
CRYSTAL PALACE PARK RD
CRYSTAL PALACE STATION RD
Crystal Palace
WESTWOOD HILL
KIRKDALE
SYDENHAM RD
Sydenham
NEWLANDS PK
PENGE
Penge East
Penge West
HIGH ST
GREEN LA
PARISH LA
ANERLEY HILL
ANERLEY RD
Anerley
CROYDON RD
ELMERS END RD
Birkbeck
Avenue Road
Croydon Tramlink
Elmers End
Mayow Park
South Norwood Lake
Betts Park
Orchard School Sp Ctr
Anerley Prim Sch
Anerley Sch for Boys
James Dixon Prim Sch
Malcolm Prim Sch
Royston Prim Sch
Churchfields Prim Sch
Alexandra Jun Sch
Green Chain Walk
Hospice
Lewisham
Bromley
A212
A213
A214
A234
A2216

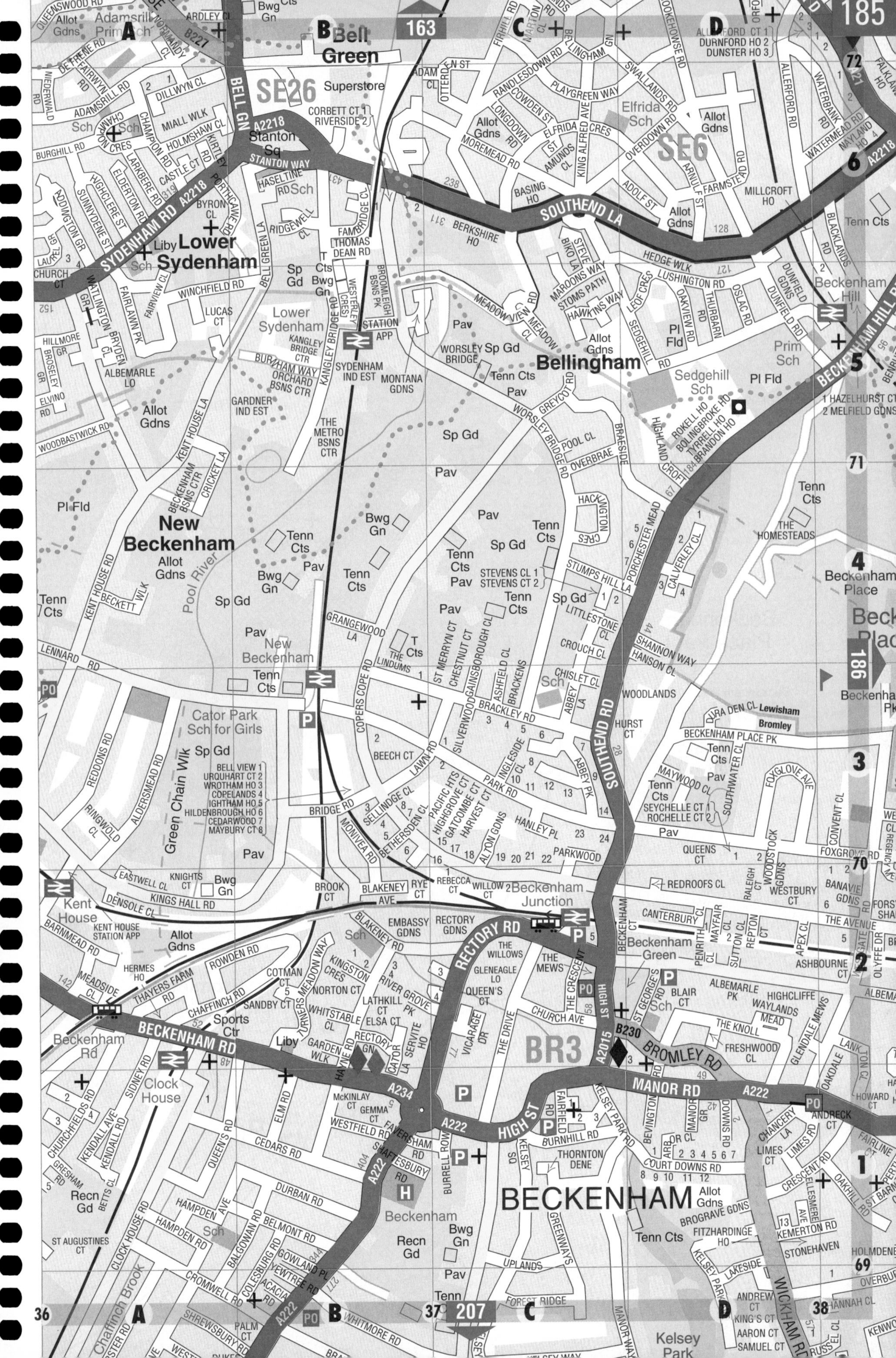

Bell Green
163
SE26
Superstore
Stanton Sq
STANTON WAY
SYDENHAM RD
A2218
BELL GN
Lower Sydenham
Lower Sydenham
SOUTHEND LA
Bellingham
SE6
Elfrida Sch
Sedgehill Sch
Beckenham Hill
BECKENHAM HILL RD
New Beckenham
New Beckenham
Pool River
Beckenham Place
186
Lewisham
Bromley
SOUTHEND RD
Cator Park Sch for Girls
Green Chain Wlk
Kent House
Beckenham Junction
RECTORY RD
BECKENHAM RD
Beckenham Rd
Clock House
Sports Ctr
BR3
HIGH ST
MANOR RD
BROMLEY RD
A222
A234
A2015
B230
BECKENHAM
Beckenham
Kelsey Park
Chaffinch Brook
36
37
207
38
A
B
C
D
1
2
3
4
5
6
69
70
71
72

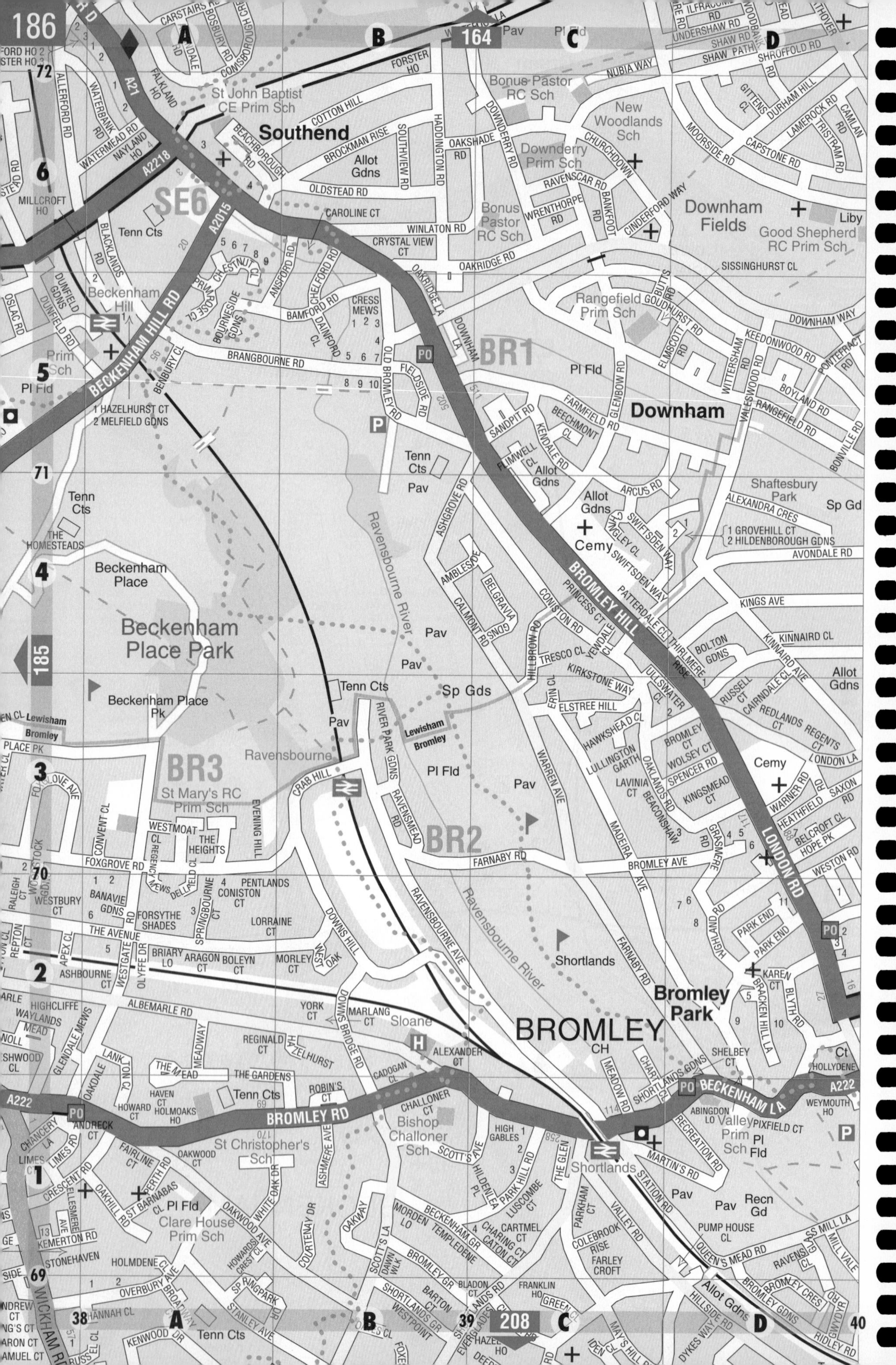
Southend
SE6
BR1
BR2
BR3
Downham
Downham Fields
New Woodlands Sch
Bonus Pastor RC Sch
Downderry Prim Sch
St John Baptist CE Prim Sch
Beckenham Hill
Beckenham Place
Beckenham Place Park
Beckenham Place Pk
Ravensbourne
Ravensbourne River
St Mary's RC Prim Sch
Rangefield Prim Sch
Good Shepherd RC Prim Sch
Shaftesbury Park
BROMLEY HILL
LONDON RD
BECKENHAM HILL RD
BROMLEY RD
BECKENHAM LA
BROMLEY
Bromley Park
Shortlands
Sloane
Bishop Challoner Sch
St Christopher's Sch
Clare House Prim Sch
Valley Prim Sch
Lewisham
Bromley
164
185
208
A
B
C
D
1
2
3
4
5
6
38
39
40
69
70
71
72

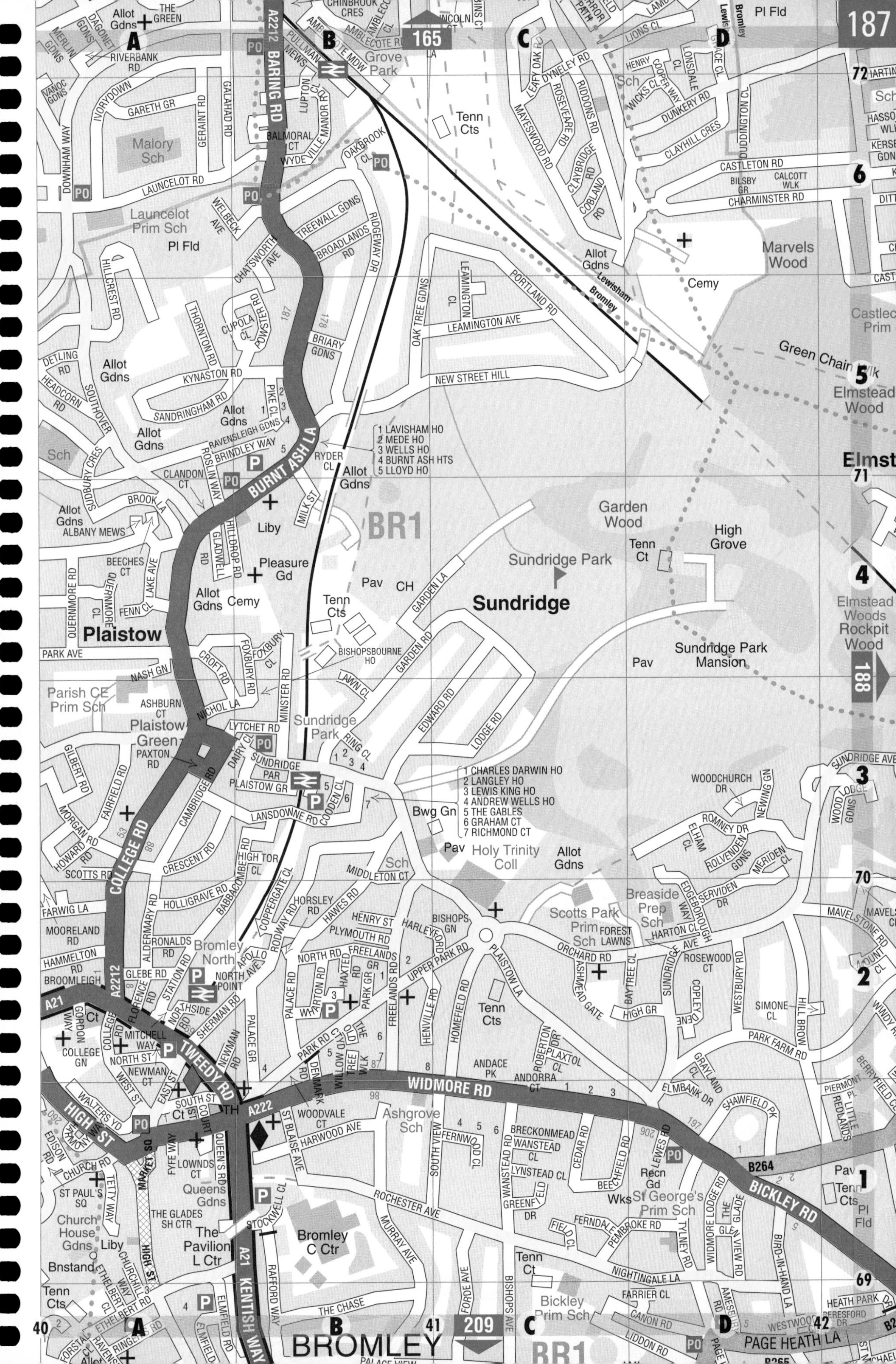

165
A
B
C
D
Grove Park
BARING RD
A2212
Malory Sch
LAUNCELOT RD
Launcelot Prim Sch
Pl Fld
Tenn Cts
Allot Gdns
Lewisham
Bromley
Cemy
Marvels Wood
Green Chain Wk
Elmstead Wood
6
5
4
3
2
1
72
71
70
69
BURNT ASH LA
NEW STREET HILL
LEAMINGTON AVE
1 LAVISHAM HO
2 MEDE HO
3 WELLS HO
4 BURNT ASH HTS
5 LLOYD HO
BR1
Garden Wood
High Grove
Sundridge Park
Sundridge
Plaistow
Sundridge Park Mansion
Elmstead Woods
Rockpit Wood
188
Plaistow Green
Parish CE Prim Sch
COLLEGE RD
1 CHARLES DARWIN HO
2 LANGLEY HO
3 LEWIS KING HO
4 ANDREW WELLS HO
5 THE GABLES
6 GRAHAM CT
7 RICHMOND CT
Holy Trinity Coll
Bromley North
Breaside Prep Sch
Scotts Park Prim Sch
WIDMORE RD
A222
A21
TWEEDY RD
HIGH ST
Ashgrove Sch
ROCHESTER AVE
Bromley C Ctr
The Pavilion L Ctr
THE GLADES SH CTR
Queens Gdns
Church House Gdns
St George's Prim Sch
BICKLEY RD
B264
Bickley Prim Sch
NIGHTINGALE LA
KENTISH WAY
PAGE HEATH LA
40
41
42
209
BROMLEY

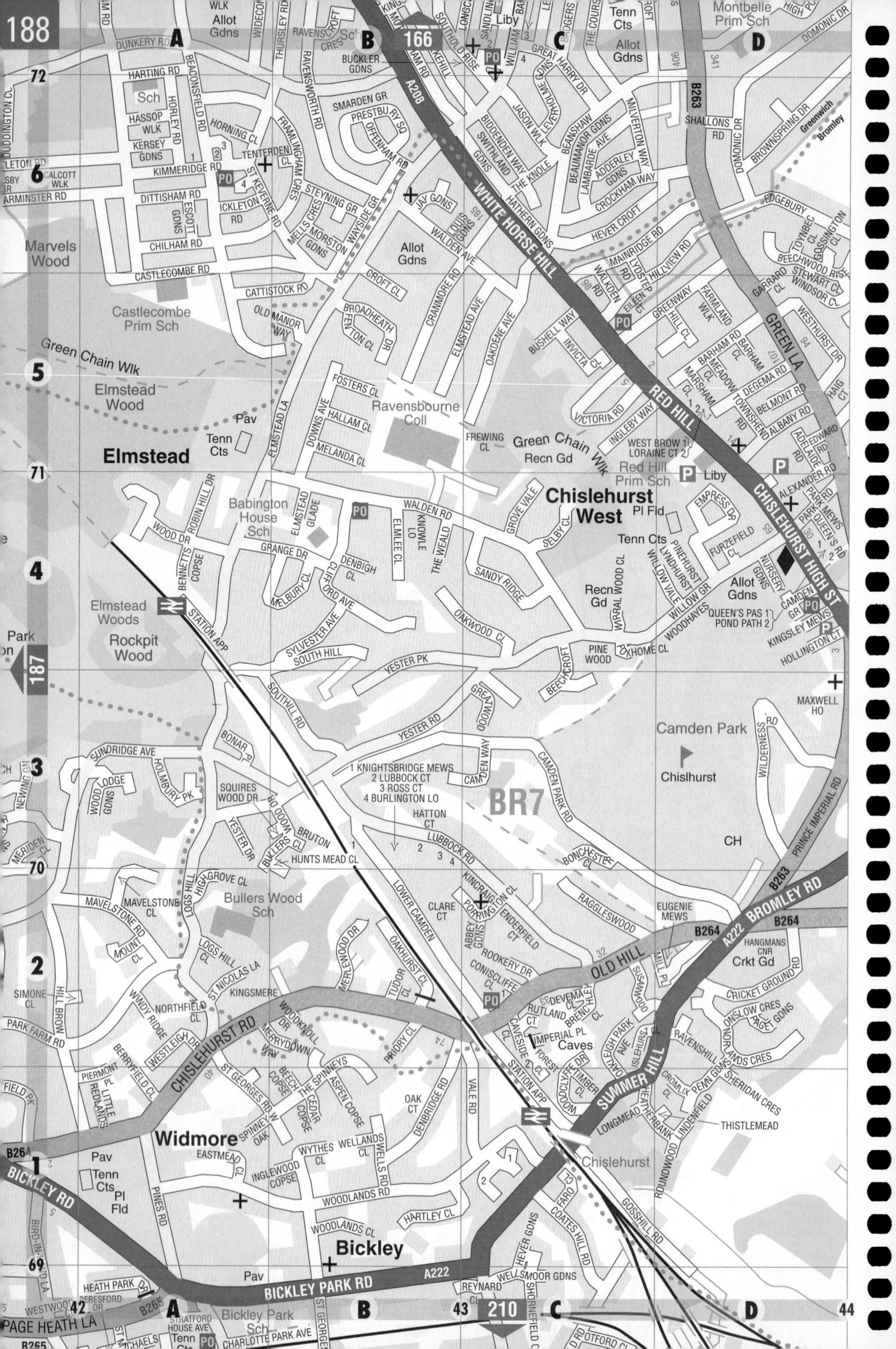

166
210
187
A
B
C
D
Elmstead
Chislehurst West
Widmore
Bickley
BR7
Marvels Wood
Castlecombe Prim Sch
Green Chain Wlk
Elmstead Wood
Elmstead Woods
Rockpit Wood
Ravensbourne Coll
Babington House Sch
Bullers Wood Sch
Red Hill Prim Sch
Camden Park
Chislhurst
Chislehurst
Caves
Montbelle Prim Sch
WHITE HORSE HILL
RED HILL
CHISLEHURST HIGH ST
BROMLEY RD
OLD HILL
SUMMER HILL
CHISLEHURST RD
BICKLEY PARK RD
BICKLEY RD
GREEN LA
PRINCE IMPERIAL RD
A208
A222
B263
B264
B265
Greenwich
Bromley

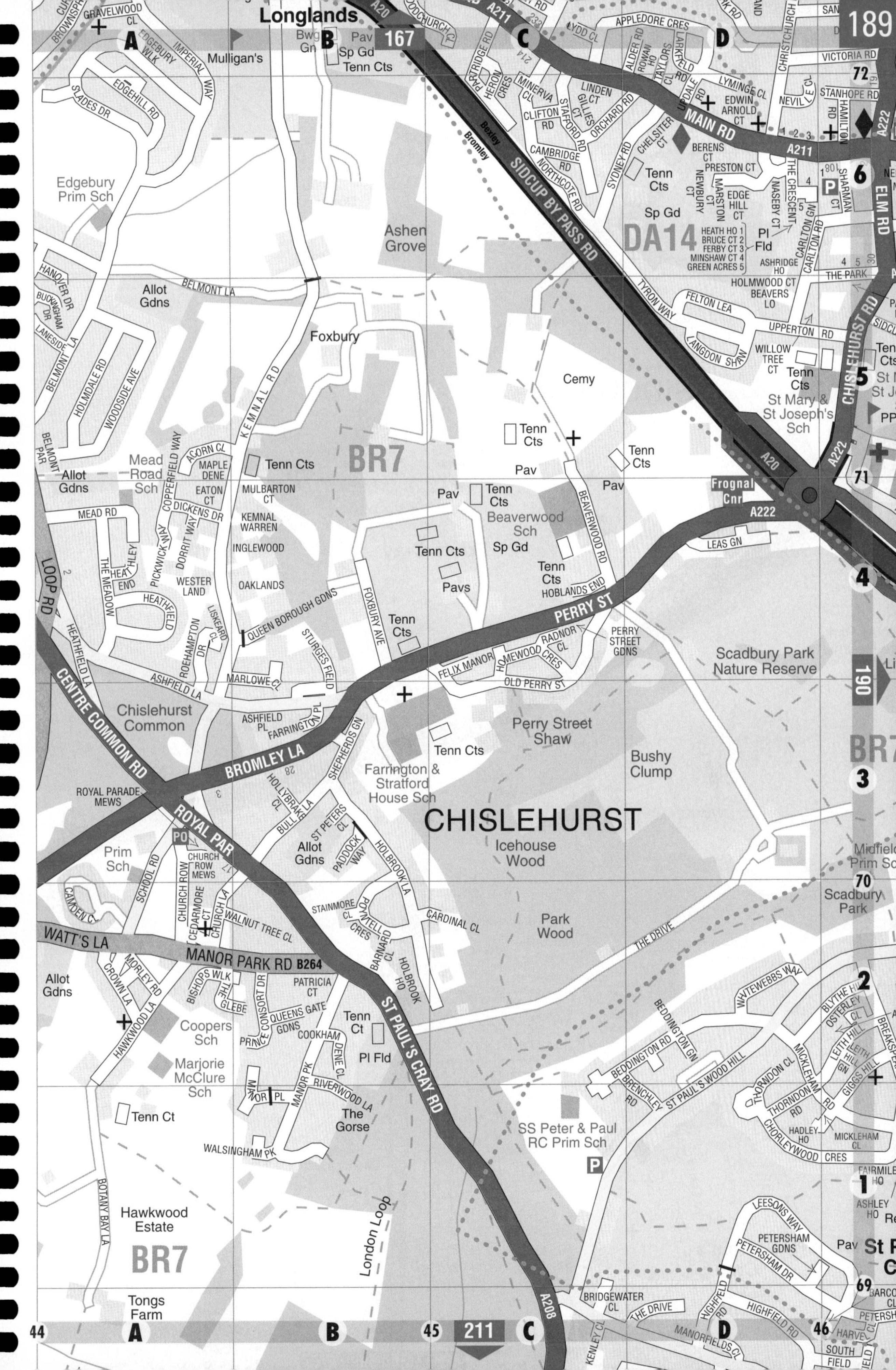
Longlands
Mulligan's
Edgebury Prim Sch
Ashen Grove
Allot Gdns
Foxbury
BR7
DA14
Cemy
Mead Road Sch
Beaverwood Sch
Chislehurst Common
Perry Street Shaw
Bushy Clump
Scadbury Park Nature Reserve
Farrington & Stratford House Sch
CHISLEHURST
Icehouse Wood
Park Wood
Coopers Sch
Marjorie McClure Sch
Hawkwood Estate
Tongs Farm
SS Peter & Paul RC Prim Sch
St Mary & St Joseph's Sch
Scadbury Park
Midfield Prim Sch
SIDCUP BY PASS RD
MAIN RD
PERRY ST
BROMLEY LA
CENTRE COMMON RD
ROYAL PAR
MANOR PARK RD B264
ST PAUL'S CRAY RD
KEMNAL RD
CHISLEHURST RD
ELM RD
LOOP RD
WATT'S LA
London Loop
167
190
211

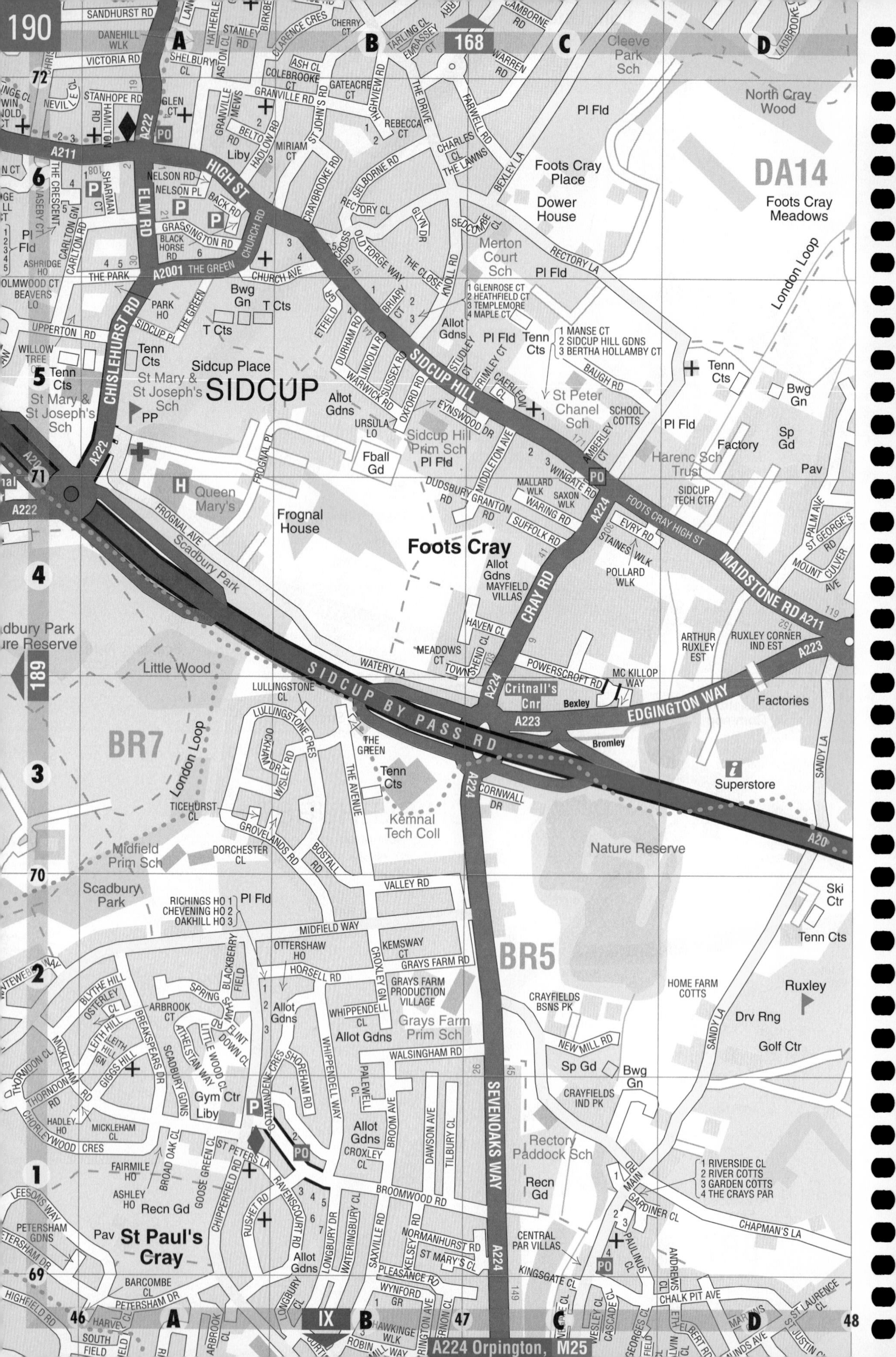
SIDCUP
Foots Cray
St Paul's Cray
Sidcup Place
Frognal House
Foots Cray Place
Dower House
Foots Cray Meadows
North Cray Wood
Nature Reserve
Ruxley
BR7
BR5
DA14
SIDCUP BY PASS RD
SIDCUP HILL
MAIDSTONE RD
EDGINGTON WAY
SEVENOAKS WAY
CRAY RD
HIGH ST
ELM RD
CHISLEHURST RD
FOOTS CRAY HIGH ST
Scadbury Park
Little Wood
Kemnal Tech Coll
Queen Mary's
London Loop
168
189
A224 Orpington, M25

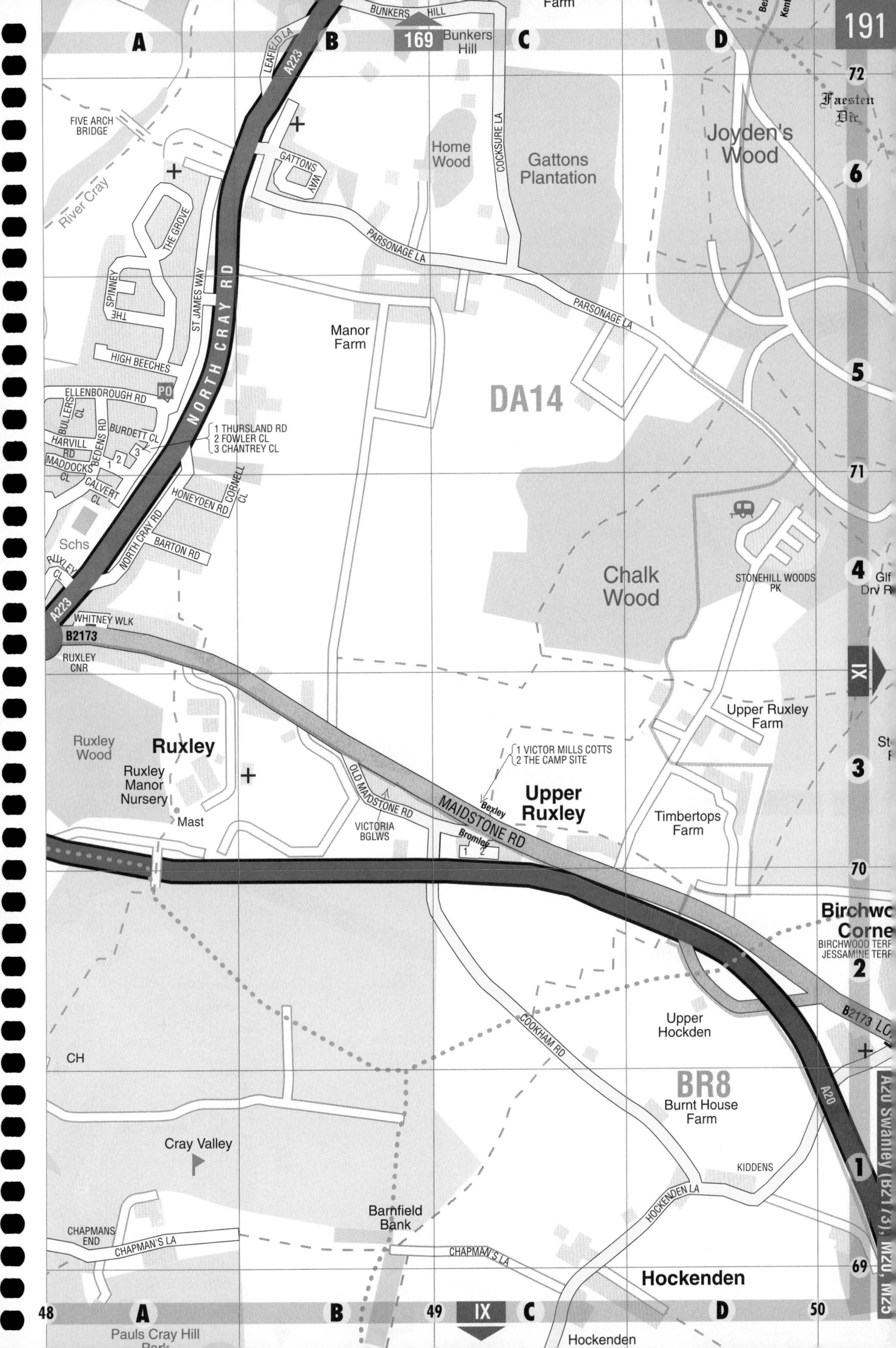
169
Bunkers Hill
BUNKERS HILL
LEAFIELD LA
A223
FIVE ARCH BRIDGE
River Cray
GATTONS WAY
Home Wood
COCKSURE LA
Gattons Plantation
Joyden's Wood
Faesten Dic
THE GROVE
THE SPINNEY
ST JAMES WAY
NORTH CRAY RD
PARSONAGE LA
Manor Farm
HIGH BEECHES
PO
ELLENBOROUGH RD
BULLERS CL
DA14
BEDENS RD
BURDETT CL
HARVILL RD
MADDOCKS CL
1 THURSLAND RD
2 FOWLER CL
3 CHANTREY CL
CALVERT CL
HONEYDEN RD
CORNELL CL
Schs
BARTON RD
RUXLEY CL
STONEHILL WOODS PK
Chalk Wood
WHITNEY WLK
B2173
RUXLEY CNR
Upper Ruxley Farm
Ruxley Wood
Ruxley
Ruxley Manor Nursery
Mast
1 VICTOR MILLS COTTS
2 THE CAMP SITE
OLD MAIDSTONE RD
VICTORIA BGLWS
MAIDSTONE RD
Bexley
Bromley
Upper Ruxley
Timbertops Farm
Birchwood Corner
BIRCHWOOD TERR
JESSAMINE TERR
COOKHAM RD
Upper Hockden
B2173 LO
CH
BR8
Burnt House Farm
A20
A20 Swanley (B2173), M20, M25
Cray Valley
KIDDENS
HOCKENDEN LA
Barnfield Bank
CHAPMANS END
CHAPMAN'S LA
Hockenden
IX
Pauls Cray Hill Park
A
B
C
D
48
49
50
69
70
71
72
1
2
3
4
5
6

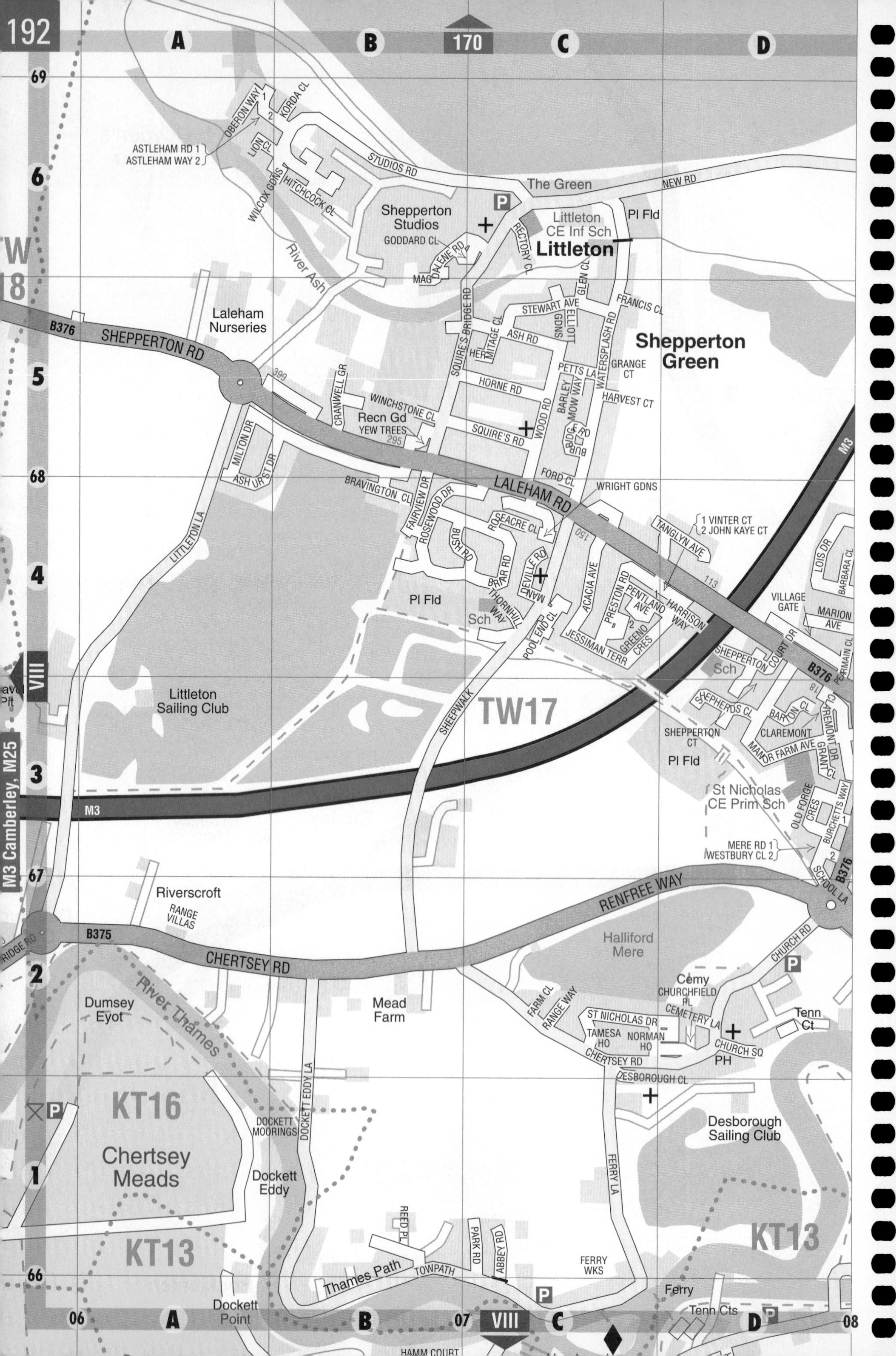

A
B
170
C
D
Shepperton Studios
The Green
Littleton CE Inf Sch
Littleton
Pl Fld
Laleham Nurseries
SHEPPERTON RD
B376
Shepperton Green
LALEHAM RD
Recn Gd
Littleton Sailing Club
TW17
M3
Riverscroft
RENFREE WAY
CHERTSEY RD
B375
Halliford Mere
Dumsey Eyot
River Thames
Mead Farm
Cemy
KT16
Chertsey Meads
Dockett Eddy
Desborough Sailing Club
KT13
Thames Path
Dockett Point
Ferry
Tenn Cts
St Nicholas CE Prim Sch
M3 Camberley, M25
VIII

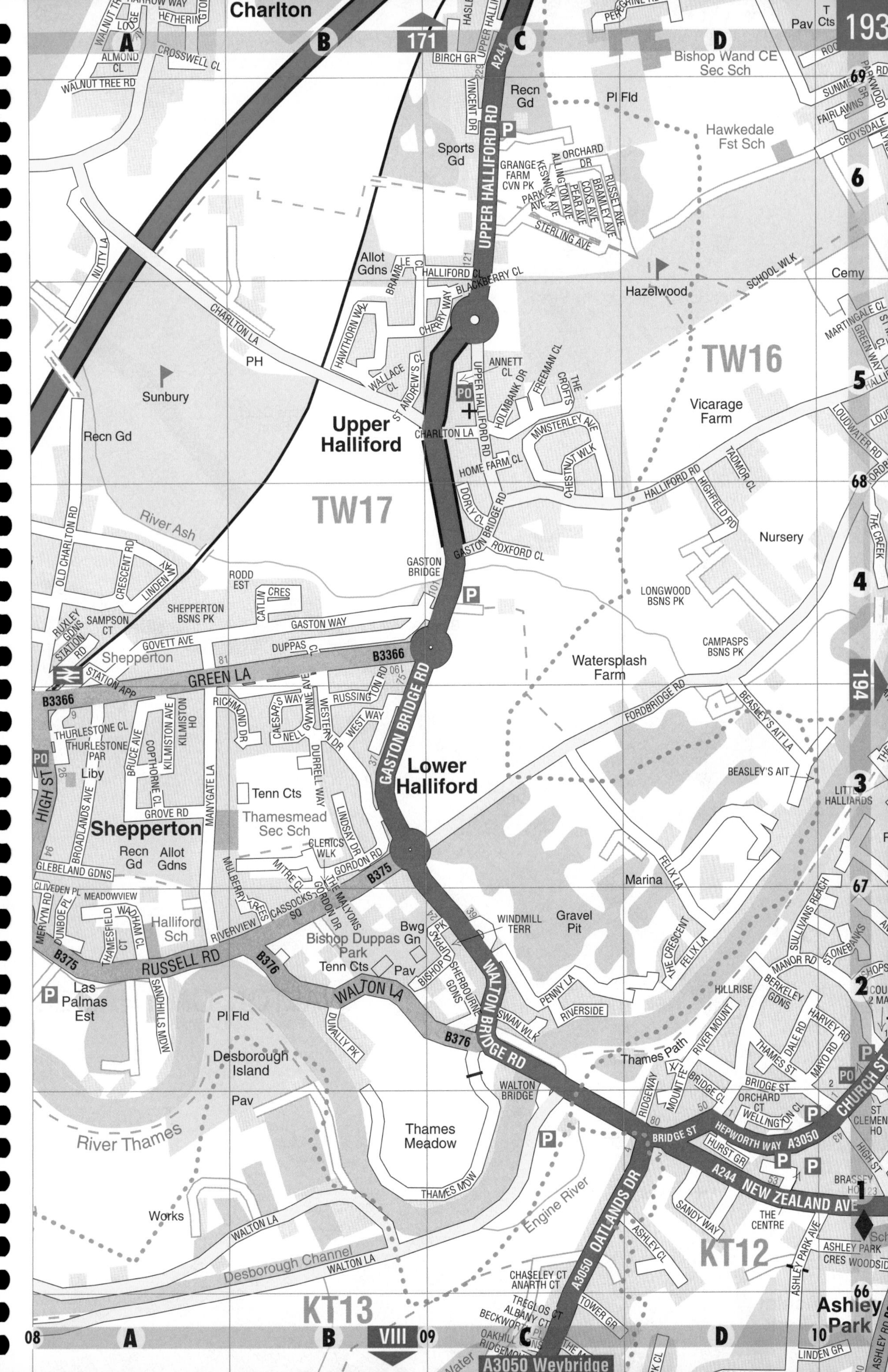
Charlton
171
Bishop Wand CE Sec Sch
Hawkedale Fst Sch
Sports Gd
Recn Gd
Pl Fld
UPPER HALLIFORD RD
A244
Allot Gdns
Hazelwood
SCHOOL WLK
Cemy
CHARLTON LA
PH
Sunbury
Recn Gd
TW16
Upper Halliford
Vicarage Farm
TW17
River Ash
HALLIFORD RD
Nursery
GASTON BRIDGE
SHEPPERTON BSNS PK
LONGWOOD BSNS PK
CAMPASPS BSNS PK
Shepperton
GREEN LA
B3366
Watersplash Farm
FORDBRIDGE RD
194
GASTON BRIDGE RD
Lower Halliford
HIGH ST
Liby
Tenn Cts
Thamesmead Sec Sch
Shepperton
Recn Gd
Allot Gdns
Marina
Halliford Sch
Bishop Duppas Park
Gravel Pit
RUSSELL RD
B375
WALTON LA
B376
WALTON BRIDGE RD
Las Palmas Est
Pl Fld
Desborough Island
Thames Path
Pav
WALTON BRIDGE
Thames Meadow
BRIDGE ST
A3050
River Thames
NEW ZEALAND AVE
Works
Engine River
OATLANDS DR
KT12
Desborough Channel
KT13
Ashley Park
VIII
A3050 Weybridge

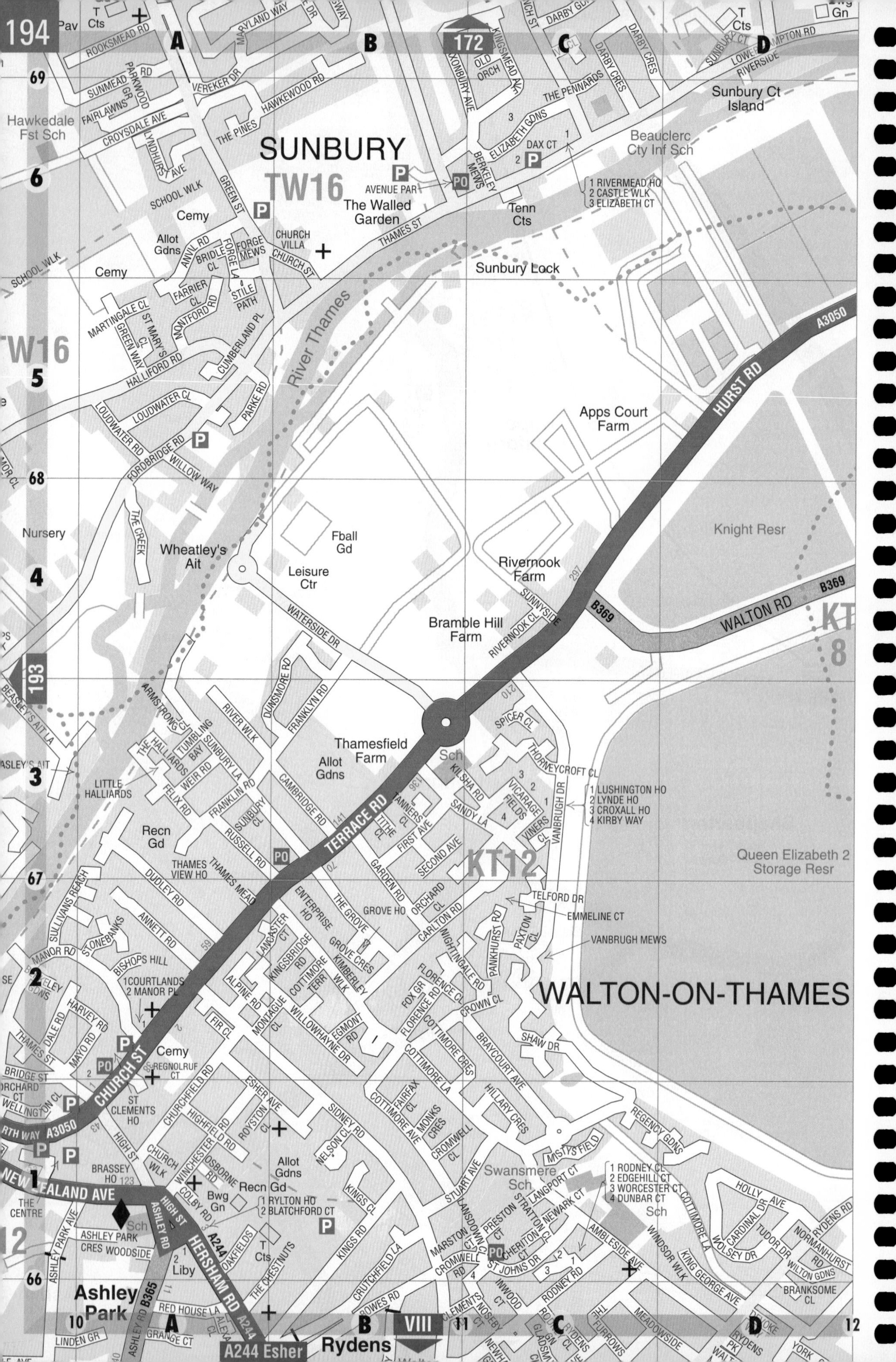
SUNBURY
TW16
The Walled Garden
River Thames
Sunbury Lock
Sunbury Ct Island
Beauclerc Cty Inf Sch
Hawkedale Fst Sch
Cemy
Allot Gdns
CHURCH VILLA
Tenn Cts
AVENUE PAR
1 RIVERMEAD HO
2 CASTLE WLK
3 ELIZABETH CT
Apps Court Farm
HURST RD
A3050
Knight Resr
WALTON RD
B369
KT 8
Rivernook Farm
Bramble Hill Farm
Nursery
Wheatley's Ait
Leisure Ctr
Fball Gd
Thamesfield Farm
TERRACE RD
KT12
1 LUSHINGTON HO
2 LYNDE HO
3 CROXALL HO
4 KIRBY WAY
Queen Elizabeth 2 Storage Resr
WALTON-ON-THAMES
TELFORD DR
EMMELINE CT
VANBRUGH MEWS
Recn Gd
THAMES VIEW HO
LITTLE HALLIARDS
1 COURTLANDS
2 MANOR PL
CHURCH ST
NEW ZEALAND AVE
ST CLEMENTS HO
BRASSEY HO
THE CENTRE
Swansmere Sch
1 RODNEY CL
2 EDGEHILL CT
3 WORCESTER CT
4 DUNBAR CT
1 RYLTON HO
2 BLATCHFORD CT
Ashley Park
HERSHAM RD
A244
B365
Liby
Rydens
A244 Esher
172
193
VIII
A
B
C
D
69
6
5
68
4
3
67
2
1
66
10
11
12

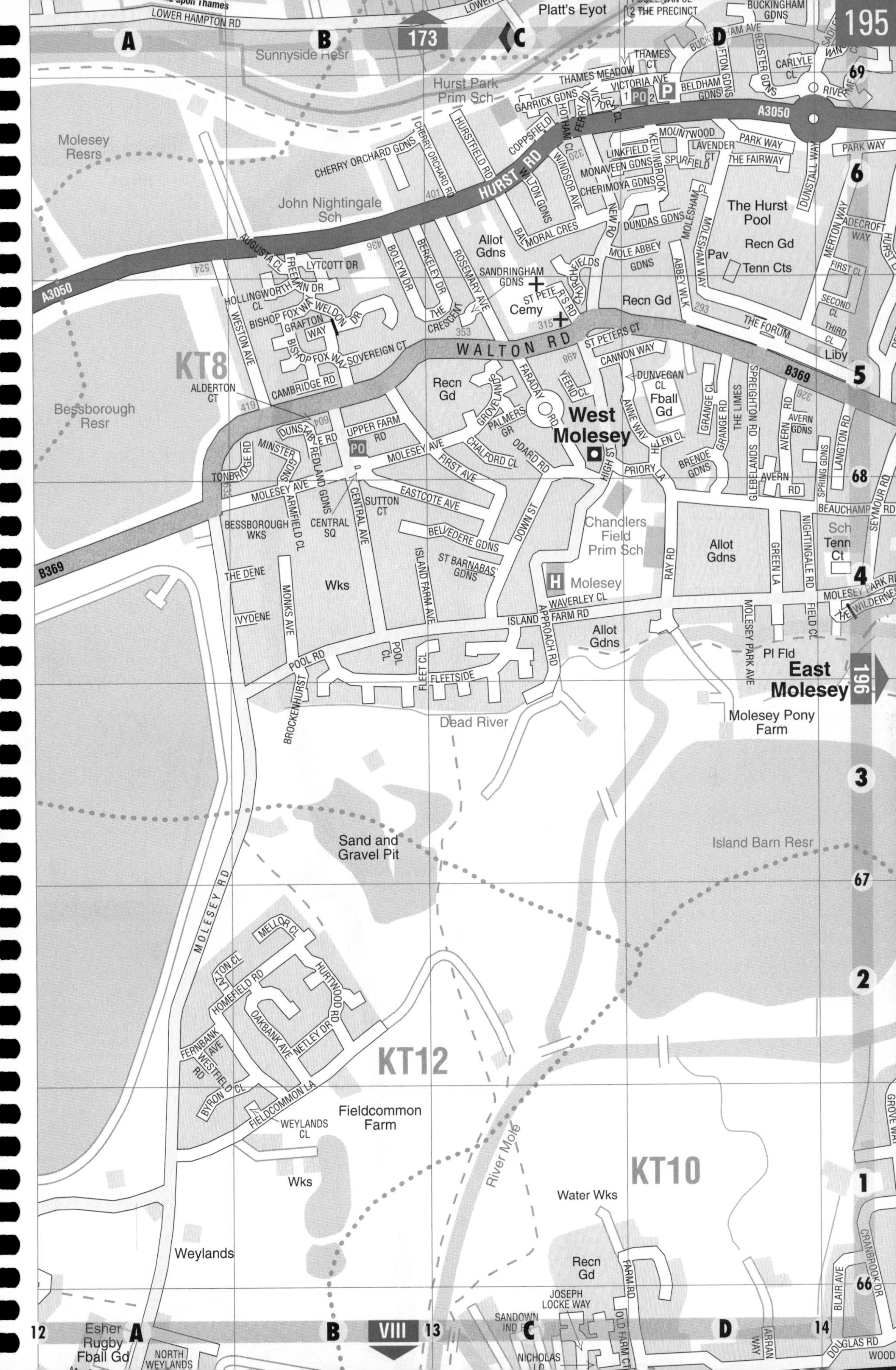
Platt's Eyot
LOWER HAMPTON RD
Sunnyside Resr
Hurst Park Prim Sch
Molesey Resrs
John Nightingale Sch
HURST RD
A3050
WALTON RD
B369
KT8
Bessborough Resr
West Molesey
The Hurst Pool
Recn Gd
Allot Gdns
Cemy
Chandlers Field Prim Sch
Molesey
Wks
East Molesey
Molesey Pony Farm
Dead River
Sand and Gravel Pit
Island Barn Resr
MOLESEY RD
KT12
Fieldcommon Farm
River Mole
KT10
Water Wks
Weylands
Esher Rugby Fball Gd
173
196
VIII

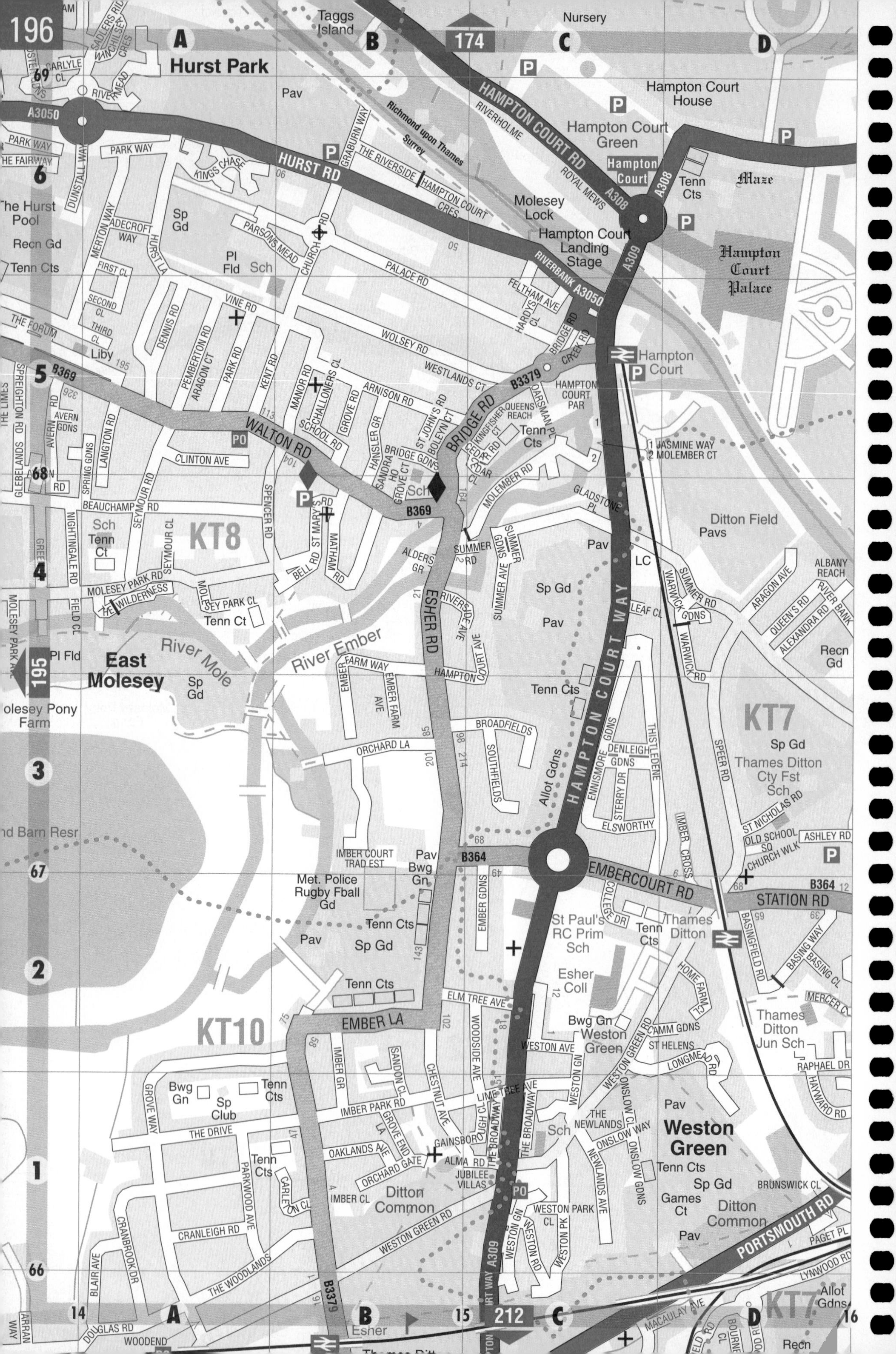

Taggs Island
174
Nursery
Hurst Park
Hampton Court House
Hampton Court Green
HAMPTON COURT RD
HURST RD
A3050
Richmond upon Thames
Surrey
Maze
Molesey Lock
Hampton Court Landing Stage
Hampton Court Palace
Hampton Court
The Hurst Pool
Recn Gd
KT8
WALTON RD
B369
B3379
BRIDGE RD
ESHER RD
HAMPTON COURT WAY
A309
A308
Ditton Field
East Molesey
River Mole
River Ember
Molesey Pony Farm
195
KT7
Thames Ditton Cty Fst Sch
EMBERCOURT RD
B364
STATION RD
Thames Ditton
St Paul's RC Prim Sch
Esher Coll
Met. Police Rugby Fball Gd
IMBER COURT TRAD EST
KT10
EMBER LA
Weston Green
Ditton Common
PORTSMOUTH RD
Thames Ditton Jun Sch
WESTON GREEN RD
Esher
212

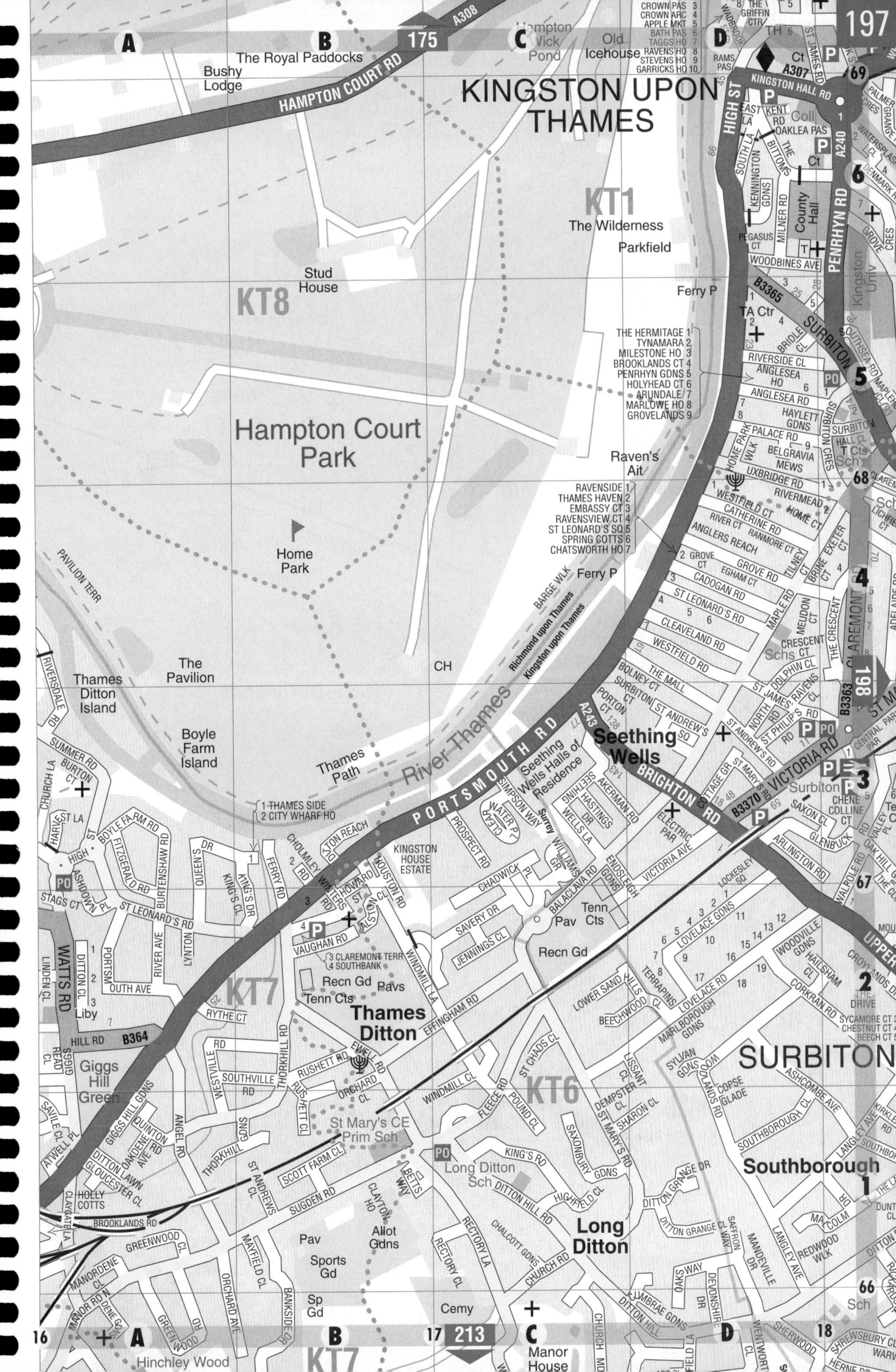
KINGSTON UPON THAMES
Hampton Court Park
Home Park
KT8
KT1
KT7
KT6
The Royal Paddocks
Bushy Lodge
Hampton Wick Pond
Old Icehouse
Stud House
The Wilderness
Parkfield
Raven's Ait
Thames Ditton Island
The Pavilion
Boyle Farm Island
Thames Path
River Thames
HAMPTON COURT RD
PORTSMOUTH RD
BRIGHTON RD
VICTORIA RD
PENRHYN RD
HIGH ST
Seething Wells
Seething Wells Halls of Residence
Kingston House Estate
Thames Ditton
Giggs Hill Green
St Mary's CE Prim Sch
Long Ditton Sch
Long Ditton
SURBITON
Southborough
Hinchley Wood
Manor House
CROWN PAS 3
CROWN ARC 4
APPLE MKT 5
BATH PAS 6
TAGGS HO 7
RAVENS HO 8
STEVENS HO 9
GARRICKS HO 10
THE HERMITAGE 1
TYNAMARA 2
MILESTONE HO 3
BROOKLANDS CT 4
PENRHYN GDNS 5
HOLYHEAD CT 6
ARUNDALE 7
MARLOWE HO 8
GROVELANDS 9
RAVENSIDE 1
THAMES HAVEN 2
EMBASSY CT 3
RAVENSVIEW CT 4
ST LEONARD'S SQ 5
SPRING COTTS 6
CHATSWORTH HO 7
1 THAMES SIDE
2 CITY WHARF HO
3 CLAREMONT TERR
4 SOUTHBANK
SYCAMORE CT 3
CHESTNUT CT 4
BEECH CT 5
175
198
213

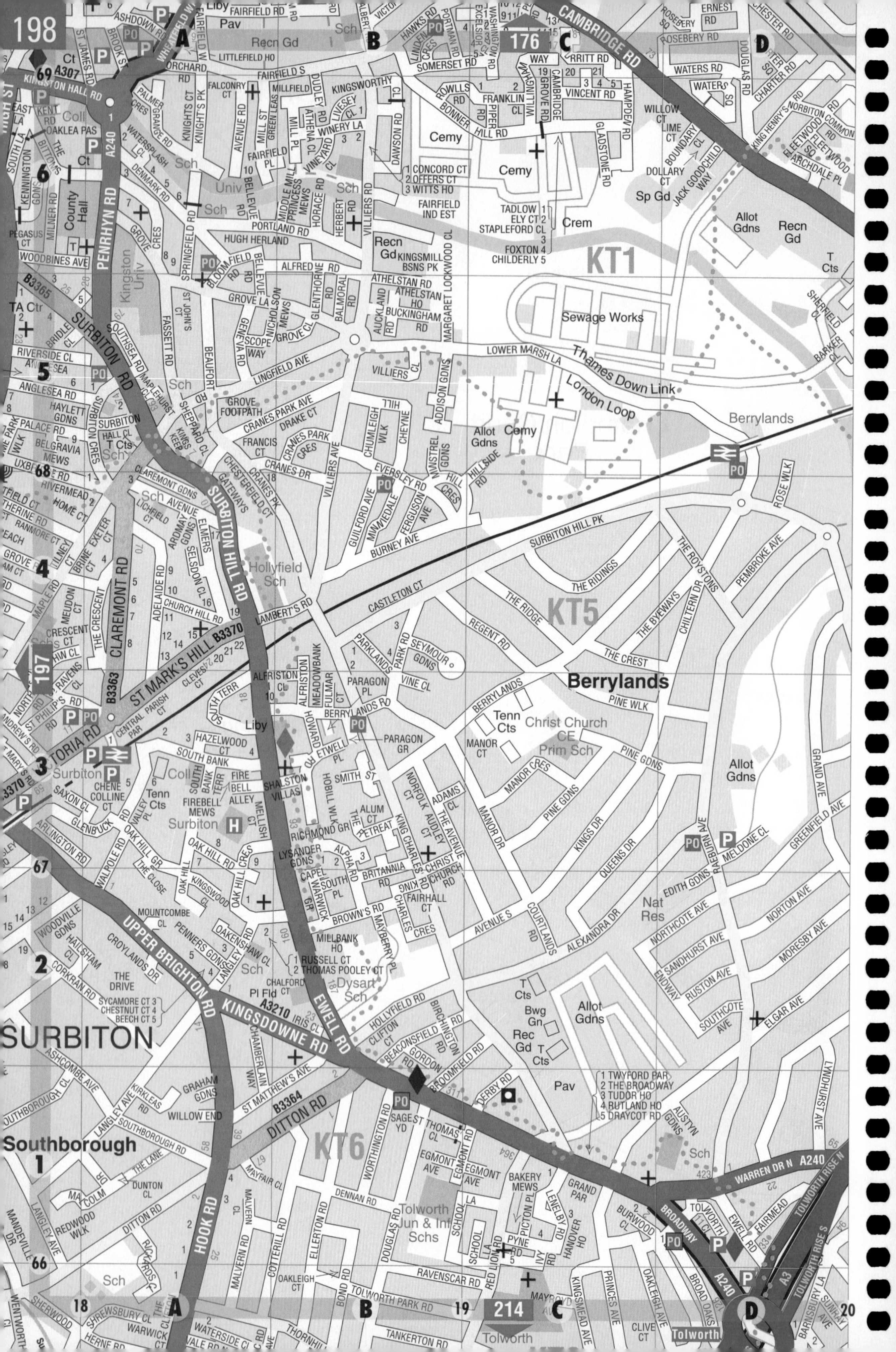
176
KT1
KT5
KT6
Berrylands
SURBITON
Southborough
Surbiton
197
214
Tolworth
A
B
C
D
6
5
4
3
2
1
69
68
67
66
18
19
20
CAMBRIDGE RD
KINGSTON HALL RD
PENRHYN RD
SURBITON RD
SURBITON HILL RD
SURBITON HILL PK
ST MARK'S HILL
CLAREMONT RD
VICTORIA RD
UPPER BRIGHTON RD
KINGSDOWNE RD
EWELL RD
DITTON RD
HOOK RD
BROADWAY
WARREN DR N
TOLWORTH RISE N
TOLWORTH RISE S
A240
A307
A3210
B3364
B3370
B3363
B3365
A3
Recn Gd
Cemy
Crem
Sewage Works
Thames Down Link
London Loop
LOWER MARSH LA
Allot Gdns
Sp Gd
Hollyfield Sch
Christ Church CE Prim Sch
Tolworth Jun & Inf Schs
Dysart Sch
County Hall
Kingston Univ
Nat Res
FAIRFIELD IND EST
KINGSMILL BSNS PK
FAIRFIELD RD
PORTLAND RD
VILLIERS RD
VILLIERS AVE
ALFRED RD
ATHELSTAN RD
BUCKINGHAM RD
MARGARET LOCKWOOD CL
LINGFIELD AVE
CRANES PARK AVE
CRANES DR
EVERSLEY RD
BURNEY AVE
CASTLETON CT
LAMBERT'S RD
THE RIDINGS
THE RIDGE
REGENT RD
THE BYEWAYS
THE ROYSTONS
CHILTERN DR
PEMBROKE AVE
THE CREST
PINE WLK
PINE GDNS
BERRYLANDS RD
MANOR DR
KINGS DR
QUEENS DR
ALEXANDRA DR
RAEBURN AVE
GRAND AVE
GREENFIELD AVE
NORTON AVE
MORESBY AVE
ELGAR AVE
SOUTHCOTE AVE
RUSTON AVE
SANDHURST AVE
NORTHCOTE AVE
EDITH GDNS
MELDONE CL
LYNDHURST AVE
ROSE WLK
AVENUE S
COURTLANDS RD
THE AVENUE
KING CHARLES RD
NORFOLK CT
AUDLEY CT
HOLLYFIELD RD
BIRCHINGTON RD
BEACONSFIELD RD
GORDON RD
BROOMFIELD RD
DERBY RD
WORTHINGTON RD
DOUGLAS RD
ELLERTON RD
COTTERILL RD
MALVERN RD
BOND RD
TOLWORTH PARK RD
RAVENSCAR RD
TANKERTON RD
RED LION RD
HANOVER HO
KINGSMEAD AVE
PRINCES AVE
OAKLEIGH AVE
BROAD OAKS
FAIRMEAD
EWELL RD
1 TWYFORD PAR
2 THE BROADWAY
3 TUDOR HO
4 RUTLAND HO
5 DRAYCOT RD
1 RUSSELL CT
2 THOMAS POOLEY CT
1 CONCORD CT
2 OFFERS CT
3 WITTS HO
TADLOW 1
ELY CT 2
STAPLEFORD CL
FOXTON 4
CHILDERLY 5
SYCAMORE CT 3
CHESTNUT CT 4
BEECH CT 5
ASHCOMBE AVE
SOUTHBOROUGH CL
SOUTHBOROUGH RD
LANGLEY AVE
KIRKLEAS RD
WILLOW END
ST MATTHEW'S AVE
CHAMBERLAIN WAY
GRAHAM GDNS
MAYFAIR CL
DENNAN RD
EGMONT AVE
BAKERY MEWS
PICTON PL
LENELBY RD
GRAND PAR
BURWOOD CL
SHREWSBURY CL
WARWICK
HERNE RD
WATERSIDE CL
SHERWOOD
WENTWORTH
MANDEVILLE DR
REDWOOD WLK
DUNTON CL
THE LANE
RICKARDS CL
CROYLANDS DR
HAILSHAM CL
WOODVILLE GDNS
CORKRAN RD
THE DRIVE
ARLINGTON RD
WALPOLE RD
OAK HILL
OAK HILL CRES
OAK HILL GR
KINGSWOOD CL
MOUNTCOMBE CL
PENNERS GDNS
OAKENSHAW CL
LANGLEY GR
GLENBUCK RD
SAXON CL
SOUTH BANK
SOUTH TERR
HAZELWOOD CT
FIREBELL MEWS
BELL ALLEY
MELLISH CT
SHALSTON VILLAS
HOWARD RD
ETWELL PL
HOBILL WLK
SMITH ST
RICHMOND GR
LYSANDER GDNS
CAPEL
WARWICK GR
BROWN'S RD
MAYBERRY PL
MILLBANK HO
FAIRHALL CT
KING CHARLES CRES
CHRIST CHURCH RD
ALFRISTON CL
MEADOWBANK
FULMAR CT
PARAGON PL
PARAGON GR
VINE CL
SEYMOUR GDNS
PARKLANDS
PARK RD
MANOR CT
MANOR CRES
ADAMS CL
ADELAIDE RD
CHURCH HILL RD
CLEVES CT
CENTRAL PARISH
CHENE COLLINE CT
GUILFORD AVE
MINNIEDALE
FERGUSON AVE
CHUMLEIGH WLK
CHEYNE HILL
ADDISON GDNS
MINSTREL GDNS
HILL CRES
HILLSIDE RD
FRANCIS CT
DRAKE CT
CRANES PARK CRES
CRANES PK
CHESTERFIELD CT
GATEWAYS
ELMERS
SELSDON CL
AROMA GDNS
AVENUE ELMERS
LICHFIELD CT
CLAREMONT GDNS
SHEPPARD CL
KINGS KEEP
GROVE FOOTPATH
BEAUFORT RD
FASSETT RD
ST JOHN'S CT
GENEVA RD
SCOPE WAY
NICHOLSON MEWS
GROVE CL
GLENTHORNE RD
BALMORAL RD
AUCKLAND RD
GROVE LA
BLOOMFIELD RD
BELLEVUE RD
HUGH HERLAND
SPRINGFIELD RD
GROVE CRES
DENMARK RD
WATERSPLASH CL
AVENUE RD
MILL ST
KNIGHTS CT
KNIGHT'S PK
FALCONRY CT
PALMER CRES
GRANGE RD
ORCHARD RD
LITTLEFIELD HO
ASHDOWN RD
BROOK ST
ST JAMES RD
WHEATFIELD WAY
DUDLEY RD
ATHENA CL
MILL PL
WINERY LA
VINEYARD CL
LIVESEY CL
KINGSWORTHY CL
DAWSON RD
HERBERT RD
HORACE RD
PRINCESS MEWS
MIDDLE MILL
SOMERSET RD
HAWKS RD
LINDEN CRES
PORTMAN RD
EXCELSIOR CL
WASHINGTON RD
ROWLLS RD
BONNER HILL RD
PIPER RD
FRANKLIN CL
WILLINGHAM WAY
GROVE RD
CAMBRIDGE GDNS
VINCENT RD
GLADSTONE RD
HAMPDEN RD
WILLOW CT
LIME CT
DOLLARY CT
BOUNDARY CT
JACK GOODCHILD WAY
WATERS RD
WATERS SQ
ROSEBERY RD
ROSEBERY SQ
ERNEST RD
CHESTER RD
DOUGLAS RD
PORTER SQ
CHARTER RD
KING HENRY'S RD
NORBITON COMMON RD
FLEETWOOD CL
FLEETWOOD SQ
ARCHDALE PL
SHERFIELD CL
BARKER CL
HIGH ST
EAST LA
KENT RD
OAKLEA PAS
BITTOMS CT
SOUTH LA
KENNINGTON GDNS
MILNER RD
PEGASUS CT
WOODBINES AVE
TA Ctr
RIVERSIDE CL
ANGLESEA RD
HAYLETT GDNS
PALACE RD
BELGRAVIA MEWS
UXBRIDGE RD
RIVERMEAD
HOME CT
SURBITON HALL CL
SURBITON CRES
SOUTHSEA RD
MAPLEHURST CL
BRIDLE CL
BRINE CT
EXETER CT
TILNEY
GROVE RD
MAPLE RD
MEUDON CT
CRESCENT CT
THE CRESCENT
RAVENS
ST PHILIP'S RD
SAGE YD
ST THOMAS' CL
EGMONT RD
SCHOOL LA
PYNE RD
MAYBOYD AVE
CLIVE CT
TOLWORTH CT
IRIS CL
CHALFORD CL
Pl Fld
Tenn Cts
Bwg Gn
Rec Gd
Pav
Liby
Sch
Coll
Univ
PO
P
T Cts

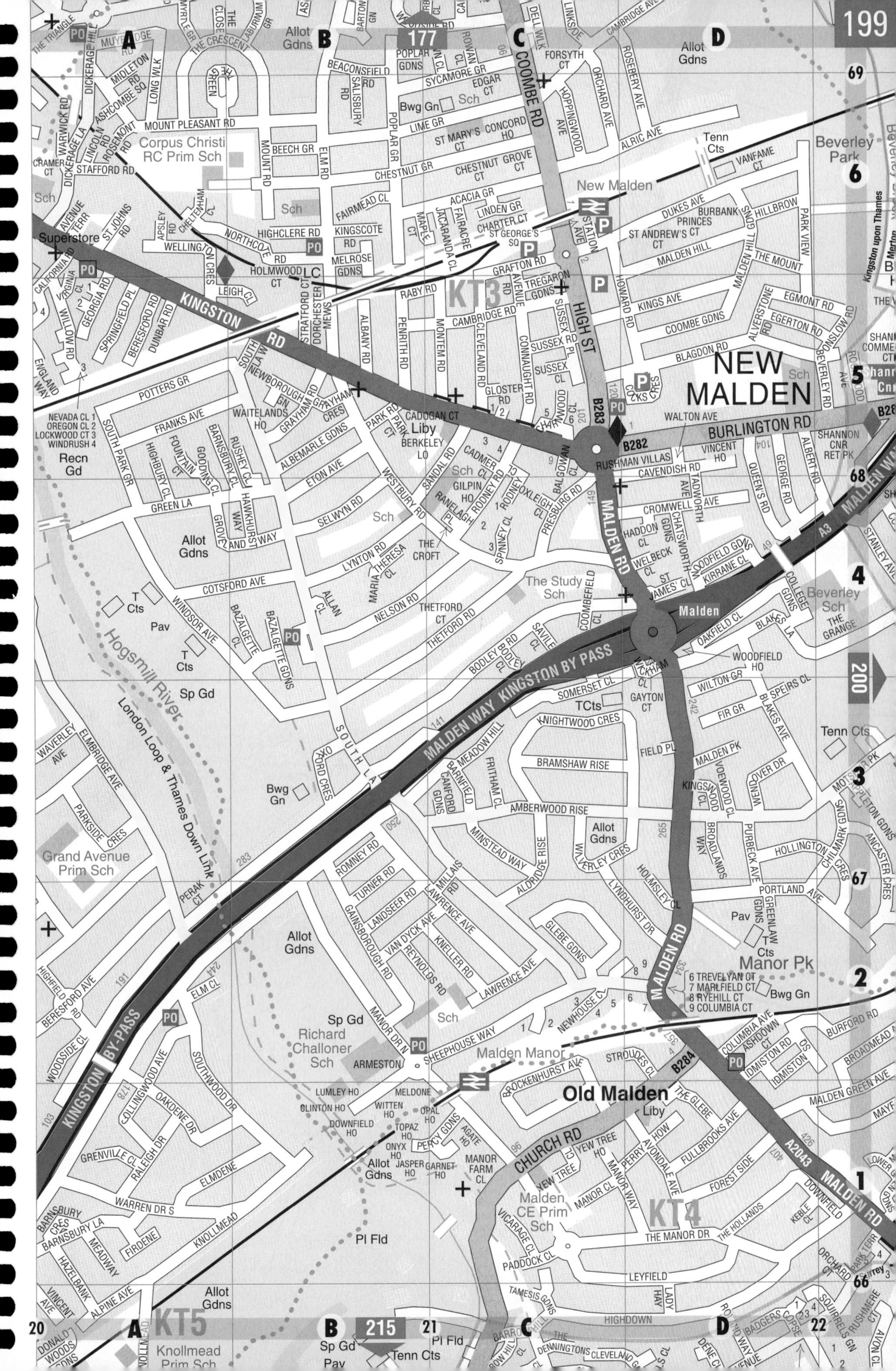
NEW MALDEN
Old Malden
New Malden
Malden Manor
KT3
KT4
KT5
KINGSTON RD
KINGSTON BY PASS
MALDEN WAY
MALDEN RD
HIGH ST
COOMBE RD
BURLINGTON RD
CHURCH RD
Hogsmill River
London Loop & Thames Down Link
Corpus Christi RC Prim Sch
The Study Sch
Beverley Sch
Grand Avenue Prim Sch
Richard Challoner Sch
Malden CE Prim Sch
Knollmead Prim Sch
Kingston upon Thames
177
200
215
20
21
22

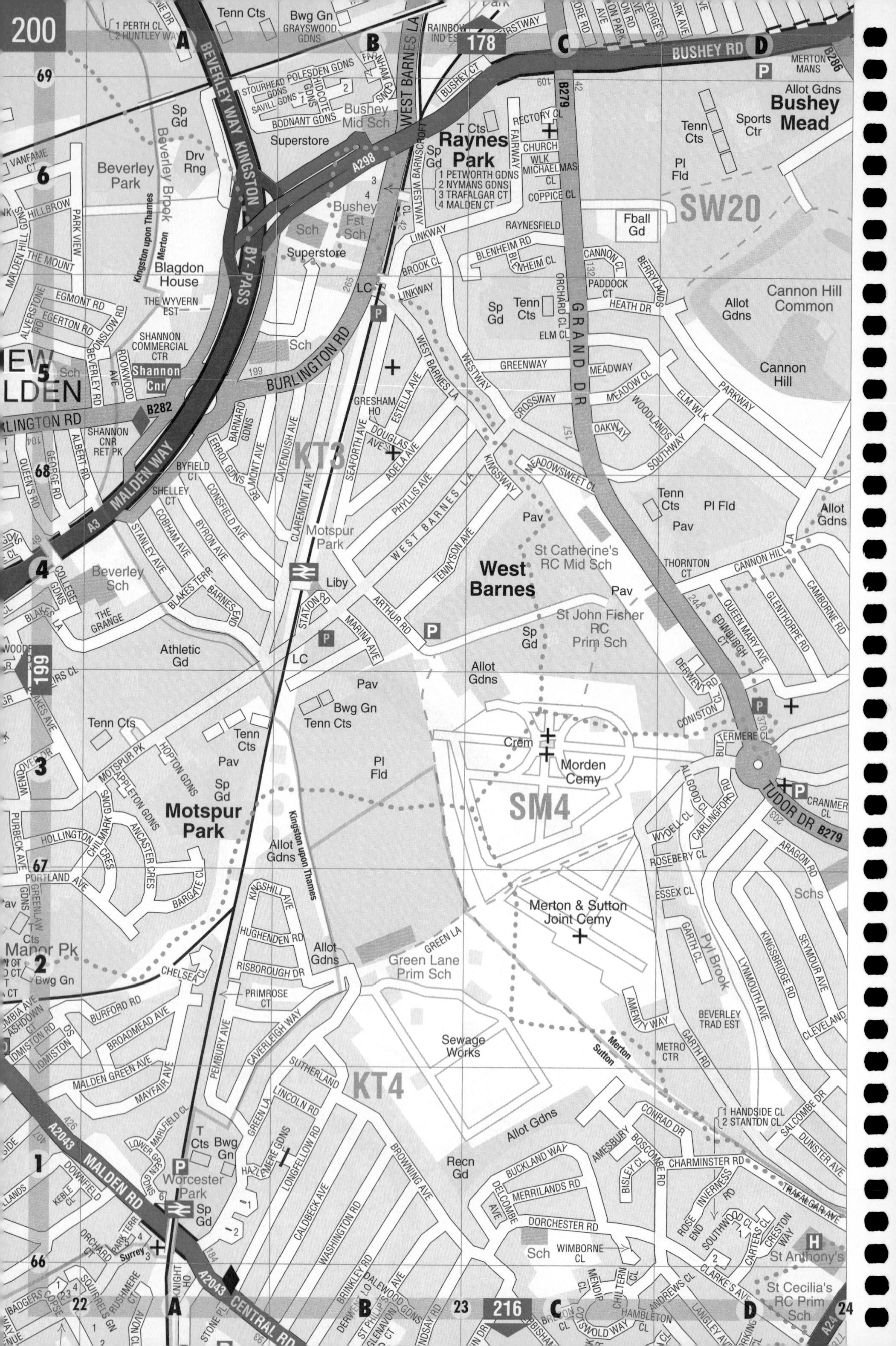

Raynes Park
West Barnes
Motspur Park
Bushey Mead
Cannon Hill Common
Cannon Hill
Beverley Park
Blagdon House
Manor Pk
Worcester Park
SW20
KT3
SM4
KT4
BEVERLEY WAY KINGSTON BY-PASS
MALDEN WAY
BURLINGTON RD
WEST BARNES LA
GRAND DR
TUDOR DR
BUSHEY RD
MALDEN RD
CENTRAL RD
St Catherine's RC Mid Sch
St John Fisher RC Prim Sch
Morden Cemy
Merton & Sutton Joint Cemy
Green Lane Prim Sch
Sewage Works
Beverley Sch
Motspur Park
Bushey Mid Sch
Bushey Fst Sch
Shannon Cnr
St Anthony's
St Cecilia's RC Prim Sch
Beverley Trad Est
Metro Ctr
178
199
216

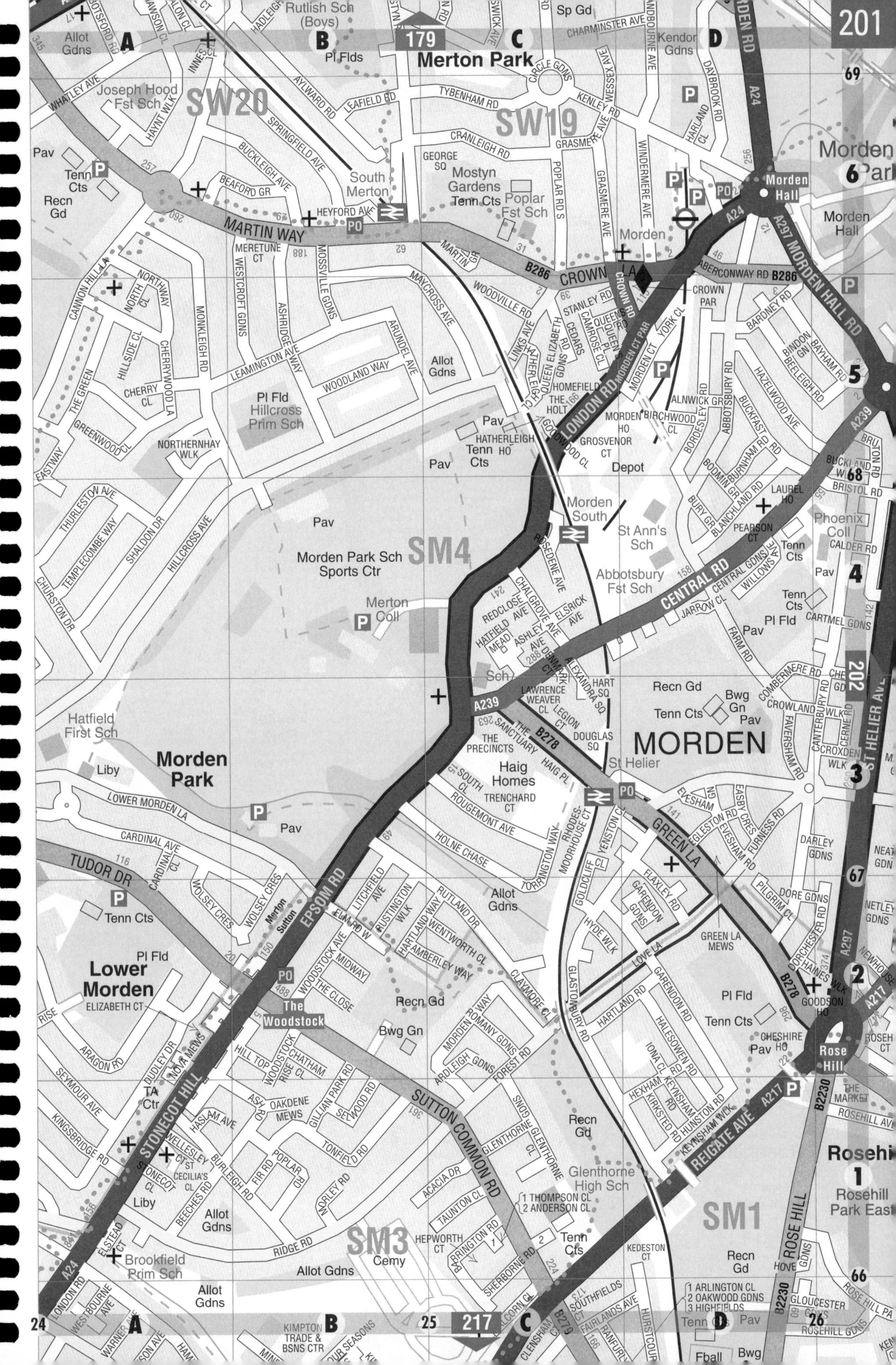
Merton Park
SW20
SW19
SM4
SM1
SM3
MORDEN
Morden Park
Lower Morden
Rosehill
Morden Hall
MARTIN WAY
CROWN LA
LONDON RD
EPSOM RD
CENTRAL RD
GREEN LA
SUTTON COMMON RD
STONECOT HILL
TUDOR DR
REIGATE AVE
ROSE HILL
MORDEN HALL RD
ST HELIER AVE
South Merton
Morden South
St Helier
Morden
The Woodstock
Morden Park Sch Sports Ctr
Merton Coll
Hillcross Prim Sch
Joseph Hood Fst Sch
Abbotsbury Fst Sch
St Ann's Sch
Glenthorne High Sch
Hatfield First Sch
Brookfield Prim Sch
Haig Homes
Mostyn Gardens
179
217
202
A
B
C
D
24
25
26

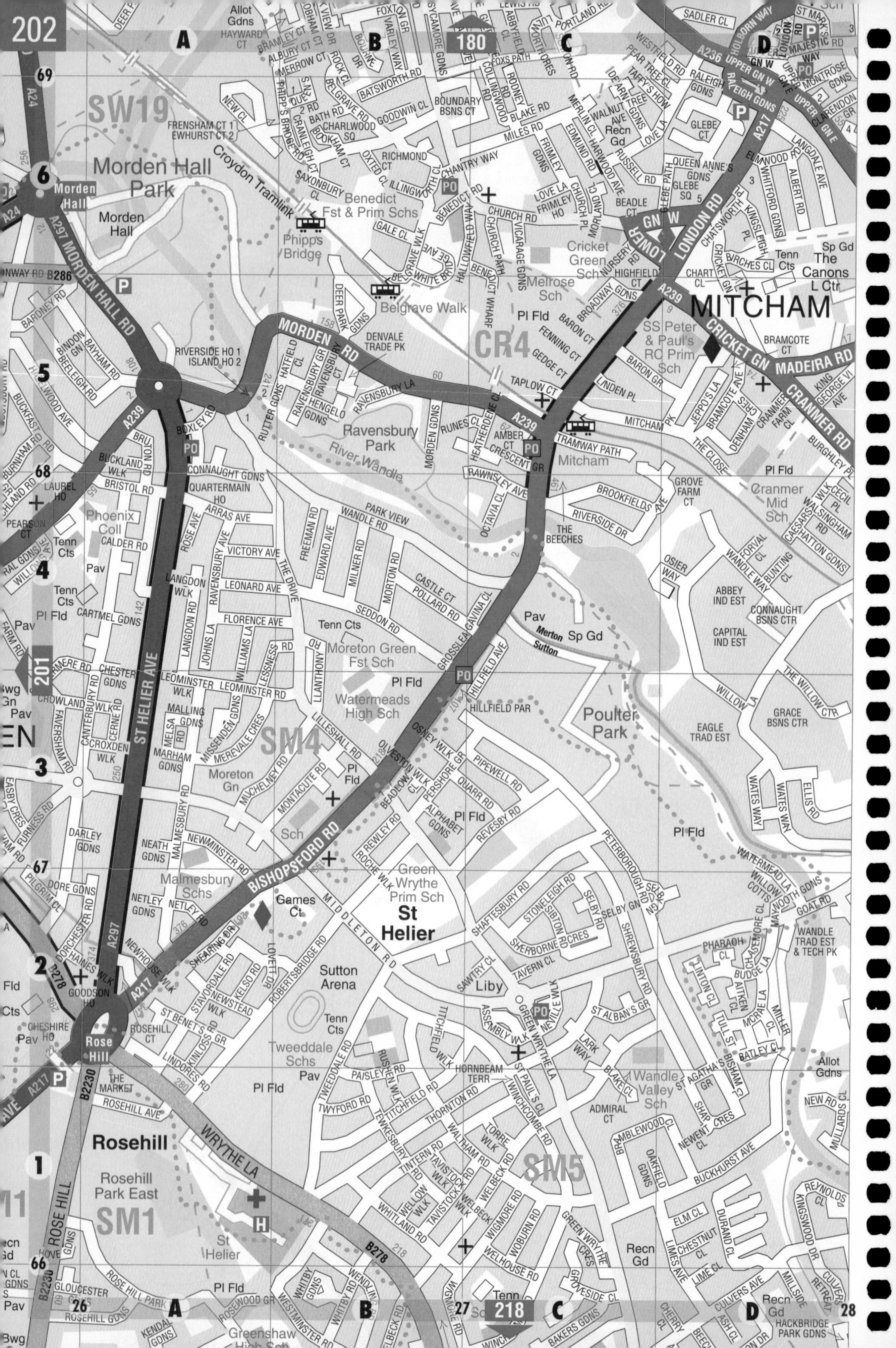

A
B
C
D
180
218
201
SW19
CR4
SM4
SM5
SM1
MITCHAM
St Helier
Rosehill
Morden Hall Park
Morden Hall
Morden Hall
Croydon Tramlink
Phipps Bridge
Belgrave Walk
Benedict Fst & Prim Schs
Ravensbury Park
River Wandle
Mitcham
Melrose Sch
Cricket Green Sch
SS Peter & Paul's RC Prim Sch
Cranmer Mid Sch
The Canons L Ctr
Poulter Park
Phoenix Coll
Moreton Green Fst Sch
Watermeads High Sch
Moreton Gn
Malmesbury Schs
Green Wrythe Prim Sch
Sutton Arena
Tweeddale Schs
Wandle Valley Sch
Rosehill Park East
Rose Hill
MORDEN HALL RD
MORDEN RD
ST HELIER AVE
BISHOPSFORD RD
LONDON RD
CRICKET GN
MADEIRA RD
CRANMER RD
WRYTHE LA
ROSE HILL
MIDDLETON RD
BUCKHURST AVE
WILLOW LA
RAVENSBURY LA
CHURCH RD
MILES RD
ABBEY IND EST
CAPITAL IND EST
EAGLE TRAD EST
GRACE BSNS CTR
WANDLE TRAD EST & TECH PK
DENVALE TRADE PK
A24
A297
A239
A217
A236
B278
B2230
B286

MITCHAM
CR4
CR0
SM6
Mitcham Common
Mitcham Junction
Croydon Tramlink
Beddington Lane
Beddington Corner
Beddington Sewage Treatment Works
Beddington Farm
Hackbridge
Mill House
Sherwood Prim Sch
Greenwood Sch
The Alfred Mizen Sch
William Morris Sch
Tamworth Manor Sch
Rowan High Sch
CROYDON RD
WINDMILL RD
MANOR RD
CARSHALTON RD
LONDON RD
BEDDINGTON LA
COMMONSIDE EAST
UPPER GN E
MITCHAM GARDEN VILLAGE
MILL GREEN BSNS PK
BROOKMEAD IND EST
PIONEERS IND PK
FELNEX TRAD EST
Soho Mills
181
204
219

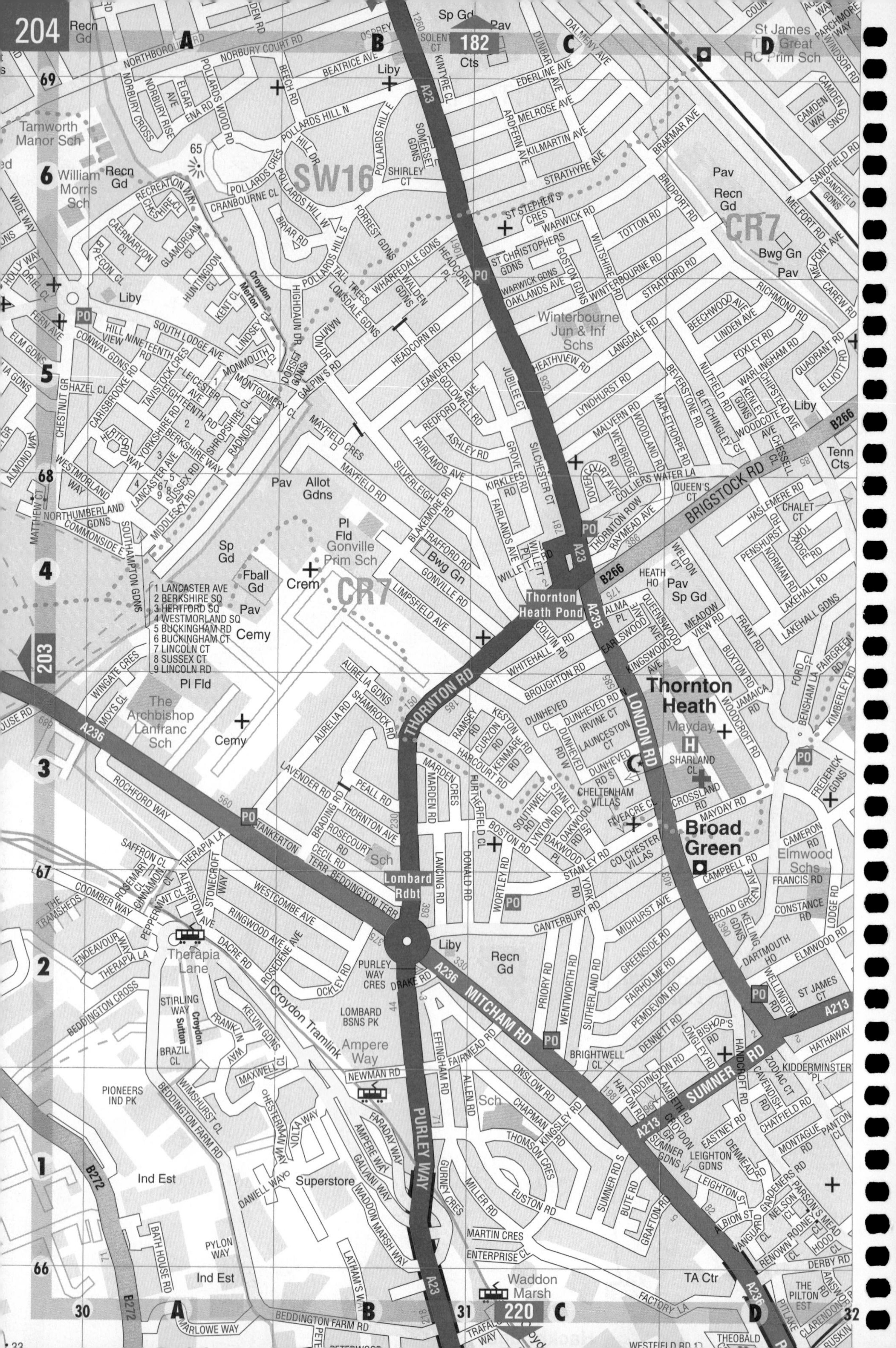

204
Recn Gd
A
B
C
D
182
Sp Gd
Pav
Cts
SOLENT CT
KINTYRE CL
NORTHBOROUGH RD
NORBURY COURT RD
OSPREY
BEATRICE AVE
Liby
DALMENY AVE
DUNBAR AVE
EDERLINE AVE
St James The Great RC Prim Sch
PARCHMORE WAY
WINDSOR RD
NORBURY CROSS
NORBURY RISE
ELGAR AVE
ENA RD
POLLARDS WOOD RD
BEECH RD
POLLARDS HILL N
POLLARDS HILL E
SOMERSET GDNS
A23
ARDFERN AVE
MELROSE AVE
KILMARTIN AVE
STRATHYRE AVE
BRAEMAR AVE
CAMDEN WAY
CAMDEN GDNS
SANDFIELD RD
SANDFIELD GDNS
Tamworth Manor Sch
William Morris Sch
Recn Gd
65
POLLARDS CRES
HILL DR
SW16
SHIRLEY CT
POLLARDS HILL W
FORREST GDNS
BRIAR RD
POLLARDS HILL S
RECREATION WAY
CHESHIRE CL
CRANBOURNE CL
CAERNARVON CL
GLAMORGAN CL
BRECON CL
HUNTINGDON CL
WIDE WAY
HOLLY WAY
ORIEL CL
FERN AVE
ELM GDNS
Liby
PO
HILL VIEW
NINETEENTH RD
CONWAY GDNS
SOUTH LODGE AVE
KENT CL
LINDSEY CL
Croydon
Merton
ST STEPHEN'S CRES
WARWICK RD
TOTTON RD
BRIDPORT RD
Recn Gd
CR7
Bwg Gn
Pav
MELFORT RD
MELFONT AVE
CAREW RD
ST CHRISTOPHERS GDNS
WARWICK GDNS
OAKLANDS AVE
GOSTON GDNS
WILTSHIRE RD
WINTERBOURNE RD
STRATFORD RD
RICHMOND RD
BEECHWOOD AVE
LINDEN AVE
FOXLEY RD
QUADRANT RD
ELLIOTT RD
WHARFEDALE GDNS
HEADCORN PL
TALL TREES
WALDEN GDNS
LONSDALE GDNS
HIGHDAUN DR
NAMTON DR
HEADCORN RD
Winterbourne Jun & Inf Schs
HEATHVIEW RD
LANGDALE RD
LYNDHURST RD
BEVERSTONE RD
BLETCHINGLEY CL
NUTFIELD RD
WARLINGHAM RD
CHIPSTEAD AVE
KENLEY GDNS
WOODCOTE AVE
CHESSELL CL
Liby
B266
Tenn Cts
MONMOUTH CL
MONTGOMERY CL
DORSET GDNS
GALPIN'S RD
TAVISTOCK CRES
LEICESTER AVE
EIGHTEENTH RD
CARISBROOKE RD
HAZEL CL
CHESTNUT GR
YORKSHIRE RD
SHROPSHIRE CL
RADNOR CL
BERKSHIRE WAY
HERTFORD WAY
LANCASTER AVE
SUSSEX RD
MIDDLESEX RD
WESTMORLAND WAY
NORTHUMBERLAND GDNS
COMMONSIDE E
MATTHEW CT
ALMOND WAY
LEANDER RD
REDFORD AVE
GOLDWELL RD
ASHLEY RD
JUBILEE CT
GROVE RD
SILCHESTER CT
MALVERN RD
WEYBRIDGE RD
WOODLAND RD
MAPLETHORPE RD
DOVERCOURT AVE
COLLIERS WATER LA
QUEEN'S CT
BRIGSTOCK RD
HASLEMERE RD
CHALET CT
MAYFIELD CRES
MAYFIELD RD
SILVERLEIGH RD
FAIRLANDS AVE
KIRKLEES RD
Pav
Allot Gdns
Pl Fld
Gonville Prim Sch
BLAKEMORE RD
TRAFFORD RD
Bwg Gn
GONVILLE RD
LIMPSFIELD AVE
WILLETT PL
WILLETT RD
THORNTON ROW
RAYMEAD AVE
WELDON CT
PENSHURST RD
NORMAN RD
TORRIDGE RD
LAKEHALL RD
LAKEHALL GDNS
Sp Gd
Fball Gd
Crem
CR7
Pav
Cemy
Thornton Heath Pond
A235
HEATH HO
Pav
Sp Gd
ALMA PL
QUEENSWOOD AVE
MEADOW VIEW RD
FRANT RD
1 LANCASTER AVE
2 BERKSHIRE SQ
3 HERTFORD SQ
4 WESTMORLAND SQ
5 BUCKINGHAM RD
6 BUCKINGHAM CT
7 LINCOLN CT
8 SUSSEX CT
9 LINCOLN RD
SOUTHAMPTON GDNS
203
COLVIN RD
WHITEHALL RD
EARLSWOOD AVE
KINGSWOOD AVE
BUXTON RD
FORD CL
FAIRGREEN RD
BENSHAM LA
KIMBERLEY RD
WINGATE CRES
MOYS CL
Pl Fld
The Archbishop Lanfranc Sch
Cemy
A236
AURELIA GDNS
SHAMROCK RD
AURELIA RD
THORNTON RD
BROUGHTON RD
DUNHEVED CL
DUNHEVED RD N
IRVINE CT
LAUNCESTON CT
DUNHEVED RD W
DUNHEVED RD S
LONDON RD
Thornton Heath
Mayday
SHARLAND CL
JAMAICA RD
WOODCROFT RD
PO
FREDERICK GDNS
RAMSEY RD
CURZON RD
KESTON RD
KENMARE RD
HARCOURT RD
MARDEN RD
MARDEN CRES
FURTHERFIELD CL
CHELTENHAM VILLAS
CROSSLAND RD
MAYDAY RD
Broad Green
ROCHFORD WAY
LAVENDER RD
PEALL RD
BRADING RD
THORNTON AVE
ROSECOURT RD
CECIL RD
BEDDINGTON TERR
Sch
SOUTHWELL RD
STANLEY GR
LYNTON RD
OAKWOOD RD
OAKWOOD PL
BOSTON RD
FIVEACRE CL
COLCHESTER VILLAS
STANLEY RD
YORK RD
CAMPBELL RD
CAMERON RD
Elmwood Schs
FRANCIS RD
STANKERTON
THERAPIA LA
SAFFRON CL
ROSEMARY CL
CINNAMON CL
ALFRISTON AVE
STONECROFT WAY
WESTCOMBE AVE
PEPPERMINT CL
COOMBER WAY
THE TRAMSHEDS
RINGWOOD AVE
ROSEDENE AVE
DACRE RD
Lombard Rdbt
LANCING RD
DONALD RD
WORTLEY RD
CANTERBURY RD
MIDHURST AVE
BROAD GREEN AVE
KELLING GDNS
CONSTANCE RD
LODGE RD
ELMWOOD RD
DARTMOUTH HO
ENDEAVOUR WAY
THERAPIA LA
Therapia Lane
OCKLEY RD
PURLEY WAY CRES
DRAKE RD
Liby
Recn Gd
PRIORY RD
WENTWORTH RD
SUTHERLAND RD
GREENSIDE RD
FAIRHOLME RD
WELLINGTON RD
ST JAMES CT
A213
BEDDINGTON CROSS
STIRLING WAY
Sutton
Croydon
FRANKLIN WAY
KELVIN GDNS
BRAZIL CL
Croydon Tramlink
LOMBARD BSNS PK
Ampere Way
MITCHAM RD
PEMDEVON RD
DENNETT RD
BISHOP'S RD
LONGLEY RD
HATHAWAY
KIDDERMINSTER PL
PIONEERS IND PK
MAXWELL CL
WIMSHURST CL
BEDDINGTON FARM RD
CHESTERMAN WAY
VOLTA WAY
NEWMAN RD
EFFINGHAM RD
FAIRMEAD RD
ALLEN RD
ONSLOW RD
Sch
CHAPMAN RD
THOMSON CRES
KINGSLEY RD
BRIGHTWELL CL
HATTON RD
ADDINGTON RD
LAMBETH RD
HANDCROFT RD
SUMNER RD
ZODIAC CT
CAVENDISH RD
CHATFIELD RD
PANTON CL
FARADAY WAY
AMPERE WAY
GALVANI WAY
PURLEY WAY
GURNEY CRES
MILLER RD
EUSTON RD
SUMNER RD S
BUTE RD
GRAFTON RD
SUMNER GDNS
CROYDON GR
EASTNEY RD
LEIGHTON GDNS
DENMEAD RD
MONTAGUE RD
GARDENERS RD
PARSON'S MEAD
NELSON CL
RODNEY CL
HOOD CL
RENOWN CL
VANGUARD CL
LEIGHTON ST
ALBION ST
DERBY RD
Ind Est
Superstore
DANIELL WAY
WADDON MARSH WAY
B272
BATH HOUSE RD
PYLON WAY
Ind Est
LATHAM'S WAY
MARTIN CRES
ENTERPRISE CL
Waddon Marsh
FACTORY LA
TA Ctr
THE PILTON EST
PITLAKE
CLARENDON RD
AINSWORTH RD
30
31
220
32
BEDDINGTON FARM RD
MARLOWE WAY
THEOBALD
WESTFIELD RD
69
68
67
66
6
5
4
3
2
1

A
B
C
D
183
221
206
South Norwood
Selhurst
SE25
CR0
Thornton Heath
West Croydon
East Croydon
Norwood Junction
Selhurst Park (Crystal Palace & Wimbledon Fball Clubs)
Grangewood Park
Beulah Schs
Bensham Manor Sch
Ecclesbourne Jun & Inf Schs
Queen's
Cemy
Allot Gdns
Recn Gd
Croydon Coll
Performing Arts & Tech Sch
Broadmead Jun & Inf Schs
St Chad's Sch
Heavers Farm Prim Sch
Selhurst Works
Davidson Jun & Inf Schs
Woodside Jun & Inf Sch
Oval Prim Sch
St Mary's Jun & Inf Schs
High Sch
Wellesley Road
PARCHMORE RD
GRANGE RD
WHITEHORSE RD
WHITEHORSE LA
SELHURST RD
SOUTH NORWOOD HILL
HIGH ST
NORTHCOTE RD
WINDMILL RD
ST JAMES'S RD
LOWER ADDISCOMBE RD
CHERRY ORCHARD RD
WELLESLEY RD
MORLAND RD
BENSHAM MANOR RD
A212
A213
A215
A222
B243
B266
B273
THISTLEDOWN CT 1
KILRAVOCK HO 2
ROSEMOUNT CT 3
1 DECIMUS CL
2 PALACE CT
3 RESERVOIR CL
1 HOMEWOOD GDNS
2 CHERITON CT
3 CLIFTON CT
4 MEDWAY CT
5 LAUREL CT
6 COLLETTE CT
ASHMILL CT 1
SMOCK WLK 2
32
33
34

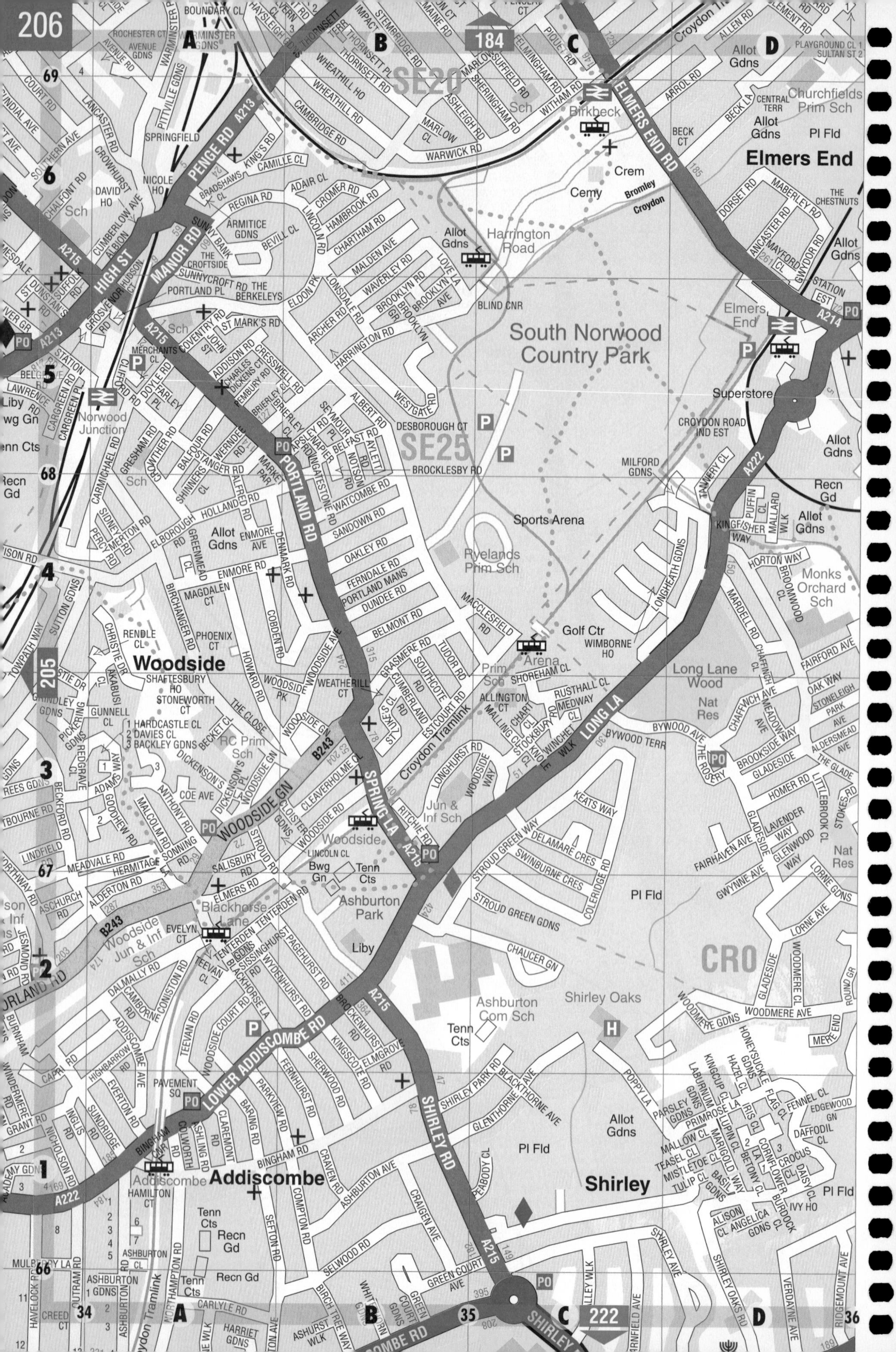
184
SE20
Birkbeck
Elmers End
Churchfields Prim Sch
Crem
Cemy
Bromley
Croydon
Harrington Road
South Norwood Country Park
SE25
Norwood Junction
Superstore
CROYDON ROAD IND EST
Sports Arena
Ryelands Prim Sch
Golf Ctr
Arena
Monks Orchard Sch
Woodside
Long Lane Wood
Nat Res
Croydon Tramlink
Ashburton Park
Blackhorse Lane
Ashburton Com Sch
Shirley Oaks
CR0
Addiscombe
Shirley
205
222
PENGE RD
HIGH ST
MANOR RD
PORTLAND RD
ELMERS END RD
LONG LA
SPRING LA
WOODSIDE GN
LOWER ADDISCOMBE RD
SHIRLEY RD
A213
A215
A214
A222
B243
A
B
C
D
1
2
3
4
5
6
34
35
36

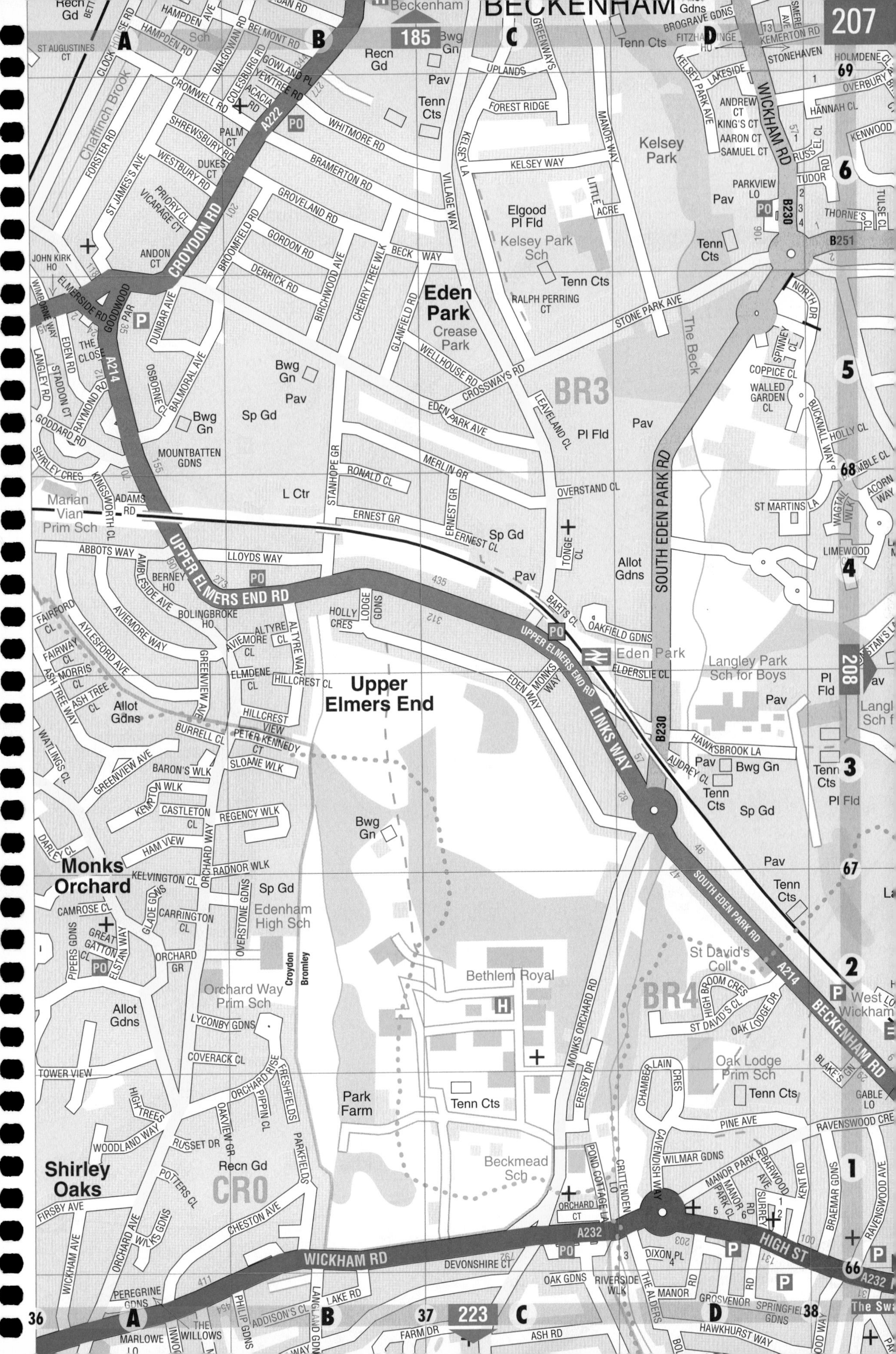

BECKENHAM
Beckenham
185
Eden Park
Crease Park
Kelsey Park
Kelsey Park Sch
Elgood Pl Fld
BR3
Upper Elmers End
Monks Orchard
Shirley Oaks
CR0
BR4
Bethlem Royal
Edenham High Sch
Orchard Way Prim Sch
Marian Vian Prim Sch
Langley Park Sch for Boys
St David's Coll
Oak Lodge Prim Sch
Beckmead Sch
Park Farm
West Wickham
CROYDON RD
UPPER ELMERS END RD
LINKS WAY
SOUTH EDEN PARK RD
WICKHAM RD
BECKENHAM RD
HIGH ST
STONE PARK AVE
CROSSWAYS RD
EDEN PARK AVE
KELSEY LA
KELSEY WAY
BRAMERTON RD
WHITMORE RD
CROMWELL RD
208
223
36
37
38

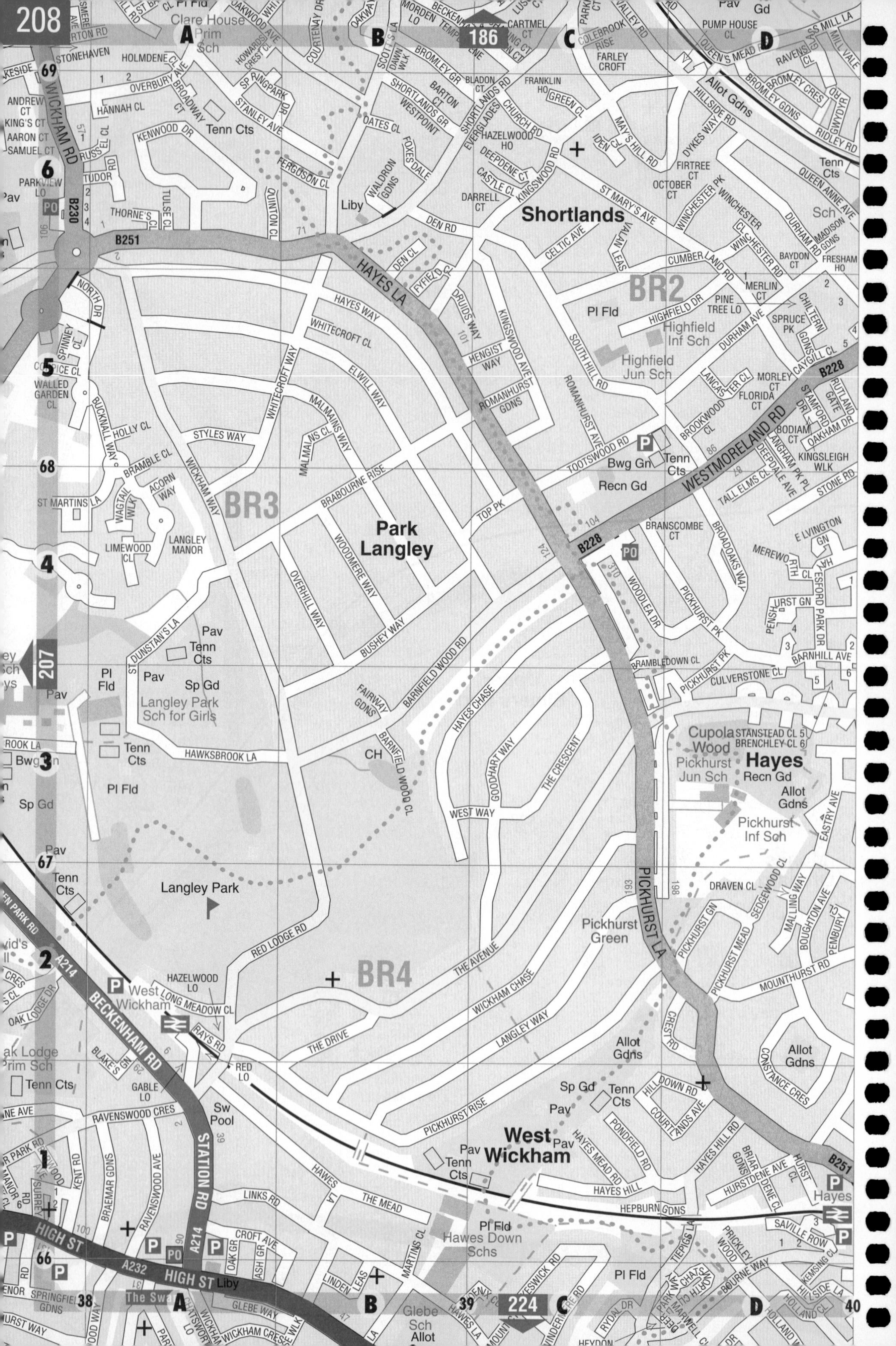
186
224
207
Shortlands
Park Langley
Hayes
West Wickham
BR2
BR3
BR4
HAYES LA
PICKHURST LA
WESTMORELAND RD
WICKHAM RD
BECKENHAM RD
STATION RD
HIGH ST
B251
B228
B230
A214
A232
Langley Park
Langley Park Sch for Girls
Highfield Inf Sch
Highfield Jun Sch
Pickhurst Jun Sch
Pickhurst Inf Sch
Cupola Wood
Pickhurst Green
Hawes Down Schs
Glebe Sch
Clare House Prim Sch
Oak Lodge Prim Sch
West Wickham
Hayes
WICKHAM WAY
WHITECROFT WAY
HAYES WAY
BUSHEY WAY
BARNFIELD WOOD RD
HAYES CHASE
THE AVENUE
WICKHAM CHASE
LANGLEY WAY
PICKHURST RISE
THE DRIVE
RED LODGE RD
HAWKSBROOK LA
ST DUNSTAN'S LA
SOUTH HILL RD
KINGSWOOD AVE
KINGSWOOD RD
ST MARY'S AVE
SHORTLANDS RD
DEN RD
BROADOAKS WAY
PICKHURST PK
WOODLEA DR
HAYES HILL RD
HEPBURN GDNS
MOUNTHURST RD
HAWES LA
LINKS RD
RAVENSWOOD CRES
QUEEN ANNE AVE
DURHAM AVE
DURHAM RD
1
2
3
4
5
6
A
B
C
D
38
39
40
66
67
68
69

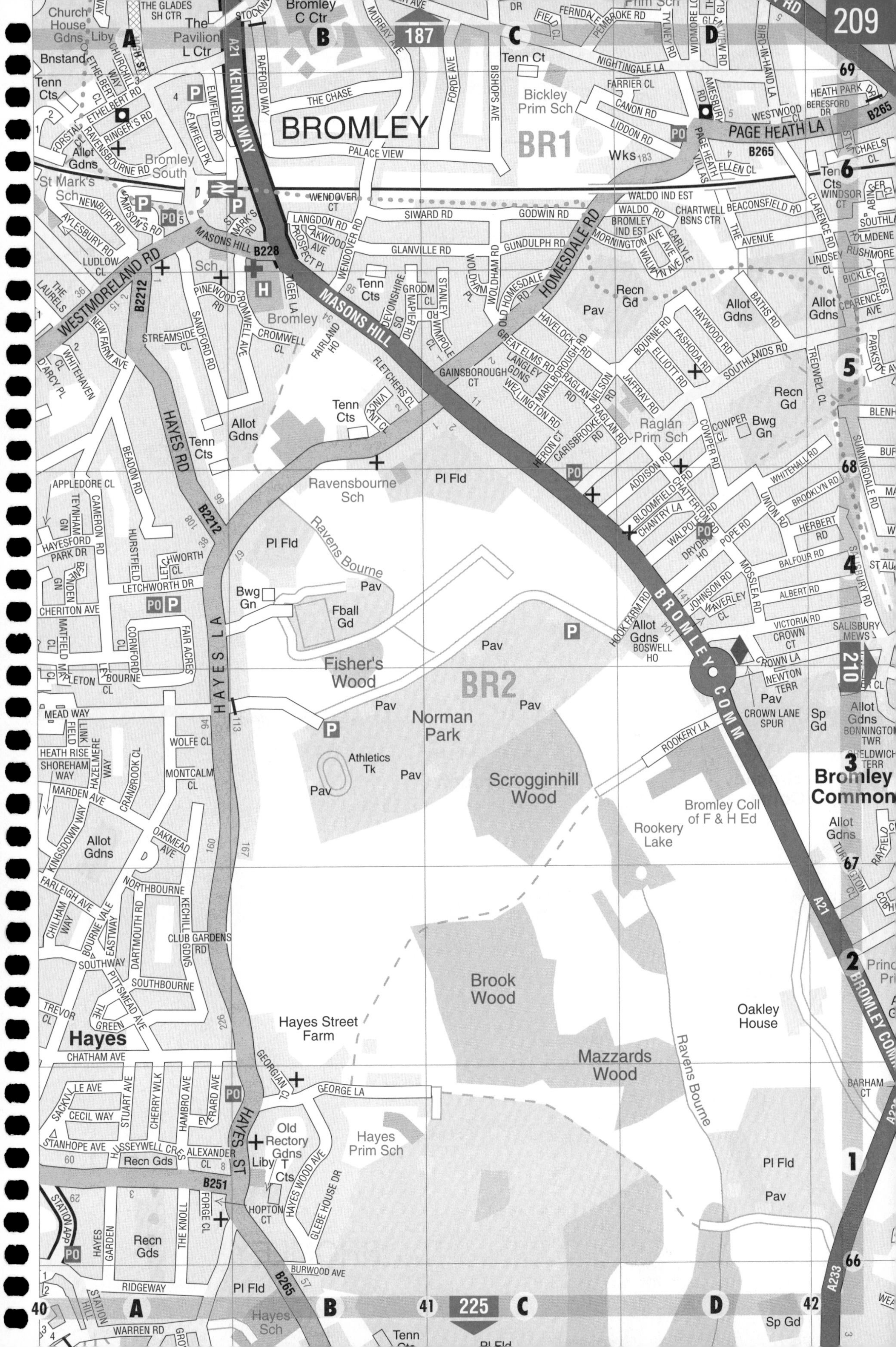
BROMLEY
BR1
BR2
Hayes
Bromley Common
Norman Park
Scrogginhill Wood
Brook Wood
Mazzards Wood
Fisher's Wood
Ravensbourne Sch
Bromley Coll of F & H Ed
Rookery Lake
Hayes Street Farm
Oakley House
Hayes Prim Sch
Raglan Prim Sch
Bickley Prim Sch
Bromley South
KENTISH WAY
MASONS HILL
BROMLEY COMM
HAYES LA
HAYES RD
HAYES ST
WESTMORELAND RD
HOMESDALE RD
PAGE HEATH LA
187
225
210

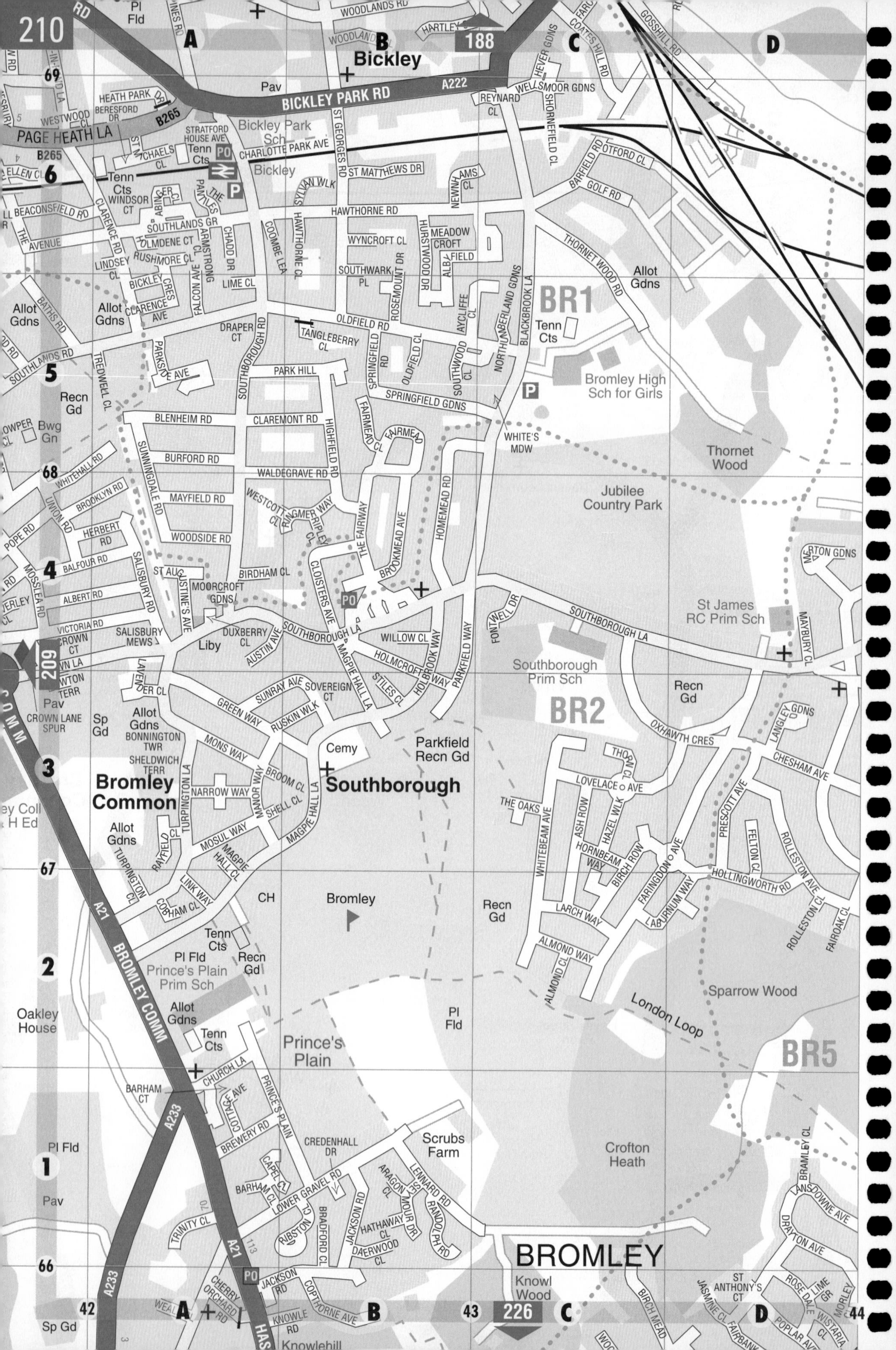
Bickley
BICKLEY PARK RD
A222
PAGE HEATH LA
B265
Bickley Park Sch
CHARLOTTE PARK AVE
ST GEORGES RD
HAWTHORNE RD
OLDFIELD RD
BR1
Bromley High Sch for Girls
Thornet Wood
Jubilee Country Park
SOUTHBOROUGH LA
St James RC Prim Sch
Southborough Prim Sch
BR2
Bromley Common
Southborough
Parkfield Recn Gd
Bromley
Sparrow Wood
London Loop
BR5
Prince's Plain
Prince's Plain Prim Sch
Crofton Heath
Scrubs Farm
BROMLEY COMM
A21
A233
BROMLEY
Knowl Wood
Oakley House
188
209
226

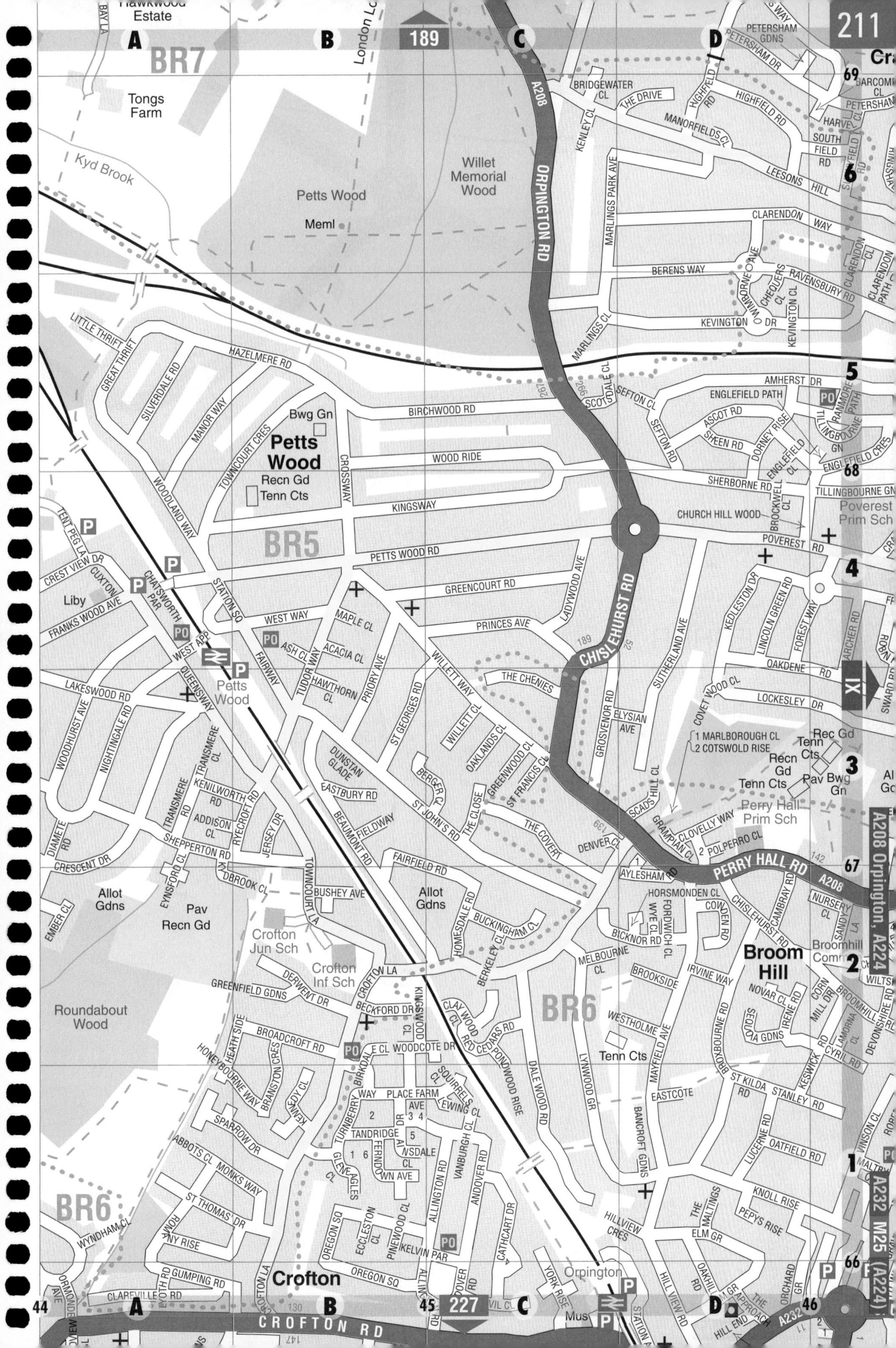

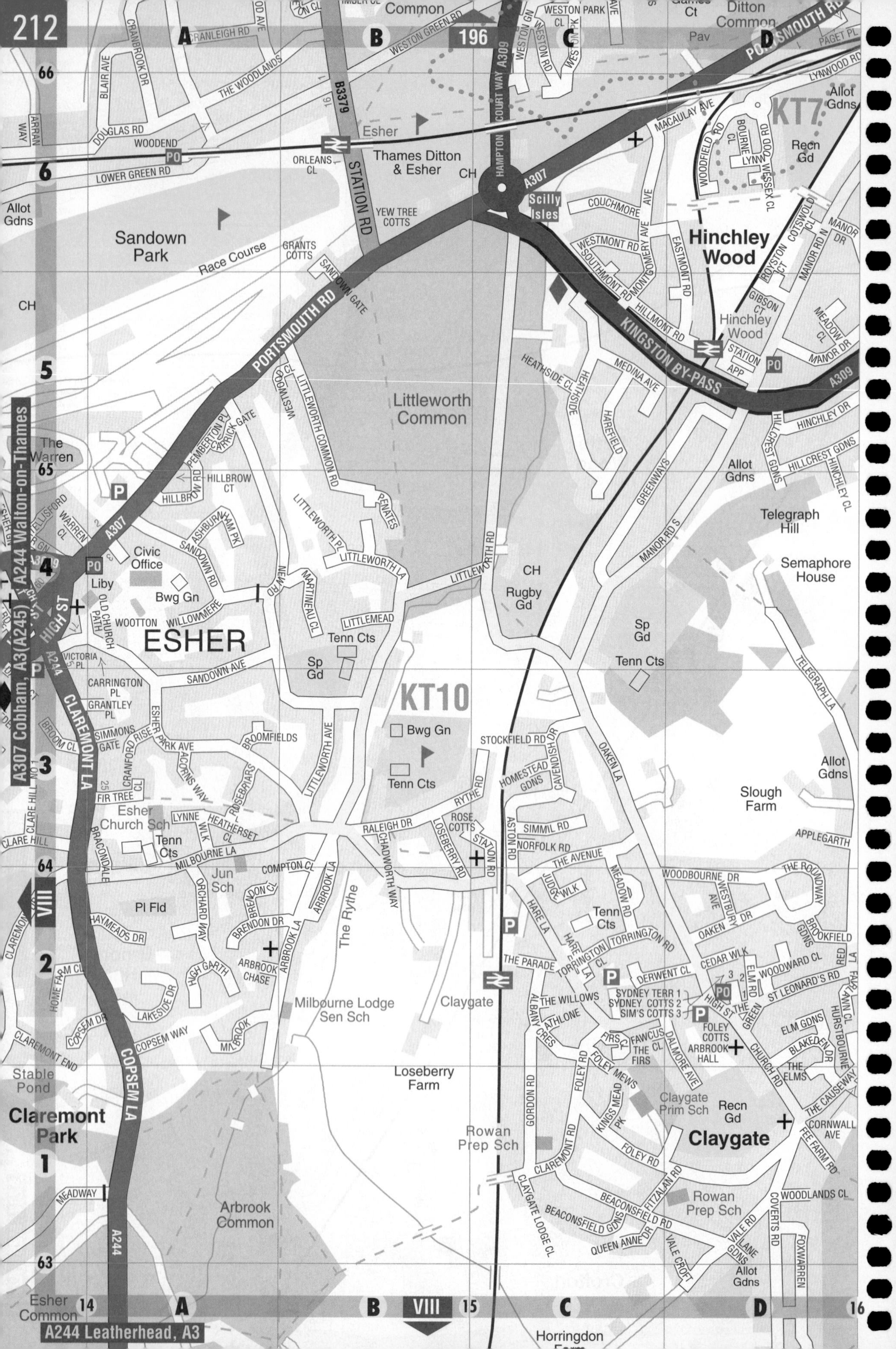

196
Portsmouth Rd
Sandown Park
Race Course
Thames Ditton & Esher
Station Rd
Hampton Court Way A309
Scilly Isles
Hinchley Wood
Kingston By-Pass
KT7
Littleworth Common
Littleworth Common Rd
Littleworth Rd
Telegraph Hill
Semaphore House
ESHER
KT10
Civic Office
Sandown Ave
Esher Park Ave
Milbourne La
Claremont La
Copsem La
Slough Farm
Milbourne Lodge Sen Sch
Claygate
Loseberry Farm
Claygate Prim Sch
Rowan Prep Sch
Claremont Park
Arbrook Common
Horringdon Farm
The Rythe
A307 Walton-on-Thames
A307 Cobham, A3(A245) A244
A244 Leatherhead, A3
Esher Common
VIII

Long Ditton
A
B
C
D
197
66
65
64
63
6
5
4
3
2
1
KT7
KT6
KT10
KT9
Pav
Allot Gdns
Sports Gd
Sp Gd
Cemy
Manor House
Sch
Hinchley Wood Sch
Hinchley Wood Prim Sch
Hill Park Nurseries
Ditton Hill Nurseries
KINGSTON BY-PASS
A309
A3
A243
Bwg Gn
Tenn Cts
Recn Gd
Allot Gdns
HOOK RD
St Paul's Sch
Sp Gd
Pl Fld
Nursery
The Waffrons
CH
Surbiton
Pl Fld
Pav
Lovelace Prim Sch
Manor Farm
Elm Farm
Lower Wood
Kingston upon Thames
Surrey
Liby
PO
214
St Philip's Sch
Ellingham Prim Sch
Chessington South
Chessington Com Coll
Chessington
Claygate Common
Barwell
Tenn Cts
Recn Gd
Allot Gdns
BARWELL BSNS PK
LEATHERHEAD RD
WOODSTOCK LA N
WOODSTOCK LA S
CLAYTON RD
SOMERSET AVE
VALLIS WAY
SELWOOD RD
MANSFIELD RD
RED LA
OLD CLAYGATE LA
COMMON LA
COMMON RD
RUXLEY CRES
HILL VIEW RD
MOUNT VIEW RD
LOWER WOOD RD
BRIDLE RD
SEVERN DR
HINCHLEY WAY
CLAYGATE LA
CHESTERFIELD DR
CUMBERLAND DR
MANOR DR
AVONDALE AVE
SOUTHWOOD GDNS
HILLCREST GDNS
THE OAKS
LOVE LA
SUMMERFIELD LA
CHURCH RD
MERLING CL 1
GOLDING CL 2
NICHOLS CL 3
WITHERS CL 4
MITFORD CL 5
VIDLER CL 6
SMEATON CL 7
HUBBARD DR 8
WHITEHALL CRES 1
TREWENNA DR 2
CHESSINGTON PAR 3
16
17
18
VIII
Sp Gd
A3 Guildford, M25
A243 Leatherhead, M25

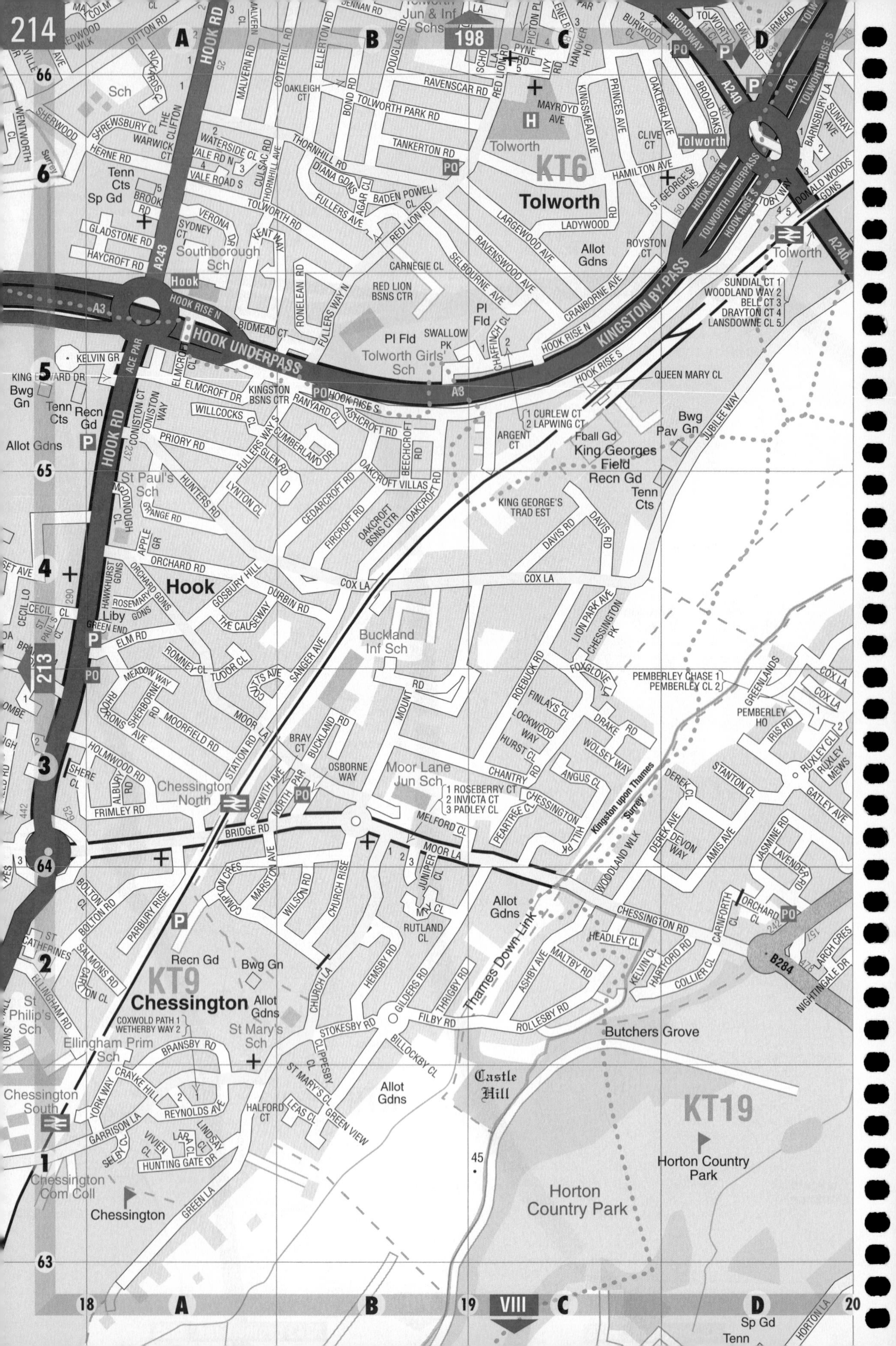
A
B
C
D
198
213
VIII
18
19
20
66
65
64
63
6
5
4
3
2
1
KT6
KT9
KT19
Tolworth
Hook
Chessington
HOOK RD
A243
A3
A240
B284
HOOK UNDERPASS
HOOK RISE N
HOOK RISE S
KINGSTON BY-PASS
TOLWORTH UNDERPASS
TOLWORTH RISE N
TOLWORTH RISE S
BROADWAY
DITTON RD
MALVERN RD
COTTERILL RD
ELLERTON RD
DOUGLAS RD
RED LION RD
IVY RD
HANOVER HO
PYNE RD
PICTON PL
RAVENSCAR RD
TOLWORTH PARK RD
TANKERTON RD
OAKLEIGH CT
BOND RD
MAYROYD AVE
KINGSMEAD AVE
PRINCES AVE
OAKLEIGH AVE
BROAD OAKS
CLIVE CT
HAMILTON AVE
ST GEORGE'S GDNS
LADYWOOD RD
LARGEWOOD AVE
RAVENSWOOD AVE
SELBOURNE AVE
CRANBORNE AVE
ROYSTON CT
Allot Gdns
CARNEGIE CL
RED LION BSNS CTR
Pl Fld
SWALLOW PK
CHAFFINCH CL
Tolworth Girls' Sch
BADEN POWELL CL
FULLERS AVE
AGAR CL
DIANA GDNS
THORNHILL RD
THORNHILL AVE
CULSAC RD
WATERSIDE CL
VALE RD N
VALE ROAD S
TOLWORTH RD
KENT WAY
RONELEAN RD
FULLERS WAY N
BIDMEAD CT
VERONA DR
SYDNEY CT
Southborough Sch
GLADSTONE RD
HAYCROFT RD
BROOK RD
Tenn Cts
Sp Gd
HERNE RD
WARWICK CT
SHREWSBURY CL
THE CLIFTON
SHERWOOD
WENTWORTH CL
Sch
RICHARDS CL
KELVIN GR
KING EDWARD DR
Bwg Gn
Recn Gd
ACE PAR
ELMCROFT CL
ELMCROFT DR
KINGSTON BSNS CTR
RANYARD CL
ASHCROFT RD
WILLCOCKS CL
CONISTON CT
CONISTON WAY
PRIORY RD
FULLERS WAY S
CUMBERLAND DR
GLEN RD
HUNTERS RD
LYNTON CL
BEECHCROFT RD
OAKCROFT VILLAS
OAKCROFT RD
CEDARCROFT RD
FIRCROFT RD
OAKCROFT BSNS CTR
St Paul's Sch
MCDONOUGH CL
GRANGE RD
APPLE GR
ORCHARD RD
HAWKHURST GDNS
ORCHARD GDNS
ROSEMARY GDNS
GOSBURY HILL
DURBIN RD
THE CAUSEWAY
COX LA
Liby
GREEN END
ELM RD
ROMNEY CL
TUDOR CL
MEADOW WAY
SHERBORNE RD
RHODRONS AVE
MOORFIELD RD
MOOR LA
STATION RD
COVERTS AVE
SANGER AVE
HOLMWOOD RD
SHERE CL
ALBURY RD
FRIMLEY RD
Chessington North
SOPWITH AVE
NORTH PAR
BRIDGE RD
BRAY CT
BUCKLAND RD
OSBORNE WAY
Buckland Inf Sch
MOUNT RD
Moor Lane Jun Sch
1 ROSEBERRY CT
2 INVICTA CT
3 PADLEY CL
MELFORD CL
JUNIPER CL
MAY CL
RUTLAND CL
QUEEN MARY CL
1 CURLEW CT
2 LAPWING CT
ARGENT CT
Fball Gd
King Georges Field Recn Gd
Bwg Gn
Pav
Tenn Cts
JUBILEE WAY
KING GEORGE'S TRAD EST
DAVIS RD
LION PARK AVE
CHESSINGTON PK
FOXGLOVE LA
ROEBUCK RD
FINLAYS CL
LOCKWOOD WAY
HURST CL
CHANTRY RD
DRAKE RD
WOLSEY WAY
ANGUS CL
CHESSINGTON HILL PK
PEARTREE CL
SUNDIAL CT 1
WOODLAND WAY 2
BELL CT 3
DRAYTON CT 4
LANSDOWNE CL 5
TOBY WAY
DONALD WOODS GDNS
Kingston upon Thames
Surrey
PEMBERLEY CHASE 1
PEMBERLEY CL 2
PEMBERLEY HO
GREENLANDS
COX LA
IRIS RD
RUXLEY CL
RUXLEY MEWS
STANTON CL
GATLEY AVE
DEREK CL
DEREK AVE
DEVON WAY
AMIS AVE
JASMINE RD
LAVENDER RD
ORCHARD CL
WOODLAND WLK
Thames Down Link
CHESSINGTON RD
HEADLEY CL
KELVIN CL
HARFORD RD
CARNFORTH CL
COLLIER CL
LARCH CRES
NIGHTINGALE DR
ASHBY AVE
MALTBY RD
ROLLESBY RD
FILBY RD
THRIGBY RD
GILDERS RD
HEMSBY RD
Butchers Grove
Castle Hill
Horton Country Park
BOLTON CL
BOLTON RD
PARBURY RISE
COMPTON CRES
MARSTON AVE
WILSON RD
CHURCH RISE
CHURCH LA
ST CATHERINES
SALMONS RD
CARLTON CL
ELLINGHAM RD
St Philip's Sch
Recn Gd
Bwg Gn
COXWOLD PATH 1
WETHERBY WAY 2
Ellingham Prim Sch
St Mary's Sch
STOKESBY RD
BILLOCKBY CL
CLIPPESBY CL
ST MARY'S CL
BRANSBY RD
CRAYKE HILL
YORK WAY
REYNOLDS AVE
LINDSAY RD
GARRISON LA
SELBY CL
VIVIEN CL
LARA CL
HUNTING GATE DR
HALFORD CT
LEAS CL
GREEN VIEW
GREEN LA
Chessington South
Chessington Com Coll
Chessington
45
Sp Gd
Tenn
HORTON LA

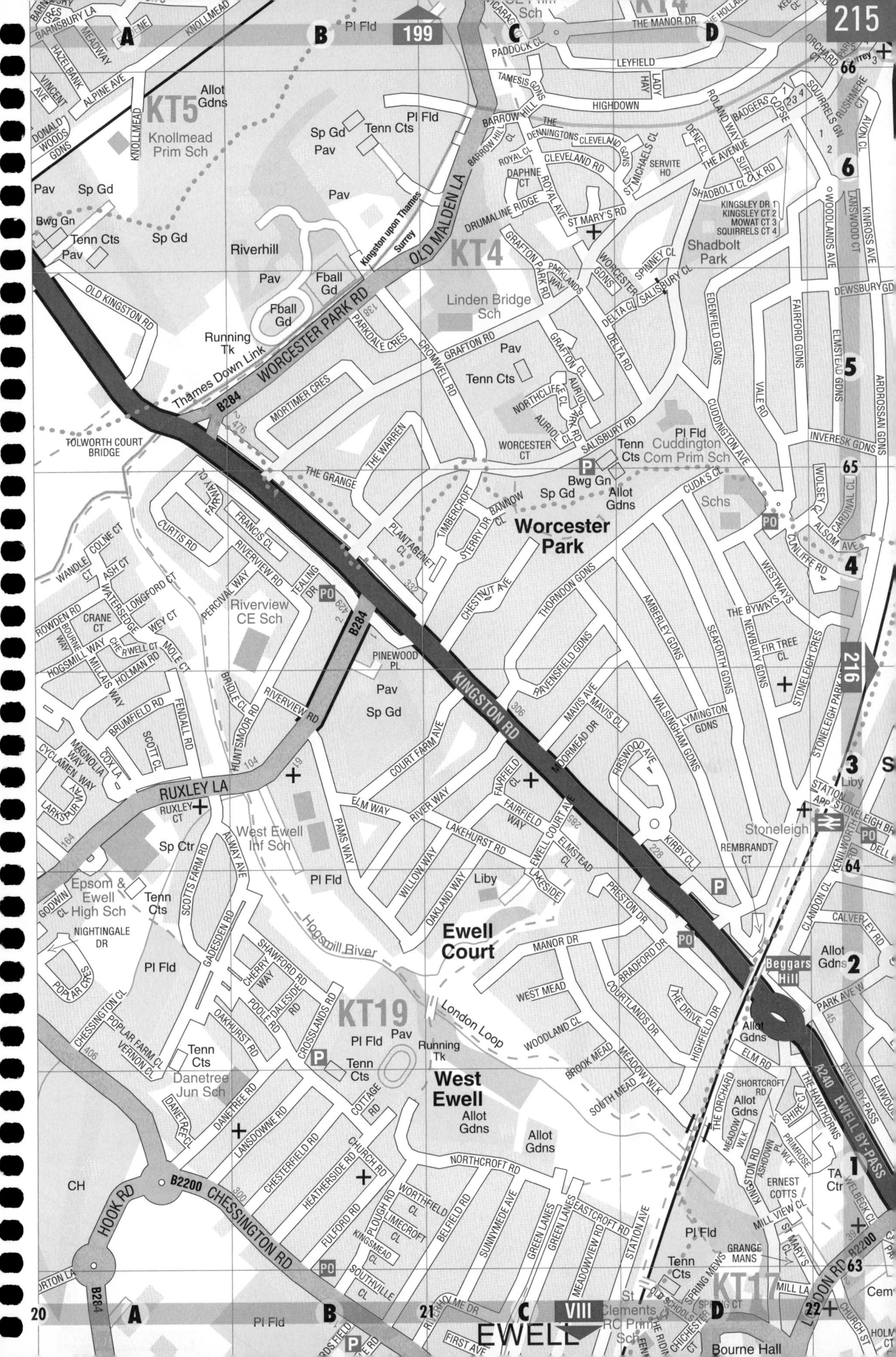

199
A
B
C
D
KT5
KT4
KT19
KT17
Knollmead Prim Sch
Riverhill
Linden Bridge Sch
Worcester Park
Cuddington Com Prim Sch
Shadbolt Park
Riverview CE Sch
West Ewell Inf Sch
Epsom & Ewell High Sch
Danetree Jun Sch
Ewell Court
West Ewell
Stoneleigh
Beggars Hill
St Clements RC Prim Sch
Bourne Hall
EWELL
WORCESTER PARK RD
OLD MALDEN LA
KINGSTON RD
RUXLEY LA
CHESSINGTON RD
HOOK RD
EWELL BY-PASS
A240
B284
B2200
Thames Down Link
London Loop
Hogsmill River
TOLWORTH COURT BRIDGE
Kingston upon Thames
Surrey
216
VIII
20
21
22
63
64
65
66
1
2
3
4
5
6

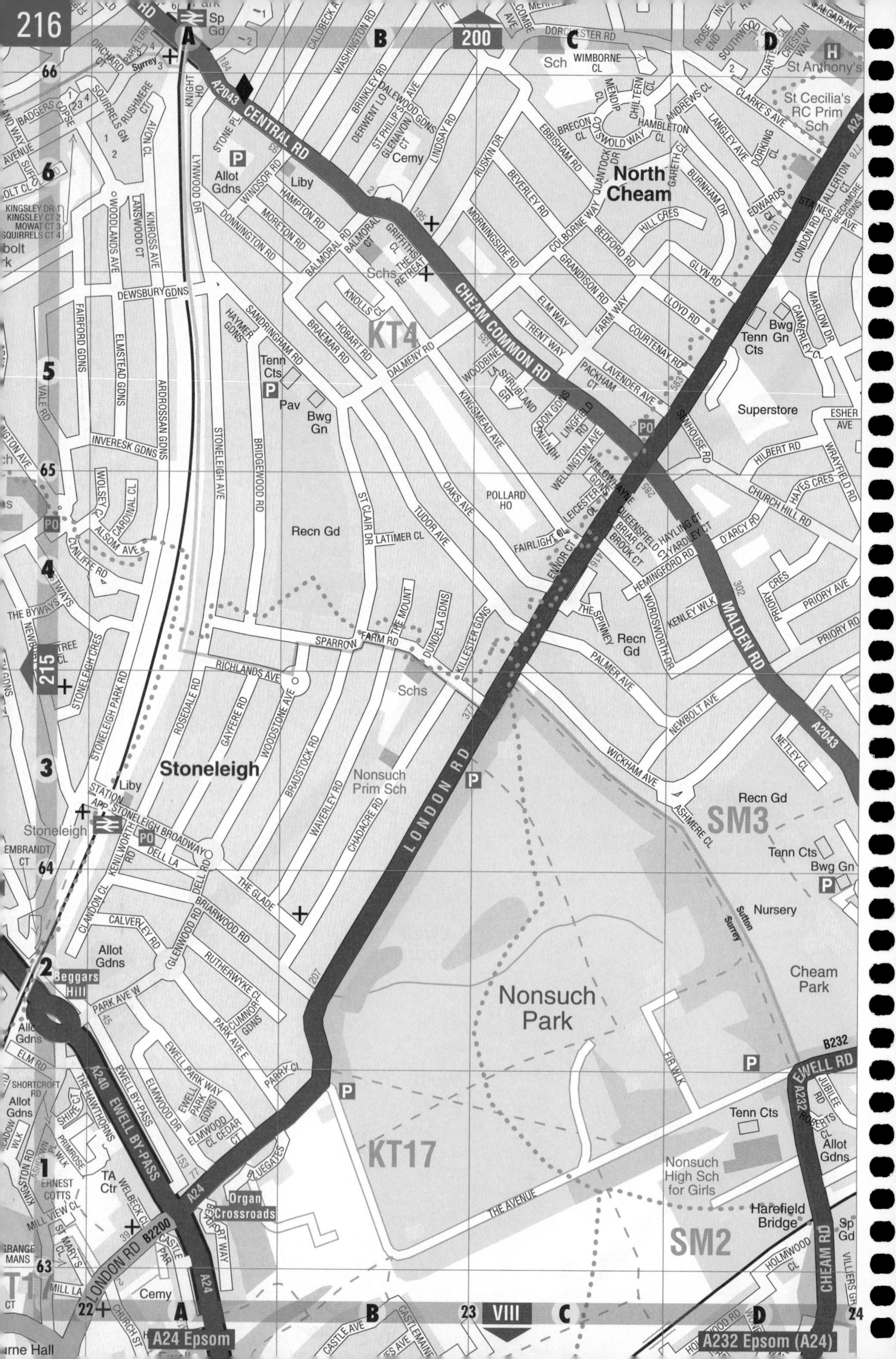
North Cheam
Stoneleigh
Nonsuch Park
Cheam Park
KT4
KT17
SM3
SM2
CENTRAL RD
CHEAM COMMON RD
MALDEN RD
LONDON RD
EWELL BY-PASS
EWELL RD
CHEAM RD
Nonsuch Prim Sch
Nonsuch High Sch for Girls
St Cecilia's RC Prim Sch
St Anthony's
Superstore
Beggars Hill
Organ Crossroads
Harefield Bridge
A24 Epsom
A232 Epsom (A24)

200
215
VIII

SM3
SM1
SM2
201
218
VIII
A
B
C
D
24
25
26
66
6
5
65
4
3
64
2
1
63
Brookfield Prim Sch
Allot Gdns
Cemy
Recn Gd
Tenn Cts
Fball Gd
Bwg Gn
Pav
Sutton Common
SUTTON COMMON RD
ROSE HILL
ANGEL HILL
KIMPTON TRADE & BSNS CTR
KIMPTON LINK BSNS CTR
FOUR SEASONS CRES
MINDEN RD
SANDIFORD RD
KIMPTON RD
WEALDSTONE RD
Superstore
Cheam Park Farm Inf Sch
Cheam Park Farm Jun Sch
OLDFIELDS RD
A217
B279
B2230
A232
A2043
B283
WESTBOURNE AVE
WARNER AVE
WATSON AVE
HAMILTON AVE
CAVERSHAM AVE
EGHAM CL
EGHAM CRES
CHERTSEY DR
MOLESEY DR
BROCKS DR
HENLEY AVE
SUNBURY RD
THE MEADS
ESHER AVE
FROGMORE CL
FROGMORE GDNS
ST MARGARET'S AVE
KINGSTON AVE
KEW CRES
WALTON AVE
WINDSOR AVE
ALDRICH GDNS
CHARTWELL PL
CHARTWELL GDNS
BUXTON CRES
CARLTON CRES
ABBOTTS RD
MATLOCK CRES
NORTHFIELD CRES
PRIORY CT
CHURCH HILL RD
CHATSWORTH RD
MATLOCK PL
MATLOCK GDNS
Cheam High Sch
Cheam Fields Prim Sch
STOUGHTON AVE
TILEHURST RD
KINGSDOWN RD
FROMONDES RD
LUMLEY RD
TUDOR CL
POND HILL GDNS
MALDEN RD
CHEAM PARK WAY
MICKLEHAM GDNS
SPRING CLOSE LA
CHURCH FARM LA
STAFFORD CL
RUSHMON PL
PARK LA
PARKSIDE
THE BROADWAY
Cheam Village
HIGH ST
St Dunstans
ST DUNSTAN'S HILL
ALMA CRES
ALBERTA AVE
THE MAISONETTES
Cheam
WESTFIELD RD
SUNNINGDALE RD
WARWICK LO
WILLOW MANOR
ELMBROOK RD
ST ALBANS RD
SALTASH CL
SILVERDALE CL
WARE CT
FREDERICK GDNS
FREDERICK RD
PRIORY CT
HILLDALE RD
DENBIGH CL
ASHTON CL
West Sutton
F Ball Gd
Recn Gd
Westbourne Prim Sch
WHEELER'S LA
OLDFIELDS TRAD EST
NORTHSPUR RD
ANTON CRES
ALEXANDRA AVE
CHAUCER GDNS
MILTON RD
COLLINGWOOD RD
ANDREWES HO 1
BALAAM HO 2
DENNIS HO 3
GIBSON HO 4
KILLICK HO
SYDNEY RD
BEULAH RD
BEAUCHAMP RD
ORCHARD RD
ORCHARD GDNS
STRATHEARN RD
ST JAMES AVE
ST JAMES RD
NORMAN RD
PETERSHAM CL
TATE RD
Pl Fld
Homefield Prep Sch
WESTERN RD
BEECHWOOD CT
CYPRESS CT
SHERWOOD PARK RD
CAMDEN GDNS
CAMDEN RD
CHEAM RD
CARLTON HO
WRIGHTON CT
KINGFISHER CT
OSPREY CL
TEAL PL
KITTIWAKE PL
HERON CL
SHEARWATER RD
BOURNE WAY
CORMORANT CL
SANDPIPER RD
GREBE CT
Works
ANTROBUS CL
QUARRY PARK RD
QUARRY RISE
REVELL RD
FAIRHOLME RD
CARLISLE RD
ROSEBERY RD
CECIL RD
DERBY RD
BRIDGEFIELD RD
LANDSEER RD
BEGGAR'S ROOST LA
GROVE AVE
TORMEAD CL
STANSTEAD MANOR
Games Ct
HOMEFIELD PK
SUTTON PARK RD
Sch
Liby
Coll
C Ctr
GIBSON RD
HILL RD
THROWLEY WAY
THROWLEY RD
ST NICHOLAS WAY
ST NICHOLAS CTR
SUTTON ARC
TIMES SQ
Manor Park
MANOR PARK
GREENFORD RD
BENHILL AVE
BENHILL WOOD
LODGE RD
LENHAM RD
HIGH ST
EDWINA CT
LEWIS RD
JENGAR CL
BURNELL RD
BELSIZE GDNS
ROSEBERY GDNS
MARSHALL'S RD
ELM GR
CROWN RD
WILCOX RD
BRANDON RD
BURGESS RD
HADDON RD
CLARENCE RD
THORNCROFT RD
THOMAS WALL CL
WEST ST
BEECH TREE PL
FALCOURT CL
RECTORY RD
VICARAGE RD
BUSHEY RD
BUSHEY LA
VALE RD
SORRENTO RD
ELMSLEIGH CT
DEANS RD
THE GREEN
BISHOPSBROOK
PYLBROOK RD
HALLMEAD RD
VERMONT RD
COOMBE WLK
AYSGARTH CT
BLENHEIM RD
STAYTON RD
SUNNYHURST CL
MARLBOROUGH RD
DIBDIN RD
DIBDIN CL
BURFORD RD
MINSTER AV
LEAFIELD RD
CHESTER CL
BROOMLOAN LA
LYMESCOTE GDNS
CLENSHAM LA
CLENSHAM CT
FAIRLANDS AVE
SOUTHFIELDS CT
RANFURLY RD
HURSTCOURT RD
ST JOHN'S RD
ALCORN CL
SHERBORNE RD
BARRINGTON RD
RIDGE RD
KEDESTON CT
1 ARLINGTON CL
2 OAKWOOD GDNS
3 HIGHFIELDS
CONIFER GDNS
CRANLEIGH GDNS
ASHLEIGH GDNS
GLOUCESTER GDNS
ROSEHILL GDNS
ROSE HILL PARK
HOVE GDNS
HORSE SHOE GN
WAVERLEY AVE
MONTROSE GDNS
MONKSDENE GDNS
HAWTHORNE CL
WOODEND
ANGEL HILL DR
CALTHORPE GDNS
LYMINGTON CT
ALL SAINTS RD
CLAYGATE CT
HUNTING GATE MEWS
KIRK RISE
BENHILTON GDNS
ALVERNIA LO
BENWOOD CT
DOVERCOURT LA
WOODSIDE RD
REGENCY CT
BOULLEN CT
BRUNSWICK MANOR
CRESSINGHAM GR
CRANFORD CL
RIPLEY GDNS
MILFORD GR
LITCHFIELD RD
BENHILL AVE
LODGE PL
MANOR PL
MASON RD
Schs
BANK MEWS
CHALK PIT
SUTTON COURT
Sutton
THE QUADRANT
WELLESLEY RD
BRIGHTON RD
GREENSLEEVES MANOR
MULGRAVE CHAMBERS
MULGRAVE HALL
MULGRAVE MANOR
BRIDGE RD
GROVE RD
WOODLAND CT
TANDRIDGE CT
CADOGAN CT
GLYNDALE GRANGE
CONWAY DR
MULGRAVE RD
JUNIPER CT
CASTLE CT
LESLIE GDNS
HEYWARD CT
HEATHER GDNS
SALISBURY AVE
VILLAGE ROW
OVERTON RD
WORCESTER RD
VALERIE CT
THE FIRS
MALVERN CT
STANLEY CT
STANLEY RD
FAIRFORD CT
WEYMOUTH CT
BRAMBLE ACRES CL
CHALCOT CL
EVESHAM CL
YORK RD
FRAMPTON CL
GRANGE RD
UPTON DENE
ABBOTSLEIGH CL
ORMSBY
REDRUTH HO
TAPESTRY CL
CAMBORNE RD
EASTLEIGH CL
GRANGE VALE
COPSE HILL
EFFINGHAM CL
BLACKBUSH CL
BONCHURCH CL
VENTNOR RD
WESTMORELAND DR
BASINGHALL GDNS
SWIFT CT
SUMMERS CL
CHANCTONBURY GDNS
BRANDY WAY
WYNDHAM CL
SACKVILLE RD
PENSHURST WAY
LYNDHURST WAY
AUDLEY PL
HOLLAND AVE
CORNWALL RD
BERESFORD RD
Belmont
MANOR RD
BELMONT RISE
ARUNDEL RD
HILLSIDE RD
BURDON PK
BURDON LA
SANDY LA
GLEBE RD
PEACHES CL
OLD BARN CL
Bwg Gn
Tenn Cts
THE LAWNS
CHAMPNEYS CL
UPPER MULGRAVE RD
STATION WAY
STATION APP
Cheam
FARRIERS CT
ANNE BOLEYN'S WLK
QUEENS ACRE
FORGE LA
KINGSWAY RD
NONSUCH CT
SCOTSDALE CL
CHEAM MAWS
TABOR GDNS
DALLAS RD
SUMMERVILLE GDNS
1 STEPHENSON CT
2 FROBISHER CT
3 CARISBROOKE CT
Cuddington Croft Cty Fst & Mid Sch
WEST DR
THE GLADE
Ambleside Sch
A217 Banstead, M25
Pav
SINCLAIR DR
CHIPSTEAD CL
Henderson
CAREW
Sp Gd
MELTON CT
LUTEA HO
WALNUT MEWS
DEVONSHIRE
PENARTH CT
KEMPSTON HO
THE DOWN
TRICKEY HO
FELBRIDGE
ARGYLE HO
SUTTON CT
BRENDON HO

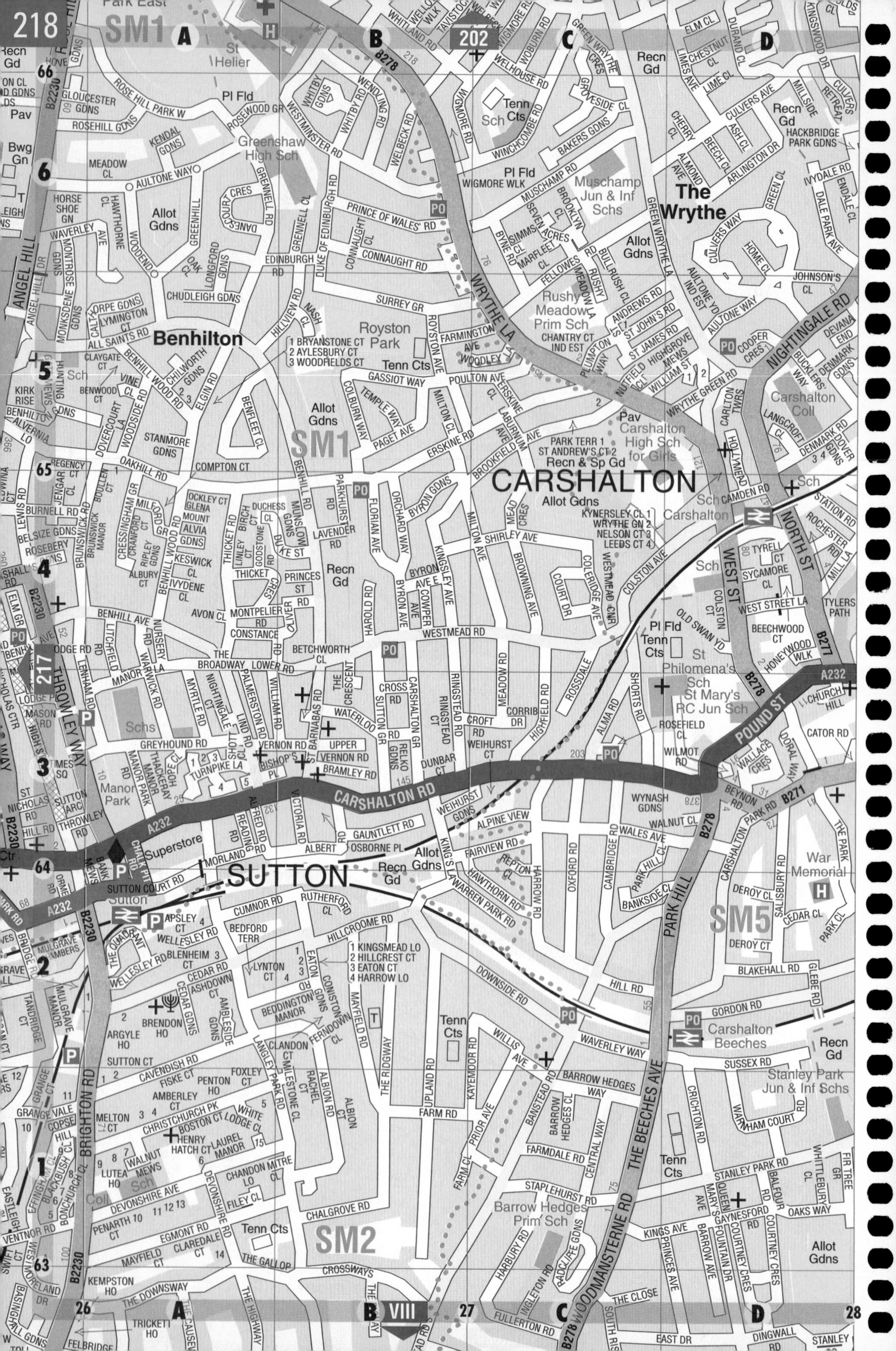

218
SM1
A
B
C
D
202
St Helier
Benhilton
Royston Park
The Wrythe
CARSHALTON
SUTTON
SM5
SM2
Carshalton
Carshalton Beeches
Greenshaw High Sch
Muschamp Jun & Inf Schs
Rushy Meadow Prim Sch
Carshalton High Sch for Girls
Carshalton Coll
St Philomena's Sch
St Mary's RC Jun Sch
Barrow Hedges Prim Sch
Stanley Park Jun & Inf Schs
War Memorial
Manor Park
Superstore
WRYTHE LA
CARSHALTON RD
NIGHTINGALE RD
WEST ST
NORTH ST
POUND ST
PARK HILL
THE BEECHES AVE
WOODMANSTERNE RD
BRIGHTON RD
ANGEL HILL
THROWLEY WAY
A232
B278
B2230
B277
B271
217
VIII
26
27
28

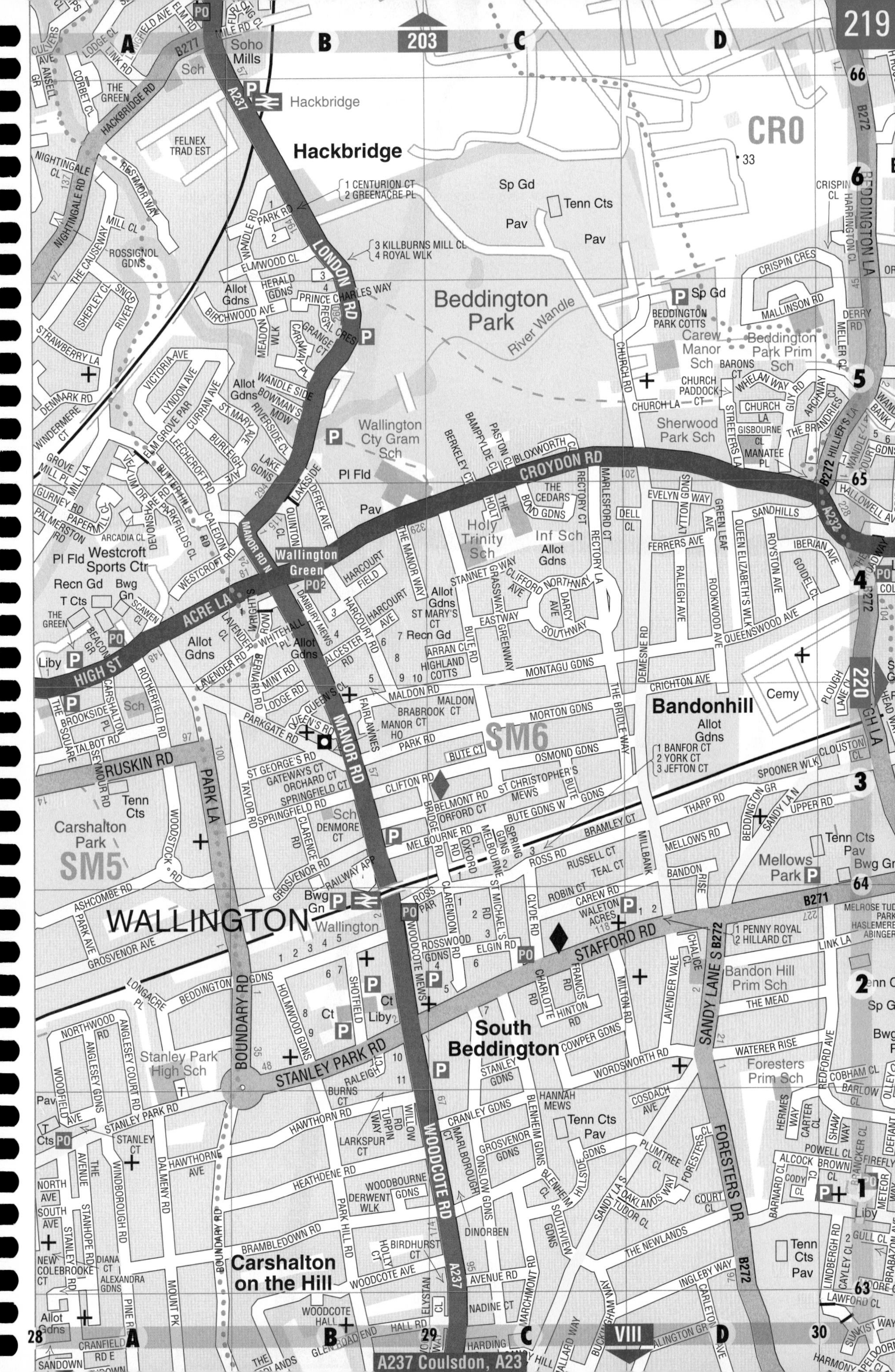

Hackbridge
Beddington Park
River Wandle
Wallington Cty Gram Sch
Holy Trinity Sch
Wallington Green
Westcroft Sports Ctr
Carshalton Park
SM5
SM6
CR0
WALLINGTON
Wallington
Bandonhill
South Beddington
Carshalton on the Hill
Stanley Park High Sch
Bandon Hill Prim Sch
Foresters Prim Sch
Mellows Park
Carew Manor Sch
Beddington Park Prim Sch
Sherwood Park Sch
Soho Mills
FELNEX TRAD EST
LONDON RD
MANOR RD
CROYDON RD
STAFFORD RD
WOODCOTE RD
STANLEY PARK RD
HIGH ST
ACRE LA
RUSKIN RD
PARK LA
BOUNDARY RD
SANDY LANE S
FORESTERS DR
BEDDINGTON LA
HACKBRIDGE RD
NIGHTINGALE RD
203
220
A237 Coulsdon, A23
VIII

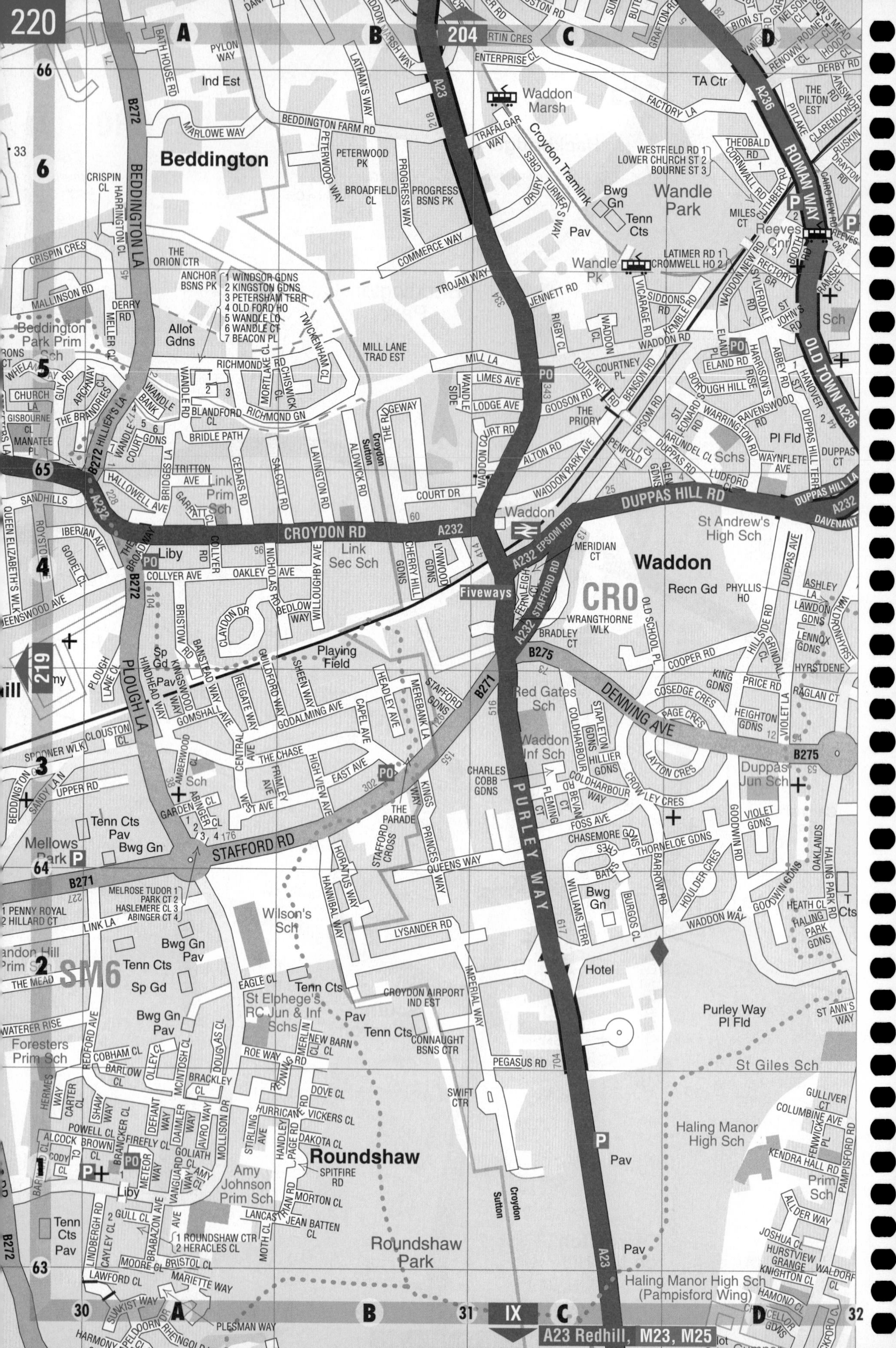

Beddington
Waddon
Roundshaw
Wandle Park
CR0
SM6
DUPPAS HILL RD
CROYDON RD
PURLEY WAY
STAFFORD RD
DENNING AVE
ROMAN WAY
BEDDINGTON LA
PLOUGH LA
204
219
IX
A23 Redhill, M23, M25

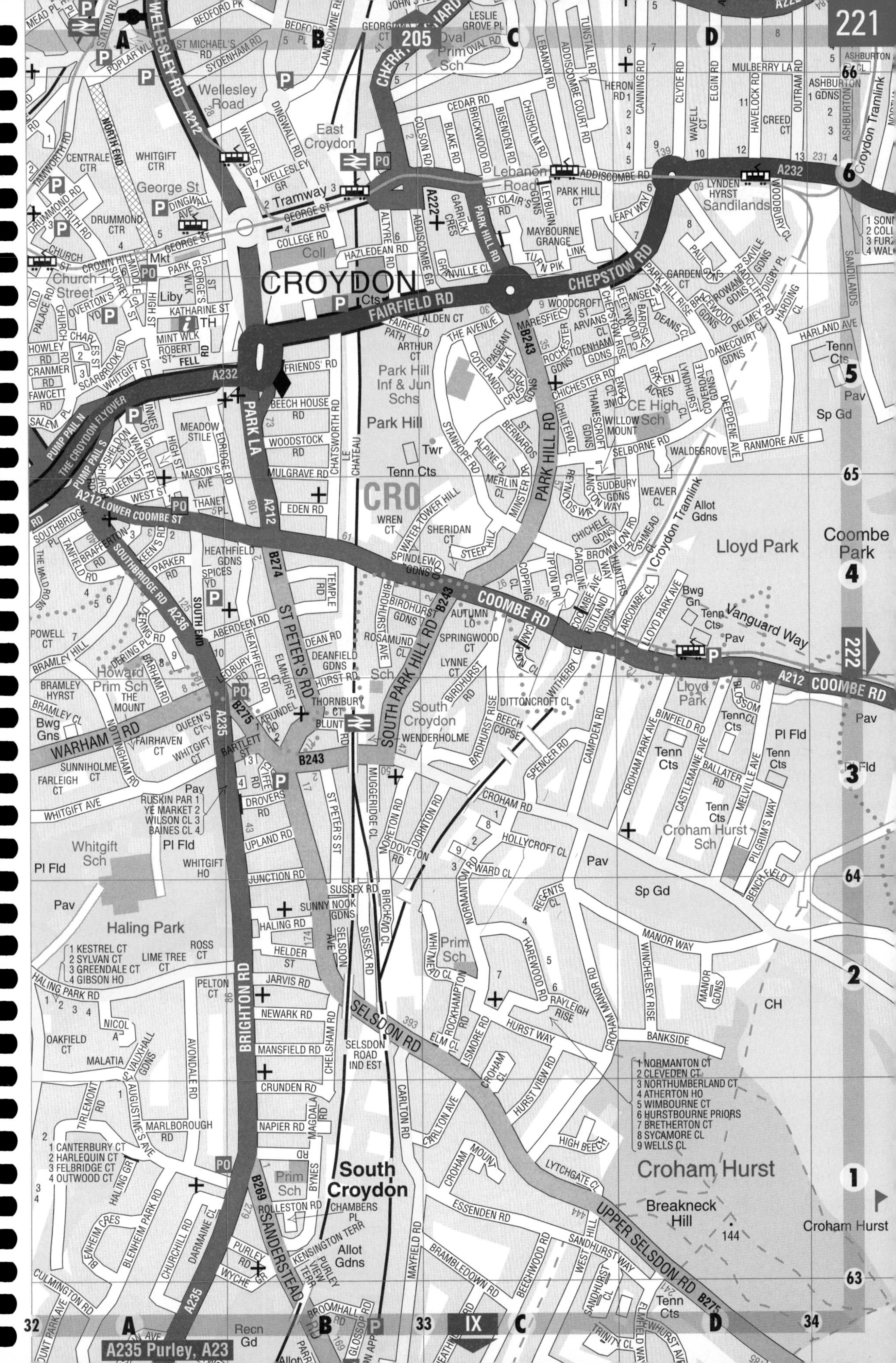

CROYDON
South Croydon
East Croydon
Wellesley Road
George St
Church Street
Lebanon Road
Sandilands
Lloyd Park
Coombe Park
Croham Hurst
Breakneck Hill
Park Hill
Haling Park
Whitgift Sch
Howard Prim Sch
Park Hill Inf & Jun Schs
CE High Sch
Croham Hurst Sch
Oval Prim Sch
CENTRALE CTR
WHITGIFT CTR
DRUMMOND CTR
Croydon Tramlink
Vanguard Way
WELLESLEY RD
ADDISCOMBE RD
FAIRFIELD RD
CHEPSTOW RD
PARK LA
PARK HILL RD
SOUTH PARK HILL RD
COOMBE RD
LOWER COOMBE ST
SOUTHBRIDGE RD
ST PETER'S RD
BRIGHTON RD
SELSDON RD
UPPER SELSDON RD
SANDERSTEAD RD
WARHAM RD
CROHAM RD
CROHAM MANOR RD
CROHAM PARK AVE
MANOR WAY
PARK HILL RISE
THE CROYDON FLYOVER
A232
A212
A222
A235
A236
B243
B274
B275
B269
A235 Purley, A23
1 NORMANTON CT
2 CLEVEDEN CT
3 NORTHUMBERLAND CT
4 ATHERTON HO
5 WIMBOURNE CT
6 HURSTBOURNE PRIORS
7 BRETHERTON CT
8 SYCAMORE CL
9 WELLS CL
1 KESTREL CT
2 SYLVAN CT
3 GREENDALE CT
4 GIBSON HO
1 CANTERBURY CT
2 HARLEQUIN CT
3 FELBRIDGE CT
4 OUTWOOD CT
RUSKIN PAR 1
YE MARKET 2
WILSON CL 3
BAINES CL 4
205
222
IX
A
B
C
D
32
33
34
63
64
65
66

A
B
C
D
206
A215
Addiscombe Rd
Shirley Rd
Wickham Rd
A232
Croydon Tramlink
Recn Gd
Tenn Cts
CH
Trinity Sch
Pl Fld
Pav
Shirley Park
Oaks Farm
Bwg Gn
Windmill (dis)
Coloma Convent Girls' Sch
Shirley High Sch
CE Prim Sch
Upper Shirley
Coombe Park
Coombe Farm
Lloyd Park
Vanguard Way
Addington Hills
CR0
Oaks Rd
Coombe Rd
A212
Hotel
Coombe Lane
Coombe La
Royal Russell Sch
Sp Gd
Heathfield
Bramley Bank
Nat Res
London Loop
Croham Hurst
Littleheath Woods
CR2
Selsdon High Sch
Sp Ctr
Ballards Way
Ballards Farm Rd
Croham Valley Rd
Shirley Hills Rd
Sunken Rd
Gravel Hill
Broadcoombe
Edgecoombe
221
IX
34
35
36
63
64
65
66

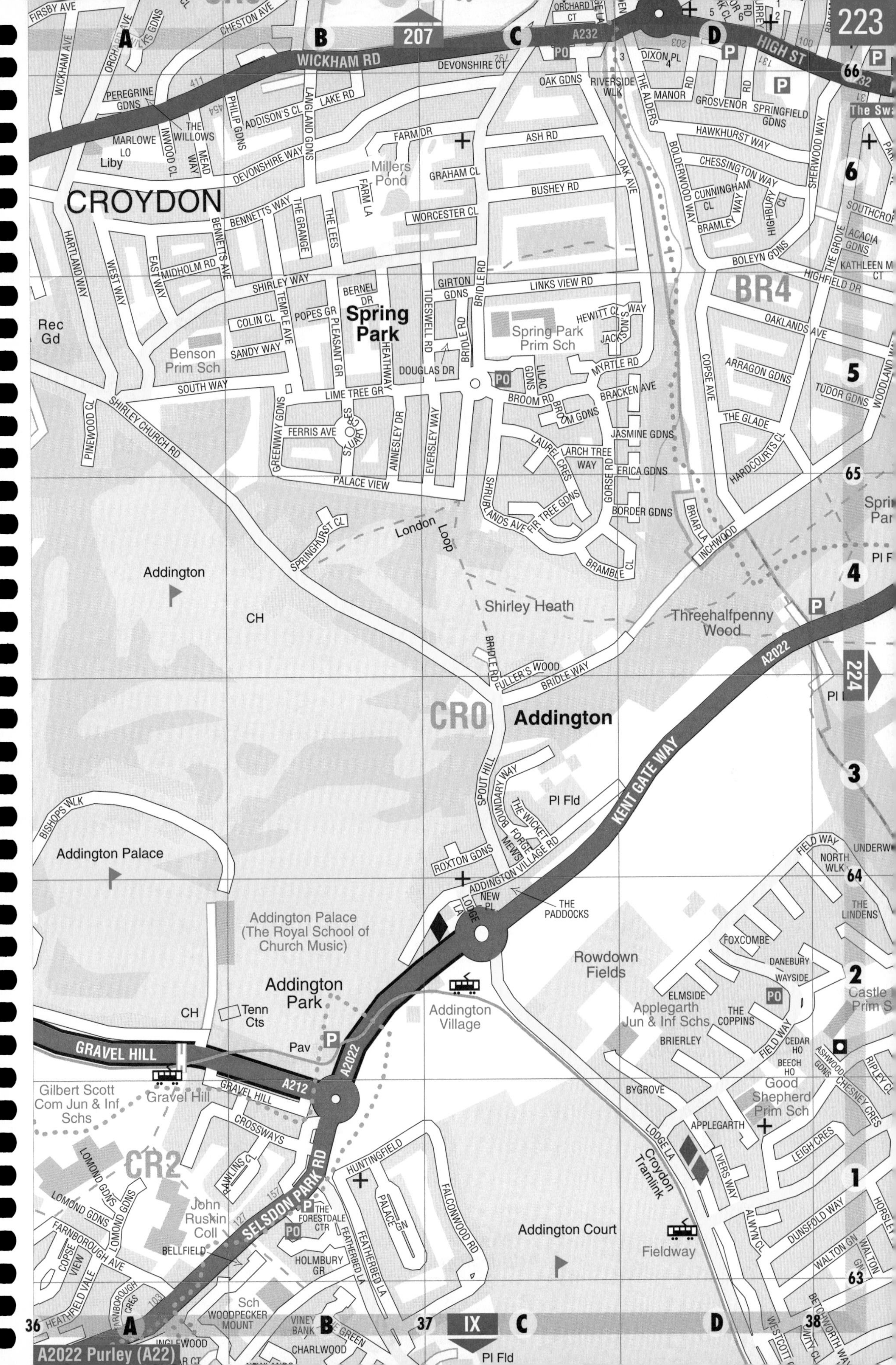
A
B
C
D
207
A232
HIGH ST
FIRSBY AVE
CHESTON AVE
ORCHARD AVE
WILKS GDNS
ORCHARD CT
WICKHAM RD
WICKHAM AVE
PEREGRINE GDNS
DEVONSHIRE CT
OAK GDNS
RIVERSIDE WLK
DIXON PL
THE ALDERS
MANOR RD
GROSVENOR RD
SPRINGFIELD GDNS
HAWKHURST WAY
CHESSINGTON WAY
BOLDERWOOD WAY
CUNNINGHAM CL
BRAMLEY WAY
HIGHBURY CL
SHERWOOD WAY
BOLEYN GDNS
THE GROVE
ACACIA GDNS
KATHLEEN M CT
HIGHFIELD DR
SOUTHCROFT
The Swa
LAKE RD
LANGLAND GDNS
ADDISON'S CL
PHILIP GDNS
THE WILLOWS
MARLOWE LO
INWOOD CL
MEAD WAY
Liby
DEVONSHIRE WAY
FARM DR
Millers Pond
FARM LA
GRAHAM CL
ASH RD
BUSHEY RD
WORCESTER CL
OAK AVE
CROYDON
BENNETTS WAY
BENNETTS AVE
THE GRANGE
THE LEES
HARTLAND WAY
WEST WAY
EAST WAY
MIDHOLM RD
SHIRLEY WAY
TEMPLE AVE
BERNEL DR
GIRTON GDNS
BRIDLE RD
LINKS VIEW RD
BR4
OAKLANDS AVE
Rec Gd
COLIN CL
POPES GR
Spring Park
HEWITT CL
JACKSON'S WAY
Spring Park Prim Sch
Benson Prim Sch
SANDY WAY
PLEASANT GR
HEATHWAY
TIDESWELL RD
DOUGLAS DR
MYRTLE RD
COPSE AVE
ARRAGON GDNS
TUDOR GDNS
WOODLAND WAY
SOUTH WAY
LIME TREE GR
PO
LILAC GDNS
BROOM RD
BROOM GDNS
BRACKEN AVE
THE GLADE
HARDCOURTS CL
PINEWOOD CL
SHIRLEY CHURCH RD
GREENWAY GDNS
FERRIS AVE
ST JAMES
ANNESLEY DR
EVERSLEY WAY
LAUREL CRES
LARCH TREE WAY
JASMINE GDNS
GORSE RD
ERICA GDNS
PALACE VIEW
SHRUBLANDS AVE
FIR TREE GDNS
BORDER GDNS
BRIAR LA
INCHWOOD
SPRINGHURST CL
London Loop
BRAMBLE CL
Addington
CH
Shirley Heath
Threehalfpenny Wood
A2022
224
FULLER'S WOOD
BRIDLE WAY
CR0
Addington
KENT GATE WAY
SPOUT HILL
BOUNDARY WAY
THE WICKET
Pl Fld
BISHOPS WLK
Addington Palace
ROXTON GDNS
FORGE MEWS
ADDINGTON VILLAGE RD
NEW PL
LODGE LA
THE PADDOCKS
FIELD WAY
NORTH WLK
UNDERWOOD
THE LINDENS
Addington Palace (The Royal School of Church Music)
Rowdown Fields
FOXCOMBE
DANEBURY
WAYSIDE
ELMSIDE
Addington Park
Addington Village
Applegarth Jun & Inf Schs
THE COPPINS
Castle Prim S
CH
Tenn Cts
GRAVEL HILL
Pav
BRIERLEY
CEDAR HO
BEECH HO
ASHWOOD GDNS
CHESNEY CRES
RIPLEY CL
A212
BYGROVE
Good Shepherd Prim Sch
Gilbert Scott Com Jun & Inf Schs
Gravel Hill
CROSSWAYS
APPLEGARTH
LEIGH CRES
CR2
LOMOND GDNS
RAWLINS CL
HUNTINGFIELD
LODGE LA
Croydon Tramlink
IVERS WAY
SELSDON PARK RD
PALACE GN
FALCONWOOD RD
John Ruskin Coll
THE FORESTDALE CTR
ALWYN CL
DUNSFOLD WAY
HORSLEY
FARNBOROUGH AVE
BELLFIELD
FEATHERBED LA
Addington Court
Fieldway
WALTON GN
COPSE VIEW
HOLMBURY GR
HEATHFIELD VALE
FARNBOROUGH CRES
Sch
WOODPECKER MOUNT
VINEY BANK
THE GREEN
WESTCOTT
BETCHWORTH WAY
TRINITY CL
36
37
38
IX
A2022 Purley (A22)
INGLEWOOD
CHARLWOOD
Pl Fld
6
5
4
3
2
1
66
65
64
63

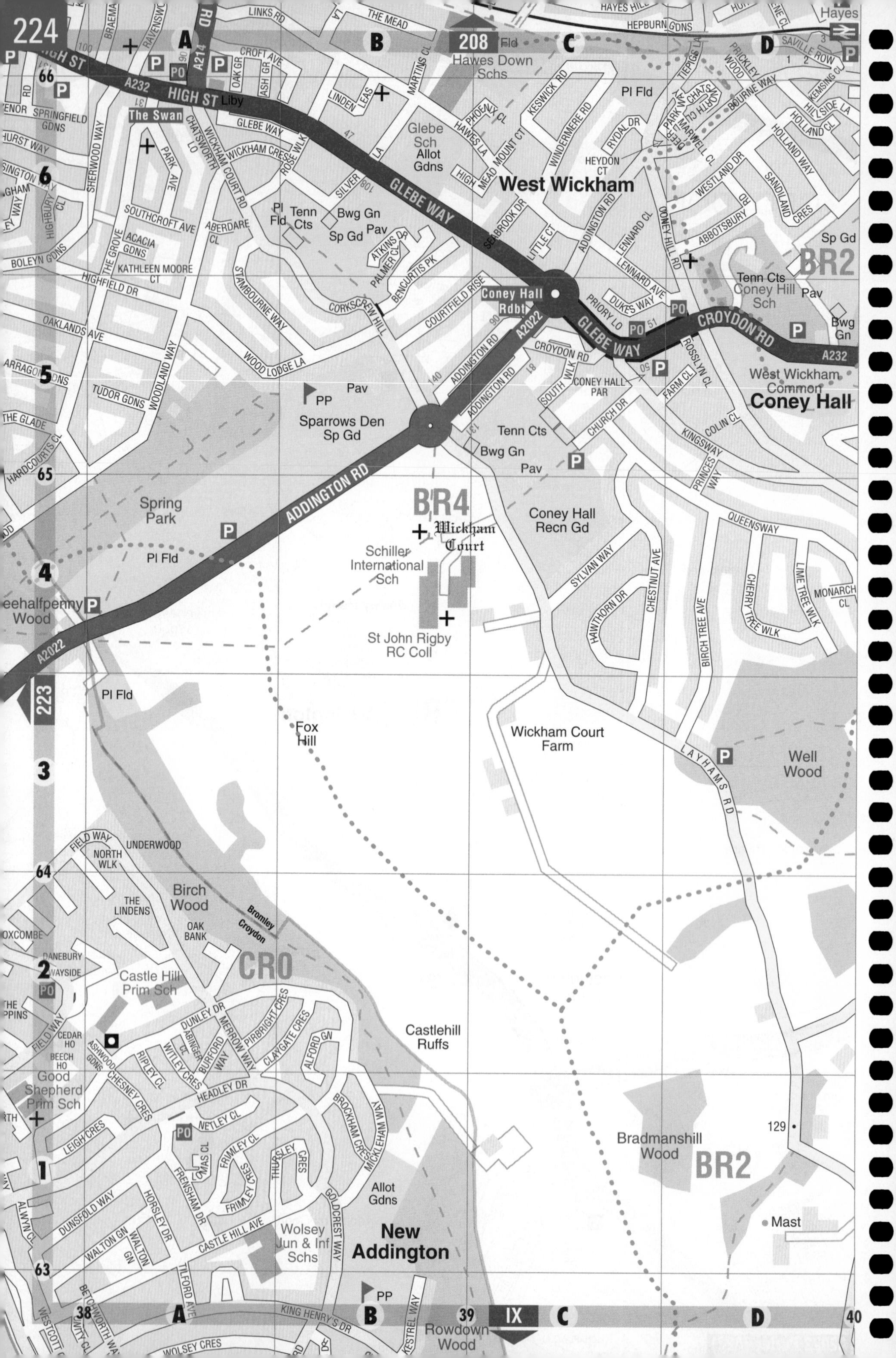
West Wickham
Coney Hall
New Addington
BR4
BR2
CR0
HIGH ST
GLEBE WAY
CROYDON RD
ADDINGTON RD
A232
A2022
A214
Coney Hall Rdbt
Sparrows Den Sp Gd
Spring Park
Coney Hall Recn Gd
Wickham Court
Schiller International Sch
St John Rigby RC Coll
Fox Hill
Wickham Court Farm
Well Wood
Birch Wood
Castle Hill Prim Sch
Castlehill Ruffs
Bradmanshill Wood
Good Shepherd Prim Sch
Wolsey Jun & Inf Schs
Rowdown Wood
Glebe Sch
Hawes Down Schs
Coney Hill Sch
West Wickham Common
LAYHAMS RD
KING HENRY'S DR
Hayes
208
223
IX

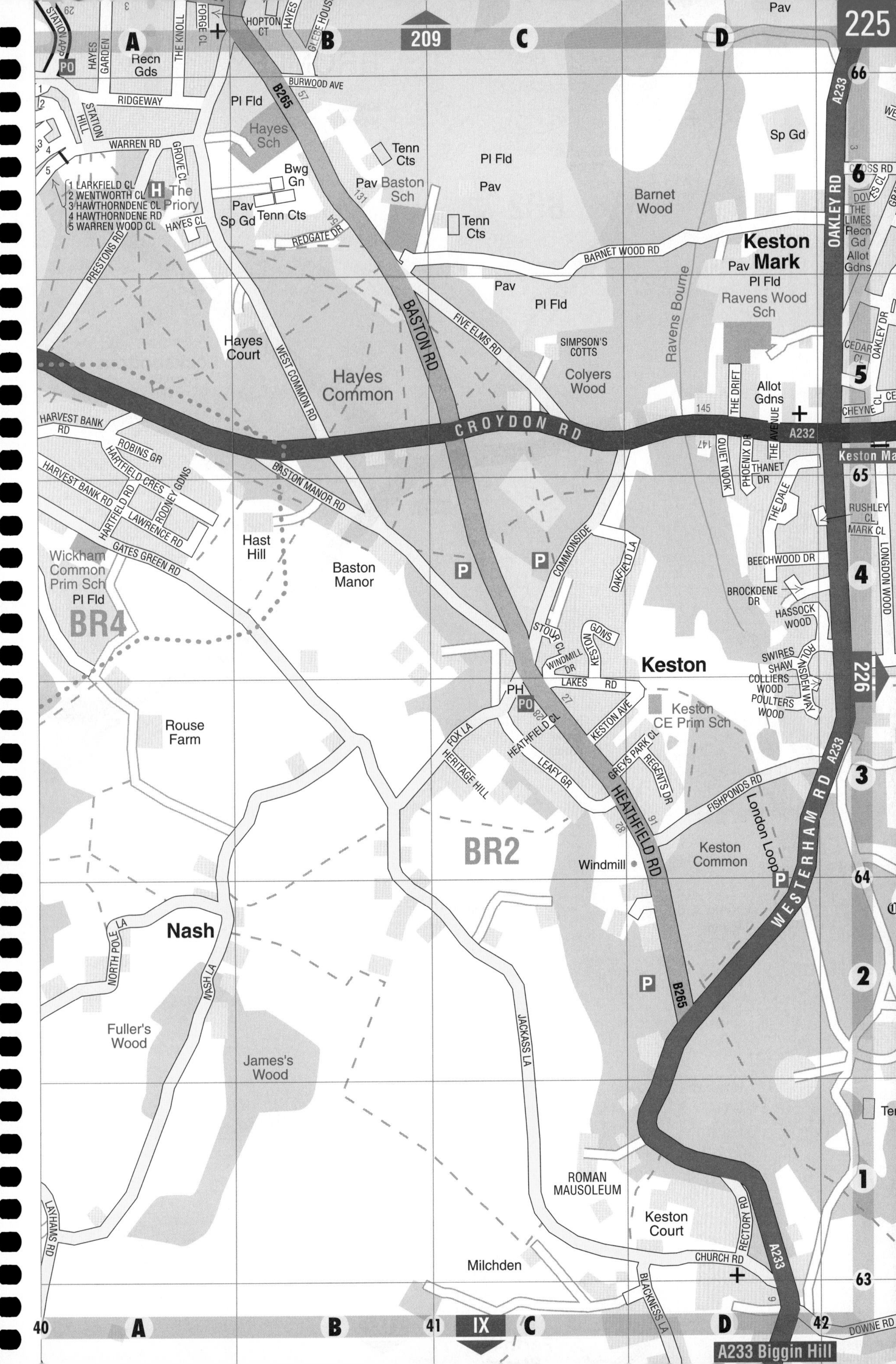

A B **209** C D

66

6

Keston Mark

Barnet Wood

Ravens Wood Sch

5

Keston Ma

65

4

226

3

64

2

1

63

Pav

OAKLEY RD A233

CROSS RD

THE LIMES Recn Gd Allot Gdns

CEDAR CL

OAKLEY DR

CHEYNE CL

Sp Gd

Pav

Pl Fld

Allot Gdns

THE DRIFT

PHOENIX DR

THANET DR

QUIET NOOK

THE DALE

The AVENUE A232

RUSHLEY CL

MARK CL

BEECHWOOD DR

BROCKDENE DR

HASSOCK WOOD

SWIRES SHAW

COLLIERS WOOD

POULTERS WOOD

RANSDEN WAY

LONGDON WOOD

WESTERHAM RD A233

STATION APP 29

The KNOLL

FORGE CL 3

HOPTON CT

HAYES

GLEBE HOUSE

BURWOOD AVE

B265

HAYES GARDEN

Recn Gds

RIDGEWAY

PO

STATION HILL

WARREN RD

1 LARKFIELD CL
2 WENTWORTH CL
3 HAWTHORNDENE CL
4 HAWTHORNDENE RD
5 WARREN WOOD CL

GROVE CL

Pl Fld

Hayes Sch

H The Priory

HAYES CL

Tenn Cts

Bwg Gn

Pav Sp Gd

Tenn Cts

Pav Baston Sch

REDGATE DR

BASTON RD 131

FIVE ELMS RD

Pl Fld

Pav

Pl Fld

SIMPSON'S COTTS

Colyers Wood

Ravens Bourne

145

147

Hayes Court

WEST COMMON RD

Hayes Common

HARVEST BANK RD

ROBINS GR

HARTFIELD RD

HARTFIELD CRES

RODNEY GDNS

LAWRENCE RD

GATES GREEN RD

PRESTONS RD

Wickham Common Prim Sch

Pl Fld

BR4

Hast Hill

Baston Manor RD

Baston Manor

P

P

COMMONSIDE

OAKFIELD LA

STOUR CL

WINDMILL DR

KESTON GDNS

KESTON LAKES RD 27

Keston

Keston CE Prim Sch

Rouse Farm

PH

PO 382

FOX LA

HERITAGE HILL

HEATHFIELD CL

LEAFY GR

HEATHFIELD RD

KESTON AVE

GREYS PARK CL

REGENT'S DR 28

FISHPONDS RD

London Loop

Keston Common

BR2

Windmill

P 91

Nash

NORTH POLE LA

NASH LA

Fuller's Wood

James's Wood

JACKASS LA

P B265

ROMAN MAUSOLEUM

Keston Court

RECTORY RD

CHURCH RD

A233

LAYHAMS RD

Milchden

BLACKNESS LA

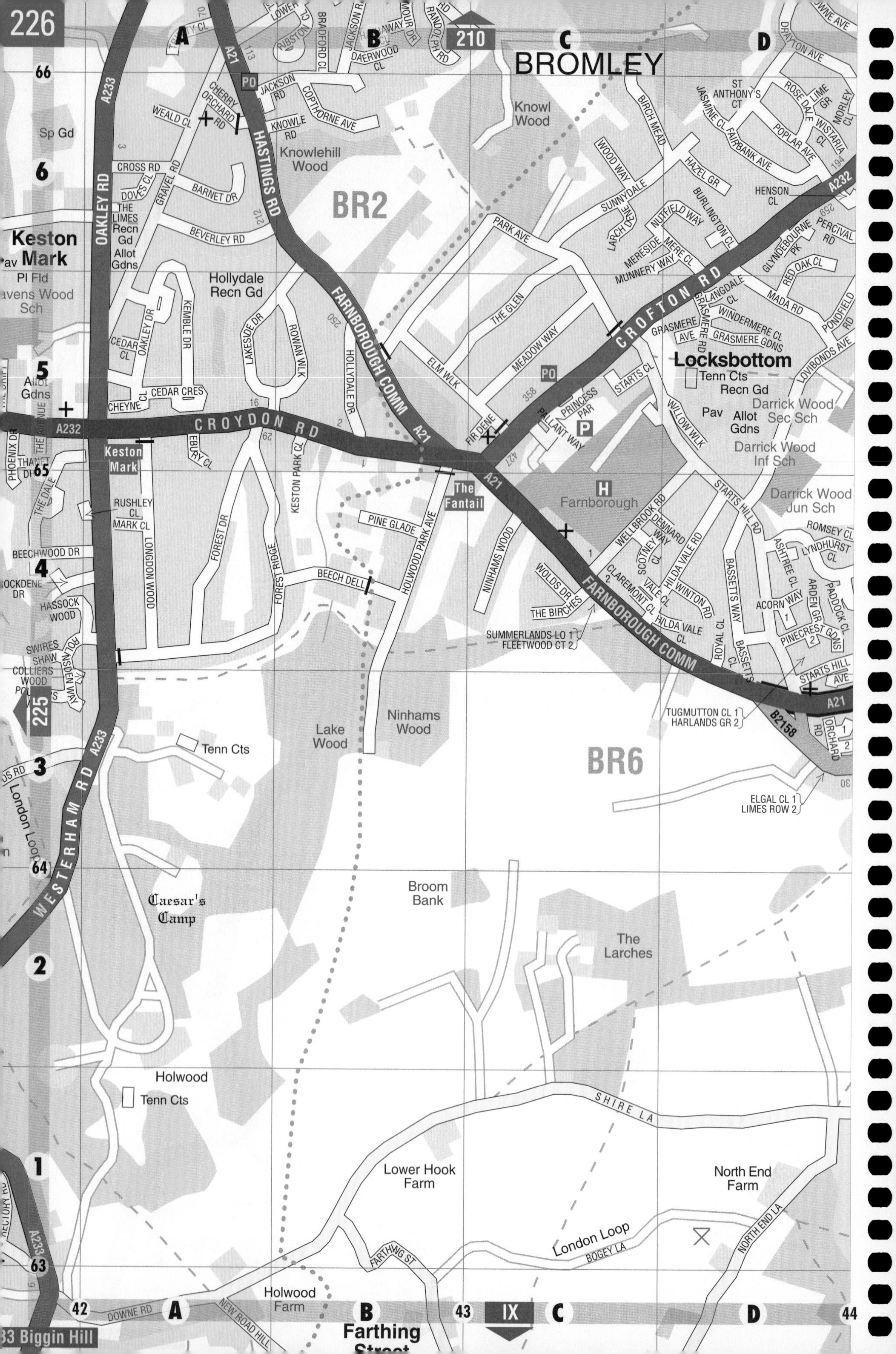
BROMLEY
210
A
B
C
D
66
6
5
65
4
3
64
2
1
63
225
Keston Mark
Locksbottom
BR2
BR6
OAKLEY RD
WESTERHAM RD
A233
A21
A232
A2158
HASTINGS RD
FARNBOROUGH COMM
CROYDON RD
CROFTON RD
Knowl Wood
Knowlehill Wood
Hollydale Recn Gd
Sp Gd
THE LIMES Recn Gd
Allot Gdns
Pl Fld
Ravens Wood Sch
Tenn Cts
Recn Gd
Pav
Darrick Wood Sec Sch
Darrick Wood Inf Sch
Darrick Wood Jun Sch
Farnborough
The Fantail
Lake Wood
Ninhams Wood
Broom Bank
Caesar's Camp
The Larches
Holwood
Lower Hook Farm
North End Farm
Holwood Farm
London Loop
SHIRE LA
BOGEY LA
NORTH END LA
FARTHING ST
DOWNE RD
NEW ROAD HILL
PARK AVE
THE GLEN
MEADOW WAY
ELM WLK
FIR DENE
PALLANT WAY
PRINCESS PAR
STARTS CL
STARTS HILL RD
WILLOW WLK
WELLBROOK RD
DENNARD WAY
SCOTNEY CL
HILDA VALE RD
WINTON RD
CLAREMONT CL
VALE CL
HILDA VALE CL
WOLDS DR
THE BIRCHES
SUMMERLANDS LO 1
FLEETWOOD CT 2
TUGMUTTON CL 1
HARLANDS GR 2
ELGAL CL 1
LIMES ROW 2
NINHAMS WOOD
PINE GLADE
HOLWOOD PARK AVE
BEECH DELL
FOREST RIDGE
FOREST DR
KESTON PARK CL
HOLLYDALE DR
ROWAN WLK
LAKESIDE DR
LONGDON WOOD
EBURY CL
CEDAR CRES
CEDAR CL
CHEYNE CL
OAKLEY DR
KEMBLE DR
BEVERLEY RD
BARNET DR
GRAVEL RD
CROSS RD
DOVES CL
WEALD CL
CHERRY ORCHARD RD
JACKSON RD
KNOWLE RD
COPTHORNE AVE
DAERWOOD CL
BRADFORD CL
RIBSTON CL
TRINITY CL
RANDOLPH RD
DRAYTON AVE
BIRCH MEAD
WOOD WAY
SUNNYDALE
LARCH DENE
HAZEL GR
BURLINGTON CL
NUTFIELD WAY
MERESIDE
MERE CL
MUNNERY WAY
ST ANTHONY'S CT
JASMINE CL
ROSE DALE
LIME GR
FAIRBANK AVE
POPLAR AVE
WISTARIA CL
MORLEY CL
HENSON CL
GLYNDEBOURNE PK
PERCIVAL RD
RED OAK CL
MADA RD
PONDFIELD RD
LANGDALE CL
WINDERMERE CL
GRASMERE AVE
GRASMERE RD
GRASMERE GDNS
LOVIBONDS AVE
ROMSEY CL
LYNDHURST CL
ASHTREE CL
ARDEN GR
PADDOCK CL
ACORN WAY
PINECREST GDNS
BASSETTS WAY
BASSETTS CL
ROYAL CL
STARTS HILL AVE
ORCHARD RD
PHOENIX DR
THANET DR
THE DALE
THE AVENUE
RUSHLEY CL
MARK CL
BEECHWOOD DR
HASSOCK WOOD
ROLINSDEN WAY
SWIRES SHAW
COLLIERS WOOD
London Loop
RECTORY RD

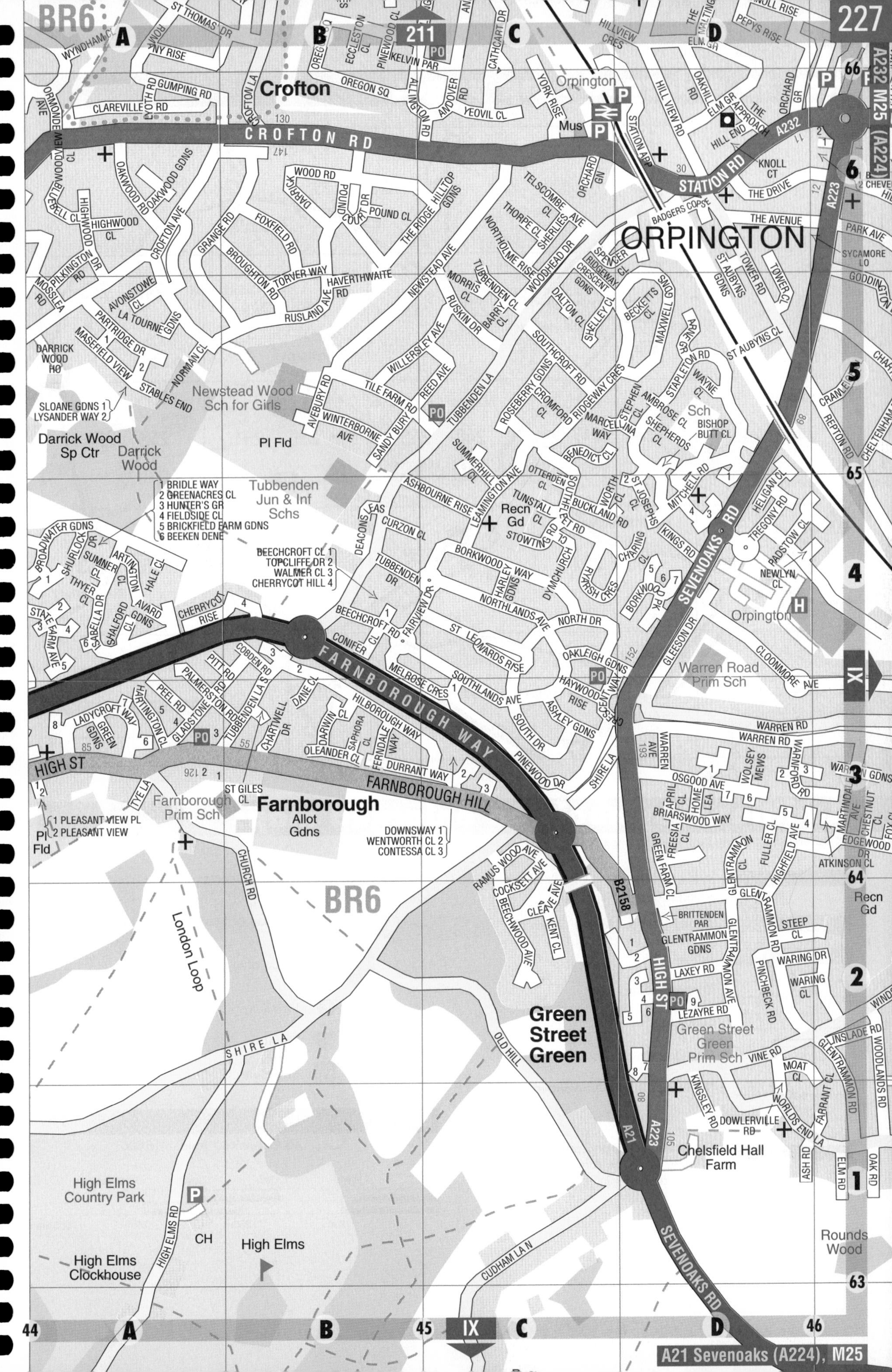
BR6
A
B
211
C
D
227
A232 M25 (A224)
Crofton
CROFTON RD
ST THOMAS DR
WYNDHAM CL
NY RISE
ORMONDE AVE
GUMPING RD
CLAREVILLE RD
LYOTH RD
CROFTON LA
ECCLESTON CL
PINEWOOD CL
KELVIN PAR
OREGON SQ
ALLINGTON RD
ANDOVER RD
YEOVIL CL
CATHCART DR
HILLVIEW CRES
THE MALTINGS
ELM GR
KNOLL RISE
PEPYS RISE
Orpington
YORK RISE
Mus
STATION APP
HILL VIEW RD
OAKHILL RD
ORCHARD GR
THE APPROACH
HILL END
A232
STATION RD
KNOLL CT
THE DRIVE
ORCHARD GN
BADGERS COPSE
THE AVENUE
ORPINGTON
PARK AVE
SYCAMORE LO
GODDINGTON LA
A223
CHEVENING RD
WOODVIEW CL
BLUEBELL CL
OAKWOOD RD
OAKWOOD GDNS
HIGHWOOD DR
HIGHWOOD CL
CROFTON AVE
GRANGE RD
FOXFIELD RD
BROUGHTON RD
WOOD RD
DARRICK CL
POUND COURT DR
POUND CL
THE RIDGE
HILLTOP GDNS
TORVER WAY
HAVERTHWAITE RD
RUSLAND AVE
TELSCOMBE CL
THORPE CL
SHERLIES AVE
NORTHOLME RISE
WOODHEAD DR
NEWSTEAD AVE
MORRIS CL
TUBBENDEN CL
BARRY CL
RUSKIN DR
SPENCER CL
RIDGEWAY CRESCENT GDNS
DALTON CL
SHELLEY CL
BECKETTS CL
MAXWELL GDNS
ST AUBYNS GDNS
TOWER RD
TOWER CL
ST AUBYNS CL
PILKINGTON RD
MOSSLEA RD
AVONSTOWE CL
LA TOURNE GDNS
PARTRIDGE DR
MASEFIELD VIEW
NORMAN CL
STABLES END
DARRICK WOOD HO
SLOANE GDNS 1
LYSANDER WAY 2
Newstead Wood Sch for Girls
AVEBURY RD
WILLERSLEY AVE
TILE FARM RD
REED AVE
WINTERBORNE AVE
SANDY BURY
TUBBENDEN LA
SOUTHCROFT RD
ROSEBERRY GDNS
CROMFORD CL
RIDGEWAY CRES
MARCELLINA WAY
STEPHEN CL
AMBROSE CL
SHEPHERDS CL
STAPLETON RD
WAYNE CL
Sch
BISHOP BUTT CL
CRANLEIGH
REPTON RD
CHELTENHAM
Darrick Wood Sp Ctr
Darrick Wood
Pl Fld
Tubbenden Jun & Inf Schs
SUMMERHILL CL
ASHBOURNE RISE
LEAMINGTON AVE
OTTERDEN CL
BENEDICT CL
ST JOSEPHS CL
WORTH CL
MITCHELL RD
HELIGAN CL
TREGONY RD
PADSTOW CL
Recn Gd
TUNSTALL CL
BUCKLAND RD
SOUTHFLEET RD
STOWTING RD
KINGS RD
SEVENOAKS RD
1 BRIDLE WAY
2 GREENACRES CL
3 HUNTER'S GR
4 FIELDSIDE CL
5 BRICKFIELD FARM GDNS
6 BEEKEN DENE
DEACONS LEAS
CURZON CL
BORKWOOD WAY
HARLEY GDNS
DYMCHURCH CL
RYARSH CRES
CHARING CL
BORKWOOD PK
NEWLYN CL
BROADWATER GDNS
SHURLOCK DR
SUMNER CL
ARTINGTON CL
HALE CL
THYER CL
BEECHCROFT CL 1
TOPCLIFFE DR 2
WALMER CL 3
CHERRYCOT HILL 4
TUBBENDEN DR
FAIRVIEW DR
NORTHLANDS AVE
NORTH DR
Orpington
STATE FARM AVE
SABELLA DR
SHALFORD CL
AVARD GDNS
CHERRYCOT RISE
BEECHCROFT RD
CONIFER
ST LEONARDS RISE
OAKLEIGH GDNS
GLEESON DR
CLOONMORE AVE
Warren Road Prim Sch
IX
FARNBOROUGH WAY
COBDEN RD
PITT RD
MELROSE CRES
SOUTHLANDS AVE
HAYWOOD RISE
CRESCENT WAY
LADYCROFT WAY
HARTINGTON RD
PEEL RD
PALMERSTON RD
TUBBENDEN LA S
CHARTWELL DR
DANE CL
DARWIN CL
SAPHORA CL
HILBOROUGH WAY
FERNDALE WAY
SOUTH DR
ASHLEY GDNS
WARREN RD
WARREN AVE
GREEN GDNS
GLADSTONE RD
OLEANDER CL
DURRANT WAY
PINEWOOD DR
SHIRE LA
WOLSEY MEWS
WARNFORD RD
WARREN GDNS
HIGH ST
FARNBOROUGH HILL
ST GILES CL
OSGOOD AVE
HOME LEA
APRIL CL
BRIARSWOOD WAY
FULLER CL
HIGHFIELD AVE
MARTINDALE AVE
CHESTNUT CL
FOX CL
EDGEWOOD
TYE LA
Farnborough Prim Sch
Farnborough
Allot Gdns
DOWNSWAY 1
WENTWORTH CL 2
CONTESSA CL 3
1 PLEASANT VIEW PL
2 PLEASANT VIEW
Pl Fld
RAMUS WOOD AVE
COCKSETT AVE
FREESIA CL
GREEN FARM CL
GLENTRAMMON CL
ATKINSON CL
CHURCH RD
BR6
BEECHWOOD AVE
CLEAVE AVE
KENT CL
B2158
BRITTENDEN PAR
GLENTRAMMON RD
Recn Gd
STEEP CL
GLENTRAMMON GDNS
PINCHBECK RD
WARING DR
WARING CL
London Loop
LAXEY RD
GLENTRAMMON AVE
LEZAYRE RD
Green Street Green
Green Street Green Prim Sch
SHIRE LA
OLD HILL
VINE RD
KINGSLEY RD
MOAT CL
GLENTRAMMON RD
GLUNSLADE RD
WOODLANDS RD
FARRANT CL
WORLDS END LA
DOWLERVILLE RD
A21
A223
Chelsfield Hall Farm
ASH RD
ELM RD
OAK RD
High Elms Country Park
HIGH ELMS RD
CH
High Elms
High Elms Clockhouse
CUDHAM LA N
SEVENOAKS RD
Rounds Wood
44
45
46
A21 Sevenoaks (A224), M25

Key to enlarged map pages

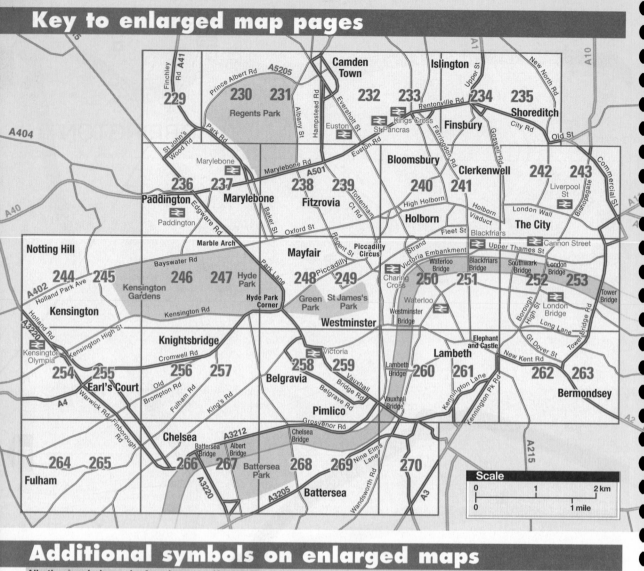

Scale
| 0 | | 1 | | 2 km |
| 0 | | | 1 mile | |

Additional symbols on enlarged maps

All other symbols can be found on page X

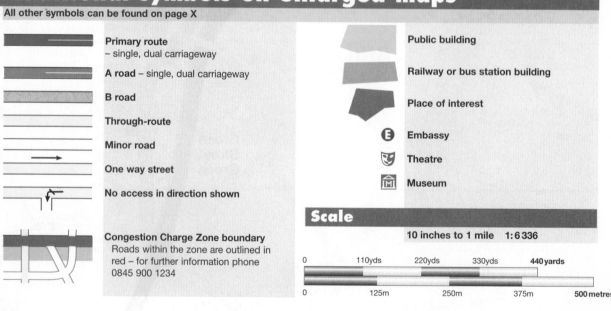

Primary route
– single, dual carriageway

A road – single, dual carriageway

B road

Through-route

Minor road

One way street

No access in direction shown

Congestion Charge Zone boundary
Roads within the zone are outlined in red – for further information phone 0845 900 1234

Public building

Railway or bus station building

Place of interest

E Embassy

Theatre

Museum

Scale

10 inches to 1 mile   1:6 336

| 0 | 110yds | 220yds | 330yds | 440 yards |
| 0 | 125m | 250m | 375m | 500 metres |

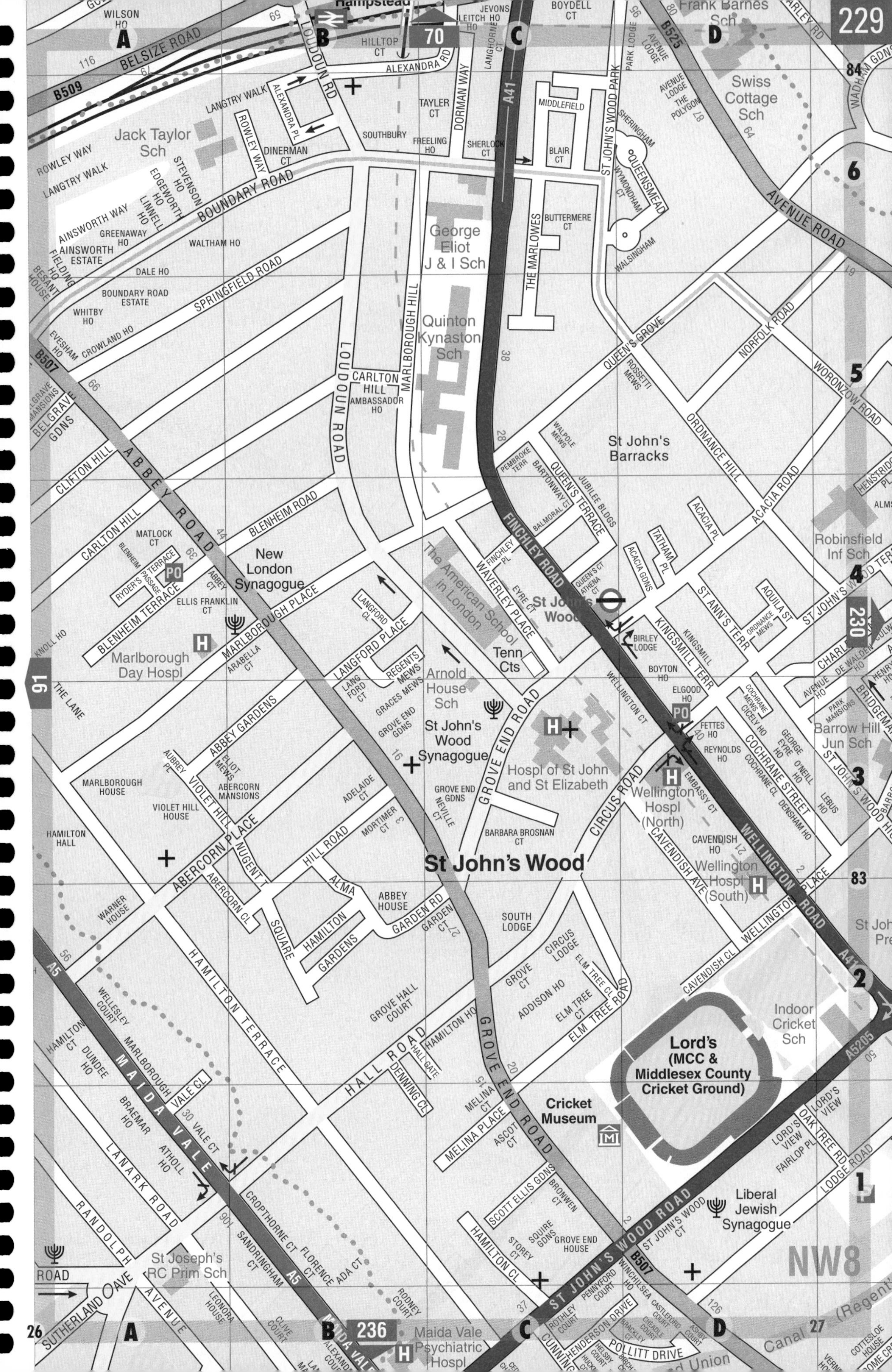
Hampstead
70
WILSON HO
BELSIZE ROAD
B509
LOUDOUN RD
HILLTOP CT
ALEXANDRA RD
JEVONS
LEITCH HO
LANGHORNE CT
BOYDELL CT
Frank Barnes Sch
B525
AVENUE LODGE
PARK LODGE
ST JOHN'S WOOD PARK
A41
LANGTRY WALK
ALEXANDRA PL
DORMAN WAY
TAYLER CT
MIDDLEFIELD
AVENUE LODGE
THE POLYGON
Swiss Cottage Sch
WADHAM GDNS
Jack Taylor Sch
ROWLEY WAY
DINERMAN CT
SOUTHBURY
FREELING HO
SHERLOCK CT
BLAIR CT
SHERINGHAM
QUEENSMEAD
WYMONDHAM CT
ROWLEY WAY
LANGTRY WALK
STEVENSON HO
EDGEWORTH HO
LINNELL HO
BOUNDARY ROAD
AINSWORTH WAY
GREENAWAY HO
AINSWORTH ESTATE
FIELDING HO
BESANT HOUSE
WALTHAM HO
DALE HO
BOUNDARY ROAD ESTATE
WHITBY HO
SPRINGFIELD ROAD
EVESHAM HO
CROWLAND HO
THE MARLOWES
BUTTERMERE CT
WALSINGHAM
AVENUE ROAD
George Eliot J & I Sch
Quinton Kynaston Sch
MARLBOROUGH HILL
LOUDOUN ROAD
CARLTON HILL
AMBASSADOR HO
QUEEN'S GROVE
NORFOLK ROAD
ROSSETTI MEWS
WORONZOW ROAD
B507
BELGRAVE MANSIONS
BELGRAVE GDNS
CLIFTON HILL
ABBEY ROAD
St John's Barracks
WALPOLE MEWS
ORDNANCE HILL
PEMBROKE TERR
BARTONWAY CT
QUEEN'S TERRACE
JUBILEE BLDGS
BALMORAL CT
ACACIA ROAD
HENSTRIDGE PL
ALMS
BLENHEIM ROAD
CARLTON HILL
MATLOCK CT
BLENHEIM
RYDER'S TERRACE
PASSAGE
ABBEY CT
New London Synagogue
ELLIS FRANKLIN CT
BLENHEIM TERRACE
MARLBOROUGH PLACE
The American School in London
WAVERLEY PLACE
FINCHLEY PL
EYRE CT
FINCHLEY ROAD
QUEEN'S CT
ATHENA CT
St John's Wood
ACACIA GDNS
TATHAM PL
ACACIA PL
ST ANN'S TERR
ORDNANCE MEWS
AQUILA ST
ST JOHN'S WOOD TERR
Robinsfield Inf Sch
230
KNOLL HO
Marlborough Day Hospl
ARABELLA CT
LANGFORD CL
LANGFORD PLACE
REGENTS MEWS
LANGFORD CT
GRACES MEWS
Arnold House Sch
Tenn Cts
BIRLEY LODGE
KINGSMILL TERR
KINGSMILL
BOYTON HO
WELLINGTON CT
ELGOOD HO
CHARLBERT
DE WALDEN
HENRY
AVENUE HO
PARK MANSIONS
BRIDGEMAN
Barrow Hill Jun Sch
91
THE LANE
ABBEY GARDENS
GROVE END GDNS
St John's Wood Synagogue
GROVE END ROAD
Hospl of St John and St Elizabeth
FETTES HO
REYNOLDS HO
COCHRANE MEWS
CICELY HO
GEORGE EYRE HO
O'NEILL HO
COCHRANE STREET
COCHRANE CL
DENSHAM HO
LEBUS HO
ST JOHN'S WOOD HIGH
AUBREY PL
ELIOT MEWS
VIOLET HILL
MARLBOROUGH HOUSE
ABERCORN MANSIONS
VIOLET HILL HOUSE
ADELAIDE CT
GROVE END GDNS
NEVILLE CT
CIRCUS ROAD
Wellington Hospl (North)
EMBASSY CT
CAVENDISH AVE
HAMILTON HALL
MORTIMER CT
HILL ROAD
BARBARA BROSNAN CT
CAVENDISH HO
Wellington Hospl (South)
WELLINGTON ROAD
WELLINGTON PLACE
ABERCORN PLACE
NUGENT T
ALMA
St John's Wood
83
ABBEY HOUSE
GARDEN RD
GARDEN CT
WARNER HOUSE
ABERCORN CL
SQUARE
HAMILTON GARDENS
SOUTH LODGE
CIRCUS LODGE
WELLINGTON PL
CAVENDISH CL
St John's Pre
A5
HAMILTON TERRACE
GROVE CT
ELM TREE CL
ELM TREE ROAD
Indoor Cricket Sch
WELLESLEY COURT
GROVE HALL COURT
ADDISON HO
ELM TREE CT
A41
A5205
HAMILTON CT
DUNDEE HO
MARLBOROUGH
MAIDA VALE
HALL ROAD
HAMILTON HO
HALL GATE
DENNING CL
GROVE END ROAD
Lord's (MCC & Middlesex County Cricket Ground)
VALE CL
BRAEMAR HO
MELINA CT
MELINA PLACE
Cricket Museum
LORD'S VIEW
OAK TREE RD
FAIRLOP PL
VALE CT
ATHOLL HO
LANARK ROAD
ASCOT CT
SCOTT ELLIS GDNS
BRONWEN CT
LODGE ROAD
RANDOLPH
CROPTHORNE CT
SANDRINGHAM CT
FLORENCE CT
ADA CT
HAMILTON CL
STOREY CT
SQUIRE GDNS
GROVE END HOUSE
ST JOHN'S WOOD ROAD
ST JOHN'S WOOD CT
Liberal Jewish Synagogue
ROAD
St Joseph's RC Prim Sch
RODNEY COURT
PENNYFORD COURT
WINCHILSEA HO
B507
NW8
SUTHERLAND AVE
AVENUE
LEONORA HOUSE
CLIVE COURT
236
Maida Vale Psychiatric Hospl
ROTHLEY COURT
HENDERSON DRIVE
BRACKLEY CT
CASTLEFORD COURT
CHEADLE COURT
ASHBY COURT
POLLITT DRIVE
Canal (Regent's)
COTTESLOE HOUSE
Union
CUNNINGHAM

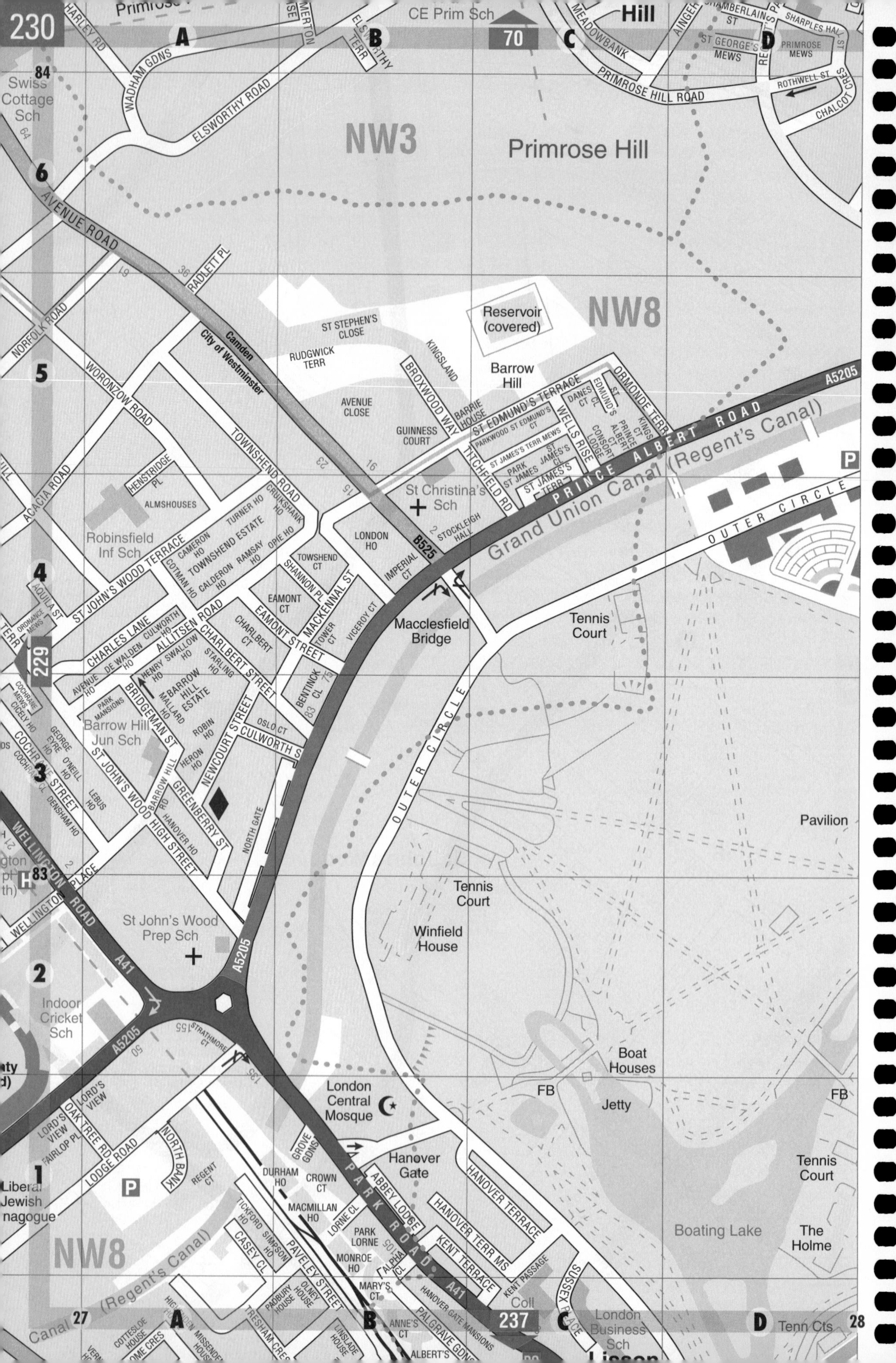
NW3
Primrose Hill
NW8
Reservoir (covered)
Barrow Hill
PRINCE ALBERT ROAD
Grand Union Canal (Regent's Canal)
OUTER CIRCLE
AVENUE ROAD
ELSWORTHY ROAD
PRIMROSE HILL ROAD
CE Prim Sch
Swiss Cottage Sch
St Christina's Sch
Robinsfield Inf Sch
Barrow Hill Jun Sch
St John's Wood Prep Sch
Macclesfield Bridge
Tennis Court
Winfield House
Pavilion
Boat Houses
Jetty
Boating Lake
The Holme
London Central Mosque
Hanover Gate
PARK ROAD
ST JOHN'S WOOD HIGH STREET
ST JOHN'S WOOD TERRACE
WELLINGTON ROAD
WELLINGTON PLACE
LODGE ROAD
Indoor Cricket Sch
Liberal Jewish Synagogue
London Business Sch
HANOVER TERRACE
KENT TERRACE
SUSSEX PLACE
TOWNSHEND ROAD
TOWNSHEND ESTATE
CHARLBERT STREET
ALLITSEN ROAD
NEWCOURT STREET
ACACIA ROAD
WORONZOW ROAD
NORFOLK ROAD
ST EDMUND'S TERRACE
Camden
City of Westminster
A5205
A41
B525

70
229
237

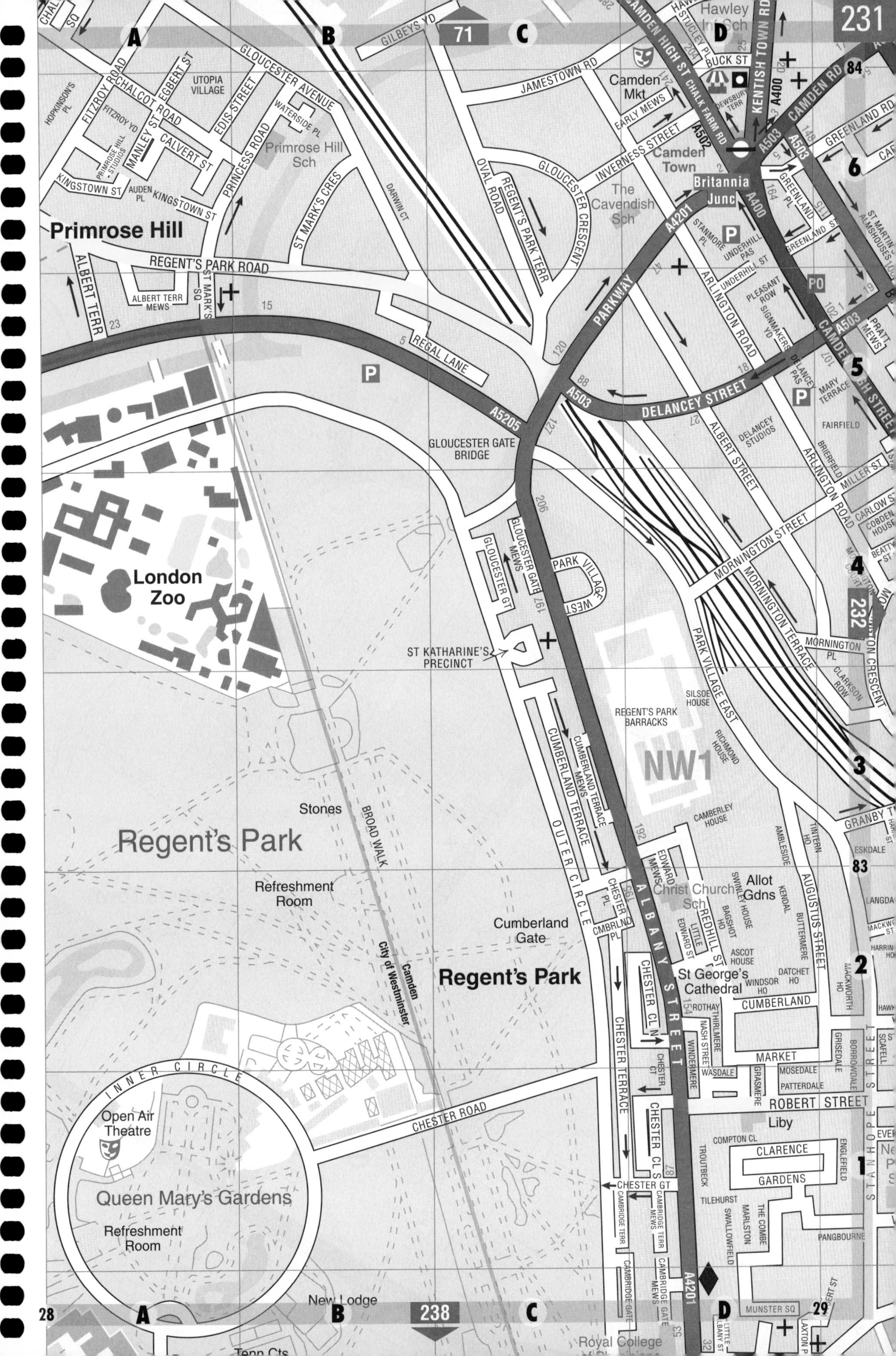
Primrose Hill
Regent's Park Road
Gloucester Avenue
Utopia Village
Primrose Hill Sch
Jamestown Rd
Camden Mkt
Camden High St
Chalk Farm Rd
Kentish Town Rd
Camden Rd
Camden Town
Britannia Junc
The Cavendish Sch
Parkway
Arlington Road
Albert Street
Delancey Street
Regal Lane
Oval Road
Regent's Park Terr
Gloucester Crescent
Inverness Street
Gloucester Gate Bridge
London Zoo
Park Village West
St Katharine's Precinct
Mornington Street
Mornington Terrace
Mornington Crescent
Park Village East
Regent's Park Barracks
NW1
Cumberland Terrace
Outer Circle
Stones
Broad Walk
Regent's Park
Refreshment Room
Cumberland Gate
Camden
City of Westminster
Christ Church Sch
Allot Gdns
Albany Street
Augustus Street
St George's Cathedral
Cumberland Market
Robert Street
Liby
Clarence Gardens
Chester Terrace
Chester Road
Inner Circle
Open Air Theatre
Queen Mary's Gardens
Refreshment Room
New Lodge
Royal College
Stanhope Street
71
238
232
84
83
29
28

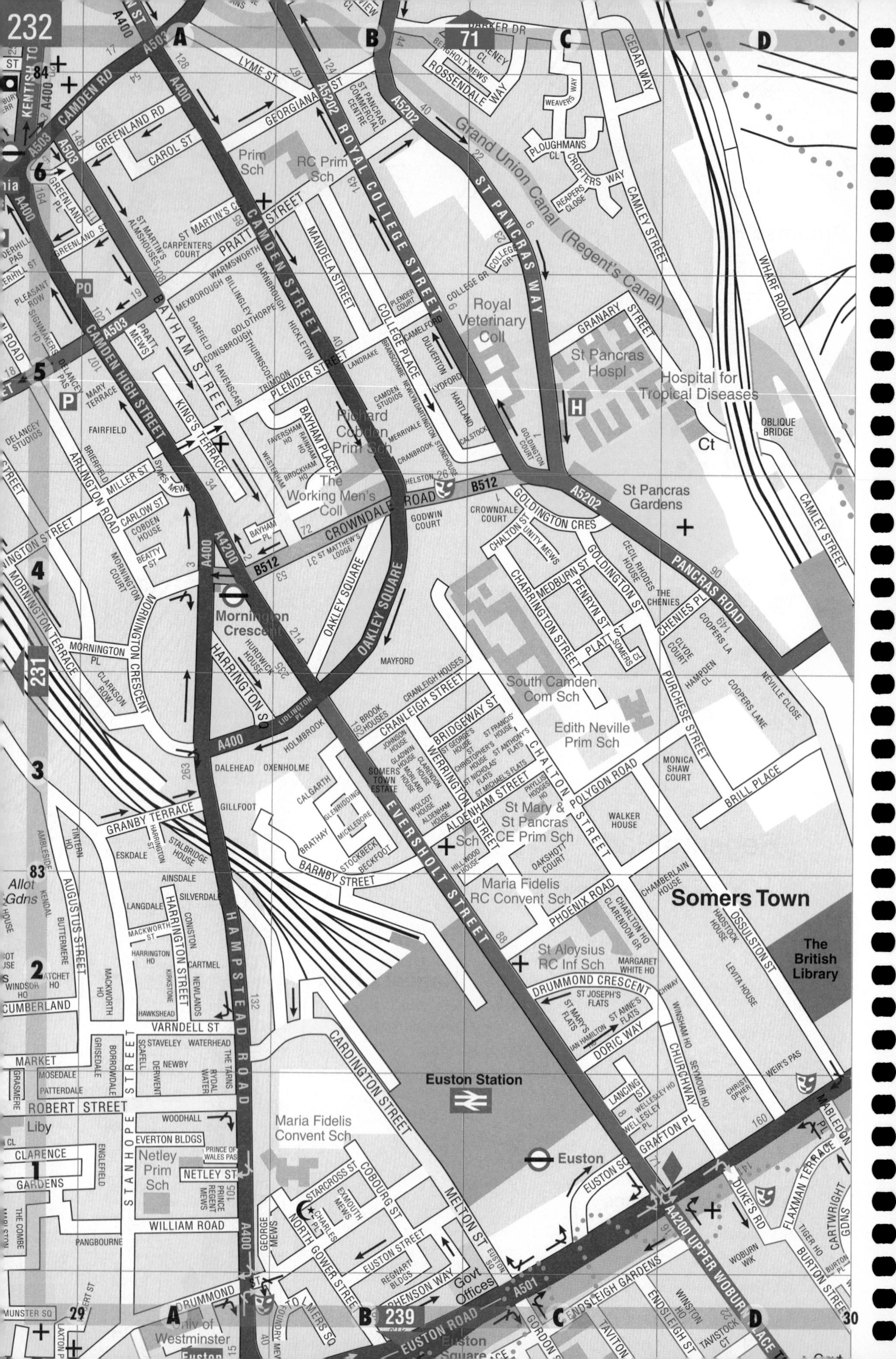
A
B
C
D
71
239
231
Camden Rd
Kentish Town
Camden High Street
Lyme St
Georgiana St
Greenland Rd
Carol St
Royal College Street
St Pancras Commercial Centre
Rossendale Way
Cedar Way
Weavers Way
Ploughmans Cl
Crofters Way
Reapers Close
Camley Street
Wharf Road
Grand Union Canal (Regent's Canal)
St Pancras Way
Prim Sch
RC Prim Sch
Camden Street
Pratt Street
Mandela Street
St Martin's Almshouses
Carpenters Court
Bayham Street
Plender Street
College Place
Royal Veterinary Coll
Granary Street
St Pancras Hospl
Hospital for Tropical Diseases
Oblique Bridge
Richard Cobden Prim Sch
The Working Men's Coll
Crowndale Road
St Pancras Gardens
Goldington Cres
Pancras Road
Mornington Crescent
Oakley Square
Harrington Sq
King's Terrace
Arlington Road
Miller St
Carlow St
Mornington Terrace
Mornington Pl
Charrington Street
Medburn St
Penryn St
Platt St
Goldington St
Chenies Pl
Coopers La
South Camden Com Sch
Edith Neville Prim Sch
Purchese Street
Brill Place
Monica Shaw Court
Polygon Road
Chalton Street
Cranleigh Street
Bridgeway St
Werrington Street
Aldenham Street
Eversholt Street
Somers Town Estate
St Mary & St Pancras CE Prim Sch
Maria Fidelis RC Convent Sch
Walker House
Somers Town
Phoenix Road
The British Library
Ossulston St
St Aloysius RC Inf Sch
Drummond Crescent
Doric Way
Churchway
Euston Station
Euston
Granby Terrace
Barnby Street
Hampstead Road
Harrington Street
Augustus Street
Varndell St
Robert Street
Stanhope Street
Clarence Gardens
Netley Prim Sch
William Road
Cardington Street
Maria Fidelis Convent Sch
Cobourg St
Melton St
Euston Street
North Gower Street
Euston Sq
Euston Road
Govt Offices
Upper Woburn Place
Endsleigh Gardens
Duke's Rd
Flaxman Terrace
Univ of Westminster
Drummond St
Allot Gdns
Liby
Sch
30

233
72
240
A
B
C
D
Freightliner Terminal
Depot
Bingfield Park
Recn Gd
Liby
Barnard Park
Battlebridge Basin
London Canal Museum
King's Cross
ISLINGTON
Pentonville
St Pancras
St Pancras Station
King's Cross Station
King's Cross St Pancras
King's Cross (Thameslink) Station
St Pancras International Station under construction
Blessed Sacrament RC Prim Sch
Copenhagen Prim Sch
St Andrew's CE Prim Sch
Vittoria Prim Sch
Winton Prim Sch
Elizabeth Garrett Anderson Language Coll
Argyle Prim Sch
Royal National TNE Hospl
Magistrates Court
Westminster Kingsway Coll
Eastman Dental Hospl
St Andrew's Gardens
St George's Gdns
Univ College London
Univ of London
Town Hall
RNIB
Tenn Cts
YORK WAY
CALEDONIAN ROAD
PENTONVILLE ROAD
KING'S CROSS ROAD
COPENHAGEN STREET
WHARFDALE ROAD
GOODSWAY
PANCRAS ROAD
MIDLAND ROAD
SWINTON STREET
ACTON STREET
ARGYLE STREET
JUDD STREET
GRAY'S INN ROAD
RICHMOND AVENUE
CARNEGIE STREET
WYNFORD ROAD
BINGFIELD STREET
TWYFORD STREET
CALEDONIA ST
RAILWAY ST
NORTHDOWN STREET
CALSHOT STREET
RODNEY STREET
PENTON RISE
LLOYD BAKER STREET
CUBITT STREET
SIDMOUTH ST
REGENT SQUARE
CROMER STREET
HARRISON STREET
LEIGH STREET
HASTINGS STREET
BIDBOROUGH STREET
TONBRIDGE STREET
CARTWRIGHT GDNS
TAVISTOCK PL
HEATHCOTE ST
MECKLENBURGH
PERCY CIRCUS
GREAT PERCY STREET
WHARTON STREET
FREDERICK STREET
WICKLOW STREET
BRITANNIA STREET
LEEKE STREET
DONEGAL STREET
COLLIER STREET
CUMMING ST
PULTENEY TERRACE
HEMINGFORD ROAD
MATILDA STREET
PRICE'S YARD
THORNHILL SQ
HAVELOCK STREET
BEMERTON STREET
RANDELL'S ROAD
MALDEN LANE BRIDGE
BATTLE BRIDGE RD
ALL SAINTS ST
CRINAN ST
BALFE STREET
TREATY STREET
NEW WHARF ROAD
A5200
A5203
A501
A201
A5202
B503
B504
B502
B514
30
31
83
84
1
2
3
4
5
6

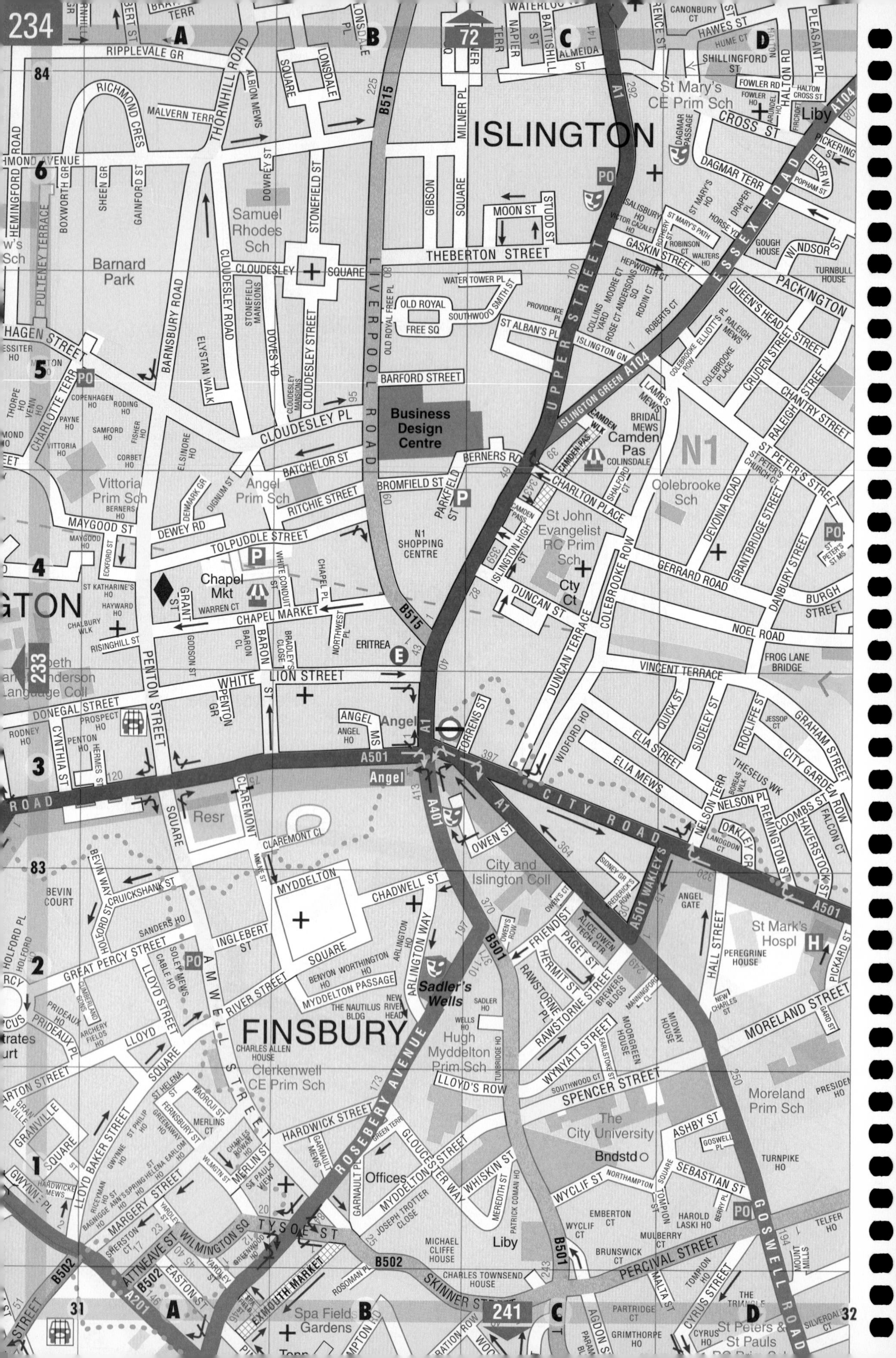

72
233
241
A
B
C
D
84
83
6
5
4
3
2
1
31
32
ISLINGTON
FINSBURY
N1
RIPPLEVALE GR
RICHMOND CRES
MALVERN TERR
THORNHILL ROAD
ALBION MEWS
LONSDALE SQUARE
LONSDALE PL
LIVERPOOL ROAD
MILNER PL
GIBSON SQUARE
MOON ST
STUDD ST
THEBERTON STREET
ALMEIDA ST
BATTISHILL ST
NAPIER TERR
CANONBURY CT
HAWES ST
HUME CT
SHILLINGFORD ST
FOWLER RD
HALTON RD
HALTON CROSS ST
PLEASANT PL
St Mary's CE Prim Sch
CROSS ST
Liby
DAGMAR PASSAGE
DAGMAR TERR
PICKERING ST
ELDER WK
POPHAM ST
ESSEX ROAD
UPPER STREET
PO
SALISBURY HO
VICTOR CAZALET HO
ST MARY'S PATH
ST MARY'S HO
HORSE YD
DRAPER PL
GOUGH HOUSE
WINDSOR ST
TURNBULL HOUSE
PACKINGTON
GASKIN STREET
HEPWORTH CT
ROBINSON CT
WALTERS HO
RICHMOND AVENUE
BOXWORTH GR
SHEEN GR
GAINFORD ST
DOWREY ST
STONEFIELD ST
PULTENEY TERRACE
Samuel Rhodes Sch
Barnard Park
BARNSBURY ROAD
CLOUDESLEY ROAD
CLOUDESLEY SQUARE
STONEFIELD MANSIONS
DOVES YD
CLOUDESLEY STREET
CLOUDESLEY MANSIONS
ELYSTAN WALK
OLD ROYAL FREE PL
OLD ROYAL FREE SQ
WATER TOWER PL
SOUTHWOOD SMITH ST
PROVIDENCE PL
ST ALBAN'S PL
COLLINS YARD
MOORE CT
ROSE CT
ANDERSONS SQ
RODIN CT
ROBERTS CT
ISLINGTON GN
ISLINGTON GREEN
A104
QUEEN'S HEAD STREET
ELLIOTT'S PL
RALEIGH MEWS
COLEBROOKE ROW
COLEBROOKE PLACE
CRUDEN STREET
CHANTRY STREET
RALEIGH STREET
COPENHAGEN STREET
ESSITER HO
MILTON HO
CHARLOTTE TERR
COPENHAGEN HO
RODING HO
PAYNE HO
SAMFORD HO
FISHER HO
VITTORIA HO
CORBET HO
THORPE HO
VENN HO
BARFORD STREET
Business Design Centre
CLOUDESLEY PL
BATCHELOR ST
ELSINORE HO
Vittoria Prim Sch
Angel Prim Sch
RITCHIE STREET
BROMFIELD ST
PARKFIELD ST
BERNERS RD
CAMDEN WLK
CAMDEN PAS
Camden Pas
COLINSDALE
LAMB'S MEWS
BRIDAL MEWS
ST PETER'S STREET
ST PETER'S CHURCH CT
Colebrooke Sch
DENMARK GR
DIGNUM ST
BERNERS HO
MAYGOOD ST
MAYGOOD HO
DEWEY RD
TOLPUDDLE STREET
N1 SHOPPING CENTRE
CHARLTON PLACE
SHALFORD CT
CAMDEN PASS
St John Evangelist RC Prim Sch
ISLINGTON HIGH ST
DEVONIA ROAD
GRANTBRIDGE STREET
DANBURY STREET
ST PETER'S ST MS
ECKFORD ST
ST KATHARINE'S HO
HAYWARD HO
Chapel Mkt
GRANT ST
WARREN CT
WHITE CONDUIT ST
CHAPEL PL
CHAPEL MARKET
B515
City Ct
DUNCAN ST
GERRARD ROAD
COLEBROOKE ROW
BURGH STREET
GTON
CHALBURY WLK
RISINGHILL ST
PENTON STREET
GODSON ST
BARON CL
BARON ST
BRADLEY'S CLOSE
NORTHWEST PL
ERITREA
NOEL ROAD
DUNCAN TERRACE
FROG LANE BRIDGE
VINCENT TERRACE
Lambeth Anderson Language Coll
WHITE LION STREET
DONEGAL STREET
PROSPECT HO
RODNEY HO
CYNTHIA ST
PENTON HO
HERMES ST
PENTON GR
ANGEL MS
ANGEL HO
Angel
TORRENS ST
QUICK ST
SUDELEY ST
ROCLIFFE ST
JESSOP CT
GRAHAM STREET
WIDFORD HO
ELIA STREET
ELIA MEWS
CITY GARDEN ROW
THESEUS WK
BOREAS WK
NELSON TERR
NELSON PL
A501
ROAD
A1
A401
Resr
CLAREMONT
CLAREMONT CL
SQUARE
OWEN ST
CITY ROAD
REMINGTON ST
COOMBS ST
HAVERSTOCK ST
FALCON CT
OAKLEY CR
LANGDON CT
BEVIN WAY
BEVIN COURT
CRUICKSHANK ST
HOLFORD ST
MYDDELTON
CHADWELL ST
City and Islington Coll
SIDNEY GR
FREDERICK'S ROW
WAKLEY ST
ANGEL GATE
OWEN'S CT
OWEN'S ROW
FRIEND ST
ALICE OWEN TECH CTR
PAGET ST
HALL STREET
St Mark's Hospl
PEREGRINE HOUSE
PICKARD ST
SANDERS HO
INGLEBERT ST
MYDDELTON SQUARE
ARLINGTON WAY
ARLINGTON HO
B501
HERMIT ST
GREAT PERCY STREET
HOLFORD PL
CUMBERLAND GDNS
SOLEY MEWS
CABLE HO
LLOYD STREET
AMWELL STREET
RIVER STREET
BENYON HO
WORTHINGTON HO
MYDDELTON PASSAGE
Sadler's Wells
RAWSTORNE PL
RAWSTORNE STREET
BREWERS BLDGS
MANNINGFORD CL
PRIDEAUX PL
ARCHERY FIELDS HO
LLOYD SQUARE
THE NAUTILUS BLDG
NEW RIVER HEAD
SADLER HO
WELLS HO
MIDWAY HOUSE
NEW CHARLES ST
MORELAND STREET
GARD ST
CHARLES ALLEN HOUSE
Clerkenwell CE Prim Sch
Hugh Myddelton Prim Sch
TUNBRIDGE HO
WYNYATT STREET
EARLSTOKE ST
MOORGREEN HOUSE
ROSEBERY AVENUE
LLOYD'S ROW
SOUTHWOOD CT
SPENCER STREET
Moreland Prim Sch
PRESIDENT HO
GRANVILLE SQUARE
LLOYD BAKER STREET
ST HELENA HO
NAOROJI ST
FERNSBURY ST
GREENAWAY HO
MERLINS CT
HARDWICK STREET
GREEN TERR
GARNAULT MEWS
GLOUCESTER WAY
The City University
ASHBY ST
GOSWELL PL
Bndstd
TURNPIKE HO
GWYNNE PL
HARDWICKE MEWS
RICEYMAN HO
BAGNIGGE HO
GWYNNE HO
ANN'S ST
ST PHILIP HO
SPRING HO
ST HELENA HO
EARLOM HO
MARGERY STREET
CHARLES ROWAN HO
MERLIN ST
WLMGTN ST
ST PAULS VIEW
Offices
MYDDELTON STREET
GARNAULT PL
WHISKIN ST
WYCLIF ST
NORTHAMPTON SQUARE
SEBASTIAN ST
TOMPION ST
BERRY PL
GOSWELL ROAD
SHERSTON CT
YARDLEY ST
WILMINGTON SQ
TYSOE ST
JOSEPH TROTTER CLOSE
MEREDITH ST
PATRICK COMAN HO
MICHAEL CLIFFE HOUSE
Liby
EMBERTON CT
WYCLIF CT
HAROLD LASKI HO
MULBERRY CT
BRUNSWICK CT
PERCIVAL STREET
TELFER HO
MOUNT MILLS
B502
ATTNEAVE ST
EASTON ST
A201
EXMOUTH MARKET
ROSOMAN PL
CHARLES TOWNSEND HOUSE
SKINNER STREET
TOMPION HO
MALTA ST
CYRUS STREET
THE TRIANGLE
PARTRIDGE CT
GRIMTHORPE HO
Spa Fields Gardens
CYRUS HO
St Peters & St Pauls
SILVERDALE CT
AGDON ST

A
B
C
D
73
DOWNHAM RD
DOWNHAM CT
84
HEDINGHAM CL
GREENMAN ST
ISLINGTON ESTATE
Charles Lamb Prim Sch
DIBDEN ST
POPHAM ROAD
MALDON CL
QUEENSBURY ST
ELIZABETH AVE
ROTHERFIELD STREET
Rotherfield Prim Sch
ROTHERFIELD COURT
HULLBRIDGE MEWS
SHERBORNE ST
Tenn Cts
Rosemary Gardens
SOUTHGATE ROAD
B102
ST LAWRENCE CT
BENYON RD
ST AUBINS CT
ST BRELADES CT
DORLESTON CT
PORTELET CT
CULFORD RD
BALMES ROAD
6
GRANVILLE CT
CORBIERE HOUSE
ST HELIER CT
A1200
SHEPPERTON ROAD
BASIRE STREET
BISHOP STREET
ISLEDEN HOUSE
POPHAM ST
FINNEMORE HOUSE
BRITANNIA ROW
City & Islington Coll
ROSEMARY MEWS
CANAL WALK
WILTON SQUARE
WILTON VILLAS
RYDON ST
ST PHILIP'S WAY
PREBEND STREET
COLEMAN FIELDS
ST PAUL STREET
STRANG HOUSE
PRICE HOUSE
HOLDEN HO
ADA CT
STREET
CANON ST
RECTOR ST
UNION SQ
MARY ST
LINTON STREET
ARBON COURT
REES STREET
ARLINGTON SQUARE
ARLINGTON AVENUE
BEVAN STREET
CLOCK TOWER MEWS
NEW NORTH ROAD
BARING STREET
BARING CT
ROSEMARY BRANCH BRIDGE
BRANCH PLACE
ROSEMARY HO
FELTON ST
FELTON HO
LUCAN HO
HARWOOD CT
JORDAN HO
KELLETT HO
SILLITOE HO
HARVEY HO
ROY HO
KENNING HOUSE
HIGGINS HOUSE
WILTSHIRE ROW
BRIDPORT HO
BRIDPORT PLACE
IMBER ST
AVEBURY ST
AVEBURY CT
BURBAGE HO
PENN STREET
NORTHPORT ST
GIRLING HO
FULCHER HO
FRANCIS HOUSE
HYDE ROAD
5
NEW NORTH ROAD BRIDGE
POOLE STREET
GOPSALL STREET
Whitmore Comm Sch
L Ctr
GRANGE ST
Islington Green Sch
RHEIDOL TERRACE
RHEIDOL MEWS
ST PAUL ST
THE PRECINCT
PACKINGTON SQUARE
Grand Union Canal (Regent's Canal)
B144
EAGLE WHARF ROAD
BRACKLYN ST
BRACKLYN CT
Shoreditch Park
Tenn Cts
Dorothy Thurtle Garden
ALLINGHAM ST
FROME ST
DAME ST
CLUSE CT
PROVENCE ST
BALDWIN TERR
HANOVER YD
PACKINGTON STREET BRIDGE
PARR ST
PARR CT
Thomas Fairchild Comm Sch
RUSHTON ST
BRIDPORT PL
4
PITFIELD STREET
CANAL BLDG
BLETSOE WK
NIAGARA CL
FORSTON ST
GODWIN CL
WIMBOURNE STREET
WIMBOURNE CT
MINTERN STREET
DANIELL HO
KINDER HO
WINDSOR HO
WHARF ROAD BRIDGE
Hanover Prim Sch
Shepherdess Walk
NAPIER GROVE
NAPIER CT
CROPLEY STREET
CROPLEY CT
SHAFTESBURY STREET
SHAFTESBURY CT
CAVENDISH ST
TRAFFORD HO
MARSHALL HO
BUCKLAND CT
BUCKLAND ST
NEVITT HO
WILKINSON HO
VINSON HO
CLUNBURY ST
GRAND JUNCTION WHARF
WHARF ROAD
Wenlock Basin
TA Centre
SYLVIA CT
WENLOCK CT
EVELYN WALK
EVELYN CT
95
CRONDALL CT
CHERBURY ST
CHERBURY CT
City Road Basin
PICKFORDS WHARF
WENLOCK ROAD
THE BREWERY IND EST
STURT ST
WENLOCK STREET
SHEPHERDESS WALK
BLETCHLEY CT
BLETCHLEY ST
Liby
St John the Baptist CE Prim Sch
3
CRONDALL ST
Islington
Hackney
PRESTWOOD ST
TAPLOW STREET
ALFORD CT
ALFORD PL
LINALE HO
MARIE LLOYD HO
MURRAY GROVE
CUSTANCE HO
THAXTED CT
ALLERTON HO
HALSTEAD CT
B101
BRITANNIA WK
CATHERWOOD CT
MARSOM HO
SHOREDITCH
83
BARLOW HO
MONEYER HO
ST LEONARD'S CT
MICAWBER STREET
UNDERWOOD STREET
Crusoe House Sch
RHODES HO
CUSTANCE ST
ALLERTON ST
FULL WOOD'S MEWS
HABERDASHER PL
BEVENDEN STREET
FINN HOUSE
261
KESTREL HO
BUXTON CT
THORESBY ST
WINDSOR TERR
MICAWBER CT
WELLESLEY TERRACE
UNDERWOOD ROW
JASPER WLK
PROVOST STREET
NILE HO
EAST ROAD
NILE STREET
HABERDASHER STREET
2
SERAPH CT
MASON'S PL
MACCLESFIELD ROAD
WESTLAND PLACE
BRITANNIA WALK
DELTA HO
VESTRY ST
EDWARD DODD CT
ASHFORD
RAHERE HO
CITY FORUM
CITY ROAD
SHEPHERDESS PL
EBENEZER STREET
ANTHONY COPE CT
BUTTESLAND ST
Tenn Ct
HOFFMAN SQ
ROYAL OAK CT
PRESIDENT ST
NELSON PAS
EAGLE DWELLINGS
SILBURY ST
CHART STREET
BOWLING G
A1200
SYMISTER
SAMUEL CT
KING SQUARE
CENTRAL STREET
DINGLEY ROAD
HULL ST
LAGONIER HO
DINGLEY PL
MORA ST
GAMBLER HO
B502
CAYTON ST
CAYTON PL
Inst
TOUCHARD HO
LEVER STREET
BARNABAS HO
CHADWORTH HO
EUROPA PL
IRONMONGER ROW
GASTIGNY HO
GUINNESS CT
City & Islington Coll
BATH STREET
Moorfields Eye Hospl
PEERLESS ST
BALDWIN ST
CORSHAM ST
HUDSONS HO
BACHE'S ST
BRUNSWICK PLACE
CHARLES SQUARE
VINCE COURT
1
CITY CENTRAL EST
GALWAY ST
GALWAY HO
GRAYSON HO
PATERSON CT
CRANWOOD ST
GADDESDEN HO
ADEYFIELD HO
KENSWORTH HO
CRANWOOD CT
CHAULDEN HO
VINCE ST
A5201
BURNHILL HO
PATON ST
NORMAN ST
RADNOR STREET
LIZARD ST
St Luke's CE Prim Sch
GODFREY HO
BATH CT
A501
Old Street
SINGER ST
Mem
A1202
SEWARD STREET
L Ctr
HELMET
IRONMONGER PAS
BARTHOLOMEW SQ
COPE HO
BARTHOLOMEW CT
NEWLAND CT
OLD STREET
WILLOW
32
PEARTREE STREET
MITCHELL
ROW
ST LUKE'S
VICKERY CT
STEADMAN CT
242
MARTHA
MALLOW
COWPER STREET
Central Foundation Sch
33
BLACKALL
ROBY HO
PRIESTLEY HO
City Ct

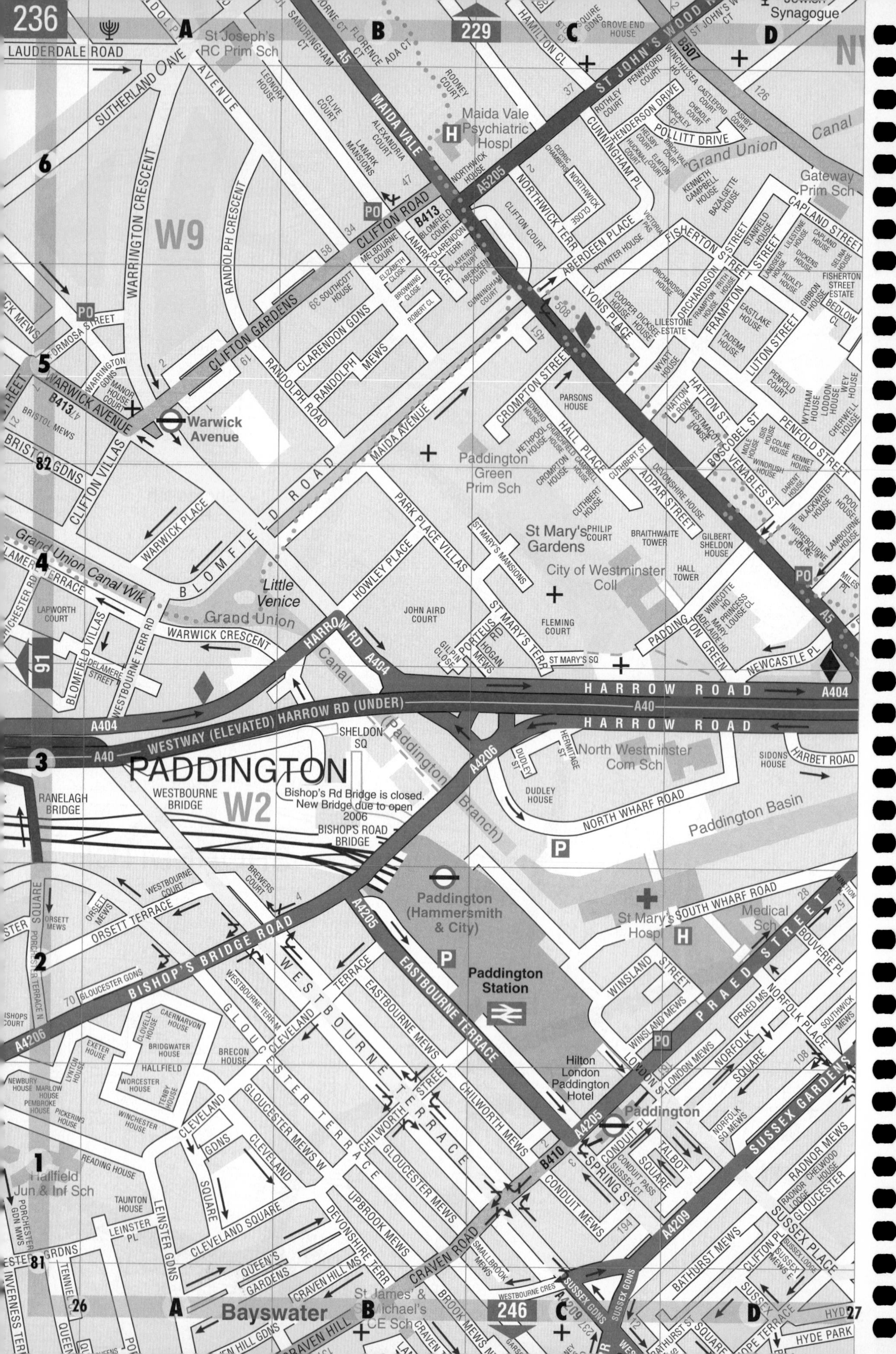

A
B
C
D
229
LAUDERDALE ROAD
St Joseph's RC Prim Sch
SUTHERLAND AVE
AVENUE
LEONORA HOUSE
SANDRINGHAM CT
CLIVE COURT
MAIDA VALE
A5
FLORENCE CT
ADA CT
RODNEY COURT
Maida Vale Psychiatric Hospl
ALEXANDRIA COURT
LANARK MANSIONS
HAMILTON CL
GROVE END HOUSE
ST JOHN'S WOOD ROAD
B507
Synagogue
ROTHLEY COURT
PENNYFORD COURT
WINCHILSEA HO
HENDERSON DRIVE
CASTLEFORD COURT
CHEADLE COURT
ASHBY COURT
POLLITT DRIVE
Grand Union Canal
CUNNINGHAM PL
NORTHWICK HOUSE
A5205
NORTHWICK TERR
NORTHWICK CLOSE
CEDRIC CHAMBERS
KENNETH CAMPBELL HOUSE
BAZALGETTE HOUSE
Gateway Prim Sch
CAPLAND STREET
6
W9
WARRINGTON CRESCENT
RANDOLPH CRESCENT
CLIFTON ROAD
B413
BLOMFIELD COURT
LANARK PLACE
CLARENDON TERR
MELBOURNE COURT
ELIZABETH CLOSE
BROWNING CLOSE
ROBERT CL
CLIFTON COURT
ABERDEEN PLACE
POYNTER HOUSE
VICTORIA PAS
FISHERTON STREET
STANFIELD HOUSE
LILESTONE HOUSE
CAPLAND HOUSE
DICKENS HOUSE
SELINA HOUSE
FISHERTON STREET ESTATE
BEDLOW CL
PO
FORMOSA STREET
CLIFTON GARDENS
SOUTHCOTT HOUSE
CLARENDON GDNS
RANDOLPH MEWS
RANDOLPH ROAD
CUNNINGHAM COURT
LYONS PLACE
COOPER HOUSE
DICKSEE HOUSE
ORCHARDSON HOUSE
ORCHARDSON STREET
FRAMPTON STREET
EASTLAKE HOUSE
TADEMA HOUSE
LUTON STREET
LILESTONE ESTATE
5
WARWICK AVENUE
WARRINGTON GDNS
MANOR HOUSE COURT
BRISTOL MEWS
BRISTOL GDNS
Warwick Avenue
CLIFTON VILLAS
MAIDA AVENUE
CROMPTON STREET
PARSONS HOUSE
HALL PLACE
WYATT HOUSE
HATTON ST
HATTON ROW
BOSCOBEL ST
PENFOLD STREET
PENFOLD COURT
WYTHAM HOUSE
LODDON HOUSE
WEY HOUSE
CHERWELL HOUSE
Paddington Green Prim Sch
CUTHBERT ST
ADPAR STREET
DEVONSHIRE HOUSE
VENABLES ST
BLACKWATER HOUSE
POOL HOUSE
INGREBOURNE HOUSE
LAMBOURNE HOUSE
WARWICK PLACE
BLOMFIELD ROAD
PARK PLACE VILLAS
ST MARY'S MANSIONS
St Mary's Gardens
PHILIP COURT
BRAITHWAITE TOWER
GILBERT SHELDON HOUSE
HALL TOWER
City of Westminster Coll
4
Grand Union Canal Wlk
DELAMERE TERRACE
LAPWORTH COURT
Little Venice
Grand Union
HOWLEY PLACE
JOHN AIRD COURT
FLEMING COURT
PADDINGTON GREEN
NEWCASTLE PL
WARWICK CRESCENT
HARROW RD
A404
Canal
PORTEUS RD
HOGAN MEWS
GILPIN CLOSE
ST MARY'S TERR
ST MARY'S SQ
91
BLOMFIELD VILLAS
WESTBOURNE TERR RD
HARROW ROAD
A40
WESTWAY (ELEVATED) HARROW RD (UNDER)
SHELDON SQ
3
PADDINGTON
W2
WESTBOURNE BRIDGE
RANELAGH BRIDGE
(Paddington Branch)
A4206
DUDLEY ST
HERMITAGE ST
North Westminster Com Sch
DUDLEY HOUSE
SIDONS HOUSE
HARBET ROAD
NORTH WHARF ROAD
Paddington Basin
Bishop's Rd Bridge is closed. New Bridge due to open 2006
BISHOPS ROAD BRIDGE
BREWERS COURT
WESTBOURNE COURT
ORSETT MEWS
ORSETT TERRACE
PORCHESTER SQUARE
A4205
Paddington (Hammersmith & City)
St Mary's Hospl
SOUTH WHARF ROAD
Medical Sch
PRAED STREET
BOUVERIE PL
2
BISHOP'S BRIDGE ROAD
GLOUCESTER GDNS
WESTBOURNE TERRACE
EASTBOURNE TERRACE
EASTBOURNE MEWS
Paddington Station
WINSLAND STREET
WINSLAND MEWS
PRAED MS
NORFOLK PLACE
SOUTHWICK MEWS
CAERNARVON HOUSE
CLOVELLY HOUSE
BRIDGWATER HOUSE
HALLFIELD
EXETER HOUSE
LYNTON HOUSE
WORCESTER HOUSE
TENBY HOUSE
BRECON HOUSE
GLOUCESTER TERRACE
CLEVELAND TERRACE
WESTBOURNE TERR M
CHILWORTH STREET
CHILWORTH MEWS
Hilton London Paddington Hotel
LONDON ST
LONDON MEWS
NORFOLK SQUARE
Paddington
NEWBURY HOUSE
MARLOW HOUSE
PEMBROKE HOUSE
PICKERING HOUSE
WINCHESTER HOUSE
CLEVELAND GDNS
GLOUCESTER MEWS W
GLOUCESTER MEWS
B410
CONDUIT PL
SPRING ST
SUSSEX CT
CONDUIT PASS
TALBOT SQUARE
NORFOLK SQ MEWS
SUSSEX GARDENS
RADNOR MEWS
CHELWOOD HOUSE
GLOUCESTER
RADNOR LODGE
1
READING HOUSE
Hallfield Jun & Inf Sch
TAUNTON HOUSE
CLEVELAND SQUARE
LEINSTER PL
LEINSTER GDNS
PORCHESTER GDN MWS
UPBROOK MEWS
DEVONSHIRE TERR
CONDUIT MEWS
CRAVEN ROAD
SMALLBROOK MEWS
A4209
BATHURST MEWS
CLIFTON PL
SUSSEX PLACE
SUSSEX LODGE
SUSSEX MEWS E
81
QUEEN'S GARDENS
CRAVEN HILL MS
WESTBOURNE CRES
SUSSEX GDNS
26
Bayswater
St James' & St Michael's CE Sch
246
CRAVEN HILL
BROOK MEWS
BATHURST ST
HYDE PARK
27
INVERNESS TER
TENNIEL CT

W8
A
B
C
D
230
Boating Lake
The Holme
(Regent's Canal)
Lisson Green
London Business Sch
Tenn Cts
NW1
Coll
PO
Lisson Grove
Alfie's Antq Mkt
Univ of Westminster
Sylvia Young Theatre Sch
St Edward's RC Prim Sch
Marylebone Station
Marylebone
Govt Offices
The Charter Nightingale Hosp
The Landmark Hotel
The Western Eye Hosp
Samaritan Hosp for Women
Courts
Liby
North Westminster Com Sch
Edgware Rd (Bakerloo)
Edgware Road
Marylebone Flyover
Francis Holland CE Sch
Sherlock Holmes Mus
Baker Street
University of Westminster
Regent's Coll
Hampden Gurney CE Prim Sch
Macready House
L Ctr
Tonga
Sweden
Switzerland
Seychelles
Honduras
Kyrgyzstan
Lithuania
Angola
W1
W2
Courtauld Inst of Art
West London Synagogue
West End Great Synagogue
Cumberland Hotel
Marble Arch
Tyburn Tree (site of)
Sri Lanka
Brazil
238
247
Lisson Grove
Rossmore Road
Marylebone Road
Edgware Road
Old Marylebone Road
Chapel St
Crawford Street
George Street
Seymour Street
Connaught Street
Upper Berkeley Street
Gloucester Place
Baker Street
Portman St
Park Road
Sussex Place
Outer Circle
Allsop Place
Dorset Square
Harewood Avenue
Church Street
Broadley Street
Bell Street
Sussex Gardens
Hyde Park Street
Hyde Park Crescent
Hyde Park Sq
Oxford Square
Cambridge Square
Norfolk Crescent
Connaught Square
Bryanston Square
Montagu Square
Portman Square
Marble Arch
A41
A40
A501
A404
A4205
A4209
A5
A5204
A402
B507
B524
1
2
3
4
5
6
27
28

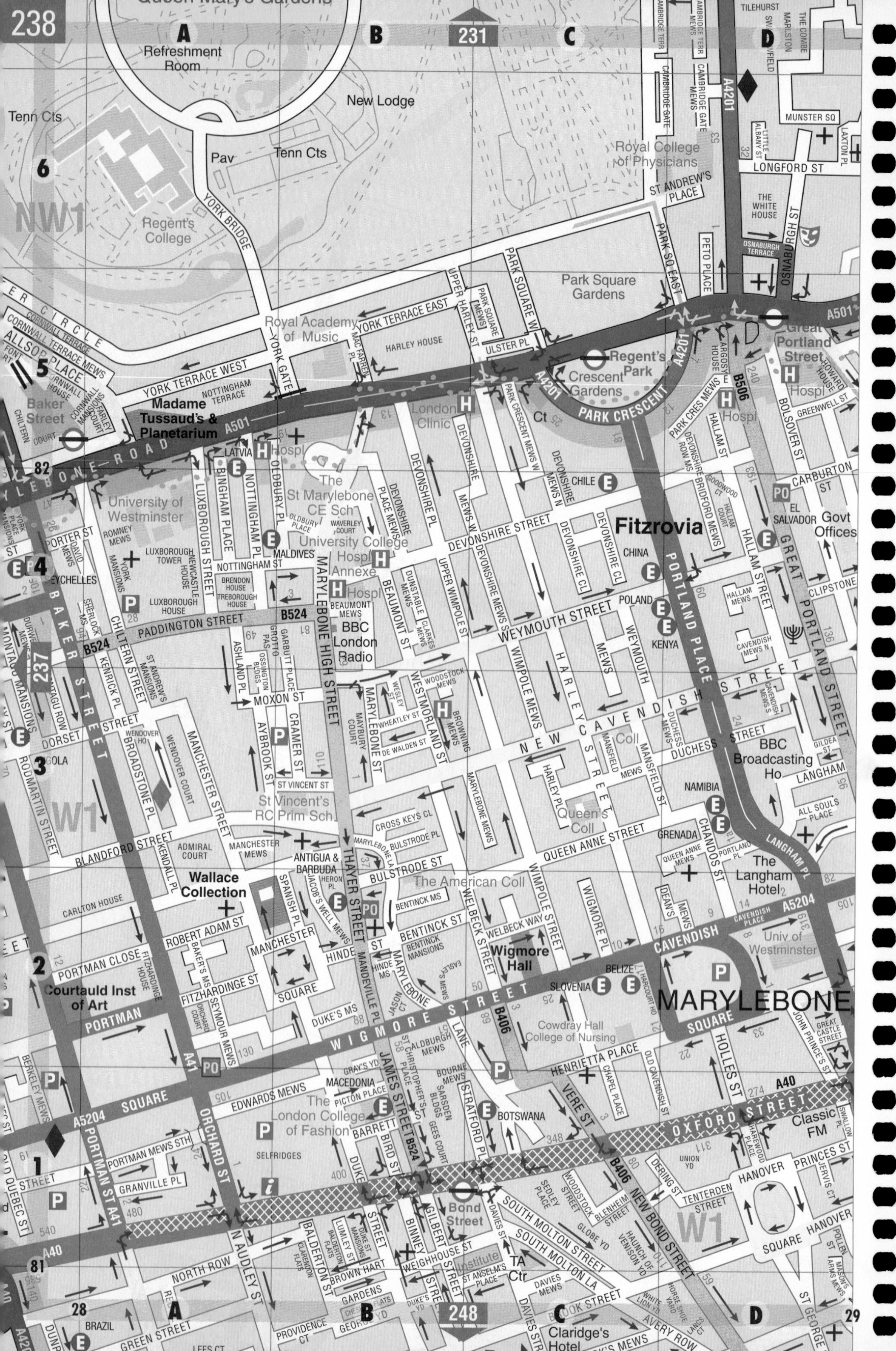
A
B
231
C
D
Queen Mary's Gardens
Refreshment Room
New Lodge
Tenn Cts
Pav
Tenn Cts
6
NW1
Regent's College
York Bridge
Royal College of Physicians
St Andrew's Place
Cambridge Terr
Cambridge Terr Mews
Cambridge Gate
Cambridge Gate Mews
A4201
Tilehurst
Marlston
The Combe
Munster Sq
Little Albany St
Laxton Pl
Longford St
The White House
Osnaburgh St
Osnaburgh Terrace
Peto Place
Park Sq East
Park Square Gardens
Park Square W
Upper Harley St
Park Square Mews
Ulster Pl
York Terrace East
Harley House
Royal Academy of Music
York Gate
Mac Farren Pl
Outer Circle
Cornwall Terrace
Cornwall Terrace Mews
Allsop Place
5
York Terrace West
Nottingham Terrace
Madame Tussaud's & Planetarium
Baker Street
Chiltern Court
A501
Marylebone Road
82
Regent's Park
Crescent Gardens
Park Crescent
Park Crescent Mews W
Park Cres Mews E
Argosy House
B506
Great Portland Street
Hospl
Howard House
Bolsover St
Greenwell St
London Clinic
Latvia
Hospl
The St Marylebone CE Sch
University of Westminster
Luxborough St
Bingham Place
Nottingham Pl
Oldbury Pl
Devonshire Place Mews
Devonshire Pl
Devonshire Mews W
Devonshire Mews N
Chile
Devonshire St
Hallam St
Carburton St
Goodwood Ct
Devonshire Row Ms
Bridford Mews
Hallam Court
El Salvador
Govt Offices
Fitzrovia
Devonshire Street
Devonshire Cl
Porter St
York Place Mansions
David Mews
Romney Mews
York Mansions
Luxborough Tower
Newcastle House
Nottingham St
Maldives
Oldbury Place
Waverley Court
University College Hospl Annexe
Hospl
Beaumont Mews
Beaumont St
Dunstable Mews
Upper Wimpole St
Devonshire Mews S
China
Portland Place
Hallam Street
Clipstone
4
Seychelles
Brendon House
Treborough House
Luxborough House
Poland
Kenya
Weymouth Street
Weymouth Mews
Hallam Mews
Cavendish Mews N
Sherlock Ms
Chiltern Street
Paddington Street
B524
Ossington Bldgs
Grotto Pas
Garbutt Place
Marylebone High Street
BBC London Radio
Clarkes Mews
Wimpole Mews
Harley Street
Great Portland Street
Montagu Mansions
237
Kenrick Pl
Baker Street
St Andrew's Mansions
Ashland Pl
Moxon St
Aybrook St
Cramer St
Wesley St
Westmorland St
Woodstock Mews
Browning Mews
New Cavendish Street
Cavendish Mews S
Duchess Mews
Duchess Street
BBC Broadcasting Ho
Gildea St
Dorset Street
Wendover Ho
Broadstone Pl
Wendover Court
Manchester Street
Maybury Court
Wheatley St
Marylebone St
De Walden St
Mansfield Mews
Mansfield St
Coll
Langham
Gola
3
Rodmartin Street
St Vincent St
St Vincent's RC Prim Sch
Marylebone Mews
Harley Pl
Queen's Coll
Namibia
Chandos St
All Souls Place
W1
Blandford Street
Kendall Pl
Admiral Court
Manchester Mews
Cross Keys Cl
Bulstrode Pl
Marylebone La
Antigua & Barbuda
Queen Anne Street
Grenada
Queen Anne Mews
Portland Pl
Langham Pl
Wallace Collection
Spanish Pl
Jacob's Well Mews
Heron Pl
Bulstrode St
The American Coll
Wimpole Street
Wigmore Pl
Dean's Mews
The Langham Hotel
Carlton House
Thayer Street
Bentinck Ms
Bentinck St
Welbeck Street
Welbeck Way
A5204
Cavendish Place
Univ of Westminster
Robert Adam St
Baker's Ms
Manchester Square
Hinde St
Hinde Ms
Bentinck Mansions
Marylebone Lane
Easley's Mews
Wigmore Hall
Cavendish
2
Portman Close
Fitzhardinge House
Fitzhardinge St
Orchard Court
Seymour Mews
Courtauld Inst of Art
Duke's Ms
Mandeville Pl
Jason Ct
Wigmore Street
B406
Slovenia
Belize
Harcourt Ho
MARYLEBONE
Square
Holles St
John Prince's St
Great Castle Street
Portman
Berkeley Mews
A41
PO
St Christopher's Place
Aldburgh Mews
Bourne Mews
Cowdray Hall College of Nursing
Henrietta Place
Chapel Place
Old Cavendish St
A40
A5204
Square
Edwards Mews
Orchard St
Gray's Yd
Macedonia
Picton Place
The London College of Fashion
James Street
Barrett St
Gees Court
Sarsden Bldgs
Stratford Pl
Botswana
Vere St
Oxford Street
Classic FM
Swallow Pl
Portman Mews Sth
Portman St
1
Quebec St
Street
Granville Pl
Selfridges
Bird St
B524
Dering St
Union Yd
Harewood Place
Princes St
Hanover
Tenterden Street
Jervis Ct
Duke Street
Bond Street
Davies St
South Molton Street
Sedley Place
Woodstock Street
Blenheim Street
New Bond Street
W1
Hanover Square
North Audley St
Balderton St
Clarendon Flats
Lumley St
Duke St Mansions
Binney St
Gilbert Street
Weighhouse St
Institute
TA Ctr
South Molton La
Globe Yd
Haunch of Venison Yd
Pollen St
Mason's Arms Mews
81
North Row
Brown Hart Gardens
St Anselm's Place
Davies Mews
Horse Shoe Yard
White Lion Yd
St George St
28
Brazil
A
Green Street
Providence Ct
B
Chesterfield Flats
George Yd
Duke's Yd
248
Davies St
C
Brook Street
Claridge's Hotel
Avery Row
Lancs Ct
D
29
Lees Ct
Dunraven St

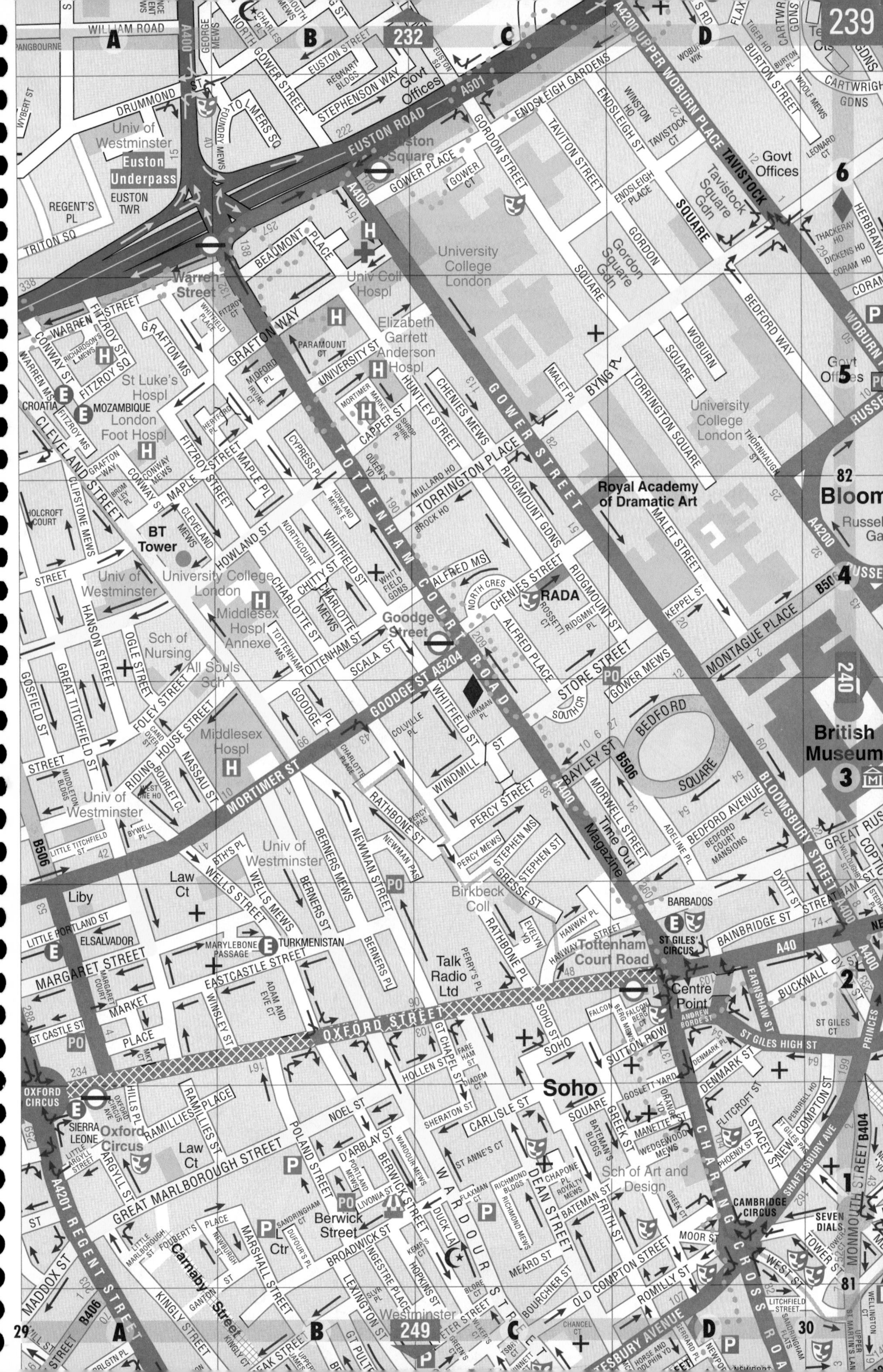
232
A
B
C
D
WILLIAM ROAD
DRUMMOND
Univ of Westminster
Euston Underpass
EUSTON TWR
REGENT'S PL
TRITON SQ
Warren Street
NORTH GOWER STREET
EUSTON STREET
STEPHENSON WAY
Govt Offices
EUSTON ROAD
Euston Square
GOWER PLACE
ENDSLEIGH GARDENS
TAVITON STREET
ENDSLEIGH ST
UPPER WOBURN PLACE
TAVISTOCK SQUARE
Tavistock Square Gdn
Govt Offices
BURTON STREET
CARTWRIGHT GDNS
6
BEAUMONT PLACE
Univ Coll Hospl
University College London
Gordon Square Gdn
GORDON SQUARE
BEDFORD WAY
WOBURN SQUARE
WARREN STREET
FITZROY SQ
CONWAY ST
GRAFTON WAY
GRAFTON MS
St Luke's Hospl
London Foot Hospl
Elizabeth Garrett Anderson Hospl
UNIVERSITY ST
HUNTLEY STREET
CHENIES MEWS
GOWER STREET
MALET PL
BYNG PL
TORRINGTON SQUARE
University College London
5
CROATIA
MOZAMBIQUE
CLEVELAND STREET
MAPLE STREET
FITZROY STREET
TOTTENHAM COURT ROAD
TORRINGTON PLACE
RIDGMOUNT GDNS
Royal Academy of Dramatic Art
MALET STREET
Bloom
Russell
82
BT Tower
Univ of Westminster
University College London
Middlesex Hospl Annexe
HOWLAND STREET
WHITFIELD ST
CHARLOTTE STREET
ALFRED MS
CHENIES STREET
RADA
RIDGMOUNT ST
KEPPEL ST
MONTAGUE PLACE
4
Sch of Nursing
All Souls Sch
Goodge Street
TOTTENHAM ST
SCALA ST
ALFRED PLACE
STORE STREET
GOWER MEWS
240
British Museum
HANSON STREET
OGLE STREET
FOLEY STREET
RIDING HOUSE STREET
Middlesex Hospl
GOODGE ST A5204
WHITFIELD ST
WINDMILL ST
BEDFORD SQUARE
BAYLEY ST
3
GREAT TITCHFIELD ST
GOSFIELD ST
NASSAU ST
MORTIMER ST
RATHBONE ST
PERCY STREET
MORWELL STREET
Time Out Magazine
BEDFORD AVENUE
BLOOMSBURY STREET
Univ of Westminster
Univ of Westminster
WELLS STREET
BERNERS MEWS
NEWMAN STREET
STEPHEN ST
Birkbeck Coll
GREAT RUSSELL
Liby
Law Ct
LITTLE PORTLAND ST
ELSALVADOR
TURKMENISTAN
MARYLEBONE PASSAGE
EASTCASTLE STREET
BERNERS ST
BERNERS PL
Talk Radio Ltd
RATHBONE PL
HANWAY ST
Tottenham Court Road
ST GILES' CIRCUS
BARBADOS
BAINBRIDGE ST
A40
MARGARET STREET
MARKET PLACE
GT CASTLE ST
OXFORD STREET
SOHO ST
Centre Point
BUCKNALL ST
2
EARNHAM ST
ST GILES HIGH ST
OXFORD CIRCUS
SIERRA LEONE
Oxford Circus
RAMILLIES PLACE
NOEL ST
HOLLEN ST
SHERATON ST
CARLISLE ST
Soho
SOHO SQUARE
SUTTON ROW
DENMARK ST
FLITCROFT ST
Law Ct
GREAT MARLBOROUGH STREET
POLAND STREET
D'ARBLAY ST
BERWICK STREET
WARDOUR STREET
ST ANNE'S CT
DEAN STREET
FRITH ST
GREEK ST
Sch of Art and Design
CHARING CROSS ROAD
SHAFTESBURY AVE
NEW COMPTON ST
MONMOUTH STREET
1
CAMBRIDGE CIRCUS
SEVEN DIALS
Berwick Street
BROADWICK ST
MEARD ST
OLD COMPTON STREET
ROMILLY ST
MOOR ST
WEST ST
81
A4201 REGENT STREET
MADDOX ST
Carnaby Street
KINGLY STREET
MARSHALL STREET
LEXINGTON ST
Westminster
BOURCHIER ST
SHAFTESBURY AVENUE
29
249
30

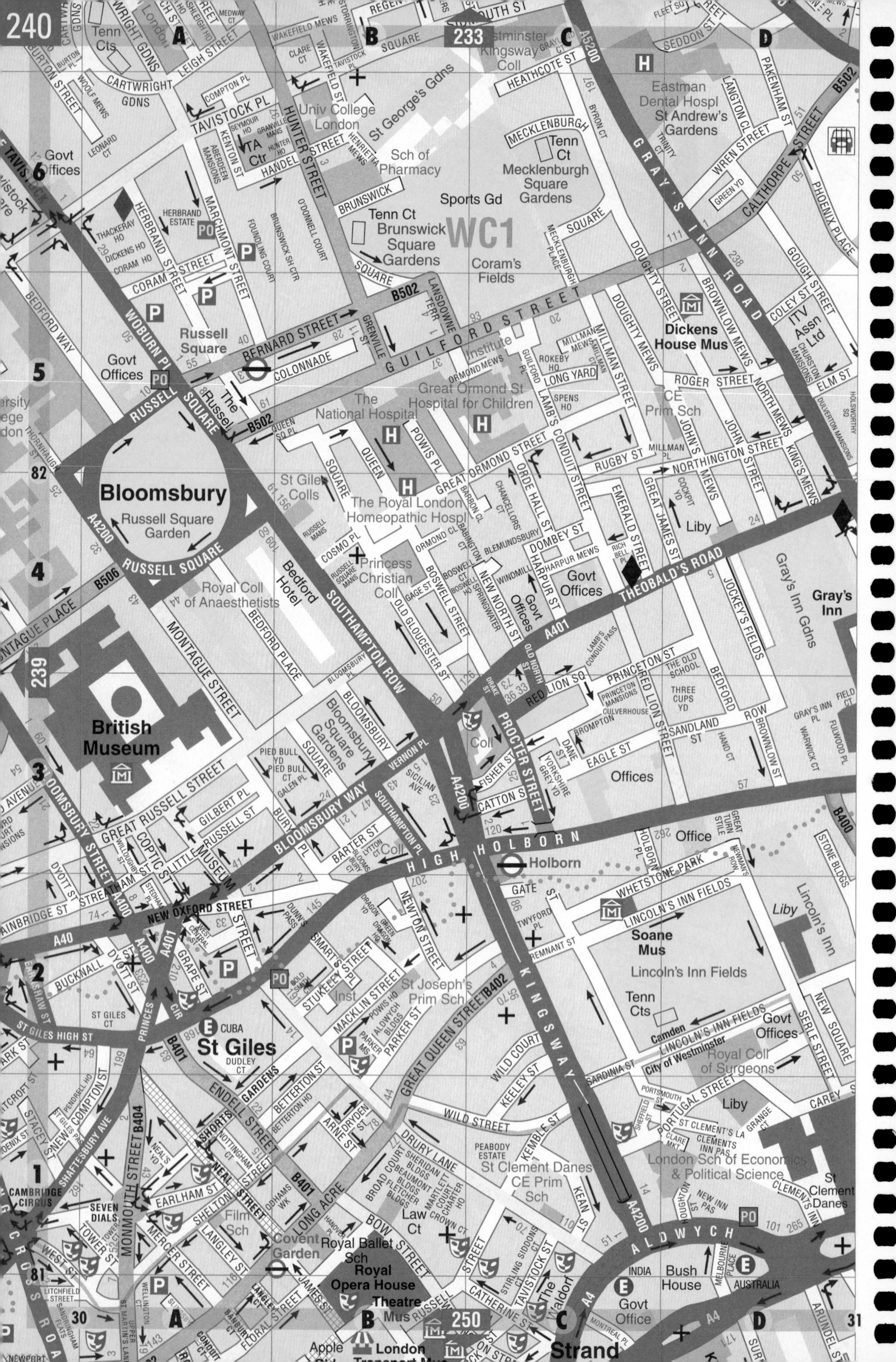
A
B
C
D
233
Tenn Cts
CARTWRIGHT GDNS
LEIGH STREET
WAKEFIELD MEWS
WAKEFIELD ST
TAVISTOCK SQUARE
Westminster Kingsway Coll
HEATHCOTE ST
SEDDON ST
Eastman Dental Hospl
St Andrew's Gardens
LANGTON CL
PAKENHAM ST
BURTON STREET
WOLF MEWS
COMPTON PL
TAVISTOCK PL
Univ College London
St George's Gdns
MECKLENBURGH
Tenn Ct
Mecklenburgh Square Gardens
GRAY'S INN ROAD
WREN STREET
CALTHORPE STREET
B502
A5200
Govt Offices
6
LEONARD CT
KENTON ST
TA Ctr
HANDEL
HUNTER STREET
Sch of Pharmacy
BRUNSWICK
Sports Gd
Tenn Ct
Brunswick Square Gardens
WC1
Coram's Fields
SQUARE
DOUGHTY STREET
BROWNLOW MEWS
GOUGH STREET
PHOENIX PLACE
THACKERAY HO
DICKENS HO
CORAM HO
HERBRAND STREET
HERBRAND ESTATE
MARCHMONT STREET
FOUNDLING COURT
BRUNSWICK SH CTR
O'DONNELL COURT
CORAM STREET
BEDFORD WAY
WOBURN PL
Russell Square
BERNARD STREET
COLONNADE
GRENVILLE ST
LANSDOWNE TERR
GUILFORD STREET
Institute
DOUGHTY MEWS
MILLMAN STREET
Dickens House Mus
COLEY ST
ITV Assn Ltd
5
Govt Offices
PO
RUSSELL SQUARE
The Russell
ORMOND MEWS
ROKEBY HO
LONG YARD
ROGER STREET
NORTH MEWS
ELM ST
Great Ormond St Hospital for Children
The National Hospital
SPENS HO
CE Prim Sch
QUEEN SQ PL
POWIS PL
GREAT ORMOND STREET
LAMB'S CONDUIT STREET
RUGBY ST
MILLMAN PL
NORTHINGTON STREET
JOHN STREET
JOHN'S MEWS
KING'S MEWS
82
Bloomsbury
Russell Square Garden
St Giles Colls
QUEEN SQUARE
The Royal London Homeopathic Hospl
BARBON CL
ORDE HALL ST
EMERALD STREET
GREAT JAMES ST
COCKPIT YD
Liby
A4200
COSMO PL
Princess Christian Coll
ORMOND CL
BLEMUNDSBURY
DOMBEY ST
HARPUR MEWS
RICH BELL PL
THEOBALD'S ROAD
Gray's Inn Gdns
Gray's Inn
4
RUSSELL SQUARE
B506
Royal Coll of Anaesthetists
Bedford Hotel
GAGE ST
BOSWELL STREET
NEW NORTH ST
Govt Offices
HARPUR ST
A401
JOCKEY'S FIELDS
MONTAGUE PLACE
239
MONTAGUE STREET
BEDFORD PLACE
SOUTHAMPTON ROW
OLD GLOUCESTER ST
RED LION SQ
PRINCETON ST
THE OLD SCHOOL
THREE CUPS YD
BEDFORD ROW
British Museum
Bloomsbury Square Gardens
BLOOMSBURY SQUARE
PROCTER STREET
Coll
DANE ST
BROMPTON
SANDLAND ST
BROWNLOW ST
GRAY'S INN PL
FIELD CT
WARWICK CT
FULWOOD PL
3
BLOOMSBURY STREET
GREAT RUSSELL STREET
GILBERT PL
PIED BULL YD
PIED BULL CT
GALEN PL
VERNON PL
SICILIAN AVE
FISHER ST
EAGLE ST
Offices
RED LION STREET
CATTON ST
B400
COPTIC ST
LITTLE RUSSELL ST
MUSEUM
BURY PL
BLOOMSBURY WAY
SOUTHAMPTON PL
BARTER ST
Coll
HIGH HOLBORN
HOLBORN PL
Office
STONE BLDGS
Holborn
DYOTT ST
STREATHAM ST
NEW OXFORD STREET
DUNN'S PASS
NEWTON STREET
GATE ST
WHETSTONE PARK
LINCOLN'S INN FIELDS
Liby
Lincoln's Inn
BAINBRIDGE ST
A40
A400
SMART'S PL
TWYFORD PL
REMNANT ST
Soane Mus
2
BUCKNALL ST
GRAPE ST
SHAFTESBURY AVE
PO
STUKELEY ST
MACKLIN STREET
St Joseph's Prim Sch
KINGSWAY
Lincoln's Inn Fields
NEW SQUARE
ST GILES HIGH ST
PRINCES CIR
CUBA
St Giles
DUDLEY CT
ENDELL STREET
BETTERTON ST
GREAT QUEEN STREET
B402
PARKER ST
WILD COURT
KEELEY ST
SARDINIA ST
Tenn Cts
Camden
City of Westminster
Royal Coll of Surgeons
Govt Offices
SERLE STREET
STACEY ST
NEW COMPTON ST
MONMOUTH STREET
B404
SHORTS GARDENS
ARNE ST
DRYDEN ST
WILD STREET
PORTUGAL STREET
Liby
CAREY ST
1
CAMBRIDGE CIRCUS
SEVEN DIALS
EARLHAM ST
NEAL STREET
DRURY LANE
PEABODY ESTATE
KEMBLE ST
St Clement Danes CE Prim Sch
ST CLEMENT'S LA
London Sch of Economics & Political Science
St Clement Danes
SHELTON ST
Film Sch
B401
LONG ACRE
Law Ct
KEAN ST
ALDWYCH
PO
MERCER STREET
LANGLEY ST
Covent Garden
Royal Ballet Sch
BOW STREET
CATHERINE ST
81
Royal Opera House
Theatre Mus
INDIA
Bush House
AUSTRALIA
ARUNDEL ST
30
A
B
C
D
31
250
Govt Office
Strand
A4
London Transport Mus

241
234
242
251
31
32
A
B
C
D
1
2
3
4
5
6
EC1
EC4
Clerkenwell
Holborn
Mt. Pleasant Post Office
Spa Fields Gardens
Exmouth Market
Skinner Street
Percival Street
Goswell Road A1
St John Street
Clerkenwell Road
Farringdon Road
Farringdon
Farringdon Lane
Farringdon Street
Charterhouse Street
Charterhouse Square
Smithfield Market
The Medical College of St Bartholomew's Hospl
St Bartholomew's Hospl
National Postal Museum
Barbican
Long Lane
Cloth Fair
Aldersgate
Holborn
Holborn Circus
Holborn Viaduct
Hatton Garden
Leather Lane
Chancery Lane
Gray's Inn Square
Central Sch of Ballet
The London Inst
St Alban's CE Prim Sch
Gresham Coll
Public Record Office
Newgate Street
Central Criminal Court (Old Bailey)
St Sepulchre
City Thameslink
Ludgate Circus
Ludgate Hill
St Paul's Cathed
Fleet Street
New Bridge Street
Dr Johnson's House Mus
St Dunstan-in-the-West
Royal Courts of Justice
Temple Bar
Inner Temple
Middle Temple Lane
Fetter Lane
New Fetter Lane
Shoe Lane
St Bride St
Cowcross Street
Turnmill Street
Smithfield Street
Snow Hill
Cock Lane
Giltspur Street
Warner Street
Rosebery Avenue
Bowling Green Lane
Northampton Rd
Compton St
Great Sutton Street
Dallington Sch
St Peters & St Pauls RC Prim Sch
Aylesbury St
Clerkenwell Green
Britton Street
St John's Lane
Hatton Wall
Greville Street
Saffron Hill
Kirby Street
St Cross Street
Ely Place
Brooke Street
Furnival Street
Cursitor Street
Bream's Buildings
Blackfriars Lane
Carter Lane
Tudor Street
Whitefriars Street
Bouverie Street
Temple Lane
Essex Street
Liby

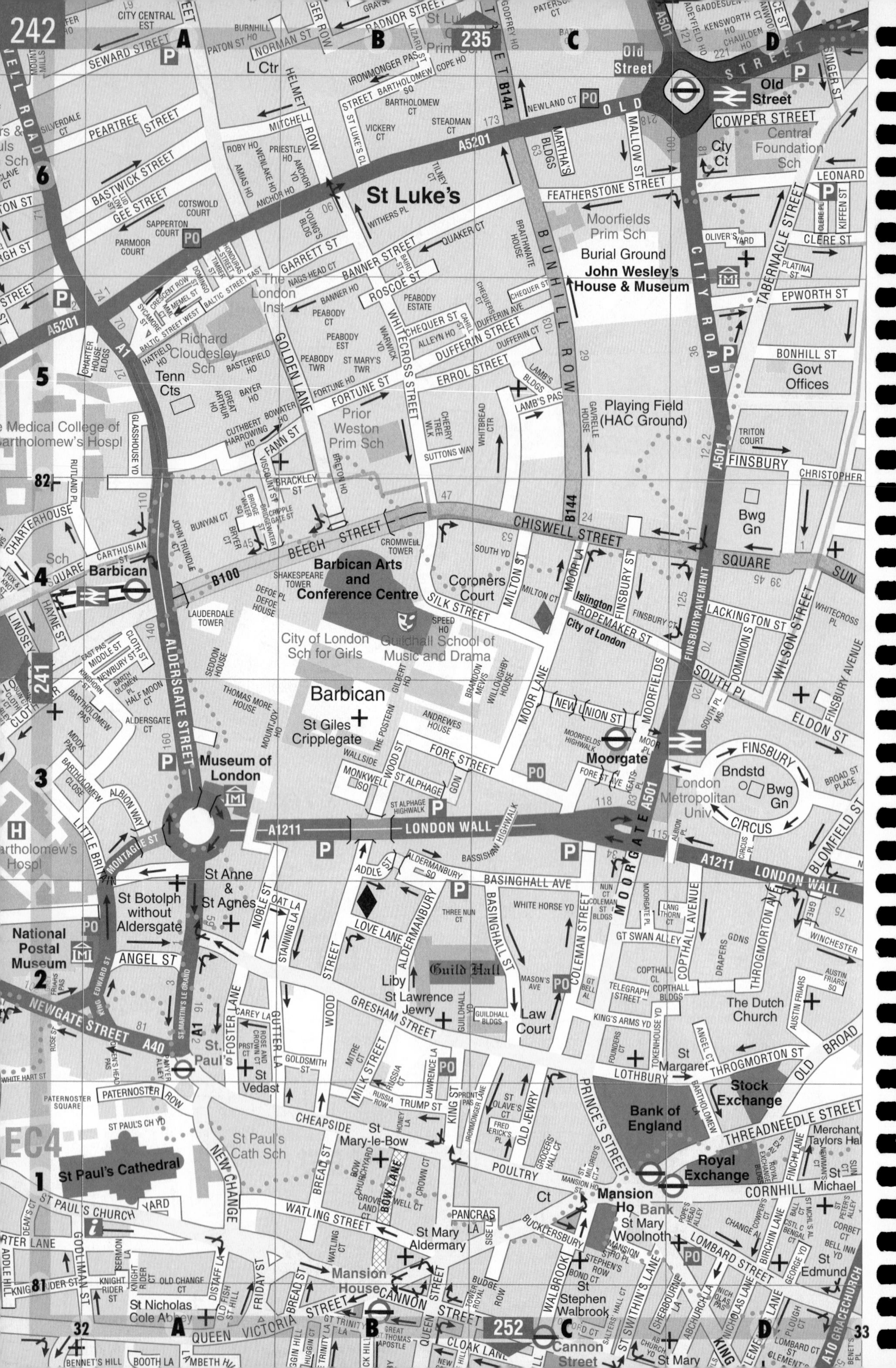

St Luke's
Old Street
Barbican
Barbican Arts and Conference Centre
Museum of London
St Paul's Cathedral
Bank of England
Royal Exchange
Stock Exchange
Guild Hall
Moorgate
Mansion House
Cannon Street
National Postal Museum
John Wesley's House & Museum
Playing Field (HAC Ground)
City of London Sch for Girls
Guildhall School of Music and Drama
St Giles Cripplegate
London Metropolitan Univ
The Dutch Church
St Mary-le-Bow
St Paul's Cath Sch
St Botolph without Aldersgate
St Anne & St Agnes
St Lawrence Jewry
St Mary Aldermary
St Mary Woolnoth
St Stephen Walbrook
St Nicholas Cole Abbey
Coroners Court
Law Court
Moorfields Prim Sch
Prior Weston Prim Sch
Central Foundation Sch
Govt Offices
Richard Cloudesley Sch
Burial Ground
OLD STREET
CITY ROAD
BUNHILL ROW
CHISWELL STREET
BEECH STREET
ALDERSGATE STREET
LONDON WALL
MOORGATE
CHEAPSIDE
NEWGATE STREET
GRESHAM STREET
THREADNEEDLE STREET
QUEEN VICTORIA STREET
CANNON STREET
WATLING STREET
FINSBURY PAVEMENT
FINSBURY CIRCUS
EC4
235
241
252
A B C D
1 2 3 4 5 6

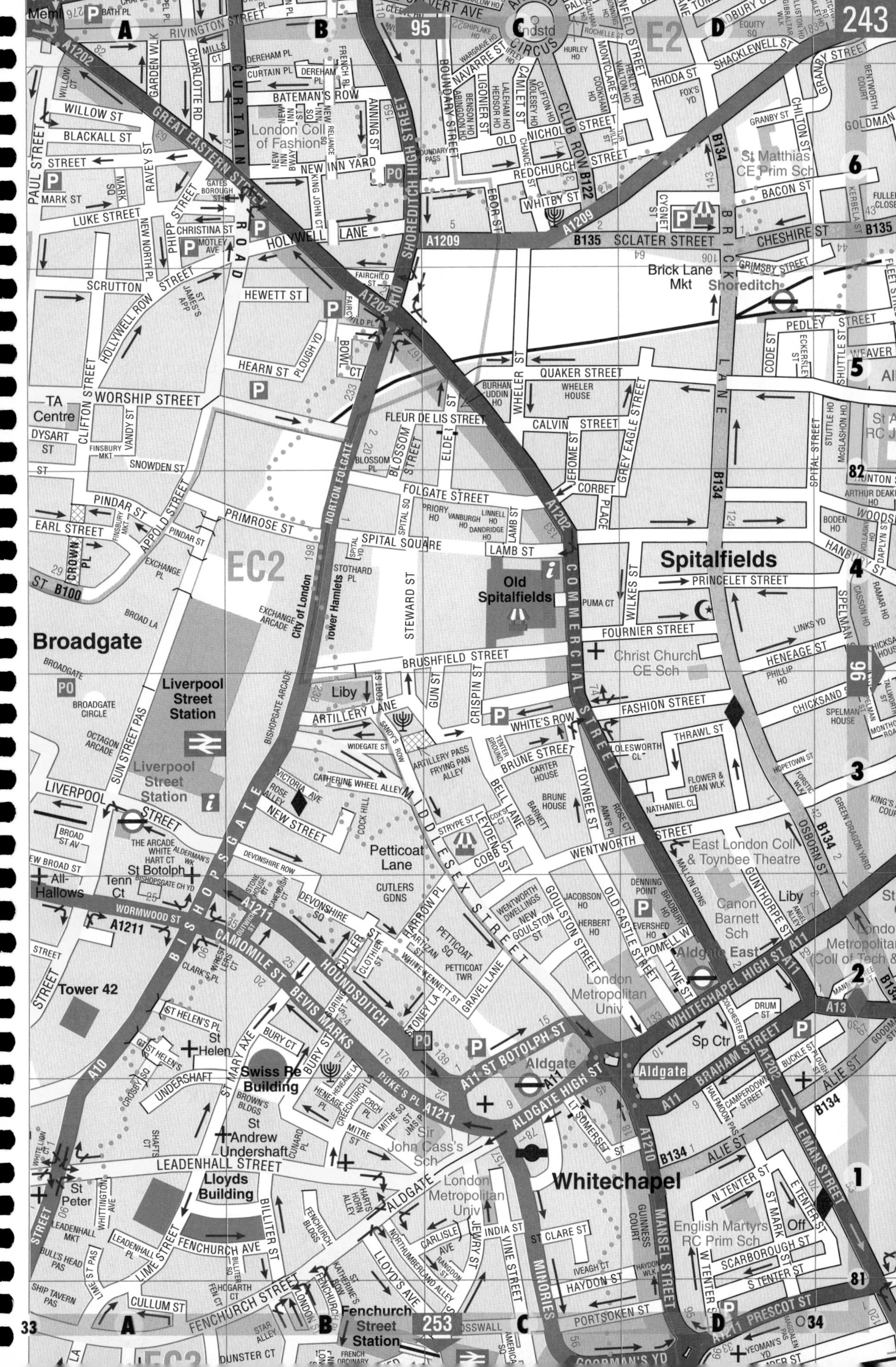

95
253
96
A
B
C
D
1
2
3
4
5
6
33
34
E2
EC2
Broadgate
Spitalfields
Whitechapel
Petticoat Lane
Shoreditch
Aldgate
Aldgate East
Brick Lane Mkt
Old Spitalfields
Liverpool Street Station
Fenchurch Street Station
London Coll of Fashion
St Matthias CE Prim Sch
Christ Church CE Sch
East London Coll & Toynbee Theatre
Canon Barnett Sch
London Metropolitan Univ
English Martyrs RC Prim Sch
Swiss Re Building
Lloyds Building
Tower 42
Sir John Cass's Sch
TA Centre
Liby
Sp Ctr
St Botolph
All-Hallows
Tenn Ct
St Helen
St Andrew Undershaft
St Peter
City of London
Tower Hamlets
RIVINGTON STREET
CALVERT AVE
ARNOLD CIRCUS
SHACKLEWELL ST
GREAT EASTERN STREET
CURTAIN ROAD
SHOREDITCH HIGH STREET
BOUNDARY STREET
OLD NICHOL STREET
CLUB ROW
REDCHURCH STREET
BATEMAN'S ROW
NEW INN YARD
HOLYWELL LANE
SCLATER STREET
CHESHIRE ST
BRICK LANE
WORSHIP STREET
QUAKER STREET
CALVIN STREET
FOLGATE STREET
NORTON FOLGATE
SPITAL SQUARE
PRIMROSE ST
LAMB ST
PRINCELET STREET
FOURNIER STREET
BRUSHFIELD STREET
FASHION STREET
COMMERCIAL STREET
WENTWORTH STREET
BISHOPSGATE
LIVERPOOL STREET
WORMWOOD ST
CAMOMILE ST
HOUNDSDITCH
BEVIS MARKS
MIDDLESEX STREET
ST BOTOLPH ST
ALDGATE HIGH ST
WHITECHAPEL HIGH ST
LEADENHALL STREET
FENCHURCH AVE
FENCHURCH STREET
MINORIES
MANSEL STREET
LEMAN STREET
ALIE ST
PRESCOT ST

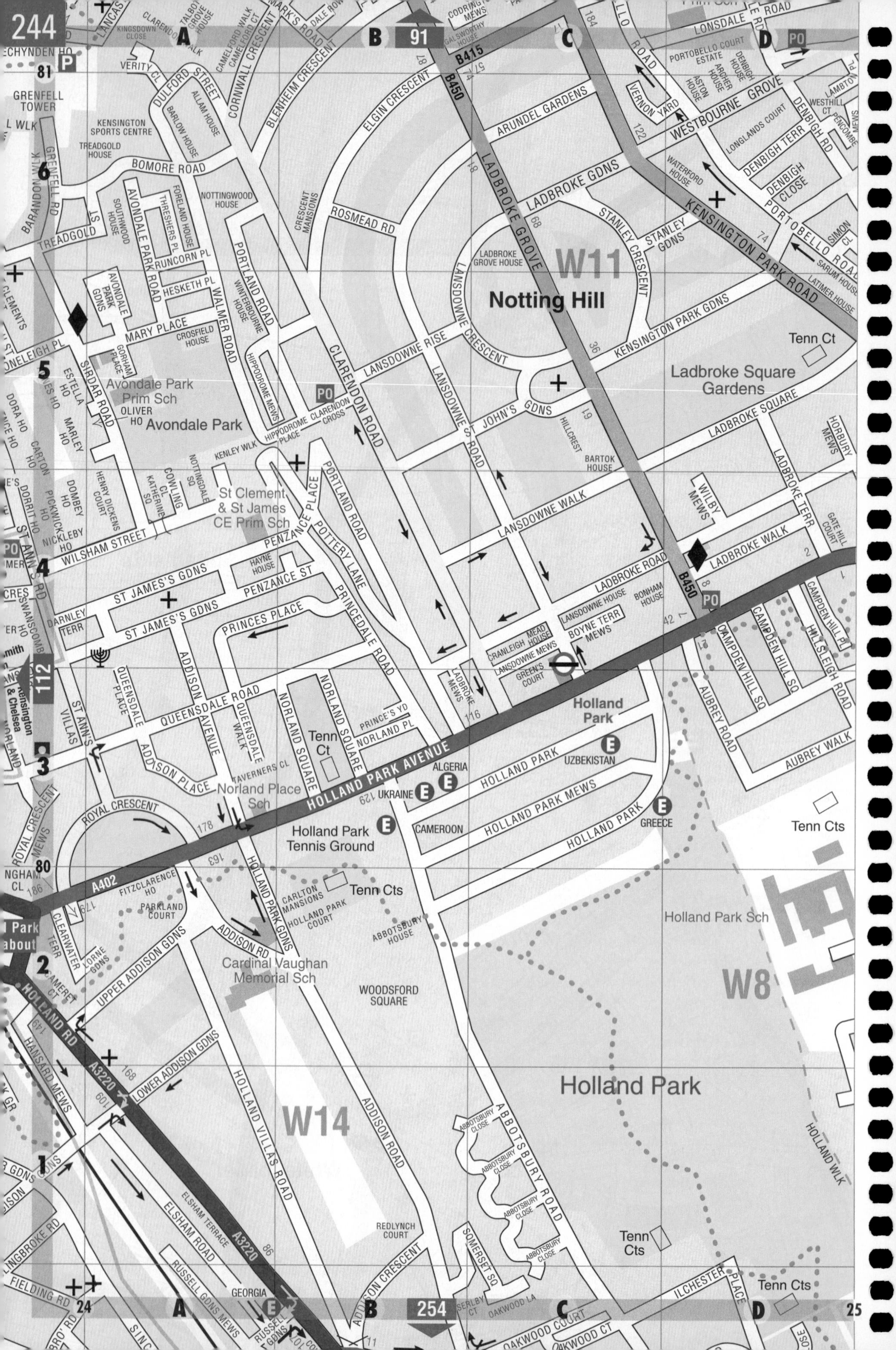

244
A
B
91
C
D
81
80
24
254
25
6
5
4
3
2
1
112
Kensington & Chelsea
W11
Notting Hill
W14
W8
Holland Park
GRENFELL TOWER
KENSINGTON SPORTS CENTRE
TREADGOLD HOUSE
BOMORE ROAD
DULFORD STREET
ALLAM HOUSE
BARLOW HOUSE
VERITY CL
CORNWALL CRESCENT
CAMELFORD WALK
CAMELFORD CT
BLENHEIM CRESCENT
ELGIN CRESCENT
ARUNDEL GARDENS
LADBROKE GDNS
LADBROKE GROVE
B450
B415
WESTBOURNE GROVE
LONSDALE ROAD
PORTOBELLO COURT ESTATE
DENBIGH HOUSE
ARCHER HOUSE
ASTON HOUSE
VERNON YARD
LONGLANDS COURT
DENBIGH TERR
DENBIGH RD
DENBIGH CLOSE
WATERFORD HOUSE
KENSINGTON PARK ROAD
PORTOBELLO ROAD
STANLEY GDNS
STANLEY CRESCENT
LADBROKE GROVE HOUSE
LANSDOWNE CRESCENT
LANSDOWNE RISE
LANSDOWNE ROAD
KENSINGTON PARK GDNS
Tenn Ct
Ladbroke Square Gardens
LADBROKE SQUARE
ST JOHN'S GDNS
HILLCREST
BARTOK HOUSE
WILBY MEWS
LADBROKE TERR
LADBROKE WALK
LADBROKE ROAD
LANSDOWNE WALK
LANSDOWNE HOUSE
BONHAM HOUSE
BOYNE TERR MEWS
CRANLEIGH MEAD HOUSE
LANSDOWNE MEWS
GREEN'S COURT
LADBROKE MEWS
Holland Park
CAMPDEN HILL SQ
CAMPDEN HILL PL
HILLSLEIGH ROAD
AUBREY ROAD
AUBREY WALK
CRESCENT MANSIONS
ROSMEAD RD
CLARENDON ROAD
CLARENDON CROSS
HIPPODROME PLACE
HIPPODROME MEWS
PORTLAND ROAD
WINTERBOURNE HOUSE
WALMER ROAD
NOTTINGWOOD HOUSE
FORELAND HOUSE
THRESHERS PL
AVONDALE PARK ROAD
SOUTHWOOD HOUSE
TREADGOLD ST
BARANDON WLK
GRENFELL RD
RUNCORN PL
HESKETH PL
AVONDALE PARK GDNS
MARY PLACE
CROSFIELD HOUSE
GORHAM PLACE
Avondale Park Prim Sch
OLIVER HO
Avondale Park
SIRDAR ROAD
ESTELLA HO
MARLEY HO
DOMBEY HO
PICKWICK HO
NICKLEBY HO
HENRY DICKENS COURT
KATHERINE SQ
COWLING CL
NOTTINGDALE SQ
KENLEY WLK
St Clement & St James CE Prim Sch
WILSHAM STREET
PENZANCE PLACE
PENZANCE ST
POTTERY LANE
HAYNE HOUSE
ST JAMES'S GDNS
PRINCES PLACE
PRINCEDALE ROAD
DARNLEY TERR
ST ANN'S RD
ADDISON AVENUE
QUEENSDALE ROAD
QUEENSDALE PLACE
QUEENSDALE WALK
NORLAND SQUARE
PRINCE'S YD
NORLAND PL
ST ANN'S VILLAS
ADDISON PLACE
TAVERNERS CL
Norland Place Sch
ROYAL CRESCENT
ROYAL CRESCENT MEWS
HOLLAND PARK AVENUE
A402
ALGERIA
UKRAINE
HOLLAND PARK
UZBEKISTAN
HOLLAND PARK MEWS
CAMEROON
GREECE
Holland Park Tennis Ground
Tenn Cts
FITZCLARENCE HO
PARKLAND COURT
CLEARWATER TERR
LORNE GDNS
CAMERET CT
CARLTON MANSIONS
HOLLAND PARK COURT
ABBOTSBURY HOUSE
HOLLAND PARK GDNS
ADDISON RD
UPPER ADDISON GDNS
Cardinal Vaughan Memorial Sch
WOODSFORD SQUARE
Holland Park Sch
HOLLAND RD
A3220
HANSARD MEWS
LOWER ADDISON GDNS
HOLLAND VILLAS ROAD
ADDISON ROAD
ABBOTSBURY CLOSE
ABBOTSBURY ROAD
HOLLAND WLK
ELSHAM TERRACE
ELSHAM ROAD
RUSSELL GDNS MEWS
RUSSELL GDNS
GEORGIA
FIELDING RD
REDLYNCH COURT
ADDISON CRESCENT
SOMERSET SQ
SERLBY CT
OAKWOOD LA
OAKWOOD COURT
ILCHESTER PLACE

A
B
C
D
91
College Park Sch
Cinema
LEDBURY ROAD
LEDBURY MEWS N
LEDBURY MEWS W
WESTBOURNE GROVE MEWS
ROSEHART MEWS
LIBERIA
CHEPSTOW PLACE
REDE PLACE
HEREFORD ROAD
GARWAY ROAD
LEINSTER SQUARE
PRINCE'S SQUARE
KENSINGTON GDNS SQUARE
PORCHESTER COURT
PORCHESTER GARDENS
PORCHESTER GDN MEWS
PO
81
CHEPSTOW VILLAS
CHEPSTOW COURT
CHEPSTOW CRES
PEMBRIDGE VILLAS
PEMBRIDGE PLACE
THORNBURY COURT
RODNEY HOUSE
PEMBRIDGE MEWS
PEMBRIDGE CRES
PRINCE'S SQ
QUEEN'S MEWS
SALEM RD
BEAUMANOR MANSIONS
QUEENSWAY
INVERNESS TERRACE
TENNIEL CL
QUEENSBOROUGH TERRACE
QUEENSBORO MEWS
PORCHESTER TERRACE
FULTON MS
6
BURNHAM COURT
WINDSOR COURT
MOSCOW PL
ILCHESTER GDNS
Bayswater
PRINCE'S MS
DAWSON PLACE
PALACE COURT
MOSCOW ROAD
CHENIES HOUSE
SHAFTESBURY HOUSE
INVERNESS MEWS
INVERNESS PLACE
POPLAR PLACE
PRINCE EDWARD MANSIONS
PEMBRIDGE SQUARE
BARK PLACE
PRINCESS COURT
OLYMPIA YD
ST PETERSBURGH PLACE
ST PETERSBURGH MEWS
CHAPEL SIDE
LOMBARDY PL
CAROLINE PL
PORTOBELLO MEWS
PRINCES HOUSE
OSSINGTON CL
OSSINGTON STREET
CLANRICARDE GARDENS
QUEEN'S COURT
CONSORT HOUSE
FOSBURY MEWS
B411
PORCHESTER GATE
LINDEN GARDENS
THE LIMES
LANCASTER CLOSE
SAXON HALL
ST OLAVES COURT
ORME LA
New West End Synagogue
ORME CT
ORME CT MS
CAROLINE PL MS
CAROLINE CL
CAROLINE HO
ORME SQUARE
KELVIN COURT
Liby
PEMBRIDGE RD
PEMBRIDGE GARDENS
GARDEN MEWS
VICTORIA GROVE MEWS
GUYANA
5
A402
Inverness Terrace Gate
Queensway Black Lion Gate
HORBURY CRES
BAYSWATER ROAD
Orme Square Gate
LINDEN MEWS
LINDEN GDNS
B415
CZECH REPUBLIC
SLOVAK REPUBLIC
Pav
Notting Hill Gate
BULMER MEWS
CAMPTON HILL TOWERS
VICTORIA GDNS
A4206
IVY LODGE
NOTTING HILL GATE
WEST MALL
RABBIT ROW
A4204
PO
KENSINGTON ML
B405
UXBRIDGE STREET
FARMER ST
JAMESON ST
NEWCOMBE STREET
HILLGATE PLACE
HILLGATE ST
CALLCOTT ST
FARM PL
LUCERNE MS
STRATHMORE GARDENS
PALACE GARDEN MEWS
KENSINGTON PALACE GARDENS
Clock Tower
4
LEBANON
NEPAL
RUSSIA
KENSINGTON PLACE
EDGE STREET
CAMPDEN HILL MANSIONS
Fox Prim Sch
CAMPDEN HILL GDNS
PALMERSTON HOUSE
MELBOURNE HOUSE
PEEL STREET
PEEL PASS
CAMPDEN HOUSES
CAMPDEN STREET
KENSINGTON CHURCH STREET
PALACE GARDENS TERRACE
BRUNSWICK GARDENS
BERKELEY GARDENS
Diana, Princess of Wales Memorial Walk
THE BROAD WALK
246
WATER TOWER HOUSE
KENSINGTON HEIGHTS
BEDFORD GARDENS
BEDFORD GARDENS HO
THE MOUNT
3
Kensington Palace
Queen Victoria Statue
AIRLIE GDNS
LAURIE HOUSE
SHEFFIELD TERRACE
CAMPDEN HOUSE
INVERNESS GARDENS
VICARAGE GATE
VICARAGE GARDENS
PHILIPPINES
80
Tenn Cts
TOR GDNS
TOR COURT
GLOUCESTER WALK
MELON PL
WINCHESTER COURT
VICARAGE GATE
VICARAGE COURT
HAMILTON HOUSE
W8
PALACE GREEN
Kensington Palace Green
CAMPDEN HILL
CAMPDEN HILL ROAD
NICARAGUA
CAMPDEN HO CL
CAMPDEN GROVE
Tenn Ct
CHURCH CLOSE
YORK HOUSE
ROMANIA
PALACE AVENUE
THE DIAL WALK
2
Kensington Chelsea
City of Westminster
Kings College London
OBSERVATORY GDNS
HORNTON STREET
GORDON PLACE
BULLINGHAM MANSIONS
DUKES LANE
YORK HOUSE PL
LANCER SQUARE
SHELDRAKE PLACE
DUCHESS OF BEDFORD HOUSE
CAMPDEN HILL COURT
PITT ST
CARMEL CT
HOLLAND PL
GREGORY PL
ISRAEL
Tenn Ct
CAMPDEN HILL GATE
HOLLAND STREET
INGELOW HOUSE
KENSINGTON HOUSE
OLD COURT PL
DUCHESS OF BEDFORD'S WALK
OLD COURT HOUSE
P
AZERBAIJAN
A315
TH
DRAYSON MEWS
St Mary Abbots CE Prim Sch
UPPER PHILLIMORE GARDENS
JORDAN
KENSINGTON
KENSINGTON CHURCH CT
CHURCH WK
BELARUS
GAMBIA
PRINCE OF WALES TERR
KENSINGTON CT
MONGOLIA
PHILLIMORE PLACE
ARGYLL ROAD
Liby
HORNTON PLACE
GEORGIA
Associated Newspapers Ltd
DERRY ST
YOUNG ST
KENSINGTON CT MANS
KENSINGTON COURT
ST CHRISTOPHER & NEVIS / ST VINCENT & THE GRENADINES
1
PHILLIMORE GARDENS
ESSEX VILLAS
HORNTON COURT
High Street Kensington
KENSINGTON SQUARE
CAMBRIDGE PL
ALBERT PL
DE VERE GARDENS
STAFFORD TERRACE
PHILLIMORE WALK
PHILLIMORE COURT
KENSINGTON HIGH STREET
THACKERAY ST
ESMOND CT
ANSDELL ST
KENSINGTON CT PLACE
KENSINGTON CT MEWS
VIETNAM
CANNING PASSAGE
VICTORIA ROAD
DE VERE COTTS
Commonwealth Institute
25
STAFFORD CT
IVERNA CT
WRIGHT'S LA
255
DOURO PLACE
26
Richmond Coll
CANNING
PHILLIMORE GDNS CL
ALLEN HO
ADAM AND EVE MEWS
ST ALBANS MANS
ANSDELL TERR
Richmond

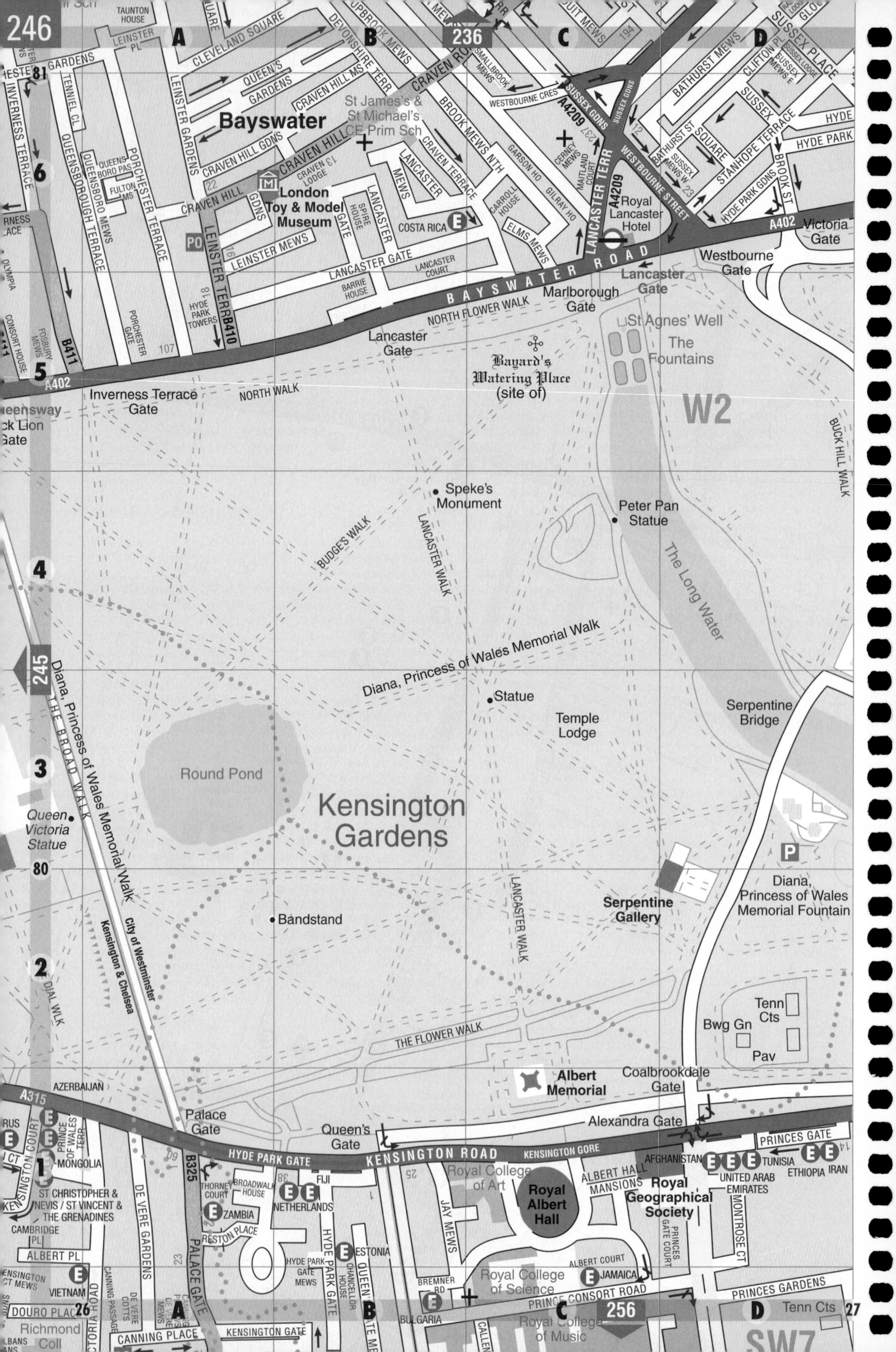

A
B
236
C
D
Bayswater
London Toy & Model Museum
St James's & St Michael's CE Prim Sch
Royal Lancaster Hotel
BAYSWATER ROAD
A402
Victoria Gate
Westbourne Gate
Lancaster Gate
Marlborough Gate
Lancaster Gate
St Agnes' Well
The Fountains
Bayard's Watering Place (site of)
Inverness Terrace Gate
NORTH WALK
NORTH FLOWER WALK
W2
BUCK HILL WALK
Speke's Monument
Peter Pan Statue
The Long Water
BUDGE'S WALK
LANCASTER WALK
Diana, Princess of Wales Memorial Walk
Statue
Temple Lodge
Serpentine Bridge
Round Pond
Kensington Gardens
Queen Victoria Statue
THE BROAD WALK
Serpentine Gallery
Diana, Princess of Wales Memorial Fountain
Bandstand
City of Westminster
Kensington & Chelsea
DIAL WALK
THE FLOWER WALK
Tenn Cts
Bwg Gn
Pav
Albert Memorial
Coalbrookdale Gate
Alexandra Gate
Palace Gate
Queen's Gate
HYDE PARK GATE
KENSINGTON ROAD
KENSINGTON GORE
PRINCES GATE
Royal College of Art
Royal Albert Hall
ALBERT HALL MANSIONS
Royal Geographical Society
Royal College of Science
PRINCE CONSORT ROAD
Royal College of Music
PRINCES GARDENS
256
SW7
245
6
5
4
3
2
1
80
81
LEINSTER GARDENS
PORCHESTER TERRACE
QUEENSBOROUGH TERRACE
INVERNESS TERRACE
CRAVEN HILL
LEINSTER TERR
LANCASTER TERR
WESTBOURNE STREET
SUSSEX GDNS
A4209
LANCASTER GATE
PALACE GATE
B325
DE VERE GARDENS
JAY MEWS
QUEEN'S GATE MEWS
ALBERT PL
Richmond Coll
CANNING PLACE
KENSINGTON GATE
Tenn Cts

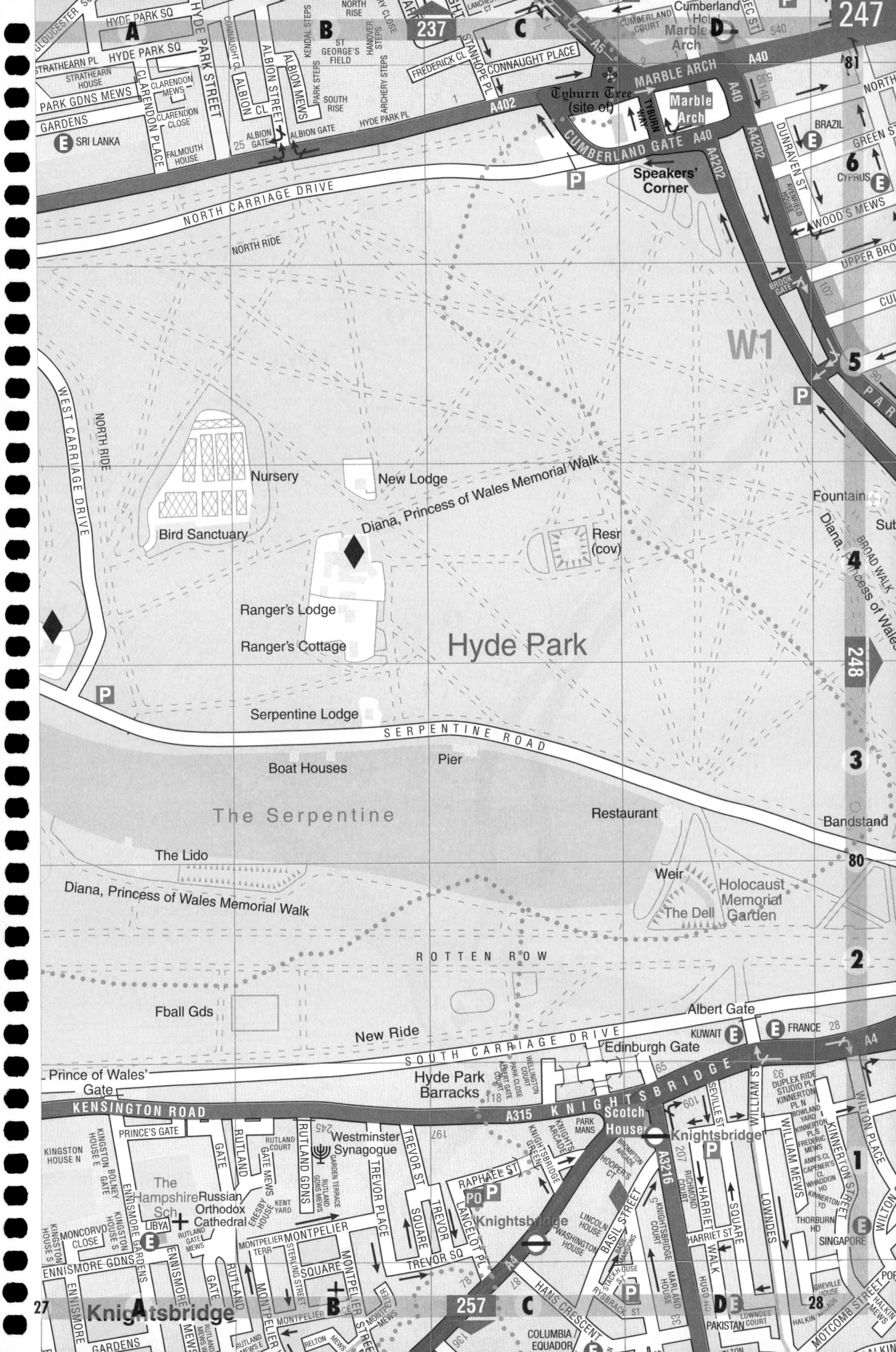
Hyde Park
The Serpentine
W1
Marble Arch
Tyburn Tree (site of)
Speakers' Corner
Cumberland Hotel
North Carriage Drive
North Ride
West Carriage Drive
Nursery
New Lodge
Bird Sanctuary
Diana, Princess of Wales Memorial Walk
Resr (cov)
Ranger's Lodge
Ranger's Cottage
Serpentine Lodge
Serpentine Road
Boat Houses
Pier
Restaurant
The Lido
Weir
Holocaust Memorial Garden
The Dell
Rotten Row
Fball Gds
New Ride
Albert Gate
Edinburgh Gate
South Carriage Drive
Prince of Wales' Gate
Hyde Park Barracks
Kensington Road
Knightsbridge
Scotch House
Westminster Synagogue
The Hampshire Sch
Russian Orthodox Cathedral
Fountain
Bandstand
Broad Walk
Hyde Park Sq
Hyde Park Street
Connaught Place
Cumberland Gate
Brook Gate
Sri Lanka
Kuwait
France
Libya
Singapore
Brazil
Cyprus
Pakistan
Columbia
Equador
Trevor Square
Montpelier Square
Hans Crescent
Basil Street
Lowndes
Wilton Place
Motcomb Street
Ennismore Gardens
Rutland Gate

237
248
257

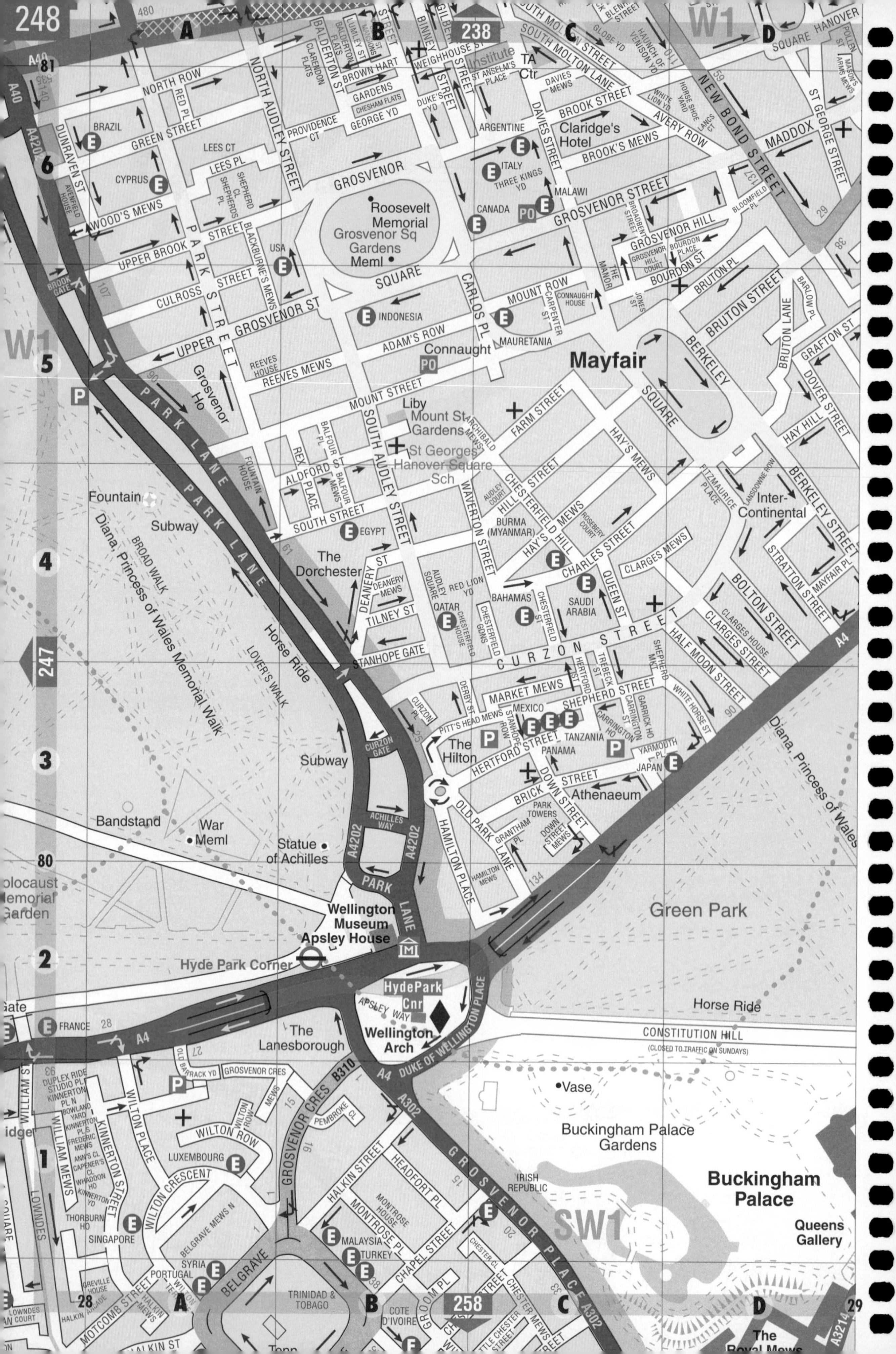
A
B
C
D
238
W1
North Row
Green Street
Brazil
Dunraven St
Cyprus
Lees Ct
Lees Pl
Shepherds Pl
Wood's Mews
Upper Brook
Street
Park Street
USA
Blackburne's Mews
Culross
Upper Grosvenor St
North Audley Street
Providence Ct
Balderton St
Balderton Flats
Clarendon Flats
Brown Hart Gardens
Chesham Flats
George Yd
Weighhouse St
Binney Street
Gilbert Street
Duke's Yd
St Anselm's Place
Institute
TA Ctr
Argentine
South Molton Street
South Molton Lane
Davies Mews
Davies Street
Brook Street
Claridge's Hotel
Brook's Mews
Avery Row
New Bond Street
Maddox
St George Street
Square Hanover
Grosvenor
Roosevelt Memorial
Grosvenor Sq Gardens
Meml
Square
Italy
Three Kings Yd
Canada
Malawi
PO
Grosvenor Street
Grosvenor Hill
Bourdon Place
Bourdon St
Bruton Pl
Bruton Street
Bruton Lane
Barlow Pl
Grafton St
Indonesia
Adam's Row
Carlos Pl
Mount Row
Carpenter St
Connaught House
Mauretania
Connaught
Mayfair
Berkeley Square
Jones St
The Manor
Dover Street
Hay Hill
Reeves House
Reeves Mews
Mount Street
Grosvenor Ho
Park Lane
Liby
Mount St Gardens
St Georges Hanover Square Sch
Farm Street
Archibald Mews
Hay's Mews
Fitzmaurice Place
Lansdowne Row
Inter-Continental
Berkeley Street
Fountain House
Balfour Pl
Rex Place
Aldford St
Balfour Mews
South Audley Street
South Street
Egypt
Audley Court
Hill Street
Chesterfield Hill
Burma (Myanmar)
Waverton Street
Hay's Mews
Rosebery Court
Charles Street
Clarges Mews
Stratton Street
Mayfair Pl
Fountain
Subway
Diana, Princess of Wales Memorial Walk
Broad Walk
The Dorchester
Deanery St
Deanery Mews
Tilney St
Audley Square
Red Lion Yd
Qatar
Chesterfield House
Bahamas
Chesterfield Gdns
Chesterfield St
Saudi Arabia
Queen St
Bolton Street
Clarges House
Clarges Street
Half Moon Street
Curzon Street
Shepherd Mkt
White Horse St
Horse Ride
Lover's Walk
Stanhope Gate
Market Mews
Derby St
Hertford St
Trebeck St
Shepherd Street
Curzon Pl
Pitt's Head Mews
Stanhope Row
Mexico
Carrington St
Garrick Ho
Carrington Ho
Tanzania
Hertford Street
Panama
Yarmouth Pl
Japan
The Hilton
Curzon Gate
Subway
Brick Street
Down Street
Athenaeum
Park Towers
Down Street Mews
Grantham Pl
Old Park Lane
Hamilton Place
Hamilton Mews
Achilles Way
A4202
A4
A40
Bandstand
War Meml
Statue of Achilles
olocaust emorial Garden
Wellington Museum
Apsley House
Hyde Park Corner
Green Park
HydePark Cnr
Apsley Way
Wellington Arch
Duke of Wellington Place
Horse Ride
Constitution Hill
(Closed to traffic on Sundays)
Gate
France
The Lanesborough
Old Barrack Yd
Grosvenor Cres
Mews
Grosvenor Cres
B310
A302
Vase
Buckingham Palace Gardens
Duplex Ride
Studio Pl
Kinnerton Pl N
Bowland Yard
Kinnerton Pl S
Frederic Mews
Ann's Cl
Capener's Cl
Whaddon Ho
Kinnerton Yd
William St
William Mews
Kinnerton Street
Wilton Place
Wilton Row
Luxembourg
Wilton Crescent
Pembroke Cl
Halkin Street
Headfort Pl
Irish Republic
Buckingham Palace
Thorburn Ho
Singapore
Belgrave Mews N
Montrose House
Montrose Pl
Malaysia
Turkey
Chapel Street
Grosvenor Place
SW1
Queens Gallery
Syria
Portugal
Wilton Ter
Belgrave
Greville House
Halkin Arcade
Motcomb Street
Halkin Mews
Trinidad & Tobago
Cote d'Ivoire
Groom Pl
258
Chester Cl
Chester Mews
Chester Street
Lowndes Square
Lowndes Court
The Royal Mews
A3214
247
6
5
4
3
2
1
81
80
28
29

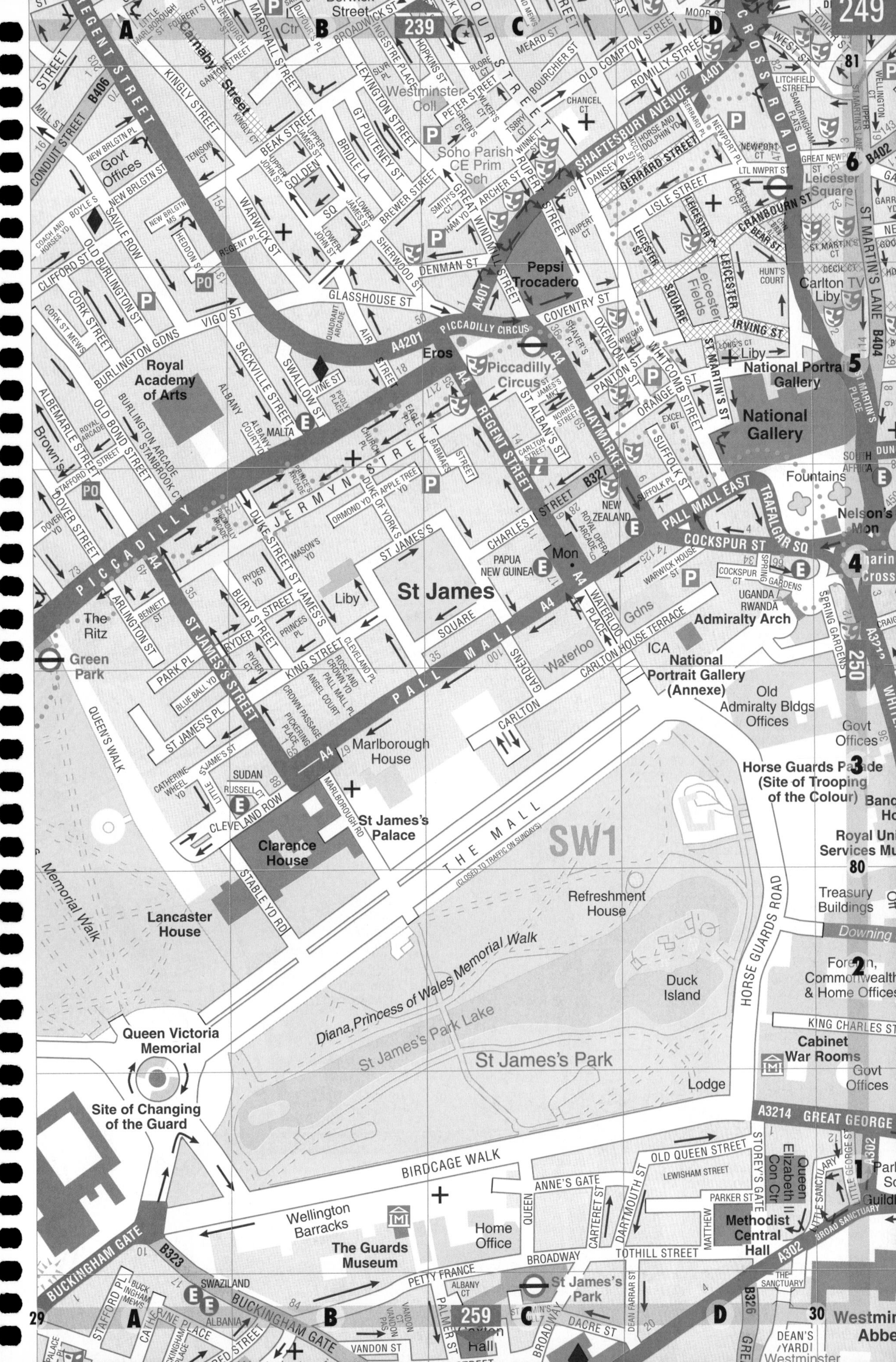

239
A
B
C
D
Regent Street
Carnaby Street
Kingly Street
Marshall Street
Broadwick Street
Lexington Street
Old Compton Street
Romilly Street
Shaftesbury Avenue
Charing Cross Road
Westminster Coll
Soho Parish CE Prim Sch
Govt Offices
Golden Sq
Beak Street
Gt Pulteney St
Brewer Street
Great Windmill St
Rupert Street
Gerrard Street
Lisle Street
Leicester Square
Leicester Fields
Cranbourn St
St Martin's Lane
Pepsi Trocadero
Denman St
Glasshouse St
Coventry St
Vigo St
Savile Row
Old Burlington St
Cork Street
Burlington Gdns
Royal Academy of Arts
Albany
Sackville Street
Swallow St
Vine St
Piccadilly Circus
Eros
Haymarket
Oxendon St
Panton St
Whitcomb Street
Orange St
Irving St
Carlton TV
Liby
National Portrait Gallery
National Gallery
Fountains
Nelson's Mon
Charing Cross
Jermyn Street
Duke of York's
St Alban's St
Charles II Street
Suffolk St
Pall Mall East
Trafalgar Sq
Cockspur St
Spring Gardens
Admiralty Arch
Uganda
Rwanda
Papua New Guinea
New Zealand
Mon
St James Square
Pall Mall
Piccadilly
Albemarle Street
Dover Street
Brown's
Arlington St
The Ritz
Green Park
Bury Street
Duke Street St James's
Ryder Street
King Street
St James's Street
St James's Pl
Park Pl
Blue Ball Yd
Queen's Walk
Waterloo Place
Waterloo Gdns
Carlton House Terrace
ICA
National Portrait Gallery (Annexe)
Old Admiralty Bldgs Offices
Govt Offices
Horse Guards Parade (Site of Trooping of the Colour)
Royal United Services Museum
Treasury Buildings
Downing St
Foreign, Commonwealth & Home Offices
King Charles St
Cabinet War Rooms
Marlborough House
St James's Palace
Marlborough Rd
Clarence House
Cleveland Row
Sudan
Stable Yd Rd
Lancaster House
The Mall
(Closed to traffic on Sundays)
SW1
Refreshment House
Duck Island
Horse Guards Road
Memorial Walk
Diana, Princess of Wales Memorial Walk
St James's Park Lake
St James's Park
Queen Victoria Memorial
Site of Changing of the Guard
Lodge
A3214 Great George St
Birdcage Walk
Old Queen Street
Lewisham Street
Queen Anne's Gate
Carteret St
Dartmouth St
Storey's Gate
Queen Elizabeth II Con Ctr
Methodist Central Hall
Broad Sanctuary
Wellington Barracks
The Guards Museum
Home Office
Broadway
Tothill Street
Petty France
Buckingham Gate
Swaziland
Albania
St James's Park
Dacre St
Caxton Hall
Westminster Abbey
259
29
30

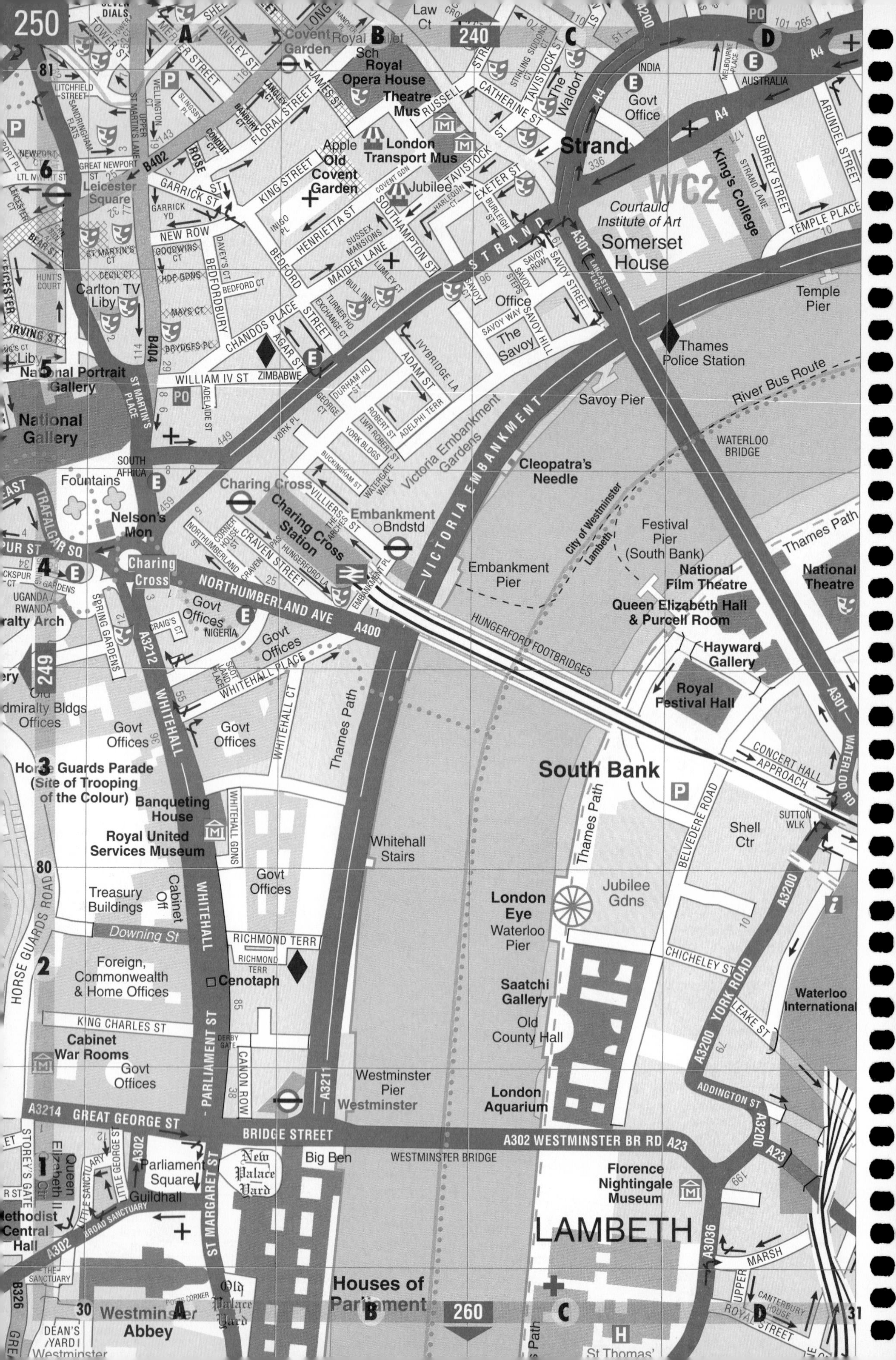
240
260
249
Covent Garden
Royal Opera House
Theatre Mus
London Transport Mus
Old Covent Garden
Jubilee
Leicester Square
Strand
WC2
Courtauld Institute of Art
Somerset House
King's College
Temple Pier
Thames Police Station
National Portrait Gallery
National Gallery
Carlton TV
The Savoy
Savoy Pier
River Bus Route
WATERLOO BRIDGE
Cleopatra's Needle
Victoria Embankment Gardens
VICTORIA EMBANKMENT
Charing Cross Station
Embankment
Trafalgar Sq
Nelson's Mon
Fountains
NORTHUMBERLAND AVE
Festival Pier (South Bank)
National Film Theatre
National Theatre
Embankment Pier
Queen Elizabeth Hall & Purcell Room
Hayward Gallery
Royal Festival Hall
HUNGERFORD FOOTBRIDGES
South Bank
WHITEHALL
Horse Guards Parade (Site of Trooping of the Colour)
Banqueting House
Royal United Services Museum
Treasury Buildings
Downing St
Foreign, Commonwealth & Home Offices
Cenotaph
Cabinet War Rooms
London Eye
Waterloo Pier
Jubilee Gdns
Shell Ctr
Saatchi Gallery
Old County Hall
London Aquarium
Waterloo International
YORK ROAD
Westminster Pier
Westminster
GREAT GEORGE ST
BRIDGE STREET
A302 WESTMINSTER BR RD
WESTMINSTER BRIDGE
Big Ben
New Palace Yard
Parliament Square
Guildhall
Methodist Central Hall
Florence Nightingale Museum
LAMBETH
Houses of Parliament
Westminster Abbey
Old Palace Yard
ST MARGARET ST
PARLIAMENT ST

RIVER THAMES
King's Reach
CITY OF LONDON
Blackfriars Station
Blackfriars Bridge
Tate Modern
Waterloo Station
Waterloo East
Southwark
Lambeth North
Blackfriars Road
Stamford Street
Waterloo Road
The Cut
Union Street
Southwark Street
Borough Road
Westminster Bridge Road
St George's Circus
Inner Temple
Middle Temple
Temple
Thames Path
Blackfriars Underpass
Oxo Tower
HQS Wellington
President
Chrysanthemum
Mermaid Theatre
BFI London Imax Cinema
Cornwall House Govt Offices
The London Nautical Sch
Southwark Coll
Crown Court
London Amb Service HQ
St George's Cathedral RC J & I Sch
SE1

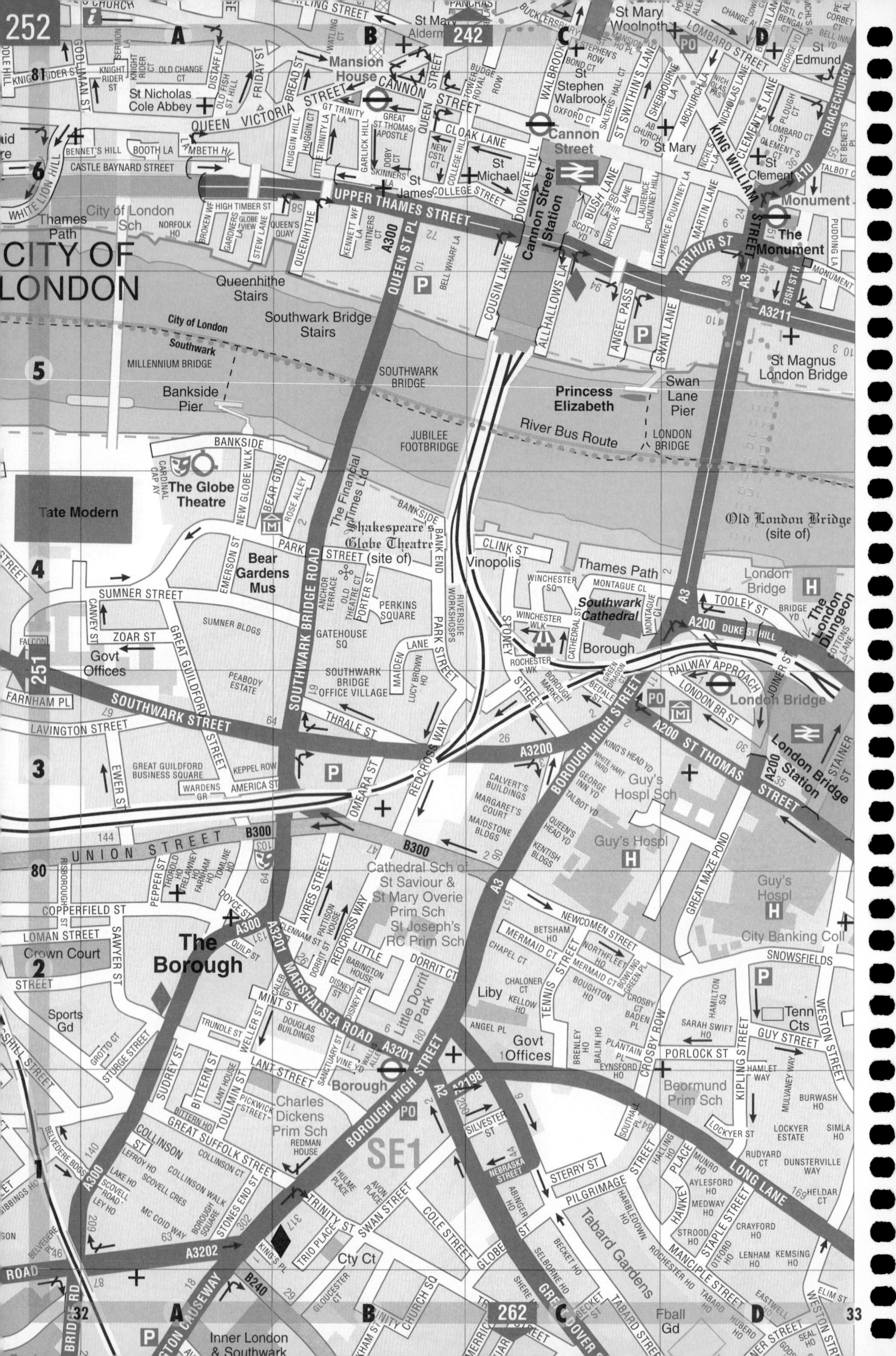
242
A
B
C
D
St Mary Aldermary
St Mary Woolnoth
Mansion House
CANNON STREET
QUEEN VICTORIA STREET
St Nicholas Cole Abbey
Cannon Street
St Stephen Walbrook
LOMBARD STREET
St Edmund
KING WILLIAM STREET
GRACECHURCH
St Clement
Monument
The Monument
St James
St Michael
UPPER THAMES STREET
CASTLE BAYNARD STREET
WHITE LION HILL
Thames Path
City of London Sch
Cannon Street Station
CITY OF LONDON
Queenhithe Stairs
Southwark Bridge Stairs
City of London
Southwark
MILLENNIUM BRIDGE
SOUTHWARK BRIDGE
Bankside Pier
Princess Elizabeth
Swan Lane Pier
River Bus Route
JUBILEE FOOTBRIDGE
LONDON BRIDGE
St Magnus London Bridge
BANKSIDE
The Globe Theatre
Tate Modern
The Financial Times Ltd
Shakespeare's Globe Theatre (site of)
Old London Bridge (site of)
Vinopolis
CLINK ST
Thames Path
Bear Gardens Mus
SUMNER STREET
PARK STREET
Southwark Cathedral
Borough
London Bridge
TOOLEY ST
The London Dungeon
DUKE ST HILL
RAILWAY APPROACH
London Bridge
London Bridge Station
Govt Offices
SOUTHWARK BRIDGE ROAD
SOUTHWARK STREET
GREAT GUILDFORD STREET
BOROUGH HIGH STREET
ST THOMAS STREET
Guy's Hospl Sch
Guy's Hospl
UNION STREET
Cathedral Sch of St Saviour & St Mary Overie Prim Sch
St Joseph's RC Prim Sch
GREAT MAZE POND
Guy's Hospl
City Banking Coll
SNOWSFIELDS
The Borough
Crown Court
Sports Gd
MARSHALSEA ROAD
Little Dorrit Park
Liby
Govt Offices
NEWCOMEN STREET
TENNIS STREET
CROSBY ROW
Tenn Cts
GUY STREET
WESTON STREET
Beormund Prim Sch
Borough
Charles Dickens Prim Sch
GREAT SUFFOLK STREET
SE1
LONG LANE
PILGRIMAGE STREET
Tabard Gardens
CAUSEWAY
Cty Ct
Fball Gd
Inner London & Southwark
262
32
33
251
5
4
3
2
6
81
80
1

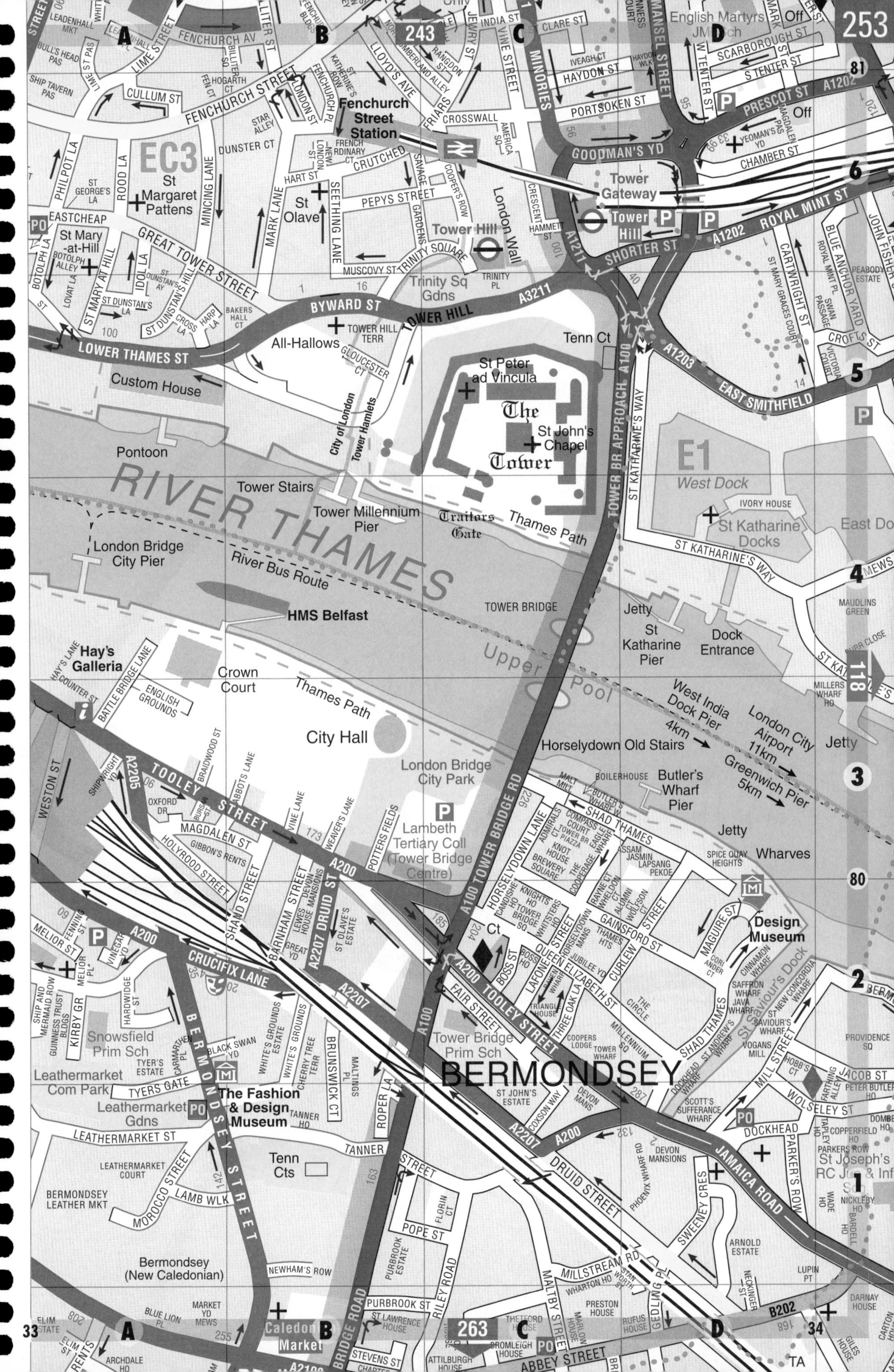
243
263
118
33
34
A
B
C
D
6
5
4
3
2
1
81
80
EC3
E1
BERMONDSEY
RIVER THAMES
Upper Pool
Fenchurch Street Station
Tower Gateway
Tower Hill
The Tower
St Peter ad Vincula
St John's Chapel
Traitors Gate
Tower Stairs
Tower Millennium Pier
London Bridge City Pier
River Bus Route
HMS Belfast
TOWER BRIDGE
Thames Path
Custom House
Pontoon
All-Hallows
Trinity Sq Gdns
St Margaret Pattens
St Olave
St Mary -at-Hill
City of London
Tower Hamlets
London Wall
Tenn Ct
West Dock
St Katharine Docks
IVORY HOUSE
East Do
Jetty
St Katharine Pier
Dock Entrance
West India Dock Pier 4km
London City Airport 11km
Greenwich Pier 5km
Horselydown Old Stairs
Butler's Wharf Pier
Wharves
Design Museum
Hay's Galleria
Crown Court
City Hall
London Bridge City Park
Lambeth Tertiary Coll (Tower Bridge Centre)
Snowsfield Prim Sch
Leathermarket Com Park
Leathermarket Gdns
The Fashion & Design Museum
Tower Bridge Prim Sch
Tenn Cts
Bermondsey (New Caledonian)
Caledon Market
St Joseph's RC Jun & Inf Sch
English Martyrs JMI Sch
FENCHURCH ST
FENCHURCH AV
LIME STREET
CULLUM ST
PHILPOT LA
ROOD LA
MINCING LANE
MARK LANE
SEETHING LANE
PEPYS STREET
CRUTCHED FRIARS
GREAT TOWER STREET
EASTCHEAP
BYWARD ST
TOWER HILL
LOWER THAMES ST
MINORIES
MANSELL STREET
GOODMAN'S YD
ROYAL MINT ST
PRESCOT ST
SHORTER ST
EAST SMITHFIELD
ST KATHARINE'S WAY
TOWER BR APPROACH A100
TOWER BRIDGE RD
TOOLEY STREET
SHAD THAMES
JAMAICA ROAD
BERMONDSEY STREET
CRUCIFIX LANE
DRUID STREET
MILLSTREAM RD
ABBEY STREET
LEATHERMARKET ST
MOROCCO STREET
WESTON ST
BATTLE BRIDGE LANE
MAGDALEN ST
HOLYROOD STREET
SHAND STREET
QUEEN ELIZABETH ST
GAINSFORD ST
CURLEW STREET
HORSELYDOWN LANE
MILL STREET
WOLSELEY ST
DOCKHEAD
PARKER'S ROW
JACOB ST
ROPER LA
RILEY ROAD
PURBROOK ST
POPE ST
TANNER STREET
A1211
A1202
A1203
A3211
A100
A200
A2205
A2207
B202

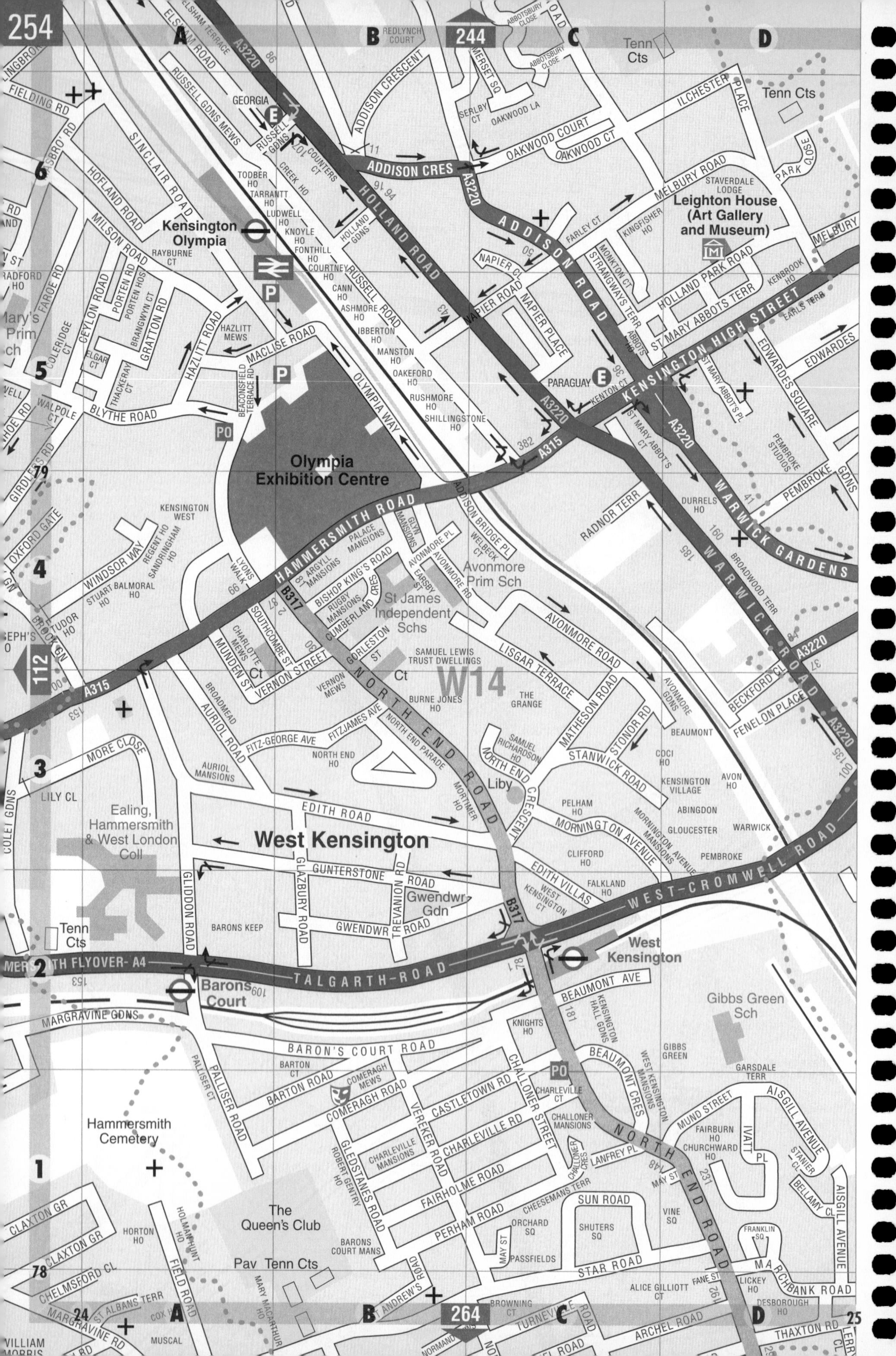
244
264
112
Kensington Olympia
Olympia Exhibition Centre
Leighton House (Art Gallery and Museum)
West Kensington
W14
Holland Road
Addison Road
Kensington High Street
Warwick Road
Warwick Gardens
Hammersmith Road
North End Road
West Cromwell Road
Talgarth Road
Hammersmith Flyover A4
Barons Court
Ealing, Hammersmith & West London Coll
Hammersmith Cemetery
The Queen's Club
St James Independent Schs
Avonmore Prim Sch
Gibbs Green Sch
Edith Road
Avonmore Road
Lisgar Terrace
Blythe Road
Addison Cres
Edwardes Square
Pembroke Gdns
Melbury Road
Ilchester Place
Barons Court Road
Comeragh Road
Castletown Rd
Charleville Rd
Fairholme Road
Perham Road
Star Road
Margravine Gdns
Gliddon Road
Gunterstone Road
Gwendwr Road
Glazbury Road
Trevanion Rd
Mornington Avenue
Stanwick Road
Matheson Road
Challoner Street
Vereker Road
Gledstanes Road
Palliser Road
Aisgill Avenue
Beaumont Cres
Beaumont Ave
Vernon Street
North End Crescent
Fitz-George Ave
Auriol Road
Sinclair Road
Russell Road
Olympia Way
Maclise Road
Napier Road
Radnor Terr
Fenelon Place
Beckford Cl
Tenn Cts
West Kensington
Pav Tenn Cts

High Street Kensington
Commonwealth Institute
Kensington High Street
Cromwell Road
West Cromwell Road
Earl's Court Road
Warwick Road
Old Brompton Road
Earl's Court
Earl's Court Exhibition Centre
West Brompton
W8
SW5
Allendale Sch
Richmond Coll
Cromwell Hospl
Bousfield Prim Sch
St Barnabas & St Philip CE Prim Sch
Lexham Gardens
Cornwall Gardens
Courtfield Gardens
Collingham Gardens
Bolton Gardens
Redcliffe Gardens
Finborough Road
Philbeach Gardens
Nevern Square
Pembroke Road
Earl's Court Square
Kensington Square
Victoria Road
Launceston Place

245
256
265

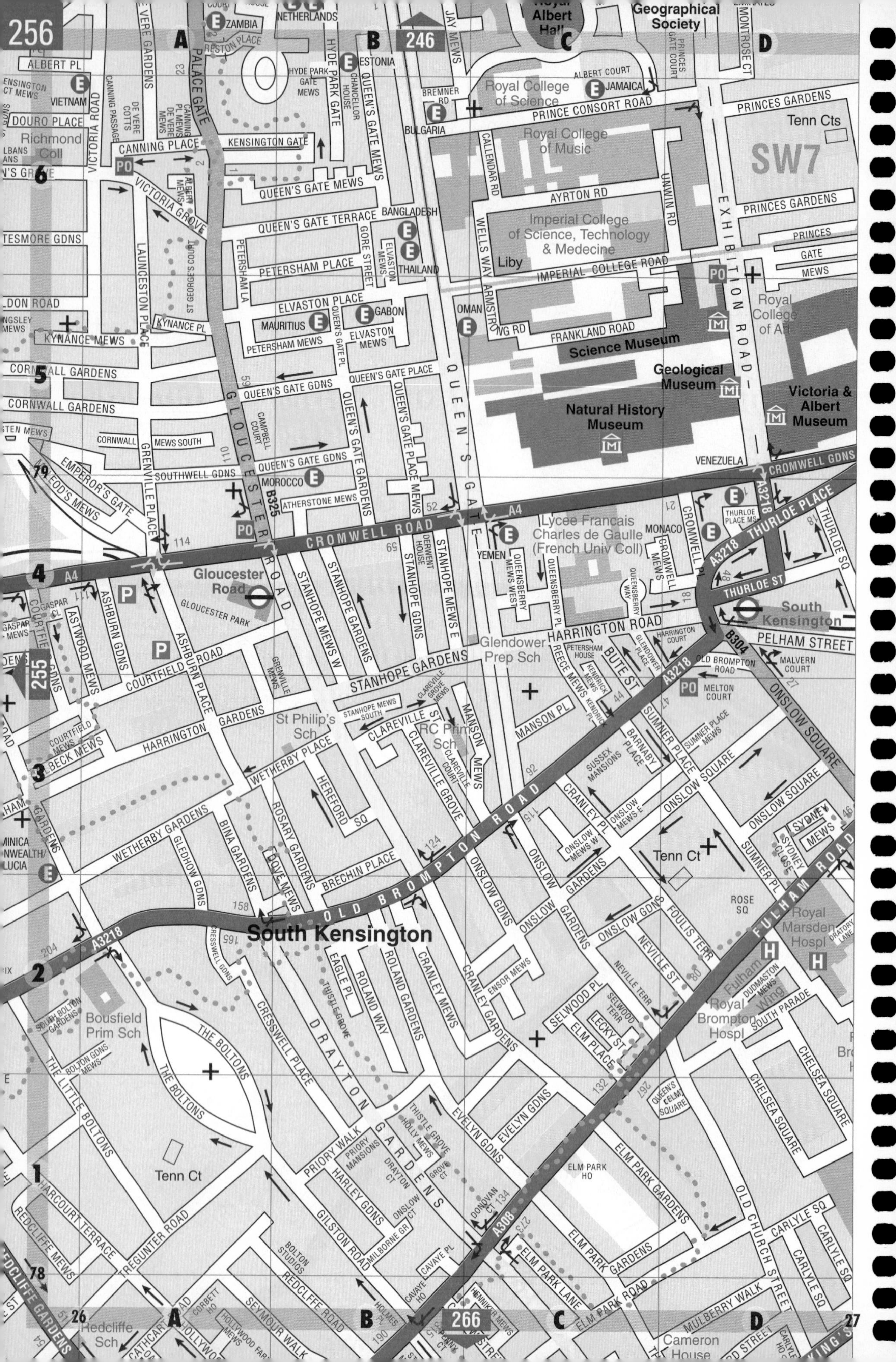

246
Royal Albert Hall
Geographical Society
A
B
C
D
SW7
ZAMBIA
NETHERLANDS
ESTONIA
JAMAICA
BULGARIA
VIETNAM
BANGLADESH
THAILAND
GABON
MAURITIUS
OMAN
MOROCCO
YEMEN
MONACO
VENEZUELA
Richmond Coll
Royal College of Science
Royal College of Music
Imperial College of Science, Technology & Medecine
Liby
Royal College of Art
Science Museum
Geological Museum
Natural History Museum
Victoria & Albert Museum
Lycee Francais Charles de Gaulle (French Univ Coll)
Gloucester Road
South Kensington
Glendower Prep Sch
St Philip's Sch
RC Prim Sch
Bousfield Prim Sch
Royal Marsden Hospl
Royal Brompton Hospl
Fulham Wing
Tenn Cts
Tenn Ct
Cameron House
Redcliffe Sch
PALACE GATE
KENSINGTON GATE
HYDE PARK GATE
QUEEN'S GATE MEWS
QUEEN'S GATE TERRACE
PRINCE CONSORT ROAD
PRINCES GARDENS
EXHIBITION ROAD
IMPERIAL COLLEGE ROAD
FRANKLAND ROAD
CROMWELL ROAD
CROMWELL GDNS
THURLOE PLACE
THURLOE ST
HARRINGTON ROAD
PELHAM STREET
ONSLOW SQUARE
OLD BROMPTON ROAD
FULHAM ROAD
GLOUCESTER ROAD
QUEEN'S GATE
STANHOPE GARDENS
VICTORIA ROAD
VICTORIA GROVE
CANNING PLACE
DOURO PLACE
KYNANCE MEWS
CORNWALL GARDENS
COURTFIELD ROAD
ASHBURN PLACE
HARRINGTON GARDENS
WETHERBY GARDENS
DRAYTON GARDENS
THE BOLTONS
CRESSWELL PLACE
REDCLIFFE GARDENS
REDCLIFFE ROAD
TREGUNTER ROAD
ELM PARK GARDENS
ELM PARK ROAD
OLD CHURCH STREET
SYDNEY STREET
MULBERRY WALK
CHELSEA SQUARE
CARLYLE SQ
266
255

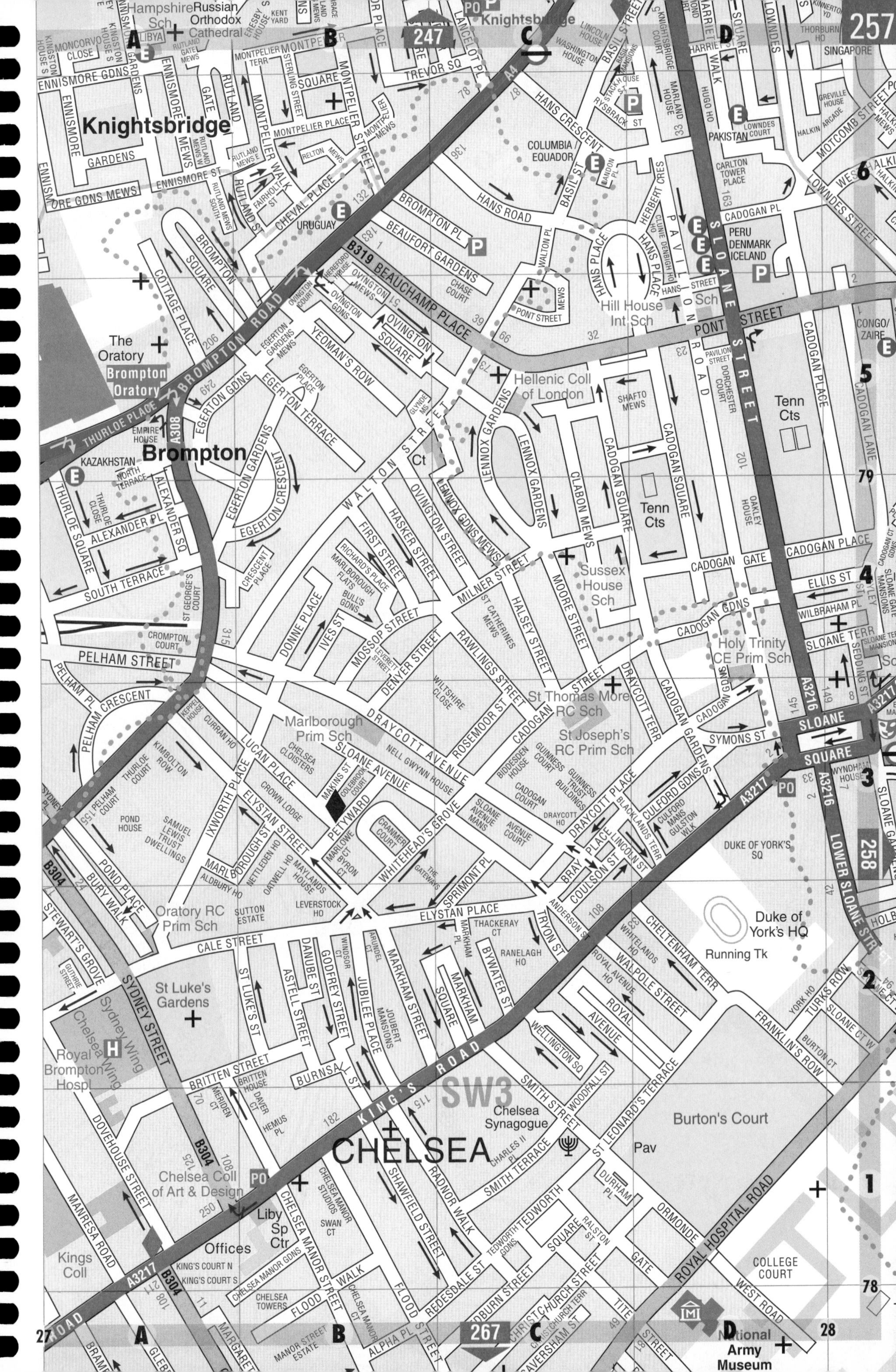
Knightsbridge
Brompton
CHELSEA
SW3
Hampshire Sch
Russian Orthodox Cathedral
The Oratory
Brompton Oratory
Kazakhstan
Uruguay
Columbia / Equador
Pakistan
Peru
Denmark
Iceland
Congo/ Zaire
Singapore
Libya
Hill House Int Sch
Hellenic Coll of London
Tenn Cts
Sussex House Sch
Holy Trinity CE Prim Sch
St Thomas More RC Sch
St Joseph's RC Prim Sch
Marlborough Prim Sch
Oratory RC Prim Sch
St Luke's Gardens
Sydney Wing
Chelsea Wing
Royal Brompton Hospl
Chelsea Coll of Art & Design
Liby
Sp Ctr
Offices
Kings Coll
Chelsea Synagogue
Burton's Court
Pav
Duke of York's HQ
Running Tk
Duke of York's Sq
College Court
National Army Museum
ENNISMORE GDNS
ENNISMORE GARDENS
MONTPELIER SQUARE
MONTPELIER STREET
MONTPELIER WALK
MONTPELIER PLACE
RUTLAND GATE
TREVOR SQ
LANCELOT PL
HANS CRESCENT
HANS ROAD
HANS PLACE
BASIL ST
BROMPTON ROAD
BROMPTON SQUARE
BROMPTON PL
BEAUFORT GARDENS
BEAUCHAMP PLACE
CHEVAL PLACE
OVINGTON SQUARE
OVINGTON GDNS
YEOMAN'S ROW
EGERTON GARDENS
EGERTON TERRACE
EGERTON CRESCENT
EGERTON GDNS
COTTAGE PLACE
THURLOE PLACE
THURLOE SQUARE
ALEXANDER PL
ALEXANDER SQ
SOUTH TERRACE
PELHAM STREET
PELHAM CRESCENT
PONT STREET
WALTON STREET
WALTON PL
LENNOX GARDENS
LENNOX GDNS MEWS
MILNER STREET
OVINGTON STREET
HASKER STREET
FIRST STREET
MOSSOP STREET
DENYER STREET
DONNE PLACE
IVES ST
RAWLINGS STREET
HALSEY STREET
MOORE STREET
CLABON MEWS
CADOGAN SQUARE
CADOGAN GATE
CADOGAN GDNS
CADOGAN PLACE
CADOGAN LANE
CADOGAN STREET
CADOGAN GARDENS
SLOANE STREET
SLOANE SQUARE
SLOANE AVENUE
SLOANE TERR
LOWER SLOANE STREET
PAVILION ROAD
DRAYCOTT AVENUE
DRAYCOTT PLACE
DRAYCOTT TERR
ROSEMOOR ST
LUCAN PLACE
IXWORTH PLACE
ELYSTAN STREET
ELYSTAN PLACE
MARLBOROUGH ST
PETYWARD
WHITEHEAD'S GROVE
SPRIMONT PL
CALE STREET
SYDNEY STREET
KING'S ROAD
BURY WALK
POND PLACE
ST LUKE'S ST
DANUBE ST
ASTELL STREET
GODFREY STREET
JUBILEE PLACE
MARKHAM STREET
MARKHAM SQUARE
BYWATER ST
TRYON ST
COULSON ST
BRAY PLACE
LINCOLN ST
CULFORD GDNS
SYMONS ST
CHELTENHAM TERR
WALPOLE STREET
ROYAL AVENUE
WELLINGTON SQ
SMITH STREET
SMITH TERRACE
ST LEONARD'S TERRACE
FRANKLIN'S ROW
TURKS ROW
ROYAL HOSPITAL ROAD
BRITTEN STREET
BURNSALL ST
SHAWFIELD STREET
RADNOR WALK
FLOOD STREET
FLOOD WALK
CHELSEA MANOR STREET
TEDWORTH SQUARE
CHRISTCHURCH STREET
REDESDALE ST
ORMONDE GATE
WEST ROAD
DOVEHOUSE STREET
MANRESA ROAD
A4
A308
B319
A3216
A3217
B304
247
258
267
A
B
C
D
1
2
3
4
5
6
27
28
78
79

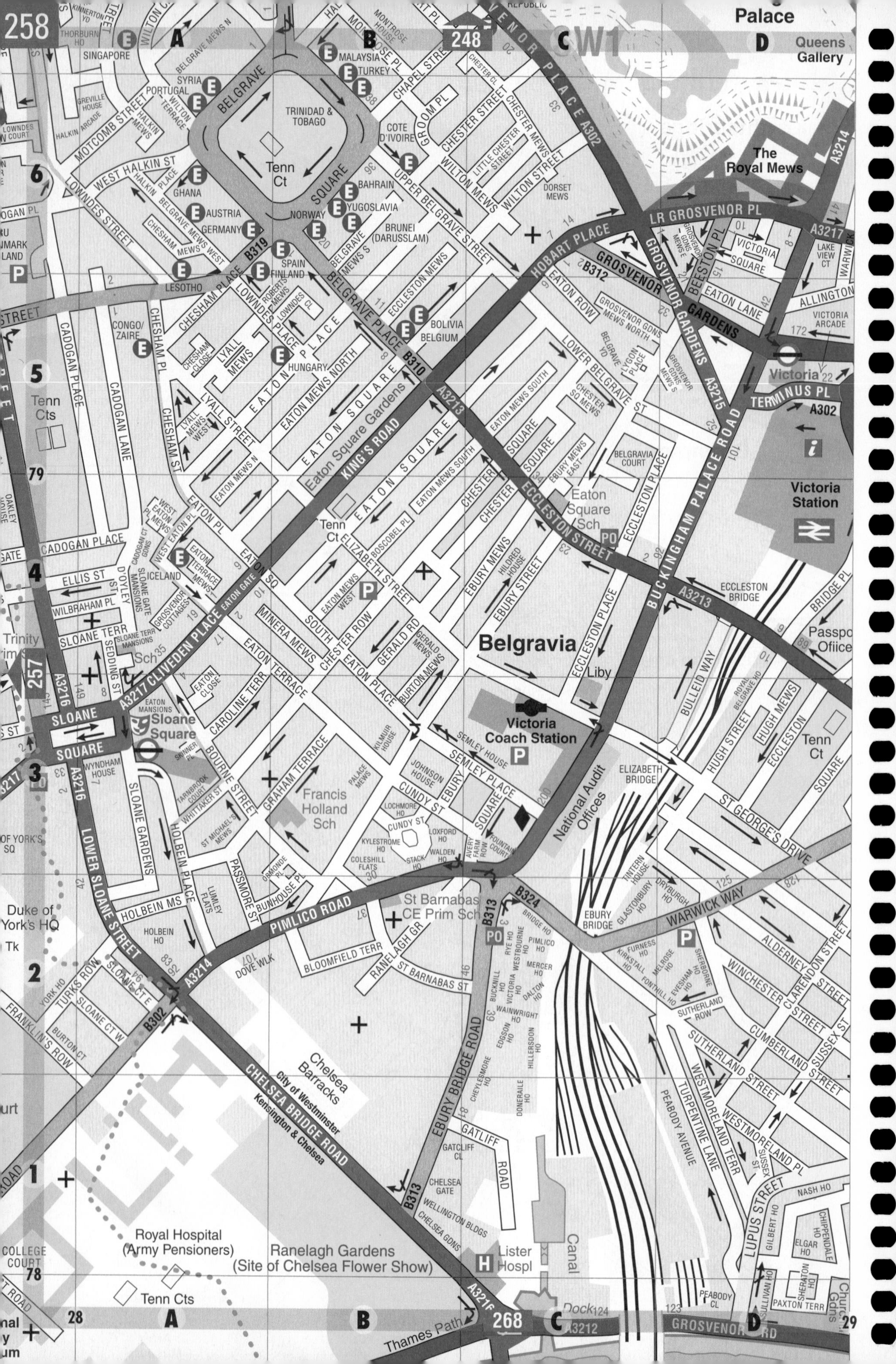
Palace
Queens Gallery
The Royal Mews
Victoria Station
Belgravia
Victoria Coach Station
Eaton Square Gardens
Francis Holland Sch
Sloane Square
Chelsea Barracks
Royal Hospital (Army Pensioners)
Ranelagh Gardens (Site of Chelsea Flower Show)
Lister Hospl
National Audit Offices
BELGRAVE SQUARE
EATON SQUARE
KING'S ROAD
BUCKINGHAM PALACE ROAD
ECCLESTON STREET
GROSVENOR GARDENS
HOBART PLACE
PIMLICO ROAD
LOWER SLOANE STREET
CHELSEA BRIDGE ROAD
EBURY BRIDGE ROAD
WARWICK WAY
ST GEORGE'S DRIVE
CLIVEDEN PLACE
Thames Path
Canal
Dock
City of Westminster
Kensington & Chelsea

248
268
257

A
B
C
D
249
Wellington Barracks
The Guards Museum
Home Office
Methodist Central Hall
Buckingham Gate
B323
Swaziland
Albania
Petty France
Albany Ct
Queen
Carteret St
Dartmouth
Parker St
Matthew
Broadway
Tothill Street
A302
The Sanctuary
St James's Park
Stafford Pl
Buckingham Mews
Catherine Place
Wilfred Street
Buckingham Place
Palace
Vandon Ct
Vandon Pas
Vandon St
Palmer St
Caxton Hall
St Ermin's Hill
Dacre St
Dean Farrar St
B326
Great Smith Street
Dean's Yard
Westminster Abbey
Westminster Abbey Choir Sch
Row
Palace Pl
Stag Place
Govt Offices
Castle Lane
Pine Ct
Westminster Coll
St James' Ct
Seaforth Pl
Caxton Street
PO
South Bldg
SW1
Roebuck Ho
Spenser St
Korea
Brewer's Green
Butler Pl
New Scotland Yard
Abbey Orchard St
St Ann's St
Abbey Orchard St Estate
Liby
Morrison Ct
Little Smith St
Great College
Barton St
Slovenia
Bressenden Place
Stag Place
Glen Ho
Westminster City Sch
Westminster City Hall
Victoria Street
Artillery Mans
Strutton Gd
Old Pye Street
St Matthews Sch Westminster
St Matthew St
Old Pye St Estate
William Gibbs Ct
Perkin's Rents
St Ann's Lane
Cowley
Great Peter St
Lord North Street
Gayfere St
Tufton Ct
Tufton Street
St
Govt Offs
Wilcox Pl
Howick Place
Artillery Row
Strutton Ground
Great Peter Street
Horseferry Road Estate
Elizabeth Ct
Westminster Cathedral
Thirleby Road
Spencer Pl
Greycoat Pl
B323
Chadwick St
Channel 4 TV Corp
Monck Street
Govt Offices
Bennett's Yd
Dean Trench St
Smith Sq
Westminster
Ashley Pl
P
B324
The Grey Coat Hosp CE Sch
RHS (Lawrence Hall & Conf Ctr)
TA Ctr
Medway St
Romney St
Ct
A202
St Vincent De Paul RC Prim Sch
Ambrosden Avenue
Greencoat Row
Greycoat St
Carlisle Place
King's Scholar's Passage
Morpeth Terr
Emery Hill St
Rochester St
Arneway St
Horseferry Road
Westminster Cath Choir Sch
Windsor Place
Coburg Cl
Greencoat Place
Rochester Row
Sch
Westminster Coll
Elverton St
Cobbold Ct
Coroner's Court
Abady House
Edric House
Bennett House
Marsham Street
St John's Gdns
Hudson's Pl
Wilton Road
Neathouse Place
Francis Street
Stillington St
Vane St
Vincent Square
RHS (Lindley Hall)
Maunsel St
Silverton
Rutherford St
Page Street
Fynes St
Coleridge Ct
Norfolk Ho
Probyn Ho
Jessel Ho
Schomberg Ho
Tothill Ho
Rogers Ho
Marsham Ct
Westminster Gdns
Offices
Gillingham Mews
Gillingham Street
Gillingham Row
Peabody Estate
Willow Place
Pav
Pl Fld
Tenn Cts
Upper Tachbrook St
Tachbrook Mews
Vauxhall Bridge Road
Walcott St
Hatherley St
Udall St
Vincent Street
Princess Mary Ho
Duke's Ho
Reynolds Ho
Dalkeith Ct
Brunswick Ct
Gladstone Ct
Marsham
260
Civil Service Coll
Charlotte Pl
Longmoore St
Guildhouse St
B324
George Eliot House
Aubrey Beardsley House
Bloomburg St
H
Vincent Sq
The Gordon Hospl
Tenn Ct
Vincent Ho
Hide Place
Hide Tower
TA Ctr
Regency Street
Esterbrooke St
The Regency
Chapter St
Offices
Millbank Prim Sch
Hogarth Ho
Erasmus Street
Rossetti Ho
Ruskin Ho
Bulinga St
John Islip St
Eccleston Sq Mews
Warwick Pl N
Warwick
Way
Churton Pl
Denbigh Mews
Dells Mews
Churton St
Joseph Conrad House
Noel Coward House
Fairchild House
Henry Wise House
Stanford St
Osbert St
Douglas Street
The Grey Coat Hospl St Michaels (Sch)
Shrubs Ho
Turner Ho
Oswulf St
Herrick Street
Tate Britain
West Warwick Place
Warwick Square Mews
Belgrave Road
Charlwood Pl
Tachbrook Street
Repton House
Morgan House
Charlwood House
Thorndike St
Gainsborough Ho
Landseer Ho
Lawrence Ho
Atterbury St
West Mews
Warwick Square
Tenn Ct
Gloucester Street
Denbigh Street
Denbigh Place
Forsyth House
Garden Terr
Thorndike Ho
Carey Place
Rampayne St
Fairley House Sch
Causton Street
Cureton St
Wilkie Ho
Royal Army Medical Coll
St George's Drive
Cambridge St
Charlwood
Street
Moreton Place
Moreton St
Longleat Ho
Wisley Ho
Priory Ho
Rampayne Street
PO
B326
Ponsonby Place
Ponsonby Terr
A3212
Thames Path
Moreton Terr Ms N
Moreton Terr
St George's Square
Liby
Pimlico
Bessborough St
A3213
Drummond Gate
Salisbury Ho
Harrington Ho
Devonshire Ho
Bessborough Gdns
Winchester Street
Russell House
Gloucester Street
Pimlico
Moreton Terr Ms S
Buonaparte Mews
Bessborough Place
Westminster Cath RC Prim Sch
Lindsay Sq
Ashgrove Ho
Hale Ho
A202
Lupus Street
Pimlico Sch
St George's Square Gdns
St George's Square
Kent Ho
Wren Ho
Founders Ho
Beaufort Ho
Abbots Ho
Tuttle Ho
Tachbrook Estate
Aylesford Street
Duncannon Ho
Crown Reach
Vauxhall Bridge
Liby
PO
Glasgow Terr
Johnson's Pl
Ranelagh Rd
Churchill Gardens Prim Sch
Chichester Street
Claverton Street
P
Cowper Ho
Malcolmson Ho
Thomson Ho
Balvaird Pl
Wharves
Wedgewood House
Seldon Ho
Black Stone Ho
Gifford Ho
Langdale Ho
Martineau Ho
Marryat Ho
Campbell Ho
Coleridge Ho
Hallam Ho
Moyle Ho
Lenthall Ho
Lowther Ho
Lutyens House
Erskine Ho
Chaucer House
Hawthorne Ho
Dolphin Square
St George's Square Mews
Cockburn Ho
Marsh Ho
Harvey Ho
St Gabriel's CE Prim Sch
Bramwell Ho
Churchill Gardens Road
Moyle House
Whitley House
Wilkins House
Ripley Ho
Keats House
Tyrrell House
Wharves
City of Westminster
Lambeth
Wandsworth
Maitland House
Shelley House
269
Thames Path
Tenn
Churchill Gardens
Telford Terrace
Hungerford House
Road
Westminster
1
2
3
4
5
6

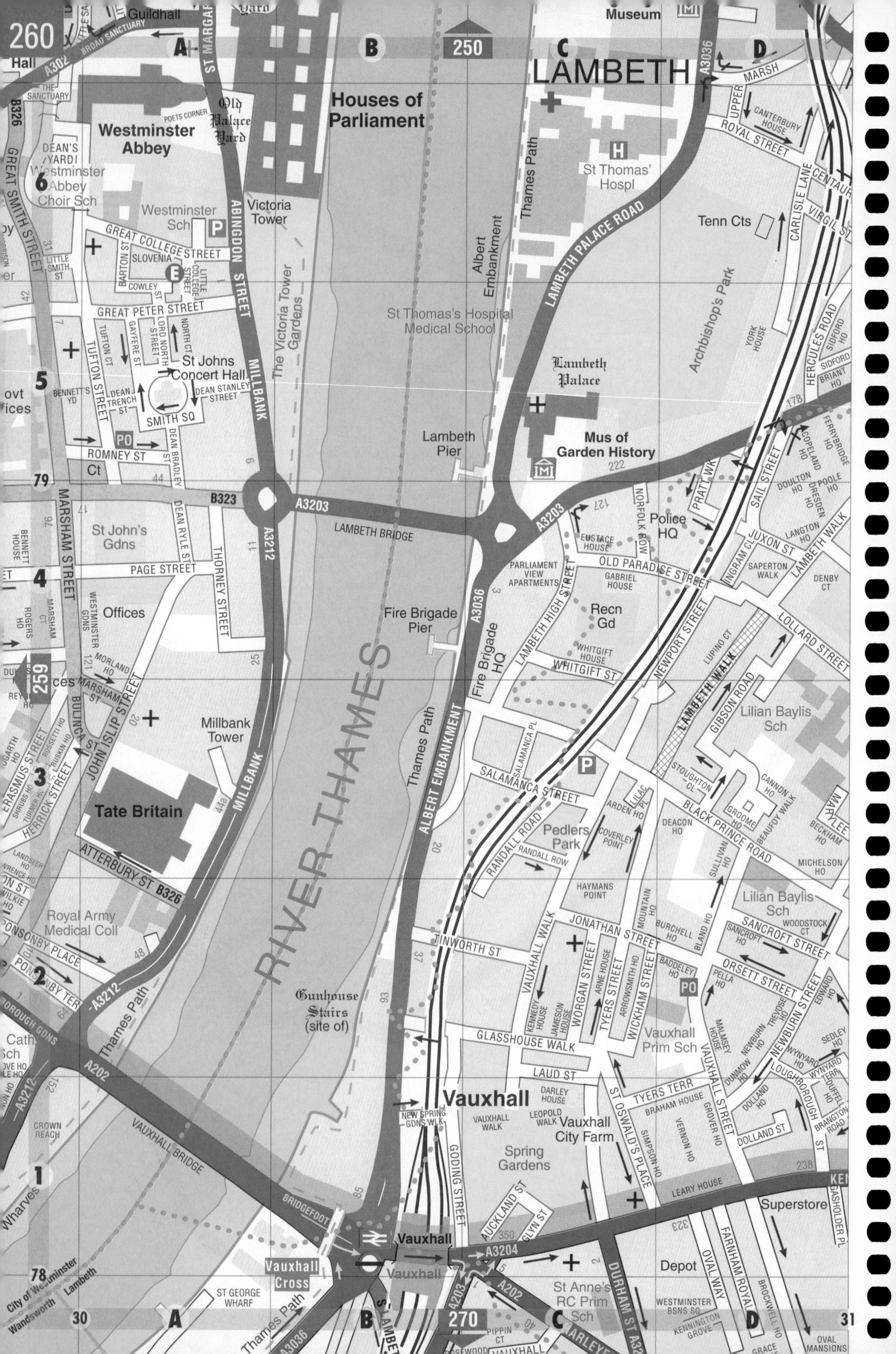
LAMBETH
Houses of Parliament
Westminster Abbey
Old Palace Yard
Victoria Tower
The Victoria Tower Gardens
St Thomas's Hospital Medical School
St Thomas' Hospl
Lambeth Palace
Mus of Garden History
Archbishop's Park
Lambeth Pier
LAMBETH BRIDGE
Fire Brigade Pier
Fire Brigade HQ
Police HQ
Millbank Tower
Tate Britain
Royal Army Medical Coll
RIVER THAMES
Gunhouse Stairs (site of)
Vauxhall
Vauxhall City Farm
Spring Gardens
Pedlers Park
Lilian Baylis Sch
Vauxhall Prim Sch
St Johns Concert Hall
St John's Gdns
Westminster Sch
Westminster Abbey Choir Sch
Superstore
Depot
St Anne's RC Prim Sch
VAUXHALL BRIDGE
Thames Path
Albert Embankment
ALBERT EMBANKMENT
LAMBETH PALACE ROAD
MILLBANK
ABINGDON STREET
GREAT SMITH STREET
MARSHAM STREET
PAGE STREET
GREAT PETER STREET
GREAT COLLEGE STREET
HORSEFERRY ROAD
LAMBETH HIGH STREET
OLD PARADISE STREET
BLACK PRINCE ROAD
KENNINGTON LANE
LAMBETH WALK
SALAMANCA STREET
JONATHAN STREET
VAUXHALL WALK
GLASSHOUSE WALK
VAUXHALL STREET
NEWBURN STREET
SANCROFT STREET
ORSETT STREET
LOLLARD STREET
ROYAL STREET
UPPER MARSH
DURHAM ST
SOUTH LAMBETH
ATTERBURY ST
PONSONBY PLACE
A3036
A3203
A3212
A202
A3204
B323
B326
250
259
270
30
31
A
B
C
D
1
2
3
4
5
6
78
79

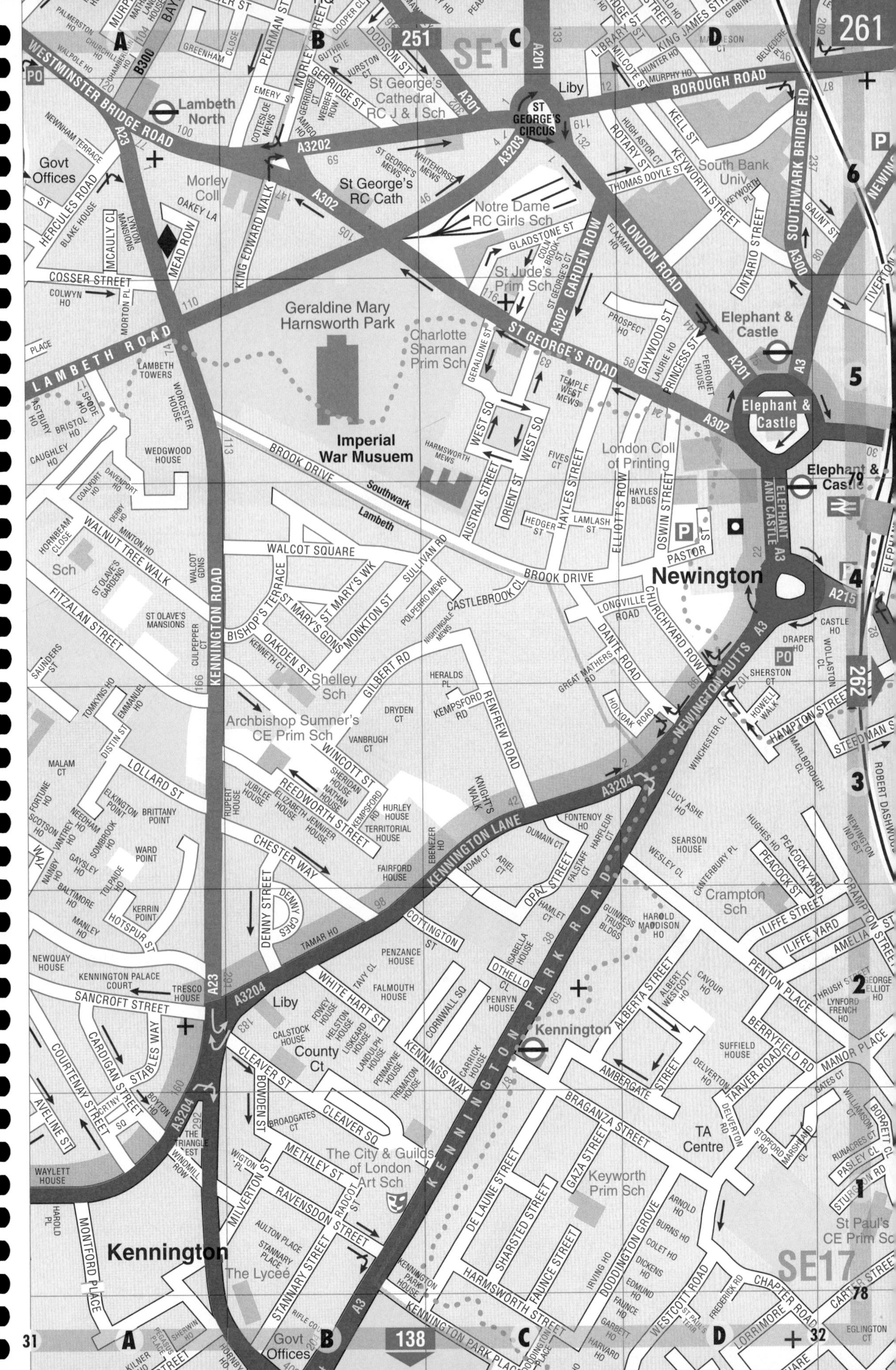

261
251
138
262
SE1
SE17
A
B
C
D
6
5
4
3
2
1
31
32
78
79
Westminster Bridge Road
Lambeth North
Govt Offices
Hercules Road
Morley Coll
Oakey La
Mead Row
King Edward Walk
St George's Cathedral RC J & I Sch
St George's RC Cath
St George's Circus
Borough Road
Library St
King James St
Liby
Notre Dame RC Girls Sch
St Jude's Prim Sch
Garden Row
London Road
Keyworth Street
South Bank Univ
Southwark Bridge Rd
Ontario Street
Elephant & Castle
Cosser Street
Lambeth Road
Geraldine Mary Harmsworth Park
Charlotte Sharman Prim Sch
St George's Road
Imperial War Musuem
West Sq
London Coll of Printing
Brook Drive
Southwark
Lambeth
Austral Street
Orient St
Hayles Street
Elliott's Row
Oswin Street
Walcot Square
Walnut Tree Walk
Fitzalan Street
Kennington Road
St Mary's Gdns
Monkton St
Newington
Longville Road
Dante Road
Churchyard Row
Newington Butts
Shelley Sch
Gilbert Rd
Archbishop Sumner's CE Prim Sch
Renfrew Road
Lollard St
Reedworth Street
Chester Way
Kennington Lane
Crampton Sch
Iliffe Street
Penton Place
Berryfield Rd
Manor Place
Kennington Park Road
Kennington
Cleaver St
Cleaver Sq
County Ct
The City & Guilds of London Art Sch
Keyworth Prim Sch
Braganza Street
De Laune Street
Sharsted Street
Faunce Street
Harmsworth Street
Doddington Grove
TA Centre
Westcott Road
Chapter Road
St Paul's CE Prim Sch
Kennington Park Place
Ravensdon Street
Milverton St
Stannary Street
The Lyceé
Montford Place
Sancroft Street
Courtenay Street
Cardigan Street
Stables Way
Aveline St
Waylett House
A3204
A302
A3202
A23
A201
A3
A215
A300
B300

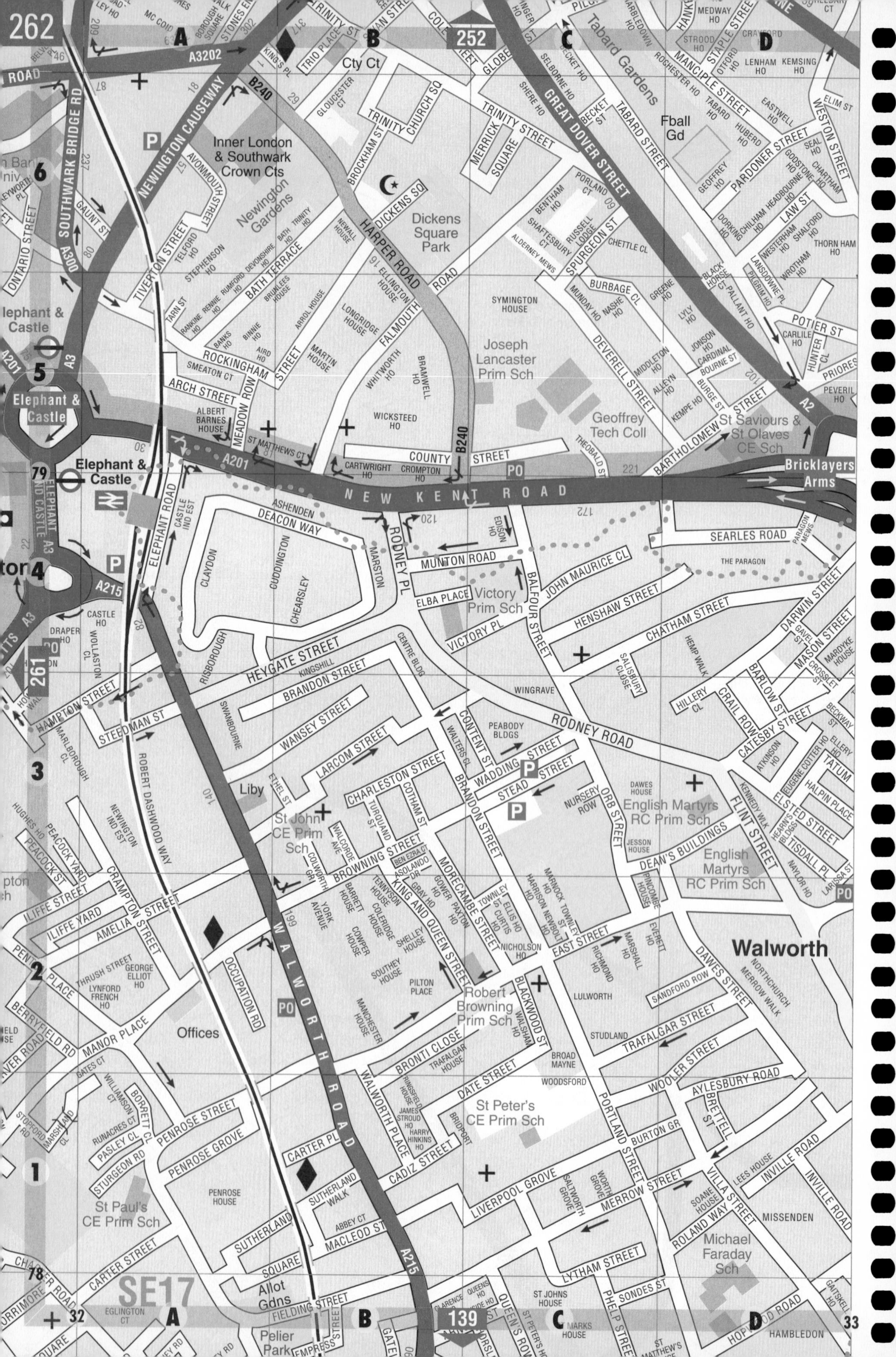
252
A
B
C
D
A3202
B240
TRINITY ST
TRIO PLACE
KING'S PL
Cty Ct
GLOUCESTER CT
TRINITY CHURCH SQ
GLOBE ST
TRINITY STREET
MERRICK SQUARE
GREAT DOVER STREET
Tabard Gardens
TABARD STREET
Fball Gd
MEDWAY HO
STROOD HO
CRAYFORD HO
LENHAM HO
KEMSING HO
MANCIPLE STREET
STAPLE STREET
OTFORD HO
EASTWELL HO
WESTON STREET
ELIM ST
HUBERD HO
TABARD HO
PARDONER STREET
GEOFFREY HO
SEAL HO
GODSTONE HO
CHARTHAM HO
HEADBOURNE HO
CHILHAM HO
DORKING HO
LAW ST
WESTERHAM HO
SHALFORD HO
THORN HAM HO
WROTHAM HO
LANSDOWNE PL
PILGRIM HO
POTIER ST
CARLILE HO
HUNTER CL
PRIORESS
PEVERIL HO
NEWINGTON CAUSEWAY
Inner London & Southwark Crown Cts
Newington Gardens
SOUTHWARK BRIDGE RD
A300
GAUNT ST
ONTARIO STREET
AVONMOUTH STREET
TIVERTON STREET
TELFORD HO
STEPHENSON HO
RENNIE HO
RUMFORD HO
DEVONSHIRE HO
BATH TERRACE
TRINITY HO
BRUNLEES HOUSE
TARN ST
RANKINE HO
BANKS HO
BINNIE HO
AIRD HO
ARROL HOUSE
ROCKINGHAM STREET
SMEATON CT
ARCH STREET
MEADOW ROW
ALBERT BARNES HOUSE
MARTIN HOUSE
LONGRIDGE HOUSE
NEWALL HOUSE
BROCKHAM ST
DICKENS SQ
HARPER ROAD
ELLINGTON HOUSE
FALMOUTH ROAD
WHITWORTH HO
BRAMWELL HO
WICKSTEED HO
Dickens Square Park
SYMINGTON HOUSE
Joseph Lancaster Prim Sch
BENTHAM HO
PORLAND CT
SHAFTESBURY CT
RUSSELL LODGE
ALDERNEY MEWS
SPURGEON ST
CHETTLE CL
BURBAGE CL
MUNDAY HO
NASHE HO
GREENE HO
LYLY HO
DEVERELL STREET
MIDDLETON HO
ALLEYN HO
KEMPE HO
JONSON HO
CARDINAL BOURNE ST
BURGE ST
BLACK HORSE CT
PALLANT HO
Geoffrey Tech Coll
BARTHOLOMEW STREET
St Saviours & St Olaves CE Sch
A2
Bricklayers Arms
THEOBALD ST
COUNTY STREET
B240
CARTWRIGHT HO
CROMPTON HO
ST MATTHEWS CT
A201
PO
NEW KENT ROAD
Elephant & Castle
A201
A3
5
6
Elephant & Castle
79
ELEPHANT AND CASTLE A3
4
A215
P
ELEPHANT ROAD
CASTLE IND EST
ASHENDEN
DEACON WAY
CLAYDON
CUDDINGTON
CHEARSLEY
MARSTON
RODNEY PL
MUNTON ROAD
EDISON HO
ELBA PLACE
Victory Prim Sch
VICTORY PL
BALFOUR STREET
JOHN MAURICE CL
HENSHAW STREET
CHATHAM STREET
SEARLES ROAD
PARAGON MEWS
THE PARAGON
DARWIN STREET
GAVEL ST
MASON STREET
MARDYKE HOUSE
HEMP WALK
SALISBURY CLOSE
WINGRAVE
RISBOROUGH
HEYGATE STREET
KINGSHILL
BRANDON STREET
CENTRE BLDG
CASTLE HO
DRAPER HO
WOLLASTON CL
261
HAMPTON STREET
STEEDMAN ST
SWANBOURNE
WANSEY STREET
LARCOM STREET
ETHEL ST
Liby
CONTENT ST
WALTERS CL
PEABODY BLDGS
WADDING STREET
STEAD STREET
P
RODNEY ROAD
HILLERY CL
CRAIL ROW
BARLOW ST
CROSSLET ST
BECKWAY ST
CATESBY STREET
ATKINSON HO
EUGENE COTTER HO
ELLERY ST
TATUM ST
HALPIN PLACE
KENNEDY WLK
HEARN'S BLDGS
ELSTED STREET
TISDALL PL
NAYLOR HO
LARISSA ST
PO
DAWES HOUSE
English Martyrs RC Prim Sch
NURSERY ROW
ORB STREET
JESSON HOUSE
DEAN'S BUILDINGS
FLINT STREET
English Martyrs RC Prim Sch
3
MARLBOROUGH CL
ROBERT DASHWOOD WAY
NEWINGTON IND EST
HUGHES HO
PEACOCK YARD
PEACOCK ST
CRAMPTON STREET
ILIFFE STREET
ILIFFE YARD
AMELIA STREET
CHARLESTON STREET
TURQUAND ST
COTHAM ST
St John CE Prim Sch
WALCORDE AVE
COLWORTH GR
BROWNING STREET
BEN EZRA CT
ASOLANDO DR
MORECAMBE STREET
BRANDON STREET
YORK AVENUE
BARRETT HOUSE
TENNYSON HOUSE
COLERIDGE HOUSE
GRAY HO
GOWER HO
PAXTON HO
TOWNLEY ST
ELLIS HO
CURTIS HO
HARRISON HO
NEWBOLT HO
MARNOCK HO
TOWNLEY ST
COWPER HOUSE
SHELLEY HOUSE
KING AND QUEEN STREET
NICHOLSON HO
EAST STREET
MARSHALL HO
EVERETT HO
RICHMOND HO
PINCOMBE HOUSE
Walworth
NORTHCHURCH
MERROW WALK
DAWES STREET
SANDFORD ROW
2
THRUSH STREET
GEORGE ELLIOT HO
LYNFORD FRENCH HO
PENTON PLACE
BERRYFIELD RD
MANOR PLACE
OCCUPATION RD
Offices
PO
WALWORTH ROAD
SOUTHEY HOUSE
PILTON PLACE
MANCHESTER HOUSE
Robert Browning Prim Sch
BLACKWOOD ST
WALSHAM HO
LULWORTH
STUDLAND
TRAFALGAR STREET
WOOLER STREET
AYLESBURY ROAD
BRETTELL ST
BRONTI CLOSE
TRAFALGAR HOUSE
BROAD MAYNE
WOODSFORD
PORTLAND STREET
DATE STREET
RINGSFIELD HOUSE
JAMES STROUD HO
HARRY HINKINS HO
BRIDPORT
St Peter's CE Prim Sch
BURTON GR
WALWORTH PLACE
CADIZ STREET
CARTER PL
BATES CT
WILLIAMSON CT
BORRETT CL
PENROSE STREET
PENROSE GROVE
RUNACRES CT
PASLEY CL
STURGEON RD
STOPFORD RD
MARSHLAND CL
1
PENROSE HOUSE
St Paul's CE Prim Sch
SUTHERLAND WALK
SUTHERLAND SQUARE
ABBEY CT
MACLEOD ST
LIVERPOOL GROVE
SALTWORTH GROVE
WORTH GROVE
MERROW STREET
VILLA STREET
LEES HOUSE
INVILLE ROAD
SOANE HOUSE
ROLAND WAY
MISSENDEN
Michael Faraday Sch
LYTHAM STREET
SONDES ST
CARTER STREET
78
SE17
Allot Gdns
FIELDING STREET
A215
ST JOHNS HOUSE
PHELP STREET
QUEEN'S ROW
HOPWOOD ROAD
GAITSKELL HO
32
EGLINGTON CT
A
B
139
C
D
MARKS HOUSE
HAMBLEDON
33
Pelier Park
EMPRESS ST
ST MATTHEW'S

Bermondsey
(New Caledonian)
Caledonian
Market
TOWER BRIDGE ROAD
ABBEY STREET
GRANGE ROAD
Grange Prim Sch
Southwark Coll
(Grange Centre)
Bermondsey Spa Gdns
Boutcher CE Prim Sch
Aylwin Girls Sch
MANDELA WAY
OLD KENT ROAD
DUNTON ROAD
Superstore
Surrey Square Jun & Inf Schs
SE17
Surrey Square Park
ROLLS ROAD
Walworth Sch
Burgess Park
ALBANY ROAD
SE5
SE 15
TRAFALGAR AVENUE
Cobourg Jun & Inf Sch
WAITE STREET
LONCROFT ROAD

253
139
118

The Queen's Club
A
B
C
D
254
HORTON HO
BARONS COURT MANS
ORCHARD SQ
SHUTERS SQ
VINE SQ
PASSFIELDS
MAY ST
STAR ROAD
Pav Tenn Cts
CLAXTON GR
78
CHELMSFORD CL
ST ALBANS TERR
COX HO
MARGRAVINE RD
MUSCAL
WILLIAM MORRIS HO
GASTEIN RD
6
GREYHOUND ROAD
SPENCER MEWS
FIELD ROAD
MARY MACARTHUR HO
ST ANDREW'S ROAD
BROWNING CT
TURNEVILLE ROAD
NORMAND MEWS
ALICE GILLIOTT CT
FANE ST
LICKEY HO
MARCHBANK ROAD
DESBOROUGH HO
ARCHEL ROAD
THAXTON RD
CHESSON ROAD
QUEEN'S CLUB GDNS
NORMAND ROAD
QUEEN'S CLUB GARDENS
Tenn Cts
B317
A3218
BRAMBER ROAD
Normand Park Prim Sch
BEAUFORT MEWS
GEORGE'S SQUARE
PEABODY ESTATE
W6
TASSO ROAD
KINNOUL ROAD
MUSARD ROAD
OAKLEY WLK
CRAMMOND CL
ABBEY GARDENS
P
Pav
MULGRAVE RD
CHESTNUT CT
CHESTNUT ALLEY
CHUTER EDE HO
TASSO YD
Normand Park
Bwg Gn
WENTWORTH CT
ADENEY CL
St Augustine's RC Prim Sch
LILLIE ROAD
Liby
JIM GRIFFITHS HO
STAFFORD CRIPPS HO
PAYENS WLK
DISBROWE ROAD
MOYLAN ROAD
TOM WILLIAMS HO
HUGH GAITSKELL CL
ELLEN WILKINSON HO
MANNY HINWELL HO
MARGARET HERBISON HO
LAMPETER SQ
LITTLE ROAD MANS
5
ANCILL CL
LAUNDRY RD
HUMBOLT ROAD
BRECON ROAD
TILTON ST
CLEM ATTLEE CT
HAROLD WILSON HO
COOMER MEWS
COOMER PL
CROWTHER CL
CREFELD CL
LINTAINE CL
HERBERT MORRISON HO
DOUGLAS JOHNSTONE HO
JOHN WHEATLEY HO
JOHN STRACHEY HO
FRANK BESWICK HO
FRANK SOSKICE HO
A3218
CAROLINE WLK
BAYONNE RD
Sir John Lillie Prim Sch
DELAFORD STREET
RYLSTON ROAD
P
MARGARET INGRAM CL
LEN FREEMAN PL
KENNETH YOUNGER HO
BUCKLER'S ALLEY
HALDANE ROAD
PURCELL CRES
TWYNHOLM MANS
PO
A3219
Recn Ground
CHALDON ROAD
WILLIAMS CL
PELLANT ROAD
MENDORA ROAD
JOHN SMITH AVE
GEORGE LINDGREN HO
EDITH SUMMERSKILL HO
NYE BEVAN HO
ST THOMAS'S WAY
TOURNAY ROAD
HARTOPP POINT
CHASEMORE HO
PROTHERO ROAD
ROCQUE HO
CLYDE FLATS
MATON HO
STRODE ROAD
4
DONNELLY CT
LANNOY POINT
ESTCOURT ROAD
FABIAN ROAD
MIRABEL ROAD
HARTISMERE ROAD
EPIRUS ROAD
ROYAL PAR
BEDFORD PAS
St Thomas of Canterbury RC Prim Sch
HANNELL ROAD
Fulham Cross Sec Sch
DAWES ROAD
PO
SHORROLDS ROAD
PALACE MEWS
BATHS APP
134
MUNSTER ROAD
AINTREE STREET
ROSALINE ROAD
ROSALINE TERR
SHERBROOKE TERR
SHERBROOKE ROAD
LETTERSTONE RD
SALISBURY MEWS
PARKVILLE ROAD
HOMESTEAD ROAD
GIRONDE ROAD
GOATER'S ALLEY
MABLETHORPE ROAD
Cemetery
ROWALLAN ROAD
VARNA ROAD
ROSAVILLE ROAD
BURNTHWAITE ROAD
BRONSART ROAD
ALLESTREE ROAD
ORBAIN ROAD
ST OLAF'S ROAD
BROOKVILLE ROAD
WHEATSHEAF TERR
LANCASTER CT
3
THE QUADRANGLE
KILMAINE ROAD
ST PETER'S TERR
FILMER ROAD
BLOOM PARK RD
MARVILLE ROAD
ATALANTA ST
BRANKSEA ST
KINGWOOD ROAD
WYFOLD ROAD
REPORTON RD
DARLAN ROAD
KELVEDON RD
77
MARRAYAT SQ
THE CODA CTR
FERNHURST RD
MUNSTER RESIDENCES
BISHOPS RD
ARUNDEL MANSIONS
Henry Compton Sec Sch
DANEHURST ST
FLORENCE MANS
HAZELWOOD MANSIONS
CHESILTON RD
RADIPOLE RD
LILYVILLE RD
WINCHENDON RD
CLONMEL RD
Kensington Prep Sch
2
CHILDERLEY ST
CONNAUGHT MANS
ROSTREVOR MANS
PENHURST MANS
AVONDALE MANS
Liby
A304
A219
SIDBURY ST
St John's CE Prim Sch
FILMER HO
DEEPDENE MANS
FILMER ROAD STUDIOS
QUENTINGTON MANSIONS
Al-Muntada Islamic Sch
LAMBROOK TERR
WARDO AVE
GOWAN AVE
SW6
SWIFT ST
ROSTREVOR RD
FULHAM RD
PURSERS CROSS RD
EPPLE RD
FINLAY ST
FULHAM PALACE RD
FULHAM
THE COURTYARD
VERA RD
FELDEN ST
ST MAUR RD
ELLERBY ST
KIMBELL GDNS
PARK MANSIONS
PO
WHITTINGSTALL MANSIONS
WHITTINGSTALL RD
EDGARLEY TERR
COLEHILL LA
HORDER RD
MUNSTER RD
MIMOSA ST
BEACONSFIELD WLK
1
DONERAILE ST
FIRTH GDNS
BURNFOOT AVE
CROOKHAM RD
ELY COURT FLATS
RINGMER AVE
DANCER RD
LETTICE ST
WOODLAWN RD
WALDEMAR AVENUE MANSIONS
HESTERCOMBE AVE
HEATHMAN'S RD
COLEHILL GDNS
DURRELL RD
CLARIDGE CT
WILLIAM BANFIELD HO
CLONCURRY ST
BISHOP'S PARK RD
Tenn Cts
LALOR ST
WALDEMAR AVE
WILSTON CT
ARTHUR HENDERSON HOUSE
PLATO PL
ST DIONIS RD
BISHOP'S MANSIONS
24
A
B
135
C
MUNSTER CT
MUSTOW PL
D
25
Pav
OXBERRY
DORNCLIFFE RD
FULHAM
EDISCO
GUION
DORIA

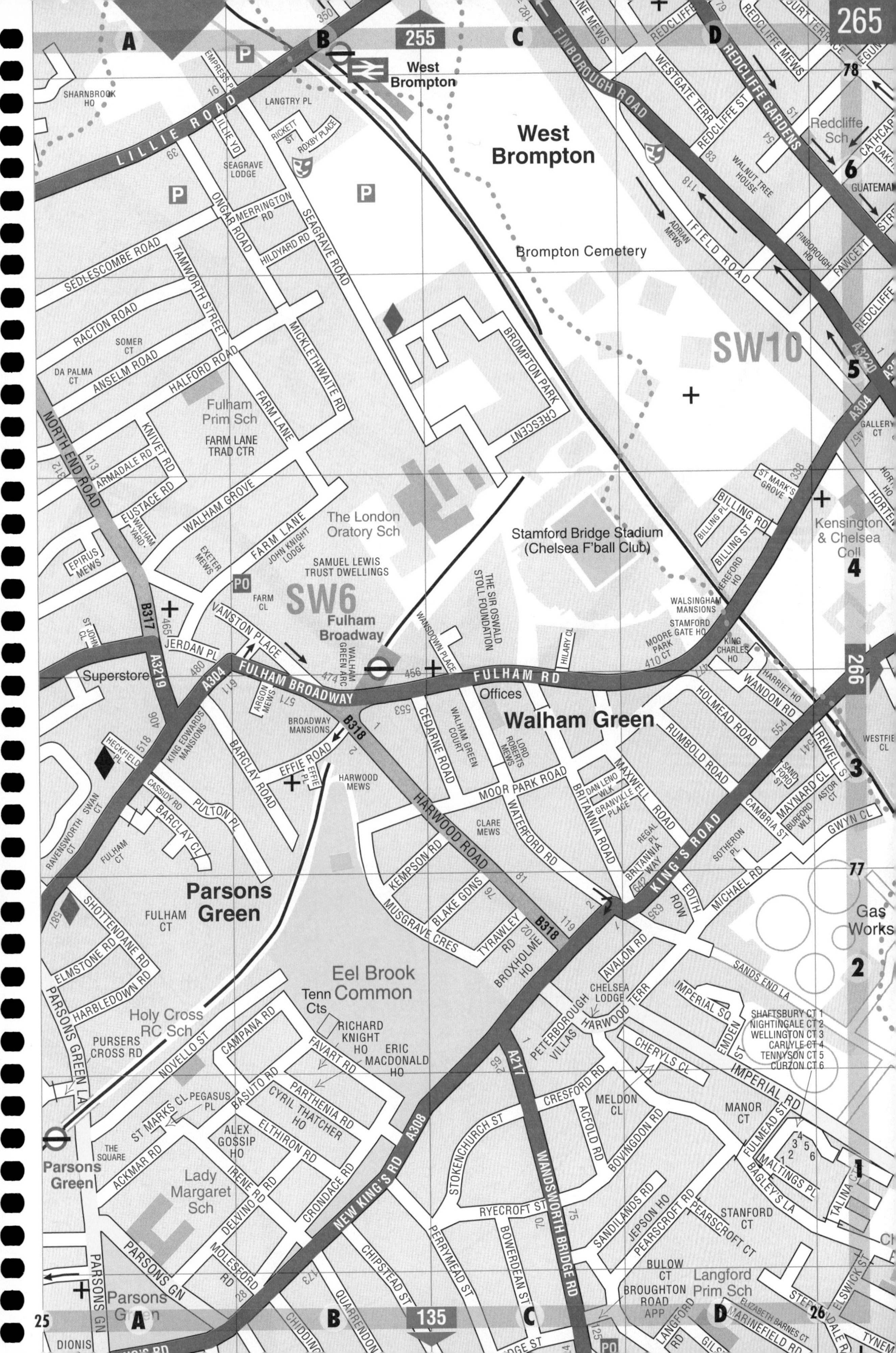

West Brompton
West Brompton
Brompton Cemetery
SW10
SW6
Fulham Broadway
Stamford Bridge Stadium (Chelsea F'ball Club)
The London Oratory Sch
Walham Green
Parsons Green
Eel Brook Common
Fulham Prim Sch
Holy Cross RC Sch
Lady Margaret Sch
Langford Prim Sch
Kensington & Chelsea Coll
Redcliffe Sch
Gas Works
LILLIE ROAD
FINBOROUGH ROAD
REDCLIFFE GARDENS
FULHAM RD
FULHAM BROADWAY
NORTH END ROAD
KING'S ROAD
NEW KING'S RD
HARWOOD ROAD
WANDSWORTH BRIDGE RD
IMPERIAL RD
PARSONS GREEN LA
SEAGRAVE ROAD
255
135
266

256
FULHAM ROAD
KING'S ROAD
CHEYNE WALK
CREMORNE ROAD
GUNTER GROVE
EDITH GROVE
REDCLIFFE GARDENS
BEAUFORT STREET
LOTS ROAD
RIVER THAMES
SW10
Chelsea & Westminster Hospl
Park Walk Prim Sch
Ashburnham Com Sch
Kensington & Chelsea Coll
Westfield Park
Cremorne Gdns
Old Ferry Wharf
Chelsea Wharf
Cremorne Wharf
Heatherley Sch of Fine Art
Gas Works
Chelsea Coll of Art & Design
Chelsea Harbour Pier
Royal Academy of Dance
Thomas's London Day Schs
Lindsey House
Cameron House Sch
Redcliffe Sch
Servite RC Prim Sch
Thames Path
Hammersmith & Fulham
Wandsworth
Kensington & Chelsea
265
136

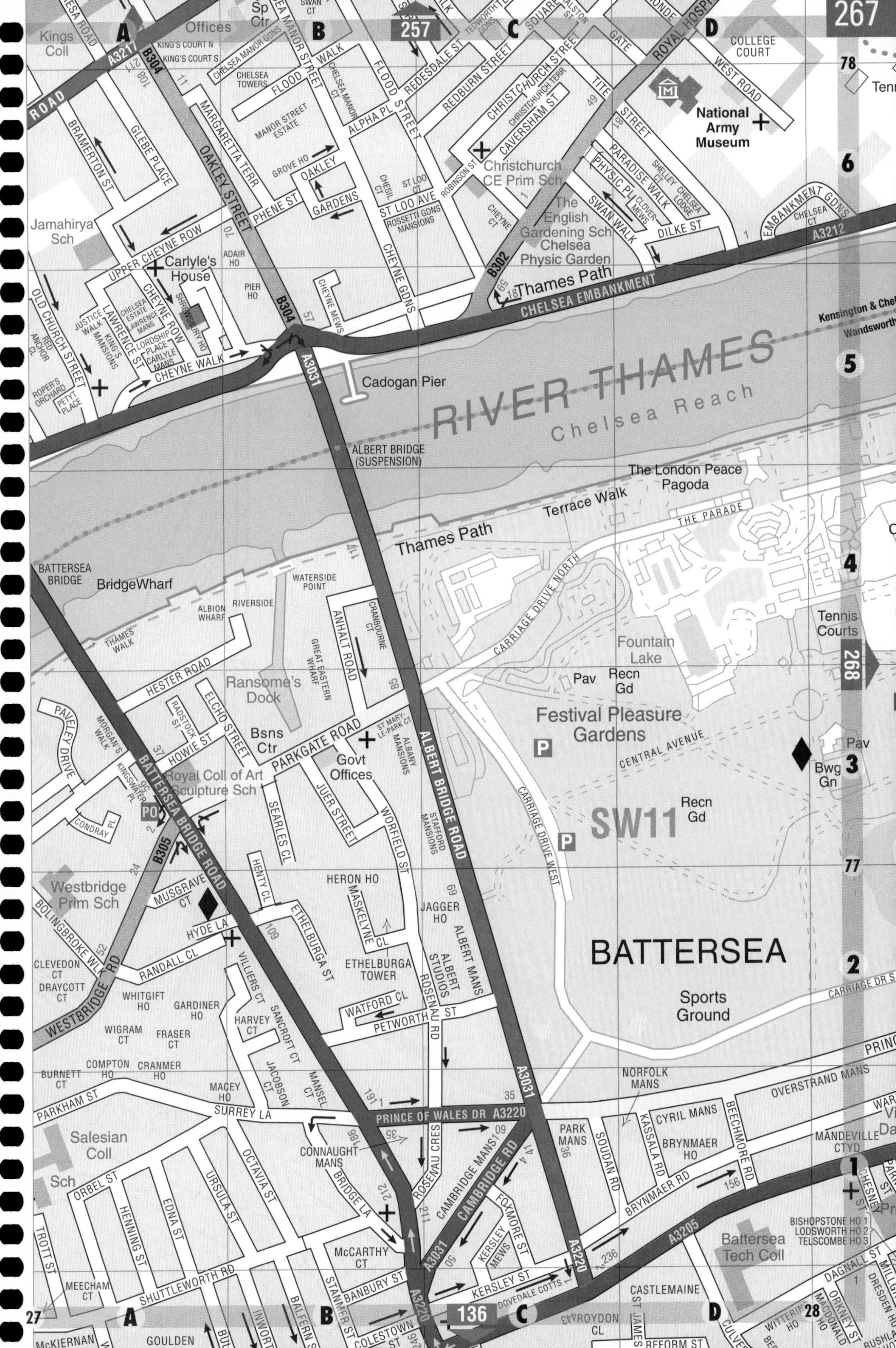

257
Kings Coll
Offices
OAKLEY STREET
CHELSEA EMBANKMENT
CHEYNE WALK
Carlyle's House
Christchurch CE Prim Sch
The English Gardening Sch
Chelsea Physic Garden
National Army Museum
Thames Path
Cadogan Pier
RIVER THAMES
Chelsea Reach
ALBERT BRIDGE (SUSPENSION)
The London Peace Pagoda
Terrace Walk
THE PARADE
BATTERSEA BRIDGE
BridgeWharf
Ransome's Dock
Fountain Lake
Festival Pleasure Gardens
CENTRAL AVENUE
CARRIAGE DRIVE NORTH
CARRIAGE DRIVE WEST
ALBERT BRIDGE ROAD
BATTERSEA BRIDGE ROAD
PARKGATE ROAD
HESTER ROAD
Royal Coll of Art Sculpture Sch
Govt Offices
Bsns Ctr
SW11
BATTERSEA
Sports Ground
Westbridge Prim Sch
WESTBRIDGE RD
PRINCE OF WALES DR A3220
CAMBRIDGE RD
SURREY LA
PARKHAM ST
Salesian Coll
SHUTTLEWORTH RD
Battersea Tech Coll
268
136
Kensington & Chelsea
Wandsworth

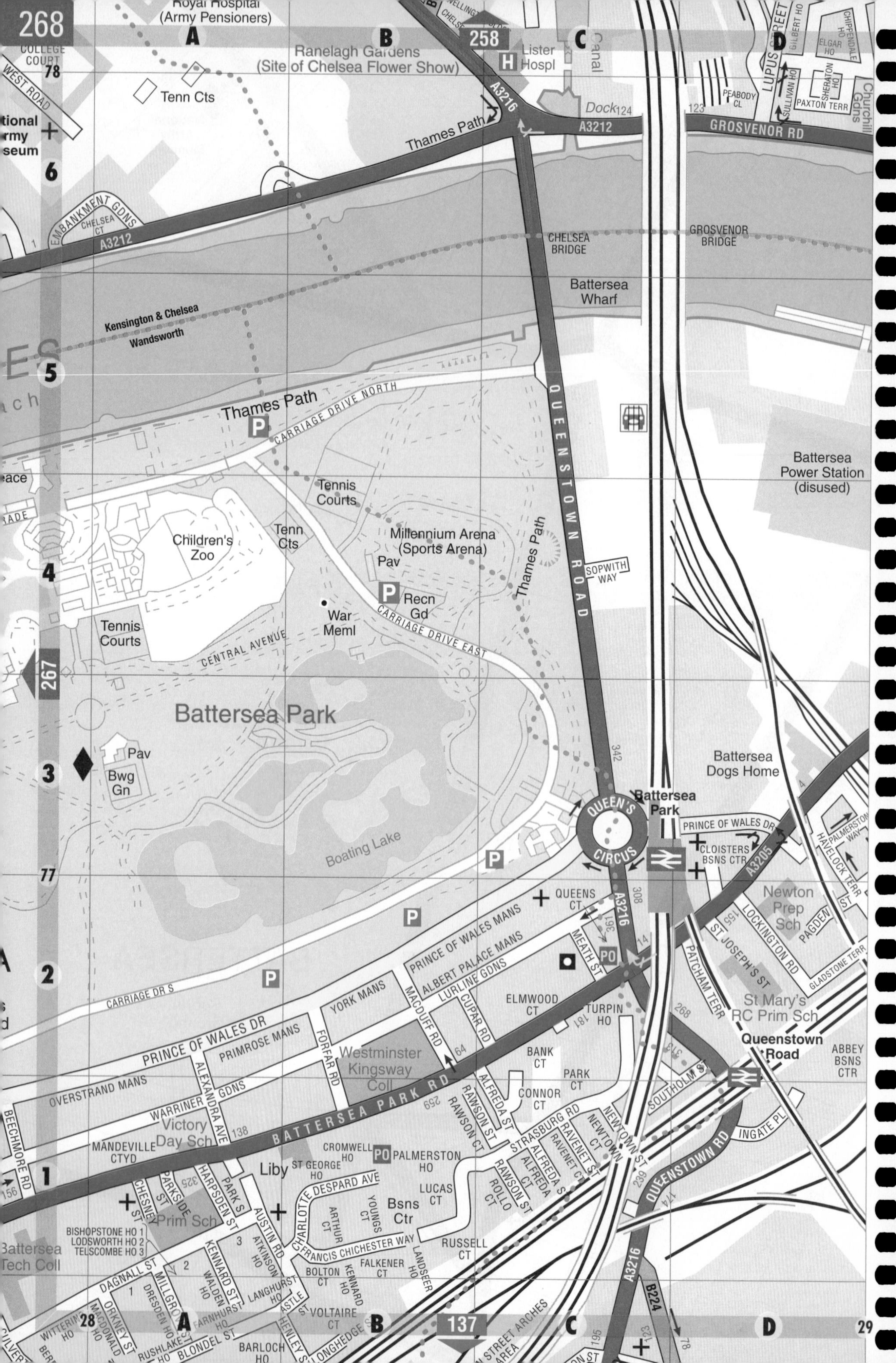
Royal Hospital (Army Pensioners)
Ranelagh Gardens (Site of Chelsea Flower Show)
Lister Hospl
Tenn Cts
Thames Path
A3216
A3212
Dock
GROSVENOR RD
LUPUS STREET
PEABODY CL
PAXTON TERR
Churchill Gdns
EMBANKMENT GDNS
CHELSEA CT
CHELSEA BRIDGE
GROSVENOR BRIDGE
Battersea Wharf
Kensington & Chelsea
Wandsworth
CARRIAGE DRIVE NORTH
QUEENSTOWN ROAD
Battersea Power Station (disused)
Tennis Courts
Children's Zoo
Tenn Cts
Millennium Arena (Sports Arena)
Pav
SOPWITH WAY
Recn Gd
War Meml
CARRIAGE DRIVE EAST
CENTRAL AVENUE
Battersea Park
Pav
Bwg Gn
Battersea Dogs Home
Battersea Park
QUEEN'S CIRCUS
PRINCE OF WALES DR
CLOISTERS BSNS CTR
Boating Lake
A3205
Newton Prep Sch
QUEENS CT
LOCKINGTON RD
PRINCE OF WALES MANS
ALBERT PALACE MANS
LURLINE GDNS
MEATH ST
ST JOSEPH'S ST
PATCHAM TERR
GLADSTONE TERR
St Mary's RC Prim Sch
CARRIAGE DR S
YORK MANS
ELMWOOD CT
TURPIN HO
Queenstown Road
ABBEY BSNS CTR
PRINCE OF WALES DR
PRIMROSE MANS
FORFAR RD
MACDUFF RD
CUPAR RD
Westminster Kingsway Coll
BANK CT
PARK CT
CONNOR CT
SOUTHOLM ST
OVERSTRAND MANS
ALEXANDRA AVE
WARRINER GDNS
BATTERSEA PARK RD
RAWSON ST
ALFREDA ST
STRASBURG RD
RAVENET ST
NEWTOWN CT
QUEENSTOWN RD
INGATE PL
Victory Day Sch
MANDEVILLE CTYD
CROMWELL HO
PALMERSTON HO
Liby
ST GEORGE HO
CHARLOTTE DESPARD AVE
LUCAS CT
ROLLO CT
BEECHMORE RD
Prim Sch
AUSTIN RD
ARTHUR CT
YOUNGS CT
Bsns Ctr
RUSSELL CT
BISHOPSTONE HO
LODSWORTH HO
TELSCOMBE HO
KENNARD ST
ATKINSON HO
FRANCIS CHICHESTER WAY
FALKENER CT
LANDSEER HO
Battersea Tech Coll
DAGNALL ST
MILLGROVE ST
WALDEN HO
LANGHURST HO
BOLTON CT
KENNARD HO
DRESDEN HO
FARNHURST HO
ASTLE ST
VOLTAIRE CT
RUSHLAKE HO
BLONDEL ST
BARLOCH HO
LONGHEDGE ST
HENLEY ST
STREET ARCHES
B224
ORKNEY ST
MACDONALD HO
WITTERING HO
A B C D
1 2 3 4 5 6
77 78

258
267
137

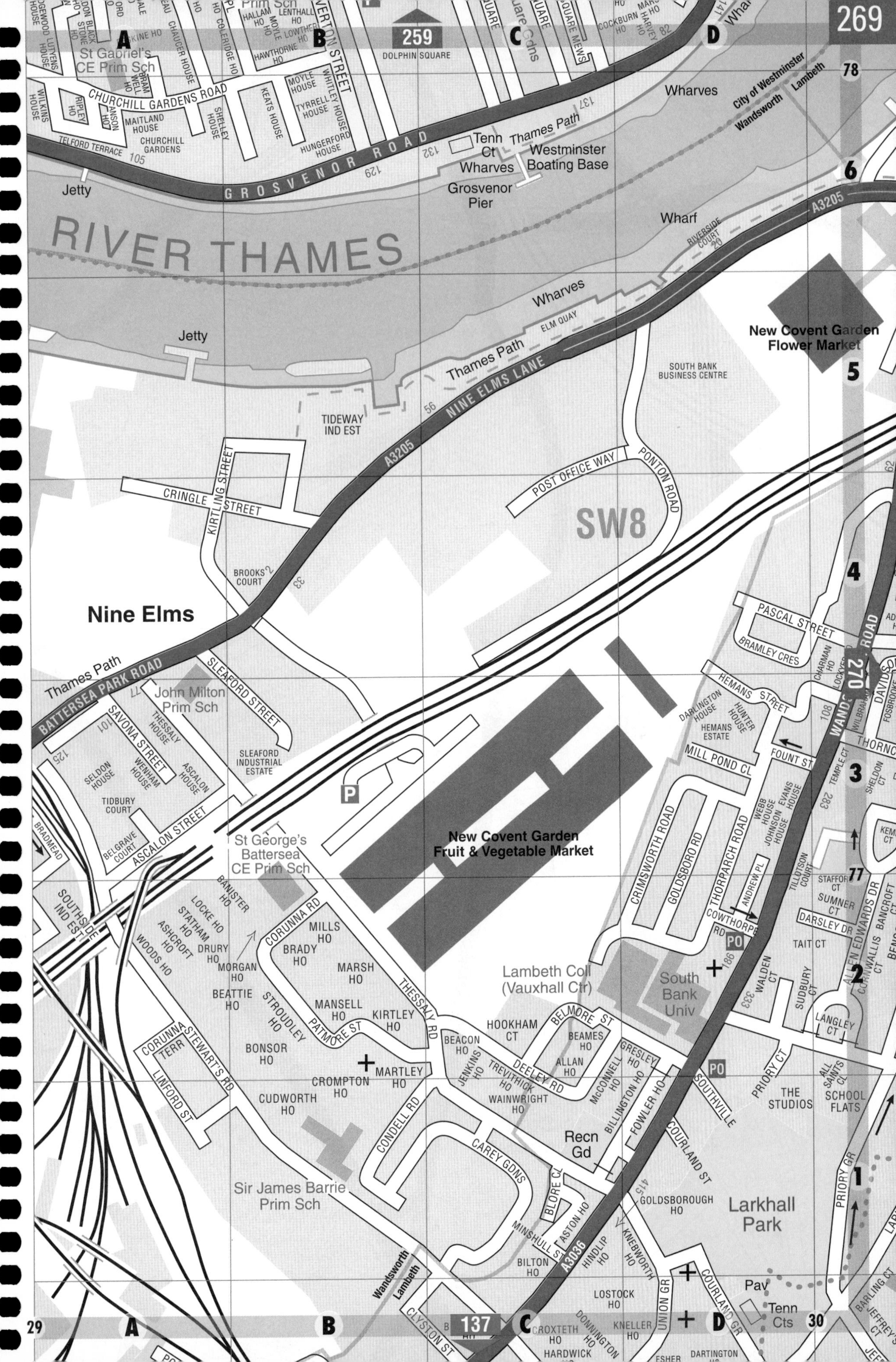

RIVER THAMES
GROSVENOR ROAD
NINE ELMS LANE
A3205
BATTERSEA PARK ROAD
Nine Elms
SW8
New Covent Garden Flower Market
New Covent Garden Fruit & Vegetable Market
SOUTH BANK BUSINESS CENTRE
TIDEWAY IND EST
POST OFFICE WAY
PONTON ROAD
CRINGLE STREET
KIRTLING STREET
BROOKS COURT
Thames Path
Jetty
Wharves
Wharf
Tenn Ct
Westminster Boating Base
Grosvenor Pier
ELM QUAY
RIVERSIDE COURT
DOLPHIN SQUARE
CHURCHILL GARDENS ROAD
CHURCHILL GARDENS
TELFORD TERRACE
St Gabriel's CE Prim Sch
City of Westminster
Lambeth
Wandsworth
John Milton Prim Sch
SLEAFORD STREET
SLEAFORD INDUSTRIAL ESTATE
SAVONA STREET
ASCALON STREET
St George's Battersea CE Prim Sch
SOUTHSIDE IND EST
Lambeth Coll (Vauxhall Ctr)
South Bank Univ
PASCAL STREET
BRAMLEY CRES
HEMANS STREET
HEMANS ESTATE
MILL POND CL
FOUNT ST
CRIMSWORTH ROAD
GOLDSBORO RD
THORPARCH ROAD
COWTHORPE RD
THESSALY RD
PATMORE ST
CORUNNA RD
CONDELL RD
CAREY GDNS
DEELEY RD
BELMORE ST
STEWART'S RD
LINFORD ST
CORUNNA TERR
Sir James Barrie Prim Sch
Recn Gd
COURLAND ST
Larkhall Park
PRIORY CT
PRIORY GR
THE STUDIOS
SCHOOL FLATS
ALLEN EDWARDS DR
WANDSWORTH ROAD
A3036
UNION GR
COURLAND GR
CLYSTON ST
Pav
Tenn Cts
A
B
C
D
1
2
3
4
5
6
29
30
77
78
137
259
270

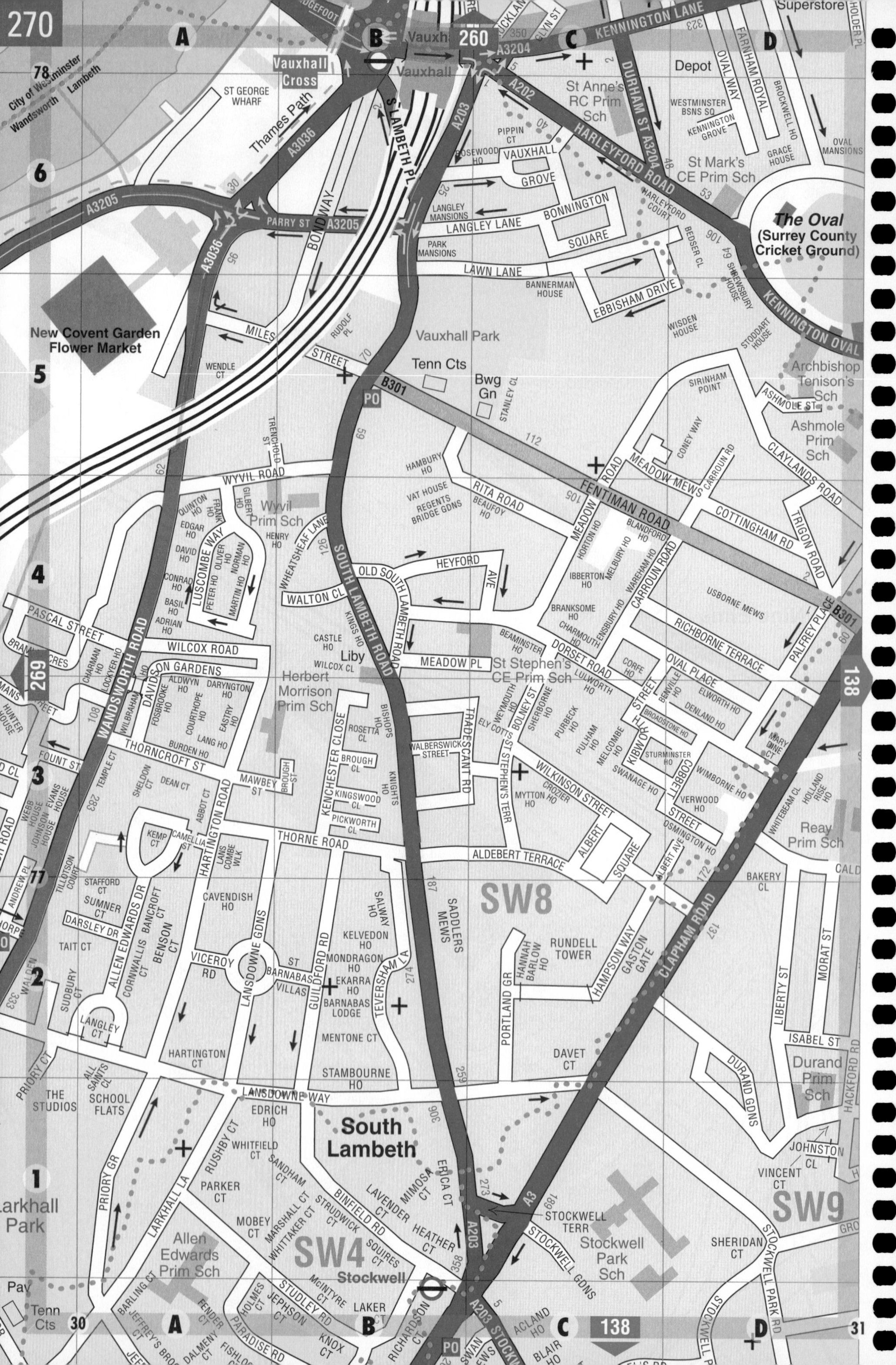
270
A
B
C
D
260
138
269
Vauxhall Cross
Vauxhall
KENNINGTON LANE
Superstore
Depot
ST GEORGE WHARF
City of Westminster
Lambeth
Wandsworth
Thames Path
A3036
A3205
A3204
A202
A203
S LAMBETH PL
St Anne's RC Prim Sch
DURHAM ST A3204
OVAL WAY
FARNHAM ROYAL
BROCKWELL HO
WESTMINSTER BSNS SQ
KENNINGTON GROVE
HARLEYFORD ROAD
St Mark's CE Prim Sch
GRACE HOUSE
OVAL MANSIONS
The Oval
(Surrey County Cricket Ground)
PIPPIN CT
ROSEWOOD HO
VAUXHALL GROVE
BONNINGTON SQUARE
LANGLEY MANSIONS
LANGLEY LANE
PARK MANSIONS
LAWN LANE
PARRY ST
BOND WAY
HARLEYFORD COURT
BEDSER CL
SHREWSBURY HOUSE
BANNERMAN HOUSE
EBBISHAM DRIVE
KENNINGTON OVAL
New Covent Garden Flower Market
MILES STREET
RUDOLF PL
WENDLE CT
Vauxhall Park
Tenn Cts
Bwg Gn
STANLEY CL
WISDEN HOUSE
STODDART HOUSE
Archbishop Tenison's Sch
ASHMOLE ST
Ashmole Prim Sch
SIRINHAM POINT
CONEY WAY
CARROUN RD
CLAYLANDS ROAD
B301
PO
TRENCHOLD ST
WYVIL ROAD
Wyvil Prim Sch
HAMBURY HO
VAT HOUSE
REGENTS BRIDGE GDNS
RITA ROAD
BEAUFOY HO
MEADOW ROAD
MEADOW MEWS
FENTIMAN ROAD
COTTINGHAM RD
TRIGON ROAD
QUINTON HO
FRANK HO
GILBERT HO
EDGAR HO
DAVID HO
LUSCOMBE WAY
OLIVER HO
NORMAN HO
HENRY HO
WHEATSHEAF LANE
SOUTH LAMBETH ROAD
OLD SOUTH LAMBETH ROAD
HEYFORD AVE
HORTON HO
BLANDFORD HO
MELBURY HO
WAREHAM HO
CARROUN ROAD
USBORNE MEWS
PALFREY PLACE
CONRAD HO
PETER HO
MARTIN HO
BASIL HO
ADRIAN HO
WALTON CL
KINGS HO
IBBERTON HO
BRANKSOME HO
CHARMOUTH HO
ENSBURY HO
RICHBORNE TERRACE
PASCAL STREET
WANDSWORTH ROAD
WILCOX ROAD
CHARMAN HO
LOCKYER HO
CASTLE HO
Liby
WILCOX CL
MEADOW PL
BEAMINSTER HO
St Stephen's CE Prim Sch
DORSET ROAD
CORFE HO
OVAL PLACE
ELWORTH HO
DAVIDSON GARDENS
ALDWYN HO
DARYNGTON HO
Herbert Morrison Prim Sch
LULWORTH HO
DENLAND HO
WILBRAHAM HO
FOSBROOKE HO
COURTHOPE HO
EASTRY HO
BISHOPS HO
ROSETTA CL
WALBERSWICK STREET
TRADESCANT RD
WEYMOUTH HO
BOLNEY ST
ELY COTTS
SHERBORNE HO
PURBECK HO
KIBWORTH STREET
BROADSTONE HO
BENVILLE HO
STURMINSTER HO
MARY DINE CT
LANG HO
BURDEN HO
THORNCROFT ST
FOUNT ST
TEMPLE CT
SHELDON CT
DEAN CT
MAWBEY ST
BROUGH ST
KENCHESTER CLOSE
BROUGH CL
KINGSWOOD CL
KNIGHTS HO
ST STEPHEN'S TERR
WILKINSON STREET
PULHAM HO
MELCOMBE HO
SWANAGE HO
COBBETT STREET
WIMBORNE HO
VERWOOD HO
WHITEBEAM CL
HOLLAND RISE HO
MYTTON HO
CROZIER HO
Reay Prim Sch
HUNTER HOUSE
WEBB HOUSE
JOHNSON HOUSE
EVANS HOUSE
KEMP CT
CAMELLIA ST
ABBOT CT
HARTINGTON ROAD
LANSCOMBE WLK
PICKWORTH CL
THORNE ROAD
ALDEBERT TERRACE
ALBERT SQUARE
ALBERT AVE
OSMINGTON HO
BAKERY CL
TILLOTSON COURT
ANDREW PL
STAFFORD CT
SUMNER CT
DARSLEY DR
ALLEN EDWARDS DR
BANCROFT CT
CAVENDISH HO
SALWAY HO
SADDLERS MEWS
SW8
TAIT CT
CORNWALLIS CT
BENSON CT
LANSDOWNE GDNS
GUILDFORD RD
KELVEDON HO
MONDRAGON HO
EKARRA HO
TEVERSHAM LA
HANNAH BARLOW HO
RUNDELL TOWER
HAMPSON WAY
GASTON GATE
CLAPHAM ROAD
LIBERTY ST
MORAT ST
VICEROY RD
ST BARNABAS VILLAS
BARNABAS LODGE
PORTLAND GR
WALDEN
SUDBURY CT
LANGLEY CT
MENTONE CT
ISABEL ST
HACKFORD RD
HARTINGTON CT
DAVET CT
DURAND GDNS
Durand Prim Sch
PRIORY CT
ALL SAINTS CL
THE STUDIOS
SCHOOL FLATS
STAMBOURNE HO
LANSDOWNE WAY
EDRICH HO
South Lambeth
JOHNSTON CL
VINCENT CT
RUSHBY CT
WHITFIELD CT
SANDHAM CT
MIMOSA CT
ERICA CT
Larkhall Park
PRIORY GR
LARKHALL LA
PARKER CT
MOBEY CT
MARSHALL CT
WHITTAKER CT
STRUDWICK CT
BINFIELD RD
LAVENDER CT
HEATHER CT
A3
STOCKWELL TERR
SW9
SW4
SQUIRES CT
STOCKWELL GDNS
Stockwell Park Sch
SHERIDAN CT
STOCKWELL PARK RD
Allen Edwards Prim Sch
Stockwell
Pay
BARLING CT
HOLMES CT
STUDLEY RD
MCINTYRE CT
LAKER CT
RICHARDSON CT
JEPHSON CT
Tenn Cts
FENDER CT
PARADISE RD
KNOX CT
DALMENY CT
JEFFREY'S RD
ACLAND HO
BLAIR HO
STOCKWELL
30
31

Index

Church Rd [6] Beckenham BR2.........**53** C6 **228** C6

Place name	**Location number**	**Locality, town or village**	**Postcode district**	**Standard scale reference**	**Enlarged scale reference**
May be abbreviated on the map	Present when a number indicates the place's position in a crowded area of mapping	Shown when more than one place (outside London postal districts) has the same name	District for the indexed place	Page number and grid reference for the standard mapping	Page number and grid reference for the central London enlarged mapping, underlined in red

Public and commercial buildings are highlighted in magenta

Places of interest are highlighted in blue with a star★

Index of Localities, towns and villages

A

Abbey Wood 124 B3
Acton 111 B5
Acton Green 111 A2
Addington 223 C3
Addiscombe 206 A1
Aldborough Hatch 57 C5
Aldersbrook 77 C6
Alperton 88 A6
Anerley 184 B2
Arkley 12 A6
Ashford 170 B4
Ashford Common 171 B4
Avery Hill 167 B5

B

Balham 159 A3
Bandonhill 219 D3
Barbican 95 A2
Barking 79 B1
Barkingside 57 A6
Barnes 133 D4
Barnet 13 B6
Barnet Gate 11 D5
Barnsbury 72 A1
Battersea 136 D4
Bayswater 114 A6
Beckenham 185 C1
Beckton 100 D2
Becontree 81 A4
Beddington 220 A6
Beddington Corner ...203 A2
Bedford Park 111 C3
Belgravia 115 B2
Bell Green 163 B1
Bellingham 185 C5
Belmont 25 B2
Belsize Park 70 C3
Belvedere 125 D2
Benhilton 218 A5
Benhurst 118 A4
Berrylands 198 C3
Bethnal Green 96 B4
Bexley 146 B1
Bexleyheath 147 B2
Bickley 188 B1
Blackfen 168 A5
Blackheath 142 C2
Blackheath Park 143 A1
Blackheath Vale 142 D3
Blackwall 120 B6
Bloomsbury 93 D2
Borehamwood 11 C5
Borough The 117 A4
Bow 97 B5
Bow Common 97 D2
Bowes Park 32 A4
Brent Cross 46 D2
Brentford 131 B6
Brentford End 131 C4
Brimsdown 7 B3
Brixton 138 C2
Broad Green 204 D3
Broadgate 95 C2
Brockley 141 B1

C

Camberwell 139 A4
Camden Town 71 B1
Canary Wharf 119 D5
Canning Town 99 B1
Canonbury 73 A2
Canons Park 26 A3
Carshalton 218 C4
Carshalton Beeches .218 D1
Carshalton on
    the Hill 219 B1
Castle Green 102 C6
Catford 163 C3
Chadwell Heath 58 D4
Charlton
    (Greenwich) 143 D6
Charlton (Surrey) ...171 B1
Chattern Hill 170 D6
Cheam 217 B3
Chelsea 114 C1
Chertsey Meads 192 A1
Chessington 214 A2
Child's Hill 69 C6
Chingford 20 C3
Chingford Green 20 A4
Chingford Hatch 36 B6
Chipping Barnet 1 B1
Chislehurst 189 C3
Chislehurst West 188 C4
Chiswick 111 D1
Church End (Barnet) ..29 C1
Church End (Brent) ...67 D2
City of London 117 A6
Clapham 137 B2
Clapham Common 137 B1
Clapham Junction ...136 C1
Clapham Park 159 D6
Clapton Park 74 D4
Clay Hill 5 A6
Claygate 212 D1
Clayhall 56 B6
Clerkenwell 94 D3
Cockfosters 2 D1
Colham Green 82 C2
Colindale 45 C6
College Park 90 B4
Collier's Wood 180 C4
Colney Hatch 30 C4
Coney Hall 224 D5

Bromley 186 C2
Bromley
    (Tower Hamlets) ...97 D4
Bromley Common 210 A3
Bromley Park 186 D2
Brompton 114 B3
Brondesbury 69 A2
Brondesbury Park 90 D6
Brook Green 112 D2
Broom Hill 211 D2
Brunswick Park 15 A1
Buckhurst Hill 21 C2
Burnt Oak 27 B3
Bush Hill Park 17 C5
Bushey 8 A2
Bushey Heath 8 C4
Bushey Mead 200 D6

D

Dagenham 81 D1
Dalston 74 A2
Dartmouth Park 71 B5
De Beauvoir Town 73 C1
Deacons Hill 10 C5
Deptford 140 D6
Dollis Hill 68 B5
Dormer's Wells 107 C6
Downham 186 C5
Ducks Island 12 D5
Dudden Hill 68 A3
Dulwich 161 C1
Dulwich Village 161 C4

E

Ealing 109 D6
Earl's Court 113 C1
Earlsfield 158 A3
East Acton 111 C5
East Barnet 14 D4
East Bedfont 149 C3
East Dulwich 162 A6
East Finchley 48 B5
East Ham 100 A5
East Molesey 196 A4
East Sheen 133 B1
East Wickham 146 A5
Eastbury 22 A5
Eastcote 40 C3
Eastcote Village 40 B4
Eden Park 205 C5
Edgware 26 C6
Edgware Bury 10 B3
Edmonton 33 D6
Elmers End 206 D6
Elmstead 188 A5
Elstree 10 A5
Eltham 166 B6
Enfield 6 B2
Enfield Highway 6 C3
Enfield Lock 7 B6
Enfield Town 5 B1
Enfield Wash 6 D5
Erith 147 D6
Esher 212 A4

Coombe 177 B3
Copse Hill 178 B3
Cottenham Park 178 B2
Covent Garden 116 A6
Cowley Peachy 82 A2
Cranbrook 56 C1
Cranford 128 C4
Cranley Gardens 49 B5
Creekmouth 101 D2
Cricklewood 68 D4
Crofton 227 B6
Crooked Billet 178 C4
Crouch End 49 D3
Croydon 221 B5
Crystal Palace 184 A5
Cubitt Town 120 A2
Custom House 121 C6
Cyprus 122 C6

F

Fair Cross 79 D3
Falconwood 145 C1
Farnborough 227 B3
Farthing Street 226 B1
Feltham 150 A3
Felthamhill 171 D5
Finchley 29 D3
Finsbury 94 C4
Finsbury Park 50 D1
Fitzrovia 93 C1
Foots Cray 190 B4
Forest Gate 77 A3
Forest Hill 163 A3
Fortis Green 48 D5
Forty Hill 5 D4
Friday Hill 20 C1
Friern Barnet 31 A6
Fulham 134 D4
Furzedown 181 B6

G

Gants Hill 56 C3
Globe Town 96 D4
Golders Green 47 B4
Goodmayes 58 B1
Gospel Oak 70 D2
Grahame Park 27 C2
Grange Park 16 C6
Green Street Green ..227 C2
Greenford 86 A4
Greenhill 42 D4
Greenwich 142 C6
Grove Park
    (Hounslow) 133 A4
Grove Park
    (Lewisham) 165 B1
Gunnersbury 110 D2

H

Hackbridge 219 B6
Hackney 74 B2
Hackney Wick 75 C2
Hadley 1 B2
Hadley Wood 2 B5
Haggerston 95 D5
Hale End 36 C4
Ham 153 C1
Hammersmith 112 C2
Hampstead 70 A3
Hampstead Garden
    Suburb 47 D4
Hampton 173 C1
Hampton Court 196 C5
Hampton Hill 174 A5
Hampton Wick 175 D3
Hanwell 108 D5
Hanworth 172 D6
Harlesden 89 C6
Harlington 127 A6

Euston 93 C4
Ewell 215 C1

Harmondsworth 126 A6
Harringay 50 D4
Harrow 42 B3
Harrow on the Hill ...42 C1
Harrow Weald 24 B2
Hatch End 23 A3
Hatton 127 D1
Hayes (Bromley) 209 A2
Hayes (Hillingdon) ...83 C1
Hayes End 83 B3
Hayes Town 106 B5
Headstone 41 D5
Hendon 46 C3
Herne Hill 161 A6
Heston 129 B5
High Barnet 1 A2
Higham Hill 35 A2
Highams Park 36 A3
Highbury 72 D4
Highgate 49 A2
Hillingdon 82 D5
Hillingdon Heath 82 D2
Hinchley Wood 212 D6
Hither Green 164 C5
Holborn 94 C2
Homerton 74 D1
Honor Oak 162 C6
Hook 214 A4
Hornsey 50 A5
Hornsey Vale 50 B4
Hounslow 129 C3
Hounslow West 128 D2
Hoxton 95 C5
Hurst Park 174 A1
Hyde Park 114 D5
Hyde The 45 D4

I

Ickenham 60 C4
Ilford 78 D6
Isle of Dogs 120 A2
Isleworth 131 B2
Islington 72 D2

K

Kennington 116 C1
Kensal Green 90 C4
Kensal Rise 91 A5
Kensal Town 91 A3
Kensington 113 C4
Kentish Town 71 C3
Kenton 43 C3
Keston 225 D4
Keston Mark 225 D6
Kew 132 C6
Kidbrooke 143 C3
Kilburn 91 B6
King's Cross 94 A5
Kingsbury 45 B3
Kingsland 73 C2
Kingston Upon
    Thames 197 C6
Kingston Vale 177 B6
Kitts End 1 A5
Knightsbridge 114 C4

L

Ladywell 163 C6
Lambeth 116 B4
Lampton 129 D4
Lea Bridge 74 D5
Lee 74 D5
Lessness Heath 125 D1
Lewisham 142 A1
Leyton 76 B5
Leytonstone 54 D1
Limehouse 119 A6
Lisson Green 92 C3
Lisson Grove 92 B2
Little Heath 58 B5
Little Ilford 78 C3
Little Stanmore 26 B2
Littleton 192 C6
Littleton Common ...171 B3
Locksbottom 226 D5
London City Airport .122 B5
Long Ditton 197 C1
Longlands 167 B1
Loughton 21 D5
Lower Clapton 74 C4
Lower Edmonton 18 B1
Lower Feltham 149 D1
Lower Green 195 D1
Lower Halliford 193 C3
Lower Holloway 72 A3
Lower Morden 201 A2
Lower Place 89 A5
Lower Sydenham 185 A6
Loxford 79 A3

M

Maida Vale 91 D4
Maitland Park 71 A2
Manor Park 78 A4
Marylebone 93 B1
Mayfair 115 B6
Merton 179 C2
Merton Park 179 C1
Mile End 97 A3
Mill Hill 28 B5
Mill Meads 98 B5
Millwall 119 C3
Mitcham 202 D5
Monken Hadley 1 A3
Monks Orchard 207 A3
Morden 201 D3
Morden Park 201 A3
Mortlake 133 A2
Motspur Park 200 A3
Mottingham 165 D2
Muswell Hill 49 A6

N

Nash 225 A2
Neasden 67 B4
New Addington 224 B1
New Barnet 14 A6
New Beckenham 185 A4
New Charlton 121 C2

New Cross 141 B4
New Cross Gate 140 D4
New Eltham 167 A2
New Malden 199 D5
New Southgate 31 C6
Newbury Park 57 B3
Newham 98 D4
Newington 116 D2
Newyears Green 38 B3
Nine Elms 137 C5
Noel Park 32 D1
Norbiton 176 C1
Norbury 182 C2
North Acton 89 B4
North Cheam 216 C6
North Cray 169 B1
North End 70 A6
North Feltham 150 B6
North Finchley 30 A6
North Harrow 41 D2
North Hillingdon 61 A2
North Hyde 107 A1
North Kensington 90 D2
North Sheen 132 C3
North Wembley 65 C6
North Woolwich 122 D4
Northolt 63 C1
Northwood 22 A3
Northwood Hills 22 A1
Norwood Green 107 C2
Norwood New Town 183 A4
Notting Hill 113 B6
Nower Hill 41 B6
Nunhead 140 C1

O

Oakleigh Park 14 B3
Oakwood 15 D6
Old Bexley 169 D4
Old Ford 97 B6
Old Malden 199 C1
Old Oak Common 89 D3
Orpington 227 D6
Osidge 15 C3
Osterley 130 B5

P

Paddington 92 A2
Palmers Green 16 A1
Park Langley 208 B4
Park Royal 88 D4
Parsons Green 135 C4
Peckham 140 A4
Penge 184 D4
Pentonville 94 B5
Perivale 87 B5
Petersham 153 D3
Petts Wood 211 B5
Pimlico 115 C1
Pinner 41 A6
Pinner Green 22 C1
Pinnerwood Park 22 C3
Plaistow (Bromley) 187 A4
Plaistow (Newham) 99 B4
Plashet 78 A2
Plumstead 123 C2
Plumstead Common 145 D6
Ponders End 18 D6
Poplar 97 C1
Preston 44 A1
Primrose Hill 70 D1
Putney 156 C6
Putney Heath 156 C6
Putney Vale 156 A1

Q

Queensbury 44 B6

R

Ratcliff 118 D6
Rayners Lane 41 B1
Raynes Park 200 C6
Redbridge 55 D3
Regent's Park 93 B4
Richmond 154 A6
Richmond Hill 154 A5
Richmond Park 155 A3
Roehampton 155 C4
Romford 59 C5
Rosehill 202 A1
Rotherhithe 118 D3
Roundshaw 220 B1
Roxeth 64 A6
Ruislip 39 B2
Ruislip Common 39 B4
Ruislip Gardens 61 D5
Ruislip Manor 40 A1
Ruxley 191 A3

S

Sands End 136 A2
Seething Wells 197 D3
Selhurst 205 B4
Selsdon 223 A1
Seven Kings 57 D2
Sewardstonebury 20 C6
Shacklewell 73 D4
Shadwell 118 C6
Shepherd's Bush 112 B5
Shepperton 193 A3
Shepperton Green 192 D5
Shirley 206 C1
Shooters Hill 145 A4
Shoreditch 95 B5
Shortlands 208 C6
Sidcup 190 A5
Silvertown 121 C4
Sipson 126 C6
Snaresbrook 54 D6
Soho 93 D1
Somers Town 93 D4
South Acton 110 D3
South Bank 116 B4
South Beddington 219 C2
South Bromley 98 B2
South Croydon 221 B1
South Hackney 96 C6
South Hampstead 70 A1
South Harrow 63 D5
South Kensington 114 A1
South Lambeth 138 A4
South Norwood 205 C6
South Oxhey 22 B6
South Ruislip 62 D4
South Tottenham 51 D4
South Wimbledon 179 D4
Southall 107 A5
Southborough (Bromley) 210 B3
Southborough (Kingston Upon Thames) 197 D1
Southend 186 B6
Southfields 157 C3
Southgate 16 B4
Southwark 117 B5
Spitalfields 95 D2
Spring Grove 130 C3
Spring Park 223 B5
St George in the East 118 A6
St Giles 94 A1
St Helier 202 B2
St James 115 C5
St John's 141 C3
St John's Wood 92 B5
St Luke's 95 A3
St Margarets 153 A5
St Pancras 94 A4
St Paul's Cray 190 A1
Stamford Hill 51 C1
Stanmore 25 B2
Stanwell 148 A3
Stepney 96 D2
Stockwell 138 A2
Stoke Newington 73 C6
Stonebridge 89 A6
Stoneleigh 216 A3
Strand 116 B6
Strand on the Green 132 C6
Stratford 76 A1
Stratford Marsh 97 D6
Stratford New Town 76 A3
Strawberry Hill 152 D1
Streatham 182 A4
Streatham Hill 160 A3
Streatham Park 181 C6
Streatham Vale 181 D3
Stroud Green 50 C3
Sudbury 65 A4
Summerstown 158 A1
Sunbury 194 B6
Sunbury Common 171 D3
Sundridge 187 C4
Surbiton 198 A2
Sutton 218 A1
Syon Park 131 B4

T

Teddington 175 C5
Temple Mills 75 D3
Thames Ditton 197 B2
Thamesmead 124 A5
Thornton Heath 204 D3
Tokyngton 66 D2
Tolworth 214 C6
Tooting 180 D4
Tooting Graveney 180 B5
Tottenham 33 D1
Tottenham Hale 52 A6
Totteridge 13 C3
Tower Hamlets 97 B2
Tufnell Park 71 D4
Tulse Hill 160 D4
Twickenham 152 D4

U

Underhill 13 C6
Upper Clapton 52 B1
Upper Edmonton 34 B5
Upper Elmers End 207 B4
Upper Halliford 193 B5
Upper Holloway 71 D6
Upper Norwood 183 C3
Upper Ruxley 191 C3
Upper Shirley 222 D4
Upper Sydenham 184 A6
Upper Tooting 158 D1
Upper Walthamstow 54 C6
Upton 77 B1
Upton Park 99 D6
Uxbridge 82 A6

V

Vale of Health 70 B5
Vauxhall 116 A1

W

Waddon 220 D4
Walham Green 135 D5
Wallend 100 C6
Wallington 219 A2
Walthamstow 53 D6
Walton-on-Thames 194 C2
Walworth 117 B1
Wandsworth 157 C5
Wanstead 55 C3
Wapping 118 B5
Waterloo 116 C4
Wealdstone 42 D6
Welling 146 B2
Welsh Harp 45 C1
Wembley 66 A2
Wembley Park 66 C5
West Acton 88 C1
West Barnes 200 C4
West Bedfont 148 C4
West Brompton 135 D6
West Drayton 104 B4
West Dulwich 161 A2
West Ealing 109 B5
West Ewell 215 C1
West Green 51 A5
West Ham 99 B6
West Hampstead 69 C4
West Harrow 42 A2
West Heath 146 D6
West Hendon 45 D3
West Hill 157 B5
West Kensington 113 A2
West Kilburn 91 A4
West Molesey 195 C5
West Norwood 161 A1
West Ruislip 61 B6
West Wickham 224 C6
Westbourne Green 91 D3
Westminster 115 C4
Weston Green 196 D1
Whetstone 14 A2
Whitechapel 95 D1
Whitton 152 A4
Widmore 188 A1
Willesden 68 A4
Willesden Green 90 B6
Wimbledon 179 B4
Wimbledon Park 157 B2
Winchmore Hill 16 D4
Wood End 83 D1
Wood End Green 83 C2
Wood Green 32 B2
Woodford 37 D5
Woodford Green 37 B3
Woodford Wells 21 B1
Woodlands 130 C2
Woodside 206 A4
Woodside Park 29 C6
Woolwich 122 D3
Worcester Park 215 C4
World's End 4 C1
Wrythe The 218 D6

Y

Yeading 84 D3
Yiewsley 104 A6

Abbreviations used in the index

Abbreviation	Meaning
Acad	Academy
App	Approach
Arc	Arcade
Art Gall	Art Gallery
Ave	Avenue
Bglws	Bungalows
Bldgs	Buildings
Bsns Ctr	Business Centre
Bsns Pk	Business Park
Bvd	Boulevard
Cath	Cathedral, Catholic
CE	Church of England
Cemy	Cemetery
Cir	Circus
Circ	Circle
Cl	Close
Cnr	Corner
Coll	College
Com	Community
Comm	Common
Comp	Comprehensive
Con Ctr	Conference Centre
Cotts	Cottages
Cres	Crescent
Cswy	Causeway
Ct	Court
Ctr	Centre
Crkt	Cricket
Ctry Pk	Country Park
Cty	County
Ctyd	Courtyard
Dr	Drive
Ent Ctr	Enterprise Centre
Ent Pk	Enterprise Park
Est	Estate
Ex Ctr	Exhibition Centre
Ex Hall	Exhibition Hall
Fst	First
Gdn	Garden
Gdns	Gardens
Gn	Green
Gr	Grove
Gram	Grammar
Her Ctr	Heritage Centre
Ho	House
Hospl	Hospital
Hts	Heights
Ind Est	Industrial Estate
Inf	Infant
Inst	Institute
Int	International
Intc	Interchange
Jun	Junior
Junc	Junction
La	Lane
L Ctr	Leisure Centre
Liby	Library
Mans	Mansions
Mdw/s	Meadow/s
Meml	Memorial
Mid	Middle
Mix	Mixed
Mkt	Market
Mon	Monument
Mus	Museum
Obsy	Observatory
Orch	Orchard
Par	Parade
Pas	Passage
Pav	Pavilion
Pk	Park
Pl	Place
Prec	Precinct
Prep	Preparatory
Prim	Primary
Prom	Promenade
RC	Roman Catholic
Rd	Road
Rdbt	Roundabout
Ret Pk	Retail Park
Sch	School
Sec	Secondary
Sh Ctr	Shopping Centre
Sp	Sports
Specl	Special
Sports Ctr	Sports Centre
Sq	Square
St	Street, Saint
Sta	Station
Stad	Stadium
Tech	Technical/Technology
Terr	Terrace
Trad Est	Trading Estate
Twr/s	Tower/s
Univ	University
Wlk	Walk
Yd	Yard

A

Aaron Ct BR3 207 D6
Aaron Hill Rd E6 100 C2
Abady Ho SW1 259 D4
Abberley Mews 9 SW8 137 B2
Abberton IG8 37 C5
Abbess Cl 11 E6 100 A2
Streatham SW2 160 D3
Abbeville Mews 3 SW4 137 D1
Abbeville Rd N8 49 D5
SW4 159 C6
Abbey Ave HA0 88 A5
Abbey Bsns Ctr SW8 137 B4 268 D2
Abbey Cl Hayes UB3 106 B5
Northolt UB5 85 B4
Pinner HA5 40 C6
Abbey Cres DA17 125 C2
Abbey Ct N3 47 C6
NW8 229 A4
SE17 262 B1
6 W12 111 C3
Abbeydale Ct 6 UB1 85 D1
Abbeydale Rd HA0 88 C6
Abbey Dr SW17 181 A5
Abbeyfield UB4 83 D2
Abbeyfield Rd SE16 118 C2
Abbeyfields Cl NW10 88 C5
Abbey Gdns NW8 92 A5 229 B3
9 SE16 118 A2
W6 135 A6 264 A5
Chislehurst BR7 188 C2
Abbey Gr SE2 124 B2
Abbeyhill Rd DA15 168 C2
Abbey Ho E15 98 C5
NW8 229 B2
Abbey Ind Est CR4 202 D4
Abbey La E15 98 B5
Beckenham BR3 185 C3
Abbey Lane Commercial Est E15 98 C5
Abbey Lo NW8 230 B1
1 Ealing W5 109 C6
Abbey Manufacturing Est HA0 88 B6
Abbey Mews E17 53 C4
Abbey Mount DA17 125 B1
Abbey Orchard St SW1 115 D3 259 D6
Abbey Orchard Street Est SW1 259 D6
Abbey Par Ealing NW10 88 B4
Merton SW19 180 A3
Abbey Park Ind Est IG11 101 A6
Abbey Pk BR3 185 C3
Abbey Prim Sch SE2 124 C3
Abbey Rd E15 98 C5
NW8 92 A5 229 A4
Barking IG11 100 D6
Bexley DA6,DA7 147 A1
Croydon CR0 220 D5
Enfield EN1 17 C6
Erith DA17 125 A3
Ilford IG2 57 B4
Lower Halliford TW17 192 C1
Merton SW19 180 A2
Wembley NW10 88 D5
Abbey St E13 99 A3
SE1 117 D3 263 C6
Abbey Terr SE2 124 C2
Abbey Tutorial Coll W2 91 C1
Abbey View NW7 11 D1
Abbey Wlk KT8 195 D5
Abbey Wood Rd SE2 124 C2
Abbey Wood Sch SE2 124 A3
Abbey Wood Sta SE2 124 C3
Abbot Cl HA4 62 D5
Abbot Ct SW8 270 A3
Abbot Ho 13 E14 119 D6
Abbotsbury Cl E15 98 A5
W14 113 B4 244 C1
Abbotsbury Fst Sch SM4 201 D4
Abbotsbury Gdns HA5 40 C3
Abbotsbury Ho W14 244 B2
Abbotsbury Mews SE15 140 C2
Abbotsbury Rd W14 113 B4 244 C1
Coney Hall BR2,BR4 224 D6
Morden SM4 201 D5
Abbots Cl BR5 211 A1
Abbots Ct SE25 205 C6
Abbots Dr HA2 63 C6
Abbotsfield Sch UB10 82 D5
Abbotsford Ave N15 51 A5
Abbotsford Gdns IG8 37 A3
Abbotsford Rd IG3 80 B6
Abbots Gdns N2 48 B5
Abbots Gn CR0,CR2 222 D2
Abbotshade Rd 15 SE16 118 D5
Abbotshall Ave N14 15 C1
Abbotshall Rd SE6 164 B2
Abbots Ho E17 35 B1
SW1 259 C1
W14 254 C5
Abbots La SE1 117 C5 253 B3
Abbotsleigh Cl SM2 217 D1
Abbotsleigh Rd SW16 181 C5
Abbotsmede Cl TW1 152 D2
Abbots Pk SW2 160 C3
Abbot's Pl NW6 91 D6
Abbots Rd E6 99 D6
HA8 27 B3
Abbot St E8 73 D2
Abbots Terr N8 50 A3
Abbotstone Ho 4 E5 74 A6
Abbotstone Rd SW15 134 C2
Abbots Way BR3 207 A4
Abbotswell Rd SE4 163 B6
Abbotswood Cl 7 DA17 125 A3
Abbotswood Gdns IG5 56 B6
Abbotswood Rd SE22 139 C1
Streatham SW16 159 D1
Abbotswood Way UB3 106 B5
Abbott Ave SW20 178 D2
Abbott Cl Hampton TW12 173 A4
Northolt UB5 63 B2
Abbott Ho SW12 158 D4
Abbott Rd E14 98 B1
Abbotts Cl N1 73 A2
Romford RM7 59 D6
Woolwich SE28 124 C6
Abbotts Cres Chingford E4 36 B6
Enfield EN2 4 D3
Abbotts Ct HA2 64 B6
Abbotts Dr HA0 65 B6
Abbotts Park Rd E10 54 A2
Abbotts Rd Barnet EN5 1 D1
Cheam SM3 217 A4
Mitcham CR4 203 C5
Southall UB1 107 A5
Abbott's Wlk DA7 146 D5
Abbyfield Cl CR4 180 C1
Abchurch La EC2,EC4 117 B6 252 D6
Abchurch Yd EC4 252 C6
Abdale Rd W12 112 B5
Abel Ho 7 SE11 138 C6
Abenglen Ind Est UB3 105 B4
Aberavon Rd E3 97 A4
Abercairn Rd SW16 181 C3
Aberconway Rd SM4 201 D5
Abercorn Cl NW7 29 A3
NW8 92 A4 229 A2
Abercorn Cres HA2 41 D1
Abercorn Gdns
Harrow HA3 43 D2
Ilford RM6 58 B3
Abercorn Gr HA4 39 B5
Abercorn Ho SE10 141 D5
Abercorn Mans NW8 229 B3
Abercorn Mews 10 TW10 132 B1
Abercorn Pl NW8 92 A5 229 A3
Abercorn Rd NW7 29 A3
Stanmore HA7 25 C3
Abercorn Trad Est HA0 87 D6
Abercorn Way SE1 118 A1
Abercrombie Dr EN1 6 A4
Abercrombie Ho 1 W12 112 B6
Abercrombie St SW11 136 C3
Aberdale Ct 22 SE16 118 D4
Aberdare Cl BR4 224 A6
Aberdare Gdns NW6 69 D1
NW7 28 D3
Aberdare Rd EN3 6 C1
Aberdeen Ct N5 73 A3
W2 236 C5
Aberdeen La N5 73 A3
Aberdeen Mans WC1 240 A6
Aberdeen Par N18 34 B5
Aberdeen Pk N5 73 A3
Aberdeen Pl NW8 92 B3 236 C6
Aberdeen Rd N5 73 A4
NW10 67 D3
Croydon CR0 221 B4
Edmonton N18 34 B5
Harrow HA3 24 D1
Aberdeen Terr SE3 142 B3
Aberdour Rd IG3 80 B6
Aberdour St SE1 117 C3 263 A4
Aberfeldy Ho SE5 138 D5
Aberfeldy St E14 98 A1
Aberford Gdns SE18 144 A4
Aberfoyle Rd SW16 181 D4
Abergeldie Rd SE12 165 B5
Abernethy Rd SE13 142 C1
Abersham Rd E8 73 D3
Abery St SE18 123 C2
Abingdon W14 254 D3
Abingdon Cl NW1 71 D2
SE1 263 D2
Hillingdon UB10 82 B6
Wimbledon SW19 180 A4
Abingdon Ct W8 255 B5
Edgware HA8 26 A6
Abingdon Gdns W8 255 B5
Abingdon Ho E2 243 C6
Abingdon Lo BR2 186 D1
Abingdon Mans W8 255 A6
Abingdon Rd N3 30 A1
W8 113 C3 255 B5
Thornton Heath SW16 182 A2
Abingdon St SW1 116 A3 260 A6
Abingdon Villas W8 113 C3 255 B5
Abinger Cl BR1 210 A6
Barking IG11 80 A4
New Addington CR0 224 A2
Wallington SM6 220 A3
Abinger Ct 3 Ealing W5 109 C6
Wallington SM6 220 A3
Abinger Gdns TW7 130 C2
Abinger Gr SE8 141 B6
Abinger Ho SE1 252 C1
2 Kingston KT2 176 D3
Abinger Mews W9 91 C3
Abinger Rd W4 111 C3
Abington Ho NW11 48 A3
Ablett St SE16 118 C1
Abney Gdns 5 N16 73 D6
Abney Park Cemetery* N16 73 C6
Abney Park Ct N16 73 D6
Aborfield 6 NW5 71 C3
Aboyne Dr SW20 178 A1
Aboyne Rd NW10 67 C5
Wandsworth SW17 158 B1
Abraham Cl WD19 22 B6
Abridge Way IG11 102 B5
Abyssinia Cl SW11 136 C1
Abyssinia Rd SW11 136 C1
Acacia Ave N2 47 D6
Brentford TW8 131 B5
Hayes UB3 83 D1
Littleton TW17 192 C4
Ruislip HA4 40 B2
Tottenham N17 33 B3
Wembley HA9 66 A3
Yiewsley UB7 104 B6
Acacia Bsns Ctr 1 E11 76 C5
Acacia Cl BR5 211 B4
SE8 119 A2
Penge SE20 184 A1
Stanmore HA7 24 C4
Acacia Ct Harrow HA1 41 D3
5 West Norwood SW16 182 C5
Acacia Dr SM3 201 C1
Acacia Gdns NW8 229 D4
West Wickham BR4 224 A6
Acacia Gr Dulwich SE21 161 B2
Kingston KT3 199 C6
Acacia Ho N16 73 B6
1 New Malden KT3 199 C5
Wood Green N22 32 C2
Acacia Pl NW8 92 B5 229 D4
Acacia Rd E11 76 C6
E17 53 A3
NW8 92 B5 229 D4
W3 111 A6
Beckenham BR3 207 B6
Enfield EN2 5 B4
Hampton TW12 173 C4
Mitcham CR4 181 B1
Thornton Heath SW16 182 A2
Wood Green N22 32 C2
Acacias Lo EN4 14 B6
Acacias The EN4 14 B6
Acacia Way DA15 167 D3
Acacia Wlk SW10 266 B3
Academy Ct 13 E2 96 C4
Academy Gdns
Croydon CR0 205 D1
Northolt UB5 84 D5
Academy Pl SE18 144 C4
Academy Rd SE18 144 B5
Academy The 2 N19 49 C1
Acanthus Dr SE1 118 A1
Acanthus Rd SW11 137 A2
Accadia Ct NW9 67 A6
Accommodation Rd NW11 47 B1
Ace Par KT9 214 A5
Acer Ave UB4 85 A2
Acer Ct NW2 68 D4
Acfold Rd SW6 265 C1
Achilles Cl SE1 118 A1
Achilles Ho 16 E2 96 B5
Achilles Rd NW6 69 C3
Achilles St SE14 141 A5
Achilles Way W1 248 B3
Acklam Rd W10 91 B2
Acklington Dr NW9 27 C2
Ackmar Rd SW6 135 C4 265 A1
Ackroyd Dr E3 97 C2
Ackroyd Rd SE23 163 A4
Acland Burghley Sch NW5 71 B4
Acland Cl SE18 145 B5
Acland Cres SE5 139 B2
Acland Ho SW9 138 B3
Acock Gr UB5 64 A4
Acol Cres HA4 62 B3
Acol Ct 3 NW6 69 C1
Acol Rd NW6 69 D1
Aconbury Rd RM9 102 B6
Acorn Cl Chingford E4 35 D5
Chislehurst BR7 189 A5
Enfield EN2 4 D4
1 Hampton TW12 173 D4
Stanmore HA7 25 B3
Acorn Ct E6 78 A1
Ilford IG2 57 C4
Acorn Gdns W3 89 B2
South Norwood SE19 183 D2
Acorn Gr Harlington UB3 127 D5
Ruislip HA4 61 D4
Acorn Par 7 SE15 140 B5
Acorn Production Ctr N7 72 A1
Acorns The 21 SW19 156 D3
Acorns Way KT10 212 A3
Acorn Way
Beckenham BR3 208 A4
Forest Hill SE23 162 D1
Orpington BR6 226 D4
Acorn Wharf SE1 140 A6
Acorn Wlk SE16 119 A5
Acre Dr SE22 140 A1
Acrefield Ho 4 NW4 46 D5
Acre La SW2 138 B1
Wallington SM5 219 A4
Acre Path UB5 63 A2
Acre Rd Dagenham RM10 81 D1
Kingston KT2 176 B2
Mitcham SW19 180 B4
Acre Way HA6 22 A2
Acris St SW18 158 A6
Action Ct TW15 171 A2
Acton Bsns Ctr NW10 89 B3
Acton Central Ind Est 4 W3 110 D5
Acton Central Sta W3 111 B5
Acton Cl N9 18 A2
Acton High Sch W3 110 C4
Acton Hill Mews W3 110 D5
Acton Ho 16 E8 95 D6
5 W3 89 A1
Acton Hospl W3 110 C4
Acton La Acton NW10 89 B5
Acton W3 111 A4
Acton W4 111 A2
Acton Main Line Sta W3 89 A1
Acton Mews E8 95 D6
Acton Park Est W3 111 B4
Acton St WC1 94 B4 233 C1
Acton Town Sta W3 110 C4
Acton Vale Ind Pk W3 111 D5
Acuba Ho SW18 157 D3
Acuba Rd SW18 157 D2
Acworth Cl N9 18 C4
Acworth Ho 1 SE18 144 D6
Ada Ct N1 235 A5
W9 92 A4 229 B1
Ada Gdns E15 98 D6
South Bromley E14 98 B1
Ada Ho 23 E2 96 A6
Adair Cl SE25 206 B6
Adair Ho SW3 267 B6
Adair Rd W10 91 A3
Adair Twr 7 W10 91 A3
Ada Kennedy Ct 6 SE10 142 A5
Ada Lewis Ho HA9 66 B4
Adam Cl SE6 185 C6
Adam Ct SE11 261 C3
Adam & Eve Ct W1 239 B2
Adam & Eve Mews W8 113 C3 255 B6
Adamfields NW3 70 B1
Adam Lo N21 16 B6
Adam Rd E4 35 B4
Adams Cl N3 29 C3
NW9 66 D6
Surbiton KT5 198 B3
Adams Ct E17 53 A3
Adams Gardens Est 5 SE16 118 C4
Adams Ho
3 South Bromley E14 98 B1
3 Streatham SW16 181 C5
Adams Mews N22 32 B3
Adamson Ct N2 48 C6
Adamson Rd E16 99 A1
NW3 70 B1
Adams Pl N7 72 B3
Adams Rd
Beckenham BR3 207 A4
Tottenham N17 33 B1
Adamsrill Cl EN1 17 B5
Adamsrill Prim Sch SE26 163 A1
Adamsrill Rd SE26 185 A6
Adam's Row W1 115 A6 248 B5
Adams Sq DA6 147 A2
Adam St WC2 116 A6 250 B5
Adams Way CR0 206 A3
Adams Wlk 11 KT1 176 A1
Adam Wlk SW6 134 C5
Ada Pl E2 96 A6
Ada Rd SE5 139 C5
Wembley HA0,HA9 65 D5
Adare Wlk SW16,SW2 160 B2
Ada St E8 96 B6
Adcot Wlk 6 BR6 227 D4
Adderley Gdns SE9 188 C6
Adderley Gr SW11 159 A6
Adderley Rd HA3 24 D2
Adderley St E14 98 A1
Addey Ho SE8 141 B5
Addey & Stanhope Sch SE14 141 C4
Addington Ct 7 SW14 133 B2
Addington Dr N12 30 B4
Addington Gr SE26 185 A6
Addington Ho 13 SW9 138 B3
Addington Palace (The Royal Sch of Church Music) CR9 223 B2
Addington Rd E16 98 C3
E3 97 C4
N4 50 C3
Thornton Heath CR0 204 C1
West Wickham BR4 224 C6
West Wickham BR4,CR0 224 B4
Addington Sq SE5 139 B5
Addington St SE1 116 B4 250 D1
Addington Village Rd CR0 223 C3
Addington Village Sta CR0 223 C2
Addis Cl EN3 6 D4
Addiscombe Ave CR0 206 A2
Addiscombe Cl HA3 43 C4
Addiscombe Court Rd CR0 221 C6
Addiscombe Ct UB10 83 A3
Addiscombe Rd CR0 222 B6
Addiscombe Sta CR0 206 A1
Addison Ave W11 113 A5 244 A3
Hounslow TW3 130 A4
Southgate N14 15 C5
Addison Bridge Pl W14 113 B2 254 C4
Addison Cl
Northwood HA6 22 A2
Orpington BR5 211 A3
Addison Cres W14 113 A3 254 B6
Addison Ct W5 110 C6
Addison Dr SE12 165 B6
Addison Gdns W14 112 D3
Kingston KT5 198 B5
Addison Gr W4 111 C3
Addison Ho NW8 92 B4 229 C2
Addison Park Mans 12 W14 112 D4
Addison Pl W11 113 A5 244 A3
Southall UB1 107 C6
Addison Prim Sch W14 112 D3
Addison Rd BR2 209 D4
E17 54 A4
W14 113 B3 254 C6
Croydon SE25 206 A5
Enfield EN3 6 D4
Teddington TW11 175 B4
Wanstead E11 55 A3
Addison's Cl CR0 223 B6
Addison Way NW11 47 C5
Hayes UB3 84 A1
Northwood HA6 22 A2
Addle Hill EC4 241 D1
Addle St EC2 242 B3
Addlestone Ho W10 90 C2
Addy Ho SE16 118 C2
Adecroft Way KT8 196 A6
Adela Ave KT3 200 B5
Adela Ho 9 W6 112 C1
Adelaide Ave SE4 141 C1
Adelaide Cl SW9 138 C1
Enfield EN1 5 C5
Stanmore HA7 25 A6
Adelaide Ct NW8 229 B3
W7 108 D4
15 Beckenham BR3 185 C3
Adelaide Gdns RM6 59 A4
Adelaide Gr W12 112 A5
Adelaide Ho E17 53 B6
Adelaide Rd E10 76 A5
NW3 70 C1
2 SW18 157 C6
Ashford TW15 170 A6
Chislehurst BR7 188 D5
Ealing W13 109 A4
Heston TW5 129 A4
Ilford IG1 78 D6
Kingston KT6 198 A4
Richmond TW9 132 B1
Southall UB2 107 A2
Teddington TW11 174 D4
Adelaide St WC2 250 A5
Adelaide Terr TW8 109 D1
Adela St W10 91 A3
Adelina Gr E1 96 C2
Adelina Mews SW12 159 D3
Adeline Pl WC1 93 D2 239 D3
Adeliza Cl IG11 79 A1
Adelphi Cres UB4 83 D4
Adelphi Ct 20 SE16 118 D4
Adelphi Terr WC2 250 B5
Adelphi Way UB4 83 D4
Adeney Cl W6 134 D6
Aden Gr N16 73 B4
Aden Ho 12 E1 96 D2
Aden Lo N16 73 B4
Adenmore Rd SE6 163 C4
Aden Rd Enfield EN3 7 A1
Ilford IG1 57 A2
Adeyfield Ho EC1 235 D1
Adhara Rd HA6 22 A5
Adie Rd W6 112 C3
Adine Rd E13 99 B3
Adisham Ho 4 E5 74 B3
Adler Ind Est UB3 105 B4
Adler St E1 96 A1
Adley St E5 75 A3
Adlington Cl N18 33 C5
Admaston Rd SE18 145 A6
Admiral Ct NW4 46 A4
SW10 136 A4 266 B2
W1 238 A3
Barking IG11 102 C5
Carshalton SM5 202 C1
Admiral Ho TW11 175 A6
Admiral Hyson Ind Est SE16 118 B1
Admiral Mews W10 90 D3
Admiral Pl SE16 119 A5
Admirals Cl E18 55 B5
Admirals Ct 3 E6 100 D1
SE1 253 C3
32 Putney SW19 156 D3
Admiral Seymour Rd SE9 144 B1
Admirals Gate SE10 141 D4
Admiral Sq SW10 136 A4 266 B2
Admiral St SE8 141 C4
Admirals Way E14 119 C4
Admiral's Wlk NW3 70 A5
Admiralty Arch* SW1 249 D4
Admiralty Cl 1 SE8 141 C4
Admiralty Rd TW11 174 D4
Admiralty Way TW11 174 D4
Admiral Wlk W9 91 C2
Adolf St SE6 185 D6
Adolphus Rd N4 50 D1
Adolphus St SE8 141 B5
Adomar Rd RM8 81 A5
Adpar St W2 92 B2 236 C4
Adrian Ave NW2 46 B1
Adrian Bolt Ho 2 E2 96 B4
Adrian Ho N1 233 D5
SW8 270 A4
Adrian Mews SW10 265 D6
Adriatic Bldg 18 E14 119 A6
Adriatic Ho 18 E1 96 D3
Adrienne Ave UB1 85 B4
Adron Ho 9 SE16 118 C2
Adstock Ho 5 N1 72 D1
ADT Coll SW15 157 B6
Advance Rd SE27 183 A6
Adventurers Ct 4 E14 120 B6
Advent Way N18 34 D5
Adys Lawn NW2 68 B2
Adys Rd SE15 139 D2
Aerodrome Rd NW4,NW9 45 D6
Aerodrome Way TW5 128 C6
Aeroville NW9 27 C1
Affleck St N1 233 D3
Afghan Rd SW11 136 C3
Agamemnon Rd NW6 69 B3
Agar Cl KT6 214 B6
Agar Gr NW1 71 D1
Agar Ho 6 KT1 198 A6
Agar Pl NW1 71 C1
Agar St WC2 250 B5
Agate Cl E16 99 D1
Agate Ho
New Malden KT4 199 C1
12 Penge SE26 184 B5
Agate Rd W6 112 C3
Agatha Cl E1 118 C5
Agaton Rd BR7,SE9 167 A2
Agave Rd NW2 68 C4
Agdon St EC1 94 D3 241 C6
Agincourt E11 54 D3
Agincourt Rd NW3 70 D4
Agnes Ave IG1 78 D4
Agnes Cl E6 122 C6
Agnes Ct 11 SW18 136 B1
Agnesfield Cl N12 30 C4
Agnes Gdns RM8 80 D4
Agnes Ho 13 W11 112 D6
Agnes Rd W3 111 D4
Agnes St E14 97 B1
Agnew Rd SE23 162 D4
Agricola Pl EN1 17 D6
Aidan Cl RM8 81 A4
Aidans Ct N12 30 C5
Aigburth Mans 5 SW9 138 C5
Ailantus Ct HA8 26 B5
Aileen Wlk E15 76 D1
Ailsa Ave TW1 153 B6
Ailsa Rd TW1 153 B6
Ailsa St E14 98 A2
Ainger Rd NW3 70 D1
Ainsdale NW1 232 A2
Ainsdale Cl BR6 211 B1
Ainsdale Cres HA5 41 C6
Ainsdale Dr SE1 118 A1
Ainsdale Rd W5 87 D3
Ainsley Ave RM7 59 D3
Ainsley Cl N9 17 C3
Ainsley St E2 96 B4
Ainsley Wood Prim Sch E4 35 D5
Ainslie Ct 2 HA0 88 A5
Ainslie Wood Cres E4 35 D5
Ainslie Wood Gdns E4 35 D5
Ainslie Wood Rd E4 35 D5
Ainsty St 14 SE16 118 C4
Ainsworth Cl NW2 68 A5
SE5 139 C3
Ainsworth Est NW8 92 A6 229 A6
Ainsworth Ho NW8 91 D6
Ainsworth Rd E9 74 C1
Croydon CR0 220 D6
Ainsworth Way NW8 92 A6 229 A6
Aintree Ave E6 100 A6
Aintree Cl UB8 82 D2
Aintree Ho SE26 184 B4
Aintree Rd UB6 87 B5
Aintree St SW6 135 A5 264 B4
Airborne Ho 10 SM6 219 B4
Air Call Bsns Ctr NW9 45 C6
Aird Ho SE1 262 A5
Airdrie Cl N1 72 B1
Hayes UB4 85 A2
Airedale Ave W4 111 D1
Airedale Ave S W4 111 D1
Airedale Rd W5 109 D3
Balham SW12 158 D4
Airlie Gdns W8 113 C5 245 A3
Ilford IG1 56 D1
Airlinks Ind Est TW5 106 C1
Air Park Way TW13 150 B2
Airport Gate Bsns Ctr UB7 126 B5
Airport Rdbt E16 121 D5
Air St W1 249 B5
Airthrie Rd IG3 80 B6
Aisgill Ave SW5 113 B1 254 D1
Aisher Rd SE28 124 C6
Aislibie Rd SE12 142 C1
Aislobie Ho N21 17 B5
Aiten Pl W6 112 A2
Aithan Ho 9 E14 97 B1
Aitken Cl E8 96 A6
Carshalton CR4 202 D2
Aitken Rd Barnet EN5 12 C6
Catford SE6 163 D2
Ajax Ave NW9 45 C6
Ajax Ho 15 E2 96 B5
Ajax Rd NW6 69 C3
Akabusi Cl SE25 206 A3
Akbar Ho 7 E14 119 D2
Akehurst St SW15 156 A4
Akenside Ct 3 NW3 70 B3
Akenside Rd NW3 70 B3
Akerman Rd SW9 138 D4
Kingston KT6 197 C3

Akintaro Ho 7 SE8 141 B6
Akiva Sch N3 29 D1
Alabama St SE18 145 C5
Alacross Rd W5 109 D4
Alamaro Lo SE10 120 D3
Alandale Dr HA5 22 B2
Aland Ct SE16 119 A3
Alander Mews E17 54 A5
Alan Dr EN5 13 A5
Alan Gdns RM7 59 C2
Alan Hocken Way E15 98 C5
Alan Lo N3 29 C2
Alan Preece Ct NW6 68 D1
Alan Rd SW19 179 A5
Alanthus Cl SE12 165 A5
Alaska St SE1 251 A3
Alba Cl UB4 84 D3
Albacore Cres SE13 163 D5
Alba Gdns NW11 47 A3
Albain Cres TW15 148 A2
Alba Mews SW18, SW19 157 C2
Alban Ho NW3 70 A2
Albans Cl SW16 160 A1
Albany N12 29 D4
W1 249 A5
Albany Cl N15 50 D5
Bushey WD23 8 B5
Ickenham UB10 60 C3
Mortlake SW14 132 D1
Sidcup DA5 168 D4
Albany Coll The NW4 46 C4
Albany Cres
Claygate KT10 212 C2
Edgware HA8 26 C3
Albany Ct E10 53 C2
HA8 27 B2
NW10 90 B4
SW1 259 C6
Kingston KT2 176 A4
Richmond TW10 153 B1
Chingford E4 19 D5
Albany Ctyd W1 249 B5
Albany Ho E5 74 C6
6 Brentford TW8 132 A6
Albany Mans SW11 267 B3
Albany Mews BR1 187 A4
N1 72 C1
SE5 139 A6
Kingston KT2 175 D4
Sutton SM1 217 D3
Albany Par 4 TW8 132 A6
Albany Park Ave EN3 6 D4
Albany Park Rd KT2 176 A4
Albany Park Sta DA14 168 D2
Albany Pas 12 TW10 154 A6
Albany Pl N7 72 C4
Brentford TW8 131 D6
Albany Rd E10 53 C2
E12 77 D4
E17 53 A3
N18 34 C5
N4 50 C3
SE5 139 C6
Brentford TW8 131 D6
Chislehurst BR7 188 D5
Dagenham RM6 59 B3
Ealing W13 109 B6
Enfield EN3 6 D5
Erith DA17 147 B6
New Malden KT3 199 B5
Richmond TW10 154 A6
Sidcup DA5 168 C4
Wimbledon SW19 179 D5
Albany Reach KT7 196 D4
Albany Sch EN3 6 D5
Albany St NW1 93 B4 231 D2
Albany Terr 6 TW10 154 B6
Albany The Kingston KT2 175 D4
Woodford IG8 36 D6
Albany View IG9 21 A3
Albany Wlk N15 50 D5
Alba Pl W11 91 B1
Albatross 31 NW9 27 D1
Albatross St SE18 145 C5
Albemarle SW19 156 D2
Albemarle App IG2 56 D3
Albemarle Ave TW2 151 B3
Albemarle Gdns
Ilford IG2 56 D3
New Malden KT3 199 B5
Albemarle Ho SE8 119 B2
Albemarle Lo SE26 185 A5
Albemarle Mans NW3 69 D4
Albemarle Pk
Beckenham BR3 185 D2
Stanmore HA7 25 C5
Albemarle Prim Sch
SW19 157 A2
Albemarle Rd
Beckenham BR2,BR3 186 A2
East Barnet EN4 14 C4
Albemarle St
W1 115 C6 249 A5
Albemarle Way EC1 241 C5
Albermarle Ho 3 SW9 138 C2
Alberon Gdns NW11 47 B5
Alberta Ave SM1 217 B3
Alberta Ct 1 TW10 154 B6
Alberta Ho E14 120 A5
Hayes UB4 84 B4
Alberta Rd Bexley DA7 147 D4
Enfield EN1 18 A5
Alberta St SE17 116 D1 261 D2
Albert Ave SW8 270 C3
Chingford E4 35 C6
Albert Barnes Ho SE1 262 A5
Albert Bigg Point E15 98 A6
Albert Bridge Rd
SW11 136 D5 267 C3
Albert Carr Gdns SW16 182 A5
Albert Cl 11 E9 96 B6
N22 31 D2
Albert Cotts 2 E1 96 A2
Albert Cres E4 35 C6
Albert Ct SW7 246 C1
9 Putney SW19 157 A3
Albert Dr SW19 157 A3
Albert Emb SE1 116 A2 260 B3
Albert Gate Ct SW1 247 C1
Albert Gdns E1 96 D1
Albert Gr SW20 178 D2
Albert Gray Ho SW10 266 C4
Albert Hall Mans
SW7 114 B4 246 C1
Albert Ho 5 E18 55 B6
Albert Mans N8 50 A2
SW11 267 C2
Albert Memorial★
SW7 114 B4 246 C1
Albert Mews W8 256 A6
Albert Palace Mans
SW11 268 B2
Albert Pl N3 29 C2
W8 113 D4 245 D1
Albert Rd BR2 209 D4
E10 54 A1
E17 53 C4
N15 51 C3
N4 50 B2
NW4 46 D5
NW6 91 B5
NW7 27 D5
Ashford TW15 170 B5
Buckhurst Hill IG9 21 D2
Chislehurst SE9 166 A1
Croydon SE25 206 B5
Dagenham RM8 59 C1
Ealing W5 87 B3
East Barnet EN4 2 A1
Erith DA17 125 B1
Hampton TW12 174 A5
Harrow HA2 42 A6
Hayes UB3 105 C3
Hounslow TW3 129 C1
Ilford IG1 79 A5
Kingston KT1 176 B1
Mitcham CR4 202 D6
Newham E16 122 B4
New Malden KT3 199 D5
Penge SE20 184 D4
Richmond TW10 154 B6
Sidcup DA5 169 D4
Southall UB2 106 D3
Sutton SM1 218 B3
Teddington TW11 174 D4
Twickenham TW1 152 D3
4 Wanstead E18 55 B6
Wood Green N22 31 C2
Yiewsley UB7 104 A5
Albert's Ct NW1 237 B6
Albert Sq E15 76 C3
SW8 138 B5 270 C3
Albert St N12 30 A5
NW1 93 B6 231 D5
Albert Starr Ho 7 SE8 118 D2
Albert Studios SW11 267 C2
Albert Terr NW10 89 A6
NW1 93 A6 231 A5
Buckhurst Hill IG9 21 D2
Albert Terr Mews NW1 231 A5
Albert Victoria Ho N22 32 C2
Albert Way SE15 140 B5
Albert Westcott Ho
SE17 261 D2
Albert Whicher Ho 3
E17 54 A5
Albert Wlk E16 122 D4
Albion Ave N10 31 A2
SW8 137 D3
Albion Cl W2 247 B6
Albion Ct 2 SE7 122 A2
7 W6 112 B2
Sutton SM2 218 B1
Albion Dr E8 74 A1
Albion Est SE16 118 C4
Albion Gate W2 247 B6
Albion Gdns 1 W6 112 B2
Albion Gr N16 73 C4
Albion Hill IG10 21 D6
Albion Ho E16 122 D5
Albion Mews N1 234 A6
W2 114 C6 247 B6
6 W6 112 B2
Albion Pk IG10 21 D6
Albion Pl EC1 241 C4
EC2 242 D3
W6 112 B2
South Norwood SE25 206 A6
Albion Prim Sch SE16 118 C4
Albion Rd E17 54 A6
N16 73 B4
Bexley DA6 147 C1
Dagenham RM10 81 B3
Hayes UB3 83 C1
Hounslow TW3 129 C1
Kingston KT2 177 A2
Sutton SM2 218 B1
Tottenham N17 34 A1
Twickenham TW2 152 C3
Albion Sq E8 73 D1
Albion St SE16 118 C4
W2 114 C6 247 B6
Thornton Heath CR0 204 D1
Albion Terr E8 73 D1
Sewardstone E4 7 D1
Albion Villas Rd SE23,
SE26 162 C1
Albion Way EC1 242 A3
SE13 142 A1
Wembley HA9 66 C5
Albion Wharf SW11 267 A4
Albion Yd N1 233 B3
Albon Ho SE14 141 B4
Wandsworth SW18 157 D5
Albrighton Rd SE5,SE22 139 C2
Albuhera Cl EN2 4 C4
Albury Ave DA7 147 A3
Hounslow TW7 130 D5
Albury Bldgs SE1 251 D1
Albury Cl TW12 173 D4
Albury Ct
4 Croydon CR0 221 A4
Mitcham CR4 180 B1
6 Northolt UB5 84 C4
Sutton SM1 218 A4
Albury Dr HA5 22 D3
Albury Lo 7 SW2 160 B4
Albury Mews E12 77 C6
Albury Rd KT9 214 A3
Albury St SE8 141 C6
Albyfield BR1 210 B6
Albyn Rd SE8 141 C4
Alcester Cres E5 74 B6
Alcester Ct 4 SM6 219 B4
Alcester Rd SM6 219 B4
Alcock Cl SM6 219 D1
Alcock Rd TW5 128 D5
Alconbury DA6 169 D6
Alconbury Rd E5 74 A6
Alcorn Cl SM3 217 C6
Alcott Cl W7 86 D2
Aldborough Ct
Chingford E4 19 D1
Ilford IG2 57 D4
Aldborough Rd IG2 57 D6
Aldborough Rd N IG2 57 D4
Aldborough Rd S IG3 57 C2
Aldbourne Rd W12 112 A5
Aldbridge St
SE17 117 C1 263 B2
Aldburgh Mews W1 238 B2
Aldbury Ave HA9 66 D1
Aldbury Ho SW3 257 A3
Aldbury Mews N9 17 B4
Aldebert Terr
SW8 138 B5 270 C3
Aldeburgh Cl 16 E5 74 B6
Aldeburgh Pl IG8 37 A6
Aldeburgh St SE10 121 A1
Alden Ave E15 98 D4
Alden Ct
South Croydon CR0 221 C5
Wimbledon SW19 179 C4
Aldenham Ctry Pk WD6 9 B6
Aldenham Dr UB8 82 D3
Aldenham Ho NW1 232 B3
Aldenham Rd WD6 9 C6
Aldenham St
NW1 93 D5 232 C3
Alden Ho E8 96 B6
Aldensley Rd W6 112 B3
Alderbrook Prim Sch
SW12 159 B4
Alderbrook Rd SW12 159 B5
Alderbury Rd SW13 134 A6
Alder Ct N2 48 B6
3 West Norwood SW16 182 C5
Alder Gr NW2 68 B6
Aldergrove Gdns TW4 129 A3
Aldergrove Ho 3 E5 74 A6
Alder Ho 1 NW3 70 D2
SE15 139 D6
SE4 141 C2
Alderley Ho 36 SW8 137 D3
Alder Lo SW6 134 D4
Alderman Ave IG11 102 A4
Aldermanbury
EC2 95 A1 242 B2
Aldermanbury Sq EC2 242 B3
Alderman Judge Mall 6
KT1 176 A1
Alderman's Hill N13 32 B6
Alderman's Wlk EC2 243 A3
Aldermary Rd BR1 187 A2
Aldermead 2 TW3 129 D1
Alder Mews 9 N19 71 C6
Aldermoor Rd SE6 163 B1
Alderney Ave TW5 129 D5
Alderney Gdns UB5 63 B1
Alderney Ho 10 N1 73 A2
Enfield EN3 6 D5
Alderney Mews SE1 262 C6
Alderney Rd E1 96 D3
Alderney St
SW1 115 B1 258 D2
Alder Rd DA14 167 D1
Mortlake SW14 133 B2
Alders Ave IG8 36 C4
Aldersbrook Ave EN1 5 C3
Aldersbrook Dr KT2 176 B4
Aldersbrook House Coll of
Railway Tech E12 78 C5
Aldersbrook La E12 78 B5
Aldersbrook Prim Sch
E12 77 C6
Aldersbrook Rd E11,E12 77 C6
Alders Cl HA8 27 A5
W5 109 D3
Wanstead E11 77 B6
Alders Ct N17 52 B5
Aldersey Gdns IG11 79 B2
Aldersford Cl SE4 140 D1
Aldersgate Ct EC1 242 A3
Aldersgate St
EC1 95 A2 242 A3
Alders Gr KT8 196 B4
Aldersgrove Ave SE9,
SE12 165 D1
Aldershot Rd NW6 91 B6
Aldersmead Ave CR0 206 D3
Aldersmead Rd BR3 185 A3
Alderson Pl UB2 108 A5
Alderson St W10 91 A3
Alders Rd HA8 27 A5
Alders The
Feltham TW13 173 A6
Heston TW5 129 B6
Southgate N21 16 C5
Streatham SW16 181 C6
West Wickham BR4 223 D6
Alderton 9 KT2 176 D2
Alderton Cl NW10 67 B5
Alderton Cres NW4 46 B4
Alderton Ct KT8 195 B5
Alderton Rd SE24 139 A2
Croydon CR0 206 A2
Alderton Way NW4 46 B4
Alderville Rd SW6 135 B3
Alderwick Ct N7 72 B2
Alderwick Dr TW3 130 B2
Alderwood Prim Sch
SE9 167 C5
Alderwood Rd SE9 167 B5
Aldford St W1 115 A5 248 B4
Aldgate EC3 95 C1 243 B1
Aldgate East Sta
E1 95 D1 243 D2
Aldgate High St
EC3 95 D1 243 C1
Aldgate Sta EC3 95 D1 243 C1
Aldham Hall 1 E11 55 A3
Aldham Ho SE4 141 B4
Aldine Ct W12 112 C5
Aldine St W12 112 C4
Aldington Cl RM8 58 C1
Aldington Ct 1 E8 74 A1
Aldington Rd SE18 121 D3
Aldis Mews Holdbrook EN3 7 C6
Upper Tooting SW17 180 C5
Aldis St SW17 180 C5
Aldred Rd NW6 69 C3
Aldren Rd SW17 158 A1
Aldriche Way E4 36 A4
Aldrich Gdns SM3 217 B5
Aldrich Terr SW18 158 A2
Aldrick Ho N1 233 D4
Aldridge Ave
Edgware HA8 10 D1
Holdbrook EN3 7 C5
Ruislip HA4 62 D6
Stanmore HA7 26 A2
Aldridge Ct W11 91 B2
Aldridge Rd Villas W11 91 B2
Aldridge Rise KT3 199 C3
Aldridge Wlk N14 16 A4
Aldrington Rd SW16 181 C6
Aldsworth Cl W9 91 D3
Aldwick Cl BR7 167 B1
Aldwick Ct N12 30 A6
Aldwick Rd CR0 220 B4
Aldworth Gr SE13 164 A5
Aldworth Rd E15 76 C1
Aldwych WC2 94 B1 240 D1
Aldwych Ave IG6 57 A5
Aldwych Bldgs WC2 240 B2
Aldwyn Ho SW8 270 A3
Alers Rd DA6 168 D6
Alesia Cl N22 32 A3
Alestan Beck Rd E16 99 D1
Alexander Ave NW10 68 B1
Alexander Cl Barnet EN4 2 B1
Hayes BR2 209 A1
Sidcup DA15 167 C5
Southall UB2 108 A5
Twickenham TW2 152 D2
Alexander Ct SW18 158 A6
Beckenham BR3 186 B2
Greenwich SE3 143 B3
Stanmore HA7 44 B6
14 Surbiton KT6 197 D2
Alexander Evans Mews
SE23 162 D2
Alexander Ho 9 E14 119 C3
Alexander McLeod Jun Sch
SE2 124 B1
Alexander McLeod Prim Sch
SE2 124 B1
Alexander Mews 2 W2 91 D1
Alexander Pl SW7 257 A4
Alexander Rd N19 72 A6
Bexley DA16 146 D3
Chislehurst BR7 188 D5
Alexander Sq
SW3 114 C2 257 A4
Alexander St W2 91 C1
Alexander Terr SE2 124 B1
Alexandra Ave N22 31 D2
SW11 268 A1
Harrow HA2 63 C5
Southall UB1 107 B6
Sutton SM1 217 C5
Alexandra Bsns Ctr EN3 6 D1
Alexandra Cl SE8 141 B6
Ashford TW15 171 B3
Harrow HA2 63 D5
Alexandra Cotts SE14 141 B4
Penge SE20 184 D4
Alexandra Cres BR1 186 D4
Alexandra Ct 4 N16 73 C4
5 W12 112 A4
W9 236 B6
Ashford TW15 171 B4
Ealing W5 87 C2
Greenford UB6 85 D5
Hounslow TW3 129 D3
Southgate N14 15 C6
Alexandra Ct *continued*
Wembley HA9 66 B4
Alexandra Dr
Surbiton KT5 198 C2
West Norwood SE19 183 C5
Alexandra Gdns N10 49 B5
Chiswick W4 133 C5
Hounslow TW3 129 D3
Wallington SM5 219 A1
Alexandra Gr N12 29 D4
N4 50 D1
Alexandra Ho 13 W6 112 C1
Alexandra Inf Sch
Kingston KT2 176 C3
Penge BR3 184 D3
Alexandra Jun & Inf Sch
TW3 129 D3
Alexandra Jun Sch
SE26 184 D4
Alexandra Mans 6 NW6 69 C3
SW3 266 C5
Alexandra Mews N2 48 D6
Alexandra National Ho
N4 72 D6
Alexandra Palace★ N22 31 D1
Alexandra Palace Sta
N22 32 A1
Alexandra Palace Way
N10 49 C6
Alexandra Park Rd N10,
N22 31 D2
Alexandra Park Sch N22 31 C2
Alexandra Pl
NW8 92 A6 229 B6
Croydon CR0 205 C1
South Norwood SE25 205 B4
Alexandra Prim Sch N22 32 B1
Alexandra Rd E10 76 A5
E17 53 B2
N10 31 B3
N15 51 B4
N8,N22 50 C6
NW4 46 D5
NW8 70 B1
W4 111 B4
Ashford TW15 171 C4
10 Brentford TW8 131 D6
Croydon CR0 205 C2
Dagenham RM6 59 A3
Edmonton N9 18 B4
Enfield EN3 6 D1
Hounslow TW3 129 D3
Kingston KT2 176 C3
Mitcham SW19 180 C3
Mortlake SW14 133 B2
Penge SE26 184 D4
Richmond TW9 132 B3
Thames Ditton KT7 196 D4
Twickenham TW1 153 C5
Wallend E6 100 C4
Wanstead E18 55 B6
Wimbledon SW19 179 C5
Alexandra Sch HA2 63 C6
Alexandra Sq SM4 201 C4
Alexandra St E16 99 A2
5 SE14 141 A5
Alexandra Wlk 8 SE19 183 C5
Alexandria Rd W13 109 B6
Alex Gossip Ho SW6 265 A1
Alexis St SE16 118 A2
Alfearn Rd E5 74 C4
Alford Ct N1 235 B3
5 Belmont SM2 217 D1
Alford Gn CR0 224 B2
Alford Ho N6 49 C3
6 SE18 144 D6
Alford Pl N1 235 B3
Alfoxton Ave N8,N15 50 D5
Alfreda Ct SW11 268 C1
Alfreda St SW11 137 B4 268 C1
Alfred Butt Ho SW17 158 D1
Alfred Cl W4 111 B2
Alfred Findley Ho N22 32 D1
Alfred Gdns UB1 107 A6
Alfred Ho E9 75 A3
Alfred Hurley Ho SW17 180 A6
Alfred Mews W1,WC1 239 C4
Alfred Mizen Prim Sch The
CR4 203 D6
Alfred Nunn Ho NW10 89 D6
Alfred Pl WC1 93 D2 239 C4
Alfred Prior Ho 6 E12 78 C4
Alfred Rd E15 76 D3
W2 91 C2
W3 111 A5
Buckhurst Hill IG9 21 D2
Croydon SE25 206 A4
Erith DA17 125 B1
Feltham TW13 150 C2
Kingston KT1 198 B6
Sutton SM1 218 A3
Alfred Salter Ho SE1 263 D3
Alfred Salter Prim Sch
SE16 118 D4
Alfred's Gdns IG11 101 C5
Alfred St E3 97 B4
Alfred's Way (East Ham &
Barking By-Pass)
IG11 101 B5
Alfred's Way Ind Est
IG11 102 A6
Alfred Villas 9 E17 54 A5
Alfreton Cl SW19 156 D1
Alfriston KT5 198 B3
Alfriston Ave Harrow HA2 41 C2
Thornton Heath CR0 204 A2
Alfriston Cl KT5 198 B3
Alfriston Rd SW11 158 D6
Algar Cl Isleworth TW7 131 A2
Stanmore HA7 24 D5
Algar Ho SE1 251 C1
Algar Rd TW7 131 A2
Algarve Rd SW18 157 D3
Algernon Rd NW4 46 A3
NW6 91 C6
SE13 141 D1
Algers Cl IG10 21 D6
Algers Rd IG10 21 D6
Alghers Mead IG10 21 D6
Algiers Rd SE13 141 C1
Alguin Ct HA7 25 C3
Alibon Gdns RM10 81 C3
Alibon Rd RM10 81 C3
Alice Ct SW15 135 B1
Alice Gilliott Ct W14 264 D6
Alice La E3 97 B6
Alice Mews 8 TW11 174 D5
Alice Owen Tech Ctr
EC1 234 C2
Alice Shepherd Ho 7
E14 120 A4
Alice St SE1 117 C3 263 A5
Alice Thompson Cl
SE12 165 C2
Alice Walker Cl 8
SE24 138 D1
Alice Way TW3 129 D1
Alicia Ave HA3 43 C5
Alicia Cl HA3 43 C5
Alicia Gdns HA3 43 C5
Alicia Ho DA16 146 B4
Alie St E1 95 D1 243 D1
Alington Cres NW9 45 A1
Alison Cl E6 100 C1
Croydon CR0 206 D1
Alison Ct 1 SE1 118 A1
Aliwal Rd SW11 136 C1
Alkerden Rd W4 111 C1
Alkham Rd N16 73 D6
Allam Ho W11 244 A6
Allan Barclay Cl N15 51 D3
Allanbridge N16 51 C2
Allan Cl KT3 199 B4
Allandale Ave N3 47 B6
Allan Ho SW8 269 C2
Allanson Ct E10 75 C6
Allan Way W3 89 A2
Allard Cres WD23 8 A2
Allard Gdns SW4 159 D6
Allardyce St SW4,SW9 138 B1
Allbrook Cl TW11 174 C5
Allbrook Ho 4 SW15 156 A4
Allcot Cl TW14 149 D3
Allcott Ho TW7 130 D2
Allcroft Rd NW5 71 A2
Allder Way CR2 220 D1
Allenby Cl UB6 85 C4
Allenby Inf Sch UB1 85 D1
Allenby Rd
Forest Hill SE23 163 A1
Southall UB1 85 C3
Allen Cl Streatham CR4 181 C2
Sunbury TW16 172 B2
Allen Ct E17 53 C3
Allendale Ave UB1 85 C1
Allendale Cl SE5 139 B4
Forest Hill SE26 184 D5
Allendale Rd UB6 65 B2
Allendale Sch
W8 113 C3 255 B6
Allen Edwards Dr
SW8 138 A4 270 A2
Allen Edwards Prim Sch
SW4 138 A4 270 A1
Allenford Ho 1 SW15 155 D5
All England Lawn Tennis &
Croquet Club The
SW19 157 A1
Allen Ho W8 255 B6
Allen Mans W8 255 B6
Allen Rd E3 97 B5
N16 73 C4
Penge BR3 184 D1
Sunbury TW16 172 B1
Thornton Heath CR0 204 C1
Allensbury Pl NW1 72 A1
7 NW1 71 D1
Allens Rd EN3 18 C6
Allen St W8 113 C3 255 B5
Allenswood 12 SW19 157 A3
Allenswood Rd SE9 144 B3
Allerdale Ho 7 N4 51 B2
Allerford Ct Catford SE6 163 D1
Harrow HA2 42 A4
Allerford Rd SE6 185 D6
Allerton Ct 5 NW4 28 D1
North Cheam SM3 216 D6
Allerton Ho N1 235 D3
4 Merton SW19 180 A3
Allerton Rd N16 73 A6
Allerton St N1 235 D2
Allerton Wlk 11 N7 72 B6
Allestree Rd
SW6 135 A5 264 A3
Alleyn Cres SE21 161 B2
Alleyndale Rd RM8 80 C6
Alleyn Ho EC1 242 B5
SE1 262 C5
Alleyn Pk Dulwich SE21 161 C1
Southall UB2 107 C1
Alleyn Rd SE21 161 C1
Alleyn's Sch SE22 161 C6
Allfarthing La SW18 158 A5
Allfarthing Prim Sch
SW18 158 A5
Allgood Cl SM4 200 D3
Allgood St 10 E2 95 D5
Allhallows La EC4 252 C5
Allhallows Rd E6 100 A1
All Hallows Rd N17 33 C2

Alliance Cl HA0 ... 65 D4
Alliance Ct Acton W3 ... 88 D2
Ashford TW15 ... 171 A6
Alliance Rd Acton W3 ... 88 D3
Newham E16 ... 99 C2
Woolwich SE18 ... 146 A5
Allied Ind Est W3 ... 111 C5
Allied Way W3 ... 111 C4
Allingham Cl W7 ... 108 D6
Allingham Ct NW3 ... 70 C3
Allingham St N1 .. 95 A5 235 A4
Allington Ave
Tottenham N17 ... 33 C4
Upper Halliford TW17 ... 193 C6
Allington Cl
Greenford UB6 ... 64 A1
3 Wimbledon SW19 ... 178 D5
Allington Ct 6 SW8 ... 137 C3
Croydon CR0 ... 206 C3
Allington Rd NW4 ... 46 B3
W10 ... 91 A5
Harrow HA2 ... 42 A4
Orpington BR6 ... 211 C1
Allington St SW1 ... 258 D5
Allison Cl SE10 ... 142 A4
Allison Gr SE21 ... 161 C3
Allison Rd N8 ... 50 D4
W3 ... 111 A6
Alliston Ho 27 E2 ... 95 D4
Allitsen Rd NW8 .. 92 C5 230 A4
Allnutt Way SW4 ... 159 D6
Alloa Ct N14 ... 15 C2
Alloa Rd SE8 ... 119 A1
Ilford IG3 ... 80 A6
Allom Ct 11 SW4 ... 138 A3
Allonby Dr HA4 ... 38 D2
Allonby Gdns HA9 ... 43 C1
Allonby Ho E14 ... 97 A2
Alloway Rd E3 ... 97 A4
Allport Ho SE5 ... 139 B2
Allport Mews 38 E1 ... 96 C3
All Saints' Benhilton CE Prim Sch SM1 ... 217 D5
All Saints CE First Sch SW19 ... 180 A3
All Saint's CE Jun Sch SE19 ...
All Saints' CE Prim Sch
N20 ... 14 B2
NW2 ... 69 B5
SE3 ... 142 C3
All Saints CE Prim Sch SW15 ... 134 C2
All Saints' CE Prim Sch SM5 ... 219 A3
All Saints' Cl N9 ... 18 A2
All Saints Ct 9 E1 ... 118 C6
E5 ... 74 C4
Heston TW5 ... 128 D4
All Saints Dr SE3 ... 142 D3
All Saint's Inf Sch SE19 ...
All Saints Mews HA3 ... 24 C4
All Saints Pas SW18 ... 157 C6
All Saints RC Sch RM8 ... 59 C1
All Saints Rd W11 ... 91 B1
All Saints' Rd W3 ... 111 A3
All Saints Rd
Merton SW19 ... 180 A3
Sutton SM1 ... 218 A5
All Saints St N1 .. 94 B5 233 C4
All Saints Sta E14 ... 119 D6
All Saints Twr 18 E10 ... 53 D2
Allsop Pl NW1 ... 92 D3 237 D5
All Souls' Ave NW10 ... 90 B6
All Souls CE Prim Sch W1 ... 93 C2 239 A4
All Souls Pl W1 ... 238 D3
Allum La WD6 ... 10 A6
Allum Way N20 ... 14 A3
Allwood Cl SE26 ... 184 D6
Alma Ave E4 ... 36 A3
Alma Birk Ho 1 NW6 ... 69 B1
Almack Rd E5 ... 74 C4
Alma Cl N10 ... 31 B2
Alma Cres SM1 ... 217 A3
Alma Gr SE1 ... 117 D2 263 D3
Alma Ho E5 ... 74 B5
7 Brentford TW8 ... 132 A6
2 Edmonton N9 ... 34 A6
Alma Pl NW10 ... 90 B4
Penge SE19 ... 183 D3
Thornton Heath CR7 ... 204 C4
Alma Prim Sch SE16 ... 118 A2
Enfield EN3 ... 18 D6
Alma Rd N10 ... 31 B3
SW18 ... 158 A6
Carshalton SM5 ... 218 C3
Enfield EN3 ... 7 A1
Sidcup DA14 ... 168 A1
Southall UB1 ... 107 A6
Thames Ditton KT10,KT7 ... 196 C1
Alma Row HA3 ... 24 B2
Alma Sq NW8 ... 92 A4 229 B2
Alma St E15 ... 76 B2
NW5 ... 71 B2
Alma Terr W8 ... 255 B5
Wandsworth SW18 ... 158 B4
Almeida St 10 N1 ... 72 D1
Almeric Rd SW11 ... 136 D1
Almer Rd SW20 ... 178 A3
Almington St N4 ... 50 B1
Almond Ave W5 ... 110 A3
Carshalton SM5 ... 218 D6
Uxbridge UB10 ... 60 D5
West Drayton UB7 ... 104 C3
Almond Cl BR2 ... 210 C2
SE15 ... 140 A3
Charlton TW17 ... 171 A1
Hayes UB3 ... 105 C6
Ruislip HA4 ... 61 D5
Feltham TW14 ... 150 A3
Almond Gr TW8 ... 131 B5
Almond Ho SE4 ... 141 B3
Almond Rd SE16 ... 118 B2
Tottenham N17 ... 34 A3
Almonds Ave IG9 ... 21 A2
Almond Way BR2 ... 210 C2
Harrow HA2 ... 24 A1
Mitcham CR4 ... 203 D5
Almorah Rd N1 ... 73 B1
Heston TW5 ... 128 D4
Almshouse La EN1 ... 6 B6
Almshouses E10 ... 75 D6
Sunbury TW16 ... 171 D2
Almshouses The IG11 ... 79 A2
Al-Muntada Islamic Sch SW6 ... 135 B4 264 D2
Alnmouth Ct 10 UB1 ... 86 A1
Alnwick 8 N17 ... 34 B3
Alnwick Gr SM4 ... 201 D5
Alnwick Rd Eltham SE12 ... 165 B4
Newham E16 ... 99 C1
Alonso Ct 4 DA17 ... 125 C1
Alperton Com Lower Sch HA0 ... 87 D6
Alperton Com Sch HA0 ... 66 B1
Alperton La UB6 ... 87 D5
Alperton St W10 ... 91 B3
Alperton Sta HA0 ... 88 A6
Alphabet Gdns SM5 ... 202 B3
Alphabet Sq E3 ... 97 C2
Alpha Bsns Ctr E17 ... 53 B4
Alpha Cl NW8 ... 92 C4 230 B1
Alpha Ct 6 NW5 ... 71 B2
Alpha Est The UB3 ... 105 C4
Alpha Gr E14 ... 119 C4
Alpha Ho NW6 ... 91 C5
NW8 ... 237 B5
10 SW4 ... 138 B1
Alpha Pl NW6 ... 91 C5
SW3 ... 136 C6 267 B6
Alpha Rd SE14 ... 141 B4
Chingford E4 ... 19 D1
Croydon CR0 ... 205 C1
Edmonton N18 ... 34 A4
Enfield EN3 ... 7 A1
Hillingdon UB10 ... 82 D3
Surbiton KT5 ... 198 B3
Teddington TW12 ... 174 B5
Alpha St SE15 ... 140 A3
Alphea Cl SW19 ... 180 C3
Alpine Ave KT5 ... 215 A6
Alpine Bsns Ctr E6 ... 100 C2
Alpine Cl CR0 ... 221 C5
Alpine Copse 2 BR1 ... 188 C1
Alpine Gr 36 E9 ... 74 C1
Alpine Rd SE16 ... 118 D1
Walton-on-T KT12 ... 194 A2
Alpine View SM1 ... 218 C3
Alpine Way E6 ... 100 C2
Alpine Wlk HA7 ... 8 C2
Alric Ave NW10 ... 67 B1
Kingston KT3 ... 199 D6
Alroy Rd N4 ... 50 C2
Alsace Rd SE17 .. 117 C1 263 A2
Al Sadiq & Al Zahra Schs NW6 ... 91 A6
Alscot Rd SE1 .. 117 D3 263 D5
Alscot Road Ind Est SE1 ... 263 D5
Alscot Way SE1 ... 263 C4
Alsike Rd DA18 ... 125 A3
Alsom Ave KT19,KT4 ... 216 A4
Alston Cl KT7 ... 197 B2
Alston Ct EN5 ... 1 A2
Alston Rd Barnet EN5 ... 1 A2
Edmonton N18 ... 34 B5
Upper Tooting SW17 ... 180 B6
Altair Cl N17 ... 33 D4
Altash Way SE9 ... 166 C2
Altenburg Ave W13 ... 109 B3
Altenburg Gdns SW11 ... 136 D1
Alt Gr SW19 ... 179 A3
Altham Rd HA5 ... 23 A3
Althea St SW6 ... 135 D2
Althope Mews SW11 ... 266 D1
Althorne Gdns E18 ... 54 D5
Althorne Way RM10 ... 81 C6
Althorp Cl EN5 ... 12 A4
Althorpe Rd HA1 ... 42 A4
Althorp Rd SW17 ... 158 D3
Altior Ct N6 ... 49 C3
Altmore Ave E6 ... 100 B6
Altmore Inf Sch E6 ... 100 B6
Alton Ave HA7 ... 24 D3
Alton Cl DA5 ... 169 A3
Isleworth TW7 ... 130 D3
Alton Ct 18 BR3 ... 185 C3
Alton Gdns
Beckenham BR3 ... 185 C3
Twickenham TW2 ... 152 B4
Alton Ho 3 E3 ... 97 D4
Alton Rd N17 ... 51 B6
Croydon CR0 ... 220 C5
Richmond TW10,TW9 ... 132 A1
Roehampton SW15 ... 156 A3
Alton St E14 ... 97 D2
Altyre Cl BR3 ... 207 B4
Altyre Rd CR0 ... 221 B6
Altyre Way BR3 ... 207 B4
Alum Ct KT5 ... 198 B3
Alumni Ct SE1 ... 253 D2
Alvanley Ct NW3 ... 69 D3
Alvanley Gdns NW6 ... 69 D3
Alvanley Ho 14 SW9 ... 138 C4
Alverstone Ave
East Barnet EN4 ... 14 C4
Wimbledon SW18,SW19 ... 157 C2
Alverstone Gdns SE9 ... 167 A3
Alverstone Ho 11 SE11 ... 138 C6
Alverstone Rd NW2 ... 68 C1
Alverstone Rd *continued*
Little Ilford E12 ... 78 C4
New Malden KT3 ... 199 D5
Wembley HA9 ... 44 B1
Alverston Gdns SE25 ... 205 C4
Alverton St SE8 ... 141 B6
Alveston Ave HA3 ... 43 B6
Alvey St SE17 ... 263 A2
Alvia Gdns SM1 ... 218 A4
Alvington Cres E8 ... 73 D3
Alway Ave KT19 ... 215 B3
Alwen Cotts CR0 ...
Alwold Cres SE12 ... 165 C5
Alwyne Ave W4 ... 111 B1
Alwyn Cl
Borehamwood WD6 ... 10 B5
New Addington CR0 ... 223 D1
Alwyne La N1 ... 72 D1
Alwyne Pl N1 ... 73 A1
Alwyne Rd N1 ... 73 A1
Ealing W7 ... 108 C6
Wimbledon SW19 ... 179 B4
Alwyne Sq N1 ... 73 A2
Alwyne Villas N1 ... 72 D1
Alwyn Gdns NW9 ... 46 A5
Acton W3 ... 88 D1
Alyn Ct N8 ... 49 D3
Alyth Gdns NW11 ... 47 C3
Alzette Ho 11 E2 ... 96 D5
Amalgamated Dr TW8 ... 131 B6
Amanda Ct TW15 ... 148 B2
Amar Ct SE18 ... 123 D2
Amardeep Ct SE18 ... 123 D1
Amazon St E1 ... 96 B1
Ambassador Cl TW3 ... 129 A3
Ambassador Ct NW4 ... 46 D4
9 NW6 ... 69 C3
Ambassador Gdns E6 ... 100 B2
Ambassador Ho NW8 ... 229 B5
Ambassador Sq E14 ... 119 D2
Amber Ave E17 ... 35 A2
Amber Ct N7 ... 72 C2
NW9 ... 45 C6
Mitcham CR4 ... 202 C5
Amberden Ave N3 ... 47 C6
Ambergate St SE17 ... 116 D1 261 D2
Amber Gr NW2 ... 46 D1
Amberley Cl
2 Orpington BR6 ... 227 D3
Pinner HA5 ... 41 B6
Amberley Ct 2 SW9 ... 138 D2
Sidcup DA14 ... 190 C5
Sutton SM2 ... 218 A1
Amberley Gdns
Enfield EN1 ... 17 C4
Worcester Park KT19 ... 215 D4
Amberley Gr
Croydon CR0 ... 205 D2
Penge SE26 ... 184 B5
Amberley Ho EN5 ... 1 D1
Amberley Rd E10 ... 53 D2
SE2 ... 146 D6
W9 ... 91 C2
Buckhurst Hill IG9 ... 21 C3
Enfield EN1 ... 17 D5
Palmers Green N13 ... 16 B2
Amberley Way
Heston TW4 ... 150 C6
Morden SM4 ... 201 B2
Romford RM7 ... 59 D5
Uxbridge UB10 ... 82 A5
Amberside Cl TW2 ... 152 B5
Amber Wharf 29 E2 ... 95 D6
Amberwood Cl SM6 ... 220 A3
Amberwood Rise KT3 ... 199 C3
Amblecote Cl SE12 ... 165 B1
Amblecote Mdw SE12 ... 165 B1
Amblecote Rd SE12 ... 165 B1
Ambler Prim Sch N4 ... 72 D6
Ambler Rd N4 ... 72 D5
Ambleside NW1 ... 231 D3
Catford BR1 ... 186 B4
13 Putney SW19 ... 157 A3
Ambleside Ave
Beckenham BR3 ... 207 A4
Streatham SW16 ... 181 D6
Walton-on-T KT12 ... 194 C1
Ambleside Cl E10 ... 53 D2
E9 ... 74 C3
Ambleside Cres EN3 ... 6 D2
Ambleside Dr TW14 ... 149 D3
Ambleside Gdns
Redbridge IG4 ... 56 A4
Streatham SW16 ... 181 D5
Sutton SM2 ... 218 A2
Wembley HA9 ... 43 D1
Ambleside Jun Sch KT12 ... 194 C1
Ambleside Point 1 SE15 ... 140 C5
Ambleside Rd DA7 ... 147 C3
NW10 ... 67 D1
Ambrook Rd DA17 ... 125 C3
Ambrosden Ave SW1 ... 115 C3 259 B5
Ambrose Ave NW11 ... 47 B3
Ambrose Cl 6 E6 ... 100 B2
Orpington BR6 ... 227 D5
Ambrose Ho 9 E14 ... 97 C2
Ambrose Mews 2 SW11 ... 136 D3
Ambrose St SE16 ... 118 B2
Ambrose Wlk E3 ... 97 C5
AMC Bsns Ctr NW10 ... 88 D4
Amelia Cl W3 ... 110 D4
Amelia Ho 5 W6 ... 112 C1
Amelia St SE17 ... 117 A1 262 A2
Amen Cnr EC4 ... 241 D1
Streatham SW17 ... 181 A4
Amen Ct EC4 ... 94 D1 241 D1
Amenity Way SM4 ... 200 C2
American Coll The W1 ... 93 A1 238 B2
American Com Schs UB10 ... 82 B6
American Sch in London The NW8 ... 92 B5 229 C4
America Sq EC3 ... 253 C6
America St SE1 ... 252 A3
Amerland Rd SW18 ... 157 B5
Amersham Ave N18 ... 33 B4
Amersham Gr SE14 ... 141 B5
Amersham Rd SE14 ... 141 B4
Thornton Heath CR0 ... 205 B3
Amersham Vale SE14, SE8 ... 141 B5
Amery Gdns NW10 ... 90 B6
Amery Ho SE17 ... 263 B2
Amery Rd HA1 ... 65 A6
Amesbury Ave SW2 ... 160 B2
Amesbury Cl KT4 ... 200 C1
Amesbury Ct EN2 ... 4 C3
Amesbury Dr E4 ... 19 D5
Amesbury Rd BR1 ... 209 D6
Dagenham RM9 ... 80 D1
Feltham TW13 ... 150 D2
Amesbury Twr 4 SW8 ... 137 C3
Ames Cotts 14 E3 ... 97 A2
Ames Ho 10 E2 ... 96 D5
Amethyst Cl N11 ... 31 D3
Amethyst Rd E15 ... 76 B4
Amherst Ave W13 ... 87 C1
Amherst Dr BR5 ... 211 D5
Amherst Gdns 2 W13 ... 87 C1
Amherst Prim Sch E8 ... 74 A3
Amherst Rd W13 ... 87 C1
Amhurst Ct N4 ... 51 B2
Amhurst Gdns TW7 ... 131 A3
Amhurst Par N16 ... 51 D2
Amhurst Pk N4,N16 ... 51 C2
Amhurst Rd E8,N16 ... 74 A4
Amhurst Terr E8 ... 74 A4
Amhurst Wlk SE28 ... 124 A5
Amias Ho EC1 ... 242 A6
Amidas Gdns RM8 ... 80 B4
Amiel St 17 E1 ... 96 C3
Amies St SW11 ... 136 D2
Amigo Ho SE1 ... 261 B6
Amina Way SE16 ... 118 A3
Amis Ave KT19 ... 214 D3
Amity Gr SW20 ... 178 C2
Amity Rd E15 ... 76 D1
Ammanford Gn NW9 ... 45 C3
Amner Rd SW11 ... 159 A5
Amor Rd W6 ... 112 C3
Amory Ho N1 ... 233 D4
Amott Rd SE15 ... 140 A2
Amoy Pl E14 ... 119 C6
Ampleforth Rd SE2 ... 124 C4
Ampton Pl WC1 ... 233 C1
Ampton St WC1 ... 94 B4 233 C1
Amroth Cl SE23 ... 162 B3
Amroth Gn NW9 ... 45 C3
Amstel Ct 11 SE15 ... 139 D5
Amsterdam Rd E14 ... 120 A3
Amundsen Ho 5 NW10 ... 67 B1
Amwell Cl EN2 ... 17 B6
Amwell St EC1 ... 94 C4 234 A2
Amyand Cotts 12 TW1 ... 153 B5
Amyand Park Gdns 2 TW1 ... 153 B4
Amyand Park Rd TW1 ... 153 B4
Amy Cl SM6 ... 220 A1
Amy Johnson Ho HA8 ... 26 D1
Amy Johnson Prim Sch SM6 ... 220 A1
Amyruth Rd SE4 ... 163 C6
Amy Warne Cl E6 ... 100 A3
Anarth Ct KT13 ... 193 C1
Anatola Rd N19 ... 71 C6
Ancaster Cres KT3 ... 200 A3
Ancaster Rd BR3 ... 206 D6
Ancaster St SE18 ... 145 C5
Anchorage Cl SW19 ... 179 C5
Anchorage Point E14 ... 119 C4
Anchorage Point Ind Est SE7 ... 121 C3
Anchor Bsns Pk CR0, SM6 ... 220 A5
Anchor Cl IG11 ... 102 B4
Anchor Ct 5 EN1 ... 17 C6
Anchor Ho EC1 ... 242 A6
Ilford IG3 ... 80 A5
Newham E16 ... 99 C1
Anchor & Hope La SE7 ... 121 C2
Anchor Mews SW12 ... 159 B5
Anchor Ret Pk E1 ... 96 C3
Anchor St SE16 ... 118 B2
Anchor Terr SE1 ... 252 B4
Anchor Yd EC1 ... 242 B6
Ancill Cl W6 ... 135 A6 264 A5
Ancona Rd NW10 ... 90 A5
SE18 ... 123 B1
Andace Pk BR1 ... 187 C2
Andalus Rd SW9 ... 138 A2
Andaman Ho 3 E1 ... 97 A2
Ander Cl HA0 ... 65 D4
Anderson Cl W3 ... 89 B1
Morden SM3 ... 201 C1
Southgate N21 ... 16 B6
Anderson Ct NW2 ... 46 C2
Anderson Dr TW15 ... 171 A6
Anderson Ho 10 E14 ... 120 A6
Barking IG11 ... 101 B5
Upper Tooting SW17 ... 180 B5
Anderson Rd E9 ... 74 D2
Redbridge IG8 ... 55 D6
Anderson's Pl TW3 ... 129 D1
Andersons Sq N1 ... 234 C5
Anderson St SW3 ... 257 C2
Anderson Way
Erith DA17 ... 125 D4
Erith DA17 ... 125 D4
Anderton Cl SE5 ... 139 B2
Anderton Ct N22 ... 31 D1
Andhurst Ct KT2 ... 176 D2
Andon Ct BR3 ... 207 A6
Andorra Ct BR1 ... 187 C2
Andover Ave E16 ... 99 D1
Andover Cl
East Bedfont TW14 ... 149 D3
Greenford UB6 ... 85 D3
Andover Ho 5 N7 ... 72 B6
Andover Pl NW6 ... 91 D5
Andover Rd N7 ... 72 B6
Orpington BR6 ... 211 C1
Twickenham TW2 ... 152 B3
Andoversford Ct 7 SE15 ... 139 C6
Andreck Ct BR3 ... 186 A1
Andre St E8 ... 74 A3
Andrew Borde St WC2 ... 239 D2
Andrew Ct
Beckenham BR3 ... 207 D6
Forest Hill SE23 ... 162 D2
Andrewes Gdns E6 ... 100 A1
Andrewes Ho EC2 ... 242 B3
Sutton SM1 ... 217 C4
Andrew Ewing Jun & Inf Sch TW5 ... 129 B4
Andrew Ho SE4 ... 141 B3
Putney SW15 ... 156 A6
Andrew Marvell Ho 12 N16 ... 73 C4
Andrew Pl SW8 ... 269 D2
Andrew Reed Ho SW18 ... 157 A4
Andrews Cl BR5 ... 190 D1
Buckhurst Hill IG9 ... 21 C2
Harrow HA1 ... 42 B2
North Cheam KT4 ... 216 D6
Andrews Crosse WC2 ... 241 A1
Andrews Ct 2 W7 ... 108 C5
Andrew's Rd E8 ... 96 B6
Andrew St E14 ... 98 A1
Andrews Wlk SE17 ... 138 D6
Andrew Wells Ho BR1 ... 187 B3
Andringham Lo 4 BR1 ... 187 B2
Andrula Ct N22 ... 32 D2
Andwell Cl SE2 ... 124 B4
Anerley Ct SE20 ... 184 B3
Anerley Gr SE19 ... 183 D3
Anerley Hill SE19 ... 183 D4
Anerley Park Rd SE20 ... 184 B3
Anerley Pk SE20 ... 184 B3
Anerley Prim Sch SE20 ... 184 A2
Anerley Rd SE20 ... 184 B2
Anerley Sch for Boys SE20 ... 184 A2
Anerley Sta SE20 ... 184 B2
Anerley Station Rd SE20 ... 184 B2
Anerley Vale SE19 ... 184 A3
Aneurin Bevan Ct NW2 ... 68 B6
Aneurin Bevan Ho N11 ... 31 D3
Anfield Cl SW12 ... 159 C4
Angel EC1 ... 94 C5 234 B3
Angela Ct 2 SE23 ... 162 C3
Angela Davis Ind Est 21 SW9 ... 138 D1
Angel Alley E1 ... 243 D2
Angel Cl N18 ... 34 A6
Angel Corner Par 6 N18 ... 34 A6
Angel Ct EC2 ... 242 D2
SW1 ... 249 B3
Angel Edmonton N18 ... 34 A5
Angelfield TW3 ... 151 D6
Angel Gate EC1 ... 234 D2
Angel Hill SM1 ... 217 D5
Angel Hill Dr SM1 ... 217 D5
Angel Ho N1 ... 234 B3
Angelica Cl UB7 ... 82 B1
Angelica Dr E6 ... 100 C2
Angelica Gdns CR0 ... 206 D1
Angelina Ho 2 SE15 ... 140 A4
Angel La E15 ... 76 B2
Hayes UB3 ... 83 B2
Angell Park Gdns 5 SW9 ... 138 C2
Angell Rd SW9 ... 138 D2
Angel Mews N1 ... 234 B3
Putney SW15 ... 156 A4
Stepney E1 ... 118 B6
Angel Pas EC4 ... 117 B6 252 C5
Angel Pl SE1 ... 252 C2
1 Edmonton N18 ... 34 A5
Angel Prim Sch N1 ... 94 C5 234 B4
Angel Rd Harrow HA1 ... 42 C3
Thames Ditton KT7 ... 197 A1
Angel Rd (North Circular Rd) N18 ... 34 B5
Angel Rd Works N18 ... 34 C5
Angel Road Sta N18 ... 34 C5
Angel St EC1 ... 95 A1 242 A2
Angel Sta EC1 ... 94 C5 234 B3
Angel Wlk W6 ... 112 C2
Angerstein Bsns Pk SE10 ... 121 A2
Angerstein La SE3 ... 142 D4
Anglebury 5 W2 ... 91 C1
Angle Cl UB10 ... 82 C6
Angle Gn RM8 ... 58 C1
Anglers Cl TW10 ... 175 C6
Anglers La NW5 ... 71 B2
Anglers Reach KT6 ... 197 D4
Anglesea Ave 4 SE18 ... 122 D2
Anglesea Ho KT1 ... 197 D5
Anglesea Rd SE18 ... 122 D2
Kingston KT1 ... 197 D5
Anglesey Cl TW15 ... 148 C1
Anglesey Court Rd SM5 .. 219 A2
Anglesey Ct W7 ... 86 D3
Anglesey Gdns SM5 ... 219 A2
Anglesey Ho 9 E14 ... 97 C1
Anglesey Rd Enfield EN3 ... 6 B1
South Oxhey WD19 ... 22 C5
Anglesmede Cres HA5 ... 41 C6
Anglesmede Way HA5 ... 41 C6
Angles Rd SW16 ... 182 A6
Anglia Cl N17 ... 34 B3
Anglia Ho 15 E14 ... 97 A1
Anglian Ind Est IG11 ... 101 D2
Anglian Rd E11 ... 76 B5
Anglo American Laundry SW17 ... 158 A1
Anglo Rd 24 E3 ... 97 B5
Angrave Ct 4 E8 ... 95 D6
Angrave Pas 5 E8 ... 95 D6
Angus Cl KT9 ... 214 C3
Angus Dr HA4 ... 62 C4
Angus Gdns NW9 ... 27 B2
Angus Ho 12 SW12 ... 159 D4
Angus Rd E13 ... 99 C4
Angus St SE14 ... 141 A5
Anhalt Rd SW11 .. 136 C5 267 B4
Ankerdine Cres SE18 ... 144 D4
Anlaby Rd TW11 ... 174 C5
Anley Rd W14 ... 112 D4
Anmersh Gr HA7 ... 25 D2
Annabel Cl E14 ... 97 D1
Anna Cl E8 ... 95 D6
Annandale Gr UB10 ... 61 A5
Annandale Prim Sch SE10 ... 120 D1
Annandale Rd DA15 ... 167 D4
SE10 ... 120 D1
W4 ... 111 C1
Croydon CR0 ... 222 A6
Anna Neagle Cl 2 E7 ... 77 A4
Anne Boleyn's Wlk
Belmont SM3 ... 217 A1
Kingston KT2 ... 176 A5
Anne Carver Lo HA0 ... 66 A1
Anne Compton Mews SE12 ... 164 D4
Anne Goodman Ho 3 E1 ... 96 C1
Anne Kerr Ct 18 SW15 ... 156 D5
Anne's Ct NW8 ... 237 B6
Annesley Ave NW9 ... 45 B6
Annesley Cl NW10 ... 67 C5
Annesley Dr CR0 ... 223 B5
Annesley Ho 15 SW9 ... 138 C5
31 SW9 ... 138 C4
Annesley Rd SE3 ... 143 B4
Annesley Wlk N19 ... 71 C6
Anne St E13 ... 99 A3
Annett Cl TW17 ... 193 C5
Annette Cl HA3 ... 24 C1
Annette Cres 9 N1 ... 73 A1
Annette Ct N7 ... 72 B5
Annette Rd N7 ... 72 B4
Annett Rd KT12 ... 194 A2
Anne Way KT8 ... 195 D5
Annie Besant Cl E3 ... 97 B6
Annie Taylor Ho 1 E12 ... 78 C4
Anning St EC2 ... 243 B6
Annington Rd N2 ... 48 D6
Annis Rd E9 ... 75 A2
Ann La SW10 ... 136 B6 266 C5
Ann Moss Way SE16 ... 118 C3
Ann Parkes Ct TW5 ... 128 D3
Ann's Cl SW1 ... 248 A1
Ann's Pl E1 ... 243 C3
Ann St SE18 ... 123 B2
Ann Stroud Ct SE12 ... 165 A6
Annsworthy Ave CR7 ... 205 B6
Annsworthy Cres CR7 ... 183 B1
Annunciation RC Inf Sch The HA8 ... 27 B2
Annunciation RC Jun Sch The HA8 ... 27 B4
Ansar Gdns E17 ... 53 B4
Ansdell Rd SE15 ... 140 C3
Ansdell St W8 ... 113 D3 255 D6
Ansdell Terr W8 ... 113 D3 255 D6
Ansell Gr SM5 ... 203 A1
Ansell Ho E1 ... 96 C2
Ansell Rd SW17 ... 158 D1
Anselm Cl CR0 ... 221 D5
Anselm Rd SW6 .. 135 C6 265 A5
Pinner HA5 ... 23 B3
Ansford Rd BR1,SE6 ... 186 B6
Ansleigh Pl W11 ... 112 D6
Anslie Wlk 8 SW12 ... 159 B4
Anson 30 NW9 ... 27 D1
Anson Ho 6 E1 ... 97 A3
SW1 ... 269 A6
Anson Pl SE28 ...
Anson Prim Sch NW2 ... 68 D3
Anson Rd N7 ... 71 D4
NW2 ... 68 C3
Anstey Ct 6 W3 ... 110 D4
Anstey Ho 8 E9 ... 96 C6
Anstey Lo EN1 ... 17 C5
Anstey Rd SE15 ... 140 A2
Anstey Wlk N15 ... 51 A5
Anstice Cl W4 ... 133 C5
Anstridge Rd SE9 ... 167 B5
Antelope Rd SE18 ... 122 B3
Antenor Ho 11 E2 ... 96 B5
Anthony Cl NW7 ... 27 C6
Anthony Cope Ct N1 ... 235 D2
Anthony Ct TW7 ... 130 D2
Anthony Ho NW8 ... 237 A5

Anthony Rd DA16 146 A4
Croydon SE25 206 A3
Greenford UB6 86 C4
Anthony St E1 96 B1
Antigua Wlk SE19 183 B5
Antilles Bay 7 E14 120 A4
Antill Rd E3 97 A4
N15 52 A5
Antill Terr 5 E1 96 D1
Antlers Hill E4 19 D6
Anton Cres SM1 217 C5
Antoneys Cl HA5 22 D1
Anton Pl HA9 66 D5
Anton St E8 74 A3
Antony Ho 4 SE14 140 D5
2 SE16 118 C2
Antrim Gr NW3 70 D2
Antrim Ho SW11 137 A2
Antrim Mans NW3 70 D2
Antrim Rd NW3 70 D2
Antrobus Cl SM1 217 B3
Antrobus Rd W4 111 A3
Anvil Cl SW16 181 C3
Anvil Ho 10 N9 18 A1
Anvil Rd TW16 194 A6
Anworth Cl IG8 37 B4
Apex Cl BR3 185 D2
Apex Cnr NW7 27 B6
Twickenham TW13 151 B1
Apex Ct W13 87 A1
Apex Ind Est NW10 89 D3
Aphrodite Ct 2 E14 119 C2
Aplin Way TW7 130 C4
Apollo Ave BR1 187 B2
Moor Park HA6 22 A5
Apollo Bldg 20 E14 119 C2
Apollo Ho 31 E2 96 B5
N6 48 D2
SW10 266 C5
Apollo Ind Bsns Ctr 29
SE8 140 D6
Apollo Pl E11 76 C5
SW10 266 C4
Apollo Studios 18 NW5 71 D3
Apollo Way SE18 123 B3
Apostle Way CR7 182 D1
Apothecary St EC4 241 C1
Appach Rd SW2 160 C5
Appin Ct HA1 42 C2
Appleby Cl N15 51 B4
Chingford E4 36 A4
Twickenham TW2 152 B2
Appleby Gdns TW14 149 D3
Appleby Rd E16 99 A1
E8 74 A1
Appleby St E2 95 D5
Appledore Ave HA4 62 C5
Appledore Cl BR2 209 A4
Edgware HA8 26 C2
Upper Tooting SW12,
SW17 158 D2
Appledore Cres DA14,
DA15 167 D1
Appleford 8 NW5 71 C3
Appleford Ho 6 W10 91 A3
Appleford Rd W10 91 A3
Applegarth
Claygate KT10 212 D3
New Addington CR0 223 D1
Apple Garth TW8 109 D2
Applegarth Dr IG2 57 D5
Applegarth Ho SE1 251 D2
8 SE15 140 A5
Applegarth Inf Sch CR0 223 D2
Applegarth Jun Sch
CR0 223 D2
Applegarth Rd W14 112 D3
Woolwich SE28 124 C6
Apple Gr
Chessington KT9 214 A4
Enfield EN1 5 C2
Apple Lo HA0 65 C5
Apple Mkt* WC2 250 B6
Kingston KT1 175 D1
Apple Rd E11 76 C5
Appleshaw Ho 4 SE5 139 C2
Appleton Gdns KT3 200 A3
Appleton Rd SE9 144 A2
Appleton Sq CR4 180 C2
Apple Tree Ave UB7 82 B1
Appletree Cl 5 SE20 184 B2
Appletree Ct SE13 142 B1
Appletree Gdns EN4 2 C1
Apple Tree Yd SW1 249 B4
Applewood Cl N20 14 C3
NW2 68 B5
Ickenham UB10 60 A4
Applewood Dr E13 99 B3
Appold St EC2 95 C2 243 A4
Apollo Ct 7 SW9 138 C4
Apprentice Way 6 E5 74 B4
Approach Cl N16 73 C4
Approach La NW7 29 A5
Approach Rd E2 96 C5
Ashford TW15 171 A4
East Molesey KT8 195 C4
Edgware HA8 26 C4
Merton SW20 178 C1
New Barnet EN4,EN5 2 B1
Approach The BR6 227 D6
NW4 46 D4
W3 89 B1
Enfield EN1 6 B3
Aprey Gdns NW4 46 C5
April Cl Ealing W7 108 C6
Feltham TW13 150 A1
Orpington BR6 227 D3
April Ct 20 E2 96 A5
April Glen SE23 162 D1
April St E8 73 D4
Apsley Cl HA2 42 A4
Apsley Ct SM2 218 A2
Apsley Ctr The NW2 68 A6
Apsley Ho E1 96 C2
Hounslow TW4 129 B1
Apsley Rd Croydon SE25 206 B5
Kingston KT3 199 A6
Apsley Way NW2 68 A6
W1 248 B2
Aquarius TW1 153 B3
Aquarius Way HA6 22 A6
Aquila St NW8 92 B5 229 D4
Aquinas St SE1 116 C5 251 B3
Arabella Ct NW8 229 B4
Arabella Dr SW15 133 C1
Arabia Cl E4 20 B4
Arabian Ho 3 E1 97 A3
Arabin Rd SE4 141 B1
Aragon Ave KT7 196 D4
Aragon Cl BR2 210 B1
Ashford TW16 171 D3
Enfield EN2 4 B5
Aragon Ct
Beckenham BR3 186 A2
East Molesey KT8 196 A5
Aragon Dr HA4 40 D1
Aragon Rd Kingston KT2 176 A5
West Barnes SM4 200 D3
West Barnes SM4 201 A2
Aragon Twr SE8 119 B2
Arakan Ho 4 N16 73 B4
Aral Ho 14 E1 96 D3
Arandora Cres RM6 58 B2
Aranya Ct E17 35 A1
Arapiles Ho 6 E14 98 B1
Arbery Rd E3 97 A5
Arbon Ct N1 235 B5
Arbor Cl BR3 185 D1
Arbor Ct N16 73 B6
Arborfield Ho 6 E14 119 C6
Arbor Rd E4 20 B1
Arbourfield Cl SW2 160 B3
Arbour Ho 3 E1 96 D1
Arbour Rd EN3 6 D2
Arbour Sq E1 96 D1
Arbroath Rd SE9 144 A2
Arbrook Chase KT10 212 A2
Arbrook Ct BR5 190 A2
Chessington KT9 213 D3
Arbrook Hall KT10 212 D2
Arbrook La KT10 212 B2
Arbury Terr 3 SE26 162 B1
Arbuthnot La DA5 169 A5
Arbuthnot Rd SE14 140 D3
Arbutus St E8 95 D6
Arcade Ho 7 NW11 47 B4
Arcade The E17 53 C5
EC2 243 A3
1 N7 72 A4
2 SE9 166 C5
Barking IG11 79 A1
Arcadia Ave N3 29 C2
Arcadia Cl SM5 219 A4
Arcadian Ave DA5 169 A5
Arcadian Cl DA5 169 A5
Arcadian Gdns N22 32 C3
Arcadian Rd DA5 169 A5
Arcadia St E14 97 C1
Archangel St SE16 118 D4
Archbishop Lanfranc Sch The
CR0 204 A3
Archbishop Michael Ramsey
Tech Coll SE5 138 D5
Archbishop's Pl 1 SW2 160 B4
Archbishop Sumner's CE
Prim Sch SE11 116 C2 261 B3
Archbishop Tenison's CE
High Sch CR0 221 D5
Archbishop Tenison's Sch
SE11 138 B6 270 D5
Archdale Ct W12 112 B5
Archdale Ho SE1 263 A6
Archdale Pl KT3 198 D6
Archdale Rd SE22 139 D1
Archdeacon Cambridge's CE
Prim Sch TW2 152 C2
Archel Rd W14 135 B6 264 C6
Archer Cl KT2 176 A3
Archer Ho 25 N1 95 C6
1 SW11 136 B3
W11 244 D6
Ealing W13 109 B5
Archer Mews TW12 174 A4
Archer Rd SE25 206 B5
Archers Dr EN3 6 C3
Archers Lo 14 SE16 118 A1
Archer Sq SE14 141 A6
Archer St W1 249 C6
Archer Terr UB7 104 A6
Archery Cl W2 237 B1
Harrow HA3 43 A5
Archery Fields Ho WC1 234 A2
Archery Rd SE9 166 B6
Archery Steps W2 247 B6
Arches Bsns Ctr The
UB2 107 B4
Arches The WC2 250 B4
Harrow HA2 63 D6
Archibald Mews W1 248 C5
Archibald Rd N7 71 D4
Archibald St E3 97 C4
Archie Cl UB7 104 C4
Arch St SE1 117 A3 262 A5
Archway N19 71 C6
Archway Bsns Ctr 5
N19 71 D5
Archway Cl W10 90 D2
Archway Cl *continued*
Wallington SM6 220 A5
Wimbledon SW19 179 D6
Archway Hts 5 N19 49 C1
Archway Mews SW15 135 A1
Archway Rd N6 49 B2
Archway St SW13,SW14 133 C2
Archway Sta N19 71 C6
Arcola St E8 73 D3
Arctic St NW5 71 B3
Arcus Rd BR1 186 C4
Ardbeg Rd SE24 161 B6
Arden 17 SW19 156 D3
Arden Cl Bushey WD23 8 D4
Erith SE28 102 D1
Harrow HA1 64 B5
Arden Court Gdns N2 48 B3
Arden Cres E14 119 C2
Dagenham RM9 80 D1
Arden Gr BR6 226 D4
Arden Grange N12 30 A6
Arden Ho 21 N1 95 C5
SE11 260 C3
29 SW9 138 A3
Arden Mhor HA5 40 B5
Arden Rd N3 47 B6
Ealing W13 109 C6
Ardent Cl SE25 205 C6
Ardent Ho 28 E3 97 A5
Ardfern Ave SW16 204 C6
Ardfillan Rd SE6 164 B2
Ardgowan Rd SE6 164 C3
Ardilaun Rd N5 73 A4
Ardingly Cl CR0 222 D5
Ardleigh Gdns SM3 201 C2
Ardleigh Rd E17 35 B2
N1 73 C2
Ardleigh Terr E17 35 B2
Ardley Cl NW10 67 C5
Forest Hill SE6 163 A1
Ruislip HA4 39 A2
Ardlui Rd SE27 161 A2
Ardmay Gdns KT6 198 A4
Ardmere Rd SE13 164 B5
Ardmore La IG9 21 B4
Ardmore Pl IG9 21 B4
Ardoch Rd SE6 164 B2
Ardra Rd N9 18 D1
Ardrossan Gdns KT4 216 A5
Ardshiel Cl SW15 134 D2
Ardwell Ave IG6 57 A4
Ardwell Rd SW2 160 A2
Ardwick Rd NW2 69 C4
Arena Bsns Ctr N4 51 A3
Arena Est N4 50 D3
Arena Sta SE25 206 C4
Arena The EN3 7 B5
Ares Ct 8 E14 119 C2
Arethusa Ho 8 E14 119 D2
Argall Ave E10 52 D1
Argall Ho 3 DA18 125 A3
Argall Way E10 53 A1
Argenta Way NW10 66 D1
Argent Ct KT6 214 C5
Argent Ctr The UB3 106 A4
Argon Mews SW6 265 B3
Argon Rd N18 34 D5
Argos Ct 5 SW9 138 C4
Argos Ho 8 E2 96 B5
Argosy Ho SE8 119 A2
W1 238 D5
Argus Way UB5 85 A4
Argyle Cl W13 87 A3
Argyle Ho E14 120 A3
Sutton SM2 218 A2
Argyle Pl W6 112 B2
Argyle Prim Sch WC1 233 A2
Argyle Rd E1 96 D3
E15 76 C4
N12 29 C5
Ealing W13 87 A2
Edmonton N18 34 A6
Harrow HA2 41 D3
Hounslow TW3 151 D6
Ilford IG1 78 C6
Newham E16 99 B1
Tottenham N17 34 A2
Argyle Sq WC1 94 A4 233 B2
Argyle St WC1 94 A4 233 B2
Argyle Way SE16 118 A1
Argyle Wlk WC1 233 B1
Argyll Ave UB1 107 D5
Argyll Cl SW9 138 B2
Argyll Ct 15 SW2 160 A4
Argyll Gdns HA8 26 D2
Argyll Mans SW3 266 D6
W14 254 B4
Argyll Rd SE18 123 A3
W8 113 C4 245 B1
Argyll St W1 93 C1 239 A1
Arica Ho SE16 118 B3
Arica Rd SE4 141 A2
Ariel Ct SE11 261 C3
W12 112 A3
5 Belvedere DA17 125 C1
Ariel Rd NW6 69 C2
Ariel Way W12 112 C5
Hounslow TW4 128 B2
Aristotle Rd SW4 137 D2
Arkansas Ho 21 N19 49 D2
Arkell Gr SW16 182 D3
Arkindale Rd SE6 164 A1
Arkley Cres E17 53 B4
Arkley Dr EN5 12 B6
Arkley Pk EN5 11 B5
Arkley Rd E17 53 B4
Arklow Ho SE17 139 B6
Arklow Mews 4 KT6 214 A6
Arklow Rd SE14 141 B6
Arklow Road Trad Est
SE14 141 B6
Arkwright Ho 23 SW2 160 A4
Arkwright Mans NW3 70 A3
Arkwright Rd NW3 70 A3
Arlesey Cl SW15 157 A6
Arlesford Rd SW9 138 A2
Arless Ho 8 HA1 42 D4
Arlingford Rd SW2 160 C5
Arlington N12 13 C1
Arlington Ave N1 95 A6 235 B5
Arlington Cl DA15 167 C4
Sutton SM1 217 C6
Twickenham TW1 153 C5
Arlington Ct N6 49 A3
4 Twickenham TW1 153 C5
Arlington Dr
Carshalton SM5 218 D6
Ruislip HA4 39 B3
Arlington Gdns W4 111 A1
Ilford IG1 56 C1
Arlington Ho EC1 234 B2
3 SE8 141 B6
W12 112 B5
Arlington Lo SW2 138 B1
Arlington Park Mans 1
W4 111 A1
Arlington Pl 7 SE10 142 A5
Arlington Rd N14 15 C3
NW1 93 B6 231 D5
Ashford TW15 170 B5
Ealing W13 87 B1
Richmond TW10 153 D2
Surbiton KT6 197 D3
Teddington TW11 174 D6
Twickenham TW1 153 C5
Woodford IG8 37 B3
Arlington Sq N1 95 A6 235 B5
Arlington St
SW1 115 C5 249 A4
Arlington Way
EC1 94 C4 234 B2
Arliss Way UB5 84 C6
Arlow Rd N21 16 C3
Armada Ct 11 SE8 141 C6
Armadale Cl N17 52 B5
Armadale Rd SW6 265 A5
Feltham TW14 150 A6
Armada St 10 SE8 141 C6
Armada Way E6 101 A1
Armagh Rd E3 97 B6
Armeston KT3 199 B2
Armfield Cl KT8 195 B4
Armfield Cotts 3 SW19 180 D1
Armfield Cres CR4 180 D1
Armfield Rd EN2 5 B4
Arminger Rd W12 112 B5
Armitage Ho
NW1 92 C2 237 B4
Armitage Rd NW11 47 B1
SE10 120 D1
Armitice Gdns SE25 206 A6
Armour Cl N7 72 B2
Armoury Rd SE8 141 D3
Armoury Way SW18 157 C6
Armsby Ho 15 E1 96 C2
Armstead Wlk RM10 81 C1
Armstrong Ave IG8 36 C4
Armstrong Cl BR1 210 A6
Dagenham RM8 58 D2
Newham E6 100 B1
Pinner HA5 40 A3
Walton-on-T KT12 194 A3
Armstrong Cres EN4 2 B2
Armstrong Ho 8 SW15 156 D5
Armstrong Rd SW7 256 C5
W3 111 D5
Feltham TW13 173 A5
Armstrong Way UB2 107 D4
Armytage Rd TW5 128 D5
Arnal Cres SW18 157 A4
Arncliffe NW6 91 D6
Arncliffe Cl N11 31 A4
Arncroft Ct IG11 102 B4
Arne Gr BR6 227 D5
Arne Ho SE11 260 C2
Arne St WC2 94 A1 240 B1
Arnett Sq E4 35 B4
Arneways Ave RM6 58 D6
Arneway St SW1 259 D5
Arne Wlk SE3 142 D1
Arnewood Cl SW15 156 A3
Arney's La CR4 203 A3
Arngask Rd SE6 164 B4
Arnhem Pl E14 119 C3
Arnhem Way 3 SE22 161 C6
Arnhem Wharf E14 119 C3
Arnhem Wharf Prim Sch
E14 119 C3
Arnison Rd KT8 196 B5
Arnold Ave E EN3 7 C5
Arnold Ave W EN3 7 B5
Arnold Cir E2 95 D4
Arnold Cl HA3 44 B2
Arnold Cres TW7 152 B6
Arnold Ct E18 36 D2
Arnold Dr KT9 213 D2
Arnold Est SE1 253 D1
Arnold Gdns N13 32 D5
Arnold Ho 9 N16 73 C5
SE17 261 D1
Arnold House Sch
NW8 92 B5 229 C3
Arnold Rd E3 97 C4
N15 51 D6
Dagenham RM10 81 C1
Mitcham SW17 180 D3
Northolt UB5 63 A2
Arnos Gr N14 15 D1
Arnos Grove Ct 4 N11 31 C5
Arnos Grove Sta N11 31 C6
Arnos Rd N11 31 C6
Arnot Ho 27 SE5 139 A5
Arnott Cl SE28 124 C5
W4 111 B2
Arnould Ave SE5 139 B1
Arnsberg Way DA7 147 C1
Arnside Gdns HA9 43 D1
Arnside Ho 2 SE17 139 B6
Arnside Rd DA7 147 C4
Arnside St SE17 139 A6
Arnulf St SE6 185 D6
Arnull's Rd SW16 182 D4
Arodene Rd SW2 160 B5
Arosa Rd 4 TW1 153 D5
Arragon Gdns
Streatham SW16 182 A3
West Wickham BR4 223 D5
Arragon Rd E6 99 D6
Wandsworth SW18 157 C3
Arran Cl SM6 219 C4
Arran Ct NW10 67 B5
32 NW9 27 D1
Arrandene Ho 3 BR5 190 B1
Arran Dr Stanmore HA7 25 C6
Wanstead E12 77 D6
Arran Ho N16 51 D1
Arran Mews W5 110 B5
Arran Rd SE6 164 A2
Arran Wlk N1 73 A1
Arras Ave SM4 202 A4
Arras Ho SE2 146 D6
Arrol Ho SE1 262 B5
Arrol Rd BR3 206 D6
Arrowe Ct 7 E5 74 B4
Arrowhead Ct E11 54 B3
Arrow Ho 24 N1 95 C6
Arrow Rd E3 97 D4
Arrow Scout Wlk UB5 85 A4
Arrowsmith Ho SE11 260 C2
Arsenal Rd SE9 144 B2
Arsenal Sta N5 72 C5
Artemis Ct 6 E14 119 C2
Arterberry Rd SW20,
SW19 178 D2
Artesian Cl NW10 67 B1
Artesian Gr EN5 2 A1
Artesian Rd W2 91 C1
Arthingworth St E15 98 C6
Arthur Ct SW11 268 B1
10 W10 90 D1
W2 91 D1
South Croydon CR0 221 B5
Arthur Deakin Ho 1 E1 96 A2
Arthurdon Rd SE4 163 C6
Arthur Gr SE18 123 A2
Arthur Henderson Ho
9 N19 49 D2
9 Fulham SW6 135 B3
Arthur Newton Ho 20
SW11 136 B2
Arthur Rd E6 100 B5
N7 72 B4
Dagenham RM6 58 D3
Edmonton N9 17 D2
6 Kingston KT2 176 C3
West Barnes KT3 200 B4
Wimbledon SW19 179 C6
Arthur Ruxley Est DA14 190 D4
Arthur St EC4 117 B6 252 D6
Arthur Wade Ho 7 E2 95 D4
Arthur Walls Ho 3 E12 78 C5
Artichoke Hill 8 E1 118 B6
Artichoke Mews 5 SE5 139 B4
Artichoke Pl SE5 139 B4
Artillery Cl IG2 57 A3
Artillery Ho SE18 122 C1
Artillery La E1 95 C2 243 B3
W12 90 A1
Artillery Pass E1 243 B3
Artillery Pl SE18 122 C2
Harrow HA3 24 A3
Artillery Row SW1 259 C5
Artington Cl BR6 227 A4
Artisan Cl E16 122 D6
Artizan St E1 243 B2
Arton Wilson Ho 12
SW15 156 A6
Arts Educational Sch The
W4 111 C2
Arundale KT1 197 D5
Arundel Ave SM4 201 B5
Arundel Bldgs SE1 263 B5
Arundel Cl E15 76 C4
SW11 158 C6
Croydon CR0 220 D5
Hampton TW12 173 D5
Sidcup DA5 169 B5
Arundel Ct 2 DA6 147 A1
N12 30 C4
SW3 257 B2
Barnes SW13 134 B6
4 Beckenham BR2 186 C1
Harrow HA2 63 C4
Putney SW15 156 D6
Tottenham N17 34 A2
Arundel Dr Harrow HA2 63 C4
Woodford IG8 37 A3
Arundel Gdns HA8 27 B3
W11 113 B6 244 C6
Ilford IG3 80 A6
Southgate N21 16 C3
Arundel Gr N16 73 C3
Arundel Ho N1 94 D6 234 D6
3 W3 110 D4
Croydon CR0 221 B3
Arundel Lo N3 29 B1
Arundel Mans SW6 264 D2
Barnes SW13 134 B6
Arundel Pl N1,N7 72 C2
Arundel Rd Belmont SM2 217 B1
Cockfosters EN4 2 C2
Hounslow TW4 128 C2
Kingston KT1 177 A1
Thornton Heath CR0 205 B3
Arundel Sq N7 72 C2
Arundel St WC2 116 B6 250 D6
Arundel Terr SW13 134 B6
Arun Ho 5 KT2 175 D2
Arvon Rd N5 72 C3
Asa Ct UB3 105 D3
Asaph Ho SE14 141 B4
Asbaston Terr IG11 79 A2
Ascalon Ct 16 SW2 160 B4
Ascalon Ho SW8 269 A3
Ascalon St SW8 137 C5 269 A3
Ascham Dr E4 35 C3
Ascham End E17 35 A2
Ascham St NW5 71 C3
Aschurch Rd CR0 205 D2
Ascot Cl
Borehamwood WD6 10 C6
Northolt UB5 63 C3
Ascot Ct DA5 169 B4
NW8 229 C1
8 SW4 138 A1
Ascot Gdns Enfield EN3 6 C6
Southall UB1 85 C2
Ascot Ho NW1 231 D2
6 W4 111 A1
1 W9 91 C2
Penge SE26 184 B4
Ascot Lo NW6 91 D5
Ascot Par 9 SW4 138 A1
Ascot Rd E6 100 B4
N15 51 B4
East Bedfont TW14 148 D2
Edmonton N18 34 A6
Orpington BR5 211 D5
Streatham SW17 181 A4
Ascott Ave W5 110 A4
Ascott Ct HA5 40 A5
Asfil Ho EC1 241 B3
Ashbourne Ave DA7 147 A5
N20 14 D2
NW11 47 B4
Harrow HA2 64 B6
Wanstead E18 55 B5
Ashbourne Cl N12 29 D6
Ealing W5 88 C2
Ashbourne Ct E5 75 A4
11 N12 29 D6
Beckenham BR3 186 A2
Ashbourne Gr NW7 27 B5
SE22 139 D1
W4 111 C1
Ashbourne Par 2 NW11 47 B5
Ealing W5 88 B3
Ashbourne Rd Ealing W5 88 B3
Mitcham CR4 181 A3
Ashbourne Rise BR6 227 C4
Ashbourne Terr 1
SW19 179 C3
Ashbourne Way NW11 47 B4
Ashbridge Rd E11 54 D2
Ashbridge St
NW8 92 C3 237 A5
Ashbrook HA8 26 B4
Ashbrook Rd N19 71 D6
Dagenham RM10 81 D5
Ashburn Ct BR1 187 A3
Ashburn Gdns SW7 256 A4
Ashburnham Ave HA1 42 D3
Ashburnham Cl N2 48 B5
Ashburnham Com Sch
SW10 266 C4
Ashburnham Gdns HA1 42 D3
Ashburnham Gr SE10 141 D5
Ashburnham Pk KT10 212 A4
Ashburnham Pl SE10 141 D5
Ashburnham Rd NW10 90 C5
SW10 136 A5 266 B3
Richmond TW10 153 B1
Ashburnham Retreat 6
SE10 141 D5
Ashburnham Twr SW10 266 C4
Ashburn Pl SW7 114 A2 256 A3
Ashburton Ave
Croydon CR0 206 B1
Ilford IG3 79 D4
Ashburton Cl CR0 206 A1
Ashburton Com Sch
CR9 206 B2
Ashburton Gdns CR0 222 A6
Ashburton Gr N7 72 C4
Ashburton Ho EN3 6 D2
Ashburton Jun & Inf Sch
CR0 206 B3
Ashburton Mans SW10 266 B4
Ashburton Rd E16 99 A1
Croydon CR0 222 A6
Ruislip HA4 62 A6
Ashburton Terr 2 E13 99 A5
Ashbury Ct N21 16 A6
Ashbury Dr UB10 60 D5
Ashbury Gdns RM6 58 D4
Ashby Ave KT19,KT9 214 C2
Ashby Ct NW8 236 D6
Ashby Gr N1 73 A1
Ashby Grange 7 SM6 219 C2
Ashby Ho 8 N1 73 A1
6 SW9 138 D3
Ashby Mews SE4 141 B3
Ashby Rd N15 52 A4
SE4 141 B3
Ashby St EC1 94 D4 234 D1
Ashby Way UB7 126 C5
Ashby Wlk CR0 205 A3
Ashchurch Ct W12 112 A3
Ashchurch Gr W12 112 A3

Ashchurch Park Villas
W12 ....112 A3
Ashchurch Terr W12 ....112 A3
Ash Cl BR5 ....211 B4
HA8 ....27 A4
Carshalton SM5 .....218 D6
Kingston KT3 ....177 B1
Penge SE20 ....184 C1
Sidcup DA14 ....168 B1
Stanmore HA7 ....25 A4
Ashcombe Ave KT6 ....197 D2
Ashcombe Ct 4 SW15 ...157 A6
Ashcombe Gdns HA8 ...26 C6
Ashcombe Ho 39 E3 ....97 C4
Ashcombe Pk NW2 ....67 C5
Ashcombe Rd
Wallington SM5 .....219 A2
Wimbledon SW19 ....179 C5
Ashcombe Sq KT3 ....199 A6
Ashcombe St SW6 ....135 D3
Ashcroft N14 ....15 C2
Pinner HA5 ....23 C4
Ashcroft Ave DA15 ...168 A5
Ashcroft Cres DA15 ...168 A5
Ashcroft Ct N20 ......14 B2
5 SE9 ....166 C5
Ashcroft Ho 269 A2
Ashcroft Rd E3 ....97 A4
Chessington KT9 ....214 B5
Ashcroft Sq W6 ......112 C2
Ash Ct N19 ....71 C6
SE12 ....165 A4
SW11 ....159 A6
W1 ....237 C2
Chingford E4 ....20 B4
Romford RM7 ....59 D3
West Ewell KT19 ....215 A4
2 West Norwood SW16 ..182 C6
Woodford E18 ....37 C2
Ashdale Cl
Stanwell TW19 ......148 A2
Twickenham TW2 ....152 A4
Ashdale Gr HA7 ......24 D4
Ashdale Ho N4 ....51 B2
Ashdale Rd SE12 ....165 B3
Ashdale Way TW2 ....151 D4
Ashdene 6 SE15 ....140 B5
Pinner HA5 ....40 C6
Ashdene Cl TW15 ....171 A4
Ashdon Cl IG8 ....37 B4
Ashdown Ealing W13 ...87 B2
Putney SW15 ....156 D6
Ashdown Cl 13 BR3 ...185 D1
Ashdown Cres NW5 ...71 A3
Ashdown Ct
New Malden KT4 ....199 D2
Sutton SM2 ....218 A2
Ashdowne Ct N17 .....34 A2
Ashdown Ho 7 E5 ....74 A6
Ashdown Pl Ewell KT17 .215 D1
Thames Ditton KT7 ...197 A2
Ashdown Rd NW10 ...89 D6
Enfield EN3 ....6 C3
Hillingdon UB10 .....82 C5
Kingston KT1 ....176 A1
Ashdown Way SW17 ...159 A2
Ashdown Wlk 15 E14 ..119 C2
Ashe Ho 8 TW1 .....153 D5
Ashen E6 ....100 C1
Ashenden SE17 ......262 B4
Ashenden Rd E5 ......75 A3
Ashen Gr SW19 ......157 C2
Ashentree Ct EC4 ....241 B1
Asher Loftus Way N11 ..30 C1
Asher Way E1 ....118 A6
Ashfield Ave Bushey WD23 ..8 A4
Feltham TW13 ......150 B3
Ashfield Cl
Beckenham BR3 ....185 C2
Richmond TW10 ....154 A3
Ashfield Ho 5 N5 ....73 A3
Ashfield La BR7 .....189 A3
Ashfield Par N14 ....15 D3
Ashfield Pl BR7 .....189 B3
Ashfield Rd N14 .....15 C1
N4 ....51 A3
W3 ....111 D5
Ashfield St E1 ....96 C2
Ashford Ave N8 .....50 A5
Ashford TW15 ......170 D4
Hayes UB4 ....84 D1
Ashford CE Prim Sch
TW15 ....170 D4
Ashford Cl E17 ....53 B3
Ashford TW15 ......170 A4
Ashford Cres
Ashford TW15 ......148 A1
Enfield EN3 ....6 C3
Ashford Ct NW2 .....68 D4
Edgware HA8 ....10 C1
Ashford Gn WD19 ....22 D5
Ashford High Sch The
TW15 ....148 A1
Ashford Ho 11 SE8 ...141 B6
14 SW9 ....138 D1
Ashford Hospl TW15 ..148 A2
Ashford Ind Est TW15 .171 A6
Ashford Rd NW2 .....68 D4
Feltham TW13,TW15 ..171 B6
Littleton TW15,TW17 ..171 A3
Staines TW18 ......170 A4
Wallend E6 ....78 C1
Woodford E18 ......37 B1
Ashford St N1 ....95 C4
Ash Gr E8 ....96 B6
NW2 ....69 A4
W5 ....110 A3
East Bedfont TW14 ...149 C3
Edmonton N13 ....17 A1
Enfield EN1 ....17 C4

Ash Gr continued
Hayes UB3 ....105 B6
Heston TW5 ....128 D5
Penge SE20 ....184 C1
Southall UB1 ....85 C2
Wembley HA0 ......65 A4
West Wickham BR4 ..208 A1
Yiewsley UB7 ......104 B6
Ashgrove SE12 .....165 A3
Ashgrove Ct 2 W9 ...91 C2
Ashgrove Ho SW1 ...259 D2
Ashgrove Rd
Ashford TW15 ......171 B5
Catford BR1 ....186 B4
Ilford IG3 ....58 A1
Ashgrove Sch BR1 ...187 B1
Ash Hill Dr HA5 .....40 C6
Ash Ho 3 E14 ......120 A4
SE1 ....263 D3
Ashingdon Cl E4 ....20 A1
Ashington 1 NW5 ...71 B2
Ashington Ho 16 E1 ..96 B3
Ashington Rd SW6 ...135 B3
Ashlake Rd SW16 ....182 A6
Ashland Pl W1 ......238 A4
Ashlar Ct N2 ....48 C6
Ashlar Pl SE18 ......122 D2
Ashleigh Commercial Est
SE7 ....121 D3
Ashleigh Ct N14 ....15 C4
W5 ....109 D2
Penge SE26 ....184 B4
Ashleigh Gdns SM1 ..217 D6
Ashleigh Point 8 SE26 ..162 D1
Ashleigh Rd
Mortlake SW14 .....133 C2
Penge SE20 ....206 B6
Ashley Ave SM4 ....201 C4
Ashley CE Prim Sch
KT12 ....194 A1
Ashley Cl NW4 .....28 C1
Oatlands Park KT12,KT13 ..193 D1
Pinner HA5 ....22 B1
Ashley Cres SW11 ...137 A2
Wood Green N22 ....32 C1
Ashley Ct 19 N16 ...73 C3
N3 ....69 D3
NW4 ....28 C1
New Barnet EN5 ....14 A6
Northolt UB5 ......85 A6
Yiewsley UB7 ......104 A5
Ashley Dr
Borehamwood WD6 ..11 B6
Hounslow TW7 .....130 C6
Twickenham TW2 ...151 D3
Ashley Gdns
Edmonton N13 ......33 A6
Orpington BR6 .....227 C3
Richmond TW10 ....153 D2
Wembley HA9 ......66 A6
Ashley Ho BR5 .....190 A1
Ashley La NW4 .....28 C1
NW7 ....28 D3
Croydon CR0 ......220 D4
Ashley Park Ave KT12 ..193 D1
Ashley Park Cres KT12 ..194 A1
Ashley Pl SW1 ...115 C3 259 A5
Ashley Rd E7 ......77 C1
N17 ....52 A6
N19 ....50 A2
Chingford E4 ....35 C4
Enfield EN3 ....6 C3
Hampton TW12 ....173 C2
Richmond TW9 ....132 A2
Thornton Heath CR7 ..204 B5
Walton-on-T KT12 ...194 A1
Wimbledon SW19 ...179 D4
Ashley Wlk NW7 ....28 D3
Ashling Rd CR0 .....206 A1
Ashlin Rd E15 ......76 B4
Ash Lo 2 Ashford TW16 ..171 D3
Fulham SW6 ....134 D4
Ashlone Rd SW15 ...134 D2
Ashlyns Way KT9 ...213 D2
Ashmead 4 N14 ....15 C6
Ashmead Bsns Ctr E16 ..98 B3
Ashmead Gate BR1 ..187 C2
Ashmead Ho E9 ....75 A3
Ashmead Prim Sch SE8 ..141 C3
Ashmead Rd SE8 ....141 C3
East Bedfont TW14 ...150 A3
Ashmere Ave BR3 ...186 B1
Ashmere Cl SM3 ....216 D3
Ashmere Gr 11 SW2, SW4 ..138 A1
Ashmere Ho 10 SW2 ..138 A1
Ashmill St NW8 ..92 C3 237 A4
Ashmole Prim Sch
SW8 ....138 B6 270 D5
Ashmole Sch N14 ...15 C3
Ashmole St SW8 ....270 D5
Ashmoor Lo NW7 ...27 B4
Ashmore NW1 ......71 D1
Ashmore Cl SE15 ...139 C5
Ashmore Ct N11 ....30 D4
Heston TW5 ....129 C6
Ashmore Gr DA16 ...145 C2
Ashmore Ho W14 ...254 B5
Ashmore Rd W9 ....91 B4
Ashmount Prim Sch N6 ..49 C2
Ashmount Rd N15 ...51 D4
N19 ....49 C2
Ashmount Terr W5 ..109 D2
Ashneal Gdns HA1 ...64 B5
Ashness Gdns UB6 ..65 B2
Ashness Rd SW11 ...158 D6
Ashpark Ho 4 E14 ..97 B1

Ash Rd E15 ....76 D2
Cheam SM3 ....201 B1
Croydon CR0 ......223 C6
Littleton TW17 .....192 C5
Orpington BR6 .....227 D1
Ashridge Cl HA3 ....43 C3
Ashridge Cres SE18 ..145 A5
Ashridge Ct Southall UB1 ..108 A6
Southgate N14 .....15 C6
Ashridge Dr WD19 ...22 C5
Ashridge Gdns
Bowes Park N13 ....32 A5
Pinner HA5 ....59 C5
Ashridge Ho DA14 ..189 D6
Ashridge Way
Ashford TW16 ......172 A4
Merton SM4 ....201 B5
Ash Row BR2 ......210 C3
Ashtead Ct 15 SW19 ..156 D3
Ashtead Rd E5 .....52 A2
Ashton Cl SM1 .....217 C4
Ashton Ct
1 Beckenham BR3 ..185 B2
Harrow HA1 ....64 D5
Ashton Gdns
Dagenham RM6 ....59 A3
Hounslow TW4 ....129 C1
Ashton Ho 13 SW9 ..138 C5
Roehampton SW15 ..156 B4
Ashton Rd E15 .....76 B3
Ashton St E14 .....120 A6
Ashtree Ave CR4 ...180 B1
Ashtree Cl BR6 .....226 D4
Ash Tree Cl Croydon CR0 ..207 A3
1 Surbiton KT6 .....198 A1
Ash Tree Dell NW9 ..45 B4
Ash Tree Way CR0 ..207 A3
Ashurst Cl SE20 ....184 B2
Ashurst Dr Ilford IG2,IG6 ..57 A4
Littleton TW17 .....192 A4
Ashurst Lo N5 ......72 D3
Ashurst Rd N12 ....30 C5
Cockfosters EN4 ....14 D6
Ashurst Wlk CR0 ...222 B6
Ashvale Rd SW17 ...180 D5
Ashview Cl TW15 ...170 A5
Ashview Gdns TW15 ..170 A5
Ashville Rd E11 .....76 B6
Ashwater Rd SE12 ..165 A3
Ashway Ctr 5 KT2 ..176 A2
Ashwell Cl 8 E6 ....100 A1
Ashwell Ct TW15 ...148 A2
Ashwin St E8 ....73 D2
Ash Wlk HA0 ......65 C4
Ashwood Ave UB8 ...82 C1
Ashwood Gdns
Hayes UB3 ....105 D2
New Addington CR0 ..224 A2
Ashwood Ho 5 NW4 ..46 C5
Ashwood Lo N21 ...16 B5
Ashwood Pk 6 SM2 ..217 C1
Ashwood Rd E4 ....20 B1
Ashworth Cl SE5 ...139 B3
Ashworth Mans W9 ..91 C4
Ashworth Rd W9 ...91 C4
Aske Ho 2 N1 ......95 C4
Asker Ho N7 ....72 A4
Askern Cl DA6 ......146 D1
Aske St N1 ....95 C4
Askew Cres W12 ...112 A4
Askew Mans 14 W12 ..112 A4
Askew Rd W12 .....112 A4
Askham Ct W12 ....112 A5
Askham 6 SE12 ....165 A4
Askham Rd W12 ....112 A5
Askill Dr SW15 .....157 A6
Asland Rd E15 .....98 B6
Aslett St SW18 .....158 A4
Asmara Rd NW2 ....69 A3
Asmuns Hill NW11 ..47 C4
Asmuns Pl NW11 ...47 B4
Asolando Dr SE17 ..262 B3
Aspen Cl 10 N19 ...71 C6
W5 ....110 B4
Yiewsley UB7 ......104 B5
Aspen Copse BR1 ...188 B1
Aspen Ct E8 ....73 D2
Hayes UB3 ....105 C2
Richmond TW9 ....132 C5
Aspen Dr HA0 .....65 A5
Aspen Gdns W6 ....112 B1
Ashford TW15 .....171 A5
Mitcham CR4 ......203 A4
Aspen Gn DA18 ....125 B3
Aspen Ho 2 DA15 ..168 A1
4 NW3 ....70 D2
8 SE15 ....140 C6
Southgate N21 .....16 B6
Aspen La UB5 ....85 A4
Aspenlea Rd W6 ...134 D6
Aspen Way E14 ....120 A6
Feltham TW13 .....150 B1
Aspern Gr NW3 ....70 C3
Aspinall Ho SW12 ..160 A3
Aspinall Rd SE4 ....140 D2
Aspinden Rd SE16 ..118 B2
Aspire Bld SW15 ...157 B6
Aspley Rd SW18 ...157 D6
Asplins Rd N17 ....34 B2
Asquith Cl RM8 ....58 C1
Asquith Court Sch HA3 ..43 C3
Assam SE1 ....253 D3
Assam St E1 ....96 A1
Assata Mews E1 ...72 D2
Assembly Pas E1 ...96 C2
Assembly Wlk SM4 ..202 C2
Assheton-Bennett Ho 13
KT6 ....198 A4
Ass House La HA3 ...23 D6

Assisi Ct
Upper Tooting SW12 ..158 D3
Wembley HA0 ......64 D5
Astall Cl HA3 ....24 C2
Astbury Ho SE11 ...261 A5
Astbury Rd SE15 ...140 C4
Astell St SW3 ...114 C2 257 B2
Aste St E14 ....120 A4
Astey's Row 3 N1 ..73 A4
Asthall Gdns IG6 ...57 A5
Astins Ho 4 E17 ...53 D5
Astle St SW11 .....137 A3
Astley Ave NW2 ...68 C3
Astley Ho SE1 .....263 D2
39 W2 ....91 C2
8 West Norwood SE27 ..183 A6
Aston Ave HA3 .....43 C2
Aston Cl Bushey WD23 ..8 A5
Sidcup DA14 ......168 A1
Aston Gn TW5 .....128 C3
Aston Ho SW8 .....269 C1
W11 ....244 B6
Aston House Sch W5 ..87 D1
Aston Mews RM6 ...58 C2
Aston Pl SW16 .....182 D4
Aston Rd Claygate KT10 ..212 C3
Ealing W5 ....87 D1
Merton SW20 .....178 C1
Aston St E14 ......97 A2
Astonville St SW18 ..157 C3
Astor Ave RM7 ....59 D3
Astor Cl KT2 ....176 D4
Astor Ct SW6 ......266 A3
Newham E16 ......99 C1
Astoria Mans 18 SW16 ..160 A1
Astoria Par SW16 ..160 A1
Astoria Wlk SW9 ...138 C2
Astra Ct W13 ......109 A5
Astra Ho 4 E3 .....97 B4
N4 ....50 B2
Astrid Ho TW13 ....150 C2
Astrop Mews W6 ...112 C3
Astrop Terr W6 ....112 C4
Astwood Mews SW7 ..256 A4
Asylum Rd SE15 ...140 B5
Atalanta St SW6 .134 D3 264 A3
Atbara Ct TW11 ...175 B4
Atbara Rd TW11 ...175 B4
Atcham Rd TW3 ...130 A1
Atcost Rd IG11 ....102 A2
Atheldene Rd SW18 ..158 A3
Athelney Prim Sch SE6 ..163 C1
Athelney St SE6 ...163 C1
Athelstan Ct E6 ...100 C5
Athelstane Gr 2 E3 ..97 B5
Athelstane Mews N4 ..50 C1
Athelstan Gdns 6 NW6 ..69 A1
Athelstan Ho E9 ...75 B3
N16 ....73 C4
Kingston KT1 .....198 B5
Athelstan House Sch
TW12 ....173 C2
Athelstan Rd KT1 ..198 B5
Athelstan Way BR5 ..190 A2
Athelstone Rd HA3 ..24 B1
Athena Cl Harrow HA2 ..64 C6
Kingston KT1 .....198 B6
Athena Ct NW8 ....229 C4
Athenaeum Pl 3 N10 ..49 B6
Athenaeum Rd N20 ..14 B3
Athenia Ho 7 E14 ..98 B1
Athenlay Rd SE15 ..162 D6
Athenoeum Ct N5 ..73 A4
Athens Gdns W9 ...91 C3
Atherden Rd E5 ....74 C4
Atherfield Ct SE18 ..157 D5
Atherfold Rd SW9 ..138 A2
Atherley Way TW4 ..151 B4
Atherstone Ct W2 ...91 D2
Atherstone Mews
SW7 ....114 A2 256 A6
Atherton Dr SW19 ..178 D6
Atherton Ho CR2 ...221 C2
Atherton Hts HA0 ...65 C2
Atherton Mews E7 ..77 A2
Atherton Pl Harrow HA2 ..42 B4
Southall UB1 ......107 C6
Atherton Rd E7 ....76 D2
Barnes SW13 ......134 A5
Atherton St SW11 ..136 C3
Athlone KT10 ......212 C2
Athlone Cl 24 E5 ...74 B3
Athlone Ct E17 ....54 B6
Athlone Ho 9 E1 ...96 C1
16 NW5 ....71 A2
Athlone House (The Middlesex Hospl) N6 ..48 D1
Athlone Rd SW2 ...160 C4
Athlone St NW5 ....71 A2
Athlon Rd HA0 ....87 D5
Athol Cl HA5 ......22 B2
Athole Gdns EN1 ...17 C1
Athol Gdns HA5 ...22 B2
Atholl Ho W9 ......229 A1
Atholl Rd IG3 ......58 A2
Athol Sq E14 ......98 A1
Athol Way UB10 ...82 C4
Atkins Ct 8 E3 ....97 B6
Atkins Dr BR4 .....224 B4
Atkinson Ct 3 E10 ..53 D2
Atkinson Ho E13 ...98 D3
18 E2 ....96 A5
SE17 ....262 D3
SW11 ....268 A1
Atkinson Morley Hospl
SW20 ....178 B3
Atkinson Rd E16 ...99 C2

Atkins Rd E10 .....53 D3
Streatham SW4,SW12 ..159 D3
Atlanta Ct 7 ......205 A6
Atlantic Ct 6 E14 ..120 B6
Atlantic Ho 4 E1 ...97 A2
4 Putney SW15 ...157 B6
Atlantic Rd SW2,SW9, SE24 ..138 C1
Atlantis Cl IG11 ...102 A4
Atlas Bsns Ctr NW2 ..68 B6
Atlas Gdns SE7 ....121 C2
Atlas Mews E8 .....73 D2
Atlas Rd E13 ......99 A5
N11 ....31 A4
NW10 ....89 C4
Wembley HA9 ......67 A4
Atley Rd E3 ....97 C6
Atlip Rd HA0 ......88 A6
Atney Rd SW15 ....135 A1
Atria Rd HA4 ......22 A5
Atterbury Rd N4 ...50 D3
Atterbury St
SW1 ....116 A2 260 A3
9 Enfield EN1 ....17 C6
Attewood Ave NW10 ..67 C5
Attewood Rd UB5 ..63 A2
Attfield Cl N20 ....14 B2
Attilburgh Ho SE1 ..263 D6
Attleborough Ct 4
SE21 ....162 B2
Attle Cl UB10 ......82 C5
Attlee Cl Hayes UB4 ..84 B4
Thornton Heath CR7 ..205 A4
Attlee Ct 4 E3 ....84 B4
Attlee Rd SE28 ....124 B6
Hayes UB4 ....84 B4
Attlee Terr 3 E17 ..53 D5
Attneave St WC1 ...234 A1
Atwater Cl SW2 ...160 C3
Atwell Cl E10 ......53 D3
Atwell Pl KT7 .....197 A1
Atwell Rd 4 SE15 ..140 A3
Atwood Ave TW9 ..132 C3
Atwood Ho SE21 ...161 C1
Atwood Rd W6 ....112 B2
Aubert Ct N5 ......72 C4
Aubert Pk N5 .....72 C4
Aubert Rd N5 .....72 C4
Aubrey Beardsley Ho
SW1 ....259 B3
Aubrey Mans NW1 ..237 A4
Aubrey Moore Point E15 ..98 A5
Aubrey Pl NW8 ....229 A3
Aubrey Rd E17 ....53 D6
N8 ....50 A4
W14 ....113 B5 244 D3
Aubrey Wlk
W14 ....113 B5 244 D3
Auburn Cl SE14 ...141 A5
Aubyn Hill SE27 ...183 B6
Aubyn Sq SW15 ...156 A6
Auckland Cl Enfield EN1 ..6 B4
South Norwood SE19 ..183 D2
Auckland Ct UB4 ...84 C3
Auckland Gdns SE19 ..183 D2
Auckland Hill SE27 ..183 A6
Auckland Ho 11 W12 ..112 B6
Auckland Rd E10 ...75 D5
SW11 ....136 C1
South Norwood SE19 ..183 D2
Auckland Rise SE19 ..183 D2
Auckland St SE11 ..260 C1
Audax 29 NW9 ....27 D1
Auden Pl NW1 .....231 A6
Audley Cl N10 .....31 B3
Audley Ct E11,E18 ..54 C5
W1 ....248 C4
Ealing W5 ....88 C3
Northolt HA5 ......84 C4
Pinner HA5 ....22 C1
Surbiton KT5 .....198 B3
Twickenham TW2 ...152 B1
Audley Dr 3 E16 ...121 B5
Audley Gdns IG3 ...79 D6
Audley Ho 11 E5 ...74 C6
N8 ....50 A5
Audley Pl SM2 ....217 D1
Audley Rd NW4 ...46 B3
Ealing W5 ....88 C2
Enfield EN2 ....4 D3
Richmond TW10 ...154 B6
Audley Sq W1 .....248 B5
Audley St BR3 .....207 D3
Audra Cl EN2 ......4 C5
Audrey Gdns HA0 ..65 B6
Audrey Rd IG1 .....78 D5
Audrey St E2 ......96 A5
Audric Cl KT2 .....176 C2
Augurs La E13 .....99 B4
Augusta Cl KT8 ...195 B6
Augusta Rd TW2 ..152 A2
Augustas Cl W12 ..112 B3
Augustine Rd W14 ..112 D3
Harrow HA3 ....24 A2
Augustines Ct E9 ...74 C3
Augustine's Cl TW8 ..131 D5
Augustus Cl
Isleworth TW3 .....130 A1
8 Putney SW19 ...157 A3
South Norwood SE19 ..183 C3
Streatham SW16 ...159 D2
Augustus Ct SW16 ..159 D2
Augustus Rd SW19 ..157 A3
Augustus St NW1 ..93 B4 231 D2
Aultone Way
Carshalton SM5 ...218 D5
Sutton SM1 ....218 A6
Aultone Yd Ind Est SM5 ..218 D5
Aulton Pl SE11 ....261 B1
Aurelia Gdns CR0 ..204 B3
Aurelia Rd CR0 ....204 B3

Auriga Mews N1 ....73 B3
Auriol Cl KT4 ......215 C5
Auriol Dr Greenford UB6 ..64 B1
Hillingdon UB10 ....60 D2
Auriol Jun Sch KT17 ..215 D4
Auriol Mans W14 ...254 A3
Auriol Park Rd KT4 ..215 C5
Auriol Rd W14 ...113 A2 254 A3
Aurora Ct IG8 ......36 D6
Austell Gdns NW7 ..11 C1
Austell Hts NW7 ...11 C1
Austen Cl SE28 ....124 B5
Austen Ho 2 NW6 ..91 C4
Austen Rd DA8 ....147 D5
Harrow HA2 ....63 D6
Austin Ave BR1,BR2 ..210 A4
Austin Cl Forest Hill SE23 ..163 B4
Twickenham TW1 ..153 C6
Austin Ct 10 E6 ...99 C6
9 Enfield EN1 ....17 C6
Austin Friars EC2 ..242 D2
Austin Friars Sq EC2 ..242 D2
Austin Ho 1 SE14 ..141 B5
6 SW2 ....160 B6
19 Kingston KT6 ..198 A4
Austin Rd SW11 ..137 A4 268 A1
Hayes UB3 ....105 A3
Austins Ct SE15 ...140 A2
Austin's La UB10 ...61 A5
Austin St E2 ......95 D4
Austral Cl DA15 ...167 D1
Australia Rd W12 ..112 B6
Austral St SE11 ..116 D2 261 C4
Austyn Gdns KT5 ..198 D1
Autumn Cl Enfield EN1 ..6 A4
Wimbledon SW19 ...180 A4
Autumn Lo CR2 ...221 C4
Autumn St E3 .....97 C6
Avalon Cl Ealing W13 ..87 A2
Enfield EN2 ....4 C3
Merton SW20 .....179 A1
Avalon Rd SW6 ...135 D4 265 C2
Ealing W13 ....87 A3
Avard Gdns EN2 ...4 B2
Avarn Rd SW17 ...180 D4
Avebury Ct N1 .....235 C5
Avebury Rd BR6 ...227 B5
E11 ....54 B1
Merton SW19 .....179 B2
Avebury St N1 .....235 C5
Aveley Ct 15 E5 ...74 B4
Aveline St SE11 ..116 C1 261 A1
Aveley Mans 1 IG11 ..78 D1
Aveling Park Rd E17 ..35 C1
Aveling Park Sch E17 ..35 C1
Ave Maria La EC4 ..241 D1
Avenell Mans N5 ...72 C4
Avenell Rd N5 .....72 D5
Avenfield Ho W1 ...247 D6
Avening Rd SW18 ..157 C4
Avening Terr SW18 ..157 C4
Avenue Cl NW8 ..92 C6 230 B5
Cranford TW5 .....128 B4
Southgate N14 ....15 C5
Avenue Cres W3 ...110 C4
Cranford TW5 .....128 B5
Avenue Ct NW2 ....69 A5
SW3 ....257 C3
Ealing W5 ....87 D2
Penge SE20 ....184 C2
Redbridge IG5 .....56 A6
Avenue Elmers KT6 ..198 A4
Avenue Gate IG10 ..21 C5
Avenue Gdns W3 ...110 D4
Cranford TW5 .....128 B5
Mortlake SW14 ....133 C2
South Norwood SE25 ..184 A1
Teddington TW11 ..174 D6
Avenue Hall N6 ....49 D3
Avenue Ho N16 ....74 A6
NW10 ....90 B5
NW8 ....230 A3
Avenue Ind Est E4 ..35 B4
Avenue Lo 12 NW8 ..70 B1
Avenue Mans N10 ..31 C1
NW3 ....69 D3
Avenue Mews N10 ..49 B6
Avenue Par Southgate N21 ..17 A4
Sunbury TW16 ....194 B6
Avenue Park Rd SE21, SE27 ..160 D2
Avenue Prim Sch E12 ..78 A3
Avenue Rd E7 .....77 B4
N12 ....30 A6
N15 ....51 B4
N6 ....49 D2
NW10 ....89 D5
NW8 ....92 C6 230 A6
W3 ....110 D4
Bexley DA6,DA7 ...147 A2
Brentford TW8 ....109 C1
Feltham TW13 ....149 D1
Hampton TW12 ...173 D2
Hounslow TW7 ....130 D4
Ilford RM6 ....58 C2
Kingston KT1 .....198 A6
Mitcham SW16 ....181 D1
New Malden KT3 ..199 C5
Pinner HA5 ....41 A6
Southall UB1 ......107 B5
Southgate N14 ....15 C5
South Norwood SE25 ..184 A1
South Norwood, Elmers End BR3,SE20 ..184 D2
Teddington TW11 ..175 A4
Wallington SM6 ...219 C1
Wimbledon SW20 ..178 B1

Avenue Rd continued
Woodford IG8 ....37 C4
Avenue Rd Sta BR3 ....184 D1
Avenue S KT5 ....198 C2
Avenue Sch The NW6 ....69 A1
Avenue Terr Ilford IG2 ....57 C3
Kingston KT3 ....199 A6
Avenue The BR1 ....209 D6
BR6 ....227 D6
N10 ....31 C1
N11 ....31 B5
N8 ....50 C6
NW6 ....91 A6
SE10 ....142 B5
SW4 ....159 A6
W4 ....111 C3
Barnet EN5 ....1 A2
Beckenham BR3 ....186 A2
8 Buckhurst Hill IG9 ....21 C2
Chingford E4 ....36 B5
Claygate KT10 ....212 C3
Cranford TW5 ....128 A4
Ealing W13 ....87 B1
Finchley N3 ....29 C1
Hampton TW12 ....173 B4
Hounslow TW3 ....151 D6
Isleworth TW1 ....153 B6
Keston Mark BR2 ....225 D5
Loughton IG10 ....21 D5
4 New Malden KT4 ....200 A1
Pinner HA5 ....23 B4
Pinner HA5 ....41 B3
Richmond TW9 ....132 B3
Sidcup DA5 ....168 D4
South Croydon CR0 ....221 C5
Stoneleigh KT17,SM3 ....216 C1
St Paul's Cray BR5 ....190 B3
Sunbury TW16 ....172 B1
Surbiton KT5 ....198 B3
Tottenham N17 ....33 C1
Uxbridge UB10 ....60 D5
Wallington SM5 ....219 A1
Wandsworth SW18,SW12 ..158 C4
Wanstead E11 ....55 B4
Wembley HA9 ....44 B1
West Wickham BR4 ....208 C2
Worcester Park KT4 ....215 D6
Averil Gr SW16 ....182 D4
Averill St W6 ....134 D6
Avern Gdns KT8 ....195 D5
Avernons Rd E13 ....99 A3
Avern Rd KT8 ....195 D5
Avery Ct SE20 ....184 B3
Avery Farm Row SW1 ..258 C3
Avery Gdns IG2 ....56 B4
Avery Hill Coll (Mile End Annexe) E3 ....97 B3
Avery Hill Rd SE9 ....167 B3
Avery Row W1 ..115 B6 248 D6
Aviary Cl E16 ....98 D2
Aviemore Cl BR3 ....207 B4
Aviemore Way BR3 ....207 A4
Avigdor (Jewish) Prim Sch N16 ....73 B6
Avignon Rd SE4 ....140 D2
Avington Ct SE1 ....263 B3
Avington Gr SE20 ....184 C3
Avion Cres NW7,NW9 ....28 A2
Avis Sq E1 ....96 D1
Avoca Rd SW17 ....181 A6
Avocet Cl SE1 ....118 A1
Avocet Mews SE28 ....123 B3
Avon Cl Hayes UB4 ....84 C3
Sutton SM1 ....218 A4
Worcester Park KT4 ....216 A6
Avon Ct N12 ....29 D5
1 W3 ....89 A1
Greenford UB6 ....85 D3
11 Putney SW15 ....157 A6
Wembley HA0 ....65 A4
Avondale Ave N12 ....29 D5
NW2 ....67 C5
Barnet, London EN4 ....14 D3
Hinchley Wood KT10 ....213 A5
New Malden KT4 ....199 D1
Avondale Cres Enfield EN3 ..7 A2
Redbridge IG4 ....55 D4
Avondale Ct E11 ....54 C1
E16 ....98 C2
9 Sutton SM2 ....218 A1
Woodford E18 ....37 B2
Avondale Dr UB3 ....106 B5
Avondale Gdns TW4 ....151 B6
Avondale Ho 10 SE1 ....118 A1
6 Mortlake SW14 ....133 B2
Avondale Mans SW6 ....264 C2
Avondale Park Gdns W11 ....113 A6 244 A5
Avondale Park Prim Sch W11 ....113 A6 244 A5
Avondale Park Rd W11 ....113 A6 244 A6
Avondale Rd E16 ....98 C2
E17 ....53 C2
N15 ....50 D4
N3 ....30 A2
Bexley DA16 ....146 C3
Bromley BR1 ....186 D4
Chislehurst SE9 ....166 A2
Harrow HA3 ....42 D6
Mortlake SW14 ....133 B2
South Croydon CR2 ....221 A2
Southgate N13 ....16 C2
Wimbledon SW19 ....179 D5
Avondale Rise SE15 ....139 D2
Avondale Sq SE1 ....118 A1
Avonfield Ct E17 ....54 B6
Avon Ho 14 N16 ....73 B4
W14 ....254 D3
7 Kingston KT2 ....175 D2
Southgate N21 ....16 B6
Avon House Sch IG8 ....37 A6
Avonhurst Ho NW6 ....69 A1
Avonley Rd SE14 ....140 C5
Avon Mews HA5 ....23 B2
Avonmore Gdns W14 ....254 D3
Avonmore Pl W14 ....254 B4
Avonmore Prim Sch W14 ....113 A2 254 B4
Avonmore Rd W14 ....113 B2 254 C4
Avonmouth St SE1 ....262 A6
Avon Pl SE1 ....252 B1
Avon Rd E17 ....54 B6
SE4 ....141 C2
Ashford TW16 ....171 D3
Greenford UB6 ....85 D3
Avonstowe Cl BR6 ....227 A5
Avon Way E18 ....55 A6
Avonwick Rd TW3 ....129 D3
Avril Way E4 ....36 A5
Avriol Ho W12 ....112 B5
Avro Ct E9 ....75 A3
Avro Way SM6 ....220 A1
Awlfield Ave N17 ....33 B2
Awliscombe Rd DA16 ....145 D3
Axe St IG11 ....101 A6
Axford Ho SW2 ....160 D3
Axholm Ave HA8 ....26 D2
Axis Bsns Ctr E15 ....97 D6
Axminster Cres DA16 ....146 C4
Axminster Rd N7 ....72 B5
Aybrook St W1 ....93 A2 238 A3
Aycliffe Cl BR1 ....210 B5
Aycliffe Ct KT1 ....176 C1
Aycliffe Rd W12 ....112 A5
Ayerst Ct 1 E10 ....54 A2
Aylands Cl HA9 ....66 A6
Aylesbury Cl E7 ....76 D2
Aylesbury Ct SM1 ....218 A5
Aylesbury Ho 13 SE15 ....140 A6
Aylesbury Rd BR2 ....209 A6
SE17 ....117 B1 262 D1
Aylesbury St EC1 ..94 D3 241 C5
NW10 ....67 B5
Ayles Ct UB4 ....84 B4
Aylesford Ave BR3 ....207 A4
Aylesford Ho SE1 ....252 D1
Aylesford St SW1 ....115 D1 259 C1
Aylesham Cl NW7 ....28 A3
Aylesham Ctr The SE15 ..140 A4
Aylesham Rd BR6 ....211 D2
Ayles Rd UB4 ....84 B4
Aylestone Ave NW6 ....90 D6
Aylett Rd Croydon SE25 ....206 B5
Isleworth TW7 ....130 C3
Ayley Croft EN1 ....18 A6
Aylmer Cl HA7 ....25 A6
Aylmer Ct N2 ....48 D4
Aylmer Dr HA7 ....25 A6
Aylmer Ho SE10 ....120 B1
Aylmer Rd E11 ....54 D1
N2 ....48 C4
W12 ....111 D4
Dagenham RM8 ....81 A5
Ayloffe Rd RM9 ....81 B2
Aylsham Dr UB10 ....61 A6
Aylton Est 22 SE16 ....118 C4
Aylward Fst & Mid Sch HA7 ....25 D5
Aylward Rd
Forest Hill SE23 ....162 D2
Merton SW20 ....201 B6
Aylward Sch N18 ....33 B6
Aylwards Rise HA7 ....25 A6
Aylward St E1 ....96 D1
Aylwin Est SE1 ....263 B6
Aylwin Girls Sch SE1 ....117 D2 263 D4
Aynhoe Mans W14 ....112 D2
Aynhoe Rd W14 ....112 D3
Ayr Ct W3 ....88 C2
Ayres Cl E13 ....99 A4
Ayres Cres NW10 ....67 B1
Ayres St SE1 ....117 A4 252 B2
Ayrsome Rd N16 ....73 C5
Ayrton Gould Ho 9 E2 ....96 D4
Ayrton Ho HA9 ....65 D6
Ayrton Rd SW7 ..114 B3 256 C6
Aysgarth Ct SM1 ....217 D5
Aysgarth Rd SE21 ....161 C4
Ayston Ho 19 SE8 ....118 D2
Ayton Ho SE5 ....139 B5
Aytoun Ct 17 SW9 ....138 B3
Aytoun Pl SW9 ....138 B3
Aytoun Rd SW9 ....138 B3
Azalea Cl Ealing W7 ....108 D5
Ilford IG1 ....78 D3
Azalea Ct W7 ....108 D5
Azalea Ho SE14 ....141 B5
Azalea Wlk HA5 ....40 B3
Azelea Ct IG8 ....36 C3
Azenby Rd SE15 ....139 D3
Azof St SE10 ....120 C2
Azov Ho 9 E1 ....97 A3

B

Baalbec Rd N5 ....72 D3
Babbacombe Cl KT9 ....213 D3
Babbacombe Gdns IG4 ....56 A5
Babbacombe Rd BR1 ....187 A2
Baber Bridge Par TW14 ..150 C5
Baber Dr TW14 ....150 C5
Babington Ct WC1 ....240 B4
Babington Ct continued
Streatham SW16 ....181 D5
Babington Ho SE1 ....252 B2
Babington House Sch BR7 ....188 B4
Babington Rd NW4 ....46 B5
Dagenham RM8 ....80 C4
Streatham SW16 ....181 D5
Babington Rise HA9 ....66 C2
Babmaes St SW1 ....249 C5
Bacchus Wlk 12 N1 ....95 C5
Bache's St N1 ....95 B4 235 D1
Back Church La E1 ....96 A1
Back Hill EC1 ....241 B5
Backhouse Pl SE1 ....263 B3
Back La HA8 ....27 A2
N8 ....50 A4
NW3 ....70 A4
Brentford TW8 ....131 D6
Dagenham RM6 ....59 A2
Richmond TW10 ....153 C2
Sidcup DA5 ....169 C4
Backley Gdns SE25 ....206 A3
Back Rd Sidcup DA14 ....190 A6
Teddington TW11 ....174 C3
Bacon Gr SE1 ....117 D3 263 C5
Bacon La NW9 ....44 D5
Edgware HA8 ....26 C2
Bacon's Coll SE16 ....119 A4
Bacon's La N6 ....49 A1
Bacon St E2 ....95 D3 243 D6
Bacon Terr RM8 ....80 B3
Bacton NW5 ....71 A3
Bacton St E2 ....96 C4
Baddeley Cl EN3 ....7 C6
Baddeley Ho SE11 ....260 D2
Baddow Cl
Dagenham RM10 ....103 C6
Woodford IG8 ....37 D4
Baddow Wlk N1 ....235 A6
Baden Ct N11 ....31 D3
Baden Pl SE1 ....252 C2
Baden Powell Cl
Dagenham RM9 ....103 A6
Surbiton KT6 ....214 B6
Baden Powell Ho 11 DA17 ....125 C3
Baden Powell Sch E5 ....74 B5
Baden Rd N8 ....49 D5
Ilford IG1 ....78 D3
Badger Cl Feltham TW13 ..150 B1
Hounslow TW4 ....128 C2
Ilford IG2 ....57 A2
Badger Ct NW2 ....68 C5
Badgers Cl
Ashford TW15 ....170 B5
Enfield EN2 ....4 D2
Harrow HA1 ....42 B3
Hayes UB3 ....105 C6
Badgers Copse BR6 ....227 D6
Worcester Park KT4 ....215 D6
Badgers Croft SE9 ....166 C1
Barnet N20 ....13 A3
Badgers Hole CR0 ....
Badgers Wlk KT3 ....177 C1
Badlis Rd E17 ....53 C6
Badma Cl N9 ....18 C1
Badminton KT2 ....176 D2
Badminton Cl
Harrow HA1 ....42 C5
Northolt UB5 ....63 C2
Badminton Ct 9 N4 ....51 A2
Badminton Ho SE22 ....139 C1
Badminton Mews 10 E16 ....121 A5
Badminton Rd SW12 ....159 A5
Badric Ct SW11 ....136 B3
Badsworth Rd 3 SE5 ....139 A4
Bagley Cl UB7 ....104 A4
Bagley's La SW6 ....135 D4 265 D1
Bagleys Spring RM6 ....59 A5
Bagnigge Ho WC1 ....234 A1
Bagshot Ho NW1 ....231 D2
Bagshot Rd EN1 ....17 D5
Bagshot St SE17 ..117 C1 263 B1
Baildon 28 E2 ....96 C5
Baildon St SE8 ....141 B5
Bailey Cl N11 ....31 D3
Chingford E4 ....36 A6
Bailey Cres KT9 ....213 D1
Bailey Ct 9 W12 ....112 A4
4 Chingford E4 ....36 B5
Bailey Ho 11 SE26 ....184 B5
Bailey Mews W4 ....132 D6
Bailey Pl SE26 ....184 D4
Bainbridge cl KT2 ....176 A5
Bainbridge Rd RM9 ....81 B4
Bainbridge St WC1 ....239 D2
Baines Cl CR2 ....221 B3
Bain Ho 23 SW9 ....138 A3
Baird Ave UB1 ....108 A6
Baird Cl E10 ....53 C1
NW9 ....45 A3
Baird Gdns SE19 ....183 C6
Baird Ho 29 W12 ....112 B6
12 Belvedere DA17 ....125 C3
Baird Rd EN1 ....6 B1
Baird St EC1 ....242 B6
Baizdon Rd SE3 ....142 C3
Baker Beall Ct DA7 ....147 D2
Baker Ct E11 ....76 B5
Baker Ho 12 E3 ....97 D4
Ealing W7 ....108 D5
Baker La CR4 ....203 A6
Baker Rd NW10 ....89 C6
SE18 ....144 A4
Bakers' Almshouses E10 ..53 D3
Bakers Ave E17 ....53 D3
Bakers Ct SE25 ....205 C6
Bakers End SW20 ....179 A1
Bakers Field N7 ....72 A4
Bakers Gdns SM5 ....218 C6
Bakers Hall Ct EC3 ....253 B5
Bakers Hill E5 ....52 C1
Barnet EN5 ....1 D3
Bakers Ho W5 ....109 D5
Baker's La N6 ....48 D3
Bakers Mews 9 BR6 ....227 D2
Baker's Mews W1 ....238 A2
Bakers Rents 13 E2 ....95 D4
Bakers Row E15 ....98 C5
Baker's Row EC1 ..94 C3 241 A5
Baker St W1 ....92 D2 237 D4
Enfield EN1 ....5 B4
Baker Street W1 ..92 D2 237 D4
Baker Street Sta NW1 ....92 D3 237 D5
Baker's Yd EC1 ....241 A5
Bakery Cl SW9 ....270 D3
Bakery Mews KT6 ....198 C1
Bakewell Way KT3 ....177 C1
Balaam Ho SM1 ....217 C4
Balaams La N14 ....15 D2
Balaam St E13 ....99 B4
Balaclava Rd SE1 ....117 D2 263 D3
Kingston KT6 ....197 C2
Balcaskie Rd SE9 ....166 B6
Balchen Rd SE3 ....143 D3
Balchier Rd SE22 ....162 B5
Balcombe Cl DA6 ....146 D1
Balcombe Ho NW1 ....237 C6
3 Streatham SW2 ....160 B3
Balcombe St NW1 ....92 D3 237 C5
Balcon Ct W5 ....88 B1
Balcorne St E9 ....74 C1
Balder Rise SE12 ....165 B2
Balderton Flats W1 ....238 B1
Balderton St W1 ..93 A1 238 B1
Baldewyne Ct N17 ....34 A2
Baldock Ho 32 SE5 ....139 A3
Baldock St E3 ....97 D5
Baldrey Ho 1 SE10 ....120 D1
Baldry Gdns SW16 ....182 B4
Baldwin Cres SE5 ....139 A4
Baldwin Gdns TW3 ....130 A4
Baldwin Ho 15 SW2 ....160 C3
Baldwin's Gdns EC1 ....94 C2 241 A4
Baldwin St EC1 ....235 C1
Baldwin Terr N1 ..95 A5 235 A4
Baldwyn Gdns W3 ....111 B6
Bale Rd E1 ....97 A2
Bales Coll W10 ....90 D4
Balfern Gr W4 ....111 C1
Balfern St SW11 ....136 C3
Balfe St N1 ....94 A5 233 B3
Balfour Ave W7 ....108 D5
Balfour Bsns Ctr UB2 ....106 D3
Balfour Gr N20 ....14 D1
Balfour Ho W10 ....90 D2
Balfour Mews W1 ....248 B4
Edmonton N9 ....18 A1
Balfour Pl W1 ....248 B5
Putney SW15 ....134 B1
Balfour Rd BR2 ....209 D4
N5 ....73 A4
W13 ....109 B4
W3 ....89 A2
Croydon SE25 ....206 A5
Harrow HA1 ....42 B4
Hounslow TW3 ....129 D2
Ilford IG1 ....57 A1
Merton SW19 ....179 D3
Southall UB2 ....106 D3
Wallington SM5 ....218 D1
Balfour St SE17 ..117 B2 262 C4
Balfron Twr 2 E14 ....98 A1
Balgonie Rd E4 ....20 B3
Balgowan Cl KT3 ....199 C5
Balgowan Prim Sch BR3 ....185 A1
Balgowan Rd BR3 ....185 B1
Balgowan St SE18 ....123 D2
Balham Gr SW12 ....159 A4
Balham High Rd SW12, SW17 ....159 A3
Balham Hill SW12 ....159 B5
Balham New Rd SW12 ....159 B4
Balham Park Mans SW12 ....158 D3
Balham Park Rd SW12, SW17 ....159 A3
Balham Rd N9 ....18 A2
Balham Sta SW12 ....159 B3
Balham Station Rd SW12 ....159 B3
Balin Ho SE1 ....252 C2
Balkan Wlk E1 ....118 B6
Balladier Wlk E14 ....97 D2
Ballamore Rd BR1 ....165 A1
Ballance Rd E9 ....75 A2
Ballantine St SW18 ....136 A1
Ballantrae Ho NW2 ....69 B4
Ballard Cl KT2 ....177 B3
Ballard Ho SE10 ....141 D6
Ballards Cl RM10 ....103 D6
Ballards Farm Rd CR0, CR2 ....222 A2
Ballards La N3 ....29 D3
Ballards Mews HA8 ....26 C4
Ballards Rd NW2 ....68 A6
Dagenham RM10 ....103 D6
Ballards Rise CR2 ....222 A2
Ballards Way CR0,CR2 ..222 B2
Ballast Quay SE10 ....120 B1
Ballater Cl WD19 ....22 C6
Ballater Rd SW2,SW4 ....138 A1
Ballater Rd continued
South Croydon CR2 ....221 D3
Ball Ct EC3 ....242 D1
Ballina St SE23 ....162 D4
Ballin Ct 9 E14 ....120 A4
Ballingdon Rd SW11 ....159 A5
Ballinger Point 18 E3 ....97 D4
Balliol Ave E4 ....36 C6
Balliol Ho 11 SW15 ....156 D5
Balliol Rd DA16 ....146 B3
W10 ....90 D1
Tottenham N17 ....33 C2
Balloch Rd SE6 ....164 B2
Ballogie Ave NW10 ....67 C4
Ballow Cl 23 SE5 ....139 C5
Ball's Pond Pl 3 N1 ....73 B2
Ball's Pond Rd N1 ....73 C2
Balmain Cl W5 ....109 D5
Balmain Ct TW3 ....129 D4
Balman Ho 3 SE16 ....118 D2
Balmer Rd E3 ....97 B5
Balmes Rd N1 ....95 B6 235 D6
Balmoral Ave N11 ....31 B5
Beckenham BR3 ....207 A5
Balmoral Cl 1 SW15 ....156 D5
Balmoral Cres KT8 ....195 C6
Balmoral Ct NW8 ....229 C4
SE12 ....187 B6
21 SE16 ....118 D5
11 Belmont SM2 ....217 C1
Ealing W5 ....87 D1
Edgware HA8 ....26 D6
North Cheam KT4 ....216 B6
Wembley HA9 ....66 B5
West Norwood SE27 ....183 A6
Balmoral Dr
Borehamwood WD6 ....11 B6
Hayes UB4 ....83 D3
Southall UB1 ....85 B3
Balmoral Gdns DA5 ....169 B4
W13 ....109 A3
Ilford IG3 ....57 D1
Balmoral Gr N7 ....72 B2
Balmoral Ho E17 ....35 B1
N4 ....51 A1
W14 ....254 A4
Balmoral Mews W12 ....111 D3
Balmoral Rd E10 ....75 D6
E7 ....77 C3
NW2 ....68 B2
Harrow HA2 ....63 C4
Kingston KT1 ....198 B5
North Cheam KT4 ....216 B6
Balmoral Trad Est IG11 ..101 D2
Balmore Cres EN4 ....15 A6
Balmore St N19 ....71 B6
Balmuir Gdns SW15 ....134 C1
Balnacraig Ave NW10 ....67 C4
Balniel Gate SW1 ....259 D2
Balsam Ho 8 E14 ....119 D6
Baltic Cl SW19 ....180 B3
Baltic Ho 7 SE5 ....139 A3
Baltic St E EC1 ....95 A3 242 A5
Baltic St W EC1 ....95 A3 242 A5
Baltimore Ho SE11 ....261 A2
Baltimore Pl DA16 ....145 D3
Balvaird Pl SW1 ....259 D1
Balvernie Gr SW18 ....157 C4
Bamber Ho 5 IG11 ....101 A6
Bamborough Gdns 12 W12 ....112 C4
Bamburgh 9 N17 ....34 B3
Bamford Ave HA0 ....88 B5
Bamford Ct E15 ....75 D3
Bamford Rd Barking IG11 ..79 A2
Catford BR1 ....186 B5
Bampfylde Cl SM6 ....219 C5
Bampton Ct W5 ....87 D1
Bampton Dr NW7 ....28 A3
Bampton Rd SE23 ....162 D1
Banavie Gdns BR3 ....186 A2
Banbury Cl EN2 ....4 D4
Banbury Ct W13 ....109 A3
WC2 ....250 A6
8 Belmont SM2 ....217 C1
Banbury Ho 5 E9 ....74 D1
Banbury Rd E17 ....35 A3
E9 ....74 D1
Banbury St 3 SW11 ....136 C3
Banbury Wlk UB5 ....85 C5
Banchory Rd SE3 ....143 B5
Bancroft Ave N2 ....48 C4
Woodford IG9 ....21 A2
Bancroft Cl
Ashford TW15 ....170 C5
Hillingdon UB8 ....82 D2
Bancroft Ct SW8 ....270 A2
Northolt UB5 ....84 C6
Bancroft Gdns BR6 ....211 D1
Harrow HA3 ....24 A2
Bancroft Ho 10 E1 ....96 C3
Bancroft Rd E1 ....96 D3
Harrow HA3 ....24 A1
Bancrofts Sch IG8 ....21 A1
Bandon Cl UB10 ....82 B5
Bandon Hill Prim Sch SM6 ....219 D2
Bandon Rise SM6 ....219 D3
Banff Ho 1 NW3 ....70 C2
Banfield Rd SE15 ....140 B2
Banfor Ct SM6 ....219 C3
Bangabandhu Prim Sch E2 ....96 C4
Bangalore St SW15 ....134 D2
Bangor Cl UB5 ....63 D3
Banim St W6 ....112 B2
Banister Ho E9 ....74 D3
SW8 ....269 B2
15 W10 ....91 A4
Banister Rd W10 ....90 D4
Bank Ave CR4 ....180 B1
Bank Ct SW11 ....268 C2
Bank End SE1 ....252 B4
Bankfoot Rd BR1 ....186 C6
Bankhurst Rd SE6 ....163 B4
Bank La Kingston KT2 ....176 A3
Roehampton SW15 ....155 C6
Bank Mews SM1 ....218 A2
Bank of England★ EC2 ..242 C1
Bank Par N11 ....31 B5
Banks Ho SE1 ....262 A5
Isleworth TW7 ....130 C3
Banksia Rd N18 ....34 D5
Bankside SE1 ....117 A6 252 A5
SE1 ....252 B4
Enfield EN2 ....4 D4
Southall UB1 ....106 D5
South Croydon CR2 ....221 D2
Bankside Ave UB5 ....84 A5
Bankside Cl
Carshalton SM5 ....218 C2
Isleworth TW7 ....130 D1
Bankside Dr KT7 ....213 B6
Bankside Pier SE1 ....117 A6 252 A5
Bankside Pk IG11 ....102 A4
Bankside Rd IG1 ....79 B3
Bankside Way 6 SE19 ....183 C4
Banks La DA6 ....147 B1
Bank Sta EC3 ....95 B1 242 D1
Banks Way E12 ....78 C4
Bank The N6 ....49 B1
Bankton Rd SW2 ....138 C1
Bankwell Rd SE13 ....142 C1
Banner Ho EC1 ....242 B5
Bannerman Ho SW8 ....270 C5
Banner St EC1 ....95 A3 242 B6
Banning Ho 4 SW19 ....156 D3
Banning St SE10 ....120 C1
Bannister Cl
Greenford UB6 ....64 B3
Streatham SW2 ....160 C3
Bannister Ho 28 SE14 ....140 D6
Bannister Sports Ctr The HA3 ....24 A4
Bannockburn Prim Sch SE18 ....123 D2
Bannockburn Rd SE18 ....123 D2
Bannow Cl KT19 ....215 C4
Banqueting House★ SW1 ....250 A3
Banstead Ct N4 ....51 A1
Banstead Gdns N9 ....17 C1
Banstead Rd SM2,SM5 ....218 C1
Banstead St SE15 ....140 C2
Banstead Way SM6 ....220 A3
Banstock Rd HA8 ....26 D4
Banting Dr N21 ....16 B6
Banting Ho 6 NW2 ....68 A5
Bantock Ho 14 W10 ....91 A4
Banton Cl EN1 ....6 B3
Bantry Ho 13 E1 ....96 D3
Bantry St SE5 ....139 B5
Banwell Rd DA5 ....168 D5
Banyan Ho 8 NW3 ....69 D2
Banyard Rd SE16 ....118 B3
Baptist Gdns NW5 ....71 A2
Barandon Wlk 6 W11 ....112 D6
Barbanel Ho 19 E1 ....96 C3
Barbara Brosnan Ct NW8 ....229 C3
Barbara Cl TW17 ....192 D4
Barbara Hucklesbury Cl N22 ....32 D1
Barbara Martin Ho 1 N11 ....31 C5
Barbara Ward Ct 3 E11 ..76 C6
Barbauld Rd N16 ....73 C5
Barber Beaumont Ho 21 E1 ....96 D4
Barber Cl N21 ....16 C4
Barbers Alley 1 E13 ....99 B4
Barbers Rd E15 ....97 D5
Barbican★ EC2 ....95 A2 242 B3
Barbican Arts & Con Ctr★ EC2 ....95 A2 242 B4
Barbican Rd UB1 ....85 D1
Barbican Sta EC1 ..95 A2 242 A4
Barb Mews W6 ....112 C3
Barbon Cl WC1 ....240 C4
Barbot Cl N9 ....18 A1
Barbrook Ho E9 ....74 C2
Barchard St SW18 ....157 D6
Barchester Cl W7 ....108 D5
Barchester Lo N12 ....29 D6
Barchester Rd HA3 ....24 B1
Barchester St E14 ....97 D2
Barclay Cl SW6 ..135 C5 265 A3
Barclay Ct N12 ....30 A5
Barclay Ho 21 E9 ....74 C1
Barclay Jun & Inf Schs E10 ....54 B3
Barclay Oval IG8 ....37 A6
Barclay Rd E11 ....54 D1
E13 ....99 C3
E17 ....54 A4
SW6 ....135 C5 265 B3
Edmonton N18 ....33 B4
South Croydon CR0 ....221 B5
Barcombe Ave SW2 ....160 B2
Bardell Ho 14 SE1 ....118 A4
Barden St SE18 ....145 C5
Bardfield Ave RM6 ....58 D6
Bardney Rd SM4 ....201 D5
Bardolph Rd N7 ....72 A4
Richmond TW9 ....132 B2
Bard Rd W10 ....112 D6
Bardsey Pl 35 E1 ....96 C3
Bardsey Wlk 2 N1 ....73 A2
Bardsley Cl CR0 ....221 D5

Bardsley Ho 5 SE10 ..... 142 A6
Bardsley La SE10 ..... 142 A6
Barents Ho 10 E1 ..... 96 D3
Barfett St W10 ..... 91 B3
Barfield Ave N20 ..... 14 D2
Barfield Rd BR1,BR7 ..... 210 C6
E11 ..... 54 D1
Barfleur Ho SE8 ..... 119 B2
Barford Cl NW4 ..... 28 A2
Barford Ho 19 E3 ..... 97 B5
Barford St N1 ..... 94 C6 234 B5
Barforth Rd SE15 ..... 140 B2
Barfreston Way SE20 ..... 184 B2
Bargate Cl SE18 ..... 123 D1
New Malden KT3 ..... 200 A2
Bargehouse Rd E16 ..... 122 D4
Barge House St SE1 ..... 251 B4
Bargery Rd SE6 ..... 163 D3
Barge Wlk KT1,KT6,KT7 ..... 197 C3
Bargrove Cl 8 SE20 ..... 184 A3
Bargrove Cres SE6 ..... 163 B2
Barham Cl
Chislehurst BR7 ..... 188 D5
Keston Mark BR2 ..... 210 A1
Wembley HA0 ..... 65 C2
Barham Ct N12 ..... 29 B5
8 Croydon CR2 ..... 221 A4
Keston Mark BR2 ..... 210 A1
Wembley HA0 ..... 65 C2
Barham Ho SE17 ..... 263 B2
Barham Prim Sch HA0 ..... 65 C2
Barham Rd
Chislehurst BR7 ..... 188 D5
Croydon CR2 ..... 221 A3
Wimbledon SW20 ..... 178 A3
Baring Cl SE12 ..... 165 A2
Baring Ct N1 ..... 235 C5
Baring Ho 11 E14 ..... 97 C1
Baring Prim Sch SE12 ..... 165 A4
Baring Rd SE12 ..... 165 A2
Barnet EN4 ..... 2 B2
Croydon CR0 ..... 206 A1
Baring St N1 ..... 95 B6 235 C5
Barker Cl KT3 ..... 198 D5
Barker Dr NW1 ..... 71 D1
Barker Ho N15 ..... 50 D5
SE17 ..... 263 A3
Dulwich SE21 ..... 161 C1
Barker Mews SW4 ..... 137 B1
Barker St SW10 ..... 266 A6
Barker Wlk SW16 ..... 159 D1
Barkham Rd N17 ..... 33 C3
Barking Abbey Comp Sch
IG11 ..... 79 D2
Barking Abbey Comp Sch
(Lower Sch) IG11 ..... 79 C3
Barking Bsns Ctr IG11 ..... 102 A4
Barking Flyover IG11 ..... 78 D1
Barking Hospl IG11 ..... 79 D1
Barking Ind Pk IG11 ..... 102 A6
Barking Rd E13 ..... 99 B4
E6 ..... 100 B6
Barkingside Sta IG6 ..... 57 B6
Barking Sta IG11 ..... 79 A1
Bark Pl W2 ..... 113 D6 245 C6
Barkston Gdns
SW5 ..... 113 D2 255 C3
Barkway Ct N4 ..... 73 A6
Barkwith Ho 27 SE14 ..... 140 D6
Barkworth Rd SE16 ..... 118 C1
Barlborough St SE14 ..... 140 D5
Barlby Gdns W10 ..... 90 D3
Barlby Prim Sch W10 ..... 90 D3
Barlby Rd W10 ..... 90 D2
Barley Cl WD23 ..... 8 A6
Barleycorn Way E14 ..... 119 B6
Barleyfields Cl RM6 ..... 58 C2
Barley La IG3 ..... 58 B3
Barley Lane Prim Sch
RM6 ..... 58 B2
Barley Mow Pas EC1 ..... 241 D3
W4 ..... 111 B1
Barley Mow Way TW17 ..... 192 C5
Barling 6 NW1 ..... 71 B1
Barling Ct 1 SW4 ..... 138 A3
Barlings Ho 2 SE4 ..... 140 D1
Barloch Ho 13 SW11 ..... 137 A3
Barlow Cl SM6 ..... 220 A1
Barlow Dr SE18 ..... 144 A4
Barlow Ho N1 ..... 235 C2
14 SE16 ..... 118 B2
W11 ..... 244 A6
Barlow Pl W1 ..... 248 D5
Barlow Rd NW6 ..... 69 B2
Acton W3 ..... 110 D5
Hampton TW12 ..... 173 C3
Barlow St SE17 ..... 117 B2 262 D3
Barmeston Rd SE6 ..... 163 D2
Barmor Cl HA2 ..... 23 D1
Barmouth Ave UB6 ..... 86 D5
Barmouth Ho 6 N7 ..... 72 B6
Barmouth Rd SW18 ..... 158 A5
Croydon CR0 ..... 222 D6
Barnabas Ct N21 ..... 16 D6
Barnabas Ho EC1 ..... 235 A1
Barnabas Lo SW8 ..... 270 B2
Barnabas Rd E9 ..... 74 D3
Barnaby Cl HA2 ..... 64 A6
Barnaby Ct NW9 ..... 45 C6
Barnaby Pl SW7 ..... 256 C3
Barnard Cl
Chislehurst BR7 ..... 189 B2
Sunbury TW16 ..... 172 B3
Wallington SM6 ..... 219 D1
Woolwich SE18 ..... 122 C3
Barnard Ct SW16 ..... 160 B1
Barnard Gdns Hayes UB4 ..... 84 B3
West Barnes KT3 ..... 200 A5
Barnard Gr E15 ..... 76 D1
Barnard Hill N10 ..... 31 B2
Barnard Ho 17 E2 ..... 96 B4
Barnard Lo 10 W9 ..... 91 C2
New Barnet EN5 ..... 2 A1
Barnard Mews SW11 ..... 136 C1
Barnardo Dr IG6 ..... 57 A5
Barnardo Gdns 1 E1 ..... 118 D6
Barnardo St E1 ..... 96 D1
Barnard Rd SW11 ..... 136 C1
Enfield EN1 ..... 6 B3
Mitcham CR4 ..... 181 A1
Barnard's Inn EC4 ..... 241 B2
Barnbrough NW1 ..... 232 A5
Barnby Sq 1 E15 ..... 98 C6
Barnby St 2 E15 ..... 98 C6
NW1 ..... 93 C4 232 B2
Barn Cl 19 NW5 ..... 71 D3
Ashford TW15 ..... 170 D5
Northolt UB5 ..... 84 C5
Barn Cres HA7 ..... 25 C4
Barn Croft Sch E17 ..... 53 A3
Barneby Cl TW2 ..... 152 C3
Barnehurst Rd DA7 ..... 147 D3
Barnersbury Ho N7 ..... 72 A4
Barnes Ave
Barnes SW13 ..... 134 A5
Southall UB2 ..... 107 B2
Barnes Bridge Sta
SW13 ..... 133 C3
Barnes Cl E12 ..... 77 D4
Barnes Common★
SW13 ..... 134 A2
Barnes Ct N1 ..... 72 C1
Barnet EN5 ..... 1 D1
Newham E16 ..... 99 C2
South Norwood CR7 ..... 205 A6
Woodford IG8 ..... 37 D5
Wood Green N22 ..... 32 A3
Barnes End KT3 ..... 200 A4
Barnes High St SW13 ..... 133 D3
Barnes Ho 14 E2 ..... 96 C5
N19 ..... 50 A2
26 SE14 ..... 140 D6
8 Barking IG11 ..... 101 B6
Barnes Hospl SW14 ..... 133 C2
Barnes Rd N18 ..... 34 C6
Ilford IG1 ..... 79 A3
Barnes St E14 ..... 97 A1
Barnes Sta SW13 ..... 134 A2
Barnes Terr SE8 ..... 119 B1
Barnes Wallis Ct HA9 ..... 67 A5
Barnet Coll EN4 ..... 15 A3
Barnet Coll of F Ed EN5 ..... 1 B1
Barnet Dr BR2 ..... 226 A6
Barnet Gate La EN5 ..... 11 D4
Barnet Gr E2 ..... 96 A4
Barnet Hill EN5 ..... 1 C1
Barnet Hill JMI Prim Sch
EN5 ..... 13 B6
Barnet Ho 36 SE5 ..... 139 A3
Barnet La Barnet EN5,N20 ..... 13 B4
Borehamwood WD6 ..... 10 B5
Barnet Mus★ EN5 ..... 1 A1
Barnet Rd Barnet EN5 ..... 1 B5
Edgware EN5 ..... 11 C5
Barnett Ho E1 ..... 243 C3
Barnett Homestead
NW11 ..... 47 C5
Barnet Trad Est EN5 ..... 1 B2
Barnetts Ct HA2 ..... 63 D5
Barnett St 8 E1 ..... 96 B1
Barnet Way (Barnet By-Pass)
EN5,NW7,WD6 ..... 11 B3
Barnet Wood Rd BR2 ..... 225 C6
Barney Cl SE7 ..... 121 C1
Barn Field NW3 ..... 70 D3
Barnfield KT3 ..... 199 C3
Barnfield Ave
Croydon CR0 ..... 222 C6
Kingston KT2 ..... 176 A5
Mitcham CR4 ..... 203 B6
Barnfield Cl N4 ..... 50 A2
Wandsworth SW17 ..... 158 A1
Barnfield Gdns SE18 ..... 144 D6
Kingston KT2 ..... 176 A5
Barnfield Pl E14 ..... 119 C2
Barnfield Prim Sch HA8 ..... 27 A2
Barnfield Rd HA8 ..... 27 A2
SE18 ..... 144 D6
Ealing W5 ..... 87 C3
Erith DA17 ..... 147 B6
Barnfield Wood Cl BR3 ..... 208 B3
Barnfield Wood Rd BR3 ..... 208 B3
Barnham Dr SE28 ..... 123 D5
Barnham Rd UB6 ..... 86 A4
Barnham St SE1 ..... 253 B2
Barnhill HA5 ..... 40 C4
Barn Hill HA9 ..... 44 D1
Barnhill Ave BR2 ..... 208 D4
Barnhill Com High Sch
UB4 ..... 84 C4
Barnhill Ct UB4 ..... 84 B4
Barnhill La UB4 ..... 84 B3
Barnhill Rd Hayes UB4 ..... 84 C3
Wembley HA9 ..... 67 A5
Barnhurst Path WD19 ..... 22 C5
Barningham Way NW9 ..... 45 B3
Barnlea Cl TW13 ..... 151 A2
Barnmead Gdns RM9 ..... 81 B3
Barnmead Rd
Dagenham RM9 ..... 81 B3
Penge BR3 ..... 185 A2
Barn Rise HA9 ..... 66 C6
Barnsbury Cl KT3 ..... 199 A5
Barnsbury Cres KT5 ..... 199 A1
Barnsbury Gr N7 ..... 72 B1
Barnsbury Ho 12 SW4 ..... 159 D5
Barnsbury La KT5 ..... 199 A1
Barnsbury Pk N1 ..... 72 C1
Barnsbury Rd N1 ..... 94 C6 234 A5
Barnsbury Sq N1 ..... 72 C1
Barnsbury St N1 ..... 72 C1
Barnsbury Terr N1 ..... 72 B1
Barnscroft SW20 ..... 200 B6
Barnsdale Ave E14 ..... 119 C2
Barnsdale Rd W9 ..... 91 B3
Barnsley St E1 ..... 96 B3
Barn St N16 ..... 73 C6
Barnstaple Ho SE12 ..... 164 D6
Barnstaple La SE13 ..... 142 A1
Barnstaple Rd HA4 ..... 62 C5
Barnston Wlk N1 ..... 235 A6
Barnview Lo HA3 ..... 24 C2
Barn Way HA9 ..... 66 C6
Barnwell Ho 1 SE5 ..... 139 C4
Barnwell Rd SW2 ..... 160 C6
Barnwood Cl W9 ..... 91 D3
Barnet N20 ..... 13 B3
Ruislip HA4 ..... 61 B6
Baron Cl N1 ..... 234 A4
N11 ..... 31 B5
Baron Ct CR4 ..... 202 C5
Baroness Rd 5 E2 ..... 95 D4
Baronet Gr N17 ..... 34 A2
Baronet Rd N17 ..... 34 A2
Baron Gdns IG6 ..... 57 A6
Baron Gr CR4 ..... 202 C5
Baron Rd RM8 ..... 58 D1
Barons Court Mans
W14 ..... 254 B1
Baron's Court Rd
W14 ..... 113 A1 254 B2
Barons Court Sta
W14 ..... 113 A1 254 A2
Barons Ct NW9 ..... 45 B3
Ilford IG1 ..... 79 B6
Wallington SM6 ..... 219 D5
Baronsfield Rd TW1 ..... 153 B5
Barons Gate 13 W4 ..... 111 A3
East Barnet EN4 ..... 14 C5
Barons Keep
W14 ..... 113 A1 254 A2
Barons Lo 8 E14 ..... 120 A2
Barons Mead HA1 ..... 42 C5
Baronsmead Rd SW13 ..... 134 A4
Baronsmede W5 ..... 110 B4
Baronsmere Ct 7 EN5 ..... 1 A1
Baronsmere Rd N2 ..... 48 C5
Baron's Pl SE1 ..... 116 C4 251 B1
Baron St N1 ..... 94 C5 234 A4
Barons The TW1 ..... 153 B5
Baron's Wlk CR0 ..... 207 A3
Baron Wlk E16 ..... 98 D2
Barque Mews SE8 ..... 141 C6
Barrack Rd TW4 ..... 129 A1
Barra Hall Cir UB3 ..... 83 C1
Barra Hall Rd UB3 ..... 105 C6
Barras Cl EN3 ..... 7 C6
Barratt Ave N22 ..... 32 B1
Barratt Ho 15 N1 ..... 72 D1
Barratt Ind Pk E3 ..... 98 A3
Southall UB1 ..... 107 C5
Barratt Way HA3 ..... 42 B6
Barr Beacon SE23 ..... 162 C4
Barrenger Rd N10 ..... 30 D1
Barret Ho NW6 ..... 91 C6
Barrett Rd E17 ..... 54 A5
Barrett's Gr N16 ..... 73 C3
Barrett's Green Rd NW10 ..... 89 B5
Barrett St W1 ..... 93 A1 238 B1
Barrhill Rd SW2 ..... 160 A2
Barrie Ct EN5 ..... 14 A6
Barriedale SE14 ..... 141 A3
Barrie Ho 8 N16 ..... 73 C5
NW8 ..... 230 B5
W2 ..... 246 B5
Acton W3 ..... 111 A4
Edmonton N9 ..... 18 B4
Barrier Gdns Pier E16 ..... 121 D3
Barringer Sq SW17 ..... 181 A6
Barrington Cl NW5 ..... 71 A3
Barrington Ct 4 N10 ..... 31 B1
NW5 ..... 71 A3
31 SW9 ..... 138 A3
Barrington Prim Sch
DA16 ..... 146 D3
Barrington Rd N8 ..... 49 D4
SW9 ..... 138 D2
Bexley DA16 ..... 146 D3
Cheam SM3 ..... 201 C1
Little Ilford E12 ..... 78 C2
Barrington Villas SE18 ..... 144 C4
Barrington Wlk 9 SE19 ..... 183 C4
Barrow Ave SM5 ..... 218 D1
Barrow Cl N21 ..... 16 D2
Barrow Ct 6 SE6 ..... 164 D3
Barrowdene Cl HA5 ..... 23 A1
Barrowell Gn N21 ..... 17 A2
Barrowfield Cl N9 ..... 18 C1
Barrowgate Ho W4 ..... 111 B1
Barrowgate Rd W4 ..... 111 B1
Barrow Hedges Cl SM5 ..... 218 C1
Barrow Hedges Prim Sch
SM5 ..... 218 C1
Barrow Hedges Way
SM5 ..... 218 C1
Barrow Hill KT4 ..... 215 C6
Barrow Hill Cl KT4 ..... 215 C6
Barrow Hill Est
NW8 ..... 92 C5 230 A3
Barrow Hill Jun Sch
NW8 ..... 92 C5 230 A3
Barrow Hill Rd NW8 ..... 230 A3
Barrow Point Ave HA5 ..... 23 A1
Barrow Point La HA5 ..... 23 A1
Barrow Rd Croydon CR0 ..... 220 C3
Streatham SW16 ..... 181 D4
Barrow Wlk TW8 ..... 109 C1
Barrs Rd NW10 ..... 67 B1
Barry Ave DA7 ..... 147 A5
N15 ..... 51 D3
Barry Cl BR6 ..... 227 C5
Barry Ct SW4 ..... 159 C5
Barrydene N20 ..... 14 B2
Barrydene Ct EN2 ..... 4 D2
Barry Ho 4 SE16 ..... 118 B1
Barry Lo N4 ..... 50 B2
Barry Par SE22 ..... 140 A1
Barry Rd E6 ..... 100 A1
NW10 ..... 67 A1
SE22 ..... 162 A6
Barry Terr TW15 ..... 148 B2
Barset Rd SE15 ..... 140 C2
Barsons Cl SE20 ..... 184 C3
Barston Rd SE27 ..... 161 A1
Barstow Cres SW2 ..... 160 B3
Bartell Ho SW2 ..... 160 C5
Barter St WC1 ..... 94 A2 240 B3
Bartholomew Cl EC1 ..... 242 A3
SW18 ..... 136 A1
Bartholomew Ct EC1 ..... 242 B6
Edgware HA8 ..... 25 D3
5 Poplar E14 ..... 120 B6
Bartholomew Ho
23 SE5 ..... 139 A3
Enfield EN3 ..... 7 A6
Enfield EN3 ..... 7 B6
Bartholomew La EC2 ..... 242 D1
Bartholomew Pas EC1 ..... 241 D3
Bartholomew Pl EC1 ..... 242 A3
Bartholomew Rd NW5 ..... 71 C2
Bartholomew Sq 18 E1 ..... 96 B3
Bartholomew St
SE1 ..... 117 B3 262 D5
Bartholomew Villas NW5 ..... 71 C2
Barth Rd SE18 ..... 123 C2
Bartle Ave E6 ..... 100 A5
Bartle Rd W11 ..... 91 A1
Bartlett Cl E14 ..... 97 C1
Bartlett Ct EC4 ..... 241 B2
Bartletts Ho 10 RM10 ..... 81 D2
Bartlett St CR2 ..... 221 B3
Bartok Ho W11 ..... 244 C5
Bartolomew Sq EC1 ..... 242 B6
Barton Ave RM7 ..... 59 D1
Barton Cl E9 ..... 74 C3
NW4 ..... 46 A5
SE15 ..... 140 B2
Bexley DA6 ..... 169 A6
2 Newham E6 ..... 100 B1
Shepperton TW17 ..... 192 D3
Barton Ct 10 SW4 ..... 138 A3
W14 ..... 254 B2
Beckenham BR2 ..... 208 B6
Barton Gn KT3 ..... 177 B1
Barton Ho 8 E3 ..... 97 D4
N1 ..... 72 D1
SW6 ..... 135 D2
Barton Mdws IG6 ..... 57 A5
Barton Rd W14 ..... 113 A1 254 B1
Sidcup DA14 ..... 191 A4
Barton St SW1 ..... 260 A6
Bartons The WD6 ..... 9 D5
Bartonway NW8 ..... 229 C4
Bartram Cl UB8 ..... 82 D3
Bartram Rd SE4 ..... 163 A5
Bartrams La EN4 ..... 2 A5
Bartrip St E9 ..... 75 B2
Barts Cl BR3 ..... 207 C4
Barville Cl SE4 ..... 141 A1
Barwell Ho 6 E2 ..... 96 A3
Barwick Dr UB8 ..... 82 D2
Barwick Ho 7 W3 ..... 111 A4
Barwick Rd E7 ..... 77 B4
Barwood Ave BR4 ..... 207 D1
Bascome St 19 SW2 ..... 160 C5
Basden Gr TW13 ..... 151 C2
Basedale Rd RM9 ..... 80 B1
Baseing Cl E6 ..... 122 C6
Basevi Way SE8 ..... 141 D6
Bashley Rd NW10 ..... 89 B3
Basil Ave E6 ..... 100 A4
Basildene Rd TW4,TW5 ..... 128 D2
Basildon Rd SE2 ..... 124 A1
Basil Gdns Croydon CR0 ..... 206 D1
West Norwood SE27 ..... 183 A5
Basil Ho 14 E1 ..... 96 A1
SW8 ..... 270 A4
Basil Mans SW1 ..... 247 C1
Basilon Rd DA7 ..... 147 A3
Basil Spence Ho N22 ..... 32 B2
Basil St SW1 ..... 114 D3 247 C1
SW1,SW3 ..... 114 D3 257 C6
Basin App 22 E14 ..... 97 A1
Basing Cl KT7 ..... 196 D2
Basing Ct 12 SE15 ..... 139 D4
Basingdon Way SE5 ..... 139 B1
Basing Dr DA5 ..... 169 B5
Basingfield Rd KT7 ..... 196 D2
Basinghall Ave
EC2 ..... 95 B1 242 C2
Basinghall St EC2 ..... 95 B1 242 C2
Basing Hill NW11 ..... 47 B1
Wembley HA9 ..... 44 C1
Basing Ho
7 Barking IG11 ..... 101 B6
Catford SE6 ..... 185 C6
Basing House Yd 23 E2 ..... 95 C4
Basing Pl E2 ..... 95 C4
Basing St W11 ..... 91 B1
Basing Way N3 ..... 47 D6
Thames Ditton KT7 ..... 196 D2
Basire St N1 ..... 95 A6 235 B6
Baskerville Gdns NW10 ..... 67 C4
Baskerville Rd SW18 ..... 158 C4
Basket Gdns SE9 ..... 166 A6
Baslow Cl HA3 ..... 24 B2
Baslow Wlk E5 ..... 74 D4
Basnett Rd 8 SW11 ..... 137 A2
Basque Ct 21 SE16 ..... 118 D4
Bassano St SE22 ..... 161 D6
Bassant Rd SE18 ..... 145 D6
Bassein Park Rd W12 ..... 111 D4
Bassett Gdns TW7 ..... 130 A5
Bassett Ho RM9 ..... 102 B6
Bassett Rd W10 ..... 90 D1
Bassetts Cl BR6 ..... 226 D4
Bassett St NW5 ..... 71 A2
Bassetts Way BR6 ..... 226 D4
Bassett Way UB1 ..... 85 D1
Bassingbourn Ho 3 N1 ..... 72 D1
Bassingham Rd
Wandsworth SW18 ..... 158 A4
Wembley HA0 ..... 65 D2
Bassishaw Highwalk
EC2 ..... 242 C3
Basswood Cl SE15 ..... 140 B2
Bastable Ave IG11 ..... 102 A5
Basterfield Ho EC1 ..... 242 A5
Bastion Rd SE18,SE2 ..... 124 A1
Baston Manor Rd BR2,
BR4 ..... 225 B4
Baston Rd BR2 ..... 225 B5
Baston Sch BR2 ..... 225 B6
Bastwick St EC1 ..... 95 A3 242 A6
Basuto Rd SW6 ..... 135 C4 265 B1
Batavia Cl TW16 ..... 172 C2
Batavia Ho 1 SE14 ..... 141 A5
Batavia Mews 3 SE14 ..... 141 A5
Batavia Rd SE14 ..... 141 A5
Sunbury TW16 ..... 172 B2
Batchelor St N1 ..... 94 C6 234 B5
Bateman Cl IG11 ..... 79 A2
Bateman Ho 8 SE17 ..... 138 D6
Bateman Rd E4 ..... 35 C4
Bateman's Bldgs W1 ..... 239 C1
Bateman's Row
EC2 ..... 95 C3 243 B6
Bateman St W1 ..... 93 D1 239 C1
Bates Cres Croydon CR0 ..... 220 C3
Streatham SW16 ..... 181 C3
Bateson St SE18 ..... 123 C2
Bates Point E13 ..... 99 A6
Bate St 10 E14 ..... 119 B6
Bath Cl SE15 ..... 140 B5
Bath Ct EC1 ..... 235 C1
EC1 ..... 241 A5
3 Forest Hill SE26 ..... 162 A1
Bathgate Ho 8 SW9 ..... 138 D4
Bathgate Rd SW19 ..... 156 D1
Bath Gr E2 ..... 96 A5
Bath Ho E2 ..... 96 A3
SE1 ..... 262 B6
Bath House Rd CR0 ..... 204 A1
Bath Pas KT1 ..... 175 D1
Bath Pl 11 EC2 ..... 95 C4
14 W6 ..... 112 C1
Barnet EN5 ..... 1 B2
Bath Rd E7 ..... 77 D2
N9 ..... 18 C2
W4 ..... 111 C2
Cranford TW3,TW4,TW5 ..... 128 C4
Dagenham RM6 ..... 59 A3
Harlington TW6,UB7,TW5 ..... 127 B4
Harmondsworth TW6,UB7 ..... 126 B4
Baths App SW6 ..... 135 B5 264 D4
Baths Rd BR1,BR2 ..... 209 D5
Bath St EC1 ..... 95 B4 235 C1
Bath Terr SE1 ..... 117 A3 262 A6
Bathurst Ave SW19 ..... 179 D2
Bathurst Gdns NW10 ..... 90 B5
Bathurst Ho 2 W12 ..... 112 B6
Bathurst Mews
W2 ..... 114 B6 246 D6
Bathurst Rd IG1 ..... 56 D1
Bathurst St W2 ..... 246 D6
Bathway 17 SE18 ..... 122 C2
Batley Cl CR4 ..... 202 D2
Batley Pl 3 N16 ..... 73 D5
Batley Rd N16 ..... 73 D5
Enfield EN2 ..... 5 B4
Batman Cl W12 ..... 112 B5
Batoum Gdns W6 ..... 112 C3
Batson Ho 21 E1 ..... 96 A1
Batson St W12 ..... 112 A4
Batsworth Rd CR4 ..... 202 B6
Battenberg Wlk 10
SE19 ..... 183 C5
Batten Cl E6 ..... 100 B1
Batten Ho 8 E17 ..... 53 D6
7 SW4 ..... 159 C6
13 W10 ..... 91 A4
Batten St SW11 ..... 136 C2
Battersby Rd SE6 ..... 164 B1
Battersea Bridge Rd
SW11 ..... 136 C5 267 A3
Battersea Church Rd
SW11 ..... 136 B4 266 D2
Battersea Dogs Home
SW8 ..... 137 B5 268 D3
Battersea Park★
SW11 ..... 137 A5 268 A3
Battersea Park Rd
SW11,SW8 ..... 267 D1
Battersea Park Sta
SW8 ..... 137 B5 268 C3
Battersea Power
Station(dis)★
SW8 ..... 137 B6 268 D6
Battersea Rise SW11 ..... 136 C1
Battersea Sq SW11 ..... 266 D1
Battersea Tech Coll
SW11 ..... 136 D4 267 D1
Battery Rd SE28 ..... 123 C4
Battishill St 9 N1 ..... 72 D1
Battlebridge Ct NW1 ..... 233 B4
Battle Bridge Ctr NW1 ..... 233 A4
Battle Bridge La
SE1 ..... 117 C5 253 A3
Battle Bridge Rd
NW1 ..... 94 A5 233 A4
Battle Cl SW19 ..... 180 A4
Battledean Rd N5 ..... 72 D3
Battle Ho 8 SE15 ..... 140 A6
Battle of Britain Mus★
NW9 ..... 27 D1
Batty St E1 ..... 96 A1
Baty Ho SW2 ..... 160 B3
Baudwin Rd SE6 ..... 164 C2
Baugh Rd DA14 ..... 190 C5
Baulk The SW18 ..... 157 C4
Bavant Rd SW16 ..... 182 B1
Bavaria Rd N19 ..... 72 A6
Bavent Rd SE5 ..... 139 A3
Bawdale Rd SE22 ..... 161 D6
Bawdsey Ave IG2 ..... 57 D5
Bawtree Rd SE14 ..... 141 A5
Bawtry Rd N20 ..... 14 D1
Baxendale N20 ..... 14 A2
Baxendale St E2 ..... 96 A4
Baxter Cl Hillingdon UB10 ..... 82 D4
Southall UB2 ..... 107 D3
Baxter Ho 11 E3 ..... 97 D4
Baxter Rd N1 ..... 73 B2
Edmonton N18 ..... 34 B6
Ilford IG1 ..... 78 D3
Newham E16 ..... 99 C1
Bayard Ct DA7 ..... 147 D1
Baycliffe Ho 8 E9 ..... 74 D2
Baycroft Cl HA5 ..... 40 C6
Bay Ct 7 E1 ..... 96 D3
W5 ..... 110 A3
Baydene Mews NW4 ..... 46 B5
Baydon Ct BR2 ..... 208 D6
Bayer Ho EC1 ..... 242 A5
Bayes Ct NW3 ..... 70 D1
Bayeux Ho 10 SE7 ..... 143 C6
Bayfield Ho 3 SE4 ..... 140 D1
Bayfield Rd SE9 ..... 143 D1
Bayford Rd NW10 ..... 90 D4
Bayford St 5 E8 ..... 74 B1
Bayford St Ind Ctr 4 E8 ..... 74 B1
Bayham Pl NW1 ..... 93 C6 232 B5
Bayham Rd W4 ..... 111 B3
Ealing W13 ..... 109 B5
Morden SM4 ..... 202 A5
Bayham St NW1 ..... 93 C6 232 A5
Bayhurst Lo N4 ..... 51 A2
Bayhurst Wood Countryside
Park UB9 ..... 38 B4
Bayleaf Cl TW12 ..... 174 B5
Bayley St WC1 ..... 239 C3
Bayley Wlk SE2 ..... 125 A1
Baylis Mews TW1 ..... 153 A4
Baylis Rd SE1 ..... 116 C4 251 A1
Bayliss Ave SE28 ..... 124 D6
Bayliss Cl N21 ..... 16 A6
Bayne Cl E6 ..... 100 B1
Baynes Cl EN1 ..... 6 A4
Baynes Mews 2 NW3 ..... 70 B2
Baynes St NW1 ..... 71 C1
Baynham Cl DA5 ..... 169 B5
Bayon Ho 27 N19 ..... 49 D2
Bayonne Rd W6 ..... 264 A5
Bays Cl SE26 ..... 184 C5
Bays Ct HA8 ..... 26 D5
Bayshill Rise UB5 ..... 63 D2
Bayston Rd N16 ..... 73 D5
Bayswater Rd
W2 ..... 114 B6 246 C5
Bayswater Sta
W2 ..... 113 D6 245 D6
Baythorne St 8 E3 ..... 97 B2
Bayton Ct 2 E8 ..... 74 A1
Baytree Cl DA15 ..... 167 D3
Bromley BR1 ..... 187 D2
Baytree Ho E4 ..... 19 D4
Baytree Rd SW2 ..... 138 B1
Bazalgette Cl KT3 ..... 199 B4
Bazalgette Gdns KT3 ..... 199 B4
Bazalgette Ho NW8 ..... 236 D6
Bazeley Ho SE1 ..... 251 C1
Bazely St E14 ..... 120 A6
Bazile Rd N21 ..... 16 C5
BBC Television Ctr
W12 ..... 112 C5
Beacham Cl SE7 ..... 143 D6
Beachborough Rd BR1 ..... 186 A6
Beachcroft Ave UB1 ..... 107 B5
Beachcroft Rd E11 ..... 76 C5
Beach Ct SE9 ..... 166 A5
Beach Gr TW13 ..... 151 C2
Beach Ho SW5 ..... 255 A2
Beachy Rd E3 ..... 75 C1
Beaconfield Terrace Rd
W14 ..... 254 A5
Beacon Gate SE14 ..... 140 D2
Beacon Gr SM5 ..... 219 A4
Beacon Hill N7 ..... 72 A3
Beacon Ho 19 SE5 ..... 139 C5
SW8 ..... 269 C2
10 Penge SE26 ..... 184 B5
Beacon House Sch W5 ..... 110 B5
Beacon Pl CR0 ..... 220 A5
Beacon Rd SE13 ..... 164 B5
Harlington TW19,TW6 ..... 148 C5
Beacon Rdbt TW6 ..... 148 C5
Beacons Cl 10 E6 ..... 100 A2
Beaconsfield Cl N11 ..... 31 A5
SE3 ..... 143 A6
W4 ..... 111 A1
Beaconsfield Ct N11 ..... 31 A5
Beaconsfield Gdns
KT10 ..... 212 C1
Beaconsfield Par 1
SE9 ..... 188 A6
Beaconsfield Prim Sch
UB2 ..... 107 A5

Beaconsfield Rd BR1 ...209 D6
E10 ...76 A5
E16 ...98 D3
E17 ...53 B3
N11 ...31 A6
N15 ...51 C5
NW10 ...67 D2
SE17 ...117 C1 263 A1
SE9 ...188 A6
W4 ...111 B3
W5 ...109 D4
Claygate KT10 ...212 C1
Edmonton N9 ...18 A1
Enfield EN3 ...6 D6
Greenwich SE3 ...143 A5
Hayes UB4 ...106 C5
Kingston KT3 ...177 B1
Southall UB1 ...107 A5
Surbiton KT5 ...198 B2
Thornton Heath CR0 ...205 B3
Twickenham TW1 ...153 B5
Beaconsfield Wlk
SW6 ...135 B4 264 D1
Beaconshaw BR1 ...186 C3
Beacontree Ave E17 ...36 B1
Beacontree Rd E11 ...54 D2
Beadle Ct CR4 ...202 C6
Beadlow Cl SM4 ...202 B3
Beadman Pl SE27 ...182 D6
Beadman St SE27 ...182 D6
Beadnell Rd SE23 ...162 D3
Beadon Rd BR2 ...209 A4
W6 ...112 C2
Beaford Gr SW20 ...201 B6
Beagle Cl TW13 ...172 B6
Beak St W1 ...115 C6 249 B6
Beal Cl DA16 ...146 A4
Beale Cl N13 ...32 D5
Beale Ho 7 SW9 ...138 B3
Beale Pl E3 ...97 B5
Beale Rd E3 ...97 B6
Beal High Sch IG5 ...56 A5
Beal Rd IG1 ...78 C6
Beam Ave RM10 ...103 D6
Beames Ho SW8 ...269 C2
Beaminster Ct N15 ...51 B4
Beaminster Gdns IG6 ...56 D6
Beaminster Ho SW8 ...270 C4
Beamish Dr WD23 ...8 A3
Beamish Ho 5 SE16 ...118 C2
Beamish Rd N9 ...18 A3
Beanacre Cl E9 ...75 B2
Bean Rd DA6 ...146 D1
Beanshaw SE9 ...188 C6
Beansland Gr RM6 ...59 A6
Bear Alley EC4 ...241 C2
Bear Cl RM7 ...59 D3
Bear Croft Ho 6 SW6 ...135 B3
Beardell St SE19 ...183 D4
Beardow Gr N14 ...15 C5
Beard Rd TW10 ...176 B5
Beardsfield E13 ...99 A5
Beard's Hill TW12 ...173 C2
Beards Hill Cl TW12 ...173 C2
Beardsley Terr RM8 ...80 B3
Beardsley Way W3 ...111 B4
Beard's Rd TW15,TW16 ...171 C4
Bearfield Rd KT2 ...176 A3
Bear Gardens Mus★
SE1 ...117 A5 252 A4
Bear Gdns SE1 ...117 A5 252 A4
Bear La SE1 ...116 D5 251 D3
Bear Rd TW13 ...172 D6
Bear St WC2 ...249 D6
Bearstead Rise SE4 ...163 B6
Bearsted Terr 2 BR3 ...185 C2
Beasley's Ait TW17 ...193 D3
Beasley's Ait La TW16,
TW17 ...193 D3
Beaton Cl SE15 ...139 D4
Beatrice Ave
Thornton Heath SW16 ...182 B1
Wembley HA9 ...66 A3
Beatrice Cl E13 ...99 A3
Pinner HA5 ...40 A5
Beatrice Ct NW4 ...46 C4
Buckhurst Hill IG9 ...21 D2
Beatrice Ho 1 SW2 ...160 B6
4 W6 ...112 C1
Beatrice Pl W8 ...255 C5
Beatrice Rd E17 ...53 C4
N4 ...50 C2
N9 ...18 C4
SE1 ...118 A2
2 Richmond TW10 ...154 B6
Southall UB1 ...107 B5
Beatrice Tate Sch E2 ...96 B4
Beatrice Webb Ho 3 E3 ...97 A5
Beatrix Ho SW5 ...255 D2
Beatrix Potter Prim Sch
SW18 ...158 A3
Beattie Cl TW14 ...149 D3
Beattie Ho SW8 ...269 B2
Beattock Rise N10 ...49 B5
Beatty Rd N16 ...73 C4
Stanmore HA7 ...25 C4
Beatty St NW1 ...232 A4
Beattyville Gdns IG6 ...56 D5
Beauchamp Cl 16 W4 ...111 A3
Beauchamp Ct HA7 ...25 C5
Beauchamp Pl
SW3 ...114 C3 257 B5
Beauchamp Rd E7 ...77 B1
SW11 ...136 D1
East Molesey KT8 ...196 A4
South Norwood SE19 ...183 B2
Sutton SM1 ...217 C4
Beauchamp Rd *continued*
Twickenham TW1 ...153 A4
Beauchamp St EC1 ...241 A3
Beauchamp Terr SW15 ...134 B2
Beauclerc Cty Inf Sch
TW16 ...194 C6
Beauclerc Rd W6 ...112 B3
Beauclere Ho 1 SM2 ...218 A1
Beauclerk Cl TW13 ...150 B3
Beauclerk Ho 10 SW16 ...160 A1
Beaudesert Mews UB7 ...104 A4
Beaufort E6 ...100 C2
Beaufort Ave HA3 ...43 B6
Beaufort Cl Chingford E4 ...35 D4
Ealing W5 ...88 B2
Putney SW19 ...156 B4
Beaufort Ct N11 ...31 B5
New Barnet EN5 ...14 A6
Richmond TW10 ...175 C6
Beaufort Dr NW11 ...47 C5
Beaufort Gdns NW4 ...46 C3
SW3 ...114 C3 257 B6
Heston TW5 ...129 A4
Ilford IG1 ...56 C1
South Norwood SW16 ...182 B3
Beaufort Ho 7 N15 ...51 D5
NW11 ...48 A3
SW1 ...259 C1
SW11 ...136 C3
SW3 ...266 D5
1 Wimbledon SW20 ...178 D2
Beaufort Mans SW3 ...266 D5
Beaufort Mews SW6 ...264 D6
Beaufort Pk NW11 ...47 C5
Beaufort Rd Ealing W5 ...88 B2
Kingston KT1,KT5,KT6 ...198 A5
Richmond TW10 ...175 C6
Ruislip HA4 ...61 B6
Twickenham TW1 ...153 C4
Beaufort St
SW3 ...136 B6 266 C6
Beaufort Way KT17 ...216 A1
Beaufoy Ho SW8 ...270 C4
3 West Norwood SE27 ...160 D1
Beaufoy Rd 11 SW8 ...137 B2
Tottenham N17 ...33 C3
Beaufoy Wlk
SE11 ...116 B2 260 D3
Beaulieu Ave 1 E16 ...121 B5
Forest Hill SE26 ...184 B6
Beaulieu Cl NW9 ...45 C5
SE5 ...139 B2
Hounslow TW4 ...151 B6
Mitcham CR4 ...181 A2
13 Twickenham TW1 ...153 D5
Beaulieu Ct W5 ...88 A2
Beaulieu Dr HA5 ...40 D2
Beaulieu Gdns N21 ...17 A4
Beaulieu Ho NW4 ...28 D1
Beaulieu Pl W4 ...111 A3
Beaumanor Gdns SE9 ...188 C6
Beaumanor Mans W2 ...245 D6
Beaumaris 4 N11 ...32 A4
Beaumaris Dr IG8 ...37 D3
Beaumaris Gn NW9 ...45 C3
Beaumaris Twr 2 W3 ...110 D4
Beaumont W14 ...254 D3
Putney SW15 ...157 A6
Beaumont Ave
W14 ...113 B1 254 C2
Harrow HA2 ...41 D3
Richmond TW9 ...132 B2
Wembley HA0 ...65 C4
Beaumont Bldgs WC2 ...240 B1
Beaumont Cl KT2 ...176 C3
Beaumont Cres
W14 ...113 B1 254 C1
Beaumont Ct E5 ...74 B5
16 NW9 ...27 D1
10 W4 ...111 A1
6 Mitcham CR4 ...181 A1
Wembley HA0 ...65 C3
16 Wimbledon SW19 ...178 D3
Beaumont Dr TW15 ...171 B5
Beaumont Gdns NW3 ...69 C5
Beaumont Gr E1 ...96 D3
Beaumont Ho 11 E10 ...53 D2
1 Streatham SW2 ...160 A3
Wimbledon SW19 ...157 C1
Beaumont Pl
NW1,WC1,W1 ...93 C3 239 B6
Barnet EN5 ...1 B4
Isleworth TW7 ...152 D6
Beaumont Rd E10 ...53 D2
E13 ...99 B4
W4 ...111 A3
Orpington BR5,BR6 ...211 B3
Putney SW15,SW19 ...157 A4
South Norwood SE19 ...183 A4
Beaumont Rise N19 ...49 D1
Beaumont Sch The E10 ...53 D1
Beaumont Sq E1 ...96 D2
Beaumont St W1 ...238 B4
Beaumont Terr 1 SE13 ...164 C4
Beaumont Wlk NW3 ...70 D1
Beauvais Terr UB5 ...84 D4
Beauvale 6 NW1 ...71 A1
Beauval Rd SE22 ...161 D5
Beaverbank Rd DA15,
SE9 ...167 B3
Beaver Cl
Hampton TW12 ...173 D2
9 Penge SE20 ...184 A3
Beaver Gr UB5 ...85 A4
Beavers Comm Prim Sch
TW4 ...128 C2
Beavers Cres TW4 ...128 D1
Beavers La TW4 ...128 C2
Beavers Lo DA14 ...189 D5
Beaverwood Rd BR7 ...189 C4
Beaverwood Sch for Girls
BR7 ...189 C4
Beavis Ho N16 ...73 C5
Beavor La W6 ...112 A1
Bebbington Rd SE18 ...123 C2
Beblets Cl 4 BR6 ...227 D3
Bec Cl HA4 ...62 D5
Beccles Dr IG11 ...79 D2
Beccles St E14 ...119 B6
Bechervaise Ct 2 E10 ...53 D1
Beck Cl SE13 ...141 D4
Beck Ct BR3 ...206 D6
Beckenham Bsns Ctr
BR3 ...185 A4
Beckenham Ct BR3 ...185 C2
Beckenham Gdns N9 ...17 C1
Beckenham Gr BR2 ...186 B1
Beckenham Hill Rd BR3,
SE6 ...186 A5
Beckenham Hill Sta
SE6 ...186 A5
Beckenham Hospl BR3 ...185 B1
Beckenham Junction Sta
BR3 ...185 C2
Beckenham La BR1,BR2 ...186 D1
Beckenham Place Pk
BR3 ...185 D3
Beckenham Rd
Penge BR3 ...185 A2
West Wickham BR3,BR4 ...208 A2
Beckenham Rd Sta BR3 ...185 A2
Beckers The N16 ...74 A4
Becket Ave E6 ...100 C4
Becket Cl Croydon SE25 ...206 A3
2 Merton SW19 ...179 D2
Becket Fold HA1 ...42 D4
Becket Ho SE1 ...252 C1
Becket Rd N18 ...34 C6
Becket St SE1 ...262 C6
Beckett Cl DA17 ...125 B3
NW10 ...67 C2
Streatham SW16 ...159 D2
Beckett Ho 12 E1 ...96 C2
28 SW9 ...138 A3
Becketts Cl
Feltham TW14 ...150 B5
Orpington BR6 ...227 D5
Becketts Pl KT1 ...175 D2
Beckett Wlk BR3 ...185 A4
Beckfoot NW1 ...232 B3
Beckford Cl W14 ...254 D3
Beckford Dr BR5,BR6 ...211 B2
Beckford Ho 18 N16 ...73 C3
Beckford Prim Sch NW6 ...69 B3
Beckford Rd CR0 ...205 D3
Beckham Ho SE11 ...260 D3
Beck Ho N16 ...73 C5
4 Edmonton N18 ...34 A5
Beckington 18 NW5 ...71 A2
Beck La BR3 ...206 D6
Beckley Ho E3 ...97 B3
Becklow Mews 7 W12 ...112 A4
Becklow Rd W12 ...112 A4
Beckmead Sch BR3 ...207 C1
Beck Rd E8 ...96 B6
Beck River Pk 8 BR3 ...185 C2
Becks Rd DA14 ...168 A1
Beckton Alps E6 ...100 C3
Beckton Alps Ski Ctr
E6 ...100 C3
Beckton Park Sta E16 ...122 B6
Beckton Rd E16 ...98 D2
Beckton Sta E6 ...100 C2
Beckton Triangle Ret Pk
E6 ...100 D3
Beck Way BR3 ...207 B6
Beckway Rd SW16 ...181 D1
Beckway St
SE17 ...117 C2 263 A3
Beckwith Ho 22 E2 ...96 B5
Beckwith Rd SE24 ...161 B6
Beclands Rd SW17 ...181 A4
Becmead Ave Harrow HA3 ...43 B4
Streatham SW16 ...181 D6
Becondale Rd SE19 ...183 C5
Becontree Ave RM8 ...80 C5
Becontree Day RM8 ...81 A6
Becontree Prim Sch
RM8 ...80 B5
Becontree Sta RM9 ...80 D2
Bective Pl SW15 ...135 B1
Bective Rd E7 ...77 A4
Putney SW15 ...135 B1
Becton Pl Erith DA7,DA8 ...147 D5
Erith DA8 ...147 D5
Bedale Rd EN2 ...5 A5
Bedale St SE1 ...252 C3
Beddington Cross CR0 ...204 A2
Beddington Farm Rd
CR0 ...204 A1
Beddington Gdns SM5,
SM6 ...219 A2
Beddington Gn BR5 ...189 D2
Beddington Gr SM6 ...219 D3
Beddington Inf Sch
SM6 ...219 C4
Beddington La
Wallington CR0 ...220 A6
Wallington CR0 ...203 D2
Beddington Lane Sta
CR0 ...203 C3
Beddington Manor SM2 ...218 B2
Beddington Park Cotts
SM6 ...219 D5
Beddington Park Prim Sch
CR0 ...219 D5
Beddington Rd BR5 ...189 D2
Ilford IG3 ...57 D2
Beddington Terr CR0 ...204 B2
Bede Cl HA5 ...22 D2
Bedefield WC1 ...233 B1
Bede Ho SE14 ...141 B4
5 Putney SW15 ...156 D5
Bedelsford Sch KT1 ...198 A6
Bedens Rd DA14 ...191 A5
Bede Rd RM6 ...58 C3
Bedfont Cl
East Bedfont TW14 ...149 A5
Mitcham CR4 ...181 A1
Bedfont Green Cl TW14 ...149 A3
Bedfont Ind Pk N TW15 ...149 A1
Bedfont Jun Sch TW14 ...149 C5
Bedfont La TW14,TW13 ...149 D4
Bedfont Lakes Ctry Pk
TW14 ...149 A2
Bedfont Rd
East Bedfont TW13,TW14 ...149 B2
Stanwell TW19 ...148 B5
Bedford Ave
WC1 ...93 D2 239 D3
Barnet EN5 ...13 B6
Hayes UB4 ...84 B1
Bedfordbury
WC2 ...116 A6 250 A5
Bedford Cl N10 ...31 A3
Chiswick W4 ...133 D6
Bedford Cnr 3 W4 ...111 C2
Bedford Court Mans
WC1 ...239 D3
Bedford Ct WC2 ...250 A5
6 Richmond TW9 ...132 B1
South Norwood SE19 ...183 D2
Wembley HA0 ...65 D4
Bedford Gardens Ho
W8 ...245 B3
Bedford Gdns
W8 ...113 C5 245 B3
Bedford Hill SW12 ...159 B2
Bedford Ho 7 SW4 ...138 A1
2 W4 ...111 C2
Bedford Park Cnr 5
W4 ...111 C2
Bedford Park Mans W4 ...111 B2
Bedford Pas SW6 ...264 B4
Bedford Pk CR0 ...205 A1
Bedford Pl WC1 ...94 A2 240 A4
Croydon CR0 ...205 B1
Bedford Rd E17 ...53 C6
N15 ...51 C5
N2 ...48 C6
N8 ...49 D3
NW7 ...11 C1
SW2,SW4 ...138 A1
W4 ...111 C3
Barking E6 ...100 C6
Ealing W13 ...109 B6
Edmonton N9 ...18 B4
Harrow HA1 ...42 A3
Ilford IG1 ...78 D5
North Cheam KT4 ...216 C6
Ruislip HA4 ...61 D4
Sidcup DA15 ...167 C1
Twickenham TW2 ...152 B1
Woodford E18 ...37 A1
Wood Green N22 ...32 A1
Bedford Row
WC1 ...94 B2 240 D3
Bedford Sq WC1 ...93 D2 239 D3
Bedford St WC2 ...116 A6 250 B5
Bedford Terr SM2 ...218 A2
Bedford Way
WC1 ...93 D3 239 D5
Bedgebury Gdns SW19 ...157 A2
Bedgebury Rd SE9 ...143 D1
Bedivere Rd BR1 ...165 A1
Bedlow Cl NW8 ...236 D4
Bedlow Way CR0 ...220 B4
Bedonwell Inf Sch SE2 ...147 A6
Bedonwell Jun Sch
DA17 ...147 A6
Bedonwell Rd
Bexley DA7,DA17 ...147 A6
Erith DA7 ...147 C5
Bedser Cl SE11 ...270 D6
South Norwood CR7 ...205 A6
Bedser Ct 7 SW4 ...138 A3
Bedser Dr UB6 ...64 B3
Bedster Gdns KT8 ...195 D6
Bedwardine Rd SE19 ...183 C3
Bedwell Ct 4 RM6 ...58 D2
Bedwell Gdns UB3 ...105 C2
Bedwell Ho 19 SW9 ...138 C3
Bedwell Rd
Belvedere DA17 ...125 C1
Tottenham N17 ...33 C2
Beeby Rd E16 ...99 B2
Beech Ave N20 ...14 C3
W3 ...111 C5
Brentford TW8 ...131 B5
Chigwell IG9 ...21 B2
Ruislip HA4 ...40 B1
Sidcup DA15 ...168 A4
Beech Cl SE8 ...141 B6
Ashford TW15 ...171 B5
Carshalton SM5 ...218 D6
Enfield N9 ...18 B5
Putney SW15 ...156 A4
Sunbury TW16 ...172 D1
West Drayton UB7 ...104 C3
Wimbledon SW19 ...178 C4
Beech Copse BR1 ...188 B1
South Croydon CR2 ...221 C3
Beechcroft BR7 ...188 C3
3 Kingston KT2 ...176 D2
Beechcroft Ave NW11 ...47 B2
Harrow HA2 ...41 C2
Kingston KT1,KT3 ...177 A1
Beechcroft Cl BR6 ...227 B4
Heston TW5 ...129 A5
Streatham SW16 ...182 B5
Beechcroft Ct 6 N12 ...29 D6
3 NW11 ...47 B2
Beech Croft Ct N5 ...72 D4
Beechcroft Gdns HA9 ...66 B5
Beechcroft Ho W5 ...88 A3
Beechcroft Lo 6 SM2 ...218 A1
Beechcroft Mans SW16 ...182 B5
Beechcroft Rd BR6 ...227 B4
Chessington KT9 ...214 B5
Mortlake SW14 ...133 A2
Upper Tooting SW17 ...158 C2
Woodford E18 ...37 B1
Beechcroft Way N19 ...49 D1
Beech Ct E17 ...54 B6
NW2 ...69 B6
W1 ...237 C2
43 W2 ...91 C2
Beckenham BR3 ...185 B3
3 Buckhurst Hill IG9 ...21 D2
Hayes UB3 ...105 D5
6 Ilford E12 ...78 C5
Northolt UB5 ...85 A6
Surbiton KT6 ...198 A2
Teddington TW11 ...175 C4
4 West Norwood SW16 ...182 C5
Beechdale N21 ...16 B2
Beechdale Rd SW2 ...160 B5
Beech Dell BR2,BR6 ...226 B4
Beechdene 4 SE15 ...140 B4
Beech Dr N2 ...48 D6
Beechen Cliff Way TW7 ...130 D3
Beechen Gr HA5 ...41 B6
Beechen Pl SE23 ...162 C2
Beeches Ave The SM5 ...218 C1
Beeches Cl SE20 ...184 C2
Beeches Ct BR1 ...187 A4
Beeches Rd Cheam SM3 ...201 A1
Upper Tooting SW17 ...158 D1
Beeches The E12 ...78 B1
1 N19 ...50 A1
N20 ...14 C2
Hounslow TW3 ...129 D4
Mitcham CR4 ...202 C4
Beechey Ho 30 E1 ...118 B5
Beech Farm Cotts IG8 ...36 B6
Beechfield Cotts 3
BR1 ...187 C1
Beechfield Ct 7 CR2 ...221 A4
Beechfield Rd BR1 ...187 C1
N4 ...51 A3
Forest Hill SE6 ...163 B3
Beech Gdns W5 ...110 A3
Dagenham RM10 ...81 D1
Beech Gr Kingston KT3 ...199 B6
Mitcham CR4 ...203 D5
Beech Hall Cres E4 ...36 B3
Beech Hall Rd E4 ...36 B3
Beech Hill EN4 ...2 C5
Beech Hill Ave EN4 ...2 B4
Beechhill Rd SE9 ...166 C6
Beech Ho 7 DA15 ...168 A1
5 N16 ...73 B6
6 NW3 ...70 D2
16 SE16 ...118 C4
Hayes UB4 ...84 D2
Heston TW5 ...129 A5
New Addington CR0 ...223 D2
Beech House Rd CR0 ...221 B5
Beech La IG9 ...21 B2
Beech Lawns N12 ...30 B5
Beechmont Cl BR1 ...186 C5
Beechmore Gdns SM3 ...216 D6
Beechmore Rd
SW11 ...136 D4 267 D1
Beechmount Ave W7 ...86 C2
Beecholme 13 N12 ...29 D6
Beecholme Ave CR4 ...181 B2
Beecholme Est E5 ...74 B5
Beecholme Prim Sch
CR4 ...181 B2
Beech Rd Bowes Park N11 ...32 A4
East Bedfont TW14 ...149 C4
Thornton Heath SW16 ...204 B6
Beechrow KT2 ...176 A6
Beech St EC2 ...95 A2 242 B4
Beech Tree Cl N1 ...72 C1
Stanmore HA7 ...25 C5
Beech Tree Glade E4 ...20 D3
Beech Tree Pl SM1 ...217 D3
Beechvale Cl N12 ...30 C5
Beechway DA5 ...168 D5
Beech Way NW10 ...67 B1
Twickenham TW2 ...151 C1
Beech Wlk NW7 ...27 C4
Beechwood Ave N3 ...47 C6
Ashford TW16 ...172 A4
Greenford UB6 ...85 D4
Harrow HA2 ...63 D5
Hayes UB3 ...105 B6
Hillingdon UB8 ...82 C1
Orpington BR6 ...227 C2
Richmond TW9 ...132 C4
Ruislip HA4 ...61 D6
Thornton Heath CR7 ...204 D5
Beechwood Circ HA2 ...63 D5
Beechwood Cl N2 ...48 D5
NW7 ...27 C5
Surbiton KT6 ...197 D2
Beechwood Cres DA7 ...147 A2
Beechwood Ct N16 ...51 C2
Carshalton SM5 ...218 D4
Chiswick W4 ...133 B6
Sutton SM1 ...217 C3
Beechwood Dr
Keston BR2 ...225 D4
Woodford IG8 ...36 D5
Beechwood Gdns
Ealing NW10 ...88 B4
Harrow HA2 ...63 D5
Ilford IG5 ...56 C5
Beechwood Gr W3 ...111 C6
Beechwood Hall N3 ...47 B6
Beechwood Ho 22 E2 ...96 A5
Beechwood Mews 2 N9 ...18 A2
Beechwood Pk E18 ...55 A6
Beechwood Rd E8 ...73 D2
N8 ...50 A5
South Croydon CR2 ...221 C1
Beechwood Rise BR7 ...188 D6
Beechwoods Ct SE19 ...183 D5
Beechworth Cl NW3 ...69 C6
Beecroft Rd SE4 ...163 A6
Beehive Cl E8 ...73 D1
Elstree WD6 ...9 D5
Hillingdon UB10 ...60 B1
Beehive Ct IG1 ...56 B3
Beehive La IG1 ...56 B3
Beehive Pl SW9 ...138 C2
Beehive Prep Sch IG4 ...56 B4
Beeken Dene BR6 ...227 A4
Beeleigh Rd SM4 ...201 D5
Beeston Cl 5 E8 ...74 A3
South Oxhey WD19 ...22 D6
Beeston Pl SW1 ...258 D6
Beeston Rd EN4 ...14 B5
Beeston's Ho SE15 ...140 B2
Beeston Way TW14 ...150 C5
Beethoven Rd WD6 ...9 D5
Beethoven St W10 ...91 A4
Beeton Cl HA5 ...23 C3
Begbie Ho SW9 ...138 B3
Begbie Rd SE3 ...143 C4
Beggars Hill KT17 ...215 D2
Beggar's Roost La SM1,
SM2 ...217 C2
Begonia Cl E6 ...100 B3
Begonia Pl 1 TW12 ...173 C4
Begonia Wlk W12 ...89 D1
Beira St SW12 ...159 B4
Beis Rachel D'Satmar Girls
Sch N16 ...51 C2
Beis Yaakov Prim Sch
NW9 ...45 B6
Bekesbourne St 19 E14 ...97 A1
Belcroft Cl BR1 ...186 D3
Beldanes Lo NW10 ...68 A1
Beldham Gdns KT8 ...195 D6
Belenoyd Ct SW16 ...160 B1
Belfairs Dr RM6 ...58 C2
Belfairs Gn WD19 ...22 D5
Belfast Rd N16 ...73 D6
Croydon SE25 ...206 B5
Belfield Rd KT19 ...215 C1
Belfont Wlk N7 ...72 A4
Belford Gr SE18 ...122 C2
Belford Ho 7 E8 ...95 D6
Belfort Rd SE15 ...140 C3
Belfry Cl 33 SE16 ...118 B1
Belgrade Ho N16 ...73 C4
Belgrade Rd N16 ...73 C4
Hampton TW12 ...173 D2
Belgrave Cl NW7 ...27 B5
1 Acton W3 ...111 A4
Southgate N14 ...15 C6
Belgrave Cres TW16 ...172 B2
Belgrave Ct E13 ...99 C3
SE3 ...143 C5
SW8 ...269 A3
8 W4 ...111 A1
Belgrave Gdns NW8 ...91 D6
Southgate N14 ...3 D1
1 Stanmore HA7 ...25 C5
Belgrave Mans NW8 ...229 A5
Belgrave Mews N SW1 ...248 A1
Belgrave Mews S
SW1 ...115 A3 258 B6
Belgrave Mews W SW1 ...258 A6
Belgrave Pl
SW1 ...115 A3 258 B5
Belgrave Rd E10 ...54 A1
E13 ...99 C3
E17 ...53 C3
SW1 ...115 C2 259 A3
Barnes SW13 ...133 D5
Hounslow TW4 ...129 B2
Mitcham CR4 ...202 B6
Redbridge IG1 ...56 B1
South Norwood SE25 ...205 D5
Sunbury TW16 ...172 B2
Wanstead E11 ...55 A1
Belgrave Sq
SW1 ...115 A3 258 A6
Belgrave St E1 ...96 D1
Belgrave Terr IG8 ...21 A1
Belgrave Wlk CR4 ...202 B6
Belgrave Wlk Sta CR4 ...202 B5
Belgrave Yd SW1 ...258 C5
Belgravia Cl EN5 ...1 B2
Belgravia Ct SW1 ...258 C5
Belgravia Gdns BR1 ...186 C4
Belgravia Ho 11 SW4 ...159 D5
Teddington TW11 ...175 C3
Belgravia Mews KT1 ...197 D5
Belgrove St WC1 ...233 B2
Belham Wlk 13 SE5 ...139 B4
Belinda Rd 8 SW9 ...138 D2
Belitha Villas N1 ...72 C1
Bel La TW13 ...151 B1
Bellamy Cl 7 E14 ...119 C4
HA8 ...11 A1
SW5 ...254 D1
Uxbridge UB10 ...60 C5
Bellamy Ct HA7 ...25 B2
Bellamy Dr HA7 ...25 B2
Bellamy Ho Harrow HA3 ...44 A2
Heston TW5 ...129 C6
Upper Tooting SW17 ...180 B6
Bellamy Rd Chingford E4 ...35 D4
Enfield EN2 ...5 B3
Bellamy's Ct 16 SE16 ...118 D5

Bellamy St SW12 159 B4
Bellasis Ave SW2 160 A2
Bell Ave UB7 104 B3
Bell Cl Pinner HA5 40 C6
Ruislip HA4 61 D5
Bellclose Rd UB7 104 A4
Bell Ct NW4 46 C5
Tolworth KT5 214 D6
Bell Dr SW18 157 A4
Bellefields Rd SW9 138 B2
Bellegrove Cl DA16 145 D3
Bellegrove Par DA16 145 D2
Bellegrove Rd DA16 145 D3
Bellenden Rd SE15 139 D3
Bellenden Rd Ret Pk
SE15 140 A4
Bellenden Sch SE15 140 A3
Bellenden Road Bsns Ctr
SE15 139 D3
Bellerbys Coll SW15 156 A5
Bellermine Cl SE28 123 D4
Belle Staines Pleasaunce
E4 19 C2
Belleville Prim Sch
SW11 158 D6
Belleville Rd SW11 158 D6
Belle Vue UB6 86 B6
Belle Vue Gdns SW9 138 A3
Belle Vue La WD23 8 B3
Bellevue Pk CR7 205 A5
Bellevue Pl E1 96 C3
Bellevue Rd DA6 169 B6
N11 31 A5
Barnes SW13 134 A3
Ealing W13 87 B3
Kingston KT1 198 A6
Upper Tooting SW17 158 D3
Belle Vue Rd E17 36 B1
Bellew St SW17 158 A1
Bellfield CR0 223 B1
Bellfield Ave HA3 24 B4
Bellflower Cl 2 E6 100 A2
Bellgate Mews NW5 71 B5
Bell Gn SE26 185 B6
Bell Green La SE26 185 B6
Bellhill 6 CR0 221 A6
Bell Ho SE10 142 A6
SE2 124 D1
6 Dagenham RM10 81 D2
15 Streatham SW2 160 C4
Bellina Mews NW5 71 C4
Bell Ind Est 2 W4 111 A2
Bellingham 10 N17 34 B3
Bellingham Ct IG11 102 B4
Bellingham Gn SE6 163 C1
Bellingham Rd SE6 164 A1
Bellingham Sta SE6 163 D1
Bellingham Trad Est
SE6 163 D2
Bell Inn Yd EC3 242 D1
Bell La E1 95 D2 243 C3
E16 121 A5
NW4 46 D5
Enfield EN3 6 D5
Twickenham TW1 153 A3
Wembley HA9 65 D6
Bell Lane Prim Sch NW4 46 D5
Bellmaker Ct 19 E3 97 C2
Bell Mdw SE19 183 C6
Bell Moor NW3 70 A5
Bellmore Ct 5 CR0 205 D1
Bello Cl SE24,SW2 160 D3
Bellot Gdns 1 SE10 120 C1
Bellot St SE10 120 C1
Bell Rd East Molesey KT8 196 B4
Enfield EN1 5 B4
Hounslow TW3 129 D1
Bellring Cl DA17 147 C6
Bells Hill EN5 12 D6
Bell St NW1 92 C2 237 A4
SE18 144 A4
Bell The E17 53 C6
Belltrees Gr 1 SW16 182 B5
Bell View BR3 185 B3
Bell View Manor HA4 39 C2
Bellview Mews N11 31 A5
Bell Water Gate SE18 122 C3
Bell Wharf La EC4 252 B6
Bellwood Rd SE15 140 D1
Bell Yd WC2 94 C1 241 A1
Belmont Ave DA16 145 C2
N17 51 A6
Bowes Park N13 32 B5
Cockfosters EN4 14 D6
Edmonton N9 18 A3
Southall UB2 107 A3
Wembley HA0 88 B6
West Barnes KT3 200 A5
Belmont Circ HA3 25 B2
Belmont Cl N20 13 D3
SW4 137 C2
Chingford E4 36 B5
Cockfosters EN4 2 D1
Uxbridge UB8 60 A2
Woodford IG8 37 B6
Belmont Ct 6 N16 51 C1
N5 73 A4
NW11 47 B4
Belmont Gr SE13 142 B2
W4 111 B2
Belmont Hall Ct SE13 142 B2
Belmont Hill SE13 142 B2
Belmont Jun & Inf Schs
N22 51 A6
Belmont La
Chislehurst BR7 189 A5
Stanmore HA7 25 C3
Belmont Lo Harrow HA3 24 B3
Stanmore HA7 25 C6
Belmont Mews SW19 156 D2
Belmont Mid Sch HA3 24 D1
Belmont Mill Hill Jun Sch
NW7 12 A1
Belmont Par 2 NW11 47 B4
Chislehurst BR7 189 A5
Belmont Park Cl SE13 142 C1
Belmont Park Rd E10 53 D3
Belmont Pk SE13 142 C1
Belmont Prim Sch W4 111 B2
Erith DA7 147 C5
Belmont Rd N15,N17 51 A5
SW4 137 C2
W4 111 B2
Beckenham BR3 185 B1
Chislehurst BR7 188 D5
Croydon SE25 206 B4
Erith DA8 147 D4
Harrow HA3 43 A6
Ilford IG1 79 A5
Twickenham TW2 152 B2
Uxbridge UB8 60 A2
Wallington SM6 219 C3
Belmont Rise SM1,SM2 217 B1
Belmont St NW1 71 A1
Belmont Terr W4 111 B2
Belmor WD6 10 C5
Belmore Ave UB4 84 A1
Belmore Ho N7 71 D3
Belmore Prim Sch UB4 84 B4
Belmore St
SW8 137 D4 269 C2
Beloe Cl SW15 134 A1
Belsham St E9 74 C2
Belsize Ave NW3 70 C3
W13 109 B3
Bowes Park N13 32 B4
Belsize Court Garages 1
NW3 70 B3
Belsize Cres NW3 70 B2
Belsize Ct NW3 70 B3
Belsize Gdns SM1 217 D4
Belsize Gr NW3 70 C2
Belsize La NW3 70 B3
Belsize Mews NW3 70 B2
Belsize Park Gdns NW3 70 C2
Belsize Park Mews 1
NW3 70 B2
Belsize Park Sta NW3 70 C3
Belsize Pk NW3 70 B2
Belsize Pl NW3 70 B3
Belsize Rd NW6 91 D6
NW8 229 A6
Harrow HA3 24 B3
Belsize Sq NW3 70 B2
Belsize Terr NW3 70 B2
Belson Rd SE18 122 B2
Beltane Dr SW19 156 D1
Belthorn Cres SW12 159 C4
Belton Rd E11 76 C4
E7 77 B1
N17 51 C6
NW2 68 A2
Sidcup DA14 190 A6
Belton Way E3 97 C2
Beltran Rd SW6 135 D3
Belvedere Ave SW19 179 A5
Belvedere Bldgs SE1 251 D1
Belvedere Cl TW11 174 C5
Belvedere Ct DA17 125 B3
N2 48 B4
NW2 68 D2
7 SW4 159 D5
8 Kingston KT2 176 C3
Putney SW15 134 C1
Belvedere Dr SW19 179 A5
Belvedere Gdns KT8 195 C4
Belvedere Gr SW19 179 A5
Belvedere Heights NW8 237 A6
Belvedere Ho TW14 150 A3
Belvedere Jun & Inf Sch
DA17 125 D3
Belvedere Mews SE15 140 C2
SE3 143 B5
Belvedere Pl SE1 251 D1
18 SW2 138 B1
Belvedere Rd
SE1 116 B4 250 D3
W7 108 D3
Bexley DA7 147 B3
Erith SE28 124 D5
Penge SE19 183 D3
Walthamstow E10 53 A1
Belvedere Sq SW19 179 A5
Belvedere Sta DA17 125 D3
Belvedere Strand NW9 27 D1
Belvedere The SW10 266 B1
Belvedere Way HA3 44 A3
Belvoir Cl SE9 166 A1
Belvoir Lo SE22 162 A4
Belvoir Rd SE22 162 A4
Belvue Bsns Ctr UB5 63 D1
Belvue Cl UB5 63 C1
Belvue Rd UB5 63 C1
Belvue Sch UB5 85 C6
Bembridge Cl NW6 69 A1
Bembridge Gdns HA4 61 B6
Bembridge Ho 8 SE8 119 B2
Wandsworth SW18 157 D5
Bemersyde Point 6 E13 99 B4
Bemerton St N1 94 B6 233 C6
Bemish Rd SW15 134 D2
Bempton Dr HA4 62 B5
Bemsted Rd E17 53 B6
Benabo Ct 6 E8 74 A3
Benares Rd SE18,SE2 123 D2
Benbow Ct W6 112 B3
Benbow Ho 12 SE8 141 C6
Benbow Rd W6 112 B3
Benbow St SE8 141 C6
Benbury Cl BR1 186 A5
Bence Ho 13 SE8 119 A2
Bench Field CR2 221 D3
Bencroft Rd SW16 181 C3
Bencurtis Pk BR4 224 B6
Bendall Mews NW1 237 B4
Bendemeer Rd SW15 134 D2
Benden Ho SE13 164 A6
Bendish Rd E6 78 A1
Bendmore Ave SE2 124 A2
Bendon Valley SW18 157 D4
Benedict Cl BR6 227 C5
9 Erith DA17 125 A3
Benedict Ct RM9 59 B3
Benedict Dr TW14 149 B4
Benedict Fst Sch CR4 202 B6
Benedict Prim Sch CR4 202 B6
Benedict Rd SW9 138 B2
Mitcham CR4 202 B6
Benedict Way N2 48 A6
Benedict Wharf CR4 202 C6
Benenden Gn BR2 209 A4
Benenden Ho SE17 263 B2
Benett Gdns SW16 182 A1
Ben Ezra Ct SE17 262 B3
Benfleet Cl SM1 218 A5
Benfleet Ct 6 E8 95 D6
Benfleet Way N11 15 A2
Bengal Ct EC3 242 D1
Bengal Ho E1 96 D2
Bengal Rd IG1 78 D5
Bengarth Dr HA3 24 B1
Bengarth Rd UB5 85 A6
Bengeo Gdns RM6 58 C3
Bengeworth Rd SE5 139 A2
Harrow HA1 65 A5
Ben Hale Cl HA7 25 B5
Benham Cl 1 SW11 136 B2
Chessington KT9 213 C2
Benham Gdns TW3,TW4 151 B6
Benham Rd W7 86 C2
Benham's Pl 8 NW3 70 A4
Benhill Ave SM1 218 A4
Benhill Rd SE5 139 B4
Sutton SM1 218 B4
Benhill Wood Rd SM1 218 A4
Benhilton Gdns SM1 217 D5
Benhurst Ct Ealing W5 110 A6
12 Penge SE20 184 B2
West Norwood SW16 182 C5
Benhurst La SW16 182 C5
Benin St SE13 164 B4
Benjafield Cl N18 34 B6
Benjamin Cl E8 96 A6
Benjamin Ct
4 Ealing W7 108 C5
4 Erith DA17 147 B6
Littleton TW15 171 A3
Benjamin St EC1 241 C4
Ben Jonson Ct 30 N1 95 C5
Ben Jonson Prim Sch E1 97 A3
Ben Jonson Rd E1 97 A2
Benledi St E14 98 B1
Bennelong Cl W12 90 B1
Bennerley Rd SW11 158 D6
Bennetsfield Rd UB11 104 D5
Bennet's Hill EC4 251 D6
Bennets Lo EN2 5 A2
Bennett Cl DA16 146 A3
Teddington KT1 175 C2
Bennett Ct N7 72 B5
NW6 69 D2
7 W3 110 D4
Bennett Gr SE13 141 D4
Bennett Ho SW1 259 D4
2 Streatham SW4 159 D4
Bennett Pk SE3 142 D2
Bennett Rd E13 99 C3
Dagenham RM6 59 A2
Bennetts Ave
Croydon CR0 223 A6
Greenford UB6 86 C6
Bennett's Castle La RM8 80 D5
Bennetts Cl
Mitcham CR4,SW16 181 B2
Tottenham N17 33 D4
Bennetts Copse BR7 188 A4
Bennett St SW1 249 A4
W4 111 C1
Bennetts Way CR0 223 B6
Bennett's Yd SW1 259 D5
Benn Ho 7 SE7 121 C1
Benningholme Rd HA8 27 C4
Bennington Rd
Chingford IG8 36 C3
Tottenham N17 33 C2
Benn St E9 75 A2
Benns Wlk 8 TW9 132 A1
Bensbury Cl SW15 156 C4
Bensham Cl CR7 205 A5
Bensham Gr CR7 183 A1
Bensham La CR0,CR7 204 D3
Bensham Manor Rd
CR7 205 A5
Bensham Manor Sch
CR7 205 A4
Bensington Ct TW14 149 B5
Bensley Cl 7 N11 30 D5
Ben Smith Way 21 SE16 118 A3
Benson Ave E13,E6 99 D5
Benson Cl Hillingdon UB8 82 A2
Hounslow TW3 129 C1
Benson Ct 1 N19 71 C4
SW8 270 A2
Holdbrook EN3 7 C5
Benson Ho E2 243 C6
SE1 251 B3
Benson Prim sch CR0 223 A5
Benson Quay E1 118 C6
Benson Rd Croydon CR0 220 C5
Forest Hill SE23 162 C3
Bentall Sh Ctr The 10
KT2 176 A1
Bentfield Gdns SE9 165 D1
Benthal Ct N16 74 A5
Benthal Prim Sch N16 74 A5
Benthal Rd N16 74 A5
Bentham Ct 10 N1 73 A1
Bentham Ho SE1 262 C6
Bentham Rd E9 74 D2
Woolwich SE28 124 B5
Bentham Wlk NW10 67 A3
Ben Tillet Cl Barking IG11 80 A1
Newham E16 122 B5
Ben Tillet Ho N15 50 D6
Bentinck Cl NW8 230 B3
Bentinck Ho 4 W12 112 B6
Bentinck Mans W1 238 B2
Bentinck Mews W1 238 B2
Bentinck Rd UB7 104 A5
Bentinck St W1 93 A1 238 B2
Bentley Cl SW19 157 C1
Bentley Dr IG2 57 A3
Bentley Ho 4 SE5 139 C4
6 Bow E3 97 C3
Bentley Lo WD23 8 C2
Bentley Mews EN1 17 B5
Bentley Rd N1 73 C2
Bentley Way
Stanmore HA7 25 A5
Woodford IG8 21 A1
Bentley Wood High Sch
HA7 24 D5
Benton Rd Ilford IG1,IG2 57 B1
South Oxhey WD19 22 D5
Benton's La SE27 183 A6
Benton's Rise SE27 183 B5
Bentry Cl RM8 81 A6
Bentry Rd RM8 81 B6
Bentworth Ct 1 E2 96 A3
Bentworth Prim Sch
W12 90 B1
Bentworth Rd W12 90 B1
Benville Ho SW8 270 D3
Benwell Ct TW16 172 A2
Benwell Rd N7 72 C3
Benwick Cl SE16 118 B2
Benwick Ct SE20 184 C2
Benwood Ct SM1 218 A5
Benworth St E3 97 B4
Benyon Ho EC1 234 B2
Benyon Rd N1 95 B6 235 D6
Beormund Prim Sch
SE1 117 B4 252 D1
Bequerel Ct SE10 120 D3
Berberis Ct IG1 78 D2
Berberis Ho 15 E3 97 C2
Berberis Wlk UB7 104 A2
Berber Pl 15 E14 119 C6
Berber Rd SW11 158 D6
Berberry Cl HA8 27 A6
Bercta Rd SE9 167 A2
Berebinder Ho 17 E3 97 B5
Berenger Twr SW10 266 C4
Berenger Wlk SW10 266 C4
Berens Ct DA14 189 D6
Berens Rd NW10 90 D4
Berens Way BR5,BR7 211 D6
Beresford Ave N20 14 D2
Ealing W7 86 C2
Tolworth KT5 199 A2
Twickenham TW1 153 C5
Wembley HA0 88 C6
Beresford Ct E9 75 A3
11 Twickenham TW1 153 C5
Beresford Dr BR1 210 A6
Woodford IG8 37 C6
Beresford Gdns
Dagenham RM6 59 A4
Enfield EN1 5 C1
Hounslow TW4 151 B6
Beresford Ho 14 SW4 138 A1
Dulwich SE21 161 C1
Beresford Lo N4 73 B3
Beresford Rd N2 48 C6
N5 73 B3
N8 50 D4
Belmont SM2 217 B1
Chingford, Chingford Green
E4 20 C3
Chingford, Highams Park
E17 35 D2
Harrow HA1 42 B4
Kingston KT2 176 B2
New Malden KT3 199 A5
Southall UB1 106 D5
Beresford Sq 1 SE18 122 D2
Beresford St SE18 122 D3
Beresford Terr 3 N5 73 A3
Bere St E1 118 D6
Berestede Rd 4 W6 111 D1
Bergen Ho 1 SE5 139 A3
Bergen Sq SE16 119 A3
Berger Cl BR5 211 C3
Berger Prim Sch E9 74 D2
Berger Rd E9 74 D2
Berghem Mews W14 112 D3
Bergholt Ave IG4 56 A4
Bergholt Cres N16 51 C2
Bergholt Mews 4 NW1 71 D1
Berglen Ct E14 97 A1
Bering Sq E14 119 C1
Bering Wlk E16 99 D1
Berisford Mews SW18 158 A5
Berkeley Ave DA16 146 D4
Cranford TW4 128 A3
Northolt UB6 64 C2
Berkeley Cl
Borehamwood WD6 10 C6
Kingston KT2 176 A3
Orpington BR5,BR6 211 C2
Berkeley Cl *continued*
Ruislip HA4 62 A5
Berkeley Cres EN4 14 B6
Berkeley Ct N3 29 D2
NW1 237 D5
1 NW11 47 B2
Ealing W5 109 C6
Edgware HA8 26 D5
16 Streatham SW2 160 C3
Wallington SM6 219 C4
Berkeley Dr KT8 195 C6
Berkeley Gdns W8 245 B3
Claygate KT10 213 A2
Southgate N21 17 B4
Walton-on-T KT12 193 D2
Berkeley Ho 17 E3 97 C4
8 SE8 119 B1
11 Brentford TW8 131 D6
Berkeley Lo Enfield EN2 4 C2
New Malden KT3 199 C5
Berkeley Mews W1 237 D1
Sunbury TW16 194 C6
Berkeley Pl SW19 178 D4
Berkeley Prim Sch
TW5 128 D5
Berkeley Rd E12 78 A3
N15 51 B3
N8 49 D3
NW9 44 C4
Barnes SW13 134 A4
Hillingdon UB10 61 A1
Berkeley Sq W1 115 B6 248 D5
Berkeley St W1 115 B6 248 D4
Berkeleys The SE25 206 A5
Berkeley The NW11 47 D2
Berkeley Waye TW5 128 D5
Berkeley Wlk 1 N7 72 B6
Berkerley Ct SW15 156 D6
Berkhampstead Rd
DA17 125 C1
Berkhamsted Ave HA9 66 C2
Berkley Cl TW2 152 C1
Berkley Ct 6 TW1 153 A4
Berkley Gr NW1 71 A1
Berkley Rd NW1 70 D1
Berkshire Ct 1 W7 86 D3
Berkshire Gdns
Edmonton N13 32 C4
Edmonton N18 34 B5
Berkshire Ho SE6 185 C6
Berkshire Rd E9 75 B2
Berkshire Sq CR4 204 A5
Berkshire Way CR4 204 A5
Berleley Ct NW10 67 C4
Bermans Way NW10 67 D4
Bermondsey Leather Mkt
SE1 253 A1
Bermondsey Mkt★
SE1 117 C3 263 B8
Bermondsey Sq SE1 263 B6
Bermondsey St
SE1 117 C4 253 A1
Bermondsey Sta SE16 118 A3
Bermondsey Trad Est
SE16 118 C1
Bermondsey Wall E
SE16 118 B4
Bermondsey Wall W
SE1,SE16 118 A4
Bermuda Ho HA1 64 B5
Bernal Cl SE28 124 D6
Bernard Angell Ho 4
SE10 142 B6
Bernard Ashley Dr SE7 121 B1
Bernard Ave W13 109 B3
Bernard Cassidy St 4
E16 98 D2
Bernard Gdns SW19 179 B5
Bernard Rd N15 51 D4
Wallington SM5,SM6 219 B4
Bernard Shaw Ct 3
NW1 71 C1
Bernard Shaw Ho 2
NW10 89 B6
Bernard St WC1 94 A3 240 B5
Bernays Cl HA7 25 C4
Bernay's Gr SW9 138 B1
Bernel Dr CR0 223 B5
Berne Rd CR7 205 A4
Berners Dr W13 109 A6
Berners Ho N1 234 A4
Bernersmede SE3 143 A2
Berners Mews
W1 93 C2 239 B3
Berners Pl W1 239 B2
Berners Rd N1 234 C5
Wood Green N22 32 C1
Berners St W1 93 C1 239 B2
Berner Terr 30 E1 96 A1
Berney Ho BR3 207 A4
Berney Rd CR0 205 B2
Bernhart Cl HA8 27 A3
Bernwell Rd E4 20 C1
Bernwood Ho 6 N4 51 B2
Berridge Gn HA8 26 C3
Berridge Mews NW6 69 C3
Berridge Rd SE19 183 C5
Berriman Rd N7 72 B5
Berrite Works UB7 104 C4
Berriton Rd HA2 41 B1
Berrybank Cl 4 E4 20 A2
Berry Cl NW10 67 C1
Dagenham RM10 81 C3
Southgate N21 16 D3
Berry Ct TW4 151 B6
Berrydale Rd UB4 85 A3
Berryfield Cl BR1 188 A1
Berry Field Cl 8 E17 53 D5
Berryfield Rd
SE17 116 D1 261 D2
Berryhill SE9 144 D1
Berry Hill HA7 25 D6
Berryhill Gdns SE9 144 D1
Berry Ho 25 E1 96 B3
10 SW11 136 D3
Berry La SE21 183 B6
Berrylands Surbiton KT5 198 C3
West Barnes SW20 200 C5
Berrylands Ct 7 SM2 217 D1
Berrylands Rd KT5 198 B3
Berrylands Sta KT5 198 D5
Berryman Cl RM8 80 C5
Berryman's La SE26 184 D6
Berrymead Gdns W3 111 A4
Berrymede Inf Sch W3 110 D4
Berrymede Jun Sch
W3 110 D4
Berrymede Rd W4 111 B3
Berry Pl EC1 234 D1
Berry St EC1 241 D5
Berry Way W5 110 A3
Bertal Rd SW17 180 B6
Bertha Hollamby Ct
DA14 190 C5
Bertha Neubergh Ho 1
SE5 139 A4
Berthan Gdns E17 54 B4
Berthon St SE8 141 C6
Bertie Rd NW10 68 A2
Penge SE26 184 D4
Bertram Cotts SW19 179 C3
Bertram Rd NW4 46 A3
Enfield EN1 6 A1
Kingston KT2 176 C3
Bertram St N19 71 B6
Bertrand Ho 11 SW16 160 A1
Bertrand St SE13 141 D2
Bertrand Way SE28 124 C6
Bert Rd CR7 205 A4
Bert Reilly Ho 1 SE18 123 B1
Bertrum House Sch
SW17 159 A2
Bert Way EN1 5 D1
Berwick Ave UB4 106 D6
Berwick Cl HA7 24 D4
Berwick Cres DA15 167 C5
Berwick Ho 10 N2 30 B1
Berwick Rd DA16 146 B4
Newham E16 99 C1
Tottenham N22 32 D2
Berwick St W1 93 C1 239 B1
Berwyn Ave TW3 129 D4
Berwyn Ho 3 N16 51 D1
Berwyn Rd
Mortlake SW14,TW10 132 D1
Streatham SE24 160 D3
Beryl Ave E6 100 A2
Beryl Harding Ho 3
SW19 178 D3
Beryl Ho SE18 123 D1
Beryl Rd W6 112 D1
Berystede KT2 176 D3
Besant Cl NW2 69 A5
Besant Ct N1 73 B3
15 SE28 124 B6
Besant Ho NW8 229 A5
Besant Rd NW2 69 A4
Besant Way NW10 67 A3
Besant Wlk N7 72 B6
Besford Ho 25 E2 96 A5
Besley St SW16 181 C4
Bessant Dr TW9 132 D4
Bessborough Gdns
SW1 115 D1 259 D2
Bessborough Pl
SW1 115 D1 259 D2
Bessborough Rd
Harrow HA1 42 B1
Roehampton SW15 156 A3
Bessborough St
SW1 115 D1 259 C2
Bessborough Wks KT8 195 B4
Bessemer Ct 5 NW1 71 C1
Bessemer Grange Prim Sch
SE5 139 C1
Bessemer Park Ind Est 3
SE24 138 D1
Bessemer Rd SE5 139 A3
Bessie Lansbury Cl E6 100 C1
Bessingby Rd HA4 62 B6
Bessingham Wlk SE4 162 D6
Besson St SE14 140 D4
Bessy St E2 96 C4
Bestwood St SE8 118 D2
Beswick Mews 1 NW6 69 D2
Betam Rd UB3 105 B4
Beta Pl 20 SW4 138 B1
Betchworth Cl SM1 218 B3
Betchworth Ho 8 N7 71 D3
Betchworth Rd IG3 79 C5
Betham Rd UB6 86 B4
Bethany Waye TW14 149 C4
Bethecar Rd HA1 42 C4
Bethell Ave E13,E16 98 D3
Ilford IG1 56 C2
Bethel Rd DA16 146 C2
Bethersden Cl BR3 185 B3
Bethersden Ho SE17 263 B2
Bethesda Ct 8 SE20 184 C3
Beth Jacob Gram Sch
NW4 46 D5
Bethlehem Ho 13 E14 119 B6
Bethlem Royal Hospl
BR3 207 C2
Bethnal Green Mus of
Childhood★ E2 96 C4

Bethnal Green Rd
E1,E2 ....96 A4 243 D6
Bethnal Green Sta E1 ....96 B3
E2 ....96 C4
Bethnal Green Tech Coll
E2 ....95 D4
Beths Gram Sch DA5 ....169 D5
Bethune Ave N11 ....30 D6
Bethune Rd N16 ....51 C2
NW10 ....89 B3
Bethwin Rd SE5 ....139 A5
Betjeman Cl HA5 ....41 C5
Betony Cl CR0 ....206 D1
Betoyne Ave E4 ....36 C6
Betsham Ho SE1 ....252 C2
Betspath Ho 6 N11 ....31 C5
Betstyle Ho 2 N10 ....31 A3
Betstyle Rd N11 ....31 B6
Betterton Dr DA14 ....169 A2
Betterton Ho WC2 ....240 B1
Betterton St WC2 .94 A1 240 B1
Bettons Pk E15 ....98 C6
Bettridge Rd SW6 ....135 B3
Betts Cl BR3 ....185 A1
Betts Ho E1 ....118 B6
Betts Mews E17 ....53 B3
Betts Rd E16 ....121 B6
Betts St E1 ....118 B6
Betts Way
Long Ditton KT6 ....197 B1
Penge SE20 ....184 B2
Bettswood Ct 15 SE20 ....184 B2
Betty Layward Prim Sch
N16 ....73 B5
Betty May Gray Ho 1
E14 ....120 A2
Beulah Ave CR7 ....183 A1
Beulah Cl HA8 ....10 D1
Beulah Cres CR7 ....183 A1
Beulah Gr CR0 ....205 A3
Beulah Hill SE19 ....183 A3
Beulah Inf Sch CR7 ....205 A6
Beulah Jun Sch CR7 ....205 A6
Beulah Rd E17 ....53 D4
Merton SW19 ....179 B3
South Norwood CR7 ....205 A6
Sutton SM1 ....217 C4
Beuleigh Ct E17 ....54 B4
Bevan Ave IG11 ....80 A1
Bevan Ct Croydon CR0 ....220 C3
9 Twickenham TW1 ....153 D5
Bevan Rd SE2 ....124 B1
Cockfosters EN4 ....2 D1
Bevan St N1 ....95 A6 235 B5
Bev Callender Cl 4
SW8 ....137 B2
Bevenden St N1 ..95 B4 235 D2
Bevercote Wlk 1 DA17 .147 B6
Beveridge Ct 1 SE28 ....124 B6
Southgate N21 ....16 A6
Beveridge Rd 1 NW10 ....67 C1
Beverley Ave DA15 ....167 D4
Hounslow TW4 ....129 B1
Wimbledon SW20 ....177 D2
Beverley Cl 6 SW11 ....136 B1
Barnes SW13 ....134 A3
Chessington KT9 ....213 C4
Edmonton N21 ....17 A3
Enfield EN1 ....5 C1
Beverley Cotts SW15 ....155 C1
Beverley Cres IG8 ....37 B2
Beverley Ct N14 ....15 C4
N2 ....48 D5
N5 ....72 D2
SE4 ....141 B2
5 W12 ....111 C4
9 W4 ....111 A1
Harrow HA2 ....42 B6
Hounslow TW4 ....129 B1
Northolt UB5 ....84 C5
Wimbledon SW20 ....177 D2
Beverley Dr HA8 ....44 C6
Beverley Gdns NW11 ....47 A2
Barnes SW13 ....133 D2
2 New Malden KT4 ....200 A1
Stanmore HA7 ....25 A2
Wembley HA9 ....44 C1
Beverley Ho 5 BR1 ....186 B5
Beverley Hyrst 10 CR0 ....221 D6
Beverley La KT2 ....177 C3
Beverley Lo 6 TW10 ....154 A6
Beverley Mans TW4 ....129 B1
Beverley Path 9 SW13 ..133 D3
Beverley Rd BR2 ....226 A6
E6 ....99 D4
W4 ....111 D1
Barnes SW13 ....133 D2
Chingford E4 ....36 B4
Dagenham RM9 ....81 A4
Mitcham CR4 ....203 D5
North Cheam KT4 ....216 C6
Penge SE20 ....184 B1
Ruislip HA4 ....62 B6
Southall UB2 ....107 A3
Sunbury TW16 ....171 D2
Teddington KT1 ....175 C2
West Barnes KT3 ....200 A5
Beverley Sch KT3 ....200 A4
Beverley Trad Est SM4 ...200 D2
Beverley Way KT3,SW20,
KT2 ....177 D2
Beverley Way (Kingston By
Pass) KT3,SW20 ....200 A6
Beverly Ct HA3 ....43 C5
Beversbrook Rd N19 ....71 D5
Beverstone Rd SW2 ....160 B6
Thornton Heath CR7 ....204 D5
Beverston Mews NW1 ...237 C3
Bevill Allen Cl SW17 ....180 D5
Bevill Cl SE25 ....206 A6
Bevin Cl SE16 ....119 A5
Bevin Ct WC1 ....233 D2
Bevington Prim Sch
W10 ....91 A2
Bevington Rd W10 ....91 A2
Beckenham BR3 ....185 D1
Bevington St SE16 ....118 A4
Bevin Ho 35 E2 ....96 C4
7 E3 ....97 C4
Bevin Rd UB4 ....84 B4
Bevin Sq SW17 ....158 D1
Bevin Way WC1 ....234 A2
Bevis Marks EC3 ..95 C1 243 B2
Bewcastle Gdns EN2 ....4 A1
Bew Ct SE21 ....162 A4
Bewdley Ho N4 ....51 A2
Bewdley St N1 ....72 C1
Bewick Mews SE15 ....140 B5
Bewick St SW8 ....137 B3
Bewley Ct SW2 ....160 B5
Bewley Ho 7 E1 ....118 B6
Bewley St Stepney E1 ....118 B6
Wimbledon SW19 ....180 A4
Bewlys Rd SE27 ....182 D5
Bexhill Cl TW13 ....151 A2
Bexhill Rd N11 ....31 D5
SE4 ....163 B5
Mortlake SW14 ....133 A2
Bexhill Wlk 6 E15 ....98 C6
Bexley Coll SE2 ....146 D6
Bexley Coll (Erith Rd
Campus) DA17 ....125 D1
Bexley Gdns Edmonton N9 .17 B1
Ilford RM6 ....58 B4
Bexley Gram Sch DA16 .146 B1
Bexleyheath Sch DA6 ...147 C2
Bexleyheath Sta DA7 ....147 A3
Bexley High St DA5 ....169 D3
Bexley Ho SE4 ....141 A2
Bexley La DA14 ....168 C1
Bexley Rd SE9 ....167 A6
Bexley Sta DA5 ....169 C3
Beynon Rd SM5 ....218 D3
BFI London Imax Cinema
SE1 ....116 C5 251 A3
Bianca Rd SE1,SE15 ....140 A6
Bibsworth Lo N3 ....29 B1
Bibsworth Rd N3 ....29 B1
Bicester Rd TW9 ....132 D2
Bickenhall Mans W1 ....237 D4
Bickenhall St W1 .92 D2 237 D4
Bickersteth Rd SW17 ....180 D4
Bickerton Rd N19 ....71 C6
Bickley Cres BR1 ....210 A5
Bickley Ct 1 HA7 ....25 C6
Bickley Park Rd BR1,
BR7 ....210 B6
Bickley Park Sch BR1 ...210 A6
Bickley Prim Sch BR1 ...209 C6
Bickley Rd BR1 ....187 D1
E10 ....53 D2
Bickley St SW17 ....180 D5
Bickley Sta BR1 ....210 A6
Bicknell Ho 23 E1 ....96 A1
Bicknell Rd SE5 ....139 A2
Bicknoller Rd EN1 ....5 D4
Bicknor Ho 2 E5 ....74 B3
Bicknor Rd BR6 ....211 D2
Bidborough Cl 3 BR2 ...208 D4
Bidborough St
N1,WC1 ....94 A4 233 A1
Biddenden Way SE9 ....188 C6
Biddenham Ho 18 SE16 .118 D2
Bidder St E16 ....98 C2
Biddesden Ho SW3 ....257 C3
Biddestone Rd N7 ....72 B4
Biddulph Ho 23 SE18 ....122 B2
Biddulph Mans W9 ....91 D4
Biddulph Rd W9 ....91 D4
Bideford Ave UB6 ....87 B5
Bideford Cl Edgware HA8 ..26 C2
Twickenham TW13 ....151 B1
Bideford Gdns EN1 ....17 C4
Bideford Rd DA16 ....146 B5
Catford BR1 ....164 D1
Enfield EN3 ....7 B5
Ruislip HA4 ....62 B5
Bidmead Ct KT6 ....214 A5
Bidwell Gdns N11 ....31 C3
Bidwell St SE15 ....140 B4
Big Ben* SW1 ....250 B1
Bigbury Cl N17 ....33 C3
Biggerstaff Rd E15 ....98 A6
Biggerstaff St N4 ....72 C6
Biggin Ave CR4 ....180 D2
Biggin Hill SE19 ....182 D3
Biggin Hill Cl KT2 ....175 C5
Biggin Way SE19 ....183 A3
Bigginwood Rd SW16 ....182 D2
Bigg's Row SW15 ....134 D2
Big Hill E5 ....52 B1
Bigland Green Prim Sch
E1 ....96 B1
Bigland St E1 ....96 B1
Bignell Rd SE18 ....122 D1
Bignold Rd E7 ....77 A4
Bigwood Ct NW11 ....47 D4
Bigwood Rd NW11 ....47 D3
Bilberry Ho 13 E3 ....97 C2
Billet Rd E17 ....35 B2
Ilford RM6 ....58 C6
Billetts Hart Cl W7 ....108 C4
Bill Hamling Cl SE9 ....166 B2
Billingford Cl SE4 ....140 D1
Billing Ho 6 E1 ....96 D1
Billingley NW1 ....232 A5
Billing Pl SW10 ..135 D5 265 D4
Billing Rd SW10 .135 D5 265 D4
Billings Cl RM9 ....80 C1
Billingsgate Mkt E14 ....119 D5
Billing St SW10 ..135 D5 265 D4
Billington Ho SW8 ....269 D1
Billington Rd SE14 ....140 D5
Billiter Sq EC3 ....243 B1
Billiter St EC3 ....95 C1 243 B1
Bill Nicholson Way N17 ..33 D3
Billockby Cl KT9 ....214 B2
Billsley Ct SE25 ....205 C5
Billson St E14 ....120 A2
Bilsby Gr SE9 ....187 D6
Bilton Ho SW8 ....269 C1
Bilton Rd UB6 ....87 B6
Bilton Twrs W1 ....237 D1
Bilton Way Enfield EN3 ....7 B5
Hayes UB3 ....106 B4
Bina Gdns SW5 ..114 A2 256 A3
Binbrook Ho W10 ....90 C2
Bincote Rd EN2 ....4 B2
Binden Rd W12 ....111 D3
Bindon Gn SM4 ....201 D5
Binfield Ct SE5 ....139 A3
Binfield Rd SW4 .138 A4 270 B1
South Croydon CR2 ....221 D3
Bingfield St N1 ...94 B6 233 C6
Bingham Cnr CR0 ....206 A1
Bingham Pl W1 ...93 A2 238 A4
Bingham Point 11 SE18 .122 D2
Bingham Rd CR0 ....206 B1
Bingham St N1 ....73 B2
Bingley Rd
Ashford TW16 ....172 A3
Newham E16 ....99 C1
Southall UB6 ....86 A2
Binley Ho SW15 ....155 D5
Binney St W1 ....93 A1 238 B1
Binnie Ho SE1 ....262 A5
Binns Rd W4 ....111 C1
Binns Terr 3 W4 ....111 C1
Binsey Wlk 1 SE2 ....124 C4
Binstead Cl UB4 ....85 A2
Binstead Ho SW18 ....157 D5
Binyon Cres HA7 ....24 D5
Binyon Ho 8 N16 ....73 C4
Birbetts Rd SE9 ....166 B2
Bircham Path SE4 ....140 D1
Birchanger Rd SE25 ....206 A4
Birch Ave Edmonton N13 ...17 A1
Hillingdon UB7 ....82 B1
Birch Cl E16 ....98 C2
N19 ....71 C6
SE15 ....140 A3
Brentford TW8 ....131 B5
Buckhurst Hill IG9 ....21 D1
Hounslow TW3 ....130 B3
Romford RM7 ....59 D6
Teddington TW11 ....175 A5
Birch Cres UB10 ....82 B6
Birch Ct E7 ....76 D4
Chingford E4 ....35 D4
Sutton SM1 ....218 A4
9 Wallington SM6 ....219 B4
Birchdale Gdns RM6 ....58 D2
Birchdale Rd E7 ....77 C3
Birchdene Dr SE28 ....124 A5
Birchdown Ho 23 E3 ....97 D4
Birchen Cl NW9 ....67 B6
Birchend Cl CR2 ....221 B2
Birchen Gr NW9 ....67 B6
Birches Cl Mitcham CR4 ..202 D6
Pinner HA5 ....41 A4
Birches The E12 ....78 A4
SE5 ....139 C3
2 Beckenham BR2 ....208 D5
Bushey WD23 ....8 A6
Greenwich SE7 ....143 B6
Orpington BR6 ....226 C4
Southgate N21 ....16 B5
South Norwood SE25 ....183 D1
Twickenham TW4 ....151 B4
Birchfield Ho 2 E14 ....119 C6
Birchfield St E14 ....119 C6
Birch Gn NW9 ....27 C3
Birch Gr E11 ....76 C5
Acton W3 ....110 C6
Bexley DA16 ....146 A1
Lewisham SE12 ....164 D4
Upper Halliford TW17 ....171 C1
Birch Hill CR0 ....222 D3
Birch Ho SE14 ....141 B4
8 SW2 ....160 C5
Birchington Cl DA7 ....147 D4
Birchington Ct N8 ....49 D3
2 NW6 ....91 D6
Birchington Ho 1 E5 ....74 B3
Birchington Rd N8 ....49 D3
NW6 ....91 C6
Surbiton KT5 ....198 B2
Birchin La EC3 ....242 D1
Birchlands Ave SW12 ....158 D4
Birch Mead BR2,BR6 ....226 C6
Birchmead Ave HA5 ....40 C5
Birchmere Lo 18 SE16 ....118 B1
Birchmere Row SE3 ....142 D3
Birchmore Wlk N5 ....73 A5
Birch Pk HA3 ....24 A3
Birch Rd Feltham TW13 ...172 D5
Romford RM7 ....59 D6
Birch Row BR2 ....210 C3
Birch Tree Ave BR4 ....224 D4
Birch Tree Ho 16 SE7 ....143 C6
Birch Tree Way CR0 ....222 B6
Birch Vale Ct NW8 ....236 D6
Birchway UB3 ....106 A5
Birch Wlk CR4 ....181 B2
Birchwood Ave N10 ....49 A6
Beckenham BR3 ....207 B5
Hackbridge SM5,SM6 ....219 B5
Birchwood Ave *continued*
Sidcup DA14 ....168 C1
Birchwood Cl SM4 ....201 D5
Birchwood Ct HA8 ....27 A1
Edmonton N13 ....32 D5
Birchwood Dr NW3 ....69 D5
Birchwood Gr TW12 ....173 C4
Birchwood Rd
Orpington BR5 ....211 C5
Streatham SW17 ....181 B5
Birdbrook Rd SE3,SE9 ....143 C2
Birdcage Wlk
SW1 ....115 D4 249 C1
Birdham Cl BR1 ....210 A4
Birdhurst Ave CR2 ....221 B4
Birdhurst Ct SM6 ....219 C1
Birdhurst Gdns CR2 ....221 B4
Birdhurst Rd SW18 ....158 A6
Mitcham SW19 ....180 C4
South Croydon CR2 ....221 C3
Birdhurst Rise CR2 ....221 C3
Bird In Bush Rd SE15 ....140 A5
Bird-in-Hand La BR1 ....187 D1
Bird-In-Hand Pas SE23 .162 C2
Bird In Hand Yd 14 NW3 ..70 A4
Birdsall Ho 5 SE5 ....139 C2
Birdsfield La E3 ....97 B6
Bird St W1 ....238 B1
Bird Wlk TW2 ....151 B3
Birdwood Cl TW11 ....174 C6
Birkbeck Ave W3 ....111 A6
Greenford UB6 ....86 A6
Birkbeck Coll
W1 ....93 D1 239 C2
Birkbeck Ct W3 ....111 B5
Birkbeck Gdns IG8 ....21 A2
Birkbeck Gr W3 ....111 B4
Birkbeck Hill SE21 ....160 D3
Birkbeck Mews 5 E8 ....73 D3
Birkbeck Pl SE21 ....161 A2
Birkbeck Prim Sch
DA14 ....168 B1
Birkbeck Rd E8 ....73 D3
N12 ....30 A5
N8 ....50 A5
NW7 ....27 D5
W3 ....111 B5
W5 ....109 C2
Enfield EN2 ....5 B5
Ilford IG2 ....57 B4
Penge BR3 ....184 D1
Sidcup DA14 ....168 A1
Tottenham N17 ....33 D2
Wimbledon SW19 ....179 D4
Birkbeck St E2 ....96 B4
Birkbeck Sta SE20 ....206 C6
Birkbeck Way UB6 ....86 B6
Birkdale Ave HA5 ....41 C6
Birkdale Cl BR6 ....211 B2
30 SE16 ....118 B1
Erith SE28 ....102 D1
Birkdale Ct 3 UB1 ....86 A1
Birkdale Gdns CR0 ....222 D4
Birkdale Rd SE2 ....124 A2
Ealing W5 ....88 A3
Birkenhead Ave KT2 ....176 B2
Birkenhead Ho 11 N7 ....72 C3
Birkenhead St
WC1 ....94 A4 233 B2
Birkhall Rd SE6 ....164 B2
Birkwood Cl SW12 ....159 D4
Birley Lo NW8 ....229 D4
Birley Rd N20 ....14 A2
Birley St SW11 ....137 A3
Birnam Rd N4 ....72 B6
Birnbeck Ct NW11 ....47 B4
Birrell Ho 10 SW9 ....138 B3
Birse Cres NW10 ....67 C4
Birstal Gn WD19 ....22 D6
Birstall Rd N15 ....51 C4
Birtwhistle Ho 5 E3 ....97 B6
Biscay Ho 11 E1 ....96 D3
Biscay Rd W6 ....112 D1
Biscoe Cl TW5 ....129 C6
Biscoe Ho UB2 ....107 D2
Biscoe Way SE13 ....142 B2
Biscott Ho 3 E3 ....97 D3
Bisenden Rd CR0 ....221 C6
Bisham Cl CR4 ....202 D1
Bisham Gdns N6 ....49 A1
Bishop Butt Cl BR6 ....227 D5
Bishop Challoner Collegiate
Sch
E1 ....118 A6
E1 ....96 C1
Bishop Challoner Sch
BR2 ....186 B1
Bishop Ct 20 SW2 ....160 C5
Bishop Douglass RC High Sch
N2 ....48 A6
Bishop Duppa's Almshouses
7 TW10 ....154 A6
Bishop Duppas Pk
TW17 ....193 C2
Bishop Fox Way KT8 ....195 B5
Bishopgate 32 N1 ....95 C6
Bishop Gilpins Prim Sch
SW19 ....179 B5
Bishop John Robinson CE
Prim Sch SE28 ....124 C6
Bishop Ken Rd HA3 ....24 D2
Bishop King's Rd
W14 ....113 A2 254 B4
Bishop Perrin CE Prim Sch
TW2 ....151 D3
Bishop Ramsey CE Sch
HA4 ....40 A2
Bishop Ramsey CE Sch
(Annexe) HA4 ....39 D2
Bishop Rd N14 ....15 B4
Bishops Ave BR1 ....209 C6
E13 ....99 B6
Borehamwood WD6 ....10 B6
Ilford RM6 ....58 C3
Bishop's Ave SW6 ....135 A3
Bishops Ave The N2 ....48 B3
Bishopsbourne Ho BR1 .187 B3
Bishop's Bridge Rd
W2 ....92 A1 236 A2
Bishops Cl SE9 ....167 A2
W4 ....111 A1
Bishop's Cl E17 ....53 D5
N19 ....71 C5
Bishops Cl Barnet EN5 ....12 D5
Enfield EN1 ....6 B3
Richmond TW10 ....153 D1
Sutton SM1 ....217 C5
Bishop's Cl UB10 ....82 C5
Bishopscourt 8 CR0 ....221 D6
Bishops Ct N2 ....48 C5
12 W2 ....91 D1
Bishop's Ct EC4 ....241 C2
WC2 ....241 A2
Bishops Ct
1 Ashford TW16 ....171 D3
Romford RM7 ....59 D5
Bishopsdale Ho 8 NW6 ..91 C6
Bishops Dr
East Bedfont TW14 ....149 B5
Northolt UB5 ....85 A6
Bishopsford Rd SM4 ....202 B3
Bishopsgate EC2 ..95 C1 243 A2
Bishopsgate Arcade E1 .243 B3
Bishopsgate Church Yd
EC2 ....243 A2
Bishops Gn BR1 ....187 C2
Bishops Gr N2 ....48 C3
Feltham TW12 ....173 B6
Bishop's Hall KT1 ....175 D1
Bishopshalt Sch UB8 ....82 B4
Bishops Hill KT12 ....194 A2
Bishops Ho SW8 ....270 B3
Bishop's Mans SW6 ....134 D3
Bishops Mead SE5 ....139 A5
Bishops Park Rd SW16 ..182 A2
Bishop's Park Rd SW6 ...134 D3
Bishop's Pl SM1 ....218 A3
Bishops Rd N6 ....49 A3
Bishop's Rd W7 ....108 C4
Bishops Rd SW6 ....135 264 C2
Bishop's Rd Hayes UB3 ....83 A1
Thornton Heath CR0 ....204 D2
Bishop St N1 ....95 A6 235 A6
Bishop's Terr
SE11 ....116 C2 261 B4
Bishopsthorpe Rd SE26 .184 D6
Bishopstone Ho 4
SW11 ....137 A3
Bishop Stopford's Sch
EN1 ....6 B3
Bishop's Way E2 ....96 C5
Bishops Wlk
Chislehurst BR7 ....189 A2
South Croydon CR0,CR9 ...223 A3
Bishopswood Rd N6 ....48 D2
Bishop Thomas Grant RC Sec
Sch SW16 ....182 B5
Bishop Wand CE Sec Sch
TW16 ....171 D1
Bishop Way NW10 ....67 C1
Bishop Wilfred Wood Cl
SE15 ....140 A3
Bishop Wilfred Wood Ct 2
E13 ....99 C5
Bishop Winnington-Ingram
CE Sch HA4 ....39 B2
Bisley Cl KT4 ....200 C1
Bisley Ho SW19 ....156 D2
Bispham Rd NW10 ....88 B4
Bissextile Ho SE13 ....141 D3
Bisson Rd E15 ....98 A5
Bistern Ave E17 ....54 B6
Bittacy Bsns Ctr NW7 ....29 A3
Bittacy Cl NW7 ....28 D4
Bittacy Ct NW7 ....29 A3
Bittacy Hill NW7 ....28 D4
Bittacy Park Ave NW7 ....28 D5
Bittacy Rd NW7 ....28 D4
Bittacy Rise NW7 ....28 D4
Bittern Cl UB4 ....84 D2
Bittern Ct NW9 ....27 C1
8 SE8 ....141 C6
Chingford E4 ....20 B4
Bittern Ho SE1 ....252 A1
Bittern St SE1 ....252 A1
Bittoms The KT1 ....197 D6
Bixley Cl UB2 ....107 B2
Blackall St EC2 ....243 A6
Blackberry Cl TW17 ....193 C5
Blackberry Farm Cl
TW5 ....129 A5
Blackberry Field BR5 ....190 A2
Blackbird Ct NW9 ....67 B5
Blackbird Hill NW9 ....67 B5
Blackborne Rd RM10 ....81 D2
Black Boy La N15 ....51 A4
Blackbrook La BR1,BR2 ..210 C5
Blackburn 28 NW9 ....27 D1
Blackburn Ct 21 SW2 ....160 C5
Blackburne's Mews W1 .248 A5
Blackburn Rd NW6 ....69 D2
Blackburn Trad Est
TW19 ....148 B5
Blackbush Ave RM6 ....58 D4
Blackbush Cl SM2 ....217 D1
Blackcap Ct NW9 ....27 C1
Blackdown Cl N2 ....30 A1
Blackdown Ho E8 ....74 A4
Blackenham Rd SW17 ...180 D6
Blackett St SW15 ....134 D2
Black Fan Cl EN2 ....5 A4
Blackfen Par DA15 ....168 A5
Blackfen Rd DA15 ....168 B5
Blackfen Sch for Girls
DA15 ....168 B5
Blackford Rd WD19 ....22 D5
Blackfriars Bridge EC4 ..251 C5
Blackfriars Ct EC4 ....251 C6
Black Friars La
EC4 ....94 D1 241 C1
Blackfriars Pas EC4 ....251 C6
Blackfriars Pier EC4 ....251 C6
Blackfriars Rd
SE1 ....116 D4 251 C3
Blackfriars Sta
EC4 ....116 D6 251 C6
Blackfriars Underpass
EC4 ....116 C6 251 B6
Blackham Ho SW19 ....179 A4
Blackheath* SE3 ....142 C4
Blackheath Ave SE3 ....142 C5
Blackheath Bluecoat CE Sch
SE3 ....143 B5
Blackheath Bsns Est
SE10 ....142 A4
Blackheath Gr SE3 ....142 D3
Blackheath High Sch
SE3 ....143 A5
Blackheath High Sch (Girls)
SE3 ....142 D3
Blackheath High Sch GPDST
(Jun Dept) SE3 ....143 A3
Blackheath Hill SE10 ....142 A4
Blackheath Hospl SE3 ...142 C2
Blackheath Pk SE3 ....143 A2
Blackheath Rd SE10 ....141 D4
Blackheath Rise SE13 ....142 A3
Blackheath Sta SE3 ....142 D2
Blackheath Vale SE3 ....142 C3
Blackheath Village SE3 .142 D3
Black Horse Ct SE1 ....262 D6
Blackhorse La E17 ....34 D1
Croydon CR0 ....206 A2
Blackhorse La Sta CR0 ..206 A2
Blackhorse Mews E17 ....52 D6
Black Horse Par HA5 ....40 B4
Blackhorse Rd E17 ....53 A5
SE8 ....141 A6
Black Horse Rd DA14 ....190 A6
Blackhorse Road E17 ....52 D5
Blackhorse Road Sta
E17 ....52 D5
Blacklands Dr UB4 ....83 A3
Blacklands Rd SE6 ....186 A6
Blacklands Terr SW3 ....257 D3
Black Lion La W6 ....112 A2
Black Lion Mews 4
W6 ....112 A2
Blackmore Ave UB1 ....108 B5
Blackmore Ho N1 ....233 D5
2 SW18 ....157 D6
Forest Hill SE23 ....163 B3
Blackmore's Gr TW11 ....175 A4
Blackmore Twr 1 W3 ....111 A3
Blackness La BR2 ....225 D1
Blackpool Gdns UB4 ....83 C3
Blackpool Rd SE15 ....140 B3
Black Prince Intc DA5 ....169 D5
Black Prince Rd
SE1,SE11 ....116 B2 260 D3
Black Rod Cl UB3 ....105 D3
Black Roof Ho 9 SE5 ....138 D4
Blackshaw Rd SW17 ....180 B5
Blacksmith Cl RM6 ....58 C3
Blacksmiths Ho 7 E17 ....53 C5
Black's Rd W6 ....112 C2
Blackstock Ho N5 ....72 D5
Blackstock Mews N4 ....72 D5
Blackstock Rd N4,N5 ....72 D6
Blackstone Ho SW1 ....259 A1
Dulwich SE21 ....161 C1
Blackstone Rd NW2 ....68 C4
Black Swan Yd SE1 ....253 A2
Blackthorn Ave UB7 ....104 C3
Blackthorn Ct 4 E15 ....76 B4
19 SE15 ....139 D5
Heston TW5 ....129 A5
6 West Norwood SW16 ...182 C5
Blackthorne Ave CR0 ....206 C1
Blackthorne Dr E4 ....36 B6
Blackthorn Gr DA7 ....147 A2
Blackthorn St E3 ....97 C3
Blacktree Mews 12
SW9 ....138 C2
Blackwall Sta E14 ....120 A6
Blackwall Trad Est E14 ....98 B2
Blackwall Tunnel E14,
SE10 ....120 B5
Blackwall Tunnel App
SE10 ....120 C4
Blackwall Tunnel Northern
Approach E14,E3 ....98 A3
Blackwall Way E14 ....120 A6
Blackwater Cl E7 ....76 D4
Blackwater Ho NW8 ....236 D4
Blackwater St SE22 ....161 D6
Blackwell Cl 10 E5 ....74 D4
Harrow HA3 ....24 B3
Blackwell Gdns HA8 ....10 C1
Blackwell Ho 3 SW4 ....159 D5
Blackwood Ho 11 E1 ....96 B3
Blackwood St
SE17 ....117 B1 262 C2
Blade Mews SW15 ....135 B1
Bladen Ho 4 E1 ....96 D1
Blades Ct SW15 ....135 B1
Blades Ho 12 SE11 ....138 C6
Blades Lo 16 SW2 ....160 C5
Bladindon Dr DA5 ....168 D4

Bladon Ct
Beckenham BR2 208 C6
Streatham SW16 182 A4
Bladon Gdns HA2 41 D3
Blagden's Cl N14 15 D2
Blagden's La N14 15 D2
Blagdon Ct W7 108 C6
Blagdon Rd SE13 163 D5
New Malden KT3 199 D5
Blagdon Wlk TW11 175 C4
Blagrove Rd 1 W10 91 B2
Blair Ave NW9 45 C2
Thames Ditton KT10 212 A6
Blair Cl DA15 167 C6
N1 73 A2
Hayes UB3 106 A2
Blair Ct NW8 229 C6
Beckenham BR3 185 D2
7 Catford SE6 164 D3
Blairderry Rd SW2 160 A2
Blair Ho SW9 138 B3
Blair Peach Prim Sch
UB1 106 D5
Blair St E14 98 B1
Blake Ave IG11 101 D6
Blake Cl DA16 145 C4
Carshalton SM5 202 C1
Blake Ct NW6 91 C4
8 SE16 118 B1
Blakeden Dr KT10 212 D2
Blake Gdns
SW6 135 D4 265 C2
Blake Hall Cres E11 55 A1
Blakehall Rd SM5 218 D2
Blake Hall Rd E11 55 A2
Blake Ho 14 N16 73 C4
1 N19 71 D3
SE1 261 A6
2 SE8 141 C6
6 Beckenham BR3 185 D4
Blake Lo N3 29 B1
Blake Mews 14 TW9 132 C4
Blakemore Rd
Streatham SW16 160 A1
Thornton Heath CR7 204 B4
Blakemore Way DA17 125 A3
Blakeney Ave BR3 185 B2
Blakeney Cl 4 E8 74 A3
N20 14 A3
5 NW1 71 D1
Blakeney Ct EN2 17 B6
Blakeney Rd BR3 185 B2
Blakenham Ct W12 112 A5
Blakenham Rd SW17 180 D6
Blaker Ct SE7 143 C5
Blake Rd E16 98 D3
N11 31 C3
Croydon CR0 221 C6
Mitcham CR4 202 C6
Blaker Rd E15 98 A6
Blakes Ave KT3 199 D3
Blakes Cl W10 90 C2
Blake's Gn BR4 208 A1
Blakes La KT3 199 D4
Blakesley Ave W5 87 C1
Blakesley Ct W5 87 C1
Blakesley Ho 4 E12 78 C5
Blake's Rd SE15 139 D5
Blakes Terr KT3 200 A4
Blakesware Gdns N9 17 B4
Blakewood Cl TW13 172 C6
Blakewood Ct SE20 184 B3
Blanca Ho 16 N1 95 C5
Blanchard Cl SE9 166 A1
Blanchard Gr EN3 7 D5
Blanchard Ho 7 TW1 153 D5
Blanchard Way E8 74 A2
Blanch Cl SE15 140 C5
Blanchedowne SE5 139 B1
Blanche Ho NW8 237 A5
Blanche Nevile Sch The
N15 51 D6
Blanche St E16 98 D3
Blanchland Rd SM4 201 D4
Blandfield Rd SW12 159 A4
Blandford Ave
2 Beckenham BR3 185 A1
Twickenham TW2 151 D3
Blandford Cl N2 48 A5
Romford RM7 59 D5
Wallington CR0 220 A5
Blandford Cres E4 20 A4
Blandford Ct 6 N1 73 C1
NW6 69 A1
Blandford Ho SW8 270 C4
Blandford Rd W4 111 C3
W5 109 D4
Penge BR3 184 D1
Southall UB2 107 C2
Teddington TW11 174 C5
Blandford Sq NW1 237 B5
Blandford St W1 93 A2 238 A3
Blandford Waye UB4 84 C1
Bland Ho SE11 260 D2
Bland St SE9 143 D1
Blaney Cres E6 100 D4
Blanmerle Rd SE9 166 D3
Blann Cl SE9 165 D5
Blantyre St
SW10 136 B5 266 C4
Blantyre Twr SW10 266 C4
Blantyre Wlk
SW10 136 B5 266 C4
Blashford NW3 70 D1
Blashford St SE13 164 B4
Blasker Wlk E14 119 D1
Blatchford Ct KT12 194 A1
Blatchford Ho 8 RM10 81 C5
Blawith Rd HA1 42 D5
Blaxland Ho 12 W12 112 B6
Blaydon Cl HA4 39 C2
Blaydon Ct 4 UB5 63 C2
Blaydon Wlk N17 34 B3
Bleak Hill La SE18 145 D6
Blean Gr SE20 184 C3
Bleasdale Ave UB6 87 A5
Blechynden Ho 17 W10 90 D1
Blechynden St W10 112 D6
Bleddyn Cl DA15 168 C5
Bledlow Cl SE28 124 C6
Bledlow Rise UB6 86 A5
Bleeding Heart Yd EC1 241 B3
Blegborough Rd SW16 181 C4
Blemundsbury WC1 240 C4
Blendon Dr DA5 168 D5
Blendon Path 7 BR1 186 D3
Blendon Rd DA5 168 D5
Blendon Terr SE18 145 A6
Blendworth Point 4
SW15 156 B3
Blenheim 26 SW19 156 D3
Blenheim Ave IG2 56 C3
Blenheim Bsns Ctr CR4 180 D1
Blenheim Cl
Edmonton N21 17 A3
Greenford UB6 86 B5
Wallington SM6 219 C1
West Barnes SW20 200 C6
Blenheim Cres
W11 113 A6 244 B6
W11 91 A1
Ruislip HA4 61 B6
South Croydon CR2 221 A1
Blenheim Ct DA15 167 B1
N19 72 A6
N7 72 A2
17 SE16 118 D5
Harrow HA3 43 A3
Richmond TW9 132 B2
South Norwood SE19 183 C2
Sutton SM2 218 A2
Blenheim Dr DA16 145 D4
Blenheim Gdns NW2 68 C3
SW2 160 B5
Kingston KT2 176 D3
Wallington SM6 219 C1
Wembley HA9 66 A5
Blenheim Gr SE15 140 A3
Blenheim Ho
6 Edmonton N9 18 A1
Hounslow TW3 129 C2
Blenheim Par 2 UB10 82 D3
Blenheim Park Rd CR2 221 A1
Blenheim Pas NW8 229 A4
Blenheim Pl TW11 174 D5
Blenheim Rd E15 76 C4
E17 53 A6
E6 99 D4
NW8 92 A5 229 B4
W4 111 C3
Bromley BR1,BR2 210 A5
Harrow HA2 41 D3
Northolt UB5 63 D2
Penge SE20 184 C3
Sidcup DA15 168 C3
Sutton SM1 217 D5
West Barnes SW20 200 C6
Blenheim Rise N15 51 D5
Blenheim St W1 238 C1
Blenheim Terr
NW8 92 A5 229 A4
Blenheim Way TW7 131 A4
Blenkarne Rd SW11 158 D5
Bleriot 27 NW9 27 D1
Bleriot Rd TW5 128 C5
Blessbury Rd HA8 27 A2
Blessed Dominic RC Prim
Sch NW9 27 D1
Blessed John Roche RC Sch
The E14 97 C1
Blessed Sacrament RC Prim
Sch N1 94 B6 233 C5
Blessington Cl SE13 142 B2
Blessington Rd SE13 142 B1
Blessing Way IG11 102 C5
Bletchingley Cl CR7 204 D5
Bletchington Ct DA17 125 C2
Bletchley Ct N1 235 C3
Bletchley St N1 95 A5 235 B3
Bletchmore Cl
Hayes UB3 105 B1
Hayes UB3 127 B6
Bletsoe Wlk N1 235 B4
Blewbury Ho 3 SE2 124 C4
Blick Ho 1 SE16 118 C3
Bligh Ho 4 SE27 183 A6
Blincoe Cl SW19 156 D2
Blind Cnr SE25 206 C5
Blissett St SE10 142 A4
Blissland Ct N12 30 A4
Bliss Mews 17 W10 91 A4
Blisworth Cl UB4 85 A3
Blisworth Ho 12 E2 96 A6
Blithbury Rd RM9 80 B2
Blithdale Rd SE2 124 A2
Blithfield St W8 255 C5
Blockley Rd HA0 65 B6
Bloemfontein Ave W12 112 B5
Bloemfontein Rd W12 112 B6
Blomfield Ct SW11 266 D2
W9 236 B6
Blomfield Mans W12 112 C5
Blomfield Rd W9 92 A2 236 A4
Blomfield St EC2 95 B2 242 D3
Blomfield Villas W2 91 D2
W9 236 A4
Blomville Rd RM8 81 A5
Blondel St SW11 137 A3
Blondin Ave W5 109 C3
Blondin St E3 97 C5
Bloomburg St SW1 259 B3
Bloomfield Cres IG2 56 D3
Bloomfield Ct N6 49 A3
Bloomfield Ho 17 E1 96 A2
Bloomfield Pl W1 248 D6
Bloomfield Rd BR2 209 D4
N6 49 A3
SE18 122 D1
Kingston KT1 198 A6
Bloomfields The IG11 79 A2
Bloomfield Terr
SW1 115 A1 258 B2
Bloom Gr SE27 160 D1
Bloomhall Rd SE19 183 B5
Bloom Park Rd SW6 264 C3
Bloomsbury Cl NW7 28 A3
Ealing W5 110 B6
Bloomsbury Ct E11 54 B1
WC1 240 B3
Cranford TW5 128 B4
Pinner HA5 41 B6
Bloomsbury Ho 10 SW4 159 D5
Bloomsbury Pl SW18 158 A6
WC1 240 B3
Bloomsbury Sq
WC1 94 A2 240 B3
Bloomsbury St
WC1 93 D2 239 D3
Bloomsbury Way
WC1 94 A2 240 B3
Blore Cl SW8 269 C1
Blore Ct W1 249 C6
Blossom Cl W5 110 A4
Dagenham RM9 103 B6
South Croydon CR2 221 D3
Blossom La EN2 5 A4
Blossom Pl E1 243 B5
Blossom St E1 95 C3 243 B5
Blossom Way
Hillingdon UB10 60 B1
West Drayton UB7 104 C2
Blossom Waye TW5 129 A5
Blount St E14 97 A1
Bloxam Gdns SE9 166 A6
Bloxhall Rd E10 53 B1
Bloxham Cres TW12 173 B2
Bloxworth Cl SM6 219 C5
Blucher Rd SE5 139 A5
Blue Anchor Alley 4
TW9 132 A1
Blue Anchor La SE16 118 B2
Blue Anchor Yd E1 118 A6
Blue Ball Yd SW1 249 A3
Bluebell Ave E12 78 A3
Bluebell Cl 16 E9 96 C6
Forest Hill SE26 183 D6
Hackbridge SM6 203 B1
Orpington BR6 227 A6
Bluebell Way IG1 78 D2
Blueberry Cl IG8 37 A4
Bluebird La RM10 81 C1
Bluebird Way Cl SE28
Bluefield Cl TW12 173 C5
Blue Gate Fields Jun & Inf
Schs E1 118 C6
Bluegate Mews E1 118 B6
Bluegates
Stoneleigh KT17 216 A1
Wimbledon SW19 179 A5
Bluehouse Rd E4 20 C1
Blue Lion Pl SE1 263 A6
Blue Point Ct 2 HA1 42 D4
Blue Sch The TW7 131 A2
Blundell Rd HA8 27 C3
Blundell St N7 72 A2
Blunden Cl RM8 58 C1
Blunt Rd CR0 221 B3
Blunts Ave UB7 126 C5
Blunts Rd SE9 166 C6
Blurton Rd E5 74 D4
Blydon Ct N21 16 B6
Blyth Cl 4 E14 120 B2
Twickenham TW1 152 D5
Blythe Cl SE23 163 B4
Blythe Hill BR5 190 A2
Forest Hill SE6 163 B4
Blythe Hill La SE6 163 B3
Blythe Ho 8 SE11 138 C6
Blythe Mews 2 W14 112 D3
Blythendale Ho 31 E2 96 A5
Blythe Rd W14 112 D3 254 A5
Blythe St E2 96 B4
Blythe Vale SE6 163 B3
Blyth Rd E17 53 B2
Bromley BR1 186 D2
Hayes UB3 105 C4
Woolwich SE28 124 C6
Blyth's Wharf E14 119 A6
Blythswood Rd IG3 58 A2
Blythwood Pk 10 BR1 186 D2
Blythwood Rd N4 50 A2
Pinner HA5 22 D2
Boadicea St N1 233 C5
Boadoak Ho 18 NW6 91 D6
Boardman Ave E4 19 D6
Boardman Cl EN5 13 A6
Boardwalk Pl E14 120 A5
Boarhound 25 NW9 27 D1
Boarley Ho SE17 263 A3
Boathouse Ctr The W10 90 D3
Boat Lifter Way 19 SE16 119 A2
Bob Anker Cl 1 E13 99 A4
Bobbin Cl SW4 137 C2
Bobby Moore Bridge The
HA9 66 C5
Bobington Ct
WC1 94 A2 240 B4
Bob Marley Way 11
SE24 138 C1
Bockhampton Rd KT2 176 B3
Bocking St E8 96 B6
Boddicott Cl SW19 157 A2
Boddington Ho SE14 140 C4
Bodeney Ho 10 SE5 139 C4
Boden Ho 4 E1 96 A2
Bodiam Cl EN1 5 C3
Bodiam Ct BR2 208 D5
Bodiam Rd SW16 181 D3
Bodicea Mews TW4 151 C5
Bodington Ct 2 W12 112 D4
Bodley Cl KT3 199 C4
Bodley Manor Way
SE24 160 C4
Bodley Rd KT3 199 C4
Bodmin 28 NW9 27 D1
Bodmin Cl HA2 63 B5
Bodmin Gr SM4 201 D4
Bodmin St SW18 157 C3
Bodnant Gdns SW20 200 B6
Bodney Mans 14 E8 74 B3
Bodney Rd E5,E8 74 B3
Boeing Way UB2 106 B3
Boelyn Dr HA4 62 D6
Boevey Path Erith DA17 125 B1
2 Erith DA17 147 B6
Bognor Gdns WD19 22 C5
Bognor Rd DA16 146 D4
Bohemia Pl 1 E8 74 B2
Bohn Rd E1 97 A2
Bohun Gr EN4 14 D5
Boileau Par W5 88 B1
Boileau Rd Barnes SW13 134 B6
Ealing W5 88 B1
Boilerhouse SE1 253 C3
Boisseau Ho 27 E1 96 C2
Bolden St SE8 141 D3
Boldero Pl NW8 237 A5
Bolderwood Way BR4 223 D6
Boldmere Rd HA5 40 C2
Boleyn Ave EN1 6 B4
Boleyn Ct E17 53 C5
Beckenham BR3 186 A2
Buckhurst Hill IG9 21 B3
East Molesey KT8 196 B5
Boleyn Dr KT8 195 B6
Boleyn Gdns BR4 223 D6
Boleyn Ground(Upton Park)
(West Ham United FC)
E13,E6 99 D5
Boleyn Rd E6 99 D5
E7 77 B1
N16 73 C3
Boleyn Way EN5 2 A2
Bolina Rd SE16 118 C1
Bolingbroke Gr SW11 158 D5
Bolingbroke Ho
Beckenham BR3 207 A4
Catford BR3 185 D5
Bolingbroke Hospl The
SW11 158 C6
Bolingbroke Rd W14 112 D3
Bolingbroke Way UB3,
UB11 105 B5
Bolingbroke Wlk
SW11 136 C4 267 A2
Bollo Bridge Rd W3 111 A4
Bollo Ct 2 W3 111 A3
Bollo La W3 110 D3
Bolney Ct KT6 197 D4
Bolney Gate SW7 247 A1
Bolney St SW8 138 B5 270 C3
Bolsover St W1 93 B3 238 D5
Bolstead Rd CR4 181 B2
Bolster Gr N22 31 D2
Bolt Ct EC4 241 B1
Boltmore Cl NW4 46 D6
Bolton Cl
Chessington KT9 214 A2
Penge SE20 184 A1
Bolton Cres SE5 138 D5
Bolton Ct SW11 268 B1
Bolton Gdns NW10 90 D5
SW5 113 D1 255 D2
Bromley BR1 186 D4
Teddington TW11 175 A4
Bolton Gdns Mews
SW10 256 A2
Bolton Ho 4 SE10 120 C1
Bolton Rd E15 76 D2
NW10 89 C6
NW8 91 D6
Chessington KT9 214 A2
Chiswick W4 133 A5
Edmonton N18 33 D5
Harrow HA1 42 B5
Boltons Ct SW5 255 D2
Bolton's La TW6,UB7 127 A5
Bolton St W1 115 B5 248 D4
Boltons The
SW10 114 A1 256 A2
Wembley HA0 64 D4
Woodford IG8 37 A6
Bolton Studios SW10 256 B1
Bolton Wlk N7 72 B6
Bombay St SE16 118 B2
Bomer Cl UB7 126 C5
Bomore Rd
W11 113 A6 244 A6
Bonar Pl BR7 188 A3
Bonar Rd SE15 140 A5
Bonchester Cl BR7 188 C3
Bonchurch Cl SM2 217 D1
Bonchurch Rd W10 91 A2
Ealing W13 109 B5
Bond Cl UB7 82 B1
Bond Ct EC4 242 C1
Bondfield Ave UB4 84 A4
Bondfield Rd 4 E6 100 B2
Bond Fst Sch CR4 180 D1
Bond Gdns SM6 219 C4
Bond Ho 4 NW6 91 B5
Bonding Yard Wlk SE16 119 A3
Bond Rd Mitcham CR4 180 D1
Surbiton KT6 214 B6
Bond St E15 76 C3
Ealing W5 109 D6
Bond Street Sta
W1 93 B1 238 B1
Bondway SW8 138 A6 270 B6
Boneta Rd SE18 122 B3
Bonfield Rd SE13 142 A1
Bonham Gdns RM8 80 D6
Bonham Ho W11 244 C4
Bonham Rd SW2 160 B6
Dagenham RM8 80 D5
Bonheur Rd W4 111 B4
Bonhill St EC2 95 B3 242 D5
Boniface Gdns HA3 23 D3
Boniface Rd UB10 60 D5
Boniface Wlk HA3 23 D3
Bonington Ho N1 233 C3
Enfield EN1 18 A6
Bonita Mews SE15 140 D2
Bonne Marche Terr Mews 18
SE27 183 C6
Bonner Hill Rd KT1 198 C6
Bonner Ho 3 SW15 156 A6
Bonner Prim Sch E2 96 C4
Bonner Rd E2 96 C5
Bonnersfield Cl HA1 43 A3
Bonnersfield La
Harrow HA1 42 D3
Harrow HA1,HA3 43 A3
Bonner St E2 96 C5
Bonneville Gdns SW4 159 C5
Bonneville Prim Sch
SW4 159 C5
Bonnington Ct 15 UB5 84 D5
Bonnington Sq
SW8 138 B6 270 C6
Bonnington Twr BR2 210 A3
Bonny St NW1 71 C1
Bonser Rd TW1 152 D2
Bonsor Ho SW8 269 B2
Bonsor St SE5 139 C5
Bonthron Ho SW15 134 C3
Bonus Pastor RC Sch
BR1 186 C6
Bonville Gdns 17 NW4 46 A5
Bonville Rd BR1 186 D5
Bookbinder Cotts N20 14 D1
Booker Cl 15 E3 97 B2
Booker Rd 5 N18 34 A5
Bookham Ct CR4 202 B6
Boone Ct N9 18 C1
Boones Rd SE13 142 C1
Boone St SE13 142 C1
Boord St SE10 120 C3
Boothby Ct E4 20 A1
Boothby Ho 2 SW16 181 C5
Boothby Rd N19 71 D6
Booth Cl 10 E9 96 B6
SE28 124 B6
Booth Ho 2 SW2 160 C4
Booth La EC4 252 A6
Boothman Ho HA3 43 D6
Booth Rd NW9 27 C1
Croydon CR0 220 D6
Boothroyd Ho TW7 130 D2
Booth's Pl W1 239 B3
Boot Par HA8 26 C4
Boot St N1 95 C4
Bordars Rd W7 86 D2
Bordars Wlk W7 86 C2
Borden Ave EN1 17 B5
Border Cres SE26 184 B5
Border Gate CR4 180 D2
Border Gdns CR0 223 D4
Border Rd SE26 184 B5
Bordesley Rd SM4 201 D5
Bordeston Ct TW8 131 C2
Bordon Wlk 5 SW15 156 A4
Boreas Wlk N1 234 D3
Boreham Ave E16 99 A1
Boreham Cl E11 54 A1
Boreham Rd N22 33 A1
Boreman Ho 10 SE10 142 A6
Borgard Ho 3 SE18 144 A4
Borgard Rd SE18 122 B2
Borkwood Pk BR6 227 D4
Borkwood Way BR6 227 C4
Borland Rd SE15 140 C1
Teddington TW11 175 B3
Borneo St SW15 134 C2
Borough High St
SE1 117 B5 252 C2
Borough Hill CR0 220 D5
Borough Mkt* SE1 252 C3
Borough Rd
SE1 116 D3 261 D6
Hounslow TW7 130 D4
7 Kingston KT2 176 C3
Mitcham CR4 180 C1
Borough Sq SE1 252 A1
Borough Sta The
SE1 117 A4 252 B1
Borrett Cl SE17 117 A1 262 A1
Borrodaile Rd SW18 157 D5
Borrowdale NW1 232 A1
Borrowdale Ave HA3 25 A1
Borrowdale Cl IG4 56 A5
Borrowdale Ct EN2 5 A4
Borthwick Mews E15 76 C4
Borthwick Rd E15 76 C4
NW9 45 D3
Borthwick St SE8 119 C1
Borwick Ave E17 53 B6
Bosbury Rd SE6 164 A1
Boscastle Rd NW5 71 B5
Boscobel Ho 4 E8 74 B2
Boscobel Pl SW1 258 B4
Boscobel St NW8 92 B3 236 D5
Boscombe Ave E10 54 B2
Boscombe Cl E5 75 A3
Boscombe Gdns SW16 182 A4
Boscombe Ho CR0 205 B1
Boscombe Rd W12 112 A4
Merton SW19 179 D2
North Cheam KT4 200 D1
Streatham SW17 181 A4
Bose Cl N3 29 A2
Bosgrove E4 20 A2
Boss Ho SE1 253 C2
Boss St SE1 253 C2
Bostall Hill SE2 124 B1
Bostall La SE2 124 B1
Bostall Manor Way SE2 124 B2
Bostall Park Ave DA7 147 A5
Bostall Rd BR5 190 B3
Bostock Ho TW5 129 C6
Boston Bsns Pk W7 108 C3
Boston Ct
South Norwood SE25 205 D5
Sutton SM2 218 A1
Boston Gdns
Brentford TW8 109 B2
Chiswick W4 133 C6
Boston Gr HA4 39 A3
Boston Ho NW1 237 C6
25 SE5 139 A3
SW5 255 D3
Boston Manor Ho TW8 109 B1
Boston Manor Rd TW8 109 B1
Boston Manor Sta TW8 109 A2
Boston Par W7 109 A2
Boston Park Rd TW8 109 C1
Boston Pl NW1 92 D3 237 C5
Boston Rd E6 100 A4
HA8 27 A3
Ealing W7 109 A3
Thornton Heath CR0 204 C3
Bostonthorpe Rd W7 108 C4
Boston Vale W7 109 A2
Bosun Cl 8 E14 119 C4
Boswell Ct 9 W14 112 D3
WC1 240 B4
Kingston KT2 176 C2
Boswell Ho BR2 209 D4
WC1 240 B4
5 Streatham SW16 181 C5
Boswell Rd CR7 205 A5
Boswell St WC1 94 A2 240 B4
Boswood Ct TW4 129 B2
Bosworth Cl E17 35 B2
Bosworth Ho 4 W10 91 A3
Bosworth Rd N11 31 D4
W10 91 A3
Barnet EN5 1 C2
Dagenham RM10 81 C5
Botany Bay La BR7 189 A1
Botany Cl EN4 2 C1
Boteley Cl E4 20 B2
Botham Cl 6 HA8 27 A3
Botha Rd E13 99 C2
Bothwell Cl E16 98 D2
Bothwell St 4 W6 134 D6
Botolph Alley EC3 253 A6
Botolph La EC3 253 A6
Botsford Rd SW20 179 A1
Bott's Mews W2 91 C1
Botwell Common Rd
UB3 105 C6
Botwell Cres UB3 83 C1
Botwell House RC Prim Sch
UB3 105 D4
Botwell La UB3 105 C6
Boucher Cl TW11 174 D5
Bouchier Ho 6 N2 30 B1
Bough Beech Ct EN3 6 D6
Boughton Ave BR2 208 D2
Boughton Ho SE1 252 C2
Boughton Rd SE28 123 C3
Boulcott St E1 96 D1
Boulevard The 4 SW17 159 A2
Boullen Ct SM1 218 A4
Boulogne Ho SE1 263 C6
Boulogne Rd CR0 205 A3
Boulter Ho SE14 140 C4
Boulton Ho TW8 110 A1
Boulton Rd RM8 81 B6
Boultwood Rd E6 100 B1
Bounces La N9 18 B2
Bounces Rd N9 18 C2
Boundaries Mans 3
SW12 159 A3
Boundaries Rd
Feltham TW13 150 C3
Upper Tooting SW12 159 A3
Boundary Ave E17 53 B2
Boundary Bsns Ct CR4 202 B6
Boundary Cl Barnet EN5 1 B4
Ilford IG3 79 C4
Kingston KT1 198 D6
Penge SE20 184 A1
Southall UB2 107 C1
Boundary Ct 3 N18 33 D4
Boundary Ho 1 SE5 139 A5
Balham SW12 159 B3
Isleworth TW1 153 B6
Boundary La E13,E6 99 D3
SE17 139 A6
Boundary Pas E2 243 C6
Boundary Rd DA15 167 C6
E13 99 D4
E17 53 C3
N9 18 C5
NW8 92 A6 229 B6

Boundary Rd N2 ... 30 B2
Boundary Rd
Mitcham SW19 ... 180 B4
Pinner HA5 ... 40 D2
Tottenham N22 ... 33 A1
Wallington SM5,SM6 ... 219 A1
Boundary Road Est
NW8 ... 92 A6 229 A5
Boundary Row SE1 ... 251 C2
Boundary St E2 ... 95 D3 243 C6
Boundary Way CR0 ... 223 C3
Boundfield Rd SE6 ... 164 C2
Bounds Green Ct N11 ... 31 D4
Bounds Green Ind Est
N11 ... 31 C4
Bounds Green Jun & Inf Schs
N11 ... 32 A3
Bounds Green Rd N11 ... 31 D4
Wood Green N22 ... 32 A2
Bounds Green Sta N11 ... 31 D3
Bourbon Ho 9 SE6 ... 186 A6
Bourchier St W1 ... 249 C6
Bourdillon Ct 2 SE9 ... 166 A2
Bourdon Pl W1 ... 248 D6
Bourdon Rd SE20 ... 184 C1
Bourdon St W1 ... 115 B6 248 D5
Bourke Cl NW10 ... 67 C2
SW4 ... 160 A5
Bourlet Cl W1 ... 239 A3
Bourn Ave N15 ... 51 B5
Hillingdon UB8 ... 82 C3
New Barnet EN4 ... 14 B6
Bournbrook Rd SE3,SE9 ... 143 D2
Bourne Ave Hayes UB3 ... 105 B3
Palmers Green N14 ... 16 A2
Ruislip HA4 ... 62 C3
Bourne Cir UB3 ... 105 A3
Bourne Cl KT7 ... 212 D6
Bourne Ct Chiswick W4 ... 133 A6
Ruislip HA4 ... 62 B3
Wanstead E11 ... 55 A4
Woodford IG8 ... 37 D1
Bourne Dr CR4 ... 180 B1
Bourne Gdns E4 ... 35 D6
Bourne Hill N13 ... 16 B2
Bourne Ho 1 NW2 ... 68 A5
5 SW4 ... 137 C1
Ashford TW15 ... 170 C5
Buckhurst Hill IG9 ... 21 D1
Bournemead Ave UB5 ... 84 A5
Bournemead Cl UB5 ... 84 A4
Bournemead Way UB5 ... 84 B5
Bourne Mews W1 ... 238 B1
Bournemouth Cl SE15 ... 140 A3
Bournemouth Rd SE15 ... 140 A3
Merton SW19 ... 179 C2
Bourne Par DA5 ... 169 D4
Bourne Pl W4 ... 111 B1
Bourne Prim Sch HA4 ... 62 C2
Bourne Rd DA5 ... 169 D5
E7,E11 ... 76 D5
N8 ... 50 A3
Bromley BR2 ... 209 D5
Bournes Ho 4 N15 ... 51 C3
Bourneside 5 N14 ... 15 D3
Bourneside Cres 6 N14 ... 15 D3
Bourneside Gdns SE6 ... 186 A5
Bourne St SW1 ... 115 A2 258 A3
Croydon CR0 ... 220 D6
Bourne Terr W2 ... 91 D2
Bourne The N14 ... 16 A2
Bourne Vale BR2 ... 208 D1
Bournevale Rd SW16 ... 182 A6
Bourne View UB6 ... 64 D3
Bourne Way Cheam SM1 ... 217 B3
Coney Hall BR2,BR4 ... 224 D6
West Ewell KT19 ... 215 A4
Bournewood Rd SE18,
SE2 ... 146 A5
Bournville Rd SE6 ... 163 C4
Bournwell Cl EN4 ... 2 D3
Bourton Cl UB3 ... 106 A5
Bousfield Prim Sch
SW10 ... 114 A1 256 A2
Bousfield Rd SE14 ... 140 D3
Boutcher CE Prim Sch
SE1 ... 117 D2 263 C4
Boutflower Rd SW11 ... 136 C1
Bouverie Gdns HA3 ... 43 A3
Bouverie Mews N16 ... 73 C6
Bouverie Pl W2 ... 236 D2
Bouverie Rd N16 ... 73 C6
Harrow HA1 ... 42 A3
Bouverie St EC4 ... 94 C1 241 B1
Bouvier Rd EN3 ... 6 C5
Boveney Rd SE23 ... 162 D4
Bovill Rd SE23 ... 162 D4
Bovingdon Ave HA9 ... 66 C2
Bovingdon Cl 3 N19 ... 71 C6
Bovingdon La NW9 ... 27 C2
Bovingdon Rd
SW6 ... 135 D4 265 D1
Bovril Ho EN1 ... 5 C2
Bowater Cl NW9 ... 45 B4
SW2 ... 160 A5
Bowater Gdns TW16 ... 172 B2
Bowater Ho EC1 ... 242 B5
Bowater Pl SE3 ... 143 B5
Bowater Rd SE18 ... 121 D3
Bow Brook The 20 E2 ... 96 D5
Bow Church Sta E3 ... 97 C4
Bow Churchyard EC2,
EC4 ... 242 B1
Bow Common La E3 ... 97 B3
Bowden Cl TW14 ... 149 C3
Bowden Ho 23 E3 ... 97 D4
Bowden House Hospl
(Private) HA1 ... 64 C6
Bowden St SE11 ... 116 C1 261 B1
Bowditch SE8 ... 119 B1
Bowdon Rd E17 ... 53 C2
Bowen Ct 2 N5 ... 72 D4
Bowen Dr SE21 ... 161 C1
Bowen Rd HA1 ... 42 A2
Bowen St E14 ... 97 D1
Bower Ave SE3 ... 142 C5
Bower Cl UB5 ... 84 C5
Bowerdean St SW6 ... 135 D3
Bower Ho SE14 ... 140 D4
Bowerman Ave SE14 ... 141 A6
Bowerman Ct 1 N19 ... 71 D6
Bowers Ho 5 IG11 ... 78 D1
Bower St E1 ... 96 D1
Bowers Wlk 1 E6 ... 100 B1
Bowes Cl DA15 ... 168 B5
Bowes Park Sta N22 ... 32 A3
Bowes Prim Sch N11 ... 31 D5
Bowes Rd N11 ... 31 C5
W3 ... 111 C6
Dagenham RM8 ... 80 C4
Walton-on-T KT12 ... 194 B1
Bowes Rd (North Circular
Rd) N13 ... 32 A5
Bowfell Rd W6 ... 134 C6
Bowford Ave DA7 ... 147 A4
Bowhill Cl SW9 ... 138 C5
Bowie Cl SW4 ... 159 D4
Bow Ind Pk E15 ... 75 C1
Bow La EC2,EC4 ... 95 A1 242 B1
N12 ... 30 A3
Bowland Ho N4 ... 51 A2
Bowland Rd SW4 ... 137 D1
Woodford IG8 ... 37 C4
Bowland Yd SW1 ... 247 D1
Bowl Ct EC2 ... 243 B5
Bowles Ct N12 ... 30 C3
Bowles Rd 1 SE1 ... 140 A6
Bowley Cl SE19 ... 183 D4
Bowley Ho 6 SE16 ... 118 A3
Bowley La SE19 ... 183 D5
Bowling Cl UB10 ... 82 B6
Bowling Green Cl SW19 ... 156 B4
Bowling Green Ct HA9 ... 66 B6
Bowling Green Ho
SW10 ... 266 C4
Bowling Green La
EC1 ... 94 C3 241 B6
Bowling Green Pl SE1 ... 252 C2
Bowling Green Row 1
SE18 ... 122 B2
Bowling Green St SE11 ... 138 C6
Bowling Green Wlk N1 ... 95 C4
Bowls Cl HA7 ... 25 B5
Bowman Ave E16 ... 120 D6
Bowman Mews E1 ... 118 A6
Wandsworth SW18 ... 157 B3
Bowmans Cl W13 ... 109 B5
Bowmans Lea SE23 ... 162 C4
Bowman's Meadow
SM6 ... 219 B5
Bowman's Mews N7 ... 72 A5
Bowman's Pl N7 ... 72 A5
Bowmead SE9 ... 166 B2
Bowmore Wlk NW1 ... 71 D1
Bowness Cl 5 E8 ... 73 D2
Bowness Cres KT2,
SW15 ... 177 C5
Bowness Dr TW4 ... 129 A1
Bowness Ho SE15 ... 140 C5
Bowness Rd DA7 ... 147 D3
Catford SE6 ... 163 D4
Bowood Rd SW11 ... 159 A6
Enfield EN3 ... 6 D3
Bow Rd E3 ... 97 C4
Bowring Gn WD19 ... 22 C5
Bow Road Sta E3 ... 97 C4
Bowrons Ave HA0 ... 65 D1
Bowry Ho 14 E14 ... 97 B2
Bow Sch E3 ... 97 C4
Bowsley Ct TW13 ... 150 A2
Bowsprit Point 5 E14 ... 119 C3
Bow St E15 ... 76 C3
WC2 ... 94 A1 240 B1
Bowstead Ct SW11 ... 266 D1
Bow Triangle Bsns Ctr
E3 ... 97 C3
Bowyer Cl E6 ... 100 B2
Bowyer Ct 4 E4 ... 20 A3
Bowyer Ho 28 N1 ... 95 C6
Wandsworth SW18 ... 157 D5
Bowyer Pl SE5 ... 139 A5
Bowyer St 15 SE5 ... 139 A5
Boxall Rd SE21 ... 161 C5
Boxgrove Prim Sch SE2 ... 124 C3
Boxgrove Rd SE2 ... 124 C3
Box La IG11 ... 102 C5
Boxley Ho 3 E5 ... 74 B3
Boxley Rd SM4 ... 202 A5
Boxley St E16 ... 121 B5
Boxmoor Ho 16 E2 ... 96 A6
9 W11 ... 112 D5
Boxmoor Rd HA3 ... 43 B5
Boxoll Rd RM9 ... 81 B5
Boxshall Ho 7 SE18 ... 144 D6
Box Tree Ho SE8 ... 119 A1
Boxtree La HA3 ... 24 B3
Boxtree Rd HA3 ... 24 B3
Boxwood Cl UB7 ... 104 B4
Boxworth Cl N12 ... 30 B5
Boxworth Gr N1 ... 94 B6 233 D6
Boyard Rd SE18 ... 122 D1
Boyce Ho 1 W10 ... 91 B4
Streatham SW16 ... 181 C5
Boyce St SE1 ... 251 A3
Boyce Way E13 ... 99 A3
Boycroft Ave NW9 ... 45 A3
Boyd Ave UB1 ... 107 B5
Boyd Cl KT2 ... 176 C3
Boyd Ct SW15 ... 156 C5
Boydell Ct NW8 ... 70 B1
Boyden Ho 8 E17 ... 54 A6
Boyd Rd SW19 ... 180 B4
Boyd St E1 ... 96 A1
Boyfield St SE1 ... 116 D4 251 D1
Boyland Rd BR1 ... 186 D5
Boyle Ave HA7 ... 25 A4
Boyle Cl UB10 ... 82 B5
Boyle Farm Rd KT7 ... 197 A3
Boyle Ho 13 DA17 ... 125 C3
Boyle St W1 ... 249 A6
Boyne Ave NW4 ... 46 D5
Boyne Ct NW10 ... 68 A1
Boyne Ho 10 E5 ... 74 B6
Boyne Rd SE13 ... 142 B2
Dagenham RM10 ... 81 C5
Boyne Terr Mews
W11 ... 113 B5 244 C4
Boyson Rd 10 SE17 ... 139 B6
Boyton Cl E1 ... 96 D3
N8 ... 50 A6
Boyton Ho NW8 ... 229 D4
SE11 ... 261 A1
Boyton Rd N8 ... 50 A6
Brabant Rd N22 ... 32 B1
Brabazon Ave SM6 ... 220 A1
Brabazon Rd
Heston TW5 ... 128 D5
Northolt UB5 ... 85 C5
Brabazon St E14 ... 97 D2
Brabner Ho 2 E2 ... 96 A4
Brabourne Cl 7 SE19 ... 183 C5
Brabourne Cres DA7 ... 147 B6
Brabourne Hts NW7 ... 11 C1
Brabourne Rise BR3 ... 208 B4
Brabourn Gr SE15 ... 140 C3
Brabrook Ct SM6 ... 219 B3
Brabstone Ho 2 UB6 ... 86 D5
Bracer Ho 1 N1 ... 95 C5
Bracewell Ave UB6 ... 65 A2
Bracewell Rd W10 ... 90 C2
Bracewood Gdns CR0 ... 221 D5
Bracey St N4 ... 72 A6
Bracken Ave
Balham SW12 ... 159 A4
Croydon CR0 ... 223 C5
Brackenbridge Dr HA4 ... 62 D5
Brackenbury N4 ... 50 B1
Brackenbury Gdns W6 ... 112 B3
Brackenbury Prim Sch
W6 ... 112 B3
Brackenbury Rd N2 ... 48 A6
W6 ... 112 B3
Bracken Cl E6 ... 100 B2
Ashford TW16 ... 171 D4
Twickenham TW4 ... 151 C4
Brackendale
Kingston KT1 ... 176 D1
Southgate N21 ... 16 B2
Brackendale Cl TW5 ... 129 D4
Brackendale Ct 2 BR3 ... 185 C3
Bracken End TW7 ... 152 B6
Brackenfield Cl E5 ... 74 B5
Bracken Gdns SW13 ... 134 A3
Brackenhill HA4 ... 63 A4
Bracken Hill Cl 5 BR1 ... 186 D2
Bracken Hill La BR1 ... 186 D2
Bracken Ho 14 E3 ... 97 C2
Bracken Mews
Chingford E4 ... 20 A3
Romford RM7 ... 59 D3
Brackens BR3 ... 185 C3
Brackens The EN1 ... 17 C4
Bracken The E4 ... 20 A2
Brackenwood TW16 ... 172 A2
Brackenwood Lo EN5 ... 1 C1
Brackley Cl SM6 ... 220 A1
Brackley Ct NW8 ... 236 D6
Brackley Rd W4 ... 111 C1
Beckenham BR3 ... 185 C3
Brackley Sq IG8 ... 37 D3
Brackley St EC1 ... 242 B4
Brackley Terr 6 W4 ... 111 C1
Bracklyn Ct N1 ... 235 C4
Bracklyn St N1 ... 235 C4
Bracknell Cl N22 ... 32 C2
Bracknell Gate NW3 ... 69 D3
Bracknell Gdns NW3 ... 69 D4
Bracknell Way NW3 ... 69 D4
Bracondale KT10 ... 212 A3
Bracondale Rd SE2 ... 124 A2
Bradbeer Ho 24 E2 ... 96 C4
Bradbourne Rd DA5 ... 169 C4
Bradbourne St SW6 ... 135 C3
Bradbury Cl UB2 ... 107 B2
Bradbury Ct 2 SE3 ... 143 A5
Bradbury Ho E1 ... 243 D2
Bradbury St 28 N16 ... 73 C3
Bradby Ho NW8 ... 91 D5
Braddock Cl TW7 ... 130 D3
Braddock Ho 9 NW6 ... 91 D6
Braddon Rd TW9 ... 132 B2
Braddyll St SE10 ... 120 C1
Bradenham 11 SE17 ... 139 B6
Bradenham Ave DA16 ... 146 A1
Bradenham Cl SE17 ... 139 B6
Bradenham Rd
Harrow HA3 ... 43 B5
Hayes UB4 ... 83 C4
Braden St W9 ... 91 D3
Bradfield Ct 14 NW1 ... 71 B1
Bradfield Dr IG11 ... 80 A3
Bradfield Ho 15 SW8 ... 137 D3
Bradfield Rd E16 ... 121 B4
Ruislip HA4 ... 63 A3
Bradford Cl BR2 ... 210 B1
Forest Hill SE26 ... 184 B6
Bradford Cl *continued*
Tottenham N17 ... 33 D4
Bradford Dr KT19 ... 215 D2
Bradford Ho 4 W14 ... 112 D3
Bradford Rd W3 ... 111 C4
Ilford IG1 ... 57 C1
Bradgate Rd SE6 ... 163 D5
Brading Cres E11 ... 77 B6
Brading Rd
Streatham SW2 ... 160 B4
Thornton Heath CR0 ... 204 B3
Brading Terr W12 ... 112 A3
Bradiston Rd W9 ... 91 B4
Bradley Cl N7 ... 72 B2
Bradley Ct CR0 ... 220 C4
Bradley Gdns W13 ... 87 B1
Bradley Ho 4 E2 ... 96 B5
1 E3 ... 97 D4
SE16 ... 118 B2
Twickenham TW1 ... 152 D3
Bradley Mews SW12 ... 158 D3
Bradley Rd Enfield EN3 ... 7 A6
South Norwood SE19 ... 183 A4
Wood Green N22 ... 32 B1
Bradley's Cl N1 ... 234 B4
Bradley Stone Rd E6 ... 100 B2
Bradlord Ho SE21 ... 161 C1
Bradman Row 7 HA8 ... 27 A3
Bradmead SW8 ... 137 C5 269 A3
Bradmore Park Rd W6 ... 112 B2
Bradon 24 NW9 ... 27 D1
Bradshaw Cl SW19 ... 179 C4
Bradshawe Waye UB8 ... 82 B2
Bradshaws Cl SE25 ... 206 A6
Bradsole Ho 13 BR3 ... 185 C3
Brad St SE1 ... 116 C5 251 B3
Bradstock Ho E9 ... 75 A1
Bradstock Rd E9 ... 74 D2
Stoneleigh KT17 ... 216 B3
Bradwell Ave RM10 ... 81 C6
Bradwell Cl E18 ... 54 D5
Bradwell Ho 9 E17 ... 53 D6
6 NW6 ... 91 D6
Bradwell Mews 5 N18 ... 34 A6
Brady Ct RM8 ... 58 D1
Brady Ho SW4 ... 159 D6
SW8 ... 269 B2
Bradymead E6 ... 100 D1
Brady St E1 ... 96 B3
Braeburn Ct 1 EN4 ... 2 C1
Brae Ct 2 Kingston KT2 ... 176 C2
South Norwood SE25 ... 183 C2
Braefoot Ct SW15 ... 156 D6
Braemar SW15 ... 156 D5
Braemar Ave NW10 ... 67 B6
Thornton Heath CR7 ... 204 D6
Wembley HA0 ... 66 A1
Wimbledon SW18,SW19 ... 157 C2
Wood Green N22 ... 32 A2
Braemar Ct
4 Brentford TW8 ... 131 D6
5 Catford SE6 ... 164 D3
Braemar Gdns DA15 ... 167 B1
NW9 ... 27 B2
West Wickham BR4 ... 208 A1
Braemar Ho W9 ... 229 A1
Richmond TW11 ... 175 B5
Braemar Mans W8 ... 255 D5
Braemar Rd E13 ... 98 D3
N15 ... 51 C4
Brentford TW8 ... 131 D6
North Cheam KT4 ... 216 B5
Braemore Ct EN4 ... 3 A1
Braemore Ho 21 SE15 ... 140 A5
Braeside BR3 ... 185 D5
Braeside Ave SW19 ... 179 A2
Braeside Cl HA5 ... 23 C3
Braeside Rd SW16 ... 181 C3
Braeside Sch
Buckhurst Hill IG9 ... 21 B3
Buckhurst Hill IG9 ... 21 C2
Braes St N1 ... 72 D1
Braesyde Cl DA17 ... 125 B2
Brafferton Rd CR0 ... 221 A4
Braganza St
SE17 ... 116 D1 261 C1
Bragg Cl RM8 ... 80 B2
Bragg Rd TW11 ... 174 D4
Braham Ho SE11 ... 260 D1
Braham St E1 ... 243 D2
Brahma Kumaris World
Spiritual Univ NW10 ... 68 A1
Braid Ave W3 ... 89 C1
Braid Cl TW13 ... 151 B2
Braid Ho SE10 ... 142 A4
Braidwood Rd SE6 ... 164 B3
Braidwood St
SE1 ... 117 C5 253 A3
Braikenridge Ho N21 ... 17 B5
Brailsford Cl SW19 ... 180 C3
Brailsford Rd SW2 ... 160 C5
Braintcroft Prim Sch
NW2 ... 67 D5
Brainton Ave TW14 ... 150 C4
Braintree Ave IG4 ... 56 A5
Braintree Ho 5 E1 ... 96 C3
Braintree Rd
Dagenham RM10 ... 81 C5
Ruislip HA4 ... 62 B4
Braintree St E2 ... 96 C4
Braithwaite Ave RM7 ... 59 C2
Braithwaite Gdns HA7 ... 25 C2
Braithwaite Ho EC1 ... 242 C6
14 South Bromley E14 ... 98 B1
Braithwaite Rd EN3 ... 7 B2
Braithwaite Twr W2 ... 236 C4
Bramah Gn SW9 ... 138 C4
Bramall Cl E15 ... 76 D3
Bramall Ct N7 ... 72 B2
Bramber WC1 ... 233 A1
Bramber Ct TW8 ... 110 A2
Bramber Rd N12 ... 30 C5
W14 ... 135 B6 264 C6
Bramble Acres Cl SM2 ... 217 C1
Bramblebury Rd SE18 ... 123 A1
Bramble Cl N15 ... 52 A5
Beckenham BR3 ... 208 A4
Croydon CR0 ... 223 D4
Hillingdon UB8 ... 82 B1
Stanmore HA7 ... 25 D3
Upper Halliford TW17 ... 193 B6
Brambledown 4 N4 ... 50 A2
Brambledown Cl BR2,
BR4 ... 208 C4
Brambledown Rd
South Croydon CR2 ... 221 C1
Wallington SM5,SM6 ... 219 B1
Bramble Gdns W12 ... 111 D6
Bramble Ho 12 E3 ... 97 C2
Bramble La TW12 ... 173 B4
Brambles Cl TW7,TW8 ... 131 B5
Brambles Farm Dr UB10 ... 82 C4
Brambles The
West Drayton UB7 ... 104 A2
8 Wimbledon SW19 ... 179 B5
Bramblewood Cl SM5 ... 202 C1
Brambling Ct 23 SE8 ... 141 B6
Bramblings The E4 ... 36 B6
Bramcote Ave CR4 ... 202 D5
Bramcote Ct CR4 ... 202 D5
Bramcote Gr SE16 ... 118 C1
Bramcote Rd SW15 ... 134 B1
Bramdean Cres SE12 ... 165 A3
Bramdean Gdns SE12 ... 165 A3
Bramerton NW6 ... 68 D1
Bramerton Rd BR3 ... 207 B6
Bramerton St
SW3 ... 136 C6 267 A6
Bramfield Ct N4 ... 73 A6
Bramfield Rd SW11 ... 158 D6
Bramford Ct N14 ... 15 D2
Bramford Rd SW18 ... 136 A1
Bramham Gdns
SW5 ... 113 D1 255 D2
Chessington KT9 ... 213 D4
Bramham Ho SE22 ... 139 C1
Bramhope La SE7 ... 143 B6
Bramlands Cl SW11 ... 136 C2
Bramlea Cl N6 ... 49 A3
Bramley Ave TW17 ... 193 C6
Bramley Cl E17 ... 35 A1
Croydon CR2 ... 221 A3
East Barnet N14 ... 15 B6
Hayes UB3 ... 106 A6
Orpington BR6 ... 210 D1
Pinner HA5 ... 39 D6
Twickenham TW2 ... 152 A5
Woodford IG8 ... 37 C3
Bramley Cres
SW8 ... 137 D5 269 D4
Ilford IG2 ... 56 C3
Bramley Ct DA16 ... 146 B4
NW2 ... 68 B5
2 Barnet EN4 ... 2 C1
9 Chingford E4 ... 20 A3
Feltham TW14 ... 149 C5
Mitcham CR4 ... 180 B1
Southall UB1 ... 108 A6
Wallington SM6 ... 219 C3
Bramley Gdns WD19 ... 22 C5
Bramley Hill CR2 ... 221 A4
Bramley Ho 19 W10 ... 90 D1
Hounslow TW3 ... 129 B1
Ilford IG2 ... 56 C3
1 Kingston KT2 ... 176 D3
5 Roehampton SW15 ... 155 D5
Bramley House Ct EN2 ... 5 B6
Bramleyhyrst CR2 ... 221 A3
Bramley Lo HA0 ... 65 D4
Bramley Rd W10 ... 90 D1
W5 ... 109 C3
Southgate N14 ... 15 C6
Sutton SM1 ... 218 B3
Bramley Way
Hounslow TW4 ... 151 B6
West Wickham BR4 ... 223 D6
Brampton Cl 14 E5 ... 74 B6
Brampton Ct NW4 ... 46 B5
Brampton Gr NW4 ... 46 C5
Harrow HA3 ... 43 B5
Wembley HA9 ... 44 C1
Brampton La 4 NW4 ... 46 C5
Brampton Manor Sch E6 ... 99 D3
Brampton Park Rd N22 ... 50 C6
Brampton Prim Sch E6 ... 100 A4
Bexley DA16 ... 146 D3
Brampton Rd DA7 ... 147 A4
E6 ... 99 D4
N15 ... 51 A4
NW9 ... 44 C5
Croydon CR0 ... 205 D3
Hillingdon UB10 ... 82 D5
Bramshaw Gdns WD19 ... 22 D5
Bramshaw Rd E9 ... 74 D2
Bramshaw Rise KT3 ... 199 C3
Bramshill Gdns NW5 ... 71 B5
Bramshill Rd NW10 ... 89 D5
Bramshot Ave SE7 ... 143 B6
Bramshott Ct 3 KT6 ... 198 A3
Bramshurst NW8 ... 91 D6
Bramston Rd NW10 ... 90 A5
Wandsworth SW17 ... 158 A1
Bramwell Cl TW16 ... 172 D1
Bramwell Ho SE1 ... 262 B5
SW1 ... 269 A6
Bramwell Mews N1 ... 233 D6
Brancaster Dr NW7 ... 28 A3
Brancaster Ho 22 E1 ... 96 D4
N5 ... 72 D3
Brancaster Rd Ilford E12 ... 78 B4
Brancaster Rd *continued*
Ilford IG2 ... 57 C3
Streatham SW16 ... 160 A1
Brancepeth Gdns IG9 ... 21 A2
Branch Hill NW3 ... 70 A5
Branch Pl N1 ... 95 B6 235 D6
Branch Rd E14 ... 119 A6
Branch St SE15 ... 139 C5
Brancker Cl SM6 ... 220 A1
Brancker Rd HA3 ... 43 D6
Brancroft Way EN3 ... 7 B4
Brand Cl N4 ... 50 D1
Brandlehow Rd SW15 ... 135 B1
Brandon Ho BR3 ... 185 D5
Brandon Mews EC2 ... 242 C4
Brandon Rd E17 ... 54 A6
N7 ... 72 A1
Southall UB2 ... 107 B1
Sutton SM1 ... 217 D4
Brandon St
SE17 ... 117 A2 262 B3
Brandram Rd SE13 ... 142 C1
Brandrams Wharf SE16 ... 118 C4
Brandreth Ct HA1 ... 42 D3
Brandreth Rd
Newham E6 ... 100 B1
Upper Tooting SW17 ... 159 B2
Brandries The SM6 ... 219 D5
Brand St SE10 ... 142 A5
Brandville Gdns IG6 ... 56 D5
Brandville Rd UB7 ... 104 A4
Brandy Way SM2 ... 217 C1
Brangbourne Rd BR1 ... 186 A5
Brangton Rd SE11 ... 260 D1
Brangwyn Cres SW19 ... 180 B1
Brangwyn Ct W14 ... 254 A5
Branham Ho 1 SE18 ... 122 D1
Branksea St
SW6 ... 135 A3 264 A3
Branksome Ave N18 ... 33 D5
Branksome Cl KT12 ... 194 D1
Branksome Ct 6 N2 ... 48 A6
Branksome Ho SW8 ... 270 C4
Branksome Rd SW2 ... 160 A6
Merton SW19 ... 179 C2
Branksome Way
Harrow HA3 ... 44 B3
Kingston KT3 ... 177 B2
Bransby Ct 4 N16 ... 73 C4
Bransby Rd KT9 ... 214 A2
Branscombe NW1 ... 232 B5
Branscombe Ct BR2 ... 208 C4
Branscombe Gdns N21 ... 16 C4
Branscombe St SE13 ... 141 D2
Bransdale Cl NW6 ... 91 C6
Bransgrove Rd HA8 ... 26 B3
Branston Cres BR5 ... 211 B1
Branstone Ct 9 TW9 ... 132 B4
Branstone Rd TW9 ... 132 B4
Branston Ho N7 ... 72 C3
Brants Wlk W7 ... 86 C3
Brantwood Ave DA8 ... 147 D5
Isleworth TW7 ... 131 A1
Brantwood Cl E17 ... 53 D6
Brantwood Gdns
Enfield EN2 ... 16 A6
Redbridge IG4 ... 56 A5
Brantwood Ho 9 SE5 ... 139 A5
Brantwood Rd DA7 ... 147 D2
SE24 ... 161 A6
Tottenham N17 ... 34 A4
Brasenose Dr SW13 ... 134 C6
Brasher Cl UB6 ... 64 B3
Brassett Point 8 E15 ... 98 C6
Brassey Cl TW14 ... 150 A3
Brassey Ho 1 E14 ... 119 D2
Walton-on-T KT12 ... 194 A1
Brassey Rd NW6 ... 69 B2
Brassey Sq SW11 ... 137 A2
Brassie Ave W3 ... 89 C1
Brass Talley Alley 31
SE16 ... 118 D4
Brasted Cl DA6 ... 168 D6
Forest Hill SE26 ... 184 C6
Brasted Lo 11 BR3 ... 185 C3
Brathay NW1 ... 232 B3
Brathway Rd SW18 ... 157 C4
Bratley St 12 E1 ... 96 A3
Bratten Ct CR0 ... 205 B3
Braund Ave UB6 ... 85 D3
Braundton Ave DA15 ... 167 D3
Braunston Dr UB4 ... 85 A3
Bravington Cl TW17 ... 192 B4
Bravington Pl W9 ... 91 B3
Bravington Rd W9 ... 91 B4
Brawne Ho 12 SE17 ... 138 D6
Braxfield Rd SE4 ... 141 B1
Braxted Pk SW16 ... 182 B4
Bray NW3 ... 70 C1
Brayard's Rd SE15 ... 140 B3
Braybourne Dr TW7 ... 130 D5
Braybrooke Gdns SE19 ... 183 C3
Braybrook St W12 ... 89 D1
Brayburne Ave SW4 ... 137 C3
Braycourt Ave KT12 ... 194 C2
Bray Cres SE16 ... 118 D4
Bray Ct Chessington KT9 ... 214 B3
Streatham SW16 ... 182 A5
Braydon Rd N16 ... 52 A1
Bray Dr E16 ... 120 D6
Brayfield Terr N1 ... 72 C1
Brayford Sq 12 E1 ... 96 C1
Bray Pl SW3 ... 114 D2 257 C3
Bray Rd NW7 ... 28 D4
Brayton Gdns EN2 ... 3 D1
Braywick Ct 9 KT2 ... 176 C3
Braywood Rd SE9 ... 145 B1
Brazil Cl CR0 ... 204 A2
Breach La RM9 ... 103 C4
Bread St EC2,EC4 ... 242 B1

Breakspeare SE21 .... 161 D1
Breakspear Jun & Inf Schs
UB10 .... 60 C6
Breakspear Rd HA4,UB9 .... 38 D3
Breakspear Rd N UB9 .... 38 B5
Breakspear Rd S UB9,
UB10 .... 38 C1
Breakspears Dr BR5 .... 190 A2
Breakspears Mews SE4 .... 141 C3
Breakspears Rd SE4 .... 141 C2
Breakwell Ct 16 W10 .... 91 A3
Bream Cl N17 .... 52 B5
Bream Gdns E6 .... 100 C4
Breamore Cl SW15 .... 156 A3
Breamore Ct IG3 .... 80 A6
Breamore Rd IG3 .... 79 D6
Bream's Bldgs
EC4 .... 94 C1 241 A2
Bream St E3 .... 75 C1
Breamwater Gdns
TW10 .... 153 B1
Brearley Cl HA8 .... 27 A3
Uxbridge UB8 .... 60 A2
Breaside Prep Sch BR1 .... 187 D2
Breasley Cl SW15 .... 134 B1
Brechin Pl SW7 .... 114 A2 256 B3
Brecknock Prim Sch
NW1 .... 71 D2
Brecknock Rd N19 .... 71 D3
Breckonmead BR1 .... 187 C1
Breco Ho IG11 .... 102 B4
Brecon Cl Mitcham CR4 .... 204 A6
North Cheam KT4 .... 216 C6
Brecon Ct N12 .... 14 A1
7 SE9 .... 166 C5
Brecon Gn NW9 .... 45 C3
Brecon Ho N16 .... 51 D1
W2 .... 236 A2
Wandsworth SW18 .... 157 C4
Brecon Rd W6 .... 135 A6 264 B5
Enfield EN3 .... 6 C1
Brede Cl E6 .... 100 C4
Bredel Ho 1 E14 .... 97 C2
Bredgar SE13 .... 163 D6
Bredgar Rd N19 .... 71 C6
Bredhurst Cl SE20 .... 184 C4
Bredinghurst SE22 .... 162 A4
Bredinghurst Sch SE15 .... 140 D1
Bredon Ct HA8 .... 26 B6
Bredon Rd CR0 .... 205 D2
Breer St SW6 .... 135 D2
Breezer's Ct 15 E1 .... 118 A6
Breezer's Hill E1 .... 118 A6
Bremans Row SW18 .... 158 A2
Brember Rd HA2 .... 64 A6
Bremer Mews E17 .... 53 D5
Bremner Rd SW7 .... 256 B6
Brenchley Cl
Chislehurst BR7 .... 188 C2
Hayes BR2 .... 208 D3
Brenchley Gdns SE15,
SE22,SE23 .... 162 D5
Brenchley Rd BR5 .... 189 D1
Brenda Rd SW17 .... 158 D2
Brende Gdns KT8 .... 195 D5
Brendon Ave NW10 .... 67 C4
Brendon Cl Esher KT10 .... 212 A2
Harlington UB7 .... 127 A5
Brendon Ct UB2 .... 107 D2
Brendon Dr KT10 .... 212 A2
Brendon Gdns
Harrow HA2 .... 63 D4
Ilford IG2 .... 57 C4
Brendon Gr N2 .... 30 A1
Brendon H SM2 .... 218 A2
Brendon Ho W1 .... 238 A4
Brendon Rd BR7 .... 167 B2
Dagenham RM8 .... 59 C1
Brendon St W1 .... 92 C1 237 B2
Brendon Villas N21 .... 17 A3
Brendon Way EN1 .... 17 C4
Brenley Cl CR4 .... 203 A6
Brenley Gdns SE9 .... 143 D1
Brenley Ho SE1 .... 252 C2
Brent Cl DA5 .... 169 A3
Brentcot Cl W13 .... 87 B3
Brent Cres NW10 .... 88 B5
Brent Cross Flyover
NW2,NW4 .... 46 D2
Brent Cross Gdns NW4 .... 46 D3
Brent Cross Interchange
NW2,NW4 .... 46 D2
Brent Cross Sh Ctr NW4 .... 46 C2
Brent Cross Sta NW11 .... 46 D2
Brent Ct NW11 .... 46 D2
5 W12 .... 111 C3
Ealing W7 .... 108 B6
Brentfield NW10 .... 66 D1
Brentfield Cl NW10 .... 67 B2
Brentfield Gdns NW2 .... 46 D2
Brentfield Ho 6 NW10 .... 67 B1
Brentfield Prim Sch
NW10 .... 67 B2
Brentfield Rd NW10 .... 67 B2
Brentford Bsns Ctr
TW8 .... 131 C5
Brentford Cl UB4 .... 84 D3
Brentford Fountain Leisure
Centre W4 .... 110 C1
Brentford Ho 6 TW1 .... 153 B4
Brentford Sch for Girls
TW8 .... 131 D6
Brentford Sta TW8 .... 131 C6
Brent Gn NW4 .... 46 D4
Brentham Way W5 .... 87 D3
Brent Ho 19 E9 .... 74 C2
3 Catford BR1 .... 186 B5
Brenthouse Rd E9 .... 74 C2
Brenthurst Rd NW10 .... 67 D2
Brent Knoll Sch SE26 .... 162 D1
Brent Lea TW8 .... 131 C5
Brent Mans NW4 .... 46 C4
Brentmead Cl W7 .... 108 C6
Brentmead Gdns NW10 .... 88 B5
Brentmead Pl NW11 .... 46 D3
Brent New Ent Ctr NW10 .... 67 D2
Brenton Ct E9 .... 75 A3
Brenton St E14 .... 97 A1
Brent Park Ind Est UB2 .... 106 C3
Brent Park Rd NW4 .... 46 B2
Brent Pl EN5 .... 13 B6
Brent Rd E16 .... 99 A2
Brentford TW8 .... 131 C6
Southall UB2 .... 106 C3
Woolwich SE18 .... 144 D5
Brent Side TW8 .... 131 C6
Brentside Cl W13 .... 87 A3
Brentside Executive Ctr
TW8 .... 131 B6
Brentside High Sch W7 .... 86 C3
Brentside Prim Sch W7 .... 86 C3
Brent St NW4 .... 46 C4
Brent Trad Est NW10 .... 67 C3
Brentvale Ave
Southall UB1 .... 108 B5
Wembley HA0 .... 88 B6
Brent View Rd NW9 .... 46 A2
Brentwaters Bsns Pk
TW8 .... 131 C5
Brent Way N3 .... 29 C4
Brentford TW8 .... 131 D5
Wembley HA9 .... 66 D2
Brentwick Gdns TW8 .... 110 A2
Brentwood Cl SE9 .... 167 A3
Brentwood Ho 2 SE18 .... 143 D5
Brentwood Lo NW4 .... 46 D4
Brereton Ho 4 SW2 .... 160 C4
Brereton Rd N17 .... 33 D3
Bressenden Pl
SW1 .... 115 C3 259 A6
Bressey Ave EN1 .... 6 A4
Bressey Gr E18 .... 36 D1
Bretherton Ct CR2 .... 221 C2
Breton Ho EC2 .... 242 B5
SE1 .... 263 C6
Brett Cl N16 .... 73 C6
15 Northolt UB5 .... 84 D4
Brett Cres NW10 .... 89 B6
Brett Ct N9 .... 18 C2
Brettell St SE17 .... 262 D1
Brettenham Ave E17 .... 35 C2
Brettenham Prim Sch
N18 .... 34 A6
Brettenham Rd
Chingford E17 .... 35 C2
Edmonton N18 .... 34 A6
Brett Gdns RM9 .... 81 A1
Brett Ho 1 SW15 .... 156 D4
Brett House Cl 2 SW15 .... 156 D4
Brettinghurst 7 SE1 .... 118 A1
Brett Manor E8 .... 74 B3
Bretton Ho N19 .... 50 A1
Brett Pas 28 E8 .... 74 B3
Brett Rd E8 .... 74 B3
Barnet EN5 .... 12 C6
Brewers Bldgs EC1 .... 234 C2
Brewers Ct W2 .... 236 A2
Brewer's Gn SW1 .... 259 C6
Brewers La 11 TW9 .... 153 D6
Brewer St W1 .... 115 C6 249 B6
Brewery Cl HA0 .... 65 A4
Brewery Ind Est The N1 .... 235 B3
Brewery Mews Bsns Ctr 11
TW7 .... 131 A2
Brewery Rd N7 .... 72 A2
SE18 .... 123 B1
Keston Mark BR2 .... 210 A1
Brewery Sq SE1 .... 253 C3
Brewhouse La E1 .... 118 B5
Brewhouse Rd 3 SE18 .... 122 B2
Brewhouse St SW15 .... 135 A2
Brewhouse Wlk SE16 .... 119 A5
Brewhouse Yd EC1 .... 241 C6
Brewood Rd RM8 .... 80 B3
Brewster Gdns W10 .... 90 C2
Brewster Ho E14 .... 119 B6
SE1 .... 263 D4
Brewster Rd E10 .... 53 D1
Brian Ct N10 .... 31 B2
Brian Rd RM6 .... 58 C4
Briant Ho SE1 .... 260 D5
Briants Cl HA5 .... 23 B1
Briant St SE14 .... 140 D5
Briar Ave SW16 .... 182 B3
Briarbank Rd W13 .... 87 A1
Briar Cl N2 .... 30 A1
Buckhurst Hill IG9 .... 21 D2
Edmonton N13 .... 17 A1
Hampton TW12 .... 173 B5
Isleworth TW7 .... 152 D6
Briar Cres UB5 .... 63 D2
Briar Ct E11 .... 54 B2
E8 .... 73 D1
Cheam SM3 .... 216 C4
Hampton TW12 .... 173 D5
Briardale HA8 .... 27 B6
Wandsworth SW19 .... 157 B3
Briardale Gdns NW3 .... 69 C5
Briardale Ho N16 .... 51 C1
Briarfield Ave N3 .... 29 D1
Briar Gdns BR2 .... 208 D1
Briaris Cl 11 N17 .... 34 B3
Briar La CR0 .... 223 D4
Briar Lo E18 .... 37 C2
Briar Rd NW2 .... 68 C4
Harrow HA3 .... 43 C4
Littleton TW17 .... 192 C4
Thornton Heath SW16 .... 204 B6
Twickenham TW2 .... 152 C3
Briars The WD23 .... 8 C4
Briarswood Way BR6 .... 227 D3
Briarview Ct E4 .... 36 B4
Briar Way UB7 .... 104 C4
Briar Wlk HA8 .... 27 A3
W10 .... 91 A3
Putney SW15 .... 134 B1
Briarwood Cl NW9 .... 45 A3
Feltham TW13 .... 149 C1
Briarwood Ct 5 KT4 .... 200 A1
Briarwood Dr HA6 .... 22 A1
Briarwood Rd SW4 .... 159 D6
Stoneleigh KT17 .... 216 A2
Briary Cl NW3 .... 70 C1
Briary Ct DA14 .... 190 B5
Briary Gdns BR1 .... 187 B5
Briary Gr HA8 .... 26 D1
Briary La N9 .... 17 D1
Briary Lo BR3 .... 186 A2
Brickbarn Cl SW10 .... 266 B4
Brick Ct EC4 .... 241 A1
Brickett Cl HA4 .... 39 A4
Brick Farm Cl TW9 .... 132 D4
Brickfield Cl TW8 .... 131 C5
Brickfield Cotts SE18 .... 145 D6
Brickfield Farm Gdns
BR6 .... 227 A4
Brickfield La
Edgware EN5 .... 11 D5
Harlington UB3 .... 127 B6
Brickfield Rd
South Norwood CR7,
SW16 .... 182 D2
Wimbledon SW19 .... 179 D6
Brickfields HA2 .... 64 B6
Brickfields Way UB7 .... 104 B3
Brick La E1 .... 95 D3 243 D5
E2 .... 95 D4
Enfield EN1 .... 6 B3
Stanmore HA7 .... 25 D3
Bricklayers Arms SE1 .... 262 D5
Brick St W1 .... 115 B5 248 C3
Brickwall La HA4 .... 39 D1
Brickwood Cl SE26 .... 162 B1
Brickwood Rd CR0 .... 221 C6
Brickworth Ho 26 SW9 .... 138 C4
Bridal Mews N1 .... 234 C5
Brideale Cl SE15 .... 139 D6
Bride Ct EC4 .... 241 C1
Bride La EC4 .... 94 D1 241 C1
Bride St N7 .... 72 B2
Bridewain St SE1 .... 263 C6
Bridewell Pl 20 E1 .... 118 B5
EC4 .... 241 C1
Bridford Mews W1 .... 238 D4
Bridge App NW3 .... 71 A1
Bridge Ave W6 .... 112 C1
Ealing W7 .... 86 B2
Bridge Avenue Mans 1
W6 .... 112 C1
Bridge Cl 13 W10 .... 90 D1
Enfield EN1 .... 6 B3
Teddington TW11 .... 174 D6
Walton-on-T KT12 .... 193 D1
Bridge Ct E10 .... 53 B2
Bridge Dr N13 .... 32 B6
Bridge End E17 .... 36 A2
Bridge Field Ho 7 W2 .... 91 D1
Bridgefield Rd SM1,SM2 .... 217 C2
Bridgefoot SE1 .... 116 A1 260 B1
Bridge Gate N21 .... 17 A4
Bridge Gdns
East Molesey KT8 .... 196 B5
Littleton TW15 .... 171 A3
Bridge Ho E9 .... 74 D3
1 NW1 .... 71 A1
SE4 .... 141 B1
TW8 .... 109 A2
Bridge Ho S TW8 .... 109 A2
Bridge House Quay E14 .... 120 A5
Bridge La NW11 .... 47 B4
SW11 .... 136 C4 267 B1
Bridgeland Rd E16 .... 121 A6
Bridgeman Ho 19 E9 .... 74 C1
Bridgeman Rd N1 .... 72 B1
Teddington TW11 .... 175 A4
Bridgeman St
NW8 .... 92 C5 230 A3
Bridge Meadows SE14 .... 140 D6
Bridgend Rd SW18 .... 136 A1
Bridgenhall Rd EN1 .... 5 D4
Bridgen Ho 15 E1 .... 96 B1
Bridgen Rd DA5 .... 169 A4
Bridge Par N21 .... 17 A4
Bridge Pk 7 SW18 .... 157 C6
Wembley NW10 .... 66 D1
Bridge Pl SW1 .... 115 B2 258 D4
Croydon CR0 .... 205 B1
Bridgeport Pl 4 E1 .... 118 A5
Bridge Rd DA7 .... 147 A3
E15 .... 98 B6
E17 .... 53 B2
E6 .... 78 B1
NW10 .... 67 C2
Beckenham BR3 .... 185 B3
Chessington KT9 .... 214 A3
East Molesey KT8 .... 196 C5
Edmonton N9 .... 18 A1
Hounslow TW3 .... 130 B2
Isleworth TW3,TW7 .... 130 B2
Southall UB2 .... 107 C4
Sutton SM2 .... 217 D2
Twickenham TW1 .... 153 B5
Wallington SM6 .... 219 C3
Wembley HA9 .... 66 C5
Wood Green N22 .... 32 A2
Bridge Row CR0 .... 205 B1
Bridges Ct SW11 .... 136 B3
Bridges Ho 15 SE5 .... 139 B5
Bridges La CR0 .... 220 A4
Bridges Rd Stanmore HA7 .... 24 D5
Bridges Rd *continued*
Wimbledon SW19 .... 179 D4
Bridges Road Mews
SW19 .... 179 D4
Bridge St SW1 .... 116 A4 250 B1
W4 .... 111 B2
Pinner HA5 .... 41 A6
Richmond TW10 .... 153 D6
Walton-on-T KT12 .... 193 D2
Bridge Terr E15 .... 76 B1
Bridge The HA3 .... 42 D5
Bridgetown Cl 5 SE19 .... 183 C5
Bridgeview 2 W6 .... 112 C1
Bridgewater Cl BR5,BR7 .... 211 C6
Bridgewater Ct HA0 .... 65 C2
Bridgewater Gdns HA8 .... 26 B1
Bridgewater Rd E15 .... 98 A6
Ruislip HA4 .... 62 B4
Wembley HA0 .... 65 C1
Bridgewater Sq EC2 .... 242 A4
Bridgewater St EC2 .... 242 A4
Bridge Way NW11 .... 47 B4
Bridgeway Barking IG11 .... 79 D1
Wembley HA0 .... 66 B1
Bridge Way
Twickenham TW2 .... 152 A4
Uxbridge UB10 .... 60 D3
Bridgeway St
NW1 .... 93 C5 232 B3
Bridge Wharf 18 E2 .... 96 D5
Bridge Wharf Rd TW7 .... 131 B2
Bridgewood Cl SE20 .... 184 B3
Bridgewood Rd
North Cheam KT17,KT4 .... 216 A4
Streatham SW16 .... 181 D3
Bridge Yd SE1 .... 252 D4
Bridgford St SW17,
SW18 .... 158 A1
Bridgman Rd W4 .... 111 A3
Bridgnorth Ho 10 SE15 .... 140 A6
Bridgwater Ho W2 .... 236 A2
Bridle Cl Enfield EN3 .... 7 B6
Kingston KT1 .... 197 D5
Sunbury TW16 .... 194 A6
West Ewell KT19 .... 215 B3
Bridle La W1 .... 115 C6 249 B6
Twickenham TW1 .... 153 B5
Bridle Path CR0 .... 220 A5
Bridle Path The IG8 .... 36 C3
Bridlepath Way TW14 .... 149 C3
Bridle Rd Addington CR0 .... 223 C4
Claygate KT10 .... 213 B2
Croydon CR0 .... 223 C5
Pinner HA5 .... 40 C4
Bridle Way BR6 .... 227 A4
Addington CR0 .... 223 C3
Bridle Way The SM6 .... 219 C3
Bridlington Ho SW18 .... 136 A1
Bridlington Rd N9 .... 18 B4
Bridport SE17 .... 262 B1
Bridport Ave RM7 .... 59 D3
Bridport Ho N1 .... 235 D5
6 Edmonton N18 .... 34 A5
Bridport Pl N1 .... 95 B6 235 D5
Bridport Rd
Edmonton N18 .... 33 D5
Greenford UB6 .... 85 D6
Thornton Heath CR7 .... 204 D6
Bridstow Pl W2 .... 91 C1
Brief St SE5 .... 138 D4
Brierfield NW1 .... 232 A5
Brierley CR0 .... 223 D2
Brierley Ave N9 .... 18 C3
Brierley Cl SE25 .... 206 A5
Brierley Ct W7 .... 108 C6
Brierley Rd E11 .... 76 B4
Upper Tooting SW12 .... 159 C2
Brierly Gdns E2 .... 96 C5
Brigade Cl HA2 .... 64 B6
Brigade St SE3 .... 142 D3
Brigadier Ave EN2 .... 5 A4
Brigadier Hill EN2 .... 5 A5
Brigeford Cl 5 E5 .... 74 A6
Briggs Cl CR4 .... 181 B2
Briggs Ho 20 E2 .... 95 D4
Bright Cl DA17 .... 124 D2
Bright Ct 8 SE28 .... 124 C5
Brightfield Rd SE12 .... 164 D6
Brightling Rd SE4 .... 163 B5
Brightlingsea Pl 5 E14 .... 119 B6
Brightman Rd SW18 .... 158 B3
Brighton Ave E17 .... 53 B4
Brighton Bldgs SE1 .... 263 A5
Brighton Cl UB10 .... 60 D1
Brighton Ct SW15 .... 157 B5
Brighton Dr 3 UB5 .... 63 C2
Brighton Gr SE14 .... 141 A4
Brighton Ho 7 SE5 .... 139 B4
Brighton Rd N16 .... 73 C4
N2 .... 30 A1
Belmont SM2 .... 217 D1
South Croydon CR2 .... 221 B2
Surbiton KT6 .... 197 D3
Sutton SM2 .... 218 A1
Wallend E6 .... 100 C4
Brighton Terr SW9 .... 138 B1
Brightside Rd SE13 .... 164 B5
Brightside The EN3 .... 7 A4
Bright St E14 .... 97 D2
Brightwell Cl CR0 .... 204 C1
Brightwell Cres SW17 .... 180 D5
Brightwell Ct N7 .... 72 B3
Brightwells 1 SW6 .... 135 D3
Brig Mews SE8 .... 141 C6
Brigstock Ho SE5 .... 139 A3
Brigstock Rd
Belvedere DA17 .... 125 D2
Thornton Heath CR7 .... 204 D4
Brill Ho NW10 .... 67 B5
Brill Pl NW1 .... 93 D5 232 D3
Brim Hill N2 .... 48 B5
Brimpsfield Cl SE2 .... 124 B3
Brimsdown Ave EN3 .... 7 A4
Brimsdown Ho E3 .... 98 A3
Brimsdown Jun & Inf Sch
EN3 .... 6 D2
Brimsdown Sta EN3 .... 7 A3
Brimstone Ho 3 E15 .... 76 C1
Brindishe Prim Sch
SE12 .... 164 D6
Brindle Gate DA15 .... 167 C3
Brindley Cl DA7 .... 147 C2
Wembley HA0 .... 87 D6
Brindley Ho 37 W2 .... 91 C2
22 Streatham SW12 .... 160 A4
Brindley St SE14 .... 141 B4
Brindley Way BR1 .... 187 B5
Southall UB1 .... 107 D6
Brindwood Rd E4 .... 19 C1
Brine Ct KT6 .... 197 D4
Brine Ho 10 E3 .... 97 A5
Brinkburn Cl SE2 .... 124 A2
Edgware HA8 .... 44 D6
Brinkburn Gdns HA8 .... 44 C6
Brinkley 18 KT1 .... 176 C1
Brinkley Rd KT4 .... 216 B6
Brinklow Cres SE18 .... 144 D5
Brinklow Ho W2 .... 91 D2
Brinkworth Rd IG5 .... 56 A6
Brinkworth Way E9 .... 75 B2
Brinsdale Rd NW4 .... 46 D6
Brinsley Ho 17 E1 .... 96 C1
Brinsley Rd HA3 .... 24 B1
Brinsley St 29 E1 .... 96 B1
Brinsworth Cl TW2 .... 152 B2
Brinton Wlk SE1 .... 251 C3
Brion Pl E14 .... 98 A2
Brisbane Ave SW19 .... 179 D2
Brisbane Ct N10 .... 31 B3
Brisbane Ho 3 W12 .... 112 B6
Brisbane Rd E10 .... 75 D6
Ealing W13 .... 109 A4
Ilford IG1 .... 57 A1
Brisbane St SE5 .... 139 B5
Briscoe Cl E11 .... 76 D6
Briscoe Rd SW19 .... 180 B4
Briset Rd SE9 .... 143 D1
Briset St EC1 .... 94 D3 241 C5
Briset Way N7 .... 72 B6
Bristol Cl Stanwell TW19 .... 148 A5
Wallington SM6 .... 220 A1
Bristol Ct 11 TW19 .... 148 A5
Bristol Gdns W9 .... 91 D3
Bristol Ho SE11 .... 261 A5
1 Barking IG11 .... 80 A1
Bristol Mews W9 .... 91 D3
Bristol Park Rd 1 E17 .... 53 A5
Bristol Rd E7 .... 77 D2
Greenford UB6 .... 85 D6
Morden SM4 .... 202 A4
Briston Gr N8 .... 50 A3
Briston Mews NW7 .... 28 A3
Bristow Rd DA7 .... 147 A4
Hounslow TW3 .... 130 A2
Wallington CR0 .... 220 A5
West Norwood SE19 .... 183 C5
Britannia Cl SW4 .... 137 D1
Northolt UB5 .... 84 D4
Britannia Gate 12 E16 .... 121 A5
Britannia Junc NW1 .... 231 D6
Britannia La TW2 .... 152 A4
Britannia Rd 11 E14 .... 119 C2
N12 .... 14 A1
SW6 .... 135 D5 265 C3
Ilford IG1 .... 78 D5
Surbiton KT5 .... 198 B2
Britannia Row
N1 .... 95 A6 235 A6
Britannia St WC1 .... 94 B4 233 C2
Britannia Way
Acton NW10 .... 88 D3
Stanwell TW19 .... 148 A4
Britannia Wlk N1 .... 235 C2
British Gr W4 .... 111 D1
British Grove Pas 2
W4 .... 111 D1
British Grove S 3 W4 .... 111 D1
British Home & Hospl for
Incurables SE27 .... 182 D5
British Legion Rd E4 .... 20 D2
British Library (Newspaper
Library) NW9 .... 45 C6
British Library The★
WC1 .... 93 D4 232 D2
British Mus★
WC1 .... 94 A2 240 A3
British St E3 .... 97 B4
British Wharf Ind Est
SE14 .... 140 D6
Britley Ho 10 E14 .... 97 B1
Brittain Ct SE9 .... 166 A3
Brittain Ho SE9 .... 166 A3
Brittain Rd RM8 .... 81 B5
Brittany Ho SW15 .... 134 C1
Brittany Point SE11 .... 261 A3
Britten Cl NW11 .... 47 D1
Elstree WD6 .... 9 D5
Brittenden Cl 1 BR6 .... 227 D2
Brittenden Par BR6 .... 227 D2
Britten Dr UB1 .... 85 C1
Britten Ho SW3 .... 257 B2
Britten St SW3 .... 114 C1 257 A2
Britton Cl SE6 .... 164 B4
Britton St EC1 .... 94 D2 241 C5
Brixham Cres HA4 .... 40 A1
Brixham Gdns IG3 .... 79 C3
Brixham Rd DA16 .... 146 D4
Brixham St E16 .... 122 C5
Brixton Day Coll SW9 .... 138 A2
Brixton Hill SW2 .... 160 B5
Brixton Hill Ct 5 SW2 .... 160 B6
Brixton Hill Pl SW2 .... 160 A4
Brixton Mkt★ SW9 .... 138 C1
Brixton Oval 7 SW2 .... 138 C1
Brixton Rd SW9 .... 138 C4
Brixton Sta SW9 .... 138 C1
Brixton Station Rd SW9 .... 138 C2
Brixton Water La SW2 .... 160 B6
Broadacre Cl UB10 .... 60 D5
Broadbent Cl N6 .... 49 B1
Broadbent St W1 .... 248 C6
Broad Berry Ct N18 .... 34 B5
Broad Bridge Cl SE3 .... 143 A5
Broad Common Est N16 .... 52 A1
Broadcoombe CR2 .... 222 D1
Broadcroft Ave HA7 .... 25 D1
Broadcroft Rd BR5 .... 211 B2
Broad Ct WC2 .... 240 B1
Broadfield NW6 .... 69 D2
Broadfield Cl NW2 .... 68 C5
Croydon CR0 .... 220 B6
Broadfield Ct WD23 .... 8 C2
Broadfield La NW1 .... 72 A1
Broadfield Rd SE6 .... 164 C3
Broadfields Harrow HA2 .... 23 D1
Thames Ditton KT8 .... 196 C3
Broadfields Ave
Edgware HA8 .... 10 D1
Southgate N21 .... 16 C4
Broadfields Hts HA8 .... 26 D6
Broadfields Inf Sch HA8 .... 10 C2
Broadfields Jun Sch
HA8 .... 10 D2
Broadfield Sq EN1 .... 6 B3
Broadfields Way NW10 .... 67 D3
Broadfield Way IG9 .... 21 C1
Broadford Ho 11 E1 .... 97 A3
Broadgate EC2 .... 95 C2 243 A4
Broadgate Circ
EC2 .... 95 C2 243 A3
Broadgate Rd E16 .... 99 D1
Broadgates Ave EN4 .... 1 D4
Broadgates Ct SE11 .... 261 B1
Broadgates Rd SW18 .... 158 B3
Broad Green Ave CR0 .... 204 D2
Broadhead Strand NW9 .... 27 D2
Broadheath Dr BR7 .... 188 B5
Broadhinton Rd SW4 .... 137 C2
Broadhurst Ave
Edgware HA8 .... 26 D6
Ilford IG3 .... 79 D4
Broadhurst Cl NW6 .... 70 A2
9 Richmond TW10 .... 154 B6
Broadhurst Gdns NW6 .... 69 D2
Ruislip HA4 .... 62 C6
Broadhurst Mans NW6 .... 69 D2
Broad La EC2 .... 243 A4
N15 .... 51 D5
N15 .... 52 A5
N8 .... 50 B4
Hampton TW12 .... 173 C4
Broadlands N6 .... 49 A2
Feltham TW13 .... 151 C1
Broadlands Ave Enfield EN3 .... 6 B2
Shepperton TW17 .... 193 A3
Streatham SW16 .... 160 A2
Broadlands Cl N6 .... 49 A2
Enfield EN3 .... 6 C2
Streatham SW16 .... 160 A2
Broadlands Ct TW9 .... 132 C5
Broadlands Lo N6 .... 48 D2
Broadlands Mans 2
SW16 .... 160 A2
Broadlands Rd BR1 .... 187 B6
N6 .... 48 D2
Broadlands Way KT3 .... 199 D3
Broad Lawn SE9 .... 166 C3
Broadlawns Ct HA3 .... 24 D2
Broadley St NW8 .... 92 C2 237 A4
Broadley Terr
NW1 .... 92 C3 237 B5
Broadmayne SE17 .... 262 C2
Broadmead W14 .... 254 A3
Catford SE6 .... 163 C1
Broadmead Ave KT4 .... 200 A2
Broadmead Cl
Hampton TW12 .... 173 C4
Pinner HA5 .... 23 A3
Broadmead Ct 6 IG8 .... 37 A4
Broadmead Inf Sch CR0 .... 205 B2
Broadmead Jun Sch
CR0 .... 205 B3
Broadmead Rd
Northolt UB5 .... 85 A3
Woodford IG8 .... 37 B3
Broad Oak Ashford TW16 .... 171 D4
Woodford IG8 .... 37 B5
Broad Oak Cl BR5 .... 190 A1
Chingford E4 .... 35 C5
Broadoak Ct 9 SW9 .... 138 C2
Broadoak Ho 18 NW6 .... 91 D6
Broad Oaks KT6 .... 214 D6
Broadoaks Way BR2 .... 208 D4
Broad Sanctuary SW1 .... 250 A1
Broad St Dagenham RM10 .... 81 C1
Teddington TW11 .... 174 D4
Broad St Ave EC2 .... 243 A3
Broadstone Ho SW8 .... 270 C3
Broadstone Pl W1 .... 238 A3
Broad St Pl EC2 .... 242 D3
Broadview NW9 .... 44 C3
Broadview Est TW19 .... 148 C4
Broadview Ho RM8 .... 58 D1
Broadview Rd SW16 .... 181 D3
Broadwalk E18 .... 54 D6
Harrow HA2 .... 41 D4
Broadwalk Ho SW7 .... 246 A1

Broadwalk La NW11 ... 47 B2
Broadwalk Sh Ctr The HA8 ... 26 D4
Broadwall SE1 ... 116 C5 251 B4
Broadwater Farm Prim Sch N17 ... 33 B1
Broadwater Gdns BR6 ... 227 A4
Broadwater Prim Sch SW17 ... 180 C6
Broadwater Rd SE18 ... 123 B3
Tottenham N17 ... 33 C1
Upper Tooting SW17 ... 180 C6
Broadway DA6 ... 147 B1
E15 ... 76 B1
SW1 ... 115 D3 259 C6
Barking IG11 ... 101 A6
Bexley DA6,DA7 ... 147 C1
Ealing W13 ... 109 A5
Ealing W7 ... 108 C5
Tolworth KT6 ... 198 D1
Broadway Arc 3 W6 ... 112 C2
Broadway Ave
Thornton Heath CR0 ... 205 B4
Twickenham TW1 ... 153 B5
Broadway Bldgs 5 W7 ... 108 C5
Broadway Cl IG8 ... 37 B4
Broadway Ct
Beckenham BR3 ... 208 A6
Wimbledon SW19 ... 179 C4
Broadway Ctr Adult Coll SW17 ... 180 C6
Broadway Gdns
Mitcham CR4 ... 202 C5
Woodford IG8 ... 37 B4
Broadway Ho 2 E8 ... 96 B6
Broadway Mans SW6 ... 265 B3
Broadway Market E8 ... 96 B6
Broadway Market Mews 21 E8 ... 96 A6
Broadway Mews E5 ... 51 D2
Southgate N21 ... 16 D3
Bowes Park N13 ... 32 B5
Broadway Par N8 ... 50 A3
Chingford E4 ... 36 A4
Hayes UB3 ... 106 A5
West Drayton UB7 ... 104 A4
Broadway Pl SW19 ... 179 B4
Broadway Sh Ctr 5 DA6 ... 147 C1
Broadway The E13 ... 99 B5
N11 ... 31 A5
2 N14 ... 15 D3
N8 ... 50 A3
NW7 ... 27 D5
W3 ... 110 C4
Barnes SW13 ... 133 C3
Cheam SM3 ... 217 A2
Chingford E4 ... 36 B4
Dagenham RM8 ... 81 C6
Ealing W5 ... 109 D6
Edmonton N9 ... 18 A1
Greenford UB6 ... 86 A3
Harrow HA3 ... 24 D1
Merton SW19 ... 179 C3
Pinner HA5 ... 23 B3
Southall UB1 ... 107 A6
Stanmore HA7 ... 25 C5
Sutton SM1 ... 218 A4
Thames Ditton KT10 ... 196 C1
Tolworth KT6 ... 198 C1
Wallington SM6 ... 220 A4
Wembley HA9 ... 66 A5
Woodford IG8 ... 37 B4
Wood Green N22 ... 32 C1
Broadwell Ct TW5 ... 128 D4
Broadwick St W1 ... 93 C1 239 B1
Broad Wlk NW1 ... 93 A5 231 B3
W1 ... 115 A5 248 A4
Eltham SE3,SE18 ... 144 A3
Heston TW5 ... 129 A4
Richmond TW9 ... 132 B5
Southgate N21 ... 16 B3
Broad Wlk The W8 ... 113 D5 245 D3
Broadwood Ave HA4 ... 39 C3
Broadwood Terr W14 ... 254 D4
Broad Yd EC1 ... 241 C5
Brocas Cl NW3 ... 70 C1
Brockbridge Ho 11 SW15 ... 155 D5
Brockdene Dr BR2 ... 225 D4
Brockdish Ave IG11 ... 79 D3
Brockelbank Lo RM8 ... 80 D6
Brockenhurst KT8 ... 195 B3
Brockenhurst Ave KT4 ... 199 C1
Brockenhurst Gdns NW7 ... 27 C5
Ilford IG1 ... 79 A3
Brockenhurst Mews 9 N18 ... 34 A6
Brockenhurst Rd CR0 ... 206 B2
Brockenhurst Way SW16 ... 181 D1
Brocket Ho 16 SW8 ... 137 D3
Brockham Cl SW19 ... 179 B5
Brockham Cres CR0 ... 224 B1
Brockham Ct 6 SM2 ... 217 D1
Brockham Dr Ilford IG2 ... 57 A4
Streatham SW2 ... 160 B4
Brockham Ho NW1 ... 232 B5
11 Streatham SW2 ... 160 B4
Brockham St SE1 ... 262 B6
Brock Ho WC1 ... 239 C4
Brockhurst Cl HA7 ... 24 D4
Brockhurst Ho N4 ... 51 B2
Brockill Cres SE4 ... 141 A1
Brocklebank Ho 7 E16 ... 122 C5
Brocklebank Rd SE7 ... 121 B2
Brocklebank Rd *continued*
Wandsworth SW18 ... 158 A4
Brocklebank Road Ind Est SE7 ... 121 A2
Brocklehurst St SE14 ... 140 D5
Brocklesby Rd SE25 ... 206 B5
Brockley Ave HA7 ... 10 A1
Brockley Cl HA7 ... 26 A6
Brockley Cross SE4 ... 141 B2
Brockley Cross Bsns Ctr SE4 ... 141 A2
Brockley Gdns SE4 ... 141 B3
Brockley Gr SE4 ... 163 B6
Brockley Hall Rd SE4 ... 163 A6
Brockley Hill HA7,HA8 ... 9 D2
Brockley Hill Ho HA7 ... 9 C3
Brockley Ho SE17 ... 263 A2
Brockley Mews SE4 ... 163 A6
Brockley Pk SE23 ... 163 A4
Brockley Prim Sch SE4 ... 163 B6
Brockley Rd SE4 ... 163 B6
Brockley Rise SE23 ... 163 A4
Brockleyside HA7 ... 26 A6
Brockley Sta SE4 ... 141 A2
Brockley View SE23 ... 163 A4
Brockley Way SE4 ... 163 A6
Brockman Rise BR1 ... 186 B6
Brockmer Ho 5 E1 ... 118 B6
Brock Pl E3 ... 97 D3
Brock Rd E13 ... 99 B2
Brocks Dr SM3 ... 217 A5
Brockshot Cl 1 TW8 ... 131 D6
Brock St SE15 ... 140 C2
Brockway Cl E11 ... 76 C6
Brockweir 29 E2 ... 96 C5
Brockwell Cl BR5 ... 211 D4
Brockwell Ct 2 SW2 ... 160 C6
Brockwell Ho SE11 ... 270 D6
Brockwell Park* SE24 ... 160 D5
Brockwell Park Gdns SE24 ... 160 D4
Brockworth 8 KT2 ... 176 D2
Broderick Ho SE21 ... 161 C1
Brodia Rd N16 ... 73 C5
Brodick Ho 11 E3 ... 97 B5
Brodie Ho SE1 ... 263 D2
7 Wallington SM6 ... 219 B4
Brodie Rd Chingford E4 ... 20 A2
Enfield EN2 ... 5 A5
Brodie St SE1 ... 117 D1 263 D2
Brodlove La E1 ... 118 D6
Brodrick Gr SE2 ... 124 B2
Brodrick Rd SW17 ... 158 C2
Brograve Gdns BR3 ... 185 D1
Broken Wharf EC4 ... 252 A6
Brokesley St E3 ... 97 B4
Broke Wlk E8 ... 96 A6
1 E8 ... 96 A6
Bromar Rd SE5 ... 139 C2
Bromborough Gn WD19 ... 22 C5
Bromefield HA7 ... 25 C2
Bromehead St 8 E1 ... 96 C1
Brome Ho 5 SE18 ... 144 A4
Bromell's Rd SW4 ... 137 C1
Brome Rd SE9 ... 144 B2
Bromfelde Rd SW4 ... 137 D3
Bromfield Ct 20 SE16 ... 118 A3
Bromfield St N1 ... 234 B4
Bromhall Rd RM8 ... 80 B2
Bromhedge SE9 ... 166 B1
Bromholm Rd SE2 ... 124 B3
Bromleigh Ct 1 SE21, SE22 ... 162 B2
Bromleigh Ho SE1 ... 263 C6
Bromley Ave BR1 ... 186 D3
Bromley-by-Bow Sta E3 ... 97 D4
Bromley Coll of F & H Ed BR2 ... 209 D3
Bromley Comm BR2 ... 209 D4
Bromley Cres
Beckenham BR2 ... 208 D6
Ruislip HA4 ... 61 D4
Bromley Ct SE13 ... 164 B6
Bromley BR1 ... 186 D3
Bromley Gdns BR2 ... 208 D6
Bromley Gr BR2 ... 186 B1
Bromley Hall Rd E14 ... 98 A2
Bromley High Sch for Girls BR1 ... 210 C5
Bromley High St E3 ... 97 D4
Bromley Hill BR1 ... 186 C4
Bromley Hospl BR1 ... 209 B5
Bromley Ind Est BR1 ... 209 D6
Bromley La BR7 ... 189 B3
Bromley Lo 2 W3 ... 89 A1
Bromley Manor Mans 3 BR1 ... 209 A6
Bromley North Sta BR1 ... 187 A2
Bromley Pk 11 BR1 ... 186 D2
Bromley Pl W1 ... 239 A4
Bromley Rd BR7 ... 188 D2
E10 ... 53 D3
E17 ... 53 C6
Beckenham BR2,BR3 ... 186 B1
Beckenham BR3 ... 185 D2
Catford SE6 ... 163 D1
Edmonton N18 ... 17 B1
Tottenham N17 ... 34 A2
Bromley Rd Ret Pk SE6 ... 163 D2
Bromley Road Inf Sch BR3 ... 185 D2
Bromley South Sta BR2 ... 209 A6
Bromley St E1 ... 96 D1
Brompton WC1 ... 240 C3
Brompton Arc SW1 ... 247 D1
Brompton Cl
Hounslow TW4 ... 151 B6
Penge SE20 ... 184 A1
Brompton Ct 4 HA7 ... 25 C6
Brompton Gr N2 ... 48 C5
Brompton Ho 3 N9 ... 34 A6
Brompton Oratory* SW3 ... 114 C3 257 A5
Brompton Park Cres SW6 ... 135 D6 265 C5
Brompton Pl SW3 ... 114 C3 257 B6
Brompton Rd SW3 ... 114 C3 257 A5
Brompton Sq SW3 ... 114 C3 257 A6
Bromstone Ho 19 SW9 ... 138 C4
Bromwich Ave N6 ... 71 A6
Bromwich Ho 3 TW10 ... 154 A5
Bromyard Ave W3 ... 111 C6
Bromyard Ho 3 SE15 ... 140 B5
Bron Ct NW6 ... 91 C6
Brondesbury Coll for Boys NW6 ... 69 A1
Brondesbury Ct NW2 ... 68 D2
Brondesbury Mews 11 NW6 ... 69 C1
Brondesbury Park Sta NW6 ... 91 A6
Brondesbury Pk NW2 ... 68 D1
Brondesbury Rd NW6 ... 91 C5
Brondesbury Sta NW6 ... 69 B1
Brondesbury Villas NW6 ... 91 C5
Bronhill Terr N17 ... 34 A2
Bronsart Rd SW6 ... 135 A5 264 A3
Bronson Rd SW20 ... 179 A1
Bronte Cl DA8 ... 147 D5
1 E7 ... 77 A4
Ilford IG2 ... 56 C5
Bronte Ct 8 W14 ... 112 D3
Bronte Ho 6 N16 ... 73 C3
NW6 ... 91 C4
Bronti Cl SE17 ... 117 A1 262 B2
Bronwen Ct NW8 ... 229 C1
Bronze Age Way DA17 ... 125 D4
Bronze St SE8 ... 141 C5
Brook Ave
Dagenham RM10 ... 81 D1
Edgware HA8 ... 26 D4
Wembley HA9 ... 66 C5
Brook Bank EN1 ... 6 B6
Brookbank Ave W7 ... 86 B2
Brookbank Rd SE13 ... 141 D2
Brook Cl Acton W3 ... 110 C5
Finchley N12 ... 29 A3
Ruislip HA4 ... 39 C2
Stanwell TW19 ... 148 B4
Upper Tooting SW17 ... 159 A2
West Barnes SW20 ... 200 B6
Brook Cres Chingford E4 ... 35 D6
Edmonton N9 ... 34 B6
Brook Ct 2 E11 ... 76 C5
E15 ... 76 A3
E17 ... 53 A6
Beckenham BR3 ... 185 B2
5 Brentford TW8 ... 131 D6
Cheam SM3 ... 216 C4
Edgware HA8 ... 26 D5
Mortlake SW14 ... 133 C2
Brookdale N11 ... 31 C6
Brookdale Rd DA5 ... 169 A5
E17 ... 53 C6
SE6 ... 163 D5
Catford SE6 ... 163 D4
Brookdales The NW4 ... 47 A5
Brookdene N12 ... 29 D6
Brookdene Rd SE18,SE2 ... 123 D2
Brook Dr SE11 ... 116 D2 261 C4
Harrow HA1 ... 42 A5
Ruislip HA4 ... 39 C2
Brooke Ave HA2 ... 64 A5
Brooke Cl WD23 ... 8 A4
Brooke Ct 7 KT2 ... 175 D6
Brookehowse Rd SE6 ... 163 D1
Brookend Rd DA15 ... 167 C3
Brooke Rd E17 ... 54 A5
E5,N16 ... 74 A5
Brookes Ct EC1 ... 241 A4
Brookes Mkt EC1 ... 241 A4
Brooke's Mkt EC1 ... 241 B4
Brooke St EC1 ... 94 C2 241 A3
Brooke Way WD23 ... 8 A4
Brookfield 1 N4 ... 72 C6
N6 ... 71 A5
Brookfield Ave E17 ... 54 A5
NW7 ... 28 B4
Carshalton SM1,SM5 ... 218 C5
Ealing W5 ... 87 D3
Brookfield Cl NW7 ... 28 B4
Brookfield Cres NW7 ... 28 B4
Harrow HA3 ... 44 A4
Brookfield Ct 1 N12 ... 29 D6
Greenford UB6 ... 86 A4
Brookfield Gdns KT10 ... 212 D2
Brookfield House Sch IG8 ... 36 C4
Brookfield Path IG8 ... 36 C4
Brookfield Pk NW5 ... 71 B5
Brookfield Prim Sch N19 ... 71 B6
Cheam SM3 ... 201 A1
Brookfield Rd E9 ... 75 A2
W4 ... 111 B4
Edmonton N9 ... 18 B1
Brookfields EN3 ... 6 D1
Brookfields Ave CR4 ... 202 C4
Brookgate N16 ... 73 B6
Brook Gate W1 ... 114 D6 247 D5
Brook Gdns
Barnes SW13 ... 133 D2
Chingford E4 ... 35 D6
Kingston KT2 ... 177 A2
Brook Gn W6 ... 112 D2
Brook Green Flats 11 W14 ... 112 D3
Brookhill Cl SE18 ... 122 D1
East Barnet EN4 ... 14 C6
Brookhill Ct 2 EN4 ... 14 C5
Brookhill Rd SE18 ... 122 D1
East Barnet EN4 ... 14 C6
Brook Ho 3 SW4 ... 159 C6
W3 ... 110 C4
4 W6 ... 112 C2
3 Edmonton N9 ... 18 A1
3 Twickenham TW1 ... 153 A4
Brook Hos NW1 ... 232 B3
Brookhouse Gdns E4 ... 36 C6
Brook House Sixth Form Coll The E5 ... 74 B5
Brook Ind Est UB4 ... 106 C5
Brooking Cl RM8 ... 80 C5
Brooking Rd E7 ... 77 A3
Brook La BR1 ... 187 A4
DA5 ... 168 D5
Greenwich SE3 ... 143 B3
Brookland Cl NW11 ... 47 C5
Brookland Garth NW11 ... 47 D5
Brookland Hill NW11 ... 47 D5
Brookland Jun & Inf Schs NW11 ... 47 D5
Brookland Rise NW11 ... 47 C5
Brooklands Ave DA15 ... 167 B2
Wandsworth SW18 ... 157 D2
Brooklands Cl TW16 ... 171 C2
Brooklands Court Apartments 3 NW6 ... 69 B1
Brooklands Ct 2 NW6 ... 69 B1
Enfield N21 ... 17 B6
Kingston KT1 ... 197 D5
2 Mitcham CR4 ... 180 B1
Brooklands Dr UB6 ... 87 D6
Brooklands Pk SE3 ... 143 A2
Brooklands Prim Sch SE3 ... 143 A2
Brooklands Rd KT7 ... 197 A1
Brooklands The TW7 ... 130 B4
Brook Lane Bns Ctr TW8 ... 109 D1
Brooklea Cl NW9 ... 27 C2
Brook Lo N8 ... 49 D3
NW4 ... 46 D4
Brooklyn SE20 ... 184 A3
Brooklyn Ave SE25 ... 206 B5
Brooklyn Cl SM5 ... 218 C6
Brooklyn Ct W12 ... 112 C5
Brooklyn Gr SE25 ... 206 B5
Brooklyn Rd BR2 ... 210 A4
Croydon SE25 ... 206 B5
Brookmarsh Ind Est SE10 ... 141 D5
Brook Mdw N12 ... 13 D1
Brook Mead KT19 ... 215 C2
Brookmead Ave BR1, BR2 ... 210 B4
Brookmead Ct N20 ... 14 A2
Brookmead Ind Est CR4 ... 203 C3
Brook Meadow Cl IG8 ... 36 C4
Brookmead Rd CR0 ... 203 C3
Brook Mews N W2 ... 114 B6 246 B6
Brookmill Rd SE8 ... 141 C4
Brook Park Cl N21 ... 16 D6
Brook Pl EN5 ... 13 C6
Brook Rd N12 ... 30 C3
N22 ... 50 B6
N8 ... 50 A5
NW2 ... 68 A6
Buckhurst Hill IG9 ... 21 A3
Ilford IG2 ... 57 C3
South Norwood CR7 ... 205 A5
Surbiton KT6 ... 214 A6
Twickenham TW1 ... 153 A5
Brook Rd S TW8 ... 131 D6
Brooks Ave E6 ... 100 B3
Brooksbank Ho 7 E9 ... 74 C2
Brooksbank St 9 E9 ... 74 C2
Brooksby Mews N1 ... 72 C1
Brooksby St N1 ... 72 C1
Brooksby's Wlk E9 ... 74 D3
Brooks Cl SE9 ... 166 C2
Brookscroft Rd E17 ... 35 D2
Brooks Ct 3 SW4 ... 138 A3
SW8 ... 269 B4
Brookshill HA3 ... 24 B5
Brookshill Ave HA3 ... 24 C5
Brookshill Dr HA3 ... 24 B5
Brooks Ho 6 SW2 ... 160 C3
Brookside BR6 ... 211 D2
East Barnet EN4 ... 14 C5
Southgate N21 ... 16 B5
Wallington SM5 ... 219 A3
Brookside Cl Barnet EN5 ... 13 A5
Feltham TW13 ... 150 A1
Harrow HA3 ... 43 D4
South Harrow HA2,HA4 ... 63 A4
Brookside Cres 1 KT4 ... 200 A1
Brookside Ct SW16 ... 181 C3
Brookside Gdns EN1 ... 6 C6
Brookside Ho N17 ... 33 C1
Brookside Prim Sch UB4 ... 84 C4
Brookside Rd N19 ... 71 C6
NW11 ... 47 B3
Edmonton N9 ... 34 B6
Hayes UB4 ... 106 C6
Brookside S EN4 ... 15 A4
Brookside Way
Croydon CR0 ... 206 D3
Hillingdon UB10 ... 60 B1
Brooks La W4 ... 132 C6
Brook's Mans 5 IG3 ... 58 B1
Brook's Mews W1 ... 115 B6 248 C6
Brook's Par 6 IG3 ... 58 B1
Brooks Rd W4 ... 110 C1
Brook's Rd E13 ... 99 A6
Brook St DA8 ... 147 D5
W1 ... 115 B6 248 C6
W2 ... 114 B6 246 D6
Kingston KT1 ... 176 A1
5 Tottenham N17 ... 33 D1
Brookstone Ct SE15 ... 140 B1
Brooksville Ave NW6 ... 91 A6
Brook Vale DA7,DA8 ... 147 D4
Brookview Ct 11 EN1 ... 17 C6
Brookview Rd SW16 ... 181 C5
Brookville Rd SW6 ... 135 B5 264 C3
Brookway SE3 ... 143 A2
Brook Wlk HA8 ... 27 B4
N2 ... 30 B2
Brookwood Ave SW13 ... 133 D3
Brookwood Cl BR2 ... 208 D5
Brookwood Ho SE1 ... 251 D1
Brookwood Rd
Hounslow TW3 ... 129 D4
Wandsworth SW18 ... 157 C3
Broom Ave BR5 ... 190 B1
Broom Cl BR2 ... 210 A3
Teddington KT1,TW11 ... 175 D3
Broomcroft Ave UB5 ... 84 C4
Broome Ct 3 TW9 ... 132 C4
Broome Ho 7 E5 ... 74 B3
Broome Rd TW12 ... 173 B2
Broome Way SE5 ... 139 B5
Broomfield E17 ... 53 B2
7 NW1 ... 71 A1
Sunbury TW16 ... 172 A2
Broomfield Ave N13 ... 32 B5
Broomfield Cotts N13 ... 32 A5
Broomfield Ct N13 ... 32 A5
Broomfield Ho 4 BR5 ... 190 B1
SE17 ... 263 A3
Stanmore HA7 ... 9 A1
Broomfield House Sch TW9 ... 132 B4
Broomfield La N13 ... 32 B6
Broomfield Pl W13 ... 109 B5
Broomfield Rd DA6 ... 169 C6
Beckenham BR3 ... 207 B6
Bowes Park N13 ... 32 A5
Dagenham RM6 ... 58 D2
Ealing W13 ... 109 B5
Richmond TW9 ... 132 B4
Surbiton KT5 ... 198 B1
Teddington TW11 ... 175 C4
Broomfields KT10 ... 212 A3
Broomfield Sch N14 ... 31 D5
Broomfield St E14 ... 97 D2
Broom Gdns CR0 ... 223 C5
Broomgrove Gdns HA8 ... 26 C2
Broomgrove Rd SW9 ... 138 B3
Broomhill Ct 2 IG8 ... 37 A4
Broomhill Rd BR6 ... 211 D2
SW18 ... 157 C6
Ilford IG3 ... 80 A6
Woodford IG8 ... 37 A4
Broomhill Rise DA6 ... 169 C6
Broomhill Wlk IG8 ... 36 D3
Broomhouse La SW6 ... 135 C2
Broomhouse Rd SW6 ... 135 C3
Broomleigh BR1 ... 187 A2
Broomleigh Bsns Pk SE26 ... 185 B5
Broomloan La SM1 ... 217 C6
Broom Lock TW11 ... 175 C4
Broom Mead DA6 ... 169 C6
Broom Pk KT1 ... 175 D3
Broom Rd Croydon CR0 ... 223 C5
Richmond TW11 ... 175 C5
Teddington KT1,TW11 ... 175 C4
Broomsleigh St NW6 ... 69 B3
Broom Water TW11 ... 175 C5
Broom Water W TW11 ... 175 C5
Broomwood Cl CR0 ... 206 D4
Broomwood Hall Sch SW12 ... 159 A4
Broomwood Rd BR5 ... 190 B1
SW11 ... 159 A6
Broseley Gr SE26 ... 185 A5
Broster Gdns SE25 ... 205 D6
Brougham Rd E8 ... 96 A6
W3 ... 89 A1
Brougham St SW11 ... 136 D3
Brough Cl SW8 ... 270 B3
Kingston KT2 ... 175 D5
Brough St SW8 ... 270 B3
Broughton Ave N3 ... 47 A6
Richmond TW10 ... 175 C6
Broughton Ct W13 ... 109 B6
Broughton Dr 20 SW9 ... 138 D1
Broughton Gdns N6 ... 49 C3
Broughton Rd SW6 ... 135 D3
Ealing W13 ... 109 B6
Orpington BR6 ... 227 B6
Thornton Heath CR7 ... 204 C3
Broughton Road App 2 SW6 ... 135 D3
Broughton St SW8 ... 137 B3
Broughton Street Arches Ind Area SW11 ... 137 A3
Brouncker Rd W3 ... 111 A4
Browells La TW13 ... 150 B2
Brown Bear Ct TW13 ... 172 D6
Brown Cl SM6 ... 220 A1
Browne Ho 13 SE8 ... 141 C5
9 Penge SE26 ... 184 B5
Brownfield St E14 ... 98 A1
Brownflete Ho SE4 ... 141 A1
Browngraves Rd UB7 ... 127 A5
Brown Hart Gdns W1 ... 248 B6
Brownhill Rd SE6 ... 164 A4
Browning Ave
Carshalton SM1 ... 218 C4
Ealing W7 ... 86 D1
North Cheam KT4 ... 200 B1
Browning Cl DA16 ... 145 C4
E17 ... 54 A5
W9 ... 236 B5
Feltham TW12 ... 173 B6
Browning Ct W14 ... 264 C6
Browning Ho 10 N16 ... 73 C4
W12 ... 90 C1
Browning Mews W1 ... 238 B3
Browning Rd E11 ... 54 D2
E12 ... 78 B2
Enfield EN2 ... 5 B5
Browning St SE17 ... 117 A2 262 B3
Browning Way TW5 ... 128 D4
Brownlea Gdns IG3 ... 80 A6
Brownlow Cl EN4 ... 14 B6
Brownlow Ct N2 ... 48 A4
1 Bowes Park N11 ... 32 A4
Brownlow Ho 7 SE16 ... 118 A4
Brownlow Mews WC1 ... 94 B3 240 D5
Brownlow Rd 3 E7 ... 77 A4
E8 ... 96 A6
N3 ... 29 D3
NW10 ... 67 C1
Bowes Park N11 ... 32 A4
6 Ealing W13 ... 109 A5
South Croydon CR0 ... 221 D4
Brownlow St WC1 ... 94 B2 240 D3
Brownrigg Rd TW15 ... 170 C6
Brown's Bldgs EC3 ... 243 B1
Brownspring Dr SE9 ... 166 D1
Brown's Rd E17 ... 53 C6
Surbiton KT5,KT6 ... 198 B2
Brown St W1 ... 92 D1 237 C2
Brownswell Rd N2 ... 30 B1
Brownswood Rd N4 ... 73 A6
Broxash Rd SW11 ... 159 A5
Broxbourne Ave E18 ... 55 B5
Broxbourne Ho 1 E3 ... 97 D3
Broxbourne Rd BR6 ... 211 D2
Wanstead E7 ... 77 A5
Broxholme Ho SW6 ... 265 C2
Broxholm Rd SE27,SW16 ... 160 C1
Broxted Rd SE6 ... 163 B2
Broxwood Way NW8 ... 92 C6 230 B5
Bruce Ave TW17 ... 193 A3
Bruce Castle Ct N17 ... 33 C2
Bruce Castle Mus* N17 ... 33 C2
Bruce Castle Rd N17 ... 33 D2
Bruce Cl DA16 ... 146 B4
W10 ... 90 D2
Bruce Ct DA15 ... 189 D6
Bruce Gdns N20 ... 14 D1
Bruce Glasier Ho 13 N19 ... 49 D2
Bruce Gr N17 ... 33 D1
Bruce Grove N17 ... 33 D1
Bruce Grove Prim Sch N17 ... 33 D1
Bruce Grove Sta N17 ... 33 D1
Bruce Hall Mews SW17 ... 181 A6
Bruce Ho 4 SW4 ... 159 D5
W10 ... 90 D2
5 Harrow HA1 ... 42 D4
Harrow HA3 ... 44 A2
Putney SW15 ... 156 B6
Bruce Lawns SW17 ... 181 A6
Bruce Rd E3 ... 97 D4
NW10 ... 67 B1
Barnet EN5 ... 1 A2
Harrow HA3 ... 24 C1
Mitcham CR4 ... 181 A3
South Norwood SE25 ... 205 B5
Bruckner St W10 ... 91 B4
Brudenell Rd SW17 ... 181 A6
Bruffs Meadow UB5 ... 63 A2
Bruges Pl 13 NW1 ... 71 C1
Brumfield Rd KT19 ... 215 A3
Brune Ho E1 ... 243 C3
Brunel Cl Cranford TW5 ... 128 B5
Northolt UB5 ... 85 B4
Penge SE19 ... 183 D4
Brunel Ct NW10 ... 90 A4
Brunel Est W2 ... 91 C2
Brunel Ho E14 ... 119 D1
4 NW5 ... 71 B4
SW10 ... 266 D4
Hayes UB3 ... 105 D3
25 Streatham SW2 ... 160 A4
Brunel Pl 8 UB1 ... 85 D1
Brunel Rd E17 ... 53 A3
SE16 ... 118 C5
W3 ... 89 C2
Brunel St E16 ... 98 D1
Brunel Univ UB8 ... 82 A4
Brunel Univ Coll Osterley Campus TW7 ... 130 D5
Brunel Univ Coll (Twickenham Campus) TW1 ... 131 B1
Brunel Wlk N15 ... 51 C5
Twickenham TW4 ... 151 C4
Brune St E1 ... 95 D2 243 C3
Brunlees Ho SE1 ... 262 B5
Brunner Cl NW11 ... 48 A4
Brunner Ho 6 SE6 ... 186 A6
Brunner Rd E17 ... 53 B4
Ealing W5 ... 87 D3
Bruno Pl NW9 ... 67 A6
Brunswick Ave N11 ... 15 A1
Brunswick Cl DA6 ... 146 D1
Pinner HA5 ... 41 A3
Thames Ditton KT7 ... 196 D1
Twickenham TW2 ... 152 B1
Brunswick Cres N11 ... 15 A1
Brunswick Ct EC1 ... 234 C1
SE1 ... 117 C4 253 B2
SW1 ... 259 D3

Brunswick Ct *continued*
Kingston KT2 175 D4
New Barnet EN4 14 B6
2 Penge SE19 184 A3
2 Wimbledon SW19 179 A3
Brunswick Gdns
W8 113 C5 245 B3
Ealing W5 88 A3
Brunswick Gr N11 15 A1
Brunswick Ho 4 E2 95 D5
N3 29 B2
NW1 237 C6
Brunswick Lo 6 E4 20 A2
Brunswick Manor SM1 218 A4
Brunswick Mews W1 237 D2
Streatham SW16 181 D4
Brunswick Park Gdns
N11 15 A2
Brunswick Park Prim Sch
N14 15 A2
SE5 139 B5
Brunswick Park Rd N11 15 A1
Brunswick Pk SE5 139 C4
Brunswick Pl N1 95 B4 235 D1
Penge SE19 184 A3
Brunswick Quay SE16 118 D3
Brunswick Rd DA6 147 A1
E10 54 A1
E14 98 A1
N15 51 C5
Ealing W5 88 A4
Holdbrook EN3 7 C5
Kingston KT2 176 C2
Sutton SM1 217 D4
Brunswick Sh Ctr
WC1 94 A3 240 B6
Brunswick Sq
WC1 94 A3 240 B6
Tottenham N17 33 D4
Brunswick St E17 54 A4
Brunswick Villas 2
SE5 139 C4
Brunswick Way N11 31 B6
Brunton Pl E14 97 A1
Brushfield St E1 95 D2 243 C4
Brushwood Ho 4 E14 97 D2
Brushwood Lo DA17 125 C2
Brussels Rd SW11 136 B1
Bruton Cl BR7 188 B3
Bruton La W1 115 B6 248 D5
Bruton Pl W1 115 B6 248 D5
Bruton Rd SM4 202 A5
Bruton St W1 115 B6 248 D5
Bruton Way W13 87 A2
Bryan Ave NW10 68 B1
Bryan Cl TW16 172 A3
Bryan Ct W1 237 C2
Bryan Ho SE16 119 B4
Bryan Rd SE16 119 B4
Bryanston Ave TW2 151 D3
Bryanston Cl UB2 107 B2
Bryanston Ct W1 237 C2
Bryanstone Ct SM1 218 A5
Bryanstone Rd N8 49 D4
Bryanston Ho 11 SE15 139 D4
Bryanston Mans W1 237 C4
Bryanston Mews E W1 237 C3
Bryanston Mews W
W1 92 D1 237 C2
Bryanston Pl W1 92 D2 237 C3
Bryanston Sq W1 92 D1 237 C2
Bryanston St W1 92 D1 237 D1
Bryant Cl EN5 13 B6
Bryant Ct E2 95 D5
Bryant Rd UB5 84 C4
Bryant St E15 76 C1
Bryantwood Rd N5,N7 72 C3
Brycedale Cres N14 15 D1
Bryce Ho 25 SE14 140 D6
Bryce Rd RM8 80 C4
Brydale Ho 2 SE16 118 D2
Bryden Cl SE26 185 A5
Brydges Pl WC2 250 A5
Brydges Rd E15 76 B3
Brydon Wlk N1 233 B6
Bryer Ct EC2 242 A4
Bryett Rd N7 72 A5
Bryher Ho W4 111 A1
Brymay Cl E3 97 C5
Brymon Ct W1 237 D3
Brynmaer Ho SW11 267 D1
Brynmaer Rd
SW11 136 D4 267 D1
Bryn-y-Mawr Rd EN1 5 D1
Bryony Cl UB8 82 B2
Bryony Rd W12 112 A6
Bryony Way TW16 172 A4
B Sky B Hq TW7 131 A6
BT Telecom Twr*
W1 93 C2 239 A4
Buccleuch Ho E5 52 A2
Buchanan Cl N21 16 B6
Buchanan Ct 16 SE16 118 D2
Buchanan Gdns NW10 90 B5
Buchanan Ho
Dulwich SE21 161 C1
Wandsworth SW18 157 C4
Buchan Ho W3 110 D4
Buchan Rd SE15 140 C2
Bucharest Rd SW18 158 A4
Buckden Cl N2 48 D5
SE12 165 A5
Buckfast Ct W13 109 A6
Buckfast Ho N14 15 C6
Buckfast Rd SM4 201 D5
Buckfast St E2 96 A4
Buck Hill Wlk
W2 114 B6 246 D5
Buckhold Rd SW18 157 C5
Buckhurst Ave CR4,SM5 202 D1
Buckhurst Hill Ho IG9 21 B2
Buckhurst Hill Sta IG9 21 D2
Buckhurst Ho 15 N7 71 D3
Buckhurst St E1 96 B3
Buckhurst Way IG9 21 D1
Buckingham Ave DA16 145 C1
N20 14 B4
East Molesey KT8 173 D1
Feltham TW14 150 B5
South Norwood CR7 182 C2
Wembley UB6 87 A6
Buckingham Cl BR5 211 C2
Ealing W5 87 C2
Enfield EN1 5 C3
Hampton TW12 173 B5
Buckingham College Sch
HA1 42 C4
Buckingham Ct NW4 46 A6
2 Ealing W7 86 D3
Mitcham CR4 204 A4
Northolt UB5 85 A6
Wembley HA0 65 C2
Buckingham Dr BR7 189 A5
Buckingham Gate
SW1 115 C3 259 B6
Buckingham Gdns
East Molesey KT8 173 D1
Edgware HA8 26 B3
South Norwood CR7 182 C1
Buckingham Gr UB10 82 C5
Buckingham Ho N4 51 A1
1 Acton W3 88 C1
Richmond TW10 154 C6
Buckingham La SE23 163 A4
Buckingham Lo N10 49 C5
Buckingham Mans NW6 69 D3
Buckingham Mews
7 N1 73 C2
NW10 89 D5
SW1 259 A6
Buckingham Palace*
SW1 115 C4 249 A1
Buckingham Palace Rd
SW1 115 B2 258 D4
Buckingham Pl SW1 259 A6
Buckingham Prim Sch
TW12 173 B5
Buckingham Rd E10 75 D5
E15 76 D3
N1 73 C2
NW10 89 D5
Edgware HA8 26 B3
Hampton TW12,TW13 173 B5
Harrow HA1 42 B4
Ilford IG1 79 B6
Kingston KT1 198 B5
Mitcham CR4 204 A4
Richmond TW10 153 D2
Wanstead E11 55 C4
Woodford E18 36 D2
Wood Green N22 32 A2
Buckingham St WC2 250 B5
Buckingham Way SM6 219 C1
Buckingham Yd NW10 89 D5
Buck La NW9 45 B4
Buckland Cres NW3 70 B2
Buckland Ct 6 N1 95 C5
Uxbridge UB10 61 A6
Buckland Inf Sch KT9 214 B4
Buckland Rd BR6 227 C4
E10 76 A6
Chessington KT9 214 B3
Buckland Rise HA5 22 D2
Bucklands Rd TW11 175 C4
Buckland St N1 95 B5 235 D3
Buckland Way KT4 200 C1
Buckland Wlk
2 Acton W3 111 A4
Morden SM4 202 A5
Buckleigh Ave SW20 201 B6
Buckleigh Ho SW17 180 B5
Buckleigh Rd SW16 182 A3
Buckleigh Way SE19 183 D3
Buckler Gdns SE9 166 B1
Buckler's Alley SW6 264 D4
Bucklersbury EC2,EC4 242 C1
Bucklers' Way SM5 218 D5
Buckles Ct DA17 124 D2
Buckle St E1 243 D2
9 E1 96 A1
Buckley Cl SE23 162 B4
Buckley Ct 5 NW6 69 B1
Buckley Rd NW6 69 B1
Buckley St SE1 251 A3
Buckmaster Cl SE17 262 B1
1 SW9 138 C2
Buckmaster Ho 1 N7 72 B4
Buckmaster Rd SW11 136 C1
Bucknall St WC1 240 A2
Bucknall Way BR3 208 A5
Bucknell Cl SW2 138 B1
Buckner Rd SW2 138 B1
Buckrell Rd E4 20 B2
Buckridge Bldg EC1 241 A4
Buckshead Ho 10 W2 91 C2
Buck St NW1 71 B1
Buckstone Cl SE23 162 C5
Buckstone Rd N18 34 A5
Buckters Rents SE16 119 A5
Buckthorne Rd SE4 163 A6
Buckthorn Ho DA15 167 D1
Buckwheat Ct DA18 124 D3
Budd Cl N12 29 D6
Buddings Circ HA9 67 A5
Bude Cl E17 53 B4
Budge La CR4 202 D2
Budge Row EC4 242 C1
Budge's Wlk W2 114 A5 246 B4
Budleigh Cres DA16 146 C4
Budleigh Ho 19 SE15 140 A5
Budoch Ct IG3 80 A6
Budoch Dr IG3 80 A6
Buer Rd SW6 135 A3
Bugsbys Way SE10 120 D2
Bugsby's Way SE7,SE10 121 B2
Buick Ho 4 E3 97 C3
Bulbarrow NW8 91 D6
Bulganak Rd CR7 205 A5
Bulinca St SW1 115 D2 259 D3
Bullace Row SE5 139 B4
Bull Alley DA16 146 B2
Bullard Rd TW11 174 D4
Bullards Pl 18 E2 96 D4
Bull Dog The (Juct)
TW15 148 A2
Bulleid Way
SW1 115 B2 258 D3
Bullen Ho 13 E1 96 B3
Bullen St SW11 136 C3
Buller Cl SE15 140 A5
Buller Rd NW10 90 D4
Barking IG11 79 C1
South Norwood CR7 205 B6
Tottenham N17 34 A1
Wood Green N22 32 C1
Bullers Cl DA14 191 A5
Bullers Wood Dr BR7 188 B3
Bullers Wood Sch BR7 188 B2
Bullescroft Rd HA8 10 D1
Bullfinch Ct 3 SE21 161 B2
Bullingham Mans W8 245 B2
Bull Inn Ct WC2 250 B5
Bullivant St 9 E14 120 A6
Bull La BR7 189 B3
Dagenham RM10 81 D5
Edmonton N18 33 C5
Bull Rd E15 98 D5
Bullrush Cl
Carshalton SM5 218 D6
Thornton Heath CR0 205 C3
Bulls Alley SW14 133 B3
Bulls Bridge Ind Est
UB2 106 B2
Bulls Bridge Rd UB2 106 B2
Bullsbrook Rd UB4 106 C5
Bull's Cross EN1,EN2 6 A6
Bull's Gdns SW3 257 B4
Bulls Head Pas EC3 243 A1
Bull Yd SE15 140 A4
Bulmer Gdns HA3 43 D2
Bulmer Mews
W11 113 C5 245 A4
Bulow Ct 3 SW6 135 D3
Bulstrode Ave TW3 129 C2
Bulstrode Gdns TW3 129 C2
Bulstrode Pl W1 238 B3
Bulstrode Rd TW3 129 C2
Bulstrode St W1 93 A1 238 B2
Bulwer Court Rd E11 54 B1
Bulwer Ct E11 54 B1
Bulwer Gdns EN5 2 A1
Bulwer Rd E11 54 B1
Edmonton N18 33 C6
New Barnet EN5 2 A1
Bulwer St W12 112 C5
Bunbury Ho SE15 140 A5
Bunces La IG8 36 D3
Bungalow Rd SE25 205 C5
Bungalows The E10 54 A3
Mitcham SW16 181 B3
Bunhill Row EC1 95 B3 242 C5
Bunhouse Pl SW1 258 B2
Bunkers Hill DA14 169 B1
NW11 48 A2
Bunker's Hill DA17 125 C2
Bunning Ho N7 72 A4
Bunning Way N7 72 B1
Bunn's La NW7 27 D4
Bunsen Ho 1 E3 97 A5
Bunsen St 2 E3 97 A5
Buntingbridge Rd IG2 57 B4
Bunting Cl N9 18 D3
Mitcham CR4 202 D4
Bunting Ct NW9 27 C1
Bunton St SE18 122 C3
Bunyan Ct EC2 242 A4
Bunyan Rd E17 53 A6
Buonaparte Mews SW1 259 C2
BUPA Bushey Hospl
WD23 8 D3
Burbage Cl SE1 117 B3 262 C5
Hayes UB3 83 B1
Burbage Ho N1 235 D5
16 SE14 140 D6
Burbage Rd SE21,SE24 161 B4
Burbage Sch N1 95 C5
Burbank KT3 199 D6
Burberry Cl KT3 177 C1
Burbidge Rd TW17 192 C5
Burbridge Way N17 34 A1
Burcham St E14 98 A1
Burcharbro Rd SE2 146 D6
Burchell Ct WD23 8 A4
Burchell Ho SE11 260 D2
Burchell Rd E10 53 D1
SE15 140 B4
Burchetts Way TW17 192 D3
Burchett Way RM6 59 B3
Burcote Rd SW18 158 B4
Burden Cl TW8 109 C1
Burden Ho SW8 270 A3
Burdenshott Ave TW10 132 D1
Burden Way E11 77 B6
Burder Cl N1 73 C2
Burder Rd N1 73 C2
Burdett Ave SW20 178 A2
Burdett Cl DA14 191 A5
2 Ealing W7 108 D5
Burdett Coutts & Townshend
CE Prim Sch
SW1 115 D2 259 D3
Burdett Mews 4 W2 91 D1
Burdett Rd E3 97 B2
Richmond TW9 132 B2
Thornton Heath CR0 205 B3
Burdetts Rd RM9 103 B6
Burdock Cl CR0 206 D1
Burdock Rd N17 52 A6
Burdon La SM2 217 A1
Burdon Pk SM2 217 B1
Bure Ct 10 EN5 13 D6
Burfield Cl SW17 180 B6
Burford Cl Dagenham RM8 80 C5
Ickenham UB10 60 A4
Ilford IG6 57 A5
Burford Gdns N13 16 B1
Burford Ho 11 SW9 138 B3
1 Brentford TW8 110 A1
Burford Rd BR1 210 A5
E15 98 B6
E6 100 A4
Brentford TW8 110 A1
Forest Hill SE6 163 B2
New Malden KT4 200 A2
Sutton SM1 217 C6
Burford Way CR0 224 A2
Burford Wlk SW6 265 D3
Burgate Ct 10 SW9 138 C2
Burges Gr SW13 134 B5
Burges Rd E6 78 B1
Burgess Ave NW9 45 B3
Burgess Cl 4 TW13 173 A6
Burgess Ct
3 Southall UB1 85 D1
Wallend E12 78 C1
Burgess Hill NW2 69 C4
Burgess Ho 3 SE5 139 A5
Burgess Ind Pk SE5 139 B5
Burgess Mews SW19 179 D4
Burgess Park Mans NW6 69 C4
Burgess Rd E15 76 C4
Sutton SM1 217 D4
Burge St SE1 262 D5
Burghill Rd SE26 185 A6
Burghley Ave
Borehamwood WD6 11 A6
Kingston KT3 177 B2
Burghley Hall Cl SW19 157 A3
Burghley Ho SW19 157 A1
Burghley Pl CR4 202 D5
Burghley Rd E11 54 C1
N8 50 C6
NW5 71 B4
Wimbledon SW19 179 A6
Burghley Twr W3 111 D6
Burgh St N1 94 D5 234 D4
Burgon St EC4 241 D1
Burgos Cl CR0 220 C2
Burgos Gr SE10 141 D4
Burgoyne Rd N4 50 D3
SW9 138 B2
Ashford TW16 171 D4
South Norwood SE25 205 D5
Burham Cl SE20 184 C3
Burhan Uddin Ho E1 243 C5
Burhill Gr HA5 23 A1
Buriton Ho 9 SW15 156 B3
Burke Cl SW15 133 C1
Burke Ho 1 SW11 136 B1
Burke Lo E13 99 B4
Burke St E16 98 D2
Burket Cl UB2 107 B2
Burland Rd SW11 158 D6
Burleigh Ave DA15 167 D6
Hackbridge SM6 219 B5
Burleigh Ct N17 34 A4
Burleigh Gdns N14 15 C3
Ashford TW15 171 A5
Burleigh Ho SW3 266 D5
W10 90 D2
Enfield EN1 18 A6
Burleigh Par N14 15 D3
Burleigh Pl SW15 156 D6
Burleigh Rd Cheam SM3 201 A1
Enfield EN1 5 C1
Hillingdon UB10 82 D6
Burleigh St WC2 250 C6
Burleigh Way EN2 5 B2
Burleigh Wlk SE6 164 A3
Burley Cl Chingford E4 35 C5
Mitcham SW16 181 D1
Burley Ho E1 96 D1
Burley Rd E16 99 C2
Burlington Arc W1 249 A5
Burlington Ave
Richmond TW9 132 C4
Romford RM7 59 D3
Burlington Cl 5 E6 100 A1
W9 91 C3
East Bedfont TW14 149 B4
Orpington BR6 226 D6
Pinner HA5 40 B6
Burlington Ct W4 133 A5
Burlington Danes Sch
W12 90 B1
Burlington Gate SW20 179 A1
Burlington Gdns
W1 115 C6 249 A5
W3 111 A5
W4 111 A1
Dagenham RM6 59 A2
Fulham SW6 135 A3
Burlington Ho NW3 70 B3
Burlington Jun Sch
KT3 199 D5
Burlington La W4 133 B5
Burlington Lo BR7 188 B3
Burlington Mews W3 111 A5
1 Putney SW15 157 B6
Burlington Pl
Fulham SW6 135 A3
Woodford IG8 21 A1
Burlington Rd N10 49 A6
W4 111 A1
Enfield EN2 5 B4
Fulham SW6 135 A3
Hounslow TW7 130 B4
New Malden KT3 199 D5
South Norwood CR7 183 B1
Tottenham N17 34 A2
Burlington Rise EN4 14 D4
Burma Rd N16 73 B4
Burmarsh 6 NW5 71 A2
Burmarsh Ct SE20 184 C2
Burma Terr 11 SE19 183 C5
Burmester Ho SW17 158 A1
Burmester Rd SW17 158 A1
Burnaby Cres W4 133 A6
Burnaby Ct 27 SE16 118 A4
Burnaby Gdns W4 132 D6
Burnaby St
SW10 136 A5 266 B3
Burnand Ho 3 W14 112 D3
Burnaston Ho 5 E5 74 A5
Burnbrae Cl N12 29 D4
Burnbury Rd SW12 159 C3
Burncroft Ave EN3 6 C3
Burndell Way UB4 84 D2
Burne Jones Ho W14 254 B3
Burnell Ave DA16 146 A3
Richmond TW10 175 C5
Burnell Gdns HA7 25 D1
Burnell Ho 19 SW2 160 C3
Burnell Rd SM1 217 D4
Burnell Wlk SE1 263 D2
Burnels Ave E6 100 C4
Burness Cl N7 72 B2
Burne St NW1 237 A4
Burnett Cl E9 74 C3
Burnett Ct SW11 267 A1
Burnett Ho 5 SE13 142 A3
Burney Ave KT5 198 B4
Burney Ho 4 SW16 181 C5
Burney St SE10 142 A5
Burnfoot Ave
SW6 135 A4 264 B1
Burnham NW3 70 C1
Burnham Ave UB10 61 A4
Burnham Cl NW7 28 A3
SE1 263 D3
Enfield EN1 5 C5
Harrow HA3 43 A5
Burnham Cres E11 55 C5
Burnham Ct NW4 46 C5
W2 245 D6
Burnham Dr KT4 216 D6
Burnham Est 8 E2 96 C4
Burnham Gdns
Cranford TW4 128 B4
Croydon CR0 205 D2
Hayes UB3 105 B3
Burnham Rd DA14 169 A2
E4 35 B5
Dagenham RM9 102 B6
Morden SM4 201 D5
Burnham St E2 96 C4
Kingston KT2 176 C2
Burnham Way W13 109 B3
Penge SE26 185 B5
Burnhill Ho EC1 235 A1
Burnhill Rd BR3 185 C1
Burnley Cl WD19 22 C5
Burnley Rd NW10 68 A3
SW9 138 B3
Burnsall St SW3 114 C1 257 B2
Burns Ave DA15 168 B5
Feltham TW14 150 A5
Ilford RM6 58 C2
Southall UB1 107 C6
Burns Cl DA16 145 D4
Hayes UB4 84 A2
Mitcham SW17 180 B4
Burns Ct SM6 219 B1
Burns Ho 18 E2 96 C4
11 N16 73 C4
N7 72 B2
SE17 261 D1
Burn's Ho NW10 89 C6
Burnside RM8 58 C1
Burnside Ave E4 35 B4
Burnside Cl SE16 118 D5
Barnet EN5 1 C2
Twickenham TW1 153 A5
Burnside Cres HA0 87 D6
Burns Rd SW11 136 D3
W13 109 B4
Burn's Rd NW10 89 D6
Burns Rd HA0 88 A5
Burns Way TW5 128 D4
Burnt Ash Hill SE12 164 D5
Lewisham SE12 165 A3
Burnt Ash Hts BR1 187 B5
Burnt Ash La BR1,SE12 187 B5
Burnt Ash Prim Sch
BR1 187 A5
Burnt Ash Rd SE12 164 D6
Burnthwaite Rd
SW6 135 B5 264 D3
Burnt Oak Broadway
HA8 26 D2
Burnt Oak Fields HA8 27 A2
Burnt Oak Jun Sch
DA15 168 A3
Burnt Oak La DA15 168 B3
Burnt Oak Sta HA8 27 A2
Burntwood Cl SW18 158 C3
Burntwood Ct SW17 158 A1
Burntwood Grange Rd
SW18 158 C3
Burntwood La SW17 158 B2
Burntwood Sch SW17 158 B2
Burntwood View SE19 183 D5
Buross St E1 96 B1
Burpham Cl UB4 84 D2
Burrage Ct 17 SE16 118 D2
Burrage Gr SE18 123 A2
Burrage Pl SE18 122 D1
Burrage Rd SE18 123 A1
Burrard Ho 11 E2 96 C5
Burrard Rd NW6 69 C4
Newham E16 99 B1
Burr Cl DA7 147 B2
E1 118 A5
Burrel Ct HA1 42 B2
Burrell Cl Croydon CR0 207 A3
Edgware HA8 10 D2
Burrell Ho 4 TW1 153 B4
Burrell Row BR3 185 C1
Burrells 9 BR3 185 D1
Burrell St SE1 116 D5 251 C4
Burrell's Wharf Sq E14 119 D1
Burrell Twrs E10 53 C2
Burrhill Ct SE16 118 D3
Burritt Rd KT1 176 C1
Burrmead Ct NW2 67 D5
Burroughs Gdns NW4 46 B5
Burroughs The NW4 46 B5
Burrow Ho 19 SW9 138 B3
Burrow Rd SE22 139 C1
Burrows Mews SE1 251 C2
Burrows Rd NW10 90 C4
Burrow Wlk SE21 161 A4
Burr Rd SW18 157 C4
Bursar St SE1 253 A3
Bursdon Cl DA15 167 D2
Bursland Rd EN3 6 D1
Burslem St E1 96 A1
Bursted Wood Prim Sch
DA7 147 D3
Burstock Rd SW15 135 A1
Burston Rd SW15 156 D6
Burstow Rd SW20 179 A2
Burtenshaw Rd KT7 197 A3
Burtley Cl N4 51 A1
Burton Bank N1 73 B1
Burton Cl
Chessington KT9 213 D1
South Norwood CR7 205 B6
Burton Ct SW3 257 D2
Thames Ditton KT7 197 A3
Burton Dr EN3 7 C6
Burton Gdns TW5 129 B4
Burton Gr SE17 262 C1
Burton Ho 6 SE16 118 B4
SE5 138 D4
Penge SE26 184 B5
Burtonhole Cl NW7 28 D6
Burtonhole La NW7 28 D6
Burton Lo 5 SW15 157 B6
Burton Mews SW1 258 B3
Burton Pl WC1 232 D1
Burton Rd NW6 69 B1
SW9 138 D3
8 SW9 138 C3
Kingston KT2 176 A3
Wanstead E18 55 B6
Burtons Ct E15 76 B1
Burtons Rd TW12 174 A6
Burton St WC1 93 D3 239 D6
Burtonwood Ho N4 51 B2
Burt Rd E16 121 C5
Burtt Ho 6 N1 95 C4
Burtwell La SE21,SE27 183 B6
Burwash Ho SE1 252 D1
Burwash Rd SE18 123 B1
Burwell 2 KT1 176 C1
Burwell Ave UB6 64 C2
Burwell Cl 25 E1 96 B1
Burwell Rd E10 53 A1
Burwell Wlk 14 E3 97 C3
Burwood Ave BR2 225 B6
Pinner HA5 40 C4
Burwood Cl KT6 198 C1
Burwood Ct SE23 162 C4
Burwood Ho 11 SW9 138 D1
Burwood Pl W2 237 B2
Bury Ave Hayes UB4 83 C5
Ruislip HA4 39 A3
Bury Cl SE16 118 D5
Bury Ct EC3 243 B2
Bury Gr SM4 201 D4
Bury Hall Villas N9 17 D4
Bury Pl WC1 94 A2 240 B3
Bury Rd N22 50 C6
Chingford E4 20 C6
Dagenham RM10 81 D3
Buryside Cl IG2 57 D5
Bury St EC3 95 C1 243 B2
SW1 115 C5 249 B4
Edmonton N9 18 A3
Ruislip HA4 39 B3
Bury St W N9 17 C4
Bury Wlk SW3 114 C1 257 A2
Burywood Ct EN3 6 C3
Busbridge Ho 16 E14 97 C2
Busby Ho SW16 181 C6
Busby Pl NW5 71 D2
Busch Cl TW7 131 B4
Busch Cnr TW7 131 B4
Bushbaby Cl SE1 263 A5
Bushberry Rd E9 75 A2
Bush Cl IG2 57 B4
Bush Cotts 12 SW18 157 C6
Bush Ct N14 15 C3

Bush Ct *continued*
7 W12 112 D4
Bushell Cl SW2 160 B2
Bushell Gn WD23 8 B2
Bushell Ho 3 SE27 183 A6
Bushell St E1 118 A5
Bushell Way BR7 188 C5
Bushey Ave BR5 211 B2
E18 54 D6
Bushey Cl Chingford E4 20 A1
Ickenham UB10 60 C6
Bushey Ct SW20 178 B1
Bushey Down SW12 159 B2
Bushey Fst Sch KT3 200 B6
Bushey Hall SE5 139 D4
Bushey Heath Prim Sch
WD23 8 B3
Bushey Hill Rd SE5 139 D4
Bushey Ho SE12 165 C1
Bushey La SM1 217 C4
Bushey Lees DA15 167 D5
Bushey Meads Sch WD23 8 A6
Bushey Mid Sch SW20 200 B6
Bushey Rd E13 99 C5
N15 51 C3
Croydon CR0 223 C6
Hayes UB3 105 C2
Ickenham UB10 60 C6
Sutton SM1 217 C4
West Barnes SW20 178 D1
Bushey Way BR3 208 B4
Bush Fair Ct N14 15 B5
Bushfield Cl HA8 10 D2
Bushfield Cres HA8 10 D2
Bushfield Ho N5 73 A3
Bush Gr NW9 45 A2
Stanmore HA7 25 D2
Bushgrove Rd RM8 80 D5
Bush Hill N21 17 A5
Bush Hill Par EN1 17 B4
Bush Hill Park Prim Sch
EN1 18 A6
Bush Hill Park Sta EN1 17 C5
Bush Hill Rd Enfield N21 17 B5
Harrow HA3 44 B3
Bush Ind Est NW10 89 B3
Bush La EC4 117 B6 252 C6
Bushmead Cl 6 N15 51 D5
Bushmoor Cres SE18 144 D5
Bushnell Rd SW17 159 B1
Bush Rd E8 96 B6
SE8 118 D2
Littleton TW17 192 B4
Richmond TW9 132 B6
Wanstead E11 55 A2
Woodford IG9 37 D6
Bushway RM8 80 D5
Bushwood E11 55 A1
Bushwood Dr
SE1 117 D2 263 D3
Bushwood Rd TW9 132 C6
Bushy Ct KT1 175 C2
Bushy Park Gdns TW12 174 B5
Bushy Park Rd TW11 175 B3
Bushy Rd TW11 174 D3
Business Acad The
DA18 125 A4
Business Design Ctr*
N1 94 C6 234 B5
Buspace Studios 3 W10 91 A3
Butcher Row E1 96 D1
Butchers Rd E16 99 A1
Bute Ave TW10 154 A2
Bute Ct SM6 219 C3
Bute Gdns W6 112 D2
Wallington SM6 219 C3
Bute Gdns W SM6 219 C3
Bute House Prep Sch
W6 112 D2
Bute Rd Ilford IG6 56 D4
Thornton Heath CR0 204 C1
Wallington SM6 219 C4
Bute St SW7 114 B2 256 C4
Butfield Ho 6 E9 74 C2
Butler Ave HA1 42 B2
Butler Ct Dagenham RM8 81 C6
Wembley HA0 65 A4
Butler Ho 13 E14 97 B1
32 E2 96 C4
5 SW9 138 D4
Butler Pl SW1 259 C6
Butler Rd NW10 67 D1
Dagenham RM8 80 B4
Harrow HA1 42 A2
Butler's Cotts DA7 147 C3
Butler St 33 E2 96 C4
Hillingdon UB10 82 D3
Butler's Wharf W SE1 253 C3
Butley Ct 7 E3 97 A5
Butterfield Cl 1 SE16 118 B4
Tottenham N17 33 A4
Twickenham TW1 152 D5
Butterfield Row EN2 5 A2
Butterfields E17 54 A4
Butterfield Sq 10 E6 100 B1
Butterfly La SE9 166 D5
Butterfly Wlk 2 SE5 139 B4
Butter Hill SM5,SM6 219 A4
Butteridges Cl RM9 103 B6
Buttermere NW1 231 D2
Buttermere Cl E11 76 B4
SE1 263 C3
East Bedfont TW14 149 D3
West Barnes SM4 200 D3
Buttermere Ct NW8 229 C6
Buttermere Dr SW15 157 A6
Buttermere Ho 11 E3 97 B4
Buttermere Ho *continued*
N12 30 C5
Buttermere Wlk 9 E8 73 D2
Butterwick W6 112 C2
Butterworth Ct SW16 160 A1
Butterworth Gdns IG8 37 A5
Buttesland St N1 95 B4 235 D2
Buttfield Cl RM10 81 D2
Buttmarsh Cl SE18 122 D1
Buttsbury Rd IG1 79 A3
Butts Cotts TW13 151 B1
Butts Cres TW13 151 C1
Butts Ho TW13 151 C1
Butts Piece UB5 84 B5
Butts Rd BR1 186 C5
Butts The TW8 131 D6
Buxhall Cres E9 75 B2
Buxlow Prep Sch HA9 66 A5
Buxted Rd E8 73 D1
N12 30 C5
SE22 139 C1
Buxton Cl N9 18 C2
Woodford IG8 37 D4
Buxton Cres SM3 217 A4
Buxton Ct N1 235 B2
Buxton Dr E11 54 C5
Kingston KT3 177 B1
Buxton Gdns W3 110 D6
Buxton Ho E11 54 C5
3 SW11 136 B1
Buxton Lo E11 77 B6
Buxton Rd E15 76 C3
E17 53 A5
E6 100 A4
N19 49 D1
NW2 68 B2
Chingford E4 20 B4
Ilford IG2 57 C3
Mortlake SW14 133 C2
Thornton Heath CR7 204 D4
Buxton St E1 96 A3 243 D5
Buzzard Creek Ind Est
IG11 102 A2
Byam Shaw Sch of Art
N19 71 D6
Byam St SW6 136 A3
Byards Croft SW16 181 D2
Byards Ct SE16 118 D3
Byas Ho 6 E3 97 B4
Byatt Wlk TW12 173 A4
Bychurch End 9 TW11 174 D5
Bycroft Rd UB1 85 C3
Bycroft St SE20 184 D3
Bycullah Ave EN2 4 D3
Bycullah Rd EN2 4 D3
Byefield Cl SE16 119 A4
Byelands Cl 12 SE16 118 D5
Bye The W3 89 C1
Byeways TW2 151 D1
Byeways The KT5 198 D4
Byeway The SW14 133 A2
Bye Way The HA3 24 D2
Byfeld Gdns SW13 134 A4
Byfield Ct KT3 200 A5
Byfield Rd TW7 131 A2
Byford Cl E15 76 C1
Bygrove CR0 223 D1
Bygrove Ct SW19 180 B4
Bygrove Prim Sch E14 97 D1
Bygrove Rd SW19 180 B4
Bygrove St E14 97 D1
Byland Cl N21 16 B4
Bylands Cl SE2 124 B3
Byne Rd Carshalton SM5 218 C6
Forest Hill SE26 184 C5
Bynes Rd CR2 221 B1
Byng Pl WC1 93 D3 239 C5
Byng St E14 119 C4
Bynon Ave DA7 147 B2
Byre Rd N14 15 B5
Byrne Ho 11 SW2 160 B6
Byrne Rd SW12 159 B2
Byron Ave E12 78 A2
NW9 44 D6
Borehamwood WD6 10 C6
Cranford TW4 128 B3
Sutton SM1 218 B4
West Barnes KT3 200 A4
Woodford E18 36 D1
Byron Ave E SM1 218 B4
Byron Cl E8 96 A6
SE28 124 C5
Feltham TW12 173 B6
Forest Hill SE26 185 A6
Streatham SW16 182 A4
Walton-on-T KT12 195 A1
Byron Court Prim Sch
HA0 65 C6
Byron Ct 3 NW6 70 A1
SW3 257 B3
W7 109 A2
W9 91 C3
WC1 240 C6
Dulwich SE21 162 A3
Enfield EN2 4 D3
Harrow HA1 42 C3
1 Richmond TW10 175 D6
South Norwood CR7 183 A1
11 Wanstead E11 55 A5
Woodford E18 37 B2
Byron Dr DA8 147 D5
N2 48 B3
Byron Gdns SM1 218 B4
Byron Hill Rd HA1,HA2 64 C6
Byron Ho 5 BR3 185 D4
Byron Mews NW3 70 C4
Byron Par UB10 83 A3
Byron Rd E10 53 D1
E17 53 C6
NW2 68 B6
Byron Rd *continued*
NW7 28 A5
Ealing W5 110 B5
Harrow HA1 42 C3
Harrow HA3 24 D1
Wembley HA0 65 C5
Byron St E14 98 A1
Byron Way Hayes UB4 83 D3
Northolt UB5 85 A4
West Drayton UB7 104 B2
Bysouth Cl N15 51 B5
Bythorn St SW9 138 B1
Byton Rd SW17 180 D4
Byward Ave TW14 150 C5
Byward St EC3 117 C6 253 B5
Bywater Ho SE18 122 A3
Bywater Pl SE16 119 A5
Bywater St SW3 114 D1 257 C2
Byways The KT19 215 D4
Bywell Pl W1 239 A3
Bywood Ave CR0 206 D3
Bywood Terr CR0 206 C3
Byworth Wlk N19 50 A1

C

Cabbell St NW1 92 C2 237 A3
Cabinet Off SW1 250 A2
Cabinet War Rooms*
SW1 115 D4 249 D2
Cabinet Way E4 35 B4
Cable Ho WC1 234 A2
Cable Pl SE10 142 A4
Cable St E1 118 B6
Cabot Ct SE16 118 D3
Cabot Sq E14 119 C5
Cabot Way 3 E6 99 D6
Cabul Rd SW11 136 C3
Cactus Cl SE5 139 C3
Cactus Wlk W12 89 D1
Cadbury Cl
Ashford TW16 171 C3
Isleworth TW7 131 A4
Cadbury Rd TW16 171 C4
Cadbury Way 1 SE16 118 A2
Caddington Cl EN4 14 C6
Caddington Rd NW2 69 A5
Caddis Cl HA7 24 D3
Cadell Cl E2 95 D5
Cadell Ho 12 E2 95 D5
Cade Rd SE10 142 B4
Cader Rd SW18 158 A5
Cadet Dr SE1 117 D1 263 D2
Cade Tyler Ho 10 SE10 142 A4
Cadiz St SE17 117 A1 262 B1
Cadley Terr SE23 162 C2
Cadman Cl SW9 138 D5
Cadmer Cl KT3 199 C5
Cadmore Ho 4 N1 72 D1
Cadmus Cl 9 SW4 137 D2
Cadmus Ct 6 SW9 138 C4
Cadnam Lo E14 120 B3
Cadnam Point 15 SW15 156 B3
Cadogan Cl E9 75 B1
Beckenham BR3 186 B1
Harrow HA2 63 D4
Teddington TW11 174 C5
Cadogan Ct SW3 257 C3
Sutton SM2 217 D2
New Malden KT3 199 C5
Cadogan Ct Gdns SW1 258 A4
Cadogan Gate
SW1 114 D2 257 D4
Cadogan Gdns N3 29 D2
SW3 114 D2 257 D3
Southgate N21 16 C6
Wanstead E18 55 B6
Cadogan Ho SW3 266 D5
Cadogan La
SW1 115 A3 258 A5
Cadogan Pl
SW1 114 D3 257 D5
Cadogan Rd SE18 123 A3
Kingston KT6 197 D4
Cadogan Sq
SW1 114 D3 257 D5
Cadogan St
SW3 114 D2 257 C3
Cadogan Terr E9 75 B1
Cadoxton Ave 3 N15 51 D3
Cadwallon Rd SE9 167 A2
Caedmon Rd N7 72 B4
Caerleon Cl
Claygate KT10 213 B1
Sidcup DA14 190 C5
Caerleon Terr SE2 124 B2
Caernarvon Cl CR4 204 A6
Caernarvon Ct 3 KT5 198 B4
Caernarvon Ho W2 236 A2
Caesar Ct 25 E2 96 D5
Caesar's Way TW17 193 B3
Caesars Wlk CR4 202 D4
Cahill St EC1 242 B5
Cahir St E14 119 D2
Cain Ct 2 W5 87 C2
Caine Ho W3 110 D4
Cain's La TW14 149 C6
Caird St W10 91 B4
Cairn Ave W5 109 D5
Cairndale Cl BR1 186 D3
Cairnfield Ave NW2 67 D5
Cairnfield Ct NW2 67 C5
Cairns Ho 3 N7 72 B4
Cairns Mews SE18 144 A4
Cairns Rd SW11 158 C6
Cairn Way HA7 24 D4
Cairo New Rd CR0 220 D6
Cairo Rd E17 53 C5
Caister Ho N7 72 B2
Caister Ho *continued*
10 Balham SW12 159 B4
Caistor Ho 5 E15 98 D6
Caistor Mews SW12 159 B4
Caistor Park Rd E15 98 D6
Caistor Rd SW12 159 B4
Caithness Gdns DA15 167 D5
Caithness Ho N1 233 C6
Caithness Rd W14 112 D3
Mitcham CR4 181 B3
Calabria Rd N5 72 D3
Calais Gate SE5 138 D4
Calais St SE5 138 D4
Calbourne Rd SW12 159 A4
Calcott Wlk SE9 187 D6
Calcraft Ho 10 E2 96 C5
Caldbeck Ave KT4 200 B1
Caldecot Ct SE5 139 A3
Caldecote 3 KT1 176 C1
Caldecote Gdns WD23 8 C4
Caldecote La WD23 8 D5
Caldecot Rd SE5 139 A3
Caldecott Way E5 74 D5
Calder Ave UB6 86 D5
Calder Cl EN1 5 C2
Calder Ct SE16 119 B5
Calder Gdns HA8 44 C6
Calderon Ho NW8 230 A4
Calderon Pl W10 90 C2
Calderon Rd E11 76 B5
Calder Rd SM4 202 A4
Caldervale Rd SW4 159 D6
Calderwood St SE18 122 C2
Caldew Ct NW7 28 A3
Caldew St SE5 139 B5
Caldicote Gn NW9 45 C3
Caldwell Rd WD19 22 D6
Caldwell St
SW9 138 B5 270 D3
Caldy Rd DA17 125 D3
Caldy Wlk 15 N1 73 A2
Caleb St SE1 252 B2
Caledonia Ct IG11 102 C5
Caledonia Ho 17 E14 97 A1
Caledonian Cl 1 IG3 58 B1
Caledonian Market
SE1 117 C3 263 B6
Caledonian Rd
N1 94 B6 233 C5
N7 72 B2
Caledonian Road &
Barnsbury Sta N7 72 B1
Caledonian Road Sta N7 72 B2
Caledonian Wharf Rd
E14 120 B2
Caledonia Rd TW19 148 A3
Caledonia St N1 233 B3
Caledon Rd E6 78 B1
Hackbridge SM5,SM6 219 A4
Cale St SW3 114 C1 257 A2
Caletock Way SE10 120 D1
Calgarth NW1 232 B3
Calgary Ct 24 SE16 118 C4
Caliban Twr 9 N1 95 C5
Calico Ho 4 SW11 136 A2
Calico Row 5 SW11 136 A2
Calidore Cl SW2 160 B5
California La WD23 8 B3
California Rd KT3 199 A6
Callaby Terr 11 N1 73 B2
Callaghan Cl SE13 142 C1
Callahan Cotts 8 E1 96 C2
Callander Rd SE6 164 A2
Callanders The WD23 8 C3
Callard Ave N13 32 D6
Callcott Ct NW6 69 B1
Callcott Rd NW6 69 B1
Callcott St W8 245 A4
Callendar Rd SW7 256 C6
Callingham Cl 17 E14 97 B2
Callingham Ho 1 SW4 138 A2
Callis Farm Cl TW19 148 A5
Callis Rd E17 53 B3
Callonfield 3 E17 53 A5
Callow St SW3 136 B6 266 C6
Calmington Rd SE5 139 C6
Calmont Rd BR1 186 C4
Calonne Rd SW19 178 D6
Calshot Ho N1 233 C4
Calshot Rd TW6 126 D3
Calshot St N1 94 B5 233 C3
Calshot Way Enfield EN2 4 D2
Harlington TW6 126 C3
Calstock NW1 232 C5
Calstock Ho SE11 261 B2
Calthorpe Gdns
Edgware HA8 26 B5
Sutton SM1 218 A5
Calthorpe St
WC1 94 B3 240 D6
Calton Ave SE21 161 C5
Calton Rd EN5 14 B5
Calver 13 NW5 71 B4
Calver Ct E17 54 B6
Calverley Cl BR3 185 D4
Calverley Cres RM10 81 C6
Calverley Gr N19 49 D1
Calverley Rd KT17 216 A2
Calvert Ave E2 95 D4
Calvert Cl
Belvedere DA17 125 D2
Sidcup DA14 191 A4
Calvert Ct 1 N19 49 C1
5 Richmond TW9 132 B1
Calvert Ho 9 W12 112 B6
Calverton SE5 139 C6
Calverton Prim Sch E16 99 D1
Calverton Rd E6 100 C6
Calvert Rd SE10 120 D1
Calvert's Bldgs SE1 252 C3
Calvert St NW1 93 A6 231 A6
Calvin St E1 95 D3 243 C5
Calydon Rd SE7 121 B1
Calypso Cres 5 SE15 139 D5
Calypso Way SE8,SE16 119 B2
Camac Rd TW2 152 B3
Camarthen Gn NW9 45 C3
Cambalt Ho 3 SW15 156 D6
Cambalt Rd SW15 156 D6
Cambell Inf Sch RM9 80 D1
Cambell Jun Sch RM9 80 D1
Cambell Wlk N1 233 B6
Camber Ho 4 SE15 140 C6
Camberley Ave Enfield EN1 5 C1
Wimbledon SW20 178 B1
Camberley Cl SM3 216 D5
Camberley Ct 8 SM2 217 D1
Camberley Ho NW1 231 D3
Camberley Rd TW6 126 C2
Cambert Way SE9 143 B1
Camberwell Church St
SE5 139 B4
Camberwell Coll of Arts
SE15 139 D5
SE5 139 C4
Camberwell Glebe SE5 139 C4
Camberwell Gn SE5 139 B4
Camberwell Gr SE5 139 C3
Camberwell Green SE5 139 A4
Camberwell New Rd
SW9 138 D5
Camberwell Rd SE5 139 A5
Camberwell Station Rd
SE5 139 A4
Camberwell Trad Est
SE5 139 A4
Cambeys Rd RM10 81 D3
Cambisgate SW19 179 A5
Camborne Ave W13 109 C4
Camborne Cl TW6 126 C2
Camborne Cres TW6 126 C2
Camborne Rd DA16 145 D3
Belmont SM2 217 D1
Croydon CR0 206 A2
Sidcup DA14 168 C1
Wandsworth SW18 157 C4
West Barnes SM4 200 D4
Harmondsworth TW6 126 C2
Camborne Way
Harlington TW6 126 C2
Heston TW5 129 C4
Cambourne Ave N9 18 D4
Cambourne Mews 6
W11 91 A1
Cambray Rd BR6 211 D2
Streatham SW12 159 C3
Cambria 6 BR3 185 D1
Cambria Cl DA15 167 C3
Hounslow TW3 129 C1
Cambria Ct TW14 150 B4
Cambria Gdns TW19 148 A4
Cambria Ho 16 E14 97 A1
Forest Hill SE26 184 A6
Cambrian Ave IG2 57 C4
Cambrian Cl SE27 160 D1
Cambrian Ct UB2 107 D2
Cambrian Gn NW9 45 C4
Cambrian Rd E10 53 C1
Richmond TW10 154 B5
Cambria Rd SE5 139 A2
Cambria St
SW6 135 D5 265 D3
Cambridge Ave DA16 145 D1
NW6 91 C5
Greenford UB6 64 D3
Kingston KT3,SW20 177 D1
Cambridge Barracks Rd 12
SE18 122 B2
Cambridge Cir
WC2 93 D1 239 D1
Cambridge Cl E17 53 B3
NW10 67 A5
Hounslow TW4 129 A1
Wimbledon SW20 178 B2
Wood Green N22 32 C2
Cambridge Cotts TW9 132 C6
Cambridge Cres 20 E2 96 B5
Teddington TW11 175 A5
Cambridge Ct 25 E2 96 B5
N16 51 C2
2 NW6 91 C5
Wimbledon SW20 178 B2
Cambridge Dr SE12 165 A6
Ruislip HA4 62 D6
Cambridge Gate NW1 238 C6
Cambridge Gate Mews
NW1 238 D6
Cambridge Gdns N10 31 B2
NW6 91 C5
W10 91 A1
Enfield EN1 6 A3
Kingston KT1 176 C1
Southgate N21 17 B4
Tottenham N17 33 B3
Cambridge Gn SE9 166 D3
Cambridge Gr W6 112 B2
Penge SE20 184 B2
Cambridge Grove Rd
Kingston KT1 198 C6
13 Kingston KT1 176 C1
Cambridge Heath Rd E1,
E2 96 B4
Cambridge Heath Sta E2 96 B5
Cambridge Ho
Ealing W13 87 A1
Fulham SW6 135 A2
2 Teddington TW11 175 A5
7 Woolwich SE18 122 B2
Cambridge Mans SW11 267 C1
Cambridge Par EN1 6 A4
Cambridge Park Ct
TW1 153 D4
Cambridge Park Rd E11 55 A2
Cambridge Pas 9 E9 74 C1
Cambridge Pk
Twickenham TW1 153 D5
Wanstead E11 55 A3
Cambridge Pl W8 245 D1
Cambridge Rd BR1 187 A3
E11 54 D3
NW6 91 C4
NW6 91 C5
SW11 136 D4 267 C1
W7 108 D4
Barking IG11 79 A1
Barnes SW13 133 D3
Carshalton SM5 218 C3
3 Chingford E4 20 B3
East Molesey KT8 195 B5
Hampton TW12 173 B3
Harrow HA2 41 C4
Hounslow TW4 129 A1
Ilford IG3 57 C1
Kingston KT1 176 C1
Littleton TW15 171 A3
Mitcham CR4 203 C6
New Malden KT3 199 C5
Penge SE20 206 B6
Richmond TW9 132 C5
Sidcup DA14 189 C6
Southall UB1 107 B5
Teddington TW11 175 A5
Twickenham TW1 153 D5
Walton-on-T KT12 194 B3
Wimbledon SW20 178 B2
Cambridge Rd N W4 110 D1
Cambridge Rd S 3 W4 110 D1
Cambridge Row SE18 122 D1
Cambridge Sch W6 112 B2
Cambridge Sq
W2 92 C1 237 A2
Cambridge St
SW1 115 C1 259 A2
Cambridge Terr NW1 231 C1
Edmonton N9 17 D4
Cambridge Terr Mews
NW1 231 D1
Cambstone Cl N11 15 A2
Cambus Cl UB4 85 A2
Cambus Rd E16 99 A2
Cam Ct 2 SE15 139 D6
Camdale Rd SE18 145 D5
Camden Ave
Feltham TW13 150 C3
Hayes UB4 106 D6
Camden Cl BR7 189 A2
Camden Ct 9 DA17 125 C1
Camden Gdns NW1 71 B1
Sutton SM1 217 D3
Thornton Heath CR7 204 D6
Camden Gr BR7 188 D4
Camden High St
NW1 93 C6 232 A5
Camden Hill Rd SE19 183 C4
Camden Ho 6 SE8 119 B1
Camdenhurst St E14 97 A1
Camden Jun Sch SM5 218 D4
Camden Lock Pl NW1 71 B1
Camden Mews NW1 71 D2
Camden Mkt*
NW1 93 B6 231 D6
Camden Park Rd BR7 188 C3
NW1 71 D2
Camden Pas N1 94 D6 234 C5
Camden Rd DA5 169 B4
E17 53 B3
NW1 71 D2 231 D6
Carshalton SM5 218 D4
Sutton SM1 217 D3
Wanstead E11 55 B3
Camden Road Sta NW1 71 C1
Camden Row SE3 142 C3
Camden Sch for Girls The
NW5 71 C2
Camden Sq NW1 71 D2
Camden St NW1 93 C6 232 B5
Camden Studios NW1 232 B5
Camden Town Sta
NW1 93 B6 231 D6
Camden Way BR7 188 C3
Thornton Heath CR7 204 D6
Camden Wlk N1 234 C5
Cameford Ct 20 SW12 160 A4
Camel Ct HA9 66 D6
Camelford NW1 232 B5
Camelford Ct 7 W11 91 A1
Camelford Wlk 8 W11 91 A1
Camel Gr KT2 175 D5
Camelia Ct IG8 36 C4
Camellia Ct 20 BR3 185 C3
Camellia Ho SE8 141 B5
Camellia Pl TW2 151 D4
Camellia St SW8 270 A3
Camelot Cl SE18 123 B4
Wimbledon SW19 179 C6
Camelot Ho 6 NW1 71 D2
Camelot Prim Sch SE15 140 B6
Camel Rd E16 121 D5
Camera Pl SW10 266 C6
Cameret Ct 6 W11 112 D4
Cameron Cl N20 14 C2
Edmonton N18 34 B5
Cameron Ct 3 SW19 157 A3
Cameron Ho NW8 230 A4
SE5 139 A5
8 Bromley BR1 186 D2
Cameron House Sch
SW10 266 D5
Cameron Lo TW3 130 A1
Cameron Rd BR2 209 A4

Cameron Rd *continued*
Forest Hill SE6 ....163 B2
Ilford IG3 ....57 C1
Thornton Heath CR0 ....204 D3
Cameron Sq CR4 ....180 C2
Camerton Cl 8 E8 ....73 D2
Camfrey Ct N8 ....50 A5
Camgate Ctr The TW19 ..148 B4
Camilla Cl TW16 ....171 D4
Camilla Ct 14 SM2 ....217 C1
Camilla Rd SE16 ....118 B2
Camille Cl SE25 ....206 A6
Camlan Rd BR1 ....186 D6
Camlet St E2 ....243 C6
Camlet Way EN4 ....1 D4
Camley St NW1 ...93 D5 232 D4
Camm 23 NW9 ....27 D1
Camm Gdns
5 Kingston KT1 ....176 B1
Thames Ditton KT7 ....196 D2
Camomile Ave CR4 ....180 D2
Camomile St EC3 .95 C1 243 B2
Camomile Way UB7 ....82 A1
Campaign Ct W9 ....91 B3
Campana Rd
SW6 ....135 C4 265 B2
Campasps Bsns Pk
TW16 ....193 D4
Campbell Ave IG6 ....57 A5
Campbell Cl SE18 ....144 C4
Ruislip HA4 ....40 A3
Streatham SW16 ....181 D6
Twickenham TW2 ....152 B3
Campbell Croft HA8 ....26 C5
Campbell Ct NW9 ....45 A3
SW7 ....256 A5
Dulwich SE21 ....162 A3
Ealing W7 ....108 C6
Tottenham N17 ....33 D2
Campbell Gordon Way
NW2 ....68 B4
Campbell Ho SW1 ....259 A1
30 W12 ....112 B6
W2 ....236 C5
6 Wallington SM6 ....219 B4
Campbell Rd E15 ....76 D4
E17 ....53 B5
E3 ....97 C4
E6 ....100 A6
Ealing W7 ....108 C6
Thornton Heath CR0 ....204 D3
Tottenham N17 ....34 A2
Twickenham TW2 ....152 B2
Campdale Rd N7 ....71 D5
Campden Cres
Dagenham RM8 ....80 C4
Wembley HA0 ....65 B5
Campden Gr
W8 ....113 C4 245 B2
Campden Hill
W8 ....113 C4 245 A2
Campden Hill Ct W8 ....245 B2
Campden Hill Gate W8 ..245 A2
Campden Hill Gdns W8 .245 A4
Campden Hill Mans W8 .245 B4
Campden Hill Pl W14 ...244 D4
Campden Hill Rd
W8 ....113 C4 245 A2
Campden Hill Sq
W14 ....113 B5 244 D4
Campden Ho 4 NW6 ....70 B1
W8 ....245 B3
Campden Hos W8 ....245 A3
Campden House Cl W8 .245 B2
Campden Rd
Ickenham UB10 ....60 B4
South Croydon CR2 ....221 C3
Campden St W8 .113 C5 245 A3
Campe Ho 1 N10 ....31 A3
Campen Cl SW19 ....157 A2
Camperdown St E1 ....243 D1
Campfield Rd SE9 ....165 D4
Campion Cl Harrow HA3 ...44 B3
Hillingdon UB8 ....82 B2
Newham E6 ....122 B6
South Croydon CR2 ....221 C4
Campion Ct 10 HA0 ....88 A5
Campion Gdns IG8 ....37 A5
Campion Ho 15 N16 ....73 C3
Campion House (Seminary)
TW7 ....130 B4
Campion Pl SE28 ....124 B5
Campion Rd
Hounslow TW7 ....130 D4
Putney SW15 ....156 C6
Campion Terr NW2 ....68 D5
Campion Way HA8 ....27 A6
Camplin Rd HA3 ....44 A4
Camplin St SE14 ....140 D5
Camp Rd SW19 ....178 C5
Campsbourne Ho 3 N8 ..50 A5
Campsbourne Jun & Inf Schs
N8 ....50 A6
Campsbourne The N8 ....50 A5
Campsey Gdns RM9 ....80 B1
Campsey Rd RM9 ....80 B1
Campsfield Ho N8 ....50 A6
Campsfield Rd N8 ....50 A6
Campshill Pl SE13 ....164 A6
Campshill Rd SE13 ....164 A6
Camp Site The BR8 ....191 C3
Campton Hill Twrs W8 ..245 A4
Campus Rd E17 ....53 B3
Camp View SW19 ....178 B5
Cam Rd E15 ....98 B6
Camrose Ave DA8 ....147 D6
Edgware HA8 ....26 B2
Feltham TW13 ....172 C6
Camrose Cl Croydon CR0 .207 A2
Morden SM4 ....201 C5
Camrose St SE2 ....124 A2
Camsey Ho 8 SW2 ....160 B6
Canada Ave N18 ....33 A4
Canada Cres W3 ....89 A3
Canada Gdns SE13 ....164 A6
Canada Rd W3 ....89 A2
Canada Sq E14 ....119 D5
Canada St SE16 ....118 D4
Canada Way W12 ....112 B6
Canadian Ave SE6 ....163 D3
Canal App SE8 ....141 A6
Canal Bldg N1 ....235 A4
Canal Bridge SE15 ....140 A6
Canal Cl E1 ....97 A3
W10 ....90 D3
Canal Gr SE15 ....140 B6
Canal Head Public Sq
SE15 ....140 A4
Canal Path 22 E2 ....95 D6
Canalside Studios 31 N1 .95 C6
Canal St SE5 ....139 B6
Canal Way W10 ....90 D3
Canal Wlk N1 ....95 B6 235 D6
Croydon CR0 ....205 D3
Forest Hill SE26 ....184 C5
Canary Wharf* E14 ....119 D5
Canary Wharf Pier River Bus)
E14 ....119 B5
Canary Wharf Sta E14 ...119 C5
Canberra Cl NW4 ....46 A6
Canberra Dr UB4 ....84 C4
Canberra Prim Sch
W12 ....112 B6
Canberra Rd E6 ....100 B6
SE7 ....143 D6
Erith DA7 ....146 D6
Harlington TW6 ....126 C2
Canbury 2000 Bsns Pk 3
KT2 ....176 A2
Canbury Ave KT2 ....176 B2
Canbury Ct KT2 ....176 A3
Canbury Mews SE26 ....162 A1
Canbury Park Rd KT2 ....176 B2
Canbury Sch KT2 ....176 D4
Cancell Rd SW9 ....138 C4
Candahar Rd SW11 ....136 C3
Candida Ct 9 NW1 ....71 B1
Candishe Ho SE1 ....253 C2
Candler Mews TW1 ....153 A4
Candler St N15 ....51 B3
Candover St W1 ....239 A3
Candy St E3 ....97 B6
Caney Mews NW2 ....68 D6
Canfield Dr HA4 ....62 B3
Canfield Gdns NW6 ....69 D1
Canfield Ho N15 ....51 C3
Canfield Pl NW6 ....70 A2
Canford Ave UB5 ....85 A6
Canford Cl EN2 ....4 C3
Canford Gdns KT3 ....199 C3
Canford Pl TW11 ....175 C4
Canford Rd SW11 ....159 A6
Canham Rd W3 ....111 C4
South Norwood SE25 ....205 C6
Canmore Gdns SW16 ....181 C3
Cann Hall Prim Sch E11 ..76 D5
Cann Hall Rd E11 ....76 D4
Cann Ho W14 ....254 B5
Canning Cres N22 ....32 B2
Canning Cross SE5 ....139 C3
Canning Ct N22 ....32 B2
Canning Ho 23 W12 ....112 B6
Canning Pas
W8 ....114 A3 256 A6
Canning Pl W8 ..114 A3 256 A6
Canning Pl Mews W8 ...256 A6
Canning Rd E15 ....98 C5
E17 ....53 A6
N5 ....72 D5
Croydon CR0 ....221 D6
Harrow HA3 ....42 D6
Cannington 14 NW5 ....71 A2
Cannington Rd RM9 ....80 C2
Canning Town E16 ....98 C2
Canning Town Sta E16 ...98 C2
Cannizaro Rd SW19 ....178 D5
Cannock Ho N4 ....51 B2
Cannock Lo EN1 ....17 C5
Cannonbury Ave HA5 ....40 D3
Cannon Cl
Hampton TW12 ....173 D4
West Barnes SW20 ....200 C6
Cannon Dr E14 ....119 C6
Cannon Hill NW6 ....69 C3
Palmers Green N14 ....16 A1
Cannon Hill La SM4,
SW20 ....201 A5
Cannon Hill Mews N14 ...16 A1
Cannon Ho SE11 ....260 D3
Penge SE26 ....184 B4
Cannon La NW3 ....70 B5
Pinner HA5 ....41 A3
Cannon Pl NW3 ....70 B5
SE7 ....122 A1
Cannon Rd DA7 ....147 B4
Palmers Green N14 ....16 A1
Cannon St EC4 ...117 B6 252 B6
Cannon Street Rd E1 ....96 B1
Cannon Street Sta
EC4 ....117 B6 252 C6
Cannon Trad Est HA9 ....66 D4
Cannon Way KT8 ....195 D5
Cannon Wharf Bsns Ctr 12
SE8 ....119 A2
Canon Ave RM6 ....58 C4
Canon Barnett CE Prim Sch
E1 ....95 D1 243 D2
Canon Beck Rd SE16 ....118 C4
Canonbie Rd SE23 ....162 C4
Canonbury Cres N1 ....73 A1
Canonbury Ct 21 N1 ....72 D1
Canonbury Gr N1 ....73 A1
Canonbury La N1 ....72 D1
Canonbury Pk N N1 ....73 A2
Canonbury Pk S N1 ....73 A2
Canonbury Pl N1 ....72 D2
Canonbury Prim Sch N1 .72 D2
Canonbury Rd N1 ....72 D1
Enfield EN1 ....5 C4
Canonbury Sq N1 ....72 D1
Canonbury St N1 ....73 A1
Canonbury Sta N1,N5 ....73 A3
Canonbury Villas N1 ....72 D1
Canon Lane Fst & Mid Schs
HA5 ....40 D3
Canon Mohan Cl N14 ....15 B5
Canon Murnane Rd SE1 .263 C5
Canon Palmer RC Sch
IG3 ....57 C1
Canon Rd BR1 ....209 D6
Canon Row
SW1 ....116 A4 250 A1
Canons Cl N2 ....48 B2
Edgware HA8 ....26 B4
Canons Cnr HA8 ....26 A6
Canons Ct HA8 ....26 B4
Canons Dr HA8 ....26 B4
Canons High Sch HA8 ....26 B1
Canons L Ctr The CR4 ...202 D5
Canonsleigh Rd RM9 ....80 B1
Canons Park Cl HA8 ....26 A3
Canons Park Sta HA8 ....26 A3
Canon St N1 ....95 A6 235 A5
Canon's Wlk CR0 ....222 D5
Canopus Way
Moor Park HA6 ....22 A6
Stanwell TW19 ....148 A4
Canrobert St E2 ....96 B4
Cantelowes Ho EN5 ....12 D6
Cantelowes Rd NW1 ....71 D2
Canterbury SE13 ....164 A6
Canterbury Ave
DA14,DA15 ....168 C2
Redbridge IG1 ....56 A2
Canterbury Cl 16 SE5 ....139 A3
Beckenham BR3 ....185 D2
7 Newham E6 ....100 B1
Southall UB6 ....85 D2
Canterbury Cres SW9 ...138 C2
Canterbury Ct NW11 ....47 A3
NW6 ....91 C5
15 NW9 ....27 D1
W3 ....111 C5
Ashford TW15 ....170 B6
South Croydon CR2 ....221 A1
Canterbury Gr SE27,
SW16 ....160 C1
Canterbury Ho 6 E3 ....97 D4
SE1 ....260 D6
2 Barking IG11 ....80 A1
Canterbury Ind Pk 15
SE15 ....140 C6
Canterbury Mans NW6 ...69 D2
Canterbury Pl SE17 ....261 D3
Canterbury Rd E10 ....54 A3
NW6 ....91 C5
Feltham TW13 ....151 A2
Harrow HA1,HA2 ....42 A4
Morden SM4 ....202 A3
Thornton Heath CR0 ....204 C2
Canterbury Terr NW6 ....91 C5
Cantium Ret Pk SE1 ....140 A6
Cantley Gdns Ilford IG2 ...57 A3
South Norwood SE19 ....183 D2
Cantley Rd W7 ....109 A3
Canton St E14 ....97 C1
Cantrell Rd E3 ....97 C3
Cantwell Ho SE18 ....144 D5
Cantwell Rd SE18 ....144 D5
Canute Ct SW16 ....160 C1
Canute Gdns SE16 ....118 D2
Canvey St SE1 ....252 A4
Cape Cl IG11 ....78 D1
Cape Henry Ct 7 E14 ....120 B6
Capel KT5 ....198 B2
Capel Ave SM6 ....220 B3
Capel Cl N20 ....14 A1
Keston Mark BR2 ....210 A1
Capel Ct SE20 ....184 C2
Capel Gdns Ilford IG3 ....79 D4
Pinner HA5 ....41 B5
Capel Ho 17 E9 ....74 C1
South Oxhey WD19 ....22 D6
Capella Ho SE7 ....143 B6
Capel Lo
5 Richmond TW9 ....132 B4
12 Streatham SW2 ....160 B4
Capel Point E7 ....77 B4
Capel Rd E7,E12 ....77 C4
East Barnet EN4 ....14 C5
Capener's Cl SW1 ....248 A1
Cape Rd N17 ....52 A6
Capern Rd SW18 ....158 A3
Capital Bsns Ctr HA0 ....87 D5
Capital Ind Est
Belvedere DA17 ....125 D3
Mitcham CR4 ....202 D4
Capital Interchange Way
TW8 ....110 C1
Capital Wharf 13 E1 ....118 A5
Capitol Way NW9 ....45 A6
Capland Ho NW8 ....236 D6
Capland St NW8 ..92 B3 236 D6
Caplan Est CR4 ....181 C2
Caple Ho SW10 ....266 B4
Caple Rd NW10 ....89 D5
Capper St WC1 ...93 C3 239 B5
Caprea Cl UB4 ....84 D2
Capricorn Ctr RM8 ....59 B2
Capri Ho E17 ....35 B1
Capri Rd CR0 ....205 D2
Capstan Cl RM6 ....58 B3
Capstan Ho 5 E14 ....120 A2
Capstan Rd SE8 ....119 B2
Capstan Ride EN2 ....4 C3
Capstan Sq E14 ....120 A4
Capstan Way SE16 ....119 A5
Capstone Rd BR1 ....186 D6
Capthorne Ave HA2 ....41 B1
Capuchin Cl HA7 ....25 B4
Capulet Mews 1 E16 ...121 A5
Capworth St E10 ....53 D2
Caradoc Cl W2 ....91 C1
Caradoc Evans Cl 1 N11 .31 B5
Caradoc St SE10 ....120 C1
Caradon Ct E11 ....54 C1
7 Twickenham TW1 ....153 C5
Caradon Way N15 ....51 B5
Caranday Villas 5 W11 .112 D5
Caravel Cl E14 ....119 C3
Caravelle Gdns 1 UB5 ...84 D4
Caravel Mews 14 SE8 ...141 C6
Caraway Cl E13 ....99 B2
Caraway Hts E14 ....120 A6
Caraway Pl SM6 ....219 B5
Carberry Rd 12 SE19 ....183 C4
Carbery Ave W3 ....110 B4
Carbis Cl E4 ....20 B3
Carbis Rd E14 ....97 B1
Carbroke Ho 10 E9 ....96 C6
Carburton St W1 ..93 B3 238 D5
Cardale St 1 E14 ....120 A3
Cardamom Ct 7 E12 ....78 C4
Carden Rd SE15 ....140 B2
Cardiff Ho 9 SE15 ....140 A6
Cardiff Rd Ealing W7 ....109 A3
Enfield EN3 ....6 B1
Cardiff St SE18 ....145 C5
Cardigan Ct 3 W7 ....86 D3
Cardigan Gdns IG3 ....80 A6
Cardigan Rd E3 ....97 B5
Barnes SW13 ....134 A3
Richmond TW10 ....154 A5
Wimbledon SW19 ....180 A4
Cardigan St
SE11 ....116 C1 261 A2
Cardigan Wlk 12 N1 ....73 A1
Cardinal Ave
Kingston KT2 ....176 A4
West Barnes SM4 ....201 A3
Cardinal Bourne St SE1 .262 D5
Cardinal Cap Alley SE1 ..252 A4
Cardinal Cl HA8 ....27 B3
Chislehurst BR7 ....189 B2
West Barnes SM4 ....201 A3
Worcester Park KT19,KT4 .216 A4
Cardinal Cres KT3 ....177 A1
Cardinal Dr KT12 ....194 D1
Cardinal Hinsey Cl NW10 .90 A5
Cardinal Hinsley RC High Sch
(Boys) NW10 ....90 A6
Cardinal Pl SW15 ....134 D1
Cardinal Pole RC Sch E9 .75 A3
E9 ....74 D1
Cardinal Rd
Feltham TW13 ....150 B3
Ruislip HA4 ....40 D1
Cardinal Road Inf Sch
TW13 ....150 B3
Cardinals Way N19 ....49 D1
Cardinal's Wlk
Ashford TW16 ....171 C4
Hampton TW12 ....174 A3
Cardinal Vaughan Memorial
Sch W14 ....244 A2
Cardinal Way HA3 ....42 C6
Cardinal Wiseman RC High
Sch UB6 ....86 A3
Cardinal Wiseman RC Sch
The UB6 ....86 A2
Cardine Mews SE15 ....140 B5
Cardington Sq TW4 ....128 D1
Cardington St
NW1 ....93 C4 232 B1
Cardozo Rd N7 ....72 A3
Cardrew Ave N12 ....30 B5
Cardrew Cl N12 ....30 B5
Cardrew Ct N12 ....30 B5
Cardross St W6 ....112 B3
Cardwell Prim Sch
SE18 ....122 B2
Cardwell Rd N7 ....72 A4
Career Ct 11 SE16 ....118 D4
Carew Cl N7 ....72 B6
Carew Ct 15 SE14 ....140 D6
Carew Ho 24 SE18 ....122 B2
West Norwood SW16 ....160 C1
Carew Manor Sch SM6 ..219 D5
Carew Rd W13 ....109 C4
Ashford TW15 ....171 A4
Mitcham CR4 ....181 A1
Thornton Heath CR7 ....204 D5
Tottenham N17 ....34 A1
Wallington SM6 ....219 C2
Carew St SE5 ....139 A3
Carey Ct DA6 ....169 D6
20 SE5 ....139 A5
Carey Gdns
SW8 ....137 D4 269 C1
Carey Ho E5 ....74 B5
Carey La EC2 ....242 A2
Carey Pl SW1 ....259 C3
Carey Rd RM9 ....81 A4
Carey St WC2 ....94 B1 240 D1
Carey Way HA9 ....66 D4
Carfax Pl SW4 ....137 D1
Carfax Rd UB3 ....106 A2
Carfree Cl 3 N1 ....72 C1
Cargill Rd SW18 ....158 A3
Cargreen Pl SE25 ....205 D5
Cargreen Rd SE25 ....205 D5
Cargrey Ho 9 HA7 ....25 C5
Carholme Rd SE23 ....163 B3
Carillon Ct W5 ....109 D6
Carinthia Ct 5 SE8 ....119 A2
Carisbrook 2 N10 ....31 B1
Carisbrook Cl EN1 ....5 D4
Carisbrook Ct 1 SW16 ...160 B1
Carisbrooke Ave DA5 ....168 D3
Carisbrooke Cl HA7 ....25 D1
Carisbrooke Ct
Acton W3 ....111 A4
Belmont SM2 ....217 B1
Northolt UB5 ....85 B6
Carisbrooke Gdns SE15 .139 D5
Carisbrooke Ho TW10 ....154 C6
Carisbrooke Rd E17 ....53 A4
Bromley BR2 ....209 C5
Mitcham CR4 ....204 A5
Carleton Ave SM6 ....219 D1
Carleton Cl KT10 ....196 B1
Carleton Gdns N19 ....71 C3
Carleton Rd N7 ....71 D4
Carlile Cl E3 ....97 B5
Carlile Ho SE1 ....262 D5
Carlina Gdns IG8 ....37 B5
Carlingford Gdns CR4 ...181 A3
Carlingford Rd N15 ....50 D6
NW3 ....70 B4
West Barnes SM4 ....200 D3
Carlisle Ave EC3 ....243 C1
W3 ....89 C1
Carlisle Cl KT2 ....176 C2
Carlisle Gdns Harrow HA3 .43 D2
Redbridge IG1 ....56 A3
Carlisle Ho IG1 ....56 A3
Carlisle La SE1 ..116 B3 260 D6
Carlisle Pl N11 ....31 B6
SW1 ....115 C3 259 A5
Carlisle Prim Sch TW12 .173 D4
Carlisle Rd E10 ....53 C1
N4 ....50 C2
NW6 ....91 A6
NW9 ....45 A6
Cheam SM1 ....217 B2
Hampton TW12 ....173 D3
Carlisle St W1 ...93 D1 239 C1
Carlisle Way SW17 ....181 A5
Carlisle Wlk 6 E8 ....73 D2
Carlos Pl W1 ...115 B6 248 C5
Carlow St NW1 ....232 A4
Carlton Ave
Feltham TW14 ....150 C5
Harrow HA3 ....43 B4
Hayes UB3 ....105 C2
South Croydon CR2 ....221 C1
Southgate N14 ....15 D6
Carlton Ave E HA9 ....44 A1
Carlton Ave W HA0 ....65 B6
Carlton Cl NW3 ....69 C6
Chessington KT9 ....213 D2
Edgware HA8 ....26 C5
Northolt UB5 ....64 A3
Carlton Cres SM3 ....217 A4
Carlton Ct NW2 ....68 C2
NW6 ....91 D5
SW9 ....138 D4
Ilford IG6 ....57 B6
11 Penge SE20 ....184 B2
South Norwood SE19 ....183 D2
Carlton Dr Ilford IG6 ....57 B6
Putney SW15 ....157 A6
Carlton Gdns
SW1 ....115 D5 249 C3
Ealing W5 ....109 C6
Carlton Gn DA14 ....189 D6
Carlton Gr SE15 ....140 B4
8 SE15 ....140 B5
Carlton Hill NW8 ..92 A5 229 A4
Carlton Ho NW6 ....91 C5
8 NW6 ....91 B5
W1 ....237 D2
Cheam SM1 ....217 B2
Edmonton N21 ....17 A3
Hounslow TW4 ....151 C5
Carlton House Terr
SW1 ....115 D5 249 D4
Carlton Lo N4 ....50 C2
Carlton Mans N16 ....51 D1
7 NW6 ....69 C1
SW9 ....138 C1
W14 ....244 B2
W9 ....91 D4
Carlton Par HA9 ....44 A1
Carlton Park Ave SW20 .178 D1
Carlton Prim Sch NW5 ...71 A3
Carlton Rd DA14 ....189 D6
DA16 ....146 B2
DA8 ....147 D6
E11 ....54 D1
E12 ....77 D4
E17 ....35 A2
N11 ....31 A5
N4 ....50 C2
W4 ....111 B4
Ashford TW16 ....171 D3
Ealing W5 ....87 C1
Kingston KT3 ....177 C1
Mortlake SW14 ....133 A1
South Croydon CR2 ....221 B1
Walton-on-T KT12 ....194 B2
Carlton Sq E1 ....96 D3
Carlton St SW1 ....249 C5
Carltons The 5 SW15 ....157 A6
Carlton Terr E7 ....77 C1
Edmonton N18 ....33 B6
Forest Hill SE26 ....162 C1
Wanstead E11 ....55 B4
Carlton Tower Pl SW1 ...257 D6
Carlton Twrs SM5 ....218 D5
Carlton Vale NW6 ....91 C5
Carlton Vale Inf Sch
NW6 ....91 B4
Carlwell St SW17 ....180 C5
Carlyle Ave BR1 ....209 D6
Southall UB1 ....107 B6
Carlyle Cl N2 ....48 A3
NW10 ....89 B6
East Molesey KT8 ....173 D1
Carlyle Ct SW6 ....265 D1
Carlyle Gdns UB1 ....107 B6
Carlyle Ho 12 N16 ....73 C5
4 SE5 ....139 A5
SW3 ....266 D6
W5 ....109 D2
Carlyle Mans SW3 ....267 A5
Carlyle Mews E1 ....96 D3
Carlyle Pl SW15 ....134 D1
Carlyle Rd E12 ....78 A4
W5 ....109 C2
Croydon CR0 ....222 A6
Woolwich SE28 ....124 C6
Carlyle's Ho* SW3 ....267 A5
Carlyle Sq SW3 ..114 B1 256 D1
Carlyon Ave HA2 ....63 C4
Carlyon Cl HA0 ....88 A6
Carlyon Ct HA0 ....88 B6
Carlyon Mans 1 HA0 ....88 A5
Carlyon Rd HA0 ....88 A6
Carlys Cl BR3 ....184 D1
Carmalt Gdns SW15 ....134 C1
Carmarthen Ct 4 W7 ....86 D3
Carmarthen Ho 8
SW15 ....156 C4
Carmarthen Pl SE1 ....253 A2
Carmel Ct W8 ....245 C2
Carmelite Cl HA3 ....24 A2
Carmelite Rd HA3 ....24 A1
Carmelite St
EC4 ....116 C6 251 B6
Carmelite Way HA3 ....24 A1
Carmelite Wlk HA3 ....24 A2
Carmen St E14 ....97 D1
Carmichael Cl 9 SW11 ..136 B2
Ruislip HA4 ....62 A4
Carmichael Ct 5 SW13 ..133 D3
Carmichael Ho 6 E14 ...120 A6
17 Dulwich SE21 ....183 C6
Carmichael Mews
SW18 ....158 B4
Carmichael Rd SE25 ....206 A5
Carminia Rd SW17 ....159 B2
Carnaby St* W1 .93 C1 239 A1
Carnac St SE21,SE27 ....161 B1
Carnanton Rd E17 ....36 B2
Carnarvon Ave EN1 ....5 D3
Carnarvon Dr UB3 ....105 A3
Carnarvon Rd E10 ....54 A4
E15 ....76 D2
Barnet EN5 ....1 A2
Woodford E18 ....36 D2
Carnation St SE2 ....124 B1
Carnbrook Rd SE3 ....143 D2
Carnecke Gdns SE9 ....166 A6
Carnegie Cl Holdbrook EN3 ..7 D5
Surbiton KT6 ....214 B6
Carnegie Ho NW3 ....70 B5
Carnegie Pl SW19 ....156 D1
Carnegie St N1 ...94 B6 233 D5
Carnforth Cl KT19 ....214 D2
Carnforth Rd SW16 ....181 D3
Carnicot Ho 9 SE15 ....140 B4
Carnoustie Cl SE28 ....102 D1
Carnoustie Dr N1 ....72 B1
Carnwath Ho SW6 ....135 D2
Carnwath Rd SW6 ....135 D2
Caroe Ct N9 ....18 B3
Carole Ho 13 SE20 ....184 B2
Carolina Cl E15 ....76 C3
Carolina Rd CR7 ....183 A2
Caroline Cl N10 ....31 B1
W2 ....245 D5
Hounslow TW7 ....130 C5
South Croydon CR0 ....221 C4
Streatham SW16 ....160 B1
Caroline Ct NW11 ....47 A3
Ashford TW15 ....170 D4
Catford SE6 ....186 B6
Stanmore HA7 ....25 A4
17 Surbiton KT6 ....197 D2
Caroline Gdns E2 ....95 C4
Caroline Ho W2 ....245 D5
20 W6 ....112 C1
Caroline Martyn Ho 8
N19 ....49 D2
Caroline Pl SW11 ....137 A3
W2 ....245 D5
Harlington UB3 ....127 C5
Caroline Pl Mews W2 ...245 D5
Caroline Rd SW19 ....179 B3
Caroline St E1 ....96 D1
Caroline Terr
SW1 ....115 A2 258 A3
Caroline Wlk W6 ....264 A5
Carol St NW1 ....93 C6 232 A6
Caronia Ct 4 SE16 ....119 A2
Carpenter Gdns N21 ....16 D2
Carpenter Ho 10 E14 ....97 C2
6 N19 ....71 D4
NW11 ....48 A3
Carpenters Bsns Pk E15 ..75 D1
Carpenters Cl EN5 ....13 D5
Carpenters Ct NW1 ....232 A6
5 Dagenham RM10 ....81 D2
Twickenham TW2 ....152 C2
Carpenter's Pl SW4 ....137 D1

Carpenters Prim Sch
E15 98 A6
Carpenter's Rd E15 75 D1
Carpenter St W1 248 C5
Carrara Wharf SW6 135 A2
Carrara Wlk 19 SW9 138 D1
Carr Gr SE18 122 A2
Carriage Dr E
SW11 137 A5 268 B4
Carriage Drive E
SW11 137 A5 268 B4
Carriage Drive N
SW11,SW8 137 A6 268 B5
Carriage Dr N
SW8,SW11 136 D5 267 C4
SW8,SW11 137 A6 268 B5
Carriage Dr S
SW11 137 A4 268 A2
Carriage Dr W
SW11 136 D5 267 C3
Carriage Mews IG1 79 A6
Carrick Cl TW7 131 A2
Carrick Gate KT10 212 A5
Carrick Gdns N17 33 C3
Carrick Ho N7 72 B2
SE11 261 C2
Carrick Mews SE8 141 C6
Carrill Way DA17 124 D3
Carrington Ave
Borehamwood WD6 10 D6
Hounslow TW3 151 D6
Carrington Cl Barnet EN5 12 A6
Borehamwood WD6 11 A6
Croydon CR0 207 A2
Carrington Ct SW11 136 C1
Carrington Gdns 4 E7 77 A4
Carrington Ho W1 248 C3
Wimbledon SW19 179 C3
Carrington Lo 3 TW10 154 A6
Carrington Pl KT10 212 A4
Carrington Rd TW10 132 C1
Carrington Sq HA3 24 A3
Carrington St W1 248 C3
Carrol Cl NW5 71 B4
Carroll Cl E15 76 D3
Carroll Ho W2 246 C6
Carronade Pl SE18 123 B3
Carron Cl E14 97 D1
Carroun Rd
SW8 138 B5 270 C4
Carroway La UB6 86 B4
Carrow Rd RM9 80 B1
Carr Rd Chingford E17 35 C1
Northolt UB5 64 A1
Carrs La N21 17 B6
Carr St E14 97 A2
Carshalton, Beddington &
Wallington War Memorial
Hospl SM5 218 D2
Carshalton Beeches Sta
SM5 218 D2
Carshalton Coll SM5 218 D5
Carshalton Gr SM1 218 B3
Carshalton High Sch for Boys
SM5 218 C6
Carshalton High Sch for Girls
SM5 218 C5
Carshalton Park Rd
SM5 218 D3
Carshalton Pl SM5 219 A3
Carshalton Rd
Mitcham CR4 203 A4
Sutton SM1,SM5 218 B3
Carshalton Sta SM5 218 D4
Carslake Rd SW15 156 C5
Carson Rd E16 99 A2
Cockfosters EN4 2 D1
Dulwich SE21 161 B2
Carstairs Rd SE6 164 A1
Carswell Cl IG4 55 D5
Carswell Rd SE6 164 A4
Carter Cl SM6 219 D1
Carter Ct EC4 241 D1
Carteret Ho 8 W12 112 B6
Carteret St SW1 249 C1
Carteret Way SE8 119 A2
Carterhatch Jun & Inf Schs
EN1 6 B4
Carterhatch La EN1 6 A4
Carterhatch Rd EN3 6 D4
Carter Ho E1 243 C3
11 SW2 160 C6
Carter La EC4 94 D1 241 D1
Carter Pl SE17 117 A1 262 B1
Carter Rd E13 99 B6
Mitcham SW19 180 B4
Carters Cl 2 NW5 71 D2
North Cheam KT4 200 D1
Carters Hill Cl SE9 165 C3
Carters Rd N2 30 C3
Carter St SE17 117 A1 262 A1
Carter's Yd SW18 157 C6
Carthew Rd W6 112 B3
Carthew Villas W6 112 B3
Carthusian St EC1 242 A4
Cartier Circ E14 120 A5
Carting La WC2 116 A6 250 B5
Cart La E4 20 C3
Cartmel NW1 232 A2
Cartmel Cl N17 34 B3
Cartmel Ct
Beckenham BR2 186 C1
Northolt UB5 63 A2
Cartmel Gdns SM4 202 A4
Cartmel Rd DA7 147 C4
Carton Ho 2 NW2 68 A5
4 SE16 118 A3
Carton Ho *continued*
12 W11 112 D6
Cartwright Gdns
WC1 94 A4 233 A1
Cartwright Ho SE1 262 B5
Cartwright Rd RM9 81 B1
Cartwright St
E1 117 D6 253 D5
Cartwright Way SW13 134 B5
Carvel Ho E14 120 A1
Carver Cl 15 W4 111 A3
Carver Rd SE24 161 A5
Carville Cres TW8 110 A2
Caryl Ho 6 SW19 156 D3
Cary Rd E11 76 C5
Carysfort Rd N16 73 B4
N8 49 D4
Casby Ho 7 SE16 118 A3
Cascade Ave N10 49 C5
Cascade Cl IG9 21 D2
Cascade Rd IG9 21 D2
Casella Rd SE14 140 D5
Casewick Rd SE27 182 D6
Casey Cl NW8 92 C4 230 B1
Casimir Rd E5 74 C5
Casino Ave SE24 161 B6
Caspian Ho 7 E1 96 D2
Caspian St SE5 139 B5
Caspian Wlk E16 99 D1
Cassandra Cl UB5 64 B4
Cassanora Ct NW2 68 C2
Casselden Rd NW10 67 B1
Cassel Hospl TW10 175 D6
Cassell Ho 21 SW9 138 A3
Casserley Ho W4 111 B3
Cass Ho 23 E9 74 D2
Cassidy Rd SW6 265 A3
Cassilda Rd SE2 124 A2
Cassilis Rd TW1 153 B5
Cassinghurst SE24 161 B6
Cassiobury Ave TW14 149 D4
Cassiobury Rd E17 53 A4
Cassland Rd E9 74 D2
South Norwood CR7 205 B5
Casslee Rd SE6 163 B4
Cassocks Sq TW17 193 B2
Casson Ho 10 E1 96 A2
Casson St E1 96 A2
Castalia Sq 6 E14 120 A4
Castellain Mans W9 91 D3
Castellain Rd W9 91 D3
Castellane Cl HA7 24 D3
Castell Ho 11 SE8 141 C5
Castello Ave SW15 156 C6
Castelnau SW13 134 B5
Casterbridge NW6 91 D6
3 W11 91 C1
Casterbridge Rd SE3 143 A2
Casterton St E8 74 B2
Castile Rd SE18 122 C2
Castilion Prim Sch
SE28 102 C1
Castillon Rd SE6 164 C2
Castlands Rd SE6 163 B2
Castleacre W2 237 A1
Castle Ave Chingford E4 36 B5
Yiewsley UB7 104 B6
Castlebar Ct 5 W5 87 C2
Castlebar Hill W5 87 C2
Castlebar Mews W5 87 C2
Castle Bar Park Sta W7 86 D2
Castlebar Pk W5 87 B2
Castlebar Rd W5 87 C1
Castlebar Sch W13 87 A2
Castle Baynard St
EC4 117 A6 252 A6
Castlebrook Cl
SE11 116 D2 261 C4
Castle Cl E9 75 A3
W3 110 D4
Ashford TW16 171 C3
Beckenham BR2 208 C6
Wimbledon SW19 156 D1
Castlecombe Dr SW19 156 D4
Castlecombe Prim Sch
SE9 188 A5
Castlecombe Rd SE9 188 A6
Castle Ct EC3 242 D1
Belmont SM2 217 C2
Forest Hill SE26 185 A6
Morden SM4 202 B4
Castleden Ho NW6 70 B1
Castledine Rd SE20 184 B3
Castle Dr IG4 56 A3
Castleford Ave SE9 166 D3
Castleford Cl N17 33 D4
Castleford Ct NW8 236 D6
Castlefrank Ho 21 N1 95 C4
Castlegate TW9 132 B2
Castlehaven Rd NW1 71 B1
Castle Hill Ave CR0 224 A1
Castle Hill Prim Sch
CR0 224 A2
Castle Ho SE1 262 A4
SW8 270 B4
10 Belmont SM2 217 C1
3 Chingford E4 36 B5
Castleigh Ct EN2 17 B6
Castle Ind Est SE17 262 A4
Castle La SW1 115 C3 259 A6
Castlemaine 8 SW11 136 D3
Castlemaine Ave CR2 221 D3
Castle Mead SE5 139 A5
Castle Mews N12 30 A5
NW1 71 B2
Castlenau Gdns SW13 134 B6
Castlenau Mans SW13 134 B6
Castlenau Row SW13 134 B6
Castle Par KT17 216 A1
Castle Pl 8 W4 111 C2
Castle Point 3 E13 99 C5
Castle Rd N12 30 B5
NW1 71 B2
Dagenham RM9 102 B6
Enfield EN3 7 A5
Isleworth TW7 130 D3
Northolt UB5 63 D1
Southall UB2 107 B3
Castlereagh St W1 237 C2
Castle St E6 99 C5
Kingston KT2 176 A1
Castleton Ave HA9 66 A4
Castleton Cl CR0 207 A3
Castleton Ct KT5 198 B4
Castleton Gdns HA9 66 A5
Castleton Ho 2 E14 120 A2
Castleton Rd SE12,SE9 187 D6
Chingford E17 36 B1
Ilford IG3 58 B1
Mitcham CR4 203 D5
Ruislip HA4 40 D1
Castletown Rd
W14 113 A1 254 B1
Castleview Cl N4 73 A6
Castle View Gdns IG1 56 B3
Castle Way
Feltham TW13 172 C6
Wimbledon SW19 156 D1
Castle Wlk TW16 194 C6
Castlewood Day Hospl
SE18 144 C4
Castlewood Dr SE9 144 B3
Castlewood Rd N16 52 A3
Barnet EN4 2 B2
Castle Yd N6 49 A2
SE1 251 D4
17 Richmond TW10 153 D6
Castor La E14 119 D6
Catalina Rd TW6 126 C2
Caterham Rd SE13 142 B2
Catesby Ho 25 E9 74 C1
Catesby St SE17 117 B2 262 D3
Catford Br SE6 163 C4
Catford Bridge Sta SE6 163 C4
Catford Broadway SE6 163 D4
Catford Girls' Sch SE6 164 A1
Catford Gyratory SE6 163 D4
Catford Hill SE6 163 C3
Catford Rd SE6 163 C4
Catford Sta SE6 163 C4
Cathall Rd E11 76 B5
Cathay Ho SE16 118 B4
Cathay St 9 SE16 118 B4
Cathay Wlk UB5 85 C5
Cathcart Dr BR6 211 C1
Cathcart Hill N19 71 C5
Cathcart Rd
SW10 136 A6 266 A6
Cathcart St NW5 71 B2
Cathedral Ct EC4 241 D1
Cathedral Sch of St Saviour
& St Mary Overie Prim Sch
SE1 117 A4 252 B2
Cathedral St
SE1 117 B5 252 C4
Catherall Rd N5,N16 73 A5
Catherine Baird Ct 12
SW12 159 B4
Catherine Ct 1 Ilford IG2 57 A3
2 Southgate N14 15 C6
3 Wimbledon SW19 179 B5
Catherine Dr
Ashford TW16 171 D4
Richmond TW9 132 A1
Catherine Gdns TW3 130 B1
Catherine Godfrey Ho
RM9 103 B6
Catherine Gr SE10 141 D4
Catherine Griffiths Ct
EC1 241 B6
Catherine Ho 16 N1 95 C6
Isleworth TW7 131 B4
Catherine Pl
SW1 115 C3 259 A6
Harrow HA1 42 D4
Catherine Rd Enfield EN3 7 A6
Kingston KT6 197 D4
Catherine St
WC2 116 B6 250 C6
Catherine Wheel Alley
E1 243 B3
Catherine Wheel Rd
TW8 131 D5
Catherine Wheel Yd
SW1 249 A3
Catherwood Ct N1 235 C3
Cat Hill EN4 14 D6
Cathles Rd SW12 159 B5
Cathnor Rd W12 112 B4
Catisfield Rd EN3 7 A6
Catlin Cres TW17 193 B4
Catling Cl SE23 162 D1
Catlin's La HA5 40 B5
Catlin St SE16 118 B1
Catman Ho N4 50 B1
Caton Ct BR2 186 C1
Cato Rd SW4 137 D1
Cator La BR3 185 B2
Cator Park Sch for Girls
BR3 185 A3
Cator Rd
Penge SE20,SE26 184 D5
Wallington SM5 218 D3
Cator St SE15 139 D5
SE15 139 D6
Cato St W1 92 C1 237 B2
Catsey La WD23 8 A4
Catsey Wood WD23 8 A4
Catterick Cl N11 31 A4
Cattistock Rd SE9 188 B5
Cattley Cl EN5 1 A1
Catton St WC1 240 C3
Caughley Ho SE11 261 A5
Caulfield Ct 12 NW1 71 C1
Caulfield Rd E6 78 B1
SE15 140 B3
Causeway TW14,TW4 128 B1
Causeway The N2 48 C5
SW18 157 D6
Carshalton SM5 219 A6
Chessington KT9 214 A4
Claygate KT10 212 D1
Teddington TW11 174 D4
Wimbledon SW19 178 C5
Causeyware Rd N9 18 C4
Causton Cotts 3 E14 97 A1
Causton Ho SE5 139 A5
Causton Rd N6 49 B2
Causton Sq RM10 81 C1
Causton St SW1 115 D1 259 D2
Cautley Ave SW4 159 C6
Cavalier Cl RM6 58 D5
Cavalier Gdns UB3 83 B1
Cavalry Cres TW4 128 D1
Cavalry Gdns SW15 157 B6
Cavan Pl HA5 23 B2
Cavaye Ho SW10 266 B6
Cavaye Pl SW10 256 B1
Cavell Dr EN2 4 C3
Cavell Ho 8 N1 95 C6
Cavell Rd N17 33 B3
Cavell St E1 96 B2
Cavendish Ave DA16 145 D2
N3 29 C1
NW8 92 B5 229 D3
Ealing W13 87 A1
Harrow HA1 64 C4
Ruislip HA4 62 B3
Sidcup DA15 168 A4
West Barnes KT3 200 B5
Woodford IG8 37 B3
Cavendish Cl NW6 69 B2
NW8 92 B4 229 D2
Ashford TW16 171 D4
Edmonton N18 34 B5
Hayes UB4 83 C2
3 Putney SW15 157 A6
Cavendish Cres
Borehamwood WD6 10 C6
Borehamwood WD6 10 C6
Cavendish Ct EC2 243 B2
Ashford TW16 171 D4
5 Chingford E4 20 C4
Cavendish Dr E11 54 B1
Claygate KT10 212 C3
Edgware HA8 26 B4
Cavendish Gdns SW4 159 C5
Barking IG11 79 D3
Dagenham RM6 59 A4
Ilford IG1 56 C1
Cavendish Ho N12 30 A6
NW8 229 D3
SW8 270 A2
Twickenham TW1 153 A5
Cavendish Mans E5 74 C3
EC1 241 A5
8 NW6 69 C3
2 SW12 159 C5
Cavendish Mews N W1 238 D4
Cavendish Mews S W1 238 D3
Cavendish Par
Balham SW12 159 B5
Hounslow TW4 129 A3
Cavendish Pl W1 238 D2
Cavendish Prim Sch
W4 133 C5
Cavendish Rd N4 50 D3
NW6 69 B1
SW12 159 C5
Ashford TW16 171 D4
Chingford E4 36 A4
Chiswick W4 133 A4
Edmonton N18 34 B5
Mitcham SW19 180 C3
New Malden KT3 199 D5
Sutton SM2 218 A1
Thornton Heath CR0 204 D1
Cavendish Sch The
NW1 93 B6 231 D6
Cavendish Sq W1 93 B1 238 D2
Cavendish St N1 95 B5 235 C3
Cavendish Terr 10 E3 97 B4
Feltham TW13 150 A2
Cavendish The NW11 47 D2
Cavendish Way BR4 207 D1
Cavenham Gdns IG1 79 B5
Cave Rd E13 99 B4
Richmond TW10 175 C6
Caverleigh Way KT4 200 B2
Caverley Gdns HA3 43 D2
Caversham Ave
Cheam SM3 217 A6
Palmers Green N13 16 C1
Caversham Ct N11 15 A1
Caversham Ho N15 51 A5
7 SE15 140 A6
8 Kingston KT1 176 A1
Caversham Rd N15 51 A5
NW5 71 C2
Kingston KT1 176 B1
Caversham St
SW3 136 D6 267 C6
Caverswall St W12 90 C1
Caveside Cl BR7 188 C2
Cavour Ho SE17 261 D2
Cawdor Cres W7 109 A2
Cawnpore St SE19 183 C5
Cawston Ct 6 BR1 186 D3
Caxton Gr E3 97 C4
Caxton Hall SW1 259 C6
Caxton Rd W12 112 D4
Southall UB2 106 D3
Wimbledon SW19 180 A5
Wood Green N22 32 B1
Caxton St SW1 115 D3 259 C6
Caxton St N E16 98 D1
Caxton Trad Est UB3 105 C5
Cayford Ho 1 NW3 70 D3
Caygill Cl BR2 208 D5
Cayley Cl SM6 220 A1
Cayley Prim Sch E14 97 A1
Cayley Rd UB2 107 D3
Cayton Pl EC1 235 C1
Cayton Rd UB6 86 C5
Cayton St EC1 235 C1
Cazenove Mans 1 N16 74 A6
Cazenove Rd N16 74 A6
Chingford E17 35 C2
Cearns Ho E6 99 D6
Cecil Ave Barking IG11 79 B1
Enfield EN1 5 D1
Wembley HA9 66 B3
Cecil Cl Chessington KT9 213 D4
Ealing W5 87 D2
Littleton TW15 171 A3
Cecil Ct NW6 69 D1
SW10 266 A6
WC2 250 A5
12 Croydon CR0 221 D6
Ealing W5 87 D2
Cecile Pk N8 50 A3
Cecil Ho 6 E5 74 C6
Chingford E17 35 C2
Cecilia Cl N2 48 A6
Cecilia Rd E8 74 A3
Cecil Lo KT9 213 D4
Cecil Mans 2 SW17 159 A2
Cecil Pk HA5 41 A5
Cecil Pl CR4 202 D4
Cecil Rd E11 76 C5
E13 99 A6
N10 31 B1
N14 15 C3
NW10 89 C6
NW9 45 C6
W3 89 A2
Ashford TW15 171 A4
Cheam SM1,SM2 217 B2
Chingford E17 35 C2
Dagenham RM6 58 D2
Enfield EN2 5 B1
Harrow HA3 42 C6
Hounslow TW3 130 A3
Ilford IG1 78 D4
Merton SW19 179 D3
Thornton Heath CR0 204 B3
Cecil Rhodes Ho NW1 232 C4
Cecil Rosen Ct HA0 65 B5
Cecil Way BR2 209 A1
Cedar Ave Dagenham RM6 59 A4
East Barnet EN4 14 C4
Enfield EN3 6 C3
Hayes UB3 84 A1
Ruislip HA4 62 C3
Sidcup DA15 168 A4
Twickenham TW2 152 A5
Yiewsley UB7 104 B6
Cedar Cl Bow E3 97 B6
Buckhurst Hill IG9 21 D2
East Molesey KT8 196 C5
Keston Mark BR2 226 A5
Kingston KT2 177 B6
Wallington SM5 218 D2
West Norwood SE21 161 A2
Cedar Copse BR1 188 B1
Cedar Cres BR2 226 A5
Cedarcroft Rd KT9 214 B4
Cedar Ct HA8 11 A1
1 N10 31 B1
N1 73 A1
5 N11 31 C5
N20 14 B3
N3 29 C3
19 SE7 143 C6
W1 237 B2
7 Brentford TW8 131 D6
Eltham SE9 166 A5
Mortlake SW14 133 A1
Stoneleigh KT17 216 A1
3 Sutton SM2 218 A2
6 Wanstead E11 55 B4
Wimbledon SW19 156 D1
5 Woodford E18 37 A2
Cedar Dr N2 48 C5
Pinner HA5 23 C4
Cedar Gdns SM2 218 A2
Cedar Gr DA5 168 D5
W5 110 A3
Southall UB1 85 C2
Cedar Grange 10 EN1 17 C6
Cedar Ho 5 E14 120 A4
SE14 140 D4
16 SE16 118 D4
W8 255 C6
Ashford TW16 171 D3
Hayes UB4 84 C3
New Addington CR0 223 D2
Wood Green N22 32 C2
Cedar Hts NW2 69 B2
Richmond TW10 154 A3
Cedarhurst Dr SE9 165 C6
Cedar Lawn Ave EN5 13 A6
Cedar Lo SW6 134 D4
Cedarmore Ct BR7 189 A2
Cedar Mount SE9 165 D3
Cedarne Rd
SW6 135 D5 265 C3
Cedar Park Gdns RM6 58 D2
Cedar Park Rd EN2 5 A5
Cedar Pl 3 SE7 121 C1
Cedar Rd BR1 187 C1
NW2 68 C4
Cranford TW5 128 C3
Croydon CR0 221 C6
East Bedfont TW14 149 B3
East Molesey KT8 196 C5
Enfield EN2 5 A5
Sutton SM2 218 A2
Tottenham N17 33 D2
Cedar Rise N14 15 A4
Cedars Ave E17 53 C4
Mitcham CR4 203 A6
Cedars Cl NW4 46 D6
SE13 142 B2
Cedars Ct Edmonton N9 17 D2
Putney SW15 156 A5
Cedars Dr UB10 82 C5
Cedars Fst & Mid Schs
HA3 24 A2
Cedars Ho 15 E17 53 D6
21 SW2 138 B1
5 West Norwood SW27 182 D5
Cedars Mews SW4 137 B1
Cedars Prim Sch The
TW5 128 A5
Cedars Rd E15 76 C2
SW4 137 B1
W4 111 C1
Barnes SW13 134 A3
Beckenham BR3 185 B1
Edmonton N21 16 D2
4 Edmonton N9 18 A2
Morden SM4 201 C5
Teddington KT8 175 C2
Wallington CR0 220 A4
Cedars The E9 74 D1
Buckhurst Hill IG9 21 A3
Ealing W13 87 C1
4 Kingston KT2 176 D2
Teddington TW11 174 D4
Wallington SM6 219 C4
Cedar Terr
9 Dagenham RM8 58 D2
Richmond TW9 132 A1
Cedar Tree Ct SE5 139 A4
Cedar Tree Gr SE27 182 D5
Cedarville Gdns SW16 182 B4
Cedar Way NW1 71 D1 232 C6
Ashford TW16 171 C3
Cedar Wlk KT10 212 D2
Cedarwood BR3 185 B3
Cedarwood Ho EN2 4 D3
Cedra Ct N16 52 A1
Cedric Chambers NW8 236 C6
Cedric Rd SE9 167 A1
Celadon Cl EN3 7 A2
Celandine Cl E3,E14 97 C2
Celandine Dr E8 73 D1
Woolwich SE28 124 B5
Celandine Way E15 98 C4
Celbridge Mews W2 91 D1
Celendine Ct E4 19 D1
Celestial Gdns SE13 142 B1
Celia Ct 7 TW9 132 B4
Celia Ho 10 N1 95 C5
Celia Rd N19 71 C4
Celtic Ave BR2 208 C6
Celtic St E14 97 D2
Cemetery La
Lower Halliford TW17 192 D2
Woolwich SE7 144 A6
Cemetery Rd E7 76 D4
Tottenham N17 33 C3
Woolwich SE2 146 B5
Cenacle Cl NW3 69 C5
Cenotaph★ SW1 250 A2
Centaur Ct 3 TW8 110 A1
Centaurs Bsns Pk TW7 131 A6
Centaur St SE1 116 B3 260 D6
Centenary Rd EN3 7 B1
Centennial Ave WD6 9 C4
Centennial Ct WD6 9 C4
Centennial Pk HA7,WD6 9 C4
Central Ave DA16 146 A3
E11 76 B6
N2 30 B1
N2 47 D6
SW11 136 D5 267 D3
East Molesey KT8 195 B4
Edmonton N9 17 D1
Enfield EN1 6 B3
Hayes UB3 106 A6
Isleworth TW3,TW7 130 A1
Pinner HA5 41 B2
Wallington SM6 220 A3
Central Bsns Ctr NW10 67 C3
Central Cir NW4 46 B4
Central Criminal Court (Old
Bailey)★ EC4 94 D1 241 D2
Central Ct 2 SE18 122 D2
Centrale Ctr CR0 221 A6
Central Foundation Lower
Sch E3 97 A4
Central Foundation Sch
EC2 95 B3 242 D6
Central Foundation Upper
Sch E3 97 B4
Central Gdns SM4 201 D4
Central Hill SE19 183 B4
Central Mans 8 NW4 46 B4
Central Middlesex Hospl
NW10 89 A4
Central Par 8 E17 53 C5
W3 110 D4
Ealing UB6 87 A4
Enfield EN3 6 C3
Feltham TW14 150 C4
Harrow HA1 42 D4
Heston TW5 129 C5
Ilford IG2 57 B3

Central Par continued
Penge SE20 ....184 D3
Surbiton KT6 ....198 A3
Central Park Ave RM10 ..81 D5
Central Park Prim Sch
E6 ....99 D5
Central Park Rd E6 ....99 D5
Central Par Villas BR5 ..190 C1
Central Pk Est TW4 ....128 D1
Central Public Health Laboratories NW9 ....45 C6
Central Rd Morden SM4 ..201 D4
Wembley HA0 ....65 B3
Worcester Park KT4 ....216 A6
Central Sch of Speech & Drama The NW3 ....70 B1
Central School of Ballet
EC1 ....94 C3 241 B5
Central Sq NW11 ....47 D3
East Molesey KT8 ....195 B5
4 Wembley HA9 ....66 A3
Central St EC1 ....95 A4 235 A1
Central St Martins Coll of Art & Design (The London Inst)
WC1 ....94 B2 240 C3
Central St Martin's Sch of Art & Design W1 ....93 D1 239 D1
Central Terr BR3 ....206 D6
Central Way NW10 ....89 A4
SE28 ....124 B6
Feltham TW14 ....150 B6
Sutton SM5 ....218 C1
Centre Ave N2 ....30 C1
NW10 ....90 C4
W3 ....111 B5
Centre Bldg SE17 ....262 B4
Centre Common Rd
BR7 ....189 A3
Centre Ct N20 ....14 B2
Centre Dr E7 ....77 C4
Centre Hts 5 NW3 ....70 B1
Centre Point 3 SE1 ....118 A1
Centre Rd
Dagenham RM10 ....103 D5
Wanstead E7,E11 ....77 A6
Centre St E2 ....96 B5
Centre The
Feltham TW13 ....150 B2
Walton-on-T KT12 ....193 D1
Centre Way N9 ....18 D2
Centreway IG1 ....79 A6
Centurian Way DA18 ....125 C3
Centurion Cl N7 ....72 B1
Centurion Ct SM6 ....219 B6
Centurion Ho 2 RM10 ....81 D2
Centurion La E3 ....97 B5
Century Cl NW4 ....46 D4
Century Ho SE13 ....141 D3
Wembley HA9 ....66 B6
Century Rd E17 ....53 A6
Century Yd SE23 ....162 C2
Cephas Ave E1 ....96 C3
Cephas Ho 8 E1 ....96 C3
Cephas St E1 ....96 C3
Ceres Rd SE18 ....123 D2
Cerise Rd SE15 ....140 A4
Cerne Cl UB4 ....106 C6
Cerne Rd SM4 ....202 A3
Cerney Mews W2 ....246 C6
Cervantes Ct 11 W2 ....91 D1
Ceylon Rd W14 ....254 A5
6 W14 ....112 D3
Chace Com Sch EN1 ....5 C4
Chadacre Ave IG5 ....56 B6
Chadacre Ho 10 SW9 ....138 D1
Chadacre Rd KT17 ....216 B3
Chadbourn St E14 ....97 D2
Chadbury Ct NW7 ....28 A2
Chad Cres N9 ....18 C1
Chadd Dr BR1 ....210 A6
Chadd Gn E13 ....99 A6
Chadston Ho 17 N1 ....72 D1
Chadswell WC1 ....233 B1
Chadview Ct 2 RM6 ....58 D2
Chadville Gdns RM6 ....58 D4
Chadway RM8 ....58 C1
Chadwell Ave RM6 ....58 B2
Chadwell Heath Foundation Sch The RM6 ....58 B3
Chadwell Heath Hospl
RM6 ....58 B4
Chadwell Heath Ind Pk
RM8 ....58 D1
Chadwell Heath La RM6 ..58 C3
Chadwell Heath Sta RM6 ..58 D2
Chadwell Prim Sch RM6 ..58 C2
Chadwell St EC1 ..94 C4 234 B2
Chadwick Ave
Chingford E4 ....36 B6
Wimbledon SW19 ....179 C4
Chadwick Cl 12 Ealing W7 .86 D2
Roehampton SW15 ....
Teddington TW11 ....175 A4
Chadwick Ct 4 SE28 ....124 B5
Chadwick Pl KT6 ....197 C3
Chadwick Rd E11 ....54 D3
NW10 ....89 D6
SE15 ....139 D3
Ilford IG1 ....78 D5
Chadwick St
SW1 ....115 D3 259 C5
Chadwick Way SE28 ....124 D6
Chadwin Rd E13 ....99 B2
Chadworth Ho EC1 ....235 A1
N4 ....51 A1
Chadworth Way KT10 ....212 B3
Chaffey Ho 6 SE7 ....121 C1
Chaffinch Ave CR0 ....206 D3
Chaffinch Cl N9 ....18 D3
Croydon CR0 ....206 D3
Chaffinch Cl continued
Tolworth KT6 ....214 C5
Chaffinch Rd BR3 ....185 A2
Chafford Way RM6 ....58 C5
Chagford Ct SW19 ....180 C3
Chagford Ho 33 E3 ....97 D4
NW1 ....237 C5
Chagford St NW1 .92 D3 237 D5
Chailey Ave EN1 ....5 D3
Chailey Cl TW5 ....128 D4
Chailey Ind Est UB3 ....106 A4
Chailey St E5 ....74 C5
Chalbury Ho 8 SW9 ....138 B1
Chalbury Wlk N1 ....234 A4
Chalcombe Rd SE2 ....124 B3
Chalcot Cl SM2 ....217 C1
Chalcot Cres
NW1 ....92 D6 230 D6
Chalcot Gdns NW3 ....70 D2
Chalcot Mews SW16 ....160 A1
Chalcot Rd NW1 ..93 A6 231 A6
Chalcot Sch NW1 ....71 B1
Chalcot Sq NW1 ....71 A1
Chalcott Gdns KT6 ....197 C1
Chalcroft Rd SE13 ....164 C6
Chaldon Rd
SW6 ....135 A5 264 B4
Chale Rd SW2 ....160 A5
Chalet Ct CR7 ....204 D4
Chalfont Ave HA9 ....66 D2
Chalfont Ct NW1 ....237 D5
NW9 ....45 D6
3 Belvedere DA17 ....125 C1
12 Harrow HA1 ....42 D3
Chalfont Gn N9 ....17 C1
Chalfont Ho NW10 ....67 B5
2 SE16 ....118 B3
Chalfont Rd Edmonton N9 .17 D1
Hayes UB3 ....106 A4
South Norwood SE25 ....205 D6
Chalfont Way W13 ....109 B3
Chalfont Wlk 3 HA5 ....22 C1
Chalford 7 NW3 ....70 A2
Chalford Cl KT8 ....195 C5
Chalford Ct Ilford IG2 ....56 D4
15 Putney SW15 ....156 D5
Surbiton KT6 ....198 B2
Chalford Rd SE21 ....183 B6
Chalford Wlk IG8 ....37 D3
Chalgrove Ave SM4 ....201 C4
Chalgrove Gdns N3 ....47 A6
Chalgrove Prim Sch N3 ..47 A6
Chalgrove Rd
Sutton SM2 ....218 B1
Tottenham N17 ....34 B2
Chalice Cl SM6 ....219 D2
Chalice Ct N2 ....48 C5
Chalkenden Cl SE20 ....184 B3
Chalkers Cnr TW9 ....132 D2
Chalk Farm Rd
NW1 ....71 A1 231 D6
Chalk Farm Sta NW3 ....71 A1
Chalkhill Prim Sch HA9 ..66 D5
Chalk Hill Rd W6 ....112 D2
Chalkhill Rd HA9 ....67 A5
Chalk La EN4 ....2 D1
Chalklands HA9 ....67 A5
Chalkley Cl CR4 ....181 A1
Chalkmill Dr EN1 ....6 B2
Chalk Pit Ave BR5 ....190 C1
Chalk Pit Rd SM1 ....218 A3
Chalk Rd E13 ....99 C2
Chalkstone Cl DA16 ....146 A4
Chalkwell Ho 9 E1 ....96 D1
Chalkwell Park Ave EN1 ....5 C1
Challenge Cl NW10 ....89 C6
Challenge Rd TW15 ....149 B1
Challenger Ho 7 E14 ....119 A6
Challice Way SW2 ....160 B3
Challiner Ct HA1 ....43 A4
Challin St 1 SE20 ....184 C2
Challis Rd TW8 ....109 D1
Challoner Cl N2 ....30 B1
Challoner Cres W14 ....254 C1
Challoner Ct BR2 ....186 B1
Challoner Mans W14 ....254 C1
Challoners Cl KT8 ....196 B5
Challoner St
W14 ....113 B1 254 C1
Chalmers Ho E17 ....53 D4
13 SW11 ....136 A2
Chalmers Rd TW15 ....170 D5
Chalmers Rd E TW15 ....171 A5
Chalmers Way TW14 ....150 B6
Chalmer's Wlk 14 SE17 ....138 D6
Chalner Ho SW2 ....160 C3
Chaloner Ct SE1 ....252 C2
Chalsey Rd SE4 ....141 B1
Chalton Dr N2 ....48 B3
Chalton St NW1 ..93 D5 232 C3
Chamberlain Cl SE18 ....123 B3
Chamberlain Cotts SE5 ..139 B4
Chamberlain Cres BR4 ..207 D1
Chamberlain Gdns TW3 ..130 A4
Chamberlain Ho 5 E1 ..118 C6
Chamberlain La HA5 ....40 A5
Chamberlain Pl E17 ....53 A6
Chamberlain Rd N2 ....30 A1
Ealing W13 ....109 A4
Edmonton N9 ....18 A2
Chamberlain St 7 NW1 ..70 D1
Chamberlain Way
Pinner HA5 ....40 B6
Surbiton KT6 ....198 A2
Chamberlain Wlk 5
TW13 ....173 A6
Chamberlayne Mans 3
NW10 ....90 D4
Chamberlayne Rd NW10 .90 C6
Chambers Gdns N2 ....30 B2
Chambers Ho 2 SW16 ..181 C6
Chambers La NW10 ....68 C1
Chambers Pl CR2 ....221 B1
Chambers Rd N7 ....72 A4
Chambers St SE16 ....118 A4
Chamber St E1 ..117 D6 253 D6
Chambon Pl 17 W6 ....112 A2
Chambord Ho 24 E2 ....95 D4
Chambord St E2 ....95 D4
Chamomile Ct E17 ....53 C3
Champion Cres SE26 ....185 A6
Champion Gr SE5 ....139 B2
Champion Hill SE5 ....139 B2
Champion Pk SE5 ....139 B3
Champion Rd SE26 ....185 A6
Champlain Ho 26 W12 ..112 B6
Champness Cl 9 SE27 ..183 B6
Champness Rd IG11 ....79 D1
Champneys Cl SM2 ....217 B1
Chancel Ct W1 ....249 C6
Chancellor Gr SE21 ....161 A1
Chancellor Ho 29 E1 ....118 B5
SW7 ....256 B6
Chancellor Pas E14 ....119 C5
Chancellor Pl NW9 ....27 D1
Chancellors' Ct WC1 ....240 C4
Chancellor's Rd W6 ....112 C1
Chancellors St W6 ....112 C1
Chancellors Wharf 21
W6 ....112 C1
Chancelot Rd SE2 ....124 B2
Chancel St SE1 ..116 D5 251 C3
Chancery Bldgs 13 E1 ....118 C6
Chancery La EC4 ..94 C1 241 A2
Beckenham BR3 ....185 D1
Chancery Lane Sta
WC1 ....94 C2 241 A3
Chance St E2 ....243 C6
Chanctonbury Cl SE9 ....166 D1
Chanctonbury Gdns
SM2 ....217 D1
Chanctonbury Way N12 ..29 C6
Chandler Ave E16 ....99 A2
Chandler Cl TW12 ....173 C2
Chandler Ct
Feltham TW14 ....150 A5
2 Tolworth KT5 ....198 D1
8 Wallington SM6 ....219 B2
Chandlers Cl TW14 ....149 D4
Chandlers Field Prim Sch
KT8 ....195 C4
Chandlers Mews E14 ....119 C4
Chandler St E1 ....118 B5
Chandlers Way 11 SE24 .160 C4
Chandler Way SE15 ....139 D5
Chandon Lo SM2 ....218 A1
Chandos Ave N14 ....15 C1
N20 ....14 B3
W5 ....109 D2
Chingford E17 ....35 C1
Chandos Cl IG9 ....21 B2
Chandos Cres HA8 ....26 C3
Chandos Ct N14 ....15 D2
Chandos Pl
WC2 ....116 A6 250 A5
Chandos Rd E15 ....76 B3
N2 ....30 C1
NW10 ....89 C3
NW2 ....68 C3
Harrow HA1 ....42 A4
Pinner HA5 ....40 D2
Tottenham N17 ....33 C1
Chandos St W1 ..93 B2 238 D3
Chandos Way NW11 ....47 D1
Change Alley EC3 ....242 D1
Channel Cl TW5 ....129 C4
Channel Ho E14 ....97 A2
Channelsea Bsns Ctr E15 .98 B5
Channing Sch N6 ....49 B1
Channon Ct 3 KT6 ....198 A4
Chantrey Cl DA14 ....191 A5
Chantrey Rd SW9 ....138 B2
Chantries The HA7 ....25 A5
Chantry Cl W9 ....91 B3
Edgware NW7 ....11 D4
Enfield EN2 ....5 A5
Harrow HA3 ....44 B4
Sunbury TW16 ....172 A3
Chantry Cres NW10 ....67 D2
Chantry Ct SW6 ....135 A2
Chantry Ct Ind Est SM5 ..218 C5
Chantry La BR2 ....209 D4
Chantry Pl HA3 ....23 D2
Chantry Rd
Chessington KT9 ....214 C3
Harrow HA3 ....23 D2
Chantry Sch UB7 ....104 A6
Chantry Sq W8 ..113 D3 255 C5
Chantry St N1 ....94 D6 234 D5
Chantry The
3 Chingford E4 ....20 A3
Hillingdon UB8 ....82 B4
Chantry Way CR4 ....202 B6
Chant Sq E15 ....76 B1
Chant St E15 ....76 B1
Chapel Cl NW10 ....67 D2
Chapel Ct 12 EC2 ....95 C4
N2 ....48 C6
SE1 ....252 C2
Hayes UB3 ....105 D6
Chapel End Ho E17 ....35 D2
Chapel End Inf Sch E17 ..35 D2
Chapel End Jun Sch E17 ..35 D2
Chapel Farm Rd SE9 ....166 B2
Chapel Hill N2 ....30 C1
Chapel House St E14 ....119 D2
Chapel La
5 Dagenham RM6 ....58 D2
Hillingdon UB8 ....82 C1
Pinner HA5 ....40 D6
Chapel Market
N1 ....94 C5 234 A4
Chapel Pl 13 EC2 ....95 C4
N1 ....234 B4
W1 ....238 C1
Tottenham N17 ....33 D3
Chapel Rd DA7 ....147 C1
Ealing W13 ....109 B5
Hounslow TW3 ....129 D2
Ilford IG1 ....78 D5
Twickenham TW1 ....153 B4
West Norwood SE27 ....182 D6
Chapel Side W2 .113 D6 245 C5
Chapel St NW1 ....92 C2 237 A3
SW1 ....115 A4 248 B1
Enfield EN2 ....5 B2
Chapel View CR2 ....222 C1
Chapel Wlk NW4 ....46 C5
Chapleton Ho SW2 ....160 C6
Chaplin Cl SE1 ....251 C2
Chaplin Cres TW16 ....171 C4
Chaplin Ho 6 SW9 ....138 C1
Chaplin Rd E15 ....98 D6
2 N17 ....51 D6
NW2 ....68 A2
Dagenham RM9 ....81 A1
Wembley HA0 ....65 D2
Chapman Cl UB7 ....104 B3
Chapman Cres HA3 ....44 B4
Chapman Gn N22 ....32 C2
Chapman Ho 26 E1 ....96 B1
2 West Norwood SE27 ....160 D1
Chapman Rd E9 ....75 B2
Belvedere DA17 ....125 D1
Thornton Heath CR0 ....204 C1
Chapmans End BR5 ....191 A1
Chapman's La BR5 ....190 D1
Chapmans Park Ind Est
NW10 ....67 D2
Chapman Sq SW19 ....156 D2
Chapman St E1 ....118 B6
Chapone Pl W1 ....239 C1
Chapter Cl 15 W4 ....111 A3
Hillingdon UB10 ....60 B1
Chapter Rd NW2 ....68 A3
SE17 ....116 D1 261 D1
Chapter St SW1 ....259 C3
Chapter Way TW12 ....173 C6
Chara Pl W4 ....133 B6
Charcot Ho 9 SW15 ....155 D5
Charcroft Ct 11 W14 ....112 D4
Charcroft Gdns EN3 ....6 D1
Chard Ho 7 N7 ....72 B6
Chardin Ho 30 SW9 ....138 C4
Chardin Rd 11 W4 ....111 C2
Chardmore Rd N16 ....52 A1
Chardwell Cl E6 ....100 B1
Charecroft Way W12 ....112 D4
Charfield Ct W9 ....91 D3
Charford Rd E16 ....99 A2
Chargeable La E13 ....99 A3
Chargeable St E16 ....98 D3
Chargrove Cl 24 SE16 ....118 D4
Charing Cl BR6 ....227 D4
Charing Cross
SW1 ....116 A5 250 A4
Charing Cross Hospl
W6 ....112 D1
Charing Cross Rd
WC2 ....93 D1 239 D1
Charing Cross Sta
WC2 ....116 A5 250 B4
Charing Ct BR2 ....186 C1
Charing Ho SE1 ....251 B2
Charlbert Ct NW8 ....230 A4
Charlbert St NW8 ..92 C5 230 A4
Charlbury Ave HA7 ....25 D5
Charlbury Gdns IG3 ....79 D6
Charlbury Gr W5 ....87 C1
Charlbury Ho 1 E12 ....78 C5
Charlbury Rd UB10 ....60 B5
Charldane Rd SE9 ....166 D1
Charlecote Gr SE26 ....162 B1
Charlecote Rd RM8 ....81 A5
Charlemont Rd E6 ....100 C4
Charles Allen Ho EC1 ....234 A2
Charles Auffray Ho 26
E1 ....96 C2
Charles Babbage Cl
KT9 ....213 C1
Charles Barry Cl SW4 ....137 C2
Charles Bradlaugh Ho 2
N17 ....34 B3
Charles Burton Ct E5 ....75 A4
Charles Cl DA14 ....190 B6
Charles Cobb Gdns CR0 .220 C3
Charles Coveney Rd 4
SE15 ....139 D4
Charles Cres HA1 ....42 B2
Charles Ct N3 ....29 C1
Charles Darwin Ho 8 E2 .96 B4
Bromley BR1 ....187 B3
Charles Dickens Ct
SE25 ....206 A5
Charles Dickens Ho 1
E2 ....96 B4
Charles Dickens Prim Sch
SE1 ....117 A4 252 A1
Charles Edward Brooke Sch
SW9 ....138 D4
Charlesfield SE12 ....165 C1
Charles Grinling Wlk
SE18 ....122 C2
Charles Haller St 25
SW2 ....160 C4
Charles Harrod Ct
SW13 ....134 C6
Charles Ho 1 N17 ....33 D3
Charles Hobson Ho
NW10 ....67 C1
Charles Hocking Ho 8
W3 ....111 A4
Charles II Pl
SW3 ....114 D1 257 C1
Charles II St
SW1 ....115 D5 249 C4
Charles La NW8 ..92 C5 230 A4
Charles Lamb Prim Sch
N1 ....95 A6 235 A6
Charles Lesser KT9 ....213 D3
Charles Mackenzie Ho 7
SE16 ....118 A2
Charles Mills Ct SW16 ....182 A4
Charles Pl NW1 ....232 B1
Charles Rd E7 ....77 C1
Dagenham RM6 ....58 D3
Ealing W13 ....87 A1
Merton SW19 ....179 C2
Charles Rowan Ho WC1 .234 A1
Charles Sevright Dr
NW7 ....28 D5
Charles Sq N1 ....95 B4 235 D1
Charles St E16 ....121 C5
W1 ....115 B5 248 C4
Barnes SW13 ....133 C3
Croydon CR0 ....221 A5
Enfield EN1 ....17 D6
Hillingdon UB10 ....82 D3
Hounslow TW3 ....129 B3
Charles Staunton Ho 3
SE27 ....183 B6
Charleston Cl TW13 ....150 A1
Charleston St SE17 ....262 B3
Charles Townsend Ho
EC1 ....241 C6
Charles Winchup Rd 2
E16 ....121 B5
Charlesworth Ho 2 E14 ..97 C1
Charleville Cir SE26 ....184 A5
Charleville Ct SW5 ....254 C1
Charleville Mans W14 ....254 B1
Charleville Rd
W14 ....113 A1 254 C1
Charlie Browns Rdbt
E18 ....37 C1
Charlmont Rd SW17 ....180 D4
Charlotte Cl DA6 ....169 A6
Charlotte Ct N8 ....49 D3
Ilford IG2 ....56 C3
5 Wembley HA0 ....66 A2
Charlotte Ho 12 W6 ....112 C1
Charlotte Mews W10 ....90 D1
W1 ....239 B4
W14 ....254 A4
Charlotte Park Ave BR1 .210 A6
Charlotte Pl SW1 ....259 A3
W1 ....239 B3
Charlotte Rd EC2 .95 C3 243 A6
Barnes SW13 ....133 D4
Dagenham RM10 ....81 D2
Wallington SM6 ....219 C2
Charlotte Row SW4 ....137 C2
Charlotte Sharman Prim Sch
SE11 ....116 D3 261 C5
Charlotte Sq 5 TW10 ....154 B5
Charlotte St W1 ..93 C2 239 B4
Charlotte Terr
N1 ....94 B6 233 D5
Charlow Cl SW6 ....136 A3
Charlton Church La
SE7 ....121 C1
Charlton Cl UB10 ....60 D6
Charlton Cres IG11 ....101 D5
Charlton Ct 25 E2 ....95 D6
E6 ....100 B4
17 N7 ....71 D3
Charlton Dene SE7 ....143 D5
Charlton Ho NW1 ....232 C2
5 Brentford TW8 ....132 A6
Charlton King's Rd NW5 ..71 D3
Charlton La SE7 ....121 D1
Upper Halliford TW17 ....193 B5
Upper Halliford TW17 ....193 C5
Charlton Lo 1 NW11 ....47 B3
Charlton Manor Prim Sch
SE7 ....143 D5
Charlton Park La SE7 ....144 A6
Charlton Park Rd SE7 ....143 D6
Charlton Park Sch SE7 ..144 A6
Charlton Pl N1 ....94 D5 234 C4
Charlton Rd N9 ....18 D4
NW10 ....89 C6
SE3,SE7 ....143 B6
Charlton TW17 ....171 A1
Harrow HA3 ....43 D5
Wembley HA9 ....44 B1
Charlton Way SE10,SE3 ..142 C4
Charlwood Cl HA3 ....24 C4
Charlwood Ho SW1 ....259 C3
1 Streatham SW2 ....160 B3
Charlwood Pl
SW1 ....115 C2 259 B3
Charlwood Rd SW15 ....134 D1
Charlwood Sq CR4 ....202 B6
Charlwood St
SW1 ....115 C1 259 B2
Charlwood Terr 5
SW15 ....134 D1
Charman Ho 18 SW2 ....160 C5
SW8 ....270 A4
Charmian Ave HA7 ....25 D1
Charmian Ho 19 N1 ....95 C5
Charminster Ave SW19 .179 D1
Charminster Ct 3 KT6 ..197 D2
Charminster Rd
SE12,SE9 ....187 D6
North Cheam KT4 ....200 D1
Charmouth Ct TW10 ....154 B6
Charmouth Ho SW8 ....270 C4
Charmouth Rd DA16 ....146 C4
Charnock Ho 22 W12 ....112 B6
Charnock Rd E5 ....74 B5
Charnwood Ave SW19 ..179 D1
Charnwood Cl KT3 ....199 C5
Charnwood Dr E18 ....55 B5
Charnwood Gdns E14 ..119 C2
Charnwood Ho 9 E5 ....74 B6
Charnwood Pl N20 ....14 A1
Charnwood Rd
Hillingdon UB10 ....82 C5
South Norwood SE25 ....205 B5
Charnwood St E5 ....74 B6
Charrington Rd 2 CR0 ..221 A6
Charrington St
NW1 ....93 D5 232 C4
Charsley Rd SE6 ....163 D2
Chart Cl Bromley BR2 ....186 C2
Croydon CR0 ....206 C3
Mitcham CR4 ....202 D5
Charter Ave IG2 ....57 B2
Charter Cres TW4 ....129 A1
Charter Ct N4 ....50 C1
W1 ....237 B3
Kingston KT3 ....199 C6
Southall UB1 ....107 C5
Charter Dr DA5 ....169 A4
Charter Ho WC2 ....240 B1
Charterhouse Ave HA0 ..65 C3
Charterhouse Bldgs
EC1 ....242 A5
Charterhouse Mews
EC1 ....241 D4
Charterhouse Rd E8 ....74 A3
Charterhouse Sq
EC1 ....94 D2 241 D4
Charterhouse Square Prim Sch The EC1 ....94 D2 241 D3
Charterhouse St EC1 ....241 C3
Charteris Rd N4 ....50 C1
NW6 ....91 B6
Woodford IG8 ....37 B4
Charter Nightingale Hospl The NW1 ....92 C2 237 B4
Charter Rd KT1 ....198 D6
Charter Rd The IG8 ....36 D4
Charter Sch The SE24 ..161 B6
Charters Cl SE19 ....183 C5
Charter Sq KT1 ....176 D1
Charter Way NW3 ....47 B5
Southgate N14 ....15 D5
Chartes Ho SE1 ....263 B6
Chartfield Ave SW15 ....156 C6
Chartfield Sch SW15 ....156 B6
Chartfield Sq SW15 ....156 D6
Chartham Ct 13 SW9 ....138 C2
Chartham Gr SE27 ....160 D1
Chartham Ho SE1 ....262 D6
Chartham Rd SE25 ....206 B6
Chart Hills Cl SE28 ....103 A1
Chartley Ave NW2 ....67 C5
Harrow HA7 ....24 D4
Charton Cl 5 DA17 ....147 B6
Chartres Ct UB6 ....86 B5
Chartridge SE17 ....139 B6
Chartridge Cl Barnet EN5 ..12 A6
Bushey WD23 ....8 A5
Chartridge Ct 6 HA7 ....25 C5
Chart St N1 ....95 B4 235 D2
Chartwell 25 SW19 ....156 D3
Chartwell Bsns Ctr BR1 .209 D6
Chartwell Cl
2 Croydon CR0 ....205 B1
Greenford UB6 ....85 D6
Sidcup BR7,DA15 ....167 B2
Chartwell Ct 8 Barnet EN5 .1 A1
2 Woodford IG8 ....37 A3
Chartwell Dr BR6 ....227 B3
Chartwell Gdns SM3 ....217 A4
Chartwell Lo 5 BR3 ....185 C3
Chartwell Pl Cheam SM3 .217 B4
Harrow HA2 ....64 B6
Chartwell Way 3 SE20 ..184 B2
Charville Ct 8 HA1 ....42 D3
Charville La UB4 ....83 C5
Charville La W UB10 ....82 D4
Charville Prim Sch UB4 ..83 C5
Charwood SW16 ....182 C6
Chase Bridge Prim Sch
TW2 ....152 C5
Chase Court Gdns EN2 ....5 A2
Chase Ct SW3 ....257 C5
Isleworth TW7 ....131 A3
Merton SW20 ....179 A1
Southgate N14 ....15 C5
Wembley HA0 ....65 D2
Chase Ctr The NW10 ....89 A4
Chase Farm Hospl EN2 ....4 C5
Chasefield Rd SW17 ....180 D6
Chase Gdns Chingford E4 .35 C6
Twickenham TW2 ....152 B4
Chase Gn EN2 ....5 A2
Chase Green Ave EN2 ....5 A3
Chase Hill EN2 ....5 A2
Chase La IG6 ....57 B4
Chase Lane Inf Sch E4 ..35 B6
Chase Lane Jun Sch E4 ..35 B6
Chaseley Ct W4 ....110 D1
Oatlands Park KT13 ....193 C1
Chaseley St E14 ....97 A1
Chasemore Cl CR4 ....202 D2
Chasemore Gdns CR0 ....220 C3
Chasemore Ho SW6 ....264 B4
Chase Rd NW10 ....89 B3
Southgate N14 ....15 D5
Chase Ridings EN2 ....4 C3

Chase Road Trad Est NW10 89 B3
Chase Side N14 15 B4
Enfield EN2 5 A3
Chaseside Ave SW20 179 A1
Chase Side Ave EN2 5 A3
Chase Side Cres EN2 5 A4
Chase Side Pl EN2 5 A3
Chase Side Prim Sch EN2 5 A3
Chase The DA7 147 D2
E12 77 D4
SW4 137 B2
Bromley BR1 209 B6
Edgware HA8 26 D2
Ickenham UB10 60 C3
Loughton IG10 21 D4
Pinner HA5 40 C3
Pinner HA5 41 B5
South Norwood SW16 182 C3
Stanmore HA7 25 A4
Sunbury TW16 172 B2
Wallington CR0,SM6 220 B3
Dagenham RM6 59 A3
Chaseville Par N21 16 B6
Chaseville Park Rd N21 16 B6
Chase Way N14 15 C3
Chasewood Ave EN2 4 D3
Chasewood Ct NW7 27 B5
Chasewood Pk HA1 64 C5
Chater Ho 6 E2 96 D4
Chatfield Rd SW11 136 A2
Thornton Heath CR0 204 D1
Chatham Ave BR2 209 A2
Chatham Cl NW11 47 C4
Cheam SM3 201 B2
Chatham Ct SW11 158 D6
Chatham Ho 22 SE18 122 B2
7 SE5 139 C3
Chatham Pl E9 74 C2
Chatham Rd E17 53 A6
SW11 158 D6
Kingston KT1,KT2 176 C1
1 Woodford E18 36 D1
Chatham St SE17 117 B2 262 D4
Chatsfield Pl W5 88 A1
Chatsworth Ave BR1 187 B6
DA15 168 A3
NW4 28 C1
Merton SW20 179 A1
Wembley HA9 66 B3
Chatsworth Cl NW4 28 C1
Coney Hall BR2,BR4 224 D6
Chatsworth Cres TW3, TW7 130 B2
Chatsworth Ct E5 74 D4
W8 255 A4
5 Stanmore HA7 25 C5
Chatsworth Dr EN1 18 A5
Chatsworth Est E5 74 D4
Chatsworth Gdns
Acton W3 110 D5
Harrow HA2 41 D1
New Malden KT3 199 D4
Chatsworth Ho 2 BR2 209 A5
Kingston KT6 197 D4
Chatsworth Inf Sch DA15 168 A3
Isleworth TW3 130 A1
Chatsworth Jun Sch TW3 130 A1
Chatsworth Lo 1 W4 111 B1
West Wickham BR4 224 A6
Chatsworth Par BR5 211 A4
Chatsworth Pl
Mitcham CR4 202 D6
Teddington TW11 175 A6
Chatsworth Rd E15 76 D3
E5 74 D4
NW2 68 D2
Cheam SM3 217 A4
Chiswick W4 133 A6
Ealing W5 88 B3
Hayes UB4 84 B3
South Croydon CR0 221 B5
Chatsworth Rise W5 88 B3
Chatsworth Way SE27 161 A1
Chattenden Ho 8 N4 51 B2
Chattern Hill TW15 170 D6
Chattern Rd TW15 171 A6
Chatterton Ct TW9 132 B3
Chatterton Rd BR2 209 D4
N4 72 D5
Chatton Ct 5 NW9 46 A5
Chatto Rd SW11 158 D6
Chaucer Ave
Cranford TW4 128 B3
Hayes UB4 84 A2
Richmond TW9 132 C3
Chaucer Cl N11 31 D5
Chaucer Ct 17 N16 73 C4
12 New Barnet EN5 13 D6
Chaucer Dr SE1 117 D2 263 D3
Chaucer Gdns SM1 217 C5
Chaucer Gn CR0 206 C2
Chaucer Ho SW1 259 A1
Harrow HA2 41 D4
Sutton SM1 217 C5
2 West Norwood SE27 183 A6
Chaucer Rd DA16 145 D4
E7 77 A2
SE24 160 D6
W3 111 A5
Ashford TW15 170 B6
Chingford E17 36 A1
Sidcup DA15 168 C3
Sutton SM1 217 C4
Chaucer Rd *continued*
Wanstead E11 55 A3
Chaucer Way SW17 180 B5
Chaulden Ho EC1 235 D1
Chauncey Cl N9 18 A1
Chaundrye Cl SE9 166 B5
Chauntler Cl E16 121 B6
Chaville Ct N11 31 A6
Cheadle Ct NW8 236 D6
Cheadle Ho 11 E14 97 B1
Cheam Common Inf Sch KT4 216 B6
Cheam Common Jun Sch KT4 216 B6
Cheam Common Rd KT4 216 C5
Cheam Court Flats 1 SM3 217 A2
Cheam Fields Prim Sch SM3 217 A3
Cheam High Sch SM3 217 A4
Cheam Mans SM3 217 A1
Cheam Park Farm Inf Sch SM3 217 A5
Cheam Park Farm Jun Sch SM3 217 A5
Cheam Park Way SM3 217 A2
Cheam Rd
Belmont SM2,SM3 216 D1
Cheam SM1 217 C2
Cheam St 4 SE15 140 B2
Cheam Sta SM2 217 A1
Cheam Village SM3 217 A2
Cheapside EC2 95 A1 242 B1
Edmonton N13 33 A6
Chearsley SE17 262 B4
Cheddar Cl N11 31 A4
Cheddar Rd TW6 126 C3
Cheddar Waye UB4 84 B1
Cheddington Ho 9 E2 96 A6
Cheddington Rd N18 33 C6
Chedworth Cl E16 98 D1
Chedworth Ho 2 E5 74 A6
N15 51 B5
Cheeseman Cl TW12 173 A4
Cheesemans Terr W14 254 C1
Chelford Rd BR1 186 B5
Chelmer Cres IG11 102 B5
Chelmer Rd E9 74 D3
Chelmsford Cl W6 134 D6
Newham E6 100 B1
Chelmsford Ct N14 15 D4
Chelmsford Gdns IG1 56 B2
Chelmsford Ho 5 N7 72 B4
Chelmsford Rd E11 54 B1
E17 53 C3
N14 15 C4
Woodford E18 36 D2
Chelmsford Sq NW10 90 C6
Chelsea Barracks★ SW1 115 A1 258 B1
Chelsea Bridge SW1 137 B6 268 C6
Chelsea Bridge Rd SW1 115 A1 258 B1
Chelsea Cl NW10 89 B6
Edgware HA8 26 C1
Hampton TW12 174 A5
New Malden KT4 200 A2
Chelsea Cloisters SW3 257 B3
Chelsea Coll of Art & Design SW3 114 C1 257 A1
W12 112 C4
Chelsea Cres SW10 266 B1
Chelsea Ct SW3 268 A6
8 Chingford E4 20 A3
Chelsea Emb SW3 136 D6 267 C5
Chelsea Est SW3 267 A5
Chelsea Farm Ho SW10 266 D5
Chelsea Fields SW19 180 B2
Chelsea Gate SW1 258 B1
Chelsea Gdns SW1 258 B1
Cheam SM3 217 A4
Ealing W13 86 D2
Chelsea Harbour Design Ctr SW10 266 B2
Chelsea Harbour Dr SW10 136 A4 266 B2
Chelsea Harbour Pier SW10 266 C1
Chelsea Lo SW3 267 D6
SW6 265 C2
Chelsea Manor Ct SW3 267 B6
Chelsea Manor Gdns SW3 257 B1
Chelsea Manor St SW3 114 C1 257 B1
Chelsea Manor Studios SW3 257 B1
Chelsea Park Gdns SW3 136 B6 266 C6
Chelsea Physic Gdn★ SW1 267 C6
Chelsea Reach Twr SW10 266 C4
Chelsea Sq SW3 114 B1 256 D1
Chelsea Twrs SW3 267 B6
Chelsea & Westminster Hospl SW10 136 A6 266 B5
Chelsfield Ave N9 18 D4
Chelsfield Gdns SE26 162 C1
Chelsfield Gn N9 18 D4
Chelsfield Ho SE17 263 A3
Chelsfield Point 3 E9 74 D1
Chelsham Ho 1 SW4 137 D2
Chelsham Rd SW4 137 D2
South Croydon CR2 221 B2
Chelsiter Ct DA14 189 D6
Chelston Ct 2 E11 55 B4
Chelston Rd HA4 40 A1
Chelsworth Dr SE18 145 B6
Cheltenham Ave 8 TW1 153 A4
Cheltenham Cl
Kingston KT3 199 A6
Northolt UB5 63 D2
Cheltenham Ct 8 HA7 25 C5
Cheltenham Gdns E6 100 A5
Cheltenham Ho UB3 105 A3
Cheltenham Pl 1 W3 110 D4
Harrow HA3 44 A5
Cheltenham Rd E10 54 A3
SE15 162 C6
Cheltenham Terr SW3 114 D1 257 D2
Cheltenham Villas CR7 204 C3
Chelverton Ct SW15 134 D1
Chelverton Rd SW15 134 D1
Chelwood N20 14 B2
NW5 71 A3
Chelwood Cl E4 19 D5
Chelwood Ct SW11 266 D2
Chelwood Gdns TW9 132 C3
Chelwood Ho W2 236 D1
Chenappa Cl E13 99 A4
Chenduit Way HA7 24 D5
Chene Colline Ct KT6 198 A3
Cheney Ct SE23 162 D3
Cheney Row E17 35 B2
Cheneys Rd E11 76 C5
Cheney St HA5 40 C4
Chenies Ho W2 245 C6
Chenies Mews WC1 239 C5
Chenies Pl NW1 232 D4
Chenies St WC1 93 D2 239 C4
Chenies The NW1 232 D4
Orpington BR5,BR6 211 C3
Cheniston Gdns W8 255 C6
Chennestone Cty Prim Sch TW16 172 B1
Chepstow Cl SW15 157 A6
Chepstow Cres W11 113 C6 245 A6
Ilford IG3 57 C3
Chepstow Ct W11 245 A6
Chepstow Gdns UB1 85 B1
Chepstow Pl W2 113 C6 245 B6
Chepstow Rd W2 91 C1
Croydon CR0 221 D6
Ealing W7 109 A3
Chepstow Rise CR0 221 C5
Chepstow Villas W11 113 C6 245 A6
Chequers IG9 21 B3
Chequers Cl NW9 45 C6
Orpington BR5 211 D5
Chequers Ct EC1 242 C5
7 Croydon CR0 205 D1
Chequers Ho NW8 237 A6
Chequers La RM9 103 C5
Chequers Par
Dagenham RM9 103 C6
Edmonton N13 33 A5
Chequer St EC1 95 A3 242 B5
Chequers The HA5 40 D6
Chequers Way N13 32 D5
Cherbury Cl SE28 102 D1
Cherbury Ct N1 235 D3
Cherbury St N1 95 B5 235 D3
Cherchefelle Mews HA7 25 B5
Cherimoya Gdns KT8 195 D6
Cherington Rd W7 108 D5
Cheriton Ave BR2 209 A4
Cheriton Cl
Cockfosters EN4 2 D1
10 Ealing W5 87 C2
Cheriton Ct 4 SE12 165 A4
South Norwood SE25 205 C4
Walton-on-T KT12 194 C1
Cheriton Dr SE18 145 B6
Cheriton Ho 9 E5 74 B3
Cheriton Sq SW17 159 A2
Cherry Ave UB1 106 D5
Cherry Blossom Cl N13 32 D5
Cherry Cl E17 53 D4
W5 109 D3
Carshalton SM5 218 D6
Merton SM4 201 A5
Ruislip HA4 61 D5
7 Streatham SW2 160 C4
Cherrycot Hill BR6 227 B4
Cherrycot Rise BR6 227 A4
Cherry Cres TW8 131 B5
Cherry Croft Gdns 2 HA5 23 B3
Cherry Ct W3 111 C5
Ilford IG6 56 D6
Pinner HA5 22 D2
Sidcup DA14 168 B1
Cherrydeal Ct E11 54 B2
Cherrydown Ave E4 19 C1
Cherrydown Cl E4 19 C1
Cherrydown Rd DA14 168 D2
Cherry Garden Ho 5 SE16 118 B4
Cherry Garden Sch SE16 118 A2
Cherry Garden St SE16 118 B4
Cherry Garth TW8 109 D1
Cherry Gdns
Dagenham RM9 81 B3
Northolt UB5 63 D1
Cherry Gr Hayes UB3 106 B5
Hillingdon UB8 83 A2
Cherry Hill
New Barnet EN5 13 D5
Stanmore HA3 24 C4
Cherry Hill Gdns CR0 220 B4
Cherry Hills WD19 23 A5
Cherry La UB7 104 C2
Cherrylands Cl NW9 67 A6
Cherry Lane Jun & Inf Schs UB7 104 B2
Cherry Laurel Wlk SW2 160 B5
Cherry Orch SE7 143 C6
West Drayton UB7 104 A4
Cherry Orchard Gdns
7 Croydon CR0 205 B1
East Molesey KT8 195 B6
5 South Croydon CR0 221 B6
Cherry Orchard Prim Sch SE7 143 C5
Cherry Orchard Rd BR2 226 A6
Croydon CR0 205 C1
East Molesey KT8 195 C6
Cherry Rd EN3 6 C5
Cherry Tree Ave UB7 82 B1
Cherry Tree Cl 17 E9 96 C6
Wembley HA0 65 A4
Cherrytree Ct NW9 45 A5
Cherry Tree Ct 17 SE7 143 C6
3 Woodford E18 36 D1
Cherry Tree Dr SW16 160 A1
Cherrytree Ho 8 W10 90 D4
Cherry Tree Ho SE14 141 B3
Cherry Tree Rd E15 76 C3
N2 48 D5
Cherry Tree Rise IG9 37 D6
Cherry Trees Sch The E3 97 C4
Cherry Tree Terr SE1 253 B2
Cherry Tree Way HA7 25 B4
Cherry Tree Wlk EC1 242 B5
Beckenham BR3 207 B5
Coney Hall BR4 224 D4
Cherry Way
Upper Halliford TW17 193 C5
West Ewell KT19 215 B2
Cherry Wlk BR2 209 A1
Cherrywood Cl E3 97 A4
Kingston KT2 176 C3
Cherrywood Ct 1 TW11 175 A5
Cherrywood Dr SW15 156 D6
Cherrywood La SM4, SW20 201 A5
Cherry Wood Way W5 88 C2
Chertsey Ct SW14 132 D2
Chertsey Dr SM3 217 A6
Chertsey Ho 37 E2 95 D4
Feltham TW13 151 C1
Chertsey Rd E11 76 B6
Ashford TW15,TW16 171 B4
Feltham TW13,TW16 171 C6
Ilford IG1 79 B4
Lower Halliford TW17 192 C2
Shepperton TW17 192 A2
Twickenham TW2 152 B4
Chertsey St SW17 181 A5
Chervil Cl TW13 150 A1
Chervil Mews SE28 124 B5
Cherwell Ct
Teddington KT1 175 D3
West Ewell KT19 215 A4
Cherwell Ho NW8 236 D5
Cherwell Way HA4 39 A3
Cheryls Cl SW6 135 D4 265 D2
Cheseman St SE26 162 B1
Chesfield Rd KT2 176 A3
Chesham Ave BR2,BR5 210 D3
Chesham Cl SW1 258 A5
Chesham Cres SE20 184 C2
Chesham Ct SW18 158 B4
Chesham Flats W1 248 B6
Chesham Mews SW1 258 A6
Chesham Pl SW1 115 A3 258 A5
Chesham Rd
Kingston KT1,KT2 176 C1
Penge SE20 184 C2
Chesham St NW10 67 B5
SW1 115 A3 258 A5
Chesham Terr W13 109 B4
Cheshire Cl
Chingford, Highams Park E17 35 D2
Mitcham CR4,SW16 204 A6
Cheshire Gdns KT9 213 D2
Cheshire Ho SM4 201 D2
Cheshire Rd N22 32 B4
Cheshire St E2 95 D3 243 D6
Cheshir Ho NW4 46 C5
Cheshold Rd N16 73 C5
Cheshunt Ho 7 NW6 91 D6
Cheshunt Rd E7 77 B2
Belvedere DA17 125 C1
Chesil Ct 18 E2 96 C5
SW3 267 B6
Chesilton Rd SW6 135 B4 264 C2
Chesil Way UB4 83 D4
Chesley Gdns E6 100 A4
Chesney Cres CR0 224 A1
Chesney Ct W9 91 C3
Chesney Ho SE13 142 B1
Chesney St SW11 268 A1
Chesnut Gr N17 51 D6
Chesnut Rd N17 51 D6
Chessell Cl CR7 204 D5
Chessholme Ct TW16 171 C3
Chessholme Rd TW15 171 A4
Chessing Ct N2 48 D6
Chessington Ave DA7 147 A5
N3 47 B6
Chessington Cl KT19 215 A2
Chessington Com Coll KT9 213 D1
Chessington Ct N3 47 B6
Pinner HA5 41 B5
Chessington Hall Gdns KT9 213 D1
Chessington Hill Pk KT9 214 C3
Chessington Ho 19 SW8 137 D3
Chessington Lo N3 47 B6
Chessington Mans E10 53 C2
E11 54 C2
Chessington North Sta KT9 214 A3
Chessington Par KT9 213 D3
Chessington Park KT9 214 C4
Chessington Pk KT9 214 C4
Chessington Rd KT19 215 B1
Chessington South Sta KT9 213 D1
Chessington Way BR4 223 D6
Chesson Rd W14 135 B6 264 D6
Chesswood Way HA5 22 D1
Chestbrook Ct 12 EN1 17 C6
Chester Ave
Richmond TW10 154 B5
Twickenham TW2 151 B3
Chester Cl SW1 248 C1
Ashford TW15 171 B5
Barnes SW13 134 B2
Hayes UB8 82 D1
1 Richmond TW10 154 B5
Sutton SM1 217 C6
Chester Close N NW1 231 D2
Chester Close S NW1 231 D1
Chester Cres E8 73 D3
Chester Ct NW1 231 D1
NW5 71 A4
4 SE5 139 B5
SE8 118 D1
2 Acton W3 88 C1
Chester Dr HA2 41 C3
Chesterfield Ct KT6 198 A4
Chesterfield Dr KT10 213 A6
Chesterfield Flats EN5 12 D6
Chesterfield Gdns N4 50 D4
SE10 142 B5
W1 248 C4
Chesterfield Gr SE22 161 D6
Chesterfield Hill W1 115 B5 248 C4
Chesterfield Ho W1 248 B4
6 Streatham SW16 181 C5
Chesterfield Jun & Inf Sch EN3 7 A6
Chesterfield Lo N21 16 B4
Chesterfield Mews N4 50 D4
Ashford TW15 170 A6
Chesterfield Rd E10 54 A3
N3 29 C4
Ashford TW15 170 A5
Barnet EN5 12 D6
Chiswick W4 133 A6
Enfield EN3 7 A6
West Ewell KT19 215 B1
Chesterfield St W1 248 C4
Chesterfield Way SE15 140 C5
Hayes UB3 106 A4
Chesterford Gdns NW3 69 D4
Chesterford Ho 4 SE18 143 D5
Chesterford Rd E12 78 B3
Chester Gate NW1 231 D1
Chester Gdns Ealing W13 87 B1
Enfield EN3 18 B5
Morden SM4 202 A3
Chester Ho N19 71 B6
1 SE8 141 B6
Kingston KT1 176 D1
Chesterman Ct W4 133 C5
Chester Mews SW1 258 C6
Chester Pl NW1 231 C2
Chester Rd DA15 167 C6
E16 98 C3
E17 52 D4
E7 77 D1
N17 51 C6
N19 71 B6
NW1 93 B4 231 C2
Edmonton N9 18 B3
Harlington TW6 126 C2
Hounslow TW4 128 B2
Ilford IG3 57 D2
Wanstead E11 55 B3
Wimbledon SW19,SW20 178 C4
Chester Row SW1 115 A2 258 B4
Chester Sq SW1 115 B2 258 C4
Chester Sq Mews SW1 258 C5
Chester St E2 96 A3
E2 96 A6
SW1 115 A3 258 B6
Chesters The KT3 177 C2
Chester Terr NW1 93 B4 231 C2
Chesterton Cl SW18 157 C6
Greenford UB6 85 D5
Chesterton Dr TW19 148 B3
Chesterton Ho 21 SW11 136 B2
3 W10 91 A2
Chesterton Prim Sch SW11 137 A4 268 A1
Chesterton Rd E13 99 A4
W10 91 A2
Chesterton Sq W8 255 A3
Chesterton Terr E13 99 A4
6 Kingston KT1 176 C1
Chester Way SE11 116 C2 261 B3
Chesthunte Rd N17 33 A2
Chestnut Alley SW6 264 D5
Chestnut Ave E7 77 B4
N8 50 A4
Chestnut Ave *continued*
Brentford TW8 109 D2
Buckhurst Hill IG9 21 D1
Coney Hall BR4 224 C4
Edgware HA8 26 B4
Hampton TW12 173 C3
Hampton, Hampton Court KT8,KT11 174 D2
11 Mortlake SW14 133 B2
Thames Ditton KT10 196 B1
Wembley HA0 65 B3
Worcester Park KT19 215 C4
Yiewsley UB7 104 B6
Chestnut Ave N E17 54 B5
Chestnut Ave S E17 54 B4
Chestnut Cl DA15 168 A2
1 N16 73 B6
SE14 141 B4
Ashford TW15 170 D6
Ashford TW16 171 D4
Buckhurst Hill IG9 21 D2
Carshalton SM5 202 D1
Catford SE6 186 A6
Harlington UB7 126 D5
Hayes UB3 105 C6
Southgate N14 15 D6
West Norwood SW16 182 C6
Chestnut Ct N8 49 D3
N8 50 A4
SW6 264 D6
Beckenham BR3 185 C3
5 Croydon CR0 221 A4
Feltham TW13 172 D5
Hounslow TW3 129 C2
Kingston KT3 199 C6
Surbiton KT6 198 A2
Wembley HA0 65 B3
Chestnut Dr DA7 147 A2
Harrow HA3 24 D2
Pinner HA5 41 A3
Wanstead E11 55 A3
Chestnut Gr W5 109 D3
Cockfosters EN4 14 D6
Isleworth TW7 131 A1
Kingston KT3 199 B6
Mitcham CR4 203 D5
Penge SE20 184 C3
South Croydon CR2 222 B1
Upper Tooting SW12 159 A3
Wembley HA0 65 B3
Chestnut Grove Sch SW12 159 A3
Chestnut Ho 7 NW3 70 D2
SE4 141 B2
1 W4 111 C2
West Norwood SE27 161 A1
Chestnut La N20 13 A3
Chestnut Pl SE19 183 D6
Chestnut Rd
Ashford TW15 170 D6
Kingston KT2 176 A3
Twickenham TW2 152 C2
West Barnes SW20 178 D1
West Norwood SE21,SE27 161 A1
Chestnut Rise SE18 123 C1
Chestnut Row N3 29 C3
Chestnuts Ct 3 E17 54 A6
Chestnuts The N2 48 D4
1 N5 72 D4
NW9 45 C6
SE18 144 D4
3 Erith DA17 125 B1
Penge BR3 206 D6
Uxbridge UB10 60 A1
Walton-on-T KT12 194 B1
Chestnut Way TW13 150 B1
Chestnut Wlk
Upper Halliford TW17 193 C5
Woodford IG8 37 A5
Cheston Ave CR0 207 B1
Chestwood Gr UB10 60 B1
Chettle Cl SE1 262 C6
Chettle Ct N8 50 C3
Chetwode Ho NW8 237 A6
Chetwode Rd SW17 158 D1
Chetwood Wlk 13 E6 100 A2
Chetwynd Ave EN4 14 D3
Chetwynd Dr UB10 82 B5
Chetwynd Rd NW5 71 B5
Cheval Ct SW15 134 B1
Chevalier Cl HA7 26 A6
Cheval Pl SW7 114 C3 257 B6
Cheval St E14 119 C3
Cheveney Wlk 2 BR2 209 A6
Chevening Ho BR5 190 A2
Chevening Rd NW6 91 A6
SE10 120 D1
South Norwood SE19 183 B4
Chevenings The DA14 168 C1
Cheverell Ho 24 E2 96 A5
Cheverton Rd N19 49 D1
Chevet St E9 75 A3
Chevington NW2 69 B2
Cheviot 4 N17 34 B3
Cheviot Cl Bushey WD23 8 A5
Enfield EN1 5 B3
Harlington UB3 127 B5
Cheviot Ct 16 SE14 140 C5
Enfield EN2 5 B3
Southall UB2 107 D2
Cheviot Gate NW2 69 A6
Cheviot Gdns NW2 69 A6
West Norwood SE27 182 D6
Cheviot Ho N16 51 D1
Cheviot Rd SE27 182 D5
Cheviots Hostel EN1 5 B3
Cheviot Way IG2 57 C5
Chevron Cl E16 99 A1
Chevy Rd UB2 108 A4
Chewton Rd E17 53 A5

Cheylesmore Ho SW1 ...258 C2
Cheyne Ave E18 ...54 D6
Twickenham TW2 ...151 B3
Cheyne Cl 6 NW4 ...46 B4
Keston Mark BR2 ...226 A5
Cheyne Ct SW3 ...267 C6
1 Croydon CR0 ...221 D6
4 Wallington SM6 ...219 B2
Cheyne Gdns
SW3 ...136 C6 267 B5
Cheyne Hill KT5 ...198 B5
Cheyne Mews
SW3 ...136 C6 267 B5
Cheyne Path W7 ...86 D1
Cheyne Rd TW15 ...171 B4
Cheyne Row
SW3 ...136 C6 267 A5
Cheyne Wlk NW4 ...46 C3
SW10 ...136 B5 266 C4
Croydon CR0 ...222 A6
Southgate N21 ...16 D6
Cheyney Ho 2 E9 ...74 D2
Cheyneys Ave HA8 ...25 D4
Chichele Gdns CR0 ...221 C4
Chichele Rd NW2 ...68 D3
Chicheley Gdns HA3 ...24 A3
Chicheley Rd HA3 ...24 A3
Chicheley St SE1 ...250 D2
Chichelle Ho HA8 ...26 B6
Chichester Ave HA4 ...61 B6
Chichester Cl E6 ...100 A1
SE3 ...143 C4
Hampton TW12 ...173 B4
Chichester Ct
Edgware HA8 ...26 C4
Harrow HA2 ...41 B1
Northolt UB5 ...85 A6
3 Sidcup DA5 ...169 C4
Stanmore HA7 ...44 A6
Stanwell TW19 ...148 A3
Chichester Gdns IG1 ...56 B2
Chichester Ho NW6 ...91 C5
2 Kingston KT2 ...176 D2
Chichester Mews SE27 ...182 C6
Chichester Rd E11 ...76 C5
NW6 ...91 C5
W2 ...91 D2
Edmonton N9 ...18 A3
South Croydon CR0 ...221 C5
Chichester Rents WC2 ...241 A2
Chichester St
SW1 ...115 C1 259 B1
Chichester Way E14 ...120 B2
Feltham TW14 ...150 C4
Chicksand Ho 13 E1 ...96 A2
Chicksand St E1 ...95 D2 243 D3
Chiddingfold N12 ...13 C1
Chiddingstone SE13 ...164 A6
Chiddingstone Ave DA7 ...147 B5
Chiddingstone St SW6 ...135 C3
Chieveley Par DA7 ...147 D2
Chieveley Rd DA7 ...147 D1
Chignell Pl 7 W13 ...109 A5
Chigwell Hill E1 ...118 B6
Chigwell Hurst Ct HA5 ...40 D6
Chigwell Rd
Wanstead E18 ...55 B6
Woodford IG8 ...37 D3
Chilam Ho 5 SE15 ...140 C6
Chilchester Ct 3 BR3 ...207 D6
Chilcombe Ho 6 SW15 ...156 A4
Chilcot Cl 13 E14 ...97 D1
Chilcott Cl HA0 ...65 C4
Child Ct E11 ...54 B2
Childebert Rd SW17 ...159 B2
Childeric Prim Sch
SE14 ...141 A5
Childeric Rd SE14 ...141 A5
Childerley St
SW6 ...135 A4 264 A2
Childerly KT1 ...198 C6
Childers St SE8 ...141 B6
Child La SE10 ...120 D3
Childs Ct UB3 ...106 A6
Child's Hill Prim Sch
NW2 ...69 A5
Childs La 11 SE19 ...183 C4
Child's Pl SW5 ...255 B3
Child's St SW5 ...255 B3
Childs Way NW11 ...47 B4
Child's Wlk SW5 ...255 B3
Chilham Cl DA5 ...169 B4
Wembley UB6 ...87 A5
Chilham Ct 14 SW9 ...138 C2
Chilham Ho SE1 ...262 D6
Chilham Rd SE9 ...188 A6
Chilham Way BR2 ...209 A2
Chillerton Rd SW17 ...181 B5
Chillingford Ho SW17 ...180 A6
Chillingworth Gdns
TW1 ...152 D1
Chillingworth Rd N7 ...72 C3
Chilmark Gdns KT3 ...200 A3
Chilmark Rd SW16 ...181 D2
Chiltern Ave Bushey WD23 ...8 A5
Twickenham TW2 ...151 C3
Chiltern Cl
Ickenham UB10 ...60 C6
North Cheam KT4 ...216 C6
South Croydon CR0 ...221 C5
Bushey WD23 ...8 A5
Chiltern Ct N10 ...31 A1
NW1 ...237 D5
15 SE14 ...140 C5
11 SE9 ...166 C5
Harrow HA1 ...42 B4
Hillingdon UB8 ...82 D3
New Barnet EN5 ...14 A6
Chiltern Dene EN2 ...4 B1
Chiltern Dr KT5 ...198 D4
Chiltern Gdns NW2 ...68 D5
Beckenham BR2 ...208 D5
Chiltern Ho 5 N16 ...51 D1
SE17 ...139 B6
4 W10 ...91 A2
Ealing W5 ...88 A2
5 Edmonton N9 ...18 A1
Chiltern Rd Bow E3 ...97 C3
Ilford IG2 ...57 C4
Pinner HA5 ...40 C4
Chiltern St W1 ...93 A2 238 A4
Chiltern Way IG8 ...21 A1
Chilthorne Cl SE6 ...163 B4
Chilton Ave W5 ...109 D2
Chilton Gr SE8 ...119 A2
Chiltonian Ind Est SE12 ...164 D5
Chilton Rd Edgware HA8 ...26 C4
Richmond TW9 ...132 C2
Chilton St E2 ...95 D3 243 D6
Chiltons The 1 E18 ...37 A1
Chilvers Cl TW2 ...152 C2
Chilver St SE10 ...120 D1
Chilwell Gdns WD19 ...22 C6
Chilworth Ct 8 SW19 ...156 D3
Chilworth Gdns SM1 ...218 A5
Chilworth Mews
W2 ...92 B1 236 C1
Chilworth St W2 ...92 A1 236 B1
Chimes Ave N13 ...32 D6
Chimney Ct 23 E1 ...118 B5
Chimneys Ct 2 SW19 ...178 C3
China Ct 1 E1 ...118 B5
China Mews 17 SW2 ...160 B4
Chinbrook Cres SE12 ...165 B1
Chinbrook Rd SE12 ...165 B1
Chinchilla Dr TW4 ...128 C3
Chindit Ho 11 N16 ...73 B4
Chine The N10 ...49 C5
Southgate N21 ...16 D6
Wembley HA0 ...65 B3
Ching Ct E4 ...20 C1
Chingdale Rd E4 ...20 C1
Chingford Ave E4 ...19 D2
Chingford CE Inf Sch E4 ...20 B3
Chingford CE Jun Sch
E4 ...20 B3
Chingford Foundation Sch
E4 ...19 D3
Chingford Hall Com Prim Sch
E4 ...35 B4
Chingford Hospl E4 ...20 A1
Chingford Ind Ctr E4 ...35 A5
Chingford La IG8 ...36 D5
Chingford Mount Rd E4 ...35 C5
Chingford Rd
Chingford E17 ...35 D1
Chingford E4 ...35 C3
Chingford Sch E4 ...19 D3
Chingford Sta E4 ...20 C4
Chingley Cl BR1 ...186 C4
Ching Way E4 ...35 B4
Chinnery Cl EN1 ...5 D4
Chinnocks Wharf E14 ...119 A6
Chinnor Cres UB6 ...86 A5
Chipka St E14 ...120 A4
Chipley St SE14 ...141 A6
Chipmunk Gr UB5 ...85 A4
Chippendale Ho SW1 ...258 D1
Chippendale St E5 ...74 D5
Chippenham 4 KT1 ...176 B1
Chippenham Ave HA9 ...66 D3
Chippenham Cl HA5 ...39 D5
Chippenham Gdns NW6 ...91 C4
Chippenham Mews W9 ...91 C3
Chippenham Rd W9 ...91 C3
Chipperfield Rd BR5 ...190 A1
Chipping Cl EN5 ...1 A2
Chip St SW4 ...137 D1
Chipstead Ave CR7 ...204 D5
Chipstead Cl SE19 ...183 D3
Chipstead Gdns NW2 ...68 B6
Chipstead Ho 4 SW2 ...160 A3
Chipstead St SW6 ...135 C3
Chirk Cl UB4 ...85 A3
Chisenhale Prim Sch E3 ...97 A5
Chisenhale Rd E3 ...97 A5
Chisholm Ct W6 ...112 A1
Chisholm Rd
Croydon CR0 ...221 C6
13 Richmond TW10 ...154 B5
Chisledon Wlk E9 ...75 B2
Chislehurst Ave N12 ...30 A3
Chislehurst High St
BR7 ...188 D4
Chislehurst Rd BR6 ...211 D2
Bromley BR1,BR7 ...188 A2
Orpington,Petts Wood
BR5,BR6,BR7 ...211 C4
Richmond TW10 ...154 A6
Sidcup DA14 ...190 A5
Chislehurst & Sidcup Gram
Sch DA15 ...168 B2
Chislehurst Sta BR7 ...188 C1
Chislehurst St Nicholas CE
Prim Sch BR7 ...189 A3
Chislet 5 NW5 ...71 A2
Chislet Cl BR3 ...185 C3
Chisley Rd 5 N15 ...51 C3
Chiswell Sq SE3 ...143 B3
Chiswell St EC1 ...95 B2 242 C4
Chiswick & Bedford Park
Prep Sch W4 ...111 C2
Chiswick Cl CR0 ...220 B5
Chiswick Common Rd
W4 ...111 B2
Chiswick Com Sch W4 ...133 B5
Chiswick Ct HA5 ...41 B6
Chiswick Green Studios 1
W4 ...111 A2
Chiswick High Rd W4 ...111 C2
Chiswick High Road (North
Circular Rd) W4 ...110 C1
Chiswick Ho★ W4 ...133 B6
Chiswick La W4 ...111 C1
Chiswick La S W4 ...133 D6
Chiswick Mall W4 ...111 D1
Chiswick Maternity Hospl
W4 ...111 D1
Chiswick Park Sta W4 ...111 A2
Chiswick Pier W4 ...133 D5
Chiswick Pk W4 ...110 D2
Chiswick Plaza W4 ...133 A6
Chiswick Quay W4 ...133 A4
Chiswick Rd Acton W4 ...111 A2
Edmonton N9 ...18 A2
Chiswick Rdbt W4 ...110 C1
Chiswick Sq W4 ...133 C6
Chiswick Sta W4 ...133 A5
Chiswick Staithe W4 ...133 A4
Chiswick Terr 6 W4 ...111 A2
Chiswick Village W4 ...132 D6
Chiswick Wharf W4 ...133 D6
Chitterfield Gate UB7 ...126 C5
Chitty's La RM8 ...80 D6
Chitty St W1 ...93 C2 239 B4
Chivalry Rd SW11 ...158 C6
Chivelston 27 SW19 ...156 D3
Chivenor Gr KT2 ...175 D5
Chivers Rd E4 ...35 D6
Choats Rd IG11 ...102 D4
Chobham Gdns SW19 ...156 D2
Chobham Rd E15 ...76 B3
Cholmeley Cres N6 ...49 B2
Cholmeley Ct N12 ...30 A6
Cholmeley Lo N6 ...49 B1
Cholmeley Pk N6 ...49 B2
Cholmley Gdns NW6 ...69 C3
Cholmley Rd KT7 ...197 B3
Cholmondeley Ave
NW10 ...90 A5
Cholmondeley Wlk
TW9 ...153 C6
Chopin's Ct 18 E1 ...118 B5
Chopwell Cl E15 ...76 B1
Chorleywood Cres BR5 ...190 A1
Choumert Gr SE15 ...140 A3
Choumert Mews SE15 ...140 A3
Choumert Rd SE15 ...139 D3
Choumert Sq 2 SE15 ...140 A3
Chow Sq 2 E8 ...73 D3
Chrisp Ho SE10 ...142 C6
Chrisp St E14 ...97 D1
Christabel Cl TW7 ...130 C2
Christchurch Ave N12 ...30 A4
NW6 ...69 A1
Harrow HA3 ...42 D5
Harrow HA3 ...43 A5
4 Teddington TW11 ...175 A5
Wembley HA0 ...66 A2
Christ Church Bentinck CE
Prim Sch NW1 ...92 C2 237 B4
Christ Church CE Mid Sch
W5 ...109 D6
Christchurch CE Prim Sch
SW3 ...136 D6 267 C6
Christ Church CE Prim Sch
NW6 ...69 B1
SE10 ...120 C1
SE18 ...144 C4
SW11 ...136 C2
Forest Hill SE23 ...162 D2
Kingston KT3 ...199 C6
Christ Church CE Sch
E1 ...95 D2 243 D3
Christ Church CE Sec Sch
N12 ...30 B5
Christchurch Cl N12 ...30 B3
Enfield EN2 ...5 A3
Mitcham SW19 ...180 B3
Christ Church Ct NW10 ...89 C6
NW6 ...69 A1
Christchurch Ct UB4 ...84 C3
Christchurch Gdns HA3 ...43 A5
Christchurch Gn HA0 ...66 A2
Christchurch Hill NW3 ...70 B4
Christchurch Ho 2
SW2 ...160 A3
Christ Church La EN5 ...1 A3
Christchurch Lo EN4 ...2 D1
Christchurch Pas NW3 ...70 A5
Christchurch Pk SM2 ...218 A1
Christ Church Prim Sch,
Hampstead NW3 ...70 B5
Christchurch Rd DA15 ...167 D1
Christ Church Rd N8 ...50 A3
Christchurch Rd
Harlington TW6 ...126 C2
Ilford IG1 ...57 A1
Mitcham SW19 ...180 B3
Mortlake SW14 ...155 A6
Surbiton KT5 ...198 B3
Christ Church Rd 1
BR3 ...185 C1
Christ Church Sch
NW1 ...93 B4 231 D2
Christ Church Sq 4 E9 ...96 C6
Christchurch St
SW3 ...136 D6 267 C6
Christ Church Streatham CE
Prim Sch SW2 ...160 B3
Christchurch Terr SW3 ...267 C6
Christchurch Way SE10 ...120 C1
Christian Ct SE16 ...119 B5
Christian Fields SW16 ...182 C3
Christian St E1 ...96 A1
Christie Ct 1 N19 ...72 A6
NW3 ...70 C3
Christie Dr SE25 ...206 A4
Christie Gdns RM6 ...58 B2
Christie Ho DA6 ...169 D6
Christie Ho *continued*
2 SE10 ...120 D1
4 West Wickham BR4 ...207 D1
Christie Rd E9 ...75 A2
Christina Sq N4 ...50 D1
Christina St EC2 ...243 A6
Christine Worsley Cl
N21 ...16 D3
Christopher Ave W7 ...109 A3
Christopher Boone's
Almshouses SE13 ...142 B1
Christopher Cl DA15 ...167 D6
SE16 ...118 D4
Christopher Ct
Ashford TW15 ...170 A5
Barnet EN5 ...1 D1
6 Croydon CR0 ...206 A1
Christopher Gdns RM9 ...80 D3
Christopher Hatton Prim Sch
EC1 ...94 C3 241 A5
Christopher Lo 2 N6 ...49 D2
Christopher Pl NW1 ...232 D1
Christopher Rd UB2 ...106 B2
Christopher St
EC2 ...95 B3 242 D5
Christ's Coll NW11 ...47 D6
SE3 ...143 A4
Christ's Coll Upper Sch
N3 ...29 B1
Christ's Sch (East Side)
TW10 ...154 C6
Christ's Sch (West Side)
TW10 ...154 B6
Christ the King RC Fst Sch
TW19 ...148 A5
Christ the King RC Prim Sch
N4 ...72 B6
Christ the King RC Sixth
Form Coll SE13 ...142 B2
Chryssell Rd SW9 ...138 C5
Chubworthy St SE14 ...141 A6
Chudleigh 1 DA14 ...190 B6
Chudleigh Cres IG3 ...79 C4
Chudleigh Gdns SM1 ...218 A5
Chudleigh Rd NW6 ...68 D1
SE4 ...163 C6
Twickenham TW1,TW2 ...152 D4
Chudleigh St E1 ...96 D1
Chudleigh Way HA4 ...40 A1
Chulsa Rd SE26 ...184 B5
Chumleigh Gdns SE5 ...139 C6
Chumleigh St SE5 ...139 C6
Chumleigh Wlk KT5 ...198 B5
Church App SE21 ...161 B1
Church Ave DA14 ...190 B5
N2 ...30 B2
NW1 ...71 B2
Beckenham BR3 ...185 C2
Chingford E4 ...36 B4
Mortlake SW14 ...133 B2
Northolt UB5 ...63 B1
Pinner HA5 ...41 B3
Ruislip HA4 ...39 B1
Southall UB2 ...107 A3
Churchbank E17 ...53 C5
Churchbury Cl EN1 ...5 C3
Churchbury La EN1 ...5 C3
Churchbury Rd SE9 ...165 D4
Enfield EN1 ...5 C3
Church Cl HA8 ...27 A5
N20 ...14 C1
W8 ...245 C2
Hayes UB4 ...83 B2
Hounslow TW4 ...129 B3
West Drayton UB7 ...104 A3
Church Cres E9 ...74 D1
N10 ...49 B5
N20 ...14 C1
N3 ...29 B2
Churchcroft Cl SW12 ...159 A4
Church Ct EC4 ...241 B1
N2 ...48 B6
Forest Hill SE26 ...185 A5
27 Richmond TW10 ...153 D6
Churchdale Ct 1 W4 ...110 D1
Churchdown BR1 ...186 C6
Church Dr NW9 ...45 B1
Coney Hall BR4 ...224 C5
Harrow HA2 ...41 C3
Church Elm La RM10 ...81 C2
Church End E17 ...53 D5
Hendon NW4 ...46 B6
Church Entry EC4 ...241 D1
Church Estate Almshouses 8
TW9 ...132 B1
Church Farm House Mus★
NW4 ...46 B6
Church Farm La SM3 ...217 A2
Churchfield Ave N12 ...30 B4
Churchfield Cl
Harrow HA2 ...42 A5
Hayes UB3 ...105 D6
Churchfield Ho W2 ...236 C5
Churchfield Mans 5
SW6 ...135 B3
Churchfield Pl TW17 ...192 D2
Churchfield Prim Sch
N9 ...17 D3
Churchfield Rd DA16 ...146 A2
W3 ...111 A5
W7 ...108 C4
Ealing W13 ...109 C5
Walton-on-T KT12 ...194 A1
Churchfields SE10 ...142 A6
East Molesey KT8 ...195 C6
Woodford E18 ...37 A2
Churchfields Ave TW13 ...151 C1
Churchfields Sch SE2 ...124 A2
Churchfields Inf Sch E18 ...37 A2
Churchfields Prim Sch
BR3 ...206 D6
Churchfields Rd BR3 ...185 A1
Churchfield Way N12 ...30 A4
Church Garth 18 N19 ...71 D6
Church Gate N20 ...14 C2
Fulham SW6 ...135 A2
Church Gdns W5 ...109 D4
Wembley HA0 ...65 A4
Church Gn 4 SW9 ...138 C3
Hayes UB3 ...83 D1
Church Gr SE13 ...163 D6
Teddington KT1 ...175 C1
Church Hill E17 ...53 D5
SE18 ...122 B3
Harrow HA1 ...42 C1
Southgate N21 ...16 C4
Wallington SM5 ...218 D3
Wimbledon SW19 ...179 B5
Church Hill Prim Sch
EN4 ...14 D4
Church Hill Rd E17 ...53 D5
Cheam SM1,SM3 ...217 A4
East Barnet EN4 ...14 D4
Kingston KT6 ...198 A4
Church Hill Wood BR5 ...211 D4
Church Hyde SE18 ...145 C6
Churchill Ave Harrow HA3 ...43 B3
Hillingdon UB10 ...82 D4
Churchill Cl
East Bedfont TW14 ...149 D3
Hillingdon UB10 ...82 D4
Churchill Ct 4 BR6 ...227 A3
N4 ...50 C2
NW2 ...68 B3
Edmonton N9 ...17 B3
Harrow HA2 ...41 D4
7 Ilford IG1 ...78 D5
Northolt UB5 ...63 C3
Churchill Gardens Prim Sch
SW1 ...115 C1 259 B1
Churchill Gdns
SW1 ...137 C6 269 A6
Acton W3 ...88 C1
Churchill Gdns Rd
SW1 ...137 C6 269 A6
Churchill Ho TW8 ...109 C1
Churchill Lo IG8 ...36 D4
Churchill Mews IG8 ...36 D4
Churchill Pl E14 ...119 D5
Harrow HA1 ...42 C5
Churchill Rd NW2 ...68 B2
NW5 ...71 B4
Edgware HA8 ...26 C4
Newham E16 ...99 C1
South Croydon CR2 ...221 A1
Churchill Terr E4 ...19 C1
Churchill Way BR1 ...187 A1
Ashford TW16 ...172 A4
Churchill Wlk E9 ...74 C3
Church La E11 ...54 C1
E17 ...53 D5
N2 ...48 B6
N8 ...50 B5
NW9 ...45 B2
W5 ...109 D4
Chessington KT9 ...214 B2
Chislehurst BR7 ...189 A2
Dagenham RM10 ...81 D1
Edmonton N9 ...18 A2
Enfield EN1 ...5 B2
Harrow HA3 ...24 D2
Keston Mark BR2 ...210 A1
Pinner HA5 ...41 B6
Teddington TW11 ...174 D5
Thames Ditton KT7 ...197 A3
Tottenham N17 ...33 C2
Twickenham TW1 ...153 A3
Upper Tooting SW17 ...181 A5
Wallington SM6 ...219 D5
Merton SW19 ...179 C2
Churchley Rd SE26 ...184 B6
Churchley Villas SE26 ...184 B6
Church Lo UB5 ...63 B1
Church Manor Way
SE18,SE2 ...124 A2
Church Mdw KT6 ...213 C6
Church Mead SE5 ...139 A5
Churchmead Cl EN4 ...14 C5
Church Mead Inf Sch
E10 ...53 C1
Church Mead Jun Sch
E10 ...53 C1
Churchmead Rd NW10 ...68 A2
Churchmore Rd SW16 ...181 D2
Church Mount N2 ...48 B4
Church Paddock Ct
SM6 ...219 D5
Church Par TW15 ...170 B6
Church Path E17 ...53 D5
W4 ...111 A3
Merton SW19 ...179 C1
Mitcham CR4 ...202 C6
Wanstead E11 ...55 A4
Church Pl SW1 ...249 B5
W5 ...109 D4
Mitcham CR4 ...202 C6
Uxbridge UB10 ...61 A5
Church Rd BR1,BR2 ...187 A1
BR6 ...227 B3
DA16 ...146 B3
E10 ...75 C6
E12 ...78 A3
E17 ...35 A1
21 N1 ...73 A2
N6 ...49 A3
NW10 ...67 C1
NW4 ...46 C5
Acton W3 ...111 A4
Ashford TW15 ...170 B6
Church Rd *continued*
Barking IG11 ...79 A2
Barnes SW13 ...134 A4
Beckenham BR2 ...208 C6
Bexley DA6,DA7 ...147 B2
Buckhurst Hill IG9 ...21 B3
Cheam SM3 ...217 A2
Claygate KT10 ...212 D1
Croydon CR0 ...221 A5
Ealing W7 ...108 C6
East Molesey KT8 ...196 B6
Enfield EN3 ...18 C6
Feltham TW13 ...172 D5
Hayes UB3 ...105 D6
Heston TW5 ...128 B6
Heston TW5 ...129 C5
Hillingdon UB8 ...82 A3
Hounslow TW7 ...130 C5
Ilford IG2 ...57 C3
Keston BR2 ...225 D1
Kingston KT1 ...176 B1
Long Ditton KT6 ...197 C1
Lower Halliford TW17 ...192 D2
Mitcham CR4,SW19 ...180 B1
New Malden KT4 ...199 C1
Northolt UB5 ...85 A6
Richmond TW10,TW9 ...154 A6
Richmond, Ham Common
TW10 ...176 A6
Sidcup DA14 ...190 A6
Southall UB2 ...107 B3
South Norwood SE19 ...183 C3
Stanmore HA7 ...25 B5
Teddington TW11 ...174 D5
Tottenham N17 ...33 D3
Wallington SM6 ...219 D5
West Drayton UB7 ...104 A3
West Ewell KT19 ...215 B1
Wimbledon SW19 ...179 A6
Mitcham CR4 ...202 C6
Church Rd N N2 ...30 B2
Church Rd S N2 ...30 B2
Church Rise
Chessington KT9 ...214 B2
Forest Hill SE23 ...162 D2
Church Row NW3 ...70 A4
Chislehurst BR7 ...189 A2
Church Row Mews BR7 ...189 A3
Church Sq TW17 ...192 D2
Church St E15 ...98 D6
E16 ...122 D5
NW8 ...92 C3 237 A5
Chiswick W4 ...133 D6
Croydon CR0 ...221 A6
Dagenham RM10 ...81 D2
Edmonton N9 ...17 C2
Enfield EN2 ...5 B2
Hampton TW12 ...174 A2
Isleworth TW7 ...131 B3
Kingston KT1 ...175 D1
Sunbury TW16 ...194 B6
Twickenham TW1 ...153 A3
Walton-on-T KT12 ...194 A2
Church St N E15 ...98 C6
Church Stretton Rd
TW3 ...152 A6
Church St Sta CR0 ...221 A6
Church Terr SE13 ...142 C2
Hendon NW4 ...46 B6
20 Richmond TW10 ...153 D6
Church Vale N2 ...48 D6
Forest Hill SE23 ...162 D2
Churchview Rd TW2 ...152 B2
Church Villa TW16 ...194 B6
Churchward Ho SE17 ...138 D6
SW5 ...254 D1
Churchway NW1 ...232 D2
Church Way N20 ...14 C1
Churchway EN4 ...2 D1
Church Wlk N16 ...73 B4
NW2 ...69 B5
NW9 ...67 B6
Barnes SW13 ...134 A4
Brentford TW8 ...131 C6
Hayes UB3 ...83 D1
Mitcham SW16 ...181 C1
15 Richmond TW10 ...153 D6
Thames Ditton KT7 ...196 D3
Walton-on-T KT12 ...194 A1
West Barnes SW20 ...200 C6
Churchwood Gdns IG8 ...37 A6
Churchyard Row
SE11 ...116 D2 261 D4
Churnfield 2 N4 ...72 C6
Churston Ave E13 ...99 B6
Churston Cl 17 SW2 ...160 C3
Churston Dr SM4 ...201 A4
Churston Gdns N11 ...31 C4
Churston Mans WC1 ...240 D5
Churton Pl SW1 ...259 B3
Brentford W4 ...132 D6
Churton St SW1 ...115 C2 259 B3
Chute Ho 18 SW9 ...138 C3
Chuter Ede Ho SW6 ...264 D5
Chyngton Cl DA15 ...167 D1
Chyngton Ct HA1 ...64 C6
Cibber Rd SE23 ...162 D2
Cicada Rd SW18 ...158 A6
Cicely Ho NW8 ...229 D3
Cicely Rd SE15 ...140 A4
Cinderford Way BR1 ...186 C6
Cinema Par RM8 ...81 B6
Cinnabar Wharf Central 17
E1 ...118 A5
Cinnabar Wharf East 16
E1 ...118 A5

Cinnabar Wharf West 18 E1 ....118 A5
Cinnamon Cl 8 SE15 ....139 D5
Thornton Heath CR0 ....204 A2
Cinnamon Row 3 SW11 ....136 A2
Cinnamon St E1 ....118 B5
Cinnamon Wharf SE1 ..253 D2
Cinque Cotts SW19 ....178 C4
Cintra Ct SE19 ....183 D4
Cintra Pk SE19 ....183 D3
Circle Ct HA0 ....65 D4
Circle Gdns SW19 ....179 C1
Circle Ho 18 E14 ....98 B1
Circle The NW2 ....67 C5
NW7 ....27 B4
SE1 ....253 D2
Circuit Rd SE28 ....124 A4
Circuits The HA5 ....40 C5
Circular Rd N17 ....51 D6
N2 ....30 B2
Circular Way SE18 ....144 C6
Circus Lo NW8 ....229 C2
Circus Mews W1 ....237 C4
Circus Pl EC2 ....242 D3
Circus Rd NW8 ....92 B5 229 C3
Circus St SE10 ....142 A5
Cirencester St W2 ....91 D2
Cirrus 17 NW9 ....27 D1
Cissbury Ho 6 SE26 ....162 A1
Cissbury Rd N15 ....51 B4
Cissbury Ring N N12 ....29 C5
Cissbury Ring S N12 ....29 B5
Citizen Ho N7 ....72 C4
Citizen Rd N7 ....72 C4
Citron Terr 3 SE15 ....140 B2
Citrus Ho 14 SE8 ....119 B1
City Airport Pier E16 ....120 D5
City and Islington Coll
EC1 ....94 D4 234 C1
City Banking Coll
SE1 ....117 B4 252 D2
City Bsns Ctr 26 SE16 ....118 C4
City Central Est EC1 ....235 A1
City Forum EC1 ....95 A4 235 A2
City Garden Row
N1 ....94 D5 234 D3
City Gate E1 ....96 C3
City & Guilds of London Art Sch The SE11 ....116 C1 261 B1
City Harbour E14 ....119 D3
City & Islington Coll
N1 ....95 B6 235 C6
N4 ....72 D6
City Literature Inst The
WC2 ....94 A1 240 B2
City of London Sch
EC4 ....117 A6 252 A6
City of London Sch for Girls
EC2 ....95 A2 242 B4
City of Westminster Coll
NW1 ....92 C2 237 B4
W2 ....92 B2 236 C4
City of Westminster Coll, Maida Vale Ctr W9 ....91 D4
City of Westminster Coll, Queens Park Ctr W9 ....91 C4
City Prospect 5 SE19 ....183 C4
City Rd EC1 ....95 A4 235 B2
City Thameslink Sta
EC4 ....94 D1 241 C1
City Wharf Ho KT7 ....197 B3
Civic Way Ilford IG6 ....57 A5
Ruislip HA4 ....62 D3
Civil Service Coll
SW1 ....115 C2 259 A3
Clabon Mews
SW1 ....114 D2 257 C4
Clack St SE16 ....118 C4
Clacton Rd E17 ....53 A3
E6 ....99 D4
Tottenham N17 ....33 D1
Claigmar Gdns N3 ....29 D2
Claire Ct N12 ....14 A1
NW2 ....69 A2
Bushey WD23 ....8 B3
Claire Gdns HA7 ....25 C5
Claire Pl E14 ....119 C3
Clairvale Rd TW5 ....129 A4
Clairview Rd SW16 ....181 B5
Clairville Gdns W7 ....108 C5
Clairville Point 12 SE23 ....162 D1
Clamp Hill HA7 ....24 C5
Clancarty Rd SW6 ....135 C3
Clandon Cl W3 ....110 D4
Stoneleigh KT17 ....216 A2
Clandon Ct BR1 ....187 A4
Sutton SM2 ....218 B2
Clandon Gdns N3 ....47 C6
Clandon Ho N3 ....47 C6
12 Kingston KT2 ....176 D4
Clandon Rd IG3 ....79 C6
Clandon St SE8 ....141 C3
Clanfield Ho 12 SW15 ....156 A3
Clanricarde Gdns
W2 ....113 C6 245 B5
Clapham Common*
SW4 ....137 C1
Clapham Common North Side SW4 ....137 A1
Clapham Common South Side SW4 ....159 C6
Clapham Common Sta
SW4 ....137 C1
Clapham Common West Side
SW11 ....159 A6
SW4,SW11 ....136 D1
Clapham Court Terr 2
SW4 ....160 A6
Clapham Cres SW4 ....137 D1
Clapham Ct 3 SW4 ....160 A6
Clapham High St SW4 ....137 D1
Clapham High Street Sta
SW4 ....137 D2
Clapham Junction Est
SW11 ....136 C1
Clapham Junction Sta
SW11 ....136 C1
Clapham Manor Ct 1
SW4 ....137 C2
Clapham Manor Prim Sch
SW4 ....137 C2
Clapham Manor St
SW4 ....137 D2
Clapham Mans SW4 ....159 B5
Clapham North Sta
SW4 ....138 A2
Clapham Park Rd SW4 ....137 D1
Clapham Park Terr 4
SW2 ....160 A6
Clapham Rd
SW9 ....138 B4 270 D2
Clapham South Sta
SW4 ....159 B5
Claps Gate La E6 ....100 D3
Clapton Comm E5 ....52 A2
Clapton Girls Tec Coll
E5 ....74 C4
Clapton Ho 7 E5 ....74 C6
Clapton Pas E5 ....74 C3
Clapton Sq E5 ....74 C3
Clapton Sta E5 ....74 B6
Clapton Terr E5 ....52 A1
Clapton Way E5 ....74 A5
Clara Grant Prim Sch The
E3 ....97 C3
Clara Pl SE18 ....122 C2
Clare Cl N2 ....48 A6
Borehamwood WD6 ....10 B5
Clare Cnr SE9 ....166 D4
Clare Ct BR7 ....188 B2
WC1 ....233 B1
Wimbledon SW19 ....179 A4
Claredale Ct SM2 ....218 A1
Claredale Ho 3 E2 ....96 B5
Claredale St E2 ....96 A5
Clare Gdns E7 ....77 A4
W11 ....91 A1
Barking IG11 ....80 A1
Clare Grant Ho 3 E14 ....119 C3
Clare Ho 6 E3 ....97 B6
4 HA8 ....27 A1
SE1 ....263 D2
Clare House Prim Sch
BR3 ....186 A1
Clare La N1 ....73 A1
Clare Lawn Ave SW14 ....155 B6
Clare Mews SW6 ....265 C3
Clare Mkt WC2 ....240 D1
Claremont
1 Putney SW15 ....157 A6
Shepperton TW17 ....192 D3
Claremont Ave
Harrow HA3 ....44 A4
Sunbury TW16 ....172 B2
West Barnes KT3 ....200 B4
Claremont Cl E16 ....122 C5
N1 ....94 C5 234 B3
Orpington BR6 ....226 C4
4 Streatham SW2 ....160 B3
Claremont Ct 1 W9 ....91 B5
Claremont Dr TW17 ....192 D3
Claremont Gdns
Ilford IG3 ....79 C6
Kingston KT6 ....198 A4
Claremont Gr
Chiswick W4 ....133 C5
Woodford IG8 ....37 C4
Claremont High Sch HA3 ....44 A4
Claremont Hts EN2 ....4 D1
Claremont La KT10 ....212 A3
Claremont Pk N3 ....29 A2
Claremont Rd BR1 ....210 B5
E17 ....35 A1
E7 ....76 B5
E7 ....77 C3
N6 ....49 C2
W9 ....91 B5
Claygate KT10 ....212 C1
Croydon CR0 ....206 A1
Ealing W13 ....87 A2
Hadley Wood EN4 ....2 B6
Harrow HA3 ....24 C1
Hendon NW2 ....68 D6
Kingston KT6 ....198 A4
Teddington TW11 ....174 D6
Twickenham TW1 ....153 C5
Claremont Sq N1 ....94 C5 234 A3
Claremont St E16 ....122 C4
SE10 ....141 D6
Edmonton N18 ....34 A4
Claremont Terr KT7 ....197 B2
Claremont Way NW2 ....46 C1
Claremont Way Ind Est
NW2 ....46 C1
Clarence Ave SW4 ....159 D5
Bromley BR1,BR2 ....210 A5
Ilford IG2 ....56 C3
Kingston KT3 ....177 B1
Clarence Cl Bushey WD23 ....8 D4
New Barnet EN4 ....14 B6
Clarence Cres DA14 ....168 B1
Clarence Ct NW7 ....27 D5
10 W6 ....112 B2
Clarence Gate Gdns
NW1 ....237 D5
Clarence Gdns
NW1 ....93 B4 231 D1
Clarence Ho SE17 ....139 A6
Clarence Ho*
SW1 ....115 C5 249 B3
Clarence La SW15 ....155 D5
Clarence Mews E5 ....74 B3
1 SE16 ....118 D5
Balham SW12 ....159 B4
Clarence Pl 25 E5 ....74 B3
Clarence Rd DA6 ....147 A1
E12 ....77 D3
E16 ....98 C3
E17 ....34 D1
E5 ....74 B4
N15 ....51 A4
NW6 ....69 B1
W4 ....110 C1
Bromley BR1,BR2 ....210 A6
Chislehurst SE9 ....166 A2
Enfield EN3 ....18 C6
Richmond TW9 ....132 C4
Sidcup DA14 ....168 B1
Sutton SM1 ....217 D3
Teddington TW11 ....175 A4
Thornton Heath CR0 ....205 B2
Wallington SM6 ....219 B3
Wimbledon SW19 ....179 D4
Wood Green N22 ....32 A3
Clarence St
Kingston KT1,KT2 ....176 A1
5 Richmond TW9 ....132 A1
Southall UB2 ....106 D3
Clarence Terr NW1 ....237 D6
Hounslow TW3 ....129 D1
Clarence Way NW1 ....71 B1
Clarence Wlk 9 SW4 ....138 A3
Clarendon CE Infants Sch
TW15 ....170 B6
Clarendon Cl W2 ....247 A6
37 Hackney E9 ....74 C1
Clarendon Cres TW2 ....152 B1
Clarendon Cross W11 ....244 B5
Clarendon Ct NW11 ....47 B5
NW2 ....68 C1
W9 ....236 B6
1 Richmond TW9 ....132 C4
Clarendon Dr SW15 ....134 C1
Clarendon Flats W1 ....238 B1
Clarendon Gdns
W9 ....92 A3 236 B5
Hendon NW4 ....46 B6
Redbridge IG1 ....56 B2
Wembley HA9 ....66 A4
Clarendon Gr NW1 ....232 C2
Mitcham CR4 ....202 D6
Clarendon Ho N12 ....30 A5
NW1 ....232 B3
Clarendon Mews DA5 ....169 D3
W2 ....247 A6
Clarendon Pl
W2 ....114 C6 247 A6
Clarendon Rd E11 ....54 B1
E17 ....53 D3
N15 ....51 A5
N8 ....50 B6
W11 ....113 A6 244 B5
Ashford TW15 ....170 B6
Croydon CR0 ....220 D6
Ealing W5 ....88 A3
Edmonton N18 ....34 A5
Harrow HA1 ....42 C3
Hayes UB3 ....105 D4
Mitcham SW19 ....180 C3
Wallington SM6 ....219 C2
Wanstead E18 ....55 A6
Wood Green N22 ....32 B1
Clarendon Rise SE13 ....142 A1
Clarendon Sch TW12 ....173 D4
Clarendon St
SW1 ....115 B1 258 D2
Clarendon Terr W9 ....236 B6
Clarendon Way
BR5,BR7 ....211 D6
Enfield N21 ....17 A5
Clarendon Wlk 10 W11 ....91 A1
Clarens St SE6 ....163 B2
Clare Pl SW15 ....
Clare Point NW2 ....46 D1
Clare Rd E11 ....54 B3
NW10 ....68 A1
SE14 ....141 B4
Hounslow TW4 ....129 B2
Northolt UB6 ....64 B2
Stanwell TW19 ....148 A4
Clare St E2 ....96 B5
Claret Gdns SE25 ....205 C5
Clareville Ct SW7 ....256 B3
Clareville Gr
SW7 ....114 A2 256 B3
Clareville Grove Mews
SW7 ....256 B3
Clareville Rd BR5,BR6 ....227 A6
Clareville St
SW7 ....114 A2 256 B3
Clare Way DA7 ....147 A4
Clarewood Ct W1 ....237 C3
Clarewood Wlk SW9 ....138 C1
Clarges Ho W1 ....248 D4
Clarges Mews
W1 ....115 B5 248 C4
Clarges St W1 ....115 B5 248 D4
Claribel Rd SW9 ....138 D3
Clarice Ct NW4 ....46 B6
Claridge Ct SW6 ....264 C1
Claridge Rd RM8 ....58 D1
Clarissa Ho 7 E14 ....97 D1
Clarissa Rd RM6 ....58 D2
Clarissa St E8 ....95 D6
Clark Ct NW10 ....67 A1
Clarke Ho 2 SW4 ....137 C2
Clarke Mans 8 IG11 ....79 D1
Clarke Mews N9 ....18 B1
Clarke Path N16 ....52 A1
Clarke's Ave KT4,SM3 ....216 D6
Clarkes Dr UB8 ....82 A2
Clarkes Mews W1 ....238 B4
Clark Lawrence Ct 11
SW11 ....136 B2
Clarks Mead WD23 ....8 B4
Clarkson Ho SW11 ....136 B1
Clarkson Rd E16 ....98 D1
Clarkson Row NW1 ....232 A3
Clarkson St E2 ....96 B4
Clarksons The IG11 ....101 A5
Clark's Pl EC2 ....243 A2
Clark's Rd IG1 ....79 B6
Clark St E1 ....96 C2
Clark Way TW5 ....128 D5
Classic Mans 33 E9 ....74 C1
Classinghall Ho 14
SW15 ....156 D5
Classon Cl UB7 ....104 A4
Claude Rd E10 ....54 A1
E13 ....99 B6
SE15 ....140 B3
Claude St E14 ....119 C2
Claudia Jones Way
SW2 ....160 A5
Claudia Pl SW19 ....157 A3
Claughton Rd E13 ....99 C5
Clauson Ave UB5 ....64 A3
Clavell St 7 SE10 ....142 A6
Claverdale Rd SW2 ....160 C4
Clavering Ave SW13 ....134 B6
Clavering Cl TW1 ....175 A6
Clavering Ho SE13 ....142 B1
Clavering Rd E12 ....77 D6
Claverings Ind Est N9 ....18 C2
Claverley Gr N3 ....29 D2
Claverley Villas N3 ....29 D3
Claverton St
SW1 ....115 C1 259 B1
Clave St E1 ....118 C5
Claxton Gr W6 ....112 D1 254 A1
Clay Ave CR4 ....181 B1
Claybank Gr SE13 ....141 D2
Claybourne Mews 2
SE19 ....183 D3
Claybridge Rd SE12 ....187 C6
Claybrook Cl N2 ....48 B6
Claybrook Rd W6 ....134 D6
Claybury Broadway IG5 ....56 A6
Clay Ct E17 ....54 B6
Claydon SE17 ....262 A4
Claydon Dr CR0 ....220 A4
Claydon Ho NW4 ....28 D1
Claydown Mews SE18 ....122 C1
Clayfarm Rd SE9 ....167 A2
Claygate Cres CR0 ....224 B2
Claygate La
Hinchley Wood KT10 ....213 A6
Thames Ditton KT7 ....197 A1
Claygate Lodge Cl KT10 ....212 C1
Claygate Prim Sch
KT10 ....212 C1
Claygate Rd W13 ....109 B3
Claygate Sta KT10 ....212 C2
Clayhall Ct 16 E3 ....97 B5
Clay Hill EN2 ....5 B6
Clayhill Cres SE12,SE9 ....187 D6
Clay La WD23 ....8 C4
Claylands Ct SE19 ....183 B5
Claylands Pl SW8 ....138 C5
Claylands Rd
SW8 ....138 B6 270 D5
Claymill Ho 2 SE18 ....123 A1
Claymore Cl SM3,SM4 ....201 C2
Claypole Ct E17 ....53 C4
Claypole Dr TW5 ....129 A4
Claypole Rd E15 ....98 A5
Clayponds Ave TW8 ....110 A2
Clayponds Gdns W5 ....109 D2
Clayponds Hospl & Day Treatment Ctr TW8 ....110 A2
Clayponds La TW8 ....110 A1
Clays Ct N16 ....51 D1
Clays La E15 ....75 D3
Clays Lane Cl E15 ....75 D3
Clay St W1 ....92 D2 237 D3
Clayton 22 NW9 ....27 D1
Clayton Ave HA0 ....66 A1
Clayton Bsns Ctr UB3 ....105 C4
Clayton Cl 3 E6 ....100 B1
Clayton Cres TW8 ....109 D1
Clayton Ct E17 ....35 A1
N16 ....52 A2
Clayton Field NW9 ....27 C2
Clayton Ho 22 E9 ....74 C1
Long Ditton KT7 ....197 B1
Clayton Mews SE10 ....142 B4
Clayton Rd SE15 ....140 A4
Chessington KT10,KT9 ....213 D4
Hayes UB3 ....105 C4
Isleworth TW7 ....130 C2
Clayton St SE11 ....138 C6
Clayton Terr UB4 ....84 D2
Claytonville Terr DA17 ....125 D4
Clay Wood Cl BR6 ....211 C2
Clayworth Cl DA15 ....168 B5
Cleanthus Cl SE18 ....144 D4
Cleanthus Rd SE18 ....144 D4
Clearbrook Way 13 E1 ....96 C1
Clearmont Ho UB2 ....107 C3
Clearwater Ho 3 TW10 ....154 A6
Clearwater Pl KT6 ....197 C3
Clearwater Terr 4
W11 ....112 D4
Clearwell Dr W9 ....91 D3
Cleave Ave Hayes UB3 ....105 C2
Cleave Ave *continued*
Orpington BR6 ....227 C2
Cleaveland Rd KT6 ....197 D4
Cleaver Ho 6 NW3 ....70 D1
Cleaverholme Cl SE25 ....206 B3
Cleaver Sq SE11 ....116 C1 261 B1
Cleaver St SE11 ....116 C1 261 B2
Cleave's Almshos 1
KT2 ....176 A1
Cleeve Ct N10 ....31 B3
East Bedfont TW14 ....149 C3
Cleeve Hill SE23 ....162 B3
Cleeve Ho 16 E2 ....95 C4
Cleeve Park Gdns DA14 ....168 B2
Cleeve Park Sch DA14 ....168 C1
Cleeve Way SW15 ....
Clegg Ho SE3 ....143 B1
Clegg St 16 E1 ....118 B5
E13 ....99 A5
Cleland Ho 20 E2 ....96 C5
Clematis Gdns IG8 ....37 A5
Clematis St W12 ....112 A6
Clem Attlee Ct
SW6 ....135 B6 264 D5
Clemence St E14 ....97 B2
Clement Attlee Ho NW10 ....67 D1
Clement Ave SW4 ....137 D1
Clement Cl NW6 ....68 C1
W4 ....111 B2
Clement Gdns UB3 ....105 C2
Clement Ho 14 SE8 ....119 A2
W10 ....90 C2
Clementhorpe Rd RM9 ....80 C2
Clementina Rd E10 ....53 B1
Clementine Churchill Hospl The HA1 ....64 D5
Clementine Cl W13 ....109 B4
Clement Rd Penge BR3 ....184 D1
Wimbledon SW19 ....179 A5
Clements Ave 1 E16 ....121 A6
Clements Ct
Hounslow TW4 ....128 D1
5 Ilford IG1 ....78 D5
Clements Inn
WC2 ....94 B1 240 D1
Clements Inn Pas WC2 ....240 D1
Clement's La
EC2,EC4 ....117 B6 252 D6
Clements La IG1 ....78 D5
Clements Pl TW8 ....109 D1
Clements Rd E6 ....78 B1
Clement's Rd SE16 ....118 B3
Clements Rd IG1 ....78 D5
Clemson Ho 9 E8 ....95 D6
Clendon Way SE18 ....123 B2
Clenham St SE1 ....252 B2
Clensham Ct SM3 ....217 C6
Clensham La SM1 ....217 C6
Clenston Mews W1 ....237 C2
Clent Ho 4 N16 ....51 D1
Cleopatra's Needle*
WC2 ....116 B5 250 C5
Clephane Rd 6 N1 ....73 A2
Clephane Rd N N1 ....73 A2
Clephane Rd S N1 ....73 B2
Clere Pl EC2 ....242 D6
Clere St EC2 ....95 B3 242 D6
Clerics Wlk TW17 ....193 B3
Clerkenwell Cl
EC1 ....94 C3 241 B5
Clerkenwell Gn
EC1 ....94 D3 241 C5
Clerkenwell Parochial CE Prim Sch EC1 ....94 C4 234 A2
Clerkenwell Rd
EC1 ....94 D3 241 C5
Clermont Rd E9 ....96 C6
Clevedon Ct CR2 ....221 C3
Clevedon Ct SW11 ....267 A2
Dulwich SE21 ....161 B1
Clevedon Gdns
Cranford TW5 ....128 B4
Hayes UB3 ....105 B3
Clevedon Mans NW5 ....71 A4
Clevedon Rd
Kingston KT1 ....176 C1
Penge SE20 ....184 D2
Twickenham TW1 ....153 D5
Cleve Ho NW6 ....69 D1
Cleveland Ave W4 ....111 D2
Hampton TW12 ....173 B3
Merton SW20 ....179 B1
Cleveland Cres WD6 ....11 A6
Cleveland Ct Ealing W13 ....87 B2
Southall UB2 ....107 D2
Cleveland Gdns N4,N15 ....51 A4
W2 ....92 A1 236 A1
Barnes SW13 ....133 D3
Hendon NW2 ....68 D6
Worcester Park KT4 ....215 D6
Cleveland Gr 33 E1 ....96 C3
Cleveland Ho 7 N2 ....30 B1
Cleveland Inf Sch IG1 ....78 D5
Cleveland Jun Sch IG1 ....78 D5
Cleveland Mans 4 NW6 ....69 B1
8 SW9 ....138 C5
W9 ....91 C3
Cleveland Mews W1 ....239 A4
Cleveland Park Ave E17 ....53 C5
Cleveland Park Cres E17 ....53 C5
Cleveland Pk TW19 ....148 A5
Cleveland Pl SW1 ....249 B4
Cleveland Rd DA16 ....145 D3
N1 ....73 B1
14 W4 ....111 A3
Barnes SW13 ....133 D3
Ealing W13 ....87 B2
Edmonton N9 ....18 B4
Ilford IG1 ....78 D5
Isleworth TW7 ....131 A1
Cleveland Rd *continued*
New Malden KT3 ....199 C5
Wanstead E18 ....55 A6
Worcester Park KT4 ....215 C6
Cleveland Rise SM4 ....200 D2
Cleveland Row
SW1 ....115 C5 249 B3
Cleveland Sq W2 ....92 A1 236 A1
Cleveland St W1 ....93 C3 239 A5
Clevelands The IG11 ....79 A2
Cleveland Terr
W2 ....92 A1 236 B2
Cleveland Way E1 ....96 C3
Cleveley Cres W5 ....88 B5
Cleveleys Rd E5 ....74 B5
Clevely Cl SE7 ....121 D2
Clevendon Cl N16 ....73 D5
Cleve Rd DA14 ....168 D1
NW6 ....69 D1
Cleverly Cotts W12 ....111 D5
Cleverly Est W12 ....112 A6
Cleves Ct KT6 ....198 A3
Cleves Prim Sch E6 ....99 D6
Cleves Rd E6 ....99 D5
Richmond TW10 ....153 C1
Cleves Way
Ashford TW16 ....171 D4
Hampton TW12 ....173 B3
Ruislip HA4 ....40 D1
Clewer Cres HA3 ....24 B2
Clewer Ct 2 E10 ....53 C1
Clewer Ho 8 SE2 ....124 D4
Cley Ho SE4 ....140 D1
Clichy Ho 22 E1 ....96 C2
Clifden Centre (Richmond Adult & Com Coll)
TW1 ....152 D3
Clifden Ho 6 TW8 ....131 D6
Clifden Rd E5 ....74 D3
Brentford TW8 ....131 D6
Twickenham TW1 ....152 D3
Cliff Ct 5 NW1 ....71 D2
Cliffe Ho 4 SE10 ....120 D1
Cliffe Rd CR2 ....221 B3
Cliffe Wlk 2 SM1 ....218 A3
Clifford Ave BR7 ....188 B4
Mortlake SW14 ....133 A3
Wallington SM6 ....219 C4
Clifford Cl UB5 ....85 A6
Clifford Ct NW10 ....67 C4
W2 ....91 D2
Wandsworth SW18 ....158 B4
Clifford Dr SW9 ....138 D1
Clifford Gdns NW10 ....90 C5
Hayes UB3 ....105 B2
Clifford Gr TW15 ....170 C6
Clifford Haigh Ho SW6 ....134 D5
Clifford Ho W14 ....254 C3
2 Beckenham BR3 ....185 D4
Clifford Rd E16 ....98 D3
N9 ....18 C5
Barnet EN5 ....1 D2
Chingford E17 ....36 A1
Croydon SE25 ....206 A5
Hounslow TW4 ....128 D2
Richmond TW10 ....153 D2
Wembley HA0 ....87 D6
Clifford's Inn Pas EC4 ....241 A1
Clifford St W1 ....115 C6 249 A5
Clifford Way NW10 ....67 D4
Cliff Rd NW1 ....71 D2
Cliffsend Ho 23 SW9 ....138 C4
Cliff Terr SE8 ....141 C3
Cliffview Rd SE13 ....141 C2
Cliff Villas NW1 ....71 D2
Cliff Wlk E16 ....98 D2
Clifton Ave E17 ....52 D6
N3 ....29 B2
Feltham TW13 ....150 C1
Shepherd's Bush W12 ....111 D5
Stanmore HA7 ....25 B1
Wembley HA9 ....66 B2
Clifton Cl 8 BR6 ....227 A3
Clifton Cres SE15 ....140 B5
Clifton Ct N4 ....72 C6
NW8 ....236 C6
SE15 ....140 B5
2 Beckenham BR3 ....185 D2
Putney SW15 ....156 D6
South Norwood SE25 ....205 C4
9 Stanwell TW19 ....148 A5
Surbiton KT5 ....198 B2
3 Woodford IG8 ....37 A4
Clifton Gate SW10 ....266 A6
Clifton Gdns N15 ....51 D3
2 NW11 ....47 B3
W4 ....111 B2
W9 ....92 A3 236 A5
Enfield EN2 ....16 A6
Hillingdon UB10 ....82 D5
Clifton Gr E8 ....74 A2
Clifton Hill NW8 ....92 A6 229 A5
Clifton Ho E11 ....76 C6
E2 ....243 C6
Clifton Lodge (Brunel Univ Coll Twickenham Campus)
TW1 ....153 B6
Clifton Mans 4 SW9 ....138 C1
Clifton Mews SE25 ....205 C5
Clifton Par TW13 ....172 C6
Clifton Park Ave SW20 ....178 C1
Clifton Pl SE16 ....118 C4
W2 ....236 D1
Clifton Prim Sch UB2 ....107 A2
Clifton Rd E16 ....98 C2
E7 ....77 D2
N3 ....30 A2
N8 ....49 D3
NW10 ....90 A5
W9 ....92 A3 236 B6

Clifton Rd *continued*
Bexley DA16 ... 146 C2
Greenford UB6 ... 86 B3
Harlington TW6 ... 126 D2
Harrow HA3 ... 44 B4
Ilford IG2 ... 57 B3
Isleworth TW7 ... 130 C3
Kingston KT2 ... 176 B2
Sidcup DA14 ... 189 C6
Southall UB2 ... 107 A2
South Norwood SE25 ... 205 C5
Teddington TW11 ... 174 C6
Wallington SM6 ... 219 B3
Wimbledon SW19 ... 178 D4
Wood Green N22 ... 31 C2
Clifton Rise SE14 ... 141 A5
Cliftons Roundabout
SE9,SE12 ... 165 C5
Clifton St EC2 ... 95 C3 243 A5
Clifton Terr N4 ... 72 C6
Clifton The KT6 ... 214 A6
Clifton Villas W9 ... 92 A2 236 A4
Cliftonville Ct SE12 ... 165 A3
Clifton Way SE15 ... 140 C5
Wembley HA0 ... 88 A6
Climsland Ho SE1 ... 251 B4
Clinch Ct 11 E16 ... 99 A2
Cline Ho SW15 ... 156 A6
Cline Rd N11 ... 31 C4
Clinger Ct N1 ... 95 C6
Clink St SE1 ... 117 B5 252 C4
Clinton Ave Bexley DA16 ... 146 A1
East Molesey KT8 ... 196 A5
Clinton Ho
New Malden KT3 ... 199 B1
6 Surbiton KT6 ... 197 D2
Clinton Rd E3 ... 97 A4
E7 ... 77 A4
N15 ... 51 B5
Clipper Cl 3 SE16 ... 118 D4
Clipper Ho E14 ... 120 A1
Clipper Way SE13 ... 142 A1
Clippesby Cl KT9 ... 214 B2
Clipstone Ho 10 SW15 ... 156 A6
Clipstone Mews W1 ... 239 A4
Clipstone Rd TW3 ... 129 C2
Clipstone St W1 ... 93 C2 239 A4
Clissold Cl N2 ... 48 D6
Clissold Cres N16 ... 73 B4
Clissold Ct N4 ... 73 A6
Clissold Ho 4 N16 ... 73 B6
Clissold Rd N16 ... 73 B5
Clitheroe Ave HA2 ... 41 C1
Clitheroe Gdns WD19 ... 22 D6
Clitheroe Rd SW9 ... 138 A3
Clitherow Ave W7 ... 109 A3
Clitherow Rd TW8 ... 109 C1
Clitterhouse Cres NW2 ... 46 C1
Clitterhouse Jun & Inf Schs
NW2 ... 68 D6
Clitterhouse Rd NW2 ... 46 C1
Clive Ave N18 ... 34 A4
Clive Ct W9 ... 236 B6
Streatham SW16 ... 181 D5
Tolworth KT6 ... 214 C6
Cliveden Cl N12 ... 30 A6
Cliveden Pl
SW1 ... 115 A2 258 A4
Shepperton TW17 ... 193 A3
Cliveden Rd SW19 ... 179 B2
Clivedon Ct W13 ... 87 B2
Clivedon Rd E4 ... 36 C5
Clive Ho SE10 ... 142 A6
18 SW8 ... 137 D3
3 Croydon CR0 ... 205 D1
Clive Lloyd Ho N15 ... 51 A4
Clive Lo NW4 ... 46 D3
Clive Rd Belvedere DA17 ... 125 C2
Enfield EN1 ... 6 A1
Feltham TW14 ... 150 A5
Mitcham SW19 ... 180 C4
Teddington TW1 ... 175 A6
West Norwood SE21,SE27 ... 161 B1
Clivesdale Dr UB3 ... 106 B5
Clive Way EN1 ... 6 A1
Cloak La EC4 ... 117 B6 252 C6
Clochar Ct NW10 ... 89 D6
Clock Ct E11 ... 55 B5
Clock Ho E17 ... 54 B5
N16 ... 51 D2
Clock Ho The EN2 ... 5 D6
Clockhouse Ave IG11 ... 101 A6
Clockhouse Cl SW19 ... 156 C2
Clock House Ct 1 BR3 ... 185 A1
Clockhouse Junc N13 ... 32 C5
Clockhouse La TW14,
TW15 ... 148 D2
Clockhouse Par N13 ... 32 C5
Clock House Par E11 ... 55 B3
Clockhouse Pl SW15 ... 157 A5
Clock House Rd BR3 ... 185 A1
Clockhouse Rdbt TW14 ... 149 A3
Clock House Sta BR3 ... 185 A2
Clockhouse The SW19 ... 156 C1
Clock Tower Mews N1 ... 235 B5
Thamesmead SE28 ... 124 B6
Clock Tower Pl N7 ... 72 A2
Clock Tower Rd TW7 ... 130 D2
Cloister Cl TW11 ... 175 B5
Cloister Gdns HA8 ... 27 A5
Croydon SE25 ... 206 B3
Cloister Rd NW2 ... 69 B6
W3 ... 89 A2
Cloisters Ave BR1,BR2 ... 210 B4
Cloisters Ct DA7 ... 147 D2
N6 ... 49 B1
Cloisters The 22 SW9 ... 138 C4
Clonard Way HA5 ... 23 C4
Clonbrock Rd N16 ... 73 C4
Cloncurry St SW6 ... 134 D3
Clone Ct 4 W12 ... 111 C3
Clone The 5 KT2 ... 176 D3
Clonmel Cl HA2 ... 42 B1
Clonmell Rd N17 ... 51 B6
Clonmel Rd TW11 ... 174 B6
Fulham SW6 ... 135 B4 264 D2
Clonmore St SW18 ... 157 B3
Cloonmore Ave BR6 ... 227 D4
Clorane Gdns NW3 ... 69 C5
Close The BR5 ... 211 C3
DA14 ... 190 B5
N10 ... 31 B1
N14 ... 15 D2
N20 ... 13 B2
Beckenham BR3 ... 207 A5
Cheam SM3 ... 201 B2
Chingford E4 ... 36 A3
Cockfosters EN4 ... 14 D6
Croydon SE25 ... 206 A3
Dagenham RM6 ... 59 A3
Hillingdon UB10 ... 82 C6
Hounslow TW7 ... 130 B3
Ilford IG2 ... 57 C3
Kingston KT3 ... 177 A1
Mitcham CR4 ... 202 D5
Mortlake TW9 ... 132 D2
Pinner HA5 ... 40 C2
Pinner HA5 ... 41 B2
1 Sidcup DA5 ... 169 C4
Surbiton KT6 ... 198 A3
Wembley HA0 ... 66 A2
Wembley HA9 ... 67 A5
Cloth Ct EC1 ... 241 D3
Cloth Fair EC1 ... 94 D2 241 D3
Clothier Ho SE7 ... 122 A1
Clothier St EC3 ... 243 B2
Cloth St EC1 ... 95 A2 242 A4
Clothworkers Rd SE18 ... 145 B5
Cloudesdale Rd SW17 ... 159 B2
Cloudesley Mans N1 ... 234 B5
Cloudesley Pl N1 ... 94 C6 234 B5
Cloudesley Rd DA7 ... 147 B4
N1 ... 94 C6 234 A5
Cloudesley Sq
N1 ... 94 C6 234 B6
Cloudesley St N1 ... 94 C6 234 B5
Clouston Cl SM6 ... 220 A3
Clova Rd E7 ... 77 A3
Clove Cres E14 ... 120 B6
Clovelly Ave NW9 ... 45 D5
Uxbridge UB10 ... 61 A4
Clovelly Cl Pinner HA5 ... 40 C6
Uxbridge UB10 ... 61 A4
Clovelly Ct NW2 ... 68 C3
Clovelly Gdns EN1 ... 17 C4
Clovelly Ho W2 ... 236 A2
Clovelly Rd DA7 ... 147 A6
N8 ... 49 D5
W4 ... 111 B4
W5 ... 109 C4
Hounslow TW3 ... 129 C3
Clovelly Way BR6 ... 211 D3
E1 ... 96 C1
Harrow HA2 ... 63 B6
Clover Cl E11 ... 76 B6
Cloverdale Gdns DA15 ... 167 D5
Clover Ho TW3 ... 130 A4
Cloverleys IG10 ... 21 D6
Clover Mews SW3 ... 267 D6
Clover Way SM6 ... 203 A1
Clove St 9 E13 ... 99 A3
Clowders Rd SE6 ... 163 B1
Clowes Ho 3 SW4 ... 138 A1
Clowser Cl 4 SM1 ... 218 A3
Cloysters Gn E1 ... 118 A5
Cloyster Wood HA8 ... 25 D4
Club Gardens Rd BR2 ... 209 A2
Club Row E2 ... 95 D3 243 C6
Clumps The TW15 ... 171 B6
Clunbury Ave UB2 ... 107 B1
Clunbury St N1 ... 235 D3
Clunie Ho SW1 ... 257 D6
Cluny Mews SW5 ... 255 A3
Cluny Pl SE1 ... 117 C3 263 A6
Cluse Ct N1 ... 235 A4
Clutton St E14 ... 97 D2
Clydach Rd EN1 ... 5 D1
Clyde Cir N15 ... 51 C5
Clyde Ct NW1 ... 232 D4
Clyde Flats SW6 ... 264 C4
Clyde Ho 9 KT2 ... 175 D2
Clyde Pl E10 ... 53 D2
Clyde Rd N15 ... 51 C5
N22 ... 31 D2
Croydon CR0 ... 221 D6
Stanwell TW19 ... 148 A3
Sutton SM1 ... 217 C3
Wallington SM6 ... 219 C2
Clydesdale EN3 ... 6 D1
Clydesdale Ave HA7 ... 43 D6
Clydesdale Cl
Borehamwood WD6 ... 11 B6
Isleworth TW7 ... 130 D2
Clydesdale Ct N20 ... 14 B3
Clydesdale Gdns TW10 ... 132 D1
Clydesdale Ho DA18 ... 125 A4
4 W11 ... 91 B1
Clydesdale Path WD6 ... 11 B6
Clydesdale Rd W11 ... 91 B1
Clyde St SE8 ... 141 B6
Clyde Terr SE23 ... 162 C2
Clyde Vale SE23 ... 162 C2
Clyfford Rd HA4 ... 61 D4
Clymping Dene TW14 ... 150 B4
Clynes Ho 3 E2 ... 96 D4
6 Dagenham RM10 ... 81 C5
Hayes UB4 ... 84 A4
Clyro Ct N4 ... 50 B1
Clyston St SW8 ... 137 C3
Clytha Ct SE27 ... 183 A6
Coach & Horses Yd W1 ... 249 A6
Coach House La N5 ... 72 D4
Wimbledon SW19 ... 156 D1
Coach House Mews
SE23 ... 162 D5
Coach House Yd NW3 ... 70 B4
Coachmaker Mews 5
SW9 ... 138 A2
Coachman Lo N12 ... 30 A5
Coalbrook Mans 3
SW12 ... 159 B3
Coaldale Wlk SE21 ... 161 A4
Coalecroft Rd SW15 ... 156 C6
Coalport Ho SE11 ... 261 A4
Coal Wharf Rd W12 ... 112 D5
Coates Ave SW18 ... 158 C5
Coates Ct NW3 ... 70 C3
Coates Hill Rd BR1 ... 188 C1
Coates Rd WD6 ... 9 D4
Coate St E2 ... 96 A5
Coates Wlk TW8 ... 110 A1
Cobbett Rd SE9 ... 144 A2
Twickenham TW2 ... 151 C3
Cobbetts Ave IG4 ... 55 D4
Cobbett St SW8 ... 138 B5 270 D3
Cobble La N1 ... 72 D1
Cobble Mews N4,N5 ... 73 A5
Cobbler's Wlk
Teddington KT1,TW11 ... 175 A2
Teddington TW11 ... 174 D3
Cobblestone Pl CR0 ... 205 A1
Cobbold Ct SW1 ... 259 C4
Cobbold Ind Est NW10 ... 67 D2
Cobbold Mews W12 ... 111 D4
Cobbold Rd E11 ... 76 D5
NW10 ... 67 D2
W12 ... 111 D4
Cobb's Hall 1 SW6 ... 134 D6
Cobbs Rd TW4 ... 129 B1
Cobb St E1 ... 243 C3
Cob Cl WD6 ... 11 A6
Cobden Bldgs WC1 ... 233 C2
Cobden Ct 9 SE28 ... 124 C5
Cobden Ho 7 E2 ... 96 A4
NW1 ... 232 A4
Cobden Mews SE26 ... 184 B5
Cobden Rd BR6 ... 227 B4
E11 ... 76 C6
Croydon SE25 ... 206 A4
Cobham 21 NW9 ... 27 D1
Cobham Ave KT3 ... 200 A4
Cobham Cl 2 DA15 ... 168 B5
SW11 ... 158 C5
Bromley BR2 ... 210 A2
Edgware HA8 ... 26 D1
Enfield EN1 ... 6 A2
Wallington SM6 ... 220 A2
Cobham Ct CR4 ... 180 B1
Cobham Ho IG11 ... 101 A6
Cobham Mews 3 NW1 ... 71 D1
Cobham Pl DA6 ... 168 D6
Cobham Rd N22 ... 50 D6
Chingford E17 ... 36 A2
Heston TW5 ... 128 C5
Ilford IG3 ... 79 C5
Kingston KT1,KT2 ... 176 C1
Cobland Rd SE12 ... 187 C6
Coborn Mews 9 E3 ... 97 B4
Coborn Rd E3 ... 97 B4
Coborn St E3 ... 97 B4
Cobourg Prim Sch SE5 ... 139 D6
Cobourg Rd SE5 ... 139 D6
Cobourg St NW1 ... 93 C4 232 B1
Coburg Cl SW1 ... 259 B4
Coburg Cres SW2 ... 160 C3
Coburg Dwellings 10
E1 ... 118 C6
Coburg Gdns IG5 ... 37 D1
Coburg Rd N22 ... 32 B1
Cochrane Cl NW8 ... 229 D3
Cochrane Ct 3 E10 ... 53 C1
Cochrane Mews
NW8 ... 92 B5 229 D3
Cochrane Rd SW19 ... 179 B3
Cochrane St
NW8 ... 92 B5 229 D3
Coci Ho W14 ... 254 D3
Cockburn Ho SW1 ... 259 D1
Cockerell Rd E17 ... 53 A3
Cockfosters Par EN4 ... 3 A1
Cockfosters Rd EN4 ... 2 D3
Cockfosters Sta EN4 ... 3 A1
Cock Hill E1 ... 243 B3
Cock La EC1 ... 94 D2 241 D3
Cockpit Yd WC1 ... 240 D4
Cocks Cres KT3 ... 199 D5
Cocksett Ave BR6 ... 227 C2
Cockspur Ct SW1 ... 249 D4
Cockspur St
SW1 ... 115 D5 249 D4
Cocksure La DA14 ... 191 C6
Coda Ctr The
SW6 ... 135 A4 264 B2
Code St E1 ... 95 D3 243 D5
Codicote Ho 22 SE8 ... 118 D2
Codicote Terr N4 ... 73 A6
Codling Cl 13 E1 ... 118 A5
Codling Way HA0 ... 65 D4
Codrington Ct SE16 ... 119 A5
Codrington Hill SE23 ... 163 A4
Codrington Ho 7 E1 ... 96 B3
Codrington Mews W11 ... 91 A1
Cody Cl Harrow HA3 ... 43 D6
Wallington SM6 ... 219 D1
Cody Rd E16 ... 98 B3
Coe Ave SE25 ... 206 A3
Coerdale Ct EN3 ... 7 A6
Coe's Alley EN5 ... 1 A1
Cofers Circ HA9 ... 66 D5
Coffey St SE8 ... 141 C5
Cogan Ave E17 ... 35 A2
Cohen Ho NW7 ... 28 A6
Cohen Lo E5 ... 75 A3
Coin St SE1 ... 116 C5 251 A4
Coity Rd NW5 ... 71 A2
Cokers La SE21 ... 161 B3
Coke St E1 ... 96 A1
Colab Ct N22 ... 32 C2
Colas Mews 7 NW6 ... 91 C6
Colbeck Mews
SW5 ... 113 D2 255 D3
Colbeck Rd HA1 ... 42 A2
Colberg Pl N16 ... 51 D2
Colbert 1 SE5 ... 139 D4
Colborne Ho 7 E14 ... 119 C6
Colborne Way KT4 ... 216 C6
Colbrook Ave UB3 ... 105 B3
Colbrook Cl UB3 ... 105 B3
Colburn Ave HA5 ... 23 A4
Colburn Way SM1 ... 218 B5
Colby Rd
Walton-on-T KT12 ... 194 A1
West Norwood SE19 ... 183 C5
Colchester Ave E12 ... 78 B5
Colchester Dr HA5 ... 40 D4
Colchester Ho 17 SW8 ... 137 D3
Colchester Rd E10 ... 54 A2
E17 ... 53 C3
HA8 ... 27 A3
Pinner HA6 ... 22 A1
Colchester St E1 ... 243 D2
Colchester Villas CR7 ... 204 C3
Coldbath Sq EC1 ... 241 A6
Coldbath St SE13 ... 141 D3
Coldblow La SE14 ... 140 D6
Coldershaw Rd W13 ... 109 A4
Coldfall Ave N10 ... 31 A1
Coldfall Prim Sch N10 ... 30 D1
Coldham Ct N22 ... 32 D2
Coldham Gr EN3 ... 7 A6
Coldharbour E14 ... 120 A5
Coldharbour Crest SE9 ... 166 C1
Coldharbour Ind Est
SE5 ... 139 A3
Coldharbour La SW9 ... 138 D2
Bushey WD23 ... 8 A6
Hayes UB3 ... 106 A5
Coldharbour Lane Ho
UB3 ... 106 A5
Coldharbour Pl SE5 ... 139 B3
Coldharbour Rd CR0 ... 220 C3
Coldharbour Sports Ctr
SE9 ... 166 C2
Coldharbour Way CR0 ... 220 C3
Coldstream Gdns SW18 ... 157 B5
Colebeck Mews N1 ... 72 D2
Colebert Ave E1 ... 96 C3
Colebert Ho 20 E1 ... 96 C3
Colebrook Cl SW19 ... 156 D4
Colebrook Ct SW3 ... 257 B3
Colebrooke Ave W13 ... 87 B1
Colebrooke Ct DA14 ... 190 B6
Colebrooke Dr E11 ... 55 C2
Colebrooke Pl N1 ... 234 D5
Colebrooke Row
N1 ... 94 D5 234 C4
N1 ... 234 C5
Colebrooke Sch
N1 ... 94 D5 234 D4
Colebrook Ho 1 E14 ... 97 D1
Colebrook Rd SW16 ... 182 A2
Colebrook Rise BR2 ... 186 C1
Colebrook Way N11 ... 31 B5
Coleby Path 21 SE5 ... 139 B5
Colechurch Ho 8 SE1 ... 118 A1
Cole Cl SE28 ... 124 B5
Cole Court Lo 7 TW1 ... 153 A4
Coledale Dr HA7 ... 25 C2
Coleford Rd SW18 ... 158 A6
Cole Gdns TW5 ... 128 A5
Colegrave Prim Sch E15 ... 76 B3
Colegrave Rd E15 ... 76 B3
Colegrove Rd SE15 ... 139 D6
Coleherne Ct
SW10 ... 113 D1 255 D1
Coleherne Mans SW5 ... 255 D2
Coleherne Mews
SW10 ... 113 D1 255 C1
Coleherne Rd
SW10 ... 113 D1 255 C1
Colehill Gdns SW6 ... 264 A1
Colehill La SW6 ... 135 A4 264 B1
Cole Ho SE1 ... 251 B1
Coleman Cl SE25 ... 184 A1
Coleman Ct SW18 ... 157 C4
Coleman Fields
N1 ... 95 A6 235 B6
Coleman Mans N19 ... 50 A2
Coleman Rd SE5 ... 139 C5
Belvedere DA17 ... 125 C2
Dagenham RM9 ... 81 A2
Colemans Heath SE9 ... 166 D1
Coleman St EC2 ... 95 B1 242 C2
Coleman St Bldgs EC2 ... 242 C2
Colenso Dr NW7 ... 28 A3
Colenso Rd E5 ... 74 C4
Ilford IG2 ... 57 C2
Cole Park Gdns TW1 ... 153 A5
Cole Park Rd TW1 ... 153 A5
Cole Park View 2 TW1 ... 153 A5
Colepits Wood Rd SE9 ... 167 B6
Coleraine Park Prim Sch
N17 ... 34 B2
Coleraine Rd N8,N22 ... 50 C6
SE3 ... 142 D6
Cole Rd TW1 ... 153 A5
Coleridge Ave E12 ... 78 A2
Carshalton SM1 ... 218 C4
Coleridge Cl SW8 ... 137 B3
Coleridge Ct W14 ... 112 D3
Coleridge Ct *continued*
11 New Barnet EN5 ... 13 D6
2 Richmond TW10 ... 175 D6
Coleridge Gdns NW6 ... 70 A1
Coleridge Ho SE17 ... 262 B2
SW1 ... 259 B1
Coleridge Prim Sch N8 ... 49 D2
Coleridge Rd E17 ... 53 B5
N12 ... 30 A5
N4,N7 ... 72 C6
N8 ... 49 D3
Ashford TW15 ... 170 B6
Croydon CR0 ... 206 C2
Coleridge Sq W13 ... 87 A1
Coleridge Way Hayes UB4 ... 84 A1
West Drayton UB7 ... 104 B2
Coleridge Wlk NW11 ... 47 C5
Colerne Ct NW4 ... 29 A1
Colesburg Rd BR3 ... 185 B1
Coles Cres HA2 ... 63 D6
Coles Ct SW11 ... 266 D1
Coles Gn WD23 ... 8 A3
Coles Green Ct NW2 ... 68 A6
Coles Green Rd NW2 ... 68 B6
Coleshill Flats SW1 ... 258 B3
Coleshill Rd TW11 ... 174 C4
Cole St SE1 ... 117 A4 252 B1
Colestown St 4 SW11 ... 136 C3
Coleswood N20 ... 14 C3
Colesworth Ho 1 HA8 ... 27 A1
Colet Cl N13 ... 32 D4
Colet Gdns W14 ... 112 D2
Colet Ho SE17 ... 261 D1
Colette Ct 5 SE16 ... 118 D4
Coley St WC1 ... 94 B3 240 D5
Colfe & Hatchcliffe's Glebe
SE13 ... 163 D6
Colfe Rd SE23 ... 163 A3
Colfe's Prep Sch SE12 ... 165 A5
Colfe's Sch SE12 ... 165 B5
Colgate Ct EN5 ... 13 A6
Colgate Ho SE13 ... 141 D3
Colgate Pl EN3 ... 7 C6
Colham Ave UB7 ... 104 A5
Colham Green Rd UB8 ... 82 C2
Colham Manor Jun & Inf
Schs UB8 ... 82 C1
Colham Rd UB8 ... 82 B3
Colina Mews N8,N15 ... 50 D5
Colina Rd N8,N15 ... 50 D4
Colin Blanchard Ho
SE4 ... 141 C3
Colin Cl NW9 ... 45 C5
Coney Hall BR4 ... 224 D5
Croydon CR0 ... 223 B5
Colin Cres NW9 ... 45 D5
Colin Ct SW16 ... 159 D2
Colindale Ave NW9 ... 45 C6
Colindale Hospl NW9 ... 45 C6
Colindale Prim Sch NW9 ... 45 D5
Colindale Sta NW9 ... 45 C6
Colindeep Gdns NW4 ... 46 A5
Colindeep La NW9,NW4 ... 45 D5
Colin Dr NW9 ... 45 D4
Colinette Rd SW15 ... 134 C1
Colin Gdns NW9 ... 45 D5
Colin Par NW9 ... 45 C5
Colin Park Rd NW9 ... 45 C5
Colin Rd NW10 ... 68 A2
Colinsdale N1 ... 234 C5
Colinton Rd IG3 ... 80 B6
Colin Winter Ho 37 E1 ... 96 C3
Coliston Pass SW18 ... 157 C4
Coliston Rd SW18 ... 157 C4
Collamore Ave SW18 ... 158 C3
Collapit Cl HA1 ... 41 D3
Collard Pl NW1 ... 71 B1
College App SE10 ... 142 A6
College Ave HA3 ... 24 C2
College Cl E5 ... 74 C3
Edmonton N18 ... 33 D5
Harrow HA3 ... 24 C3
Twickenham TW2 ... 152 B3
College Cres NW3 ... 70 B2
College Cross N1 ... 72 C1
College Ct NW3 ... 70 B2
SW3 ... 114 D1 257 D1
3 W6 ... 112 C1
Croydon CR0 ... 222 A6
Ealing W5 ... 110 A6
Enfield EN3 ... 18 C6
College Dr Ruislip HA4 ... 40 A2
Thames Ditton KT7 ... 196 C2
College Fields Bsns Ctr
SW19 ... 180 C2
College Gdns
Chingford E4 ... 20 A3
Dulwich SE21 ... 161 C3
Edmonton N18 ... 34 A5
Enfield EN2 ... 5 B4
New Malden KT3 ... 199 D4
Redbridge IG4 ... 56 A4
Upper Tooting SW17 ... 158 C2
College Gn BR1 ... 187 A2
South Norwood SE19 ... 183 C3
College Gr NW1 ... 232 C6
College Hill EC4 ... 252 B6
College Hill Rd HA3 ... 24 C3
College La NW5 ... 71 B4
College Park Cl SE13 ... 142 B1
College Park Rd N17 ... 33 D4
College Park Sch W2 ... 91 D1
College Pl E17 ... 54 C5
NW1 ... 93 C6 232 B5
SW10 ... 266 A4
College Pt E15 ... 76 D2
College Rd BR1 ... 187 A3
E17 ... 54 A4
NW10 ... 90 C5
Dulwich SE19,SE21 ... 161 C2
College Rd *continued*
Ealing W13 ... 87 B1
Enfield EN2 ... 5 B3
Harrow HA1 ... 42 C3
Harrow HA3 ... 24 C2
Hounslow TW7 ... 130 D4
Mitcham SW19 ... 180 B4
South Croydon CR0 ... 221 B6
Southgate N21 ... 16 C2
Tottenham N17 ... 33 D4
Wembley HA9 ... 43 D1
College Rdbt 1 KT1 ... 198 A6
College St EC4 ... 117 A6 252 B6
College Terr E3 ... 97 B4
N3 ... 29 B1
College View SE9 ... 165 D3
College Way
Ashford TW15 ... 170 B6
Hayes UB3 ... 106 A6
College Wlk 10 KT1 ... 198 A6
Collent Ho 12 E9 ... 74 C2
Collent St E9 ... 74 C2
Collerston Ho SE10 ... 120 D1
Colless Rd N15 ... 51 D4
Collette Ct SE25 ... 205 C4
Collette Ho N16 ... 51 D1
Collett Rd SE16 ... 118 A3
Collett Way UB2 ... 107 D4
Colley Ho 12 N7 ... 71 D3
Collier Cl E16 ... 122 D6
West Ewell KT19 ... 214 D2
Collier Dr HA8 ... 26 C1
Collier St N1 ... 94 B5 233 C3
Colliers Water La CR7 ... 204 C4
Colliers Wood BR2 ... 225 D3
Mitcham SW19 ... 180 B3
Collier's Wood Sta
SW19 ... 180 B3
Collindale Ave DA15 ... 168 A3
DA8 ... 147 D6
Collingbourne Rd W12 ... 112 B5
Collingham Gdns
SW5 ... 113 D2 255 D3
Collingham Pl
SW5 ... 113 D2 255 D4
Collingham Rd
SW5 ... 113 D2 255 D3
Collings Cl N22 ... 32 B4
Collington Ho SE7 ... 143 B6
Collington St SE10 ... 120 B1
Collingtree Rd SE26 ... 184 C6
Collingwood Ave N10 ... 49 A5
Tolworth KT5 ... 199 A1
Collingwood Cl
2 Penge SE20 ... 184 B2
Twickenham TW2,TW4 ... 151 C4
Collingwood Ct NW4 ... 46 C4
New Barnet EN5 ... 13 D6
Collingwood Ho 27 E1 ... 96 B3
Collingwood Rd N15 ... 51 C5
Hillingdon UB8 ... 82 D3
Mitcham CR4 ... 202 C6
Sutton SM1 ... 217 C4
Collingwood Sch SM6 ... 219 B3
Collingwood St E1 ... 96 B3
Collins Ave HA7 ... 26 A1
Collins Ct E8 ... 74 A2
Collins Dr HA4 ... 62 C6
Collins Ho 4 E14 ... 120 A6
6 SE10 ... 120 D1
8 Barking IG11 ... 78 D1
Collinson Ct SE1 ... 252 A1
Edgware HA8 ... 26 B6
Collinson Ho 13 SE15 ... 140 A5
Collinson St SE1 ... 252 A1
Collinson Wlk SE1 ... 252 A1
Collins Rd N5,N16 ... 73 A4
Collins Sq SE3 ... 142 D3
Collins St SE3 ... 142 C3
Collins Yd N1 ... 234 C5
Collinwood Ave EN3 ... 6 C2
Collinwood Gdns IG5 ... 56 C5
Collis Prim Sch TW11 ... 175 B4
Coll of Liberal Arts
SM1 ... 217 D3
Coll of North East London
The
N11 ... 31 D3
N15 ... 51 D5
Coll of NW London
(Willesden Centre) The
NW10 ... 67 D3
Coll Sharp Ct 42 E2 ... 95 D4
Coll's Rd SE15 ... 140 C4
Collyer Ave CR0 ... 220 A4
Collyer Pl SE15 ... 140 A4
Collyer Rd CR0 ... 220 A4
Colman Ct N12 ... 30 A4
Stanmore HA7 ... 25 B4
Colman Rd E16 ... 99 C2
Colmans Wharf 6 E14 ... 97 D2
Colmar Cl 3 E1 ... 96 D3
Colmer Pl HA3 ... 24 B3
Colmer Rd SW16 ... 182 A3
Colmore Mews SE15 ... 140 B4
Colmore Rd EN3 ... 6 C1
Colnbrook Ct SW17 ... 180 B6
Colnbrook St SE1 ... 261 C6
Colne Ct Ealing W7 ... 86 B1
West Ewell KT19 ... 215 A4
Colne Ho NW8 ... 236 D5
Barking IG11 ... 78 D2
Colne Rd E5 ... 75 A4
Southgate N21 ... 17 B4
Twickenham TW1,TW2 ... 152 C3
Colne St E13 ... 99 A4
Colney Hatch N10 ... 31 A3

Colney Hatch La N10 ...31 A3
Cologne Rd SW11 ...136 B1
Coloma Convent Girls Sch
CR0 ...222 D5
Colombo Rd IG1 ...57 A2
Colombo St SE1 ...251 C3
Colomb St SE10 ...120 C1
Colonades The 4 SE5 ...139 B4
Colonels Wlk EN2 ...4 D2
Colonial Ave TW2 ...152 A5
Colonial Dr W4 ...111 A2
Colonial Rd TW14 ...149 C4
Colonnade WC1 ...240 B5
Colonnades The 6 E8 ...74 B2
Colonnade The 11 SE8 ...119 B2
Colosseum Ct N3 ...29 B1
Colroy Ct NW4 ...47 A4
Colson Rd CR0 ...221 C6
Colson Way SW16 ...181 C6
Colstead Ho 23 E1 ...96 B1
Colsterworth Rd N15 ...51 D5
Colston Ave SM1,SM5 ...218 C4
Colston Ct SM5 ...218 D4
Colston Rd E7 ...77 D2
Mortlake SW14 ...133 A1
Colthurst Cres N4 ...73 A6
Colthurst Dr N9 ...18 B1
Coltman Ho 1 E14 ...97 A1
SE10 ...142 A6
Colt Mews EN3 ...7 C6
Coltness Cres SE2 ...124 B1
Colton Gdns N17 ...51 A6
Colton Rd HA1 ...42 C4
Coltsfoot Dr UB7 ...82 A1
Columba Ho SE14 ...141 B4
Columbas Dr NW3 ...48 B1
Columbia Ave
Edgware HA8 ...26 D2
New Malden KT4 ...199 D2
Ruislip HA4 ...40 B1
Columbia Ct KT3 ...199 D2
Columbia Ho 16 E3 ...97 C4
Columbia Point 7
SE16 ...118 C3
Columbia Prim Sch E2 ...95 D4
Columbia Rd E13 ...98 D3
E2 ...95 D4
Columbine Ave E6 ...100 A2
Croydon CR2 ...220 D1
Columbus Gdns HA6 ...22 A2
Colveiw Ct SE9 ...165 D3
Colverson Ho 11 E1 ...96 C2
Colvestone Cres E8 ...73 D3
Colvestone Prim Sch E8 ...73 D3
Colville Gdns W11 ...91 B1
Colville Ho 33 E2 ...96 C5
W11 ...91 B1
Colville Mews W11 ...91 B1
Colville Pl W1 ...239 B3
Colville Prim Sch W11 ...91 B1
Colville Rd E11 ...76 A5
E17 ...35 A1
W11 ...91 B1
W3 ...110 D3
Edmonton N9 ...18 B3
Colville Sq W11 ...91 B1
Colville Sq Mews 6 W11 ...91 B1
Colville Terr W11 ...91 B1
Colvin Cl SE26 ...184 C5
Colvin Gdns Chingford E4 ...20 A1
Wanstead E11 ...55 B5
Colvin Rd E6 ...78 A1
Thornton Heath CR7 ...204 C4
Colwall Gdns IG8 ...37 A5
Colwall Ho 18 SW9 ...138 B3
Colwell Rd SE22 ...161 D6
Colwick Cl N6 ...49 D2
Colwith Rd W6 ...134 C6
Colwood Gdns SW19 ...180 B3
Colworth Gr SE17 ...262 B3
Colworth Rd E11 ...54 C2
Croydon CR0 ...206 A1
Colwyn Ave UB6 ...86 D5
Colwyn Cl SW16 ...181 C5
Colwyn Cres TW3 ...130 A4
Colwyn Gn NW9 ...45 C3
Colwyn Ho SE1 ...261 A5
Colwyn Rd NW2 ...68 B5
Colyer Cl SE9 ...166 D2
Colyer Ho SE2 ...124 D1
Colyton Cl DA16 ...146 D4
Wembley HA0 ...65 C2
Colyton Rd SE22 ...162 B6
Colyton Way N18 ...34 A5
Combe Ave SE3 ...142 D5
Combedale Rd SE10 ...121 A1
Combe Ho 20 W2 ...91 C2
Mortlake SW14 ...133 A3
Combe Hurst KT2 ...177 A5
Combe Lane Sta CR0 ...222 C3
Combemartin Rd SW18 ...157 A3
Combe Mews 4 SE3 ...142 D5
Comber Cl NW2 ...68 B6
Comber Gr SE5 ...139 A5
Comber Grove Prim Sch
SE5 ...139 A5
Comber Ho SE5 ...139 A5
Combermere Rd SW9 ...138 B2
Morden SM4 ...201 D4
Comberton 10 KT1 ...176 C1
Comberton Rd E5 ...74 B6
Combeside SE18 ...145 D5
Combes Rd RM9 ...81 B1
Combe The NW1 ...231 D1
Combwell Cres SE2 ...124 A3
Comely Bank Rd E17 ...54 A4
Comeragh Mews W14 ...254 B1
Comeragh Rd
W14 ...113 A1 254 B1
Comer Cres UB2 ...108 A4
Comerford Rd SE4 ...141 B1
Comet Cl E12 ...77 D4
Comet Pl SE8 ...141 C5
Comet St SE8 ...141 C5
Comins Ho SW4 ...159 C6
Commerce Est E18 ...37 C1
Commerce Rd
Brentford TW8 ...131 C5
Wood Green N22 ...32 B2
Commerce Way CR0 ...220 B6
Commercial Rd E1 ...96 C1
Edmonton N18 ...33 C4
Commercial St
E1 ...95 D2 243 C4
Commercial Way SE15 ...140 A5
Wembley NW10 ...88 D5
Commerell Pl SE10 ...120 D1
Commerell St SE10 ...120 C1
Commodore Ct SE8 ...141 C4
Commodore Ho 7 E14 ...120 A6
Commodore St E1 ...97 A3
Commondale SW15 ...134 C2
Common La KT10 ...213 A1
Common Rd
Barnes SW13 ...134 A2
Claygate KT10 ...213 A1
Stanmore HA7 ...8 C1
Commonside BR2 ...225 C4
Commonside Ct SW16 ...182 A4
Commonside E CR4 ...203 B6
Common The Ealing W5 ...110 A5
Southall UB2 ...106 D2
Stanmore HA7 ...8 D2
Common View SW15 ...134 C2
Commonwealth Ave
21 W12 ...112 B6
Hayes UB3 ...83 B1
Commonwealth Rd N17 ...34 A3
Commonwealth Way
SE2 ...124 C1
Community Cl
Cranford TW5 ...128 B4
Uxbridge UB10 ...61 A5
Community Coll The E9 ...74 D3
E9 ...96 D6
Community Rd E15 ...76 B3
Greenford UB6 ...86 A6
Como Rd SE23 ...163 A2
Compania Bldg 12 E1 ...118 D6
Compass Ct SE1 ...253 C3
Compass Hill TW10 ...153 D5
Compass Ho SE8 ...141 D3
W2 ...91 D1
Compass Point 9 E14 ...119 C6
Compayne Gdns NW6 ...69 D1
Compton Ave E6 ...99 D5
N1 ...72 D2
N6 ...48 C2
Wembley HA0 ...65 C4
Compton Cl 5 HA8 ...27 A3
NW1 ...231 D1
NW11 ...68 D5
SE15 ...139 D5
Ealing W13 ...87 A1
Esher KT10 ...212 B3
Compton Cres
Chessington KT9 ...214 A2
Chiswick W4 ...133 A6
Northolt UB5 ...84 D6
Tottenham N17 ...33 A3
Compton Ct Sutton SM1 ...218 A4
9 West Norwood SE19 ...183 C5
Compton High Sch & Sports
Coll UB5 ...85 A6
Compton Ho SW11 ...267 A2
Compton Lo N21 ...16 D3
Compton Pas EC1 ...241 D6
Compton Pl WC1 ...240 A6
South Oxhey WD19 ...23 A6
Compton Rd N1 ...72 D2
NW10 ...90 D4
Croydon CR0 ...206 B1
Hayes UB3 ...105 D6
Southgate N21 ...16 D3
Wimbledon SW19 ...179 B4
Compton Rise HA5 ...41 B4
Compton Sch The N12 ...30 C4
Compton St EC1 ...94 D3 241 D6
Compton Terr N1 ...72 D2
Southgate N21 ...16 C3
Comreddy Cl EN2 ...4 D4
Comus Ho SE17 ...263 A3
Comus Pl SE17 ...117 C2 263 A3
Comyn Rd SW11 ...136 C1
Comyns Cl E16 ...98 D2
Comyns Rd RM9 ...81 C1
Comyns The WD23 ...8 A3
Conal Ct SW16 ...181 D5
Conant Ho SE11 ...138 D6
Conant Mews 1 E1 ...118 A6
Concanon Rd SW2,SW4 ...138 B1
Concert Hall App
SE1 ...116 B5 250 D3
Concord Bsns Ctr W3 ...88 D2
Concord Cl UB5 ...85 A4
Concord Ct KT1 ...198 B6
Concord Ctr W12 ...112 D4
Concorde Cl
Hounslow TW3 ...129 D3
Uxbridge UB10 ...82 A5
Concorde Dr E6 ...100 B2
Concord Ho
Kingston KT3 ...199 C6
5 Tottenham N17 ...33 D3
Concordia Wharf E14 ...120 A5
Concord Rd Acton W3 ...88 D3
Enfield EN3 ...18 C6
Concourse The 7 N9 ...18 A2
Condell Rd SW8 ...137 C4 269 B1
Conder St E14 ...97 A1
Condor Path UB5 ...85 C5
Condover Cres SE18 ...144 D5
Condray Pl SW11 ...267 A3
Conduit Ct WC2 ...250 A6
Conduit Ho SE10 ...142 B4
Conduit La N18 ...34 C5
South Croydon CR0 ...222 A3
Conduit Mews
W2 ...92 B1 236 C1
Conduit Pas W2 ...236 C1
Conduit Pl W2 ...236 C1
Conduit Rd SE18 ...122 D1
Conduit St W1 ...115 C6 249 A6
Conduit Way NW10 ...67 A1
Conewood St N5 ...72 D5
Coney Acre SE21 ...161 A3
Coney Burrows E4 ...20 C2
Coney Gr UB8 ...82 C4
Coneygrove Path UB5 ...63 A2
Coney Hall Par BR4 ...224 C5
Coney Hall Rdbt BR4 ...224 C5
Coney Hill Rd BR4 ...224 D6
Coney Hill Sch BR2 ...224 D5
Coney Way SW8 ...270 D5
Conference Cl 3 E4 ...20 A2
Conference Ho UB8 ...83 A1
Conference Rd SE2 ...124 C2
Congers Ho SE8 ...141 C5
Congleton Gr SE18 ...123 A1
Congo Rd SE18 ...123 B1
Congress Rd SE2 ...124 C2
Congreve Ho 10 N16 ...73 C3
Congreve Rd SE9 ...144 B2
Congreve St
SE17 ...117 C2 263 A3
Congreve Wlk 6 E16 ...99 D2
Conical Cnr EN2 ...5 A3
Conifer Cl BR6 ...227 B4
Conifer Ct Ilford IG1 ...78 D2
23 Putney SW19 ...156 D3
Conifer Gdns Enfield EN1 ...17 C5
Streatham SW16 ...160 B1
Sutton SM1 ...217 D6
Conifer Ho SE4 ...141 B1
Conifers Cl TW11 ...175 C3
Conifer Way Hayes UB3 ...106 A6
Wembley HA0 ...65 C5
Coniger Rd SW6 ...135 C3
Coningham Ct SW10 ...266 B4
Coningham Mews W12 ...112 A5
Coningham Rd W12 ...112 B4
Coningsby Cotts W5 ...109 D4
Coningsby Ct 4 CR4 ...181 A1
Coningsby Gdns E4 ...35 D4
Coningsby Rd N4 ...50 D2
W5 ...109 D4
Conington Rd SE13 ...142 A3
Conisbee Ct 3 N14 ...15 C6
Conisborough Cres SE6 ...164 A1
Conisbrough NW1 ...232 A5
Coniscliffe Cl BR7 ...188 C2
Coniscliffe Rd N13 ...17 A1
Coniston NW1 ...232 A2
Coniston Ave DA16 ...145 C2
Barking IG11 ...79 C1
Ealing UB6 ...87 B4
Coniston Cl N20 ...14 A1
Barking IG11 ...79 C1
Barnes SW13 ...133 D5
Chiswick W4 ...133 A5
West Barnes SM4 ...200 D3
Coniston Ct 6 SE16 ...118 D4
W2 ...237 B1
Beckenham BR3 ...186 A2
Chessington KT9 ...214 A5
Edgware HA8 ...26 B5
Penge SE26 ...184 B4
3 Wallington SM6 ...219 B4
Conistone Way N7 ...72 A1
Coniston Gdns N9 ...18 C3
NW9 ...45 B4
Pinner HA5 ...40 A5
Redbridge IG4 ...56 A5
Sutton SM2 ...218 B2
Wembley HA9 ...43 C1
Coniston Ho 13 E3 ...97 B4
18 SE5 ...139 A5
Coniston Rd N10 ...31 B1
Catford BR1 ...186 C4
Croydon CR0 ...206 A2
Tottenham N17 ...34 A4
Twickenham TW2 ...151 D5
Coniston Way KT9 ...214 A5
Coniston Wlk E9 ...74 C3
Conlan St W10 ...91 A3
Conley Rd NW10 ...67 C2
Conley St SE10 ...120 C1
Connaught Ave
Ashford TW15 ...170 A6
Barnet, London EN4 ...14 D3
Chingford E4 ...20 B4
Enfield EN1 ...5 C3
Hounslow TW4 ...129 A1
Mortlake SW14 ...133 A1
Connaught Bsns Ctr
NW9 ...45 D4
Mitcham CR4 ...202 D4
Wallington CR0 ...220 B2
Connaught Cl E10 ...75 A6
W2 ...237 B1
Carshalton SM1 ...218 B6
Enfield EN1 ...5 C3
Hillingdon UB8 ...83 A3
Connaught Ct 10 E17 ...53 D5
1 Chingford E4 ...20 C4
Connaught Day Hospl
E11 ...54 C3
Connaught Dr NW11 ...47 C5
Connaught Gdns N10 ...49 B4
Edmonton N13 ...32 D6
Morden SM4 ...202 A5
Connaught Grange N13 ...32 D6
Connaught Ho N10 ...49 B4
NW10 ...90 B4
W1 ...248 C5
Connaught La IG1 ...79 B6
Connaught Lo N4 ...50 C2
Connaught Mans 15 N16 ...73 B4
SW11 ...267 B1
SW6 ...264 A2
3 SW9 ...138 C1
Connaught Mews SE18 ...122 C1
Ilford IG1 ...79 B6
Connaught Pl W2 ...237 C1
Connaught Rd E11 ...54 B1
E16 ...121 D5
E17 ...53 C4
N4 ...50 C2
NW10 ...89 C5
SE18 ...122 D1
Barnet EN5 ...12 D5
Carshalton SM1 ...218 B6
Chingford, Chingford Green
E4 ...20 C3
Ealing W13 ...109 B6
Harrow HA3 ...24 D2
Ilford IG1 ...79 B6
New Malden KT3 ...199 C5
5 Richmond TW10 ...154 B6
Teddington TW11,TW12 ...174 B5
Connaught Sch for Girls
E11 ...54 C1
Connaught Sch for Girls
(Annexe) E11 ...76 C6
Connaught Sq
W2 ...92 D1 237 C1
Connaught St
W2 ...92 C1 237 B1
Connaught Way N13 ...32 D6
Connell Cres W5 ...88 B3
Connell Ct 6 SE14 ...140 D6
Connell Ho 6 SM6 ...219 C2
Connemara Cl WD6 ...11 B5
Connett Ho 5 E2 ...96 B5
Connington 5 KT1 ...176 C1
Connington Cres E4 ...20 B1
Connoly Ct NW2 ...68 B5
Connop Rd EN3 ...6 D5
Connor Cl E11 ...54 C2
Connor Ct SW11 ...268 C1
Connor Rd RM9 ...81 B4
Connor St E9 ...96 D6
Conolly Rd W7 ...108 C5
Conrad Dr KT4 ...200 D1
Conrad Ho 12 N16 ...73 C3
8 SE16 ...119 A6
SW8 ...270 A4
Consfield Ave KT3 ...200 A4
Consolata Missionary Coll
N20 ...13 C1
Consort Ho NW7 ...27 D5
W2 ...245 D5
Consort Lo NW8 ...230 C5
Consort Mews TW7 ...152 B6
Consort Rd SE15 ...140 B3
Cons St SE1 ...251 B2
Constable Ave E16 ...121 B5
Constable Cl NW11 ...47 D3
Hayes UB4 ...83 A5
Constable Cres N15 ...52 A4
Constable Ct 11 SE16 ...118 B1
Constable Gdns
Edgware HA8 ...26 C1
Isleworth TW7 ...152 B6
Constable Ho NW3 ...70 D1
Enfield EN1 ...18 A6
14 Northolt UB5 ...84 D5
Constable Mews RM8 ...80 B4
Constable Wlk SE21 ...161 C1
Constance Cres BR2 ...208 D1
Constance Rd Enfield EN1 ...17 C5
Sutton SM1 ...218 A4
Thornton Heath CR0 ...204 D2
Twickenham TW2 ...151 D4
Constance St E16 ...122 A5
Constant Ho 23 E14 ...119 D6
Constantine Ho SW2 ...160 D3
Constantine Pl UB10 ...82 B6
Constantine Rd NW3 ...70 C4
Constitution Hill
SW1,W1 ...115 B4 248 D2
Constitution Rise SE18 ...144 C4
Consul Ho 5 E3 ...97 C3
Content St SE17 ...117 B2 262 C3
Contessa Cl BR6 ...227 C3
Control Tower Rd TW6 ...126 D2
Convair Wlk 11 UB5 ...84 D4
Convent Cl BR3 ...186 A3
Convent Gdns W11 ...91 B1
W5 ...109 C2
Convent Hill SE19 ...183 A4
Convent Lo TW15 ...170 D5
Convent of Jesus & Mary
Language Coll NW10 ...89 D6
Convent of Jesus & Mary RC
Inf Sch NW2 ...68 C2
Convent Rd TW15 ...170 D5
Convent Way UB2 ...106 D2
Conway Cl HA7 ...25 A4
Conway Cres
Dagenham RM6 ...58 C3
Greenford UB6 ...86 C5
Conway Dr
Ashford TW15 ...171 A4
Hayes UB3 ...105 A3
Sutton SM2 ...217 D2
Conway Gdns Enfield EN2 ...5 C5
Conway Gdns *continued*
Mitcham CR4 ...204 A5
Wembley HA9 ...43 C2
Conway Gr W3 ...89 B2
Conway Ho 5 E14 ...119 D2
6 Streatham SW2 ...160 A3
Conway Mews W1 ...239 A5
Conway Prim Sch SE18 ...123 C2
Conway Rd N15 ...51 A4
NW2 ...68 C6
SE18 ...123 C2
Feltham TW13 ...172 D5
Harlington TW6 ...126 D2
Palmers Green N14 ...16 A1
Twickenham TW4 ...151 C4
Wimbledon SW20 ...178 C2
Conway St W1 ...93 C3 239 A5
Conway Wlk TW12 ...173 B4
Conybeare NW3 ...70 C1
Conyers Cl IG8 ...36 C4
Conyer's Rd SW16 ...181 D5
Conyer St 19 E3 ...97 A5
Cooden Cl BR1 ...187 B3
Cookes Cl E11 ...76 D6
Cookes La SM3 ...217 A2
Cookham Cl UB2 ...107 D4
Cookham Cres SE16 ...118 D4
Cookham Dene Cl BR7 ...189 B2
Cookham Ho E2 ...243 C6
Cookham Rd BR8 ...191 C2
Cookhill Rd SE2 ...124 B3
Cooks Ferry N18 ...34 D5
Cook's Hole Rd EN2 ...5 A5
Cookson Gr DA8 ...147 D5
Cook's Rd E15 ...97 D5
SE17 ...138 D6
Coolfin Rd E16 ...99 B1
Coolgardie Ave E4 ...36 B5
Coolgardie Rd TW15 ...171 A5
Coolhurst Rd N8 ...49 D3
Cool Oak La NW9 ...45 D2
Coomassie Rd W9 ...91 B3
Coombe Ave CR0 ...221 C4
Coombe Bank KT2,KT3 ...177 C2
Coombe Cl Edgware HA8 ...26 B1
Hounslow TW3 ...129 C1
Coombe Cnr N21 ...16 D3
Coombe Cres TW12 ...173 A3
Coombe Ct
2 Beckenham BR3 ...185 B2
3 Croydon CR0 ...221 B4
Coombe Dr HA4 ...40 B1
Coombe End KT2 ...177 B3
Coombefield Cl KT3 ...199 C4
Coombe Gdns
New Malden KT3 ...199 D5
Wimbledon SW20 ...178 A2
Coombe Girls Sch KT3 ...177 B1
Coombe Hill Glade KT2 ...177 C3
Coombe Hill Inf Sch
KT3 ...177 B2
Coombe Hill Jun Sch
KT3 ...177 B2
Coombe Hill Rd KT2 ...177 C3
Coombe Ho 13 N7 ...71 D3
Coombe House Chase
KT3 ...177 B2
Coombehurst Cl EN4 ...2 D3
Coombe La CR0 ...222 B3
Coombe Lane Flyover
SW20 ...177 D2
Coombe La W KT2 ...177 B2
Coombe Lea BR1 ...210 A6
Coombe Lo SE7 ...143 C6
Coombe Neville KT2 ...177 B3
Coombe Pk KT2 ...177 B5
Coombe Pl KT2 ...177 A5
Coombe Rd NW10 ...67 B5
W13 ...109 B3
W4 ...111 C1
Bushey WD23 ...8 B4
Forest Hill SE26 ...184 B6
Hampton TW12 ...173 B4
Kingston KT2 ...176 C2
Kingston KT3 ...199 C6
South Croydon CR0,CR2 ...221 C4
Wood Green N22 ...32 C2
Coomber Ho SW6 ...135 D2
Coombe Ridings KT2 ...177 A5
Coombe Rise KT2 ...177 A2
Coombes Rd RM9 ...103 B6
Coombe Wlk SM1 ...217 D5
Coombewood Dr RM6 ...59 B3
Coombe Wood Rd KT2 ...177 A5
Coombs St N1 ...234 D3
Coomer Mews SW6 ...264 D5
Coomer Pl SW6 ...135 B6 264 D5
Cooms Wlk HA8 ...27 A2
Cooperage Cl 5 N17 ...33 D4
Cooperage The SE1 ...253 C3
Cooper Ave E17 ...35 A2
Cooper Cl SE1 ...251 B1
Cooper Cres SM5 ...218 D5
Cooper Ct E15 ...76 A3
SE18 ...144 D6
Cooper Ho NW8 ...236 C5
Hounslow TW4 ...129 B2
7 West Norwood SW27 ...182 D5
Cooper Rd NW10 ...68 A3
NW4 ...46 D3
Croydon CR0,CR9 ...220 D4
Coopersale Cl 3 IG8 ...37 C3
Coopersale Rd E9 ...74 D3
Coopers Cl E1 ...96 C3
Dagenham RM10 ...81 D2
Coopers Ct E3 ...97 B3
9 W3 ...111 A5
Isleworth TW7 ...130 D3
Coopers La NW1 ...232 D3
SE12 ...165 B2
Cooper's La E10 ...54 A1
Coopers' Lane Prim Sch
SE12 ...165 B2
Coopers Lodge SE1 ...253 C2
Cooper's Rd
SE1 ...117 D1 263 D2
Cooper's Row
EC3 ...117 D6 253 C6
Coopers Sch BR7 ...189 A2
Cooper St 10 E16 ...98 D2
Cooper's Yd SE19 ...183 C4
Coote Gdns RM8 ...81 B5
Coote Rd DA7 ...147 B4
Dagenham RM8 ...81 B5
Cope Ho EC1 ...235 B1
Copeland Dr E14 ...119 C2
Copeland Ho SE11 ...260 D5
Upper Tooting SW17 ...180 B6
Copeland Rd E17 ...53 D3
SE15 ...140 B3
Copelands BR3 ...185 B3
Copeman Cl SE26 ...184 C5
Copenhagen Gdns W4 ...111 B4
Copenhagen Ho N1 ...234 A5
Copenhagen Pl E14 ...97 B1
Copenhagen Prim Sch
N1 ...94 B6 233 C5
Copenhagen St
N1 ...94 B6 233 C5
Cope Pl W8 ...113 C3 255 A5
Copers Cope Rd BR3 ...185 B3
Cope St SE16 ...118 D2
Copeswood Ct UB7 ...126 C5
Cope Yd 6 E1 ...118 A5
Copford Wlk N1 ...235 A6
Copinger Wlk HA8 ...26 D2
Copland Ave HA0 ...65 D3
Copland Cl HA0 ...65 C3
Copland Com Sch & Tech Ctr
HA9 ...66 B3
Copland Mews 3 HA0 ...66 A2
Copland Rd HA0 ...66 A2
Copleston Rd SE15 ...139 D2
Copley Cl 15 SE17 ...138 D6
Ealing W7 ...86 D2
Copley Dene BR1 ...187 D2
Copley Pk SW16 ...182 B4
Copley Rd HA7 ...25 C5
Coppard Gdns KT9 ...213 C2
Coppedhall 1 SE21 ...161 B2
Coppelia Rd SE3 ...142 D1
Coppen Rd RM8 ...59 B2
Copperas St SE8 ...141 D6
Copper Beech N6 ...49 A2
Copperbeech Cl NW3 ...70 B3
Copper Beech Ct N20 ...14 A1
Copper Beeches TW7 ...130 B4
Copper Cl SE19 ...183 D3
Copperdale Rd UB3 ...106 A4
Copperfield Ave UB8 ...82 C3
Copperfield Dr N15 ...51 D5
Copperfield Ho 10 SE1 ...118 A4
Copperfield Mews N18 ...33 C5
Copperfield Rd SE28 ...102 C1
Stepney E3 ...97 A2
Copperfields
5 Beckenham BR3 ...186 A2
Harrow HA1 ...42 C2
Copperfields Ct W3 ...110 C4
Copperfield St
SE1 ...117 A4 252 A2
Copperfield Way BR7 ...189 A4
Pinner HA5 ...41 B5
Coppergate Cl BR1 ...187 B2
Coppermead Cl NW2 ...68 C5
Copper Mill Dr TW7 ...130 D3
Coppermill La E17 ...52 D4
Copper Mill La SW17 ...180 A6
Coppermill Prim Sch
E17 ...52 D4
Copperwood Lo EN2 ...4 D3
Coppetts Cl N12 ...30 D3
Coppetts Ctr* N12 ...30 D3
Coppetts Rd N10 ...30 D2
Coppetts Wood Prim Sch
N10 ...31 A2
Coppice Cl
Beckenham BR3 ...207 D5
Harrow HA7 ...24 D4
Ruislip HA4 ...39 B3
West Barnes SW20 ...200 C6
Coppice Dr SW15 ...156 B5
Coppice The
Ashford TW15 ...170 D4
Enfield EN2 ...4 D1
Hillingdon UB7 ...82 A1
New Barnet EN5 ...13 D5
Coppice Way E18 ...54 D6
Coppice Wlk N20 ...13 C1
Coppies Gr N11 ...31 B6
Copping Cl CR0 ...221 C4
Coppinger Ct UB7 ...104 A4
Coppin Ho SW2 ...160 D3
Coppins The
New Addington CR0 ...223 D2
Stanmore HA3 ...24 C4
2 Ilford RM6 ...58 B2
Coppock Cl SW11 ...136 C3
Coppsfield KT8 ...195 C6
Copse Ave BR4 ...223 D5
Copse Cl SE7 ...143 B6
Copse Ct SW15 ...157 A6
Copse Glade KT6 ...197 D1
Copse Hill Belmont SM2 ...217 D1
Wimbledon SW20 ...178 B3
Copsem Dr KT10 ...212 A2
Copsem La KT10 ...212 A1
Copsem Way KT10 ...212 A2
Copse The N2 ...48 D6
Chingford E4 ...20 D3

Copse View CR2 223 A1
Coptefield Dr DA17 125 A3
Copthall Ave EC2 95 B1 242 D2
Copthall Bldgs EC2 242 D2
Copthall Cl EC2 242 C2
Copthall Dr NW7 28 A4
Copthall Gdns NW7 28 A3
Twickenham TW1 152 D3
Copthall Rd E UB10 60 C5
Copthall Rd W UB10 60 C6
Copthall Sch NW7 28 B3
Copthall Sports Ctr NW4 28 B2
Copthorne Ave BR2 226 B6
Streatham SW12 159 D4
Copthorne Chase TW15 170 B6
Copthorne Cl TW17 193 A3
Copthorne Mews UB3 105 C2
Coptic St WC1 94 A2 240 A3
Copton Cl E3 97 C2
Copwood Cl N12 30 B6
Coral Cl RM6 58 C6
Coral Ho 5 E1 97 A3
Coraline Cl UB1 85 B4
Coralline Wlk 4 SE2 124 C4
Coral Row 14 SW11 136 A2
Coral St SE1 116 C4 251 B1
Coram Ho 9 W4 111 C1
WC1 240 A6
Coram St WC1 94 A3 240 A5
Coran Cl N9 18 D4
Corban Rd TW3 129 C2
Corbar Cl EN4 2 B4
Corbden Cl SE15 139 D4
Corbet Cl CR4,SM6 219 A6
Corbet Ct EC3 242 D1
Corbet Ho N1 234 A5
Corbet Pl E1 95 D2 243 C4
Corbett Ct SE26 185 B6
Corbett Gr N22 32 A3
Corbett Ho SW10 266 A6
Corbett Rd E17 54 A6
Wanstead E11 55 C3
Corbett's La SE16 118 C2
Corbett Villas RM8 58 C1
Corbicum E11 54 C2
Corbidge Ct SE8 141 D6
Corbiere Ct SW19 178 D4
Corbiere Ho 5 N1 95 C6
Corbin Ho 7 E3 97 D4
Corbin's La HA2 63 D5
Corbridge 5 N17 34 B3
Corbridge Cres E2 96 B5
Corby Cres EN2 4 A1
Corbyland Rd DA15 167 C3
Corbylands Rd DA15 167 C4
Corbyn St N4,N19 50 A1
Corby Rd NW10 89 B5
Corby Way E3 97 C3
Cordelia Cl SE24 138 D1
Cordelia Gdns TW19 148 A4
Cordelia Ho 26 N1 95 C5
Cordelia Rd TW19 148 A4
Cordelia St E14 97 D1
Cordell Ho N15 51 D4
Cordingley Rd HA4 61 B6
Cording St E14 97 D2
Cordwainers Coll E8 74 B1
Cordwainers Ct 18 E9 74 C1
Cordwainers Wlk 9 E13 99 A5
Cordwain Ho 7 N18 34 A5
Cord Way 7 E14 119 C3
Cordwell Rd SE13 164 C6
Corefield Cl N11 15 A2
Corelli Rd SE3 144 A4
Corfe Ave HA2 63 C4
Corfe Cl UB4 84 C1
Corfe Ho SW8 270 C4
Corfe Lo SE21 161 B2
Corfe Twr 6 W3 111 A4
Corfield Rd N21 16 B6
Corfield St E2 96 B4
Corfton Lo W5 88 A2
Corfton Rd W5 88 A2
Coriander Ave E14 98 B1
Coriander Ct SE1 253 D2
Cories Cl RM8 80 D6
Corigan Ct 5 E11 76 C6
Corinium Cl HA9 66 B4
Corinne Rd N19 71 C4
Corkscrew Hill BR4 224 B5
Cork Sq E1 118 B5
Cork St W1 115 C6 249 A5
Cork St Mews W1 249 A5
Cork Tree Ho 3 SW27 182 D5
Cork Tree Ret Pk N18 35 A4
Cork Tree Way E4 35 A5
Corlett St NW1 237 A4
Cormont Rd SE5 138 D4
Cormorant Cl E17 35 A3
Cheam SM1 217 B3
Cormorant Ct 34 SE8 141 B6
12 Dulwich SE21 161 B2
Cormorant Ho EN3 18 D6
Cormorant Rd E7 76 D3
Cornbury Ho 5 SE8 141 B6
Cornbury Rd HA8 25 D3
Cornel Ho 4 DA15 168 A1
Cornelia St N7 72 B2
Cornell Cl DA14 191 A4
Cornell Ho HA2 63 B5
Corner Fielde SW2 160 B3
Corner Gn SE3 143 A3
Corner House St WC2 250 A4
Corner Mead NW9 27 D2
Cornerside TW15 171 A3
Cornerways Harrow HA1 65 A5
Putney SW15 134 A1
Corney Rd W4 133 C6
Corney Reach Way W4 133 C5
Cornflower La CR0 206 D1
Cornflower Terr SE22 162 B5
Cornford Cl BR2 209 A4
Cornford Gr SW12 159 B2
Cornhill EC3 95 B1 242 D1
Cornhill Dr EN3 7 A6
Cornick Ho 7 SE16 118 B3
Cornish Ct N9 18 B4
Cornish Gr SE20 184 B2
Cornish Ho 7 SE17 138 D6
Brentford TW8 110 B1
Cornmill La SE13 142 A2
Cornmow Dr NW10 68 A3
Cornshaw Rd RM8 58 D1
Cornthwaite Rd E5 74 C5
Cornwall Ave DA16 145 D2
E2 96 C4
N3 29 C3
Claygate KT10 212 D1
Southall UB1 85 C2
Wood Green N22 32 A2
Cornwall Cl Barking IG11 79 D2
3 Pinner HA5 23 B3
Cornwall Cres W11 91 A1
Cornwall Ct 5 W7 86 D3
Cornwall Dr BR5 190 C3
Cornwall Gdns NW10 68 B2
SW7 113 D3 255 D5
Cornwall Gdns Wlk
SW7 255 D5
Cornwall Gr W4 111 C1
Cornwall Ho NW1 237 D5
3 Putney SW15 156 C4
Cornwallis Ave DA15 167 B2
N9 18 C2
Cornwallis Ct SW8 270 A2
Cornwallis Gr N9 18 C2
Cornwallis Ho 24 W12 112 B6
Cornwallis Rd N19 72 A6
SE18 122 D3
Dagenham RM9 81 A4
Edmonton N9 18 B2
Walthamstow E17 52 D5
Cornwallis Sq N19 72 A6
Cornwallis Wlk SE9 144 B2
Cornwall Mans NW1 237 D5
SW10 266 B4
Cornwall Mews S SW7 256 A5
Cornwall Mews W SW7 255 D5
Cornwall Rd N15 51 B4
N4 50 C2
SE1 116 C5 251 B2
Belmont SM2 217 B1
Croydon CR0 220 D6
Edmonton N18 34 A5
Harrow HA1 42 A3
Pinner HA5 23 B3
Ruislip HA4 61 D6
Twickenham TW1 153 A3
Cornwall Sq SE11 261 D2
Cornwall St 4 E1 118 B6
Cornwall Terr NW1 237 D5
Cornwall Terr Mews
NW1 237 D5
Corn Way E11 76 C5
Cornwell Ct 21 E10 53 D2
Cornwood Cl N2 48 B5
Cornwood Dr E1 96 C1
Cornworthy Rd RM8 80 C3
Corona Rd SE12 165 A4
Coronation Ave 1 N16 73 D4
Coronation Cl DA5 168 D5
Ilford IG6 57 A5
Coronation Ct E15 76 D2
W10 90 C2
Coronation Rd E13 99 C4
Acton NW10 88 C3
Hayes UB3 105 D2
Coronet Par 4 HA0 66 A2
Coronet St N1 95 C4
Corporation Ave TW4 129 A1
Corporation Row EC1 241 B6
Corporation St E15 98 D5
N7 72 A3
Corpus Christi RC Prim Sch
SW2 160 B6
Kingston KT3 199 A6
Corrance Rd SW2,SW4 138 A1
Corri Ave N14 31 D6
Corrib Ct N13 16 B1
Corrib Dr SM1 218 C3
Corrib Hts N8 49 D3
Corrigan Cl NW4 46 C6
Corringham Ct NW11 47 C2
Corringham Ho 10 E1 96 D1
Corringham Rd NW11 47 C2
Wembley HA9 66 C6
Corringway NW11 47 C2
Ealing W5 88 C2
Corris Gn NW9 45 C3
Corry Dr SW9 138 D1
Corry Ho 2 E14 119 D6
Corsair Cl TW19 148 A4
Corsair Rd TW19 148 A4
Corscombe Cl KT2 177 A5
Corsehill St SW16 181 C4
Corseley Way E9 75 B2
Corsham Ho HA9 66 C2
Corsham St N1 95 B4 235 D1
Corsica St N5 72 D2
Cortayne Rd SW6 135 B3
Cortis Rd SW15 156 B5
Cortis Terr SW15 156 B5
Corunna Rd
SW8 137 C4 269 B2
Corunna Terr SW8 269 A2
Corvette Sq 5 SE10 142 B6
Corwell Gdns UB8 83 A1
Corwell La UB8 83 A1
Coryton Path W9 91 B3
Cosbycote Ave SE24 161 A6
Cosdach Ave SM6 219 D1
Cosedge Cres CR0,CR9 220 D3
Cosgrove Cl
Edmonton N21 17 A3
Hayes UB4 84 D3
Cosgrove Ho 11 E2 96 A6
Cosmo Pl WC1 240 B4
Cosmur Cl W12 111 D3
Cossall Wlk SE15 140 B4
Cossar Mews 10 SW2 160 C6
Cosser St SE1 116 C3 261 A6
Costa St SE15 140 A3
Coston Prim Sch UB6 86 A4
Costons Ave UB6 86 B4
Costons La UB6 86 B4
Coston Wlk 4 SE4 140 D1
Cosway Ho NW11 48 A3
Cosway Mans NW1 237 B4
Cosway St NW1 92 C2 237 B4
Cotall St E14 97 C2
Coteford Cl HA5 40 A4
Coteford Inf Sch HA5 40 A3
Coteford Jun Sch HA5 39 D4
Coteford St SW17 181 A6
Cotelands CR0 221 C5
Cotesbach Rd E5 74 C5
Cotes Ho NW8 237 A5
Cotesmore Gdns RM8 80 C4
Cotford Rd CR7 205 A5
Cotham St SE17 262 B3
Cotherstone Rd SW2 160 B3
Cotleigh Ave DA5 168 D2
Cotleigh Rd NW6 69 C1
Cotman Cl NW11 48 A3
Putney SW15 156 D6
Cotman Ct BR3 185 B2
Cotmandene Cres BR5 190 A1
Cotman Gdns HA8 26 C1
Cotman Ho NW8 230 A4
6 Northolt UB5 84 D5
Cotmans Cl UB3 106 A5
Coton Rd DA16 146 A2
Cotsford Ave KT3 199 B4
Cotswold Ave WD23 8 A5
Cotswold Cl
Hinchley Wood KT10 212 D6
Kingston KT2 177 A4
Cotswold Ct EC1 242 A6
N11 31 A6
3 Wembley UB6 86 D5
Cotswold Gate NW2 47 A1
Cotswold Gdns E6 99 D5
Hendon NW2 68 D6
Ilford IG2 57 B2
Cotswold Gn EN2 4 B1
Cotswold Ho N16 51 D1
Cotswold Mews SW11 266 D1
Cotswold Rd TW12 173 C4
Cotswold Rise BR6 211 D3
Cotswold St SE27 182 D6
Cotswold Way Enfield EN2 4 B2
North Cheam KT4 216 C6
Cottage Ave BR2 210 A1
Cottage Cl HA4 39 B1
Cottage Field Cl DA5,
DA15 168 C3
Cottage Gn SE5 139 B5
Cottage Gr SW9 138 A2
Surbiton KT6 197 D3
Cottage Pl SW3 114 C3 257 A5
Cottage Rd KT19 215 B1
Cottage St E14 119 D6
Cottages The UB10 60 D5
Cottage Wlk 2 N16 73 D5
Cottenham Dr NW9 45 D6
Wimbledon SW20 178 B3
Cottenham Ho 4 N19 72 A6
Cottenham Par SW20 178 B1
Cottenham Park Rd
SW20 178 C3
Cottenham Pl SW20 178 B3
Cottenham Rd E17 53 B5
Cotterill Rd KT6 198 B1
Cottesbrook St 9 SE14 141 A5
Cottesloe Ho NW8 237 A6
Cottesloe Mews SE1 261 B6
Cottesmore Ct W8 255 D6
Cottesmore Gdns
W8 113 D3 255 D6
Cottimore Ave KT12 194 B1
Cottimore Cres KT12 194 B2
Cottimore Terr KT12 194 B2
Cottingham Chase HA4 62 A5
Cottingham Rd
SW8 138 B5 270 D4
Penge SE20 184 D3
Cottington Rd TW13 172 D6
Cottington St SE11 261 C2
Cotton Ave W3 89 B1
Cotton Cl RM9 80 C1
Cottongrass Cl 1 CR0 206 D1
Cotton Hill BR1 186 B6
Cotton Ho W12 111 D4
18 Streatham SW12 160 A4
Cotton Row SW11 136 B2
Cotton's Gdns E2 95 C4
Cottons La SE1 252 D4
Cotton St E14 120 A6
Cottrell Ct SE10 120 D3
Cotts Cl 13 W7 86 D2
Couchman Ho 8 SW4 159 C5
Couchmore Ave KT10 212 C6
Coulgate St SE4 141 A2
Coulsdon Ct 3 N8 49 D4
Coulsdon Ho 5 SW2 160 A3
Coulson Cl RM8 58 C1
Coulson St SW3 114 D1 257 C2
Coulter Cl UB4 85 A3
Coulter Rd W6 112 B3
Coulthurst Ct SW16 182 A3
Coults Cres NW5 71 A5
Councillor St SE5 139 A5
Counters Ct W14 254 B6
Counter St SE1 253 A3
Countess Rd NW5 71 C3
Countisbury Ave EN1 17 D4
Countisbury Ho SE26 162 A1
Country Way TW13,
TW16 172 C5
County Gate BR7 167 A1
New Barnet EN5 13 D5
County Gr SE5 139 A4
County Ho 9 SW9 138 C4
County Par TW8 131 D5
County Rd Newham E6 100 D2
South Norwood CR7 182 D1
County St SE1 117 A3 262 B5
Coupland Pl SE18 123 A1
Courcy Rd N8,N22 50 C6
Courier Ho 17 SW2 160 C4
Courland Gr SW8 137 D3
Courland St
SW8 137 D4 269 D1
Course The SE9 166 C1
Courtauld Galleries*
WC2 250 C6
Courtauld Ho 11 E2 96 A5
Courtauld Inst of Art
W1 237 D2
Courtauld Rd N19 50 A1
Courtaulds Cl SE28 124 A5
Court Ave DA17 125 B1
Court Cl Harrow HA3 44 A6
Twickenham TW13,TW2 151 D1
Wallington SM6 219 D1
Court Close Ave TW13,
TW2 151 D1
Court Cres KT9 213 D2
Court Downs Rd BR3 185 D1
Court Dr Carshalton SM1 218 C4
Hillingdon UB10 82 C6
Stanmore HA7 26 A6
Wallington CR0 220 B4
Courtenay Ave N6 48 C2
Harrow HA3 24 A2
Courtenay Dr BR3 186 B1
Courtenay Gdns HA3 24 A1
Courtenay Mews E17 53 A4
Courtenay Pl E17 53 A4
Courtenay Rd E11 76 D5
North Cheam KT4,SM3 216 C5
Penge BR3,SE20 184 D4
Walthamstow E17 52 D5
Wembley HA9 65 D5
Courtenay Sq SE11 261 A1
Courtenay St
SE11 116 C1 261 A2
Courtens Mews HA7 25 C3
Court Farm Ave KT19 215 B3
Court Farm Ind Est
TW19 148 B5
Court Farm Rd
Chislehurst SE9 166 A1
Northolt UB5 63 C1
Courtfield W13 87 C2
Courtfield Ave HA1 42 D4
Courtfield Cres HA1 42 D4
Courtfield Gdns
SW5 113 D2 255 D3
Ealing W13 87 A1
Ruislip HA4 61 D6
Courtfield Ho EC1 241 A4
Courtfield Mews SW7 255 D3
Courtfield Rd
SW7 114 A2 256 A3
Ashford TW15 170 D4
Courtfield Rise BR4 224 B5
Court Gdns N7 72 C2
Courthill Rd SE13 142 A1
Courthope Ho 14 SE16 118 C3
SW8 270 A3
Courthope Rd NW3 70 D4
Greenford UB6 86 B5
Wimbledon SW19 179 A5
Courthope Villas SW19 179 A3
Court House Gdns N3 29 C4
Court House Rd N12 29 D4
Court La SE21 161 D4
Courtland Ave NW7 11 C1
Chingford E4 20 D2
Redbridge IG1 78 B6
South Norwood SW16 182 B3
Courtland Gr SE28 124 D6
Courtland JMI Sch NW7 11 C2
Courtland Rd E6 100 A6
Courtlands 5 E5 52 B1
11 Beckenham BR3 185 D1
10 Belmont SM2 217 D1
Ealing W5 87 C2
Richmond TW10 154 C6
Walton-on-T KT12 194 A2
Courtlands Ave SE12 165 B6
Hampton TW12 173 B4
Hayes BR2 208 D1
Richmond TW9 132 D3
Courtlands Cl HA4 39 D2
Courtlands Dr KT19 215 D2
Courtlands Rd KT5 198 C2
Court Lane Gdns SE21 161 C4
Courtleet Dr DA7 147 D4
Courtleigh 6 NW11 47 B4
Courtleigh Ave EN4 2 B5
Courtleigh Gdns NW11 47 A5
Court Lo 11 DA17 125 C1
Courtman Rd N17 33 A3
Court Mans 8 W6 112 A2
Court Mead UB5 85 B4
Courtmead Cl SE24 161 A5
Courtnell St W2 91 C1
Courtney Cl SE19 183 C4
Courtney Cres SM5 218 D1
Courtney Ct N7 72 C3
Courtney Ho 1 NW4 46 C5
W14 254 B6
Courtney Pl CR0 220 C5
Courtney Rd N7 72 C3
Croydon CR0 220 C5
Harlington TW6 126 C2
Mitcham SW19 180 C3
Courtney Way TW6 126 C2
Court Par HA0 65 B5
Courtrai Rd SE23 163 A5
Court Rd Eltham SE9 166 B4
Southall UB2 107 B1
South Norwood SE25 205 D6
Uxbridge UB10 60 D4
Court Royal SW15 157 A6
Courtside N8 49 D3
Forest Hill SE23 162 C1
Court St BR1 187 A1
E1 96 B2
Courts The SW16 182 A3
Court The N10 49 C5
Ruislip HA4 63 A4
Courtville Ho 11 W10 91 A4
Court Way NW9 45 C5
W3 89 A2
Courtway IG8 37 C5
Court Way Ilford IG6 57 A6
Twickenham TW1,TW2 152 D4
Courtyard The N1 72 B1
13 SW18 136 B1
Fulham SW6 135 A4 264 A1
Court Yd SE9 166 B5
Cousin La EC4 117 B6 252 C5
Cousins Cl 2 UB7 104 A6
Cousins Ct 2 NW9 46 A5
Couthurst Rd SE3 143 B5
Coutts Ave KT9 214 A3
Coutts Ho SE7 143 C6
Couzens Ho 9 E3 97 B2
Coval Gdns SW14 132 D1
Coval La SW14 132 D1
Coval Rd SW14 133 A1
Covelees Wall E6 100 C1
Covell Ct 15 SE8 141 C5
Covent Garden Sta
WC2 94 A1 240 B1
Covent Gdn*
WC2 116 A6 250 B6
Coventry Cl NW6 91 C6
9 Newham E6 100 B1
Coventry Rd E1 96 B3
Croydon SE25 206 A5
Ilford IG1 56 D1
Coventry St W1 249 C5
Coverack Cl
Croydon CR0 207 A2
Southgate N14 15 C5
Coverdale Cl HA7 25 B5
Coverdale Gdns CR0 221 D5
Coverdale Pl NW6 68 D1
Coverdale Rd N11 31 A4
NW2 69 A2
W12 112 B4
Coverdales The IG11 101 B5
Coverham Ho 5 SE4 140 D1
Coverley Cl E1 96 A2
Coverley Point SE11 260 C3
Coverton Rd SW17 180 C5
Coverts Rd KT10 212 D1
Covert The BR5,BR6 211 C3
Covert Way EN4 2 A3
Covet Wood Cl BR5 211 D3
Covey Cl SW19 179 D1
Covington Gdns SW16 182 D3
Covington Way
South Norwood SW16 182 C3
South Norwood SW16 182 D3
Cowan Cl E6 100 A2
Cowan Ct NW10 67 B1
Cowbridge La IG11 78 D1
Cowbridge Rd HA3 44 B5
Cowcross St EC1 94 D2 241 C4
Cowdenbeath Path N1 233 C6
Cowden Rd BR6 211 D2
Cowden St SE6 185 C6
Cowdray Hall Coll of Nursing
W1 93 B1 238 C2
Cowdray Ho 23 SE22 139 C2
Cowdray Rd UB10 83 A6
Cowdrey Cl EN1 5 C3
Cowdrey Rd SW19 180 A5
Cowdry Rd E9 75 B2
Cowell Lo E4 36 D5
Cowen Ave HA2 64 B6
Cowen Ho 4 SE18 144 D6
Cowgate Rd UB6 86 B4
Cowick Rd SW17 180 D6
Cowings Mead UB5 63 A2
Cowland Ave EN3 6 C1
Cow Leaze E6 100 C1
Cowleaze Rd KT2 176 A2
Cowley La E11 76 C5
Cowley Pl NW4 46 C4
Cowley Rd SW9 138 C4
16 SW9 138 C5
W3 111 D5
Mortlake SW14 133 C2
Redbridge IG1 56 B2
Wanstead E11 55 B4
Cowley St SW1 260 A5
Cowling Cl W11 244 A4
Cowper Ave E6 78 A1
Sutton SM1 218 B4
Cowper Cl Bexley DA16 168 A6
Bromley BR2 209 D5
Cowper Gdns
Southgate N14 15 C5
Wallington SM6 219 C2
Cowper Ho SE17 262 B2
SW1 259 D1
Cowper Rd N14 15 B3
N16 73 C4
W3 111 B5
Belvedere DA17 125 C2
Bromley BR2 209 D5
Ealing W7 108 D6
Edmonton N18 34 A5
Richmond TW10 176 B5
Wimbledon SW19 180 A4
Cowper's Ct EC3 242 D1
Cowper St EC1,
EC2 95 B3 242 D6
Cowper Terr W10 90 D2
Cowslip Cl UB10 60 A1
Cowslip Rd E18 37 B1
Cowthorpe Rd SW8 269 D2
Cox Ct 3 EN4 2 C1
Coxe Pl HA3 43 A5
Cox Ho W6 264 A6
Cox La Chessington KT9 214 B4
West Ewell KT19 215 A3
Coxmount Rd SE7 121 D1
Coxs Ave TW17 193 C6
Cox's Ct E1 243 C3
Coxson Way SE1 253 C1
Coxwell Rd SE18 123 B1
South Norwood SE19 183 C3
Coxwold Path KT9 214 A1
Coysh Ct 8 SW15 157 A6
Crabbs Croft Cl 7 BR6 227 A3
Crab Hill BR3 186 B3
Crabtree Ave
Dagenham RM6 58 D5
Wembley HA0 88 B5
Crabtree Cl E2 95 D5
Crabtree Ct E15 75 D3
Crabtree Hall SW6 134 C5
Crabtree La SW6 134 D5
Craddock Rd EN1 5 D2
Craddock St NW5 71 A2
Cradley Rd DA15,SE9 167 B3
Craig Dr UB8 82 D1
Craigen Ave CR0 206 B1
Craigerne Rd SE3 143 B5
Craig Gdns E18 36 D1
Craigholm SE18 144 C4
Craigie Ho SE1 263 D3
Craigleith SW15 156 D5
Craigmuir Pk HA0 88 B6
Craignair Rd SW2 160 C4
Craignish Ave SW16 182 B1
Craig Park Rd N18 34 B6
Craig Rd TW10 175 C6
Craig's Ct SW1 250 A4
Craigside KT2 176 D2
Craigton Rd SE9 144 B1
Craigweil Cl HA7 25 D5
Craigweil Dr HA7 25 D5
Craigwell Ave TW13 150 A1
Craik Ct NW6 91 B5
Crail Row SE17 117 B2 262 D3
Crales Ct SE18 122 A3
Cramer Ct KT3 199 A6
Cramer St W1 93 A2 238 B3
Crammond Cl W6 264 A5
Cramond Ct TW14 149 C3
Crampton Rd SE20 184 C4
Crampton Sch
SE17 116 D1 261 D2
Crampton St
SE17 117 A1 262 A2
Cranberry Cl 2 UB5 84 D5
Cranberry La E16 98 C3
Cranborne Ave
Southall UB2 107 C2
Tolworth KT6,KT9 214 C5
Cranborne Rd IG11 101 B6
Cranborne Waye
Hayes UB4 106 C6
Hayes UB4 84 B1
Cranbourn Alley WC2 249 D6
Cranbourne Cl SW16 204 A6
Cranbourne Ct N2 47 D6
SW11 267 B4
Wanstead E18 55 B5
Cranbourne Dr HA5 40 D4
Cranbourne Gdns NW11 47 B4
Ilford IG6 57 A6
Cranbourne Rd E12 78 A3
E15 76 A4
N10 31 B1
Northwood HA6 39 D6
Cranbourn Ho 4 SE16 118 B4
Cranbourn St
WC2 115 D6 249 D6
Cranbrook NW1 232 B5
Cranbrook Cl BR2 209 A3
Cranbrook Coll (Boys)
IG1 78 C6
Cranbrook Ct 8 TW8 131 D6
Cranbrook Dr
Thames Ditton KT10 196 A1
Twickenham TW2 151 D3
Cranbrook Ho 5 E5 74 B3
South Norwood SE19 183 B2
Cranbrook La N11 31 B6
Cranbrook Mews E17 53 B4
Cranbrook Pk N22 32 C2
Cranbrook Rd DA7 147 B4
SE8 141 C4
W4 111 C1
Hounslow TW4 129 B1
Ilford IG1,IG2 56 C3
New Barnet EN4 14 B5
South Norwood CR7 183 A1

Cranbrook Rd continued
Wimbledon SW19 179 A3
Cranbrook Rise IG1 56 B2
Cranbrook St E2 96 D5
Cranbury Rd SW6 135 D3
Crandale Ho 8 E5 74 B3
Crandley Ct SE8 119 A2
Crane Ave W3 111 A6
Isleworth TW7 153 A6
Cranebrook TW2 152 A2
Crane Cl Dagenham RM10 81 C2
Harrow HA2 64 A5
Crane Ct EC4 241 B1
7 W12 111 C4
West Ewell KT19 215 A4
Craneford Cl TW2 152 D4
Craneford Way TW2 152 D4
Crane Gdns UB3 105 D2
Crane Gr N7 72 C2
Crane Ho 22 E3 97 A5
9 SE15 139 D4
9 Catford BR1 186 B5
Feltham TW13 151 C1
Crane Lodge Rd TW5 128 B6
Crane Mead SE16 118 D2
Crane Mead Ct TW1 152 D4
Crane Park Prim Sch
TW13 151 B2
Crane Park Rd TW2 151 D2
Crane Rd Stanwell TW19 148 C5
Twickenham TW2 152 C3
Cranes Dr KT5 198 B5
Cranes Park Ave KT5,
KT6 198 B5
Cranes Park Cres KT5 198 B5
Cranes Pk KT5,KT6 198 A4
Crane St SE10 120 B1
5 SE15 139 D4
Craneswater TW6 127 D5
Craneswater Pk UB2 107 B1
Cranes Way WD6 11 A6
Crane Way TW2 152 A4
Cranfield Ct NW1 237 B3
2 Woodford IG8 37 A6
Cranfield Dr NW9 27 C3
Cranfield Rd SE4 141 B2
Cranford Ave
Bowes Park N13 32 A5
Stanwell TW19 148 B4
Cranford Cl
Stanwell TW19 148 A4
Wimbledon SW20 178 B3
Cranford Comm Coll
TW5 128 B6
Cranford Cotts 8 E1 118 D6
Cranford Ct SM1 218 A4
Cranford Dr UB3 105 D2
Cranford Jun Sch TW4 128 B3
Cranford La
Harlington UB3 127 C5
Hatton TW6 127 D4
Hatton, Hatton Cross
TW6 127 D2
Heston TW5 128 C5
Cranford Lo SW19 156 D2
Cranford Park Prim Sch
UB3 105 D2
Cranford Park Rd UB3 105 D2
Cranford Rise KT10 212 A3
Cranford St E1 118 D6
Cranford Way N8 50 C4
Cranhurst Rd NW2 68 C3
Cranleigh W11 244 C4
Cranleigh Cl DA5 169 D5
Penge SE20 184 B1
Cranleigh Ct 4 N16 51 C1
Mitcham CR4 202 B6
Richmond TW9 132 C2
Southall UB1 85 B1
Cranleigh Gardens Ind Est
UB1 85 B2
Cranleigh Gdns
Barking IG11 79 B2
Harrow HA3 44 A4
Kingston KT2 176 B4
Southall UB1 85 B1
Southgate N21 16 C6
South Norwood SE25 205 C6
Sutton SM1 217 D6
Cranleigh Ho SW20 178 B1
Cranleigh Hos NW1 232 B3
Cranleigh Mews SW11 136 D3
Cranleigh Rd N15 51 A4
Feltham TW13 171 D6
Merton SW19 201 C6
Thames Ditton KT10 196 A1
Cranleigh St
NW1 93 C5 232 B3
Cranley Dene Ct N10 49 B5
Cranley Dr Ilford IG2 57 A2
Ruislip HA4 61 D6
Cranley Gdns N10 49 B5
SW7 114 B1 256 C2
Palmers Green N13 16 B1
Wallington SM6 219 C1
Cranley Mews
SW7 114 A1 256 B2
Cranley Par 2 SE9 188 A6
Cranley Pl SW7 114 B2 256 C3
Cranley Rd E13 99 B2
Ilford IG2 57 A2
Cranmer Ave W13 109 B3
Cranmer Cl Ruislip HA4 40 D1
Stanmore HA7 25 C3
West Barnes SM4 200 D3
Cranmer Ct N3 29 A1
SW3 257 B3
Cranmer Ct continued
Hampton TW12 173 D5
Kingston KT2 175 D6
Cranmer Farm Cl CR4 202 D5
Cranmer Ho SW11 267 A2
Cranmer Mid Sch CR4 202 D5
Cranmer Rd E7 77 B4
SW9 138 C5
Croydon CR0 221 A5
Edgware HA8 10 D1
Hampton TW12 173 D5
Hayes UB3 83 B1
Kingston KT2 176 A5
Mitcham CR4 202 D5
Cranmer Terr SW17 180 B5
Cranmore Ave TW7 130 A5
Cranmore Rd BR7 188 B5
Catford BR1 164 D1
Cranmore Way N10 49 C5
Cranston Cl
Hounslow TW3,TW4 129 A3
Uxbridge UB10 61 B6
Cranston Gdns E4 35 D4
Cranston Rd SE23 163 A2
Cranswick Rd SE16 118 B1
Crantock Rd SE6 164 A2
Cranwell Cl E3 97 D3
Cranwell Ct 6 NW9 27 D3
Croydon CR0 222 D6
Cranwell Gr TW17 192 B5
Cranwell Rd TW6 126 D3
Cranwich Ave N21 17 B4
Cranwich Rd N16 51 C2
Cranwood Ct EC1 235 D1
Cranwood St EC1 95 B4 235 D1
Cranworth Cres 7 E4 20 B3
Cranworth Gdns SW9 138 C4
Cranworth Ho 6 N7 72 B4
Craster Rd SW2 160 B4
Craston Ho 2 SE5 139 C3
Crathie Rd SE12 165 B5
Crathorne Ho N2 30 B1
Cravan Ave TW13 150 A2
Craven Ave Ealing W5 109 C6
Southall UB1 85 B2
Craven Cl N16 52 A2
Hayes UB4 84 A1
Craven Cottage (Fulham FC)
SW6 134 D4
Craven Ct NW10 89 C6
Dagenham RM6 59 A3
Edgware HA8 26 B6
Craven Gdns
Barking IG11 101 C5
Ilford IG6 57 B6
Wimbledon SW19 179 D5
Craven Hill W2 114 A6 246 B6
Craven Hill Gdns
W2 114 A6 246 A6
Craven Hill Mews W2 246 B6
Craven Ho 13 N2 30 B1
2 Mortlake SW14 133 B2
Craven Lo W2 246 B6
Fulham SW6 134 D4
Craven Mews 6 SW11 137 A2
Craven Park Mews
NW10 89 C6
Craven Park Rd N15 52 A3
NW10 89 C6
Craven Park Sch N16 52 A3
Craven Pas WC2 250 A4
Craven Pk NW10 89 C6
Craven Rd NW10 89 B6
W2 92 A1 236 B1
Croydon CR0 206 B1
Ealing W5 109 C6
Kingston KT2 176 B2
Craven St WC2 116 A5 250 A4
Craven Terr W2 114 A6 246 B6
Craven Wlk E5,N16 52 A2
Crawford Ave HA0 65 D3
Crawford Bldgs NW1 237 B3
Crawford Cl TW7 130 C3
Crawford Gdns
Edmonton N13 16 D1
Northolt UB5 85 B4
Crawford Mews W1 237 C3
Crawford Pas EC1 241 B5
Crawford Pl W1 92 C2 237 B3
Crawford Place Dwellings
NW1 237 B3
Crawford Point 4 E16 98 D1
Crawford Prim Sch SE5 139 A4
Crawford Rd SE5 139 A3
Crawford St W1 92 D2 237 C3
Crawley Rd E10 53 D1
Enfield EN1 17 D4
Tottenham N22 33 A1
Crawshay Ct SW9 138 C4
Crawshay Ho 13 N16 73 B4
Crawthew Gr SE22 139 D1
Craybrooke Rd DA14 190 B6
Craybury End SE9 167 A2
Crayfields Bsns Pk BR5 190 C2
Crayfields Ind Pk BR5 190 C1
Crayford Cl E6 100 A1
Crayford Ho N7 72 A4
SE1 252 D1
Crayford Rd N7 72 A4
Crayke Hill KT9 214 A1
Crayle Ho EC1 241 D6
Crayonne Cl TW16 171 C2
Cray Rd DA17 147 C6
Sidcup DA14 190 C4
Crays Par The BR5 190 C1
Crealock Gr IG8 36 D5
Crealock St SW18 157 D5
Creasy Est SE1 263 A5
Crebor St SE22 162 A5
Credenhall Dr BR2 210 B1
Credenhill Ho 2 SE15 140 B5
Credenhill St SW16 181 C4
Crediton Hill NW6 69 D3
Crediton Ho EN3 6 D2
Crediton Rd E16 99 A1
NW10 90 D6
Crediton Way KT10 213 A3
Credon Rd E13 99 C5
SE16 118 B1
Creechurch La EC3 243 B1
Creechurch Pl EC3 243 B1
Creed Ho SE15 140 B2
Creed La EC4 241 D1
Creek Ho W14 254 B6
Creekmouth Ind Pk
IG11 101 D3
Creek Rd SE10,SE8 141 D6
Barking IG11 101 D4
East Molesey KT8 196 C5
Creekside SE8 141 D5
Creek The TW16 194 A4
Creeland Gr SE6 163 B3
Crefeld Cl W6 135 A6 264 A5
Creffield Rd W3,W5 110 C6
Creighton Ave E6 99 D5
N2,N10 30 D1
Creighton Cl W12 112 B6
Creighton Ho N2 48 C6
Creighton Rd NW6 90 D5
W5 109 D3
Tottenham N17 33 C3
Cremer Bsns Ctr 8 E2 95 D5
Cremer Ho 9 SE8 141 C5
Cremer St E2 95 D5
Cremorne Rd
SW10 136 B5 266 C4
Creon Ct 3 SW9 138 C4
Crescent EC3 253 C6
Crescent Court Bsns Ctr
E16 98 B3
Crescent Ct 14 DA15 168 A1
SW4 159 D6
Kingston KT6 197 D4
Crescent Dr BR5 211 A3
Crescent E EN4 2 A5
Crescent Gdns
Ruislip HA4 40 B2
Wimbledon SW19 157 C1
Crescent Gr SW4 137 C1
Mitcham CR4 202 C5
Crescent Ho SE13 141 D3
5 Wimbledon SW20 178 D2
Crescent La SW4 159 D6
Crescent Mans N5 72 D3
W11 244 B6
Crescent Par UB10 82 C4
Crescent Pl SW3 257 B4
Crescent Rd BR1 187 A3
DA15 167 D1
E10 75 D6
E13 99 A6
E6 99 C6
N11 30 D6
N15 50 D6
N22 31 D2
N3 29 B2
N8 49 D3
SE18 122 D2
Beckenham BR3 185 D1
Chingford E4 20 C4
Dagenham RM10 81 D5
East Barnet EN4 14 C6
Edmonton N9 18 A3
Enfield EN2 4 D1
Kingston KT2 176 D3
Shepperton TW17 193 A4
Wimbledon SW20 178 D2
Woodford E18 37 C2
Crescent Rise N22 31 D2
N3 29 B2
3 N3 29 C2
East Barnet EN4 14 C6
Crescent Row EC1 242 A5
Crescent St N1 72 B1
Crescent Stables SW15 157 A6
Crescent The DA14 189 D6
E17 53 A4
N11 31 A6
N2 47 D6
NW2 68 B5
W3 89 C1
Ashford TW15 170 B5
Barnes SW13 134 A3
Barnet EN5 1 D3
Beckenham BR3 185 C2
East Molesey KT8 195 C5
Harlington UB7 127 B5
Harrow HA2 42 A1
Ilford IG2 56 C3
Kingston KT3 177 A1
Kingston KT6 198 A4
Loughton IG10 21 D5
Lower Halliford TW17 193 D2
Sidcup DA5 168 C4
Southall UB1 107 A4
Sutton SM1 218 B3
Thornton Heath CR0 205 B3
Wembley HA0 65 B6
West Wickham BR4 208 C3
Wimbledon SW19 157 C1
Crescent View IG10 21 D6
Crescent W EN4 2 A5
Crescent Way N12 30 C4
SE4 141 C2
Orpington BR6 227 C3
South Norwood SW16 182 C3
Crescent Wood Rd
SE21,SE26 162 A1
Cresford Rd
SW6 135 D4 265 C1
Crespigny Rd NW4 46 B3
Cressage Cl UB1 85 C3
Cressage Ho 9 TW8 132 A6
Cressall Ho 8 E14 119 C3
Cresset Ho 8 E9 74 C2
Cresset Rd E9 74 C2
Cresset St SW4 137 D2
Cressfield Cl NW5 71 A3
Cressida Rd N19 49 D1
Cressingham Ct 1
DA17 125 C3
Cressingham Gr SM1 218 A4
Cressingham Rd HA8 27 B3
SE13 142 A2
Cressington Cl 4 N16 73 C3
Cress Mews BR1 186 B5
Cresswell Gdns SW5 256 A2
Cresswell Pk SE3 142 D2
Cresswell Pl
SW10 114 A1 256 B2
Cresswell Rd
Croydon SE25 206 A5
Feltham TW13 173 A6
Twickenham TW1 153 D5
Cresswell Way N21 16 C4
Cressy Ct 6 E1 96 C2
W6 112 B3
Cressy Ho SW13 134 B2
Cressy Hos 7 E1 96 C2
Cressy Pl E1 96 C2
Cressy Rd NW3 70 D4
Cresta Ct W5 88 B3
Cresta Ho NW6 70 B1
7 Bow E3 97 C3
Crestbrook Ave N13 16 D1
Crestbrook Pl N13 16 D1
Crest Ct NW4 46 C4
Crest Dr EN3 6 C5
Crestfield St N1,WC1 233 B2
Crest Gdns HA4 62 C5
Creston Way KT4 200 D1
Crest Rd NW2 68 A6
Hayes BR2 208 D2
South Croydon CR2 222 B1
Crest The NW4 46 C4
Edmonton N13 32 C6
Surbiton KT5 198 C4
10 West Norwood SW27 182 D5
Crestview NW5 71 B5
Crest View HA5 40 D5
Crest View Dr BR5 211 A4
Crestway SW15 156 B5
Crestwood Way TW4 151 A6
Creswick Ct W3 110 D6
Creswick Rd W3 110 D6
Creswick Wlk 6 E3 97 C4
NW11 47 B5
Creton St SE18 122 C3
Crewdson Rd SW9 138 C5
Crewe Pl NW10 89 D4
Crewkerne Ct SW11 266 D2
Crews St E14 119 C2
Crewys Rd NW2 69 B6
SE15 140 B3
Crichton Ave SM6 219 D4
Crichton Rd SM5 218 D1
Crichton St SW8 137 C3
Cricketers Arms Rd EN2 5 A3
Cricketers Cl N14 15 C4
Chessington KT9 213 D4
Cricketers Mews 4
SW18 157 D6
Cricketers Wlk SE26 184 C5
Cricketfield Rd E5 74 B4
Cricket Gn CR4 202 D5
Cricket Green Sch CR4 202 C6
Cricket Ground Rd BR7 188 D2
Cricket La BR3 185 A4
Cricket Row N2 48 B6
Cricklade Ave SW2 160 B2
Cricklewood Broadway
NW2 68 D4
Cricklewood La NW2 69 B5
Cricklewood Sta NW2 68 D4
Cridland St E15 98 D6
Crieff Ct TW11,KT8 175 C3
Crieff Rd SW18 158 A5
Criffel Ave SW2 159 D3
Crimscott St
SE1 117 C3 263 B5
Crimsworth Rd
SW8 137 D5 269 D3
Crinan St N1 94 A5 233 B4
Cringle St SW8 137 C5 269 A4
Cripplegate St EC1 242 B4
Cripps Gn UB4 84 B3
Crispe Ho N1 233 D5
Barking IG11 101 B5
Crispen Rd TW13 173 A6
Crispian Cl NW10 67 C4
Crispin Cl SM6 220 A6
Crispin Cres SM6 219 D6
Crispin Ct SE17 263 A3
Crispin Rd HA8 27 A4
Crispin St E1 95 D2 243 C3
Crisp Rd W6 112 C1
Cristowe Rd SW6 135 B3
Criterion Mews N19 71 D6
Crittall's Cnr DA14 190 C3
Crittenden Lo BR4 207 C1
Crockerton Rd SW17 158 D2
Crockham Way SE9 188 C6
Crocus Cl CR0 206 D1
Crocus Field EN5 13 B5
Croft Ave BR4 208 A1
Croft Cl BR7 188 B5
NW7 11 C1
Erith DA17 125 B1
Harlington UB7 127 A5
Hillingdon UB10 60 C1
Croft Ct HA4 39 D1
Croftdown Rd NW5 71 B5
Crofters Cl TW7 152 B6
Crofters Ct 9 SE8 119 A2
Crofters Way
NW1 93 D6 232 C6
Croft Gdns W7 109 A4
Ruislip HA4 39 D1
Croft Ho 12 W10 91 A4
Putney SW15 157 A5
Croft Lodge Cl IG8 37 B4
Croft Mews N12 14 A1
Crofton Ave Chiswick W4 133 B5
Orpington BR6 227 A6
Sidcup DA5 168 D4
Crofton Gate Way SE4 163 A6
Crofton Gr E4 36 B6
Crofton Inf Sch BR5 211 B2
Crofton Jun Sch BR5 211 B2
Crofton La BR5,BR6 211 B2
Crofton L Ctr SE4 163 C5
Crofton Park Rd SE4 163 B5
Crofton Park Sta SE4 163 B6
Crofton Rd BR6 226 C5
BR6 226 D5
E13 99 B3
SE5 139 C3
Crofton Sch SE4 163 C5
Crofton Terr E5 75 A3
Richmond TW9 132 B1
Crofton Way Enfield EN2 4 C3
New Barnet EN5 13 D5
Croft Rd BR1 187 A4
Carshalton SM1 218 C3
Enfield EN3 7 A4
Merton SW19 180 A3
South Norwood SW16 182 C3
Crofts Ho 19 E2 96 A5
Croftside The SE25 206 A6
Crofts La N22 32 C3
Crofts Rd HA1 43 A4
Crofts St E1 118 A6
Croft St SE8 119 A2
Crofts The TW17 193 C5
Croft The NW10 89 D5
Barnet EN5 1 A1
Chingford E4 20 C2
Ealing W5 88 A2
Edgware HA8 26 D3
Heston TW5 129 A5
New Malden KT3 199 C4
Pinner HA5 41 B2
Ruislip HA4 62 C4
Wembley HA0 65 C3
Croft Villas HA1 43 A3
Croft Way
Richmond TW10 153 B1
Sidcup DA15 167 C1
Crogsland Rd NW1 71 A1
Croham Cl CR2 221 C1
Croham Hurst Sch CR2 221 D3
Croham Manor Rd CR2 221 C2
Croham Mount CR2 221 C1
Croham Park Ave CR2 221 D3
Croham Rd CR2 221 C3
Croham Valley Rd CR2 222 B1
Croindene Rd SW16 182 A2
Crokesley Ho 2 HA8 27 A1
Cromartie Rd N19 49 D2
Cromarty Ct 5 BR1 187 C1
Cromarty Ho 8 E1 97 A2
Cromarty Rd HA8 10 D2
Cromberdale Ct N17 34 A2
Crombie Cl IG4 56 B4
Crombie Mews 5
SW11 136 C3
Crombie Rd DA15 167 B3
Cromdale Ct N16 51 D2
Crome Ho UB5 85 A5
Cromer Cl UB8 83 A1
Cromer Ct
7 Southall UB1 85 D1
Streatham SW16 160 A1
Wandsworth SW18 157 B5
Cromer Pl 5 BR6 211 B1
Cromer Rd E10 54 B2
Barnet EN5 2 A2
Croydon SE25 206 B6
Dagenham RM6 59 A3
Harlington TW6 126 C3
Streatham SW17 181 A4
Tottenham N17 34 A1
Woodford IG8 37 A6
Cromer Road Prim Sch
EN5 2 A2
Cromer St WC1 94 A4 233 B1
Cromer Terr E8 74 A3
Cromer Villas Rd SW18 157 B5
Cromford Cl BR6 227 C5
Cromford Path 1 E5 74 D4
Cromford Rd SW18 157 C6
Cromford Way KT3 177 B2
Cromlix Cl BR7 188 D1
Crompton Ct SW3 257 A4
Crompton Ho SE1 262 B5
SW8 269 B1
W2 236 C5
Crompton Pl EN3 7 C5
Crompton St W2 92 B3 236 C5
Cromwell Ave BR2 209 B5
N6 49 B1
W6 112 B2
New Malden KT3 199 D4
Cromwell Bsns Ctr
IG11 101 C4
Cromwell Cl N2 48 B5
W3 111 A5
2 W4 110 D1
Bromley BR2 209 B5
Walton-on-T KT12 194 B1
Cromwell Cres
SW5 113 C2 255 A4
Cromwell Ct Enfield EN3 18 D6
15 Kingston KT2 176 C3
Wembley HA0 88 A5
Cromwell Ctr NW10 89 B4
Barking IG11 102 A4
Cromwell Ctr The RM8 59 B2
Cromwell Est E10 53 A1
Cromwell Gdns
SW7 114 B3 256 D5
Cromwell Gr W6 112 C3
Cromwell Ho SW11 268 B1
Croydon CR0 220 D5
Putney SW15 134 A1
Cromwell Hospl
SW5 113 D2 255 C4
Cromwell Lo 38 E1 96 C3
Barking IG11 79 C3
Cromwell Mans SW5 255 B4
Cromwell Mews SW7 256 D4
Cromwell Pl N6 49 B1
SW7 114 B2 256 D4
5 W3 111 A5
Mortlake SW14 133 A2
Cromwell Rd E17 54 A4
E7 77 C1
N10 31 A3
N3 30 A2
SW7 256 B4
SW9 138 D4
Beckenham BR3 207 A6
Feltham TW13 150 B3
Hayes UB3 83 B1
Hounslow TW3 129 C1
Kingston KT2 176 A2
Teddington TW11 175 A4
Thornton Heath CR0 205 B2
Walton-on-T KT12 194 B1
Wembley HA0 88 A5
Wimbledon SW19 179 D5
Worcester Park KT4 215 C5
Cromwell St TW3 129 C1
Cromwell Twr EC2 242 B4
Crondace Rd
SW6 135 C4 265 B1
Crondall Ct 7 N1 95 C5
Crondall Ho SW15 156 A3
Crondall Pl 15 N1 95 C5
Crondall St N1 95 C5
Crone Ct 5 NW6 91 B5
Cronin St SE15 139 D5
Crooked Billet E4 35 C3
Crooked Billet Yd 19 E2 95 C4
Crooked Usage N3 47 A6
Crooke Rd SE8 119 A1
Crookham Rd
SW6 135 B4 264 C1
Crook Log DA6 146 D1
Crook Log Prim Sch
DA6 146 D1
Crook Log Sports Ctr
DA16 146 D2
Crookston Rd SE9 144 C2
Croombs Rd E16 99 C2
Croom's Hill SE10 142 B5
Croom's Hill Gr SE10 142 A5
Cropley Ct N1 235 C4
Cropley St N1 95 B5 235 C4
Croppath Rd RM10 81 C4
Cropthorne Ct W9 229 B1
Crosbie 10 NW9 27 D1
Crosbie Ho 20 E17 53 D6
Crosby Cl TW13 173 A6
Crosby Ct N2 48 A5
SE1 252 C2
Crosby Rd E7 77 A2
Dagenham RM10 103 D6
Crosby Row SE1 117 B4 252 C2
Crosby Sq EC3 243 A2
Crosby Wlk 3 E8 73 D2
Streatham SE24 160 C4
Crosfield Ct 3 W10 90 D1
Crosfield Ho W11 244 A5
Crosier Cl SE3 144 A3
Crosier Rd UB10 61 A4
Crosier Way HA4 61 C5
Crosland Pl 5 SW11 137 A2
Crossbow Ho 15 N1 95 C6
Ealing W13 109 B5
Crossbrook Rd SE3 144 A2
Cross Cl SE15 140 B3
Cross Ct 11 SE28 124 B6
SE5 139 B2
Cross Deep TW1 153 A2
Cross Deep Gdns TW1 152 D2
Crossfield Rd N17 51 A6
NW3 70 B2
Crossfield St SE8 141 C5
Crossford St SW9 138 B3
Crossgate Edgware HA8 10 C1
Wembley UB6 65 B2
Crossharbour & London
Arena Sta E14 119 D3
Cross Keys Cl W1 238 B3
5 Edmonton N9 18 A2
Cross La DA5 169 B4
EC3 253 A5
N8 50 B5
Cross Lances Rd TW3 129 D1
Crossland Rd CR7 204 D3
Crosslands Ave
Ealing W5 110 B5
Southall UB2 107 B1
Crosslands Rd KT19 215 B2
Crossleigh Ct 3 SE14 141 B5
Crosslet St SE17 262 D4
Crosslet Vale SE10 141 D4
Crossley St N7 72 C2
Crossman Hos 19 SW12 160 A4

Crossmead SE9 .....166 B3
Crossmead Ave UB6 .....85 C4
Crossmount Ho 13 SE5 ..139 A5
Crossness Rd IG11 .....101 D4
Cross Rd BR2 .....226 A6
N11 .....31 B5
N2 .....30 C1
SE5 .....139 C3
Chingford, Chingford Green
E4 .....20 C3
Croydon CR0 .....205 B1
Enfield EN1 .....5 C1
Feltham TW13 .....173 A6
Harrow HA1 .....42 B4
Harrow HA2 .....63 D5
Harrow HA3 .....25 A1
Ilford RM6 .....58 C2
Kingston KT2 .....176 B3
Merton SW19 .....179 C3
Romford RM7 .....59 C6
Sidcup DA14 .....190 B6
Sutton SM1 .....218 B3
Wood Green N22 .....32 C3
Cross St N1 .....94 D6 234 D6
2 Edmonton N18 .....34 A5
Hampton TW12 .....174 A5
Mortlake SW13 .....133 C2
Crossthwaite Ave SE5,
SE24 .....139 B1
Crosswall EC3 ...117 D6 253 C6
Crossway BR5 .....211 B4
E8,N16 .....73 C3
N12 .....30 B4
NW9 .....45 D5
SE28 .....102 D1
Dagenham RM8 .....80 C5
Ealing W13 .....87 A3
Enfield EN1 .....17 C4
Hayes UB3 .....106 A5
Pinner HA5 .....22 B1
Ruislip HA4 .....62 C4
West Barnes KT3,SW20 ...200 C5
Woodford IG8 .....37 C6
Crossway Ct SE4 .....141 A3
Crossway Par N22 .....32 D3
Crossways Ashford TW16 .171 D3
South Croydon CR2 .....223 B1
Sutton SM2 .....218 B1
Crossways Rd
Beckenham BR3 .....207 C5
Mitcham CR4 .....203 B6
Crossways The
Heston TW5 .....129 B5
Wembley HA9 .....66 C6
Crossway The
Chislehurst SE9 .....165 D2
Hillingdon UB10 .....82 B5
Tottenham N22 .....32 D3
Cross Way The HA3 .....24 C1
Crosswell Cl TW17 .....171 A1
Croston St E8 .....96 A6
Crothall Cl N13 .....16 B1
Crouch Ave IG11 .....102 B5
Crouch Cl BR3 .....185 C4
Crouch Croft SE9 .....166 C1
Crouch End Hill N8 .....49 D2
Crouch Hall Ct N19 .....50 A1
Crouch Hall Rd N8 .....49 D3
Crouch Hill N4,N8,N19 ....50 A2
Crouchmans Cl SE21,
SE26 .....162 A1
Crouch Rd NW10 .....67 B1
Crowborough Ct W13 ...109 C6
Crowborough Path
WD19 .....22 D6
Crowborough Rd SW17 .181 A5
Crowden Way SE28 .....124 C6
Crowder St E1 .....118 B6
Crowfield Ho N5 .....73 A4
Crowfoot Cl E9 .....75 B3
Crowhurst SE25 .....206 A6
Crowhurst Cl SW9 .....138 C3
Crowhurst Ct N17 .....34 B2
Crowhurst Ho 21 SW9 ...138 B3
Crow La RM7,RM8 .....59 D2
Crowland Ave UB3 .....105 D2
Crowland Gdns N14 .....16 A4
Crowland Ho NW8 .....229 A5
Crowland Prim Sch N15 ..52 A4
Crowland Rd N15 .....51 D4
South Norwood CR7 .....205 B5
Crowlands Ave RM7 .....59 D3
Crowland Terr N1 .....73 B1
Crowland Wlk SM4 .....202 A3
Crowley Cres CR0 .....220 C3
Crowline Wlk 1 N1 .....73 A2
Crowmarsh Gdns SE23 ..162 C4
Crown Arc KT1 .....175 D1
Crown Bldgs 4 E4 .....20 B3
Crownbourne Ct SM1 ...217 D4
Crown Cl E3 .....97 C6
NW6 .....69 D2
NW7 .....11 D2
Hayes UB3 .....105 D4
Walton-on-T KT12 .....194 C2
Crown Close Bsns Ctr E3 .97 C6
Crown Ct EC4 .....242 B1
6 N10 .....31 A3
NW8 .....230 B1
SE12 .....165 B5
WC2 .....240 B1
Bromley BR1 .....209 D4
4 Putney SW15 .....134 D1
3 Twickenham TW1 .....153 B4
Crown Dale SE19 .....183 A5
Crowndale Ct NW1 .....232 C4
Crowndale Rd
NW1 .....93 C5 232 B4
Crownfield Ave IG2 .....57 C4
Crownfield Rd E15 .....76 B4
Crown Hill CR0 .....221 A5
Crownhill Rd NW10 .....89 D6
Crown Ho HA4 .....40 A1
Crown La BR2 .....209 D4
N14 .....15 C3
Chislehurst BR7 .....189 A2
Merton SM4 .....201 C6
South Norwood SE19,
SW16 .....182 C5
Crown Lane Gdns SE27 ..182 C5
Crown Lane Prim Sch
SE27 .....182 D5
Crown Lane Spur BR2 ...209 D3
Crownleigh Ct SW2 .....160 C6
Crown Lo SW3 .....257 B3
Crownmead Way RM7 .....59 D5
Crown Mews 3 E13 .....99 C6
Crown Office Row EC4 ..251 A6
Crown Par N14 .....15 C3
Morden SM4 .....201 D5
South Norwood SE19 .....182 D4
Crown Pas SW1 .....249 B3
Kingston KT1 .....175 D1
Crown Pl EC2 .....243 A4
NW5 .....71 B2
Crown Point SE19 .....182 D4
Crown Rd N10 .....31 A3
Enfield EN1 .....6 B2
Ilford IG6 .....57 B5
Kingston KT3 .....177 A2
Morden SM4 .....201 D5
Ruislip HA4 .....62 D3
Sutton SM1 .....217 D4
Twickenham TW1 .....153 B5
Crown Reach SW1 .....259 D1
Crown St SE5 .....139 A5
Acton W3 .....110 D5
Dagenham RM10 .....81 D2
Harrow HA2 .....42 C1
Crownstone Ct 1 SW2 ..160 C6
Crownstone Rd SW2 ..160 C6
Crown Terr TW9 .....132 B1
Crown Trad Ctr UB3 .....105 C4
Crowntree Cl TW7 .....130 D6
Crown Way UB7 .....104 B5
Crown Wlk HA9 .....66 B5
Crown Woods Sch SE9 ..167 A6
Crown Woods Way SE9 ..167 B6
Crown Yard TW3 .....130 A2
Crowshott Ave HA7 .....25 D2
Crows Rd E15 .....98 B4
Barking IG11 .....78 D2
Crowther Ave TW8 .....110 A2
Crowther Cl
SW6 .....135 B6 264 D5
Crowther Rd SE25 .....206 A5
Crowthorne Cl SW18 .....157 B3
Crowthorne Rd W10 .....90 D1
Croxall Ho KT12 .....194 C3
Croxden Cl HA8 .....44 C6
Croxden Wlk SM4 .....202 A3
Croxford Gdns N22 .....32 D3
Croxley Cl BR5 .....190 B1
Croxley Gn BR5 .....190 B2
Croxley Rd W9 .....91 B4
Croxted Cl SE21 .....161 A4
Croxted Mews SE24 .....161 A5
Croxted Rd SE21,SE24 .....161 B3
Croxteth Ho 11 SW8 .....137 D3
Croxton 17 KT1 .....176 C1
Croyde Ave Greenford UB6 .86 A4
Hayes UB3 .....105 C2
Croyde Cl SE9 .....167 B4
Croydon N17 .....33 B1
Croydon Airport Ind Est
CR0 .....220 B2
Croydon Central Sta
CR0 .....221 A6
Croydon Coll CR0 .....221 B6
Croydon Coll Annexe
CR0 .....205 B1
Croydon Coll (Selhurst
Tertiary Ctr) SE25 .....205 B4
Croydon Flyover The
CR0 .....221 A5
Croydon Gr CR0 .....204 D1
Croydon Ho SE1 .....251 B2
Croydon Rd E13 .....98 D3
Beckenham BR3 .....207 A6
Coney Hall BR2,BR4 .....224 D5
Harlington TW6 .....126 D2
Keston Mark BR2,BR4,
BR6 .....225 C5
Mitcham CR0,CR4 .....203 C4
Penge SE20 .....184 C2
Wallington CR0 .....220 B4
Wallington CR0,SM5,SM6 .219 C5
Croydon Rd Ind Est
BR3 .....206 D5
Croyland Rd N9 .....18 A3
Croylands Dr KT6 .....198 A2
Croysdale Ave TW16 .....194 A6
Crozier Ho SE3 .....143 B2
SW8 .....270 C3
Crozier Terr E9 .....74 D3
Crucible Cl RM6 .....58 B3
Crucifix La SE1 ..117 C4 253 A2
Cruden Ho 23 E3 .....97 B5
11 SE17 .....138 D6
Cruden St N1 .....94 D6 234 D5
Cruickshank St WC1 .....234 A2
Cruikshank Ho NW8 .....230 B4
Cruikshank Rd E15 .....76 C3
Crummock Gdns NW9 .....45 C4
Crumpsall St SE2 .....124 C2
Crundale Ave NW9 .....44 C4
Crunden Rd CR2 .....221 B1
Crusader Gdns CR0 .....221 C5
Crusader Ind Est N4 .....51 A3
Crusoe House Sch
N1 .....95 B4 235 C2
Crusoe Mews N16 .....73 B6
Crusoe Rd CR4 .....180 D3
Crutched Friars
EC3 .....117 C6 253 B6
Crutchfield La KT12 .....194 B1
Crutchley Rd SE6 .....164 C2
Crystal Ct SE19 .....183 D5
Crystal Ctr The 1 HA1 ....42 D4
Crystal Ho SE18 .....123 D1
Crystal Palace Mus*
SE19 .....183 D4
Crystal Palace National
Sports Ctr SE20 .....184 A4
Crystal Palace Par
SE19 .....183 D5
Crystal Palace Park Rd
SE26 .....184 B5
Crystal Palace Rd SE22 ..162 A6
Crystal Palace Sta SE19 .184 A4
Crystal Palace Station Rd
SE19 .....184 A4
Crystal Terr SE19 .....183 B4
Crystal View Ct BR1 .....186 B6
Crystal Way
Dagenham RM8 .....58 C1
Harrow HA1 .....42 D4
Cuba Dr EN3 .....6 C3
Cuba St E14 .....119 C4
Cubitt Ho 4 SW4 .....159 C5
Cubitt Sq UB2 .....108 A5
Cubitt St WC1 .....94 B4 233 D1
Cubitt Terr SW4 .....137 C2
Cubitt Town Jun & Inf Sch
E14 .....120 A3
Cuckoo Ave W7 .....86 C3
Cuckoo Dene W7 .....86 B2
Cuckoo Hall La N9 .....18 D4
Cuckoo Hall Prim Sch
N9 .....18 C4
Cuckoo Hill HA5 .....40 C6
Cuckoo Hill Dr HA5 .....40 C6
Cuckoo Hill Rd HA5 .....40 D5
Cuckoo La W7 .....108 C6
Cuda's Cl KT19 .....215 D4
Cuddington SE17 .....262 B4
Cuddington Ave KT19,
KT4 .....215 D5
Cuddington Com Prim Sch
KT4 .....215 D5
Cudham La N BR6 .....227 C1
Cudham St SE6 .....164 A4
Cudworth Ho SW8 .....269 B1
Cudworth St E1 .....96 B3
Cuff Cres SE9 .....165 D5
Cuffley Ho W10 .....90 C2
Cuff Point 12 E2 .....95 D4
Culand Ho SE17 .....263 A3
Culford Gdns
SW3 .....114 D2 257 D3
Culford Gr N1 .....73 C2
Culford Mans SW3 .....257 D3
Culford Mews N1 .....73 C2
Culford Rd N1 .....73 C2
N1 .....95 C6
Culgaith Gdns EN2 .....4 A1
Culham Ho 33 E2 .....95 D4
21 W2 .....91 C2
Cullen Ho W9 .....91 B5
Cullen Way NW10 .....89 A3
Culling Rd SE16 .....118 C3
Cullington Cl HA3 .....43 A5
Cullingworth Rd NW10 ...68 B3
Culloden Cl 15 SE16 .....118 A1
Culloden Prim Sch E14 ...98 A1
Culloden Rd EN2 .....4 D3
Cullum St EC3 .....253 A6
Culmington Mans W13 ..109 C6
Culmington Par W13 ...109 C6
Culmington Rd
Ealing W13,W5 .....109 C5
South Croydon CR2 .....221 A1
Culmore Rd SE15 .....140 C5
Culmstock Rd SW11 .....159 A6
Culpepper Ct SE11 .....261 A4
Culross Bldgs NW1 .....233 A4
Culross Cl N15 .....51 A5
Culross St W1 ...115 A6 248 A5
Culsac Rd KT6 .....214 A6
Culver Ct SW18 .....157 D5
Culverden Rd SW12 .....159 C2
Culver Gr HA7 .....25 C1
Culverhouse WC1 .....240 C3
Culverhouse Gdns
SW16 .....160 B1
Culverlands Cl HA7 .....25 B6
Culverley Rd SE6 .....164 A3
Culvers Ave SM5,CR4 ...218 D6
Culvers House Prim Sch
CR4 .....203 A1
Culvers Retreat SM5 .....218 D6
Culverstone Cl BR2 .....208 D4
Culvers Way SM5 .....218 D6
Culvert Ct SW11 .....137 A3
Culverton Ct 5 DA14 .....190 A6
Culvert Pl SW11 .....137 A3
Culvert Rd N15 .....51 C4
SW11 .....136 D3
Culworth Ho NW8 .....230 A4
Culworth St NW8 .....230 A3
Cumber Ho SW18 .....157 C3
Cumberland Ave DA16 ..145 D1
Wembley NW10 .....88 D4
Cumberland Bsns Pk
NW10 .....88 D4
Cumberland Cl E8 .....73 D2
2 Twickenham TW1 .....153 B5
8 Wimbledon SW20 .....178 D3
Cumberland Cres W14 ..254 B4
Cumberland Ct W1 .....237 D1
4 Croydon CR0 .....205 B1
Woodford IG8 .....37 B3
Cumberland Dr DA7 .....147 A5
Chessington KT9 .....214 B5
Hinchley Wood KT10 .....213 A6
Cumberland Gate
W1 .....114 D6 247 D6
Cumberland Gdns NW4 ..29 A1
WC1 .....234 A2
Cumberland Ho N9 .....18 C3
Kingston KT2 .....176 D3
1 Putney SW15 .....156 C4
Cumberland Mans
7 NW6 .....69 C3
W1 .....237 C2
Cumberland Market
NW1 .....93 B4 231 D2
Cumberland Mills Sq
E14 .....120 B1
Cumberland Park Ind Est
NW10 .....90 A4
Cumberland Pk W3 .....111 A6
Cumberland Pl NW1 ...231 C2
Catford SE6 .....164 D3
Sunbury TW16 .....194 A5
Cumberland Rd E12 .....77 D4
E13 .....99 B3
E17 .....35 A1
N9 .....18 C3
W3 .....111 A6
W7 .....108 D4
Ashford TW15 .....148 A1
Barnes SW13 .....134 A4
Beckenham BR2 .....208 D6
Croydon SE25 .....206 B3
Harrow HA1 .....41 D4
Richmond TW9 .....132 C5
Stanmore HA7,HA8 .....44 B6
Wood Green N22 .....32 B1
Cumberland Sch E16 .....98 D2
Cumberland St
SW1 .....115 B1 258 D2
Cumberland Terr NW1 ..231 C3
Cumberland Terrace Mews
NW1 .....231 C3
Cumberland Villas W3 ...111 A6
Cumberlow Ave SE25 .....206 A6
Cumbernauld Gdns
TW16 .....171 D5
Cumberton Rd N17 .....33 B2
Cumbrae Gdns KT6 .....213 D6
Cumbria Ho 2 SW15 .....157 B6
Cumbrian Gdns NW2 .....69 A6
Cumming St N1 .....233 D3
Cumnor Cl 23 SW9 .....138 B3
Cumnor Gdns KT17 .....216 A2
Cumnor Rd SM2 .....218 A2
Cunard Cres N21 .....17 B5
Cunard Pl EC3 .....243 B1
Cunard Rd NW10 .....89 B4
Cunard Wlk 3 SE16 .....119 A2
Cundy Rd E16 .....99 C1
Cundy St SW1 .....115 A2 258 B3
Cunliffe Rd KT19 .....215 D4
Cunliffe St SW16 .....181 C4
Cunningham Cl
Dagenham RM6 .....58 C4
West Wickham BR4 .....223 D6
Cunningham Ct W2 .....236 C5
Cunningham Ho 16 SE5 .139 B5
Cunningham Pk HA1 .....42 B4
Cunningham Pl
NW8 .....92 B3 236 C6
Cunningham Rd N15 .....52 A5
Cunnington St W4 .....111 A2
Cupar Rd SW11 .....268 B2
Cupola Cl BR1 .....187 B5
Cureton St SW1 .115 D2 259 D3
Curie Gdns NW9 .....27 C1
Curie Ho 1 HA9 .....67 A5
Curlew Cl SE28 .....124 D6
Curlew Ct KT6 .....214 C5
Curlew Ho 6 SE15 .....139 D4
SE4 .....141 A1
Enfield EN3 .....18 D6
Curlew St SE1 ...117 D4 253 D2
Curlew Way UB4 .....84 D2
Curnick's La SE27 .....183 A6
Curran Ave DA15 .....167 D6
Hackbridge SM6 .....219 A5
Curran Ho SW3 .....257 A3
Currey Rd UB6 .....64 B2
Curricle St W3 .....111 C5
Currie Hill Cl SW19 .....179 B6
Currie Ho 13 SW12 .....159 D4
Curry Rise NW7 .....28 D4
Cursitor St EC4 ...94 C1 241 A2
Curtain Pl EC2 .....243 B6
Curtain Rd EC2 ....95 C3 243 B6
Curthwaite Gdns EN2 .....15 D6
Curtis Dr W3 .....89 B1
Curtis Field Rd SW16 .....182 C6
Curtis Ho 7 N11 .....31 C5
SE17 .....262 C2
Curtis La HA0 .....66 A3
Curtis Rd
Twickenham TW4 .....151 B4
West Ewell KT19 .....215 A4
Curtis St SE1 ...117 D2 263 C4
Curtis Way SE1 .....263 C4
7 SE28 .....124 B6
Curtlington Ho 3 HA8 .....27 A1
Curve The W12 .....112 A6
Curwen Ave E7 .....77 B4
Curwen Rd W12 .....112 A4
Curwen Sch E13 .....99 A5
Curzon Ave Enfield EN3 ...18 D6
Stanmore HA7 .....25 A2
Curzon Cl BR6 .....227 B4
Curzon Cres NW10 .....67 C1
Barking IG11 .....101 D4
Curzon Ct SE9 .....167 A1
SW6 .....265 D1
Curzon Gate W1 .....248 B3
Curzon Ho W5 .....87 B3
Curzon Pl W1 .....248 B3
Pinner HA5 .....40 C4
Curzon Rd N10 .....31 B1
Ealing W5 .....87 B3
Thornton Heath CR7 .....204 C3
Curzon St W1 ....115 B5 248 C4
Cusack Cl TW1 .....174 D6
Custance Ho N1 .....235 C3
Custance St N1 .....235 C2
Custom House*
EC3 .....117 C6 253 A5
Custom House for ExCeL Sta
E16 .....121 B6
Custom House Reach
SE16 .....119 B3
Cutbush Ho N7 .....71 D3
Cutcombe Mans 22 SE5 .139 A3
Cutcombe Rd SE5 .....139 A3
Cuthberga Cl IG11 .....79 A1
Cuthbert Gdns SE25 .....205 C6
Cuthbert Harrowing Ho
EC1 .....242 A5
Cuthbert Ho W2 .....236 C4
Cuthbert Rd E17 .....54 A6
Croydon CR0 .....220 D6
8 Edmonton N18 .....34 A6
Cuthbert St W2 .....236 C5
Cuthill Wlk 3 SE5 .....139 B4
Cutlers Gdns EC2 .....243 B2
Cutlers Sq E14 .....119 C2
Cutler St EC2 .....243 B2
Cut The SE1 .....116 C4 251 B2
Cutty Sark* SE10 .....142 A6
Cutty Sark Sta SE10 .....142 A6
Cuxton BR5 .....211 A4
Cuxton Cl DA6 .....169 A6
Cuxton Ho SE17 .....263 B2
Cyclamen Cl 4 TW12 .....173 C4
Cyclamen Way KT19 .....215 A3
Cyclops Mews 9 E14 .....119 C2
Cygnet Ave TW14 .....150 D4
Cygnet Cl NW10 .....67 B3
Cygnet St E1 .....243 D6
Cygnets The TW13 .....173 A6
Cygnet Way UB4 .....84 D2
Cygnus Bsns Ctr NW10 ...67 D2
Cymbeline Ct 6 HA1 .....42 D3
Cyns Ct 5 E11 .....55 A3
Cynthia St N1 .....233 D3
Cypress Ave N2 .....47 D6
Twickenham TW2 .....152 A4
Cypress Ct 5 E11 .....76 B4
Cheam SM1 .....217 C2
7 West Norwood SW16 ..182 C5
Cypress Gdns SE4 .....163 A6
Cypress Ho SE14 .....140 D4
Cypress Inf Sch SE25 ...183 C1
Cypress Jun Sch SE25 ...183 C1
Cypress Lo SE25 .....183 C1
Cypress Pl W1 .....239 B5
Cypress Rd Harrow HA3 ..24 B1
South Norwood SE25 .....183 C1
Cypress Tree Cl DA15 .....167 D3
Cyprus Ave N3 .....29 A1
Cyprus Cl N4 .....50 C3
Cyprus Gdns N3 .....29 A1
Cyprus Pl 24 E2 .....96 C5
E6 .....122 C6
Cyprus Rd N3 .....29 B1
Edmonton N9 .....17 D2
Cyprus St E2 .....96 C5
Cyprus Sta E6 .....122 C6
Cyrena Rd SE22 .....161 D6
Cyril Jackson Prim Sch
(North Bldg) E14 .....119 B6
Cyril Jackson Prim Sch
(South Bldg) E14 .....119 B6
Cyril Lo 2 DA14 .....190 A6
Cyril Mans SW11 .....267 D1
Cyril Rd DA7 .....147 A3
Cyril Smith Ho N13 .....32 B5
Cyril Thatcher Ho SW6 ..265 B1
Cyrus Ho EC1 .....241 D6
Cyrus St EC1 .....94 D3 241 D6
Czar St SE8 .....141 C6

D

Dabbs Hill La UB5 .....63 C3
Dabb's La EC1 .....241 B5
Dabin Cres SE10 .....142 A4
Dacca St SE8 .....141 B6
Dace Rd E3 .....97 C6
Dacre Cl UB6 .....85 D5
Dacre Gdns SE13 .....142 C1
Borehamwood WD6 .....11 B6
Dacre Ho SW3 .....266 D5
Dacre Pk SE13 .....142 C1
Dacre Pl SE13 .....142 C2
Dacre Rd E11 .....54 D1
E13 .....99 B6
Thornton Heath CR0 .....204 A2
Dacres Rd SE23 .....162 D1
Dacre St SW1 ...115 D3 259 C6
Dade Way UB2 .....107 B1
Daerwood Cl BR2 .....210 B1
Daffodil Cl CR0 .....206 D1
Daffodil Gdns IG1 .....78 D3
Daffodil Pl 7 TW12 .....173 C4
Daffodil St W12 .....111 D6
Dafforne Rd SW17 .....159 A1
Dagenham Ave RM9 .....103 A6
Dagenham Dock Sta
RM9 .....103 B5
Dagenham East Sta
RM10 .....81 D3
Dagenham Heathway Sta
RM9 .....81 B2
Dagenham Priory Comp Sch
RM10 .....103 D6
Dagenham Rd E10 .....53 B1
Dagenham RM10 .....81 D4
Dagger La WD23,WD6 .....9 A6
Dagmar Ave HA9 .....66 B4
Dagmar Ct E14 .....120 A3
Dagmar Gdns NW10 .....90 D5
Dagmar Mews UB2 .....107 A3
Dagmar Pas N1 .....234 D6
Dagmar Rd N15 .....51 B5
N22 .....31 D2
N4 .....50 C2
SE5 .....139 C4
4 Kingston KT2 .....176 C3
Southall UB2 .....107 A3
South Norwood SE25 .....205 C4
Dagmar Terr N1 ..94 D6 234 D6
Dagnall Pk SE25 .....205 C4
Dagnall Rd SE25 .....205 C4
Dagnall St
SW11 .....137 A4 268 A1
Dagnan Rd SW12 .....159 C4
Dagobert Ho 25 E1 .....96 C2
Dagonet Gdns BR1 .....165 A1
Dagonet Rd BR1 .....165 A1
Dahlia Gdns Ilford IG1 ....78 D2
Mitcham CR4 .....203 D5
Dahlia Rd SE2 .....124 B2
Dahomey Rd SW16 .....181 C4
Daiglen Sch The IG9 .....21 C2
Daimler Ho 8 E3 .....97 C3
Daimler Way SM6 .....220 A1
Daines Cl E12 .....78 B5
Dainford Cl BR1 .....186 B5
Dainton Cl 2 BR1 .....187 B2
Dainton Ho 22 W2 .....91 C2
Daintry Cl HA3 .....43 A5
Daintry Way E9 .....75 B2
Dairsie Ct 2 BR1 .....187 C1
Dairsie Rd SE9 .....144 C2
Dairy Cl BR1 .....187 B3
South Norwood CR7 .....183 A1
Dairy La SE18 .....122 B2
Dairyman Cl NW2 .....69 A5
Dairy Meadow Prim Sch
UB2 .....107 B3
Daisy Cl CR0 .....206 D1
Daisy Dormer Ct 11
SW9 .....138 B1
Daisy La SW6 .....135 C2
Daisy Rd E16 .....98 C3
Woodford E18 .....37 B1
Dakota Cl SM6 .....
Dakota Gdns
Newham E6 .....100 A3
Northolt UB5 .....85 A4
Dalberg Rd SW2 .....160 C6
Dalberg Way SE2 .....124 D3
Dalbury Ho 6 SW9 .....138 B1
Dalby Rd SW18 .....136 A1
Dalbys Cres N17 .....33 C4
Dalby St NW5 .....71 B2
Dalcross Rd TW4,TW5 ...129 A3
Dale Ave Edgware HA8 .....26 B1
Hounslow TW4 .....129 A2
Dalebury Rd SW17 .....158 D2
Dale Cl SE3 .....143 A2
New Barnet EN5 .....13 D5
Pinner HA5 .....22 B2
Dale Croft N4 .....73 A5
Dale Ct N8 .....49 C5
3 Kingston KT2 .....176 B3
Woodford E18 .....37 A1
Dale Dr UB4 .....83 D4
Dalefield IG9 .....21 D3
Dale Gdns IG8 .....37 B6
Dale Gr N12 .....30 A5
Dale Green Rd N11 .....15 B1
Dalehead NW1 .....232 A3
Daleham Dr UB8 .....82 D1
Daleham Gdns NW3 .....70 B2
Daleham Mews NW3 .....70 B2
Dale Ho NW8 .....229 A6
SE4 .....141 A1
Dale Lo N6 .....49 C3
Dalemain Ho 5 SW8 .....137 D3
Dalemain Mews 13 E16 .121 A5
Dale Park Ave SM5 .....218 D6
Dale Park Rd SE19 .....183 B2
Dale Rd NW5 .....71 A3
SE17 .....138 D6
Ashford TW16 .....171 D3
Cheam SM1 .....217 B4
Southall UB6 .....85 D2
Walton-on-T KT12 .....193 D2
Dale Row W11 .....91 A1
Daleside Rd
Streatham SW17 .....181 B5
West Ewell KT19 .....215 B2
Dales Path WD6 .....11 B6
Dales Rd WD6 .....11 B6
Dale St W4 .....111 C1
Dale The BR2 .....225 D4
Dale View Ave E4 .....20 A2
Dale View Cres E4 .....20 A1
Dale View Gdns E4 .....20 B1
Daleview Rd N15 .....51 C3
Dalewood Gdns KT4 .....216 B6
Dale Wood Rd BR6 .....211 C1
Daley Ho W12 .....90 B1

Daley St E9 ....74 D2
Daley Thompson Way 7 SW8 ....137 B2
Dalgarno Gdns W10 ....90 C2
Dalgarno Way W10 ....90 C3
Daling Way E3 ....97 A5
Dalkeith Ct SW1 ....259 D3
Dalkeith Gr HA7 ....26 A5
Dalkeith Ho 6 SW9 ....138 D4
Dalkeith Rd Ilford IG1 ....79 A5
West Norwood SE21 ....161 A4
Dallas Rd NW4 ....46 A2
Cheam SM3 ....217 A2
Ealing W5 ....88 B2
Forest Hill SE26 ....162 B1
Dallas Terr UB3 ....105 D3
Dallega Cl UB3 ....105 B6
Dallinger Rd SE12 ....164 D5
Dalling Rd W6 ....112 B2
Dallington Sch EC1 ....94 D3 241 D6
Dallington St EC1 ....94 D3 241 D6
Dallin Rd DA6 ....146 D1
Woolwich SE18 ....144 D5
Dalmain Prim Sch SE23 .163 A3
Dalmain Rd SE23 ....162 D3
Dalmally Rd CR0 ....206 A2
Dalmeny Ave N7 ....71 D4
Thornton Heath SW16 ....182 C1
Dalmeny Cl HA0 ....65 C2
Dalmeny Cres TW3 ....130 B1
Dalmeny Ct 8 SW4 ....138 A3
Dalmeny Rd DA7,DA8 ....147 D4
N7 ....71 D4
New Barnet EN5 ....14 A5
North Cheam KT4 ....216 B5
Wallington SM5 ....219 A1
Dalmeyer Rd NW10 ....67 D2
Dalmore Ave KT10 ....212 D2
Dalmore Rd SE21 ....161 A2
Dalrymple Cl N14 ....15 D4
Dalrymple Rd SE4 ....141 A1
Dalston Gdns HA7 ....26 A1
Dalston Jct E8 ....73 D2
Dalston Kingsland Sta E8 ....73 D3
Dalston La E8 ....74 A3
Dalton Ave CR4 ....180 C1
Dalton Cl BR6 ....227 C5
Hayes UB4 ....83 B3
Dalton Ho 9 E3 ....97 A5
10 SE14 ....140 D6
Dalton St SE27 ....160 D1
Dalwood St SE5 ....139 C4
Daly Ct E15 ....76 A3
Dalyell Rd SW9 ....138 B2
Damascene Wlk SE21 ....161 A3
Damask Cres E16 ....98 C3
Damer Ho 9 TW10 ....154 B5
Damer Terr SW10 ....266 B3
Dames Rd E7 ....77 A5
Dame St N1 ....95 A5 235 A4
Damien Ct 20 E1 ....96 B1
Damien St E1 ....96 B1
Damon Cl DA14 ....168 B1
Damon Ct DA14 ....168 B1
Damory Ho 1 SE16 ....118 C2
Damson Dr UB3 ....106 A6
Damsonwood Rd UB2 ....107 C3
Danbrook Rd SW16 ....182 A3
Dan Bryant Ho 5 SW12 .159 C4
Danbury Cl RM6 ....58 D6
Danbury Mans 3 IG11 ...78 D1
Danbury Mews SM5, SM6 ....219 B4
Danbury St N1 ....94 D5 234 D4
Danbury Way IG8 ....37 C4
Danby Ct EN2 ....5 A2
Danby Ho 23 E9 ....74 C1
3 W10 ....91 B4
Danby St SE15 ....139 D2
Dancer Rd
Fulham SW6 ....135 B4 264 C1
Richmond TW9 ....132 C2
Dando Cres SE3 ....143 B2
Dandridge Cl SE10 ....120 D1
Dandridge Ho E1 ....243 C4
Danebury W10 ....90 C2
New Addington CR0 ....223 D2
Danebury Ave SW15 ....155 D5
Daneby Rd SE6 ....164 A2
Dane Cl BR6 ....227 B3
Sidcup DA5 ....169 C4
Danecourt Gdns CR0 ....221 D5
Danecroft Rd SE24 ....161 B6
Danegrove Prim Sch EN4 ....14 C5
Danegrove Sch EN4 ....14 D5
Danehill Wlk DA14 ....168 A1
Dane Ho 10 SE5 ....139 A3
Danehurst TW8 ....131 C5
Danehurst Gdns IG4 ....56 B4
Danehurst St SW6 ....135 A4 264 A2
Daneland EN4 ....14 D5
Danemead Gr UB5 ....63 D3
Danemere St SW15 ....134 C2
Dane Pl E3 ....97 B5
Dane Rd N18 ....18 C1
Ashford TW15 ....171 B4
Ealing W13 ....109 C5
Ilford IG1 ....79 A3
Merton SW19 ....180 A2
Southall UB1 ....107 A6
Danesbury Rd TW13 ....150 B3
Danescombe SE12 ....165 A3
Danescourt Cres SM1 ...218 A6
Danescroft NW4 ....46 D4
Danescroft Ave NW4 ....46 D4
Danescroft Gdns NW4 ....46 D4
Danes Ct NW8 ....230 C5
Wembley HA9 ....66 D5
Danesdale Rd E9 ....75 A2
Danesfield SE5 ....139 C6
Danes Gate HA1 ....42 C6
Danes Ho W10 ....90 C2
Dane St WC1 ....240 C3
Daneswood Ave SE6 ....164 A1
Danethorpe Rd HA0 ....65 D2
Danetree Cl KT19 ....215 A1
Danetree Jun Sch KT19 .215 A1
Danetree Rd KT19 ....215 A1
Danette Gdns RM8 ....81 B6
Daneville Rd SE5 ....139 B4
Danford Ho 9 N11 ....31 C5
Dangan Rd E11 ....55 A3
Daniel Bolt Cl E14 ....97 D2
Daniel Cl N18 ....34 C6
Twickenham TW4 ....151 B4
Upper Tooting SW17 ....180 C4
Daniel Ct 8 NW9 ....27 C2
W3 ....111 C6
3 Beckenham BR3 ....185 C3
Daniel Gdns SE15 ....139 D5
Daniell Ho N1 ....235 D4
Daniell Way CR0 ....204 B1
Daniel Pl NW4 ....46 B2
Daniel Rd W5 ....110 B6
Daniel's Rd SE15 ....140 C2
Dan Leno Wlk SW6 ....265 C3
Dansey Pl W1 ....249 C6
Dansington Rd DA16 ....146 A1
Danson Cres DA16 ....146 B2
Danson Intc DA5,DA6 ....168 C5
Danson La DA16 ....146 B1
Danson Mead DA16 ....146 C2
Danson Prim Sch DA16 .146 A1
Danson Rd DA5,DA6, DA15 ....168 D6
Danson Underpass DA15 ....168 C5
Dante Rd SE11 ...116 D2 261 C4
Danube Ct 12 SE15 ....139 D5
Danube St SW3 ..114 C1 257 B2
Danvers Ho 22 E1 ....96 A1
Danvers Rd N8 ....49 D5
Danvers St SW3 .136 B6 266 D5
Da Palma Ct SW6 ....265 A5
Daphne Ct Ealing W5 ....87 C1
Worcester Park KT4 ....215 C6
Daphne Gdns E4 ....20 A1
Daphne Ho N22 ....32 C2
Daphne St SW18 ....158 A5
Daplyn St 6 E1 ....96 A2
D'arblay St W1 ....93 C1 239 B1
Darby Cres TW16 ....172 C1
Darby Gdns TW16 ....172 C1
Darcy Ave SM6 ....219 C4
Darcy Cl N20 ....14 B2
D'arcy Dr HA3 ....43 D5
D'arcy Gdns
Dagenham RM9 ....103 B6
Harrow HA3 ....44 A5
Darcy Ho E8 ....96 B6
D'arcy Pl BR2 ....209 A5
D'arcy Rd Isleworth TW7 ..131 A4
Thornton Heath SW16 ....182 A1
D'arcy Rd SM3 ....216 D4
Dare Ct 2 E10 ....54 A2
Dare Gdns RM8 ....81 A5
Darell Prim Sch TW9 ....132 C2
Darell Rd TW9 ....132 C2
Daren Ct N7 ....72 A4
Darent Ho NW8 ....236 D4
4 Catford BR1 ....186 B5
Darenth Rd DA16 ....146 A4
N16 ....51 D1
Darfield NW1 ....232 A5
Darfield Rd SE4 ....163 B6
Darfield Way W10 ....90 D1
Darfur St SW15 ....134 D2
Dargate Cl SE19 ....183 D3
Darien Ho 8 E1 ....96 D2
17 SW11 ....136 B2
Darien Rd SW11 ....136 B2
Daring Ho 23 E3 ....97 A5
Darland Ct SW15 ....157 B5
Darlands Dr EN5 ....12 D6
Darlan Rd SW6 ....135 B5 264 D3
Darlaston Rd SW19 ....179 A3
Darley Cl CR0 ....207 A3
Darley Dr KT3 ....177 B1
Darley Gdns SM4 ....201 D3
Darley Ho SE11 ....260 C1
Darley Rd SW11 ....158 D5
Edmonton N9 ....17 D3
Darling Ho 5 TW1 ....153 D5
Darling Rd SE4 ....141 C2
Darling Row E1 ....96 B3
Darlington Ct 8 SE6 ....164 D3
Darlington Ho SW8 ....269 D3
2 Surbiton KT6 ....197 D2
Darlington Rd SE27 ....182 D5
Darmaine Cl CR2 ....221 A1
Darnay Ho 3 SE16 ....118 A3
Darndale Cl E17 ....35 B1
Darnell Ho 4 SE10 ....142 A4
9 SE10 ....142 A5
Darnley Ho 9 E14 ....97 A1
Darnley Rd E9 ....74 C2
Woodford IG8 ....37 B2
Darnley Terr 12 W11 ....112 D5
Darrell Ct BR2 ....208 C6
Darrell Rd SE22 ....162 A6
Darren Cl N4 ....50 B2
Darrick Wood Ho BR6 ...227 A5
Darrick Wood Inf Sch BR6 ....226 D5
Darrick Wood Jun Sch BR6 ....226 D4
Darrick Wood Rd BR6 ...227 B6
Darrick Wood Sec Sch BR6 ....226 D5
Darrick Wood Sports Ctr BR6 ....227 C6
Darris Cl UB4 ....85 A3
Darsley Dr SW8 ..138 A4 270 A2
Dartford Ave N9 ....18 D5
Dartford Gdns RM6 ....58 B4
Dartford Ho SE1 ....263 D4
Dartford St SE17 ....139 A6
Dartington NW1 ....232 B5
Dartington Ho 7 SW8 ..137 D3
W2 ....91 D2
Dartle Ct 26 SE16 ....118 A4
Dartmoor Wlk 17 E14 ...119 C2
Dartmouth Cl W11 ....91 C1
Dartmouth Ct SE10 ....142 A4
Dartmouth Gr SE10 ....142 A4
Dartmouth Hill SE10 ....142 A4
Dartmouth Ho N19 ....71 B6
Lewisham SE10 ....142 A3
Thornton Heath CR0 ....204 D2
Dartmouth Park Ave NW5 ....71 B5
Dartmouth Park Hill N19 .71 B6
Dartmouth Park Rd NW5 .71 B5
Dartmouth Pl
Chiswick W4 ....133 C6
Forest Hill SE23 ....162 C2
Dartmouth Rd NW2 ....68 D2
NW4 ....46 A3
Forest Hill SE23,SE26 ....162 C1
Hayes BR2 ....209 A2
Ruislip HA4 ....62 A5
Dartmouth Row SE10 ...142 A4
Dartmouth St SW1 ....115 D4 249 D1
Dartmouth Terr SE10 ....142 B4
Dartnell Rd CR0 ....205 D2
Darton Ct W3 ....111 A5
Dartrey Twr SW10 ....266 C4
Dartrey Wlk SW10 ....136 A5 266 B4
Dart St W10 ....91 B4
Darville Rd N16 ....73 D5
Darwell Cl E6 ....100 C5
Darwen Pl E2 ....96 B6
Darwin Cl BR6 ....227 B3
N11 ....15 B1
Darwin Ct E13 ....99 B4
NW1 ....231 B6
SE9 ....166 C5
Darwin Dr UB1 ....85 D1
Darwin Gdns WD19 ....22 C5
Darwin Ho 2 HA9 ....67 A5
Darwin Rd DA16 ....145 D2
W5 ....109 C2
Tottenham N22 ....32 D1
Darwin St SE17 ..117 B2 262 D4
Daryngton Dr UB6 ....86 C5
Daryngton Ho SW8 ....270 A3
Dashwood Cl DA6 ....169 C6
Dashwood Ct TW3 ....130 A1
Dashwood Ho SE21 ....161 D1
Dashwood Rd N8 ....50 B3
Dassett Rd SE27 ....182 D5
Data Point Bsns Ctr E16 .98 B3
Datchelor Pl 14 SE5 ....139 B4
Datchet Ho NW1 ....231 D2
Datchet Rd SE6 ....163 B2
Datchett Ho 40 E2 ....95 D4
Datchwood Ct N4 ....73 A5
Datchworth Ct 7 EN1 ....17 C6
Datchworth Ho 8 N1 ....72 D1
Date St SE17 ....117 B1 262 C1
Daubeney Gdns N17 ....33 A3
Daubeney Pl TW12 ....173 D1
Daubeney Prim Sch E5 ...75 A4
Daubeney Rd E5 ....75 A4
Tottenham N17 ....33 A3
Daubeney Twr 2 SE8 ....119 B1
Dault Rd SW18 ....158 A5
Dauney Ho SE1 ....251 C1
Dave Adams Ho 7 E3 ....97 B5
Davenant Ho 18 E1 ....96 A2
Davenant Rd N19 ....71 D6
Croydon CR0,CR9 ....220 D4
Davenant St E1 ....96 A2
Davenport Cl TW11 ....175 A4
Davenport Ctr IG11 ....102 B5
Davenport Ho SE11 ....261 A5
Davenport Lo TW5 ....129 A5
Davenport Rd DA14 ....169 A2
SE6 ....164 A5
Daventer Dr HA7 ....24 D3
Daventry Ave E17 ....53 C3
Daventry St NW1 .92 C2 237 A4
Dave Porter Hts SW19 ...157 A4
Daver Ct SW3 ....257 B1
Ealing W5 ....87 D3
Davern Cl SE10 ....120 D2
Davet Ct SW8 ....270 C2
Davey Cl N7 ....72 B2
Bowes Park N13 ....32 B5
Davey Lo 2 N1 ....72 C1
Davey Rd E9 ....75 C1
Davey's Ct WC2 ....250 A6
Davey St SE15 ....139 D6
David Ave UB6 ....86 C5
David Cl UB3 ....127 C5
David Coffer Ct DA17 ...125 D2
David Devine Ho 7 E8 ....74 A3
Davidge Ho SE1 ....251 B1
Davidge St SE1 ..116 D4 251 D1
David Ho 3 E14 ....97 D2
David Ho *continued*
SW8 ....270 A4
8 Putney SW15 ....156 A6
South Norwood SE25 ....206 A6
David Lee Point 4 E15 ...98 C6
David Livingstone Prim Sch CR7 ....183 A2
David Mews W1 ....237 D4
David Rd RM8 ....81 A6
Davidson Gdns SW8 ....138 A5 270 A4
Davidson Ho 7 N19 ....71 C4
Davidson Inf Sch CR0 ...205 D2
Davidson Jun Sch CR0 ..205 D2
Davidson Lo CR0 ....205 C2
Davidson Rd CR0 ....205 D3
Davidson Terrs E7 ....77 B3
Davidson Twr BR1 ....187 B5
David's Rd SE23 ....162 C3
David St E15 ....76 B3
David Twigg Cl KT2 ....176 A2
Davies Cl CR0 ....206 A3
Davies La E11 ....76 D6
Davies Lane Jun & Inf Sch E11 ....76 D6
Davies Mews W1 ....248 C6
Davies St W1 ....115 B6 248 C6
Davies Walk TW7 ....130 B4
Da Vinci Ct 12 SE16 ....118 B1
Davington Gdns RM8 ....80 B3
Davington Rd RM8 ....80 B3
Davis Ho W12 ....112 B6
Davis Rd W3 ....111 D4
Chessington KT9 ....214 C4
Davis St E13 ....99 B5
Davisville Rd W12 ....112 A4
Davmor Ct TW8 ....109 C1
Davy Ho HA9 ....67 A6
Dawes Ave TW7 ....131 A1
Dawe's Cl UB10 ....82 A5
Dawes Ho SE17 ....262 C3
Dawes Rd SW6 ....135 B5 264 C4
Dawe's Rd UB10 ....82 A5
Dawes St SE17 ....117 B1 262 D2
Dawley Ave UB8 ....83 A1
Dawley Par UB3 ....105 A6
Dawley Rd Hayes UB3 ....105 B6
Hayes UB3 ....105 C2
Dawlish Ave
Bowes Park N13 ....32 A5
Wandsworth SW18 ....157 D2
Wembley UB6 ....87 A5
Dawlish Dr Ilford IG3 ....79 D4
Pinner HA5 ....41 A3
Ruislip HA4 ....62 B6
Dawlish Prim Sch E10 ....54 A1
Dawlish Rd E10 ....76 A6
N17 ....52 A6
NW2 ....68 D2
Dawnay Gdns SW18 ....158 B2
Dawnay Rd SW17,SW18 ..158 B2
Dawn Cl TW4 ....129 A2
Dawn Cres E15 ....98 B6
Dawn Wlk BR2 ....186 B1
Dawpool Rd NW2 ....67 D6
Daws Ho 35 W12 ....112 B6
Daws La NW7 ....28 A5
Dawson Ave BR5 ....190 B1
Barking IG11 ....79 D1
Dawson Cl SE18 ....123 A2
Hayes UB3 ....83 B2
Dawson Gdns 9 IG11 ....79 D1
Dawson Ho 23 E2 ....96 C4
5 SE5 ....139 C4
Dawson Pl W2 ....113 C6 245 B6
Dawson Rd NW2 ....68 C4
Kingston KT1 ....198 B6
Dawson St E2 ....95 D5
Dawson Terr N9 ....18 C4
Dax Ct TW16 ....194 C6
Daybrook Rd SW19 ....201 D6
Day Ho SE5 ....138 D5
2 SE5 ....139 A5
Daylesford Ave SW15 ....134 A1
Daymer Gdns HA5 ....40 C5
Daynor Ho 4 NW6 ....91 C6
Daysbrook Rd SW2 ....160 B3
Days La DA15 ....167 C4
Days Lane Prim Sch DA15 ....167 D5
Daytone Ho SW20 ....178 D2
Dayton Gr SE15 ....140 C4
Deaconess Ct 4 N15 ....51 D5
Deacon Ho SE11 ....260 D3
Deacon Mews N1 ....73 B1
Deacon Rd NW2 ....68 A2
Kingston KT2 ....176 B2
Deacons Cl HA5 ....22 B1
Deacon's Hill Rd WD6 ....10 C6
Deacons Hts WD6 ....10 C5
Deacons Leas BR6 ....227 B4
Deacons Rise N2 ....48 B4
Deacons Wlk TW12 ....173 C6
Deacon Way SE17 ....117 A2 262 B4
Deal Ct 13 NW9 ....27 D1
7 Southall UB1 ....86 A1
Deal Ho SE15 ....140 D6
SE17 ....263 B2
Deal Porters Way SE16 ..118 D3
Deal Rd SW17 ....181 A4
Deal St E1 ....96 A2
Dealtry Rd SW15 ....134 C1
Deal Wlk 3 SW9 ....138 C5
Dean Bradley St SW1 ....260 A5
Dean Cl E9 ....74 C3
SE16 ....118 D5
Hillingdon UB10 ....60 B1
Deancross St E1 ....96 C1
Dean Ct SW8 ....270 A3
Dean Ct *continued*
Edgware HA8 ....26 D4
10 Kingston KT2 ....176 C3
Wembley HA0 ....65 B5
Dean Dr HA7 ....26 A1
Deane Ave HA4 ....62 C3
Deane Croft Rd HA5 ....40 C3
Deanery Cl N2 ....48 C5
Deanery Mews W1 ....248 B4
Deanery Rd E15 ....76 C2
Deanery St W1 ...115 A5 248 B4
Deane Way HA4 ....40 B3
Dean Farrar St SW1 ....259 D6
Deanfield Gdns CR0 ....221 B4
Dean Gdns E17 ....54 B5
Deanhill Ct 2 SW14 ....132 D1
Deanhill Rd SW14 ....132 D1
Dean Ho 18 E1 ....96 C1
N16 ....51 D1
N4 ....51 A2
SE14 ....141 B5
Ruislip HA4 ....39 B1
Dean Rd NW2 ....68 C2
Croydon CR0 ....221 B4
Hampton TW12 ....173 C5
Hounslow TW3 ....151 D6
Thamesmead SE28 ....124 A6
Dean Ryle St SW1 ....260 A4
Dean's Bldgs SE17 ....117 B2 262 D3
Deansbrook Cl HA8 ....27 A3
Deansbrook Jun & Inf Schs HA8,NW7 ....27 A4
Deansbrook Rd HA8 ....27 B4
Edgware HA8 ....26 D3
Deans Cl HA8 ....27 A4
Chiswick W4 ....132 D6
South Croydon CR0 ....221 D5
Deanscroft Ave NW9 ....45 A1
Dean's Ct EC4 ....241 D1
Dean's Dr HA8 ....27 B5
Deans Dr N13 ....32 D4
Deansfield Prim HA4 ....62 D4
Deansfield Prim Sch SE9 ....144 C2
Deans Gate Cl SE23 ....162 D1
Deanshanger Ho 21 SE8 ....118 D2
Dean's La HA8 ....27 A4
Dean's Mews W1 ....238 D2
Dean's Rd W7 ....108 D4
Deans Rd SM1 ....217 D5
Dean St E7 ....77 A3
W1 ....93 D1 239 C1
Dean Stanley St SW1 ....260 A5
Deansway N2 ....48 B5
Deans Way HA8 ....27 A5
Deansway N9 ....17 C1
Deanswood N11 ....31 D4
Dean's Yd SW1 ....259 D6
Dean Trench St SW1 ....260 A5
Dean Way UB2 ....107 D4
Dean Wlk HA8 ....27 B3
Dearmer Ho 6 SW2 ....160 C4
Dearne Cl HA7 ....25 A5
De'arn Gdns CR4 ....202 C6
Dearsley Rd EN1 ....6 A2
Deason St E15 ....98 A6
Deauville Ct 4 SE16 ....118 D4
14 SW4 ....159 C5
Deauville Mans 13 SW4 .159 C5
De Barowe Mews N5 ....72 D3
Debdale Ho 20 E2 ....96 A6
Debden N17 ....33 B1
Debden Cl Kingston KT2 .175 D5
Woodford IG8 ....37 D3
De Beauvoir Cres N1 ....95 C6
De Beauvoir Ct N1 ....73 B1
De Beauvoir Pl 5 N1 ....73 C2
De Beauvoir Prim Sch N1 ....73 C2
De Beauvoir Rd N1 ....73 C1
De Beauvoir Sq N1 ....73 C1
Debenham Ct E8 ....96 A6
Barnet EN5 ....12 C6
Debham Ct NW2 ....68 C5
Debnams Rd SE16 ....118 C2
De Bohun Ave N14 ....15 B5
De Bohun Prim Sch N14 .15 B6
Deborah Cl TW7 ....130 C4
Deborah Cres HA4 ....39 B2
Deborah Ct 7 E18 ....55 B6
De Broome Rd TW13 ....150 C3
De Burgh Ho 10 SW19 ....180 A3
Deburgh Rd SW19 ....180 A3
Debussy 9 NW9 ....27 D1
Decimal Ctr UB2 ....107 C4
Decima St SE1 ...117 C3 263 A6
Decimus Cl CR7 ....205 B5
Deck Cl SE16 ....118 D5
Decoy Ave NW11 ....47 A5
De Crespigny Pk SE5 ....139 B3
Dedham Ho 1 SE6 ....186 A6
Dee Ct W7 ....86 B1
Deeley Rd SW8 ..137 D4 269 C2
Deena Cl W3 ....88 B1
Deepdale N4 ....72 D5
Wimbledon SW19 ....178 D6
Deepdale Ave BR2 ....208 D5
Deepdale Cl N11 ....31 A4
Deepdale Ct 4 CR0 ....221 B4
Deepdene N12 ....30 C6
Deepdene Ave CR0 ....221 D5
Deepdene Cl E11 ....55 A5
Deepdene Ct
Beckenham BR2 ....208 C6
Southgate N21 ....16 D5
Deepdene Gdns SW2 ....160 B4
Deepdene Ho N16 ....51 B1
Deepdene Lo 5 SW2 ....160 B4
Deepdene Mans SW6 ....264 C2
Deepdene Point 9 SE26 ....162 D1
Deepdene Rd DA16 ....146 A2
SE5,SE24 ....139 B1
Deepwell Cl TW7 ....131 A4
Deepwood La UB6 ....86 B4
Deerbrook Rd SE24, SW2 ....160 D3
Dee Rd TW9 ....132 B1
Deerdale Rd SE24 ....139 A1
Deerhurst 7 KT2 ....176 D2
Deerhurst Cl TW13 ....172 B6
Deerhurst Cres TW12 ....174 A5
Deerhurst Ho 6 SE15 ....140 A6
Deerhurst Rd NW2 ....68 D2
Streatham SW16 ....182 B5
Deerings Dr HA5 ....40 A4
Deerleap Gr E4 ....19 D6
Deer Lo SW6 ....135 A2
Deer Park Cl KT2 ....176 D3
Deer Park Gdns CR4 ....202 B5
Deer Park Rd SW19 ....180 A1
Deer Park Way BR4 ....224 D6
Deeside Rd SW17 ....158 B1
Dee St E14 ....98 A1
Defiance Wlk SE18 ....122 B3
Defiant 18 NW9 ....27 D1
Defiant Way SM6 ....220 A1
Defoe Ave TW9 ....132 C5
Defoe Cl SW17 ....180 C4
Defoe Ho EC2 ....242 A4
5 N16 ....73 C5
Defoe Pl EC2 ....242 A4
Upper Tooting SW17 ....180 D6
Defoe Rd N16 ....73 C5
SE16 ....119 B4
De Frene Rd SE26 ....163 A1
De Gama Pl E14 ....119 C1
Degema Rd BR7 ....188 D5
Dehar Cres NW9 ....46 A2
Dehavilland Cl UB5 ....84 D4
De Havilland Rd
Edgware HA8 ....26 D1
Heston TW5 ....128 C5
De Havilland Way TW19 .148 A5
Dekker Ho 19 SE5 ....139 B5
Dekker Rd SE21 ....161 C5
Delacourt Rd SE3 ....143 B5
Delafield Ho 18 E1 ....96 A1
Delafield Rd SE7 ....121 C1
Delaford Rd SE16 ....118 B1
Delaford St SW6 .135 B6 264 B5
Delamare Cres CR0 ....206 C3
Delamere Gdns NW7 ....27 B4
Delamere Ho 4 N4 ....51 B2
Delamere Rd W5 ....110 A4
Hayes UB4 ....106 D6
Wimbledon SW20 ....178 D2
Delamere St W2 ....236 A3
Delamere Terr W2 ....91 D2
Delancey Pas NW1 ....231 D5
Delancey St NW1 .93 B6 231 D5
Delancey Studios NW1 ..231 D5
Delany Ho SE10 ....142 A6
Delarch Ho SE1 ....251 C1
De Laune St SE17 ....116 D1 261 C1
Delaware Rd W9 ....91 D3
Delawyk Cres SE24 ....161 B5
Delcombe Ave KT4 ....200 C1
Delft Ho 8 KT2 ....176 B3
Delft Way 2 SE22 ....161 C6
Delhi Rd EN1 ....17 D4
Delhi St N1 ....94 A6 233 B5
Delia St SW18 ....157 D4
Delisle Rd SE28 ....123 C5
Delius Cl WD6 ....9 C5
Delius Gr E15 ....98 A5
Dellafield N4 ....72 C6
Della Path E5 ....74 B5
Dellbow Rd TW14 ....150 B6
Dell Cl E15 ....98 B6
Wallington SM6 ....219 D4
Woodford IG8 ....21 B1
Dellfield Cl BR3 ....186 A2
Dell La KT17 ....216 A3
Dellors Cl EN5 ....12 D6
Dellow Cl IG2 ....57 B2
Dellow Ho 6 E1 ....118 B6
Dellow St E1 ....118 B6
Dell Rd Enfield EN3 ....6 C5
Stoneleigh KT17 ....216 A2
West Drayton UB7 ....104 B3
Dells Cl Chingford E4 ....19 D4
Teddington TW11 ....174 D4
Dell's Mews SW1 ....259 B3
Dell The SE2 ....124 A1
Brentford TW8 ....131 C6
Feltham TW14 ....150 B4
Pinner HA5 ....22 D1
South Norwood SE19 ....183 D2
Wembley HA0 ....65 B3
Woodford IG8 ....21 B1
Dell Way W13 ....87 C1
Dell Wlk KT3 ....177 C1
Dellwood Gdns IG5 ....56 C6
Delme Cres SE3 ....143 B3
Delmey Cl CR0 ....221 D5
Deloraine Ho SE8 ....141 C4
Deloraine St SE8 ....141 C4
Delorme St W6 ....134 D6
Delphian Ct 5 SW16 ....182 C6
Delroy Ct N20 ....14 A4
Delta Bldg 4 E14 ....98 A1
Delta Cl KT4 ....215 D5
Delta Ct NW2 ....68 A6
Delta Gr UB5 ....84 D4
Delta Ho N1 ....235 D2
Delta Pk SW18 ....135 D1

Delta Rd KT4 ...215 C5
Delta St 3 E2 ...96 A4
De Lucy Prim Sch SE2 ...124 B4
De Lucy St SE2 ...124 B2
Delvan Cl SE18 ...144 C5
Delverton Ho SE17 ...261 D2
Delverton Rd SE17 ...261 D1
Delvino Rd SW6 .135 C4 265 B1
De Mandeville Ct E4 ...35 A6
De Mandeville Gate EN1 ...6 B1
Demesne Rd SM6 ...219 D4
Demeta Cl HA9 ...67 A5
De Montfort Par 1
SW16 ...160 A1
De Montfort Rd SW16 ...160 A2
De Morgan Rd SW6 ...135 D2
Dempster Cl KT6 ...197 C1
Dempster Rd SW18 ...158 A6
Denberry Dr DA14 ...168 B1
Denbigh Cl BR7 ...188 B4
NW10 ...67 C1
W11 ...113 B6 244 D6
Cheam SM1 ...217 B3
Ruislip HA4 ...61 D6
Southall UB1 ...85 B1
Denbigh Ct E6 ...99 D4
1 Ealing W7 ...86 D2
Denbigh Dr UB3 ...105 A4
Denbigh Gdns TW10 ...154 B6
Denbigh Ho SW1 ...257 D6
W11 ...244 D6
7 W11 ...91 B1
Denbigh Mews SW1 ...259 A3
Denbigh Pl SW1 .115 C1 259 A2
Denbigh Rd E6 ...99 D4
W11 ...113 B6 244 D6
Ealing W13 ...87 B1
Hounslow TW3 ...129 D3
Southall UB1 ...85 B1
Denbigh St SW1 .115 C1 259 B2
Denbigh Terr
W11 ...113 B6 244 D6
Denbridge Rd BR1,BR7 ..188 B1
Denbury Ho 48 E3 ...97 D4
Denby Ct SE11 ...260 D4
Dence Ho 20 E2 ...96 A4
Denchworth Ho 15 SW9 .138 C3
Den Cl BR2,BR3 ...208 B6
Dencliffe TW15 ...170 C5
Dendridge Cl EN1 ...6 B6
Dendy St SW12 ...159 A3
Dene Ave DA15 ...168 B4
Hounslow TW3 ...129 B2
Dene Cl SE4 ...141 A1
Hayes BR2 ...208 D1
Worcester Park KT4 ...215 D6
Denecroft Cres UB10 ...82 D6
Dene Ct W7 ...108 D4
Ealing W5 ...87 C2
Dene Gdns
Hinchley Wood KT7 ...213 A6
Stanmore HA7 ...25 C5
Dene Ho N14 ...15 D4
Denehurst Gdns NW4 ...46 C3
Acton W3 ...110 D5
Richmond TW10 ...132 C1
Twickenham TW2 ...152 B4
Woodford IG8 ...37 B6
Dene Mans 1 NW6 ...69 C2
Dene Rd N11 ...14 D2
Buckhurst Hill IG9 ...21 D3
Denesmead SE24 ...161 A6
Dene The Ealing W13 ...87 B2
East Molesey KT12,KT8 ...195 B4
South Croydon CR0 ...222 D4
Wembley HA9 ...66 A4
Denewood EN5 ...14 A6
Denewood Rd N6 ...48 D2
Dengie Wlk N1 ...235 A6
Denham Cl DA16 ...146 C2
Denham Cres CR4 ...202 D5
Denham Ct
Forest Hill SE26 ...162 B1
Southall UB1 ...108 A6
Denham Dr IG2 ...57 A3
Denham Ho 32 W12 ...112 B6
Denham Lo W5 ...88 A1
Denham Rd N20 ...14 D1
Feltham TW14 ...150 C4
Denham St SE10 ...121 A1
Denham Way IG11 ...101 D6
Denholme Rd W9 ...91 B4
Denise Ct HA0 ...65 C4
Denison Cl N2 ...48 A6
Denison Ho 8 E14 ...97 C1
Denison Rd Ealing W5 ...87 C3
Feltham TW13 ...171 D6
Mitcham SW19 ...180 B4
Deniston Ave DA5 ...169 A3
Denland Ho SW8 ...270 D3
Denleigh Ct N14 ...15 D4
Denleigh Gdns
Southgate N21 ...16 C4
Thames Ditton KT7 ...196 C3
Denman Dr NW11 ...47 C4
Ashford TW15 ...170 D4
Claygate KT10 ...213 A3
Denman Dr N NW11 ...47 C4
Denman Dr S NW11 ...47 C4
Denman Ho N16 ...73 C6
Denman Rd SE15 ...139 D3
Denman St W1 ...249 C5
Denmark Ave SW19 ...179 A3
Denmark Ct SM4 ...201 C4
Denmark Gdns SM5 ...218 D5
Denmark Gr N1 ...234 A4
Denmark Hill SE5 ...139 B3
Denmark Hill Dr NW9 ...46 A6
Denmark Hill Sta SE5 ...139 B3
Denmark Ho 9 SE7 ...122 A2
Denmark Mans 14 SE5 ..139 A3
Denmark Pl WC2 ...239 D2
Denmark Rd BR1 ...187 B2
N8 ...50 C5
NW6 ...91 B5
SE5 ...139 A3
Carshalton SM5 ...218 D5
Croydon SE25 ...206 B4
Ealing W13 ...109 B6
Kingston KT1 ...198 A6
Twickenham TW2 ...152 B1
Wimbledon SW19 ...178 D4
Denmark St 6 E11 ...76 C5
E13 ...99 B2
WC2 ...239 D2
Tottenham N17 ...34 B3
Denmark Terr NW2 ...48 D6
Denmead Ho 8 SW15 ...155 D5
Denmead Rd CR0 ...204 D1
Denmead Sch TW12 ...173 D3
Denmead Upper Sch
TW12 ...173 D3
Denmore Ct SM6 ...219 B3
Dennan Rd KT6 ...198 B1
Dennard Way BR6 ...226 C4
Denner Rd E4 ...19 C2
Denne Terr E8 ...95 D6
Dennett Rd CR0 ...204 C2
Dennett's Gr SE14 ...140 D3
Dennett's Rd SE14 ...140 C4
Denning Ave CR0 ...220 C3
Denning Cl NW8 ..92 A4 229 B1
Hampton TW12 ...173 B5
Denning Point E1 ...243 D2
Denning Rd NW3 ...70 B4
Dennington Cl 17 E5 ...74 B6
Dennington Park Rd
NW6 ...69 C2
Denningtons The KT4 ...215 C6
Dennis Ave HA9 ...66 B3
Dennis Cl TW15 ...171 B3
Dennis Ct E17 ...36 B1
Dennis Gdns HA7 ...25 C5
Dennis Ho 4 E3 ...97 B5
Sutton SM1 ...217 C4
Dennis La HA7 ...25 B6
Dennison Point E15 ...76 A1
Dennis Par 1 N14 ...15 D3
Dennis Park Cres SW20 .179 A2
Dennis Rd KT8 ...196 A5
Dennis Reeve Cl CR4 ...180 D2
Dennis Way SW4 ...137 D2
Denny Cl 15 E6 ...100 A2
Denny Cres SE11 ...261 B2
Denny Gdns RM9 ...80 B1
Denny Rd N9 ...18 B3
Denny St SE11 ...116 C1 261 B2
Den Rd BR2 ...208 B6
Densham Ho NW8 ...229 D3
Densham Rd E15 ...98 C6
Densole Cl BR3 ...185 A2
Denstone Ho 5 SE15 ...140 A6
Densworth Gr N9 ...18 C2
Dent Ho SE17 ...263 A3
Denton NW1 ...71 A2
Denton Cl EN5 ...12 C6
Denton Ho N1 ...72 D1
Denton Rd N8 ...50 B3
Bexley DA16 ...146 C5
Edmonton N18 ...33 C6
Twickenham TW1 ...153 D5
Denton St SW18 ...157 D5
Denton Way E5 ...74 D5
Dents Rd SW11 ...158 D5
Denvale Trade Pk CR4 ...202 B5
Denver Cl BR6 ...211 C3
Denver Rd N16 ...51 C2
Denwood SE23 ...162 D1
Denyer Ho 1 NW5 ...71 B4
Denyer St SW3 ..114 C2 257 B4
Denys Bldg EC1 ...241 A4
Denziloe Ave UB10 ...82 D4
Denzil Rd NW10 ...67 D3
Deodar Rd SW15 ...135 A1
Deodora Cl N20 ...14 D1
Depot App NW2 ...68 D4
Depot Rd W12 ...112 C6
Isleworth TW3,TW7 ...130 B2
Depot St SE5 ...139 B6
Deptford Bridge SE8 ...141 C4
Deptford Bridge Sta
SE8 ...141 C4
Deptford Broadway
SE8,SE14 ...141 C4
Deptford Church St
SE8 ...141 C5
Deptford Ferry Rd 12
E14 ...119 C2
Deptford Gn SE8 ...141 C6
Deptford Green Sch
SE14 ...141 B5
Deptford Green Sch (Annexe)
SE14 ...141 A5
Deptford High St SE8 ...141 C5
Deptford Park Prim Sch
SE8 ...119 A1
Deptford Sta SE8 ...141 C5
Deptford Trad Est SE8 ...141 A6
Deptford Wharf SE8 ...119 B2
Dept of Transport &
Environment SW1 ...259 D5
De Quincey Mews 3
E16 ...121 A5
De Quincey Rd N17 ...33 B2
Derby Ave N12 ...30 A5
Harrow HA3 ...24 B2
Romford RM7 ...59 D3
Derby Ct 8 E5 ...74 D4
Woodford E18 ...36 D2
Derby Gate SW1 ...250 A2
Derby Hill SE23 ...162 C2
Derby Hill Cres SE23 ...162 C2
Derby Ho NW4 ...46 C6
SE11 ...261 A4
Pinner HA5 ...22 D1
Derby Lo N3 ...29 B1
Derby Rd E7 ...77 D1
E9 ...96 D6
N18 ...34 C5
Cheam SM1,SM2 ...217 B2
Enfield EN3 ...18 C6
Greenford UB6 ...85 D6
Hounslow TW3 ...129 D1
Merton SW19 ...179 C3
Mortlake SW14 ...132 D1
Surbiton KT5,KT6 ...198 C1
Thornton Heath CR0 ...204 D1
Woodford E18 ...36 D2
Derby Rd Ind Est TW3 ...129 D1
Derbyshire St E2 ...96 A4
Derby St W1 ...248 B3
Dereham Ho 7 SE4 ...140 D1
Dereham Pl EC2 ...243 B6
Dereham Rd IG11 ...79 D3
Derek Ave
Chessington KT19 ...214 D3
Wallington SM6 ...219 B4
Wembley HA9 ...66 D1
Derek Cl KT19 ...214 D3
Derek Walcott Cl SE24 ..160 D6
Dericote St E8 ...96 B6
Deri Dene Cl 2 TW19 ...148 A5
Derifall Cl E6 ...100 B2
Dering Pl CR0 ...221 A4
Dering Rd CR0 ...221 A4
Dering St W1 ...238 D1
Derinton Rd SW17 ...181 A6
Derley Rd UB2 ...106 D3
Dermody Gdns SE13 ...164 B6
Dermody Rd SE13 ...164 B6
Deronda Rd SE24,SW2 ...160 D3
Deroy Cl SM5 ...218 D2
Deroy Ct SM5 ...218 D2
Derrick Gdns SE7 ...121 C2
Derrick Ho 18 SW2 ...160 C3
Derrick Rd BR3 ...207 B5
Derrycombe Ho W11 ...91 B2
18 W2 ...91 C2
Derry Rd CR0,SM6 ...220 A5
Derry St W8 ...113 D4 245 C1
Dersingham Ave E12 ...78 C4
Dersingham Inf Sch E12 ..78 C3
Dersingham Rd NW2 ...69 A5
Derwent NW1 ...232 A1
Derwent Ave NW7 ...27 B4
NW9 ...45 C4
Barnet, London EN4 ...14 D3
Edmonton N18 ...33 B5
Kingston SW15 ...177 C6
Pinner HA5 ...23 A4
Uxbridge UB10 ...60 C5
Derwent Cl
Claygate KT10 ...212 D2
East Bedfont TW14 ...149 D3
Derwent Cres DA7 ...147 C3
N20 ...14 A1
Stanmore HA7 ...25 C1
Derwent Ct N8 ...50 A3
8 SE16 ...118 D4
2 W6 ...112 A2
Derwent Dr BR5 ...211 B2
Hayes UB4 ...83 C2
Derwent Gdns
Redbridge IG4 ...56 A5
Wembley HA9 ...43 C2
Derwent Gr SE22 ...139 D1
Derwent Ho E3 ...97 B3
SW7 ...256 B4
Penge SE20 ...184 B1
Derwent Lo
Hounslow TW7 ...130 B3
North Cheam KT4 ...216 B6
Derwent Rd W5 ...109 C3
Palmers Green N13 ...16 B1
Penge SE20 ...184 B1
Southall UB1 ...85 B1
Twickenham TW2 ...151 D5
West Barnes SM4 ...200 D3
Derwent Rise NW9 ...45 C3
Derwent St SE10 ...120 C1
Derwentwater Mans 2
W3 ...111 A5
Derwentwater Prim Sch
W3 ...111 A5
Derwentwater Rd W3 ...111 A5
Derwent Wlk SM6 ...219 B1
Derwent Yd W5 ...109 C3
De Salis Rd UB10 ...83 A3
Desborough Cl W2 ...91 D2
Lower Halliford TW17 ...192 C2
Desborough Ct SE25 ...206 B5
Desborough Ho W14 ...264 D6
Desenfans Rd SE21 ...161 C5
Desford Rd E16 ...98 C3
Desford Way TW15 ...148 B2
Design Mus*
SE1 ...117 D4 253 D2
Desmond Ho 4 EN4 ...14 C5
Desmond St SE14 ...141 A6
Despard Ho SW2 ...160 C2
Despard Rd N19 ...49 C1
Dessouter 19 NW9 ...27 D1
Detherick Ct TW3 ...130 A1
Dethick Ct E3 ...97 A6
Detling Ho SE17 ...263 A3
Detling Rd BR1 ...187 A5
Detmold Rd E5 ...74 C6
Deutsche Schule TW10 .153 D3
Devalls Cl E6 ...122 C6
Devana End SM5 ...218 D5
Devas Rd SW20 ...178 C2
Devas St E3 ...97 D3
Devema Cl BR7 ...188 C2
Devenay Rd E15 ...76 D1
Devenish Rd SE2 ...124 A4
Deventer Cres 8 SE22 ..161 C6
De Vere Cotts W8 ...256 A6
De Vere Gdns
W8 ...114 A4 246 A1
Redbridge IG1 ...56 B1
Deverell St SE1 ..117 B3 262 C5
De Vere Mews W8 ...256 A6
Devereux Ct WC2 ...241 A1
Devereux Ho 7 SW15 ...156 A6
Devereux La SW13 ...134 B5
Devereux Rd SW11 ...158 D5
Deverill Ct SE20 ...184 C2
Devey Cl KT2 ...177 B5
Devitt Ho 4 E14 ...119 D6
Devizes St N1 ...235 D5
Devon Ave TW2 ...152 A3
Devon Cl N17 ...51 D6
Chigwell IG9 ...21 B2
Wembley UB6 ...87 C6
Devoncroft Gdns TW1 ...153 A4
Devon Ct 3 Acton W3 ...88 C1
2 Ealing W7 ...86 D2
Devon Gdns N4 ...50 D3
Devon Ho E17 ...35 B1
Penge SE20 ...184 B3
5 Wanstead E11 ...55 A4
Devonhurst Pl 4 W4 ...111 B1
Devonia Gdns N18 ...33 A4
Devonia Rd N1 ...94 D5 234 D4
Devon Mans SE1 ...253 B2
Devon Par HA3 ...43 C4
Devonport W2 ...237 A2
Devonport Gdns IG1 ...56 B3
Devonport Ho 23 W2 ...91 C2
Devonport Rd W12 ...112 B4
Devonport St E1 ...96 D1
Devon Rd IG11 ...101 C6
Devon Rise N2 ...48 B5
Devonshire Ave SM2 ...218 A1
Devonshire Cl E15 ...76 C4
W1 ...238 C4
Edmonton N13 ...32 C6
Devonshire Cres NW7 ...28 D3
Devonshire Ct
Croydon CR0 ...207 C1
Feltham TW13 ...150 B2
6 Richmond TW9 ...132 B4
Tottenham N17 ...33 A4
Devonshire Dr SE10 ...141 D4
Long Ditton KT6 ...213 D6
Devonshire Gdns
Chiswick W4 ...133 A5
Edmonton N21 ...17 A4
Tottenham N17 ...33 A4
Devonshire Gr SE15 ...140 B6
Devonshire Hall 14 E9 ...74 C2
Devonshire Hill La N17 ...33 A4
Devonshire Hill Prim Sch
N17 ...33 B4
Devonshire Ho N12 ...14 A1
NW6 ...69 B2
SE1 ...262 A6
SW1 ...259 D2
W2 ...236 D4
14 Balham SW12 ...159 B4
Hounslow TW3 ...130 A2
2 Putney SW15 ...156 C4
10 Sutton SM2 ...218 A1
Devonshire Hospl
W1 ...93 A2 238 B4
Devonshire House Prep Sch
NW3 ...70 B3
Devonshire House Sch
NW3 ...70 A3
Devonshire Mews 2
W4 ...111 C1
Devonshire Mews N
W1 ...238 C4
Devonshire Mews S
W1 ...238 C4
Devonshire Mews W
W1 ...238 B4
Devonshire Pl NW2 ...69 C5
W1 ...93 A2 238 B4
W8 ...255 C5
Devonshire Place Mews
W1 ...238 B4
Devonshire Prim Sch
SM2 ...218 A1
Devonshire Rd DA6 ...147 A1
E17 ...53 C3
N9 ...18 C3
NW7 ...28 D3
W4 ...111 C1
W5 ...109 C3
Chislehurst SE9 ...166 A2
Edmonton N13 ...32 C6
Feltham TW13 ...173 A6
Forest Hill SE23 ...162 C4
Hackbridge SM5,SM6 ...219 A4
Harrow HA1 ...42 B3
Ilford IG2 ...57 C2
Mitcham SW17,SW19 ...180 C3
Newham E16 ...99 B1
Pinner HA5 ...23 B2
Pinner HA5 ...40 C2
Southall UB1 ...85 C2
Sutton SM2 ...218 A1
Thornton Heath CR0 ...205 B2
Tottenham N17 ...33 A4
Devonshire Row EC2 ...243 B3
Devonshire Row Mews
W1 ...238 D5
Devonshire Sq BR2 ...209 B5
EC2 ...95 C1 243 B2
Devonshire St
W1 ...93 B2 238 C4
W4 ...111 C1
Devonshire Terr
W2 ...92 A1 236 B1
Devonshire Way
Croydon CR0,CR9 ...223 B6
Hayes UB4 ...84 B1
Devons Rd E3 ...97 D3
Devons Road Sta E3 ...97 D3
Devon St SE15 ...140 B6
Devon Way
Chessington KT19 ...214 D3
Chessington KT9 ...213 C3
Hillingdon UB10 ...82 B5
Devon Waye TW5 ...129 B5
De Walden Ho NW8 ...230 A4
De Walden St W1 ...238 B3
Dewar Ho 2 SW17 ...180 C5
Dewar St SE15 ...140 A2
Dewberry Gdns E6 ...100 A2
Dewberry St E14 ...98 A2
Dewey Rd N1 ...94 C5 234 A4
Dagenham RM10 ...81 D2
Dewey St SW17 ...180 D5
Dewhurst Rd W14 ...112 D3
Dewlands Ct NW4 ...28 D1
Dewsbury Cl HA5 ...41 A3
Dewsbury Ct 5 W4 ...111 A2
Dewsbury Gdns KT4 ...216 A5
Dewsbury Rd NW10 ...68 A3
Dewsbury Terr NW1 ...231 D6
Dexter Ho 2 DA18 ...125 A3
Dexter Rd EN5 ...12 D5
Deyncourt Rd N17 ...33 A2
Deynecourt Gdns E11 ...55 C5
D'eynsford Rd SE5 ...139 B4
Dhonau Ho SE16 ...263 D4
Diadem Ct W1 ...239 C2
Dial Wlk The
W8 ...113 D4 245 D2
Diameter Rd BR5 ...211 A3
Diamond Cl RM8 ...58 C1
Diamond Est SW17 ...158 C1
Diamond Ho 20 E3 ...97 A5
Diamond Rd HA4 ...63 A4
Diamond St SE15 ...139 C5
13 NW10 ...67 B1
Diamond Terr SE10 ...142 A4
Diana Cl 45 SE8 ...141 B6
Woodford E18 ...37 B2
Diana Ct SM5 ...219 A1
Diana Gdns KT6 ...214 B6
Diana Ho 4 SW2 ...160 B6
Diana, Princess of Wales
Mml Wlk W2 ...114 A5 246 A3
Diana Rd E17 ...53 B6
Dianne Ct SE12 ...165 A3
Dianne Way EN4 ...2 C1
Dianthus Cl SE2 ...124 B1
Dibden Ho 16 SE5 ...139 C5
Dibden St N1 ...95 A6 235 A6
Dibdin Cl SM1 ...217 C5
Dibdin Ho W9 ...91 D5
Dibdin Rd SM1 ...217 C6
Dicey Ave NW2 ...68 C4
Dickens Ave N3 ...30 A2
Hayes UB8 ...82 D1
Dickens Cl DA8 ...147 D5
Hayes UB3 ...105 C2
Richmond TW10 ...154 A2
Dickens Ct
10 Wanstead E11 ...55 A5
Wembley HA0 ...65 C5
Dickens Dr BR7 ...189 A4
Dickens Ho NW6 ...91 C4
NW8 ...236 D6
SE17 ...261 D1
WC1 ...240 A6
3 Erith DA17 ...125 B1
Hayes UB3 ...105 C2
Dickens House Mus*
WC1 ...94 B3 240 D5
Dickens La N18 ...33 C5
Dickenson Cl N9 ...18 A3
Dickenson Ho N8 ...50 B3
Dickenson Rd N8 ...50 A2
Dickenson's La SE25 ...206 A3
Dickenson's Pl SE25 ...206 A3
Dickens Rd E6 ...99 D5
Dickens Sq SE1 ..117 A3 262 B6
Dickens St SW8 ...137 B3
Dickens Wood Cl SE19 ..182 D3
Dickerage Hill
Kingston KT3 ...199 A6
Kingston KT3 ...177 A1
Dickerage La KT3 ...199 A6
Dickerage Rd KT1,KT2,
KT3 ...177 A1
Dickinson Ho 21 E2 ...96 A4
Dickinson Rd TW13 ...172 D5
Dicksee Ho NW8 ...236 C5
Dick Shepherd Ct 17
SW2 ...160 C5
Dickson Fold HA5 ...40 D5
Dickson Ho 13 E1 ...96 B1
9 SE18 ...144 A4
Dickson Rd SE9 ...144 A2
Dick Turpin Way TW14 ..127 D1
Didbin Ho N7 ...72 B6
Didsbury Cl E6 ...100 B6
Digby Bsns Ctr E9 ...74 D2
Digby Cres N4 ...73 A6
Digby Gdns RM10 ...103 C6
Digby Mans W6 ...112 C1
Digby Pl CR0 ...221 D5
Digby Rd E9 ...74 D2
Barking IG11 ...79 D1
Digby St E2 ...96 C4
Digby Stuart Coll SW15 .156 A6
Diggon St 16 E1 ...96 D2
Dighton Ct SE17 ...139 A6
Dighton Rd SW18 ...136 A1
Dignum St N1 ...234 A4
Digswell St N7 ...72 C2
Dilhorne Cl SE12 ...165 B1
Dilke St SW3 ...136 D6 267 D6
Dilloway Yd UB2 ...107 A4
Dillwyn Cl SE26 ...185 A6
Dilston Cl 1 UB5 ...84 C4
Dilston Gr SE16 ...118 C2
Dilton Gdns SW15 ...156 B3
Dilwyn Ct E17 ...35 A1
Dimes Pl 9 W6 ...112 B2
Dimmock Dr UB6 ...64 B3
Dimond Cl E7 ...77 A4
Dimsdale Dr NW9 ...45 A1
Enfield EN1 ...18 A5
Dimsdale Wlk 4 E13 ...99 A5
Dimson Cres E3 ...97 C4
Dinerman Ct NW8 ...229 B6
Dingle Cl EN5 ...11 D5
Dingle Gdns E14 ...119 C6
Dingle Rd TW15 ...170 D5
Dingle The UB10 ...82 D4
Dingley La SW16 ...159 D2
Dingley Pl EC1 ...95 A4 235 B1
Dingley Rd EC1 ...95 A4 235 A1
Dingwall Ave CR0 ...221 A6
Dingwall Gdns NW11 ...47 C3
Dingwall Rd
South Croydon CR0 ...221 B6
Wandsworth SW18 ...158 A4
Dinmont Ho 26 E2 ...96 A5
Dinmont St 1 E2 ...96 B5
Dinmore Ho 17 E9 ...96 C6
Dinnington Ho 17 E1 ...96 B3
Dinorben SM6 ...219 C1
Dinsdale Ct EN5 ...13 D6
Dinsdale Gdns
New Barnet EN5 ...13 D6
South Norwood SE25 ...205 C4
Dinsdale Rd SE3 ...142 D6
Dinsmore Rd SW12 ...159 B4
Dinton Ho NW8 ...237 A6
Dinton Rd Kingston KT2 ...176 B3
Mitcham SW19 ...180 B4
Dinwiddy Ho N1 ...233 C3
Diploma Ave N2 ...48 C5
Diploma Ct N2 ...48 C5
Dirleton Rd E15 ...98 D6
Disbrowe Rd
W6 ...135 A6 264 B5
Discovery Bsns Pk 13
SE16 ...118 A3
Discovery Ho 1 E14 ...120 A6
Dishforth La NW9 ...27 C2
Disley Ct 2 UB1 ...85 D1
Disney Pl SE1 ...252 B2
Disney St SE1 ...252 B2
Dison Cl EN3 ...6 D4
Disraeli Cl SE28 ...124 C5
W4 ...111 B2
Disraeli Gdns SW15 ...135 B1
Disraeli Rd E7 ...77 A2
Acton NW10 ...89 B5
Ealing W5 ...109 D5
Putney SW15 ...135 A1
Diss St E2 ...95 D4
Distaff La EC4 ...252 A6
Distillery La W6 ...112 C1
Distillery Rd W6 ...112 C1
Distillery Wlk 14 TW8 ...132 A6
Distin St SE11 ...116 C2 261 A3
District Rd HA0 ...65 B3
Ditchburn St E14 ...120 A6
Ditchfield Rd UB4 ...85 A3
Dittisham Rd SE9 ...188 A6
Ditton Cl KT7 ...197 A2
Dittoncroft Cl CR0 ...221 C4
Ditton Grange Cl KT6 ...197 D1
Ditton Grange Dr KT6 ...197 D1
Ditton Hill KT6 ...213 D6
Ditton Hill Rd KT6 ...197 C1
Ditton Ho 10 E5 ...74 B3
Ditton Lawn KT7 ...197 A1
Ditton Pl 6 SE20 ...184 B2
Ditton Rd Bexley DA6 ...169 A6
Southall UB2 ...107 B1
Surbiton KT6 ...198 B1
Ditton Reach KT7 ...197 B3
Divis Way SW15 ...156 B5
Dixon Cl 4 E6 ...100 B1
Dixon Clark Ct N1 ...72 D2
Dixon Ct N4 ...50 C3
Dixon Ho SE2 ...124 C1
Dixon Pl BR4 ...207 D1
Dixon Rd SE14 ...141 A4
South Norwood SE25 ...205 D6
Dobbin Cl HA3 ...25 A1
Dobell Rd SE9 ...166 B6
Dobree Ave NW10 ...68 B1
Dobson Cl NW6 ...70 B1
Dobson Ho 18 SE14 ...140 D6
SE5 ...139 B5
Doby Ct EC4 ...252 B6
Dockers Tanner Rd 19
E14 ...119 C2
Dockett Eddy La KT16,
TW17 ...192 B1
Dockett Moorings KT16 .192 B1
Dockhead SE1 ...117 D4 253 D1
Dockhead Wharf SE1 ...253 D2
Dock Hill Ave SE16 ...118 D4
Docklands Heritage Mus*
SE16 ...119 B5

Docklands Mus (Museum in Docklands)★ E14 ......119 C6
Dockland St E16 ......122 C5
Dockley Rd SE16 ......118 A3
Dockley Road Ind Est 11 SE16 ......118 A3
Dock Offices 12 SE16 ....118 C3
Dock Rd E16 ......120 D6
Brentford TW8 ......131 D5
Dockside Rd E16 ......121 D6
Dock St E1 ......118 A6
Dockwell Cl TW14 ......128 A1
Dockwell's Ind Est TW14 ......150 C6
Doctors Cl SE26 ......184 C5
Doctor Spurstowe Almshos 9 E8 ......74 B2
Docura Ho N7 ......72 B6
Docwra's Bldgs N1 ......73 C2
Dodbrooke Rd SE27 ......160 D1
Dodd Ho 18 SE16 ......118 B2
Doddington Gr SE17 ......116 D1 261 D1
Doddington Pl 4 SE17 ..138 D6
Dodsley Pl N9 ......18 C1
Dodson St SE1 ...116 C4 251 B1
Dod St E14 ......97 C1
Doebury Wlk SE18 ......146 A6
Doel Cl SW19 ......180 A3
Doggett Rd SE6 ......163 C4
Doggetts Ct EN4 ......14 C6
Doghurst Ave UB3 ......126 D5
Doghurst Dr UB7 ......126 D5
Dog Kennel Hill SE22 ....139 C2
Dog Kennel Hill Sch SE22 ......139 C2
Dog La NW10 ......67 C4
Dogrose Ct 14 NW9 ......46 A5
Doherty Rd E13 ......99 A3
Dokal Ind Est UB2 ......107 A4
Doland Ct SW17 ......180 D4
Dolben Ct SE8 ......119 B2
Dolben St SE1 ...116 D5 251 D3
Dolby Rd SW6 ......135 B3
Dolland Ho SE11 ......260 D1
Dolland St SE11 ......260 D1
Dollar Bay E14 ......120 A4
Dollary Ct KT3 ......198 D6
Dollis Ave N3 ......29 B2
Dollis Brook Wlk EN5 ......13 A5
Dollis Cres HA4 ......40 C1
Dolliscroft NW7 ......29 A3
Dollis Ct N3 ......29 B2
Dollis Hill Ave NW2 ......68 B5
Dollis Hill Est NW2 ......68 A5
Dollis Hill La NW2 ......68 A5
Dollis Hill Sta NW2 ......68 A3
Dollis Hts NW2 ......68 B5
Dollis Jun & Inf Schs NW7 ......28 C3
Dollis Mews N3 ......29 C2
Dollis Pk N3 ......29 B2
Dollis Rd N3,NW7 ......29 B3
Dollis Valley Way EN5 ......13 B5
Dolman Cl N3 ......30 A1
Dolman Rd W4 ......111 B2
Dolman St SW4 ......138 B1
Dolphin Cl 2 SE16 ......118 D4
SE28 ......102 D1
Kingston KT6 ......197 D4
Dolphin Ct N7 ......71 D4
NW11 ......47 A3
Harrow HA3 ......24 C1
Merton SW19 ......179 C3
2 Wallington SM6 ......219 B2
Dolphin Est The TW16 ...171 B2
Dolphin La E14 ......119 D6
Dolphin Rd
Charlton TW16 ......171 C2
Northolt UB5 ......85 B5
Dolphin Rd N TW16 ......171 C2
Dolphin Rd S TW16 ......171 C2
Dolphin Rd W TW16 ......171 C2
Dolphin Sch SW11 ......158 D6
Dolphin Sq SW1 ......259 B1
Dolphin St KT2 ......176 A2
Dolphin Twr 21 SE8 ......141 B6
Dombey Ho 9 SE1 ......118 A4
4 W11 ......112 D5
Dombey St WC1 ......240 C4
Dome Hill Pk SE26 ......183 D6
Domelton Ho SW18 ......157 D5
Domett Cl SE5 ......139 B1
Domfe Pl E5 ......74 C4
Domingo St EC1 ......242 A5
Dominica Cl 6 E6 ......99 D5
Dominion Bsns Pk N9 ....18 D2
Dominion Ind Est UB2 ...107 A4
Dominion Par HA1 ......42 D4
Dominion Rd
Croydon CR0 ......205 D2
Southall UB2 ......107 A3
Dominion St EC2 ..95 B2 242 D4
Dominion Wks RM8 ......59 A1
Domonic Dr SE9 ......166 D1
Domville Cl N20 ......14 B2
Donaghue Cotts 13 E14 ...97 A2
Donald Dr RM6 ......58 C4
Donald Lynch Ho CR4 ...180 D1
Donald Rd E13 ......99 B6
Thornton Heath CR0 ......204 B2
Donaldson Rd NW6 ......91 B6
SE18 ......144 C4
Donald Woods Gdns KT5 ......215 A6
Doncaster Dr UB5 ......63 B3
Doncaster Gdns N4 ......51 A3
Doncaster Gdns *continued*
Northolt UB5 ......63 B3
Doncaster Gn WD19 ......22 C5
Doncaster Rd N9 ......18 B4
Doncel Ct E4 ......20 B4
Donegal Ho 2 E1 ......96 C3
Donegal St N1 ....94 B5 233 D3
Doneraile Ho SW1 ......258 C1
Doneraile St SW6 ......134 D4
Dongola Rd E1 ......97 A2
E13 ......99 B4
N17 ......51 C6
Dongola Rd W 5 E13 ....99 B4
Donington Ave IG6 ......57 A4
Donkey Alley SE22 ......162 A5
Donkey La EN1 ......6 A3
Donkin Ho 15 SE16 ......118 B2
Donne Ct SE24 ......161 A5
Donnefield Ave HA8 ......26 A3
Donne Ho 7 E14 ......97 C1
18 N16 ......73 B4
14 SE14 ......140 D6
Donnelly Ct SW6 ......264 B4
Donne Pl SW3 ..114 C2 257 B4
Mitcham CR4 ......203 B5
Donne Rd RM8 ......80 C6
Donnington Ct NW10 ......68 B1
11 NW1 ......71 B1
Donnington Ho 12 SW8 .137 D3
Donnington Prim Sch NW10 ......90 B6
Donnington Rd NW10 ......90 B6
Harrow HA3 ......43 D3
Worcester Park KT4 ......216 A6
Donnybrook Rd SW16 ...181 D3
Donovan Ave N10 ......31 C1
Donovan Ct SW7 ......256 C1
Donovan Ho 3 E1 ......118 C6
Donovan Pl N21 ......16 B6
Don Phelan Cl SE5 ......139 B4
Doone Cl TW11 ......175 A4
Doon St SE1 ....116 C5 251 A4
Doradus Ct 20 SW19 ......156 D3
Dora Ho 1 E14 ......97 B1
11 W11 ......112 D6
Doral Way SM5 ......218 D3
Doran Ct E6 ......100 B5
Dorando Cl W12 ......112 B6
Doran Gr SE18 ......145 C5
Doran Manor N2 ......48 D4
Doran Wlk E15 ......76 A1
Dora Rd SW19 ......179 C6
Dora St E14 ......97 B1
Dorcas Ct 9 SW18 ......136 B1
Dorchester Ave
Edmonton N13 ......33 A6
Harrow HA2 ......42 A3
Sidcup DA5 ......168 D4
Dorchester Cl
Northolt UB5 ......63 D3
St Paul's Cray BR5 ......190 B3
Dorchester Ct 1 N10 ......49 B6
1 N1 ......73 C1
N14 ......15 B4
NW2 ......68 D5
SE24 ......161 A6
SW1 ......257 D5
5 Streatham SW16 ......160 A2
2 Woodford E18 ......36 D2
Dorchester Dr SE24 ......161 A6
Feltham TW14 ......149 C5
Dorchester Gdns NW11 ...47 C5
Chingford E4 ......35 C6
Dorchester Gr W4 ......111 D1
Dorchester Mews
New Malden KT3 ......199 B5
Twickenham TW1 ......153 C5
Dorchester Prim Sch KT4 ......200 C1
Dorchester Rd
Cheam SM4 ......202 A2
North Cheam KT4 ......200 C1
Northolt UB5 ......63 D3
Dorchester Way HA3 ......44 B4
Dorchester Waye
Hayes UB4 ......84 B1
Hayes UB4 ......84 C1
Dorcis Ave DA7 ......147 A3
Dordrecht Rd W3 ......111 C5
Dore Ave E12 ......78 C3
Doreen Ave NW9 ......45 B1
Doreen Capstan Ho 3 E11 ......76 C5
Dore Gdns SM4 ......201 D2
Dorell Cl UB1 ......85 B2
Doria Rd SW6 ......135 B3
Doric Ho 7 E2 ......96 D5
Doric Way NW1 ...93 D4 232 C2
Dorien Rd SW20 ......178 D1
Doris Emmerton Ct SW18 ......136 A1
Doris Rd E7 ......77 A1
Ashford TW15 ......171 B4
Dorking Cl SE8 ......141 B6
North Cheam KT4 ......216 D6
Dorking Ct N17 ......34 A2
Dorking Ho SE1 ......262 D6
Dorland Ho SE9 ......167 B5
Dorlcote Rd SW18 ......158 C4
Dorleston Ct N1 ......235 D6
Dorly Cl TW17 ......193 C4
Dorman Pl 6 N9 ......18 A2
Dorman Way NW8 ......92 B6 229 C6
Dorman Wlk NW10 ......67 B2
Dorma Trad Pk E10 ......52 D1
Dormay St SW18 ......157 D6
Dormer Cl E15 ......76 D2
Barnet EN5 ......12 D6
Dormer's Ave UB1 ......85 C1
Dormers Lo EN4 ......2 D3
Dormers Rise UB1 ......85 D1
Dormer's Wells High Sch UB1 ......85 C1
Dormers Wells Ho UB4 ...84 C2
Dormer's Wells Inf Sch UB1 ......107 D6
Dormer's Wells Jun Sch UB1 ......107 D6
Dormer's Wells La UB1 ..107 C5
Dormstone Ho SE17 ......263 A3
Dormywood HA4 ......39 D4
Dornan Wlk E15 ......98 A6
Dornberg Cl SE3 ......143 A5
Dornberg Rd SE3 ......143 B5
Dorncliffe Rd SW6 ......135 A3
Dorney NW3 ......70 C1
Dorney Ct SW6 ......135 A2
Dorney Rise BR5 ......211 D5
Dorney Way TW4 ......151 A6
Dornfell St NW6 ......69 B3
Dornoch Ho 25 E3 ......97 B5
Dornton Rd
South Croydon CR2 ......221 C3
Upper Tooting SW12, SW17 ......159 C2
Dorothy Ave HA0 ......66 A1
Dorothy Barley Inf Sch RM8 ......80 B3
Dorothy Barley Jun Sch RM8 ......80 B3
Dorothy Charrington Ho 1 SE22 ......162 A6
Dorothy Evans Cl DA7 ...147 D1
Dorothy Gdns RM8 ......80 B4
Dorothy Rd SW11 ......136 D2
Dorrien Wlk SW16 ......159 D2
Dorrington Ct SE25 ......183 C1
Dorrington Point 20 E3 ...97 D4
Dorrington St EC1 ......241 A4
Dorrit Ho 2 W11 ......112 D5
Dorrit Mews N18 ......33 C5
Dorrit St SE1 ......252 B2
Dorrit Way BR7 ......189 A4
Dorryn Ct SE26 ......184 D5
Dors Cl NW9 ......45 B1
Dorset Ave DA16 ......145 D1
Hayes UB4 ......83 C4
Southall UB2 ......107 C2
Dorset Bldgs EC4 ......241 C1
Dorset Cl NW1 ......237 C4
Hayes UB4 ......83 C4
Dorset Ct 3 N1 ......73 C1
3 Ealing W7 ......86 D2
Dorset Dr HA8 ......26 B4
Dorset Gdns SW16 ......204 B5
Dorset Ho 1 SE20 ......184 B2
Dorset Mans 2 W6 ......134 D6
Dorset Mews N3 ......29 C2
SW1 ......258 C6
Dorset Pl E15 ......76 B2
Dorset Rd E7 ......77 C1
N15 ......51 B5
SW8 ......138 B5 270 C4
W5 ......109 D3
Ashford TW15 ......148 A1
Chislehurst SE9 ......166 A2
Harrow HA1 ......42 A3
Merton SW19 ......179 C1
Mitcham CR4 ......180 C1
Penge BR3 ......206 D6
Wood Green N22 ......32 A2
Dorset Rise EC4 ...94 D1 241 C1
Dorset Road Inf Sch SE9 ......166 A2
Dorset Sq NW1 ...92 D3 237 C5
Dorset St W1 ....92 D2 237 D3
Dorset Way
Hillingdon UB10 ......82 B5
Twickenham TW2 ......152 B3
Dorset Waye TW5 ......129 B5
Dorton Cl 6 SE15 ......139 C5
Dorville Cres W6 ......112 B3
Dorville Rd SE12 ......165 A6
Dothill Rd SE18 ......145 A5
Douai Gr TW12 ......174 A2
Douay Martyrs RC Sch (Annexe) The UB10 ......60 D3
Doughty Ct 11 E1 ......118 B5
Doughty Mews WC1 ......94 B3 240 C5
Doughty St WC1 ..94 B3 240 C5
Douglas 20 NW9 ......27 D1
Douglas Ave
Chingford E17 ......35 C2
Wembley HA0 ......66 A1
West Barnes KT3 ......200 B5
Douglas Bader Ho N3 ......29 D4
Douglas Bldgs SE1 ......252 B2
Douglas Cl Stanmore HA7 ..25 A5
Wallington SM6 ......220 A2
Douglas Cres UB4 ......84 D3
Douglas Ct N3 ......29 D1
5 NW6 ......69 C1
Douglas Dr CR0 ......223 C5
Douglas Gracey Ho SW18 ......157 A4
Douglas Ho
Isleworth TW1 ......153 B6
Putney SW15 ......156 A5
Douglas Johnstone Ho SW6 ......264 C5
Douglas Mews NW2 ......69 A5
Douglas Rd DA16 ......146 B4
5 E16 ......99 A2
N1 ......73 A1
NW6 ......91 B6
Chingford, Chingford Green E4 ......20 C3
Hounslow TW3 ......129 D2
Douglas Rd *continued*
Ilford IG3 ......58 A3
Kingston KT1 ......176 D1
Stanwell TW19 ......148 A5
Surbiton KT6 ......198 B1
Thames Ditton KT10 ......212 A6
Wood Green N22 ......32 C2
Douglas Rd N N1 ......73 A2
Douglas Rd S N1 ......73 A2
Douglas Robinson Ct SW16 ......182 A3
Douglas Sq SM4 ......201 C3
Douglas St SW1 .115 D2 259 C3
Douglas Terr E17 ......35 B2
Douglas Waite Ho NW6 ...69 D1
Douglas Way SE8 ......141 B5
Doulton Ho SE11 ......260 D4
Doulton Mews 4 NW6 ...69 D2
Dounesforth Gdns SW18 ......157 D3
Douro Pl W8 ....113 D3 255 D6
Douro St E3 ......97 C5
Douthwaite Sq 12 E1 ......118 A5
Dove App E6 ......100 A2
Dove Cl NW7 ......27 D3
Northolt UB5 ......84 D3
Wallington SM6 ......
Dovecot Cl HA5 ......40 C4
Dovecote Gdns 8 SW14 ......133 B2
Dove Ct Enfield EN3 ......18 B6
Stanwell TW19 ......148 A4
Dovedale Ave HA3 ......43 C3
Dovedale Cl DA16 ......146 A3
Dovedale Cotts 6 SW11 ......136 D3
Dovedale Ho N16 ......51 B2
Dovedale Rd SE22 ......162 B5
Dovedale Rise CR4 ......180 D3
Dovedon Cl N14 ......16 A2
Dove House Gdns E4 ......19 C2
Dovehouse Mead IG11 ...101 B5
Dovehouse St SW3 ......114 C1 257 A1
Dove Mews SW7 ......114 A2 256 B2
Dove Pk HA5 ......23 C3
Dover Cl NW2 ......68 D6
Dovercourt Ave CR7 ......204 C5
Dovercourt Gdns HA7 ......26 A5
Dovercourt La SM1 ......218 A5
Dovercourt Rd SE22 ......161 D5
Dover Ct EC1 ......241 C5
SE10 ......141 D4
Dove Rd N1 ......73 B2
Doverfield Rd SW2 ......160 A4
Dover Flats SE1 ......263 B3
Dover Gdns SM5 ......218 D5
Dover Ho 11 SE15 ......140 C6
SE5 ......138 D4
7 Beckenham BR3 ......185 C3
14 Penge SE20 ......184 B2
Dover House Rd SW15 ..156 B6
Doveridge Gdns N13 ......32 D6
Dover Mans 17 SW9 ......138 C2
Dove Row E2 ......96 A6
Dover Park Dr SW15 ......156 B5
Dover Patrol SE3 ......143 C3
Dover Rd N9 ......18 C2
Dagenham RM6 ......59 A3
South Norwood SE19 ......183 B4
Wanstead E12 ......77 C6
Woolwich SE18 ......145 A3
Dover St W1 ....115 C5 249 A4
Dover Terr TW9 ......132 C3
Dover Yd W1 ......249 A4
Doves Cl BR2 ......226 A6
Doves Yd N1 ......94 C6 234 A5
Doveton Ho 6 E1 ......96 C3
Doveton Rd CR2 ......221 B3
Doveton St 7 E1 ......96 C3
Dove Wlk SW1 ......258 A2
Dowanhill Rd SE6 ......164 B3
Dowdeswell Cl SW15 ......133 C1
Dowding Ho N6 ......49 A2
Dowding Pl HA7 ......25 A4
Dowding Rd UB10 ......60 B1
Dowe Ho SE3 ......142 C2
Dowell Ho SE21 ......161 D1
Dowes Ho 13 SW16 ......160 A1
Dowgate Hill EC4 ......252 C6
Dowland Ho EN1 ......5 D5
Dowland St W10 ......91 A4
Dowlas St SE5 ......139 C5
Dowler Ct 2 KT2 ......176 B2
Dowlerville Rd BR6 ......227 D2
Dowling Ho DA17 ......125 B3
Dowman Cl 2 SW19 ......179 D3
Downage NW4 ......46 C6
Downalong WD23 ......8 B3
Down Barns Rd HA4 ......62 D5
Downbarton Ho 11 SW9 ......138 C4
Downbury Mews 13 SW18 ......157 C6
Down Cl UB5 ......84 B5
Downderry Prim Sch BR1 ......186 C6
Downderry Rd BR1 ......186 C6
Downe Cl DA16 ......146 C5
Downe Ho 9 SE7 ......143 C6
Downe Manor Prim Sch UB5 ......84 B4
Downend SE18 ......144 D5
Downend Ct 8 SE15 ......139 C6
Downe Rd CR4 ......180 D1
Downer's Cotts SW4 ......137 C1
Downes Cl TW1 ......153 B5
Downes Ct N21 ......16 C3
Downey Ho 6 E1 ......96 D3
Downfield KT4 ......200 A1
Downfield Cl W9 ......91 D3
Downfield Ho KT3 ......199 B1
Down Hall Rd KT2 ......175 D2
Downham Ct N1 ......73 B1
Downham Ent Ctr SE6 ..164 D2
Downham La BR1 ......186 B5
Downham Rd N1 ......73 B1
Downham Way BR1 ......186 C6
Downhills Ave N17 ......51 B6
Downhills Jun & Inf Schs N15 ......51 B5
Downhills Park Rd N17 ...51 A6
Downhills Way N17 ......33 A1
Downhurst Ave NW7 ......27 B5
Downhurst Ct NW4 ......46 C6
Downing Cl HA2 ......42 A6
Downing Ct N12 ......29 D5
Downing Dr UB6 ......86 C6
Downing Ho 2 W10 ......90 D1
3 Merton SW19 ......179 C3
4 Putney SW15 ......156 A6
Downing Rd RM9 ......81 B1
Downings E6 ......100 C1
Downing St★ SW1 ......116 A4 250 A2
Downland Cl N20 ......14 A3
Downland Ct E11 ......76 C6
Downleys Cl SE9 ......166 B2
Downman Rd SE9 ......144 A2
Down Pl W6 ......112 B1
Down Rd TW11 ......175 B4
Downs Ave BR7 ......188 B5
Pinner HA5 ......41 B2
Downs Bridge Rd BR3 ...186 B2
Downs Ct 16 E8 ......74 B3
12 Wimbledon SW19 ......178 D3
Downsell Jun & Inf Schs E15 ......76 B4
Downsell Rd E15 ......76 B4
Downsfield Rd E17 ......53 A3
Downshall Ave IG3 ......57 C3
Downshall Ct IG3 ......57 C3
Downs Hill BR2,BR3 ......186 B2
Downshire Hill NW3 ......70 B4
Downside
2 Putney SW15 ......157 A6
Sunbury TW16 ......172 A2
Twickenham TW1 ......152 D1
Downside Cl SW19 ......180 A4
Downside Cres NW3 ......70 C3
Ealing W13 ......87 A3
Downside Rd SM2 ......218 C2
Downside Wlk UB5 ......85 B4
Downs La 3 E5 ......74 B4
Downs Park Rd E5,E8 ......74 A3
Downs Rd E5,N16 ......74 A4
Beckenham BR3 ......185 D1
Enfield EN1 ......5 C1
South Norwood CR7 ......183 A2
Downs Side JMI Sch E5 ..74 A4
Down St W1 ....115 B5 248 C3
East Molesey KT8 ......195 C4
Downs The SW19,SW20 ..178 D3
Down St Mews W1 ......248 C3
Downs View TW7 ......131 A4
Downsview Gdns SE19 ..183 A3
Downs View Lo 9 KT6 ..198 A3
Downsview Prim Sch SE19 ......183 A3
Downsview Rd SE19 ......183 A3
Downsview Sch E5 ......74 B4
Downsway BR6 ......227 C3
Downsway The SM2 ......218 A1
Downton Ave SW2 ......160 B2
Downtown Rd SE16 ......119 A4
Downway N12 ......30 C3
Down Way UB5 ......84 B4
Dowrey St N1 ......234 A6
Dowsett Rd N17 ......34 A1
Dowson Cl SE5 ......139 B1
Dowson Ct SE13 ......142 B2
Dowson Ho 7 E1 ......96 D1
Doyce St SE1 ......252 A2
Doyle Gdns NW10 ......90 B6
Doyle Ho W3 ......110 D4
Doyle Rd SE25 ......206 A5
D'Oyley St SW1 ......258 A4
Doynton St N19 ......71 B6
Draco St SE17 ......139 A6
Dragonfly Cl E13 ......99 B4
Dragon Rd SE15 ......139 C6
Dragon Yd WC1 ......240 B2
Dragoon Rd SE8 ......119 B1
Dragor Rd NW10 ......89 A3
Drake Cl 30 SE16 ......118 D4
Drake Cres SE28 ......102 C1
Drake Croft N16 ......73 B6
Drake Ct 5 W12 ......112 B4
Dulwich SE19 ......183 D5
Kingston KT5 ......198 B5
Drakefell Rd SE4,SE14 ...140 D2
Drakefield Rd SW17 ......159 A1
Drake Ho 17 E1 ......96 C2
2 E14 ......119 A6
Drakeley Ct N5 ......72 D4
Drake Rd SE4 ......141 C2
Chessington KT9 ......214 C3
Harrow HA2 ......63 B6
Mitcham CR4 ......203 A3
Thornton Heath CR0 ......204 B2
Drakes Ct SE23 ......162 C3
Drakes Ctyd NW6 ......69 B1
Drake St WC1 ......240 C3
Enfield EN2 ......5 B4
Drakes Wlk E6 ......100 B6
Drakewood Rd SW16 ......181 D3
Draldo Ho 6 SW15 ......157 A6
Draper Cl DA17 ......125 B2
Hounslow TW7 ......130 B3
Draper Ct BR1 ......210 A5
Draper Ho SE1 ......261 D4
Draper Pl N1 ......234 D6
Drapers Almshouses 4 E3 ......97 C4
Draper's Cottage Homes NW7 ......28 A6
Drapers Gdns EC2 ......242 D2
Drapers Rd E15 ......76 B4
N17 ......51 D6
Enfield EN2 ......4 D4
Drappers Way 8 SE16 ...118 A2
Draven Cl BR2 ......208 D2
Drawell Cl SE18 ......123 C1
Drax Ave SW20 ......178 A3
Draxmont SW19 ......179 A4
Draycot Rd Tolworth KT6 .198 C1
Wanstead E11 ......55 B2
Draycott Ave
SW3 ......114 C2 257 B3
Harrow HA3 ......43 C3
Draycott Cl NW2 ......68 D5
Harrow HA3 ......43 B3
Draycott Ct SW11 ......267 A2
Draycott Ho SW3 ......257 C3
Draycott Pl
SW3 ......114 D2 257 C3
Draycott Terr
SW3 ......114 D2 257 D3
Drayford Cl W9 ......91 B3
Dray Gdns SW2 ......160 B6
Draymans Ct 4 SW9 ......138 B2
Draymans Way TW7 ......130 D2
Drayside Mews UB2 ......107 B4
Drayson Mews
W8 ......113 C4 245 B1
Drayton Ave Ealing W13 ..109 A6
Orpington BR6 ......210 D1
Drayton Bridge Rd
Ealing W13 ......87 A1
Ealing W7,W13 ......108 D6
Drayton Cl
Hounslow TW4 ......151 B6
Ilford IG1 ......57 B1
Drayton Ct SW10 ......256 B1
Tolworth KT5 ......214 D6
West Drayton UB7 ......104 B2
Drayton Gdns
SW10 ......114 A1 256 B1
Ealing W13 ......109 A6
Southgate N21 ......16 D4
West Drayton UB7 ......104 A4
Drayton Gn W13 ......109 A6
Drayton Gr W13 ......109 A6
Drayton Green Prim Sch W13 ......109 A6
Drayton Green Rd W13 ..109 B6
Drayton Green Sta W7 ...86 D1
Drayton Ho E11 ......54 B1
14 SE5 ......139 B5
Drayton Manor High Sch W7 ......86 D1
Drayton Park Prim Sch N5 ......72 C3
Drayton Park Sta N5 ......72 C3
Drayton Pk N5,N7 ......72 C4
Drayton Rd E11 ......54 B1
NW10 ......89 D6
Croydon CR0 ......220 D6
Ealing W13 ......109 B6
Tottenham N17 ......33 C1
Drayton Sch The N15 ......52 A3
Drayton Waye HA3 ......43 B3
Dreadnought St SE10 ...120 C3
Drenon Sq UB3 ......105 D6
Dresden Cl NW6 ......69 D2
Dresden Ho SE11 ......260 D4
5 SW11 ......137 A3
Dresden Rd N19 ......49 D1
Dressington Ave SE4 ....163 C5
Drew Ave NW7 ......29 A4
Drewery Ct SE3 ......142 C2
Drewett Ho 19 E1 ......96 A1
Drew Gdns UB6 ......64 D2
Drew Ho 12 SW16 ......160 A1
Drew Prim Sch E16 ......122 A5
Drew Rd E16 ......122 A5
Drewstead Rd SW16 ......159 D2
Driffield Ct 4 NW9 ......27 C2
Driffield Rd E3 ......97 A5
Drift The BR2 ......225 D5
Driftway Ho 15 E3 ......97 B5
Driftway The CR4 ......181 A2
Drinkwater Ho 11 SE5 ...139 B5
Drinkwater Rd HA2 ......63 D6
Drive Mans SW6 ......135 A3
Drive The BR6 ......227 D6
BR7 ......189 D2
DA8 ......147 D6
E17 ......53 D6
HA9 ......67 A6
N11 ......31 D4
N3 ......29 C3
N6 ......48 D4
N7 ......72 B2
NW10 ......89 D6
NW11 ......47 A2
W3 ......89 A1
Ashford TW15 ......171 B3
Barking IG11 ......79 D1
Barnet EN5 ......1 A2
Beckenham BR3 ......185 C2
Buckhurst Hill IG9 ......21 C4
Chingford E4 ......20 B4
Edgware HA8 ......26 C5
Enfield EN2 ......5 B4
Feltham TW14 ......150 C4
Harrow HA2 ......41 C2
Hounslow TW3,TW7 ......130 B3
Ickenham UB10 ......60 A5

Drive The *continued*
Kingston KT2 177 A3
Morden SM4 202 B4
New Barnet EN5 14 A5
Redbridge IG1 56 B2
Sidcup DA14 190 B6
Sidcup DA5 168 D4
South Norwood CR7 205 B5
St Paul's Cray BR7 211 D6
Surbiton KT6 198 A2
Thames Ditton KT10 196 A1
Wanstead E18 55 A6
West Ewell KT19 215 D2
West Wickham BR4 208 B2
Wimbledon SW19,SW20 178 C3
Barking IG11 80 A2
Dr Johnson Ave SW17 159 B1
Dr Johnson's House★
EC4 241 B1
Droitwich Cl SE26 162 A1
Dromey Gdns HA3 24 D3
Dromore Rd SW15 157 A5
Dronfield Gdns RM8 80 C3
Dron Ho E1 96 C2
Droop St W10 91 A3
Drovers Ct SE13 142 A2
3 Kingston KT1 176 A1
Drovers Pl SE15 140 B5
Drovers Rd CR2 221 B3
Dr Triplett's CE Prim Sch
UB3 83 D1
Druce Rd SE21 161 C5
Druid St SE1 117 D4 253 C1
Druids Way BR2 208 B5
Drumaline Ridge KT4 215 C6
Drummer Lo N7 72 B5
Drummond Castle Ct E7 76 D4
Drummond Cres
NW1 93 D4 232 C2
Drummond Ct N12 30 C3
Drummond Ctr CR0 221 A6
Drummond Dr HA7 24 D3
Drummond Gate SW1 259 D2
Drummond Ho 12 E2 96 A5
N2 30 A1
Drummond Rd SE16 118 B3
Croydon CR0 221 A6
Wanstead E11 55 C3
Drummonds Pl TW9 132 A1
Drummond St
NW1 93 C3 239 A6
Drummonds The IG9 21 B2
Drum St E1 243 D2
Drury Cres CR0 220 C6
Drury Ho SW8 269 A2
Drury La WC2 94 A1 240 B1
Drury Rd HA1 42 A2
Drury Way NW10 67 B3
Dryad St SW15 134 D2
Dryburgh Gdns NW9 44 C6
Dryburgh Ho SW1 258 D2
Dryburgh Mans SW15 134 C2
Dryburgh Rd SW15 134 C2
Dryden Ave W7 86 D1
Dryden Ct SE11 261 B3
11 Richmond TW10 175 D6
Dryden Ho BR2 209 D4
16 N16 73 C5
6 SE5 139 C4
Dryden Rd DA16,SE18 145 D4
Enfield EN1 17 D5
Harrow HA3 24 D2
Wimbledon SW19 180 A4
Dryden St WC2 240 B1
Dryer's Bldgs EC1 241 A3
Dryfield Cl NW10 67 A2
Dryfield Rd HA8 27 A4
Dryfield Wlk 1 SE8 141 C6
Dryhill Rd DA17 147 B6
Dryland Ave 5 BR6 227 D4
Drylands Rd N8 50 A3
Drysdale Ave E4 19 D5
Drysdale Flats 3 E8 73 D3
Drysdale Ho 20 E2 95 C4
Drysdale Pl N1 95 C4
Drysdale St N1 95 C4
Dublin Ave E8 96 A6
Du Burstow Terr W7 108 C4
Ducal St 25 E2 95 D4
Ducane Cl W12 90 C1
Du Cane Ct SW12 159 A3
Du Cane Rd W12 90 A1
Ducavel Ho SW2 160 B3
Duchess Cl N11 31 B5
Sutton SM1 218 A4
Duchess Gr IG9 21 B2
Duchess Mews W1 238 D3
Duchess of Bedford Ho
W8 245 A2
Duchess of Bedford's Wlk
W8 113 C4 245 A1
Duchess St W1 93 B2 238 D3
Duchy Rd EN4 2 B5
Duchy St SE1 116 C5 251 B4
Ducie Ho 8 SE7 143 C6
2 Putney SW15 156 C6
Ducie St SW4 138 B1
Duckett Mews N4 50 D3
Duckett Rd N4 50 D3
Duckett St E1 97 A2
Duck La W1 239 C1
Duck Lees La EN3 7 A1
Ducks Hill Rd HA4,HA6 39 A5
Duck's Wlk TW1 153 C6
Du Cros Dr HA7 25 D4
Du Cros Rd W3 111 C5
Dudden Hill La NW10 67 D3
Duddington Cl SE9 187 D6
Dudley Ave HA3,HA7 43 C6
Dudley Ct NW11 47 B5
Dudley Ct *continued*
W1 237 C1
WC2 240 A2
9 Wanstead E11 55 A4
Wembley HA0 65 D3
Dudley Dr Ruislip HA4 62 B3
West Barnes SM4 201 A2
Dudley Gdns W13 109 B4
Harrow HA2 42 B1
Dudley Ho 14 SW9 138 C3
W2 236 C3
Dudley Mews 14 SW2 160 C5
Dudley Rd N3 29 D1
NW6 91 B5
Ashford TW15 170 B6
Chingford E17 35 C1
East Bedfont TW14 149 B3
Harrow HA2 64 A6
Ilford IG1 78 D4
Kingston KT1 198 B6
Richmond TW9 132 B3
Southall UB2 106 D3
Walton-on-T KT12 194 A2
Wimbledon SW19 179 C4
Dudley St W2 236 C3
Dudlington Rd E5 74 C6
Dudmaston Mews SW3 256 D2
Dudsbury Rd DA14 190 B4
Dudset La TW5 128 A4
Duffell Ho SE11 260 D1
Dufferin Ave EC1 242 C5
Dufferin Ct EC1 242 C5
Dufferin St EC1 95 A3 242 B5
Duffield Cl HA1 42 D4
Duffield Dr N15 51 D5
Duffield Ho N4 51 A2
Duff St E14 97 D1
Dufour's Pl W1 239 B1
Dugdale Ho 10 N7 71 D3
Duke Gdns IG6 57 B5
Duke Humphrey Rd
SE3 142 C3
Duke Of Cambridge Cl
TW2 152 B5
Duke Of Edinburgh Rd
SM1 218 B6
Duke of Wellington Pl
SW1,W1 248 B2
Duke Of York's Sq
SW3 114 D2 258 A4
Duke of York St SW1 249 B4
Duke Rd W4 111 B1
Ilford IG6 57 B5
Dukes Ave N10 49 C6
N3 29 D2
Duke's Ave W4 111 B1
Dukes Ave Edgware HA8 26 B5
Harrow HA1 42 C5
Harrow HA2,HA5 41 B3
Hounslow TW4 129 A1
Kingston KT3 199 D6
Northolt UB5 63 A1
Richmond KT2,TW10 175 D6
Dukes Cl Ashford TW15 171 A6
Hampton TW12 173 B5
Dukes Ct SE13 142 A3
SE22 162 A3
SE22 162 B6
Barking E6 100 C6
Beckenham BR3 207 A6
Ealing W13 87 B2
Dukes Gate 4 W4 111 A2
Dukes Green Ave TW14 150 A6
Dukes Head Yd N6 49 B1
Duke's Ho SW1 259 D4
Duke Shore Wharf E14 119 B6
Dukes La W8 113 D4 245 C2
Dukes Mews N10 49 B6
Duke's Mews W1 238 B2
Duke's Pl EC3 95 C1 243 B1
Dukes Point N6 49 B1
Duke's Rd WC1 93 D4 232 D1
Dukes Rd Acton W3 88 C3
Barking E6 100 C6
Dukes Ride UB10 60 A4
Duke St W1 93 A1 238 B1
Richmond TW10,TW9 153 D6
Sutton SM1 218 B4
Duke St Hill SE1 252 D4
Dukesthorpe Rd SE26 184 D6
Duke St Mans W1 238 B1
Duke St St James's
SW1 115 C5 249 B4
Dukes Way BR4 224 C5
Duke's Yd W1 248 B6
Dulas St N4 50 B1
Dulford St W11 113 A6 244 A6
Dulka Rd SW11 158 D6
Dulverton NW1 232 B5
Dulverton Ct 12 KT6 198 A4
Dulverton Mans WC1 240 D5
Dulverton Prim Sch
DA15 167 B2
Dulverton Rd DA15,DA15 167 B2
Ruislip HA4 62 A6
Dulwich Bsns Ctr SE23 162 D3
Dulwich Coll (Endowed)
SE21 161 C2
Dulwich Coll Picture Gall★
SE21 161 C4
Dulwich Coll Prep Sch
SE21 161 C1
Dulwich Comm SE21 161 C3
Dulwich Ct SE22 162 B3
Dulwich Hamlet Jun Sch
SE21 161 B5
Dulwich High Sch for Boys
SE24 161 B6
Dulwich Hospl SE22 139 C1
Dulwich Mead SE24 161 A5
Dulwich Mews 1 SE22 139 D1
Dulwich Oaks The SE21 161 D1
Dulwich Rd SE24 160 D5
Dulwich Village SE21 161 C5
Dulwich Village CE Inf Sch
SE21 161 C5
Dulwich Wood Ave
SE19 183 C5
Dulwich Wood Pk SE19 183 C6
Dumain Ct SE11 261 C3
Du Maurier Ho 2 NW3 70 D3
Dumbarton Ct 16 SW2 160 A4
Dumbarton Rd SW2 160 A5
Dumbleton Cl KT2 176 D2
Dumbreck Rd SE9 144 C2
Dumont Rd N16 73 C5
Dumphreys Ho 5 SW4 159 D4
Dumpton Pl NW1 71 A1
Dunally Pk TW17 193 B2
Dunbar Ave
Beckenham BR3 207 A5
Dagenham RM10 81 C5
Thornton Heath SW16 182 C1
Dunbar Cl UB4 84 A2
Dunbar Ct 3 N12 29 D6
Sutton SM1 218 B3
Walton-on-T KT12 194 C1
Dunbar Gdns RM10 81 D3
Dunbar Rd E7 77 A2
New Malden KT3 199 A5
Tottenham N22 32 D2
Dunbar St SE27 161 A1
Dunbar Wharf 20 E14 119 B6
Dunblane Rd SE9 144 A3
Dunboe Pl TW17 193 A2
Dunboyne Rd NW3 70 D3
Dunbridge Ho 7 SW15 155 D5
Dunbridge St E2 96 B3
Duncan Cl EN5 2 A1
Duncan Ct 3 E14 98 A2
Southgate N21 16 D3
Duncan Gr W3 89 C1
Duncan Ho 3 NW3 70 D1
Duncannon Ho SW1 259 D1
Duncannon St WC2 250 A5
Duncan Rd E8 96 B6
Richmond TW9 132 A1
Duncan St N1 94 D5 234 C4
Duncan Terr N1 94 D5 234 C4
Dunch St 30 E1 96 B1
Dunchurch Ho RM10 81 C1
Duncombe Hill SE23 163 A4
Duncombe Ho 7 SW19 156 D3
Duncombe Prim Sch
N19 50 A1
Duncombe Rd N19 49 D1
Duncrievie Rd SE13 164 B5
Duncroft SE18 145 C5
Dundalk Ho 2 E1 96 C1
Dundalk Rd SE4 141 A2
Dundas Gdns KT8 195 D6
Dundas Ho 12 E2 96 C5
Dundas Rd SE15 140 C3
Dundee Ct 36 E1 118 B5
Dundee Ho W9 229 A2
Dundee Mews EN3 7 C6
Dundee Rd E13 99 B5
Croydon SE25 206 B4
Dundee St E1 118 B5
Dundee Way EN3 7 A2
Dundee Wharf E14 119 B6
Dundela Gdns KT17,KT4 216 B4
Dundonald Cl 6 E6 100 A1
Dundonald Prim Sch
SW19 179 B3
Dundonald Rd NW10 90 D6
Merton SW19 179 B3
Dundonald Road Sta
SW19 179 B3
Dundry Ho 8 SE26 162 A1
Duneaves HA1 64 C5
Dunedin Rd E10 75 D5
Ilford IG1 57 A1
Dunedin Way UB4 84 C3
Dunelm Gr SE27 161 A1
Dunelm St E1 96 D1
Dunfield Gdns SE6 185 D5
Dunfield Rd SE6 185 D5
Dunford Rd N7 72 B4
Dungarvan Ave SW15 134 A1
Dungeness Ho SW18 136 A1
Dunheved Cl CR7 204 C3
Dunheved Rd N CR7 204 C3
Dunheved Rd S CR7 204 C3
Dunheved Rd W CR7 204 C3
Dunhill Point 12 SW15 156 B3
Dunholme Gn N9 17 D1
Dunholme La N9 17 D1
Dunholme Rd N9 17 D1
Dunkeld Ho 13 E14 98 B1
Dunkeld Rd
Dagenham RM8 80 C6
South Norwood SE25 205 B5
Dunkery Rd SE9 166 A1
Dunkirk St 12 SE27 183 A6
Dunlace Rd E5 74 D4
Dunleary Cl TW4 151 B4
Dunley Dr CR0 224 A2
Dunlin Ct 11 SE21 161 B2
Dunlin Ho 13 SE16 118 D2
Dunloe Ave N17 51 B6
Dunloe Ct 7 E2 95 D5
Dunloe St E2 95 D5
Dunlop Pl SE16 117 D3 263 D5
Dunlop Point 10 E16 121 B5
Dunmore Point 15 E2 95 D4
Dunmore Rd NW6 91 A6
Wimbledon SW20 178 D2
Dunmow Cl
Dagenham RM6 58 C4
Dunmow Cl *continued*
3 Feltham TW13 173 A6
Dunmow Ho SE11 260 D2
Dagenham RM9 102 B6
Dunmow Rd E15 76 B4
Dunmow Wlk N1 235 A6
Dunnage Cres SE16 119 A2
Dunnet Ho 26 E3 97 B5
Dunnico Ho SE17 263 A2
Dunn Mead NW9 27 D3
Dunnock Cl N9 18 D3
Dunnock Ct 10 SE21 161 B2
Dunnock Rd E6 100 A1
Dunn's Pas WC1 240 B2
Dunn St E8 73 D3
Dunollie Pl NW5 71 C3
Dunollie Rd NW5 71 C3
Dunoon Gdns SE23 162 D4
Dunoon Ho N1 233 C5
Dunoon Rd SE23 162 C4
Dunraven Dr EN2 4 C3
Dunraven Ho 12 TW9 132 B4
Dunraven Rd W12 112 A5
Dunraven St
W1 114 D6 247 D6
Dunraven Upper Sch
SW16 160 B1
Dunrobin Ct NW3 69 D3
Dunsany Rd W14 112 D3
Dunsfold Ct 9 SM2 217 D1
Dunsfold Ho
10 Kingston KT2 176 D4
4 Streatham SW2 160 B4
Dunsfold Way CR0 223 D1
Dunsford Ct 4 HA5 23 B3
Dunsford Way SW15 156 B5
Dunsmore Cl Bushey WD23 8 B5
Hayes UB4 85 A3
Dunsmore Rd KT12 194 B3
Dunsmore Way WD23 8 B5
Dunsmure Rd N16 51 C1
Dunstable Ct 3 SE3 143 A5
Dunstable Mews W1 238 B4
Dunstable Rd
East Molesey KT8 195 B5
Richmond TW10,TW9 132 A1
Dunstall Ho 9 SE15 140 A4
Dunstall Rd SW19,SW20 178 C4
Dunstall Way KT8 195 D6
Dunstall Welling Est
DA16 146 B3
Dunstan Cl 2 N2 48 A6
Dunstan Glade BR5 211 B3
Dunstan Ho SE4 141 B3
Dunstan Hos 5 E1 96 C2
Dunstan Rd NW11 47 C1
Dunstan's Gr SE22 162 B5
Dunstan's Rd SE22 162 A5
Dunster Ave SM4 200 D1
Dunster Ct EC3 253 B6
Dunster Dr NW9 45 A1
Dunster Gdns NW6 69 B1
Dunster Ho SE6 163 D1
Dunsterville Way SE1 252 D1
Dunster Way
Carshalton CR4 203 A1
Harrow HA2 63 A5
Dunston Rd E8 95 D6
SW11 137 A3
Dunston St E8 95 D6
Dunton Cl KT6 198 A1
Dunton Ct 5 SE26 162 B2
Dunton Ho 14 SW16 160 A1
Dunton Rd E10 53 D2
SE1 117 D2 263 C3
Duntshill Rd SW18 157 D3
Dunvegan Cl KT8 195 D5
Dunvegan Rd SE9 144 B1
Dunwich Rd DA7 147 B4
Dunworth Mews W11 91 B1
Duplex Ride SW1 247 D1
Dupont Rd SW20 178 D1
Duppas Ave CR0 220 D4
Duppas Cl TW17 193 B4
Duppas Ct CR0 220 D5
Duppas Hill La CR0 220 D4
Duppas Hill Rd CR0 220 D4
Duppas Hill Terr CR0 220 D5
Duppas Jun Sch CR0 220 D3
Duppas Rd CR0 220 D5
Dupree Rd SE7 121 B1
Dura Den Cl BR3 185 D3
Durand Cl SM5 202 D1
Durand Gdns
SW9 138 B4 270 D1
Durand Prim Sch
SW9 138 B4 270 D1
Durand Way NW10 67 A1
Durants Lo EN3 6 D2
Durants Park Ave EN3 6 D1
Durants Rd EN3 6 D1
Durants Sch EN3 6 C4
Durant St E2 96 A4
Durban Ct E7 77 D1
Durban Ho 28 W12 112 B6
Durban Rd E15 98 C4
E17 35 B2
Beckenham BR3 185 B1
Ilford IG2 57 C1
Tottenham N17 33 D4
West Norwood SE27 183 B6
Durbin Ho 13 N9 18 A1
Durbin Rd KT9 214 B4
Durdans Ho 1 NW1 71 C1
Durdans Park Prim Sch
UB1 85 B2
Durdans Rd UB1 85 B1
Durell Gdns RM9 80 D3
Durell Rd RM9 80 D3
Durfey Ho SE5 139 B5
Durford Cres SW15 156 B3
Durham Ave
Beckenham BR2 208 D5
Hounslow TW5 107 B1
Woodford IG8 37 D5
Durham Cl SW20 178 B1
Durham Ct 3 NW6 91 C5
Teddington TW11 174 C6
Durham Hill BR1 186 D6
Durham Ho NW8 230 B1
3 Barking IG11 80 A1
Durham House St WC2 250 B5
Durham Pl SW3 257 C1
Ilford IG1 79 A4
Durham Rd DA14 190 B5
E12 77 D4
E16 98 C3
N2 48 D6
N4,N7 72 B6
W5 109 D3
Beckenham BR2 208 D6
Edmonton N9 18 A2
Feltham TW14 150 C4
Harrow HA1 41 D4
Wimbledon SW20 178 B2
Durham Rise SE18 123 B1
Durham Row E1 97 A2
Durham St SE11 138 B6 270 C6
Durham Terr W2 91 D1
Durley Ave HA5 41 A3
Durley Rd N16 51 C2
Durlock Ho 16 SW9 138 C4
Durlston Rd E5 74 A6
Kingston KT2 176 A4
Durnford Ho SE6 163 D1
Durnford St N15 51 C4
3 SE10 142 A6
Durning Rd SE19 183 B5
Durnsford Ave SW18,
SW19 157 C2
Durnsford Rd N11 31 D3
Wimbledon SW18,SW19 157 C1
Durrant Ct HA3 24 C2
Durrant Way BR6 227 B3
Durrell Rd SW6 264 C1
Durrell Way TW17 193 B3
Durrels Ho W14 254 D4
Durrington Ave SW20 178 C3
Durrington Park Rd
SW20 178 C2
Durrington Rd E5 75 A4
Durrington Twr 3 SW8 137 C3
Durrisdeer Ho NW2 69 B4
Dursley Cl SE3 143 C3
Dursley Gdns SE3 143 D4
Dursley Rd SE3 143 C3
Durston NW5 71 A3
Durston House Middleton's
Sch W5 87 D1
Durston House Prep Sch
W5 87 D1
Durward St E1 96 B2
Durweston Mews W1 237 D4
Durweston St W1 237 D3
Dury Rd EN5 1 B3
Dutch Gdns KT2 176 D4
Dutch Yd SW18 157 C6
Dutton Ho SW2 160 D3
Dutton St SE10 142 A4
Duxberry Cl BR2 210 A4
Duxford 21 KT1 176 C1
Duxford Ho 12 SE2 124 D4
Dwight Ct SW6 135 A3
Dycer Ho 19 E9 74 D2
Dye House La E3 97 C6
Dyer Ho TW12 173 D2
Dyers Hall Rd E11 54 C1
E11 76 B6
Dyer's La SW15 134 B1
Dykes Ct 11 SW2 160 B3
Dykes Way BR2 208 D6
Dylan Cl WD6 9 D4
Dylan Rd 2 SE24 138 D1
Belvedere DA17 125 C3
Dylan Thomas Ho N8 50 B5
Dylways SE5 139 B1
Dymchurch Cl BR6 227 C4
Ilford IG5 56 C6
Dymchurch Ho 12 E5 74 B3
Dymes Path SW19 156 D2
Dymock St SW6 135 D2
Dyneley Rd SE12 165 C1
Dyne Rd NW6 69 B1
Dynevor Rd N16 73 D5
Richmond TW10 154 A6
Dynham Rd NW6 69 C1
Dyott St WC1 239 D2
WC1,WC2 94 A1 240 A2
Dysart Ave KT2,TW10 175 C6
Dysart Sch Kingston KT2 175 D6
Surbiton KT6 198 B2
Dysart St EC2 95 C3 243 A5
Dyson Ct NW2 46 C2
Wembley HA0 65 A4
Dyson Ho 3 SE10 120 D1
Dyson Rd E11 54 C3
E15 76 D2
Dyson's Rd N18 34 B4

E

Eade Rd N4 51 A2
Eagans Cl N2 48 B6
Eagle Ave RM6 59 A3
Eagle Cl SE16 118 C1
Enfield EN3 6 C1
Wallington SM6 220 A2
Eagle Ct EC1 241 C4
9 Dulwich SE21 161 B2
Eagle Ct *continued*
Edmonton N18 33 D4
6 Wanstead E11 55 A5
Eagle Dr NW9 27 C1
Eagle Dwellings EC1 235 B2
Eagle Hill SE19 183 B4
Eagle Ho 22 E1 96 B3
Eagle Hts 10 SW11 136 C2
Eagle La E11 55 A5
Eagle Lo E11 54 D5
NW11 47 B2
Eagle Mans N16 73 D3
Eagle Mews N1 73 C2
Eagle Pl SW1 249 B5
SW7 114 A1 256 B2
Eagle Rd Hatton TW6 127 D2
Wembley HA0 65 D1
Eaglesfield Rd SE18 144 D4
Eaglesfield Sch SE18 144 C4
Eagle St WC1 94 B2 240 C3
Eagle Terr IG8 37 B3
Eagle Trad Est CR4 202 D3
Eagle Wharf SE1 253 C3
Eagle Wharf Rd
N1 95 A5 235 B4
Ealcom Ct W5 110 B5
Eldham Prim Sch SE9 143 C1
Ealdham Sq SE9 143 C1
Ealing Almshouses W5 109 D4
Ealing Broadway Ctr
W5 109 D6
Ealing Broadway Sta
W5 109 D6
Ealing Coll W13 87 B1
Ealing Common W5 110 B6
Ealing Common Sta W5 110 B5
Ealing Gn W5 109 D5
Ealing,Hammersmith & West
London Coll
W14 113 A1 254 B1
Ealing Hospl UB1,UB2 108 B4
Ealing Park Gdns W5 109 C2
Ealing Park Mans W5 109 D3
Ealing Rd Brentford TW8 109 D2
Northolt UB5 63 C1
Wembley HA0 66 A1
Ealing Road Trad Est
TW8 109 D1
Ealing Tertiary Coll
Acton W3 110 D5
Ealing W5 109 D5
Ealing Village W5 88 A1
Eamann Casey Ho 34
SW9 138 C4
Eamont Cl HA4 38 D2
Eamont Ct NW8 230 B4
Eamont St NW8 92 C5 230 B4
Eardley Cres
SW5 113 C1 255 B1
Eardley Point 9 SE18 122 D2
Eardley Prim Sch SW16 181 C4
Eardley Rd
Belvedere DA17 125 C1
Streatham SW16 181 C4
Earl Cl N11 31 B5
Earldom Rd SW15 134 C1
Earle Gdns KT2 176 A3
Earlham Gr E7 77 A3
Wood Green N22 32 B3
Earlham Prim Sch E7 76 D3
Earlham Prim Schs N22 32 C3
Earlham St WC2 94 A1 240 A1
Earl Ho NW1 237 B5
Earlom Ho WC1 234 A1
Earl Rd SW14 133 A1
Earl Rise SE18 123 B2
Earl's Court Ex Ctr SW5 255 A1
Earl's Court Gdns
SW5 113 D2 255 C3
Earl's Court Rd
SW5,W8 113 C2 255 B4
Earl's Court Sq
SW5 113 D1 255 C2
Earl's Court Sta
SW5 113 C2 255 B3
Earls Cres HA1 42 C5
Earlsdown Ho IG11 101 B5
Earlsferry Way N1 72 A1
Earlsfield Prim Sch
SW18 158 A2
Earlsfield Rd SW18 158 A4
Earlsfield Sta SW18 158 A3
Earlshall Rd SE9 144 C1
Earlsmead HA2 63 B4
Earlsmead Fst & Mid Sch
HA2 63 B4
Earlsmead Prim Sch
N15 51 D5
Earlsmead Rd N15 51 D4
NW10 90 C4
Earl St EC2 95 C2 243 A4
Earls Terr W8 254 D5
Earlsthorpe Mews 3
SW12 159 A5
Earlsthorpe Rd SE26 184 D6
Earlstoke St EC1 234 C2
Earlston Gr E9 96 B6
Earls Wlk W8 113 C3 255 A5
Dagenham RM8 80 B4
Earlswood Ave CR7 204 C4
Earlswood Cl 10 SE10 120 C1
Earlswood Gdns IG5 56 C6
Earlswood Ho 2 SW2 160 B3
Earlswood St SE10 120 C1
Early Mews NW1 231 D6
Earnshaw St WC1,WC2 239 D2
Earsby St W14 254 B4

Easby Cres SM4 ......201 D3
Easebourne Rd RM8 ......80 C3
Easedale Ho TW7 ......152 D6
Eashing Point 5 SW15 ..156 B3
Easleys Mews W1 ......238 B2
East Acton Arc W3 ......89 D1
East Acton Ct W3 ......111 C6
East Acton La W3 ......111 C6
East Acton Prim Sch
 W3 ......111 C6
East Acton Sta W12 ......89 D1
East Arbour St E1 ......96 D1
East Ave E12 ......78 A1
 E17 ......53 D5
 NW2 ......48 A6
 Croydon CR0 ......220 B3
 Hayes UB3 ......106 A5
 Southall UB1 ......107 B6
East Bank N16 ......51 C2
Eastbank Rd TW12 ......174 A5
East Barnet Main Sch
 Barnet EN4 ......2 B1
East Barnet EN4 ......14 D5
East Barnet Rd EN4 ......14 C6
East Beckton District Ctr
 E6 ......100 B2
East Block 5 E1 ......118 D6
Eastbourne Ave W3 ......89 B1
Eastbourne Gdns SW14 ..133 A2
Eastbourne Mews
 W2 ......92 A1 236 B2
Eastbourne Rd E15 ......98 C6
 N15 ......51 C3
 Brentford TW8 ......109 B1
 Chiswick W4 ......133 A6
 Feltham TW13 ......150 D2
 Streatham SW17 ......181 A4
 Walland E6 ......100 C4
Eastbourne Terr
 W2 ......92 A1 236 B2
Eastbournia Ave N9 ......18 B1
Eastbrook Ave N9 ......18 C4
Eastbrook Rd SE3 ......143 B4
Eastbury Ave
 Barking IG11 ......101 C6
 Enfield EN1 ......5 D4
 Moor Park HA6 ......22 C2
Eastbury Ct Barking IG11 .101 C6
 New Barnet EN5 ......14 A6
Eastbury Gr W4 ......111 C1
Eastbury Inf Sch IG11 ......79 D1
Eastbury Rd E6 ......100 C3
 Kingston KT2 ......176 A3
Eastbury Sq IG11 ......101 D6
Eastbury Terr E1 ......96 D3
Eastcastle St W1 ..93 C1 239 B2
Eastcheap EC3 ..117 C6 253 A6
East Churchfield Rd
 W3 ......111 B5
Eastchurch Rd TW6 ......127 C2
Eastchurch Road Rdbt
 TW6 ......127 C3
East Cl W5 ......88 C3
 Cockfosters EN4 ......3 A1
 Greenford UB6 ......86 A5
Eastcombe Ave SE7 ......143 B6
Eastcote BR6 ......211 D1
Eastcote Ave
 East Molesey KT8 ......195 C4
 Greenford UB6 ......65 A3
 Harrow HA2 ......64 A6
Eastcote Ind Est HA4 ......40 C2
Eastcote La Harrow HA2 ..63 C5
 Northolt UB5 ......63 B2
Eastcote La N UB5 ......63 C2
Eastcote Pl HA5 ......40 B3
Eastcote Prim Sch
 DA16 ......145 B2
Eastcote Rd DA16 ......145 B3
 Harrow HA2 ......64 A5
 Pinner HA5 ......40 D4
 Ruislip HA4 ......40 A3
Eastcote St SW9 ......138 B3
Eastcote Sta HA5 ......40 C2
Eastcote View HA5 ......40 C5
Eastcourt Ind Sch IG3 ......58 A1
East Cres N11 ......30 D6
 Enfield EN1 ......17 D6
Eastcroft Rd KT19 ......215 C1
East Cross Ctr E15 ......75 C2
East Cross Route E3 ......97 C6
 E9 ......75 B3
East Croydon Sta CR0 ..221 B6
East Ct HA0 ......65 C6
Eastdown Ho E8 ......74 A4
Eastdown Pk SE13 ......142 B1
East Duck Lees La EN3 ......7 B1
East Dulwich Gr SE22 ..161 C6
East Dulwich Rd SE15,
 SE22 ......140 A1
East Dulwich Sta SE22 ..139 C1
East End Rd N2 ......48 A6
 N2,N3 ......47 D6
 N3 ......29 C1
East End Way HA5 ......41 A6
East Entrance RM10 ......103 D5
Eastern Ave
 Ilford IG1,IG2,IG4, ...56 B3
 Ilford IG1,IG2,IG4 ......56 C3
 Ilford IG2 ......57 B3
 Pinner HA5 ......40 D2
 Wanstead E11 ......55 C3
Eastern Ave W RM7 ......59 C5
Eastern Bsns Pk TW16 ..127 D3
Eastern Perimeter Rd
 TW14 ......127 D3
Eastern Rd E13 ......99 B5

Eastern Rd continued
 E17 ......54 A4
 N2 ......48 D5
 SE4 ......141 C1
 Wood Green N22 ......32 A2
Easternville Gdns IG2 ..57 A3
Eastern Way SE28 ......124 B4
Eastfield Gdns RM10 ......81 C4
Eastfield Prim Sch EN3 ......6 D5
Eastfield Rd E17 ......53 C5
 Dagenham RM10 ......81 C4
 Dagenham RM9 ......81 B4
 Enfield EN3 ......6 D5
Eastfields HA5 ......40 C4
Eastfields Rd W3 ......89 A2
 Mitcham CR4 ......181 A1
Eastfield St E14 ......97 A2
East Finchley Sta N2 ......48 C5
Eastgate Cl SE28 ......102 D1
Eastgate Gdns SW1 ......180 C4
Eastglade HA5 ......41 B6
Eastham Cl EN5 ......13 A6
East Ham Ind Est E6 ..100 A2
East Ham Manor Way
 E6 ......100 C1
East Ham Meml Hosp
 E7 ......77 D1
East Ham Sta E6 ......78 A1
East Harding St EC4 ..241 B2
East Heath Rd NW3 ......70 B5
East Hill SW18 ......158 A6
 Wembley HA4 ......44 C1
Eastholm NW11 ......47 D5
Eastholme UB3 ......106 A5
East India Bldgs 8 E14 .119 C6
East India Dock Basin
 E14 ......120 C6
East India Dock Rd E14 .119 D6
East India Dock Road Tunnel
 17 E14 ......98 B1
East India Dock Wall Rd
 E14 ......120 B6
East India Sta E14 ......120 B6
East La SE16 ......118 A4
 Kingston KT1 ......197 D6
 Wembley HA0,HA9 ......65 D5
Eastlake Ho NW8 ......236 D5
Eastlake Rd SE5 ......139 A3
Eastlands Cres SE21 ..161 D5
Eastlea Com Sch E16 ..98 C3
Eastlea Mews E16 ......98 C3
Eastleigh Ave HA2 ......63 D6
Eastleigh Cl NW2 ......67 C5
 Belmont SM2 ......217 D1
Eastleigh Rd E17 ......35 B1
Eastleigh Way TW14 ..150 A3
Eastleigh Wlk 9 SW15 .156 A4
East London Coll & Toynbee
 Theatre E1 ......95 D1 243 D2
East London Stadium E3 .97 B2
Eastman Dental Hosp
 WC1 ......94 B4 240 C6
Eastman Ho 7 SW4 ......159 C5
Eastman Rd W3 ......111 B4
East Mascalls 15 SE7 ..143 C6
East Mead HA4 ......62 D5
Eastmead Ave UB6 ......85 D4
Eastmead Cl BR1 ......188 A1
Eastmearn Rd SE21,
 SE27 ......161 A2
East Molesey Inf sch
 KT8 ......196 B5
Eastmont Rd KT10 ......212 D6
Eastmoor Pl SE7 ......121 D3
Eastmoor St SE7 ......121 D3
East Mount St E1 ......96 B2
Eastney Rd CR0 ......204 D1
Eastney St SE10 ......120 B1
Eastnor Rd SE9 ......167 A3
Easton Ho 4 SE27 ......160 D1
Easton St WC1 ......241 A6
East Park Cl RM6 ......59 A4
East Parkside SE10 ......120 C4
East Pas EC1 ......242 A4
East Pl SE27 ......183 A6
East Point 4 SE1 ......118 A1
Eastpole Cotts N14 ......3 D1
East Poultry Ave EC1 ..241 C3
East Putney Sta SW15 .157 A6
East Ramp TW6 ......126 D4
East Rd DA16 ......146 B3
 E15 ......99 A6
 HA8 ......27 A2
 N1 ......95 B4 235 D2
 N2 ......30 C2
 Dagenham RM6 ......59 A4
 East Barnet EN4 ......15 A3
 Enfield EN3 ......6 C5
 Kingston KT2 ......176 A2
 West Drayton UB7 ......104 C2
 Wimbledon SW19 ......180 A4
East Rochester Way
 DA5,DA15,DA16,SE9 ..168 C5
East Row W10 ......91 A3
 Wanstead E11 ......55 A3
Eastry Ave BR2 ......208 D3
Eastry Ho SW8 ......270 A3
Eastry Rd DA8 ......147 C5
East Sheen Ave SW14 ..133 B1
East Sheen Prim Sch
 SW14 ......133 C1
Eastside Rd NW11 ......47 B5
East Smithfield
 E1 ......117 D6 253 D6
East St BR1 ......187 A1
 DA7 ......147 C1

East St continued
 SE17 ......117 B1 262 C2
 Barking IG11 ......79 A1
 Brentford TW8 ......131 C5
East Surrey Gr SE15 ..139 D5
East Tenter St
 E1 ......95 D1 243 D1
East Terr DA15 ......167 C3
EastThamesmead Bsns Pk
 DA18 ......125 B4
East Towers HA5 ......40 D3
Eastvale W3 ......111 D5
East View NW3 ......70 B6
 Barnet EN5 ......1 D1
 Chingford E4 ......36 A5
Eastview Ave SE18 ..145 C5
Eastville Ave NW11 ......47 B3
Eastway E3,E9 ......97 A6
 E9,E10 ......75 C4
 Hayes BR2 ......209 A2
 Merton SM4,SW20 ..201 A5
 Wallington SM6 ......219 C4
 Wanstead E11 ......55 B4
East Way Croydon CR0 ..223 A5
 Hayes UB3 ......106 A5
 Ruislip HA4 ......40 A1
Eastwell Cl BR3 ......185 A2
Eastwell Ho SE1 ......262 D6
Eastwick Ct 2 SW19 ..156 D3
East Wickham Inf Sch
 DA16 ......145 D4
East Wickham Jun Sch
 DA16 ......146 A4
East Wlk East Barnet EN4 ..15 A3
 Hayes UB3 ......106 A5
Eastwood Cl
 7 Tottenham N17 ......34 B3
 Woodford E18 ......37 A1
Eastwood Rd N10 ......31 A1
 Ilford IG3 ......58 A2
 West Drayton UB7 ......104 C4
 Woodford E18 ......37 A1
East Woodside SE9 ......169 A3
Eastwood St SW16 ..181 C4
Eatington Rd E10 ......54 B4
Eaton Cl SW1 ......258 A3
 Stanmore HA7 ......25 B6
Eaton Ct BR7 ......189 A4
 Ealing W5 ......87 D1
 Edgware HA8 ......26 C6
 Southall UB1 ......107 B6
 Sutton SM2 ......218 B2
Eaton Dr SW9 ......138 D1
 Kingston KT2 ......176 C3
Eaton Gate SW1 ..115 A2 258 A4
Eaton Gdns RM9 ......81 A1
Eaton Ho SW11 ......266 D1
 Ealing W5 ......87 D1
Eaton House The Manor Sch
 SW4 ......137 B1
Eaton La SW1 ..115 B3 258 D5
Eaton Mans SW1 ......258 A3
Eaton Mews N
 SW1 ......115 A3 258 A5
Eaton Mews S
 SW1 ......115 B3 258 C5
Eaton Mews W SW1 ..258 B4
Eaton Park Rd N13 ......16 C2
Eaton Pl SW1 ..115 A3 258 B5
Eaton Rd DA14 ......168 D2
 NW4 ......46 C4
 Enfield EN1 ......5 C1
 Isleworth TW3,TW7 ..130 B1
 Sutton SM2 ......218 B2
Eaton Rise Ealing W5 ..87 D1
 Wanstead E11 ......55 C4
Eaton Row SW1 ..115 B3 258 C5
Eatons Mead E4 ......19 C2
Eaton Sq SW1 ..115 A3 258 B5
Eaton Square Sch
 SW1 ......115 B2 258 C4
Eaton Terr E3 ......97 A4
 SW1 ......115 A2 258 A4
Eaton Terr Mews SW1 ..258 A4
Eatonville Rd SW17 ..158 D2
Eatonville Villas SW17 .158 D2
Ebbisham Dr
 SW8 ......138 B6 270 C5
Ebbisham Rd KT4 ......216 C6
Ebbsfleet Rd NW2 ......69 A4
Ebdon Way SE3 ......143 B2
Ebenezer Ho SE11 ......261 C3
Ebenezer Mussel Ho 5
 E2 ......96 C5
Ebenezer St N1 ......235 C2
Ebenezer Wlk CR4 ......181 C2
Ebley Cl SE15 ......139 D6
Ebner St SW18 ......157 D6
Ebony Ho 10 NW3 ......69 D2
Ebor Cotts SW15 ......155 C1
Ebor St E1,E2 ......243 C6
Ebrington Rd HA3 ......43 D3
Ebsworth St SE23 ......162 D4
Eburne Rd N7 ......72 A5
Ebury Bridge Rd
 SW1 ......115 A1 258 B1
Ebury Cl BR2 ......226 A5
Ebury Mews
 SW1 ......115 B2 258 C4
Ebury Mews E SW1 ..258 C4
Ebury Sq SW1 ......258 B3
Ebury St SW1 ..115 B2 258 C4
Ecclesbourne Cl N13 ..32 C5
Ecclesbourne Gdns N13 .32 C5
Ecclesbourne Inf Sch
 CR7 ......205 A4
Ecclesbourne Jun Sch
 CR7 ......205 A4
Ecclesbourne Prim Sch
 N1 ......73 B1

Ecclesbourne Rd N1 ......73 A1
 Thornton Heath CR7 ..205 A4
Eccleshill 3 BR2 ......208 D5
Eccles Rd SW11 ......136 D1
Eccleston Cl BR6 ......211 B1
 Cockfosters EN4 ......2 C1
Eccleston Cres RM6 ......58 B2
Ecclestone Ct HA9 ......66 A3
Ecclestone Mews HA9 ..66 A3
Ecclestone Pl HA9 ......66 B3
Eccleston Ho 1 SW2 ..160 C5
Eccleston Mews
 SW1 ......115 A3 258 B5
Eccleston Pl
 SW1 ......115 B2 258 C4
Eccleston Rd W13 ......109 A5
Eccleston Sq
 SW1 ......115 B2 258 C3
Eccleston Sq Mews
 SW1 ......259 A3
Eccleston St
 SW1 ......115 B2 258 C4
Echelford Cty Prim Sch
 TW15 ......170 D5
Echelforde Dr TW15 ..170 C6
Echo Hts E4 ......19 D3
Eckersley St E1 ......243 D5
 8 E2 ......96 A3
Eckford St N1 ......234 A4
Eckington Ho N15 ......51 B3
Eckstein Rd SW11 ......136 C1
Eclipse Rd E13 ......99 B2
Ector Rd SE6 ......164 C2
Edam Ct 11 DA14 ......168 A1
Edans Ct W12 ......111 D4
Edbrooke Rd W9 ......91 C3
Eddisbury Ho 7 SE26 ..162 A1
Eddiscombe Rd SW6 ..135 B4
Eddy Cl RM7 ......59 D3
Eddystone Rd SE4 ......163 A6
Eddystone Twr SE8 ......119 A5
Eddystone Wlk TW19 ..148 A4
Ede Cl TW4 ......129 B2
Edenbridge Cl 20 SE16 .118 B1
Edenbridge Rd E9 ......74 D1
 Enfield EN1 ......17 C5
Eden Cl NW3 ......69 C6
 W8 ......255 B6
 Wembley HA0 ......87 D6
Edencourt W5 ......88 B1
Edencourt Rd SW16 ..181 B4
Edendale W3 ......110 D6
Edenfield Gdns KT4 ..215 D5
Eden Gr E17 ......53 D4
 N7 ......72 B3
Edenham High Sch CR0 .207 B2
Edenham Way W10 ......91 B2
Eden Ho NW8 ......237 A5
 15 SW11 ......136 C2
Edenhurst Ave SW6 ..135 B2
Eden Lodge NW6 ......68 D1
Eden Mews SW17 ......158 A1
Eden Park Ave BR3 ..207 C4
Eden Park Sta BR3 ..207 C4
Eden Rd E17 ......53 D4
 Croydon CR0 ......221 B4
 Penge BR3 ......185 A2
 West Norwood SE27 ..182 D5
Edensmuir Ct SE3 ......143 A5
Edensor Gdns W4 ......133 C5
Edensor Rd W4 ......133 C5
Eden St KT1,KT2 ......176 A1
Edenvale Cl CR4 ......181 A3
Edenvale Rd CR4 ......181 A3
Edenvale St SW6 ......136 A3
Eden Way BR3 ......207 C3
Eden Wlk 6 KT1 ......176 A1
Ederline Ave SW16 ..182 C1
Edgar Ct KT3 ......199 C6
Edgar Ho E9 ......75 A3
 Wanstead E11 ......55 C2
 SW8 ......270 A4
Edgar Kail Way SE22 ..139 C1
Edgarley Terr SW6 ..264 A1
Edgar Rd E3 ......97 D4
 Dagenham RM6 ......58 D2
 Twickenham TW4 ......151 B4
 Yiewsley UB7 ......104 A5
Edgbaston Rd CR4 ......181 B6
Edgeborough Way BR1 .187 D2
Edgebury BR7,SE9 ..188 D6
Edgebury Prim Sch
 BR7 ......189 A6
Edgebury Wlk BR7 ......167 A1
Edgecombe Cl KT2 ..177 B3
Edgecombe Ho 4 SE5 .139 C3
 Putney SW19 ......157 A4
Edgecoombe CR2 ......222 C1
Edgecote Cl 7 W3 ......111 A5
Edgecumbe Ct 2 CR0 ..206 A1
Edgecot Gr N15 ......51 C4
Edgefield Ave IG11 ......79 D1
Edgefield Ct 2 IG11 ..79 D1
Edge Hill SE18 ......144 D6
 Wimbledon SW19 ......178 D3
Edge Hill Ave N3 ......47 C5
Edge Hill Ct DA14 ..189 D6
Edge Hill Ct KT12 ..194 C1
Edge Hill St SW19 ..178 D3
Edgehill Gdns RM10 ..81 C4
Edgehill Ho 4 SW9 ..138 D3
Edgehill Rd BR7 ......189 A6
 Ealing W13 ......87 C2
 Mitcham CR4 ......181 B2

Edgewood Dr BR6 ......227 D3
Edgewood Gn CR0 ......206 D1
Edgeworth Ave NW4 ..46 A4
Edgeworth Cl NW4 ......46 A4
Edgeworth Cres NW4 ..46 A4
Edgeworth Ct 10 EN4 ..2 C1
Edgeworth Ho NW8 ..229 A6
Edgeworth Rd SE9 ..143 D1
 Barnet EN4 ......2 C1
Edgington Rd SW16 ..181 D4
Edgington Way DA14 ..190 D3
Edgson Ho SW1 ......258 C2
Edgwarebury Ct HA9 ..66 A3
Edgwarebury Gdns HA8 .26 C5
Edgwarebury La HA8 ..10 C2
Edgware Community Hospl
 HA8 ......26 D3
Edgware Ct HA8 ......26 C4
Edgware Jun & Inf Schs
 HA8 ......26 C4
Edgware Rd NW2 ......68 C6
 W1,W2,NW1,NW8 ..92 C2 237 A3
Edgware Rd Burnt Oak
 Broadway HA8 ......26 D3
Edgware Rd High St HA8 .26 C4
Edgware Road Sta (Bakerloo)
 NW1 ......92 C2 237 A3
Edgware Road Sta
 (Met,Distr,Circle)
 NW1 ......237 B3
Edgware Road The Hyde
 NW9 ......45 C5
Edgware Road West Hendon
 Broadway NW9 ......46 A2
Edgware Sch The HA8 ..26 B6
Edgware Sta HA8 ......26 D4
Edgware Way (Watford
 By-Pass) HA8 ......26 C6
Edinburgh Cl 7 E2 ......96 C5
 Uxbridge UB10 ......60 D4
Edinburgh Ct E13 ......99 B5
 10 SE16 ......118 D5
 1 Catford SE6 ......164 D3
 2 Kingston KT1 ......198 A6
 West Barnes SM4 ......200 D4
Edinburgh Dr UB10 ......60 D4
Edinburgh Ho NW4 ......46 C6
 3 W3 ......89 B1
 W9 ......91 D4
Edinburgh Prim Sch E17 .53 B4
Edinburgh Rd E13 ......99 B5
 E17 ......53 C4
 W7 ......108 D4
 Carshalton SM1 ......218 B6
 Edmonton N18 ......34 A5
Edis St NW1 ......93 A6 231 B6
Editha Mans SW10 ..266 A5
Edith Cavell Cl 6 N19 ..50 A2
Edith Cavell Way SE18 .144 A4
Edith Gdns KT5 ......198 D2
Edith Gr SW10 ..136 A5 266 B4
Edith Ho 6 W6 ......112 C1
Edithna St SW9 ......138 A2
Edith Neville Prim Sch
 NW1 ......93 D5 232 C3
Edith Pond Ct SE9 ......166 D2
Edith Ramsay Ho 2 E1 ..97 A2
Edith Rd E15 ......76 B3
 E6 ......77 D1
 N11 ......31 D3
 W14 ......113 A2 254 B3
 Dagenham RM6 ......58 D2
 South Norwood SE25 ..205 B4
 Wimbledon SW19 ......179 D4
Edith Row SW6 ......265 D2
Edith St E2 ......96 A5
Edith Summerskill Ho
 SW6 ......264 D4
Edith Terr SW10 ..136 A5 266 A4
Edith Villas W14 ..113 B2 254 C2
Edith Yd SW10 ......266 B4
Edmanson's Cl N17 ..33 D2
Edmeston Cl E9 ......75 A2
Edmond Ct SE14 ......140 C4
Edmonscote W13 ......87 A2
Edmonton Coll of F Ed
 EN3 ......6 C4
Edmonton Ct 5 SE16 ..118 C3
Edmonton Cty Lower Sch
 N9 ......17 C3
Edmonton Cty Upper Sch
 EN1 ......17 C6
Edmonton Green Sh Ctr
 N9 ......18 B2
Edmonton Green Stan 9 ..18 A2
Edmonton Wharf N18 ..34 C4
Edmund Gr TW13 ......151 B2
Edmund Halley Way
 SE10 ......120 C4
Edmund Ho SE14 ......141 B4
 SE17 ......261 D1
Edmund Hurst Dr E6 ..100 D2
Edmund Rd DA16 ......146 A2
 Mitcham CR4 ......202 C6
Edmundsbury Ct Est 16
 SW9 ......138 B1

Edmunds Cl UB4 ......84 C2
Edmund St SE5 ......139 B5
Edmunds Wlk N2 ......48 C5
Edmund Waller Prim Sch
 SE14 ......140 D3
Ednam Ho SE15 ......140 A6
Edna Rd SW20 ......178 D1
Edna St SW11 ..136 C4 267 A1
Edred Ho E9 ......75 A4
Edrich Ho SW4 ......270 A1
Edric Ho 1 SW1 ......259 D4
Edrick Rd HA8 ......27 A4
Edrick Wlk HA8 ......27 A4
Edric Rd SE14 ......140 D5
Edridge Cl WD23 ......8 A6
Edridge Ho 9 SE27 ..160 D1
Edridge Rd CR0 ......221 B5
Edward Alleyn Ho SE21 .161 C4
Edward Ave Chingford E4 .35 D4
 Morden SM4 ......202 B4
Edward Betham CE Prim Sch
 UB6 ......86 A5
Edward Cl Edmonton N9 ..17 C4
 Hampton TW12 ......174 A5
Edward Ct 2 E16 ......99 A2
 2 Ealing W5 ......87 B3
 Harrow HA1 ......64 C6
Edward Dodd Ct N1 ..235 D2
Edward Edward's Ho
 SE1 ......251 C3
Edwardes Sq
 W8 ......113 B3 254 D3
Edward Friend Ho 6
 N16 ......73 C5
Edward Gr EN4 ......14 B6
Edward Harvey Ct DA17 .125 B1
Edward Ho SE11 ......260 D2
 W2 ......236 C5
Edward Kennedy Ho 18
 W10 ......91 A3
Edward Mann Cl 12 E1 ..96 D1
Edward Mans 7 IG11 ..79 D1
Edward Mews NW1 ..231 B3
Edward Pauling Ho
 TW14 ......149 D4
Edward Pauling Prim Sch
 TW13 ......149 D4
Edward Pinner Ct 5
 KT6 ......214 A6
Edward Pl SE8 ......141 B6
Edward Rd E17 ......52 D4
 Bromley BR1 ......187 C3
 Chislehurst BR7 ......188 D5
 Croydon CR0 ......205 C2
 Dagenham RM6 ......59 A3
 Hampton TW12 ......174 A5
 Harrow HA2 ......42 A4
 Hatton TW14 ......149 C6
 New Barnet EN4 ......14 B6
 Northolt UB5 ......84 C5
 Penge SE20 ......184 D4
Edward Redhead Jun & Inf
 Sch E17 ......53 C4
Edward Robinson Ho 3
 SE14 ......140 D5
Edward's Ave HA4 ......62 C2
Edwards Cl KT4 ......216 D6
Edward's Cotts 11 N1 ..72 C1
Edwards Dr N11 ......31 D3
Edward's La N16 ......73 C6
Edwards Language Sch
 W5 ......110 A6
Edwards Mews N1 ......72 C1
 W1 ......93 A1 238 A1
Edward Sq N1 ......233 C5
 SE16 ......119 A5
Edwards Rd DA17 ......125 C2
Edward St 10 E16 ......99 A1
 SE14 ......141 B5
Edward Temme Ave E15 .76 D1
Edward Tyler Rd SE12 ..165 C2
Edward VII Mans NW10 ..90 D4
Edward Way TW15 ..148 B2
Edward Wilson Prim Sch
 W2 ......91 D2
Edwina Ct SM1 ......217 D4
Edwina Gdns IG4 ......56 A4
Edwin Arnold Ct DA15 .189 D6
Edwin Ave E6 ......100 C4
Edwin Cl DA7 ......147 B6
Edwin Ho SE15 ......140 A5
Edwin Rd HA8 ......27 B4
 Twickenham TW1,TW2 ..152 C3
Edwin's Mead E9 ......75 A4
Edwin St E1 ......96 C3
 E16 ......99 A2
Edwin Stray Ho TW13 ..151 C1
Edwin Ware Ct 2 HA5 ..22 C1
Edwy Ho E9 ......75 B4
Edwyn Cl EN5 ......12 D5
Edwyn Ho SW18 ......157 D5
Eel Pie Island ★ TW1 ..153 A3
Effie Pl SW6 ......265 B3
Effie Rd SW6 ..135 C5 265 B3
Effingham Cl SM2 ......217 C2
Effingham Ct SW19 ..180 C3
Effingham Ho 87 SW8 ..137 D3
 9 Kingston KT2 ......176 B2
Effingham Lo 1 KT6 ..198 A4
Effingham Rd N8 ......50 C5
 SE12 ......164 D6
 Thames Ditton KT6,KT7 ..197 C2
 Thornton Heath CR0 ..204 B2
Effort St SW17 ......180 C5
Effra Ct SW2 ......160 B6
 South Norwood SE19 ..183 C3
Effra Mans SW2 ......160 C6
Effra Par SW2 ......160 C6
Effra Rd SW2 ......160 C6
 Wimbledon SW19 ......179 D4

Effra Road Ret Pk SW2 ..160 C6
Egan Way UB3 ....105 C6
Egbert Ho E9 ....75 A3
Egbert St NW1 ....93 A6 231 A6
Egbury Ho SW15 ....155 D5
Egerton Cl HA5 ....40 A5
Egerton Cres
SW3 ....114 C2 257 B4
Egerton Ct E11 ....54 B2
5 Richmond TW10 ....154 A6
Egerton Dr SE10 ....141 D4
Egerton Gdns NW4 ....46 B5
SW3 ....114 C3 257 A5
Ealing W13 ....87 B1
Ilford IG3 ....79 D5
Willesden NW10 ....90 C6
Egerton Gdns Mews
SW3 ....257 B5
Egerton Ho W4 ....133 A6
Egerton Pl SW3 ....257 B5
Egerton Rd N16 ....51 D2
New Malden KT3 ....199 D5
South Norwood SE25 ....205 C6
Twickenham TW2 ....152 C4
Wembley HA0 ....66 B1
Egerton Terr
SW3 ....114 C3 257 B5
Egerton Way UB3 ....126 D5
Eggardon Ct UB5 ....64 A2
Egham Cl Cheam SM3 ....217 A6
Putney SW19 ....157 A2
Egham Cres SM3 ....217 A6
Egham Ct KT6 ....197 D4
Egham Rd E13 ....99 B2
Eglantine Rd SW18 ....158 A6
Egleston Rd SM4 ....201 D3
Eglington Ct SE17 ....139 A6
Eglington Rd E4 ....20 B4
Eglinton Hill SE18 ....144 D5
Eglinton Prim Sch SE18 .144 C6
Eglinton Rd SE18 ....144 D6
Egliston Mews SW15 ....134 C2
Egliston Rd SW15 ....134 C2
Egmont Ave KT6 ....198 B1
Egmont Rd
New Malden KT3 ....199 D5
Sutton SM2 ....218 A1
Tolworth KT6 ....198 C1
Walton-on-T KT12 ....194 B2
Egmont St SE14 ....140 D5
Egremont Ho SE13 ....141 D3
Egremont Rd SE27 ....160 C1
Egret Ho 11 SE16 ....118 D2
Egret Way UB4 ....84 D2
Eider Cl E7 ....76 D3
Hayes UB4 ....84 D2
Eider Ct 39 SE8 ....141 B6
Eighteenth Rd CR4 ....204 A5
Eighth Ave Hayes UB3 ....106 A5
Ilford E12 ....78 B4
Eileen Ct BR7 ....188 C5
Eileen Rd SE25 ....205 B4
Eindhoven Cl SM5 ....203 A1
Einstein Ho HA9 ....67 A5
Eisenhower Dr E6 ....100 A2
Eisenhower Ho KT8 ....175 C2
Ekarra Ho SW8 ....270 B2
Elaine Ct 13 NW3 ....70 D2
Elaine Gr NW5 ....71 A3
Elaine Ho N4 ....50 A1
Elam Cl SE5 ....138 D3
Elam St SE5 ....138 D3
Elan Ct E1 ....96 B2
Eland Pl CR0 ....220 D5
Eland Rd SW11 ....136 D2
Croydon CR0 ....220 D5
Elba Pl SE17 ....117 A2 262 B4
Elberon Ave CR0 ....203 C3
Elbe St SW6 ....136 A3
Elborough Rd SE25 ....206 A4
Elborough St SW18 ....157 C3
Elbourne Trad Est
DA17 ....125 D3
Elbury Dr E16 ....99 A1
Elcho St SW11 ...136 C5 267 B3
Elcot Ave SE15 ....140 B5
Eldenwall Ind Est RM8 ....59 B1
Elder Ave N8 ....50 A4
Elderberry Gr 10 SE27 ....183 A6
Elderberry Rd W5 ....110 A4
Elder Cl DA15 ....167 D3
HA8 ....27 A5
Barnet N20 ....13 D3
Yiewsley UB7 ....104 A6
Elder Ct WD23 ....8 C2
Elderfield Ho 3 E14 ....119 C6
Elderfield Pl SW17 ....181 B6
Elderfield Rd E5 ....74 C4
Elderfield Wlk E11 ....55 B4
Elderflower Way E15 ....76 C1
Elder Gdns 9 SE27 ....183 A6
Elder Oak Cl SE20 ....184 B2
Elder Rd SE27 ....183 A5
Elderslie Cl BR3 ....207 D3
Elderslie Rd SE9 ....166 C6
Elder St E1 ....95 D3 243 C5
Elderton Rd SE26 ....185 A6
Eldertree Pl CR4 ....181 C2
Eldertree Way CR4 ....181 C2
Elder Wlk N1 ....234 D6
Elderwood Pl SE27 ....183 A5
Eldon Ave Croydon CR0 ...222 C6
Heston TW5 ....129 C5
Eldon Ct NW6 ....91 C6
Eldon Gr NW3 ....70 B3
Eldon Ho SW9 ....138 D2
Eldon Jun & Inf Schs N9 ..18 C3
Eldon Pk SE25 ....206 B5
Eldon Rd E17 ....53 B5
N9 ....18 C3
Eldon Rd *continued*
W8 ....113 D3 255 D5
Tottenham N22 ....32 D2
Eldon St EC2 ....95 B2 242 D3
Eldon Way NW10 ....88 D5
Eldred Rd IG11 ....101 C6
Eldrick Ct TW14 ....149 B3
Eldridge Cl TW14 ....150 A3
Eldridge Ct SE16 ....118 A3
Eleanor Cl N15 ....51 D6
SE16 ....118 D4
Eleanor Cres NW7 ....28 D6
Eleanor Ct 13 E2 ....96 A6
Eleanor Gdns Barnet EN5 ..12 D6
Dagenham RM8 ....81 B6
Eleanor Gr
Mortlake SW13 ....133 C2
Uxbridge UB10 ....60 D5
Eleanor Ho 1 NW5 ....71 C3
18 W6 ....112 C1
6 Merton SW19 ....179 D2
Eleanor Palmer Prim Sch
NW5 ....71 C4
Eleanor Rathbone Ho 1
N6 ....49 D2
Eleanor Rd E15 ....76 D2
Bowes Park N11 ....32 A4
Eleanor Smith Sch E13 ....99 B5
Eleanor St E3 ....97 C4
Eleanor Wlk 25 SE18 ....122 B2
Electra Ave TW6 ....127 D2
Electric Ave SW9 ....138 C1
Enfield EN3 ....7 B6
Electric Ho 12 E3 ....97 C4
Electric La 2 SW9 ....138 C1
Electric Mans 1 SW9 ....138 C1
Electric Par Ilford IG3 ....57 D1
Surbiton KT6 ....197 D3
Woodford E18 ....37 A1
Elephant & Castle SE1 ..261 D4
SE1 ....117 A3 261 D5
Elephant & Castle Sta
SE1 ....116 D3 261 D5
SE17 ....117 A2 262 A4
Elephant La SE16 ....118 C4
Elephant Rd
SE17 ....117 A2 262 A4
Elers Rd W13 ....109 C4
Hayes UB3 ....105 B2
Eley Rd N18 ....34 D5
Eley's Est N18 ....34 D6
Elfindale Rd SE24 ....161 A6
Elfin Gr TW11 ....174 D5
Elford Cl SE9 ....143 C1
Elfort Rd N5 ....72 C4
Elfrida Cres SE6 ....185 C6
Elfrida Prim Sch SE6 ....185 C6
Elf Row E1 ....118 C6
Elfwine Rd W7 ....86 C2
Elgal Cl BR6 ....226 D3
Elgar N8 ....50 A6
Elgar Ave NW10 ....67 B2
W5 ....110 A4
Thornton Heath SW16 ....204 A6
Tolworth KT5,KT6 ....198 D2
Elgar Cl E13 ....99 C5
SE8 ....141 C5
Buckhurst Hill IG9 ....21 D2
Elstree WD6 ....9 D4
Ickenham UB10 ....60 C6
Elgar Ct W14 ....254 A5
Elgar Ho NW6 ....70 A1
SW1 ....258 D1
Hayes UB4 ....84 C2
Isleworth TW2 ....152 B5
Elgar St SE16 ....119 A3
Elgin Ave W12 ....112 B3
W9 ....91 D3
Ashford TW15 ....171 A4
Harrow HA3 ....25 B1
Elgin Cres W11 ....113 A6 244 B6
Hatton TW6 ....127 C3
Elgin Ct W9 ....91 D3
6 Croydon CR0 ....221 A4
Elgin Ho 8 E14 ....97 D1
Northolt UB5 ....84 B5
Elgin Mans W9 ....91 D4
Elgin Mews W11 ....91 A1
Elgin Mews N W9 ....91 D4
Elgin Mews S W9 ....91 D4
Elgin Rd N22 ....31 C1
Croydon CR0 ....221 D6
Ilford IG3 ....57 C2
Sutton SM1 ....218 A5
Wallington SM6 ....219 C2
Elgood Ave HA6 ....22 A3
Elgood Ho NW8 ....229 D3
Elham Cl BR1 ....187 D3
Elham Ho 13 E5 ....74 B3
Elia Mews N1 ....94 D5 234 C3
Elias Pl SW8 ....138 C6
Elia St N1 ....94 D5 234 C3
Elibank Rd SE9 ....144 C1
Elim Est SE1 ....263 A6
Elim St SE1 ....263 A6
Elim Way E13 ....98 D4
Eliot Bank SE23,SE26 ....162 B2
Eliot Bank Prim Sch
SE23 ....162 B2
Eliot Ct SW18 ....157 D5
Eliot Dr HA2 ....63 D6
Eliot Gdns SW15 ....134 A1
Eliot Hill SE13 ....142 A3
Eliot Ho 10 TW10 ....154 B5
Eliot Mews NW8 ....229 A3
Eliot Pk SE13 ....142 A3
Eliot Pl SE3 ....142 C3
Eliot Rd RM9 ....80 D4
Eliot Vale SE3 ....142 B3
Elizabethan Ct N3 ....47 A6
Elizabeth Ave N1 ..73 B1 235 B6
Enfield EN2 ....4 D2
Ilford IG1 ....79 B6
Elizabeth Barnes Ct 5
SW6 ....135 D3
Elizabeth Blackwell Ho
N22 ....32 C2
Elizabeth Cl 12 E14 ....97 D1
W9 ....236 B5
Cheam SM1 ....217 B6
Elizabeth Clyde Cl N15 ....51 C5
Elizabeth Cotts 5 TW9 .132 C4
Elizabeth Ct NW8 ....237 B6
SE22 ....140 A1
SW10 ....266 D5
SW1 ....259 D5
Buckhurst Hill IG9 ....21 B3
Sunbury TW16 ....194 C6
3 Teddington TW11 ....174 C5
West Barnes SM4 ....201 A2
6 Woodford E18 ....37 A2
2 Woodford IG8 ....37 C3
Elizabeth Finn Ho W12 ..112 A3
Elizabeth Fry Ho UB3 ..105 D2
Elizabeth Fry Pl SE18 ..144 A4
Elizabeth Garrett Anderson
Ho 9 DA17 ....125 C3
Elizabeth Garrett Anderson
Hospl NW1 ....93 C3 239 B6
Elizabeth Garrett Anderson
Language Coll
N1 ....94 B5 233 C3
Elizabeth Gdns W3 ....111 D5
Stanmore HA7 ....25 C5
Sunbury TW16 ....194 C6
Elizabeth Ho 46 E3 ....97 D4
N20 ....14 D1
SE11 ....261 B3
15 W6 ....112 C1
Wembley HA9 ....66 B3
Elizabeth Ind Est SE14 ..140 D6
Elizabeth Kenny Ho N1 ..73 A2
Elizabeth Mews NW3 ....70 D2
Elizabeth Pl N15 ....51 B5
Elizabeth Rd E6 ....99 D6
N15 ....51 C4
Elizabeth Ride N9 ....18 B4
Elizabeth Selby Inf Sch
E2 ....96 A4
Elizabeth Sq 13 SE16 ....119 A6
Elizabeth St
SW1 ....115 A2 258 B4
Elizabeth Terr SE9 ....166 B5
Elizabeth Way
Feltham TW13 ....172 C6
South Norwood SE19 ....183 B3
Elkanette Mews N20 ....14 A2
Elkington Point SE11 ..261 A3
Elkington Rd E13 ....99 B3
Elkstone Rd W10 ....91 B2
Ellacombe Ho 1 SW2 ....160 C4
Ellaline Rd W6 ....134 D6
Ella Mews NW3 ....70 D4
Ellanby Cres N18 ....34 B5
Elland Ho 12 E14 ....97 B1
Elland Rd SE15 ....140 C1
Ella Rd N4,N8 ....50 A2
Ellement Cl HA5 ....40 D4
Ellena Ct N14 ....16 A1
Ellenborough Ct N22 ....32 D2
Ellenborough Ho 5
W12 ....112 B6
Ellenborough Pl SW15 ..134 A1
Ellenborough Rd DA14 ..191 A5
Tottenham N22 ....33 A2
Ellen Cl BR1 ....209 D6
Ellen Ct N9 ....18 C2
6 Chingford E4 ....20 A3
Ellen Miller Ho 2 E17 ....54 A4
Ellen St E1 ....96 A1
Ellen Webb Dr HA3 ....42 C6
Ellen Wilkinson Ho
7 E2 ....96 D4
SW6 ....264 D5
12 Dagenham RM10 ....81 C5
Ellen Wilkinson Prim Sch
E6 ....100 A2
Ellen Wilkinson Sch for Girls
W3 ....88 B1
Elleray Rd TW11 ....174 D4
Ellerby St SW6 ....134 D4
Ellerdale Cl 22 NW3 ....70 A4
Ellerdale Rd NW3 ....70 A3
Ellerdale St SE13 ....141 D2
Ellerdine Rd TW3 ....130 B1
Ellerker Gdns TW10 ....154 A5
Ellerman Ave TW2,TW4 ..151 B3
Ellerslie Ct 6 SM6 ....219 B2
Ellerslie Gdns NW10 ....90 A6
Ellerslie Ind Est SW2 ....160 A6
Ellerslie Rd W12 ....112 B5
Ellerton Ct W3 ....110 D4
Ellerton Gdns RM9 ....80 C1
Ellerton Lo N3 ....29 C1
Ellerton Rd
Barnes SW13 ....134 A4
Dagenham RM9 ....80 C1
Surbiton KT6 ....198 B1
Wandsworth SW17,SW18 .158 B3
Wimbledon SW20 ....178 A3
Ellery Ho SE17 ....262 D3
Ellery Rd SE19 ....183 B3
Ellery St SE15 ....140 B3
Ellesborough Cl WD19 ....22 C5
Ellesmere Ave NW7 ....11 B1
Beckenham BR3 ....185 D1
Ellesmere Cl E11 ....54 D4
Ruislip HA4 ....39 A2
Ellesmere Ct
Chiswick W4 ....133 B6
Ellesmere Ct *continued*
Lewisham SE12 ....165 A3
Penge SE20 ....184 B1
Ellesmere Gdns IG4 ....56 A3
Ellesmere Gr EN5 ....13 B6
Ellesmere Rd E3 ....97 A5
NW10 ....68 A3
Chiswick W4 ....133 B6
Greenford UB6 ....86 A3
Twickenham TW1 ....153 C5
Ellesmere St E14 ....97 D1
Ellies Mews TW15 ....148 A2
Ellingfort Rd E8 ....74 B1
Ellingham Prim Sch
KT9 ....213 D1
Ellingham Rd E15 ....76 B4
W12 ....112 A4
Chessington KT9 ....213 D2
Ellington Ct N14 ....15 D2
Ellington Ho SE1 ....262 B5
Ellington Rd N10 ....49 B5
Feltham TW13 ....171 D6
Hounslow TW3 ....129 D3
Ellington St N7 ....72 C2
Elliot Cl E15 ....76 C1
Wembley HA9 ....66 C5
Elliot Ct 5 N15 ....51 D5
Elliot Rd NW4 ....46 B3
SW9 ....138 D5
Elliott Ave HA4 ....62 B6
Elliott Gdns TW17 ....192 C5
Elliott Rd SW9 ....138 D4
W4 ....111 C2
Bromley BR2 ....209 D5
Stanmore HA7 ....25 A4
Thornton Heath CR7 ....204 D5
Elliott Sch SW15 ....156 C5
Elliott's Pl N1 ....234 D5
Elliott Sq NW3 ....70 C1
Elliott's Row
SE11 ....116 D2 261 D4
Ellis Cl HA8 ....27 C4
NW10 ....68 C2
SE9 ....167 A2
Elliscombe Mount 11
SE7 ....143 C6
Elliscombe Rd SE7 ....143 C6
Ellis Ct W7 ....86 D2
Ellisfield Dr SW15 ....156 A4
Ellis Franklin Ct NW8 ..229 A4
Ellis Ho E17 ....54 A4
SE17 ....262 C2
Ellison Gdns UB2 ....107 B2
Ellison Ho 1 SE13 ....142 A3
Ellison Rd DA15 ....167 B3
Barnes SW13 ....133 D3
Streatham SW16 ....182 A3
Ellis Rd Mitcham CR4 ....202 D3
Southall UB2 ....108 A5
Ellis St SW1 ....115 A2 258 A4
Elliston Ho 14 SE18 ....122 C2
Ellora Rd SW16 ....181 D5
Ellswood Ct 18 KT6 ....197 D2
Ellsworth St E2 ....96 B4
Ellwood Ct 1 W9 ....91 D3
Elmar Rd N15 ....51 B5
Elm Ave Ealing W5 ....110 B5
Ruislip HA4 ....40 B2
Elmbank N14 ....16 A4
Elmbank Dr BR1 ....187 D1
Elm Bank Gdns SW13 ....133 C3
Elm Bank Mans SW13 ....133 C3
Elmbank Way W7 ....86 B2
Elmbourne Dr DA17 ....125 D2
Elmbourne Rd SW17 ....159 B1
Elmbridge Ave KT5 ....199 A3
Elmbridge Cl HA4 ....40 A3
Elmbridge Dr HA4 ....40 A3
Elmbridge Wlk E8 ....74 A1
Elmbrook 2 E18 ....55 A6
Elmbrook Cl TW16 ....172 B2
Elmbrook Gdns SE9 ....144 A1
Elmbrook Rd SM1 ....217 B4
Elm Cl N19 ....71 C6
NW4 ....46 D4
Buckhurst Hill IG9 ....21 D2
Carshalton SM5 ....202 D1
Harrow HA2 ....41 D3
Hayes UB3 ....84 A1
South Croydon CR2 ....221 C2
Tolworth KT5 ....199 A2
Twickenham TW13,TW2 ....151 D2
Wanstead E11 ....55 B3
West Barnes SW20 ....200 C5
Elmcote HA5 ....22 D1
Elmcourt Rd SE21,SE27 ..160 D2
Elm Court Sch SE27 ....161 A2
Elm Cres W5 ....110 A4
Kingston KT2 ....176 A2
Elmcroft N6 ....49 C2
N8 ....50 B4
Elmcroft Ave DA15 ....168 A5
NW11 ....47 B2
Enfield N9 ....18 B5
Wanstead E11 ....55 B5
Elmcroft Cl
Chessington KT9 ....214 A5
Ealing W5 ....87 D1
Feltham TW14 ....149 D5
Wanstead E11 ....55 B5
Elmcroft Cres NW11 ....47 A2
Harrow HA2 ....41 C6
Elmcroft Dr
Ashford TW15 ....170 C5
Chessington KT9 ....214 A5
Elmcroft Gdns NW9 ....44 C4
Elmcroft St E5 ....74 C4
Elmcroft Terr UB8 ....82 C1
Elm Ct EC4 ....251 A6
4 N3 ....29 C2
Elm Ct *continued*
SE13 ....142 B2
SW9 ....138 C4
42 W2 ....91 C2
5 Ashford TW16 ....171 D3
Catford SE6 ....163 D3
Chingford E4 ....36 A4
Mitcham CR4 ....180 D1
Elmdale Rd N13 ....32 B5
Elmdene KT5 ....199 A1
Elmdene Cl BR3 ....207 B4
Elmdene Rd SE18 ....122 D1
Elmdon Rd
Hatton, Hatton Cross
TW6 ....127 D2
Hounslow TW5 ....129 A3
Elm Dr Harrow HA2 ....41 D3
Sunbury TW16 ....172 C1
Elmer Cl EN2 ....4 B2
Elmer Ct SW6 ....135 A3
Elmer Gdns Edgware HA8 ..26 D3
Isleworth TW7 ....130 B2
Elmer Ho NW1 ....237 A4
Elmer Rd SE6 ....164 A4
Elmer's Dr TW11 ....175 B4
Elmers End Rd BR3,
SE20 ....206 C6
Elmers End Sta BR3 ....206 D5
Elmerside Rd BR3 ....207 A5
Elmers Rd SE25 ....206 A2
Elmfield Ave N8 ....50 A4
Mitcham CR4 ....181 A2
Teddington TW11 ....174 D5
Elmfield Cl HA1 ....64 C6
Elmfield Ct DA16 ....146 B4
Elmfield Ho 17 N2 ....30 B1
6 N5 ....73 A3
W9 ....91 C3
Elmfield Mans 5 SW17 .159 A2
Elmfield Pk BR1 ....209 A6
Elmfield Rd BR1 ....209 A6
E17 ....52 D3
N2 ....48 B6
Chingford E4 ....20 B2
Southall UB2 ....107 A3
Upper Tooting SW17 ....159 B2
Elmfield Way W9 ....91 C2
South Croydon CR2 ....221 D1
Elm Friars Wlk NW1 ....71 D1
Elmgate Ave TW13 ....150 C1
Elmgate Gdns HA8 ....27 B6
Elm Gdns N2 ....48 A6
Claygate KT10 ....212 D2
Enfield EN2 ....5 B5
Mitcham CR4 ....203 D5
Elm Gn W3 ....89 C1
Elm Gr BR6 ....211 D1
N8 ....50 A3
NW2 ....68 D4
SE15 ....140 A3
Harrow HA2 ....41 C2
Kingston KT2 ....176 A2
Sutton SM1 ....217 D4
Wimbledon SW19 ....179 A3
Woodford IG8 ....36 D5
Yiewsley UB7 ....104 B6
Elmgreen Cl 8 E15 ....98 C6
Elmgrove Cres HA1 ....43 A4
Elmgrove Fst & Mid Schs
HA3 ....43 A5
Elmgrove Gdns HA1 ....43 A4
Elm Grove Par SM6 ....219 A5
Elm Grove Rd W5 ....110 A4
Elmgrove Rd
Croydon CR0 ....206 B2
Harrow HA1 ....42 D4
Elm Grove Rd SW13 ....134 A3
Elm Hall Gdns E11 ....55 B3
Elm Hatch HA5 ....23 B3
Elm Ho 4 E14 ....120 A4
2 Kingston KT2 ....176 B3
Elmhurst DA17 ....147 A6
Elmhurst Ave N2 ....48 B6
Mitcham CR4 ....181 B3
Elmhurst Ct CR0 ....221 B3
Elmhurst Dr E18 ....37 A1
Elmhurst Lo 3 SM2 ....218 A1
Elmhurst Mans SW4 ....137 D2
Elmhurst Prim Sch E7 ....77 B1
Elmhurst Rd E7 ....77 B1
Chislehurst SE9 ....166 A1
Enfield EN3 ....6 C6
Tottenham N17 ....33 D1
Elmhurst Sch CR2 ....221 B3
Elmhurst St SW4 ....137 D2
Elmhurst Villas SE15 ....140 C1
Elmington Cl DA5 ....169 D5
Elmington Rd SE5 ....139 B5
Elmira St SE13 ....141 D2
Elm La SE6 ....163 B2
Elm Lawn Cl UB8 ....60 A1
Elmlea Dr UB3 ....83 D2
Elmlee Cl BR7 ....188 B4
Elmley Cl 12 E6 ....100 A2
Elmley St SE18 ....123 B2
Elm Lo SW6 ....134 D4
Elmore Cl HA0 ....88 A5
Elmore Ho SW9 ....138 D3
Elmore Rd E11 ....76 B5
Enfield EN3 ....6 D5
Elmore St N1 ....73 B1
Elm Park Ave N15 ....52 A3
Elm Park Ct HA5 ....40 C6
Elm Park Gdns NW4 ....46 D4
SW10 ....114 B1 256 C1
Elm Park Ho SW10 ....256 C1
Elm Park La
SW3 ....114 B1 256 C1
Elm Park Mans SW10 ....266 B6
Elm Park Rd N3 ....29 B3
Elm Park Rd *continued*
SW3 ....136 B6 266 C6
Edmonton N21 ....17 A4
Pinner HA5 ....40 D6
South Norwood SE25 ....205 D6
Walthamstow E10 ....53 A1
Elm Pk Stanmore HA7 ....25 C5
Streatham SW2 ....160 B4
Elm Pl SW7 ....114 B1 256 C2
Elm Quay SW8 ....269 C5
Elm Rd E11 ....76 B6
E17 ....54 A4
E7 ....76 D2
Barnet EN5 ....1 B1
Beckenham BR3 ....185 B1
Chessington KT9 ....214 A4
Claygate KT10 ....212 D2
East Bedfont TW14 ....149 B4
Hackbridge SM6 ....203 A1
Kingston KT2 ....176 B2
Kingston KT3 ....199 B6
Mortlake SW14 ....133 A1
Sidcup DA14 ....190 A6
South Norwood CR7 ....205 B5
Stoneleigh KT17 ....215 D2
Tottenham N22 ....32 D2
Wembley HA9 ....66 A3
Elm Rd W SM4 ....201 B2
Elm Row NW3 ....70 A5
Elms Ave N10 ....49 B6
NW4 ....46 D4
Elmscott Gdns N21 ....17 A5
Elmscott Rd BR1 ....186 D5
Elms Cotts 1 CR4 ....180 D1
Elms Cres SW4 ....159 D5
Elms Ct Merton SW19 ....179 D3
Wembley HA0 ....65 A4
Elmsdale Rd E17 ....53 B5
Elms Gdns Dagenham RM9 .81 B4
Wembley HA0 ....65 A4
Elmshaw Rd SW15 ....156 A6
Elmshurst Cres N2 ....48 B5
Elmside CR0 ....223 D2
Elmside Rd HA9 ....66 C5
Elms La HA0 ....65 A5
Elmsleigh Ave HA3 ....43 C5
Elmsleigh Ct SM1 ....217 D5
Elmsleigh Ho TW2 ....152 B2
Elmsleigh Rd TW2 ....152 B2
Elmslie Ct SE9 ....166 C5
Elmslie Point 2 E3 ....97 B2
Elms Mews W2 ....246 C6
Elms Park Ave HA0 ....65 A4
Elms Rd SW4 ....159 C6
Harrow HA3 ....24 C3
Elm St WC1 ....94 B3 240 D5
Elmstead Ave BR7 ....188 B5
Wembley HA9 ....66 B6
Elmstead Cl N20 ....13 C2
West Ewell KT19 ....215 C3
Elmstead Gdns KT4 ....216 A5
Elmstead Glade BR7 ....188 B4
Elmstead La BR7 ....188 B5
Elmstead Rd IG3 ....79 D6
Elmstead Woods Sta
BR7 ....188 A4
Elmsted Cres DA16 ....146 C6
Elms The E12 ....78 A2
NW10 ....89 C5
NW9 ....45 A3
Ashford TW15 ....170 C5
Barnes SW13 ....133 D2
Claygate KT10 ....212 D1
Croydon CR0 ....205 A1
Elmstone Rd SW6 ....265 A2
Elmsway TW15 ....170 C5
Elmsworth Ave TW3 ....129 D3
Elm Terr NW2 ....69 C5
3 SE9 ....166 C5
Harrow HA3 ....24 B2
Elmton Ct NW8 ....236 C6
Elmton Way E5 ....74 A5
Elm Tree Ave KT10 ....196 C2
Elm Tree Cl NW8 ..92 B4 229 C2
Ashford TW15 ....170 D5
Northolt UB5 ....85 B5
Elm Tree Ct NW8 ....229 C2
5 SE5 ....139 A4
18 SE7 ....143 C6
Elm Tree Rd NW8 ..92 B4 229 C2
Elmtree Rd TW11 ....174 C5
Elm View Ct UB2 ....107 C2
Elm Way N11 ....31 A4
NW10 ....67 C4
North Cheam KT4 ....216 C5
West Ewell KT19 ....215 B3
Elm Wlk NW3 ....69 C6
Orpington BR6 ....226 B5
West Barnes SW20 ....200 D5
Elmwood Ave
Bowes Park N13 ....32 A5
Feltham TW13 ....150 B1
Harrow HA3 ....43 B3
Elmwood Cl
Hackbridge SM6 ....219 B6
Stoneleigh KT17 ....216 A1
Elmwood Cres NW9 ....45 A5
Elmwood Ct SW11 ....268 C2
Wembley HA0 ....65 A5
Elmwood Dr DA5 ....169 A4
Stoneleigh KT17 ....216 A1
Elmwood Gdns W7 ....86 C1
Elmwood Inf Sch CR0 ....204 D3
Elmwood Jun Sch CR0 ..204 D2
Elm Wood Prim Sch
SE27 ....161 B1
Elmwood Rd SE24 ....161 B6

Elmwood Rd *continued*
Chiswick W4 ...133 A6
Mitcham CR4 ...202 D6
Thornton Heath CR0 ...204 D2
Elmworth Gr SE21 ...161 B2
Elnathan Mews W9 ...91 D3
Elphinstone Ct SW16 ...182 A4
Elphinstone Rd E17 ...35 B1
Elphinstone St N5 ...72 D4
Elrington Rd E8 ...74 A2
Woodford IG8 ...37 A5
Elsa Ct BR3 ...185 B2
Elsa Rd DA16 ...146 C3
Elsa St E1 ...97 A2
Elsdale St E9 ...74 C2
Elsden Mews E2 ...96 C5
Elsden Rd N17 ...33 D2
Elsenham Rd E12 ...78 C3
Elsenham St SW18, SW19 ...157 B2
Elsfield NW5 ...71 B3
Elsham Rd E11 ...76 C4
W14 ...113 A4 244 A1
Elsham Terr W14 ...244 A1
Elsiedene Rd N21 ...17 A4
Elsie Lane Ct W2 ...91 D2
Elsiemaud Rd SE4 ...163 B6
Elsie Rd SE22 ...139 D1
Elsinge Rd EN1 ...6 B6
Elsinore Ave TW19 ...148 A4
Elsinore Gdns NW2 ...69 A5
Elsinore Ho N1 ...234 A5
12 SE5 ...139 A3
7 SE7 ...122 A2
Elsinore Rd SE23 ...163 A3
Elsinore Way TW9 ...132 D2
Elsley Ct HA9 ...66 D2
Elsley Prim Sch HA9 ...66 B2
Elsley Rd SW11 ...137 A2
Elsley Sch SW11 ...137 A2
Elspeth Rd SW11 ...136 D1
Wembley HA0 ...66 A3
Elsrick Ave SM4 ...201 C4
Elstan Way CR0 ...207 A2
Elstead Ct SM4 ...201 A1
Elstead Ho 9 SW2 ...160 B4
Elsted St SE17 ...117 B2 262 D3
Elstow Cl SE9 ...166 B6
Ruislip HA4 ...40 D2
Elstow Gdns RM9 ...103 A6
Elstow Grange NW6 ...68 D1
Elstow Rd RM9 ...103 A6
Elstree Gdns DA17 ...125 A2
Edmonton N9 ...18 B3
Ilford IG1 ...79 A3
Elstree Hill BR1 ...186 C3
Elstree Hill N WD6 ...9 D6
Elstree Hill S WD6 ...9 D4
Elstree Ho 3 HA7 ...25 C6
Elstree Pk WD6 ...11 B5
Elstree Rd Bushey WD23 ...8 C4
Elstree WD6 ...9 A5
Elswick Rd SE13 ...141 D3
Elswick St SW6 ...136 A3
Elsworth Cl TW14 ...149 C3
Elsworthy KT7 ...196 C3
Elsworthy Rd NW3 ...92 C6 230 A6
Elsworthy Rise NW3 ...70 C1
Elsworthy Terr NW3 ...70 C1
Elsynge Rd SW18 ...158 B6
Elsynge Road Mans SW18 ...158 B6
Eltham CE Prim Sch SE9 ...166 B6
Eltham Coll SE9 ...165 D2
Eltham Green Rd SE9 ...165 C6
Eltham Green Sch SE9 ...165 D5
Eltham High St SE9 ...166 B5
Eltham Hill SE9 ...166 A6
Eltham Hill Sch SE9 ...166 A5
Eltham Hill Tech Coll for Girls SE9 ...166 A5
Eltham Palace★ SE9 ...166 A4
Eltham Palace Rd SE9 ...165 D5
Eltham Park Gdns SE9 ...144 C1
Eltham Rd SE9,SE12 ...165 B6
Eltham Sta SE9 ...166 B6
Elthiron Rd SW6 ...135 C4 265 B1
Elthorne Ave W7 ...109 A4
Elthorne Ct NW9 ...45 B3
Feltham TW13 ...150 C3
Elthorne Park High Sch W7 ...108 D3
Elthorne Park Rd W7 ...109 A4
Elthorne Rd N19 ...71 D6
NW9 ...45 B2
Elthorne Way NW9 ...45 B3
Elthruda Rd SE13 ...164 B5
Eltisley Rd IG1 ...78 D4
Elton Ave Barnet EN5 ...13 B6
Wembley HA0 ...65 B3
Wembley UB6 ...64 D2
Elton Cl KT1 ...175 C3
Elton Ho 3 E3 ...97 B6
Elton Lo 4 W5 ...110 A6
Elton Pl N16 ...73 C3
Elton Rd KT2 ...176 C2
Elton St 11 N16 ...73 C3
Eltringham St SW18 ...136 A1
Elvaston Ct EN5 ...12 C6
Elvaston Mews SW7 ...256 B6
Elvaston Pl SW7 ...114 A3 256 B5
Elveden Ho 17 SW9 ...138 D1
Elveden Pl NW10 ...88 C5
Elveden Rd NW10 ...88 C5
Elvendon Rd N13 ...32 A4
Elver Gdns 6 E2 ...96 A4
Elverson Rd SE8 ...141 D3
Elverson Rd Sta SE8 ...141 D3
Elverton St SW1 ...115 D2 259 C4
Elvin Ct NW9 ...45 A2
Elvington Gn BR2 ...208 D4
Elvington La NW9 ...27 C2
Elvin Ho 2 E9 ...74 C2
Elvino Rd SE26 ...185 A5
Elvis Rd NW2 ...68 C2
Elwill Way BR3 ...208 B5
Elwin St E2 ...96 A4
Elwood Ho N5 ...72 D5
Elwood St N4,N5 ...72 D5
Elworth Ho SW8 ...270 D3
Elwyn Gdns SE12 ...165 A4
Ely Cl SW20 ...177 D1
Ely Cottages SW8 ...270 C3
Ely Court Flats SW6 ...264 A1
Ely Ct KT1 ...198 C6
Ely Gdns
Borehamwood WD6 ...11 B6
Redbridge IG1 ...56 A2
Ely Ho 22 SE15 ...140 A5
Barnet EN4 ...2 C1
Elyne Rd N4 ...50 C3
Ely Pl EC1 ...94 C2 241 B3
Ely Rd E10 ...54 A2
Hatton TW6 ...127 D3
Hounslow TW4 ...128 C2
Thornton Heath CR0 ...205 B4
Elysian Ave BR5 ...211 D3
Elysium Gate 7 SW6 ...135 B3
Elysium Pl SW6 ...135 B3
Elysium St SW6 ...135 B3
Elystan Bsns Ctr UB4 ...106 C6
Elystan Pl SW3 ...114 D1 257 C2
Elystan St SW3 ...114 C2 257 B3
Elystan Wlk N1 ...234 A5
Elyston Ct SW15 ...156 B6
Emanuel Ave W3 ...89 A1
Emanuel Ct W3 ...89 B1
Emanuel Sch SW11 ...158 C6
Embankment SW15 ...134 D3
Embankment Gdns SW3 ...136 D6 267 D6
Embankment Pier WC2 ...116 B4 250 B4
Embankment Pl WC2 ...250 B4
Embankment Sta WC2 ...116 A5 250 B4
Embankment The TW1 ...153 A3
Embassy Ct DA14 ...168 B1
Embassy Ct DA16 ...146 B2
N11 ...31 D4
NW8 ...229 D3
Kingston KT6 ...197 D4
7 Wallington SM6 ...219 B2
7 Wanstead E18 ...55 A6
Ealing W5 ...110 B6
Embassy Gdns BR3 ...185 B2
Embassy Ho 2 NW6 ...69 C1
Embassy Lo N3 ...29 B1
Emba St SE16 ...118 A4
Ember Cl BR5 ...211 A2
Embercourt Rd KT10, KT7,KT8 ...196 C3
Ember Ct 14 NW9 ...27 D1
2 W12 ...111 C3
Ember Farm Ave KT8 ...196 B3
Ember Farm Way KT8 ...196 B4
Ember Gdns KT10,KT8 ...196 C2
Ember Ho 8 BR1 ...186 B5
Ember La KT10,KT8 ...196 B2
Emberson Ho 7 E17 ...54 A5
Emberton SE5 ...139 C6
Emberton Ct EC1 ...234 C1
Embleton Rd SE13 ...141 D1
Embleton Wlk TW12 ...173 B5
Embley Point 2 E5 ...74 B4
Embry Cl HA7 ...25 A6
Embry Dr HA7 ...25 A4
Embry Way HA7 ...25 A6
Emden Cl UB7 ...104 C4
Emden St SW6 ...265 D2
Emerald Cl E16 ...100 A1
Emerald Ct N12 ...30 A6
Emerald Gdns RM8 ...59 C1
Emerald Sq UB2 ...106 D3
Emerald St WC1 ...94 B2 240 C4
Emerson Gdns HA3 ...44 B3
Emerson Ho N16 ...73 C3
Emerson Rd IG1 ...56 C2
Emerson St SE1 ...117 A5 252 A4
Emerton Cl DA6 ...147 A1
Emery Hill St SW1 ...259 B5
Emery St SE1 ...116 C3 261 B6
Emilia Cl EN3 ...18 B6
Emily Pl N7 ...72 C4
Emily St 7 E16 ...98 D1
Emlyn Gdns 3 W12 ...111 C3
Emlyn Rd W12 ...111 D3
Emmanuel CE Prim Sch NW6 ...69 C3
Emmanuel Ct 9 E10 ...53 D2
Emmanuel Ho SE11 ...261 A3
Dulwich SE21 ...161 B1
Emmanuel Rd
Streatham SW12 ...159 D3
Northwood HA6 ...22 A3
Emma Rd E13 ...98 D5
Emma St E2 ...96 B5
Emmeline Ct KT12 ...194 C2
Emminster NW6 ...91 D6
Emmott Ave IG6 ...57 A4
Emmott Cl E1 ...97 A3
NW11 ...48 A3
Emperor's Gate SW7 ...114 A2 256 A4
Empingham Ho 20 SE8 ...118 D2
Empire Ave N18 ...33 A4
Empire Ct HA9 ...66 D5
Empire Ho SW3 ...257 A5
Edmonton N18 ...33 B4
Empire Par Edmonton N18 ...33 B4
Wembley HA9 ...66 C5
Empire Rd UB6 ...65 C1
Empire Sq N19 ...72 A5
Empire Way HA9 ...66 C4
Empire Wharf E3 ...97 A6
Empire Wharf Rd E14 ...120 B2
Empress Ave Chingford E4 ...35 D3
Ilford IG1 ...78 C6
Wanstead E12 ...77 D6
Woodford IG8 ...36 D3
Empress Dr BR7 ...188 D4
Empress Mews 37 SE5 ...139 A3
Empress Par E4 ...35 C3
Empress Pl SW5 ...113 C1 255 A1
Empress St SE17 ...139 A6
Empson St E3 ...97 D3
Emsworth Cl N9 ...18 C3
Emsworth St SW2 ...160 B2
Emu Rd SW8 ...137 B3
Ena Rd SW16 ...204 A6
Enard Ho 27 E3 ...97 B5
Enbrook St W10 ...91 A4
Enclave Ct EC1 ...241 C6
Endale Cl SM5 ...218 D6
Endeavour Way
Barking IG11 ...102 A5
Thornton Heath CR0 ...204 A2
Wimbledon SW19 ...179 D6
Endell St WC2 ...94 A1 240 A1
Enderby St SE10 ...120 C1
Enderfield Ct BR7 ...188 C2
Enderley Cl HA3 ...24 C2
Enderley Ho SE19 ...183 D2
Enderley Rd HA3 ...24 C2
Endersby Rd EN5 ...12 C6
Endersleigh Gdns NW4 ...46 A5
Endlebury Ct 3 E4 ...20 B2
Endlebury Rd E4 ...20 A2
Endlesham Ct 2 SW12 ...159 A4
Endlesham Rd SW12 ...159 A4
Endsleigh Gdns
WC1 ...93 D3 239 C6
Ilford IG1 ...56 D1
Kingston KT6 ...197 C3
Endsleigh Ind Est UB2 ...107 B2
Endsleigh Mans 4 SW16 ...160 A1
Endsleigh Pl WC1 ...239 D6
Endsleigh Rd
Ealing W13 ...109 A6
Southall UB2 ...107 A2
Endsleigh St WC1 ...93 D3 239 D6
Endway KT5 ...198 D2
Endwell Rd SE4 ...141 A3
Endymion Rd N4 ...50 D2
SW2 ...160 B5
Energen Cl NW10 ...67 C1
NW10 ...67 C2
Enfield Chase Sta EN2 ...5 A2
Enfield Cloisters 7 N1 ...95 C4
Enfield Coll EN3 ...6 C2
Enfield Gram Sch EN2 ...5 B2
Enfield Gram Sch Lower EN1 ...5 B3
Enfield Ho 24 SW9 ...138 A3
Enfield Lock Sta EN3 ...7 A6
Enfield Rd E8,N1 ...73 C1
W3 ...110 D4
Brentford TW8 ...109 D1
Enfield EN2 ...4 A2
Hatton TW6 ...127 C3
Enfield Road Rdbt TW6 ...127 C3
Enfield Town Sta EN1 ...5 B2
Enfield Wlk TW8 ...109 D1
Enford St W1 ...92 D2 237 C4
Engadine Cl CR0 ...221 D5
Engadine St SW18 ...157 C3
Engate St SE13 ...142 A1
Engel Pk NW7 ...28 C4
Engineer Cl SE18 ...144 C6
Engineers Way HA9 ...66 C4
England's La NW3 ...70 D2
England Way KT3 ...199 A5
Englefield NW1 ...232 A1
Englefield Cl Enfield EN2 ...4 C3
Orpington BR5 ...211 D5
Thornton Heath CR0 ...205 A3
Englefield Path BR5 ...211 D5
Englefield Rd N1 ...73 C1
Engleheart Dr TW14 ...149 D5
Engleheart Rd SE6 ...164 A4
Englewood Rd SW12 ...159 C5
English Gardening Sch The SW3 ...136 D6 267 C6
English Grounds SE1 ...253 A3
English Martyrs RC Prim Sch E1 ...95 D1 243 D1
English St E3 ...97 B3
Enid St SE16 ...117 D3 263 D6
Enid Stacy Ho 11 N19 ...49 D2
Enmore Ave SE25 ...206 A4
Enmore Ct SW14 ...155 B6
Enmore Gdns SW14 ...155 B6
Enmore Rd
Croydon SE25 ...206 A4
Putney SW15 ...156 C6
Southall UB1 ...85 C3
Ennerdale Ave HA3,HA7 ...43 C6
Ennerdale Cl
Cheam SM1 ...217 B4
East Bedfont TW14 ...149 D3
Ennerdale Ct E11 ...55 A2
Ennerdale Dr NW9 ...45 C4
Ennerdale Gdns HA9 ...43 C1
Ennerdale Ho 3 N4 ...51 B2
Ennerdale Rd DA7 ...147 C4
Richmond TW9 ...132 B3
Ennersdale Prim Sch SE13 ...164 B6
Ennersdale Rd SE13 ...164 B6
Ennis Ho 16 E14 ...97 D1
Ennismore Ave W4 ...111 D2
Greenford UB6 ...64 C3
Ennismore Gdns SW7 ...114 C3 257 A6
Thames Ditton KT7 ...196 C3
Ennismore Gdns Mews SW7 ...114 C3 257 A6
Ennismore Mews SW7 ...114 C3 257 A6
Ennismore St SW7 ...114 C3 257 A6
Ennis Rd N4 ...50 C1
SE18 ...145 A6
Ennor Ct KT4 ...216 C4
Ensbury Ho SW8 ...270 C4
Ensign Cl TW19 ...148 A3
Ensign Ct 7 E1 ...118 A6
Ensign Dr N13 ...17 A1
Ensign St E1 ...118 A6
Ensign Way TW19 ...148 A3
Enslin Rd SE9 ...166 C4
Ensor Mews SW7 ...256 C2
Enstone Rd Enfield EN3 ...7 A2
Ickenham UB10 ...60 B5
Enterprise Cl CR0 ...204 C1
Enterprise Ho
Barking IG11 ...101 D4
Chingford E4 ...20 A4
Walton-on-T KT12 ...194 B2
Enterprise Row N15 ...51 D4
Enterprise Way NW10 ...90 A4
SW18 ...135 C1
Teddington TW11 ...174 D4
Enterprize Way SE8 ...119 B2
Enton Pl TW3 ...129 D1
Epirus Mews SW6 ...265 A4
Epirus Rd SW6 ...135 B5 264 D4
Epping Cl E14 ...119 C2
Romford RM7 ...59 D6
Epping Forest★ IG10 ...21 B6
Epping Glade E4 ...20 A6
Epping Ho E5 ...74 A6
Epping New Rd IG9 ...21 B5
Epping Pl N1 ...72 C2
Epping Way E4 ...19 D5
Epple Rd SW6 ...135 B4 264 D2
Epsom Cl DA7 ...147 D2
Northolt UB5 ...63 B3
Epsom & Ewell High Sch KT19 ...215 A3
Epsom Rd E10 ...54 A3
Croydon CR0 ...220 C4
Ilford IG3 ...57 D3
Morden SM4 ...201 B2
Epsom Sq TW6 ...127 D3
Epstein Rd SE28 ...124 B5
Epworth Rd TW7,TW8 ...131 B5
Epworth St EC2 ...95 B3 242 D5
Equity Sq 29 E2 ...95 D4
Erasmus St SW1 ...115 D2 259 D3
Erconwald St W12 ...89 D1
Erebus Dr SE28 ...123 B4
Eresby Dr BR3 ...207 C1
Eresby Ho SW7 ...247 B1
Eresby Pl NW6 ...69 C1
Erica Ct SW4 ...270 B1
Erica Gdns CR0 ...223 D5
Erica Ho SE4 ...141 B2
Wood Green N22 ...32 C2
Erica St W12 ...112 A6
Eric Cl E7 ...77 A4
Eric Clarke La IG11 ...101 A4
Ericcson Cl SW18 ...157 C6
Eric Fletcher Ct 7 N1 ...73 A1
Eric Macdonald Ho SW6 ...265 B1
Eric Rd E7 ...77 A4
NW10 ...67 D2
Dagenham RM6 ...58 D2
Eric Shipman Terr 2 E13 ...99 A3
Ericson Ho N16 ...51 D1
SE13 ...142 B1
Eric St E3 ...97 B3
Eric Wilkins Ho 13 SE1 ...118 A1
Eridge Ho SE22 ...139 D2
Eridge Rd W4 ...111 B3
Erin Cl BR1 ...186 C3
Erindale SE18 ...145 B6
Erindale Ct 1 BR3 ...185 C2
Erindale Terr SE18 ...145 B6
Erith Rd DA7 ...147 D2
Belvedere DA17 ...125 D1
Erlanger Rd SE14 ...140 D3
Erlesmere Gdns W13 ...109 A3
Ermine Cl TW4 ...128 C3
Ermine Ho 3 N17 ...33 D3
Ermine Rd N15 ...51 D3
SE13 ...141 D1
Ermine Side EN1 ...18 A6
Ermington Rd BR7,SE9 ...167 A2
Ernald Ave E6 ...100 A5
Erncroft Way TW1 ...152 D5
Ernest Ave SE27 ...182 D6
Ernest Bevin Coll SW17 ...158 C2
Ernest Cl BR3 ...207 C4
Ernest Cotts KT17 ...215 D1
Ernest Gdns W4 ...132 D6
Ernest Gr BR3 ...207 B4
Ernest Rd KT1 ...176 D1
Ernest Richards Twr E17 ...53 B3
Ernest Simmonds Ho SE14 ...140 C3
Ernest Sq KT1 ...176 D1
Ernest St E1 ...96 D3
Ernle Rd SW20 ...178 C3
Ernshaw Pl SW15 ...157 A6
Eros (Shaftesbury Meml)★ W1 ...115 D6 249 C5
Erpingham Rd SW15 ...134 C2
Erridge Rd SW19 ...179 C1
Errington Rd W9 ...91 B3
Errol Gdns Hayes UB4 ...84 B3
West Barnes KT3 ...200 A5
Errol St EC1 ...95 A3 242 B5
Erskine Cl SM1 ...218 C5
Erskine Cres N17 ...52 B5
Erskine Hill NW11 ...47 C4
Erskine Ho 7 SE7 ...143 C6
SW1 ...259 A1
Erskine Rd E17 ...53 B5
NW3 ...70 D1
Carshalton SM1,SM5 ...218 B5
Erwood Rd SE7 ...122 A1
Esam Way SW16 ...182 C5
Escot Rd TW16 ...171 C3
Escott Gdns SE9 ...188 A6
Escot Way EN5 ...12 C6
Escreet Gr SE18 ...122 C2
Escuan Lo N5 ...73 A3
Esher Ave Cheam SM3 ...216 D5
Walton-on-T KT12 ...194 A1
Esher Church Sch KT10 ...212 A3
Esher Cl DA5 ...169 A3
Esher Coll KT7 ...196 C2
Esher Cres TW6 ...127 D3
Esher Gdns SW19 ...156 D2
Esher Ho 8 SW8 ...137 D3
Esher Mews 4 CR4 ...202 D6
Esher Park Ave KT10 ...212 A3
Esher Rd
East Molesey KT8 ...196 B4
Ilford IG3 ...79 C5
Esher Sta KT10 ...212 B6
Eskdale NW1 ...232 A3
Eskdale Ave UB5 ...85 B6
Eskdale Cl HA9 ...65 D6
Eskdale Rd DA7 ...147 C4
Esk Ho E3 ...97 B3
Eskmont Ridge SE19 ...183 C3
Esk Rd E13 ...99 B3
Esmar Cres NW9 ...46 A2
Esme Ho SW15 ...133 D1
Esmeralda Rd SE1 ...118 A2
Esmond Ct W8 ...255 D6
Esmond Gdns W4 ...111 B2
Esmond Rd NW6 ...91 B6
W4 ...111 B3
Esmond St SW15 ...135 A1
Esparto St SW18 ...157 D4
Essan Ho W13 ...87 B2
Essenden Rd
Belvedere DA17 ...125 C1
South Croydon CR2 ...221 C1
Essendine Mans W9 ...91 C4
Essendine Prim Sch W9 ...91 C4
Essendine Rd W9 ...91 C4
Essex Ave TW7 ...130 C2
Essex Cl E17 ...53 A5
Romford RM7 ...59 D5
Ruislip HA4 ...40 D1
West Barnes SM4 ...200 D2
Essex Ct EC4 ...241 A1
W6 ...112 C3
Barnes SW13 ...133 D3
South Norwood SE19 ...183 B4
Essex Gdns N4 ...50 D3
Essex Gr SE19 ...183 B4
Essex Ho 2 E14 ...97 D1
4 Acton W3 ...88 C1
Essex Lo 5 N10 ...31 B1
Essex Mans E11 ...54 B2
Essex Park Mews W3 ...111 C5
Essex Pk N3 ...29 D4
Essex Pl W4 ...111 A2
Essex Place Sq W4 ...111 B2
Essex Prim Sch E12 ...78 A3
Essex Rd E10 ...54 A3
E12 ...78 A2
E17 ...53 A3
N1 ...73 A1 234 D6
NW10 ...67 C1
W3 ...111 A6
W4 ...111 B2
Barking IG11 ...79 B1
Chingford, Chingford Green E4 ...20 C3
Enfield EN2 ...5 B1
Ilford RM6 ...58 C2
Romford RM7 ...59 D5
Woodford E18 ...37 B1
Essex Rd S E11 ...54 B2
Essex Road Sta N1 ...73 A1
Essex St E7 ...77 A3
SE18 ...123 A3
WC2 ...116 C6 251 A6
Essex Twr 4 SE20 ...184 B2
Essex Villas W8 ...113 C4 245 A1
Essian St E1 ...97 A2
Essington SW15 ...157 A5
Essoldo Way HA8 ...44 B6
Estate Way E10 ...53 B1
Estcourt Rd
SW6 ...135 B5 264 C4
Croydon SE25 ...206 B3
Estella Ave KT3 ...200 B5
Estella Ho W11 ...112 D6
Estelle Rd NW3 ...70 D4
Esterbrooke St SW1 ...259 C3
Este Rd SW11 ...136 C2
Esther Cl N21 ...16 C4
Esther Rd E11 ...54 C2
Estoria Cl 22 SW2 ...160 C4
Estreham Rd SW16 ...181 D4
Estridge Cl TW3 ...129 C1
Estuary Cl IG11 ...102 B4
Eswyn Rd SW17 ...180 D5
Etal Ho N1 ...72 D1
Etchingham Ct N12 ...30 A3
Etchingham Park Rd N3 ...29 D3
Etchingham Rd E15 ...76 A4
Etfield Gr DA14 ...190 B5
Ethelbert Cl BR1 ...209 A6
Ethelbert Gdns IG2 ...56 C4
Ethelbert Ho E9 ...75 A4
Ethelbert Rd
Bromley BR1,BR2 ...209 A6
Wimbledon SW20 ...178 D2
Ethelbert St SW12 ...159 B3
Ethel Brooks Ho SE18 ...144 D6
Ethelburga St SW11 ...136 C4 267 B2
Ethelburga Twr SW11 ...267 B2
Ethel Cotts RM6 ...58 D6
Ethel Davis Sch RM6 ...58 B4
Etheldene Ave N10 ...49 C5
Ethelden Rd W12 ...112 B5
Ethel Rankin Ct 8 SW6 ...135 B3
Ethel Rd Ashford TW15 ...170 A5
Newham E16 ...99 B1
Ethel St SE17 ...262 B3
Ethelworth Ct 4 SW2 ...160 C3
Etheridge Rd NW2 ...46 C2
Etherley Rd N15 ...51 A4
Etherow St SE22 ...162 A4
Etherstone Gn SW16 ...182 C6
Etherstone Rd SW16 ...182 C6
Ethnard Rd SE15 ...140 B6
Ethronvi Rd DA7 ...147 A2
Etloe Ho E10 ...53 C1
Etloe Rd E10 ...75 C6
Eton Ave N12 ...30 A3
NW3 ...70 C1
East Barnet EN4 ...14 C5
Heston TW5 ...129 C6
New Malden KT3 ...199 B5
Wembley HA0 ...65 A4
Eton Cl SW18 ...157 D4
Eton College Rd NW3 ...70 D2
Eton Ct NW3 ...70 B1
Wembley HA0 ...65 C4
Eton Garages 11 NW3 ...70 C2
Eton Gr NW9 ...44 C5
SE13 ...142 C2
Eton Hall NW3 ...70 D2
Eton Ho N5 ...72 D4
Eton Manor Ct E10 ...75 C6
Eton Pl NW1 ...71 A1
Eton Rd NW3 ...70 D2
Harlington UB3 ...127 D5
Ilford IG1 ...79 B4
Eton Rise NW3 ...70 D2
Eton St TW10 ...154 A6
Eton Villas NW3 ...70 D2
Etta St SE8 ...141 A6
Ettrick Ho 8 E5 ...74 B6
Ettrick St E14 ...98 A1
Etwell Pl KT5 ...198 B3
Eugene Cotter Ho SE17 ...262 D3
Eugenia Rd SE16 ...118 C2
Eugenie Mews BR7 ...188 D2
Eureka Rd 8 KT1 ...176 C1
Euro Bsns Ctr 3 E15 ...98 D6
Euro Cl NW10 ...68 A2
Eurolink Bsns Ctr SW2 ...160 C6
Europa Pl EC1 ...235 A1
Europe Rd SE18 ...122 B3
Eusdon Cl N9 ...18 B1
Eustace Ho SE11 ...260 C4
Eustace Pl SE18 ...122 B2
Eustace Rd E6 ...100 A4
SW6 ...135 C5 265 A4
Dagenham RM6 ...58 D2
Euston Rd NW1 ...93 D3 239 B6
Thornton Heath CR0 ...204 C1
Euston Sq NW1 ...232 C1
Euston Square Sta WC1 ...93 C3 239 B6
Euston St NW1 ...93 C4 232 B1
Euston Sta NW1 ...93 D4 232 C1
Euston Underpass NW1 ...239 A6
Evandale Rd SW9 ...138 C3
Evangelist Rd NW5 ...71 B4
Evans Cl E8 ...73 D2
Evans Gr TW13 ...151 C2
Evans Ho SW8 ...269 D3
34 W12 ...112 B6
Evans Rd SE6 ...164 C2
Evanston Ave E4 ...36 A3
Evanston Gdns IG4 ...56 A3
Eva Rd RM6 ...58 D2
Evelina Mans 8 SE5 ...139 B5
Evelina Rd SE15 ...140 C3
Penge SE20 ...184 D3
Eveline Ct N10 ...49 B4
Eveline Lowe Prim Sch SE1 ...118 A1
Eveline Rd CR4 ...180 D2
Evelyn Ave NW9 ...45 B5
Ruislip HA4 ...39 D2
Evelyn Cl TW2 ...151 D4
Evelyn Cres TW16 ...171 D2
Evelyn Ct E8 ...74 A4
N1 ...235 C3
W1 ...237 C1
Croydon CR0 ...206 A2
Evelyn Denington Ct 2 N1 ...72 D1
Evelyn Denington Rd E6 ...100 A3
Evelyn Dr HA5 ...22 D3

Evelyn Fox Ct W10 ....90 C2
Evelyn Gdns
SW7 ....114 B1 256 C1
Richmond TW9 ....132 A1
Evelyn Gr Ealing W5 ......110 B5
Southall UB1 ....85 B1
Evelyn Ho 3 SW2 ....160 B6
W12 ....111 D4
Evelyn Rd E16 ....121 B5
E17 ....54 A5
W4 ....111 B3
Cockfosters EN4 ....2 D1
Richmond TW10 ....153 C1
Richmond TW9 ....132 A2
Wimbledon SW19 ....179 D4
Evelyns Cl UB8 ....82 C1
Evelyns Com Sch UB7 ....82 B1
Evelyn St SE8 ....119 A1
Evelyn Terr TW9 ....132 A2
Evelyn Way
Sunbury TW16 ....171 D2
Wallington SM6 ....219 D4
Evelyn Wlk N1 ....95 B5 235 C3
Evelyn Yd W1 ....239 C2
Evening Hill BR3 ....186 A3
Evenlode Ho 5 SE2 ....124 C4
Evenwood Cl SW15 ....157 A6
Everard Ave BR2 ....209 A1
Everard Ct N13 ....16 B1
Everard Ho 24 E1 ....96 A1
Everard Way HA9 ....66 A5
Everatt Cl SW18 ....157 B6
Eve Rd E11 ....76 C4
E15 ....98 C5
N17 ....51 C6
Isleworth TW7 ....131 A1
Everdale Ct N2 ....48 C5
Everdon Rd SW13 ....134 A6
Everest Ct
6 Chislehurst SE9 ....166 A2
South Norwood SE19 ......183 C2
Everest Pl E14 ....98 A2
Everest Rd SE9 ....166 B6
Stanwell TW19 ....148 A4
Everett Cl Bushey WD23 .....8 C3
Pinner HA5 ....39 D6
Everett Ho N7 ....72 C4
SE17 ....262 C2
Everett Wlk DA17 ....125 B1
Everglade Ho E17 ....35 B1
Everglades
Beckenham BR2 ....208 C6
Hounslow TW3 ....130 A2
Everglade Strand NW9 ...27 D2
Evergreen Cl SE20 ....184 C3
Evergreen Sq 3 E8 ....73 D1
Evergreen Way UB3 ....105 D6
Everilda St N1 ....233 D5
Evering Rd E5,N16 ....74 A5
Everington Rd N10 ....30 D1
Everington St W6 ....134 D6
Everitt Rd NW10 ....89 B4
Everleigh St N4 ....50 B1
Eversfield Ct SE12 ....165 B2
Eversfield Gdns HA8,NW7 .27 C3
Eversfield Rd TW9 ....132 B3
Eversfield Ho E1 ....243 D2
Evershed Wlk W4 ....111 B2
Eversholt Ct EN5 ....14 A6
Eversholt St NW1 .93 C4 232 B3
Evershot Rd N4 ....50 B1
Eversleigh Ct N3 ....29 C3
Eversleigh Rd E6 ....99 D6
N3 ....29 B3
SW11 ....137 A3
New Barnet EN5 ....14 A6
Eversley Ave HA9 ....66 C6
Eversley Cl N21 ....16 B5
Eversley Cres
Hounslow TW7 ....130 B4
Ruislip HA4 ....61 D6
Southgate N21 ....16 C5
Eversley Ho 18 E2 ....96 A4
Eversley Mount N21 ....16 B5
Eversley Park Rd N21 .....16 B5
Eversley Pk SW19 ....178 B5
Eversley Prim Sch N21 ...16 B5
Eversley Rd
Greenwich SE7 ....143 B6
Kingston KT5 ....198 B4
South Norwood SE19 .....183 B3
Eversley Way CR0 ....223 C5
Everthorpe Rd SE15 ......139 D2
Everton Bldgs NW1 ....232 A1
Everton Ct HA0 ....65 D4
Everton Dr HA7 ....44 A6
Everton Rd CR0 ....206 A1
Evesham Ave E17 ....35 C1
Evesham Cl
Belmont SM2 ....217 C1
Greenford UB6 ....85 D5
Evesham Ct
2 Ealing W13 ....109 A5
2 Richmond TW10 ....154 B5
Evesham Gn SM4 ....201 D3
Evesham Ho 1 E2 ....96 C5
NW8 ....229 A5
SW1 ....258 D2
Evesham Rd E15 ....76 D1
N11 ....31 D5
Morden SM4 ....201 D3
Evesham St W11 ....112 D6
Evesham Way SW11 ......137 A2
Ilford IG5 ....56 C6
Evesham Wlk SE5 ....139 B3
SW9 ....138 C3
Evry Rd DA14 ....190 C4
Ewald Rd SW6 ....135 B3
Ewanrigg Terr IG8 ....37 C5
Ewart Gr N22 ....32 C2
Ewart Pl 10 E3 ....97 B5
Ewart Rd SE23 ....162 D4
Ewe Cl N7 ....72 A2
Ewell By-Pass KT17 ......216 A1
Ewell Court Ave KT19 ...215 C3
Ewell Park Gdns KT17 ...216 A1
Ewell Park Way KT17 ....216 A1
Ewell Rd
Cheam SM2,SM3 ....216 D2
Surbiton KT5,KT6 ....198 B2
Thames Ditton KT6,KT7 ...197 B2
Tolworth KT6 ....198 D1
Ewelme Rd SE23 ....162 C3
Ewen Cres SW2 ....160 C4
Ewen Ho N1 ....233 C5
Ewer St SE1 ......117 A5 252 A3
Ewhurst 18 SW15 ....156 D5
Ewhurst Cl E1 ....96 C2
Ewhurst Ct CR4 ....202 B6
Ewhurst Rd SE4 ....163 B5
Exbury Ho E9 ....74 C2
4 SW9 ....138 B1
Exbury Rd SE6 ....163 C2
Excel Ct WC2 ....249 D5
Excel Ex Ctr E16 ....121 B6
Excelsior Cl KT1 ....176 C1
Excelsior Gdns SE13 .....142 A3
Excelsior Ind Est SE16 ...140 C6
Exchange Arc EC2 ....243 B4
Exchange Cl N11 ....15 A2
Exchange Ct WC2 ....250 B5
Exchange Mans 2 NW11 .47 B2
Exchange Pl EC2 ....243 A4
Exchange The IG1 ....78 D6
Exeforde Ave TW15 ....170 C6
Exeter Cl E6 ....100 B1
Exeter Ct NW6 ....91 C5
Kingston KT6 ....198 A4
Mitcham SW19 ....180 C3
Exeter Gdns IG1 ....56 B1
Exeter Ho 11 SE15 ....140 A6
W2 ....236 A2
7 Barking IG11 ....80 A1
Feltham TW13 ....151 C2
Putney SW15 ....156 C5
Exeter Mans NW2 ....69 A2
Exeter Mews SW6 ....265 A4
Exeter Rd DA16 ....145 D3
E16 ....99 A2
E17 ....53 C4
N14 ....15 B4
N9 ....18 C2
NW2 ....69 A2
Croydon CR0 ....205 D2
Dagenham RM10 ....81 D2
Enfield EN3 ....6 D2
Harrow HA2 ....63 A6
Hatton TW6 ....127 C2
Twickenham TW13 ....151 B1
Exeter St WC2 ....116 B6 250 C6
Exeter Way 2 SE14 ......141 B5
Hatton TW6 ....127 C3
Exford Ct SW11 ....266 D2
Exford Gdns SE12 ....165 B3
Exford Rd SE12 ....165 B3
Exhibition Cl W12 ....112 C6
Exhibition Rd
SW7 ....114 B3 256 D6
Exmoor Ho 23 E3 ....97 A5
Exmoor St W10 ....90 D2
Exmouth Ho 6 E14 ....119 D2
Exmouth Market
EC1 ....94 C3 241 B6
Exmouth Mews NW1 ....232 B1
Exmouth Pl E8 ....74 B1
Exmouth Rd E17 ....53 B4
Bexley DA16 ....146 C5
Hayes UB4 ....83 C4
Ruislip HA4 ....62 C5
Exmouth St E1 ....96 C1
Exning Rd E16 ....98 D3
Exonbury NW8 ....91 D6
Exon St SE17 .....117 C2 263 A3
Explorer Ave TW19 ....148 A3
Express Dr IG3 ....58 B1
Exton Cres NW10 ....67 A1
Exton Gdns RM8 ....80 C3
Exton St SE1 .....116 C5 251 A3
Eyebright Cl 3 CR0 ....206 D1
Eyhurst Cl NW2 ....68 A6
Eylewood Rd SE27 ....183 A5
Eynella Rd SE21 ....161 D4
Eynham Rd W12 ....90 C1
Eynsford Cl BR5 ....211 A3
Eynsford Cres DA5,DA14 .168 D3
Eynsford Ho SE1 ....252 C2
12 SE15 ....140 C6
SE17 ....263 A3
Eynsford Rd IG3 ....79 C6
Eynsford Terr UB7 ....82 B1
Eynsham Dr SE2 ....124 B3
Eynswood Dr DA14 ....190 C5
Eyot Gdns W6 ....111 D1
Eyot Gn W4 ....111 D1
Eyre Ct NW8 ....229 C4
Eyre St Hill EC1 ....94 C3 241 A5
Eysham Ct 8 EN5 ....13 D6
Eythorne Rd SW9 ....138 C4
Ezra St E2 ....95 D4

F

Faber Gdns NW4 ....46 A4
Fabian Rd SW6 ....135 B5 264 D4
Fabian St E6 ....100 B3
Fabyc Ho TW9 ....132 C5
Factory La Croydon CR0 ..220 D6
Tottenham N17 ....33 D1
Factory Rd E16 ....122 A5
Factory Yd W7 ....108 C5
Fagg's Rd TW14 ....150 A6
Fairacre Hounslow TW7 ...130 B4
Kingston KT3 ....199 C6
Pinner HA5 ....40 A5
Fair Acres BR2 ....209 A4
Fairacres Putney SW15 ...134 A1
Ruislip HA4 ....39 D2
Fairbairn Gn 1 SW9 ......138 D4
Fairbank Ave BR6 ....226 D6
Fairbanks Rd N17 ....52 A6
Fairbourne Ho UB3 ....105 A3
Fairbourne Rd N17 ....51 C6
Fairbridge Rd N19 ....71 D6
Fairbrook Cl N13 ....32 C5
Fairbrook Rd N13 ....32 C4
Fairburn Ct 6 SW15 ......157 A6
Fairburn Ho 9 N16 ....51 C1
SW5 ....254 D1
Fairby Ho SE1 ....263 D4
Fairby Rd SE12 ....165 B6
Faircharm Trad Est SE8 .141 D5
Fairchild Cl 6 SW11 ......136 B3
Fairchild Ho 13 E9 ....74 C1
5 N1 ....95 C4
SW1 ....259 B3
Fairchild Pl EC2 ....243 B5
Fairchild St EC2 ....243 B5
Fairclough St E1 ....96 A1
Faircourt 14 NW3 ....70 D2
Faircroft N16 ....51 B1
Forest Hill SE26 ....184 C6
Faircross Ave IG11 ....79 A2
Faircross Par IG11 ....79 C3
Fairdale Gdns
Hayes UB3 ....106 A4
Putney SW15 ....134 B1
Fairdene Ct N7 ....72 A3
Fairey Ave UB3 ....105 D3
Fairfax Cl KT12 ....194 B1
Fairfax Gdns SE3 ....143 C4
Fairfax Ho 12 SW9 ....138 C3
5 Ealing W5 ....88 A4
6 Putney SW15 ....156 A6
Fairfax Mews E16 ....121 B5
N8 ....50 D5
Putney SW15 ....134 C1
Fairfax Pl NW6 ....70 A1
Fairfax Rd N8 ....50 C5
NW6 ....70 A1
W4 ....111 C3
Teddington TW11 ....175 B3
Fairfax Way N10 ....31 A3
Fairfield 4 E1 ....96 C2
N20 ....14 B4
NW1 ....232 A5
Pinner HA6 ....22 A1
Fairfield Ave NW4 ....46 B3
Edgware HA8 ....26 D3
Ruislip HA4 ....39 A2
Twickenham TW2 ....151 D3
Fairfield Cl DA15 ....167 D5
N12 ....30 A6
Enfield EN3 ....7 A1
Mitcham SW19 ....180 C3
West Ewell KT19 ....215 C3
Fairfield Cres HA8 ....26 D4
Fairfield Ct NW10 ....90 A6
1 SW18 ....157 D6
Ruislip HA4 ....39 B1
8 Woodford IG8 ....37 A4
Fairfield Dr SW18 ....157 D6
Harrow HA2 ....42 A6
Wembley UB6 ....87 C6
Fairfield E KT1 ....176 A1
Fairfield Gdns N8 ....50 A4
Fairfield Gr SE7 ....143 D6
Fairfield Ind Est KT1 .....198 B6
Fairfield N KT1,KT2 ......176 A1
Fairfield Path CR0 ....221 B5
Fairfield Pl KT1 ....198 A6
Fairfield Rd BR1 ....187 A3
BR5 ....211 B3
E17 ....35 A1
E3 ....97 C5
N8 ....50 A4
Beckenham BR3 ....185 C1
Bexley DA7 ....147 B3
Edmonton N18 ....34 A6
Ilford IG1 ....78 D2
Kingston KT1 ....176 A1
Southall UB1 ....85 B1
South Croydon CR0 ....221 C5
Woodford IG8 ....37 A4
Yiewsley UB7 ....104 A6
Fairfields SE6 ....163 D4
Fairfield S KT1 ....176 B1
Fairfields Cl NW9 ....45 A4
Fairfields Cres NW9 ....45 A4
Fairfields Rd TW3 ....130 A2
Fairfield St SW18 ....157 D6
Fairfield W KT1 ....176 A1
Fairfield Way Barnet EN5 ..13 C6
West Ewell KT19 ....215 C3
Fairfoot Rd E3 ....97 C3
Fairford SE6 ....163 C3
Fairford Ave CR0 ....206 D4
Fairford Cl CR0 ....207 A4
Fairford Ct SM2 ....217 D1
Fairford Gdns KT4 ....215 D5
Fairford Ho SE11 ....261 B3
Fairgreen EN4 ....2 D2
Fairgreen Ct EN4 ....2 D2
Fair Green Ct 1 CR4 ......202 D6
Fairgreen E EN4 ....2 D2
Fairgreen Rd CR7 ....204 D4
Fairhall Ct KT6 ....198 B2
Fairhaven Ave CR0 ....206 D3
Fairhaven Ct CR2 ....221 A3
Fairhazel Gdns NW6 ....70 A1
Fairheathe SW15 ....156 D5
Fairholme TW14 ....149 C4
Fairholme Cl N3 ....47 A5
Fairholme Cres UB4 ....84 A3
Fairholme Gdns N3 ....47 A5
Fairholme Ho 3 KT3 ......199 C5
Fairholme Jun & Inf Schs
TW14 ....149 B3
Fairholme Rd
W14 ....113 A1 254 B1
Ashford TW15 ....170 B5
Cheam SM1 ....217 B2
Harrow HA1 ....42 D4
Ilford IG1 ....56 C2
Thornton Heath CR0 ......204 C2
Fairholt Cl N16 ....51 C1
Fairholt Rd N16 ....51 B1
Fairholt St SW7 ....257 B6
Fairhurst 4 NW6 ....70 A2
Fairland Ho BR2 ....209 B5
Fairland Rd E15 ....76 D1
Fairlands Ave
Sutton SM1 ....217 C6
Thornton Heath CR7 .....204 C4
Woodford IG9 ....21 A2
Fairlands Ct 6 SE9 ....166 C5
Fairlawn SE7 ....143 C6
Fairlawn Ave N2 ....48 C5
Acton W4 ....111 A2
Bexley DA16 ....146 D3
Fairlawn Cl
Claygate KT10 ....212 D2
Feltham TW13 ....173 B6
Kingston KT2 ....177 A4
Southgate N14 ....15 D5
Fairlawn Ct SE7 ....143 C5
3 Acton W4 ....111 A2
Fairlawn Dr IG8 ....37 A3
Fairlawnes SM6 ....219 B3
Fairlawn Gdns UB1 ......107 B6
Fairlawn Gr W4 ....111 A2
Fairlawn Mans SE14 ......140 D4
Fairlawn Pk SE26 ....185 A5
Fairlawn Prim Sch
Forest Hill SE23 ....162 C4
Forest Hill SE23 ....162 C3
Fairlawn Rd SW19 ....179 B3
Fairlawns
3 Bowes Park N11 ....32 A4
10 Chingford E4 ....20 A2
Pinner WD19 ....22 D1
Putney SW15 ....156 D6
Sunbury TW16 ....194 A6
Twickenham TW1 ....153 C5
Fairlea Pl W5 ....87 D3
Fair Lea Pl W5 ....87 C2
Fairleas 12 BR3 ....185 D1
Fairley House Sch SW1 .259 D2
Fairlie Ct 22 E3 ....97 D4
1 N7 ....71 D4
Fairlie Gdns SE23 ....162 C4
Fairlight TW12 ....173 D5
Fairlight Ave NW10 ....89 C5
Chingford E4 ....20 B2
Woodford IG8 ....37 A4
Fairlight Cl Cheam KT4 ..216 C4
Chingford E4 ....20 B2
Fairlight Ct NW10 ....89 C5
Greenford UB6 ....86 B5
Fairlight Rd SW17 ....180 B6
Fairline Ct BR3 ....186 A1
Fairlop Ct E11 ....54 C1
Fairlop Pl NW8 ....229 D1
Fairlop Rd E11 ....54 B2
Fairmark Dr UB10 ....60 C2
Fairmead BR1 ....210 B5
Tolworth KT5,KT6 ....198 D1
Fairmead Cl BR1 ....210 B5
Heston TW5 ....128 D5
Kingston KT3 ....199 B6
Fairmead Cres HA8 ....11 A1
Fairmead Ct 3 E4 ....20 C4
Fairmead Gdns IG4 ....56 A4
Fairmead Ho E9 ....75 A4
Fairmead Rd N7,N19 ....72 A5
Thornton Heath CR0 ......204 C2
Fairmeadside IG10 ....21 C6
Fairmile Ave SW16 ....181 D5
Fairmile Ho BR5 ....190 A1
Teddington TW11 ....175 A6
Fairmont Cl DA17 ....125 B1
Fairmont Ho 1 E3 ....97 C3
Fairmount Rd SW2 ....160 B5
Fairoak Cl BR5 ....210 D2
Fairoak Dr SE9 ....167 B6
Fairoaks Gr EN3 ....6 D6
Fairseat Cl WD23 ....8 C2
Fair St SE1 ....117 D4 253 C2
Hounslow TW3 ....130 A2
Fairstead Lo 4 IG8 ....37 A4
Fairstead Wlk N1 ....235 A6
Fairthorn Rd SE7,SE10 ...121 A1
Fairview Ave HA0 ....65 D2
Fair View Cl E17 ....35 A2
Fairview Cl SE26 ....185 A5
Fairview Cres HA2 ....41 C1
Fairview Ct NW4 ....28 D1
Ashford TW15 ....170 C5
Kingston KT2 ....176 D2
Fairview Dr BR6 ....227 B4
Littleton TW17 ....192 B4
Fairview Gdns IG8 ....37 B2
Fairview Ho 14 SW2 ....160 B4
Fairview Pl SW2 ....160 B4
Fairview Rd N15 ....51 D3
Carshalton SM1,SM5 .....218 C3
Enfield EN2 ....4 C4
Thornton Heath SW16 ....182 B2
Fairview Villas E4 ....35 D3
Fairview Way HA8 ....26 C6
Fairwall Ho 9 SE5 ....139 C4
Fairwater Ave DA16 ......146 A1
Fairwater Ho TW11 ....175 A6
Fairway BR5 ....211 B4
Bexley DA6 ....169 A6
West Barnes SW20 ....200 C6
Woodford IG8 ....37 C5
Fairway Ave NW9 ....44 D6
Fairway Cl NW11 ....48 A2
Croydon CR0 ....207 A4
Hounslow TW4 ....150 D6
West Ewell KT19 ....215 A4
Fairway Ct NW7 ....11 B1
13 SE16 ....118 D4
12 SE9 ....166 C5
New Barnet EN5 ....13 D5
Fairway Dr Erith SE28 ...103 A1
Greenford UB6 ....63 D1
Fairway Est TW4 ....150 C6
Fairway Gdns Ilford IG1 ...79 A3
West Wickham BR3 ....208 B3
Fairway Prim Sch NW7 ...11 B2
Fairways E17 ....54 A5
Ashford TW15 ....170 D4
4 Hounslow TW7 ....130 C4
Stanmore HA7 ....26 A1
Teddington TW11 ....175 D3
Fairways Bsns Pk E10 ...75 A6
Fairway The BR1,BR2 ....210 B4
NW7 ....11 B1
W3 ....89 C1
East Molesey KT8 ....195 D6
Edmonton N13 ....17 B1
Hillingdon UB10 ....82 B5
Kingston KT3 ....177 B2
New Barnet EN5 ....13 D5
Northolt UB5 ....64 A2
Ruislip HA4 ....62 D5
Southgate N14 ....15 C5
Wembley HA0 ....65 B6
Fairweather Cl N15 ....51 C5
Fairweather Ct N13 ....32 B6
Fairweather Ho N7 ....72 A4
Fairweather Rd N16 ....52 A3
Fairwood Ct E11 ....54 B2
Fairwyn Rd SE26 ....185 A6
Faith Ct NW2 ....68 B2
Faithfull Ho N5 ....73 A3
Fakenham Cl NW7 ....28 A3
5 Northolt UB5 ....63 C2
Fakruddin St E1 ....96 A3
Falaize Ave IG1 ....78 D4
Falcon Ave BR1 ....210 A5
Falconberg Ct W1 ....239 D2
Falconberg Mews W1 ....239 D2
Falconbrook Inf Sch
SW11 ....136 B2
Falcon Cl SE1 ....251 D4
Chiswick W4 ....133 A6
Falcon Cres EN3 ....18 D6
Falcon Ct EC4 ....241 A1
N1 ....234 D3
8 Dulwich SE21 ....161 B2
New Barnet EN5 ....2 A1
Ruislip HA4 ....61 C6
6 Wanstead E18 ....55 B6
Falcon Dr TW19 ....148 A5
Falconer Ct N17 ....33 A3
Falconer Wlk 12 N7 ....72 B6
Falcon Gr SW11 ....136 C2
Falcon Ho 10 SE15 ....139 D4
Falconhurst 4 KT6 ....198 A4
Falcon La SW11 ....136 C2
Falcon Lo NW3 ....69 D4
11 W9 ....91 C2
Falcon Pk Ind Est NW10 ..67 C3
Falcon Point SE1 ....251 D5
Falcon Rd SW11 ....136 C2
Enfield EN3 ....18 D6
Hampton TW12 ....173 B3
Falconry Ct KT1 ....198 A6
Falcon St E13 ....99 A3
Falcon Terr SW11 ....136 C2
Falcon Way E14 ....119 D2
NW9 ....27 C1
Feltham TW14 ....150 B6
Harrow HA3 ....44 A3
Sunbury TW16 ....171 C1
Wanstead E11 ....55 A5
Falconwood Ave DA16 ...145 C3
Falconwood Ct SE3 ....142 D3
Falconwood Par DA16 ...145 D1
Falconwood Rd CR0 ....223 C1
Falconwood Sta SE9 .....145 B1
Falcourt Cl SM1 ....217 D3
Falkener Ct SW11 ....268 B1
Falkirk Ct 11 SE16 ....118 D5
Falkirk Gdns WD19 ....22 D5
Falkirk Ho W9 ....91 D4
Falkirk St N1 ....95 C5
Falkland Ave N11 ....31 B6
N3 ....29 C3
Falkland Ho W14 ....254 C2
W8 ....255 C5
Catford SE6 ....186 A6
Falkland Park Ave SE25 .183 C1
Falkland Pl 2 NW5 ....71 C3
Falkland Rd N8 ....50 C5
NW5 ....71 C3
Barnet EN5 ....1 A3
Falladon Ho W11 ....91 B2
Falling La UB7 ....104 A6
Falloden Way NW11 ....47 C5
Fallodon Ho 6 SW8 ....137 D3
Fallow Court Ave N12 .....30 A4
Fallow Ct 16 SE16 ....118 A1
Fallowfield N4 ....72 B6
Stanmore HA7 ....9 A1
Fallowfield Ct HA7 ....9 A1
Fallowfields Dr N12 ....30 C4
Fallows Cl N2 ....30 B1
Fallsbrook Rd SW16 ......181 C4
Falman Cl N9 ....18 A3
Falmer Rd E17 ....53 D6
N15 ....51 B4
Enfield EN1 ....5 C1
Falmouth Ave E4 ....36 C5
Falmouth Cl SE12 ....164 D6
Wood Green N22 ....32 B3
Falmouth Gdns IG4 ....55 D5
Falmouth Ho SE11 ....261 B2
W2 ....247 A6
Falmouth Rd
SE1 ....117 A3 262 B5
Falmouth St E15 ....76 B3
Falmouth Way E17 ....53 B4
Falstaff Ct SE11 ....261 C3
Falstaff Ho 18 N1 ....95 C5
Fambridge Cl SE26 ....185 B6
Fambridge Rd RM8 ....59 C1
Fane St W14 ....264 D6
Fann St EC1 ....95 A3 242 B5
Fanshawe Ave IG11 ....79 A2
Fanshawe Cres RM9 ....81 B3
Fanshawe Rd TW10 ....175 C6
Fanshaw Ho 6 E17 ....53 D6
Fanshaw St N1 ....95 C4
Fantail The BR6 ....226 B5
Fanthorpe St SW15 ....134 C2
Faraday Ave DA14 ....168 B2
Faraday Cl N7 ....72 B2
Faraday Ho 6 E14 ....119 B6
6 NW5 ....71 B4
W10 ....91 A2
2 Balham SW12 ....159 B4
4 Belvedere DA17 ....125 C3
5 Hampton TW12 ....173 D4
Wembley HA9 ....67 A5
Faraday Lo SE10 ....120 D3
Faraday Rd DA16 ....146 A2
E15 ....76 D2
W10 ....91 A2
W3 ....111 A6
East Molesey KT8 ....195 C5
Southall UB1 ....107 D6
Wimbledon SW19 ....179 D4
Faraday Way SE18 ....121 D3
Thornton Heath CR0 ......204 B1
Fareham Ho 13 SW15 .....156 A3
Fareham Rd TW14 ....150 C4
Fareham St W1 ....239 C2
Farewell Pl CR4 ....180 C2
Faringdon Ave BR2 ....210 C3
Faringford Rd E15 ....76 C1
Farjeon Ho NW6 ....70 B1
Farjeon Rd SE3 ....143 D4
Farleigh Ave BR2 ....209 A2
Farleigh Ct CR2 ....221 A3
Farleigh Ho 7 KT2 ....176 D4
Farleigh Pl N16 ....73 D4
Farleigh Rd N16 ....73 D4
Farleycroft 1 CR0 ....206 A1
Farley Croft BR2 ....186 C1
Farley Ct NW1 ....238 A5
W14 ....254 C6
Farley Dr IG3 ....57 C1
Farley Ho SE26 ....162 B1
Farley Pl SE25 ....206 A5
Farley Rd Catford SE6 ....164 A4
South Croydon CR2 ....222 B1
Farlington Pl SW15 ....156 B4
Farlow Rd SW15 ....134 D2
Farlton Rd SW18 ....157 D4
Farman Terr HA3 ....43 D5
Farm Ave NW2 ....69 B5
Harrow HA2,HA5 ....41 C3
Streatham SW16 ....182 A6
Wembley HA0 ....65 C2
Farm Avenue Ho HA0 ....65 C2
Farmborough Cl HA1 ......42 B2
Farm Cl SW6 ....265 B4
Barnet EN5 ....12 C6
Buckhurst Hill IG9 ....21 C1
Coney Hall BR4 ....224 D5
Lower Halliford TW17 .....192 C2
Southall UB1 ....107 D6
Sutton SM2 ....218 B1
Uxbridge UB10 ....60 D6
Farmcote Rd SE12 ....165 A3
Farm Cotts E17 ....53 A6
Farm Ct NW4 ....46 A6
Farmdale Rd SE10 ....121 A1
Sutton SM5 ....218 C1
Farm Dr CR0 ....223 B6
Farm End E4 ....20 C6
Farmer Ho 4 SE16 ....118 B3
Farmer Rd E10 ....53 D1
Farmers Rd SE5 ....138 D5
Farmer St W8 ....245 A4
Farmfield Rd BR1 ....186 C5
Farm House Ct NW7 ....28 A3
Farmhouse Rd SW16 ......181 C3
Farmilo Rd E17 ....53 C2
Farmington Ave SM1 .....218 B5
Farm La SW6 ....135 C5 265 B4
Croydon CR0 ....223 B6
East Barnet N14 ....15 B5
Farmlands Enfield EN2 ......4 C4
Pinner HA5 ....40 A5
Farmlands The UB5 ....63 C2
Farmland Wlk BR7 ....188 D5
Farm Lane Trad Ctr
SW6 ....135 C6 265 B5
Farmleigh N14 ....15 C4
Farmleigh Ho SW9 ....160 D6
Farm Pl W8 ....245 A4
Farm Rd NW10 ....89 B6

Farm Rd *continued*
Edmonton N21 ... 17 A3
Morden SM4 ... 201 D4
Sutton SM2 ... 218 B1
Twickenham TW4 ... 151 A3
Thames Ditton KT10 ... 195 C1
Farm St W1 ... 115 B6 248 C5
Farmstead Rd
Catford SE6 ... 185 D6
Harrow HA3 ... 24 B1
Farm Vale DA5 ... 169 D5
Farm View N3 ... 47 B6
Farmway RM8 ... 80 C5
Farm Way
Buckhurst Hill IG9 ... 37 C6
North Cheam KT4 ... 216 C5
Farm Wlk NW11 ... 47 A4
Farnaby Ho 2 W10 ... 91 B4
Farnaby Rd SE9 ... 143 C1
Bromley BR1,BR2 ... 186 C2
Farnan Ave E17 ... 53 D6
Farnan Rd SW16 ... 182 A5
Farnborough Ave E17 ... 53 A6
South Croydon CR2 ... 223 A1
Farnborough Cl HA9 ... 66 D6
Farnborough Comm
Keston Mark BR2,BR6 ... 226 B5
Orpington BR6 ... 226 C4
Farnborough Cres
3 Hayes BR2 ... 208 D1
South Croydon CR2 ... 223 A1
Farnborough Ct 2 BR6 ... 227 A3
Farnborough Hill BR6 ... 227 C3
Farnborough Ho 1 SW15 ... 156 A3
Farnborough Hospl BR6 ... 226 C4
Farnborough Prim Sch BR6 ... 227 A3
Farnborough Way BR6 ... 227 B3
10 SE15 ... 139 C5
Farncombe St SE16 ... 118 A4
Farndale Ave N13 ... 17 A1
Farndale Cres UB6 ... 86 A4
Farndale Ho 1 NW6 ... 91 D6
Farnell Mews SW5 ... 255 C2
Farnell Pl W3 ... 110 D6
Farnell Rd TW7 ... 130 B2
Farnell's Almshouses TW7 ... 130 D3
Farnfield Ho 12 SW2 ... 160 B6
Farnham Cl N20 ... 14 A4
Farnham Ct 2 N16 ... 51 C1
2 Cheam SM3 ... 217 A2
1 Southall UB1 ... 86 A1
Farnham Gdns SW20 ... 178 B1
Farnham Green Prim Sch IG3 ... 58 A3
Farnham Ho NW1 ... 237 B5
SE1 ... 252 A3
Farnham Pl SE1 ... 251 D3
Farnham Rd
Bexley DA16 ... 146 C3
Ilford IG3 ... 57 D2
Farnham Royal SE11 ... 116 B1 260 D1
Farnhurst Ho 7 SW11 ... 137 A3
Farningham Ct SW16 ... 181 D3
Farningham Ho 9 N4 ... 51 B2
Farningham Rd N17 ... 34 A3
Farnley Ho 13 SW8 ... 137 D3
Farnley Rd Chingford E4 ... 20 C4
South Norwood SE25 ... 205 B5
Farnsworth Ho 8 SW27 ... 182 D5
Farnworth Ho 5 E14 ... 120 B2
Faro Cl BR1 ... 188 C1
Faroe Rd W14 ... 112 D3
Farorna Wlk EN2 ... 4 C4
Farquhar Rd
Dulwich SE19 ... 183 D5
Wimbledon SW19 ... 157 C1
Farquharson Rd CR0 ... 205 A1
Farrance Rd RM6 ... 59 A2
Farrance St E14 ... 97 C1
Farrans Ct HA3 ... 43 B2
Farrant Ave N22 ... 32 D1
Farrant Cl BR6 ... 227 D1
Farrant Ho 18 SW11 ... 136 B2
Farr Ave IG11 ... 102 A5
Farrell Ho E1 ... 96 C1
Farren Rd SE23 ... 163 A2
Farrer Ho SE8 ... 141 C5
Farrer Mews N8 ... 49 C5
Farrer Rd N8 ... 49 D5
Harrow HA3 ... 44 A5
Farrer's Pl CR0 ... 222 D4
Farrier Cl BR1 ... 209 D6
Hillingdon UB8 ... 82 C1
Sunbury TW16 ... 194 A5
Farrier Mews SE15 ... 140 C2
Farrier Rd UB5 ... 85 C5
Farriers Ct Belmont SM2 ... 217 A1
Wimbledon SW19 ... 179 A3
Farrier St NW1 ... 71 C1
Farriers Way WD6 ... 11 B6
Farrier Wlk SW10 ... 136 A6 266 A6
Farringdon La EC1 ... 94 C3 241 B5
Farringdon Rd EC1 ... 94 C3 241 B5
Farringdon St EC4 ... 94 D1 241 C2
Farringdon Sta EC1 ... 94 D2 241 C4
Farrington Pl BR7 ... 189 B3
Farrington & Stratford House Sch BR7 ... 189 B3
Farrins Rents SE16 ... 119 A5
Farrow La SE14 ... 140 C5
Farrow Pl SE16 ... 119 A3
Farr Rd EN2 ... 5 B4
Farthingale Wlk E15 ... 76 B1
Farthing Alley 5 SE1 ... 118 A4
Farthing Fields 8 E1 ... 118 B5
Farthings Cl Chingford E4 ... 20 C1
Pinner HA5 ... 40 B3
Farthing St BR6 ... 226 B1
Farthings The 1 KT2 ... 176 C2
Farwell Rd DA14 ... 190 C6
Farwig La BR1 ... 187 A2
Fashion & Design Museum The★ SE1 ... 253 A2
Fashion St E1 ... 95 D2 243 D3
Fashoda Rd BR2 ... 209 D5
Fassett Rd E8 ... 74 A2
Kingston KT1 ... 198 A5
Fassett Sq E8 ... 74 A2
Fauconberg Ct W4 ... 133 A6
Fauconberg Rd W4 ... 133 A6
Faulkner Cl 6 RM8 ... 58 D2
Faulkner Ho SW15 ... 134 C3
Faulkner's Alley EC1 ... 241 C4
Faulkner St SE14 ... 140 C4
Fauna Cl RM6 ... 58 C3
Faunce Ho 1 SE17 ... 138 D6
Faunce St SE17 ... 116 D1 261 C1
Favart Rd SW6 ... 135 C4 265 B2
F Ave SE18 ... 122 D3
Faversham Ave
Chingford E4 ... 20 D3
Enfield EN1 ... 17 B5
Faversham Ho NW1 ... 232 B5
SE17 ... 263 A1
Faversham Rd
Beckenham BR3 ... 185 B1
Forest Hill SE6 ... 163 B3
Morden SM4 ... 201 D3
Fawcett Cl SW11 ... 136 B3
West Norwood SW16 ... 182 C6
Fawcett Est E5 ... 52 A1
Fawcett Ho 25 SW9 ... 138 A3
Fawcett Rd NW10 ... 67 D1
Croydon CR0 ... 221 A5
Fawcett St SW10 ... 136 A6 266 A6
Fawcus Cl KT10 ... 212 C2
Fawe Park Rd SW15 ... 135 B1
Fawe St E14 ... 97 D2
Fawkham Ho SE1 ... 263 D3
Fawley Ct SE27 ... 160 D2
Fawley Lo 2 E14 ... 120 B2
Fawley Rd NW6 ... 69 D3
Fawnbrake Ave SE24 ... 161 A6
Fawn Rd E13 ... 99 C5
Fawns Manor Cl TW14 ... 149 A3
Fawns Manor Rd TW14 ... 149 B3
Fawood Ave NW10 ... 67 B1
Fayetville Ho 28 N19 ... 49 D2
Faygate Cres DA6 ... 169 C6
Faygate Rd SW2 ... 160 B2
Fayland Ave SW16 ... 181 C5
Fazal Laf IG1 ... 79 A6
Fazerley Ct 49 W2 ... 91 C2
Fearnley Cres TW12 ... 173 B4
Fearnley Ho SE5 ... 139 C3
Fearon St SE10 ... 121 A1
Featherbed La CR0 ... 223 B1
Feathers Pl SE10 ... 142 B6
Featherstone Ave 4 SE23 ... 162 C2
Featherstone Ct NW7 ... 28 A3
Featherstone Ho UB4 ... 84 C2
Featherstone Ind Est UB2 ... 107 A3
Featherstone Prim Sch UB2 ... 107 A3
Featherstone Rd NW7 ... 28 B4
Southall UB2 ... 107 A3
Featherstone St EC1 ... 95 B3 242 C6
Featherstone Terr UB2 ... 107 A3
Featley Rd SW9 ... 138 D2
Federal Rd UB6 ... 87 C5
Federation Rd SE2 ... 124 C2
Fee Farm Rd KT10 ... 212 D1
Felbridge Ave HA7 ... 25 B2
Felbridge Cl SW16 ... 182 C6
Felbridge Ct
Croydon CR2 ... 221 A1
East Bedfont TW14 ... 150 B3
Feltham TW14 ... 150 A3
Harlington UB3 ... 127 B6
Felbridge Ho 22 SE22 ... 139 C2
Felbrigge Rd IG3 ... 57 D1
Felday Rd SE13 ... 163 D5
Felden Cl HA5 ... 23 B3
Felden St SW6 ... 135 B4 264 C1
Feldman Cl N16 ... 52 A1
Felgate Mews 4 W6 ... 112 B2
Felhampton Rd SE9 ... 166 D1
Felhurst Cres RM10 ... 81 D4
Feline Ct 1 EN4 ... 14 C5
Felix Ave N8 ... 50 A3
Felix Ct E17 ... 53 D4
Felix La TW17 ... 193 D3
Felix Manor BR7 ... 189 C4
Felix Neubergh Ct EN1 ... 5 C1
Felix Rd Ealing W13 ... 109 A6
Walton-on-T KT12 ... 194 A3
Felix St 19 E2 ... 96 B5
Felixstowe Ct E16 ... 122 D5
Felixstowe Rd N17 ... 51 D6
NW10 ... 90 B4
SE2 ... 124 B3
Edmonton N9 ... 34 A6
Fellbrigg Rd SE22 ... 161 D6
Fellbrigg St 21 E1 ... 96 B3
Fellbrook TW10 ... 153 B1
Fellmongers Yd 3 CR0 ... 221 A5
Fellowes Cl UB4 ... 84 D3
Fellowes Ct UB3 ... 127 B6
Fellowes Rd SM1,SM5 ... 218 C6
Fellows Ct E2 ... 95 D5
Fellows Rd NW3 ... 70 C1
Fell Rd CR0 ... 221 A5
Fells Haugh 6 W3 ... 89 A1
Felltram Way SE7 ... 121 A1
Fell Wlk HA8 ... 26 D2
Felmersham Cl 2 SW4 ... 137 D1
Felmingham Rd SE20 ... 184 C1
Felnex Trad Est SM6 ... 219 A6
Felsberg Rd SW2 ... 160 A4
Fels Cl RM10 ... 81 D5
Felsham Ho SW15 ... 134 D2
Felsham Rd SW15 ... 134 D2
Felspar Cl SE18 ... 123 D1
Felstead Rd E11 ... 55 A2
Felstead St E9 ... 75 B2
Felstead Wharf E14 ... 120 A1
Felsted Rd E16 ... 99 D1
Feltham Ave KT8 ... 196 C5
Felthambrook Ind Est TW13 ... 150 B1
Felthambrook Way TW13 ... 172 B6
Feltham Bsns Complex TW13 ... 150 B2
Feltham Comm Sch TW13 ... 150 C2
Feltham Corporate Ctr TW13 ... 150 B1
Feltham Hill Jun Sch TW13 ... 149 D1
Feltham Hill Rd
Ashford TW15 ... 171 A4
Feltham TW13 ... 172 B6
Feltham Rd
Ashford TW15 ... 171 A6
Mitcham CR4 ... 181 A1
Feltham Sta TW13 ... 150 B3
Felton Cl BR5 ... 210 D3
Felton Gdns IG11 ... 101 C5
Felton Ho N1 ... 235 D5
SE9 ... 143 C1
Felton Lea DA14 ... 189 D5
Felton Rd W13 ... 109 C4
Barking IG11 ... 101 C5
Felton St N1 ... 95 B6 235 D5
Fenchurch 34 N1 ... 95 C6
Fenchurch Ave EC3 ... 95 C1 243 A1
Fenchurch Bldgs EC3 ... 243 B1
Fenchurch Pl EC3 ... 253 B6
Fenchurch St EC3 ... 117 C6 253 B6
Fenchurch Street Sta EC3 ... 117 C6 253 B6
Fen Ct EC3 ... 253 A6
Fendall Rd KT19 ... 215 A3
Fendall St SE1 ... 117 C3 263 B5
Fender Ct 5 SW4 ... 138 A3
Fendt Cl 8 E16 ... 98 D1
Fendyke Rd SE2,DA17 ... 124 D3
Fenelon Pl W14 ... 113 B2 254 D3
Fen Gr DA15 ... 167 D5
Fenham Rd SE15 ... 140 B5
Fenman Ct N17 ... 34 B2
Fenman Gdns IG3 ... 58 B1
Fenn Cl BR1 ... 187 A4
Fenn Ct HA1 ... 43 A4
Fennel Cl E16 ... 98 C3
Croydon CR0 ... 206 D1
Fennell St SE18 ... 144 C6
Fenner Cl SE16 ... 118 B2
Fenner Ho 25 E1 ... 118 B5
Fenner Sq 10 SW11 ... 136 B2
Fenning Ct CR4 ... 202 C5
Fenning St SE1 ... 253 A2
Fenn St E9 ... 74 C3
Fen St E16 ... 120 D6
Fenstanton Ave N12 ... 30 B5
Fenstanton Prim Sch SW2 ... 160 C3
Fentiman Rd SW8 ... 138 B5 270 C4
Fenton Cl BR7 ... 188 B5
E8 ... 73 D2
SW9 ... 138 B3
Fenton Ho SE14 ... 141 A5
Heston TW5 ... 129 C6
Fenton Rd N17 ... 33 A3
Fentons SE3 ... 142 D5
Fenton's Ave E13 ... 99 B5
Fenton St E1 ... 96 B1
Fenwick Cl 16 SE18 ... 144 C6
Fenwick Gr SE15 ... 140 A2
Fenwick Pl SW9 ... 138 A2
Croydon CR2 ... 220 D1
Fenwick Rd SE15 ... 140 A2
Ferby Ct DA15 ... 189 D6
Ferdinand Ho 1 NW1 ... 71 B1
Ferdinand Pl NW1 ... 71 A1
Ferdinand St NW1 ... 71 A1
Ferguson Ave KT5 ... 198 B4
Ferguson Cl BR2,BR3 ... 208 B6
Ferguson Dr W3 ... 89 B1
Ferguson Ho SE10 ... 142 A4
Ferguson's Cl E14 ... 119 C2
Fergus Rd N5 ... 72 D3
Fermain Ct E N1 ... 95 C6
Fermain Ct N N1 ... 95 C6
Fermain Ct W N1 ... 95 C6
Ferme Park Rd N4,N8 ... 50 B3
Fermor Rd SE23 ... 163 A3
Fermoy Rd W9 ... 91 B3
Fermoy Rd *continued*
Greenford UB6 ... 85 D3
Fern Ave CR4 ... 203 D5
Fernbank IG9 ... 21 B3
Fernbank Ave
Walton-on-T KT12 ... 195 A2
Wembley HA0 ... 64 D3
Fernbank Mews SW12 ... 159 C5
Fernbrook Dr HA2 ... 41 D2
Fernbrook Rd SE13 ... 164 C5
Fern Cl 3 N1 ... 95 C5
Ferncliff Rd E8 ... 74 A3
Ferncroft Ave N12 ... 30 D4
NW3 ... 69 C4
Ruislip HA4 ... 62 C6
Fern Ct DA7 ... 147 C1
SE14 ... 140 D2
Chingford E4 ... 36 A4
Ferndale BR1 ... 187 C1
Ferndale Ave E17 ... 54 B4
Hounslow TW4 ... 129 A2
Ferndale Cl DA7 ... 147 A4
Ferndale Ct 3 SE3 ... 142 D5
Ferndale Ho N16 ... 51 B1
Ferndale Rd E11 ... 76 D6
E7 ... 77 B1
N15 ... 51 D4
SW4,SW9 ... 138 B1
Ashford TW15 ... 170 A5
Croydon SE25 ... 206 B4
Enfield EN3 ... 7 A6
Ferndale St E6 ... 100 D1
Ferndale Way BR6 ... 227 B3
Ferndene NW9 ... 45 A4
Fern Dene W13 ... 87 B2
Ferndene Rd SE24 ... 139 A1
Fernden Way RM7 ... 59 D3
Ferndown
5 Kingston KT6 ... 198 A4
Pinner HA6 ... 22 A1
6 Wanstead E18 ... 55 A6
Ferndown Ave BR6 ... 211 B1
Ferndown Cl Pinner HA5 ... 23 A3
Sutton SM2 ... 218 B2
Ferndown Ct 6 UB1 ... 86 A1
Ferndown Lo E14 ... 120 A3
Ferndown Rd SE9 ... 165 D4
South Oxhey WD19 ... 22 C6
Ferney Meade Way TW7 ... 131 A3
Ferney Rd EN4 ... 15 A3
Fern Gr TW14 ... 150 B4
Fernhall Dr IG4 ... 55 D4
Fernham Rd CR7 ... 205 A6
Fernhead Rd W9 ... 91 B4
Fernhill Ct Chingford E17 ... 36 B1
Kingston KT2 ... 175 D5
Fernhill Gdns KT2 ... 176 A5
Fernhill Ho E5 ... 74 A6
Fern Hill Pl 3 BR6 ... 227 A3
Fern Hill Prim Sch KT2 ... 176 A4
Fernhill St E16 ... 122 B5
Fernholme Rd SE15 ... 162 D6
Fernhurst Gdns HA8 ... 26 C4
Fernhurst Rd
Ashford TW15 ... 171 A6
Croydon CR0 ... 206 B1
Fulham SW6 ... 135 A4 264 B2
Fernie Ho SE22 ... 139 D2
Fern La TW5 ... 107 B1
Fernlea Ho NW10 ... 88 B4
Fernlea Rd Balham SW12 ... 159 B3
Mitcham CR4 ... 181 A2
Fernleigh Cl W9 ... 91 B4
Croydon CR0 ... 220 C4
Fernleigh Ct Harrow HA2 ... 23 D1
Wembley HA9 ... 44 A1
Fernleigh Rd N21 ... 16 D2
Fernley Cl HA5 ... 40 A5
Fern Lo 13 SW16 ... 182 C5
Fernsbury St WC1 ... 234 A1
Fernshaw Mans SW10 ... 266 A5
Fernshaw Rd SW10 ... 136 A6 266 A5
Fernside IG9 ... 21 B3
Fernside Ave NW7 ... 11 B1
Feltham TW13 ... 172 B6
Fernside Ct NW4 ... 28 D1
Fernside Rd SW12 ... 159 A4
Ferns Rd E15 ... 76 D2
Fern St E3 ... 97 C3
Fernthorpe Rd SW16 ... 181 C4
Ferntower Rd N5 ... 73 B3
Fernways IG1 ... 78 D4
Fern Wlk 17 SE16 ... 118 A1
Fernwood
Wandsworth SW19 ... 157 B3
Wood Green N22 ... 32 A3
Fernwood Ave
Streatham SW16 ... 181 D6
Wembley HA0 ... 65 C2
Fernwood Cl BR1 ... 187 C1
Fernwood Cres N20 ... 14 D1
Ferny Hill EN4 ... 3 A5
Ferranti Cl SE18 ... 121 D3
Ferraro Cl TW5 ... 129 C6
Ferrers Ave
Wallington SM6 ... 219 D4
West Drayton UB7 ... 104 A4
Ferrers Rd SW16 ... 181 D5
Ferrestone Rd N8 ... 50 B5
Ferrey Mews 20 SW9 ... 138 C3
Ferriby Cl N1 ... 72 C1
Ferrier Ind Est SW18 ... 135 D1
Ferrier Point 6 E16 ... 99 A2
Ferrier St SW18 ... 135 D1
Ferring Cl HA2 ... 42 A1
Ferrings SE21 ... 161 C1
Ferris Ave CR0 ... 223 B5
Ferris Rd SE22 ... 140 A1
Ferron Rd E5 ... 74 B5
Ferrour Ct N2 ... 48 B6
Ferrybridge Ho SE11 ... 260 D5
Ferry Ho E5 ... 52 B1
Ferry La N17 ... 52 B5
Barnes SW13 ... 133 D6
Brentford TW8 ... 132 A6
Lower Halliford TW17 ... 192 C1
Richmond TW9 ... 132 B6
Ferry Lane Prim Sch N17 ... 52 B5
Ferrymead Ave UB6 ... 85 C5
Ferrymead Dr UB6 ... 85 C5
Ferrymead Gdns UB6 ... 86 A5
Ferrymoor TW10 ... 153 B1
Ferry Rd Barnes SW13 ... 134 A4
East Molesey KT8 ... 195 C6
Richmond TW11 ... 175 B5
Thames Ditton KT7 ... 197 B3
Twickenham TW1 ... 153 B3
Ferry Sq 1 TW8 ... 132 A6
Ferry St E14 ... 120 A1
Ferry Wks TW17 ... 192 C1
Festing Rd SW15 ... 134 D2
Festival Cl DA5 ... 168 D3
Hillingdon UB10 ... 82 D6
Festival Pier SE1 ... 116 B5 250 C4
Festival Pleasure Gdns SW11 ... 136 D5 267 C3
Fetter La EC4 ... 94 C1 241 B2
Fettes Ho NW8 ... 229 D3
Fews Lo RM6 ... 58 D5
Ffinch St SE8 ... 141 C5
Field Cl BR1 ... 187 C1
Buckhurst Hill IG9 ... 21 C1
Chessington KT9 ... 213 C3
Chingford E4 ... 35 D4
Cranford TW4 ... 128 B4
East Molesey KT8 ... 195 D4
Harlington UB7 ... 127 A5
Ruislip HA4 ... 39 A1
Uxbridge UB10 ... 60 D6
Fieldcommon La KT12 ... 195 B1
Field Ct N7 ... 72 A3
NW3 ... 70 A3
WC1 ... 240 D3
Wimbledon SW19 ... 157 C1
Field End Ruislip HA4 ... 62 C2
Twickenham TW11 ... 174 D6
Field End Jun & Inf Schs HA4 ... 62 D6
Fieldend Rd SW16 ... 181 C2
Field End Rd HA5,HA4 ... 40 C1
Fielders Cl 2 Enfield EN1 ... 5 C1
Harrow HA2 ... 42 A1
Fieldfare Rd SE28 ... 124 C6
Fieldgate Mans 23 E1 ... 96 A2
Fieldgate St E1 ... 96 A2
Field Ho 4 N9 ... 34 A6
Fieldhouse Cl E18 ... 37 B2
Fieldhouse Rd SW12 ... 159 C3
Fielding Ave TW2 ... 152 A1
Fielding Ho 3 NW6 ... 91 C4
NW8 ... 229 A6
Chiswick W4 ... 133 C6
Fielding Mews SW13 ... 134 B6
Fielding Prim Sch W13 ... 109 B3
Fielding Rd W14 ... 112 D3
W4 ... 111 C3
Fielding St SE17 ... 139 A6
Fieldings The SE23 ... 162 C3
Fielding Terr W5 ... 110 B6
Field La Brentford TW8 ... 131 C5
Teddington TW11 ... 175 A5
Field Mead NW9,NW7 ... 27 D3
Field Pl KT3 ... 199 D3
Field Point E7 ... 77 A4
Field Rd E7 ... 77 A4
N17 ... 51 C6
W6 ... 135 A6 264 A6
Feltham TW14 ... 150 B5
Fieldsend Rd SM3 ... 217 A3
Fields Est E8 ... 74 A1
Fieldside Cl BR6 ... 227 A4
Fieldside Rd BR1 ... 186 B5
Fields Park Cres RM6 ... 58 D4
Field St WC1 ... 233 C2
Fieldsway Ho N5 ... 72 C3
Fieldview SW17,SW18 ... 158 B3
Field View TW13 ... 171 B6
Fieldview Ct N5 ... 72 D3
NW9 ... 44 C3
Fieldway BR5 ... 211 B3
Field Way NW10 ... 67 A1
Fieldway RM8 ... 80 C4
Field Way Greenford UB6 ... 85 D6
New Addington CR0 ... 223 D2
Ruislip HA4 ... 39 A1
Fieldway Cres N5,N7 ... 72 C3
Fieldway Sta CR0 ... 223 D1
Fieldwick Ho 14 E9 ... 74 D2
Fiennes Cl RM8 ... 58 C1
Fife Ct 5 W3 ... 88 C1
Fifehead Cl TW15 ... 170 A4
Fife Rd E16 ... 99 A2
Kingston KT2 ... 176 A1
Mortlake SW14 ... 155 A6
Tottenham N22 ... 32 D3
Fife Terr N1 ... 233 D4
Fifield Path SE23 ... 162 D1
Fifteenpenny Fields SE9 ... 166 C6
Fifth Ave W10 ... 91 A4
Hayes UB3 ... 105 D5
Ilford E12 ... 78 B4
Fifth Cross Rd TW2 ... 152 B2
Fifth Way HA9 ... 66 D4
Figge's Rd CR4 ... 181 A3
Fig Tree Cl NW10 ... 89 C6
Filanco Ct W7 ... 108 D5
Filby Rd KT9 ... 214 B2
Filey Ave N16 ... 52 A1
Filey Cl SM2 ... 218 A1
Filey Ho SW18 ... 136 A1
Filey Waye HA4 ... 62 B6
Filigree Ct SE16 ... 119 B5
Fillebrook Ave EN1 ... 5 D3
Fillebrook Hall E11 ... 54 C2
Fillebrook Rd E11 ... 54 C1
Filmer Ho SW6 ... 264 B2
Filmer Rd SW6 ... 135 B5 264 C3
Filmer Road Studios SW6 ... 264 B2
Filston Rd DA8 ... 125 D1
Filton Ct 14 SE14 ... 140 C5
Finborough Ho SW10 ... 266 A6
Finborough Rd
SW10 ... 135 D6 265 D6
Upper Tooting SW17 ... 180 D4
Finchale Rd SE2 ... 124 A3
Fincham Cl UB10 ... 61 A5
Finch Ave SE27 ... 183 B6
Finch Cl NW10 ... 67 B2
Barnet EN5 ... 13 C6
Finchdean Ho SW15 ... 155 D4
Finch Dr TW14 ... 150 D4
Finch Gdns E4 ... 35 C5
Finch Ho 1 SE8 ... 141 D5
Finchingfield Ave IG8 ... 37 C3
Finch La EC2,EC3 ... 242 D1
Finchley Cath High Sch N12 ... 13 D1
Finchley Central Sta N3 ... 29 C2
Finchley Ct N3 ... 29 D4
Finchley La NW4 ... 46 D5
Finchley Lo N12 ... 29 D5
Finchley Memorial Hospl N12 ... 30 A3
Finchley Pk N12 ... 30 B6
Finchley Pl NW8 ... 229 C4
Finchley Rd NW11 ... 47 B3
NW3 ... 70 A2
NW8 ... 229 C4
Finchley Road & Frognal Sta NW3 ... 70 A3
Finchley Road Sta NW3 ... 70 A2
Finchley Way N3 ... 29 C3
Finch Lo 15 W9 ... 91 C2
Finch Mews 3 SE15 ... 139 D4
Finch's Ct 9 E14 ... 119 D6
Finden Rd E7 ... 77 C3
Findhorn Ave UB4 ... 84 B2
Findhorn St E14 ... 98 A1
Findon Cl SW18 ... 157 C5
Harrow HA2 ... 63 D5
Findon Rd W12 ... 112 A4
Edmonton N9 ... 18 B3
Fine Bush La HA4 ... 38 D3
Fineran Ct 16 SW11 ... 136 B1
Fingal St SE10 ... 120 D1
Fingest Ho NW8 ... 237 A6
Finians Cl UB10 ... 60 B1
Finland Rd SE4 ... 141 A2
Finland St SE16 ... 119 A3
Finlays Cl KT9 ... 214 C3
Finlay St SW6 ... 134 D4
Finley Ct 21 SE5 ... 139 A5
Finmere Ho 1 N4 ... 51 A2
Finnemore Ho N1 ... 235 A6
Finney La TW7 ... 131 A4
Finn Ho N1 ... 235 D2
Finnis St E2 ... 96 B3
Finnymore Rd RM9 ... 81 A1
Finsbury Ave EC2 ... 242 D3
Finsbury Cir EC2 ... 95 B2 242 D3
Finsbury Cotts N22 ... 32 A3
Finsbury Ct EC2 ... 242 C4
Finsbury Ho N22 ... 32 A2
Finsbury Market EC2 ... 243 A4
Finsbury Mkt EC2 ... 243 A5
Finsbury Park Ave N4 ... 51 A3
Finsbury Park Rd N4,N5 ... 72 D6
Finsbury Park Sta N4 ... 72 C6
Finsbury Pavement EC2 ... 95 B2 242 D4
Finsbury Rd N22 ... 32 B2
Finsbury Sq EC2 ... 95 B2 242 D4
Finsbury St EC2 ... 242 C4
Finsbury Way DA5 ... 169 B5
Finsen Rd SE5 ... 139 A2
Finstock Rd W10 ... 90 D1
Finton House Sch SW17 ... 158 D2
Finucane Ct TW9 ... 132 B2
Finucane Rise WD23 ... 8 A2
Finwhale Ho E14 ... 119 D3
Fiona Ct 9 NW6 ... 91 B5
Enfield EN2 ... 4 D2
Firbank Cl E16 ... 99 D2
Enfield EN2 ... 5 A1
Firbank Rd SE15 ... 140 B3
Fir Cl KT12 ... 194 A2
Fircroft N1 ... 94 D6 234 D6
Fircroft Gdns HA1 ... 64 C5
Fircroft Prim Sch SW17 ... 158 D1
Fircroft Rd
Chessington KT9 ... 214 B4
Upper Tooting SW17 ... 158 D1
Fir Dene BR6 ... 226 C5
Firdene KT5 ... 199 A1
Fire Bell Alley KT6 ... 198 A3
Firebell Mews KT6 ... 198 A3
Fire Brigade Pier SE1 ... 260 B4
Firecrest Dr NW3 ... 69 D5
Firefly 7 NW9 ... 27 D1
Firefly Cl SM6 ... 220 A1
Firefly Gdns E6 ... 100 A3
Firemans Cotts N10 ... 49 A6
Fireman's Flats N22 ... 32 A2

Firepower (The Royal Artillery Mus)★ SE18 122 D3
Fire Station Alley EN5 1 A3
Fire Station Mews 3
BR3 185 D2
Firethorn Cl HA8 27 A6
Fir Gr KT3 199 D3
Firhill Rd SE6 163 C1
Firle Ho W10 90 C2
Fir Lo SW15 134 B1
Firmston Ho 9 SW14 133 B2
Fir Rd Cheam SM3 201 B1
Feltham TW13 172 D5
Firs Ave N10 49 A5
N11 31 A4
Mortlake SW14 133 A1
Firsby Ave CR0 207 A1
Firsby Rd N16 52 A1
Firs Cl N10 49 A6
Claygate KT10 212 C2
Forest Hill SE23 163 A4
Mitcham CR4 181 B2
Firscroft N13 17 A1
Firs Dr TW5 128 B5
Firs Farm Prim Sch N13 17 B1
Firs Ho N22 32 C2
Firside Gr DA15 167 D3
Firs La N21,N13 17 A2
Firs Park Ave N21 17 B3
Firs Park Gdns N21 17 B3
First Ave E12 78 A3
E13 99 A4
E17 53 D4
N18 34 C6
NW4 46 C5
W10 91 B3
W3 111 D5
Bexley DA7 146 C5
Dagenham RM10 103 D5
Dagenham RM6 58 C4
East Molesey KT8 195 C5
Enfield EN1 17 D6
Hayes UB3 105 D5
Mortlake SW14 133 C2
Walton-on-T KT12 194 B3
Wembley HA9 65 D6
First Cl KT8 196 A6
First Cross Rd TW2 152 C2
First Dr NW10 67 A1
Firs The DA15 167 D1
E6 78 A1
N20 14 B3
Belmont SM2 217 D1
Claygate KT10 212 C2
Ealing W5 87 D2
Forest Hill SE26 184 C5
2 Penge SE26 184 B5
Wimbledon SW20 178 A3
Woodford IG8 37 C3
First St SW3 114 C2 257 B4
Firstway SW20 178 C1
First Way HA9 66 D4
Firs Wlk IG8 37 A5
Firswood Ave KT19 215 D3
Firth Gdns SW6 135 A4 264 A1
Firtree Ave CR4 181 A1
Fir Tree Ave UB7 104 C3
Fir Tree Cl Ealing W5 88 A1
Esher KT10 212 A3
5 Orpington BR6 227 D3
Streatham SW16 181 C5
Worcester Park KT19 215 D4
Firtree Ct BR2 208 D6
Fir Tree Gdns CR0 223 C4
Fir Tree Gr SM5 218 D1
Fir Tree Ho 11 SE14 140 C5
Fir Tree Rd TW4 129 A1
Fir Trees Cl SE16 119 A5
Fir Tree Wlk EN1 5 B2
Fir Wlk KT17,SM3 216 D2
Fisher Cl Croydon CR0 205 D1
Southall UB6 85 C4
Holdbrook EN3 7 C6
Fisher Ho 8 E1 118 C6
N1 234 A5
2 N19 71 C5
Fisherman Cl TW10 175 C6
Fishermans Dr SE16 118 D4
Fishermans Wlk SE28 123 C4
Fisherman's Wlk E14 119 C5
Fisher Rd HA3 24 D1
Fishers Cl SW16 159 D1
Fishers Ct SE14 140 D4
4 Teddington TW11 174 D5
Fishersdene KT10 213 A1
Fisher's La W4 111 B2
Fisher St E16 99 A2
WC1 240 C3
Fisherton St NW8 92 B3 236 D6
Fisherton Street Est
NW8 92 B3 236 D5
Fishguard Way E16 122 D5
Fishlock Ct 6 SW4 138 A3
Fishponds Rd BR2 225 D3
Upper Tooting SW17 180 C6
Fish St Hill EC3 252 D5
Fiske Ct Barking IG11 101 B5
1 Merton SW19 180 A3
Sutton SM2 218 A1
Tottenham N17 34 A2
Fitch Ct SW2 160 C6
8 Mitcham CR4 181 A1
Fitzalan Rd N3 47 B6
Claygate KT10 212 C1
Fitzalan St SE11 116 C2 261 A4
Fitzclarence Ho W11 244 A2
Fitz-George Ave W14 254 A3
Fitzgeorge Ave KT2,KT3 177 B2
Fitzgerald Ave SW14 133 C2
Fitzgerald Ct 1 E10 53 D1
Fitzgerald Ho 14 E14 97 D1
16 SW9 138 C3
Hayes UB3 106 B5
Fitzgerald Rd
Mortlake SW14 133 B2
Thames Ditton KT7 197 A3
Wanstead E11 55 A4
Fitzhardinge Ho W1 238 A2
Beckenham BR3 185 D1
Fitzhardinge St W1 238 A2
Fitzherbert Ho 11 TW10 154 B5
Fitzhugh Gr SW18 158 B5
Fitzjames Ave W14 254 B3
Croydon CR0 222 A6
Fitzjohn Ave EN5 1 B1
Fitzjohn's Ave NW3 70 B3
Fitzjohns Mans NW3 70 A2
Fitzjohns Prim Sch NW3 70 B3
Fitzmaurice Ho 17 SE16 118 B2
Fitzmaurice Pl W1 248 D4
Fitzneal St W12 89 D1
Fitzroy Cl N6 48 D1
Fitzroy Cres W4 133 B5
Fitzroy Ct N6 49 C3
W1 239 B5
Fitzroy Gdns SE19 183 C3
Fitzroy Ho 14 E14 97 B1
SE1 263 D2
Fitzroy Lo N21 16 D6
Fitzroy Mews W1 239 A5
Fitzroy Pk N6 48 D1
Fitzroy Rd NW1 93 A6 231 A6
Fitzroy Sq W1 239 A5
Fitzroy St W1 93 C3 239 A5
Fitzroy Yd NW1 231 A6
Fitzsimmons Ct 1 NW10 89 B6
Fitzstephen Rd RM8 80 C3
Fitzwarren Gdns N19 49 C1
Fitzwilliam Ave TW9 132 B3
Fitzwilliam Ho TW9 131 D1
Fitzwilliam Hts 1 SE23 162 C2
Fitzwilliam Mews E16 121 A5
Fitzwilliam Rd SW4 137 C2
Fitzwygram Cl TW12 174 A5
Five Acre NW9 27 D1
Fiveacre Cl CR7 204 C3
Five Elms Prim Sch RM8 81 B5
Five Elms Rd BR2 225 C5
Dagenham RM9 81 B5
Fives Ct SE11 261 C5
Fiveways SE9 166 D2
Croydon CR0 220 C4
Five Ways Cnr NW4 28 A2
Fiveways Rd SW9 138 C3
Five Ways Retail Pk
NW7 27 D3
Flack Ct 14 E10 53 D2
Fladbury Rd N15 51 B3
Fladgate Rd E11 54 C3
Flag Cl CR0 206 D1
Flag Wlk HA5 40 A3
Flambard Rd HA1,HA3 43 A3
Flamborough Ho 11
SE15 140 A4
Flamborough Rd HA4 62 A5
Flamborough St E14 97 A1
Flamingo Ct 2 SE8 141 C5
Flamingo Gdns UB5 85 A4
Flamstead Gdns RM9 80 C1
Flamstead Rd RM9 80 C1
Flamsted Ave HA9 66 C2
Flamsteed Ho★ SE10 142 B5
Flamsteed Rd SE7 122 A1
Flanchford Rd W12 111 D3
Flanders Cres SW17 180 D4
Flanders Ct E17 53 A3
Flanders Mans 1 W4 111 D2
Flanders Rd W4 111 C2
Wallend E6 100 C5
Flanders Way E9 74 D2
Flank St 6 E1 118 A6
Flansham Ho 2 E14 97 B1
Flash La EN2 5 A6
Flask Wlk NW3 70 B4
Flatford Ho 2 SE6 186 A6
Flavell Mews SE10 120 C1
Flaxen Cl E4 19 D1
Flaxen Rd E4 19 D1
Flaxley Rd SM4 201 D2
Flaxman Ct W1 239 C1
12 Belvedere DA17 125 C1
Flaxman Ho SE1 261 D6
10 W4 111 C1
Flaxman Rd SE5 138 D3
Flaxman Terr
WC1 93 D4 232 D1
Flaxman Villas N2 48 A6
Flaxmore Ct DA7 147 D2
South Norwood CR7 183 B1
Flaxton Rd SE18 145 C5
Flecker Cl HA7 24 D5
Flecker Ho 6 SE5 139 B5
Fleece Dr N9 34 A6
Fleecefield Prim Sch
N18 34 A6
Fleece Rd KT6 197 C1
Fleece Wlk N7 72 A2
Fleeming Cl E17 35 B1
Fleeming Rd E17 35 B1
Fleet Cl East Molesey KT8 195 B4
Ruislip HA4 39 A3
Fleet Ct 1 W12 111 C3
Fleetfield WC1 233 B2
Fleet Ho 4 E14 119 A6
6 SW2 160 C6
Fleet Pl EC4 241 C2
Fleet Prim Sch NW3 70 D3
Fleet Rd NW3 70 D3
Fleetside KT8 195 C4
Fleet Sq WC1 233 D1
Fleet St EC4 94 C1 241 B1
Fleet Street Hill 11 E1 96 A3
Fleet Terr SE6 164 A4
Fleetway WC1 233 B2
Fleetway West Bsns Pk
UB6 87 B5
Fleet Wood 6 N16 73 D6
Fleetwood Cl E16 99 D2
Chessington KT9 213 D1
South Croydon CR0 221 D5
Fleetwood Ct 1 E6 100 B2
Orpington BR6 226 C4
8 Stanwell TW19 148 A5
Fleetwood Rd NW10 68 A3
Kingston KT3 198 D6
Fleetwood Sq KT3 198 D6
Fleetwood St N16 73 C6
Fleetwood Way WD19 22 C6
Fleming Cl 3 W9 91 C3
Fleming Ct W2 236 C4
Croydon CR0 220 C3
Fleming Dr N21 16 B6
Fleming Ho N4 51 A1
8 SE16 118 A4
8 Wembley HA9 67 A5
Fleming Mead CR4 180 D3
Fleming Rd SE17 138 D6
Southall UB1 86 A1
Fleming Way SE28 124 D6
Isleworth TW7 130 D1
Fleming Wlk NW9 27 C1
Flemming Ave HA4 62 B6
Flempton Rd E10 53 A1
Fletcher Bldgs WC2 240 B1
Fletcher Cl E16 122 D6
Fletcher Ct 9 NW5 71 B4
Fletcher Ho 22 N1 95 C6
16 N16 73 C4
Fletcher La E10 54 A2
Fletcher Path 7 SE8 141 C5
Fletcher Rd W4 111 A3
Fletchers Cl BR2 209 B5
Fletcher St 10 E1 118 A6
Fletching Rd E5 74 C5
SE7 143 D6
Fletton Rd N11 32 A3
Fleur Gates 7 SW19 156 D4
Flexmere Rd N17 33 C2
Flimwell Cl BR1 186 C5
Flinders Ho 28 E1 118 B5
Flint Cl 8 BR6 227 D2
Flint Down Cl BR5 190 A2
Flintmill Cres SE3,SE9 144 A3
Flinton St SE17 117 C1 263 B2
Flint St SE17 117 B2 262 D3
Flitcroft St WC2 239 D1
Flitton Ho 7 N1 72 D1
Floathaven Cl SE28 124 A5
Flock Mill Pl SW18 157 D3
Flodden Rd SE5 139 A4
Flood La 4 TW1 153 A3
Flood St SW3 136 C6 267 B6
Flood Wlk SW3 136 C6 267 B6
Flora Cl E14 97 D1
Flora Gardens Prim Sch
W6 112 B2
Flora Gdns 2 W6 112 B2
Dagenham RM6 58 C3
Floral St WC2 116 A6 250 A6
Flora St DA17 125 B1
Florence Ave Enfield EN2 5 A2
Morden SM4 202 A4
Florence Cl KT12 194 B2
Florence Ct 4 E5 74 A5
W9 229 B1
Wanstead E11 55 C5
5 Wimbledon SW19 179 A4
Florence Dr EN2 5 A2
Florence Elson Cl E12 78 C4
Florence Gdns
Chiswick W4 133 A6
Ilford RM6 58 C2
Florence Ho 20 SE16 118 B1
2 SE18 144 B4
7 SW18 136 B1
2 SW2 160 B6
10 W11 112 D6
5 Kingston KT2 176 B3
Florence Mans 4 NW4 46 B4
SW6 264 C2
Florence Nightingale Ho 11
N1 73 A2
Florence Nightingale Mus★
SE1 250 D1
Florence Rd BR1 187 A2
E13 99 A5
8 E6 99 C6
N4 50 C2
SE14 141 B4
SE2 124 C2
W4 111 B3
5 Beckenham BR3 185 A1
Ealing W5 110 A6
Feltham TW13 150 B3
6 Kingston KT2 176 B3
Southall UB2 106 D3
Walton-on-T KT12 194 B2
Wimbledon SW19 179 D4
Florence Root Ho IG4 56 B4
Florence St E16 98 D3
N1 72 D1
NW4 46 C5
Florence Terr SE14 141 B4
Kingston SW15 155 C1
Florence Way SW12 158 D3
Florentine Ho 3 IG1 78 D6
Flores Ho 10 E1 96 D2
Florfield Rd E8 74 B2
Florian SE5 139 C4
Florian Ave SM1 218 B4
Florian Rd SW15 135 A1
Florida Cl WD23 8 B2
Florida Ct BR2 208 D5
Florida Rd CR7 182 D2
Florida St E2 96 A4
Florin Ct SE1 253 C1
Edmonton N18 33 C6
Floris Pl 7 SW4 137 C2
Floriston Ave UB10 61 A1
Floriston Cl HA7 25 B2
Floriston Ct UB5 63 D3
Floriston Gdns HA7 25 B2
Florys Ct 7 SW19 157 A3
Floss St SW15 134 C3
Flower & Dean Wlk E1 243 D3
Flower La NW7 27 D4
Flower Pot Cl N15 51 D3
Flowers Cl NW2 68 A5
Flowersmead SW17 159 A2
Flowers Mews 1 N19 71 C6
Flower Wlk The
SW7 114 A4 246 B2
Floyd Rd SE7 121 C1
Fludyer St SE13 142 C1
Fluer De Lis St E1 243 C5
Flynn Ct 12 E14 119 C6
Fogerty Cl EN3 7 C6
Foley Cotts KT10 212 D2
Foley Ho 19 E1 96 C1
Foley Mews KT10 212 C2
Foley Rd KT10 212 C1
Foley St W1 93 C2 239 A3
Folgate St E1 95 D2 243 C4
Foliot Ho N1 233 C4
Foliot St W12 89 D1
Folkestone Ct UB5 63 D3
Folkestone Rd E17 53 D5
Edmonton N18 34 A6
Wallend E6 100 C4
Folkingham La 6 NW9 27 C2
Folkington Cnr N12 29 B5
Folland 6 NW9 27 D1
Follett Ho SW10 266 C4
Follett St E14 98 A1
Folly La E17 35 A2
E4 35 B3
Folly Wall E14 120 A4
Fontaine Ct 3 BR3 185 B2
Fontaine Rd SW16 182 B3
Fontarabia Rd SW11 137 A1
Fontenelle SE5 139 C4
Fontenoy Ho SE11 261 C3
Fontenoy Rd SW12,
SW17 159 C2
Fonteyne Gdns IG8 37 D1
Fonthill Cl SE20 184 A1
Fonthill Ct SE23 162 C4
Fonthill Ho SW1 258 D2
W14 254 B6
Fonthill Mews N4 72 B6
Fonthill Rd N4 72 C6
Font Hills N2 30 A1
Fontley Way SW15 156 A4
Fontmell Cl TW15 170 C5
Fontmell Pk TW15 170 C5
Fontwell Cl Harrow HA3 24 C3
Northolt UB5 63 C2
Fontwell Dr BR2 210 C4
Football La HA1 42 C1
Footpath The SW15 156 A6
Foots Cray High St
DA14 190 D4
Foots Cray La DA5,DA14 168 C3
Footscray Rd SE9 166 D3
Forber Ho 25 E2 96 C4
Forbes Cl NW2 68 A5
Forbes Ct SE19 183 C5
Forbes Ho 2 W4 110 C1
Forbes St E1 96 A1
Forbes Way HA4 62 B6
Forburg Rd N16 52 A1
Fordbridge Ct TW15 170 A4
Fordbridge Rd
Ashford TW15 170 B5
Lower Halliford TW16,
TW17 193 D3
Sunbury TW16 194 A5
Fordbridge Rdbt TW15 170 A4
Ford Cl 11 E3 97 A5
Ashford TW15 170 A4
Harrow HA1 42 B2
Littleton TW17 192 C4
Thornton Heath CR7 204 D4
Fordcombe 13 NW5 71 A2
Forde Ave BR1 209 C6
Fordel Rd SE6 164 B3
Ford End IG8 37 B4
Fordham 4 KT1 176 C1
Fordham Cl EN4 2 C2
Fordham Rd EN4 2 C2
Fordham St 7 E1 96 A1
Ford Ho 2 SE18 122 D1
2 New Barnet EN5 13 D6
Fordhook Ave W5 110 C6
Fordingley Rd W9 91 B4
Fordington Ho 2 SE26 162 B1
Fordington Rd N6 48 D5
Fordmill Rd SE6 163 C2
Ford Rd E3 97 B5
Ashford TW15 170 B6
Dagenham RM10 81 C1
Ford's Gr N21 17 A3
Fords Park Rd E16 99 A1
Ford Sq E1 96 B2
Ford St E16 98 D1
E3 97 A5
Fordwich Cl BR6 211 D2
Fordwych Ct NW2 69 A2
Fordwych Rd NW2 69 A3
Fordyce Ho 3 SW16 181 C6
Fordyce Rd SE13 164 A6
Fordyke Rd RM8 81 B6
Foreign, Commonwealth & Home Offices SW1 250 A2
Foreland Ct NW4 29 A2
Foreland Ho W11 244 A6
Foreland St SE18 123 B2
Foreshore SE8 119 B2
Fore St EC2 95 A2 242 B3
Edmonton N18 34 A6
Pinner HA5 40 A4
Forest App Chingford E4 20 C4
Woodford IG8 37 A3
Fore St Ave EC2 242 C3
Forest Ave E4 20 C4
Forest Bsns Pk E17 52 D2
Forest Cl Chislehurst BR7 188 C2
Wanstead E11 55 A4
Woodford IG8 37 B6
Forest Croft SE23 162 B2
Forest Ct E11 54 C5
12 N12 29 D6
Chingford E4 20 D3
Forestdale N14 31 D6
Forestdale Ctr The CR0 223 B1
Forest Dene Ct 2 SM2 218 A2
Forest Dr Ashford TW16 171 D3
Chingford IG8 36 C3
Keston Mark BR2 226 A4
Wanstead E12 77 D5
Forest Dr E E11 54 B3
Forest Dr W E11 54 B2
Forest Edge IG9 21 D1
Forester Rd SE15 140 B2
Foresters Cl SM6 219 D1
Foresters Cres DA7 147 D1
Foresters Dr E17 54 B5
Wallington SM6 219 D1
Foresters Prim Sch
SM6 219 D2
Forest Gate NW9 45 C4
Forest Gate Com Sch E7 77 A3
Forest Gate Sta E7 77 A3
Forest Gdns N17 33 D1
Forest Glade E11 54 C3
Chingford E4 36 C5
Forest Gr E8 73 D2
Forest Hill SE23 162 C3
Forest Hill Bsns Ctr
SE23 162 C2
Forest Hill Ct 6 SE26 162 B1
Forest Hill Ind Est SE23 162 C2
Forest Hill Rd SE22 162 B5
Forest Hill Sec Sch
SE23 162 D1
Forest Hill Sta SE23 162 C2
Forest Ho 9 E4 20 C4
Forestholme Cl SE23 162 C2
Forest Hts IG9 21 A2
Forest La E7,E15 76 D3
Forest Lawns BR1 187 C2
Forest Lea E11 54 D2
Forest Lo 1 SE23 162 C1
Forest Mount Rd IG8 36 B3
Forest Point E7 77 B3
Forest Rd E11 54 B2
E17 53 C6
E7 77 A4
E8 73 D2
Edmonton N9 18 B3
Feltham TW13 150 C2
Morden SM3,SM4 201 C2
Richmond TW9 132 C5
Romford RM7 59 D6
Woodford IG8 21 A1
Forest Ridge BR2 226 B4
Beckenham BR3 207 C6
Forest Rise E17 54 B5
Forest Sch E17 54 C5
Forest Side E7 77 B4
Buckhurst Hill IG9 21 C3
Chingford E4 20 D3
New Malden KT4 199 D1
Forest St E7 77 A3
Forest The E11 54 C5
Forest Trad Est E17 52 D6
Forest View E11 54 D2
Chingford E4 20 B4
Forest View Ave E10 54 B4
Forest View Rd E12 78 A4
Chingford E17 36 A2
Forest Way BR5 211 D4
6 N19 71 C6
Sidcup DA15 167 B4
Woodford IG8 37 B6
Forfar Rd SW11 137 A4 268 B2
Tottenham N22 32 D2
Forge Cl BR2 209 A1
Forge Cotts W5 109 D5
Forge Dr KT10 213 A1
Forge La Belmont SM3 217 A1
Feltham TW13 173 A5
Sunbury TW16 194 A6
Forge Lane Inf Sch
TW13 173 A5
Forge Lane Jun Sch
TW13 173 A5
Forge Mews
Addington CR0 223 C3
Sunbury TW16 194 A6
Forge Pl NW1 71 A2
Forge The UB3 127 B6
Forlong Path UB5 63 A2
Forman Ct TW1 152 D3
Forman Gr 2 UB5 84 D4
Forman Ho SE4 140 D1
Forman Pl N16 73 D4
Formby Ave HA3,HA7 43 C6
Formby Ct 9 N7 72 C3
Formosa Ho 1 E1 97 A3
Formosa St W9 91 D3
Formunt Cl E16 98 D2
Forres Gdns NW11 47 C3
Forrest Ct N7 72 C2
Forrester Path SE26 184 C6
Forresters The HA5 40 B3
Forrest Gdns SW16 204 B6
Forrest Ho SW15 134 C3
Forris Ave UB3 105 D5
Forset Ct W1 237 B2
Forset St W1 92 C1 237 B2
Forstal Cl BR2 209 A6
Forster Ho SE6 164 B1
Forster Park Prim Sch
SE6 164 C1
Forster Rd E17 53 A3
N17 51 D6
Beckenham BR3 207 A6
Streatham SW2 160 A4
Thornton Heath CR0 205 A2
Forsters Cl RM6 59 B3
Forsters Way UB4 84 B1
Forstic Wlk E1 243 D3
Forston St N1 95 A5 235 B4
Forsyte Cres SE19 183 C2
Forsyte Ct KT2 176 D2
Forsyth Ct KT3 177 C1
Forsythe Shades BR3 186 A2
Forsyth Gdns SE17 138 D6
Forsyth Ho 14 E9 74 C1
SW1 259 B3
Forsythia Cl IG1 78 D3
Forsythia Ho SE4 141 A2
Forsyth Pl EN1 17 C6
Forterie Gdns IG3 80 A4
Fortescue Ave 1 E8 74 B1
Twickenham TW2 152 A1
Fortescue Rd HA8 27 B3
Mitcham SW19 180 B3
Fortess Gr NW5 71 C3
Fortess Rd NW5 71 C4
Fortess Wlk NW5 71 B3
Forthbridge Rd SW11 137 A1
Forth Ho 29 E3 97 B5
Forties The 9 NW5 71 C3
Fortior Ct N6 49 C2
Fortis Cl E16 99 C1
Fortis Ct N10 49 A6
Fortis Gn N2,N10 48 D6
Fortis Green Ave N2 48 D5
Fortis Green Cotts N2 48 D6
Fortismere Ave N10 49 A6
Fortismere Sch N10 30 D1
Fortismere Sch (South Wing)
N10 49 A6
Fortnam Rd N19 71 D6
Fortnums Acre HA7 24 D4
Fort Rd SE1 117 D2 263 D3
Northolt UB5 63 C1
Fortrose Gdns SW12,
SW2 160 A3
Fort St E1 243 B3
E16 121 B5
Fortuna Cl N7 72 B2
Fortune Ct IG11 102 B5
Fortune Gate Rd NW10 89 C6
Fortune Green Rd NW6 69 C4
Fortune Ho EC1 242 B5
SE11 261 A3
Fortune La WD6 9 D5
Fortune Mead UB5 63 A2
Fortune St EC1 95 A3 242 B5
Fortune Way NW10 90 A4
Fortune Wlk SE28 123 B3
Forty Acre La E16 99 A2
Forty Ave HA9 66 B6
Forty Cl HA9 66 B5
Forty Hall★ EN2 5 D6
Forty Hill EN2 5 D5
Forty Hill CE Prim Sch
EN2 6 A6
Forty Hill Ho EN1 5 D5
Forty La HA9 66 D6
Forumside HA8 26 C4
Forum The KT8 195 D5
Forum Way HA8 26 C4
Forval Cl CR4 202 D4
Forward Bsns Ctr The
E16 98 B3
Forward Dr HA3 42 D5
Fosbroke Ho SW8 270 A3
Fosbury Ho 7 SW9 138 B1
Fosbury Mews W2 245 D5
Foscote Mews W9 91 C2
Foscote Rd NW4 46 B3
Foskett Ho 16 N2 30 B1
Foskett Rd SW6 135 B3
Foss Ave CR0,CR9 220 C3
Fossdene Prim Sch SE7 121 B1
Fossdene Rd SE7 121 B1
Fossdyke Cl UB4 85 A2
Fosse Way W13 87 A2
Fossil Rd SE13 141 C2
Fossington Rd DA17 124 D2
Foss Rd SW17 180 B6
Fossway RM8 80 C6
Foster Ct E16 120 D6
4 NW1 71 C1
NW4 46 C5
Foster Ho SE14 141 B4
Foster La EC2 95 A1 242 A2
Foster Rd E13 99 A3
W3 111 C6
W4 111 B1
Fosters Cl BR7 188 B5
Woodford E18 37 B2
Fosters Old Sch DA16 146 B3

Foster's Prim Sch DA16 ... 146 C2
Foster St NW4 ... 46 C5
Foster Wlk NW4 ... 46 C5
Fothergill Cl E13 ... 99 A5
Fothergill Dr N21 ... 16 A6
Fotheringham Ct EN1 ... 5 D1
Fotheringham Rd EN1 ... 5 D1
Foubert's Pl W1 ... 239 A1
Foulden Rd N16 ... 73 D4
Foulden Terr N16 ... 73 D4
Foulis Terr SW7 ... 114 B1 256 D2
Foulser Rd SW17 ... 159 A1
Foulsham Rd CR7 ... 205 B6
Foundary Ho 7 E14 ... 97 D2
Founder Cl 2 E6 ... 100 D1
Founders Ct EC2 ... 242 C2
Founders Gdns SE19 ... 183 A3
Founders Ho SW1 ... 259 C2
Foundling Ct WC1 ... 240 A6
Foundry Cl SE16 ... 119 A5
Foundry Mews NW1 ... 239 B6
Foundry Pl E1 ... 96 C2
Fountain Cl UB8 ... 83 A2
Fountain Ct DA15 ... 168 B5
EC4 ... 251 A6
SW1 ... 258 C3
New Malden KT3 ... 199 A5
Penge SE26 ... 184 C4
Fountain Dr
Dulwich SE19 ... 183 D6
Wallington SM5 ... 218 D1
Fountain Green Sq 31
SE16 ... 118 A4
Fountain Ho 1 NW6 ... 69 A1
30 SE16 ... 118 A4
W1 ... 248 A4
Fountain Mews 1 N5 ... 73 A4
NW3 ... 70 D2
Fountain Pl SW9 ... 138 C4
Fountain Rd
South Norwood CR7 ... 183 A1
Upper Tooting SW17 ... 180 B6
Fountains Ave TW13 ... 151 B1
Fountains Cl TW13 ... 151 B1
Fountains Cres N14 ... 16 A4
Fountains The N3 ... 29 D3
Loughton IG10 ... 21 D4
Fountayne Bsns Ctr N15 ... 52 A5
Fountayne Rd N15 ... 52 A5
N16 ... 74 A6
Fount St SW8 ... 137 D5 269 D3
Four Acres N12 ... 29 D6
Fouracres EN3 ... 7 A4
Fourland Wlk HA8 ... 27 A4
Fournier St E1 ... 95 D2 243 D4
Four Seasons Cl E3 ... 97 C5
Four Seasons Cres SM3 ... 217 B6
Four Square Ct TW4 ... 151 C5
Fourth Ave W10 ... 91 A4
Hayes UB3 ... 105 D5
Ilford E12 ... 78 B4
Fourth Cross Rd TW2 ... 152 B2
Fourth Way Wembley HA9 ... 66 D4
Wembley HA9 ... 67 A4
Four Tubs The WD23 ... 8 B4
Fourways 2 CR0 ... 221 D6
Four Wents The E4 ... 20 B2
Fovant Ct 5 SW8 ... 137 C3
Fowey Ave IG4 ... 55 D4
Fowey Cl E1 ... 118 B5
Fowey Ho SE11 ... 261 B2
Fowler Cl DA14 ... 191 A5
SW11 ... 136 B2
Fowler Ho N1 ... 94 D6 234 D6
N15 ... 51 B4
5 SE5 ... 139 C3
SW8 ... 269 D1
Fowler Rd E7 ... 77 A4
N1 ... 94 D6 234 D6
Mitcham CR4 ... 181 A1
Fowler's Wlk W5 ... 87 D3
Fownes St SW11 ... 136 C2
Foxberry Ct SE4 ... 141 B1
Foxberry Rd SE4 ... 141 A2
Foxborough Gdns SE4 ... 163 C6
Foxbourne Rd SW17 ... 159 A2
Foxbury Ave BR7 ... 189 B4
Foxbury Cl BR1 ... 187 B4
Foxbury Rd BR1 ... 187 B4
Fox Cl E1 ... 96 C3
E16 ... 99 A2
Elstree WD6 ... 9 D5
Foxcombe CR0 ... 223 D2
Foxcombe Cl 1 E6 ... 99 D5
Foxcombe Rd 6 SW15 ... 156 A3
Foxcote SE5 ... 263 B1
Foxcroft N1 ... 233 D3
Foxcroft Rd SE18 ... 144 D4
Foxes Dale SE3 ... 143 A2
Beckenham BR2 ... 208 B6
Foxfield Prim Sch SE18 ... 123 A2
Foxfield Rd BR6 ... 227 B6
Foxglove Ave BR3 ... 185 D3
Foxglove Cl UB1 ... 107 A6
Foxglove Ct 11 HA0 ... 88 A5
Foxglove Gdns E11 ... 55 C5
Foxglove La KT9 ... 214 C4
Foxglove St W12 ... 111 D6
Foxglove Way SM6 ... 203 B1
Fox Gr KT12 ... 194 B2
Foxgrove N14 ... 16 A1
Foxgrove Path WD19 ... 22 D5
Foxgrove Rd BR3 ... 186 A3
Foxham Rd N19 ... 71 D5
Fox Hill SE19 ... 183 D3
Fox Hill Gdns SE19 ... 183 D3
Fox Ho 2 SW11 ... 136 B1
Foxhole Rd 2 SE9 ... 166 A6
Fox Hollow Cl 1 SE18 ... 123 C1
Fox Hollow Dr DA16 ... 146 D2
Foxholt Gdns NW10 ... 67 A1
Foxhome Cl BR7 ... 188 C4
Fox House Rd DA17 ... 125 D1
Fox & Knot St EC1 ... 241 D4
Fox La BR2 ... 225 C3
Ealing W5 ... 88 A3
Palmers Green N13 ... 16 B1
Foxlands Rd RM10 ... 81 D3
Foxlees HA0 ... 65 A4
Foxley Cl E8 ... 74 A3
Foxley Ct SM2 ... 218 A1
Foxley Ho 4 E3 ... 97 D4
Foxley Rd SW9 ... 138 D5
Thornton Heath CR7 ... 204 D5
Foxley Sq 3 SW9 ... 138 D4
Foxmead Cl EN2 ... 4 B2
Foxmore St SW11 ... 267 C1
Fox Prim Sch
W8 ... 113 C5 245 A3
Fox Rd E16 ... 98 D2
Foxs Path CR4 ... 180 C1
Fox's Yd E2 ... 243 D6
Foxtail Ho TW3 ... 130 A4
Foxton KT1 ... 198 C6
Foxton Gr CR4 ... 180 B1
Foxton Ho E16 ... 122 C4
Foxwarren KT10 ... 212 D1
Foxwell Mews SE4 ... 141 A2
Foxwell St SE4 ... 141 A2
Foxwood Cl NW7 ... 27 C6
Feltham TW13 ... 150 B1
Foxwood Green Cl EN1 ... 17 C5
Foxwood Rd SE3 ... 142 D1
Foyle Rd SE3 ... 142 D6
Tottenham N17 ... 34 A2
Fradel Lo N16 ... 51 B1
Framfield Cl N12 ... 13 C1
Framfield Ct EN1 ... 17 C5
Framfield Rd N5 ... 72 D3
Ealing W7 ... 86 D1
Mitcham CR4 ... 181 A3
Framlingham Cl 2 E5 ... 74 C6
Framlingham Cres SE9 ... 188 B6
Frampton NW1 ... 71 D1
Frampton Cl SM2 ... 217 C1
Frampton Ct 3 W3 ... 111 A4
Frampton Ho NW8 ... 236 D5
Frampton Park Rd E9 ... 74 C1
Frampton Rd TW4 ... 151 A6
Frampton St
NW8 ... 92 B3 236 D5
Francemary Rd SE4 ... 163 C6
Frances Ct E17 ... 53 C3
South Norwood SE25 ... 183 D1
Frances Grey Ho 13 E1 ... 96 D2
Frances Rd E4 ... 35 C4
Frances St SE18 ... 122 B2
Franche Court Rd
SW17 ... 158 A1
Francis Ave DA7 ... 147 C3
Feltham TW13 ... 150 A1
Ilford IG1 ... 79 B6
Francis Barber Cl SW16 ... 182 B6
Franciscan Prim Sch
SW17 ... 181 A5
Franciscan Rd SW17 ... 181 A6
Francis Chichester Way
SW11 ... 137 A4 268 B1
Francis Cl 6 E14 ... 120 B2
Littleton TW17 ... 192 C5
West Ewell KT19 ... 215 B4
Francis Ct NW7 ... 27 D5
12 SE14 ... 140 D6
Ealing W5 ... 110 B6
Kingston KT1 ... 198 A5
Francis Gr SW19 ... 179 B4
Francis Ho 11 N1 ... 95 C6
NW10 ... 89 D6
Francis Holland Sch
NW1 ... 92 D3 237 D5
SW1 ... 115 A2 258 B3
Francis Rd E10 ... 76 A6
N2 ... 48 D5
Harrow HA1 ... 43 A4
Hounslow TW4 ... 128 D3
Ilford IG1 ... 79 B6
Pinner HA5 ... 40 C4
Thornton Heath CR0 ... 204 D2
Wallington SM6 ... 219 C2
Wembley UB6 ... 87 C6
Francis Snary Lo 11
SW18 ... 157 C6
Francis St E15 ... 76 C3
SW1 ... 115 C2 259 B4
Ilford IG1 ... 79 B6
Francis Terr N19 ... 71 C5
Francis Wlk N1 ... 233 C6
Francklyn Gdns HA8 ... 10 C1
Franconia Rd SW4 ... 159 D6
Frank Bailey Wlk E12 ... 78 C2
Frank Barnes Prim Sch for
Deaf Children NW3 ... 70 B1
Frank Beswick Ho SW6 ... 264 D5
Frank Burton Cl 4 SE7 ... 121 B1
Frank Dixon Cl SE21 ... 161 C3
Frank Dixon Way SE21 ... 161 C3
Frank Douglas Ct W6 ... 112 A2
Frankfurt Rd SE24 ... 161 A6
Frankham Ho 8 SE8 ... 141 C5
Frankham St SE8 ... 141 C5
Frank Ho SW8 ... 270 A4
Frankland Cl SE16 ... 118 B2
Woodford IG8 ... 37 C5
Frankland Ho 4 SW12 ... 159 B4
Frankland Rd
SW7 ... 114 B3 256 C5
Chingford E4 ... 35 C5
Franklin Bldg 6 E14 ... 119 C4
Franklin Cl N20 ... 14 A4
SE13 ... 141 D4
Kingston KT1 ... 198 C6
West Norwood SE27 ... 160 D1
Franklin Cres CR4 ... 203 C5
Franklin Ho 26 E1 ... 118 B5
NW9 ... 45 D2
Beckenham BR2 ... 208 C6
Franklin Ind Est SE20 ... 184 C2
Franklin Pas SE9 ... 144 A2
Franklin Rd DA7 ... 147 A4
Penge SE20 ... 184 C3
Walton-on-T KT12 ... 194 A3
Franklins Mews HA2 ... 64 A6
Franklin Sq SW5 ... 254 D1
Franklin's Row
SW3 ... 114 D1 257 D2
Franklin St 43 E3 ... 97 D4
N15 ... 51 C3
Franklin Way CR0 ... 204 A2
Franklyn Rd NW10 ... 67 D2
Walton-on-T KT12 ... 194 B3
Franks Ave KT3 ... 199 A5
Franks Ho TW7 ... 131 B1
Frank Slater Ho 4 IG3 ... 58 B1
Frank Soskice Ho SW6 ... 264 D5
Frank St 5 E13 ... 99 A3
Franks Wood Ave BR2,
BR5 ... 211 A4
Frankswood Ave UB7 ... 82 B1
Frank Towell Ct TW14 ... 150 A3
Frank Whymark Ho 4
SE16 ... 118 C4
Franlaw Cres N13 ... 33 A6
Fransfield Gr SE26 ... 162 B1
Frans Hals Ct E14 ... 120 B3
Franshams WD23 ... 8 C2
Frant Cl SE20 ... 184 C3
Franthorne Way SE6 ... 163 D1
Frant Rd CR7 ... 204 D4
Fraserburgh Ho 28 E3 ... 97 B5
Fraser Cl 3 E6 ... 100 A1
Fraser Ct SW11 ... 267 A2
Fraser Ho 3 SE18 ... 122 C2
40 SW8 ... 137 D3
Brentford TW8 ... 110 B1
Fraser Rd E17 ... 53 D3
Edmonton N9 ... 18 B1
Wembley UB6 ... 87 C6
Fraser Regnart Ct 12
NW5 ... 70 D3
Fraser St W4 ... 111 C1
Frating Cres IG8 ... 37 B4
Frazer Ave HA4 ... 62 C3
Frazier St SE1 ... 116 C4 251 A1
Freame Ho N21 ... 17 B5
Frean St SE16 ... 118 A3
Frearson Ho WC1 ... 233 D2
Freda Corbett Cl 9
SE15 ... 140 A5
Frederica Rd E4 ... 20 B4
Frederica St 4 N7 ... 72 B1
Frederic Ho SE7 ... 122 A3
Frederick SE16 ... 119 B5
Frederick Charrington Ho 3
E1 ... 96 C3
Frederick Cl
W2 ... 114 D6 247 C6
Cheam SM1 ... 217 B3
Frederick Cres SW9 ... 138 D5
Enfield EN3 ... 6 C3
Frederick Ct SW6 ... 135 A2
Frederick Gdns
Cheam SM1 ... 217 B3
Thornton Heath CR0 ... 204 D3
Frederick Ho UB1 ... 107 B6
Frederick Pl SE18 ... 122 D1
Frederick Rd SM1 ... 217 B3
Frederick's Pl EC2 ... 242 C1
N12 ... 30 A6
Frederick Sq 11 SE16 ... 119 A6
Frederick's Row EC1 ... 234 C2
Frederick St WC1 ... 94 B4 233 C1
Frederick Terr E8 ... 73 D1
Frederic Mews SW1 ... 248 A1
Frederic St E17 ... 53 A4
Fredora Ave UB4 ... 83 D3
Fred Wigg Twr E11 ... 76 D6
Freedom Cl E17 ... 53 A5
Freedom St SW11 ... 136 D3
Freegrove Rd N7 ... 72 A3
Freehold Ind Ctr TW4 ... 150 C6
Freeland Ct W5 ... 110 B6
Freeland Pk N3 ... 29 A1
Freeland Rd W5 ... 110 B6
Freelands Ave CR2 ... 222 D1
Freelands Gr BR1 ... 187 B2
Freelands Rd BR1 ... 187 B2
Freeling Ho NW8 ... 229 C6
Freeling St 7 N1 ... 72 B1
Freeman Cl Northolt UB5 ... 63 A1
Upper Halliford TW17 ... 193 C5
Freeman Dr KT8 ... 195 B5
Freeman Ho 13 SW2 ... 160 A4
Freeman Rd SM4 ... 202 B4
Freemans La UB3 ... 105 C6
Freemantle Ave EN3 ... 18 D6
Freemantle St
SE17 ... 117 C1 263 A2
Freemasons Rd E16 ... 99 B1
Freemason's Rd CR0 ... 205 C1
Freemens Hos 1 SW9 ... 138 B1
Freesia Cl BR6 ... 227 D3
Freethorpe Cl SE19 ... 183 C2
Freezeland Way UB10 ... 60 D2
Freke Rd SW11 ... 137 A2
Fremantle Ho 14 E1 ... 96 B3
Fremantle Rd
Belvedere DA17 ... 125 C2
Fremantle Rd *continued*
Ilford IG6 ... 57 A6
Fremont St E9 ... 96 C6
French Ordinary Ct EC3 ... 253 B6
French Pl E1 ... 243 B6
French St TW16 ... 172 C1
Frendsbury Rd SE4 ... 141 A1
Frensham Cl UB1 ... 85 B4
Frensham Ct N5 ... 73 A3
4 NW9 ... 46 A5
Mitcham CR4 ... 202 B6
Frensham Dr
New Addington CR0 ... 224 A1
Roehampton SW15 ... 156 A2
Frensham Ho 7 KT6 ... 198 A4
Frensham Rd DA15 ... 167 B2
Frensham St SE15 ... 140 A6
Frere St 6 SW11 ... 136 C3
Fresham Ho BR2 ... 208 D6
Freshfield Ave E8 ... 73 D1
Freshfield Cl SE13 ... 142 B1
Freshfield Dr N14 ... 15 B4
Freshfields CR0 ... 207 B1
Freshford St SW17,
SW18 ... 158 A1
Freshwater Cl SW17 ... 181 A4
Freshwater Ct UB1 ... 85 C4
Freshwater Rd
Dagenham RM8 ... 59 A1
Streatham SW17 ... 181 A4
Freshwell Ave RM6 ... 58 C5
Fresh Wharf Est IG11 ... 100 D6
Fresh Wharf Rd IG11 ... 100 D5
Freshwood Cl BR3 ... 185 D2
Freston Gdns EN4 ... 15 A6
Freston Pk N3 ... 29 B1
Freston Rd W10,W11 ... 112 D6
Freswick Ho 6 SE8 ... 119 A2
Freta Rd DA6 ... 169 B6
Freud Mus The★ NW3 ... 70 A2
Frewell Bldg EC1 ... 241 A4
Frewing Cl BR7 ... 188 C5
Frewin Rd SW18 ... 158 B3
Friar Mews SE27 ... 160 D1
Friar Rd UB4 ... 84 D3
Friars Ave N20 ... 30 C6
Roehampton SW15 ... 155 D1
Friars Cl SE1 ... 251 D3
Chingford E4 ... 20 A1
Ilford IG1 ... 57 B1
16 Northolt UB5 ... 84 D4
Friars Ct 5 SM6 ... 219 B4
Friars Gate Cl IG8 ... 37 A6
Friars Gdns W3 ... 89 B1
Friars La TW9 ... 153 D6
Friars Mead E14 ... 120 A3
Friars Mews SE9 ... 166 C6
Friars Place La W3 ... 111 B6
Friars Prim Sch
SE1 ... 116 D4 251 D1
Friar's Rd E6 ... 99 D6
Friars Stile Pl 9 TW10 ... 154 A5
Friars Stile Rd TW10 ... 154 A5
Friar St EC4 ... 241 D1
Friars Way W3 ... 89 B1
Friars Wlk N14 ... 15 B4
SE2 ... 124 D1
Friary Cl N12 ... 30 C5
Friary La IG8 ... 37 A6
Friary Park Ct W3 ... 89 A1
Friary Rd N12 ... 30 C6
SE15 ... 140 A5
W3 ... 89 B1
Friary Way N12 ... 30 C6
Friday Hill E4 ... 20 C1
Friday Hill E E4 ... 20 C1
Friday Hill W E4 ... 20 C2
Friday Rd CR4 ... 180 D3
Friday St EC4 ... 117 A6 252 A6
Frideswide Pl NW5 ... 71 C3
Friendly Pl SE13 ... 141 D4
Friendly St SE8 ... 141 C4
Friendly Street Mews
SE8 ... 141 C3
Friendship Wlk UB5 ... 84 D4
Friends' Rd CR0 ... 221 B5
Friend St EC1 ... 94 D4 234 C2
Friern Barnet La N20 ... 30 C6
Friern Barnet Rd N11 ... 31 A5
Friern Barnet Sch N11 ... 30 D5
Friern Bridge Ret Pk
N11 ... 31 B4
Friern Ct N20 ... 14 B1
Friern Mount Dr N20 ... 14 A4
Friern Pk N12 ... 30 B5
Friern Rd SE22 ... 162 A5
Friern Watch Ave N12 ... 30 B6
Frigate Ho 6 E14 ... 120 A2
Frigate Mews SE8 ... 141 C6
Frimley Ave SM6 ... 220 B3
Frimley Cl
New Addington CR0 ... 224 A1
Putney SW19 ... 157 A2
Frimley Cres CR0 ... 224 A1
Frimley Ct DA14 ... 190 C5
Frimley Gdns CR4 ... 202 C6
Frimley Ho CR4 ... 202 C6
Frimley Rd
Chessington KT9 ... 214 A3
Ilford IG3 ... 79 C5
Frimley Way E1 ... 96 D3
Frinstead Ho 1 W10 ... 112 D6
Frinton Ct W13 ... 87 B2
Frinton Dr IG8 ... 36 B3
Frinton Mews IG2 ... 56 C3
Frinton Rd DA14 ... 169 A2
E6 ... 99 D4
N15 ... 51 C3
Streatham SW17 ... 181 A4
Friston St SW6 ... 135 D3
Friswell Pl 1 DA7 ... 147 C1
Fritham Cl KT3 ... 199 C3
Frith Ct NW7 ... 29 A3
Frith Ho E2 ... 96 A4
NW8 ... 236 D5
Frith La NW7 ... 29 A4
Frith Manor Sch N12 ... 29 B5
Frith Rd E11 ... 76 B4
Croydon CR0 ... 221 A6
Frith St W1 ... 93 D1 239 C1
Frithville Ct W12 ... 112 C5
Frithville Gdns W12 ... 112 C5
Frizlands La RM10 ... 81 D5
Frobisher Cl HA5 ... 40 D2
Frobisher Cres TW19 ... 148 A4
Frobisher Ct NW9 ... 27 C1
1 SE10 ... 142 B6
3 W12 ... 112 C4
Belmont SM2 ... 217 B1
6 Forest Hill SE23 ... 162 B2
Frobisher Gdns TW19 ... 148 A4
Frobisher Ho 27 E1 ... 118 B5
3 Ealing W5 ... 88 A4
Frobisher Mews EN2 ... 5 B1
Frobisher Pas E14 ... 119 C5
Frobisher Pl SE14 ... 140 C4
Frobisher Rd E6 ... 100 B1
N8 ... 50 C5
Frobisher St SE10 ... 142 C6
Froebel Coll SW15 ... 155 D5
Frogley Rd SE22 ... 139 D1
Frogmore SW18 ... 157 C6
Frogmore Ave UB4 ... 83 C3
Frogmore Cl SM3 ... 217 A5
Frogmore Ct UB2 ... 107 B2
Frogmore Est NW10 ... 89 A4
Frogmore Gdns
Cheam SM3 ... 217 A4
Hayes UB4 ... 83 C3
Frogmore Ind Est N5 ... 73 A4
Frognal NW3 ... 70 A3
Frognal Ave DA14 ... 190 A4
Harrow HA1 ... 42 D5
Frognal Cl NW3 ... 70 A3
Frognal Cnr BR7 ... 189 D4
Frognal Ct NW3 ... 70 A2
Frognal Gdns NW3 ... 70 A4
Frognal La NW3 ... 69 D3
Frognal Par NW3 ... 70 A2
Frognal Pl DA14 ... 190 A5
Frognal Rise NW3 ... 70 A4
Frognal Way NW3 ... 70 A4
Froissart Rd SE9 ... 166 A6
Frome Ho SE15 ... 140 C1
Frome Rd N22 ... 50 D6
Frome St N1 ... 95 A5 235 A4
Fromondes Rd SM3 ... 217 A3
Frontenac NW10 ... 68 B1
Frontier Works N17 ... 33 C4
Froude St SW8 ... 137 B3
Fruen Rd TW14 ... 149 D4
Fryatt Rd N17 ... 33 B3
Frye Ct E3 ... 97 B4
Fryent Cl NW9 ... 44 C3
Fryent Cres NW9 ... 45 C3
Fryent Ctry Park HA3,
HA9 ... 44 C2
Fryent Fields NW9 ... 45 C3
Fryent Gr NW9 ... 45 C3
Fryent Prim Sch NW9 ... 45 A2
Fryent Way HA9,NW9 ... 44 D2
Fry Ho E6 ... 77 C1
Frying Pan Alley E1 ... 243 C3
Fry Rd E6 ... 77 D1
NW10 ... 89 D6
Fryston Ave CR0 ... 222 A6
Fuchsia St SE2 ... 124 B1
Fulbeck Dr NW9 ... 27 C2
Fulbeck Ho N7 ... 72 B2
Fulbeck Way HA2 ... 24 A1
Fulbourn 9 KT1 ... 176 C1
Fulbourne Rd E17 ... 36 A1
Fulbourne St E1 ... 96 B2
Fulbrook Rd N19 ... 71 C4
Fulcher Ho 10 N1 ... 95 C6
13 SE8 ... 119 B1
Fulford Mans N19 ... 72 A5
Fulford Rd KT19 ... 215 B1
Fulford St SE16 ... 118 B4
Fulham Broadway
SW6 ... 135 C5 265 B3
Fulham Broadway Sta
SW6 ... 135 C5 265 B4
Fulham Cl UB10 ... 83 A3
Fulham Cross Sec Sch
SW6 ... 135 A5 264 B2
Fulham Ct SW6 ... 135 C4 265 A2
Fulham High St SW6 ... 135 A3
Fulham Palace★ SW6 ... 135 A3
Fulham Palace Rd W6 ... 134 D6
Fulham SW6 ... 135 A4 264 A1
Fulham Park Gdns SW6 ... 135 B3
Fulham Park Rd SW6 ... 135 B3
Fulham Prep Sch SW6 ... 135 A3
Fulham Prim Sch
SW6 ... 135 C6 265 A5
Fulham Rd
SW10 ... 136 A6 266 B6
Fulham SW6 ... 135 B4 264 D2
Fulke Ho E5 ... 74 B5
Fullbrooks Ave KT4 ... 199 D1
Fuller Cl 3 E2 ... 96 A3
Orpington BR6 ... 227 D3
Fuller Rd RM8 ... 80 C4
Fullers Ave KT6 ... 214 B6
Fuller's Ave IG8 ... 36 D3
Fullers Cotts N22 ... 32 B3
Fullers Ho 6 SW18 ... 157 C6
Fuller's Rd E18 ... 36 D3
Fuller St NW4 ... 46 C5
Fullers Way N KT6 ... 214 B5
Fullers Way S KT9 ... 214 A5
Fuller's Wood CR0 ... 223 C3
Fuller Terr IG1 ... 79 B3
Fullerton Ct TW11 ... 175 A4
Fullerton Rd SW18 ... 158 A6
Croydon CR0 ... 205 D2
Fuller Way UB3 ... 105 D1
Fullwood Prim Sch IG6 ... 57 A5
Fullwood's Mews N1 ... 235 D2
Fulmar Ct
5 Dulwich SE21 ... 161 B2
Surbiton KT5 ... 198 B3
Fulmar Ho NW8 ... 237 B5
12 SE16 ... 118 D2
Fulmead St SW6 ... 265 D1
Fulmer Cl TW12 ... 173 A5
Fulmer Rd E16 ... 99 D2
Fulmer Way W13 ... 109 B3
Fulneck 1 E1 ... 96 C2
Fulready Rd E10 ... 54 B4
Fulstone Cl TW4 ... 129 B1
Fulthorp Rd SE3 ... 143 A3
Fulton Ct EN3 ... 7 C5
Fulton Mews W2 ... 246 A6
Fulton Rd HA9 ... 66 C5
Fulwell Ct UB1 ... 108 A6
Fulwell Park Ave TW2 ... 152 A2
Fulwell Rd TW11,TW12 ... 174 B6
Fulwell Sta TW11 ... 174 B6
Fulwood Ave HA0 ... 88 B5
Fulwood Cl UB3 ... 83 D1
Fulwood Gdns TW1 ... 153 A5
Fulwood Pl WC1 ... 240 D3
Fulwood Wlk SW19 ... 157 A3
Furber St W6 ... 112 B3
Furham Field HA5 ... 23 C3
Furley Ho 7 SE15 ... 140 A5
Furley Rd SE15 ... 140 A5
Furlong Cl SM6 ... 203 B1
Furlong Rd N7 ... 72 C2
Furmage St SW18 ... 157 D4
Furneaux Ave SE27 ... 182 D5
Furness Ho SW1 ... 258 C2
Furness Lo 4 SW14 ... 132 D1
Furness Rd NW10 ... 90 A5
SW6 ... 135 D3
Harrow HA2 ... 41 D1
Morden SM4 ... 201 D3
Furnival St EC4 ... 94 C1 241 A2
Furrow La E9 ... 74 C3
Furrows The KT12 ... 194 C1
Fursby Ave N3 ... 29 C4
Fursecroft W1 ... 237 C2
Further Acre NW9 ... 27 D1
Furtherfield Cl CR0 ... 204 C3
Further Green Rd SE6 ... 164 C3
Furze Cl WD19 ... 22 C5
Furze Ct CR0 ... 222 A6
Furzedown Dr SW17 ... 181 B5
Furzedown Prim Sch
SW17 ... 181 A4
Furzedown Rd SW17 ... 181 B5
Furzefield Cl BR7 ... 188 D4
Furzefield Rd SE3 ... 143 B5
Furzeground Way UB11 ... 105 A5
Furzeham Rd UB7 ... 104 A4
Furzehill Rd WD6 ... 11 A6
Furze Inf Sch RM6 ... 59 A3
Furzeland Ho 2 KT3 ... 199 C2
Furze Rd CR7 ... 205 A6
Furze St E3 ... 97 C2
Furzewood TW16 ... 172 A2
Fuschia Ct IG8 ... 36 C4
Fyfe Way BR1 ... 187 A1
Fyfield N4 ... 72 C6
Fyfield Cl BR2,BR3 ... 208 B5
Fyfield Ct E7 ... 77 A2
Fyfield Ho RM9 ... 80 B1
Fyfield Rd E17 ... 54 B6
6 SW9 ... 138 C2
Enfield EN1 ... 5 C2
Woodford IG8 ... 37 C3
Fynes St SW1 ... 259 C4

G

Gable Cl HA5 ... 23 C3
Gable Ct SE26 ... 184 B6
Gable Ho 12 W4 ... 111 C2
Gable Lo Hadley Wood EN4 ... 2 A5
West Wickham BR4 ... 208 A1
Gables Ave TW15 ... 170 B5
Gables Cl SE5 ... 139 C4
Lewisham SE12 ... 165 A3
Gables The BR1 ... 187 B3
N10 ... 49 A6
N12 ... 29 D5
NW3 ... 70 B6
3 SW4 ... 137 C2
Barking IG11 ... 79 A2
Ealing W13 ... 87 B1
Wembley HA9 ... 66 B5
Gabriel Cl 1 TW13 ... 173 A6
Gabriel Ho SE11 ... 260 C4
Gabrielle Cl HA9 ... 66 B5
Gabrielle Ct NW3 ... 70 B2
Gabriel St SE23 ... 163 A4
Gabriel's Wharf★ SE1 ... 251 A4
Gad Cl E13 ... 99 B4
Gaddesden Ave HA9 ... 66 B2
Gaddesden Ho EC1 ... 235 D1
Gade Cl UB3 ... 106 B5
Gadesden Rd KT19 ... 215 A2
Gadsbury Cl NW9 ... 45 D3
Gadsden Ho 6 E9 ... 74 D2
8 W10 ... 91 A3
Gadwall Cl E16 ... 99 B1
Gadwall Way SE28 ... 123 B4

Gagarin Ho SW11 ...136 B2
Gage Rd E16 ...98 C2
Gage St WC1 ...240 B4
Gainford Ho 18 E2 ...96 B4
Gainford St N1 ...94 C6 234 A6
Gainsboro Gdns UB6 ...64 C3
Gainsborough Ave E12 ...78 C3
Gainsborough Cl
Beckenham BR3 ...185 C3
Thames Ditton KT10 ...196 C1
Gainsborough Ct N12 ...29 D5
6 SE16 ...118 B1
W12 ...112 C4
Barnet EN5 ...1 D1
Bromley BR2 ...209 C5
Dulwich SE21 ...161 C2
Gainsborough Gdns
NW11 ...47 B2
NW3 ...70 B5
Edgware HA8 ...26 C1
Isleworth TW7 ...152 B6
Gainsborough Ho
5 E14 ...119 A6
N4 ...50 B1
3 NW3 ...70 A4
SW1 ...259 D3
Dagenham RM8 ...80 B5
Enfield EN1 ...18 A6
Gainsborough Lo HA1 ...42 C4
Gainsborough Mews 5
SE26 ...162 B1
Gainsborough Prim Sch
E15 ...98 C4
E9 ...75 C2
Gainsborough Rd E11 ...54 C2
E15 ...98 C4
N12 ...29 D5
W4 ...111 D2
Dagenham RM8 ...80 B5
Hayes UB4 ...83 B5
New Malden KT3 ...199 B2
Richmond TW9 ...132 B2
Gainsborough Sq DA7 ...146 D2
Gainsborough Twr 8
UB5 ...84 D5
Gainsford Rd E17 ...53 B5
Gainsford St
SE1 ...117 D4 253 D2
Gairloch Ho 2 NW1 ...71 D1
Gairloch Rd SE5 ...139 C3
Gaisford St NW5 ...71 C2
Gaitskell Ct SW11 ...136 C3
Gaitskell Ho 3 E17 ...53 D6
2 E6 ...99 D6
SE17 ...139 B6
Gaitskell Rd SE9 ...167 A3
Galahad Rd BR1 ...187 A6
Galata Rd SW13 ...134 A5
Galatea Sq SE15 ...140 B2
Galba Ct 1 TW8 ...131 D5
Galbraith St E14 ...120 A3
Galdana Ave EN5 ...2 A2
Galeborough Ave IG8 ...36 B3
Gale Cl Hampton TW12 ...173 A4
Mitcham CR4 ...202 B6
Gale Ho 10 SW2 ...160 B6
Galena Ho SE18 ...123 D1
5 W6 ...112 B2
Galena Rd W6 ...112 B2
Galen Pl WC1 ...240 B3
Galesbury Rd SW18 ...158 A5
Gales Gdns E2 ...96 B4
Gale St E3 ...97 C2
Dagenham RM9 ...80 D1
Galgate Cl 4 SW19 ...157 A3
Gallants Farm Rd EN4 ...14 C3
Galleon Cl SE16 ...118 D4
Galleon Ho 7 E14 ...120 A2
Galleons Dr IG11 ...102 A4
Gallery Ct SW10 ...266 A5
Gallery Gdns UB5 ...84 D5
Gallery Rd SE21 ...161 B3
Galleywall Prim Sch
SE16 ...118 B2
Galleywall Rd SE16 ...118 B2
Galleywall Road Trad Est 12
SE16 ...118 B2
Galleywood Ho W10 ...90 C2
Gallia Rd N5 ...72 D3
Galliard Cl N9 ...18 C5
Galliard Ct N9 ...18 A5
Galliard Rd N9 ...18 A5
Gallions Cl IG11 ...102 A4
Gallions Mount Prim Sch
SE18 ...123 D1
Gallions Rd
Greenwich SE7 ...121 A2
Newham E16 ...123 A6
Gallions Reach Sta E16 ...122 D6
Gallions View Rd SE28 ...123 C4
Gallon Cl SE7 ...121 C2
Gallop The
South Croydon CR2 ...222 B1
Sutton SM2 ...218 A1
Gallosson Rd SE18 ...123 C2
Galloway Path 5 CR0 ...221 B4
Galloway Rd W12 ...112 A5
Gallus Cl N21 ...16 B5
Gallus Sq SE3 ...143 B2
Galpin's Rd CR4,CR7 ...204 B5
Galsworthy Ave E14 ...97 A2
Ilford RM6 ...58 B2
Galsworthy Cl SE28 ...124 B5
Galsworthy Cres SE3 ...143 C4
Galsworthy Ho 4 W11 ...91 A1
Galsworthy Rd NW2 ...69 A4
Kingston KT2 ...176 D2
Galton Ho 1 SE18 ...144 B4
Galton St W10 ...91 A4
Galva Cl EN4 ...3 A1
Galvani Way CR0 ...204 B1
Galveston Ho 2 E1 ...97 A3
Galveston Rd SW15 ...157 B6
Galway Cl 28 SE16 ...118 B1
Galway Ho 6 E1 ...96 D2
EC1 ...235 B1
Galway St EC1 ...95 A4 235 B1
Galy 5 NW9 ...27 D1
Gambetta St 3 SW8 ...137 B3
Gambia St SE1 ...116 D5 251 D3
Gambler Ho EC1 ...235 B1
Gambole Rd SW17 ...180 C6
Games Ho 6 SE7 ...143 C6
Games Rd EN4 ...2 D2
Gamlen Rd SW15 ...134 D1
Gamuel Cl E17 ...53 C3
Gander Green Cres
TW12 ...173 C2
Gander Green La KT4,
SM1,SM3 ...217 B5
Gandhi Cl E17 ...53 C3
Gandolfi St 5 SE15 ...139 C6
Ganley Ct 19 SW11 ...136 B2
Gannet Ct 4 SE21 ...161 B2
Gannet Ho SE15 ...139 D4
Ganton St W1 ...239 B1
Ganton Wlk WD19 ...22 D6
Gants Hill IG2 ...56 C3
Gants Hill Cres IG2 ...56 C4
Gants Hill Sta IG2 ...56 C3
Gap Rd SW19 ...179 D5
Garage Rd W3 ...88 C1
Garbett Ho 2 SE17 ...138 D6
Garbutt Pl W1 ...238 B3
Garden Ave DA7 ...147 C2
Mitcham CR4 ...181 B3
Garden City HA8 ...26 C4
Garden Cl SE12 ...165 B1
Ashford TW15 ...171 A4
Chingford E4 ...35 C5
Hampton TW12 ...173 B5
Northolt UB5 ...85 A6
Roehampton SW15 ...156 B4
Ruislip HA4 ...61 D6
Wallington SM6 ...220 A3
Garden Cotts BR5 ...190 C1
Garden Ct EC4 ...251 A6
N12 ...29 D5
NW8 ...229 C2
10 SE9 ...166 C5
12 W4 ...111 A3
5 Belmont SM2 ...217 C1
4 Richmond TW9 ...132 B4
South Croydon CR0 ...221 D5
4 Stanmore HA7 ...25 C5
Wembley HA0 ...65 C5
Gardeners Rd CR0 ...204 D1
Garden Flats SW16 ...160 A1
Garden Ho 2 N2 ...30 B1
12 SW9 ...138 A3
Garden Hospl The NW4 ...46 C6
Gardenia Ct 1 BR3 ...185 C3
Gardenia Rd EN1 ...17 C5
Gardenia Way IG8 ...37 A5
Garden La Bromley BR1 ...187 B4
Streatham SW2 ...160 B3
Garden Lodge Ct N2 ...48 B6
Garden Mews W2 ...245 B5
Garden Pl 28 E2 ...95 D6
Garden Rd NW8 ...92 A4 229 B2
Bromley BR1 ...187 B4
Penge SE20 ...184 C2
Richmond TW9 ...132 C2
Walton-on-T KT12 ...194 B2
Garden Row
SE1 ...116 D3 261 C6
Garden Royal 13 SW15 ...156 D5
Garden St E1 ...96 D2
Gardens The N16 ...51 D2
SE22 ...140 A1
Beckenham BR3 ...186 A2
East Bedfont TW14 ...149 B5
Harrow HA1,HA2 ...42 A3
Pinner HA5 ...41 B3
Garden Suburb Jun & Inf
Schs NW11 ...47 B4
Garden Terr SW1 ...259 C2
SW7 ...247 B1
Garden Way NW10 ...67 A2
Garden Wlk EC2 ...95 C3 243 A6
Beckenham BR3 ...185 B2
Gardiner Ave NW2 ...68 C3
Gardiner Cl BR5 ...190 C1
Dagenham RM8 ...80 D4
Enfield EN3 ...18 D5
Gardiner Ct NW10 ...89 B6
Gardiner Ho 3 SE18 ...144 A5
SW11 ...267 A2
Gardner Cl E11 ...55 B3
Gardner Ct N5 ...73 A4
Hounslow TW3 ...129 C2
Tottenham N22 ...32 D1
Gardner Ho
Feltham TW13 ...151 B2
Southall UB1 ...106 D6
Gardner Ind Est SE26 ...185 B5
Gardner Pl TW14 ...150 B5
Gardner Rd E13 ...99 B3
Gardners Cl N11 ...15 A2
Gardners La EC4 ...252 A6
Gardnor Mans 10 NW3 ...70 A4
Gardnor Rd NW3 ...70 B4
Gard St EC1 ...234 D2
Garendon Gdns SM4 ...201 D2
Garendon Rd SM4 ...201 D2
Garenne Ct 10 E4 ...20 A3
Gareth Cl KT4 ...216 D6
Gareth Ct SW16 ...159 D1
Gareth Gr BR1 ...187 A6
Garfield Edmonton N9 ...18 B3
Garfield *continued*
Enfield EN2 ...17 B6
Garfield Jun Sch SW19 ...180 A4
Garfield Prim Sch N11 ...31 C5
Garfield Rd E13 ...98 D3
SW11 ...137 A2
Chingford E4 ...20 B3
Enfield EN3 ...6 C1
2 Twickenham TW1 ...153 A3
Wimbledon SW19 ...180 A4
Garford St E14 ...119 C6
Garganey Ct NW10 ...67 B2
Gargany Wlk SE28 ...124 C6
Garibaldi St SE18 ...123 C2
Garland Dr TW3 ...130 A3
Garland Ho N16 ...73 B5
Garland Rd SE18 ...145 B5
Stanmore HA7 ...26 A2
Garlands Ct 2 CR0 ...221 B4
Garlands The HA1 ...42 D2
Garlick Hill EC4 ...117 A6 252 B6
Garlies Rd SE23 ...163 A1
Garlinge Ho 12 SW9 ...138 C4
Garlinge Rd NW2 ...69 B2
Garman Cl N18 ...33 B5
Garman Rd N17 ...34 C3
Garnault Mews EC1 ...234 B1
Garnault Pl EC1 ...234 B1
Garnault Rd EN1 ...5 D5
Garner Cl RM8 ...58 D1
Garner Rd E17 ...36 A2
Garner St E2 ...96 A5
Garnet Ho KT4 ...199 B1
Garnet Rd NW10 ...67 C2
South Norwood CR7 ...205 B5
Garnet St E1 ...118 C6
Garnett Cl SE9 ...144 B2
Garnett Ho 5 NW3 ...70 D3
Garnett Rd NW3 ...70 D3
Garnett Way E17 ...35 A2
Garnet Wlk 8 E6 ...100 A2
Garnham Cl 2 N16 ...73 D6
Garnham St 1 N16 ...73 D6
Garnies Cl SE15 ...139 D5
Garrad's Rd SW16 ...159 D1
Garrard Cl DA7 ...147 C2
Chislehurst BR7 ...188 D5
Garrard Wlk NW10 ...67 C2
Garratt Cl CR0 ...220 A4
Garratt Ho 8 N16 ...51 C1
Garratt La
Upper Tooting SW17,
SW18 ...180 C6
Wandsworth SW18 ...157 D3
Garratt Park Sch SW18 ...158 A1
Garratt Rd HA8 ...26 C3
Garratts Rd WD23 ...8 A4
Garratt Terr SW17 ...180 C6
Garraway Ct SW13 ...134 C5
Garraway Ho SE21 ...161 D1
Garrett Cl W3 ...89 B2
Garrett Ho W12 ...90 B1
Teddington TW11 ...175 B4
Garrett St EC1 ...95 A3 242 B6
Garrick Ave NW11 ...47 A3
Garrick Cl SW18 ...136 A1
Ealing W5 ...88 A3
1 Richmond TW9 ...153 D6
Garrick Cres CR0 ...221 C6
Garrick Ct HA8 ...26 B6
Garrick Dr NW4 ...28 C1
SE18 ...123 B3
Garrick Gdns KT8 ...195 C6
Garrick Ho W1 ...248 C3
Chiswick W4 ...133 C6
2 Kingston KT1 ...198 A5
7 Streatham SW16 ...181 C5
Garrick Ind Est NW9 ...45 D4
Garrick Pk NW4 ...28 D1
Garrick Rd NW9 ...45 D3
Greenford UB6 ...85 D3
Richmond TW9 ...132 C3
Garrick's Ait KT8 ...174 A1
Garricks Ho KT1 ...175 D1
Garrick St WC2 ...116 A6 250 A6
Garrick Way NW4 ...46 D5
Garrick Yd WC2 ...250 A6
Garrison Cl SE18 ...144 C5
Hounslow TW4 ...151 B6
Garrison La KT9 ...214 A1
Garrowsfield EN5 ...13 B6
Garsdale Cl N11 ...31 A4
Garsdale Terr SW5 ...254 D2
Garside Cl SE28 ...123 B3
Hampton TW12 ...173 D4
Garsington Mews SE4 ...141 B2
Garson Ho W2 ...246 C6
Garston Ho 6 N1 ...72 D1
Garter Way SE16 ...118 D4
Garth Cl Kingston KT2 ...176 B5
Ruislip HA4 ...40 D1
West Barnes SM4 ...200 D2
Garth Ct Chiswick W4 ...133 B6
Harrow HA1 ...42 D3
Garth Ho NW2 ...69 B6
Garthland Dr EN5 ...12 C6
Garth Mews W5 ...88 A3
Garthorne Rd SE23 ...162 D4
Garth Rd NW2 ...69 B6
8 W4 ...111 B1
Kingston KT2 ...176 B5
West Barnes SM4 ...200 D2
Garthside TW10 ...176 A5
Garth The N12 ...29 D5
Hampton TW12 ...173 D4
Harrow HA3 ...44 B3
Garthway N12 ...30 C4
Gartmoor Gdns SW19 ...157 B3
Gartmore Rd IG3 ...79 D6
Garton Ho 6 N6 ...49 D2
Garton Pl SW18 ...158 A5
Gartons Cl EN3 ...6 C1
Gartons Way SW11 ...136 A2
Garvary Rd E16 ...99 B1
Garway Rd W2 ...91 D1
Gascoigne Gdns IG8 ...36 C3
Gascoigne Pl 17 E2 ...95 D4
Gascoigne Prim Sch
IG11 ...101 A6
Gascoigne Rd IG11 ...101 A5
Gascony Ave NW6 ...69 C1
Gascoyne Ho 2 E9 ...74 D1
Gascoyne Rd E9 ...74 D1
Gaselee St E14 ...120 A6
Gasholder Pl
SE11 ...116 B1 260 D1
Gaskarth Rd HA8 ...27 A1
Balham SW12 ...159 B5
Gaskell Rd N6 ...48 D3
Gaskell St SW4 ...138 A3
Gaskin Ho N16 ...73 B5
Gaskin St N1 ...94 D6 234 C6
Gaspar Cl SW7 ...255 D4
Gaspar Mews SW5 ...255 D4
Gassiot Rd SW17 ...180 D6
Gassiot Way SM1 ...218 B5
Gasson Ho 24 SE14 ...140 D6
Gastein Rd W6 ...134 D6
Gastigny Ho EC1 ...235 B1
Gaston Bell Cl TW9 ...132 B2
Gaston Bridge Rd TW17 ...193 B3
Gaston Gate SW8 ...270 C2
Gaston Rd CR4 ...203 A6
Gaston Way TW17 ...193 B4
Gataker Ho 5 SE16 ...118 B3
Gataker St 6 SE16 ...118 B3
Gatcliff Cl SW1 ...258 B1
Gatcombe Ct BR3 ...185 C3
Gatcombe Ho 20 SE22 ...139 C2
Gatcombe Mews W5 ...110 B6
Gatcombe Rd 9 E16 ...121 A5
N19 ...71 D5
Gatcombe Way EN4 ...2 D2
Gateacre Ct DA14 ...190 B6
Gatebeck Ho 21 SE22 ...139 C2
Gate End HA6 ...22 A3
Gatefield Ct SE15 ...140 A2
Gateforth St NW8 ...237 A5
Gate Hill Ct W11 ...244 D4
Gatehill Rd HA6 ...22 A3
Gate Ho 4 KT6 ...198 A1
Gatehouse Cl KT2 ...177 A3
Gatehouse Sch E2 ...96 D5
Gatehouse Sq SE1 ...252 B4
Gateley Ho 6 SE4 ...140 D1
Gateley Rd SW9 ...138 B2
Gate Mews SW7 ...114 C4 247 B1
Gater Dr EN2 ...5 B4
Gates 4 NW9 ...27 D1
Gatesborough St EC2 ...243 A6
Gates Ct SE17 ...262 A2
Gatesden WC1 ...233 B1
Gates Green Rd
BR2,BR4 ...225 A4
Coney Hall BR4 ...224 D5
Gateside Rd SW17 ...158 D1
Gate St WC2 ...94 B1 240 C2
Gatestone Ct 10 SE19 ...183 C4
Gatestone Rd SE19 ...183 C4
Gateway SE17 ...139 A6
Gateway Mews 4 E8 ...73 D3
Gateway Prim Sch
NW8 ...92 B3 236 D6
Gateway Rd E10 ...75 D5
Gateway Ret Pk E6 ...100 D3
Gateways KT6 ...198 A4
Gateways Ct SM6 ...219 B3
Gateways The SW3 ...257 B3
Richmond TW9 ...131 D1
Gateway Trad Est NW10 ...89 D4
Gatfield Gr TW13 ...151 C2
Gatfield Ho TW13 ...151 C2
Gathorne Rd N22 ...32 C2
Gathorne St 19 E2 ...96 D5
Gatley Ave KT19 ...214 D3
Gatliff Rd SW1 ...115 B1 258 C1
Gatling Rd SE18,SE2 ...124 A1
Gatonby St SE15 ...139 D4
Gatting Cl HA8 ...27 A3
Gatting Way UB8 ...60 A2
Gatton Rd SW17 ...180 C6
Gattons Way DA14 ...191 B6
Gatward Cl N21 ...16 D5
Gatward Gn N9 ...17 D2
Gatwick Ho 3 E14 ...97 B1
Gatwick Rd SW18 ...157 B4
Gauden Cl SW4 ...137 D2
Gauden Rd SW4 ...137 D2
Gaugin Ct 13 SE16 ...118 B1
Gauntlet 1 NW9 ...27 D1
Gauntlet Cl UB5 ...63 A1
Gauntlett Ct HA0 ...65 B3
Gauntlett Rd SM1 ...218 B3
Gaunt St SE1 ...262 A6
Gautrey Rd SE15 ...140 C3
Gautrey Sq 5 E6 ...100 B1
Gavel St SE17 ...262 D4
Gaven Ho N17 ...33 C1
Gavestone Cres SE12 ...165 B4
Gavestone Rd SE12 ...165 B4
Gaviller Pl 4 E5 ...74 B4
Gavina Cl SM4 ...202 C4
Gavin Ho SE18 ...123 C2
Gavrelle Ho EC1 ...242 C5
Gawber St E2 ...96 C4
Gawsworth Cl E15 ...76 D3
Gawthorne Ave NW7 ...29 A5
Gawthorne Ct E3 ...97 C5
Gay Cl NW2 ...68 B3
Gaydon Ho W2 ...91 D2
Gaydon La NW9 ...27 C2
Gayfere Rd Redbridge IG5 ...56 B6
Stoneleigh KT17 ...216 A3
Gayfere St SW1 ...116 A3 260 A5
Gayford Rd W12 ...111 D4
Gay Ho N16 ...73 C3
Gayhurst SE17 ...139 B6
Gayhurst Ct 9 UB5 ...84 C4
Gayhurst Ho NW8 ...237 B6
Gayhurst Rd E8 ...74 A1
Gayhurst Sch E8 ...74 A1
Gaylor Rd UB5 ...63 B3
Gaymead NW8 ...91 D6
Gaynesford Rd
Forest Hill SE23 ...162 D2
Wallington SM5 ...218 D1
Gay Rd E15 ...98 B5
Gaysham Ave IG2 ...56 D4
Gaysham Hall IG5 ...56 D6
Gaysley Ho SE11 ...261 A3
Gay St SW15 ...134 D2
Gayton Cres NW3 ...70 B4
Gayton Ct 3 Harrow HA1 ...42 D3
New Malden KT3 ...199 D4
Gayton Ho E3 ...97 C3
Gayton Rd NW3 ...70 B4
SE2 ...124 C3
Harrow HA1 ...43 A3
Gayville Rd SW11 ...158 D5
Gaywood Cl SW2 ...160 C3
Gaywood Rd E17 ...53 C6
Gaywood St SE1 ...261 D5
Gaza St SE17 ...116 D1 261 C1
Gazelle Ho 10 E14 ...98 B1
Gean Ct 3 E11 ...76 B4
Gearies Inf Sch IG2 ...56 D4
Gearies Jun Sch IG2 ...56 D4
Geariesville Gdns IG6 ...56 D5
Geary Ho N7 ...72 B3
Geary Rd NW10 ...68 A3
Geary St N7 ...72 B3
GEC Est HA9 ...65 D6
Geddes Pl 3 DA7 ...147 C1
Gedeney Rd N17 ...33 A2
Gedge Ct CR4 ...202 C5
Gedling Ho SE22 ...139 D2
Gedling Pl SE1 ...263 D6
Geere Rd E15 ...98 D6
Gees Ct W1 ...238 B1
Gee St EC1 ...95 A3 242 A6
Geffrey's Ct SE9 ...166 A1
Geffrye Ct N1 ...95 C5
Geffrye Mus★ E2 ...95 D5
Geffrye St E2 ...95 D5
Geldart Rd SE15 ...140 B5
Geldeston Rd E5 ...74 A6
Gellatly Rd SE14 ...140 D3
Gell Cl UB10 ...60 B5
Gemini Bsns Ctr E16 ...98 B3
Gemini Gr UB5 ...85 A4
Gemma Ho SW15 ...134 D1
Gemma Ct BR3 ...185 B1
General Gordon Pl
SE18 ...122 D2
Generals Wlk The EN3 ...7 A6
General Wolfe Rd SE10 ...142 B4
Genesis Cl TW19 ...148 B3
Genesta Rd SE18 ...145 A6
Geneva Cl TW17 ...171 C1
Geneva Ct N16 ...51 B1
1 Putney SW15 ...156 D6
Geneva Dr SW9 ...138 C1
Geneva Gdns RM6 ...59 A4
Geneva Rd Kingston KT1 ...198 A5
Thornton Heath CR7 ...205 A4
Genever Cl E4 ...35 C5
Genista Rd N18 ...34 B5
Genoa Ave SW15 ...156 C6
Genoa Ho 19 E1 ...96 D3
Genoa Rd SE20 ...184 C2
Genotin Rd EN1 ...5 B2
Genotin Terr EN1 ...5 B2
Gentleman's Row EN2 ...5 A2
Gentry Gdns E13 ...99 A4
Geoffrey Chaucer Tech Coll
SE1 ...117 B3 262 B5
Geoffrey Cl SE5 ...139 A3
Geoffrey Ct SE4 ...141 B2
Geoffrey Gdns E6 ...100 A5
Geoffrey Ho SE1 ...262 D6
Geoffrey Jones Ct NW10 ...90 A6
Geoffrey Rd SE4 ...141 B2
Geological Mus★
SW7 ...114 B3 256 D5
George Akass Ho 3
SE18 ...123 A1
George Beard Rd 10
SE8 ...119 B2
George Beare Lo 9
SW4 ...159 C6
George Belt Ho 8 E2 ...96 D4
George Comberton Wlk 3
E12 ...78 C3
George Cres N10 ...31 A3
George Ct WC2 ...250 B5
Buckhurst Hill IG9 ...21 D2
George Downing Est
N16 ...73 D6
George Eliot Ho SW1 ...259 B3
George Eliot Jun & Inf Sch
NW8 ...92 B6 229 C6
George Elliot Ho SE17 ...262 A2
George Elliston Ho 12
SE1 ...118 A1
George Eyre Ho NW8 ...229 D3
George Gange Way HA3 ...42 D6
George Green's Sec Sch
E14 ...120 A1
George Groves Rd SE20 ...184 A2
George Ho 8 SE26 ...184 B5
George Inn Yd SE1 ...252 C3
George La SE13 ...164 A5
Hayes BR2 ...209 B1
Wanstead E18 ...55 B6
Woodford E18 ...37 A1
George Lansbury Ho
7 E3 ...97 B4
NW10 ...67 C1
Wood Green N22 ...32 C2
George Lashwood Ct 12
SW9 ...138 B1
George Leybourne Ho 9
E1 ...118 A6
George Lindgren Ho
SW6 ...264 D4
George Loveless Ho 4
E2 ...95 D4
George Lovell Dr EN3 ...7 C6
George Mews NW1 ...232 A1
George Mitchell Com Sch
E10 ...53 D1
George Orwell Sch N4 ...50 B1
George Parr Ho N21 ...16 D4
George Peabody Ct
NW1 ...237 A4
George Rd Chingford E4 ...35 C4
Kingston KT2 ...177 A3
New Malden KT3 ...199 D4
George Row SE16 ...118 A4
Georges Mead WD6 ...10 A5
George Spicer Prim Sch
EN1 ...5 D2
George Sq SW19 ...201 C6
George's Rd N7 ...72 B3
George's Sq SW6 ...264 D6
George St 6 E16 ...98 D1
W1 ...92 D1 237 D2
Barking IG11 ...79 A1
Ealing W7 ...108 C5
Hounslow TW3,TW5 ...129 B3
Richmond TW10 ...153 D6
Southall UB2 ...107 A2
South Croydon CR0 ...221 B6
George Tingle Ho SE1 ...263 D6
George Tomlinson Prim Sch
E11 ...54 C1
Georgetown Cl 4 SE19 ...183 C5
Georgette Pl SE10 ...142 A5
George Vale Ho 32 E2 ...96 A5
George V Ave HA2,HA5 ...41 C6
Georgeville Gdns IG6 ...56 D5
George V Way UB6 ...87 B6
George Walter Ho 7
SE16 ...118 C2
George Wyver Cl SW18 ...157 A4
George Yd EC3 ...242 D1
W1 ...115 A6 248 B6
Georgiana St
NW1 ...93 C6 232 B6
Georgian Cl Hayes BR2 ...209 B1
Ickenham UB10 ...60 A4
Stanmore HA7 ...25 A3
Georgian Ct 19 E9 ...96 C6
3 NW4 ...46 B4
Croydon CR0 ...205 B1
Wembley HA9 ...66 D2
Georgian Lo HA5 ...40 B4
Georgian Way HA1 ...64 B6
Georgia Rd
New Malden KT3 ...199 A5
South Norwood CR7 ...182 D2
Georgina Ct 5 TW1 ...153 C5
Georgina Gdns 10 E2 ...95 D4
Geraint Rd BR1 ...187 A6
Geraldine Ct 6 NW9 ...46 A5
Geraldine Rd SW18 ...158 A6
Brentford W4 ...132 C6
Geraldine St SE11 ...261 C5
Gerald Mews SW1 ...258 B4
Gerald Rd E16 ...98 D3
SW1 ...115 A2 258 B4
Dagenham RM8 ...59 B1
Gerard Ave TW4 ...151 C4
Gerard Ct NW2 ...68 D3
Gerard Rd Barnes SW13 ...133 D4
Harrow HA1 ...43 A3
Gerards Cl SE16 ...118 C1
Gerboa Ct 6 E4 ...36 B5
Gerda Rd SE9 ...167 A2
Germander Way E15 ...98 C4
Gernigan Ho SW18 ...158 B5
Gernon Rd E3 ...97 A5
Geron Way NW2 ...68 C6
Gerrard Gdns HA5 ...40 A4
Gerrard Ho 5 SE14 ...140 D5
Gerrard Pl W1 ...249 D6
Gerrard Rd N1 ...94 D5 234 D4
Gerrards Cl N14 ...15 C6
Gerrard's Ct W5 ...109 D3
Gerrard St W1 ...115 D6 249 D6
Gerridge Ct SE1 ...261 B6
Gerridge St SE1 ...116 C3 261 B6
Gerry Raffles Sq E15 ...76 B2
Gertrude Rd DA17 ...125 C2
Gertrude St
SW10 ...136 A6 266 B5
Gervase Cl HA9 ...67 A5
Gervase Rd HA8 ...27 B2
Gervase St SE15 ...140 B5
Ghent St SE6 ...163 C2
Ghent Way E8 ...73 D2
Giant Arches Rd SE24 ...161 A5
Giant Tree Hill WD23 ...8 B3
Gibbards Cott 1 IG11 ...79 D1
Gibbfield Cl RM6 ...59 A6
Gibbings Ho SE1 ...251 D1

Gibbins Rd E15 76 A1
Gibbon Ho NW8 236 D5
Gibbon Rd SE15 140 C3
W3 111 C6
Kingston KT2 176 A3
Gibbons Rd NW10 67 C2
Gibbon's Rents SE1 253 A3
Gibbon Wlk SW15 134 A1
Gibbs Ave SE19 183 B5
Gibbs Cl SE19 183 B5
Gibbs Gn HA8 27 A6
W14 113 B1 254 D2
Gibbs Green Sch
W14 113 B1 254 D2
Gibbs Ho
6 Balham SW12 159 B4
2 Bromley BR1 186 D2
Gibbs Rd N18 34 C6
Gibbs Sq SE19 183 B5
Gibraltar Ho NW10 89 C5
Gibraltar Wlk 28 E2 95 D4
Gibson Bsns Ctr N17 33 D3
Gibson Cl E1 96 C3
Chessington KT9 213 C3
Isleworth TW7 130 B2
Southgate N21 16 C5
Gibson Ct KT10 212 D5
Gibson Gdns N16 73 D6
Gibson Ho
South Croydon CR2 221 A2
Sutton SM1 217 C4
Gibson Rd SE11 260 D3
Dagenham RM8 58 C1
Ickenham UB10 60 B4
Sutton SM1 217 D3
Gibson's Hill
South Norwood SW16 182 C3
South Norwood SW16 182 C4
Gibson Sq N1 94 C6 234 B6
Gibson St SE10 120 C1
Gideon Cl DA17 125 D2
Gideon Mews W5 109 D4
Gideon Rd SW11 137 A2
Giesbach Rd N19 71 D6
Giffard Rd N18 33 C4
Giffen Square Mkt SE8 141 C5
Giffin St SE8 141 C5
Gifford Gdns W7 86 C2
Gifford Ho SE10 120 B1
5 SW4 137 D1
Gifford Prim Sch UB5 85 B5
Gifford St N1 72 A1
Gift La E15 98 D6
Giggs Hill BR5 190 A2
Giggs Hill Gdns KT7 197 A1
Giggs Hill Rd KT7 197 A2
Gilbert Cl SE18 144 B4
1 Merton SW19 179 D2
Gilbert Ct W5 88 B1
Gilbert Gr HA8 27 B2
Gilbert Ho 5 E17 54 A6
5 E2 96 D4
EC2 242 B3
SE8 141 C6
SW1 258 D1
SW8 270 A4
Gilbert Pl WC1 94 A2 240 A3
Gilbert Rd BR1 187 A3
SE11 116 C2 261 B4
Belvedere DA17 125 C3
Merton SW19 180 A3
Pinner HA5 40 D5
Gilbert Scott Com Inf Sch
CR2 223 A1
Gilbert Scott Com Jun Sch
CR2 223 A1
Gilbert Sheldon Ho W2 236 D4
Gilbertson Ho 4 E14 119 C3
Gilbert St E15 76 C4
W1 93 A1 238 B1
Enfield EN3 6 C6
Hounslow TW3 130 A2
Gilbey Cl UB10 60 D4
Gilbey Rd SW17 180 C5
Gilbeys Yd NW1 71 A1
Gilbourne Rd SE18 145 D6
Gilby Ho 5 E9 74 D2
Gilda Ave EN3 19 A6
Gilda Cres N16 52 A1
Gilda Ct NW7 28 A2
Gildea Cl HA5 23 C3
Gildea St W1 238 D3
Gilden Cres NW5 71 A3
Gildersome St SE18 144 C6
Gilders Rd KT9 214 B2
Giles Coppice SE19 183 D6
Giles Ho 5 SE16 118 A3
W11 91 C1
Gilesmead SE5 139 B4
Gilfrid Cl UB8 82 D1
Gilkes Cres SE21 161 C5
Gilkes Pl SE21 161 C5
Gillam Ho 6 SE16 118 C2
Gillan Ct SE12 165 B1
Gillan Gn WD23 8 A2
Gillards Mews 6 E17 53 C5
Gillards Way E17 53 C5
Gill Ave E16 99 A1
Gill Ct SE18 123 A2
Gillender St E3 98 A3
Gillespie Prim Sch N5 72 D5
Gillespie Rd N4,N5 72 D5
Gillett Ave E6 100 A5
Gillette Cnr TW7 131 A5
Gillett Ho N8 50 A6
Gillett Pl 27 E8 73 C3
Gillett Rd CR7 205 B5
Gillett St E8,N16 73 C3
Gillfoot NW1 232 A3
Gillham Terr N17 34 A3
Gillian Ho HA3 24 C4
Gillian Park Rd SM3 201 B1
Gillian St SE13 163 D6
Gillies Ct DA14 189 C6
Gillies Ho NW6 70 B1
Gilling Ct 5 NW3 70 C2
Gillingham Mews SW1 259 A4
Gillingham Rd NW2 69 A5
Gillingham Row SW1 259 A4
Gillingham St
SW1 115 C2 259 A4
Gillings Ct EN5 1 A1
Gillison Wlk 19 SE16 118 A3
Gillman Dr E15 98 D6
Gillman Ho 23 E2 96 A5
Gillray Ho SW10 266 C5
Gill St E14 119 B6
Gillum Cl EN4 14 D3
Gilmore Cl UB10 60 C5
Gilmore Cres TW15 170 C4
Gilmore Ct N11 30 D5
Gilmore Ho SW4 136 D1
Gilmore Rd SE13 142 B1
Gilpin Ave SW14 133 B1
Gilpin Cl CR4 180 C1
W1 236 B3
Gilpin Cres Edmonton N18 33 D5
Twickenham TW2 151 D4
Gilpin Ho 9 Edmonton N9 18 A1
New Malden KT3 199 C4
Gilpin Rd E5 75 A4
Gilpin Way UB3 127 B5
Gilray Ho W2 246 C6
Gilsland Rd CR7 205 B5
Gilstead Ho IG11 102 B5
Gilstead Rd SW6 135 D3
Gilston Rd
SW10 114 A1 256 B1
Gilton Rd SE6 164 C1
Giltspur St EC1 94 D1 241 D2
Gilwell Cl E4 7 D1
Gilwell Ct 8 E5 74 B4
Gippeswyck Cl HA5 22 D2
Gipsy Cnr W3 89 B2
Gipsy Hill SE19 183 C5
Gipsy Hill Sta SE19 183 C5
Gipsy La SW15 134 B2
Gipsy Moth IV★ SE10 142 A6
Gipsy Rd Bexley DA16 146 D3
West Norwood SE27 183 B6
Gipsy Road Gdns SE27 183 A6
Giralda Cl E16 99 D2
Giraud St E14 97 D1
Girdlers Rd W14 112 D2
Girdlestone Wlk N19 71 C6
Girdwood Rd SW18,
SW19 157 A4
Girling Ho 9 N1 95 C6
Girling Way TW14 128 A2
Gironde Rd SW6 135 B5 264 D3
Girtin Ho 5 UB5 84 D5
Girton Ave NW9 44 C6
Girton Cl UB5 64 A2
Girton Gdns CR0 223 C5
Girton Ho SW15 156 D5
Girton Rd
Forest Hill SE26 184 D5
Northolt UB5 64 A2
Girton Villas 6 W10 90 D1
Gisbourne Cl SM6 219 D5
Gisburn Mans N8 50 B5
Gisburn Rd N8 50 B5
Gissing Wlk N1 72 C1
Gistelword Ho 9 TW7 131 A2
Gittens Cl BR1 186 D6
Given-Wilson Wlk E13 98 D5
Glacier Way HA0 87 D5
Gladbeck Way EN2 4 D1
Gladding Rd E12 77 D4
Glade Cl KT6 213 D6
Glade Gdns CR0 207 A2
Glade La UB2 107 D4
Gladeside Croydon CR0 206 D3
Southgate N21 16 B4
Gladeside Cl KT9 213 D1
Gladesmore Com Sch
N15 52 A4
Gladesmore Rd N15 51 D3
Glades Sh Ctr The BR1 187 A1
Gladeswood Rd DA17 125 D2
Glade The BR1 187 D1
SE7 143 C5
Croydon CR0 206 D3
Enfield EN2 4 C3
Southgate N21 16 B4
Stoneleigh KT17 216 A2
West Wickham BR4 223 D5
Woodford IG8 21 B1
Gladiator St SE23 163 A4
Glading Terr N16 73 D5
Gladioli Cl 6 TW12 173 C4
Gladsdale Dr HA5 40 B5
Gladsmuir Rd N19 49 C1
Barnet EN5 1 A3
Gladstone Ave E12 78 A1
Feltham TW14 150 B5
Tottenham N22 32 D1
Twickenham TW2 152 B4
Gladstone Ct NW2 68 B3
SW1 259 D3
5 Merton SW19 179 C3
Gladstone Gdns TW3 130 A4
Gladstone Ho 14 E14 97 C1
Gladstone Mews
3 Penge SE20 184 C3
Wood Green N22 32 C1
Gladstone Par NW2 68 C5
Gladstone Park Gdns
NW2 68 B5
Gladstone Park Sch
NW10 68 B3
Gladstone Pl KT8 196 C4
Gladstone Rd BR6 227 A3
W4 111 B3
Buckhurst Hill IG9 21 C3
Kingston KT1 198 C6
Merton SW19 179 C3
Southall UB2 107 A4
Surbiton KT6 214 A6
Thornton Heath CR0 205 B2
Gladstone St SE1 261 C6
Gladstone Terr
SW8 137 B4 268 D2
Gladstone Way HA3 42 C6
Gladwell Rd BR1 187 A4
N8 50 B3
Gladwin Ho NW1 232 B3
Gladwyn Rd SW15 134 D2
Gladys Dimson Ho E7 76 D3
Gladys Rd NW6 69 C1
Glaisher St 2 SE10 142 A5
SE8 141 D6
Glamis Cres UB3 105 A3
Glamis Ct W3 110 D4
Glamis Est 3 E1 118 D6
Glamis Pl E1 118 C6
Glamis Rd E1 118 C6
Glamis Way UB5 64 A2
Glamorgan Cl CR4,SW16 204 A6
Glamorgan Ct 4 W7 86 D2
Glamorgan Rd KT1 175 C3
Glanfield Rd BR3 207 B5
Glanleam Rd HA7 25 D6
Glanville Ho 4 SW12 159 C4
Glanville Rd SW2 160 A6
Bromley BR2 209 B6
Glasbrook Ave TW2 151 B3
Glasbrook Rd SE9 165 D4
Glasbury Ho 5 SW9 138 B1
Glaserton Rd N16 51 C2
Glasford St SW17 180 D4
Glasfryn Ct HA2 64 B6
Glasgow Ho W9 91 D5
Glasgow Rd E13 99 B5
Edmonton N18 34 B5
Glasgow Terr
SW1 115 C1 259 A1
Glasse Cl W13 109 A6
Glasshill St SE1 116 D4 251 D2
Glasshouse Fields E1 118 D6
Glasshouse St
W1 115 C6 249 B5
Glasshouse Wlk
SE11 116 B1 260 C2
Glasshouse Yd EC1 242 A5
Glasslyn Rd N8 49 D4
Glassmill La BR2 186 D1
Glass St 4 E2 96 B3
Glass Yd SE18 122 C3
Glastonbury Ave IG8 37 D4
Glastonbury Ct 12 SE14 140 C5
1 Ealing W13 109 A5
Glastonbury Ho SW1 258 C2
Glastonbury Pl 25 E1 96 C1
Glastonbury Rd
Edmonton N9 18 A3
Morden SM4 201 C2
Glastonbury St NW6 69 B3
Glaston Ct W5 109 D5
Glaucus St E3 97 D2
Glazbury Rd
W14 113 A1 254 B2
Glazebrook Cl SE21 161 B2
Glazebrook Rd TW11 174 D3
Glebe Ave Enfield EN2 4 D2
Harrow HA3 44 A6
Mitcham CR4 180 C1
Ruislip HA4 62 B2
Uxbridge UB10 61 A4
Woodford IG8 37 A4
Glebe Cl 1 W4 111 C1
Uxbridge UB10 61 A4
Glebe Cotts TW13 151 C1
Glebe Cres NW4 46 C5
Harrow HA3 44 A6
Glebe Ct SE3 142 C2
Ealing W5 109 D5
Ealing W7 108 B6
Mitcham CR4 202 D6
Palmers Green N13 16 C1
Stanmore HA7 25 C5
Glebe Fst & Mid Sch
HA3 44 A5
Glebe Gdns KT3 199 C2
Glebe Ho 8 SE16 118 B3
7 SE18 122 C2
Feltham TW13 151 C1
Glebe House Dr BR2 209 B1
Glebehyrst SE19 183 C6
Glebe La Barnet EN5 12 A5
Harrow HA3 44 A5
Glebeland Gdns TW17 193 A3
Glebelands E10 75 D6
East Molesey KT8 195 D5
Glebelands Ave Ilford IG2 57 B2
Woodford E18 37 A1
Glebelands Cl SE5 139 C2
Glebelands Rd TW14 150 A4
Glebe Path CR4 202 D6
Glebe Pl SW3 136 C6 267 A6
Glebe Prim Sch UB10 61 B4
Glebe Rd BR1 187 A2
E8 73 D1
N3 30 A2
N8 50 B5
NW10 68 A2
Barnes SW13 134 A3
Glebe Rd continued
Belmont SM2 217 A1
Dagenham RM10 81 D2
Hayes UB3 105 D5
Stanmore HA7 25 C5
Wallington SM5 218 D2
Glebe Sch BR4 224 B6
Glebe Side TW1 152 D5
Glebe Sq CR4 202 D6
Glebe St W4 111 C1
Glebe Terr 15 E3 97 D4
Glebe The SE3 142 C2
Chislehurst BR7 189 A2
New Malden KT4 199 D1
Streatham SW16 181 D6
West Drayton UB7 104 B2
Glebeway IG8 37 C5
Glebe Way
Feltham TW13 151 C1
West Wickham BR4 224 B6
Gledhow Gdns SW5 256 A3
Gledstanes Rd
W14 113 A1 254 B1
Gledwood Ave UB4 84 A2
Gledwood Cres UB4 83 D2
Gledwood Ct UB4 83 D2
Gledwood Dr UB4 83 D2
Gledwood Gdns UB4 84 A2
Gleed Ave WD23 8 B2
Gleeson Dr BR6 227 D4
Glegg Pl 3 SW15 134 D1
Glenaffric Ave E14 120 B2
Glen Albyn Rd SW19 156 D2
Glenalla Rd HA4 39 D2
Glenalmond Ho
Ashford TW15 148 A1
2 Putney SW15 156 D5
Glenalmond Rd HA3 44 A5
Glenalvon Way 5 SE7 122 A2
Glena Mount SM1 218 A4
Glenarm Coll IG1 78 D6
Glenarm Rd E5 74 D4
Glen Ave TW15 170 C6
Glenavon Cl KT10 213 A1
Glenavon Ct KT4 216 B6
Glenavon Lo 4 E18 55 A6
Glenavon Rd E15 76 C1
Glenbarr Cl SE9 144 D2
Glenbow Rd BR1 186 C5
Glenbrook Inf Sch SW4 159 D5
Glenbrook Jun Sch
SW4 159 D5
Glenbrook N EN2 4 B1
Glenbrook Rd NW6 69 C3
Glenbrook S EN2 4 B1
Glenbuck Ct 6 KT6 198 A3
Glenbuck Rd KT6 198 A3
Glenburnie Rd SW17 158 D1
Glencairn Dr W5 87 C3
Glencairne Cl E16 99 D2
Glencairn Rd SW16 182 A3
Glen Cl TW17 192 C5
Glencoe Ave IG2 57 C2
Glencoe Dr RM10 81 C4
Glencoe Mans 6 SW9 138 C5
Glencoe Rd UB4 84 D3
Glencorse Gn WD19 22 D6
Glen Cres IG8 37 B4
Glen Ct 5 Bromley BR1 186 D3
9 Penge SE20 184 B2
Sidcup DA14 190 A6
Glendale Ave
Edgware HA8 26 C6
Ilford RM6 58 C2
Wood Green N22 32 C3
Glendale Cl SE9 144 C2
Glendale Dr SW19 179 B5
Glendale Gdns HA9 44 A1
Glendale Mews BR3 185 D2
Glendale Way SE28 124 C6
Glendall St SW9 138 B1
Glendarvon St SW15 134 D2
Glendevon Cl HA8 10 D1
Glendish Rd N17 34 B2
Glendor Gdns NW7 27 B6
Glendower Gdns 10
SW14 133 B2
Glendower Pl SW7 256 C4
Glendower Prep Sch
SW7 114 B2 256 D4
Glendower Rd
Chingford E4 20 B3
Mortlake SW14 133 B2
Glendown Ho 2 E8 74 A3
Glendown Rd SE2 124 A1
Glendun Ct W3 111 C6
Glendun Rd W3 111 C6
Gleneagle Lo BR3 185 C2
Gleneagle Mews SW16 181 D5
Gleneagle Rd SW16 181 D5
Gleneagles Ealing W13 87 B2
Stanmore HA7 25 B4
Gleneagles Cl BR6 211 B1
21 SE16 118 B1
South Oxhey WD19 22 D6
Gleneagles Ct 3 TW11 175 A5
Gleneagles Gn 1 BR6 211 B1
Gleneagles Twr 2 UB1 86 A1
Gleneldon Mews SW16 182 A6
Gleneldon Rd SW16 182 A6
Glenelg Rd SW2 160 A6
Glenesk Rd SE9 144 D1
Glenfarg Rd SE6 164 B3
Glenfield Cres HA4 39 B2
Glenfield Rd W13 109 B4
Ashford TW15 171 A4
Streatham SW12 159 C3
Glenfield Terr W13 109 B5
Glenfinlas Way SE5 138 D5
Glenforth St SE10 120 D1
Glengall Gr E14 120 A3
Glengall Pass 2 NW6 91 C6
Glengall Rd DA7 147 A2
NW6 91 B6
SE15 139 D6
Edgware HA8 10 D1
Woodford IG8 37 B4
Glengall Terr SE15 139 D6
Glengarnock Ave E14 120 A2
Glengarry Rd SE22 161 D6
Glen Gdns CR0 220 C4
Glenham Dr IG2 56 D4
Glenhead Cl SE9 144 D2
Glenhill Cl N3 29 C1
Glen Ho 6 E16 122 C5
SW1 259 A6
Glenhouse Rd SE9 166 C6
Glenhurst 4 BR3 186 A2
Glenhurst Ave DA5 169 B3
NW5 71 A4
Ruislip HA4 39 A1
Glenhurst Ct SE19 183 D5
Glenhurst Rd N12 30 B5
Brentford TW8 109 C1
Glenhurst Rise SE19 183 A3
Glenilla Rd NW3 70 C2
Glenister Ho UB3 106 B5
Glenister Park Rd
SW16 181 D3
Glenister Rd SE10 120 D1
Glenister St E16 122 C5
Glenlea Rd SE9 166 C6
Glenloch Ct 2 NW3 70 C2
Glenloch Rd NW3 70 C3
Enfield EN3 6 C3
Glenluce Rd SE3 143 A6
Glenlyon Rd SE9 166 C6
Glenmead IG9 21 C3
Glenmere Ave NW7 28 A4
Glen Mews E17 53 B4
Glenmill TW12 173 B5
Glenmore SW15 156 D5
Glenmore Ho 6 TW10 154 A5
Glenmore Lawns W13 87 A1
Glenmore Rd DA16 145 D4
NW3 70 C2
Glenmore Way IG11 102 A5
Glenmount Path 1
SE18 123 A1
Glennie Ct SE21 162 A3
Glennie Ho SE10 142 A4
Glennie Rd SE27,SW16 160 C1
Glenny Rd IG11 79 A2
Glenorchy Cl UB4 85 A2
Glenparke Rd E7 77 B2
Glen Rd E13 99 C3
E17 53 B4
Chessington KT9 214 A5
Glenridding NW1 232 B3
Glen Rise IG8 37 B4
Glenrosa St SW6 136 A3
Glenrose Ct DA14 190 B5
Glenroy St W12 90 C1
Glensdale Rd SE4 141 B2
Glenshaw Mans 7 SW9 138 C5
Glenshiel Rd SE9 166 C6
Glentanner Way SW17 158 B1
Glen Terr E14 120 A4
Glentham Gdns SW13 134 B6
Glentham Rd SW13 134 B6
Glen The BR6 226 C5
Beckenham BR2 186 C1
Enfield EN2 4 D1
Pinner HA5 40 B4
Pinner HA5 41 A2
Southall UB2 107 B1
South Croydon CR0 222 D5
Wembley HA9 65 D4
Glenthorne Ave CR0 206 C1
Glenthorne Cl SM3 201 C1
Glenthorne Gdns
Cheam SM3 201 C1
Ilford IG6 56 D5
Glenthorne High Sch
SM3 201 C1
Glenthorne Mews W6 112 B2
Glenthorne Rd E17 53 A4
N11 31 A5
W6 112 B2
Kingston KT1 198 B5
Glenthorpe SW15 134 A1
Glenthorpe Rd SM4 200 D4
Glenton Rd SE13 142 C1
Glentrammon Ave BR6 227 D2
Glentrammon Cl BR6 227 D3
Glentrammon Gdns
BR6 227 D2
Glentrammon Rd BR6 227 D2
Glentworth St
NW1 92 D3 237 D5
Glenure Rd SE9 166 C6
Glenview SE2 146 D6
Glen View Rd BR1 187 D1
Glenville Ave EN2 5 A5
Glenville Gr SE8 141 B5
Glenville Mews SW18 157 C4
Glenville Rd KT2 176 C2
Glen Wlk TW7 152 B6
Glenwood Ave NW9 45 C1
Glenwood Cl HA1 42 D4
Glenwood Ct
4 Sidcup DA14 190 A6
5 Wanstead E18 55 A6
Glenwood Gdns IG2 56 C4
Glenwood Gr NW9 45 A1
Glenwood Ho 3 EN5 13 D6
Glenwood Rd N15 50 D4
NW7 11 C1
Forest Hill SE6 163 C3
Hounslow TW3 130 B2
Glenwood Rd continued
Stoneleigh KT17 216 A2
Glenwood Way CR0 206 D3
Glenworth Ave E14 120 B2
Gliddon Rd W14 113 A1 254 A2
Glifford Ho SW1 259 A1
Glimpsing Gn DA18 125 A3
Glisson Rd UB10 82 C5
Globe Pond Rd SE16 119 A5
Globe Prim Sch E2 96 C4
Globe Rd E15 76 D3
E1,E2 96 C3
Woodford IG8 37 C4
Globe St SE1 117 B4 252 C1
Globe Terr 9 E2 96 C4
Globe Theatre The★
SE1 252 A5
Globe View EC4 252 A6
Globe Yd W1 238 C1
Gloster Rd KT3 199 C5
Gloucester W14 113 B2 254 D3
Gloucester Ave DA16 145 D1
NW1 93 A6 231 B6
Sidcup DA15 167 C2
Gloucester Cir SE10 142 A5
Gloucester Cl NW10 67 B1
Thames Ditton KT7 197 A1
Gloucester Cres
NW1 93 B6 231 C6
Staines TW18 170 A4
Gloucester Ct EC3 253 B5
NW11 47 B2
SE1 262 B6
SE22 162 A3
6 Acton W3 88 C1
5 Ealing W7 86 D2
Harrow HA1 42 C6
Redbridge IG1 56 B2
Richmond TW9 132 C5
8 Surbiton KT6 197 D2
Gloucester Dr N4 72 D6
NW11 47 C5
Gloucester Gate NW1 231 C4
Gloucester Gate Mews
NW1 231 C4
Gloucester Gdns NW11 47 B2
W2 236 A2
Cockfosters EN4 15 A6
Redbridge IG1 56 A2
Sutton SM1 217 D6
Gloucester Gr HA8 27 B2
Gloucester Ho NW6 91 C5
Richmond TW10 154 C6
Gloucester Lo 9 CR0 221 D6
Gloucester Mews W2 236 B1
Gloucester Mews W
W2 236 B1
Gloucester Par DA15 168 A6
Hayes UB3 105 A3
Gloucester Pk SW7 256 A4
Gloucester Pl
W1 92 D2 237 D4
Gloucester Pl Mews
W1 92 D2 237 D3
Gloucester Prim Sch
SE15 139 C5
Gloucester Rd E10 53 C2
E17 34 D1
N17 51 B6
SW7 114 A3 256 A4
W5 109 C4
Acton W3 111 A4
Croydon CR0 205 C2
Edmonton N18 33 D5
Enfield EN2 5 A5
Erith DA17 125 B1
Feltham TW13 150 C3
Hampton TW12 173 D3
Harrow HA1 41 D4
Hounslow TW4 129 A1
Ilford E12 78 B4
Kingston KT1,KT2 176 D1
New Barnet EN5 14 A6
Richmond TW9 132 C5
Teddington TW11 174 C5
Twickenham TW2 152 A3
Wanstead E11 55 C4
Gloucester Road Sta
SW7 114 A2 256 A4
Gloucester Sq 6 E2 96 A6
W2 92 C1 237 A1
Gloucester St
SW1 115 C1 259 A2
Gloucester Terr
W2 92 A1 236 B1
Gloucester Way EC1 234 B1
Gloucester Wlk
W8 113 C4 245 B2
Glover Cl SE2 124 C2
Glover Dr N18 34 C4
Glover Ho 2 NW6 70 A1
SE15 140 B1
Glover Rd HA5 40 D3
Glovers Gr HA4 38 D2
Gloxinia Wlk TW12 173 C4
Glycena Rd SW11 136 D2
Glyn Ave EN4 2 B1
Glyn Cl SE25 183 C2
Glyn Ct SE27 160 C1
Glyndale Grange SM2 217 D2
Glyndebourne Ct 5 UB5 84 C4
Glyndebourne Pk BR6 226 D6
Glynde Mews SW3 257 B5
Glynde Rd DA7 147 A2
Glynde Reach WC1 233 B1
Glynde St SE4 163 B5
Glyndon Rd SE18 123 B2
Glyn Dr DA14 190 B6
Glynfield Rd NW10 67 C1
Glyn Mans W14 254 B4

Glynne Rd N22 32 C1
Glyn Rd E5 74 D4
Enfield EN3 6 C1
North Cheam KT4,SM3 216 D6
Glyn St SE11 260 C1
Glynwood Ct SE23 162 C2
Goater's Alley SW6 264 D3
Goat La EN1 5 D5
Goat Rd CR4 202 D2
Goat Wharf TW8 132 A6
Godalming Ave SM6 220 B3
Godalming Rd E14 97 D2
Godbold Rd E15 98 C4
Goddard Cl TW17 192 B6
Goddard Ho SW19 156 D2
Goddard Pl N19 71 C5
Goddard Rd BR3 207 A5
Goddards Way IG1 57 B1
Goddarts Ho E17 53 C6
Godfrey Ave Northolt UB5 85 A6
Twickenham TW2 152 B4
Godfrey Hill SE18 122 A2
Godfrey Ho EC1 235 C1
Godfrey Rd SE18 122 B2
Godfrey St E15 98 A5
SW3 114 C1 257 B2
Godfrey Way TW4 151 B4
Goding St SE11 116 A1 260 B1
Godley Rd SW18 158 B3
Godliman St EC4 252 A6
Godman Rd SE15 140 B3
Godolphin Cl N13 32 D4
Godolphin Ho NW3 70 C1
7 Streatham SW2 160 C3
Godolphin & Latymer Sch
W6 112 B2
Godolphin Pl W3 111 B6
Godolphin Rd W12 112 B4
Godson Rd CR0 220 C5
Godson St N1 234 A4
Godstone Ct 1 N16 51 C1
Godstone Ho SE1 262 D6
1 Kingston KT2 176 D4
Godstone Rd Sutton SM1 218 A4
Twickenham TW1 153 B5
Godstow Rd SE2 124 C4
Godwin Cl N1 235 B4
West Ewell KT19 215 A2
Godwin Ct NW1 232 B4
Godwin Ho 2 E2 95 D5
NW6 91 D5
6 SE18 144 B4
Godwin Jun Sch E7 77 B4
Godwin Prim Sch RM9 81 A1
Godwin Rd BR1,BR2 209 C6
E7 77 B4
Goffers Ho SE3 142 C3
Goffers Rd SE3,SE13 142 C3
Goffs Rd TW15 171 B4
Goffton Ho 14 SW9 138 B3
Goidel Cl SM6 219 D4
Golborne Gdns W10 91 B3
5 W10 91 A3
Golborne Mews 9 W10 91 A2
Golborne Rd W10 91 A2
Golda Cl EN5 12 D5
Goldbeaters Gr HA8 27 C3
Goldbeaters Prim Sch
HA8 27 B2
Goldcliff Cl SM4 201 C2
Goldcrest Cl E16 99 D2
Woolwich SE28 124 C6
Goldcrest Mews W5 87 D2
Goldcrest Way
Bushey WD23 8 A3
New Addington CR0 224 B1
Golden Cres UB3 105 D5
Golden Cross Mews 8
W11 91 B1
Golden Ct 4 Barnet EN4 2 C1
Ealing W7 108 C6
10 Richmond TW9 153 D6
Golden Hind Pl 4 SE8 119 B2
Golden La EC1 95 A3 242 B5
Golden Manor W7 108 C6
Golden Mews SE20 184 C2
Golden Par 2 E17 54 A6
Golden Plover Cl E16 99 A1
Golden Sq W1 115 C6 249 B6
Golders Cl HA8 26 D5
Golders Ct NW11 47 B2
Golders Gdns NW11 47 B2
Golders Green Coll
NW11 47 B1
Golders Green Cres
NW11 47 C2
Golders Green Rd NW11 47 A2
Golders Green Sta NW11 47 C1
Golders Hill Sch NW11 47 C2
Goldersiea NW11 47 C1
Golders Manor Dr NW11 47 A3
Golders Park Cl NW11 47 C1
Golders Rise NW4 46 D4
Golders Way NW11 47 B2
Golderton 2 NW4 46 C5
Goldfinch Rd SE28 123 B3
Goldhawk Ind Est The
W6 112 B3
Goldhawk Mews 2
W12 112 B4
Goldhawk Rd W12 112 A3
Goldhawk Road Sta
W12 112 C4
Goldhaze Cl IG8 37 D3
Gold Hill HA8 27 B4
Goldhurst Terr NW6 70 A1
Goldie Ho N19 49 D2
Goldie Leigh Hospl SE2 146 C6
Golding Cl KT9 213 C2
Golding Ct 7 IG1 78 C5
Golding St E1 96 A1
Golding Terr 17 E1 96 A1
Goldington Cres NW1 232 C4
Goldington Ct NW1 232 C5
Goldington St
NW1 93 D5 232 C4
Gold La HA8 27 B4
Goldman Cl E2 96 A3
Goldmark Ho SE3 143 B2
Goldney Rd W9 91 C3
Goldrill Dr N11 15 A2
Goldsboro Rd
SW8 137 D5 269 D3
Goldsborough Cres E4 20 A2
Goldsborough Ho SW8 269 D1
Goldsdown Cl EN3 7 A3
Goldsdown Rd EN3 7 A3
Goldsmid St 2 SE18 123 C1
Goldsmith Ave E12 78 A2
NW9 45 C3
W3 111 B6
Dagenham RM7 59 C2
Goldsmith Cl HA2 41 D1
Goldsmith Ct WC1 240 A2
Edgware HA8 26 B6
Goldsmith Ho W3 111 B6
Goldsmith La NW9 45 A5
Goldsmith Rd E10 53 D1
E17 34 D1
N11 30 D5
SE15 140 A4
W3 111 B5
Goldsmiths Bldgs W3 111 B5
Goldsmiths Cl W3 111 B5
Goldsmith's Coll, Univ of
London SE14 141 A4
Goldsmith's Ct N6 49 B3
Goldsmith's Pl 4 NW6 91 D6
Goldsmith's Row E2 96 A5
Goldsmith's Sq 16 E2 96 A5
Goldsmith St EC2 242 B2
Goldsworthy Gdns SE16 118 C1
Goldthorpe NW1 232 A5
Goldwell Ho SE22 139 C1
Goldwell Rd CR7 204 B5
Goldwin Cl SE14 140 C4
Goldwing Cl E16 99 A1
Golf Cl
South Norwood SW16 182 C2
Stanmore HA7 25 C3
Golf Club Dr KT2 177 B3
Golfe Rd IG1 79 B5
Golf Rd BR1 210 C6
Ealing W5 88 B1
Golf Side TW2 152 B1
Golfside Cl N20 14 C1
Kingston KT3 177 C1
Goliath Cl SM6 220 A1
Gollogly Terr 9 SE7 121 C1
Gomer Gdns TW11 175 A4
Gomer Pl TW11 175 A4
Gomm Rd SE16 118 C3
Gomshall Ave SM6 220 A3
Gondar Gdns NW6 69 B3
Gondar Mans NW6 69 B3
Gonson St SE8 141 D6
Gonston Cl SW19 157 A2
Gonville Cres UB5 63 D2
Gonville Ho 6 SW15 156 D5
Gonville Prim Sch CR7 204 B4
Gonville Rd CR7 204 B4
Gonville St SW6 135 A2
Gooch Ho E5 74 B5
EC1 241 A4
Goodall Ho 10 SE4 140 D1
Goodall Rd E11 76 A5
Goodbehere Ho 7
SE27 183 A6
Gooden Ct HA1 64 C5
Goodenough Rd SW19 179 B3
Goodey Rd IG11 79 D1
Goodfaith Ho 16 E14 119 D6
Goodge Pl W1 239 B3
Goodge St W1 93 C2 239 B3
Goodge Street Sta
W1 93 D2 239 C4
Goodhall St NW10 89 D4
Good Hart Pl E14 119 A6
Goodhart Way BR4 208 C3
Goodhew Rd CR0 206 A3
Goodhope Ho 15 E14 119 D6
Gooding Cl KT3 199 A4
Goodinge Cl N7 72 A2
Goodinge Rd N7 72 A2
Gooding Ho 4 SE7 121 C1
Goodison Cl WD23 8 A6
Goodland Ho 1 KT3 199 C2
Goodman Cres SW2 159 D2
Goodman Rd E10 54 A2
Goodmans Ct HA0 65 D4
Goodman's Stile 12 E1 96 A1
Goodman's Yd
E1,EC3 117 D6 253 C6
Goodmayes Ave IG3 58 A1
Goodmayes Hospl IG3 58 A4
Goodmayes La IG3 80 A5
Goodmayes Prim Sch
IG3 58 B1
Goodmayes Rd IG3 58 A1
Goodmayes Ret Pk RM6 58 B2
Goodmayes Sta IG3 58 A1
Goodrich Com Sch
SE22 162 A5
Goodrich Ct 9 W10 90 D1
Goodrich Ho 21 E2 96 C5
N16 51 C2
Goodrich Rd SE22 162 A5
Goodridge Ho E17 36 A3
Good Shepherd RC Prim Sch
Catford BR1 186 D6
Good Shepherd RC Prim Sch
continued
New Addington CR0 223 D1
Good Shepherd RC Prim Sch
The W12 111 D4
Goodson Ho SM4 202 A2
Goodson Rd NW10 67 C1
Goodsway NW1 94 A5 233 A4
Goodway Gdns E14 98 B1
Goodwill Ho 19 E14 119 D6
Goodwin Cl
SE16 117 D3 263 D5
Mitcham CR4 202 B6
Goodwin Ct N8 50 A6
East Barnet EN4 14 C5
Goodwin Dr DA14 168 D2
Goodwin Gdns CR0,CR2 220 D2
Goodwin Ho N9 18 C3
2 SE15 140 B2
Goodwin Rd N9 18 D3
W12 112 A4
Croydon CR0 220 D3
Goodwins Ct WC2 250 A6
Goodwin St N4 72 C6
Goodwood Ave EN3 6 C6
Goodwood Cl
Morden SM4 201 C5
11 Stanmore HA7 25 C5
Goodwood Ct W1 238 D4
Goodwood Dr UB5 63 C2
Goodwood Ho 3 W4 111 A1
Penge SE26 184 B4
Goodwood Mans 4
SW9 138 C2
Goodwood Par BR3 207 A5
Goodwood Rd SE14 141 A5
Goodwyn Ave NW7 27 C5
Goodwyn Sch NW7 28 A5
Goodwyn's Vale N10 31 B2
Goodyear Ho 8 N2 30 B1
Goodyers Gdns NW4 46 D4
Goosander Ct 24 NW9 27 D1
Goosander Way SE18,
SE28 123 B3
Gooseacre La HA3 43 D4
Goose Green Cl BR5 190 A1
Goose Green Trad Est
SE22 140 A1
Gooseley La E6 100 C4
Goose Sq 8 E6 100 B1
Goossens Cl 1 SM1 218 A3
Gophir La EC4 252 C6
Gopsall St N1 95 B6 235 D5
Gordon Ave Chingford E4 36 C4
Isleworth TW1 153 B6
Mortlake SW14 133 C1
Stanmore HA7 25 A4
Gordonbrock Prim Sch
SE4 163 C6
Gordonbrock Rd SE4 163 C6
Gordon Cl E17 53 C3
Gordon Cres
Croydon CR0 205 D1
Hayes UB3 106 A2
Gordon Ct W12 90 C1
17 Wimbledon SW20 178 D3
Gordondale Rd SW18,
SW19 157 C2
Gordon Dr TW17 193 B2
Gordon Gdns HA8 26 D1
Gordon Gr SE5 138 D3
Gordon Hill EN2 5 A4
Gordon Hill Sta EN2 4 D4
Gordon Ho 18 E1 118 C6
3 SE10 141 D5
SE12 165 A4
2 Ealing W5 88 A4
Gordon Hospl The
SW1 115 D2 259 C3
Gordon House Rd NW5 71 A4
Gordon Inf Sch IG1 79 B5
Gordon Lo N16 51 D1
Gordon Pl W8 113 C4 245 B2
Gordon Prim Sch SE9 144 B1
Gordon Rd DA15 167 C6
E15 76 A4
N11 31 D3
N3 29 B3
SE15 140 B3
Ashford TW15 148 A1
Barking IG11 101 C6
Beckenham BR3 207 B6
Chingford E4 20 C4
Chiswick W4 132 D6
Claygate KT10 212 C1
Dagenham RM6 59 B3
Ealing W13 109 C6
Edmonton N9 18 B2
Enfield EN2 5 B3
Harrow HA3 42 C6
Ilford IG1 79 B5
Isleworth TW3 130 A1
Kingston KT2 176 B2
Richmond TW9 132 B3
Shepperton TW17 193 B3
Southall UB2 107 A2
Surbiton KT5 198 B2
Wallington SM5 218 D2
Wanstead E11 55 A3
Woodford E18 37 B2
Yiewsley UB7 104 A6
Gordon Sq WC1 93 D3 239 D6
Gordon St E13 99 A4
WC1 93 D3 239 C6
Gordon Way BR1 187 A2
Barnet EN5 1 B1
Gore Ct NW9 44 C4
Gorefield Ho NW6 91 C5
Gorefield Pl NW6 91 C5
Gore Rd E9 96 C6
Gore Rd *continued*
Merton SW20 178 C1
Goresbrook Rd RM9 102 D6
Gore St SW7 114 A3 256 B6
Gorham Ho 12 SW4 159 C5
Gorham Pl W11 244 A5
Goring Gdns RM8 80 C4
Goring Rd N11 32 A4
Goring St EC3 243 B2
Goring Way UB6 86 A5
Gorleston Rd N15 51 B4
Gorleston St
W14 113 A2 254 B4
Gorman Rd SE18 122 B2
Gorringe Park Ave CR4 181 A3
Gorringe Park Prim Sch
CR4 181 A2
Gorse Cl E16 99 A1
Gorsefield Ho 5 E14 119 C6
Gorse Rd CR0 223 C5
Gorse Rise SW17 181 A5
Gorse Wlk UB7 82 A1
Gorst Rd NW10 89 B3
SW11 158 D5
Gorsuch Pl 1 E2 95 D4
Gorsuch St E2 95 D4
Gosberton Rd SW12 159 A3
Gosbury Hill KT9 214 A4
Gosfield Rd RM8 59 C1
Gosfield St W1 93 C2 239 A3
Gosford Gdns IG4 56 B4
Gosford Ho 21 E3 97 B5
Goshawk Gdns UB4 83 C5
Goslett Yd WC2 239 D2
Gosling Cl UB6 85 C4
Gosling Ho 1 E1 118 C6
Gosling Way SW9 138 C4
Gospatrick Rd N17 33 A2
Gospel Oak Prim Sch
NW5 71 A4
Gospel Oak Sta NW5 71 A4
Gosport Ho 9 SW15 156 A3
Gosport Rd E17 53 B4
Gosport Wlk N17 52 B5
Gossage Rd SE18 123 B1
Hillingdon UB10 60 B1
Gosset St E2 96 A4
Gosshill Rd BR7 188 C1
Gossington Cl BR7 188 D6
Gosterwood St SE8 141 A6
Gostling Rd TW2 151 C3
Goston Gdns CR7 204 C6
Goswell Pl EC1 234 D1
Goswell Rd EC1 94 D4 234 D2
Gothic Ct 17 SE5 139 A5
Harlington UB3 127 B6
Gothic Rd TW2 152 B2
Gottfried Mews NW5 71 C4
Goudhurst Ho 10 SE20 184 C3
Goudhurst Rd BR1 186 D5
Gough Ho N1 234 D6
4 Kingston KT1 176 A1
Gough Rd E15 76 D4
Enfield EN1 6 B3
Gough Sq EC4 94 C1 241 B2
Gough St WC1 94 B3 240 D5
Gough Wlk 10 E14 97 C1
Gould Ct SE19 183 C5
Goulden Ho SW11 136 C3
Goulding Ct N8 50 B5
Goulding Gdns CR7 183 A1
Gouldman Ho 30 E1 96 C3
Gould Rd
East Bedfont TW14 149 C4
Twickenham TW2 152 C3
Gould's Gn UB8 104 D6
Gould Terr 26 E8 74 B3
Goulston St E1 95 D1 243 C2
Goulton Rd E5 74 B4
Gourley Pl N15 51 C4
Gourley St N15 51 C4
Gourock Rd SE9 166 C6
Govan St E2 96 A6
Gover Ct 8 SW4 138 A3
Government Row EN3 7 C6
Govett Ave TW17 193 A4
Govier Cl E15 76 C1
Gowan Ave SW6 135 A4 264 A2
Gowan Ho 22 E2 95 D4
Gowan Lea 4 E18 55 A5
Gowan Rd NW10 68 B2
Gower Cl SW4 159 C5
Gower Ct WC1 239 C6
Gower Ho 12 E17 53 D6
SE17 262 B2
Barking IG11 79 A1
Hayes UB3 105 C6
Upper Tooting SW17 180 B4
Gower House Sch NW9 67 A6
Gower Mews WC1 239 D4
Gower Pl NW1,
WC1 93 D3 239 C6
Gower Rd E7 77 A2
Hounslow TW7 130 D6
Gower St WC1 93 D3 239 C5
Gower's Wlk E1 96 A1
Gowland Pl BR3 185 B1
Gowlett Rd SE15 140 A2
Gowrie Rd SW11 137 A2
Graburn Way KT8 196 B6
Grace Ave DA7 147 B3
Grace Bsns Ctr CR4 202 D3
Gracechurch St EC2,
EC4 252 D6
Grace Cl HA8 27 A3
SE9 165 D1
Gracedale Rd SW16 181 B5
Gracefield Gdns SW16 160 A1
Gracehill 2 E1 96 C2
Grace Ho SE11 270 D6
Grace Ho *continued*
Penge SE26 184 B5
Grace Jones Cl E8 74 A2
Grace Path SE26 184 C6
Grace Pl E3 97 D4
Grace Rd CR0 205 A3
Graces Mews NW8 229 B3
Grace's Mews SE5 139 C3
Grace's Rd SE5 139 C3
Grace St E3 97 D4
Gradient The SE26 184 A6
Graeme Rd EN1 5 C3
Graemesdyke Ave
SW14 132 D1
Grafton Cl Ealing W13 87 A1
Twickenham TW4 151 B3
Worcester Park KT4 215 C5
Grafton Cres NW1 71 B2
Grafton Ct 10 E8 74 A3
East Bedfont TW14 149 B3
Grafton Gdns N4 51 A3
Dagenham RM8 81 A6
Grafton Ho 15 E3 97 C4
12 SE8 119 B1
Grafton Inf Sch RM8 81 B6
Grafton Jun Sch RM8 81 B6
Grafton Mews W1 239 A5
Grafton Park Rd KT4 215 C6
Grafton Pl NW1 93 D4 232 D1
Grafton Prim Sch N7 72 A5
Grafton Rd NW5 71 A3
W3 111 A6
Dagenham RM8 81 A6
Enfield EN2 4 B2
Harrow HA1 42 A4
Kingston KT3 199 C6
Thornton Heath CR0 204 C1
Worcester Park KT4 215 C5
Grafton Sq SW4 137 C2
Grafton St W1 115 B6 248 D5
Grafton Terr NW5 71 A3
Grafton Way W1 239 B5
East Molesey KT8 195 B5
Grafton Yd NW5 71 B2
Graham Ave W13 109 B4
Mitcham CR4 181 A2
Graham Cl CR0 223 C6
Graham Ct BR1 187 B3
5 SE14 140 D6
Northolt UB5 63 B3
Grahame Park Way NW7,
NW9 27 D2
Grahame White Ho HA3 43 D6
Graham Gdns KT6 198 A1
Graham Ho 7 N19 71 D4
N9 18 C3
5 Balham SW12 159 B4
Woolwich SE18 144 D5
Graham Lo NW4 46 B3
Graham Mans 2 E8 74 B2
11 Barking IG11 80 A1
Graham Rd DA7 147 C1
E13 99 A3
E8 74 A2
N15 50 D6
NW4 46 B3
W4 111 B3
Hampton TW12 173 C6
Harrow HA3 42 C6
Merton SW19 179 B3
Mitcham CR4 181 A2
Graham St N1 94 D5 234 D3
Graham Terr
SW1 115 A2 258 B3
Grainger Cl UB5 64 A3
Grainger Ct 22 SE5 139 A5
Grainger Rd
Isleworth TW7 130 D3
Tottenham N22 33 A2
Gramer Cl E11 76 B6
Grampian Cl BR6 211 D3
Harlington UB3 127 B5
15 Sutton SM2 218 A1
Grampian Gdns NW2 47 A1
Grampians The 10 W14 112 D4
Granada St SW17 180 D5
Granard Ave SW15 156 B6
Granard Bsns Ctr NW7 27 C4
Granard Ho 20 E9 74 D2
Granard Prim Sch
SW15 156 B5
Granard Rd SW11,SW12 158 D4
Granary Cl N9 18 C4
Granary Ct 3 RM6 58 D2
Granary Rd E1 96 B3
Granary St NW1 93 D6 232 C5
Granby Ho 14 SE18 122 B2
Granby Pl SE1 251 A1
Granby Rd SE18 122 D3
SE9 144 B2
Granby St E2 96 A3 243 D6
Granby Terr NW1 93 C5 232 A3
Grand Arc N12 30 A5
Grand Ave EC1 241 D4
N10 49 A5
Tolworth KT5 198 D3
Wembley HA9 66 C3
Grand Ave E HA9 66 D3
Grand Avenue Prim Sch
KT5 199 A3
Grand Ct RM8 81 A5
Grand Depot Rd SE18 122 C1
Grand Dr Southall UB2 108 A4
West Barnes SM4,SW20 200 C5
Granden Rd SW16 182 A1
Grandfield Ct W4 133 B6
Grandison Rd SW11 158 D6
North Cheam KT4 216 C5
Grand Junction Wharf
N1 235 A3
Grand Par N4 50 D3
Mortlake SW14 133 A1
Tolworth KT6 198 C1
Wembley HA9 66 C6
Grand Union Cl W9 91 B2
Grand Union Cres E8 96 A6
Grand Union Ind Est
NW10 88 D5
Grand Union Way UB2 107 C4
Grand Vitesse Ind Est
SE1 251 D3
Granfield St SW11 266 D1
Grange Ave N12 30 A5
Barnet N20 13 A4
Barnet, London EN4 14 D3
South Norwood SE25 183 C1
Stanmore HA7 25 C1
Twickenham TW2 152 C2
Woodford IG8 37 A3
Grange Cl DA15 168 A1
HA8 27 A5
East Molesey KT8 195 D5
Hayes UB3 83 C2
Heston TW5 129 B6
Woodford IG8 37 A3
Grangecliffe Gdns SE25 183 C1
Grangecourt Rd N16 51 C1
Grange Cres SE28 102 C1
Grange Ct SE15 139 D3
WC2 240 D1
Belmont SM2 217 D1
Hackbridge SM6 219 B5
Littleton TW17 192 C5
Loughton IG10 21 D6
Northolt UB5 84 C5
Pinner HA5 41 A6
Harrow HA1 64 D5
Grange Dr BR7 188 B4
Grange Farm Cl HA2 64 A6
Grange Farm Cvn Pk
TW17 193 C6
Grangefield NW1 72 A1
Grange Fst & Mid Schs
HA2 41 D1
Grange Gdns N14 15 D3
NW3 69 D5
Pinner HA5 41 A5
South Norwood SE25 183 C1
Grange Gr N1 73 A2
Grange Hill HA8 27 A5
South Norwood SE25 183 C1
Grangehill Pl SE9 144 B2
Grangehill Rd SE9 144 B1
Grange Ho NW10 68 B1
SE1 263 C5
6 Barking IG11 101 B6
Grange Inf Sch E13 98 D4
Grange La SE21 161 D2
Grange Lo SW19 178 D4
Grange Mans KT17 215 D1
Grangemill 11 NW5 71 B4
Grangemill Rd SE6 163 C2
Grange Mills SW12 159 C3
Grangemill Way SE6 163 C2
Grange Mus of Community
History The★ NW10 67 C4
Grange Park Ave N21 17 A5
Grange Park Jun & Inf Schs
UB4 83 D3
Grange Park Pl SW20 178 B3
Grange Park Prep Sch
N21 16 D5
Grange Park Rd E10 53 D1
South Norwood CR7 205 B6
Grange Park Sta N21 16 D5
Grange Pk W5 110 A5
Grange Pl NW6 69 C1
Grange Prim Sch
SE1 117 C3 263 A5
W5 109 D4
Grange Rd E10 53 C1
E13 98 D4
E17 53 A4
HA8 27 B4
N6 49 A3
NW10 68 B2
SE1 117 D3 263 C5
W4 110 D1
Barnes SW13 134 A4
Belmont SM2 217 C1
Borehamwood WD6 10 B6
Chessington KT9 214 A4
Ealing W5 110 A5
East Molesey KT8 195 D5
Harrow HA1 43 A4
Harrow HA2 64 B6
Hayes UB3 83 C1
Ilford IG1 79 A4
Kingston KT1 198 A6
Orpington BR6 227 A6
Southall UB1 107 A4
South Norwood SE19,
SE25 183 B1
Tottenham N17 34 A4
Grange St N1 235 D5
Grange The 3 E17 53 A4
19 NW3 70 D2
SE1 117 D3 263 C5
W12 112 B3
W14 113 B2 254 C3
W3 110 D4
7 W4 110 D1
Cockfosters EN4 2 D2
Croydon CR0 223 B6
Ealing W13 87 C2
3 Wanstead E18 55 A6
Wembley HA0 66 C1

Grange The continued
West Barnes KT3 ....**200** A4
West Ewell KT19 ....**215** B4
Wimbledon SW19 ....**178** D4
Grange The(Eltham Coll Jun
Sch) SE9 ....**165** D3
Grange Vale SM2 ....**217** D1
Grangeview Rd N20 ......**14** A3
Grangeway N12 ....**29** D6
NW6 ....**69** C1
Woodford IG8 ....**37** C6
Grangeway Gdns IG4 .....**56** A4
Grangeway The N21 ......**16** D5
Grange Wlk SE1 ..**117** D3 **263** C5
Grangewood DA5 ....**169** B3
Grangewood Ind Est E7 .**77** D1
Grangewood La BR3 ......**185** B4
Grangewood Sch HA5 ....**39** D4
Grange Yd SE1 ...**117** D3 **263** C5
Granham Gdns N9 ....**17** D2
Granite St SE18 ....**123** D1
Granleigh Rd E11 ....**76** C6
Gransden Ave E8 ....**74** B1
Gransden Ho 1 SE8 .....**119** B1
Gransden Rd W12 ....**111** D4
Grantbridge St
N1 ....**94** D5 **234** D4
Grantchester 12 KT1 ....**176** C1
Grantchester CI HA1 .....**64** D5
Grant CI N14 ....**15** C4
Shepperton TW17 ....**192** D3
Grant Ct 11 NW9 ....**27** D1
2 Chingford E4 ....**20** A3
Grantham CI HA8 ....**10** A1
Grantham Ct 9 SE16 ....**118** D4
Dagenham RM6 ....**59** B2
Grantham Gdns RM6 .....**59** B2
Grantham Gn WD6 ....**11** A6
Grantham Ho 12 SE15 ...**140** A6
Ashford TW16 ....**171** C3
Grantham PI W1 ....**248** C2
Grantham Rd SW9 ....**138** A3
Chiswick W4 ....**133** C5
Little Ilford E12 ....**78** C4
Grant Ho 38 SW8 ....**137** D3
Grantley Ho 2 SE14 ....**140** D6
5 Putney SW19 ....**156** B3
Grantley PI KT10 ....**212** A3
Grantley Rd TW4,TW5 ...**128** C3
Grantley St E1 ....**96** D3
Grantock Rd E17 ....**36** B2
Granton Prim Sch
SW16 ....**181** D3
Granton Rd Ilford IG3 ....**58** A1
Sidcup DA14 ....**190** C4
Streatham SW16 ....**181** C2
Grant PI 2 CR0 ....**205** D1
Grant Rd SW11 ....**136** C2
Croydon CR0 ....**205** D1
Harrow HA3 ....**42** D6
Grants CI NW7 ....**28** D3
Grants Cotts KT10 ......**212** B6
Grant St E13 ....**99** A4
N1 ....**234** A4
Grantully Rd W9 ....**91** D4
Grant Way TW7 ....**131** A6
Feltham TW13 ....**150** A2
Hounslow TW3,TW4 ......**151** C6
Granville Ave N9 ....**18** C1
Feltham TW13 ....**150** A2
Hounslow TW3,TW4 ......**151** C6
Granville CI CR0 ....**221** C6
Granville Ct N1 ....**235** D6
N4 ....**50** B3
8 SE14 ....**141** A5
Granville Gdns
Ealing W5 ....**110** B5
South Norwood SW16 ....**182** B3
Granville Gr SE13 ....**142** A2
Granville Ho 13 E14 .....**97** C1
Granville Mans 8 W12 ..**112** C4
WC1 ....**240** A6
Granville Mews
Sidcup DA14 ....**190** A6
Stanmore HA7 ....**25** A5
Granville Pk SE13 ....**142** B2
Granville PI N12 ....**30** A3
SW6 ....**265** C3
W1 ....**93** A1 **238** A1
Pinner HA5 ....**40** D6
Granville Point NW2 ......**69** B6
Granville Rd E17 ....**53** D3
N12 ....**30** A3
N4,N8 ....**50** B3
NW2 ....**69** B6
NW6 ....**91** C5
Bexley DA16 ....**146** C2
Bowes Park N13 ....**32** B4
Hayes UB3 ....**105** D2
Hillingdon UB10 ....**60** D2
Ilford IG1 ....**78** D6
Merton SW19 ....**179** C3
Sidcup DA14 ....**190** B6
Tottenham N22 ....**32** D2
Wandsworth SW18 ....**157** B4
Woodford E18 ....**37** B1
Granville Sq 8 SE15 ....**139** C5
WC1 ....**94** B4 **233** D1
Granville St WC1 ....**233** D1
Granwood Ct 5 TW7 ....**130** C4
Grape St WC2 ....**240** A2
Grapsome CI KT9 ....**213** C1
Grasdene Rd SE18,SE2 ..**146** A5
Grasmere NW1 ....**231** D1
Grasmere Ave BR6 ......**226** D5
W3 ....**111** B6
Kingston SW15 ....**177** C6

Grasmere Ave continued
Merton SW19 ....**201** C6
Ruislip HA4 ....**39** A2
Twickenham TW3 ....**151** D5
Wembley HA9 ....**43** D1
Grasmere CI TW14 ....**149** D3
Grasmere Ct
Barnes SW13 ....**134** A6
Bowes Park N22 ....**32** B4
Forest Hill SE26 ....**184** A5
Grasmere Gdns BR6 ....**226** D5
Harrow HA3 ....**25** A1
Redbridge IG4 ....**56** B4
Grasmere Ho 19 N16 .....**73** B4
Jarman JMI Sch N16 .....**73** B4
Grasmere Point 2
SE15 ....**140** C5
Grasmere Rd BR6 ....**226** D5
N10 ....**31** B2
Bromley BR1 ....**186** D3
Croydon SE25 ....**206** B4
Streatham SW16 ....**182** B5
Tottenham N17 ....**34** A4
Grasshaven Way SE28 ..**123** D5
Grassington CI N11 ......**31** A4
Grassington Rd DA14 ...**190** A6
Grassmere Ct 6 EN1 ....**17** C6
Grassmount SE23 ....**162** B2
Grass Pk N3 ....**29** B2
Grassway SM6 ....**219** C4
Grasvenor Ave EN5 .....**13** C5
Grasvenor Avenue Inf Sch
EN5 ....**13** C5
Grately Ho 10 SW15 .....**156** B3
Gratton Rd W14 ..**113** A3 **254** A1
Gratton Terr NW2 ....**68** D3
Graveley 16 KT1 ....**176** C1
Graveley Ave WD6 ....**11** A6
Graveley Ho 7 SE8 ......**119** A2
N3 ....**29** B1
South Croydon CR0,CR2 ..**223** B1
Gravel Hill DA6 ....**169** D6
DA6 ....**169** D6
Gravel Hill CI DA5,DA6 ..**169** D6
Gravel Hill Prim Sch
DA6 ....**169** D6
Gravel Hill Sta CR0 .....**223** A2
Gravel La E1 ....**95** D1 **243** C2
Gravel Rd BR2 ....**226** A6
Twickenham TW2 ....**152** C3
Gravelwood CI BR7 ......**167** A1
Gravenel Gdns SW17 ...**180** C5
Graveney Gr SE20 ....**184** C3
Graveney Rd SW17 ......**180** C6
Graveney St SW17 ....**181** B5
Gravesend Rd W12 ......**112** A6
Graves Est DA16 ....**146** B3
Gray Ave RM8 ....**59** B1
Gray Ct 8 KT2 ....**175** D6
Grayfriars Pas EC1 .....**241** D2
Grayham Cres KT3 ......**199** B5
Grayham Rd KT3 ....**199** B5
Gray Ho SE17 ....**262** B2
Grayland CI BR1 ....**187** D2
Grayland Ct WC1 ....**233** C1
Grayling CI E16 ....**98** C3
Grayling Ct N17 ....**52** B5
Ealing W5 ....**109** D5
Grayling Rd N16 ....**73** B6
Grayling Sq 2 E2 ....**96** A4
Grays Cotts SW9 ....**38** C1
Grayscroft Rd SW16 ....**181** D3
Grays Farm Prim Sch
BR5 ....**190** B2
Grays Farm Production
Village BR5 ....**190** B2
Grays Farm Rd BR5 .....**190** B2
Grayshott Rd SW11 .....**137** A2
Gray's Inn * WC1 .**94** B3 **240** D4
Gray's Inn PI WC1 ....**240** D3
Gray's Inn Rd
WC1 ....**94** B3 **240** D6
Gray's Inn Sq
WC1 ....**94** C2 **241** A4
Grays La TW15 ....**170** D6
Grayson Ho EC1 ....**235** B1
Gray's Rd UB10 ....**60** A1
Gray St SE1 ....**116** D4 **251** D3
Grayswood Gdns SW20 .**178** B1
Grayswood Point 14
SW15 ....**156** A3
Gray's Yd W1 ....**238** B2
Graywood Ct N12 ....**30** A3
Grazebrook Prim Sch
N16 ....**73** C6
Grazebrook Rd N16 ......**73** B6
Grazeley Ct SE19 ....**183** C5
Great Arthur Ho EC1 ....**242** A5
Great Bell Alley EC2 ....**242** C2
Great Benty RM7 ....**104** A2
Great Brownings SE21 ..**183** D6
Great Bushey Dr N20 ...**13** D3
Great Cambridge Ind Est
EN1 ....**18** B6
Great Cambridge Junction
N13,N18 ....**33** B6
Great Cambridge Rd
Edmonton N9,N18 ....**17** C3
Enfield EN1 ....**6** A3
Great Castle St W1 ......**239** A2
Great Central Ave HA4 ..**62** C3
Great Central St
NW1 ....**92** D2 **237** C4
Great Central Way NW10 **67** B4
Great Chapel St
W1 ....**93** D1 **239** C2
Great Chertsey Rd
Chiswick SW14,W4 ....**133** B4
Feltham TW13,TW2 ....**151** C1
Great Church La W6 .....**112** D1

Great College St
SW1 ....**116** A3 **260** A6
Great Croft WC1 ....**233** B1
Great Cumberland Mews
W1 ....**237** C1
Great Cumberland PI
W1 ....**92** D1 **237** D2
Great Dover St SE1 ...**117** B3 **262** C6
Greatdown Rd W7 ....**86** D2
Great Eastern Bldgs 10
E8 ....**74** B2
Great Eastern Ent Ctr
E14 ....**119** D4
Great Eastern Pier E14 ..**119** C1
Great Eastern Rd E15 ...**76** B2
Great Eastern St
EC2 ....**95** C3 **243** A6
Great Eastern Wharf
SW11 ....**267** B3
Great Elms Rd BR2 ......**209** C5
Great Field 7 NW5 ......**71** C3
NW9 ....**27** D2
Greatfield Ave E6 ....**100** B3
Greatfield CI 4 N19 .....**71** C4
SE4 ....**141** C1
Greatfields Dr UB8 ......**82** C2
Greatfields Rd IG11 .....**101** B5
Great Fleete Way IG11 ..**102** C4
Great Galley CI IG11 .....**102** C4
Great Gatton CI CR0 ....**207** A2
Great George St
SW1 ....**116** A4 **250** A1
Great Guildford St SE1 ..**117** A5 **252** A3
Great Guilford Bsns Sq
SE1 ....**252** A3
Greatham Wlk 8 SW15 ..**156** A3
Great Harry Dr SE9 ......**166** C1
Great James St WC1 ....**240** C4
Great Marlborough St
W1 ....**93** C1 **239** A1
Great Mathers Rd SE11 .**261** C4
Great Maze Pond
SE1 ....**117** B4 **252** D2
Great Newport St WC2 ..**250** A6
Great New St EC4 .**94** C1 **241** B2
Great North Rd N2 ......**48** C5
Barnet EN5 ....**1** A4
New Barnet EN5 ....**13** D6
Great North Way (Barnet
By-Pass) NW4 ....**46** D6
Greatorex Ho 12 E1 .....**96** A2
Greatorex St E1 ....**96** A2
Great Ormond St
WC1 ....**94** B3 **240** C3
Great Ormond St Hospl for
Children * WC1 ..**94** B3 **240** C5
Great Percy St
WC1 ....**94** C4 **234** A2
Great Peter St
SW1 ....**115** D3 **259** D5
Great Portland St
W1 ....**93** B3 **238** D5
Great Portland Street Sta
W1 ....**93** B3 **238** D5
Great Pulteney St W1 ..**249** B6
Great Queen St
WC2 ....**94** A1 **240** B2
Great Russell St
WC1 ....**94** A2 **240** A3
Great Scotland Yd
SW1,WC2 ....**116** A5 **250** A4
Great Smith St
SW1 ....**115** D3 **259** D6
Great South West Rd
TW6,TW14,TW4 ....**126** B4
Great South-West Rd
TW5 ....**128** B2
Great Spilmans SE22 ...**161** C6
Great St Helen's EC3 ...**243** A2
Greatstone Ho 13 SE20 .**184** C3
Great Strand NW9 ....**27** D1
Great St Thomas Apostle
EC4 ....**252** B6
Great Suffolk St
SE1 ....**116** D4 **251** D3
Great Sutton St
EC1 ....**94** D3 **241** D5
Great Swan Alley EC2 ...**242** C2
Great Thrift BR5 ....**211** A5
Great Titchfield St
W1 ....**93** C2 **239** A3
Great Tower St
EC3 ....**117** C6 **253** A6
Great Trinity La EC4 .....**252** B6
Great Turnstile WC2 ....**240** D3
Great Western Ind Pk
UB2 ....**108** A4
Great Western Rd W2,
W9 ....**91** B2
Great West Rd
Brentford TW7,TW8 .....**131** B4
Chiswick W4,W6 ....**133** B6
Heston TW5,TW7 ....**129** B4
Hounslow TW5 ....**129** B4
Hounslow TW5,TW7 .....**130** B3
Great West Road Cedars Rd
W4 ....**133** A6
Great West Road Hogarth La
W4 ....**133** A6
Great West Trad Est
TW8 ....**131** B6
Great Winchester St
EC2 ....**95** B1 **242** D2
Great Windmill St
W1 ....**115** D6 **249** C6
Greatwood BR7 ....**188** C3
Great Yd SE1 ....**253** B2
Greaves CI IG11 ....**79** C1

Greaves Cotts 12 E14 ...**97** A2
Greaves PI SW17 ....**180** C6
Greaves Twr SW10 ......**266** B4
Grebe 3 NW9 ....**27** D1
Grebe Ave UB4 ....**84** D1
Grebe CI E17 ....**35** A3
E7 ....**76** D3
Barking IG11 ....**102** A3
Grebe Terr 4 KT1 ....**198** A6
Grecian Cres SE19 ......**182** D4
Greek St W1 ....**239** D1
Greek St W1 ....**93** D1 **239** D1
Greenacre CI Barnet EN5 ..**1** B5
Northolt UB5 ....**63** B3
Greenacre Ct E8 ....**74** A3
Greenacre Gdns E17 ....**54** A5
Greenacre PI SM6 ......**219** B6
Greenacres N3 ....**29** A1
SE9 ....**166** C5
Green Acres DA14 ......**189** D6
Green Acres WD23 ......**8** B2
Green Acres CR0 ....**221** D5
Greenacres Ave UB10 ...**60** C5
Greenacres CI BR6 ......**227** A4
Greenacres Dr HA7 .....**25** B3
Greenacres Prim Sch
SE9 ....**166** C2
Greenacre Sq 20 SE16 ..**118** D4
Greenacre Wlk N14 .....**15** D1
Green Arbour Ct EC1 ...**241** C2
Green Ave NW7 ....**27** C6
W13 ....**109** B3
Greenaway Gdns NW3 ..**69** D4
Greenaway Ho NW8 .....**229** A6
WC1 ....**234** A1
Greenaway Terr TW19 ..**148** A3
Green Bank E1 ....**118** B5
N12 ....**29** D6
Greenbank Ave HA0 .....**65** A3
Greenbank CI E4 ....**20** A2
Greenbank Cres NW4 ...**47** A5
Greenbank Lo 2 BR7 ....**188** C2
Greenbanks HA1 ....**64** C4
Greenbay Rd SE7 ....**143** D5
Greenberry St NW8 .....**230** A3
Greenbrook Ave EN4 ....**2** A4
Green CE Prim Sch The
N17 ....**51** D6
Green CE Sch Holy Trinity
(Infants' Annexe) The
N15 ....**51** D5
Green CI NW11 ....**48** A2
NW9 ....**45** A3
Beckenham BR2 ....**208** C6
Carshalton SM5 ....**218** D6
Feltham TW13 ....**173** A5
Greencoat Ho 13 KT1 ...**176** A1
Greencoat PI
SW1 ....**115** C2 **259** B4
Greencoat Row SW1 ....**259** B5
Greencourt Ave HA8 ....**26** D2
Green Court Ave CR0 ...**222** B6
Green Court Gdns CR0 ..**222** B6
Greencourt Ho E1 ....**96** D3
Greencourt Rd BR5 .....**211** C4
Greencroft HA8 ....**27** A5
Greencroft Ave HA4 ....**62** C6
Greencroft CI E16 ....**99** D2
Greencroft Gdns NW6 ...**70** A1
Enfield EN1 ....**5** C2
Greencroft Rd TW5 ......**129** B4
Green Ct TW16 ....**171** D4
Green Dale NW7 ....**27** C6
Green Dale SE22 ....**161** C6
Greendale CI SE22 ......**161** C6
Greendale Ct CR2 ....**221** A2
Green Dr UB1 ....**107** C5
Green Dragon Ct SE1 ...**252** C3
Green Dragon Ho WC1 ..**240** B2
Green Dragon Jun & Inf Sch
TW8 ....**132** A6
Green Dragon La
Brentford TW8 ....**110** B1
Southgate N21 ....**16** D5
Green Dragon Yd 21 E1 ..**96** A2
Greene Ct 20 SE14 .....**140** D6
Greene Ho SE1 ....**262** C5
Green Elms IG6 ....**57** A6
Green End
Chessington KT9 ....**214** A4
Edmonton N21 ....**16** D2
Greenend Rd W4 ....**111** C4
Greener Ho 3 SW4 ......**137** D2
Green Farm CI BR6 ......**227** D3
Greenfell Mans SE8 .....**141** D6
Greenfield Ave KT5 .....**198** D3
Greenfield Dr BR1 ....**187** C1
N2 ....**48** D5
Greenfield Gdns BR5 ...**211** B2
NW2 ....**69** A5
Dagenham RM9 ....**102** D6
Greenfield Ho 28 SW19 ..**156** D3
Greenfield Rd E1 ....**96** A1
N15 ....**51** C4
Dagenham RM9 ....**102** C6
Greenfields UB1 ....**85** C1
Greenfields JMI Sch
WD19 ....**22** C5
Greenfields Sch N10 .....**30** D2
Greenfield Way HA2 .....**41** D6
Greenford Ave Ealing W7 ..**86** C1
Southall UB1 ....**107** B6
Greenford Gdns UB6 ....**86** A4
Greenford High Sch UB6 ..**85** C4
Greenford Ind Est UB6 ..**85** D6
Greenford Rd
Greenford UB6 ....**86** A3

Greenford Rd continued
Greenford,Harrow HA1,
UB6 ....**64** C3
Sutton SM1 ....**217** D4
Greenford Rdbt UB6 .....**86** B5
Greenford Sta UB6 ....**86** B6
Greengate UB6 ....**65** B2
Greengate St E13 ......**99** B4
Green Gdns BR6 ....**227** A3
Cheam SM1 ....**217** B3
Grebe Terr 4 KT1 ....**198** A6
Greenhalgh Wlk N2 .....**48** A5
Greenham CI SE1 ....**251** A1
Greenham Cres E4 ......**35** C4
Greenham Ho 6 E9 ......**96** C6
Isleworth TW7 ....**130** B2
Greenham Rd N10 ....**31** A1
Greenhaven Dr SE28 ....**102** B1
Greenheath Bsns Ctr 3
E2 ....**96** B3
Green Hedges 8 TW1 ...**153** C5
Greenheys Dr E18 ....**54** D6
Greenhill HA9 ....**66** C6
NW3 ....**70** B4
Buckhurst Hill IG9 ....**21** C3
Sutton SM1 ....**218** A6
Green Hill SE18 ....**122** B1
Greenhill Cts SE7 ....**122** B1
Greenhill Gdns UB5 .....**85** B5
Greenhill Gr E12 ....**78** A4
Greenhill Par EN5 ....**13** D6
Greenhill Pk NW10 ......**89** C6
New Barnet EN5 ....**13** D6
Greenhill Rd NW10 ......**89** C6
Harrow HA1 ....**42** C3
Greenhill's Rents EC1 ...**241** C4
Greenhills Terr 16 N1 ....**73** B2
Greenhill Terr
Northolt UB5 ....**85** B5
Woolwich SE18 ....**122** B1
Greenhithe CI SE9 ......**167** C4
Greenholm Rd SE9 ......**166** D6
Green Ho The 5 SW19 ..**157** A3
Green Hundred Rd
SE15 ....**140** A6
Greenhurst Rd SE27 ....**182** C5
Greening St SE2 ....**124** C2
Green La NW4 ....**46** D4
SE9 ....**166** D1
W7 ....**108** C4
Ashford TW16 ....**171** D4
Chessington KT9 ....**214** A1
Dagenham RM8 ....**81** B6
East Molesey KT8 ....**195** D4
Edgware HA8 ....**26** C5
Feltham TW13 ....**173** A5
Hillingdon UB8 ....**83** A2
Hounslow TW4 ....**128** C1
Ilford IG1 ....**79** C6
Ilford IG3 ....**79** C6
Morden SM4 ....**201** D3
New Malden KT3 ....**199** A4
New Malden KT4 ....**200** A1
Penge SE20 ....**184** D3
Shepperton TW17 ....**193** A4
South Norwood CR7,
SW16 ....**182** C2
Stanmore HA7 ....**25** B5
Greenland Cres UB2 ....**106** D3
Greenland Ho 4 E1 ......**97** A3
SE8 ....**118** D1
Greenland Mews SE8 ...**118** D1
Greenland PI NW1 ......**231** D1
Greenland Quay SE16 ..**118** D2
Greenland Rd
NW1 ....**93** D6 **232** A6
Barnet EN5 ....**12** C5
Greenlands
Borehamwood WD6 .....**11** B5
Chessington KT19 ....**214** B3
Greenland St NW1 ......**231** D6
Green Lane Bsns Pk
SE9 ....**166** C2
Green Lane Cotts HA7 ...**25** B6
Green Lane Gdns CR7 ..**183** A1
Green Lane Mews SM4 .**201** D3
Green Lane Prim Sch
KT4 ....**200** B2
Green Lanes N4,N8,N15 ..**50** C2
Palmers Green N13 ....**16** C1
West Ewell KT19 ....**215** C1
Greenlaw Ct W5 ....**87** D1
Greenlaw Gdns KT3 .....**199** D2
Greenlawns N12 ....**29** D4
Green Lawns 8 SE18 ....**122** D2
Ruislip HA4 ....**40** C1
Greenlaw St SE18 ....**122** C3
Green Leaf Ave SM6 ....**219** D4
Greenleaf CI 8 SW2 ....**160** C4
Greenleafe Dr IG6 ....**56** D6
Greenleaf Rd E17 ....**53** B6
E6 ....**99** C6
Greenleaf Prim Sch E17 ..**53** B6
Greenlea Pk SW19 ......**180** C2
Green Leas
Ashford TW16 ....**171** D4
Kingston KT1 ....**198** A6
Green Leas CI TW16 .....**171** D4
Greenleaves Ct TW15 ...**170** D4
Green Man Gdns W13 ...**109** A6
Green Man Intc E11 .....**54** C2
Green Man La
Ealing W13 ....**109** A5
Hatton TW14 ....**128** A1
Greenman St N1 ...**95** A6 **235** A6
Greenmead SE25 ....**206** A4
Greenmead Sch SW15 ..**156** B6
Green Moor Link N21 ....**16** D4
Greenmoor Rd EN3 ......**6** C3
Greenoak PI EN4 ....**2** D3

Green Oaks UB2 ....**106** D2
Greenoak Way SW19 ...**178** D6
Greenock Rd 11 W3 .....**111** A3
Mitcham SW16 ....**181** D2
Greeno Cres TW17 ......**192** C4
Green Park *
SW1,W1 ....**115** B4 **248** D2
Green Park Sta
W1 ....**115** C5 **249** A4
Green Pond CI E17 ....**53** B6
Green Pond Rd E17 ......**53** A6
Green Pt E15 ....**76** C2
Green Rd N20 ....**14** A1
East Barnet N14 ....**15** B5
Green Ride IG10,E4 ......**21** A6
Greenrigg Wlk HA9 ......**66** D6
Greenroof Way SE10 ...**120** D3
Green Sch for Girls The
TW7 ....**131** A4
Greens Ct W1 ....**249** C6
Green's Ct W11 ....**244** C3
Greens Ct HA9 ....**65** D5
Greens End SE18 ....**122** D2
Greenshank CI E17 ......**35** A3
Greenshields Ind Est
E16 ....**121** B5
Greenside DA5 ....**169** A3
Dagenham RM8 ....**58** C1
Greenside CI N20 ....**14** B2
Catford SE6 ....**164** B2
Greenside Prim Sch
W12 ....**112** A4
Greenside Rd W12 ......**112** A4
Thornton Heath CR0 .....**204** C2
Greenslade Prim Sch
SE18 ....**145** B6
Greenslade Rd IG11 .....**79** B1
Greensleeves Ho UB2 ..**107** D2
Greensleeves Manor
SM2 ....**217** D2
Green St E13 ....**99** C6
E7 ....**77** C1
W1 ....**115** A6 **248** A6
Enfield EN3 ....**6** D3
Sunbury TW16 ....**172** A1
Greenstead Ave IG8 .....**37** C4
Greenstead CI IG8 ......**37** C5
Greenstead Gdns
Putney SW15 ....**156** B6
Woodford IG8 ....**37** C4
Greenstone Mews E11 ...**55** A3
Green Street Green Prim Sch
BR6 ....**227** D2
Greenstreet Hill SE4 .....**140** C2
Green Terr EC1 ....**234** B1
Green The BR1 ....**165** A1
DA16 ....**145** C1
DA7 ....**147** C4
E15 ....**76** D2
N14 ....**15** D1
W3 ....**89** C4
Chingford E4 ....**20** B3
Claygate KT10 ....**212** D2
Ealing W5 ....**109** D6
Edmonton N9 ....**18** A2
Feltham TW13 ....**150** B2
Hackbridge SM6 ....**219** A6
Hayes BR2 ....**209** A2
Heston TW5 ....**129** C6
Kingston KT3 ....**177** A1
Merton SM4 ....**201** A3
7 Richmond TW9 ....**153** D6
Sidcup DA14 ....**190** A6
Southall UB2 ....**107** B4
Southgate N21 ....**16** A4
St Paul's Cray BR5 ....**190** B3
Sutton SM1 ....**217** D6
Tottenham N17 ....**33** A4
Twickenham TW2 ....**152** C2
Uxbridge UB10 ....**61** D6
Wallington SM5 ....**219** A4
Wanstead E11 ....**55** B3
Wembley HA0 ....**65** A6
Wimbledon SW19 ....**178** D5
Woodford IG8 ....**37** A5
Buckhurst Hill IG9 ....**21** B3
Green Vale DA6 ....**168** D6
Ealing W5 ....**88** B1
Greenvale Specl Sch
SE23 ....**163** A1
Green Verges HA7 ....**25** D3
Green View KT9 ....**214** B1
Greenview Ave CR0 .....**207** A3
Greenview CI W3 ....**111** C5
Greenview Ct TW15 .....**170** B6
Greenway N20 ....**13** C2
Green Way BR2 ....**210** A3
Greenway
Chislehurst BR7 ....**188** D5
Dagenham RM8 ....**58** C1
Harrow HA3 ....**44** A4
Hayes UB4 ....**84** B3
Palmers Green N14 ......**16** A2
Pinner HA5 ....**22** B1
Wallington SM6 ....**219** C4
West Barnes SW20 ......**200** C5
Woodford IG8 ....**37** C5
Green Way Eltham SE9 ..**165** D6
Sunbury TW16 ....**194** A3
Greenway Ave E17 ......**54** B5
Greenway CI N11 ....**31** A4
11 N15 ....**51** D5
N20 ....**13** C2
N4 ....**73** A4
NW9 ....**27** B1
Greenway Ct Hayes UB4 ..**84** B3
Ilford IG1 ....**56** D1
Greenway Gdns NW9 ....**27** B1
Croydon CR0 ....**223** B5

Gun Wharf *continued*
E3 ... 97 A6
Gurdon Ho 3 E14 ... 97 C1
Gurdon Rd SE7 ... 121 A1
Gurnell Gr W13 ... 86 D3
Gurney Cl E15 ... 76 C3
E17 ... 34 D2
Barking IG11 ... 78 D2
Gurney Cres CR0 ... 204 B1
Gurney Dr N2 ... 48 A5
Gurney Ho 14 E2 ... 96 A5
3 W2 ... 91 D1
Hayes UB3 ... 105 C2
Gurney Rd E15 ... 76 C3
SW6 ... 136 A2
Northolt UB5 ... 84 C4
Wallington SM5 ... 219 A4
Guru Nanak Sikh Coll UB4 ... 106 C5
Guthrie Ct SE1 ... 251 B1
Guthrie St SW3 ... 257 A2
Gutter La EC2 ... 95 A1 242 A2
Guyatt Gdns CR4 ... 181 A1
Guy Barnett Gr SE3 ... 143 A2
Guy Rd CR0,SM6 ... 219 D5
Guyscliff Rd SE13 ... 164 A6
Guy's Hospl SE1 ... 117 B5 252 D2
Guy's Hospl Sch SE1 ... 117 B5 252 D3
Guy's Retreat IG9 ... 21 C4
Guy St SE1 ... 117 B4 252 D2
Gwalior Ho N14 ... 15 C5
Gwalior Rd SW15 ... 134 D2
Gwendolen Ave SW15 ... 156 D6
Gwendolen Cl SW15 ... 156 D6
Gwendoline Ave E13 ... 99 B6
Gwendwr Rd W14 ... 113 A1 254 B2
Gwent Ct 13 SE16 ... 118 D5
Gwillim Cl DA15 ... 168 A6
Gwilym Maries Ho 11 E2 ... 96 B4
Gwydor Rd BR3 ... 206 D6
Gwydyr Rd BR2 ... 208 D6
Gwyn Cl SW6 ... 136 A5 266 A3
Gwyn Jones Prim Sch E11 ... 54 B2
Gwynne Ave CR0 ... 206 D2
Gwynne Cl W4 ... 133 D6
Gwynne Ho WC1 ... 234 A1
6 Streatham SW2 ... 160 B3
3 Wanstead E11 ... 55 A4
Gwynne Pl WC1 ... 233 D1
Gwynne Rd SW11 ... 136 B3
Gye Ho 2 SW4 ... 138 A1
Gylcote Cl SE5 ... 139 B1
Gyles Pk HA7 ... 25 C2
Gyllyngdune Gdns IG3 ... 79 D5

H

Haarlem Rd 12 W14 ... 112 D3
Haberdasher Pl 4 N1 ... 95 C4
Haberdasher St N1 ... 95 B4 235 D2
Habington Ho 9 SE5 ... 139 B5
Haccombe Rd SW19 ... 180 A4
Hackbridge Park Gdns SM5 ... 218 D6
Hackbridge Prim Sch SM5 ... 203 A1
Hackbridge Rd SM5, SM6 ... 219 A6
Hackbridge Sta SM6 ... 219 B6
Hackett Cl SE8 ... 119 B2
Hackford Rd SW9 ... 138 C4 270 D2
Hackford Wlk SW9 ... 138 C4
Hackforth Cl EN5 ... 12 B6
Hackington Cres BR3 ... 185 C4
Hackney Central Sta E8 ... 74 B2
Hackney Cl WD6 ... 11 B6
Hackney Coll (Poplar Ctr) E3 ... 97 D3
Hackney Com Coll N1 ... 95 C4
N4 ... 51 A2
Hackney Downs Sch E5, E8 ... 74 A3
Hackney Downs Sta E8 ... 74 B3
Hackney Free & Parochial CE Sch (Secondary) E9 ... 74 C2
Hackney Gr E8 ... 74 B2
Hackney Hospl E9 ... 75 A3
Hackney Rd E2 ... 96 A5
Hackney Wick E9 ... 75 B2
Hackney Wick Sta E9 ... 75 C2
Hackworth Point 24 E3 ... 97 D4
Haddenham Ct SW17 ... 180 B6
Hadden Rd SE28 ... 123 C3
Hadden Way UB6 ... 64 B2
Haddington Ct 4 SE10 ... 141 D5
Haddington Rd BR1 ... 186 B6
Haddo Ho NW5 ... 71 B4
SE10 ... 141 D6
Haddon Cl Enfield EN1 ... 18 A5
New Malden KT3 ... 199 D4
Haddon Ct NW4 ... 46 C6
W3 ... 111 D6
Haddon Gr DA15 ... 168 A4
Haddon Rd SM1 ... 217 D4
Haddo St SE10 ... 142 A6
Haden Ct N4 ... 72 C6
Hadfield Cl UB1 ... 85 B4
Hadfield Ho 26 E1 ... 96 A1
Hadleigh Cl 16 E1 ... 96 C3
Merton SW20 ... 179 B1
Hadleigh Ct 8 E4 ... 20 C4
Hadleigh Ho 15 E1 ... 96 C3
Hadleigh Lo 5 IG8 ... 37 A4
Hadleigh Rd N9 ... 18 B4
Hadleigh St E2 ... 96 C4
Hadleigh Wlk 1 E6 ... 100 A1
Hadley Cl
Borehamwood WD6 ... 10 B5
Southgate N21 ... 16 C5
Hadley Ct N16 ... 52 A1
Hadley Gdns W4 ... 111 B1
Southall UB2 ... 107 B1
Hadley Gn EN5 ... 1 B3
Hadley Gn W EN5 ... 1 B3
Hadley Gr EN5 ... 1 A3
Hadley Green Rd EN5 ... 1 B3
Hadley Hall N21 ... 16 C3
Hadley Highstone EN5 ... 1 B4
Hadley Ho BR5 ... 189 D1
Hadley Rd DA17 ... 125 B2
Barnet EN5 ... 1 D2
Enfield EN2 ... 4 A5
Mitcham CR4 ... 203 D5
Hadley Ridge EN5 ... 1 B2
Hadley St NW1 ... 71 B2
Hadleyvale Ct EN5 ... 1 D2
Hadley Way N21 ... 16 C5
Hadley Wood Prim Sch EN4 ... 2 A5
Hadley Wood Rd
Barnet EN4 ... 2 A3
Barnet EN5 ... 1 C3
Hadley Wood Sta EN4 ... 2 A5
Hadlow Coll (Mottingham Ctr) SE12 ... 165 C3
Hadlow Ho SE17 ... 263 B2
Hadlow Pl SE19 ... 184 A3
Hadlow Rd Bexley DA16 ... 146 C5
Sidcup DA14 ... 190 A6
Hadrian Cl TW19 ... 148 A4
Hadrian Ct SE4 ... 141 C2
Barnet EN5 ... 1 D1
1 Belmont SM2 ... 217 D1
Hadrian Est 30 E2 ... 96 A5
Hadrian's Ride EN1 ... 17 D6
Hadrian St SE10 ... 120 C1
Hadrian Way TW19 ... 148 A4
Hadstock Ho NW1 ... 232 D2
Hadyn Park Ct 13 W12 ... 112 A4
Hadyn Park Rd W12 ... 112 A4
Hafer Rd SW11 ... 136 D1
Hafton Rd SE6 ... 164 C2
Haggard Rd TW1 ... 153 B4
Hagger Ct E17 ... 54 B6
Haggerston Rd E8 ... 95 D6
Haggerston Sch E2 ... 95 D5
Hague Prim Sch E2 ... 96 B3
Hague St 12 E2 ... 96 A4
Ha-Ha Rd SE7,SE18 ... 144 B6
Haig Ct BR7 ... 188 D5
Haig Ho 4 E2 ... 96 A5
Haig Pl SM4 ... 201 C3
Haig Rd Hillingdon UB8 ... 83 A2
Stanmore HA7 ... 25 C5
Haig Rd E E13 ... 99 C5
Haig Rd W E13 ... 99 C4
Haigville Gdns IG6 ... 56 D5
Hailes Cl SW19 ... 180 A4
Haileybury Ave EN1 ... 17 D5
Hailey Rd DA18 ... 125 C4
Hailey Rd Bsns Pk DA18 ... 125 C4
Hailsham Ave SW2 ... 160 B2
Hailsham Cl KT6 ... 197 D2
Hailsham Dr HA1 ... 42 B6
Hailsham Ho NW8 ... 237 A5
Hailsham Rd SW17 ... 181 A4
Hailsham Terr N18 ... 33 B5
Haimo Prim Sch SE9 ... 165 D6
Haimo Rd SE9 ... 165 D6
Hainault Bldgs E10 ... 54 A1
Hainault Bridge Par 4 IG1 ... 78 D6
Hainault Ct E17 ... 54 B5
Hainault Gore RM6 ... 59 A4
Hainault Rd E11 ... 54 B2
Dagenham RM6 ... 59 B3
Ilford RM6 ... 58 B6
Hainault St SE9 ... 166 D3
Ilford IG1 ... 78 D6
Haines Wlk SM4 ... 201 D2
Hainford Cl SE4 ... 140 D1
Haining Cl 3 W4 ... 110 C1
Hainthorpe Rd SE27 ... 182 D6
Hainton Cl E1 ... 96 B1
Halberd Mews E5 ... 74 B6
Halbutt Gdns RM9 ... 81 B5
Halcomb St N1 ... 95 C6
Halcot Ave DA6 ... 169 D6
Halcrow St E1 ... 96 B2
Halcyon 3 EN1 ... 17 C6
Halcyon Wharf 19 E1 ... 118 A5
Haldane Cl N10 ... 31 B3
Holdbrook EN3 ... 7 D5
Haldane Pl SW18 ... 157 D3
Haldane Rd E6 ... 100 A4
SE28 ... 124 D6
SW6 ... 135 B6 264 D5
Southall UB1 ... 86 A1
Haldan Rd E4 ... 36 A4
Haldon Rd SW18 ... 157 B5
Hale Cl BR6 ... 227 A4
HA8 ... 27 A5
Chingford E4 ... 20 A1
Hale Ct HA8 ... 27 A5
Hale Dr NW7 ... 27 B4
Hale End Cl HA4 ... 40 A3
Hale End Rd E17 ... 36 B2
Halefield Rd N17 ... 34 B2
Hale Gdns N17 ... 52 A6
Acton W3 ... 110 C5
Hale Grove Gdns NW7 ... 27 C5
Hale Ho SW1 ... 259 D2
Enfield EN3 ... 6 D6
Hale La NW7,HA8 ... 27 B5
Hale Lo HA1 ... 42 C2
Hale Rd N17 ... 52 A6
Newham E6 ... 100 A3
Hales Ct 5 TW11 ... 175 A5
Hales Ho 3 SW12 ... 159 B4
Halesowen Rd SM4 ... 201 D2
Hales Prior N1 ... 233 C3
Hales St SE8 ... 141 C5
Hale St E14 ... 119 D6
Halesworth Cl 3 E5 ... 74 C6
Halesworth Rd SE13 ... 141 D2
Hale The N17 ... 52 A6
Chingford E4 ... 36 B3
Hale Wlk W7 ... 86 C2
Haley Rd NW4 ... 46 C3
Half Acre TW8 ... 131 D6
Half Acre Mews TW8 ... 131 D6
Half Acre Rd W7 ... 108 C5
Half Moon Ct EC1 ... 242 A3
Half Moon La SE24 ... 161 A5
Halfmoon Pas E1 ... 243 D1
Half Moon St W1 ... 115 B5 248 D3
Halford Cl HA8 ... 26 D1
Halford Ct KT9 ... 214 A1
Halford Ho 9 SW15 ... 156 D6
Halford Rd E10 ... 54 B4
SW6 ... 135 C6 265 A5
Ickenham UB10 ... 60 C3
Richmond TW10 ... 154 A6
Halfway St DA15 ... 167 C3
Haliburton Rd TW1,TW7 ... 131 A1
Haliday Ho N1 ... 73 B2
Haliday Wlk 4 N1 ... 73 B2
Halidon Cl E9 ... 74 C3
Halifax 8 NW9 ... 27 D1
Halifax Cl TW11 ... 174 C4
Halifax Rd Enfield EN2 ... 5 B3
Greenford UB6 ... 85 D6
Halifax St SE26 ... 162 B1
Halifield Dr DA17 ... 125 A3
Haling Gr CR2 ... 221 A1
Haling Manor High Sch CR2 ... 220 D1
Haling Park Gdns CR2 ... 220 D2
Haling Park Rd CR2 ... 221 A2
Haling Rd CR2 ... 221 B2
Haliwell Ho 8 NW6 ... 91 D6
Halkett Ho 1 E2 ... 96 C6
Halkin Arc SW1 ... 114 D3 257 D6
Halkin Mews SW1 ... 258 A6
Halkin Pl SW1 ... 258 A6
Halkin St SW1 ... 115 A4 248 B1
Hallam Cl BR7 ... 188 B5
Hallam Ct W1 ... 238 D4
Hallam Gdns HA5 ... 23 A3
Hallam Ho SW1 ... 259 B1
17 SW9 ... 138 C4
Hallam Mews W1 ... 238 D4
Hallam Rd N15 ... 50 D5
Barnes SW13 ... 134 B2
Hallam St W1 ... 93 B2 238 D4
Hallane Ho SE27 ... 183 A5
Hall Cl W5 ... 88 A2
Hall Ct TW11 ... 174 D5
Hall Dr Ealing W7 ... 86 C1
Forest Hill SE26 ... 184 C5
Halley Gdns SE13 ... 142 B1
Halley Ho 15 E2 ... 96 A5
8 SE10 ... 120 D1
Halley Prim Sch E14 ... 97 A2
Halley Rd E7,E12 ... 77 D2
Halley St E14 ... 97 A2
Hall Farm Cl HA7 ... 25 B6
Hall Farm Dr TW2 ... 152 B4
Hallfield W2 ... 236 A1
Hallfield Jun & Inf Schs W2 ... 91 D1
Hallgate SE3 ... 143 A2
Hall Gate NW8 ... 92 A4 229 B2
Hall Gdns E4 ... 35 B6
Halliards The KT12 ... 194 A3
Halliday Ho 29 E1 ... 96 A1
Halliday Sq UB2 ... 108 B5
Halliford Cl TW17 ... 193 C6
Halliford Rd
Sunbury TW16 ... 194 A5
Upper Halliford TW16, TW17 ... 193 D5
Halliford Sch TW17 ... 193 A2
Halliford St N1 ... 73 B1
Halling Ho SE1 ... 252 D1
Halliwell Ct 4 SE22 ... 162 A6
Halliwell Rd SW2 ... 160 B5
Halliwick Court Par 2 N12 ... 30 D5
Halliwick Ct 1 N12 ... 30 D5
Halliwick Ho N21 ... 17 B5
Halliwick Rd N10 ... 31 A2
Hall La E4 ... 35 B5
NW4 ... 28 A1
Harlington UB3 ... 127 B5
Hall Lane E4 ... 35 A5
Hallmark Trad Ctr HA9 ... 67 A4
Hallmead Rd SM1 ... 217 D5
Hall Oak Wlk NW6 ... 69 B2
Hallowell Ave CR0 ... 220 A4
Hallowell Cl CR4 ... 203 A6
Hallowfield Way CR4 ... 202 C6
Hall Pl W2 ... 92 B3 236 C5
Hall Rd E15 ... 76 B4
E6 ... 100 B6
NW8 ... 92 A4 229 B2
Dagenham RM6 ... 58 D3
Isleworth TW7 ... 152 B6
Hall Sch SW20 ... 178 D2
Hall Sch The NW3 ... 70 B2
Hall Sch Wimbledon SW15 ... 156 A1
Hallside Rd EN1 ... 5 D5
Hall St EC1 ... 94 D4 234 D2
N12 ... 30 A5
Halls Terr UB10 ... 82 D3
Hallsville Prim Sch E16 ... 99 A1
Hallsville Rd E16 ... 98 D1
Hallswelle Par 1 NW11 ... 47 B4
Hallswelle Rd NW11 ... 47 B4
Hall The SE3 ... 143 A2
Hall Twr W2 ... 236 D4
Hall View SE9 ... 165 D2
Hallywell Cres E6 ... 100 B2
Halons Rd SE9 ... 166 C4
Halpin Pl SE17 ... 117 B2 262 D3
Halsbrook Rd SE3 ... 143 D2
Halsbury Cl HA7 ... 25 B6
Halsbury Ct HA7 ... 25 B6
Halsbury Ho 4 N7 ... 72 B4
Halsbury Rd W12 ... 112 B5
Halsbury Rd E UB5 ... 64 A4
Halsbury Rd W UB5 ... 63 D3
Halsend UB3 ... 106 B5
Halsey St SW3 ... 114 D2 257 C4
Halsham Cres IG11 ... 79 D3
Halsmere Rd SE5 ... 138 D4
Halstead Cl 2 CR0 ... 221 A5
Halstead Ct N1 ... 235 D3
Halstead Gdns N21 ... 17 B3
Halstead Rd
Edmonton N21 ... 17 B3
Enfield EN1 ... 5 C1
Wanstead E11 ... 55 B4
Halston Cl SW11 ... 158 D5
Halstow 12 NW5 ... 71 A2
Halstow Prim Sch SE10 ... 121 A1
Halstow Rd NW10 ... 90 D4
SE3,SE10 ... 121 A1
Halsway UB3 ... 106 A5
Halter Cl WD6 ... 11 B6
Halton Cl N11 ... 30 D4
Halton Cross St N1 ... 94 D6 234 D6
Haltone Ho 1 SW4 ... 137 D3
Halton Ho 23 N1 ... 72 D1
Halton Mans N1 ... 72 D1
Halton Pl N1 ... 235 A6
Halton Rd N1 ... 72 D1 234 D6
Halt Robin La DA17 ... 125 D2
Halt Robin Rd DA17 ... 125 D2
Halyard Ho E14 ... 120 A3
Hamara Ghar 5 E13 ... 99 C6
Hambalt Rd SW4 ... 159 C6
Hamble Cl HA4 ... 61 C6
Hamble Ct KT1 ... 175 D3
Hambledon SE17 ... 139 B6
Hambledon Chase N4 ... 50 A2
Hambledon Cl UB8 ... 82 D3
Hambledon Ct
5 Ealing W5 ... 110 A6
9 Wallington SM6 ... 219 B2
Hambledon Gdns SE25 ... 205 D6
Hambledon Ho E5 ... 74 B4
2 Kingston KT2 ... 176 D4
Hambledon Pl SE21 ... 161 D3
Hambledon Rd SW18 ... 157 B4
Hambledown Rd SE9 ... 167 C4
Hamble St SW6 ... 135 D2
Hambleton Cl KT4 ... 216 C6
Hamble Wlk UB5 ... 85 C5
Hambley Ho 5 SE16 ... 118 B2
Hamblin Ho UB1 ... 107 A6
Hamblyn Ct N16 ... 51 D2
Hambridge Way SW2 ... 160 C4
Hambro Ave BR2 ... 209 A1
Hambrook Ct 12 NW5 ... 71 B4
Hambrook Rd SE25 ... 206 B6
Hambro Rd SW16 ... 181 D5
Hambrough Ho UB4 ... 84 C2
Hambrough Prim Sch UB1 ... 107 B5
Hambrough Rd UB1 ... 107 A5
Hambury Ho SW8 ... 270 B5
Ham Cl TW10 ... 153 C1
Ham Comm TW10 ... 153 D1
Ham Ct 12 NW9 ... 27 D1
Hamden Cres RM10 ... 81 D5
Hamel Cl HA3 ... 43 D5
Hamelton Terr RM9 ... 80 C1
Hamers Ho 19 SW2 ... 160 C4
Hameway E6 ... 100 C3
Ham Farm Rd KT2,TW10 ... 176 A6
Hamfrith Rd E15 ... 76 D2
Ham Gate Ave TW10 ... 176 A6
Ham Ho★ TW10 ... 153 C2
Hamilton Ave
Cheam SM3 ... 217 A6
Edmonton N9 ... 18 A4
Ilford IG6 ... 57 A4
Tolworth KT6,SM3 ... 214 C6
Hamilton Cl N17 ... 51 D6
NW8 ... 92 B4 229 C1
SE16 ... 119 A4
Ashford TW13 ... 171 D5
Cockfosters EN4 ... 2 D1
Teddington TW11 ... 175 B4
Hamilton Cres
Edmonton N13 ... 32 C6
Harrow HA2 ... 63 B5
Hounslow TW3 ... 151 D6
Hamilton Ct W9 ... 229 A2
9 Catford SE6 ... 164 D3
Croydon CR0 ... 206 A1
Ealing W5 ... 110 B6
Hamilton Gdns NW8 ... 92 A4 229 B2
Hamilton Hall NW8 ... 92 A5 229 A3
Hamilton Ho 1 E14 ... 119 B6
19 E3 ... 97 B4
NW8 ... 229 C2
W8 ... 245 C2
Chiswick W4 ... 133 C6
Putney SW15 ... 156 A6
10 Richmond TW9 ... 132 C4
Hamilton La N5 ... 72 D4
Hamilton Lo 32 E1 ... 96 C3
Hamilton Mews W1 ... 248 C2
Hamilton Par TW13 ... 172 A6
Hamilton Pk N5 ... 72 D4
Hamilton Pk W N5 ... 72 D4
Hamilton Pl W1 ... 115 A5 248 B3
Sunbury TW16 ... 172 B3
Tottenham N17 ... 33 D1
Hamilton Rd DA7 ... 147 A3
E15 ... 98 C4
E17 ... 35 A1
N2 ... 48 A6
NW10 ... 68 A3
NW11 ... 47 A2
W4 ... 111 C4
Barnet EN4 ... 2 C1
Brentford TW8 ... 131 D6
Ealing W5 ... 110 A6
Edmonton N9 ... 18 A4
Feltham TW13 ... 171 D6
Harrow HA1 ... 42 C4
Hayes UB3 ... 106 B6
Ilford IG1 ... 78 D4
Merton SW19 ... 179 D3
Sidcup DA15 ... 190 A6
Southall UB1 ... 107 B5
South Norwood CR7 ... 205 B6
Twickenham TW2 ... 152 C3
West Norwood SE27 ... 183 B6
Hamilton Road Ctr E15 ... 98 C4
Hamilton Road Ind Est SE27 ... 183 B6
Hamilton Road Mews 1 SW19 ... 179 D3
Hamilton Sq N12 ... 30 A4
SE1 ... 252 D2
Hamilton St SE8 ... 141 C6
Hamilton Terr NW8 ... 92 A4 229 B2
Hamilton Way N3 ... 29 C4
Edmonton N13 ... 32 D6
Hamlea Cl SE12 ... 165 A6
Hamlet Cl SE13 ... 142 C1
Hamlet Ct SE11 ... 261 C2
1 W6 ... 112 A2
14 Enfield EN1 ... 17 C6
Hamlet (Day) Hospl The TW9 ... 132 A2
Hamlet Gdns W6 ... 112 A2
Hamlet Ho SE9 ... 166 C6
Hamlet Ind Est E9 ... 75 C1
Hamlet Rd SE19 ... 184 A3
Hamlet Sq NW2 ... 69 A5
Hamlets Way E3 ... 97 B3
Hamlet The SE5 ... 139 B2
Hamlet Way SE1 ... 252 D2
Hamlin Cres HA5 ... 40 C4
Hamlyn Cl HA8 ... 10 A1
Hamlyn Gdns SE19 ... 183 C3
Hammelton Ct 4 BR1 ... 186 D2
Hammelton Gn 2 SW9 ... 138 D4
Hammelton Rd BR1 ... 187 A2
Hammers La NW7 ... 28 A6
Hammersley Ho 8 SE14 ... 140 C5
Hammersmith Bridge Rd W6,SW13 ... 112 C1
Hammersmith Broadway 5 W6 ... 112 C2
Hammersmith Flyover W6 ... 112 C1
Hammersmith Gr W6 ... 112 C3
Hammersmith Hospl W12 ... 90 B1
Hammersmith Rd W14 ... 254 B4
W6 ... 112 D2
Hammersmith Sta W6 ... 112 C2
Hammersmith Terr W6 ... 112 A1
Hammet Cl UB4 ... 84 D2
Hammett St EC3 ... 253 C6
Hammond Ave CR4 ... 181 B1
Hammond Cl Barnet EN5 ... 13 B6
Greenford UB6 ... 64 B3
Hampton TW12 ... 173 C2
Hammond Ct 1 E10 ... 75 D6
1 E17 ... 53 A4
Hammond Ho E14 ... 119 D3
10 SE14 ... 140 C5
Hammond Lo 6 W9 ... 91 C2
Hammond Rd Enfield EN1 ... 6 B3
Southall UB2 ... 107 A3
Hammonds Cl RM8 ... 80 C5
Hammond St NW5 ... 71 C2
Hammond Way 2 SE28 ... 124 B6
Hamonde Cl HA8 ... 10 D2
Hamond Sq N1 ... 95 C5
Ham Park Rd E15 ... 76 D1
Hampden Ave BR3 ... 185 A1
Hampden Cl NW1 ... 232 D4
Hampden Ct 5 N10 ... 31 A3
Hampden Gurney CE Prim Sch W1 ... 92 C1 237 B2
Hampden Gurney St W1 ... 237 C1
Hampden Ho SW9 ... 138 C3
Hampden La N17 ... 34 A2
Hampden Rd N10 ... 31 A3
N19 ... 71 D6
N8 ... 50 C5
Beckenham BR3 ... 185 A1
Harrow HA3 ... 24 A1
Kingston KT1 ... 198 C6
Hampden Rd *continued*
Tottenham N17 ... 34 A2
Hampden Sq N14 ... 15 B3
Hampden Way N14 ... 15 B2
Hampshire Cl N18 ... 34 B5
Hampshire Ct 6 SW13 ... 133 D3
Hampshire Hog La 11 W6 ... 112 B2
Hampshire Rd N22 ... 32 B3
Hampshire Sch The SW7 ... 114 C4 247 B1
Hampshire St NW5 ... 71 D2
Hampson Way SW8 ... 138 B4 270 C2
Hampstead Cl SE28 ... 124 B5
Hampstead Garden Suburb Inst NW11 ... 47 D4
Hampstead Gate NW3 ... 70 A3
Hampstead Gdns NW11 ... 47 C3
Hampstead Gn NW3 ... 70 C3
Hampstead Gr NW3 ... 70 A5
Hampstead Heath★ NW3 ... 70 B6
Hampstead Heath Sta NW3 ... 70 C4
Hampstead High St NW3 ... 70 B4
Hampstead Hill Gdns NW3 ... 70 C4
Hampstead Hill Sch NW3 ... 70 C3
Hampstead Hts N2 ... 48 A6
Hampstead La N6 ... 48 C2
Hampstead Parochial CE Prim Sch NW3 ... 70 A4
Hampstead Rd NW1 ... 93 C4 232 A2
Hampstead Sch NW2 ... 69 A4
Hampstead Sq NW3 ... 70 A5
Hampstead Sta NW3 ... 70 A4
Hampstead Way NW11 ... 47 C3
Hampstead West 4 NW6 ... 69 C2
Hampstead Wlk 1 E3 ... 97 B6
Hampton Cl N11 ... 31 B5
NW6 ... 91 C4
Wimbledon SW20 ... 178 C3
Hampton Com Coll TW12 ... 173 C5
Hampton Court KT8 ... 196 C6
Hampton Court Ave KT8 ... 196 C3
Hampton Court Cres KT8 ... 196 B6
Hampton Court Landing Stage KT8 ... 196 C6
Hampton Court Palace★ KT8 ... 196 D6
Hampton Court Par KT8 ... 196 C5
Hampton Court Rd KT1, KT8 ... 197 B6
Hampton Court Sta KT8 ... 196 C5
Hampton Court Way KT10,KT7,KT8 ... 196 C3
Hampton Ct N1 ... 72 D2
19 SE16 ... 118 D5
Wood Green N22 ... 31 C2
Hampton Farm Ind Est TW13 ... 151 A1
Hampton Hill Bsns Pk TW12 ... 174 A5
Hampton Hill Jun Mix Sch TW12 ... 174 A5
Hampton Ho DA7 ... 147 D3
Hampton Inf Sch TW12 ... 173 C3
Hampton Jun Sch TW12 ... 173 C2
Hampton La TW13 ... 173 A6
Hampton Rd E11 ... 54 B1
E4 ... 35 B5
E7 ... 77 C3
Ilford IG1 ... 79 A4
North Cheam KT4 ... 216 B6
Teddington TW11,TW12 ... 174 C5
Thornton Heath CR0 ... 205 A3
Twickenham TW2 ... 152 B1
Hampton Rd E TW13 ... 151 B1
Hampton Rd W TW13 ... 151 A1
Hampton Rise HA3 ... 44 A3
Hampton Road Ind Pk CR0 ... 205 A3
Hampton Sch TW12 ... 173 C5
Hampton St SE1 ... 116 D2 261 D3
Hampton Sta TW12 ... 173 C2
Hampton Wick Inf Sch KT1 ... 175 D3
Hampton Wick Sta KT1 ... 175 C2
Ham Ridings TW10 ... 176 B5
Ham Shades Cl 1 DA15 ... 168 A1
Ham St TW10 ... 153 C1
Ham The TW8 ... 131 C5
Ham View CR0 ... 207 A3
Ham Yd W1 ... 249 C6
Hanameel St 6 E16 ... 121 A5
7 E16 ... 121 B5
10 E16 ... 121 B5
Hana Mews E5 ... 74 B4
Hanbury Cl NW4 ... 46 C6
Hanbury Ct HA1 ... 42 D3
Hanbury Dr N21 ... 16 B6
Hanbury Ho 8 E1 ... 96 A2
Hanbury Rd W3 ... 110 D4
Tottenham N17 ... 34 B1
Hanbury St E1 ... 96 A2 243 D4
Hancocke Ho 4 E17 ... 53 D6
Hancock Nunn Ho 1 NW3 ... 70 D1
Hancock Rd E3 ... 98 A4
South Norwood SE19 ... 183 B4

Handa Wlk 3 N1 ... 73 A2
Handcroft Rd CR0 ... 204 D1
Hand Ct WC1 ... 240 D3
Handel Cl HA8 ... 26 B4
Handel Ho TW2 ... 152 B5
Handel Mans SW13 ... 134 C5
Handel Pl NW10 ... 67 B2
Handel St WC1 ... 94 A3 240 B6
Handel Way HA8 ... 26 C3
Handen Rd SE12 ... 164 D6
Handforth Rd SW9 ... 138 C5
6 Ilford IG1 ... 78 D5
Handley Gr NW2 ... 68 D5
Handley Page Rd SM6 ...
Handley Rd E9 ... 96 C6
Handowe Cl NW4 ... 46 A5
Handside Cl KT4 ... 200 D1
Hands Wlk E16 ... 99 A1
Handsworth Ave E4 ... 36 B4
Handsworth Prim Sch
E4 ... 36 B4
Handsworth Rd N17 ... 51 B6
Handtrough Way IG11 ... 100 D5
Hanford Cl SW18 ... 157 C3
Hanger Ct W5 ... 88 C3
Hanger Gn W5 ... 88 C3
Hanger Lane Sta W5 ... 88 A4
Hanger La (North Circular
Rd) W5 ... 88 B2
Hanger Vale La W5 ... 88 B1
Hanger View Way W3 ... 88 C2
Hangmans Cnr BR7 ... 188 D2
Hankey Pl SE1 ... 117 B4 252 D1
Hankins La NW7 ... 11 C1
Hanley Gdns N4 ... 50 B1
Hanley Pl BR3 ... 185 C3
Hanley Rd N4,N19 ... 50 A1
Hanmer Wlk N7 ... 72 B6
Hannah Cl BR3 ... 208 A6
Hannah Ct SW19 ... 178 D3
Hannah Mary Way 15
SE1 ... 118 A2
Hannah Mews SM6 ... 219 C1
Hannan Cl NW10 ... 67 A4
Hannay La N8 ... 49 D2
Hannay Wlk SW16 ... 159 D2
Hannell Rd SW6 ... 135 A5 264 B4
Hannen Ho SE5 ... 139 B2
Hannen Rd SE27 ... 160 D1
Hannibal Rd E1 ... 96 C2
Stanwell TW19 ... 148 A4
Hannibal Way CR0 ... 220 B2
Hanning Lo TW3 ... 130 A1
Hannington Rd SW4 ... 137 B2
Hanover Ave E16 ... 121 A5
Feltham TW13 ... 150 A2
Hanover Circ UB3 ... 83 B1
Hanover Cl Cheam SM3 ... 217 B4
Richmond TW9 ... 132 C5
Hanover Ct N16 ... 51 D2
NW9 ... 45 C6
W12 ... 112 A5
1 Penge SE19 ... 184 A3
Hanover Dr BR7 ... 189 A6
Hanover Gate Mans
NW1 ... 237 B6
Hanover Gdns SE11 ... 138 C6
Hanover Ho NW8 ... 230 A3
New Barnet EN5 ... 2 A1
Tolworth KT6 ... 198 C1
Hanover Mans 5 SW2 ... 160 C6
Hanover Mead NW11 ... 47 A3
Hanover Pk SE15 ... 140 A4
Hanover Pl 12 E3 ... 97 B4
WC2 ... 240 B1
Hanover Prim Sch N1 ... 235 B4
Hanover Rd N15 ... 51 D5
Merton SW19 ... 180 A3
Willesden NW10 ... 90 C6
Hanover Sq W1 ... 93 B1 238 D1
Hanover St W1 ... 93 B1 238 D1
Croydon CR0 ... 220 D5
Hanover Steps W2 ... 237 B1
Hanover Terr
NW1 ... 92 D4 230 C1
Isleworth TW7 ... 131 A4
Hanover Terr Mews
NW1 ... 92 C4 230 B1
Hanover Way DA7 ... 146 D2
Hanover West Ind Est
NW10 ... 89 B4
Hanover Yd N1 ... 235 A4
Hansard Mews W14 ... 112 D4
Hansart Way EN2 ... 4 C4
Hanscomb Mews 3
SW4 ... 137 C1
Hans Cres SW1 ... 114 D3 257 C6
Hanselin Cl HA7 ... 24 D5
Hansen Dr N21 ... 16 B6
Hanshaw Dr HA8 ... 27 B2
Hansler Gr KT8 ... 196 B5
Hansler Rd SE22 ... 161 D6
Hansol Rd DA6 ... 169 A6
Hansom Terr 1 BR1 ... 187 B2
Hanson Cl Balham SW12 ... 159 B4
Beckenham BR3 ... 185 D4
Mortlake SW14 ... 133 A2
West Drayton UB7 ... 104 B3
Hanson Ct E17 ... 53 D3
Hanson Gdns UB1 ... 107 A4
Hanson Ho 2 E1 ... 118 A6
Hanson St W1 ... 93 C2 239 A4
Hans Pl SW1 ... 114 D3 257 C6
Hans Rd SW3 ... 114 D3 257 C6
Hans St SW1 ... 114 D3 257 D5
Hanway Ho 25 SW9 ... 138 C4
Hanway Pl W1 ... 239 C2
Hanway Rd W7 ... 86 C1
Hanway St W1 ... 239 C2
Hanwell Ho 24 W2 ... 91 C2
Hanwell Sta W7 ... 108 C6
Hanworth Ho SE5 ... 138 D5
Hanworth Rd
Ashford TW16 ... 172 A3
Feltham TW13 ... 150 B3
Hampton TW12 ... 173 C5
Hounslow TW3,TW4 ... 129 D1
Twickenham TW4 ... 151 B4
Hanworth Terr TW3 ... 129 D1
Hanworth Trad Est
TW13 ... 151 A1
Hapgood Cl UB6 ... 64 B3
Harben Rd NW6 ... 70 A1
Harberson Rd E15 ... 98 D6
Balham SW12 ... 159 B3
Harberton Rd N19 ... 49 C1
Harbet Rd N18 ... 35 A4
W2 ... 92 B2 236 D3
Harbex Cl DA5 ... 169 D4
Harbinger Prim Sch
E14 ... 119 D2
Harbinger Rd E14 ... 119 D2
Harbin Ho 5 SW2 ... 160 C3
Harbledown Ho SE1 ... 252 C1
Harbledown Rd SW6 ... 265 A2
Harbord Cl SE5 ... 139 B3
Harbord Ho 5 SE16 ... 118 D2
Harbord St SW6 ... 134 D4
Harborne Cl WD19 ... 22 C5
Harborough Ave DA15 ... 167 D4
Harborough Rd SW16 ... 182 B6
Harborough Sch N19 ... 71 D6
Harbour Ave
SW10 ... 136 A4 266 B1
Harbour Exchange Sq
E14 ... 119 D4
Harbour Rd SE5 ... 139 A2
Harbridge Ave SW15 ... 156 A4
Harbury Rd SM5 ... 218 C1
Harbut Rd SW11 ... 136 B1
Harcastle Cl UB4 ... 85 A3
Harcombe Rd N16 ... 73 C5
Harcourt Ave DA5,DA15 ... 168 C4
E12 ... 78 B3
HA8 ... 11 A1
Wallington SM6 ... 219 B4
Harcourt Cl TW7 ... 131 A2
Harcourt Field SM6 ... 219 B4
Harcourt Ho 27 SW8 ... 137 D3
W1 ... 238 C2
5 Chingford E4 ... 36 B5
Harcourt Lo 2 SM6 ... 219 B4
Harcourt Rd E15 ... 98 D5
N22 ... 31 D2
SE4 ... 141 B2
Bexley DA6,DA7 ... 147 A1
Bushey WD23 ... 8 A6
Merton SW19 ... 179 C3
Thornton Heath CR7 ... 204 C3
Wallington SM6 ... 219 B4
Harcourt St W1 ... 92 C2 237 B3
Harcourt Terr
SW10 ... 113 D1 255 D1
Hardcastle Cl SE25 ... 206 A3
Hardcastle Ho 8 SE15 ... 140 A4
Hardcourts Cl BR4 ... 223 D5
Hard Ct IG8 ... 37 C4
Hardel Rise SW2 ... 160 D3
Hardel Wlk SE24,SW2 ... 160 C4
Harden Ct 1 SE7 ... 122 A2
Harden Ho SE5 ... 139 C3
Harders Rd SE15 ... 140 B3
Hardess St SE24 ... 139 A2
Hardham Ho 5 SW2 ... 160 C5
Hardie Cl NW10 ... 67 B3
Harding Cl SE17 ... 139 A6
South Croydon CR0 ... 221 D5
Harding Ct SE25 ... 183 D1
Hardinge Cl UB8 ... 82 D1
Hardinge Rd
Edmonton N18 ... 33 C4
Willesden NW10 ... 90 C6
Hardinge St E1 ... 96 C1
SE18 ... 122 D3
Harding Ho 16 SE18 ... 122 B2
Barnes SW13 ... 134 B6
Hayes UB3 ... 84 B1
Harding Pl SE23 ... 163 A4
Harding Rd DA7 ... 147 B3
Hardings Cl KT2 ... 176 B2
Hardings La SE20 ... 184 D4
Hardington 2 NW1 ... 71 A1
Hardman Rd SE7 ... 121 B1
Kingston KT2 ... 176 A1
Hardwick Cl 7 HA7 ... 25 C5
Hardwick Ct 8 E11 ... 55 A3
Hardwicke Ave TW5 ... 129 C4
Hardwicke Ho 14 E3 ... 97 D4
Hardwicke Mews WC1 ... 233 D1
Hardwicke Rd W4 ... 111 B2
Bowes Park N13 ... 32 A4
Richmond TW10 ... 175 C6
Hardwicke St IG11 ... 101 A6
Hardwick Gn W13 ... 87 B2
Hardwick Ho NW8 ... 237 B6
14 SW8 ... 137 D3
Hardwick St EC1 ... 94 C4 234 B1
Hardwick's Way SW18 ... 157 C6
Hardwidge St SE1 ... 253 A2
Hardy Ave 4 E16 ... 121 A5
Ruislip HA4 ... 62 B3
Hardy Cl SE16 ... 118 D4
Barnet EN5 ... 13 A6
Pinner HA5 ... 40 D2
Hardy Cotts 2 SE10 ... 142 B6
Hardy Ct SE3 ... 142 D6
9 Wanstead E11 ... 55 A5
Hardyng Ho 4 E17 ... 53 A5
Hardy Pas N22 ... 32 C1
Hardy Rd E4 ... 35 B4
Hardy Rd *continued*
SE3 ... 142 D6
Merton SW19 ... 179 D3
Hardys Cl KT8 ... 196 C5
Hardy Way EN2 ... 4 C4
Harebell Dr E6 ... 100 C2
Hare & Billet Rd SE3 ... 142 B3
Harecourt Rd N1 ... 73 A2
Hare Ct EC4 ... 241 A1
Haredale Ho 22 SE16 ... 118 A4
Haredale Rd SE24 ... 139 A1
Haredon Cl SE23 ... 162 D4
Harefield KT10 ... 212 C5
Harefield Cl EN2 ... 4 C4
Harefield Ct 6 SW19 ... 179 C3
Harefield Mews SE4 ... 141 B2
Harefield Rd DA14 ... 168 D1
N8 ... 49 D4
SE4 ... 141 B2
South Norwood SW16 ... 182 B3
Uxbridge UB8 ... 60 A3
Hare La KT10 ... 212 C2
Hare Marsh E2 ... 96 A3
Harenc Sch Trust DA14 ... 190 C5
Hare Pl EC4 ... 241 B1
Hare Row E2 ... 96 B5
Haresfield Rd RM10 ... 81 C2
Hare St SE18 ... 122 C3
Hare Wlk N1 ... 95 C5
Harewood Ave
NW1 ... 92 C3 237 B5
Northolt UB5 ... 63 B1
Harewood Cl UB5 ... 63 B1
Harewood Ct HA3 ... 24 C2
Harewood Pl W1 ... 238 D1
Harewood Rd
Hounslow TW7 ... 130 D4
Mitcham SW19 ... 180 C4
South Croydon CR2 ... 221 C2
Harewood Row NW1 ... 237 B4
Harewood Terr UB2 ... 107 B2
Harfield Gdns 1 SE5 ... 139 C2
Harfield Rd TW16 ... 172 D1
Harfleur Ct SE11 ... 261 C3
Harford Cl E4 ... 19 D4
Harford Ho SE5 ... 139 A6
W11 ... 91 B2
Harford Rd E4 ... 19 D4
Harford St E1 ... 97 A3
Harford Wlk N2 ... 48 B5
Hargood Cl HA3 ... 44 A3
Hargood Rd SE3 ... 143 C4
Hargrave Mans 2 N19 ... 71 D6
Hargrave Park Prim Sch
N19 ... 71 C6
Hargrave Pk N19 ... 71 C6
Hargrave Pl N7 ... 71 D3
Hargrave Rd N19 ... 71 C6
Hargraves Ho 14 W12 ... 112 B6
Hargwyne St SW9 ... 138 B2
Haringey Pk N8 ... 50 A3
Haringey Rd N8 ... 50 A5
Harington Terr N18 ... 17 B1
Harkett Cl HA3 ... 24 D1
Harkness Ho 20 E1 ... 96 A1
Harland Ave
Sidcup DA15 ... 167 C2
South Croydon CR0 ... 222 A5
Harland Cl SW19 ... 201 D6
Harland Fst Sch CR4 ... 180 B1
Harland Rd SE12 ... 165 A3
Harlands Gr BR6 ... 226 D4
Harlech Ct 1 SE23 ... 162 C3
Harlech Gdns TW5 ... 128 C5
Harlech Rd N14 ... 16 A1
Harlech Twr 5 W3 ... 111 A4
Harlequin Ave TW8 ... 131 A6
Harlequin Cl Hayes UB4 ... 84 D2
Isleworth TW7 ... 152 C6
Harlequin Ct NW10 ... 67 B2
Croydon CR2 ... 221 A1
Ealing W5 ... 109 C6
Harlequin Ho 1 DA18 ... 125 A3
Harlequin Rd TW11 ... 175 B3
Harlescott Rd SE15 ... 140 D1
Harlesden Gdns NW10 ... 89 D6
Harlesden Plaza 2
NW10 ... 89 D5
Harlesden Prim Sch
NW10 ... 89 C5
Harlesden Rd NW10 ... 90 A6
Harlesden Sta NW10 ... 89 B5
Harleston Cl 4 E5 ... 74 C6
Harley Cl HA0 ... 65 D2
Harley Cres HA1 ... 42 B5
Harley Ct N20 ... 14 A1
Wanstead E11 ... 55 A2
Harleyford BR1 ... 187 C2
Harleyford Ct SW8 ... 270 C6
Harleyford Manor 8
W3 ... 111 A5
Harleyford Rd
SE11 ... 138 B6 270 C6
Harleyford St SE11 ... 138 C6
Harley Gdns BR6 ... 227 C4
SW10 ... 114 A1 256 B1
Harley Gr E3 ... 97 B4
Harley Ho E11 ... 54 B2
NW1 ... 238 B5
Harley Pl W1 ... 93 B2 238 C3
Harley Rd NW10 ... 89 C5
NW3 ... 70 B1
Harrow HA1 ... 42 B5
Harley St W1 ... 93 B2 238 C3
Harley Villas NW10 ... 89 C5
Harling Ct 3 SW11 ... 136 D3
Harlinger St SE18 ... 122 A3
Harlington Bridge UB3 ... 105 C1
Harlington Cl UB7 ... 127 A5
Harlington Cnr UB3 ... 127 B4
Harlington Com Sch
UB3 ... 105 B2
Harlington Rd DA7 ... 147 A2
Hillingdon UB8 ... 82 C3
Harlington Rd E TW13,
TW14 ... 150 C3
Harlington Rd W TW14 ... 150 B5
Harlowe Ho 12 E8 ... 95 D6
Harlow Mans 2 IG11 ... 78 D1
Harlow Rd N13 ... 17 B1
Harlyn Dr HA5 ... 40 B6
Harlyn Prim Sch HA5 ... 40 B6
Harlynwood 18 SE5 ... 139 A5
Harman Ave IG8 ... 36 D4
Harman Cl NW2 ... 69 A5
9 SE1 ... 118 A1
Chingford E4 ... 36 B6
Harman Dr DA15 ... 167 D5
NW2 ... 69 A4
Harman Rd EN1 ... 17 D6
Harmondsworth La UB7 ... 126 B6
Harmondsworth Rd
UB7 ... 104 A2
Harmon Ho 6 SE8 ... 119 B2
Harmony Cl NW11 ... 47 A4
Harmony Way BR1 ... 187 A1
NW4 ... 46 C5
Harmood Gr NW1 ... 71 B1
Harmood Ho 2 NW1 ... 71 B1
Harmood St NW1 ... 71 B1
Harmsworth St
SE17 ... 116 D1 261 C1
Harmsworth Way N20 ... 13 C3
Harness Rd SE28 ... 124 A4
Harold Ave Erith DA17 ... 125 B1
Hayes UB3 ... 105 D3
Harold Ct 14 SE16 ... 118 D4
Harold Est SE1 ... 263 B5
Harold Gibbons Ct 12
SE7 ... 143 C6
Harold Ho 16 E2 ... 96 D5
Harold Laski Ho EC1 ... 234 D1
Harold Maddison Ho
SE17 ... 261 D2
Harold Pl SE11 ... 261 A1
Harold Rd E11 ... 54 C1
E13 ... 99 B6
N15 ... 51 D4
N8 ... 50 B5
NW10 ... 89 B4
Chingford E4 ... 20 A1
South Norwood SE19 ... 183 B3
Sutton SM1 ... 218 B4
Woodford IG8 ... 37 A2
Haroldstone Rd E17 ... 53 A4
Harold Wilson Ho SW6 ... 264 D5
Harp Alley EC4 ... 241 C2
Harp Bsns Ctr The NW2 ... 68 A6
Harpenden Rd
Wanstead E12 ... 77 C6
West Norwood SE27,
SW16 ... 160 D2
Harpenmead Point NW2 ... 69 B6
Harper Cl N14 ... 15 C6
Harper Ho 3 SW9 ... 138 D2
Harper Mews SW17 ... 158 A1
Harper Rd SE1 ... 117 A3 262 B6
Newham E6 ... 100 B1
Harper's Yd N17 ... 33 D2
Harp Island Cl NW10 ... 67 B6
Harp La EC3 ... 253 A5
Harpley Sq E1 ... 96 D3
Harpour Rd IG11 ... 79 A2
Harp Rd W7 ... 86 D3
Harpsden St SW11 ... 268 A1
Harpur Mews WC1 ... 240 C4
Harpur St WC1 ... 94 B2 240 C4
Harraden Rd SE3 ... 143 C4
Harrier Ave E11 ... 55 B3
Harrier Ct TW4 ... 129 A3
Harrier Ho 9 SW11 ... 136 C2
Harrier Mews SE28 ... 123 B4
Harrier Rd NW9 ... 27 C1
Harriers Cl W5 ... 110 A6
Harrier Way E6 ... 100 B2
Harries Rd UB4 ... 84 C3
Harriet Cl E8 ... 96 A6
Harriet Gdns CR0 ... 222 A6
Harriet Ho SW6 ... 265 D3
Harriet St SW1 ... 114 D4 247 D1
Harriet Tubman Cl 21
SW2 ... 160 C4
Harriet Way WD23 ... 8 B4
Harriet Wlk
SW1 ... 114 D4 247 D1
Harringay Gdns N8 ... 50 D5
Harringay Green Lanes Sta
N4 ... 50 D3
Harringay Rd N15 ... 50 D5
Harringay Sta N4 ... 50 C3
Harrington Cl NW10 ... 67 B5
Wallington CR0 ... 220 A6
Harrington Ct SW7 ... 256 D4
9 W9 ... 91 B4
6 South Croydon CR0 ... 221 B6
Harrington Gdns
SW7 ... 114 A2 256 A3
Harrington Hill E5 ... 52 B1
Harrington Hill Prim Sch
E5 ... 52 B1
Harrington Ho E5 ... 52 C1
NW1 ... 232 A2
SW1 ... 259 D2
Harrington Rd E11 ... 54 C1
SW7 ... 114 B2 256 C4
Croydon SE25 ... 206 B5
Harrington Rd Sta SE25 ... 206 C6
Harrington Sq
NW1 ... 93 C5 232 A3
Harrington St
NW1 ... 93 C4 232 A2
Harrington Way SE18 ... 121 D3
Harriott Cl SE10 ... 120 D2
Harriott Ho 11 E1 ... 96 C1
Harris City Tech Coll
SE19 ... 183 D2
Harris Cl Enfield EN2 ... 4 D4
Heston TW5 ... 129 C4
Harris Cotts 1 E15 ... 98 D6
Harris Ho 10 E3 ... 97 C4
8 SW9 ... 138 C2
Harris Lo SE6 ... 164 A3
Harrison Cl N20 ... 14 C3
Harrison Ho SE17 ... 262 C2
Harrison Rd RM10 ... 81 D2
Harrisons Ct 1 SE14 ... 140 D6
Harrison's Rise CR0 ... 220 D5
Harrison St WC1 ... 94 A4 233 B1
Harrison Way TW17 ... 192 D4
Harris Rd DA7 ... 147 B4
Dagenham RM9 ... 81 B3
Harris St E17 ... 53 B2
SE5 ... 139 B5
Harris Way TW16 ... 171 C2
Harrodian Sch The
SW13 ... 133 D5
Harrogate Ct 2 SE26 ... 162 A1
Harrold Ho 1 NW3 ... 70 A1
Harrold Rd RM8 ... 80 B3
Harrow Ave EN1 ... 17 D5
Harroway Rd SW11 ... 136 B3
Harrowby St W1 ... 92 C1 237 B2
Harrow Cl KT9 ... 213 D1
Harrow Coll HA1 ... 42 C2
Harrow Coll (Harrow Weald
Campus) HA3 ... 24 C4
Harrowdene Cl HA0 ... 65 D4
Harrowdene Ct SW19 ... 179 A5
Harrowdene Gdns
TW11 ... 175 A3
Harrowdene Rd HA0 ... 65 D4
Harrow Dr N9 ... 17 D3
Harrowes Meade HA8 ... 10 C1
Harrow Fields Gdns HA1 ... 64 C5
Harrowgate Ho 22 E9 ... 74 D2
Harrowgate Rd E9 ... 75 A1
Harrow Gn E11 ... 76 C5
Harrow High Sch HA1 ... 43 A3
Harrow Hospl HA2 ... 64 C6
Harrow La E14 ... 120 A6
Harrow Lo SM2 ... 218 B2
Harrow Manor Way
SE2 ... 124 C3
Harrow Mus & Her Ctr*
HA2 ... 42 A6
Harrow-on-the-Hill Sta
HA1 ... 42 C3
Harrow Pk HA1 ... 64 C6
Harrow Pl E1 ... 95 C1 243 B2
Harrow Rd E11 ... 76 D5
2 E6 ... 100 A6
W2 ... 92 A2 236 B3
W2,W9 ... 91 C3
Ashford TW15 ... 148 C2
Barking IG11 ... 101 C6
Carshalton SM1,SM2,SM5 ... 218 C2
Ilford IG1 ... 79 A4
Wembley HA0 ... 65 A4
Wembley HA0 ... 65 D3
Wembley HA9 ... 66 C2
Harrow Sch HA1 ... 42 C1
Harrow St NW1 ... 237 A4
Harrow View
Harrow HA1,HA2 ... 42 B5
Hayes UB3 ... 84 A1
Hillingdon UB10 ... 83 A4
Harrow View Rd W5 ... 87 B3
Harrow Way
Charlton TW17 ... 171 A1
South Oxhey WD19 ... 23 A6
Harrow Weald Pk HA3 ... 24 B4
Harrow & Wealdstone Sta
HA1 ... 42 C5
Harry Ct 15 NW9 ... 46 A5
Harry Gosling Prim Sch
E1 ... 96 A1
Harry Hinkins Ho SE17 ... 262 B1
Harry Lambourn Ho 10
SE15 ... 140 B5
Harston 15 KT1 ... 176 C1
Harston Dr EN3 ... 7 C5
Hart Ct E12 ... 78 C1
Harte Rd TW3 ... 129 B3
Hartfield Ave
Borehamwood WD6 ... 10 C6
Northolt UB5 ... 84 B5
Hartfield Cl WD6 ... 10 C6
Hartfield Cres BR4 ... 225 A5
Merton SW19 ... 179 B3
Hartfield Gr SE20 ... 184 C2
Hartfield Ho UB5 ... 84 B5
Hartfield Rd
Chessington KT9 ... 213 D3
Hayes BR4 ... 225 A4
Merton SW19 ... 179 C3
Hartfield Terr E3 ... 97 C5
Hartford Ave HA3 ... 43 B6
Hartford Rd DA5 ... 169 C5
West Ewell KT19 ... 214 D2
Hart Gr Ealing W5 ... 110 C5
Southall UB1 ... 85 C2
Hart Grove Ct 3 W5 ... 110 C5
Hartham Cl N7 ... 72 A3
Isleworth TW7 ... 131 A4
Hartham Rd N7 ... 72 A3
Isleworth TW7 ... 131 A4
Tottenham N17 ... 33 D1
Hart Ho SW2 ... 160 C3
Harting Rd SE9 ... 166 A1
Hartington Cl BR6 ... 227 A3
Harrow HA1 ... 64 C4
Hartington Ct SW8 ... 270 A2
Chiswick W4 ... 132 D5
Hartington Rd E17 ... 53 A3
SW8 ... 138 A5 270 A3
Chiswick W4 ... 133 A4
Ealing W13 ... 109 B6
Newham E16 ... 99 B1
Southall UB2 ... 107 A3
Twickenham TW1 ... 153 B5
Hartismere Rd
SW6 ... 135 B5 264 D4
Hartlake Rd E9 ... 75 A2
Hartland NW1 ... 232 B5
Hartland Cl Edgware HA8 ... 10 C2
Enfield N21 ... 17 A5
Hartland Ct 5 N11 ... 30 D5
Hartland Dr Edgware HA8 ... 10 C2
Ruislip HA4 ... 62 B4
Hartland Rd E15 ... 76 D1
N11 ... 30 D5
NW1 ... 71 B1
NW6 ... 91 B6
Cheam SM4 ... 201 D2
Hampton TW12 ... 173 D6
Isleworth TW7 ... 131 A2
Hartlands Cl DA5 ... 169 B5
Hartlands Cvn Pk The
TW5 ... 128 B6
Hartland Way
Croydon CR0 ... 223 A6
Morden SM4 ... 201 B2
Hartlepool Ct E16 ... 122 D5
Hartley Ave E6 ... 100 A6
NW7 ... 27 D5
Hartley Cl BR1 ... 188 B1
NW7 ... 27 D5
Hartley Ct W5 ... 110 C5
Hartley Ho N3 ... 29 D4
SE1 ... 263 D4
Putney SW15 ... 156 A6
Hartley Prim Sch E6 ... 100 A6
Hartley Rd E11 ... 54 D1
Bexley DA16 ... 146 C5
Thornton Heath CR0 ... 205 A2
Hartley St E2 ... 96 C4
Hart Lo EN5 ... 1 A2
Hartmann Rd E16 ... 122 A5
Hartmoor Mews EN3 ... 6 D6
Hartnoll Ho 4 N7 ... 72 C3
Hartnoll St N7 ... 72 B3
Harton Cl BR1 ... 187 D2
Harton Lo 2 SE8 ... 141 C4
Harton Rd N9 ... 18 B2
Harton St SE8 ... 141 C4
Hartopp Ct N16 ... 73 C5
Hartopp Point SW6 ... 264 B4
Hartsbourne Ave WD23 ... 8 B2
Hartsbourne Cl WD23 ... 8 B2
Hartsbourne Ct 5 UB1 ... 86 A1
Hartsbourne Pk WD23 ... 8 C2
Hartsbourne Prim Sch
WD23 ... 8 B2
Hartsbourne Rd WD23 ... 8 B2
Harts Gr IG8 ... 37 A5
Hartshill Cl UB10 ... 60 D2
Hartshorn Alley EC3 ... 243 B1
Hartshorn Gdns E6 ... 100 C3
Hart's La SE14 ... 141 A4
Harts La IG11 ... 78 D2
Hartslock Dr SE2 ... 124 D4
Hartsmead Rd SE9 ... 166 B2
Hart Sq SM4 ... 201 C3
Hart St EC3 ... 253 B6
Hartsway EN3 ... 6 C1
Hartswood Gn WD23 ... 8 B2
Hartswood Ho 10 SW2 ... 160 A3
Hartswood Rd W12 ... 111 D3
Hartsworth Cl E13 ... 98 D5
Hartville Rd SE18 ... 123 C2
Hartwell Dr E4 ... 36 A4
Hartwell Ho 2 SE7 ... 121 B1
Hartwell St E8 ... 73 D2
Harvard Ct NW6 ... 69 D3
9 SE9 ... 166 C5
Harvard Hill W4 ... 132 D6
Harvard Ho 3 SE17 ... 138 D6
Putney SW15 ... 156 D5
Harvard Mans 18 SW11 ... 136 B1
Harvard Rd SE13 ... 164 A6
W4 ... 110 D1
11 W4 ... 111 A1
Hounslow TW7 ... 130 C4
Harvel Cres SE2 ... 124 D1
Harvest Bank Rd BR4 ... 225 A5
Harvest Ct
Beckenham BR3 ... 185 C3
Littleton TW17 ... 192 C5
Harvesters Cl TW7 ... 152 B6
Harvest La Loughton IG10 ... 21 D4
Thames Ditton KT7 ... 197 A3
Harvest Rd TW13 ... 150 A1
Harvey Ct E17 ... 53 C4
SW11 ... 267 B2
Harvey Dr TW12 ... 173 C2
Harvey Gdns E11 ... 54 D1
SE7 ... 121 C1
Harvey Ho 10 E1 ... 96 B3
N1 ... 235 D5
N8 ... 50 A6
SW1 ... 259 D1
Barking IG11 ... 79 A1
Brentford TW8 ... 110 A1
Dagenham RM6 ... 58 D5
Harvey Lo 8 W9 ... 91 C2
Harvey Mews N8 ... 50 B4

Harvey Point 7 E16 ......99 A2
Harvey Rd E11 ....54 D1
N8 ....50 B4
15 SE5 ....139 B4
Hillingdon UB10 ....82 C5
Ilford IG1 ....78 D3
Ruislip UB5 ....62 C1
Twickenham TW4 ....151 B4
Walton-on-T KT12 ....194 A2
Harvey St N1 ....235 D5
Harvill Rd DA14 ....191 A5
UB9 ....38 A2
Harvil Rd UB9,UB10 ......38 A2
Harvington Sch W5 ....87 D1
Harvington Wlk E8 ....74 A1
Harvist Rd NW6 ....91 A5
Harwell Cl HA4 ....39 B1
Harwick Mans SE18 .....122 A3
Harwood Ave BR1 ....187 B1
Mitcham CR4 ....202 C6
Harwood Cl N12 ....30 C4
Wembley HA0 ....65 D4
Harwood Ct N1 ....235 D5
Putney SW15 ....134 C1
Harwood Dr UB10 ....82 B6
Harwood Point SE16 ....119 B4
Harwood Rd
SW6 ....135 D5 265 C3
Harwoods Yd N21 ....16 C4
Harwood Terr
SW6 ....135 D4 265 C2
Hascombe Ho 11 SW15 ..156 B3
Hascombe Terr 2 SE5 ...139 B3
Haselbury Rd N9 ....17 C1
Haseley End SE23 ....162 C4
Haselrigge Rd SW4 ......137 D1
Haseltine Prim Sch
SE26 ....185 B6
Haseltine Rd SE26 ....185 B6
Haselwood Dr EN2 ....4 D1
Haskard Rd RM9 ....80 D4
Hasker St SW3 ..114 C2 257 B4
Haslam Ave SM3 ....201 A1
Haslam Cl N1 ....72 C1
Uxbridge UB10 ....61 A6
Haslam Ct N11 ....31 B6
Haslam Ho 1 N1 ....73 A1
Haslam St SE15 ....139 D4
Haslemere Ave NW4 ......46 D3
W13 ....109 A3
Barnet, London EN4 ....14 D3
Cranford TW5 ....128 C3
Mitcham CR4,SW19 ....180 B1
Wandsworth SW18 ....157 D2
Haslemere Cl
Hampton TW12 ....173 B5
Wallington SM6 ....220 A3
Haslemere Ct 5 N16 .....51 C1
Haslemere Fst Sch CR4 .180 B1
Haslemere Gdns N3 ......47 B5
Haslemere & Heathrow Est
The TW4 ....128 B2
Haslemere Ind Est
Feltham TW14 ....150 A6
Wandsworth SW18 ....157 D2
Haslemere Rd DA7 ....147 C3
N8 ....50 A2
Ilford IG3 ....79 D6
Southgate N21 ....16 D3
Thornton Heath CR7 .....204 D4
Hasler Cl SE28 ....124 C6
Hasler Ct E12 ....78 A4
Haslett Rd TW17 ....171 C1
Hasluck Gdns EN5 ....14 A5
Hasmonean High Sch (Boys)
NW4 ....28 D1
Hasmonean High Sch (Girls)
NW7 ....28 A2
Hasmonean Prim Sch
NW4 ....46 D4
Hassard St E2 ....95 D5
Hassendean Rd SE3 .....143 B5
Hassett Rd E9 ....75 A2
Hassocks Cl SE23,SE26 ..162 B1
Hassocks Rd SW16 ......181 D2
Hassop Rd NW2 ....68 D4
Hassop Wlk SE9 ....188 A6
Hasted Rd SE7 ....121 D1
Hastings Ave IG6 ....57 A5
Hastings Cl 16 SE15 .....140 A5
New Barnet EN5 ....2 A1
Wembley HA0 ....65 C4
Hastings Dr KT6 ....197 C3
Hastings Ho 11 SE18 ....122 B2
18 W12 ....112 B6
Ealing W13 ....109 B6
Enfield EN3 ....6 C3
Tottenham N17 ....34 A2
Hastings Hos WC1 ....233 A1
Hastings Pl 1 CR0 ....205 D1
Hastings Rd BR2 ....226 A6
N11 ....31 D5
N17 ....51 B6
Croydon CR0 ....205 D1
Ealing W13 ....109 B6
Hastings St WC1 ..94 A4 233 A1
Hastingwood Ct E17 ......53 D4
Hastingwood Trad Est
N18 ....34 D4
N18 ....35 A4
Hastoe Cl UB4 ....85 A3
Hatcham Mews Bsns Ctr
SE14 ....140 D4
Hatcham Park Mews
SE14 ....140 D4
Hatcham Park Rd SE14 .140 D4
Hatcham Rd SE15 ....140 C6
Hatchard Rd N19 ....72 A6
Hatchcroft NW4 ....46 B6
Hatch End High Sch HA3 .23 D2
Hatch End Sta HA5 ....23 C3
Hatchett Rd TW14 ....149 A3
Hatchfield Ho 8 N15 .....51 C3
Hatch Gr RM6 ....59 A5
Hatch La E4 ....20 C1
Hatch Pl TW10 ....176 B5
Hatch Rd SW16 ....182 A1
Hatch The EN3 ....6 D4
Hatchwoods IG8 ....36 D6
Hatcliffe Almshouses 8
SE10 ....120 C1
Hatcliffe Cl SE3 ....142 D2
Hatcliffe St SE10 ....120 D1
Hatfield Cl SE14 ....140 D5
Ilford IG6 ....56 D6
Mitcham CR4 ....202 B5
Hatfield Ct
Greenwich SE3 ....143 A5
8 Northolt UB5 ....84 C4
Hatfield First Sch SM4 ..201 A3
Hatfield Ho E11 ....54 D2
EC1 ....242 A5
16 Kingston KT6 ....198 A4
Hatfield Mead SM4 ......201 C4
Hatfield Rd E15 ....76 C3
W4 ....111 B4
Dagenham RM9 ....81 A1
10 Ealing W13,W7 ....109 A5
Hatfields SE1 ....116 C5 251 B4
Hathaway Cl BR2 ....210 B1
Ruislip HA4 ....61 D4
Stanmore HA7 ....25 A5
Hathaway Cres E12 ....78 C2
Hathaway Gdns
Ealing W13 ....87 A2
Ilford RM6 ....58 D4
Hathaway Ho 3 N1 ....95 C4
Hathaway Prim Sch W13 .86 D2
Hathaway Rd CR0 ....204 D2
Hatherleigh Cl
Chessington KT9 ....213 D3
Morden SM4 ....201 C5
Hatherleigh Ho SM4 .....201 C5
Hatherleigh Rd HA4 ......62 A6
Hatherley Cres DA14 ...168 A2
Hatherley Ct 6 W2 ....91 D1
Hatherley Gdns E6 ....99 D4
N8 ....50 A3
Hatherley Gr W2 ....91 D1
Hatherley Ho 2 E17 ......53 C5
Hatherley Mews E17 ......53 C5
Hatherley Rd E17 ....53 C5
Richmond TW9 ....132 B4
Sidcup DA14 ....168 A1
Hatherley St SW1 ....259 B3
Hathern Gdns SE9 ....188 C6
Hatherop Rd TW12 ......173 B3
Hathersage Ct N1 ....73 B3
Hathersley Ho 3 SW2 ..160 C4
Hathorne Cl 3 SE15 ....140 B3
Hathway Ho 3 SE15 ....140 C3
Hathway St 4 SE15 ......140 C3
Hatley Ave IG6 ....57 A5
Hatley Cl N11 ....30 D5
Hatley Rd N4,N7 ....72 B6
Hat & Mitre Ct EC1 .....241 D5
Hatteraick St 6 SE16 ...118 C4
Hattersfield Cl DA17 ....125 B2
Hatton Cl SE18 ....145 B5
Hatton Cross Rdbt TW6 .127 D2
Hatton Cross Sta TW6 ..127 D1
Hatton Ct BR7 ....188 B3
Hatton Gdn EC1 ...94 C2 241 B4
Hatton Gdns CR4 ....202 D4
Hatton Gn TW14 ....128 A1
Hatton Ho 13 E1 ....118 A6
Hatton Pl EC1 ....241 B4
Hatton Rd
Hatton TW14,TW6 ....149 C6
Thornton Heath CR0 .....204 C1
Hatton Rd N TW6 ....127 B4
Hatton Row NW8 ....236 D5
Hatton Sch IG8 ....55 D6
Hatton St NW8 ....236 D5
Hatton Wall EC1 ..94 C2 241 B4
Haughmond 4 N12 ....29 D6
Haunch of Venison Yd
W1 ....238 C1
Hauteville Court Gdns 2
W6 ....111 D3
Havana Rd SW18,SW19 ..157 C2
Havannah St E14 ....119 C4
Havant Rd E17 ....54 A6
Havelock Cl 13 W12 ....112 B6
Havelock Ct UB2 ....107 B3
Havelock Hall 8 CR0 ...205 D1
Havelock Ho
4 Croydon CR0 ....205 D1
Forest Hill SE23 ....162 C3
Havelock Pl HA1 ....42 C3
Havelock Prim Sch UB2 .107 B3
Havelock Rd DA17 ....125 B2
Bromley BR2 ....209 C5
Croydon CR0 ....221 D6
Harrow HA3 ....42 C6
Southall UB2 ....107 C3
Tottenham N17 ....34 A1
Wimbledon SW19 ....180 A5
Havelock St N1 ...94 A6 233 B6
Ilford IG1 ....78 D6
Havelock Terr
SW8 ....137 B5 268 D3
Havelock Wlk SE23 .....162 C2
Haven Cl SE9 ....166 B1
Hayes UB4 ....83 C3
Sidcup DA14 ....190 C4
Wimbledon SW19 ....156 D1
Haven Ct BR3 ....186 A1
Haven Gn W5 ....87 D1
Haven Green Ct W5 ......87 D1
Havenhurst Rise EN2 ....4 C3
Haven La W5 ....88 A1
Haven Lo NW11 ....47 B4
7 SE18 ....122 D2
13 Enfield EN1 ....17 C6
Haven Pl W5 ....109 D6
Havenpool NW8 ....91 D6
Haven Rd TW15 ....148 D1
Haven St 17 NW1 ....71 B1
Haven The Ashford TW16 .172 A3
East Barnet N14 ....15 B5
Richmond TW9 ....132 C2
Havenwood HA9 ....66 D5
Havercourt 3 NW3 ....70 C2
Haverfield Gdns TW9 ...132 C5
Haverfield Rd E3 ....97 A4
Haverford Way HA8 ....26 B2
Havergal Villas N15 ......50 D6
Haverhill Rd Chingford E4 .20 A3
Streatham SW12 ....159 C3
Havering 8 NW1 ....71 B1
Havering Gdns RM6 ......58 D4
Havering Ho N4 ....51 A2
Havering St E1 ....96 D1
Havering Way IG11 ......102 B4
Haverley 14 SW20 ....178 D3
Haversham Cl TW1 ......153 D5
Haversham Ct UB6 ....64 D2
Haversham Lo NW2 ......68 D3
Haversham Pl N6 ....70 D6
Haverstock Ct 2 BR5 ..190 B1
Haverstock Hill NW3 .....70 D2
Haverstock Rd NW5 ......71 A3
Haverstock Sch NW1 .....71 A2
Haverstock St
N1 ....94 D5 234 D3
Haverthwaite Rd BR6 ...227 B5
Havilland Ct HA8 ....26 B6
Havil St SE5 ....139 C4
Havisham Ho 23 SE16 ..118 A4
Havisham Pl SW16 ......182 D3
Hawarden Gr SE24 ......161 A4
Hawarden Hill NW2 ....68 A5
Hawarden Rd E17 ....52 D5
Hawberry Ho N7 ....72 A2
Hawbridge Rd E11 ....54 B1
Hawes Down Inf Sch BR4 ....
Hawes Down Jun Sch
BR4 ....208 B1
Hawes La BR4 ....224 C6
Hawes Rd BR1 ....187 B2
Edmonton N18 ....34 B4
Hawes St N1 ....72 D1
Haweswater Ho TW1 ....152 D6
Hawfinch 29 NW9 ....27 D2
Hawgood St E3 ....97 C2
Hawkdene E4 ....20 A5
Hawke Ct UB4 ....84 C3
Hawkedale Fst Sch
TW16 ....193 D6
Hawke Ho 20 E1 ....96 D3
Hawke Park Rd N22 ......50 D6
Hawke Pl 29 SE16 ....118 D4
Hawker 28 NW9 ....27 D2
Hawker Ct 14 KT2 ....176 C3
Hawke Rd SE19 ....183 C4
Hawkesbury Rd SW15 ..156 B6
Hawkesfield Rd SE23 ...163 B2
Hawkesley Cl TW1 ......175 A6
Hawkes Rd
Feltham TW14 ....150 A4
Mitcham CR4 ....180 D2
Hawkesworth Ho 5
SW4 ....159 C5
Hawke Twr 4 SE14 ......141 A6
Hawkewood Rd TW16 ..194 A6
Hawkfield Ct TW7 ....130 C3
Hawk Ho 7 SW11 ....136 C2
Hawkhurst Gdns KT9 ..214 A4
Hawkhurst Rd SW16 ....181 D2
Hawkhurst Way
New Malden KT3 ....199 B4
West Wickham BR4 .....223 D6
Hawkinge N17 ....33 B1
Hawkins Cl NW7 ....27 B5
Harrow HA1 ....42 B2
Hawkins Ho 3 SE8 ......141 C6
Hawkins Rd TW11 ....175 B4
Hawkins Way SE6 ....185 C5
Hawkley Gdns SE27 ....160 D2
Hawkridge 19 NW5 ....71 A2
Hawkridge Cl RM6 ....58 C3
Hawksbrook La BR3 ....208 A3
Hawkshead NW1 ....232 A2
Hawkshead Cl BR1 ......186 C3
Hawkshead Rd NW10 ....67 D1
W4 ....111 C4
Hawkslade Rd SE15 ....162 D6
Hawksley Rd N16 ....73 C5
Hawks Mews 10 SE10 ..142 A5
Hawksmoor Cl 2 E6 ....100 A1
SE18 ....123 C1
Hawksmoor Mews E1 ...118 B6
Hawksmoor Sch SE28 ..124 B6
Hawksmoor St 5 W6 ...134 D6
Hawksmouth E4 ....20 A4
Hawks Rd KT1 ....176 B1
Hawkstone Rd SE16 ....118 C2
Hawkswood Sch E4 ......20 A6
Hawkwell Ct E4 ....20 A1
Hawkwell Ho RM8 ....81 C6
Hawkwell Wlk N1 ....235 B6
Hawkwood Cres E4 ....19 D5
Hawkwood La BR7 ......189 A2
Hawkwood Mount 1 E5 ..52 B1
Hawlands Dr HA5 ....41 A2
Hawley Cl TW12 ....173 B4
Hawley Cres NW1 ....71 B1
Hawley Inf Sch NW1 .....71 B1
Hawley Mews 4 NW1 ....71 B1
Hawley Rd N18 ....34 D5
3 NW1 ....71 B1
Hawley St NW1 ....71 B1
Hawley Way TW15 ......170 D5
Haworth Ct E15 ....76 A3
Haworth Ho 7 SW2 ....160 C5
Hawstead Rd SE6 ......163 D5
Hawsted IG9 ....21 B4
Hawthorn Ave Bow E3 ....97 B6
Bowes Park N13 ....32 A5
South Norwood CR7 .....182 D2
Hawthorn Cl BR5 ....211 B3
Cranford TW5 ....128 B5
Hampton TW12 ....173 C5
Hawthorn Cres SW17 ..181 A5
Hawthorn Ct
Putney SW15 ....134 B2
Richmond TW9 ....132 D4
8 West Norwood SW16 ..182 C5
Hawthorn Ctr HA1 ....43 A4
Hawthornden Cl N12 ....30 C4
Hawthorndene Cl BR2 ..225 A6
Hawthorndene Rd BR2 ..225 A6
Hawthorn Dr
Coney Hall BR4 ....224 C4
Harrow HA2 ....41 C3
Hawthorne Ave
Harrow HA3 ....43 A3
Mitcham CR4 ....180 B1
Ruislip HA4 ....40 B2
Wallington SM5 ....219 A1
Hawthorne Cl BR1 ....210 B6
N1 ....73 C2
Sutton SM1 ....218 A6
Hawthorne Cres UB7 ...104 B4
Hawthorne Ct
Chingford E4 ....35 D4
Ealing W5 ....110 A5
Pinner HA6 ....22 A1
Hawthorne Gr NW9 ....45 A2
Hawthorne Ho SW1 .....259 B1
Hawthorne Mews UB6 ...86 A4
Hawthorne Rd BR1 ......210 B6
E17 ....53 C6
Edmonton N18 ....33 D5
Feltham TW14 ....150 A3
Hawthorne Way N9 ....17 D2
Hawthorn Farm Ave UB5 .85 A6
Hawthorn Gdns W5 .....109 D3
Hawthorn Gr
Edgware EN5 ....11 D5
Enfield EN2 ....5 B5
Penge SE20 ....184 B2
Hawthorn Hatch TW8 ...131 B5
Hawthorn Mews NW7 ....29 A2
Hawthorn Pl UB3 ....105 D6
Hawthorn Rd DA6 ....147 B1
N8 ....50 A6
NW10 ....68 A1
Brentford TW8 ....131 B5
Carshalton SM1,SM2,SM5 .218 C2
Wallington SM5,SM6 ....219 B1
Woodford IG9 ....37 D6
Hawthorns IG8 ....21 A1
Hawthorns The KT17 ....216 A1
Hawthorn Terr DA15 ....167 D6
Hawthorn Way TW17 ...193 B5
Hawthorn Wlk W10 ....91 A3
Hawtrey Ave UB5 ....84 D5
Hawtrey Dr HA4 ....40 A2
Hawtrey Rd NW3 ....70 C1
Haxted Rd BR1 ....187 B2
Haybridge Ho 1 E5 ......74 C6
Hay Cl E15 ....76 D1
Haycroft Gdns NW10 ....90 B6
Haycroft Mans NW10 ....90 A6
Haycroft Rd SW2 ....160 A6
Surbiton KT6 ....214 A6
Hay Currie St E14 ....97 D1
Hayday Rd E16 ....99 A2
Hayden's Pl W11 ....91 B1
Haydock Ave UB5 ....63 C2
Haydock Gn UB5 ....63 C2
Haydock Green Flats 2
UB5 ....63 C2
Haydon Cl NW9 ....45 A5
Enfield EN1 ....17 C6
Haydon Ct NW9 ....45 A5
Haydon Dr HA5 ....40 A5
Haydon Ho Ealing W7 ...108 D5
Teddington TW11 ....175 C3
Haydon Park Rd SW19 ..179 D5
Haydon Rd RM8 ....80 C6
Haydon Sch HA5 ....39 D6
Haydon's Rd SW19 .....180 A4
Haydons Road Sta
SW19 ....180 A5
Haydon St E1,
EC3 ....117 D6 253 C6
Haydon Way SW11 ......136 B1
Haydon Wlk E1 ....243 D1
Hayes Bridge Ret Pk
UB4 ....106 D6
Hayes Chase BR4 ....208 C3
Hayes Cl BR2 ....225 A6
Hayes Cres NW11 ....47 B4
Cheam SM3 ....216 D4
Hayes Ct 23 SE5 ....139 A5
Streatham SW12 ....160 A3
Wimbledon SW19 ....179 A4
Hayes End Cl UB4 ....83 B2
Hayes End Dr UB4 ....83 B3
Hayesend Ho SW17 .....180 A6
Hayes End Rd UB4 ....83 B3
Hayesford Park Dr BR2 .208 D4
Hayes Garden BR2 ......209 A1
Hayes & Harlington Sta
UB3 ....105 D3
Hayes Hill BR2 ....208 C1
Hayes Hill Rd BR2 ......208 D1
Hayes La BR2 ....209 A4
Beckenham BR2,BR3 ....208 B5
Hayes Manor Sch UB3 ....83 C1
Hayes Mead Rd BR2 ....208 C1
Hayes Park Sch UB4 .....83 D3
Hayes Pl NW1 ....237 B5
Hayes Prim Sch BR2 ....209 B1
Hayes Rd BR2 ....209 A5
Southall UB2 ....106 B2
Hayes Sch BR2 ....225 B6
Hayes St BR2 ....209 B1
Hayes Sta BR2 ....208 D1
Hayes Way BR3 ....208 B5
Hayes Wood Ave BR2 ..209 B1
Hayfield Pas E1 ....96 C3
Hayford Ct NW2 ....68 D5
Haygarth Pl 2 SW19 ...178 D5
Haygreen Cl KT2 ....176 D4
Hay Hill W1 ......115 B6 248 D5
Hay La NW9 ....45 B5
Hayland Cl NW9 ....45 B5
Hay Lane Sch NW9 ....45 A5
Hayles Bldgs SE11 .....261 D4
Hayles St SE11 ...116 D3 261 C4
Haylett Gdns KT1 ....197 D5
Hayling Ave TW13 ......150 A1
Hayling Cl 20 N16 ....73 C3
Hayling Ct SM3 ....216 C4
Haymaker Cl UB10 ....60 B1
Hayman Cres UB4 ....83 B5
Haymans Point SE11 ...260 C2
Haymarket SW1 .115 D6 249 C5
Haymeads Dr KT10 .....212 A2
Haymer Gdns KT4 ......216 A5
Haymerle Ho 6 SE15 ...140 A5
Haymerle Rd SE15 ......140 A6
Haymerle Sch SE15 .....140 A6
Haymill Cl UB6 ....86 D4
Hayne Ho W11 ....244 A4
Hayne Rd BR3 ....185 B2
Haynes Cl N11 ....15 A1
SE3 ....142 C2
Tottenham N17 ....34 B3
Haynes Dr N9 ....18 B1
Haynes Ho 5 E9 ....74 D2
Haynes La SE19 ....183 C4
Haynes Rd HA0 ....66 A1
Hayne St EC1 ......94 D2 241 D4
Haynt Wlk SW20 ....201 A6
Hay's Galleria SE1 .....253 A4
Hay's La SE1 ....253 A4
Haysleigh Gdns SE20 ..184 A1
Haysleigh Ho SE20 ......184 B1
Hay's Mews W1 ..115 B6 248 C4
Hay St E2 ....96 A6
Haystall Cl UB4 ....83 C5
Haystocks E18 ....55 C6
Hayter Ho W12 ....112 A6
Hayter Rd SW2 ....160 B6
Haythorn Ho
SW11 ....136 B4 266 D1
Hayton Cl 11 E8 ....73 D2
Hayward Cl SW19 ....179 D2
Hayward Ct 14 SW4 ....138 A3
Mitcham CR4 ....180 B1
Hayward Gallery*
SE1 ....116 B5 250 D4
Hayward Gdns SW15 ...156 C5
Hayward Ho E5 ....74 B5
N1 ....234 A4
Hayward Rd N20 ....14 A2
Thames Ditton KT7 ....196 D1
Haywards Cl RM6 ....58 C4
Haywards Pl EC1 ....241 C6
Haywood Cl HA5 ....22 D1
Haywood Lo N11 ....31 D4
23 N7 ....71 D3
Haywood Rd BR2 ....209 D5
Haywood Rise BR6 ......227 C3
Hazel Ave UB7 ....104 C3
Hazelbank KT5 ....199 A1
Hazel Bank SE25 ....183 C1
Hazelbank Rd SE6 ......164 C2
Hazelbourne Rd SW12 ..159 B5
Hazelbury Cl SW19 .....179 C1
Hazelbury Gn N9 ....17 C1
Hazelbury Inf Sch N9 ....17 C1
Hazelbury Jun Sch N9 ...17 C1
Hazelbury La N9 ....17 C1
Hazel Cl N19 ....71 C6
NW9 ....27 D1
SE15 ....140 A3
Brentford TW8 ....131 B5
Croydon CR0 ....206 D1
Edmonton N13 ....17 B1
Mitcham CR4 ....203 D5
Twickenham TW2 ....152 A4
Hazelcroft HA5 ....23 D4
Hazelcroft Cl UB10 ....60 B1
Hazel Ct Ealing W5 ......110 A6
9 West Norwood SW16 ..182 C5
Hazeldean Rd NW10 ......67 B1
Hazeldene Dr HA5 ....40 C6
Hazeldene Gdns UB10 ...83 A6
Hazeldene Rd
Bexley DA16 ....146 C3
Ilford IG3 ....80 B6
Hazeldon Rd SE4 ....163 A6
Hazel Gdns HA8 ....26 D6
Hazel Gr Dagenham RM6 ..59 A6
Enfield EN1 ....18 A5
Feltham TW14 ....150 A3
Forest Hill SE26 ....184 D6
Orpington BR6 ....226 D6
Wembley HA0 ....88 A6
Hazelgreen Cl N21 ....16 D3
Hazel Ho 12 NW3 ....70 D2
SE4 ....141 B2
Hazelhurst BR3 ....186 B2
Hazelhurst Ct SE6 ......186 A5
Hazelhurst Rd SW17 ...180 B6
Hazellville Rd N19 ....49 D1
Hazel Mead EN5 ....12 B6
Hazelmere Cl
Feltham TW14 ....149 C5
Northolt UB5 ....85 B5
Hazelmere Ct 10 SW2 ..160 B3
Hazelmere Dr UB5 ....85 B5
Hazelmere Rd BR5 .....211 B5
NW6 ....91 B6
Northolt UB5 ....85 B5
Hazelmere Way BR2 ....209 A3
Hazelmere Wlk UB5 ......85 B5
Hazel Rd E15 ....76 C3
NW10 ....90 C4
Hazeltree La UB5 ....85 A4
Hazel Way E4 ....35 B4
SE1 ....263 C4
Hazel Wlk BR2 ....210 C3
Hazelwood IG10 ....21 D6
Hazelwood Ave SM4 ....201 D5
Hazelwood Cl E5 ....75 A5
W5 ....110 A4
Harrow HA2 ....41 D5
Hazelwood Cres N13 ....32 C6
Hazelwood Ct 1 NW10 ..67 C5
Surbiton KT6 ....198 A3
Hazelwood Dr HA5 ....22 B1
Hazelwood Ho 11 SE8 ..119 A2
Beckenham BR2 ....208 C6
Edmonton N13 ....32 D6
Hazelwood Jun & Inf Schs
N13 ....32 C6
Hazelwood La N13 ....32 C6
Hazelwood Lo BR4 .....208 A2
Hazelwood Mans SW6 ..264 C2
Hazelwood Rd E17 ....53 A4
Enfield EN1 ....17 D5
Hazlebury Rd SW6 ......135 D3
Hazledean Rd CR0 ......221 B6
Hazledene Rd W4 ....133 A6
Hazlemere Bsns Ctr EN1 ..18 B6
Hazlemere Gdns KT4 ...200 A1
Hazlewell Rd SW15 .....156 C6
Hazlewood Cres W10 .....91 A3
Hazlewood Twr W10 .....91 B3
Hazlitt Cl TW13 ....173 A6
Hazlitt Ct 4 SE28 ....124 C5
Hazlitt Mews W14 ....254 A5
Hazlitt Rd W14 ...113 A3 254 A5
Heacham Ave UB10 ......61 A5
Headbourne Ho SE1 ....262 D6
Headcorn 10 NW5 ....71 A2
Headcorn Pl CR7 ....204 B5
Headcorn Rd BR1 ....187 A5
Thornton Heath CR7 .....204 B5
Tottenham N17 ....33 D3
Headfort Pl
SW1 ....115 A4 248 B1
Headington Rd SW18 ...158 A2
Headlam Rd SW4 ....159 D4
Headlam St E1 ....96 B3
Headley App IG2 ....56 D4
Headley Ave CR0,SM6 ..220 B3
Headley Cl KT19 ....214 C2
Headley Ct SE26 ....184 C5
Headley Dr Ilford IG2 .....56 D3
New Addington CR0 .....224 A1
Headley Ho 5 BR5 ......190 B1
Heads Mews W11 ....91 C1
Head St E1 ....96 D1
Headstone Dr HA1,HA3 ...42 C6
Headstone Gdns HA2 .....42 A5
Headstone La
Harrow HA2 ....41 D5
Harrow HA2,HA3 ....23 D2
Headstone Lane Sta HA3 .23 D3
Headstone Rd HA1 ....42 C3
Headway Cl TW10 ....175 C6
Heald St SE8,SE14 ......141 C4
Healey St NW1 ....71 B2
Healy Ct EN5 ....12 D5
Healy Dr 1 BR6 ....227 D4
Healy Ho 2 E3 ....97 C3
12 SW9 ....138 C5
Heanor Ct 4 E5 ....74 D4
Hearne Rd W4 ....132 C6
Hearn Rise UB5 ....84 D6
Hearn's Bldgs SE17 ....262 D3
Hearn St EC2 ....95 C3 243 B5
Hearnville Rd SW12 ....159 A3
Heart Hospl The
W1 ....93 A2 238 B4
Heatham Pk TW2 ....152 D4
Heath Ave DA7 ....146 D6
Heathbourne Rd WD23,
HA7 ....8 D3
Heathbrook Prim Sch
SW4 ....137 C3
Heath Brow NW3 ....70 A5
Heath Bsns Ctr The
TW3 ....130 A1
Heath Cl NW11 ....47 D2
Croydon CR2 ....220 D2
Ealing W5 ....88 B3
Harlington UB3 ....127 B5
Heathcote Gr E4 ....20 A2
Heathcote Rd TW1 ......153 B6
Heathcote Sch E4 ....20 C2
Heathcote St
WC1 ....94 B4 233 C1
Heathcroft NW11 ....47 D1
Ealing W5 ....88 B3
Heathcroft Ave TW16 ...171 D3
Heathcroft Gdns E4 ......36 B2
Heath Ct E11 ....54 D3

Heath Ct continued
N16 51 B1
2 NW3 70 A2
Uxbridge UB8 60 A1
Heathdale Ave TW4 129 A2
Heathdene N14 15 C4
Heathdene Dr DA17 125 D2
Heathdene Rd
South Norwood SW16 182 B3
Wallington SM5,SM6 219 B1
Heath Dr SW20 200 C5
Heathedge SE23,SE26 162 B2
Heatherbank BR7 188 C1
SE9 144 B3
Heather Cl E6 100 C1
SW8 137 B2
Hampton TW12 173 B2
Hillingdon UB8 82 B2
Isleworth TW7 152 B6
Heather Ct SW4 270 B1
Heatherdale Cl KT2 176 D3
Heatherdene Cl N12 30 A2
Mitcham CR4 202 C5
Heatherdene Mans 2
TW1 153 D5
Heather Dr EN2 4 D3
Heatherfold Way HA5,
HA6 39 D6
Heather Gdns NW11 47 A3
Belmont SM2 217 C2
Heather Ho 7 E14 98 A1
Heather La UB7 82 A1
Heatherlands TW16 172 A4
Heatherley Ct N16 74 A5
Heatherley Dr IG5 56 B6
Heatherley Sch of Fine Art
SW10 266 B3
Heather Lo N16 51 C1
Heather Park Dr HA0 66 C1
Heather Park Par HA0 66 B1
Heather Rd E4 35 B4
NW2 67 D6
Lewisham SE12 165 A3
Heatherset Cl KT10 212 A3
Heatherset Gdns SW16 182 B3
Heatherside Rd
Sidcup DA14 168 C1
West Ewell KT19 215 B1
Heathers The TW19 148 B4
Heather Way HA7 24 D4
Heather Wlk W10 91 A3
Edgware HA8 26 D5
Twickenham TW4 151 C4
Heatherwood Cl E12 77 C6
Heatherwood Dr UB4 83 B5
Heathfield BR7 189 A4
Chingford E4 20 A1
Heathfield Ave SW18 158 B4
Heathfield Cl BR2 225 C3
E16 99 D2
Heathfield Ct DA14 190 B5
5 W4 111 B1
Ashford TW15 148 A1
Penge SE20 184 C3
Wandsworth SW18 158 B4
Heathfield Dr CR4 180 C2
Heathfielde N2 48 A4
Heathfield Gdns NW11 46 D3
SW18 158 B5
W4 111 A1
Croydon CR0 221 B4
Heathfield Ho SE3 142 C3
Heathfield Inf Sch TW2 151 D3
Heathfield Jun Sch
TW2 151 C3
Heathfield La BR7 189 A4
Heathfield N TW1,TW2 152 D4
Heathfield Park Dr RM6 58 B4
Heathfield Pk NW2 68 C2
Heathfield Rd BR2 225 D3
DA6 147 B1
SW18 158 B5
W3 110 D4
Bromley BR1 186 D3
Croydon CR0 221 B4
Heathfield Rise HA4 39 A2
Heathfield S TW1,TW2 152 D4
Heathfield Sch HA5 40 D2
Heathfield Sq SW18 158 B4
Heathfield Terr SE18 145 D6
W4 111 B1
Heathfield Vale CR2 223 A1
Heathgate NW11 47 D3
Heathgate Pl NW3 70 D4
Heath Gdns TW1 152 D2
Heath Gr Ashford TW16 171 D3
Penge SE20 184 C3
Heath Ho DA15 189 D6
Thornton Heath CR7 204 C4
Uxbridge UB10 60 D4
Heath Hurst Rd NW3 70 C4
Heath La SE3 142 B3
Heathland Rd N16 51 C1
Heathland Sch SW19 156 D1
Heathland Sch The
TW4 151 B5
Heathlands Cl
Sunbury TW16 172 A1
Twickenham TW1 152 D3
Heathlands Ct
Hounslow TW4 151 A6
Mitcham CR4 203 A6
Heathlands Way TW4 151 A6
Heathlee Rd SE3 142 D1
Heathley End BR7 189 A4
Heath Lo WD23 8 B3
Heath Mans 4 NW3 70 A4
Putney SW15 156 D5
Heathman's Rd
SW6 135 B4 264 D1
Heath Mead SW19 156 D1
Heathmere Prim Sch
SW15 156 A3
Heath Park Dr BR1 210 A6
Heath Park Gdns NW3 69 D5
Heathpool Ct 8 E1 96 B3
Heath Rd SW8 137 B3
Dagenham RM6 59 A2
Harrow HA1 42 A2
Hillingdon UB10 83 A3
Isleworth TW3,TW7 130 A1
South Norwood CR7 205 A6
Twickenham TW1 152 D3
Heath Rise Hayes BR2 209 A3
Putney SW15 156 D5
Heathrow Airport London
TW6 126 D3
Heathrow Bvd UB7 126 B5
Heathrow Causeway Est
TW4 128 B2
Heathrow International Trad
Est TW4 128 B2
Heathrow Sch UB7 126 B6
Heathrow Terminal 4 Sta
TW6 149 A5
Heathrow Terminals 1,2,3
TW6 126 D2
Heath Royal SW15 156 D5
Heath's Cl EN1 5 C3
Heathshot 8 TW10 154 A5
Heathside NW3 70 B4
Heath Side BR5 211 A2
Heathside
Hinchley Wood KT10 212 C5
Twickenham TW4 151 B4
Heathside Ave DA7 147 A3
Heathside Cl
Hinchley Wood KT10 212 C5
Ilford IG2 57 B4
Heathside Prep Sch
NW3 70 A4
Heath St NW3 70 A5
Heathstan Rd W12 90 A1
Heath Terr RM6 58 D2
Heath The W7 108 C5
Heath View N2 48 A5
NW5 71 A4
Heath View Cl N2 48 A5
Heathview Ct SW19 156 D2
Heath View Dr SE2 146 D6
Heathview Gdns SW15 156 C4
Heathview Rd CR7 204 C5
Heath Villas SE18 123 D1
Heathville Rd N4,N19 50 A2
Heathwall St SW11 136 D2
Heathway 6 SE3 142 D5
Croydon CR0 223 B5
Greenwich SE3 143 A5
Woodford IG8 37 C5
Heathway Ct NW3 69 C6
Heathwood Ct
1 Hounslow TW3 129 D1
Streatham SW12 159 C3
Heathwood Gdns SE7 122 A1
Heathwood Point 7
SE26 162 D1
Heaton Cl E4 20 A1
Heaton Ho 6 SE15 140 B3
SW10 266 B6
Heaton Rd SE15 140 B3
Mitcham CR4 181 A3
Heaver Rd 24 SW11 136 B2
Heavers Farm Prim Sch
SE25 205 D4
Heavitree Cl SE18 123 B1
Heavitree Rd SE18 123 B1
Hebden Ct 24 E2 95 D6
Hebden Terr N17 33 C4
Hebdon Rd SW17 158 C1
Heber Prim Sch SE22 161 D5
Heber Rd NW2 68 D4
SE22 161 D5
Hebron Rd W6 112 B3
Hecham Cl E17 35 A2
Heckfield Pl
SW6 135 C5 265 A3
Heckford St E1 118 D6
Hector 31 NW9 27 D2
Hector Ct 1 SW9 138 C4
Putney SW15 156 D6
Hector Ho 14 E2 96 B5
Hector St SE18 123 C2
Heddington Gr N7 72 B3
Heddon Cl TW7 131 A1
Heddon Court Ave EN4 14 D6
Heddon Court Par EN4 15 A6
Heddon Ct EN4 15 A6
Heddon Rd EN4 14 D6
Heddon St W1 249 A6
Hedge Hill EN2 4 D4
Hedge La N13 17 A1
Hedgeley IG4 56 B5
Hedgemans Rd RM9 81 A1
Hedgemans Way RM9 81 A2
Hedgemoor Ct 1 E4 36 B5
Hedgerley Gdns UB6 86 A5
Hedgerow La EN5 12 B6
Hedger's Gr E9 75 A2
Hedger St SE11 261 C4
Hedge Wlk SE6 185 D6
Hedgewood Gdns IG5 56 C4
Hedgewood Specl Sch
UB4 83 C4
Hedgley Mews SE12 164 D6
Hedgley St SE12 164 D6
Hedingham Cl 6 N1 73 A1
Hedingham Rd RM8 80 B3
Hedley Ct SW15 156 D5
Hedley Ho E14 120 A3
Hedley Rd TW4 151 C4
Hedley Row N5,N16 73 B3
Hedsor Ho E2 243 C6
Heenan Cl IG11 79 A2
Heene Rd EN2 5 B4
Heidegger Cres SW13 134 B5
Heigham Rd E6 78 A1
Heighton Gdns CR0 220 D3
Heights Cl SW20 178 B3
Heights The N4 50 C3
NW3 70 A4
SE7 121 C1
Beckenham BR3 186 A3
Northolt UB5 63 C3
Heiron St SE17 138 D6
Helby Rd SW4 159 D5
Heldar Ct SE1 252 D1
Helder Gr SE12 164 D4
Helder St CR2 221 B2
Heldmann Cl TW7 130 B1
Helena Cl EN4 2 B5
Helena Ct W5 87 D2
Helena Rd E13 99 A5
E17 53 C4
NW10 68 B3
Ealing W5 87 D2
Helena Sq 12 SE16 119 A6
Helen Ave TW14 150 B4
Helen Cl N2 48 A6
East Molesey KT8 195 D5
Helen Ct N3 47 A6
Helen Gladstone Ho
SE1 251 C2
Helen Ho 9 E2 96 B5
Helen Mackay Ho 9 E14 98 B1
Helen Peele Cotts 10
SE16 118 C3
Helenslea Ave NW11 47 C1
Helen's Pl E2 96 C4
Helen St SE18 122 D2
Helen Taylor Ho 5
SE16 118 A2
Helford Cl HA4 61 C6
Helgiford Gdns TW16 171 C3
Heligan Cl BR6 227 D4
Helios Rd CR4 203 A1
Heliport Est The SW11 136 B3
Helix Gdns SW2 160 B5
Helix Ho TW7 131 B3
Helix Rd SW2 160 B5
Hellenic Coll of London
SW1 114 D3 257 C5
Hellings St E1 118 A5
Helme Cl SW19 179 B5
Helmet Row EC1 242 B6
Helmore Rd IG11 79 D1
Helmsdale Cl UB4 85 A3
Helmsdale Ho NW6 91 D5
Helmsdale Rd SW16 181 D2
Helmsley 10 E18 55 A6
Helmsley Pl E8 74 B1
Helmsley St 7 E8 74 B1
Helperby Rd NW10 67 C1
Helsby Ct NW8 236 C6
Helsinki Sq SE16 119 A3
Helston NW1 232 B4
Helston Cl HA5 23 B3
Helston Ct N15 51 C4
Helston Ho SE11 261 B2
Helvetia St SE6 163 B2
Helwys Ct E4 36 A4
Hemans Est
SW8 137 D5 269 D3
Hemans St SW8 137 D5 269 D3
Hemberton Rd SW9 138 A2
Hemery Rd UB6 64 B3
Hemingford Cl N12 30 B5
Hemingford Rd
N1 72 B1 233 D6
Cheam SM3 216 C4
Heming Rd HA8 26 D3
Hemington Ave N11 30 D5
Hemlock Rd W12 111 D6
Hemmen La UB3 83 D1
Hemming Cl 5 TW12 173 C2
Hemmings Cl DA14 168 B2
Hemmings Ct HA8 27 A3
Hemming St E1 96 A3
Hempstead Cl IG9 21 A2
Hempstead Rd E17 36 B1
Hemp Wlk SE17 262 D4
Hemsby Rd KT9 214 B2
Hemstal Rd NW6 69 C1
Hemswell Dr NW9 27 C2
Hemsworth Ct N1 95 C5
Hemsworth St N1 95 C5
Hemus Pl SW3 257 B1
Henchman St W12 89 D1
Hendale Ave NW4 46 B6
Hendale Ho 13 E5 74 B6
Henderson Cl NW10 67 A2
Henderson Ct NW3 70 B3
8 SE14 140 D6
Henderson Dr
NW8 92 B3 236 C6
Henderson Ho 7 RM10 81 C5
Henderson Rd E7 77 C2
Edmonton N9 18 B3
Hayes UB4 84 A4
Thornton Heath CR0 205 B3
Wandsworth SW18 158 C4
Hendfield Ct 5 SM6 219 B2
Hendham Rd SW17 158 D2
Hendon Ave N3 29 A2
Hendon Central NW4 46 B4
Hendon Central Sta NW4 46 B4
Hendon Coll NW9 27 D2
Hendon Coll of F Ed
NW4 46 A3
Hendon Hall Ct NW4 46 D6
Hendon Ho NW4 46 D4
Hendon La N3 29 B1
Hendon Lo NW4 46 B6
Hendon Park Mans NW4 46 C4
Hendon Park Row NW11 47 B3
Hendon Prep Sch NW4 46 D6
Hendon Rd N9 18 A2
Hendon Sch NW4 46 D3
Hendon Sta NW4 46 A3
Hendon Terr TW15 171 B4
Hendon Way NW2 46 C3
NW2,NW4 46 C3
Hendon Wood La NW7 12 A3
Hendre Ho SE1 263 B3
Hendren Cl UB6 64 B3
Hendre Rd SE1 117 C2 263 B3
Hendrick Ave SW12 158 D4
Heneage La EC3 243 B1
Heneage Pl EC3 243 B1
Heneage St E1 95 D2 243 D4
Henfield Cl DA5 169 C5
N19 49 C1
Henfield Rd SW19,SW20 179 B2
Hengelo Gdns CR4 202 B5
Hengist Rd DA8 147 D5
Eltham SE12 165 B4
Hengist Way BR2,BR3 208 C5
Hengrave Rd SE23 162 D4
Hengrove Ct DA5 169 A3
Henley Ave SM3 217 A5
Henley Cl SE16 118 C4
Greenford UB6 86 A5
Hounslow TW7 130 D4
Henley Ct N14 15 C4
NW2 68 D2
NW4 46 A6
SE15 140 A2
Mitcham CR4 203 A6
Henley Dr SE1 117 D2 263 D4
Kingston KT2 177 D3
Henley Gdns
Dagenham RM6 59 A4
Pinner HA5 40 B6
Henley Ho E2 243 D6
N12 30 B5
Henley Lo E17 53 B4
South Norwood SE25 205 D5
Henley Prior N1 233 C3
Henley Rd Edmonton N18 33 C6
Ilford IG1 79 B4
Newham E16 122 B4
Willesden NW10 90 C6
Henleys Cnr NW11 47 B5
Henley St SW11 137 A3
Henley Way TW13 172 D5
Henlow Pl TW10 153 D2
Henlys Rdbt TW5 128 C3
Hennel Cl SE23 162 C1
Hennessy Rd N9 18 C2
Henniker Gdns E6 100 A4
Henniker Mews SW3 266 C6
Henniker Point E15 76 C3
Henniker Rd E15 76 B3
Henningham Rd N17 33 B2
Henning St
SW11 136 C4 267 A1
Henrietta Barnett Sch
NW11 47 D3
Henrietta Cl SE8 141 C6
Henrietta Ho 3 N15 51 C3
11 W6 112 C1
Henrietta Mews WC1 240 B6
Henrietta Pl W1 93 B1 238 C2
Henrietta St E15 76 A3
WC2 116 A6 250 B6
Henriques St E1 96 A1
Henry Addlington Cl E6 100 D2
Henry Cavendish Prim Sch
SW12 159 C3
Henry Cl EN2 5 C5
Henry Compton Sec Sch
SW6 135 A4 264 A2
Henry Cooper Way
SE12 187 D6
Henry Darlot Dr NW7 29 A5
Henry Dent Cl SE5 139 B2
Henry Dickens Ct W11 244 A4
Henry Doulton Dr SW17 181 B6
Henry Fawcett Prim Sch
SE11 138 C6
Henry Green Prim Sch
RM8 80 D6
Henry Hatch Ct SM2 218 A1
Henry Ho NW8 230 A4
SE1 251 B3
SW8 270 A4
Henry Jackson Ho
SW15 134 D2
Henry Jackson Rd
SW15 134 D2
Henry Maynard Inf Sch
E17 54 A4
Henry Maynard Jun Sch
E17 54 A4
Henry Peters Dr TW11 174 C5
Henry Rd E6 100 A5
N4 51 A1
New Barnet EN4 14 B6
Henry's Ave IG8 36 D5
Henryson Rd SE4 163 C6
Henry St BR1 187 B2
Henry Tate Mews SW16 182 C5
Henry Wise Ho SW1 259 B3
Hensford Gdns SE26 184 B6
Henshall Point 19 E3 97 D4
Henshall St N1 73 B2
Henshawe Rd RM8 80 D5
Henshaw St
SE17 117 B2 262 C4
Henslowe Rd SE22 162 A6
Henslow Ho 11 SE15 140 A5
Henson Ave NW2 68 C3
Henson Cl BR6 226 D6
Henson Ct 3 N5 73 A4
Henson Path HA3 43 D6
Henson Pl UB5 84 C6
Henty Cl SW11 136 C4 267 B2
Henty Wlk SW15 156 B6
Henville Rd BR1 187 B2
Henwick Prim Sch SE9 144 A2
Henwick Rd SE9 144 A2
Hepburn Gdns BR2 208 D1
Hepburn Mews SW11 158 D6
Hepple Cl TW7 131 B3
Hepplestone Cl SW15 156 B5
Hepscott Rd E9 75 C1
Hepworth Ct N1 234 D6
Barking IG11 80 A3
Cheam SM3 201 C1
Hepworth Gdns IG11 80 A3
Hepworth Ho IG8 21 A1
Hepworth Rd SW16 182 A3
Hepworth Way KT12 193 D1
Heracles 30 NW9 27 D2
Heracles Cl SM6 220 A1
Hera Ct 7 E14 119 C2
Herald Gdns SM6 219 B5
Heralds Pl SE11 261 C4
Herald St 5 E2 96 B3
Herbal Hill EC1 241 B5
Herbert Chapman Ct N5 72 D4
Herbert Cres SW1 257 D6
Herbert Gdns NW10 90 B5
Chiswick W4 132 D6
Dagenham RM6 58 D2
Herbert Ho E1 243 C2
Herbert Mews 15 SW2 160 C5
Herbert Morrison Ho
SW6 264 C5
Herbert Morrison Prim Sch
SW8 138 A5 270 B3
Herbert Pl SE18 144 D6
Herbert Rd BR2 210 A4
DA7 147 A3
E12 78 A4
E17 53 B2
N15 51 D4
NW9 46 A3
SE18 144 D6
Ilford IG3 79 C6
Kingston KT1 198 B6
Merton SW19 179 B3
Southall UB1 107 B5
Wood Green N11 32 A3
Herbert St E13 99 A5
NW5 71 A2
Herbrand Est
WC1 94 A3 240 A6
Herbrand St WC1 94 A3 240 A6
Hercies Rd UB10 60 C2
Hercules Pl N7 72 A5
Hercules Rd
SE1 116 B3 260 D5
Hercules St N7 72 A5
Hereford Ave EN4 14 D3
Hereford Bldgs SW3 266 D6
Hereford Ct
12 Belmont SM2 217 C1
6 Croydon CR0 205 D1
6 Ealing W7 86 D2
Harrow HA1 42 C6
Hereford Gdns SE13 164 C6
Pinner HA5 41 A4
Redbridge IG1 56 A2
Twickenham TW2 152 A3
Hereford Ho 26 SE5 139 A3
SW10 265 D4
5 SW2 138 C1
SW3 257 B6
7 Acton W3 88 C1
Hereford Mans 10 W2 91 C1
Hereford Mews 11 W2 91 C1
Hereford Pl SE14 141 B5
Hereford Rd W2 91 C1 245 B6
W3 111 A6
W5 109 C3
Feltham TW13 150 C3
Wanstead E11 55 B4
Hereford Retreat 5
SE15 140 A5
Hereford Sq
SW7 114 A2 256 B3
Hereford St E2 96 A3
Hereford Way KT9 213 D3
Herent Dr IG5 56 B6
Hereward Gdns N13 32 C5
Hereward House Sch
NW3 70 B2
Hereward Rd SW17 180 D6
Herga Ct HA1 64 C6
Herga Rd HA3 42 D5
Heriot Ave E4 19 C2
Heriot Rd NW4 46 C4
Heriots Cl HA7 25 A6
Heritage Cl SW9 138 D2
Heritage Ct SE8 118 D1
Heritage Hill BR2 225 C3
Heritage Ho 22 SW19 156 D3
Heritage View HA1 64 D5
Herlwyn Ave HA4 61 C5
Herlwyn Gdns SW17 180 D6
Herm Cl TW7 130 A5
Hermes Cl 4 W9 91 C3
Hermes Ct 4 SW9 138 C4
Hermes Ho BR3 185 A2
Hermes St N1 234 A3
Hermes Way SM6 219 D1
Hermes Wlk UB5 85 C5
Herm Ho 10 N1 73 A2
Enfield EN3 6 D5
Hermiston Ave N8 50 A4
Hermitage Cl E18 54 D5
Claygate KT10 213 A2
Enfield EN2 4 D3
Littleton TW17 192 C5
Hermitage Ct 14 E1 118 A5
2 NW2 69 C5
3 Wanstead E18 55 A5
Hermitage Gdns NW2 69 C5
South Norwood SE19 183 A3
Hermitage La NW2 69 C5
Croydon CR0 206 A3
South Norwood SW16 182 B3
Hermitage Prim Sch E1 118 A5
Hermitage Rd N4,N15 51 A3
South Norwood SE19 183 B4
Hermitage Row 9 E8 74 A3
Hermitage St W2 236 C3
Hermitage The
Barnes SW13 133 D4
Feltham TW13 149 D1
Forest Hill SE23 162 C3
Kingston KT1 197 D5
Richmond TW10 154 A6
Uxbridge UB8 60 A2
Hermitage Wall E1 118 A5
Hermitage Way HA7 25 A2
Hermitage Wlk E18 54 D5
Hermit Pl NW6 91 D6
Hermit Rd E16 98 D3
Hermit St EC1 234 C2
Hermon Gr UB3 106 A5
Hermon Hill E11 55 A5
Herndon Rd SW18 158 A6
Herne Cl NW10 67 B3
Herne Ct WD23 8 A4
Herne Hill SE24 139 A1
Herne Hill Ho SE24 160 D5
Herne Hill Mans SE24 161 A5
Herne Hill Rd SE24 139 A1
Herne Hill Sta SE24 160 D5
Herne Hill Stad SE24 161 B5
Herne Mews N18 34 A6
Herne Pl SE24 160 D6
Herne Rd KT6 214 A6
Heron Cl E17 35 B1
NW10 67 C2
Buckhurst Hill IG9 21 A3
Cheam SM1 217 B3
Heron Cres DA14 189 C6
Heron Ct 14 E14 120 A3
Bromley BR2 209 C5
6 Dulwich SE21 161 B2
9 Forest Hill SE23 162 C3
Ilford IG1 78 D6
5 Kingston KT1 198 A6
Ruislip HA4 61 B6
Stanwell TW19 148 A3
Herondale Ave SW18 158 C3
Heron Dr N4 73 A6
Herongate N1 235 B6
Herongate Rd E12 77 C6
Heron Hill DA17 125 B2
Heron Ho NW8 230 A3
SE15 139 D4
SW11 267 B2
Ealing W13 87 A3
Teddington KT1 175 C2
Heron Ind Est E15 97 D5
Heron Mead EN3 7 C5
Heron Mews IG1 78 D6
Heron Pl SE16 119 A5
W1 238 B2
Heron Quays E14 119 C5
Heron Quays Sta E14 119 C5
Heron Rd SE24 139 A1
Croydon CR0 221 C6
Isleworth TW1 131 B1
Heronsforde W13 87 C1
Heronsgate HA8 26 C5
Heronsgate Prim Sch
SE28 123 B3
Heron's Lea N6 48 D3
Heronslea Dr HA7 26 A5
Herons Pl TW7 131 B2
Heron Sq 23 TW10 153 D6
Herons Rise EN4 2 C1
Herons The E11 54 D3
Heron Trad Est W3 88 D2
Heronway IG8 37 C6
Heron Way TW14 128 A1
Herrick Ct 4 TW10 175 D6
Herrick Ho 17 N16 73 B4
18 SE5 139 B5
Herrick Rd N5 73 A5
Herrick St SW1 115 D2 259 D3
Herries St W10 91 A5
Herringham Rd SE7 121 C3
Herrongate Cl EN1 5 D3
Hersant Cl NW10 90 A6
Herschell Rd SE23 163 A4
Herschell's Mews SE5 139 A2
Hersham Cl SW15 156 A4
Hersham Rd KT12 194 A1
Hershell Ct 1 SW14 132 D1
Hertford Ave SW14 133 C1
Hertford Cl EN4 2 B2
Hertford Ct E6 100 B4
16 SW11 136 C2
Palmers Green N13 16 C1
Hertford Lo 10 SW19 157 A3
Hertford Pl W1 239 B5
Hertford Rd N1 95 C6
N2 48 C6
Barking IG11 78 D1
Barnet EN4 2 A2
Edmonton N9 18 B3
Enfield EN3 6 C5

Hertford Rd *continued*
Ilford IG2 57 C3
Hertford Rd High St EN3 18 C6
Hertford Sq CR4 204 A5
Hertford St W1 115 B5 248 C3
Hertford Way CR4 204 A5
Hertford Wlk 13 DA17 125 C1
Hertmitage The 4
SE13 142 A3
Hertslet Rd N7 72 B5
Hertsmere Rd E14 119 C6
Hertswood Ct 1 EN5 1 A1
Hervey Cl N3 29 C2
Hervey Park Rd E17 53 A5
Hervey Rd SE3 143 B4
Hesa Rd UB3 106 A6
Hesewall Cl SW4 137 C3
Hesketh Pl W11 244 A5
Hesketh Rd E7 77 A5
Heslop Ct 1 SW12 159 A3
Heslop Rd SW12 158 D3
Hesper Mews
SW5 113 D2 255 C3
Hesperus Cres E14 119 D2
Hessel Rd W13 109 B4
Hessel St E1 96 B1
Hestercombe Ave
SW6 135 B4 264 B1
Hesterman Way CR0 204 B1
Hester Rd SW11 136 C5 267 A3
Edmonton N18 34 A5
Hester Terr TW9 132 C2
Heston Ave TW5 129 A5
Heston Com Sch TW5 129 C5
Heston Ctr The TW5 106 C1
Heston Grange TW5 129 B6
Heston Grange La TW5 129 B6
Heston Ho 5 SE8 141 C4
W4 110 D1
Heston Ind Mall TW5 129 B5
Heston Inf Sch TW5 129 C5
Heston Jun Sch TW5 129 C5
Heston Phoenix Distribution
Pk TW5 128 C6
Heston Rd TW5 129 C5
Heston St SE14 141 C4
Hetherington Rd
SW2,SW4 138 A1
Charlton TW17 171 A1
Hetherington Way UB10 60 A4
Hethpool Ho W2 236 C5
Hetley Gdns 1 SE19 183 D3
Hetley Rd W12 112 B4
Heton Gdns NW4 46 A5
Hevelius Cl SE10 120 D1
Hever Croft SE9 188 C6
Heverfield Ct CR4 180 D3
Hever Gdns BR1 188 C1
Heverham Rd SE18 123 C2
Hever Ho SE15 140 D6
Heversham Ho SE15 140 C6
Heversham Rd DA7 147 C4
Hewens Rd UB4 83 A3
Hewer Ho 6 SW4 159 C6
Hewer St W10 90 D2
Hewes Ho E17 52 D5
Hewett Cl HA7 25 B6
Hewett Ho 7 SE18 122 D1
Hewett Rd RM8 80 D4
Hewett St EC2 95 C3 243 B5
Hewish Rd N18 33 C6
Hewison St E3 97 B5
Hewitt Ave N22 32 D1
Hewitt Cl CR0 223 C5
Hewitt Ho 2 E4 36 B5
Hewitt Rd N8 50 D4
Hewlett Rd E3 97 A5
Hewling Ho 1 N16 73 C3
Hewtt Ho SW15 134 C3
Hexagon The N6 48 D1
Hexal Rd SE6 164 C1
Hexham Gdns TW7 131 A5
Hexham Rd Barnet EN5 1 D1
Cheam SM4 201 D1
West Norwood SE27 161 A2
Heybourne Rd N17 34 B3
Hey Bridge 9 NW1 71 B2
Heybridge Ave SW16 182 B4
Heybridge Dr IG6 57 B6
Heybridge Way E10 53 B1
Heydon Ct BR4 224 C6
Heydon Ho SE14 140 C4
Heyford Ave
SW8 138 A5 270 B4
Merton SW20 201 B6
Heyford Rd CR4 180 C1
Heygate St SE17 117 A2 262 B4
Heylyn Sq E3 97 B4
Heynes Rd RM8 80 C4
Heysham Dr WD19 22 D5
Heysham La NW3 69 D5
Heysham Rd N15 51 B3
Heythorp St SW18 157 B2
Heythrop Dr UB10 60 B4
Heyward Ct SM2 217 C2
Heywood Ave NW9 27 C2
Heywood Ct 2 HA7 25 C5
Heywood Ho 11 SE14 140 D6
6 SW2 160 C5
Heyworth Rd E15 76 D4
E5 74 B4
Hibbert Rd E17 53 B2
Harrow HA3 24 D1
Hibbert St SW11 136 B2
Hibernia Gdns TW3 151 C6
Hibernia Point 11 SE2 124 D4
Hibernia Rd TW3 129 C1
Hibiscus Cl HA8 27 A6
Hibiscus Lo E15 76 C1
Hichisson Rd SE15 162 C6
Hickes Ho 6 NW6 70 B1
Hickey's Almshouses 7
TW9 132 B1
Hickin Cl SE7 121 D2
Hickin St 2 E14 120 A3
Hickleton NW1 232 B5
Hickling Ho 10 SE16 118 B3
Hickling Rd IG1 78 D3
Hickman Ave E4 36 A4
Hickman Cl E16 99 D2
Hickman Rd RM6 58 C2
Hickmore Wlk SW4 137 C2
Hickory Cl N9 18 A4
Hicks Ave UB6 86 C4
Hicks Cl SW11 136 C2
Hicks Ct RM10 81 D5
Hicks St SE8 119 A1
Hidaburn Ct 7 SW16 181 C6
Hidcote Gdns SW20 200 B6
Hidcote Ho 11 SM2 218 A1
Hide E6 100 C1
Hide Pl SW1 115 D2 259 C3
Hide Rd HA1 42 B5
Hide Twr SW1 259 C3
Hieover SE21 161 A2
Higgins Ho 7 N1 95 C6
Higginson Ho 2 NW3 70 D1
Higgins Wlk TW12 173 A4
Higgs Ind Est 9 SE24 138 D2
High Acre EN2 4 D2
Higham Ct 9 IG8 37 A4
Higham Hill Ho E17 34 D2
Higham Hill Rd E17 35 A1
Higham Ho E4 35 C4
Higham Pl E17 53 A6
Higham Rd N17 51 B6
Woodford IG8 37 A4
Highams Lodge Bsns Ctr
E17 52 D6
Highams Park Sch E4 36 B4
Highams Park Sta E4 36 B4
Higham St E17 53 A6
Higham Station Ave E4 35 D4
Highams The E17 36 A2
High Ashton 11 KT2 176 D3
Highbanks Cl DA16 146 B5
Highbanks Rd HA5 23 D4
Highbank Way N8 50 C3
High Barnet Sta EN5 1 C1
Highbarrow Rd CR0 206 A1
High Beech
South Croydon CR2 221 C1
Southgate N21 16 B5
High Beeches DA14 191 A5
High Birch Ct 7 EN4 2 C1
Highbridge Ct 13 SE14 140 C5
Highbridge Rd IG11 100 D6
High Bridge Wharf
SE10 120 B1
Highbrook Rd SE3 143 D2
High Broom Cres BR4 207 D2
Highbury (Arsenal FC)
N5 72 D5
Highbury Ave CR7 182 D1
Highbury Cl
New Malden KT3 199 A4
West Wickham BR4 223 D6
Highbury Cnr N5 72 D2
Highbury Corner N5 72 D2
Highbury Cres N5 72 C3
Highbury Fields Sch N5 72 D3
Highbury Gdns IG3 79 C6
Highbury Gr N5 72 D3
Highbury Grange N5 73 A4
Highbury Grove Ct N5 72 D2
Highbury Grove Sch N5 73 A3
Highbury Hill N5 72 D4
Highbury & Islington Sta
N1 72 D2
Highbury New Pk N5 73 A4
Highbury Pk N5 72 D4
Highbury Pl N5 72 D3
Highbury Quadrant N5 73 A5
Highbury Quadrant Prim Sch
N5 73 A4
Highbury Rd SW19 179 A5
Highbury Station Rd N1 72 C2
Highbury Terr N5 72 D3
Highbury Terrace Mews
N5 72 D3
High Cedar Dr SW20 178 B3
Highclere Rd KT3 199 B6
Highclere St SE26 185 A6
Highcliffe
Beckenham BR3 185 D2
Ealing W13 87 B2
Highcliffe Dr SW15 155 D5
Highcliffe Gdns IG4 56 A4
Highcombe SE7 143 B6
Highcombe Cl SE9 166 A3
High Coombe Pl KT2 177 B3
Highcroft N6 49 A3
NW9 45 C4
2 Kingston KT5 198 B4
Highcroft Ave HA0 88 C6
Highcroft Gdns NW11 47 B3
Highcroft Rd N19 50 A2
High Cross Ctr The N15 52 A5
High Cross Rd N17 52 A6
Highcross Way 4
SW15 156 A3
Highdaun Dr SW16 204 B5
High Dene EN2 4 D2
Highdown KT4 215 D6
Highdown Rd SW15 156 B5
High Dr KT2,KT3 177 A1
High Elms IG8 37 A5
High Elms Rd BR6 227 A1
Highenden Ho NW8 237 A6
Highfield WD23 8 C2
Highfield Ave DA8 147 D6
NW11 47 A2
NW9 45 A4
Greenford UB6 64 D3
Orpington BR6 227 D3
Pinner HA5 41 B4
Wembley HA9 66 B5
Highfield Cl NW9 45 A4
SE13 164 B5
Long Ditton KT6 197 C1
Wood Green N22 32 C2
Highfield Ct NW11 47 A3
Mitcham CR4 202 C5
Southgate N14 15 C5
Wanstead E12 77 C6
Highfield Dr
Beckenham BR2 208 D5
Ickenham UB10 60 A5
West Ewell KT19 215 D2
West Wickham BR4 224 A5
Highfield Gdns NW11 47 A3
Highfield Gr N6 48 D1
Highfield Hill SE19 183 C3
Highfield Ho N21 16 D3
Highfield Inf Sch BR2 208 C5
Highfield Jun Sch BR2 208 C5
Highfield Prim Sch
Edmonton N21 17 A3
Hillingdon UB10 82 D4
Highfield Rd BR1 210 B5
BR5,BR7 211 D6
DA6 169 B6
NW11 47 A3
W3 89 A2
Carshalton SM1 218 C3
Edmonton N21 16 D2
Feltham TW13 150 A2
Hounslow TW7 130 D4
Tolworth KT5 199 A2
Upper Halliford TW16 193 D4
Walton-on-T KT12 194 A1
Highfields SM1 217 C6
Highfield Sch SW18 158 C4
High Foleys KT10 213 B1
High Gables
Beckenham BR2 186 C1
Loughton IG10 21 D6
High Garth KT10 212 A2
Highgate Archway N6 49 C1
Highgate Ave N6 49 B2
Highgate Ballet Sch
NW11 47 D5
Highgate Cemetery★
N19 71 B6
Highgate Cl N6 49 A2
High Gate Edge N2 48 C4
Highgate High St N6 49 B1
Highgate Hill N19 49 C1
Highgate Ho 11 SE26 162 A1
Highgate Hts N6 49 C3
Highgate Jun Sch N6 48 D2
Highgate Prim Sch N6 48 D3
Highgate Private Hospl
N6 48 D3
Highgate Rd NW5 71 B4
Highgate Sch N6 49 A2
Highgate Spinney N8 49 D3
Highgate Sta N6 49 B3
Highgate West Hill N6 71 A6
Highgate Wlk SE23 162 C2
Highgate Wood Sch N8 49 C4
High Gr Bromley BR1 187 D2
Woolwich SE18 145 B4
Highgrove Cl BR7 188 A2
N11 31 A5
Highgrove Ct BR3 185 C3
Highgrove Ho HA4 40 A3
Highgrove Mews SM5 218 D5
Highgrove Point 2 NW3 70 A4
Highgrove Rd RM8 80 C4
Highgrove Way HA4 40 A2
High Hill Ferry 3 E5 52 B1
High Holborn
WC1 94 B2 240 C3
High La W7 86 B1
Highland Ave W7 86 C1
Highland Cotts SM6 219 C4
Highland Croft BR3 185 D4
Highland Ct E18 37 B2
Highland Dr WD23 8 A4
Highland Lo 3 SE19 183 D3
Highland Pk TW13 171 D6
Highland Rd Bexley DA6 147 C1
Bromley BR1 186 D2
Pinner HA6 22 A1
West Norwood SE19 183 C4
Highlands N20 14 B2
Highlands Ave W3 111 A6
Southgate N21 16 B6
Highlands Cl N4 50 A2
Hounslow TW3 129 D4
Highlands Ct SE19 183 C4
Highlands Gdns IG1 56 B1
Highlands Heath SW15 156 C4
Highlands Prim Sch IG1 56 B1
Highlands Rd EN5 13 C6
Highlands Sch N21 6 C1
Highlands The Barnet EN5 1 D1
Edgware HA8 26 D1
Highlawn Hall HA1 64 C5
Highlea Cl NW9 27 C2
High Level Dr SE26 184 A6
Highlever Rd W10 90 C2
High Limes 2 SE19 183 C4
High London 5 N6 49 D2
Highmead SE18 145 D5
9 Edmonton N18 34 A5
High Mead Harrow HA1 42 D4
West Wickham BR4 224 C6
Highmead Cres HA0 66 B1
High Meadow Cl HA5 40 C5
High Meadow Cres NW9 45 B4
High Meads Rd E16 99 D1
Highmore Rd SE3 142 C5
High Mount NW4 46 A3
High Oaks EN2 4 B5
High Park Ave TW9 132 C4
High Park Rd TW9 132 C4
High Par The SW16 160 A1
High Path SW19 180 A2
High Point N6 49 A2
SE9 166 D1
Highpoint EN5 14 A6
High Range SW20 178 C3
High Rd E10 53 D3
N11 31 B5
N15,N17 51 D5
N20 14 A4
N2 48 C6
N2,N12 30 A3
NW10 68 A2
Buckhurst Hill IG9,IG10 21 C5
Bushey WD23 8 B3
Harrow HA3 24 C3
Ilford IG1 78 D6
Ilford IG1,IG3 79 C6
Ilford IG3 57 D1
Ilford RM6 58 B2
Tottenham N17 33 D2
Wembley HA0,HA9 66 A3
Woodford E18 37 A2
Wood Green N22 32 B3
High Ridge N10 31 B2
High Road Eastcote HA5 40 B4
High Road, Ickenham
UB10 61 A6
High Road Leyton E10 75 D6
High Road Leytonstone
E11 76 C6
High Road Woodford Gn
IG8 37 A6
High Sheldon N6 48 D3
Highshore Rd SE15 139 D3
Highshore Sch SE15 139 D4
High Silver IG10 21 D6
High St BR1 187 A1
BR6 227 A3
BR6 227 D2
E13 99 A5
E15 98 A6
E17 53 B5
N14 15 D2
N8 50 B5
NW7 28 B5
Acton W3 110 D5
Barnet EN5 1 B1
Beckenham BR3 185 C1
Brentford TW8 132 A6
Cheam SM1,KT17 217 A2
Claygate KT10 212 D2
Cranford TW5 128 B5
Croydon CR0 221 A5
Croydon SE25 206 A5
Ealing W5 109 D6
East Molesey KT8 195 C5
Elstree WD6 9 D5
Feltham TW13 150 A2
Hampton TW12 174 A4
Harlington UB3 127 B6
Harrow HA1 42 C1
Harrow HA3 42 C6
Hounslow TW3 129 D2
Ilford IG6 57 A6
Kingston KT1 197 D6
New Malden KT3 199 C5
Penge SE20 184 D3
Pinner HA5 41 A6
Ruislip HA4 39 C1
Shepperton TW17 193 A3
Sidcup DA14 190 A6
Southall UB1 107 B5
South Norwood CR7 205 B5
Sutton SM1 217 D4
Sutton SM1,SM2 217 D3
Teddington KT1 175 D2
Teddington TW11 175 A5
Thames Ditton KT7 197 A3
Twickenham TW2 152 A4
Wallington SM5 219 A4
Walton-on-T KT12 194 A1
Wanstead E11 55 A4
Wembley HA9 66 B4
West Wickham BR4 207 D1
Wimbledon SW19 178 D5
Yiewsley UB7 104 A6
High St Mews SW19 179 A5
High St N E12 78 A2
E6 100 A6
Highstone Ave E11 55 A3
Highstone Ct E11 54 D3
High Street Collier's Wood
SW17,SW19 180 B4
High Street Harlesden
NW10 89 D5
High Street Harlington
TW6 127 B5
High Street Kensington Sta
W8 113 D3 245 C1
High St S E6 100 B4
High The SW16 160 A1
High Timber St EC4 252 A6
High Tor Cl BR1 187 B3
High Tor View SE28 123 C5
High Trees N20 14 A1
Croydon CR0 207 A1
East Barnet EN4 14 C6
Streatham SW2 160 C3
High Trees *continued*
Uxbridge UB10 61 A6
Hightrees Ct W7 108 C6
Hightrees Ho SW12 159 A5
Highview N8 50 A2
Northolt UB5 85 A4
Woolwich SE18 144 D5
High View
6 Penge SE19 183 D3
Pinner HA5 40 C6
Highview Ave HA8 27 A6
High View Ave CR0,SM6 220 B3
High View Cl
Loughton IG10 21 C6
South Norwood SE19 183 D1
Highview Ct 2 SW19 157 A3
High View Ct HA3 24 C3
Highview Gdns HA8 27 A6
N11 31 C5
N3 47 A6
High View Par 1 IG4 56 B4
High View Prim Sch
SW11 136 B1
Wallington SM6 220 A3
High View Rd E18 54 D6
N10 30 D2
Highview Rd Ealing W13 87 A1
Sidcup DA14 190 B6
High View Rd SE19 183 B4
Highway Bsns Pk The 7
E1 118 D6
Highway The E1 118 C6
Stanmore HA7 25 A3
Highway Trad Ctr The 6
E1 118 D6
High Wigsell TW11 175 A5
Highwood Ave N12 30 A6
Highwood Cl BR6 227 A6
Highwood Ct N12 14 A1
Barnet EN5 13 C6
Highwood Dr BR6 227 A6
Highwood Gdns IG5 56 B5
Highwood Gr NW7 27 B5
Highwood Hill NW7 11 D2
Highwood Rd N19 72 A5
High Worple HA2 41 B1
Highworth Rd N11 31 D5
Highworth St NW1 237 B4
Hilary Ave CR4 203 A6
Hilary Cl SW6 265 C4
Bexley DA7 147 D4
Hilary Ct N9 18 D3
Hilary Rd W12 111 D6
Hilbert Rd SM3 216 D5
Hilborough Cl SW19 180 A3
Hilborough Ct 1 E8 95 D6
Hilborough Rd 1 E8 73 D1
Hilborough Way BR6 227 B3
Hilda Rd E16 98 C3
E6 77 D1
Hilda Terr 2 SW9 138 C3
Hilda Vale Cl BR6 226 D4
Hilda Vale Rd BR6 226 D4
Hildenborough Gdns
BR1 186 D4
Hildenborough Ho BR3 185 B3
Hildenlea Pl BR2 186 C1
Hilditch Ho 7 TW10 154 B5
Hildred Ho SW1 258 C4
Hildreth St SW12 159 B3
Hildreth Street Mews 2
SW12 159 B3
Hildyard Rd SW6 265 B6
Hiley Rd NW10 90 C4
Hilfield La WD23 8 C6
Hilfield La S WD23 8 D5
Hilgrove Rd NW6 70 A1
Hiliary Gdns HA7 25 C1
Hillard Ct SM6 219 D2
Hillary Cres KT12 194 C1
Hillary Ct
3 Chislehurst SE9 166 A2
Stanwell TW19 148 A3
Hillary Dr TW7 152 D6
Hillary Ho E14 98 A2
Hillary Rd UB2 107 C3
Hillary Rise EN5 1 C1
Hillbeck Cl SE15 140 C5
SE15 140 C6
Hillbeck Way UB6 86 B6
Hillborne Cl UB3 106 A1
Hillboro Ct E11 54 B2
1 Woodford E18 36 D2
Hillbrook Rd SW17 181 A6
Hillbrook Sch SW17 181 A6
Hillbrow Kingston KT3 199 D6
7 Richmond TW10 154 A5
Hill Brow BR1 187 D2
Hillbrow Ct KT10 212 A4
Hillbrow Rd Catford BR1 186 C4
Esher KT10 212 A4
Hill Bunker's DA17 125 C2
Hillbury Ave HA3 43 B4
Hillbury Rd SW17 159 B1
Hill Cl NW11 47 C3
NW2 68 B5
Barnet EN5 12 C6
Chislehurst BR7 188 D5
Harrow HA1 64 C5
Stanmore HA7 25 B6
Hillcote Ave SW16 182 C3
Hillcourt Ave N12 29 D4
Hillcourt Rd SE22 162 B5
Hill Cres N20 13 D2
Harrow HA1 43 A4
Kingston KT5 198 B4
North Cheam KT4 216 C6
Hillcrest N6 49 A2
SE24 139 B1
W11 244 C5
Hill Crest DA15 168 B4
Hillcrest N21 16 C4
Hillcrest Ave NW11 47 B4
Edgware HA8 26 D6
Pinner HA5 40 D5
Hillcrest Cl
Beckenham BR3 207 B3
Forest Hill SE26 184 A6
Hillcrest Ct NW2 69 A3
Sutton SM2 218 B2
Hillcrest Gdns N3 47 A5
NW2 68 A5
Hinchley Wood KT10 212 D5
Hillcrest Hts W5 88 A3
Hillcrest Rd BR1 187 A6
Acton W3 110 D5
Chingford E17 36 B1
Ealing W5 88 A2
Loughton IG10 21 D5
Woodford E18 37 A1
Hillcrest View BR3 207 B3
Hillcroft Ave HA5 41 B3
Hillcroft Coll KT6 198 A3
Hillcroft Cres Ealing W5 87 D1
Ruislip HA4 62 D5
Wembley HA9 66 B4
Hillcroft Rd E6 100 D2
Hillcroome Rd SM2 218 B2
Hillcross Ave SM4 201 A4
Hillcross Prim Sch SM4 201 B5
Hill Ct NW3 70 C4
Barnet EN4 2 C1
Ealing W5 88 B3
8 Kingston KT2 176 D3
14 Kingston KT6 198 A4
Northolt UB5 63 C3
Putney SW15 156 D6
Hilldale Rd SM1 217 B4
Hilldown Ct SW16 182 A3
Hilldown Rd Hayes BR2 208 D1
South Norwood SW16 182 B3
Hill Dr NW9 45 A1
Thornton Heath SW16 204 B6
Hilldrop Cres N7 71 D3
Hilldrop Est 4 N7 71 D4
Hilldrop La N7 71 D3
Hilldrop Rd N7 71 D3
Bromley BR1 187 B4
Hill End BR6 227 D6
SE18 144 C4
Hillersdon Ave
Barnes SW13 134 A3
Edgware HA8 26 B5
Hillersdon Ho SW1 258 C2
Hillery Cl SE17 262 D3
Hill Farm Rd W10 90 D2
Hillfield Ave N8 50 A5
NW9 45 C5
Mitcham SM4 202 C4
Wembley HA0 66 B1
Hillfield Cl HA2 42 A5
Hillfield Ct NW3 70 C3
Hillfield Ho N5 73 A3
Hillfield Mans NW3 70 C3
Hillfield Par SM4 202 B3
Hillfield Park Mews N10 49 B5
Hillfield Pk N10 49 B5
Southgate N21 16 C2
Hillfield Rd NW6 69 C3
Hampton TW12 173 B2
Hillgate Pl W8 113 C5 245 A4
Balham SW12 159 B4
Hillgate St W8 245 A4
Hill Gr TW13 151 B2
Hill Ho E5 52 B1
Stanmore HA7 9 A1
Hill House Ave HA7 24 D3
Hill House Cl N21 16 C4
Hill House Dr TW12 173 C2
Hill House Rd SW16 182 B5
Hill House Sch
SW1 114 D3 257 D5
Hilliard Ho 15 E1 118 B5
Hilliard's Ct E1 118 C5
Hillier Cl EN5 13 D5
Hillier Gdns CR0 220 C3
Hillier Ho 1 NW1 71 D1
Hillier Lo TW12 174 B5
Hillier Pl KT9 213 D2
Hillier Rd SW11 158 D5
Hilliers Ave UB8 82 C4
Hillier's La CR0,SM6 220 A5
Hillingdon Ave TW19 148 A3
Hillingdon Circus UB10 60 D2
Hillingdon Hill UB10 82 B4
Hillingdon Hospl UB8 82 B2
Hillingdon Par 6 UB10 82 D3
Hillingdon Prim Sch
UB10 82 D4
Hillingdon Rd UB10 82 A5
Hillingdon St SE17 138 D6
Hillingdon Sta UB10 60 D3
Hillington Gdns IG8 37 D1
Hill La HA4 39 A1
Hill Lo SW11 136 B1
Hillman Cl UB8 60 A3
Hillman St E8 74 B2
Hillmarton Rd N7 72 A3
Hillmead Dr SW9 138 D1
Hill Mead Prim Sch
SW9 138 D1
Hillmont Rd KT10 212 C5
Hillmore Ct SE13 142 B2
Hillmore Gr SE26 185 A5
Hill Rd N10 30 D2
NW8 92 A5 229 B3
Carshalton SM5 218 C2
Harrow HA1 43 A4
Mitcham CR4 181 B3
Pinner HA5 41 A3

Hill Rd *continued*
Sutton SM1 217 D3
Wembley HA0 65 B5
Hillreach SE7,SE18 122 B1
Hill Rise NW11 47 D5
Hillrise KT12 193 D2
Hill Rise Enfield N9 18 B5
Forest Hill SE23 162 B3
Greenford UB6 86 A6
Hinchley Wood KT10 213 B6
Richmond TW10 153 D6
Ruislip HA4 39 B1
Hillrise Mans N19 50 A2
Hillrise Rd N19 50 A2
Hillsboro Rd SE22 161 C6
Hillsborough Ct 11 NW6 91 D6
Hillsgrove Cl DA16 146 C5
Hillsgrove Prim Sch
DA16 146 C5
Hillside N8 49 D3
NW10 89 B6
NW9 45 B5
Barnet EN5 14 A6
Wimbledon SW19 178 D4
Hill Side EN5 14 A6
Hillside Ave N11 30 D4
Wembley HA9 66 B4
Woodford IG8 37 C5
Hillside Cl NW8 91 D5
Merton SM4 201 A5
Woodford IG8 37 C5
Hillside Cres Enfield EN2 5 B5
Harrow HA2 42 A1
Northwood HA6 22 A2
Hillside Ct NW3 69 D3
7 Kingston KT2 176 D3
Hillside Dr HA8 26 C5
Hillside Gdns E17 54 B6
N6 49 B3
Barnet EN5 1 A1
Barnet N11 31 C4
Edgware HA8 26 B6
Harrow HA3 44 A2
Northwood HA6 22 B2
Streatham SW2 160 C2
Wallington SM6 219 C1
Hillside Gr N14 15 D4
NW7 28 A3
Hillside Jun Inf Schs
HA6 22 A3
Hillside La BR2 224 D6
Hillside Mans EN5 1 B1
Hillside Rd N15 51 C3
Beckenham BR2 208 D6
Belmont SM2 217 B1
Croydon CR0 220 D4
Ealing W5 88 A2
Northwood HA6,HA5 22 B3
Southall UB1 85 C3
Streatham SW2 160 C2
Surbiton KT5 198 C4
Hillside Rise HA6 22 A3
Hillsleigh Rd
W14 113 B5 244 D4
Hills Mews 2 W5 110 A6
Hills Pl W1 239 A1
Hill's Rd IG9 21 B3
Hill St W1 115 B6 248 C4
Richmond TW10 153 D6
Hillstone Ct 5 E3 97 D3
Hillstowe St E5 74 C5
Hilltop 7 E17 53 D6
Hill Top NW11 47 D5
Cheam SM3 201 B2
Hilltop Ct NW8 70 A1
12 SW18 136 B1
South Norwood SE19 183 B2
Hilltop Gdns BR6 227 C6
Hilltop Ho 7 N6 49 D2
Hilltop Rd NW6 69 C1
Hilltop Way HA7 9 A1
Hillview SW20 178 B3
Hill View CR4 204 A5
Hillview Ave HA3 44 A4
Hillview Cl Pinner HA5 23 B4
Wembley HA9 66 B6
Hillview Cres BR6 211 D1
Hill View Cres IG1 56 B3
Hillview Ct SE19 183 C6
Hill View Dr DA16 145 C3
Woolwich SE28 123 C5
Hillview Gdns NW4 46 D5
Hill View Gdns NW9 45 B4
Hillview Gdns HA2 41 C5
Hillview Rd BR7 188 D6
NW7 28 D6
Hill View Rd BR6 227 D6
Hillview Rd
Carshalton SM1 218 B5
Pinner HA5 23 B4
Hill View Rd
Claygate KT10 213 A1
Twickenham TW1 153 A5
Hillway N6 71 A6
NW9 45 C1
Hill Wood Ho NW1 232 C3
Hillworth 7 BR3 185 D1
Hillworth Rd SW2 160 C4
Hillyard Rd W7 86 C2
Hillyard St SW9 138 C4
Hillyfield E17 35 A1
Hillyfield Cl E9 75 A3
Hilly Fields Cres SE4 141 C2
Hilly Mead SW19 179 A3
Hilsea Point 7 SW15 156 B3
Hilsea St E5 74 C4
Hilton Ave N12 30 B5
Hilton Ho N7 72 A4
9 SE4 140 D1
4 Ealing W13 87 C1
Hilversum Cres 10 SE22 161 C6
Himley Rd SW17 180 D4
Hinchley Cl KT10 212 D5
Hinchley Dr KT10 212 D5
Hinchley Way KT10 213 A5
Hinchley Wood Prim Sch
KT10 213 A6
Hinchley Wood Sch
KT10 213 A6
Hinchley Wood Sta
KT10 212 D5
Hinckley Rd SE15 140 A1
Hind Ct EC4 241 B1
Hinde Mews W1 238 B2
Hindes Rd HA1 42 C4
Hinde St W1 93 A1 238 B2
Hind Gr E14 97 C1
Hindhead Cl UB8 82 D2
Hindhead Gdns UB5 85 A6
Hindhead Gn WD19 22 C5
Hindhead Point 6
SW15 156 B3
Hindhead Way SM6 220 A3
Hind Ho N7 72 C4
13 SE14 140 D6
Hindhurst Ct NW9 45 A5
Hindle Ho E8 73 D3
Hindley Ho N7 72 B5
Hindlip Ho SW8 269 C1
Hindmans Rd SE22 162 A6
Hindmans Way RM9 103 B3
Hindmarsh Cl E1 118 A6
Hindrey Rd E5 74 B3
Hindsley's Pl SE23 162 C2
Hines Ct HA1 43 A4
Hinkler Rd HA3 43 D6
Hinksey Path SE2 124 D3
Hinstock NW6 91 D6
Hinstock Rd SE18 145 A5
Hinton Ave TW4 128 D1
Hinton Cl SE9 166 A3
Hinton Ct 3 E10 75 D6
Hinton Rd SE24 138 D2
Edmonton N18 33 C6
Wallington SM6 219 C2
Hippodrome Mews
W11 244 A5
Hippodrome Pl W11 244 B5
Hiscocks Ho NW10 67 A1
Hitcham Rd E17 53 B2
Hitchcock Cl TW17 192 B6
Hitchin Sq E3 97 A5
Hitherbroom Rd UB3 106 A6
Hither Farm Rd SE3 143 C2
Hitherfield Prim Sch
SW2 160 C2
Hitherfield Rd
Dagenham RM8 81 A6
Streatham SW16,SW27 160 C1
Hither Green La SE13 164 B5
Hither Green Prim Sch
SE13 164 B5
Hither Green Sta SE13 164 C5
Hitherlands SW12 159 B2
Hitherwell Dr HA3 24 B2
Hitherwood Ct SE21 183 D6
Hitherwood Dr SE19 183 D6
Hive Cl WD23 8 B2
Hive Rd WD23 8 C2
HM Prison Wormwood
Scrubs W12 90 A1
HMS Belfast* SE1 253 B4
Hoadly Rd SW16 159 D2
Hobart Cl N20 14 C2
Hayes UB4 84 D3
Hobart Ct Harrow HA1 42 C2
Woodford IG8 36 D6
Hobart Dr UB4 84 D3
Hobart Gdns CR7 205 B6
Hobart La UB4 84 D3
Hobart Pl SW1 115 B3 258 C6
Richmond TW10 154 B4
Hobart Rd Dagenham RM9 80 D4
Hayes UB4 84 D3
North Cheam KT4 216 B5
Hobbayne Prim Sch W7 86 D1
Hobbayne Rd W7 86 B1
Hobbes Wlk SW15 156 B6
Hobb's Ct SE1 253 D2
Hobbs Gn N2 48 A6
Hobbs Mews IG3 79 D6
Hobbs' Pl N1 95 C6
Hobbs Rd 5 SE27 183 A6
Hobday St E14 97 D1
Hobill Wlk KT5 198 B3
Hoblands End BR7 189 C4
Hobsons Pl 7 E1 96 A2
Hobury St SW10 136 B6 266 C5
Hockenden La BR5,BR8 191 D1
Hocker St 41 E2 95 D4
Hockington Ct 7 EN5 13 D6
Hockley Ave E6 100 A5
Hockley Ct 2 E18 37 A2
Hockley Ho 4 E9 74 C2
Hockley Mews IG11 101 C5
Hockliffe Ho W10 90 C2
Hockney Ct 11 SE16 118 B1
Hockworth Ho 7 N16 51 C1
Hocroft Ave NW2 69 B5
Hocroft Ct NW2 69 B5
Hocroft Rd NW2 69 B5
Hocroft Wlk NW2 69 B5
Hodder Dr UB6 86 D5
Hoddesdon Rd DA17 125 C1
Hodford Rd NW11 47 B1
Hodgkins Cl SE28 124 D6
Hodister Cl 28 SE5 139 A5
Hodnet Gr SE16 118 D2
Hodson Cl HA2 63 B5
Hodson Pl EN3 7 C5
Hoecroft Ct EN3 6 C5
Hoe La EN1 6 B5
Hoe St E17 53 C4
Hoffman Sq N1 235 D2
Hofland Rd W14 113 A3 254 A6
Hogan Mews W2 236 C4
Hogan Way E5 74 A6
Hogarth Ave TW15 171 A4
Hogarth Bsns Pk W4 133 C6
Hogarth Cl E16 99 D2
Ealing W5 88 A2
Hogarth Cres
Mitcham SW19 180 B2
Thornton Heath CR0 205 A2
Hogarth Ct 15 E1 96 A1
EC3 253 B6
6 NW1 71 C1
Dulwich SE19 183 D6
Heston TW5 129 A5
Hogarth Gdns TW5 129 C5
Hogarth Hill NW11 47 B5
Hogarth Ho SW1 259 D3
Enfield EN1 18 A6
13 Northolt UB5 84 D5
6 West Norwood SE27 183 A6
Hogarth Ind Est NW10 90 A3
Hogarth La W4 133 C6
Hogarth Pl SW5 255 C3
Hogarth Prim Sch W4 111 C1
Hogarth Rd
SW5 113 D2 255 C3
Barking RM8 80 B3
Edgware HA8 26 C1
Hogarth Roundabout
W4 133 C6
Hogarth Way TW12 174 A2
Hogsmill Way KT19 215 A4
Holbeach Gdns DA15 167 D5
Holbeach Mews 1
SW12 159 B3
Holbeach Prim Sch SE6 163 C4
Holbeach Rd SE6 163 D4
Holbeck Row SE15 140 A5
Holbein Ho SW1 258 A2
10 Stanmore HA7 25 C5
Holbein Mews
SW1 115 A1 258 A2
Holbein Pl SW1 115 A2 258 A3
Holberry Ho 5 SE21 183 C6
Holberton Gdns NW10 90 B4
Holborn EC1 94 C2 241 B3
Holborn Cir EC1 94 C2 241 B3
Holborn Pl WC1 240 C3
Holborn Rd E13 99 B3
Holborn Sta WC1 94 B2 240 C3
Holborn Way CR4 180 D1
Holbrook Cl N19 49 B1
Enfield EN1 6 A5
Holbrooke Ct N7 72 A4
Holbrooke Pl 28 TW10 153 D6
Holbrook Ho W3 89 B2
Chislehurst BR7 189 B2
5 Streatham SW2 160 B3
Holbrook La BR7 189 B3
Holbrook Rd E15 98 D5
Holbrook Way BR2 210 B4
Holburn 33 N1 95 C6
Holburne Cl SE3 143 C4
Holburne Gdns SE3 143 D4
Holburne Rd SE3 143 D4
Holburn Viaduct
EC1 94 D2 241 C3
Holcombe Hill NW7 12 A1
Holcombe Ho SW9 138 A2
Holcombe Rd N17 52 A6
1 N17 51 D6
Ilford IG1 56 C2
Holcombe St W6 112 B2
Holcote Cl DA17 125 A3
Holcroft Ct W1 239 A4
Holcroft Ho SE10 142 A4
SW11 136 B2
Holcroft Rd E9 74 C1
Holden Ave N12 29 D5
NW9 45 A1
Holdenby Rd SE4 163 A6
Holden Cl RM8 80 B5
Holden Ho N1 235 A5
12 SE8 141 C5
Holden Hts N12 13 D1
Holdenhurst Ave N12 30 A3
Holden Lo N11 31 C5
Holden Rd N12 29 D6
Holden St SW11 137 A3
Holdernesse Rd
Isleworth TW7 131 A4
6 Upper Tooting SW17 159 A2
Holderness Ho SE5 139 C2
Holderness Way SE27 182 D5
Holders Hill Ave NW4 46 D6
Holders Hill Cres NW4 28 D1
Holders Hill Dr NW4 28 D1
Holders Hill Gdns NW4 29 A1
Holders Hill Par NW7 29 A2
Holders Hill Rd NW4 28 D1
NW4,NW7 29 A2
Holdsworth Ho 5 SW2 160 C4
Holford Ho 6 SE16 118 B2
WC1 233 D2
Holford Pl WC1 233 D2
Holford Rd NW3 70 A5
Holford St WC1 234 A2
Holgate Ave SW11 136 B2
Holgate Ct HA8 26 B6
Holgate Gdns RM10 81 C2
Holgate Rd RM10 81 C3
Holgate St SE7 121 D3
Hollam Ho N8 50 B5
Holland Ave
Belmont SM2 217 C1
Holland Ave *continued*
Wimbledon SW20 177 D2
Holland Cl
Coney Hall BR2 224 D6
New Barnet EN5 14 B4
Stanmore HA7 25 B5
Holland Ct 6 E17 54 A5
NW7 28 A4
Holland Dr SE23 163 A1
Holland Gdns W14 254 B6
Holland Gr SW9 138 C5
Holland Ho E4 36 A6
Holland House Sch HA8 26 D6
Holland Park
W11 113 B5 244 C3
Holland Park Ave
W11 113 A5 244 B3
Ilford IG3 57 D4
Holland Park Ct W14 244 B2
Holland Park Gdns
W14 113 A4 244 A2
Holland Park Mews
W11 113 B5 244 C3
Holland Park Rd
W14 113 B3 254 D5
Holland Park Rdbt W12 112 D4
Holland Park Sch
W8 113 B4 244 D2
Holland Park Sta
W11 113 B5 244 C3
Holland Pl W8 245 C2
Holland Rd E15 98 C4
NW10 90 B5
W14 113 A3 254 B6
Croydon SE25 206 A4
Wallend E6 78 C1
Wembley HA0 65 D2
Holland Rise Ho SW9 270 D3
Holland St SE1 116 D5 251 D4
W8 113 C4 245 B2
Hollands The
Feltham TW13 172 D6
New Malden KT4 199 D1
Holland Villas Rd
W14 113 A4 244 A1
Holland Way BR2 224 D6
Holland Wlk N19 49 D1
W14 113 B4 244 D1
Stanmore HA7 25 A5
Hollar Rd N16 73 D5
Hollen St W1 239 C2
Holles Cl TW12 173 C5
Holles Ho 9 SW9 138 C3
Holles St W1 93 B1 238 D2
Holley Rd W3 111 C4
Hollickwood Ave N12 30 D4
Hollickwood Prim Sch
N10 31 B3
Holliday Sq 7 SW11 136 B2
Hollidge Way RM10 81 D1
Hollies Ave DA15 167 D3
Hollies Cl
South Norwood SW16 182 C4
Twickenham TW1 152 D2
Hollies End NW7 28 B5
Hollies Rd W5 109 C2
Hollies The N20 14 B3
7 Harrow HA3 43 A5
2 Wanstead E11 55 A4
Hollies Way 1 SW12 159 A4
Holligrave Rd BR1 187 A2
Hollingbourne Ave DA7 147 B4
Hollingbourne Gdns
W13 87 B2
Hollingbourne Rd SE24 161 A6
Hollingbury Ct 1 E17 53 D6
Hollingsworth Rd CR0 222 B2
Hollington Cres KT3 199 D3
Hollington Ct BR7 188 D4
Hollington Rd E6 100 B4
Tottenham N17 34 A1
Hollingworth Cl KT8 195 B5
Hollingworth Ct 7 KT6 197 D2
Hollingworth Rd BR2,
BR5 210 D2
Hollins Ho N7 72 A4
Hollisfield WC1 233 B1
Hollman Gdns SW16 182 D4
Holloway Cl UB7 104 A1
Holloway La UB7 104 B1
Holloway Rd E11 76 B5
E6 100 B4
N19 71 D6
N7 72 B4
Holloway Road Sta N7 72 B3
Holloway Sch N7 71 D3
Holloway St TW3 129 D2
Hollowfield Wlk UB5 63 A2
Hollow The IG8 36 D6
Holly Ave N2 47 D6
Stanmore HA7 26 A1
Walton-on-T KT12 194 D1
Hollybank Cl TW12 173 C5
Holly Berry La 6 NW3 70 A4
Hollybrake Cl BR7 189 B3
Hollybush Cl Harrow HA3 24 C2
Wanstead E11 55 A4
Hollybush Gdns E2 96 B4
Hollybush Hill E11 54 D3
Holly Bush Hill 23 NW3 70 A4
Hollybush Ho 23 E2 96 B4
Holly Bush La TW12 173 C3
Hollybush Pl E2 96 B4
Hollybush Rd KT2 176 A4
Hollybush St E13 99 B4
Holly Bush Vale 9 NW3 70 A4
Holly Cl NW10 67 C1
Beckenham BR3 208 A5
Buckhurst Hill IG9 21 D1
Feltham TW13 173 A5
Holly Cott KT7 197 A1
Holly Cottage Mews UB8 82 C2
Holly Cres
Beckenham BR3 207 B4
Chingford IG8 36 B3
Hollycroft Ave NW3 69 C5
Wembley HA9 66 B5
Hollycroft Cl
Harmondsworth UB7 126 C6
South Croydon CR2 221 C3
Hollycroft Gdns UB7 126 C6
Holly Ct N15 51 C5
9 Belmont SM2 217 C1
4 Sidcup DA14 190 B6
Wallington SM6 219 B1
Hollydale Cl UB5 63 D4
Hollydale Dr BR2 226 B5
Holly Dale Prim Sch
SE15 140 C3
Hollydale Rd SE15 140 C3
Hollydene SE13 164 B5
5 SE15 140 B4
Bromley BR1 186 D2
Hollydown Way E11 76 B5
Holly Dr E4 19 D4
Holly Farm Rd UB2 107 A1
Hollyfield Ave N11 30 D5
Hollyfield Rd KT5 198 B2
Hollyfield Sch KT6 198 A4
Holly Gdns UB7 104 B4
Holly Gr NW9 45 A2
SE15 140 A3
Pinner HA5 23 A2
Hollygrove WD23 8 B4
Hollygrove Cl TW3 129 B1
Holly Hedge Terr SE13 164 B6
Holly Hill NW3 70 A4
Southgate N21 16 B5
Holly Hill Rd DA8,DA17 125 D1
Holly Ho TW8 131 C6
Holly House Hospl IG9 21 B2
Holly Lo SE13 142 B1
Harrow HA1 42 B4
Southgate N21 16 C3
4 Wimbledon SW19 179 A4
Wimbledon SW20 178 B1
Holly Lodge Gdns N6 49 A1
Holly Lodge Mans N6 71 A6
Hollymead SM5 218 D5
Holly Mews SW10 256 B1
Holly Mount NW3 70 A4
Hollymount Cl 9 SE10 142 A4
Hollymount Prim Sch
SW20 178 C2
Holly Park Est N4 50 B2
Holly Park Gdns N3 47 C6
Holly Park Prim Sch N11 31 A5
Holly Park Rd N11 31 A5
Ealing W7 108 D5
Holly Pk N3 47 C6
N4 50 B2
Holly Pl NW3 70 A4
Holly Rd E11 54 D2
W4 111 B2
Hampton TW12 174 A4
Hounslow TW3 129 D1
Twickenham TW1 153 A3
Holly St E8 73 D1
Holly Terr N6 49 A1
Hollytree Cl SW19 156 D3
Holly Tree Ho SE4 141 B2
Holly Tree Lo EN2 4 D3
Hollyview Cl NW4 46 A3
Holly Village N6 71 B6
Holly Way CR4 203 D6
Hollywell Row
EC2 95 C3 243 A5
Holly Wlk NW3 70 A4
Enfield EN2 5 B2
Hollywood Ct W5 110 B6
Hollywood Gdns UB4 84 B1
Hollywood Mews SW10 266 A6
Hollywood Rd E4 35 A5
SW10 136 A6 266 A6
Hollywood Way IG8 36 B4
Holman Ho 2 E2 96 D4
Holman Hunt Ho W14 254 A1
Holman Rd SW11 136 B3
West Ewell KT19 215 A3
Holmbank Dr TW17 193 C5
Holmbridge Gdns EN3 6 D1
Holmbrook NW1 232 B3
Holmbrook Dr NW4 46 D4
Holmbury Cl WD23 8 C2
Holmbury Ct
Mitcham SW19 180 C3
Upper Tooting SW17 158 D1
Holmbury Gdns UB3 105 D5
Holmbury Gr CR0 223 B1
Holmbury Ho SW9 160 D6
Holmbury Manor 6
DA14 190 A6
Holmbury Pk BR7 188 A3
Holmbury View 2 E5 52 B1
Holmbush Ct NW4 46 D4
Holmbush Rd SW15 157 A5
Holmcote Gdns N5 73 A3
Holmcroft Ho 9 E17 53 D5
Holmcroft Way BR2 210 B4
Holm Ct SE12 165 B1
Holmdale Gdns NW4 46 D4
Holmdale Rd NW6 69 C3
Chislehurst BR7 189 A5
Holmdale Terr N15 51 C3
Holmdene N12 29 D5
Holmdene Ave NW7 28 A4
SE24 161 A6
Harrow HA2 41 D6
Holmdene Cl BR3 186 A1
Holmdene Ct BR1 210 A6
Holmead Rd
SW6 135 D5 265 D3
Holmefield Ho W10 91 A3
Holme Lacey Rd SE12 164 D5
Holmeleigh Ct EN3 6 C1
Holme Rd E6 100 A6
Holmes Ave E17 53 B6
NW7 29 A5
Holmes Ct 18 SW4 138 A3
17 W4 111 A3
5 Chingford E4 20 B2
Holmesdale Ave SW14 132 D1
Holmesdale Cl SE25 205 D6
Holmesdale Ho 12 NW6 91 C6
Holmesdale Rd N6 49 B2
Bexley DA16 146 D3
Richmond TW9 132 B4
South Norwood SE25 205 C5
Teddington TW11 175 C4
Thornton Heath CR0 205 B4
Holmesley Rd SE23 163 A5
Holmes Pl SW10 266 B6
Holmes Rd NW5 71 B3
Merton SW19 180 A3
Twickenham TW1 152 D2
Holmes Terr SE1 251 A2
Holmeswood Ct 3 N22 32 C1
Holme Way HA7 24 D4
Holmewood Gdns SW2 160 B4
Holmewood Rd
South Norwood SE25 205 C6
Streatham SW2 160 B4
Holmfield Ave NW4 46 D4
Holmfield Ct 4 NW3 70 C2
Holmfield Ho E17 54 B5
Holm Gr UB10 60 C1
Holmhurst SE13 164 B5
Holmhurst Rd DA17 125 D1
Holmlea Ct 1 CR0 221 B4
Holmleigh Prim Sch N16 51 C1
Holmleigh Rd N16 51 C1
Holm Oak Cl SW15 157 B5
Holmoaks Ho BR3 186 A1
Holmsbury Ho 6 N7 71 D3
Holmsdale Ho 21 E14 119 D6
6 N11 31 B6
Holmshaw Cl SE26 185 A6
Holmside Ct SW12 159 A5
Holmside Rd SW12 159 A5
Holmsley Cl KT3 199 D2
Holmsley Ho SW15 155 D4
Holmstall Ave HA8 27 A1
Holmstall Par HA8 27 A1
Holm Wlk SE3 143 A3
Holmwood 2 KT5 198 B3
Holmwood Cl
Cheam SM2 216 D1
Harrow HA2 42 A6
Northolt UB5 63 D2
Holmwood Ct DA14 189 D5
3 N16 51 D2
Kingston KT3 199 B6
Holmwood Gdns N3 29 C1
Wallington SM6 219 B2
Holmwood Gr NW7 27 B5
Holmwood Mans W3 110 C5
Holmwood Rd
Chessington KT9 214 A3
Ilford IG3 79 C6
Holne Chase N2 48 A3
Morden SM4 201 C3
Holness Rd E15 76 D2
Holocaust Meml Gdn*
W2 114 D4 247 D2
Holroyd Rd SW15 156 C6
Holsgrove Ct W3 111 C5
Holstein Way 6 DA18 125 A3
Holst Mans SW13 134 C5
Holstock Rd IG1 79 A6
Holsworth Cl HA2 42 A4
Holsworthy Ho 49 E3 97 D4
Holsworthy Way KT9 213 C3
Holt Cl N10 49 A5
Woolwich SE28 124 C6
Holt Ct E15 76 A3
Holt Ho SW2 160 C5
Holtoake Ct 1 W5 87 C3
Holtoake Ho 3 W5 87 C3
Holton St E1 96 D3
Holt Rd E16 122 A5
Wembley HA0 65 C5
Holt The Morden SM4 201 C5
Wallington SM6 219 C4
Holtwhite Ave EN2 5 A3
Holtwhite's Hill EN2 4 D4
Holwell Pl HA5 41 A5
Holwood Park Ave BR2,
BR6 226 B4
Holwood Pl 7 SW4 137 D1
Holybourne Ave SW15 156 A4
Holy Cross RC Sch
SW6 135 C4 265 A2
Holy Cross Sch The
KT3 199 C4
Holy Family RC Prim Sch
E14 119 C6
SE9 143 C1
Holy Ghost RC Prim Sch
SW12 159 A4
Holyhead Cl E3 97 C4
6 E6 100 B2
Holyhead Ct KT1 197 D5
Holy Innocents RC Prim Sch
BR6 227 D5
Holyoake Ct SE16 119 B4
Holyoake Wlk N2 48 A6
Ealing W5 87 C3

Holyoak Rd
SE11 116 D2 261 D3
Holyport Rd SW6 134 D5
Holyrood Ave HA2 63 B4
Holyrood Gdns HA8 26 D1
Holyrood Ho N4 50 D1
Holyrood Mews 11 E16 121 A5
Holyrood Rd EN5 14 B5
Holyrood St SE1 117 C5 253 A3
Holy Trinity CE First Sch
SW19 179 D4
Holy Trinity CE Inf Sch
SW17 158 D2
Holy Trinity CE JMI Sch
E8 73 D2
Holy Trinity CE Jun Sch
Richmond TW10 132 C1
Wallington SM6 219 C4
Holy Trinity CE Prim Sch
DA15 168 A3
N2 48 B6
NW3 70 A2
SW1 114 D2 257 D4
SW1 115 A2 258 A4
Forest Hill SE23 162 C2
Streatham SW2 160 B4
Holy Trinity Coll BR1 187 C2
Holy Trinity & St Silas CE
Prim Sch NW1 71 B1
Holywell Cl 35 SE16 118 B1
2 SE3 143 A6
Stanwell TW19 148 A3
Holywell La EC2 243 B6
Holywell Way TW19 148 A3
Homan Ct N12 30 A6
Homan Ho 6 SW4 159 D4
Homebush Ho E4 19 D4
Home Cl Carshalton SM5 218 D6
Northolt UB5 85 B4
Homecoppice Ho 1
BR1 186 D3
Homecroft Rd
Forest Hill SE26 184 C5
Tottenham N22 33 A2
Home Ct KT6 197 D4
Home Farm Cl
Thames Ditton KT7 196 D2
Upper Halliford TW17 193 C5
Home Farm Cotts BR5 190 D2
Homefarm Rd W7 86 D1
Homefield SM4 201 C5
Home Field EN5 13 B6
Homefield Ave IG2 57 C4
Homefield Cl NW10 67 A2
Hayes UB4 84 D3
Homefield Ct NW4 46 C5
Homefield Gdns N2 48 B6
Mitcham CR4,SW19 180 B1
Homefield Ho SE23 162 D1
Homefield Pk SM1,SM2 217 D2
Homefield Pl 4 SW19 178 D5
Homefield Prep Sch
SM1 217 C3
Homefield Rd BR1 187 C2
HA8 27 B4
W4 111 D1
Walton-on-T KT12 195 A2
Wembley HA0 65 B4
Wimbledon SW19 179 A4
Homefield St 14 N1 95 C5
Homefirs Ho HA9 66 B5
Homelands Dr SE19 183 C3
Home Lea BR6 227 D3
Homeleigh Ct 8 SW16 160 A1
Homeleigh Rd SE15 162 D6
Homemead SW12 159 B2
Home Mead HA7 25 C2
Homemead Rd BR2 210 B4
Wallington CR0 203 C3
Home Office SW1 249 C1
Home Park Rd SW19 157 B1
Home Park Terr KT1 175 D1
Home Park Wlk KT1 197 D5
Home Rd SW11 136 C3
Homer Dr E14 119 C2
Homer Rd E9 75 A2
Croydon CR0 206 D3
Homer Row W1 237 B3
Homersham Rd KT1 176 D1
Homer St W1 92 C2 237 B3
Homerton Coll of Technology
E9 74 C3
Homerton Gr E9 74 D3
Homerton High St E9 74 D3
Homerton Hospl E9 74 D3
Homerton Rd E9 75 B3
Homerton Row E9 74 C3
Homerton Sta E9 74 D2
Homerton Terr E9 74 C2
Homesdale Cl E11 55 A4
Homesdale Rd BR1,BR2 209 C6
Orpington BR5,BR6 211 C2
Homesfield NW11 47 C4
Homes Of Rest (CE
Temperance Society)
IG1 79 B5
Homestall Rd SE22 162 C6
Homestead Ct EN5 13 C6
Homestead Gdns KT10 212 C3
Homestead Paddock
N14 15 B6
Homestead Pk NW2 67 D5
Homestead Rd
SW6 135 B5 264 D3
Dagenham RM8 81 B6
Homesteads The BR3 185 D4
Homestead The N11 31 B6
Homewalk Ho SE26 184 C6
Homewaters Ave TW16 171 D2
Homewillow Cl N21 16 D5
Homewood Cl TW12 173 B4
Homewood Cres BR7 189 C4
Homewood Gdns SE25 205 C4
Homewoods 2 SW12 159 C4
Homildon Ho 10 SE26 162 A1
Homington Ct KT2 176 A3
Honduras St EC1 242 A6
Honeybourne Rd NW6 69 D3
Honeybourne Way BR5 211 B1
Honeybrook Rd SW12,
SW4 159 C4
Honey Cl RM10 81 D2
Honeycroft Hill UB10 60 A1
Honeyden Rd DA14 191 A4
Honeyfield N4 72 C6
Honey Hill UB10 60 B1
Honey La EC2 242 B1
Honeyman Cl NW6 68 D1
Honeypot Bsns Ctr HA7 26 A2
Honeypot Cl NW9 44 B5
Honeypot La HA3,HA7,
NW9 44 B6
Honeysett Rd 1 N17 33 D1
Honeysuckle Cl UB1 107 A6
Honeysuckle Ct
2 SE12 165 A4
Ilford IG1 78 D2
Honeysuckle Gdns CR0 206 D1
Honeywell Jun & Inf Schs
SW11 158 D5
Honeywell Rd SW11 158 D5
Honeywood Ho 5 SE15 140 A4
Honeywood Rd NW10 89 D5
Isleworth TW7 131 A1
Honeywood Wlk SM5 218 D4
Honister Cl HA7 25 B2
Honister Gdns HA7 25 B2
Honister Pl HA7 25 B2
Honiton Gdns 1 SE15 140 C3
Honiton Ho 30 SE5 139 A3
Honiton Rd DA16 145 D3
NW6 91 B5
Honley Rd SE6 163 D4
Honnor Gdns TW7 130 B3
Honor Oak Park Sta
SE23 162 D5
Honor Oak Pk SE23 162 D5
Honor Oak Rd SE23 162 C4
Honor Oak Rise SE23 162 C5
Honwell Ho W2 91 C2
Hood Ave East Barnet N14 15 B5
Mortlake SW14 155 A6
Hood Cl CR0 204 D1
Hoodcote Gdns N21 16 D4
Hood Ct N7 72 B5
Hood Ho 17 SE5 139 B5
Hood Lo E11 77 B6
Hood Rd SW20 177 D3
Hook KT6 214 A5
Hooke Ct SE10 142 A4
Hooke Ho 30 E3 97 A5
Hooker's Rd E17 52 D6
Hook Farm Rd BR2 209 D4
Hookham Ct SW8 269 C2
Hook Ho 9 SW27 182 D5
Hooking Gn HA2 41 D4
Hook La DA16 146 A1
Hook Lane Prim Sch
DA16 146 A2
Hook Rd KT19,KT17 215 A1
Hook Rise N
Surbiton KT6 214 A5
Tolworth KT6,KT9 214 D6
Hook Rise S KT6,KT9 214 D6
Hook Rise South KT6 214 A5
Hooks Cl SE15 140 B4
Hookstone Way IG8 37 D3
Hook The EN5 14 B5
Hook Underpass KT6 214 A5
Hook Wlk HA8 27 A4
Hooper Ho 8 SW18 157 B6
Hooper Rd E16 99 A1
Hooper's Ct SW1 247 C1
Hooper's Mews 4 W3 111 A5
Hooper St E1 96 A1
Hoop La NW11 47 C2
Hoover Ho 5 SE6 186 A6
Hope Cl N1 73 A2
SE12 165 B1
2 Brentford TW8 110 A1
Dagenham RM6 58 D5
Sutton SM1 218 A3
1 Woodford IG8 37 C4
Hopedale Rd SE7 143 B6
Hopefield 3 W7 108 D5
Hopefield Ave NW6 91 A5
Hope Pk BR1 186 D3
Hopes Cl TW5 129 C6
Hope St SW11 136 B2
Hopetown St E1 243 D3
Hopewell St SE5 139 B5
Hop Gdns WC2 250 A5
Hopgood St W12 112 C5
Hopkins Cl N10 31 A3
Hopkins Ho 12 E14 97 C1
Hopkins Mews E15 98 D6
Hopkinson Ho 1 SW11 137 A3
Hopkinson's Pl NW1 231 A6
Hopkins St W1 93 D1 239 C1
Hoppers Rd N21 16 C2
Hoppett Rd E4 20 C2
Hopping La N1 72 D2
Hoppingwood Ave KT3 199 C6
Hoppner Rd UB4 83 B5
Hop St SE10 120 D3
Hopton Ct BR2 209 A1
Hopton Gdns KT3 200 A3
Hopton Ho 5 SW9 138 D3
Hopton Rd SW16 182 A5
Hopton's Gdns SE1 251 D4
Hopton St SE1 116 D5 251 D4
Hoptree Cl N12 29 D6
Hopwood Cl SW17 158 A1
Hopwood Rd SE17 139 B6
Hopwood Wlk E8 74 A1
Horace Rd E7 77 B4
Ilford IG6 57 A6
Kingston KT1 198 B6
Horatio Ho 13 E2 95 D5
Horatio Pl E14 120 A5
Horatio St 11 E2 95 D5
Horatius Way CR0 220 B2
Horbury Cres
W11 113 C6 245 A5
Horbury Mews
W11 113 B6 244 D5
Horder Rd SW6 135 A4 264 B1
Hordle Prom E 14 SE15 139 D5
Hordle Prom N 3 SE15 139 D5
Hordle Prom S 7 SE15 139 D5
Hordle Prom W 13
SE15 139 C5
Horizon Bldg 14 E14 119 C6
Horizon Sch N16 73 C4
Horle Wlk SE5 138 D3
Horley Cl DA6 169 C6
Horley Rd SE9 188 A6
Hormead Rd W9 91 B3
Hornbeam Cl NW7 11 D1
SE11 261 A4
Barking IG11 102 B3
Buckhurst Hill IG9 21 D1
Northolt UB5 63 B3
Hornbeam Cres TW8 131 B5
Hornbeam Gr E4 20 D1
Hornbeam Ho 6 DA15 168 A1
2 NW3 70 D2
Buckhurst Hill IG9 21 D1
Hornbeam La E4 20 C6
Hornbeam Rd
Buckhurst Hill IG9 21 D1
Hayes UB4 84 C2
Hornbeams Rise N11 31 A4
Hornbeam Terr SM5 202 C1
Hornbeam Twr E11 76 B5
Hornbeam Way BR2 210 C3
Hornblower Cl 2 SE16 119 A2
Hornbuckle Cl HA2 64 B6
Hornby Cl NW3 70 B1
Hornby Ho 6 SE11 138 C6
Horncastle Cl SE12 165 A4
Horncastle Rd SE12 165 A4
Hornchurch N17 33 B1
Hornchurch Cl KT2 175 D6
Horndean Cl 3 SW15 156 A3
Horne Ho 7 SE18 144 A4
Horner Ct E11 76 B5
Horne Rd TW17 192 C5
Horner Hos 18 N1 95 C6
Horner La 3 CR4 180 B1
Horne Way SW15 134 C3
Hornfair Rd SE7 143 D5
Horniman Dr SE23 162 C4
Horniman Grange 7
SE23 162 C3
Horniman Mus & Gdns★
SE23 162 B3
Horniman Sch SE23 162 B3
Horning Cl SE9 188 A6
Horn La SE10 121 A2
W3 89 A1
Woodford IG8 37 A3
Horn Link Way SE10 121 A2
Horn Park Cl SE12 165 B6
Horn Park La SE12 165 B5
Horn Park Prim Sch
SE12 165 B4
Hornsby House Sch
SW12 159 A3
Horns End Pl HA5 40 C4
Hornsey Central Hospl
N8 49 D4
Hornsey La N6 49 C2
Hornsey Lane Gdns N6 49 C2
Hornsey Park Rd N8 50 B6
Hornsey Rd N7,N19 72 B6
Hornsey Rise Gdns N19 50 A2
Hornsey Sch for Girls N8 50 B4
Hornsey St N7 72 B3
Hornsey Sta N8 50 B5
Hornshay St SE15 140 C6
Horns Rd IG2,IG6 57 A4
Hornton Ct W8 245 B1
Hornton Pl W8 245 B1
Hornton St W8 113 C4 245 B2
Horrocks Ho SW15 156 B6
Horsa Rd DA8 147 D5
Eltham SE12 165 C4
Horsebridge Cl RM9 103 A6
Horsecroft Rd HA8 27 B3
Horse & Dolphin Yd
W1 249 D6
Horse Fair KT1 175 D1
Horseferry Pl SE10 142 A6
Horseferry Rd E14 119 A6
SW1 115 D2 259 D4
Horseferry Rd Est SW1 259 C5
Horseguards Ave
SW1 116 A5 250 A3
Horse Guards Par★
SW1 115 D5 249 D3
Horse Guards Rd
SW1 115 D4 249 D2
Horse Leaze E6 100 C1
Horsell Rd BR5 190 B2
N5 72 C3
Horselydown La
SE1 117 D5 253 C3
Horselydown Mans SE1 253 C2
Horsenden Ave UB6 64 D3
Horsenden Cres UB6 64 D3
Horsenden La N UB6 64 D1
Horsenden La S UB6 87 A6
Horsenden Prim Sch
UB6 64 C2
Horsendon Ho 11 N7 71 D3
Horseshoe Cl E14 120 A1
NW2 68 B6
Horse Shoe Cres UB5 85 C5
Horseshoe Dr UB8 82 C1
Horse Shoe Gn SM1 217 D6
Horseshoe La Barnet N20 12 D3
Enfield EN2 5 A2
Horse Shoe Yd W1 248 D6
Horse Yd N1 234 D6
Horsfeld Gdns 1 SE9 166 A6
Horsfeld Rd SE9 165 D6
Horsfield Ho 2 N1 73 A1
Horsford Rd SW2 160 B6
Horsham Ave N12 30 C5
Horsham Ct N17 34 A2
Horsham Rd DA6 169 C6
East Bedfont TW14 149 A5
Horsley Dr Kingston KT2 175 D5
New Addington CR0 224 A1
Horsley Ho 11 SE4 140 D1
Horsley Rd BR1 187 B2
Chingford E4 20 A2
Horsley St 3 SE17 139 B6
Horsman Ho SE5 139 A6
Horsman St SE5 139 A6
Horsmonden Cl BR6 211 D2
Horsmonden Rd SE4 163 B5
Horston Ho N4 51 A2
Hortensia Ho SW10 266 A4
Hortensia Rd
SW10 136 A5 266 A4
Horticultural Pl 6 W4 111 B1
Horton Ave NW2 69 A4
Horton Bridge Rd UB7 104 B5
Horton Cl UB7 104 B5
Horton Ctry Pk KT19 214 C1
Horton Ho 13 SE15 140 C6
SW8 270 C4
W14 254 A1
Horton Ind Pk UB7 104 B5
Horton La KT19 215 A1
Horton Par UB7 104 A5
Horton Rd E8 74 B2
Yiewsley UB7 104 B5
Horton Road Ind Est
UB7 104 B5
Horton St SE13 141 D2
Horton Way CR0 206 D4
Hortus Rd Chingford E4 20 A2
Southall UB2 107 B4
Horwood Ho 24 E2 96 B4
NW8 237 B6
Hosack Rd SW12,SW17 159 A2
Hoser Ave SE12 165 A2
Hosier La EC1 94 D2 241 D3
Hoskins Cl UB3 105 D1
Hoskin's Cl E16 99 C1
Hoskins St SE10 120 B1
Hospital Bridge Rd
TW2 151 D3
Hospital Bridge Rdbt
TW2 151 D2
Hospital of the Holy Trinity
(Almshouses) 5 CR0 221 A6
Hospital Rd TW3 129 C2
Hospl for Tropical Diseases
NW1 232 C5
Hospl of St John & St
Elizabeth NW8 92 B5 229 C3
Hotham Cl KT8 195 C6
Hotham Prim Sch
SW15 134 D1
Hotham Rd
Merton SW19 180 A3
Putney SW15 134 C2
Hotham Road Mews 12
SW19 180 A3
Hotham St E15 98 C6
Hothfield Pl SE16 118 C3
Hotspur Ind Est N17 34 B4
Hotspur Rd UB5 85 C5
Hotspur St SE11 116 C1 261 A2
Houblon Rd TW10 154 A6
Houghton Cl 10 E8 73 D2
Hampton TW12 173 A4
Houghton Rd N15 51 D5
Houghton St WC2 240 D1
Houlder Cres CR0 220 D2
Houndsden Rd N21 16 C5
Houndsditch EC3 95 C1 243 B2
Houndsfield Prim Sch
N9 18 B4
Houndsfield Rd N9 18 B4
Hounslow Ave TW3 151 D6
Hounslow Bsns Pk TW3 129 D1
Hounslow Central Sta
TW3 129 D2
Hounslow Ctr The TW3 129 D2
Hounslow East Sta
TW3 130 A3
Hounslow Ed Ctr (Specl Sch)
The TW4 129 A2
Hounslow Gdns TW3 151 D6
Hounslow Heath Jun & Inf
Schs TW4 129 A2
Hounslow Heath Nature
Reserve TW4 151 A5
Hounslow Manor Sch
TW3 130 A2
Hounslow Rd
Feltham TW13 151 A2
Twickenham TW2,TW3 152 A5
Feltham TW14 150 B4
Hounslow Sta TW3 151 D6
Hounslow Town Prim Sch
TW3 130 B2
Hounslow West Sta
TW3 129 A3
Houseman Way 20 SE5 139 B5
Houses of Parliament★
SW1 116 A3 260 B6
Houston Ct 3 CR0 205 C1
Houston Rd
Forest Hill SE23 163 A1
Thames Ditton KT6 197 B3
Houstoun Ct TW5 129 B5
Hove Ave E17 53 B4
Hoveden Rd NW2 69 A3
Hove Gdns SM1 201 D1
Hovenden Ho 6 SE21 183 C6
Hoveton Rd SE28 102 C1
Howard Ave DA5 168 C4
Howard Cl N11 15 A2
NW2 69 A4
Acton W3 88 D1
Ashford TW16 171 D4
Bushey WD23 8 C4
Hampton TW12 174 A4
Howard Ct SE15 140 A2
12 Barking IG11 101 B6
Beckenham BR3 186 A1
Howard Ho 8 E5 74 C6
14 SE8 141 B6
7 SW9 138 C2
W1 238 D5
Penge SE20 184 C2
Howard Mans E17 53 D6
Howard Prim Sch CR0 221 A4
Howard Rd BR1 187 A3
E11 76 C5
E17 53 D6
E6 100 B5
N15 51 C3
N16 73 B4
NW2 68 D4
Barking IG11 101 B6
Croydon SE25 206 A3
Ilford IG1 78 D4
Isleworth TW7 130 D2
New Malden KT3 199 D5
Penge SE20 184 C2
Southall UB1 85 D1
Surbiton KT5 198 B3
Howards Cl HA5 22 B1
Howards Crest Cl BR3 186 A1
Howard's La SW15 134 C1
Howard's Rd E13 99 A4
Howard St KT7 197 B3
Howard Way EN5 12 D6
Howard Wlk N2 48 B5
Howarth Rd SE2 124 A2
Howberry Cl HA8 25 D4
Howberry Rd
South Norwood CR7 183 B1
Stanmore HA7,H8 25 D4
Howbury Rd SE15 140 C2
Howcroft Cres N3 29 C3
Howcroft Ho 3 E3 97 B4
Howcroft La UB6 86 B4
Howden Cl SE28 124 D6
Howden Ct SE25 183 D1
Howden Rd SE25 183 D1
Howden St SE15 140 A2
Howell Cl RM6 58 D4
Howell Ct 2 E10 53 D2
Howell Ho 5 N7 71 D3
Howell Wlk SE1 261 D3
Howerd Way SE18 144 A4
Howes Cl N3 47 C6
Howfield Pl N17 51 D6
Howgate Rd SW14 133 B2
Howick Pl SW1 115 C3 259 B5
Howie St SW11 136 C5 267 A3
Howitt Cl 6 NW3 70 C2
Howitt Rd NW3 70 C2
Howland Ho 9 SW16 160 A1
Howland Mews E W1 239 B4
Howland St W1 93 C2 239 B4
Howland Way SE16 119 A4
Howletts La HA4 39 A3
Howletts Rd SE24 161 A5
Howley Pl W2 92 A2 236 B4
Howley Rd CR0 221 A5
Howmic Ct 1 TW1 153 C5
Howsman Rd SW13 134 A6
Howson Rd SE4 141 A1
Howson Terr TW10 154 A5
How's St E2 95 D5
Howton Pl WD23 8 B3
Hoxton Mkt 10 N1 95 C4
Hoxton Point EC1 95 C4
Hoxton Sq N1 95 C4
Hoxton St N1 95 C5
Hoylake Cres UB10 60 D6
Hoylake Gdns
Mitcham CR4 203 C6
Ruislip HA4 40 B1
South Oxhey WD19 22 D6
Hoylake Rd W3 89 C1
Hoyland Cl 4 SE15 140 B5
Hoyle Rd SW17 180 C5
Hoy St E16 98 D1
Huan Ct N20 14 C2
Hubbard Dr KT9 213 D2
Hubbard Rd SE27 183 A6
Hubbards Cl UB8 82 D1
Hubbard St E15 98 C6
Hub Buildings The 4
SW12 159 B3
Huberd Ho SE1 262 D6
Hubert Gr SW9 138 A2
Hubert Ho NW8 237 A5
Hubert Rd E6 99 D4
Hucknall Ct NW8 236 C6
Huddart St E3 97 B2
Huddleston Cl E2 96 C5
Huddlestone Rd E7 76 D4
NW2 68 B2
Huddleston Rd N7 71 C4
Hudson 27 NW9 27 D2
Hudson Cl 15 W12 112 B6
Hudson Ct Croydon SE25 206 A5
4 Merton SW19 179 D2
3 Millwall E14 119 C1
Hudson Ho SW10 266 A4
5 W11 91 A1
Hudson Pl SE18 123 A1
Hudson Rd DA7 147 B4
Harlington UB7 127 B6
Hudsons Ho N1 235 D1
Hudson's Pl
SW1 115 C2 259 A4
Hudson Way N9 18 C2
Huggin Ct EC4 252 B6
Huggin Hill EC4 252 B6
Huggins Ho 8 E3 97 C4
Huggins Pl SW2 160 B3
Hughan Rd E15 76 B3
Hugh Astor Ct SE1 261 D6
Hugh Clark Ho W13 109 A5
Hughenden Ave HA3 43 B4
Hughenden Gdns UB5 84 C4
Hughenden Rd KT4 200 A2
Hughendon EN5 1 D1
Hughendon Terr E15 76 A4
Hughes Cl N12 30 A5
Hughes Ho 26 E2 96 C4
SE17 261 D3
SE5 139 A4
15 SE8 141 C6
Hughes Mans E1 96 A3
Hughes Rd
Ashford TW15 171 A4
Hayes UB3 106 B6
Hughes Terr 6 E16 98 D2
Hughes Wlk CR0 205 A2
Hugh Gaitskell Cl SW6 264 C5
Hugh Gaitskell Ho N16 73 D6
NW10 67 D1
Hugh Herland KT1 198 A6
Hugh Mews SW1 258 D3
Hugh Morgan Ho 5
SW4 137 D2
Hugh Myddelton Prim Sch
EC1 94 C4 234 B1
Hugh Platt Ho 29 E2 96 B5
Hugh St SW1 115 B2 258 D3
Hugo Ho SW1 257 D6
Hugon Rd SW6 135 D2
Hugo Rd N19 71 C4
Huguenot Pl SW18 158 A6
Huguenot Sq SE15 140 B2
Hullbridge Mews N1 235 C6
Hull Cl SE16 118 D5
Hull Ct SE5 139 B3
Hull Pl E16 123 A5
Hull St EC1 235 A1
Hulme Pl SE1 252 B1
Hulse Ave IG11 79 C2
Humber Ct W7 86 B1
Humber Dr W10 90 D3
Humber Rd NW2 68 B6
SE3 142 D6
Humberstone Rd E13 99 C4
Humberton Cl E9 75 A3
Humbolt Rd W6 135 A6 264 A5
Hume Ct N1 72 D1
Hume Ho 14 W11 112 D5
Humes Ave W7 108 D4
Hume Terr E16 99 B1
Hume Way HA4 40 A3
Humphrey Ct SW11 266 D1
Humphrey St
SE1 117 D1 263 C2
Humphries Cl RM9 81 B4
Humphry Ho 10 SW15 156 D6
Hundred Acre NW9 27 D1
Hungerdown E4 20 A3
Hungerford Bridge
WC2 250 C4
Hungerford Ho SW1 269 B6
Hungerford Inf Sch N7 72 A2
Hungerford Jun & Inf Schs
N7 71 D2
Hungerford La WC2 250 B4
Hungerford Prim Sch N7 72 A2
Hungerford Rd N7 72 A3
4 N7 71 D2
Hungerford St 24 E1 96 B1
Hunsdon Cl RM9 81 A2
Hunsdon Ho E5 74 B5
Hunsdon Rd SE14 140 D5
Hunslett St 27 E2 96 C5
Hunstanton Ho NW1 237 B4
Hunston Rd SM4 201 D1
Hunt Ct N14 15 B4
11 Northolt UB5 84 D5
Hunter Cl SE1 262 D5
Borehamwood WD6 11 A6
Upper Tooting SW12 159 A3
Huntercrombe Gdns
WD19 22 C5
Hunter Ct 8 SE5 139 B1
27 Streatham SW2 160 C4
Hunter Ho 1 N19 71 C5
SE1 251 D1
SW5 255 B1
SW8 269 D3
WC1 240 B6

Hunter Ho *continued*
Feltham TW14 ...150 A3
Hunter Lo 9 W9 ...91 C2
Hunter Rd
South Norwood CR7 ...205 B6
Wimbledon SW20 ...178 C2
Hunters Ct 5 TW9 ...153 D6
Hunter's Gr BR6 ...227 A4
Hunters Gr Harrow HA3 ...43 C5
Hayes UB3 ...106 A4
Hunters Hall Prim Sch
RM10 ...81 D3
Hunters Hall Rd RM10 ...81 C3
Hunters Hill HA4 ...62 D5
Hunters Lo 10 DA15 ...168 A1
Hunters Mdw SE19 ...183 C6
Hunters Rd
Chessington KT9 ...214 A4
Ilford IG1 ...78 D3
Hunters Sq RM10 ...81 C4
Hunter St WC1 ...94 A3 240 B6
Hunters The 2 BR3 ...186 A2
Hunters Way Enfield EN2 ...4 C4
South Croydon CR0 ...221 C4
Hunter Wlk E13 ...99 A5
Borehamwood WD6 ...11 B6
Huntingdon Cl CR4,
SW16 ...204 A5
Huntingdon Ct SW14 ...133 A2
Huntingdon Gdns
Chiswick W4 ...133 A5
North Cheam KT4 ...216 C5
Huntingdon Ho SW5 ...255 B4
Huntingdon Rd N2 ...48 C6
N9 ...18 C3
Huntingdon St E16 ...98 D1
N1 ...72 B1
Huntingfield CR0 ...223 B1
Huntingfield Rd SW15 ...156 A6
Huntingford Ho SW15 ...134 C3
Hunting Gate Cl EN2 ...4 C2
Hunting Gate Dr KT9 ...214 A1
Hunting Gate Mews
Sutton SM1 ...217 D5
Twickenham TW2 ...152 C3
Huntings Farm IG1 ...79 C6
Huntings Rd RM10 ...81 C2
Huntley Ho 3 SE21 ...183 C6
Huntley St WC1 ...93 D3 239 C5
Huntley Way SW20 ...178 A1
Huntly Dr N3 ...29 C4
Huntly Rd SE25 ...205 C5
Hunton St E1 ...96 A2
Hunt Rd UB2 ...107 C3
Hunts Cl SE3 ...143 A3
Hunt's Ct WC2 ...249 D5
Huntshaw Ho 37 E3 ...97 D4
Hunt's La E15 ...98 A5
Huntsman Cl TW13 ...172 B6
Huntsman St SE17 ...263 A3
Hunts Mead EN3 ...6 D2
Hunts Mead Cl BR7 ...188 B3
Huntsmoor Rd KT19 ...215 B3
Huntspill St SW17 ...158 A1
Hunts Slip Rd SE21 ...161 C2
Huntsworth Ct SE6 ...163 C3
Huntsworth Mews
NW1 ...92 D3 237 C5
Hurdwick Ho NW1 ...232 A4
Hurleston Ho 11 SE8 ...119 B1
Hurley Cres SE16 ...118 D4
Hurley Ct 1 W5 ...87 C1
Hurley Ho 34 E2 ...95 D4
SE11 ...261 B3
Hurley Lo SE22 ...162 C5
Hurley Rd UB6 ...85 D2
Hurlingham Bsns Pk
SW6 ...135 C2
Hurlingham & Chelsea Sec
Sch SW6 ...135 C2
Hurlingham Court Mans
SW6 ...135 C3
Hurlingham Ct SW6 ...135 B2
Hurlingham Gdns SW6 ...135 B2
Hurlingham Rd DA7 ...147 B5
Fulham SW6 ...135 B3
Hurlingham Sq SW6 ...135 D2
Hurlock Ho N5 ...72 D5
Hurlock St N5 ...72 D5
Hurlstone Rd SE25 ...205 C4
Hurn Court Rd TW5 ...128 D3
Hurn Ct TW5 ...128 D3
Huron Cl 5 BR6 ...227 D2
Huron Rd SW17 ...159 A1
Hurren Cl SE3 ...142 C2
Hurricane Rd SM6 ...220 B1
Hurry Cl E15 ...76 C1
Hursley Ct 11 KT6 ...197 D2
Hurst Ave N6 ...49 C3
Chingford E4 ...19 C1
Hurstbourne KT10 ...212 D2
Hurstbourne Cotts DA5 ...169 D4
Hurstbourne Gdns IG11 ...79 C2
Hurstbourne Ho 12
SW15 ...155 D5
Hurstbourne Priors
CR2 ...221 C2
Hurstbourne Rd SE23 ...163 A3
Hurst Cl NW11 ...47 D3
Chessington KT9 ...214 C3
Chingford E4 ...19 C1
Hayes BR2 ...208 D1
Northolt UB5 ...63 B3
Hurstcombe IG9 ...21 A2
Hurstcourt Rd SM1 ...217 D6
Hurst Ct Beckenham BR3 ...185 C3
South Norwood SE25 ...205 D5
Woodford IG8 ...37 B4
Hurstdene Ave BR2 ...208 D1
Hurstdene Gdns N15 ...51 C2
Hurstfield BR2 ...209 A4
Hurstfield Cres UB4 ...83 C2
Hurstfield Rd KT8 ...195 C6
Hurst Gr KT12 ...193 D1
Hurst Ho N1 ...233 D3
SE2 ...124 D1
7 Penge SE26 ...184 B5
Hurst La SE2 ...124 D1
East Molesey KT8 ...196 A6
Hurst Lo N8 ...49 D3
Hurstmead Ct HA8 ...26 D6
Hurstmere Foundation Sch
for Boys DA15 ...168 C3
Hurst Park Prim Sch
KT8 ...195 C6
Hurst Pl SE2 ...146 D6
Hurst Prim Sch DA5 ...168 D3
Hurst Rd DA5,DA15 ...168 C3
E17 ...53 D6
Buckhurst Hill IG9 ...21 D3
Croydon CR0 ...221 B3
East Molesey KT8,KT12 ...195 C6
Southgate N21 ...16 C3
Walton-on-T KT8&KT12 ...194 D5
Hurst Rise EN5 ...1 C2
Hurst Springs DA5 ...169 A3
Hurst St SE24 ...160 D5
Hurstview Grange CR2 ...220 D1
Hurst View Rd CR2 ...221 C1
Hurst Way CR2 ...221 C2
Hurstway Wlk 2 W11 ...112 D6
Hurstwood Ave DA5 ...169 A3
Wanstead E18 ...55 B5
Hurstwood Ct N12 ...30 C4
NW11 ...47 B5
Hurstwood Dr BR1 ...210 B6
Hurstwood Rd NW11 ...47 B5
Hurtwood Rd KT12 ...195 B2
Husbourne Ho 8 SE8 ...119 A2
Huson Cl NW3 ...70 C1
Hussain Cl HA1 ...64 D4
Hussars Cl TW4 ...129 A2
Husseywell Cres BR2 ...209 A1
Hutching's St E14 ...119 C4
Hutchings Wlk NW11 ...47 D5
Hutchins Cl E15 ...76 A1
Hutchins Ho 8 SW4 ...159 D4
Hutchinson Ct RM6 ...58 D5
Hutchinson Ho 9 SE14 ...140 C5
Hutchinson Terr HA9 ...65 D5
Hutchins Rd SE28 ...124 A5
Thamesmead SE28 ...124 A6
Hutton Cl Greenford UB6 ...64 B3
Woodford IG8 ...37 B4
Hutton Ct 3 N4 ...50 B1
N9 ...18 C4
1 Ealing W5 ...87 C2
Hutton Gdns HA3 ...24 A3
Hutton Gr N12 ...29 D5
Hutton Ho 22 E2 ...96 A4
Hutton La HA3 ...24 A3
Hutton Row 4 HA8 ...27 A3
Hutton St EC4 ...241 B1
Hutton Wlk HA3 ...24 A3
Huxbear St SE4 ...163 B6
Huxley Cl UB5 ...85 A6
Huxley Dr RM6 ...58 B2
Huxley Gdns NW10 ...88 B5
Huxley Ho NW8 ...236 D5
SE2 ...124 D1
4 SW9 ...138 B3
Huxley Par N18 ...33 B5
Huxley Pl N13 ...16 D1
Huxley Rd DA16 ...145 D2
E10 ...76 A6
Edmonton N18 ...33 C6
Huxley Sayze N18 ...33 B5
Huxley South N18 ...33 B5
Huxley St W10 ...91 A4
Hyacinth Cl
3 Hampton TW12 ...173 C4
Ilford IG1 ...78 D2
Hyacinth Dr UB10 ...60 A1
Hyacinth Rd SW15 ...156 A3
Hyde Cl E13 ...99 A5
Ashford TW16 ...171 C4
Barnet EN5 ...1 B2
Hyde Cres NW9 ...45 C4
Hyde Ct N20 ...14 B1
NW9 ...45 B2
Hounslow TW4 ...151 B6
Hyde Estate Rd NW9 ...45 D4
Hyde Farm Mews SW12 ...159 D3
Hydefield Cl N21 ...17 B3
Hydefield Ct N9 ...17 C2
Hyde Ho TW3 ...130 A2
Hyde La SW11 ...136 C4 267 A2
Hyde Park*
W2 ...114 D5 247 C3
Hyde Park Ave N21 ...17 B3
Hyde Park Cnr SW1 ...248 B2
Hyde Park Corner Sta
SW1 ...115 A4 248 B2
Hyde Park Cres
W2 ...92 C1 237 A1
Hyde Park Gate Mews
SW7 ...246 B1
Hyde Park Gdns
W2 ...114 C6 246 D6
Edmonton N21 ...17 A3
Hyde Park Gdns Mews
W2 ...114 C6 247 A6
Hyde Park Mans NW1 ...237 A3
Hyde Park Pl W2 ...247 B6
Hyde Park Sq
W2 ...92 C1 237 A1
Hyde Park Square Mews
W2 ...237 A1
Hyde Park St W2 ...92 C1 237 A1
Hyde Park Twrs W2 ...246 A5
Hyderabad Way E15 ...76 C1
Hyde Rd N1 ...95 C6
Bexley DA7 ...147 B3
Richmond TW10 ...154 B6
Hyde Sch The NW9 ...45 D3
Hydeside Gdns N9 ...17 D2
Hyde's Pl 12 N1 ...72 D1
Hyde St SE8 ...141 C6
Hyde Terr TW15,TW16 ...171 C4
Hydethorpe Ave N9 ...17 D2
Hydethorpe Rd SW12 ...159 C3
Hyde Vale SE10 ...142 A5
Hyde Way Edmonton N9 ...17 D2
Hayes UB3 ...105 D2
Hyde Wlk SM4 ...201 C2
Hydon Ct N11 ...30 D5
Hyh Ho E17 ...35 D2
Hyland House Sch E17 ...36 B1
Hylands Rd E17 ...36 B1
Hylda Ct NW5 ...71 A5
Hyleford Sch IG3 ...79 C4
Hylton St SE18 ...123 D2
Hyndewood 14 SE23 ...162 D1
Hyndman Ho 5 N19 ...71 D4
5 Dagenham RM10 ...81 C5
Hyndman St SE15 ...140 B6
Hynton Rd RM8 ...80 C6
Hyperion Ho 25 E3 ...97 A5
Streatham SW2 ...160 B4
Hyrstdene CR0 ...220 D4
Hyson Rd SE16 ...118 B1
Hythe Ave DA7 ...147 B5
Hythe Cl N18 ...34 A6
Hythe Ho 7 SE16 ...118 C4
Hythe Rd NW10 ...90 A3
South Norwood CR7 ...183 B1
Hythe Road Ind Est
NW10 ...90 A3
Hyver Hill NW7 ...11 B4

I

Ian Ct SE23 ...162 C2
Ian Hamilton Ho NW1 ...232 C2
Ian Sq EN3 ...6 D4
Ibberton Ho SW8 ...270 C4
W14 ...254 B6
Ibbotson Ave E16 ...98 D1
Ibbott St 22 E1 ...96 C3
Iberia Ho 17 N19 ...49 D2
Iberian Ave CR0,SM6 ...220 A4
Ibis Ct 16 SE8 ...141 B6
Ibis La W4 ...133 A4
Ibis Way UB4 ...84 D1
Ibrox Ct 3 IG9 ...21 C2
Ibsley Gdns SW15 ...156 A3
Ibsley Way EN4 ...2 C1
Ibstock Place Sch
SW15 ...155 C5
Icarus Ho 16 E3 ...97 B4
Iceland Rd E3 ...97 C6
Iceland Wharf SE16 ...119 A2
Ice Wharf NW1 ...233 B4
Ickburgh Est E5 ...74 B6
Ickburgh Rd E5 ...74 B5
Ickburgh Sch E5 ...74 B5
Ickenham Cl HA4 ...61 B6
Ickenham Rd HA4 ...39 B1
Ickenham Sta UB10 ...61 A4
Ickleton Rd SE9 ...188 A6
Icknield Dr IG2 ...56 D4
Ickworth Park Rd E17 ...53 A5
Icough Ct SE3 ...143 B5
Ida Rd N15 ...51 B5
Ida St E14 ...98 A1
Iden Cl BR2 ...208 C6
Idlecombe Rd SW17 ...181 A4
Idmiston Rd E15 ...76 D3
New Malden KT4 ...199 D2
West Norwood SE21,SE27 ...161 A2
Idmiston Sq KT4 ...199 D2
Idol La EC3 ...117 C6 253 A5
Idonia St SE8 ...141 C5
Iffley Ho 47 E2 ...95 D4
Iffley Rd W6 ...112 B3
Ifield Ho SE17 ...263 B2
Ifield Rd SW10 ...135 D6 265 D6
Ifor Evans Pl E1 ...96 D3
Ightham Ho SE17 ...263 A3
Beckenham BR3 ...185 B3
Ightham Rd DA8 ...147 C5
Ilbert St W10 ...91 A4
Ilchester Gdns W2 ...245 C6
Ilchester Mans W8 ...255 A6
Ilchester Pl
W14 ...113 B3 254 D6
Ilchester Rd RM8 ...80 C3
Ildersly Gr SE21 ...161 B2
Ilderton Prim Sch SE16 ...118 C1
Ilderton Rd SE15,SE16 ...140 C6
Ilex Cl TW16 ...172 C1
Ilex Rd NW10 ...67 D2
Ilex Way SW16 ...182 C5
Ilford Hill IG1 ...78 C5
Ilford Ho 14 N1 ...73 B2
Ilford Interchange IG1 ...78 C5
Ilford Jewish Prim Sch
IG6 ...57 B6
Ilford La IG1 ...78 D4
Ilford Prep Sch IG3 ...58 A1
Ilford Ret Pk IG1 ...79 A6
Ilford Sta IG1 ...78 D6
Ilford Ursuline High Sch
IG1 ...78 D6
Ilfracombe Gdns RM6 ...58 B2
Ilfracombe Rd BR1 ...164 D1
Iliffe St SE17 ...116 D1 261 D2
Iliffe Yd SE17 ...116 D1 261 D2
Ilkeston Ct 7 E5 ...74 D4
Ilkley Cl SE19 ...183 B4
Ilkley Ct N11 ...31 A4
Ilkley Rd Newham E16 ...99 C2
South Oxhey WD19 ...22 D5
Illingworth Cl CR4 ...202 B6
Illingworth Way EN1 ...17 C6
Ilmington Rd HA3 ...43 D3
Ilminster Gdns SW11 ...136 C1
Ilsley Ct 8 SW8 ...137 C3
Imber Cl N14 ...15 C4
Thames Ditton KT7 ...196 B1
Imber Court Trad Est
KT8 ...196 B3
Imber Cross KT7 ...196 D3
Imber Ct 4 SE9 ...166 C5
Imber Gr KT10 ...196 B2
Imber Park Rd KT10 ...196 B1
Imber St N1 ...235 C5
Immanuel Coll WD23 ...8 C4
Immanuel & St Andrew CE
Prim Sch SW16 ...182 A4
Impact Ct SE20 ...184 B1
Imperial Ave 5 N16 ...73 C4
Imperial Cl HA2 ...41 C3
Imperial College Rd
SW7 ...114 B3 256 C6
Imperial Coll of Science,
Technology & Medicine
SW7 ...114 B3 256 C6
Imperial Ct N20 ...14 A1
NW8 ...230 B4
Wembley HA9 ...66 C5
Harrow HA2 ...41 C2
Imperial Dr HA2 ...41 C3
Imperial Gdns CR4 ...203 B6
Imperial Ho 2 E14 ...119 B6
E3 ...97 A4
Imperial Mews 5 E6 ...99 D5
Imperial Pl BR7 ...188 C2
Imperial Rd SW6 ...265 D1
East Bedfont TW14 ...149 C4
Wood Green N22 ...32 A2
Imperial Sq SW6 ...265 D2
Imperial St E3 ...98 A4
Imperial Twrs 3 NW3 ...70 A2
Imperial War Mus*
SE1,SE11 ...116 C3 261 B5
Imperial Way BR7,SE9 ...167 A1
Croydon CR0,CR9 ...220 C2
Harrow HA3 ...44 A3
Impington 10 KT1 ...176 C1
Imre Cl W12 ...112 B5
Inca Dr SE9 ...166 D4
Inchmery Rd SE6 ...164 A3
Inchwood BR4,CR0 ...223 D4
Independant Jewish Day Sch
NW4 ...46 D4
Independant Pl E8 ...73 D3
Independents Rd SE3 ...142 D2
Inderwick Rd N8 ...50 B4
Indescon Ct E14 ...119 D4
India St EC3 ...243 C1
India Way W12 ...112 B6
Indigo Mews N16 ...73 B5
Indus Ct 15 SE15 ...139 D5
Indus Rd SE7 ...143 C5
Ingal Rd E13 ...99 A3
Ingate Pl SW8 ...137 B4 268 D1
Ingatestone Rd
Croydon SE25 ...206 B5
Wanstead E12 ...55 C1
Woodford IG8 ...37 B3
Ingelow Ho W8 ...245 C2
Ingelow St SW8 ...137 B3
Ingersoll Rd W12 ...112 B5
Enfield EN3 ...6 C5
Ingestre Pl W1 ...239 B1
Ingestre Rd E7 ...77 A4
NW5 ...71 B4
Ingham Rd NW6 ...69 C4
Inglebert St EC1 ...94 C4 234 A2
Ingleborough Ct N17 ...51 D6
Ingleborough St SW9 ...138 C3
Ingleby Dr HA1 ...64 B5
Ingleby Rd N7 ...72 A5
Dagenham RM10 ...81 D2
Ilford IG1 ...56 D1
Ingleby Way BR7 ...188 C5
Wallington SM6 ...219 D1
Ingle Cl HA5 ...41 B6
Ingledew Rd SE18 ...123 B1
Inglefield Sq 12 E1 ...118 B5
Ingle Ho 3 SW12 ...159 D3
Inglehurst Gdns IG4 ...56 B4
Inglemere Ct CR4,SW17 ...180 D3
Inglemere Rd
Forest Hill SE23 ...162 D1
Mitcham CR4,SW17 ...180 D3
Ingleshaw Wlk E9 ...75 B2
Ingleside Cl BR3 ...185 C3
Ingleside Gr SE3 ...142 D6
Inglethorpe Ho 6 E5 ...74 A6
Inglethorpe St SW6 ...134 D4
Ingleton Ave DA16 ...168 A6
Ingleton Rd N18 ...34 A4
Ingleton St SW9 ...138 C3
Ingle Way N12 ...30 C4
Inglewood BR7 ...189 B4
Inglewood Cl E14 ...119 C2
Inglewood Copse BR1 ...188 B1
Inglewood Ct 3 BR1 ...186 D3
Inglewood Mans 11 NW6 ...69 C3
Inglewood Rd NW6 ...69 C3
Inglis Ct W5 ...110 B6
Inglis Ho 1 SW15 ...156 C6
Inglis Rd Croydon CR0 ...205 D1
Ealing W5 ...110 B6
Inglis St SE5 ...138 D4
Ingram Ave NW11 ...48 A2
Ingram Cl SE11 ...260 D4
Ingram Cl *continued*
Stanmore HA7 ...25 C5
Ingram Ct EN1 ...17 D5
Ingram Ho E3 ...97 A6
7 Harrow HA1 ...42 D4
Teddington KT8 ...175 C2
Ingram Lo 8 SW4 ...159 D5
Ingram Rd N2 ...48 C5
South Norwood CR7 ...183 A2
Ingram Way UB6 ...86 B6
Ingrave Ho RM9 ...102 B6
Ingrave St SW11 ...136 C2
Ingrebourne Ct E4 ...19 D2
Ingrebourne Ho NW8 ...236 D4
2 Catford BR1 ...186 B5
Ingress St 4 W4 ...111 C1
Inigo Jones Rd SE7 ...144 A5
Inigo Pl WC2 ...250 A6
Inkerman Rd NW5 ...71 B2
Inkerman Terr W8 ...255 B5
Inks Gn E4 ...36 A5
Inkster Ho 8 SW11 ...136 C2
Inkwell Cl N12 ...14 A1
Inman Rd NW10 ...89 C6
Wandsworth SW18 ...158 A4
Inmans Row IG8 ...37 A6
Inner Circ NW1 ...93 A4 231 A2
Inner Park Rd SW19 ...156 D2
Inner Ring E TW6 ...126 D2
Inner Ring W TW6 ...126 C2
Inner Temple* EC4 ...251 A6
Inner Temple La EC4 ...241 A1
Innes Cl SW20 ...179 A1
Innes Gdns SW15 ...156 B5
Innes Lo SE23 ...162 D1
Innes Yd CR0 ...221 A5
Innis Ho SE17 ...263 A2
Inniskilling Rd E13 ...99 C5
Innovation Cl HA0 ...88 A6
Inskip Cl E10 ...75 D6
Inskip Rd RM8 ...58 D1
Insley Ho 13 E3 ...97 D4
Inst for Child Health
WC1 ...94 B3 240 C5
Institute Pl E8 ...74 B3
Instituto Espanol Vicente
Canada Blanch W10 ...91 A2
Inst of Ophthalmology
EC1 ...235 D2
Integer Gdns E11 ...54 B2
Interchange The NW5 ...71 B3
International Ave TW5 ...106 C1
International Sch of London
W3 ...110 C2
International Trad Est
UB2 ...106 B3
Inveagh Cl E9 ...96 D6
Inverary Pl SE18 ...145 B6
Inver Cl E5 ...74 C6
Inverclyde Gdns RM6 ...58 D5
Inver Ct W2 ...91 D1
Inveresk Gdns KT4 ...216 A5
Inverforth Cl NW3 ...70 A6
Inverforth Ho NW3 ...70 A6
Inverforth Rd N11 ...31 B5
Invergarry Ho NW6 ...91 D5
Inverine Rd SE7 ...121 B1
Invermore Pl SE18 ...123 A2
Inverness Ave EN1 ...5 C4
Inverness Ct 8 Acton W3 ...88 C1
10 Catford SE6 ...164 D3
Inverness Gdns W8 ...245 C3
Inverness Mews E16 ...122 D5
W2 ...245 D6
North Woolwich E16 ...123 A5
Inverness Pl W2 ...245 D6
Inverness Rd
Edmonton N18 ...34 B5
Hounslow TW3 ...129 C1
North Cheam KT4 ...200 D1
Southall UB2 ...107 A2
Inverness St NW1 ...231 D6
Inverness Terr
W2 ...113 D6 245 D6
Inverton Rd SE15 ...140 D1
Invicta Cl BR7 ...188 C5
18 E3 ...97 C2
East Bedfont TW14 ...149 D3
Invicta Ct KT9 ...214 B3
Invicta Ctr The IG11 ...102 A6
Invicta Gr UB5 ...85 B4
Invicta Plaza SE1 ...251 C4
Invicta Prim Sch SE3 ...143 A5
Invicta Rd SE3,SE7 ...143 A6
Inville Rd SE17 ...117 B1 262 D1
Inwen Ct SE8 ...119 A1
Inwood Ave TW3 ...130 A2
Inwood Bsns Pk TW3 ...129 D1
Inwood Cl CR0 ...223 A6
Inwood Ct 10 NW1 ...71 C1
Inwood Ho 19 SE22 ...139 C2
Inwood Rd TW3 ...130 A1
Inworth St SW11 ...136 C3
Inworth Wlk N1 ...235 A6
Iona Cl Catford SE6 ...163 C4
Morden SM4 ...201 D2
Ion Ct 8 E2 ...96 A5
Ionian Bldg 19 E14 ...119 A6
Ionian Ho 22 E1 ...96 D3
Ipsden Bldgs SE1 ...251 B2
Ipswich Ho SE4 ...162 D6
Ipswich Rd SW17 ...181 A4
Irby Ho SW2 ...160 C5
Ireland Cl E6 ...100 B2
Ireland Pl N22 ...32 A3
Ireland Yd EC4 ...241 D1
Irene Rd BR6 ...211 D2
SW6 ...135 C4 265 B1
Ireton Cl N10 ...31 A3
Ireton Ho SW9 ...138 C3
Ireton St 12 E3 ...97 C3
Iris Ave DA5 ...169 A5
Iris Cl Croydon CR0 ...206 D1
Newham E6 ...100 A3
Surbiton KT6 ...198 B2
Iris Cres DA7 ...147 B6
Iris Rd KT19 ...214 D3
Iris Way E4 ...35 B4
Iris Wlk 1 HA8 ...27 A6
Irkdale Ave EN1 ...5 D4
Iroko Ho 7 NW3 ...69 D2
Iron Bridge Cl NW10 ...67 C3
Southall UB2 ...108 A5
Iron Bridge Ho NW3 ...70 D1
Iron Bridge Rd N UB11 ...104 C5
Iron Bridge Rd S UB7 ...104 C4
Iron Mill Pl SW18 ...157 D5
Iron Mill Rd SW18 ...157 D5
Ironmonger La
EC2 ...95 B1 242 C1
Ironmonger Pas EC1 ...235 B1
Ironmonger Row
EC1 ...95 A4 235 B1
Ironmonger's Pl 13 E14 ...119 C2
Ironside Cl SE16 ...118 D4
Ironside Ho E9 ...75 A4
Irvine Ave HA3 ...43 B6
Irvine Cl N20 ...14 C2
Irvine Ct W1 ...239 B5
Thornton Heath CR7 ...204 C3
Irvine Ho 2 E14 ...97 D2
N7 ...72 B2
Irvine Way BR6 ...211 D2
Irving Ave UB5 ...84 D6
Irving Ct N22 ...32 D2
Irving Gr SW9 ...138 B3
Irving Ho SE17 ...261 C1
Irving Mews N1 ...73 A2
Irving Rd W14 ...112 D3
Irving St WC2 ...249 D5
Irwell Ct W7 ...86 B1
Irwell Est 25 SE16 ...118 C4
Irwin Ave SE18 ...145 C5
Irwin Cl UB10 ...60 C5
Irwin Gdns NW10 ...90 B6
Isabel Hill Cl TW12 ...173 C2
Isabella Cl N14 ...15 C4
Isabella Ct 8 TW10 ...154 B5
Isabella Dr BR6 ...227 A4
Isabella Ho SE11 ...261 C2
19 W6 ...112 C1
Isabella Rd E9 ...74 C3
Isabella St SE1 ...251 C3
Isabel St SW9 ...270 D2
Isambard Mews E14 ...120 A3
Isambard Pl SE16 ...118 C5
Iseldon Ct N7 ...72 A4
Isel Way 4 SE22 ...161 C6
Isham Rd SW16 ...182 A1
Isis Cl Putney SW15 ...134 C1
Ruislip HA4 ...39 A3
Isis Ct W4 ...132 D5
Isis Ho NW8 ...236 D5
2 Edmonton N18 ...33 D4
Isis St SW18 ...158 A2
Islamia Girls' High Sch
NW6 ...91 A6
Islamia Prim Sch NW6 ...91 A6
Islamic Coll for Advanced
Studies NW10 ...68 B2
Island Centre Way EN3 ...7 C6
Island Farm Ave KT8 ...195 B4
Island Farm Rd KT8 ...195 C4
Island Gardens Sta E14 ...120 A1
Island Ho SW19 ...202 A5
Island Rd CR4 ...180 D3
Island Row E14 ...97 B1
Isla Rd SE18 ...145 A6
Islay Gdns TW4 ...150 D6
Isleden Ho N1 ...235 A6
Isledon Rd N4,N7 ...72 C5
Islehurst Cl BR7 ...188 C2
Isleworth Bsns Complex
TW7 ...130 D3
Isleworth Sta TW7 ...130 D3
Isleworth & Syon Sch for
Boys TW7 ...130 C5
Isleworth Town Sch
TW7 ...131 A3
Islington Est N1 ...95 A6 235 A6
Islington Gn N1 ...94 D6 234 C5
Islington Green Sch
N1 ...95 A6 235 A5
Islington High St
N1 ...94 D5 234 C4
Islington Park Mews 1
N1 ...72 D1
Islington Park St N1 ...72 D1
Islington Sixth Form Ctr
N7 ...72 C4
Islip Gdns HA8 ...27 B3
Northolt UB5 ...63 A1
Islip Manor Rd UB5 ...63 A1
Islip St NW5 ...71 C3
Ismailia Rd E7 ...77 B1
Isobel Ho
10 Ashford TW16 ...171 D3
Harrow HA1 ...42 D4
Isokon Flats 3 NW3 ...70 D3
Isom Cl E13 ...99 B4
Ivanhoe Dr HA3 ...25 B1
Ivanhoe Ho 32 E3 ...97 A5
11 Balham SW12 ...159 B4
Ivanhoe Rd SE5 ...139 D2
Hounslow TW4 ...128 D2
Ivatt Pl W14 ...113 B1 254 D1
Ivatt Way N17 ...50 D6

Iveagh Ave NW10 ....88 C5
Iveagh Cl NW10 ....88 C5
Iveagh Ct EC3 ....243 C1
4 Beckenham BR3 ....207 D6
Iveagh Ho SW10 ....266 B4
2 SW9 ....138 D3
Ivebury Ct W10 ....90 C1
Ivedon Rd DA16 ....146 C3
Ive Farm Cl E10 ....75 C6
Ive Farm La E10 ....75 C6
Iveley Rd SW4 ....137 C3
Iver Ct N1 ....73 A2
Ivere Dr EN5 ....13 D5
Iverhurst Cl DA6 ....168 D6
Iverna Ct W8 ....255 B6
Iverna Gdns W8 .113 C3 255 B6
Hatton TW14 ....149 B6
Iverson Rd NW6 ....69 C2
Ivers Way CR0 ....223 D1
Ives Rd E16 ....98 C2
Ives St SW3 ....114 C2 257 B4
Ivestor Terr SE23 ....162 C4
Ivimey St E2 ....96 A4
Ivinghoe Cl EN1 ....5 C4
Ivinghoe Ho 14 N7 ....71 D3
Ivinghoe Rd Barking RM8 ..80 B3
Bushey WD23 ....8 B4
Ivor Ct N8 ....50 A3
NW1 ....237 C6
Ivor Gr SE9 ....166 D3
Ivories The N1 ....73 A1
Ivor Pl NW1 ....92 D3 237 C5
Ivor St NW1 ....71 C1
Ivory Ct TW13 ....150 A3
Ivorydown BR1 ....187 A6
Ivory Ho E1 ....253 D4
9 SW11 ....136 A2
Ivybridge Cl
2 Twickenham TW1 ....153 A4
Uxbridge UB8 ....82 A4
Ivybridge Ct 1 BR7 ....188 C2
Ivybridge Ho 18 SE22 ....139 C2
Ivybridge La WC2 ....250 B5
Ivybridge Prim Sch
TW1 ....152 D5
Ivybridge Ret Pk TW7 ...152 D6
Ivychurch Cl SE20 ....184 C3
Ivy Church La SE1,SE17 ..263 C2
Ivy Cl Harrow HA2 ....63 B4
Pinner HA5 ....40 C2
Sunbury TW16 ....172 C1
Ivy Cotts UB10 ....82 C4
Ivy Cres W4 ....111 A2
Ivy Ct SE13 ....163 C6
18 SE16 ....118 A1
SE3 ....142 D1
Ivydale Prim Sch SE15 ..140 D1
Ivydale Rd SE15 ....140 D1
Carshalton SM5 ....218 D6
Ivyday Gr SW16 ....160 B1
Ivydene KT12,KT8 ....195 B4
Ivydene Cl SM1 ....218 A4
Ivy Gdns N8 ....50 A3
Mitcham CR4 ....203 D6
Ivy Ho 6 E5 ....52 B1
Croydon CR0 ....206 D1
Ivyhouse Rd
Dagenham RM9 ....81 A2
Uxbridge UB10 ....60 D5
Ivy La TW4 ....129 B1
Ivy Lo W8 ....245 A4
Ivymount Rd SE27 ....160 C1
Ivy Rd E16 ....99 A1
E17 ....53 C3
N14 ....15 D4
NW2 ....68 C4
SE4 ....141 C1
Hounslow TW3 ....129 D1
Tolworth KT6 ....198 C1
Upper Tooting SW17 ....180 C5
Ivy St N1 ....95 C5
Ivy Terr 3 IG2 ....57 A3
Ivy Wlk RM9 ....81 A2
Ixworth Pl SW3 ..114 C2 257 A3
Izane Rd DA6 ....147 B1

J

Jacaranda Cl KT3 ....199 C6
Jacaranda Gr E8 ....73 D1
Jack Ashley Ct 5 NW9 ...27 C2
Jackass La BR2 ....225 C2
Jack Barnett Way N22 ...32 B1
Jack Clow Rd E15 ....98 C5
Jack Cook Ho 9 IG11 ...78 D1
Jack Cornwell St E12 ...78 C4
Jack Goodchild Way
KT3 ....198 D6
Jacklin Gn IG8 ....37 A6
Jackman Ho 24 E1 ....118 B5
Jackman Mews NW2 ....67 C5
Jackman St E8 ....96 B6
Jackson Cl E9 ....74 D1
Uxbridge UB10 ....60 A1
Jackson Ct E7 ....77 B2
Wanstead E11 ....55 B1
Jackson Ho 10 SW11 ....136 B2
Jackson Rd BR2 ....226 B6
N7 ....72 B4
Barking IG11 ....101 B6
East Barnet EN4 ....14 C5
Uxbridge UB10 ....60 A1
Jackson's La N6 ....49 B2
Jackson's Pl CR0 ....205 C1
Jackson St SE18 ....144 C6
Jackson's Way CR0 ....223 C5
Jackson Way UB2 ....107 D4
Jack Taylor Sch
NW8 ....92 A6 229 A6
Jack Tizard Sch SW6 ....134 D4
Jack Walker Ct N5 ....72 D4
Jacob Ho 5 DA18 ....124 D4
Jacobin Lo N7 ....72 A3
Jacob Mans 1 E1 ....96 B1
Jacobs Cl RM10 ....81 D4
Jacobs Ho E13 ....99 C4
Jacobson Ct SW11 ....267 B1
Jacobson Ho E1 ....243 C2
Jacob St SE1 ....118 A4
Jacob's Well Mews W1 ..238 B2
Jacotts Ho W10 ....90 C3
Jacqueline Cl UB5 ....85 A6
Jade Cl E16 ....99 D1
NW2 ....46 D2
Dagenham RM8 ....58 C1
Jaffe Rd IG1 ....57 B1
Jaffray Rd BR2 ....209 D5
Jaggard Way SW12 ....158 D4
Jagger Ho SW11 ....267 C2
Jago Cl SE18 ....145 A6
Jago Wlk 22 SE5 ....139 B5
Jamahirya Sch
SW3 ....136 C6 267 A6
Jamaica Rd SE1 ....253 D1
SE16 ....118 B3
Thornton Heath CR7 ....204 D3
Jamaica St E1 ....96 C2
James Allen's Girls' Sch
SE22 ....161 C6
James Anderson Ct 29
E2 ....95 C5
James Ave NW2 ....68 C3
Dagenham RM8 ....59 B1
James Bedford Cl HA5 ...22 C1
James Boswell Cl 1
SW16 ....182 C6
James Brine Ho 6 E2 ....95 D4
James Campbell Ho 2
E2 ....96 C5
James Cl 8 E13 ....99 A5
NW11 ....47 A3
James Collins Cl W9 ....91 B3
James Ct N12 ....30 C3
NW9 ....27 C1
4 Chingford E4 ....20 B2
Northolt UB5 ....85 A5
3 Woodford E18 ....37 B1
James Dixon Prim Sch
SE20 ....184 B3
James Docherty Ho 4
E2 ....96 C5
James Dudson Ct NW10 ..67 A1
James Est CR4 ....180 D1
James Gdns N22 ....32 D3
James Hammett Ho 9
E2 ....95 D5
James Ho E1 ....97 A3
33 SE16 ....118 D4
James Joyes Wlk 7
SE24 ....138 D1
James La E10,E11 ....54 B3
James Lee Sq EN3 ....7 C5
James Leicester Hall of
Residence N7 ....72 A2
James Lind Ho 5 SE8 ..119 B2
James Middleton Ho 20
E2 ....96 B4
James Newman Ct SE9 .166 C1
Jameson Ct 6 E2 ....96 C5
Jameson Ho SE11 ....260 C2
Jameson Lo N6 ....49 C3
Jameson Pl 11 W3 ....111 A4
Jameson St W8 ....245 B4
James Pl N17 ....33 D2
James St W1 ....93 A1 238 B1
WC2 ....116 A6 250 B6
Barking IG11 ....79 A1
Enfield EN1 ....17 D6
Hounslow TW3 ....130 B2
James Stewart Ho NW6 ..69 B1
James Stroud Ho SE17 ..262 B1
Jamestown Rd
NW1 ....93 B6 231 C6
Jamestown Way E14 ....120 B6
James Wolfe Prim Sch
SE10 ....142 A5
Jamieson Ho TW4 ....151 B5
Jamuna Cl E14 ....97 A2
Jane Sabina Colard's
Almshouses 1 E17 ....54 A4
Jane St E1 ....96 B1
Janet Ct 4 DA7 ....147 C1
Janet St E14 ....119 C3
Janeway Pl 2 SE16 ....118 B4
Janeway St SE16 ....118 A4
Janice Mews 3 IG1 ....78 D5
Jansen Wlk SW11 ....136 B1
Janson Cl E15 ....76 C3
NW10 ....67 C5
Janson Rd E15 ....76 C3
Jansons Rd N15 ....51 C6
Japan Cres N4 ....50 B1
Japanese Sch The W3 ...110 C6
Japan Rd RM6 ....58 D3
Jaquets Ct DA5 ....169 C2
Jardine Rd E1 ....118 D6
Jarman Ho 13 E1 ....96 C2
SE16 ....118 D2
Jarret Ho 1 E3 ....97 C4
Jarrett Cl SW2 ....160 D3
Jarrow Cl SM4 ....201 D4
Jarrow Rd N17 ....52 B5
SE16 ....118 C1
Dagenham RM6 ....58 C3
Jarrow Way E9 ....75 A4
Jarvis Cl 1 Barking IG11 .101 B6
Jarvis Cl *continued*
Barnet EN5 ....12 D6
Jarvis Ct 2 SE10 ....142 A4
Jarvis Ho 3 SE15 ....140 A4
Jarvis Rd SE22 ....139 C1
South Croydon CR2 ....221 B2
Jashada Ho SE18 ....122 C1
Jasmin SE1 ....253 D3
Jasmine Cl Ilford IG1 ....78 D3
Orpington BR6 ....226 D6
Southall UB1 ....107 A6
Jasmine Ct SE12 ....165 A5
11 Wallington SM6 ....219 B2
Jasmine Gdns
Harrow HA2 ....63 C6
West Wickham CR0 ....223 D5
Jasmine Gr SE20 ....184 B2
Jasmine Rd KT19 ....214 D3
Jasmine Terr UB7 ....104 C4
Jasmine Way KT7 ....196 C5
Jasmin Ho SE4 ....141 B2
Jasmin Lo 17 SE16 ....118 B1
Jason Ct 2 SW9 ....138 C4
W1 ....238 B2
Jason Ho UB5 ....84 B4
Jason Wlk SE9 ....188 C6
Jasper Cl EN3 ....6 C5
Jasper Ho KT4 ....199 B1
Jasper Rd E16 ....99 D1
Penge SE19 ....183 D4
Jasper Wlk N1 ....235 C2
Java Wharf SE1 ....253 D2
Javelin Way UB5 ....84 D4
Jawahar Bagh SW16 ....182 D4
Jaycroft EN2 ....4 C4
Jay Gdns BR7 ....188 B6
Jay Ho SW15 ....134 C3
Jay Mews SW7 ..114 A4 246 B1
Jayson Ct 7 CR0 ....206 A1
Jean Batten Cl SM6 ....220 B1
Jean Darling Ho SW10 ..266 C5
Jean Ho 3 SW17 ....180 C5
Jean Humbert Ho 2
SE27 ....183 B6
Jean Pardies Ho 21 E1 ...96 C2
Jebb Ave SW2 ....160 A5
Jebb St E3 ....97 C5
Jedburgh Rd E13 ....99 C4
Jedburgh St SW11 ....137 A1
Jeddo Mews W12 ....111 D4
Jeddo Rd W12 ....111 D4
Jefferies Ho 12 NW10 ....67 B1
Jefferson Bldg 3 E14 ...119 C4
Jefferson Cl W13 ....109 B3
Ilford IG2 ....56 D4
Jefferson Wlk 13 SE18 ..144 C6
Jeffrey Row SE12 ....165 B6
Jeffrey's Ct 2 SW4 ....138 A3
Jeffrey's Pl NW1 ....71 C1
Jeffrey's Rd SW4 ....138 A3
Jeffreys Rd EN3 ....7 B1
Jeffrey's St NW1 ....71 C1
Jeffs Cl TW12 ....173 D4
Jeffs Rd SM1 ....217 B4
Jefton Ct SM6 ....219 C3
Jeger Ave E2 ....95 D6
Jeken Rd SE9 ....143 C1
Jelf Rd SW2 ....160 C6
Jellicoe Ct E4 ....36 B4
Jellicoe Gdns HA7 ....25 A4
Jellicoe Ho 5 E2 ....96 A5
11 Putney SW15 ....156 D6
Jellicoe Rd 4 E13 ....99 A3
Tottenham N17 ....33 B3
Jemmett Cl KT2 ....176 D2
Jemotts Ct 9 SE14 ....140 D6
Jem Paterson Ct HA1 ....64 C4
Jengar Cl SM1 ....217 D4
Jenkins Ho SW8 ....269 C2
Jenkins La IG11 ....101 A4
Jenkinson Ho 12 E2 ....96 D4
Jenkins Rd E13 ....99 B3
Jenner Ave W3 ....89 B2
Jenner Ct N21 ....16 A6
Jenner Ho SE3 ....142 C6
5 Belvedere DA17 ....125 C3
Jenner Pl SW13 ....134 B6
Jenner Rd N16 ....73 D5
Jennett Rd CR0 ....220 C5
Jennifer Ho SE11 ....261 B3
Jennifer Rd BR1 ....164 D1
Jennings Cl KT6 ....197 C2
Jennings Ho SE10 ....120 B1
Jennings Rd SE22 ....161 D5
Jenny Hammond Cl E11 ..76 D5
Jenny Hammond Sch
E11 ....76 C4
Jensen Ho 10 E3 ....97 C3
Jenson Way SE19 ....183 D3
Jenton Ave DA7 ....147 A3
Jephson Ct 17 SW4 ....138 A3
Jephson Ho 2 SE17 ....138 D6
Jephson Rd E7 ....77 C1
Jephson St SE5 ....139 B4
Jephtha Rd SW18 ....157 C5
Jeppo's La CR4 ....202 D5
Jerdan Pl SW6 ....265 A4
Jeremiah St 11 E14 ....97 D1
Jeremy Bentham Ho 9
E2 ....96 A4
Jeremy's Gn N18 ....34 C6
Jermyn St SW1 ..115 C5 249 B4
Jerningham Ct SE14 ....141 A4
Jerningham Rd SE14 ....141 A4
Jerome Cres
NW8 ....92 C3 237 A6
Jerome Ct 2 N11 ....31 C5
Jerome Ho NW1 ....237 B4
Kingston KT1 ....175 D1
Jerome Pl KT1 ....175 D1
Jerome St E1 ....95 D3 243 C5
Jerome Twr 5 W3 ....110 D4
Jerrard St SE13 ....141 D2
Jerrold Lo SW15 ....134 C2
Jerrold St 24 N1 ....95 C5
Jersey Ave HA7 ....25 C1
Jersey Ct UB2 ....107 B3
Jersey Dr BR5 ....211 B3
Jersey Ho 12 N1 ....73 A2
Enfield EN3 ....6 D5
Jersey Rd E11 ....54 B1
N1 ....73 A2
W7 ....109 A4
Hounslow TW5,TW7 ....130 B5
Ilford IG1 ....78 D4
Mitcham SW17 ....181 B4
Newham E16 ....99 C1
Jersey St E2 ....96 B4
Jerusalem Pas EC1 ....241 C5
Jervis Bay Ho 8 E14 ....98 B1
Jervis Ct W1 ....238 D1
9 Dagenham RM10 ....81 D2
Jerviston Gdns SW16 ...182 C4
Jesmond Ave HA9 ....66 B2
Jesmond Cl CR4 ....203 B6
Jesmond Rd CR0 ....205 D2
Jesmond Way HA7 ....26 A5
Jessam Ave E5 ....52 B1
Jessamine Rd W7 ....108 D5
Jessel Ho SW1 ....259 D4
WC1 ....233 A1
Jesse Rd E10 ....54 A1
Jessica Rd SW18 ....158 A6
Jessie Blythe La 2 N19 ..50 A2
Jessie Duffett Ho 11
SE5 ....139 A5
Jessie's Cotts E17 ....53 A3
Jessiman Terr TW17 ....192 C4
Jesson Ho SE17 ....262 C3
Jessop Ave UB2 ....107 B2
Jessop Ct N1 ....234 D3
Jessop Prim Sch SE24 ...139 A1
Jessop Sq E14 ....119 C5
Jessops Way CR0 ....203 C3
Jessup Cl SE18 ....123 A2
Jeston Ho 10 SE27 ....160 D1
Jethou Ho 13 N1 ....73 A2
Jetstar Way UB5 ....85 A4
Jevington Way SE12 ....165 B3
Jevons Ho 9 NW8 ....70 B1
Jewell Ho 3 SW12 ....159 C4
Jewel Rd E17 ....53 C6
Jewish Prep Sch The
NW6 ....91 D5
Jewry St EC3 ....95 D1 243 C1
Jews Coll NW4 ....46 D5
Jews Free Sch NW1 ....71 D2
Jews Row SW18 ....136 A1
Jews Wlk SE26 ....184 B6
Jeymer Ave NW2 ....68 C3
Jeymer Dr UB6 ....86 A6
Jeypore Rd SW18 ....158 A5
JFS Sch NW9 ....44 C3
Jillian Cl TW12 ....173 C3
Jim Bradley Cl 16 SE18 ..122 C2
Jim Griffiths Ho SW6 ....264 D5
Joan Cres SE9 ....165 D4
Joan Gdns RM8 ....81 A6
Joanna Ho 7 W6 ....112 C1
Joan Player Ho EN3 ....6 D6
Joan Rd RM8 ....81 A6
Joan St SE1 ....116 D5 251 C3
Jocelin Ho N1 ....233 D5
Jocelyn Rd TW9 ....132 A2
Jocelyn St SE15 ....140 A4
Jockey's Fields
WC1 ....94 B2 240 D4
Jodane Rd SE8 ....119 B2
Jodrell Cl TW7 ....131 A4
Jodrell Rd E3 ....75 B1
Joe Hunte Ct 2 SW27 ...182 D5
Joel St HA5,HA6 ....40 A5
Johanna Prim Sch
SE1 ....116 C4 251 A1
Johanna St SE1 ....251 A1
John Adam St
WC2 ....116 A6 250 B5
John Aird Ct W2 ..92 A2 236 B4
John Archer Way SW18 ..158 B5
John Ashby Cl SW2 ....160 A5
John Austin Cl KT2 ....176 B2
John Baird Ct SE26 ....184 D6
John Baird Ho 14 SE20 ..184 C3
John Ball Prim Sch SE3 .142 C3
John Barker Ct NW6 ....69 A1
John Barker Ho IG1 ....79 B6
John Barnes Wlk E15 ....76 D2
John Barter Ho TW3 ....129 B3
John Betts' Ho W12 ....112 A3
John Betts Prim Sch
W6 ....112 B3
John Bond Ho 2 E3 ....97 B5
John Bradshaw Rd N14 ..15 D3
John Brent Ho 8 SE8 ...118 D2
John Buck Ho NW10 ....89 D6
John Burns Dr IG11 ....79 C1
John Burns Prim Sch
SW11 ....137 A3
John Busch Sch TW7 ....131 B4
Johnby Cl EN3 ....7 A6
John Campbell Rd 26
N16 ....73 C3
John Carpenter St EC4 ..251 C6
John Cartwright Ho 7
E2 ....96 B4
John Chilton Sch UB5 ....63 A1
John Clifford Ho N8 ....50 A3
John Conwey Ho 23
SW2 ....160 C5
John Cornwell VC Ho 6
E12 ....78 C4
John Dee Ho 8 SW14 ...133 B2
John Donne Prim Sch
SE15 ....140 B4
John Drinkwater Cl E11 ..54 D2
John Dwight Ho SW6 ...135 D2
John Felton Rd 16 SE16 .118 A4
John Fielden Ho 10 E2 ...96 B4
John Fisher St E1 ....118 A6
John F. Kennedy Specl Sch
E15 ....98 B6
John Glynes Ct SW15 ...134 B1
John Gooch Dr EN2 ....4 D4
John Harris Ho SE15 ...140 A2
John Harrison Way
SE10 ....120 D3
John Hunt Ct 5 SE9 ...166 A2
John Islip St
SW1 ....116 A2 260 A3
John Kaye Ct TW17 ....192 C4
John Keall Ho SW15 ....134 D2
John Keats Lo EN2 ....5 B4
John Keble CE Prim Sch
NW10 ....89 D6
John Kelly Tech Colls
NW2 ....67 D5
John Kennedy Ct 1 N1 ...73 B2
John Kennedy Ho 1
SE16 ....118 D2
John Kennedy Lo 2 N1 ..73 B2
John King Ct 4 N19 ....71 D6
John Kirk Ho 22 SW11 ...136 B2
Beckenham BR3 ....207 A5
5 Streatham SW16 ....160 A1
John Knight Lo SW6 ....265 B4
John Lamb Ct HA3 ....24 C2
John Loughborough Sch The
N17 ....33 D1
John Lyon Sch The HA2 ...42 B1
John Masefield Ho N15 ...51 B3
John Maurice Cl
SE17 ....117 B2 262 C4
John McDonald Ho 3
E14 ....120 A3
John McKenna Wlk 17
SE16 ....118 A3
John Milton Prim Sch
SW8 ....137 C5 269 A3
John Nettleford Ho 14
E2 ....96 B4
John Newton Ct DA16 ...146 B2
John Nightingale Sch
KT8 ....195 B6
John Orwell Sports Ctr
E1 ....118 B5
John Parker Cl RM10 ....81 D1
John Parker Sq 8
SW11 ....136 B2
John Parry Ct 28 N1 ....95 C5
John Paul II Sch SW19 ..156 D4
John Penn St SE13 ....141 D4
John Perrin Pl HA3 ....44 A2
John Perryn Prim Sch
W3 ....89 C1
John Prince's St W1 ....238 D2
John Pritchard Ho 14 E1 .96 A3
John Ratcliffe Ho 5
NW6 ....91 C4
John Rennie Wlk 1 E1 ..118 C5
John Roan Sch The
SE3 ....142 C5
John Roll Way SE16 ....118 A3
John Ruskin Coll CR2 ...223 A1
John Ruskin Prim Sch
SE5 ....139 A6
John Ruskin St SE5 ....139 A6
John's Ave NW4 ....46 C5
Johns Cl TW15 ....171 A6
John Scurr Ho 20 E14 ....97 A1
John Scurr Prim Sch E1 ..96 C3
John Silkin La SE8 ....118 D1
Johns La SM4 ....202 A4
John's Mews
WC1 ....94 B3 240 D5
John Smith Ave
SW6 ....135 B5 264 C4
Johnson Cl E8 ....96 A6
Johnson Ct 10 SW18 ....136 B1
Johnson Ho 14 E2 ....96 A4
NW1 ....232 B3
SW1 ....258 B3
SW8 ....269 D3
Johnson Lo 12 W9 ....91 C2
Johnson Rd BR2 ....209 D4
NW10 ....89 B6
Heston TW5 ....128 C5
Thornton Heath CR0 ....205 B2
Johnson's Cl SM5 ....218 D5
Johnsons Ct EC4 ....241 B1
Johnsons Dr TW12 ....174 A2
Johnson's Ind Est UB3 ...106 A3
Johnson's Pl
SW1 ....115 C1 259 A1
Johnson St E1 ....96 C1
Southall UB2 ....106 D3
Johnsons Way NW10 ....88 D3
John Spencer Sq N1 ....72 D2
John's Pl E1 ....96 B1
John St E15 ....98 D6
WC1 ....94 B3 240 D5
Croydon SE25 ....206 A5
Enfield EN1 ....17 D6
Hounslow TW3,TW5 ....129 A3
John Stainer Com Prim Sch
SE4 ....141 A2
John's Terr CR0 ....205 C1
Johnston Cl SW9 ....270 D1
Johnstone Ho SE13 ....142 B2
Johnstone Rd E6 ....100 B4
Johnston Rd IG8 ....37 A5
Johnston Terr NW2 ....68 D5
John Strachey Ho SW6 ..264 D5
John Strype Ct E10 ....53 D1
John Trundle Ct EC2 ....242 A4
John Tucker Ho 2 E14 ..119 C3
John Walsh Twr E11 ....76 D6
John Wesley Ct 5 TW1 .153 A3
John Wesley's House &
Mus★ EC1 ....242 D6
John Wheatley Ho
14 N19 ....49 D2
SW6 ....264 D5
John Williams Cl SE14 ..140 D6
12 Kingston KT2 ....175 D2
John Wilson St SE18 ....122 C2
John Wooley Cl SE13 ....142 C1
Johnsen Ho 5 SW15 ....156 A6
Joiners Arms Yd 1 SE5 .139 B4
Joiner St SE1 ....252 D3
Joint Rd N10 ....30 C2
Jolles Ho 9 E3 ....97 D4
Jollys La Harrow HA2 ....42 B1
Hayes UB4 ....84 D2
Jonathan Ct 9 W4 ....111 C2
Jonathan St
SE11 ....116 B1 260 C2
Jones Ho N16 ....51 C1
4 South Bromley E14 ....98 B1
Jones Rd E13 ....99 B3
Jones St W1 ....248 C5
Jones Wlk 6 TW10 ....154 B5
Jonquil Gdns 5 TW12 ...173 C4
Jonson Cl Hayes UB4 ....84 A2
Mitcham CR4 ....203 B6
Jonson Ho 16 N16 ....73 B4
SE1 ....262 D5
Jordan Cl HA2 ....63 B5
Jordan Ct SW15 ....134 D1
Jordan Hill N10 ....30 C2
Jordan ho N1 ....235 D5
12 SE4 ....140 D1
Jordan Rd UB6 ....87 C6
Jordans Cl RM10 ....81 D4
Jordans Ho NW8 ....237 A5
Jordans Mews TW11 ....152 C2
Jo Richardson Com Sch
RM9 ....80 C2
Joscoyne Ho 14 E1 ....96 B1
Josef Perrin Ho 1
SE27 ....183 B6
Joseph Ave W3 ....89 B1
Joseph Clarke Sch E4 ....36 B4
Joseph Conrad Ho SW1 .259 B3
Joseph Ct N16 ....51 C2
Joseph Hood Fst Sch
SW20 ....201 A6
Josephine Ave SW2 ....160 B6
Joseph Irwin Ho 11 E14 .119 B6
Joseph Lancaster Prim Sch
SE1 ....117 B3 262 C5
Joseph Lister Ct E7 ....77 A1
Joseph Lister Lo E11 ....55 B1
Joseph Powell Cl 1
SW12 ....159 C5
Joseph Priestley Ho 12
E2 ....96 B4
Joseph Ray Rd E11 ....76 C6
Joseph St E3 ....97 B3
Joseph Trotter Cl EC1 ....234 B1
Joshua Cl N10 ....31 B3
Croydon CR2 ....220 D1
Joshua St E14 ....98 A1
Joslings Cl W12 ....112 A6
Joslyn Cl EN3 ....7 C5
Josseline Ct 8 E3 ....97 A5
Joubert Mans SW3 ....257 B2
Joubert St SW11 ....136 D3
Jowett Ho 27 SW9 ....138 A3
Jowett St SE15 ....139 D5
Joyce Ave N18 ....33 D5
Joyce Butler Ho N22 ....32 B2
Joyce Dawson Way
SE28 ....124 A6
Joyce Page Cl SE7 ....143 D6
Joy Ct NW2 ....68 D5
Joydon Dr RM6 ....58 B3
Joyners Cl RM9 ....81 B4
Joystone Ct 8 EN4 ....2 C1
Jubb Powell Ho N15 ....51 C3
Jubet Ho 9 N16 ....73 B4
Jubilee Ave Chingford E4 ..36 A4
Romford RM7 ....59 D4
Twickenham TW2 ....152 A3
Jubilee Bldgs NW8 ....229 C4
Jubilee Cl NW9 ....45 B3
Pinner HA5 ....22 C1
Romford RM7 ....59 D4
Teddington KT1 ....175 C2
Jubilee Cres E14 ....120 A3
Edmonton N9 ....18 A3
Jubilee Ct Harrow HA3 ....44 A2
Hounslow TW3 ....129 D2
Thornton Heath CR7 ....204 C5
Jubilee Ctry Pk BR2 ....210 D4
Jubilee Dr HA4 ....63 A4
Jubilee Gdns UB1 ....85 C1
Jubilee Ho SE11 ....261 B3
3 Hampton TW12 ....173 C2
Jubilee Mans 10 E1 ....96 C1
Jubilee Mkt WC2 ....250 B6
Jubilee Par IG8 ....37 C4
Jubilee Pl SW3 ..114 C1 257 B2
Jubilee Prim Sch N16 ....52 A1
SW2 ....160 C5
Woolwich SE28 ....124 C6
Jubilee Rd Cheam SM3 ...216 D1
Wembley UB6 ....87 B6
Jubilee St E1 ....96 C2
Jubilee The 2 SE10 ....141 D5

Jubilee Villas KT10 ....196 C1
Jubilee Way DA14 ....168 A2
East Bedfont TW14 ....150 A3
Merton SW19 ....179 D2
Tolworth KT4,KT9 ....214 D5
Jubilee Wks SW19 ....180 A1
Jubilee Yd SE1 ....253 C2
Judd St WC1 ....94 A4 233 A1
Jude St E16 ....98 D1
Judge Heath La UB3 ....83 B1
Judges' Wlk NW3 ....70 A5
Judge Wlk KT10 ....212 C2
Juer St SW11 ....136 C5 267 B3
Jules Thorn Ave EN1 ....6 A1
Julia Ct E17 ....53 D4
Julia Garfield Mews 4
E16 ....121 B5
Julia Gdns IG11 ....102 D5
Juliana Cl N2 ....48 A6
Julian Ave W3 ....110 D6
Julian Cl EN5 ....1 D2
Julian Hill HA1 ....64 C6
Julian Ho SE21 ....183 C6
Julian Pl E14 ....119 D1
Julians Prim Sch SW16 ....182 C6
Julian Taylor Path 7
SE23 ....162 B2
Julia St NW5 ....71 A3
Julie Garfield Mews 4
E16 ....121 B5
Julien Rd W5 ....109 C3
Juliet Ho 11 N1 ....95 C5
Juliette Rd E13 ....99 A5
Julius Ct TW8 ....132 A5
Julius Nyerere Cl N1 ....233 C5
Junction App SE13 ....142 A2
SW11 ....136 C2
Junction Mews W2 ....237 A2
Junction Pl W2 ....236 D2
Junction Rd E13 ....99 B5
N17 ....52 A6
N19 ....71 C5
Ashford TW15 ....171 B5
Brentford TW8 ....109 D2
Croydon CR2 ....221 B3
Edmonton N9 ....18 A3
Harrow HA1 ....42 C3
Junction Rd E RM6 ....59 A2
Junction Rd W RM6 ....59 A2
Juniper Cl Barnet EN5 ....12 D6
Chessington KT9 ....214 B3
Wembley HA9 ....66 C3
Juniper Cres NW1 ....71 A1
Juniper Ct N16 ....73 B6
Belmont SM2 ....217 C2
Dagenham RM6 ....58 C3
12 Ealing W5 ....87 C2
Harrow HA3 ....24 D2
Hounslow TW3 ....129 D1
Juniper Gdns
Ashford TW16 ....171 D4
Streatham CR4 ....181 C2
Juniper La E6 ....100 A2
Juniper Rd IG1 ....78 D4
Juniper St 15 E1 ....118 C6
Juniper Way UB3 ....105 C6
Juno Ct 11 SW9 ....138 C5
Juno Way SE14 ....140 D6
Juno Way Ind Est SE14 ....140 D6
Jupiter Ct 10 SW9 ....138 C5
8 Northolt UB5 ....84 D4
Jupiter Hts UB10 ....82 B6
Jupiter Way N7 ....72 B2
Jupp Rd E15 ....76 B1
Jupp Rd W E15 ....98 B6
Jura Ho SE16 ....119 A2
Jurston Ct SE1 ....251 B1
Justice Wlk SW3 ....267 A5
Justin Cl TW8 ....131 D5
Justin Rd E4 ....35 B4
Jute La EN3 ....7 A2
Jutland Cl N19 ....50 A1
Jutland Ho 4 SE5 ....139 A3
10 SE7 ....122 A2
Jutland Rd E13 ....99 A3
Catford SE6 ....164 A4
Jutsums Ave RM7 ....59 D3
Jutsums Ct RM7 ....59 D3
Jutsums La RM7 ....59 D2
Juxon Cl HA3 ....23 D2
Juxon St SE11 ....116 B2 260 D4
JVC Bsns Pk NW2 ....46 A1

K

Kaduna Cl HA5 ....40 B4
Kale Rd DA18 ....125 A4
Kambala Rd SW11 ....136 B2
Kangley Bridge Ctr
SE26 ....185 B5
Kangley Bridge Rd
SE26 ....185 B5
Kaplan Dr N21 ....16 B6
Kara Way NW2 ....68 D4
Karen Ct 2 SE5 ....139 C2
Bromley BR1 ....186 D2
Karen Ho 7 N16 ....73 B4
Karens Ct EN3 ....6 D6
Karen Terr E11 ....76 D6
Ilford IG2 ....57 B4
Karenza Ct HA9 ....43 C2
Kariba Cl N9 ....18 C1
Karoline Gdns UB6 ....86 B5
Kashgar Rd SE18 ....123 D2
Kashmir Rd SE7 ....143 D5
Kasmin Ct NW10 ....68 A1
Kassala Rd
SW11 ....136 D4 267 D1
Katella Trad Est IG11 ....101 C4
Kates Cl EN5 ....12 A6
Katharine Rd 1 TW1 ....153 A3
Katharine St CR0 ....221 A5
Katherine Cl 3 SE16 ....118 D5
Katherine Ct
10 Forest Hill SE23 ....162 C3
Penge SE20 ....184 C2
Katherine Gdns SE9 ....143 D1
Katherine Ho 15 W10 ....91 A3
Katherine Rd E6,E7 ....77 C1
Katherine Sq W11 ....244 A4
Kathleen Ave W3 ....89 A2
Wembley HA0 ....66 A1
Kathleen Ferrier Ct 4
N17 ....33 D3
Kathleen Moore Ct BR4 ....224 A6
Kathleen Rd SW11 ....136 D2
Katrine Ct NW2 ....68 C5
Kayemoor Rd SM2 ....218 C2
Kay Rd SW9 ....138 B3
Kays Ct EN3 ....6 D1
Kay St DA16 ....146 B4
E2 ....96 A5
Kean Ho 5 SE17 ....138 D6
Kean St WC2 ....94 B1 240 C1
Keates Est N16 ....73 D6
Keatley Gn E4 ....35 B4
Keats Ave E16 ....121 B5
Keats Cl NW3 ....70 C4
SE1 ....263 C3
Enfield EN3 ....18 D6
Hayes UB4 ....84 A2
Mitcham SW19 ....180 B4
Wanstead E11 ....55 B4
Keats Ct HA0 ....65 C5
Keats Gr NW3 ....70 C4
Keats Ho 22 E2 ....96 C4
30 SE5 ....139 A5
SW1 ....269 B6
7 Beckenham BR3 ....185 D4
Keats House Mus* NW3 ....70 C4
Keats Par 3 N9 ....18 A2
Keats Pl EC2 ....242 C3
Keats Rd DA16 ....145 D4
Keats Way Croydon CR0 ....206 C3
Southall UB6 ....85 D2
West Drayton UB7 ....104 B2
Kebbell Terr E7 ....77 B3
Keble Cl New Malden KT4 ....199 D1
Northolt UB5 ....64 A3
Keble Ho 4 SW15 ....156 D5
Keble Pl SW13 ....134 B6
Keble Prep Sch N21 ....16 C4
Keble St SW17 ....180 A6
Kechill Gdns BR2 ....209 A2
Kedeston Ct SM3 ....201 D1
Kedge Ho 10 E14 ....119 C3
Kedleston Ct E5 ....75 A4
Kedleston Dr BR5 ....211 D4
Kedleston Wlk 21 E2 ....96 B4
Kedyngton Ho 5 HA8 ....27 A1
Keeble Cl SE18 ....144 D6
Keedonwood Rd BR1 ....186 D5
Keel Cl SE16 ....118 D5
Barking IG11 ....102 C5
Keeley St WC2 ....94 B1 240 C1
Keeling Ho 2 TW11 ....174 C5
Keeling Rd SE9 ....165 D6
Keely Cl EN4 ....14 C6
Keemor Cl SE18 ....144 C5
Keens Cl SW16 ....181 D5
Keen's Rd CR0 ....221 A4
Keen's Yd N1 ....72 D2
Keepers Mews TW11 ....175 C4
Keeper Wharf E1 ....118 D6
Keepier Wharf 15 E1 ....118 D6
Keep The SE3 ....143 A3
Forest Hill SE6 ....163 C3
Kingston KT2 ....176 B3
Keeton's Rd SE16 ....118 B3
Keevil Dr SW19 ....157 A4
Keighley Cl N7 ....72 A4
Keightley Dr SE9 ....167 A3
Keilder Cl UB10 ....82 C5
Keildon Rd SW11 ....136 D1
Keir Hardie Est E5 ....52 B1
Keir Hardie Ho 15 N19 ....49 D2
NW10 ....67 D1
W6 ....134 D6
Keir Hardie Way
Barking IG11 ....80 A1
Hayes UB4 ....84 A4
Keir Hardy Ho 6 DA17 ....125 C3
Keir The SW19 ....178 C5
Keith Connor Cl 5
SW8 ....137 B2
Keith Gr W12 ....112 A5
Keith Ho NW6 ....91 D5
Keith Park Rd UB10 ....60 B1
Keith Rd E17 ....35 B2
Barking IG11 ....101 B5
Hayes UB3 ....105 C3
Keith Sutton Ho 3 SE9 ....167 A2
Kelbrook Rd SE3 ....144 A2
Kelby Ho N7 ....72 B2
Kelceda Cl NW2 ....68 A6
Kelf Gr UB3 ....83 D1
Kelfield Ct 1 W10 ....90 D1
Kelfield Gdns W10 ....90 D1
Kelfield Mews W10 ....90 D1
Kelham Ho 10 SE18 ....144 D6
Kelland Cl 1 N8 ....49 D4
Kelland Rd E13 ....99 A3
Kellaway Rd SE3 ....143 D3
Keller Cres E12 ....77 D4
Kellerton Rd SE13 ....164 C6
Kellett Ho N1 ....235 D5
Kellett Rd SW2 ....138 C1
Kelling Gdns CR0 ....204 D2
Kellino St SW17 ....180 D6
Kellner Rd SE28 ....123 D3
Kellow Ho SE1 ....252 C2
Kell St SE1 ....116 D3 261 D6
Kelly Ave SE15 ....139 D4
Kelly Cl NW10 ....67 B5
Upper Halliford TW17 ....171 C1
Kelly Ct 11 E14 ....119 C6
Kelly Rd NW7 ....29 A4
Kelly St NW1 ....71 B2
Kelly Way RM6 ....59 A3
Kelman Cl SW4 ....137 D3
Kelmore Gr SE22 ....140 A1
Kelmscott 5 SE23 ....162 D1
Kelmscott Cl E17 ....35 B2
Kelmscott Ct 2 HA7 ....25 C6
Kelmscott Gdns W12 ....112 A3
Kelmscott L Ctr E17 ....53 B3
Kelmscott Rd SW11 ....158 D6
Kelmscott Sch E17 ....53 B3
Kelross Rd N5 ....73 A4
Kelsall Cl SE3 ....143 B3
Kelsey Gate 8 BR3 ....185 D1
Kelsey La BR3 ....207 C6
Kelsey Park Ave BR3 ....185 D1
Kelsey Park Rd BR3 ....185 C1
Kelsey Park Sch BR3 ....207 C6
Kelsey Rd BR5 ....190 B1
Kelsey Sq BR3 ....185 C1
Kelsey St E2 ....96 A3
Kelsey Way BR3 ....207 C6
Kelshall Ct N4 ....73 A6
Kelso Ct SE20 ....184 B3
Kelso Lo E18 ....37 B1
Kelson Ho E14 ....120 A3
Kelso Pl W8 ....113 D3 255 D6
Kelso Rd SM5 ....202 A2
Kelvedon Cl KT2 ....176 C4
Kelvedon Ho SW8 ....270 B2
Kelvedon Rd
SW6 ....135 B5 264 D3
Kelvin Ave N13 ....32 B4
Kelvinbrook KT8 ....195 D6
Kelvin Cl KT19 ....214 C2
Kelvin Cres HA3 ....24 C3
Kelvin Ct W11 ....245 A5
Chiswick W4 ....133 A5
Isleworth TW7 ....130 C3
7 Penge SE20 ....184 B2
8 Twickenham TW1 ....153 B5
Kelvin Dr TW1 ....153 B5
Kelvin Gdns Southall UB1 ....85 C1
Thornton Heath CR0 ....204 A2
Kelvin Gr Forest Hill SE26 ....162 B1
Surbiton KT6 ....214 A5
Kelvin Grove Prim Sch
SE26 ....162 B1
Kelvington Cl CR0 ....207 A2
Kelvington Rd SE15 ....162 D6
Kelvin Ho 3 DA17 ....125 C3
Kelvin Par BR6 ....211 C1
Kelvin Rd DA16 ....146 A2
N5 ....73 A4
Kelyway Ho 20 SW2 ....160 C4
Kember St N1 ....72 B1
Kemble Dr BR2 ....226 A5
Kemble Ho SW9 ....138 D2
Kemble Rd Croydon CR0 ....220 D5
Forest Hill SE23 ....162 D3
Tottenham N17 ....34 A2
Kemble St WC2 ....94 B1 240 C1
Kemerton Rd SE5 ....139 A2
Beckenham BR3 ....185 D1
Croydon CR0 ....205 D2
Kemey's St E9 ....75 A3
Kemnal Rd BR7 ....189 B5
Kemnal Tech Coll BR5 ....190 B3
Kemnal Warren BR7 ....189 B4
Kemp 24 NW9 ....27 D2
Kemp Ct SW8 ....270 A3
Kempe Ho SE1 ....262 D5
Kempe Rd NW6 ....90 D5
Kemp Gdns CR0 ....205 A3
Kemp Ho 1 E2 ....96 D5
Wallend E6 ....78 C2
Kempis Way 5 SE22 ....161 C6
Kemplay Rd NW3 ....70 B4
Kemp Rd RM8 ....58 D1
Kemps Ct NW2 ....68 D5
Kemp's Ct W1 ....239 C1
Kemps Dr E14 ....119 C6
Kempsford Gdns
SW5 ....113 C1 255 B1
Kempsford Rd SE11 ....261 B3
Kemps Gdns SE13 ....164 A6
Kempshott Rd SW16 ....182 A3
Kempson Rd
SW6 ....135 C5 265 B3
Kempthorne Rd SE8 ....119 B2
Kempton Ave
Northolt UB5 ....63 C3
Sunbury TW16 ....172 B2
Kempton Cl UB10 ....61 A4
Kempton Ct E1 ....96 B2
Sunbury TW16 ....172 B2
Kempton Ho 13 N1 ....95 C6
Kempton Park Race Course
TW16 ....172 C3
Kempton Park Sta
TW16 ....172 B3
Kempton Rd E6 ....100 B6
Kempton Wlk CR0 ....207 A3
Kempt St SE18 ....144 C6
Kemsford Rd SE11 ....261 C3
Kemsing Cl DA5 ....169 A4
Coney Hall BR2 ....224 D6
South Norwood CR7 ....205 A5
Kemsing Ho SE1 ....252 D1
Kemsing Rd SE10 ....121 A1
Kemsley SE13 ....163 D6
Kemsley Ct W13 ....109 C5
Kemsway Ct BR5 ....190 B2
Kenbrook Ho 5 NW5 ....71 C3
W14 ....254 D5
Kenbury Cl UB10 ....60 C5
Kenbury Gdns 10 SE5 ....139 A3
Kenbury Mans 18 SE5 ....139 A3
Kenbury St SE5 ....139 A3
Kenchester Cl
SW8 ....138 A5 270 B3
Kencot Cl DA18 ....125 B4
Erith DA18 ....125 B4
Kendal NW1 ....231 D2
Kendal Ave Acton W3 ....88 D2
Barking IG11 ....101 C6
Edmonton N18 ....33 B6
Kendal Cl SE5 ....138 D5
East Bedfont TW14 ....149 D3
Hayes UB4 ....83 C5
Woodford IG8 ....20 D2
Kendal Ct NW2 ....69 A3
Acton W3 ....88 C2
11 Chingford E4 ....20 A3
7 Croydon CR0 ....205 C1
Kendale Rd BR1 ....186 C5
Kendal Gdns
Edmonton N18 ....33 B6
Sutton SM1 ....218 A6
Kendal Ho 32 E9 ....74 C1
N1 ....233 D4
5 Croydon CR0 ....205 C1
Penge SE20 ....184 B1
Kendall Ave BR3 ....185 A1
Kendall Ct DA15 ....168 A1
3 SE22 ....162 A6
Mitcham SW19 ....180 B4
5 Penge SE19 ....183 D3
Kendall Ho SE12 ....164 D4
Kendall Lo 5 BR1 ....187 B2
Kendall Pl W1 ....238 A3
Kendall Rd SE18 ....144 A4
Beckenham BR3 ....185 A1
Isleworth TW7 ....131 A3
Kendalmere Cl N10 ....31 B2
Kendal Par N18 ....33 B6
Kendal Pl SW15 ....157 B6
Kendal Rd NW10 ....68 A4
Kendal St W2 ....92 C1 237 B1
Kendal Steps W2 ....237 B1
Kender Prim Sch SE14 ....140 C4
Kender St SE14 ....140 C4
Kendoa Rd 1 SW4 ....137 D1
Kendon Cl E11 ....55 B4
Kendra Hall Rd CR2 ....220 D1
Kendrey Gdns TW2 ....152 C4
Kendrick Ct 11 SE15 ....140 B4
Kendrick Mews SW7 ....256 C3
Kendrick Pl SW7 ....256 C3
Kenelm Cl HA1 ....65 A5
Kenerne Dr EN5 ....13 A6
Kenilford Rd SW12 ....159 B4
Kenilworth Ave E17 ....53 C6
Harrow HA2 ....63 B4
Wimbledon SW19 ....179 C6
Kenilworth Cres EN1 ....5 C4
Kenilworth Ct
7 Chingford E4 ....20 A2
Fulham SW6 ....135 A2
Twickenham TW2 ....152 C2
Kenilworth Gdns
Hayes UB4 ....83 D2
Ilford IG3 ....79 D6
Southall UB1 ....85 B4
South Oxhey WD19 ....22 C5
Woolwich SE18 ....144 D3
Kenilworth Rd E3 ....97 A5
HA8 ....11 A1
NW6 ....91 B6
Ashford TW15,TW19 ....148 A1
Ealing W5 ....110 A5
Orpington BR5 ....211 A3
Penge SE20 ....184 D2
Stoneleigh KT17 ....216 A3
Kenilworth Terr 3 SM2 ....217 C1
Kenley N17 ....33 B1
Kenley Ave NW9 ....27 C1
Kenley Cl Barnet EN4 ....2 C1
Sidcup DA5 ....169 C4
St Paul's Cray BR7 ....211 C6
Kenley Gdns CR7 ....204 D5
Kenley Ho 6 BR5 ....190 B1
5 Croydon CR0 ....206 A1
Kenley Rd
Kingston KT1,KT3 ....176 D1
Merton SW19 ....201 C6
Twickenham TW1 ....153 B5
Kenley Wlk W11 ....244 A5
Cheam SM3 ....216 D4
Kenlor Rd SW17 ....180 B5
Kenmare Ct 5 HA7 ....25 C6
Kenmare Dr CR4 ....180 D3
Kenmare Gdns N13 ....33 A6
Kenmare Mans NW6 ....69 B3
Kenmare Rd CR7 ....204 C3
Kenmere Gdns HA0 ....88 C6
Kenmere Mans W5 ....87 C3
Kenmere Rd DA16 ....146 C3
Kenmont Gdns NW10 ....90 B4
Kenmont Prim Sch
NW10 ....90 B4
Kenmore Ave HA3 ....43 A6
Kenmore Cl TW9 ....132 C5
Kenmore Cres UB4 ....83 D4
Kenmore Ct NW6 ....69 C1
Kenmore Gdns HA8 ....26 D1
Kenmore Park Fst & Mid
Schs HA3 ....44 A6
Kenmore Rd HA3 ....43 D5
Kenmure Rd E8 ....74 B3
Kenmure Yd E8 ....74 B3
Kennacraig Cl 7 E16 ....121 A5
Kennard Ho 11 SW11 ....137 A3
Kennard Mans 6 N11 ....30 D5
Kennard Rd E15 ....76 B1
N11 ....30 D5
Kennard St 9 SW11 ....137 A3
Newham E16 ....122 B5
Kennedy Ave EN3 ....18 C5
Kennedy Cl BR5 ....211 B1
E13 ....99 A5
1 Mitcham CR4 ....181 A1
Pinner HA5 ....23 B4
Kennedy Cox Ho 9 E16 ....98 D2
Kennedy Ct TW15 ....171 A5
Kennedy Ho SE11 ....260 C2
Kennedy Path W7 ....86 D3
Kennedy Rd
Barking IG11 ....101 C6
Ealing W7 ....86 C2
Kennedy Wlk SE17 ....262 D3
Kennet Cl SW11 ....136 B1
Kennet Ct 47 W2 ....91 C2
Kennet Dr UB4 ....85 A2
Kenneth Ave IG1 ....78 D4
Kenneth Campbell Ho
NW8 ....236 D6
Kenneth Cres NW2 ....68 B3
Kenneth Ct SE11 ....261 B4
Kenneth Gdns HA7 ....25 A4
Kenneth Moor Rd 4 IG1 ....78 D5
Kennet Ho NW8 ....236 D5
Kenneth Rd RM6 ....59 A2
Kenneth Robbins Ho 1
N17 ....34 B3
Kenneth Younger Ho
SW6 ....264 D5
Kennet Rd W9 ....91 B3
Isleworth TW7 ....130 D2
Kennet Sq CR4 ....180 C2
Kennet St E1 ....118 A5
Kennet Wharf La EC4 ....252 B6
Kenninghall N18 ....34 C5
Kenninghall Rd E5 ....74 B5
N18 ....34 C5
Kenning Ho 6 N1 ....95 C6
Kenning St 12 SE16 ....118 C4
Kennings Way
SE11 ....116 C1 261 B2
Kennington Gdns KT1 ....197 D6
Kennington Gr SE11 ....270 D6
Kennington La
SE11 ....116 C1 260 D1
Kennington Oval
SE11 ....138 C6 270 D5
Kennington Palace Ct
SE11 ....261 A2
Kennington Park Gdns
SE17 ....138 D6
Kennington Park Ho
SE11 ....261 B1
Kennington Park Pl
SE11 ....138 D6
Kennington Park Rd
SE11 ....116 D1 261 C2
Kennington Rd
SE11 ....116 C2 261 A3
Kennington Sta
SE17 ....116 D1 261 C2
Kennoldes SE21 ....161 B2
Kennyland Lo NW4 ....46 B3
Kenny Rd NW7 ....29 A5
Kenrick Pl W1 ....238 A3
Kensal Green Cemy (All
Souls)* NW10 ....90 C4
Kensal Green Sta NW10 ....90 C4
Kensal Ho W10 ....90 D3
Kensal Rd W10 ....91 A3
Kensal Rise Prim Sch
NW6 ....90 D5
Kensal Rise Sta NW10 ....90 D5
Kensington Ave E12 ....78 B2
South Norwood CR7 ....182 C2
Kensington Avenue Inf Sch
CR7 ....182 C2
Kensington Avenue Jun Sch
CR7 ....182 C2
Kensington & Chelsea Coll
SW10 ....136 A5 266 A4
W10 ....91 A2
Kensington Church Ct
W8 ....245 C1
Kensington Church St
W8 ....113 C5 245 B3
Kensington Church Wlk
W8 ....245 C1
Kensington Cl N11 ....31 A4
Kensington Court Mans
W8 ....245 D1
Kensington Court Mews
W8 ....255 D6
Kensington Court Pl
W8 ....113 D3 255 D6
Kensington Ct 2 NW7 ....27 B5
W8 ....113 D4 245 D1
Enfield EN2 ....5 C5
Kensington Ct Gdns
W8 ....255 D6
Kensington Dr IG8 ....37 D1
Kensington Gardens*
W2 ....114 A5 246 B3
Kensington Gate
W8 ....114 A3 256 A6
Kensington Gdns IG1 ....56 B1
Kensington Gdns Sq W2 ....91 D1
Kensington Gore
SW7 ....114 B4 246 C1
Kensington Hall Gdns
W14 ....254 C2
Kensington Hgts HA1 ....42 D3
Kensington High St
W8 ....113 C3 255 B6
Kensington Ho 3 NW5 ....71 C3
Kensington Hts W8 ....245 A3
Kensington Mall W8 ....245 B4
Kensington Mans SW5 ....255 B2
Kensington Olympia Sta
W14 ....113 A3 254 A6
Kensington Palace*
W8 ....113 D5 245 D3
Kensington Palace Gdns
W8 ....113 D5 245 C4
Kensington Park Gdns
W11 ....113 B6 244 D5
Kensington Park Mews
W11 ....91 B1
Kensington Park Rd
W11 ....113 B6 244 D6
Kensington Pl
W8 ....113 C5 245 A4
Kensington Prep Sch
SW6 ....135 B4 264 D2
Kensington Prim Sch
E12 ....78 B2
Kensington Rd
SW7 ....114 C4 246 B1
Northolt UB5 ....85 C5
Kensington Sports Ctr
W11 ....244 A6
Kensington Sq
W8 ....113 D4 245 C1
Kensington Terr CR2 ....221 B1
Kensington Village
W14 ....113 B2 254 D3
Kensington W W14 ....254 A4
Kensworth Ho EC1 ....235 D1
Kent Ave Bexley DA16 ....167 D6
Dagenham RM9 ....103 C3
Ealing W13 ....87 B2
Kent Cl
Mitcham CR4,SW16 ....204 A5
Orpington BR6 ....227 C2
Kent Ct 3 E2 ....95 D5
NW9 ....27 C1
Acton W3 ....88 B1
Kent Dr Cockfosters EN4 ....15 A6
Teddington TW11 ....174 C5
Kentford Way UB5 ....85 A6
Kent Gate Way CR0 ....223 D3
Kent Gdns Ealing W13 ....87 B2
Ruislip HA4 ....40 B3
Kent Ho SE1 ....263 D1
SW1 ....259 C1
13 W4 ....111 C1
Richmond TW10 ....154 C6
Kent House La BR3 ....185 A5
Kent House Rd BR3 ....185 A4
Kent House Sta BR3 ....185 A2
Kent House Station App
BR3 ....184 D2
Kentish Bldgs SE1 ....252 C3
Kentish Rd DA17 ....125 C2
Kentish Town CE Prim Sch
NW5 ....71 C3
Kentish Town Rd NW1 ....71 B2
Kentish Town Sta NW5 ....71 C3
Kentish Town West Sta
NW5 ....71 B2
Kentish Way BR1,BR2 ....209 B6
Kentlea Rd SE28 ....123 C4
Kent Lo 9 SW19 ....156 D3
Kentmere Ho SE15 ....140 C6
Kentmere Rd SE18 ....123 C2
Kenton Ave Harrow HA1 ....42 D2
Southall UB1 ....107 C6
Sunbury TW16 ....173 A1
Kenton Ct W14 ....254 C5
2 Forest Hill SE26 ....185 A6
Harrow HA3 ....43 B3
3 Richmond TW10 ....153 D5
Kenton Gdns HA3 ....43 C4
Kenton Ho 21 E1 ....96 C3
N5 ....72 C5
Kenton La Harrow HA3 ....24 D3
Harrow HA3 ....43 C6
Kenton Park Ave HA3 ....43 D5
Kenton Park Cl HA3 ....43 C4
Kenton Park Cres HA3 ....43 D5
Kenton Park Par HA3 ....43 D4
Kenton Park Rd HA3 ....43 C5
Kenton Rd E9 ....74 D2
Harrow HA3 ....43 C4
Kenton St WC1 ....240 A6
Kenton Sta HA3 ....43 B3
Kenton Way UB4 ....83 C4
Kent Pas NW1 ....237 C6
Kent Rd W4 ....111 A3
Dagenham RM10 ....81 D3
East Molesey KT8 ....196 A5
Kingston KT1 ....197 D6
Richmond TW9 ....132 C5
Southgate N21 ....17 B4
West Wickham BR4 ....207 D1
Kent St E13 ....99 B4
E2 ....95 D5
Kent Terr NW1 ....92 C4 230 B1
Kent Twr SE20 ....184 B3
Kent View Gdns IG3 ....79 C6
Kent Way KT6 ....214 B6
Kentwell Cl SE4 ....141 A1
Kentwode Gn SW13 ....134 A5
Kent Yard SW7 ....247 B1
Kenver Ave N12 ....30 B4
Kenward Rd SE9 ....165 D6
Ken Way HA9 ....67 A5
Kenway Rd SW5 ....113 D2 255 C3
Ken Wilson Ho 17 E2 ....96 A5
Kenwood EN1 ....17 C5
Kenwood Ave N14 ....15 D6

Kenwood Cl NW3 ...48 B1
Harmondsworth UB7 ...126 C6
Kenwood Ct NW9 ...45 A5
Kenwood Dr BR3 ...208 A6
Kenwood Gdns Ilford IG2 .56 C4
2 Wanstead E18 ...55 B6
Kenwood Ho★ NW3 ...48 C1
15 SW9 ...138 D1
Kenwood Rd N6 ...48 D3
Edmonton N9 ...18 A3
Kenworthy Rd E9 ...75 A2
Kenwrick Ho N1 ...233 D5
Kenwyn Dr NW2 ...67 D5
Kenwyn Rd SW4 ...137 D1
Wimbledon SW20 ...178 C2
Kenya Rd SE7 ...143 D5
Kenyngton Dr TW16 ...172 A5
Kenyngton Manor Prim Sch
TW16 ...172 A4
Kenyngton Pl HA3 ...43 C4
Kenyon Ho 31 SE5 ...139 A5
Kenyon St SW6 ...134 D4
Keogh Rd E15 ...76 D2
Kepler Ho 9 SE10 ...120 D1
Kepler Rd SW2,SW4 ...138 A1
Keppel Ho 5 SE8 ...119 B1
SW3 ...257 A3
Keppel Rd E6 ...100 B6
Dagenham RM9 ...81 A4
Keppel Row SE1 ...252 A3
Keppel St WC1 ...239 D4
Kerala Ct N17 ...33 D2
Kerbela St 2 E2 ...96 A3
Kerbey St E14 ...97 D1
Kerem Sch N2 ...48 B4
Kerfield Cres SE5 ...139 B4
Kerfield Pl SE5 ...139 B4
Kerridge Ct N1 ...73 C2
Kerrier Ho SW10 ...266 B3
Kerrington Ct 7 W12 ...112 C4
Kerrin Point SE11 ...261 A2
Kerrison Pl W5 ...109 D5
Kerrison Rd E15 ...98 B6
SW11 ...136 C2
Ealing W5 ...109 D5
Kerrison Villas W5 ...109 D5
Kerry N7 ...72 A2
Kerry Ave HA7 ...25 D6
Kerry Cl Newham E16 ...99 B1
Palmers Green N13 ...16 B2
Kerry Ct HA7 ...25 D6
Kerry Ho 5 E1 ...96 C1
Kerry Path SE8 ...141 B6
Kerry Rd SE8 ...141 B6
Kerscott Ho 30 E3 ...97 D4
Kersey Gdns SE9 ...188 A6
Kersfield Ho SW15 ...156 D5
Kersfield Rd SW15 ...156 D5
Kershaw Cl SW18 ...158 B5
Kershaw Ho 7 SE27 ...160 D1
Kershaw Rd RM10 ...81 C5
Kersley Mews SW11 ...267 C1
Kersley Rd N16 ...73 C5
Kersley St SW11 ...136 D3
Kerstin Cl UB3 ...105 D6
Kerswell Cl N15 ...51 C4
Kerwick Cl 1 N7 ...72 B1
Keslake Mans NW10 ...90 D5
Keslake Rd NW6 ...90 D5
Kessock Cl N17 ...52 B4
Kestlake Rd DA5 ...168 C5
Keston Ave BR2 ...225 C3
Keston CE Prim Sch
BR2 ...225 D3
Keston Cl Bexley DA16 ...146 C5
Edmonton N18 ...17 B1
Keston Ct DA5 ...169 B4
Keston Gdns BR2 ...225 C4
Keston Ho SE17 ...263 B2
Keston Mark BR2 ...226 A5
Keston Park Cl BR2 ...226 B5
Keston Rd N17 ...51 B5
SE15 ...140 A2
Thornton Heath CR7 ...204 C3
Kestral Ho EC1 ...235 A2
Kestrel Ave E6 ...100 A2
SE24 ...161 A6
Kestrel Cl NW10 ...67 B3
NW9 ...27 C1
Kingston KT2 ...175 D6
Kestrel Ct E17 ...34 D1
Ruislip HA4 ...61 B6
South Croydon CR2 ...221 A2
Kestrel Ho 4 SW11 ...136 C2
Enfield EN3 ...19 A6
Kestrel Pl SE14 ...141 A6
Kestrel Way UB3 ...105 B4
Keswick Ave
Kingston KT2,SW15 ...177 C5
Merton SW19 ...179 C1
Upper Halliford TW17 ...193 C6
Keswick Cl SM1 ...218 A4
Keswick Ct 2 SE22 ...162 A6
13 Catford SE6 ...164 D3
Keswick Dr EN3 ...6 C6
Keswick Gdns
Redbridge IG4 ...56 A5
Ruislip HA4 ...39 B3
Wembley HA9 ...66 A4
Keswick Ho 8 SE5 ...139 A4
Keswick Hts 9 SW15 ...157 A6
Keswick Lo E8 ...73 D2
Keswick Mews W5 ...110 A5
Keswick Rd BR6 ...211 D1
DA7 ...147 C4
Putney SW15 ...157 A6
Twickenham TW2 ...152 A5
Keswick Rd *continued*
West Wickham BR4 ...224 C6
Kettering Ct CR7 ...205 A5
Kettering Rd EN3 ...6 D6
Kettering St SW16 ...181 C4
Kett Gdns SW2 ...160 B6
Kettlebaston Rd E10 ...53 B1
Kettleby Ho SW9 ...138 D2
Kettlewell Cl N11 ...31 A4
Ketton Ho W10 ...90 C3
Kevan Ct 6 E17 ...53 A5
Kevan Ho SE5 ...139 A5
Kevelioc Rd N17 ...33 A2
Kevin Cl TW4 ...128 D3
Kevington Cl BR5 ...211 D5
Kevington Dr BR5,BR7 ...211 D5
Kew Bridge TW8 ...110 B1
Kew Bridge Ct 3 W4 ...110 C1
Kew Bridge Distribution Ctr
TW8 ...110 B1
Kew Bridge Rd TW8 ...110 B1
Kew Bridge Sta TW8 ...110 B1
Kew Bridge Steam Mus★
TW8 ...110 B1
Kew Cres SM3 ...217 B5
Kew Foot Rd TW9 ...132 A2
Kew Gardens Rd TW9 ...132 C4
Kew Gardens(Royal
Botanic)★ TW9 ...132 A4
Kew Gardens Sta TW9 ...132 C4
Kew Gn TW9 ...132 B6
Kew Green TW9 ...132 C6
Kew Lo 11 TW9 ...132 B4
Kew Obsy★ TW9 ...131 C2
Kew Palace★ TW9 ...132 A5
Kew Pier TW9 ...132 C6
Kew Rd N2 ...30 C2
Richmond TW9,W4 ...132 B4
Kew Ret Pk TW9 ...132 D4
Key Cl E1 ...96 B3
Keyes Ct SE22 ...162 A6
Keyes Rd NW2 ...68 D3
Keyham Ho 31 W2 ...91 C2
Key Ho 9 SE11 ...138 C6
Keymer Rd SW2 ...160 B2
Keynes Cl N2 ...48 D6
Keynes Ct 9 SE28 ...124 B6
Keynsham Ave IG8 ...36 C6
Keynsham Gdns SE9 ...166 A6
Keynsham Ho 2 N4 ...51 A2
Keynsham Rd SE9 ...166 A6
Cheam SM4 ...201 D1
Keynsham Wlk SM4 ...201 D1
Keyse Rd SE1 ...117 D3 263 C5
Keysham Ave TW5 ...128 A4
Keystone Cres N1 ...233 B3
Keywood Dr TW16 ...172 A4
Keyworth Cl E5 ...75 A4
Keyworth Pl SE1 ...261 D6
Keyworth Prim Sch
SE17 ...116 D1 261 C2
Keyworth St
SE1 ...116 D3 261 D6
Kezia St SE8 ...119 A1
Khalsa Ct N22 ...32 D2
Khama Rd SW17 ...180 C6
Khartoum Rd E13 ...99 B4
Ilford IG1 ...78 D3
Upper Tooting SW17 ...180 B6
Khyber Rd SW11 ...136 C3
Kibworth St
SW8 ...138 B5 270 C3
Kidbrooke Gdns SE3 ...143 A4
Kidbrooke Gr SE3 ...143 B4
Kidbrooke Interchange
SE3 ...143 C2
Kidbrooke La SE9 ...144 A1
Kidbrooke Park Cl SE3 ...143 B4
Kidbrooke Park Prim Sch
SE3 ...143 C4
Kidbrooke Park Rd
SE12,SE3 ...143 B2
Kidbrooke Sch SE3 ...143 D3
Kidbrooke Sta SE3 ...143 B2
Kidbrooke Way SE3 ...143 B3
Kiddens BR8 ...191 D1
Kidderminster Pl CR0 ...204 D1
Kidderminster Rd CR0 ...205 A2
Kidderpore Ave NW3 ...69 C4
Kidderpore Gdns NW3 ...69 C4
Kidd Ho RM9 ...81 B4
Kidd Pl SE7 ...122 A1
Kidlington Way NW9 ...27 C2
Kierbeck Bsns Complex
E16 ...121 B4
Kiffen St EC2 ...242 D6
Kilberry Cl TW7 ...130 B4
Kilbrennan Ho 8 E14 ...98 A1
Kilburn Bridge 14 NW6 ...91 C6
Kilburn Gate NW6 ...91 D5
Kilburn High Rd NW6 ...91 C6
Kilburn High Road Sta
NW6 ...91 D6
Kilburn Ho 13 W9 ...91 B4
Kilburn La W10 ...91 A5
Kilburn Park Jun Sch
NW6 ...91 B5
Kilburn Park Rd NW6 ...91 C4
Kilburn Park Sta NW6 ...91 C5
Kilburn Pl NW6 ...91 C6
Kilburn Priory NW6 ...91 D6
Kilburn Sq NW6 ...91 C6
Kilburn Sta NW2 ...69 B2
Kilburn Vale NW6 ...91 D6
Kilburn Vale Est 13 NW6 ...91 C6
Kildare Cl HA4 ...40 C1
Kildare Ct W2 ...91 C1
Kildare Gdns W2 ...91 C1
Kildare Rd E16 ...99 A2
Kildare Terr W2 ...91 C1
Kildare Wlk E14 ...97 C1
Kildoran Rd SW2 ...160 A6
Kildowan Rd IG3 ...58 A1
Kilgour Rd SE23 ...163 A5
Kilkie St SW6 ...136 A3
Killarney Rd SW18 ...158 A5
Killburns Mill Cl SM6 ...219 B6
Killearn Rd SE6 ...164 B3
Killester Gdns KT17,KT4 ...216 B4
Killick Ho SM1 ...217 D4
Killick St N1 ...94 B5 233 C3
Killieser Ave SW2 ...160 A2
Killigrew Ho TW16 ...171 C3
Killip Cl E16 ...98 D1
Killowen Ave UB5 ...64 A3
Killowen Rd E9 ...74 D2
Killross Rd TW14 ...149 B3
Killyon Rd SW8 ...137 C3
Kilmaine Rd
SW6 ...135 A5 264 B3
Kilmarnock Gdns RM8 ...80 C5
Kilmarnock Rd WD19 ...22 D6
Kilmarsh Rd W6 ...112 C2
Kilmartin Ave SW16 ...204 C6
Kilmartin Rd IG3 ...80 A6
Kilmington Rd SW13 ...134 A6
Kilmiston Ave TW17 ...193 A3
Kilmiston Ho TW17 ...193 A3
Kilmore Ho 17 E14 ...97 D1
Kilmorey Gdns TW1 ...131 B1
Kilmorey Rd TW1 ...131 B1
Kilmorie Prim Sch SE23 .163 A2
Kilmorie Rd SE23 ...163 A2
Kilmuir Ho SW1 ...258 B3
Kiln Cl UB3 ...127 B6
Kiln Ct E14 ...119 B6
Kilner Ho 3 SE11 ...138 C6
Kilner St E14 ...97 C2
Kiln Mews SW17 ...180 B5
Kiln Pl NW5 ...71 A3
Kilnside KT10 ...213 A1
Kiloh Ct 1 SW11 ...136 C2
Kilpatrick Ct N16 ...51 D1
Kilpatrick Way UB4 ...85 A2
Kilpeck Ho 3 N4 ...51 A2
Kilravock Ho SE25 ...205 C6
Kilravock St W10 ...91 A4
Kilronan 5 W3 ...89 B1
Kilross Rd TW14 ...149 C3
Kilsby Wlk RM9 ...80 B2
Kilsha Rd KT12 ...194 C3
Kilvinton Dr EN2 ...5 B5
Kimbell Gdns
SW6 ...135 A4 264 A1
Kimbell Pl SE9 ...143 C1
Kimber Ctr The SW18 ...157 C4
Kimber Ho 11 SE18 ...144 D6
Kimberley Ave E6 ...100 A5
SE15 ...140 C2
Ilford IG2 ...57 C2
Kimberley Dr DA14 ...168 D2
Kimberley Gate 2 BR1 ...186 D3
Kimberley Gdns N4 ...50 D4
Enfield EN1 ...5 D2
Kimberley Ho 7 E14 ...120 A3
Kimberley Ind Est E17 ...35 B2
Kimberley Rd E11 ...76 B6
E16 ...98 D3
E17 ...35 B2
NW6 ...91 A6
SW9 ...138 A2
Chingford, Chingford Green
E4 ...20 C3
Edmonton N18 ...34 B4
Penge BR3 ...184 D1
Thornton Heath CR0 ...204 D3
Tottenham N17 ...34 A1
Kimberley Way E4 ...20 C3
Kimberley Wlk KT12 ...194 B2
Kimber Rd SW18 ...157 D4
Kimble Cres WD23 ...8 A4
Kimble Ho 1 N7 ...72 A3
NW8 ...237 B6
Kimble Rd
Mitcham SW17 ...180 B4
Upper Tooting SW17 ...180 B5
Kimbolton Cl SE12 ...164 D5
Kimbolton Row SW3 ...257 A3
Kimmeridge Gdns 3
SE9 ...188 A6
Kimmeridge Rd SE9 ...188 A6
Kimm Ho 10 E17 ...53 D6
Kimpton Ct 12 SE5 ...139 B4
Kimpton Ho SW15 ...156 A4
Kimpton Link Bsns Ctr
SM3 ...217 B6
Kimpton Rd SE5 ...139 B4
Cheam SM3 ...217 B6
Kimpton Trade & Bsns Ctr
SM3 ...217 B6
Kinburn St SE16 ...118 D4
Kincaid Rd SE15 ...140 B5
Kincardine Gdns W9 ...91 C3
Kinch Gr HA3,HA9 ...44 B2
Kincraig BR7 ...188 C2
Kindell Ho 4 SW14 ...133 B2
Kinder Cl SE28 ...124 D6
Kinder Ho N1 ...235 D4
Kindersley Ho 27 E1 ...96 A1
Kinder St 9 E1 ...96 B1
Kinefold Ho N7 ...72 A2
Kinetic Cres EN3 ...7 B6
Kinfauns Rd Ilford IG3 ...58 A2
Streatham SW2 ...160 C2
King Alfred Ave SE6 ...185 C6
King Alfred Sch NW11 ...47 D1
King Arthur Cl SE15 ...140 C5
King Athelstan Prim Sch
KT1 ...198 B6
King Charles Cres KT5 ..198 B2
King Charles Ho SW6 ...265 D4
King Charles' Rd KT5,
KT6 ...198 B3
King Charles St
SW1 ...116 A4 250 A2
King Charles Wlk 6
SW19 ...157 A3
King Ct 15 E10 ...53 D2
Kingcup Cl CR0 ...206 D1
King David La E1 ...118 C6
Kingdon Ho 8 E14 ...120 A3
Kingdon Rd NW6 ...69 C2
King Edward Dr KT6 ...214 A5
King Edward Mans 12 E8 .96 B6
King Edward Mews
SW13 ...134 A4
King Edward Rd E10 ...54 A1
E17 ...53 A6
Barnet EN5 ...1 D1
King Edward's Gdns
W3 ...110 C5
King Edward's Gr TW11 .175 C4
King Edwards Mans
SW6 ...265 A3
King Edward's Rd E9 ...96 C6
Barking IG11 ...101 B5
Edmonton N9 ...18 B4
Enfield EN3 ...6 D1
Ruislip HA4 ...39 B1
King Edward St EC1 ...242 A2
King Edward The Third Mews
8 SE16 ...118 B4
King Edward Wlk
SE1 ...116 C3 261 B6
King Fahad Acad The
W5 ...109 C2
King Fahed Acad W3 ...111 D6
Kingfield Rd W5 ...87 D3
Kingfield St E14 ...120 A2
Kingfisher Ave E11 ...55 B3
Kingfisher Cl Harrow HA3 .24 D3
Woolwich SE28 ...124 C6
Kingfisher Ct 12 E14 ...120 A4
11 SW11 ...136 C2
Cheam SM1 ...217 B3
East Molesey KT8 ...196 C5
Enfield EN2 ...4 B5
Hounslow TW3 ...151 D6
Merton SW19 ...179 B3
Putney SW19 ...157 A2
Kingfisher Dr TW10 ...175 B6
Kingfisher Ho SE15 ...139 D4
W14 ...254 C6
Kingfisher Lo TW11 ...175 A6
Kingfisher Mews SE13 ..163 D6
Kingfisher Sports Ctr The 12
KT1 ...176 A1
Kingfisher Sq 19 SE8 ...141 B6
Kingfisher St E6 ...100 A2
Kingfisher Way NW10 ...67 B3
Croydon CR0 ...206 D4
Kingfisher Wlk NW9 ...27 C1
King Frederick IX Ct
SE16 ...119 B3
King Garth Mews SE23 ..162 C2
King Gdns CR0 ...220 D3
King George Ave E16 ...99 D1
Ilford IG2 ...57 B3
Walton-on-T KT12 ...194 D1
King George Cl TW16 ...171 C5
King George Hospl IG3 ...58 A4
King George Sq TW10 ...154 B5
King George St SE10 ...142 A5
King George's Trad Est
KT9 ...214 C4
King George VI Ave
CR4 ...202 D5
Kingham Cl 3 W11 ...112 D4
Wandsworth SW18 ...158 A4
King Harolds Way DA7 ..147 A5
King Henry Mews 7
BR6 ...227 D3
King Henry's Mews EN3 ...7 C6
King Henry's Rd NW3 ...70 C1
Kingston KT1,KT3 ...198 D6
King Henry's Reach W6 .134 C6
King Henry St N16 ...73 C3
King Henry's Wlk N1 ...73 C2
King Henry's Yd 5 N16 ...73 C3
King Ho W12 ...90 B1
Kinghorn St EC1 ...242 A3
King James St
SE1 ...116 D4 251 D1
King John Ct EC2 ...243 B6
King John St E1 ...96 D2
King John's Wlk SE9 ...166 A5
Kinglake St
SE17 ...117 C1 263 B2
Kingly Ct W1 ...249 B6
Kingly St W1 ...115 C6 249 A6
King & Queen Cl 4
SE9 ...188 A6
King & Queen St
SE17 ...117 A1 262 B2
Kingsand Rd SE12 ...165 A2
Kings Arbour UB2 ...107 A1
King's Arms Ct 22 E1 ...96 A2
King's Arms Yd EC2 ...242 C2
Kingsash Dr UB4 ...85 A3
Kings Ave N10 ...49 A6
SW4 ...160 A5
Bromley BR1 ...186 D4
Dagenham RM6 ...59 B3
Ealing W5 ...87 D1
New Malden KT3 ...199 D5
Wallington SM5 ...218 D1
King's Ave Ashford TW16 .171 D4
Buckhurst Hill IG9 ...21 D2
Hounslow TW3,TW5 ...129 D4
Southall UB1 ...85 D1
King's Ave *continued*
Southgate N21 ...16 D3
Woodford IG8 ...37 C5
Kings Avenue Sch SW4 .160 A6
King's Bench St
SE1 ...116 D4 251 D2
King's Bench Wlk EC4 ...241 B1
Kingsbridge N16 ...51 B1
Kingsbridge Ave W3 ...110 B4
Kingsbridge Cres UB1 ...85 B2
Kingsbridge Ct E14 ...119 C2
Edmonton N21 ...16 D2
Kingsbridge Ho 10 SE20 .184 B2
Kingsbridge Ind Est
IG11 ...101 C4
Kingsbridge Rd W10 ...90 C1
Barking IG11 ...101 B5
Southall UB2 ...107 B2
Walton-on-T KT12 ...194 B2
West Barnes SM4 ...200 D2
Kingsbridge Way UB4 ...83 C4
Kingsbury Green Prim Sch
NW9 ...44 D4
Kingsbury High Sch Annexe
NW9 ...44 D5
Kingsbury Rd N1 ...73 C2
NW9 ...44 D4
Kingsbury Sta NW9 ...44 C4
Kingsbury Terr N1 ...73 C2
Kingsbury Trad Est NW9 ..45 B3
Kings Chace View EN2 ...4 C3
Kings Chase KT8 ...196 A6
Kings Cl NW4 ...46 D5
King's Cl E10 ...53 D2
Kings Cl KT12 ...194 B1
King's Cl KT7 ...197 A2
Kingsclere Cl SW15 ...156 A4
Kingsclere Ct N12 ...30 C5
New Barnet EN5 ...14 A6
Kingsclere Pl EN2 ...5 A3
Kingscliffe Gdns SW19 ...157 B3
King's Coll SE24 ...161 B5
WC2 ...116 B6 250 D6
Kings College Ct NW3 ...70 C1
King's College Hospl
SE5 ...139 B3
King's College London
NW3 ...69 C4
Kings College Rd NW3 ...70 B1
Ruislip HA4 ...39 D3
Kings Coll London W8 ...245 A2
Kings Coll London (Chelsea
Campus) SW3 ..114 C1 257 A1
King's Coll Sch SW19 ...178 D4
Kingscote NW11 ...47 B1
Kingscote Rd W4 ...111 B3
Croydon CR0 ...206 B2
Kingston KT3 ...199 B6
Kingscote St EC4 ...251 C6
King's Court N SW3 ...257 A1
Kingscourt Rd SW16 ...160 A1
King's Court S SW3 ...257 A1
King's Cres N4,N5 ...73 A5
Kingscroft SW4 ...160 A5
Kingscroft Rd NW2 ...69 B2
King's Cross WC1 .94 A4 233 B2
King's Cross Bridge
WC1 ...233 B2
King's Cross Rd
WC1 ...94 B4 233 D1
King's Cross Sta
N1 ...94 A5 233 B2
King's Cross, St Pancras
N1 ...233 A2
King's Cross (Thames Link)
Sta WC1 ...233 B2
Kings Ct E13 ...99 B6
HA9 ...66 D6
6 N7 ...72 B1
NW8 ...230 C5
SE22 ...140 A1
W6 ...112 A2
2 Buckhurst Hill IG9 ...21 D2
16 Kingston KT2 ...176 C3
10 Putney SW15 ...156 A4
3 Wallington SM6 ...219 B2
King's Ct Beckenham BR3 .207 D6
9 Ealing W5 ...87 C2
Wimbledon SW19 ...179 C4
Kingsdale Gdns W11 ...112 D5
Kingsdale Rd SE18 ...145 D6
Penge SE20 ...184 D3
Kingsdale Sec Sch
SE21 ...161 C1
Kingsdown 1 SW19 ...178 D3
Kingsdown Ave W13 ...109 B4
W3 ...111 C6
Kingsdown Cl 26 SE16 ...118 B1
W10 ...90 D1
11 W11 ...91 A1
Kingsdown Ct SW11 ...158 C5
Kingsdowne Rd KT6 ...198 B2
Kingsdown Ho 1 E8 ...74 A3
Kingsdown Rd E11 ...76 C5
3 N19 ...72 A6
Cheam SM3 ...217 A3
Kingsdown Way BR2 ...209 A3
Kings Dr HA9 ...66 D6
Edgware HA8 ...26 B6
Surbiton KT5 ...198 C3
King's Dr KT7 ...197 B2
Kingsend HA4 ...39 C1
Kings Farm E17 ...35 D2
Kings Farm Ave TW10 ...132 C1
Kingsfield Ave HA1,HA2 ...42 A4
Kingsfield Ho 18 N16 ...73 C5
SE9 ...165 D1
Kingsfield Rd HA1 ...42 B2
Kingsford Com Sch E13 ..99 C3
Newham E6 ...100 B1
Kingsford St NW5 ...70 D3
Kingsford Way E6 ...100 B2
Kingsgate HA9 ...67 A5
Kingsgate Ave N3 ...47 C6
Kingsgate Bsns Ctr KT2 .176 A2
Kingsgate Cl BR5 ...190 C1
DA7 ...147 A4
Kingsgate Est N1 ...73 C2
Kingsgate Ho 29 SW9 ...138 C4
Kingsgate Pl NW6 ...69 C1
Kingsgate Prim Sch
NW6 ...69 C1
Kingsgate Rd NW6 ...69 C1
Kingston KT2 ...176 A2
Kings Gdns 6 NW6 ...69 C1
Kings Gdns IG1 ...57 B1
King's Gr SE15 ...140 B4
SE15 ...140 B5
Kings Grange HA4 ...39 D1
Kingsground SE9 ...166 A5
Kings Hall Mews SE13 ...142 A2
Kings Hall Rd BR3 ...185 A2
Kings Head Hill E4 ...19 D4
King's Head Yd SE1 ...252 C3
King's Highway SE18,
SE2 ...145 D6
Kingshill SE17 ...262 B4
Kingshill Ave Harrow HA3 .43 B5
Hayes UB4 ...83 D4
New Malden KT4 ...200 B2
Northolt UB5 ...84 B4
Kingshill Ct 6 EN5 ...1 A1
Kingshill Dr HA3 ...43 B6
Kings Ho 19 E14 ...119 B6
SW8 ...270 B4
Kingshold Rd E9 ...74 C1
Kingsholm Gdns SE9 ...144 A1
King's House Jun Sch
TW10 ...154 B6
King's House Prep Sch
TW10 ...154 B6
Kingshurst Rd SE12 ...165 A4
Kings Keep KT6 ...198 A5
Kings Keep 6 SW15 ...156 D6
King's La SM1,SM2 ...218 B3
Kingsland NW8 ...92 C6 230 B5
Kingsland Gn 1 E8,N1 ...73 C2
Kingsland High St E8 ...73 D3
Kingsland Pas 2 E8 ...73 C2
Kingsland Rd E13 ...99 C4
E2 ...95 C5
Kingsland Sch E8 ...73 D3
Kingsland Sh Ctr E8 ...73 D2
Kingslawn Cl SW15 ...156 B6
Kingslee Ct 12 SM2 ...217 D1
Kingsleigh Pl CR4 ...202 D6
Kingsleigh Wlk BR2 ...208 D5
Kingsley Ave Ealing W13 ...87 A1
Hounslow TW3 ...130 A3
Southall UB1 ...107 C6
Sutton SM1 ...218 B4
Kingsley Cl N2 ...48 A4
Dagenham RM10 ...81 D4
Kingsley Ct E11 ...54 D3
NW2 ...68 B2
1 SE28 ...124 C5
Bexley DA6 ...147 C1
Edgware HA8 ...10 D2
Wood Green N22 ...32 B3
2 Worcester Park KT4 ...215 D6
Kingsley Dr 1 KT4 ...215 D6
Kingsley Flats SE1 ...263 B3
Kingsley Gdns E4 ...35 C5
Kingsley Grange 1 E11 ...55 A4
Kingsley Ho NW11 ...48 A3
SW3 ...266 D5
3 SW4 ...137 D3
8 Kingston KT6 ...198 A4
Kingsley Mews BR7 ...188 D4
W8 ...255 D5
Dagenham RM9 ...80 D4
Kingsley Pl N6 ...49 A2
Kingsley Prim Sch CR9 .204 C1
Kingsley Rd E7 ...77 A1
NW6 ...91 B6
Chingford E17 ...36 A1
Edmonton N13 ...32 D6
Harrow HA2 ...64 A5
Hounslow TW3 ...130 A3
Orpington BR6 ...227 D1
Pinner HA5 ...41 B5
Thornton Heath CR0 ...204 C1
Wimbledon SW19 ...179 D5
Kingsley St SW11 ...136 D2
Kingsley Way N2 ...48 A4
Kingsley Wood Dr SE9 ..166 B1
Kings Lo HA4 ...39 C1
Kingslyn Cres SE19 ...183 C2
Kings Mall W6 ...112 C2
Kingsman Par SE18 ...122 B3
King's Mans SW3 ...267 A5
Kingsman St SE18 ...122 B2
Kingsmead Barnet EN5 ...1 C1
Richmond TW10 ...154 B5
Kingsmead Ave NW9 ...45 B2
Edmonton N9 ...18 B3
Mitcham CR4 ...203 C6
North Cheam KT4 ...216 B5
Sunbury TW16 ...172 C1
Tolworth KT6 ...214 C6
Kingsmead Cl DA15 ...168 A2
Teddington TW11 ...175 B4
West Ewell KT19 ...215 B1
Kingsmead Ct N6 ...49 D2
Bromley BR1 ...186 D3
Kingsmead Dr UB5 ...63 B1
Kingsmead Ho E9 ...75 A4
Kingsmead Lo
9 Chingford E4 ...20 A2
Sutton SM2 ...218 B2

Kings Mead Pk KT10 ...212 C1
Kingsmead Prim Sch E9 .75 A4
Kingsmead Rd SW2 ...160 C2
Kingsmead Sch EN1 ...6 A2
Kingsmead Way E5,E9 ...75 A4
Kingsmere BR7 ...188 A2
Catford SE6 ...163 D3
Kingsmere Cl SW15 ...134 D2
Kingsmere Ct NW9 ...44 D1
Kingsmere Pk NW9 ...45 A1
Kingsmere Pl N16 ...51 B1
Kingsmere Rd SW19 ...156 D2
King's Mews 1 SW4 ...160 A6
WC1 ...94 B3 240 D5
Kingsmill NW8 ...92 B5 229 D4
Kingsmill Bsns Pk KT1 ..198 B6
Kingsmill Gdns RM9 ...81 B3
Kingsmill Rd RM9 ...81 B3
Kingsmill Terr
NW8 ...92 B5 229 D4
Kingsnorth Ho 12 W10 ...90 D1
Kingsnympton Pk KT2 ..176 D4
Kings Oak RM7 ...59 C6
Kings Oak Hospl (Private)
The EN2 ...4 C5
King's Orch SE9 ...166 A5
King's Paddock TW12 ..174 A2
King's Par W12 ...112 A3
Willesden NW10 ...90 C6
Kingspark Ct E18 ...55 A6
King's Pas KT2 ...175 D2
King's Pl SE1 ...252 A1
Kings Pl Acton W4 ...111 A2
Buckhurst Hill IG9 ...21 D2
Loughton IG10 ...21 D4
King Sq EC1 ...95 A4 235 A1
King's Quay SW10 ...266 B2
Kings Rd BR6 ...227 D4
NW10 ...68 B1
King's Rd E11 ...54 C2
E6 ...99 C6
SW10 ...136 B6 266 C5
SW3 ...257 B1
Kings Rd Ealing W5 ...87 D2
Feltham TW13 ...150 C3
Harrow HA2 ...63 B6
Mitcham CR4 ...203 A6
Richmond TW10,TW9 ...154 B6
Walton-on-T KT12 ...194 B1
West Drayton UB7 ...104 B4
Wood Green N22 ...32 B2
King's Rd Barking IG11 ...79 A1
Chingford E4 ...20 B3
Edmonton N18 ...34 A6
Kingston KT2 ...176 B3
Long Ditton KT6 ...197 C1
Mortlake SW14 ...133 B2
South Norwood SE25 ...206 A6
Teddington TW11,TW12 ...174 B5
Tottenham N17 ...33 D2
Twickenham TW1 ...153 B5
Wimbledon SW19 ...179 C4
Kings Ride Gate TW10 ..132 C1
Kingsridge SW19 ...157 A2
Kings Road Bglws HA2 ...63 B5
King's Scholars' Pas
SW1 ...259 A4
King St E13 ...98 D3
E13 ...99 A3
EC2 ...95 A1 242 B1
N2 ...48 B6
SW1 ...115 C5 249 B4
W3 ...111 A5
W6 ...112 A2
WC2 ...250 A6
Richmond TW9 ...153 D6
Southall UB2 ...107 A3
Tottenham N17 ...33 D2
Twickenham TW1 ...153 A3
King Stairs Cl SE16 ...118 B4
King's Terr NW1 ...93 C6 232 A5
8 Isleworth TW7 ...131 A2
Kingsthorpe Rd SE26 ...184 D6
Kingston Ave
Cheam SM3 ...217 A5
Feltham TW14 ...149 D5
Yiewsley UB7 ...104 B6
Kingston Bsns Ctr KT9 ..214 B5
Kingston By-Pass KT6,
KT7,KT9 ...213 C5
Kingston By - Pass KT6 .214 C5
Kingston Cl
Dagenham RM6 ...59 A6
Northolt UB5 ...85 B6
Teddington TW11 ...175 B4
Kingston Coll of F Ed
KT1 ...197 D6
Kingston Coll of F Ed (M V
Annex) KT2 ...176 A2
Kingston Cres BR3 ...185 B2
Kingston Gdns CR0 ...220 A5
Kingston Gram Sch KT2 .176 B1
Kingston Hall Rd KT1 ...197 D6
Kingston Hill KT2 ...177 A5
Kingston Hill Ave RM6 ...59 A6
Kingston Hill Pl KT2,
TW10 ...177 A6
Kingston Ho 2 NW6 ...69 A1
Kingston Ho E SW7 ...247 A1
Kingston Ho N SW7 ...247 A1
Kingston Ho S SW7 ...247 A1
Kingston Hospl KT2 ...176 D2
Kingston House Estate
KT6 ...197 B3
Kingston La
Teddington TW11 ...175 B4
Uxbridge UB8 ...82 A4
West Drayton UB7 ...104 B4
Kingston Lo 2 KT3 ...199 C5
Kingston Mus KT1 ...176 A1
Kingston Pl HA3 ...24 D3
Kingston Rd SW15,SW19 .156 B3
Ashford TW15 ...170 A4
Ashford TW15,TW17 ...170 B4
Edmonton N9 ...18 A2
Ilford IG1 ...79 A4
Kingston KT1,KT3 ...199 A5
Merton SW19,SW20 ...179 B1
New Barnet EN4 ...14 B6
Southall UB2 ...107 B4
Teddington TW11 ...175 B4
Ewell KT17 ...215 D1
Kingston Sq SE19 ...183 B5
Kingston Sta KT2 ...176 A2
Kingston Univ
Kingston KT1 ...198 A6
Kingston KT2 ...177 B5
Kingston Univ Annex
KT1 ...176 B1
Kingston Univ Roehampton
Vale Ctr SW15 ...155 D1
Kingston Vale SW15 ...155 C1
Kingstown St
NW1 ...93 A6 231 A6
King Street Cloisters 8
W6 ...112 B2
King Street Coll W12 ...112 C4
W6 ...112 C2
King Street Par 6 TW1 .153 A3
Kings View Ct 1 SW20 .178 D3
Kingswater Pl SW11 ...267 A3
Kingsway BR5 ...211 B4
N12 ...30 A4
WC2 ...94 B1 240 C2
Coney Hall BR4 ...224 D5
Enfield EN3 ...18 B6
Hayes UB3 ...83 A2
Mortlake SW14,TW9 ...132 D2
Stanwell TW19 ...148 A3
Wembley HA9 ...66 A4
West Barnes KT3 ...200 C4
Woodford IG8 ...37 C5
Kings Way Croydon CR0 ..220 B3
Harrow HA1 ...42 C5
Kingsway Bsns Pk
TW12 ...173 B2
Kingsway Coll NW5 ...71 B2
Kingsway Cres HA2 ...42 A5
Kingsway Est N18 ...34 D4
Kingsway Pl EC1 ...241 C6
Kingsway Rd SM3 ...217 A1
Kingswear Ho 5 SE23 ..162 C2
Kingswear Rd NW5 ...71 B5
Ruislip HA4 ...62 A6
Kingswood 32 E2 ...96 C5
Kingswood Ave DA17 ...125 B2
NW6 ...91 A5
Beckenham BR2,BR3 ...208 C5
Hampton TW12 ...173 D4
Hounslow TW3,TW5 ...129 B3
Thornton Heath CR7 ...204 C4
Kingswood Cl BR6 ...211 B2
N20 ...14 A4
SW8 ...270 B3
Enfield EN1 ...17 D6
New Malden KT3 ...199 D3
Surbiton KT6 ...198 A2
Kings Wood Ct 4 NW6 ...69 C1
Kingswood Ct
Chingford E4 ...35 C5
7 Richmond TW10 ...154 B6
Kingswood Dr
Carshalton SM5 ...202 D1
Dulwich SE19,SE21 ...183 D6
Kingswood Ho 8 KT2 ...176 D4
Kingswood Pk N3 ...29 B1
Kingswood Pl SE13 ...142 C1
Kingswood Prim Sch
SE27 ...183 B5
Kingswood Rd E11 ...54 C2
W4 ...111 A3
Beckenham BR2 ...208 C6
Ilford IG3 ...58 A2
Merton SW19 ...179 B2
Penge SE20 ...184 C4
Streatham SW2 ...160 A4
Kingswood Terr W4 ...111 A3
Kingswood Way SM6 ...220 A3
Kingsworth Cl BR3 ...207 A4
Kingsworthy Cl KT1 ...198 B6
Kings Yd E15 ...75 C2
Kingthorpe Rd NW10 ...67 B1
Kingthorpe Terr 1
NW10 ...67 B1
Kington Ho 10 NW6 ...91 D6
Kingward Ho E1 ...96 A2
Kingwell Rd EN4 ...2 B5
King William IV Gdns
SE20 ...184 C4
King William La 3
SE10 ...120 C1
King William St
EC4 ...117 B6 252 D6
King William Wlk SE10 ..142 A6
Kingwood Rd
SW6 ...135 A5 264 A3
Kinlet Rd SE18 ...145 A4
Kinloch Dr NW9 ...45 C2
Kinloch St N7 ...72 B5
Kinloss Ct NW3 ...47 B5
Kinloss Gdns NW3 ...47 B5
Kinloss Rd SM5 ...202 A2
Kinnaird Ave
Bromley BR1 ...186 D4
Chiswick W4 ...133 A5
Kinnaird Cl BR1 ...186 D4
Kinnear Ct 2 SW20 ...178 D2
Kinnear Rd W12 ...111 D4
Kinnerton Pl N SW1 ...247 D1
Kinnerton Pl S SW1 ...247 D1
Kinnerton St
SW1 ...115 A4 248 A1
Kinnerton Yd SW1 ...248 A1
Kinnoull Mans 10 E5 ...74 B4
Kinnoul Rd W6 ..135 A6 264 A6
Kinross Ave KT4 ...216 A6
Kinross Cl Ashford TW16 .171 D5
Harrow HA3 ...44 B4
Kinross Ct 1 SE6 ...164 D2
Kinross Dr TW16 ...171 D5
Kinross Ho N1 ...233 C6
Kinross Terr E17 ...35 B1
Kinsale Rd SE15 ...140 A2
Kinsella Gdns SW19 ...178 B5
Kinsey Ho SE21 ...183 C6
Kinsham Ho 4 E2 ...96 A3
Kintore Way SE1 ...263 C4
Kintyre Cl SW16 ...204 B6
Kintyre Ct 17 SW2 ...160 A4
Kinveachy Gdns SE7 ...122 A1
Kinver Ho N4 ...51 B2
Kinver Rd SE26 ...184 C6
Kipling Ct W7 ...108 D6
Kipling Dr SW17 ...180 B4
Kipling Ho 29 SE5 ...139 A5
Kipling Pl HA7 ...24 D4
Kipling Rd DA7 ...147 A4
Kipling St SE1 ...117 B4 252 D2
Kipling Terr N9 ...17 B2
Kipling Twr 3 W3 ...111 A3
Kippington Dr SE9 ...165 D3
Kirby Cl KT19 ...215 D3
Kirby Est SE16 ...118 B3
Kirby Gr SE1 ...117 C4 253 A2
Kirby St EC1 ...94 C2 241 B4
Kirby Way KT12 ...194 C3
Kirchen Rd W13 ...109 B6
Kirkby Cl N11 ...31 A4
Kirkdale SE26 ...162 B1
Kirkdale Rd E11 ...54 C2
Kirkeby Bldg EC1 ...241 A4
Kirkfield Cl W13 ...109 B5
Kirkham Rd E6 ...100 A1
Kirkham St SE18 ...145 C6
Kirk La SE18 ...145 A6
Kirkland Cl DA15 ...167 C5
Kirkland Dr EN2 ...5 A4
Kirkland Wlk 4 E8 ...73 D2
Kirkleas Rd KT6 ...198 A1
Kirklees Rd
Dagenham RM8 ...80 C3
Thornton Heath CR7 ...204 C4
Kirkley Ho N16 ...51 C1
Kirkley Rd SW19 ...179 C2
Kirkman Pl W1 ...239 C3
Kirkmichael Rd E14 ...98 A1
Kirk Rd E17 ...53 B3
Kirk Rise SM1 ...217 D5
Kirkside Rd SE3 ...143 A6
Kirk's Pl E3 ...97 B2
Kirkstall Ave N17 ...51 B5
Kirkstall Gdns SW2 ...160 A3
Kirkstall Ho SW1 ...258 C2
Kirkstall Rd SW2 ...160 A3
Kirkstead Ct E5 ...75 A4
Kirksted Rd SM4 ...201 D1
Kirkstone NW1 ...232 A2
Kirkstone Way BR1 ...186 C3
Kirkton Lo SW18 ...157 D5
Kirkton Rd N15 ...51 C5
Kirkwall Pl E2 ...96 C4
Kirkwood Rd SE15 ...140 B3
Kirn Rd W13 ...109 B6
Kirrane Cl KT3 ...199 D4
Kirtley Ho SW8 ...269 B2
Kirtley Rd SE26 ...185 A6
Kirtling St SW8 ..137 C5 269 A4
Kirton Cl W4 ...111 B2
Kirton Rd E13 ...99 C5
Kirton Wlk HA8 ...27 A3
Kirwin Way SE5 ...138 D5
Kisharon Day Sch NW11 ..47 B3
Kitcat Terr E3 ...97 C4
Kitchener Rd E7 ...77 B2
N17 ...51 C6
N2 ...48 C6
Chingford, Highams Park
E17 ...35 D2
Dagenham RM10 ...81 D2
South Norwood CR7 ...205 B6
Kite Ho 5 SW11 ...136 C2
Kitley Gdns SE19 ...183 D2
Kitson Rd SE5 ...139 A5
Barnes SW13 ...134 A4
Kittiwake Ct 26 SE8 ...141 B6
Kittiwake Pl SM1 ...217 B3
Kittiwake Rd UB5 ...84 D4
Kittiwake Way UB4 ...84 D2
Kitto Rd SE14 ...140 D3
Kitt's End Rd EN5 ...1 A6
Kiver Rd N19 ...72 A6
Klea Ave SW4 ...159 C5
Kleffens Ct 2 SE3 ...142 D5
Knaggs Ho 1 TW11 ...174 C5
Knapdale Cl SE23 ...162 B2
Knapmill Rd SE6 ...163 D2
Knapmill Way SE6 ...163 D2
Knapp Cl NW10 ...67 C2
Knapp Rd Ashford TW15 ..170 B6
Bow E3 ...97 C3
Knapton Mews SW17 ...181 A4
Knaresborough Dr
SW18 ...157 D3
Knaresborough Ho 4
N4 ...51 A2
Knaresborough Pl
SW5 ...113 D2 255 C4
Knatchbull Rd NW10 ...89 B6
SE5 ...138 D4
Knebworth Ave E17 ...35 C2
Knebworth Ho 2 N16 ...73 C4
SW8 ...269 D1
Chingford E17 ...35 C2
Knebworth Rd 3 N16 ...73 C4
Knee Hill SE2 ...124 C1
Knee Hill Cres SE2 ...124 C2
Kneller Gdns TW7 ...152 B5
Kneller Ho 9 SW8 ...137 D3
4 Northolt UB5 ...84 D5
Kneller Rd SE4 ...141 A1
Isleworth TW2 ...152 B5
New Malden KT3 ...199 C2
Knight Cl RM8 ...80 C6
Knight Ct N15 ...51 C4
1 Chingford E4 ...20 A3
Knighten St E1 ...118 B5
Knighthead Point E14 ...119 C4
Knight Ho SE17 ...263 A3
Knightland Ho E5 ...74 B6
Knightland Rd E5 ...74 B6
Knightleas Ct NW2 ...68 C2
Knighton Cl
Croydon CR2 ...220 D1
Woodford IG8 ...37 B6
Knighton Dr IG8 ...37 B6
Knighton Gn IG9 ...21 B2
Knighton La IG9 ...21 B2
Knighton Park Rd SE26 .184 D5
Knighton Rd E7 ...77 A4
Knightrider Ct EC4 ...252 A6
Knightrider St EC4 ...251 D6
Knights Arc SW1 ...247 C1
Knight's Ave W5 ...110 A4
Knightsbridge
SW1,SW7 ...114 D4 247 C1
Knightsbridge Ct SW1 ..247 D1
Knightsbridge Gn SW1 ..247 C1
Knightsbridge Mews
BR7 ...188 B3
Knights Cl E9 ...74 C3
Knights Ct Bushey WD23 ...8 B4
Kingston KT1 ...198 A6
Penge BR3 ...185 A2
Knightshayes Ho NW4 ...28 D1
Knight's Hill SE19,SE27 ..182 D6
Knight's Hill Sq SE27 ...182 D6
Knights Ho SE1 ...253 C2
SW5 ...254 C2
SW8 ...270 B3
Knight's Ho SW10 ...266 A4
Knight's La N9 ...18 A1
Knight's Pk KT1 ...198 A6
Knight's Pl TW2 ...152 C3
Knights Rd Newham E16 .121 A4
Stanmore HA7 ...25 C6
Knight's Wlk SE11 ...261 C3
Knightswood Cl HA8 ...11 A2
Knightswood Ct N6 ...49 D2
Knightswood Ho N12 ...30 A4
Knightwood Cres KT3 ...199 C3
Knivet Rd SW6 ...265 A5
Knobs Hill Rd E15 ...97 D6
Knockholt Rd SE9 ...165 D6
Knole Cl CR0 ...206 C3
Knole Ct UB5 ...84 C4
Knole Gate DA15 ...167 C1
Knole The SE9 ...188 C6
Knoll Ct BR6 ...227 D6
Dulwich SE19 ...183 D5
Knoll Dr N14 ...15 A4
Knoll Ho NW8 ...229 A4
Knollmead KT4,KT5 ...199 A1
Knollmead Prim Sch
KT5 ...215 A6
Knoll Rd DA5 ...169 C5
SW18 ...158 A6
Sidcup DA14 ...190 B6
Knoll Rise BR6 ...211 D1
Knolls Cl KT4 ...216 B5
Knoll The
Beckenham BR3 ...185 D2
Ealing W13 ...87 C2
Hayes BR2 ...209 A1
Knolly's Cl SE27,SW16 ...160 C1
Knolly's Rd SE27,SW16 ...160 C1
Knot Ho SE1 ...253 C3
Knottisford St E2 ...96 C4
Knotts Green Mews E10 ..54 A3
Knotts Green Rd E10 ...54 A3
Knowlden Ho 4 E1 ...118 C6
Knowle Ave DA7 ...147 B5
Knowle Cl SW9 ...138 C2
Knowle Lo BR7 ...188 B4
Knowle Rd BR2 ...226 A6
Twickenham TW2 ...152 C3
Knowles Cl UB7 ...104 A5
Knowles Ct 7 HA1 ...42 D3
Knowles Hill Cres SE13 ..164 B6
Knowles Ho NW10 ...90 A6
Wandsworth SW18 ...157 D5
Knowles Wlk SW4 ...137 C2
Knowl Pk WD6 ...10 A6
Knowlton Gn 1 BR2 ...208 D4
Knowlton Ho 32 SW9 ...138 C4
Knowl Way WD6 ...10 B6
Knowsley Ave UB1 ...107 D5
Knowsley Rd SW11 ...136 D3
Knox Ct 10 SW4 ...138 A3
Knox Ho SW15 ...134 C3
Knox Rd E7 ...77 A2
Knox St W1 ...92 D2 237 C4
Knoyle Ho W14 ...254 B5
Knoyle St SE14 ...141 A6
Kobi Nazrul Prim Sch E1 .96 A1
Koblenz Ho N8 ...50 A6
Kohat Rd SW19 ...179 D5
Korda Cl TW17 ...192 B6
Kossuth St SE10 ...120 C1
Kotree Way 16 SE1 ...118 A2
Kramer Mews SW5 ...255 C1
Kreedman Wlk 8 E8 ...74 A3
Kreisel Wlk TW9 ...132 B6
Kuala Gdns SW16 ...182 B2
Kubrick Bsns Est E7 ...77 B4
Kuhn Way E7 ...77 A3
Kwesi Johnson Ct 4
N22 ...32 C1
Kydbrook Cl BR5 ...211 A2
Kylemore Cl 3 E6 ...99 D5
Kylemore Ct 4 W12 ...112 A4
Kylemore Rd NW6 ...69 C1
Kylestrome Ho SW1 ...258 B3
Kymberley Rd HA1 ...42 C3
Kynance Gdns HA7 ...25 C2
Kynance Mews
SW7 ...113 D3 255 D5
Kynance Pl SW7 ...256 A5
Kynaston Ave CR7 ...205 A4
Kynaston Cl HA3 ...24 B3
Kynaston Cres CR7 ...205 A4
Kynaston Ho 7 SW2 ...160 B3
Kynaston Rd BR1 ...187 A5
N16 ...73 C5
Enfield EN2 ...5 B4
Thornton Heath CR7 ...205 A4
Kynaston Wood HA3 ...24 B3
Kynersley Cl SM5 ...218 D5
Kynoch Rd N18 ...34 D6
Kyrle Rd SW11 ...159 A5
Kyverdale Rd N16 ...51 D1

L

Laburnam Ct 12 SW16 ...182 C5
Laburnham Cl 5 SE15 ...140 C5
Laburnham Ct NW2 ...69 B6
Laburnham Ho SE4 ...141 B3
Laburnham Pl SE9 ...166 C6
Laburnum Ave
Carshalton SM1 ...218 C5
Edmonton N9 ...17 D2
Tottenham N17 ...33 B3
Yiewsley UB7 ...104 B6
Laburnum Cl E4 ...35 B4
N11 ...31 A4
Laburnum Cres TW16 ...172 B2
Laburnum Ct 26 E2 ...95 D6
Harrow HA1 ...41 D3
5 Mitcham CR4 ...181 A1
Stanmore HA7 ...25 C6
Laburnum Gdns
Croydon CR0 ...206 D1
Edmonton N21 ...17 A2
Laburnum Gr NW9 ...45 A2
Edmonton N21 ...17 A2
Hounslow TW3 ...129 B1
Kingston KT3 ...177 B1
Ruislip HA4 ...39 B3
Southall UB1 ...85 B3
Laburnum Ho 6 N16 ...73 B6
Dagenham RM10 ...81 C6
Laburnum JMI Sch E2 ...95 D6
Laburnum Lo N3 ...29 B1
Laburnum Rd
Hayes UB3 ...105 D2
Merton SW19 ...180 A3
Mitcham CR4 ...181 A1
Laburnum St E2 ...95 D6
Laburnums The E6 ...100 A3
Laburnum Way BR2 ...210 D2
Stanwell TW19 ...148 B3
Lacebark Cl DA15 ...167 D4
Lacey Cl N9 ...18 A2
Lacey Dr Dagenham RM8 ...80 C5
Edgware HA8 ...26 B6
Hampton TW12 ...173 B2
Lacey Ho 6 SE13 ...142 A3
Lacey Wlk E3 ...97 C5
Lacine Ct 12 SE16 ...118 D4
Lackington St EC2 ...242 D4
Lackland Ho SE1 ...263 D2
Lacland Ho SW10 ...266 C4
Lacock Cl SW19 ...180 A4
Lacock Ct 3 W13 ...109 A5
Lacon Rd SE22 ...140 A1
Lacrosse Way SW16 ...181 D2
Lacy Rd SW15 ...134 D1
Ladas Rd SE27 ...183 A5
Ladbroke Cres W11 ...91 A1
Ladbroke Gdns
W11 ...113 B6 244 C6
Ladbroke Gr W10 ...91 A2
W11 ...113 B6 244 C6
Ladbroke Grove Ho
W11 ...244 C6
Ladbroke Grove Sta W10 .91 A1
Ladbroke Mews W11 ...244 B3
Ladbroke Rd
W11 ...113 B5 244 C4
Enfield EN1 ...17 D5
Ladbroke Sq
W11 ...113 B6 244 D5
Ladbroke Terr
W11 ...113 B5 244 D4
Ladbroke Wlk
W11 ...113 B5 244 D4
Ladbrook Cl HA5 ...41 B4
Ladbrooke Cres DA14 ...168 D1
Ladbrook Rd SE25 ...205 B5
Ladderstile Ride KT2,
TW10 ...176 D5
Ladderswood Way N11 ...31 C5
Ladlands SE22 ...162 A4
Lady Aylesford Ave HA7 ..25 B5
Lady Bankes Jun & Inf Schs
HA4 ...62 A6
Lady Booth Rd 7 KT1 ...176 A1
Ladybower Ct 5 E5 ...74 D4
Ladycroft Gdns 6 BR6 ...227 A3
Ladycroft Rd SE13 ...141 D2
Ladycroft Way BR6 ...227 A3
Ladycroft Wlk HA7 ...25 D1
Lady Eleanor Holles Sch The
(Jun Girls) TW12 ...173 D5
Lady Eleanor Holles Sch The
(Senior Girls) TW12 ...173 D5
Lady Elizabeth Ho
SW14 ...133 A2
Lady Florence Ctyd 14
SE8 ...141 C5
Ladygate La HA4 ...39 A3
Lady Hay KT4 ...215 D6
Lady Margaret Prim Sch
UB1 ...85 B2
Lady Margaret Rd NW5 ...71 C3
Southall UB1 ...85 B2
Lady Margaret Sch
SW6 ...135 C4 265 A1
Lady Shaw Ct N13 ...16 B1
Ladysmith Ave E6 ...100 A5
Ilford IG2 ...57 C2
Ladysmith Cl NW7 ...28 A3
Ladysmith Rd E16 ...98 D4
SE9 ...166 C5
Edmonton N18 ...34 B5
Enfield EN1 ...5 D3
Harrow HA3 ...24 C1
Tottenham N17 ...34 A1
Lady Somerset Rd NW5 ..71 B4
Ladywell Cl SE4 ...141 C1
Ladywell Ho 7 BR5 ...190 B1
Ladywell Hts SE4 ...163 B5
Ladywell Rd SE13 ...163 D6
Ladywell St 4 E15 ...98 D6
Ladywell Sta SE13 ...163 D6
Ladywell Water Twr
SE4 ...163 C6
Ladywood Ave BR5 ...211 C4
Ladywood Rd KT6 ...214 C6
Lafitte Ho 22 N19 ...49 D2
Lafone Ave TW13 ...150 C2
Lafone Ho 11 SW2 ...160 A4
Lafone St SE1 ...117 D4 253 C2
Lagado Mews SE16 ...118 D5
Lagonda Ho 11 E3 ...97 C3
Lagonier Ho EC1 ...235 B1
Laidlaw Dr N21 ...16 B6
Laindon Ho 6 N16 ...51 D1
Laing Dean UB5 ...84 C6
Laing Ho SE5 ...139 A5
Laings Ave CR4 ...180 D1
Laings Cnr CR4 ...180 D2
Lainlock Pl TW3 ...129 D4
Lainson St SW18 ...157 C4
Lairdale Cl SE21 ...161 A4
Laird Ho SE5 ...139 A5
Lairs Cl N7 ...72 A2
Laitwood Rd SW12 ...159 B3
Lakanal 14 SE5 ...139 C4
Lake Ave BR1 ...187 A4
Lake Bsns Ctr N17 ...34 A3
Lake Cl Dagenham RM8 ...80 D5
6 Wimbledon SW19 ...179 B5
Lakedale Rd SE18 ...123 C1
Lake Dr WD23 ...8 B2
Lakefield Cl SE20 ...184 B3
Lakefield Rd N22 ...32 D1
Lake Gdns
Dagenham RM10 ...81 C3
Hackbridge SM6 ...219 B5
Richmond TW10 ...153 B2
Lakehall Gdns CR7 ...204 D4
Lakehall Rd CR7 ...204 D4
Lake Ho SE1 ...252 A1
4 West Norwood SW27 ..182 D5
Lake House Rd E11 ...77 A6
Lakehurst Rd KT19 ...215 C3
Lakeland Cl HA3 ...24 B4
Lakeman Ct CR7 ...183 A1
Lakenheath N14 ...15 D6
Laker Ct SW4 ...138 A3
Lake Rd Croydon CR0 ...223 B6
Dagenham RM6 ...58 D5
Dagenham RM9 ...103 D4
Wimbledon SW19 ...179 B5
Laker Pl SW15 ...157 A5
Lakeside Beckenham BR3 .207 D6
Borehamwood WD6 ...10 C6
Ealing W13 ...87 C1
Enfield EN2 ...3 D1
10 Kingston KT2 ...176 D3
Wallington SM6 ...219 B4
West Ewell KT19 ...215 C2
Lakeside Ave SE28 ...124 A5
Redbridge IG4 ...55 D5
Lakeside Cl Ruislip HA4 ...39 B5
Sidcup DA15 ...168 C6
South Norwood SE25 ...184 A1
Lakeside Complex The
SE2 ...124 D5
Lakeside Cres EN4 ...14 D6
Lakeside Ct N4 ...51 A1
Lakeside Dr Esher KT10 ..212 A2
Keston Mark BR2 ...226 A5
Lakeside Lo NW4 ...47 A5
Lakeside Rd W14 ...112 D3
Palmers Green N13 ...16 B1
Lakeside Way HA9 ...66 C4
Lakes Rd BR2 ...225 C3
Lakeswood Rd BR5 ...211 A3
Lake The WD23 ...8 B3
Lakeview 23 E3 ...96 D5
Lake View HA8 ...26 B5
Lake View Ct SW1 ...258 D6
Lakeview Ct E4 ...36 B4
Lakeview Rd DA16 ...146 B1

Lakeview Rd *continued*
West Norwood SE27 ....182 D5
Lake View Terr N18 ....33 D6
Lakis Cl NW3 ....70 A4
Laleham Ave NW7 ....11 B1
Laleham Ho E2 ....243 C6
Laleham Rd Catford SE6 ..164 A4
Littleton TW17 ....192 C4
Lambarde Ave SE9 ....188 C6
Lamb Ct 10 E14 ....119 A6
Lamberhurst Ho 14
SE15 ....140 C6
Lamberhurst Rd
Dagenham RM8 ....59 B1
West Norwood SE27 ....182 C5
Lambert Ave TW9 ....132 D2
Lambert Ho 19 N19 ....49 D2
17 SW9 ....138 C3
Lambert Lo TW8 ....109 D1
Lambert Rd N12 ....30 B5
SW2 ....160 B6
Newham E16 ....99 B1
Lambert's Pl CR0 ....205 B1
Lambert's Rd KT6 ....198 B4
Lambert St N1 ....72 C1
Lambert Way N12 ....30 A5
Lambert Wlk HA9 ....65 D5
Lambeth Coll (Brixton Ctr)
SW2 ....160 B6
Lambeth Coll (Clapham Ctr)
SW4 ....159 C6
Lambeth Coll (Tower Bridge
Ctr) SE1 ....117 C5 253 B3
Lambeth Coll (Vauxhall Ctr)
SW8 ....137 D4 269 C2
Lambeth Ct 8 SW18 ....157 C6
Lambeth High St
SE1 ....116 B2 260 C4
Lambeth Hill EC4 ....252 A6
Lambeth Hospl SW9 ....138 B2
Lambeth Inst Strand Ctr
SW2 ....160 B4
Lambeth North Sta
SE1 ....116 C3 261 A6
Lambeth Palace*
SE1 ....116 B3 260 C5
Lambeth Palace Rd
SE1 ....116 B3 260 C6
Lambeth Pier SE1 ....260 B5
Lambeth Prospect SE19 ..183 B4
Lambeth Rd SE1 .116 C3 261 B5
Thornton Heath CR0 ....204 D1
Lambeth Twrs SE11 ....261 A5
Lambeth Wlk
SE11 ....116 B2 260 D4
Lambfold Ho N7 ....72 A2
Lamb Ho SE10 ....142 A6
11 SE5 ....139 B4
28 SE5 ....139 A5
Lamb La E8 ....74 B1
Lamble St NW5 ....71 A4
Lambley Rd RM9 ....80 B2
Lambolle Pl NW3 ....70 C2
Lambolle Rd NW3 ....70 C2
Lambourn Cl 9 NW5 ....71 C4
W7 ....108 D4
Lambourne Ave SW19 ..179 B6
Lambourne Ct 5 IG8 ....37 C3
Lambourne Gdns
4 Barking IG11 ....79 D1
Chingford E4 ....19 C2
Enfield EN1 ....5 D3
Lambourne Gr KT1 ....176 D1
Lambourne Ho NW8 ....236 D4
SE16 ....118 D2
Lambourne Pl SE3 ....143 B4
Lambourne Rd E11 ....54 A2
Barking IG11 ....79 D1
Ilford IG3 ....79 C6
Lambourn Rd SW4 ....137 B2
Lambrook Ho 12 SE15 ....140 A4
Lambrook Terr
SW6 ....135 A4 264 A2
Lamb's Bldgs EC1 ....242 C5
Lamb's Cl N9 ....18 A2
Lamb's Conduit Pas
WC1 ....240 C4
Lamb's Conduit St
WC1 ....94 B3 240 C5
Lambscroft Ave SE9,
SE12 ....165 D1
Lambs Mdw IG8 ....37 D1
Lamb's Mews N1 ....234 C5
Lamb's Pas EC1 ...95 B3 242 C5
Lamb St E1 ....95 D2 243 C4
Lamb's Terr N9 ....17 B2
Lambs Wlk EN2 ....5 A3
Lambton Ct 2 N19 ....50 A1
Lambton Pl W11 ....244 D6
Lambton Rd N19 ....50 A1
Wimbledon SW20 ....178 C2
Lamb Wlk SE1 ....253 A1
Lamerock Rd BR1 ....186 D6
Lamerton Lo 10 TW9 ....132 B4
Lamerton St 9 SE8 ....141 C6
Lamford Cl N17 ....33 B3
Lamington St 3 W6 ....112 B2
Lamlash St SE11 ....261 C4
Lamley Ho SE10 ....141 D5
Lammas Ave CR4 ....181 A1
Lammas Gn SE26 ....162 B1
Lammas Park Gdns W5 ..109 C5
Lammas Park Rd W5 ....109 D4
Lammas Rd E9 ....74 D1
Richmond TW10 ....175 C6
Walthamstow E10 ....53 A1
Lammas Sch The E10 ....53 B1
Lammermoor Rd SW12 .159 B4
Lamont Rd
SW10 ....136 B6 266 C5
Lamont Rd Pas SW10 ....266 C5
Lamorbey Cl DA15 ....167 D2
Lamorna Cl E17 ....36 A2
Lamorna Gr HA7 ....25 D1
Lampard Gr N16 ....51 D1
Lampern Sq 8 E2 ....96 A4
Lampeter Cl NW9 ....45 C3
Lampeter Sq W6 ....264 A5
Lamplighter Cl 31 E1 ....96 C3
Lampmead Rd SE12 ....142 D1
Lamport Cl SE18 ....122 B2
Lampson Ho 6 N19 ....71 C4
Lampton Ave TW5 ....129 D4
Lampton Ct TW5 ....129 D4
Lampton House Cl
SW19 ....178 D6
Lampton Park Rd TW3 ..129 D3
Lampton Rd TW3,TW5 ..129 D3
Lampton Sch TW5 ....129 C4
Lanacre Ave NW9 ....27 C2
Lanain Ct SE12 ....164 D4
Lanark Cl W5 ....87 C2
Lanark Ct UB5 ....63 C3
Lanark Ho 11 SE1 ....118 A1
Lanark Mans 6 W12 ....112 C4
W9 ....236 B6
Lanark Pl W9 ....92 A3 236 B6
Lanark Rd W9 ....92 A4 229 A1
Lanark Sq E14 ....119 D3
Lanata Wlk UB4 ....84 D3
Lanbury Rd SE15 ....140 D1
Lancashire Ct W1 ....248 D6
Lancaster Ave
Barking IG11 ....101 C6
Hadley Wood EN4 ....2 B5
Wanstead E18 ....55 B5
West Norwood SE21,SE27 .161 A2
Wimbledon SW19 ....178 D5
Lancaster Cl 9 N1 ....73 C1
NW9 ....27 D3
W2 ....245 C5
Beckenham BR2 ....208 D5
Kingston KT2 ....175 D5
Stanwell TW19 ....148 A5
Tottenham N17 ....34 A3
Lancaster Cotts 1
TW10 ....154 A5
Lancaster Ct SW6 ....264 D3
W2 ....246 B6
1 Belmont SM2 ....217 C1
Stanwell TW19 ....148 A3
Walton-on-T KT12 ....194 B2
West Norwood SE27 ....160 D2
Lancaster Dr E14 ....120 A5
NW3 ....70 C2
Lancaster Gate
W2 ....114 A6 246 B6
Lancaster Gate Sta
W2 ....114 B6 246 C6
Lancaster Gdns W13 ....109 B4
Kingston KT2 ....175 D5
Wimbledon SW19 ....179 A5
Lancaster Gr NW3 ....70 C2
Lancaster Ho Enfield EN2 ....5 B4
Putney SW15 ....134 C3
Wandsworth SW18 ....157 D4
Lancaster House SW1 ....249 A2
Lancasterian Inf Sch
N17 ....33 D2
Lancaster Lo 2 W11 ....91 A1
Lancaster Mews
3 SW18 ....157 D6
W2 ....114 A6 246 B6
2 Richmond TW10 ....154 A5
Lancaster Pk TW10 ....154 A6
Lancaster Pl
WC2 ....116 B6 250 C5
Hounslow TW5 ....128 D3
Ilford IG1 ....79 A4
Twickenham TW1 ....153 A4
1 Wimbledon SW19 ....178 D5
Lancaster Rd E11 ....76 C6
E17 ....34 D1
E7 ....77 A1
N11 ....31 D4
N4 ....50 C2
NW10 ....68 A3
W11 ....91 A1
Edmonton N18 ....33 D5
Enfield EN2 ....5 B4
Harrow HA2 ....41 C4
New Barnet EN4 ....14 B6
Northolt UB5 ....64 A2
Southall UB1 ....107 A6
South Norwood SE25 ....206 A6
Wimbledon SW19 ....178 D5
Lancaster Road Ind Est 2
EN4 ....14 B6
Lancaster St
SE1 ....116 D4 251 D1
Lancaster Stables 10
NW3 ....70 C2
Lancaster Terr
W2 ....114 B6 246 C6
Lancaster Wlk
W2 ....114 A5 246 B4
Hayes UB3 ....83 A1
Lancastrian Rd SM6 ....220 B1
Lancefield Ct 1 NW6 ....91 A5
Lancefield Ho SE15 ....140 B2
Lancefield St W10 ....91 B4
Lancell St N16 ....73 C6
Lancelot Ave HA0 ....65 D4
Lancelot Cres HA0 ....65 D4
Lancelot Gdns EN4 ....15 A4
Lancelot Par 4 HA0 ....65 D3
Lancelot Pl
SW7 ....114 D4 247 C1
Lancelot Rd DA16 ....146 A2
Wembley HA0 ....65 D3
Lance Rd HA1 ....42 A2
Lancer Sq W8 ....245 C2
Lancey Cl SE7 ....122 A2
Lanchester Ct W2 ....237 C1
Lanchester Rd N6 ....48 D4
Lancing Gdns N9 ....17 D3
Lancing Rd Ealing W13 ..109 B6
Feltham TW13 ....149 D2
Ilford IG2 ....57 B2
Thornton Heath CR0 ....204 B2
Lancing St NW1 ....232 C1
Lancresse Ct N1 ....95 C6
Landale Ho 13 SE16 ....118 C3
Landcroft Rd SE22 ....161 D5
Landells Rd SE22 ....162 A5
Lander Ct EN5 ....14 A6
Landford Rd SW15 ....134 C2
Landgrove Rd SW19 ....179 C5
Landin Ho 1 E14 ....97 C1
Landleys Field 21 N7 ....71 D3
Landmann Ho 16 SE16 ....118 B2
Landmann Way SE14 ....118 D1
Landmark Commercial Ctr
N18 ....33 C4
Landon Pl SW1 ....257 C6
Landons Cl E14 ....120 A5
Landon Way TW15 ....170 D4
Landon Wlk 14 E14 ....119 D6
Landor Ct N16 ....73 C3
Landor Ho 7 SE5 ....139 B5
Landor Rd SW9 ....138 A2
Landor Wlk 11 W12 ....112 A4
Landra Gdns N21 ....16 D5
Landrake NW1 ....232 B5
Landridge Dr EN1 ....6 B5
Landridge Rd SW6 ....135 B3
Landrock Rd N8 ....50 B3
Landscape Rd IG8 ....37 B3
Landseer Ave E12 ....78 C3
Landseer Cl Edgware HA8 .26 C1
Mitcham SW19 ....180 B2
Landseer Ct UB4 ....83 B5
Landseer Ho NW8 ....236 D6
SW1 ....259 D3
SW11 ....268 B1
17 Northolt UB5 ....84 D5
Landseer Rd N19 ....72 A6
Cheam SM1,SM2 ....217 C2
Enfield EN1 ....18 A6
New Malden KT3 ....199 B2
Lands' End WD6 ....9 D5
Landstead Rd SE18 ....145 B5
Landulph Ho SE11 ....261 B2
Landward Ct W1 ....237 B2
Lane Cl NW2 ....68 B5
Lane Ct SW11 ....158 D4
Lane End DA7 ....147 D2
Lane Gdns Bushey WD23 ....8 C4
Claygate KT10 ....212 D1
Lane Mews E12 ....78 B5
Lanercost Cl SW2 ....160 C2
Lanercost Gdns N14 ....16 A4
Lanercost Rd SW2 ....160 C2
Laneside HA8 ....27 A5
Chislehurst BR7 ....189 A5
Laneside Ave RM8 ....59 B2
Lane The NW8 ....92 A5 229 A3
SE3 ....143 A2
Laneway SW15 ....156 B6
Laney Bldg EC1 ....241 A4
Lanfranc Ct HA1 ....64 D5
Lanfranc Rd E3 ....97 A5
Lanfrey Pl W14 ....254 C1
Langbourne Ave N6 ....71 A6
Langbourne Ct E17 ....53 A3
Langbourne Ho 7 SW2 .160 C6
Langbourne Mans N6 ....71 A6
Langbourne Pl E14 ....119 D1
Langbourne Prim Sch
SE21 ....161 C1
Langbourne Way KT10 ..213 A2
Langbrook Rd SE3 ....143 D3
Langcroft Cl SM5 ....218 D5
Langdale NW1 ....232 A2
Langdale Ave CR4 ....202 D6
Langdale Cl BR6 ....226 D5
SE17 ....139 A6
Dagenham RM8 ....58 C1
Mortlake SW14 ....132 D1
Langdale Cres DA7 ....147 C4
Langdale Ct 3 Ealing W5 ..87 C2
9 Ilford IG1 ....78 D5
Langdale Dr UB4 ....83 C5
Langdale Gdns UB6 ....87 B4
Langdale Ho SW1 ....259 A1
Langdale Rd SE10 ....142 A5
Thornton Heath CR7 ....204 C5
Langdale St 3 E1 ....96 B1
Langdon Cres E6 ....100 C5
Langdon Ct EC1 ....234 D3
NW10 ....89 C6
Langdon Dr NW9 ....45 A1
Langdon Ho 1 E14 ....98 A1
Langdon Park Rd N6 ....49 C2
Langdon Park Sec Sch
E14 ....98 A1
Langdon Pl SW14 ....133 A2
Langdon Rd Barking E6 ..100 C6
Bromley BR2 ....209 B6
Morden SM4 ....202 A4
Langdon Sch E6 ....100 D6
Langdons Ct UB2 ....107 C3
Langdon Shaw DA14 ....189 D5
Langdon Way 14 SE1 ....118 A2
Langdon Wlk SM4 ....202 A4
Langford Cl E8 ....74 A3
Langford Cl *continued*
7 N15 ....51 C3
NW8 ....229 B4
Langford Cres EN4 ....2 D1
Langford Ct NW8 ....229 B3
Langford Gn SE5 ....139 C2
Langford Ho 5 SE8 ....141 C6
Langford Pl NW8 ..92 A5 229 B4
Sidcup DA14 ....168 A1
Langford Prim Sch
SW6 ....135 D3
Langford Rd 4 SW6 ....135 D3
Cockfosters EN4 ....2 D1
Woodford IG8 ....37 C4
Langfords IG9 ....21 D2
Langham Cl N15 ....50 D6
Langham Ct NW4 ....46 D4
Merton SW20 ....178 C1
4 Putney SW15 ....156 D6
Ruislip HA4 ....62 B3
12 Twickenham TW1 ....153 C5
Langham Dr RM6 ....58 B3
Langham Gdns HA8 ....27 A3
Ealing W13 ....109 B6
Richmond TW10 ....175 C6
Southgate N21 ....16 D6
Wembley HA0 ....65 C6
Langham Ho SW4 ....159 C6
Langham House Cl
TW10 ....175 D6
Langham Mans SW5 ....255 C1
Langham Park Pl BR2 ....208 D5
Langham Pl N15 ....50 D6
W1 ....93 B2 238 D3
Chiswick W4 ....133 C6
Langham Rd HA8 ....27 A4
N15 ....51 A6
Teddington TW11 ....175 B4
Wimbledon SW20 ....178 C2
Langham Sch The N15 ....51 A5
Langham St W1 ....93 B2 238 D3
Langhedge Cl N18 ....33 D4
Langhedge La N18 ....33 D4
Langhedge Lane Ind Est
N18 ....33 D4
Lang Ho 3 N19 ....71 C5
SW8 ....270 A3
Langholm Cl SW12 ....159 D4
Langholme WD23 ....8 A3
Langhorn Dr TW2 ....152 C4
Langhorne Ct 10 NW8 ....70 B1
Langhorne Ho 5 SE7 ....143 C6
Langhorne Rd RM10 ....81 C1
Langhurst Ho 10 SW11 ..137 A3
Langland Cres HA7 ....25 D1
Langland Dr HA5 ....23 A3
Langland Gdns NW3 ....69 D3
Croydon CR0 ....223 B6
Langland Ho 10 SE5 ....139 B5
Upper Tooting SW17 ....180 B5
Langler Rd NW10 ....90 C5
Langley Ave
North Cheam KT4,SM3 ....216 D6
Ruislip HA4 ....62 B6
Surbiton KT6 ....198 A1
Langley Cres HA8 ....11 A1
Dagenham RM9 ....80 D1
Harlington UB3 ....127 D5
Wanstead E11 ....55 C2
Langley Ct SW8 ....270 A2
WC2 ....250 A6
Langley Dr W3 ....110 D4
Wanstead E11 ....55 B2
Langley Gdns BR5 ....210 D3
Bromley BR2 ....209 C5
Dagenham RM9 ....80 D1
Langley Gr KT3 ....177 C1
Langley Ho BR1 ....187 B3
11 E5 ....74 B3
36 W2 ....91 C2
Langley La SW8 ..138 A6 270 B6
Langley Manor BR3 ....208 A4
Langley Mans SW8 ....270 B6
Langley Park Rd SM1,
SM2 ....218 A1
Langley Park Sch for Boys
BR3 ....207 D3
Langley Park Sch for Girls
BR3 ....208 A3
Langley Pk NW7 ....27 C4
Langley Rd DA16 ....146 C6
Beckenham BR3 ....207 A5
Isleworth TW7 ....130 D3
Merton SW19 ....179 C2
Surbiton KT6 ....198 A2
Langley Row EN5 ....1 B4
Langley St WC2 ....94 A1 240 A1
Langley Way BR4 ....208 C2
Langmead Dr WD23 ....8 B3
Langmead Ho 34 E3 ....97 D4
Langmead St SE27 ....183 A6
Langmore Ct DA7 ....146 D2
Langmore Ho 28 E1 ....96 A1
Langport Ct KT12 ....194 C1
Langport Ho 1 SW9 ....138 D3
Langridge 18 NW5 ....71 A2
Langridge Mews TW12 ..173 B4
Langroyd Rd SW17 ....158 D2
Langside Ave SW15 ....134 A1
Langside Cres N14 ....15 D1
Lang St E1 ....96 C3
Langston Hughes Cl 5
SE24 ....138 D1
Langthorn Ct EC2 ....242 D2
Langthorne Ct 4 SE6 ....186 A6
Langthorne Ho UB3 ....105 C2
Langthorne Lo 30 SW2 ..160 C4
Langthorne Rd E11 ....76 B5
Langthorne St SW6 ....134 D5
Langton Ave N20 ....14 B4
Langton Ave *continued*
Wallend E6 ....100 C4
Langton Cl WC1 ...94 B3 240 D6
Langton Ct SW15 ....157 B5
Langton Ho SE11 ....260 D4
5 Streatham SW16 ....181 C6
Langton Pl SW18 ....157 C3
Langton Rd NW2 ....68 C5
SW9 ....138 D5
East Molesey KT8 ....196 A5
Harrow HA3 ....24 A3
Langton Rise SE22,SE23 .162 B4
Langton St
SW10 ....136 A6 266 B5
Langton Way
Greenwich SE3 ....143 A5
South Croydon CR0 ....221 C4
Langtry Pl SW6 ....265 B6
Langtry Rd NW8 ....91 D6
Northolt UB5 ....84 D5
Langtry Wlk NW8 .92 A6 229 A6
NW8 ....91 D6
Langwood Chase TW11 .175 C4
Langworth Dr UB4 ....84 B1
Langworthy HA5 ....23 C4
Lanherne Ho 7 SW19 ...178 D3
Lanhill Rd W9 ....91 C3
Lanier Rd SE13 ....164 B5
Lanigan Dr TW3 ....151 D6
Lankaster Gdns N2 ....30 B2
Lankers Dr HA2 ....41 B3
Lankton Cl BR3 ....186 A2
Lanner Ho 2 SW11 ....136 C2
Lannock Rd UB3 ....105 D5
Lannoy Point SW6 ....264 B4
Lannoy Rd SE9 ....167 A3
Lanrick Rd E14 ....98 C1
Lanridge Rd SE2 ....124 D3
Lansbury Ave
Barking IG11 ....80 A1
Dagenham RM6 ....59 A4
Edmonton N18 ....33 C5
Feltham TW14 ....150 B5
Lansbury Cl NW10 ....67 A3
Lansbury Ct 4 SE28 ....124 B6
Lansbury Dr UB4 ....83 D3
Lansbury Gdns 1 E14 ....98 B1
Lansbury Ho 5 DA17 ....125 B1
Lansbury Rd EN3 ....6 D4
Lansbury Way N18 ....33 C5
Lanscombe Wlk SW8 ....270 A3
Lansdell Rd CR4 ....181 A1
Lansdown Cl KT12 ....194 C1
Lansdowne Ave DA7 ....146 D5
Orpington BR6 ....210 D1
Lansdowne Cl
Tolworth KT5 ....214 D6
Twickenham TW1 ....152 D3
Wimbledon SW20 ....178 D3
Lansdowne Copse 1
KT4 ....216 A6
Lansdowne Cres
W11 ....113 A6 244 B5
Lansdowne Ct 2 KT4 ....216 A6
Lansdowne Dr E8 ....74 A1
Lansdowne Gdns
SW8 ....138 A4 270 A2
Lansdowne Gr NW10 ....67 C4
Lansdowne Hill SE27 ....160 D1
Lansdowne Ho W11 ....244 C4
Enfield EN2 ....4 C3
Lansdowne La SE7 ....121 D1
Lansdowne Mews SE7 ..121 D1
W11 ....244 C4
Lansdowne Pl SE1 ....262 D6
Penge SE19 ....183 D3
Lansdowne Rd BR1 ....187 B3
E11 ....76 D6
E17 ....53 C3
E8 ....74 A2
N10 ....31 C1
N3 ....29 C3
W11 ....113 A6 244 B5
Chingford E4 ....19 C2
Croydon CR0 ....205 B1
Harrow HA1 ....42 C2
Hayes UB8 ....83 A1
Hounslow TW3 ....129 D2
Ilford IG3 ....57 D2
Stanmore HA7 ....25 C4
Tottenham N17 ....34 A2
Wanstead E18 ....55 A6
West Ewell KT19 ....215 B1
Wimbledon SW19,SW20 ..178 C3
Lansdowne Rise
W11 ....113 A6 244 B5
Lansdowne Row W1 ....248 D4
Lansdowne Sch SW9 ....138 B2
Lansdowne Terr WC1 ....240 B5
Lansdowne Way
SW4,SW8 ....138 A4 270 B1
Lansdowne Wlk
W11 ....113 B5 244 C4
Lansdowne Wood Cl 11
SE27 ....160 D1
Lansdown Ho 29 SE5 ....139 A3
Lansdown Rd E7 ....77 C1
Sidcup DA14 ....168 B1
Lansfield Ave N18 ....34 A6
Lanson Ct E11 ....76 D6
Lanson Ho HA8 ....26 C4
Lanswood Ct KT4 ....216 A6
Lantern Cl Putney SW15 ..134 A1
Wembley HA0 ....65 D3
Lantern Ct 4 SW20 ....178 D2
Lantern Ho E14 ....119 C4
Lanterns Ct E14 ....119 C3
Lanterns The N12 ....29 D4
Lantern Way UB7 ....104 B4
Lant Ho SE1 ....252 A1
Lantry Ct 1 W3 ....110 D5
Lant St SE1 ....117 A4 252 B1
Lanvanor Rd SE15 ....140 C3
Lanyard Ho 3 SE8 ....119 B2
Lapford Cl W9 ....91 B3
Lapponum Wlk UB4 ....84 D2
Lapsang SE1 ....253 D3
Lapse Wood Wlk SE22 ...162 B3
Lapstone Gdns HA3 ....43 C3
Lapwing Ct NW9 ....27 C1
Tolworth KT6 ....214 C5
Lapwing Twr 31 SE8 ....141 B6
Lapwing Way UB4 ....84 D1
Lapworth 2 N11 ....31 B6
Lapworth Ct W2 ....91 D2
Lara Cl SE13 ....164 A5
Chessington KT9 ....214 A1
Larbert Rd SW16 ....181 C3
Larch Ave W3 ....111 C5
Larch Cl E13 ....99 C3
N11 ....31 A3
7 N19 ....71 C6
15 SE8 ....141 B6
Balham SW12 ....159 B2
Larch Cres Hayes UB4 ....84 D2
West Ewell KT19 ....214 D2
Larch Ct 41 W2 ....91 C2
Larch Dene BR6 ....226 C6
Larches Ave SW14 ....133 B1
Larches The
Edmonton N13 ....17 A1
Hillingdon UB10 ....82 D5
Larchfield Ho 2 N5 ....73 A3
Larch Gn NW9 ....27 C2
Larch Gr DA15 ....167 D3
Larch Ho 17 SE16 ....118 C4
Hayes UB4 ....84 C2
Larchmore Ct N19 ....72 A6
Larch Rd E10 ....75 C6
NW2 ....68 C4
Larch Tree Way CR0 ....223 C5
Larchvale Ct 4 SM2 ....217 D1
Larch Way BR2 ....210 C2
Larchwood Rd SE9 ....166 D2
Larcombe Cl CR0 ....221 D4
Larcom St SE17 ..117 A2 262 B3
Larden Rd W3 ....111 C4
La Retraite RC Girls Sch
SW12 ....159 C4
Largewood Ave KT6 ....214 C6
Larissa St SE17 ....262 D3
Larix Ct NW10 ....90 A6
Larkbere Rd SE26 ....185 A6
Larken Cl WD23 ....8 A3
Larken Dr WD23 ....8 A3
Larkfield Ave HA3 ....43 B6
Larkfield Cl BR2 ....225 A6
Larkfield Rd DA14 ....167 D1
Richmond TW9 ....132 A1
Lark Hall Inf Sch SW4 ..137 D3
Lark Hall Jun Sch SW4 ..138 A3
Larkhall La SW4 .138 A4 270 A1
Larkhall Rise SW4 ....137 D3
Larkham Cl TW13 ....149 C1
Lark Row E2 ....96 C6
Larksfield Gr EN1 ....6 B4
Larks Gr IG11 ....79 C1
Larkshall Bsns Ctr 2 E4 ..20 B2
Larkshall Cres E4 ....36 A6
Larkshall Ct E4 ....36 A5
Larkshall Rd E4 ....36 B6
Larkspur Cl 4 E6 ....100 A2
NW9 ....44 D4
Ruislip HA4 ....39 A2
Tottenham N17 ....33 B3
Larkspur Ct SM6 ....219 B1
Larkspur Gr HA8 ....27 A6
Larkspur Way KT19 ....215 A3
Larkswood Ct E4 ....36 B5
Larkswood Jun & Inf Sch
E4 ....35 D6
Larkswood Rd E4 ....35 D6
Larkswood Rise HA5 ....40 C5
Lark Way SM5 ....202 C2
Larkway Cl NW9 ....45 B5
Larmenier & Sacred Heart RC
Prim Sch W6 ....112 D2
Larnaca Ho SE1 ....263 C6
Larnach Rd W6 ....134 D6
Larne Rd HA4 ....39 D2
Larpent Ave SW15 ....156 C6
Larwood Cl UB6 ....64 B3
La Saint Union Rc Sec Sch
NW5 ....71 A5
Lascelles Ave HA1 ....42 B2
Lascelles Cl E11 ....76 B6
Lascelles Ho NW1 ....237 B5
Lascott's Rd N22 ....32 B4
Lashford Ho HA8 ....27 A4
Lassa Rd SE9 ....166 B6
Lassell St SE10 ....120 B1
Lasseter Pl SE3 ....142 D6
Latchett Rd E18 ....37 B2
Latchingdon Ct E17 ....52 D5
Latchmere Cl KT2,TW10 .176 A5
Latchmere Jun & Inf Schs
KT2 ....176 B4
Latchmere La KT2,TW10 .176 B5
Latchmere Rd SW11 ....136 D3
Kingston KT2 ....176 B4
Latchmere St 5 SW11 ..136 D3
Lateward Rd TW8 ....131 D6
Latham Cl E6 ....100 A1
4 Twickenham TW1 ....153 A4
Latham Ct
2 Bowes Park N11 ....32 A4
7 Northolt UB5 ....84 D4
Latham Ho E1 ....96 D1
18 E17 ....53 D6
Latham Rd DA6 ....169 C6

Latham Rd *continued*
Twickenham TW1 ...152 D4
Latham's Way CR0 ...220 B6
Lathkill Cl EN1 ...18 A4
Lathkill Ct BR3 ...185 B2
Lathom Jun Sch E6 ...78 A1
Lathom Rd E6 ...78 B1
Lathwood Ho 6 SE26 ...184 B5
Latimer SE17 ...263 A1
Latimer Ave E6 ...100 B6
Latimer Cl
North Cheam KT4 ...216 B4
Pinner HA5 ...22 C2
Latimer Gdns HA5 ...22 C2
Latimer Ho 11 E9 ...74 D2
W11 ...244 D5
Latimer Pl W10 ...90 C1
Latimer Rd E7 ...77 B4
N15 ...51 C3
W10 ...90 C1
Barnet EN5 ...1 D2
Croydon CR0 ...220 D5
Teddington TW11 ...174 D5
Wimbledon SW19 ...179 D4
Latimer Road Sta W10 ...112 D6
Latona Rd SE15 ...140 A6
La Tourne Gdns BR6 ...227 A5
Lattimer Pl W4 ...133 C6
Latton Cl KT12 ...195 A2
Latymer All Saints CE Prim Sch N9 ...17 D2
Latymer Ct W6 ...112 D2
Latymer Rd N9 ...17 D3
Latymer Sch The N9 ...17 C2
Latymer Upper Sch W6 ...112 A1
Latymer Way N9 ...17 C2
Lauder Cl UB5 ...84 D5
Lauder Ct N14 ...16 A4
Lauderdale Dr TW10 ...153 D1
Lauderdale Mans W9 ...91 D4
Lauderdale Rd W9 ...91 D4
Lauderdale Twr EC2 ...242 A4
Laud St SE11 ...116 B1 260 C2
Croydon CR0 ...221 A5
Laughton Ho 11 SW2 ...160 C5
Laughton Rd UB5 ...84 D6
Launcelot Prim Sch BR1 ...187 A6
Launcelot Rd BR1,SE12 ...187 A6
Launcelot St SE1 ...251 A1
Launceston Ct CR7 ...204 C3
Launceston Gdns UB6 ...65 C1
Launceston Pl W8 ...114 A3 256 A5
Launceston Rd UB6 ...87 C6
Launch St E14 ...120 A3
Laundress La N16 ...74 A5
Laundry La 15 N1 ...73 A1
Laundry Mews SE23 ...162 D4
Laundry Rd W6 ...135 A6 264 A5
Laura Cl Enfield EN1 ...17 C6
Wanstead E11 ...55 C4
Lauradale Rd N2 ...48 D5
Laura Pl E5 ...74 C4
Laurel Ave TW1 ...152 D3
Laurel Bank Gdns 3 SW6 ...135 B3
Laurel Bank Rd EN2 ...5 B4
Laurel Cl 5 N19 ...71 C6
Sidcup DA14 ...168 A1
Upper Tooting SW17 ...180 C5
Laurel Cres CR0 ...223 C5
Laurel Ct E8 ...73 D2
2 Putney SW15 ...156 D6
South Norwood SE25 ...205 C4
8 Wembley HA0 ...88 A5
Laurel Dr N21 ...16 C4
Laurel Gdns NW7 ...11 B1
Chingford E4 ...19 D4
Ealing W7 ...108 C5
Hounslow TW4 ...129 A1
Laurel Gr
Forest Hill SE26 ...185 A6
Penge SE20 ...184 C3
Laurel Ho 5 NW3 ...69 D2
9 SE8 ...141 B6
Morden SM4 ...201 D4
Laurel La UB7 ...104 A2
Laurel Manor SM2 ...218 A1
Laurel Mead Ct 8 E18 ...37 A2
Laurel Pk HA3 ...24 D3
Laurel Rd Barnes SW13 ...134 A3
Teddington TW12 ...174 B5
Wimbledon SW20 ...178 B2
Laurel St E8 ...73 D2
Laurels The 8 BR1 ...187 B2
BR2 ...209 A5
N3 ...29 D4
Bushey WD23 ...8 C2
8 Belvedere DA17 ...125 C1
Buckhurst Hill IG9 ...21 C3
Laurel View N12 ...13 D1
Laurel Way E18 ...54 D5
N20 ...13 C1
Laurence Ct E10 ...53 D2
Laurence Mews 12 W12 ...112 A4
Laurence Pountney Hill EC4 ...252 C6
Laurence Pountney La EC4 ...252 D6
Laurie Gr SE14 ...141 A4
Laurie Ho SE1 ...261 D5
W8 ...113 C5 245 A3
Laurie Rd W7 ...86 C2
Laurier Rd NW5 ...71 B5
Croydon CR0 ...205 D2
Laurimel Cl HA7 ...25 B4
Laurino Pl WD23 ...8 A2
Lauriston Lo NW6 ...69 B2
Lauriston Rd E9 ...74 D1
Lauriston Rd *continued*
Wimbledon SW19 ...178 D4
Lauriston Sch E9 ...96 D6
Lausanne Rd N8 ...50 C5
SE15 ...140 C4
Lavehham Ho E17 ...35 D2
Lavell St N16 ...73 B4
Lavender Ave NW9 ...45 A1
Mitcham CR4 ...180 D2
North Cheam KT4,SM3 ...216 C5
Lavender Cl BR2 ...210 A3
SW3 ...266 D5
Wallington SM5 ...219 B4
Lavender Ct SW4 ...270 B1
East Molesey KT8 ...195 D6
Lavender Gdns SW11 ...136 D1
Enfield EN2 ...4 D4
Stanmore HA3 ...24 C4
Lavender Gr E8 ...74 A1
Mitcham CR4 ...180 C2
Lavender Hill SW11 ...137 A2
Enfield EN2 ...4 D4
Lavender Ho 14 SE16 ...118 D5
Lavender Pl IG1 ...78 D3
Lavender Prim Sch EN2 ...5 C5
Lavender Rd SE16 ...119 A5
SW11 ...136 B2
Enfield EN2 ...5 B4
Hillingdon UB8 ...82 B2
Sutton SM1 ...218 B4
Thornton Heath CR0 ...204 B3
Wallington SM5 ...219 A4
West Ewell KT19 ...214 D2
Lavender Rise UB7 ...104 C4
Lavender St E15 ...76 C2
Lavender Sweep SW11 ...136 D1
Lavender Terr 12 SW11 ...136 C2
Lavender Vale SM6 ...219 D2
Lavender Way CR0 ...206 D3
Lavender Wlk SW11 ...136 D1
Lavendon Ho NW8 ...237 B6
Lavengro Rd SE27 ...161 A2
Lavenham Ho E17 ...35 D2
Lavenham Rd SW18 ...157 C3
Lavernock Rd DA7 ...147 C3
Lavers Rd N16 ...73 C5
Laverstoke Gdns SW15 ...156 A4
Laverton Mews SW5 ...255 D3
Laverton Pl SW5 ...255 D3
Lavidge Rd SE9 ...166 B2
Lavina Gr N1 ...233 C4
Lavington Cl E9 ...75 B2
Lavington Rd Ealing W13 ...109 B5
Wallington CR0 ...220 B4
Lavington St SE1 ...116 D5 251 D3
Lavinia Ct BR1 ...186 C3
Lavisham Ho BR1 ...187 B5
Lawdale Jun Sch E2 ...96 A4
Lawdon Gdns CR0 ...220 D4
Lawford Cl SM6 ...220 A1
Lawford Rd N1 ...73 C1
NW5 ...71 C2
Chiswick W4 ...133 A5
Lawfords Wharf 15 NW1 ...71 C1
Lawless Ho 5 E14 ...120 A6
Lawless St 11 E14 ...119 D6
Lawley Ho 10 TW1 ...153 D5
Lawley Rd N14 ...15 B4
Lawley St E5 ...74 C4
Lawman Ct 2 TW9 ...132 B4
Lawn Cl BR1 ...187 B3
Edmonton N9 ...17 D4
Kingston KT3 ...177 C1
Ruislip HA4 ...61 D5
Lawn Cres TW9 ...132 C3
Lawn Farm Gr RM6 ...59 A5
Lawnfield NW6 ...68 D1
Lawn Gdns W7 ...108 C5
Lawn House Cl E14 ...120 A4
Lawn La SW8 ...138 B6 270 C6
Lawn Rd NW3 ...70 D3
Beckenham BR3 ...185 B3
Lawns Ct HA9 ...66 C6
Lawnside SE3 ...142 D1
Lawns The N16 ...73 C3
SE3 ...142 D2
Belmont SM2 ...217 A1
Chingford E4 ...35 C5
Harrow HA5 ...23 D3
Sidcup DA14 ...190 B6
South Norwood SE19 ...183 B2
1 Wimbledon SW19 ...179 B5
Lawn Terr SE3 ...142 C2
Lawn The UB2 ...107 C1
Lawn Vale HA5 ...23 A1
Lawrence Ave E17 ...34 D2
NW7 ...27 D6
Edmonton N13 ...32 D6
Little Ilford E12 ...78 C4
New Malden KT3 ...199 C2
Lawrence Camp Ct N20 ...14 B1
Lawrence Cl E3 ...97 C5
N15 ...51 C5
6 W12 ...112 B6
Lawrence Cres
Dagenham RM10 ...81 D5
Edgware HA8 ...26 C1
Lawrence Ct N10 ...49 C6
N16 ...73 C5
NW7 ...27 C5
4 W3 ...111 A3
Lawrence Dr UB10 ...61 A4
Lawrence Est TW4 ...128 C1
Lawrence Gdns NW7 ...11 D1
Lawrence Hill E4 ...19 C2
Lawrence Ho SW1 ...259 D3
Bowes Park N22 ...32 B4
Lawrence La EC2 ...242 B2
Lawrence Mans SW3 ...267 A5
Lawrence Pl N1 ...233 B6
Lawrence Rd DA8 ...147 D5
E13 ...99 B6
E6 ...100 A6
N15 ...51 C5
W5 ...109 D2
Edmonton N18 ...34 B6
Hampton TW12 ...173 B3
Hayes BR4 ...225 A4
Hayes UB4 ...83 A5
Hounslow TW4 ...128 C1
Pinner HA5 ...40 D4
Richmond TW10 ...175 C6
South Norwood SE25 ...205 D5
Lawrence's Bldgs 1 N16 ...73 D5
Lawrence St E16 ...98 D2
NW7 ...27 D6
SW3 ...136 C6 267 A5
Lawrence Trad Est SE10 ...120 C2
Lawrence Way NW10 ...67 B5
Lawrence Weaver Cl SM4 ...201 C3
Lawrence Yd N15 ...51 C5
Lawrie Ct HA3 ...24 D3
Lawrie Park Ave SE26 ...184 B5
Lawrie Park Cres SE26 ...184 B5
Lawrie Park Gdns SE26 ...184 B5
Lawrie Park Rd SE26 ...184 C5
Lawson Cl Newham E16 ...99 C2
Wimbledon SW19 ...156 D1
Lawson Ct 1 N4 ...50 B1
13 Surbiton KT6 ...197 D2
Lawson Gdns HA5 ...40 B6
Lawson Ho 1 SE18 ...144 C6
17 W12 ...112 B6
Lawson Rd Enfield EN3 ...6 C4
Southall UB1 ...85 C3
Law St SE1 ...117 B3 262 D6
Lawton Rd E10 ...54 A1
E3 ...97 A4
Barnet EN4 ...2 B2
Laxcon Cl NW10 ...67 B3
Laxey Rd BR6 ...227 D2
Laxfield Ct E8 ...96 A6
Laxley Cl SE5 ...138 D5
Laxton Ct CR7 ...205 A5
Laxton Path 1 SE4 ...140 D1
Laxton Pl NW1 ...238 D6
Layard Rd SE16 ...118 B2
Enfield EN1 ...5 D4
South Norwood CR7 ...183 B1
Layard Sq SE16 ...118 B2
Laycock Prim Sch N1 ...72 D2
Laycock St N1 ...72 C2
Layer Gdns W3 ...110 C6
Layfield Cl NW4 ...46 B2
Layfield Cres NW4 ...46 B2
Layfield Ho 1 SE10 ...121 A1
Layfield Rd NW4 ...46 B2
Laymarsh Cl DA17 ...125 B3
Laymead Cl UB5 ...63 A2
Laystall Ct EC1 ...241 A5
Laystall St EC1 ...241 A5
Layton Cres CR0 ...220 D3
Layton Ct TW8 ...109 D1
Layton Pl TW9 ...132 C4
Layton Rd Brentford TW8 ...109 D1
Hounslow TW3 ...129 D1
Layton's La TW16 ...171 D1
Layzell Wlk SE9 ...165 D3
Lazar Wlk 2 N7 ...72 B6
Leabank Cl HA1 ...64 C5
Leabank Sq E9 ...75 C2
Leabank View N15 ...52 A3
Leabourne Rd N16 ...52 A2
Lea Bridge Rd E10 ...53 C2
Lea Cl TW2 ...151 B4
Lea Cres HA4 ...61 D4
Leacroft Ave SW12 ...158 D4
Leacroft Cl Southgate N21 ...16 D2
3 Yiewsley UB7 ...104 A6
Lea Ct 2 E13 ...99 A4
3 W12 ...111 C4
1 Chingford E4 ...20 A2
3 Hillingdon UB10 ...82 D3
Leadale Ave E4 ...19 C2
Leadale Rd N16 ...52 A3
Leadbeaters Cl N11 ...30 D5
Leadbetter Ct 10 NW10 ...67 B1
Leadenhall Mkt EC3 ...243 A1
Leadenhall Pl EC3 ...243 A1
Leadenhall St EC3 ...95 C1 243 A1
Leadenham Ct 15 E3 ...97 C3
Leader Ave E12 ...78 C3
Leadings The HA9 ...67 A5
Leaf Cl KT7,KT8 ...196 C4
Leaf Gr SE27 ...182 C5
Leaf Ho 9 HA1 ...42 D4
Leafield Cl SW16 ...182 D4
Leafield La DA14 ...169 B1
Leafield Rd
Merton SW19,SW20 ...201 B6
Sutton SM1 ...217 C6
Leafy Gr BR2 ...225 C3
Leafy Oak Rd SE12 ...165 C1
Leafy Way CR0 ...221 D6
Lea Gdns HA9 ...66 B4
Leagrave St E5 ...74 C5
Lea Hall Gdns E10 ...53 C1
Lea Hall Rd E10 ...53 C1
Lea Ho E5 ...52 C1
NW8 ...237 A5
2 Edmonton N9 ...18 A1
Leaholme Waye HA4 ...39 A3
Leahurst Rd SE13 ...164 C6
Lea Int E9 ...75 C3
Leake St SE1 ...116 B4 250 D2
SE1 ...251 A1
Lealand Rd N15 ...51 D3
Leamington Ave BR6 ...227 C4
E17 ...53 C4
Bromley BR1 ...187 C5
Merton SM4 ...201 B5
Leamington Cl E12 ...78 A3
Bromley BR1 ...187 C5
Hounslow TW3 ...152 A6
Leamington Cres HA2 ...63 B5
Leamington Ct W3 ...89 B2
4 Forest Hill SE26 ...162 A1
Leamington Gdns IG3 ...79 D6
Leamington Ho 3 W11 ...91 B2
Edgware HA8 ...26 B5
Leamington Pk W3 ...89 B2
Leamington Pl UB4 ...83 D3
Leamington Rd UB2 ...106 D2
Leamington Rd Villas W11 ...91 B2
Leamington Villas SE13 ...164 C6
Leamore St W6 ...112 C2
Leamouth Rd E6 ...100 A2
South Bromley E14 ...98 B1
Leander Ct 27 E9 ...74 C1
7 NW9 ...27 C2
SE8 ...141 C4
5 Surbiton KT6 ...197 D2
Leander Rd SW2 ...160 C5
Northolt UB5 ...85 C5
Thornton Heath CR7 ...204 B5
Lea Rd
2 Beckenham BR3 ...185 C1
Enfield EN2 ...5 B4
Southall UB2 ...107 A2
Learner Dr HA2 ...63 C6
Learoyd Gdns E6 ...122 C6
Leary Ho SE11 ...260 D1
Leas Cl KT9 ...214 B1
Leas Dale SE9 ...166 C1
Leas Gn BR7 ...189 D4
Leaside Ave N10 ...49 A5
Leaside Bsns Ctr EN3 ...7 B3
Leaside Ct UB10 ...82 D4
Leaside Ho 4 E5 ...52 B1
Leaside Mans N10 ...49 A6
Leaside Rd E5 ...52 C1
Leasowes Rd E10 ...53 C1
Leas The SE18 ...144 D4
Leatherbottle Gn DA18 ...125 B3
Leather Cl CR4 ...181 A1
Leatherdale St 29 E1 ...96 C3
Leather Gdns E15 ...98 C6
Leatherhead Cl N16 ...51 D1
Leatherhead Rd KT9 ...213 D1
Leather La EC1 ...94 C2 241 B4
Leathermarket Ct SE1 ...253 A1
Leathermarket St SE1 ...117 C4 253 A1
Leathersellers Cl EN5 ...1 A2
Leathsale Rd HA2 ...63 D5
Leathwaite Rd SW11 ...158 D6
Leathwell Rd SE8 ...141 D3
Lea Valley Prim Sch N17 ...34 A3
Lea Valley Rd EN3 ...19 B5
Lea Valley Riding Sch E10 ...52 D1
Lea Valley Technopark N17 ...52 A6
Lea Valley Trad Est N18 ...34 D5
Leaveland Cl BR3 ...207 C5
Leaver Gdns UB6 ...86 C5
Leavesden Rd HA7 ...25 A4
Leaview Ct 7 E4 ...20 A3
Lea View Ho E5 ...52 B1
Lebanon Ave TW13 ...172 D5
Lebanon Ct 10 TW1 ...153 B4
Lebanon Gdns SW18 ...157 C5
Lebanon Pk TW1 ...153 B4
Lebanon Rd SW18 ...157 C6
Croydon CR0 ...205 C1
Lebanon Road Sta CR0 ...221 C6
Lebrun Sq SE3 ...143 B2
Lebus Ho NW8 ...230 A3
Le Chateau CR0 ...221 B5
Lechmere App IG8 ...37 D1
Lechmere Ave IG8 ...37 D1
Lechmere Rd NW2 ...68 B2
Leckford Rd SW18 ...158 A3
Leckhampton Pl 23 SW2 ...160 C4
Leckwith Ave DA17 ...147 A6
Lecky St SW7 ...114 B1 256 C2
Leclair Ho SE3 ...143 B2
L'Ecole des Petits SW6 ...135 D3
Leconfield Ave SW13, SW15 ...133 D2
Leconfield Ho SE5 ...139 C2
Leconfield Rd N5 ...73 B4
Leda Ave EN3 ...6 D5
Leda Ct 9 SW9 ...138 C5
Ledalle Ho NW2 ...68 B5
Ledam Bldg EC1 ...241 A4
Leda Rd SE18 ...122 B3
Ledbury Ho 12 SE22 ...139 C2
Ledbury Mews N W11 ...91 C1
Ledbury Mews W W11 ...245 A6
Ledbury Pl 10 CR0 ...221 A4
Ledbury Rd W11 ...91 C1
Croydon CR0 ...221 B4
Ledbury St SE15 ...140 A5
Ledo Ho 1 N16 ...73 B4
Ledrington Rd SE19 ...184 A4
Ledway Dr HA9 ...44 B2
Lee Ave RM6 ...59 A3
Leechcroft Ave DA15 ...167 D6
Leechcroft Rd SM6 ...219 A5
Lee Church St SE13 ...142 C1
Lee Cl E17 ...34 D2
New Barnet EN5 ...2 A1
Lee Conservancy Rd E9 ...75 B3
Leecroft Rd EN5 ...1 A1
Leeds Ct EC1 ...241 C5
Carshalton SM5 ...218 D5
Catford SE6 ...163 D1
Leeds Rd IG1 ...57 B1
Leeds St N18 ...34 A5
Leegate SE12 ...164 D6
Lee Green SE12 ...142 D1
Lee High Rd SE12,SE13 ...142 C1
Lee Ho 3 N19 ...71 D3
Leeke St WC1 ...94 B4 233 C2
Leeland Mans W13 ...109 A5
Leeland Rd W13 ...109 A5
Leeland Terr W13 ...109 A5
Leeland Way NW10 ...67 D4
Lee Manor Sch SE13 ...164 C5
Leemount Cl NW4 ...46 D5
Lee Park Way N9,N18 ...19 A1
Lee Pk SE3 ...142 D2
Lee Rd NW7 ...28 D3
SE3 ...142 D1
Enfield EN1 ...18 A5
Merton SW19 ...179 D2
Wembley UB6 ...87 C6
Leerdam Dr E14 ...120 A3
Lees Ct W1 ...248 A6
Lees Ho SE17 ...262 D1
Leeside EN5 ...13 A5
Leeside Cres NW11 ...47 B4
Leeside Ind Est N17 ...34 B3
Leeside Rd N17 ...34 B4
Leeside Trad Est N17 ...34 C3
Leeside Works N17 ...34 C3
Leeson Ho 7 TW1 ...153 B4
Leeson Rd 12 SE24 ...138 C1
Leesons Hill BR5,BR7 ...211 D6
Leesons Way BR5 ...189 D1
Lees Par UB10 ...82 D3
Lees Pl W1 ...115 A6 248 A6
Lees Rd UB8 ...82 D3
Lee St E8 ...95 D6
Lee Sta SE12 ...165 A5
Lees The CR0 ...223 B6
Leet Ct N16 ...73 B4
Lee Terr SE3 ...142 C2
Lee Valley L Ctr N9 ...19 A3
Lee Valley Sp Ctr E15 ...75 D4
Leeve Ho 7 W9 ...91 B4
Lee View EN2 ...4 D4
Leeward Ct 3 E1 ...118 A5
Leeward Gdns SW19 ...179 B5
Leeway SE8 ...119 B1
Leeway Cl HA5 ...23 B3
Leewood Cl SE12 ...165 A5
Lefevre Wlk E3 ...97 B6
Leffern Rd W12 ...112 A4
Left Ho 7 NW6 ...69 A1
Lefroy Ho SE1 ...252 A1
Lefroy Rd W12 ...111 D4
Legard Rd N5 ...72 D5
Legat Ct N4 ...51 A4
Legatt Rd SE9 ...165 D6
Leggatt Rd E15 ...98 A5
Legge St SE13 ...164 A6
Leghorn Rd NW10 ...90 A5
SE18 ...123 B1
Legion Cl N1 ...72 C1
Legion Ct SM4 ...201 C3
Legion Rd UB6 ...86 A5
Legion Terr E3 ...97 C6
Legion Way N12 ...30 C3
Legrace Ave TW4,TW5 ...128 D3
Leicester Ave CR4 ...204 A5
Leicester Cl KT4 ...216 C4
Leicester Ct 46 W2 ...91 C2
WC2 ...249 D6
11 Twickenham TW1 ...153 D5
Leicester Gdns IG3 ...57 C2
Leicester Ho 4 SW9 ...138 D2
5 Putney SW15 ...156 C4
2 Thames Ditton KT7 ...197 A2
Leicester Mews N2 ...48 C6
Leicester Pl WC2 ...249 D6
Leicester Rd N2 ...48 C6
NW10 ...67 B1
Barnet EN5 ...1 D1
Croydon CR0 ...205 C2
Wanstead E11 ...55 B4
Leicester Sq★ WC2 ...115 D6 249 D5
Leicester Square Sta WC2 ...115 D6 249 D6
Leicester St WC2 ...249 D6
Leigham Ave SW16 ...160 A1
Leigham Cl SW16 ...182 B6
Leigham Court Rd SW16 ...182 C6
Leigham Dr TW7 ...130 C5
Leigham Hall 3 SW16 ...160 A1
Leigham Hall Par 2 SW16 ...160 A1
Leigham Vale SE27, SW16,SW2 ...160 C2
Leigh Ave IG4 ...55 D5
Leigh Cl KT3 ...199 B5
Leigh Cres CR0 ...223 D1
Leigh Ct 22 SW2 ...160 C5
Harrow HA2 ...42 C1
3 Woodford E18 ...37 A1
Leighfield Ho 5 N4 ...51 A2
Leigh Gdns NW10 ...90 C5
Leigh Ho
4 Kingston KT2 ...176 D4
9 Putney SW15 ...156 A6
Leigh Hunt Dr N14 ...15 D3
Leigh Orchard Cl SW16 ...160 B1
Leigh Pl DA16 ...146 A3
EC1 ...241 A4
Leigh Rd E10 ...54 A2
N5 ...72 D4
Leigh Rd *continued*
Isleworth TW3 ...130 B1
Wallend E6 ...78 C2
Leigh St WC1 ...94 A4 233 A1
Leigh The KT2 ...177 C3
Leighton Ave
Little Ilford E12 ...78 C3
Pinner HA5 ...41 A6
Leighton Cl HA8 ...26 C1
Leighton Cres NW5 ...71 C3
Leighton Gdns NW10 ...90 C5
Thornton Heath CR0 ...204 D1
Leighton Gr NW5 ...71 C3
Leighton Ho 7 KT6 ...198 A3
Leighton House (Art Gall & Mus)★ W14 ...254 D6
Leighton Pl NW5 ...71 C3
Leighton Rd NW5 ...71 C3
Ealing W13 ...109 A4
Enfield EN1 ...18 A6
Harrow HA3 ...24 B1
Leighton St CR0 ...204 D1
Leila Parnell Pl 14 SE7 ...143 C6
Leinster Ave SW14 ...133 A1
Leinster Ct NW6 ...91 C4
Leinster Gdns W2 ...114 A6 246 A6
Leinster Mews W2 ...246 A6
Leinster Pl W2 ...236 A1
Leinster Rd N10 ...49 B5
Leinster Sq W2 ...91 D1
Leinster Terr W2 ...246 A6
Leisure Way N12 ...30 B3
Leitch Ho 8 NW8 ...70 B1
Leith Cl NW9 ...45 B1
Leithcote Gdns SW16 ...182 B6
Leithcote Path SW16 ...160 B1
Leith Hill BR5 ...190 A2
Leith Hill Gn BR5 ...190 A2
Leith Ho 7 N7 ...71 D3
13 Streatham SW2 ...160 B4
Leith Mans W9 ...91 D4
Leith Rd N22 ...32 D2
Leith Towers 11 SM2 ...217 D1
Leith Yd 3 NW6 ...91 C6
Lela Ave TW4,TW5 ...128 C3
Lelitia Cl E8 ...96 A6
Lelland Ho 8 SE7 ...122 A2
Lely Ho 3 UB5 ...84 D5
Leman St E1 ...96 A1
Lemark Cl HA7 ...25 C4
Le May Ave SE12 ...165 B1
Lemmon Rd SE10 ...142 C6
Lemna Ct E11 ...54 C2
Lemna Rd E11 ...54 C2
Le Moal Ho 23 E1 ...96 C2
Lemon Gr TW14 ...150 A3
Lemonwell Ct SE9 ...167 A6
Lemonwell Dr SE9 ...167 A6
Lemsford Cl N15 ...52 A4
Lemsford Ct N4 ...73 A6
Lena Cres N9 ...18 C2
Lena Gardens Prim Sch W6 ...112 C3
Lena Gdns W6 ...112 C3
Lena Kennedy Cl E4 ...36 A4
Len Clifton Ho 13 SE18 ...122 B2
Lendal Terr 7 SW4 ...137 D2
Lenelby Rd KT6 ...198 C1
Len Freeman Pl SW6 ...264 C5
Lenham 11 NW5 ...71 A2
Lenham Ho SE1 ...252 D1
Lenham Rd DA7 ...147 B6
SE12 ...142 D1
South Norwood CR7 ...183 B1
Sutton SM1 ...218 A3
Lennard Ave BR4 ...224 C6
Lennard Cl BR4 ...224 C6
Lennard Rd BR2 ...210 B1
Croydon CR0 ...205 A1
Penge BR3 ...185 A4
Lennon Rd NW2 ...68 C2
Lennox Gdns NW10 ...67 D4
SW1 ...114 D3 257 C5
Croydon CR0 ...220 D4
Redbridge IG1 ...56 B1
Lennox Gdns Mews SW1 ...257 C4
Lennox Ho 10 E9 ...74 C2
7 Belvedere DA17 ...125 C3
Lennox Rd E17 ...53 C3
N4,N7 ...72 C6
Lenor Cl DA6 ...147 A1
Lensbury Way SE2 ...124 D3
Lens Rd E7 ...77 C1
Lenthall Ho SW1 ...259 B1
Lenthall Rd E8 ...74 A1
Lenthorp Rd SE10 ...120 D2
Lentmead Rd BR1 ...164 D1
Lenton Rise TW9 ...132 A2
Lenton St SE18 ...123 B2
Len Williams Ct NW6 ...91 C5
Leo Ct 4 TW8 ...131 D5
Leof Cres SE6 ...185 D5
Leominster Rd SM4 ...202 A3
Leominster Wlk SM4 ...202 A3
Leonard Ave SM4 ...202 A4
Leonard Ct W8 ...255 A6
WC1 ...240 A6
Leonard Day Ho 3 NW5 ...71 B2
Leonard Pl 6 N16 ...73 C4
Leonard Rd E7 ...77 A4
Chingford E4 ...35 C4
Edmonton N9 ...18 A1
Mitcham CR4,SW16 ...181 C2
Southall UB2 ...106 D2

Leonard Robbins Path 3 SE28 124 B6
Leonard St E16 122 A5
EC2 95 B3 242 D6
Leonora Ho W9 236 A6
Leontine Cl SE15 140 A5
Leopards Ct EC1 241 A4
Leopold Ave SW19 179 B5
Leopold Bldgs 14 E2 95 D4
Leopold Mews E9 96 C6
Leopold Prim Sch NW10 67 D1
Leopold Rd E17 53 C4
N2 48 B6
NW10 67 C1
Ealing W5 110 B5
Edmonton N18 34 B5
Wimbledon SW19 179 B5
Leopold St E3 97 B2
Leopold Terr SW19 179 C5
Leopold Wlk SE11 260 C1
Leo St SE15 140 B5
Leo Yd EC1 241 D5
Leppoc Rd SW4 159 D6
Leroy St SE1 117 C2 263 A4
Lerry Cl W14 264 D6
Lerwick Ct 4 EN1 17 C6
Lerwick Ho SW18 136 A1
Lescombe Cl SE23 163 A1
Lescombe Rd SE23,SE6 163 A1
Lesley Cl DA5 169 D4
Lesley Ct 8 SM6 219 B4
Leslie Gdns SM2 217 C1
Leslie Gr CR0 205 C1
Leslie Grove Pl CR0 205 C1
Leslie Park Rd CR0 205 C1
Leslie Rd E11 76 B4
N2 48 B6
Newham E16 99 B1
Leslie Smith Sq 7
SE18 144 C6
Lessar Ave SW4 159 C5
Lessar Ct SW4 159 C5
Lessingham Ave
Ilford IG5 56 C6
Upper Tooting SW17 181 A6
Lessing St SE23 163 A4
Lessness Ave DA7 146 D5
Lessness Heath Prim Sch
DA17 125 C1
Lessness Pk DA17 125 C1
Lessness Rd
Belvedere DA17 125 C1
Morden SM4 202 A4
Lester Ave E16 98 C3
Lester Ct 42 E3 97 D4
Lester Ho IG8 36 B3
Lestock Ho SE3 143 D4
Lestor Ct TW7 130 D2
Leswin Pl N16 73 D5
Leswin Rd N16 73 D5
Letchford Gdns NW10 90 A4
Letchford Mews NW10 90 A4
Letchmore Ho W10 90 C3
Letchworth Ave TW14 149 D4
Letchworth Cl BR2 209 A4
South Oxhey WD19 22 D5
Letchworth Dr BR2 209 A4
Letchworth St SW17 180 D6
Lethaby Ho 15 SW4 138 B1
Lethbridge Cl SE13 142 A3
Letterstone Rd SW6 264 C3
Lettice St SW6 135 B4 264 D1
Lett Rd E15 76 B1
Lettsom St SE5 139 C3
Lettsom Wlk 1 E13 99 A5
Leucha Rd E17 53 A4
Levana Cl SW19 157 A3
Levant Ho 17 E1 96 D3
Levehurst Ho SE27 183 A5
Levehurst Way SW4,
SW9 138 A3
Leven Cl WD19 22 D5
Levendale Rd SE23 163 B2
Leven Rd E14 98 B1
Leven Way UB3 83 C1
Lever Ct 15 E9 74 D2
Leverett St SW3 257 B4
Leverholme Gdns SE9 188 C6
Leverington Pl N1 235 D1
Leverson St SW16 181 C4
Lever St EC1 95 A4 235 A1
Leverstock Ho SW3 257 B2
Leverton Pl NW5 71 C3
Leverton St NW5 71 C3
Levett Gdns IG3 80 A5
Levett Ho 8 SW16 181 C5
Levett Rd IG11 79 C2
Levine Gdns IG11 102 D5
Levison Way 2 N19 49 D1
Levita Ho NW1 232 D2
Levyne Ct EC1 241 A6
Lewes Cl UB5 63 C2
Lewes Ct 3 CR4 202 D6
Lewesdon Cl 13 SW19 156 D3
Lewes Ho SE1 253 B2
SE15 140 A6
Lewes Rd BR1 187 D1
N12 30 C5
Leweston Pl N16 51 D2
Lewey Ho E3 97 B3
Lewgars Ave NW9 45 A3
Lewin Ct SW16 182 A4
Lewing Cl BR6 211 C1
Lewin Rd DA6 147 A1
Mortlake SW14 133 B2
Streatham SW16 181 D4
Lewis Ave E17 35 C2
Lewis Cl N14 15 C4
Lewis Cres NW10 67 B3
Lewis Ct 5 SE16 118 B1
Lewis Gdns N2 30 B1
Lewis Gr SE13 142 A2
Lewisham Bridge Prim Sch
SE13 141 D2
Lewisham Bsns Ctr
SE14 140 D6
Lewisham Coll SE4 141 C3
Lewisham Ctr SE13 142 A2
Lewisham High St SE13 163 D6
Lewisham Hill SE13 142 A3
Lewisham Hospl SE13 163 D6
Lewisham Pk SE13 164 A5
Lewisham Rd SE13 142 A3
Lewisham St SW1 249 D1
Lewisham Sta SE13 142 A2
Lewisham Way SE4,SE14 141 B4
Lewis King Ho BR1 187 B3
Lewis Pl E8 74 A3
Lewis Rd Bexley DA16 146 C2
Mitcham CR4 180 C1
18 Richmond TW10 153 D6
Sidcup DA14 168 C1
Southall UB1 107 A4
Sutton SM1 217 D4
Lewis Silkin Ho 9 SE15 140 C6
Lewis Sports & L Ctr
SE19 183 D2
Lewis St NW1 71 B2
Lewis Way RM10 81 D2
Lexden Dr RM6 58 B3
Lexden Rd Acton W3 110 D5
Mitcham CR4 203 D5
Lexfield Ho N5 73 A4
Lexham Gardens Mews
W8 255 D5
Lexham Gdns
W8 113 D2 255 C4
Lexham Ho 9 IG11 101 B6
Lexham Mews
W8 113 C2 255 B4
Lexham Wlk W8 255 D5
Lexington St
W1 115 C6 249 B6
Lexton Gdns SW12 159 D3
Leyborne Ave W13 109 C4
Leyborne Pk TW9 132 C4
Leybourne Cl BR2 209 A3
Leybourne Ho 15 E14 97 B1
19 SE15 140 C6
Leybourne Rd E11 54 D1
16 NW1 71 B1
NW9 44 C4
Hillingdon UB10 83 A6
Leybourne St 5 NW1 71 B1
Leybridge Ct SE12 165 A6
Leyburn Cl E17 53 D5
Leyburn Gdns CR0 221 C6
Leyburn Gr N18 34 A4
Leyburn Ho 1 SE18 144 A5
Leyburn Rd N18 34 B4
Leyden Mans 3 N19 50 A2
Leyden St E1 95 D2 243 C3
Leydon Cl SE16 118 D5
Leyes Rd E16 99 D1
Leyfield KT4 199 D1
Ley Ho SE1 252 A1
Leyland Ave EN3 7 A3
Leyland Gdns IG8 37 C5
Leyland Ho 5 E14 119 D6
Leyland Rd SE12 165 A6
Leylands SW18 157 B5
Leylang Rd SE14 140 D5
Leys Cl HA1 42 B4
Leys Ct 10 SW9 138 C3
Leysdown 9 NW5 71 A2
Leysdown Ho SE17 263 B2
Leysdown Rd SE9 166 B2
Leysfield Rd W12 112 A4
Leys Gdns EN4 15 A6
Leyspring Rd E11 54 D1
Leys Rd E EN3 7 A4
Leys Rd W EN3 7 A4
Ley St Ilford IG1 78 D6
Ilford IG1,IG2 57 B1
Leys The N2 48 A5
Harrow HA3 44 B3
Leyswood Dr IG2 57 C4
Leythe Rd W3 111 A4
Leyton Bsns Ctr E10 75 C6
Leyton Ct SE23 162 C3
Leyton Grange E10 53 C1
Leyton Green Rd E10 54 A3
Leyton Ind Village E10 52 D2
Leyton Midland Road Sta
E10 54 A2
Leyton Park Rd E10 76 A5
Leyton Rd E15 76 B2
Merton SW19 180 A3
Leyton Sixth Form Coll
E10 54 B3
Leyton Sta E11 76 A5
Leyton Stadium (Leyton
Orient FC) E10 75 D5
Leytonstone High Road Sta
E11 76 C6
Leytonstone Rd E15 76 C3
Leytonstone Sch E11 54 C3
Leytonstone Sta E11 54 C1
Leyton Town Ctr E10 76 A5
Leywick St E15 98 C5
Lezayre Rd BR6 227 D2
Liardet St SE14 141 A6
Liberia Rd N5 72 D2
Liberty Ave SW19 180 B2
Liberty Ct IG11 102 C5
Liberty Ctr HA0 88 B6
Liberty Mews SW12 159 B5
Liberty Mid Sch CR4 180 C1
Liberty Pl 18 E1 118 A6
Liberty St SW9 138 B4 270 D2
Libra Ct E4 35 C6
Libra Rd E13 99 A5
6 E3 97 B5
Library Ct N17 51 D6
Library Mans 4 W12 112 C4
Library Par NW10 89 C6
Library Pl E1 118 B6
Library St SE1 116 D4 251 D1
Lichen Ct IG6 56 D6
Lichfield Cl EN4 2 D2
Lichfield Ct Kingston KT6 198 A4
Richmond TW9 132 A1
Lichfield Gdns TW10,
TW9 154 A6
Lichfield Gr N3 29 C1
Lichfield Ho 28 SE5 139 A3
Lichfield Rd E3 97 A4
E6 99 D4
NW2 69 A4
Dagenham RM8 80 C5
Edmonton N9 18 A2
Hounslow TW4 128 C2
Northwood HA6 40 A6
Richmond TW9 132 B4
Woodford IG8 36 C6
Lichfield Terr 1 TW9 154 A6
Lichlade Cl 7 BR6 227 D4
Lichport Ct N4 50 D1
Lickey Ho W14 264 D6
Lidbury Rd NW7 29 A4
Lidcote Gdns 22 SW9 138 B3
Liddall Way UB7 104 B5
Liddell Cl HA3 43 D6
Liddell Gdns NW10 90 C5
Liddell Rd NW6 69 C2
Lidding Rd HA3 43 D4
Liddington Rd E15 98 D6
Liddlesdale Ho E 6
KT2 176 D2
Liddlesdale Ho W 5
KT2 176 D2
Liddon Rd BR1 209 D6
E13 99 B4
Liden Cl E10,E17 53 B1
Lidfield Rd N16 73 B4
Lidgate Rd 21 SE15 139 D5
Lidiard Rd SW18 158 A2
Lidlington Pl NW1 232 B3
Lido Sq N17 33 B1
Lidyard Rd N19 49 C1
Liffey Ct NW10 68 A1
Liffler Rd SE18 123 C1
Liffords Pl SW13 133 D3
Lifford St SW15 134 D1
Lightcliffe Rd N13 16 C1
Lighter Cl 16 SE16 119 A2
Lighterman Mews 13 E1 96 D1
Lighterman's Rd E14 119 D4
Lighterman's Wlk SW18 135 C1
Lightfoot Rd N8 50 A4
Lightley Cl HA0 88 B6
Ligonier St E2 243 C6
Lilac Cl E4 35 B4
Lilac Ct 4 E13 99 C6
Lilac Gdns W5 109 D3
Croydon CR0 223 C5
Hayes UB3 83 C1
Lilac Ho SE4 141 B2
Lilac Pl SE11 116 B2 260 C3
Yiewsley UB7 104 B6
Lilac St W12 112 A6
Lilburn Ct SW15 134 D2
Lilburne Gdns SE9 166 A6
Lilburne Rd SE9 166 A6
Lilburne Wlk NW10 67 A2
Lile Cres W7 86 C2
Lilestone Est NW8 236 D5
Lilestone Ho NW8 236 D6
Lilestone St NW8 92 C3 237 A6
Lilford Ho 21 SE5 139 A3
Lilford Rd SE5 138 D3
Lilian Barker Cl SE12 165 A6
Lilian Baylis Ho N1 73 A2
Lilian Baylis Sch
SE11 116 B1 260 C2
Lilian Board Way UB6 64 B3
Lilian Gdns IG8 37 B2
Lilian Rd SW16 181 C2
Lilian Rolfe Ho 5 SE27 183 B6
Lillechurch Rd RM8 80 C2
Lilleshall Rd SM4 202 B3
Lilley Cl E1 118 A5
Lilliam Ave W3 110 C4
Lillian Cl 14 N16 73 C5
Lillian Rd SW13 134 B6
Lillie Ho N5 72 C3
Lillie Rd SW6 135 B6 264 C5
Lillieshall Rd SW4 137 C2
Lillie Yd SW6 135 C6 265 A6
Lillingston Ho N7 72 C4
Lilliput Ave UB5 85 B6
Lillywhite 21 NW9 27 D2
Lily Cl W14 112 D2
Lily Gdns HA0 87 C5
Lily Pl EC1 241 B4
Lily Rd E17 53 C3
Lilyville Rd SW6 135 B4 264 C2
Limavady Ho 18 SE18 122 C2
Limberg Ho SE8 119 B2
Limborough Ho 5 E14 97 C2
Limbourne Ave RM8 59 B2
Limburg Rd SW11 136 C1
Lime Ave UB7 104 B6
Limeburner La
EC4 94 D1 241 C2
Lime Cl BR1 210 A5
E1 118 A5
Lime Cl *continued*
Buckhurst Hill IG9 21 D2
Carshalton SM5 218 D6
Harrow HA3 25 A1
Pinner HA5 39 D6
Lime Cres TW16 172 C1
Limecroft Cl KT19 215 B1
Lime Ct 8 E11 76 C6
9 Harrow HA1 42 D3
Kingston KT3 198 D6
Mitcham CR4 180 B1
Putney SW15 134 B2
Limedene Cl HA5 22 D2
Lime Gr DA15 167 D5
W12 112 C4
Barnet N20 13 B3
Hayes UB3 105 B6
Kingston KT3 199 C6
Orpington BR6 226 D6
Ruislip HA4 40 B2
Twickenham TW1 153 A5
Limeharbour E14 119 D4
Limehouse Cswy E14 119 B6
Limehouse Cut 5 E14 97 D2
Limehouse Fields Est
E14 97 A2
Limehouse Link (Tunnel)
E14 119 B6
Limehouse Sta E14 97 A1
Lime Kiln Dr SE7 143 B6
Limekiln Pl SE19 183 D3
Limekiln Wharf 21 E14 119 B6
Lime Lo 3 TW16 171 D3
Limerick Cl SW12 159 C4
Limerick Ct 1 SW12 159 C4
Lime Row DA18 125 B3
Limerston St
SW10 136 A6 266 B5
Limes Ave N12 30 A6
NW11 47 A2
NW7 27 C4
Barnes SW13 133 D3
Carshalton SM5 202 D1
Croydon CR0 220 C5
Penge SE20 184 B3
Wanstead E11 55 B5
Limes Ave The N11 31 C5
Limes Cl 3 N11 31 C5
Ashford TW15 170 C5
Limes Ct NW6 68 D1
Beckenham BR3 185 D1
Limesdale Gdns HA8 27 A1
Limes Field Rd SW14 133 C2
Limesford Rd SE15 140 D1
Limes Gdns SW18 157 C5
Limes Gr SE13 142 A1
Limes Rd
Beckenham BR3 185 D1
Thornton Heath CR0 205 B2
Limes Row BR6 226 D3
Lime St E17 53 A5
EC3 95 C1 243 A1
Limes The BR2 226 A6
SE5 139 C2
W2 245 B5
East Molesey KT8 195 D5
Lime St Pas EC3 253 A6
Limes Wlk SE15 140 C1
W5 109 D4
Lime Terr W7 108 C6
Lime Tree Ave KT10,KT7 196 C1
Limetree Cl SW2 160 B3
Lime Tree Ct N2 47 D6
Limetree Ct HA5 23 C3
Lime Tree Ct CR2 221 A2
Lime Tree Gr CR0 223 B5
Lime Tree Pl CR4 181 B2
Lime Tree Rd TW5 129 D4
Limetree Wlk 2 SW17 181 A5
Lime Tree Wlk
Bushey WD23 8 C2
Coney Hall BR4 224 D4
Enfield EN2 5 A5
Lime Wlk 11 E15 98 C6
Limewood Cl E17 53 B5
Beckenham BR3 208 A4
Ealing W13 87 B1
Limewood Ct IG4 56 B4
Limpsfield Ave
Putney SW19 156 D2
Thornton Heath CR7 204 B4
Limscott Ho 35 E3 97 D4
Linacre Cl SE15 140 B2
Linacre Ct W6 112 D1
Linacre Rd NW2 68 B2
Linale Ho N1 235 C3
Linberry Wlk 2 SE8 119 B2
Linchmere Rd SE12 164 D4
Lincoln Ave N14 15 C2
Twickenham TW2 152 A2
Wimbledon SW19 156 D1
Lincoln Cl Croydon SE25 206 B3
Greenford UB6 86 A6
Harrow HA2 41 B4
Lincoln Cres EN1 17 D6
Lincoln Ct N16 51 B2
NW4 46 B5
SE12 165 C1
Borehamwood WD6 11 B6
Enfield EN2 5 B1
Hampton TW12 173 B5
2 Ilford IG2 57 A3
Mitcham CR4 204 A4
Redbridge IG1 56 B2
Lincoln Gdns IG1 56 A2
Lincoln Green Rd BR5 211 D4
Lincoln Ho SW1 247 C1
10 Putney SW15 157 A6
Lincoln Lo 10 BR3 185 D1
Lincoln Mews NW6 91 B6
Lincoln Rd DA14 190 B5
E13 99 B3
E7 77 D2
N2 48 C6
Croydon SE25 206 B6
Enfield EN1,EN3 18 B6
Harrow HA2,HA5 41 B4
Kingston KT3 199 A6
Mitcham CR4 204 A4
North Cheam KT4 200 B1
Northwood HA6 39 D6
Twickenham TW13 151 B1
Wembley HA0 65 D2
Woodford E18 37 A2
Lincoln's Inn*
WC2 94 B1 240 D2
Lincoln's Inn Fields
WC2 94 B1 240 D2
Lincoln St E11 76 C6
SW3 257 C3
Lincolns The NW7 11 D1
Lincoln Terr 4 SM2 217 C1
Lincoln Way
Charlton TW16 171 C2
Enfield EN1 18 B6
Lincombe Rd BR1 164 D1
Linda Ct KT9 213 D4
Lindal Cres EN2 4 B1
Lindal Ct 1 E18 37 A2
Lindale SW19 157 A2
Lindales The N17 33 D4
Lindal Rd SE4 163 B6
Lindbergh Rd SM6 220 A1
Linden Ave NW10 90 D5
Enfield EN1 6 A4
Hounslow TW3 151 D6
Ruislip HA4 40 A1
Thornton Heath CR7 204 D5
Wembley HA9 66 B3
Linden Bridge Sch KT4 215 C5
Linden Cl Ruislip HA4 40 A1
Southgate N14 15 C5
Stanmore HA7 25 B5
Thames Ditton KT7 197 A2
Linden Cotts 6 SW19 179 A4
Linden Cres
Kingston KT1 176 B1
Wembley UB6 64 D2
Woodford IG8 37 B4
Linden Ct NW7 27 B5
8 SW18 136 B1
W12 112 C5
1 Beckenham BR3 207 D6
Penge SE20 184 B3
Sidcup DA14 189 C6
Lindenfield BR7 188 D1
Linden Gdns
W2 113 C6 245 B5
W4 111 B1
Enfield EN1 6 A4
Linden Gr SE15 140 C2
Kingston KT3 199 C6
Penge SE20 184 C4
Teddington TW11 174 D5
Linden Ho 10 SE8 141 B6
Linden Lawns HA9 66 B4
Linden Lea N2 48 A4
Lindenlea Ct E17 53 B5
Linden Leas BR4 224 B6
Linden Lodge Sch
SW19 157 A3
Linden Mans N6 49 B1
Linden Mews N1 73 B3
W2 245 B5
Linden Pl CR4 202 C5
Linden Rd N10 49 B5
N11 15 A2
N15 51 A5
Hampton TW12 173 C2
Lindens The 5 E17 53 D5
N12 30 B5
Chiswick W4 133 A4
New Addington CR0 224 A2
Linden Way
Shepperton TW17 193 A4
Southgate N14 15 C5
Lindeth Cl HA7 25 B4
Lindfield Gdns NW3 70 A3
Lindfield Hts NW3 70 A3
Lindfield Rd
Croydon CR0 205 D3
Ealing W5 87 C3
Lindfield St E14 97 C1
Lindhill Cl EN3 6 D3
Lindholme Ct 3 NW9 27 C2
Lindisfarne Rd
Dagenham RM8 80 C5
Wimbledon SW20 178 A3
Lindisfarne Way E9 75 A4
Lindley Ct KT1 175 C2
Lindley Ho 12 SE15 140 A5
Lindley Pl TW9 132 C4
Lindley Rd E10 76 A6
Lindley St E1 96 C2
Lindon Bennett Sch
TW13 172 D5
Lindop Ho 7 E3 97 A3
Lindore Rd SW11 136 D1
Lindores Rd SM5 202 A1
Lindo St SE15 140 C3
Lind Rd SM1 218 A3
Lindrop St SW6 136 A3
Lindsay Cl KT9 214 A1
Lindsay Ct SW11 266 D1
Lindsay Dr Harrow HA3 44 B4
Shepperton TW17 193 B3
Lindsay Ho 2 SE18 122 C2
Lindsay Rd
Hampton TW12 173 D6
North Cheam KT4 216 B6
Lindsay Sq SW1 115 D1 259 D2
Lindsell St 6 SE10 142 A4
Lindsey Cl BR1 210 A6
Mitcham CR4,SW16 204 A5
Lindsey Ct N13 16 C1
Lindsey Gdns TW14 149 B4
Lindsey Ho* SW10 266 D4
W5 109 D2
Lindsey Mews 13 N1 73 A1
Lindsey Rd RM8 80 C5
Lindsey St EC1 94 D2 241 D4
Lind St SE8 141 D3
Lindum Rd TW11 175 C3
Lindums The BR3 185 B4
Lindway SE27 182 D5
Lindwood Cl 8 E6 100 B2
Linfield WC1 233 C1
Linfield Cl NW4 46 C5
Linford Ct 1 CR4 180 C2
Linford Ho 17 E2 96 A6
Linford Rd E17 54 A6
Linford St SW8 137 C4 269 A1
Lingard Ho 9 E14 120 A3
Lingards Rd SE13 142 A1
Lingey Cl DA15 167 D2
Lingfield Ave KT1,KT5 198 B5
Lingfield Ct EN1 17 C5
Lingfield Cres SE9,DA16 145 B1
Lingfield Ct Northolt UB5 85 C5
Wimbledon SW19 178 D4
Lingfield Gdns N9 18 B4
Lingfield Ho SE1 251 D1
5 W4 111 A1
Penge SE26 184 B4
Lingfield Rd
North Cheam KT4 216 C5
Wimbledon SW19 178 D4
Lingham St SW9 138 B3
Lingholm Way EN5 12 D6
Ling Rd E16 99 A2
Lingrove Gdns IG9 21 B2
Ling's Coppice SE21 161 B2
Lingwell Rd SW17 158 C1
Lingwood DA7 147 D3
Lingwood Gdns TW7 130 C5
Lingwood Rd E5 52 A2
Linhope St NW1 92 D3 237 C5
Linkenholt Mans 3 W6 111 D2
Linkfield KT8 195 D6
Link Field BR2 209 A3
Linkfield Rd TW7 130 D3
Link La SM6 220 A2
Linklea Cl NW9 27 C3
Link Prim Sch CR0 220 A4
Link Rd N11 31 A6
Dagenham RM9 103 D5
East Bedfont TW14 149 D4
Hackbridge SM6 203 A1
Links Ave SM4 201 C5
Linkscroft Ave TW15 170 D4
Links Ct N20 14 B1
Links Dr N20 13 D3
Link Sec Sch CR0 220 B4
Links Gdns SW16 182 C3
Linkside N12 29 C4
Kingston KT3 177 C1
Linkside Cl EN2 4 C2
Linkside Gdns EN2 4 B2
Links Ind Est TW13 151 A1
Links Prim Sch SW17 181 A4
Links Rd NW2 67 D6
Acton W3 88 C1
Ashford TW15 170 A5
Mitcham SW16,SW17 181 A4
West Wickham BR4 208 A1
Woodford IG8 37 A5
Links Side EN2 4 C2
Link St E9 74 C2
Links The E17 53 A5
Linksview N2 48 D4
Links View N3 29 B3
SE18 144 D4
Links View Cl HA7 25 A4
Links View Rd
Croydon CR0 223 C5
Hampton TW12 174 A6
Linksway NW4 28 D1
Links Way
Beckenham BR3 207 C3
Streatham SW17 181 A4
Links Yd E1 243 D4
9 E1 96 A2
Link The NW2 46 A1
SE9 166 C1
Acton W3 88 D1
Enfield EN3 7 A4
Northolt UB5 63 B3
Pinner HA5 40 C2
Teddington TW11 174 D4
Wembley HA0 43 C1
Linkway N4 51 A2
Dagenham RM8 80 C4
Pinner HA5 22 D2
West Barnes SW20 200 B6
Link Way Bromley BR2 210 A2
Richmond TW10 153 B2
Linkway The EN5 13 D5
Linkwood Wlk NW1 71 D1
Linley Cres RM7 59 D6
Linley Ct
1 Dulwich SE21 183 C6
Sutton SM1 218 A4
Linley Rd N17 33 C1
Linnell Cl NW11 47 D3
Linnell Dr NW11 47 D3
Linnell Ho E1 243 C4
NW8 229 A6
Linnell Rd SE5 139 C3
Edmonton N18 34 A5
Linnet Cl N9 18 D3

Linnet Cl *continued*
Bushey WD23 ....8 A3
Woolwich SE28 ....124 C6
Linnet Mews SW12 ....159 A4
Linnett Cl E4 ....36 A6
Linom Rd SW4 ....138 A1
Linscott Rd E5 ....74 C4
Linsdell Rd IG11 ....101 A6
Linsey St SE16 ....118 A2
SE16 ....118 A3
Linslade Cl
Hounslow TW4 ....151 A6
Pinner HA5 ....40 B6
Linslade Ho 10 E2 ....96 A6
NW8 ....237 B6
Linstead St 1 NW6 ....69 C1
Linstead Way SW18,
SW19 ....157 A4
Linsted Ct SE9,DA15 ....167 C5
Linster Gr WD6 ....11 A6
Lintaine Cl W6 ....264 B5
Linthorpe Ave HA0 ....65 C2
Linthorpe Rd N16 ....51 C2
Cockfosters EN4 ....2 C2
Linton Cl DA16 ....146 B4
2 SE7 ....121 C1
Carshalton CR4 ....202 D2
Linton Gdns E6 ....100 A1
Linton Gr SE27 ....183 A5
Linton Ho 2 E3 ....97 C2
Linton Mead Prim Sch
SE28 ....124 B6
Linton Rd IG11 ....79 A1
Linton St N1 ....95 A6 235 B5
Lintons The IG11 ....79 A1
Linver Rd SW6 ....135 C3
Linwood Cl SE5 ....139 D3
Linwood Cres EN1 ....6 A4
Linzee Rd N8 ....50 A5
Lion Ave TW1 ....152 D3
Lion Cl SE4 ....163 C5
Littleton TW17 ....192 A6
Lion Ct 12 NW9 ....46 A5
Lion Ctr The TW13 ....151 A1
Lionel Gdns SE9 ....165 D6
Lionel Ho 5 W10 ....91 A2
Bowes Park N22 ....32 B4
Lionel Mans 14 W14 ....112 D3
Lionel Mews W10 ....91 A2
Lionel Rd SE9 ....165 D6
Lionel Road Jun & Inf Sch
TW8 ....110 A2
Lionel Road N TW8 ....110 A2
Lionel Road S TW8 ....110 B1
Lion Gate Gdns TW9 ....132 B2
Lion Gate Mews SW18 ....157 C4
Lion Mills 33 E2 ....96 A5
Lion Park Ave KT9 ....214 C4
Lion Rd DA6 ....147 B1
E6 ....100 B2
Edmonton N9 ....18 A2
Thornton Heath CR0 ....205 A4
Twickenham TW1,TW2 ....152 D3
Lions Cl SE12 ....165 D1
Lion Way TW8 ....131 D5
Lion Wharf Rd TW7 ....131 B2
Lion Yd SW4 ....137 D1
Liphook Cres SE23 ....162 C4
Liphook Rd WD19 ....22 D6
Lipton Cl SE28 ....124 C6
Lipton Rd 8 E1 ....96 D1
Lisa Lo 5 EN5 ....13 D6
Lisbon Ave TW2 ....152 A2
Lisbon Cl E17 ....35 B1
Lisburne Rd NW3 ....70 D4
Lisford St SE15 ....139 D4
Lisgar Terr W14 ....113 B2 254 C4
Liskeard Cl BR7 ....189 A4
Liskeard Gdns SE3 ....143 A4
Liskeard Ho SE11 ....261 B2
Lisle Cl SW17 ....181 B6
Lisle Ct NW2 ....69 A5
Lisle St WC2 ....115 D6 249 D6
Lismirrane Ind Pk WD6 ....9 B5
Lismore 9 SW19 ....179 B5
Lismore Cl TW7 ....131 A3
Lismore Rd N17 ....51 B6
South Croydon CR2 ....221 C2
Lismore Wlk 4 N1 ....73 A2
Lissant Cl KT6 ....197 D2
Lisselton Ho 3 NW4 ....46 D5
Lissenden Gdns NW5 ....71 A4
Lissenden Mans NW5 ....71 A4
Lisson Cotts NW1 ....237 B4
Lisson Gr NW1,
NW8 ....92 C3 237 A6
Lisson Ho NW1 ....237 A4
Lisson St NW1 ....92 C2 237 A4
Lister Cl W3 ....89 B2
Mitcham SW19 ....180 C2
Lister Com Sch E13 ....99 B5
Lister Ct N16 ....73 C6
NW9 ....27 C1
Lister Gdns N18 ....33 A5
Lister Ho E1 ....96 A2
SE2 ....124 D1
SE3 ....142 C6
Hayes UB3 ....105 C2
9 Wembley HA9 ....67 A5
Lister Hospl
SW1 ....115 B1 258 C1
Lister Mews N7 ....72 B4
Lister Rd E11 ....54 D1
Lister Wlk SE28 ....124 D6
Liston Ho N21 ....16 B6
Liston Rd SW4 ....137 C2
Tottenham N17 ....34 A2
Liston Way 1 IG8 ....37 C3
Listowel Cl 2 SW9 ....138 C5
Listowel Rd RM10 ....81 C5
Listria Lo N16 ....73 D6
Listria Pk N16 ....73 D6
Litcham Ho 23 E1 ....96 D4
Litchfield Ave E15 ....76 C2
Morden SM4 ....201 B2
Litchfield Ct E17 ....53 C3
Litchfield Gdns NW10 ....68 A2
Litchfield Rd SM1 ....218 A4
Litchfield St WC2 ....249 D6
Litchfield Way NW11 ....48 A4
Lithgow's Rd TW14,TW6 ....127 D1
Lithos Rd NW3 ....70 A2
Little Acre BR3 ....207 C6
Little Albany St NW1 ....238 D6
Little Argyll St W1 ....239 A1
Little Birches DA15 ....167 C2
Little Boltons The
SW10 ....255 D1
Little Bornes SE21 ....183 C6
Littlebourne 2 SE13 ....164 C4
Little Britain EC1 ....242 A3
Littlebrook Cl CR0 ....206 D3
Little Brownings SE23 ....162 B2
Littlebury Rd SW4 ....137 D2
Little Bury St N9 ....17 C4
Little Bushey La WD23 ....8 B5
Little Cedars N12 ....30 A6
Little Chelsea Ho SW10 ....266 B5
Little Chester St SW1 ....258 C6
Little College St SW1 ....260 A6
Littlecombe SE7 ....143 B6
Little Combe Cl 13
SW15 ....156 D5
Little Common HA7 ....9 A1
Littlecote Cl SW19 ....157 A4
Littlecote Pl HA5 ....23 B2
Littlecroft SE9 ....144 C2
Little Ct BR4 ....224 C6
Littledale SE2 ....146 A6
Little Dimocks SW12 ....159 B2
Little Dorrit Ct SE1 ....252 B2
Little Ealing La W5 ....109 C2
Little Ealing Prim Sch
W5 ....109 C3
Little Edward St NW1 ....231 D2
Little Elms UB3 ....127 B5
Little Essex St WC2 ....251 A6
Little Ferry Rd TW1 ....153 B3
Littlefield Cl N19 ....71 C4
9 Kingston KT1 ....176 A1
Littlefield Ct UB7 ....126 A5
Littlefield Ho KT1 ....176 A1
Littlefield Rd HA8 ....27 A3
Little Friday Rd E4 ....20 C2
Little Gearies IG6 ....56 D5
Little George St SW1 ....250 A1
Little Gn TW9 ....131 D1
Little Grange UB6 ....87 A4
Little Green St NW5 ....71 B4
Littlegrove EN4 ....14 C5
Littlegrove Ct 3 EN4 ....14 C5
Little Halliards KT12 ....194 A3
Little Heath SE7 ....122 A1
Ilford RM6 ....58 B5
Little Heath Rd DA7 ....147 B5
Littleheath Rd CR2 ....222 B1
Little Heath Sch RM6 ....58 B5
Little Holt 8 E11 ....55 A4
Little Ilford La E12 ....78 B4
Little Ilford Sch E12 ....78 B3
Littlejohn Rd W7 ....86 D1
Little Larkins EN5 ....13 A5
Little Marlborough St
W1 ....239 A1
Littlemead KT10 ....212 B4
Littlemede SE9 ....166 B1
Littlemoor Rd IG1 ....79 B5
Littlemore Rd SE2 ....124 A4
Little Moss La HA5 ....23 A1
Little Newport St WC2 ....249 D6
Little New St EC4 ....241 B2
Little Orchard Cl HA5 ....23 A1
Little Oxhey La WD19 ....23 A6
Little Park Dr TW13 ....151 A2
Little Park Gdns EN2 ....5 B2
Little Pluckett's Way IG9 ....21 D3
Little Portland St W1 ....239 A2
Little Potters WD23 ....8 C4
Little Queens Rd TW11 ....174 D4
Little Rd UB3 ....105 D4
Little Redlands BR1 ....188 A1
Little Road Mans SW6 ....264 B5
Littlers Cl SW19 ....180 B2
Little Russell St WC1 ....240 A3
Little Sanctuary SW1 ....250 A1
Little Smith St SW1 ....259 D6
Little Somerset St E1 ....243 C1
Little Stanmore Fst & Mid
Sch HA8 ....26 B2
Little St James's St
SW1 ....249 A3
Little St Leonards
SW14 ....133 A2
Littlestone Cl BR3 ....185 C4
Little Strand NW9 ....27 D1
Little Thrift BR5 ....211 A5
Little Titchfield St W1 ....239 A3
Littleton Ave E4 ....20 D3
Littleton CE Inf Sch
TW17 ....192 C6
Littleton Cres HA1 ....64 D6
Littleton La TW17,TW18 ....192 A4
Littleton Rd Harrow HA1 ....64 D6
Littleton TW15,TW17 ....171 A3
Littleton St SW18 ....158 A2
Little Trinity La EC4 ....252 B6
Little Venice★
W9 ....92 A2 236 A4
Littlewood SE13 ....164 A5
Littlewood Cl W13 ....109 B3
Little Wood Cl BR5 ....190 A2
Littleworth Ave KT10 ....212 B3
Littleworth Common Rd
KT10 ....212 B5
Littleworth La KT10 ....212 B4
Littleworth Pl KT10 ....212 B4
Littleworth Rd KT10 ....212 C4
Livermere Ct 3 E8 ....95 D6
Livermere Rd E8 ....95 D6
Liverpool Gr
SE17 ....117 B1 262 C1
Liverpool Ho N7 ....72 C2
Liverpool Rd E10 ....54 A3
E16 ....98 C2
N1 ....234 B5
N1,N7 ....72 C1
W5 ....109 D4
Kingston KT2 ....176 C3
South Norwood CR7 ....205 A6
Liverpool St EC2 ....95 C2 243 A3
Liverpool Street Sta
EC2 ....95 C2 243 A3
Livesey Cl KT1 ....198 B6
Livesey Mus★ SE15 ....140 B6
Livesey Pl SE15 ....140 A6
Livingstone Ct E10 ....54 A3
Barnet EN5 ....1 A3
Stanwell TW19 ....148 A3
Livingstone Ho 16 SE5 ....139 A5
Livingstone Lo 13 W9 ....91 C2
Livingstone Pl E14 ....120 A1
Livingstone Prim Sch EN4 ....2 B2
Livingstone Rd E15 ....98 A6
E17 ....53 D3
14 SW11 ....136 B2
Bowes Park N13 ....32 A5
Isleworth TW3 ....130 A1
Southall UB1 ....106 D6
South Norwood CR7 ....183 B1
Livity Sch The SW2 ....160 A6
Livonia St W1 ....239 B1
Lizard St EC1 ....95 A4 235 B1
Lizban St SE3 ....143 B5
Llandovery Ho 1 E14 ....120 A4
Llanelly Rd NW2 ....69 B6
Llanover Ct HA9 ....65 D4
Llanover Rd SE18 ....144 C5
Wembley HA9 ....65 D5
Llanthony Rd SM4 ....202 B4
Llanvanor Rd NW2 ....69 B6
Llewellyn Ct SE20 ....184 C2
Llewellyn St SE16 ....118 A4
Lloyd Ave SW16 ....182 A2
Lloyd Baker St
WC1 ....94 C4 234 A1
Lloyd Ct SE13 ....163 D6
Pinner HA5 ....40 D4
6 West Norwood SE27 ....160 D1
Lloyd Ho N16 ....73 B5
3 Beckenham BR3 ....185 D4
Bromley BR1 ....187 B5
Lloyd Mews EN3 ....7 C5
Lloyd Park Ave CR0 ....221 D4
Lloyd Park Ho E17 ....53 C6
Lloyd Park Sta CR0 ....221 D4
Lloyd Rd E6 ....100 B6
Dagenham RM9 ....81 B1
North Cheam KT4,SM3 ....216 D5
Walthamstow E17 ....52 D5
Lloyd's Ave EC3 ....243 B1
Lloyd's Bldg★
EC3 ....95 C1 243 A1
Lloyd's Pl SE3 ....142 C3
Lloyd Sq WC1 ....94 C4 234 A2
Lloyd's Row EC1 ....94 D4 234 C1
Lloyd St WC1 ....94 C4 234 A2
Lloyds Way BR3 ....207 B4
Lloyd Villas SE4 ....141 C3
Loampit Hill SE13 ....141 D3
Loampit Vale SE13 ....142 A2
Loanda Cl 17 E8 ....95 D6
Loanda Ho SE15 ....140 C2
Loats Rd SW2 ....160 A5
Lobelia Cl 5 E6 ....100 A2
Locarno Rd 6 W3 ....111 A5
Greenford UB6 ....86 B3
Lochaber Rd SE13 ....142 C1
Lochaline St W6 ....134 C6
Lochan Cl UB4 ....85 A3
Lochbie 5 N4 ....50 A2
Lochinvar St SW12 ....159 B4
Lochleven Ho 9 N2 ....30 B1
Lochmere Cl DA8 ....147 D6
Lochmore Ho SW1 ....258 B3
Lochnagar St E14 ....98 A2
Lockbridge Ct 3 W9 ....91 C2
Lock Chase SE3 ....142 C2
Lock Cl UB2 ....108 A4
Locke Ho SW8 ....269 A2
Lockesfield Pl E14 ....119 D1
Lockesley Dr BR5 ....211 D3
Lockesley Sq KT6 ....197 D3
Locket Rd HA3 ....24 D1
Lockfield Ave EN3 ....7 B4
Lockgate Cl E9 ....75 B3
Lockhart Cl N7 ....72 B2
Enfield EN3 ....18 B6
Lockhart Lo 4 E4 ....20 C4
Lockhart St E3 ....97 B3
Lock Ho N16 ....51 D1
Lockhurst St E5 ....74 D4
Lockier Wlk HA9 ....65 D5
Lockington Rd
SW8 ....137 B4 268 D2
Lockmead Rd N15 ....52 A3
SE13 ....142 A2
Lock Rd TW10 ....175 C6
Lockside 17 E14 ....119 A6
Lock's La CR4 ....181 A1
Locksley St E14 ....97 B2
Locksmeade Rd TW10 ....175 C6
Lock View Ct 9 E14 ....119 A6
Lockwood Cl SE26 ....184 D6
Lockwood Ct KT3 ....199 A5
Lockwood Ho 10 SE11 ....138 C6
Lockwood Ind Pk N17 ....52 B6
Lockwood Sq SE16 ....118 B3
Lockwood Way E17 ....34 D1
Chessington KT9 ....214 C3
Lockyer Est SE1 ....252 D1
Lockyer Ho 7 SE10 ....120 D1
SW8 ....270 A4
Putney SW15 ....134 D2
Lockyer St SE1 ....252 D1
Locomotive Dr TW14 ....150 A3
Locton Gn 4 E3 ....97 B6
Lodden Lo 13 SM2 ....218 A1
Loddiges Ho 5 E9 ....74 C1
Loddiges Rd E9 ....74 C1
Loddon Ho NW8 ....236 D5
Loder St SE15 ....140 C5
Lodge Ave
Borehamwood WD6 ....10 B6
Croydon CR0 ....220 C5
Dagenham RM8,RM9,IG11 ....80 B3
Harrow HA3 ....44 A5
Lodge Cl Edgware HA8 ....26 C4
Edmonton N18 ....33 A5
Hackbridge SM6 ....203 A1
Isleworth TW7 ....131 B4
Lodge Ct 3 HA0 ....66 A3
Lodge Dr N13 ....32 C6
Lodge Gdns BR3 ....207 B4
Lodge Hill DA16 ....146 B5
Redbridge IG4 ....56 A5
Lodgehill Park Cl HA2 ....63 D6
Lodge La DA5 ....168 D5
N12 ....30 A5
New Addington CR0 ....223 D1
Lodge Pl SM1 ....217 D3
Lodge Rd NW4 ....46 C5
NW8 ....92 C4 230 A1
Bromley BR1 ....187 C3
Sutton SM1 ....217 D3
Thornton Heath CR0 ....204 D2
Wallington SM6 ....219 B3
Lodge Villas IG8 ....36 D4
Lodge Way
Charlton TW17 ....171 A1
Stanwell TW15 ....148 A2
Lodore Gdns NW9 ....45 C4
Lodore Gn UB10 ....60 A5
Lodore St E14 ....98 A1
Lodsworth Ho SW11 ....268 A1
Lofthouse Pl KT9 ....213 C2
Loftie St SE16 ....118 A4
Lofting Rd N1 ....72 C1
Lofts on the Park 24 E9 ....74 D2
Loftus Rd W12 ....112 B5
Loftus Rd (Queens Park
Rangers FC) W12 ....112 B5
Logan Cl Enfield EN3 ....6 D4
Hounslow TW4 ....129 B2
Logan Mews W8 ....255 A4
Logan Pl W8 ....113 C2 255 A4
Logan Rd Edmonton N9 ....18 B2
Wembley HA9 ....66 A6
Loggetts SE21 ....161 C2
Logs Hill BR1,BR7 ....188 A2
Logs Hill Cl BR7 ....188 A2
Lohmann Ho 5 SE11 ....138 C6
Lois Dr TW17 ....192 D4
Lolesworth Cl E1 ....243 D3
Lollard St SE11 ....116 C2 261 A3
Loman St SE1 ....116 D4 251 D2
Lomas Cl CR0 ....224 A1
Lomas St E1 ....96 A2
Lombard Ave Enfield EN3 ....6 C4
Ilford IG3 ....57 C1
Lombard Bsns Pk
Merton SW19 ....179 D1
Thornton Heath CR0 ....204 B2
Lombard Ct EC3 ....252 D6
Lombard Ho 4 SE10 ....142 A5
Lombard La EC4 ....241 B1
Lombard Rd N11 ....31 B5
SW11 ....136 B3
Merton SW19 ....179 D1
Lombard Rdbt CR0 ....204 B2
Lombard St EC3 ....95 B1 242 D1
Lombard Trad Est SE7 ....121 B2
Lombard Wall SE7 ....121 B2
Lombardy Pl W2 ....245 D5
Lombardy Ret Pk UB3 ....106 B6
Lomley Ho 10 SW2 ....160 C5
Lomond Cl N15 ....51 C4
Wembley HA0 ....66 B1
Lomond Ct HA3 ....42 D6
Lomond Gdns CR2 ....223 A1
Lomond Gr SE5 ....139 B5
Lomond Ho 10 SE5 ....139 B4
Loncroft Rd SE5 ....139 C6
Londale Ct SE10 ....142 A4
Londesborough Ho 1
N16 ....73 C4
Londesborough Rd N16 ....73 C4
London Aquarium★
SE1 ....250 C1
London Bridge
EC4,SE1 ....117 B6 252 D5
London Bridge City Pier
SE1 ....117 C5 253 A4
London Bridge Hospl
SE1 ....117 B5 252 D4
London Bridge St
SE1 ....117 B5 252 D3
London Bridge Sta
SE1 ....117 B5 252 D3
London Business Sch
NW1 ....92 D3 237 C6
London Butterfly Ho★
TW8 ....131 B4
London Canal Mus★
N1 ....94 A5 233 B4
London Central Mosque★
NW8 ....92 C4 230 B1
London Chest Hospl E2 ....96 C5
London City Airport
E16 ....122 B5
London Clinic
NW1 ....93 A3 238 B5
London Coll of Fashion
EC2 ....95 C3 243 B6
London Coll of Fashion The
W1 ....238 B1
London Coll of International
Business Studies WC1 ....240 B3
London Coll of Printing
SE11 ....116 D3 261 D5
London Ct 3 SW18 ....157 C6
London Docklands Visitor Ctr
E14 ....120 A4
London Dungeon The★
SE1 ....117 B5 252 D4
London Eye (Millennium
Wheel)★ SE1 ....116 B4 250 C2
London Fields East Side
E8 ....74 B1
London Fields Prim Sch
E8 ....96 B6
London Fields Sta E8 ....74 B1
London Fields West Side
E8 ....74 A1
London Foot Hospl
W1 ....93 C3 239 A5
London Gas Mus The★
E3,E16 ....98 B3
London Group Bsns Pk
NW2 ....46 A1
London Ho NW8 ....230 B4
Edgware HA8 ....26 A6
London Hospital Dental Inst
E1 ....96 B2
London Independent Hospl
The E1 ....96 D2
London Ind Pk The E6 ....100 C2
London Inst The W1 ....238 C1
Streatham SW17 ....181 B5
London International Film
Sch WC2 ....94 A1 240 B1
London La E8 ....74 B1
Bromley BR1 ....186 D3
London Metropolitan Univ
E1 ....95 D1 243 D2
London Metropolitan Univ
(Carleton Grange Hall) 2
N7 ....71 D4
London Metropolitan Univ
(Central Ho) E1 ....96 A1
London Metropolitan Univ
(Coll of Tech & Design)
E1 ....96 A1
London Metropolitan Univ
(Commercial Rd) E1 ....96 A1
London Metropolitan Univ
(Ladbrook Ho) N5 ....72 D3
London Metropolitan Univ
(Moorgate) EC2 ....95 B2 242 C3
London Metropolitan Univ
(North London Campus)
N7 ....72 C3
London Metropolitan Univ
(Tufnel Park Hall) N7 ....71 C5
London Metropolitan Univ
(Spring Ho) N7 ....72 C2
London Mews W2 ....236 D2
London Nautical Sch The
SE1 ....116 C5 251 B4
London Oratory Sch The
SW6 ....135 C5 265 B4
London Peace Pagoda★
SW3 ....267 D4
London Rd E13 ....99 A5
SE1 ....116 D3 261 D6
Ashford TW15,TW18,
TW19,TW14 ....148 B2
Brentford TW7,TW8 ....131 B4
Bromley BR1 ....186 D3
Enfield EN2 ....5 B1
Forest Hill SE22,SE23 ....162 C3
Hackbridge SM6,CR4 ....219 B6
Harrow HA1 ....64 C6
Hounslow TW3,TW7,TW1,
TW8 ....130 B3
Kingston KT1,KT2 ....176 B1
Morden SM4 ....201 C5
Romford RM7,RM8 ....59 C3
Stanmore HA7 ....25 D6
Stoneleigh KT17 ....216 B3
Stoneleigh KT17,KT4,SM3 ....216 B3
Thornton Heath CR0,CR7,
SW16 ....204 C3
Twickenham TW1 ....153 A4
Wembley HA9 ....66 A2
Carshalton CR4 ....203 A2
London Road Rdbt TW1 ....153 A5
London Sch of Economics &
Political Science
WC2 ....94 B1 240 D1
London St EC3 ....253 B6
W2 ....92 B1 236 C1
London Stile 5 W4 ....110 C1
London Terr 1 E2 ....96 A5
London Theological
Seminary at Kensit
Memorial Coll N3 ....29 A1
London Toy & Model Mus★
W2 ....114 A6 246 A6
London Transport Mus★
WC2 ....250 B6
London Wall EC2 ....95 B2 242 D3
London Wharf 4 E2 ....96 B6
London Zoo★
NW1 ....93 A5 231 A4
Lonesome Prim Sch
CR4 ....181 B1
Lonesome Way CR4 ....181 C2
Long Acre WC2 ....94 A1 240 B1
Long Acre Ct W13 ....87 A2
Longacre Pl SM5 ....219 A2
Longacre Rd E17 ....36 B2
Longbeach Rd SW11 ....136 D2
Longberrys NW2 ....69 B5
Longboat Row UB1 ....85 B1
Longbow Ho 20 N1 ....95 C6
Longbridge Ho RM8 ....80 B4
Longbridge Rd
Barking IG11 ....79 C3
Dagenham RM8 ....80 B4
Longbridge Way SE13 ....164 A6
Longbury Dr BR5 ....190 B1
Longcliffe Ho SW18 ....157 D6
Longcroft SE9 ....166 C1
Longcrofte Rd HA8 ....25 D3
Longdale Sq N1 ....234 B6
Long Deacon Rd E4 ....20 C3
Long Ditton Cty Inf Sch
KT6 ....197 C1
Longdon Wood BR2 ....226 A4
Longdown Rd SE6 ....185 C6
Long Dr W3 ....89 C1
Greenford UB6 ....85 D6
Ruislip HA4 ....62 D4
Long Elmes HA3 ....24 A2
Longfellow Rd E17 ....53 B3
North Cheam KT4 ....200 B1
Longfellow Way SE1 ....263 D3
Long Field NW9 ....27 D3
Longfield
3 Bromley BR1 ....186 D2
Loughton IG10 ....21 C6
Longfield Ave E17 ....53 A5
NW7 ....28 A3
Ealing W5 ....109 C6
Enfield EN3 ....6 C5
Hackbridge SM6 ....203 A1
Wembley HA9 ....44 A1
Longfield Cres SE23,
SE26 ....162 C1
Longfield Ct 4 N2 ....48 A6
Longfield Dr
Mitcham SW19 ....180 C2
Mortlake SW14 ....154 D6
Longfield Est SE1 ....263 D3
Longfield Fst & Mid Schs
HA2 ....41 C3
Longfield Ho E17 ....53 B4
Ealing W5 ....109 C6
Longfield Rd W5 ....87 C1
Longfield St SW18 ....157 C4
Longford Ave
Feltham TW14 ....149 D5
Southall UB1 ....107 D6
Stanwell TW19 ....148 A3
Longford Cl
Feltham TW13 ....151 A1
Hampton TW12 ....173 C6
Hayes UB4 ....106 D6
Longford Ct 2 E5 ....74 D4
6 NW4 ....46 C5
1 W12 ....111 C4
Southall UB1 ....107 C5
West Ewell KT19 ....215 A4
Longford Gdns
Hayes UB4 ....106 D6
Sutton SM1 ....218 A6
Longford Ho 7 E1 ....96 C1
1 Catford BR1 ....186 B5
Hampton TW12 ....173 C6
Longford Ind Est TW12 ....173 D4
Longford Rd TW2 ....151 D3
Longford Sch TW14 ....149 D4
Longford St NW1 ....93 B3 238 D6
Longford Way TW19 ....148 A3
Longford Wlk 9 SW2 ....160 C4
Longhayes Ave RM6 ....58 D5
Longhayes Ct RM6 ....58 D5
Longheath Gdns CR0 ....206 C4
Longhedge Ho SE26 ....184 A6
Longhill Rd SE6 ....164 B1
Longhook Gdns UB5 ....84 B4
Longhope Cl SE15 ....139 D6
Longhurst Ho 8 W9 ....91 B4
Longhurst Rd SE13 ....164 C6
Croydon CR0 ....206 B3
Long La DA7 ....147 B4
EC1 ....94 D2 241 D4
N2 ....48 B6
N3 ....29 D2
SE1 ....117 B4 252 D1
Croydon CR0 ....206 C3
Hillingdon UB10 ....60 D1
Stanwell TW15,TW19 ....148 B3
Longland Ct E9 ....75 A3
SE1 ....118 A1
Longland Dr N20 ....13 D2
Longlands Ct DA15 ....167 D1
E17 ....35 A2
W11 ....244 D6
Mitcham CR4 ....181 A2
Longlands Park Cres
DA15 ....167 C2
Longlands Prim Sch
DA15 ....167 C1
Longlands Rd DA15 ....167 D1
Longleat Ho SW1 ....259 C2
Longleat Rd EN1 ....17 C6

Longleat Villas 3 DA6 ... 147 A1
Longleat Way TW14 ... 149 B4
Longleigh Ho 8 SE5 ... 139 C4
Longleigh La SE2 ... 146 C6
Longlents Ho 3 NW10 ... 89 B6
Longley Ave HA0 ... 88 A5
Longley Ho 5 N19 ... 71 C4
Longley Rd Harrow HA1 ... 42 B5
Thornton Heath CR0 ... 204 D2
Upper Tooting SW17 ... 180 D4
Long Leys E4 ... 36 A4
Longley St SE1 ... 118 A2
Longley Way NW2 ... 68 C5
Longman Ho 9 E2 ... 96 D5
10 E8 ... 95 D6
Long Mark Rd 5 E16 ... 99 D2
Longmead BR7 ... 188 C1
Long Mead NW9 ... 27 D2
Longmead Dr DA14 ... 168 D2
Longmead Ho SE27 ... 183 A5
Long Meadow 20 N7 ... 71 D3
Long Meadow Cl BR3, BR4 ... 208 A2
Longmeadow Rd DA15 ... 167 C3
Longmead Prim Sch UB7 ... 104 A2
Longmead Rd
Hayes UB3 ... 105 D6
Thames Ditton KT7 ... 196 D2
Upper Tooting SW17 ... 180 D5
Longmoor Point 14 SW15 ... 156 B3
Longmore Ave EN4,EN5 ... 14 B5
Longmore St SW1 ... 115 C2 259 A3
Longnor Rd E1 ... 96 D4
Long Pond Rd SE3 ... 142 C4
Long Rd SW4 ... 137 C1
Longreach Ct IG11 ... 101 B5
Long Reach Rd IG11 ... 101 D3
Longridge Ho SE1 ... 262 B5
Longridge La UB1 ... 85 D1
Longridge Rd SW5 ... 113 C2 255 B3
Long Ridges N2 ... 49 A6
Long's Ct W1 ... 249 D5
Longs Ct 2 TW9 ... 132 B1
Longshaw Prim Sch E4 ... 20 B1
Longshaw Rd E4 ... 20 B1
Longshore SE8 ... 119 B2
Long St E2 ... 95 D4
Longstaff Cres SW18 ... 157 C4
Longstaff Rd SW18 ... 157 C5
Longstone Ave NW10 ... 89 D6
Longstone Rd SW17 ... 181 B5
Longthorne Ho 20 E3 ... 97 B4
Longthornton Rd SW16 ... 181 D1
Longton Ave SE26 ... 184 A6
Longton Gr SE26 ... 184 B6
Longville Rd SE11 ... 261 D4
Longwalk Rd UB11 ... 104 D5
Long Wlk SE1 ... 263 B6
SE18 ... 144 D6
Kingston KT3 ... 199 A6
Longwood Bsns Pk TW16 ... 193 D4
Longwood Dr SW15 ... 156 A5
Longwood Gdns IG2,IG6, IG5 ... 56 C6
Longwood Par IG6 ... 56 D6
Longworth Cl SE28 ... 102 D1
Long Yd WC1 ... 94 B3 240 C5
Loning The NW9 ... 45 D5
Enfield EN3 ... 6 C5
Lonsdale Ave
Newham E6 ... 100 A3
Wembley HA9 ... 66 A3
Lonsdale Cl SE12 ... 165 D1
Edgware HA8 ... 26 B5
Hillingdon UB8 ... 83 A2
Newham E6 ... 100 A3
Pinner HA5 ... 23 A2
Lonsdale Cres IG2 ... 56 D3
Lonsdale Dr EN2 ... 16 A6
Lonsdale Dr N EN2 ... 4 A1
Lonsdale Gdns CR7, SW16 ... 204 B5
Lonsdale Ho 6 N4 ... 51 A2
SW6 ... 135 C2
Lonsdale Mews W11 ... 91 B1
4 Richmond TW9 ... 132 C4
Lonsdale Pl N1 ... 72 C1
Lonsdale Rd E11 ... 54 D2
NW6 ... 91 B6
W11 ... 91 B1
W4 ... 111 D2
Barnes SW13 ... 133 D5
Bexley DA7 ... 147 B3
Croydon SE25 ... 206 B5
Southall UB2 ... 106 D3
Lonsdell Ho 9 SW2 ... 160 C5
Loobert Rd N15 ... 51 C6
Looe Gdns IG6 ... 56 D6
Loop Rd BR7 ... 189 A4
Lopen Rd N18 ... 33 C6
Lopen Works N18 ... 33 C6
Lopez Ho 4 SW9 ... 138 A2
Lorac Ct 12 SM2 ... 217 C1
Loraine Cl EN3 ... 18 C6
Loraine Ct BR7 ... 188 D5
Loraine Ho 1 SM5 ... 219 B4
Loraine Rd N7 ... 72 B4
Chiswick W4 ... 132 D6
Lord Ave IG5 ... 56 B6
Lord Chancellor Wlk KT2 ... 177 A2
Lord David Pitt Ho 8 SE24 ... 138 C1
Lordell Pl SW19 ... 178 C4
Lorden Wlk 25 E2 ... 96 A4
Lord Gdns IG5 ... 56 B5
Lord Hills Rd W2 ... 91 D2
Lord Holland La 5 SW9 ... 138 C3
Lord Knyvetts Ct 3 TW19 ... 148 A5
Lord Napier Pl W6 ... 112 A1
Lord North St SW1 ... 260 A5
Lord Roberts Mews SW6 ... 265 C3
Lord Roberts Terr SE18 ... 122 C1
Lords Cl Feltham TW13 ... 151 A2
West Norwood SE21 ... 161 A2
Lord's Cricket Mus★ NW8 ... 92 B4 229 D1
Lords Ct 3 HA8 ... 27 A3
Lordship Gr N16 ... 73 B6
Lordship Ho 3 N16 ... 73 B6
Lordship La SE22 ... 161 D5
Tottenham N22 ... 33 B2
Lordship Lane Prim Sch N22 ... 33 A2
Lordship Park Mews N16 ... 73 A6
Lordship Pk N16 ... 73 B6
Lordship Pl SW3 ... 267 A5
Lordship Rd N16 ... 73 B6
Northolt UB5 ... 63 A1
Lordship Terr N16 ... 73 B6
Lord's Indoor Cricket Sch NW8 ... 229 D2
NW8 ... 230 A2
Lord's (MCC & Middlesex Cty Cricket Ground)★ NW8 ... 92 B4 229 D2
Lordsmead Rd N17 ... 33 C1
Lord St E16 ... 122 A5
Lord's View NW8 ... 229 D1
Lord Warwick St SE18 ... 122 B3
Loreburn Ho 2 N7 ... 72 B4
Lorenzo St N1,WC1 ... 233 C2
Loretto Gdns HA3 ... 44 A5
Lorian Cl N12 ... 29 D6
Loring Rd N20 ... 14 C2
Isleworth TW7 ... 130 D3
Loris Rd W6 ... 112 C3
Lorn Ct SW9 ... 138 C3
Lorne Ave CR0 ... 206 D2
Lorne Cl NW8 ... 92 C4 230 B1
Lorne Ct SW15 ... 156 D5
Lorne Gdns 5 W11 ... 112 D4
Croydon CR0 ... 206 D2
Wanstead E11 ... 55 C5
Lorne Ho 7 E1 ... 97 A2
3 N11 ... 31 B5
Lorne Rd E17 ... 53 C4
E7 ... 77 C4
N4 ... 50 B1
Harrow HA3 ... 24 D1
3 Richmond TW10 ... 154 B6
Lorn Rd SW9 ... 138 C3
Lorraine Ct 10 NW1 ... 71 B1
Beckenham BR3 ... 186 A2
Lorraine Pk HA3 ... 24 C3
Lorrimore Rd SE17 ... 138 D6
Lorrimore Sq SE17 ... 138 D6
Lorton Ho 9 NW6 ... 91 C6
Loseberry Rd KT10 ... 212 B3
Lostock Ho 10 SW8 ... 137 D3
Lothair Rd W5 ... 109 D4
Lothair Rd N N4 ... 50 B3
Lothair Rd S N4 ... 50 D2
Lothbury EC2 ... 95 B1 242 C2
Lothian Ave UB4 ... 84 B2
Lothian Cl HA0 ... 65 A5
Lothian Rd SW9 ... 138 D4
Lothrop St W10 ... 91 A4
Lots Rd SW10 ... 136 A5 266 B3
Loubet St SW17 ... 180 D4
Loudoun Ave IG6 ... 56 D4
Loudoun Rd NW8 ... 92 A6 229 B5
Loudwater Cl TW16 ... 194 A5
Loudwater Rd TW16 ... 194 A5
Loughborough Ct 7 SW9 ... 138 D2
Loughborough Junction Sta SW9 ... 138 D2
Loughborough Pk SW9 ... 138 D1
Loughborough Prim Sch SW9 ... 138 D3
Loughborough Rd SE5, SW9 ... 138 D3
Loughborough St SE11 ... 116 B1 260 D1
Lough Rd N7 ... 72 B2
Loughton Way IG9 ... 21 D3
Louisa Cl E9 ... 96 D6
Louisa Ct TW2 ... 152 C2
Louisa Gdns E1 ... 96 D3
Louisa Ho SW15 ... 133 D1
Louisa St E1 ... 96 D3
Louis Ct 3 RM10 ... 81 D2
Louise Bennett Cl 9 SE24 ... 138 D1
Louise Ct
4 Wanstead E11 ... 55 B4
Wood Green N22 ... 32 C2
Louise De Marillac Ho 18 E1 ... 96 C2
Louise Graham Ho 5 IG11 ... 101 B6
Louise Rd E15 ... 76 C2
Louise White Ho 1 N19 ... 49 D1
Louis Gdns BR7 ... 188 B6
Louis Mews N10 ... 31 B2
Louisville Rd SW17 ... 159 A1
Lousada Lo N14 ... 15 C5
Louvaine Rd SW11 ... 136 B1
Lovage App E6 ... 100 A2
Lovat Cl NW2 ... 67 D5
Lovat La EC3 ... 253 A5
Lovatt Cl HA8 ... 26 D4
Lovatt Ct SW12 ... 159 B3
Lovatt Dr HA4 ... 39 D4
Lovat Wlk TW5 ... 129 A5
Loveday Ho 2 SW2 ... 160 C3
Loveday Rd W13 ... 109 B5
Lovegrove St SE1 ... 140 A6
Lovegrove Wlk E14 ... 120 A5
Lovekyn Cl KT2 ... 176 B1
Love La DA5 ... 169 C5
EC2 ... 95 A1 242 B2
SE18 ... 122 D2
Cheam SM3 ... 217 A2
Cheam SM4 ... 201 D2
Croydon SE25 ... 206 B6
Long Ditton KT6 ... 213 D6
Mitcham CR4 ... 202 C6
Pinner HA5 ... 41 A6
Tottenham N17 ... 33 D3
Lovelace Ave BR2 ... 210 C3
Lovelace Gdns
Barking IG11 ... 80 A4
Surbiton KT6 ... 197 D2
Lovelace Gn SE9 ... 144 B2
Lovelace Ho 12 E8 ... 95 D6
Lovelace Prim Sch KT9 ... 213 C3
Lovelace Rd
East Barnet EN4 ... 14 C4
Surbiton KT6 ... 197 D2
West Norwood SE21 ... 161 A3
Loveland Mans 6 IG11 ... 79 D1
Lovel Ave DA16 ... 146 A3
Lovelinch Cl SE15 ... 140 C6
Lovell Ho E8 ... 96 A6
4 Merton SW19 ... 180 A2
Lovell Pl SE16 ... 119 A3
Lovell Rd
Richmond TW10 ... 153 C1
Southall UB1 ... 85 D1
Loveridge Mews NW6 ... 69 B2
Loveridge Rd NW6 ... 69 B2
Lover's Wlk W1 ... 115 A5 248 A3
Lovett Dr SM5 ... 202 B2
Lovette Ho 3 E3 ... 97 C4
Lovett Way NW10 ... 67 A3
Love Wlk SE5 ... 139 B3
Lovibonds Ave BR6 ... 226 D5
Hillingdon UB7 ... 82 B1
Lowbrook Rd IG1 ... 78 D4
Low Cross Wood La SE21 ... 161 D1
Lowdell Cl UB7 ... 82 A1
Lowden Rd SE24 ... 139 A1
Edmonton N9 ... 18 B3
Southall UB1 ... 107 A6
Lowder Ho 6 E1 ... 118 B5
Lowe Ave E16 ... 99 A2
Lowell Ho 10 SE5 ... 139 A5
Lowell St E14 ... 97 A1
Lower Addiscombe Rd CR0 ... 205 C1
Lower Addison Gdns W14 ... 113 A4 244 A1
Lower Belgrave St SW1 ... 115 B3 258 C5
Lower Boston Rd W7 ... 108 C4
Lower Broad St RM10 ... 103 C6
Lower Camden BR7 ... 188 B2
Lower Church St CR0 ... 220 D6
Lower Clapton Rd E5 ... 74 C4
Lower Clarendon Wlk 12 W11 ... 91 A1
Lower Comm S SW15 ... 134 B2
Lower Coombe St CR0 ... 221 A4
Lower Downs Rd SW20 ... 178 D2
Lower Fosters NW4 ... 46 C4
Lower George St 13 TW10 ... 153 D6
Lower Gn W CR4 ... 202 C6
Lower Gravel Rd BR2 ... 210 B1
Lower Green Gdns KT4 ... 200 A1
Lower Green Rd KT10 ... 212 A6
Lower Grosvenor Pl SW1 ... 115 B3 258 D6
Lower Grove Rd TW10 ... 154 B6
Lower Hall La E4 ... 35 A6
Lower Hampton Rd TW12,TW16 ... 172 D1
Lower Ham Rd KT2 ... 175 D4
Lower James St W1 ... 249 B6
Lower John St W1 ... 249 B6
Lower Kenwood Ave EN2 ... 16 A6
Lower Lea Crossing E14,E16 ... 120 C6
Lower Maidstone Rd N11 ... 31 C4
Lower Mall W6 ... 112 B1
Lower Marsh SE1 ... 116 C4 251 A1
Lower Marsh La KT1, KT5 ... 198 C5
Lower Merton Rise NW3 ... 70 C1
Lower Morden La SM4 ... 201 A3
Lower Mortlake Rd TW9 ... 132 B2
Lower Park Rd N11 ... 31 C5
Belvedere DA17 ... 125 C2
Loughton IG10 ... 21 D6
Lower Pk 5 SW15 ... 156 D6
Lower Place Bsns Ctr NW10 ... 89 A5
Lower Queen's Rd IG9 ... 21 D2
Lower Rd N2 ... 30 B2
SE16 ... 118 C4
Lower Rd *continued*
Belvedere DA17 ... 125 D3
Harrow HA2 ... 42 B1
Sutton SM1 ... 218 A4
Lower Richmond Rd
Mortlake SW14,TW9 ... 132 D2
Putney SW15 ... 134 C2
Lower Robert St WC2 ... 250 B5
Lower Sand Hills KT6 ... 197 C2
Lower Sloane St SW1 ... 115 A1 258 A2
Lower Strand NW9 ... 27 D1
Lower Sunbury Rd TW12 ... 173 C1
Lower Sydenham Sta SE26 ... 185 B5
Lower Teddington Rd KT1 ... 175 D2
Lower Terr NW3 ... 70 A5
Lower Thames St EC3 ... 117 C6 253 A5
Lower Tub WD23 ... 8 B4
Lowerwood Ct W11 ... 91 A1
Lower Wood Rd KT10 ... 213 B2
Lowestoft Cl 5 E5 ... 74 C6
Lowestoft Mews E16 ... 122 D4
Loweswater Cl HA9 ... 65 D6
Loweswater Ho E3 ... 97 B3
Lowfield Rd NW6 ... 69 C1
W3 ... 89 A1
Low Hall Cl E4 ... 19 D4
Low Hall La E17 ... 53 A3
Low Ho IG11 ... 102 A5
Lowick Rd HA1 ... 42 C4
Lowland Gdns RM7 ... 59 D3
Lowlands NW3 ... 70 C2
Lowlands Rd Harrow HA1 ... 42 C2
Pinner HA5 ... 40 C3
Lowman Rd N7 ... 72 B4
Lowndes Cl SW1 ... 258 B5
Lowndes Ct SW1 ... 257 D6
Lowndes Lo EN5 ... 1 D2
Lowndes Pl SW1 ... 115 A3 258 A5
Lowndes Sq SW1 ... 114 D4 247 D1
Lowndes St SW1 ... 115 A3 258 A6
Lownds Ct BR1 ... 187 A1
Lowood Ct SE19 ... 183 D5
Lowood Ho 11 E1 ... 118 C6
Lowood St E1 ... 118 B6
Lowry Cres CR4 ... 180 C1
Lowry Ct 3 SE16 ... 118 B1
Lowry Ho N17 ... 33 D2
Lowry Lo 2 HA0 ... 65 D3
Lowry Rd RM8 ... 80 B3
Lowther Cl WD6 ... 10 B6
Lowther Dr EN2 ... 4 A1
Lowther Hill SE23 ... 163 A4
Lowther Ho 11 E8 ... 95 D6
SW1 ... 259 B1
Lowther Prim Sch SW13 ... 134 A6
Lowther Rd E17 ... 35 A1
N7 ... 72 C3
Barnes SW13 ... 133 D4
Kingston KT2 ... 176 B2
Stanmore HA7 ... 44 B6
Lowth Rd SE5 ... 139 A3
Loxdon Ct RM6 ... 58 B3
Loxford Ave E6 ... 99 D5
Loxford Ho SW1 ... 258 B3
Loxford La IG1 ... 79 B3
Loxford Rd IG11 ... 78 D2
Loxford Sch of Science & Tech IG1 ... 79 B3
Loxham Rd E4 ... 35 D3
Loxham St WC1 ... 233 B1
Loxley Cl SE26 ... 184 D5
Loxley Rd Feltham TW12 ... 173 B6
Wandsworth SW18 ... 158 B3
Loxton Rd SE23 ... 163 A3
Loxwood Cl TW14 ... 149 C3
Loxwood Rd N17 ... 51 C6
Loyola Prep Sch IG9 ... 21 C3
Lubavitch House Gram Sch N2 ... 48 A4
Lubbock Ct BR7 ... 188 B3
Lubbock Ho 18 E14 ... 119 D6
Lubbock Rd BR7 ... 188 B3
Lubbock St SE14 ... 140 C5
Lucan Ho N1 ... 235 D5
Lucan Pl SW3 ... 114 C2 257 B3
Lucan Rd EN5 ... 1 A2
Lucas Ave E13 ... 99 B6
Harrow HA2 ... 63 C6
Lucas Ct SW11 ... 268 B1
Forest Hill SE26 ... 185 A5
Lucas Gdns N2 ... 30 A1
Lucas Ho 2 SW8 ... 137 C3
Lucas Rd SE20 ... 184 C4
Lucas Sq NW11 ... 47 C3
Lucas St SE4,SE8 ... 141 C4
Lucas Vale Prim Sch SE8 ... 141 C4
Lucerne Cl N14 ... 16 A1
Lucerne Ct 5 DA18 ... 125 A3
8 Beckenham BR3 ... 185 C3
Lucerne Gr E17 ... 54 B5
Lucerne Mews W8 ... 245 B4
Lucerne Rd BR6 ... 211 D1
N5 ... 72 D4
South Norwood CR7 ... 205 A5
Lucey Rd SE16 ... 118 A3
Lucey Way SE16 ... 118 A2
Lucie Ave TW15 ... 170 D4
Lucien Rd
Upper Tooting SW17 ... 181 A6
Wandsworth SW18 ... 157 D2
Lucille Ho SE26 ... 184 B4
Lucknow St SE18 ... 145 C5
Lucorn Cl SE12 ... 164 D5
Lucraft Ho 12 SW2 ... 160 A4
Luctons Ave IG9 ... 21 C3
Lucy Ashe Ho SE17 ... 261 D3
Lucy Brown Ho SE1 ... 252 B3
Lucy Cres W3 ... 89 A3
Lucy Gdns RM8 ... 81 A5
Luddesdon Rd DA8 ... 147 C5
Ludford Cl NW9 ... 27 C1
Croydon CR0 ... 220 D4
Ludgate Broadway EC4 ... 241 D1
Ludgate Cir EC4 ... 94 D1 241 C1
Ludgate Hill EC4 ... 94 D1 241 D1
Ludgate Sq EC4 ... 241 D1
Ludham NW5 ... 70 D3
Ludham Cl SE28 ... 102 C1
Ludlow Cl BR2 ... 209 A6
Harrow HA2 ... 63 B4
Ludlow Ct W3 ... 111 A4
Ludlow Rd Ealing W5 ... 87 C3
Feltham TW13 ... 172 A6
Ludlow St EC1 ... 242 A6
Ludlow Way N2 ... 48 A5
Ludovick Wlk SW15 ... 133 C1
Ludwell Ho W14 ... 254 B6
Ludwick Mews SE14 ... 141 A5
Luffield Rd SE2 ... 124 B3
Luffman Rd SE12 ... 165 B1
Lugard Ho W12 ... 112 B5
Lugard Rd SE15 ... 140 B4
Lugg App E12 ... 78 C5
Luke Ho 31 E1 ... 96 B1
Lukes Ct N3 ... 47 C6
Luke St EC2 ... 95 C3 243 A6
Lukin Cres E4 ... 20 B1
Lukin St E1 ... 96 C1
Lullingstone Cl BR5 ... 190 B3
Lullingstone Cres BR5 ... 190 B3
Lullingstone Ho 20 SE15 ... 140 C6
Lullingstone La SE13 ... 164 B5
Lullingstone Rd 3 DA17 ... 147 B6
Lullington Garth N12 ... 29 B5
Borehamwood WD6 ... 10 D6
Bromley BR1 ... 186 C3
Lullington Rd
Dagenham RM9 ... 81 A1
Penge SE20 ... 184 A3
Lulot Gdns N19 ... 71 B6
Lulworth NW1 ... 71 D1
SE17 ... 262 C2
Lulworth Ave
Hounslow TW5,TW7 ... 130 A5
Wembley HA9 ... 43 C2
Lulworth Cl HA2 ... 63 B5
Lulworth Cres CR4 ... 180 C1
Lulworth Ct N14 ... 16 A1
Lulworth Dr HA5 ... 41 A2
Lulworth Gdns HA2 ... 63 B6
Lulworth Ho SW8 ... 270 C3
Lulworth Rd DA16 ... 145 D3
SE15 ... 140 B3
Chislehurst SE9 ... 166 A2
Lulworth Waye UB4 ... 84 B1
Lumen Rd HA9 ... 65 D6
Lumiere Bldg The E7 ... 77 D3
Lumiere Ct SW17 ... 159 A2
Lumley Cl DA17 ... 125 C1
Lumley Ct WC2 ... 250 B5
Lumley Flats SW1 ... 258 A2
Lumley Gdns SM3 ... 217 A3
Lumley Ho KT3 ... 199 B1
Lumley Rd SM1,SM3 ... 217 A3
Lumley St W1 ... 238 B1
Lumsdon NW8 ... 91 D6
Lunan Ho 12 E3 ... 97 B5
Luna Rd CR7 ... 205 A6
Lundin Wlk WD19 ... 22 D6
Lund Point E15 ... 98 A6
Lundy Dr UB3 ... 105 C2
Lunham Rd SE19 ... 183 C4
Lupin Cl Croydon CR0 ... 206 D1
Streatham SW2 ... 160 D2
Lupin Cres IG11 ... 78 D2
Lupino Ct SE11 ... 260 C4
Lupin Point SE1 ... 253 D1
Lupton Cl SE12 ... 187 B6
Lupton St NW5 ... 71 C4
Lupus Ct SE19 ... 183 B2
Lupus St SW1 ... 115 C1 259 B1
Luralda Gdns E14 ... 120 B1
Lurgan Ave W6 ... 134 D6
Lurline Gdns SW11 ... 137 A4 268 B2
Luscombe Ct BR2 ... 186 C1
Luscombe Ho SW18 ... 157 B6
Luscombe Way SW8 ... 138 A5 270 A4
Lusher Ho SW15 ... 156 D5
Lushington Ho KT12 ... 194 C3
Lushington Rd NW10 ... 90 B5
Catford SE6 ... 185 D5
Lushington Terr 11 E8 ... 74 A3
Lutea Ho SM2 ... 218 A1
Luther Cl HA8 ... 11 A2
Luther King Cl E17 ... 53 A3
Luther Rd TW11 ... 174 D5
Luton Pl SE10 ... 142 A5
Luton Rd E13 ... 99 A3
E17 ... 53 B6
Sidcup DA14 ... 168 C1
Luton St NW8 ... 92 B3 236 D5
Luttrell Ave SW15 ... 156 B6
Lutwyche Rd SE6 ... 163 B2
Lutyens Ho SW1 ... 259 A1
Luxborough Ho W1 ... 238 A4
Luxborough St W1 ... 93 A2 238 A4
Luxborough Twr W1 ... 238 A4
Luxemburg Gdns W6 ... 112 D2
Luxfield Rd SE9 ... 166 A3
Luxford St SE16 ... 118 D2
Luxmore St SE4 ... 141 B4
Luxor St SE5 ... 139 A2
Lyall Ave SE21 ... 183 D6
Lyall Mews SW1 ... 115 A3 258 A5
Lyall Mews W SW1 ... 258 A5
Lyall St SW1 ... 115 A3 258 A5
Lyal Rd E3 ... 97 A5
Lyceé Francais Charles de Gaulle (French Univ Coll) SW7 ... 114 B2 256 C4
Lyceé The SE11 ... 116 C1 261 B1
Lycett Ho 10 SW2 ... 160 A4
Lycett Pl 3 W12 ... 112 A4
Lychgate Manor HA1 ... 42 C2
Lych Gate Wlk UB3 ... 105 D6
Lyconby Gdns CR0 ... 207 A2
Lydd Cl DA15 ... 167 C1
Lydden Ct SE9 ... 167 C5
Lydden Gr SW18 ... 157 D4
Lydden Rd SW18 ... 157 D4
Lydd Rd DA7 ... 147 B5
Lydeard Rd E6 ... 78 B1
Lydford NW1 ... 232 B5
Lydford Cl 22 N16 ... 73 C3
Lydford Rd N15 ... 51 B4
NW2 ... 68 D2
W9 ... 91 B3
Lydgate Ho 8 N16 ... 73 C3
Lydhurst Ave SW2 ... 160 B2
Lydia Lo HA1 ... 64 C4
Lydney Cl SE15 ... 139 C5
Putney SW19 ... 157 A2
Lydon Rd SW4 ... 137 C2
Lydstep Rd BR7 ... 188 C6
Lydwell Ho 29 SW8 ... 137 D3
Lyford Rd SW18 ... 158 C3
Lyford St SE7 ... 122 A2
Lygoe Ho 18 N6 ... 49 D2
Lygoe Rd N2 ... 30 B2
Lygon Ho 1 E2 ... 96 A4
Lygon Pl SW1 ... 258 C5
Lyham Cl SW2 ... 160 A5
Lyham Rd SW2 ... 160 A5
Lyle Cl CR4 ... 203 A2
Lyly Ho SE1 ... 262 D5
Lyme Farm Rd SE12 ... 143 B1
Lyme Gr E9 ... 74 C1
Lyme Grove Ho 2 E9 ... 74 C1
Lymer Ave SE19 ... 183 D5
Lyme Rd DA16 ... 146 B4
Lymescote Gdns SM1 ... 217 C6
Lyme St NW1 ... 71 C1 232 A6
Lyminge Cl DA14 ... 189 D6
Lyminge Gdns SW17, SW18 ... 158 C3
Lymington Ave N22 ... 32 D1
Lymington Cl 2 E6 ... 100 B2
Mitcham SW16 ... 181 D1
Lymington Ct SM1 ... 218 A5
Lymington Dr HA4 ... 61 B6
Lymington Gdns KT19 ... 215 D3
Lymington Mans NW6 ... 69 D2
Lymington Rd NW6 ... 69 D2
Dagenham RM8 ... 58 D1
Lyminster Cl UB4 ... 85 A2
Lympne N17 ... 33 B1
Lympstone Gdns SE15 ... 140 A5
Lynbridge Gdns N13 ... 32 D6
Lynch Cl SE3 ... 142 D3
Lynchen Cl TW5 ... 128 B4
Lynch Wlk 2 SE8 ... 141 B6
Lyncott Cres SW4 ... 137 B1
Lyncourt SE3 ... 142 B3
Lyncroft Ave HA5 ... 41 A4
Lyncroft Gdns NW6 ... 69 C3
Ealing W13 ... 109 C5
Hounslow TW3 ... 152 A6
Lyncroft Mans 4 NW6 ... 69 C3
Lyndale NW2 ... 69 B5
Lyndale Ave NW2 ... 69 B5
Lyndale Cl SE3 ... 142 D6
Lyndean Ind Est SE2 ... 124 C3
Lynde Ho 2 SW4 ... 137 D2
Walton-on-T KT12 ... 194 C3
Lynden Gate SW15 ... 156 B4
Lynden Hyrst CR0 ... 221 D6
Lyndhurst BR7 ... 188 D4
Lyndhurst Ave N12 ... 30 D4
NW7 ... 27 C4
Mitcham SW16 ... 181 D1
Pinner HA5 ... 22 B2
Southall UB1 ... 107 D5
Sunbury TW16 ... 194 A6
Tolworth KT5 ... 198 D1
Twickenham TW2,TW4 ... 151 C3
Lyndhurst Cl DA7 ... 147 D2
NW10 ... 67 B5
Orpington BR6 ... 226 D4
South Croydon CR0 ... 221 D5
Lyndhurst Ct
7 Belmont SM2 ... 217 C1
11 Woodford E18 ... 37 A2
Lyndhurst Dr E10 ... 54 A2
New Malden KT3 ... 199 D2
Lyndhurst Gdns N3 ... 29 A2
NW3 ... 70 B3
Barking IG11 ... 79 C2
Enfield EN1 ... 5 C1
Ilford IG2 ... 57 B3
Pinner HA5 ... 22 B2
Lyndhurst Gr SE5,SE15 ... 139 D3
Lyndhurst Ho 2 SW15 ... 156 A4
Lyndhurst House Prep Sch NW3 ... 70 B3

Lyndhurst Lo 3 E14 ... 120 B2
Lyndhurst Rd DA7 ... 147 D2
NW3 ... 70 B3
Chingford E4 ... 36 A3
Edmonton N18 ... 34 A6
Greenford UB6 ... 85 D3
Thornton Heath CR7 ... 204 C5
Tottenham N22 ... 32 C4
Lyndhurst Sch SE5 ... 139 B3
Lyndhurst Sq SE15 ... 139 D4
Lyndhurst Terr NW3 ... 70 B3
Lyndhurst Way SE15 ... 139 D3
Belmont SM2 ... 217 C1
Lyndon Ave DA15 ... 167 D6
Hackbridge SM6 ... 219 A5
Pinner HA5 ... 23 A4
Lyndon Rd DA17 ... 125 C2
Lyndon Yd SW17 ... 179 D6
Lyndum Ct N22 ... 32 C2
Lyne Cres E17 ... 35 B2
Lyne Ct NW9 ... 45 B2
Lynegrove Ave TW15 ... 171 A5
Lyneham Wlk E5 ... 75 A3
Pinner HA5 ... 39 D6
Lynette Ave SW4 ... 159 C5
Lynfield Ct SE23 ... 162 D4
Lynford Cl HA8 ... 27 A2
Edgware EN5 ... 11 D6
Lynford French Ho
SE17 ... 262 A2
Lynford Gdns
Edgware HA8 ... 10 D1
Ilford IG3 ... 79 D6
Lynford Terr N9 ... 17 D3
Lynhurst Cres UB10 ... 61 B1
Lynhurst Rd UB10 ... 61 A1
Lynmere Rd DA16 ... 146 B3
Lynmouth Ave
Enfield EN1 ... 17 D5
West Barnes SM4 ... 200 D2
Lynmouth Dr HA4 ... 62 B5
Lynmouth Gdns
Heston TW5 ... 128 D4
Wembley UB6 ... 65 B1
Lynmouth Rd E17 ... 53 A4
N16 ... 51 D1
N2 ... 48 D5
Wembley UB6 ... 87 B6
Lynn Cl Ashford TW15 ... 171 B5
Harrow HA3 ... 24 B1
Lynn Ct SW16 ... 181 D5
Lynne Cl 7 BR6 ... 227 D2
Lynne Ct NW6 ... 69 D1
Forest Hill SE23 ... 163 B4
South Croydon CR2 ... 221 C4
Wimbledon SW20 ... 178 B2
Lynnett Ct E9 ... 75 A2
Lynnett Rd RM8 ... 58 D1
Lynne Way NW10 ... 67 C2
Northolt UB5 ... 84 D5
Lynne Wlk KT10 ... 212 A3
Lynn Ho SE15 ... 140 A6
Lynn Mews E11 ... 76 C6
Lynn Rd E11 ... 76 C5
Balham SW12 ... 159 B4
Ilford IG2 ... 57 B2
Lynn St EN2 ... 5 B4
Lynstead Cl BR1 ... 187 C1
Lynsted Cl DA6 ... 169 D6
Lynsted Ct 4 BR3 ... 185 A1
Lynsted Gdns SE9 ... 143 D2
Lynton KT7 ... 197 A2
Lynton Ave N12 ... 30 B6
NW9 ... 45 D5
Ealing W13 ... 87 A1
Lynton Cl NW10 ... 67 D3
Chessington KT9 ... 214 A4
Isleworth TW7 ... 130 D1
Lynton Cres IG2 ... 56 D3
Lynton Ct 9 W3 ... 89 A1
Bowes Park N13 ... 32 A5
Penge SE20 ... 184 B2
Sutton SM2 ... 218 A2
Lynton Est SE1 ... 118 A2
Lynton Gdns N11 ... 31 D4
Enfield EN1 ... 17 C4
Lynton Grange N2 ... 48 D6
Lynton Ho 15 W2 ... 91 D1
Lynton Lo N5 ... 72 D3
Lynton Mans SE1 ... 261 A6
Lynton Mead N20 ... 13 D2
Lynton Rd N8 ... 50 A4
NW6 ... 91 B5
SE1 ... 118 D3 263
Acton W3 ... 110 D6
Chingford E4 ... 35 D5
Harrow HA2 ... 63 A6
New Malden KT3 ... 199 B4
Thornton Heath CR0 ... 204 C3
Lynton Terr 4 W3 ... 89 A1
Lynton Wlk UB4 ... 83 C4
Lynwood Cl Harrow HA2 ... 63 A5
Woodford E18 ... 37 C2
Lynwood Dr KT4 ... 216 A6
Lynwood Gdns
Southall UB1 ... 85 B1
Wallington CR0 ... 220 B4
Lynwood Gr
Orpington BR6 ... 211 C1
Southgate N21 ... 16 C3
Lynwood Rd Ealing W5 ... 88 A3
Thames Ditton KT7 ... 196 D1
Upper Tooting SW17 ... 180 D6
Lyon Bsns Pk IG11 ... 101 C5
Lyon Ct HA4 ... 39 D1
Lyon Ho NW8 ... 237 A5
Lyon Meade HA7 ... 25 C2
Lyon Park Ave HA0 ... 66 B2
Lyon Park Jun & Inf Schs
HA0 ... 66 B1
Lyon Rd Harrow HA1 ... 42 D3
Merton SW19 ... 180 A2
Lyonsdown Ave EN5 ... 14 A5
Lyonsdown Ct EN5 ... 14 A6
Lyonsdown Rd EN5 ... 14 A6
Lyonsdown Sch EN5 ... 14 A6
Lyons Pl NW8 ... 92 B3 236 C5
Lyon St N1 ... 72 B1
Lyons Wlk W14 ... 254 A4
Lyon Way UB6 ... 86 C6
Lyoth Rd BR5 ... 227 A6
Lyric Dr UB6 ... 85 D3
Lyric Mews SE26 ... 184 C6
Lyric Rd SW13 ... 133 D4
Lysander 20 NW9 ... 27 D2
Lysander Gdns KT5 ... 198 B3
Lysander Gr N19 ... 49 D1
Lysander Ho 10 E2 ... 96 B5
Lysander Rd Ruislip HA4 ... 61 B6
Wallington CR0 ... 220 B2
Lysander Way BR6 ... 227 A5
Lysia Ct SW6 ... 134 D5
Lysias Rd SW12 ... 159 B5
Lysia St SW6 ... 134 D5
Lysons Wlk SW15 ... 156 A6
Lytchet Rd BR1 ... 187 B3
Lytchet Way EN3 ... 6 C4
Lytchgate Cl CR2 ... 221 C1
Lytcott Dr KT8 ... 195 B6
Lytcott Gr SE22 ... 161 D6
Lytham Ave WD19 ... 22 D5
Lytham Cl SE28 ... 103 A1
Lytham Ct 5 UB1 ... 85 D1
Lytham Gr W5 ... 88 B4
Lytham St SE17 ... 117 B1 262 C1
Lyttelton Cl NW3 ... 70 C1
Lyttelton Ct N2 ... 48 A4
Lyttelton Rd E10 ... 76 A5
N2 ... 48 A4
Lytten Ct 6 W12 ... 112 A4
Lyttleton Ct UB4 ... 84 C3
Lyttleton Ho 10 E9 ... 74 C1
Lyttleton Rd N8 ... 50 C6
Lytton Ave Enfield EN3 ... 7 A5
Southgate N13 ... 16 C2
Lytton Cl N2 ... 48 B4
Northolt UB5 ... 63 B1
Lytton Ct WC1 ... 240 B3
Lytton Gdns SM6 ... 219 D4
Lytton Gr SW15 ... 157 A5
Lytton Ho 3 TW12 ... 173 D4
Lytton Rd E11 ... 54 C2
New Barnet EN5 ... 2 A1
Pinner HA5 ... 23 A3
Lytton Strachy Path 8
SE28 ... 124 B6
Lyveden Rd SE3 ... 143 B5
Mitcham SW17,SW19 ... 180 D4

M

Mabbett Ho 2 SE18 ... 144 C6
Mabel Evetts Ct UB3 ... 106 B6
Mabel Thornton Ho 12
N16 ... 73 B4
Maberley Cres SE19 ... 184 A3
Maberley Ct SE19 ... 184 A3
Maberley Rd SE19 ... 182 C2
Mabledon Pl NW1,WC1 ... 232 D1
Mablethorpe Rd SW6 ... 264 A3
Mabley St E9 ... 75 A3
Mcadam Dr EN2 ... 4 D3
Macallister Ho 8 SE18 ... 144 D6
Macaret Cl N20 ... 14 A4
Macarthur Cl E7 ... 77 A2
MacArthur Ho 4 SW2 ... 160 A4
Macaulay Ave KT10 ... 212 C6
Macaulay CE Prim Sch
SW4 ... 137 B1
Macaulay Ct SW4 ... 137 B2
Macaulay Ho 10 N16 ... 73 C5
2 W10 ... 91 A2
Macaulay Rd E6 ... 99 D5
SW4 ... 137 B2
Macaulay Sq SW4 ... 137 B1
Macaulay Way 2 SE28 ... 124 B5
McAuley Cl SE1 ... 116 C3 261 A6
SE9 ... 166 C6
Macbean St SE18 ... 122 D3
Macbeth Ho 4 N1 ... 95 C5
Macbeth St W6 ... 112 B1
McBride Ho 5 E3 ... 97 B5
McCall Cl SW4 ... 138 A3
McCall Cres SE7 ... 122 A1
McCall Ho N7 ... 72 A4
Mccarthy Ct SW11 ... 267 B1
McCarthy Rd TW13 ... 172 D5
Macclesfield Rd
EC1 ... 95 A4 235 A2
Croydon SE25 ... 206 C4
Macclesfield St W1 ... 249 D6
McClintock Pl EN3 ... 7 C6
McCoid Way SE1 ... 252 A1
Mcconnell Ho SW8 ... 269 C1
McCormick Ho 9 SW2 ... 160 C3
McCrone Mews 3 NW3 ... 70 B2
McCullum Rd E3 ... 97 B6
McDermott Cl SW11 ... 136 C2
McDermott Rd SE15 ... 140 A2
Macdonald Ave RM10 ... 81 D5
Macdonald Ct TW3 ... 130 A1
Macdonald Ho 2 SW11 ... 137 A3
McDonald Ho 1 KT2 ... 176 B3
Macdonald Rd E7 ... 77 A4
N11 ... 30 D5
N19 ... 71 C6
Chingford E17 ... 36 A1
McDonough Cl KT9 ... 214 A4
McDougall Ct TW9 ... 132 C3
McDowall Cl E16 ... 98 D2
McDowall Rd SE5 ... 139 A4
Macduff Rd
SW11 ... 137 A4 268 B2
Mace Cl E1 ... 118 B5
Mace Gateway E16 ... 121 B6
Mace Ho 2 E17 ... 53 D6
McEntee Ave E17 ... 35 A2
Mace St E2 ... 96 D5
McEwan Way E15 ... 98 B6
Macey Ho 9 SE10 ... 142 A6
SW11 ... 267 A1
Macfarlane La TW7 ... 131 A6
Macfarlane Rd W12 ... 112 C5
Macfarren Ho 9 W10 ... 91 A4
MacFarren Pl NW1 ... 238 B5
McGlashon Ho 10 E1 ... 96 A3
McGrath Rd E15 ... 76 D2
McGregor Ct 8 N1 ... 95 C4
MacGregor Ho 2
SW12 ... 159 D3
McGregor Rd W11 ... 91 B2
Macgregor Rd E16 ... 99 C2
Mcguffie Ct E17 ... 53 B6
Machell Rd SE15 ... 140 C2
McIndoe Ct N1 ... 235 C6
McIntosh Cl SM6 ... 220 A1
McIntosh Ho 11 SE16 ... 118 C2
McIntyre Ct 19 SW4 ... 138 A3
Mackay Ho 33 W12 ... 112 B6
Mackay Rd SW4 ... 137 B2
McKay Rd SW20 ... 178 C4
McKellar Cl WD23 ... 8 A2
McKenna Ho 3 E3 ... 97 B5
Mackennal St
NW8 ... 92 C5 230 B4
Mackenzie Cl 7 W12 ... 112 B6
Mackenzie Ct 1 N8 ... 50 A5
Mackenzie Ho 5 NW2 ... 68 A5
Mackenzie Rd N7 ... 72 B2
Penge BR3 ... 184 D1
Mackenzie Wlk E14 ... 119 C5
McKerrell Rd SE15 ... 140 A4
Mackeson Rd NW3 ... 70 D4
Mackie Ho SW2 ... 160 C4
Mackie Rd 18 SW2 ... 160 C4
McKiernan Ct 2 SW11 ... 136 C3
Mc Killop Way DA14 ... 190 C3
McKinlay Ct BR3 ... 185 B1
McKinnon Wood Ho 23
E2 ... 96 A4
Mackintosh La E9 ... 74 D3
Macklin Ho SE23 ... 162 B2
Macklin St WC2 ... 94 A1 240 B2
Mackonochie Ho EC1 ... 241 A4
Mackrow Wlk 11 E14 ... 120 A6
Macks Rd SE16 ... 118 A2
Mackworth Ho NW1 ... 232 A2
Mackworth St NW1 ... 232 A2
Maclean Rd SE23 ... 163 A5
Mcleod Ct SE21 ... 162 A3
Macleod Ho 4 SE18 ... 144 A4
McLeod Ho 3 SE23 ... 162 C2
McLeod Rd SE2 ... 124 B2
Macleod Rd N21 ... 16 A6
McLeod's Mews
SW7 ... 113 D2 255 D4
Macleod St
SE17 ... 117 A1 262 B1
Maclise Rd W14 ... 113 A3 254 A5
McManus Ho 3 SW11 ... 136 B2
McMillan Ct 2 SE6 ... 164 D3
Macmillan Ct HA2 ... 41 C1
Mcmillan Ho SE4 ... 141 A2
Macmillan Ho NW4 ... 68 B4
NW8 ... 230 A1
McMillan St SE8 ... 141 C6
Macmillan Way SW17 ... 181 B6
Mcmorran Ho N7 ... 72 A4
McNair Rd UB2 ... 107 D3
Macnamara Ho SW10 ... 266 C4
Mcneil Rd SE5 ... 139 C3
McNicol Dr NW10 ... 89 A5
Macoma Rd SE18 ... 145 B6
Macoma Terr SE18 ... 145 B6
Maconochies Rd E14 ... 119 D1
Macquarie Way E14 ... 119 D2
McRae La CR4 ... 202 D2
Macready Ho W1 ... 237 B3
Macready Pl 2 N7 ... 72 A4
Macroom Ho W9 ... 91 B4
Macroom Rd W9 ... 91 B4
Mac's Pl EC4 ... 241 B2
Madame Tussaud's★
NW1 ... 93 A3 238 A5
Mada Rd BR6 ... 226 D5
Maddams St E3 ... 97 D3
Maddison Cl TW11 ... 174 D4
Maddocks Cl DA14 ... 191 A5
Maddocks Ho 3 E1 ... 118 B6
Maddock Way SE17 ... 138 D6
Maddox Ct 1 E4 ... 20 B3
Maddox St W1 ... 248 D6
Madeira Ave BR1 ... 186 C3
Madeira Gr IG8 ... 37 C4
Madeira Rd E11 ... 54 C1
Edmonton N13 ... 16 D1
Mitcham CR4 ... 202 D5
Streatham SW16 ... 182 A5
Madeley Ct W5 ... 88 A1
Madeley Rd W5 ... 88 A1
Madeline Gr IG1 ... 79 B3
Madeline Rd SE20 ... 184 A3
Madge Gill Way 4 E6 ... 100 A6
Madge Hill W7 ... 108 C6
Madinah Rd E8 ... 74 A3
Madingley 11 KT1 ... 176 C1
Madingley Ct TW1 ... 153 C6
Madison Cres DA7 ... 146 C5
Madison Gdns
Beckenham BR2 ... 208 D6
Bexley DA7 ... 146 C5
Madison Ho E3 ... 98 A4
Madras Ho IG1 ... 78 D4
Madras Pl N7 ... 72 C2
Madras Rd IG1 ... 78 D4
Madrid Rd SW13 ... 134 A5
Madron St SE17 ... 117 C1 263 B2
Mafeking Ave E6 ... 100 A5
Brentford TW8 ... 132 A6
Ilford IG2 ... 57 B2
Mafeking Rd E16 ... 98 D3
Enfield EN1 ... 5 D2
Tottenham N17 ... 34 A1
Magdala Ave N19 ... 71 C6
Magdala Rd
Isleworth TW7 ... 131 A2
South Croydon CR2 ... 221 B1
Magdalen Ct SE25 ... 206 A4
Magdalene Cl 7 SE15 ... 140 B3
Magdalene Gdns E6 ... 100 C3
Magdalene Ho 7 SW15 ... 156 D5
Magdalene Rd TW17 ... 192 B6
Magdalen Pas E1 ... 253 D6
Magdalen Rd SW18 ... 158 B3
Magdalen St SE1 ... 253 A3
Magee St SE11 ... 138 C6
Magellan Ct 9 NW10 ... 67 B1
Magellan Ho 16 E1 ... 96 D3
Magellan Pl 10 E14 ... 119 C2
Magnaville Rd WD23 ... 8 D4
Magnet Rd HA9 ... 65 D6
Magnin Cl 5 E8 ... 96 A6
Magnolia Cl E10 ... 75 C6
Kingston KT2 ... 176 D4
Magnolia Ct 2 N12 ... 29 D6
SW11 ... 158 D5
3 Belmont SM2 ... 217 D1
Feltham TW14 ... 150 A3
Forest Hill SE26 ... 184 C5
Harrow HA3 ... 44 B2
Hillingdon UB10 ... 60 D2
Northolt UB5 ... 85 A3
Richmond TW9 ... 132 D4
Magnolia Ho 13 SE8 ... 141 B6
Magnolia Lo E4 ... 19 D1
Magnolia Pl SW4 ... 160 A6
Ealing W5 ... 87 D2
Magnolia Rd W4 ... 132 D6
Magnolia Way KT19 ... 215 A3
Magnolia Wharf W4 ... 132 D6
Magpie Cl E7 ... 76 D3
NW9 ... 27 C1
Enfield EN1 ... 6 A4
Magpie Hall Cl BR2 ... 210 A3
Magpie Hall La BR2 ... 210 B3
Magpie Hall Rd WD23 ... 8 C2
Magpie Ho 7 E3 ... 97 B6
Magpie Pl SE14 ... 141 A6
Maguire Dr TW10 ... 175 C6
Maguire St SE1 ... 117 D4 253 D2
Mahatma Gandhi Ind Est 1
SE24 ... 138 D1
Mahlon Ave HA4 ... 62 B2
Mahogany Cl SE16 ... 119 A5
Mahon Cl EN1 ... 5 D4
Mahoney Ho SE14 ... 141 B4
Maida Ave W2 ... 92 A3 236 B5
Chingford E4 ... 19 D4
Maida Rd DA17 ... 125 C3
Maida Vale W9 ... 92 A4 229 A1
Maida Vale Psychiatric Hospl
W9 ... 92 A3 236 B6
Maida Vale Sta W9 ... 91 D4
Maida Way E4 ... 19 D4
Maiden Erlegh Ave DA5 ... 169 A3
Maiden La NW1 ... 71 D1
SE1 ... 117 A5 252 B4
WC2 ... 116 A6 250 B6
Maiden Rd E15 ... 76 C1
Maidenstone Hill SE10 ... 142 A4
Maids of Honour Row 4
TW9 ... 153 D6
Maidstone Bldgs SE1 ... 252 C3
Maidstone Ho 4 E14 ... 97 D1
Maidstone Rd N11 ... 31 D4
Ruxley DA14 ... 191 C3
Mail Coach Yd 24 E2 ... 95 C4
Main Ave EN1 ... 17 D6
Main Dr HA9 ... 65 D5
Main Rd BR5 ... 190 C1
Sidcup DA14,DA15 ... 167 C1
Mainridge Rd BR7,SE9 ... 188 C6
Main St TW13 ... 172 D5
Mainwaring Ct 3 CR4 ... 181 A1
Main Yd E9 ... 75 C2
Mais Ho SE26 ... 162 B2
Maismore St SE15 ... 140 A6
Maison Alfort HA3 ... 24 C2
Maisonettes The SM1 ... 217 B3
Maitland Cl 5 SE10 ... 141 D5
Hounslow TW4 ... 129 B2
Maitland Ct W2 ... 246 C6
Maitland Ho 17 E2 ... 96 C5
SW1 ... 269 A6
Maitland Park Rd NW3 ... 70 D2
Maitland Park Villas
NW3 ... 70 D2
Maitland Pl E5 ... 74 C4
Maitland Rd E15 ... 76 D2
Penge SE26 ... 184 D4
Majendie Rd SE18 ... 123 B1
Majestic Ct N4 ... 50 D1
Majestic Way CR4 ... 180 D1
Major Rd E15 ... 76 B3
22 SE16 ... 118 A3
Makepeace Ave N6 ... 71 A6
Makepeace Mans N6 ... 71 A6
Makepeace Rd
Northolt UB5 ... 85 A6
Wanstead E11 ... 55 A5
Makinen Ho IG9 ... 21 C3
Makins St SW3 ... 257 B3
Malabar Ct 20 W12 ... 112 B6
Malabar St E14 ... 119 C4
Malam Ct SE11 ... 261 A3
Malam Gdns 3 E14 ... 119 D6
Malatia CR2 ... 221 A2
Malay Ho 2 E1 ... 118 C5
Malbrook Rd SW15 ... 134 B1
Malcolm Cl SE20 ... 184 C3
Malcolm Cres NW4 ... 46 A3
Malcolm Ct E7 ... 76 D2
NW4 ... 46 A3
Ealing W5 ... 88 B3
Stanmore HA7 ... 25 C5
Malcolm Dr KT6 ... 198 A1
Malcolm Gavin Cl SW17 ... 158 C2
Malcolm Ho 13 N1 ... 95 C5
Malcolm Pl E2 ... 96 C3
Malcolm Prim Sch
SE20 ... 184 C3
Malcolm Rd E1 ... 96 C3
Croydon SE25 ... 206 A3
Ickenham UB10 ... 60 B4
Penge SE20 ... 184 C3
Wimbledon SW19 ... 179 A4
Malcolmson Ho SW1 ... 259 D1
Malcolms Way N14 ... 15 C6
Malcolm Way E11 ... 55 A5
Malden Ave
Croydon SE25 ... 206 B6
Northolt UB6 ... 64 C2
Malden CE Prim Sch
KT4 ... 199 C1
Malden Cres NW1 ... 71 A2
Malden Ct N4 ... 51 A3
West Barnes KT3 ... 200 B6
Malden Green Ave KT4 ... 200 A1
Malden Hill KT3 ... 199 D6
Malden Hill Gdns KT3 ... 199 D6
Malden Junc KT3 ... 199 D4
Malden Manor Prim Sch
KT3 ... 199 C2
Malden Manor Sta KT3 ... 199 C2
Malden Pk KT3 ... 199 D3
Malden Pl NW5 ... 71 A3
Malden Rd NW5 ... 71 A2
Cheam KT4,SM3 ... 216 D4
New Malden KT3,KT4 ... 199 D2
Malden Way KT3 ... 200 A5
Malden Way (Kingston By
Pass) KT3,KT5 ... 199 C4
Maldon Cl E15 ... 76 B3
N1 ... 235 B6
SE5 ... 139 C2
Maldon Ct Barking E6 ... 100 C6
Wallington SM6 ... 219 C3
Maldon Rd W3 ... 111 A6
Edmonton N9 ... 17 D1
Wallington SM6 ... 219 B3
Maldon Wlk IG8 ... 37 C4
Malet Pl WC1 ... 239 C5
Malet St WC1 ... 93 D2 239 D4
Maley Ave SE27 ... 160 D2
Malford Ct E18 ... 37 A1
Malford Gr E18 ... 54 D6
Malfort Rd SE5 ... 139 C2
Malham Cl N11 ... 31 A4
Malham Rd SE23 ... 162 D3
Malham Road Ind Est
SE23 ... 162 D3
Malins Cl EN5 ... 12 C6
Mallams Mews 1 SW9 ... 138 D2
Mallard Cl E9 ... 75 B2
NW6 ... 91 C6
W7 ... 108 C4
New Barnet EN5 ... 14 B5
Twickenham TW4 ... 151 C4
Mallard Ct E12 ... 78 B3
E17 ... 54 B6
NW9 ... 45 A2
Chingford E4 ... 20 B4
Ilford IG1 ... 79 A6
15 Richmond TW10 ... 153 D5
Mallard Ho NW8 ... 230 A3
7 SE15 ... 139 D4
Mallard Path SE28 ... 123 B3
Mallard Pl TW1 ... 153 A1
Mallard Point 5 E3 ... 97 C4
Mallards E11 ... 55 A2
Mallards Rd
Barking IG11 ... 102 A3
Woodford IG8 ... 37 B3
Mallard Way NW9 ... 45 A2
Mallard Wlk
Beckenham BR3 ... 206 D4
Sidcup DA14 ... 190 C4
Mall Ct W5 ... 110 A6
Mallet Dr UB5 ... 63 B3
Mallet Ho 11 SW15 ... 156 A6
Mallet Rd SE13 ... 164 B5
Malling SE13 ... 163 D6
Malling Cl CR0 ... 206 C3
Malling Gdns SM4 ... 202 A3
Malling Ho 9 BR3 ... 185 C3
Malling Way BR2 ... 208 D2
Mallinson Ct 2 E11 ... 76 C6
Mallinson Rd SW11 ... 158 D6
Wallington SM6 ... 219 D5
Mallon Gdns E1 ... 243 D3
Mallord St SW3 ... 136 B6 266 D6
Mallory Bldgs EC1 ... 241 C5
Mallory Cl SE4 ... 141 A1
Mallory Gdns EN4 ... 15 A4
Mallory Ho E14 ... 98 A2
Mallory St NW8 ... 92 C3 237 B6
Mallow Cl CR0 ... 206 D1
Mallow Mead NW7 ... 29 A3
Mallow St EC1 ... 242 C6
Mallows The UB10 ... 60 D5
Mall Rd W6 ... 112 B1
Mall Studios 9 NW3 ... 70 D3
Mall The 4 BR1 ... 209 A6
SW1 ... 115 D5 249 C3
6 Bexley DA6 ... 147 C1
Brentford TW8 ... 131 D6
Ealing W5 ... 110 A6
Harrow HA3 ... 44 B3
Kingston KT6 ... 197 D4
Mortlake SW14 ... 155 A6
Palmers Green N14 ... 16 A1
Mall The (Prep Sch)
TW2 ... 152 B1
Malmains Cl BR3 ... 208 B5
Malmains Way BR3 ... 208 B5
Malmesbury 31 E2 ... 96 C5
Malmesbury Cl HA5 ... 40 A5
Malmesbury Fst Sch
SM4 ... 202 A2
Malmesbury Mid Sch
SM4 ... 202 A3
Malmesbury Prim Sch
E3 ... 97 B4
Malmesbury Rd E16 ... 98 C2
E3 ... 97 B5
Morden SM4 ... 202 A3
Woodford E18 ... 36 D2
Malmesbury Terr E16 ... 98 D2
Malmsey Ho SE11 ... 260 D2
Malmsmead Ho E9 ... 75 A3
Malorees Jun & Inf Schs
NW6 ... 68 D1
Malory Sch BR1 ... 187 A6
Malpas Dr HA5 ... 40 D4
Malpas Rd E8 ... 74 B2
SE4 ... 141 B3
Dagenham RM9 ... 80 D2
Malta Rd E10 ... 53 C2
Malta St EC1 ... 241 D6
Maltby Dr EN1 ... 6 B5
Maltby Rd KT9 ... 214 C2
Maltby St SE1 ... 117 D3 263 C6
Maltham Terr N18 ... 34 B4
Malthouse Dr
Chiswick W4 ... 133 D6
Feltham TW13 ... 172 D5
Malthouse Pas SW13 ... 133 C3
Malthus Path 7 SE28 ... 124 C5
Malting Ho E14 ... 119 B6
Maltings W4 ... 110 C1
Maltings Cl SW13 ... 133 C3
Maltings Lo W4 ... 133 C5
Maltings Pl SE1 ... 253 B2
SW6 ... 265 D1
Maltings The BR6 ... 211 D1
Malting Way TW7 ... 130 D2
Malt Mill SE1 ... 253 C3
Malton Ho SE25 ... 205 C5
Malton Mews SE18 ... 145 C6
1 W10 ... 91 A1
Malton Rd W10 ... 91 A1
Malton St SE18 ... 145 C6
Maltravers St WC2 ... 251 A6
Malt St SE1 ... 140 A6
Malva Cl SW18 ... 157 D6
Malvern Ave DA7 ... 147 A5
Chingford E4 ... 36 B3
Harrow HA2 ... 63 B5
Malvern Cl W10 ... 91 B2
Ickenham UB10 ... 60 C6
Mitcham CR4 ... 203 C6
Penge SE20 ... 184 A1
Surbiton KT6 ... 198 A1
Malvern Court SW7 ... 256 D4
Malvern Ct Belmont SM2 ... 217 C1
3 Surbiton KT6 ... 198 A1
Malvern Dr
Feltham TW13 ... 172 D5
Ilford IG3 ... 79 D4
Woodford IG8 ... 37 C6
Malvern Gdns NW2 ... 69 A6
Harrow HA3 ... 44 A5
Malvern Ho N16 ... 51 D1
Malvern Lo N12 ... 30 B6
Malvern Mews NW6 ... 91 C4
Malvern Pl NW6 ... 91 B4
Malvern Rd E11 ... 76 D6
E6 ... 100 A6
E8 ... 74 A1
N17 ... 52 A6
N19 ... 49 D1
N8 ... 50 C6
NW6 ... 91 C4
Enfield EN3 ... 7 A6
Hampton TW12 ... 173 C3
Harlington UB3 ... 127 C5
Surbiton KT6 ... 198 A1
Thornton Heath CR7 ... 204 C5
Malvern Terr N1 ... 234 A6
Edmonton N9 ... 17 D3
Malvern Way W13 ... 87 B2
Malwood Rd SW12 ... 159 B5
Malyons Rd SE13 ... 163 D6
Malyons Terr SE13 ... 163 D6
Malyons The TW17 ... 193 B3
Managers St E14 ... 120 A5
Manatee Pl SM6 ... 219 D5
Manaton Cl SE15 ... 140 B2
Manaton Cres UB1 ... 85 C1
Manbey Gr E15 ... 76 C2
Manbey Park Rd E15 ... 76 C2
Manbey Rd E15 ... 76 C2
Manbey St E15 ... 76 C2
Manbre Rd W6 ... 134 C6

Manbrough Ave E6 ... 100 C4
Manchester Ct E16 ... 99 B1
Manchester Dr W10 ... 91 A3
Manchester Gr E14 ... 120 A1
Manchester Ho SE17 ... 262 B2
Manchester Mans N19 ... 49 D2
Manchester Mews W1 ... 238 A3
Manchester Rd E14 ... 120 A3
N15 ... 51 B3
South Norwood CR7 ... 205 A6
Manchester Sq
W1 ... 93 A1 238 B2
Manchester St
W1 ... 93 A2 238 A3
Manchester Way RM10 ... 81 D4
Manchuria Rd SW11 ... 159 A5
Manciple St SE1 ... 117 B3 262 D6
Mandalay Ho 6 N16 ... 73 B4
Mandalay Rd SW4 ... 159 C6
Mandarin Ct NW10 ... 67 B2
6 SE8 ... 141 C6
Mandarin Way UB4 ... 84 D1
Mandela Cl NW10 ... 67 A1
36 W12 ... 112 B6
Mandela Ho 18 E2 ... 95 D4
Mandela Rd E16 ... 99 A1
Mandela St NW1 ... 93 C6 232 B6
SW9 ... 138 C5
Mandela Way
SE1 ... 117 C2 263 B4
Manderville Ho SE1 ... 263 D2
Mandeville Cl 5 SE3 ... 142 D5
Merton SW19 ... 179 A2
Mandeville Ct NW3 ... 69 D3
Mandeville Ctyd SW11 ... 268 A1
Mandeville Dr KT6 ... 197 D1
Mandeville Ho 8 SW4 ... 159 C6
Mandeville Pl W1 ... 238 B2
Mandeville Prim Sch E5 ... 74 D5
Mandeville Rd N14 ... 15 C2
Enfield EN3 ... 7 A6
Isleworth TW7 ... 131 A3
Littleton TW17 ... 192 C4
Northolt UB5 ... 63 C1
Mandeville Sch UB5 ... 63 B2
Mandeville St E5 ... 75 A5
Mandrake Rd SW17 ... 158 D1
Mandrake Way 2 E15 ... 76 C1
Mandrell Rd SW2 ... 160 A6
Manesty Ct N14 ... 15 D4
Manette St W1 ... 239 D1
Manfred Ct 6 SW15 ... 157 B6
Manfred Rd SW15 ... 157 B6
Manger Rd N7 ... 72 A2
Mangold Way 4 DA18 ... 125 A3
Manilla St E14 ... 119 C4
Manister Rd SE2 ... 124 A3
Manitoba Ct 23 SE16 ... 118 C4
Manitoba Gdns 6 BR6 ... 227 D2
Manley Ct N16 ... 73 D5
Manley Ho SE11 ... 261 A2
Manley St NW1 ... 231 A6
Manly Dixon Dr EN3 ... 7 A6
Mann Cl 1 CR0 ... 221 A5
Mannebury Prior N1 ... 233 D3
Mannering Ho 16 SW2 ... 160 B6
Manning Ct 3 SE28 ... 124 B5
Manningford Cl EC1 ... 234 C2
Manning Gdns HA3 ... 43 D2
Manning Ho 6 E17 ... 54 A6
3 W11 ... 91 A1
Manning Pl TW10 ... 154 B5
Manning Rd E17 ... 53 A4
Dagenham RM10 ... 81 C1
Manningtree Cl SW19 ... 157 A3
Manningtree Rd HA4 ... 62 B4
Manningtree St 1 E1 ... 96 A1
Mannin Rd RM6 ... 58 B2
Mannock Rd N22 ... 50 D6
Mann's Cl TW7 ... 152 D6
Manns Rd HA8 ... 26 C4
Manny Shinwell Ho
SW6 ... 264 D5
Manoel Rd TW2 ... 152 A2
Manor Ave SE4 ... 141 B3
Hounslow TW4 ... 128 D3
Northolt UB5 ... 63 B1
Manorbrook SE12,SE3 ... 143 A1
Manor Circus TW9 ... 132 C2
Manor Cl E17 ... 35 A1
NW7 ... 27 B5
NW9 ... 44 D4
SE28 ... 102 C1
Barnet EN5 ... 1 A1
New Malden KT4 ... 199 C1
Ruislip HA4 ... 39 D1
Manor Cottages App N2 ... 30 A1
Manor Cotts N2 ... 30 A1
Manor Court Rd W7 ... 108 C6
Manor Cres KT5 ... 198 C3
Manor Ct E10 ... 53 D1
N14 ... 15 D2
N20 ... 14 D1
N2 ... 48 D4
SE15 ... 139 D4
7 SW2 ... 160 B6
SW6 ... 265 D1
W3 ... 110 C2
3 Barking IG11 ... 79 D1
Chingford, Chingford Green
E4 ... 20 C3
Harrow HA1 ... 42 D3
Kingston KT2 ... 176 C2
Streatham SW16 ... 160 A1
Surbiton KT5 ... 198 C3
Twickenham TW2 ... 152 A2
5 Wembley HA9 ... 66 A3
Manordene Cl KT7 ... 197 A1
Manordene Rd SE28 ... 102 D1
Manor Dr N14 ... 15 B3
N20 ... 14 D1
NW7 ... 27 B5
Feltham TW13 ... 172 D5
Hinchley Wood KT10 ... 213 A5
Sunbury TW16 ... 172 A1
Surbiton KT5 ... 198 C3
Wembley HA9 ... 66 B4
West Ewell KT19 ... 215 C2
Manor Dr N KT3,KT4 ... 199 B2
Manor Dr The KT4 ... 199 D1
Manor Farm Ave TW17 ... 192 D3
Manor Farm Cl KT4 ... 199 C1
Manor Farm Ct E6 ... 100 B4
Manor Farm Dr E4 ... 20 C1
Manor Farm Rd
Thornton Heath CR7,
SW16 ... 182 C1
Wembley HA0 ... 87 D5
Manorfield Cl 3 N19 ... 71 C4
Manorfield Prim Sch
E14 ... 97 D2
Manorfields Cl BR7 ... 211 D6
Manor Gate UB5 ... 63 A1
Manorgate Rd KT2 ... 176 C2
Manor Gdns N7 ... 72 A5
SW4 ... 137 C3
W3 ... 110 C2
8 W4 ... 111 C1
Hampton TW12 ... 174 A3
Merton SW20 ... 179 B1
Richmond TW10,TW9 ... 132 B1
Ruislip HA4 ... 62 C3
South Croydon CR2 ... 221 D2
Sunbury TW16 ... 172 A1
Manor Gr SE15 ... 140 C6
Beckenham BR3 ... 185 D1
Richmond TW9 ... 132 C2
Manor Gt SW15 ... 157 A6
Manor Hall Ave NW4 ... 28 D1
Manor Hall Dr NW4 ... 28 D1
Manor Hall Gdns E10 ... 53 C1
Manor Ho E12 ... 77 D4
N14 ... 15 D3
NW1 ... 237 B4
Brentford TW8 ... 109 C1
Wallington SM6 ... 219 B3
Manor House Ct W9 ... 236 A5
Manor House Dr NW6 ... 68 D1
Manor House Est HA7 ... 25 B5
Manor House Sch W7 ... 108 C6
Manor House Way TW7 ... 131 B2
Manor Inf Sch IG11 ... 79 D2
Manor Jun Sch IG11 ... 79 D2
Manor La SE12 ... 164 C5
Feltham TW13 ... 150 A2
Harlington UB3 ... 127 B6
Sunbury TW16 ... 172 B1
Sutton SM1 ... 218 A3
Manor Lane Terr SE13 ... 164 C6
Manor Lodge NW2 ... 68 D2
Manor Mans N7 ... 72 A5
7 NW3 ... 70 C2
Manor Mead Sch TW17 ... 192 D4
Manor Mews NW6 ... 91 C5
SE4 ... 141 B3
Manor Mount SE23 ... 162 C3
Manor Oak Mans SE22 ... 162 B5
Manor Par N16 ... 73 D6
Harrow HA1 ... 42 D3
Manor Park Cl BR4 ... 207 D1
Manor Park Cres HA8 ... 26 C4
Manor Park Dr HA2 ... 41 D6
Manor Park Gdns HA8 ... 26 C4
Manor Park Prim Sch
SM1 ... 218 A3
Manor Park Rd E12 ... 77 D4
N2 ... 48 B6
NW10 ... 89 D6
Chislehurst BR7 ... 189 B2
Sutton SM1 ... 218 A3
West Wickham BR4 ... 207 D1
Manor Park Sta E12 ... 77 D4
Manor Pk SE13 ... 164 C6
Chislehurst BR7 ... 189 B2
Richmond TW9 ... 132 B1
Manor Pl BR7 ... 189 B1
SE17 ... 117 A1 262 A2
East Bedfont TW14 ... 150 A3
Mitcham CR4 ... 203 C6
Sutton SM1 ... 217 D4
Walton-on-T KT12 ... 194 A2
Manor Prim Sch E15 ... 98 C5
Manor Rd DA15 ... 168 A1
DA5 ... 169 D3
E10 ... 53 C2
E15,E16 ... 98 C4
E17 ... 35 A1
N16 ... 51 C1
Ashford TW15 ... 170 C5
Barking IG11 ... 79 D2
Barnet EN5 ... 1 A1
Beckenham BR3 ... 185 D1
Belmont SM2 ... 217 B1
Bowes Park N22 ... 32 A4
Dagenham RM6 ... 58 D3
Ealing W13 ... 109 A6
East Molesey KT8 ... 196 B5
Enfield EN2 ... 5 B2
Harrow HA1 ... 43 A3
Hayes UB3 ... 84 A1
Loughton IG10 ... 21 B5
Merton SW20 ... 179 B1
Mitcham CR4 ... 203 C6
Richmond TW10,TW9 ... 132 B1
Richmond TW11 ... 175 B5
Ruislip HA4 ... 39 B1
South Norwood SE25 ... 206 A6
Manor Rd *continued*
Tottenham N17 ... 34 B2
Twickenham TW2 ... 152 B2
Wallington SM5,SM6 ... 219 B3
Walton-on-T KT12 ... 193 D2
West Wickham BR4 ... 223 D6
Manor Rd N
Hinchley Wood KT7 ... 213 A6
Wallington SM5,SM6 ... 219 B4
Manor Rd S KT10 ... 212 C4
Manor Sch NW10 ... 90 C6
Manorside EN5 ... 1 A1
Manorside Cl SE2 ... 124 D2
Manorside Prim Sch N3 ... 30 A2
Manor Sq RM8 ... 80 C6
Manor Street Est SW3 ... 267 B6
Manor The W1 ... 248 C5
Manor Vale TW8 ... 109 C1
Manor View N3 ... 29 D1
Manor Way BR2 ... 210 A3
BR5 ... 211 A5
DA5 ... 169 C3
NW9 ... 45 C5
W3 ... 110 C2
Manorway Enfield EN1 ... 17 C4
Woodford IG8 ... 37 C5
Manor Way
Beckenham BR3 ... 207 C6
Chingford E4 ... 36 B6
Greenwich SE3 ... 143 A1
Harrow HA2 ... 41 D5
Mitcham CR4 ... 203 C6
New Malden KT4 ... 199 D1
Ruislip HA4 ... 39 D1
Southall UB2 ... 106 D2
South Croydon CR2 ... 221 D2
Manor Waye UB8 ... 82 A6
Manor Way The SM6 ... 219 B4
Manpreet Ct E12 ... 78 B3
Manresa Rd
SW3 ... 114 C1 257 A1
Mansard Beeches
SW17 ... 181 A5
Mansard Cl HA5 ... 40 D6
Mansard Manor 4 SM2 ... 218 A1
Manse Cl UB3 ... 127 B6
Manse Ct DA14 ... 190 C5
Mansel Ct SW11 ... 267 B1
Mansel Gr E17 ... 35 C2
Mansell Ho SW8 ... 269 B2
Mansell Rd W3 ... 111 B4
Southall UB6 ... 85 D2
Mansell St E1 ... 95 D1 243 D1
Mansel Rd SW19 ... 179 B4
Manse Rd N16 ... 73 D5
Mansergh Cl SE18 ... 144 A5
Mansfield Ave N15 ... 51 B5
East Barnet EN4 ... 15 A5
Ruislip HA4 ... 40 B1
Mansfield Cl N9 ... 18 A5
Mansfield Ct 27 E2 ... 95 D6
Mansfield Dr UB4 ... 83 C3
Mansfield Hill E4 ... 19 D3
Mansfield Ho SW15 ... 156 D5
Mansfield Hts N2 ... 48 D4
Mansfield Mews W1 ... 238 C3
Mansfield Pl 11 NW3 ... 70 A4
Mansfield Rd E17 ... 53 B5
NW3 ... 70 D4
Acton W3 ... 88 D3
Chessington KT9 ... 213 D3
Ilford IG1 ... 78 C6
South Croydon CR2 ... 221 B2
Wanstead E11 ... 55 B3
Mansfield St W1 ... 93 B2 238 C3
Mansford St E2 ... 96 A5
Manship Rd CR4 ... 181 A2
Mansion Cl SW9 ... 138 C4
Mansion Gdns NW3 ... 69 D5
Mansion House* EC4 ... 242 C1
Mansion House Pl EC3,
EC4 ... 242 C1
Mansion House St EC2 ... 242 C1
Mansion House Sta
EC4 ... 117 A6 252 B6
Mansions The NW6 ... 69 B3
Manson Mews
SW7 ... 114 B2 256 C3
Manson Pl SW7 ... 114 B2 256 C3
Manstead Gdns RM6 ... 58 C2
Manston NW1 ... 71 C1
Tottenham N17 ... 33 B1
Manston Ave UB2 ... 107 C2
Manston Cl SE20 ... 184 C2
Manstone Rd NW2 ... 69 A3
Manston Gr KT2 ... 175 D5
Manston Ho W14 ... 254 B5
Mantell Ho SW4 ... 159 C6
Manthorpe Rd SE18 ... 123 A1
Mantilla Rd SW17 ... 181 A6
Mantle Rd SE4 ... 141 A2
Mantlet Cl SW16 ... 181 C3
Mantle Way E15 ... 76 C1
Manton Ave W7 ... 109 A4
Manton Cl UB3 ... 105 C6
Manton Ho N16 ... 73 B5
Manton Rd SE2 ... 124 A2
Holdbrook EN3 ... 7 C5
Mantua St 23 SW11 ... 136 B2
Mantus Cl E1 ... 96 C3
Mantus Rd E1 ... 96 C3
Manus Way N20 ... 14 A3
Manville Gdns SW17 ... 159 B1
Manville Rd SW17 ... 159 B1
Manwood Rd SE4 ... 163 B5
Manwood St E16 ... 122 B5
Manygate La TW17 ... 193 A3
Many Gates SW12 ... 159 B2
Mapesbury Ct NW2 ... 69 A3
Mapesbury Rd NW2 ... 69 A2
Mapeshill Pl NW2 ... 68 C2
Mapes Ho 5 NW6 ... 69 A1
Mape St E2 ... 96 B3
Maple Ave E4 ... 35 B4
W3 ... 111 C5
Harrow HA2 ... 63 D6
Yiewsley UB7 ... 104 B6
Maple Cl BR5 ... 211 B4
N16 ... 52 A3
N3 ... 29 C4
SW4 ... 159 D5
Buckhurst Hill IG9 ... 21 D1
Hampton TW12 ... 173 B4
Hayes UB4 ... 84 D4
Mitcham CR4 ... 181 B2
Ruislip HA4 ... 40 B3
Maple Cres DA15 ... 168 A5
Maplecroft Cl E6 ... 100 A1
Maple Ct E6 ... 100 C2
NW2 ... 68 D4
Catford SE6 ... 163 D3
2 Croydon CR0 ... 221 A4
7 Dagenham RM8 ... 58 D2
Kingston KT3 ... 199 B6
4 Pinner HA5 ... 22 C1
Sidcup DA14 ... 190 B5
11 West Norwood SW16 ... 182 C5
Mapledale Ave CR0 ... 222 A5
Mapledene BR7 ... 189 A5
Mapledene Est E8 ... 74 A1
Mapledene Rd E8 ... 74 A1
Mapledown Sch NW2 ... 46 C2
Maple Gdns HA8 ... 27 C3
Stanwell TW19 ... 148 A2
Maple Gr NW9 ... 45 A2
W5 ... 109 D3
Brentford TW8 ... 131 B5
Southall UB1 ... 85 B2
Maple Gr Bsns Ctr TW4 ... 128 D1
Maple Ho 13 E17 ... 53 D6
11 NW3 ... 70 D2
5 SE8 ... 141 B5
2 Kingston KT6 ... 198 A4
Maplehurst 2 BR2 ... 186 C1
Maplehurst Cl KT1 ... 198 A5
Maple Ind Est TW13 ... 150 A1
Maple Inf Sch KT6 ... 197 D4
Maple Leaf Dr DA15 ... 167 D3
Mapleleafe Gdns IG6 ... 56 D6
Maple Leaf Sq 27 SE16 ... 118 D4
Maple Lo NW9 ... 67 B6
Putney SW15 ... 157 A5
Maple Mews NW6 ... 91 D5
Streatham SW16 ... 182 B5
Maple Pl W1 ... 239 B5
Tottenham N17 ... 34 A3
Yiewsley UB7 ... 104 B6
Maple Rd E11 ... 54 C3
Hayes UB4 ... 84 D4
Kingston KT6 ... 197 D4
Penge SE20 ... 184 C2
Maples Pl E1 ... 96 B2
Maple St W1 ... 93 C3 239 B5
Maplestead Rd
Dagenham RM9 ... 102 B6
Streatham SW2 ... 160 B4
Maples The KT8 ... 175 C3
Maplethorpe Rd CR7 ... 204 D5
Mapleton Cl BR2 ... 209 A3
Mapleton Cres Enfield EN3 ... 6 C5
Wandsworth SW18 ... 157 D5
Mapleton Rd Chingford E4 ... 20 A1
Enfield EN1 ... 6 B3
Wandsworth SW18 ... 157 D5
Maple Way TW13 ... 150 B1
Maple Wlk W10 ... 90 D3
Maplin Cl N21 ... 16 B5
Maplin Ho 9 SE2 ... 124 D4
Maplin Rd E16 ... 99 B1
Maplin St E3 ... 97 B4
Mapperley Cl 3 E11 ... 55 A3
Mapperley Dr IG8 ... 36 C3
Marada Ho NW6 ... 69 A1
Marais W4 ... 133 A5
Maran Way DA18 ... 124 D3
Marathon Way SE28 ... 123 D4
Marban Rd W9 ... 91 B4
Marble Arch*
W1 ... 114 D6 247 D6
Marble Arch Sta
W1 ... 92 D1 237 D1
Marble Cl W3 ... 110 D5
Marble Dr NW2 ... 46 D2
Marbleford Ct 4 N6 ... 49 D2
Marble Hill* TW1 ... 153 C4
Marble Hill Cl TW1 ... 153 B4
Marble Hill Gdns TW1 ... 153 B4
Marble Ho SE18 ... 123 D1
W9 ... 91 B3
Marbrook Ct SE12 ... 165 C1
Marcella Rd SW9 ... 138 C3
Marcellina Way BR6 ... 227 D5
March 23 NW9 ... 27 D2
Marchant Ct SE1 ... 263 D2
Marchant Ho 13 SW2 ... 160 B6
Marchant Rd E11 ... 76 B6
Marchant St SE14 ... 141 A6
Marchbank Rd
W14 ... 135 B6 264 D6
March Ct SW15 ... 134 B1
Marchmont Ho 10
SW16 ... 181 C5
Marchmont Rd
Richmond TW10 ... 154 B6
Wallington SM6 ... 219 C1
Marchmont St
WC1 ... 94 A3 240 A6
March Rd 5 TW1 ... 153 A4
Marchside Cl TW5 ... 128 D4
Marchwood Cl 17 SE5 ... 139 C5
Marchwood Cres W5 ... 87 D1
Marcia Rd SE1 ... 117 C2 263 B3
Marcilly Rd SW18 ... 158 B6
Marcon Ct 29 E8 ... 74 B3
Marconi Pl N11 ... 31 B6
Marconi Rd E10 ... 53 C1
Marconi Way UB1 ... 85 D1
Marcon Pl E8 ... 74 B3
Marco Rd W6 ... 112 C3
Marcourt Lawns W5 ... 88 A3
Marcus Ct E15 ... 98 C6
Brentford TW8 ... 132 A5
Marcus Garvey Mews
SE22 ... 162 B6
Marcus Garvey Way 9
SE24 ... 138 C1
Marcus Ho 13 SE15 ... 139 D4
Marcus St E15 ... 98 D6
Wandsworth SW18 ... 157 D5
Marcus Terr SW18 ... 157 D5
Mardale Ct NW7 ... 28 A3
Mardale Dr NW9 ... 45 B4
Mardell Rd CR0 ... 206 D4
Marden Ave BR2 ... 209 A3
Marden Cres CR0 ... 204 B3
Marden Ho 6 E8 ... 74 B3
Marden Rd
Thornton Heath CR0 ... 204 B3
Tottenham N17 ... 33 C1
Marden Sq SE16 ... 118 B3
Marder Rd W13 ... 109 A4
Mardyke Ho SE17 ... 262 D4
Marechal Niel Ave
DA15 ... 167 B1
Marechal Niel Par DA15 ... 167 B1
Maresby Ho E4 ... 19 D2
Maresfield CR0 ... 221 C5
Maresfield Gdns NW3 ... 70 A2
Mare St E8 ... 74 B2
E8,E2 ... 96 B6
Marfleet Cl SM5 ... 218 C6
Margaret Ave E4 ... 19 D5
Margaret Bondfield Ave
IG11 ... 80 A1
Margaret Bondfield Ho
4 E3 ... 97 A5
22 N7 ... 71 D3
Margaret Ct W1 ... 239 A2
Barnet EN4 ... 2 B1
Margaret Gardner Dr
SE9 ... 166 B2
Margaret Herbison Ho
SW6 ... 264 D5
Margaret Hill Ho N8 ... 50 A4
Margaret Ho 16 W6 ... 112 C1
Margaret Ingram Cl
SW6 ... 264 C5
Margaret Lockwood Cl
KT5 ... 198 B5
Margaret Mcmillan Ho 10
N19 ... 49 D2
Margaret Rd DA5 ... 168 D5
N16 ... 51 D1
Barnet EN4 ... 2 B1
Margaret's Ct E11 ... 54 B2
SE1 ... 252 C3
Margarets Ct HA8 ... 26 D5
Margaret St W1 ... 93 C1 239 A2
Margaretta Terr
SW3 ... 136 C6 267 B6
Margaretting Rd E12 ... 55 C1
Margaret Way IG4 ... 56 A3
Margaret White Ho
NW1 ... 232 C2
Margate Rd SW2 ... 160 A6
Margery Fry Ct N7 ... 72 A5
Margery Park Rd E7 ... 77 A2
Margery Rd RM8 ... 80 D5
Margery St WC1 ... 94 C4 234 A1
Margetson Ho N16 ... 51 D3
Margin Dr SW19 ... 178 D6
Margravine Gdns W14 ... 254 A2
W6 ... 112 D1
Margravine Rd
W6 ... 112 D1 264 A6
Marham Gdns
Morden SM4 ... 202 A3
Wandsworth SW17,SW18 ... 158 C3
Mar Ho 4 SE7 ... 143 C6
Maria Cl 10 SE1 ... 118 A2
Maria Fidelis RC Convent Sch
NW1 ... 93 D4 232 C2
Maria Ho 13 SW9 ... 138 C4
Marian Cl UB4 ... 84 D3
Marian Ct E9 ... 74 C3
Sutton SM1 ... 217 D3
Marian Lo 5 SW20 ... 178 D3
Marian Pl E2 ... 96 B5
Marian Rd SW16 ... 181 C2
Marian Sq E2 ... 96 B5
Marian St 2 E2 ... 96 B5
Marian Vian Prim Sch
BR3 ... 207 A4
Marian Way NW10 ... 67 D1
Maria Terr E1 ... 96 D3
Maria Theresa Cl KT3 ... 199 B4
Maribor 13 SE10 ... 142 A5
Maricas Ave HA3 ... 24 B2
Marie Curie SE5 ... 139 C4
Marie Lloyd Ct 13 SW9 ... 138 B1
Marie Lloyd Gdns 1 N19 ... 50 A2
Marie Lloyd Ho N1 ... 235 C3
Marien Ct E4 ... 36 B5
Marigold Cl UB1 ... 107 A6
Marigold Rd N17 ... 34 C3
Marigold St SE16 ... 118 B4
Marigold Way CR0 ... 206 D1
Marilea Ct W5 ... 109 D4
Marina App UB4 ... 85 A2
Marina Ave KT3 ... 200 B4
Marina Cl 1 BR2 ... 209 A6
Marina Ct 11 E3 ... 97 C4
Marina Dr DA16 ... 145 C3
Marina Gdns RM7 ... 59 D4
Marina Way TW11 ... 175 D3
Marine Dr 5 SE18 ... 122 B2
Barking IG11 ... 102 B4
Marinefield Rd SW6 ... 135 D3
Marinel Ho 25 SE5 ... 139 A5
Mariner Gdns TW10 ... 153 C1
Mariner Rd E12 ... 78 C4
Mariners Mews E14 ... 120 B2
Marine St SE16 ... 118 A3
Marine Twr 23 SE8 ... 141 B6
Marion Ave TW17 ... 192 D4
Marion Ct 4 SW17 ... 180 C5
Marion Gr IG8 ... 36 C6
Marion Rd NW7 ... 28 A5
Thornton Heath CR0 ... 205 B4
Marion Richardson Prim Sch
E1 ... 96 D1
Marischal Rd SE13 ... 142 B2
Maritime Ho 5 SW4 ... 137 C2
Maritime Ind Est SE7 ... 121 B2
Maritime Quay 6 E14 ... 119 C1
Maritime St E3 ... 97 B3
Marius Mans 3 SW17 ... 159 A2
Marius Rd SW17 ... 159 A2
Marjorie Gr SW11 ... 136 D1
Marjorie McClure Sch
BR7 ... 189 A2
Marjory Kinnon Sch
TW14 ... 149 C6
Markab Rd HA6 ... 22 A5
Mark Ave E4 ... 19 D5
Mark Cl BR2 ... 226 A4
DA7 ... 147 A4
Southall UB1 ... 107 D5
Markeston Gn WD19 ... 22 D6
Market Ct W1 ... 239 A2
Market Ctr The UB2 ... 106 B2
Market La HA8 ... 27 A2
Market Mews
W1 ... 115 B5 248 C3
Market Par E10 ... 53 D3
E17 ... 53 B6
Croydon SE25 ... 206 A5
1 Edmonton N9 ... 18 A2
Feltham TW13 ... 151 A2
Market Pl 2 DA7 ... 147 C1
N2 ... 48 C6
1 SE16 ... 118 B2
W1 ... 239 A2
3 W3 ... 111 A5
Brentford TW8 ... 131 C5
Enfield EN2 ... 5 B2
Kingston KT1 ... 175 D1
Market Pl The NW11 ... 47 D5
Market Rd N7 ... 72 A2
Richmond TW9 ... 132 C2
Market Sq BR1 ... 187 A1
E14 ... 97 D1
Market Sq The N9 ... 18 B2
Market St SE18 ... 122 C2
Wallend E6 ... 100 C5
Market The SM1,SM5 ... 202 A1
Market Way E14 ... 97 D1
1 Wembley HA0 ... 66 A3
Market Yd Mews SE1 ... 263 A6
Markfield Gdns E4 ... 19 D4
Markfield Ho N15 ... 52 A5
Markfield Rd N15 ... 52 A4
Markham Ct NW4 ... 46 C6
Markham Ho
1 Dagenham RM10 ... 81 C5
9 Dulwich SE21 ... 183 C6
Markham Pl SW3 ... 257 C2
Markham Sq
SW3 ... 114 D1 257 C2
Markham St
SW3 ... 114 C1 257 B2
Mark Ho 3 E2 ... 96 D5
Markhole Cl TW12 ... 173 B3
Markhouse Ave E17 ... 53 A3
Markhouse Pas E17 ... 53 B3
Markhouse Rd E17 ... 53 B3
Mark La EC3 ... 117 C6 253 B6
Markland Ho W10 ... 112 D6
Mark Lo 9 EN4 ... 2 C1
Markmanor Ave E17 ... 53 B2
Mark Mans W12 ... 112 A4
Mark Rd N22 ... 32 D1
Marksbury Ave TW9 ... 132 C2
Marks Gate Inf Sch RM6 ... 59 A6
Marks Gate Jun Sch
RM6 ... 59 A6
Mark Sq EC2 ... 243 A6
Mark St E15 ... 76 C1
EC2 ... 243 A6
Markstone Ho SE1 ... 251 C1
Mark Wade Cl E12 ... 55 D1
Markway The TW16 ... 172 C1
Markwell Cl SE26 ... 184 B6
Markyate Ho W10 ... 90 C3
Markyate Rd RM8 ... 80 B3
Marland Ho SW1 ... 257 D6
Marlands Rd IG5 ... 56 B6
Marlang Ct BR3 ... 186 B2
Marlborough W9 ... 229 A2
11 Putney SW19 ... 156 D3
Marlborough Ave 3 E8 ... 96 A6
N14 ... 15 C1
Edgware HA8 ... 10 D1
Ruislip HA4 ... 39 B3
Marlborough Cl BR6 ... 211 D3
N20 ... 14 D1
SE17 ... 261 D3
Mitcham SW19 ... 180 C4
Marlborough Cres W4 ... 111 C3
Harlington UB3 ... 127 B5

Marlborough Ct W8 .... 255 A4
7 Buckhurst Hill IG9 .... 21 C2
Harrow HA1 .... 42 B5
Wallington SM6 .... 219 C1
Marlborough Day Hospl NW8 .... 92 A5 229 A4
Marlborough Dr IG5 .... 56 A6
Marlborough Flats SW3 .... 257 B4
Marlborough Fst & Mid Sch HA1 .... 42 C5
Marlborough Gdns N20 .... 14 D1
Surbiton KT6 .... 197 D2
Marlborough Gr SE1 .... 118 A1
Marlborough Hill NW8 .... 92 A6 229 B5
Harrow HA1 .... 42 C5
Marlborough Ho N4 .... 51 A1
NW8 .... 229 A3
Richmond TW10 .... 154 C6
Wimbledon SW19 .... 156 D1
Marlborough House SW1 .... 249 B3
Marlborough La SE7 .... 143 C5
Marlborough Mans 5 NW6 .... 69 C3
Marlborough Mews SW2 .... 138 B1
Marlborough Par 1 UB10 .... 82 D3
Marlborough Park Ave DA15 .... 168 A3
Marlborough Pl NW8 .... 92 A5 229 B4
Marlborough Prim Sch SW3 .... 114 C2 257 B3
Marlborough Rd DA16 .... 146 D2
E15 .... 76 C4
E7 .... 77 C1
N19 .... 72 A6
SE18 .... 123 A3
SW1 .... 115 C5 249 B3
W4 .... 111 A1
W5 .... 109 D4
Ashford TW15 .... 170 A5
Bowes Park N22 .... 32 B4
Brentford TW7 .... 131 B5
Bromley BR2 .... 209 C5
Chingford E4 .... 35 D4
Dagenham RM8 .... 80 C4
Edmonton N9 .... 18 A3
Feltham TW13 .... 150 D2
Hampton TW12 .... 173 C4
Hillingdon UB10 .... 82 D4
Mitcham SW19 .... 180 C4
Richmond TW10 .... 154 B5
Romford RM7 .... 59 D5
Southall UB2 .... 106 C3
South Croydon CR2 .... 221 A1
Sutton SM1 .... 217 C6
Wanstead E18 .... 55 A6
Marlborough Sch Isleworth TW7 .... 131 A4
Sidcup DA15 .... 168 A4
Marlborough St SW3 .... 114 C2 257 B3
Marlborough Trad Est TW9 .... 132 D4
Marlborough Yd N19 .... 71 D6
Marlbury NW8 .... 91 D6
Marler Rd SE23 .... 163 B3
Marlesford Ct SM6 .... 219 C4
Marley Ave DA7 .... 146 D6
Marley Cl N15 .... 50 D5
Southall UB6 .... 85 C4
Marley Ho 14 W11 .... 112 D6
Marley Wlk NW2 .... 68 C3
Marlfield Cl KT4 .... 200 A1
Marlfield Ct KT3 .... 199 D2
Marlin Cl TW16 .... 171 C4
Marling Ct TW12 .... 173 B4
Marlingdene Cl TW12 .... 173 C4
Marlings Cl BR7 .... 211 C5
Marlings Park Ave BR7 .... 211 C6
Marlin Ho SW15 .... 157 A6
Marlins Cl 3 SM1 .... 218 A3
Marloes Cl HA0 .... 65 D4
Marloes Rd W8 .... 113 D3 255 C5
Marlow Cl SE20 .... 206 B6
Marlow Cres TW1 .... 152 D5
Marlow Ct N14 .... 15 C4
NW6 .... 68 D1
NW9 .... 45 D6
1 Ealing W7 .... 108 C5
Marlow Dr SM3 .... 216 D5
Marlowe Bsns Ctr 2 SE14 .... 141 A5
Marlowe Cl BR7 .... 189 B4
Marlowe Ct SW3 .... 257 B3
Dulwich SE19 .... 183 D5
6 Kingston KT2 .... 175 D6
Marlowe Gdns SE9 .... 166 C5
Marlowe Ho 15 N16 .... 73 C4
SE8 .... 119 B1
Kingston KT1 .... 197 D5
Marlowe Lo CR0 .... 223 A6
Marlowe Rd E17 .... 54 A5
Marlowe Sq CR4 .... 203 C5
Marlowes The NW8 .... 92 B6 229 C6
Marlowe Way CR0 .... 220 A6
Marlow Gdns UB3 .... 105 B3
Marlow Ho 44 E2 .... 95 D4
SE1 .... 263 C6
14 W2 .... 91 D1
Teddington TW11 .... 175 A6
Marlow Rd E6 .... 100 B4
Penge SE20 .... 184 B1
Southall UB2 .... 107 B3
Marlow Studio Workshops 43 E2 .... 95 D4
Marlow Way SE16 .... 118 D4
Marl Rd SW18 .... 136 A1
Marlston NW1 .... 231 D1
Marlton St SE10 .... 120 D1
Marlwood Cl DA15 .... 167 C2
Marmadon Rd SE18,SE2 .... 123 D2
Marmion App E4 .... 35 C6
Marmion Ave E4 .... 35 B6
Marmion Cl E4 .... 35 B6
Marmion Ho 13 SW12 .... 159 B4
Marmion Mews 4 SW11 .... 137 A2
Marmion Rd SW11 .... 137 A1
Marmont Rd SE15 .... 140 A5
Marmora Ho E1 .... 97 A2
Marmora Rd SE22 .... 162 C5
Marmot Rd TW4 .... 128 D2
Marne Ave DA16 .... 146 A2
N11 .... 31 B6
Marnell Way TW4 .... 128 D2
Marner Prim Sch E3 .... 97 D3
Marne St W10 .... 91 A4
Marney Rd SW11 .... 137 A1
Marnfield Cres SW2 .... 160 B3
Marnham Ave NW2 .... 69 A4
Marnham Cres UB6 .... 85 D5
Marnham Ct HA0 .... 65 C3
Marnock Ho SE17 .... 262 C2
Marnock Rd SE4 .... 163 B6
Maroon St E14 .... 97 A2
Maroons Way SE6 .... 185 C5
Marqueen Twrs SW16 .... 182 B3
Marquess Rd N1 .... 73 B2
Marquess Rd N N1 .... 73 B2
Marquess Rd S 17 N1 .... 73 A2
Marquis Cl HA0 .... 66 B1
Marquis Ct N4 .... 50 B1
Barking IG11 .... 79 C3
1 Kingston KT1 .... 198 A5
Marquis Rd N4 .... 50 C1
NW1 .... 71 D2
Bowes Park N22 .... 32 B4
Marrabon Cl DA15 .... 168 A3
Marrayat Sq SW6 .... 264 A2
Marrick Cl SW15 .... 134 A1
Marrick Ho 17 NW6 .... 91 D6
Marrilyne Ave EN3 .... 7 B5
Marriner Ct UB3 .... 105 C6
Marriott Cl TW14 .... 149 B5
Marriott Ho 8 SE6 .... 186 A6
Marriott Rd E15 .... 98 C6
N10 .... 30 D2
N4 .... 50 B1
Marriotts Cl NW9 .... 45 D3
Marryat Ct 12 W6 .... 112 B2
Marryat Ho SW1 .... 259 A1
Marryat Pl SW19 .... 179 A6
Marryat Rd SW19 .... 179 A6
Marryatt Ct W5 .... 88 B1
Marsala Rd SE13 .... 141 D1
Marsalis Ho 2 E3 .... 97 C4
Marsden Rd SE15 .... 139 D2
Edmonton N9 .... 18 B2
Marsden St NW5 .... 71 A2
Marsden Way 2 BR6 .... 227 D4
Marshall Cl N11 .... 15 B1
SW18 .... 158 A5
Harrow HA1 .... 42 B2
Hounslow TW4 .... 151 B6
Marshall Ct SW4 .... 270 B1
Marshall Dr UB4 .... 83 D2
Marshall Ho N1 .... 235 D4
NW6 .... 91 B5
SE17 .... 262 C2
4 New Malden KT3 .... 199 C5
Marshall Path 10 SE28 .... 124 B6
Marshall Rd Leyton E10 .... 75 D4
Tottenham N17 .... 33 B2
Marshalls Gr SE18 .... 122 A2
Marshall's Pl SE16 .... 263 D5
Marshall's Rd SM1 .... 217 D4
Marshall St W1 .... 93 C1 239 B1
Marshalsea Rd SE1 .... 117 A4 252 B2
Marsham Cl BR7 .... 188 D5
Marsham Ct SW1 .... 259 D4
19 Putney SW19 .... 156 D3
Marsham St SW1 .... 115 D2 259 D4
Marsh Ave CR4 .... 181 A1
Marshbrook Cl SE3 .... 143 D2
Marsh Cl NW7 .... 11 D1
Marsh Ct E8 .... 74 A2
3 Merton SW19 .... 180 A2
Marsh Dr NW9 .... 45 D3
Marsh Farm Rd TW2 .... 152 D3
Marshfield St E14 .... 120 A3
Marshgate Bsns Ctr E15 .... 98 A5
Marshgate Ctr The E15 .... 97 D6
Marshgate La E15 .... 75 D1
Marsh Green Prim Sch RM10 .... 103 C5
Marsh Green Rd RM10 .... 103 C6
Marsh Hall HA9 .... 66 B5
Marsh Hill E9 .... 75 A3
Marsh Ho SW1 .... 259 D1
SW8 .... 269 B2
Marsh La E10 .... 75 C6
NW7 .... 11 C1
Stanmore HA7 .... 25 C4
Tottenham N17 .... 34 B2
Marsh Rd Pinner HA5 .... 41 A5
Wembley HA0 .... 87 D5
Marshside Cl N9 .... 18 C3
Marsh St E14 .... 119 D2
Marsh Wall E14 .... 119 D4
Marshwood Ho 10 NW6 .... 91 C6
Marsland Cl SE17 .... 261 D1
Marsom Ho N1 .... 235 C3
Marston SE17 .... 262 B4
Marston Ave Chessington KT9 .... 214 A2
Dagenham RM10 .... 81 C5
Marston Cl NW6 .... 70 A1
Dagenham RM10 .... 81 C5
Marston Ct DA14 .... 189 D6
Walton-on-T KT12 .... 194 C1
Marston Ho SW9 .... 138 C3
Marston Rd TW11 .... 175 B5
Marston Way SE19 .... 183 A3
Marsworth Ave HA5 .... 22 D2
Marsworth Cl UB4 .... 85 A2
Marsworth Ho 8 E2 .... 96 A6
Martaban Rd N16 .... 73 D6
Martello St E8 .... 74 B1
Martello Terr E8 .... 74 B1
Martell Rd SE21 .... 161 B1
Martel Pl E8 .... 73 D2
Marten Rd E17 .... 35 C1
Martens Ave DA7 .... 147 D1
Martham Cl SE28 .... 124 D6
Martha Rd E15 .... 76 C2
Martha's Bldgs EC1 .... 242 C6
Martha St E1 .... 96 C1
Marthorne Cres HA3 .... 24 B1
Martin Bowes Rd SE9 .... 144 B2
Martinbridge Trad Est EN1 .... 18 B6
Martin Cl N9 .... 18 D3
Uxbridge UB10 .... 82 A5
Martin Cres CR0 .... 204 C1
Martin Ct 10 E14 .... 120 A4
Merton SW19 .... 179 C3
Southall UB2 .... 107 B4
Martindale SW14 .... 155 A6
Martindale Ave 2 E16 .... 121 A6
Martindale Ho 20 E14 .... 119 D6
Martindale Rd Balham SW12 .... 159 B4
Hounslow TW4 .... 129 A2
Martin Dene DA6 .... 169 B6
Martin Dr UB5 .... 63 B3
Martineau Cl KT10 .... 212 B4
Martineau Ho SW1 .... 259 A1
Martineau Mews N5 .... 72 D4
Martineau Rd N5 .... 72 D4
Martingale Cl TW16 .... 194 A5
Martingales Cl TW10 .... 153 D1
Martin Gdns RM8 .... 80 D4
Martin Gr SM4 .... 201 C6
Martin Ho SE1 .... 262 B5
SW8 .... 270 A4
6 New Malden KT3 .... 199 C5
Martini Dr EN3 .... 7 C6
Martin La EC4 .... 252 D6
Martin Prim Sch N2 .... 30 C1
Martin Rd RM8 .... 80 D4
Martin Rise DA6 .... 169 B6
Martins Cl BR4 .... 224 B6
Martins Mount EN5 .... 1 D1
Martin's Rd BR2 .... 186 D1
Martin St SE28 .... 123 C5
Martins The Penge SE26 .... 184 B5
Wembley HA9 .... 66 B5
Martins Wlk N10 .... 31 A2
Woolwich SE28 .... 123 C5
Martin Way SW19,SW20, SM4 .... 201 B6
Martlesham N17 .... 33 C1
Martlet Gr 5 UB5 .... 84 D4
Martlett Ct WC2 .... 240 B1
Martlett Lo NW3 .... 69 D4
Martley Dr IG2 .... 56 D4
Martley Ho SW8 .... 269 B2
Martock Cl HA3 .... 43 A5
Martock Ct 10 SE15 .... 140 B4
Martock Gdns N11 .... 31 A5
Marton Cl SE6 .... 163 C1
Marton Rd 2 N16 .... 73 C5
Martyn Ct HA8 .... 26 B6
Martyn Ho SE2 .... 146 D6
Martynside 22 NW9 .... 27 D2
Marvel Ho 5 SE5 .... 139 B5
Marvell Ave UB4 .... 84 A2
Marvels Cl SE12 .... 165 B2
Marvels La SE12 .... 165 C1
Marvels Lane Prim Sch SE12 .... 187 D6
Marville Ho SW18 .... 158 B5
Marville Rd SW6 .... 135 B5 264 C3
Marvin Ho 9 SE18 .... 144 D6
Marvin St 3 E8 .... 74 B2
Marwell Cl BR4 .... 224 D6
Marwick Rd UB7 .... 104 B4
Marwood Cl DA16 .... 146 B2
Mary Adelaide Cl Kingston SW15 .... 155 C1
Kingston SW15 .... 177 C6
Mary Adelaide Ho W2 .... 236 D4
Mary Ann Bldgs SE8 .... 141 C6
Maryatt Ave HA2 .... 63 D6
Marybank SE18 .... 122 B2
Mary Batchelor Sch (Girls) SE5 .... 139 B4
Mary Cl HA7 .... 44 B5
Mary Datchelor Cl SE5 .... 139 B4
Mary Dine Ct SW8 .... 270 D3
Mary Gn NW8 .... 91 D6
Marygold Ho TW3 .... 130 A4
Mary Ho 6 SW9 .... 138 B3
8 W6 .... 112 C1
Mary James Ho 29 E2 .... 96 A5
Mary Jones Ho 18 E14 .... 119 C6
Maryland Ct KT1 .... 176 D1
Maryland Pk E15 .... 76 C3
Maryland Point E15 .... 76 C2
Maryland Prim Sch E15 .... 76 C3
Maryland Rd E15 .... 76 B3
W9 .... 91 C3
Maryland Rd *continued* South Norwood CR7 .... 182 D2
Tottenham N22 .... 32 C4
Marylands Ind Est E15 .... 76 C3
Maryland Sq E15 .... 76 C3
Marylands Rd W9 .... 91 D3
Maryland St E15 .... 76 C3
Maryland Sta E15 .... 76 C2
Maryland Way TW16 .... 172 A1
Maryland Wlk N1 .... 235 A6
Mary Lawrenson Pl 1 SE3 .... 143 A5
Marylebone Flyover NW1 .... 92 C2 237 A3
Marylebone High St W1 .... 93 A2 238 B4
Marylebone La W1 .... 93 A1 238 B2
Marylebone Mews W1 .... 238 C3
Marylebone Pas W1 .... 239 B2
Marylebone Rd NW1 .... 92 D2 237 D4
Marylebone St W1 .... 93 A2 238 B3
Marylebone Sta NW1 .... 92 D3 237 C5
Marylee Way SE11 .... 116 B2 260 D3
Mary Macarthur Ho 15 E2 .... 96 D4
W14 .... 264 A6
8 Belvedere DA17 .... 125 C3
11 Dagenham RM10 .... 81 C5
Mary McArthur Ho 12 N19 .... 49 D2
Marymount International Sch KT2 .... 177 A3
Maryon Gr SE7 .... 122 A2
Maryon Mews NW3 .... 70 C4
Maryon Rd SE7 .... 122 A2
Mary Peters Dr UB6 .... 64 B3
Mary Pl W11 .... 113 A6 244 A5
Mary Rose Cl TW12 .... 173 C2
Mary Rose Mall E6 .... 100 B2
Maryrose Way N20 .... 14 B3
Mary's Ct NW8 .... 237 B6
Mary Secole Cl 21 E8 .... 95 D6
Mary St 5 E16 .... 98 D2
N1 .... 95 A6 235 B5
Mary's Terr TW1 .... 153 A4
Mary Terr NW1 .... 232 A5
Maryville DA16 .... 145 D3
Mary Wharrie Ho 4 NW3 .... 70 D1
Masbro' Rd W14 .... 112 D3
Mascalls Ct 13 SE7 .... 143 C6
Mascalls Rd SE7 .... 143 C6
Mascotte Rd 2 SW15 .... 134 D1
Mascotts Cl NW2 .... 68 B5
Masefield Ave Borehamwood WD6 .... 10 D6
Southall UB1 .... 107 C6
Stanmore HA7 .... 24 D5
Masefield Cres N14 .... 15 C5
Masefield Ct N5 .... 73 B3
New Barnet EN5 .... 2 A1
19 Surbiton KT6 .... 197 D2
Masefield Gdns E6 .... 100 C3
Masefield Ho 1 NW6 .... 91 C4
Masefield La UB4 .... 84 C3
Masefield Rd TW13 .... 173 B6
Masefield View BR6 .... 227 A5
Masefield Way TW19 .... 148 B3
Masham Ho 6 DA18 .... 124 D4
Mashie Rd W3 .... 89 C1
Maskall Cl SW2 .... 160 C3
Maskani Wlk SW16 .... 181 C3
Maskell Rd SW17 .... 158 A1
Maskelyne Cl SW11 .... 136 C4 267 B2
Mason Cl DA7 .... 147 D2
E16 .... 121 A6
SE16 .... 118 A1
Hampton TW12 .... 173 B2
Wimbledon SW20 .... 178 D2
Mason Ct 4 Penge SE19 .... 183 D3
Wembley HA9 .... 66 C6
Mason Ho 18 E9 .... 74 C1
8 N11 .... 31 C5
13 SE1 .... 118 A2
Mason Rd Sutton SM1 .... 217 D3
Woodford IG8 .... 36 C6
Mason's Arms Mews W1 .... 248 D6
Mason's Ave EC2 .... 242 C2
Masons Ave HA3 .... 42 D5
Mason's Ave CR0 .... 221 A5
Masons Hill BR2 .... 209 B5
SE18 .... 122 D2
Mason's Pl EC1 .... 235 A2
Mitcham CR4 .... 180 D2
Mason St SE17 .... 117 B2 262 D4
Mason's Yd SW1 .... 249 B4
Wimbledon SW19 .... 178 D5
Massey Cl N11 .... 31 B5
Massey Ct 7 E6 .... 99 C6
Massie Rd E8 .... 74 A2
Massingberd Way SW17 .... 181 B6
Massinger St SE1,SE17 .... 263 A3
Massingham St E1 .... 96 D3
Masson Ave HA4 .... 62 C2
Mast Ct 17 SE16 .... 119 A2
Master Gunner's Pl 1 SE18 .... 144 A4
Masterman Ho 1 SE5 .... 139 B5
Masterman Rd E6 .... 100 A4
Masters Cl SW16 .... 181 C4
Masters Ct HA4 .... 61 C6
Masters Dr SE16 .... 118 B1
Masters Lo 22 E1 .... 96 C1
Master's St 13 E1 .... 96 D2
Mast House Terr E14 .... 119 C2
Mastin Ho SW18 .... 157 C3
Mastmaker Rd E14 .... 119 C4
Maswell Park Cres TW3 .... 152 A6
Maswell Park Rd TW3 .... 130 A1
Matcham Rd E11 .... 76 D5
Matching Ct 18 E3 .... 97 C4
Matchless Dr SE18 .... 144 C5
Matfield Cl BR2 .... 209 A4
Matfield Rd DA17 .... 147 C6
Matham Gr SE22 .... 139 D1
Matham Rd KT8 .... 196 B4
Mathart Ct E4 .... 36 B4
Matheson Lang Ho SE1 .... 251 A1
Matheson Rd W14 .... 113 B2 254 C3
Mathews Ave E6 .... 100 C5
Mathews Park Ave E15 .... 76 D2
Mathieson Ct SE1 .... 251 D1
Mathieson Ho 10 E4 .... 20 C4
Matilda Cl SE19 .... 183 B3
Matilda Ho E1 .... 118 A5
Matilda Marks-Kennedy Jewish Prim Sch NW7 .... 27 B5
Matilda St N1 .... 94 B6 233 D6
Matlock Cl SE24 .... 139 A1
Barnet EN5 .... 12 D6
Matlock Cres SM3 .... 217 A4
Matlock Ct NW8 .... 229 A4
7 SE5 .... 139 B1
Matlock Gdns SM1,SM3 .... 217 A4
Matlock Pl SM1,SM3 .... 217 A4
Matlock Rd E10 .... 54 A3
Matlock St E14 .... 97 A1
Matlock Way KT3 .... 177 B2
Maton Ho SW6 .... 264 C4
Matson Ct IG8 .... 36 C3
Matson Ho 16 E9 .... 74 D2
9 SE16 .... 118 B3
Matthew Cl W10 .... 90 D3
Matthew Ct 4 E17 .... 54 A6
Mitcham CR4 .... 203 D4
Matthew Parker St SW1 .... 249 D1
Matthews Ct N5 .... 73 A4
Matthews Ho 3 E14 .... 97 C2
Matthews Rd UB6 .... 64 B3
Matthews St SW11 .... 136 D3
Matthias Ct 12 TW10 .... 154 A5
Matthias Ho 2 N16 .... 73 C3
Matthias Rd N16 .... 73 C3
Mattingly Way 4 SE15 .... 139 D5
Mattison Rd N4 .... 50 D3
Mattock La W5,W13 .... 109 C5
Maud Cashmore Way SE18 .... 122 B3
Maude Ho 3 E2 .... 96 A5
Maude Rd E17 .... 53 A4
SE5 .... 139 C4
Maudesville Cotts W7 .... 108 C5
Maude Terr E17 .... 53 A5
Maud Gdns E13 .... 98 D5
Barking IG11 .... 101 D5
Maudlins Gn E1 .... 118 A5
Maud Rd E10 .... 76 A5
E13 .... 98 D5
Maudsley Rd SE9 .... 144 B2
Maudsley Ho TW8 .... 110 A1
Maudsley Hospl The SE5 .... 139 B3
Maud St E16 .... 98 D2
Maugham Ct 5 W3 .... 111 A3
Mauleverer Rd SW2 .... 160 A6
Maundeby Wlk NW10 .... 67 C2
Maunder Rd 4 W7 .... 108 D5
Maunsel St SW1 .... 115 D2 259 C4
Mauretania Bldg 11 E1 .... 118 D6
Maurice Ave N22 .... 32 D1
Maurice Browne Cl NW7 .... 28 D4
Maurice Ct 3 TW8 .... 131 D5
Maurice Ho 1 SW9 .... 138 B3
Maurice St W12 .... 90 B1
Maurice Wlk NW11 .... 48 A5
Maurier Cl UB5 .... 84 C6
Mauritius Rd SE10 .... 120 C2
Maury Rd N16 .... 74 A5
Mauveine Gdns TW3 .... 129 C1
Mavelstone Cl BR1 .... 188 A2
Mavelstone Rd BR1 .... 188 A2
Maverton Rd E3 .... 97 C6
Mavery Ct 4 BR1 .... 186 D3
Mavis Ave KT19 .... 215 C3
Mavis Cl KT19 .... 215 C3
Mavis Ct 33 NW9 .... 27 D1
Mavis Wlk 9 E6 .... 100 A2
Mavor Ho N1 .... 233 D5
Mawbey Ho SE1 .... 263 D1
Mawbey Pl SE1 .... 117 D1 263 D1
Mawbey Rd SE1 .... 263 D1
Mawbey St SW8 .... 270 A3
Mawdley Ho SE1 .... 251 B1
Mawney Cl RM7 .... 59 D6
Mawney Rd RM7 .... 59 D6
Mawson Cl SW20 .... 179 A1
Mawson Ho EC1 .... 241 A4
Mawson La W4 .... 133 D6
Maxden Ct SE15 .... 140 A2
Maxey Gdns RM9 .... 81 A4
Maxey Rd SE18 .... 123 A2
Dagenham RM9 .... 81 A4
Maxfield Cl N20 .... 14 A4
Maxim Rd N21 .... 16 C5
Maxted Pk HA1 .... 42 C2
Maxted Rd SE15 .... 139 D2
Maxwell Cl Croydon CR0 .... 204 A1
Hayes UB3 .... 106 A6
Maxwell Ct SE21 .... 162 A3
Maxwell Gdns BR6 .... 227 D5
Maxwell Ho 12 SE18 .... 144 D6
Bowes Park N22 .... 32 B4
Chislehurst BR7 .... 188 D3
Maxwell Rd DA16 .... 146 A2
SW6 .... 135 D5 265 D3
Ashford TW15 .... 171 A4
West Drayton UB7 .... 104 B2
Maxwelton Ave NW7 .... 27 B5
Maxwelton Cl NW7 .... 27 B5
Maya Cl SE15 .... 140 B3
Mayall Cl EN3 .... 7 C5
Mayall Rd SE24 .... 160 D6
Maya Pl N11 .... 31 D3
Maya Rd N2 .... 48 A5
Maybank Ave Wembley HA0 .... 65 A3
Woodford E18 .... 37 B1
Maybank Gdns HA5 .... 40 A4
Maybank Rd E18 .... 37 C2
May Bate Ave KT2 .... 175 D2
Maybells Commercial Est IG11 .... 102 D5
Mayberry Pl KT5 .... 198 B2
Maybourne Cl SE26 .... 184 B5
Maybourne Grange CR0 .... 221 C6
Maybury Cl BR5 .... 210 D4
Enfield EN1 .... 6 B5
Maybury Ct W1 .... 238 B3
Beckenham BR3 .... 185 B3
Harrow HA1 .... 42 B3
Maybury Gdns NW10 .... 68 B2
Maybury Mews N6 .... 49 C2
Maybury Rd E13 .... 99 C3
Barking IG11 .... 102 A5
Maybury St SW17 .... 180 C5
Maychurch Cl HA7 .... 25 D3
May Cl KT9 .... 214 B2
Maycroft 2 Hayes BR2 .... 208 D1
Pinner HA5 .... 22 B1
Maycross Ave SM4 .... 201 C5
May Ct 2 SW19 .... 180 A2
Mayday Gdns SE3 .... 144 A3
Mayday Rd CR0,CR7 .... 204 D3
Mayday University Hospl CR7 .... 204 D3
Maydeb Ct RM6 .... 59 B3
Maydew Ho SE16 .... 118 C2
Maydwell Ho 6 E14 .... 97 C2
Maye Angelou Ct E4 .... 36 A6
Mayefield Rd CR7 .... 204 B4
Mayerne Rd SE9 .... 165 D6
Mayers Ct E8 .... 74 A4
Mayesbrook Rd Barking IG11 .... 101 D6
Dagenham RM8,IG3 .... 80 B5
Mayesford Rd RM6 .... 58 C2
Mayespark Prim Sch IG3 .... 80 A5
Mayeswood Rd SE12 .... 187 C6
Mayfair Ave DA16 .... 146 D4
Dagenham RM6 .... 58 D3
Ilford IG1 .... 56 C1
New Malden KT4 .... 200 A1
Twickenham TW2 .... 152 A4
Mayfair Cl Beckenham BR3 .... 185 D2
Surbiton KT6 .... 198 A1
Mayfair Ct 1 Beckenham BR3 .... 185 D2
7 Croydon CR0 .... 221 D6
1 Wimbledon SW19 .... 179 A3
Mayfair Gdns Tottenham N17 .... 33 B4
Woodford IG8 .... 37 A3
Mayfair Pl W1 .... 248 D4
Mayfair Terr N14 .... 15 D4
Mayfield DA7 .... 147 B2
Mayfield Ave BR6 .... 211 D2
N12 .... 30 B6
N14 .... 15 D2
W13 .... 109 B4
W4 .... 111 C2
Harrow HA3 .... 43 B4
Woodford IG8 .... 37 A4
Mayfield Cl E8 .... 73 D2
SW4 .... 159 D6
Ashford TW15 .... 170 D4
Hillingdon UB10 .... 82 D4
Long Ditton KT7 .... 197 B1
Penge SE20 .... 184 C2
Mayfield Cres Enfield N9 .... 18 B5
Thornton Heath CR7 .... 204 B4
Mayfield Ct SM2 .... 218 A1
Mayfield Dr HA5 .... 41 B5
Mayfield Gdns NW4 .... 46 D3
Ealing W7 .... 86 C2
Mayfield Ho 30 E2 .... 96 B5
N16 .... 51 C2
Mayfield Mans SW15 .... 157 B6
Mayfield Prim Sch W7 .... 86 B1
Mayfield Rd BR1 .... 210 A4
E13 .... 98 D3
E17 .... 35 A1
E8 .... 73 D1
N8 .... 50 B3
W12 .... 111 C4
Acton W3 .... 110 D6
Chingford E4 .... 20 B2
Dagenham RM8 .... 58 C1
Enfield EN3 .... 6 D3
Merton SW19 .... 179 B2
South Croydon CR2 .... 221 B1
Sutton SM2 .... 218 B2
Mayfields HA9 .... 66 C6
Mayfield Sch & Coll RM8 .... 58 C1

Mayfields Cl HA9 .66 C6
Mayfield Villas DA14 .190 C4
Mayflower Cl SE16 .118 D2
Ruislip HA4 .39 A3
Mayflower Ho 2 IG11 .101 B6
Mayflower Lo N10 .31 A2
N3 .47 B6
Mayflower Prim Sch E14 .97 D1
Mayflower Rd SW9 .138 A2
Mayflower St 1 SE16 .118 C4
Mayfly Cl HA5 .40 C2
Mayfly Gdns 12 UB5 .84 D4
Mayford NW1 .232 B4
Mayford Cl
Balham SW12 .158 D4
Penge BR3 .206 D6
Mayford Rd SW12 .159 A4
May Gdns Elstree WD6 .9 D5
Wembley HA0 .87 C4
Maygood Ho N1 .234 A4
Maygood St N1 .94 C5 234 A4
Maygrove Rd NW6 .69 B2
Mayhew Cl E4 .19 C1
Mayhew Ct 2 SE5 .139 B1
Mayhill Rd Barnet EN5 .13 A5
Greenwich SE7 .143 B6
Mayland Mans 4 IG11 .78 D1
Maylands Dr DA14 .168 D1
Maylands Ho SW3 .257 B3
Maylands Rd WD19 .22 C6
Maynard Cl N15 .51 C4
SW6 .135 D5 265 D3
Maynard Ct EN3 .7 C5
Maynard Ho E1 .97 A4
SE18 .123 A2
Maynard Rd E17 .54 A4
Maynards Quay E1 .118 C6
Maynooth Gdns CR4 .202 D2
Mayo Ct W13 .109 B3
Mayola Rd E5 .74 C4
Mayo Rd NW10 .67 C2
Thornton Heath CR0 .205 B4
Walton-on-T KT12 .194 A2
Mayow Rd SE23,SE26 .184 D6
Mayplace Cl DA7 .147 D2
Mayplace La SE18 .144 D6
Mayplace Rd W DA7 .147 C1
Maypole Ct UB2 .107 B4
May Rd E13 .99 A5
Chingford E4 .35 C4
Twickenham TW2 .152 C3
Mayroyd Ave KT6 .214 C6
May's Buildings Mews
SE10 .142 B5
Mays Ct WC2 .250 A5
May's Ct SE10 .142 B5
May's Hill Rd BR2 .208 C6
Mays La EN5 .12 C5
Maysoule Rd SW11 .136 B1
Mays Rd TW11,TW12 .174 B5
Mayston Mews 3 SE10 .121 A1
May Terr IG1 .78 D4
Maythorne Cotts SE13 .164 B5
Maytime Prep Sch IG1 .78 C5
Mayton St N7 .72 B5
Maytree Cl HA8 .11 A1
Maytree Ct Mitcham CR4 .203 A6
Northolt UB5 .85 A4
May Tree Ho SE4 .141 B2
Maytree La HA7 .24 D3
Maytree Wlk SW2 .160 C2
Mayville Prim Sch E11 .76 C6
Mayville Rd E11 .76 C6
Ilford IG1 .78 D3
Mayward Ho 7 SE5 .139 C4
May Wlk E13 .99 B5
Maywood Cl BR3 .185 D3
May Wynne Ho E16 .99 B1
Maze Hill SE10,SE3 .142 C6
Maze Hill Lo 8 SE10 .142 B6
Maze Hill Specl Sch
SE10 .142 A5
Maze Hill Sta SE10 .142 C6
Mazenod Ave NW6 .69 C1
Maze Rd TW9 .132 C5
Mead Cl 3 NW1 .71 A1
Harrow HA3 .24 B2
Mead Cres
Carshalton SM1 .218 C4
Chingford E4 .36 A6
Meadcroft Ho 4 KT3 .199 C2
Meadcroft Rd SE17 .138 D6
Mead Ct NW9 .45 B4
Meade Cl W4 .132 C6
Meader Ct SE14 .140 D5
Meadfield HA8 .10 D2
Mead Field HA2 .63 B5
Meadfield Gn HA8 .10 D2
Meadfoot Rd SW16 .181 C2
Mead Gr RM6 .58 D6
Mead Ho W11 .244 C4
Mead House La UB4 .83 B3
Meadhurst Pk TW16 .171 C4
Mead Inf Sch The KT19 .215 D4
Meadlands Dr TW10 .153 D2
Meadlands Prim Sch
TW10 .175 C6
Mead Lo W4 .111 B4
Meadow Ave CR0 .206 D3
Meadowbank NW3 .70 D1
SE3 .142 D2
Southgate N21 .16 B5
Surbiton KT5 .198 B3
Meadow Bank 7 SW15 .157 B6
Meadowbank Cl SW6 .134 C5
Meadowbank Gdns
TW5 .128 B4
Meadowbank Rd NW9 .45 B2
Meadowbanks EN5 .12 A6
Meadowbrook Ct TW7 .130 D2
Meadow Cl DA6 .169 B6
E9 .75 B3
Barnet EN5 .13 B5
Catford SE6 .185 C5
Chingford E4 .19 D3
Chislehurst BR7 .188 D5
Enfield EN3 .7 A5
Hinchley Wood KT10 .212 D5
Northolt UB5 .85 C5
Richmond TW10 .154 A3
Ruislip HA4 .39 D3
Sutton SM1 .218 A6
West Barnes SW20 .200 C5
Hounslow TW4 .151 C5
Meadowcourt Rd SE3 .142 D1
Meadowcroft 9 W4 .110 C1
Meadow Croft BR1 .210 B6
Meadowcroft Rd N13 .16 C2
Meadow Dr N10 .49 B6
NW4 .28 C1
Meadowford Cl SE28 .124 A6
Meadow Garth NW10 .67 B2
Meadowgate Sch SE4 .141 A2
Meadow Gdns HA8 .27 A4
Meadow High Sch UB8 .82 A2
Meadow Hill KT3 .199 C3
Meadow La SE12 .165 B1
Meadow Mews SW8 .270 C5
Meadow Pl SW8 .138 A5 270 B4
Chiswick W4 .133 C5
Meadow Rd
SW8 .138 B5 270 C4
Ashford TW15 .171 B5
Barking IG11 .80 A1
Beckenham BR2 .186 C1
Carshalton SM1 .218 C3
Claygate KT10 .212 C2
Dagenham RM9 .81 B2
Feltham TW13 .151 A2
Loughton IG10 .21 D6
Merton SW19 .180 A3
Pinner HA5 .41 A5
Southall UB1 .107 B6
Meadow Row SE1 .262 A5
Meadows Cl E10 .75 C6
Meadows Ct DA14 .190 B4
Meadows End TW16 .172 A2
Meadowside SE9 .143 C1
Twickenham TW1 .153 D4
Meadow Stile CR0 .221 A5
Meadowsweet Cl 3 E16 .99 D2
West Barnes KT3 .200 C5
Meadow The BR7 .189 A4
Meadow View DA15 .168 B4
Meadowview TW17 .193 A2
Meadow View HA1 .42 C1
Meadowview Rd
Catford SE6 .185 C5
Sidcup DA5 .169 B5
West Ewell KT19 .215 C1
Meadow View Rd
Hayes UB4 .83 B3
Thornton Heath CR7 .204 D4
Meadow Way BR6 .226 C5
NW9 .45 B4
Chessington KT9 .214 A3
Ruislip HA4 .40 B3
Wembley HA9 .65 D4
Meadow Waye TW5 .129 A5
Meadow Way The HA3 .24 C2
Meadow Wlk
Dagenham RM9 .81 B2
Ewell KT17 .215 D1
Hackbridge SM6 .219 B5
Wanstead E18 .55 A5
West Ewell KT17,KT19 .215 D1
Meadow Wood Sch WD23 .8 A6
Mead Pl E9 .74 C2
Croydon CR0 .205 A1
Mead Plat NW10 .67 A2
Mead Rd BR7 .189 A4
Edgware HA8 .26 C4
Richmond TW10 .153 C1
Mead Road Inf Sch BR7 .189 A4
Mead Row SE1 .116 C3 261 A6
Meads Ct E15 .76 D2
Meadside Cl BR3 .185 A2
Meads La IG3 .57 D2
Meads Rd Enfield EN3 .7 A4
Tottenham N22 .32 D1
Meads The HA8 .27 B4
Cheam SM3 .217 A5
Hillingdon UB8 .82 A3
Mead The N2 .30 A1
Beckenham BR3 .186 A2
Ealing W13 .87 B2
Ickenham UB10 .60 C6
Wallington SM6 .219 D2
West Wickham BR4 .208 B1
Meadvale Rd
Croydon CR0 .206 A3
Ealing W5 .87 C3
Meadway NW11 .47 D3
Ashford TW15 .170 C6
Barnet EN5 .1 C1
Beckenham BR3 .186 A2
Enfield EN3 .6 D6
Palmers Green N14 .16 A2
Tolworth KT5 .199 A1
Twickenham TW2 .152 B3
West Barnes SW20 .200 C5
Woodford IG8 .37 C5
Mead Way CR0 .223 A6
Meadway KT10 .212 A1
Mead Way Hayes BR2 .209 A3
Hayes BR2,BR4 .208 D3
Ilford IG3 .79 C4
Mead Way *continued*
Ruislip HA4 .39 B3
Meadway Cl NW11 .47 D3
Barnet EN5 .1 C1
Pinner HA5 .23 D4
Meadway Ct NW11 .47 D3
Dagenham RM8 .81 B6
Ealing W5 .88 B2
Meadway Gate NW11 .47 C3
Meadway Gdns HA4 .39 B3
Meadway The SE3 .142 B3
Buckhurst Hill IG9 .21 D3
Meaford Way SE20 .184 B3
Meakin Est SE1 .263 A6
Meakin Ho N7 .72 B3
Meanley Rd E12 .78 A3
Meard St W1 .239 C1
Meath Ho SE24 .160 D5
Meath Rd E15 .98 D5
Ilford IG1 .79 A5
Meath St SW11 .137 B4 268 C2
Mecklenburgh Pl WC1 .240 C6
Mecklenburgh Sq
WC1 .94 B3 240 C6
Medburn St NW1 .232 C4
Medcalf Rd EN3 .7 B6
Medcroft Gdns SW14 .133 A1
Medebourne Cl SE3 .143 A2
Mede Ho BR1 .187 B5
Medesenge Way N13 .32 D4
Medfield St SW15 .156 B4
Medhurst Cl 17 E3 .97 A5
Median Rd E5 .74 C3
Medical Coll of St
Bartholomew's Hospl The
EC1 .94 D3 241 D5
Medina Ave KT10 .212 C5
Medina Ct N7 .72 C5
Medina Gr N7 .72 C5
Medina Ho SE15 .140 C1
Medina Rd N7 .72 C5
Medland Cl CR4 .203 A1
Medlar Cl 1 UB5 .84 D5
Medlar Ho 3 DA15 .168 A1
Medlar St SE5 .139 A4
Medley Rd NW6 .69 C2
Medora Rd SW2 .160 B4
Medresco Ho NW3 .70 B3
Medusa Rd SE6,SE13 .163 D5
Medway Bldgs E3 .97 A5
Medway Cl Croydon CR0 .206 C3
Ilford IG1 .79 A3
Medway Ct WC1 .233 A1
South Norwood SE25 .205 C4
Medway Dr UB6 .86 D5
Medway Gdns HA0 .65 A4
Medway Ho N16 .73 B3
NW8 .237 A4
SE1 .252 D1
6 Kingston KT2 .175 D2
Medway Mews 33 E3 .97 A5
Medway Par 1 UB6 .86 D5
Medway Rd E3 .97 A5
Medway St SW1 .115 D3 259 D5
Medwin St SW4 .138 B1
Meecham Ct 1 SW11 .136 C3
Meerbrook Rd SE3,SE9 .143 C2
Meeson Rd E15 .76 D1
Meeson St E5 .75 A4
Meeting House Alley 7
E1 .118 B5
Meeting House La SE15 .140 B5
Mehetabel Rd E9 .74 C3
Meister Cl IG1 .57 B1
Melanda Cl BR7 .188 B5
Melanie Cl DA7 .147 A4
Melba Ct E8 .73 D1
Melbourne Ave
Bowes Park N13 .32 B4
Ealing W13 .109 A5
Pinner HA2,HA5 .41 D6
Melbourne Cl BR6 .211 C2
Ickenham UB10 .60 C4
Wallington SM6 .219 C3
Melbourne Ct E5 .75 A4
N10 .31 B3
W9 .236 B6
Penge SE20 .184 A3
Twickenham TW2 .152 B3
Melbourne Gdns RM6 .59 A4
Melbourne Gr SE22 .139 D1
Melbourne Ho W8 .245 A3
Hayes UB4 .84 C3
Melbourne Mews SW9 .138 C4
Catford SE6 .164 A4
Melbourne Pl WC2 .240 D1
Melbourne Rd E10 .53 D2
E17 .53 A5
E6 .100 B5
Ilford IG1 .56 D1
Merton SW19 .179 C2
Teddington TW11 .175 C4
Wallington SM6 .219 C3
Melbourne Sq 21 SW9 .138 C4
Melbourne Way EN1 .17 D5
Melbrook Ho 11 SE22 .139 C2
Melbury Ave UB2 .107 D3
Melbury Cl BR7 .188 B4
Claygate KT10 .213 B2
Melbury Ct W8 .113 B3 254 D6
Melbury Dr SE5 .139 C5
Melbury Gdns SW20 .178 B2
Melbury Ho SW8 .270 C4
Twickenham TW2 .152 B2
Melbury Rd
W14 .113 B3 254 D6
Harrow HA3 .44 B4
Melchester 3 W11 .91 B1
Melchester Ho 1 N19 .71 D5
Melcombe Ct NW1 .237 C4
Melcombe Gdns HA3 .44 B3
Melcombe Ho SW8 .270 C3
Melcombe Pl NW1 .237 C4
Melcombe Prim Sch
W6 .134 D6
Melcombe St
NW1 .92 D3 237 D5
Meldex Cl NW7 .28 C4
Meldon Cl SW6 .265 D2
Meldone KT3 .199 B1
Meldone Cl KT5 .198 D3
Meldrum Rd IG3 .80 A6
Melfield Gdns SE6 .186 A5
Melfont Ave CR7 .204 D6
Melford Ave IG11 .79 D2
Melford Cl KT9 .214 B3
Melford Ct E5 .74 B5
Dulwich SE22 .162 A4
2 Sutton SM2 .218 A1
Melford Rd E11 .76 C6
E17 .53 B5
E6 .100 B4
Dulwich SE21,SE22 .162 A3
Ilford IG1 .79 B6
Melfort Rd CR7 .204 D6
Melgund Rd N5 .72 C3
Melina Cl UB3 .83 B2
Melina Ct NW8 .229 C1
Putney SW15 .134 A2
Melina Pl NW8 .92 B4 229 C1
Melina Rd W12 .112 B4
Melior Ct N6 .49 C3
Melior Pl SE1 .253 A2
Melior St SE1 .117 C4 253 A2
Meliot Rd SE6 .164 B2
Melisa Ct N6 .49 D2
Meller Cl SM6 .220 A5
Melling Dr EN1 .6 A4
Melling St SE18 .145 C6
Mellington Ct 2 N16 .74 A5
Mellis Ave TW9 .132 D4
Mellish Cl IG11 .101 D6
Mellish Ct KT6 .198 A3
Mellish Flats E10 .53 C2
Mellish Gdns IG8 .37 A5
Mellish Ho 12 E1 .96 B1
Mellish Ind Est E16 .121 D3
Mellish St E14 .119 C3
Mellison Rd SW17 .180 C5
Mellitus St W12 .89 D1
Mellor Cl KT12 .195 B2
Mellor Ct 2 SW19 .180 A3
Mellor Ho 2 SE21 .183 C6
Mellow La E UB4 .83 A3
Mellow Lane Sch UB4 .83 A3
Mellow La W UB10 .83 A4
Mellows Rd Redbridge IG5 .56 B6
Wallington SM6 .219 D3
Mells Cres SE9 .188 B6
Mell St 6 SE10 .120 C1
Melody Rd SW18 .158 A6
Melon Pl W8 .245 B2
Melon Rd E11 .76 C5
SE15 .140 A4
Melrose Ave NW2 .68 C3
Borehamwood WD6 .10 D6
Greenford UB6 .85 D5
Mitcham CR4 .181 B3
Thornton Heath SW16 .204 C6
Tottenham N22 .32 D2
Twickenham TW2 .151 D4
Wimbledon SW19 .157 C1
Melrose Cl SE12 .165 B3
Greenford UB6 .85 D5
Hayes UB4 .84 A2
Melrose Cres BR6 .227 B3
Melrose Ct
5 Ealing W13 .109 A5
Wandsworth SW18 .157 B5
Melrose Dr UB1 .107 C5
Melrose Gdns W6 .112 C3
Edgware HA8 .26 D1
Kingston KT3 .199 B6
Melrose Ho NW6 .91 C4
SW1 .258 D2
Melrose Rd
1 Barnes SW13 .133 D3
Merton SW19 .179 C2
Pinner HA5 .41 B5
Wandsworth SW18 .157 B5
Melrose Sch CR4 .202 C6
Melrose Terr W6 .112 C3
Melrose Tudor SM6 .220 A3
Melsa Rd SM4 .202 A3
Melthorne Dr HA4 .62 C5
Melthorpe Gdns SE3 .144 A4
Melton Cl HA4 .40 C1
Melton Ct SW7 .256 D3
11 Croydon CR0 .221 D6
Sutton SM2 .218 A1
1 Twickenham TW1 .153 B4
Melton Ho E5 .74 A6
Melton St NW1 .93 D4 232 C1
Melville Ave
Greenford UB6 .64 D3
South Croydon CR2 .221 D3
Wimbledon SW20 .178 A3
Melville Cl UB10 .61 B5
Melville Court Flats
W12 .112 B4
Melville Ct SE8 .119 A2
4 W4 .110 C1
Melville Gdns N13 .32 D5
Melville Ho SE10 .142 A4
New Barnet EN5 .14 B5
Melville Pl 4 N1 .73 A1
Melville Rd E17 .53 B6
NW10 .67 B1
Barnes SW13 .134 A4
Sidcup DA14 .168 C2
Melville Villas Rd W3 .111 B5
Melvin Ct 11 TW9 .132 C4
Melvin Rd SE20 .184 C2
Melwood Ho 22 E1 .96 B1
Melyn Cl N7 .71 C4
Memel Ct EC1 .242 A5
Memel St EC1 .242 A5
Memess Path 4 SE18 .144 C6
Memorial Ave E15 .98 C4
Memorial Cl TW5 .129 B6
Memorial Hospl SE18 .144 C3
Mendham Ho SE1 .263 A6
Mendip Cl
Forest Hill SE26 .184 C6
Harlington UB3 .127 B5
North Cheam KT4 .216 C6
Mendip Ct SE14 .140 C6
12 SW11 .136 A2
Mendip Dr NW2,NW11 .69 A6
Mendip Ho 2 N4 .51 B2
Mendip Hos 12 E2 .96 C4
Mendip Rd SW11 .136 A2
Bushey WD23 .8 A5
Ilford IG2 .57 C4
Mendora Rd
SW6 .135 B5 264 C4
Menelik Rd NW2 .69 B4
Menlo Gdns SE19 .183 B3
Mennie Ho 5 SE18 .144 B4
Menon Dr N9 .18 B1
Menora Foundation Sch
HA8 .27 A3
Menorah Gram Sch
NW11 .47 A2
Menorah Prim Sch
NW11 .47 A2
Menotti St 6 E2 .96 A3
Menteath Ho 5 E14 .97 C1
Mentmore Cl HA3 .43 C3
Mentmore Terr E8 .74 B1
Mentone Ct SW8 .270 B2
Meon Ct TW7 .130 C3
Meon Rd W3 .111 A4
Meopham Rd CR4,SW16 .181 C2
Mepham Cres HA3 .24 A3
Mepham Gdns HA3 .24 A3
Mepham St SE1 .116 C5 251 A3
Mera Dr DA7 .147 D1
Merantun Way SW19 .180 A2
Merbury Cl SE13 .164 B6
Merbury Rd SE28 .123 C4
Merbury St SE18 .122 D3
Mercator Pl E14 .119 C1
Mercator Rd SE13 .142 B1
Mercer Cl KT7 .196 D2
Merceron Ho 3 E2 .96 C4
Merceron St E1 .96 B3
Mercer Pl HA5 .22 C1
Mercers Cl SE10 .120 D2
Mercer's Cotts 10 E3 .97 A1
Mercers Pl W6 .112 D2
Mercers Rd N19 .71 D5
Mercer St WC2 .94 A1 240 A1
Merchant Ct E1 .118 C5
Merchants Cl SE25 .206 A5
Merchants Lo 5 E17 .53 C5
Merchant St E3 .97 B4
Merchant Taylors'
Almshouses SE13 .142 C1
Merchant Taylors Hall★
EC3 .242 D1
Merchiston Rd SE6 .164 B2
Merchland Rd SE9 .167 A3
Merchon Ho N7 .71 C4
Mercia Gr SE13 .142 A1
Mercia Ho 9 SE5 .139 A3
Mercier Rd SW15 .157 A6
Mercury 25 NW9 .27 D2
Mercury Ct 3 E14 .119 C2
8 SW9 .138 C4
Mercury Ctr TW14 .150 B6
Mercury Ho TW8 .109 D1
Mercury Rd TW8 .109 C1
Mercury Way SE14 .140 D6
Mercy Terr SE13 .163 D6
Merebank La CR0,SM6 .220 B3
Mere Cl Orpington BR6 .226 D6
Putney SW15,SW19 .156 D4
Meredith Ave NW2 .68 C3
Meredith Cl HA5 .22 D3
Meredith Ho 17 N16 .73 C3
Meredith Mews SE4 .141 B1
Meredith St E13 .99 A4
EC1 .234 C1
Meredyth Rd SW13 .134 A3
Mere End CR0 .206 D2
Mere Rd TW17 .192 D3
Mereside BR6 .226 C6
Meretone Cl SE4 .141 A1
Meretune Ct SM4 .201 B6
Merevale Cres SM4 .202 A3
Mereway Industry TW2 .152 C3
Mereway Rd TW2 .152 C3
Merewood Cl 1 BR1 .188 C1
Mereworth Cl BR2 .208 D4
Mereworth Dr SE18 .145 A5
Mereworth Ho 3 SE15 .140 C6
Merganser Ct 17 SE8 .141 B6
Merganser Gdns SE28 .123 B3
Meridan Ct SE13 .142 B1
Meriden Cl BR1 .187 D3
Meriden Ct SW3 .257 A1
Meriden Ho 26 N1 .95 C6
3 Barnet EN5 .1 A1
Meridian Building SE10 .142 B5
Meridian Ct
4 Catford SE6 .164 D3
Croydon CR0 .220 C4
Meridian Ho SE10 .120 C2
Meridian Pl E14 .120 A4
Meridian Prim Sch
SE10 .142 B6
Meridian Rd SE7 .143 D5
Meridian Sq E15 .76 B1
Meridian Trad Est SE7 .121 B2
Meridian Way N9,N18 .18 D1
Enfield EN3 .19 A5
Meridian Wlk N17 .33 C4
Merifield Rd SE9 .143 C1
Merino Cl E11 .55 C5
Merino Pl DA15 .168 A6
Merioneth Ct 7 W7 .86 D2
Merivale Rd Harrow HA1 .42 A2
Putney SW15 .135 A1
Merlewood Dr BR7 .188 B2
Merley Ct NW9 .45 A1
Merlin 26 NW9 .27 D2
Merlin Cl Mitcham CR4 .202 C6
4 Northolt UB5 .84 C4
South Croydon CR0 .221 C4
Wallington SM6 .220 B2
Merlin Cres HA8 .26 B2
Merlin Ct
Beckenham BR2 .208 D5
6 Ealing W7 .86 D3
Ruislip HA4 .61 B6
Wood Green N22 .32 C2
Merling Cl KT9 .213 D3
Merlin Gdns BR1 .165 A1
Merlin Gr BR3 .207 C4
Merlin Ho NW3 .69 D4
7 W4 .111 B1
Enfield EN3 .18 D6
Merlin Prim Sch BR1 .165 A1
Merlin Rd Bexley DA16 .146 A1
Wanstead E12 .77 D6
Merlin Rd N DA16 .146 A1
Merlins Ave HA2 .63 B5
Merlins Ct WC1 .234 A1
Merlin St EC1 .94 C4 234 A1
Mermaid Ct N4 .50 C3
SE1 .117 B4 252 C2
SE16 .119 B5
Mermaid Ho 8 E14 .120 A6
Mermaid Twr 22 SE8 .141 B6
Meroe Ct N16 .73 C6
Merredene St SW2 .160 B5
Merriam Ave 3 E9 .75 B2
Merriam Cl E4 .36 A5
Merrick Rd UB2 .107 B3
Merricks Ct 5 SW14 .132 D1
Merrick Sq SE1 .117 B3 262 C6
Merridale SE12 .164 D6
Merridene N21 .16 D5
Merrielands Cres RM9 .103 B5
Merrielands Ret Pk
RM9 .103 B5
Merrilands Rd KT4 .200 C1
Merrilees Rd DA15 .167 C4
Merrilyn Cl KT10 .213 A2
Merriman Rd SE3 .143 C4
Merrington Rd SW6 .265 B6
Merrion Ave HA7 .25 D5
Merritt Gdns KT9 .213 C2
Merritt Rd SE4 .163 B6
Merrivale NW1 .232 B5
Southgate N14 .15 D6
Merrivale Ave IG4 .55 D5
Merrow Ct CR4 .180 B1
Merrow St SE17 .117 B1 262 C1
Merrow Way CR0 .224 A2
Merrow Wlk SE17 .262 D2
Merrydown Way BR7 .188 B2
Merry Fiddlers RM8 .81 B6
Merryfield SE3 .142 D3
Merryfield Gdns HA7 .25 C5
Merryfield Ho SE12 .165 C1
Merryhill Cl E4 .19 D4
Merry Hill Rd WD23 .8 A3
Merry Hill Sch WD23 .8 A4
Merryhills Ct N14 .15 C6
Merryhills Dr EN2 .4 A1
Merryhills Prim Sch EN2 .4 B1
Merryweather Ct 1
KT3 .199 C4
Mersea Ho IG11 .78 D2
Mersey Ct 10 KT2 .175 D2
Mersey Ho 10 N7 .72 C3
Mersey Rd E17 .53 B6
Mersey Wlk UB5 .85 C5
Mersham Dr NW9 .44 D4
Mersham Pl Penge SE20 .184 B2
South Norwood CR7 .183 B1
Mersham Rd CR7 .183 B1
Merstone Ho SW18 .157 D5
Merten Rd RM6 .59 A2
Merthyr Terr SW13 .134 B6
Merton Abbey Mills
Merton SW19 .180 A2
Wandsworth SW18 .157 D3
Merton Abbey Prim Sch
SW19 .179 D2
Merton Ave W4 .111 D2
Hillingdon UB10 .60 D1
Northolt UB5 .64 A3
Merton Coll SM4 .201 B4
Merton Court Sch DA14 .190 C6
Merton Ct DA16 .146 B3
Merton Gdns BR5 .210 D4
Merton Hall Gdns SW20 .179 A2
Merton Hall Rd SW19 .179 A2
Merton High St SW19 .180 A3
Merton Ho SW18 .157 C3
Merton Ind Pk SW19 .180 A2
Merton La N6 .70 D6
Merton Lo EN5 .14 A6
Merton Mans SW20 .178 D1
Merton Park Fst Sch
SW19 .179 C1
Merton Park Par SW19 .179 B2

Merton Park Sta SW19 ...179 C2
Merton Pl 9 SW19 ...180 A3
Merton Rd E17 ...54 A3
Barking IG11 ...79 D1
Croydon SE25 ...206 A4
Enfield EN2 ...5 B5
Harrow HA2 ...42 A1
Ilford IG3 ...57 D2
Merton SW19 ...179 D3
Wandsworth SW18 ...157 C4
Merton Rise NW3 ...70 C1
Merton Road Ind Est
SW18 ...157 C4
Merton Way
East Molesey KT8 ...196 A6
Hillingdon UB10 ...60 D1
Merttins Rd SE15 ...162 D6
Meru Cl NW5 ...71 A3
Mervan Rd SW2 ...138 C1
Mervyn Ave BR7,SE9 ...167 A2
Mervyn Rd W13 ...109 A3
Shepperton TW17 ...193 A2
Mervyn Stockwood Ho 1
SE9 ...167 A2
Messaline Ave W3 ...89 A1
Messent Rd SE9 ...165 D6
Messeter Pl SE9 ...166 C5
Messina Ave NW6 ...69 C1
Messiter Ho N1 ...233 D5
Metcalfe Ho 28 SW8 ...137 D3
Metcalfe Wlk 2 TW13 ...173 A6
Metcalf Rd TW15 ...170 D5
Meteor St SW11 ...137 A1
Meteor Way SM6 ...220 A1
Metford Cres EN3 ...7 C5
Metherell Ho N21 ...17 B5
Metheringham Way NW9 ...27 C2
Methley Ho 8 N7 ...72 B6
Methley St SE11 ...116 C1 261 B1
Methodist Central Hall*
SW1 ...115 D4 249 D1
Methuen Cl HA8 ...26 C3
Methuen Pk N10 ...49 B6
Methuen Rd DA6 ...147 B1
Belvedere DA17 ...125 D2
Edgware HA8 ...26 C3
Methwold Rd W10 ...90 D2
Metro Bsns Ctr The
SE26 ...185 B5
Metro Ctr Hayes UB4 ...106 C6
West Barnes SM4 ...200 D2
Metro Ind Ctr TW7 ...130 C3
Metropolitan Benefit
Societies Almshs 3 N1 ...73 C2
Metropolitan Cl 17 E14 ...97 C2
Metropoliton Police Cadet
Training Sch NW9 ...45 C6
Metro Trad Ctr HA9 ...66 D4
Meudon Ct KT6 ...197 D4
Mews Pl IG8 ...37 A6
Mews St E1 ...118 A5
Mews The N8 ...50 C5
Beckenham BR3 ...185 C2
Redbridge IG4 ...55 D4
Thornton Heath SW16 ...182 B2
Mexborough NW1 ...232 A5
Mexfield Rd SW15 ...157 B6
Meyer Gn EN1 ...6 A5
Meyer Ho 1 SW12 ...159 B4
Meymott St SE1 ...116 D5 251 C3
Meynell Cres E9 ...74 D1
Meynell Gdns E9 ...74 D1
Meynell Rd E9 ...74 D1
Meyrick Ho 8 E14 ...97 C2
Meyrick Rd NW10 ...68 A2
SW11 ...136 C2
Miah Terr 10 E1 ...118 A5
Miall Wlk SE26 ...185 A6
Micawber Ave UB8 ...82 C3
Micawber Ct N1 ...235 B2
Micawber Ho 24 SE16 ...118 A4
Micawber St N1 ...95 A4 235 B2
Michael Cliffe Ho EC1 ...234 B1
Michael Faraday Ho
SE17 ...262 D1
Michael Faraday Sch
SE17 ...117 B1 262 D1
Michael Gaynor Cl W7 ...108 D5
Michael Marshall Ho 2
SE9 ...167 A2
Michaelmas Cl SW20 ...200 C6
Michael Rd E11 ...54 D1
SW6 ...135 D4 265 D2
South Norwood SE25 ...205 C6
Michaels Cl SE13 ...142 C1
Michael Sobell Sinai Sch
HA3 ...44 C3
Michaelson Ho 4 SE21 ...183 C6
Michelangelo Ct 14
SE16 ...118 B1
Micheldever Rd SE12 ...164 D5
Michelham Gdns TW1 ...152 D1
Michelle Ct N12 ...30 A5
W3 ...111 B6
Michell Ho TW1 ...152 D3
Michels Almshouses 11
TW10 ...154 A6
Michelsdale Dr 3 TW9 ...132 A1
Michelson Ho SE11 ...260 D3
Michel's Row 2 TW9 ...132 A1
Michigan Ave E12 ...78 B4
Michigan Ho E14 ...119 C3
Michleham Down N12 ...29 B6
Mickledore NW1 ...232 B3
Mickleham Cl BR5 ...190 A1
Mickleham Gdns SM3 ...217 A2
Mickleham Rd BR5 ...190 A1
Mickleham Way CR0 ...224 B1
Micklethwaite Rd
SW6 ...135 C6 265 B5
Mickleton Ho 30 W2 ...91 C2
Midas Bsns Ctr RM10 ...81 D4
Midcroft HA4 ...39 C1
Middle Dene NW7 ...11 B1
Middlefield NW8 ...92 B6 229 C6
Middlefield W13 ...87 B2
Middlefield Gdns IG2 ...56 D3
Middle Green Cl 8 KT5 ...198 B3
Middleham Gdns N18 ...34 A4
Middleham Rd N18 ...34 A4
Middle La N8 ...50 A4
Teddington TW11 ...174 D4
Middle Lane Mews N8 ...50 A4
Middle Mill KT5 ...198 B6
Middle Park Ave SE9 ...165 D4
Middle Park Prim Sch
SE9 ...165 D4
Middle Rd 12 E13 ...99 A5
N10 ...30 C2
East Barnet EN4 ...14 C5
Harrow HA2 ...42 B1
Mitcham SW16 ...181 D1
Middle Row W10 ...91 A3
Middle Row Prim Sch
W10 ...91 A3
Middlesborough Rd N18 ...34 A4
Middlesex Bsns Ctr
UB2 ...107 B4
Middlesex Coll of Computing
& Tech HA9 ...66 A3
Middlesex Ct 5 W4 ...111 D2
Harrow HA1 ...42 D4
Middlesex Cty Cricket Sch
N3 ...29 D1
Middlesex Ho 6 SE20 ...184 C3
Middlesex Hospl
W1 ...93 C2 239 B3
Middlesex Hospl Annexe
W1 ...239 B4
Middlesex Pas EC1 ...241 D3
Middlesex Pl 13 E9 ...74 C2
Middlesex Rd CR4 ...204 A4
Middlesex St E1 ...95 D2 243 C2
Middlesex Univ N17 ...33 D4
Middlesex Univ (Bounds
Green) N11 ...31 C4
Middlesex Univ (Cat Hill)
EN4 ...15 A6
Middlesex Univ (Enfield
Campus) EN3 ...18 C6
Middlesex Univ (Hendon
Campus) NW4 ...46 B5
Middlesex Univ Trent Park
EN4 ...3 C3
Middle St EC1 ...242 A4
Croydon CR0 ...221 A5
Middle Temple*
EC4 ...116 C6 251 A6
Middle Temple La
EC4 ...116 C6 251 A6
Middleton Ave E4 ...19 B1
Greenford UB5 ...86 B5
Sidcup DA14 ...190 C5
Middleton Bldgs W1 ...239 A3
Middleton Cl E4 ...19 B1
Middleton Ct BR1 ...187 B3
Middleton Dr SE16 ...118 D4
Pinner HA5 ...40 A6
Middleton Gdns IG2 ...56 D3
Middleton Gr N7 ...72 A3
Middleton Ho E8 ...73 D1
SE1 ...262 C5
Middleton Mews N7 ...72 A3
Middleton Rd E8 ...73 D1
NW11 ...47 C2
Carshalton CR4,SM5 ...202 B2
Hayes UB3 ...83 B2
Middleton St E2 ...96 B4
Middleton Way SE13 ...142 B1
Middleway NW11 ...47 D4
Middle Way Hayes UB4 ...84 C3
Mitcham SW16 ...181 D1
Middle Way The HA3 ...24 D1
Midfield Prim Sch BR5 ...190 A3
Midfield Way BR5 ...190 B2
Midford Ho 1 NW4 ...46 D5
Midford Pl W1 ...239 B5
Midholm NW11 ...47 D5
Wembley HA9 ...44 C1
Midholm Cl NW11 ...47 D5
Midholm Rd CR0 ...223 A6
Midhope Ho WC1 ...233 B1
Midhope St WC1 ...233 B1
Midhurst SE26 ...184 C4
Midhurst Ave N10 ...49 A6
Thornton Heath CR0 ...204 C2
Midhurst Ct N8 ...50 A2
Midhurst Gdns UB10 ...61 A1
Midhurst Hill DA6 ...169 C6
Midhurst Ho 6 E14 ...97 B1
Midhurst Par N10 ...49 A6
Midhurst Rd W13 ...109 A3
Midhurst Way E5 ...74 A4
Midland Pl E14 ...120 A1
Midland Rd E10 ...54 A2
NW1 ...94 A5 233 A3
Midland Terr NW10 ...89 C3
NW2 ...68 D5
Midleton Rd KT3 ...177 A1
Midlothian Rd E3 ...97 B3
Midmoor Rd
Merton SW19 ...179 A2
Streatham SW12 ...159 C3
Midship Cl SE16 ...118 D5
Midship Point E14 ...119 C4
Midstrath Rd NW10 ...67 C4
Midsummer Apmts 15
SM2 ...217 C1
Midsummer Ave TW4 ...129 B1
Midsummer Ct SE12 ...143 A1
Midway SM3 ...201 B2
Midway Ho EC1 ...234 D2
Midwinter Cl 3 DA16 ...146 A2
Midwood Cl NW2 ...68 B5
Mighell Ave IG4 ...55 D4
Milan Ct N11 ...31 D2
Milan Rd UB1 ...107 B4
Milborne Gr SW10 ...256 B1
Milborne Ho 11 E9 ...74 C2
Milborne St E9 ...74 C2
Milborough Cres SE12 ...164 C5
Milbourne La KT10 ...212 A3
Milbourne Lodge Jun Sch
KT10 ...212 B2
Milbourne Lodge Sen Sch
KT10 ...212 B2
Milbrook KT10 ...212 A2
Milburn Dr 1 UB7 ...104 A6
Milburn Ho SW20 ...178 B1
Milcote St SE1 ...251 D1
Milday Gr N N1 ...73 B3
Mildenhall Rd E5 ...74 C5
Mildmay Ave N1 ...73 B2
Mildmay Ct N1 ...73 B3
Mildmay Gr N N1 ...73 B3
Mildmay Ho 6 SW15 ...156 C6
Mildmay Mission Hospl
E2 ...95 D4
Mildmay Pk N1 ...73 B3
Mildmay Rd N1 ...73 C3
Ilford IG1 ...78 D5
Mildmay St N1 ...73 B2
Mildon Ho EN3 ...6 C3
Mildred Ave Hayes UB3 ...105 B3
Northolt UB5 ...63 D3
Mildura Ct N8 ...50 B5
Mile End Pl E1 ...96 D3
Mile End Rd E1,E3 ...96 D3
Mile End Sta E3 ...97 B4
Mile End The E17 ...34 D2
Mile Rd Hackbridge SM6 ...203 A1
Wallington CR0, CR4, CR9 ...203 D1
Miles Bldgs NW1 ...237 A4
Miles Coverdale Prim Sch
W12 ...112 C4
Miles Ct E1 ...96 B1
Croydon CR0 ...220 D6
Miles Dr SE28 ...123 C5
Miles Ho 5 SE10 ...120 C1
Miles Lo E15 ...76 B3
Harrow HA1 ...42 B4
Milespit Hill NW7 ...28 C5
Miles Pl NW8 ...236 D4
Miles Rd N8 ...50 A6
Mitcham CR4 ...202 C6
Miles St SW8 ...138 A6 270 B5
Milestone Cl Edmonton N9 ...18 A2
Sutton SM2 ...218 B1
Milestone Ct TW7 ...131 A4
Milestone Green SW14 ...133 B1
Milestone Ho KT1 ...197 D5
Milestone Rd SE19 ...183 D4
Miles Way N20 ...14 C2
Milfoil St W12 ...112 A6
Milford Cl SE2 ...147 A6
Milford Ct 3 N16 ...51 C1
Southall UB1 ...107 C5
Milford Gdns
Croydon CR0 ...206 D4
Edgware HA8 ...26 C3
Wembley HA0 ...65 D3
Milford Gr SM1 ...218 A4
Milford La WC2 ...116 C6 251 A6
Milford Mews SW16 ...160 B1
Milford Rd Ealing W13 ...109 B5
Southall UB1 ...107 C6
Milk St E16 ...122 D5
EC2 ...95 A1 242 B2
Bromley BR1 ...187 B4
Milkwell Gdns IG8 ...37 B3
Milkwell Yd SE5 ...139 A4
Milkwood Rd SE24 ...138 D1
Milk Yd E1 ...118 C6
Millais Ave E12 ...78 C3
Millais Ct 10 UB5 ...84 D5
Millais Gdns HA8 ...26 C1
Millais Rd E11 ...76 B4
Enfield EN1 ...17 D6
New Malden KT3 ...199 C2
Millais Way KT19 ...215 A4
Millard Ho 11 SW15 ...156 A3
Millard Cl 21 N16 ...73 C3
Millard Ho SE8 ...119 B1
Millard Terr RM10 ...81 C2
Millbank SW1 ...116 A2 260 A3
Wallington SM6 ...219 D3
Millbank Ho KT6 ...198 B2
Millbank Prim Sch
SW1 ...115 D2 259 D3
Millbank Way SE12 ...165 A6
Millbourne Rd TW13 ...173 A6
Mill Bridge EN5 ...13 B5
Millbrook 1 E18 ...55 A6
Millbrook Ave DA16 ...145 B1
Millbrooke Ct 7 SW15 ...157 A6
Millbrook Gdns RM6 ...59 A3
Millbrook Ho 4 SE15 ...140 A6
Millbrook Rd SW9 ...138 D2
Edmonton N9 ...18 B3
Mill Cl SM5 ...219 A6
Mill Cnr EN5 ...1 B4
Millcroft Ho SE6 ...185 D6
Mill Ct E10 ...76 A5
NW7 ...29 A2
14 SE28 ...124 B6
Millender Wlk SE16 ...118 C2
Millennium Bsns Ctr NW2 ...68 B6
Millennium Bridge*
SE1,EC4 ...252 A5
Millennium Dome*
SE10 ...120 C5
Millennium Dr E14 ...120 B2
Millennium Harbour
E14 ...119 C4
Millennium Pl 27 E2 ...96 B5
Millennium Prim Sch
SE10 ...120 D3
Millennium Sq SE1 ...253 D2
Millennium Way SE10 ...120 C3
Miller Ave EN3 ...7 C5
Miller Cl Carshalton CR4 ...202 D2
Pinner HA5 ...22 C1
Miller Ct DA7 ...147 D2
8 NW9 ...46 A5
Miller Ho N15 ...50 D5
9 Streatham SW2 ...160 A4
Miller Rd Mitcham SW19 ...180 B4
Thornton Heath CR0 ...204 C1
Miller's Ave E8,N16 ...73 D3
Millers Cl NW7 ...28 A6
Miller's Ct 1 W4 ...111 D1
Millers Ct 3 HA0 ...88 A5
Millers Green Cl EN2 ...4 D2
Millers Mead Ct SW19 ...180 B3
Miller St NW1 ...232 A4
Miller's Terr 1 E8 ...73 D3
Miller's Way W6 ...112 C4
Millers Wharf Ho E1 ...118 A5
Millers Yd N3 ...29 D3
Miller Wlk SE1 ...251 B3
Millet Rd UB6 ...85 D5
Mill Farm Ave TW16 ...171 C3
Millfarm Bsns Pk TW4 ...151 A4
Mill Farm Cl HA5 ...22 C1
Mill Farm Cres TW4 ...151 A3
Millfield N4 ...72 C6
Charlton TW16 ...171 B2
Kingston KT1 ...198 B6
Millfield Ave E17 ...35 B2
Millfield La N6 ...70 D6
Millfield Pl N6 ...71 A6
Millfield Rd HA8 ...27 A1
Twickenham TW4 ...151 B3
Millfields Com Sch E5 ...74 C4
Millfields Rd E5 ...74 C5
Mill Gdns SE26 ...162 B1
Mill Gn CR4 ...203 A2
Mill Green Bsns Pk CR4 ...203 A2
Mill Green Rd CR4 ...203 A2
Millgrove St 6 SW11 ...137 A3
Millharbour E14 ...119 D4
Millhaven Cl RM6 ...58 B3
Mill Hill SW13 ...134 A2
Mill Hill Broadway Sta
NW7 ...27 C4
Mill Hill Circus NW7 ...27 D5
Mill Hill Cty High Sch
NW7 ...11 C2
Mill Hill East Sta NW7 ...29 A3
Mill Hill Gr 11 W3 ...110 D5
Mill Hill Ind Est NW7 ...27 D4
Mill Hill Rd W3 ...110 D4
Barnes SW13 ...134 A3
Mill Hill Sch NW7 ...28 B6
Mill Hill Terr 9 W3 ...110 D5
Mill Ho IG8 ...36 D5
Millhouse Pl SE27 ...182 D6
Millicent Fawcett Ct N17 ...33 D2
Millicent Preston Ho 4
IG11 ...101 B6
Millicent Rd E10 ...53 B1
Milligan St E14 ...119 B6
Milling Rd HA8 ...27 B3
Millington Ho N16 ...73 B5
Millington Rd UB3 ...105 C3
Mill La NW6 ...69 B3
SE18 ...122 C1
Carshalton SM5 ...219 A5
Croydon CR0 ...220 C5
Dagenham RM6 ...59 A3
Sewardstone E4 ...7 D2
Woodford IG8 ...36 D5
Mill Lane Trad Est CR0 ...220 B5
Millman Ct SE3 ...143 B5
WC1 ...240 C5
Millman Mews WC1 ...240 C5
Millman Pl WC1 ...240 C5
Millman St WC1 ...94 B3 240 C5
Millmark Gr SE14 ...141 A3
Millmarsh La EN3 ...7 B3
Millmead Bsns Ctr N17 ...52 B6
Millmead Ind Ctr N17 ...52 B6
Mill Mead Rd N17 ...52 B6
Millner Ct SE4 ...141 B3
Mill Pl BR7 ...188 D2
E14 ...97 A1
Kingston KT1 ...198 B6
Mill Plat TW7 ...131 A3
Mill Plat Ave TW7 ...131 A3
Mill Pond Cl
SW8 ...137 D5 269 D3
Millpond Est SE16 ...118 B4
Mill Rd E16 ...121 B5
Ilford IG1 ...78 C5
Merton SW19 ...180 A3
Twickenham TW2 ...152 A2
Mill Ridge HA8 ...26 C5
Mill River Trad Est EN3 ...7 A1
Mill Row N1 ...95 C6
Mills Cl UB10 ...82 C5
Mills Ct 7 E11 ...76 C5
Mills Gr 1 E14 ...98 A2
NW4 ...46 D6
Mills Ho E17 ...54 B6
SW8 ...269 B2
Millshot Cl SW6 ...134 C4
Millside SM5 ...218 D6
Millside Pl TW7 ...131 B3
Millson Cl N20 ...14 B2
Mills Row W4 ...111 B2
Mill St SE1 ...117 D4 253 D2
W1 ...249 A6
Kingston KT1 ...198 A6
Millstream Cl N13 ...32 C5
Millstream Rd
SE1 ...117 D4 253 C1
Mill Trad Est The NW10 ...89 A4
Mill Vale BR2 ...186 D1
Mill View Cl KT17 ...215 D1
Mill View Gdns CR0 ...222 D5
Millwall Dock Rd E14 ...119 C3
Millward Wlk 14 SE18 ...144 C6
Mill Way NW7 ...27 C5
Feltham TW14 ...150 B6
Millway Gdns UB5 ...63 B2
Millwood Rd TW3,TW7 ...152 A6
Millwood St 10 W10 ...91 A2
Mill Yd E1 ...118 A6
Milman Cl HA5 ...40 D6
Milman Rd NW6 ...91 A5
Milman's Ho SW10 ...266 C5
Milman's St
SW10 ...136 B6 266 C5
Milne Ct 4 E18 ...37 A2
Milne Field HA5 ...23 C3
Milne Gdns SE9 ...166 A6
Milne Ho 15 SE18 ...122 B2
Milner Dr TW2 ...152 B4
Milner Ho 2 SW11 ...136 B2
Hayes UB4 ...84 B4
Milner Pl N1 ...94 C6 234 B6
Milner Rd E15 ...98 C4
Dagenham RM8 ...80 C6
Kingston KT1 ...197 D6
Merton SW19 ...179 D2
Morden SM4 ...202 B4
South Norwood CR7 ...205 B6
Milner Sq N1 ...72 D1
Milner St SW3 ...114 D2 257 C4
Milner Wlk DA15 ...167 B3
Milnthorpe Rd W4 ...133 B6
Milo Rd SE22 ...161 D5
Milrood Ho 4 E1 ...96 D2
Milroy Wlk SE1 ...251 C4
Milson Rd W14 ...112 D3 254 A6
Milsted Ho 23 E5 ...74 B3
Milton Ave E6 ...78 A1
N6 ...49 C2
NW10 ...89 B6
NW9 ...45 A6
Barnet EN5 ...13 B6
Carshalton SM1 ...218 C4
Thornton Heath CR0 ...205 B2
Milton Cl N2 ...48 A3
SE1 ...117 D2 263 C3
Carshalton SM1 ...218 B5
Hayes UB4 ...84 A1
Milton Court Rd SE14 ...141 A6
Milton Cres IG2 ...57 A3
Milton Ct EC2 ...242 C4
NW11 ...47 A3
SE14 ...141 A6
9 SW18 ...157 C6
Fulham SW6 ...135 A2
Ilford RM6 ...58 C2
Kingston KT2 ...176 A6
Twickenham TW2 ...152 C1
Uxbridge UB10 ...60 D5
Milton Dr
Borehamwood WD6 ...10 D6
Littleton TW17 ...192 A5
Milton Gdns TW19 ...148 B3
Milton Gr N11 ...31 D5
N16 ...73 C4
Milton Ho 19 E2 ...96 C4
2 SE5 ...139 B5
12 Beckenham BR3 ...185 C3
5 Kingston KT2 ...176 D4
Sutton SM1 ...217 C5
Milton House Mans E8 ...73 D4
Milton Lo
3 Sidcup DA14 ...190 A6
Southgate N21 ...16 D3
Twickenham TW1 ...152 D4
Milton Pk N6 ...49 C2
Milton Pl 3 N7 ...72 C3
Milton Rd DA16 ...145 D4
E17 ...53 C5
N15 ...50 D6
N6 ...49 C2
NW7 ...28 A5
1 NW9 ...46 A2
SE24 ...160 D6
W3 ...111 B5
Belvedere DA17 ...125 C2
Ealing W7 ...108 D6
Harrow HA1 ...42 C5
Mitcham CR4 ...181 A3
Mortlake SW14 ...133 B2
Sutton SM1 ...217 C4
Thornton Heath CR0 ...205 B2
Uxbridge UB10 ...60 D4
Wallington SM6 ...219 D2
Wimbledon SW19 ...180 A4
Hampton TW12 ...173 C3
Milton St EC1,EC2 ...95 B2 242 C4
Milton Way UB7 ...104 B2
Milverton NW5 ...71 A3
Milverton Dr UB10 ...61 A4
Milverton Gdns IG3 ...79 D6
Milverton Ho SE23 ...163 A1
Milverton Rd NW6 ...68 C1
Milverton St
SE11 ...116 C1 261 B1
Milverton Way SE9 ...188 C6
Milward St E1 ...96 B2
Mimosa N15 ...51 B4
Mimosa Ct SW4 ...270 B1
Mimosa Ho UB4 ...84 C2
Mimosa Rd UB4 ...84 C2
Mimosa St SW6 ...135 B4 264 D1
Mina Rd SE17 ...117 C1 263 B2
Merton SW19 ...179 C2
Minard Rd SE6 ...164 C3
Minchenden Cres N14 ...15 D1
Minchenden Ct N14 ...15 D2
Minchin Ho 6 E14 ...97 C1
Mincing La EC3 ...117 C6 253 A6
Minden Rd Cheam SM3 ...217 B6
Penge SE20 ...184 B2
Minehead Ct HA2 ...63 C6
Minehead Rd Harrow HA2 ...63 C5
Streatham SW16 ...182 B5
Mineral St SE18 ...123 C2
Minera Mews SW1 ...258 B4
Minerva Cl SW9 ...138 C5
Sidcup DA14 ...189 C6
Minerva Rd NW10 ...89 B4
Chingford E4 ...35 D3
Kingston KT1 ...176 B1
Minerva St E2 ...96 B5
Minerva Wlk EC1 ...241 D2
Minet Ave NW10 ...89 C5
Minet Dr UB3 ...106 A5
Minet Gdns NW10 ...89 C5
Hayes UB3 ...106 B5
Minet Jun & Inf Schs
UB3 ...106 B5
Minet Rd SE5,SW9 ...138 D3
Minford Gdns W14 ...112 D4
Mingard Wlk N7 ...72 B5
Ming St E14 ...119 C6
Minimax Cl TW14 ...150 A5
Ministry Way SE9 ...166 B2
Mink Ct TW4 ...128 C3
Minniedale KT5 ...198 B4
Minnow Wlk SE17 ...263 B3
Minories EC3 ...117 D6 253 C6
Minshaw Ct DA14 ...189 D6
1 Sidcup DA14 ...190 A6
Minshull Pl 23 BR3 ...185 C3
Minshull St SW8 ...269 C1
Minson Rd E9 ...96 D6
Minstead Gdns SW15 ...155 D4
Minstead Way KT3 ...199 C3
Minster Ave SM1 ...217 C6
Minster Dr CR0 ...221 C4
Minster Gdns KT8 ...195 B5
Minsterley Ave TW16,
TW17 ...193 C5
Minster Rd BR1 ...187 B3
NW2 ...69 A3
Minster Wlk N8 ...50 A5
Minstrel Ct HA3 ...24 C1
Minstrel Gdns KT5 ...198 B5
Mint Bsns Pk 12 E16 ...99 A2
Mint Cl UB10 ...82 D4
Mintern Cl N13 ...16 D1
Minterne Ave UB2 ...107 C2
Minterne Rd HA3 ...44 B4
Minterne Waye UB4 ...84 C1
Mintern St N1 ...95 B5 235 D4
Minton Ho SE11 ...261 A4
Minton Mews 1 NW6 ...69 D2
Mint Rd SM5,SM6 ...219 B4
Mint St SE1 ...252 B2
Mint Wlk CR0 ...221 A5
Mirabel Rd SW6 ...135 B5 264 D4
Mirage Ctr The HA9 ...66 D4
Miranda Cl 16 E1 ...96 C2
Miranda Ct W3 ...88 B1
Miranda Ho 17 N1 ...95 C5
6 Belvedere DA17 ...125 C1
Miranda Rd N19 ...49 C1
Mirfield Ct SE20 ...184 A1
Mirfield St SE7 ...121 D3
Miriam Ct DA14 ...190 B6
Miriam Rd SE18 ...123 C1
Mirravale Trad Est RM6 ...59 A2
Mirren Cl HA2 ...63 B5
Mirror Path SE12 ...165 C1
Misbourne Rd UB10 ...82 C6
Missenden SE17 ...262 D1
Missenden Cl TW14 ...149 D3
Missenden Gdns SM4 ...202 A3
Missenden Ho NW8 ...237 A6
Mission Gr E17 ...53 A4
Mission Grove Prim Sch
E17 ...53 B5
Mission Pl SE15 ...140 A4
Mission Sq 18 TW8 ...132 A6
Misterton Ct SW11 ...266 D2
Mistletoe Cl CR0 ...206 D1
Mistley Thorn IG1 ...56 C2
Mistral SE5 ...139 C4
Mistral Ct E4 ...19 D1
Mistys Field KT12 ...194 C1
Mitali Pas 13 E1 ...96 A1
Mitcham Garden Village
CR4 ...203 A4
Mitcham Ho 9 SE5 ...139 A4
Mitcham Ind Est CR4 ...181 A2
Mitcham Junction Sta
CR4 ...203 A4
Mitcham La SW16 ...181 C5
Mitcham Pk CR4 ...202 D5
Mitcham Rd E6 ...100 A4
Ilford IG3 ...57 D2
Upper Tooting SW17 ...180 D5
Mitcham Sta CR4 ...202 C5
Mitcham Vale High Sch
CR4 ...181 B1
Mitchell 19 NW9 ...27 D2
Mitchell Brook Prim Sch
NW10 ...67 C2

Mitchellbrook Way
NW10 ....67 B2
Mitchell CI SE2 ....124 C2
Belvedere DA17 ....125 D3
Mitchell CI E10 ....53 D2
Mitchell Ho 31 W12 ....112 B6
W4 ....110 D1
Mitchell Rd BR6 ....227 D4
Edmonton N13 ....33 A5
Mitchell's PI SE21 ....161 C4
Mitchell St EC1 ....95 A3 242 B6
Mitchell Way NW10 ......67 A2
Bromley BR1 ....187 A2
Mitchell Wlk E6 ....100 B2
Mitchison Rd N1 ....73 B2
Mitchley Rd N17 ....52 A6
Mitford CI KT9 ....213 C2
Mitford Rd N19 ....72 A6
Mitre Bridge Ind Pk W10 ..90 B3
Mitre CI
Shepperton TW17 ....193 B3
Sutton SM2 ....218 B1
Mitre Ct EC2 ....242 B2
Belvedere DA17 ....125 C1
1 Ilford RM6 ....58 B2
9 Woodford E18 ....37 A2
Mitre Ho RM7 ....59 D5
Mitre Rd E15 ....98 C5
SE1 ....116 C4 251 B2
Mitre Sq EC3 ....243 B1
Mitre St EC3 ....95 C1 243 B1
Mitre The 9 E14 ....119 B6
Mitre Way W10 ....90 B2
Moatbridge Sch SE9 ....165 D5
Moat CI BR6 ....227 D2
Moat Cres N3 ....47 D6
Moat Croft DA16 ....146 C2
Moat Ct DA15 ....167 D1
9 DA15 ....168 A1
SE9 ....166 B5
Moat Dr 4 E13 ....99 C5
Harrow HA1 ....42 B5
Ruislip HA4 ....39 C2
Moat Farm Rd UB5 ....63 B1
Moatfield NW6 ....69 A1
Moat Lo The HA1 ....64 C6
Moat PI SW9 ....138 B2
Acton W3 ....88 D1
Moat Side Enfield EN3 ....6 D1
Feltham TW13 ....172 C6
Moat The KT3 ....177 C2
Moberly Rd SW4 ....159 D4
Mobey Ct SW4 ....270 A1
Moblin Lo IG9 ....21 C3
Moby Dick RM6 ....59 B5
Mocatta Ho 9 E1 ....96 B3
Modbury Gdns NW5 ......71 A2
Modder PI SW15 ....134 D1
Model Cotts SW14 ....133 A2
Model Farm CI SE9 ....166 A1
Modling Ho 8 E2 ....96 D5
Moelwyn Hughes Ct N7 ..71 D3
Moelyn Mews HA1 ....43 A4
Moffat Ct
Upper Tooting SW17 ....180 C6
Wimbledon SW19 ....179 C5
Moffat Ho 24 SE5 ....139 A5
Moffat Rd Bowes Park N13 ..32 A4
South Norwood CR7 .....183 B1
Upper Tooting SW17 ....180 D6
Mogden La TW7 ....152 D6
Mohawk Ho 31 E3 ....97 A5
Mohmmad Khan Rd E11 ..54 D1
Mohr Ct E2 ....32 B3
Moineau 18 NW9 ....27 D2
Moira CI N17 ....33 C1
Moira Ct SW17 ....159 A2
Moira Rd SE9 ....144 B1
Moland Mead SE16 ....118 D1
Molasses Ho 1 SW11 ...136 A2
Molasses Row 2 SW11 ..136 A2
Mole Abbey Gdns KT8 ..195 D6
Mole Ct 2 W12 ....111 C4
West Ewell KT19 ....215 A4
Mole Ho NW8 ....236 D5
Molember Ct KT7 ....196 C5
Molember Rd KT8 ....196 C4
Molescroft SE9 ....167 A1
Molesey Ave KT12,KT8 ..195 B4
Molesey Dr SM3 ....217 A5
Molesey Ho E2 ....243 C6
Molesey Hospl KT8 ....195 C4
Molesey Park Ave KT8 ..195 D4
Molesey Park CI KT8 ....196 A4
Molesey Park Rd KT8 ....196 A4
Molesey Rd KT12 ....195 A2
Molesford Rd SW6 ....265 A1
Molesham CI KT8 ....195 D6
Molesham Way KT8 ....195 D6
Molesworth Ho 9 SE17 ..138 D6
Molesworth St SE13 .....142 A2
Moliner Ct 4 BR3 ....185 C3
Mollie Davis Ct SE19 ....183 D4
Mollison Ave EN3 ....7 B5
Mollison Dr SM6 ....220 A1
Mollison Way HA8 ....26 C1
Molly Huggins CI SW12 ..159 C4
Molton Ho N1 ....233 D5
Molyneux Dr SW17 ....181 B6
Molyneux St W1 ...92 C2 237 B3
Monarch CI
Coney Hall BR4 ....224 D4
East Bedfont TW14 ....149 C4
Monarch Ct N2 ....48 A4
Ealing W5 ....87 C2
Monarch Dr E16 ....99 D2
Monarch Mews E17 ....53 D3

Monarch Mews continued
West Norwood SW16 ....182 C5
Monarch Par CR4 ....180 D1
Monarch PI IG9 ....21 C2
Monarch Rd DA17 ....125 C3
Monarchs Ct 1 NW7 ....27 B5
Mona Rd SE15 ....140 C3
Mona St E16 ....98 D2
Monastery Gdns EN2 ....5 B3
Monaveen Gdns KT8 .....195 D6
Monck St SW1 ...115 D3 259 D5
Monclar Rd SE5 ....139 B1
Moncorvo CI
SW7 ....114 C4 247 A1
Moncrieff CI 4 E6 ....100 A1
Moncrieff St SE15 ....140 A3
Mondial Way UB7 ....127 A5
Mondragon Ho 3 SW8 ..270 B2
Monega Rd E7,E12 ....77 D2
Monega Prim Sch E12 ....77 D2
Monet Ct 15 SE16 ....118 B1
Moneyer Ho N1 ....235 C2
Monica James Ho 12
DA14 ....168 A1
Monica Shaw Ct NW1 ..232 D3
Monier Rd E3 ....75 C1
Monivea Rd BR3 ....185 B3
Monk Ct W12 ....112 A5
Monk Dr E16 ....121 A6
Monken Hadley CE Prim Sch
EN4 ....1 C4
Monkfrith Ave N14 ....15 B5
Monkfrith CI N14 ....15 B4
Monkfrith Prim Sch N14 ..15 A4
Monkfrith Way N14 ....15 A4
Monkham's Ave IG8 ....37 B5
Monkham's Dr IG8 ....37 B5
Monkham's La IG8 ....37 B6
Monkleigh Rd SM4,
SW20 ....201 A5
Monkridge 3 N8 ....49 D2
Monks Ave
East Molesey KT8 ....195 B4
New Barnet EN5 ....14 A5
Monks CI SE2 ....124 C2
Enfield EN2 ....5 A3
Harrow HA2 ....63 D6
Ruislip HA4 ....62 D4
Monks Cres KT12 ....194 B1
Monksdene Gdns SM1 ..217 D5
Monks Dr W3 ....88 C1
Monksfield N4 ....72 C6
Monks Orchard Rd BR3,
CR0 ....207 C2
Monks Orchard Sch
CR0 ....206 B4
Monks Park Gdns HA9 ..66 D1
Monks Pk HA9 ....67 A2
Monks Rd EN2 ....5 A3
Monk St SE18 ....122 C2
Monks Way BR5 ....211 B1
NW11 ....47 B5
Beckenham BR3 ....207 C3
Harmondsworth UB7 ....126 A6
Monkswell Ct N10 ....31 A2
Monkswood Gdns
Borehamwood WD6 ....11 B6
Ilford IG5 ....56 C6
Monkton Ct W14 ....254 C6
Monkton Ho 22 SE16 ....74 B1
32 SE16 ....118 D4
Monkton Rd DA16 ....145 D3
Monkton St
SE11 ....116 C2 261 B4
Monkville Ave NW11 ......47 B5
Monkville Par 1 NW11 ..47 B5
Monkwell Sq EC2 ....242 B3
Monmouth Ave
Teddington KT1 ....175 C3
Wanstead E18 ....55 B4
Monmouth CI W4 ....111 B3
Bexley DA16 ....146 A1
Mitcham CR4,SW16 .....204 A5
Monmouth Ct 9 W7 ....86 D5
Monmouth Gr TW8 ....110 A2
Monmouth Ho 5 NW5 ....71 B2
SW18 ....157 C5
Monmouth PI W2 ....91 D1
Monmouth Rd E6 ....100 B4
N9 ....18 C2
W2 ....91 C1
Dagenham RM9 ....81 B3
Hayes UB3 ....105 D2
Monmouth St
WC2 ....94 A1 240 A1
Monnery Rd N19 ....71 C5
Monnow Rd SE1 ....118 A2
Mono La TW13 ....150 B2
Monoux Almshouses
E17 ....53 D5
Monoux Gr E17 ....35 C2
Monro Dr N11 ....31 C4
Monroe Cres EN1 ....6 B4
Monroe Dr SW14 ....154 D6
Monroe Ho 16 N19 ....49 D2
NW8 ....230 A1
Monro Gdns HA3 ....24 C3
Monro Ho 21 NW3 ....70 A4
Putney SW15 ....156 B6
Monro way E5 ....74 A4
Monsal Ct E5 ....75 A4
Monsell Rd N4,N5 ....72 D5
Monson Prim Sch SE14 ..140 D5
Monson Rd NW10 ....90 B5
SE14 ....140 D5
Mons Way BR2 ....210 A3
Montacute Rd
Bushey WD23 ....8 C4

Montacute Rd continued
Carshalton SM4 ....202 B3
Forest Hill SE6 ....163 B4
Montagu Cres N18 ....34 A6
Montagu Ct W1 ....237 D3
Montague Ave SE4 ....141 C1
Ealing W7 ....108 D5
Montague CI SE1 ....252 C4
Walton-on-T KT12 ....194 A2
Montague Fell HA0 ....65 A4
Montague Gdns W3 .....110 C6
Montague PI
WC1 ....93 D2 239 D2
Montague Rd E11 ....76 D6
E8 ....74 A3
N15 ....52 A5
N8 ....50 B4
W7 ....108 D4
Ealing W13 ....87 B1
Hounslow TW3 ....129 D2
Merton SW19 ....179 D3
Richmond TW10 ....154 A5
Southall UB2 ....107 A2
Thornton Heath CR0 .....204 D1
Uxbridge UB8 ....60 A1
Montague Sq SE14 ......140 C5
Montague St
WC1 ....94 A3 240 A4
Montague Street EC1 ....242 A3
Montague Terr 1 BR2 ....209 A5
Montague Way UB2 ......107 A5
Montagu Gdns
Edmonton N18 ....34 B6
Wallington SM6 ....219 C4
Montagu Ind Est N18 .....34 C6
Montagu Mans
W1 ....92 D3 237 D3
Montagu Mews N W1 ....237 D3
Montagu Mews S W1 ....237 D2
Montagu Mews W W1 ....237 D2
Montagu PI W1 ...92 D2 237 D3
Montagu Row W1 ....237 D3
Montagu Sq W1 ...92 D1 237 D2
Montagu St W1 ...92 D1 237 D2
Montalt Ho IG8 ....36 D6
Montalt Rd IG8 ....36 D5
Montana Gdns
Penge SE26 ....185 B5
5 Sutton SM1 ....218 A3
Montana Rd
Upper Tooting SW17 ....159 A1
Wimbledon SW20 ....178 C2
Montbelle Prim Sch
SE9 ....166 D1
Montbelle Rd SE9 ....166 D1
Montcalm CI Hayes BR2 ..209 A5
Hayes UB4 ....84 B4
Montcalm Ho E14 ....119 C3
Montcalm Rd SE7 ....143 D5
Montclare St E2 ...95 D3 243 C6
Monteagle Ave IG11 ....79 A3
Monteagle Ct 27 N1 ....95 C5
Monteagle Prim Sch
RM9 ....102 B6
Monteagle Way E5 ....74 A5
SE15 ....140 B2
Montefiore Ct 2 N16 ......51 D1
Montefiore St 2 SW8 ....137 B3
Montem Prim Sch N7 .....72 B5
Montem Rd
Forest Hill SE23 ....163 B4
New Malden KT3 ....199 C5
Montem St N4 ....50 B1
Montenotte Rd N8 ....49 B4
Montesole Ct 5 HA5 ......22 C1
Montesquieu Terr 3
E16 ....98 B1
Montessori Coll SW19 ..179 C4
Montford PI
SE11 ....116 C1 261 A1
Montford Rd TW16 ....194 A5
Montfort Ho E14 ....120 A3
4 E2 ....96 C4
Montfort PI SW19 ....156 D3
Montgo CI 10 SW2 ....160 C1
Montgolfier Wlk UB5 ......85 A4
Montgomery CI DA15 ...167 D5
Mitcham CR4 ....204 A5
Montgomery Ct W4 ......133 A6
Montgomery Ho 5
SW14 ....133 B2
Montgomery Lo 34 E1 ....96 C3
Montgomery Rd
Acton W4 ....111 A2
Edgware HA8 ....26 A4
Montholme Rd SW11 ....158 D5
Monthorpe Rd 18 E1 ......96 A2
Montolieu Gdns SW15 ..156 B6
Montpelier Ave Ealing W5 ..87 D2
Sidcup DA5 ....168 D4
Montpelier Ct
5 Beckenham BR2 ......208 D5
Ealing W5 ....87 D2
Montpelier Gdns E6 ....99 D4
Ilford RM6 ....58 C2
Montpelier Gr NW5 ....71 C3
Montpelier PI 21 E1 ....96 C1
SW7 ....257 B6
Montpelier Prim Sch
W5 ....87 D2
Montpelier Rd N3 ....30 A2
SE15 ....140 B4
Ealing W5 ....87 D2
Sutton SM1 ....218 A4
Montpelier Rise NW11 ...47 A2

Montpelier Rise continued
Wembley HA9 ....43 D1
Montpelier Row SE3 .....142 D1
Twickenham TW1 ....153 C4
Montpelier Sq
SW7 ....114 C4 247 B1
Montpelier St
SW7 ....114 C3 257 B6
Montpelier Terr SW7 ....247 B1
Montpelier Vale SE3 .....142 D3
Montpelier Way NW11 ...47 A2
Montpelier Wlk
SW7 ....114 C3 257 B6
Montrave Rd SE20 ....184 C3
Montreal Ho UB4 ....84 B4
Montreal PI WC2 ....250 C6
Montreal Rd IG1 ....57 A2
Montrell Rd SW2 ....160 A3
Montrose Ave DA16 .....145 C2
HA8 ....27 B2
NW6 ....91 A5
Sidcup DA15 ....168 A4
Twickenham TW2 ....152 A4
Montrose CI DA16 ....145 D2
Ashford TW15 ....171 A5
Woodford IG8 ....37 A6
Montrose Cres N12 ....30 A4
N10 ....49 B5
Montrose Ct NW11 ....47 B5
NW9 ....27 A1
SW7 ....114 B4 246 D1
2 Catford SE6 ....164 C2
Montrose Gdns
Mitcham CR4 ....180 D1
Sutton SM1 ....217 D6
Montrose Ho E14 ....119 C3
SW1 ....248 B1
Montrose PI
SW1 ....115 A4 248 B1
Montrose Rd
East Bedfont TW14 ....149 B5
Harrow HA3 ....24 D1
Montrose Villas W6 ......112 A1
Montrose Way SE23 .....162 D3
Montserrat Ave IG8 ....36 B3
Montserrat CI SE19 ......183 B5
Montserrat Rd SW15 ....135 A1
Montway Hts SW19 ......179 D3
Monument Gdns SE13 ..164 A6
Monument St
EC3 ....117 B6 252 D6
Monument Sta
EC3 ....117 B6 252 D6
Monument The ★ EC3 ..252 D6
Monument Way N17 ......51 D6
Monza St E1 ....118 C6
Moodkee St SE16 ....118 C3
Moody Rd SE15 ....139 D4
Moody St E1 ....96 D4
Moon Ct SE12 ....143 A1
Moon La EN5 ....1 B2
Moon St N1 ....94 D6 234 C6
Moorcroft HA8 ....26 D2
Moorcroft Gdns BR1 ....210 A4
Moorcroft La UB8 ....82 C2
Moorcroft Rd SW16 .....160 A1
Moorcroft Sch UB8 ....82 D2
Moorcroft Way HA5 ....41 A4
Moordown SE18 ....144 D4
Moore CI Mitcham CR4 ..181 B3
Mortlake SW14 ....133 A2
Wallington SM6 ....220 A1
Moore Cres RM9 ....102 B6
Moore Ct 3 N1 ....234 C5
Moorefield Rd N17 ....33 D1
Moore Ho 6 E1 ....118 C6
16 E2 ....96 C4
N8 ....50 A5
5 SE10 ....120 D1
Wandsworth SW17 ....158 B1
1 West Norwood SE27 ..183 A6
Mooreland Rd BR1 ....187 A2
Moore Park Ct SW6 .....265 D6
Moore Park Rd
SW6 ....135 D5 265 C3
Moore Rd SE19 ....183 A4
Moore St SW3 ....114 D2 257 C4
Montgolfier Wlk UB5 ......77 A4
Moorey CI 2 E15 ....98 D6
Moorfield Ave W5 ....87 D3
Moorfield Rd
Chessington KT9 ....214 A3
Enfield EN3 ....6 C4
Moorfields EC2 ...95 B2 242 C3
Moorfields Eye Hospl
EC1 ....95 B3 235 C1
Moorfields Highwalk
EC2 ....242 C3
Moorfields Prim Sch
EC1 ....95 B3 242 C6
Moorgate EC2 ....95 B2 242 C3
Moorgate PI EC2 ....242 C2
Moorgate Sta
EC2 ....95 B3 242 C3
Moorgreen Ho EC1 ....234 C2
Moorhead Way SE3 .....143 B2
Moorhouse 17 NW9 ......27 D2
Moorhouse Rd W2 ....91 C1
Harrow HA3 ....43 D6
Moorings The E16 ....99 C2
Moor La EC2 ......95 B2 242 C3
Chessington KT9 ....214 A3
Moorland CI TW4 ....151 C4
Moorland Rd SW9 ....138 D1
Moorlands Ave NW7 ......28 B4
Moor Lane Jun Sch
KT9 ....214 B3
Moormead Dr KT19 ......215 C3

Moor Mead Rd TW1 .....153 A5
Moor Park Gdns KT2 ...177 C3
Moor PI EC2 ....242 C3
Moorside Rd BR1 ....186 D6
Moor St W1 ....239 D1
Moortown Rd WD19 ....22 C6
Moot Ct NW9 ....44 C4
Morant Ho SW9 ....138 B1
Morant PI N22 ....32 B2
Morant St E14 ....119 C6
Mora Prim Sch NW2 .....68 C4
Mora Rd NW2 ....68 C4
Mora St EC1 ....95 A4 235 A3
Morat St SW9 ....138 B4 270 D2
Moravian CI SW3 ....266 D5
Moravian PI
SW10 ....136 B6 266 D5
Moravian St 10 E2 ....96 C4
Moray Ave UB3 ....105 C5
Moray CI HA8 ....10 C2
Moray Ho 8 E1 ....97 A3
11 Kingston KT6 ....198 A4
Moray Mews N4,N7 ....72 B6
Moray Rd N4,N7 ....72 B6
Mordaunt Gdns RM9 .....81 A1
Mordaunt Ho 4 NW10 ..89 B6
34 SW8 ....137 D3
Mordaunt Rd NW10 ....89 B6
Mordaunt St SW9 ....138 B2
Morden Court Par SM4 ..201 D5
Morden Ct SM4 ....201 D5
Morden Gdns
Greenford UB6 ....64 D3
Mitcham CR4 ....202 B5
Morden Hall SW19 ....201 D6
Morden Hall Rd SM4 ....202 A5
Morden Hill SE13 ....142 A3
Morden Ho 19 SW2 ......160 C5
Morden Mead 201 C5
Morden La SE13 ....142 A4
Morden Lo 8 BR2 ....186 B1
Morden Mount Prim Sch
SE13 ....141 D3
Morden Park Sch Sports Ctr
SM4 ....201 C4
Morden Prim Sch SM4 ..201 C4
Morden Rd SE3 ....143 A3
Dagenham RM6 ....59 A2
Merton SW19 ....179 D1
Mitcham CR4,SM4 ....202 B5
Morden Road Mews
SE3 ....143 A3
Morden Road Sta SW19 ..201 D6
Morden South Sta SM4 ..201 C4
Morden St SE13 ....141 D4
Morden Sta SW19 ....201 D6
Morden Way SM3 ....201 C2
Morden Wharf Rd SE10 ..120 C3
Mordern Ho NW1 ....237 B5
Mordon Rd IG3 ....57 D2
Mordred Rd SE6 ....164 C2
Morecambe CI 2 E1 ......96 D2
Morecambe Gdns HA7 ..25 D6
Morecambe St
SE17 ....117 B2 262 B2
Morecambe Terr N18 .....33 B6
More CI E16 ....98 D1
W14 ....113 A2 254 A3
Morecoombe CI KT2 ....176 D3
Moredown Ho 3 E8 ....74 A3
Moree Way N18 ....34 A6
More House Sch
SW1 ....114 D3 257 D5
Moreland Ct 3 NW2 ....69 C5
Moreland Prim Sch
EC1 ....95 A4 234 D2
Moreland St EC1 ..94 D4 234 D2
Moreland Way E4 ....20 A1
Morella Rd SW11,SW12 ..158 D4
Morell Ho 5 SW9 ....138 B3
Morello Ave UB8 ....82 D2
Morello CI HA9 ....66 B5
Moremead Rd SE6 ....185 C6
Morena St SE6 ....163 D4
Moresby Ave KT5 ....198 D2
Moresby Rd E5 ....52 B1
Moresby Wlk 6 SW8 .....137 B3
More's Gdn SW3 ....266 D5
Moreton Ave TW7 ....130 C4
Moreton CI E5 ....52 C1
N15 ....51 B3
NW7 ....28 C4
Moreton Green Fst Sch
SM4 ....202 B4
Moreton Ho SE16 ....118 B3
Upper Tooting SW17 ....180 B6
Moreton PI SW1 ...115 C2 259 B2
Moreton Rd N15 ....51 B3
South Cheam KT4 ....216 B6
Moreton St
SW1 ....115 D1 259 C2
Moreton Terr
SW1 ....115 C1 259 B2
Moreton Terr Mews N
SW1 ....259 B2
Moreton Terr Mews S
SW1 ....259 B2
Moreton Twr 3 W3 ....110 D5
Morford CI HA4 ....40 B2
Morford Way HA4 ....40 B2
Morgan Ave E17 ....54 B5
Morgan Ct RM10 ....81 C1
Morgan Ct 5 SW11 ....136 B3
Ashford TW15 ....170 D5
Morgan Ho SW1 ....259 B3
SW8 ....269 B2
Morgan Rd BR1 ....187 A3
N7 ....72 C3
W10 ....91 B2

Morgan Rd continued
Teddington TW11 ....174 C4
Morgan's La UB3 ....83 B2
Morgan St E16 ....98 D2
E3 ....96 D4
Morgan's Wlk SW11 ....267 A3
Moriah Jewish Day Sch The
HA5 ....41 A1
Moriatry CI N7 ....72 A4
Morie St SW18 ....157 D6
Morieux Rd E10 ....53 B1
Moring Rd SW17 ....181 A6
Moriss Ho 5 E5 ....74 B6
Morkyns Wlk SE21 ....161 C1
Morland Ave CR0 ....205 C1
Morland CI NW11 ....47 D1
Hampton TW12 ....173 B5
Mitcham CR4 ....202 C6
Morland Ct W12 ....112 B4
Morland Est E8 ....74 A1
Morland Gdns NW10 .....67 B3
Southall UB1 ....107 D5
Morland Ho NW1 ....232 B3
NW6 ....91 C6
SW1 ....260 A4
W11 ....91 A1
Morland Mews N1 ....72 C1
Morland Rd E17 ....52 D4
Croydon CR0 ....205 D2
Dagenham RM10 ....81 C1
Harrow HA3 ....44 A5
Ilford IG1 ....78 D6
Penge SE20 ....184 D4
Sutton SM1 ....218 A3
Morland Road Day Hospl
RM10 ....103 C6
Morley Ave Chingford E4 ..36 B3
Edmonton N18 ....34 A6
Tottenham N22 ....32 D1
Morley CI BR6 ....226 D6
Morley Coll SE1 ..116 C3 261 B6
Morley Cres HA8 ....11 A2
Ruislip HA4 ....62 C6
Morley Cres E HA7 ....43 D6
Morley Cres W HA7 ......43 C6
Morley Ct E4 ....35 B5
Beckenham BR2 ....208 D5
Beckenham BR3 ....186 B2
Morley Hill EN2 ....5 B5
Morley Ho N16 ....74 A6
Streatham SW2 ....160 A4
Morley Rd E10 ....54 A1
SE13 ....142 A1
Barking IG11 ....101 B6
Cheam SM3 ....201 B3
Chislehurst BR7 ....189 A2
Dagenham RM6 ....59 A4
Twickenham TW1 ....153 D5
Morley St SE1 ....116 C3 251 B1
Morna Rd SE5 ....139 A3
Morning La E9 ....74 C2
Morningside Prim Sch
E9 ....74 C2
Morningside Rd KT4 .....216 C6
Mornington Ave BR1 ....209 D6
W14 ....113 B2 254 C3
Ilford IG1 ....56 C2
Mornington Avenue Mans
W14 ....254 C3
Mornington CI IG8 ....37 A6
Mornington Cres
NW1 ....93 C5 232 A4
Cranford TW5 ....128 A3
Mornington Crescent Sta
NW1 ....93 C5 232 A4
Mornington Gr E3 ....97 C4
Mornington Mews 2
SE5 ....139 A4
Mornington PI NW1 ......232 A4
4 SE8 ....141 B5
Mornington Rd E11 ....54 D1
SE14,SE8 ....141 B5
Ashford TW15 ....171 A5
Chingford E4 ....20 B4
Greenford UB6 ....85 D3
Woodford IG8 ....36 D6
Mornington St
NW1 ....93 B5 231 D5
Mornington Terr
NW1 ....93 B5 231 D5
Mornington Wlk TW10 ..175 C4
Morocco St SE1 ..117 C4 253 A1
Morpeth Gr E9 ....96 D6
Morpeth Rd E9 ....96 D6
Morpeth Sec Sch E2 ......96 C4
Morpeth St E2 ....96 D4
Morpeth Terr
SW1 ....115 C3 259 A4
Morpeth Wlk N17 ....34 B3
Morrab Gdns IG3 ....79 D5
Morrel CI EN5 ....2 A2
Morrel CI 10 E2 ....96 A5
Morris Ave E12 ....78 B3
Morris Blitz Ct 2 N16 .....73 D4
Morris CI BR6 ....227 C6
Croydon CR0 ....207 A4
Morris Ct 3 SE5 ....139 B1
Chingford E4 ....19 D1
Morris Gdns SW18 ....157 C4
Morris Ho 17 E2 ....96 C4
10 N19 ....71 C4
NW8 ....237 A5
1 SW4 ....138 A1
Morrish Rd SW2 ....160 A4
Morrison Ave N17 ....51 C6
Morrison Bldgs 3 E1 .....96 A1
Morrison Ct N12 ....30 C3

Morrison Ct continued
5 Barnet EN5 ...1 A1
Morrison Ho SW2 ...160 C3
Morrison Rd
Barking IG11 ...103 A5
Hayes UB4 ...84 B4
Morrison St SW11 ...137 A2
Morrison Yd N17 ...33 D1
Morris Pl N4 ...72 C6
Morris Rd E15 ...76 C4
Dagenham RM8 ...81 B6
Isleworth TW7 ...130 D2
Morriss Ho 7 SE16 ...118 B4
Morris St E1 ...96 B1
E14 ...97 D2
Morriston Cl WD19 ...22 C5
Morritt Ho 3 HA0 ...65 D3
Morse Cl E13 ...99 A4
Morshead Mans W9 ...91 C4
Morshead Rd W9 ...91 C4
Morson Rd EN3 ...19 A5
Morston Gdns SE9 ...188 B6
Mortain Ho 9 SE16 ...118 B2
Morten Cl SW4 ...159 D5
Morteyne Rd N17 ...33 B2
Mortgramit Sq SE18 ...122 C3
Mortham St E15 ...98 C6
Mortimer Cl 1 NW2 ...69 B5
Streatham SW16 ...159 D2
Mortimer Cres NW6 ...91 D6
Worcester Park KT4 ...215 B5
Mortimer Ct NW8 ...229 B3
Mortimer Dr EN1 ...17 C6
Mortimer Est NW6 ...91 D6
Mortimer Ho 6 W11 ...112 D5
W14 ...254 B3
Mortimer Lo 11 SW19 ...157 A3
Mortimer Market WC1 ...239 B5
Mortimer Pl NW6 ...91 D6
Mortimer Rd E6 ...100 B4
N1 ...73 C1
NW10 ...90 C4
Ealing W13 ...87 C1
Mitcham CR4 ...180 D2
Mortimer Sq W11 ...112 D6
Mortimer St W1 ...93 C2 239 B3
Mortimer Terr NW5 ...71 B4
Mortlake Cl CR0 ...220 A5
Mortlake Dr CR4 ...180 C2
Mortlake High St SW14 ...133 B2
Mortlake Rd Ilford IG1 ...79 B4
Newham E16 ...99 B1
Richmond SW14,TW9 ...132 C4
Mortlake Sta SW14 ...133 A2
Mortlock Cl SE15 ...140 B4
Mortlock Ct E12 ...77 D4
Morton Cl SM6 ...220 B1
Morton Cres N14 ...31 D6
Morton Ct UB5 ...64 A3
Morton Gdns SM6 ...219 C3
Morton Ho SE17 ...138 D6
West Norwood SE27 ...183 B5
Morton Mews SW5 ...255 C3
Morton Pl SE1 ...261 A5
Morton Rd E15 ...76 D1
N1 ...73 A1
Morden SM4 ...202 B4
Morton Way N14 ...31 D6
Morvale Cl DA17 ...125 B2
Morval Rd SW2 ...160 C6
Morven Rd SW17 ...158 D1
Morville St E3 ...97 C5
Morwell St WC1 ...239 D3
Moscow Pl W2 ...245 C6
Moscow Rd W2 ...113 D6 245 C6
Mosedale NW1 ...231 D1
Moseley Way SE10 ...120 D3
Moselle Ave N22 ...32 C1
Moselle Cl N8 ...50 B6
Moselle Ho 2 N17 ...33 D3
Moselle Pl N17 ...33 D3
Moselle Sch N17 ...51 A6
Tottenham N17 ...33 C1
Moselle St N17 ...33 D3
Mosque Terr E1 ...96 A2
Mosque Tower 24 E1 ...96 A2
Mossborough Cl N12 ...29 D4
Mossbury Rd SW11 ...136 C2
Moss Cl E1 ...96 A2
Pinner HA5 ...23 A1
Mossdown Cl DA17 ...125 C2
Mossford Ct IG6 ...56 D6
Mossford Gn IG6 ...57 A6
Mossford St E3 ...97 B3
Moss Gdns
Feltham TW13 ...150 A2
South Croydon CR2 ...222 D1
Moss Hall Cres N12 ...30 A4
Moss Hall Ct N12 ...29 D4
Moss Hall Gr N12 ...29 D4
Moss Hall Jun & Inf Schs
N12 ...29 D4
Mossington Gdns SE16 ...118 C2
Moss La HA5 ...23 A1
Mosslea Rd BR2 ...209 D4
BR6 ...227 A5
Penge SE20 ...184 C4
Mossop St SW3 ...114 C2 257 B4
Moss Rd RM10 ...81 C1
Mossville Gdns SM4 ...201 B5
Mosswell Ho 4 N10 ...31 A3
Moston Cl UB3 ...105 D1
Mostyn Ave HA9 ...66 B3
Mostyn Gdns NW10 ...90 D5
Mostyn Gr E3 ...97 C5
Mostyn Lo N5 ...73 A4
Mostyn Rd HA8 ...27 C3
SW9 ...138 C4
Bushey WD23 ...8 A6
Merton SW19 ...179 B1
Mosul Way BR2 ...210 A3
Motcomb St
SW1 ...115 A3 258 A6
Moth Cl SM6 ...220 A1
Mothers Sq The 13 E5 ...74 B4
Motley Ave EC2 ...243 A6
Motley St SW8 ...137 C3
Motspur Park Sta KT3 ...200 B4
Motspur Pk KT3 ...200 A3
Mottingham Ct SE9 ...166 B3
Mottingham Gdns SE9 ...165 D3
Mottingham Prim Sch
SE9 ...166 B1
Mottingham Rd N9 ...18 D4
SE9 ...166 B1
Mottingham Sta SE9 ...166 B3
Mottisfont Rd SE2 ...124 B2
Moules Ct SE5 ...139 A5
Moulins Rd E9 ...74 C1
Moulsford Ho 5 N7 ...72 A3
32 W2 ...91 C2
Moulton Ave TW3,TW5 ...129 B3
Moundfield Rd N16 ...52 A3
Mound The SE9 ...166 C1
Mounsey Ho 10 W10 ...91 A4
Mountacre Cl SE26 ...183 D6
Mount Adon Pk SE21,
SE22 ...162 A4
Mountague Pl 2 E14 ...120 A6
Mountain Ho SE11 ...260 C2
Mountaire Ct NW9 ...45 B4
Mount Angelus Rd
SW15 ...155 D4
Mount Ararat Rd TW10 ...154 A6
Mount Arlington 3
BR2 ...186 C1
Mount Ash Rd SE26 ...162 B1
Mount Ave Chingford E4 ...19 D1
Ealing W5 ...87 D2
Southall UB1 ...85 C1
Mountbatten Cl SE18 ...145 C6
6 West Norwood SE19 ...183 C5
Mountbatten Ct IG9 ...21 D2
Mountbatten Gdns BR3 ...207 A5
Mountbatten Ho N6 ...49 A2
Mountbatten Mews
SW18 ...158 A3
Mountbel Rd HA7 ...25 A1
Mount Carmel RC Coll
N19 ...49 D1
Mount Carmel RC Sec Sch
N7 ...72 B3
Mount Cl BR1 ...188 A2
Cockfosters EN4 ...3 A1
Ealing W5 ...87 C2
Mountcombe Cl KT6 ...198 A2
Mountcombe Ho SW17 ...180 B5
Mount Ct
6 Kingston KT2 ...176 D3
West Wickham BR4 ...224 C6
Mount Culver Ave DA14 ...190 D4
Mount Dr HA9 ...67 A6
Bexley DA6 ...169 A6
Harrow HA2,HA5 ...41 B4
Mountearl Gdns SW16,
SW2 ...160 B1
Mount Eaton Ct W5 ...87 C2
Mount Echo Ave E4 ...19 D3
Mount Echo Dr E4 ...19 D3
Mount Ephraim La
SW16 ...159 D1
Mount Ephraim Rd
SW16 ...159 D1
Mount Felix KT12 ...193 D1
Mountfield NW2 ...69 B6
Mountfield Cl SE6 ...164 B4
Mountfield Ct SE13 ...164 B5
Mountfield Rd N3 ...47 C6
Ealing W5 ...88 A1
Wallend E6 ...100 C4
Mountford Ho EN2 ...4 D1
Mountford St 4 E1 ...96 A1
Mountfort Cres N1 ...72 C1
Mountfort Terr 1 N1 ...72 C1
Mount Gdns SE26 ...162 B1
Mount Gr HA8 ...27 B6
Mountgrove Rd N5 ...73 A5
Mount House (St Martha's
Senior Sch) The EN4 ...1 C4
Mounthurst Rd BR2 ...208 D2
Mountington Park Cl
HA3 ...43 D3
Mountjoy Cl SE2 ...124 B4
Mountjoy Ho EC2 ...242 A3
Mount Lo N6 ...49 C3
Mount Lodge SW4 ...137 D1
Mount Mews TW12 ...173 D2
Mount Mills EC1 ...234 D1
Mount Nod Rd SW16,
SW2 ...160 B1
Mount Olive Ct W7 ...108 C4
Mount Park Ave HA1 ...64 C6
Mount Park Cres W5 ...87 D1
Mount Park Rd Ealing W5 ...87 D1
Harrow HA1 ...64 B5
Pinner HA5 ...40 A4
Mount Pk SM5 ...219 A1
Mount Pl 7 W3 ...110 D5
Mount Pleasant N14 ...15 D4
WC1 ...94 C3 241 A5
Cockfosters EN4 ...2 D1
Ilford IG1 ...79 A3
Ruislip HA4 ...62 D6
Wembley HA0 ...88 B6
West Norwood SE27 ...183 A6
Mount Pleasant Cres N4 ...50 B2
Mount Pleasant Hill E5 ...74 C6
Mount Pleasant La E5 ...52 B1
Mount Pleasant Pl SE18 ...123 B2
Mount Pleasant Rd E17 ...35 A1
Mount Pleasant Rd continued
SE13 ...164 A5
Ealing W5 ...87 C3
Kingston KT3 ...199 A6
Tottenham N17 ...33 C1
Willesden NW10 ...90 C6
Mount Pleasant Villas
N4 ...50 B2
Mount Prim Sch The
KT3 ...199 A6
Mount Rd NW2 ...68 C5
NW4 ...46 A3
Bexley DA6 ...169 A6
Chessington KT9 ...214 B3
Dagenham RM8 ...59 B1
East Barnet EN4 ...14 C6
Feltham TW13 ...151 A1
Hayes UB3 ...106 A4
Kingston KT3 ...199 B6
Mitcham CR4 ...180 C1
South Norwood SE19 ...183 B4
Wimbledon SW18,SW19 ...157 D2
Mount Row W1 ...115 B6 248 C5
Mount Sch NW7 ...28 C5
Mountside HA7 ...25 A2
Mounts Pond Rd SE3,
SE13 ...142 B3
Mount Sq The NW3 ...70 A5
Mount St W1 ...115 A6 248 B5
Mount Stewart Ave HA3 ...43 D2
Mount Stewart Jun & Inf
Schs HA3 ...43 D2
Mount Terr E1 ...96 B2
Mount The DA6 ...169 D6
E5 ...74 B6
HA9 ...67 A6
N20 ...14 A2
N2 ...30 C1
NW3 ...70 A5
W8 ...245 A3
Croydon CR2 ...221 A3
Kingston KT3 ...199 D6
North Cheam KT4 ...216 B4
Northolt UB5 ...63 D3
Mount Tyndal NW3 ...48 B1
Mount Vernon NW3 ...70 A4
Mountview NW7 ...11 B1
5 Streatham SW16 ...160 B1
Mount View Ealing W5 ...87 D3
Enfield EN2 ...4 B5
Southall UB2 ...106 D2
Northwood HA6 ...22 A4
Mountview Cl NW11 ...48 A1
Mountview Ct N8 ...50 D5
Mount View Rd N4 ...50 B3
NW9 ...45 B4
Chingford E4 ...20 B4
Claygate KT10 ...213 B1
Mountview Theatre Sch
N8 ...50 A3
Mount Villas SE27 ...160 D1
Mountwood KT8 ...195 D6
Mountwood Ho W5 ...87 D3
Mourne Ho NW3 ...70 A2
Movers La IG11 ...101 C6
Mowat Ct 3 KT4 ...215 D6
Mowatt Cl N19 ...49 D1
Mowbray Ct
South Norwood SE19 ...183 D2
Wood Green N22 ...32 C2
Mowbray Gdns UB5 ...85 C6
Mowbray Ho 5 N2 ...30 B1
Mowbray Rd NW6 ...69 A1
Edgware HA8 ...26 C6
New Barnet EN5 ...14 A6
Richmond TW10 ...153 C1
South Norwood SE19 ...183 D2
Mowlem Prim Sch E2 ...96 C5
Mowlem St E2 ...96 B5
Mowlem Trad Est N17 ...34 C3
Mowll St SW9 ...138 C5
Moxon Cl E13 ...98 D5
Moxon St W1 ...93 A2 238 A3
Barnet EN5 ...1 B2
Moye Cl 9 E2 ...96 A5
Moyers Rd E10 ...54 A2
Moylan Rd W6 ...135 A6 264 B5
Moyle Ho SW1 ...269 B6
Moyne Ho 10 SW9 ...138 D1
Moyne Pl NW10 ...88 C5
Moynihan Dr N21 ...16 A6
Moys Cl CR0 ...204 A3
Moyser Rd SW16 ...181 B5
Mozart St W10 ...91 B4
Mt Carmel RC Prim Sch
W5 ...109 C3
Muchelney Rd SM4 ...202 A3
Mudchute Sta E14 ...119 D2
Mudie Ho 8 SW2 ...160 A4
Muggeridge Cl CR2 ...221 B3
Muggeridge Rd RM10 ...81 D4
Muir Cl SW18 ...158 C5
Muirdown Ave SW14 ...133 B1
Muirfield W3 ...89 C1
Muirfield Cl 23 SE16 ...118 B1
South Oxhey WD19 ...22 C6
Muirfield Cres E14 ...119 D3
Muirfield Gn WD19 ...22 C6
Muirfield Rd WD19 ...22 C6
Muirkirk Rd SE6 ...164 A3
Muir Rd E5 ...74 A5
Muir St E16 ...122 A5
Mulbarton Ct BR7 ...189 B4
Mulberry Ave TW19 ...148 A3
Mulberry Bsns Ctr SE16 ...118 D4
Mulberry Cl N8 ...50 A4
NW3 ...70 B4
NW4 ...46 C6
SE22 ...162 A5
SE7 ...143 D6
Mulberry Cl continued
SW3 ...266 D5
Barnet EN4 ...2 B1
Chingford E4 ...19 C2
Northolt UB5 ...85 A5
Streatham SW16 ...181 C6
Mulberry Cres
Brentford TW8 ...131 C5
West Drayton UB7 ...104 C4
Mulberry Ct 1 E11 ...76 B4
EC1 ...234 D1
N5 ...72 D3
NW10 ...67 B2
10 W9 ...91 B4
Barking IG11 ...79 D1
4 Surbiton KT6 ...197 D2
Twickenham TW1 ...152 D1
Mulberry Ho 1 E2 ...96 C4
8 SE8 ...141 B6
Mulberry House Sch
NW2 ...69 A3
Mulberry La CR0 ...205 D1
Mulberry Mews SE14 ...141 B4
2 Wallington SM6 ...219 C2
Mulberry Par UB7 ...104 C4
Mulberry Pl W6 ...112 A1
Mulberry Rd E8 ...73 D1
Mulberry Sch for Girls
E1 ...96 B1
Stepney E1 ...118 B6
Mulberry St 5 E1 ...96 A1
Mulberry Trees TW17 ...193 B2
Mulberry Way Ilford IG6 ...57 A5
Woodford E18 ...37 B1
Mulberry Wlk
SW3 ...136 B6 266 D6
Mulgrave Chambers
SM2 ...217 D2
Mulgrave Hall SM2 ...217 D2
Mulgrave Ho 20 SE18 ...122 B2
Mulgrave Manor SM2 ...217 D2
Mulgrave Prim Sch
SE18 ...122 D3
Mulgrave Rd NW10 ...67 D4
SE18 ...122 C2
W14 ...264 C6
Belmont SM2 ...217 C2
Ealing W5 ...87 D3
Harrow HA1 ...65 A6
South Croydon CR0 ...221 B5
Mulholland Cl CR4 ...181 B1
Mulkern Rd N19 ...49 D1
Mullard Ho WC1 ...239 C4
Mullards Cl CR4 ...202 D1
Mullens Ho 7 SW15 ...156 C6
Mullen Twr EC1 ...241 A5
Muller Ho SE18 ...122 C1
Mullet Gdns 5 E2 ...96 A4
Mulletsfield WC1 ...233 B1
Mull Ho 13 E3 ...97 B5
Mullins Path SW14 ...133 B2
Mullion Cl HA3 ...23 D2
Mullion Wlk WD19 ...22 D6
Mulready St NW8 ...237 A5
Multi Way W3 ...111 C4
Multon Ho E9 ...74 C1
Multon Rd SW18 ...158 B4
Mulvaney Way SE1 ...252 D1
Mumford Rd SE24 ...160 D6
Muncaster Cl TW15 ...170 C6
Muncaster Rd SW11 ...159 A6
Ashford TW15 ...170 D5
Muncies Mews SE6 ...164 A2
Mundania Ct SE22 ...162 B5
Mundania Rd SE22 ...162 C5
Munday Ho SE1 ...262 C5
Munday Rd E16 ...121 A6
Munden Ho 5 E3 ...97 D4
Munden St W14 ...113 A2 254 A4
Mundesley Cl WD19 ...22 C6
Mundford Rd E5 ...74 C6
Mundon Gdns IG1 ...57 B1
Mund St W14 ...113 B1 254 D1
Mundy Ho 8 W10 ...91 A4
Mundy St N1 ...95 C4
Mungo-Park Cl WD23 ...8 A2
Munnery Way BR6 ...226 D6
Munnings Gdns TW7 ...152 B6
Munro Ho SE1 ...251 A1
SE1 ...252 D1
Munro Mews W10 ...91 A2
Munro Rd WD23 ...8 A6
Munslow Gdns SM1 ...218 B4
Munstead Ct 12 SM2 ...218 A1
Munster Ave TW4 ...151 A6
Munster Ct Fulham SW6 ...135 B3
Teddington TW11 ...175 C4
Munster Gdns N13 ...33 A6
Munster Rd
SW6 ...135 A4 264 B2
Teddington TW11 ...175 C4
Munster Residences
SW6 ...264 B2
Munster Sq NW1 ...93 B3 238 D6
Munton Rd SE1,
SE17 ...117 A2 262 B4
Murchison Ave DA5 ...169 A3
Murchison Ho 1 W10 ...91 A2
Murchison Rd E10 ...76 A6
Murdoch Ho 4 SE16 ...118 C3
Murdock Cl E16 ...98 D1
Murdock St SE15 ...140 B6
Murfett Cl SW19 ...157 A2
Muriel Ct 17 E10 ...53 D2
Muriel St N1 ...94 B6 233 D4
Murillo Rd SE13 ...142 C1
Murley Ct N21 ...17 A4
Murphy Ho SE1 ...261 D6
Murphy St SE1 ...116 C4 251 A1
Murray Ave BR1 ...187 B1
Murray Ave continued
Hounslow TW3 ...151 D6
Murray Cres HA5 ...22 D2
Murray Ct 5 HA1 ...42 D3
Murray Gr N1 ...95 B5 235 C3
Murray Ho 21 SE18 ...122 B2
Murray Mews NW1 ...71 D1
Murray Rd W5 ...109 C2
Richmond TW10 ...153 C2
Wimbledon SW19 ...178 D4
Murray Sq E16 ...121 B6
Murray St NW1 ...71 D1
Murray Terr NW3 ...70 B4
Musard Rd W6 ...135 A6 264 B6
Musbury St E1 ...96 C1
Muscal W6 ...264 A6
Muscatel Pl SE5 ...139 C4
Muschamp Inf Sch SM5 ...218 C6
Muschamp Jun Sch
SM5 ...218 C6
Muschamp Rd SE15 ...139 D2
Carshalton SM1,SM5 ...218 C6
Muscott Ho 15 E2 ...96 A6
Muscovy Ho DA18 ...125 A4
Muscovy St EC3 ...253 B6
Museum Ho 7 E2 ...96 C4
Museum in Docklands*
E14 ...119 C6
Museum St WC1 ...94 A1 240 A2
Musgrave Cl EN4 ...2 A4
Musgrave Cres
SW6 ...135 C4 265 B2
Musgrave Ct SW11 ...267 A2
Musgrave Rd TW7 ...130 D4
Musgrove Ho 1 E9 ...74 D2
Musgrove Rd SE14 ...141 A4
Musical Mus The*
TW8 ...132 A6
Musjid Rd 7 SW11 ...136 B3
Muslim Coll The W5 ...110 C6
Mus of Garden History*
SE1 ...260 C5
Mus of London*
EC2 ...95 A2 242 A3
Mus of Richmond*
TW10 ...153 D6
Mus of the Great Eastern
Railway* E16 ...122 C4
Musquash Way TW4 ...128 C3
Muston Rd E5 ...74 B6
Mustow Pl 2 SW6 ...135 B3
Muswell Ave N10 ...31 B1
Muswell Hill N10 ...49 C6
Muswell Hill Bdwy N10 ...49 B6
Muswell Hill Jun & Inf Schs
N10 ...49 B6
Muswell Hill Pl N10 ...49 B5
Muswell Hill Rd N10 ...49 A4
Muswell Mews N10 ...49 B6
Muswell Rd N10 ...31 B1
Mutrix Rd NW6 ...91 C6
Mutton Pl NW1 ...71 A2
Muybridge Rd KT3 ...177 A1
Myatt Ct SE4 ...141 B3
Myatt Garden Prim Sch
SE4 ...141 B3
Myatt Ho SE5 ...138 D3
Myatt Rd SW9 ...138 D4
Myatts Field Ct SE5 ...139 A4
Mycenae Rd SE3 ...143 A6
Mychell Ho 8 SW19 ...180 A3
Myddelton Ave EN1 ...5 C5
Myddelton Cl EN1 ...5 D4
Myddelton Gdns N21 ...17 A4
Myddelton Ho N8 ...50 A6
Myddelton Pas
EC1 ...94 C4 234 B2
Myddelton Pk N20 ...14 B2
Myddelton Rd N8 ...50 A5
Myddelton Sq
EC1 ...94 C4 234 B2
Myddelton St
EC1 ...94 C4 234 B1
Myddleton Ave N4 ...73 A6
Myddleton Mews N22 ...32 A3
Myddleton Rd N22 ...32 A3
Myers Ho 5 SE5 ...139 A5
Myers La SE14 ...140 D6
Mylis Cl SE26 ...184 B6
Mylius Cl SE14 ...140 C4
Mylne Cl W6 ...112 A1
Mylne Ho TW7 ...17 B5
Mylne St EC1 ...234 A3
Mynterne Ct 16 SW19 ...156 D3
Myra St SE2 ...124 A2
Myrdle Ct 8 E1 ...96 A1
Myrdle St E1 ...96 A1
Myrna Cl SW19 ...180 C3
Myron Pl SE13 ...142 A2
Myrtle Alley SE18 ...122 C3
Myrtle Ave Hatton TW14 ...149 C6
Ruislip HA4 ...40 B2
Myrtle Cl
Barnet, London EN4 ...14 D3
Hillingdon UB8 ...82 B2
West Drayton UB7 ...104 B3
Myrtledene Rd SE2 ...124 A1
Myrtle Gdns W7 ...108 C5
Myrtle Gr Enfield EN2 ...5 B5
Kingston KT3 ...177 A1
Myrtle Ho SE14 ...140 D4
Myrtle Rd E17 ...53 A3
E6 ...100 A6
W3 ...111 A5
Croydon CR0 ...223 C5
Edmonton N13 ...17 B1
Hampton TW12 ...174 A4
Hounslow TW3 ...130 A3
Ilford IG1 ...78 D6
Sutton SM1 ...218 A3
Myrtle Wlk 20 N1 ...95 C5
Mysore Rd SW11 ...136 D1
Myton Rd SE21 ...161 B1
Mytton Ho SW8 ...270 C3

N

N1 Shopping Ctr
N1 ...94 C5 234 B4
Nadine St SE7 ...121 C1
Nadir Ct E11 ...55 A2
Naffenton Rise IG10 ...21 D6
Nagle Cl E17 ...36 B1
Nags Head N7 ...72 B4
Nags Head Ct EC1 ...242 B5
Nag's Head La DA16 ...146 B2
Nags Head Rd EN3 ...6 D1
Nainby Ho SE11 ...261 A3
Nairn Ct
3 Wallington SM6 ...219 C2
Wimbledon SW19 ...179 D4
Nairne Gr SE5,SE24 ...139 B1
Nairn Rd HA4 ...62 C2
Nairn St E14 ...98 A2
Naish Ct N1 ...233 B6
Nallhead Rd TW13 ...172 C5
Nalton Ho 4 NW6 ...70 A1
Namba Roy Cl SW16 ...182 B6
Namton Dr CR7,SW16 ...204 B5
Nan Clark's La NW7 ...11 D2
Nankin St E14 ...97 C1
Nansen Ct 1 E11 ...76 C6
Nansen Ho 7 NW10 ...67 B1
Nansen Rd SW11 ...137 A2
Nansen Village 5 N12 ...29 D6
Nant Ct NW2 ...69 B6
Nantes Cl SW18 ...136 A1
Nant Rd NW2 ...69 B6
Nant St E2 ...96 B4
Naoroji St WC1 ...234 A1
Napier 15 NW9 ...27 D2
Napier Ave E14 ...119 C1
Fulham SW6 ...135 B2
Napier Cl SE14,SE8 ...141 B5
W14 ...254 C6
West Drayton UB7 ...104 B3
Napier Ct N1 ...235 C4
SE12 ...165 B1
13 Croydon CR0 ...221 D6
Fulham SW6 ...135 B2
Hayes UB4 ...84 C3
1 Surbiton KT6 ...197 D2
Napier Gr N1 ...95 A5 235 B4
Napier Lo TW15 ...171 B4
Napier Pl W14 ...113 B3 254 C5
Napier Rd BR2 ...209 B5
DA17 ...125 B2
E11 ...76 C5
E15 ...98 C5
N17 ...51 C6
NW10 ...90 B4
W14 ...113 B3 254 C5
Ashford TW15 ...171 B3
Croydon SE25 ...206 B5
Enfield EN3 ...18 D6
Isleworth TW7 ...131 A1
South Croydon CR2 ...221 B1
Wallend E6 ...100 C5
Wembley HA0 ...65 D2
Napier Terr N1 ...72 D1
Napier Wlk TW15 ...171 B3
Napoleon Rd E5 ...74 B5
Twickenham TW1 ...153 B4
Napton Cl UB4 ...85 A3
Narbonne Ave SW4 ...159 C6
Narborough Cl UB10 ...61 A6
Narborough St SW6 ...135 D3
Narcissus Rd NW6 ...69 C3
Nardini 12 NW9 ...27 D2
Naresby Fold HA7 ...25 C4
Narford Rd E5 ...74 A6
Narrow Boat Cl SE28 ...123 B4
Narrow St E14 ...119 A6
6 Acton W3 ...110 D5
Narrow Way BR2 ...210 A3
Nascot St W12 ...90 C1
Naseby Cl NW6 ...70 A1
Hounslow TW7 ...130 C4
Naseby Ct DA14 ...189 D6
Naseby Rd
Dagenham RM10 ...81 C5
South Norwood SE19 ...183 B4
Nash Cl SM1 ...218 B5
Nash Ct HA3 ...43 B3
Nashe Ho SE1 ...262 C5
Nash Gn BR1 ...187 A4
Nash Ho 1 E17 ...53 D5
SW1 ...258 D1
Nash La BR2 ...225 A2
Nash Rd N9 ...18 C2
SE4 ...163 A6
Dagenham RM6 ...58 D5
Nash Street NW1 ...231 D2
Nash Way HA3 ...43 B3
Nasmyth St W6 ...112 B3
Nassau Path 6 SE28 ...124 C5
Nassau Rd SW13 ...133 D4
Nassau St W1 ...239 A3
Nassington Rd NW3 ...70 D4
Natalie Cl TW14 ...149 B4
Natalie Mews TW2 ...152 B1
Natal Rd Bowes Park N11 ...32 A4
Ilford IG1 ...78 D4
South Norwood CR7 ...205 B6
Streatham SW16 ...181 D4
Nathan Ct N9 ...18 C4

Nathan Ho SE11 ...261 B3
Nathaniel Cl E1 ...243 D3
Nathaniel Ct E17 ...53 A3
Nathans Rd HA0 ...65 C6
Nathan Way SE28,SE18 ...123 D3
National Army Mus★ SW3 ...136 D6 267 D6
National Fan Mus★ SE10 ...142 A5
National Film Theatre★ SE1 ...250 D4
National Gallery★ W1 ...115 D6 249 D5
National Hospital for Neurology & Neurosurgery N2 ...48 C5
National Hospl The WC1 ...94 A3 240 B5
National Maritime Mus★ SE10 ...142 B6
National Physical Laboratory TW11 ...174 C4
National Portrait Gallery★ W1 ...115 D6 249 D5
National Portrait Gallery (Annexe)★ SW1 ...115 D5 249 D4
National Postal Mus★ EC1 ...95 A1 242 A2
National Theatre SE1 ...116 B5 250 D4
National Wks TW4 ...129 B2
Nation Way E4 ...20 A3
Natural History Mus★ SW7 ...114 B3 256 C5
Nat West Twr★ EC2 ...243 A2
Nautilus Bldg The EC1 ...234 B2
Naval Row E14 ...120 A6
Navarino Gr E8 ...74 A2
Navarino Mans E8 ...74 A2
Navarino Rd E8 ...74 A2
Navarre Rd E6 ...100 A5
Navarre St E2 ...243 C6
Navenby Wlk 13 E3 ...97 C3
Navestock Cl E4 ...20 A1
Navestock Ho IG11 ...102 B5
Navigator Dr UB2 ...108 A4
Navy St SW4 ...137 D2
Nayland Ho SE6 ...186 A6
Naylor Gr EN3 ...18 D6
Naylor Ho SE17 ...262 D2
33 SW8 ...137 D3
5 W10 ...91 B4
Naylor Rd N20 ...14 A2
SE15 ...140 B5
Nazareth Cl SE15 ...140 B3
Nazrul St E2 ...95 D4
Neal Ave UB1 ...85 B3
Neal Cl HA6 ...22 A2
Nealden St SW9 ...138 B2
Neale Cl N2 ...48 A6
Neale Ct N10 ...31 B3
Neal St WC2 ...94 A1 240 A1
Neal's Yd WC2 ...240 A1
Near Acre NW9 ...27 D2
Neasden Cl NW10 ...67 C3
Neasden Junc NW10 ...67 C4
Neasden La NW10 ...67 B5
NW10 ...67 C3
Neasden La N NW10 ...67 C5
Neasden Sta NW10 ...67 C3
Neasham Rd RM8 ...80 B3
Neate St SE5 ...139 C6
SE5 ...139 D6
Neath Gdns SM4 ...202 A3
Neathouse Pl SW1 ...259 A4
Neats Acre HA4 ...39 B2
Neatscourt Rd E16 ...99 D2
Nebraska St SE1 ...117 B4 252 C1
Neckinger SE16 ...117 D3 263 D6
Neckinger Est SE16 ...263 D6
Neckinger St SE1 ...263 D6
Nectarine Way SE13 ...141 D3
Nedahall Ct 4 NW11 ...47 B2
Needham Ho SE11 ...261 A3
Needham Rd W11 ...91 C1
Needham Terr NW2 ...68 D5
Needleman St SE16 ...118 D4
Needwood Ho N4 ...51 A1
Neela Cl UB10 ...60 D4
Neeld Cres NW4 ...46 B4
Wembley HA9 ...66 C3
Neeld Ct HA9 ...66 C3
Neeld Par HA9 ...66 B3
Neil Cl TW15 ...171 A5
Neilson-Terry Ct 9 SW9 ...138 B1
Neil Wates Cres 18 SW2 ...160 C3
Nelgarde Rd SE6 ...163 C4
Nelland Ct SE6 ...163 B2
Nella Rd W6 ...134 D6
Nelldale Rd SE16 ...118 C2
Nellgrove Rd UB10 ...82 D3
Nell Gwynne Ave TW17 ...193 B3
Nell Gwynn Ho SW3 ...257 B3
Nello James Gdns SE27 ...183 B6
Nelson Cl 9 NW6 ...91 C4
East Bedfont TW14 ...149 D3
Hillingdon UB10 ...82 D4
Thornton Heath CR0 ...204 D1
Walton-on-T KT12 ...194 B1
Nelson Ct SE16 ...119 B5
Carshalton SM5 ...218 D5
Nelson Gdns E2 ...96 A4
Twickenham TW3,TW4 ...151 C5
Nelson Grove Rd SW19 ...180 A2
Nelson Ho 1 W5 ...88 A4
Nelson Hospl SW20 ...179 B1
Nelson La UB10 ...82 D4
Nelson Mandela Cl N10 ...31 A1
Nelson Mandela Rd SE3 ...143 C2
Nelson Pas EC1 ...235 B2
Nelson Pl N1 ...234 D3
Sidcup DA14 ...190 A6
Nelson Prim Sch
Twickenham TW2 ...151 D5
Wallend E6 ...100 C5
Nelson Rd N15 ...51 C5
N8 ...50 B3
SE10 ...142 A6
Ashford TW15 ...170 A5
Bromley BR2 ...209 C5
Chingford E4 ...35 D4
Edmonton N9 ...18 B2
Enfield EN3 ...18 D5
Erith DA17 ...125 B1
Harmondsworth TW6 ...126 B4
Harrow HA1 ...42 C1
Hillingdon UB10 ...82 D4
Merton SW19 ...180 A3
New Malden KT3 ...199 B4
Sidcup DA14 ...190 A6
Stanmore HA7 ...25 C4
Twickenham TW2,TW4 ...151 C5
Wanstead E11 ...55 B5
Nelson's Monument★ WC2 ...250 A4
Nelson Sq SE1 ...116 D4 251 C2
Nelsons Row SW4 ...137 D1
Nelson St E1 ...96 B1
E16 ...120 D6
E6 ...100 B5
Barking E6 ...100 C6
Nelson Terr N1 ...234 D3
Nelson Trad Est SW19 ...179 D2
Nemoure Rd W3 ...111 A6
Nene Gdns TW13 ...151 B2
Nene Rd TW6,UB7 ...126 D4
Nene Road Rdbt TW6 ...126 D4
Nepaul Rd 17 SW11 ...136 C2
Nepean St SW15 ...156 A4
Neptune Ct 6 E14 ...119 C2
Neptune Ho 14 N16 ...73 C3
2 SE16 ...118 C3
Neptune Rd
Harlington TW6 ...127 A4
Harrow HA1 ...42 B3
Neptune St SE16 ...118 C3
Nero Ct 6 TW8 ...131 D5
Nesbit Cl SE3 ...142 C2
Nesbit Rd SE9 ...143 D1
Nesbitt Ho DA6 ...169 D6
Nesbitt Sq SE19 ...183 C3
Nesham Ho 14 N1 ...95 C6
Nesham St E1 ...118 A5
Ness St 9 SE16 ...118 A3
Nesta Rd IG8 ...36 D4
Nestle's Ave UB3 ...105 D3
Nestor Ave N21 ...16 D5
Nestor Ho 13 E2 ...96 B5
Netheravon Rd W4 ...111 D1
Ealing W7 ...108 D5
Netheravon Rd S W4 ...111 D1
Netherbury Rd W5 ...109 D3
Netherby Gdns EN2 ...4 A1
Netherby Ho 23 SW8 ...137 D3
Netherby Rd SE23 ...162 C4
Nether Cl N3 ...29 C3
Nethercombe Ho 1 SE3 ...143 A6
Nethercott Ho 27 E3 ...97 D4
Nethercourt Ave N3 ...29 C4
Netherfield Gdns IG11 ...79 B1
Netherfield Rd N12 ...29 D5
Upper Tooting SW17 ...159 A1
Netherford Rd SW4 ...137 C3
Netherhall Gdns NW3 ...70 A3
Netherhall Way NW3 ...70 A3
Netherlands Rd EN5 ...14 B5
Netherleigh Cl N6 ...49 B1
Nether St N12 ...30 A5
N3 ...29 D4
Netherton Gr SW10 ...136 A6 266 B5
Netherton Rd N15 ...51 B3
Isleworth TW1 ...153 B6
Netherwood 19 N2 ...30 B1
Netherwood Rd W14 ...112 D4
Netherwood St NW6 ...69 C2
Nethewode Ct DA17 ...125 D3
Netley 18 SE5 ...139 C4
Netley Cl Cheam SM3 ...216 D3
New Addington CR0 ...224 A1
Netley Ct IG2 ...57 B4
Netley Dr KT12 ...195 B2
Netley Gdns SM4 ...202 A2
Netley Prim Sch NW1 ...93 C4 232 A1
Netley Rd E17 ...53 B4
Brentford TW8 ...132 A6
Cheam SM4 ...202 A2
Ilford IG2 ...57 B4
Netley Rd (W) TW6 ...127 B4
Netley St NW1 ...93 C4 232 A1
Nettlecombe NW1 ...71 D1
Nettleden Ave HA9 ...66 C2
Nettleden Ho SW3 ...257 B3
Nettlefold Pl SE27 ...160 D1
Nettlestead Cl 16 BR3 ...185 C3
Nettleton Rd SE14 ...140 D4
Harlington TW6 ...126 D4
Ickenham UB10 ...60 B4
Nettlewood Rd SW16 ...181 D3
Neuchatel Rd SE6 ...163 B2
Nevada Cl KT3 ...199 A5
Nevada St SE10 ...142 A6
Nevena Ct 3 SW2 ...160 C6
Nevern Mans SW5 ...255 A2
Nevern Pl SW5 ...113 C2 255 B3
Nevern Rd SW5 ...255 A3
Nevern Sq SW5 ...113 C2 255 B3
Nevil Ho 7 SW9 ...138 D3
Nevill Ct SW10 ...266 A4
Neville Ave KT3 ...177 B2
Neville Cl DA15 ...189 D6
E11 ...76 D5
NW1 ...232 D3
NW6 ...91 B5
SE15 ...140 A4
17 SE15 ...140 A5
Acton W3 ...111 A4
Hounslow TW3 ...129 D3
Neville Ct 10 SW12 ...159 C4
Neville Dr N2 ...48 A3
Neville Gdns RM8 ...80 D5
Neville Gill Cl SW18 ...157 D5
Neville Ho N11 ...31 A6
Neville Pl N22 ...32 B2
Neville Rd E7 ...77 B1
NW6 ...91 B5
Dagenham RM8 ...80 D5
Ealing W5 ...87 D3
Kingston KT1 ...176 C1
Richmond TW10 ...153 C2
Thornton Heath CR0 ...205 B2
Neville's Ct NW2 ...68 A5
Neville St SW7 ...114 B1 256 C2
Neville Terr SW7 ...256 C2
Neville Wlk SM5 ...202 C2
Nevill Rd N16 ...73 C5
Nevin Dr E4 ...19 D3
Nevin Ho UB3 ...105 A3
Nevinson Cl SW18 ...158 B5
Nevis Rd SW17 ...159 A2
Nevitt Ho N1 ...235 D3
New Acres Rd SE28 ...123 C5
Newall Ho SE1 ...262 B6
Newall Rd TW6 ...127 A4
Newark Cres NW10 ...89 B4
Newark Ct KT12 ...194 C1
Newark Ho 3 SW9 ...138 D3
Newark Knok E6 ...100 C2
Newark Par NW4 ...46 A6
Newark Rd CR2 ...221 B2
Newark St E1 ...96 B2
Newark Way NW4 ...46 A6
New Ash Cl N2 ...48 B6
New Barn Cl SM6 ...220 B2
New Barnet Sta EN5 ...14 B6
New Barns Ave CR4 ...203 D5
New Barn St E13 ...99 B3
New Beckenham Sta BR3 ...185 B3
New Belmont Ho 4 SE23 ...162 C3
New Bentham Ct 11 N1 ...73 A1
Newbery Ho N1 ...73 A1
Newbiggin Path WD19 ...22 C6
Newbold Cotts 4 E1 ...96 C1
Newbolt Ave SM3 ...216 D3
Newbolt Ho SE17 ...262 C2
Newbolt Rd HA7 ...24 D5
New Bond St W1 ...115 B6 248 D6
Newborough Gn KT3 ...199 B5
Newborough Ho SW19 ...180 B3
New Brent St NW4 ...46 C4
Newbridge Ct SW17 ...180 A6
Newbridge Point 3 SE23 ...162 D1
New Bridge St EC4 ...94 D1 241 C1
New Broad St EC2 ...95 C2 243 A3
New Broadway
Ealing W5 ...109 D6
7 Hillingdon UB10 ...82 D3
Teddington TW12 ...174 B5
New Bsns Ctr The NW10 ...89 D4
Newburgh Rd W3 ...111 A5
Newburgh St W1 ...239 B1
New Burlington Mews W1 ...249 A6
New Burlington Pl W1 ...249 A6
New Burlington St W1 ...249 A6
Newburn Ho SE11 ...260 D2
Newburn St SE11 ...116 B1 260 D2
Newbury Ave EN3 ...7 B6
Newbury Cl UB5 ...63 B2
Newbury Cotts 4 IG2 ...57 A3
Newbury Ct DA14 ...189 D6
E5 ...75 A3
7 Wanstead E11 ...55 A5
Newbury Gdns KT19 ...215 D4
Newbury Ho SW9 ...138 D3
13 W2 ...91 D1
Wood Green N22 ...32 A2
Newbury Mews NW5 ...71 A2
Newbury Park Prim Sch IG2 ...57 B3
Newbury Park Sta IG2 ...57 B3
Newbury Rd BR2 ...209 A6
Chingford E4 ...36 A4
Harmondsworth TW6 ...126 B4
Ilford IG2 ...57 C3
Newbury St EC1 ...242 A4
Newbury Way UB5 ...63 B2
New Butt La SE8 ...141 C5
Newby NW1 ...232 A2
Newby Cl EN1 ...5 C3
Newby Pl E14 ...120 A6
Newby St SW8 ...137 B2
New Caledonian Wharf SE16 ...119 B3
New Campden Ct 7 NW3 ...70 A4
Newcastle Cl EC4 ...241 C2
Newcastle Ct EC4 ...252 B6
Newcastle Ho W1 ...238 A4
Newcastle Pl W2 ...92 B2 236 D4
Newcastle Row EC1 ...241 B5
New Cavendish St W1 ...93 B2 238 C3
New Change EC4 ...95 A1 242 A1
New Chapel Sq TW13 ...150 B3
New Charles St EC1 ...234 D2
New Church Ct 3 SE19 ...184 A3
New Church Rd SE5 ...139 B6
32 SE5 ...139 A5
New City Prim Sch E13 ...99 C4
New City Rd E13 ...99 C4
New Cl Feltham TW13 ...173 A5
Morden SW19 ...202 A6
New Colebrooke Ct SM5 ...219 A1
New College Ct 6 NW3 ...70 A2
New College Mews 4 N1 ...72 C1
New College Par 1 NW3 ...70 B1
Newcombe Ho N5 ...73 A3
Newcombe Pk NW7 ...27 C5
Wembley HA0 ...88 B6
Newcombe Rise UB7 ...82 A1
Newcombe St W8 ...245 B4
Newcome Gdns SW16 ...182 A6
Newcome Ho E5 ...74 B5
Newcomen Ho 5 NW5 ...71 B4
Newcomen Rd E11 ...76 D5
SW11 ...136 B2
Newcomen St SE1 ...117 B4 252 C2
New Compton St WC2 ...94 A1 240 A1
New Concordia Wharf SE1 ...253 D2
Newcourt Ho 26 E2 ...96 B4
Newcourt St NW8 ...92 C5 230 A3
New Covent Garden Flower Market SW8 ...138 A6 270 A5
New Covent Garden Fruit & Vegetable Mkt SW8 ...137 D5 269 C3
New Crescent Yd 1 NW10 ...89 D5
Newcroft Cl UB8 ...82 B2
New Cross SE14 ...141 B5
New Cross Gate SE14 ...140 D4
New Cross Gate Sta SE14 ...141 A5
New Cross Hospl SE14 ...140 C5
New Cross Rd SE14 ...141 A4
New Cross Sta SE14 ...141 B5
New Ct EC4 ...241 A1
N16 ...51 B1
13 NW3 ...70 A4
Northolt UB5 ...63 D3
Newdales Cl N9 ...18 A2
Newdene Ave UB5 ...84 D5
New Den (Millwall FC) The SE16 ...118 C1
Newdigate Ho 5 E14 ...97 B1
6 Kingston KT2 ...176 D4
Newell St E14 ...97 B1
New Eltham Sta SE9 ...166 D3
New End NW3 ...70 A5
New End Prim Sch NW3 ...70 A4
New End Sq NW3 ...70 B4
New England Est IG11 ...101 A5
Newent Cl SE15 ...139 C5
Carshalton SM5 ...202 D1
New Farm Ave BR2 ...209 A5
New Ferry App SE18 ...122 C3
New Fetter La EC4 ...94 C1 241 B2
Newfield Cl TW12 ...173 C2
Newfield Prim Sch NW10 ...67 D1
Newfield Rise NW2 ...68 B5
New Furness Prim Sch The NW10 ...90 A5
Newgale Gdns HA8 ...26 B2
New Garden Dr UB7 ...104 A4
Newgate CR0 ...205 A1
Newgate Cl TW13 ...151 A1
Newgate St EC1 ...94 D1 241 D2
Chingford E4 ...20 C1
New Globe Wlk SE1 ...252 A4
New Goulston St E1 ...243 C2
New Green Pl SE19 ...183 C4
Newham Acad of Music E6 ...100 A6
Newham Coll of FE E6 ...100 B5
Newham Coll of F Ed (Royal Docks Campus) E16 ...123 A5
Newham Ctr for Mental Health E16 ...99 D3
Newham General Hospl E13 ...99 C3
Newham Gn N22 ...32 C2
Newham Ho IG10 ...21 D5
Newham Sch of Nursing E3 ...97 D3
Newham Sixth Form Coll E13 ...99 A3
Newham's Row SE1 ...253 B1
Newham Way E13 ...99 B2
E6 ...100 B3
Newhaven Cl UB3 ...105 D2
Newhaven Cres TW15 ...171 B5
Newhaven Gdns SE9 ...143 D1
Newhaven La 3 E16 ...99 A2
Newhaven Rd SE25 ...205 B4
New Heston Rd TW5 ...129 B5
Newhouse 5 KT3 ...199 C2
Newhouse Ave RM6 ...58 D6
Newhouse Cl KT3 ...199 C2
Newhouse Wlk SM4 ...202 A2
Newick Cl DA5 ...169 D5
Newick Rd E5 ...74 C5
Newing Gn BR1 ...187 D3
Newington Barrow Way N7 ...72 B5
Newington Butts SE1,SE11 ...116 D2 261 D3
Newington Cswy SE1 ...117 A3 262 A6
Newington Green Mans N16 ...73 B3
Newington Green Prim Sch N16 ...73 B3
Newington Green Rd N1 ...73 B3
Newington Ind Est SE17 ...262 A3
New Inn Broadway EC2 ...243 B6
New Inn Pas WC2 ...240 D1
New Inn Sq EC2 ...243 B6
New Inn St EC2 ...243 B6
New Inn Yd EC2 ...95 C3 243 B6
New James Ct SE15 ...140 B2
New Jubilee Ct 1 IG8 ...37 A3
New Kelvin Ave TW11 ...174 C4
New Kent Rd SE1 ...117 A2 262 B4
New King's Prim Sch SW6 ...135 B3
New Kings Rd SW6 ...135 C3
New King's Rd SW6 ...135 C3 265 B1
New King St SE8 ...141 C6
Newland Cl HA5 ...23 B4
Newland Ct EC1 ...242 C6
Wembley HA9 ...66 C6
Newland Dr EN1 ...6 B4
Newland Gdns W13 ...109 A4
Newland Ho N8 ...50 A6
17 SE14 ...140 D6
Newland House Sch TW1 ...174 D6
Newland House Sch Annex TW1 ...174 D6
Newland Rd N8 ...50 A6
Newlands NW1 ...232 A2
Newlands Ave KT7 ...196 C1
Newlands Cl Edgware HA8 ...10 A1
Southall UB2 ...107 A1
Wembley HA0 ...65 C2
Newlands Croft SE20 ...184 D4
Newlands Ct 8 SE9 ...166 C5
Streatham SW16 ...182 A5
Newlands Pk SE26 ...184 D5
Newlands Pl EN5 ...12 D6
Newlands Quay E1 ...118 C6
Newlands Rd
Thornton Heath SW16 ...182 A1
Woodford IG8 ...20 D2
Newland St E16 ...122 B5
Newlands The
Thames Ditton KT7 ...196 C1
Wallington SM6 ...219 D1
Newlands Way KT9 ...213 C3
Newling Cl E6 ...100 B1
New London St EC3 ...253 B6
New Lydenburg Commercial Est E16 ...121 C3
New Lydenburg St SE7 ...121 C3
Newlyn NW1 ...232 B5
Newlyn Cl Hillingdon UB8 ...82 C2
Orpington BR6 ...227 D4
Newlyn Gdns HA2 ...41 B2
Newlyn Rd DA16 ...145 D3
Barnet EN5 ...1 B1
Tottenham N17 ...33 D2
New Malden Sta KT3 ...199 C6
Newman Ct BR1 ...187 A2
Newman Pas W1 ...239 B3
Newman Rd BR1 ...187 A2
E13 ...99 B4
E17 ...52 D4
Hayes UB3 ...106 B6
Thornton Heath CR0 ...204 B1
Newman's Ct EC3 ...242 D1
Newman's Row WC2 ...240 D3
Newman St W1 ...93 C2 239 B3
Newman's Way EN4 ...2 A4
Newmarket Ave UB5 ...63 D3
Newmarket Gn SE9 ...165 D4
Newmarsh Rd SE28 ...123 D5
Newmill Ho E3 ...98 A3
New Mill Rd BR5 ...190 C2
Newminster Rd SM4 ...202 A3
Newmount NW3 ...70 B3
New Mount St E15 ...76 B1
Newnes Path SW15 ...134 B1
Newnham Ave HA4 ...40 C1
Newnham Cl
Loughton IG10 ...21 D5
Northolt UB5 ...64 A2
South Norwood CR7 ...183 A1
Newnham Gdns UB5 ...64 A2
Newnham Ho
Catford SE6 ...164 A1
9 Putney SW15 ...156 D5
Newnham Jun & Inf Schs HA4 ...40 C1
Newnham Lo 10 DA17 ...125 C1
Newnham Rd N22 ...32 C2
Newnhams Cl BR1 ...210 B6
Newnham Terr SE1 ...261 A6
Newnham Way HA3 ...44 A4
New North Pl EC2 ...243 A6
New North Rd N1 ...95 B6 235 C5
New North Road Bridge N1 ...235 C5
New North St WC1 ...94 B2 240 C4
Newnton Cl N4 ...51 B2
New Oak Rd N2 ...30 A1
New Oxford St WC1 ...94 A1 240 A2
New Palace Yd SW1 ...116 A4 250 A1
New Par Ashford TW15 ...170 B6
Yiewsley UB7 ...104 A5
New Park Ave N13 ...17 B1
New Park Cl UB5 ...63 A2
New Park Ct 26 SW2 ...160 A4
New Park Est N18 ...34 C5
New Park Ho N13 ...32 B6
New Park Par 14 SW2 ...160 A4
New Park Rd
Ashford TW15 ...171 A5
Streatham SW2 ...160 A4
New Pl CR0 ...223 C2
New Place Sq SE16 ...118 B3
New Plaistow Rd E15 ...98 C6
New Pond Par HA4 ...62 A5
Newport Ave E13 ...99 B3
E14 ...120 B6
Newport Cl EN3 ...7 A6
Newport Ct WC2 ...249 D6
Newport Ho E3 ...97 A4
Newport Jun & Inf Schs E10,E11 ...76 A6
Newport Lo 2 EN1 ...17 C6
Newport Mead WD19 ...22 D6
Newport Pl WC2 ...249 D6
Newport Rd E10 ...76 B6
E17 ...53 A5
Barnes SW13 ...134 A4
Harmondsworth TW6 ...126 C4
Hayes UB4 ...83 B2
Newport St SE11 ...116 B2 260 D4
New Priory Ct 9 NW6 ...69 C1
Newquay Cres HA2 ...63 A6
Newquay Ho SE11 ...261 A2
Newquay Rd SE6 ...164 A2
New Quebec St W1 ...237 D1
New Rd DA16 ...146 B3
E1 ...96 B2
N10 ...30 C2
N8 ...50 A4
NW7 ...29 A3
SE2 ...124 D1
Brentford TW8 ...109 D1
Carshalton CR4 ...203 A1
Chingford E4 ...36 A6
Dagenham RM10 ...103 D5
East Bedfont TW14 ...149 B5
East Bedfont TW14 ...150 B3
East Molesey KT8 ...195 C6
Edmonton N9 ...18 A2
Elstree WD6 ...9 D5
Esher KT10 ...212 A4
Feltham TW13 ...173 A5
Harlington TW6,UB7 ...127 A5
Harrow HA1 ...64 D4
Hillingdon UB8 ...83 A2
Hounslow TW3 ...129 D1
Ilford IG3 ...79 C6
Kingston KT2 ...176 C3
Littleton TW17 ...192 D6
Richmond TW10 ...175 C6
Tottenham N22 ...33 A2
New Rd Units TW3 ...129 D1
New River Cres N13 ...32 D6
New River Ct N5 ...73 B4
New River Sports & Recreation Ctr N22 ...32 D3
New River Way N4 ...51 B2
New Row WC2 ...116 A6 250 A6
Newry Rd TW1 ...153 A6
Newsam Ave N15 ...51 B4
New Scotland Yard★ SW1 ...115 D3 259 C6
Newsholme Dr N21 ...16 B6
New Southgate Ind Est 10 N11 ...31 C5
New Southgate Sta N11 ...31 B5
New Spring Gdns Wlk SE11 ...260 B1
New Sq WC2 ...94 B1 240 D2
East Bedfont TW14 ...149 A3
New Sq Pas WC2 ...241 A2
New St EC2 ...95 C2 243 B3
New Stanford Prim Sch SW16 ...181 D2
Newstead Ave BR6 ...227 C6
Newstead Cl N12 ...30 C4
Newstead Ct UB5 ...85 A4
Newstead Rd SE12 ...164 D4
Newstead Way SW19 ...178 D6
Newstead Wlk SM5 ...202 A2
Newstead Wood Sch for Girls BR6 ...227 B5
New Street Hill BR1 ...187 C5
New St Sq EC4 ...94 C1 241 B2
Newton Ave N10 ...31 B2
Acton W3 ...111 A4
Newton Cl E17 ...53 A3
Harrow HA2 ...63 C6
Newton Farm Fst & Mid Sch HA2 ...63 B6
Newton Gr W4 ...111 C2
Newton Ho 10 E17 ...54 A6
NW8 ...91 D6
22 SW8 ...137 D3
1 Stepney E1 ...118 B6
Newton Pl E14 ...119 C2
Newton Point 1 E16 ...98 D1

Newton Prep Sch
SW8 ....137 B4 268 D2
Newton Rd DA16 ....146 A2
E15 ....76 B3
N15 ....52 A4
NW2 ....68 C5
W2 ....91 D1
Harrow HA3 ....24 C1
Isleworth TW7 ....130 D3
Wembley HA0 ....66 B1
Wimbledon SW19 ....179 A3
Newton St WC2 ..94 A1 240 B2
Newton's Yd 14 SW18 ....157 C6
Newton Terr BR2 ....209 D3
Newton Way N18 ....33 A5
Newton Wlk HA8 ....26 D2
New Tower Bldgs 21 E1 .118 B5
Newtown Ct SW11 ....268 C1
SW4 ....159 B6
New Trinity Rd 1 N2 ....30 B1
New Union Cl E14 ....120 A3
New Union St EC2 ....242 C3
New Victoria Hospl KT3 .177 C2
New Wanstead E11 ....55 A3
New Way Rd NW9 ....45 C5
New Wharf Rd
N1 ....94 A5 233 B4
New Woodlands Sch
BR1 ....186 C6
Newyears Green La UB9 ..38 B3
New Zealand Ave KT12 .193 D1
Niagara Ave W5 ....109 C2
Niagara Cl N1 ....235 B4
Niagara Ct 6 SE16 ....118 C3
Niagara Ho W5 ....109 C2
Nibthwaite Rd HA1 ....42 C4
Nicholas Cl UB6 ....85 D5
Nicholas Ct Chiswick W4 .133 C5
Lewisham SE12 ....165 A3
Nicholas Gdns W5 ....109 D4
Nicholas Ho Ealing W13 ..87 C1
Penge SE26 ....184 B4
2 Putney SW15 ....156 A6
Nicholas La EC2,EC4 ....252 D6
Nicholas Pas EC3 ....252 D6
Nicholas Rd E1 ....96 C3
Borehamwood WD6 ....10 B6
Dagenham RM8 ....81 B5
Wallington CR0 ....220 A4
Nicholas Stacey Ho 3
SE7 ....121 B1
Nicholay Rd N19 ....49 D1
Nichol Cl N14 ....15 D3
Nicholes Rd TW3 ....129 C1
Nichol La BR1 ....187 A3
Nicholl Ho N4 ....51 A1
Nicholls Ave UB8 ....82 C3
Nicholls Point E15 ....99 A6
Nicholl St E2 ....96 A6
Nichols Cl N4 ....50 C1
Chessington KT9 ....213 C2
Nichols Ct E2 ....95 D5
Nichols Gn W5 ....88 A2
Nicholson Dr WD23 ....8 A2
Nicholson Ho SE17 ....262 C2
2 SE18 ....144 A4
Nicholson Rd CR0 ....205 D1
Nicholson St SE1 ....251 C3
Nickelby Cl SE28 ....102 C1
Nickleby Cl UB8 ....82 D1
Nickleby Ho 15 SE1 ....118 A4
7 W11 ....112 D5
Nicola Cl Harrow HA3 ....24 B1
South Croydon CR2 ....221 A2
Nicola Terr DA7 ....147 A4
Nicol Cl 6 TW1 ....153 B5
Nicole Ho SE25 ....206 A4
Nicoll Ct N10 ....31 B3
NW10 ....89 C6
Nicoll Pl NW4 ....46 B2
Nicoll Rd NW10 ....89 C6
Nicoll Way WD6 ....11 B6
Nicolson 14 NW9 ....27 D2
Nicosia Rd SW18 ....158 C4
Niederwald Rd SE26 ....185 A6
Nield Rd UB3 ....105 D4
Nigel Bldg EC1 ....241 A4
Nigel Cl UB5 ....85 A6
Nigel Ct N3 ....29 D3
Nigel Fisher Way KT9 ....213 D1
Nigel Mews IG1 ....78 D4
Nigel Playfair Ave W6 ...112 B1
Nigel Rd E7 ....77 C3
SE15 ....140 A2
Nigeria Rd SE7 ....143 D5
Nighthawk 16 NW9 ....27 D2
Nightingale Ave
Chingford E4 ....36 C5
Harrow HA1 ....43 B1
Nightingale Cl
Carshalton SM5 ....219 A6
Chingford E4 ....36 C6
Chiswick W4 ....133 A6
Pinner HA5 ....40 C4
Nightingale Ct 12 E14 ....120 A3
N4 ....72 B6
SW6 ....265 D1
1 Harrow HA1 ....42 D3
Penge SE19 ....183 D4
Sutton SM1 ....218 A3
1 Wanstead E11 ....55 B4
Nightingale Dr KT19 ....214 D2
Nightingale Gr SE13 ....164 B6
Nightingale Ho 7 E1 ....118 A5
21 E1 ....95 C6
SE18 ....122 C1
W12 ....90 C1
Hayes UB3 ....105 D2
Nightingale La BR1 ....187 D1
N8 ....50 A6
Nightingale La *continued*
Balham SW11,SW12 ....159 A5
Richmond TW10 ....154 A4
Wanstead E11 ....55 B4
Nightingale Lo 5 W9 ....91 C2
Nightingale Mews SE11 .261 D4
Nightingale Pl SE18 ....144 D6
SW10 ....136 A6 266 B6
Nightingale Prim Sch
SE18 ....122 D1
Wanstead E18 ....55 C5
Wood Green N22 ....32 B2
Nightingale Rd E5 ....74 B5
N9 ....18 C4
NW10 ....89 D5
Carshalton SM5 ....219 A6
Ealing W7 ....108 D5
East Molesey KT8 ....195 D4
Hampton TW12 ....173 C4
Orpington BR5 ....211 A3
Walton-on-T KT12 ....194 B2
Wood Green N22 ....32 B3
Nightingale Sch SW17 ..158 C2
Nightingale Sq SW12 ....159 A4
Nightingales The TW19 ..148 B3
Nightingale Vale SE18 ...144 C6
Nightingale Way E6 ....100 A2
Nightingale Wlk SW18,
SW4 ....159 B5
Nile Cl N16 ....73 D5
Nile Dr N9 ....18 C2
Nile Ho N1 ....235 C2
Nile Path 6 SE18 ....144 C6
Nile Rd E13 ....99 C5
Nile St N1 ....95 B4 235 C2
Nile Terr SE1,
SE15 ....117 D1 263 D1
Nimegen Way 9 SE22 ...161 C6
Nimmo Dr WD23 ....8 B4
Nimrod 9 NW9 ....27 C2
Nimrod Cl UB5 ....84 D4
Nimrod Pas 4 N1 ....73 C2
Nimrod Rd SW16 ....181 B5
Nina Mackay Cl 10 E15 ...98 C6
Nine Acres Cl E12 ....78 A3
Nine Elms Cl TW14 ....149 D3
Nine Elms La
SW8 ....137 D6 269 C5
Nineteenth Rd CR4 ....204 A5
Ninhams Wood BR6 ....226 C4
Ninth Ave UB3 ....106 A6
Nisbet 10 NW9 ....27 C2
Nisbet Ho E9 ....74 D3
Nita Ct SE12 ....165 A3
Nithdale Rd SE18 ....145 A5
Nithsdale Gr UB10 ....61 A5
Niton Cl EN5 ....12 D5
Niton Rd TW9 ....132 C2
Niton St SW6 ....134 D5
No 1 St SE18 ....122 D3
Noam Prim Sch N12 ....29 D6
Nobel Dr TW6 ....127 C5
Nobel Ho 8 SE5 ....139 A3
Nobel Rd N18 ....34 C6
Noble Cnr TW5 ....129 C4
Noble Ct Mitcham CR4 ....180 B1
Stepney E1 ....118 B6
Noblefield Hts N2 ....48 D4
Noble Ho 12 E1 ....118 A6
Noble St EC2 ....95 A1 242 A2
Noel 13 NW9 ....27 D2
Noel Baker Ct 4 E11 ....76 C6
Noel Coward Ho SW1 ...259 B3
Noel Ct TW4 ....129 B2
Noel Dene W5 ....109 C1
Noel Ho 3 NW3 ....70 B1
Noel Park Prim Schs
N22 ....32 C1
Noel Park Rd N22 ....32 C1
Noel Rd N1 ....94 D5 234 D4
Acton W3 ....88 D1
Newham E6 ....100 A3
Noel Sq RM8 ....80 C4
Noel St W1 ....93 C1 239 B1
Noel Terr SE23 ....162 C2
Nolan Way E5 ....74 A4
Noll Ho N7 ....72 B6
Nolton Pl HA8 ....26 B2
Nonsuch Ct SM3 ....217 A2
Nonsuch High Sch for Girls
SM3 ....216 D1
Nonsuch Prim Sch
KT17 ....216 B3
Noor Ul Islam Prim Sch
E10 ....76 A6
Nora Gdns NW4 ....46 D5
Norbiton Ave KT1,KT2 ...176 C1
Norbiton Common Rd
KT1,KT3 ....198 D6
Norbiton Hall KT2 ....176 B1
Norbiton Rd E14 ....97 B1
Norbiton Sta KT1 ....176 C1
Norbreck Gdns NW10 ....88 B4
Norbreck Par NW10 ....88 B4
Norbroke St W12 ....111 D6
Norburn St W10 ....91 A2
Norbury Ave
Isleworth TW3 ....130 B1
Thornton Heath CR7,
SW16 ....182 C1
Norbury Cl SW16 ....182 D2
Norbury Court Rd
SW16 ....182 A1
Norbury Cres SW16 ....182 C1
Norbury Cross SW16 ....204 A6
Norbury Gdns RM6 ....58 D4
Norbury Gr NW7 ....11 C1
Norbury Hill SW16 ....182 D3
Norbury Manor Girls High
Sch CR7 ....182 C2
Norbury Manor Prim Sch
SW16 ....182 A2
Norbury Rd Chingford E4 ..35 C5
South Norwood CR7 ....205 A6
Norbury Rise SW16 ....204 A6
Norbury Sch HA1 ....42 C4
Norbury Sta SW16 ....182 B2
Norbury Trad Est SW16 ..182 B1
Norcombe Gdns HA3 ....43 C4
Norcombe Ho 2 N19 ....71 D5
Norcott Cl UB4 ....84 C3
Norcott Rd N16 ....74 A5
Norcroft Gdns SE22 ....162 A4
Norcutt Rd TW2 ....152 C3
Norden Ho 25 E2 ....96 B4
Norden Point NW2 ....46 C1
Nore Ct NW10 ....68 A1
Norfolk Ave N15 ....51 D3
Edmonton N13 ....32 D4
Norfolk Cl N2 ....48 C6
Cockfosters EN4 ....3 A1
Edmonton N13 ....32 D4
5 Twickenham TW1 ....153 B5
Norfolk Cres DA15 ....167 C4
W2 ....92 C1 237 B2
Norfolk Ct 4 Barnet EN5 ....1 A1
Surbiton KT5 ....198 B3
Wembley HA0 ....65 C2
Norfolk Gdns DA7 ....147 B4
Norfolk Ho E8 ....73 D4
EC4 ....252 A6
SE3 ....142 C6
SE8 ....141 C4
SW1 ....259 D4
13 Acton W3 ....88 C1
11 Merton SW19 ....180 A3
Penge SE20 ....184 C2
4 Putney SW15 ....156 C4
Richmond TW10 ....154 C6
2 South Croydon CR0 ....221 B6
3 Stanmore HA7 ....25 C5
Norfolk House Rd
SW16 ....160 A1
Norfolk House Sch N10 ...31 B1
Norfolk Mans SW11 ....267 D1
10 SW18 ....157 C6
Norfolk Mews 12 W10 ....91 A2
Norfolk Pl DA16 ....146 A3
W2 ....92 B1 236 D2
Norfolk Rd E17 ....34 D1
E6 ....100 B6
NW10 ....67 C1
NW8 ....92 B6 229 D5
Barking IG11 ....79 C1
Barnet EN5 ....1 C2
Claygate KT10 ....212 C3
Dagenham RM10 ....81 D3
Enfield EN3 ....18 B6
Feltham TW13 ....150 C3
Harrow HA1 ....41 D4
Ilford IG3 ....57 C2
Mitcham SW19 ....180 C4
South Norwood CR7 ....205 A6
Norfolk Row
SE1,SE11 ....116 B2 260 C4
Norfolk Sq W2 ...92 B1 236 D2
Norfolk Sq Mews W2 ...236 D1
Norfolk St E7 ....77 A3
Norgrove St SW12 ....159 A4
Norhyrst Ave SE25 ....205 D6
Norland Ho 13 W11 ....112 D5
Norland Pl W11 ..113 A5 244 B3
Norland Place Sch
W11 ....113 A5 244 A3
Norland Rd W11 ....112 D5
Norlands Cres BR7 ....188 D2
Norland Sq W11 .113 A5 244 B3
Norley Vale SW15 ....156 A3
Norlington Rd E10,E11 ....54 B1
Norlington Sch for Boys
E10 ....54 B1
Norman Ave
Feltham TW13 ....151 B2
Southall UB1 ....107 A6
Tottenham N22 ....33 A2
Twickenham TW1 ....153 C4
Norman Butler Ho 10
W10 ....91 A3
Normanby Cl SW15 ....157 B6
Normanby Rd NW10 ....67 D4
Norman Cl BR6 ....227 A5
Tottenham N22 ....33 A2
Norman Cres
Heston TW5 ....128 D5
Pinner HA5 ....22 C2
Norman Ct N4 ....50 C2
NW10 ....68 A1
Dulwich SE22 ....162 A4
7 Hampton TW12 ....173 C2
Ilford IG2 ....57 B2
West Norwood SW16 ....182 C5
Woodford IG8 ....37 B5
Normand Mews W14 ....264 B6
Normand Park Prim Sch
W14 ....135 B6 264 D6
Normand Rd
W14 ....135 B6 264 C6
Normandy Ave EN5 ....1 B1
Normandy Cl SE26 ....163 A1
Normandy Dr UB3 ....83 A1
Normandy Ho 4 NW4 ....28 D1
Normandy Rd SW9 ....138 C4
Normandy Terr E16 ....99 B1
Norman Gr E3 ....97 A5
Norman Ho 6 E11 ....76 C6
SW8 ....270 A4
Feltham TW13 ....151 B2
Lower Halliford TW17 ....192 C2
Normanhurst TW15 ....170 C5
Normanhurst Ave DA16 .146 D4
Normanhurst Dr TW1 ....153 B6
Normanhurst Rd BR5 ....190 B1
Streatham SW2 ....160 B2
Walton-on-T KT12 ....194 D1
Normanhurst Sch E4 ....20 B4
Norman Par DA14 ....168 D2
Norman Rd E11 ....76 C6
E6 ....100 B3
N15 ....51 D4
SE10 ....141 D5
Ashford TW15 ....171 B4
Ilford IG1 ....78 D3
Merton SW19 ....180 A3
Sutton SM1 ....217 C3
Thornton Heath CR7 ....204 D4
Normans Cl NW10 ....67 B2
Hillingdon UB8 ....82 A2
Normansfield Ave KT1,
KT8 ....175 C3
Normanshire Dr E4 ....35 D6
Normans Mead NW10 ....67 B2
Norman St EC1 ....95 A4 235 B1
Normanton Ave SW18,
SW19 ....157 C2
Normanton Ct CR2 ....221 C3
Normanton Ho 6 SW4 ..159 C5
Normanton Pk E4 ....20 C2
Normanton Rd CR2 ....221 C2
Normanton St SE23 ....162 D2
Norman Way Acton W3 ....88 D1
Palmers Green N14 ....16 A2
Normington Cl SW16 ....182 C5
Norrice Lea N2 ....48 B4
Norris 11 NW9 ....27 D2
Norris Ho 22 E9 ....96 C6
12 N1 ....95 C6
Norris St SW1 ....249 C5
Norroy Rd SW15 ....134 D1
Norrys Cl EN4 ....2 D1
Norrys Rd EN4 ....2 D1
Norse Ho 13 SE5 ....139 A3
Norseman Cl 3 IG3 ....58 B1
Norseman Way UB6 ....85 D6
Norstead Pl SW15 ....156 A2
North Access Rd E17 ....52 D3
North Acre NW9 ....27 C2
North Acton Rd NW10 ....89 B4
North Acton Sta W3 ....89 B2
Northampton Gr N1 ....73 B3
Northampton Pk N1 ....73 B2
Northampton Rd
EC1 ....94 C3 241 B6
Croydon CR0 ....222 A6
Enfield EN3 ....7 A1
Northampton Sq
EC1 ....94 D4 234 C1
Northampton St N1 ....73 A1
Northanger Rd SW16 ....182 A4
North Audley St
W1 ....115 A6 248 A6
North Ave Ealing W13 ....87 B2
Edmonton N18 ....34 A6
Harrow HA2 ....41 D3
Hayes UB3 ....106 A6
8 Richmond TW9 ....132 C4
Southall UB1 ....107 B6
Wallington SM5 ....219 A1
Northaw Ho W10 ....90 C3
North Bank NW8 ..92 C4 230 A1
Northbank Rd E17 ....36 A1
North Beckton Prim Sch
E6 ....100 B2
North Birkbeck Rd E11 ...76 B5
North Block 18 E1 ....118 C6
Northborough Rd SW16 .182 A1
Northbourne BR2 ....209 A2
Northbourne Ho 21 E5 ....74 B3
N14 ....15 D4
Northbourne Rd SW4 ....159 D6
North Branch Ave NW10 ..90 C4
Northbrook CE Sch
SE12 ....164 D6
Northbrook Rd SE13 ....164 C6
Barnet EN5 ....13 A5
Ilford IG1 ....78 C6
Thornton Heath CR0 ....205 B4
Wood Green N22 ....32 A3
Northburgh St
EC1 ....94 D3 241 D6
Northbury Jun & Inf Sch
IG11 ....79 A2
North Carriage Dr
W2 ....114 C6 247 B6
Northchurch SE17 ....262 D2
North Church Ho 19 E2 ...96 A6
Northchurch Rd N1 ....73 B1
Wembley HA9 ....66 C2
Northchurch Terr N1 ....73 C1
North Circular Rd N2 ....30 B2
N3,NW2,NW4 ....47 A4
NW10 ....67 C3
NW2 ....67 C3
Chingford, Highams Park
E17 ....35 D2
Edmonton N13 ....32 C5
Ilford IG1,E12 ....78 C4
Woodford E18 ....37 C1
North Cl DA6 ....146 D1
Barnet EN5 ....12 C6
Dagenham RM10 ....103 C6
East Bedfont TW14 ....149 B5
Merton SM4 ....201 A5
Northcliffe Cl KT4 ....215 C5
Northcliffe Dr N20 ....13 B3
North Colonnade E14 ....119 C5
North Common Rd
Ealing W5 ....110 A6
Uxbridge UB8 ....60 A3
Northcote 1 HA5 ....22 C1
Northcote Ave
Ealing W5 ....110 A6
Isleworth TW7 ....153 A6
Southall UB1 ....107 A6
Tolworth KT5 ....198 D2
Northcote Ho UB4 ....84 D2
Northcote Lodge Sch
SW11 ....158 D5
Northcote Rd E17 ....53 A5
NW10 ....67 C1
SW11 ....158 D6
Isleworth TW7 ....153 A6
Kingston KT3 ....199 B6
Sidcup DA14 ....189 C6
Thornton Heath CR0 ....205 B3
Northcott Ave N22 ....32 A2
North Countess Rd E17 ...35 B2
Northcourt W1 ....239 B4
North Cray Prim Sch
DA14 ....191 A4
North Cray Rd DA14 ....191 A5
North Cres E16 ....98 B3
N3 ....29 B1
WC1 ....239 C4
Northcroft Ct 8 W12 ....112 A4
Northcroft Rd W13 ....109 B3
West Ewell KT19 ....215 C1
North Crofts SE21 ....162 B3
North Cross Rd SE22 ....162 A6
Ilford IG6 ....57 A5
North Ct SW1 ....260 A5
North Dene NW7 ....11 B1
Hounslow TW5 ....129 D4
Northdene Gdns N15 ....51 D3
Northdown Cl HA4 ....61 D5
Northdown Gdns IG2 ....57 C4
Northdown Rd DA16 ....146 C3
Northdown St N1 .94 B5 233 C3
North Dr BR6 ....227 C4
Beckenham BR3 ....207 D5
Hounslow TW3,TW7 ....130 A3
Ruislip HA4 ....39 C2
Streatham SW16 ....181 C6
North Dulwich Sta SE21 .161 B6
North Ealing Prim Sch
W5 ....87 B3
North Ealing Sta W3 ....88 B1
North End NW3 ....70 A6
Buckhurst Hill IG9 ....21 C4
Croydon CR0 ....221 A6
North End Ave NW3 ....70 A6
North End Cres
W14 ....113 B2 254 C3
North End Ho
W14 ....113 A2 254 B3
North End La BR6 ....226 D1
North End Par W14 ....254 B3
North End Rd NW11 ....47 D1
W14 ....113 B1 254 D1
Wembley HA9 ....66 D5
North End Way NW3 ....70 A6
Northern Ave N9 ....17 D2
Northernhay Wlk SM4 ....201 A5
Northern Hts N8 ....49 D2
Northern Perimeter Rd
TW6 ....127 C4
Northern Perimeter Road
(W) TW6 ....126 B4
Northern Rd E13 ....99 B5
Northern Relief Rd IG11 ..79 A2
Northesk Ho 6 E1 ....96 B3
North Eyot Gdns 5 W6 .111 D1
Northey St E14 ....119 A6
North Farm IG10 ....21 C5
North Feltham Trad Est
TW14 ....128 B1
Northfield IG10 ....21 D6
Northfield Ave W13,W5 ..109 B4
Pinner HA5 ....40 D5
Northfield Cl BR1 ....188 A2
Hayes UB3 ....105 D3
Northfield Cres SM3 ....217 A4
Northfield Gdns RM9 ....81 B4
Northfield Hall N6 ....49 A2
Northfield Ho 3 SE15 ....140 A6
Northfield Ind Est HA0 ....88 C6
Northfield Par UB3 ....105 D3
Northfield Path RM9 ....81 B4
Northfield Pk UB3 ....105 D3
Northfield Rd E6 ....78 B1
N16 ....51 C2
W13 ....109 B4
Cockfosters EN4 ....2 C2
Dagenham RM9 ....81 B4
Enfield EN3 ....18 B6
Heston TW5 ....128 D5
Northfields SW18 ....135 C1
Northfields Prospect
SW18 ....135 C1
Northfields Rd W3 ....89 A2
Northfields Sta W5 ....109 C3
Northfleet Ho SE1 ....252 C2
North Flower Wlk
W2 ....114 246 C5
North Gate NW8 ..92 C5 230 A3
Northgate Bsns Ctr EN1 ....6 B1
Northgate Ct 15 SW9 ....138 C2
Northgate Dr NW9 ....45 C3
North Gates N12 ....30 A2
North Gdns SW19 ....180 B3
North Glade DA5 ....169 B3
North Gn NW9 ....27 C3
North Gower St
NW1 ....93 C4 232 B1
North Gr N15 ....51 B4
N6 ....49 A2
North Greenwich Sta
SE10 ....120 C4
North Haringay Jun & Inf Sch
N8 ....50 C5
North Harrow Sta HA2 ....41 D4
North Hill N6 ....49 A3
North Hill Ave N6 ....48 D3
North Hill Ct N6 ....49 A2
North Ho 3 SE8 ....119 B1
North Hyde Gdns UB3 ..106 A2
North Hyde La UB2 ....107 A1
North Hyde Rd UB3 ....105 D3
Northiam N12 ....29 C6
WC1 ....233 B1
Northiam St E9 ....96 B6
Northington St
WC1 ....94 B3 240 D5
North La TW11 ....174 D4
Northlands Ave BR6 ....227 C4
Northlands St SE5 ....139 A3
Northleigh Ho 38 E3 ....97 D4
North Lo N22 ....31 D1
New Barnet EN5 ....14 A6
North Lodge Cl SW15 ....156 D6
North London Boys Sch
N16 ....52 A1
North London Collegiate Sch
HA7,HA8 ....26 A5
North London Collegiate Sch
The HA7,HA8 ....26 A5
North London Nuffield Hospl
EN2 ....4 C3
North Mall The N9 ....18 B2
North Mews WC1 .94 B3 240 D5
North Middlesex Hospl
N18 ....33 C5
Northmoor 4 SE23 ....162 D1
North Mount N20 ....14 A2
Northolm HA8 ....27 B6
Northolme Gdns HA8 ....26 C2
Northolme Rd N5 ....73 A4
Northolme Rise BR6 ....227 C6
Northolt N17 ....33 C1
Northolt Ave HA4 ....62 B3
Northolt Gdns UB6 ....64 D3
Northolt High Sch UB5 ....63 B2
Northolt Park Inf Sch
UB5 ....63 D3
Northolt Park Sta HA2 ....63 D4
Northolt Prim Sch UB5 ....63 A1
Northolt Rd
Harmondsworth TW6 ....126 A4
Harrow HA2 ....64 A5
Northolt Sta UB5 ....63 C2
Northover BR1 ....164 D1
North Par
Chessington KT9 ....214 B3
Edgware HA8 ....26 C1
Southall UB1 ....85 C1
North Pas SW18 ....157 C6
North Pk SE9 ....166 C5
North Pl Mitcham SW19 ..180 D3
Teddington TW11 ....174 D4
Northpoint BR1 ....187 A2
North Point UB7 ....104 A5
North Pole La BR2 ....225 A2
North Pole Rd W10 ....90 C2
Northport St N1 ....235 D5
North Prim Sch UB1 ....107 B6
North Rd BR1 ....187 B2
N2 ....30 C2
N6 ....49 A2
N7 ....72 A2
SE18 ....123 C2
W5 ....109 D3
Brentford TW8 ....132 A6
Dagenham RM6 ....59 A4
East Bedfont TW14 ....149 B5
Edgware HA8 ....26 D2
Edmonton N9 ....18 B3
Erith DA17 ....125 D4
Hayes UB3 ....83 B2
Heston TW5 ....128 C6
Ilford IG3 ....79 C6
Richmond TW9 ....132 C3
Southall UB1 ....107 C6
Surbiton KT6 ....197 D3
West Drayton UB7 ....104 B3
1 West Wickham BR4 ....207 D1
Wimbledon SW19 ....180 A4
North Residence IG3 ....58 B4
North Ride W2 ..114 C6 247 A5
North Rise W2 ....237 B1
Northrop Rd TW6 ....127 C4
North Row W1 ....115 A6 248 A6
North Sheen Sta TW10 ....132 C1
Northside Prim Sch N12 .30 A5
Northside Rd BR1 ....187 A2
North Side Wandsworth
Comm SW18 ....158 B6
Northspur Rd SM1 ....217 C5
North Sq NW11 ....47 C4
Edmonton N9 ....18 B2
North St BR1 ....187 A2
DA7 ....147 C1
E13 ....99 B5
NW4 ....46 C4
SW4 ....137 C2
Barking IG11 ....79 A1
Carshalton SM5 ....218 D4
Isleworth TW7 ....131 A2
Northstead Rd SW2 ....160 C2
North Tenter St E1 ....243 D1
North Terr SW3 ....257 A5
Northumberland Alley
EC3 ....243 B1
Northumberland Ave
DA16 ....145 C2
WC2 ....116 A5 250 A4
Enfield EN1 ....6 B4
Hounslow TW7 ....130 D4

Northumberland Ave *continued*
Wanstead E12 55 C1
Northumberland Cl
TW19 148 A5
Northumberland Cres
TW14 149 C5
Northumberland Ct
3 Hounslow TW3 129 D1
South Croydon CR2 221 C3
Northumberland Gdns
BR1 210 C5
Brentford TW7 131 A5
Edmonton N9 17 D1
Mitcham CR4 203 D4
Northumberland Gr N17 34 B3
Northumberland Heath Prim Sch DA8 147 D5
Northumberland Ho
NW5 71 C2
Northumberland Mans
E5 74 C4
Northumberland Park Com Sch N17 34 A3
Northumberland Park Ind Est N17 34 B3
Northumberland Park Sports Ctr N17 34 A3
Northumberland Park Sta N17 34 B3
Northumberland Pk
DA8 147 D5
Tottenham N17 34 A3
Northumberland Pl W2 91 C1
26 Richmond TW10 153 D6
Northumberland Rd E17 53 C2
E6 100 A1
Harrow HA2 41 C4
New Barnet EN5 14 A4
Northumberland St
WC2 250 A4
Northumbria St E14 97 C1
North Verbena Gdns
W6 112 A1
Northview 1 N7 72 A5
North View Ealing W5 87 C3
Pinner HA5 40 C2
Wimbledon SW19 178 C5
Northview Cres NW10 67 D4
Northview Dr IG8 37 D1
Northview Prim Sch
NW10 67 D3
North View Rd N8 49 D6
North Villas NW1 71 D2
Northway NW11 47 D4
North Way N11 31 C4
N9 18 D2
NW9 44 D6
Northway Merton SM4 201 A5
Wallington SM6 219 C4
North Way Pinner HA5 40 D5
Uxbridge UB10 60 A1
Northway Cir NW7 27 B6
Northway Cres NW7 27 C6
Northway Ct NW11 47 D4
NW7 27 B6
Northway Rd SE5 139 A2
Croydon CR0 205 D2
Northway Sch NW7 11 B1
Northways Par 2 NW3 70 B1
Northweald La KT2 175 D5
North Wembley Sta HA0, HA9 65 D5
North Western Ave (Watford By-Pass) WD6 9 B5
North Westminster Com Sch
W2 92 B2 236 D4
W9 91 C3
Northwest Pl N1 234 B4
North Wharf Rd
W2 92 B2 236 C3
Northwick Ave HA3 43 B3
Northwick Circ HA3 43 C3
Northwick Cl
NW8 92 B3 236 C6
Harrow HA1 65 B6
Northwick Ho NW8 236 B6
Northwick Park Hospl
HA1 43 A2
Northwick Park Rd HA1 42 D3
Northwick Park Sta HA3 43 B2
Northwick Rd
South Oxhey WD19 22 C6
Wembley HA0 87 D6
Northwick Terr
NW8 92 B3 236 C6
North Wlk W2 114 A6 246 A5
New Addington CR0 224 A3
Northwold Dr HA5 40 C6
Northwold Prim Sch E5 74 A6
Northwold Rd E5,N16 74 A6
Northwood Comp Sch
HA6 22 B2
Northwood Gdns N12 30 B5
Greenford UB6 64 D3
Ilford IG5 56 C5
Northwood Hills Cir HA6 22 A2
Northwood Hills Sta HA6 22 A1
North Wood Lo NW3 69 D4
Northwood & Pinner Com Hospl HA6 22 A2
Northwood Pl DA18 125 B3
Northwood Prim Sch
DA18 125 B3
Northwood Rd N6 49 B2
Forest Hill SE23 163 B3
South Norwood CR7 183 A1
Wallington SM5 219 A2
Northwood Twr 1 E17 54 A5
Northwood Way
Northwood HA6 22 A3
1 West Norwood SE19 183 C4
North Woolwich Rd
E16 121 B5
North Woolwich Rdbt
E16 121 D5
North Woolwich Sta
E16 122 C4
North Worple Way
SW14 133 B2
Norton Ave KT5 198 D2
Norton Cl Chingford E4 35 C5
Enfield EN1 6 B3
Norton Ct
Beckenham BR3 185 B2
Ilford IG2 57 B3
Norton Folgate E1 243 B4
Norton Gdns SW16 182 A1
Norton Ho 33 E1 96 B1
14 E2 96 D5
16 SW9 138 B3
5 New Malden KT3 199 C5
Norton Rd E10 53 B1
Wembley HA0 65 D2
Norval Gn 1 SW9 138 C3
Norval Rd HA0 43 B1
Norvic Ho 5 SE5 139 A3
Norway Gate SE16 119 A3
Norway Pl E14 97 B1
Norway St SE10 141 D6
Norwegian Sch SW19 178 C3
Norwich Ho 6 E14 97 D1
Norwich Mews IG3 58 A1
Norwich Pl 7 DA6 147 C1
Norwich Rd E7 77 A3
Greenford UB6 85 D6
Northwood HA6 39 D6
South Norwood CR7 205 A6
Norwich St EC4 94 C1 241 A2
Norwich Wlk HA8 27 A3
Norwood Ave HA0 88 B5
Norwood Cl Southall UB2 107 C2
Twickenham TW2 152 B2
Norwood Dr HA2 41 C3
Norwood Gdns
Hayes UB4 84 C3
Southall UB2 107 B2
Norwood Green Inf Sch
UB2 107 B1
Norwood Green Jun Sch
UB2 107 A1
Norwood Green Rd
UB2 107 C2
Norwood Heights Sh Ctr 13
SE19 183 C4
Norwood High St SE27 183 A6
Norwood Ho 22 E14 119 D6
Norwood Hospl SE19 183 B4
Norwood Junction Sta
SE25 206 A5
Norwood Park Rd SE27 183 A5
Norwood Rd
Southall UB2 107 C2
West Norwood SE24,SE27 160 D3
Norwood Terr UB2 107 D2
Notley St SE5 139 B5
Notre Dame RC Girls Sch
SE1 116 D3 261 D5
Notson Rd SE25 206 B5
Notting Barn Rd W10 90 D3
Nottingdale Sq W11 244 A4
Nottingham Ave E16 99 C1
Nottingham Ct WC2 240 A1
Nottingham Ho N4 51 A1
34 SE5 139 A3
Nottingham Pl
W1 93 A2 238 A4
Nottingham Rd E10 54 A3
Croydon CR2 221 A3
Isleworth TW7 130 D3
Upper Tooting SW17 158 D3
Nottingham St W1 238 A4
Nottingham Terr NW1 238 A5
Notting Hill & Ealing High Sch W13 87 B2
Notting Hill Gate
W11 113 C5 245 A4
Notting Hill Gate Sta
W11 113 C5 245 A4
Nottingwood Ho W11 244 A6
Nova Bldg 21 E14 119 C2
Nova Mews SM4 201 A2
Novar Cl BR6 211 D2
Nova Rd CR0 205 A2
Novar Rd SE9 167 A3
Novello St SW6 135 C4 265 A2
Nowell Rd SW13 134 A6
Nower Ct HA5 41 B5
Nower Hill HA5 41 B5
Nower Hill High Sch
HA5 41 C5
Noyna Rd SW17 158 D1
Nubia Way SE6 164 C1
Nuding Cl SE13 141 C2
Nuffield Ct TW5 129 B5
Nuffield Lo 14 W9 91 C2
Nugent Ct SW16 181 C6
Nugent Rd N19 50 A1
South Norwood SE25 205 D6
Nugents Ct HA5 23 A2
Nugent's Pk HA5 23 B2
Nugent Terr NW8 92 A5 229 B3
Numa Ct TW8 131 D5
Nun Ct EC2 242 C2
Nuneaton Rd RM9 81 A1
Nuneham SW16 181 D6
Nunhead Cres SE15 140 B2
Nunhead Gr SE15 140 C2
Nunhead La SE15 140 B2
Nunhead Sta SE15 140 C3
Nunnington Cl SE9 166 A1
Nunn's Rd EN2 5 A3
Nupton Dr EN5 12 C5
Nurse Cl HA8 27 A2
Nursery Ave DA7 147 B2
N3 30 A1
Croydon CR0 222 D6
Nursery Cl BR6 211 D2
SE4 141 B3
Croydon CR0 222 D6
Dagenham RM6 58 D3
Enfield EN3 6 D4
Feltham TW14 150 B4
Putney SW15 134 D1
Woodford IG8 37 B5
Nursery Ct Ealing W13 87 A2
7 Tottenham N17 33 D3
Nursery Gdns BR7 188 D4
Enfield EN3 6 D4
Hampton TW13 173 B6
Hounslow TW4 151 B6
Sunbury TW16 171 D1
Nursery La E2 95 D6
E7 77 A2
W10 90 C2
Nurserymans Rd N11 15 A2
Nursery Rd E9 74 C2
N14 15 C4
N2 30 B2
SW9 138 B1
Loughton IG10 21 C6
Merton SW19 179 D1
Mitcham CR4 202 C6
Pinner HA5 40 C6
South Norwood CR7 205 B5
Sunbury TW16 171 D1
Sutton SM1 218 A4
Wimbledon SW19 179 A3
Nursery Row SE17 262 C3
Nursery St N17 33 D3
Nursery Walk Ct NW4 46 B6
Nursery Wlk NW4 46 C6
Nurstead Rd DA8 147 C5
Nutborn Ho SW19 178 D4
Nutbourne St W10 91 A4
Nutbrook St SE15 140 A2
Nutbrowne Rd RM9 103 B6
Nutcroft Rd SE15 140 B5
Nutfield Cl
Carshalton SM5 218 C5
Edmonton N18 34 A4
Nutfield Gdns Ilford IG3 80 A6
Northolt UB5 84 C5
Nutfield Rd E15 76 A4
NW2 68 A5
SE22 139 D1
Thornton Heath CR7 204 D5
Nutfield Way BR6 226 D6
Nutford Pl W1 92 D1 237 C2
Nuthatch Cl TW19 148 B3
Nuthatch Gdns SE28 123 B4
Nuthurst Ave SW2 160 B2
Nutkin Wlk UB8 60 A1
Nutley Terr NW3 70 B2
Nutmeg Cl E16 98 C3
Nutmeg La E14 98 B1
Nuttall St N1 95 C5
Nutter La E11 55 C4
Nutt Gr HA8 9 D2
Nutt St SE15 139 D5
Nutty La TW17 193 A6
Nutwell St SW17 180 C5
Nuxley Rd DA17 125 C1
NW London Jewish Day Sch
NW6 69 A1
Nyanza St SE18 145 B6
Nye Bevan Est E5 74 D5
Nye Bevan Ho SW6 264 C4
Nye's Wharf SE15 140 A6
Nylands Ave TW9 132 C3
Nymans Gdns SW20 200 B6
Nynehead St SE14 141 A5
Nyon Gr SE6 163 B2
Nyton Cl N19 50 A1

O

Oak Apple Ct SE12 165 A3
Oak Ave N10 31 B3
N8 50 A5
Croydon CR0 223 D6
Enfield EN2 4 B5
Hampton TW12,TW13 173 A4
Heston TW5 129 A5
Tottenham N17 33 C3
Uxbridge UB10 60 D6
West Drayton UB7 104 C3
Oak Bank CR0 224 A2
Oakbank Ave KT12 195 B2
Oakbank Gr SE24 139 A1
Oakbrook 3 BR3 185 D1
Oakbrook Cl BR1 187 B6
Oakbury Rd SW6 135 D3
Oak Cl N14 15 B4
Sutton SM1 218 A6
Oakcombe Cl KT3 177 C2
Oak Cottage Cl 11 SE6 164 D3
Oak Cotts W7 108 C4
Oakcourt 16 SE15 139 D5
Oak Cres E16 98 C2
Oakcroft SE12 165 B1
Oakcroft Bsns Ctr KT9 214 B4
Oakcroft Cl HA5 22 B1
Oakcroft Ho 3 KT3 199 C2
Oakcroft Rd SE13 142 B3
Chessington KT9 214 B4
Oakcroft Villas KT9 214 B4
Oak Ct BR1 188 B1
Chingford E4 35 D4
Oakdale N14 15 B3
Beckenham BR3 186 A1
Oakdale Ave Harrow HA3 44 A4
Pinner HA6 22 A1
Oakdale Cl WD19 22 C6
Oakdale Ct N19 72 A6
Oakdale Gdns E4 36 A5
Oakdale Inf Sch E18 37 B1
Oakdale Jun Sch E18 37 B1
Oakdale Lo NW4 29 A2
Oakdale Rd E11 76 B6
E7 77 B1
N4 51 B3
SE15 140 C2
South Oxhey WD19 22 C6
Streatham SW16 182 A5
Woodford E18 37 B1
Oakdale Way CR4 203 A2
Oakdene 3 SE15 140 B4
1 West Norwood SE19 183 C5
Oak Dene W13 87 B2
Oakdene Ave BR7 188 C5
Thames Ditton KT7 197 A1
Oakdene Cl HA5 23 B3
Oakdene Dr KT5 199 A1
Oakdene Ho N16 51 C1
Enfield EN2 4 D2
Oakdene Lo SE20 184 B3
Oakdene Mews SM3 201 B1
Oakdene Pk N3 29 B3
Oakdene Rd BR5 211 D4
Hillingdon UB10 82 D5
Oakden St SE11 116 C2 261 B4
Oake Ct SW15 157 A6
Oakeford Ho W14 254 B5
Oakend Ho 10 N4 51 B2
Oaken Dr KT10 212 D2
Oakenholt Ho 1 SE2 124 D4
Oaken La KT10 212 C3
Oakenshaw Cl KT6 198 A2
Oakes Cl E6 100 B1
Oakeshott Ave N6 71 A6
Oakey La SE1 261 A6
Oak Farm WD6 11 A6
Oak Farm Jun & Inf Schs
UB10 82 D6
Oakfield E4 35 D5
Oakfield Ave HA3 43 B6
Oakfield Cl
New Malden KT3 199 D4
Ruislip HA4 39 D3
Oakfield Ct N3 29 D2
N8 50 A2
NW2 46 D2
SW4 160 A5
2 Ealing W5 110 C5
South Croydon CR2 221 A2
Oakfield Gdns
Beckenham BR3 207 C4
Carshalton SM5 202 D1
Edmonton N18 33 C6
Greenford UB6 86 B4
3 West Norwood SE19 183 C5
Oakfield Ho 2 IG1 78 D5
Oakfield La BR2 225 C4
Oakfield Lo 8 IG1 78 D5
Oakfield Prep Sch SE21 161 B3
Oakfield Rd E17 35 A1
E6 100 A6
N3 29 D2
N4 50 C2
Ashford TW15 170 D5
Croydon CR0 205 A1
Ilford IG1 78 D5
Palmers Green N14 16 A2
Penge SE20 184 B3
Wimbledon SW19 156 D1
Oakfields KT12 194 A1
Oakfields Rd NW11 47 A3
Oakfield St
SW10 136 A6 266 A6
Oakford Rd NW5 71 C4
Oak Gdns HA8 27 A1
Croydon CR0 223 C6
Oak Gr NW2 69 A4
Ruislip HA4 40 B1
Sunbury TW16 172 B3
West Wickham BR4 208 A1
Oak Grove Rd SE20 184 C1
Oakhall Ct Ashford TW16 171 D5
Wanstead E11 55 B3
Oakhall Dr TW16 171 D5
Oak Hall Rd E11 55 B3
Oakham Cl SE6 163 B2
Oakham Dr BR2 208 D5
Oakham Ho W10 90 C3
Oakhampton Rd NW7 28 D3
Oakhill KT10 213 A2
Oak Hill Chingford IG8 36 C3
Surbiton KT6 198 A2
Oakhill Ave NW3 69 D4
Pinner HA5 23 A1
Oak Hill Cl IG8 36 B3
Oak Hill Coll N14 15 A5
Oak Hill Cres
Chingford IG8 36 C3
Surbiton KT6 198 A2
Oakhill Ct SE23 162 C5
Putney SW15 157 B6
8 Surbiton KT6 198 A3
Wimbledon SW19 178 D3
Oak Hill Ct IG8 36 C3
Oak Hill Gdns E4 36 C2
Oak Hill Gr KT6 198 A3
Oakhill Ho BR5 190 A2
Oak Hill Lo NW3 69 D4
Oak Hill Park Mews NW3 70 A4
Oak Hill Pk NW3 69 D4
Oakhill Pl SW15 157 C6
Oakhill Prim Sch IG8 36 C4
Oakhill Rd BR6 227 D6
Beckenham BR3 186 A1
Putney SW15 157 B6
Sutton SM1 218 A5
Thornton Heath SW16 182 B2
Oak Hill Rd KT6 198 A3
Oak Hill Way NW3 70 A4
Oak Ho 13 DA15 168 A1
8 E14 120 A4
N16 73 B6
11 N2 30 B1
8 NW3 70 D2
Penge SE20 184 B1
Wood Green N22 32 A3
Oakhouse Rd DA6 169 C6
Oakhurst Ave DA7 147 A5
East Barnet EN4 14 C4
Oakhurst Cl BR7 188 B2
E17 54 C5
4 Teddington TW11 174 C5
Oakhurst Ct E17 54 C5
Oakhurst Gdns DA7 147 A5
E11,E17 54 C5
Chingford E4 20 D3
Oakhurst Gr SE22 140 A1
Oakhurst Rd KT19 215 B2
Oakington 14 KT1 176 C1
Oakington Ave
Harrow HA2 41 C2
Hayes UB3 105 B2
Wembley HA9 66 B5
Oakington Dr TW16 172 C1
Oakington Manor Dr
HA9 66 C3
Oakington Manor Prim Sch
HA9 66 D3
Oakington Rd W9 91 C3
Oakington Way N8 50 A2
Oak La E14 119 B6
N11 31 D4
N2 30 B1
Isleworth TW7 130 C1
Twickenham TW1 153 A4
Woodford IG8 36 D6
Oakland Pl IG9 21 A2
Oakland Rd E15 76 C4
Oaklands BR7 189 B4
Croydon CR0 220 D3
Ealing W13 87 A2
Southgate N21 16 B2
Oaklands Ave DA15 167 D4
Enfield N9 18 B5
Hounslow TW7 130 D6
Thames Ditton KT10 196 B1
Thornton Heath CR7 204 C5
West Wickham BR4 223 D5
Oaklands Cl BR5 211 C3
DA6 169 B6
Chessington KT9 213 C4
Wembley HA0 65 D3
Oaklands Ct NW10 89 C6
1 Wembley HA0 65 D3
Oaklands Dr TW2 152 A4
Oaklands Gr W12 112 A5
Oaklands Ho SE4 141 B2
Oaklands Mews NW2 68 D4
Oaklands Park Ave IG1 79 A6
Oaklands Pas NW2 68 D4
Oaklands Pl 8 SW4 137 D1
Oaklands Prim Sch W7 108 D4
Oaklands Rd DA6 169 B6
NW2 68 D4
W7,W13 109 A4
Barnet N20 13 B4
Bromley BR1 186 C3
Ealing W7 108 D4
Mortlake SW14 133 B2
Oaklands Sch
Hounslow TW3 130 B2
Loughton IG10 21 C6
Oaklands Sec Sch E2 96 B4
Oaklands Way SM6 219 D1
Oakland Way KT19 215 C2
Oakleafe Gdns IG6 56 D6
Oaklea Pas KT1 197 D6
Oakleigh Ave N20 14 C3
Edgware HA8 26 D2
Tolworth KT6 214 D6
Oakleigh Cl N20 14 D1
Oakleigh Cres N20 14 C1
Oakleigh Ct HA8 27 A1
East Barnet EN4 14 C5
Penge SE20 184 B3
Southall UB1 107 B5
Surbiton KT6 214 B6
Oakleigh Gdns BR6 227 C4
N20 14 B3
Edgware HA8 26 B5
Oakleigh Lo IG3 80 A5
Oakleigh Mews N20 14 A2
Oakleigh Park Ave BR7 188 C2
Oakleigh Park Sta EN4 14 C4
Oakleigh Pk N N20 14 B3
Oakleigh Pk S N20 14 C3
Oakleigh Rd
Hillingdon UB10 61 A1
Pinner HA5 23 B4
Oakleigh Rd N N20 14 C2
Oakleigh Rd S N11 31 A6
Oakleigh Sch N20 14 D1
Oakleigh Way
Mitcham CR4 181 B2
1 Tolworth KT6 198 D1
Oakley Ave Barking IG11 79 D1
Ealing W5 110 C6
Wallington CR0 220 A4
Oakley Cl 7 E6 100 A1
Chingford E4 20 A1
Oakley Cl *continued*
Ealing W7 108 C6
Hounslow TW7 130 B4
Oakley Cres EC1 234 D3
Oakley Ct CR4 203 A2
Oakley Dr DA15 167 B3
SE13 164 B5
Keston Mark BR2 226 A5
Oakley Gdns N8 50 B4
SW3 136 C6 267 B6
Oakley Ho SW1 257 D4
Ealing W5 110 C6
Oakley Pk DA5,DA15 168 C4
Oakley Pl SE1 117 D1 263 C1
Oakley Rd N1 73 B1
Croydon SE25 206 B4
Harrow HA1 42 C3
Keston Mark BR2 226 A6
Oakley Sq NW1 93 C5 232 B4
Oakley St SW3 136 C6 267 A6
Oakley Wlk W6 134 D6
Oak Lo 4 Ashford TW16 171 D3
Southgate N21 16 B5
Wanstead E11 55 A2
Oak Lodge Cl HA7 25 C5
Oak Lodge Dr BR4 207 D2
Oak Lodge Sch N2 48 A5
Balham SW12 159 A4
Oaklodge Way NW7 27 D4
Oakman Ho 29 SW19 156 D3
Oakmead Ave BR2 209 A3
Oakmead Ct HA7 25 C6
Oakmeade HA5 23 C4
Oakmead Gdns HA8 27 B6
Oakmead Pl CR4 180 C2
Oakmead Rd
Balham SW12 159 B3
Wallington CR0 203 D3
Oakmere Rd SE2 146 A6
Oakmont Pl 6 BR6 211 B1
Oak Park Gdns SW19 156 D3
Oak Park Mews N16 73 D5
Oak Rd Ealing W5 109 D6
Kingston KT3 177 B1
Oakridge Dr N2 48 B6
Oakridge La BR1 186 B5
Oakridge Rd BR1 186 C6
Oak Rise IG9 21 D1
Oak Row CR4 181 C1
Oaks Ave Feltham TW13 151 A2
North Cheam KT4 216 B4
West Norwood SE19 183 C5
Oaksford Ave SE26 162 B1
Oaks Gr E4 20 C2
Oakshade Rd BR1 186 B6
Oakshaw Rd SW18 157 D4
Oakshott Ct NW1 232 C3
Oaks La Ilford IG2 57 C5
South Croydon CR0 222 C5
Oaks Park High Sch IG2 57 C4
Oaks Rd CR0 222 C4
Oaks Sh Ctr The W3 111 A5
Oaks The BR2 210 C3
N12 29 D6
NW10 68 B1
NW6 68 D1
SE18 123 A1
Chingford IG8 36 C3
Enfield EN2 4 D2
Hayes UB4 83 A5
Long Ditton KT6 213 C5
Ruislip HA4 39 C2
Wimbledon SW19 179 A4
Oaks Way Surbiton KT6 197 D1
Wallington SM5 218 D1
Oakthorpe Ct N13 33 A5
Oakthorpe Prim Sch N13 33 A5
Oakthorpe Rd N13 32 C5
Oak Tree Ave N2 47 D6
Oaktree Ave N13 16 D1
Oak Tree Cl Ealing W5 87 C1
Stanmore HA7 25 C3
Oak Tree Ct 6 SW4 160 A6
Acton W3 110 D6
Elstree WD6 9 D5
Oak Tree Dell NW9 45 B4
Oak Tree Dr N20 13 D3
Oak Tree Gdns BR1 187 B5
Oaktree Gr IG1 79 B3
Oak Tree Ho W9 91 D3
Oak Tree Rd
NW8 92 C4 230 A1
Oaktree Sch EN4 15 A5
Oakview Gdns N2 48 B5
Oakview Gr CR0 207 A1
Oakview Lo NW11 47 B2
Oakview Rd SE6 185 D5
Oak Village NW5 71 A4
Oak Way N14 15 B4
W3 111 C5
Oakway Beckenham BR2 186 B1
West Barnes SW20 200 C5
Oak Way Croydon CR0 206 D3
East Bedfont TW14 149 C3
Oakway Cl DA5 169 A5
Oakways SE9 166 D5
Oakwell Ho 24 SW8 137 D3
Oak Wlk CR4 203 A1
Oakwood Ave N14 15 D4
Beckenham BR2,BR3 186 A1
Bromley BR2 209 B6
Mitcham CR4 180 B1
Southall UB1 107 C6
Oakwood Cl BR7 188 C4
Southgate N14 15 C5
Oakwood Cres
Southgate N21 16 B5
Wembley UB6 65 B2
Oakwood Ct 1 E6 100 A6
W14 113 B3 254 C6

Oakwood Ct *continued*
Beckenham BR3 ....186 A1
6 Chingford E4 ....20 C4
Oakwood Dr HA8 ....27 A4
West Norwood SE19 ....183 C4
Oakwood Gdns Ilford IG3 .79 D6
Orpington BR6 ....227 A6
Sutton SM1 ....217 C6
Oakwood La
W14 ....113 B3 254 C6
Oakwood Park Rd N14 ...16 A5
Oakwood Pl CR0 ....204 C3
Oakwood Rd NW11 ....47 D4
Orpington BR6 ....227 A6
Pinner HA5 ....22 B1
Thornton Heath CR0 ....204 C3
Wimbledon SW20 ....178 A2
Oakwood Sta N14 ....15 C6
Oakwood View N14 ....15 D4
Oakworth Rd W10 ....90 D2
Oarsman Pl KT8 ....196 C5
Oasis The 4 BR1 ....187 C1
Oast Ct 8 E14 ....119 B6
Oast Lo W4 ....133 C5
Oates Cl BR2 ....208 B6
Oatfield Ho 1 N15 ....51 C3
Oatfield Rd BR6 ....211 D1
Oat La EC2 ....95 A1 242 B2
Oatland Rise E17 ....35 A1
Oatlands Ct 8 SW19 ....156 D3
Oatlands Dr KT13 ....193 C1
Oatlands Rd EN3 ....6 C4
Oatwell Ho SW3 ....257 B3
Oban Cl E13 ....99 C3
Oban Ho Barking IG11 ...101 B5
South Bromley E14 ....98 B1
Oban Rd E13 ....99 C4
South Norwood SE25 ....205 B5
Oban St E14 ....98 B1
Oberon Ho 5 N1 ....95 C5
Oberon Way TW17 ....192 A6
Oberstein Rd 15 SW11 ...136 B1
Oborne Cl SE24 ....160 D6
O'Brian Ho 10 E1 ....96 D4
Observatory Gdns W8 ..245 B2
Observatory Mews E14 .120 B2
Observatory Rd SW14 ...133 A1
Occupation La SE18 ....144 D4
W5 ....109 D2
Occupation Rd
SE17 ....117 A1 262 A2
W13 ....109 B4
Ocean St E1 ....96 D2
Ocean Wharf E14 ....119 C4
Ockbrook 3 E1 ....96 C2
Ockendon Rd N1 ....73 B2
Ockham Dr BR5 ....190 A3
Ockley Ct SM1 ....218 A4
Ockley Ho 8 KT2 ....176 D4
Ockley Rd
Streatham SW16 ....160 A1
Thornton Heath CR0 ....204 B2
Octagon Arc EC2 ....243 A3
Octagon The NW3 ....69 C4
Octavia Cl CR4 ....202 C4
Octavia Ho W10 ....91 A3
Octavia Rd TW7 ....130 D2
Octavia St SW11 .136 C4 267 B1
Octavia Way 12 SE28 ....124 B6
Octavius St SE8 ....141 C5
October Ct BR2 ....208 D6
October Pl NW4 ....46 D6
Odard Rd KT8 ....195 C5
Odell Cl IG11 ....79 D1
Odeon Ct 1 E16 ....99 A2
NW10 ....89 C6
Odeon Par SE9 ....144 A1
Wembley UB6 ....65 B2
Odessa Inf Sch E7 ....77 A3
Odessa Rd E7 ....76 D4
NW10 ....90 A5
Odessa St SE16 ....119 B3
Odette Ct N20 ....14 A1
Odette Duval Ho 24 E1 ....96 C2
Odette Ho 6 SE27 ....183 B6
Odger St SW11 ....136 D3
Odhams Wlk WC2 ....240 B1
Odin Ho 6 SE5 ....139 A3
O'Donnell Ct WC1 ....240 B6
O'Driscoll Ho W12 ....90 B1
Odyssey Bsns Pk HA4 ...62 B3
Offa's Mead E9 ....75 A4
Offenbach Ho 12 E2 ....96 D5
Offenham Rd BR7,SE9 ...188 B6
Offers Ct KT1 ....198 B6
Offerton Rd SW4 ....137 C2
Offham Ho SE17 ....263 A3
Offham Slope N12 ....29 B5
Offley Ho 10 E9 ....74 D2
Offley Pl TW7 ....130 B3
Offley Rd SW9 ....138 C5
Offord Cl N17 ....34 A4
Offord Rd N1 ....72 B1
Offord St N1 ....72 B1
Ogden Ho TW13 ....173 A6
Ogilby St SE18 ....122 B2
Ogilvie Ho 11 E1 ....96 D1
Oglander Rd SE15 ....139 D2
Ogle St W1 ....93 C2 239 A4
Oglethorpe Rd RM10 ....81 C5
O'Gorman Ho SW10 ....266 B4
O'Grady Ho 17 E17 ....53 D6
Ohio Rd E13 ....98 D3
Oil Mill La W6 ....112 A1
Okeburn Rd SW17 ....181 A5
Okehampton Cl N12 ....30 B5
Okehampton Cres DA16 .146 C4
Okehampton Rd NW10 ...90 D6
Okeover Manor SW4 ....137 B1
Olaf Palme Ho TW13 ....150 B1
Olaf St W11 ....112 D6
Old Bailey EC4 ..94 D1 241 D1
Old Barn Cl SM2 ....217 A1
Old Barrack Yd SW1 ....248 A1
Old Bellgate Wharf E14 .119 C3
Oldberry Rd HA8 ....27 B4
Old Bethnal Green Rd E2 .96 B4
Old Bexley Bsns Pk
DA5 ....169 D4
Old Bexley CE Prim Sch
DA5 ....169 B3
Old Bldgs WC2 ....241 A2
Old Bond St W1 .115 C6 249 A5
Oldborough Rd HA0 ....65 C5
Old Borrowfield 7 E15 ..98 C6
Old Brewery Mews NW3 .70 B4
Old Bridge Cl UB5 ....85 C5
Old Bridge St KT1 ....175 D1
Old Broad St EC2 .95 B1 242 D2
Old Bromley Rd BR1 ....186 B5
Old Brompton Rd
SW5,SW7 ....114 A1 256 B3
Old Burlington St
W1 ....115 C6 249 A5
Oldbury Ct E9 ....75 A3
Oldbury Pl W1 ...93 A2 238 B4
Oldbury Rd EN1 ....6 A3
Old Castle St E1 ..95 D1 243 D2
Old Cavendish St W1 ....238 C1
Old Change Ct EC4 ....242 A1
Old Chapel Pl 2 N10 ....49 B6
Old Charlton Rd TW17 ..193 A4
Old Chiswick Yd W4 ....133 C6
Old Church Ct N11 ....31 B5
Old Church La NW9 ....67 B6
Ealing UB6 ....87 A4
Stanmore HA7 ....25 C4
Old Church Path KT10 ..212 A4
Old Church Rd E1 ....96 D1
Chingford E4 ....19 C1
Old Church St SW3 ....256 D1
Old Claygate La KT10 ...213 A3
Old Clem Sq 12 SE18 ....144 C6
Old Compton St
W1 ....93 D1 239 C1
Old Cote Dr TW5 ....129 C6
Old County Hall SE1 ....250 C2
Old Court Ho W8 ....245 C1
Old Court (Mus & Liby)
HA0 ....65 C3
Old Court Pl
W8 ....113 D4 245 C1
Old Covent Garden
WC2 ....250 B6
Old Ctyd The BR1 ....187 B2
Old Dairy Mews 4 NW5 ..71 B2
5 Balham SW12 ....159 A3
Old Deer Park Gdns
TW9 ....132 A2
Old Devonshire Rd
SW12 ....159 B4
Old Dock Cl TW9 ....132 C6
Old Dover Rd SE3 ....143 B5
Oldegate Ho 1 E6 ....99 D6
Old Farm Ave N14 ....15 C4
Sidcup DA15 ....167 C2
Old Farm Cl TW4 ....129 B1
Old Farm Ct UB2 ....107 D2
Old Farm Rd N2 ....30 B2
Hampton TW12 ....173 C4
Old Farm Rd E DA15 ....168 A2
Old Farm Rd W DA15 ....167 D2
Oldfield Cl BR1 ....210 B5
Stanmore HA7 ....25 A5
Oldfield Farm Gdns UB6 ..86 B6
Oldfield Gr SE16 ....118 D2
Oldfield Ho 14 W4 ....111 C1
Streatham SW16 ....181 B6
Oldfield House Sch
TW12 ....173 B2
Oldfield Mews N6 ....49 C2
Oldfield Prim Sch UB6 ...86 B5
Oldfield Rd BR1 ....210 B5
DA7 ....147 A3
N16 ....73 C5
NW10 ....67 D1
W3,W12 ....111 D4
Hampton TW12 ....173 B2
Wimbledon SW19 ....179 A4
Oldfields Cir UB5 ....64 A2
Oldfields Rd SM1,SM3 ..217 C6
Oldfields Trad Est SM1 ..217 C5
Old Fish St Hill EC4 ....252 A6
Old Fleet La EC4 ....241 C2
Old Fold Cl EN5 ....1 B4
Old Fold La EN5 ....1 B4
Old Ford Ho CR0 ....220 A5
Old Ford Prim Sch E3 ....97 B5
Old Ford Rd E2,E3 ....96 D5
Old Ford Trad Ctr E3 ....97 C6
Old Forge Cl HA7 ....25 A6
Old Forge Cres TW17 ....192 D3
Old Forge Mews W12 ....112 B4
Old Forge Rd EN1 ....5 D5
Old Forge Way DA14 ....190 B6
Old Gloucester St
WC1 ....94 A2 240 B4
Old Hall Cl HA5 ....23 A2
Old Hall Dr HA5 ....23 A2
Oldham Ho 10 SE21 ....183 C6
Oldham Terr W3 ....111 A5
Old Hatch Manor HA4 ....40 A2
Old Hill Chislehurst BR7 ..188 C2
Orpington BR6 ....227 C2
Oldhill St N16 ....52 A1
Old Homesdale Rd BR2 .209 C5
Old Hospital Cl SW12,
SW17 ....158 D3
Old House Cl SW19 ....179 A5
Old House Gdns 9
TW1 ....153 C5
Old Howlett's La HA4 ....39 B3
Olding Ho 6 SW12 ....159 C4
Old Jamaica Bsns Est 23
SE16 ....118 A3
Old Jamaica Rd SE16 ....118 A3
Old James St SE15 ....140 B2
Old Jewry EC2 ....95 B1 242 C1
Old Kenton La NW9 ....44 D4
Old Kent Rd SE1 .117 C1 263 B2
SE1,SE15 ....140 B6
Old Kingston Rd KT4 ....215 A5
Old Laundry The 14
SW18 ....136 B1
Old Lodge Pl 7 TW1 ....153 B5
Old Lodge Way HA7 ....25 A5
Old Maidstone Rd BR8,
DA14 ....191 B3
Old Malden La KT4 ....215 C6
Oldman Ct SE12 ....165 B2
Old Manor Dr TW7 ....152 A5
Old Manor Rd UB2 ....106 D2
Old Manor Way BR7,SE9 .188 B5
Old Manor Yd SW5 ....255 C3
Old Market Sq 11 E2 ....95 D4
Old Marylebone Rd
NW1 ....92 C2 237 B3
Oldmead Ho 8 RM10 ....81 D2
Old Mill Ct E18 ....55 C6
Old Mill Rd SE18 ....145 B6
Old Mitre Ct EC4 ....241 B1
Old Montague St E1 ....96 A2
Old Nichol St E2 ..95 D3 243 C6
Old North St WC1 ....240 C4
Old Nursery Pl TW15 ...170 D5
Old Oak Common La
NW10 ....89 C3
Old Oak La NW10 ....89 D4
Old Oak Prim Sch W12 ...89 D1
Old Oak Rd W3 ....111 D6
Old Orch TW16 ....172 C1
Old Orchard Cl
Hadley Wood EN4 ....2 B5
Hillingdon UB8 ....82 C1
Old Orch The NW3 ....70 D4
Old Palace La TW9 ....153 C6
Old Palace Prim Sch E3 ..97 D4
Old Palace Rd CR0 ....221 A5
Old Palace Sch of John
Whitgift CR9 ....220 D5
Old Palace Terr 8 TW9 .153 D6
Old Palace Yd 2 TW9 ..153 D6
Old Paradise St
SE11 ....116 B2 260 C4
Old Park Ave SW12 ....159 A5
Enfield EN2 ....5 A1
Old Park Gr EN2 ....5 A1
Old Park Ho N13 ....32 B6
Old Park La W1 .115 B5 248 C3
Old Park Mews TW5 ....129 B5
Old Park Rd SE2 ....124 A1
Enfield EN2 ....4 D2
Palmers Green N13 ....32 B6
Old Park Rd S EN2 ....4 D1
Old Park Ridings N21 ....17 A6
Old Park View EN2 ....4 D2
Old Perry St BR7 ....189 C3
Old Pound Cl TW7 ....131 A4
Old Priory UB9 ....38 D2
Old Pye St SW1 ....259 C6
Old Pye Street Est SW1 .259 C5
Old Quebec St W1 ....237 D1
Old Queen St
SW1 ....115 D4 249 D1
Old Rd SE13 ....142 C1
Enfield EN3 ....6 C4
Old Rectory Gdns HA8 ...26 C4
Old Redding HA3 ....24 A6
Oldridge Rd SW12 ....159 B4
Old Royal Free Pl N1 ....234 B5
Old Royal Free Sq
N1 ....94 C6 234 B5
Old Royal Observatory
Greenwich (National
Maritime Mus Annexe)★
SE10 ....142 B5
Old Ruislip Rd UB5 ....84 C5
Old School Cl
3 Beckenham BR3 ....185 A1
Merton SW19 ....179 C1
Old School Cres E7 ....77 A2
Old School Ho The EN2 ...4 D2
Old School Pl CR0 ....220 C4
Old School Rd UB8 ....82 B3
Old School Sq 19 E14 ....97 C1
Thames Ditton KT7 ....196 D3
Old School The WC1 ....240 C4
Old Seacoal La EC4 ....241 C1
Old South Lambeth Rd
SW8 ....138 A5 270 B4
Old Spitalfields Mkt
E1 ....95 D2 243 D2
Old Sq WC2 ....241 A2
Old St E13 ....99 B5
EC1 ....95 B3 242 B6
Old Stable Mews N5 ....73 A5
Old St Andrews Mans
NW9 ....67 B6
Old Station Rd UB3 ....105 D3
Oldstead Rd BR1 ....186 B6
Old Street Sta
EC1 ....95 B3 242 D6
Old Sun Wharf E14 ....119 A6
Old Swan Wharf SW11 ..266 D2
Old Swan Yd SM5 ....218 D4
Old Theatre Ct SE1 ....252 B4
Old Town SW4 ....137 C2
Croydon CR0 ....220 D5
Old Tramyard SE18 ....123 C2
Old Woolwich Rd SE10 ..120 B1
Old York Rd SW18 ....157 D6
Oleander Cl BR6 ....227 B3
O'Leary Sq E1 ....96 C2
Olga Prim Sch E3 ....97 A5
Olga St 18 E3 ....97 A5
Olinda Rd N16 ....51 D3
Oliphant St W10 ....91 A4
Olive Blythe Ho 14 W10 ..91 A3
Oliver Ave SE25 ....205 D6
Oliver Bsns Pk NW10 ....89 A5
Oliver Cl W4 ....132 D6
Oliver Ct SE18 ....123 A2
Isleworth TW7 ....130 D2
Olive Rd E13 ....99 C4
NW2 ....68 C4
W5 ....109 D3
3 Merton SW19 ....180 A3
Oliver Gdns E6 ....100 A2
Oliver Goldsmith Prim Sch
NW9 ....45 B4
Oliver Goldsmith Prim Schs
SE5 ....139 D4
Oliver Gr SE25 ....205 D5
Oliver Ho 19 SE16 ....118 A4
SW8 ....270 A4
W11 ....244 B5
Oliver Mews SE15 ....140 A3
Oliver Rd E10 ....75 D5
E17 ....54 A4
Kingston KT3 ....177 A1
Sutton SM1 ....218 B4
Oliver's Yd EC1 ....242 D6
Olive Tree Ho N4 ....50 C3
7 SE15 ....140 C6
Olivette St 1 SW15 ....134 D1
Olive Waite Ho NW6 ....69 D1
Ollard's Gr IG10 ....21 D6
Ollerton Gn E3 ....97 B6
Ollerton Rd N11 ....31 D5
Olley Cl SM6 ....220 A2
Ollgar Cl W12 ....111 D5
Olliffe St E14 ....120 A3
Olmar St SE1 ....140 A6
Olmar Wharf SE1 ....140 A6
Olney Ho NW8 ....237 B6
Olney Rd SE17 ....139 A6
Olron Cres DA6 ....169 A6
Olven Rd SE18 ....145 A6
Olveston Wlk SM5 ....202 B3
Olwen Mews HA5 ....22 D1
Olyffe Ave DA16 ....146 A3
Olyffe Dr BR3 ....186 A2
Olympia Ex Ctr★
W14 ....112 D3 254 A6
Olympian Ct 1 E14 ....119 C2
Olympia Way
W14 ....113 A3 254 B5
Olympia Yd W2 ....245 D5
Olympic Ho W10 ....90 C1
Olympic Ret Pk HA9 ....66 D4
Olympic Way
Greenford UB6 ....85 D6
Wembley HA9 ....66 C4
Olympus Sq E5 ....74 A5
Oman Ave NW2 ....68 C4
Oman Ct NW4 ....68 B4
Ombersley Ho N4 ....51 A2
Omeara St SE1 ....252 B3
Omega Cl E14 ....119 D3
Omega Ho SW10 ....266 B4
Omega Pl N1 ....233 B3
Omega St SE14 ....141 C4
Ommaney Rd SE14 ....141 A4
Omnibus Way E17 ....35 C1
Ondine Rd SE15 ....139 D1
Onedin Point 17 E1 ....118 A6
Onega Gate SE16 ....119 A3
O'Neill Ho NW8 ....229 D3
O'Neill Path 11 SE18 ....144 C6
One Tree Cl SE23 ....162 C5
Ongar Cl RM6 ....58 C4
Ongar Ho 15 N1 ....73 B2
Ongar Rd SW6 ..135 C6 265 B6
Onra Rd E17 ....53 C2
Onslow Ave TW10 ....154 A6
Onslow Avenue Mans 10
TW10 ....154 A6
Onslow Cl Chingford E4 ....20 B2
Thames Ditton KT7 ....196 C1
Onslow Cres BR7 ....188 D2
Onslow Ct SW10 ....256 B1
Onslow Dr DA14 ....168 D2
Onslow Gdns N10 ....49 B4
SW7 ....114 B1 256 C2
Southgate N21 ....16 C6
Thames Ditton KT7 ....196 C1
Wallington SM6 ....219 C1
Wanstead E18 ....55 C6
Onslow Ho 1 KT2 ....176 B2
Onslow Lo 28 SW2 ....160 C4
Onslow Mews E SW7 ....256 C3
Onslow Mews W SW7 ....256 C3
Onslow Par N14 ....15 B3
Onslow Rd
Richmond TW10 ....154 A5
Thornton Heath CR0 ....204 C1
West Barnes KT3 ....200 A5
Onslow Sq SW7 .114 B2 256 D3
Onslow St EC1 ....241 B5
Onslow Way KT7 ....196 C1
Ontario St SE1 ..116 D3 261 D6
Ontario Way E14 ....119 C6
Onyx Ho KT4 ....199 B1
Opal Cl E16 ....99 D1
Opal Ho KT4 ....199 B1
Opal Mews 2 IG1 ....78 D6
Opal St SE11 ...116 D1 261 C2
Open Air Theatre, Regent's
Park NW1 ....231 A1
Openshaw Rd SE2 ....124 B2
Openview SW17,SW18 ...158 B2
Operating Theatre Mus &
Herb Garret★
SE1 ....117 B5 252 D3
Ophelia Gdns NW2 ....69 A5
Ophir Terr SE15 ....140 A4
Opie Ho NW8 ....230 B4
Opossum Way TW4 ....128 C2
Oppenheim Rd SE13 ....142 A3
Oppidans Rd NW3 ....70 D1
Orange Hill Rd HA8 ....27 A3
Orange Pl SE16 ....118 C3
Orangery La SE9 ....166 B6
Orangery The TW10 ....153 C2
Orange St WC2 ..115 D6 249 D5
Orange Yd WC2 ....239 D1
Oratory La SW3 ....256 D2
Oratory RC Prim Sch
SW3 ....114 C1 257 A2
Oratory The★
SW7 ....114 C3 257 A5
Orbain Rd SW6 ..135 A5 264 B3
Orbel St SW11 ..136 C4 267 A1
Orb St SE17 ....117 B2 262 C3
Orchard Ave N14 ....15 C4
N20 ....14 B2
N3 ....47 C6
Ashford TW15 ....171 A4
Carshalton CR4 ....203 A1
Croydon CR0 ....207 A1
Erith DA17 ....147 B6
Hatton TW14 ....149 B6
Heston TW5 ....129 A5
Hinchley Wood KT7 ....213 A6
Kingston KT3 ....199 C6
Southall UB1 ....107 B5
Orchard Bsns Ctr SE26 ..185 B5
Orchard Cl DA7 ....147 A4
N1 ....73 A1
NW2 ....68 A5
SE23 ....162 C5
W10 ....91 A2
Ashford TW15 ....171 A4
Bushey WD23 ....8 B3
Chingford E4 ....35 C6
Edgware HA8 ....26 A4
Northolt UB5 ....64 A2
Ruislip HA4 ....39 A2
Thames Ditton KT7 ....197 B2
Walton-on-T KT12 ....194 B2
Wanstead E11 ....55 B5
Wembley HA0 ....88 A6
West Barnes SW20 ....200 C5
West Ewell KT19 ....214 D2
Orchard Cotts UB3 ....105 C4
Orchard Cres HA8 ....27 A5
Enfield EN1 ....5 D4
Orchard Ct E10 ....53 D1
W1 ....238 A2
Barnes SW13 ....133 D2
Croydon BR3 ....207 C1
Edgware HA8 ....26 B5
Hounslow TW7 ....130 B5
New Malden KT4 ....200 A1
Southgate N14 ....15 C5
Wallington SM6 ....219 B3
Walton-on-T KT12 ....193 D1
Wood Green N22 ....32 A3
Orchard Dr SE3 ....142 C3
Edgware HA8 ....26 B5
Upper Halliford TW17 ..193 C6
Orchard Gate NW9 ....45 C5
Thames Ditton KT10 ....196 B1
Wembley UB6 ....65 B2
Orchard Gdns
Chessington KT9 ....214 A4
Sutton SM1 ....217 C3
Orchard Gn BR6 ....227 C6
Orchard Gr BR6 ....211 D1
BR6 ....227 D6
Croydon CR0 ....207 A2
Edgware HA8 ....26 D2
Harrow HA3 ....44 B4
Penge SE20 ....184 A3
Orchard Hill SE13 ....141 D4
Orchard Ho 11 SE16 ....118 C3
SE5 ....139 A4
W12 ....112 A5
Orchard Jun & Inf Sch The
TW3 ....151 C6
Orchard La
Thames Ditton KT8 ....196 B3
Wimbledon SW20 ....178 B2
Woodford IG8 ....37 C6
Orchardleigh Ave EN3 ....6 C3
Orchard Lo N12 ....14 A1
Orchard Mead Ho NW11 .69 C6
Orchardmede N21 ....17 B5
Orchard Mews N1 ....73 B1
Orchard Pl E14 ....120 C6
Tottenham N17 ....33 D3
Orchard Prim Sch E9 ....74 C1
Orchard Rd BR1 ....187 C2
BR6 ....226 D3
DA16 ....146 B2
N6 ....49 B2
Barnet EN5 ....1 B1
Belvedere DA17 ....125 C2
Brentford TW8 ....131 C6
Carshalton CR4 ....203 A1
Chessington KT9 ....214 A4
Dagenham RM10 ....103 C6
Enfield EN3 ....18 C6
Feltham TW14 ....150 A3
Hampton TW12 ....173 B3
Hayes UB3 ....106 A6
Hounslow TW4 ....151 C6
Isleworth TW1 ....153 B6
Kingston KT1 ....176 A1
Orchard Rd *continued*
Richmond TW9 ....132 C2
Sidcup DA14 ....189 C6
Sunbury TW16 ....172 B3
Sutton SM1 ....217 C4
Orchard Rise
Croydon CR0 ....207 B1
Kingston KT2 ....177 A2
Mortlake TW10 ....132 D1
Pinner HA5 ....39 D6
Orchard Rise E DA15 ....167 D6
Orchard Rise W DA15 ....167 C6
Orchard School Sports Ctr
SE20 ....184 A2
Orchardson Ho NW8 ....236 D5
Orchardson St
NW8 ....92 B3 236 D5
Orchard Sq W14 ....254 C1
Orchard St E17 ....53 A5
W1 ....238 A1
Orchard Terr EN1 ....18 A5
Orchard The N20 ....13 D3
NW11 ....47 C4
SE3 ....142 B3
W4 ....111 B2
Ealing W5 ....87 D2
East Barnet N14 ....15 B6
Enfield N21 ....17 B5
Ewell KT17 ....215 D1
Hounslow TW3 ....130 A3
Orchard Way
Ashford TW15 ....148 B2
Croydon BR3,CR0 ....207 A3
Enfield EN1 ....5 C2
Esher KT10 ....212 A2
Sutton SM1 ....218 B4
Orchard Way Prim Sch
CR0 ....207 A2
Orchid Cl 1 E6 ....100 A2
Chessington KT9 ....213 C1
Southall UB1 ....85 A1
Orchid Ct HA9 ....66 A6
Orchid Grange N14 ....15 C4
Orchid Lo N14 ....15 C4
Orchid Rd N14 ....15 C4
Orchid St W12 ....112 A6
Orde 6 NW9 ....27 D2
Orde Hall St WC1 .94 B2 240 C4
Orde Ho 10 N16 ....73 B4
Ordell Ct 30 E3 ....97 B5
Ordell Rd E3 ....97 B5
Ordnance Cl TW13 ....150 A2
Ordnance Cres SE10 ....120 C4
Ordnance Hill
NW8 ....92 B6 229 D5
Ordnance Mews NW8 ....229 D4
Ordnance Rd E16 ....98 D2
SE18 ....144 C6
Enfield EN3 ....7 B6
Oregano Cl UB7 ....104 B6
Oregano Dr E14 ....98 B1
Oregon Ave E12 ....78 B4
Oregon Cl KT3 ....199 A5
Oregon Sq BR6 ....211 B1
Orestes Ct 8 E18 ....55 A6
Orestes Mews 1 NW6 ....69 C3
Orford Ct Stanmore HA7 ..25 C4
Wallington SM6 ....219 C3
West Norwood SE27 ....160 D2
Orford Gdns TW1 ....152 D2
Orford Rd E17 ....53 D4
Catford SE6 ....163 D1
Wanstead E18 ....55 B6
Organ Crossroads KT17 .216 A1
Oriana Ho 3 E14 ....119 B6
Oriel Cl CR4 ....203 D6
Oriel Ct NW3 ....70 A4
6 Croydon CR0 ....205 B1
Oriel Dr SW13 ....134 C6
Oriel Gdns IG5 ....56 B6
Oriel Jun & Inf Sch
TW13 ....151 A1
Oriel Rd E9 ....74 D2
E9 ....75 A2
Oriel Way UB5 ....63 D1
Oriental City NW9 ....45 B6
Oriental Rd E16 ....121 D5
Orient Ind Pk E10 ....75 C6
Orient St SE11 ...116 D2 261 C4
Orient Way E5 ....74 D5
Oriole Way SE28 ....124 B6
Orion Bsns Ctr SE14 ....118 D1
Orion Ctr The CR0 ....220 A6
Orion Ho 20 E1 ....96 B3
Orion Prim Sch The
NW9 ....27 D2
Orion Rd N11 ....31 A4
Orion Way HA6 ....22 A6
Orissa Rd SE18 ....123 C1
Orkney Ho N1 ....233 C6
Orkney St SW11 ....137 A3
Orlando Rd SW4 ....137 C2
Orleans Cl KT10 ....212 B6
Orleans Ct 9 TW1 ....153 B4
Orleans Inf Sch TW1 ....153 B4
Orleans Park Sec Sch
TW1 ....153 B4
Orleans Rd
South Norwood SE19 ....183 B4
Twickenham TW1 ....153 C4
Orleston Mews N7 ....72 C2
Orleston Rd N7 ....72 C2
Orley Farm Rd HA1 ....64 C5
Orley Farm Sch HA1 ....64 B5
Orlop St SE10 ....120 C1
Ormanton Rd SE26 ....184 A6
Orme Ct W2 ....113 D6 245 C5

Orme Ct Mews W2 245 D5
Orme Ho 8 E8 95 D6
Orme La W2 113 D6 245 C5
Ormeley Rd SW12 159 B3
Orme Rd
Kingston KT1,KT3 176 D1
Sutton SM1 217 D2
Ormerod Gdns CR4 181 A2
Ormesby Cl SE28 124 D6
Ormesby Way HA3 44 B4
Orme Sq W2 245 C5
Ormiston Gr W12 112 B5
Ormiston Rd SE10 121 A1
Ormond Ave
Hampton TW12 173 D2
22 Richmond TW10 153 D6
Ormond Cl WC1 240 B4
Ormond Cres TW12 173 D2
Ormond Dr TW12 173 D3
Ormonde Ave BR6 227 A6
Ormonde Ct SW15 134 C1
Ormonde Gate
SW3 114 D1 257 D1
Ormonde Pl SW1 258 B3
Ormonde Rd SW14 133 A2
Ormonde Rise IG9 21 C3
Ormonde Terr
NW8 92 D6 230 C5
Ormond Ho 7 N16 73 B6
Ormond Mews WC1 240 B5
Ormond Rd N4,N19 50 A1
Richmond TW10 153 D6
Ormond Yd SW1 249 B4
Ormrod Ct W11 91 B1
Ormsby SM2 217 D1
Ormsby Gdns UB6 86 A5
Ormsby Lo 7 W4 111 C3
Ormsby Pl N16 73 D5
Ormsby Point 6 SE18 122 D2
Ormsby St E2 95 D5
Ormside St SE15 140 C6
Ormskirk Rd WD19 22 D5
Ornan Rd NW3 70 C3
Oronsay Rd 18 N1 73 A2
Orpheus Ho 25 N19 49 D2
Orpheus St SE5 139 B4
Orpington Gdns N18 17 C1
Orpington Hospl BR6 227 D4
Orpington Mans N21 16 C3
Orpington Rd
Southgate N21 16 D3
St Paul's Cray BR7 211 C6
Orpington Sta BR6 227 C6
Orpwood Cl TW12 173 B4
Orsett Mews W2 91 D1 236 A2
Orsett St SE11 116 B1 260 D2
Orsett Terr W2 92 A1 236 A2
Woodford IG8 37 C3
Orsman Rd N1 95 C6
Orton St E1 118 A5
Orville Rd SW11 136 B3
Orwell Cl UB3 105 C6
Orwell Ct E8 96 A6
N5 73 A4
Orwell Ho W12 112 A6
Orwell Lo 2 E18 55 A5
Orwell Rd E13 99 C6
Osbaldeston Rd N16 52 A1
Osberton Rd SE12 165 A6
Osbert St SW1 259 C3
Osborn Cl E8 96 A6
Osborne Ave TW19 148 B3
Osborne Cl
Beckenham BR3 207 A5
Cockfosters EN4 2 D2
Feltham TW13 172 D5
Osborne Ct 16 E10 53 D2
Ealing W5 88 A2
10 Surbiton KT6 198 A3
Osborne Gdns CR7 183 A1
Osborne Gr E17 53 B5
Osborne Mews E17 53 B5
Osborne Pl SM1 218 B3
Osborne Rd E10 75 D6
E7 77 B3
E9 75 B2
N4 50 C1
NW2 68 B2
W3 110 D4
Buckhurst Hill IG9 21 B3
Dagenham RM9 81 B3
Enfield EN3 7 A3
Erith DA17 147 B6
Hounslow TW3,TW4 129 B2
Kingston KT2 176 A3
Palmers Green N13 16 C1
Southall UB1 86 A1
South Norwood CR7 183 A1
Walton-on-T KT12 194 A1
Osborne Sq RM9 81 B4
Osborne Way KT9 214 B3
Osborn Gdns NW7 28 D3
Osborn La SE23 163 A4
Osborn St E1 95 D2 243 D2
Osborn Terr SE3 142 D1
Osbourne Ct HA2 41 D5
Osbourne Ho TW10 154 C6
Osbourne Terr 1 SW17 181 A5
Oscar Faber Pl 8 N1 73 C1
Oscar St SE8 141 C4
Oseney Cres NW5 71 D2
Osgood Ave BR6 227 D3
Osgood Gdns 1 BR6 227 D3
O'Shea Gr E3 97 B6
Osidge JMI Sch N14 15 C3
Osidge La N14 15 B3
Osier Cres N10 30 D2
Osier Ct E1 96 D3
Osier Mews W4 133 D6
Osiers Ct 3 KT1 175 D2
Osiers Rd SW18 135 C1
Osier St E1 96 C3
Osier Way E10 75 D5
Mitcham CR4 202 D4
Oslac Rd SE6 185 D5
Oslo Ct NW8 230 A3
Mitcham SW19 180 B3
Oslo Ho 2 SE5 139 A3
Oslo Sq SE16 119 A3
Osman Cl N15 51 B3
Osmani Prim Sch E1 96 A2
Osman Rd W6 112 C3
Edmonton N9 18 A1
Osmington Ho SW8 270 D3
Osmond Cl HA2 64 A6
Osmond Gdns SM6 219 C3
Osmund St W12 89 D2
Osnaburgh St
NW1 93 B3 238 D6
Osnaburgh Terr NW1 238 D6
Osney Ho 4 SE2 124 D4
Osney Wlk SM5 202 B3
Osprey 7 NW9 27 D2
Osprey Cl E17 35 A3
E6 100 A2
Cheam SM1 217 B3
Wanstead E11 55 A5
West Drayton UB7 104 A4
Osprey Ct NW3 69 D3
7 Ealing W7 86 D3
Thornton Heath SW16 182 B1
Osprey Ho 3 E14 119 A6
E4 35 B4
SE15 139 D4
Osprey Mews EN3 18 B6
Ospringe Cl 9 SE20 184 C3
Ospringe Ct SE9 167 B5
Ospringe Ho SE1 251 B3
Ospringe Rd NW5 71 C4
Osram Ct W6 112 C3
Osram Rd HA9 65 D5
Osric Path 8 N1 95 C5
Ossian Rd N4 50 B2
Ossie Garvin Rdbt UB4 106 C6
Ossington Bldgs W1 238 A3
Ossington Cl W2 245 B5
Ossington St
W2 113 D6 245 C5
Ossory Rd SE1 140 A6
Ossulston St
NW1 93 D4 232 D2
Ossultan Pl N2 48 A6
Ossulton Way N2 48 A5
Ostade Rd SW2 160 B4
Ostell Cres EN3 7 C5
Osten Mews
SW7 113 D3 255 D5
Osterley Ave TW7 130 B5
Osterley Cl BR5 190 A2
Osterley Cres TW7 130 D4
Osterley Ct
Hounslow TW7 130 B4
7 Northolt UB5 84 C4
Osterley Gdns UB2 108 A4
Osterley Ho 5 E14 97 D1
Osterley La
Isleworth TW7 108 C1
Southall UB2,TW7 107 D1
Osterley Lo 1 TW7 130 C4
Osterley Park* TW7 108 B1
Osterley Park Rd UB2 107 B3
Osterley Park View Rd
W7 108 C4
Osterley Rd N16 73 C4
Hounslow TW7 130 C4
Osterley Sta TW7 130 B5
Osterley Views UB2 108 B4
Osterly Gdns CR7 183 A1
Oster Terr E17 52 D4
Ostliffe Rd N13 33 A5
Oswald Rd UB1 107 A5
Oswald's Mead E9 75 A4
Oswald St E5 74 D5
Oswald Terr NW2 68 C5
Osward Pl N9 18 B2
Osward Rd SW12,SW17 158 D2
Oswell Ho 9 E1 118 B5
Oswin St SE11 116 D2 261 D4
Oswyth Rd SE5 139 C3
Otford Cl BR1 210 C6
DA5 169 D5
Penge SE20 184 C2
Otford Cres SE4 163 B5
Otford Ho SE1 252 D1
6 SE15 140 C6
Otha Ho 18 SW9 138 A3
Othello Cl SE11 261 C2
Otho Ct 5 TW8 131 D5
Otis St E3 98 A4
Otley App IG2 56 D3
Otley Ct N11 31 A4
Otley Dr IG2 56 D3
Otley Ho N5 72 D5
Otley Rd E16 99 C1
Otley Terr E5 74 D5
Ottawa Ho 4 HA4 40 C1
Ottaway Ct E5 74 A5
Ottaway St E5 74 A5
Otterbourne Rd
Chingford E4 20 B1
1 Croydon CR0 221 A6
Otterburn Gdns TW7 131 A5
Otterburn Ho 12 SE5 139 A5
Otterburn St SW17 180 D4
Otterden Cl BR6 227 C4
Otterden St SE6 185 C6
Otterfield Rd UB7 104 A6
Otter Rd UB6 86 A3
Ottershaw Ho BR5 190 B2
Ottoman Ct W5 109 D2
Otto St SE17 138 D6
Otway Ct N4 50 B3
Otway Gdns WD23 8 C4
Oulton Cl E5 74 C6
Erith SE28 102 C1
Oulton Cres IG11 79 D3
Oulton Rd N15 51 B4
Oulton Way WD19 23 B6
Oundle Ave WD23 8 A5
Our Lady Immaculate RC
Prim Sch KT6 198 D1
Our Lady of Dolours RC Prim
Sch W2 91 D2
Our Lady of Grace RC Inf Sch
NW2 68 C6
Our Lady of Grace RC Jun
Sch NW2 68 B5
Our Lady of Grace Sch
SE7 143 B6
Our Lady of Lourdes RC Prim
Sch
N11 31 C5
N12 30 A2
SE13 142 B2
Our Lady of Lourdes RC Sch
NW10 89 A6
Our Lady of Lourds RC Prim
Sch E11 55 A3
Our Lady of Muswell Prim
Sch N10 49 A6
Our Lady of Muswell RC Prim
Sch N10 31 A1
Our Lady of the Assumption
RC Prim Sch E2 96 C5
Our Lady of the Rosary RC
Prim Sch DA15 167 C5
Our Lady of the Sacred Heart
RC Prim Sch (Annexe)
N7 72 B2
Our Lady of the Sacred Heart
RC Sch N7 72 B3
Our Lady of the Visitation RC
Prim Sch UB6 86 A3
Our Lady of Victories RC
Prim Sch
SW7 114 A2 256 B3
Putney SW15 134 D1
Our Lady Queen of Heaven
RC Sch SW19 156 D4
Our Lady RC Prim Sch
E14 97 B1
NW1 93 C6 232 B5
Our Lady's Convent High Sch
N15,N16 51 C2
Our Lady & St John's RC Jun
& Inf Sch TW8 109 C1
Our Lady & St Joseph RC
Prim Sch N1 73 C2
Our Lady & St Philip Neri RC
Prim Sch SE26 185 A6
Our Lady & St Philip Neri RC
Sch SE26 185 A6
Ouseley Rd SW12 158 D3
Outer Circ NW8 92 C4 230 B3
Outgate Rd NW10 67 D1
Outram Pl N1 94 A6 233 B6
Outram Rd E6 100 A6
N22 31 D2
Croydon CR0 221 D6
Outwich St EC3 243 B2
Outwood Ct CR2 221 A1
Outwood Ho 3 SW2 160 B4
Oval Ct HA8 27 A3
Oval Mans SE11 270 D6
Oval Pl SW8 138 B5 270 D4
Oval Prim Sch CR0 205 C1
Oval Rd NW1 93 B6 231 C6
Croydon CR0 205 C1
Oval Rd N RM10 103 D6
Oval Rd S RM10 103 D5
Oval Sta SE11 138 C6
Oval The E2 96 B5
Sidcup DA15 168 A4
Oval The (Surrey Cnty Crkt
Gd) SE11 138 C6
Oval Way SE11 116 B1 260 D1
Overbrae BR3 185 C5
Overbrook Wlk HA8 26 C3
Overbury Ave BR3 208 A6
Overbury Ct 1 BR3 208 A6
Overbury Ho 3 E5 74 D4
Overbury Rd N4,N15 51 B3
Overbury St E5 74 D4
Overcliff Rd SE13 141 C2
Overcourt Cl DA15 168 B5
Overdale Ave KT3 177 B1
Overdale Rd W5 109 C3
Overdown Rd SE6 185 D6
Overhill Rd SE21,SE22 162 A4
Overhill Way BR3 208 B4
Overlea Rd E5 52 A2
Overmead SE9 167 B4
Oversley Ho 17 W2 91 C2
Overstand Cl BR3 207 C4
Overstone Gdns CR0 207 B2
Overstone Ho 17 E14 97 C1
Overstone Rd W6 112 C2
Overstrand Mans SW11 268 A1
Overton Cl NW10 67 A2
Hounslow TW7 130 D4
Overton Ct E11 55 A2
Overton Dr Ilford RM6 58 C2
Wanstead E11 55 B2
Overton Grange Sch
SM2 217 D1
Overton Ho SW15 155 D4
Overton Rd SE2 124 D3
Overton Rd *continued*
SW9 138 C3
Belmont SM2 217 C1
Southgate N14 16 A6
Walthamstow E10 53 A1
Overton's Yd CR0 221 A5
Overy Ho SE1 251 C1
Ovesdon Ave HA2 41 B1
Ovett Cl SE19 183 C4
Ovex Cl E14 120 A4
Ovington Ct SW3 257 B5
Ovington Gdns SW3 257 B5
Ovington Mews SW3 257 B5
Ovington Sq
SW3 114 C3 257 B5
Ovington St
SW3 114 C2 257 B4
Owen Cl SE28 124 C5
Hayes UB4 84 B4
Thornton Heath CR0 205 B3
Owen Ct UB4 84 B4
Owen Ho 11 N19 71 C4
Feltham TW14 150 A4
5 Twickenham TW1 153 B4
Owenite St SE2 124 B2
Owen Rd Edmonton N13 33 A5
Hayes UB4 84 B4
Owen's Ct EC1 234 C2
Owen's Row EC1 234 C2
Owen St EC1 234 C3
Owens Way SE23 163 A4
Owen Way NW10 67 A3
Owen Wlk 7 SE20 184 A3
Owgan Cl SE5 139 B5
Oxberry Ave SW6 135 A3
Oxbridge Ct 4 W4 110 D1
Oxendon St
SW1,W1 115 D6 249 C5
Oxenford St SE15 139 D2
Oxenham Ho 13 SE8 141 C6
Oxenholme NW1 232 B3
Oxenpark Ave HA9 44 A2
Oxestalls Rd SE8 119 A1
Oxford Ave NW10 90 C4
Harlington TW6 127 D5
Hounslow TW5 107 C1
Merton SW20 179 A1
Oxford & Cambridge Mans
NW1 237 B3
Oxford Cir W1 93 C1 239 A1
Oxford Circus Ave W1 239 A1
Oxford Circus Sta
W1 93 C1 239 A1
Oxford Cl Edmonton N9 18 B2
Littleton TW15,TW17 171 A3
Mitcham CR4 203 C6
Oxford Cres KT3 199 B3
Oxford Ct EC4 252 C6
48 W2 91 C2
W4 110 D1
16 Acton W3 88 C1
8 Ealing W7 86 D2
17 Kingston KT6 198 A4
Oxford Dr SE1 253 B1
Ruislip HA4 62 C6
Oxford Gardens Prim Sch
W10 90 D1
Oxford Gate W6 112 D2
Oxford Gdns N20 14 B3
W10 90 D1
Brentford W4 132 C6
Edmonton N21 17 A4
Oxford Mews DA5 169 C4
Oxford Rd DA14 190 B5
E15 76 B2
N4 50 C1
NW6 91 C5
Carshalton SM2,SM5 218 C3
Ealing W5 109 D6
Edmonton N9 18 B2
Enfield EN3 18 B6
Harrow HA1 42 A3
Harrow HA3 42 D6
Ilford IG1 79 A3
Putney SW15 135 A1
South Norwood SE19 183 B4
Teddington TW11,TW12 174 B5
Wallington SM6 219 C3
Woodford IG8 37 D5
Oxford Rd N W4 110 D1
Oxford Rd S W4 110 D1
Oxford Sq W2 92 C1 237 B1
Oxford St W1 93 B1 238 D1
Oxford Way TW13 172 D6
Oxford Wlk UB1 107 B5
Oxgate Ct Par NW2 68 A6
Oxgate Ctr NW2 68 B6
Oxgate Gdns NW2 68 B6
Oxgate La NW2 68 B6
Oxhawth Cres BR2 210 D3
Oxhey Dr HA6,WD19 22 B6
Oxhey La HA5 23 C5
Oxhey Ridge Cl HA6 22 B5
Oxhey Wood JMI Schs
WD19 22 C6
Oxleas E6 100 D1
Oxleas Cl DA16 145 B3
Oxleay Rd HA2 41 C1
Oxleigh Cl KT3 199 C4
Oxley Cl SE1 118 A1
Oxleys Rd NW2 68 B5
Oxlip Cl 2 CR0 206 D1
Oxlow La RM10 81 C4
Oxonian St SE22 139 D1
Oxo Tower SE1 251 B5
Oxo Tower Wharf SE1 251 B5
Oxted Cl CR4 202 B6
Oxted Ct N16 51 C1
Oxtoby Way SW16 181 D2
Oyster Catchers Cl E16 99 B1
Oyster Catcher Terr IG5 56 C6
Oyster Row E1 96 C1
Ozolins Way E16 99 A1

P

Pablo Neruda Cl 4
SE24 138 D1
Pace Pl E1 96 B1
Pacific Cl TW14 149 D3
Pacific Ho 15 E1 96 D3
Pacific Hts BR3 185 C3
Pacific Rd E16 99 A1
Pacific Wharf SE16 118 D5
Packenham Ho 21 E2 95 D4
24 N19 49 D2
Packham Ct KT4 216 C5
Packington Ho 22 SW9 138 A3
Packington Sq
N1 95 A6 235 A6
Packington St
N1 94 D6 234 D5
Packmores Rd SE9 167 B6
Padbury SE17 263 B1
Padbury Cl TW14 149 B3
Padbury Ct E2 95 D4
Padbury Ho NW8 237 B6
Paddenswick Ct W6 112 B3
Paddenswick Rd W6 112 A3
Paddington Cl UB4 84 D3
Paddington Com Hospl
W9 91 C2
Paddington Ct 10 W7 86 D2
Paddington Gn
W2 92 B2 236 C4
Paddington Green Prim Sch
NW8 92 B3 236 C5
Paddington St W1 238 A4
Paddington Sta
W2 92 B1 236 C2
Paddock Cl SE3 143 A3
Forest Hill SE26 184 D6
New Malden KT4 199 C1
Northolt UB5 85 C5
Orpington BR6 226 D4
Paddock Ct SW20 200 C5
Paddock Gdns SE19 183 C4
Paddock Lo 13 EN1 17 C6
Paddock Rd DA6 147 A1
NW2 68 A6
Ruislip HA4 62 D5
Paddock Sch SW15 133 D1
Paddocks Cl HA2 63 D4
Paddocks Gn NW9 44 D1
Paddocks The HA9 66 D6
Addington CR0 223 C2
Cockfosters EN4 2 D2
Paddock The UB10 60 D4
Paddock Way BR7 189 B3
Padfield Ct HA9 66 B5
Padfield Rd SE5 139 A2
Padley Cl KT9 214 B3
Padnall Ct RM6 58 D6
Padnall Rd RM6 58 D5
Padstow Cl BR6 227 D4
Padstow Ho 12 E14 119 B6
Padstow Rd EN2 4 D4
Padstow Wlk TW14 149 D3
Padua Rd SE20 184 C2
Pagden St SW8 268 D2
Pageant Ave NW9 27 C2
Pageant Cres SE16 119 B5
Pageantmaster Ct EC4 241 C1
Pageant Wlk CR0 221 C5
Page Cl Dagenham RM9 81 A3
Hampton TW12 173 A4
Harrow HA3 44 B3
Page Cres CR0 220 D3
Page Ct NW7 28 A3
Page Green Rd N15 52 A4
Page Green Terr N15 51 D4
Page Heath La BR1 209 D6
Page Heath Villas BR1 209 D6
Page High N22 50 C6
Page Ho SE10 142 A6
Pagehurst Rd CR0 206 B2
Page Mdw NW7 28 A3
Page Rd TW14 149 B5
Page's Ct N10 31 A1
Page's Hill N10 31 A1
Page's La N10 31 A1
Page St NW7 28 A3
SW1 115 D2 259 D4
Page's Wlk SE1 117 C3 263 B5
Page's Yd W4 133 C6
Paget Ave SM1 218 B5
Paget Cl TW12 174 B6
Paget Ct UB7 104 A4
Paget Gdns BR7 188 D2
Paget Ho 15 E2 96 C5
Paget La TW7 130 C2
Paget Pl Kingston KT2 177 A4
Thames Ditton KT7 196 D1
Paget Rd N16 51 B1
Hillingdon UB10 83 A3
Ilford IG1 78 D4
Paget Rise SE18 144 C5
Paget St EC1 234 C2
Paget Terr SE18 144 D6
Pagham Ho W10 90 C3
Pagin Ho N15 51 C4
Pagitts Gr EN4 1 D4
Pagnell St SE14 141 B5
Pagoda Ave TW9 132 B2
Pagoda Gdns SE3 142 B3
Paignton Rd N15 51 C3
Ruislip HA4 62 A5
Paine Ct SE3 142 D6
Paines Cl HA5 41 A6
Paine's La HA5 23 A1
Pain's Cl CR4 181 B1
Painsthorpe Rd 3 N16 73 C5
Painswick Ct 1 SE15 139 D5
Painters Mews SE16 118 A2
Painters Rd IG2,RM6 58 A6
Paisley Rd
Carshalton SM5 202 B1
Tottenham N22 32 D2
Pakeman Ho SE1 251 D2
Pakeman Prim Sch N7 72 B5
Pakeman St N7 72 B5
Pakenham Cl SW12 159 A3
Pakenham St
WC1 94 B3 240 D6
Palace Ave W8 113 D4 245 D2
Palace Court Gdns N10 49 C6
Palace Ct NW3 69 D3
SE9 166 B1
W2 113 D6 245 C5
Harrow HA3 44 A3
South Norwood CR7 205 B5
Streatham SW2 160 C2
Palace Garden Mews
W8 245 B4
Palace Gardens Terr
W8 113 D5 245 C3
Palace Gate W8 114 A4 246 A1
Palace Gates Rd N22 31 D2
Palace Gdns
Buckhurst Hill IG9 21 D3
Enfield EN2 5 B1
Palace Gdns Mews
W8 113 D5 245 D3
Palace Gn W8 113 D5 245 C3
New Addington CR0 223 B1
Palace Gr BR1 187 B2
Penge SE19 183 D3
Palace Mans W14 254 B4
Palace Mews E17 53 B5
SW1 258 B3
SW6 264 D4
Palace of Ind HA9 66 C4
Palace Par E17 53 C5
Palace Pl SW1 259 A6
Palace Rd BR1 187 B2
N8 49 D4
East Molesey KT8 196 B6
Kingston KT1 197 D5
Penge SE19 183 D3
Ruislip HA4 63 A4
Streatham SE27,SW16,
SW2 160 C2
Wood Green N11 32 A3
Palace Sq SE19 183 D3
Palace St SW1 115 C3 259 A6
Palace View SE12 165 A2
Bromley BR1 209 B6
Croydon CR0 223 B4
Palace View Rd E4 35 D5
Palamon Ct SE1 263 D2
Palamos Rd E10 53 C1
Palatine Ave N16 73 C4
Palatine Rd N16 73 C4
Palemead Cl SW6 134 D4
Palermo Rd NW10 90 A5
Palestine Gr SW19 180 B2
Palewell Cl BR5 190 B1
Palewell Common Dr
SW14 155 B6
Palewell Pk SW14 133 B1
Palfrey Pl SW8 138 B5 270 D4
Palgrave Ave UB1 107 C6
Palgrave Gdns NW1 237 A5
Palgrave Ho 4 NW3 70 D3
7 SE5 139 A5
Twickenham TW2 152 A4
Palgrave Rd W12 111 D3
Palissy St 33 E2 95 D4
Pallant Ho SE1 262 D5
Pallant Way BR6 226 C5
Pallet Way SE18 144 A4
Palliser Ct W14 254 A1
Palliser Ho 21 E1 96 D3
3 SE10 142 B6
Palliser Rd W14 113 A1 254 A1
Pallister Terr SW15 155 D2
Pall Mall SW1 115 D5 249 C3
Pall Mall E SW1 115 D5 249 D4
Pall Mall Pl SW1 249 B3
Palmar Cres DA7 147 C3
Palmar Rd DA7 147 C3
Palm Ave DA14 190 D4
Palm Cl E10 75 D5
Palm Ct N16 73 B6
17 SE15 139 D5
Beckenham BR3 207 B6
Wood Green N22 32 B3
Palmeira Rd DA16 146 D2
Palmer Ave KT4,SM3 216 C4
Palmer Cl Heston TW5 129 C4
West Wickham BR4 224 B6
Palmer Cres KT1 198 A6
Palmer Ct NW10 89 B6
Palmer Gdns EN5 12 D6
Palmer Ho 5 N19 71 C5
8 NW5 71 C4
6 SE14 140 D5
Palmer Pl N7 72 C3
Palmer Rd E13 99 B3
Dagenham RM8 58 D1
Palmer's Ct 11 N11 31 C5
Palmers Gr KT8 195 C5
Palmers Green High Sch
N21 16 C2
Palmers Green Sta N13 32 B6
Palmers La EN3 6 C4
Palmers Rd E2 96 B5
Palmer's Rd N11 31 C5

Palmers Rd
Mortlake SW14 ....133 A2
Thornton Heath SW16 ....182 B1
Palmer St SW1 ....259 C6
Palmerston Cres SE18 ..145 A6
Bowes Park N13 ....32 B5
Palmerston Ct E17 ....53 B5
22 E3 ....96 D5
2 Buckhurst Hill IG9 ....21 C2
9 Surbiton KT6 ....197 D2
Palmerston Ctr HA3 ....42 D6
Palmerston Gr 4 SW19 .179 C3
Palmerston Ho SW11 ....268 B1
W8 ....245 A3
Palmerston Rd BR6 ....227 A3
E17 ....53 B5
E7 ....77 B2
NW6 ....69 B1
NW6 ....69 C1
W3 ....111 A3
Bowes Park N22 ....32 B4
Buckhurst Hill IG9 ....21 C3
Harrow HA3 ....42 D6
Hounslow TW3 ....130 A4
Merton SW19 ....179 C3
Mortlake SW14 ....133 A1
Sutton SM1 ....218 A3
Thornton Heath CR0 ....205 B4
Twickenham TW2 ....152 C5
Wallington SM5 ....219 A4
Palmerston Way SW8 ..268 D3
Palm Gr W5 ....110 A3
Palm Tree Ct 3 N17 ....33 D1
Palm Tree Ho 2 SE14 ....140 D5
Pamela Ct N12 ....29 D4
NW10 ....68 A1
Pamela Gdns HA5 ....40 B4
Pamela Ho 14 E8 ....95 D6
Pamlion Ct N4 ....50 A2
Pams Way KT19 ....215 B3
Panama Ho 5 E1 ....96 D2
Panbro Ho 7 SE18 ....144 B4
Pancras La EC2 ....242 C1
Pancras Rd NW1 ..93 D5 232 D4
Pandora Ct 4 KT6 ....198 A3
Pandora Rd NW6 ....69 C2
Panfield Mews IG2 ....56 C3
Panfield Rd SE2 ....124 A3
Pangbourne NW1 ....232 A1
Pangbourne Ave W10 ....90 C2
Pangbourne Ct N20 ....14 A4
Upper Tooting SW17 ....180 A6
Pangbourne Dr HA7 ....26 A5
Pangbourne Ho 4 N7 ....72 A3
Panhard Pl UB1 ....107 D6
Pank Ave EN5 ....14 A6
Pankhurst Cl 7 SE14 ....140 D5
Isleworth TW7 ....130 D2
Pankhurst Rd KT12 ....194 C2
Panmuir Rd SW20 ....178 B2
Panmure Cl N5 ....72 D4
Panmure Ct 11 UB1 ....86 A1
Panmure Rd SE26 ....162 B1
Panorama Ct N6 ....49 C3
Pansy Gdns W12 ....112 A6
Panther Dr NW10 ....67 B3
Pantiles Cl N13 ....32 D5
Pantiles The BR1 ....210 A6
DA7 ....147 B5
NW11 ....47 B4
Bushey WD23 ....8 B3
Panton Cl CR0 ....204 D1
Panton St SW1 ....249 C5
Panyer Alley EC2 ....242 A2
Papermill Cl SM5 ....219 A4
Paper Mill Wharf E14 ..119 A6
Papillons Wlk SE3 ....143 A2
Papworth Gdns N7 ....72 B3
Papworth Way SW2 ....160 C4
Parade Mans 2 NW4 ....46 B4
19 SE5 ....139 A3
Parade Mews SE27,SW2 .160 D2
Parade The
SW11 ....136 D5 267 D4
Ashford TW16 ....171 D3
Claygate KT10 ....212 C2
Croydon CR0 ....220 B3
Greenford UB6 ....65 B3
2 Kingston KT2 ....176 A1
Paradise Pas N7 ....72 C3
Paradise Pl 15 SE7 ....122 A2
Paradise Rd SW4 ....138 A3
Richmond TW10 ....154 A6
Paradise Row E2 ....96 B4
Paradise St SE16 ....118 B4
Paradise Wlk
SW3 ....136 D6 267 D6
Paragon Cl E16 ....99 A1
Paragon Ct NW4 ....29 A2
Paragon Gr KT5 ....198 B3
Paragon Mews SE1 ....262 D4
Paragon Pl SE3 ....142 D3
Surbiton KT5 ....198 B3
Paragon Rd E9 ....74 C2
Paragon The SE17 ....262 C4
SE3 ....143 A3
Paramount Bldg EC1 ....241 C6
Paramount Ct WC1 ....239 B5
Paramount Ho 8 E11 ....76 C5
Parayhouse Sch W12 ....112 B5
Parbury Rd SE23 ....163 A5
Parbury Rise KT9 ....214 A2
Parchmore Rd CR7 ....205 A6
Parchmore Way CR7 ....182 D1
Pardes House & Beis Yaakov Sch (Boys) N3 ....29 B1
Pardoner St
SE1 ....117 B3 262 D6
Pardon St EC1 ....241 D6
Parfett St E1 ....96 A1
Parfew Ct 2 SE22 ....162 B2
Parfitt Cl NW3 ....48 A1
Parfrey St W6 ....134 C6
Pargraves Ct HA9 ....66 C6
Parham Dr IG2 ....56 D4
Paris Gdn SE1 ...116 D5 251 C4
Parish CE Prim Sch
BR1 ....187 A3
Parish Church CE Inf & Jun Schs CR0 ....220 D5
Parish Ct KT6 ....198 A3
Parish Gate Dr DA15 ....167 C5
Parish La SE20 ....184 D3
Paris Ho 12 E2 ....96 B5
Parish Wharf 6 SE7 ....122 A2
Park App DA16 ....146 B1
Park Ave BR1 ....187 A4
BR6 ....226 C6
E15 ....76 C2
N3 ....29 D2
NW11 ....47 D1
NW2 ....68 C2
Barking IG11 ....79 A2
Edmonton N18 ....34 A6
Enfield EN1 ....17 C5
Ilford IG1 ....56 C1
Mitcham CR4 ....181 B3
Mortlake SW14 ....133 B1
Palmers Green N13 ....16 C1
Ruislip HA4 ....39 C3
Southall UB1 ....107 C5
Twickenham TW3 ....151 D5
Upper Halliford TW17 ....193 C6
Wallend E6 ....100 C5
Wallington SM5 ....219 A2
West Wickham BR4 ....224 A6
Woodford IG8 ....37 B5
Wood Green N22 ....32 B2
Park Ave E KT17 ....216 A2
Park Ave N N8 ....49 D5
NW10 ....68 B3
Park Avenue Mews CR4 .181 B3
Park Avenue Rd N17 ....34 B3
Park Ave S N8 ....49 D5
Park Ave W KT17 ....216 A2
Park Bsns Ctr 4 NW6 ....91 C4
Park Chase HA9 ....66 B4
Park Cl 20 E9 ....96 C6
N12 ....30 B6
NW2 ....68 B5
SW1 ....247 C1
W14 ....113 B3 254 D6
Ealing NW10 ....88 B4
Hampton TW12 ....174 A2
Harrow HA3 ....24 C2
Isleworth TW3,TW7 ....152 A6
Kingston KT2 ....176 C2
Wallington SM5 ....218 D2
Park Cotts 10 TW1 ....153 B5
Park Cres N3 ....30 A3
W1 ....93 B3 238 C5
Enfield EN2 ....5 B1
Harrow HA3 ....24 C2
Twickenham TW2 ....152 B3
Park Cres Mews E W1 ..238 D5
Park Cres Mews W W1 ..238 C5
Park Croft HA8 ....27 A2
Parkcroft Rd SE12 ....164 D4
Park Ct E17 ....53 D4
N11 ....31 D3
N12 ....30 B5
SW11 ....268 C2
SW4 ....159 D6
2 Beckenham BR3 ....207 D6
2 Chingford E4 ....20 A2
Dulwich SE21 ....161 B1
New Barnet EN5 ....14 B4
New Malden KT3 ....199 B5
Teddington KT1 ....175 C2
Upper Tooting SW12 ....159 A3
Wallington SM6 ....220 A3
Wembley HA9 ....66 A3
Parkdale N11 ....31 D4
Parkdale Cres KT4 ....215 B5
Parkdale Rd SE18 ....123 C1
Park Dr NW11 ....47 D1
Acton W3 ....110 C3
Enfield N21 ....17 A5
Harrow HA2 ....41 C2
Mortlake SW14 ....133 B1
Stanmore HA3 ....24 C4
Woolwich SE7 ....144 A6
Park Dwellings 7 NW3 ....70 D3
Park End NW3 ....70 C4
Bromley BR1 ....186 D2
Parker Cl E16 ....122 A5
Parker Ct N1 ....235 B6
SW4 ....270 A1
Wimbledon SW19 ....179 A3
Parke Rd Barnes SW13 ..134 A4
Sunbury TW16 ....194 A5
Parker Ho 4 SE18 ....122 D1
Parker Mews WC2 ....240 B2
Parker Rd CR0 ....221 A4
Parkers Rd N10 ....30 C2
Parkers Row 12 SE16 ....118 A4
Parker's Row SE1 ....253 D1
Parker St E16 ....122 A5
WC2 ....94 A1 240 B2
Park Farm SE7 ....144 A6
Park Farm Cl N2 ....48 A6
Pinner HA5 ....40 B4
Park Farm Ct UB3 ....105 C6
Park Farm Rd
Bromley BR1 ....187 D2
Kingston KT2 ....176 A3
Parkfield 3 TW7 ....130 C4
Parkfield Ave
Feltham TW13 ....150 A1
Harrow HA2 ....24 A1
Parkfield Ave continued
Hillingdon UB10 ....82 D4
Mortlake SW14 ....133 C1
Northolt UB5 ....84 D5
Parkfield Cl Edgware HA8 .26 D4
Northolt UB5 ....85 A5
Parkfield Cres
Feltham TW13 ....150 A1
Harrow HA2 ....24 A1
Ruislip HA4 ....63 A5
Parkfield Dr UB5 ....84 D5
Parkfield Gdns HA2 ....41 D6
Parkfield Ho HA2 ....23 D2
Parkfield Ind Est SW11 ..137 A3
Parkfield Par TW13 ....150 A1
Parkfield Prim Sch NW4 ..46 B2
Parkfield Rd NW10 ....68 B1
SE14 ....141 B4
Feltham TW13 ....150 A1
Harrow HA2 ....64 A5
Northolt UB5 ....85 A5
Uxbridge UB10 ....60 D6
Parkfields Croydon CR0 ..207 B1
Putney SW15 ....134 C1
Parkfields Ave NW9 ....45 B1
Wimbledon SW20 ....178 B1
Parkfields Cl SM5 ....219 A4
Parkfields Rd TW10 ....176 B5
Parkfield St N1 ....94 C5 234 B4
Parkfield Way BR2 ....210 B4
Park Flats N6 ....48 C2
Parkgate SE3 ....142 D2
Park Gate N2 ....48 B6
Ealing W5 ....87 D2
Southgate N21 ....16 B4
Parkgate Ave EN4 ....2 A4
Parkgate Cl KT2 ....176 D4
Parkgate Cres EN4 ....2 A4
Park Gate Ct TW12 ....174 A5
Parkgate Gdns SW14 ....155 B6
Parkgate House Sch
SW11 ....137 A1
Park Gate Mans N2 ....48 B6
Parkgate Mews N6 ....49 C2
Parkgate Rd
SW11 ....136 C5 267 B3
Wallington SM5,SM6 ....219 B3
Park Gates HA2 ....63 C4
Park Gdns NW9 ....44 D6
Kingston KT2 ....176 B5
Park Gr BR1 ....187 B2
E15 ....99 A6
N11 ....31 D3
Edgware HA8 ....26 B5
Park Grove Rd E11 ....76 C6
Park Hall Rd N2 ....48 C5
Dulwich SE21 ....161 B1
Park Hall Road Trad Est
SE21 ....161 B1
Parkham Ct BR2 ....186 C1
Parkham St
SW11 ....136 C4 267 A1
Parkham Way N10 ....31 C1
Park High Sch HA7 ....25 D1
Park Hill BR1 ....210 B5
SW4 ....159 D6
Ealing W5 ....87 D2
Forest Hill SE23 ....162 C3
Loughton IG10 ....21 D6
Richmond TW10 ....154 B5
Wallington SM5 ....218 D2
Park Hill Cl SM5 ....218 C3
Park Hill Ct Croydon CR0 .221 C6
Ealing W5 ....87 D2
Upper Tooting SW17 ....158 D1
Parkhill Inf Sch IG5 ....56 C6
Park Hill Inf Sch CR0 ....221 C5
Parkhill Jun Sch IG5 ....56 C6
Park Hill Jun Sch CR0 ....221 C5
Parkhill Rd DA5 ....169 B4
NW3 ....70 D3
Chingford E4 ....20 A4
Sidcup DA15 ....167 C1
Park Hill Rd
Beckenham BR2 ....186 C1
South Croydon CR0 ....221 C5
Wallington SM6 ....219 B1
Park Hill Rise CR0 ....221 C6
Park Hill Sch KT2 ....176 C3
Park Hill Wlk 10 NW3 ....70 D3
Park Ho 35 E9 ....74 C1
N4 ....72 D6
8 SE5 ....139 B4
Forest Hill SE26 ....184 A5
Sidcup DA14 ....190 A5
Southgate N21 ....16 B4
Parkholme Rd E8 ....74 A2
Park House Gdns TW1 ..153 C6
Park House Mid Sch
SW19 ....179 B6
Parkhouse St SE5 ....139 B5
Parkhurst Ct N7 ....72 A4
Parkhurst Gdns 2 DA5 ..169 C4
Parkhurst Rd E17 ....53 A5
N11 ....31 A5
N7 ....72 A4
Bowes Park N22 ....32 B4
Little Ilford E12 ....78 C4
Sidcup DA5 ....169 C4
Sutton SM1 ....218 B4
Tottenham N17 ....34 A1
Parkin Ho SE20 ....184 D3
Parkinson Ct EC1 ....235 D2
N1 ....235 C1
Parkinson Ho 6 E9 ....74 C1
Park La E15 ....98 B6
W1 ....115 A6 248 A5
Cheam SM3 ....217 A2
Cranford TW5 ....128 A5
Dagenham RM6 ....58 D3
Park La continued
Edmonton N9 ....17 D1
Harrow HA2 ....63 D5
Hayes UB4 ....83 C3
Richmond TW9 ....131 D1
South Croydon CR0 ....221 B5
Stanmore HA7 ....9 A1
Teddington TW11 ....174 D4
Tottenham N17 ....34 A3
Wallington SM5,SM6 ....219 A3
Wembley HA9 ....66 A4
Parkland Ct E15 ....76 C3
W14 ....244 A2
Parkland Gdns 12
SW19 ....156 D3
Parkland Gr
Ashford TW15 ....170 C6
Hounslow TW7 ....130 D4
Parkland Rd
Ashford TW15 ....170 C6
Woodford IG8 ....37 B3
Wood Green N22 ....32 B1
Parklands N6 ....49 B2
SE22 ....162 B6
Bushey WD23 ....8 A5
Kingston KT5 ....198 B4
Parklands Cl
Hadley Wood EN4 ....2 B5
Ilford IG2 ....57 A2
Mortlake SW14 ....155 A6
Parklands Ct TW5 ....128 D3
Parklands Dr N3 ....47 A6
Parklands Par TW5 ....128 D3
Parklands Rd SW16 ....181 B5
Parklands Way KT4 ....215 C6
Parkland Wlk N4,N8 ....50 B2
Park Lane Cl N17 ....34 A3
Park Lane Prim Sch HA9 .66 A3
Park Lawn CR7 ....183 A1
Parklea Cl NW9 ....27 C2
Park Lea Ct N16 ....51 C2
Parkleigh Ct SW19 ....179 D1
Parkleigh Rd SW19 ....179 D1
Parkleys
Richmond KT2,TW10 ....175 D6
Richmond, Ham Common
TW10 ....176 A6
Park Lo 10 E1 ....118 B5
N12 ....30 A5
NW2 ....68 C4
11 NW8 ....70 B1
3 Ealing W5 ....87 B3
Park Lofts 7 SW4 ....160 A6
Park Lorne NW8 ....230 B1
Park Mans 5 NW4 ....46 B4
NW8 ....230 A3
SW1 ....247 C1
SW11 ....267 C1
SW6 ....264 B1
SW8 ....270 B6
W6 ....111 D3
Forest Hill SE26 ....162 C1
Park Mead DA15 ....168 B5
Parkmead SW15 ....156 B5
Park Mead HA2 ....63 D5
Parkmead Gdns NW7 ....27 D4
Park Mews BR7 ....188 D4
W10 ....91 A5
Stanwell TW19 ....148 B4
Parkmore Cl IG8 ....37 A6
Park Nook Gdns EN2 ....5 B6
Park Par NW10 ....89 D5
NW9 ....45 B6
Acton W3 ....110 C3
Hayes UB3 ....83 C1
Park Pl E14 ....119 C5
SW1 ....115 C5 249 A4
W3 ....110 C2
Ealing W5 ....109 D5
Hampton TW12 ....174 A4
Wembley HA9 ....66 B4
Park Place Dr W3 ....110 C3
Park Place Villas W2 ....236 B4
Park Prim Sch E15 ....76 D1
Park Rd BR1 ....187 B2
BR7 ....188 D4
E10 ....53 C1
E15 ....99 A6
E17 ....53 B4
E6 ....99 C6
N11 ....31 D3
N14 ....15 D4
N2 ....48 B6
N8 ....49 D4
N8,N15 ....50 D5
NW10 ....89 C6
NW1,NW8 ....92 C3 237 B6
NW4 ....46 B3
NW9 ....45 B2
Ashford TW15 ....170 D5
Barnet EN4 ....2 C1
Barnet EN5 ....1 B1
Beckenham BR3 ....185 C3
Cheam SM3 ....217 A2
Chiswick W4 ....133 B6
Ealing W7 ....108 D6
East Molesey KT8 ....196 A5
Edmonton N18 ....34 A6
Feltham TW13 ....172 D6
Hackbridge SM6 ....219 B6
Hampton TW12 ....174 A5
Hayes UB4 ....83 C2
Ilford IG1 ....79 B5
Isleworth TW3,TW7 ....152 A6
Isleworth TW7 ....131 B3
Kingston KT2,TW10 ....176 C3
Lower Halliford TW17 ....192 C1
Mitcham SW19 ....180 C4
New Malden KT3 ....199 B5
Richmond TW10 ....154 B5
Park Rd continued
South Norwood SE25 ....205 C5
Sunbury TW16 ....172 B3
Teddington KT1 ....175 C2
Teddington TW11 ....174 D4
Twickenham TW1 ....153 C5
Uxbridge UB8 ....60 A2
Wallington SM6 ....219 B3
Wanstead E12 ....77 B6
Wembley HA0 ....66 A2
Park Rd E Acton W3 ....111 A4
Uxbridge UB10 ....82 A5
Park Rd N W3 ....110 D4
W4 ....111 B1
Park Ridings N8 ....50 C6
Park Rise
Forest Hill SE23 ....163 A3
Harrow HA3 ....24 C2
Park Rise Rd SE23 ....163 A3
Park Road Ho 3 KT2 ....176 C3
Park Row SE10 ....142 B6
Park Royal NW10 ....88 D6
Park Royal Bsns Ctr
NW10 ....89 A3
Park Royal Metro Ctr
NW10 ....88 D3
Park Royal Rd NW10,W3 ..89 A3
Park Royal Sta W5 ....88 C3
Park S SW11 ....268 A1
Park Sch IG1 ....56 D1
Park Sheen 3 SW14 ....132 D1
Parkshot TW9 ....132 A1
Parkside DA14 ....168 B2
N3 ....29 D3
NW7 ....28 A4
SE3 ....142 D5
W3 ....111 C5
Park Side NW2 ....68 B4
Parkside
1 Beckenham BR3 ....185 D1
Cheam SM3 ....217 A2
Ealing W5 ....110 A6
Hampton TW12 ....174 A5
Hayes UB3 ....105 C6
Wimbledon SW19 ....178 D6
Park Side IG9 ....21 B2
Parkside Ave BR1 ....210 A5
Wimbledon SW19 ....178 D5
Parkside Cl SE20 ....184 C3
Parkside Cres N7 ....72 C5
Tolworth KT5 ....199 A3
Parkside Ct
Bowes Park N22 ....32 B4
2 Wanstead E11 ....55 A3
Parkside Dr HA8 ....10 C1
Parkside Est E9 ....96 D6
Parkside Gdns
East Barnet EN4 ....15 A4
Wimbledon SW19 ....178 D6
Parkside Lo DA17 ....125 D1
Parkside Rd
Belvedere DA17 ....125 D2
Hounslow TW3 ....151 D6
Parkside St SW11 ....268 A1
Parkside Terr N18 ....33 B6
Parkside Way HA2 ....42 A5
Park Sq E NW1 ....93 B3 238 D6
Park Sq Mews NW1 ....238 C5
Park Sq W NW1 ....93 B3 238 C5
Park St SE1 ....117 A5 252 B4
W1 ....115 A6 248 A5
Croydon CR0 ....221 A6
Teddington TW11 ....174 C4
Parkstead Rd SW15 ....156 B6
Park Steps W2 ....247 B6
Park St James NW8 ....230 C5
Parkstone Ave N18 ....33 D5
Parkstone Rd E17 ....54 A6
3 SE15 ....140 A3
Park Terr
Carshalton SM5 ....218 C5
Enfield EN3 ....7 A5
New Malden KT4 ....200 A1
Park The N6 ....49 A3
NW11 ....47 D1
Ealing W5 ....109 D5
Forest Hill SE23 ....162 C3
Sidcup DA14 ....190 A5
Wallington SM5 ....218 D3
Parkthorne Cl HA2 ....41 D3
Parkthorne Dr HA2 ....41 D3
Parkthorne Rd SW12 ....159 D4
Park Twrs W1 ....248 C3
Park View N5 ....73 A4
NW2 ....68 C4
W3 ....89 A2
Parkview UB6 ....87 A4
Park View Kingston KT3 ..199 D6
Morden SM4 ....202 B4
Pinner HA5 ....23 B2
Southgate N21 ....16 B4
Wembley HA9 ....66 D3
Yiewsley UB7 ....104 A6
Park View Cres N11 ....31 B6
Park View Ct N12 ....30 C6
NW9 ....45 A5
SW18 ....157 C5
Parkview Ct Fulham SW6 .135 A3
Penge SE20 ....184 B2
Park View Dr CR4 ....180 B1
Park View Gdns NW4 ....46 D4
Redbridge IG4 ....56 B5
Wood Green N22 ....32 C2
Park View Ho SE24 ....160 D5
Parkview Lo BR3 ....207 D6
Park View Mews 24
SW9 ....138 B3
Park View Rd DA16 ....146 D2
N3 ....29 D2
NW10 ....67 D4
Park View Rd continued
SE9 ....166 D2
Parkview Rd CR0 ....206 A1
Park View Rd Ealing W5 ....88 A2
Hillingdon UB8 ....82 C1
Pinner HA5 ....22 B3
Southall UB1 ....107 C5
Tottenham N17 ....34 A1
Park Village E
NW1 ....93 B5 231 D3
Park Village W
NW1 ....93 B5 231 C4
Park Villas RM6 ....58 D3
Parkville Rd
SW6 ....135 B5 264 C3
Park Vista SE10 ....142 B6
Park Walk Prim Sch
SW10 ....136 B6 266 C5
Parkway DA18 ....125 A3
NW1 ....93 B6 231 C5
Park Way N20 ....30 D6
NW11 ....47 A4
W3 ....110 C2
Parkway Hillingdon UB10 ..60 D1
Ilford IG3 ....79 D5
Palmers Green N14 ....16 A2
West Barnes SW20 ....200 D5
Woodford IG8 ....37 C5
Park Way
East Molesey KT8 ....195 D6
Edgware HA8 ....26 D2
Enfield EN2 ....4 C3
Feltham TW14 ....150 B4
Ruislip HA4 ....40 A1
Park Way Ct HA4 ....39 D1
Parkway Prim Sch
DA18 ....125 A3
Parkway The
Cranford TW5 ....128 B5
Hayes UB2,UB3,UB4,TW5 .106 B3
Hayes UB4 ....84 D2
Parkway Trad Est TW5 ..128 C6
Park West W2 ....92 C1 237 B1
Park West Pl W1,
W2 ....92 C1 237 B2
Park Wlk SW10 ..136 B6 266 C6
Parkwood N20 ....14 D2
NW8 ....230 C5
Beckenham BR3 ....185 C3
Parkwood Ave KT10 ....196 A1
Parkwood Gr TW16 ....194 A6
Parkwood Mews N6 ....49 B3
Parkwood Prim Sch N4 ..72 D6
Parkwood Rd DA5 ....169 B4
Hounslow TW7 ....130 D4
Wimbledon SW19 ....179 B5
Parliament Ct NW3 ....70 C4
Parliament Hill NW3 ....70 C4
Parliament Hill Mans
NW5 ....71 A4
Parliament Hill Sch NW5 .71 A4
Parliament Mews SW14 .133 A3
Parliament Sq★
SW1 ....116 A4 250 A1
Parliament St
SW1 ....116 A4 250 A2
Parliament View Apartments
SE11 ....260 B4
Parma Cres SW11 ....136 D1
Parminter Ind Est 23 E2 ..96 B5
Parmiter St E2 ....96 B5
Parmoor Ct EC1 ....242 A6
Parnall Ho 11 SE19 ....183 C6
Parnell Cl HA8 ....27 A6
W12 ....112 B3
Parnell Rd E3 ....97 B6
Parnham St E14 ....97 A1
Parolles Rd N19 ....49 C1
Paroma Rd DA17 ....125 C3
Parr Cl N9 ....34 B6
Parr Ct N1 ....235 C4
Feltham TW13 ....172 C6
Parrington Ho 1 SW4 ..159 D5
Parr Pl W4 ....111 D2
Parr Rd E6 ....99 D6
Stanmore HA7 ....26 A2
Parr's Pl TW12 ....173 C3
Parr St N1 ....95 B5 235 C4
Parry Ave E6 ....100 B1
Parry Cl KT17 ....216 A1
Parry Ho 32 E1 ....118 B5
Parry Pl SE18 ....122 D2
Parry Rd W10 ....91 A4
South Norwood SE25 ....205 C6
Parry St SW8 ....138 A6 270 B6
Parsifal Coll NW3 ....69 C4
Parsifal Ho NW3 ....69 C4
Parsifal Rd NW6 ....69 C3
Parsley Gdns CR0 ....206 D1
Parsloes Ave RM9 ....81 A3
Parsloes Prim Sch RM9 ..81 B2
Parsonage Cl UB3 ....83 D1
Parsonage Gdns EN2 ....5 A3
Parsonage La DA14 ....191 B6
Enfield EN2 ....5 B3
Parsonage Manorway
DA8,DA17 ....147 C6
Parsonage St E14 ....120 A2
Parson Ct SE13 ....141 D2
Parsons Gn
SW6 ....135 C3 265 A1
Parsons Gr HA8 ....10 C1
Parsons Green La
SW6 ....135 C4 265 A2
Parsons Green Sta
SW6 ....135 C4 265 A1
Parsons Hill SE18 ....122 C3

Parsons Ho W2 236 C5
21 Streatham SW12 160 A4
Parsons Lo NW6 69 D1
Parsons Mead KT8 196 A6
Parson's Mead CR0 204 D1
Parsons Rd E13 99 C5
Edgware HA8 10 C1
Parson St NW4 46 C6
Parthenia Rd
SW6 135 C4 265 B1
Partingdale La NW7 28 D5
Partington Cl N19 49 D1
Partridge Cl 1 E16 99 D2
Barnet EN5 12 C5
Bushey WD23 8 A3
Stanmore HA7 26 A6
Partridge Ct EC1 241 C6
Partridge Dr BR6 227 A5
Partridge Gn SE9 166 C1
Partridge Ho 20 E3 97 B5
Partridge Rd
8 Hampton TW12 173 C4
Sidcup DA14 189 C6
Partridge Sq 3 E6 100 A2
Partridge Way N22 32 A2
Pasadena Cl UB3 106 B4
Pascall Ho SE17 139 A6
Pascal St SW8 137 D5 269 D4
Pascoe Rd SE13 164 B6
Pasley Cl SE17 262 A1
Pasquier Rd E17 53 A6
Passey Pl SE9 166 B5
Passfield Dr E14 97 D2
Passfield Ho SE18 123 B2
Passfield Path 13 SE28 124 B6
Passfields W14 254 C1
Catford SE6 164 A1
Passing Alley EC1 241 D5
Passingham Ho TW5 129 C6
Passmore Gdns N11 31 D4
Passmore Ho 12 N9 18 A1
Passmores Edwards Ho
N11 31 D3
Passmore St
SW1 115 A1 258 A2
Pasteur Cl NW9 27 C1
Pasteur Gdns N18 33 A5
Paston Cl SM6 219 C5
Paston Cres SE12 165 B4
Pastor Ct N6 49 C3
Pastor St SE1,
SE11 116 D2 261 D4
Pasture Cl Bushey WD23 8 A4
Wembley HA0 65 B5
Pasture Rd Catford SE6 164 D3
Dagenham RM9 81 B3
Wembley HA0 65 B5
Pastures Mead UB10 60 C2
Pastures The N20 13 B3
Patcham Terr SW8 268 D2
Patch Cl UB10 82 B6
Patching Way UB4 85 A2
Patent Ho E14 97 D2
Paternoster Row
EC2,EC4 95 A1 242 A1
Paternoster Sq
EC4 94 D1 241 D2
Pater St W8 113 C3 255 A5
Pates Manor Dr TW14 149 B4
Pathfield Rd SW16 181 D4
Path The SW19 179 D2
Patience Rd SW11 136 C3
Patio Cl SW4 159 D5
Patmore Ho 9 N16 73 C3
Patmore St SW8 137 C4 269 B2
Paton Cl E3 97 C4
Paton Ho 5 SW9 138 B3
Paton St EC1 235 A1
Patricia Ct
Chislehurst BR7 189 B2
Woolwich SE2 146 B5
Patricia Villas N17 34 B2
Patrick Coman Ho EC1 234 C1
Patrick Connolly Gdns 41
E3 97 D4
Patrick Rd E13 99 C4
Patriot Sq E2 96 B5
Patrol Pl SE6 163 D5
Pat Shaw Ho 2 E1 96 D3
Patshull Pl NW5 71 C2
Patshull Rd NW5 71 C2
Patson Cl E5 74 D5
Pattenden Rd SE6 163 B3
Patten Ho N4 51 A1
Patten Rd SW18 158 C4
Patterdale NW1 231 D1
Patterdale Cl BR1 186 C4
Patterdale Rd SE15 140 C5
Patterson Ct SE19 183 D4
Patterson Rd SE19 183 D4
Pattina Wlk SE16 119 A5
Pattinson Point 10 E16 99 A2
Pattison Ho 1 E1 96 D1
SE1 252 B2
Pattison Rd NW2 69 C5
Pattison Wlk SE18 123 A1
Paul Byrne Ho 3 N2 48 A6
Paul Cl E15 76 C1
Paul Ct N3 29 A1
7 Edmonton N18 34 A6
Paulet Rd SE5 138 D4
Paul Gdns CR0 221 D6
Paulhan Rd HA3 43 D5
Paul Ho 13 W10 91 A3
Paulin Dr N21 16 C4
Pauline Cres TW2 152 A3
Pauline Ho 19 E1 96 A2
Paulinus Cl BR5 190 C1
Paul Julius Cl E14 120 B6
Paul Robeson Cl E6 100 C4
Paul's Ho E3 97 B2
Paulson Ho 7 IG11 78 D1
Paul St E15 98 C6
EC2 95 C3 243 A6
Paultons Ho SW3 266 D6
Paultons Sq
SW3 136 B6 266 D6
Paultons St
SW3 136 B6 266 D5
Pauntley Ho 6 N19 49 C1
Pauntley St 4 N19 49 C1
Pavan Ct 29 E2 96 C4
Paved Ct 9 TW9 153 D6
Paveley Dr
SW11 136 C5 267 A3
Paveley Ho N1 233 C3
Paveley St NW8 92 C3 237 B6
Pavement Mews 1 RM6 58 D2
Pavement Sq CR0 206 A1
Pavement The E11 54 A1
SW4 137 C1
W5 110 A3
11 West Norwood SE27 183 A6
Pavet Cl RM10 81 D2
Pavilion Ct NW3 70 B3
5 NW3 70 A4
8 NW6 91 C4
3 Wimbledon SW19 179 A3
Pavilion L Ctr The BR1 187 A1
Pavilion Lo HA2 42 B1
Pavilion Mans 10 SW9 138 B1
Pavilion Mews N3 29 C1
Pavilion Rd
SW1 114 D3 257 D5
Redbridge IG1 56 B2
Pavilion St SW1 257 D5
Pavilion Terr W12 90 C1
Hampton KT1 197 A4
Pavilion Way HA8 27 A3
Ruislip HA4 62 C6
Pawleyne Cl SE20 184 C3
Pawsey Cl E13 99 A6
Pawson's Rd CR0 205 A4
Paxford Rd HA0 65 B6
Paxton Cl Richmond TW9 132 B3
Walton-on-T KT12 194 C2
Paxton Ct SE9 165 C1
1 Forest Hill SE26 185 A6
Mitcham CR4 180 D1
Paxton Ho SE17 262 B2
Paxton Pl SE27 183 C6
Paxton Prim Sch SE19 183 C4
Paxton Rd BR1 187 A3
Forest Hill SE23 163 A1
Tottenham N17 34 A3
Chiswick W4 133 C6
Paxton Terr SW1 268 D6
Payens Wlk W6 135 A6 264 A5
Paymal Ho 28 E1 96 C2
Payne Cl IG11 79 D1
Payne Ho N1 233 D5
Paynell Ct SE3 142 C2
Payne Rd E3 97 D5
Paynesfield Ave SW14 133 B2
Paynesfield Rd WD23 8 D4
Payne St SE8 141 B6
Payzes Gdns IG8 36 D5
Peabody Ave
SW1 115 B1 258 D1
Peabody Bldgs SE17 262 C3
6 SE5 139 B4
Peabody Cl SW1 268 D6
Croydon CR0 206 C1
Peabody Cotts N17 33 C2
Peabody Ct EC1 242 B5
9 SE5 139 B4
Peabody Est E1 118 A6
4 E1 118 D6
18 E2 96 B5
EC1 241 B5
EC1 242 B5
SE1 251 B3
SE1 252 A3
SW1 259 B4
SW6 135 B6 264 D6
W10 90 C2
17 W6 112 C1
WC2 240 C1
Streatham SE24 161 A4
Peabody Hill SE21 161 A3
Peabody Sq SE1 251 C1
Peabody Twr EC1 242 B5
Peabody Yd N1 235 A6
Peace Cl East Barnet N14 15 B6
Greenford UB6 86 B6
South Norwood SE25 205 C5
Peace Ct 10 NW9 46 A5
Peace Gr HA9 66 D6
Peace St SE18 144 C6
Peaches Cl SM2 217 A1
Peach Rd W10 91 A4
Feltham TW14 150 A3
Peach Tree Ave UB7 82 B1
Peachum Rd SE3 142 D6
Peach Walk Mews 23 E3 96 D5
Peacock Ave TW14 149 B3
Peacock Cl RM8 80 C6
Peacock Est N17 33 D3
Peacock St
SE17 116 D2 261 D3
Peacock Wlk E16 99 B1
Peacock Yd SE17 261 D3
Peaketon Ave IG4 55 D4
Peak Hill SE26 184 C6
Peak Hill Ave SE26 184 C6
Peak Hill Gdns SE26 184 C6
Peak Ho N4 51 A1
Peak The SE26 162 C1
Peal Gdns W13 87 A3
Peall Rd CR0 204 B3
Pear Ave TW17 193 C6
Pearce Cl 2 CR4 181 A1
Pearcefield Ave 5
SE23 162 C3
Pearce Ho N19 71 C5
7 Streatham SW2 160 A4
Pear Cl NW9 45 B5
SE14 141 A5
Pearcroft Rd E11 76 B6
Pear Ct 20 SE15 139 D5
Peardon St SW8 137 B3
Peareswood Gdns HA7 25 D2
Pearfield Ho 1 N5 73 A3
Pearfield Rd SE23 163 A1
Pearl Cl E6 100 C1
NW2 46 D2
Pearl Ct 18 NW9 46 A5
Pearl Rd E17 53 C6
Pearl St E1 118 B5
Pearlstones Ct RM10 103 C6
Pearmain Cl TW17 192 D4
Pearman St SE1 116 C4 251 B1
Pear Pl SE1 251 A2
Pear Rd E11 76 C5
Pearscroft Ct
SW6 135 D4 265 D1
Pearscroft Rd
SW6 135 D4 265 D1
Pearse St 3 SE15 139 C6
Pearson Ct SM4 201 D4
Pearson Ho SW15 134 C3
Pearson's Ave SE8,SE14 141 C4
Pearson St E2 95 D5
Pears Rd TW3 130 A2
Peartree Ave SW17 158 A1
Pear Tree Ave UB7 82 B1
Pear Tree Cl 23 E2 95 D6
Peartree Cl KT9 214 C3
Pear Tree Cl CR4 180 C1
Pear Tree Ct EC1 241 B5
Putney SW15 134 B1
Peartree Gdns RM8 80 B4
Pear Tree Ho SE4 141 B1
Hayes UB8 83 A1
Peartree La E1 118 C6
Peartree Rd EN1 5 C2
Pear Tree Rd TW15 171 A5
Peartree St EC1 95 A3 242 A6
Peartree Way SE10 121 A2
Peary Ho 3 NW10 67 B1
Peary Pl E2 96 C4
Peas Mead Terr E4 36 A6
Peatfield Cl DA15 167 C1
Pebworth Lo SE25 205 D5
Pebworth Rd HA1 65 A6
Peckarmans Wood
SE21,SE26 162 A1
Peckett Sq 3 N5 72 D4
Peckford Pl SW9 138 C3
Peckham Gr SE15 139 C5
Peckham High St SE15 140 A4
Peckham Hill St SE15 140 A5
Peckham Park Prim Sch
SE15 140 A5
Peckham Park Rd SE15 140 A5
Peckham Rd SE5 139 C4
Peckham Rye SE22 140 A1
Peckham SE15,SE22 140 B1
Peckham Rye Prim Sch
SE15 140 B2
Peckham Rye Sta SE15 140 A3
Peckwater St NW5 71 C3
Pedlars Wlk N7 72 A3
Pedley Rd RM8 58 C1
Pedley St E1 95 D3 243 D5
Pedro St E5 74 D4
Pedworth Gdns 4 SE16 118 C2
Peebles Ct UB1 86 A1
Peek Cres SW19 178 D5
Peel Centre (Metropolitan
Police Training
Establishment) NW9 45 D6
Peel Cl Chingford E4 19 D2
Edmonton N9 18 A1
Peel Ct UB6 86 A4
Peel Dr NW9 45 D6
Redbridge IG5 56 A6
Peel Gr E2 96 C5
Peel Pass W8 245 A3
Peel Pl IG5 37 D1
Peel Prec NW6 91 C5
Peel Rd BR6 227 A3
NW6 91 B4
Harrow HA3 42 D6
Wembley HA0,HA9 65 D5
Woodford E18 36 D2
Peel St W8 113 C5 245 A3
Peel Way UB8 82 A2
Peel Yates Ho 13 SE7 122 A2
Peerglow Est EN3 18 C6
Peerless St EC1 95 B4 235 C1
Pegamoid Rd N18 18 C1
Pegasus Ct NW10 90 B4
Brentford TW8 110 B1
Kingston KT1 197 D6
Pegasus Ho 9 E1 96 D3
Pegasus Rd CR0,CR9 220 C2
Pegasus Way N11 31 B4
Peggotty Way UB8 82 D1
Pegg Rd TW5 128 D5
Peggy Quirke Ct 2 HA0 66 A2
Pegley Gdns SE12 165 A2
Pegwell Ho 19 E5 74 B3
Pegwell St SE18 145 C5
Pekin St E14 97 C1
Pekoe SE1 253 D3
Peldon Ct TW10 154 B6
Pele Ct N17 33 B3
Pelham Ave IG11 101 D6
Pelham Cl SE5 139 C2
Pelham Cotts DA5 169 D3
Pelham Cres SW7 257 A3
Pelham Ct SW3 257 A3
Pelham Ho W14 254 C3
Pelham Pl SW7 257 A3
8 Ealing W7 86 D3
Pelham Prim Sch DA7 147 C2
Pelham Rd DA7 147 C2
N15 51 D5
Ilford IG1 79 B6
Merton SW19 179 C3
Penge BR3,SE20 184 C1
Wanstead E18 55 B6
Wood Green N22 32 C1
Pelham St SW7 114 B2 256 D4
Pelican Ho 7 SE8 119 B2
Pelier St SE17 139 A6
Pelinore Rd SE6 164 C2
Pella Ho SE11 260 D2
Pellant Rd SW6 135 A5 264 B4
Pellatt Gr N22 32 C2
Pellatt Rd SE22 161 D6
Wembley HA9 66 A6
Pellerin Rd N16 73 C3
Pellew Ho 15 E1 96 B3
Pelling St E14 97 C1
Pellipar Cl N13 16 C1
Pellipar Gdns SE18 122 B1
Pellipar Rd SE18 122 B1
Pelly Ct 4 E17 54 A5
Pelly Rd E13 99 A5
Pelter St E2 95 D4
Pelton Ct CR2 221 A2
Pelton Rd SE10 120 C1
Pembar Ave E17 53 A6
Pemberley Chase KT19 214 D3
Pemberley Cl KT19 214 D3
Pemberley Ho KT19 214 D3
Pember Rd NW10 90 D4
Pemberton Ct 18 E1 96 D4
Pemberton Gdns N19 71 C5
Dagenham RM6 59 A4
Pemberton Ho SE26 184 A6
Pemberton Pl 2 E8 74 B1
Esher KT10 212 A5
Pemberton Rd N4 50 D4
East Molesey KT8 196 A5
Pemberton Row EC4 241 B2
Pemberton Terr N19 71 C5
Pembridge Ave TW4 151 B3
Pembridge Cres
W11 113 C6 245 A6
Pembridge Gdns
W2 113 C6 245 A5
Pembridge Mews
W11 113 C6 245 A6
Pembridge Pl 1 SW15 157 C6
W2 113 C6 245 B6
Pembridge Rd
W11 113 C6 245 A5
Pembridge Sq
W2 113 C6 245 B5
Pembridge Villas
W11 113 C6 245 A6
Pembroke W14 254 D3
Pembroke Ave Enfield EN1 6 B4
Harrow HA3 43 B6
Surbiton KT5 198 D4
Pembroke Bldgs NW10 90 A4
Pembroke Cl SW1 248 B1
Pembroke Ct 11 W7 86 D2
Pembroke Gdns
W8 113 C3 254 D4
Dagenham RM10 81 D5
Pembroke Gdns Cl W8 255 A5
Pembroke Hall NW4 46 C6
Pembroke Ho 16 W2 91 D1
Acton W3 111 A4
Putney SW15 156 A6
Upper Tooting SW17 180 B5
Pembroke Mews N10 31 A2
W8 255 A5
Pembroke Pl W8 255 A5
Edgware HA8 26 C3
Isleworth TW7 130 C3
Pembroke Rd BR1 187 D1
E17 53 D4
E6 100 B2
N10 31 A3
N15 51 D4
N8 50 A5
W8 113 C2 255 A4
Edmonton N13 17 A1
Greenford UB6 85 D3
Ilford IG3 57 D2
Mitcham CR4 181 A1
Ruislip HA4 39 D1
South Norwood SE25 205 C5
Wembley HA9 65 D5
Pembroke Sq
W8 113 C3 255 A5
Pembroke St N1 72 A1 233 B6
Pembroke Studios W8 254 D5
Pembroke Terr NW8 229 C5
Pembroke Villas W8 255 A4
Richmond TW9 131 D1
Pembroke Way UB3 105 A3
Pembroke Wlk W8 255 A4
Pembrook Lo 2 SW16 160 B1
Pembury Ave KT4 200 A2
Pembury Cl E5 74 B3
Hayes BR2 208 D2
Pembury Cres DA14 169 A2
Pembury Ct UB3 127 B6
Pembury Ho SE5 139 C3
Pembury Pl 15 E5,E8 74 B3
Pembury Rd DA7 147 A6
Pembury Rd *continued*
E5 74 B3
Croydon SE25 206 A5
Tottenham N17 33 D1
Pemdevon Rd CR0 204 C2
Pemell Cl 27 E1 96 C3
Pemell Ho 28 E1 96 C3
Pemerich Cl UB3 105 D1
Pempath Pl HA9 65 D6
Penally Pl N1 235 D6
Penang St E1 118 B5
Penard Rd UB2 107 D3
Penarth Ct SM2 218 A1
Penarth St SE15 140 C6
Penates KT10 212 B4
Penberth Rd SE6 164 A3
Penbury Rd UB2 107 B1
Penceat Ct SE20 184 C1
Pencombe Mews W11 244 D6
Pencraig Way SE15 140 B6
Pendall Cl EN4 2 C1
Penda Rd DA8 147 D5
Pendarves Rd SW20 178 C2
Penda's Mead E9 75 A4
Pendell Ave UB3 127 D5
Pendennis Ho 15 SE8 119 A2
Pendennis Rd N17 51 B6
Streatham SW16 182 A6
Penderel Rd TW3 151 C6
Penderry Rise SE6 164 B2
Penderyn Way N7 71 D4
Pendlebury Gn 8 SE18 144 A4
Pendle Ho 13 SE26 162 A1
Pendle Rd SW16 181 B5
Pendlestone Rd E17 53 D4
Pendley Ho 18 E2 96 A6
Pendragon Rd BR1 165 A1
Pendragon Sec Sch
BR1 165 A1
Pendrell Ho WC2 239 D1
Pendrell Rd SE4 141 A3
Pendrell St SE18 145 B6
Pendula Dr UB4 84 D3
Penelope Ho 20 SW9 138 C4
Penerley Rd SE6 163 D3
Penfield Lo 7 W9 91 C2
Penfields Ho N7 72 A2
Penfold Cl CR0 220 C5
Penfold Ct NW8 236 D5
7 Mitcham CR4 181 A1
Penfold Ho 14 SE18 144 D6
Penfold La DA5 168 D3
Penfold Pl NW1 92 C2 237 A4
Penfold Rd N9 18 D3
Penfold St NW8 92 B3 236 D5
Penford Gdns SE9 143 D2
Penford St SE5 138 D3
Pengarth Rd DA5 168 D5
Penge East Sta SE20 184 C4
Penge La SE20 184 D3
Penge Rd E13 99 C6
South Norwood SE25 206 A6
Penge West Sta SE20 184 B4
Penhall Rd SE7 121 D2
Penhill Rd DA5 168 C4
Penhurst Mans SW6 264 C2
Penifather La UB6 86 B4
Peninsula Ct E14 119 D3
Peninsular Cl TW14 149 C5
Peninsular Park Rd SE7 121 A2
Penistone Rd SW16 182 A3
Penketh Dr HA1 64 B5
Penmayne Ho SE11 261 B2
Penmon Rd SE2 124 A3
Pennack Rd SE15 139 D6
Penn Almshouse 1
SE10 142 A4
Pennant Mews
W8 113 D2 255 C4
Pennant Terr E17 35 B1
Pennard Mans 5 W12 112 C4
Pennard Rd W12 112 C4
Pennards The TW16 194 C6
Penn Cl Greenford UB6 85 D5
Harrow HA3 43 C5
Penn Ct NW9 45 B6
Penner Cl SW19 157 A2
Penners Gdns KT6 198 A2
Pennethorne Cl E9 96 C6
Pennethorne Ho SW11 136 B2
Pennethorne Rd SE15 140 B5
Penn Gdns BR7 188 D1
Penn Ho NW8 237 A5
7 Edmonton N9 18 A1
Pennine Dr NW2 68 D6
Pennine La NW2 69 A6
Pennine Mans NW2 69 A6
Pennine Par NW2 69 A6
Pennine Way UB7 127 B5
Pennington Cl 10 SE27 183 B6
Pennington Ct 16 E1 118 A6
SE16 119 A5
Pennington Dr N21 16 A6
Pennington Lo 18 KT5 198 A4
Pennington St E1 118 B6
Pennington Way SE12 165 B2
Penniston Cl N17 33 A1
Penn La DA5 169 A5
Penn Rd N7 72 A4
Penn St N1 95 B6 235 D5
Penny Ct SW10 266 B6
Pennyfields E14 119 C6
Pennyford Ct NW8 236 C6
Penny La TW17 193 C2
Penny Mews SW12 159 B4
Pennymore Wlk W9 91 B3
Penny Rd NW10 88 D4
Penny Royal SM6 219 D2
Pennyroyal Ave E6 100 C1
Penpoll Rd E8 74 B2
Penpool La DA16 146 B2
Penrhyn Ave E17 35 C2
Penrhyn Cres
Chingford E17 35 C2
Mortlake SW14 133 A1
Penrhyn Gdns KT1 197 D5
Penrhyn Gr E17 35 C2
Penrhyn Rd KT1 198 A6
Penrith Cl
Beckenham BR3 185 D2
Putney SW15 157 A6
Penrith Pl SE27 160 D2
Penrith Rd N15 51 B4
New Malden KT3 199 B5
South Norwood CR7 183 A1
Penrith St SW16 181 C4
Penrose Gr
SE17 117 A1 262 A1
Penrose Ho SE17 262 A1
Southgate N21 16 B6
Penrose St
SE17 117 A1 262 A1
Penryn Ho SE11 261 C2
Penryn St NW1 93 D5 232 C4
Penry St SE1 263 B3
Pensbury Pl SW8 137 C3
Pensbury St SW8 137 C3
Pensford Ave TW9 132 C3
Penshurst 2 NW5 71 A2
Penshurst Ave DA15 168 A5
Penshurst Gdns HA8 26 D5
Penshurst Gn BR2 208 D4
Penshurst Ho 1 SE15 140 C6
Penshurst Rd DA7 147 B4
E9 74 D1
Thornton Heath CR7 204 D4
Tottenham N17 33 D3
Penshurst Way SM2 217 C1
Penshurst Wlk 4 BR2 208 D4
Pensilver Cl EN4 2 C1
Penstemon Cl N3 29 C4
Pentelow Gdns TW14 150 A5
Pentire Rd E17 36 B2
Pentland Ave
Edgware HA8 10 D2
Littleton TW17 192 C4
Pentland Cl N9 18 C2
NW11 69 A6
Pentland Ho 7 N16 51 D1
17 NW5 71 A2
Pentland Pl UB5 85 A6
Pentland Rd WD23 8 A5
Pentlands BR3 186 A2
Pentlands Cl CR4 203 B6
Pentland St SW18 158 A5
Pentland Way UB10 61 A5
Pentlow St SW15 134 C2
Pentney Rd
5 Chingford E4 20 B3
Merton SW19,SW20 179 A2
Streatham SW12 159 C3
Penton Gr N1 234 A3
Penton Ho N1 234 A3
3 SE2 124 D4
Sutton SM2 218 A1
Penton Pl SE17 116 D1 261 D2
Penton Rise WC1 94 B4 233 D2
Penton St N1 94 C5 234 A3
Pentonville Rd
N1 94 B5 233 C3
Pentrich Ave EN1 6 A5
Pentridge St SE15 139 D5
Pentyre Ave N18 33 B5
Penwerris Ave TW5,
TW7 130 A5
Penwerris Ct TW7 130 A5
Penwith Rd SW18 157 D2
Penwood Ho 4 SW15 155 D5
Penwortham Ct 1 N22 32 C1
Penwortham Prim Sch
SW17 181 B4
Penwortham Rd SW16 181 C4
Penylan Pl HA8 26 C3
Penywern Rd
SW5 113 C1 255 B2
Penzance Ho SE11 261 B2
Penzance Pl
W11 113 A5 244 B4
Penzance St
W11 113 A5 244 A4
Peony Ct IG8 36 C3
Peony Gdns W12 112 A6
Peperfield WC1 233 C1
Pepler Ho 17 W10 91 A3
Pepler Mews SE1 263 C1
Peploe Rd NW6 90 D5
Pepper Cl E6 100 B2
Peppermead Sq SE13 163 C6
Peppermint Cl CR0 204 A2
Peppermint Pl 5 E11 76 C5
Pepper St E14 119 D3
SE1 252 A2
Peppie Cl N16 73 C6
Pepsi Trocadero W1 249 C5
Pepys Cl UB10 60 D4
Pepys Cres 2 E16 121 A5
Barnet EN5 12 C6
Pepys Ct SW20 178 C1
Pepys Ent Ctr 12 SE8 119 B2
Pepys Ho 14 E2 96 C4
SW4 159 D6
Pepys Rd SE14 140 D3
Wimbledon SW20 178 C2
Pepys Rise BR6 211 D1
Pepys St EC3 117 C6 253 B6
Perak Ct KT5 199 A2
Perceval Ave NW3 70 C3
Perceval Ct UB5 63 C3
Percheron Cl TW7 130 D2
Percheron Ct 3 SW9 138 B2

Percheron Rd WD6 .... 11 B5
Perch St E8 .... 73 D4
Percival Ct N17 .... 33 D3
Percival Gdns RM6 .... 58 C3
Percival Rd Enfield EN1 ..... 5 D1
Feltham TW13 .... 149 D2
Mortlake SW14 .... 133 A1
Orpington BR6 .... 226 D6
Percival St EC1 ... 94 D4 234 D1
Percival Way KT19 .... 215 B4
Percy Ave TW15 .... 170 C5
Percy Bilton Ct TW5 ..... 129 D4
Percy Bryant Rd TW16 .. 171 C3
Percy Bush Rd UB7 ...... 104 B3
Percy Cir WC1 ... 94 B4 233 D2
Percy Ct 1 KT5 .... 198 B3
Percy Gdns Enfield EN3 ... 18 D6
Hayes UB4 .... 83 C4
3 Isleworth TW7 .... 131 A2
New Malden KT4 .... 199 C1
Percy Ho 4 SW16 .... 181 C6
Percy Mews W1 .... 239 C3
Percy Pas W1 .... 239 C3
Percy Rd DA7 .... 147 A3
E11 .... 54 C2
E16 .... 98 C2
N12 .... 30 A5
W12 .... 112 A4
Carshalton CR4 .... 203 A2
Croydon SE25 .... 206 A4
Edmonton N21 .... 17 A4
Hampton TW12 .... 173 C3
Ilford IG3 .... 58 A2
Isleworth TW7 .... 131 A1
Penge SE20 .... 184 D2
Romford RM7 .... 59 D6
Twickenham TW2 .... 152 A3
Percy St W1 .... 93 D2 239 C3
Percy Way TW2 .... 152 A3
Peregrine Cl NW10 .... 67 B3
Peregrine Ct DA16 .... 145 D4
Streatham SW16 .... 182 B6
Peregrine Gdns CR0 ..... 223 A6
Peregrine Ho EC1 .... 234 D2
6 SW11 .... 136 C2
Peregrine Rd TW16 ..... 171 D1
Peregrine Way SW19,
SW20 .... 178 C3
Performing Arts & Tech Sch
SE25 .... 205 B3
Perham Rd W14 . 113 B1 254 B1
Peridot St E6 .... 100 A2
Perifield SE21 .... 161 A3
Perimeade Rd UB6 .... 87 C5
Periton Rd SE9 .... 143 D1
Perivale UB6 .... 86 D5
Perivale Fst & Mid Schs
UB6 .... 87 C5
Perivale Gdns W13 .... 87 B3
Perivale Grange UB6 ..... 87 A4
Perivale Ind Pk UB6 ...... 87 B5
Perivale La UB6 .... 87 A4
Perivale Lo UB6 .... 87 A4
Perivale New Bsns Ctr
UB6 .... 87 C5
Perivale Sta UB6 .... 87 A5
Perkin Cl Hounslow TW3 .. 129 D1
Wembley HA0 .... 65 B3
Perkins Ct TW15 .... 170 B5
Perkins Ho 18 E14 .... 97 B2
Perkins Rd IG2 .... 57 B4
Perkins Rents SW1 ..... 259 C5
Perkins Sq SE1 .... 252 B4
Perks Cl SE3 .... 142 C2
Perley Ho 10 E3 .... 97 B2
Perotti Ho SW6 .... 135 D2
Perpins Rd SE9 .... 167 C5
Perran Rd SE24,SW2 ..... 160 D2
Perren St NW5 .... 71 B2
Perrers Rd W6 .... 112 B2
Perrin Cl TW15 .... 170 B5
Perring Est E3 .... 97 C2
Perrin Grange HA9 .... 66 B6
Perrin Rd HA0 .... 65 B4
Perrin's Ct 17 NW3 .... 70 A4
Perrin's La NW3 .... 70 A4
Perrin's Wlk NW3 .... 70 A4
Perronet Ho SE1 .... 261 D5
Perry Ave W3 .... 89 B1
Perry Cl UB8 .... 82 D1
Perry Ct 2 N15 .... 51 C3
5 Millwall E14 .... 119 C1
Perryfield Way NW9 ..... 45 D3
Richmond TW10 .... 153 B2
Perry Garth UB5 .... 84 C6
Perry Gdns N9 .... 17 C1
Perry Hall Prim Sch
BR6 .... 211 D3
Perry Hill SE6 .... 163 B1
Perry Ho 24 SW2 .... 160 A4
Perry How KT4 .... 199 D1
Perryman Ho IG11 .... 101 A6
Perrymans Farm Rd IG2 .. 57 B4
Perry Mead Bushey WD23 ... 8 A5
Enfield EN2 .... 4 D3
Perrymead St
SW6 .... 135 D3 265 C1
Perrymount Prim Sch
SE23 .... 162 D2
Perryn Ct 1 TW1 .... 153 A4
Perryn Ho W3 .... 111 C6
Perryn Rd 1 SE16 .... 118 B3
W3 .... 111 B6
Perry Rise SE23 .... 163 A1
Perry's Pl W1 .... 239 C2
Perry St BR7 .... 189 C4
Perry Street Gdns BR7 .. 189 C4
Perry Vale SE23 .... 162 D2
Perrywood Ho 17 E5 ...... 74 B3
Persant Rd SE6 .... 164 C2
Perserverance Pl SW9 .. 138 C5
Perseverance Works 18
E2 .... 95 C4
Pershore Cl IG2 .... 56 D4
Pershore Gr SM5 .... 202 B3
Pert Cl N10 .... 31 B4
Perth Ave NW9 .... 45 B2
Hayes UB4 .... 84 C3
Perth Cl SW20 .... 178 A1
Perth Ct 5 SE5 .... 139 B1
Perth Ho N1 .... 72 B1
12 Acton W3 .... 88 C1
Perth Rd E10 .... 53 B1
E13 .... 99 B5
N4 .... 50 C1
Barking IG11 .... 101 B6
Beckenham BR3 .... 186 A1
Ilford IG2 .... 56 D3
Tottenham N22 .... 32 D2
Perth Terr IG2 .... 57 A2
Perwell Ave HA2 .... 41 B1
Perystreete SE23 .... 162 C2
Petavel Rd TW11 .... 174 C4
Peter Ave NW10 .... 68 B1
Peter Best Ho 6 E1 .... 96 B1
Peterboat Cl SE10 ...... 120 C2
Peterborough Ct EC4 ... 241 B1
Peterborough Gdns IG1 .. 56 A2
Peterborough Mews
SW6 .... 135 C3
Peterborough Prim Sch
SW6 .... 135 C3
Peterborough Rd E10 .... 54 B3
SW6 .... 135 C2
Carshalton SM5 .... 202 C3
Harrow HA1 .... 42 D2
Peterborough Villas
SW6 .... 265 C2
Peter Bradley Ct RM9 ..... 81 B1
Peter Butler Ho 6 SE1 .. 118 A4
Peterchurch Ho SE15 ... 140 B6
Petergate SW11 .... 136 A1
Peterhead Ct 12 UB1 ..... 86 A1
Peter Hills Ho 6 SE16 ... 118 A2
Peter Hills with St Mary's &
St Paul's CE Prim Sch
SE16 .... 118 D5
Peter Ho SW8 .... 270 A4
Peter James Bsns Ctr
UB3 .... 106 A4
Peter Kennedy Ct CR0 ... 207 B3
Peterley Bsns Ctr 21 E2 ... 96 B5
Peters Cl DA16 .... 145 C3
Dagenham RM8 .... 58 D1
Stanmore HA7 .... 25 D4
Peters Ct 9 W2 .... 91 D1
Peter's Ct SW4 .... 160 A5
Petersfield Cl N18 .... 33 A5
Petersfield Rd W3 ...... 111 A4
Petersfield Rise SW15 ... 156 B3
Petersham Cl
Richmond TW10 .... 153 D2
Sutton SM1 .... 217 C3
Petersham Dr BR5 ...... 190 A1
Petersham Gdns BR5 ... 189 D1
Petersham Ho SW7 ..... 256 C4
Petersham La SW7 ..... 256 A6
Petersham Mews
SW7 .... 114 A3 256 B5
Petersham Pl
SW7 .... 114 A3 256 B6
Petersham Rd TW10 .... 154 A3
Petersham Terr CR0 .... 220 A5
Peter's La EC1 .... 241 D4
Peter's Lo HA8 .... 26 B4
Peter's Path SE26 .... 184 B6
Peter St W1 ...... 115 D6 249 C6
Peterstone Rd SE2 ...... 124 B4
Peterstow Cl SW19 ...... 157 A2
Peterwood Pk CR9 ...... 220 B6
Peterwood Way CR0 .... 220 B6
Petherton Ct NW10 .... 90 D6
10 Harrow HA1 .... 42 D3
Petherton Ho N4 .... 51 A1
Petherton Rd N5 .... 73 A3
Petiver Cl 26 E9 .... 74 C1
Petley Rd W6 .... 134 D5
Peto Pl NW1 .... 238 D6
Peto St N E16 .... 98 D1
Petrel Ct 7 SE21 .... 161 B2
Petrie Cl NW2 .... 69 A2
Petrie Ho 3 SE18 .... 144 C6
Petros Gdns 1 NW3 ...... 70 A2
Petticoat Lane Mkt★
EC2 .... 95 D2 243 C3
Petticoat Sq E1 .... 243 C2
Petticoat Twr E1 .... 243 C2
Pettit's Pl RM10 .... 81 C3
Pettit's Rd RM10 .... 81 C3
Pettiward Cl SW15 ...... 134 C1
Pettman Cres SE18,SE28 . 123 B3
Pettsgrove Ave HA0 ...... 65 C3
Pett's Hill UB5 .... 63 D3
Petts La TW17 .... 192 C5
Pett St SE7 .... 122 A2
Petts Wood Rd BR5 ..... 211 B4
Petts Wood Sta BR5 .... 211 A4
Petty France
SW1 .... 115 C3 259 C6
Petworth Cl UB5 .... 63 B1
Petworth Gdns
Hillingdon UB10 .... 83 A6
West Barnes SW20 ..... 200 B6
Petworth Ho 16 SE22 ... 139 C2
Petworth Rd DA6 .... 169 C6
N12 .... 30 C5
Petworth St
SW11 .... 136 C4 267 B2
Petyt Pl SW3 ..... 136 C6 267 A5
Petyward SW3 ... 114 C2 257 B3
Pevensey Ave N11 .... 31 D5
Enfield EN1 .... 5 C3
Pevensey Cl TW7 .... 130 A5
Pevensey Ct 4 W3 ...... 110 D4
West Norwood SW16 ..... 160 C1
10 Woodford E18 .... 37 A2
Pevensey Ho 5 E1 .... 97 A2
Pevensey Rd E7 .... 77 A4
Feltham TW13 .... 151 A3
Upper Tooting SW17 .... 180 B6
Peverel E6 .... 100 C1
Peverel Ho RM10 .... 81 C6
Peverett Cl N11 .... 31 B5
Peveril Dr TW11 .... 174 B5
Peveril Ho SE1 .... 262 D5
Pewsey Cl E4 .... 35 C5
Pewsham Ho N4 .... 51 A1
Pewterers Ct N3 .... 29 B2
Peyton Ho N11 .... 31 A6
Peyton Pl SE10 .... 142 A5
Pharamond NW2 .... 68 D2
Pharaoh Cl CR4 .... 202 D2
Pheasant Cl E16 .... 99 B1
Phelps Ho SW15 .... 134 D2
Phelp St SE17 .... 139 B6
Phelps Way UB3 .... 105 D2
Phene St SW3 ... 136 C6 267 B6
Philadelphia Ct SW10 ... 266 B3
Philbeach Gdns
SW5 .... 113 C1 255 A2
Phil Brown Pl 3 SW8 ... 137 B2
Philchurch Pl 25 E1 .... 96 A1
Phildor Ct NW11 .... 47 A3
Philia Ho 2 NW1 .... 71 C1
Philimore Cl SE18 .... 123 C1
Philip Ct W2 .... 236 C4
Enfield EN2 .... 5 B4
Philip Gdns CR0 .... 223 B6
Philip Ho N20 .... 14 D2
10 NW6 .... 91 D6
Philip La N15 .... 51 C6
Philipot Almshouse SE9 166 B5
Philipot Path SE9 .... 166 B5
Philippa Gdns SE9 ...... 165 D6
Philip Rd SE15 .... 140 A2
Philips Cl CR4 .... 203 A1
Philip St E13 .... 99 A3
Philip Turner Est 28 E9 ... 74 C1
Philip Wlk SE15 .... 140 B2
Phillimore Ct W8 .... 245 B1
Phillimore Gardens Cl
W8 .... 113 C3 255 A6
Phillimore Gdns
W8 .... 113 C4 245 A1
Willesden NW10 .... 90 C6
Phillimore Pl
W8 .... 113 C4 245 A1
Phillimore Terr W8 ...... 255 B6
Phillimore Wlk
W8 .... 113 C3 255 B6
Phillip Ho E1 .... 243 D3
Phillipp St N1 .... 95 C6
Phillips Ct Edgware HA8 .. 26 C4
Hayes UB4 .... 84 B4
Philpot La EC3 .... 253 A6
Philpot Sq SW6 .... 135 D2
Philpot St E1 .... 96 B1
Phineas Pett Rd SE9 .... 144 A2
Phipp's Bridge Rd CR4,
SW19 .... 202 B6
Phipps Bridge Sta CR4 .. 202 B6
Phipps Hatch La EN2 .... 5 A5
Phipps Ho 1 SE7 .... 121 B1
16 W12 .... 112 B6
Phipp St EC2 ..... 95 C3 243 A6
Phoebeth Rd SE4 .... 163 C6
Phoenix Bsns Ctr E3 ...... 97 C2
Phoenix Cl E17 .... 35 B1
18 E8 .... 95 D6
West Wickham BR4 ...... 224 C6
Phoenix Coll SM4 .... 202 A4
Phoenix Ct E14 .... 119 C2
2 SE14 .... 141 A6
4 Brentford TW8 .... 110 A1
Chingford E4 .... 19 D1
Croydon SE25 .... 206 A4
Enfield EN3 .... 6 C5
Phoenix Dr BR2 .... 225 D5
Phoenix High Sch W12 .. 112 A6
Phoenix Ind Est HA1 ...... 42 D5
Phoenix Lodge Mans 1
W6 .... 112 C2
Phoenix Pk NW2 .... 68 A6
Phoenix Pl WC1 ... 94 B3 240 D6
Phoenix Rd NW1 .. 93 D4 232 C2
Penge SE20 .... 184 C4
Phoenix Sch E3 .... 97 B4
Phoenix Sch The NW3 .... 70 A2
Phoenix St WC2 .... 239 D1
Phoenix Trad Est UB6 .... 87 D6
Phoenix Trad Pk TW8 .... 109 D1
Phoenix Way TW5 .... 128 D6
Phoenix Wharf Rd SE1 .. 253 D1
Phyllis Ave KT3 .... 200 B4
Phyllis Ho CR0 .... 220 D4
Phyllis Hodges Ho
NW1 .... 93 D5 232 C3
Physic Pl SW3 ... 136 D6 267 C6
Picador Ho 1 RM10 ...... 81 D2
Picardy Manorway
DA17 .... 125 D4
Picardy Rd DA17 .... 125 C2
Picardy St DA17 .... 125 C3
Piccadilly W1 .... 115 C5 249 A4
Piccadilly Arc SW1 ..... 249 A4
Piccadilly Cir★
W1 .... 115 D6 249 C5
Piccadilly Circus Sta
SW1 .... 115 D6 249 C5
Piccadilly Pl W1 .... 249 B5
Pickard St EC1 .... 234 D2
Pickering Ave E6 .... 100 C4
Pickering Gdns N11 ...... 31 A4
Croydon SE25 .... 205 D3
Pickering Ho N4 .... 51 B2
4 SE18 .... 122 C2
17 W2 .... 91 D1
W5 .... 109 C2
Pickering Mews W2 ...... 91 D1
Pickering Pl SW1 .... 249 B3
Pickering St N1 .... 234 D6
Pickets Cl WD23 .... 8 C3
Pickets St SW12 .... 159 B4
Pickett Croft HA7 .... 25 D2
Pickett's Lock La N9 ..... 18 D2
Pickford Cl DA7 .... 147 A3
Pickford La DA7 .... 147 A3
Pickford Rd DA7 .... 147 A2
Pickfords Wharf N1 ..... 235 A3
Pickhurst Gn BR2 .... 208 D2
Pickhurst Inf Sch BR2 .. 208 D3
Pickhurst Jun Sch BR2 .. 208 D3
Pickhurst La BR2,BR3,
BR4 .... 208 C2
Pickhurst Mead BR2 .... 208 D2
Pickhurst Pk BR2 .... 208 D4
Pickhurst Rise BR4 ..... 208 B1
Pickwick Cl TW4 .... 151 A6
Pickwick Ct SE9 .... 166 B3
Pickwick Ho 18 SE16 .... 118 A4
3 W11 .... 112 D5
Pickwick Mews N18 ...... 33 C5
Pickwick Pl HA1 .... 42 C2
Pickwick Rd SE21 .... 161 C4
Pickwick St SE1 .... 252 A1
Pickwick Way BR7 ...... 189 A4
Pickworth Cl SW8 .... 270 B3
Picton Ho 1 SW4 .... 160 A4
Picton Pl W1 .... 238 B1
Tolworth KT6 .... 198 C1
Picton St SE5 .... 139 B5
Pied Bull Ct WC1 .... 240 B3
Pied Bull Yd WC1 .... 240 B3
Piedmont Rd SE18 ...... 123 B1
Pield Heath Ave UB8 ..... 82 C3
Pield Heath Rd UB8 ...... 82 B3
Pield Heath Sch UB8 ..... 82 B3
Pierhead Wharf 37 E1 ... 118 B5
Pier Ho SW3 .... 267 B5
Piermont Pl BR1 .... 188 A1
Piermont Rd SE22 ...... 162 B6
Pier Par 3 E16 .... 122 C5
Pierpoint Bldg 5 E14 ... 119 C4
Pier Rd E16 .... 122 C4
Feltham TW14 .... 150 B6
Pierrepoint SE25 .... 205 C6
Pierrepoint Rd W3 ...... 110 D6
Pierson Ho 12 SE19 ..... 183 C6
Pier St E14 .... 120 A2
Pier Terr SW18 .... 136 A1
Pier Way SE18 .... 123 B3
Pigeon Ct E4 .... 36 A4
Pigeon La TW12 .... 173 C6
Piggott Ho 2 E2 .... 96 D5
Pigott St E14 .... 97 C1
Pike Cl BR1 .... 187 B5
Hillingdon UB10 .... 82 B6
Pike Rd NW7 .... 27 B6
Pike's End HA5 .... 40 B5
Pikestone Cl UB4 .... 85 A3
Pikethorne SE23 .... 162 D2
Pilgrimage St
SE1 .... 117 B4 252 C1
Pilgrim Cl SM4 .... 201 D2
Pilgrim Hill SE27 .... 183 A6
Pilgrim Ho SE1 .... 262 D5
Pilgrims Cl Northolt UB5 ... 64 A3
Palmers Green N13 .... 32 B6
Pilgrims Cloisters 18
SE5 .... 139 C5
Pilgrims Ct SE3 .... 143 A4
Enfield EN1 .... 5 B3
Pilgrim's La NW3 .... 70 B4
Pilgrims Mews E14 ...... 120 B6
Pilgrim's Rise EN4 .... 14 C6
Pilgrim St EC4 .... 241 C1
Pilgrims Way 5 E6 ...... 100 A6
N19 .... 49 D1
Wembley HA9 .... 44 D1
Pilgrim's Way CR2 ...... 221 D3
Pilgrims Way Prim Sch
SE15 .... 140 C6
Pilkington Ct 1 NW9 ..... 46 A5
Pilkington Rd 4 SE15 ... 140 B3
Orpington BR6 .... 227 A6
Pillar of Fire Society Church
& Bible Sch NW4 .... 46 D4
Pillions La UB4 .... 83 B3
Pilot Ind Ctr NW10 .... 89 C3
Pilsden Cl SW19 .... 156 D3
Piltdown Rd WD19 .... 22 D6
Pilton Est The CR0 ..... 220 D6
Pilton Pl SE17 .... 262 B2
Pimento Ct W5 .... 109 D3
Pimilico Sta
SW1 .... 115 D1 259 C2
Pimlico Rd SW1 . 115 A1 258 B2
Pimlico Sch
SW1 .... 115 C1 259 B1
Pimlico Wlk 1 N1 .... 95 C4
Pinchbeck Rd BR6 ...... 227 D2
Pinchin St E1 .... 118 A6
Pincombe Ho SE17 ...... 262 C2
Pincott Pl SE4 .... 140 D2
Pincott Rd
8 Bexley DA6 .... 147 C1
Merton SW19 .... 180 A2
Pindar St EC2 ..... 95 C2 243 A4
Pindock Mews W9 .... 91 D3
Pine Apple Ct SW1 ..... 259 A6
Pine Ave E15 .... 76 B3
West Wickham BR4 ..... 207 D1
Pine Cl N14 .... 15 C4
8 N19 .... 71 C6
E10 .... 75 D6
3 Penge SE20 .... 184 C2
Stanmore HA7 .... 25 B6
Pine Coombe CR0 .... 222 D4
Pinecrest Gdns BR6 .... 226 D4
Pinecroft DA16 .... 146 A5
Harrow HA3 .... 44 B4
Pinecroft Cres EN5 .... 1 A1
Pine Ct UB5 .... 85 A4
Pinedene 2 SE15 .... 140 B4
Pinefield Cl E14 .... 119 C6
Pine Gdns Ruislip HA4 ..... 62 B6
Surbiton KT5 .... 198 C3
Pine Glade BR6 .... 226 B4
Pine Gr N20 .... 13 C3
N4,N19 .... 72 B6
Wimbledon SW19 .... 179 B5
Pine Ho 15 SE16 .... 118 C4
Pinehurst BR7 .... 188 D4
Pinehurst Ct 1 W11 ...... 91 B1
Pinehurst Wlk 4 BR6 ... 211 B1
Pinelands Cl 7 SE3 .... 142 D5
Pine Lo SW15 .... 157 A5
Pinemartin Cl NW2 ...... 68 C5
Pine Pl UB4 .... 83 D3
Pine Rd N11 .... 15 A2
NW2 .... 68 D4
Pine Ridge SM5 .... 219 A1
Pines Ct 14 SW19 ...... 156 D3
Pines Rd BR1 .... 188 A1
Pine St EC1 ...... 94 C3 241 A6
Pines The Southgate N14 .. 15 C6
South Norwood SE19 .... 182 D4
Sunbury TW16 .... 194 A6
Woodford IG8 .... 21 A1
Pine Tree Cl TW5 .... 128 B4
Pine Tree Ho SE14 ...... 140 D5
Pine Tree Lo BR2 .... 208 D5
Pine Trees Dr UB10 ...... 60 A4
Pineview Ct 5 E4 .... 20 A3
Pine Wlk KT5 .... 198 C3
Pinewood BR7 .... 188 C4
Pine Wood TW16 .... 172 A2
Pinewood Ave DA15 .... 167 C3
Hillingdon UB8 .... 82 B1
Pinner HA5 .... 23 D4
Pinewood Cl BR6 .... 211 B1
Croydon CR0 .... 223 A5
Pinner HA5 .... 23 D4
Pinewood Ct SW4 ...... 159 D5
Enfield EN2 .... 4 D2
Pinewood Dr BR6 ...... 227 C3
Pinewood Gr W5 .... 87 C1
Pinewood Pl KT19 ...... 215 B4
Pinewood Rd BR2 ...... 209 A5
SE2 .... 146 D6
Feltham TW13 .... 150 B1
Pinfold Rd SW16 .... 182 A6
Pinglestone Cl UB7 .... 126 A5
Pinkcoat Cl TW13 .... 150 B1
Pinkerton Ct KT2 .... 176 D1
Pinkerton Pl SW16 ..... 181 D6
Pinkham Mans W4 ..... 110 C1
Pinkham Way (North Circular
Rd)
N12 .... 30 D3
N12 .... 31 A4
Pinkwell Ave UB3 .... 105 B2
Pinkwell Jun & Inf Schs
UB3 .... 105 A2
Pinkwell La UB3 .... 105 B2
Pinley Gdns RM9 .... 102 B6
Pinnacle Hill DA7 ...... 147 D1
Pinnacle Hill N DA7 .... 147 D1
Pinnacle Ho E14 .... 120 A3
Pinnell Rd SE9 .... 143 D1
Pinner Ct HA5 .... 41 C5
Pinner Gn HA5 .... 22 C1
Pinner Gr HA5 .... 41 A4
Pinner Hill HA5 .... 22 B3
Pinner Hill Rd HA5 .... 22 C1
Pinner Ho 31 SE5 .... 139 A3
Pinner Park Ave HA2 .... 24 A1
Pinner Park Fst & Mid Schs
HA5 .... 41 D6
Pinner Park Gdns HA2 ... 24 A1
Pinner Rd
Harrow HA1,HA2 .... 42 A3
Harrow, Pinner HA2,HA5 ... 41 C5
Pinner HA6 .... 22 A1
Pinner Sta HA5 .... 41 A5
Pinner View HA1,HA2 .... 42 A4
Pinner Wood Fst & Mid Schs
HA5 .... 22 C2
Pinn Way HA4 .... 39 C2
Pintail Cl E6 .... 100 A2
Pintail Ct 40 SE8 .... 141 B6
Pintail Rd IG8 .... 37 B3
Pintail Way UB4 .... 84 D2
Pinter Ho 30 SW9 ...... 138 A3
Pinto Cl WD6 .... 11 B5
Pinto Way SE3 .... 143 B1
Pioneer Cl W12 .... 90 B1
Pioneers Ind Pk CR0 ... 204 A1
Pioneer St SE15 .... 140 A4
Pioneer Way W12 .... 90 C1
Piper Cl N7 .... 72 B2
Piper Rd KT1 .... 198 C6
Pipers Gdns CR0 .... 207 A2
Pipers Gn NW9 .... 45 A4
Pipers Green La HA8 ..... 10 A1
Pipewell Rd SM5 .... 202 C3
Pippenhall SE9 .... 166 D5
Pippin Cl NW2 .... 68 B5
Croydon CR0 .... 207 B1
Pippin Ct 5 EN4 .... 2 C1
Pippins Ct TW15 .... 170 D4
Piquet Rd SE20 .... 184 C1
Pirbright Cres CR0 ..... 224 A2
Pirbright Ho 11 KT2 .... 176 D4
Pirbright Rd SW18 ...... 157 C3
Pirie St 6 E16 .... 121 B5
Pitcairn Cl RM7 .... 59 C5
Pitcairn Ho 1 E9 .... 74 C1
Pitcairn Rd CR4 .... 180 D3
Pitchford St E15 .... 76 C1
Pitfield Cres SE28 ...... 124 A5
Pitfield Ho N5 .... 73 A3
Pitfield St N1 .... 95 C5
Pitfield Way NW10 .... 67 A2
Enfield EN3 .... 6 C4
Pitfold Cl SE12 .... 165 B5
Pitfold Rd SE12 .... 165 A4
Pit Ho NW10 .... 67 B5
Pitlake CR0 .... 220 D6
Pitman Ho 4 SE8 .... 141 C4
Southgate N21 .... 16 B6
Pitmans Coll HA0 .... 65 D2
Pitman St SE5 .... 139 A5
Pitmaston Ho 2 SE13 ... 142 A3
Pitsea Pl E1 .... 96 D1
Pitsea St E1 .... 96 D1
Pitshanger Ct 2 W5 ...... 87 C3
Pitshanger La W5 .... 87 C3
Pitshanger Manor Mus & Art
Gallery★ W5 .... 109 D5
Pitt Cres SW19 .... 179 D6
Pitt Ho 4 SW11 .... 136 B1
Pittman Gdns IG1 .... 79 A3
Pitt Rd BR6 .... 227 A4
Harrow HA2 .... 64 A6
Thornton Heath CR0,CR7 .. 205 A4
Pitt's Head Mews W1 ... 248 B3
Pittsmead Ave BR2 ..... 209 A2
Pitt St W8 .... 113 C4 245 B2
Pittville Gdns SE25 ..... 206 A6
Pixfield Ct BR2 .... 186 D1
Pixley St E14 .... 97 B1
Pixton 11 NW9 .... 27 C2
Pixton Way CR2 .... 223 B1
Place Farm Ave BR5,
BR6 .... 211 B1
Plains The 7 E4 .... 20 C4
Plaistow Gr BR1 .... 187 B3
E15 .... 98 D6
Plaistow Hospl E13 ...... 99 C5
Plaistow La BR1 .... 187 C2
Plaistow Park Rd E13 .... 99 B5
Plaistow Prim Sch E13 ... 99 B5
Plaistow Rd E13,E15 ..... 98 D5
Plaistow Sta E13 .... 98 D5
Plane St SE26 .... 162 B1
Planetarium The★
NW1 .... 93 A3 238 A5
Plane Tree Cres TW13 ... 150 B1
Planetree Ct W6 .... 112 D2
Plane Tree Ho SE7 ..... 121 D1
SE8 .... 141 A6
Plane Tree Wlk 4 SE19 .. 183 C4
Plantagenet Cl KT19 .... 215 B4
Plantagenet Gdns RM6 ... 58 D2
Plantagenet Ho SE18 ... 122 B3
Plantagenet Pl RM6 ...... 58 D2
Plantagenet Rd EN5 .... 2 A1
Plantain Pl SE1 .... 252 C2
Plantation The SE3 ..... 143 A3
Plasel Ct E13 .... 99 B6
Plashet Gr E6 .... 77 D1
Plashet Rd E13 .... 77 B1
Plashet Sch E6 .... 78 A1
Plassy Rd SE6 .... 163 D4
Platina St EC2 .... 242 D6
Plato Pl 1 SW6 .... 135 B3
Plato Rd SW2 .... 138 A1
Platt Halls (a) 35 NW9 .... 27 D1
Platt Halls (b) 37 NW9 .... 27 D1
Platt Halls (c) 38 NW9 .... 27 D1
Platt's Eyot TW12 ...... 173 C1
Platt's La NW3 .... 69 C5
Platts Rd EN3 .... 6 C4
Platt St NW1 .... 232 C4
Plaxdale Ho SE17 .... 263 A3
Plaxtol Cl BR1 .... 187 C2
Plaxtol Rd DA8 .... 147 C5
Plaxton Ct E11 .... 76 D5
Playfair St W6 .... 112 C1
Playfield Cres SE22 .... 161 D6
Playfield Rd HA8 .... 27 A1
Playford Rd N4 .... 72 B6
N4 .... 72 C6
Playgreen Way SE6 .... 185 C6
Playground Cl BR3 ..... 184 D1
Playhouse Yd EC4 .... 241 C1
Plaza Bsns Ctr EN3 .... 7 B3
Pleasance Rd BR5 ...... 190 B1
Putney SW15 .... 156 B6
Pleasance The SW15 ... 134 B1
Pleasant Gr CR0 .... 223 B5
Pleasant Pl N1 .... 72 D1
Pleasant Row NW1 ..... 231 D5
Pleasant View BR6 ..... 227 A3
Pleasant View Pl BR6 .. 227 A3
Pleasant Way HA0 .... 87 C5
Pleasaunce Ct SE9 ..... 144 B1
Plender Ct NW1 .... 232 B5
Plender St NW1 ... 93 C6 232 B5
Pleshey Rd N7 .... 71 D4
Plevna Cres N15 .... 51 C3
Plevna Ho 1 N9 .... 18 A1
Plevna Rd Edmonton N9 ... 18 B1
Hampton TW12 .... 173 D2
Plevna St E14 .... 120 A3
Pleydell Ave W6 .... 111 D2

Pleydell Ave continued
Penge SE19 ....**183** D3
Pleydell Ct EC4 ....**241** B1
Pleydell Gdns SE19 ....**183** D4
Pleydell St EC4 ....**241** B1
Plimsoll Cl E14 ....**97** C1
Plimsoll Rd N4 ....**72** D5
Plough Ct EC3 ....**252** D6
Plough Farm Cl HA4 ......**39** B3
Plough La SE22 ....**161** D5
Wallington CR0,SM6 ......**220** A3
Wimbledon SW17,SW19 ..**180** A6
Plough Lane Cl CR0,
SM6 ....**220** A3
Ploughmans Cl NW1 .....**232** C6
Ploughmans End TW7 ..**152** B6
Plough Pl EC4 ....**241** B2
Plough Rd SW11 ....**136** B1
West Ewell KT19 ....**215** B1
Plough St E1 ....**96** A1
Plough Terr SW11 ....**136** B1
Plough Way SE16 ....**119** A2
Plough Yd EC2 ....**243** B5
Plover Ho SW9 ....**138** C5
Plover Way SE16 ....**119** A3
Hayes UB4 ....**84** D2
Plowman Cl N18 ....**33** B5
Plowman Ho SW19 ......**156** D2
Plowman Way RM8 ....**58** C1
Plumbers Row E1 ....**96** A1
Plumbridge St 7 SE10 ..**142** A4
Plum Cl TW14 ....**150** A3
Plumcroft Prim Sch
SE18 ....**145** A6
Plume Ho SE10 ....**141** D6
Plum Garth TW8 ....**109** D2
Plum La SE18 ....**145** A5
Plummer Ct SE13 ....**163** D5
Plummer La CR4 ....**180** C1
Plummer Rd SW4 ....**159** D4
Plumpton Cl UB5 ....**63** C2
Plumpton Way SM5 ......**218** C5
Plumstead Common Rd
SE18 ....**145** A6
Plumstead High St
SE18,SE2 ....**123** C2
Plumstead Manor Sch
SE18 ....**145** B6
Plumstead Rd SE18,
SE28 ....**123** A2
Plumstead Sta SE18 ....**123** B2
Plumtree Cl
Dagenham RM10 ....**81** D4
Wallington SM6 ....**219** D1
Plumtree Ct EC4 ....**241** C2
Plymouth Ho IG11 ....**80** A1
Plymouth Rd BR1 ....**187** B2
E16 ....**99** A2
Plymouth Wharf E14 ....**120** B2
Plympton Ave NW6 ....**69** B1
Plympton Cl DA17 ....**125** A3
Plympton Pl NW1 ....**237** A5
Plympton Rd NW6 ....**69** B1
Plympton St NW8 ....**237** A5
Plymstock Rd DA16 .....**146** C5
Pocklington Cl NW9 ....**27** C1
Pocklington Ct SW15 ...**156** A3
Pocock Ave UB7 ....**104** B3
Pocock St SE1 ...**116** D4 **251** D2
Podmore Rd SW18 ....**136** A1
Poets Corner SW1 ....**260** A6
Poet's Rd N5 ....**73** B3
Poets Way HA1 ....**42** C5
Pointalls Cl N3 ....**30** A1
Point Cl SE10 ....**142** A4
Pointer Cl SE28 ....**102** D1
Pointer Sch The SE3 ....**143** A5
Pointers Cl E14 ....**119** D1
Point Hill SE10 ....**142** A4
Point Pl HA9 ....**66** D1
Point Pleasant SW18 ...**135** C1
Point Terr E7 ....**77** B3
Poland St W1 .....**93** C1 **239** B1
Polebrook Rd SE3 ....**143** C2
Polecroft La SE6 ....**163** B2
Polehamptons The
TW12 ....**174** A2
Pole Hill Rd Chingford E4 ..**20** A4
Hillingdon UB4 ....**83** A4
Polesden Gdns SW20 ...**178** B1
Polesworth Ho 16 W2 ....**91** C2
Polesworth Rd RM9 ....**80** D1
Polish Univ Abroad W6 ..**112** A2
Polish War Meml HA4 .....**62** C2
Pollard Cl E16 ....**121** A6
N7 ....**72** B4
Pollard Ho N1 ....**233** C3
Cheam KT4 ....**216** C4
Pollard Rd N20 ....**14** C2
Morden SM4 ....**202** B4
Pollard Row E2 ....**96** A4
Pollards Cl IG10 ....**21** C6
Pollards Cres SW16 .....**204** A6
Pollards Hill E SW16 ....**204** B6
Pollards Hill N SW16 ....**204** A6
Pollards Hill S SW16 ....**204** B6
Pollards Hill W SW16 ...**204** A6
Pollard St E2 ....**96** A4
Pollards Wood Rd
SW16 ....**204** A6
Pollard Wlk DA14 ....**190** C4
Pollen St W1 ....**238** D1
Pollitt Dr NW8 ...**92** B3 **236** D6
Pollock Ho W10 ....**91** A3
Polperro Cl EN3 ....**211** D3
Polperro Mans 3 NW6 ...**69** C3
Polperro Mews SE11 ....**261** D4

Polsted Rd SE6 ....**163** B4
Polsten Mews EN3 ....**7** C6
Polthorne Gr SE18 ....**123** B2
Polworth Rd SW16 ....**182** A5
Polygon Rd NW1 ..**93** D5 **232** C3
Polygon The NW8 ....**229** D6
1 SW4 ....**137** C1
Polytechnic St SE18 ....**122** C2
Pomell Way E1 ....**243** D2
Pomeroy Ct W11 ....**91** A1
Pomeroy Ho 5 E2 ....**96** D5
Pomeroy St SE14 ....**140** C4
Pomfret Rd SE5 ....**138** D2
Pomoja La N19 ....**72** A6
Pomona Ho 10 SE8 ....**119** A2
SE3 ....**143** A3
Pond Cl N12 ....**30** C4
Pond Cottage La BR3,
BR4 ....**207** C1
Pond Cotts SE21 ....**161** C3
Ponders End Ind Est EN3 ..**19** A6
Ponders End Sta EN3 .....**19** A6
Ponder St 5 N7 ....**72** B1
Pondfield Ho 6 N5 ....**73** A3
West Norwood SE27 ....**183** A5
Pondfield Rd BR6 ....**226** D5
Dagenham RM10 ....**81** D3
West Wickham BR2 ....**208** C1
Pond Gn HA4 ....**61** C6
Pond Hill Gdns SM3 .....**217** A2
Pond Ho SW3 ....**257** A3
Pond Mead SE21 ....**161** B5
Pond Path BR7 ....**188** D4
Pond Pl SW3 ....**114** C2 **257** A3
Pond Rd E15 ....**98** C5
SE3 ....**142** D3
Pondside Cl UB3 ....**127** B6
Pond Sq N6 ....**49** A1
Pond St NW3 ....**70** C3
Pond Way TW11 ....**175** C4
Pondwood Rise BR6 .....**211** C2
Ponler St E1 ....**96** B1
Ponsard Rd NW10 ....**90** B4
Ponsford St E9 ....**74** C2
Ponsonby Pl
SW1 ....**115** D1 **259** D2
Ponsonby Rd SW15 ......**156** B4
Ponsonby Terr SW1 .....**259** D2
Pontefract Ct UB5 ....**63** D3
Pontefract Rd BR1 ....**186** D5
Ponton Ho SW2 ....**160** C3
Ponton Rd SW8 ..**137** D6 **269** D5
Pont St SW1 .....**114** D3 **257** D5
Pont St Mews SW1 ......**257** C5
Pontypool Pl SE1 ....**251** C2
Pool Cl Beckenham BR3 .**185** C5
East Molesey KT8 ....**195** B4
Pool Ct SE6 ....**163** C2
Poole Cl N1 ....**73** C1
Hounslow TW5 ....**129** A3
Poole Ho SE11 ....**260** D5
Pool End Cl TW17 ....**192** C4
Poole Rd E9 ....**74** D2
West Ewell KT19 ....**215** B2
Pooles Bldgs EC1 ....**241** A5
Pooles Ct IG3 ....**80** A5
Pooles La SW10 ....**266** A3
Pooles Park Prim Sch
N4 ....**72** B6
Pooles Pk N4 ....**72** C6
Poole St N1 ....**95** B6 **235** C5
Poole Way UB4 ....**83** C4
Pool Ho NW8 ....**236** A5
Poolmans St SE16 ....**118** D4
Pool Rd
East Molesey KT12,KT8 ..**195** B4
Harrow HA1 ....**42** B2
Poolsford Rd NW9 ....**45** C5
Poonah St E1 ....**96** C1
Pope Cl
East Bedfont TW14 ....**149** D3
Mitcham SW17,SW19 .....**180** B4
Pope Ct 10 KT2 ....**175** D6
Pope Ho 7 SE16 ....**118** B2
3 SE5 ....**139** B5
Pope John RC Prim Sch
W12 ....**112** B6
Pope Rd BR2 ....**209** D4
Pope's Ave TW2 ....**152** C4
Popes Dr N3 ....**29** C2
Popes Gr CR0 ....**223** B5
Pope's Gr TW1,TW2 .....**152** D2
Pope's Head Alley EC3 ..**242** D1
Pope's La W5 ....**110** A3
Pope's Rd SW9 ....**138** C2
Pope St SE1 ....**253** B1
Pope Street St SE9 ....**166** B3
Popham Ct TW13 ....**151** B1
Popham Gdns TW9 ....**132** D2
Popham Rd N1 ...**95** A5 **235** A6
Popham St N1 ....**234** D6
N1 ....**95** A6 **235** A6
Poplar Ave Mitcham CR4 ..**180** D2
Orpington BR6 ....**226** D6
Southall UB2 ....**107** D3
Yiewsley UB7 ....**104** B6
Poplar Bath St 10 E14 ..**119** D6
Poplar Bsns Pk E14 ......**120** A6
Poplar Cl E9 ....**75** B3
Pinner HA5 ....**22** D2
Poplar Cres KT19 ....**215** A2
Poplar Ct Chingford E4 ....**35** D4

Poplar Ct continued
Wimbledon SW19 ....**179** C5
Poplar Farm Cl KT19 ....**215** A2
Poplar Fst Sch SW19 ....**201** C6
Poplar Gdns KT3 ....**177** B1
Poplar Gr N11 ....**31** A4
W6 ....**112** C4
Kingston KT3 ....**199** B6
Wembley HA9 ....**67** A5
Poplar High St E14 ....**119** D6
Poplar Ho 19 SE16 ....**118** D4
SE4 ....**141** B1
Poplar Mews W12 ....**112** C5
Poplar Mount DA17 ......**125** D2
Poplar Pl W2 ....**113** D6 **245** D6
Hayes UB3 ....**106** A6
Woolwich SE28 ....**124** C6
Poplar Rd SE24 ....**139** A1
Ashford TW15 ....**171** A5
Cheam SM3 ....**201** B1
Merton SW19 ....**179** C1
Poplar Rd S SW19 ....**201** C6
Poplars Cl HA4 ....**39** C1
Poplars Ho 14 E17 ....**53** D6
Poplars Rd E17 ....**53** D3
Poplar Sta E14 ....**119** D6
Poplars The NW5 ....**71** C3
East Barnet N14 ....**15** B6
Poplar View HA9 ....**65** D6
Poplar Way
Feltham TW13 ....**150** B1
Ilford IG6 ....**57** A5
Poplar Wlk SE24 ....**139** A1
Croydon CR0 ....**205** A1
Poppins Ct EC4 ....**241** C1
Poppleton Rd E11 ....**54** C3
Poppy Cl Belvedere DA17 .**125** D4
Hackbridge SM6 ....**203** A1
Poppy La CR0 ....**206** C1
Porchester Ct W2 ....**245** D6
Porchester Gate W2 .....**246** A5
Porchester Gdn Mews
W2 ....**91** D1
Porchester Gdns
W2 ....**113** D6 **245** D6
Porchester Mead BR3 ..**185** C4
Porchester Mews W2 .....**91** D1
Porchester Pl W2 ....**237** B1
Porchester Rd W2 ....**91** D1
Kingston KT1 ....**176** D1
Porchester Sq W2 ....**91** D1
Porchester Terr
W2 ....**114** A6 **246** A6
Porchester Terr N W2 .....**91** D1
Porch Way N20 ....**14** D1
Porcupine Cl SE9 ....**166** A2
Porden Rd SW2 ....**138** B1
Porland Ct SE1 ....**262** C6
Porlock Ave HA1,HA2 .....**42** A1
Porlock Ho 5 SE5 ....**162** A1
Porlock Rd EN1 ....**17** D4
Porlock St SE1 ..**117** B4 **252** B2
Porrington Cl BR7 ....**188** C2
Portal Cl Hillingdon UB10 ..**60** B1
Ruislip HA4 ....**62** B4
West Norwood SE27 ......**160** C1
Portbury Cl 15 SE15 .....**140** A4
Portchester Cl SE24 .....**139** B1
Portchester St W2 ....**91** D1
Port Cres E13 ....**99** B3
Portcullis Lodge Rd EN1 ...**5** B2
Porte Ho 10 NW9 ....**27** D2
Portelet Ct 1 N1 ....**95** C6
Portelet Rd E1 ....**96** D4
Porten Hos W14 ....**254** A5
Porten Rd W14 ....**254** A5
Porter Rd E6 ....**100** B1
Porter Sq N19 ....**50** A1
Porter St SE1 ...**117** A5 **252** B4
W1 ....**237** D4
Porters & Walters
Almshouses N22 ....**32** B3
Porters Ave RM8,RM9 .....**80** C3
Porters Way UB7 ....**104** B4
Porteus Rd W2 ....**236** B4
Portgate Cl W9 ....**91** B3
Porthcawe Rd SE26 ......**185** B6
Porthkerry Ave DA16 ....**146** A1
Port Ho 6 SW11 ....**136** A2
Portia Ct 12 IG11 ....**80** A1
Portia Way E3 ....**97** B3
Porticos The SW3 ....**266** C5
Portinscale Rd SW15 ....**157** B6
Portishead Ho 20 W2 .....**91** C2
Portland Ave DA15 ....**168** A5
N16 ....**51** D2
New Malden KT3 ....**199** D2
Portland Cl RM6 ....**59** A4
Portland Commercial Est
IG11 ....**102** C5
Portland Cotts CR0 ....**203** D2
Portland Cres
1 Chislehurst SE9 ....**166** A2
Feltham TW13 ....**171** B6
Southall UB6 ....**86** A2
Stanmore HA7 ....**25** D1
Portland Cres W HA7 .....**43** D6
Portland Ct 7 N1 ....**73** C1
1 SE14 ....**141** A6
Portland Dr EN2 ....**5** C3
Portland Gdns N4 ....**50** D3
Ilford RM6 ....**58** D4
Portland Gr
SW8 ....**138** B4 **270** C2
Portland Hosp for Women &
Children The W1 ....**238** D5
Portland Mans SE25 .....**206** B4
Portland Mews W1 ....**239** B1
Portland Pl W1 ...**93** B2 **238** D3

Portland Pl continued
Croydon SE25 ....**206** A5
Portland Rd N15 ....**51** D5
W11 ....**113** A6 **244** A6
W11 ....**113** A5 **244** B4
Ashford TW15 ....**148** A1
Bromley BR1 ....**187** C5
Chislehurst SE9 ....**166** A2
Croydon SE25 ....**206** B4
Hayes UB4 ....**83** C4
Kingston KT1 ....**198** B6
Mitcham CR4 ....**180** C1
Southall UB2 ....**107** B3
Portland Rise N4 ....**51** A1
Portland Sq 4 E1 ....**118** B5
Portland St
SE17 ....**117** B1 **262** C1
Portland Terr TW9 ....**131** D1
Portland Village W6 ......**112** C3
Portman Ave SW14 ....**133** B2
Portman Cl DA7 ....**147** A2
W1 ....**93** A1 **238** A2
Portman Dr IG8 ....**37** D1
Portman Gate NW1 ....**237** B5
Portman Gdns NW9 ....**27** B1
Hillingdon UB10 ....**60** C1
Portman Hts 1 NW3 ....**69** C5
Portman Lo N21 ....**16** D6
Portman Mews S W1 .....**238** A1
Portman Pl E2 ....**96** C4
Portman Rd KT1 ....**176** B1
Portman Sq W1 ..**93** A1 **238** A2
Portman St W1 ..**93** A1 **238** A1
Portman The NW11 ....**47** C2
Portman Twrs W1 ....**237** D2
Portmeadow Wlk SE2 ...**124** D4
Portmeers Cl E17 ....**53** D3
Portnall Rd W9 ....**91** B4
Portobello Ct Est W11 ....**91** A1
Portobello Ho 1 SW27 ..**182** D5
Portobello Mews W11 ...**245** A5
Portobello Rd W10 ....**91** A2
W11 ....**113** B6 **244** D6
Portobello Road Mkt ★
W10 ....**91** A2
Porton Ct KT6 ....**197** B6
Portpool La EC1 ..**94** C2 **241** A4
Portree Cl 2 N22 ....**32** B3
Portree St E14 ....**98** B1
Port Royal Pl 3 N16 ....**73** C3
Portrush Ct 9 UB1 ....**86** A1
Portsdown HA8 ....**26** C5
Portsdown Ave NW11 .....**47** B3
Portsdown Mews NW11 ...**47** B3
Portsea Hall W2 ....**237** A1
Portsea Ho 3 SW15 ......**156** B3
Portsea Mews W2 ....**237** B1
Portsea Pl W2 ....**237** B1
Portslade Rd SW8 ....**137** C3
Portsmouth Ave KT7 .....**197** A3
Portsmouth Rd
Esher KT10 ....**212** A5
Putney SW15 ....**156** C4
Thames Ditton KT6,KT7 .**197** C3
Portsmouth St WC2 ......**240** C1
Portsoken St E1,EC3 .....**253** C6
Portswood Pl 10 SW15 ..**155** D5
Portugal Gdns TW2 ......**152** A2
Portugal St WC2 ..**94** B1 **240** C1
Portway E15 ....**98** D6
Portway Gdns SE18 ......**143** D5
Portway Sch E13 ....**98** D6
Poseidon Ct 4 E14 ....**119** C2
Postern Gn EN2 ....**4** C2
Postern The EC2 ....**242** B3
Post La TW2 ....**152** B3
Postmill Cl CR0 ....**222** D5
Post Office App E7 ....**77** B3
Post Office Way
SW8 ....**137** D5 **269** C4
Post Rd UB2 ....**107** D4
Postway Mews 1 IG1 ......**78** D5
Potier St SE1 ....**262** D5
Potter Cl CR4 ....**181** B1
Potterhill Ct TW11 ....**175** B3
Potteries The EN5 ....**13** C6
Potterne Cl 5 SW19 ......**156** B3
Potters Cl CR0 ....**207** A1
Pottersfield EN1 ....**5** C1
Potters Fields
SE1 ....**117** C5 **253** B3
Potters Gr KT3 ....**199** A5
Potters Heights Cl HA5 ...**22** B3
Potter's La Barnet EN5 ......**1** C1
Streatham SW16 ....**181** D4
Potters Lo E14 ....**120** A1
Potters Mews WD6 ....**9** D5
Potters Rd SW6 ....**136** A3
Potter's Rd EN5 ....**1** D1
Potters Mews E2 ....**22** B2
Potter Street Hill HA5 .....**22** B3
Pottery La W11 ..**113** A5 **244** B4
Pottery Rd TW8 ....**132** A6
Pottery St SE16 ....**118** B4
Pott St E2 ....**96** B4
Poulett Gdns TW1 ....**153** A3
Poulett Rd E6 ....**100** B5
Poullett Ho SW2 ....**160** D3
Poulters Wood BR2 ....**225** D3
Poulton Ave SM1,SM5 ...**218** B5
Poulton Cl E8 ....**74** B2
Poultry EC2 ....**95** B1 **242** C1
Pound Cl Long Ditton KT6 .**197** C1
Orpington BR6 ....**227** B6
Pound Court Dr BR6 .....**227** B6
Pound Green 8 DA5 ....**169** C4
Pound La NW10 ....**68** A2
Pound Park Rd SE7 ......**121** D2
Pound Pl SE9 ....**166** C5
Pound St SM5 ....**218** D3

Pountney Rd SW11 ......**137** C2
Poverest Rd BR5 ....**211** D4
Povey Ho SE17 ....**263** A3
SW2 ....**160** C5
Powder Mill La TW2,
TW4 ....**151** C3
Powell Cl
Chessington KT9 ....**213** D3
Edgware HA8 ....**26** B4
Wallington SM6 ....**220** A1
Powell Ct 19 E17 ....**53** D6
Powell Gdns RM10 ....**81** C5
Powell Rd E5 ....**74** B5
Buckhurst Hill IG9 ....**21** C4
Powell's Wlk W4 ....**133** D6
Powergate Bsns Pk
NW10 ....**89** B4
Power Ho 12 TW9 ....**132** C4
Power Ho The W4 ....**111** D2
Power Rd W4 ....**110** C2
Powerscroft Rd E5 ....**74** C4
Sidcup DA14 ....**190** C4
Powers Ct TW1 ....**153** D4
Powis Ct Bushey WD23 ....**8** B3
Edgware HA8 ....**26** B6
Powis Gdns NW11 ....**47** B2
W11 ....**91** B1
Powis Ho WC2 ....**240** B2
Powis Mews W11 ....**91** B1
Powis Pl WC1 .....**94** A3 **240** B5
Powis Rd E3 ....**97** C4
Powis Sq W11 ....**91** B1
Powis St SE18 ....**122** D2
Powis Terr W11 ....**91** B1
Powle Terr 1 IG11 ....**79** B3
Powlett Ho NW1 ....**71** B2
Powlett Pl NW1 ....**71** B1
Pownall Gdns TW3 ....**129** D1
Pownall Rd E8 ....**96** A6
Hounslow TW3 ....**129** D1
Pownsett Terr IG1 ....**79** A3
Powrie Ho 4 SW11 ....**136** B3
Powster Rd BR1 ....**187** B5
Powys Cl DA7 ....**146** D6
Powys Ct N11 ....**32** A5
Powys La Bowes Park N13 ..**32** A5
Palmers Green N11 ....**32** A6
Poynder Ct 8 N7 ....**72** A3
Poynder Lo TW7 ....**131** A4
Poynders Ct 9 SW4 ....**159** C5
Poynders Gdns SW12 ...**159** C4
Poynders Rd SW12,SW4 .**159** C4
Poynings Rd N19 ....**71** C5
Poynings Way N12 ....**29** C5
Poyntell Cres BR7 ....**189** B2
Poynter Ct 12 UB5 ....**84** D5
Poynter Ho NW8 ....**236** C6
10 W11 ....**112** D5
Poynter Rd EN1 ....**18** A6
Poynton Rd N17 ....**34** A1
Poyntz Rd SW11 ....**136** D3
Poyser St E2 ....**96** B5
Praed Mews W2 ....**236** D2
Praed St W2 ....**92** B1 **236** D2
Pragel St E13 ....**99** C5
Pragnell Rd SE12 ....**165** B2
Prague Pl SW2 ....**160** A6
Prah Rd N4 ....**72** C6
Prairie St SW8 ....**137** B3
Pratt Mews NW1 ....**232** A5
Pratt St NW1 ....**93** C6 **232** A6
Pratt Wlk SE1,
SE11 ....**116** B2 **260** D4
Prayle Gr NW2 ....**46** D1
Prebend Gdns W4,W6 ...**111** C2
Prebend Mans 4 W4 .....**111** C2
Prebend St N1 ...**95** A6 **235** A6
Precinct Rd UB3 ....**106** A6
Precincts The SM4 ....**201** C3
Precinct The N1 ....**235** A5
N5 ....**72** D3
East Molesey KT8 ....**195** D6
Preedy Ho N1 ....**233** D4
Premier Cl EN3 ....**6** D5
Premier Ho TW9 ....**132** B1
Premier Lo N3 ....**29** C2
Premier Park Rd NW10 ...**88** D5
Premier Pl E14 ....**119** C6
Prendergast Ho 7
SW4 ....**159** D4
Prendergast Rd SE3 ......**142** C2
Prendergast Sch SE4 ....**141** C1
Prentice Ct 2 SW19 ......**179** B5
Prentis Rd SW16 ....**181** D6
Prentiss Ct SE7 ....**121** D2
Presburg Rd KT3 ....**199** C4
Prescelly Pl HA8 ....**26** B2
Prescot St E1 ...**117** D6 **253** D6
Prescott Ave BR5 ....**210** D3
Prescott Ho 19 SE17 ....**138** C6
Prescott Pl SW4 ....**137** D1
Presentation Mews
SW2 ....**160** B3
President Dr E1 ....**118** B5
President Ho EC1 ....**234** D1
President St EC1 ....**235** A2
Prespa Cl N9 ....**18** C2
Press Ho NW10 ....**67** B5
Press Rd NW10 ....**67** B5
Prestage Way E14 ....**120** A6
Prestbury Rd E7 ....**77** C1
Prestbury Sq SE9 ....**188** B6
Prested Rd SW11 ....**136** C1
Preston Ave E4 ....**36** A4
Preston Cl SE1 ....**263** A4
Twickenham TW2 ....**152** C1
Preston Ct DA14 ....**189** D6
Walton-on-T KT12 ....**194** C1
Preston Dr DA16 ....**146** D4

Preston Dr continued
Wanstead E11 ....**55** C4
West Ewell KT19 ....**215** D2
Preston Gdns NW10 ....**67** C2
Enfield EN3 ....**7** A6
Redbridge IG1 ....**56** A3
Preston Hill HA3 ....**44** B3
Preston Ho SE1 ....**263** A4
SE1 ....**263** C6
1 SE18 ....**122** C2
3 Dagenham RM10 ....**81** C5
Preston Manor High Sch
HA9 ....**66** B6
Preston Park Prim Sch
HA9 ....**43** D1
Preston Pl NW2 ....**68** A2
Richmond TW10 ....**154** A6
Preston Rd E11 ....**54** C3
Littleton TW17 ....**192** C4
South Norwood SE19 .....**182** D4
Wembley HA3,HA9 ....**66** A6
Wimbledon SW20 ....**177** D3
Preston Road Sta HA3 ....**44** A1
Prestons Rd BR2 ....**225** A4
Preston's Rd E14 ....**120** A5
Preston Waye HA3 ....**44** A1
Prestwich Terr SW4 ......**159** D6
Prestwick Cl UB2 ....**107** A1
Prestwick Ct UB1 ....**108** A1
Prestwick Rd WD19 ....**22** D6
Prestwood Ave HA3 ....**43** B5
Prestwood Cl SE18 ....**146** A6
Harrow HA3 ....**43** B5
Prestwood Gdns CR0 ....**205** A2
Prestwood Ho 3 SE16 ...**118** B3
Prestwood St N1 ....**235** B3
Pretoria Ave E17 ....**53** A5
Pretoria Cres E4 ....**20** A3
Pretoria Ho 3 HA4 ....**40** C1
Pretoria Rd E11 ....**54** B1
E16 ....**98** D3
Chingford E4 ....**20** B3
Ilford IG1 ....**78** D3
Streatham SW16 ....**181** C5
Tottenham N17 ....**33** D4
Pretoria Rd N N18 ....**33** D4
Pretty Cnr HA6 ....**22** A5
Prevost Rd N11 ....**15** A2
Priam Ho 17 E2 ....**96** B5
Price Cl NW7 ....**29** A4
Upper Tooting SW17 ......**158** D1
Price Ct HA1 ....**43** A4
Price Ho N1 ....**235** A5
Price Rd CR0 ....**220** D3
Prices Ct SW11 ....**136** B2
Price's St SE1 ....**251** D4
Price's Yd N1 ....**233** D4
Price Way TW12 ....**173** A4
Prichard Ct N7 ....**72** B3
SW11 ....**266** D1
Pricklers Hill EN5 ....**13** D5
Prickley Wood BR2 ....**208** D1
Priddy's Yd 4 CR0 ....**221** A6
Prideaux Ho WC1 ....**233** D2
Prideaux Pl W3 ....**111** B6
WC1 ....**94** A4 **233** D2
Prideaux Rd SW9 ....**138** A2
Pridham Rd CR7 ....**205** B5
Priestfield Rd SE23 ......**163** A1
Priestlands Park Rd
DA15 ....**167** D1
Priestley Cl N16 ....**51** D2
Priestley Gdns RM6 ....**58** B3
Priestley Ho EC1 ....**242** B6
2 NW5 ....**71** B2
6 Wembley HA9 ....**67** A5
Priestley Rd CR4 ....**181** A1
Priestley Way E17 ....**52** B6
NW2 ....**45** A6
Priestman Point 28 E3 ....**97** D4
Priestmead Fst & Mid Schs
HA3 ....**43** B6
Priest Park Ave HA2 ....**63** C6
Priests Bridge SW14 .....**133** C2
Priest's Ct EC2 ....**242** C2
Prima Rd SW9 ....**138** C5
Primrose Ave Enfield EN2 ...**5** C4
Ilford RM6 ....**58** D3
Primrose Cl Catford SE6 .**186** A5
Hackbridge SM6 ....**203** B1
Harrow HA2 ....**63** B5
Primrose Ct
New Malden KT4 ....**200** A2
11 Streatham SW12 .....**159** C4
Primrose Gdns NW3 ....**70** C2
Ruislip HA4 ....**62** C3
Primrose Hill EC4 ....**241** B1
Primrose Hill ★
NW1,NW3 ....**92** D6 **230** C6
Primrose Hill Ct NW3 ......**70** D1
Primrose Hill Rd
NW1,NW3 ....**70** D1 **230** C6
Primrose Hill Sch
NW1 ....**93** A6 **231** B6
Primrose Hill Studios
NW1 ....**231** A6
Primrose Ho 15 SE15 ....**140** A4
1 Richmond TW9 ....**132** B4
Primrose La CR0 ....**206** D1
Primrose Mans SW11 ....**268** A2
Primrose Mews 9 NW1 ...**70** D1
Primrose Rd E10 ....**53** D1
Woodford E18 ....**37** B1
Primrose Sq E9 ....**96** C6
Primrose St EC2 ...**95** C3 **243** B4
Primrose Way HA0 ....**87** D5
Primrose Wlk 6 SE14 ....**141** A4
Ewell KT17 ....**215** D1
Primula St W12 ....**90** A1
Prince Albert Ct NW8 ....**230** C5

Prince Albert Ct *continued*
Sunbury TW16 ....171 C3
Prince Albert Rd
NW8 ....92 D5 230 C5
Prince Arthur Ct 19 NW3 .70 A4
Prince Arthur Mews 20
NW3 ....70 A4
Prince Arthur Rd NW3 ...70 A3
Prince Charles Dr NW2 ...46 C2
Prince Charles Rd SE3 ..142 D4
Prince Charles Way
SM6 ....219 B5
Prince Consort Dr BR7 ..189 B2
Prince Consort Rd
SW7 ....114 B3 256 C6
Princedale Rd
W11 ....113 A5 244 B4
Prince Edward Mans
W2 ....245 B6
Prince Edward Rd E9 ....75 B2
Prince George Ave N14 ...15 D6
Prince George Rd N16 ...73 C4
Prince George's Ave
SW20 ....178 C1
Prince Georges Rd
SW19 ....180 B2
Prince Henry Rd SE7 ....143 D5
Prince Imperial Rd
SE18 ....144 B4
Chislehurst BR7 ....188 D3
Prince John Rd SE9 ....166 A6
Princelet St E1 ...95 D2 243 D4
Prince of Orange La 3
SE10 ....142 A5
Prince Of Wales Cl NW4 ..46 B5
Prince of Wales Dr
SW11 ....137 A4 268 A2
Prince of Wales Mans
SW11 ....268 B2
SW4 ....159 B6
Prince of Wales Pas
NW1 ....232 A1
Prince of Wales Prim Sch
EN3 ....7 B6
Prince Of Wales Rd NW5 .71 A2
SE3 ....142 D4
Newham E16 ....99 C1
Prince Of Wales' Rd
SM1 ....218 B6
Prince Of Wales Terr
W4 ....111 C1
W8 ....245 D1
Prince Rd SE25 ....205 C4
Prince Regent E16 ....99 C2
Prince Regent Ct SE16 ..119 A5
Prince Regent La E13 ....99 C3
Prince Regent Mews
NW1 ....232 A1
Prince Regent Rd TW3 ..130 A2
Prince Regent Sta E16 ..121 C6
Prince Rupert Rd SE9 ...144 B1
Princes Arc SW1 ....249 B4
Princes Ave BR5 ....211 C4
N10 ....49 B6
N22 ....31 D2
N3 ....29 D2
NW9 ....44 D5
Acton W3 ....110 C3
Edmonton N13 ....32 C5
Tolworth KT6 ....214 C6
Wallington SM5 ....218 D1
Woodford IG8 ....37 C6
Prince's Ave UB1 ....85 D1
Princes Cir WC2 ..94 A1 240 A2
Princes Cl DA14 ....168 D1
N4 ....50 D1
NW9 ....44 C5
Edgware HA8 ....26 C5
Prince's Cl TW11,TW12 ...174 B6
Princes Ct NW2 ....69 A3
NW3 ....70 B4
Prince's Ct SE16 ....119 B3
Princes Ct Kingston KT3 ..199 D6
Stepney E1 ....118 B6
Wembley HA9 ....66 A3
Princes Dr HA1 ....42 C6
Princes Gate
SW7 ....114 C4 246 D1
Prince's Gate
SW7 ....114 C4 247 A1
Princes Gate Ct SW7 ....246 D1
Princes Gate Mews
SW7 ....114 B3 256 D6
Princes Gdns
SW7 ....114 B3 256 D6
Acton W3 ....88 C2
Ealing W5 ....87 C3
Princes Ho W11 ....245 A5
Princes La N10 ....49 B6
Prince's Mews
W2 ....113 D6 245 C6
W6 ....112 B1
Princes Mews TW3 ....129 C1
Princes Par NW11 ....47 A3
Princes Park Ave NW11 ...47 A4
Hayes UB3 ....105 B6
Princes Park Circ UB3 ...105 B6
Princes Park Cl UB3 ....105 B6
Princes Park La UB3 ....105 B6
Princes Park Par UB3 ...105 B6
Princes Pl SW1 ....249 B4
W11 ....113 A5 244 A4
Prince's Plain BR2 ....210 A1
Prince's Plain Prim Sch
BR2 ....210 A2
Princes Rd N18 ....34 C6
Ashford TW15 ....170 B5
Buckhurst Hill IG9 ....21 C2
Ealing W13 ....109 B5
Feltham TW13 ....149 D1
Princes Rd *continued*
Ilford IG6 ....57 B5
Kingston KT2 ....176 C3
Penge SE20 ....184 D4
Richmond TW10 ....154 B6
Richmond TW9 ....132 B4
Prince's Rd
Mortlake SW14 ....133 B2
Teddington TW11,TW12 ...174 B6
Wimbledon SW19 ....179 C4
Princes Rise SE13 ....142 A3
Princes Riverside Rd 7
SE16 ....118 D5
Princessa Ct EN2 ....17 B6
Princess Alexandra School of Nursing The E1 ....96 B2
Princess Alice Ho W10 ...90 C3
Princess Alice Way
SE28 ....123 B4
Princess Ave HA9 ....66 A6
Princess Beatrice Ho
SW10 ....255 C1
Princess Christian Coll
WC1 ....94 A2 240 B4
Princess Cres N4 ....72 D6
Princess Ct NW6 ....69 D1
W1 ....237 C3
W2 ....245 D6
Catford BR1 ....186 C4
3 Croydon CR0 ....221 D6
11 Wimbledon SW19 ....178 D3
Princess Frederica CE Prim Sch NW10 ....90 C5
Princess Grace Hospl The
W1 ....93 A3 238 A5
Princess La HA4 ....39 C1
Princess Louise Cl W2 ..236 D4
Princess Louise Hospl
W10 ....90 C2
Princess Mary Ho SW1 ..259 D3
Princess May Prim Sch
N16 ....73 D4
Princess May Rd N16 ....73 C4
Princess Mews NW3 ....70 B2
Kingston KT1 ....198 B6
Princess Par BR6 ....226 C5
Dagenham RM10 ....103 C5
Princess Park Manor
N11 ....31 A5
Prince's Sq W2 ..113 D6 245 C6
Princess Rd NW1 .93 A6 231 B6
NW6 ....91 C5
Thornton Heath CR0 ....205 A3
Princess St SE1 ....261 D5
Princes St DA7 ....147 B2
W1 ....238 D1
Prince's St EC2 ...95 B1 242 C1
Princes St Sutton SM1 ...218 B4
Tottenham N17 ....33 C4
Prince's St TW10,TW9 ...154 A6
Princes St SE8 ....141 B6
Prince's Terr E13 ....99 B6
Princes Way Acton W3 ...110 C3
Buckhurst Hill IG9 ....21 C2
Coney Hall BR4 ....224 D5
Croydon CR0 ....220 B3
Putney SW15,SW19 ....157 A3
Ruislip HA4 ....63 A4
Princes Yd W11 ....244 B3
Princethorpe Ho W2 ....91 D2
Princethorpe Rd SE26 ..184 D6
Princeton Ct SW15 ....134 D2
Princeton Mans WC1 ....240 C3
Princeton Mews 3 KT2 .176 C2
Princeton St
WC1 ....94 B2 240 C4
Prince William Ct TW15 .170 B5
Pringle Gdns SW16 ....181 C6
Printers Mews E3 ....97 A6
Printer St EC4 ....241 B2
Printinghouse La UB3 ...105 C4
Printing House Yd 17 E2 ..95 C4
Printon Ho 12 E3 ....97 B2
Print Village Ind Est
SE15 ....139 D3
Priolo Rd SE7 ....121 C1
Prior Ave SM2,SM5 ....218 C1
Prior Bolton St N1 ....72 D2
Prioress Ho 2 E3 ....97 D4
Prioress Rd SE27 ....160 D1
Prioress St SE1 ....262 D5
Prior Rd IG1 ....78 C5
Priors Croft E17 ....35 B1
Priors Field UB5 ....63 A2
Priors Gdns HA4 ....62 C3
Priors Lo 4 TW10 ....154 A5
Priors Mead EN1 ....5 C4
Prior St SE10 ....142 A5
Priorty Ct SE15 ....140 C1
Prior Weston Prim Sch
EC1 ....95 A3 242 B5
Priory Ave BR5 ....211 B3
E17 ....53 C4
N8 ....49 D5
W4 ....111 C3
Cheam SM3 ....216 D4
Chingford E4 ....19 C1
Wembley HA0 ....64 D4
Priory CE Prim Sch
SW19 ....179 D5
Priory Cl BR7 ....188 B2
E4 ....19 B1
N3 ....29 B2
Ashford TW16 ....172 A3
Barnet N20 ....13 B4
Beckenham BR3 ....207 A6
East Barnet N14 ....15 B6
Hampton TW12 ....173 B2
Hayes UB3 ....106 B6
3 Merton SW19 ....179 D2
Priory Cl *continued*
Ruislip HA4 ....39 D1
Stanmore HA7 ....8 D1
Wembley HA0 ....64 D4
Woodford E18 ....37 A2
Priory Cres Cheam SM3 ..216 D4
South Norwood SE19 ....183 A3
Wembley HA0 ....65 A5
Priory Ct E17 ....35 B1
E17 ....53 B6
E6 ....99 D6
E9 ....74 D3
EC4 ....241 D1
SW8 ....137 D4 269 D2
Bushey WD23 ....8 A3
Cheam SM1 ....217 B3
Cheam SM3 ....217 A4
Hounslow TW3 ....129 D2
Ilford RM6 ....58 B3
Putney SW15 ....156 C5
Roehampton SW15 ....133 D1
4 Wembley HA0 ....88 A5
Priory Dr SE2 ....124 D1
Stanmore HA7 ....8 D1
Priory Field Dr HA8 ....26 D6
Priory Gdns N6 ....49 B3
6 W4 ....111 C2
Ashford TW15 ....171 B5
Barnes SW13 ....133 D2
Ealing W5 ....88 A4
Hampton TW12 ....173 B2
South Norwood SE25 ....205 D5
Wembley HA0 ....65 A4
Priory Gn N1 ....233 C4
Priory Gr SW8 ...138 A4 270 A1
Priory Grange N2 ....48 D6
Priory Heights N1 ....233 D4
Priory Hill HA0 ....65 A4
Priory Ho E1 ....243 C4
EC1 ....241 C6
3 SE7 ....143 C6
SW1 ....259 C2
Priory Hospl Hayes Grove The BR2 ....225 A6
Priory Hospl The SW15 ..133 D1
Priory House Ct SE6 ....163 D3
Priory La
East Molesey KT8 ....195 D5
Roehampton SW15 ....155 D6
Priory Leas SE9 ....166 A3
Priory Lo 7 W4 ....110 C1
Coney Hall BR4 ....224 C5
Ealing W5 ....87 C1
Priory Mans 17 NW3 ....70 D2
SW10 ....256 B1
Priory Park Rd NW6 ....91 B6
Wembley HA0 ....65 A4
Priory Pk SE3 ....142 D2
Priory Rd E6 ....99 D5
N8 ....49 D5
NW6 ....69 D1
W4 ....111 B3
Barking IG11 ....79 B1
Cheam SM3 ....216 D4
Chessington KT9 ....214 A5
Hampton TW12 ....173 C3
Hounslow TW3 ....152 A6
Mitcham SW19 ....180 B3
Richmond TW9 ....132 C5
Thornton Heath CR0 ....204 C2
Priory Ret Pk SW19 ....180 B3
Priory Sch SE25 ....205 D5
Priory St 16 E3 ....97 D4
Priory Terr NW6 ....91 D6
Priory The N8 ....49 D5
SE1 ....251 C1
SE3 ....142 D1
Croydon CR0 ....220 C5
21 Kingston KT6 ....198 A4
Priory View WD23 ....8 C4
Priory Villas N11 ....30 D5
Priory Way
Harmondsworth UB7 ....126 A6
Harrow HA2 ....41 D5
Southall UB2 ....106 D3
Priory Wlk
SW10 ....114 A1 256 B1
Priscilla Ho 8 TW16 ....171 D3
Pritchard Ho 34 E2 ....96 A5
Pritchard's Rd E2 ....96 A5
Pritchett Cl EN3 ....7 C6
Priter Rd SE16 ....118 A3
Priter Road Hostel 14
SE16 ....118 A3
Private Rd EN1 ....17 C6
Probert Rd SW2 ....160 C6
Probyn Ho SW1 ....259 D4
Probyn Rd SW2 ....160 D2
Procter Ho 12 SE5 ....139 B5
Procter St WC1 ...94 B2 240 C3
Proctor Cl CR4 ....181 A2
Proctor Ho 5 SE1 ....118 A1
Proctors Cl TW14 ....150 A3
Prodger 8 NW9 ....27 D2
Progress Bsns Pk CR9 ...220 B6
Progress Way
Croydon CR0 ....220 B6
Enfield EN1 ....18 A6
Wood Green N22 ....32 C2
Prologis Pk TW4 ....128 C1
Prome Ho 8 N16 ....73 B4
Promenade Approach Rd
W4 ....133 C5
Promenade Mans HA8 ....26 C5
Promenade The W4 ....133 C4
Pronto Trad Est UB4 ....83 C2
Prospect Cl
Belvedere DA17 ....125 C2
Forest Hill SE26 ....184 B6
Hounslow TW5 ....129 B4
Prospect Cl *continued*
Ruislip HA4 ....40 D2
Prospect Cotts SW18 ....135 C1
Prospect Cres TW2 ....152 A5
Prospect Hill E17 ....53 D5
Prospect Ho 9 E17 ....54 A6
1 E8 ....73 D2
N1 ....234 A3
SE1 ....261 D5
14 W10 ....90 D1
Prospect House Sch
SW15 ....156 D4
Prospect Pl E1 ....118 C5
N2 ....48 B5
4 NW2 ....69 B5
24 NW3 ....70 A4
6 SE8 ....141 B6
2 W4 ....111 B1
Bromley BR2 ....209 B6
Tottenham N17 ....33 C3
Wimbledon SW20 ....178 B3
Prospect Quay SW18 ....135 C1
Prospect Rd NW2 ....69 C5
Barnet EN5 ....1 D1
Kingston KT6 ....197 C3
Woodford IG8 ....37 C5
Prospect Ring N2 ....48 B6
Prospect St SE16 ....118 B4
Prospect Vale SE7,SE18 ..122 A2
Prospect Wharf E1 ....118 C6
Prospero Ho 7 DA17 ....125 C1
Prospero Rd N19 ....49 D1
Protea Cl E16 ....98 D3
Protheroe Ho 4 N17 ....51 D6
Prothero Gdns NW4 ....46 B4
Prothero Ho NW10 ....67 B1
Prothero Rd
SW6 ....135 B5 264 C4
Prout Gr NW10 ....67 D4
Prout Rd E5 ....74 B5
Provence St N1 ....235 A4
Providence Ct W1 ....248 B6
Providence Ho E9 ....96 D6
Providence La UB3 ....127 B5
Providence Pl N1 ....234 C5
Providence Rd UB7 ....104 B5
Providence Row N1 ....233 C3
Providence Sq 4 SE1 ...118 A4
Providence Twr 1
SE16 ....118 A4
Provident Ind Est UB3 ...106 A4
Provincial Terr 2 SE20 ..184 D3
Provost Ct NW3 ....70 D2
Provost Rd NW3 ....70 D2
Provost St N1 ....95 B4 235 C2
Prowse Ave WD23 ....8 A2
Prowse Pl NW1 ....71 C1
Pruden Cl N14 ....15 C2
Prudent Pas EC2 ....242 B1
Prusom's Island 8 E1 ...118 C5
Prusom St E1 ....118 B5
Pryors The NW3 ....70 B5
Public Record Office
EC4,WC2 ....94 C1 241 A2
Richmond TW9 ....132 D5
Public Record Office Mus★
EC4,WC2 ....241 A2
Pudding La EC3 ....252 D6
Pudding Mill La E15 ....97 D6
Pudding Mill Lane Sta
E15 ....97 D6
Puddle Dock
EC4 ....116 D6 251 D6
Puffin Cl Barking IG11 ....102 B4
Beckenham BR3 ....206 D4
Puffin Terr IG5 ....56 C6
Pugin Ct N1 ....72 C1
Pulborough Rd SW18 ....157 B4
Pulborough Way TW4 ...128 C1
Pulford Rd N15 ....51 B3
Pulham Ave N2 ....48 B5
Pulham Ho SW8 ....270 C3
Puller Rd EN5 ....1 A3
Pulleyns Ave E6 ....100 A4
Pullman Ct SW2 ....160 B3
Pullman Gdns SW15 ....156 C5
Pullman Mews SE12 ....165 B1
Pullman Pl SE9 ....166 A6
Pulross Rd SW9 ....138 B2
Pulteney Cl 13 E3 ....97 B6
Pulteney Gdns 9 E18 ....55 B6
Pulteney Rd E18 ....55 B6
Pulteney Terr N1 ..94 B6 233 D6
Pulton Ho SE4 ....141 A1
Pulton Pl SW6 ....135 C5 265 A3
Puma Ct E1 ....243 C4
Pump Alley 8 TW8 ....131 D5
Pump Cl UB5 ....85 C5
Pump Ct EC4 ....241 A1
Pump House Cl SE16 ....118 C4
Bromley BR2 ....186 D1
Pumping Station Rd
W4 ....133 C6
Pump La SE14 ....140 C5
Hayes UB3 ....106 A4
Pump Pail N CR0 ....221 A5
Pump Pail S CR0 ....221 A5
Punchard Cres EN3 ....7 D5
Punderson's Gdns E2 ....96 B4
Puran Ho E13 ....99 C5
Purbeck Ave KT3 ....199 D3
Purbeck Dr NW2 ....68 D6
Purbeck Ho SW8 ....270 C3
Purbrook Est SE1 ....253 B1
Purbrook Ho 2 SW15 ....156 B3
Purbrook St SE1 ....263 B6
Purcell Cres
SW6 ....135 A5 264 A4
Purcell Ho SW10 ....266 C5
Isleworth TW2 ....152 B5
Purcell Ho *continued*
Southall UB1 ....85 C1
Purcell Mews NW10 ....67 C1
Purcell Rd UB6 ....85 D2
Purcells Ave HA8 ....26 C5
Purcell St N1 ....95 C5
Purchese St
NW1 ....93 D5 232 D3
Purday Ho 4 W10 ....91 B4
Purdey Ct 3 KT4 ....200 A1
Purdon Ho 10 SE15 ....140 A4
Purdy St E3 ....97 D3
Purland Cl RM8 ....59 B1
Purland Rd SE28,SE18 ...123 D4
Purley Ave NW2 ....69 A6
Purley Oaks Prim Sch
CR2 ....221 B1
Purley Pl N1 ....72 D1
Purley Rd Edmonton N9 ....17 C1
South Croydon CR2 ....221 B1
Purley View Terr CR2 ....221 B1
Purley Way
Croydon CR0,CR9 ....220 C3
Thornton Heath CR0 ....204 B1
Purley Way Cres CR0 ....204 B2
Purneys Rd SE9 ....143 D1
Purrett Rd SE18 ....123 D1
Purser Ho 3 SW2 ....160 C5
Pursers Cross Rd
SW6 ....135 B4 264 D2
Pursewardens Cl W13 ...109 C5
Pursley Rd NW7 ....28 B3
Purves Rd NW10 ....90 C5
Purvis Ho CR0 ....205 B2
Pusey Ho 16 E14 ....97 C1
Puteaux Ho 6 E2 ....96 D5
Putney Bridge App
SW6 ....135 A2
Putney Bridge Rd SW15 .135 B1
Putney Bridge Sta SW6 .135 B2
Putney Comm SW15 ....134 C2
Putney Gdns RM6 ....58 B4
Putney Heath SW15 ....156 C5
Putney Heath La SW15 ..156 D5
Putney High Sch SW15 ..156 D6
Putney High St SW15 ....135 A1
Putney Hill SW15 ....156 D6
Putney Hospl SW15 ....134 C2
Putney Park Ave SW15 ..134 A1
Putney Park La SW15 ....156 B6
Putney Pier SW15 ....135 A2
Putney School of Art & Design SW15 ....135 A1
Putney Sta SW15 ....135 A1
Putney Wharf Twr
SW15 ....135 A2
Pycombe Cnr N12 ....29 B6
Pycroft Way N9 ....34 A6
Pylbrook Rd SM1 ....217 D5
Pylon Trad Est E16 ....98 B2
Pylon Way CR0 ....204 A1
Pym Cl EN4 ....14 B6
Pymers Mead SE21 ....161 A3
Pymmes Brook Ho 3
N10 ....31 A3
Pymmes Cl
Bowes Park N13 ....32 B5
Tottenham N17 ....34 B2
Pymmes Gdns N N9 ....17 D1
Pymmes Gdns S N9 ....17 D1
Pymmes Green Rd N11 ...15 C1
Pymmes Rd N13 ....32 A5
Pymms Brook Dr EN4 ....2 C1
Pynchester Cl UB10 ....60 C6
Pyne Rd KT6 ....198 C1
Pynfolds SE16 ....118 B4
Pynham Cl SE2 ....124 B3
Pynnacles Cl HA7 ....25 B5
Pynnersmead SE24 ....161 A6
Pyramid Ho N12 ....30 A6
Pyrford Ho 12 SW9 ....138 D1
Pyrland Rd N5 ....73 B3
Richmond TW10 ....154 B5
Pyrmont Gr SE27 ....160 D1
Pyrmont Rd W4 ....132 C6
Pytchley Cres SE19 ....183 A4
Pytchley Rd SE22 ....139 C2

Q

Quadrangle Cl SE1 ....263 A4
Quadrangle Lo SW19 ....179 C4
Quadrangle The E17 ....35 B1
SE24 ....161 A6
SW10 ....266 B2
SW6 ....264 A3
W12 ....90 C1
W2 ....237 A2
Stanmore HA7 ....25 C3
Quadrant Arc W1 ....249 B5
Quadrant Bsns Pk NW6 ...91 A6
Quadrant Cl NW4 ....46 B4
Quadrant Gr NW5 ....70 D3
Quadrant Ho E15 ....98 C4
Quadrant Rd
Richmond TW9 ....131 D1
Thornton Heath CR7 ....204 D5
Quadrant The DA7 ....146 D5
4 W10 ....90 D4
Richmond TW9 ....132 A1
Sutton SM2 ....218 A2
Wimbledon SW20 ....179 A2
Quad Rd HA9 ....65 D5
Quaggy Wlk SE3 ....143 A1
Quainton Hall Sch HA1 ...42 C4
Quainton St NW10 ....67 B5
Quaker Ct EC1 ....242 B6
Quaker La UB2 ....107 C3
Quakers Course NW9 ....27 D2
Quaker's Pl E7 ....77 D3
Quaker St E1 ....95 D3 243 C5
Quakers Wlk N21 ....17 B5
Quality Ct WC2 ....241 A2
Quantock Cl UB3 ....127 B5
Quantock Ct UB6 ....64 C3
Quantock Dr KT4 ....216 C6
Quantock Gdns NW2 ....68 D6
Quantock Ho N16 ....51 D1
Quarrendon St SW6 ....135 C3
Quarr Rd SM5 ....202 C3
Quarry Park Rd SM1 ....217 B2
Quarry Rd SW18 ....158 A5
Quarry Rise SM1 ....217 B2
Quarterdeck The E14 ....119 C4
Quartermain Ho SM4 ....202 A4
Quartermile La E10,E15 ...75 D4
Quayside Ct 6 SE16 ....118 D5
Quay West TW11 ....175 B5
Quebec & Crown Wharves
E14 ....97 B1
Quebeck Ind Est SE16 ...119 A3
Quebec Mews W1 ....237 D1
Quebec Rd Hayes UB4 ....84 C1
Ilford IG1 ....56 D2
Quebec Way SE16 ....119 A4
Quedgeley Ct 3 SE15 ....139 D6
Queen Adelaide Ct
SE20 ....184 C4
Queen Adelaide Rd
SE20 ....184 C3
Queen Alexandra Mans
WC1 ....233 A1
Queen Alexandra's Ct 5
SW19 ....179 B5
Queen Anne Ave BR2 ....208 D6
Queen Anne Dr KT10 ....212 C1
Queen Anne Gate DA7 ..146 D2
Queen Anne Mews W1 ..238 D3
Queen Anne Rd E9 ....74 D2
Queen Annes Cl TW2 ....152 B1
Queen Anne's Gate
SW1 ....115 D4 249 C1
Queen Anne's Gdns W4 .111 C3
W5 ....110 A4
Enfield EN1 ....17 C5
Mitcham CR4 ....202 D6
Queen Anne's Gr W4 ....111 C3
W5 ....110 A4
Enfield EN1 ....17 C5
Queen Anne's Pl EN1 ....17 C5
Queen Anne St
W1 ....93 B2 238 C3
Queen Borough Gdns
BR7 ....189 B4
Queenborough Gdns IG2 .56 C5
Queen Caroline St W6 ..112 C1
Queen Charlottes & Chelsea Hospl W12 ....90 A1
Queen Elizabeth College 15
SE10 ....142 A5
Queen Elizabeth Ct EN5 ....1 B1
Queen Elizabeth Gdns
SM4 ....201 C5
Queen Elizabeth Hall & Purcell Room SE1 ....250 D4
Queen Elizabeth Hospital for Children The E2 ....96 A5
Queen Elizabeth Hospl
SE7 ....144 A5
Queen Elizabeth II Con Ctr
SW1 ....249 D1
Queen Elizabeth II Jubilee Sch W9 ....91 B3
Queen Elizabeth II Pier
SE10 ....120 D5
Queen Elizabeth Rd E17 ...53 A6
Kingston KT2 ....176 B1
Queen Elizabeth's Cl N16 .73 B6
Queen Elizabeth's Dr
N14 ....16 A3
Queen Elizabeth's Girls Sch
EN5 ....1 B1
Queen Elizabeth's Hunting Lodge Mus★ E4 ....20 D4
Queen Elizabeth St
SE1 ....117 D4 253 C2
Queen Elizabeth's Wlk
N16 ....73 B6
Wallington SM6 ....219 D4
Queen Elizabeth Wlk
SW13 ....134 B4
Queenhithe EC4 ....252 B6
Queen Margaret Flats 22
E2 ....96 B4
Queen Margarets Ct N1 ..73 C3
Queen Margaret's Gr N1 .73 C3
Queen Mary Ave SM4 ...200 D4
Queen Mary Cl KT9 ....214 C5
Queen Mary Rd
Charlton TW17 ....171 A1
South Norwood SE19 ....182 D4
Queen Mary's Ave SM5 ..218 D1
Queen Mary's Gdns★
NW1 ....231 A1
Queen Mary's Hospl
DA14 ....190 A4
NW3 ....70 A5
Queen Mary's Univ Hospl
SW15 ....156 A5
Queen Mary, Univ of London
E1 ....97 A3
Queen of Denmark Ct
SE16 ....119 B3
Queens Acre SM3 ....217 A1
Queens Ave N10 ....49 B6
N20 ....14 B2

Queen's Ave N3 ...30 A2
Queens Ave
Feltham TW13 ...172 C6
Stanmore HA7 ...25 C1
Queen's Ave Southall UB1 ..86 A1
Southgate N21 ...16 D3
Woodford IG8 ...37 B5
Queensberry Ho 6
TW9 ...153 D6
Queensberry Mews W
SW7 ...256 C4
Queensberry Pl E12 ...78 A3
SW7 ...114 B2 256 C4
Queensberry Way SW7 ..256 C4
Queensborough Ct N3 ...47 B5
Queensborough Mews
W2 ...246 A6
Queensborough Pas
W2 ...246 A6
Queensborough Terr
W2 ...113 D6 245 D6
Queensbridge Ct 1 E2 ...95 D5
Queensbridge Inf Sch
E8 ...73 D1
Queensbridge Pk TW7 ..152 C6
Queensbridge Rd E2,E8 ..95 D6
E8 ...73 D1
Queensbury IG9 ...21 B3
Queensbury Circ Par
HA3 ...44 A6
Queensbury Ct CR7 ...183 A1
Queensbury Rd NW9 ...45 B2
Wembley HA0 ...88 B5
Queensbury St N1 ...73 A1
Queensbury Sta HA7,HA8 .44 B6
Queensbury Station Par
HA8 ...44 B6
Queen's CE Prim Sch The
TW9 ...132 C5
Queen's Cir
SW11 ...137 B5 268 C3
Queen's Cl Edgware HA8 ..26 C5
Wallington SM6 ...219 B3
Queen's Club Gdns
W14 ...135 A6 264 B6
Queen's Club The★
W14 ...113 A1 254 B1
Queen's Coll W1 ..93 B2 238 C3
Queenscourt HA9 ...66 A4
Queen's Cres NW5 ...71 A2
Queens Cres TW10 ...154 B6
Queenscroft Rd SE9 ...165 D5
Queens Ct E10 ...53 C2
4 E14 ...119 B6
E17 ...53 C4
8 NW11 ...47 B4
SE5 ...139 C3
SW11 ...268 C2
Queen's Ct E11 ...54 C2
NW11 ...47 C4
NW8 ...229 C4
W2 ...245 D5
Queens Ct
Beckenham BR3 ...185 D3
5 Buckhurst Hill IG9 ...21 C2
Stanmore HA7 ...25 B1
Queen's Ct Barnes SW13 .134 A2
Beckenham BR3 ...185 C2
Croydon CR2 ...221 A3
8 Ealing W5 ...87 C2
1 Kingston KT2 ...176 C3
3 Richmond TW10 ...154 B5
Thornton Heath CR7 ...204 C4
Queensdale Cres W11 ..112 D5
Queensdale Pl W11 ...244 A3
Queensdale Rd
W11 ...113 A5 244 A3
Queensdale Wlk W11 ...244 A3
Queens Down Rd E5 ...74 B4
Queens Dr E10 ...53 C2
Queen's Dr N4 ...72 D6
Queens Dr KT5 ...198 C3
Queen's Dr Acton W3 ...88 C1
Thames Ditton KT7 ...197 A3
Queen's Elm Sq SW3 ...256 D1
Queensferry Wlk N17 ...52 B5
Queensfield Ct SM3 ...216 C4
Queen's Gallery The★
SW1 ...115 B4 248 D1
Queen's Gate
SW7 ...114 A3 256 B5
Queens Gate IG4 ...56 B5
Queensgate Ct N12 ...29 D5
Queen's Gate Gdns
SW7 ...114 A3 256 B5
Queensgate Gdns SW15 .134 B1
Queens Gate Gdns BR7 ..189 B2
Queen's Gate Mews
SW7 ...114 A3 256 B6
Queensgate Pl 10 NW6 ...69 C1
Queen's Gate Pl
SW7 ...114 A3 256 B5
Queen's Gate Pl Mews
SW7 ...114 A3 256 B5
Queen's Gate Terr
SW7 ...114 A3 256 B6
Queens Gate Villas E9 ...75 A1
Queens Gdns NW4 ...46 C4
Queen's Gdns
W2 ...114 A6 246 A6
Ealing W5 ...87 C3
Heston TW5 ...129 A4
Queen's Gr NW8 ..92 B6 229 D5
Queen's Grove Rd E4 ...20 B3
Queen's Head Pas EC2 ..242 A2
Queen's Head St
N1 ...94 D6 234 D5
Queen's Head Yd SE1 ...252 C3
Queens Ho 1 SE17 ...139 B6
Queen's Ho TW11 ...174 D4
Queen's Hospl CR0 ...205 A3
Queen's House The★
SE10 ...142 B6
Queens Keep 10 TW1 ...153 C5
Queens La N10 ...49 B6
Queensland Ave
Edmonton N18 ...33 A4
Merton SW19 ...179 D2
Queensland Cl E17 ...35 B1
Queensland Ct N10 ...31 B3
Queensland Ho 2 E16 ..122 C5
Queensland Pl N7 ...72 C4
Queensland Rd N7 ...72 C4
Queens Manor Prim Sch
SW6 ...134 D5
Queens Mans NW4 ...46 B4
NW6 ...69 D3
Queen's Mans W6 ...112 D2
Queensmead
NW8 ...92 B6 229 D6
Queen's Mead Rd BR2 ...186 D1
Queensmead Sch HA4 ...62 D4
Queensmere Cl SW19 ...156 D2
Queensmere Ct SW13 ...134 A6
Queensmere Rd SW19 ..156 D2
Queen's Mews
W2 ...113 D6 245 C6
Queensmill Rd SW6 ...134 D5
Queensmill Sch SW6 ...135 C3
Queen's Mkt 1 E13 ...99 C6
Queens Par NW2 ...68 C2
7 NW4 ...46 B4
Queen's Par 3 N11 ...30 D5
Queens Par W5 ...88 B1
Queen's Par N11 ...32 A3
Queens Parade Cl N11 ...30 D5
Queens Park Com Sch
NW6 ...90 D6
Queens Park Ct 5 W10 ..90 D4
Queens Park Gdns
TW13 ...149 D1
Queen's Park Prim Sch
W10 ...91 A3
Queen's Park Sta NW6 ...91 B5
Queen's Pas BR7 ...188 D4
Queen's Pl SM4 ...201 C5
Queen Sq WC1 ...94 A2 240 B4
Queen Sq Pl WC1 ...240 B5
Queen's Quay EC4 ...252 B6
Queen's Rd BR1 ...187 A1
BR7 ...188 D4
DA16 ...146 B3
E11 ...54 C2
E13 ...99 C6
E17 ...53 C3
N3 ...30 A2
NW4 ...46 C4
SE14,SE15 ...140 C4
Queens Rd Hayes UB3 ...83 C1
Morden SM4 ...201 C5
Twickenham TW1 ...153 A3
West Drayton UB7 ...104 B4
Queen's Rd Barking IG11 ...79 A2
Beckenham BR3 ...185 A1
Bowes Park N11 ...32 A4
Buckhurst Hill IG9 ...21 C2
Ealing W5 ...88 A1
Edmonton N9 ...18 B2
Enfield EN1 ...5 C1
Feltham TW13 ...150 B3
Hampton TW12 ...173 D6
Hounslow TW3 ...129 D2
Kingston KT2 ...176 C3
Mitcham CR4 ...202 B6
Mortlake SW14 ...133 B2
New Malden KT3 ...199 D4
Richmond TW10 ...154 B5
Richmond, Richmond Park
KT2,TW10 ...176 C5
Southall UB2 ...107 A4
Teddington TW11 ...174 D4
Thames Ditton KT7 ...196 D4
Thornton Heath CR0 ...205 A3
Wallington SM6 ...219 B3
Wimbledon SW19 ...179 C4
Queen's Rd W E13 ...99 B5
Queens Reach KT8 ...196 C5
Queen's Ride SW13 ...134 B2
Queen's Rise TW10 ...154 B5
Queen's Road Sta SE15 ..140 C4
Queens Row SE17 ...139 B6
Queen St DA7 ...147 B2
EC4 ...117 A6 252 B6
W1 ...115 B5 248 C4
Croydon CR0 ...221 A4
Tottenham N17 ...33 C4
Queens Terr E13 ...99 B6
NW8 ...92 B5 229 C4
Queen's Terr TW7 ...131 A1
Queensthorpe Rd SE26 .184 D6
Queenstown Rd
SW8 ...137 B5 268 C4
Queenstown Road Sta
SW8 ...137 B4 268 D2
Queen St Pl EC4 ...252 B6
Queensville Rd SW12,
SW4 ...159 D4
Queens Walk Ho W5 ...87 C2
Queensway W2 .113 D6 245 D6
Queens Way NW4 ...46 C4
Queensway
Coney Hall BR4 ...224 D4
Enfield EN3 ...6 C1
Orpington BR5 ...211 A3
Sunbury TW16 ...172 B1
Queens Way
Croydon CR0 ...220 B3
Queens Way *continued*
Feltham TW13 ...172 C6
Queensway Sta
W2 ...113 D6 245 D5
Queens Well Ave N20 ...30 C6
Queenswell Jun & Inf Schs
N20 ...14 B2
Queens Wlk NW9 ...67 A6
Queen's Wlk
SW1 ...115 C5 249 A3
Queens Wlk
Ashford TW15 ...170 A6
Chingford E4 ...20 B3
Harrow HA1 ...42 C5
Ruislip HA4 ...62 C5
Queen's Wlk W5 ...87 C2
Queenswood Ave
Chingford E17 ...36 A2
Hampton TW12 ...173 D4
Hounslow TW3,TW5 ...129 B3
Thornton Heath CR7 ...204 C4
Wallington CR0,SM6 ...219 D4
Queenswood Ct
5 SW4 ...160 A6
11 West Norwood SE27 ..183 B6
Queenswood Gdns E11 ...55 B1
Queenswood Pk N3 ...29 A2
Queenswood Rd DA15 ...167 D5
Queen's Wood Rd N6 ...49 B3
Queenswood Rd SE23 ...163 A1
Queens Yd E9 ...75 C2
Queen's Yd W1 ...239 B5
Queen Terr Cotts W7 ...108 C4
Queen Victoria Ave HA0 ..65 D1
Queen Victoria Mon★
SW1 ...249 A2
Queen Victoria St
EC4 ...117 A6 252 A6
Quelch Ho 2 N19 ...71 D3
Quemerford Rd N7 ...72 B3
Quendon Ho W10 ...90 C3
Quenington Ct 5 SE15 ..139 D6
Quennel Ho 7 SW12 ...159 C4
Quentington Mans SW6 .264 C2
Quentin Pl SE13 ...142 C2
Quentin Rd SE13 ...142 C2
Quernmore Cl BR1 ...187 A4
Quernmore Rd BR1 ...187 A4
N4 ...50 C3
Querrin St SW6 ...136 A3
Quested Ct 27 E8 ...74 B3
Quex Mews NW6 ...91 C6
Quex Rd NW6 ...91 C6
Quick Rd W4 ...111 C1
Quicks Rd SW19 ...179 D3
Quick St N1 ...94 D5 234 D3
Quickswood NW3 ...70 C1
Quiet Nook BR2 ...225 D5
Quill La SW15 ...134 D1
Quill St N4 ...72 C5
Ealing W5 ...88 A5
Quilp St SE1 ...252 A2
Quilter Ho 11 W9 ...91 B4
Quilter St E2 ...96 A4
SE18 ...123 D1
Quilting Ct 23 SE16 ...118 D4
Quinta Dr EN5 ...12 C6
Quintin Ave SW20 ...179 B2
Quintin Ct W4 ...133 A5
Quintock Ho 2 TW9 ...132 C4
Quinton Cl
Beckenham BR3 ...208 A6
Cranford TW5 ...128 B5
Wallington SM6 ...219 B4
Quinton Ho SW8 ...270 A4
Quinton Kynaston Sch
NW8 ...92 B6 229 C5
Quinton Rd KT7 ...197 A1
Quinton St SW18 ...158 A2
Quixley St E14 ...120 B6
Quorn Rd SE22 ...139 C2

R

Rabbit Row W8 ...245 B4
Rabbits Rd E12 ...78 A4
Rabbs Farm Prim Sch
UB7 ...104 A6
Rabournmead Dr UB5 ...63 A3
Raby Rd KT3 ...199 B5
Raby St E14 ...97 A1
Raccoon Way TW4 ...128 C3
Rachel Cl IG6 ...57 B6
Rachel Ct SM2 ...218 B1
Rachel Point E5 ...74 A4
Racine 15 SE5 ...139 C4
Rackham Cl DA16 ...146 B3
Rackham Mews SW16 ...181 C4
Racton Rd SW6 ..135 C6 265 A5
Radbourne Ave W5 ...109 C2
Radbourne Cl E5 ...74 D4
Radbourne Cres E17 ...36 B1
Radbourne Ct HA3 ...43 B3
Radbourne Rd SW12 ...159 D3
Radcliff Bldg EC1 ...241 A4
Radcliffe Ave NW10 ...90 A5
Enfield EN2 ...5 A4
Radcliffe Gdns SM5 ...218 C1
Radcliffe Ho 10 SE16 ...118 B2
Radcliffe Mews TW12 ...174 A5
Radcliffe Path 5 SW8 ...137 B3
Radcliffe Rd SE1 ...263 B6
Harrow HA3 ...25 A1
South Croydon CR0 ...221 D5
Southgate N21 ...16 D3
Radcliffe Sq SW15 ...156 D5
Radcliffe Way UB5 ...84 D4
Radcot Point 2 SE23 ...162 D1
Radcot St SE11 ...261 B1
Raddington Rd W10 ...91 A2
Radfield Way SE9 ...167 B4
Radford Ho 8 E14 ...97 D2
N7 ...72 B3
Radford Rd SE13 ...164 A5
Radford Way IG11 ...101 D4
Radipole Rd
SW6 ...135 B4 264 C2
Radius Pk TW6 ...127 D1
Radland Rd E16 ...99 A1
Radlet Ave SE23 ...162 B2
Radlett Cl E7 ...76 D2
Radlett Pl NW8 ...92 C6 230 A6
Radley Ave IG3 ...80 A4
Radley Cl TW14 ...149 D3
Radley Ct 25 SE16 ...118 D4
3 Catford BR1 ...186 A6
Radley Gdns HA3 ...44 A5
Radley Ho NW1 ...237 C6
13 SE2 ...124 D4
Radley Lo 30 SW19 ...156 D3
Radley Mews W8 ...255 B5
Radley Rd N17 ...33 C1
Radley's La E18 ...37 A1
Radleys Mead RM10 ...81 D2
Radley Sq E5 ...74 C6
Radley Terr 1 E16 ...98 D2
Radlix Rd E10 ...53 C1
Radnor Ave DA16 ...168 B6
Harrow HA1 ...42 C4
Radnor Cl BR7 ...189 C4
Mitcham CR4 ...204 A5
Radnor Cres
Redbridge IG4 ...56 B4
Woolwich SE18 ...146 A5
Radnor Ct Ealing W7 ...86 D1
6 Forest Hill SE23 ...162 D1
Harrow HA3 ...24 D2
Radnor Gdns Enfield EN1 ...5 C4
Twickenham TW1 ...152 D2
Radnor Gr UB10 ...82 C5
Radnor Lo W2 ...236 D1
Radnor Mews
W2 ...92 B1 236 D1
Radnor Pl W2 ...92 C1 237 A1
Radnor Rd NW6 ...91 A6
SE15 ...140 A5
Twickenham TW1 ...152 D2
Radnor St EC1 ...95 A4 235 B1
Radnor Terr
W14 ...113 B2 254 C4
Radnor Way NW10 ...88 D3
Radnor Wlk 14 E14 ...119 C2
SW3 ...114 D1 257 C1
Croydon CR0 ...207 A3
Radstock Ave HA3 ...43 B6
Radstock Cl N11 ...31 A4
Radstock St SW11 ...267 A3
Radway Ho 38 W2 ...91 C2
Radwell Ho SW2 ...160 C6
Raebarn Ct 6 SW16 ...160 A1
Raebarn Gdns EN5 ...12 B6
Raeburn Ave
Surbiton KT5 ...198 D3
Tolworth KT5,KT6 ...198 D3
Raeburn Cl NW11 ...48 A3
Teddington KT1 ...175 D3
Raeburn Ho 7 UB5 ...84 D5
Raeburn Rd Edgware HA8 .26 C2
Hayes UB4 ...83 B5
Sidcup DA15 ...167 C5
Raeburn St SW2 ...138 A1
Raffles Ct HA8 ...26 B6
Raffles Ho NW4 ...46 B5
Rafford Way BR1 ...209 B6
RAF Mus★ NW9 ...28 A1
Ragate Ho E5 ...74 A5
Ragged School Mus The★
E3 ...97 A2
Raggleswood BR7 ...188 C2
Raglan Cl TW4 ...151 B6
Raglan Ct SE12 ...165 A6
SW9 ...138 C2
Croydon CR0,CR2 ...220 D3
Wembley HA9 ...66 C5
Raglan Jun & Inf Schs
EN1 ...17 C4
Raglan Prim Sch BR2 ...209 D5
Raglan Rd DA17 ...125 B2
E17 ...54 B4
SE18 ...123 A1
Bromley BR2 ...209 C5
Enfield EN1 ...17 D4
Raglan St NW5 ...71 B2
Raglan Terr HA2 ...63 D4
Raglan Way UB5 ...64 A2
Ragley Cl W3 ...111 A4
Ragwort Ct 1 SE26 ...184 B5
Rahere Ho EC1 ...235 A2
Railey Mews NW5 ...71 C3
Railshead Rd TW1,TW7 ...131 B1
Railton Rd SE24 ...160 D6
Railway App N4 ...50 C3
SE1 ...252 D4
Harrow HA1,HA3 ...42 D5
9 Twickenham TW1 ...153 A4
Wallington SM6 ...219 B3
Railway Ave SE16 ...118 C4
Railway Cotts W6 ...112 C4
Railway Gr SE14 ...141 B5
Railway Pl DA17 ...125 C3
Railway Rd TW11 ...174 D6
Railway Rise SE22 ...139 C1
Railway Side SW13 ...133 C2
Railway St N1 ...233 B3
Ilford RM6 ...58 C2
Railway Terr SE13 ...163 D6
Chingford E17 ...36 A2
Feltham TW13,TW14 ...150 A3
Rainborough Cl NW10 ...67 A2
Rainbow Ave E14 ...119 D1
Rainbow Ct 3 SE14 ...141 A6
Rainbow Ind Est SW20 ..178 B1
Rainbow Quay SE16 ...119 A3
Rainbow St SE5 ...139 C5
Rainbow Works N15 ...52 A4
Raine's Foundation Sch
E2 ...96 B4
Raines Foundation Sec Sch
E2 ...96 C5
Raine St E1 ...118 B5
Rainford Ho 9 N7 ...72 B6
Rainham Cl SE9 ...167 C5
SW11 ...158 C5
Rainham Ho NW1 ...232 B5
Rainham Rd NW10 ...90 C4
Rainham Rd N RM10 ...81 D6
Rainham Rd S RM10 ...81 D4
Rainhill Way E3 ...97 C4
Rainsborough Ave SE8 ..119 A2
Rainsford Cl HA7 ...25 C5
Rainsford Ct NW10 ...88 D5
Rainsford Ho 14 SW2 ...160 B6
Rainsford Rd NW10 ...88 D5
Rainsford St W2 ...237 A2
Rainstar Est N18 ...34 C6
Rainton Rd SE7 ...121 A1
Rainville Rd W6 ...134 C6
Raisins Hill HA5 ...40 C6
Raith Ave N14 ...15 D1
Raleigh Ave Hayes UB4 ...84 B2
Wallington SM6 ...219 D4
Raleigh Cl NW4 ...46 C4
Pinner HA5 ...40 D2
Ruislip HA4 ...61 D6
Raleigh Ct 2 SE16 ...118 D5
Beckenham BR3 ...185 D2
Dulwich SE19 ...183 D5
Ealing W13 ...87 B2
Wallington SM6 ...219 B2
Raleigh Dr N20 ...14 C1
Esher KT10 ...212 B3
Tolworth KT5 ...199 A1
Raleigh Gdns SW2 ...160 B5
Mitcham CR4 ...202 D6
Raleigh Ho 30 SW8 ...137 D3
1 Thames Ditton KT7 ...197 A2
Raleigh Mews N1 ...234 D5
6 Orpington BR6 ...227 D3
Raleigh Rd N10 ...30 C2
N8 ...50 C5
Enfield EN2 ...5 B1
Feltham TW13 ...149 D2
Penge SE20 ...184 D3
Richmond TW9 ...132 B2
Southall UB2 ...107 A1
Raleigh St N1 ...94 D6 234 D5
Raleigh Way
Feltham TW13 ...172 C5
Southgate N14 ...16 A3
Ralph Ct 8 W2 ...91 D1
Ralph Perring Ct BR3 ...207 C5
Ralston St SW3 ...257 C1
Ramac Ind Est SE7 ...121 B1
Rama Cl SW16 ...182 A3
Rama Ct HA1 ...64 C6
Ramac Way SE7 ...121 B1
Rama La SE19 ...183 D3
Ramar Ho 11 E1 ...96 A2
Rambler Cl SW16 ...181 C6
Rambler Ct 11 NW9 ...46 A5
Rame Cl SW17 ...181 A5
Ramilles Cl SW2 ...160 A5
Ramillies Pl W1 ...93 C1 239 A1
Ramillies Rd DA15 ...168 B5
NW7 ...11 C2
W4 ...111 B3
Ramillies St W1 ...239 A1
Ramney Dr EN3 ...7 A6
Rampart St E1 ...96 B1
Rampayne St SW1 ...259 C2
Rampton Cl E4 ...19 C1
Ramsay Ho NW8 ...230 A4
Ramsay Rd E7 ...76 D4
Acton W3 ...111 A4
Ramscroft Cl N9 ...17 C4
Ramsdale Rd SW17 ...181 A5
Ramsdean Ho 1 SW15 ..156 B3
Ramsden Rd N11 ...30 D5
Balham SW12 ...159 A4
Ramsey Cl NW9 ...45 D3
Greenford UB6 ...64 B3
Ramsey Ct N8 ...49 D4
Croydon CR0 ...220 D6
Ramsey Ho 14 SW9 ...138 C5
7 Merton SW19 ...179 D2
Ramsey Rd CR7 ...204 B3
Ramsey St E2 ...96 A3
Ramsey Way N14 ...15 C4
Ramsfort Ho 4 SE16 ...118 B2
Ramsgate Cl 8 E16 ...121 B5
11 E16 ...121 B5
Ramsgate St E8 ...73 D2
Ramsgill App IG2 ...57 D5
Ramsgill Dr IG2 ...57 D5
Rams Gr RM6 ...59 A5
Rams Pas KT1 ...175 D1
Ram St SW18 ...157 D6
Ramulis Dr UB4 ...84 D3
Ramus Wood Ave BR6 ...227 C3
Rance Ho 16 SE7 ...122 A2
Rancliffe Gdns SE9 ...144 A1
Rancliffe Rd E6 ...100 A5
Randal Cremer JMI Sch
E2 ...95 D5
Randall 9 NW9 ...27 D2
Randall Ave NW2 ...67 D5
Randall Cl
SW11 ...136 C4 267 A2
Randall Ct NW7 ...28 A3
Randall Pl SE10 ...142 A5
Randall Rd SE11 .116 B2 260 C3
Randall Row SE11 ...260 C3
Randell's Rd N1 ...94 A6 233 B6
Randisbourne Gdns
SE6 ...163 D1
Randle Rd TW10 ...175 C6
Randlesdown Rd SE6 ...163 D1
Randmore Ct 6 BR3 ...185 C3
Randolph App E16 ...99 C1
Randolph Ave
W9 ...92 A4 229 A1
Randolph Cl KT2 ...177 A5
Randolph Cres
W9 ...92 A3 236 A6
Randolph Ct HA5 ...23 C3
Randolph Gdns NW6 ...91 D5
Randolph Gr RM6 ...58 C4
Randolph Mews
W9 ...92 A3 236 B5
Randolph Rd BR2 ...210 B1
E17 ...53 D4
W9 ...92 A3 236 B5
Southall UB1 ...107 B4
Randolph St NW1 ...71 C1
Randon Cl HA2 ...23 D1
Ranelagh Ave
Barnes SW13 ...134 A3
Fulham SW6 ...135 B2
Ranelagh Cl HA8 ...26 C6
Ranelagh Dr Edgware HA8 .26 C6
Twickenham TW1 ...153 C6
Ranelagh Gardens Mans
SW6 ...135 A2
Ranelagh Gardens (site of
Chelsea Flower Show)★
SW1 ...115 A1 258 B1
Ranelagh Gdns 3 W6 ...111 D3
Chiswick W4 ...133 A5
Fulham SW6 ...135 B2
Ilford IG1 ...56 C1
Wanstead E11 ...55 C4
Ranelagh Gr
SW1 ...115 A1 258 B2
Ranelagh Ho SW3 ...257 C2
Ranelagh Mans 4 SW6 .135 B3
Ranelagh Pl KT3 ...199 C4
Ranelagh Prim Sch E15 ...98 C5
Ranelagh Rd E11 ...76 C4
E15 ...98 C5
N17 ...51 C6
NW10 ...89 D5
SW1 ...115 C1 259 B1
W5 ...109 D4
Southall UB1 ...106 D5
Wallend E6 ...100 C5
Wembley HA0 ...65 D2
Wood Green N22 ...32 B2
Ranfurly Rd SM1 ...217 C6
Rangdon St EC3 ...243 C1
Rangefield Prim Sch
BR1 ...186 C5
Rangefield Rd BR1 ...186 D5
Rangemoor Rd N15 ...51 D4
Ranger's Rd
Buckhurst Hill IG9,IG10 ...21 A4
Chingford E4 ...20 D4
Rangers Sq SE10 ...142 B4
Range Villas TW17 ...192 A2
Range Way TW17 ...192 C2
Rangeworth Pl DA15 ...167 D1
Rangoon Ho 5 N16 ...73 B4
Rankin Cl NW9 ...45 C6
Rankine Ho SE1 ...262 A5
Ranleigh Gdns DA7 ...147 B5
Ranmere St SW12 ...159 B3
Ranmoor Cl HA1 ...42 B5
Ranmoor Gdns HA1 ...42 C5
Ranmore Ave CR0 ...221 D5
Ranmore Ct
Kingston KT6 ...197 D4
3 Wimbledon SW20 ...178 D2
Rann Ho 1 SW14 ...133 B2
Rannoch Cl HA8 ...10 D2
Rannoch Ct 9 KT6 ...198 A4
Rannoch Rd W6 ...134 D6
Rannock Ave NW9 ...45 C2
Ransford Ho 16 SE21 ...183 C6
Ransom Rd 1 SE7 ...121 C1
Ranston St NW1 ...237 A4
Ranulf Rd NW2 ...69 B4
Ranwell Cl 11 E3 ...97 B6
Ranwell Ho 10 E3 ...97 B6
Ranworth Rd N9 ...18 C2
Ranyard Cl KT9 ...214 B5
Raphael Ct 5 SE16 ...118 B1
Raphael Dr KT7 ...196 D2
Raphael St SW7 ...247 C1
Rapide 12 NW9 ...27 C2
Rapley Ho 19 E2 ...96 A4
Rashleigh Ct 8 SW8 ...137 B2
Rashleigh Ho WC1 ...233 A1
Rasper Rd N20 ...14 A2
Rastell Ave SW12 ...159 D3
Ratcliffe Cl SE12 ...165 A4
Ratcliffe Cross St E1 ...96 D1
Ratcliffe Ho 12 E14 ...97 A1
Ratcliffe La 18 E14 ...97 A1
Ratcliffe Orch 9 E1 ...118 D6
Ratcliff Rd E7 ...77 C3
Rathbone Ho 5 E16 ...98 D1
NW6 ...91 C6
10 Wimbledon SW19 ...178 D3
Rathbone Mkt 2 E16 ...98 D2
Rathbone Pl W1 ..93 D1 239 C2
Rathbone Point E5 ...74 A4
Rathbone St E16 ...98 D1
W1 ...93 C2 239 B3
Rathcoole Ave N8 ...50 B4
Rathcoole Gdns N8 ...50 B4

Rathfern Prim Sch
SE23 163 B3
Rathfern Rd SE6 163 B3
Rathgar Ave W13 109 C5
Rathgar Cl N3 29 B1
Rathgar Rd SW9 138 D2
Rathmell Dr SW4 159 D5
Rathmore Rd SE7 121 B1
Ratier 13 NW9 27 C2
Rattray Ct 3 SE6 164 D2
Rattray Rd SW2 160 C6
Raul Rd SE15 140 A4
Raveley St NW5 71 C4
Raven Cl NW9 27 C1
Ravendale Rd TW16 171 D1
Ravenet Ct SW11 268 C1
SW4 159 B6
Ravenet St
SW11 137 B4 268 C1
Ravenfield Rd SW17 158 D1
Ravenhill Rd E13 99 C5
Raven Ho 10 SE16 118 D2
Ravenings Par IG3 58 A1
Ravenna Rd SW15 156 D6
Ravenor Ct UB6 85 D3
Ravenor Park Rd UB6 86 A4
Ravenor Prim Sch UB6 85 C4
Raven Rd E18 37 C1
Raven Row E1 96 B2
Ravensbourne 3 TW1 153 C5
Ravensbourne Ave
Bromley BR2,BR3 186 C2
Catford BR2 186 B3
Stanwell TW19 148 A3
Ravensbourne Coll of Design & Communication
BR7 188 B5
Ravensbourne Ct SE6 163 C4
Ravensbourne Gdns W13 87 B2
Ravensbourne Ho NW8 237 A4
10 Catford BR1 186 B5
Ravensbourne Park Cres
SE6 163 B4
Ravensbourne Pk SE6 163 C4
Ravensbourne Pl SE13 141 D3
Ravensbourne Rd
Bromley BR1,BR2 209 A6
Forest Hill SE23 163 B3
Twickenham TW1 153 C5
Ravensbourne Sch The
BR2 209 B4
Ravensbourne Sta BR3 186 B3
Ravensbury Ave SM4 202 A4
Ravensbury Ct CR4 202 B5
Ravensbury Gr CR4 202 B5
Ravensbury La CR4 202 B5
Ravensbury Rd
Orpington BR5 211 D5
Wandsworth SW18 157 D2
Ravensbury Terr SW18 157 D2
Ravenscar NW1 232 A5
Ravenscar Lo 13 SW19 178 D3
Ravenscar Rd
Catford BR1 186 C6
Surbiton KT6 214 B6
Ravens Cl Bromley BR2 186 D1
Enfield EN1 5 C3
Kingston KT6 197 D3
Ravenscourt 1 N16 74 A5
Sunbury TW16 171 D2
Ravenscourt Ave W6 112 A2
Ravenscourt Cl HA4 39 A2
Ravenscourt Gdns W6 112 A2
Ravenscourt Park Mans
W6 112 B3
Ravenscourt Park Prep Sch
W6 112 A2
Ravenscourt Park Sta
W6 112 B2
Ravenscourt Pk W6 112 A2
Ravenscourt Pl W6 112 B2
Ravenscourt Rd BR5 190 B1
W6 112 B2
Ravenscourt Sq W6 112 A3
Ravenscourt Theatre Sch
W6 112 B2
Ravenscraig Rd N11 31 C6
Ravenscroft Ave NW11 47 B2
Wembley HA9 44 B2
Ravenscroft Cl 4 E16 99 A2
Ravenscroft Cres SE9 166 B1
Ravenscroft Ct NW11 47 B2
Ravenscroft Prim Sch
E16 99 A3
Ravenscroft Rd E16 99 A2
Acton W4 111 A2
Penge BR3 184 D1
Ravenscroft Sch N20 13 B4
Ravenscroft St E2 95 D4
Ravensdale Ave N12 30 B6
Ravensdale Com Est N16 52 A3
Ravensdale Gdns
Hounslow TW4 129 A2
South Norwood SE19 183 B3
Ravensdale Mans N8 50 A3
Ravensdale Rd N16 51 D3
Hounslow TW4 129 A2
Ravensdon St
SE11 116 C1 261 B1
Ravensfield Cl RM9 80 D4
Ravensfield Gdns KT19 215 C4
Ravenshaw St NW6 69 B3
Ravenshill BR7 188 D2
Ravens Ho KT1 175 D1
Ravenshurst Ave NW4 46 C5
Ravenside KT6 197 D4
Ravenside Cl N18 34 D5
Ravenslea Rd SW11,
SW12 158 D4
Ravensleigh Gdns BR1 187 B5
Ravensmead Rd BR2 186 B3
Ravensmede Way W4 111 D2
Ravensroost SE19 183 B2
Ravenstone
SE17 117 C1 263 B1
Ravenstone Prim Sch
SW12 159 A2
Ravenstone Rd N8 50 C6
NW9 45 D3
Ravenstone St SW12 159 A3
Ravensview Ct KT6 197 D4
Ravens Way SE3,SE12 165 A6
Ravenswood DA5 169 A3
Ravenswood Ave
Tolworth KT6 214 C6
West Wickham BR4 208 A1
Ravenswood Cres
Harrow HA2 63 B6
West Wickham BR4 208 A1
Ravenswood Gdns TW7 130 C4
Ravenswood Pk HA6 22 A4
Ravenswood Rd E17 54 A5
Balham SW12 159 B4
Croydon CR0 220 D5
Ravenswood Road Ind Est 5
E17 54 A5
Ravens Wood Sch BR2 225 D5
Ravensworth Ct SW6 265 A3
Ravensworth Rd NW10 90 B4
SE9 188 B6
Raven Wharf SE1 253 C2
Ravey St EC2 95 C3 243 A6
Ravine Gr SE18 145 C6
Rav Pinter Cl N16 51 C2
Rawlings Cl 3 BR6 227 D3
Rawlings Cres HA9 66 D5
Rawlings St
SW3 114 D2 257 C4
Rawlins Cl N3 47 A6
South Croydon CR2 223 B1
Rawlinson Ct NW2 46 C2
Rawlinson Ho SE13 142 B1
Rawlinson Point 8 E16 98 D2
Rawnsley Ave CR4 202 C4
Rawreth Wlk N1 235 B6
Rawson Ct SW11 268 B1
Rawson St
SW11 137 B4 268 C1
Rawsthorne Cl E16 122 B5
Rawstone Wlk 5 E13 99 A5
Rawstorne Pl EC1 234 C2
Rawstorne St
EC1 94 D4 234 C2
Raybell Ct TW7 130 D3
Rayburne Ct W14 254 A6
Buckhurst Hill IG9 21 C3
Ray Cl KT9 213 C2
Ray Ct Ealing W13 109 B5
Woodford IG8 37 D4
Raydean Rd EN5 13 D6
Raydons Gdns RM9 81 A3
Raydons Rd RM9 81 A3
Raydon St N19 71 B6
Rayfield Cl BR2 210 A3
Rayford Ave SE12 164 D4
Ray Gdns Barking IG11 102 A5
Stanmore HA7 25 B5
Ray Ho 7 W10 90 D1
Rayleas Cl SE18 144 D4
Rayleigh Ave TW11 174 C4
Rayleigh Cl N13 17 B1
Rayleigh Ct
2 Kingston KT1 176 B1
Tottenham N22 33 A2
Rayleigh Rd 5 E16 121 B5
7 E16 121 B5
Edmonton N13 17 B1
Merton SW19 179 B2
Woodford IG8 37 C3
Rayleigh Rise CR2 221 C2
Ray Lodge Prim Sch IG8 37 D4
Ray Lodge Rd IG8 37 D4
Ray Massey Way 3 E6 100 A6
Raymead Ave CR7 204 C4
Raymede Twr W10 90 D2
Raymere Gdns SE18 145 C5
Raymond Ave W13 109 A3
Woodford E18 36 D1
Raymond Cl SE26 184 C5
Raymond Ct N10 31 A3
Raymond Postgate Ct 5
SE28 124 B6
Raymond Rd E13 99 C6
Beckenham BR3 207 A5
Ilford IG2 57 B2
Wimbledon SW19 179 A4
Raymond Way KT10 213 A2
Raymouth Rd SE16 118 B2
Raynald Ho 15 SW16 160 A1
Rayne Ct E18 54 D5
SE1 253 C2
Rayne Ho 1 SW12 159 A5
W9 91 D3
Rayner Ct 10 W12 112 C4
Rayners Cl HA0 65 D3
Rayners Cres UB5 84 B4
Rayners Gdns UB5 84 B4
Rayners La Harrow HA2 63 D6
Pinner HA5 41 B3
Rayners Lane Sta HA5 41 B2
Rayner's Rd SW15 157 A6
Rayner Twrs E10 53 C2
Raynes Ave E11 55 C2
Raynes Ct NW2 69 A4
Raynesfield SW20 200 C6
Raynes Park High Sch
KT3 200 B6
Raynes Park Sta SW20 178 C1
Raynham W2 237 A2
Raynham Ave N18 34 A5
Raynham Ho 1 E1 96 D3
Raynham Prim Sch N18 34 A5
Raynham Rd W6 112 B2
Edmonton N18 34 A5
Raynham Terr N18 34 A5
Raynor Cl UB1 107 B5
Raynor Pl N1 235 B6
Raynton Cl Harrow HA2 41 A2
Hayes UB4 83 D3
Raynton Dr Hayes UB4 83 C5
Hayes UB4 83 D3
Raynton Rd EN3 6 D6
Ray Rd KT8 195 D4
Rays Ave N18 34 C6
Rays Rd N18 34 C6
West Wickham BR4 208 A2
Ray St EC1 241 B5
Ray Wlk N7 72 B6
Raywood Cl UB7 127 A5
Reachview Cl 14 NW1 71 C1
Read Cl KT7 197 A2
Read Ct E17 53 D3
Reade Ct 6 W3 111 A3
Reade Ho 7 SE10 142 B6
Reade Wlk NW10 67 C1
Read Ho N11 30 D6
4 SE11 138 C6
Reading Ho SE15 140 A6
W2 236 A1
Reading La E8 74 B2
Reading Rd Northolt UB5 64 A3
Sutton SM1 218 A3
Reading Way NW7 29 A5
Readman Ct 8 SE20 184 B2
Reads Cl IG1 78 D5
Reapers Cl NW1 232 C6
Reapers Way TW7 152 B6
Reardon Ho 5 E1 118 B5
Reardon Path 31 E1 118 B5
Reardon St E1 118 B5
Reaston St SE14 140 D5
Reay Prim Sch
SW9 138 B5 270 D3
Rebecca Ct
Beckenham BR3 185 C2
Sidcup DA14 190 B6
Rebecca Ho 10 N12 29 D6
Reckitt Rd W4 111 C1
Record St SE16 140 C6
Recovery St SW17 180 C5
Recreation Rd
Bromley BR2 186 D1
Forest Hill SE26 184 D6
Southall UB2 107 A2
Recreation Way CR4,
SW16 204 A6
Rector St N1 95 A6 235 A5
Rectory Bsns Ctr 5
DA14 190 B6
Rectory Cl N3 29 B2
Chingford E4 19 C1
Littleton TW17 192 C6
Long Ditton KT6 197 C1
Sidcup DA14 190 B5
Stanmore HA7 25 B5
West Barnes SW20 200 C6
Rectory Cres E11 55 C3
Rectory Ct E11 76 D5
Cranford TW5 128 C3
Feltham TW13 172 C6
Wallington SM6 219 C4
Woodford E18 36 D2
Rectory Field Cres SE7 143 C5
Rectory Gdns N8 50 A5
SW4 137 C2
Beckenham BR3 185 C2
Northolt UB5 85 B6
Rectory Gn BR3 185 B2
Rectory Gr SW4 137 C2
Croydon CR0 220 D6
Hampton TW12,TW13 173 B6
Rectory La DA14 190 C6
Edgware HA8 26 C4
Long Ditton KT6 197 C1
Stanmore HA7 25 B5
Upper Tooting SW17 181 A5
Wallington SM6 219 C4
Rectory Orch SW19 179 A6
Rectory Paddock Sch
BR5 190 C1
Rectory Park Ave UB5 85 B4
Rectory Pl SE18 122 C2
Rectory Rd E12 78 B3
E17 53 D5
N16 73 D5
1 W3 111 A5
Barnes SW13 134 A3
Beckenham BR3 185 C2
Cranford TW5 128 C3
Dagenham RM10 81 D1
Hayes UB3 84 A1
Keston BR2 225 D1
Southall UB2 107 B3
Sutton SM1 217 D5
Rectory Road Sta N16 73 D5
Rectory Sq E1 96 D2
Rectory Way UB10 60 D5
Reculver Ho 2 SE15 140 C6
Reculver Mews N18 34 A6
Reculver Rd SE16 118 D1
Red Anchor Cl SW3 267 A5
Redan Pl W2 91 D1
Redan St W14 112 D3
Redan Terr SE5 138 D3
Red Barracks Rd 4
SE18 122 B2
Redberry Gr SE23,SE26 162 C1
Redbourne Ave N3 29 C2
Redbourne Dr SE28 102 D1
Redbourne Ho 7 E14 97 B1
Redbourne Ho *continued*
N3 29 C2
Redbourn Ho W10 90 C3
Redbridge Coll RM6 58 B4
Redbridge Ent Ctr IG1 79 A6
Redbridge Gdns SE5 139 C5
Redbridge Inf Sch IG4 56 A4
Redbridge Jun Sch IG4 56 A4
Redbridge La E IG4 56 A4
Redbridge La W E11 55 C3
Redbridge Rdbt IG4 55 D3
Redbridge Sta IG4 55 D3
Redburn St
SW3 136 D6 267 C6
Redburn Trad Est EN3 18 D5
Redcar Cl UB5 63 D2
Redcar Ho SE26 184 B4
Redcar St SE5 139 A5
Redcastle Cl E1 118 C6
Red Cedars Rd BR6 211 C2
Redchurch St E2 95 D3 243 C6
Redcliffe Cl SW5 255 C1
Redcliffe Gdns
SW10 135 D6 265 D6
Chiswick W4 132 D5
Ilford IG1 56 C1
Redcliffe Mews SW10 255 D1
Redcliffe Pl SW10 266 A5
Redcliffe Rd
SW10 136 A6 266 B6
Redcliffe Sch
SW10 136 A6 266 B6
Redcliffe Sq
SW10 113 D1 255 D1
Redcliffe St SW10 265 D6
Redcliffe Wlk HA9 66 D5
Redclose Ave SM4 201 C4
Redclyffe Rd E6 99 C6
Redclyffe Terr 2 SM2 217 C1
Redclyf Ho 12 E1 96 C3
Redcroft 5 NW6 69 C2
Redcroft Rd UB1 86 A1
Redcross Way
SE1 117 A5 252 B3
Redding Ho SE18 122 A3
Reddings Ave WD23 8 A6
Reddings Cl NW7 27 D6
Reddings The NW7 11 D1
Reddins Rd SE15 140 A6
Reddons Rd BR3 185 A3
Rede Ho 2 E12 78 C3
Rede Pl W2 113 C6 245 B6
Redesdale Gdns TW7 131 A5
Redesdale St SW3 267 C6
Redfern Ave TW2,TW4 151 C4
Redfern Ho 6 E13 98 D6
Redfern Rd NW10 67 C1
Catford SE6 164 A4
Redfield La
SW5 113 D2 255 C4
Redfield Mews SW5 255 B4
Redfiff Est SE16 119 B3
Redford Ave
Thornton Heath CR7 204 B5
Wallington SM6 220 A2
Redford Cl TW13 149 D2
Redford Wlk N1 235 A6
Redgate Dr BR2 225 B6
Red Gates Sch CR9 220 C3
Redgate Terr SW15 156 D5
Redgrave Cl SE25 205 D3
Redgrave Rd SW15 134 D2
Red Hill BR7 188 D5
Redhill Ct SW2 160 C2
Redhill Dr HA8 27 A1
Red Hill Prim Sch BR7 188 D5
Redhill St NW1 93 B4 231 D2
Red House La DA6 147 A1
Red House Rd CR0 203 D3
Redif Ho RM10 81 D4
Redington Gdns NW3 69 D4
Redington Ho N1 233 D4
Redington Rd NW3 69 D4
Redknap Ho TW10 153 C1
Red La KT10 213 A2
Redland Gdns KT8 195 B5
Redlands N15 51 B5
Teddington TW11 175 A4
Redlands Ct BR1 186 D3
Redlands Prim Sch E1 96 C2
Redlands Rd EN3 7 A4
Redlands The 5 BR3 185 D1
Redlands Way SW2 160 B4
Redleaf Cl DA17 147 C6
Redleaves Ave TW15 170 D4
Redlees Cl TW7 131 A1
Red Leys UB8 60 A1
Red Lion Bsns Ctr KT6 214 B5
Red Lion Cl 9 SE17 139 B6
Red Lion Ct EC4 241 B1
Red Lion Hill N2 30 B1
Red Lion La SE18 144 C4
Red Lion Pl SE18 144 C4
Red Lion Rd KT6 214 C6
Red Lion Row SE17 139 A6
Red Lion Sq WC1 94 B2 240 C3
Red Lion St WC1 94 B2 240 C3
Richmond TW10 153 D6
Red Lion Yd W1 248 B4
Red Lo BR4 208 A2
Red Lodge Rd BR3,BR4 208 B2
Redlynch Ct
W14 113 A4 244 B1
Redlynch Ho 27 SW9 138 C4
Redman Bldg EC1 241 A4
Redman Cl UB5 84 C5
Redman Ho SE1 252 B1
Redman's Rd E1 96 C2
Redmayne Ho 15 SW9 138 B3
Redmead La E1 118 A5
Redmead Rd UB3 105 C2
Redmill Ho 24 E1 96 B3
Redmond Ho N1 233 D5
Redmore Rd W6 112 B2
Red Oak Cl BR6 226 D6
Red Pl W1 248 A6
Redpoll Way DA18 124 D3
Red Post Hill SE21,SE24 161 B6
Red Post Ho E6 77 D1
Redriffe Rd E13 98 D6
Redriff Prim Sch SE16 119 A4
Redriff Rd SE16 119 A3
Redroofs Cl BR3 185 D2
Redrose Trad Ctr 1 EN4 14 B6
Red Rover SW13 134 A2
Redrup Ho 21 SE14 140 D6
Redruth Cl N22 32 B3
Redruth Ho SM2 217 D1
Redruth Rd E9 96 C6
Red Sq The N16 73 B5
Redstart Cl E6 100 A2
SE14 141 A5
Redston Rd N8 49 D5
Redvers Rd N22 32 C1
Redvers St E2 95 C4
Redway Dr TW2 152 A4
Redwing Path SE28 123 B4
Redwood Cl DA15 168 A3
N14 15 D4
SE16 119 A5
Chigwell IG9 21 B2
Hillingdon UB10 82 D5
South Oxhey WD19 22 D6
Redwood Ct N19 49 D2
NW6 69 A1
Northolt UB5 85 A4
10 Surbiton KT6 197 D2
Redwood Est TW5 128 B6
Redwood Gdns E4 19 D5
Redwood Mews 2 SW4 137 B2
Ashford TW15 171 B3
Redwoods SW15 156 A3
Redwood Twr E11 76 B5
Redwood Way EN5 12 D6
Redwood Wlk KT6 197 D1
Reece Mews SW7 256 C4
Reed Ave BR6 227 C5
Reed Cl E16 99 A2
SE12 165 A6
Reede Gdns RM10 81 D3
Reede Rd RM10 81 D2
Reede Way RM10 81 D2
Reedham Cl N17 52 B5
Reedham St SE15 140 A2
Reed Ho SW15 156 A5
Reedholm Villas N16 73 B4
Reed Mans 6 E11 55 A3
Reed Pl Bsns Pk TW17 192 B1
Reed Rd N17 33 D1
Reedsfield Cl TW15 148 D1
Reedsfield Rd TW15 170 D6
Reed's Pl NW1 71 C1
Reedworth St
SE11 116 C2 261 B3
Reef Ho E14 120 A3
Reenglass Rd HA7 25 D6
Rees Dr HA7 26 A6
Rees Gdns CR0 205 D3
Rees Ho 6 N17 33 D3
Reesland Cl E12 78 C2
Rees St N1 95 A6 235 B5
Reets Farm Cl NW9 45 C3
Reeves Ave NW9 45 B2
Reeves Cnr CR0 220 D6
Reeves Cnr Sta CR0 220 D6
Reeves Ho SE1 251 A1
W1 248 A5
Reeves Mews
W1 115 A6 248 B5
Reeves Rd E3 97 D3
SE18 144 D6
Reflection The E16 122 D4
Reform Row N17 33 D1
Reform St SW11 136 D3
Regal Cl E1 96 A2
Ealing W5 87 D2
Regal Cres SM6 219 B5
Regal Ct Edmonton N18 33 D5
2 Mitcham CR4 202 D6
Wembley HA0 65 D4
Regal Dr N11 31 B5
Regal La NW1 231 B5
Regal Pl 8 E3 97 B4
SW6 265 D3
Regal Way HA3 44 A3
Regan Ho 1 N18 33 D4
Regan Way N1 95 C5
Regatta Ho TW11 175 A6
Regatta Point TW8 132 B6
Regency Cl Ealing W5 88 A1
Hampton TW12 173 B5
Regency Cres 3 NW4 28 D1
Regency Ct 21 E9 96 C6
Enfield EN1 17 B6
4 Kingston KT5 198 B4
4 Penge SE19 184 A3
Sutton SM1 217 D4
Wimbledon SW19 179 B3
Regency Dr HA4 39 C1
Regency Gdns KT12 194 C1
Regency Ho N3 29 B1
Regency Lo NW3 70 B1
1 Buckhurst Hill IG9 21 D2
Regency Mews 1 NW10 68 A2
Beckenham BR3 186 A2
Isleworth TW7 152 C6
Regency St
SW1 115 D2 259 D3
Regency Way DA7 147 A2
Regency Wlk
Croydon CR0 207 B3
8 Richmond TW10 154 A6
Regent Ave UB10 60 D1
Regent Bsns Ctr UB3 106 A4
Regent Cl N12 30 A5
Cranford TW4 128 B4
Harrow HA3 44 A3
Regent Ct 1 N16 51 D2
N3 29 D3
NW8 230 A1
South Norwood SE19 182 D4
Regent Gdns IG3 58 A2
Regent Ho W14 254 A4
Regent Lo 9 SW2 160 B3
Regent Pl W1 249 B6
Croydon CR0 205 D1
Wimbledon SW19 180 A5
Regent Rd SE24 160 D6
Surbiton KT5 198 C4
Regents Ave N13 32 C5
Regents Bridge Gdns
SW8 270 B4
Regents Canal Ho 21
E14 97 A1
Regents Cl Hayes UB4 83 C2
South Croydon CR2 221 C2
Regent's Coll
NW1 93 A3 238 A6
Regents Ct E8 96 A6
22 Beckenham BR3 185 C3
Bromley BR1 186 D3
Edgware HA8 26 A6
1 Kingston KT2 176 A2
Regents Dr BR2 225 D3
Regents Gate Ho 20
E14 119 A6
Regents Mews
NW8 92 A5 229 B4
Regent's Park*
NW1 93 A4 231 A3
Regent's Park Barracks
NW1 231 D3
Regent's Park Rd N3 47 B6
NW1 93 A6 231 A6
Regent's Park Sta
NW1 93 B3 238 C5
Regent's Park Terr
NW1 231 C6
Regent's Pl SE3 143 A3
Regents Pl IG10 21 D4
Regents Plaza 2 NW6 91 D5
Regent Sq 23 E3 97 D4
WC1 94 A4 233 B1
Belvedere DA17 125 D2
Regent's Row E8 96 A6
Regent St W1 115 C6 249 A6
W4 110 C1
Regents Wharf 3 E2 96 B6
N1 233 C4
Regina Coeli RC Prim Sch
CR2 220 D1
Reginald Ct BR3 186 A2
Reginald Pl 6 SE8 141 C5
Reginald Rd E7 77 A2
SE8 141 C5
Reginald Sorenson Ct
E11 54 B2
Reginald Sq SE8 141 C5
Regina Point SE16 118 C3
Regina Rd N4 50 B1
Ealing W13 109 A5
Southall UB2 107 A2
South Norwood SE25 206 A6
Regina Terr W13 109 B5
Regis Ct N8 50 B5
NW1 237 C4
East Bedfont TW14 149 B5
Mitcham SW19 180 C2
Regis Pl 17 SW2 138 B1
Regis Rd NW5 71 B3
Regnart Bldgs NW1 232 B1
Regnolruf Ct KT12 194 A2
Reid Cl HA5 40 A5
Reid Ct SW14 133 A3
Reidhaven Rd SE18 123 C2
Reigate Ave SM3,SM4 201 D1
Reigate Rd BR1,SE12 165 A2
Catford BR1 164 D1
Ilford IG3 79 D6
Reigate Way SM6 220 A3
Reighton Rd E5 74 A6
Reizel Cl N16 51 C1
Relay Rd W12 112 C5
Relf Rd SE15 140 A2
Reliance Sq E2 243 A6
Relko Gdns SM1 218 B3
Relton Mews SW7 257 B6
Rembrandt Cl E14 120 B3
Rembrandt Ct 10 SE16 118 B1
West Ewell KT19 215 D2
Rembrandt Rd SE13 142 C1
Edgware HA8 26 C1
Remembrance Ave N2 47 D6
Remington Rd E6 100 A1
N15 51 B3
Remington St N1 94 D5 234 D3
Remnant St WC2 240 C2
Remsted Ho 5 NW6 91 D6
Remus Rd E3 75 C1
Renbold Ho 5 SE10 142 A4
Rendlebury Ho 17 SE18 122 B2
Rendle Cl CR0 206 A4
Rendlesham Ho 3 E5,
N16 74 A5
Rendlesham Rd E5 74 A5
Enfield EN2 4 D4

Renforth St SE16 ... 118 C4
Renfree Way TW17 ... 192 C2
Renfrew Cl E6 ... 122 C6
Renfrew Ct TW5 ... 129 A3
Renfrew Ho E17 ... 35 B1
NW6 ... 91 D5
Renfrew Rd
SE11 ... 116 D2 261 C3
Hounslow TW5 ... 129 A3
Kingston KT2 ... 177 A3
Renmuir St SW17 ... 180 D4
Rennell Ho 18 E9 ... 74 D2
Rennell St SE13 ... 142 A2
Renness Rd E17 ... 53 A6
Rennets Cl SE9 ... 167 C6
Rennets Wood Rd SE9 ... 167 B6
Rennie Cotts 24 E1 ... 96 C3
Rennie Ct SE1 ... 251 C4
Holdbrook EN3 ... 7 C5
Rennie Ho SE1 ... 262 A5
Rennie St SE1 ... 116 D5 251 C4
Renoir Ct 7 SE16 ... 118 B1
Renovation The E16 ... 122 D4
Renown Cl CR0 ... 204 D1
Rensburg Rd E17 ... 52 D3
Rensburg Villas E17 ... 52 D4
Renshaw Cl 7 DA17 ... 147 B6
Renshaw Ct SW19 ... 179 A6
Renshaw Ho 11 SW27 ... 182 D5
Renters Ave NW4 ... 46 C3
Renton Cl SW2 ... 160 B5
Renwick Rd IG11 ... 102 B4
Repens Way UB4 ... 84 D3
Rephidim St SE1 ... 263 A5
Replingham Rd SW18 ... 157 C3
Reporton Rd
SW6 ... 135 A5 264 B3
Repository Rd SE7,SE18 ... 122 B1
Repton Ave Hayes UB3 ... 105 B2
Wembley HA0 ... 65 C4
Repton Cl SM1,SM5 ... 218 C3
Repton Ct BR3 ... 185 D2
Repton Ho 2 E14 ... 97 A1
SW1 ... 259 B3
Repton Rd Harrow HA3 ... 44 B5
Orpington BR6 ... 227 D5
Repton St E14 ... 97 A1
Re Sassoon Ho SE15 ... 140 C4
Reservoir Cl CR7 ... 205 B5
Reservoir Rd SE4 ... 141 A3
Ruislip HA4 ... 39 B5
Southgate N14 ... 15 C6
Resolution Wlk SE18 ... 122 B3
Restell Cl SE3 ... 142 C6
Restmor Way SM5,SM6 ... 219 A6
Reston Pl SW7 ... 246 A1
Restons Cres DA15,SE9 ... 167 C5
Restoration Sq SW11 ... 266 D1
Restormel Cl TW3 ... 151 C6
Retcar Pl N19 ... 71 B6
Retford St E2 ... 95 C5
Retingham Way E4 ... 19 D2
Retreat Cl HA3 ... 43 C4
Retreat Ho 5 E9 ... 74 C2
Retreat Pl E9 ... 74 C2
Retreat Rd TW9 ... 153 D6
Retreat The NW9 ... 45 B4
Harrow HA2 ... 41 C2
Mortlake SW14 ... 133 C2
North Cheam KT4 ... 216 B6
South Norwood CR7 ... 205 B5
Surbiton KT5 ... 198 B3
Reunion Row E1 ... 118 B6
Reveley Sq SE16 ... 119 A4
Revell Rd Cheam SM1 ... 217 B2
Kingston KT1 ... 176 D2
Revell Rise SE18 ... 145 D6
Revelon Rd SE4 ... 141 A2
Revelstoke Rd SW18,
SW19 ... 157 C2
Reventlow Rd SE9 ... 167 A3
Reverdy Rd SE1 ... 118 A2
Reverend Cl HA2 ... 63 D5
Revesby Rd SM5 ... 202 C3
Review Rd NW2 ... 67 D6
Dagenham RM10 ... 103 D6
Rewell St SW6 ... 136 A5 266 A3
Rewley Rd SM4 ... 202 B3
Rex Ave TW15 ... 170 C5
Rex Ho TW13 ... 151 A1
Rex Par 2 IG8 ... 37 C4
Rex Pl W1 ... 115 A5 248 B4
Reydon Ave E11 ... 55 C3
Reygate Ct N4 ... 51 A3
Reynard Cl BR1 ... 210 C6
SE4 ... 141 A2
Reynard Dr SE19 ... 183 D3
Reynard Mills Trad Est
TW8 ... 109 C1
Reynard Pl SE14 ... 141 A6
Reynardson Rd N17 ... 33 B3
Reynardson's Ct 3 N17 ... 51 D6
Reynolds Ave
Chessington KT9 ... 214 A1
Ilford RM6 ... 58 C2
Little Ilford E12 ... 78 C3
Reynolds Cl NW11 ... 47 D2
Carshalton SM5 ... 202 D1
Mitcham SW19 ... 180 B2
Reynolds Ct E11 ... 76 D5
Ilford RM6 ... 58 D6
Reynolds Dr HA8 ... 44 B6
Reynolds Ho 19 E2 ... 96 C5
N4 ... 50 A1
NW8 ... 229 D3
SW1 ... 259 D3
Enfield EN1 ... 18 A6
Reynolds Pl SE3 ... 143 B5
12 Richmond TW10 ... 154 B5
Reynolds Rd SE15 ... 140 C1
W4 ... 111 A3
Hayes UB4 ... 84 C3
New Malden KT3 ... 199 B2
Reynolds Way CR0 ... 221 C4
Rheidol Mews N1 ... 235 A4
Rheidol Terr N1 ... 95 A6 235 A5
Rhein Ho N8 ... 50 A6
Rheola Cl N17 ... 33 D2
Rhoda St E2 ... 95 D3 243 D6
Rhodes Ave N22 ... 31 C2
Rhodes Avenue Prim Sch
N22 ... 31 C2
Rhodes Ho N1 ... 235 C2
Rhodesia Rd E11 ... 76 B6
SW9 ... 138 A3
Rhodes-Moorhouse Ct
SM4 ... 201 C3
Rhodes St N7 ... 72 B3
Rhodeswell Rd E14 ... 97 A2
Rhodrons Ave KT9 ... 214 A3
Rhondda Gr E3 ... 97 B4
Rhyl Prim Sch NW5 ... 71 A2
Rhyl Rd UB6 ... 86 D5
Rhyl St NW5 ... 71 A2
Rhys Ave N11 ... 31 D3
Rialto Rd CR4 ... 181 A1
Ribble Cl IG8 ... 37 C4
Ribblesdale Ave N11 ... 31 A4
Northolt UB5 ... 63 D2
Ribblesdale Ho 11 NW6 ... 91 C6
Ribblesdale Rd N8 ... 50 B5
Streatham SW16 ... 181 B5
Ribbon Dance Mews
SE5 ... 139 B4
Ribchester Ave UB6 ... 86 D4
Ribston Cl BR2 ... 210 B1
Ribstone Ho 12 E9 ... 74 D2
Ricardo Path 5 SE28 ... 124 C5
Ricardo St E14 ... 97 D1
Ricards Lodge High Sch
SW19 ... 179 B5
Ricards Rd SW19 ... 179 B5
Riccal Ct 2 NW9 ... 27 C2
Riceyman Ho WC1 ... 234 A1
Richard Alibon Prim Sch
RM10 ... 81 C3
Richard Anderson Ct 1
SE14 ... 140 D5
Richard Atkins Prim Sch
SW2 ... 160 A4
Richard Burbidge Mans
SW13 ... 134 C6
Richard Burton Ct 4
IG9 ... 21 C2
Richard Challoner Sch
KT3 ... 199 B2
Richard Cl SE18 ... 122 A2
Richard Cloudesley Sch
EC1 ... 95 A3 242 A5
Richard Cobden Prim Sch
NW1 ... 93 C6 232 B5
Richard Ct EN5 ... 1 A2
Richard Fell Ho 2 E12 ... 78 C4
Richard Fox Ho N4 ... 73 A5
Richard Ho 8 SE16 ... 118 C2
Richard House Dr E16 ... 99 D1
E6 ... 100 A1
Richard Knight Ho SW6 ... 265 B2
Richard Neale Ho 2 E1 ... 118 B6
Richards Cl Bushey WD23 ... 8 B4
Harlington UB3 ... 127 B6
Harrow HA1 ... 43 A4
Hillingdon UB10 ... 82 C6
Richards Ct BR3 ... 184 D2
Richardson Cl 15 E8 ... 95 D6
Richardson Ct 20 SW4 ... 138 A3
Richardson Gdns 12
RM10 ... 81 D2
Richardson Ho TW7 ... 130 D2
Richardson Rd E15 ... 98 C5
Richardson's Mews W1 ... 239 A5
Richards Pl E17 ... 53 C6
Richard's Pl SW3 ... 257 B4
Richard St 10 E1 ... 96 B1
Richard Thornton Ho
SW19 ... 179 C1
Richbell Pl WC1 ... 240 C4
Richborne Terr
SW8 ... 138 B5 270 D4
Richborough Ho 14 E5 ... 74 B4
10 SE15 ... 140 C6
Richborough Rd NW2 ... 69 A4
Richens Cl TW3 ... 130 B3
Riches Rd IG1 ... 79 A6
Richfield Ct 4 BR3 ... 185 B2
Richfield Rd WD23 ... 8 A4
Richford Gate W6 ... 112 C3
Richford Rd E15 ... 98 D6
Richford St W6 ... 112 C3
Richings Ho BR5 ... 190 A2
Rich La SW5 ... 255 C2
Richland Ho 4 SE15 ... 140 A4
Richlands Ave KT17 ... 216 A4
Richman Ho 10 SE8 ... 119 B1
Richmond Adult & Com Coll
TW9 ... 131 D1
Richmond Ave
N1 ... 94 B6 233 D6
NW10 ... 68 C2
Chingford E4 ... 36 B5
Feltham TW14 ... 149 C5
Hillingdon UB10 ... 60 D2
Wimbledon SW20 ... 179 A2
Richmond Bldgs W1 ... 239 C1
Richmond Bridge TW1 ... 153 D5
Richmond Bridge Mans 1
TW1 ... 153 D5
Richmond Circus TW9 ... 132 A1
Richmond Cl E17 ... 53 B3
Borehamwood WD6 ... 11 B6
Richmond Coll
W8 ... 113 D3 255 D6
Richmond TW10 ... 154 A4
Richmond Cres
N1 ... 94 C6 234 A6
Chingford E4 ... 36 B5
Edmonton N9 ... 18 A3
Richmond Ct BR1 ... 187 B3
SW1 ... 247 D1
12 Kingston KT2 ... 176 C3
Mitcham CR4 ... 202 B6
Wembley HA9 ... 66 B6
Wimbledon SW20 ... 178 B1
Richmond Dr TW17 ... 193 B3
Richmond Gdns NW4 ... 46 A4
Harrow HA3 ... 24 D3
Richmond Gn CR0 ... 220 A5
Richmond Gr N1 ... 72 D1
Surbiton KT5 ... 198 B3
Richmond Hill TW10 ... 154 A5
Richmond Hill Ct 5
TW10 ... 154 A5
Richmond Ho NW1 ... 231 D3
SE17 ... 262 C2
12 Forest Hill SE26 ... 162 A1
Richmond Ho(Annexe of
Rectory Sch) TW12 ... 173 B5
Richmond International Bsns
Ctr 9 TW9 ... 132 B1
Richmond Mans SW5 ... 255 C2
Putney SW15 ... 135 A2
14 Twickenham TW1 ... 153 D5
Richmond Mews W1 ... 239 C1
Richmond Park★
TW10 ... 155 A3
Richmond Park Rd
Kingston KT2 ... 176 A3
Mortlake SW14 ... 133 B1
Richmond Pk IG10 ... 21 D4
Richmond Pl SE18 ... 123 A2
Richmond Rd E11 ... 76 B6
E7 ... 77 B3
E8 ... 74 A1
N15 ... 51 C3
N2 ... 30 A1
W5 ... 110 A4
Bowes Park N11 ... 32 A4
Chingford E4 ... 20 B3
Ilford IG1 ... 79 A5
Isleworth TW7 ... 131 A2
Kingston KT2 ... 176 A4
New Barnet EN5 ... 14 A6
Thornton Heath CR7 ... 204 D5
Twickenham TW1 ... 153 C4
Wallington CR0 ... 220 A5
Wimbledon SW20 ... 178 B2
Richmond St E13 ... 99 A5
Richmond Sta TW9 ... 132 A1
Richmond Terr
SW1 ... 116 A4 250 A2
Richmond upon Thames Coll
TW2 ... 152 C4
Richmond Way
W12,W14 ... 112 D4
Wanstead E11 ... 77 A6
Richmount Gdns SE3 ... 143 A2
Rich St E14 ... 119 B6
Rickard Cl NW4 ... 46 A5
Streatham SW2 ... 160 C3
Rickards Cl KT6 ... 214 A6
Rickett St SW6 ... 265 B6
Rickman Ho 26 E2 ... 96 C3
Rickman St 25 E1 ... 96 C3
Rickmansworth Rd HA5 ... 22 C1
Rick Roberts Way E15 ... 98 B5
Rickthorne Rd 6 N19 ... 72 A6
Rickyard Path SE9 ... 144 A1
Riddell Ct SE1 ... 263 C2
Ridding La UB6 ... 64 D3
Riddons Rd SE12 ... 187 C6
Rideout St SE18 ... 122 B2
Rider Cl DA15 ... 167 C5
Ride The Brentford TW8 ... 109 C1
Enfield EN3 ... 6 D2
Ridgdale St E3 ... 97 D5
Ridge Ave N21 ... 17 B4
Ridgebrook Rd SE3,SE9 ... 143 D2
Ridge Cl NW4 ... 28 D1
NW9 ... 45 B5
SE28 ... 123 B4
Ridge Crest EN2 ... 4 B4
Ridge Hill NW11 ... 47 A1
Ridge Ho 4 KT2 ... 176 D3
Ridgemead Cl N13,N14 ... 16 A2
Ridgemont Gdns HA8 ... 27 A6
Ridgemount Ave CR0 ... 222 D6
Ridgemount Cl SE20 ... 184 B3
Ridgemount Gdns EN2 ... 4 D3
Ridgeon Ct N22 ... 32 B4
Ridge Rd N8 ... 50 B3
NW2 ... 69 B5
Cheam SM3 ... 201 B1
Edmonton N21 ... 17 B3
Mitcham CR4 ... 181 B3
Ridges The E4 ... 35 C6
Ridge Terr N21 ... 17 A4
Ridge The DA5 ... 169 B4
Barnet EN5 ... 13 B6
Orpington BR6 ... 227 B6
Surbiton KT5 ... 198 C4
Twickenham TW2 ... 152 B4
Ridgeview Cl EN5 ... 12 D5
Ridgeview Rd N20 ... 14 A1
Ridgeway BR2 ... 225 A6
11 Richmond TW10 ... 154 A5
Walton-on-T KT12 ... 193 D1
Woodford IG8 ... 37 C6
Ridge Way
Feltham TW13 ... 151 A1
7 West Norwood SE19 ... 183 C4
Ridgeway Ave EN4 ... 14 D5
Ridgeway Cres BR6 ... 227 C5
Ridgeway Crescent Gdns
BR6 ... 227 C5
Ridgeway Ct HA5 ... 23 C3
Ridgeway Dr BR1 ... 187 B6
Acton W3 ... 110 C3
Ridgeway E DA15 ... 167 D6
Ridgeway Gdns N6 ... 49 C2
Redbridge IG4 ... 56 A4
Ridgeway Rd TW7 ... 130 C4
Ridgeway Rd N TW7 ... 130 C5
Ridgeway The N11 ... 30 D6
N3 ... 29 D3
NW11 ... 47 B1
NW7 ... 28 B6
NW9 ... 45 B5
Acton W3 ... 110 C3
Chingford E4 ... 20 A3
Enfield EN2 ... 4 B5
Harrow HA2 ... 41 B4
Harrow HA2 ... 41 D3
Harrow HA3 ... 43 C3
Palmers Green N14 ... 16 A2
Ruislip HA4 ... 40 A2
Stanmore HA7 ... 25 C4
Wallington CR0 ... 220 B5
Ridgeway W DA15 ... 167 C6
Ridgeway Wlk UB5 ... 63 A2
Ridgewell Cl N1 ... 235 B6
Dagenham RM10 ... 103 D6
Forest Hill SE26 ... 185 B6
Ridgmount Gdns
WC1 ... 93 D2 239 C4
Ridgmount Pl WC1 ... 239 C4
Ridgmount Rd SW18 ... 157 D6
Ridgmount St
WC1 ... 93 D2 239 C4
Ridgway SW19,SW20 ... 178 D4
Ridgway Ct SW19 ... 178 D4
Ridgway Gdns SW19 ... 178 D3
Ridgway Pl SW19 ... 179 A4
Ridgway Rd SW9 ... 138 D2
Ridgway The SM2 ... 218 B1
Ridgwell Rd E16 ... 99 C2
Riding House St
W1 ... 93 C2 239 A3
Ridings Ave N21 ... 17 A6
Ridings Cl N6 ... 49 C2
Ridings The EN4 ... 14 B4
Ealing W5 ... 88 B3
Sunbury TW16 ... 172 A2
Surbiton KT5 ... 198 C4
Riding The NW11 ... 47 B2
Ridler Rd EN1 ... 5 C5
Ridley Ave W13 ... 109 B3
Ridley Cl IG11 ... 79 D1
Ridley Ct SW16 ... 182 A4
Ridley Ho 14 SW11 ... 136 C2
Ridley Rd DA16 ... 146 B4
E7 ... 77 C4
E8 ... 73 D3
NW10 ... 90 A5
Beckenham BR2 ... 208 D6
Merton SW19 ... 179 D3
Ridley Road Mkt E8 ... 73 D3
Ridsdale Rd SE20 ... 184 B2
Riefield Rd SE9 ... 167 A6
Riesco Dr CR0 ... 222 C2
Riffel Rd NW2 ... 68 C3
Rifle Ct SE11 ... 138 C6
Rifle Pl W11 ... 112 D5
Rifle Range La HA1 ... 42 D1
Rifle St E14 ... 97 D2
Rigault Rd SW6 ... 135 A3
Rigby Cl CR0 ... 220 C5
Rigby La UB3 ... 105 A4
Rigby Mews IG1 ... 78 C6
Rigby Pl EN3 ... 7 C6
Rigden St E14 ... 97 D1
Rigeley Rd NW10 ... 90 A4
Rigg App E10 ... 53 A1
Rigge Pl SW4 ... 137 D1
Rigg Ho 2 SW4 ... 160 A4
Riggindale Rd SW16 ... 181 D6
Rigold Ho 6 SE5 ... 139 C3
Rigo Ho 9 E1 ... 96 D2
Riley Ho SW10 ... 266 C5
9 Bow E3 ... 97 C3
1 Streatham SW4 ... 159 D4
Riley Rd SE1 ... 117 D3 263 C6
Enfield EN3 ... 6 C5
Riley St SW10 ... 136 B5 266 C4
Rill Ho 24 SE5 ... 139 C5
Rimini Ct SW12 ... 158 D3
Rinaldo Rd SW12 ... 159 B4
Ring Cl BR1 ... 187 B3
Ringcroft St N7 ... 72 C3
Ring Cross Prim Sch N7 ... 72 B3
Ringer's Rd BR1 ... 209 A6
Ringford Ho SW18 ... 157 B6
Ringford Rd SW18 ... 157 C5
Ring Ho 14 E1 ... 118 C6
Ringlet Cl E16 ... 99 B2
Ringlewell Cl EN1 ... 6 B3
Ringmer Ave
SW6 ... 135 A4 264 B1
Ringmer Gdns 2 N19 ... 72 A6
Ringmer Ho 15 SE22 ... 139 C2
Ringmer Pl N21 ... 17 B6
Ringmer Way BR1 ... 210 B4
Ringmore Rise SE23 ... 162 B4
Ringsfield Ho SE17 ... 262 B1
Ringslade Rd N22 ... 32 B1
Ringstead Ct SM1 ... 218 B3
Ringstead Rd
Catford SE6 ... 163 D4
Ringstead Rd *continued*
Sutton SM1 ... 218 B3
Ring Way N11 ... 31 C4
Ringway UB2 ... 107 A1
Ringwold Cl BR3 ... 185 A3
Ringwood Ave N2 ... 48 D6
Thornton Heath CR0 ... 204 A2
Ringwood Cl HA5 ... 40 C6
Ringwood Gdns 18 E14 ... 119 C2
Roehampton SW15 ... 156 A3
Ringwood Rd E17 ... 53 B3
Ringwood Way
Hampton TW12 ... 173 C6
Southgate N21 ... 16 D4
Ripley Cl BR1 ... 210 B4
New Addington CR0 ... 224 A2
Ripley Ct 1 CR4 ... 180 B1
Ripley Gdns
Mortlake SW14 ... 133 B2
Sutton SM1 ... 218 A4
Ripley Ho SW1 ... 269 A6
13 Kingston KT2 ... 176 D4
Mortlake SW14 ... 133 C2
5 Penge SE26 ... 184 B5
Ripley Mews E11 ... 54 C3
Ripley Rd
Belvedere DA17 ... 125 C2
Enfield EN2 ... 5 A4
Hampton TW12 ... 173 C3
Ilford IG3 ... 79 D6
Newham E16 ... 99 C1
Riplington Ct SW15 ... 156 B4
Ripon Cl UB5 ... 63 C2
Ripon Gdns
Chessington KT9 ... 213 D3
Redbridge IG1 ... 56 A2
Ripon Rd N17 ... 51 B6
SE18 ... 144 D6
Edmonton N9 ... 18 B4
Ripon Way WD6 ... 11 B6
Rippersley Rd DA16 ... 146 A4
Ripple Ct 10 IG11 ... 101 B6
Ripple Rd Barking IG11 ... 101 C6
Barking RM9 ... 102 A6
Rippleside Commercial Est
IG11 ... 102 C5
Ripplevale Gr N1 ... 72 B1
Rippolson Rd SE18 ... 123 D1
Ripston Rd TW15 ... 171 B5
Risborough SE17 ... 262 A4
Risborough Cl 4 N10 ... 49 B6
Risborough Dr KT4 ... 200 A2
Risborough Ho NW8 ... 237 B6
Risborough St SE1 ... 251 D2
Risdon Ho 20 SE16 ... 118 C4
Risdon St 21 SE16 ... 118 C4
Risedale Rd DA7 ... 147 D2
Riseholme Ho 14 SE22 ... 139 C2
Riseldine Rd SE23 ... 163 A5
Rise The NW10 ... 67 B5
NW7 ... 27 D4
Borehamwood WD6 ... 10 B6
Buckhurst Hill IG9 ... 21 D4
Chingford, Chingford Green
E4 ... 20 C3
Edgware HA8 ... 26 D5
Edmonton N13 ... 32 C6
Greenford HA0,UB6 ... 65 A3
Hillingdon UB10 ... 82 B5
Sidcup DA5 ... 168 C4
Wanstead E11 ... 55 A4
Risinghill St N1 ... 234 A4
Risingholme Cl HA3 ... 24 C2
Risingholme Rd HA3 ... 24 C1
Risings The E17 ... 54 B5
Rising Sun Ct EC1 ... 241 D3
Risley Ave N17 ... 33 B2
Risley Avenue Prim Sch
N17 ... 33 C2
Risley Ho 7 E9 ... 74 D2
Rita Rd SW8 ... 138 B5 270 C4
Ritches Rd N15 ... 51 A4
Ritchie Ho N19 ... 49 D2
8 SE16 ... 118 C3
11 South Bromley E14 ... 98 B1
Ritchie Rd CR0 ... 206 B3
Ritchie St N1 ... 94 C5 234 B4
Ritchings Ave E17 ... 53 A5
Ritherdon Rd SW17 ... 159 B2
Ritson Ho N1 ... 233 C5
Ritson Rd E8 ... 74 A2
Ritter St SE18 ... 144 C6
Ritz Par W5 ... 88 B3
Rivaz Pl E9 ... 74 C2
Riven Ct 10 W2 ... 91 D1
Rivenhall Gdns E11,E18 ... 54 D5
Riverains The SW11 ... 266 C1
River Ave Southgate N13 ... 16 D2
Thames Ditton KT7 ... 197 A2
Riverbank KT8 ... 196 C5
River Bank Edmonton N21 ... 17 A4
Thames Ditton KT7 ... 196 D4
Riverbank Rd BR1 ... 165 A1
Riverbank Way TW8 ... 131 C6
River Barge Cl E14 ... 120 A4
River Brent Bsns Pk
W7 ... 108 C3
River Cl Ruislip HA4 ... 39 D3
Southall UB2 ... 108 A4
Wanstead E11 ... 55 C3
River Cotts BR5 ... 190 C1
Rivercourt Rd W6 ... 112 B1
River Crane Way TW13 ... 151 B2
River Ct SE1 ... 251 C3
Kingston KT6 ... 197 D4
Wanstead E11 ... 55 C3
Riverdale Dr SW18 ... 157 D3
Riverdale Gdns TW1 ... 153 C6
Riverdale Rd SE18 ... 123 D1
Erith DA8 ... 125 D1
Riverdale Rd *continued*
Feltham TW13 ... 173 B6
Sidcup DA5 ... 169 B5
Twickenham TW1 ... 153 C5
Riverdene HA8 ... 11 A1
Riverdene Rd IG1 ... 78 D5
Riverfleet WC1 ... 233 B2
Riverford Ho 28 W2 ... 91 C2
River Front EN1 ... 5 C2
River Gdns
Carshalton SM5 ... 219 A5
Feltham TW14 ... 150 B6
River Gdns Bsns Ctr
TW14 ... 128 B1
River Grove Pk BR3 ... 185 B2
Riverhead Cl E17 ... 34 D1
River Ho Barnes SW13 ... 133 C3
1 Forest Hill SE26 ... 162 B1
Riverholme KT8 ... 196 C6
Riverhope Mans SE18 ... 122 A3
Riverine Lo HA7 ... 25 A5
River La TW10 ... 153 D3
Rivermead
East Molesey KT8 ... 196 A6
Kingston KT6 ... 197 D4
Rivermead Cl TW11 ... 175 B5
Rivermead Ct Ealing UB6 ... 87 A4
Fulham SW6 ... 135 B2
Rivermead Ho E9 ... 75 A3
Sunbury TW16 ... 194 C6
Rivermeads Ave TW13,
TW2 ... 151 D1
River Mount KT12 ... 193 D2
Rivernook Cl KT12 ... 194 C4
River Park Gdns BR2 ... 186 B3
River Park Rd N22 ... 32 B1
River Pl N1 ... 73 A1
River Rd Barking IG11 ... 101 D3
Buckhurst Hill IG9 ... 21 D3
River Reach TW11 ... 175 C5
River Road Bsns Pk
IG11 ... 101 D4
Riversdale Gdns N22 ... 32 C2
Riversdale Prim Sch
SW18 ... 157 C3
Riversdale Rd N5 ... 73 A5
Thames Ditton KT7 ... 197 A3
Riversdene N5 ... 73 A5
Riversfield Rd EN1 ... 5 C2
Rivers Ho 11 TW8 ... 110 C1
Riverside NW4 ... 46 B2
SW11 ... 267 B4
WC1 ... 233 B2
Forest Hill SE6 ... 185 B6
Greenwich SE7 ... 121 B3
Oatlands Park TW17 ... 193 C2
Sunbury TW16 ... 172 D1
Twickenham TW1 ... 153 B3
Riverside Apartments
N13 ... 32 B5
Riverside Ave KT8 ... 196 B4
Riverside Bsns Ctr
SW18 ... 157 D3
Riverside Bsns Pk
SW19 ... 180 A2
Riverside Cl BR5 ... 190 C1
E5 ... 74 C6
Ealing W7 ... 86 C3
Hackbridge SM6 ... 219 B5
Kingston KT1 ... 197 D5
Riverside Cotts IG11 ... 101 B5
Riverside Ct SE12 ... 142 D1
SW8 ... 269 D6
Chingford E4 ... 19 D5
Richmond TW11 ... 175 C5
Riverside Dr NW11 ... 47 A3
Chiswick W4 ... 133 C4
Mitcham CR4 ... 202 C4
Richmond TW10 ... 153 B1
Riverside Est EN3 ... 19 A5
Riverside Gdns N3 ... 47 A6
W6 ... 112 B1
Enfield EN2 ... 5 A3
Wembley HA0 ... 88 A5
Riverside Ho N12 ... 29 D6
Morden SW19 ... 202 A5
Riverside Ind Est IG11 ... 102 A4
Riverside Mans 4 E1 ... 118 C5
Riverside Pl N11 ... 15 C1
Stanwell TW19 ... 148 A5
Riverside Prim Sch
SE16 ... 118 A4
Riverside Rd DA14 ... 169 A2
E15 ... 98 A5
N15 ... 52 A3
Stanwell TW19 ... 148 A5
Wandsworth SW17,SW19 ... 158 A1
Riverside The KT8 ... 196 B6
Riverside West SW18 ... 135 D1
Riverside Wlk
Isleworth TW7 ... 130 C2
3 West Wickham BR4 ... 207 D1
Riverside Works IG11 ... 78 D1
Riverside Workshops
SE1 ... 252 B4
River St EC1 ... 94 C4 234 A2
Riverstone Ct KT2 ... 176 B2
Riverston Sch SE12 ... 165 A6
River Terr W6 ... 112 C1
Riverton Cl W9 ... 91 B4
Riverview TW17 ... 193 B2
River View EN2 ... 5 A2
Riverview CE Sch KT19 ... 215 B4
Riverview Ct 14 DA17 ... 125 C1
Riverview Gdns
Barnes SW13 ... 134 B6
Twickenham TW1 ... 152 D2
Riverview Gr W4 ... 132 D6
Riverview Hts SE18 ... 144 D5
Riverview Lo NW9 ... 67 B6

Riverview Pk SE6 ....163 C2
Riverview Prim Sch
KT19 ....215 B4
Riverview Rd
Chiswick W4 ....132 C6
West Ewell KT19 ......215 B4
River Way SE10 ....120 D3
Riverway N13 ....32 C6
River Way
Twickenham TW13,TW2 ..151 D2
West Ewell KT19 ......215 C3
River Wlk KT12 ....194 A3
Riverwood La BR7 ....189 B2
Rivet Ho SE1 ....263 D2
Rivington Ave IG8 ....37 D1
Rivington Cres NW7 ......27 D3
Rivington Ct NW10 ....90 A6
Rivington Pl EC2 ....95 C4
Rivington St EC2 ....95 C4
Rivington Wlk 4 E8 ......96 A6
Rivulet Rd N17 ....33 A3
Rixon Ho SE18 ....144 D6
Rixon St N7 ....72 C5
Rixsen Rd E12 ....78 A3
Roach Rd E3 ....75 C1
Roach Works E3 ....75 C1
Roads Pl N19 ....72 A6
Roan Ind Est CR4 ......180 D2
Roan St SE10 ....142 A6
Robarts Cl HA5 ....40 B4
Robbins Hall EN3 ....18 D5
Robb Rd HA7 ....25 A4
Robert Adam St W1 .....238 A2
Roberta St E2 ....96 A4
Robert Bell Ho 2 SE16 .118 A2
Robert Blair Prim Sch
N7 ....72 A2
Robert Browning Prim Sch
SE17 ....117 B1 262 C2
Robert Burns Ho N17 ....34 B3
Robert Cl W9 ....236 B5
Robert Clack Lower Sch
RM8 ....81 B6
Robert Clack Upper Sch
RM8 ....59 C1
Robert Dashwood Way
SE17 ....262 A3
Robert Gentry Ho W14 ..254 B1
Robert Gerard Ho 7
SE27 ....183 B6
Robert Jones Ho 3
SE16 ....118 A2
Robert Keen Cl 17 SE15 .140 A4
Robert Lowe Cl SE14 ...140 D5
Roberton Dr BR1 ....187 C2
Robert Owen Ho 8 E2 ....95 D4
Fulham SW6 ....134 D4
Robert Owen Lo 6 E5 ....74 B4
Robertsbridge Rd SM5 ..202 B2
Roberts Cl SE9 ....167 B3
Cheam SM3 ....216 D1
Yiewsley UB7 ....104 A5
Roberts Ct N1 ....234 D5
NW10 ....67 C2
Chessington KT9 ......213 D3
Ealing W5 ....88 A1
Penge SE20 ....184 C2
Roberts Ho 2 N11 ....31 B5
10 SE18 ....144 A4
5 West Norwood SE27 ..160 D1
Roberts Mews SW1 .....258 A5
Robertson Ho 11 SE10 ..142 A4
4 SE18 ....144 B4
1 Upper Tooting SW17 ..180 C5
Robertson Rd E15 ....98 A6
Robertson St SW8 ......137 B3
Robert's Pl EC1 ....241 B6
Roberts Rd NW7 ....29 A4
Belvedere DA17 ....125 C1
Chingford, Highams Park
E17 ....35 D2
Robert St E16 ....122 D5
NW1 ....93 B4 231 D1
SE18 ....123 B2
WC2 ....250 B5
Croydon CR0 ....221 A5
Robert Sutton Ho 20 E1 ..96 C1
Robeson St 8 E3 ....97 B2
Robina Cl DA6 ....146 D1
Northwood HA6 ....22 A2
Robin Cl NW7 ....11 C1
Hampton TW12 ....173 A5
Robin Cres E6 ....99 D2
Robin Ct 13 E14 ....120 A3
Wallington SM6 ....219 C2
Robin Gr N6 ....71 A6
Brentford TW8 ....131 C6
Harrow HA3 ....44 B3
Robin Hill Dr BR7 .....188 A4
Robin Ho NW8 ....230 A3
Robin Hood SW15 ......155 C1
Robinhood Cl CR4 ......203 C6
Robin Hood Ct SM1 ....217 C3
Robin Hood Dr HA3 .....24 D3
Robin Hood Gdns 12
E14 ....120 A6
Robin Hood Inf Sch
SM1 ....217 C3
Robin Hood Jun Sch
SM1 ....217 C3
Robin Hood La E14 ....120 A6
Robinhood La CR4 .....203 C6
Robin Hood La
Bexley DA6 ....169 A6
Kingston SW15 ....177 C6
Sutton SM1 ....217 C2
Robin Hood Prim Sch
SW15 ....177 C5
Robin Hood Way UB6 ....64 D2

Robin Hood Way (Kingston
By Pass) KT2,SW15,
SW20 ....177 C5
Robinia Cl SE20 ......184 A2
Robinia Cres E10 ....75 D6
Robinscroft Mews SE10 .141 D4
Robins Ct SE12 ....165 C1
Robin's Ct SW4 ....160 A5
Robin's Ct SW10 ......154 A5
Robin's Ct BR3 ....186 B1
Robinsfield Inf Sch
NW8 ....92 C5 230 A4
Robins Gr BR4 ....225 A5
Robinson Cres WD23 .....8 A3
Robinson Ct N1 ....234 D6
4 Richmond TW9 ......132 B1
Robinson Ho 11 E14 .....97 C2
4 W10 ....90 D1
Robinson Rd E2 ....96 C5
Dagenham RM10 ....81 C4
Mitcham SW19 ....180 C4
Robinson's Cl W13 ......87 A2
Robinson St SW3 ......267 C6
Robinwood Gr UB8 ......82 B3
Robinwood Pl SW15 ....177 B6
Robsart St SW9 ....138 C3
Robson Ave NW10 ....68 A1
Robson Cl E6 ....100 A1
Enfield EN2 ....4 D3
Robson Ct N12 ....30 A5
Robson Rd SE21,SE27 ..161 A1
Roby Ho EC1 ....242 A6
Roch Ave HA8 ....26 B1
Rochdale SE19 ....183 C4
Rochdale Rd E10 ....53 C2
SE2 ....124 B2
Rochdale Way 4 SE8 ...141 C5
Roche Ho 15 E14 ......119 B6
Rochelle Cl SW11 .....136 B1
Rochelle Ct 14 E1 ......96 C1
Beckenham BR3 ....185 D3
Rochelle St 31 E2 ......95 D4
Rochemont Wlk 2 E8 ....96 A6
Roche Rd SW16 ....182 C1
Rochester Ave BR1 ....187 B1
E13 ....99 C6
Rochester Cl 1 DA15 ..168 B5
SE3 ....143 C2
Enfield EN1 ....5 C4
Streatham SW16 ......182 A3
Rochester Ct 1 E2 ......96 B3
7 NW1 ....71 C1
NW9 ....45 B4
South Norwood SE25 ..184 A1
Rochester Dr DA5 .....169 C5
Pinner HA5 ....40 D4
Rochester Gdns
Redbridge IG1 ....56 B2
South Croydon CR0 ...221 C5
Rochester Ho SE1 .....252 D1
18 SE15 ....140 C6
Rochester Mews NW1 ...71 C1
Rochester Par TW13 ...150 A1
Rochester Pl 1 NW1 ....71 C1
Rochester Rd NW1 ......71 C2
Carshalton SM5 ......218 D4
Northwood HA6 ....39 C6
Rochester Row
SW1 ....115 C2 259 B4
Rochester Sq NW1 ......71 C1
Rochester St SW1 .....259 C5
Rochester Terr NW1 ....71 C2
Rochester Way SE3,SE9 .143 D2
SE9 ....144 C2
Rochester Wlk SE1 ....252 C4
Roche Wlk SM5 ....202 B3
Rochford N17 ....33 C1
Rochford Ave RM6 ......58 C4
Rochford Cl 2 E6 ....99 D5
Rochford Way CR0 .....204 A3
Rochford Wlk 3 E8 ......74 A1
Rochfort Ho 4 SE8 ....119 B1
Rock Ave 13 SW14 .....133 B2
Rockbourne Rd SE23 ...162 D3
Rock Cl CR4 ....180 B1
Rockell's Pl SE22 .....162 B5
Rockfield Ho 2 NW4 ....46 D5
SE10 ....142 A6
Rockford Ave UB6 ......87 B5
Rock Gdns RM10 ....81 D3
Rock Grove Way SE16 ..118 A2
Rockhall Rd NW2 ....68 D4
Rockhampton Cl 4
SE27 ....182 C6
Rockhampton Rd
South Croydon CR2 ...221 C2
West Norwood SE27,
SW16 ....182 C6
Rock Hill SE19 ....183 D6
Rockingham Cl SW15 ...133 D1
Rockingham St 15 BR3 ..185 B1
Rockingham Gate WD23 ...8 A3
Rockingham St
SE1 ....117 A3 262 A6
Rockland Rd SW15 .....135 A1
Rocklands N3 ....29 B3
Rocklands Dr HA7 ......25 C1
Rockley Ct 9 W14 .....112 D4
Rockley Rd W14 ....112 D4
Rockliffe Manor Prim Sch
SE18 ....145 D6
Rockmount Prim Sch
SE19 ....183 B4
Rockmount Rd
SE18,SE2 ....123 D1
South Norwood SE19 ..183 B4
Rocks La SW13 ....134 A2
Rock St N4 ....72 C6
Rockstraw Ho 5 NW3 ...70 D1

Rockware Ave UB6 ......86 C6
Rockways EN5 ....11 D5
Rockwell Gdns SE19 ...183 C6
Rockwell Rd RM10 ......81 D3
Rockwood Ct N16 ....52 A2
Rocliffe St N1 ....94 D5 234 D3
Rocombe Cres SE23 ...162 C4
Rocque Ho SW6 ....264 C4
Rocque La 3 SE3 ......142 D2
Rodborough Rd NW11 ...47 C1
Rodd Est TW7 ....131 A1
Roden Gdns CR0 ......205 C3
Rodenhurst Ct SW4 ....159 D6
Rodenhurst Rd SW4 ...159 D5
Roden St N7 ....72 B5
Ilford IG1 ....78 C5
Roderick Ho 3 SE16 ...118 C2
Roderick Rd NW3 ......70 D4
Rodgers Cl WD6 ....9 D5
Rodgers Ho 4 SW4 ....159 D4
Rodin Ct N1 ....234 C5
Roding Ct 6 W12 ......111 C4
Roding Ho N1 ....234 A5
Roding Hospl IG4 ......55 B6
Roding La N IG8 ....21 D3
Roding La N IG8 ....37 D1
Roding La S IG4 ....55 D5
Roding Lo IG1 ....55 D3
Roding Mews E1 ....118 A5
Roding Prim Sch RM8 ...80 C3
Roding Rd E5 ....75 A3
Newham E6 ....100 D2
Rodings Ct E4 ....36 B5
Rodings The Barnet EN5 ..1 A1
6 Woodford IG8 ....37 C4
Roding Valley Sta IG9 ...37 B6
Roding View IG11 ......21 D3

Rodmarton St
W1 ....92 D2 237 D3
Rodmell WC1 ....233 B1
Rodmell Cl UB4 ....85 A3
Rodmell Slope N12 ....29 B5
Rodmere St SE10 ......120 C1
Rodmill La SW2 ....160 A4
Rodney Cl
New Malden KT3 ....199 C4
Pinner HA5 ....41 A2
Thornton Heath CR0 ..204 D1
Walton-on-T KT12 ....194 C1
Rodney Ct NW8 ....236 B6
Rodney Gdns Hayes BR4 .225 A4
Pinner HA5 ....40 C4
Rodney Ho 4 E14 .....119 D2
N1 ....233 D3
W11 ....245 A6
Rodney Pl E17 ....35 B1
SE17 ....117 A2 262 B4
Merton SW19 ....180 A2
Rodney Rd SE17 ..117 B2 262 C3
Mitcham CR4 ....202 C6
New Malden KT3 .....199 C4
Twickenham TW4 .....151 C4
Walton-on-T KT12 ....194 C1
Wanstead E11 ....55 B5
Rodney St N1 ....94 B5 233 D3
Rodway Rd BR1 ....187 B2
Putney SW15 ....156 A4
Rodwell Cl 2 HA4 ......40 C1
Rodwell Rd SE22 .....161 D5
Roe 5 NW9 ....27 D2
Roebourne Way E16 ...122 C4
Roebuck Cl
Feltham TW13 ....172 B6
Tottenham N17 ....33 D4
Roebuck Ct Chingford E4 ..36 A3
2 New Malden KT3 ....199 C4
Roebuck La IG9 ....21 C3
Roebuck Rd KT9 ......214 C3
Roedean Ave EN3 ......6 C5
Roedean Cl EN3 ....6 C4
Roedean Cres SW15 ...155 C6
Roe End NW9 ....45 A5
Roe Gn NW9 ....45 A4
Roe Green Jun & Inf Schs
NW9 ....44 D5
Roe La NW9 ....45 A5
Roe Way SM6 ....220 A2
Roffey St E14 ....120 A4
Roffey Sch E14 ....120 A4
Roger Ascham Prim Sch
E17 ....35 B2
Roger Dowley Ct 8 E2 ...96 C5
Roger's Almshouses 2
SW9 ....138 B1
Rogers Est 28 E2 ......96 C4
Rogers Gdns RM10 .....81 C3
Rogers Ho SW1 ....259 D4
9 Dagenham RM10 .....81 C5
Rogers Rd E16 ....98 D1
Dagenham RM10 ....81 C3
Upper Tooting SW17 ..180 C6
Roger St WC1 ....94 B3 240 D5
Roger Stone Ct NW10 ...67 B6
Rogers Wlk N12 ....13 D1
Rojack Rd SE23 ....162 D3

Rokeby Gdns IG8 ....37 A2
Rokeby Ho WC1 ....240 C5
9 Balham SW12 ....159 B4
Rokeby Pl SW20 ......178 B3
Rokeby Rd SE4 ....141 B3
Rokeby Sch E15 ....76 B1
Kingston KT2 ....177 A3
Rokeby St E15 ....98 C6
Rokeland Ho SE4 .....141 A1
Rokell Ho BR3 ....185 D5
Roker Park Ave UB10 ...60 A4
Rokesby Cl DA16 .....145 B3
Rokesby Pl HA0 ....65 D3
Rokesly Ave N8 ....50 A4
Rokesly Jun & Inf Schs
N8 ....50 A4
Roland Ct SE19 ......183 D2
Roland Gdns
SW7 ....114 A1 256 B2
Roland Mews 1 E1 ......96 D2
Roland Rd E17 ....54 B5
Roland Way SE17 .....262 D1
SW7 ....114 A1 256 B2
Worcester Park KT4 ..215 B6
Roles Gr RM6 ....59 A5
Rolfe Cl EN4 ....2 C1
Rolfe Ho N11 ....30 D6
Rolinsden Way BR2 ...225 D4
Rolland Ho W7 ....86 C2
Rollesby Rd KT19,KT9 ..214 C2
Rollesby Way SE28 ....102 C1
Rolleston Ave BR5 ....210 D3
Rolleston Cl BR5 .....210 D2
Rolleston Rd CR2 .....221 B1
Roll Gdns IG2 ....56 C4
Rollins St SE15 ....140 C6
Rollit Cres TW3 ......151 C6
Rollit Ho N7 ....72 C3
Rollit St N7 ....72 C3
Rollo Ct SW11 ....268 C1
Rolls Bldgs EC4 .....241 B2
Rollscourt Ave SE24 ..161 A6
Rolls Park Ave E4 .....35 C5
Rolls Park Rd E4 ......35 D5
Rolls Pas EC4 ....241 A2
Rolls Rd SE1 ....118 A1 263 D2
Rolt St SE8 ....141 A6
Rolvenden Gdns BR1 ..187 D3
Rolvenden Pl N17 ......34 A2
Roman Cl W3 ....110 D4
Feltham TW14 ....150 C6
Romanfield Rd SW2 ...160 B4
Romanhurst Ave BR2 ..208 C5
Romanhurst Gdns BR2,
BR3 ....208 C5
Roman Ind Est CR0 ...205 C2
Roman Rd E2,E3 ....96 D5
E3 ....97 B6
N10 ....31 B3
N12 ....30 C2
W4 ....111 D2
Ilford IG1 ....78 D2
Newham E6 ....100 A3
Roman Rise SE19 .....183 B4
Roman Road Prim Sch
E6 ....99 D3
Roman Sq SE28 ......124 A5
Roman Square Mkt 1
E3 ....97 B5
Roman Way N7 ....72 B2
4 SE15 ....140 C5
Croydon CR0 ....220 D6
Enfield EN1 ....17 D6
Romany Gdns E17 ......35 A2
Cheam SM3 ....201 C2
Romany Ho 8 N9 ......18 A1
Romany Prospect SE19 ..183 B4
Romany Rise BR5 .....211 A1
Roma Rd E17 ....53 A6
Roma Read Cl SW15 ...156 A4
Romayne Ho SW4 .....137 D2
Romberg Rd SW17 ....159 A1
Romborough Gdns
SE13 ....164 A6
Romborough Way SE13 .164 A6
Romeland WD6 ....9 C5
Romer Ho 9 SW2 .....160 B6
12 W10 ....91 B4
Romero Cl SW9 ......138 B2
Romero Sq SE7 ....143 C1
Romey Mews W1 ......238 A4
Romeyn Rd SW16 .....160 B1
Romford Ho 17 N1 .....73 B2
Romford Rd E15 ....76 D2
E7,E12 ....77 C3
Romford St E1 ....96 B2
Romilly Dr WD19 ......23 A6
Romilly Rd N4 ....72 C6
Romilly St W1 ....249 D6
Romily Ct SW6 ....135 A3
Rommany Ct SE27 ....183 B6
Rommany Rd SE27 ....183 B6
Romney Cl NW11 ......48 A1
7 SE14 ....140 C5
Ashford TW15 ....171 A5
Chessington KT9 ....214 A4
Harrow HA2 ....41 C2
Tottenham N17 ....34 B2
Romney Ct 9 NW3 .....70 C2
9 W12 ....112 C4
18 Northolt UB5 ......63 B4
Romney Dr Bromley BR1 .187 D3
Harrow HA2 ....41 C2
Romney Gdns DA7 ....147 B4
Romney Ho EN1 ......18 A6
Romney Par HA2 ......83 B5
Romney Rd SE10 .....142 B6
Hayes UB4 ....83 B5
New Malden KT3 .....199 B3
Romney Row NW2 ......68 D6

Romney St SW1 ..116 A3 260 A5
Romola Rd SE24,SW2 ..160 D3
Romsey Cl BR6 ....227 A4
Romsey Gdns RM9 .....102 C6
Romsey Rd
Dagenham RM9 ....102 C6
Ealing W13 ....109 A6
Romulus Ct 7 TW8 ....131 D5
Ronald Ave E15 ....98 C4
Ronald Cl BR3 ....207 B4
Ronald Ho SE9 ....143 C1
SW19 ....157 A3
Ronaldshay N4 ....50 C1
Ronald Rd BR1 ....187 A2
N5 ....72 C3
Ronaldstone Rd DA15 ..167 C5
Rona Rd NW3 ....71 A4
Ronart St HA3 ....42 D6
Rona Wlk 7 N1 ....73 B2
Rondu Rd NW2 ....69 A3
Ronelean Rd KT6 .....214 B5
Ron Leighton Way E6 ..100 A6
Ronver Lo E4 ....20 C1
Ronver Rd SE12 ......164 D3
Rood La EC3 ....117 C6 253 A6
Rookby Ct N21 ....16 D2
Rook Cl HA9 ....66 D5
Rookeries Cl TW13 ...150 C1
Rookery Cl NW9 ....45 C4
Rookery Cotts EN4 .....3 B2
Rookery Cres RM10 ....81 D1
Rookery Dr BR7 ......188 C2
Rookery La BR2 ......209 D3
Rookery Rd SW4 .....137 C1
Rookery Way NW9 .....45 D4
Rookes Heath High Sch
HA2 ....63 C3
Rooke Way SE10 ......120 D1
Rookfield Ave N10 .....49 C5
Rookfield Cl N10 ......49 C5
Rook Lo IG1 ....55 D3
Rooksmead Rd TW16 ..172 A1
Rooks Terr UB7 ....104 A4
Rookstone Rd SW17 ...180 D5
Rook Wlk E6 ....100 A1
Rookwood Ave
Wallington SM6 ......219 D4
West Barnes KT3 ....200 A5
Rookwood Gdns E4 .....20 D2
Rookwood Ho IG11 ...101 B5
Rookwood Rd N16 .....52 A2
Rootes Dr W10 ....90 D2
Ropemaker Rd SE16 ...119 A3
Ropemaker's Fields 7
E14 ....119 B6
Ropemaker St
EC2 ....95 B2 242 C4
Roper Ho 13 SE21 ....183 C6
7 Wembley HA0 ....88 A5
Roper La SE1 ....117 C4 253 B1
Ropers Ave E4 ....36 A5
Roper's Orchard SW3 ..267 A5
Roper St 1 SE9 ......166 C5
Ropers Wlk 13 SE24 ..160 C4
Roper Way CR4 ....181 A1
Ropery Bsns Est SE7 ..121 C2
Ropery St E3 ....97 B3
Rope St SE16 ....119 A3
Ropewalk Gdns 16 E1 ...96 A1
Rope Yard Rails SE18 ..122 D3
Ropley St 6 E2 ....96 A5
Rosa Alba Mews N5 ....73 A4
Rosa Ave TW15 ....170 C6
Rosalind Ct 6 IG11 ....80 A1
Rosalind Ho 25 N1 .....95 C5
Rosaline Rd
SW6 ....135 A5 264 B3
Rosaline Terr SW6 ...264 B3
Rosamond St SE26 ...162 B1
Rosamund Cl CR2 ....221 B4
Rosamun St UB2 .....107 A2
Rosa Parks Ho 8 SW9 .138 B3
Rosary Cl TW3,TW5 ...129 A3
Rosary Gdns
SW7 ....114 A2 256 B3
Ashford TW15 ....170 D6
Bushey WD23 ....8 C4
Rosary RC Inf Sch TW5 .129 C6
Rosary Sq SE1 ....129 C6
Rosary RC Jun Sch
TW5 ....129 C6
Rosary RC Prim Sch
NW3 ....70 C3
Rosaville Rd
SW6 ....135 B5 264 C3
Rosbury SW15 ....157 D4
Roscoe St EC1 ...95 A3 242 B5
Roscoff Cl HA8 ....27 A2
Roscommon Ho 2 NW3 ..70 B3
Roseacre Cl Ealing W13 ..87 B2
Littleton TW17 ......192 C4
Roseacre Lo EN3 ......6 C1
Roseacre Rd DA16 ...146 B2
Rose Alley EC2 ......243 B3
SE1 ....252 C4
Rose Ave Mitcham CR4 .180 C2
Morden SM4 ....202 A4
Woodford E18 ....37 B1
Rosebank SW6 ....134 C5
Penge SE20 ....184 B3
Rosebank Ave HA0 ....64 D4
Rose Bank Cl N12 .....30 C5
Rosebank Cl N11 .....175 A4
Rosebank Gdns E3 ....97 B5
1 W3 ....89 B1
Rosebank Gr E17 .....53 D5
W7 ....108 C4

Rosebank Villas E17 ...53 C5
Rosebank Way W3 ......89 B1
Rosebank Wlk NW1 .....71 C1
14 SE7 ....122 A2
Rose Bates Dr NW9 ....44 C5
Roseberry Gdns BR6 ..227 C5
N4 ....50 D3
Roseberry Pl E8 ....73 D2
Roseberry St SE16 ...118 B2
Roseberry Ave DA15 ..167 C4
E12 ....78 B2
EC1 ....94 C4 234 B1
Harrow HA2 ....63 B4
Kingston KT3 ....199 D6
South Norwood CR7 ..183 A1
Tottenham N17 ......34 A1
Roseberry Cl SM4 ....200 D3
Rosebery Ct EC1 .....241 A6
W1 ....248 C6
Chessington KT9 ....214 B3
Rosebery Gdns N8 .....50 A4
Ealing W13 ....87 A1
Sutton SM1 ....217 D4
Rosebery Ho 22 E2 ....96 C5
Rosebery Ind Pk N17 ...34 B1
Rosebery Mews N10 ...31 C1
Rosebery Rd N10 .....31 C1
SW2 ....160 A5
Cheam SM1,SM2 ......217 B2
Edmonton N9 ....18 A2
Isleworth TW3,TW7 ..152 A6
Kingston KT1 ....176 D1
Rosebery Sq EC1 ....241 A5
Kingston KT1 ....176 D1
Rosebine Ave TW2 ...152 B4
Rosebriars KT10 .....212 A3
Rose Bruford Coll SE8 .141 C6
Rose Bruford Coll of Speech
& Drama SE8 ....168 A3
Rosebury Rd SW6 ....135 D3
Rosebury Vale HA4 ....62 A6
Rose Bush Ct NW3 ....70 D3
Rose Cotts NW10 .....212 B3
Rosecourt Rd CR0 ....204 B3
Rosecroft N22 ....32 B2
Rosecroft Ave NW3 ...69 C5
Rosecroft Gdns NW2 ..68 A5
Twickenham TW2 ....152 B3
Rosecroft Rd UB1 ....85 C3
Rosecroft Wlk Pinner HA5 .40 D4
Wembley HA0 ....65 D3
Rose & Crown Ct EC2 ..242 A2
Rose & Crown Yd SW1 ..249 B3
Rose Ct E1 ....243 D3
E14 ....234 D6
Harrow HA2 ....64 A6
Ilford IG1 ....78 D2
7 Wembley HA0 ......88 A5
10 Wimbledon SW19 ..179 B5
Rose Dale BR6 ....226 D6
Rosedale Ave UB3 ....83 B2
Rosedale Cl SE2 ......124 B3
W7 ....108 D4
Stanmore HA7 ....25 B4
Rosedale Ct N5 ....72 D4
Rosedale Gdns RM9 ...80 B1
Rosedale Ho N16 .....51 B1
Rosedale Lo N14 .....15 B4
Rosedale Rd E7 ....77 C3
Dagenham RM9 ....80 B1
Richmond TW9 ......132 A1
Stoneleigh KT17 ....216 A3
Rosedale Terr W6 ....112 B3
Rosedene NW6 ....90 D6
Rosedene Ave
Morden SM4 ....201 C4
Southall UB6 ....85 C4
Streatham SW16 ....160 B1
Thornton Heath CR0 .204 A2
Rosedene Gdns IG2 ...56 C5
Rosedene Terr E10 ....75 D6
Rosedew Rd W6 ......134 D6
Rose End KT4 ....200 D1
Rosefield Cl SM5 ....218 C3
Rosefield Ct EN4 ......2 D1
Rosefield Gdns E14 ..119 C6
Rose Garden Cl HA8 ..26 A4
Rose Gdns W5 ....109 D3
Feltham TW13 ....150 A2
Southall UB1 ....85 C3
Rose Glen NW9 ....45 B5
Rosehart Mews 8 W11 .91 C1
Rose Hatch Ave RM6 ..58 D6
Roseheath Rd TW4 ...151 B6
Rosehill Claygate KT10 .213 A4
Hampton TW12 ......173 C2
Rose Hill
Carshalton SM4,SM5 .202 A2
Cheam SM1 ....201 D1
Rosehill Ct SM4 .....202 A2
Rosehill Gdns
Greenford UB6 ....64 D3
Sutton SM1 ....218 A6
Rose Hill Park W SM1 .218 A6
Rosehill Rd SW18 ....158 A6
Rose La RM6 ....59 A5
Roseland Cl N17 .....33 B3
Roseland Ho SW6 ....135 A2
Rose Lawn WD23 ......8 A3
Roseleigh Ave N5 ....72 D4
Roseleigh Cl 12 TW1 .153 D5
Roselle Ct W5 ....88 A1
Rosemary Ave N3 ....29 D1
NW2 ....47 D5
East Molesey KT8 ...195 C6
Edmonton N9 ....18 B3

Rosemary Ave *continued*
Enfield EN2 .....5 C4
Hounslow TW4 .....128 D3
Rosemary Branch Bridge
N1 .....235 C6
Rosemary Cl
Hillingdon UB8 .....82 C2
Thornton Heath CR0 .....204 A3
Rosemary Cotts 3
SW19 .....178 C3
Rosemary Ct 43 SE8 .....141 B6
Rosemary Dr
Redbridge IG4 .....55 D4
15 South Bromley E14 .....98 B1
Rosemary Gdns
Chessington KT9 .....214 A4
Dagenham RM8 .....59 B1
Mortlake SW14 .....133 A2
Rosemary Ho N1 .....235 D5
Rosemary La SW14 .....133 A2
Rosemary Mews N1 .....235 D6
Rosemary Rd DA16 .....145 D4
SE15 .....139 D5
Wandsworth SW17 .....158 A1
Rosemary Works Sch
N1 .....235 D5
Rosemead NW9 .....46 A2
Rosemead Ave
Feltham TW13 .....149 D2
Mitcham CR4 .....181 C1
Wembley HA9 .....66 A3
Rosemead Prep Sch
SE27 .....161 A2
Rose Mews N18 .....34 B6
Rosemont Ave N12 .....30 A4
Rosemont Mans 11 NW3 .69 D2
Rosemont Rd NW3 .....70 A2
Acton W3 .....110 D6
Kingston KT3 .....199 A6
Richmond TW10 .....154 A5
Wembley HA0 .....88 A6
Rosemoor St
SW3 .....114 D2 257 C3
Rosemount Ct
2 Acton W3 .....110 D5
South Norwood SE25 .....205 C6
Rosemount Dr BR1 .....210 B5
Rosemount Lo W3 .....110 D6
Rosemount Point 10
SE23 .....162 D1
Rosemount Rd W13 .....87 A1
Rosemount Towers 5
SM6 .....219 C2
Rosenau Cres SW11 .....267 C1
Rosenau Rd
SW11 .....136 D4 267 C2
Rosendale Prim Sch
SE21 .....161 A4
Rosendale Rd SE21,SE24 161 A3
Roseneath Ave N21 .....16 D3
Roseneath Rd SW11 .....159 A5
Roseneath Wlk EN1 .....5 C1
Rosens Wlk HA8 .....10 D1
Rosenthal Rd SE6 .....164 A5
Rosenthorpe Rd SE15 ...162 D6
Roserton St E14 .....120 A4
Rosery The CR0 .....206 D3
Rose Sq SW7 .....256 D2
Rose St EC4 .....241 D1
WC2 .....116 A6 250 A6
Roses The IG8 .....36 D3
Rosethorn Cl SW12 .....159 D4
Rosetta Cl SW8 .....270 B3
Rosetta Ct SE19 .....183 C3
Rosetta Prim Sch E16 .....99 B2
Rosetti Terr RM8 .....80 B4
Roseveare Rd SE12 .....187 C6
Roseville N21 .....16 C3
Roseville Ave TW3,TW4 ..151 C6
Roseville Rd UB3 .....106 A2
Rosevine Rd SW20 .....178 C2
Roseway SE21 .....161 B5
Rose Way HA8 .....27 A6
SE12 .....165 A6
Rosewell Cl SE20 .....184 B3
Rose Wlk Surbiton KT5 ...198 D4
West Wickham BR4 .....224 B6
Rosewood Ave UB6 .....65 A2
Rosewood Cl DA14 .....168 C1
Rosewood Ct 2 E11 .....76 B4
Bromley BR1 .....187 D2
Dagenham RM6 .....58 C4
Kingston KT2 .....176 C3
Rosewood Dr TW17 .....192 B4
Rosewood Gr SM1 .....218 A6
Rosewood Sq W12 .....90 A1
Rosher Cl E15 .....76 B1
Roshni Ho SW17 .....180 C4
Rosh Pinah Prim Sch
HA8 .....10 D1
Rosina Ct SW17 .....180 C5
Rosina St E9 .....74 D2
Roskeen Ct 1 SW19 .....178 C3
Roskell Rd SW15 .....134 D2
Roskild Ct HA9 .....66 B4
Roslin Ho 2 E1 .....118 D6
Roslin Rd W3 .....110 D3
Roslin Way BR1 .....187 A5
Roslyn Cl CR4 .....180 B1
Roslyn Rd N15 .....51 C4
Rosmead Rd
W11 .....113 A6 244 B6
Rosoman Pl EC1 .....241 B6
Rossal Ct SE20 .....184 B3
Rossall Cres NW10 .....88 B4
Rossanne Ho N3 .....29 D3
Ross Ave NW7 .....29 A5
Ross Ave *continued*
Dagenham RM8 .....59 B1
Ross Cl Harrow HA3 .....24 A3
Hayes UB3 .....105 B2
Ross Ct BR7 .....188 B3
NW9 .....45 C6
Ealing W13 .....87 B2
4 Putney SW15 .....156 D4
South Croydon CR2 .....221 A2
Rossdale SM1 .....218 C3
Rossdale Dr N9 .....18 C5
NW9 .....45 A1
Rossdale Rd SW15 .....134 C1
Rosse Mews SE3 .....143 B4
Rossendale Cl EN2 .....4 D6
Rossendale Ho 7 E5 .....74 B6
Rossendale St E5 .....74 B6
Rossendale Way
NW1 .....93 C6 232 B6
Rossendon Ct 1 SM6 ...219 C2
Rossetti Ct WC1 .....239 C4
Rossetti Gdns Mans
SW3 .....267 C6
Rossetti Ho SW1 .....259 D3
Rossetti Mews NW8 .....229 D5
Rossetti Rd SE16 .....118 B1
Ross Ho 18 E1 .....118 B5
6 SE18 .....144 A4
Twickenham TW2 .....151 D2
Rossignol Gdns SM5 .....219 A6
Rossindel Rd TW3 .....151 C6
Rossington Cl EN1 .....6 B5
Rossington St E5 .....74 A6
Rossiter Fields EN5 .....13 B5
Rossiter Rd SW12 .....159 B3
Rossland Cl DA6 .....169 D6
Rosslyn Ave
Barnes SW13 .....133 D2
Chingford E4 .....20 D2
Dagenham RM8 .....59 C2
East Barnet EN4 .....14 C5
Feltham TW14 .....150 A5
Rosslyn Cl Ashford TW16 .171 C4
Coney Hall BR4 .....224 D5
Hayes UB3 .....83 B2
Rosslyn Cres Harrow HA1 .42 D5
Wembley HA9 .....66 A4
Rosslyn Ct NW3 .....70 C3
Rosslyn Hill NW3 .....70 B3
Rosslyn Ho 8 TW9 .....132 B4
Rosslyn Mans NW6 .....70 A2
Rosslyn Park Mews NW3 .70 B3
Rosslyn Rd E17 .....54 A5
Barking IG11 .....79 B1
Twickenham TW1 .....153 C5
Rossmore Ct NW1 .....237 C6
Rossmore Rd
NW1 .....92 C3 237 B6
Ross Par SM6 .....219 B2
Ross Rd
South Norwood SE25 .....205 C6
Twickenham TW2 .....152 A3
Wallington SM6 .....219 C3
Ross Way SE9 .....144 A2
Rossway Dr WD23 .....8 B6
Rosswood Gdns SM6 ....219 C2
Rosswood Lo CR0 .....222 D6
Rostella Rd SW17 .....180 B6
Rostrever Gdns UB3 .....105 C5
Rostrevor Ave N15 .....51 D3
Rostrevor Gdns UB2 .....107 A1
Rostrevor Mans SW6 .....264 C2
Rostrevor Rd
Fulham SW6 .....135 B4 264 C2
Wimbledon SW19 .....179 C5
Rotary St SE1 .....261 D6
Rothay NW1 .....231 D2
Rothbury Gdns TW7 .....131 A5
Rothbury Rd E9 .....75 C1
Rothbury Wlk N17 .....34 A3
Rotherfield Ct N1 .73 B1 235 C6
Rotherfield Prim Sch
N1 .....95 A6 235 B6
Rotherfield Rd Enfield EN3 ..6 D6
Wallington SM5 .....219 A3
Rotherfield St N1 .73 A1 235 B6
Rotherham Wlk SE1 .....251 C3
Rotherhill Ave SW16 .....181 D4
Rotherhithe SE16 .....119 B5
Rotherhithe Holiday Inn Pier
SE16 .....119 B5
Rotherhithe New Rd
SE16 .....118 B1
Rotherhithe Old Rd
SE16 .....118 D2
Rotherhithe Prim Sch
SE16 .....118 D2
Rotherhithe St SE16 .....118 C4
10 SE16 .....118 B4
Rotherhithe Sta SE16 ...118 C4
Rotherhithe Tunnel
SE16 .....118 D5
Rother Ho SE15 .....140 B1
Rotherwick Hill W5 .....88 B3
Rotherwick Rd NW11 .....47 C2
Rotherwood Cl SW20 ...179 A2
Rotherwood Rd SW15 ...134 D2
Rothery St N1 .....234 D6
Rothesay Ave
Merton SW20 .....179 A1
Mortlake SW14,TW10 .....132 D1
Northolt UB6 .....64 B2
Rothesay Ct 13 SE11 .....138 C6
SE12 .....165 B1
4 Catford SE6 .....164 D2
Rothesay Rd SE25 .....205 C5
Rothley Ct NW8 .....236 C6
Rothsay Rd E7 .....77 C2
Rothsay St SE1 ..117 C3 263 A5
Rothsay Wlk 16 E14 .....119 C2
Rothschild Rd W4 .....111 A3
Rothschild St SE27 .....182 D6
Rothwell Ct HA1 .....42 D4
Rothwell Gdns RM9 .....102 C6
Rothwell Ho TW5 .....129 C6
Rothwell Rd RM9 .....102 C6
Rothwell St NW1 .....230 D6
10 NW1 .....70 D1
Roth Wlk N7 .....72 B6
Rotten Row★
SW1 .....114 D4 247 C2
Rotterdam Dr E14 .....120 A3
Rotunda Mus★ SE18 .....122 B1
Rouel Rd SE16 .....118 A2
SE16 .....118 A3
Rougemont Ave SM4 .....201 C3
Roundabout Ho HA6 .....22 A2
Roundacre SW19 .....156 D2
Roundel Cl SE4 .....141 B1
Roundell Ho 14 SE21 .....183 C6
Rounders Ct 7 RM10 .....81 D2
Round Gr CR0 .....206 D2
Roundhay Cl SE23 .....162 D2
Roundhedge Way EN2 .....4 B5
Round Hill SE23 .....162 C1
Roundhill Dr EN2 .....4 B1
Roundshaw Ctr SM6 .....220 A1
Roundtable Rd BR1 .....164 D1
Roundtree Rd HA0 .....65 B3
Roundways HA4 .....61 D5
Roundway The
Claygate KT10 .....212 D2
Tottenham N17 .....33 B2
Roundwood BR7 .....188 D1
Roundwood Ave UB11 ...105 A5
Roundwood Cl HA4 .....39 B2
Roundwood Rd NW10 .....67 D1
Rounton Rd E3 .....97 C3
Roupell Ho 7 KT2 .....176 B3
Roupell Rd SW2 .....160 B3
Roupell St SE1 ...116 C5 251 B3
Rousden St NW1 .....71 C1
Rouse Gdns SE21 .....183 C6
Routemaster Cl E13 .....99 B4
Routh Ct TW14 .....149 B3
Routh Rd SW18 .....158 C4
Routh St E6 .....100 B2
Rover Ho 27 N1 .....95 C6
Rowallan Ct 3 SE6 .....164 D3
Rowallan Rd
SW6 .....135 A5 264 A3
Rowallen Par RM8 .....58 C1
Rowan N10 .....31 B1
Rowan Ave E4 .....35 B4
Rowan Cl W5 .....110 A4
Harrow HA7 .....24 D4
Kingston KT3 .....177 C1
Streatham SW16 .....181 C2
Wembley HA0 .....65 A5
Rowan Cres SW16 .....181 C2
Rowan Ct 18 SE15 .....139 D5
SW11 .....158 D5
Forest Hill SE26 .....184 C6
11 Kingston KT2 .....176 C3
Wimbledon SW20 .....178 B1
Rowan Dr NW9 .....46 A6
Rowan Gdns CR0 .....221 D5
Rowan High Sch SW16 ..181 C1
Rowan Ho DA14 .....167 D1
NW10 .....89 C3
5 NW3 .....70 D2
East Bedfont TW14 .....149 B5
Ilford IG1 .....79 B3
Rowan Pl UB3 .....105 D6
Rowan Rd DA7 .....147 A2
W6 .....112 D2
Brentford TW8 .....131 B5
Mitcham SW16 .....181 C1
West Drayton UB7 .....104 A2
Rowans The
Ashford TW16 .....171 D5
Edmonton N13 .....17 A1
Rowan Terr W6 .....112 D2
Rowantree Cl N21 .....17 B3
Rowantree Rd
Edmonton N21 .....17 B3
Enfield EN2 .....4 D3
Rowan Way RM6 .....58 C6
Rowan Wlk BR2 .....226 B5
N19 .....71 C6
N2 .....48 A4
W10 .....91 A3
1 New Barnet EN5 .....13 D6
Rowanwood Ave DA15 ..168 A3
Rowanwood Mews EN2 .....4 D3
Rowben Cl N20 .....13 D3
Rowberry Cl SW6 .....134 C5
Rowcross St
SE1 .....117 D1 263 D2
Rowdell Rd UB5 .....85 C6
Rowden Par E4 .....35 C4
Rowden Park Gdns E4 ....35 C4
Rowden Rd
Beckenham BR3 .....185 B2
Chingford E4 .....35 D4
West Ewell KT19 .....215 A4
Rowditch La SW11 .....137 A3
Rowdon Ave NW10 .....68 B1
Rowdowns Rd RM9 .....81 B1
Rowe Gdns IG11 .....102 A5
Rowe La E9 .....74 C3
Rowena Cres SW11 .....136 C3
Rowe Wlk HA2 .....63 C5
Rowfant Rd SW12,SW17 .159 A2
Rowhill Mans 11 E5 .....74 B4
Rowhill Rd E5 .....74 B4
Rowington Cl W2 .....91 D2
Rowland Ave HA3 .....43 C6
Rowland Ct E16 .....98 D3
Rowland Gr SE26 .....162 B1
Rowland Hill Almshouses
TW15 .....170 C5
Rowland Hill Ave N17 .....33 B4
Rowland Hill Ho SE1 .....251 C2
Rowland Hill St NW3 .....70 C3
Rowlands Ave HA5 .....23 D4
Rowlands Cl N6 .....49 A3
NW7 .....28 A3
Rowlands Rd RM8 .....81 B6
Rowland Way
Ashford TW15 .....171 B3
Merton SW19 .....179 D2
Rowley Ave DA15 .....168 B4
Rowley Cl HA0 .....66 B1
Rowley Gdns N4 .....51 A2
Rowley Green Rd EN5 .....12 A6
Rowley Ho SE8 .....141 C6
Rowley Ind Pk W3 .....110 D3
Rowley La EN5 .....11 D6
Rowley Rd N15 .....51 A4
Rowlheys Pl UB7 .....104 A3
Rowlls Rd KT1 .....198 B6
Rowney Gdns RM9 .....80 C2
Rowney Rd RM9 .....80 B2
Rowntree Cl NW6 .....69 C2
Rowntree Clifford Cl 7
E13 .....99 B4
Rowntree Path 1 SE28 .124 B5
Rowntree Rd TW2 .....152 C3
Rowse Cl E15 .....98 A6
Rowsham Ct HA1 .....64 C5
Rowsley Ave NW4 .....46 C6
Rowstock 1 NW5 .....71 D2
Rowstock Gdns N7 .....71 D3
Rowton Rd SE18 .....145 A5
Roxborough Ave
Harrow HA1 .....42 C2
Hounslow TW7 .....130 D5
Roxborough Pk HA1 .....42 C2
Roxborough Rd HA1 .....42 B3
Roxbourne Cl UB5 .....62 D2
Roxbourne Fst & Mid Schs
HA2 .....63 A6
Roxburgh Rd SE27 .....182 D5
Roxburn Way HA4 .....61 D5
Roxby Pl SW6 ...135 C6 265 B6
Roxeth Ct TW15 .....170 C5
Roxeth Fst & Mid Sch
HA2 .....64 B6
Roxeth Gr HA2 .....63 D4
Roxeth Green Ave HA2 .....63 D6
Roxeth Hill HA2 .....64 C6
Roxeth Manor Fst & Mid Schs
HA2 .....63 C5
Roxeth Mead Sch HA2 .....64 B6
Roxford Cl TW17 .....193 C4
Roxford Ho 2 E3 .....97 D3
Roxley Rd SE13 .....163 D5
Roxton Gdns CR0 .....223 C3
Roxwell 10 NW1 .....71 B2
Roxwell Rd W12 .....112 A4
Barking IG11 .....102 A5
Roxwell Trad Pk E10 .....53 A2
Roxwell Way IG8 .....37 C3
Roxy Ave RM6 .....58 C2
Royal Academy of Dramatic
Art★ WC1 .....93 D2 239 C4
Royal Acad of Arts★
W1 .....115 C6 249 A5
Royal Acad of Dance
SW11 .....266 D1
Royal Acad of Music
NW1 .....238 B5
Royal Albert Hall★
SW7 .....114 B4 246 C1
Royal Albert Rd E16 .....122 D6
Royal Albert Sta E16 .....122 A6
Royal Albert Way E16 .....122 B6
Royal Arc W1 .....249 A5
Royal Army Medical Coll
SW1 .....116 A1 260 A2
Royal Ave SW3 ..114 D1 257 C2
Worcester Park KT4 .....215 C6
Royal Avenue Ho SW3 ...257 C2
Royal Ballet Sch The
WC2 .....240 B1
Royal Brompton Hospl
SW3 .....114 B1 256 C2
SW3 .....114 C1 257 B1
Royal Cir SE27 .....160 D1
Royal Cl BR6 .....226 D4
N16 .....51 C1
SE8 .....141 B6
Hillingdon UB7 .....82 B1
Ilford IG3 .....58 A2
Putney SW19 .....156 D2
Worcester Park KT4 .....215 C6
Royal College St
NW1 .....93 C6 232 B6
Royal Coll of Anaesthetists
WC1 .....94 A2 240 B4
Royal Coll of Art
SW7 .....114 B4 246 C1
Royal Coll of Art Sculpture
Sch SW11 .....136 C5 267 A3
Royal Coll of Midwives
W1 .....93 B2 238 C3
Royal Coll of Music
SW7 .....114 B3 256 C6
Royal Coll of Obstetricians &
Gynaecologists
NW1 .....92 D3 237 C6
Royal Coll of Physicians
NW1 .....93 B3 238 D6
Royal Coll of Science
SW7 .....114 B3 256 C6
Royal Coll of Surgeons
WC2 .....94 B1 240 D2
Royal Connaught Apps
E16 .....121 D5
Royal Courts of Justice
WC2 .....94 C1 241 A1
Royal Cres W11 ..113 A5 244 A3
Ruislip HA4 .....63 A5
Royal Crescent Mews
W11 .....112 D5
Royal Ct SE16 .....119 B3
SE9 .....166 B3
Enfield EN1 .....17 C5
9 Kingston KT2 .....176 D3
Royal Docks Rd E6 .....100 D2
Royal Duchess Mews
SW12 .....159 B4
Royal Exchange★ EC3 ..242 D1
Royal Exchange Ave
EC3 .....242 D1
Royal Exchange Bldgs
EC3 .....242 D1
Royal Festival Hall★
SE1 .....116 B5 250 D3
Royal Free Hospl NW3 ...70 C3
Royal Gdns W7 .....109 A3
Royal Geographical Society
SW7 .....114 B4 246 D1
Royal Hill SE10 .....142 A5
Royal Horticultural Society
(Lawrence Hall & Conf Ctr)
SW1 .....259 D5
Royal Horticultural Society
(Lindley Hall) SW1 .....259 C4
Royal Hospital (Army
Pensioners)★
SW1 .....115 A1 258 A1
Royal Hospital Rd
SW3 .....114 D1 257 D1
Royal Hospl and Home
SW15 .....157 A5
Royal La Hillingdon UB7 ....82 B1
Hillingdon UB8 .....82 B3
Royal Langford 3 NW6 ..91 D5
Royal London Est N17 ....34 B4
Royal London Est The
NW10 .....89 B5
Royal London Homeopathic
Hospl The WC1 ..94 A2 240 B4
Royal London Hospl (Mile
End) The E2 .....96 D4
Royal London Hospl (St
Clements) The E3 .....97 B4
Royal London Hospl
(Whitechapel) The E1 ...96 B2
Royal Marsden Hospl
SW3 .....114 B1 256 D2
Royal Mews KT8 .....196 C6
Royal Mews The★
SW1 .....115 B3 258 D6
Royal Military Sch of Music
(Kneller Hall) TW2 .....152 B5
Royal Mint Pl 5 E1 .....118 A6
Royal Mint St
E1 .....117 D6 253 D6
Royal National Orthopaedic
Hospl
W1 .....93 B3 238 D5
Stanmore HA7 .....9 C2
Royal National TNE Hospl
The WC1 .....94 B4 233 C2
Royal Nat TN&E Hospl The
W5 .....87 C2
Royal Naval Pl SE14 .....141 B5
Royal Oak Ct 9 N1 .....95 C4
Dagenham RM8 .....80 C6
Royal Oak Pl SE22 .....162 B5
Royal Oak Rd 5 E8 .....74 B2
Bexley DA6 .....147 C1
Royal Oak Sta W2 .....91 D2
Royal Opera Arc SW1 ...249 C4
Royal Orchard Cl SW18 .157 A4
Royal Par BR7 .....189 A3
SE3 .....142 D3
SW6 .....264 A4
Ealing W5 .....88 A4
11 Dagenham RM10 .....81 D2
Royal Parade Mews
BR7 .....189 A3
Royal Park Prim Sch
DA14 .....169 A1
Royal Pl 11 SE10 .....142 A5
Royal Rd DA14 .....168 D1
E16 .....99 D1
SE17 .....138 D6
Teddington TW11 .....174 B5
Royal Route HA9 .....66 B4
Royal Russell Sch (Ballards)
CR0 .....222 B3
Royal Sch Hampstead The
NW3 .....70 B4
Royal St SE1 .....116 B3 260 D6
Royalty Mews W1 .....239 C1
Royalty Studios W11 .....91 A1
Royal United Services Mus★
SW1 .....250 A3
Royal Veterinary Coll
NW1 .....93 D6 232 C5
Royal Victoria Pl E16 .....121 B5
Royal Victoria Sta E16 ...121 A6
Royal Victor Pl E3 .....96 D5
Royal Wlk SM6 .....219 B5
Roycraft Ave IG11 .....101 D5
Roycroft Cl
Streatham SW2 .....160 C3
Woodford E18 .....37 B2
Roydene Rd SE18 .....123 C1
Roydon Cl 7 SW11 .....136 D3
Roy Gdns IG2 .....57 D4
Roy Gr TW12 .....173 D4
Roy Ho N1 .....235 D5
Royle Cres W13 .....87 A3
Roymount Ct TW2 .....152 C1
Roy Ridley Ho 6 SW4 ....137 D2
Roy Sq E14 .....119 A6
Royston Ave
Carshalton SM1 .....218 B5
Chingford E4 .....35 D5
Wallington SM6 .....219 D4
Royston Cl Cranford TW5 .128 B4
Walton-on-T KT12 .....194 A1
Royston Ct 1 E13 .....99 A6
Hinchley Wood KT10 .....212 D6
Redbridge IG1 .....55 D3
3 Richmond TW9 .....132 B4
Tolworth KT6 .....214 C6
Royston Gdns IG1 .....55 D3
Royston Gr HA5 .....23 C4
Royston Ho N11 .....31 A6
14 SE15 .....140 A6
Royston Par IG1 .....55 D3
Royston Park Rd HA5 .....23 C5
Royston Prim Sch SE20 .184 D2
Royston Rd Penge SE20 ..184 D2
Richmond TW10 .....154 A6
Royston St 25 E2 .....96 C5
Roystons The KT5 .....198 D4
Rozel Ct 3 N1 .....95 C6
Rozel Rd SW4 .....137 C2
Rubastic Rd UB2 .....106 C3
Rubens Rd UB5 .....84 D5
Rubens St SE6 .....163 B2
Rubin Pl EN3 .....7 C6
Ruby Rd E17 .....53 C6
Ruby St NW10 .....67 A1
SE15 .....140 B6
Ruby Triangle SE15 .....140 B6
Ruckholt Cl E10 .....75 D5
Ruckholt Rd E10 .....75 D5
Rucklidge Ave NW10 .....90 A5
Rudall Cres NW3 .....70 B4
Rudbeck Ho 10 SE15 .....140 A5
Ruddington Cl E5 .....75 A4
Ruddock Cl HA8 .....27 A3
Ruddstreet Cl SE18 .....123 A2
Rudge Ho 1 SE16 .....118 A3
Rudgwick Terr
NW8 .....92 C6 230 B5
Rudhall Ho 4 SW2 .....160 C5
Rudland Rd DA7 .....147 D2
Rudloe Rd SW12 .....159 C4
Rudolf Pl SW8 .....270 B5
Rudolph Ct SE22 .....162 B4
Rudolph Rd E13 .....98 D5
NW6 .....91 C5
Rudstone Ho 10 E3 .....97 D4
Rudyard Ct SE1 .....252 D1
Rudyard Gr NW7 .....27 A4
Ruegg Ho 5 SE18 .....144 C6
Ruffetts Cl CR2 .....222 B1
Ruffetts The CR2 .....222 B1
Ruffle Cl UB7 .....104 B4
Rufford Cl HA3 .....43 A3
Rufford St N1 .....94 A6 233 B6
Rufford Street Mews N1 .72 A1
Rufford Twr 5 W3 .....110 D5
Rufforth Ct 1 NW9 .....27 C2
Rufus Bsns Ctr SW18 ....157 D2
Rufus Cl HA4 .....63 A5
Rufus Ho SE1 .....263 D6
Rufus St N1 .....95 C4
Rugby Ave Edmonton N9 ...17 D3
Northolt UB6 .....64 B2
Wembley HA0 .....65 C4
Rugby Cl HA1 .....42 C5
Rugby Gdns RM9 .....80 C2
Rugby Mans W14 .....254 B4
Rugby Rd NW9 .....44 D5
W4 .....111 C4
Dagenham RM9 .....80 C2
Twickenham TW1,TW2,
TW7 .....152 C5
Rugby St WC1 .....94 B3 240 C5
Rugg St E14 .....119 C6
Rugless Ho 2 E14 .....120 A4
Rugmere 4 NW1 .....71 A1
Ruislip Cl UB6 .....85 D3
Ruislip Ct HA4 .....61 D6
Ruislip Gardens Prim Sch
HA4 .....61 D4
Ruislip Gardens Sta HA4 .62 A4
Ruislip Lido★ HA4,HA5 ...39 B5
Ruislip Lido Railway★
HA4 .....39 B5
Ruislip Manor Sta HA4 ...40 A1
Ruislip Rd UB6,UB5 .....85 C4
Ruislip Rd E
Ealing UB6,W7 .....86 D3
Greenford UB6 .....86 B3
Ruislip St SW17 .....180 D6
Ruislip Sta HA4 .....39 D1
Rumball Ho 22 SE5 .....139 C5
Rumbold Rd
SW6 .....135 D5 265 D3
Rum Cl E1 .....118 C6
Rumford Ho SE1 .....262 A5
Rumsey Cl TW12 .....173 B4
Rumsey Rd SW9 .....138 B2
Runacres Ct SE17 .....262 A1
Runbury Circ NW9 .....67 B6
Runcorn Cl N17 .....52 B5
Runcorn Pl W11 .....244 A6
Rundell Cres NW4 .....46 B4
Rundell Twr SW8 .....270 C2
Runes Cl CR4 .....202 C5
Runnelfield HA1 .....64 C5
Running Horse Yd 12
TW8 .....132 A6
Runnymede SW19 .....180 B2
Runnymede Cl TW2 .....151 D4
Runnymede Cres SW16 .182 A2
Runnymede Ct 1 SM6 ..219 B2
Runnymede Gdns
Greenford UB6 .....86 C5

Runnymede Gdns *continued*
Twickenham TW2 ....151 D4
Runnymede Ho E9 ....75 A4
Richmond TW10 ....154 C6
Runnymede Rd TW2 ....151 D5
Runway The HA4 ....62 C3
Rupack St 3 SE16 ....118 C4
Rupert Ave 6 HA9 ....66 A3
Rupert Ct W1 ....249 C6
Rupert Gdns SW9 ....138 D3
Rupert Ho SE11 ....261 B3
Rupert Rd N19 ....71 D6
NW6 ....91 B5
W4 ....111 C3
Rupert St W1 ....115 D6 249 C6
Rural Way SW16 ....181 B3
Rusbridge Cl E8 ....74 A3
Ruscoe Ho 12 SW27 ....182 D5
Ruscoe Rd E16 ....98 D1
Ruscombe Way TW14 ....149 D4
Rusham Rd SW12 ....158 D4
Rushbrook Cres E17 ....35 B2
Rushbrook Ho 20 SW8 ....137 D3
Rushbrook Rd SE9 ....167 A2
Rushbury Ct 4 TW12 ....173 C2
Rushby Ct SW4 ....270 A1
Rush Common Mews 18
SW2 ....160 B4
Rushcroft Rd SW2,SW9 ....138 C1
Chingford E4 ....35 D3
Rush Croft Sch E4 ....35 D3
Rushcutters Ct 18 SE16 ....119 A2
Rushden Cl SE19 ....183 B3
Rushdene SE2 ....124 D3
Rushdene Ave EN4 ....14 C4
Rushdene Cl UB5 ....84 C5
Rushdene Cres UB5 ....84 C4
Rushdene Rd HA5 ....40 B3
Rushden Gdns NW7 ....28 C4
Ilford IG5 ....56 C6
Rushen Wlk SM5 ....202 B1
Rushet Rd BR5 ....190 A1
Rushett Cl KT7 ....197 B2
Rushett Rd KT7 ....197 B2
Rushey Cl KT3 ....199 B5
Rushey Gn SE6 ....163 D4
Rushey Green Prim Sch
SE6 ....163 D3
Rushey Hill EN2 ....4 B1
Rushey Mead SE4 ....163 C6
Rushford Rd SE4 ....163 B5
Rush Green Rd RM7,RM8,
RM10 ....59 D1
Rushgrove Ave NW9 ....45 D5
Rushgrove Ct NW9 ....45 C4
Rushgrove St SE18 ....122 B2
Rush Hill Mews 3
SW11 ....137 A2
Rush Hill Rd SW11 ....137 A2
Rushlake Ho 3 SW11 ....137 A3
Rushley Cl BR2 ....226 A4
Rushman Villas KT3 ....199 D5
Rushmead 5 E2 ....96 B4
Richmond TW10 ....153 B1
Rushmead Cl CR0 ....221 D4
Rushmere Ct KT4 ....216 A6
Rushmere Ho 2 SW15 ....156 A3
Rushmere Pl SW19 ....178 D5
Rushmon Pl SM3 ....217 A2
Rushmoor Cl HA5 ....40 B5
Rushmore Cl BR1 ....210 A6
Rushmore Cres 9 E5 ....74 D4
Rushmore Ho 9 N7 ....71 D3
W14 ....254 B5
Rushmore Prim Sch E5 ....74 D4
Rushmore Rd E5 ....74 D4
E5 ....75 A4
Rusholme Ave RM10 ....81 C5
Rusholme Gr SE19 ....183 C5
Rusholme Rd SW15 ....157 A5
Rushout Ave HA3 ....43 B3
Rush The SW20 ....179 B2
Rushton Ho 26 SW8 ....137 D3
Rushton St N1 ....95 B5 235 D4
Rushworth St
SE1 ....116 D4 251 D1
Rushy Meadow La SM5 ....218 C5
Rushy Meadow Prim Sch
SM5 ....218 C5
Ruskin Ave DA16 ....146 A3
E12 ....78 A2
Feltham TW14 ....149 D5
Richmond TW9 ....132 C5
Ruskin Cl NW11 ....47 D3
Ruskin Ct SE5 ....139 B2
SE9 ....166 B5
Southgate N21 ....16 B4
Ruskin Dr BR6 ....227 C5
DA16 ....146 A2
North Cheam KT4 ....216 C6
Ruskin Gdns Ealing W5 ....87 D3
Harrow HA3 ....44 B5
Ruskin Gr DA16 ....146 A3
Ruskin Ho SW1 ....259 D3
Ruskin Par CR0 ....221 B3
Ruskin Park Ho SE5 ....139 B2
Ruskin Rd
Belvedere DA17 ....125 C2
Croydon CR0 ....220 D6
Isleworth TW7 ....130 D2
Southall UB1 ....107 A6
Tottenham N17 ....33 D2
Wallington SM5 ....219 A3
Ruskin Way SW19 ....180 B2
Ruskin Wlk BR2 ....210 B3
SE24 ....161 A6
Edmonton N9 ....18 A2
Rusland Ave BR6 ....227 B5
Rusland Hts HA1 ....42 C5
Rusland Park Rd HA1 ....42 C5
Rusper Cl NW2 ....68 C5
Stanmore HA7 ....25 C6
Rusper Ct SW9 ....138 A3
Rusper Rd N17,N22 ....51 A6
Dagenham RM9 ....80 C2
Russel Cl BR3 ....208 A6
Russel Ct N14 ....15 D6
Russell Ave N22 ....32 D1
Russell Cl DA7 ....147 C1
NW10 ....67 A1
SE7 ....143 C5
Chiswick W4 ....133 D6
Ruislip HA4 ....62 C6
Russell Ct 4 E10 ....53 D2
5 SE15 ....140 B3
SW1 ....249 B3
SW11 ....268 B1
Bromley BR1 ....186 D3
New Barnet EN5 ....2 A1
Streatham SW16 ....182 B5
Surbiton KT6 ....198 A2
Wallington SM6 ....219 C3
Wembley HA0 ....66 A1
Russell Gdns N20 ....14 C2
NW11 ....47 A3
W14 ....113 A3 254 A6
Ilford IG2 ....57 B2
Richmond TW10 ....153 C2
West Drayton UB7 ....104 C1
Russell Gdns Mews
W14 ....113 A3 254 A6
Russell Gr NW7 ....27 C6
33 SW9 ....138 C4
Russell Ho 15 E14 ....97 C1
SW1 ....259 A2
Russell Kerr Cl W4 ....133 A5
Russell La N20 ....14 D2
Russell Lo 5 E4 ....20 A2
Russell Lodge SE1 ....262 C6
Russell Mans WC1 ....240 B4
Russell Par NW11 ....47 A3
Russell Pickering Ho 2
SW4 ....138 A2
Russell Pl NW3 ....70 C3
SE16 ....119 A3
Russell Prim Sch The
TW10 ....153 D3
Russell Rd E10 ....53 D3
E17 ....53 B6
E4 ....35 B6
N15 ....51 C4
N20 ....14 C2
N8 ....49 D3
NW9 ....45 D3
W14 ....113 A3 254 B5
Bowes Park N13 ....32 B4
Buckhurst Hill IG9 ....21 C3
Enfield EN1 ....5 D5
Merton SW19 ....179 C3
Mitcham CR4 ....202 C6
Newham E16 ....99 B1
Northolt UB5 ....64 A3
Shepperton TW17 ....193 A2
Twickenham TW1,TW2 ....152 D5
Walton-on-T KT12 ....194 A3
Russell Sch The TW10 ....153 D2
Russell Sq WC1 ....94 A3 240 A5
Russell Square Mans
WC1 ....240 B4
Russell Square Sta
WC1 ....94 A3 240 A5
Russell St WC2 ....116 A6 250 B6
Russell's Wharf 2 W9 ....91 B3
Russell Way SM1 ....217 D3
Russell Wlk 4 TW10 ....154 B5
Russet Ave TW16,TW17 ....193 C6
Russet Cl UB10 ....83 A3
Russet Cres N7 ....72 B3
Russet Ct NW2 ....68 B5
6 Barnet EN4 ....2 C1
Russet Dr CR0 ....207 A1
Russet Ho TW3 ....129 B1
Russet House Sch EN1 ....6 B4
Russets Cl E4 ....36 B6
Russett Way SE13 ....141 D3
Russia Ct EC2 ....242 B2
Russia Dock Rd SE16 ....119 A5
Russia La E2 ....96 C5
Russian Submarine
SE18 ....121 D3
Russia Row EC2 ....242 B1
Russington Rd TW17 ....193 B3
Rusthall Ave W4 ....111 B3
Rusthall Cl CR0 ....206 C3
Rusthall Mans W4 ....111 B2
Rustic Ave SW16 ....181 B3
Rustic Pl HA0 ....65 D4
Rustic Wlk E16 ....99 B1
Rustington Wlk SM4 ....201 B2
Ruston Ave KT5 ....198 D2
Ruston Gdns N14 ....15 A5
Ruston Mews W11 ....91 A1
Ruston Rd SE18 ....122 A3
Ruston St E3 ....97 B6
Rust Sq SE5 ....139 B5
Rutford Rd SW16 ....182 A5
Ruth Cl HA7 ....44 B5
Ruth Ct 14 E3 ....97 A5
Rutherford Cl
Hillingdon UB8 ....82 B3
Sutton SM2 ....218 B2
Rutherford Ho 12 E1 ....96 B3
Teddington TW11 ....174 D5
7 Wembley HA9 ....67 A5
Rutherford St
SW1 ....115 D2 259 C4
Rutherford Twr 10 UB1 ....85 D1
Rutherford Way
Bushey WD23 ....8 C3
Wembley HA9 ....66 C4
Rutherglen Rd SE2 ....146 A6
Rutherwyke Cl KT17 ....216 A2
Ruth Ho W10 ....91 A3
Ruthin Cl NW9 ....45 C3
Ruthin Rd SE3 ....143 A6
Ruthven St E9 ....96 D6
Rutland Ave DA15 ....168 A4
Rutland Cl DA5 ....168 D3
Chessington KT9 ....214 B2
Mitcham SW19 ....180 C3
Mortlake SW14 ....133 A2
Rutland Ct SE5 ....139 B1
SW7 ....247 B1
15 Acton W3 ....88 C1
Chislehurst BR7 ....188 C2
Enfield EN3 ....18 B6
Sidcup BR7 ....167 A2
Rutland Dr Morden SM4 ....201 C2
Richmond TW10 ....154 A3
Rutland Gate
SW7 ....114 C4 247 B1
Beckenham BR2 ....208 D5
Belvedere DA17 ....125 D1
Rutland Gate Mews
SW7 ....247 A1
Rutland Gdns N4 ....51 A3
SW7 ....114 C4 247 B1
Dagenham RM8 ....80 C3
Ealing W13 ....87 A2
South Croydon CR0 ....221 C4
Rutland Gdns Mews
SW7 ....247 B1
Rutland Gr W6 ....112 B1
Rutland Ho 18 SE18 ....122 B2
W8 ....255 C5
6 Northolt UB5 ....63 C2
2 Penge SE20 ....184 C2
10 Putney SW15 ....156 C4
Tolworth KT6 ....198 C1
Rutland Lo SE6 ....163 B2
Rutland Mews E SW7 ....257 B6
Rutland Mews S SW7 ....257 A6
Rutland Mews W SW7 ....257 A6
Rutland Park Gdns NW2 ....68 C2
Rutland Park Mans NW2 ....68 C2
Rutland Pk NW2 ....68 C2
Forest Hill SE6 ....163 B2
Rutland Pl EC1 ....241 D4
Bushey WD23 ....8 B3
Rutland Rd E17 ....53 C3
E7 ....77 D1
E9 ....96 D6
Harrow HA1 ....42 A3
Hayes UB3 ....105 B2
Ilford IG1 ....78 D5
Mitcham SW19 ....180 C3
Southall UB1 ....85 C2
Twickenham TW2 ....152 B2
Wanstead E11 ....55 B4
Rutland St SW7 ....257 B6
Rutland Studios NW10 ....90 A4
Rutland Wlk SE6 ....163 B2
Rutley Cl SE11 ....138 D6
Rutlish Rd SW19 ....179 C2
Rutlish Sch (Boys)
SW20 ....179 B1
Rutter Gdns CR4 ....202 B5
Rutters Cl UB7 ....104 C4
Rutt's Terr SE14 ....140 D4
Rutts The WD23 ....8 B3
Ruvigny Gdns SW15 ....134 D2
Ruvigny Mans SW15 ....134 D2
Ruxbury Ct TW15 ....148 A1
Ruxley Cl
Chessington KT19 ....214 D3
Sidcup DA14 ....191 A4
Ruxley Cnr DA14 ....191 A4
Ruxley Corner Ind Est
DA14 ....190 D4
Ruxley Cres KT10 ....213 B1
Ruxley Ct KT19 ....215 A3
Ruxley Gdns TW17 ....193 A4
Ruxley La KT19 ....215 B3
Ruxley Mews KT19 ....214 D3
Ruxley Ridge KT10 ....213 A1
Ryall's Ct N20 ....14 D1
Ryan Cl SE9 ....143 C1
Ruislip HA4 ....40 B1
Ryan Ct SW16 ....182 A3
Ryan Dr TW8 ....131 A6
Ryan Ho 3 HA1 ....42 D4
Ryarsh Cres BR6 ....227 C4
Rycott Path SE22 ....162 A4
Rycroft Way N17 ....51 D6
Ryculff Sq SE3 ....142 D3
Rydal Cl NW4 ....29 A2
Rydal Cres UB6 ....87 C5
Rydal Ct Edgware HA8 ....26 B5
Wembley HA9 ....44 A2
Rydal Dr DA7 ....147 C4
West Wickham BR4 ....224 C6
Rydal Gdns NW9 ....45 C4
Kingston SW15 ....177 C5
Twickenham TW2,TW3 ....151 D5
Wembley HA9 ....43 C1
Rydal Ho 25 SW8 ....137 D3
Rydal Lo N17 ....34 A3
Rydal Rd SW16 ....181 D6
Rydal Water NW1 ....232 A1
Rydal Way Enfield EN3 ....18 C5
Ruislip HA4 ....62 C4
Ryde Ho 1 NW6 ....91 C6
Rydens Ho SE9 ....165 C1
Rydens Rd KT12 ....194 D1
Ryde Pl TW1 ....153 D5
Ryder Cl BR1 ....187 B5
Ryder Ct E10 ....75 D6
SW1 ....249 B4
Ryder Dr SE16 ....118 B1
Ryder Ho 14 E1 ....96 C3
Ryder Ho *continued*
5 Merton SW19 ....179 D2
Ryder St SW1 ....249 B4
Ryder's Terr NW8 ....92 A5 229 A4
Ryder Yd SW1 ....249 B4
Ryde Vale Rd SW12 ....159 C2
Rydon Mews SW19 ....178 C3
Rydons Cl SE9 ....144 A2
Rydon St N1 ....235 B6
Rydston Cl 2 N7 ....72 B1
Rye Cl DA5 ....169 D5
Ryecotes Mead SE21 ....161 C3
Ryecroft Ave TW2 ....151 D3
Ryecroft Cres EN5 ....12 B6
Ryecroft Rd BR5 ....211 B3
SE13 ....164 A6
South Norwood SW16 ....182 C4
Ryecroft St
SW6 ....135 D4 265 C1
Rye Ct BR3 ....185 B2
Ryedale SE22 ....162 B5
Ryedale Ct 6 TW12 ....173 C2
Ryefield Ave UB10 ....60 D1
Ryefield Cres HA5,HA6 ....22 A1
Ryefield Ct HA6 ....22 A1
Ryefield Path 7 SW15 ....156 A3
Ryefield Prim Sch UB10 ....83 B6
Ryefield Rd SE19 ....183 A4
Ryegates 2 SE15 ....140 B3
Ryehill Ct KT3 ....199 D2
Rye Hill Pk SE15 ....140 C1
Rye La SE15 ....140 A3
Ryeland Cl UB7 ....82 A1
Ryelands Cres SE12 ....165 C5
Ryelands Prim Sch
SE25 ....206 B4
Rye Rd SE15 ....140 D1
Rye The N14 ....15 C4
Rye Way HA8 ....26 B4
Rye Wlk SW15 ....156 D6
Ryfold Rd SW19 ....157 C1
Ryhope Rd N11 ....31 B6
Ryland Cl TW13 ....171 D6
Ryland Ct EN2 ....5 B1
Rylandes Rd NW2 ....68 A5
Ryland Ho 11 SW16 ....181 C5
Ryland Rd NW5 ....71 B2
Rylett Cres W12 ....111 D3
Rylett Rd W12 ....111 D3
Rylston Rd SW6 ....135 B6 264 C5
Edmonton N13 ....17 B1
Rylton Ho KT12 ....194 A1
Rymer Rd CR0 ....205 C2
Rymer St SE24 ....160 D5
Rymill St E16 ....122 C5
Rysbrack St SW1 ....257 C6
Rythe Cl KT9 ....213 C1
Rythe Ct KT7 ....197 A2
Rythe Ho 7 BR1 ....186 B5
Rythe Rd KT10 ....212 C3

S

Saatchi Gallery★ SE1 ....250 C2
Sabah Ct TW15 ....170 C6
Sabbarton St 9 E16 ....98 D1
Sabella Ct E3 ....97 B5
Sabine Rd SW11 ....137 A2
Sable Cl TW4 ....128 C2
Sable Ct 3 KT3 ....199 C4
Sable St N1 ....72 D1
Sach Rd E5 ....74 B6
Sacketts Ho 24 SW9 ....138 C4
Sackville Ave BR2 ....209 A1
Sackville Cl HA2 ....64 B5
Sackville Gdns IG1 ....56 B1
Sackville Ho N8 ....50 A5
16 Streatham SW16 ....160 A1
Sackville Rd SM2 ....217 C1
Sackville St W1 ....115 C6 249 B5
Sacred Heart High Sch
W6 ....112 C2
Sacred Heart Jun Sch
W6 ....112 D2
Sacred Heart Prim Sch,
Battersea SW11 ....136 C3
Sacred Heart RC High Sch
The HA3 ....24 C1
Sacred Heart RC Prim Sch
N20 ....14 C2
Putney SW15 ....156 A6
Ruislip HA4 ....61 C6
Teddington TW11 ....175 B3
West Barnes KT3 ....200 A5
Sacred Heart RC Sch The
SE5 ....139 A4
Saddlebrook Pk TW16 ....171 C3
Saddlers Cl Barnet EN5 ....12 B6
Borehamwood WD6 ....11 B5
Pinner HA5 ....23 C5
Saddlers Mews SW8 ....270 B2
Teddington KT1 ....175 C2
Wembley HA0 ....64 D4
Saddlers Path WD6 ....11 B6
Saddlescombe Way N12 ....29 C5
Sadler Cl CR4 ....180 D1
Sadler Ho 17 E3 ....97 D4
EC1 ....234 C2
Sadlers Ride KT8 ....174 A1
Saffron Ave E14 ....120 B6
Saffron Cl NW11 ....47 B3
Thornton Heath CR0 ....204 A3
Saffron Ct E15 ....76 C3
10 N1 ....73 B2
Saffron Hill EC1 ....94 C2 241 B4
Saffron St EC1 ....241 B4
Saffron Way KT6 ....197 D1
Saffron Wharf SE1 ....253 D2
Sage Cl 7 E6 ....100 B2
Sage Mews SE22 ....161 D6
Sage St E1 ....118 C6
Sage Way WC1 ....233 C1
Sage Yd KT6 ....198 B1
Sahara Ct UB1 ....107 A6
Saigasso Cl E16 ....99 D1
Sailmakers Ct SW6 ....136 A2
Sail St SE11 ....116 C3 260 D4
Saimet 3 NW9 ....27 D2
Sainfoin Rd SW17 ....159 A2
Sainsbury Rd SE19 ....183 C5
St Agatha's Dr KT2 ....176 B4
St Agatha's Gr SM5 ....202 D1
St Agatha's RC Prim Sch
KT2 ....176 B4
St Agatha's RC Sch KT2 ....176 B3
St Agnes Cl E9 ....96 C6
St Agnes Pl SE11 ....138 D6
St Agnes RC Prim Sch
E3 ....97 D4
St Agnes RC Sch NW2 ....69 A5
St Aidans Ct IG11 ....102 B5
St Aidan's Prim Sch N4 ....50 C2
St Aidan's RC Prim Sch
IG1 ....57 B1
St Aidan's Rd SE22 ....162 B6
W13 ....109 B4
St Albans Ave W4 ....111 B3
Feltham TW13 ....172 D5
St Alban's Ave E6 ....100 C4
St Alban's CE Prim Sch
EC1 ....94 C2 241 A4
St Alban's Cl NW11 ....47 C1
St Albans Cres N22 ....32 C2
St Alban's Cres IG8 ....37 A2
St Alban's Gdns TW11 ....175 A5
St Alban's Gr
W8 ....113 D3 255 D6
Carshalton SM5 ....202 C2
St Albans Ho 2 SW16 ....182 C6
St Albans La NW11 ....47 C1
St Albans Mans W8 ....255 D6
St Alban's Pl N1 ....94 D6 234 C5
St Alban's RC Prim Sch
KT8 ....196 A4
St Alban's Rd NW10 ....89 C6
NW5 ....71 B5
St Albans Rd Barnet EN5 ....1 A3
Cheam SM1 ....217 B4
Ilford IG3 ....57 D2
Kingston KT2 ....176 A4
St Alban's Rd IG8 ....37 A3
St Alban's St SW1 ....249 C5
St Albans Studios W8 ....255 D6
St Albans Terr W6 ....264 A6
St Alban's Villas NW5 ....71 A5
St Alfege Pas SE10 ....142 A6
St Alfege Rd SE7 ....143 D6
St Alfege with St Peter's CE
Prim Sch SE10 ....142 A6
St Aloysius RC Inf Sch
NW1 ....232 D1
St Aloysius' RC Jun & Inf Sch
NW1 ....232 C2
St Aloysius RC Jun Sch
NW1 ....93 D5 232 D3
St Alphage Ct NW9 ....45 B6
St Alphage Gdn EC2 ....242 B3
St Alphage Highwalk
EC2 ....242 B3
St Alphage Wlk HA8 ....27 A1
St Alphege Rd N9 ....18 C4
St Alphonsus Rd SW4 ....137 D1
St Amunds Cl SE6 ....185 C6
St Andrews Ave HA0 ....65 A4
St Andrew's CE Prim Sch
N1 ....94 B6 233 D6
N14 ....15 D3
SW9 ....138 A3
Enfield EN1 ....5 C3
St Andrew's CE Sch N20 ....13 B2
St Andrews Cl 25 SE16 ....118 B1
St Andrew's Cl N12 ....30 A6
NW2 ....68 B5
St Andrews Cl
Erith SE28 ....102 D1
Hinchley Wood KT7 ....197 B1
Ruislip HA4 ....62 D6
Stanmore HA7 ....25 C1
St Andrew's Cl
2 Hounslow TW7 ....130 C4
Upper Halliford TW17 ....193 B5
St Andrew's Ct E17 ....35 A1
St Andrews Ct W4 ....133 A4
St Andrew's Ct
Kingston KT3 ....199 D6
Wandsworth SW18 ....158 A2
St Andrews Dr HA7 ....25 C2
St Andrew's Gr N16 ....51 B1
St Andrew's Greek Sch
NW1 ....71 C2
St Andrew's High Sch
CR0 ....220 D4
St Andrew's Hill
EC4 ....94 D1 241 D1
St Andrews Ho 11 SE16 ....118 B3
St Andrew's Hospl E3 ....97 D3
St Andrew's Mans W1 ....238 A3
St Andrew's Mews N16 ....51 C1
St Andrews Mews
Greenwich SE3 ....143 A5
4 Streatham SW12 ....159 D3
St Andrew's Pl NW1 ....238 D6
St Andrews RC Prim Sch
SW16 ....182 A5
St Andrews Rd DA14 ....168 D1
E17 ....35 A1
N9 ....18 C4
NW9 ....45 B1
St Andrew's Rd E11 ....54 C3
St Andrew's Rd *continued*
E13 ....99 B4
NW11 ....47 B3
NW2 ....68 B2
W14 ....264 B6
W3 ....89 C1
W7 ....108 C4
St Andrews Rd SM5 ....218 C5
St Andrew's Rd
3 Croydon CR0 ....221 A4
Enfield EN1 ....5 B2
Hillingdon UB10 ....82 B6
Redbridge IG1 ....56 B2
Surbiton KT6 ....197 D3
St Andrew's Sq W11 ....91 A1
Surbiton KT6 ....197 D3
St Andrew's & St Mark's CE
Jun Sch KT6 ....197 D4
St Andrew St EC4 ....241 B3
St Andrews Terr WD19 ....22 C5
St Andrew & St Francis CE
Prim Sch NW2 ....68 A2
St Andrew's Twr UB1 ....108 A6
St Andrews Way E3 ....97 D3
St Andrew's Wharf SE1 ....253 D2
St Angela's Ursuline Convent
Sch E7 ....77 B2
St Anna Rd EN5 ....12 D6
St Anne RC Prim Sch E1 ....96 A3
St Annes Catholic High Sch
for Girls (Upper) N13 ....32 C6
St Anne's CE Prim Sch
SW18 ....157 D6
St Anne's Cl N6 ....71 A5
St Annes Cl WD19 ....22 C6
St Anne's Ct NW6 ....91 A6
W1 ....239 C1
St Anne's Flats NW1 ....232 C2
St Annes Gdns NW10 ....88 B4
St Anne's Pas E14 ....97 B1
St Anne's Prim Sch
TW19 ....148 A4
St Anne's RC Prim Sch
SE11 ....138 B6 270 C6
St Anne's Rd E11 ....76 B6
Wembley HA0 ....65 D3
St Anne's Row E14 ....97 B1
St Anne St E14 ....97 B1
St Anne's Trad Est E14 ....97 B1
St Ann's IG11 ....101 A6
St Ann's CE Prim Sch
N15 ....51 B4
St Ann's Cres SW18 ....158 A5
St Ann's Ct NW4 ....46 B6
St Ann's Ctr HA1 ....42 C3
St Ann's Gdns NW5 ....71 A2
St Ann's General Hospl
N4,N15 ....51 A4
St Ann's Hill SW18 ....158 A5
St Ann's Ho WC1 ....234 A1
St Ann's La SW1 ....259 D5
St Ann's Park Rd SW18 ....158 A5
St Ann's Rd N15 ....51 B4
W11 ....112 D6
St Anns Rd SW13 ....133 D4
St Ann's Rd
2 Barking IG11 ....101 A6
Edmonton N9 ....17 D3
Harrow HA1 ....42 C3
St Ann's Sch Ealing W7 ....108 C5
Morden SM4 ....201 D4
St Ann's St SW1 ....115 D3 259 D6
St Ann's Terr
NW8 ....92 B5 229 D4
St Ann's Villas
W11 ....112 D5 244 A3
St Ann's Way CR2 ....220 D2
St Anselm RC Prim Sch
UB2 ....107 B3
St Anselm's Ct SW16 ....182 A5
St Anselm's Pl W1 ....248 C6
St Anselm's RC Prim Sch
Harrow HA1 ....42 C2
Upper Tooting SW17 ....159 A1
St Anselms Rd UB3 ....105 D4
St Anthony's Ave IG8 ....37 C3
St Anthony's Cl 8 E1 ....118 A5
St Anthonys Cl SW17 ....158 C2
St Anthony's Ct
2 SW12 ....159 A5
Orpington BR6 ....226 D6
Upper Tooting SW17 ....159 A2
St Anthony's Flats NW1 ....232 C3
St Anthony's Hospl KT4 ....200 D1
St Anthony's RC Prim Sch
E7 ....77 B1
SE22 ....162 A5
Penge SE20 ....184 B2
St Anthony's Way TW14 ....127 D1
St Antony's RC Prim Sch
IG8 ....37 A6
St Antony's Rd E7 ....77 B1
St Arvans Cl CR0 ....221 C5
St Asaph Ct SE4 ....140 D2
St Asaph Rd SE4 ....140 D2
St Aubins Ct N1 ....235 D6
St Aubyns E18 ....54 D5
St Aubyn's Ave
Hounslow TW3,TW4 ....151 C6
Wimbledon SW19 ....179 B5
St Aubyns Cl BR6 ....227 D5
St Aubyn's Ct SW19 ....179 A4
St Aubyns Gdns BR6 ....227 D6
St Aubyn's Prep Sch IG8 ....36 D3
St Aubyn's Rd SE19 ....183 D4
St Aubyn's Sch IG8 ....36 D3
St Audrey Ave DA7 ....147 C3

St Augustine's Ave
BR1,BR2 210 A4
Ealing W5 88 A4
South Croydon CR2 221 A1
Wembley HA9 66 A5
St Augustine's CE High Sch NW6 91 C5
St Augustine's CE Prim Sch NW6 91 D5
St Augustine's Ct E11 54 D1
St Augustines Ct BR3 185 A1
St Augustine's Prim Sch DA17 125 B2
St Augustine's RC Prim Sch W6 135 A6 264 B5
Ilford IG2 56 D4
St Augustine's Rd DA17 125 B2
NW1 71 D1
St Augustines's RC Prim Sch SE6 186 A5
St Austell Cl HA8 26 B1
St Austell Rd SE13 142 B3
St Awdry's Rd IG11 79 B1
St Barnabas CE Prim Sch SW1 115 A1 258 B2
St Barnabas Cl 11 SE22 161 C6
Beckenham BR3 186 A1
St Barnabas Ct HA3 24 A2
St Barnabas' Gdns KT8 195 C4
St Barnabas Rd E17 53 C3
Mitcham CR4 181 A3
Sutton SM1 218 B3
Woodford IG8 37 C3
St Barnabas St SW1 258 B2
St Barnabas & St Philip's CE Prim Sch W8 113 C3 255 A5
St Barnabas Terr E9 74 D3
St Barnabas Villas SW8 138 A4 270 B2
St Bartholomews CE Prim Sch SE26 162 C1
St Bartholomew's CE Prim Sch SE26 184 C6
St Bartholomew's Cl SE26 184 C6
St Bartholomew's Hospl EC1 94 D2 241 D3
St Bartholomew's Rd E6 100 B5
St Bede's RC Inf Sch SW12 159 D3
St Bede's RC Prim Sch RM6 58 C4
St Benedict's Cl SW17 181 A5
St Benedict's Jun Sch W5 87 C2
St Benedict's Sch W5 87 D2
St Benets Cl SW17 158 C2
St Benet's Gr SM5 202 A2
St Benet's Pl EC3 252 D6
St Bernadette RC Jun Sch SW12 159 C4
St Bernadette's RC Fst & Mid Sch HA3 44 B5
St Bernadette's RC Prim Sch UB10 82 D6
St Bernard Ho 6 E14 120 A3
St Bernards CR0 221 C5
St Bernards Cl 8 SE27 183 B6
St Bernards Ho 1 KT6 214 A6
St Bernard's Rd E6 99 D6
St Blaise Ave BR1 187 B1
St Bonaventure's RC Sec Sch E7 77 A1
St Boniface Catholic Prim Sch SW17 180 D5
St Botolph St E1, EC3 95 D1 243 C2
St Brelades Ct N1 235 D6
St Bride's Ave EC4 241 C1
Edgware HA8 26 B2
St Brides Cl DA18 124 D4
St Bride's Pas EC4 241 C1
St Bride St EC4 94 D1 241 C2
St Catherines Cl
Chessington KT9 213 D2
Upper Tooting SW17 158 C2
St Catherine's Convent Girls Prep & Senior Schs TW1 153 A2
St Catherine's Ct 8 W4 111 C3
St Catherines Ct TW13 150 A3
St Catherine's Dr SE14 140 D3
St Catherines Farm Ct HA4 39 A3
St Catherines Mews SW3 257 C4
St Catherine's RC Mid Sch SW20 200 C4
St Catherine's RC Prim Sch EN5 1 C1
St Catherine's RC Sch for Girls DA6 169 D6
St Catherines Rd
Chingford E4 19 C2
Ruislip HA4 39 B3
St Cecilia's Cl SM3 201 A1
St Cecilia's RC Prim Sch SM3 216 D6
St Chads Cl KT6 197 C2
St Chad's Gdns RM6 59 A2
St Chad's Pl WC1 233 C2
St Chad's RC Prim Sch SE25 205 C4
St Chad's Rd RM6 59 A2
St Chad's St WC1 233 B2
St Charles' Hospl W10 90 D2
St Charles Pl W10 91 A2
St Charles RC Prim Sch W10 90 D2
St Charles RC Sixth Form Coll W10 90 D2
St Charles Sq W10 90 D2
St Christina's Sch NW8 92 C5 230 A3
St Christopher's Cl TW7 130 C4
St Christophers Dr UB3 106 B6
St Christophers Gdns CR7 204 C6
St Christopher's Ho NW1 232 C3
St Christopher's Hospice SE26 184 C5
St Christopher's Mews SM6 219 C3
St Christopher's Pl W1 238 B2
St Christopher's Sch NW3 70 B3
Beckenham BR3 186 A1
Wembley HA9 66 B5
St Clair Dr KT4 216 B4
St Clair Ho 14 E3 97 B4
St Clair Rd E13 99 B5
St Clair's Rd CR0 221 C6
St Clare Bsns Pk TW12 174 A4
St Clare St EC3 243 C1
St Clement Danes CE Prim Sch WC2 94 B1 240 C1
St Clements Ct N7 72 B2
7 SE14 140 D6
8 W11 112 D6
St Clement's Ct EC3 252 D6
St Clements Ho KT12 194 A2
St Clement's Hts SE26 184 A6
St Clement's La WC2 240 D1
St Clements Mans 3 SW6 134 D6
St Clements St N7 72 C1
St Clement & St James CE Prim Sch W11 112 D5 244 A3
St Cloud Rd SE27 183 B6
St Columba's Ct E15 76 C4
St Columbas Ho 2 E17 53 D5
St Columba's RC Sch for Boys DA6 169 D6
St Columb's Ho 11 W10 91 A2
St Crispins Cl NW3 70 C4
St Crispin's Cl UB1 85 B1
St Cross St EC1 94 C2 241 B4
St Cuthberts Gdns 1 HA5 23 B3
St Cuthbert's Rd NW2 69 B2
St Cuthberts Rd N13 32 C4
St Cuthbert with St Matthias Prim Sch SW5 113 D1 255 C2
St Cyprian's Greek Orthodox Prim Sch CR7 183 A2
St Cyprian's St SW17 180 D6
St Davids Cl 27 SE16 118 B1
Wembley HA9 67 A5
St David's Cl BR4 207 D2
St David's Coll BR4 207 D2
St David's Ct 1 E17 54 A6
St Davids Ct 5 E11 55 B4
St David's Ct 8 UB1 86 A1
St David's Dr HA8 26 B2
St David's Pl NW4 46 B2
St David's Sch TW15 148 B1
St David's Sq E14 119 D1
St Denis Rd SE27 183 B6
St Dionis Rd SW6 135 B3
St Domingo Ho SE18 122 B3
St Dominic RC Prim Sch NW5 70 D3
St Dominics RC Prim Sch E9 75 A2
St Dominic's Sixth Form Coll (RC) HA1 64 C6
St Donatt's Rd SE14 141 B4
St Dunstans SM1 217 B2
St Dunstan's Alley EC3 253 A5
St Dunstan's Ave W3 111 B6
St Dunstan's CE Prim Sch SM3 217 A1
St Dunstans Cl UB3 105 D2
St Dunstan's Coll SE6 163 C3
St Dunstan's Ct EC4 241 B1
St Dunstan's Gdns W3 111 B6
St Dunstan's Hill EC3 253 A5
Cheam SM1,SM3 217 A3
St Dunstan's La EC3 253 A5
Beckenham BR3 208 A4
St Dunstans Rd E7 77 C2
St Dunstan's Rd W6 112 D1
W7 108 C4
Cranford TW5 128 B3
Feltham TW13 149 D1
South Norwood SE25 205 D5
St Edmund RC Sch E14 119 C2
St Edmunds Ave HA4 39 B3
St Edmunds Cl DA18 124 D4
St Edmund's Cl NW8 230 C5
St Edmunds Cl SW17 158 C2
St Edmund's Ct NW8 230 C5
St Edmunds Dr HA7 25 A2
St Edmund's La TW2 151 D4
St Edmund's RC Prim Sch
Edmonton N9 18 B3
Twickenham TW2 151 D4
St Edmunds Rd N9 18 A4
St Edmund's Rd IG1 56 B3
St Edmund's Sq SW13 134 C6
St Edmund's Terr NW8 92 D6 230 C5
St Edward's CE Comp Sch RM7 59 C3
St Edward's Cl NW11 47 C3
St Edwards Ct 3 E10 54 A2
St Edward's Ct NW11 47 C3
St Edward's RC Prim Sch E6 99 C6
St Edward's RC Prim Sch NW1 92 C3 237 B5
St Egberts Way E4 20 A3
St Elizabeth Ct 8 E10 53 D2
St Elizabeth's RC Prim Sch N12 30 A6
St Elizabeth's RC Prim Sch TW10 154 B5
St Elmo Rd W12 111 D4
St Elmos Rd SE16 119 A4
St Elphege's RC Inf Sch SM6 220 A2
St Elphege's RC Jun Sch SM6 220 A2
St Erkenwald Mews IG11 101 B6
St Erkenwald Rd IG11 101 B6
St Ermin's Hill SW1 259 C6
St Ervan's Rd W10 91 B2
St Eugene de Mazenod RC Prim Sch NW6 91 C6
St Faith's CE Prim Sch SW18 158 A6
St Faith's Cl EN2 5 A4
St Faith's Rd SE24 160 D3
St Fillans Rd SE6 164 A4
St Francesca Cabrini Prim Sch SE23 162 C5
St Francis Cl BR6 211 C3
St Francis de Sales RC Jun Sch N17 33 D3
St Francis' Ho NW1 232 C3
St Francis Lo HA0 64 D5
St Francis of Assisi RC Prim Sch W11 112 D6
St Francis RC Prim Sch E15 76 C3
SE15 140 A5
St Francis Rd SE22 139 C1
St Francis Way IG1 79 B4
St Francis Xavier Sixth Form Coll SW12 159 B5
St Gables Ct N11 31 D3
St Gabriel's CE Prim Sch SW1 115 C1 259 A1
St Gabriel's Cl E11 55 B1
St Gabriel's Rd NW2 68 D3
St George Ho SW11 268 B1
St George's Ave E7 77 B1
N7 71 D4
NW9 45 B5
W5 109 D4
Southall UB1 107 B6
St George's Battersea CE Prim Sch SW8 137 C5 269 B3
St George's Bickley CE Prim Sch BR1 187 D1
St George's Cath NW1 231 D2
St George's Cath RC Jun & Inf Sch SE1 116 D3 261 C6
St George's CE Prim Sch SE5 139 C5
St George's Circ SE1 116 D3 261 C6
St George's Cl NW11 47 B3
St Georges Cl Erith SE28 102 D1
Wembley HA0 65 A5
St Georges Ct E17 54 B4
E6 100 B3
St George's Ct SE1 261 C5
SW3 257 A4
SW7 256 A5
St Georges Ct
Harrow HA3 43 A3
Penge SE20 184 B2
Putney SW15 135 B1
St George's Dr SW1 115 C1 259 A2
Ickenham UB10 60 B6
South Oxhey WD19 23 A6
St George's Field W2 92 C1 237 B1
St George's Gdns KT6 214 D6
St George's Gr SW17 158 B1
St Georges Hanover Sq Sch W1 115 A6 248 B5
St George's Ho NW1 232 B3
St George's Hospl SW17 180 B5
St Georges Ind Est
Kingston KT2 175 D5
Tottenham N22 32 D3
St George's La EC3 253 A6
St Georges Lo N10 49 C5
St Georges Mews 11 NW1 70 D1
St George's Mews SE1 261 B6
St George's RC Cath SE1 116 C3 261 B6
St George's RC Prim Sch
Enfield EN2 5 B3
Harrow HA1 64 D5
St George's RC Sec Sch W9 91 D5
St Georges Rd BR1 210 B6
BR5 211 B3
W4 111 B4
St George's Rd DA14 190 D4
E10 76 A5
E7 77 B2
NW11 47 B3
SE1 116 D3 261 C5
St Georges Rd RM9 81 A4
St George's Rd
Beckenham BR3 185 D2
Ealing W7 108 D5
Edmonton N9 18 A1
St George's Rd *continued*
Enfield EN1 5 D5
Feltham TW13 172 D6
Isleworth TW1 153 B6
2 Kingston KT2 176 C3
Mitcham CR4 203 B6
Palmers Green N13 16 B2
Redbridge IG1 56 B2
Richmond TW9 132 B2
Wallington SM6 219 B3
Wimbledon SW19 179 B4
St Georges Rd W BR1 188 A1
St George's Residences 4 SW2 160 C6
St Georges's Ct EC4 241 C2
St Georges Sh & L Ctr HA1 42 C3
St Georges Sq 1 E14 119 A6
St George's Sq E7 77 B1
SE8 119 B2
SW1 115 D1 259 C1
Kingston KT3 199 C6
St George's Square Mews SW1 259 C1
St George St W1 115 B6 248 D6
St Georges Terr NW1 70 D1
St George's Way SE15 139 C6
St George's Wlk CR0 221 A5
St George the Martyr CE Prim Sch WC1 94 B3 240 D5
St Gerards Cl SW4 159 C6
St German's Pl SE3 143 A4
St German's Rd SE23 163 A3
St Gildas' RC Jun Sch N8 50 A3
St Giles Ave
Dagenham RM10 81 D1
Uxbridge UB10 61 A4
St Giles Cir WC1 93 D1 239 D2
St Giles Cl BR6 227 B3
Dagenham RM10 81 D1
St Giles Colls WC1 94 A2 240 B4
St Giles Ct WC2 240 A2
Ealing W13 109 C5
St Giles High St WC2 93 D1 239 D2
St Giles Hospl SE5 139 C4
St Giles Pas WC2 239 D1
St Giles Rd SE5 139 C4
St Giles' Sch CR2 220 D2
St Giles Twr 3 SE5 139 C4
St Gilles Ho 15 E2 96 D5
St Gothard Rd SE21, SE27 183 B6
St Gregory Cl HA4 62 C4
St Gregory RC High Sch HA3 43 D4
St Gregory's RC Prim Sch W5 87 D2
St Helena Ho WC1 234 A1
St Helena Pier TW9 153 D6
St Helena Rd SE16 118 D2
St Helena St WC1 234 A1
St Helena Terr 23 TW9 153 D6
St Helens KT7 196 D2
Saint Helens Coll UB10 60 C1
St Helen's Cres SW16 182 B2
St Helen's Gdns W10 90 D1
St Helen's Pl EC3 243 A2
St Helen's RC Inf Sch E17 54 A4
St Helen's RC Prim Sch E13 99 A3
SW9 138 C2
St Helens Rd 7 DA18 124 D4
St Helen's Rd
Ealing W13 109 C5
Redbridge IG1 56 B3
Thornton Heath SW16 182 B2
St Helens Sch UB10 60 C1
St Helier Ave SM4 202 A3
St Helier Ct 4 N1 95 C6
St Helier Hospl SM5 202 A1
St Heliers Ave TW3,TW4 151 C6
St Helier's Rd E10 54 A3
St Helier Sta SM4 201 C3
St Hilda's Ave TW15 170 A5
St Hilda's Cl NW6 68 D1
St Hildas Cl SW17 158 C2
St Hilda's Rd SW13 134 B6
St Hildas Wharf E1 118 C5
St Hubert's Ho 1 E14 119 C3
St Hughes Cl SW17 158 C2
St Hugh's Rd SE20 184 B3
St Ignatius Coll EN1 6 B6
St Ignatius' RC Prim Sch N15 51 D3
St Ignatius RC Prim Sch TW16 172 A2
St Ivian Ct 3 N10 31 B1
St James Apartments 2 E17 53 A4
St James Ave N20 14 C1
Sutton SM1 217 C3
St James' Ave W13 109 A5
St James CE Jun Sch E7 77 A3
St James CE Prim Sch EN3 6 C3
St James Cl N20 14 C1
Barnet EN4 2 B1
St James' Cl
New Malden KT3 199 D4
Ruislip HA4 62 C6
St James Ct 11 E2 96 A4
SE3 143 B4
10 W4 110 C1
St James' Ct SW1 259
W4 111 B3
St James Ct
Thornton Heath CR0 204 D2
Wanstead E12 77 C6
St James' Ct 7 KT1 198 A6
St James Gate IG9 21 B3
St James Gdns IG6 58 B5
St James' Gdns HA0 66 A1
St James Hatcham CE Prim Sch SE14 141 A4
St James Independent Schs W14 113 A2 254 A4
St James Ind Mews SE1 118 A1
St James' Mans NW6 69 C1
St James Mews E14 120 A3
St James RC Prim Sch BR5 210 D4
St James' Rd E15 76 D3
St James Rd
Carshalton SM5 218 C5
Kingston KT1 175 D1
Sutton SM1,SM2 217 C3
St James' Rd
Edmonton N9 18 B2
Mitcham CR4 181 A3
Surbiton KT6 197 D3
St James's SE14 141 A4
St James's App EC2 243 A5
St James's Ave E2 96 C5
Beckenham BR3 207 A6
Hampton TW12 174 A5
St James's CE Prim Sch N10 49 A5
SE16 118 A3
St James School Flats 5 N7 72 C3
St James's Cl NW8 230 C5
SE18 123 A1
Upper Tooting SW17 158 D2
St James's Cloisters 2 SE22 139 D1
St James's Cotts 14 TW10 153 D6
St James's Cres SW9 138 C2
St James's Ct 8 N18 34 A5
St James's Dr
Balham SW12,SW17 158 D4
Upper Tooting SW17 158 D3
St James's Gdns W11 113 A5 244 A4
St James's Gr SW11 136 D3
St James's La N10 49 B5
St James's Lo 4 CR0 205 C1
St James's Market SW1 249 C5
St James's Mews E17 53 A4
St James's Palace* SW1 115 C5 249 B3
St James's Park* SW1 249 C2
St James's Park Sta SW1 115 D3 259 C6
St James's Pas EC3 243 B1
St James's Pk CR0 205 A2
St James's Pl SW1 115 C5 249 A3
St James's RC High Sch NW9 27 D2
St James's RC Prim Sch TW2 152 C1
St James's Rd SE1,SE16 118 A2
Hampton TW12 173 D5
Thornton Heath CR0 205 B2
St James's Sq SW1 115 C5 249 B4
St James's St E17 53 A4
SW1 115 C5 249 A4
St James's & St Michael's CE Prim Sch W2 114 A6 246 A6
St James St W6 112 C1
St James's Terr NW8 230 C4
2 Upper Tooting SW12 159 A3
St James's Terrace Mews NW8 230 C5
St James Street Sta E17 53 A4
St James's Wlk EC1 241 C6
St James The Great RC Prim Sch SE15 139 D4
South Norwood CR7 182 D1
St James Way DA14 191 A5
St Jerome's Gr UB3 83 A1
St Joachim's RC Prim Sch E16 99 C1
St Joan of Arc RC Prim Sch N5 73 A4
St Joan's Rd N9 17 D2
St John Baptist CE Prim Sch BR1 186 A6
St John CE Prim Sch SE17 117 A2 262 B3
St John Cl SW6 265 A4
St John Evangelist RC Prim Sch N1 94 D5 234 C4
St John Fisher RC Fst & Mid Sch HA5 41 C5
St John Fisher RC Prim Sch DA18 125 A3
Wembley UB6 87 C4
West Barnes SW20 200 D4
St John of Jerusalem CE Prim Sch E9 74 C1
St John Rigby RC Coll BR4 224 B4
St John's Angell Town CE Prim Sch SW9 138 C3
St John's Ave N11 30 D5
NW10 89 D6
Putney SW15 156 D6
St Johns CE Fst Sch HA7 25 B6
St John's CE Inf Sch NW4 46 B4
St John's CE JMI Sch N11 30 D6
St Johns CE Mid Sch HA7 25 A6
St John's CE Prim Sch E2 96 C5
N20 14 A2
Buckhurst Hill IG9 21 B3
Fulham SW6 135 A4 264 B1
Kingston KT1 198 A6
Penge SE20 184 C3
St John's Church Rd E9 74 C3
St John's Cl N20 14 A1
St Johns Cl N14 15 C5
St Johns Cl HA9 66 A3
St Johns Concert Hall SW1 260 A5
St John's Cotts 2 SE20 184 C3
St John's Cres SW9 138 C2
St Johns Ct 39 E1 118 B5
St John's Ct E11 54 D1
N4 72 D6
N5 72 D4
5 NW3 70 A2
SE13 142 A3
W6 112 B2
Buckhurst Hill IG9 21 B3
2 Harrow HA1 42 D3
Isleworth TW7 130 D3
Kingston KT1 198 A5
St Johns Dr KT12 194 C1
St John's Dr SW18 157 D3
St John's Est SE1 253 C1
St John's Gdns W11 113 B6 244 C5
St John's Gr N19 71 C6
3 Barnes SW13 133 D3
1 Richmond TW9 132 A1
St John's (Highbury Vale) CE Prim Sch N5 72 D5
St John's Hill SW11 136 B1
St John's Hill Gr SW11 136 B1
St Johns Ho 5 SE17 139 B6
St John's La EC1 94 D2 241 D4
St John's Mans E5 74 C3
St John's Par Ealing W13 109 B5
3 Sidcup DA14 190 B6
St John's Park Mans N19 71 C5
St John's Path EC1 241 C5
St John's Pk SE3 143 A5
St John's Pl EC1 241 C5
St John's Prim Sch W13 109 A6
St John's RC Prim Sch SE16 119 A4
St John's Rd DA16 146 B2
E16 99 A1
E6 100 A6
N15 51 C3
NW11 47 B3
SW11 136 C1
St Johns Rd Ilford IG2 57 C2
Kingston KT3 199 A6
St John's Rd
Barking IG11 101 C6
Carshalton SM5 218 C5
Chingford E17 36 A1
Chingford E4 35 D6
Croydon CR0 220 D5
East Molesey KT8 196 B5
Feltham TW13 173 B6
Harrow HA1 42 D3
Isleworth TW7 130 D3
Orpington BR5,BR6 211 C3
Penge SE20 184 C4
Richmond TW9 132 A1
Sidcup DA14 190 B6
Southall UB2 107 A3
Sutton SM1 217 D6
Teddington KT1 175 C1
Wembley HA9 66 A3
Wimbledon SW19 179 A4
St John's (Shirley) CE Prim Sch CR0 222 D5
St John's Sq EC1 94 D3 241 C5
St Johns Sta SE8 141 C3
St John's & St Clements CE Prim Sch SE15 140 A2
St John St EC1 94 D3 241 C6
St John's Terr E7 77 B2
SE18 145 B6
W10 90 D3
Enfield EN2 5 B6
St John & St James CE Prim Sch E9 74 C3
Edmonton N18 33 D5
St Johnstone Ho 15 N12 29 D6
St John's (Upper Holloway) Prim Sch N19 71 D6
St John's Vale SE8 141 C3
St John's Village 2 N11 30 D5
St John's Villas N19 71 D6
W8 255 D5
St John's Way N19 49 D1
St John's Wood Ct NW8 229 D1
St John's Wood High St NW8 92 C5 230 A3
St John's Wood Park NW8 92 B6 229 C6
St John's Wood Prep Sch NW8 92 C4 230 A1
St John's Wood Rd NW8 92 B4 229 D1
St John's Wood Sta NW8 92 B5 229 C4
St John's Wood Terr NW8 92 C5 230 A4

St John the Baptist CE Jun Sch KT1 175 D3
St John the Baptist CE Prim Sch N1 95 C5
St John the Divine CE Jun & Inf Sch SE5 138 D5
St John Vianney RC Prim Sch N8 50 D5
St Joseph RC Prim Sch W7 108 C5
St Joseph's Acad SE3 142 C2
St Josephs Cl BR6 227 D4
St Joseph's Cl W10 91 A2
St Joseph's Coll Mill Hill Missionaries NW7 27 D6
St Joseph's Convent Prep Sch KT8 196 A4
St Joseph's Convent Prim Sch NW4 46 B5
St Joseph's Convent Sch E11 55 A3
St Josephs Ct 19 E10 53 D2
3 NW10 89 D5
St Joseph's Ct E4 20 B4
St Joseph's Dr UB1 107 B5
St Joseph's Flats NW1 232 C2
St Josephs Gr NW4 46 B5
St Joseph's Ho W6 112 D2
St Joseph's Hospice E9, E8 96 B6
St Joseph's RC Coll SW16 182 D4
St Josephs RC Fst & Mid Sch HA3 25 A1
St Joseph's RC Inf Sch E10 75 C6
South Norwood SE19 183 A4
St Joseph's RC Jun & Inf Sch SE1 117 A4 252 B2
SE16 118 A4
SE16 118 C3
St Joseph's RC Jun & Inf Schs HA9 66 B3
St Joseph's RC Jun Sch E10 53 D1
SE5 139 A5
South Norwood SE19 183 A4
St Joseph's RC Prim Sch N19 49 B1
NW10 67 C1
SE10 120 C1
SE8 141 C5
SW18 157 C6
SW3 114 D2 257 C3
W9 92 A4 229 A1
WC2 94 A1 240 B2
Barking IG11 101 A6
Dagenham RM9 81 B4
Kingston KT1 176 B1
St Joseph's RC Sch BR1 187 B3
St Joseph's Rd N9 18 C3
St Joseph's St SW8 268 D2
St Joseph's Vale SE3 142 B2
St Jude's CE Prim Sch SE24 160 D6
St Judes Ho 6 W10 91 B4
St Jude's Prim Sch SE1 116 D3 261 C5
St Jude's Rd E2 96 B5
St Jude's & St Paul's Prim Sch N1 73 C2
St Jude St N16 73 C3
St Julian's Cl SW16 182 C6
St Julian's Farm Rd SE27,SW16 182 D6
St Julian's Rd NW6 91 C6
St Katharine Docks★ E1 117 D5 253 D4
St Katharine's Ho N1 234 A4
St Katharine's Pier E1 117 D5 253 D4
St Katharine's Way E1 117 D5 253 D4
St Katherine's Prec NW1 231 C4
St Katherines Rd DA18 124 D4
St Katherine's Row EC3 243 B1
St Katherine's Wlk 1 W11 112 D5
St Keverne Rd SE9 188 A6
St Kilda Rd BR6 211 D1
Ealing W13 109 A4
St Kilda's Rd N16 51 C1
Harrow HA1 42 C3
St Kitts Terr SE19 183 C5
St Laurence's Cl NW6 90 D6
St Lawrence CE Jun & Mid Sch KT8 196 B5
St Lawrence Cl HA8 26 B3
St Lawrence Ct N1 235 D6
St Lawrence Dr HA5 40 B4
St Lawrence Ho SE1 263 B6
St Lawrence RC Sch TW13 150 B2
St Lawrence St E14 120 A5
St Lawrence Terr W10 91 A2
St Lawrence Way SW9 138 C3
St Leonards Ave HA3 43 C4
St Leonard's Ave E4 36 B4
St Leonards CE Prim Sch SW16 181 D5
St Leonards Cl 4 DA16 146 A2
St Leonard's Ct N1 235 D2
St Leonards Ct SW14 133 A2
St Leonards Gdns IG1 79 A3
St Leonard's Gdns TW5 129 A4
St Leonard's Hospl N1 95 C5
St Leonard's Rd E14 98 A2
NW10 89 B3
St Leonards Rd SW14 133 A2
St Leonard's Rd
Claygate KT10 212 D2
Croydon CR0 220 D5
Ealing W13 109 C6
Kingston KT6 197 D4
Thames Ditton KT7 197 A2
St Leonards Rise BR6 227 C4
St Leonard's Sq NW5 71 A2
Kingston KT6 197 D4
St Leonard's St E3 97 D4
St Leonard's Terr SW3 114 D1 257 D1
St Leonard's Wlk SW16 182 B3
St Loo Ave SW3 136 C6 267 B6
St Loo Ct SW3 267 C6
St Louis Rd SE27 183 B6
St Loy's Rd N17 51 D6
St Lucia Dr E15 98 D6
St Luke Ct 5 E10 53 D2
St Luke's Ave SW4 137 D1
Enfield EN2 5 B5
Ilford IG1 78 D3
St Luke's CE Prim Sch E14 120 B2
St Luke's CE Prim Sch EC1 235 A2
W9 91 B4
Kingston KT2 176 B2
Richmond TW9 132 C4
West Norwood SE27 183 A5
St Luke's Cl EC1 95 A3 242 B6
Croydon SE25 206 B3
St Luke's Ct W11 91 B1
St Luke's Hospl W1 93 C3 239 A5
St Luke's Mews W11 91 B1
St Luke's Path 1 IG1 78 D3
St Luke's Prim Sch E16 98 D1
St Luke's Rd W11 91 B2
Uxbridge UB10 60 A1
St Luke's Sq E16 98 D1
St Luke's St SW3 257 B2
St Luke's Woodside Hospl N10 49 A5
St Malo Ave N9 18 C1
St Margaret Clitherow RC Prim Sch NW10 67 A4
Woolwich SE28 124 B5
St Margarets IG11 101 B6
St Margarets Ave DA15 167 B1
N20 14 A3
St Margaret's Ave N8, N15 50 D5
St Margarets Ave Ashford TW15 170 D5
Hillingdon UB8 82 C3
St Margaret's Ave Cheam SM3 217 A5
Harrow HA2 64 A5
St Margarets Bsns Ctr 11 TW1 153 B5
St Margaret's CE Prim Sch SE18 123 A1
Barking IG11 79 A1
St Margaret's Cres SW15 156 B6
St Margaret's Ct E15 76 C4
Putney SW15 134 B1
9 Twickenham TW1 153 B5
St Margaret's Dr TW1 153 B6
St Margaret's Gr E11 76 D5
SE18 145 A6
Twickenham TW1 153 A5
St Margaret's La W8 113 D3 255 C5
St Margaret's Lee CE Prim Sch SE13 142 C1
St Margarets Lo W3 110 D4
St Margaret's Rd N17 51 C6
NW10 90 C4
SE4 141 B1
W7 108 C4
St Margarets Rd Edgware HA8 26 D5
Ruislip HA4 39 B3
St Margaret's Rd Isleworth TW1 153 B6
Wanstead E12 77 C6
St Margarets Rdbt TW1 153 B6
St Margaret's Sch NW3 69 D4
St Margaret's Sta TW1 153 B5
St Margaret St SW1 250 A1
St Margaret's Terr SE18 123 A1
St Mark's CE Prim Sch BR2 209 A6
SE11 138 B6 270 D6
Croydon SE25 206 A5
St Marks Cl 5 SE10 142 A5
St Mark's Cl Barnet EN5 1 D2
Harrow HA1 43 B1
St Mark's Cres NW1 93 A6 231 B6
St Mark's Ct 7 E10 53 D2
W7 108 C4
St Mark's Fst Sch CR4 180 D1
St Marks Gate E9 75 B1
St Mark's Gr SW10 135 D5 265 D4
St Mark's Hill KT6 198 A3
St Marks Ho 6 SE17 139 B6
St Mark's Ho 8 E17 54 A5
St Mark's Hospl EC1 94 D4 234 D2
St Marks Ind Est E16 121 D5
St Mark's Pl W11 91 A1
Wimbledon SW19 179 B4
St Mark's Prim Sch N19 72 A6
W7 108 C4
St Mark's RC Sch TW3 129 C2
St Mark's Rd W10 90 D2
W11 91 A1
W7 108 C4
Bromley BR2 209 B6
Croydon SE25 206 A5
Ealing W5 110 A5
Enfield EN1 17 D6
Mitcham CR4 181 A1
Teddington TW11 175 B3
St Mark's Rise E8 73 D3
St Mark's Sq NW1 231 A5
St Mark St E1 95 D1 243 D1
St Martha's Convent Jun Sch for Girls EN5 1 A1
St Martin-in-the-Fields High Sch for Girls SW2 160 C3
St Martin of Porres RC Prim Sch N11 31 C4
St Martin's Almshos NW1 232 A6
St Martin's App HA4 39 C2
St Martin's Ave E6 99 D5
St Martins Cl DA18 124 D4
St Martin's Cl NW1 232 A6
St Martins Cl WD19 22 C6
St Martin's Cl EN1 6 B4
St Martins Ct N1 95 C6
St Martin's Ct WC2 250 A6
West Norwood SE27 160 D2
St Martin's La WC2 116 A6 250 A5
St Martins La BR3 207 D4
St Martin's Le Grand EC1 242 A2
St Martin's Pl WC2 250 A5
St Martin's Rd N2 30 B2
SW9 138 B3
Edmonton N9 18 B2
St Martin's Sch NW7 27 B5
St Martin's St WC2 249 D5
St Martin's Way SW17 158 A1
St Mary Abbots CE Prim Sch W8 113 D4 245 C1
St Mary Abbot's Ct W14 254 C5
St Mary Abbot's Pl W8 254 D5
St Mary Abbots Terr W14 254 D5
St Mary at Hill EC3 117 C6 253 A5
St Mary Ave SM6 219 B5
St Mary Axe EC3 95 C1 243 B2
St Marychurch St SE16 118 C4
St Mary Graces Ct E1 253 D5
St Marylebone CE Sch The W1 93 A2 238 A3
St Mary le Bow Church★ EC2 242 B1
St Mary- le-Park Ct SW11 267 B3
St Mary Magdalene CE Prim Sch N7 72 C2
SE15 140 B3
W2 91 D2
St Mary Magdalens RC Prim Sch SE4 141 A1
St Mary Magdalen's RC Prim Sch SW14 133 B2
St Mary Magdelen's RC Jun Sch NW2 68 B2
St Mary Newington Cl SE17 263 B2
St Mary of the Angels RC Prim Sch W2 91 C1
St Mary RC Prim Sch W10 91 A3
St Mary Rd E17 53 D5
St Marys IG11 101 B6
St Mary's App E12 78 B3
St Mary's Ave N3 29 B1
St Marys Ave UB2 107 D2
St Mary's Ave Beckenham BR2 208 C6
Teddington TW11 174 D4
Wanstead E11 55 B2
St Mary's Bryanston Square CE Sch W1 92 D2 237 C4
St Mary's CE High Sch (Lower & Upper) NW4 46 C6
St Mary's CE High Sch (Middle) NW4 46 C6
St Mary's CE Inf Sch N8 50 B5
St Mary's CE Jun Sch N8 50 A5
NW4 46 B4
St Mary's CE Prim Sch E17 53 D5
N1 94 D6 234 D6
N3 29 B3
NW10 67 C2
SE18 122 C2
Chessington KT9 214 B2
East Barnet EN4 14 C5
Long Ditton KT7 197 B1
Putney SW15 134 D2
St Mary's CE Sch TW19 148 A4
St Mary's Church Sch TW1 153 A4
St Mary's Cl BR5 190 B1
Chessington KT9 214 B1
Ewell KT17 215 D1
Sunbury TW16 194 A5
Tottenham N17 34 A2
St Mary's Coll TW1 152 D1
St Mary's Cottage Hospl TW12 173 B2
St Mary's Cres Hayes UB3 105 D6
Hendon NW4 46 B6
Hounslow TW7 130 C5
St Marys Ct E6 100 B3
St Marys Ct *continued*
SE7 143 D5
St Mary's Ct E11 54 D1
N12 30 A3
W5 109 D4
W6 111 D3
Kingston KT3 199 C6
Wallington SM6 219 C4
St Mary's Dr TW14 149 A4
St Mary's Est 2 SE16 118 C4
St Mary's Flats NW1 232 C2
St Mary's Gate W8 255 C5
St Mary's Gdns SE11 261 B4
St Mary's Gn 1 N2 48 A6
St Mary's Gr N1 72 D2
Barnes SW13 134 B2
Chiswick W4 132 D6
Richmond TW10,TW9 132 B1
St Mary's Ho N1 234 D6
W5 109 D3
St Mary's Hospl W2 92 B1 236 D2
St Mary's Inf Sch E17 53 D5
St Mary's Kilburn CE Prim Sch NW6 91 C6
St Mary's Lewisham CE Prim Sch SE13 163 D6
St Mary's Lo E11 55 B3
St Mary's Mans NW10 89 C6
W2 92 B2 236 C4
St Mary's Medical Sch W2 92 B1 236 D2
St Mary's Mews NW6 69 D1
St Mary's Path N1 234 D6
St Mary's Pl SE9 166 C5
W5 109 D4
W8 113 D3 255 C5
St Mary's RC High Sch CR0 205 A1
St Mary's RC Inf Sch CR0 205 B1
St Mary's RC Jun & Inf Schs N15 51 B4
St Mary's RC Jun Sch E17 54 A6
Croydon CR0 205 B1
Wallington SM5 218 D3
St Mary's RC Prim Sch NW6 91 C5
SE9 166 C6
SW4 159 C6
SW8 137 B4 268 D2
W14 112 D3
Beckenham BR3 186 A3
Chingford E4 20 B3
Chiswick W4 133 C6
Enfield EN3 6 D1
Isleworth TW7 131 A2
Merton SW19 179 C3
St Mary's RC Sch TW7 131 A2
St Mary's Rd E10 76 A6
E13 99 B5
N2 30 B2
N8 50 A5
N9 18 C3
NW10 89 C6
NW11 47 A2
SE15 140 C3
St Marys Rd IG1 79 B6
St Mary's Rd Ealing W5 109 D5
East Barnet EN4 14 D4
East Molesey KT8 196 B4
Hayes UB3 105 D6
Long Ditton KT6 197 C1
South Norwood SE25 205 C6
Surbiton KT6 197 D3
Wimbledon SW19 179 B5
Worcester Park KT4 215 C6
St Mary's Roman Catholic Inf Sch SM5 218 D4
St Mary's Sch Hampstead NW3 70 B3
St Mary's Sq W2 236 C4
W5 109 D4
St Mary's Stoke Newington CE Prim Sch N16 73 C6
St Mary's & St Peter's CE Prim Sch TW11 174 D5
St Mary St SE18 122 C2
St Mary's Terr W2 236 C4
St Mary & St Joseph's Sch DA14 190 A5
St Mary & St Michael Prim Sch E1 96 C1
St Mary & St Pancras CE Prim Sch NW1 93 D5 232 C3
St Mary's Twr EC1 242 B5
St Marys View HA3 43 C4
St Mary's Wlk SE11 261 B4
Hayes UB3 105 D6
St Matthew's Ave KT6 198 B1
St Matthew's CE Fst Sch SW20 178 A2
St Matthew's CE Prim Sch Enfield EN3 18 C6
Surbiton KT6 198 A2
Yiewsley UB7 104 A5
St Matthews Ct 6 E10 53 D2
E15 76 D1
N10 31 A1
SE1 262 A5
St Matthew's Ct TW15 170 C5
St Matthews Dr BR1 210 B6
St Matthew's Ho 8 SE17 139 B6
St Matthew's Lo NW1 232 B4
St Matthew's Rd SW2 160 B6
Ealing W5 110 A5
St Matthew's Row E2 96 A3
St Matthews Sch Westminster SW1 115 D3 259 D6
St Matthew St SW1 259 C5
St Matthias CE Prim Sch E2 95 D3 243 D6
St Matthias Cl NW9 45 D4
St Matthias's CE Prim Sch N16 73 C4
St Maur Rd SW6 135 B4 264 D1
St Mellion Cl SE28 102 D1
St Merryn Cl SE18 145 B5
St Merryn Ct BR3 185 C3
St Michael-at-Bowes CE Jun Sch N13 32 C4
St Michael's Alley EC3 242 D1
St Michaels Ave N9 18 C4
St Michael's Ave HA9 66 C2
St Michael's CE Jun & Inf Sch N22 32 B2
St Michael's CE Prim Sch N6 49 A2
NW1 93 C6 232 A6
Enfield EN2 5 A4
Forest Hill SE26 185 A6
Wandsworth SW18 157 B4
St Michaels Cl BR1 210 A6
4 E16 99 D2
St Michael's Cl DA18 124 D4
N12 30 C5
N3 29 B1
St Michaels Cl KT4 215 D6
St Michael's Cres HA5 41 A3
St Michaels Ct E14 98 A2
St Michael's Ct N11 15 A1
NW11 47 B2
St Michael's East Wickham CE Sch DA16 146 C4
St Michael's Flats NW1 232 C3
St Michael's Gdns W10 91 A2
St Michael's Hospl EN2 5 B4
St Michael's RC Gram Sch N12 30 A5
St Michael's RC Prim Sch E6 100 B5
Ashford TW15 170 C5
St Michael's RC Sch SE16 118 A4
St Michael's Rd DA16 146 B2
NW2 68 C4
SW9 138 B3
St Michaels Rd TW15 170 C5
St Michael's Rd Croydon CR0 205 A1
Wallington SM6 219 C2
St Michael's Rise DA16 146 B4
St Michael's St W2 92 C1 237 A2
St Michael's Terr N22 32 A2
St Michael & St Martin RC Prim Sch TW4 129 B2
St Michael Twr E17 53 B4
St Mildred's Ct EC2 242 C1
St Mildreds Rd SE12, SE6 164 D4
St Mirren Ct EN5 14 A6
St Monica's RC Prim Sch N1 95 C4
St Nicholas CE JMI Sch WD6 9 D5
St Nicholas CE Prim Sch TW17 192 D3
St Nicholas Cl WD6 9 D5
St Nicholas Ct SE18 123 D1
St Nicholas Ctr SM1 217 D3
St Nicholas Dr TW17 192 C2
St Nicholas Elstree CE Prim Sch WD6 9 D5
St Nicholas' Flats NW1 232 C3
St Nicholas Glebe SW17 181 A4
St Nicholas Ho SE8 141 C6
St Nicholas Rd SE18 123 D2
Sutton SM1 217 D3
Thames Ditton KT7 196 D3
St Nicholas Sch NW9 67 A6
St Nicholas St SE8 141 C4
St Nicholas Way SM1 217 D3
St Nicolas La BR7 188 A2
St Ninian's Ct N20 14 D1
St Norbert Gn SE4 141 A1
St Norbert Rd SE4 141 A1
St Olaf's Rd SW6 135 A5 264 B3
St Olaves Ct W2 245 C5
St Olave's Ct EC2 242 C1
St Olave's Est SE1 253 B2
St Olave's Gdns SE11 261 A4
St Olave's Mans SE11 261 A4
St Olaves Prep Sch SE9 166 D2
St Olave's Rd E6 100 C6
St Olave's Wlk SW16 181 D1
St Olav's Sq 27 SE16 118 C4
St Osmund's RC Prim Sch SW13 133 D4
St Oswald's Pl SE11 116 B1 260 C1
St Oswald's Rd SW16 182 D2
St Oswulf St SW1 259 D3
St Owen Ho SE1 263 B6
St Pancras Almshouses 13 NW5 70 D3
St Pancras Commercial Ctr NW1 232 B6
St Pancras Ct N2 30 B1
St Pancras Hospl NW1 93 D6 232 C5
St Pancras Sta WC1 94 A4 233 A2
St Pancras Way NW1 93 C6 232 C6
St Patrick's RC Inf Sch E1 118 B5
St Patrick's RC Prim Sch E17 53 A5
NW5 71 B3
SE18 123 B2
St Paul's & All Hallows CE Jun & Inf Sch N17 34 A3
St Paul's Ave NW2 68 C2
SE16 118 D5
Harrow HA3 44 B5
St Paul's Cath★ EC4 95 A1 242 A1
St Paul's Catholic Coll TW16 172 A2
St Pauls Catholic Sch TW16 172 A2
St Paul's Cath Sch EC4 95 A1 242 A1
St Paul's CE Jun Sch KT2 176 C3
St Paul's CE Prim Sch N11 31 B5
NW3 70 D1
NW7 28 B6
SE17 262 B2
W6 112 C1
St Pauls CE Prim Sch TW8 131 D6
St Paul's CE Prim Sch Chessington KT9 214 A4
Southgate N21 16 D4
St Paul's Church Yd EC4 95 A1 242 A1
St Pauls Cl W5 110 B4
St Paul's Cl SE7 121 D1
St Pauls Cl UB3 105 B1
St Paul's Cl Ashford TW15 171 A5
Carshalton SM5 202 C1
Chessington KT9 213 D4
Hounslow TW3,TW4 129 A3
St Paul's Cray Rd BR7 189 B2
St Pauls Cres NW1 71 D1
St Paul's Ct 5 N19 72 A6
SW4 137 D1
Hounslow TW4 129 A2
St Paul's Dr E15 76 B3
St Paul's Girls' Sch W6 112 D2
St Pauls Mews NW1 71 D1
St Paul's Pl N1 73 B2
St Paul's RC Prim Sch Thames Ditton KT7 196 C2
Wood Green N22 32 B1
St Paul's RC Sec Sch SE2 146 A6
St Paul's Rd N1 73 A2
St Pauls Rd Barking IG11 101 A6
Richmond TW9 132 B2
St Paul's Rd Brentford TW8 131 D6
South Norwood CR7 205 A6
Tottenham N17 34 A2
St Pauls Rise N13 32 D4
St Paul's Sch SW13 112 A1
St Paul's Sq BR2 187 A1
St Paul's Sta EC2 95 A1 242 A2
St Paul St N1 235 B5
St Paul's Terr SE17 138 D6
St Paul's Twr 13 E10 53 D2
St Pauls View WC1 234 A1
St Paul's Way E3 97 C2
N3 29 D3
St Paul's Way Com Sch E3 97 C2
St Paul's Whitechapel CE Prim Sch E1 118 A6
St Paul's with St Michael's Prim Sch E8 96 A6
St Paul's Wood Hill BR5,BR7 189 D1
St Paul with St Luke CE Prim Sch E3 97 B2
St Peter Chanel RC Prim Sch DA14 190 C5
St Peter in Chains RC Inf Sch N8 50 A3
SS Peter & Paul RC Prim Sch BR5 189 C1
SS Peter & Paul's RC Prim Sch Ilford IG1 79 B5
Mitcham CR4 202 D5
St Peter's Alley EC3 242 D1
St Peters Ave N12 30 C3
St Peter's Ave N18 34 A6
St Petersburgh Mews W2 245 C6
St Petersburgh Pl W2 113 D6 245 C5
St Peter's CE Prim Sch SE17 262 D1
W9 91 C3
St Peter's Church Ct N1 234 D5
St Peters Cl BR7 189 B3
St Peter's Cl E2 96 A5
St Peters Cl Ilford IG2 57 D5
Upper Tooting SW17 158 C2
St Peter's Cl Barnet EN5 12 B6
Bushey WD23 8 B3
Ruislip HA4 62 D6
St Peters Ct SE12 164 D6
SE4 141 B3
St Peter's Ct NW4 46 C4

St Peters Ct KT8 ....195 C5
St Peter's Eaton Square CE Sch SW1 ....115 B3 258 D5
St Peter's Gdns SE27 ....160 C1
St Peter's Gr W6 ....112 A2
St Peters Ho N15 ....52 A5
WC1 ....233 B1
St Peter's Ho N16 ....51 C2
4 SE17 ....139 B6
St Peters La BR5 ....190 A1
St Peter's London Docks CE Prim Sch E1 ....118 C5
St Peter's Path E17 ....54 C5
St Peter's Pl W9 ....91 D3
St Peter's Prim Sch W6 ....112 A1
South Croydon CR2 ....221 C2
St Peter's RC Prim Sch
SE18 ....122 D2
Dagenham RM9 ....103 B6
St Peter's Rd W6 ....112 A1
St Peters Rd KT1 ....176 C1
St Peter's Rd
Croydon CR0 ....221 B4
East Molesey KT8 ....195 C5
Edmonton N9 ....18 B3
Isleworth TW1 ....153 B6
Southall UB1 ....85 C2
St Peter's Sq E2 ....96 A5
W6 ....111 D1
St Peter's St N1 ....94 D6 234 D5
Croydon CR2 ....221 B3
St Peters & St Pauls RC Prim Sch EC1 ....94 D3 241 D6
St Peter's Street Mews
N1 ....234 D4
St Peter's Terr SW6 ....264 B3
St Peter's Villas 5 W6 ....112 A2
St Peter's Way N1 ....73 C1
St Peters Way UB3 ....105 B1
St Peter's Way W5 ....87 D2
St Philip Ho WC1 ....234 A1
St Philip's Ave KT4 ....216 B6
St Philip Sq 1 SW8 ....137 B3
St Philip's Rd E8 ....74 A2
Surbiton KT6 ....197 D3
St Philip's Sch SW7 ....256 B4
Chessington KT9 ....213 D2
St Philip St SW8 ....137 B3
St Philip's Way N1 ....235 B5
St Philomena's Sch
SM5 ....218 C3
St Quentin Ho SW18 ....158 B5
St Quentin Rd DA16 ....145 D2
St Quintin Ave W10 ....90 D2
St Quintin Gdns W10 ....90 C2
St Quintin Rd E13 ....99 B5
St Raphael's RC Prim Sch
UB5 ....84 B5
St Raphael's Way NW10 ....67 A3
St Regis Cl N10 ....31 B1
St Regis Hts NW3 ....69 D5
St Richard of Chichester RC Sec Sch NW1 ....71 C1
St Richards Ct TW10 ....153 B1
St Richard's with St Andrew's CE Prim Sch TW10 ....153 B1
St Ronan's 2 N3 ....29 C2
St Ronans Cl EN4 ....2 B5
St Ronans Cres IG8 ....37 A3
St Rule St SW8 ....137 C3
St Savior's CE Inf Sch
W5 ....109 D6
St Saviours SW4 ....137 B1
St Saviour's CE Prim Sch
E14 ....97 D2
E17 ....53 B2
SE24 ....139 A2
W9 ....91 D3
St Saviour's Coll SE27 ....183 B6
St Saviours Ct N22 ....31 D1
Harrow HA1 ....42 C4
St Saviours Ho 4 SE1 ....118 A4
St Saviour's RC Prim Sch
SE13 ....142 A1
St Saviour's Rd SW2 ....160 B6
Thornton Heath CR0 ....205 A3
St Saviours & St Olaves CE Sch SE1 ....117 B3 262 D5
St Saviour's Wharf SE1 ....253 D2
St Scholastica's RC Prim Sch
E5 ....74 A5
Saints Cl SE27 ....182 D6
Saints Dr E7 ....77 D3
St Silas Pl NW5 ....71 A2
St Simon's Ave SW15 ....156 C6
St Stephen's Ave E17 ....54 A4
W12 ....112 B4
Ealing W13 ....87 B1
St Stephen's CE Prim Sch
SE8 ....141 C3
SW8 ....138 B5 270 C4
W12 ....112 C4
W2 ....91 C2
St Stephen's Cl E17 ....53 D4
NW5 ....70 D3
NW8 ....230 B5
Southall UB1 ....85 C2
St Stephen's Cres W2 ....91 C1
Thornton Heath CR7 ....204 C6
St Stephens Ct N8 ....50 B3
Ealing W13 ....87 B1
St Stephen's Gdns W2 ....91 C1
3 Putney SW15 ....157 B6
Twickenham TW1 ....153 C5
St Stephen's Gr SE13 ....142 A2
St Stephens Ho 7 SE17 ....139 B6
St Stephen's Mews 34
W2 ....91 C2
St Stephens Par E6 ....77 C1
St Stephens Prim Sch
E6 ....77 C1
St Stephen's RC Prim Sch
DA16 ....146 A3
St Stephens Rd E6 ....77 C1
St Stephen's Rd E17 ....53 D4
E3 ....97 B5
St Stephens Rd EN5 ....12 D6
St Stephen's Rd
Ealing W13 ....87 C1
Enfield EN3 ....6 D6
Hounslow TW3,TW4 ....151 C6
Yiewsley UB7 ....104 A5
St Stephen's Row EC4 ....242 C1
St Stephen's Terr SW8 ....270 C3
St Swithin's La
EC4 ....117 B6 252 C6
St Swithun's Rd SE13 ....164 B6
St Swithun Wells RC Prim Sch HA4 ....62 D5
St Teresa RC Prim Sch The
RM8 ....80 C4
St Teresa's RC Fst & Mid Sch
HA3 ....24 A2
St Teresa's RC Prim Sch
SM4 ....202 B3
St Theresa Ct E4 ....20 B4
St Theresa's RC Sch N3 ....47 D6
St Theresa's Rd TW14 ....127 D1
St Thomas a Beckett RC Prim Sch SE2 ....124 A3
St Thomas Becket RC Prim Sch SE25 ....206 A3
St Thomas' CE Prim Sch
N16 ....52 A1
W10 ....91 A3
St Thomas' Cl KT6 ....198 B1
St Thomas Ct 10 E10 ....53 D2
Sidcup DA5 ....169 C4
St Thomas' Dr BR5 ....211 A1
Pinner HA5 ....23 A2
St Thomas' Gdns NW5 ....71 A2
St Thomas Gdns IG1 ....79 A2
St Thomas Ho 2 E1 ....96 D1
St Thomas More RC Prim Sch
SE9 ....144 A2
Bexley DA7 ....147 B3
St Thomas More RC Sch
SE9 ....166 C5
SW3 ....114 D2 257 C3
East Molesey KT8 ....196 A4
St Thomas More Sch
N22 ....32 C3
St Thomas of Canterbury RC Mid Sch CR4 ....203 A6
St Thomas of Canterbury RC Prim Sch SW6 ....135 B5 264 C4
St Thomas Rd E16 ....99 A1
N14 ....15 D4
St Thomas' Rd W4 ....133 A6
St Thomas's Hospl
SE1 ....116 B3 260 C6
St Thomas's Hospl Medical Sch SE1 ....116 B3 260 C5
St Thomas's Pl 20 E9 ....74 C1
St Thomas's Rd N4,N5 ....72 C5
NW10 ....89 C6
St Thomas's Sq E9 ....74 C1
St Thomas St
SE1 ....117 B5 252 D3
St Thomas's Way
SW6 ....135 B5 264 D4
St Thomas the Apostle Coll The SE15 ....140 C4
St Timothy's Mews 3
BR1 ....187 B2
St Ursula Gr HA5 ....41 A4
St Ursula Rd UB1 ....85 C1
St Ursula's Convent Sch
SE10 ....142 B5
St Vincent Cl SE27 ....182 D5
St Vincent De Paul Ho 20
E1 ....96 C2
St Vincent De Paul RC Prim Sch SW1 ....115 C3 259 B6
St Vincent Ho SE1 ....263 C6
St Vincent Rd TW2 ....152 A5
St Vincent's Hospl HA5 ....39 D6
St Vincents RC Prim Sch
SE9 ....188 A6
St Vincent's RC Prim Sch
W1 ....93 A2 238 B3
Acton W3 ....110 D6
Dagenham RM8 ....80 C6
St Vincent's RC Sch NW7 ....28 C5
St Vincent St W1 ....238 B3
St Wilfrid's Cl EN4 ....14 C6
St Wilfrid's Rd EN4 ....14 C6
St William of York RC Prim Sch SE23 ....163 A3
St William of York RC Sec Boys Sch (Upper) N1 ....72 A1
St Winefride's Ave E12 ....78 B3
St Winefride's RC Prim Sch
E12 ....78 B3
St Winifred's RC Inf Sch
SE12 ....164 C6
St Winifred's RC Jun Sch
SE12 ....164 D4
St Winifred's Rd TW11 ....175 B4
Sala Ho SE3 ....143 B1
Salamanca Pl SE1 ....260 C3
Salamanca St
SE1,SE11 ....116 B2 260 C3
Salamander Cl KT2 ....175 C5
Salamander Quay KT1 ....175 D2
Salcombe Dr
Dagenham RM6 ....59 B3
North Cheam SM4 ....200 D1
Salcombe Gdns NW7 ....28 C4
SW4 ....137 B1
Salcombe Ho 6 SE23 ....162 C2
Salcombe Lo NW5 ....71 A4
Salcombe Pk IG10 ....21 D6
Salcombe Prep Sch N14 ....15 B4
Salcombe Rd E17 ....53 B2
23 N16 ....73 C3
Ashford TW15 ....148 A1
Salcombe Villas 13
TW10 ....154 A6
Salcombe Way
Hayes UB4 ....83 C4
Ruislip HA4 ....62 A6
Salcot N4 ....72 B6
Salcott Rd SW11 ....158 D6
Wallington CR0 ....220 B4
Salehurst Cl HA3 ....44 A4
Salehurst Rd SE4 ....163 B5
Salem Ho 13 E9 ....74 D2
Salem Pl CR0 ....221 A5
Salem Rd W2 ....113 D6 245 D6
Sale Pl W2 ....92 C1 237 A2
Salesian Coll
SW11 ....136 C4 267 A1
Sale St E2 ....96 A3
Salford Ho 4 E14 ....120 A2
Salford Rd SW12,SW2 ....159 D3
Salhouse Cl SE28 ....102 C1
Salisbury Ave N3 ....47 B6
Barking IG11 ....79 C1
Cheam SM1,SM2 ....217 B2
Salisbury Cl SE17 ....262 C4
Worcester Park KT4 ....215 D5
Salisbury Ct E9 ....75 A3
EC4 ....241 C1
N3 ....29 B1
15 SE16 ....118 A3
W4 ....111 C2
Edgware HA8 ....26 B6
Enfield EN2 ....5 B1
Northolt UB5 ....63 D3
Salisbury Gdns
Buckhurst Hill IG9 ....21 D2
Wimbledon SW19 ....179 A3
Salisbury Hall Gdns E4 ....35 C4
Salisbury Ho 3 E14 ....97 D1
N1 ....234 C6
SW1 ....259 D2
1 Ruislip HA4 ....40 C1
Stanmore HA7 ....25 A4
Wimbledon SW19 ....156 D1
Salisbury Lower Sch N9 ....18 C4
Salisbury Mans N4,N15 ....50 D4
Salisbury Mews BR2 ....210 A4
SW6 ....264 C3
Salisbury Pl SW9 ....138 D5
W1 ....237 C4
Salisbury Prim Sch E12 ....78 A3
Salisbury Rd BR2 ....210 A4
DA5 ....169 C3
E10 ....76 A6
E12 ....77 D3
E17 ....54 A4
E7 ....77 A2
N4 ....50 D4
W13 ....109 B4
Barnet EN5 ....1 A2
Chingford E4 ....19 C1
Croydon SE25 ....206 A3
Dagenham RM10 ....81 D2
East Bedfont TW6 ....149 A5
Edmonton N9 ....18 A1
Enfield EN3 ....7 B6
Feltham TW13 ....150 C3
Harrow HA1 ....42 B4
Hounslow TW4 ....128 C2
Ilford IG3 ....79 C6
Kingston KT3 ....199 B6
Pinner HA5 ....40 A5
Richmond TW9 ....132 A1
Southall UB2 ....107 A2
Tottenham N22 ....32 D1
Wallington SM5 ....218 D2
Wimbledon SW19 ....179 A3
Worcester Park KT4 ....215 C5
Salisbury Sq EC4 ....241 B1
Salisbury St NW8 ....237 A5
10 Acton W3 ....111 A4
Salisbury Terr SE15 ....140 C2
Salisbury Upper Sch N9 ....18 C4
Salisbury Wlk N19 ....71 C6
Salix Cl TW16 ....172 B3
Salix Ct N3 ....29 C4
Salliesfield TW2 ....152 B5
Sally Murray Cl E12 ....78 C4
Salmen Rd E13 ....98 D5
Salmond Cl HA7 ....25 A4
Salmon La E14 ....97 A1
Salmon Rd DA17 ....125 C1
Salmons Rd
Chessington KT9 ....214 A2
Edmonton N9 ....18 A3
Salmon St 6 E14 ....97 B1
NW9 ....45 A2
Salomons Rd E13 ....99 C2
Salop Rd E17 ....52 D3
Saltash Cl SM1 ....217 B4
Saltash Rd DA16 ....146 C4
Saltcoats Rd W4 ....111 C4
Saltcroft Cl HA9 ....44 D1
Saltdene N4 ....50 B1
Salter Cl HA2 ....63 B4
Salterford Rd SW17 ....181 A4
Salter Ho 8 SW16 ....181 C6
Salter Rd SE16 ....119 A5
Salters' Hall Ct EC4 ....252 C6
Salter's Hill SE19 ....183 B5
Salters Rd E17 ....54 B5
W10 ....90 D3
Salter St 10 E14 ....119 C6
NW10 ....90 A4
Salterton Rd N7 ....72 B5
Salt Hill Cl UB8 ....60 A3
Saltley Cl E6 ....100 A1
Saltoun Rd SW2,SW9 ....138 C1
Saltram Cl N15 ....51 D5
Saltram Cres W9 ....91 C4
Saltwell St E14 ....119 C6
Saltwood Gr SE17 ....262 C1
Salusbury Prim Sch NW6 ....91 B6
Salusbury Rd NW6 ....91 A6
Salutation Rd SE10 ....120 C2
Salvador SW17 ....180 D5
Salvatorian RC Coll HA3 ....24 C1
Salvia Gdns UB6 ....87 A5
Salvin Rd SW15 ....134 D2
Salway Cl IG8 ....37 A3
Salway Ho E10 ....75 D6
SW8 ....270 B2
Salway Pl E15 ....76 C2
Salway Rd E15 ....76 B2
Salween Ho 2 N16 ....73 B4
Samantha Cl E17 ....53 B2
Samantha Ct E11 ....54 C2
Samaritan Hospl for Women
NW1 ....237 C4
Sam Bartram Cl SE7 ....121 C1
Sambrooke Ct EN1 ....17 D6
Sambrook Ho 19 E1 ....96 C2
Sambruck Mews SE6 ....163 D3
Samels Ct W6 ....112 A1
Samford Ho N1 ....234 A5
Samford St NW8 ....92 C3 237 A5
Samira Cl E17 ....53 C3
Sam Manners Ho 7
SE10 ....120 C1
Sam March Ho 5 E14 ....98 B1
Samos Rd SE20 ....184 B1
Sampson Ave EN5 ....12 D6
Sampson Cl DA17 ....125 A3
Sampson Ct TW17 ....193 A4
Sampson St E1 ....118 A5
Samson Ho SE18 ....123 A2
Samson St E13 ....99 C5
Samuel Cl E8 ....95 D6
SE14 ....140 D6
SE18 ....122 A2
Samuel Ct BR3 ....207 D6
Samuel Gray Gdns KT2 ....175 D2
Samuel Ho 15 E8 ....95 D6
Samuel Johnson Cl
SW16 ....182 B6
Samuel Jones Ind Est 15
SE15 ....139 C5
Samuel Lewis Bldgs N1 ....72 C2
Samuel Lewis Trust Dwellings
6 SE5 ....139 A4
SW3 ....257 A3
SW6 ....135 C5 265 B4
W14 ....254 B4
Samuel Lewis Trust Est
N15 ....51 C3
Samuel Rhodes Sch
N1 ....94 C6 234 A6
Samuel Richardson Ho
W14 ....254 C3
Samuel's Cl 2 W6 ....112 C2
Samuel St 6 SE15 ....139 D5
SE18 ....122 B2
Sancroft Cl NW2 ....68 B5
Sancroft Ct SW11 ....267 B2
Sancroft Rd HA3 ....25 A1
Sancroft St
SE11 ....116 C1 260 D2
Sanctuary Rd TW19,TW6 ....148 C5
Sanctuary St SE1 ....252 B2
Sanctuary The DA5 ....168 D5
35 E1 ....118 B5
SW1 ....115 D3 259 D6
Morden SM4 ....201 C3
Sandale Cl N16 ....73 B5
Sandall Cl W5 ....88 A3
Sandall Ho 6 E3 ....97 A5
Sandall Rd NW5 ....71 C2
Ealing W5 ....88 A3
Sandal Rd Edmonton N18 ....34 A5
New Malden KT3 ....199 C5
Sandal St E15 ....98 C6
Sandalwood Cl 10 E1 ....97 A3
Sandalwood Dr HA4 ....39 A2
Sandalwood Ho DA15 ....167 D1
6 NW3 ....69 D2
Sandalwood Rd TW13 ....150 B1
Sandbach Pl SE18 ....123 A1
Sandbourne 12 NW8 ....91 D6
4 W11 ....91 C1
Sandbourne Ave SW19 ....179 D1
Sandbourne Rd SE4 ....141 A3
Sandbrook Cl NW7 ....27 B4
Sandbrook Rd N16 ....73 C5
Sandby Ct BR3 ....185 B2
Sandby Gn SE9 ....144 A2
Sandby Ho 6 NW6 ....91 C6
11 SE5 ....139 C4
Sandcroft Cl N13 ....32 D4
Sandcroft Ho SE11 ....260 D2
Sandells Ave
Ashford TW15 ....171 A6
Ashford TW15 ....171 A6
Sandell St SE1 ....251 A2
Sanderling Ct 20 SE8 ....141 B6
Woolwich SE28 ....124 C6
Sanders Cl TW12 ....174 A5
Sanders Ho WC1 ....234 A2
Streatham SW16 ....182 A4
Sanders La NW7 ....28 C3
Sanderson Cl NW5 ....71 B4
Sanderson Ho 7 SE8 ....119 B1
Sanderstead Ave NW2 ....69 A6
Sanderstead Cl SW12 ....159 C4
Sanderstead Rd
South Croydon CR2 ....221 B1
Walthamstow E10 ....53 A1
Sanders Way 3 N19 ....49 D1
Sandfield WC1 ....233 B1
Sandfield Gdns CR7 ....204 D6
Sandfield Pl CR7 ....205 A6
Sandfield Rd CR7 ....204 D6
Sandford Ave N22 ....33 A2
Sandford Cl E6 ....100 B3
Sandford Ct N16 ....51 C1
Barnet EN5 ....1 D2
Sandford Rd BR2 ....209 A5
E6 ....100 B4
Bexley DA6,DA7 ....147 A2
Sandford Row SE17 ....262 D2
Sandford St SW6 ....265 D3
Sandford Wlk 4 N16 ....73 D6
SE14 ....141 A6
Sandgate Ho 15 E5 ....74 B4
14 Beckenham BR3 ....185 C3
Ealing W5 ....87 C2
Sandgate La SW17,
SW18 ....158 C3
Sandgate Rd DA16 ....146 C5
Sandgate St SE15 ....140 B6
Sandgate Trad Est SE15 ....140 B6
Sandham Ct SW4 ....270 B1
Sandham Point 10 SE18 ....122 D2
Sandhills CR0,SM6 ....219 D4
Sandhills Mdw TW17 ....193 A2
Sandhills The SW10 ....266 B6
Sandhurst Ave
Harrow HA2 ....41 D3
Tolworth KT5 ....198 D2
Sandhurst Cl NW9 ....44 C6
South Croydon CR2 ....221 C1
Sandhurst Ct SW2 ....138 A1
Sandhurst Dr IG3 ....79 D4
Sandhurst Ho 10 E1 ....96 C2
Sandhurst Jun & Inf Sch
SE6 ....164 C3
Sandhurst Mkt SE6 ....164 A3
Sandhurst Rd DA15 ....168 A1
HA8,NW9 ....44 C6
N9 ....18 D5
Bexley DA5 ....168 D6
Catford SE6 ....164 B3
Sandhurst Way CR2 ....221 C1
Sandifer Dr NW2,NW11 ....68 D5
Sandiford Rd SM3 ....217 B6
Sandiland Cres BR2 ....224 D6
Sandilands CR0 ....222 A5
Sandilands Rd
SW6 ....135 D4 265 C1
Sandilands Sta CR0 ....221 D6
Sandison St SE15 ....140 A2
Sandland St WC1 ....240 D3
Sandling Rise SE9 ....166 C1
Sandlings Cl SE15 ....140 B3
Sandlings The N22 ....50 D6
5 Wood Green N22 ....32 C1
Sandmartin Way CR4 ....203 A1
Sandmere Rd SW4 ....138 A1
Sandon Cl KT10 ....196 B1
Sandon Ct IG3 ....80 A5
Sandon Ho 2 SW2 ....160 A4
Sandow Cres UB3 ....105 D3
Sandown Ave KT10 ....212 A3
Sandown Cl TW5 ....128 A4
Sandown Gate KT10 ....212 B5
Sandown Ho 2 W4 ....111 A1
Penge SE26 ....184 B4
Sandown Park KT10 ....212 A6
Sandown Rd
Croydon SE25 ....206 B4
Esher KT10 ....212 A4
Sandown Way UB5 ....63 B3
Sandpiper Cl E17 ....34 D3
SE16 ....119 B4
Sandpiper Ct 11 E14 ....120 A3
1 SE8 ....141 C5
Sandpiper Rd SM1 ....217 B3
Sandpiper Terr IG5 ....56 D6
Sandpit Pl SE7 ....122 A1
Sandpit Rd BR1 ....186 C5
Sandpits Rd
Richmond TW10 ....153 D2
South Croydon CR0 ....222 D4
Sandra Cl Hounslow TW3 ....151 D6
Tottenham N17 ....33 A2
Sandra Ho KT8 ....196 B4
Sandridge Cl HA1 ....42 C5
Sandridge Ct N4 ....73 A6
Sandridge St 2 N19 ....71 C6
Sandringham Ave
SW20 ....179 A1
Sandringham Cl
Enfield EN1 ....5 C3
Ilford IG6 ....57 A6
1 Putney SW19 ....156 D3
Sandringham Cres HA2 ....63 D6
Sandringham Ct
18 SE16 ....118 D5
W1 ....239 B1
W9 ....229 B1
3 Beckenham BR3 ....186 A2
Edgware HA8 ....26 D6
Hillingdon UB10 ....83 A3
Putney SW15 ....156 D5
Sandringham Dr DA16 ....145 C3
Ashford TW15 ....170 A6
Sandringham Flats
WC2 ....249 D6
Sandringham Gdns N12 ....30 B4
Sandringham Gdns *continued*
N8 ....50 A3
Cranford TW5 ....128 A4
East Molesey KT8 ....195 C5
Ilford IG6 ....57 A6
Sandringham Ho W14 ....254 A4
Richmond TW10 ....154 C6
Sandringham Prim Sch
E7 ....77 C3
Sandringham Rd BR1 ....187 A5
E10 ....54 B3
E7 ....77 C3
E8 ....73 D3
NW11 ....47 A2
NW2 ....68 B2
Barking IG11 ....79 D2
Northolt UB5 ....63 C1
Stanwell TW19,TW6 ....148 A6
Thornton Heath CR0 ....205 A4
Tottenham N22 ....33 A1
Worcester Park KT4 ....216 A5
Sandrock Pl CR0 ....222 D4
Sandrock Rd SE13 ....141 C2
Sands End La
SW6 ....135 D4 265 D2
Sandstone TW9 ....132 C5
Sandstone Pl N19 ....71 B6
Sandstone Rd SE12 ....165 B2
Sandtoft Rd SE7 ....143 B6
Sandways 6 TW9 ....132 C4
Sandwell Cres 2 NW6 ....69 C2
Sandwell Mans 3 NW6 ....69 C2
Sandwich Ho 9 SE16 ....118 C4
WC1 ....233 A1
Sandwich St
WC1 ....94 A4 233 A1
Sandwick Cl NW7 ....28 A3
Sandy Bury BR6 ....227 B5
Sandycombe Rd
East Bedfont TW14 ....150 A3
Richmond TW9 ....132 C3
Sandycoombe Rd TW1 ....153 C5
Sandycroft SE2 ....146 A6
Sandy Dr TW14 ....149 C3
Sandy Hill Ave SE18 ....122 D1
Sandy Hill La SE18 ....122 D2
Sandy Hill Rd SE18 ....122 D1
Sandyhill Rd IG1 ....78 D4
Sandy La BR5 ....190 D2
Belmont SM2 ....217 A1
Harrow HA3 ....44 C3
Mitcham CR4 ....181 A2
Moor Park HA6 ....22 A6
Richmond TW10 ....153 D2
Teddington KT8,TW11 ....175 B3
Walton-on-T KT12 ....194 C3
Sandy La N SM6 ....219 D3
Sandy La S SM6 ....219 C1
Sandy Lo N6 ....49 C2
Sandymount Ave HA7 ....25 D5
Sandy Rd NW3 ....69 D6
Sandy Ridge BR7 ....188 C4
Sandy's Row E1 ....243 B3
Sandy Way Croydon CR0 ....223 B5
Walton-on-T KT12 ....193 D1
Sanford La 3 N16 ....73 D6
Sanford St SE14,SE8 ....141 A6
Sanford Terr N16 ....73 D5
Sanger Ave KT9 ....214 B4
Sangley Rd Catford SE6 ....164 A3
South Norwood SE25 ....205 C5
Sangora Rd 17 SW11 ....136 B1
Sankey Ho 23 E2 ....96 C5
Sansom Rd E11 ....76 D6
Sansom St SE5 ....139 B4
20 SE5 ....139 B5
Sans Wlk EC1 ....94 D3 241 C6
Santana Ho SE18 ....144 D5
Santley Ho SE1 ....251 B1
Santley St SW4 ....138 B1
Santos Rd SW18 ....157 C6
Sapcote Trad Ctr NW10 ....67 D2
Saperton Wlk SE11 ....260 D4
Saphora Cl BR6 ....227 B3
Sapperton Ct EC1 ....242 A6
Sapphire Cl E6 ....100 C1
Dagenham RM8 ....58 C1
Sapphire Ct 8 E1 ....118 A6
Sapphire Rd SE8 ....119 A2
Saracen Cl CR0 ....205 B3
Saracen St E14 ....97 C1
Sarah Bonnell Sch E15 ....76 C2
Sarah Ct UB5 ....85 B6
Sarah Ho 11 E1 ....96 B1
Roehampton SW15 ....133 D1
Sarah Swift Ho SE1 ....252 D2
Sara Lane Ct 31 N1 ....95 C5
Saratoga Rd E5 ....74 C4
Sara Turnbull Ho 2
SE18 ....122 B2
Sardeson Ho 13 SW27 ....182 D5
Sardinia St WC2 ....240 C2
Sargents Hill N2 ....30 C2
Sarita Cl HA3 ....24 B1
Sarjant Path SW19 ....156 D2
Sark Cl TW5 ....129 C5
Sark Ho 5 N1 ....73 A2
Enfield EN3 ....6 D5
Sark Wlk E16 ....99 B1
Sarnersfield Ho SE15 ....140 B6
Sarnes Ct 4 N11 ....31 B6
Sarnesfield Rd EN2 ....5 B2
Sarratt Ho W10 ....90 C2
Sarre Rd NW2 ....69 B3
Sarsden Bldgs W1 ....238 B1
Sarsen Ave TW3 ....129 C3
Sarsfield Rd SW12,SW17 ....158 D3
Sarsfield Rd UB6 ....87 C5
Sartor Rd SE15 ....140 D1
Sarum Hall Sch NW3 ....70 C1

Sarum Ho W11 ... 244 D5
Sassoon 4 NW9 ... 27 D2
Satanita Cl E16 ... 99 D1
Satchell Mead NW9 ... 27 D2
Satchwell Rd 24 E2 ... 96 A4
Saul Ct 4 SE15 ... 139 D6
Sauls Gn E11 ... 76 C5
Saunders Cl 14 E14 ... 119 B6
Saunders Ho 11 SW2 ... 160 C3
Saunders Ness Rd E14 ... 120 B2
Saunders Rd SE18 ... 123 D1
Hillingdon UB10 ... 82 B6
Saunders St SE11 ... 261 A4
Saunders Way SE28 ... 124 B6
Saunderton Rd HA0 ... 65 B3
Saunton Ave UB3 ... 127 D5
Saunton Ct UB1 ... 108 A6
Savage Gdns EC3 ... 253 B6
Newham E6 ... 100 B1
Savana N16 ... 73 C6
Savannah Cl 9 SE15 ... 139 D5
Savernake Ct HA7 ... 25 B4
Savernake Ho N4 ... 51 B2
Savernake Rd NW3 ... 70 D4
Enfield N9 ... 18 A5
Savery Dr KT6 ... 197 C2
Savile Cl
New Malden KT3 ... 199 C4
Thames Ditton KT7 ... 197 A1
Savile Gdns CR0 ... 221 D6
Saville Cres TW15 ... 171 B4
Saville Rd E16 ... 122 A5
W4 ... 111 B3
Dagenham RM6 ... 59 B2
Twickenham TW1 ... 152 D3
Saville Row W1 ... 115 C6 249 A6
Enfield EN3 ... 6 D3
Hayes BR2 ... 208 D1
Savill Gdns SW20 ... 200 A6
Savill Ho E16 ... 122 D5
2 SW4 ... 159 D5
Savill Row IG8 ... 36 D4
Savin Lo 7 SM2 ... 218 A1
Savona Cl 15 SW19 ... 178 D3
Savona Ct SW20 ... 178 D2
Savona St SW8 ... 137 C5 269 A3
Savoy Ave UB3 ... 105 C1
Savoy Bldgs W12 ... 111 D6
Savoy Circus W3 ... 111 D6
Savoy Cl E15 ... 98 C6
Edgware HA8 ... 26 C5
Savoy Ct SW5 ... 255 B4
WC2 ... 250 B5
Savoy Hill WC2 ... 250 C5
Savoy Par EN1 ... 5 C2
Savoy Pier WC2 ... 250 C5
Savoy Pl WC2 ... 116 B6 250 C5
Savoy Row WC2 ... 250 C6
Savoy St WC2 ... 116 B6 250 C5
Savoy Steps WC2 ... 250 C5
Savoy Way WC2 ... 250 C5
Sawbill Cl UB4 ... 84 D2
Sawkins Cl SW19 ... 157 A2
Sawley Rd W12 ... 112 A5
Sawmill Yd E3 ... 97 A6
Sawtry Cl SM5 ... 202 C2
Sawyer Cl N9 ... 18 A2
Sawyer Ho 15 SE21 ... 183 C6
Sawyer's Hill TW10 ... 154 B4
Sawyers Lawn W13 ... 87 A1
Sawyer St SE1 ... 117 A4 252 A2
Saxby Rd SW2 ... 160 A4
Saxham Rd IG11 ... 101 D5
Saxlingham Rd E4 ... 20 B1
Saxon Ave TW13 ... 151 B2
Saxon Bsns Ctr SW19 ... 180 A2
Saxonbury Ave TW16 ... 172 B1
Saxonbury Cl CR4 ... 202 B6
Saxonbury Ct 2 N7 ... 72 A3
16 N7 ... 71 D3
Saxonbury Gdns KT6 ... 197 C1
Saxon Cl E17 ... 53 C2
Hillingdon UB8 ... 82 A2
Surbiton KT6 ... 197 D3
Saxoncroft Ho SW16 ... 159 D1
Saxon Cty Jun Sch
TW17 ... 192 C4
Saxon Dr W3 ... 88 D2
Saxonfield Cl SW2 ... 160 B4
Saxon Gdns UB1 ... 107 A6
Saxon Hall W2 ... 245 C5
Saxon Ho 4 SW4 ... 137 D1
Feltham TW13 ... 151 B2
Saxon Rd E3 ... 97 B5
E6 ... 100 B3
Ashford TW15 ... 171 B4
Bromley BR1 ... 186 D3
Ilford IG1 ... 78 D3
Kingston KT2 ... 176 A2
Southall UB1 ... 107 A6
South Norwood SE25 ... 205 B4
Tottenham N22 ... 32 D2
Wembley HA9 ... 67 A5
Saxon Way N14 ... 15 D5
Saxon Wlk DA14 ... 190 C4
Saxony Par UB3 ... 83 A2
Saxton Cl SE13 ... 142 B2
Saxville Rd BR5 ... 190 B1
Sayer Ho SE4 ... 141 A1
Sayers Ho 4 N2 ... 30 B1
Sayer's Wlk TW10 ... 154 B4
Sayesbury La N18 ... 34 A5
Sayes Court St SE8 ... 141 B6
Sayes Ct SE8 ... 141 B6
Scadbury Gdns BR5 ... 190 A1
Scadbury Park Nature
Reserve* BR7 ... 189 D4
Scads Hill Cl BR5,BR6 ... 211 D3
Scafell NW1 ... 232 A2
Scala St W1 ... 239 B4
Scales Rd N17 ... 52 A6
Scampston Mews 5
W10 ... 90 D1
Scandrett St 33 E1 ... 118 B5
Scarba Wlk N1 ... 73 B2
Scarborough Rd E11 ... 54 B1
N4 ... 50 C1
N9 ... 18 C4
East Bedfont TW6 ... 149 A5
Scarborough St E1 ... 243 D1
Scarbrook Rd CR0 ... 221 A5
Scardale Ho 12 E5 ... 74 B6
Scarle Rd HA0 ... 65 D2
Scarlet Rd SE6 ... 164 C1
Scarlette Manor Wlk 10
SE24 ... 160 C4
Scarsbrook Ho 2 SW2 ... 160 C5
Scarsbrook Rd SE3 ... 143 D2
Scarsdale Pl W8 ... 255 C6
Scarsdale Rd HA2 ... 64 A5
Scarsdale Villas
W8 ... 113 C3 255 B5
Scarth Rd SW13 ... 133 D2
Scawen Cl SM5 ... 219 A4
Scawen Rd SE8 ... 119 A1
Scawfell St E2 ... 95 D5
Scaynes Link N12 ... 29 C6
Sceptre Ho 9 E1 ... 96 C3
Sceptre Rd E2 ... 96 C4
Schiller International Sch
BR4 ... 224 B4
Schofield Wlk SE3 ... 143 A5
Sch of Nursing
W1 ... 93 C2 239 A4
Sch of Pharmacy
WC1 ... 94 A3 240 B6
Sch of the Douay Martyrs
UB10 ... 60 D4
Scholars Ho 6 E4 ... 20 B3
Scholars Rd Chingford E4 ... 20 B3
Streatham SW12 ... 159 C3
Scholefield Rd N19 ... 71 D6
Scholey Ho SW11 ... 136 C2
Schomberg Ho SW1 ... 259 D4
Schonfeld Sq N16 ... 51 B1
School App 22 E2 ... 95 C4
Schoolbank Rd SE10 ... 120 D3
School Bell Cloisters 15
E3 ... 97 A5
Schoolbell Mews 16 E3 ... 97 A5
School Cotts DA14 ... 190 C5
School Flats SW8 ... 270 A1
School Ho SE1 ... 263 A4
Schoolhouse La E1 ... 118 D6
School House La TW11 ... 175 C3
School La DA16 ... 146 B2
Lower Halliford TW17 ... 192 D2
Pinner HA5 ... 41 A5
Surbiton KT6 ... 198 B1
Teddington KT1 ... 175 C2
School of Finance &
Management N7 ... 72 B2
School of St David & St
Katharine The N8 ... 50 A5
School Pas
3 Kingston KT1 ... 176 B1
Southall UB1 ... 107 B6
School Rd BR7 ... 189 A3
NW10 ... 89 B3
Ashford TW15 ... 170 D4
Dagenham RM10 ... 103 D6
East Molesey KT8 ... 196 B5
Hampton TW12 ... 174 A4
Hounslow TW3 ... 130 A2
Ilford E12 ... 78 B4
Littleton TW15 ... 170 D3
Teddington KT1 ... 175 C2
School Road Ave TW12 ... 174 A4
School Sq SE10 ... 120 D3
Schoolway N12 ... 30 B4
School Way RM8 ... 80 C5
School Wlk TW16 ... 193 D6
Schooner Cl E14 ... 120 B3
1 SE16 ... 118 D4
Barking IG11 ... 102 B4
Schubert Rd Elstree WD6 ... 9 D5
Putney SW15 ... 157 B6
Science Mus*
SW7 ... 114 B3 256 C5
Scilly Isles KT10 ... 212 C6
Sclater St E1 ... 243 D6
Scoles Cres SW2 ... 160 C3
Scope Way KT1 ... 198 A5
Scoresby St SE1 ... 251 C3
Scoresdale SE19 ... 183 C2
Scorton Ave UB6 ... 87 A5
Scorton Ho 2 N1 ... 95 C5
Scotch Comm W13 ... 87 B2
Scotch Ho SW1 ... 114 D4 247 C1
Scoter Cl IG8 ... 37 B3
Scoter Ct 23 SE8 ... 141 B6
Scot Gr HA5 ... 22 D3
Scotia Bldg 10 E1 ... 118 D6
Scotia Ct 3 SE16 ... 118 C3
Scotia Rd 24 SW2 ... 160 C4
Scotland Gn N17 ... 33 D1
Scotland Green Rd EN3 ... 18 D6
Scotland Green Rd N EN3 ... 7 A1
Scotland Pl SW1 ... 250 A3
Scotland Rd IG9 ... 21 C3
Scotney Ho E9 ... 74 C2
Scots Cl TW19 ... 148 A3
Scotsdale Cl BR5,BR7 ... 211 C5
Belmont SM3 ... 217 A1
Scotsdale Rd SE12 ... 165 B6
Scotson Ho SE11 ... 261 A3
Scotswood St
EC1 ... 94 C3 241 B6
Scotswood Wlk N17 ... 34 A3
Scott Cl
Thornton Heath SW16 ... 182 B2
West Drayton UB7 ... 104 B2
West Ewell KT19 ... 215 A3
Scott Ct 17 N16 ... 73 C5
4 SW11 ... 137 B3
W4 ... 111 B4
Scott Ellis Gdns
NW8 ... 92 B4 229 C1
Scottes La RM8 ... 58 D1
Scott Farm Cl KT7 ... 197 B1
Scott Gdns TW5 ... 128 D5
Scott Ho 6 E13 ... 99 A5
N1 ... 235 C6
N7 ... 72 B2
2 NW10 ... 67 B1
NW8 ... 237 A5
3 Edmonton N18 ... 34 A5
4 Erith DA17 ... 125 B1
Richmond TW10 ... 153 C2
Scott Lidgett Cres SE16 ... 118 A4
Scott's Ave
Ashford TW16 ... 171 C3
Beckenham BR2 ... 186 B1
Scotts Ct 6 W12 ... 112 B4
Scotts Dr TW12 ... 173 D3
Scotts Farm Rd KT19 ... 215 A2
Scott's La BR2,BR3 ... 186 B1
Scotts Park Prim Sch
BR1 ... 187 C2
Scotts Rd BR1 ... 187 A3
Scott's Rd E10 ... 54 A1
W12 ... 112 B4
Scotts Rd UB2 ... 106 D3
Scott's Sufferance Wharf
SE1 ... 253 D1
Scott St E1 ... 96 B3
Scott's Way TW16 ... 171 C3
Scott's Yd EC4 ... 252 C6
Scott Trimmer Way
TW3 ... 129 A3
Scottwell Dr NW9 ... 45 D4
Scott Wilkie Prim Sch
E16 ... 99 C1
Scoulding Ho 6 E14 ... 119 C3
Scoulding Rd E16 ... 99 A1
Scouler St E14 ... 120 B6
Scout App NW10 ... 67 C4
Scout Way NW7 ... 27 B6
Scovell Cres SE1 ... 252 A1
Scovell Rd SE1 ... 252 A1
Scrattons Terr IG11 ... 103 A5
Scriven Ct 2 E8 ... 95 D6
Scriven St E8 ... 95 D6
Scrooby St SE6 ... 163 D5
Scrope Bldg EC1 ... 241 A4
Scrubs La NW10,W10,W12 ... 90 B3
Scrutton Cl SW12 ... 159 D4
Scrutton St EC2 ... 95 C3 243 A5
Scudamore La NW9 ... 45 A5
Scutari Rd SE22 ... 162 C6
Scylla Cres TW6&TW14 ... 148 D4
Scylla Rd SE15 ... 140 B2
East Bedfont TW14,TW6 ... 148 D5
Seabright St 27 E2 ... 96 B4
Seabrook Dr BR4 ... 224 C6
Seabrook Gdns RM7 ... 59 C2
Seabrook Rd RM8 ... 80 D5
Seacole Cl W3 ... 89 B2
Seacole Ct N15 ... 51 D4
Seacole Lo N21 ... 16 B6
Seacourt Rd SE2 ... 124 D4
Seacroft Gdns WD19 ... 22 D6
Seafield Rd N11 ... 31 D6
Seaford Cl HA4 ... 61 B6
Seaford Ho 8 SE16 ... 118 C4
Seaford Rd E17 ... 53 D6
N15 ... 51 C4
Ealing W13 ... 109 B5
Enfield EN1 ... 5 C1
Seaford St WC1 ... 233 B1
Seaforth Ave KT3 ... 200 B5
Seaforth Cres N5 ... 73 A3
Seaforth Gdns
Southgate N21 ... 16 C3
Woodford IG8 ... 37 C5
Worcester Park KT19 ... 215 D3
Seaforth Lo 2 SW13 ... 133 D3
Seaforth Pl SW1 ... 259 B6
Seager Pl E3 ... 97 B2
Seagrave Lo SW6 ... 265 B6
Seagrave Rd
SW6 ... 135 C6 265 B6
Seagrove Cl E1 ... 96 D2
Seagry Rd E11 ... 55 B2
Seagull Cl IG11 ... 102 A4
Sealand Rd TW6 ... 148 C5
Sealand Wlk UB5 ... 85 A4
Seal Ho SE1 ... 262 D6
Seal St E8 ... 73 D4
Searle Ct 2 CR4 ... 180 C2
Searle Pl N4 ... 50 B1
Searles Cl SW11 ... 136 C5 267 B3
Searles Dr E6 ... 100 D2
Searles Rd SE1 ... 262 D4
Searson Ho SE17 ... 261 D3
Sears St SE5 ... 139 B5
Seasalter Ho 10 SW9 ... 138 C4
Seasprite Cl 10 UB5 ... 84 D4
Seath Ho 4 SE26 ... 184 B5
Seaton Ave IG3 ... 79 D3
Seaton Cl 6 E13 ... 99 A3
Isleworth TW2 ... 152 B5
Roehampton SW15 ... 156 B4
Seaton Dr TW15 ... 148 A2
Seaton Gdns HA4 ... 62 A6
Seaton Point E5 ... 74 A4
Seaton Rd Bexley DA16 ... 146 C5
Hayes UB3 ... 105 B3
Mitcham CR4 ... 180 C1
Seaton Rd *continued*
Twickenham TW2 ... 152 A5
Wembley HA0 ... 88 A5
Seaton Sq NW7 ... 28 D3
Seaton St N18 ... 34 A5
Seavington Ho 3 SE5 ... 139 C2
Sebastian Ct 10 IG11 ... 79 D1
Sebastian Ho 22 N1 ... 95 C5
Sebastian St EC1 ... 94 D4 234 D1
Sebastopol Rd N9 ... 34 A6
Sebbon St N1 ... 72 D1
Sebergham Gr NW7 ... 28 A3
Sebert Rd E7 ... 77 B4
Sebright Ho 21 E2 ... 96 A5
Sebright Rd EN5 ... 1 A2
Sebright Sch E2 ... 96 A5
Secker Cres HA3 ... 24 A2
Secker Ho SW9 ... 138 D3
Secker St SE1 ... 251 A3
Second Ave E12 ... 78 A3
E13 ... 99 A4
E17 ... 53 C4
N18 ... 34 C6
NW4 ... 46 D5
W10 ... 91 A3
W3 ... 111 D5
Dagenham RM10 ... 103 D5
Dagenham RM6 ... 58 C4
Enfield EN1 ... 17 D6
Hayes UB3 ... 105 D5
Mortlake SW14 ... 133 C2
Walton-on-T KT12 ... 194 B3
Wembley HA9 ... 65 D6
Second Cl KT8 ... 196 A5
Second Cross Rd TW2 ... 152 C2
Second Way HA9 ... 66 D4
Sedan Way
SE17 ... 117 C1 263 A2
Sedcombe Cl DA14 ... 190 C6
Sedcote Rd EN3 ... 18 D6
Sedding St SW1 ... 258 A4
Seddon Ho EC2 ... 242 A4
Seddon Rd SM4 ... 202 B4
Seddon St WC1 ... 94 B4 233 D1
Sedgebrook Rd SE3 ... 143 D2
Sedgecombe Ave HA3 ... 43 C4
Sedgefield Ct UB5 ... 63 D3
Sedgeford Rd W12 ... 111 D5
Sedgehill Rd SE6 ... 185 D5
Sedgehill Sch SE6 ... 185 D5
Sedgemere Ave N2 ... 48 A6
Sedgemere Rd SE2 ... 124 C3
Sedgemoor Dr RM10 ... 81 C4
Sedge Rd N17 ... 34 C3
Sedgeway SE6 ... 164 D3
Sedgewick Ho SW19 ... 156 D2
Sedgewood Cl BR2 ... 208 D2
Sedgley Ho N4 ... 72 B6
Sedgmoor Pl SE5 ... 139 C5
Sedgwick Ave UB10 ... 60 D1
Sedgwick Rd E10 ... 76 A6
Sedgwick St E9 ... 74 D3
Sedleigh Rd SW18 ... 157 B5
Sedlescombe Rd
SW6 ... 135 C6 265 A6
Sedley Cl EN1 ... 6 B5
Sedley Ct SE26 ... 162 B2
Sedley Ho SE11 ... 260 D2
Sedley Pl W1 ... 238 C1
Sedum Cl NW9 ... 44 D4
Seeley Dr SE21 ... 183 C6
Seelig Ave NW9 ... 46 A2
Seely Rd SW17 ... 181 A4
Seething La EC3 ... 117 C6 253 B6
Seething Wells Halls of
Residence KT6 ... 197 C3
Seething Wells La KT6 ... 197 C3
Sefton Ave NW7 ... 27 B5
Harrow HA3 ... 24 B2
Sefton Cl BR5 ... 211 D5
Sefton Ct TW5 ... 129 D4
Sefton Lo 2 TW1 ... 153 C5
Sefton Rd Croydon CR0 ... 206 A1
Orpington BR5 ... 211 D5
Sefton St SW15 ... 134 C2
Segal Cl SE23 ... 163 A4
Sekforde St EC1 ... 94 D3 241 C6
Sekhon Terr TW13 ... 151 C1
Selan Gdns UB4 ... 84 B2
Selbie Ave NW10 ... 67 D3
Selborne 2 SW11 ... 137 A2
Selborne Ave DA5 ... 169 A3
E17 ... 53 B5
Little Ilford E12 ... 78 C4
Selborne Gdns NW4 ... 46 A5
Wembley UB6 ... 87 A5
Selborne Ho SE1 ... 252 C1
Selborne Prim Sch UB6 ... 86 D5
Selborne Rd E17 ... 53 C4
1 SE5 ... 139 B3
Ilford IG1 ... 78 C6
Kingston KT3 ... 177 C1
Palmers Green N14 ... 16 A1
Sidcup DA14 ... 190 B6
South Croydon CR0 ... 221 D5
Wood Green N22 ... 32 B2
Selborne Wlk E17 ... 53 B5
Selbourne Ave KT6 ... 214 C5
Selby Chase HA4 ... 62 B6
Selby Cl BR7 ... 188 C4
14 E6 ... 100 A2
Chessington KT9 ... 214 A1
Selby Ct TW2 ... 152 B2
Selby Gdns UB1 ... 85 C3
Selby Gn SM5 ... 202 C2
Selby Ho 10 SW4 ... 159 C5
6 W10 ... 91 A4
Selby Rd E11 ... 76 C5
E13 ... 99 B2
Ashford TW15 ... 171 A4
Selby Rd *continued*
Carshalton SM5 ... 202 C2
Ealing W5 ... 87 C3
Penge SE20 ... 184 A1
Tottenham N17 ... 33 C4
Selby St E1 ... 96 A3
Selden Ho 2 SE15 ... 140 C3
Selden Rd SE15 ... 140 C3
Selden Wlk N7 ... 72 B6
Seldon Ho SW1 ... 259 A1
SW8 ... 269 A3
Selena Ct N20 ... 14 D1
Selfridges W1 ... 238 B1
Selhurst Cl SW19 ... 156 D3
Selhurst New Ct SE25 ... 205 C3
Selhurst New Rd SE25 ... 205 C3
Selhurst Park (Crystal Palace
FC) SE25 ... 205 C5
Selhurst Pl SE25 ... 205 C3
Selhurst Rd Edmonton N9 ... 17 C1
South Norwood SE25 ... 205 C4
Selhurst Sta SE25 ... 205 C4
Selina Ho NW8 ... 236 D6
Selinas La RM8 ... 59 B2
Selkirk Ct N17 ... 33 C1
Selkirk Ho N1 ... 233 C6
4 N16 ... 73 C5
Selkirk Rd
Twickenham TW2 ... 152 A3
Upper Tooting SW17 ... 180 C6
Sellers Hall Cl N3 ... 29 C3
Sellincourt Inf Sch
SW17 ... 180 C4
Sellincourt Jun Sch
SW17 ... 180 C4
Sellincourt Rd SW17 ... 180 C4
Sellindge Cl BR3 ... 185 B3
Sellons Ave NW10 ... 89 D6
Sellsby Ct N11 ... 31 B5
Selwood Dr EN5 ... 12 D6
Selma Ho W12 ... 90 B1
Selman Ho 3 E9 ... 75 A2
Selsdon Ave CR2 ... 221 B2
Selsdon Cl KT6 ... 198 A4
Selsdon Ct 4 UB1 ... 85 D1
Selsdon High Sch CR2 ... 222 D1
Selsdon Park Rd CR0,
CR2 ... 223 B1
Selsdon Rd E13 ... 99 C5
NW2 ... 67 D6
South Croydon CR2 ... 221 B2
Wanstead E11 ... 55 A2
West Norwood SE27 ... 182 D6
Selsdon Road Ind Est
CR2 ... 221 B2
Selsdon Way E14 ... 119 D3
Selsea Pl N16 ... 73 C3
Selsey Cres DA16 ... 146 D4
Selsey St E14 ... 97 C2
Selvage La NW7 ... 27 B6
Selway Cl HA5 ... 40 B6
Selwood Ho 1 N4 ... 51 B2
Selwood Pl SW7 ... 114 B1 256 C2
Selwood Rd Cheam SM3 ... 201 B1
Chessington KT9 ... 213 D4
Croydon CR0 ... 206 B1
Selwood Terr SW7 ... 256 C2
Selworthy Cl E11 ... 55 A4
Selworthy Ho SW11 ... 266 D2
Selworthy Rd SE6 ... 163 B1
Selwyn Ave Chingford E4 ... 36 A4
Ilford IG3 ... 57 D3
Richmond TW9 ... 132 B2
Selwyn Cl TW4 ... 129 A1
Selwyn Cres DA16 ... 146 B1
Selwyn Ct E17 ... 53 C4
SE3 ... 142 D2
Edgware HA8 ... 26 D3
8 Richmond TW10 ... 154 B6
Selwyn Ho 3 SW15 ... 156 D5
Selwyn Inf Sch E4 ... 36 A4
Selwyn Jun Sch E4 ... 36 A4
Selwyn Prim Sch E13 ... 99 A6
Selwyn Rd E13 ... 99 B6
E3 ... 97 B5
NW10 ... 67 C1
New Malden KT3 ... 199 B4
Semley Gate E9 ... 75 B2
Semley Ho SW1 ... 258 C3
Semley Pl SW1 ... 115 B2 258 C3
Semley Rd SW16 ... 182 A1
Senate St SE15 ... 140 C3
Senators Lo 29 E3 ... 97 A5
Senator Wlk SE28 ... 123 B3
Sencler Ho SE2 ... 146 D6
Sendall Ct 13 SW11 ... 136 B2
Seneca Rd CR7 ... 205 A5
Senga Rd SM6 ... 203 A1
Senhouse Rd SM3 ... 216 D5
Senior St W2 ... 91 D2
Senlac Rd SE12 ... 165 B3
Sennen Rd EN1 ... 17 D4
Sennen Wlk SE9 ... 166 A1
Senrab St E1 ... 96 D1
Sentinel Cl UB5 ... 85 A3
Sentinel Ho NW4 ... 46 C5
Sentinel Sq NW4 ... 46 C5
September Ct UB1 ... 107 D5
September Way HA7 ... 25 B4
Sequoia Cl WD23 ... 8 B3
Sequoia Gdns BR6 ... 211 D2
Sequoia Pk HA5 ... 23 D4
Seraph Ct EC1 ... 95 A4 235 A2
Serbin Cl E10 ... 54 A2
Serenaders Rd 21 SW9 ... 138 C3
Sergeant Ind Est The
SW18 ... 157 D5
Serica Ct 14 SE10 ... 142 A5
Serjeants' Inn EC4 ... 241 B1
Serlby Ct W14 ... 254 C6
Serle St WC2 ... 94 B1 240 D2
Sermon La EC4 ... 242 A1
Serpentine Ct 10 SE16 ... 118 D4
Serpentine Gallery*
W2 ... 114 B4 246 D2
Serpentine Rd
W2 ... 114 D5 247 C3
Serpentine The*
W2 ... 114 C5 247 B3
Service Route No 1 E15 ... 76 B1
Service Route No 2 E15 ... 76 B1
Service Route No 3 E15 ... 76 B1
Serviden Dr BR1 ... 187 D2
Servite Ho SE13 ... 141 D4
Beckenham BR3 ... 185 B2
East Barnet N14 ... 15 B6
Penge SE26 ... 184 C4
Worcester Park KT4 ... 215 D6
Servite RC Prim Sch
SW10 ... 136 A6 266 A6
Servius Ct 2 TW8 ... 131 D5
Setchell Rd SE1 ... 117 D2 263 C4
Setchell Way SE1 ... 263 C4
Seth St 18 SE16 ... 118 C4
Seton Ct 3 NW9 ... 46 A5
Seton Gdns RM9 ... 80 C1
Settle Point 11 E13 ... 99 A5
Settlers Ct 2 E14 ... 120 B6
Settles St E1 ... 96 A1
Settrington Rd SW6 ... 135 D3
Seven Acres
Carshalton SM5 ... 218 C6
Northwood HA6 ... 22 A4
Seven Dials WC2 ... 94 A1 240 A1
Seven Kings High Sch
IG2 ... 57 B2
Seven Kings Rd IG3 ... 79 D6
Seven Kings Sta IG3 ... 57 C1
Seven Kings Way KT2 ... 176 A2
Seven Mills Prim Sch
E14 ... 119 C4
Sevenoaks Rd BR6 ... 227 D4
SE4 ... 163 B5
Sevenoaks Way BR5 ... 190 C1
Seven Sisters N15 ... 51 D4
Seven Sisters Inf Sch
N15 ... 51 B4
Seven Sisters Rd N4,N7,
N15 ... 51 A2
Seven Sisters Sta N15 ... 51 C4
Seven Stars Cnr W12 ... 112 A3
Seventh Ave Hayes UB3 ... 106 A5
Ilford E12 ... 78 B4
Seven Ways Par IG2 ... 56 C4
Severnake Cl E14 ... 119 C2
Severn Ct 11 KT2 ... 175 D2
Severn Dr Enfield EN1 ... 6 A5
Hinchley Wood KT10 ... 213 A6
Severn Way NW10 ... 67 D3
Severus Rd SW11 ... 136 C1
Seville Ho 11 E1 ... 118 A5
Seville Mews N1 ... 73 C1
Seville St SW1 ... 247 D1
Sevington Rd NW4 ... 46 B3
Sevington St W9 ... 91 D3
Seward Rd W7 ... 109 A4
Penge BR3 ... 184 D1
Seward St EC1 ... 95 A4 235 A1
Sewardstone Gdns E4 ... 19 D6
Sewardstone Rd E2 ... 96 C5
Chingford E4 ... 19 D6
Sewdley St E5 ... 74 D5
Sewell Ho 7 N16 ... 73 C3
Sewell Rd SE28 ... 124 B4
Sewell St E13 ... 99 A4
Sextant Ave E14 ... 120 B2
Sexton's Ho 4 SE13 ... 142 A6
Seychelle Ct BR3 ... 185 D3
Seymour Ave
Tottenham N17 ... 34 A1
West Barnes SM4 ... 200 D2
Seymour Cl
East Molesey KT8 ... 196 A4
Pinner HA5 ... 23 B2
Seymour Ct N10 ... 31 A1
N16 ... 52 A1
NW2 ... 68 B6
Chingford E4 ... 20 D2
Putney SW15 ... 134 B1
Southgate N21 ... 16 B5
Seymour Dr BR2 ... 210 B1
Seymour Gdns SE4 ... 141 A2
Feltham TW13 ... 172 C6
Kingston KT5 ... 198 B4
Redbridge IG1 ... 56 B1
Ruislip HA4 ... 40 D1
Twickenham TW1 ... 153 B4
Seymour Ho NW1 ... 232 D1
1 SW8 ... 137 C3
WC1 ... 240 A6
Seymour Mews W1 ... 238 A2
Seymour Pl W1 ... 92 D1 237 C2
Croydon SE25 ... 206 B5
Seymour Rd E10 ... 53 B1
E6 ... 99 D6
N3 ... 29 D3
N8 ... 50 D4
Acton W4 ... 111 A2
Carshalton CR4 ... 203 A2
Chingford E4 ... 19 D3
East Molesey KT8 ... 196 A4
Edmonton N9 ... 18 B2
Hampton TW12 ... 174 A5
Teddington KT1 ... 175 D2
Wallington SM5 ... 219 A3
Wandsworth SW18 ... 157 B5
Wimbledon SW19 ... 156 D1

Seymour St SE18 ... 123 A3
W1 ... 92 D1 237 D1
Seymour Terr SE20 ... 184 B2
Seymour Villas SE20 ... 184 A2
Seymour Way TW16 ... 171 C3
Seymour Wlk
SW10 ... 136 A6 266 A6
Seyssel St E14 ... 120 A2
Shaa Rd W3 ... 111 B6
Shacklegate La TW11 ... 174 C6
Shackleton Cl SE23 ... 162 B2
Shackleton Ct 4 W12 ... 112 B4
2 Dulwich SE21 ... 161 B2
4 Millwall E14 ... 119 C1
7 Stanwell TW19 ... 148 A5
Shackleton Ho 5 E1 ... 118 C5
4 NW10 ... 67 B1
Shackleton Rd UB1 ... 107 B6
Shacklewell Ho 3 E8 ... 73 D4
Shacklewell La E8 ... 73 D4
Shacklewell Prim Sch
E8 ... 73 D4
Shacklewell Rd N16 ... 73 D4
Shacklewell Row E8 ... 73 D4
Shacklewell St 30 E2 ... 95 D4
Shadbolt Cl KT4 ... 215 D6
Shad Thames
SE1 ... 117 D4 253 D2
Shadwell Ct UB5 ... 85 B5
Shadwell Dr UB5 ... 85 B4
Shadwell Gdns E1 ... 118 C6
Shadwell Pierhead E1 ... 118 C6
Shadwell Sta E1 ... 118 B6
Shady Bush Cl WD23 ... 8 A4
Shaef Way TW11 ... 175 A3
Shafter Rd RM10 ... 81 D2
Shaftesbury Ave
W1 ... 115 D6 249 D6
Enfield EN3 ... 6 D3
Feltham TW14 ... 150 A5
Harrow HA1,HA2 ... 42 A1
Harrow HA3 ... 44 A3
New Barnet EN5 ... 2 A1
Southall UB2 ... 107 C3
Shaftesbury Circ HA2 ... 42 A1
Shaftesbury Ct N1 ... 235 C3
SE1 ... 262 C6
3 SE28 ... 124 C5
1 SE5 ... 139 B1
Ilford RM6 ... 58 C2
Shaftesbury Gdns NW10 ... 89 C3
Shaftesbury Ho 18 N16 ... 73 C5
W2 ... 245 D6
Croydon SE25 ... 206 A3
Shaftesbury Lo 9 E14 ... 97 D1
Shaftesbury Mews W8 ... 255 B5
Shaftesbury Park Chambers
1 SW11 ... 137 A2
Shaftesbury Prim Sch
E7 ... 77 C1
Shaftesbury Rd E10 ... 53 C1
E17 ... 53 D3
E7 ... 77 C1
N4,N19 ... 50 A1
Beckenham BR3 ... 185 B1
Carshalton SM5 ... 202 C2
Chingford E4 ... 20 B3
Edmonton N18 ... 33 D4
Richmond TW9 ... 132 A2
Shaftesbury Sch HA3 ... 23 D2
Shaftesbury St N1 ... 235 C3
Shaftesburys The IG11 ... 101 A5
Shaftesbury Way TW2 ... 152 B1
Shaftesbury Waye UB4 ... 84 C1
Shafteswood Ct SW17 ... 158 D1
Shafto Mews SW1 ... 257 D5
Shafton Rd E9 ... 96 D6
Shaftsbury Ct E6 ... 100 C1
SW6 ... 265 D1
Shaftsbury Mews 2
SW4 ... 159 C6
Shaftsbury Park Prim Sch
SW11 ... 137 A3
Shafts Ct EC3 ... 243 A1
Shahjalal Ho 18 E2 ... 96 A5
Shakespeare Ave N11 ... 31 C5
NW10 ... 89 B6
Feltham TW14 ... 150 A5
Hayes UB4 ... 84 B2
Shakespeare Cl HA3 ... 44 C2
Shakespeare Cres E12 ... 78 B2
NW10 ... 89 B6
Shakespeare Dr HA3 ... 44 B3
Shakespeare Gdns N2 ... 48 D5
Shakespeare Ho 3 E9 ... 74 C1
N14 ... 15 D2
1 Erith DA17 ... 125 B1
Shakespeare Rd DA7 ... 147 A4
E17 ... 34 D1
N3 ... 29 C2
NW7 ... 28 A6
SE24 ... 138 D1
W3 ... 111 A5
Ealing W7 ... 108 D6
Shakespeares Globe Theatre
(site of)* SE1 ... 252 B4
Shakespeare Twr EC2 ... 242 B4
Shakespeare Way
TW13 ... 172 C6
Shakspeare Mews 7
N16 ... 73 C4
Shakspeare Wlk N16 ... 73 C4
Shalbourne Sq E9 ... 75 B2
Shalcomb St
SW10 ... 136 A6 266 B5
Shalden Ho 6 SW15 ... 155 D5
Shaldon Dr Ruislip HA4 ... 62 C5
Shaldon Dr *continued*
West Barnes SM4 ... 201 A4
Shaldon Rd HA8 ... 26 B1
Shalfleet Dr W10 ... 112 D6
Shalford NW10 ... 90 A6
3 Woodford IG8 ... 37 C4
Shalford Cl BR6 ... 227 A4
Shalford Ct N1 ... 234 C4
Shalford Ho SE1 ... 262 D6
Shalimar Gdns W3 ... 111 A6
Shalimar Lo W3 ... 111 A6
Shalimar Rd W3 ... 111 A6
Shallons Rd SE9 ... 188 D6
Shalstone Rd SW14,
TW9 ... 132 D2
Shalston Villas KT5,KT6 ... 198 B3
Shamrock Ho SE26 ... 184 A6
Shamrock Rd CR0 ... 204 B3
Shamrock St SW4 ... 137 D2
Shamrock Way N14 ... 15 B3
Shandon Rd SW4 ... 159 C5
Shand St SE1 ... 117 C4 253 B2
Shandy St E1 ... 96 D3
Shanklin Gdns WD19 ... 22 C6
Shanklin Ho E17 ... 35 B1
Shanklin Rd N15 ... 52 A5
N8 ... 49 D4
Shannon Cl NW2 ... 68 D5
Southall UB2 ... 106 D1
Shannon Cnr KT3 ... 200 A5
Shannon Cnr Ret Pk
KT3 ... 200 A5
Shannon Commercial Ctr
KT3 ... 200 A5
Shannon Ct N16 ... 73 C5
NW10 ... 68 A2
Croydon CR0 ... 205 A1
Shannon Gr SW9 ... 138 B1
Shannon Pl NW8 ... 92 C5 230 B4
Shannon Way BR3 ... 185 D4
Shanti Ct SW18 ... 157 C3
Shap Cres SM5 ... 202 D1
Shapland Way N13 ... 32 B5
Shapla Prim Sch E1 ... 118 A6
Shapwick Cl N11 ... 30 D5
Shardcroft Ave SE24 ... 160 D6
Shardeloes Rd SE14 ... 141 B3
Shard's Sq SE15 ... 140 A6
Sharebourne Ho SW2 ... 160 C6
Sharland Cl CR7 ... 204 C3
Sharman Ct DA14 ... 190 A6
Sharnbrooke Cl DA16 ... 146 C2
Sharnbrook Ho W6 ... 265 A6
Sharon Cl KT6 ... 197 C1
Sharon Gdns E9 ... 96 C6
Sharon Rd W4 ... 111 B1
Enfield EN3 ... 7 A3
Sharpe Cl W7 ... 86 D2
Sharp Ho SW8 ... 137 B2
Sharples Hall St 8 NW1 ... 70 D1
Sharpness Cl UB4 ... 85 A2
Sharpness Ct 2 SE15 ... 139 D5
Sharps La HA4 ... 39 B2
Sharratt St SE15 ... 140 C6
Sharstead St
SE17 ... 116 D1 261 C1
Sharvel La UB5 ... 84 B6
Sharwell Ho SW18 ... 157 D5
Sharwood WC1 ... 233 D3
Shaver's Pl SW1 ... 249 C5
Shaw Ave IG11 ... 103 A5
Shawbrooke Rd SE9 ... 143 D1
Shawbury Ct SE22 ... 161 D6
Shawbury Rd SE22 ... 161 D6
Shaw Cl Bushey WD23 ... 8 C2
Woolwich SE28 ... 124 B5
Shaw Ct N19 ... 72 A6
12 SW11 ... 136 B2
8 W3 ... 111 A3
Shaw Dr KT12 ... 194 C2
Shawfield Ct UB7 ... 104 A3
Shawfield Pk BR1 ... 187 D1
Shawfield St
SW3 ... 114 C1 257 B1
Shawford Ct 8 SW15 ... 156 A4
Shawford Rd KT19 ... 215 B2
Shaw Gdns IG11 ... 103 A5
Shaw Ho 5 E16 ... 122 C5
6 Erith DA17 ... 125 B1
Shaw Path BR1 ... 164 D1
Shaw Rd SE22 ... 139 C1
Catford BR1 ... 164 D1
Enfield EN3 ... 6 D4
Shaws Sq E17 ... 35 A2
Shaws Wood Cotts EN4 ... 3 C3
Shaw Way SM6 ... 220 A1
Shearing Dr SM4 ... 202 A2
Shearling Way N7 ... 72 A2
Shearman Rd SE3 ... 142 D2
Shears Ct TW16 ... 171 C3
Shearsmith Ho 14 E1 ... 118 A6
Shears The TW16 ... 171 C3
Shearwater Cl IG11 ... 102 A4
Shearwater Ct 24 SE8 ... 141 B6
Shearwater Rd SM1 ... 217 B3
Shearwater Way UB4 ... 84 D1
Sheaveshill Ave NW9 ... 45 C5
Sheaveshill Ct NW9 ... 45 C5
Sheaveshill Par NW9 ... 45 C5
Sheen Common Dr
SW14,TW10 ... 154 C6
Sheen Court Rd TW10 ... 132 C1
Sheen Ct TW10 ... 132 C1
Sheendale Rd TW9 ... 132 B1
Sheenewood SE26 ... 184 B6
Sheen Gate Gdns SW14 ... 133 A1
Sheen Gr N1 ... 94 C6 234 A6
Sheen La SW14 ... 133 A1
Sheen Mount JMI Sch
SW14 ... 154 D6
Sheen Pk TW10,TW9 ... 132 A1
Sheen Rd Orpington BR5 ... 211 D5
Richmond TW10,TW9 ... 132 B1
Sheen Way SM6 ... 220 B3
Sheen Wood SW14 ... 155 A6
Sheepcote Cl TW5 ... 128 A5
Sheepcote La SW11 ... 136 D3
Sheepcote Rd HA1 ... 42 D3
Sheepcotes Rd RM6 ... 59 A5
Sheephouse Way KT3 ... 199 C2
Sheep La E8 ... 96 B6
Sheepwalk TW17 ... 192 B3
Sheep Walk Mews 7
SW19 ... 179 A4
Sheerness Mews E16 ... 122 D4
Sheerwater Rd E16 ... 99 D2
Sheffield Ho 14 SE15 ... 139 D4
Sheffield Rd TW14,TW6 ... 149 A6
Sheffield Sq 2 E3 ... 97 B4
Sheffield St WC2 ... 240 C1
Sheffield Terr
W8 ... 113 C5 245 B3
Sheffield Way TW14,
TW6 ... 149 B6
Shefton Rise HA6 ... 22 A3
Shelbey Ct BR1 ... 186 D2
Shelbourne Cl HA5 ... 41 B6
Shelbourne Ho 20 N19 ... 49 D2
Shelbourne Rd N17 ... 34 B2
Shelburne Ct SW15 ... 156 D6
Shelburne Dr TW4 ... 151 C5
Shelburne Ho 9 SW16 ... 181 C5
Shelburne Rd N7 ... 72 B4
Shelbury Cl DA14 ... 168 A1
Shelbury Rd SE22 ... 162 B6
Sheldon Ave N6 ... 48 D3
Sheldon Cl SE12 ... 165 B6
Penge SE20 ... 184 B2
Sheldon Ct SW8 ... 270 A3
Barnet EN5 ... 1 D1
Sheldon Ho 9 E9 ... 74 D2
Chingford E4 ... 36 C4
Teddington TW11 ... 175 A4
Sheldon Rd DA7 ... 147 B4
NW2 ... 68 D4
Dagenham RM9 ... 81 A1
Edmonton N18 ... 33 C6
Sheldon St CR0 ... 221 A5
Sheldrake Cl E16 ... 122 B5
Sheldrake Ho 15 SE16 ... 118 D2
Sheldrake Pl
W8 ... 113 C4 245 A2
Sheldrick Cl CR4 ... 180 B1
Shelduck Cl E15 ... 76 D3
Shelduck Ct 36 SE8 ... 141 B6
Sheldwich Terr BR2 ... 210 A3
Shelford 20 KT1 ... 176 C1
Shelford Ct 7 E5 ... 52 B1
Shelford Pl N16 ... 73 B5
Shelford Rd EN5 ... 12 C5
Shelford Rise SE19 ... 183 D3
Shelgate Rd SW11 ... 158 D6
Shell Cl BR2 ... 210 A3
Shell Ctr SE1 ... 250 D3
Shellduck Cl NW9 ... 27 C1
Shelley N8 ... 50 A6
Shelley Ave E12 ... 78 A2
Greenford UB6 ... 86 B4
Shelley Cl BR6 ... 227 C5
SE15 ... 140 B3
Edgware HA8 ... 26 C6
Greenford UB6 ... 86 B4
Hayes UB4 ... 84 A2
Shelley Cres
Heston TW5 ... 128 D4
Southall UB1 ... 85 B1
Shelley Ct 12 E10 ... 53 D2
N4 ... 50 B1
SW3 ... 267 D6
5 Kingston KT2 ... 175 D6
8 Wanstead E11 ... 55 A5
Wembley HA0 ... 65 C4
West Barnes KT3 ... 200 A4
Shelley Dr DA16 ... 145 C4
Shelley Gdns HA0 ... 65 C6
Shelley Ho 21 E2 ... 96 C4
9 N16 ... 73 C4
SE17 ... 262 B2
SW1 ... 269 A6
Shelley Rd NW10 ... 89 B6
Shelley Sch
SE11 ... 116 C2 261 B3
Shelley Way SW17 ... 180 B4
Shellgrove Rd N16 ... 73 C3
Shellness Rd E5 ... 74 B3
Shell Rd SE13 ... 141 D2
Shellwood Rd SW11 ... 136 D3
Shelly Lo EN2 ... 5 B4
Shelmerdine Cl E3 ... 97 C2
Shelson Ave TW13 ... 171 D6
Shelton Rd SW19 ... 179 C2
Shelton St WC2 ... 94 A1 240 A1
Shene Bldg EC1 ... 241 A4
Shene Int Sch SW14 ... 133 C1
Shenfield Ho 3 SE18 ... 143 D5
Shenfield Rd IG8 ... 37 B3
Shenfield St N1 ... 95 C5
Shenley Ave HA4 ... 39 D1
Shenley Rd SE5 ... 139 C4
Heston TW5 ... 129 A4
Shenstone W13 ... 109 C5
Shenstone Gdns IG2 ... 57 D4
Shenstone Ho SW16 ... 181 C5
Shepherd Cl W1 ... 248 A6
Feltham TW13 ... 173 A6
Shepherdess Pl N1 ... 235 B2
Shepherdess Wlk
N1 ... 95 A5 235 B3
Shepherd Ho 10 E14 ... 97 D1
N7 ... 72 A2
Shepherd Mkt W1 ... 248 C3
Shepherd's Bush (Central
Line) Sta W12 ... 112 D4
Shepherd's Bush Gn
W12 ... 112 C4
Shepherd's Bush (Hamm &
City) Sta W12 ... 112 C5
Shepherd's Bush Market
W12 ... 112 C4
Shepherd's Bush Pl
W12 ... 112 D4
Shepherd's Bush Rd
W6 ... 112 C3
Shepherds Cl N6 ... 49 B3
Shepherds Cl
Dagenham RM6 ... 58 D5
Orpington BR6 ... 227 D5
Shepperton TW17 ... 192 D3
Shepherds Ct 8 W12 ... 112 D4
Shepherds Gn BR7 ... 189 B3
Shepherd's Hill N6 ... 49 C3
Shepherd's La E9 ... 74 D2
Shepherds Leas SE9 ... 145 B1
Shepherds Path UB5 ... 63 A2
Shepherds Pl W1 ... 248 A6
Shepherd St
W1 ... 115 B5 248 C3
Shepherds Way CR2 ... 222 D1
Shepherds Wlk NW2 ... 68 A6
Shepherd's Wlk NW3 ... 70 B4
Shepherds Wlk WD23 ... 8 B2
Shepiston La UB3 ... 105 A1
Shepley Cl SM5 ... 219 A5
Shepley Ct SW16 ... 181 C6
Shepley Mews EN3 ... 7 C6
Sheppard Cl Enfield EN1 ... 6 B5
Kingston KT6 ... 198 A5
Sheppard Dr SE16 ... 118 B1
Sheppard Ho 28 E2 ... 96 A5
18 SW11 ... 136 B2
8 Streatham SW2 ... 160 C3
Sheppard's Ct
Harrow HA1 ... 42 C2
Wembley UB6 ... 64 D2
Sheppard St E16 ... 98 D3
Shepperton Bsns Park
TW17 ... 193 A4
Shepperton Court Dr
TW17 ... 192 D4
Shepperton Ct TW17 ... 192 D3
Shepperton Rd
N1 ... 95 B6 235 C6
Littleton TW17,TW18 ... 192 A5
Orpington BR5 ... 211 A3
Shepperton Sta TW17 ... 193 A4
Shepperton Studios
TW17 ... 192 B6
Sheppey Gdns RM9 ... 80 C1
Sheppey Ho 16 E5 ... 74 B4
Sheppey Rd RM9 ... 80 C1
Sheppey Wlk N1 ... 73 A1
Shepton Ct SW11 ... 266 D2
Shepton Hos 11 E2 ... 96 C4
Sherard Ct N19 ... 72 A5
Sherard Ho 24 E9 ... 74 C1
Sherard Rd SE9 ... 166 A6
Sheraton Bsns Ctr UB6 ... 87 C5
Sheraton Cl WD6 ... 10 B6
Sheraton Ho SW1 ... 268 D6
Sheraton Lo HA3 ... 42 C6
Sheraton St W1 ... 239 C1
Sheraton The 22 KT6 ... 198 A4
Sherborne Ave Enfield EN3 ... 6 C3
Southall UB2 ... 107 C2
Sherborne Cl UB4 ... 84 C1
Sherborne Cres SM5 ... 202 C2
Sherborne Ct SE20 ... 184 C1
Sherborne Gdns NW9 ... 44 C6
Ealing W13 ... 87 B2
Sherborne Ho SW1 ... 258 D2
SW8 ... 270 C3
Sherborne La EC4 ... 252 D6
Sherborne Rd BR5 ... 211 D4
Cheam SM3 ... 201 C1
Chessington KT9 ... 214 A3
East Bedfont TW14 ... 149 B3
Sherborne St N1 ... 95 B6 235 C6
Sherboro Rd 1 N15 ... 51 D3
Sherbourne Ct 1 TW12 ... 173 C2
Sherbourne Gdns TW17 ... 193 C2
Sherbourne Pl HA7 ... 25 A4
Sherbrooke Cl DA7 ... 147 C1
Sherbrooke Ho 9 E2 ... 96 C5
Sherbrooke Rd
SW6 ... 135 A5 264 B3
Sherbrooke Terr SW6 ... 264 B3
Sherbrook Gdns N21 ... 16 D4
Shere Cl KT9 ... 213 D3
Sheredan Rd E4 ... 36 C5
Shere Ho SE1 ... 262 C6
Shere Rd IG2 ... 56 C4
Sherfield Cl KT3 ... 198 D5
Sherfield Gdns SW15 ... 155 D5
Sheridan N8 ... 50 C5
Sheridan Bldgs WC2 ... 240 B1
Sheridan Cl UB10 ... 83 A3
Sheridan Cres BR7 ... 188 D1
Sheridan Ct NW6 ... 70 A1
SW9 ... 270 D1
Ealing W7 ... 108 D6
Harrow HA1 ... 42 B3
Hounslow TW4 ... 151 A6
Sheridan Gdns HA3 ... 43 D3
Sheridan Ho 16 E1 ... 96 C1
7 N16 ... 73 C5
SE11 ... 261 B3
Sheridan Lo EN5 ... 1 D1
Sheridan Mews E11 ... 55 B3
Sheridan Pl
Barnes SW13 ... 133 D2
Sheridan Pl *continued*
Hampton TW12 ... 174 A2
Harrow HA1 ... 42 C2
Sheridan Rd DA7 ... 147 A2
E12 ... 78 B3
E7 ... 76 D5
Belvedere DA17 ... 125 C2
Merton SW19 ... 179 B2
Richmond TW10 ... 153 C1
Sheridan St 28 E1 ... 96 B1
Sheridan Terr UB5 ... 63 D3
Sheridan Way 5 BR3 ... 185 B2
Sheridan Wlk NW11 ... 47 C3
Sheridon Ct SW5 ... 255 C3
Sheringdale Prim Sch
SW18 ... 157 B3
Sheringham NW8 ... 229 D6
Sheringham Ave E12 ... 78 B3
Southgate N14 ... 15 D5
Twickenham TW2 ... 151 C3
Sheringham Dr IG11 ... 80 A3
Sheringham Ho NW1 ... 237 B4
Sheringham Jun Sch
E12 ... 78 B4
Sheringham Rd N7 ... 72 C2
Penge SE20 ... 206 C6
Sheringham Twr UB1 ... 107 D6
Sherington Ave HA5 ... 23 C3
Sherington Prim Sch
SE7 ... 143 B6
Sherington Rd SE7 ... 143 B6
Sherland Rd TW1 ... 152 D3
Sherleys Ct HA4 ... 61 C6
Sherlies Ave BR6 ... 227 C6
Sherlock Ct NW8 ... 229 C6
Sherlock Holmes Mus*
NW1 ... 92 D3 237 D5
Sherlock Mews W1 ... 238 A4
Sherman Gdns RM6 ... 58 C3
Sherman Rd BR1 ... 187 A2
Shernwood Ho 1 E18 ... 55 A5
Sherrard Rd E7,E12 ... 77 D2
Sherrards Way EN5 ... 13 D5
Sherrick Green Rd NW10 ... 68 B3
Sherriff Ct NW6 ... 69 C2
Sherriff Rd NW6 ... 69 C2
Sherringham Ave
Feltham TW13 ... 150 A1
Tottenham N17 ... 34 A1
Sherringham Ct 1 N3 ... 29 C2
Sherrin Rd E10 ... 75 D4
Sherrock Gdns NW4 ... 46 A5
Sherry Mews IG11 ... 79 B1
Sherston Ct SE1 ... 261 D4
WC1 ... 234 A1
Sherwin Ho 1 SE11 ... 138 C6
Sherwin Rd SE14 ... 140 D4
Sherwood NW6 ... 69 A1
Long Ditton KT6 ... 213 D6
Sherwood Ave
Greenford UB6 ... 64 C3
Hayes UB4 ... 84 B3
Mitcham SW16 ... 181 D2
Ruislip HA4 ... 39 C3
Wanstead E18 ... 55 B6
Sherwood Cl DA5 ... 168 C5
E17 ... 35 B1
Barnes SW13 ... 134 B2
Ealing W13 ... 109 B5
Sherwood Ct SE13 ... 141 D3
11 SW11 ... 136 A2
W1 ... 237 C3
5 West Wickham BR4 ... 207 D1
Sherwood Gdns E14 ... 119 C2
SE16 ... 118 B1
Barking IG11 ... 79 B1
Sherwood Hall 7 N2 ... 48 A6
Sherwood Ho N4 ... 51 A2
Sherwood Park Ave
DA15 ... 168 B5
Sherwood Park Prim Sch
DA15 ... 168 B5
Sherwood Park Rd
Mitcham CR4 ... 203 D5
Sutton SM1 ... 217 C3
Sherwood Park Sch
SM6 ... 219 D5
Sherwood Prim Sch
CR4 ... 203 C5
Sherwood Rd DA16 ... 145 C2
NW4 ... 46 C6
Croydon CR0 ... 206 B1
Hampton TW12 ... 174 A5
Harrow HA2 ... 64 A6
Ilford IG6 ... 57 B5
Merton SW19 ... 179 B3
Sherwood St N20 ... 14 B1
W1 ... 249 B6
Sherwood Terr N20 ... 14 B1
Sherwood Way BR4 ... 224 A6
Shetland Cl WD6 ... 11 B5
Shetland Rd E3 ... 97 B5
East Bedfont TW6 ... 149 A5
Shield Dr TW8 ... 131 A6
Shieldhall St SE2 ... 124 C2
Shield Rd TW15 ... 171 B6
Shifford Path SE23 ... 162 D1
Shillaker Ct W3 ... 111 D5
Shillibeer Pl W1 ... 237 B3
Shillingford Ho 40 E3 ... 97 D4
Shillingford St 22 N1 ... 72 D1
Shillingstone Ho W14 ... 254 B5
Shinfield St W12 ... 90 C1
Shinglewell Rd DA8 ... 147 C5
Shinners Cl SE25 ... 206 A4
Shipka Rd SW12 ... 159 B3
Ship La SW14 ... 133 A3
Shiplake Ct SW17 ... 180 B6
Shiplake Ho 45 E2 ... 95 D4
Shipley Ct SE20 ... 184 A1
Shipley Ho 32 SW8 ... 137 D3
Shipman Par SE23 ... 163 A2
Shipman Rd
Forest Hill SE23 ... 162 D2
Newham E16 ... 99 C1
Ship & Mermaid Row
SE1 ... 253 A2
Ship St SE8 ... 141 C4
Ship Tavern Pas EC3 ... 253 A6
Shipton Cl RM8 ... 80 D5
Shipton Ho 14 E2 ... 95 D5
7 NW5 ... 71 A2
Shipton Rd UB8 ... 60 B4
Shipton St E2 ... 95 D4
Shipwright Rd SE16 ... 119 A4
Shipwright Yd SE1 ... 253 A3
Shirburn Cl SE23 ... 162 C4
Shirbutt St E14 ... 119 D6
Shirebrook Rd SE3 ... 143 D2
Shire Ct DA18 ... 124 D3
Ewell KT17 ... 215 D1
Shirehall Cl NW4 ... 46 D3
Shirehall Gdns NW4 ... 46 D3
Shirehall La NW4 ... 46 D3
Shirehall Pk NW4 ... 46 D3
Shire Ho E11 ... 76 D5
Shire Horse Way TW7 ... 130 D2
Shire La
Farthing Street BR6,BR2 ... 227 B2
Orpington BR6 ... 227 C3
Shiremeade WD6 ... 10 B6
Shire Pl SW18 ... 158 A4
Shires The TW10 ... 176 A6
Shirland Mews W9 ... 91 B4
Shirland Rd W9 ... 91 C3
Shirley Ave DA5 ... 168 D3
Carshalton SM1 ... 218 C4
Croydon CR0 ... 206 D1
Shirley Church Rd CR0 ... 223 A5
Shirley Cl TW3 ... 152 A6
Shirley Cres BR3 ... 207 A5
Shirley Ct NW9 ... 45 B4
8 Ealing W13 ... 109 A5
Ilford IG2 ... 57 B4
Thornton Heath SW16 ... 204 B6
Shirley Dr TW3 ... 152 A6
Shirley Gdns Barking IG11 ... 79 C2
Ealing W7 ... 108 D5
Shirley Gr N9 ... 18 D4
SW11 ... 137 A2
Shirley High Sch CR0 ... 222 D5
Shirley Hills Rd CR0 ... 222 D3
Shirley Ho 18 SE5 ... 139 B5
Shirley House Dr SE7 ... 143 C5
Shirley Lo 4 SE26 ... 185 A6
Shirley Oaks Hospl CR0 ... 206 C2
Shirley Oaks Rd CR0 ... 222 D6
Shirley Park Rd CR0 ... 206 C1
Shirley Rd E15 ... 76 C1
W4 ... 111 B4
Croydon CR0 ... 206 B1
Enfield EN2 ... 5 A2
Sidcup DA15 ... 167 C1
Shirleys Cl E17 ... 53 D4
Shirley St E16 ... 98 D1
Shirley Way CR0 ... 223 B5
Shirlock Rd NW3 ... 70 D4
Shobden Rd N17 ... 33 B2
Shobroke Cl NW2 ... 68 C5
Shoebury Rd E6 ... 78 B1
Shoe La EC4 ... 94 C1 241 B2
Shoelands Ct NW9 ... 45 B6
Shooters Ave HA3 ... 43 C5
Shooters Hill SE18 ... 144 C4
Shooters Hill Rd
SE18,SE3,SE7 ... 143 D5
SE3,SE10 ... 142 C4
Shooters Rd EN2 ... 4 D4
Shoot-Up Hill NW2 ... 69 A2
Shore Bsns Ctr 31 E9 ... 74 C1
Shore Cl Feltham TW14 ... 150 A4
Hampton TW12 ... 173 A5
Shorediche Cl UB10 ... 60 B5
Shoreditch Ct 2 E8 ... 73 D1
Shoreditch High St
E2 ... 95 C3 243 B6
Shoreditch Sta
E1 ... 95 D3 243 D5
Shore Gr TW13 ... 151 C2
Shoreham Cl DA5 ... 168 D3
SW18 ... 157 D6
Croydon CR0 ... 206 C3
Shoreham Rd BR5 ... 190 B1
Shoreham Rd (E) TW6 ... 148 A6
Shoreham Rd (W) TW6 ... 148 A6
Shoreham Way BR2 ... 209 A3
Shore Ho SW8 ... 137 B2
Shore Mews 30 E9 ... 74 C1
Shore Pl E9 ... 74 C1
Shore Rd E9 ... 74 C1
Shorncliffe Rd
SE1 ... 117 D1 263 C2
Shorndean St SE6 ... 164 A3
Shorne Cl 3 DA15 ... 168 B5
Shornefield Cl BR1 ... 210 C6
Shornells Way SE2 ... 124 C1
Shorrolds Rd
SW6 ... 135 B5 264 D4
Shortcroft Mead Ct
NW10 ... 68 A3
Shortcroft Rd KT17 ... 215 D1
Shortcrofts Rd RM9 ... 81 B2
Shorter St EC3 ... 117 D6 253 D6
Shortgate N12 ... 29 B6
Short La TW15,TW19 ... 148 B3
Shortlands W6 ... 112 D2
Harlington UB3 ... 127 B6
Shortlands Cl DA17 ... 125 B3
Edmonton N18 ... 17 B1
Shortlands Gdns BR2 ... 186 C1

Shortlands Gr BR2 ... 208 B6
Shortlands Rd E10 ... 53 D2
Beckenham BR2,BR3 ... 208 C6
Kingston KT2 ... 176 B3
Shortlands Sta BR2 ... 186 C1
Short Path SE18 ... 144 D6
Short Rd E11 ... 76 C6
Chiswick W4 ... 133 C6
Stanwell TW19 ... 148 A5
Shorts Croft NW9 ... 44 D5
Shorts Gdns WC2 . 94 A1 240 A1
Shorts Rd SM5 ... 218 C3
Short St 7 NW4 ... 46 C5
SE1 ... 251 B2
Shortway SE9 ... 144 A2
Short Way N12 ... 30 C4
Twickenham TW2 ... 152 A4
Shotfield SM6 ... 219 B2
Shott Cl SM1 ... 218 A3
Shottendane Rd
SW6 ... 135 C4 265 A2
Shottery Cl SE9 ... 166 A1
Shottfield Ave SW14 ... 133 C1
Shottsford 1 W11 ... 91 C1
Shoulder of Mutton Alley 10
E14 ... 119 A6
Shouldham St
W1 ... 92 C2 237 B3
Showers Way UB3 ... 106 A5
Shrapnel Cl SE18 ... 144 A5
Shrapnel Rd SE9 ... 144 B2
Shreveport Ho 23 N19 ... 49 D2
Shrewsbury Ave
Harrow HA3 ... 44 A5
Mortlake SW14 ... 133 B1
Shrewsbury Cl KT6 ... 214 A6
Shrewsbury Cres NW10 ... 89 B6
Shrewsbury Ho SE11 ... 270 D5
SW3 ... 267 A5
Shrewsbury House Sch
KT6 ... 214 A6
Shrewsbury La SE18 ... 144 D4
Shrewsbury Mews 33
W2 ... 91 C2
Shrewsbury Rd E7 ... 77 D2
N11 ... 31 D4
W2 ... 91 C1
Beckenham BR3 ... 207 A6
Carshalton SM5 ... 202 C2
Harlington TW14,TW6 ... 149 B5
Shrewsbury St W10 ... 90 C3
Shrewsbury Wlk 7
TW7 ... 131 A2
Shrewton Rd SW17 ... 180 D3
Shroffold Rd BR1 ... 164 D1
Shropshire Cl CR4 ... 204 A5
Shropshire Ct W7 ... 86 D1
Shropshire Pl WC1 ... 239 B5
Shropshire Rd N22 ... 32 B3
Shroton St NW1 ... 92 C2 237 B4
Shrubberies The
Ilford IG2 ... 57 D4
Woodford E18 ... 37 A1
Shrubbery Gdns N21 ... 16 D4
Shrubbery Rd
Edmonton N9 ... 18 A1
Southall UB1 ... 107 C5
Streatham SW16 ... 182 A6
Shrubbery The
2 Surbiton KT6 ... 198 A1
7 Wanstead E11 ... 55 B4
Shrubland Gr KT4 ... 216 C5
Shrubland Rd E10 ... 53 C2
E8 ... 96 A6
Walthamstow E10 ... 53 C4
Shrublands Ave CR0 ... 223 C4
Shrublands Cl N20 ... 14 B2
Forest Hill SE26 ... 162 C1
Shrubsall Cl SE9 ... 166 A3
Shrubs Ho SW1 ... 259 D3
Shubbery Cl N1 ... 235 B5
Shurland Ave EN4 ... 14 B5
Shurland Gdns SE15 ... 139 D5
Shurlock Dr BR6 ... 227 A4
Shuters Sq W14 ... 254 C1
Shuttle Cl DA15 ... 167 D4
Shuttlemead DA5 ... 169 B4
Shuttle St E1 ... 96 A3
Shuttleworth Rd SW11 ... 136 C3
Sibella Rd SW4 ... 137 D3
Sibford Ct 5 CR4 ... 202 D6
Sibley Cl DA6 ... 169 A6
Sibley Ct UB8 ... 83 A2
Sibley Gr E12 ... 78 A1
Sibthorpe Rd SE12 ... 165 C4
Sibthorp Rd 2 CR4 ... 180 D1
Sibton Rd SM5 ... 202 C2
Sicilian Ave WC1 ... 240 B3
Sidbury St SW6 . 135 A4 264 A2
Sidcup By Pass Rd
Sidcup DA14 ... 189 C6
St Paul's Cray BR5,BR7 ... 190 B3
Sidcup Hill DA14 ... 190 B5
Sidcup Hill Gdns DA14 ... 190 C5
Sidcup Hill Prim Sch
DA14 ... 190 B5
Sidcup Pl DA14 ... 190 A5
Sidcup Rd SE9 ... 166 A3
Sidcup Sta DA14,DA15 ... 168 A2
Sidcup Tech Ctr DA14 ... 190 D4
Siddeley Dr TW4 ... 129 A3
Siddons Ct WC2 ... 240 C1
Siddons Ho 8 NW3 ... 70 D3
W2 ... 236 D3
Siddons La NW1 . 92 D3 237 D5
Siddons Rd Croydon CR0 . 220 D5
Forest Hill SE23 ... 163 A2
Tottenham N17 ... 34 A2
Side Rd E17 ... 53 B4
Sidewood Rd DA15,SE9 ... 167 B3
Sidford Ho SE1 ... 260 D5
Sidford Pl SE1 ... 116 B3 260 D5
Sidgwick Ho 26 SW9 ... 138 A3
Sidings Mews N7 ... 72 C4
Sidings The E11 ... 54 A1
Sidlaw Ho N16 ... 51 D1
Sidmouth Ave TW7 ... 130 C3
Sidmouth Dr HA4 ... 62 A5
Sidmouth Ho 18 SE15 ... 140 A5
W1 ... 237 B2
26 Streatham SW2 ... 160 C4
Sidmouth Par NW2 ... 68 C1
Sidmouth Rd E10 ... 76 A5
NW2 ... 68 C1
Bexley DA16 ... 146 C5
Sidmouth St WC1 . 94 B4 233 C1
Sidney Ave N13 ... 32 B5
Sidney Boyd Ct NW6 ... 69 C1
Sidney Elson Way E6 ... 100 C5
Sidney Gdns TW8 ... 131 D6
Sidney Godley (VC) Ho 31
E2 ... 96 C4
Sidney Gr EC1 ... 234 C3
Sidney Ho 4 E2 ... 96 D5
3 SE18 ... 144 B4
Sidney Miller Ct 8 W3 ... 110 D5
Sidney Rd SW9 ... 138 B3
Beckenham BR3 ... 185 A1
Croydon SE25 ... 206 A4
Harrow HA2 ... 42 A6
Twickenham TW1 ... 153 B5
Walton-on-T KT12 ... 194 B1
Wanstead E7 ... 77 A5
Wood Green N22 ... 32 B3
Sidney Sq E1 ... 96 C2
Sidney St E1 ... 96 C2
Sidworth St 6 E8 ... 74 B1
Siebert Rd SE3 ... 143 A6
Siedle Ho 9 SE18 ... 144 C6
Siege Ho 21 E1 ... 96 B1
Siemens Rd SE18 ... 121 D3
Sierra Dr RM9 ... 103 D5
Sigdon Rd E8 ... 74 A3
Sigers The HA5 ... 40 B3
Signmakers Yd NW1 ... 231 D5
Sigrist Sq 4 KT2 ... 176 A2
Silbury Ave CR4 ... 180 C2
Silbury Ho 9 SE26 ... 162 A1
Silbury St N1 ... 235 C2
Silchester Ct
Stanwell TW15 ... 148 A2
Thornton Heath CR7 ... 204 C5
Silchester Rd W10 ... 90 D1
Silecroft Rd DA7 ... 147 C4
Silesia Bldgs E8 ... 74 B1
Silex St SE1 ... 116 D4 251 D1
Silicone Bsns Ctr UB6 ... 87 C5
Silk Cl SE12 ... 165 A5
Silkfield Rd NW9 ... 45 C4
Silk Ho NW9 ... 45 B6
Silk Mills Path SE13 ... 142 A2
Silk Mills Sq E9 ... 75 B2
Silks Ct E11 ... 54 C1
Silk St EC2 ... 95 A2 242 B4
Silkstream Par HA8 ... 27 A2
Silkstream Rd HA8 ... 27 A2
Sillitoe Ho N1 ... 235 D5
Silsoe Ho NW1 ... 231 D3
Silsoe Rd N22 ... 50 B6
Silver Birch Ave E4 ... 35 B4
Silver Birch Cl N11 ... 31 A4
Forest Hill SE6 ... 163 B1
Ickenham UB10 ... 60 A4
Silver Birch Ct EN3 ... 18 D6
Silver Birch Gdns E6 ... 100 B3
Silver Birch Rd SE28 ... 124 A5
Silverbirch Wlk 1 NW3 ... 71 A2
Silverburn Ho 4 SW9 ... 138 D4
Silver Cl SE14 ... 141 A5
Harrow HA3 ... 24 B3
Silvercliffe Gdns EN4 ... 2 C1
Silver Cres W4 ... 110 D2
Silver Ct N19 ... 71 C5
Silverdale NW1 ... 232 A2
Enfield EN2 ... 4 A1
Forest Hill SE26 ... 184 C6
Silverdale Ave IG3 ... 57 D4
Silverdale Cl Cheam SM1 . 217 B4
1 Ealing W7 ... 108 D5
Northolt UB5 ... 63 B3
Silverdale Ct EC1 ... 241 D6
Silverdale Dr
Chislehurst SE9 ... 166 A2
Sunbury TW16 ... 172 B1
Silverdale Factory Ctr
UB3 ... 106 A4
Silverdale Gdns UB3 ... 106 A4
Silverdale Par IG3 ... 57 D4
Silverdale Rd BR5 ... 211 A5
DA7 ... 147 D3
Chingford E4 ... 36 B4
Hayes UB3 ... 106 A4
Silverhall St TW7 ... 131 A2
Silverholme Cl HA3 ... 44 A2
Silver Ind Est N17 ... 33 D1
Silver Jubilee Way TW4 . 128 B3
Silver La BR4 ... 224 B6
Silverland St E16 ... 122 B5
Silverleigh Rd CR7 ... 204 B4
Silvermead 7 E18 ... 37 A2
Silvermere Rd SE6 ... 163 D5
Silver Pl W1 ... 249 B6
Silver Rd W12 ... 112 D6
Silvers IG9 ... 21 C3
Silver Spring Cl DA8 ... 147 D6
Silver St Edmonton N18 ... 33 C6
Enfield EN1 ... 5 B2
Silverstone Ct 6 BR1 ... 187 C1
Silverston Way HA7 ... 25 C4
Silver Street Sta N18 ... 33 D5
Silverthorn 15 NW6 ... 91 D6
Silverthorne Rd SW8 ... 137 B3
Silverthorn Gdns E4 ... 19 C2
Silverton Lo SE19 ... 183 C3
Silverton Rd W6 ... 134 D6
Silvertown Sta E16 ... 122 A5
Silvertown Way E16 ... 121 A5
Silvertree La UB6 ... 86 B4
Silver Way
Hillingdon UB10 ... 82 D5
Romford RM7 ... 59 D6
Silver Wlk SE16 ... 119 B5
Silverwood Cl BR3 ... 185 C3
Silvester Ho 17 E1 ... 96 B1
27 E2 ... 96 C4
2 W11 ... 91 B1
Pinner HA5 ... 40 A5
Silvester Rd SE22 ... 161 D6
Silvester St SE1 ... 252 C1
Silwood St SE16 ... 118 C1
Simba Ct TW1 ... 152 D3
Simla Ho SE1 ... 252 D1
Simmil Rd KT10 ... 212 C3
Simmons Cl N20 ... 14 C3
Chessington KT9 ... 213 C2
Simmons Gate KT10 ... 212 A3
Simmons Ho 16 E2 ... 96 A4
N7 ... 72 B6
Simmons La E4 ... 20 B2
Simmons Rd SE18 ... 122 D1
Simmons' Way N20 ... 14 C2
Simms Cl SM5 ... 218 C6
Simms Ct SW6 ... 135 A2
Simms Gdns N2 ... 30 A1
Simms Rd SE1 ... 118 A2
Simnel Rd SE12 ... 165 B4
Simon Cl W11 ... 113 B6 244 D6
Simon Ct W9 ... 91 C4
5 Woolwich SE28 ... 124 B5
Simonds Rd E10 ... 75 C6
Simone Cl BR1 ... 187 D2
Simon Lo 31 SW19 ... 156 D3
Simon Marks (Jewish) Prim
Sch N16 ... 73 D6
Simon Peter Ct EN2 ... 4 D3
Simons Wlk E15 ... 76 B3
Simpson Cl N21 ... 16 B6
Simpson Dr W3 ... 89 B1
Simpson Ho NW8 ... 230 A1
SE11 ... 260 C1
Wembley HA9 ... 65 D6
Simpson Rd
Hounslow TW4 ... 151 B5
Richmond TW10 ... 175 C6
Simpson's Cotts BR2 ... 225 C5
Simpson's Rd BR2 ... 209 A6
E14 ... 119 D6
Simpson St SW11 ... 136 C3
Simpson Way KT6 ... 197 C3
Sim's Cotts KT10 ... 212 D2
Sims Wlk SE3 ... 142 D1
Sinclair Ct N5 ... 73 A2
21 Beckenham BR3 ... 185 C3
5 Croydon CR0 ... 221 D6
Sinclair Gdns W14 ... 112 D4
Sinclair Gr NW11 ... 46 D3
Sinclair Ho 1 SW12 ... 159 D3
Sinclair Mans 13 W12 ... 112 D4
Sinclair Rd E4 ... 35 B5
W14 ... 113 A3 254 A6
Sinclairs Ho 14 E3 ... 97 B5
Sinclare Cl EN1 ... 5 D4
Singapore Rd W13 ... 109 A5
Singer St EC2 ... 235 D1
Singlegate First Sch
SW19 ... 180 B3
Singleton Cl
Mitcham SW17,SW19 ... 180 D3
Thornton Heath CR0 ... 205 A2
Singleton Rd RM9 ... 81 B3
Singleton Scarp N12 ... 29 C5
Sinnott Rd E17 ... 34 D2
Sion Ct TW1 ... 153 B3
Sion-Manning RC Sch for
Girls
W10 ... 90 D2
W10 ... 91 A2
Sion Rd TW1 ... 153 B3
Sippetts Ct IG1 ... 57 B1
Sipson Cl UB7 ... 126 C6
Sipson La UB3,UB7 ... 126 D6
Sipson Rd
Harmondsworth UB7 ... 126 C6
West Drayton UB7 ... 104 B2
West Drayton UB7 ... 104 C1
Sipson Way UB7 ... 126 C5
Sir Abraham Dawes Cotts
SW15 ... 135 A1
Sir Alexander Cl W3 ... 111 D5
Sir Alexander Rd W3 ... 111 D5
Sir Cyril Black Way 2
SW19 ... 179 C3
Sirdar Rd W11 ... 113 A6 244 A5
Mitcham CR4 ... 181 A4
Tottenham N22 ... 33 A1
Sir Francis Drake Prim Sch
SE8 ... 119 A1
Sir George Monoux Sixth
Form Coll E17 ... 35 D1
Sir Henry Floyd Ct HA7 ... 9 B2
Sirinham Point SW8 ... 270 D5
Sirius Bldg 13 E1 ... 118 D6
Sir James Barrie Prim Sch
SW8 ... 137 C4 269 B1
Sir John Cass Foundation &
Redcoat CE Sec Sch E1 . 96 D2
Sir John Cass's Prim Sch
EC3 ... 95 C1 243 A1
Sir John Heron Prim Sch
E12 ... 78 B4
Sir John Kirk Cl 33 SE5 .. 139 A5
Sir John Lillie Prim Sch
SW6 ... 135 A6 264 B5
Sir Martin Bowes Ho 15
SE18 ... 122 C2
Sir Oswald Stoll Foundation
The SW6 ... 265 C4
Sir Thomas Abney Sch
N16 ... 51 B1
Sir Thomas More Est
SW3 ... 136 B6 266 D5
Sirus Rd HA6 ... 22 A5
Sir William Burrough Prim
Sch E14 ... 97 A1
Sir William Powell's Almshos
SW6 ... 135 A2
Sise La EC4 ... 242 C1
Siskin Ho 14 SE16 ... 118 D2
Sisley Rd IG11 ... 101 D6
Sispara Gdns SW18 ... 157 B5
Sissinghurst Cl BR1 ... 186 C5
Sissinghurst Ho 17
SE15 ... 140 C6
Sissinghurst Rd CR0 ... 206 A2
Sissulu Ct 9 E6 ... 99 C6
Sister Mabel's Way 14
SE15 ... 140 A5
Sisters Ave SW11 ... 136 D1
Sistova Rd SW12 ... 159 B3
Sisulu Pl SW9 ... 138 C2
Site of Changing of the
Guard★ SW1 ... 249 A1
Sittingbourne Ave EN1 ... 17 B5
Sitwell Gr HA7 ... 24 D5
Siverst Cl UB5 ... 63 D2
Sivill Ho 9 E2 ... 95 D4
Siviter Way RM10 ... 81 D1
Siward Rd Bromley BR2 .. 209 C6
Tottenham N17 ... 33 B2
Wandsworth SW17 ... 158 A1
Six Bridges Ind Est SE1 . 118 A1
Sixth Ave W10 ... 91 A4
Hayes UB3 ... 105 D5
Ilford E12 ... 78 B4
Sixth Cross Rd TW2 ... 152 A1
Skardu Rd NW2 ... 69 A3
Skeena Hill SW18,SW19 . 157 A4
Skeffington Rd E6 ... 100 B6
Skeggs Ho 5 E14 ... 120 A3
Skegness Ho 3 N7 ... 72 B1
Skelbrook St SW18 ... 158 A2
Skelgill Rd SW15 ... 135 B1
Skelley Rd E15 ... 76 D1
Skelton Cl 7 E8 ... 73 D2
Skelton Ho N16 ... 73 C3
Skelton Rd E7 ... 77 A2
Skelton's La E10 ... 53 D2
Skelwith Rd W6 ... 134 C6
Skenfrith Ho SE15 ... 140 B6
Skerne Rd KT2 ... 175 D2
Sketchley Gdns SE16 ... 118 D1
Sketty Rd EN1 ... 5 D2
Skiers St E15 ... 98 C6
Skiffington Cl SW2 ... 160 C3
Skinner Ct E17 ... 53 C4
Skinner Pl SW1 ... 258 A3
Skinners Almshouses
N13 ... 16 C1
Skinners Company Sch
(Upper) N16 ... 51 D2
Skinner's Company's Lower
Sch E5 ... 52 B1
Skinners La EC4 ... 252 B6
Hounslow TW5 ... 129 D4
Skinner St EC1 ... 94 C3 241 B6
Skipsea Ho SW18 ... 158 B5
Skipsey Ave E6 ... 100 B4
Skipton Cl N11 ... 31 A4
Skipton Dr UB3 ... 105 A3
Skipton Ho SE4 ... 141 A1
Skipwith Bldg EC1 ... 241 A4
Skipworth Rd E9 ... 96 C6
Skua Ct 42 SE8 ... 141 B6
Skyline Ct SE1 ... 263 C5
Skylines E14 ... 120 A4
Sky Peals Rd IG8 ... 36 B3
Sladebrook Rd SE3 ... 143 D2
Slade Ct NW2 ... 69 A3
Barnet EN5 ... 1 D2
Sladedale Rd SE18 ... 123 C1
Slade Ho TW4 ... 151 B5
Sladen Pl 12 E5 ... 74 B4
Slades Cl EN2 ... 4 C2
Slades Dr BR7 ... 189 A6
Slades Gdns EN2 ... 4 C2
Slades Hill EN2 ... 4 C2
Slades Rise EN2 ... 4 C2
Slade The SE18 ... 145 C6
Slade Twr E10 ... 75 C6
Slade Wlk SE17 ... 139 A6
Slagrove Pl SE13 ... 163 D6
Slaidburn St
SW10 ... 136 A6 266 B5
Slaithwaite Rd SE13 ... 142 A1
Slaney Ct NW10 ... 68 C1
Slaney Pl 1 N7 ... 72 C3
Slater Cl 13 SE18 ... 122 C2
Slater Ho 4 N16 ... 51 D3
Slatter 1 NW9 ... 27 D2
Slattery Rd TW13 ... 150 C3
Sleaford Ho 16 E3 ... 97 C3
Sleaford Ind Est
SW8 ... 137 C5 269 B3
Sleaford St SW8 . 137 C5 269 B3
Sleat Ho 9 E3 ... 97 B5
Sledmere Ct TW14 ... 149 C3
Slievemore Cl 8 SW4 ... 137 D2
Sligo Ho 8 E1 ... 96 D3
Slingsby Pl WC2 ... 250 A6
Slippers Pl SE16 ... 118 B3
Sloane Ave SW3 . 114 C2 257 B3
Sloane Avenue Mans
SW3 ... 257 C3
Sloane Ct E SW3 ... 258 A2
Sloane Ct W SW3 ... 258 A2
Sloane Gate Mans SW1 . 258 A4
Sloane Gdns BR6 ... 227 A5
SW1 ... 115 A2 258 A3
Sloane Ho 7 E9 ... 74 C1
Sloane Hospl BR3 ... 186 B2
Sloane Sq SW1 ... 257 D3
Sloane Square Sta
SW1 ... 115 A2 258 A3
Sloane St SW1 .. 114 D3 257 D5
Sloane Terr SW1 ... 258 A4
Sloane Terr Mans SW1 .. 258 A4
Sloane Wlk CR0 ... 207 B3
Slocum Cl SE28 ... 124 C6
Slomon Ho 2 W10 ... 91 A4
Slough La NW9 ... 45 A3
Sly St 7 E1 ... 96 B1
Smaldon Cl UB7 ... 104 C3
Smallberry Ave TW7 ... 130 D3
Smallberry Green Prim Sch
TW7 ... 131 A4
Smallbrook Mews W2 .. 236 C1
Smalley Cl N16 ... 73 D5
Smallwood Prim Sch
SW17 ... 180 B6
Smallwood Rd SW17 ... 180 B6
Smarden Cl DA17 ... 125 C1
Smarden Gr SE9 ... 188 B6
Smart's Pl WC1,WC2 ... 240 B2
Edmonton N18 ... 34 A5
Smart St E2 ... 96 D4
Smeaton Cl KT9 ... 213 D2
Smeaton Ct SE1 ... 262 A5
Smeaton Rd Holdbrook EN3 . 7 C6
Wandsworth SW18 ... 157 C4
Smeaton St E1 ... 118 B5
Smedley St SW4 ... 137 D3
Smeed Rd E3 ... 75 C1
Smiles Pl SE13 ... 142 A3
Smith Cl SE16 ... 118 D5
Smithers Ho 3 SE20 ... 184 D3
Smithfield Mkt EC1 ... 241 D3
Smithfield St
EC1 ... 94 D2 241 C3
Smithies Ct E15 ... 76 A3
Smithies Rd SE2 ... 124 B2
Smith's Ct W1 ... 249 C6
Smithson Rd N17 ... 33 B2
Smiths Point E13 ... 99 A6
Smith Sq SW1 ... 116 A3 260 A5
Smith St SW3 ... 114 D1 257 C1
Surbiton KT5 ... 198 B3
Smith's Yd SW18 ... 158 A2
Smith Terr SW3 .. 114 D1 257 C1
Smithwood Cl SW19 ... 157 A2
Smithy St E1 ... 96 C2
Smithy Street Sch E1 ... 96 C2
Smock Wlk CR0 ... 205 A3
Smoothfield TW3 ... 129 C1
Smugglers Way SW18 ... 135 D1
Smyrk's Rd SE17 . 117 C1 263 B1
Smyrna Mans 8 NW6 ... 69 C1
Smyrna Rd NW6 ... 69 C1
Smythe St E14 ... 119 D6
Snakes La EN4,N14 ... 3 C1
Snakes La E IG8 ... 37 C4
Snakes La W IG8 ... 37 B4
Snaresbrook Dr HA7 ... 26 A6
Snaresbrook Hall 11 E18 . 55 A6
Snaresbrook Ho E18 ... 54 D5
Snaresbrook Prim Sch
E18 ... 55 A5
Snaresbrook Rd E11 ... 54 D5
Snaresbrook Sta E11 ... 55 A4
Snarsgate St W10 ... 90 C2
Sneath Ave NW11 ... 47 B2
Snell's Pk N18 ... 33 D4
Sneyd Rd NW2 ... 68 C4
Snowberry Cl E11 ... 76 B4
Snowbury Rd 6 SW6 ... 135 D3
Snow Ct 6 HA0 ... 65 D3
Snowden Ave UB10 ... 82 D5
Snowden St EC2 .. 95 C3 243 A5
Snowdon Cres UB3 ... 105 A3
Snowdon Dr NW9 ... 45 C3
Snowdon Rd TW6 ... 149 A5
Snowdown Cl SE20 ... 184 D2
Snowdrop Cl 2 TW12 ... 173 C4
Snow Hill EC1 ... 94 D2 241 C3
Snow Ho SE27 ... 160 D1
Snowman Ho NW6 ... 91 D6
Snowsfield Prim Sch
SE1 ... 117 C4 253 A2
Snowsfields
SE1 ... 117 B4 252 D2
Snowshill Rd E12 ... 78 A3
Snowy Fielder Waye
TW7 ... 131 B3
Soames St SE15 ... 139 D2
Soames Wlk KT3 ... 177 C2
Soane Cl W5 ... 109 D4
Soane Ct 8 NW1 ... 71 C1
Soane Ho SE17 ... 262 D1
Soane Mus★
WC2 ... 94 B1 240 C2
Soaphouse La TW8 ... 132 A5
Soham Rd EN3 ... 7 B6
Soho★ W1 ... 93 D1 239 C2
Soho Mills SM6 ... 203 B1
Soho Parish CE Prim Sch
W1 ... 115 D6 249 C6
Soho Sq W1 ... 93 D1 239 C2
Soho St W1 ... 239 C2
Sojourner-Truth Cl 11
E8 ... 74 B2
Solander Gdns 12 E1 ... 118 C6
Solander Gdns *continued*
Stepney E1 ... 118 B6
Solar Ct N3 ... 29 D3
Soldene Ct N7 ... 72 B2
Solebay St E1 ... 97 A3
Solent Ct SW16 ... 182 B1
Solent Ho 6 E1 ... 97 A2
Solent Rd NW6 ... 69 C3
Solent Rise E13 ... 99 A4
Soley Mews WC1 ... 234 A2
Solna Ave SW15 ... 156 C6
Solna Rd N21 ... 17 B4
Solomon Ave N9 ... 34 A6
Solomon's Pas SE15 ... 140 B1
Solon New Rd SW4 ... 138 A1
Solon Rd SW2 ... 138 A1
Solway Cl TW4 ... 129 A2
Solway Ho 12 E1 ... 96 D3
Solway Lo 4 IG8 ... 37 A3
Solway Rd SE22 ... 140 A1
Tottenham N22 ... 32 D2
Somaford Gr EN4 ... 14 B5
Somali Rd NW2 ... 69 B3
Somborne Ho SW15 ... 156 A4
Sombrook Ho SE11 ... 261 A3
Somerby Rd IG11 ... 79 B1
Somercoates Cl EN4 ... 2 C2
Somer Ct SW6 ... 265 A5
Somerfield Ho SE16 ... 118 D1
Somerfield Rd N4 ... 72 D6
Somerford Cl HA5 ... 40 A5
Somerford Gr N16 ... 73 D4
Tottenham N17 ... 34 A3
Somerford Grove Est
N16 ... 73 D4
Somerford St E1 ... 96 B3
Somerford Way SE16 ... 119 A4
Somerhill Ave DA15 ... 168 B4
Somerhill Rd DA16 ... 146 B3
Somerleyton Rd SW9 ... 138 C1
Somersby Est SE20 ... 184 C3
Somersby Gdns IG4 ... 56 B4
Somers Cl NW1 ... 232 C4
Somers Cres W2 ... 237 A1
Somerset Ave DA16 ... 145 D1
Chessington KT9 ... 213 D4
Wimbledon SW20 ... 178 B1
Somerset Cl
New Malden KT3 ... 199 C3
Tottenham N17 ... 33 B1
Woodford IG8 ... 37 A2
Somerset Ct Ealing W7 ... 86 D1
2 Hampton TW12 ... 173 C2
Somerset Gdns N6 ... 49 A2
SE13 ... 141 D3
Teddington TW11 ... 174 C5
Thornton Heath SW16 ... 204 B6
Tottenham N17 ... 33 C3
Somerset Hall N17 ... 33 C3
Somerset Ho★
WC2 ... 116 B6 250 D6
Wimbledon SW19 ... 157 A1
Somerset Lo
9 Brentford TW8 ... 131 D6
Putney SW15 ... 134 B1
Somerset Rd E17 ... 53 C3
N17 ... 51 D6
NW4 ... 46 C5
W4 ... 111 B3
Brentford TW8 ... 131 C6
Ealing W13 ... 109 C5
Edmonton N18 ... 33 D5
Harrow HA1 ... 42 A4
Holdbrook EN3 ... 7 C5
Kingston KT1 ... 176 B1
New Barnet EN5 ... 14 A6
Southall UB1 ... 85 C2
Teddington TW11 ... 174 C5
Wimbledon SW19 ... 157 A1
Somerset Sq
W14 ... 113 B4 244 C1
Somerset Waye TW5 ... 129 A5
Somersham Rd DA7 ... 147 A3
Somers Pl SW2 ... 160 B4
Somers Rd E17 ... 53 B5
SW2 ... 160 B5
Somers Town Est
NW1 ... 93 C5 232 B3
Somers Way WD23 ... 8 A4
Somerton Ave TW9 ... 132 D2
Somerton Rd NW2 ... 69 A5
SE15 ... 140 B1
Somertrees Ave SE12 ... 165 B2
Somervell Rd HA2 ... 63 C3
Somerville Ave SW13 ... 134 C6
Somerville Ct SW16 ... 181 D4
Somerville Ho 10 SW15 ... 156 D5
Somerville Point SE16 ... 119 B4
Somerville Rd
Dagenham RM6 ... 58 C4
Penge SE20 ... 184 D3
Sonderburg Rd 13 N7 ... 72 B6
Sondes St SE17 ... 139 B6
Sonia Ct N12 ... 30 A6
Edgware HA8 ... 26 B3
Sonia Gdns N12 ... 30 A6
NW10 ... 67 D4
Heston TW5 ... 129 C5
Sonning Ct CR0 ... 222 A6
Sonning Gdns TW12 ... 173 A4
Sonning Ho 32 E2 ... 95 D4
Sonning Rd CR0 ... 206 A3
Soper Cl E4 ... 35 B5
4 Forest Hill SE23 ... 162 D2
Soper Mews EN3 ... 7 C5
Sophia Cl N7 ... 72 B2
Sophia Ho N15 ... 51 D5

Sophia Ho continued
10 W6 ...112 C1
Sophia Rd E10 ...53 D1
E13 ...99 B2
Sophia Sq 14 SE16 ...119 A6
Sopwith 2 NW9 ...27 D2
Sopwith Ave KT9 ...214 A3
Sopwith Cl TW10 ...176 B5
Sopwith Rd TW5 ...128 C5
Sopwith Way SW11 ...268 C4
Kingston KT2 ...176 A2
Sorbus Ct EN2 ...4 D3
Sorenson Ct 2 E10 ...75 D6
Sorrel Cl SE28 ...124 A5
Sorrel Gdns E6 ...100 A2
Sorrel Ho TW3 ...130 A4
Sorrel La 16 E14 ...98 B1
Sorrell Cl SE14 ...141 A5
7 SW9 ...138 C3
Sorrento Rd SM1 ...217 D5
Sotheby Rd N5 ...73 A4
Sotheran Cl E8 ...96 A6
Sotheron Pl SW6 ...265 D3
Soudan Rd
SW11 ...136 D4 267 C1
Souldern Rd 10 W14 ...112 D3
South Access Rd E17 ...53 A3
South Acre NW9 ...27 D1
Southacre Way HA5 ...22 C2
South Acton Sta W3,W4 .111 A3
South Africa Rd W12 ...112 B6
Southall Ct UB1 ...107 B6
Southall Ent Ctr UB2 ...107 C4
Southall La TW5 ...106 B1
Southall Norwood Hospl
UB2 ...107 B3
Southall Pl SE1 ...252 C1
Southall Sta UB1 ...107 B4
Southall & West London Coll
UB1 ...107 A5
Southam Ho 9 W10 ...91 A3
Southampton Bldgs
WC2 ...241 A3
Southampton Gdns
CR4 ...204 A4
Southampton Pl WC1 ...240 B3
Southampton Rd NW5 ...70 D3
Stanwell TW19,TW6 ...148 B5
Southampton Row
WC1 ...94 A2 240 B4
Southampton St WC2 ...250 B6
Southampton Way SE5 ..139 C5
Southam St W10 ...91 A3
South Audley St
W1 ...115 A5 248 B4
South Ave NW11 ...47 D5
Chingford E4 ...20 A4
Richmond TW9 ...132 C3
Southall UB1 ...107 B6
Wallington SM5 ...219 A1
South Avenue Gdns
UB1 ...107 B6
Southbank KT7 ...197 B2
South Bank KT6 ...198 A3
South Bank Bsns Ctr
SW8 ...137 D6 269 D5
South Bank Lo 2 KT6 ...198 A3
South Bank Terr KT6 ...198 A3
South Bank Univ
SW8 ...137 D4 269 D2
SE1 ...116 D3 261 D6
South Bermondsey Sta
SE16 ...118 C1
South Birkbeck Rd E11 ...76 B5
South Black Lion La
W6 ...112 A1
South Bldg SW1 ...259 B5
South Block 19 E1 ...118 C6
South Bolton Gdns
SW10 ...255 D2
Southborough Cl KT6 ...197 D1
Southborough Ho SE17 ..263 B2
Southborough La BR1,
BR2 ...210 B4
Southborough Prim Sch
BR2 ...210 C4
Southborough Rd E9 ...96 D6
Bromley BR1,BR2 ...210 A5
Surbiton KT6 ...198 A1
Southborough Rd (The Lane)
KT6 ...198 A1
Southborough Sch KT6 .214 A5
Southbourne BR2 ...209 A2
Southbourne Ave NW9 ...27 B1
Southbourne Cl HA5 ...41 A2
Southbourne Cres NW4 ...47 A5
Southbourne Ct NW9 ...27 A1
Southbourne Gdns
SE12 ...165 B6
Ilford IG1 ...79 A3
Ruislip HA4 ...40 B1
Southbridge Pl CR0 ...221 A4
Southbridge Rd CR0 ...221 A4
Southbridge Way UB2 ...107 A4
Southbrook Mews SE12 .164 D5
Southbrook Rd SE12 ...164 D5
Thornton Heath SW16 ...182 A2
South Building SE10 ...142 B5
Southbury NW8 ...229 B6
Southbury Ave EN1 ...6 A1
Southbury Prim Sch EN3 ..6 C1
Southbury Rd Enfield EN1 ...5 D1
Enfield EN1,EN3 ...6 B1
Southbury Sta EN3 ...6 B1
South Camden Com Sch
NW1 ...93 D5 232 C3
South Carriage Dr
SW1,SW7 ...114 D4 247 C2
South Church Ct E6 ...100 B5
Southchurch Rd E6 ...100 B5
South Cl DA6 ...146 D1
N6 ...49 B3
Barnet EN5 ...1 B2
Dagenham RM10 ...103 C6
Morden SM4 ...201 C3
Pinner HA5 ...22 D2
Pinner HA5 ...41 B2
Twickenham TW2 ...151 C1
West Drayton UB7 ...104 C3
South Colonnade E14 ...119 C5
Southcombe St W14 ...254 A4
South Common Rd UB8 ..60 A2
Southcote Ave
Feltham TW13 ...150 A2
Tolworth KT5 ...198 D2
Southcote Rd E17 ...53 A4
N19 ...71 C4
Croydon SE25 ...206 B3
Southcote Rise HA4 ...39 B2
Southcott Ho 31 E3 ...97 D4
W9 ...236 B5
South Cres E16 ...98 B3
WC1 ...239 C3
Southcroft Ave DA16 ...145 C2
West Wickham BR4 ...224 A6
Southcroft Rd BR6 ...227 C5
Streatham SW17 ...181 A4
South Cross Rd IG6 ...57 A4
South Croxted Rd SE21 ...183 B6
South Croydon Sta CR2 .221 B3
South Ct 17 SW15 ...156 D5
Southdean Gdns SW19 ...157 B2
South Dene NW7 ...11 B1
Southdene Ct N11 ...15 C1
Southdown N7 ...72 A2
Southdown Ave W7 ...109 A3
Southdown Cres
Harrow HA2 ...42 A1
Ilford IG2 ...57 C4
Southdown Dr SW20 ...178 D3
Southdown Rd SW20 ...178 D2
South Dr Orpington BR6 .227 C3
Ruislip HA4 ...39 C1
South Ealing Cemy W5 .109 D2
South Ealing Rd W5 ...109 D3
South Ealing Sta W5 ...109 D3
South Eastern Ave N9 ...17 D1
South Eaton Pl
SW1 ...115 A2 258 B4
South Eden Park Rd
BR3 ...207 D4
South Edwardes Sq W8 .255 A5
South End W8 ...113 D3 255 D6
Croydon CR0 ...221 A4
Southend Cl SE9 ...166 D5
South End Cl NW3 ...70 C4
Southend Cres SE9 ...166 D5
South End Gn NW3 ...70 C4
Southend La SE6 ...185 C6
Southend Rd E6 ...78 B1
South End Rd NW3 ...70 C4
Southend Rd
Beckenham BR3 ...185 C2
Woodford IG8 ...37 D1
Southend Road (North
Circular Rd) E17,E18 ...36 C2
South End Row
W8 ...113 D3 255 D6
Southern Ave
East Bedfont TW14 ...150 A3
South Norwood SE25 ...205 D6
Southerngate Way
SE14 ...141 A5
Southern Gr E3 ...97 B3
Southernhay IG10 ...21 D6
Southern Perimeter Rd
Harlington TW14,TW6 ...149 B6
Harlington TW19,TW6 ...148 C5
Stanwell TW6 ...148 C5
Southern Rd E13 ...99 B5
N2 ...48 D5
Southern Road Inf Sch
E13 ...99 B5
Southern Road Prim Sch
E13 ...99 B5
Southern Row W10 ...91 A3
Southern St N1 ...233 C4
Southern Way SE10 ...120 D3
Romford RM7 ...59 C3
Southerton Rd W6 ...112 C2
South Esk Rd E7 ...77 C2
Southey Ho SE17 ...262 B2
Southey Rd N15 ...51 C4
SW9 ...138 C4
Merton SW19 ...179 C3
Southey St SE20 ...184 D3
Southfield EN5 ...12 D5
Southfield Cl UB8 ...82 C4
Southfield Cotts W7 ...108 D4
Southfield Gdns TW1,
TW2 ...174 D6
Southfield Pk HA2 ...41 D5
Southfield Prim Sch
W4 ...111 C4
Southfield Rd W4 ...111 B4
Enfield EN3 ...18 C5
St Paul's Cray BR7 ...211 D6
Southfields Hendon NW4 ..46 B6
Thames Ditton KT8 ...196 C3
Southfields Ave TW15 ...170 D4
Southfields Com Coll
SW18 ...157 C3
Southfields Ct SM3 ...217 C6
Southfields Rd SW18 ...157 C5
Southfields Sta SW18 ...157 B3
Southfleet Rd BR6 ...227 C4
South Gate Ave TW13 ...171 B6
Southgate Cir 3 N14 ...15 D3
Southgate Coll N14 ...15 D2
Southgate Ct N1 ...73 B1
Southgate Gr N1 ...73 B1
Southgate Ho 7 E17 ...54 A6
Southgate Rd N1 .73 B1 235 D6
Southgate Sch EN4 ...15 B6
Southgate Sta N14 ...15 D3
Southgate Way N2 ...30 C2
South Gdns
Mitcham SW19 ...180 B3
Wembley HA9 ...66 C6
South Gipsy Rd DA16 ...146 D2
South Glade DA5 ...169 B3
South Gn NW9 ...27 C2
South Gr E17 ...53 B4
N15 ...51 B4
N6 ...49 A1
South Greenford Sta
UB6 ...86 C4
South Grove Ho N6 ...49 A1
South Grove Prim Sch
E17 ...53 B3
South Hampstead High Sch
NW3 ...70 B2
South Hampstead Jun Sch
NW3 ...70 A2
South Hampstead Sta
NW8 ...70 A1
South Harringay Jun & Inf
Schs N4 ...50 D4
South Harrow Sta HA2 ...64 A5
South Hill BR7 ...188 B4
South Hill Ave HA1,HA2 ...64 B5
South Hill Gr HA1 ...64 C4
South Hill Pk NW3 ...70 C4
South Hill Pk Gdns NW3 ..70 C4
South Hill Rd BR2 ...208 C5
Southholme Cl SE19 ...183 C2
Southill La HA5 ...40 B5
Southill Rd BR7 ...188 B3
Southill St E14 ...97 D1
South Island Pl SW9 ...138 C5
South Kensington Sta
SW7 ...114 B2 256 D4
South Kenton Sta HA9 ...43 C1
South La Kingston KT1 ...197 D6
New Malden KT3 ...199 B3
Southlake Prim Sch
SE2 ...124 D4
South Lambeth Pl SW8 ..270 B6
South Lambeth Rd
SW8 ...138 A5 270 B4
Southland Rd SE18 ...145 D5
Southlands Ave BR6 ...227 C3
Southlands Coll SW15 ...156 A6
Southlands Dr SW19 ...156 D2
Southlands Gr BR1 ...210 A6
Southlands Rd BR1,BR2 .209 D5
Southland Way TW7 ...152 B6
South La W KT3 ...199 B5
South Lo NW8 ...229 C2
6 New Barnet EN5 ...13 D6
Twickenham TW2 ...152 A5
South Lodge Ave CR4,
CR7,SW16 ...204 A5
South Lodge Cres EN2 ...3 D1
South Lodge Dr N14 ...15 D6
South London Montessori
Sch SW11 ...267 A1
South London Tamil Sch
CR0 ...205 A2
South Mall The N9 ...18 A1
South Mead NW9 ...27 D2
West Ewell KT19 ...215 D1
Southmead Prim Sch
SW19 ...157 A3
Southmead Rd SW19 ...157 A3
South Merton Sta SW20 .201 B6
South Molton La
W1 ...93 B1 238 C1
South Molton Rd E16 ...99 A1
South Molton St
W1 ...93 B1 238 C1
Southmont Rd KT10 ...212 C5
Southmoor Way E9 ...75 B3
South Mount N20 ...14 A2
South Norwood Ctry Pk★
SE25 ...206 C5
South Norwood Hill
SE19,SE25 ...183 D1
South Norwood Prim Sch
SE25 ...206 A5
South Oak Rd SW16 ...182 B6
Southold Rise SE9 ...166 B1
Southolm St
SW11 ...137 B4 268 D1
South Ordnance Rd EN3 ...7 C5
Southover BR1 ...187 A5
N12 ...29 C6
South Par W4 ...111 B2
Edgware HA8 ...26 C1
South Parade
SW3 ...114 B1 256 D2
South Park Cres
Catford SE6 ...164 D3
Ilford IG1 ...79 C5
South Park Ct 24 BR3 ...185 C3
South Park Dr
Barking IG11 ...79 C4
Ilford IG3 ...79 C5
South Park Gr KT3 ...199 A5
South Park Hill Rd CR2 ..221 B4
South Park Mews SW6 ..135 D2
South Park Prim Sch
IG3 ...79 C5
South Park Rd Ilford IG1 ..79 B5
Wimbledon SW19 ...179 D4
South Park Terr IG1 ...79 C5
South Park Villas IG3 ...79 C4
South Park Way HA4 ...62 C3
South Pl EC2 ...95 B2 242 D3
Enfield EN3 ...18 C6
Surbiton KT5 ...198 B2
South Pl Mews EC2 ...242 D3
Southport Rd SE18 ...123 B2
South Quay Plaza E14 ...119 D4
South Quay Sta E14 ...119 D4
South Rd W5 ...109 D2
Edgware HA8 ...26 D2
Edmonton N9 ...18 A3
Feltham TW13 ...172 D5
Forest Hill SE23 ...162 D2
Hampton TW12 ...173 B4
Mitcham SW19 ...180 B4
Southall UB1 ...107 B5
Twickenham TW2 ...152 B1
West Drayton UB7 ...104 C3
Heston TW5 ...128 D6
South Residence IG3 ...58 B4
Southridge Pl SW20 ...178 D3
South Rise W2 ...247 B6
South Rise Prim Sch
SE18 ...123 B1
South Rise Way SE18 ...123 B2
South Row SE3 ...142 D3
South Ruislip Sta HA4 ...62 C3
Southsea Rd KT1 ...198 A5
South Sea St SE16 ...119 B3
Southside N7 ...71 D4
South Side W6 ...111 D3
Southside Comm SW19 .178 D4
Southside Ind Est SW8 ..269 A2
Southside Quarter 4
SW11 ...136 D3
Southspring SE9 ...167 B4
South Sq NW11 ...47 D3
WC1 ...241 A3
South St BR1 ...187 A1
W1 ...115 A5 248 B4
Enfield EN3 ...18 D6
Isleworth TW7 ...131 A2
South Tenter St
E1 ...95 D1 243 D1
South Terr N22 ...31 D1
SW7 ...114 C2 257 A4
Surbiton KT6 ...198 A3
South Thames Coll
SW18 ...157 D6
Putney SW15 ...156 D6
South Tottenham Sta
N15 ...51 D4
South Vale Harrow HA1 ...64 C4
West Norwood SE19 ...183 C4
Southvale Rd SE3 ...142 C3
South View BR1 ...187 C1
Wimbledon SW19 ...178 D4
Southview Ave NW10 ...67 D3
Southview Cl SW17 ...181 A5
South View Cl DA5 ...169 B5
South View Cres IG2 ...56 D3
South View Ct
8 Forest Hill SE23 ...162 C3
South Norwood SE19 ...183 A3
Southview Dr E18 ...55 B6
Southview Gdns SM6 ...219 C1
South View Rd N8 ...50 A6
Southview Rd BR1 ...186 B6
South View Rd HA5 ...22 B4
South Villas NW1 ...71 D2
Southville SW8 ..137 D4 269 D1
Southville Cl
East Bedfont TW14 ...149 C3
West Ewell KT19 ...215 B1
Southville Cres TW14 ...149 C3
Southville Jun Sch
TW14 ...149 D3
Southville Rd
East Bedfont TW14 ...149 C4
Thames Ditton KT7 ...197 B2
Southwark Bridge
SE1,EC4 ...117 A6 252 B5
Southwark Bridge Office
Village SE1 ...252 B3
Southwark Bridge Rd
SE1 ...117 A5 252 B3
Southwark Cath★
SE1 ...117 B5 252 C4
Southwark Coll
SE1 ...116 D4 251 C2
SE15 ...140 B5
Southwark Coll (Blackfriars
Ctr) SE1 ...251 C3
Southwark Coll (Camberwell
Ctr) SE5 ...139 C5
Southwark Coll (Grange Ctr)
SE1 ...263 B5
Southwark Coll (Surrey
Docks Ctr) SE16 ...118 B3
Southwark Park Est 11
SE16 ...118 B2
Southwark Park Prim Sch
SE16 ...118 B3
Southwark Park Rd
SE16 ...118 A2 263 D4
Southwark Pk BR1 ...210 B6
Southwark St
SE1 ...117 A5 252 A3
Southwater Cl 8 E14 ...97 B1
Beckenham BR3 ...185 D3
Southway N20 ...13 C2
NW11 ...47 D4
South Way N11 ...31 C4
N9 ...18 C2
Southway Hayes BR2 ...209 A2
Wallington SM6 ...219 C4
West Barnes SW20 ...200 D5
South Way Croydon CR0 ...223 A5
Harrow HA2 ...41 C5
South Way continued
Wembley HA9 ...66 C3
Southwell Ave UB5 ...63 C2
Southwell Gdns SW7 ...256 A3
Southwell Grove Rd E11 ..76 C6
Southwell Ho 13 N16 ...73 C3
8 SE16 ...118 B2
Southwell Rd SE5 ...139 A2
Harrow HA3 ...43 D3
Thornton Heath CR0 ...204 C3
South Western Rd TW1 .153 B5
Southwest Rd E11 ...54 B1
South Wharf Rd
W2 ...92 B1 236 D2
Southwick Mews W2 ..236 D2
Southwick Pl W2 ...237 A1
Southwick St W2 .92 C1 237 A2
Southwick Yd W2 ...237 A1
South Wimbledon Sta
SW19 ...179 D3
South Wlk
Coney Hall BR4 ...224 C5
Hayes UB3 ...83 B2
Southwold Dr IG11 ...80 A3
Southwold Mans W9 ...91 C4
Southwold Prim Sch E5 ..74 B6
Southwold Rd DA5 ...169 D5
E5 ...74 C6
Southwood Ave N6 ...49 B2
Kingston KT2,KT3 ...177 A2
Southwood Cl BR1 ...210 B5
North Cheam KT4 ...200 D1
Southwood Ct EC1 ...234 C1
NW11 ...47 D4
Southwood Dr KT5 ...199 A1
South Woodford Sta E18 .37 B1
Southwood Gdns
Hinchley Wood KT10 ...213 A5
Ilford IG2 ...56 D5
Southwood Hall N6 ...49 B3
Southwood Ho SE9 ...166 D2
W11 ...244 A6
Southwood Hospl (Geriatric)
N6 ...49 A2
Southwood Hts N6 ...49 B2
Southwood La N6 ...49 A2
Southwood Lawn Rd N6 ..49 B2
Southwood Mans N6 ...49 B3
Southwood Park N6 ...49 A2
Southwood Prim Sch
RM9 ...81 A4
Southwood Rd SE9 ...166 D2
Woolwich SE28 ...124 B5
Southwood Smith Ho 4
E2 ...96 B4
Southwood Smith St
N1 ...234 C5
South Worple Way
SW14 ...133 B2
Southwyck Ho SW9 ...138 C1
South Yd EC1 ...242 C4
Sovereign Bsns Ctr EN3 ...7 B2
Sovereign Cl Ealing W5 ...87 C2
Ruislip HA4 ...39 C1
Stepney E1 ...118 B6
Sovereign Cres SE16 ...119 A6
Sovereign Ct BR2 ...210 B3
East Molesey KT8 ...195 B5
Harlington UB7 ...126 D5
3 Richmond TW9 ...132 B1
Stepney E1 ...118 B6
Sovereign Gr HA0 ...65 D5
Sovereign Ho 23 E1 ...96 B3
NW7 ...27 B6
SE18 ...122 B3
Ashford TW15 ...170 A6
3 Wimbledon SW19 ...179 A4
Sovereign Mews 6 E2 ...95 D5
Barnet EN4 ...2 D2
Sovereign Pk NW10 ...88 D3
Sovereign Pl HA1 ...42 D4
Sovereign Rd IG11 ...102 C4
Sowerby Cl SE9 ...166 B6
Space Waye TW14 ...150 B6
Spa Cl SE19 ...183 C2
Spa Ct 12 SE16 ...118 A3
Spafield St EC1 ...241 A6
Spa Hill CR7,SE19 ...183 B2
Spalding Cl HA8 ...27 C3
Spalding Ct HA8 ...26 B6
Spalding Ho SE4 ...163 A6
Spalding Rd NW4 ...46 C3
Streatham SW17 ...181 B5
Spanby Rd E3 ...97 C3
Spangate SE3 ...142 D2
Spaniards Cl NW11 ...48 B1
Spaniards End NW3 ...48 B1
Spaniards Rd NW3 ...70 A6
Spanish Pl W1 ...238 B2
Spanish Rd SW18 ...158 A6
Spa Rd SE16 ...117 D3 263 D5
Sparkbridge Rd HA1 ...42 C5
Sparke Terr 2 E16 ...98 D1
Sparkford Gdns N11 ...31 A5
Sparkford Ho SW11 ...266 D2
Sparks Cl W3 ...89 B1
Dagenham RM8 ...80 C6
Hampton TW12 ...173 A4
Sparrow Cl TW12 ...173 A4
Sparrow Dr BR5 ...211 B1
Sparrow Farm Com Jun Sch
KT17 ...216 B4
Sparrow Farm Dr TW14 .150 D4
Sparrow Farm Inf Sch
TW14 ...150 C4
Sparrow Farm Jun Sch
TW14 ...150 C4
Sparrow Farm Rd KT17,
KT4 ...216 B4
Sparrow Gn RM10 ...81 D5
Sparrow's Farm L Ctr
SE9 ...167 A4
Sparrows Herne WD23 ...8 A4
Sparrows La SE9 ...167 A3
Sparrows Way WD23 ...8 A4
Sparsholt Rd N19 ...50 B1
Barking IG11 ...101 C6
Sparta St SE10 ...142 A4
Spa Sch SE1 ...118 A2
Spa View 6 SW16 ...160 B1
Speakers' Corner★
W1 ...114 D6 247 D6
Speaker's Ct 3 CR0 ...205 B1
Speakman Ho SE4 ...141 A2
Spearman St 8 SE18 ...144 C6
Spear Mews
SW5 ...113 C2 255 B3
Spearpoint Gdns IG2 ...57 D5
Spears Rd N19 ...50 A1
Speart La TW5 ...129 A5
Spectrum Ho NW5 ...71 A4
Spedan Cl NW3 ...70 A5
Speechly Mews E8 ...73 D3
Speed Ho EC2 ...242 B4
Speedwell Ct 7 N12 ...29 D6
Speedwell Ho 9 N12 ...29 D6
Speedwell St 5 SE8 ...141 C5
Speedy Pl WC1 ...233 A1
Speer Rd KT7 ...196 D3
Speirs Cl KT3 ...199 D3
Spekehill SE9 ...166 B1
Speke Rd CR7 ...183 B1
Speldhurst Cl 2 BR2 ...208 D4
Speldhurst Rd E9 ...74 D1
W4 ...111 B3
Spellbrook Wlk N1 ...235 B6
Spelman Ho 14 E1 ...96 A2
Spelman St E1 ...96 A2
Spelthorne Coll TW15 ...170 B6
Spelthorne Cty Inf Sch
TW15 ...171 B4
Spelthorne Gr TW16 ...171 D3
Spelthorne La TW15,
TW17 ...171 A2
Spence Cl SE16 ...119 B4
Spencer Ave
Bowes Park N13 ...32 B4
Hayes UB4 ...84 A2
Spencer Cl BR6 ...227 D6
N3 ...29 C1
Ealing NW10 ...88 B4
Woodford IG8 ...37 C5
Spencer Ct 5 BR6 ...227 A3
Wimbledon SW20 ...178 B2
Spencer Dr N2 ...48 A3
Spencer Gdns SW14 ...155 A6
Spencer Hill SW19 ...179 A3
Spencer Hill Rd SW19 ...179 A3
Spencer Ho NW3 ...70 B5
NW4 ...46 B4
31 SW8 ...137 D3
24 Putney SW19 ...156 D3
Wimbledon SW19 ...156 D1
Spencer Mews W6 ...264 A6
Spencer Park Ct SW18 ...158 B6
Spencer Pk SW18 ...158 B6
Spencer Pl 16 N1 ...72 D1
SW1 ...259 B5
Thornton Heath CR0 ...205 B2
Spencer Rd E6 ...99 D6
N11 ...31 B6
N8 ...50 B4
SW18 ...158 B6
W3 ...111 A5
Bromley BR1 ...186 D3
Carshalton CR4 ...203 A2
Chingford E17 ...36 A1
Chiswick W4 ...133 A5
East Molesey KT8 ...196 A4
Harrow HA3 ...24 C1
Hounslow TW3,TW5,TW7 .130 A4
Ilford IG3 ...57 D1
Mitcham CR4 ...203 A6
South Croydon CR2 ...221 C3
Tottenham N17 ...34 A2
Twickenham TW2 ...152 C2
Wembley HA0 ...65 C6
Wimbledon SW20 ...178 B2
Spencer Rise NW5 ...71 B5
Spencer St EC1 ...94 D4 234 C1
Southall UB2 ...106 D4
Spencer Wlk 15 NW3 ...70 A4
Putney SW15 ...134 D1
Spenlow Ho 2 SE16 ...118 A3
Spenser Ct 5 TW10 ...175 D6
Spenser Gr N16 ...73 C4
Spenser Mews SE21 ...161 B3
Spenser Rd SE24 ...160 D6
Spenser St SW1 ...259 B6
Spens Ho WC1 ...240 C5
Spensley Wlk N16 ...73 B5
Speranza St SE18 ...123 D1
Sperling Rd N17 ...33 C1
Spert St E14 ...119 A6
Speyside N14 ...15 C5
Spey St E14 ...98 A2
Spezia Rd NW10 ...90 A5
Spice Ct 2 E1 ...118 A5
10 SW11 ...136 A2
Spice Quay Heights
SE1 ...253 D3
Spicer Cl SE5,SW9 ...138 D3
Walton-on-T KT12 ...194 C3
Spicer Ct EN1 ...5 C2
Spices Yd CR0 ...221 A4
Spigurnell Rd N17 ...33 B2
Spikes Bridge Rd UB1 ...107 A6
Spilsby Cl NW9 ...27 C1
Spindle Cl SE18 ...122 A3
Spindle Ho 8 DA15 ...168 A1

Spindlewood Gdns CR0 221 C4
Spindrift Ave E14 119 D2
Spinel Cl SE18 123 D1
Spinnaker Cl IG11 102 B4
Spinnaker Ct 2 KT1 175 D2
Spinnaker Ho E14 119 C4
Spinnells Rd HA2 41 B1
Spinney Cl
Beckenham BR3 207 D5
New Malden KT3 199 C4
Worcester Park KT4 215 D6
Yiewsley UB7 104 A6
Spinney Dr TW14 149 A4
Spinney Gdns
Dagenham RM9 81 A3
Dulwich SE19 183 D5
Spinney Oak BR1 188 A1
Spinneys The BR1 188 B1
Spinney The DA14 191 A5
Barnes SW13 134 B6
Barnet EN5 1 D3
Cheam SM3 216 C4
Southgate N21 16 C4
Stanmore HA7 26 A6
Streatham SW16 159 D1
Sunbury TW16 172 A2
Wembley HA0 65 A5
Spire Ct 10 TW10 154 A5
Spire Ho W2 246 B6
Spires The EN5 1 A2
Spirit Quay E1 118 B5
Spital Sq E1 95 C2 243 B4
Spital St E1 96 A2
Spital Yd E1 243 B4
Spitfire Est The TW5 106 C1
Spitfire Rd SM6 220 B1
Spitfire Way TW5 106 C1
Splendour Wlk SE16 118 C1
Spode Ho SE11 261 A5
Spode Wlk NW3 69 D3
Spondon Rd N15 52 A5
Spoonbill Way UB4 84 D2
Spooner 8 NW9 27 D3
Spooner Ho TW5 129 C6
Spooner Wlk SM6 219 D3
Sporle Ct 6 SW11 136 B2
Sportsbank St SE6 164 A4
Spottons Gr N17 33 A2
Spout Hill CR0 223 C3
Spratt Hall Rd E11 55 A3
Spray St SE18 122 D2
Spreighton Rd KT8 195 D5
Sprewell SW15 157 A5
Spriggs Ho 14 N1 72 D1
Sprimont Pl
SW3 114 D2 257 C2
Springall St 9 SE15 140 B5
Springalls Wharf 2
SE16 118 A4
Springbank N21 16 B5
Springbank Rd SE13 164 C5
Springbank Wlk NW1 71 D1
Springbourne Ct BR3 186 A2
Spring Bridge Rd W5 109 D6
Spring Cl Barnet EN5 12 D6
Dagenham RM8 58 D1
Springclose La SM3 217 A2
Spring Cnr TW13 149 D1
Spring Cott 10 W12 112 A4
Spring Cotts KT6 197 D4
Spring Court Rd EN2 4 C5
Springcroft Ave N2 48 D5
Spring Ct Ealing W7 108 B6
10 Wanstead E18 55 B6
Springdale Rd N16 73 B4
Spring Dr HA5 40 A3
Springett Ho 15 SW2 160 B6
Springfield E5 52 B1
Bushey WD23 8 B3
South Norwood SE25 206 A6
Springfield Ave N10 49 C6
Hampton TW12 173 D4
Merton SW20 201 B6
Springfield Cl N12 29 D5
Stanmore HA7 9 A1
Springfield Ct E5 52 B1
NW3 70 C1
7 W3 89 A1
2 Ilford IG1 78 D3
9 Kingston KT1 198 A6
Wallington SM6 219 B3
Springfield Dr IG2 57 A3
Springfield Gdns BR1 210 B5
E5 52 B1
NW9 45 B4
Ruislip HA4 40 B1
West Wickham BR4 223 D6
Woodford IG8 37 C3
Springfield Gr SE7 143 C6
Sunbury TW16 172 A2
Springfield Ho 1 SE5 139 C3
W3 111 A5
Springfield Hospl SW17 158 C1
Springfield La NW6 91 D6
Springfield Mount NW9 45 C4
Springfield Pl KT3 199 A5
Springfield Rd BR1 210 B5
DA16 146 B2
DA7 147 D1
E15 98 C4
E17 53 B3
E6 78 B1
N11 31 C5
N15 52 A5
NW8 92 A6 229 B5
Ashford TW15 170 B5
Chingford E4 20 C4
Ealing W7 108 C5
Harrow HA1 42 C3
Hayes UB4 106 C5
Springfield Rd *continued*
Kingston KT1 198 A6
Penge SE26 184 B5
South Norwood CR7 183 A2
6 Teddington TW11 175 A5
Twickenham TW2 151 C3
Wallington SM6 219 B3
Wimbledon SW19 179 B5
Springfield Rise SE26 162 B1
Springfields 9 EN5 13 D6
Springfield Wlk 3 BR6 211 B1
NW6 91 D6
Spring Gdns N5 73 A3
SW1 116 A5 250 A4
East Molesey KT8 196 A5
Wallington SM6 219 C3
Woodford IG8 37 C3
Spring Gr Brentford W4 132 C6
Hampton TW12 173 D2
Loughton IG10 21 D5
Mitcham CR4 181 A2
Spring Grove Cres TW3,
TW5 130 A4
Spring Grove Prim Sch
TW7 130 B3
Spring Grove Rd
Hounslow TW3,TW5,TW7 130 A4
Richmond TW10 154 B6
Springhallow Sch W13 87 A1
Spring Hill E5 52 A2
Forest Hill SE26 184 C6
Springhill Cl SE5 139 B2
Spring Ho WC1 234 A1
Merton SW19 179 B2
Springhurst Cl CR0 223 B4
Spring La E5 52 B1
N10 49 A6
Croydon SE25 206 B3
Spring Lake HA7 25 B6
Spring Mews W1 237 D4
Spring Park Ave CR0 222 D6
Springpark Dr N4 51 A1
Beckenham BR3 208 A6
Spring Park Prim Sch
CR0 223 C5
Spring Park Rd CR0 222 D6
Spring Pl N3 47 C6
NW5 71 B3
Springpond Rd RM9 81 A3
Spring Rd TW13 149 D1
Springrice Rd SE13 164 B5
Spring Shaw Rd BR5 190 A2
Spring St W2 92 B1 236 C1
Spring Terr TW10 154 A6
Spring Vale DA7 147 D1
Springvale Ave TW8 110 A1
Springvale Ct SE12 143 A1
Springvale Terr 5 W14 112 D3
Spring Villa Rd HA8 26 C3
Springwater WC1 240 C4
Springwater Cl SE18 144 C4
Springway HA1 42 B2
Springwell Ave NW10 89 D6
Springwell Cl SW16 182 B6
Springwell Ct TW5 128 D3
Springwell Jun & Inf Schs
TW5 129 A5
Springwell Rd
Heston TW5 128 D4
West Norwood SW16 182 C5
Spring Wlk E1 96 A2
Springwood Cres HA8 11 A2
Springwood Ct CR2 221 C4
Sprowston Mews E7 77 A3
Sprowston Rd E7 77 A3
Spruce Ct W5 110 A3
Sprucedale Gdns CR0 222 D4
Spruce Hills Rd E17 36 A1
Spruce Ho 15 SE16 118 D4
Spruce Pk BR2 208 D5
Sprules Rd SE4 141 A3
Spurfield KT8 195 D6
Spurgeon Ave SE19 183 B2
Spurgeon Rd SE19 183 B3
Spurgeon's Coll SE25 183 C1
Spurgeon St
SE1 117 B3 262 C6
Spurling Rd SE22 139 D1
Dagenham RM9 81 B2
Spur Rd N15 51 B5
SE1 116 C4 251 A2
Brentford TW7 131 B5
Edgware HA8 26 A6
Feltham TW14 128 B1
Wallend IG11 101 A4
Spurstowe Rd E8 74 B2
Spurstowe Terr E8 74 B3
Spurway Par 2 IG2 56 B4
Square Rigger Row 7
SW11 136 A2
Square The SW6 265 A1
W6 112 C1
Hayes UB11 105 B5
Ilford IG1 56 C2
12 Richmond TW10 153 D6
Wallington SM5 219 A3
Woodford IG8 37 A5
Squarey St SW17 158 A1
Squire Ct 2 CR0 205 C1
Squire Gdns NW8 229 C1
Squire's Almshouses 7
E17 53 D5
Squires Bridge Rd KT17 192 B5
Squires Ct N3 30 A2
SW4 270 B1
Wimbledon SW19 179 C6
Squires Ho 3 SE18 144 D6
Squires La N3 30 A2
Squire's Mount NW3 70 B5
Squire's Rd TW17 192 C5
Squires The RM7 59 D3
Squires Wlk TW15 171 B3
Squires Wood Dr BR7 188 B3
Squirrel Cl TW4 128 C2
Squirrel Mews W13 109 A6
Squirrels Cl N12 30 A6
Hillingdon UB10 60 C1
Orpington BR6 211 C1
Squirrels Ct 4 KT4 215 D6
Squirrels Gn KT4 216 A6
Squirrel's La IG9 21 D1
Squirrels The SE13 142 B2
Bushey WD23 8 B5
Pinner HA5 41 B6
Squirrels Trad Est UB3 105 D3
Squirries St E2 96 A4
Stable Cl UB5 85 C5
Stable Mews SE27 183 A5
Stables End BR6 227 A5
Stables The IG9 21 C4
Stables Way
SE11 116 C1 261 A2
Stable Way W10 90 C1
Stable Wlk N2 30 B2
Stable Yd Rd
SW1 115 C4 249 B2
Staburn Ct HA8 27 A1
Stacey Ave N18 34 C6
Stacey Cl E10 54 B4
Stacey St N7 72 C5
WC2 93 D1 239 D1
Stack Ho SW1 258 B3
Stackhouse St SW1 257 C6
Stacy Path 21 SE5 139 C5
Staddon Ct BR3 207 A5
Stadium Bsns Ctr HA9 66 D5
Stadium Rd SE7,SE18 144 B6
Stadium Ret Pk HA9 66 C5
Stadium St
SW10 136 A5 266 B3
Stadium Way HA9 66 C4
Staffa Rd E10 53 A1
Stafford Cl E17 53 B3
NW6 91 C4
Cheam SM3 217 A2
Southgate N14 15 C6
Stafford Cripps Ho 30 E2 96 C4
SW6 264 D5
Stafford Cross CR0 220 B3
Stafford Ct SW8 270 A2
W8 255 B6
Ealing W7 86 D1
Stafford Gdns CR0 220 B3
Stafford Ho SE1 263 D2
Stafford Mans SW11 267 C3
13 SW4 138 A1
13 W14 112 D3
Stafford Morris Ho 9
E15 98 C6
Stafford Pl SW1 115 C3 259 A6
Richmond TW10 154 B4
Stafford Rd E3 97 B5
E7 77 D2
NW6 91 C4
Croydon CR0 220 C4
Harrow HA3 24 A3
Kingston KT3 199 A6
Ruislip HA4 61 D4
Sidcup DA14 189 C6
Wallington CR0,SM6 220 A3
Staffordshire St SE15 140 A4
SE15 140 B4
Stafford St W1 249 A4
Stafford Terr
W8 113 C3 255 A6
Stag Cl HA8 27 A1
Stagg Hill EN4 2 C6
Stag La Chigwell IG9 21 B2
Edgware HA8,NW9 45 A6
Roehampton SW15 155 D2
Stag Lane Fst & Mid Schs
HA8 26 C1
Stag Pl SW1 115 C3 259 A6
Stags Ct KT7 197 A2
Stagshaw Ho 17 SE22 139 C2
Stags Way TW7 130 D6
Stainbank Rd CR4 203 B6
Stainby Cl UB7 104 A3
Stainby Rd N15 51 D5
Stainer Ho SE9 143 C1
Stainer St SE1 252 D3
Staines Ave SM3 216 D6
Staines By-Pass TW15 170 A4
Staines Rd
East Bedfont TW14 149 B4
Feltham TW14,TW3 150 C6
Ilford IG1 79 B4
Twickenham TW13,TW2 151 D1
Hounslow TW3 129 C1
Twickenham TW2 152 A1
Staines Rd E TW12,
TW16 172 C2
Staines Rd W TW15 171 B3
Staines Wlk DA14 190 C4
Stainford Cl TW15 171 B5
Stainforth Rd E17 53 C5
Ilford IG2 57 B2
Staining La EC2 242 B2
Stainmore Cl BR7 189 B2
Stainsbury St 26 E2 96 C5
Stainsby Pl E14 97 C1
Stainsby Rd E14 97 C1
Stainton Rd Enfield EN3 6 C4
Lewisham SE13 164 B4
Stalbridge Ho NW1 232 A3
Stalbridge St NW1 237 B4
Stalham St SE16 118 B3
Stambourne Ho SW8 270 B2
Stambourne Way
Penge SE19 183 D3
Stambourne Way *continued*
West Wickham BR4 224 A5
Stamford Bridge Stadium
(Chelsea FC)
SW6 135 D5 265 C4
Stamford Brook Ave
W6 111 D3
Stamford Brook Gdns 1
W6 111 D3
Stamford Brook Mans 2
W6 111 D2
Stamford Brook Rd W6 111 D3
Stamford Brook Sta
W6 111 D2
Stamford Cl N15 52 A5
2 NW3 70 A5
Harrow HA3 24 C3
Southall UB1 107 C6
Stamford Ct W6 112 A2
Edgware HA8 26 B6
Stamford Dr BR2 208 D5
Stamford Gdns RM9 80 C1
Stamford Grove E 1
N16 52 A1
Stamford Grove W 4
N16 52 A1
Stamford Hill N16 51 D1
Stamford Hill Mans 1
N16 51 D1
Stamford Hill Prim Sch
N15 51 B3
Stamford Hill Sta N16 51 C2
Stamford Ho N15 52 A5
Stamford Hospl W6 112 A2
Stamford Lo 2 N16 51 D2
Stamford Mans 2 N16 52 A1
Stamford Rd E6 100 A6
N1 73 C2
N15 52 A4
Dagenham RM9 80 C1
Stamford St SE1 116 C5 251 B4
Stamp Pl E2 95 D4
Stanard Cl N16 51 C2
Stanborough Cl TW12 173 B4
Stanborough Ho 4 E3 97 D3
Stanborough Pas E8 73 D2
Stanborough Rd TW3,
TW7 130 B2
Stanbridge Mans SW15 134 C2
Stanbridge Pl N21 16 D2
Stanbridge Rd SW15 134 C2
Stanbrook Ct W1 249 A4
Stanbrook Rd SE2 124 B4
Stanburn Fst & Mid Schs
HA7 25 C3
Stanbury Ct 16 NW3 70 D2
Stanbury Rd SE15 140 B3
SE15 140 C3
Stancroft NW9 45 C4
Standale Gr HA4 39 A4
Standard Ind Est E16 122 B4
Standard Pl 14 EC2 95 C4
Standard Rd DA6 147 A1
NW10 89 B3
Belvedere DA17 125 C1
Enfield EN3 7 A6
Hounslow TW4 129 A2
Standen Rd SW18 157 C4
Standfield Gdns RM10 81 C2
Standfield Rd RM10 81 C3
Standish Ho SE9 143 B1
6 W6 112 A2
Standish Rd W6 112 A2
Standlake Point 1
SE23 162 D1
Stane Cl SW19 179 D3
Stanedge Ct SW16 182 A5
Stanesgate Ho 20 SE15 140 A5
Stanetto Ct 3 RM6 58 B2
Stane Way SE18 144 A5
Stanfield Ho NW8 236 D6
9 Northolt UB5 84 D5
Stanfield Rd 13 E3 97 A5
Stanford Cl
Hampton TW12 173 B4
Romford RM7 59 D3
Ruislip HA4 39 A3
Stanford Ct N11 31 A5
SW6 265 D1
W8 255 D5
Stanford Ho IG11 102 B5
Stanford Pl SE1 117 C2 263 A3
Stanford Rd N11 30 D5
W8 113 D3 255 D6
Thornton Heath SW16 182 A1
Stanford St SW1 259 C3
Stanford Way SW16 181 D1
Stangate Cres WD6 11 C6
Stangate Gdns HA7 25 B6
Stangate Lo N21 16 B4
Stangate Mansi TW1 152 D1
Stanger Rd SE25 206 A5
Stanhope Ave N3 47 B6
Harrow HA3 24 B2
Hayes BR2 209 A1
Stanhope Cl 28 SE16 118 D4
Stanhope Ct N3 29 B1
Stanhope Gate W1 248 B4
Stanhope Gdns N4 51 A3
N6 49 C3
NW7 27 D5
SW7 114 A2 256 B4
Dagenham RM8 81 B5
Redbridge IG1 56 B1
Stanhope Gr BR3 207 B5
Stanhope Ho 5 N11 31 B6
N6 49 C3
SE8 141 B5
4 Putney SW15 156 C6
Stanhope Mews E
SW7 114 A2 256 B4
Stanhope Mews S SW7 256 B3
Stanhope Mews W
SW7 114 A2 256 B4
Stanhope Park Rd UB6 86 A3
Stanhope Pl W2 237 C1
Stanhope Prim Sch UB6 86 A3
Stanhope Rd DA7 147 A3
E17 53 D4
N12 30 A5
N6 49 C2
Barnet EN5 12 D5
Dagenham RM8 81 B5
Sidcup DA15 190 A6
Southall UB6 86 A2
South Croydon CR0 221 C5
Wallington SM5 219 A1
Stanhope Row W1 248 C3
Stanhope St NW1 93 C4 232 A1
Stanhope Terr
W2 114 B6 246 D6
Stanier Cl SW5 254 D1
Stanlake Rd W12 112 C5
Stanlake Villas W12 112 C5
Stanley Ave
Barking IG11 101 D5
Beckenham BR2,BR3 208 A6
Dagenham RM8 59 B2
Greenford UB6 86 A6
Wembley HA0 66 A1
West Barnes KT3 200 A4
Stanley Bldgs NW1 233 A3
Stanley Cl SW8 270 C5
Wembley HA0 66 A1
Stanley Cres
W11 113 B6 244 C6
Stanleycroft Cl TW7 130 C4
Stanley Ct Belmont SM2 217 D1
11 Ealing W5 87 C2
Wallington SM5 219 A1
Wimbledon SW19 179 C4
Stanley Gardens Rd
TW11 174 C5
Stanley Gdns NW2 68 C3
W11 244 C6
W3 111 C4
Mitcham CR4 181 A4
Wallington SM6 219 C2
Stanley Gr SW11 137 A3
Thornton Heath CR0 204 C3
Stanley Ho E11 54 C3
18 E14 97 C1
35 SW8 137 D3
Stanley Horstead Twr
E10 75 D6
Stanley Inf Sch TW2 174 C6
Stanley Jun Sch TW2 174 C6
Stanley Mans SW10 266 B6
Upper Tooting SW17 158 D2
Stanley Park Dr HA0 88 B6
Stanley Park High Sch
SM5 219 A2
Stanley Park Inf Sch
SM5 218 D1
Stanley Park Jun Sch
SM5 218 D1
Stanley Park Rd SM5,
SM6 219 A1
Stanley Rd BR6 211 D1
E10 53 D3
E12 78 A3
E15 98 B6
N10 31 B3
N11 31 D5
N15 50 D5
N2 48 B6
2 NW9 46 A2
W3 111 A3
Ashford TW15 170 A5
Belmont SM2 217 D1
Bromley BR2 209 C5
Chingford E4 20 B3
Edmonton N9 17 D2
Enfield EN1 5 C2
Harrow HA2 64 A6
Ilford IG1 79 B6
Isleworth TW3 130 A1
Mitcham CR4 181 A3
Morden SM4 201 C5
Mortlake SW14 132 D1
Northwood HA6 22 A2
Sidcup DA14 168 A1
Southall UB1 107 A6
Teddington TW11,TW2 174 C5
Thornton Heath CR0 204 C3
Twickenham TW2 152 B1
Wallington SM5 219 A1
Wembley HA9 66 B2
Wimbledon SW19 179 C4
Woodford E18 36 D2
Stanley St SE14,SE8 141 B5
Stanley Studios SW10 266 B6
Stanley Tech High Sch for
Boys SE25 205 D6
Stanley Terr 7 N19 72 A6
Stanmer St SW11 136 C3
Stanmore Coll HA7 25 C4
Stanmore Gdns
Richmond TW9 132 B2
Sutton SM1 218 A5
Stanmore Hill HA7 25 A6
Stanmore Ho 21 SW8 137 D3
Stanmore Lo HA7 25 B6
Stanmore Pl NW1 231 D6
Stanmore Rd E11 54 D1
N15 50 D5
Richmond TW9 132 B2
Stanmore St N1 94 B6 233 C6
Stanmore Sta HA7 25 D6
Stanmore Terr 3 BR3 185 C1
Stannard Cotts 23 E1 96 C3
Stannard Mews E8 74 A2
Stannard Rd E8 74 A2
Stannary Pl SE11 261 B1
Stannary St
SE11 116 C1 261 B1
Stannet Way SM6 219 C4
Stansbury Ho 3 W10 91 A4
Stansfeld Ho SE1 263 D3
Stansfeld Rd E6 99 D1
Stansfield Rd SW9 138 B2
Cranford TW4,TW5 128 B3
Stansgate Rd RM10 81 C5
Stanstead Cl BR2 208 D3
Stanstead Gr SE23 163 B3
Stanstead Ho E3 98 A3
Stanstead Manor SM1 217 C2
Stanstead Rd
Forest Hill SE23,SE6 163 A3
Wanstead E11 55 B4
Stansted Cres DA5 168 D3
Stansted Rd TW6 148 B5
Stanswood Gdns SE5 139 C5
Stanthorpe Cl SW16 182 A5
Stanthorpe Rd SW16 182 A5
Stanton Ave TW11 174 C4
Stanton Cl
Chessington KT19 214 D3
North Cheam KT4 200 D1
Stanton Ct 5 DA15 168 A1
N16 51 B2
N3 29 C2
Stanton Ho 8 SE10 142 A6
Stanton Rd Barnes SW13 133 D3
Thornton Heath CR0 205 A2
Wimbledon SW20 178 D2
Stanton Sq SE26 185 B6
Stanton Way SE26 185 B6
Stanway Ct 23 N1 95 C5
Stanway Gdns HA8 27 A5
Acton W3 110 C5
Stanway St N1 95 C5
Stanwell Rd
Ashford TW15 170 A6
East Bedfont TW14,TW19,
TW6 148 D4
Stanwell TW15 148 A1
Ashford TW15 148 A1
Stanwick Rd
W14 113 B2 254 C3
Stanworth Ct TW5 129 C5
Stanworth St SE1 253 D1
Stanyhurst SE23 163 A3
Stapelhurst Ho 18 E5 74 B3
Stapenhill Rd HA0 65 B5
Staplefield Cl Pinner HA5 23 A3
3 Streatham SW2 160 A3
Stapleford N17 33 C1
Stapleford Ave IG2 57 C4
Stapleford Cl
Chingford E4 20 A1
Kingston KT1 198 C6
Putney SW19 157 A4
Stapleford Rd HA0 65 D1
Stapleford Way IG11 102 B4
Staplehurst Ct SW11 158 D5
Staplehurst Rd SE13 164 C6
Sutton SM5 218 C1
Staple Inn WC2 241 A3
Staple Inn Bldgs WC2 241 A3
Staples Cl SE16 119 A5
Staples Corner Bsns Pk
NW2 46 B1
Staples Corner (East)
NW2 46 B1
Staples Corner (West)
NW2 46 B1
Staple St SE1 117 B4 252 D1
Stapleton Gdns CR0 220 C3
Stapleton Hall N4 50 B2
Stapleton Hall Rd N4 50 B2
Stapleton Ho 10 E2 96 B4
Stapleton Rd DA7 147 B6
Orpington BR6 227 D5
Upper Tooting SW17 159 A1
Stapley Rd DA17 125 C1
Staplyton Rd EN5 1 A2
Star Alley EC3 253 B6
Star and Garter Hill
TW10 154 A4
Starboard Way E14 119 C3
Starcross St NW1 93 C4 232 B1
Star Ct UB10 83 A3
Starfield Rd W12 112 A4
Star & Garter Mans
SW15 134 D2
Star La E16 98 C3
Starliner Ct N7 72 C2
Starling Cl
Buckhurst Hill IG9 21 A3
Pinner HA5 40 C6
Starling Ho NW8 230 A4
Starling Wlk TW12 173 A5
Starmans Cl RM9 103 A6
Star Path UB5 85 C5
Star Pl E1 118 A6
Star Prim Sch E16 98 C3
Star Rd W14 113 B1 254 C1
Hillingdon UB10 83 A3
Hounslow TW7 130 B3
Star St W2 92 C1 237 A2
Starts Cl BR6 226 C5
Starts Hill Ave BR6 226 D4
Starts Hill Rd BR6 226 D4
Starveall Cl UB7 104 B3
Star Works NW10 90 A4

Star Yd WC2 94 C1 241 A2
State Farm Ave BR6 227 A4
Staten Gdns TW1 152 D3
Statham Gr N16 73 B5
Edmonton N18 33 C5
Statham Ho SW8 269 A2
Stathard Ho 18 E1 96 C3
Station App BR6 227 D6
BR7 188 A4
BR7 188 C1
DA16 146 A3
DA7 147 A3
E17 53 C4
E7 77 B4
N11 31 B5
N12 29 D6
NW10 89 D4
SE3 143 B2
SE9 166 B3
Ashford TW15 170 B6
5 Beckenham BR3 185 C2
Belmont SM2 217 A1
Fulham SW6 135 A2
Greenford UB6 64 B1
Hampton TW12 173 C2
Hayes BR2 209 A1
Hayes UB3 105 D3
Hinchley Wood KT10 212 D5
4 Kingston KT1,KT2 176 C2
New Barnet EN5 2 A1
6 New Malden KT4 200 A1
Penge SE26 185 B5
Pinner HA5 41 A6
Richmond TW9 132 C4
Ruislip HA4 39 D1
Ruislip HA4 62 B3
Shepperton TW17 193 A4
3 South Croydon CR0 221 B6
Streatham SW16 181 D5
Sunbury TW16 172 A2
1 Surbiton KT6 198 A3
Wanstead E11 55 A4
Wembley HA0 65 B2
2 Woodford E18 37 B1
Woodford IG9 37 D6
Worcester Park KT19 216 A3
Yiewsley UB7 104 A5
Station App Rd
SE1 116 C4 251 A2
Station Approach Rd
W4 133 A5
Station Ave 5 SW9 138 D2
Kingston KT3 199 C6
13 Richmond TW9 132 C4
West Ewell KT19 215 D1
Station Bldgs SW20 178 C1
Station Blgs W5 110 B5
Station Cl N3 29 C2
Hampton TW12 173 D2
Station Cres N15 51 B5
SE3 121 A1
Ashford TW15 170 A6
Wembley HA0 65 B2
Station Ct 1 E10 53 D2
5 SE15 140 C3
Stationers Hall Ct EC4 241 D1
Station Est
Beckenham BR3 206 D5
1 Woodford E18 37 B1
Station Estate Rd TW14 150 B3
Station Gdns W4 133 A5
Station Hill BR2 225 A6
Station House Mews N9 34 A6
Station Par 4 N14 15 D3
NW2 68 C2
Acton W3 88 C1
Ashford TW15 170 B6
Barking IG11 79 A1
Cockfosters EN4 3 A1
Dagenham RM10 81 C2
Ealing W5 110 B5
Edgware HA8 26 A3
Feltham TW14 150 B4
Harrow HA2 63 D4
Harrow HA3 25 A1
Richmond TW9 132 C4
Ruislip HA4 61 B6
4 Upper Tooting SW12 159 A3
2 Wanstead E11 55 A4
Woodford IG9 37 D6
Station Pas SE15 140 C4
Woodford E18 37 B1
Station Pl N4 72 C6
Station Rd BR1 187 A2
BR6 227 D6
DA7 147 A2
E10 76 A5
E12 78 A4
E17 53 A4
E7 77 A4
N11 31 B5
N17 52 A6
N19 71 C5
N3 29 C1
NW10 89 D5
NW4 46 A4
NW7 27 C4
SE13 142 A2
Ashford TW15 170 B6
Ashford TW16 172 A3
Barnes SW13 133 D3
Beckenham BR2 186 C1
Belvedere DA17 125 C3
Carshalton SM5 218 D4
Chessington KT9 214 A3
Chingford E4 20 B3
Claygate KT10 212 C3
Station Rd *continued*
Croydon CR0 205 A1
Dagenham RM6 58 D2
Ealing W5 88 B1
Ealing W7 108 C5
Edgware HA8 26 C4
Esher KT10 212 B6
Hampton TW12 173 D2
Harrow HA1 42 D4
Harrow HA1,HA2 41 D4
Hayes UB3 105 C2
Hounslow TW3 129 D1
Ilford IG1 78 D5
Ilford IG6 57 B6
Kingston KT2 176 C2
Merton SW19 180 A2
New Barnet EN5 13 D6
Penge SE20 184 C4
Shepperton TW17 193 A4
Sidcup DA14,DA15 168 A1
Southgate N21 16 D3
South Norwood SE25 205 D5
Teddington KT1 175 D2
Teddington TW11 175 A4
Thames Ditton KT7 196 D2
Twickenham TW1 152 D4
West Barnes KT3 200 B4
West Drayton UB7 104 A4
West Wickham BR4 208 A1
Wood Green N22 32 B1
Station Rd N DA17 125 D3
Station Rise SE27 160 D2
Station Sq BR5 211 A4
Station St E15 76 B1
E16 122 D5
Station Terr NW10 90 D5
SE5 139 A4
Station View UB6 86 B6
Station Way
Cheam SM2,SM3 217 A1
Woodford IG9 37 D6
Station Yd TW1 153 A4
Staunton Ho SE17 263 A3
Staunton Rd KT2 176 B3
Staunton St SE8 141 B6
Staveley NW1 232 A2
Staveley Cl E9 74 C3
N7 72 A4
SE15 140 C4
8 SE15 140 B4
Staveley Ct 4 E11 55 A4
Staveley Gdns W4 133 B4
Staveley Rd
Ashford TW15 171 B4
Chiswick W4 133 B5
Staverdale Lo W14 254 D6
Stavers Ho 18 E3 97 B5
Staverton Rd NW2 68 C1
Stave Yard Rd SE16 119 A5
Stavordale Rd N5 72 D4
Carshalton SM5 202 A2
Stayner's Rd E1 96 D3
Stayton Rd SM1 217 C5
Steadfast Rd KT1 175 D2
Steadman Ct EC1 242 B6
Steadman Ho 4 RM10 81 C5
Stead St SE17 117 B2 262 C3
Steam Farm La TW14 127 D1
Stean St E8 95 D6
Stebbing Ho 8 W11 112 D5
Stebbing Way IG11 102 A5
Stebondale St E14 120 A2
Stebon Prim Sch E14 97 C2
Stedham Pl WC1 240 A2
Stedman Cl UB10 60 C5
Steedman St
SE17 117 A2 262 A3
Steeds Rd N10 30 D2
Steele App IG11 102 B5
Steele Rd E11 76 C4
N17 51 C6
NW10 89 A5
W4 111 A3
Isleworth TW7 131 A1
Steele's Mews N NW3 70 D2
Steele's Mews S NW3 70 D2
Steele's Rd NW3 70 D2
Steele Wlk DA8 147 D5
Steel's La 23 E1 96 C1
Steen Way 7 SE22 161 C6
Steep Cl BR6 227 D2
Steep Hill
South Croydon CR0 221 C4
Streatham SW16 159 D1
Steeple Cl Fulham SW6 135 A3
Wimbledon SW19 179 A6
Steeple Ct 19 E1 96 B3
Steeplestone Cl N18 33 A5
Steeple Wlk N1 235 B6
Steerforth St SW18 158 A2
Steers Mead CR4 180 D2
Steers Way SE16 119 A4
Steetley Ct 14 SM2 218 A1
Steinman Ct TW7 130 D2
Stelfax Ho WC1 233 D2
Stella Rd SW17 180 D4
Stellar Ho 4 N17 33 D4
Stellman Cl E5 74 A5
Stembridge Rd SE20 184 B1
Sten Cl EN3 7 C6
Stephan Cl E8 96 A6
Stephen Cl BR6 227 D5
Stephen Ct 18 SW19 156 D3
Stephendale Rd SW6 136 A3
Stephen Fox Ho 7 W4 111 C1
Stephen Hawking Sch
E14 97 A1
Stephen Mews W1 239 C3
Stephen Pl SW4 137 C2
Stephen Saunders Ct
SW11 158 C6
Stephens Ct E16 98 D3
SE4 141 A2
Stephens Lo N12 14 A1
Stephenson Ct SM2 217 B1
Stephenson Ho 6 NW3 70 D3
2 NW5 71 B4
SE1 262 A6
SE2 124 D1
Stephenson Rd E17 53 A4
Ealing W7 86 D1
Twickenham TW4 151 C4
Stephenson St E16 98 C2
NW10 89 D4
Stephenson Way
NW1 93 C3 239 B6
Stephen's Rd E15 98 C6
Stephen St W1 239 C3
Stepney Cswy E1 96 D1
Stepney Day Hospl E1 96 C1
Stepney Gn E1 96 D2
Stepney Greencoat CE Prim
Sch The E14 97 B1
Stepney Green Ct 3 E1 96 D2
Stepney Green Sch E1 96 D2
Stepney Green Sta E1 96 D3
Stepney High St E1 96 D2
Stepney Way E1 96 C2
Sterling Ave Edgware HA8 26 B6
Upper Halliford TW17 193 C6
Sterling Cl NW10 68 A1
Sterling Gdns SE14 141 A6
Sterling Ho SE9 143 B1
Sterling Ind Est RM10 81 D4
Sterling Pl W5 110 A2
Sterling Rd EN2 5 B5
Sterling St SW7 257 B6
Sterling Way (North Circular
Rd) N18 33 C5
Stern Cl IG11 102 C5
Sterndale Rd W14 112 D3
Sterne St W12 112 D4
Sternhall La SE15 140 A2
Sternhold Ave SW12,
SW2 159 D2
Sterry Cres RM10 81 C3
Sterry Dr
Thames Ditton KT7 196 C3
Worcester Park KT19 215 C4
Sterry Gdns RM10 81 C2
Sterry Rd Barking IG11 101 D6
Dagenham RM10 81 C3
Sterry St SE1 252 C1
Steucers La SE23 163 A3
Stevanne Ct 1 DA17 125 C1
Steve Biko Ct W10 90 D3
Steve Biko La SE6 185 C6
Steve Biko Rd N7 72 C5
Steve Biko Way TW3 129 C2
Stevedale Rd DA16 146 C3
Stevedore St 3 E1 118 B5
Stevenage Rd
Fulham SW6 134 D4
Wallend E6 78 C2
Stevens Ave E9 74 C2
Stevens Cl
Beckenham BR3 185 C4
Hampton TW12 173 B4
Pinner HA5 40 C4
Stevens Ct BR3 185 C4
Stevens Gn WD23 8 A3
Stevens Ho KT1 175 D1
Stevens' La KT10 213 A2
Stevenson Cl EN5 14 B5
Stevenson Cres SE16 118 B1
Stevenson Ho NW8 229 A6
1 SW11 136 D3
Wembley HA9 65 D6
Stevens Rd RM8 80 C5
Stevens St SE1 263 B6
Steventon Rd W12 111 D6
Stewards Holte Wlk 3
N11 31 B6
Steward St E1 95 C2 243 B4
Stewart Ave TW17 192 C5
Stewart Cl BR7 188 D6
NW9 45 A3
Hampton TW12 173 A4
Stewart Fleming Prim Sch
SE20 206 C6
Stewart Headlam Prim Sch
E1 96 B3
Stewart Ho SE1 263 A5
Stewart Quay UB3 105 C4
Stewart Rainbird Ho 1
E12 78 C3
Stewart Rd E15 76 B4
Stewartsby Cl N18 33 A5
Stewart's Gr
SW3 114 C1 257 A2
Stewart's Rd
SW8 137 C4 269 A2
Stewart St E14 120 A4
Stew La EC4 252 A6
Steyne Rd W3 110 D5
Steyning Gr SE9 188 B6
Steynings Way N12 29 C5
Steyning Way TW4 128 C1
Steynton Ave DA5 168 D2
Stickland Rd DA17 125 C2
Stickleton Cl UB6 85 D4
Stifford Ho E1 96 C2
Stilecroft Gdns HA0 65 B5
Stile Hall Gdns W4 110 C1
Stile Hall Par 6 W4 110 C1
Stileman Ho 4 E3 97 B2
Stile Path TW16 194 A5
Stiles Cl BR2 210 B3
Erith DA8 125 D1
Stillingfleet Rd SW13 134 A6
Stillington St
SW1 115 C2 259 B4
Stillness Jun & Inf Schs
SE23 163 A5
Stillness Rd SE23 163 B5
Stilwell Dr UB8 82 B3
Stilwell Rdbt UB8 104 D6
Stipularis Dr UB4 84 D3
Stirling Ave Pinner HA5 41 A2
Wallington SM6 220 A1
Stirling Cl SW16 181 C2
Stirling Cnr EN5,WD6 11 B5
Stirling Ct EC1 241 C6
WC2 240 C1
Ealing W13 109 B6
Stirling Gr TW3 130 A3
Stirling Ho 5 SE18 122 D1
Stirling Mans NW6 70 A2
Stirling Rd E13 99 B5
E17 53 A6
SW9 138 A3
W3 110 D3
Harrow HA3 42 D6
Hayes UB3 106 B6
Stanwell TW19,TW6 148 B5
Tottenham N17 34 A2
Tottenham N22 32 D2
Twickenham TW2 151 D4
Stirling Way
Borehamwood WD6 11 B6
Thornton Heath CR0 204 A2
Stiven Cres HA2 63 B5
Stoatley Ho 10 SW15 156 A3
Stockbeck NW1 232 B3
Stockbridge Ho EN2 4 D3
Stockbury Rd CR0 206 C3
Stockdale Rd RM8 81 B6
Stockdove Way UB6 86 D4
Stocker Gdns RM9 80 C1
Stock Exchange* EC2 242 D1
Stockfield Rd
Claygate KT10 212 C3
Streatham SW16 160 B1
Stockholm Ho E1 118 A6
Stockholm Rd SE16 118 C1
Stockholm Way 9 E1 118 A5
Stockhurst Cl SW15 134 D3
Stockingswater La EN3 7 B2
Stockleigh Hall NW8 230 B4
Stockley Cl UB7 104 D4
Stockley Ctry Pk UB7 104 C6
Stockley Farm Rd UB7 104 D3
Stockley Park Bsns Pk
UB11 105 A5
Stockley Rd UB7,UB8,
UB11 104 D4
Stock Orchard Cres N7 72 B3
Stock Orchard St N7 72 B3
Stockport Rd SW16 181 D2
Stocks Ct 5 E1 96 D3
Stocksfield Rd E17 54 A6
Stocks Pl 16 E14 119 B6
Hillingdon UB10 82 C6
Stock St E13 99 A5
Stockton Cl EN5 2 A1
Stockton Gdns NW7 11 C1
Tottenham N17 33 A3
Stockton Ho 16 E2 96 B4
Harrow HA2 41 C1
Stockton Rd
Edmonton N18 34 B4
Tottenham N17 33 A3
Stockwell Ave SW9 138 B2
Stockwell Cl BR1 187 B1
Stockwell Gdns
SW9 138 B4 270 C1
Stockwell Gn SW9 138 B3
Stockwell La SW9 138 B3
Stockwell Park Cres
SW9 138 B3
Stockwell Park Rd
SW9 138 B4 270 D1
Stockwell Park Sch
SW9 138 B4 270 C1
Stockwell Park Wlk
SW9 138 C2
Stockwell Prim Sch
SW9 138 B2
Stockwell Rd SW9 138 B3
Stockwell St SE10 142 A6
Stockwell Sta SW4 138 A3
Stockwell Terr SW9 270 C1
Stodart Rd SE20 184 C2
Stoddart Ho SW8 270 D5
Stodmarsh Ho 28 SW9 138 C4
Stofield Gdns SE9 165 D1
Stoford Cl SW19 157 A4
Stokenchurch St
SW6 135 D4 265 C1
Stoke Newington Church St
N16 73 C6
Stoke Newington Comm
N16 73 D6
Stoke Newington High St
N16 73 D5
Stoke Newington Rd
N16 73 D4
Stoke Newington Sch
N16 73 B5
Stoke Newington Sta N16 73 D6
Stoke Pl NW10 89 D4
Stoke Rd KT2 177 A3
Stokesby Rd KT9 214 B2
Stokes Ct N2 48 C5
Stokesley St W12 89 D1
Stokes Rd Croydon CR0 206 D3
Newham E6 100 A3
Stokley Ct N8 50 A5
Stoll Cl NW2 68 C5
Stoms Path SE6 185 C5
Stonard Rd
Dagenham RM8 80 B4
Palmers Green N13 16 C1
Stondon Pk SE23 163 A5
Stondon Wlk E6 100 A5
4 E6 99 D5
Stonebanks KT12 194 A2
Stone Bldgs WC2 94 B2 240 D3
Stonebridge Ct 8 NW10 67 B1
Stonebridge Ctr The N15 52 A4
Stonebridge Park HA9 66 D1
Stonebridge Park Sta
NW10 66 D1
Stonebridge Pk NW10 67 B1
Stonebridge Rd N15 51 D4
Stonebridge Sch The
NW10 89 B6
Stonebridge Sh Ctr 6
NW10 89 B6
Stonebridge Way HA9 66 D2
Stonechat Sq 6 E6 100 A2
Stone Cl SW4 137 C3
Dagenham RM8 81 B6
Yiewsley UB7 104 B5
Stonecot Cl SM3 201 A1
Stonecot Hill SM4 201 A1
Stone Cres TW14 149 D4
Stonecroft Way CR0 204 A2
Stonecutter St EC4 241 C2
Stonefield N4 72 B6
Stonefield Cl DA7 147 C2
Ruislip HA4 63 A3
Stonefield Mans N1 234 A5
Stonefield St N1 94 C6 234 B6
Stonefield Way SE7 143 D5
Ruislip HA4 63 A3
Stone Gate 8 NW5 71 A2
Stone Gr HA8 26 B5
Stone Grove Ct HA8 26 B5
Stonegrove Gdns HA8 26 A5
Stonehall Ave IG1 56 A3
Stone Hall Rd N21 16 C4
Stoneham Rd N11 31 C5
Stonehaven BR3 185 D1
Stonehill Cl SW14 155 B6
Stonehill Ct E4 19 D4
Stonehill Rd W4 110 C1
Mortlake SW14 155 B6
Stonehills Ct SE21 161 C1
Stonehill's Mans 3
SW16 160 A2
Stonehill Woods Pk
DA14 169 D3
Stonehorse Rd EN3 18 C6
Stonehouse NW1 232 B5
Stonehouse Ct EC2 243 B2
Stonehouse Ho 27 W2 91 C2
Stone Lake Ind Pk SE7 121 C2
Stone Lake Ret Pk SE7 121 C2
Stoneleigh Ave Enfield EN1 6 B4
North Cheam KT17,KT4 216 A5
Stoneleigh Broadway
KT17 216 A3
Stoneleigh Cres KT19 215 D3
Stoneleigh Ct
Redbridge IG5 56 A6
4 Tottenham N17 33 D1
Stoneleigh Fst Sch
KT17 216 B4
Stoneleigh Lo 13 TW9 132 B4
Stoneleigh Park Ave
CR0 206 D3
Stoneleigh Park Rd
KT19,KT4 216 A3
Stoneleigh Pl W11 112 D6
Stoneleigh Rd
Carshalton SM5 202 C2
Redbridge IG5 56 B6
Tottenham N17 33 D1
Stoneleigh St W11 112 D6
Stoneleigh Sta KT19 216 A3
Stoneleigh Terr N19 71 B6
Stonell's Rd SW11 158 D6
Stonemasons Cl N15 51 B5
Stonenest St N4 50 B1
Stone Park Ave BR3 207 D5
Stone Pl KT4 216 A6
Stone Rd BR2 208 D4
Stones End St SE1 252 A1
Stonewall E6 100 C2
Stoneworth Ct SE25 206 A3
Stoney Alley SE18 144 C3
Stoneyard La E14 119 D6
Stoneycroft Cl SE12 164 D4
Stoney Deep TW11 175 A6
Stoneydown E17 53 A5
Stoneydown Ave E17 53 A5
Stoneydown Ho 2 E17 53 A5
Stoneydown Park Sch
E17 53 A5
Stoneyfields Gdns HA8 27 A6
Stoneyfields La HA8 27 A6
Stoney La E1 243 B2
Penge SE19 183 D4
Stoney St SE1 117 B5 252 C4
Stonhouse St SW4 137 D1
Stonor Rd W14 113 B2 254 C3
Stonycroft Cl EN3 7 A3
Stopes St SE15 139 D5
Stopford Rd E13 99 A6
SE17 261 D1
Stopher Ho SE1 251 D1
Storace Ho 6 SW4 138 A1
Store Rd E16 122 C4
Storers Quay E14 120 B2
Store St E15 76 B3
WC1 93 D2 239 C4
Storey Ct NW8 229 C1
Storey Ho 12 E14 119 D6
Storey Prim Sch E16 122 D5
Storey Rd E17 53 B5
N6 48 D3
Storey's Gate
SW1 115 D4 249 D1
Storey St E16 122 C4
Stories Rd SE5 139 C2
Stork Rd E7 77 A2
Storksmead Rd HA8 27 C3
Storks Rd SE16 118 A3
Stormont House Sch E5 74 B4
Stormont Rd N6 48 D2
SW11 137 A1
Stormont Way KT9 213 C3
Stormount Dr UB3 105 A4
Storrington WC1 233 B1
Storrington Rd CR0 205 D1
Story St N1 72 B1
Stothard Pl E1 243 B4
Stothard St 11 E1 96 C3
Stott Cl SW18 158 B5
Stoughton Ave SM3 217 A3
Stoughton Cl SE11 260 D3
Roehampton SW15 156 A3
Stour Ave UB2 107 C3
Stour Cl BR2 225 C4
Stourcliffe Cl W1 237 C2
Stourcliffe St W1 237 C1
Stourhead Cl 6 SW19 156 D4
Stourhead Gdns SW20 200 A6
Stour Rd E3 75 C1
Dagenham RM10 81 C6
Stourton Ave TW13 173 B6
Stowage SE8 141 D6
Stow Cres E17 35 A3
Stowe Cres HA4 39 A3
Stowe Gdns N9 17 D3
Stowe Ho 11 N16 73 C5
NW11 48 A3
Stowell Ho 2 N8 50 A5
Stowe Pl N15 51 C6
Stowe Rd W12 112 B4
Stowford Coll SM2 218 A1
Stowting Rd BR6 227 C4
Stox Mead HA3 24 B2
Stracey Rd E7 77 A4
NW10 89 B6
Strachan Pl SW19,SW20 178 C4
Stradbroke Gr
Buckhurst Hill IG9 21 D3
Redbridge IG5 56 B6
Stradbroke Rd N5 73 A4
Stradbrook Cl HA2 63 B5
Stradella Rd SE24 161 A5
Straffan Lo 8 NW3 70 C2
Strafford Ho 9 SE8 119 B1
Strafford Rd Acton W3 111 A4
Barnet EN5 1 A2
Hounslow TW3 129 B2
Twickenham TW1 153 A4
Strafford St E14 119 C4
Strahan Rd E3 97 A4
Straightsmouth SE10 142 A5
Straight The UB2 107 A4
Strait Rd E6 122 B6
Straker's Rd SE15 140 B1
Strale Ho 17 N1 95 C6
Strand WC2 116 B6 250 C6
Strandfield Cl SE18 123 C1
Strand La WC2 250 D6
Strand-on-the-Green
W4 132 C6
Strand-on-the-Green Sch
W4 132 C6
Strand Pl N18 33 C6
Strang Ho N1 235 A5
Strangways Terr W14 254 C5
Stranraer Way N1 72 A1
1 Stanwell TW6 148 A5
Strasburg Rd
SW11 137 B4 268 C1
Stratfield Ho SE12 165 A2
Stratfield Park Cl N21 16 D4
Stratford Ave UB10 82 B5
Stratford Bus Sta E15 76 B1
Stratford Cir E15 76 B2
Stratford Cl IG11 80 A1
Stratford Ct KT3 199 B5
Stratford Ctr E15 76 B1
Stratford Gr SW15 134 D1
Stratford House Ave
BR1 210 A6
Stratford Office Village The
1 E15 76 C1
Stratford Pl W1 238 C1
Stratford Rd E13 99 A6
W8 113 C3 255 B5
Harlington TW6 149 A6
Hayes UB4 84 B3
Southall UB2 107 A2
Thornton Heath CR7 204 D6
Stratford Sta E15 76 B1
Stratford Studios W8 255 C5
Stratford Villas NW1 71 D1
Stratford Workshops
E15 98 B6
Strathan Cl SW18 157 A5
Strathaven Rd SE12 165 B5
Strathblaine Rd SW11 136 B1
Strathbrook Rd SW16 182 B3
Strathcona Rd HA9 65 D6
Strathdale SW16 182 B5
Strathdon Dr SW17 158 B1
Strathearn Ave
Harlington UB3 127 D5
Twickenham TW2 152 A3
Strathearn House W2 247 A6
Strathearn Pl
W2 114 C6 247 A6

Strathearn Rd
Sutton SM1 ....217 C3
Wimbledon SW19 ....179 C6
Stratheden Par SE3 ....143 A5
Stratheden Rd SE3 ....143 A5
Strathfield Gdns IG11 ....79 B2
Strathleven Rd SW2 ....160 A6
Strathmore Ct NW8 ....230 A2
Strathmore Gdns N3 ....29 D2
W8 ....245 B4
Edgware HA8 ....26 D1
Strathmore Rd
Teddington TW11,TW2 ....174 C6
Thornton Heath CR0 ....205 B2
Wimbledon SW19 ....157 C1
Strathmore Sch TW10 ....153 D2
Strathnairn St SE1 ....118 A2
Strathray Gdns NW3 ....70 C2
Strath Terr SW11 ....136 C1
Strathville Rd SW18 ....157 D2
Strathyre Ave SW16 ....204 C6
Stratton Ave EN2 ....5 B6
Stratton Cl DA7 ....147 A2
Edgware HA8 ....26 B4
Heston TW5 ....129 C4
Merton SW19 ....179 C1
Walton-on-T KT12 ....194 C1
Stratton Ct 4 N1 ....73 C1
10 Kingston KT6 ....198 A4
Strattondale St E14 ....120 A3
Stratton Dr IG11 ....79 D2
Stratton Gdns UB1 ....85 C1
Stratton Ho HA8 ....26 B6
Stratton Rd DA7 ....147 A2
Merton SW19 ....179 C1
Sunbury TW16 ....171 D1
Stratton St W1 ....115 B5 248 D4
Strauss Rd W4 ....111 B4
Strawberry Hill Cl TW1 ....152 D1
Strawberry Hill Rd TW1 ....152 D1
Strawberry Hill Sta
TW2 ....152 D1
Strawberry La SM5 ....219 A5
Strawberry Terr N10 ....30 D2
Strawberry Vale N2 ....30 B2
Twickenham TW1 ....153 A1
Strayfield Rd EN2 ....4 D6
Streakes Field Rd NW2 ....68 A6
Streamdale SE2 ....146 B6
Streamline Mews SE22 ....162 A3
Streamside Cl BR2 ....209 A5
Edmonton N9 ....17 D3
Stream Way DA17 ....147 C6
Streatfield Ave E6 ....100 B6
Streatfield Rd HA3,HA7 ....43 D6
Streatham Cl SW16 ....160 A2
Streatham & Clapham High
Sch SW16 ....159 D1
Streatham Comm N
SW16 ....182 B5
Streatham Common Sta
SW16 ....181 D3
Streatham Comm S
SW16 ....182 B4
Streatham Ct SW16 ....160 A1
Streatham High Rd
SW16,SW2 ....182 A5
Streatham Hill SW2 ....160 A3
Streatham Hill & Clapham
High Sch SW2 ....160 B3
Streatham Hill Sta SW2 ....160 A2
Streatham Pl SW2 ....160 A4
Streatham Rd CR4 ....181 A2
Streatham St WC1 ....240 A2
Streatham Sta SW16 ....181 D5
Streatham & Tooting Adult
Inst SW16 ....160 B2
Streatham Vale SW16 ....181 D3
Streathbourne Rd
SW17 ....159 A1
Streathem Wells Prim Sch
SW2 ....160 C2
Streatleigh Par 4
SW16 ....160 A2
Streatley Pl NW3 ....70 B4
12 NW3 ....70 A4
Streatley Rd NW6 ....69 B1
Streeters La SM6 ....219 D5
Streetfield Mews SE3 ....143 A2
Streimer Rd E15 ....98 A5
Strelley Way W3 ....111 C6
Stretton Lo W13 ....109 B6
Stretton Mans 16 SE8 ....141 C6
Stretton Rd Croydon CR0 ....205 C2
Richmond TW10 ....153 C2
Strickland Ct SE15 ....140 A2
Strickland Ho 26 E2 ....95 D4
Strickland Row SW18 ....158 B4
Strickland St SE8 ....141 C4
Strickland Way 4 BR6 ....227 D4
Stride Rd E13 ....98 D5
Strimon Cl N9 ....18 C2
Stringer Hos 19 N1 ....95 C6
Strode Cl N10 ....31 A3
Strode Ho 3 SW2 ....160 C3
Strode Rd E7 ....77 A4
NW10 ....68 A2
SW6 ....135 A5 264 A4
Tottenham N17 ....33 C1
Strome Ho NW6 ....91 D5
Strone Rd E7,E12 ....77 D2
Strone Way UB4 ....85 A3
Strongbow Cres SE9 ....166 B6
Strongbow Rd SE9 ....166 B6
Strongbridge Cl HA2 ....41 C1
Stronsa Rd W12 ....111 D4
Strood Ho SE1 ....252 D1
12 Penge SE20 ....184 C3
Stroud Cres SW15 ....156 A1
Stroudes Cl KT4 ....199 D2
Stroud Field UB5 ....63 A2
Stroud Gate HA2 ....63 D4
Stroud Green Gdns CR0 ....206 C2
Stroud Green JMI Sch
N4 ....50 C1
Stroud Green Rd N4 ....50 C1
Stroud Green Way CR0 ....206 C3
Stroudley Ho SW8 ....269 B2
Stroudley Wlk E3 ....97 D4
Stroud Rd Croydon SE25 ....206 A3
Wimbledon SW19 ....157 C1
Strouds Cl RM6 ....58 B4
Stroud Way TW15 ....171 A4
Strout's Pl 2 E2 ....95 D4
Struan Ho 11 E11 ....55 A4
Strudwick Ct SW4 ....270 B1
Strutton Ground
SW1 ....115 D3 259 C5
Strype St E1 ....243 C3
Stuart Ave NW9 ....46 A2
W5 ....110 B4
Harrow HA2 ....63 B5
Hayes BR2 ....209 A1
Walton-on-T KT12 ....194 B1
Stuart Cl UB10 ....60 C2
Stuart Cres Croydon CR0 ....223 B5
Hayes UB3 ....83 A1
Wood Green N22 ....32 B2
Stuart Ct Chingford E4 ....20 D2
2 Elstree WD6 ....9 D5
Stuart Evans Cl DA16 ....146 C2
Stuart Gr TW11 ....174 C5
Stuart Ho 1 E9 ....74 D1
5 SW4 ....138 A1
W14 ....254 A4
Stuart Lo SE25 ....183 C1
Stuart Mill Ho N1 ....233 C3
Stuart Pl CR4 ....180 D2
Stuart Rd DA16 ....146 B4
NW6 ....91 C4
SE15 ....140 C1
W3 ....111 A5
East Barnet EN4 ....14 D4
Harrow HA3 ....42 D6
Richmond TW10 ....153 B1
South Norwood CR7 ....205 A5
Wimbledon SW19 ....157 C1
Stubbs Cl NW9 ....45 A4
Stubbs Dr SE16 ....118 B1
Stubbs Ho 1 E2 ....96 D4
N4 ....50 B1
Stubbs Mews RM8 ....80 B4
Stubbs Point E13 ....99 B3
Stubbs Way SW19 ....180 B2
Stucley Pl 18 NW1 ....71 B1
Stucley Rd TW5,TW7 ....130 A5
Studdridge St SW6 ....135 C3
Studd St N1 ....94 D6 234 C6
Studholme Ct NW3 ....69 C4
Studholme St SE15 ....140 B5
Studio Pl SW1 ....247 D1
Studios Rd TW17 ....192 B6
Studios The 4 SW4 ....137 C1
SW8 ....269 D1
Studland SE17 ....262 C2
Studland Cl DA15 ....167 D1
Studland Ho E14 ....97 A1
Studland Rd Ealing W7 ....86 C1
Forest Hill SE26 ....184 D5
Kingston KT2 ....176 A4
Studland St W6 ....112 B2
Studley Ave E4 ....36 B3
Studley Cl E5 ....75 A3
Studley Ct DA14 ....190 B5
9 Poplar E14 ....120 B6
Redbridge IG4 ....55 D3
Studley Dr IG4 ....55 D3
Studley Grange Rd W7 ....108 D4
Studley Rd E7 ....77 B2
SW4 ....138 A3
Dagenham RM9 ....80 D1
Study Prep Sch The
SW19 ....178 C5
Study Sch The KT3 ....199 C4
Stukeley Rd E7 ....77 B1
Stukeley St WC2 ....94 A1 240 B2
Stumps Hill La BR3 ....185 C4
Stunnell Ho 23 SE14 ....140 D6
Sturdee Ho 2 E2 ....96 A5
Sturdy Ho 26 E3 ....97 A5
Sturdy Rd SE15 ....140 B3
Sturge Ave E17 ....35 D1
Sturgeon Rd
SE17 ....117 A1 262 A1
Sturges Field BR7 ....189 B4
Sturgess Ave NW4 ....46 B2
Sturge St SE1 ....117 A4 252 A2
Sturmer Way N7 ....72 B3
Sturminster Cl UB4 ....84 C1
Sturminster Ho SW8 ....270 D3
Sturrock Cl N15 ....51 B5
Sturry St E14 ....97 D1
Sturt St N1 ....235 B3
Stutfield St E1 ....96 A1
Stuttle Ho 9 E1 ....96 A3
Styles Gdns SW9 ....138 D2
Styles Ho SE1 ....251 C3
Styles Way BR3 ....208 A5
Sudbourne Prim Sch
SW2 ....160 B6
Sudbourne Rd SW2 ....160 B6
Sudbrooke Rd SW12 ....159 A5
Sudbrook Gdns TW10 ....154 A1
Sudbrook La TW10 ....154 A2
Sudbury E6 ....100 C1
Sudbury Ave HA0 ....65 D4
Sudbury Court Dr HA1 ....65 A5
Sudbury Court Rd HA1 ....65 A5
Sudbury Cres BR1 ....187 A5
Wembley HA0 ....65 B3
Sudbury Croft HA0 ....64 D4
Sudbury Ct E5 ....75 A4
SW8 ....269 D2
Sudbury Gdns CR0 ....221 C4
Sudbury & Harrow Road Sta
HA0 ....65 B3
Sudbury Heights Ave
UB6 ....65 A3
Sudbury Hill HA1 ....64 C5
Sudbury Hill Cl HA0 ....64 D5
Sudbury Hill Harrow Sta
HA1 ....64 C4
Sudbury Hill Sta HA1 ....64 C4
Sudbury Ho SW18 ....157 D6
Sudbury Jun & Inf Schs
HA0 ....65 B4
Sudbury Rd IG11 ....79 D3
Sudbury Town Sta UB6 ....65 B2
Sudeley St N1 ....94 D5 234 D3
Sudlow Rd SW18 ....157 C6
Sudrey St SE1 ....252 A1
Suez Ave UB6 ....86 D5
Suez Rd EN3 ....7 A2
Suffield Ho SE17 ....261 D2
Suffield Rd 2 N15 ....51 D4
Chingford E4 ....35 D6
Penge SE20 ....184 C1
Suffolk Cl WD6 ....11 B6
Suffolk Ct Ilford IG3 ....57 C3
3 West Norwood SW16 ....182 C6
Suffolk Ho 11 Acton W3 ....88 C1
Penge SE20 ....184 C2
4 South Croydon CR0 ....221 B6
Suffolk La EC4 ....252 C6
Suffolk Park Rd E17 ....53 A5
Suffolk Pl SW1 ....249 D4
Suffolk Rd 4 E13 ....99 A4
N15 ....51 B3
NW10 ....67 C1
Barking IG11 ....79 B1
Barnes SW13 ....134 A5
Dagenham RM10 ....81 D3
Enfield EN3 ....18 B6
Harrow HA2 ....41 B4
Ilford IG3 ....57 C3
Sidcup DA14 ....190 C4
South Norwood SE25 ....205 D5
Worcester Park KT4 ....215 D6
Suffolks Prim Sch EN1 ....6 B3
Suffolk St E7 ....77 A4
SW1 ....115 D5 249 D4
Sugar House La E15 ....98 A5
Sugar Loaf Wlk 6 E2 ....96 C4
Sugden Rd SW11 ....137 A1
Long Ditton KT7 ....197 B1
Sugden Way IG11 ....101 D5
Sulby Ho SE4 ....141 A1
Sulgrave Gdns 11 W6 ....112 C4
Sulgrave Rd W6 ....112 C3
Sulina Rd SW2 ....160 A4
Sulivan Ct SW6 ....135 C3
Sulivan Ent Ctr SW6 ....135 C2
Sulivan Prim Sch SW6 ....135 C3
Sulivan Rd SW6 ....135 C2
Sulkin Ho 11 E2 ....96 D4
Sullivan Ave E16 ....99 D2
Sullivan Cl SW11 ....136 C2
East Molesey KT8 ....195 D6
Northolt UB4 ....84 C2
Sullivan Ct N16 ....51 D1
SW5 ....255 B4
4 Croydon CR0 ....206 A1
Sullivan Ho SE11 ....260 D3
SW1 ....268 D6
Isleworth TW2 ....152 B5
Sullivan Rd
SE11 ....116 C2 261 B4
Sullivans Reach KT12 ....193 D2
Sullivan Way WD6 ....9 C5
Sultan Rd E11 ....55 B5
Sultan St SE5 ....139 A5
Penge BR3 ....184 D1
Sumal Ct E9 ....76 B6
Sumatra Rd NW6 ....69 C2
Sumburgh Rd SW12 ....159 A5
Summer Ave KT8 ....196 C4
Summercourt Rd E1 ....96 C1
Summerene Cl SW16 ....181 C3
Summerfield 6 BR1 ....187 B2
Summerfield Ave N12 ....30 C4
NW6 ....91 A5
Summerfield La KT6 ....213 D6
Summerfield Rd
Ealing W5 ....87 B3
Loughton IG10 ....21 D5
Summerfield St SE12 ....164 D4
Summer Gdns KT8 ....196 C4
Summer Gr WD6 ....9 D5
Summer Hill BR7 ....188 C1
Borehamwood WD6 ....10 C6
Summerhill Cl BR6 ....227 C5
Summerhill Gr EN1 ....17 C5
Summerhill Rd N15 ....51 B5
Summerhill Way CR4 ....181 A2
Summer Ho SE13 ....142 B1
Summerhouse Ave
TW5 ....129 A4
Summerhouse Rd N16 ....73 C6
Summerland Gdns N10 ....49 B6
Summerland Grange
N10 ....49 B6
Summerlands Ave W3 ....111 A6
Summerlands Lo BR6 ....226 C4
Summerlee Ave N2 ....48 D5
Summerlee Gdns N2 ....48 D5
Summerley St SW18 ....157 D2
Summer Rd
East Molesey KT8 ....196 B4
Thames Ditton KT7,KT8 ....196 D4
Summersby Rd N6 ....49 B3
Summers Cl
Belmont SM2 ....217 C1
Wembley HA9 ....44 D1
Summersell Ho SE27 ....183 B5
Summerside Prim Sch
N12 ....30 B4
Summerskille Cl N9 ....18 B2
Summers La N12 ....30 B3
Summers Row N12 ....30 C4
Summers St EC1 ....241 A5
Summerstown SW17 ....180 A6
Summerton Way SE28 ....102 D1
Summer Trees TW16 ....172 B2
Summerville Gdns SM1 ....217 B2
Summerwood Rd TW1,
TW7 ....152 D5
Summit Ave NW9 ....45 B4
Summit Bsns Pk The
TW16 ....172 A3
Summit Cl N14 ....15 C2
NW9 ....45 B5
Edgware HA8 ....26 C3
Summit Ct NW2 ....69 A3
Summit Dr IG8 ....37 D1
Summit Est N16 ....52 A2
Summit Rd E17 ....53 D5
Northolt UB5 ....63 C1
Summit The TW16 ....172 A3
Summit Way N14 ....15 B2
South Norwood SE19 ....183 C3
Sumner Ave SE15 ....139 D4
Sumner Bldgs SE1 ....252 A4
Sumner Cl BR6 ....227 A4
Sumner Ct SW8 ....270 A2
Sumner Gdns CR0 ....204 C1
Sumner Ho 1 E3 ....97 D2
Sumner Pl SW7 ....114 B2 256 D3
Sumner Place Mews
SW7 ....256 D3
Sumner Rd SE15 ....139 D5
Harrow HA1 ....42 A2
Thornton Heath CR0 ....204 D1
Sumner Rd S CR0 ....204 C1
Sumner St SE1 ....117 A5 252 A4
Sumpter Cl NW3 ....70 A2
Sun Alley 6 TW9 ....132 A1
Sunbeam Cres W10 ....90 C3
Sunbeam Rd NW10 ....89 B3
Sunbury Ave NW7 ....27 B6
Mortlake SW14 ....133 B1
Sunbury Cl KT12 ....194 A3
Sunbury Court Island
TW16 ....194 D6
Sunbury Court Rd
TW16 ....172 C1
Sunbury Cres TW13 ....171 D6
Sunbury Cross TW16 ....172 A3
Sunbury Cross Ctr 9
TW16 ....171 D3
Sunbury Ct 3 SE14 ....140 D6
2 Barnet EN5 ....1 A1
Sunbury TW16 ....172 D1
Sunbury Ct (Con Ctr)
TW16 ....172 D1
Sunbury Gdns NW7 ....27 B5
Sunbury Ho 38 E2 ....95 D4
Sunbury Int Bsns Ctr
TW16 ....171 C2
Sunbury La
SW11 ....136 B4 266 D2
Walton-on-T KT12 ....194 A3
Sunbury Manor Sch
TW16 ....171 D2
Sunbury Rd Cheam SM3 ....217 A5
Feltham TW13 ....171 D6
Sunbury St SE18 ....122 B3
Sunbury Sta TW16 ....172 A2
Sunbury Way TW13 ....172 C5
Sunbury Workshops 39
E2 ....95 D4
Suncroft Pl SE26 ....162 C1
Sun Ct EC3 ....242 D1
Sunderland Ct
Dulwich SE22 ....162 A4
12 Stanwell TW19 ....148 A5
Sunderland Ho 26 W2 ....91 C2
Sunderland Mount
SE23 ....162 D2
Sunderland Pt E16 ....123 A5
Sunderland Rd W5 ....109 D3
Forest Hill SE23 ....162 D2
Sunderland Terr W2 ....91 D1
Sunderland Way E12 ....77 D6
Sundew Ave W12 ....112 A6
Sundew Ct 9 HA0 ....88 A5
Sundial Ave SE25 ....205 D6
Sundial Ct KT5 ....214 D6
Sundorne Rd SE7 ....121 C1
Sundown Rd TW15 ....171 A5
Sundridge Ave DA16 ....145 B2
Bromley BR1,BR7 ....188 A3
Sundridge Ho 4 E9 ....74 D1
Sundridge Par BR1 ....187 B3
Sundridge Park Sta
BR1 ....187 B3
Sundridge Rd CR0 ....206 A1
Sunfields Pl SE3 ....143 B5
Sun in the Sands SE3 ....143 B5
Sunken Rd CR0 ....222 C3
Sun La SE3 ....143 B5
Sunland Ave DA6 ....147 A1
Sunleigh Ct HA0 ....88 A6
Sunleigh Rd HA0 ....88 A6
Sunley Gdns UB6 ....87 A6
Sun Life Trad Est TW14 ....128 A2
Sunlight Cl SW19 ....180 A4
Sunlight Sq 29 E2 ....96 B4
Sunmead Rd TW16 ....194 A6
Sunna Gdns TW16 ....172 B1
Sunniholme Ct CR2 ....221 A3
Sunningdale N14 ....31 D5
Ealing W13 ....87 B2
Sunningdale Ave W3 ....111 C6
Barking IG11 ....79 B1
Feltham TW13 ....151 A2
Ruislip HA4 ....40 C1
Sunningdale Cl E6 ....100 B4
22 SE16 ....118 B1
Erith SE28 ....103 A1
Stanmore HA7 ....25 A3
3 Surbiton KT6 ....214 A6
Sunningdale Ct
13 Kingston KT2 ....176 C3
13 Southall UB1 ....86 A1
Sunningdale Gdns NW9 ....45 A4
W8 ....255 B5
Sunningdale Rd
BR1,BR2 ....210 A4
Cheam SM1 ....217 B4
Sunningfields Cres NW4 ....28 B1
Sunningfields Rd NW4 ....46 B6
Sunninghill Ct 9 W3 ....111 A4
Sunninghill Gdns IG2 ....57 D4
Sunninghill Rd SE13 ....141 D3
Sunny Bank SE25 ....206 A6
Sunny Cres NW10 ....67 A1
Sunnycroft Rd
Hounslow TW3 ....129 D3
Southall UB1 ....85 C2
South Norwood SE25 ....206 A6
Sunnydale BR6 ....226 C6
Sunnydale Gdns NW7 ....27 C4
Sunnydale Rd SE12 ....165 B6
Sunnydene Ave
Chingford E4 ....36 B5
Ruislip HA4 ....62 A6
Sunnydene Gdns HA0 ....65 C2
Sunnydene St SE26 ....185 A6
Sunnyfield NW7 ....27 D6
Sunnyfields Prim Sch
NW4 ....46 B6
Sunny Gardens Par NW4 ....28 B1
Sunny Gardens Rd NW4 ....46 C6
Sunny Hill NW4 ....46 B6
Sunnyhill Cl E5 ....75 A4
Sunny Hill Ct NW4 ....28 B1
Sunnyhill Prim Sch
SW16 ....182 B6
Sunnyhill Rd SW16 ....182 A6
Sunnyhurst Cl SM1 ....217 C5
Sunnymead Ave CR4 ....203 D6
Sunnymead Ct W5 ....109 D6
Sunnymead Rd NW9 ....45 B2
Putney SW15 ....156 B6
Sunnymede Ave KT19 ....215 C1
Sunnymede Dr IG6 ....56 D5
Sunny Nook Gdns CR2 ....221 B2
Sunny Pl NW4 ....46 C5
Sunny Rd The EN3 ....6 D4
Sunnyside 3 NW2 ....69 B5
Walton-on-T KT12 ....194 C4
Wimbledon SW19 ....179 A4
Sunnyside Dr E4 ....20 A4
Sunnyside Ho 2 NW2 ....69 B5
Sunnyside Pl SW19 ....179 A4
Sunnyside Rd E10 ....53 C1
N19 ....49 D2
Ealing W5 ....109 D5
Ilford IG1 ....79 B5
Teddington TW11 ....174 B6
Sunnyside Rd E N9 ....18 A1
Sunnyside Rd N N9 ....18 A1
Sunnyside Rd S N9 ....18 A1
Sunny View NW9 ....45 B4
Sunny Way N12 ....30 C3
Sun Pas 8 SE16 ....118 A3
Sunray Ave BR2 ....210 B3
SE5,SE24 ....139 B1
Tolworth KT5 ....214 D6
Sun Rd W14 ....113 B1 254 C1
Sunrise Cl TW13 ....151 B1
Sunrise View NW7 ....27 D4
Sunset Ave Chingford E4 ....19 D3
Woodford IG8 ....36 D6
Sunset Ct 4 IG8 ....37 C3
Sunset Gdns SE25 ....183 D1
Sunset Rd SE28 ....124 A5
SE5 ....139 B1
Wimbledon SW19 ....178 B5
Sunset View EN5 ....1 A3
Sunshine Way CR4 ....180 D1
Sun St EC2 ....95 B2 242 D4
Sun St Pas EC2 ....95 C2 243 A3
Sunwell Cl SE15 ....140 B4
Superior Dr 4 BR6 ....227 D2
Surbiton Cres KT1,KT6 ....198 A5
Surbiton Ct KT6 ....197 D3
Surbiton Hall Cl KT1 ....198 A5
Surbiton High Sch KT1 ....198 A5
Surbiton High Sch Jun Sch
for Girls KT1 ....198 A5
Surbiton Hill Pk KT5 ....198 C4
Surbiton Hill Rd KT6 ....198 A4
Surbiton Hospl KT6 ....198 A3
Surbiton Prep Sch KT6 ....198 A4
Surbiton Rd KT1 ....198 A5
Surbiton Sta KT6 ....198 A3
Surcot Ho 2 SW4 ....137 D3
Surlingham Cl SE28 ....124 D6
Surma Cl E1 ....96 A3
Surmans Cl RM9 ....102 C6
Surrendale Pl W9 ....91 C3
Surrey Canal Rd SE14,
SE16,SE8 ....140 D6
Surrey Cres 1 W4 ....110 C1
Surrey Ct N3 ....47 A6
Surrey Gdns N4 ....51 A3
Surrey Gr SE17 ....263 A1
Carshalton SM1 ....218 B5
Surrey Ho 6 SE16 ....118 D5
Surrey La SW11 ....136 C4 267 B1
Surrey Lo SW20 ....178 C1
Surrey Mews SE27 ....183 C6
Surrey Mount SE23 ....162 B3
Surrey Quays Rd SE16 ....118 D4
Surrey Quays Sh Ctr
SE16 ....118 D3
Surrey Quays Sta SE16 ....118 D2
Surrey Rd SE15 ....162 D6
Barking IG11 ....79 C1
Dagenham RM10 ....81 D3
Harrow HA1 ....42 A4
West Wickham BR4 ....207 D1
Surrey Row SE1 ....116 D4 251 D2
Surrey Sq SE17 ....117 C1 263 B2
Surrey Square Inf Sch
SE17 ....117 C1 263 A2
Surrey Square Jun Sch
SE17 ....117 C1 263 A2
Surrey St 4 E13 ....99 B4
WC2 ....116 B6 250 D6
Croydon CR0 ....221 A5
Surrey Terr SE17 ....263 B2
Surrey Water Rd SE16 ....118 D5
Surrey Wharf SE1 ....140 A6
Surridge Ct 15 SW9 ....138 A3
Surridge Gdns SE19 ....183 B4
Surr St N7 ....72 A3
Sury Basin KT2 ....176 A2
Susan Constant Ct 3
E14 ....120 B6
Susan Lawrence Ho 3
E12 ....78 C4
Susan Lawrence Prim Schs
E14 ....97 D1
Susannah St E14 ....98 A1
Susan Rd SE3 ....143 B3
Susan Wood BR7 ....188 C2
Sussex Ave TW7 ....130 C2
Sussex Cl N19 ....72 A6
New Malden KT3 ....199 C5
Redbridge IG4 ....56 B4
4 Twickenham TW1 ....153 B5
Sussex Cres UB5 ....63 C2
Sussex Ct SE10 ....142 A6
W2 ....236 C1
4 Barnes SW13 ....133 D3
Mitcham CR4 ....204 A4
Sussex Gate N6 ....48 D4
Sussex Gdns N4 ....51 A4
N6 ....48 D4
W2 ....92 B1 236 D1
Chessington KT9 ....213 D2
Sussex Ho NW3 ....70 C2
Richmond TW9 ....132 B3
Sussex House Sch
SW3 ....114 D2 257 C3
Sussex Lo W2 ....236 D1
Sussex Mans SW7 ....256 C3
WC2 ....250 B6
Sussex Mews SE6 ....163 C3
Sussex Mews E W2 ....236 D1
Sussex Mews W W2 ....246 D6
Sussex Pl NW1 ....92 D3 237 C6
W2 ....92 B1 236 D1
22 W6 ....112 C1
New Malden KT3 ....199 C5
Sussex Rd DA14 ....190 B5
DA8 ....147 D5
Barking IG11 ....100 C6
Harrow HA1 ....42 A4
Mitcham CR4 ....204 A4
New Malden KT3 ....199 C5
Southall UB2 ....106 D3
South Croydon CR2 ....221 B2
Uxbridge UB10 ....61 A3
Wallington SM5 ....218 D2
2 West Wickham BR4 ....207 D1
Sussex Ring N12 ....29 C5
Sussex Sq W2 ....114 B6 246 D6
Sussex St E13 ....99 B4
SW1 ....258 D2
Sussex Way N19 ....49 D1
N7,N19 ....72 A6
Cockfosters EN4 ....15 B6
Sutcliffe Cl NW11 ....47 D4
Sutcliffe Ho UB3 ....84 A1
Sutcliffe Rd SE18 ....145 C6
Bexley DA16 ....146 C3
Sutherland Ave BR5 ....211 D4
DA16 ....145 C1
W9 ....92 A3 236 A6
Ealing W13 ....87 B1
Hayes UB3 ....106 A2
Sunbury TW16 ....171 D1
Sutherland Cl EN5 ....1 A1
Sutherland Ct N16 ....73 B5
NW9 ....44 D4
2 W9 ....91 C3
Sutherland Dr SW19 ....180 B2
Sutherland Gdns
Mortlake SW14 ....133 C2
North Cheam KT4 ....200 B1
Sunbury TW16 ....171 D1
Sutherland Gr
Putney SW18,SW19 ....157 B4
Teddington TW11 ....174 C5
Sutherland Ho 9 NW6 ....70 A2
8 SE18 ....144 B4
W8 ....255 C5
Ealing W13 ....109 A6
7 Putney SW15 ....156 C4
Richmond TW10 ....153 C2
Sutherland Pl W2 ....91 C1
Sutherland Point 1 E5 ....74 B4
Sutherland Rd E17 ....53 A6
E3 ....97 B5

Sutherland Rd *continued*
Belvedere DA17 .... 125 C3
Chiswick W4 .... 133 C6
Ealing W13 .... 87 A1
Edmonton N9 .... 18 B3
Enfield EN3 .... 18 D6
Southall UB1 .... 85 B1
Thornton Heath CR0 .... 204 C2
Tottenham N17 .... 34 A2
Sutherland Row SW1 ... 258 D2
Sutherland Sq
SE17 .... 117 A1 262 A1
Sutherland St
SW1 .... 115 B1 258 D2
Sutherland Wlk SE17 ... 262 B1
Sutlej Rd SE7 .... 143 C5
Sutterton St N7 .... 72 B2
Sutton Arc SM1 .... 217 D3
Sutton Cl
Beckenham BR3 .... 185 D2
Pinner HA5 .... 40 A4
Sutton Common Rd
Cheam SM3 .... 201 C1
Sutton SM1,SM3 .... 217 D6
Sutton Common Sta
SM1 .... 217 D6
Sutton Courtenay Ho
SW17 .... 180 B6
Sutton Court Rd E13 ...... 99 C4
Chiswick W4 .... 133 A6
Hillingdon UB10 .... 82 D6
Sutton SM1,SM2 .... 218 A2
Sutton Cres EN5 .... 12 D6
Sutton Ct 9 E5 .... 74 B4
Chiswick W4 .... 133 A6
Ealing W5 .... 110 A5
East Molesey KT8 .... 195 B4
Penge SE19 .... 183 D3
Sutton SM2 .... 218 A2
Sutton Dene TW3 .... 129 D4
Sutton Est SW3 .. 114 C1 257 B2
Sutton Est The W10 ...... 90 C2
Sutton Gdns
Barking IG11 .... 101 C5
Croydon CR0 .... 205 D4
Sutton Gn IG11 .... 101 C6
Sutton Gr SM1 .... 218 B3
Sutton Gram Sch For Boys
SM1 .... 218 A3
Sutton Hall Rd TW5 ...... 129 C5
Sutton High Sch SM1 ... 217 D2
Sutton Ho N21 .... 16 B6
Sutton La TW3,TW4,TW5 . 129 B3
Sutton La N W4 .... 111 A1
Sutton La S W4 .... 133 A6
Sutton Par NW4 .... 46 C5
Sutton Park Rd SM1,
SM2 .... 217 D2
Sutton Pl E9 .... 74 C3
Sutton Rd E13 .... 98 D3
E17 .... 34 D2
N10 .... 31 A2
Barking IG11 .... 101 C6
Heston TW5 .... 129 C4
Sutton Row W1 .... 239 D2
Sutton Sq E9 .... 74 C3
Hounslow TW5 .... 129 B4
Sutton St E1 .... 96 C1
Sutton Sta SM2 .... 218 A2
Suttons Way EC1 .... 242 B5
Sutton Way W10 .... 90 C2
Hounslow TW5 .... 129 B4
Sutton Wlk SE1 .. 116 B5 250 D3
Swaby Rd SW17,SW18 ... 158 A2
Swaffield Prim Sch
SW18 .... 158 A4
Swaffield Rd SW18 ...... 158 A4
Swain Cl SW16 .... 181 B4
Swain Rd CR7 .... 205 A4
Swains Cl UB7 .... 104 A4
Swain's La N6 .... 71 B6
Swainson Ho N7 .... 72 C4
Swainson Rd W3 .... 111 D4
Swains Rd CR4,SW17,
SW19 .... 180 D3
Swakeleys Dr UB10 ...... 60 C3
Swakeleys Rd UB10 ...... 60 C5
Swakeleys Rdbt UB8,
UB10 .... 60 A4
Swakeleys Sch UB10 ...... 82 D5
Swaledale Cl N11 .... 31 A4
Swallands Rd SE6 ...... 163 C1
Swallowbrook Bsns Ctr
UB4 .... 106 D5
Swallow Cl SE14 .... 140 D4
Bushey WD23 .... 8 A3
Swallow Ct 1 SE12 ...... 165 A4
4 W9 .... 91 C2
Chingford IG8 .... 36 B3
Ilford IG2 .... 56 D4
5 Ruislip HA4 .... 40 C1
Swallow Dr NW10 .... 67 B2
Northolt UB5 .... 85 C5
Swallowfield NW1 ...... 231 D1
Swallowfield Rd SE7 ...... 121 B1
Swallowfield Way UB3 .. 105 B4
Swallow Gdns SW16 ...... 181 D5
Swallow Ho N8 .... 50 B6
NW8 .... 230 A4
Swallow Pk KT6 .... 214 B5
Swallow Pl W1 .... 238 D1
Swallows Ct 5 SE20 ...... 184 D3
Swallow St E6 .... 100 A2
W1 .... 115 C6 249 B5
Swaminarayan Sch The
NW10 .... 67 B2
Swanage Ct 5 N1 .... 73 C1
Swanage Ho SW8 .... 270 C3
Swanage Rd SW18 ...... 158 A5
Chingford E4 .... 36 A3
Swanage Waye UB4 ...... 84 C1
Swan App E6 .... 100 A2
Swanbourne SE17 .... 262 A3
Swanbourne Ho NW8 .. 237 A6
Swanbridge Rd DA7 ...... 147 C4
Swan Cl E17 .... 35 A3
Croydon CR0 .... 205 C2
Feltham TW13 .... 173 A6
Swan Ct E14 .... 97 B1
N20 .... 14 A2
SW3 .... 257 B1
SW6 .... 265 A3
Swan Ctr SW17 .... 158 A1
Swandon Way SW18 ...... 135 D1
Swan Dr NW9 .... 27 C1
Swanfield St E2 .... 95 D4
Swan Ho N1 .... 73 B1
Enfield EN3 .... 18 C6
Swan La EC4 ..... 117 B6 252 D5
N20 .... 14 A1
Loughton IG10 .... 21 C4
Swan Lane Pier
EC4 .... 117 B6 252 C5
Swanlea Sec Sch E1 ...... 96 B3
Swanley Ho SE17 .... 263 B2
Swanley Rd DA16 .... 146 C4
Swan Mead SE1 . 117 C3 263 A5
Swan Mews SW9 .... 138 B3
Swanmore Ct SW18 ...... 158 A5
Swann Ct 6 TW7 .... 131 A2
Swanne Ho 12 SE10 ...... 142 A5
Swan Pas 4 E1 .... 118 A6
Swan Pl SW13 .... 133 D3
Swan Rd SE16 .... 118 C4
SE18 .... 121 D3
Feltham TW13 .... 173 A6
Southall UB1 .... 85 D1
West Drayton UB7 .... 104 A4
Swanscombe Ho
1 BR5 .... 190 B1
11 W11 .... 112 D5
Swanscombe Point 7
E16 .... 98 D2
Swanscombe Rd W11 ... 112 D5
5 W4 .... 111 C1
Swansea Ct E16 .... 122 D5
Swansea Rd Enfield EN3 ..... 6 C1
Harlington TW14,TW6 ...... 149 B5
Swansland Gdns E17 ...... 35 A2
Swansmere Sch KT12 ... 194 C1
Swan St SE1 ..... 117 A4 252 B1
Isleworth TW7 .... 131 B2
Swan The BR4 .... 224 A6
Swanton Gdns SW19 ... 156 D3
Swanton Rd DA8 .... 147 D5
Swan Way EN3 .... 6 D3
Swanwick Cl SW15 ...... 155 D4
Swan Wlk SW3 .. 136 D6 267 C6
Oatlands Park TW17 ...... 193 C2
Swan Yd N1 .... 72 D2
Swaton Rd E3 .... 97 C3
Swaylands Rd DA17 ...... 147 C6
Swaythling Cl N18 .... 34 B6
Swaythling Ho 2 SW15 . 155 D5
Swedenborg Gdns E1 ... 118 B6
Swede Gate SE16 .... 119 A2
Swedish Sch The SW13 . 133 D6
Sweeney Cres SE1 .... 253 D1
Sweet Briar Gn N9 .... 17 D1
Sweet Briar Gr N9 .... 17 D1
Sweet Briar Wlk N18 ...... 33 D6
Sweetcroft La UB10 ...... 60 C1
Sweetmans Ave HA5 ...... 40 D6
Sweets Way N20 .... 14 B2
Swell Ct E17 .... 53 D3
Swetenham Wlk SE18 ... 123 A1
Swete St E13 .... 99 A5
Sweyn Pl SE3 .... 143 A3
Swift Cl E17 .... 35 A3
Harrow HA2 .... 63 D6
Hayes UB3 .... 83 D1
Swift Ct SM2 .... 217 D1
Swift Ctr CR0 .... 220 B1
Swift Ho 24 E1 .... 96 C1
15 N16 .... 73 C5
1 SW9 .... 138 C5
8 Wanstead E18 .... 55 B6
Swift Rd Feltham TW13 ... 173 A6
Southall UB2 .... 107 B3
Swiftsden Way BR1 ...... 186 C4
Swift St SW6 ...... 135 B4 264 C2
Swinbrook Rd W10 .... 91 A2
Swinburne Cres CR0 .... 206 C3
Swinburne Ct 4 SE5 ...... 139 B1
Swinburne Ho 15 E2 ...... 96 C4
Swinburne Rd SW15 ...... 134 A1
Swinderby Rd HA0 .... 66 A2
Swindon Cl IG3 .... 57 C1
Swindon Rd TW6 .... 149 A6
Swindon St W12 .... 112 C5
Swinfield Cl TW13 .... 173 A6
Swinford Gdns SW9 ...... 138 D2
Swingate La SE18 .... 145 C5
Swingfield Ho 5 E9 ...... 96 C6
Swinley Ho NW1 .... 231 D2
Swinnerton St E9 .... 75 A3
Swinton Cl HA9 .... 44 D1
Swinton Ho 17 E2 .... 96 A4
Swinton Pl WC1 .... 233 C2
Swinton St WC1 .... 94 B4 233 C2
Swires Shaw BR2 .... 225 D4
Swiss Cottage NW3 ...... 70 B1
Swiss Cottage Sch
NW8 .... 92 B6 229 D6
Swiss Cottage Sta NW3 .. 70 B1
Swiss Re Building★
EC2 .... 243 B2
Swiss Terr 7 NW3 .... 70 B1
Swithland Gdns SE9 ...... 188 C6
Swyncombe Ave W5 ...... 109 B2
Swynford Gdns 7 NW4 ... 46 A5
Sybil Elgar Sch UB2 ...... 107 B3
Sybil Mews N4 .... 50 D3
Sybil Phoenix Cl SE8 .... 118 D1
Sybil Thorndike Casson Ho
SW5 .... 255 B1
Sybil Thorndike Ho 7
N1 .... 73 A2
Sybourn Inf Sch Annexe
E10 .... 53 A1
Sybourn Jun & Inf Schs
E17 .... 53 B2
Sybourn St E17 .... 53 B2
Sycamore Ave DA15 ...... 167 D5
N3 .... 47 D6
W5 .... 109 D3
Bow E3 .... 97 B6
Hayes UB3 .... 105 C6
Sycamore Cl E16 .... 98 C3
W3 .... 111 C5
2 HA8 .... 27 A6
Carshalton SM5 .... 218 D4
Chislehurst SE9 .... 166 A2
Edmonton N9 .... 34 A6
Feltham TW13 .... 150 A1
New Barnet EN4 .... 14 B5
Northolt UB5 .... 85 A6
South Croydon CR2 .... 221 C3
Yiewsley UB7 .... 104 B6
Sycamore Ct E7 .... 77 A2
N19 .... 71 D5
NW6 .... 91 C6
SE12 .... 164 D5
4 SE5 .... 139 A4
Forest Hill SE26 .... 184 C6
Hillingdon UB8 .... 82 C3
Hounslow TW4 .... 129 A1
Surbiton KT6 .... 198 A2
10 West Norwood SW16 . 182 C5
Sycamore Gdns N15 ...... 51 D5
W6,W12 .... 112 B3
Mitcham CR4 .... 180 B1
Sycamore Gr NW9 .... 45 A2
SE6 .... 164 A5
Kingston KT3 .... 199 C6
Penge SE20 .... 184 A2
Sycamore Hill N11 .... 31 A4
Sycamore Ho 2 N16 ...... 73 B6
18 N2 .... 30 B1
10 NW3 .... 70 D2
17 SE16 .... 118 D4
3 W6 .... 112 B4
4 Buckhurst Hill IG9 ...... 21 D2
Penge SE20 .... 184 D4
Sycamore Lo
7 Ashford TW16 .... 171 D3
Putney SW15 .... 134 B2
Sycamore Mews 4
SW4 .... 137 C2
Sycamore Rd SW19,
SW20 .... 178 C4
Sycamore St EC1 .... 242 A5
Sycamore Way TW11 ...... 175 C4
Sycamore Wlk 1 W10 .... 91 A3
Ilford IG6 .... 57 A5
Sydenham Ave
Penge SE26 .... 184 B5
Southgate N21 .... 16 B6
Sydenham High Sch For Girls
SE26 .... 184 B6
Sydenham Hill SE21,
SE22,SE23,SE26,SE19 ... 162 A1
Sydenham Hill Sta
SE21 .... 161 D1
Sydenham Ho 16 KT6 ... 197 D2
Sydenham Ind Est SE26 . 185 B5
Sydenham Park Mans 2
SE26 .... 162 C1
Sydenham Park Rd
SE23,SE26 .... 162 C1
Sydenham Pk SE26 ...... 162 C1
Sydenham Rd
Forest Hill SE26 .... 184 D5
Forest Hill SE26 .... 185 A6
Thornton Heath CR0 ...... 205 B2
Sydenham Rise SE23 ... 162 B2
Sydenham Sec Sch
SE26 .... 162 B1
Sydenham Sta SE26 ...... 184 C6
Sydenham Station App
SE26 .... 184 C6
Sydmons Ct SE23 .... 162 C4
Sydner Mews N16 .... 73 D4
Sydner Rd N16 .... 73 D4
Sydney Cl SW3 .... 256 D3
Sydney Cotts KT10 ...... 212 D2
Sydney Cres TW15 ...... 170 D4
Sydney Ct Hayes UB4 ..... 84 C3
Surbiton KT6 .... 214 A6
Sydney Gr NW4 .... 46 C4
Sydney Ho 4 W4 .... 111 C2
Sydney Mews SW3 ...... 256 D3
Sydney Pl SW7 .... 257 A3
Sydney Rd DA6 .... 146 D1
N10 .... 31 B3
N8 .... 50 C5
SE2 .... 124 D3
Ealing W13 .... 109 A4
East Bedfont TW14 .... 150 A3
Enfield EN2 .... 5 B1
Richmond TW10,TW9 ...... 132 A1
Sidcup DA14 .... 189 C6
Sutton SM1 .... 217 C4
Teddington TW11 .... 174 D5
Wanstead E11 .... 55 B3
West Barnes SW20 .... 178 D1
Woodford IG8 .... 37 A6
Sydney Russell Sch The
RM9 .... 80 D3
Sydney St SW3 .. 114 C1 257 A2
Sydney Terr KT10 .... 212 D2
Sylva Ct 3 SW15 .... 156 D4
Sylvana Cl UB10 .... 82 B6
Sylvan Ave N3 .... 29 C1
NW7 .... 27 D4
Dagenham RM6 .... 59 B3
Wood Green N22 .... 32 C3
Sylvan Ct N12 .... 29 D6
South Croydon CR2 ...... 221 A2
Sylvan Gdns KT6 .... 197 D2
Sylvan Gr NW2 .... 68 D4
SE15 .... 140 B6
Sylvan Hill SE19 .... 183 C2
Sylvan Ho N21 .... 16 B6
Sylvan Rd E17 .... 53 C4
E7 .... 77 B2
Ilford IG1 .... 79 A6
South Norwood SE19 ..... 183 D2
Wanstead E11 .... 55 A4
Sylvan Way
Coney Hall BR4 .... 224 C4
Dagenham RM8 .... 80 B5
Sylvan Wlk BR1 .... 210 B6
Sylverdale Rd CR0 ...... 220 D5
Sylvester Ave BR7 ...... 188 B4
Sylvester Ho 7 E8 ...... 74 B2
Sylvester Path 8 E8 ...... 74 B2
Sylvester Rd E17 .... 53 B2
E8 .... 74 B2
N2 .... 30 B1
Wembley HA0 .... 65 C3
Sylvestrus Cl KT1 .... 176 C1
Sylvia Ave HA5 .... 23 B4
Sylvia Cotts 3 SE8 ...... 141 C4
Sylvia Ct N1 .... 235 C3
Wembley HA9 .... 66 D1
Sylvia Gdns HA9 .... 66 D1
Sylvia Pankhurst Ho
14 E2 .... 96 D4
10 Dagenham RM10 ...... 81 C5
Sylvia Young Theatre Sch
NW1 .... 237 B5
Symes Mews NW1 ...... 232 A4
Symington Ho SE1 ...... 262 C5
Symington Mews E9 ...... 74 D3
Symister Mews N1 .... 95 C4
Symons St SW3 . 114 D2 257 D3
Symphony Mews 16 W10 . 91 A4
Syon Gate Way
Brentford TW7,TW8 ...... 131 A5
Brentford TW8 .... 131 B5
Syon Ho TW8 .... 131 C2
Syon La
Brentford TW7,TW8 ...... 131 B5
Hounslow TW7 .... 130 D6
Syon Lane Sta TW7 ...... 131 A5
Syon Lo 6 SE12 .... 165 A4
Syon Park Cotts TW8 .... 131 C2
Syon Park Gdns TW7 .... 130 D5
Syringa Ho SE4 .... 141 B2

T

Tabard Ct 3 E14 .... 98 A1
Tabard Ho SE1 .... 262 D6
Teddington KT1 .... 175 C2
Tabard St SE1 .... 117 B3 262 C6
Tabernacle Ave 7 E13 .... 99 A3
Tabernacle St
EC2 .... 95 B3 242 D6
Tableer Ave SW4 .... 159 D6
Tabley Rd N7 .... 72 A4
Tabor Ct 3 SM3 .... 217 A2
Tabor Gdns SM2,SM3 .... 217 B1
Tabor Gr SW19 .... 179 B3
Tabor Rd W6 .... 112 B3
Tachbrook Est
SW1 .... 115 D1 259 D1
Tachbrook Mews SW1 .. 259 A4
Tachbrook Rd
East Bedfont TW14 ...... 149 D4
Southall UB2 .... 106 D2
Tachbrook St
SW1 .... 115 C2 259 B3
Tack Mews SE4 .... 141 C2
Tadbourne Ct 1 HA8 ..... 27 A3
Tadema Ho NW8 .... 236 D5
Tadema Rd
SW10 .... 136 A5 266 B3
Tadlow KT1 .... 198 C6
Tadmor Cl TW16 .... 193 D5
Tadmor St W12 .... 112 D5
Tadworth Ave KT3 ...... 199 D4
Tadworth Ho SE1 .... 251 C1
Tadworth Rd NW2 .... 68 A6
Taeping St E14 .... 119 D2
Taffy's How CR4 .... 202 C6
Taft Way 44 E3 .... 97 D4
Taggs Ho KT1 .... 175 D1
Tailworth St 15 E1 ...... 96 A2
Tait 7 NW9 .... 27 D3
Tait Ct 9 E3 .... 97 B6
SW8 .... 269 D2
Tait Ho 2 N19 .... 71 C4
SE1 .... 251 B3
Tait Rd CR0 .... 205 C2
Tait Rd Ind Est CR0 ...... 205 C2
Takhar Mews SW11 ...... 136 C3
Talacre Rd NW5 .... 71 A2
Talbot Ave N2 .... 48 B6
Talbot Cl N15 .... 51 D5
Talbot Cres NW4 .... 46 A4
Talbot Ct EC3 .... 252 D6
NW9 .... 67 B5
Talbot Gdns IG3 .... 80 A6
Talbot Grove Ho 9 W11 .. 91 A1
Talbot Ho E14 .... 97 D1
N7 .... 72 C5
Talbot Pl SE3 .... 142 C3
Talbot Rd E7 .... 77 A4
N15 .... 51 D5
N6 .... 49 A3
SE22 .... 139 C1
W11 .... 91 B1
W2 .... 91 C1
Ashford TW15 .... 170 A5
Dagenham RM9 .... 81 B1
Ealing W13 .... 109 A5
Harrow HA3 .... 24 D1
Isleworth TW1,TW7 ...... 131 A1
Southall UB2 .... 107 A2
South Norwood CR7 ...... 205 B5
Twickenham TW2 .... 152 D3
Wallend E6 .... 100 C5
Wallington SM5 .... 219 A3
Wembley HA0 .... 65 D2
Wood Green N22 .... 31 C2
Talbot Sq W2 ..... 92 B1 236 C1
Talbot Wlk NW10 .... 67 C2
W11 .... 91 A1
Talbot Yd SE1 .... 252 C3
Talcott Path 12 SW2 ..... 160 C3
Talfourd Pl SE15 .... 139 D4
Talfourd Rd SE15 .... 139 D4
Talgarth Rd
W14 .... 113 A1 254 B2
W6 .... 112 D1
Talgarth Wlk NW9 .... 45 C4
Talia Ho E14 .... 120 A3
Talina Ctr SW6 .... 266 A1
Talisman Cl 2 IG3 .... 58 B1
Talisman Sq SE26 .... 184 A6
Talisman Way HA9 .... 66 B5
Tallack Cl HA3 .... 24 C3
Tallack Rd E10 .... 53 B1
Tall Elms Cl BR2 .... 208 D4
Talleyrand Ho SE5 ...... 139 A3
Tallis Cl E16 .... 99 B1
Tallis Gr SE7 .... 143 B6
Tallis St EC4 .... 251 B6
Tallis View NW10 .... 67 B2
Tall Trees SW16 .... 204 B6
Talma Gdns TW2 .... 152 C4
Talmage Cl SE23 .... 162 C4
Talman Gr HA7 .... 25 D4
Talma Rd SW2 .... 138 C1
Talmudical Coll N16 ...... 51 B2
Talmud Torah Sch N16 ... 51 D2
Talwin St E3 .... 97 D4
Tamar Cl E3 .... 97 B6
Tamar Ho SE11 .... 261 B2
Tamarind Ct 8 W3 .... 89 A1
Tamarind Ho 4 SE15 ...... 140 A5
Tamarind Yd 5 E1 .... 118 A5
Tamarisk Sq W12 .... 111 D6
Tamar Sq IG8 .... 37 B4
Tamar St SE7 .... 122 A2
Tamar Way N17 .... 52 A6
Tamesa Ho TW17 .... 192 C2
Tamesis Gdns KT4 .... 215 C6
Tamian Ind Est TW4 ...... 128 C1
Tamian Way TW4 .... 128 C1
Tamworth N7 .... 72 A2
Tamworth Ave IG8 .... 36 C4
Tamworth La CR4 .... 203 B6
Tamworth Manor High Sch
CR4 .... 203 D6
Tamworth Pk CR4 .... 203 B6
Tamworth Pl 3 CR0 ...... 221 A6
Tamworth Rd CR0 .... 221 A6
Tamworth St
SW6 .... 135 C6 265 A5
Tancred Rd N4 .... 50 D3
Tandem Ctr SW19 .... 180 B2
Tandridge Ct SM2 .... 217 D2
Tandridge Dr BR5,BR6 ... 211 B1
Tandridge Pl 2 BR6 ...... 211 B1
Tanfield Ave NW2 .... 67 D5
Tanfield Rd CR0 .... 221 A4
Tangier Rd TW10 .... 132 D2
Tangleberry Cl BR1 ...... 210 B5
Tangle Tree Cl N3 .... 29 D1
Tanglewood Cl
Hillingdon UB10 .... 82 C3
South Croydon CR0 ...... 222 C5
Stanmore HA7 .... 8 C2
Tanglewood Way TW13 . 150 B1
Tangley Gr SW15 .... 155 D4
Tangley Park Rd TW12 . 173 B4
Tanglyn Ave TW17 .... 192 D4
Tangmere WC1 .... 233 C1
Tottenham N17 .... 33 B1
Tangmere Gdns UB5 ...... 84 C5
Tangmere Gr KT2 .... 175 D5
Tangmere Way NW9 ...... 27 C1
Tanhurst Ho 27 SW2 ...... 160 A4
Tankerton Rd KT6 .... 214 B6
Tankerton St WC1 .... 233 B1
Tankerton Terr CR0 ...... 204 B3
Tankerville Rd SW16 ... 182 A3
Tankridge Rd NW2 .... 68 B6
Tanner Ho SE1 .... 253 B1
1 Merton SW19 .... 180 A2
Tanner Point E13 .... 99 A6
Tanners Cl KT12 .... 194 B3
Tanners End La N18 ...... 33 C5
Tanner's Hill SE8 .... 141 C4
Tanners La IG6 .... 57 A6
Tanner St SE1 .... 117 C4 253 B1
Barking IG11 .... 79 A2
Tanners Yd 32 E2 .... 96 B5
Tannery Cl
Beckenham BR3,CR0 ...... 206 D4
Dagenham RM10 .... 81 D5
Tannery Ho 20 E1 .... 96 A2
Tannington Terr N5 ...... 72 C5
Tannsfeld Rd SE26 ...... 184 D5
Tansley Cl N7 .... 71 D3
Tanswell St SE1 .... 251 A1
Tansy Cl E6 .... 100 C1
Tantallon Rd SW12 ...... 159 A3
Tant Ave E16 .... 98 D1
Tantony Gr RM6 .... 58 D6
Tanworth Gdns HA5 ...... 22 C1
Tan Yard La DA5 .... 169 C4
Tanza Rd NW3 .... 70 D4
Tapestry Cl SM2 .... 217 D1
Tapley Ho 11 SE1 .... 118 A4
Taplow NW3 .... 70 B1
Taplow Ct CR4 .... 202 C5
Taplow Ho 36 E2 .... 95 D4
Taplow Rd N13 .... 33 A6
Taplow St N1 ...... 95 A5 235 B3
Tappesfield Rd SE15 ...... 140 C2
Tapping Cl 5 KT2 .... 176 C3
Tapp St E1 .... 96 B3
Tapster St EN5 .... 1 B2
Tara Ct
4 Beckenham BR3 ...... 185 D1
9 Buckhurst Hill IG9 ...... 21 C2
Taranto Ho 11 E1 .... 96 D2
Tarbert Rd SE22 .... 161 C6
Tarbert Wlk E1 .... 118 C6
Target Cl TW14 .... 149 C5
Target Ho W13 .... 109 B5
Target Rdbt UB5 .... 85 B6
Tariff Rd N17 .... 34 A4
Tarleton Ct 2 N22 .... 32 C1
Tarleton Gdns SE23 ...... 162 B3
Tarling Cl DA14 .... 168 B1
Tarling Ho 27 E1 .... 96 B1
Tarling Rd E16 .... 98 D1
N2 .... 30 A1
Tarling St E1 .... 96 C1
Tarnbank EN2 .... 16 A6
Tarnbrook Ct SW1 .... 258 A3
Tarn St SE1 ...... 117 A3 262 A5
Tarns The NW1 .... 232 A2
Tarnwood Pk SE9 .... 166 B3
Tarplett Ho 22 SE14 ...... 140 D6
Tarquin Ho SE26 .... 184 A6
Tarragon Cl SE14 .... 141 A5
Tarragon Gr SE26 .... 184 D4
Tarranbrae NW6 .... 69 A1
Tarrant Ho E2 .... 96 C4
Tarrant Pl W1 .... 237 C3
Tarrantt Ho W14 .... 254 B5
Tarriff Cres SE8 .... 119 B2
Tarrington Cl SW16 ...... 159 D1
Tartan Ho 8 E14 .... 98 A1
Tarver Rd SE17 .. 116 D1 261 D2
Tarves Way SE10 .... 141 D5
Tash Pl N11 .... 31 B5
Tasker Cl UB7 .... 127 A5
Tasker Ho 18 E14 .... 97 B2
Barking IG11 .... 101 B5
Tasker Rd NW3 .... 70 D3
Tasman Ct 9 E14 .... 119 D2
Ashford TW16 .... 171 C3
Tasman Ho 17 E1 .... 118 B5
Tasmania Terr N18 .... 33 A4
Tasman Rd SW9 .... 138 A2
Tasman Wlk E16 .... 99 D1
Tasso Rd W6 ..... 135 A6 264 A6
Tasso Yd W6 .... 264 A5
Tatchbury Ho 3 SW15 . 155 D5
Tate Britain★
SW1 .... 116 A2 260 A3
Tate Gdns WD23 .... 8 C4
Tate Ho 13 E2 .... 96 D5
Tate Modern★
EC4 .... 116 D5 251 C3
Tate Rd Newham E16 ..... 122 B5
Sutton SM1 .... 217 C3
Tatham Pl NW8 .... 92 B5 229 D4
Tatnell Rd SE23 .... 163 A5
Tattersall Cl SE9 .... 166 A6
Tatton Cres E5,N16 ...... 51 D2
Tatum Rd NW10 .... 67 B1
Tatum St SE17 ... 117 C2 262 D3
Tauheed Cl N4 .... 73 A6
Taunton Ave
Hounslow TW3 .... 130 A3
Wimbledon SW20 .... 178 B1
Taunton Cl SM3 .... 201 C1
Taunton Dr N2 .... 30 A1
Enfield EN2 .... 4 C2
Taunton Ho W2 .... 236 A1
Taunton Mews NW1 ...... 237 C5
Taunton Pl NW1 .. 92 D3 237 C6
Taunton Rd SE12 .... 164 D6
Greenford UB6 .... 85 D6
Taunton Way HA7 .... 26 A1
Tavern Cl SM5 .... 202 C2
Taverner Ho N16 .... 73 B5
Taverners Cl W11 .... 244 A3
Taverners Ct HA9 .... 66 B6
Taverner Sq 4 N5 .... 73 A4
Taverners Way E4 .... 20 C3
Tavern La SW9 .... 138 C3
Tavistock Ave E17 .... 53 A6
NW7 .... 28 D3
Wembley UB6 .... 87 A5
Tavistock Cl N16 .... 73 C3
Tavistock Cres W11 ...... 91 B2
Mitcham CR4 .... 204 A5
Tavistock Ct WC1 .... 239 D6
1 Croydon CR0 .... 205 B1
Tavistock Gdns IG3 ...... 79 C4
Tavistock Gr CR0 .... 205 B2
Tavistock Ho 2 W11 ...... 91 B2
Tavistock Mews 1 W11 .. 91 B1
Tavistock Pl WC1 .. 94 A3 240 A6
East Barnet N14 .... 15 B5
Tavistock Rd DA16 ...... 146 C4
E15 .... 76 D2

Tavistock Rd *continued*
E7 76 D4
N4,N15 51 B3
NW10 89 D5
W11 91 B2
4 Beckenham BR2 208 D5
Carshalton SM5 202 B1
Croydon CR0 205 B1
Edgware HA8 26 C2
Uxbridge UB10 61 A3
Wanstead E18 55 A6
Tavistock Sq
WC1 93 D3 239 D6
Tavistock St
WC2 116 A6 250 B6
Tavistock Terr N19 71 D5
Tavistock Twr SE16 119 A3
Tavistock Wlk SM5 202 B1
Taviton St WC1 93 D3 239 C6
Tavy Bridge SE2 124 C4
Tavy Cl SE11 261 B2
Tawney Rd SE28 124 B6
Tawny Cl Ealing W13 109 B5
Feltham TW13 150 A1
Tawny Way SE16 118 D2
Tayben Ave TW2 152 C5
Taybridge Rd SW11 137 A1
Tayburn Cl E14 98 A1
Tayfield Cl UB10 61 A5
Tay Ho 8 E3 97 B5
Tayler Ct NW8 229 C6
Taylor Ave TW9 132 D3
Taylor Cl 3 BR6 227 D4
Hampton TW12 174 A5
Hounslow TW3 130 A4
Tottenham N17 34 A3
Taylor Ct E15 76 A3
Ealing W13 109 C5
Penge SE20 184 C1
Taylor Ho 10 SW2 160 C3
Taylor Rd Mitcham CR4 180 C3
Wallington SM6 219 B3
Taylor's Bldgs SE18 122 D2
Taylors Cl DA14 167 D1
Taylors Ct TW13 150 A2
Taylor's Gn W3 89 C1
Taylor's La NW10 67 C1
Barnet EN5 1 B4
Forest Hill SE26 184 B6
Taylorsmead NW7 28 A5
Taymount Grange 2
SE23 162 C2
Taymount Rise SE23 162 C2
Tayport Cl N1 72 A1
Tayside Ct 6 SE5 139 B1
Tayside Dr HA8 10 D2
Taywood Rd UB5 85 B4
Teak Cl SE16 119 A5
Tealby Ct N7 72 B2
Teal Cl E16 99 D2
Teal Ct NW10 67 B2
30 SE8 141 B6
Wallington SM6 219 C3
Teale St E2 96 A5
Tealing Dr KT19 215 B4
Teal Pl SM1 217 B3
Teasel Cl CR0 206 D1
Teasel Way E15 98 C4
Teather St 20 SE5 139 C5
Tebbs Ho 14 SW2 160 C4
Tebworth Rd N17 33 D3
Teck Cl TW7 131 A3
Tedder 5 NW9 27 D3
Tedder Cl
Chessington KT9 213 C3
Hillingdon UB10 60 B1
Tedder Rd CR2 222 D1
Teddington Memorial Hospl
TW11 174 C4
Teddington Park Rd
TW11 174 D6
Teddington Pk TW11 174 D5
Teddington Sch TW11 175 C4
Teddington Sta TW11 175 A4
Ted Hennem Ho RM10 81 D5
Ted Roberts Ho 24 E2 96 B5
Tedworth Gdns SW3 257 C1
Tedworth Sq
SW3 114 D1 257 C1
Tees Ave UB6 86 D5
Tees Ct W7 86 B1
Teesdale Ave TW7 131 A4
Teesdale Cl E2 96 B5
Teesdale Gdns
Isleworth TW7 131 A4
South Norwood SE25 183 C1
Teesdale Rd E11 54 D2
Teesdale St E2 96 B5
Teesdale Yd 33 E2 96 B5
Teeswater Ct DA18 124 D3
Tee The W3 89 C1
Teevan Cl CR0 206 A2
Teevan Rd CR0 206 A2
Teignmouth Cl 6 SW4 137 D1
Edgware HA8 26 B1
Teignmouth Gdns UB6 87 A4
Teignmouth Rd NW2 68 D2
Bexley DA16 146 C3
Telcote Way HA4 40 C2
Telegraph Hill NW3 69 D5
Telegraph La KT10 212 D3
Telegraph Mews IG3 58 A1
Telegraph Pl E14 119 D2
Telegraph Rd SW15 156 C4
Telegraph St EC2 242 C2
Telemann Sq SE3 143 B2
Telfer Cl 4 W3 111 A4
Telfer Ho EC1 234 D1
8 Dulwich SE21 183 C6
Telferscot JMI Sch
SW12 159 D3
Telferscot Prim Sch
SW12 159 D3
Telferscot Rd SW12 159 D3
Telford Ave SW12,SW2 160 A3
Telford Avenue Mans 7
SW2 160 A3
Telford Cl E17 53 A2
Penge SE19 183 D4
Telford Dr KT12 194 C2
Telford Ho SE1 262 A6
8 W10 91 A2
2 Belvedere DA17 125 C3
Telford Parade Mans 8
SW2 160 A3
Telford Rd 2 NW9 46 A3
W10 91 A2
Sidcup BR7,DA15 167 B2
Southall UB1 85 D1
Twickenham TW4 151 C4
Telford Rd (North Circular Rd) N11 31 C5
Telford Terr SW1 269 A6
Telford Way W3 89 C2
Hayes UB4 85 A2
Telham Rd E6 100 C5
Tell Gr SE22 139 D1
Tellson Ave SE18 144 A4
Telscombe Cl BR6 227 C6
Telscombe Ho SW11 268 A1
Temair Ho 1 SE10 142 A5
Temeraire St SE16 118 C4
Temperley Rd SW12 159 A4
Templar Ct RM7 59 D5
Templar Dr SE28 102 D1
Templar Ho 9 E5 74 C6
NW2 69 B2
Templar Pl TW12 173 C3
Templars Ave NW11 47 B3
Templars Cres N3 29 C1
Templars Dr HA3 24 B4
Templars Ho E15 75 D3
Templar St SE5 138 D3
Temple Ave EC4 116 C6 251 B6
N20 14 B4
Croydon CR0 223 B5
Dagenham RM8 59 C1
Temple Cl E11 54 C2
N3 29 B1
SE18 123 A3
Templecombe Rd E9 96 C6
Templecombe Way
SM4 201 A4
Templecroft TW15 171 B4
Temple Ct SW8 270 A3
Templedene BR2 186 B1
Temple Dwellings 7 E2 96 B5
Temple Fortune Ct 9
NW11 47 B4
Temple Fortune Hill
NW11 47 C4
Temple Fortune Ho 3
NW11 47 B4
Temple Fortune La
NW11 47 C3
Temple Fortune Par 5
NW11 47 B4
Temple Gdns NW11 47 B3
Dagenham RM8 80 D5
Edmonton N21 16 D2
Temple Gr NW11 47 C3
Enfield EN2 4 D2
Temple Hall Ct 1 E4 20 B2
Temple Ho 11 E17 53 D6
4 N7 71 C5
13 SW11 136 C2
Templehof Ave NW2 46 C2
Temple La EC4 94 C1 241 B1
Temple Lo EN5 14 B4
Templeman Rd W7 86 D2
Templemead Cl W3 89 C1
Temple Mead Cl HA7 25 B4
Templemead Ho E9 75 A4
Temple Mills La E10,E15 76 A4
Temple Mills Rd E9 75 C4
Templemore DA14 190 B5
Temple Par EN5 14 B4
Temple Pk UB8 82 C4
Temple Pl WC2 116 B6 250 D6
Temple Rd E6 100 A6
N8 50 B5
NW2 68 C5
W4 111 A3
W5 109 D3
Croydon CR0 221 B4
Isleworth TW3 130 A1
Richmond TW9 132 B2
Temple Sheen SW14 155 A6
Temple Sheen Rd
SW14 133 A1
Temple St E2 96 B5
Temple Sta
WC2 116 C6 251 A6
Temple Terr N22 32 C1
Templeton Ave E4 35 D6
Templeton Cl 25 N16 73 C3
South Norwood SE19 183 B2
Templeton Ct E10 53 D1
Templeton Pl
SW5 113 C2 255 B3
Templeton Rd N4,N15 51 B3
Temple Way SM1 218 B5
Temple West Mews
SE11 261 C5
Templewood W13 87 B2
Templewood Ave NW3 69 D5
Templewood Gdns NW3 69 D5
Templewood Point NW2 69 B6
Tempsford Cl EN2 5 A2
Tempsford Ct HA1 42 D3
Temsford Cl HA2 24 A1
Tenbury Cl E7 77 D3
Tenbury Ct SW12 159 D3
Tenby Ave HA3 25 B1
Tenby Cl N15 51 D5
Dagenham RM6 59 A3
Tenby Ct E17 53 A4
Tenby Gdns UB5 63 C2
Tenby Ho N7 72 C4
W2 236 A1
Hayes UB3 105 A3
Tenby Rd DA16 146 D4
E17 53 A4
Dagenham RM6 59 A3
Edgware HA8 26 B1
Enfield EN3 6 C1
Tench St E1 118 B5
Tenda Rd SE16 118 B2
Tendring Ho SW2 160 C5
Tendring Way RM6 58 C4
Tenham Ave SW2 159 D2
Tenison Ct W1 249 A6
Tenison Way SE1 251 A3
Tenniel Cl W2 245 D6
Tennison Ave WD6 10 D6
Tennison Rd SE25 205 D4
Tennis St SE1 117 B4 252 C2
Tenniswood Rd EN1 5 C4
Tennyson Ave E12 78 A1
NW9 45 A6
Twickenham TW1 152 D3
Wanstead E11 55 A2
West Barnes KT3 200 B4
Tennyson Cl DA16 145 D4
Enfield EN3 18 D6
Feltham TW14 150 A5
Tennyson Ct SW6 265 D1
3 Richmond TW10 175 D6
Tennyson Ho SE17 262 B2
2 Erith DA17 125 B1
Tennyson Rd E10 75 D6
E15 76 C1
E17 53 B3
NW6 91 B6
NW7 28 A5
Ashford TW15 170 A5
Ealing W7 108 D6
Hounslow TW3 130 A3
Penge SE20 184 D3
Wimbledon SW19 180 A4
Tennyson St SW8 137 B3
Tensing Ct TW19 148 A3
Tensing Ho N1 72 D2
Tensing Rd UB2 107 C3
Tentelow La UB2 107 D3
Tenterden Cl NW4 46 D6
SE9 188 B6
Tenterden Dr NW4 46 D6
Tenterden Gdns NW4 46 D6
Croydon CR0 206 A2
Tenterden Gr NW4 46 D6
Tenterden Ho SE17 263 B2
Tenterden Rd
Croydon CR0 206 A2
Dagenham RM8 81 B6
Tottenham N17 33 D3
Tenterden St W1 238 D1
Tenter Ground E1 243 C3
Tent Peg La BR5 211 A4
Tent St E1 96 B3
Tenzing Ct 4 SE9 166 A2
Terborah Way 6 SE22 161 C6
Terence Ct 6 DA17 147 B6
Terence Messenger Twr
E10 75 D6
Teresa Mews E17 53 C5
Teresa Wlk N10 49 B4
Terling Cl E11 76 D5
Terling Ho W10 90 C2
Terling Rd RM8 81 C6
Terling Wlk N1 235 A6
Terminal Rdbt TW6 149 A5
Terminus Pl SW1 258 D5
Tern Ho 8 SE15 139 D4
Terrace Ave NW10 90 C4
Terrace Gdns SW13 133 D3
Terrace La TW10 154 A5
Terrace Rd E13 99 B6
E9 74 C1
Walton-on-T KT12 194 B3
Terraces The 6 SW20 178 D3
Terrace The EC4 241 B1
N2 49 A5
NW6 91 C6
9 SE8 119 B2
SW13,SW14 133 C3
Chingford E4 20 C1
1 Woodford IG8 37 A4
Terrace Wlk RM9 81 A3
Terrapin Ct SW17 159 B1
Terrapin Rd SW17 159 B1
Terrapins KT6 197 D2
Terrick Rd N22 32 A2
Terrick St W12 90 B1
Terrilands HA5 41 B6
Territorial Ho SE11 261 B3
Terront Rd N15 51 A5
Terry Ho SW2 160 C3
Tersha St TW9 132 B1
Tessa Sanderson Pl 6
SW8 137 B2
Tessa Sanderson Way
UB6 64 B3
Testerton Wlk 3 W11 112 D6
Testwood Ct W7 108 C6
Tetcott Rd
SW10 136 A5 266 A3
Tetherdown N10 49 A6
Tetherdown Prim Sch
N10 49 A5
Tetty Way BR1,BR2 187 A1
Teversham La
SW8 138 A4 270 B2
Teviot Cl DA16 146 B4
Teviot St E14 98 A2
Tewkesbury Ave
Forest Hill SE23 162 B4
Pinner HA5 41 A4
Tewkesbury Cl N15 51 B3
Tewkesbury Gdns NW9 44 D6
Tewkesbury Rd N15 51 B3
Carshalton SM5 202 B1
Ealing W13 109 A6
Tewkesbury Terr N11 31 D4
Tewson Rd SE18 123 C1
Teyham Ct SW11 158 D5
Teynham Ave EN1 17 B5
Teynham Gn BR2 209 A4
Teynham Ho SE9 167 B5
Teynton Terr N17 33 A2
Thackeray Ave N17 34 A1
Thackeray Cl Harrow HA2 41 C1
Hayes UB8 82 D1
Isleworth TW7 131 A3
Wimbledon SW19 178 D3
Thackeray Ct SW3 257 C2
W14 254 A5
Ealing W5 88 B1
Thackeray Dr RM6 58 B2
Thackeray Ho WC1 240 A6
Thackeray Manor SM1 218 A3
Thackeray Mews E8 74 A2
Thackeray Rd E6 99 D5
SW8 137 B3
Thackeray St W8 255 D6
Thackery Lo TW14 149 B5
Thackran Cl N2 30 A1
Thakeham Cl SE26 184 B5
Thalia Cl SE10 142 B6
Thame Rd SE16 118 D4
Thames Ave
SW10 136 A4 266 B2
Dagenham RM9,RM13 103 D3
Wembley UB6 86 D5
Thames Bank SW14 133 A3
Thamesbank Pl SE28 102 C1
Thames Barrier Visitor Ctr*
SE18 121 D3
Thames Circ E14 119 C2
Thames Cl TW12 173 D1
Thames Cres W4 133 C5
Thames Ct 10 SE15 139 D5
West Molesey KT8 173 D1
Thames Ditton Cty Fst Sch
KT7 196 D3
Thames Ditton Island
KT7 197 A4
Thames Ditton Jun Sch
KT7 196 D2
Thames Ditton Sta KT7 196 D2
Thames Dr HA4 39 A3
Thames Eyot 7 TW1 153 A3
Thamesfield Ct TW17 193 A2
Thamesgate Cl TW10 175 B6
Thames Gateway Pk
RM9 103 B4
Thames Haven KT6 197 D4
Thames Hts SE1 253 C2
Thameside TW11 175 D3
Thameside Ctr TW8 132 B6
Thameside Ind Est E16 121 D4
Thames Link Ho 7
TW9 132 A1
Thames Mead KT12 194 A2
Thames Meadow
East Molesey KT8 195 C6
Lower Halliford KT12,
TW17 193 C1
Thamesmead Sec Sch
TW17 193 B3
Thamesmead Sh Ctr
SE28 124 A6
Thamesmere Dr SE28 124 A6
Thames Pl SW15 134 D2
Thamespoint TW11 175 D3
Thames Quay E14 119 D4
SW10 266 B1
Thames Rd E16 121 D5
Barking IG11 102 A4
Chiswick W4 132 D6
Thames Reach W6 134 C6
Thames Road Ind Est
E16 121 D4
Thames Side
Teddington KT1 175 D2
Thames Ditton KT7 197 B3
Thames St SE10 141 D6
Hampton TW12 173 D1
Kingston KT1,KT2 175 D1
Sunbury TW16 194 B6
Walton-on-T KT12 193 D2
Thamesvale Cl TW3 129 C3
Thames Valley Univ
W5 109 D5
Thames View Ho TW12 194 A3
Thames View Inf Sch
IG11 102 A5
Thames View Jun Sch
IG11 101 D5
Thames View Lodge
IG11 101 C4
Thames Village W4 133 A4
Thames Wlk
SW11 136 C5 267 A4
Thane Mans N7 72 B5
Thanescroft Gdns CR0 221 C5
Thanet Ct 14 W3 88 C1
Thanet Dr BR2 225 D5
Thanet Ho WC1 233 A1
1 West Norwood SE27 160 D1
Thanet Lo NW2 69 A2
Thanet Pl CR0 221 A4
Thanet Rd DA5 169 C4
Thanet St WC1 94 A4 233 A1
Thane Villas N7 72 B5
Thane Works N7 72 B5
Thanington Ct DA15 167 C5
Thant Cl E10 75 D5
Tharp Rd SM6 219 D3
Thatcham Ct N20 14 A4
Thatcham Gdns N20 14 A4
Thatcher Cl UB7 104 A4
Thatchers Way TW7 152 B6
Thatches Gr RM6 59 A5
Thavie's Inn EC4 241 B2
Thaxted Ct N1 235 D3
Thaxted Ho SE16 118 C2
Dagenham RM10 81 D1
Thaxted Lo 8 E18 55 B6
Thaxted Pl 9 SW20 178 D3
Thaxted Rd SE9 167 A2
Buckhurst Hill IG9 21 D4
Thaxton Rd
W14 135 B6 264 D6
Thayers Farm Rd BR3 185 A2
Thayer St W1 93 A2 238 B2
Theatre Mus* WC2 250 B6
Theatre Sq E15 76 B2
Theatre St SW11 136 D2
Theberton St N1 94 D6 234 C6
Theed St SE1 116 C5 251 B3
Thelbridge Ho 28 E3 97 D4
Thelma Gdns SE3 144 A4
Thelma Gr TW11 175 A4
Theobald Cres HA3 24 A2
Theobald Rd E17 53 C2
Croydon CR0 220 D6
Theobalds Av N12 30 A6
Theobalds Ct N4 73 A6
Theobalds Park Rd EN2 4 D6
Theobald's Rd
WC1 94 B2 240 C4
Theobald St SE1 262 C5
Theodora Way HA5 39 D6
Theodore Ho 1 SW15 156 A6
Theodore Rd SE13 164 B5
Therapia La
Thornton Heath CR0 204 A2
Thornton Heath CR0 204 A3
Wallington CR0 203 D2
Therapia Lane Sta CR0 204 A2
Therapia Rd SE22 162 C5
Theresa Rd W6 112 A2
Therfield Ct N4 73 A6
Thermopylae Gate E14 119 D2
Theseus Ho 2 E14 98 B1
Theseus Wlk N1 234 D3
Thesiger Rd SE20 184 D3
Thessaly Ho SW8 269 A3
Thessaly Rd
SW8 137 C4 269 B2
Thesus Ho 2 E14 98 B1
Thetford Cl N13 32 D4
Thetford Ct
3 Dulwich SE21 162 B2
New Malden KT3 199 C4
Thetford Gdns RM9 103 A6
Thetford Ho SE1 263 C6
Thetford Rd
Ashford TW15 148 A1
Dagenham RM9 80 D1
New Malden KT3 199 C4
Thetis Terr TW9 132 C6
Theydon Gr IG8 37 C4
Theydon Rd E5 74 C6
Theydon St E17 53 B2
Thicket Cres SM1 218 A4
Thicket Gr Dagenham RM9 80 C2
Penge SE20 184 A3
Thicket Rd Penge SE20 184 B3
Sutton SM1 218 A4
Thicket The UB7 82 A1
Third Ave E12 78 B3
3 E13 99 A4
E17 53 C4
W10 91 A4
W3 111 D5
Dagenham RM10 103 D5
Dagenham RM6 58 C3
Enfield EN1 17 D6
Hayes UB3 105 D5
Wembley HA9 65 D6
Third Cl KT8 196 A5
Third Cross Rd TW2 152 B2
Third Way HA9 66 D4
Thirleby Rd HA8 27 B2
SW1 115 C3 259 B5
Thirlestone Ct N10 31 A1
Thirlmere NW1 231 D2
Thirlmere Ave UB6 87 C4
Thirlmere Gdns HA9 43 D1
Thirlmere Ho 20 N16 73 B4
Isleworth TW1 152 D6
Thirlmere Rd N10 31 B2
Streatham SW16 181 D6
Thirlmere Rise BR1 186 D4
Thirsk Cl UB5 63 C2
Thirsk Rd SW11 137 A1
Mitcham CR4 181 A3
South Norwood SE25 205 B5
Thisilefield Cl DA5 168 D3
Thistlebrook SE2 124 C4
Thistlecroft Gdns HA7 25 D1
Thistle Ct N17 52 B5
Thistledene KT7 196 C3
Thistledene Ave HA2 63 A5
Thistledown Ct SE25 205 C6
Thistle Gr SW7 256 B1
Thistle Ho 6 E14 98 A1
Thistlemead BR7 188 D1
Thistlewaite Rd E5 74 B5
Thistlewood Cl 3 N7 72 B6
Thistleworth Cl TW7 130 B5
Thistley Cl N12 30 C4
Thistly Ct SE8 141 D6
Thomas a' Beckett Cl
HA0 64 D4
Thomas Arnold Prim Sch
RM9 81 B1
Thomas Baines Rd
SW11 136 B2
Thomas Burt Ho 9 E2 96 B4
Thomas Buxton Jun & Inf Sch
E1 96 A3
Thomas Cribb Mews E6 100 B1
Thomas Ct E17 53 D4
Dagenham RM8 80 C6
Ealing W7 86 C1
Thomas Dean Rd SE26 185 B6
Thomas Dinwiddy Rd
SE12 165 B2
Thomas Doyle St SE1 261 D6
Thomas Fairchild Comm Sch
N1 95 A5 235 B4
Thomas Gamuel Prim Sch
E17 53 C3
Thomas Hardy Ho N22 32 B2
Thomas Hewlett Ho HA1 64 C4
Thomas Ho 3 E9 74 C2
4 SW4 138 A1
Thomas Hollywood Ho 3
E2 96 C5
Thomas Jones Prim Sch
W11 91 A1
Thomas' La SE6 163 C4
Thomas More Ho EC2 242 A3
Thomas More Sq E1 118 A6
Thomas More St E1 118 A5
Thomas More Way N2 48 A6
Thomas North Terr 3
E16 98 D2
Thomas Pl W8 255 C5
Thomas Pooley Ct KT6 198 A2
Thomas Rd E14 97 C2
Thomas Road Ind Est
E14 97 C1
Thomas's London Day Schs
SW11 136 B4 266 D2
Thomas's Prep Sch Clapham
SW11 158 D6
Thomas St SE18 122 D2
Thomas Tallis Sch SE3 143 B2
Thomas Wall Cl SM1 217 D3
Thomas Watson Cottage
Homes The EN5 13 A6
Thompson Ave TW9 132 C2
Thompson Cl Ilford IG1 79 A6
Morden SM3 201 C1
Thompson Ho SE14 140 D6
11 W10 91 A3
Thompson Rd SE22 161 D5
Dagenham RM9 81 B5
Hounslow TW3 129 D1
Uxbridge UB10 60 A1
Thompson's Ave 6 SE5 139 A5
Thomson Cres CR0 204 C1
Thomson Ho SE17 263 A3
SW1 259 D1
Southall UB1 107 A6
Thomson Rd HA3 42 C6
Thorburn Ho SW1 248 A1
Thorburn Sq SE1 118 A2
Thorburn Way SW19 180 B2
Thoresby Ho N16 73 B5
Thoresby St N1 95 A4 235 B2
Thorkhill Gdns KT7 197 B1
Thorkhill Rd KT7 197 B2
Thornaby Gdns N18 34 B5
Thornaby Ho 15 E2 96 B4
Thorn Ave WD23 8 A3
Thornbill Ho 1 SE15 140 A5
Thornbury 3 NW4 46 C5
Thornbury Ave TW7 130 B5
Thornbury Cl N16 73 C3
Thornbury Ct W11 245 A6
Croydon CR2 221 B3
Hounslow TW7 130 C5
Thornbury Ho N6 49 C1
Thornbury Rd SW2 160 A5
Hounslow TW7 130 B4
Thornbury Sq N6 49 C1
Thornby Rd E5 74 C5
Thorn Cl BR2 210 C3
Northolt UB5 85 B4
Thorncliffe Ct SW2 160 A5
Thorncliffe Rd SW2 160 A5
Southall UB2 107 B1
Thorncombe Rd SE22 161 C6
Thorncroft Rd SM1 217 D4
Thorncroft St
SW8 138 A5 270 A3
Thorndale Ho N16 51 C1
Thorndean St SW18 158 A2
Thorndene Ave N11 15 A3
Thorndike Ave UB5 84 D6
Thorndike Cl
SW10 136 A5 266 A4
Thorndike Ho SW1 259 C2
Thorndike St
SW1 115 D2 259 C3
Thorndon Cl BR5 189 D1
Thorndon Gdns KT19 215 C4
Thorndon Rd BR5 189 D1
Thorndyke Ct HA5 23 B3
Thorne Cl DA8 147 D6

Thorne Cl continued
E11 76 C4
E16 99 A1
Littleton TW15 171 A3
Thorne Ho 4 E14 120 A3
34 E2 96 C4
Thorneloe Gdns CR0,
CR9 220 D3
Thorne Pas 7 SW13 133 D3
Thorne Rd SW8 138 A5 270 B3
Thorne's Cl BR3 208 A6
Thorness Ct SW18 158 A5
Thorne St SW13,SW14 133 C2
Thornet Wood Rd BR1 210 C6
Thornewill Ho 7 E1 118 C6
Thorney Cres
SW11 136 B5 266 D3
Thorneycroft Cl KT12 194 C3
Thorneycroft Dr EN3 7 C6
Thorneycroft Ho 11 W4 111 C1
Thorney Ct W8 246 A1
Thorney Hedge Rd W4 110 D2
Thorney St SW1 116 A2 260 A4
Thornfield Ave NW7 29 A2
Thornfield Ct NW7 29 A2
Thornfield Ho 4 E14 119 C6
Thornfield Par NW7 29 A3
Thornfield Rd W12 112 B4
Thornford Rd SE13 164 A6
Thorngate Rd W9 91 C3
Thorngrove Rd E13 99 B6
Thornham Gr E15 76 B3
Thorn Ham Ho SE1 262 D6
Thornham St SE10 141 D6
Thornhaugh St WC1 239 D5
Thornhill Ave SE18 145 C5
Surbiton KT6 214 A6
Thornhill Bridge Wharf
N1 233 C5
Thornhill Cres N1 72 B1
Thornhill Ct N8 49 D3
Thornhill Gdns E10 75 D6
Barking IG11 79 C1
Thornhill Gr N1 72 C1
Thornhill Ho N1 72 C1
12 W4 111 C1
Thornhill Prim Sch N1 72 C1
Thornhill Rd E10 75 D6
N1 72 C1 234 A6
Ickenham UB10 60 C4
Surbiton KT6 214 B6
Thornton Heath CR0 205 A2
Thornhill Sq N1 72 B1
Thornhill Way TW17 192 C4
Thornicroft Ho 12 SW9 138 B3
Thornlaw Rd SE27 182 D6
Thornley Cl N17 34 A3
Thornley Dr HA2 63 D6
Thornley Pl 2 SE10 120 C1
Thornsbeach Rd SE6 164 A2
Thornsett Pl SE20 184 B1
Thornsett Rd
Penge SE20 184 B1
Wandsworth SW18 157 D3
Thornsett Terr SE20 184 B1
Thornton Ave W4 111 C2
Streatham SW2 159 D3
Thornton Heath CR0 204 B3
West Drayton UB7 104 B3
Thornton Cl UB7 104 B3
Thornton Ct N7 72 A3
West Barnes SW20 200 D4
Thornton Dene BR3 185 C1
Thornton Gdns SW12 159 D3
Thornton Gr HA5 23 C4
Thornton Heath Pond
CR7 204 C4
Thornton Heath Sta
CR7 205 A5
Thornton Hill SW19 179 A3
Thornton Ho SE17 263 A3
7 Wanstead E11 55 A3
Thornton Lo CR7 205 A6
Thornton Pl W1 237 D4
Thornton Rd BR1 187 A5
E11 76 B6
N18 18 C1
Barnet EN5 1 A2
Belvedere DA17 125 D2
Carshalton SM5 202 B1
Ilford IG1 78 D4
Mortlake SW14 133 B2
Streatham SW12,SW2 159 D3
Thornton Heath CR0,CR7 204 B3
Wimbledon SW19 178 D3
Thornton Rd E SW19 178 D4
Thornton Row CR7 204 C4
Thornton St SW9 138 C3
Thornton Way NW11 47 D4
Thorntree Ct W5 88 A2
Thorntree Rd SE7 121 D1
Thorntree Sch SE7 121 B1
Thornville Gr CR4 180 B1
Thornville St SE8 141 C4
Thornwell Ct W7 108 C4
Thornwood Cl E18 37 B1
Thornwood Rd SE13 164 C6
Thornycroft Ct TW9 132 B3
Thorogood Gdns E15 76 C3
Thorold Ho SE1 252 A2
6 Streatham SW2 160 A4
Thorold Rd Ilford IG1 57 A1
Wood Green N22 32 A3
Thorparch Rd
SW8 137 D5 269 D3
Thorpebank Rd W12 112 A5
Thorpe Cl BR6 227 C6
Thorpe Cl continued
W10 91 A1
Forest Hill SE26 184 D6
Thorpe Coombe Hospl
E17 54 A6
Thorpe Cres E17 35 B1
Thorpe Ct EN2 4 D2
Thorpedale Gdns IG6 56 D5
Thorpedale Rd N4 50 B1
Thorpe Hall W5 87 D2
Thorpe Hall Rd E17 36 A2
Thorpe Ho N1 233 D5
Thorpe Rd E6 100 B6
E7 76 D4
N15 51 C3
Barking IG11 79 B1
Chingford E17 36 A1
Kingston KT2 176 A3
Thorpewood Ave SE23,
SE26 162 B2
Thorpland Ave UB10 61 A5
Thorsden Way 2 SE19 183 C5
Thorverton Rd NW2 69 A5
Thoydon Rd E3 97 A5
Thrale Almhouses
SW16 182 A5
Thrale Rd SW16 181 C5
Thrale St SE1 252 B3
Thrasher Cl 20 E8 95 D6
Thrawl St E1 95 D2 243 D3
Thrayle Ho 2 SW9 138 B2
Threadgold Ho 8 N1 73 B2
Threadneedle St
EC2,EC3 95 B1 242 D1
Three Bridges Bsns Ctr
UB2 108 A4
Three Bridges Prim Sch
UB2 107 D3
Three Colts La E2 96 B3
Three Colt St E14 119 B6
Three Corners DA7 147 D3
Three Cups Yd WC1 240 D3
Three Kings Yd W1 248 C6
Three Meadows Mews
HA7 24 D2
Three Mill La E3 98 A4
Three Nun Ct EC2 242 B2
Three Oak La SE1 253 C2
Three Oaks Cl UB10 60 B5
Threshers Pl W11 244 A6
Thriffwood SE23,SE26 162 D1
Thrigby Rd KT9 214 B2
Thring Ho 2 SW9 138 B3
Throckmorten Rd E16 99 B1
Throgmorton Ave
EC2 95 B1 242 D2
Throgmorton St
EC2 95 B1 242 D2
Throwley Cl SE2 124 C3
Throwley Rd SM1 217 D3
Throwley Way SM1 217 D3
Thrupp Cl CR4 181 B1
Thrush Gn HA2 41 C5
Thrush St SE17 262 A2
Thunderer Rd RM9 103 B3
Thunder Rd RM9 103 B3
Thurbarn Rd SE6 185 D5
Thurland Ho 3 SE16 118 B2
Thurland Rd SE16 118 A3
Thurlby Cl HA1 43 A3
Thurlby Croft NW4 46 C6
Thurlby Rd Wembley HA0 65 D2
West Norwood SE27 182 C6
Thurleigh Ave SW12 159 A5
Thurleigh Ct SW12 159 A5
Thurleigh Rd SW12 159 A5
Thurleston Ave SM4 201 A4
Thurlestone Ave N12 30 D4
Ilford IG3 79 D4
Thurlestone Cl TW17 193 A3
Thurlestone Ct 1 UB1 85 D1
Thurlestone Par TW17 193 A3
Thurlestone Rd SE27 182 C6
Thurloe Cl SW7 257 A4
Thurloe Ct SW3 257 A3
Thurloe Pl SW7 114 B2 256 D4
Thurloe Place Mews
SW7 256 D4
Thurloe Sq SW7 114 C2 257 A4
Thurloe St SW7 114 B2 256 D4
Thurlow Cl E4 35 D4
Thurlow Ct 6 E11 55 A4
Thurlow Gdns HA0 65 D3
Thurlow Hill SE21 161 A2
Thurlow Ho 17 SW16 160 A1
Thurlow Park Rd SE21,
SE24 161 A2
Thurlow Rd NW3 70 B3
W7 109 A4
Thurlow St
SE17 117 C1 263 A1
Thurlow Terr NW5 71 A3
Thurlow Twrs SE27 160 C1
Thurlston Rd HA4 62 A5
Thurnby Ct TW2 152 C1
Thurnscoe NW1 232 A5
Thursland Rd DA14 191 A5
Thursley Cres CR0 224 B1
Thursley Gdns SW19 156 D2
Thursley Ho
3 Kingston KT2 176 D3
10 Streatham SW2 160 B4
Thursley Rd SE9 166 B1
Thurso Ho NW6 91 D5
Thurso St SW17 180 B6
Thurstan Rd SW20 178 B3
Thurston Ho 4 BR3 185 D4
Thurston Ind Est SE13 141 D2
Thurston Rd SE8,SE13 141 D3
Southall UB1 85 B1
Thurtle Rd E2 95 D5
Thurza Ct TW7 130 D3
Thyer Cl BR6 227 A4
Thyra Gr N12 29 D4
Tibbatt's Rd E3 97 D3
Tibbenham Pl SE6 163 C2
Tibbenham Wlk E13 98 D5
Tibbets Cl SW19 156 D3
Tibbet's Corner SW19 156 D4
Tibbet's Ride SW19 156 D4
Tiber Gdns N1 233 B5
Ticehurst Cl BR5 190 A3
Ticehurst Rd SE23 163 A2
Tickford Cl SE2 124 C4
Tickford Ho NW8 230 A1
Tidal Basin Rd E16 120 D6
Tidbury Ct SW8 269 A3
Tidemill Prim Sch SE8 141 C5
Tidenham Gdns CR0 221 C5
Tideside Ct SE18 122 A3
Tideswell 10 NW5 71 B4
Tideswell Rd
Croydon CR0 223 C5
Putney SW15 134 C1
Tideway Cl TW10 175 C6
Tideway Ct 9 SE16 118 D5
Tideway Ho E14 119 C4
Tideway Ind Est
SW8 137 C6 269 B5
Tideway Wharf SW13 133 C3
Tideway Yd SW13 133 C3
Tidey St E3 97 C2
Tidford Rd DA16 145 D3
Tidworth Ho 13 SE22 139 C2
Tidworth Rd E3 97 C3
Tiepigs La BR2,BR4 208 D1
Tierney Ct 4 CR0 221 D6
Tierney Rd SW2 160 A3
Tierney Terr SW2 160 A3
Tiffin Girls' Sch KT2 176 A4
Tiffin Sch KT2 176 B1
Tiger Ho WC1 232 D1
Tiger La BR2 209 B5
Tiger Way E5 74 B4
Tigris Cl N9 18 C2
Tilbrook Rd SE3,SE9 143 C2
Tilbury Cl BR5 190 B1
13 SE15 139 D5
Tilbury Ho 4 SE14 140 D6
Tilbury Rd E10 54 A2
E6 100 B5
Tildesley Rd SW15 156 C5
Tile Farm Rd BR6 227 B5
Tilehurst NW1 231 D1
Tilehurst Point 2 SE2 124 C4
Tilehurst Rd Cheam SM3 217 A3
Wandsworth SW17,SW18 158 B3
Tile Kiln La N6 49 C1
Edmonton N13 33 A5
Harefield UB9 38 D2
Tileyard Rd N7 72 A1
Tilford Ave CR0 224 A1
Tilford Gdns SW19 156 D3
Tilford Ho 8 SW2 160 B4
Tilia Rd E5 74 B4
Tilia Wlk 21 SW9 138 D1
Tilleard Ho 4 W10 91 A4
Tiller Ho 30 N1 95 C6
Tiller Rd E14 119 C3
Tillet Sq SE16 119 A4
Tillett Cl NW10 67 A2
Tillet Way 4 E2 96 A4
Tilley Rd TW14 150 A3
Tillingbourne Gdns N3 47 B6
Tillingbourne Way N3 47 B5
Tillingham Way N12 29 D6
Tilling Ho 1 SE15 140 B2
Tilling Rd NW2 46 C2
Tilling Way HA9 65 D6
Tillman Ho 8 SW2 160 B3
Tillman St E1 96 B1
Tillotson Ct SW8 269 D3
Tillotson Rd Edmonton N9 17 D2
Harrow HA3 23 D3
Ilford IG1 56 C2
Tilney Ct EC1 242 B6
Kingston KT6 197 D4
Woodford IG9 21 A2
Tilney Dr IG9 21 A2
Tilney Gdns 12 N1 73 B2
Tilney Rd Chigwell IG9 21 B2
Dagenham RM9 81 B2
Southall UB2 106 C2
Tilney St W1 248 B4
Tilson Cl 2 SE15 139 C5
Tilson Gdns SW2,SW4 160 A4
Tilson Ho SW2 160 A4
Tilson Rd N17 34 A2
Tilston Cl E11 76 D5
Tilton St SW6 264 B5
Tiltwood The W3 111 A6
Tilt Yard App SE9 166 B5
Timber Cl BR7 188 C1
Timbercroft KT19 215 C4
Timbercroft La SE18 145 C5
Timbercroft Prim Sch
SE18 145 C5
Timberdene NW4 28 D1
Timberland Cl 15 SE15 140 A5
Timberland Rd E1 96 B1
Timber Mill Way SW4 137 D2
Timber Pond Rd SE16 118 D4
Timber St EC1 242 A6
Timberwharf Rd N16 52 A3
Time Sq E8 73 D3
Times Sq SM1 217 D3
Timothy Cl 1 SW4 159 C6
Bexley DA6 169 A6
Timothy Ho DA18 125 A4
Timothy Rd E3 97 B2
Timsbury Wlk 5 SW15 156 A3
Tina Ct SW16 160 C1
Tindal St SW9 138 D4
Tinniswood Cl N5 72 C3
Tinsley Rd E1 96 C2
Tintagel Cres SE22 139 D1
Tintagel Ct EC1 241 C6
Tintagel Dr HA7 25 D6
Tintagel Ho SE20 184 A3
Tintern Ave NW9 44 D6
Tintern Cl Putney SW15 157 A6
Wimbledon SW19 180 A4
Tintern Ct W13 109 A6
Tintern Gdns N14 16 A4
Tintern Ho NW1 231 D3
SW1 258 C3
Tintern Path NW9 45 C3
Tintern Rd
Carshalton SM5 202 B1
Tottenham N22 33 A2
Tintern St SW4 138 A1
Tintern Way HA2 41 D1
Tinto Rd E16 99 A3
Tinwell Mews WD6 11 B6
Tinworth St
SE11 116 A1 260 B2
Tippett Ct E6 100 B5
Tippetts Cl EN2 5 A4
Tipthorpe Rd SW11 137 A2
Tipton Dr CR0 221 C4
Tiptree 7 NW1 71 B1
Tiptree Cl E4 20 A1
Tiptree Cres IG5 56 C6
Tiptree Ct EN2 5 B1
Tiptree Dr EN2 5 B1
Tiptree Rd HA4 62 B4
Tirlemont Rd CR2 221 A1
Tirrell Rd CR0 205 A3
Tisbury Ct W1 249 C6
Tisbury Rd SW16 182 A1
Tisdall Pl SE17 117 B2 262 D3
Tissington Ct 4 SE16 118 D2
Titan Bsns Est 3 SE8 141 C5
Titan Ct TW8 110 B1
Titchborne Row W2 237 B1
Titchfield Rd
NW8 92 D6 230 C4
Carshalton SM5 202 B1
Enfield EN3 7 A6
Titchfield Wlk SM5 202 B2
Titchwell Rd SW18 158 B3
Tite St SW3 136 D6 267 C6
Tithe Barn Cl KT2 176 B2
Tithe Barn Way UB5 84 B5
Tithe Cl NW7 28 A2
Hayes UB4 83 D2
Walton-on-T KT12 194 B3
Tithe Ct NW4 28 A2
Tithe Farm Ave HA2 63 C5
Tithe Farm Cl HA2 63 C5
Tithe Wlk NW7 28 A2
Titian Ave WD23 8 C4
Titley Cl E4 35 C5
Titmus Cl UB8 83 A1
Titmuss Ave SE28 124 B6
Titmuss St W12 112 C4
Tivendale N8 50 A6
Tiverton Ave IG5 56 C6
Tiverton Dr SE9 167 A3
Tiverton Prim Sch N15 51 B3
Tiverton Rd N4,N15 51 B3
NW6,NW10 90 D6
Edgware HA8 26 B1
Edmonton N18 33 C5
Hounslow TW3 130 A3
Ruislip HA4 62 A5
Wembley HA0 88 A5
Tiverton St SE1 117 A3 262 A6
Tiverton Way KT9 213 D3
Tivoli Ct SE16 119 B5
Tivoli Gdns 11 SE7 122 A2
Tivoli Rd N8 49 D4
Hounslow TW4 129 A1
West Norwood SE27 183 A5
Toad La TW4 129 B1
Tobago St E14 119 C4
Tobin Cl NW3 70 C1
Toby Ct N9 18 C4
Toby La E1 97 A3
Toby Way KT5,KT6 214 D6
Todber Ho W14 254 B5
Todd Ho 3 N2 30 B1
Todds Wlk N7 72 B6
Tokenhouse Yd EC2 242 C2
Tokyngton Ave HA9 66 C2
Toland Sq SW15 156 A6
Tolcairn Ct 2 DA17 125 C1
Tolcarne Dr HA5 40 B6
Tolchurch 2 W11 91 C1
Toley Ave HA3,HA9 44 A2
Tollbridge Cl W10 91 A3
Tollesbury Gdns IG6 57 B6
Tollet St E1 96 D3
Tollgate Dr Dulwich SE21 161 C2
Hayes UB4 106 D6
Tollgate Ho 1 NW6 91 D5
Tollgate Prim Sch E13 99 C3
Croydon CR0 206 C3
Tollgate Rd E6 100 A2
Tollhouse Way N19 71 C6
Tollington Ct N4 72 B6
Tollington Pk N4 72 B6
Tollington Pl N4 72 B6
Tollington Rd N7 72 B4
Tollington Way N7 72 A5
Tolmers Sq NW1 93 C3 239 B6
Tolpaide Ho SE11 261 A3
Tolpuddle Ave 2 E13 99 C6
Tolsford Rd E5 74 B3
Tolson Ho 2 TW7 131 A2
Tolson Rd TW7 131 A2
Tolverne Rd SW20 178 C2
Tolworth Cl KT6 198 D1
Tolworth Gdns RM6 58 D4
Tolworth Girls' Sch KT6 214 B5
Tolworth Hospl KT6 214 C6
Tolworth Inf Sch KT6 198 B1
Tolworth Junc KT6 214 D6
Tolworth Jun Sch KT6 198 B1
Tolworth Par RM6 59 A4
Tolworth Park Rd KT6 214 B6
Tolworth Rd KT6 214 A6
Tolworth Rise N KT5 198 D1
Tolworth Rise S KT5 198 D1
Tolworth Sta KT5 214 D6
Tolworth Underpass
KT5,KT6 214 D6
Tomahawk Gdns 4 UB5 84 D4
Tom Coombs Cl SE9 144 A1
Tom Cribb Rd SE18,SE28 123 B3
Tom Groves Cl E15 76 B3
Tom Hood Cl E15 76 B3
Tom Hood Sch E11 76 D5
Tom Jenkinson Rd 5
E16 121 A5
Tomkyns Ho SE11 261 A3
Tomline Ho SE1 252 A3
Tomlin's Gr E3 97 C4
Tomlinson Cl E2 95 D4
5 W4 110 D1
Tomlins Orch IG11 101 A6
Tomlin's Terr E14 97 A1
Tomlins Wlk 4 N7 72 B6
Tom Mann Cl IG11 101 C6
Tom Nolan Cl E15 98 C5
Tompion Ho EC1 241 D6
Tompion St EC1 234 D1
Tom Smith Cl SE10 142 C6
Tom Smith Ho 3 E17 54 A4
Tomson Ho SE1 263 C6
Tom Williams Ho SW6 264 C5
Tonbridge Cres HA3 44 A5
Tonbridge Hos WC1 233 A1
Tonbridge Rd KT12,KT8 195 B5
Tonbridge St
WC1 94 A4 233 A1
Toneborough 14 NW8 91 D6
Tonfield Rd SM3 201 B1
Tonge Cl BR3 207 C4
Tonsley Hill SW18 157 D6
Tonsley Pl SW18 157 D6
Tonsley Rd SW18 157 D6
Tonsley St SW18 157 D6
Tonstall Rd CR4 181 A1
Tooke Cl HA5 23 A2
Tookey Cl HA3 44 B2
Took's Ct EC4 241 A2
Tooley St SE1 117 C5 253 A3
Toorack Rd HA3 24 B1
Tooting Bec SW17 159 A1
Tooting Bec Gdns
SW16 181 D6
Tooting Bec Rd
Streatham SW16 181 C5
Upper Tooting, Furzedown
SW17 181 B6
Tooting Bec Sta SW17 159 A1
Tooting Broadway
SW17 180 D5
Tooting Broadway Sta
SW17 180 C5
Tooting Gr SW17 180 C5
Tooting High St SW17,
SW19 180 C5
Tooting Sta SW17 180 D4
Tootswood Rd BR2,BR3 208 C5
Topaz Ho KT4 199 B1
Topaz Wlk NW2 46 D2
Topcliffe Dr BR6 227 B4
Topham Ho 8 SE10 142 A5
Topham Sq N17 33 A2
Topham St EC1 241 A6
Top House Rise E4 20 A4
Topiary Sq TW9 132 B2
Topley St SE9 143 D1
Topmast Point E14 119 C4
Top Pk BR3 208 C4
Topsfield Cl N8 49 D4
Topsfield Par N8 50 A3
Topsfield Rd N8 50 A4
Topsham Rd SW17 181 A6
Torbay Ct 13 NW1 71 B1
Torbay Mans NW6 91 B6
Torbay Rd NW6 69 B1
Harrow HA2 63 A6
Torbay St 15 NW1 71 B1
Torbitt Way IG2 57 D4
Torbridge Cl HA8 26 A3
Torbrook Cl DA5 169 A5
Torcross Dr SE23 162 C2
Torcross Rd HA4 62 C5
Tor Ct W8 245 B2
Torfell 5 E18 36 D1
Tor Gdns W8 113 C4 245 A2
Tor Ho N6 49 B3
Tormead Cl SM1 217 C2
Tormount Rd SE18 145 C6
Tornay Ho E9 74 C1
N1 233 C4
Toronto Ave E12 78 B4
Toronto Rd IG1 57 A1
Torquay Gdns IG4 55 D5
Torquay St W2 91 D2
Tor Rd DA16 146 C4
Torrens Ct SE5 139 B2
Torrens Rd E15 76 D2
SW2 160 B6
Torrens Sq E15 76 D2
Torrens St EC1 94 D5 234 C3
Torres Sq E14 119 C1
Torre Wlk SM5 202 C1
Torriano Ave NW5 71 D3
Torriano Cotts NW5 71 C3
Torriano Jun & Inf Schs
NW5 71 D3
Torridge Gdns SE15 140 C1
Torridge Rd CR7 204 D4
Torridon Ho NW6 91 D5
Torridon Inf Sch SE6 164 B2
Torridon Jun Sch SE6 164 B2
Torridon Rd SE13,SE6 164 B3
Torrington Ave N12 30 B5
Torrington Cl N12 30 B6
Claygate KT10 212 C2
Torrington Ct N12 30 B6
Forest Hill SE26 184 A5
Harrow HA2 63 D5
Torrington Dr HA2 63 D5
Torrington Gdns N11 31 C4
Wembley UB6 65 C1
Torrington Gr N12 30 C5
Torrington Pk N12 30 B6
Torrington Pl E1 118 A5
WC1 93 D2 239 C4
Torrington Rd
Claygate KT10 212 C2
Dagenham RM8 59 B1
Ruislip HA4 62 A5
Wanstead E18 55 A6
Wembley UB6 87 C6
Torrington Sq
WC1 93 D3 239 D5
Thornton Heath CR0 205 B2
Torrington Way SM4 201 C3
Torr Rd SE20 184 D3
Tortington Ho 1 SE15 140 B5
Torver Rd HA1 42 C5
Torver Way BR6 227 B5
Torwood Rd SW15 156 A6
Totham Lo SW20 178 B2
Tothill Ho SW1 259 D4
Tothill St SW1 115 D4 249 D1
Totland Ho SW18 157 D5
Totnes Rd DA16 146 C5
Totnes Villas N11 31 C5
Totnes Wlk N2 48 B5
Tottan Terr E1 96 D1
Tottenhall 5 NW1 71 A1
Tottenhall Inf Sch N13 32 C4
Tottenhall Rd N13 32 D4
Tottenham Court Rd
W1 93 C2 239 B4
Tottenham Court Road Sta
W1 93 D1 239 D2
Tottenham Gn E 2 N15 51 D5
Tottenham Gn E South Side
3 N15 51 D5
Tottenham Hale N15 52 A5
Tottenham Hale Ret Pk
N15 52 A5
Tottenham Hale Sta N17 52 B6
Tottenham La N8 50 B4
Tottenham Mews W1 239 B4
Tottenham Rd N1 73 C2
Tottenham St W1 93 C2 239 B4
Totterdown St SW17 180 D5
Totteridge Comm N20 12 C3
Totteridge Ho SW11 136 B3
Totteridge La N20 13 D3
Totteridge Rd EN3 6 D6
Totteridge Village N20 13 B3
Totteridge & Whetstone Sta
N20 14 A2
Totternhoe Cl HA3 43 C4
Totton Rd CR7 204 C6
Touchard Ho N1 235 D1
Toulmin St SE1 117 A4 252 A1
Toulon St SE5 139 A5
Toulouse Ct 2 SE16 118 B1
Tournay Rd
SW6 135 B5 264 D4
Toussaint Wlk 18 SE16 118 A3
Tovil Cl SE20 184 B1
Tovy Ho 6 SE1 118 A1
Towcester Rd E3 98 A3
Tower 42★ EC2 243 A2
Tower Bldgs 22 E1 118 B5
Tower Br App E1,EC3 253 C5
Tower Bridge★
E1,EC3,SE1 117 D5 253 C4
Tower Bridge Bsns Complex
SE16 118 B3
Tower Bridge Bsns Sq
SE16 118 B2
Tower Bridge Piazza
SE1 253 C3
Tower Bridge Prim Sch
SE1 117 D4 253 C2
Tower Bridge Rd
SE1 117 C4 253 C3
Tower Bridge Sq SE1 253 C2
Tower Cl NW3 70 B3
Orpington BR6 227 D5
Penge SE20 184 B3
Tower Ct E5 51 D2
NW8 230 B4
WC2 240 A1
Tower Gardens Rd N17 33 B2
Towergate SE1 263 A4
Towergate Cl UB8 60 A3
Tower Gateway Sta
EC3 117 D6 253 C6
Tower Gdns KT10 213 A1
Tower Gr KT13 193 C1
Tower Hamlets Coll E1 96 C2
E1 96 D1
E14 119 D6
E14 97 D1
Tower Hamlets Rd E17 53 C6
E7 76 D3

Tower Hill EC3 117 D6 253 C5
Tower Hill Sta EC3 117 D6 253 C6
Tower Hill Terr EC3 253 B5
Tower La HA9 65 D5
Tower Mans SE1 263 C5
Tower Mews E17 53 C5
E5 75 A3
Tower Millennium Pier EC3 117 C5 253 B4
Tower Mill Rd 1 SE15 139 C5
Tower Rd DA7 147 D1
NW10 68 A1
Orpington BR6 227 D5
Twickenham TW1,TW2 152 D1
Tower Rise TW9 132 A2
Tower Royal EC4 252 C6
Towers Ave UB10 83 A4
Towers Ct UB10 83 A4
Towers Pl TW10 154 A6
Towers Rd Pinner HA5 23 A2
Southall UB1 85 C3
Tower St WC2 240 A1
Towers The NW5 71 B5
1 Richmond TW9 132 B1
Tower Terr SE4 141 A1
Wood Green N22 32 B1
Tower The* EC3 117 D6 253 C5
Tower View CR0 207 A2
Tower Wharf SE1 253 C2
Tower Wlk SE1 263 A4
Towfield Ct TW13 151 B2
Towfield Rd TW13 151 B2
Towncourt Cres BR5 211 B5
Towncourt La BR5 211 B2
Towncourt Path N4 51 A1
Townend Ct 6 BR1 186 D2
Towney Mead UB5 85 B5
Towney Mead Ct UB5 85 B5
Townfield Rd UB3 105 D5
Townfield Sq UB3 105 D6
Town Field Way TW7 131 A3
Town Hall Approach Rd N15 51 D5
Townhall Ave 3 W4 111 B1
Town Hall Rd SW11 136 D2
Townholm Cres W7 108 D3
Town La TW19 148 A2
Townley Ct E15 76 D2
Townley Gram Sch for Girls DA5 169 B6
Townley Rd DA6 169 B6
SE22 161 C6
Townley St SE17 117 B1 262 C2
Townmead Bsns Ctr SW6 136 A2
Town Meadow TW8 131 D5
Townmead Rd SW6 136 A3
Richmond TW9 132 D3
Town Quay IG11 100 D6
Town Quay Wharf IG11 100 D6
Town Rd N9 18 B2
Townsend Ave N14 31 D6
Townsend Ho 12 SE1 118 A2
Townsend Ind Est NW10 89 A5
Townsend La NW9 45 B3
Townsend Prim Sch SE17 117 C2 263 A4
Townsend Rd N15 51 D4
Ashford TW15 170 A5
Southall UB1 107 A5
Townsend St SE1,SE17 117 C2 263 A4
Townsend Way HA6 22 A3
Townsend Yd N6 49 B1
Townshend Cl DA14 190 C4
Townshend Ct NW8 230 B4
Townshend Est NW8 92 C5 230 A4
Townshend Ho 19 SE18 122 B2
Townshend Rd NW8 92 C6 230 A5
Chislehurst BR7 188 D5
Richmond TW9 132 B1
Townshend Terr TW9 132 B1
Towns Ho 4 SW4 137 D2
Townson Ave UB5 84 B5
Townson Way UB5 84 A5
Town The EN2 5 B2
Town Tree Rd TW15 170 C5
Towpath TW17 192 B1
Towpath Way CR0 205 D4
Towton Rd SE27 161 A2
Toxteth Ho N4 51 A2
Toynbec Cl BR7 188 D6
Toynbee Rd SW19,SW20 179 A2
Toynbee St E1 95 D2 243 C3
Toyne Way N6 48 D3
Tracey Ave NW2 68 C3
Tracy Ct HA7 25 C3
Tracy Ho 12 E3 97 B4
Trade Cl N13 32 C6
Trader Rd E6 100 D1
Tradescant Ho 15 E9 74 C1
Tradescant Rd SW8 138 A5 270 B3
Trade Twr 8 SW11 136 A2
Trade Winds Ct 1 E1 118 A5
Trading Estate Rd NW10 89 A3
Traemore Ct SW16 160 C1
Trafalgar Ave SE15 139 D6
North Cheam KT4,SM3, SM4 200 D1
Tottenham N17 33 C4
Trafalgar Bsns Ctr IG11 101 D3
Trafalgar Cl 1 SE16 119 A2
Trafalgar Ct Barking E6 100 C6
Hounslow TW3 129 B2
Trafalgar Ct continued
West Barnes KT3 200 B6
Trafalgar Gdns E1 96 D2
W8 255 D6
Trafalgar Gr SE10 142 B6
Trafalgar Ho SE17 262 B2
Barking IG11 102 B4
Trafalgar Inf Sch TW2 152 B2
Trafalgar Jun Sch TW2 152 B2
Trafalgar Mews E9 75 B2
Trafalgar Pl
Edmonton N18 34 A5
Wanstead E11 55 A5
Trafalgar Rd SE10 120 C1
Merton SW19 180 A3
Twickenham TW2 152 B2
Trafalgar Sq* SW1 115 D5 249 D4
Trafalgar St SE17 117 B1 262 D2
Trafalgar Terr HA1 42 C1
Trafalgar Trad Est EN3 7 A1
Trafalgar Way E14 120 A5
Croydon CR0 220 C6
Trafford Cl E15 75 D3
Trafford Ho N1 235 D4
Trafford Rd CR7 204 B4
Tragail SW15 157 A6
Traherne Lo 3 TW11 174 D5
Traitors Gate* EC3 117 D5 253 C4
Tralee Ct 31 SE16 118 B1
Tramsheds The CR0, CR4 203 D2
Tramway Ave E15 76 B1
N9 18 C4
Tramway Path CR4 202 C5
Trance Way W3 110 C3
Tranmere Ct 5 SM2 218 A1
Tranmere Ho 7 N7 72 C3
Tranmere Rd
Edmonton N9 17 D4
Twickenham TW2 151 D4
Wandsworth SW17,SW18 158 A2
Tranquil Pass SE3 142 D3
Tranquil Vale SE3 142 C3
Transept St NW1 237 B3
Transmere Cl BR5 211 A3
Transmere Rd BR5 211 A3
Transom Cl SE16 119 A2
Transom Sq E14 119 D1
Transport Ave TW8 131 B6
Tranton Rd SE16 118 B3
Trappes Ho 2 SE16 118 B2
Traps La KT2,KT3 177 C2
Travel Clinic, Hospl for Tropical Diseases WC1 93 C3 239 B5
Travellers Way TW5 128 C3
Travers Cl E17 34 D2
Travers Ho 6 SE10 142 B6
Travers Rd N7 72 C5
Travis Ho SE10 142 A4
Treacy Cl WD23 8 A2
Treadgold Ho 7 W11 112 D6
Treadgold St W11 112 D6
Treadway St E2 96 B5
Treasury Buildings SW1 250 A2
Treaty Ctr TW3 129 D2
Treaty St N1 94 B6 233 C5
Trebeck St W1 248 C3
Treborough Ho W1 238 A4
Trebovir Rd SW5 113 C2 255 B3
Treby St E3 97 B3
Trecastle Way 3 N7 71 D4
Tredegar Rd E3 97 B5
N11 31 D3
Tredegar Sq E3 97 B4
Tredegar Terr E3 97 B4
Trederwen Rd E8 96 A6
Tredown Rd SE26 184 C5
Tredwell Cl BR2 210 A5
Tredwell Rd SE27 182 D6
Tree Cl TW10 153 D3
Treen Ave SW13 133 D2
Tree Rd E16 99 C1
Trees The N16 51 B2
Tree Tops 1 IG8 37 A6
Treetops Cl SE2 125 A1
Treetops Ct CR7 205 A4
Treetops View IG10 21 D4
Treeview Cl SE19 183 C2
Treewall Gdns BR1 187 B6
Trefgarne Rd RM10 81 C6
Trefil Wlk N7 72 A4
Trefoil Ho DA18 125 A4
Trefoil Rd SW18 158 A6
Trefusis Ct TW5 128 B4
Tregaron Ave N8 50 A3
Tregaron Gdns KT3 199 C5
Tregarvon Rd SW11 137 A1
Tregenna Ave HA2 63 C4
Tregenna Cl 1 N14 15 C6
Tregenna Ct HA2 63 C4
Tregony Rd BR6 227 D4
Trego Rd E9 75 C1
Tregothnan Rd SW9 138 A2
Tregunter Rd SW10 114 A1 256 A1
Treherne Ct SW9 138 D4
Upper Tooting SW17 181 A6
Trehern Rd 12 SW14 133 B2
Trehurst St E5 75 A3
Trelawney Est E9 74 C2
Trelawney Ho SE1 252 A2
Trelawn Rd E10 76 A5
SW2 160 C6
Trelawny Cl E17 53 D5
Trellis Ho SW19 180 A3
Trellis Sq 1 E3 97 B4
Treloar Gdns SE19 183 B4
Tremadoc Rd SW4 137 D1
Tremaine Cl SE4 141 C3
Tremaine Rd SE20 184 B1
Trematon Ho SE11 261 B2
Trematon Pl TW11 175 C3
Tremlett Gr N19 71 C5
Tremlett Mews N19 71 C5
Trenance Gdns IG3 80 A5
Trenchard Ave HA4 62 B4
Trenchard Cl NW9 27 C2
Stanmore HA7 25 B4
Trenchard Ct SM4 201 C3
Trenchard St SE10 120 B1
Trenchold St SW8 138 A6 270 A5
Trend Ct W13 109 B5
Trendell Ho 4 E14 97 C1
Trenholme Cl SE20 184 B3
Trenholme Rd SE20 184 B3
Trenholme Terr SE20 184 B3
Trenmar Gdns NW10 90 B4
Trenmar Lo NW10 90 B4
Trent Ave W5 109 C3
Trent CE Prim Sch EN4 2 D1
Trent Ct E11 55 A4
Trent Ctry Pk EN4 3 A3
Trent Gdns N14 15 B5
Trentham Lo 8 EN1 17 C6
Trentham St SW18 157 C3
Trent Ho SE15 140 C1
4 Kingston KT2 175 D2
Trent Rd SW2 160 B6
Buckhurst Hill IG9 21 B3
Trent Way Hayes UB4 83 C4
North Cheam KT4 216 C5
Trentwood Side EN2 4 B2
Treport St SW18 157 D4
Tresco Cl BR1 186 C4
Trescoe Gdns HA2 41 A2
Tresco Gdns IG3 80 A6
Tresco Ho SE11 261 A2
Tresco Rd SE15 140 B1
Tresham Cres NW8 92 C3 237 A6
Tresham Rd IG11 79 D1
Tresham Wlk E9 74 C3
Tresidder Ho 10 SW4 159 D4
Tresilian Ave N21 16 B6
Tressel Cl 20 N1 72 D1
Tressillian Cres SE4 141 C2
Tressillian Rd SE4 141 C2
Trestis Cl UB4 84 D2
Treswell Rd RM9 103 A6
Tretawn Gdns NW7 11 C1
Tretawn Pk NW7 27 C6
Trevallyn Lo 1 KT2 176 D2
Trevanion Rd W14 254 B2
Treve Ave HA1 42 B2
Trevelayan Rd SW17 180 D4
Trevelyan Ave E12 78 B4
Trevelyan Cres HA3 43 D2
Trevelyan Ct KT3 199 D2
Trevelyan Gdns NW10 90 C6
Trevelyan Ho 16 E2 96 D4
SE5 138 D5
6 Twickenham TW1 153 C5
Trevelyan Rd E15 76 D4
Trevenna Ho 18 SE23 162 D1
Treveris St SE1 251 D3
Treversh Ct 7 BR1 186 D2
Treverton St W10 90 D3
Treverton Twr W10 90 D2
Treves Cl N21 16 B6
Treves Ho E1 96 A3
Treville St SW15 156 B4
Treviso Rd SE23 163 A2
Trevithick Cl TW14 149 D3
Trevithick Ho 3 NW5 71 B4
13 SE16 118 B2
SW8 269 C2
Trevithick St SE8 141 C6
Trevone Gdns HA5 41 A3
Trevor Cl Harrow HA3 24 D3
Hayes BR2 209 A2
Isleworth TW7 152 D6
New Barnet EN4 14 B5
Northolt UB5 84 C5
Trevor Cres HA4 61 D4
Trevor Gdns HA8 27 B2
Northolt UB5 84 C5
Trevor Pl SW7 114 C4 247 B1
Trevor Rd HA8 27 B2
Hayes UB3 105 C4
Wimbledon SW19 179 A3
Woodford IG8 37 A3
Trevor Roberts Tutorial Coll NW8 70 B1
Trevor Sq SW7 114 C4 247 B1
Trevor St SW7 114 C4 247 B1
Trevose Ho SE11 260 D2
Trevose Rd E17 36 B2
Trewenna Dr KT9 213 D3
Trewince Rd SW20 178 C2
Trewint St SW18 158 A2
Trewsbury Ho 2 SE2 124 D4
Trewsbury Rd SE26 184 D5
Triandra Way UB4 84 D2
Triangle Ct E16 99 C2
Triangle Ctr UB1 108 B5
Triangle Est The SE11 261 A1
Triangle Ho SE1 253 C2
Triangle Pl SW4 137 D1
Triangle Rd 7 E8 96 B6
Triangle The E8 96 B6
EC1 241 D6
N19 49 D2
Barking IG11 79 A2
Triangle The continued
Kingston KT3 177 A1
Tribune Ct 16 NW9 46 A5
Trident Gdns 6 UB5 84 D4
Trident Ho 9 E14 98 A1
Trident St SE16 118 D2
Trident Way UB2 106 B3
Trieste Ct SW12 158 D3
Trigon Rd SW8 138 B5 270 D4
Trilby Rd SE23 162 D2
Trillo Ct IG1 57 C2
Trimdon NW1 232 B5
Trimmer Ct TW7 130 D2
Trimmer Wlk 11 TW8 132 A6
Trim St SE8 141 B6
Trinder Gdns N19 50 A1
Trinder Rd N4,N19 50 A1
Barnet EN5 12 C6
Tring Ave Ealing W5 110 B5
Southall UB1 85 B1
Wembley HA9 66 C2
Tring Cl IG2 57 B4
Tring Ct TW1 175 A6
Trinidad Ho 17 E14 119 B6
Trinidad St E14 119 B6
Trinity Ave N2 48 B6
Enfield EN1 17 D5
Trinity Church Rd SW13 134 B6
Trinity Church Sq SE1 117 A3 262 B6
Trinity Cl E11 76 C6
SE13 142 B1
3 SW4 137 C1
Hounslow TW4 129 A1
Keston Mark BR2 210 A1
Trinity Cotts TW9 132 B2
Trinity Cres SW17 159 A2
Trinity Ct 2 N1 95 C6
SE16 119 A4
SE9 166 D5
WC1 240 C6
8 Chingford E4 20 A2
Edmonton N18 33 D4
Forest Hill SE23 162 C1
Southgate N21 16 D3
Thornton Heath SE25 205 C3
Twickenham TW2 152 C2
Trinity Gdns E16 98 D2
SW2,SW9 138 B1
11 Wanstead E18 55 B6
Trinity Gn E1 96 C2
Trinity Gr 8 SE10 142 A4
Trinity Ho 5 E17 53 D6
SE1 262 B6
Trinity Homes 14 SW2 138 B1
Trinity Mews SE9 167 B5
Penge SE20 184 B2
Wandsworth SW18 157 C3
Trinity Par TW3 129 D2
Trinity Pl DA6 147 B1
EC3 253 C5
Trinity RC High Sch (Lower) IG8 37 A6
Trinity RC High Sch (Upper Sch) IG8 36 D6
Trinity RC High Sch (Upper) IG8 37 A6
Trinity Rd N2 48 B6
Ilford IG6 57 A6
Richmond TW9 132 B2
Southall UB1 107 A5
Wandsworth SW17,SW18 158 C4
Wimbledon SW19 179 C4
Wood Green N22 32 A3
Wood Green N22 32 B2
Trinity Rise SE24,SW2 160 D4
Trinity Sch Croydon CR0 222 C6
Dagenham RM10 81 C4
Trinity Sq EC3 117 C6 253 B6
Trinity St 9 E16 99 A2
SE1 117 B3 262 C6
Enfield EN2 5 A3
Trinity St Mary's CE Prim Sch SW12 159 A3
Trinity Terr IG9 21 B4
Trinity Way E4 35 B4
W3 111 D6
Trio Pl SE1 117 A4 252 B1
Triscott Ho UB3 106 A5
Tristan Ct 21 SE8 141 B6
Tristan Sq SE3 142 C2
Tristram Cl E17 54 B6
Tristram Rd BR1 186 D6
Triton Ct EC2 242 D5
Triton Ho 2 E14 119 D2
Triton Sq NW1 239 A6
Tritton Ave CR0 220 A4
Tritton Ho N21 17 B5
Tritton Rd SE21,SE27 161 B1
Triumph Cl UB7 127 A4
Triumph Ho IG11 102 A4
Triumph Rd E6 100 B1
Triumph Trad Est N17 34 A4
Trocette Mans SE1 263 B6
Trojan Ct NW6 69 A1
9 Ealing W7 109 A5
Trojan Ind Est NW10 67 D2
Trojan Way CR0 220 B5
Troon Cl 34 SE16 118 B1
Erith SE28 102 D1
Troon Ho 11 E14 97 A1
Troon St E1 97 A1
Tropical Ct 2 W10 90 D4
Trosley Rd DA17 147 C6
Trossachs Rd SE22 161 C6
Trothy Rd SE1 118 A2
Trotman Ho SE14 140 C4
Trott Rd N10 31 A3
Trott St SW11 136 C4 267 A1
Trotwood Ho 3 SE16 118 B4
Troubridge Ct 12 W4 111 A1
Troughton Rd SE7 121 B1
Troutbeck NW1 231 D1
Troutbeck Rd SE14 141 A4
Trouville Rd SW4 159 C5
Trowbridge Rd E9 75 B2
Trower Ho 5 E9 75 A2
Trowlock Ave TW11 175 C4
Trowlock Island TW11 175 D4
Trowlock Way TW11 175 D4
Troy Ct 5 SE18 122 D2
W8 255 A6
Troyes Ho NW3 70 D3
Troy Rd SE19 183 B4
Troy Town SE15 140 A2
Troy Town Flats SE15 140 A2
Trubshaw Rd UB2 107 D3
Truesdale Rd E6 100 B1
Trulock Ct N17 34 A3
Trulock Rd N17 34 A3
Truman Cl 2 HA8 27 A3
Truman's Rd 24 N16 73 C3
Trumpers Way W7 108 D3
Trumpeters Inn TW9 153 C6
Trumpington Rd E7 76 D4
Trump St EC2 242 B1
Trundlers Way WD23 8 C3
Trundle St SE1 252 A2
Trundleys Rd SE8 141 A6
Trundley's Rd SE8 118 D1
Trundley's Terr SE8 118 D2
Truro Gdns IG1 56 A2
Truro Ho 25 W2 91 C2
Truro Rd E17 53 B5
Wood Green N22 32 B3
Truro St NW5 71 A2
Truro Way UB4 83 C4
Truslove Rd SE27 182 D5
Trussley Rd W6 112 C3
Trust Wlk SE21 160 D3
Tryfan Cl IG4 55 D4
Tryon Cres E9 96 C6
Tryon St SW3 114 D1 257 C2
Trystings Cl KT10 213 A2
Tuam Rd SE18 145 B6
Tubbenden Cl BR6 227 C5
Tubbenden Dr BR6 227 B4
Tubbenden Jun & Inf Schs BR6 227 B4
Tubbenden La BR6 227 C5
Tubbenden La S BR6 227 B3
Tubbs Rd NW10 89 D5
Tudor Ave
Hampton TW12 173 C3
North Cheam KT4 216 B4
Tudor Cl BR7 188 B2
N6 49 C2
NW3 70 C2
NW7 28 A4
NW9 67 A6
SW2 160 B5
Ashford TW15 170 A6
Cheam SM3 217 A2
Chessington KT9 214 A3
Hampton TW12 174 A5
Pinner HA5 40 A4
Wallington SM6 219 C1
Woodford IG8 37 B5
Tudor Cres EN2 5 A4
Tudor Ct E17 53 B2
N1 73 C2
5 SE16 118 D5
W5 110 C4
Feltham TW13 172 C6
Sidcup DA14 168 A1
4 Stanwell TW19 148 A5
Teddington TW11 174 D4
3 Ealing W13 87 C1
Tudor Ct N HA9 66 C3
Tudor Ct S HA9 66 C3
Tudor Dr Kingston KT2 176 A5
Walton-on-T KT12 194 D1
West Barnes SM4 201 A3
Tudor Ent Pk HA3 42 B6
Tudor Est NW10 88 D5
Tudor Gables NW7 27 D6
Tudor Gdns NW9 67 A6
Acton W3 88 C1
Harrow HA3 24 B1
Mortlake SW14 133 C2
Twickenham TW1 152 D3
West Wickham BR4 224 A5
Tudor Gr E9 74 C1
Tudor Ho 38 E9 74 C1
W14 112 D2
Tolworth KT6 198 C1
Tudor Mews 2 NW10 68 A2
Tudor Par SE9 144 A1
Dagenham RM6 58 D2
Tudor Pl SW19 180 C3
Tudor Prim Sch N3 30 A2
Southall UB1 107 A6
West Barnes SM4 200 D2
Tudor Rd E6 99 C6
E9 96 B6
N9 18 C4
Ashford TW15 171 B4
Barking IG11 101 D6
Barnet EN5 1 D2
Beckenham BR3 208 A6
Chingford E4 35 D4
Croydon SE25 206 B4
Hampton TW12 173 C3
Harrow HA3 24 B1
Hayes UB3 83 B1
Isleworth TW3 130 B1
Kingston KT2 176 C3
Penge SE19 183 D3
Pinner HA5 22 C1
Southall UB1 107 A6
Tudor Sq UB3 83 B2
Tudor St EC4 116 C6 251 B6
Tudors The 2 BR3 185 D1
Tudor Way BR5 211 B3
N14 15 D3
W3 110 C4
Hillingdon UB10 60 C2
Tudor Well Cl HA7 25 B5
Tudor Wlk DA5 169 A5
Tudway Rd SE3,SE9 143 C1
Tufnell Ct 12 E3 97 B6
Tufnell Park Mans 2 N7 72 A5
Tufnell Park Prim Sch N7 71 D4
Tufnell Park Rd N19,N7 71 D4
Tufnell Park Sta N19 71 C4
Tufton Ct SW1 260 A5
Tufton Gdns KT8 173 D1
Tufton Rd E4 35 C6
Tufton St SW1 116 A3 260 A5
Tugboat St SE28 123 C4
Tugela Rd CR0 205 B3
Tugela St SE6 163 B2
Tugmutton Cl BR6 226 D4
Tuke Sch SE15 140 B4
Tulip Cl 5 E6 100 B2
Croydon CR0 206 D1
Hampton TW12 173 B4
Southall UB2 108 A4
Tulip Gdns Chingford E4 20 B1
Ilford IG1 78 D2
Tullis Ho 12 E9 74 C1
Tull St CR4 202 D2
Tulse Cl BR3 208 A6
Tulse Hill
Streatham SW2 160 D2
Streatham SW2,SE24 160 C4
Tulse Hill Sta SE27 160 D2
Tulse Ho SW2 160 C5
Tulsemere Rd SE21, SE27 161 A2
Tumbling Bay KT12 194 A3
Tummons Gdns SE25 183 C1
Tunbridge Ct 1 SE26 162 A1
Tunbridge Ho EC1 234 C2
Tuncombe Rd N18 33 C6
Tunis Rd W12 112 B5
Tunley Gn 16 E14 97 B2
Tunley Rd NW10 89 C6
Upper Tooting SW12, SW17 159 A2
Tunmarsh La E13 99 C4
Tunnan Leys E6 100 C1
Tunnel Avenue Trad Est SE10 120 B4
Tunnel Gdns N11 31 C3
Tunnel Link Rd TW6 148 C6
Tunnel Rd SE16 118 C4
Tunnel Rd E TW6 126 D4
Tunnel Rd W TW6 126 D4
Tunstall Cl BR6 227 C4
Tunstall Ct 14 TW9 132 B4
Tunstall Rd SW9 138 B1
Croydon CR0 205 C1
Tunstall Wlk 10 TW8 132 A6
Tunstock Way DA17 125 A3
Tunworth Cl NW9 45 A3
Tunworth Cres SW15 155 D5
Tupelo Rd E10 75 D6
Tupman Ho 21 SE16 118 A4
Turberville Ho 1 SW9 138 B2
Turene Cl SW18 136 A1
Turin Rd N9 18 C4
Turin St E2 96 A4
Turkey Oak Cl SE19 183 C2
Turkey St Enfield EN1 6 B6
Enfield EN3 6 B6
Turkey Street Sta EN3 6 C6
Turks Cl UB8 82 C4
Turk's Head Yd EC1 241 C4
Turks Row SW3 114 D1 257 D2
Turle Rd N4 72 B6
Thornton Heath SW16 182 A1
Turlewray Cl N4 50 B1
Turley Cl E15 98 C6
Turnagain La EC4 241 C2
Turnage Rd RM8 59 A1
Turnant Rd N17 33 A2
Turnberry Cl NW4 28 D1
24 SE16 118 B1
Turnberry Way BR6 211 B1
Turnbull Ho N1 234 D6
Turnbury Cl SE28 102 D1
Turnchapel Mews 1 SW4 137 B2
Turner Ave N15 51 C5
Mitcham CR4 180 D2
Twickenham TW2 152 A1
Turner Cl NW11 47 D3
7 SW9 138 D4
Hillingdon UB4 83 A4
Wembley HA0 65 D2
Turner Ct 19 SE16 118 C4
9 SE5 139 B1
Turner Dr NW11 47 D3
Turner Ho N4 50 B1
NW8 230 A4
SW1 259 D3
WC2 250 B5
6 Twickenham TW1 153 D5
Turner Lo 10 SW19 156 D3
Turner Pl SW11 158 C6
Turner Rd E17 54 A6
Edgware HA8 26 B1
New Malden KT3 199 B2
Turners Meadow Way BR3 185 B2

Turner's Rd E3 ... 97 B2
Turner St E1 ... 96 B2
E16 ... 98 D1
Turners Way CR0 ... 220 C6
Turneville Rd
W14 ... 135 B6 264 C6
Turney Rd SE21 ... 161 B4
Turney Sch SE21 ... 161 A4
Turnham Green Sta W4 ... 111 C2
Turnham Green Terr
W4 ... 111 C2
Turnham Ho SE4 ... 141 A1
Turnham Prim Sch SE4 ... 141 A1
Turnham Rd SE4 ... 141 A1
Turnmill Ho 8 SW2 ... 160 C6
Turnmill St EC1 ... 94 D2 241 C4
Turnour Ho 32 E1 ... 96 B1
Turnpike Cl SE8 ... 141 B5
Turnpike Ct DA6 ... 146 D1
Turnpike Ho EC1 ... 234 D1
Turnpike La N8 ... 50 C6
Sutton SM1 ... 218 A3
Uxbridge UB10 ... 82 A5
Turnpike Lane Sta N15 ... 50 D6
Turnpike Link CR0 ... 221 C6
Turnpike Way TW7 ... 131 A4
Turnpin La 2 SE10 ... 142 A6
Turnstone Cl E13 ... 99 A4
NW9 ... 27 C1
Uxbridge UB10 ... 60 D3
Turpentine La
SW1 ... 115 B1 258 D1
Turpin Cl EN3 ... 7 C6
Turpington Cl BR2 ... 210 A2
Turpington La BR2 ... 210 A3
Turpin Ho SW11 ... 268 C2
Turpin Rd TW14 ... 149 D5
Turpin Way N19 ... 49 D1
Wallington SM6 ... 219 B1
Turquand St SE17 ... 262 B3
Turret Gr SW4 ... 137 C2
Turret Ho KT2 ... 176 A4
Turton Ho 5 SE18 ... 144 D6
Turton Rd HA0 ... 66 A3
Turville Ho NW8 ... 237 A6
Turville St E2 ... 243 C6
Tuscan Ho 30 E2 ... 96 C4
Tuscan Rd SE18 ... 123 B1
Tuskar St SE10 ... 120 C1
Tutorial Coll of West London
UB1 ... 107 B5
Tuttlebee La IG9 ... 21 A2
Tuttle Ho SW1 ... 259 D1
Tweedale Ct E15 ... 76 A3
Tweed Ct W7 ... 86 C1
Tweeddale Gr UB10 ... 61 A5
Tweeddale Jun & Inf Schs
SM5 ... 202 B2
Tweeddale Rd SM5 ... 202 B1
Tweed Ho E14 ... 98 A3
Tweedmouth Rd E13 ... 99 B5
Tweedy Cl EN1 ... 17 D6
Tweedy Rd BR1 ... 187 A2
Tweezer's Alley WC2 ... 251 A6
Twelve Acre Ho 5 E12 ... 78 C5
Twelvetrees Cres E3 ... 98 A3
Twentyman Cl IG8 ... 37 A5
Twickenham Bridge
TW9 ... 153 C6
Twickenham Cl CR0 ... 220 B5
Twickenham Gdns
Greenford UB6 ... 65 A3
Harrow HA3 ... 24 C3
Twickenham Rd E11 ... 76 B6
Isleworth TW1,TW7 ... 131 A2
Richmond TW1,TW9 ... 131 C1
Teddington TW11 ... 175 A6
Twickenham TW13 ... 151 B1
Twickenham Rugby Football
Union Ground★ TW2 ... 152 C5
Twickenham Sta TW1 ... 153 A4
Twickenham Trad Ctr
TW1 ... 152 D5
Twig Folly Cl E2 ... 96 D5
Twilley St SW18 ... 157 D4
Twine Cl IG11 ... 102 B4
Twine Ct E1 ... 118 C6
Twineham Gn N12 ... 29 C6
Twining Ave TW2 ... 152 B1
Twinn Rd NW7 ... 29 A4
Twisden Rd NW5 ... 71 B4
Twiss Ho 6 SE18 ... 122 D1
Twybridge Way NW10 ... 67 A1
Twyford Abbey Rd NW10 ... 88 B4
Twyford Ave N2 ... 48 D6
Acton W3 ... 110 C6
Twyford CE High Sch
W3 ... 110 D5
Twyford Cres W3 ... 110 C5
Twyford Ct N10 ... 49 A6
Acton W3 ... 110 C6
6 Wembley HA0 ... 88 A5
Twyford Ho 6 N15 ... 51 C3
N5 ... 72 D5
Twyford Par KT6 ... 198 C1
Twyford Pl WC2 ... 240 C2
Twyford Rd
Carshalton SM5 ... 202 B1
Harrow HA2 ... 41 D2
Ilford IG1 ... 79 A3
Twyford St N1 ... 94 B6 233 C6
Twynholm Mans SW6 ... 264 A4
Tyas Rd E16 ... 98 D3
Tybenham Rd SW19 ... 201 C6
Tyberry Rd EN3 ... 6 C2
Tyburn La HA1 ... 42 D2
Tyburn Tree (site of)★
W2 ... 247 C6
Tyburn Way W1 ... 247 D6
Tye La BR6 ... 227 A3
Tyer's Est SE1 ... 253 A2
Tyers Gate SE1 ... 117 C4 253 A1
Tyers Ho 1 SW16 ... 181 C5
Tyers St SE11 ... 116 B1 260 C2
Tyers Terr SE11 ... 116 B1 260 D1
Tyeshurst Cl SE2 ... 125 A1
Tylecroft Rd SW16 ... 182 A1
Tylehurst Gdns IG1 ... 79 A3
Tyler Cl E2 ... 95 D5
Tyler Rd UB2 ... 107 D3
Tylers Ct 4 E17 ... 53 C5
5 Wembley HA0 ... 88 A5
Tylers Gate HA3 ... 44 A3
Tylers Path SM5 ... 218 D4
Tyler St SE10 ... 120 C1
Tylers Way WD23 ... 8 C6
Tylney Ave SE19 ... 183 D5
Tylney Ho 19 E1 ... 96 B1
Tylney Rd BR1 ... 187 D1
E7 ... 77 C4
Tymperley Ct SW19 ... 157 A3
Tynamara KT1 ... 197 D5
Tynan Cl TW14 ... 150 A3
Tyndale Ct E14 ... 119 D1
Tyndale La N1 ... 72 D1
Tyndale Mans N1 ... 72 D1
Tyndale Terr 13 N1 ... 72 D1
Tyndall Gdns E10 ... 76 A6
Tyndall Rd DA16 ... 145 D2
E10 ... 76 A6
Tyne Ct W7 ... 86 C1
Tynedale Ct E14 ... 119 D1
Tyneham Cl 10 SW11 ... 137 A2
Tyne Ho 8 KT2 ... 175 D2
Tynemouth Cl E6 ... 100 D1
Tynemouth Dr EN1 ... 6 A5
Tynemouth Rd N15 ... 51 D5
SE18 ... 123 C1
Mitcham CR4 ... 181 A3
Tynemouth St SW6 ... 136 A3
Tynemouth Terr 8 N15 ... 51 D5
Tyne St E1 ... 243 D2
Tynsdale Rd NW10 ... 67 C2
Tynte Ct E9 ... 75 A3
Tynwald Ho 14 SE26 ... 162 A1
Type St E2 ... 96 D5
Tyrawley Rd SW6 ... 265 C2
Tyrell Cl HA1 ... 64 C4
Tyrell Ct SM5 ... 218 D4
Tyrols Rd SE23 ... 162 D3
Tyrone Rd E6 ... 100 B4
Tyron Way DA14 ... 189 D5
Tyrrell Ave DA16 ... 168 B6
Tyrrell Ho SW1 ... 269 B6
Catford BR3 ... 185 D5
Tyrrell Rd SE22 ... 140 A1
Tyrrell Sq CR4 ... 180 C2
Tyrrel Way NW9 ... 46 A2
Tyrwhitt Rd SE4 ... 141 C2
Tysoe Ave EN3 ... 7 B6
Tysoe St EC1 ... 234 B1
Tyson Rd SE23 ... 162 C4
Tyssen Rd N16 ... 73 D5
Tyssen Sch N16 ... 52 A1
Tyssen St E8 ... 73 D2
N1 ... 95 C5
Tytherton 30 E2 ... 96 C5
Tytherton Rd N19 ... 71 D5

U

Uamvar St E14 ... 97 D2
Uckfield Gr CR4 ... 181 A2
Uckfield Rd EN3 ... 6 D6
Udall St SW1 ... 259 B3
Udimore Ho W10 ... 90 C2
Udney Park Rd TW11 ... 175 A4
Uffington Rd NW10 ... 90 B6
West Norwood SE27 ... 182 C6
Ufford Cl HA3 ... 23 D3
Ufford Rd HA3 ... 23 D3
Ufford St SE1 ... 116 C4 251 B2
Ufton Ct UB5 ... 84 D4
Ufton Gr N1 ... 73 B1
Ufton Rd N1 ... 73 C1
Uhura Sq 19 N16 ... 73 C5
Ujima Ct N19 ... 50 A1
Streatham SW16 ... 182 A6
Ujima Ho SW16 ... 182 A6
Uk Cotts UB3 ... 105 B4
Ullathorne Rd SW16 ... 181 C6
Ulleswater Rd N14 ... 16 B1
Ullin St E14 ... 98 A2
Ullswater SW15 ... 156 D5
Ullswater Cl
Bromley BR1 ... 186 C3
Hayes UB4 ... 83 C5
Kingston KT2,SW15 ... 177 B6
Ullswater Cres SW15 ... 177 B6
Ullswater Ct
2 Woodford E18 ... 37 A1
Harrow HA2 ... 41 C2
Ullswater Ho SE15 ... 140 C6
Ullswater Rd
Barnes SW13 ... 134 A5
West Norwood SE27,
SW16 ... 160 D2
Ulster Ct KT2 ... 175 D4
Ulster Gdns N13 ... 33 A6
Ulster Pl NW1 ... 238 C5
Ulundi Rd SE3 ... 142 C6
Ulva Rd SW15 ... 134 D1
Ulverscroft Rd SE22 ... 162 A6
Ulverstone Rd SE27 ... 160 D2
Ulverston Rd E17 ... 36 B1
Ulysses Rd NW6 ... 69 B3
Umberston St E1 ... 96 B1
Umbria St SW15 ... 156 A5
Umfreville Rd N4 ... 50 D3
Una Ho 7 NW5 ... 71 B2
Under Cliff SE10 ... 142 A4
Undercliff Rd SE13 ... 141 D2
Underhill EN5 ... 13 C6
Underhill Ct EN5 ... 13 C6
Underhill Ho 7 E14 ... 97 C2
Underhill Jun & Inf Schs
EN5 ... 13 A6
Underhill Pas NW1 ... 231 D6
Underhill Rd SE21,SE22 ... 162 B4
Underhill St NW1 ... 231 D5
Underne Ave N14 ... 15 B2
Undershaft EC3 ... 95 C1 243 A1
Undershaw Rd BR1 ... 164 D1
Underwood CR0 ... 224 A3
Underwood Ct 3 E10 ... 53 D1
Underwood Ho W6 ... 112 B3
Underwood Rd E1 ... 96 A3
Chingford E4 ... 35 D5
Woodford IG8 ... 37 D3
Underwood Row N1 ... 235 B2
Underwood St
N1 ... 95 A4 235 B2
Underwood The SE9 ... 166 B2
Undine Rd E14 ... 119 D2
Undine St SW17 ... 180 D5
Uneeda Dr UB6 ... 86 B6
Unicorn Bldg 14 E1 ... 118 D6
Unicorn Sch TW9 ... 132 B4
Unicorn Works N17 ... 34 C3
Union Cl E11 ... 76 B4
Union Ct SW4 ... 138 A3
45 W2 ... 91 C2
2 Richmond TW10 ... 154 A6
Union Dr E1 ... 97 A3
Union Gr SW8 ... 137 D3
Union Mews SW9 ... 138 A3
Union Rd BR2 ... 209 D4
N11 ... 31 D4
SW8 ... 137 D3
Northolt UB5 ... 85 C5
Thornton Heath CR0 ... 205 A2
Wembley HA0 ... 66 A2
Union Sq N1 ... 95 A6 235 B5
Union St E15 ... 98 B6
SE1 ... 117 A5 252 A3
Barnet EN5 ... 1 A2
Kingston KT1 ... 175 D1
Union Wlk E2 ... 95 C4
Union Yd W1 ... 238 D1
Unity Cl NW10 ... 68 A2
West Norwood SE19 ... 183 A5
Unity Mews NW1 ... 232 C4
Unity Rd EN3 ... 6 C6
Unity Way SE18 ... 121 D3
Univ College Hospl (Annexe)
W1 ... 93 A2 238 B4
Univ Coll Jun Sch NW3 ... 70 A4
Univ Coll London
W1 ... 93 C2 239 B4
WC1 ... 93 D3 239 C6
WC1 ... 94 A3 240 B6
University Cl NW7 ... 27 D3
University Coll Hospl
WC1 ... 93 C3 239 B5
University Coll Sch NW3 ... 70 A3
University Gdns DA5 ... 169 B4
University Mans SW15 ... 134 D2
University of North London
(Tufnel Park Hall) N7 ... 71 C5
University Pl DA8 ... 147 D5
University Rd SW19 ... 180 B4
University St
WC1 ... 93 C3 239 B5
University Way E16 ... 122 D6
Univ of East London E15 ... 76 C2
E15 ... 98 B6
E6 ... 122 C6
Barking RM8 ... 80 A4
Univ of East London
(Holbrook Ctr) E15 ... 98 D5
Univ of Greenwich Avery Hill
Campus Mansion Site
SE9 ... 167 A5
Univ of Greenwich Avery Hill
Campus Southwood Site
SE9 ... 167 B4
Univ of Greenwich Rachel
Mcmillan Campus SE8 ... 141 C6
Univ of Greenwich Riverside
Ho Annexe SE18 ... 122 C3
Univ of Greenwich The
SW15 ... 156 A4
Univ of London
WC1 ... 94 A4 233 A1
Univ of London (King's Coll
Hall) SE5 ... 139 B2
Univ of London Observatory
NW7 ... 27 D4
Univ of London (Queen Mary
& Westfield Coll) E1 ... 97 A3
Univ of Westminster
NW1 ... 93 C3 239 A6
NW8 ... 92 C3 237 A5
W1 ... 93 A2 238 A4
W1 ... 93 B1 238 D2
Univ of Westminster (Harrow
Campus) HA1 ... 43 A2
Unwin Ave TW14 ... 149 B6
Unwin Cl SE15 ... 140 A6
Unwin Rd SW7 ... 114 B3 256 D6
Isleworth TW7 ... 130 C2
Upbrook Mews
W2 ... 92 A1 236 B1
Upcerne Rd
SW10 ... 136 A5 266 B3
Upchurch Cl SE20 ... 184 B3
Upcott Ho 33 E3 ... 97 D4
4 E9 ... 74 C1
Upcroft Ave HA8 ... 27 A6
Updale Rd DA14 ... 189 D6
Upfield CR0 ... 222 B5
Upfield Rd W7 ... 86 D2
Upgrove Manor Way 12
SE24 ... 160 C4
Uphall Prim Sch IG1 ... 78 D3
Uphall Rd IG1 ... 78 D3
Upham Park Rd W4 ... 111 C2
Uphill Dr NW7 ... 27 C5
NW9 ... 45 A4
Uphill Gr NW7 ... 27 C6
Uphill Rd NW7 ... 27 C6
Upland Ct SE23 ... 162 C2
Upland Inf Sch DA7 ... 147 B2
Upland Jun Sch DA7 ... 147 B2
Upland Rd DA7 ... 147 B2
8 E13 ... 99 A3
SE22 ... 162 A5
Croydon CR2 ... 221 B3
Sutton SM2 ... 218 B1
Uplands BR3 ... 185 C1
Uplands Ave E17 ... 34 D1
Uplands Bsns Pk E17 ... 52 D6
Uplands Cl SW14 ... 154 D6
Uplands Ct N21 ... 16 C4
Uplands Park Rd EN2 ... 4 C3
Uplands Rd N8 ... 50 B4
East Barnet EN4 ... 15 A3
Ilford RM6 ... 58 D6
Woodford IG8 ... 37 D3
Uplands The HA4 ... 40 A1
Uplands Way N21 ... 16 C6
Upnall Ho 16 SE15 ... 140 C6
Upney La IG11 ... 79 D1
Upney Sta IG11 ... 79 D1
Upnor Way SE17 ... 263 B2
Uppark Dr IG2 ... 57 A3
Upper Abbey Rd DA17 ... 125 C2
Upper Addison Gdns
W14 ... 113 A4 244 A2
Upper Belgrave St
SW1 ... 115 A3 258 B6
Upper Berkeley St
W1 ... 92 D1 237 D1
Upper Beulah Hill SE19 ... 183 C2
Upper Brighton Rd KT6 ... 198 A2
Upper Brockley Rd SE4 ... 141 B3
Upper Brook St
W1 ... 115 A6 248 A6
Upper Butts TW8 ... 131 C6
Upper Caldy Wlk 14 N1 ... 73 A2
Upper Cavendish Ave N3 ... 47 C6
Upper Cheyne Row
SW3 ... 136 C6 267 A6
Upper Clapton Rd E5 ... 74 B6
Upper Clarendon Wlk 13
W11 ... 91 A1
Upper Dengie Wlk N1 ... 235 A6
Upper Elmers End Rd
BR3 ... 207 A4
Upper Farm Rd KT8 ... 195 B5
Upper Fosters NW4 ... 46 C5
Upper Gn E CR4 ... 203 A6
Upper Gn W CR4 ... 180 D1
Upper Gr SE25 ... 205 D5
Upper Grosvenor St
W1 ... 115 A6 248 A5
Upper Grotto Rd TW1 ... 152 D2
Upper Ground
SE1 ... 116 C5 251 A4
Upper Grove Rd DA17 ... 147 B6
Upper Gulland Wlk 19
N1 ... 73 A2
Upper Halliford Rd
TW17 ... 193 C6
Upper Halliford Sta
TW16 ... 171 C1
Upper Ham Rd KT2,
TW10 ... 175 D6
Upper Harley St NW1 ... 238 B5
Upper Hawkwell Wlk
N1 ... 235 B6
Upper Holloway Sta N19 ... 71 D6
Upper Holly Hill Rd
DA17 ... 125 D1
Upper James St W1 ... 249 B6
Upper John St W1 ... 249 B6
Upper Lodge Mews
TW12 ... 174 A4
Upper Mall W6 ... 112 B1
Upper Marsh
SE1 ... 116 B4 260 D6
Upper Montague St
W1 ... 92 D2 237 C3
Upper Mulgrave Rd
SM2 ... 217 A1
Upper North St E3,E14 ... 97 C2
Upper Park Rd BR1 ... 187 C2
N11 ... 31 C5
NW3 ... 70 D3
Belvedere DA17 ... 125 D2
Kingston KT2 ... 176 C4
Upper Phillimore Gdns
W8 ... 113 C4 245 A1
Upper Pk IG10 ... 21 D6
Upper Rawreth Wlk N1 ... 235 B6
Upper Rd E13 ... 99 A4
N2 ... 30 C2
Wallington SM6 ... 219 D3
Upper Richmond Rd
SW15 ... 134 C1
Upper Richmond Rd W
TW10,SW14,SW15 ... 133 A1
Upper Selsdon Rd CR2 ... 221 D1
Upper Sheridan Rd
DA17 ... 125 C2
Upper Shirley Rd CR0 ... 222 D5
Upper Sq TW7 ... 131 A2
Upper St N1 ... 94 D6 234 C5
Upper St Martin's La
WC2 ... 250 A6
Upper Sunbury Rd
TW12 ... 173 C2
Upper Sutton La TW5 ... 129 C4
Upper Tachbrook St
SW1 ... 259 B4
Upper Teddington Rd
KT1,KT8 ... 175 C2
Upper Terr NW3 ... 70 A5
Upper Thames St
EC4 ... 117 A6 252 B6
Upper Tollington Pk N4 ... 50 C1
Upperton Rd DA14 ... 189 D5
Upperton Rd E E13 ... 99 C4
Upperton Rd W E13 ... 99 C4
Upper Tooting Park Mans 1
SW17 ... 159 A2
Upper Tooting Pk
SW17 ... 158 D2
Upper Tooting Rd
SW17 ... 158 D1
Upper Town Rd UB6 ... 85 D3
Upper Tulse Hill SW2 ... 160 B3
Upper Vernon Rd SM1 ... 218 B3
Upper Walthamstow Rd
E17 ... 54 B6
Upper Wickham La
DA16 ... 146 B4
Upper Wimpole St
W1 ... 93 A2 238 B4
Upper Woburn Pl
NW1,WC1 ... 93 D4 232 D1
Uppingham Ave HA7 ... 25 C1
Upsdell Ave N13 ... 32 C4
Upshire Ho E17 ... 35 B1
Upstall St SE5 ... 138 D4
Upton Ave E7 ... 77 A1
Upton Cl NW2 ... 69 A5
Sidcup DA5 ... 169 B5
Upton Cross E13 ... 99 A6
Upton Cross Prim Sch
E13 ... 99 B6
Upton Ct Penge SE20 ... 184 C3
Southall UB1 ... 107 D5
4 Wimbledon SW19 ... 178 D3
Upton Day Hospl DA6 ... 147 A1
Upton Dene SM2 ... 217 D1
Upton Gdns HA3 ... 43 C3
Upton La E7 ... 77 A1
Upton Lodge Cl WD23 ... 8 A4
Upton Park Rd E7 ... 77 B1
Upton Park Sta E13 ... 99 C6
Upton Prim Sch DA5 ... 169 B6
Upton Rd SE18 ... 145 A6
Bexley DA6 ... 169 A6
Edmonton N18 ... 34 A5
Hounslow TW3 ... 129 C2
South Norwood CR7 ... 183 B1
Upton Rd S DA5 ... 169 B5
Upton Villas 4 DA6 ... 147 A1
Upway N12 ... 30 C4
Upwood Rd SE12 ... 165 A5
Thornton Heath SW16 ... 182 A2
Urlwin St SE5 ... 139 A6
Urlwin Wlk SW9 ... 138 D4
Urmston Dr SW19 ... 157 A3
Urmston Ho 3 E14 ... 120 A2
Urquhart Ct BR3 ... 185 B3
Ursula Lo DA14 ... 190 B5
Ursula Mews N4 ... 51 A1
Ursula St SW11 ... 136 C4 267 A1
Ursuline High Sch
SW20 ... 178 D2
Urswick Gdns RM9 ... 81 A1
Urswick Rd E5,E9 ... 74 C3
Dagenham RM9 ... 81 A1
Usborne Mews SW8 ... 270 D4
Usher Rd E3 ... 97 B5
Usk Rd SW11 ... 136 A1
Usk St E2 ... 96 D4
Utopia Village
NW1 ... 71 A1 231 A6
Uvedale Rd
Dagenham RM10 ... 81 C5
Enfield EN2 ... 17 B6
Uverdale Rd
SW10 ... 136 A5 266 B3
Uxbridge Coll
Hayes UB3 ... 106 A6
Uxbridge UB8 ... 60 A2
Uxbridge High Sch UB8 ... 82 A5
Uxbridge Rd W12 ... 112 B5
Acton W3,W5 ... 110 C5
Ealing W13 ... 109 C6
Feltham TW13 ... 150 D2
Hampton TW12,TW13 ... 173 D5
Hayes UB4 ... 106 C6
Hillingdon UB10,UB4 ... 83 C2
Kingston KT1,KT6 ... 197 D4
Southall UB1,UB2,W5,W7 ... 108 B5
Stanmore HA7 ... 25 A5
Uxbridge Road (Harrow
Weald) HA3 ... 24 B3
Uxbridge Road (Hatch End)
HA5 ... 23 B3
Uxbridge St W8 ... 113 C5 245 A4
Uxendon Cres HA3,HA9 ... 44 A1
Uxendon Hill HA9 ... 44 B2
Uxendon Manor Prim Sch
HA3 ... 44 A4

V

Vaine Ho 4 E9 ... 75 A2
Valance Ave E4 ... 20 D3
Valan Leas BR2 ... 208 C6
Vale Ave WD6 ... 10 D6
Vale Cl N2 ... 48 D6
W9 ... 92 A4 229 A1
Orpington BR6 ... 226 C4
Twickenham TW1 ... 153 A1
Vale Cres SW15 ... 177 C6
Vale Croft Claygate KT10 ... 212 D1
Pinner HA5 ... 41 A4
Vale Ct W3 ... 111 D5
W9 ... 92 A4 229 A1
Barnet EN5 ... 1 D1
Wembley HA0 ... 65 C5
Vale Dr EN5 ... 13 C6
Vale End SE22 ... 139 D1
Vale Est The W3 ... 111 C5
Vale Farm Sports Ctr
HA0 ... 65 B4
Vale Gr N4 ... 51 A2
W3 ... 111 B5
Vale La W3 ... 88 C2
Vale Lo SE23 ... 162 C2
Valence Ave RM8 ... 80 D6
Valence Cir RM8 ... 81 A5
Valence House Mus★
RM8 ... 81 A6
Valence Inf Sch RM8 ... 80 D6
Valence Jun Sch RM8 ... 80 D6
Valence Wood Rd RM8 ... 81 A5
Valencia Rd HA7 ... 25 C6
Valens Ho 1 SW2 ... 160 C3
Valentia Pl SW9 ... 138 C1
Valentine Ave DA5 ... 169 A3
Valentine Ct SE23 ... 162 D2
Valentine Ho 11 SW4 ... 159 C5
Valentine Pl
SE1 ... 116 D4 251 C2
Valentine Rd E9 ... 74 D2
Harrow HA2 ... 64 A5
Valentine Row SE1 ... 251 C1
Valentines High Sch IG2 ... 56 C3
Valentines Rd IG1 ... 56 D1
Vale of Health NW3 ... 70 B5
Vale Rd BR1 ... 188 C1
E7 ... 77 B2
N4 ... 51 A2
Claygate KT10 ... 212 D1
Mitcham CR4 ... 203 D5
Sutton SM1 ... 217 D4
Worcester Park KT19,KT4 ... 215 D5
Vale Rd N KT6 ... 214 A6
Vale Rd S KT6 ... 214 A6
Valerian Way E15 ... 98 C4
Valerie Ct Belmont SM2 ... 217 D1
Bushey WD23 ... 8 A4
Vale Rise NW11 ... 47 B1
Vale Row N5 ... 72 D5
Vale Royal N7 ... 72 A1
Valery Pl TW12 ... 173 C3
Vale Sch The N4 ... 51 B3
Valeswood Rd BR1 ... 186 D5
Vale Terr N4 ... 51 A3
Vale The N10 ... 31 A2
NW11 ... 69 A6
SW3 ... 136 B6 266 D6
W3 ... 111 C5
Ashford TW16 ... 172 A4
Croydon CR0 ... 222 D6
Feltham TW14 ... 150 B5
Heston TW5 ... 129 A6
Ruislip HA4 ... 62 C4
Southgate N14 ... 16 A4
Woodford IG8 ... 37 A3
Valetta Gr E13 ... 99 A5
Valetta Rd W3 ... 111 D4
Valette Ct N10 ... 49 B5
Valette Ho E9 ... 74 C2
Valette St E8 ... 74 B2
Valiant Cl 13 UB5 ... 84 D4
Valiant Ho 5 SE7 ... 121 C1
SW11 ... 266 D1
Valiant Way E6 ... 100 B2
Vallance Rd E1 ... 96 A3
N22 ... 31 C1
Vallentin Rd E17 ... 54 A5
Valley Ave N12 ... 30 B6
Valley (Charlton Athletic FC)
The SE7 ... 121 C1
Valley Cl HA5 ... 22 B1
Valley Ct IG8 ... 37 B3
Valley Dr NW9 ... 44 D3
Valleyfield Rd SW16 ... 182 B5
Valley Fields Cres EN2 ... 4 C3
Valley Gdns
Mitcham SW19 ... 180 B3
Wembley HA0 ... 66 B1
Valley Gr SE7 ... 121 C1
Valley Ho E5 ... 52 C1
4 Edmonton N9 ... 18 A1
Valley L Ctr SE9 ... 167 A4
Valleylink Est EN3 ... 19 A5
Valley Mews TW1 ... 153 A2
Valley Pl KT6 ... 198 A3
Valley Prim Sch BR2 ... 186 D1
Valley Prospect 3
SE19 ... 183 C4
Valley Rd BR5 ... 190 B2
Beckenham BR2 ... 186 C1
Streatham SW16 ... 182 B6
Uxbridge UB10 ... 82 A5
Valleyside SE7 ... 121 D1
Valley Side E4 ... 19 C3
Valley Side Par E4 ... 19 C2
Valley View EN5 ... 13 A5
Valley Wlk CR0 ... 222 C6
Valliere Rd NW10 ... 90 A4
Valliers Wood Rd DA15 ... 167 C3
Vallis Way
Chessington KT9 ... 213 D4
Ealing W13 ... 87 A2
Valmar Rd SE5 ... 139 A4

Valmar Trad Est 7 SE5 ..139 A4
Valnay St SW17 ....180 D5
Valognes Ave E17 ....35 A2
Valois Ho SE1 ....263 C6
Valonia Gdns SW18 ....157 B5
Vambery Rd SE18 ....145 A6
Vanbern Ho NW5 ....71 A2
Vanborough Ct 4 SM2 ..218 A2
Vanbrough Cres UB5 ....84 C6
Vanbrugh Cl 2 E16 ....99 D2
Vanbrugh Ct SE11 ....261 B3
Vanbrugh Dr KT12 ....194 C3
Vanbrugh Fields SE3 ..142 D5
Vanbrugh Hill SE10,SE3 ..142 D6
Vanbrugh Ho 8 E9 ....74 C1
Vanbrugh Mews KT12 ..194 C2
Vanbrugh Park Rd SE3 ..142 D5
Vanbrugh Park Rd W
SE3 ....142 D5
Vanbrugh Pk SE3 ....142 D5
Vanbrugh Rd W4 ....111 B3
Vanbrugh Terr SE3 ....142 D4
Vanburgh Cl BR6 ....211 C1
Vanburgh Ho E1 ....243 C4
Vancouver Rd
Edgware HA8 ....26 D2
Forest Hill SE23 ....163 B2
Hayes UB4 ....84 B3
Richmond TW10 ....175 C6
Vancover Ho 33 E1 ....118 B5
Vanderbilt Rd SW18 ....158 A3
Vanderbilt Villas 1
W12 ....112 D4
Vanderville Gdns N2 ....30 B1
Vandome Cl E16 ....99 B1
Vandon Ct SW1 ....259 B6
Vandon Pas SW1 ....259 B6
Vandon St SW1 ....259 B6
Van Dyck Ave KT3 ....199 B2
Vandyke Cl SW15 ....156 D5
Vandyke Cross SE9 ....166 A6
Vandy St EC2 ....243 A5
Vane Cl NW3 ....70 B4
Harrow HA3 ....44 B3
Vane Ho 15 N2 ....30 B1
Vanessa Cl DA17 ....125 C1
Vane St SW1 ....259 B4
Vanfame Ct KT3 ....199 D6
Vangaurd Way TW6 ....127 C2
Vange Ho W10 ....90 C2
Van Gogh Ct E14 ....120 B3
Vanguard Bldg 12 E14 ...119 C4
Vanguard Cl E16 ....99 B2
Thornton Heath CR0 ....204 D1
Vanguard Ho
7 Merton SW19 ....180 A3
6 Stanwell TW19 ....148 A5
Vanguard St SE8 ....141 C4
Vanguard Trad Ctr E15 ....98 A6
Vanguard Way SM6 ....220 A1
Vanneck Sq SW15 ....156 A6
Vanoc Gdns BR1 ....187 A6
Vansittart Rd E7 ....77 A4
Vansittart St 7 SE14 ....141 A5
Vanston Pl SW6 ..135 C5 265 B4
Vantage Mews E14 ....120 A5
Vant Rd SW17 ....180 D5
Vantrey Ho SE11 ....261 A3
Varcoe Rd SE16 ....118 C1
Vardens Rd SW11 ....136 B1
Varden St E1 ....96 B1
Vardon Cl W3 ....89 B1
Vardon Ho SE10 ....142 A4
Varey Ho E1 ....97 A4
Varley Ho 5 NW6 ....91 C6
Varley Par NW9 ....45 C5
Varley Rd E16 ....99 B1
Varley Way CR4 ....180 B1
Varna Rd SW6 ..135 B5 264 C3
Hampton TW12 ....173 D2
Varndell St NW1 ..93 C4 232 A2
Varsity Dr TW1,TW7 ....152 D5
Varsity Row SW14 ....133 A3
Vartry Rd N15 ....51 C3
Vassal Ho E3 ....97 A4
Vassall Rd SW9 ....138 C5
Vat Ho SW8 ....270 B4
Vauban Est SE16 ....263 D5
Vauban St SE16 ..117 D3 263 D5
Vaudeville Ct N4 ....72 C6
Vaughan Almshouses
TW15 ....170 D5
Vaughan Ave NW4 ....46 A4
W6 ....111 D2
Vaughan Est 3 E2 ....95 D4
Vaughan Fst & Mid Sch
HA1 ....42 A3
Vaughan Gdns IG1 ....56 B2
Vaughan Ho SE1 ....251 C2
Vaughan Rd DA16 ....145 D3
E15 ....76 D2
SE5 ....139 A2
Harrow HA1 ....42 B3
Thames Ditton KT7 ....197 B2
Vaughan St SE16 ....119 B4
Vaughan Way E1 ....118 A5
Vaughan Williams Cl
SE8 ....141 C5
Vauxhall Bridge Rd
SW1 ....115 C2 259 B3
Vauxhall Cross
SE1,SW8 ....116 A1 260 B1
Vauxhall Gdns CR2 ....221 A2
Vauxhall Gr
SW8 ....138 B6 270 C6
Vauxhall Prim Sch
SE11 ....116 B1 260 D2
Vauxhall St
SE11 ....116 B1 260 D2
Vauxhall Sta
SE11 ....116 A1 260 B1
Vauxhall Wlk SE11 ....260 C2
Vawdrey Cl E1 ....96 C3
Vaynor Ho N7 ....72 A4
Veals Mead CR4 ....180 C2
Vectis Ct SW18 ....157 D5
Vectis Gdns SW17 ....181 B4
Vectis Rd SW17 ....181 B4
Veda Rd SE13 ....141 C1
Vega Cres HA6 ....22 A5
Vega Rd WD23 ....8 A4
Veitch Cl TW14 ....149 D4
Veldene Way HA2 ....63 B5
Velde Way 1 SE22 ....161 C6
Vellacott Ho W12 ....90 B1
Velletri Ho 17 E2 ....96 D5
Vellum Dr SM5 ....219 A5
Venables Cl RM10 ....81 D4
Venables St NW8 ..92 B2 236 D4
Vencourt Pl W6 ....112 A2
Venetian Rd SE5 ....139 A3
Venetia Rd N4 ....50 D3
W5 ....109 D4
Venice Ct 14 SE5 ....139 A5
Venita Manor SE27 ....182 C5
Venmead Ct DA17 ....125 C2
Venner Rd SE26 ....184 C5
Venn Ho N1 ....233 D5
Venn St SW4 ....137 C1
Ventnor Ave HA7 ....25 B1
Ventnor Dr N20 ....13 D2
Ventnor Gdns IG11 ....79 C2
Ventnor Mans IG11 ....79 C2
Ventnor Rd SE14 ....140 D5
Belmont SM2 ....217 D1
Ventnor Terr N15 ....52 A5
Venture Cl DA5 ....169 A4
Venture Ct 3 SE12 ....165 A4
Venue St E14 ....98 A2
Venus Rd SE18 ....122 B3
Vera Ave N21 ....16 C6
Vera Ct 1 W2 ....91 D1
Vera Lynn Cl 5 E7 ....77 A4
Vera Rd SW6 ....135 A4 264 B2
Verbena Cl E16 ....98 D3
Verbena Gdns W6 ....112 A1
Verdant Ct 3 SE6 ....164 C4
Verdant La SE6 ....164 C3
Verdayne Ave CR0 ....222 D6
Verdi Ho 2 NW6 ....91 A5
Verdun Rd SE18,SE2 ....146 A6
Barnes SW13 ....134 A5
Vere Bank SW19 ....157 B3
Vereker Dr TW16 ....194 A6
Vereker Rd W14 ....254 B1
Vere St W1 ....93 B1 238 C1
Verity Cl W11 ....91 A1
Verity Ct N9 ....18 D3
Verity Ho 15 E3 ....97 B4
Vermeer Ct E14 ....120 B3
Vermont Cl EN2 ....4 D1
Vermont Ho E17 ....35 B1
Vermont Rd Sutton SM1 ..217 D5
Wandsworth SW18 ....157 D5
West Norwood SE19 ....183 C4
Verne Ct 9 W3 ....111 A3
Verney Gdns RM9 ....81 A4
Verney Ho NW8 ....237 A6
Isleworth TW3 ....130 A1
Verney Rd SE16 ....118 B1
Dagenham RM9 ....81 A4
Verney St NW10 ....67 B5
Verney Way SE16 ....118 B1
Vernham Rd SE18 ....145 A6
Vernon Ave Ilford E12 ....78 B4
West Barnes SW20 ....178 D1
Woodford IG8 ....37 B3
Vernon Cl KT19 ....215 A2
Vernon Cres EN4 ....15 A5
Vernon Ct NW2 ....69 B5
Ealing W5 ....109 C6
Stanmore HA7 ....25 B2
Vernon Dr HA7 ....25 A2
Vernon Ho NW9 ....45 D4
Vernon House Sch NW10 .67 B3
Vernon Mews W14 ....254 B3
Vernon Pl WC1 ....240 B3
Vernon Rd E11 ....54 C1
E15 ....76 C1
E17 ....53 B4
E3 ....97 B5
N8 ....50 C6
Feltham TW13 ....149 D2
Ilford IG3 ....57 D1
Mortlake SW14 ....133 B2
Sutton SM1 ....218 B3
Vernon Rise WC1 ....233 D2
Greenford UB6 ....64 B3
Vernon Sq WC1 ....233 D2
Vernon St W14 ..113 A2 254 B3
Vernon Yd W11 ..113 B6 244 C6
Veroan Rd DA7 ....147 A3
Verona Ct 10 SE14 ....140 D6
W4 ....111 C1
Verona Dr KT6 ....214 A6
Verona Rd E7 ....77 A1
Veronica Gdns CR4,
SW16 ....181 C2
Veronica Ho SE4 ....141 B2
Veronica Rd SW17 ....159 B2
Veronique Gdns IG6 ....57 A4
Verran Rd SW12 ....159 B4
Versailles Rd SE20 ....184 A3
Verulam Ave E17 ....53 B2
Verulam Ct NW9 ....46 A2
4 Southall UB1 ....86 A1
Verulam Ho 1 W6 ....112 C4
Verulam Rd UB6 ....85 C3
Verulam St EC1 ..94 C2 241 A4
Vervain Ho 2 SE15 ....140 A5
Verwood Dr EN4 ....2 D2
Verwood Ho SW8 ....270 D3
Verwood Lo 1 E14 ....120 B2
Verwood Rd HA2 ....24 A1
Veryan Ct 2 N8 ....49 D4
Vesage Ct EC1 ....241 B3
Vesey Path 15 E14 ....97 D1
Vespan Rd W12 ....112 A4
Vesta Rd SE4,SE14 ....141 A3
Vestris Rd SE23 ....162 D2
Vestry House (Mus)★
E17 ....53 D5
Vestry Mews 12 SE5 ....139 C4
Vestry Rd E17 ....53 D5
SE5 ....139 C4
Vestry St N1 ....95 B4 235 C2
Vevey St SE23,SE6 ....163 B2
Veysey Gdns RM10 ....81 C5
Viaduct Pl 28 E2 ....96 B4
Viaduct Rd N2 ....30 C1
Viaduct St E2 ....96 B4
Viaduct The Harrow HA2 ..64 A5
Woodford E18 ....37 B1
Vian St SE13 ....141 D2
Viant Ho 11 NW10 ....67 B1
Vibart Gdns SW2 ....160 B4
Vibart Wlk N1 ....233 B6
Vicarage Ave SE3 ....143 A5
Vicarage Cl
New Malden KT4 ....199 C1
Northolt UB5 ....63 B1
Ruislip HA4 ....39 B2
Vicarage Cres
SW11 ....136 B4 266 C1
Vicarage Ct N12 ....29 D5
W8 ....245 C2
Beckenham BR3 ....207 A6
East Bedfont TW14 ....149 A4
7 Putney SW15 ....156 A4
Vicarage Dr Barking IG11 ..79 A1
Beckenham BR3 ....185 C2
Mortlake SW14 ....155 B6
Vicarage Farm Ct TW5 ..129 B5
Vicarage Farm Rd TW3,
TW4,TW5 ....129 A4
Vicarage Fields KT12 ...194 C3
Vicarage Fields Sh Ctr The
IG11 ....79 A1
Vicarage Gate
W8 ....113 D5 245 C3
Vicarage Gdns W8 ....245 B3
Mitcham CR4 ....202 C6
Mortlake SW14 ....155 B6
Vicarage Gr SE5 ....139 B4
Vicarage Ho 1 KT1 ....176 B1
Vicarage La E15 ....76 D1
Ilford IG1 ....57 B1
Wallend E6 ....100 C4
Vicarage Pk SE18 ....123 A1
Vicarage Prim Sch E6 ...100 B4
Vicarage Rd DA5 ....169 D3
E10 ....53 D1
E15 ....76 D1
NW4 ....46 A3
SE18 ....123 A1
Ashford TW16 ....171 D4
Croydon CR0 ....220 C5
Dagenham RM10 ....81 D1
Kingston KT1,KT2 ....175 D1
Mortlake SW14 ....155 B6
Sutton SM1 ....217 D5
Teddington KT1,KT8 ....175 C2
Teddington TW11 ....175 A5
Tottenham N17 ....34 A2
Vicarage Way NW10 ....67 B5
Harrow HA2 ....41 C2
Vicarage Wlk
SW11 ....136 B4 266 D2
Vicars Bridge Cl HA0 ....88 A5
Vicar's Cl E15 ....99 A6
E9 ....96 C6
Enfield EN1 ....5 C3
Vicar's Green Prim Sch
HA0 ....87 C5
Vicars Hill SE13 ....141 D1
Vicar's Moor La N21 ....16 D4
Vicars Oak Rd SE19 ....183 C4
Vicar's Rd NW5 ....71 A3
Vicar's Wlk RM8 ....80 B5
Viceroy Cl N2 ....48 C6
Viceroy Ct NW8 ....230 B4
5 Croydon CR0 ....205 B1
Viceroy Lo 6 KT6 ....198 A4
Viceroy Par N2 ....48 C6
Viceroy Rd SW8 ..138 A4 270 A2
Vic Johnson Ho 14 E3 ....97 B6
Vickers Cl SM6 ....220 B1
Vickers Ct 10 TW19 ....148 A5
Vickery Ct EC1 ....242 B6
Vickery Ho 12 SW4 ....138 A1
Victor Cazalet Ho N1 ....234 C6
Victor Gr HA0 ....66 A1
Victor Ho N20 ....14 D1
Victoria & Albert Mus★
SW7 ....114 B3 256 D5
Victoria Arc SW1 ....258 D5
Victoria Ave E6 ....99 D6
EC2 ....243 B3
N3 ....29 B2
Barnet EN4 ....2 B1
East Molesey KT8 ....195 D6
Hackbridge SM5,SM6 ....219 A5
Hillingdon UB10 ....60 D1
Hounslow TW3,TW4 ....151 C6
Surbiton KT6 ....197 D3
Wembley HA9 ....66 D2
Victoria Bglws DA14 ....191 B3
Victoria Bldgs 18 E8 ....96 B6
Victoria Bsns Ctr DA16 ..146 B3
Victoria Cl Barnet EN4 ....2 B1
East Molesey KT8 ....195 C6
Harrow HA1 ....42 D3
Hayes UB3 ....83 B1
Victoria Coach Sta
SW1 ....115 B2 258 C3
Victoria Cotts N10 ....31 A1
3 E1 ....96 A2
Ilford IG6 ....57 A4
7 Richmond TW9 ....132 C4
Victoria Cres N15 ....51 C4
Merton SW19 ....179 B3
West Norwood SE19 ....183 C4
Victoria Ct 3 E1 ....118 A6
5 SW4 ....159 D5
W3 ....110 C4
Penge SE26 ....184 C4
1 Wanstead E18 ....55 B6
Wembley HA9 ....66 C2
Victoria Dock Rd E16 ....121 B6
Victoria Dr SW19 ....156 D3
Victoria Emb
WC2 ....116 C6 251 A5
Victoria Gdns
W11 ....113 C5 245 A4
Heston TW5 ....129 A4
Victoria Gr N12 ....30 B5
W8 ....114 A3 256 A6
Victoria Gr Mews W2 ...245 C5
Victoria Ho SW1 ....258 C2
6 SW4 ....159 D5
2 W12 ....112 A4
Edgware HA8 ....26 D4
Victoria Ind Est W3 ....89 C2
Victoria Jun Sch The
TW13 ....150 B3
Victoria La Barnet EN5 ....1 B1
Hayes UB3 ....105 B1
Victoria Lo 4 SW19 ....178 C3
Victoria Mans 8 N7 ....72 C3
NW10 ....68 B1
Victoria Mews NW6 ....91 C6
Wandsworth SW18 ....158 A3
Victorian Gr N16 ....73 C5
Victorian Rd N16 ....73 D5
Victoria Park Ct 11 E9 ....74 C1
Victoria Park Ind Ctr E3 ..75 B1
Victoria Park Lofts E9 ....96 D6
Victoria Park Rd E9 ....74 D1
Victoria Park Sq E2 ....96 C4
Victoria Pas NW8 ....236 C6
Victoria Pl 18 TW10 ....153 D6
Victoria Point 10 E13 ....99 A5
Victoria Rd BR2 ....209 D4
BR7 ....188 C5
DA15 ....168 A1
E11 ....76 C4
E13 ....99 A5
N15 ....52 A5
N22 ....31 D2
N4 ....50 B1
NW10 ....89 C3
NW4 ....46 D5
NW6 ....91 B6
NW7 ....27 D5
W8 ....114 A3 256 A6
Barking IG11 ....78 D2
Barnet EN4 ....2 B1
Bexley DA6 ....147 C1
Buckhurst Hill IG9 ....21 D2
Chingford E17 ....36 A1
Chingford, Chingford Green
E4 ....20 C3
Dagenham RM10 ....81 D3
Ealing W5 ....87 B2
Edmonton N18 ....33 D6
Edmonton N9 ....17 D1
Feltham TW13 ....150 B3
Kingston KT1 ....176 B1
Mitcham CR4 ....180 D3
Mortlake SW14 ....133 B2
Ruislip HA4 ....62 B4
Southall UB2 ....107 B3
Surbiton KT6 ....197 D3
Sutton SM1 ....218 B3
Teddington TW11 ....175 A4
Twickenham TW1 ....153 B4
Wanstead E18 ....55 B6
Victoria Ret Pk HA4 ....62 D3
Victoria Rise SW4 ....137 B2
Victoria Sq SW1 ....258 D6
Victoria St E15 ....76 C1
SW1 ....115 C3 259 B5
Erith DA17 ....125 B1
Victoria Sta
SW1 ....115 B2 258 D4
Victoria Terr N4 ....50 C1
NW10 ....89 C3
Harrow HA1 ....42 C1
Victoria Villas TW9 ....132 B1
Victoria Way SE7 ....143 C6
Victoria Yd 31 E1 ....96 A1
Victor Mills Cotts BR8 ..191 C3
Victor Rd NW10 ....90 B4
Harrow HA2 ....42 A6
Penge SE20 ....184 D3
Teddington TW11 ....174 C6
Victors Dr TW12 ....173 A4
Victor Seymour Inf Sch
SM5 ....218 D4
Victors Way EN5 ....1 B2
Victor Villas N9 ....17 B1
Victory Ave SM4 ....202 A4
Victory Bsns Ctr The
TW7 ....130 D1
Victory Ct IG11 ....102 B4
Victory Day Sch
SW11 ....137 A4 268 A1
Victory Pl 6 E14 ....119 A6
Victory Pl *continued*
SE17 ....117 B2 262 C4
West Norwood SE19 ....183 C4
Victory Prim Sch
SE17 ....117 A2 262 B4
Victory Rd Merton SW19 .180 A3
Wanstead E11 ....55 B5
Victory Road Mews 5
SW19 ....180 A3
Victory Way SE16 ....119 A4
Hounslow TW5 ....106 C1
Victory Wharf E14 ....119 A6
Victory Wlk SE8 ....141 C4
Video Ct N4 ....50 A2
Vidler Cl KT9 ....213 C2
Vienna Cl IG5 ....37 D1
View Cl N6 ....48 D2
Harrow HA1 ....42 B5
View Cres N8 ....49 D4
Viewfield Cl HA3 ....44 A2
Viewfield Rd DA5 ....168 C3
Wandsworth SW18 ....157 B5
Viewland Rd SE18 ....123 D1
View Point SE3 ....142 D2
View Rd N6 ....48 D3
Viewside Lo N6 ....49 C3
View The SE2 ....125 A1
Viga Rd N21 ....16 C5
Vigilant Cl SE26 ....184 A6
Vignoles Rd RM7 ....59 C2
Vigo St W1 ....115 C6 249 A5
Vi & John Rubens Ho
IG2 ....56 C3
Viking Cl 12 E3 ....97 A5
Viking Ct TW12 ....173 D2
Viking Fst & Mid Sch
UB5 ....84 D4
Viking Gdns E6 ....100 A3
Viking Ho 3 SE5 ....139 A3
3 SE7 ....122 A2
Viking Pl E10 ....53 B1
Viking Rd UB1 ....107 A6
Villacourt Rd SE18,SE2 ..146 A6
Village Arc The 2 E4 ....20 B3
Village Cl NW3 ....70 B3
Chingford E4 ....36 A5
Village Ct E17 ....53 D4
SE3 ....142 C2
Village Gate TW17 ....192 D4
Village Home The IG6 ....57 A6
Village Hts IG8 ....36 D5
Village Inf Sch RM10 ....81 C1
Village Mount 18 NW3 ....70 A4
Village Park Cl EN1 ....17 C5
Village Rd N3 ....29 A1
Enfield EN1 ....17 C6
Village Row SM2 ....217 C1
Village Sch The NW3 ....70 D2
Village The SE7 ....143 D6
SW11 ....136 D2
Village Way NW10 ....67 B4
SE21 ....161 B5
Ashford TW15 ....170 C6
Beckenham BR3 ....207 C6
Pinner HA5 ....41 B2
Village Way E HA2 ....41 C2
Villa Rd SW9 ....138 C2
Villas Rd SE18 ....123 A2
Villa St SE17 ....117 B1 262 D1
Villiers Ave Kingston KT5 .198 B5
Twickenham TW2 ....151 B3
Villiers Cl E10 ....75 C6
Kingston KT5 ....198 B5
Villiers Ct N20 ....14 A4
SW11 ....267 B2
Villiers High Sch UB1 ....107 B5
Villiers Ho W5 ....109 D6
Villiers Rd NW2 ....68 A2
Isleworth TW7 ....130 C3
Kingston KT1 ....198 B6
Penge BR3 ....184 D1
Southall UB1 ....107 B5
Villiers St WC2 ....250 B4
Vincam Cl TW2 ....151 C4
Vince Ct N1 ....235 D1
Vincent Ave KT5 ....215 A6
Vincent Cl BR2 ....209 B5
DA15 ....167 C3
Barnet EN5 ....1 D2
Harmondsworth UB7 ....126 C6
Vincent Ct N4 ....50 A1
NW4 ....46 D5
SW9 ....270 D1
W1 ....237 C2
Vincent Dr
Hillingdon UB10 ....82 B6
Upper Halliford TW17 ....193 C6
Vincent Gdns NW2 ....67 D5
Vincent Ho KT3 ....199 D5
Vincent Rd N15 ....51 A5
SE18 ....122 D2
W3 ....111 A3
Chingford E4 ....36 B4
Croydon CR0 ....205 C2
Dagenham RM9 ....81 A1
Hounslow TW4 ....128 D2
Hounslow TW7 ....130 B4
Kingston KT1 ....198 C6
Wembley HA0 ....66 B1
Wood Green N22 ....32 C1
Vincent Row TW12 ....174 A5
Vincents Cl SE16 ....119 A4
Vincents Path UB5 ....63 A2
Vincent Sq SW1 .115 D2 259 C4
Wood Green N22 ....32 C1
Vincent St E16 ....98 D2
SW1 ....115 D2 259 D4
Vincent Terr N1 ..94 D5 234 D4
Vince St EC1 ....95 B4 235 D1
Vine Cl Surbiton KT5 ....198 B3
Vine Cl *continued*
Sutton SM1 ....218 A5
West Drayton UB7 ....104 C2
Vine Cotts 3 Ealing W7 ..108 C5
Southall UB2 ....107 D2
Vine Ct E1 ....96 A2
Harrow HA3 ....44 A3
Vinegar St E1 ....118 B5
Vinegar Yd SE1 ....253 A2
Vine Gdns IG1 ....79 A3
Vine Gr UB10 ....60 C1
Vine Hill EC1 ....241 A5
Vine La SE1 ....117 C5 253 B3
Hillingdon UB10 ....82 B6
Uxbridge UB10 ....60 B1
Vine Lo N12 ....30 A4
Vine Pl Ealing W5 ....110 A5
Hounslow TW3 ....129 D1
Vine Rd BR6 ....227 D2
E15 ....76 D1
Barnes SW13 ....133 D2
East Molesey KT8 ....196 A5
Vineries Bank NW7 ....28 B5
Vineries Cl
Dagenham RM9 ....81 B2
Harmondsworth UB7 ....126 C6
Vineries The Enfield EN1 ....5 C2
Southgate N14 ....15 C5
Viners Cl KT12 ....194 C3
Vines Ave N3 ....29 D2
Vine Sq W14 ....254 D1
Vines Sch The SW11 ....137 A1
Vine St EC3 ....95 D1 243 C1
W1 ....249 B5
Vine St Bridge EC1 ....241 B5
Vinewood Ct E17 ....54 B4
Vineyard Ave NW7 ....29 A3
Vineyard Cl
Forest Hill SE6 ....163 C3
Kingston KT1 ....198 B6
Vineyard Gr N3 ....29 D2
Vineyard Hill Rd SW19 ..179 C6
Vineyard Path SW14 ....133 B2
Vineyard Rd TW13 ....150 A1
Vineyard Row KT1,KT8 ..175 C2
Vineyard Sch The TW10 .154 A5
Vineyards The TW13 ....150 A1
Vineyard The TW10 ....154 A6
Vineyard Wlk EC1 ....241 A6
Viney Ct 9 SW4 ....159 D5
Vine Yd SE1 ....252 B2
Viney Rd SE13 ....141 D2
Vining St SW2,SW9 ....138 C1
Vinlake Ave UB10 ....60 C5
Vinson Ho N1 ....235 D3
Vinter Ct TW17 ....192 C4
Vintners Ct EC4 ....252 B6
Vintry Mews 3 E17 ....53 C5
Viola Ave SE2 ....124 B1
Feltham TW14 ....150 C5
Stanwell TW19 ....148 A3
Viola Sq W12 ....111 D6
Violet Ave Enfield EN2 ....5 B5
Hillingdon UB8 ....82 B2
Violet Cl E16 ....98 C3
44 SE8 ....141 B6
Hackbridge SM6 ....203 A1
Violet Gdns CR0 ....220 D3
Violet Hill NW8 ..92 A5 229 A3
Violet Hill Ho NW8 ....229 A3
Violet La CR0 ....220 D3
Violet Rd E17 ....53 C3
E3 ....97 D3
Woodford E18 ....37 B1
Violet St E2 ....96 B3
Violet Terr UB8 ....82 C2
Violette Szabo Ho 4
SE27 ....183 B6
VIP Trad Est SE7 ....121 C2
Virgil Pl W1 ....237 C3
Virgil St SE1 ....116 B3 260 D6
Virginia Cl KT3 ....199 A5
Virginia Ct 7 SE16 ....118 D4
Virginia Ho 3 E14 ....120 A6
Teddington TW11 ....175 A5
Virginia Prim Sch E2 ....95 D4
Virginia Rd 19 E2 ....95 D4
South Norwood CR7 ....182 D2
Virginia St E1 ....118 A6
Virginia Wlk SW2 ....160 B5
Viscount Cl N11 ....31 B5
Viscount Ct 9 W11 ....91 C1
Viscount Dr E6 ....100 B2
Viscount Gr 3 UB5 ....84 D4
Viscount Point 7 SW19 .179 C3
Viscount Rd TW19 ....148 A3
Viscount St EC1 ....242 A4
Viscount Way TW6 ....127 C1
Vista Ave EN3 ....6 D3
Vista Dr IG4 ....55 D4
Vista The SE9 ....165 D4
Vista Way HA3 ....44 A3
Vita Et Pax Sch N14 ....15 B6
Vittoria Ho N1 ....233 D5
Vittoria Prim Sch
N1 ....94 C5 234 A4
Viveash Cl UB3 ....105 D3
Vivian Ave NW4 ....46 B4
Wembley HA9 ....66 C2
Vivian Ct N12 ....29 D5
Vivian Gdns HA9 ....66 C3
Vivian Ho N4 ....51 B2
Vivian Mans 1 NW4 ....46 B4
Vivian Rd E3 ....97 A5
Vivian Sq SE15 ....140 B2
Vivian Way N2 ....48 B4
Vivien Cl KT9 ....214 A1

Vivienne Cl TW1 153 D5
Voce Rd SE18 145 B5
Voewood Cl KT3 199 D3
Vogans Mill SE1 253 D2
Vogler Ho 2 E1 118 C6
Vollasky Ho 5 E1 96 A2
Volta Cl N9 18 C1
Voltaire 2 SE5 139 D4
15 Richmond TW9 132 B4
Voltaire Ct 12 SW11 137 A3
Voltaire Rd SW4 137 D2
Voltaire Way UB3 105 C6
Volt Ave NW10 89 C4
Volta Way CR0 204 B1
Voluntary Pl E11 55 A3
Vorley Rd N19 71 C6
Voss Ct SW16 182 A4
Voss St E2 96 A4
Voyager Bsns Est 10 SE16 118 A3
Voyagers Cl IG11 102 C1
Voysey Cl N3 47 A6
Vulcan Cl E6 100 C1
Vulcan Gate EN2 4 C3
Vulcan Rd SE4 141 B3
Vulcan Sq E14 119 C2
Vulcan Terr SE4 141 B3
Vulcan Way N7 72 B2
Vyner Ct E5 74 A6
Vyner Rd W3 111 B6
Vyners Sch UB10 60 B4
Vyner St E2 96 B6
Vyners Way UB10 60 C3
Vyne The DA7 147 D2
Vyvyan Ho SE18 144 C4

W

Wadbrook St KT1 175 D1
Wadding St SE17 117 B2 262 C3
Waddington Cl EN1 5 C1
Waddington Rd E15 76 B2
Waddington St E15 76 B2
Waddington Way SE19 183 B2
Waddon Cl CR0 220 C5
Waddon Court Rd CR0 220 C5
Waddon Inf Sch CR9 220 C3
Waddon Marsh Sta CR0 220 C6
Waddon Marsh Way CR0 204 B1
Waddon New Rd CR0 220 D6
Waddon Park Ave CR0 220 C5
Waddon Rd CR0 220 D5
Waddon Sta CR0 220 C4
Waddon Way CR0,CR2, CR9 220 D2
Wade Ct N10 31 B3
Wembley HA0 65 D5
Wade Ho 13 SE1 118 A4
1 Enfield EN1 17 C6
Wade's Gr N21 16 C4
Wade's Hill N21 16 C4
Wade's La TW11 175 A5
Wadeson St E2 96 B5
Wade's Pl E14 119 D6
Wadeville Ave RM6 59 B2
Wadeville Cl DA17 125 C1
Wadham Ave E17 35 D3
Wadham Cl TW17 193 A2
Wadham Gdns NW3 70 C1 230 A6
Wadham Rd
Chingford, Highams Park E17 35 D2
Putney SW15 135 A1
Wadhurst Cl SE20 184 B1
Wadhurst Ct E6 100 C5
Wadhurst Rd W4 111 B3
Wadley Rd E11 54 C2
Wadsworth Bsns Ctr UB6 87 C5
Wadsworth Cl Enfield EN3 18 D6
Wembley UB6 87 C5
Wadsworth Rd UB6 87 C5
Wager St E3 97 B3
Waggoners Rdbt TW5 128 B4
Waggon Mews N14 15 C3
Waghorn Rd E13 99 C6
Harrow HA3 43 D6
Waghorn St SE15 140 A2
Wagner St SE15 140 C5
Wagon Rd EN4,EN5 1 D6
Wagstaff Gdns RM9 80 C1
Wagtail Cl NW9 27 C1
Wagtail Wlk BR3 208 A4
Waights Ct KT2 176 A2
Waikato Lo IG9 21 C3
Wainford Cl SW19 156 D3
Wainwright Gr TW7 130 B1
Wainwright Ho 3 E1 118 C5
Waite Davies Rd SE12 164 D4
Waitelands Ho KT3 199 B5
Waite St SE15 139 D6
Waithman St EC4 241 C1
Wakefield Gdns
Redbridge IG1 56 A3
South Norwood SE19 183 C3
Wakefield Ho 6 SE15 140 A4
Dulwich SE22 162 B3
Wakefield Mews WC1 233 B1
Wakefield Rd N11 31 D5
N15 51 D4
19 Richmond TW10 153 D6
Wakefield St E6 100 A6
WC1 94 A4 233 B1
Wakefield St *continued*
Edmonton N18 34 A5
Wakeford Cl SW4 159 C6
Wakehams Hill HA5 41 B6
Wakeham St 9 N1 73 B2
Wakehurst Rd SW11 158 D6
Wakeling Ho 8 SE27 160 D1
Wakeling Rd W7 86 D2
Wakeling St 13 E14 97 A1
Wakelin Ho 19 N1 72 D1
Forest Hill SE23 163 A4
Wakelin Rd E15 98 C5
Wakeman Ho HA8 26 A6
Wakeman Rd NW10 90 D4
Wakemans Hill Ave NW9 45 B4
Wakering Rd IG11 79 A1
Wakerings The IG11 79 A2
Wakerly Cl 6 E6 100 B1
Wakley St EC1 94 D4 234 C2
Walberswick St SW8 270 B3
Walbrook EC4 252 C6
9 Wanstead E18 55 A6
Walbrook Ct 32 N1 95 C5
Walburgh St E1 96 B1
Walcorde Ave SE17 262 B3
Walcot Ct CR0 222 A6
Walcot Gdns SE11 261 A4
Walcot Ho 9 SE22 139 C2
Walcot Rd EN3 7 B3
Walcot Sq SE11 116 C2 261 B4
Walcott St SW1 259 B4
Waldair Ct E16 122 D4
Waldeck Gr SE27 160 D1
Waldeck Rd N15 50 D6
Brentford W4 132 C6
Ealing W13 87 B1
Mortlake SW14 133 A2
Waldeck Terr SW14 133 A2
Waldegrave Ct
11 Barking IG11 101 B6
1 Teddington TW11 174 D5
Waldegrave Gdns TW1 152 D1
Waldegrave Ho 5 SW15 156 C6
Waldegrave Pk TW1 174 D6
Waldegrave Rd BR1 210 B5
N8 50 C6
Dagenham RM8 80 C6
Ealing W5 110 B6
Penge SE19 183 D3
Teddington TW11 174 D6
Waldegrave Sch TW2 152 B1
Waldegrove CR0 221 D5
Waldemar Ave
Ealing W13 109 C5
Fulham SW6 135 A3
Waldemar Avenue Mans SW6 264 A1
Waldemar Rd SW19 179 C5
Walden Ave BR7 188 B6
Edmonton N13 33 A6
Walden Cl DA17 125 B1
Walden Ct SW8 269 D2
Walden Gdns CR7,SW16 204 B5
Walden Ho SW1 258 B3
8 SW11 137 A3
Barnet EN4 2 C1
Walden Rd BR7 188 B4
Tottenham N17 33 B2
Waldenshaw Rd SE23 162 C3
Walden St E1 96 B1
Walden Way NW7 28 D4
Waldo Cl SW4 159 C6
Waldo Ind Est BR1 209 D6
Waldo Pl SW19 180 C3
Waldo Rd BR1 209 D6
NW10 90 B4
Waldorf Cl CR2 220 D1
Waldram Cres SE23 162 C3
Waldram Park Rd SE23 162 D3
Waldram Pl 6 SE23 162 C3
Waldrist Way DA18 125 B4
Waldron Gdns BR2 208 B6
Waldron Ho 17 SW2 160 B6
Waldronhyrst CR0,CR2 220 D4
Waldron Mews SW3 266 D6
Waldron Rd
Harrow HA1,HA2 42 C1
Wandsworth SW18 158 A1
Waldrons The CR0 221 A4
Waldron's Yd HA2 64 B6
Waldstock Rd SE28 124 A6
Waleran Cl HA7 24 D4
Walerand Rd SE13 142 A3
Waleran Flats SE1 263 A4
Wales Ave SM5 218 C3
Wales Cl SE15 140 B6
Wales Farm Rd W3 89 B2
Waleton Acres SM6 219 C2
Waley St 1 E1 97 A2
Walfield Ave N20 13 D4
Walford Ct SE1 263 B6
Walford Ho 4 E1 96 B1
Walford Rd N16 73 C4
Walfrey Gdns RM9 81 A1
Walham Ct 15 NW3 70 D2
Walham Gr SW6 135 C5 265 A4
Walham Green Arc SW6 265 B4
Walham Rise 1 SW19 179 A4
Walham Yd SW6 265 A4
Walkden Hall (Hall of Residence) KT2 177 B6
Walkden Rd BR7 188 C5
Walker Cl N11 31 C6
SE18 123 A2
Ealing W7 108 C5
East Bedfont TW14 149 D4
Hampton TW12 173 B4
Walker Ho NW1 232 C3
Walker Mews SW2 160 C6
Walker Prim Sch N14 15 D2
Walkerscroft Mead SE21 161 A3
Walker's Ct W1 249 C6
Walkers Lo 7 E14 120 A4
Walkers Pl SW15 135 A1
Walkinshaw Ct 14 N1 73 A1
Walks The N2 48 B6
Walk The Ashford TW16 171 D3
Palmers Green N13 16 C1
Walkynscroft 1 SE15 140 B3
Wallace Cl SE28 124 D6
Upper Halliford TW17 193 B5
Uxbridge UB10 82 A5
Wallace Collection★ W1 238 A2
Wallace Cres SM5 218 D3
Wallace Ho N7 72 B2
Wallace Rd N1,N5 73 A2
Wallasey Cres UB10 60 C5
Wallbrook Bsns Ctr TW4 128 B2
Wallbrook Ho N9 18 C2
Wallbutton Rd SE4 141 A3
Wallcote Ave NW2 46 D1
Wall Ct N4 50 B1
Walled Garden Cl BR3 207 D5
Walled Gdn The TW16 194 B6
Wall End Ct E6 100 C6
Wall End Rd E6 78 C1
Waller Dr HA6 22 A2
Waller Rd SE14 140 D3
Wallers Cl RM9 103 B6
Wallett Ct 9 NW1 71 C1
Wallflower St W12 111 D6
Wallgrave Rd SW5 255 C3
Wallingford Ave W10 90 D1
Wallington Cl HA4 39 A3
Wallington Ct 10 SM6 219 B2
Wallington Cty Gram Sch SM6 219 B5
Wallington Green SM6 219 B4
Wallington Rd IG3 57 D2
Wallington Sq 4 SM6 219 C2
Wallington Sta SM6 219 B2
Wallis Alley SE1 252 B2
Wallis Cl SW11 136 B2
Wallis Rd E9 75 C2
Southall UB1 85 D1
Wallorton Gdns SW14 133 B1
Wallside EC2 242 B3
Wall St N1 73 B2
Wallwood Rd E11 54 B2
Wallwood St E14 97 B2
Walmar Cl EN4 2 B4
Walmer Cl BR6 227 B4
Chingford E4 19 D2
Walmer Gdns W13 109 A4
Walmer Ho 8 W10 90 D1
11 Penge SE20 184 C3
Walmer Pl W1 237 C4
Walmer Rd W10 90 C1
W11 113 A6 244 A5
Walmer St NW1 237 C4
Walmer Terr SE18 123 B2
Walmgate Rd UB6 87 B6
Walmington Fold N12 29 C4
Walm La NW2 68 C2
Walmsley Ho 1 SW16 181 C6
Walnut Ave UB7 104 C3
Walnut Cl SE8 141 B6
Hayes UB3 105 C6
Ilford IG6 57 A5
Wallington SM5 218 D3
Walnut Ct 2 E17 54 A5
Walnut Gdns E15 76 C3
Walnut Gr EN1 17 B6
Walnut Mews SM2 218 A1
Walnut Rd E10 75 D6
Walnut Tree Ave CR4 202 C6
Walnut Tree Cl
Barnes SW13 133 D4
Chislehurst BR7 189 A2
Walnut Tree Cotts SW19 179 A5
Walnut Tree Ho SW10 265 D6
Walnut Tree Rd SE10 120 C1
Brentford TW8 132 A6
Charlton TW17 171 A1
Dagenham RM8 81 A6
Heston TW5 129 B6
Walnut Tree Walk Prim Sch SE11 116 C2 261 A4
Walnut Tree Wlk SE11 116 C2 261 A4
Walnut Way
Buckhurst Hill IG9 21 D1
Ruislip HA4 62 C2
Walpole Ave TW9 132 B3
Walpole Cl W13 109 C4
Pinner HA5 23 C4
Walpole Cres 7 TW11 174 D5
Walpole Ct NW6 70 A1
7 W14 112 D3
Ealing W5 109 D5
Twickenham TW2 152 C2
Walpole Gdns W4 111 A1
Twickenham TW2 152 C1
Walpole Lo W13 109 C5
Walpole Mews NW8 229 C5
Walpole Pl 3 SE18 122 D2
6 Teddington TW11 174 D5
Walpole Rd BR2 209 D4
E17 53 A5
E6 77 C1
N17 51 A6
Mitcham SW19 180 B4
South Croydon CR0 221 B6
Walpole Rd *continued*
Surbiton KT6 198 A3
Teddington TW11 174 D5
Tottenham N17 33 A1
Twickenham TW2 152 C2
Woodford E18 36 D2
Walpole St SW3 114 D1 257 D2
Walrond Ave HA9 66 A3
Walsham Cl N16 52 A1
SE28 124 D6
Walsham Ho SE14 140 D3
SE17 262 C2
Walsham Rd SE14 140 D3
Feltham TW14 150 B4
Walsingham NW8 229 D6
Walsingham Gdns KT19 215 D3
Walsingham Ho E4 20 B4
Walsingham Lo SW13 134 A4
Walsingham Mans SW6 265 D4
Walsingham Pk BR7 189 B1
Walsingham Pl SW4, SW11 159 A5
Walsingham Rd BR5 190 B2
E5 74 A5
Ealing W13 109 A5
Enfield EN2 17 B6
Mitcham CR4 202 D4
Walsingham Wlk DA17 147 C6
Walter Besant Ho 20 E1 96 D4
Walter Ct 3 W3 89 A1
Walter Green Ho SE15 140 C4
Walter Ho SW10 266 C4
Walter Hurford Par 4 E12 78 C4
Walter Northcott Ho 2 NW6 69 C3
Walter Savill Twr E17 53 C3
Walters Cl SE17 262 B3
Hayes UB3 105 D4
Walters Ho N1 234 D5
10 SE17 138 D6
3 SE5 139 C3
Walters Rd EN3 6 C1
Walter's Rd SE25 205 C5
Walter St E2 96 D4
2 Kingston KT2 176 A2
Walters Way SE23 162 D5
Walters Yd BR1 187 A1
Walter Terr E1 96 D1
Walterton Rd W9 91 C3
Walter Wlk HA8 27 A4
Waltham Ave NW9 44 C3
Hayes UB3 105 B3
Waltham Ct E17 36 A2
Waltham Dr HA8 44 C6
Waltham Forest Coll E17 35 D1
Waltham Gdns EN3 6 C6
Waltham Green Ct SW6 265 C3
Waltham Ho NW8 229 A6
10 SW9 138 B3
Waltham Park Way E17 35 C3
Waltham Pk E17 35 C2
Waltham Rd
Carshalton SM5 202 C1
Southall UB2 107 A3
Walthamstow Ave E4 35 C3
Walthamstow Ave (North Circular Rd) E4 35 B4
Walthamstow Bsns Ctr E17 36 A1
Walthamstow Central Sta E17 53 C4
Walthamstow Queens Road Sta E17 53 C4
Walthamstow Sch for Girls E17 53 D5
Waltham Way E4 19 C2
Waltheof Ave N17 33 B2
Waltheof Gdns N17 33 B2
Walton Ave Cheam SM3 217 B5
Harrow HA2 63 B4
New Malden KT3 199 D5
Wembley HA9 66 D5
Walton Bridge Rd KT12, TW17 193 C2
Walton Cl E5 74 D5
NW2 68 B6
SW8 138 A5 270 B4
Harrow HA1 42 B5
Walton Croft HA1 64 C4
Walton Ct EN5 14 A6
Walton Dr NW10 67 B2
Harrow HA1 42 B5
Walton Gdns Acton W3 88 D2
Feltham TW13 171 D6
Wembley HA9 66 A6
Walton Gn CR0 224 A1
Walton Ho 10 E17 53 D6
E2 243 D6
N7 72 B5
SW18 157 C5
1 Edmonton N9 34 A6
Kingston KT2 176 A3
Walton La
Oatlands Park KT13,TW17 193 B1
Shepperton TW17 193 B2
Walton Pl SW3 257 C6
Walton Rd E13 99 C5
N15 51 D5
East Molesey KT8,KT12 195 C5
Harrow HA1 42 B5
Little Ilford E12 78 C4
Sidcup DA14 168 C1
Walton-on-T KT12&KT8 194 D4
Walton St SW3 114 C3 257 B5
Enfield EN2 5 B4
Walton Way Acton W3 88 D2
Mitcham CR4 203 C5
Walt Whitman Cl 6 SE24 138 D1
Walworth Pl SE17 117 A1 262 B1
Walworth Rd SE17 117 A1 262 B2
Walworth Sch SE17 117 C1 263 B1
Walwyn Ave BR1 209 D6
Wanborough Dr SW15 156 B3
Wanderer Dr IG11 102 C4
Wandle Bank
Mitcham SW19 180 B3
Wallington CR0 220 A5
Wandle Court Gdns CR0 220 A5
Wandle Ct 4 W12 111 C4
Wallington CR0 220 A5
West Ewell KT19 215 A4
Wandle Ho NW8 237 A4
6 Catford BR1 186 B5
Wandsworth SW18 157 D4
Wandle Lo CR0 220 A5
Wandle Pk Sta CR0 220 C6
Wandle Prim Sch SW18 157 D3
Wandle Rd Croydon CR0 221 A5
Hackbridge SM6 219 B6
Morden SM4 202 B4
Upper Tooting SW17 158 C2
Wallington CR0 220 A5
Wandle Side
Hackbridge SM6 219 B5
Wallington CR0 220 B5
Wandle Tech Pk CR4 202 D2
Wandle Trad Est CR4 202 D2
Wandle Valley Sch SM5 202 C2
Wandle Way
Mitcham CR4 202 D4
Wandsworth SW18 157 D3
Wandon Rd SW6 135 D5 265 D3
Wandsworth Bridge Rd SW6 135 D2 265 C1
Wandsworth Common Sta SW12 158 D4
Wandsworth Common West Side SW18 158 A6
Wandsworth Gyratory SW18 157 D6
Wandsworth High St SW18 157 D6
Wandsworth Plain SW18 157 D6
Wandsworth Rd SW8 138 A5 270 A3
Wandsworth Road Sta SW4 137 C3
Wandsworth Town Sta SW18 135 D1
Wangey Rd RM6 58 D2
Wangford Ho 13 SW9 138 D1
Wanless Rd SE24 139 A2
Wanley Rd SE5 139 B1
Wanlip Rd E13 99 B3
Wansbeck Ct EN2 4 D2
Wansbeck Rd E3,E9 75 B1
Wansdown Pl SW6 135 D5 265 C4
Wansey St SE17 117 A2 262 B3
Wansford Rd IG8 37 C2
Wanstead Church Sch E11 55 A4
Wanstead Cl BR1 187 C1
Wanstead High Sch E11 55 C3
Wanstead Hospl E11 55 B5
Wanstead La IG1 56 A3
Wanstead Park Ave E12 77 D6
Wanstead Park Rd IG1 56 A1
Wanstead Park Sta E7 77 B4
Wanstead Pl E11 55 A4
Wanstead Rd BR1 187 C1
Wanstead Sta E11 55 B3
Wantage Rd SE12 164 D6
Wantz Rd RM10 81 D3
Wapping Dock St 19 E1 118 B5
Wapping High St E1 118 B5
Wapping La E1 118 B5
Wapping Sta E1 118 C5
Wapping Wall E1 118 C5
Warbank La KT2 177 D3
Warbeck Rd W12 112 B4
Warberry Rd N22 32 B1
Warboys App KT2 176 D4
Warboys Cres E4 36 A5
Warboys Rd KT2 176 D4
Warburton Cl 6 N1 73 C2
Stanmore HA3 24 B4
Warburton Ct SE15 140 A2
Ruislip HA4 62 A6
Warburton Ho 5 E8 96 B6
Warburton Rd 8 E8 96 B6
Twickenham TW2 151 D3
Warburton St 6 E8 96 B6
Warburton Terr E17 35 D1
Wardalls Ho 12 SE8 141 B6
Ward Cl CR2 221 C3
Ward Cotts TW19 148 B4
Wardell Cl NW7 27 C3
Wardell Ct N2 48 B6
Wardell Ho 5 SE10 142 A6
Warden Ave HA2 41 B1
Warden Rd NW5 71 A2
Wardens Field Cl 2 BR6 227 D2
Wardens Gr SE1 252 A3
Wardle St E9 74 D3
Wardley Lo E11 54 D3
Wardley St SW18 157 D4
Wardlow 8 NW5 71 B4
Wardo Ave SW6 135 A4 264 A2
Wardour Mews W1 239 B1
Wardour St W1 93 D1 239 C1
Ward Point SE11 261 A3
Ward Rd E15 98 B6
N19 71 C5
Wardrobe Pl EC4 241 D1
Wardrobe Terr EC4 251 D6
Wardrobe The 3 TW9 153 D6
Wards Rd IG2 57 B2
Ware Ct Cheam SM1 217 B4
Edgware HA8 26 A6
Wareham Cl TW3 129 D1
Wareham Ct 2 N1 73 C1
Wareham Ho SW8 270 C4
Waremead Rd IG2 56 D4
Ware Point Dr SE28 123 B4
Warfield Rd NW10 90 D4
East Bedfont TW14 149 C4
Hampton TW12 173 D2
Warfield Yd 6 NW10 90 D4
Wargrave Ave N15 51 D3
Wargrave Ho 46 E2 95 D4
Wargrave Rd HA2 64 A5
Warham Rd N4 50 D4
Croydon CR2 221 A3
Harrow HA3 24 D1
Warham St SE5 138 D5
Waring Cl BR6 227 D2
Waring Dr BR6 227 D2
Waring Ho 10 E2 96 A4
Waring Rd DA14 190 C4
Waring St SE27 183 A6
Warkworth Gdns TW7 131 A5
Warkworth Rd N17 33 B3
Warland Rd SE18 145 C5
Warley Ave
Dagenham RM8 59 B2
Hayes UB4 84 A1
Warley Cl E10 53 B1
Warley Ho N1 73 B2
Warley Rd N9 18 C2
Hayes UB4 84 A2
Woodford IG8 37 B3
Warley St E2 96 D4
Warlingham Rd CR7 204 D5
Warlock Rd W9 91 C3
Warlow Cl EN3 7 C6
Warlters Cl N7 72 A4
Warlters Rd N7 72 A4
Warltersville Mans N19 50 A2
Warltersville Rd N4,N8, N19 50 A2
War Memorial Homes W4 133 B5
Warming Cl E5 74 D5
Warmington Rd SE24 161 A5
Warmington St 3 E13 99 A3
Warminster Gdns SE25 184 A1
Warminster Rd SE25 184 A1
Warminster Sq SE25 184 A1
Warminster Way CR4 181 B1
Warmsworth NW1 232 A6
Warncliffe Ho 3 SW15 156 C6
Warndon St SE16 118 C2
Warneford Rd HA3 44 A6
Warneford St E9 96 B6
Warne Pl 4 DA15 168 B5
Warner Ave SM3 217 A6
Warner Cl E15 76 C3
NW9 46 A2
Hampton TW12 173 B5
Harlington UB3 127 B5
Warner Ct SM3 217 A6
Warner Ho 4 E9 74 D2
NW8 229 A2
SE13 141 D3
1 Beckenham BR3 185 D4
Warner Pl E2 96 A4
Warner Rd E17 53 A5
N8 49 D5
SE5 139 A4
Bromley BR1 186 D3
Warners Cl IG8 37 A5
Warner St EC1 94 C3 241 A5
Warner Yd EC1 241 A5
Warnford Ho SW15 155 C5
Warnford Ind Est UB3 105 C4
Warnford Rd BR6 227 D3
Warnham WC1 233 C1
Warnham Court Rd SM5 218 D1
Warnham Ho 6 SW2 160 B4
Warnham Rd N12 30 C5
Warple Mews W3 111 C4
Warple Way W3,W12 111 C4
Warren Ave E11 76 B5
Bromley BR1 186 C3
Mortlake SW14,TW10 132 D1
Orpington BR6 227 D3
South Croydon CR2 222 D1
Warren Cl DA6 169 C6
N9 18 D4
Hayes UB4 84 C2
Wembley HA9 65 D6
West Norwood SE21 161 A4
Esher KT10 212 A4
Warren Comp Sch RM6 59 B4
Warren Cres N9 17 D4
Warren Ct N1 234 A4
N17 52 A6
17 Beckenham BR3 185 C3
6 Croydon CR0 205 C1
6 Ealing W5 87 C2
Warren Cutting KT2 177 B3
Warrender Prim Sch HA4 39 D2
Warrender Rd N19 71 C4
Warrender Way HA4 40 A2
Warren Dr Greenford UB6 86 A3
Ruislip HA4 40 D2
Warren Dr N KT5,KT6 198 D1
Warren Dr S KT5 199 A1

Warren Dr The E11 55 C2
Warren Fields HA7 25 C6
Warren Gdns E15 76 B3
Warren Hill IG10 21 C6
Warren Ho 21 E3 97 D4
Warren Jun Sch RM6 59 B4
Warren La SE18 122 D3
Stanmore HA7 9 A2
Warren Mews W1 239 A5
Warren Park Rd SM1, SM2 218 C2
Warren Pk KT2 177 A4
Warren Pond Rd E4 20 D4
Warren Rd BR2 225 A6
DA6 169 C6
E10 76 A5
NW2 67 D6
Ashford TW15 171 C3
Bushey WD23 8 B3
Chingford E4 20 A2
Croydon CR0 205 D1
Ickenham UB10 60 B4
Ilford IG6 57 B4
Isleworth TW2 152 B5
Kingston KT2 177 A4
Mitcham SW19 180 C4
Sidcup DA14 168 C1
Wanstead E11 55 C2
Warren Rise KT3 177 B2
Warren Road Prim Sch BR6 227 D4
Warrens Shawe La HA8 10 D2
Warren St W1 93 C3 239 A5
Warren Street Sta NW1 93 C3 239 B6
Warren Terr RM6 58 D5
Warren The E12 78 A4
Hayes UB4 84 A1
Heston TW5 129 B5
Worcester Park KT19 215 B5
Warren Way NW7 29 A4
Warren Wlk 1 SE7 143 C6
Warren Wood Cl BR2 225 A6
Warriner Dr N9 18 A1
Warriner Gdns SW11 137 A4 268 A1
Warrington Cres W9 92 A3 236 A6
Warrington Gdns W9 236 A5
Warrington Pl E14 120 A5
Warrington Rd
Croydon CR0 220 D5
Dagenham RM8 81 A6
Harrow HA1 42 C4
21 Richmond TW10 153 D6
Warrington Sq RM8 80 D6
Warrior Sq E12 78 C4
Warsaw Cl HA4 62 B2
Warspite Ho 3 E14 119 D2
Warspite Rd SE18 122 A3
Warton Rd E15 98 A6
Warwall E6 100 D1
Warwick W14 113 B2 254 D3
Warwick Ave HA8 11 A1
W9 92 A3 236 A5
Harrow HA2 63 B4
Warwick Avenue Sta W9 92 A3 236 A5
Warwick Chambers W8 255 A6
Warwick Cl DA5 169 B4
Bushey WD23 8 C4
Hampton TW12 174 A3
New Barnet EN4 14 B6
Warwick Cres W2 92 A2 236 A4
Hayes UB4 83 D3
Warwick Ct 3 E5 74 B6
N11 31 D4
5 N2 48 A6
NW2 69 A3
WC1 240 D3
1 Beckenham BR2 186 C1
Ealing W7 86 D1
Harrow HA1 42 C6
Merton SW19 179 C2
Northolt UB5 63 C3
Surbiton KT6 214 A6
Warwick Dene W5 110 A5
Warwick Dr SW15 134 B2
Warwick Gdns N4 51 A4
W14 113 B2 254 D4
Ilford IG1 56 D1
Thames Ditton KT7 196 D4
Thornton Heath CR7 204 C5
Warwick Gr E5 52 B1
Surbiton KT5 198 B2
Warwick Ho 10 E5 74 C6
N4 51 A1
11 SW9 138 C3
9 Acton W3 88 C1
6 Kingston KT2 176 A2
6 Putney SW15 156 C4
Warwick House St SW1 249 D4
Warwick La EC4 94 D1 241 D1
Warwick Lo Cheam SM1 217 B4
Twickenham TW2 151 D1
Warwick Mans SW5 255 A4
Warwick Park Sch SE15 139 D4
Warwick Pas EC4 241 D2
Warwick Pl W5 109 D4
W9 92 A2 236 A4
Warwick Pl N SW1 259 A3
Warwick Rd DA14 190 B5
E12 78 A3
E15 76 D2
E17 35 B1
N11 31 D4
W14,SW5 113 B2 254 D4
Ashford TW15 170 A5
Warwick Rd *continued*
Barnet EN5 1 D1
Bexley DA16 146 C2
Chingford E4 35 C5
Ealing W5 110 A5
Edmonton N18 33 D6
Enfield EN3 7 B6
Hounslow TW4 128 B2
Kingston KT3 199 A6
Penge SE20 206 B6
Southall UB2 107 B3
Sutton SM1 218 A3
Teddington KT1 175 C2
Thames Ditton KT7 196 D4
Thornton Heath CR7 204 C6
Twickenham TW2 152 C3
Wanstead E11 55 B4
Yiewsley UB7 104 A5
Warwick Row SW1 115 B3 258 D6
Warwick Sch for Boys E17 54 A5
Warwickshire Path SE8 141 B5
Warwickshire Rd N16 73 C4
Warwick Sq EC4 241 D2
SW1 115 C1 259 A2
Warwick Sq Mews SW1 259 A3
Warwick St W1 115 C6 249 B6
Warwick Terr E17 54 B4
SE18 145 B6
Warwick Way SW1 115 B2 258 D2
Warwick Yd EC1 242 B5
Wasdale NW1 231 D1
Washbrook Ho SW2 160 C5
Washington Ave E12 78 B4
Washington Cl 45 E3 97 D4
Washington Ct SW17 180 D4
Washington Ho E17 35 B1
SW1 247 C1
Washington Rd E6 77 C1
Barnes SW13 134 A5
Kingston KT1 176 C1
North Cheam KT4 200 B1
2 Woodford E18 36 D1
Wastdale Rd SE23 162 D3
Watchfield Ct 7 W4 111 A1
Watcombe Cotts TW9 132 C6
Watcombe Rd SE25 206 B4
Waterbank Rd SE6 186 A6
Waterbeach Rd RM9 80 C2
Water Brook La NW4 46 C4
Watercress Pl N1 73 C1
Waterdale Rd SE2 146 A6
Waterden Cres E9 75 C3
Waterden Rd E15 75 C2
Waterer Ho 7 SE6 186 A6
Waterer Rise SM6 219 D2
Waterfall Cl N14 15 C1
Waterfall Cotts SW19 180 B4
Waterfall Rd N11,N14 15 C1
Mitcham SW19 180 B4
Waterfall Terr SW17 180 C4
Waterfield Cl
Belvedere DA17 125 C3
Woolwich SE28 124 B5
Waterfield Gdns SE25 205 C4
Waterford Rd SW6 135 D5 265 C3
Watergardens The KT2 177 A4
Watergate EC4 251 C6
Watergate Ho 5 SE18 122 C2
Watergate Sch SE13 141 D1
Watergate St SE8 141 C6
Watergate Wlk WC2 250 B4
Water Gdns HA7 25 B4
Water Gdns The W2 92 C1 237 B2
Waterglade Ctr The W5 109 D6
Waterhall Ave E4 36 C6
Waterhall Cl E17 34 D2
Waterhead NW1 232 A2
Waterhedge Mews EN1 17 D6
Waterhouse Cl E16 99 D2
NW3 70 B3
W6 112 D1
Waterhouse Ct 5 TW11 174 D5
Wateridge Cl E14 119 C3
Wateringbury Cl BR5 190 B1
Water La E15 76 C2
SE14 140 C5
Edmonton N9 18 B4
Ilford IG3 79 D5
Richmond TW10,TW9 153 D6
Sidcup DA14 169 B2
Teddington KT1 175 D2
Twickenham TW1 153 A3
Water Lily Cl UB2 108 A4
Waterloo Bridge SE1,WC2 116 B6 250 D5
Waterloo Cl E9 74 C3
East Bedfont TW14 149 D3
Waterloo East Sta SE1 116 C5 251 B3
Waterloo Gdns E2 96 C5
Waterloo Int Sta SE1 116 B4 250 D2
Waterloo Pier SE1 250 C2
Waterloo Pl SW1 115 D5 249 C4
Waterloo Rd E10 53 C2
E6 77 C1
E7 76 D3
NW2 68 A6
SE1 116 C4 251 B2
Sutton SM1 218 B3
Waterloo Sta SE1 116 C4 251 A2
Waterloo Terr N1 72 D1
Waterlow Ct NW11 47 D2
Waterlow Rd N19 49 C1
Waterman Bldg 4 E14 119 C4
Watermans Mews 1 W5 110 A6
Waterman St SW15 134 D2
Waterman Way E1 118 B5
Watermead TW14 149 C3
Watermead Ho E9 75 B3
Watermead La CR4 202 D2
Watermeadow La SW6 136 A3
Watermead Rd SE6 186 A6
Watermeads High Sch SM4 202 B3
Watermead Way N17 34 B1
Watermen's Sq 1 SE20 184 C3
Water Mews SE15 140 C1
Watermill Bsns Ctr EN3 7 B3
Watermill Cl TW10 153 C1
Watermill La N18 33 C5
Watermill Way
Feltham TW13 151 C2
Merton SW19 180 A2
Watermint Quay N16 52 A2
Water Rd HA0 88 B6
Watersedge KT19 215 A4
Water's Edge SW6 134 C4
Watersfield Way HA8 26 A3
Waters Gdns RM10 81 C3
Watership Down Ho E11 54 D2
Waterside E17 52 C3
4 Beckenham BR3 185 C2
Waterside Cl E3 97 B6
28 SE16 118 A4
Barking IG11 80 A4
Northolt UB5 85 B4
Surbiton KT6 214 A6
Waterside Ct SE13 142 B1
Waterside Dr KT12 194 B4
Waterside Pl NW1 231 B6
Waterside Point SW11 267 B4
Waterside Rd UB2 107 C3
Waterside Sch SE18 123 B1
Waterside Trad Ctr W7 108 C3
Waterside Way SW17 180 A5
Watersmeet Way SE28 102 D1
Waterson St E2 95 D4
Waters Pl SW15 134 C3
Watersplash Cl KT1 198 A6
Watersplash La
Hayes UB3 106 A2
Southall TW5 106 B1
Watersplash Rd TW17 192 C5
Waters Rd Catford SE6 164 C1
Kingston KT1 176 D1
Waters Sq KT1 198 D6
Water St WC2 251 A6
Water Tower Cl UB8 60 A3
Water Tower Hill CR0 221 B4
Water Tower Ho W8 245 A3
Water Tower Pl N1 234 C5
Waterview Ho E14 97 A2
Waterworks Cnr E17 36 C1
Waterworks La E5 74 D6
Waterworks Rd SW2 160 B5
Watery La DA14 190 B4
Hayes UB3 105 B1
Merton SW19,SW20 179 B1
Northolt UB5 84 C5
Wates Way CR4 202 D3
Wateville Rd N17 33 A2
Watford Cl SW11 267 B2
Watford Rd E16 99 A2
Elstree WD6 9 C5
Harrow HA0,HA1 65 A5
Harrow HA1 43 A1
Northwood HA6 22 A4
Watford Way NW4 46 A5
Watford Way (Barnet By-Pass) NW9 27 D3
Watkin Ho N16 51 D2
Watkin Rd HA9 66 D5
Watkinson Rd N7 72 B2
Watling Ave HA8 27 B2
Watling Ct EC4 242 B1
1 Elstree WD6 9 D5
Watling Gate NW9 45 C5
Watling Gdns NW2 69 A2
Watling Ho 10 SE18 144 C6
Watlings Cl CR0 207 A3
Watling St DA6,DA7 147 D1
EC4 95 A1 242 B1
4 SE15 139 C6
Watlington Gr SE26 185 A5
Watney Cotts SW14 133 A2
Watney Mkt E1 96 B1
Watney Rd SW14 133 A2
Watneys Rd CR4 203 D4
Watney St E1 96 B1
Watson Ave Cheam SM3 217 A6
Wallend E6 78 C1
Watson Cl N16 73 B3
Mitcham SW19 180 C3
Watson Ho 3 SW2 160 A4
Watsons Lo 4 RM10 81 D2
Watson's Mews W1 237 B3
Watsons Rd N22 32 B2
Watson's St SE8 141 C5
Watson St E13 99 B5
Wattisfield Rd E5 74 C5
Watts Cl N15 51 C4
Watts Gr E3 97 D2
Watts Ho 6 W10 91 A2
Watt's La Chislehurst BR7 189 A2
Teddington TW11 175 A5
Watts Point E13 99 A6
Watts Rd KT7 197 A2
Watts St E1 118 B5
SE15 139 D4
Wat Tyler Ho N8 50 A6
Wat Tyler Rd SE10 142 B4
Wauthier Cl N13 32 D5
Wavel Ct 7 E1 118 C5
7 Streatham SW16 160 A1
Wavell Dr DA15 167 C5
Wavell Ho N6 49 A3
Wavel Mews N8 49 D5
NW6 69 D1
Wavel Pl SE26 183 D6
Wavendon Ave W4 111 B1
Waveney Ave SE15 140 B1
Waveney Cl E1 118 A5
Waveney Ho SE15 140 B1
Waverley Ave E17 54 B6
E4 35 B6
Sutton SM1 217 D6
Tolworth KT5 199 A3
Twickenham TW2,TW4 151 C3
Wembley HA9 66 B3
Waverley Cl BR2 209 D4
East Molesey KT8 195 C4
Hayes UB3 105 B2
Woodford E18 37 C1
Waverley Cres SE18 123 B1
Waverley Ct 3 NW6 69 A1
W1 238 B4
Enfield EN2 5 A2
Waverley Gdns E6 100 A2
Barking IG11 101 C5
Ealing NW10 88 B5
Ilford IG6 57 B6
Northwood HA6 22 A2
Waverley Gr N3 47 A6
Waverley Ind Pk HA1 42 B6
Waverley Pl N4 50 D1
NW8 92 B5 229 C4
Waverley Rd E17 54 A6
N8 50 A2
SE18 123 B1
Croydon SE25 206 B6
Enfield EN2 4 D2
Harrow HA2 41 A1
Southall UB1 107 C6
Stoneleigh KT17,KT4 216 B3
Tottenham N17 34 B3
Woodford E18 37 C2
Waverley Sch EN3 6 C1
Waverley Sch (lower) SE22 162 B6
Waverley Sch (Upper) SE15 162 C6
Waverley Way SM2,SM5 218 C2
Waverly Ct NW3 70 D2
Waverton Ho 2 E3 97 B6
Waverton Rd SW18 158 A4
Waverton St W1 115 B5 248 C4
Wavertree Ct 9 SW2 160 A3
Wavertree Rd
Streatham SW2 160 B3
Woodford E18 37 A1
Waxham NW5 70 D3
Waxlow Cres UB1 85 C1
Waxlow Ho UB4 84 C2
Waxlow Rd NW10 89 B5
Waxwell Cl HA5 22 D1
Waxwell La HA5 22 D1
Wayborne Gr HA4 39 A3
Waye Ave TW5 128 A4
Wayfarer Rd UB5 85 A4
Wayfield Link SE9 167 B5
Wayford St SW11 136 C3
Wayland Ave E8 74 A3
Wayland Ho 13 SW9 138 C3
Waylands UB3 83 B2
Waylands Ct IG1 79 B4
Waylands Mead BR3 185 D2
Waylett Ho SE11 261 A1
Waylett Pl Wembley HA0 65 D4
West Norwood SE27 160 D1
Wayman Ct E8 74 B2
Wayne Cl BR6 227 D5
Waynflete Ave CR0 220 D5
Waynflete Sq 16 W10 112 D6
18 W10 90 D1
Waynflete St SW18 158 A2
Wayside NW11 47 A1
Mortlake SW14 155 A6
New Addington CR0 223 D2
Wayside Ave WD23 8 B5
Wayside Cl N14 15 C5
Wayside Commercial Est IG11 102 A5
Wayside Ct
Isleworth TW7 130 C3
Twickenham TW1 153 C5
Wembley HA9 66 C5
Wayside Gdns RM10 81 C3
Wayside Gr BR7,SE9 188 B6
Wayside Mews IG2 56 C4
Weald Cl BR2 226 A6
16 SE16 118 B1
Weald Fst & Mid Schs HA3 24 D3
Weald La HA3 24 B2
Weald Rd UB10 82 C5
Weald Rise HA3 24 D2
Weald Sq E5 74 B6
Wealdstone Rd SM3 217 B6
Weald The BR7 188 B4
Weald Way Hayes UB4 83 C4
Romford RM7 59 D3
Wealdwood Gdns HA5 23 D4
Weale Rd E4 20 B1
Weall Ct HA5 41 A5
Weardale Ct EN5 12 C6
Weardale Gdns EN2 5 B4
Weardale Ho N4 51 A2
Weardale Rd SE13 142 B1
Wearmouth Ho 1 E3 97 B2
Wear Pl 13 E2 96 B4
Wearside Rd SE13 141 D1
Weatherbury 6 W2 91 C1
Weatherbury Ho 3 N19 71 D5
Weatherill Ct SE25 206 B3
Weatherley Cl E3 97 B2
Weathersfield Ct SE9 166 B5
Weaver Cl E16 122 D6
South Croydon CR0 221 D4
Weaver Ct 2 E2 96 B3
Weaver Ho 13 E1 96 A3
Weavers Cl TW7 130 C1
Weavers Ho 4 E11 55 A3
Weaver's La SE1 117 C5 253 B3
Weaver St E1 96 A3
Weavers Way NW1 232 C6
6 NW1 71 D1
Weaver Wlk SE27 182 D6
Webb Ct 6 SE28 124 B6
W3 110 D4
Webber Cl WD6 9 D5
Webber Ho 6 IG11 78 D1
Webber Row SE1 116 D4 251 C1
Webber St SE1 116 D4 251 C1
Webb Est E5 52 A2
Webb Gdns 1 E13 99 A3
Webb Ho SW8 269 D3
2 Dagenham RM10 81 C5
Feltham TW13 151 A1
Webb Pl NW10 89 D4
Webb Rd SE3 142 D6
Webbscroft Rd RM10 81 D4
Webb's Rd SW11 158 D6
Webbs Rd UB4 84 B4
Webb St SE1 117 C3 263 A5
Webheath 6 NW6 69 B1
Webster Gdns W5 109 D5
Webster Ho 10 N16 73 C3
Webster Rd E11 76 A5
SE16 118 A3
Weddell Ho 23 E1 96 D3
Wedderburn Rd NW3 70 B3
Barking IG11 101 C6
Wedgewood Ct DA5 169 B4
1 Beckenham BR2 208 D5
Wedgewood Ho SW1 259 A1
Wedgewood Mews W1 239 D1
Wedgewood Wlk NW3 69 D3
Wedgwood Ho 17 E2 96 D4
SE11 261 A5
Wedgwood Way SE19 183 A3
Wedlake St W10 91 A3
Wedmore Gdns N19 71 D6
Wedmore Rd UB6 86 B4
Wedmore St N19 71 D5
Weech Rd NW6 69 C4
Weedington Rd NW5 71 A3
Weedon Ho W12 90 A1
Weekley Sq SW11 136 B2
Weeks Ho TW10 175 C6
Weigall Rd SE12,SE3 143 A1
Weighhouse St W1 238 B1
Weighton Rd Harrow HA3 24 B2
Penge SE20 184 B1
Weihurst Ct SM1 218 C3
Weihurst Gdns SM1 218 B3
Weimar St SW15 135 A2
Weirdale Ave N20 14 D2
Weir Hall Ave N18 33 B4
Weir Hall Gdns N18 33 B5
Weir Hall Rd N18 33 B4
Weir Ho 8 SW12 159 C4
Weir Rd Sidcup DA5 169 D4
Streatham SW12 159 C4
Walton-on-T KT12 194 A3
Wimbledon SW18,SW19 157 D1
Weir's Pas NW1 232 D2
Weiss Rd SW15 134 D2
Welbeck Ave BR1 187 B6
DA15 168 A3
Hayes UB4 84 B3
Welbeck Cl N12 30 B5
New Malden KT3 199 D4
Stoneleigh KT17 216 A1
Welbeck Ct W14 254 C4
Hayes UB4 84 B3
Welbeck Mans 10 NW6 69 C3
Welbeck Rd E6 99 D4
Carshalton SM1,SM5 218 B6
East Barnet EN4 14 C5
Harrow HA2 41 D1
Carshalton SM5 202 C1
Welbeck St W1 93 B1 238 C2
Welbeck Villas N21 17 A3
Welbeck Way W1 238 C2
Welbeck Wlk SM5 202 B1
Welbourne Prim Sch N17 52 A6
Welby Ho N19 49 D2
Welby St SE5 138 D4
Welch Pl HA5 22 C2
Welcome Ct E17 53 C2
Weldon Cl HA4 62 B2
Weldon Ct Southgate N21 16 B6
Thornton Heath CR7 204 D4
Weldon Dr KT8 195 B5
Weld Pl N11 31 B5
Welfare Rd E15 76 C1
Welford Cl E5 74 D5
Welford Ct 12 NW1 71 B1
7 SW8 137 C3
Welford Pl SW19 179 A6
Welham Rd SW16,SW17 181 B4
Welhouse Rd SM5 202 C1
Wellacre Rd HA3 43 B3
Wellan Cl DA15,DA16 168 B6
Welland Gdns UB6 86 D5
Welland Ho SE15 140 C1
Welland Mews E1 118 A5
Wellands Cl BR1 188 B1
Welland St SE10 142 A6
Well App EN5 12 C6
Wellbrook Rd BR6 226 C4
Wellby Ct 1 E13 99 C5
Well Cl Ruislip HA4 63 A5
Streatham SW16 182 B6
Wellclose Sq E1 118 A6
Wellclose St 11 E1 118 A6
Well Cottage Cl E11 55 C2
Well Ct EC4 242 B1
Wellday Ho 2 E9 75 A2
Welldon Cres HA1 42 C3
Welldon Park Fst Sch HA2 64 A4
Welldon Park Mid Sch HA2 64 A4
Weller Ho 20 SE16 118 A4
Weller St SE1 252 A2
Wellesley Ave W6 112 B3
Wellesley Cl 8 SE7 121 C1
Wellesley Court Rd 1 CR0 221 B6
Wellesley Cres TW2 152 C1
Wellesley Ct W9 92 A4 229 A2
Cheam SM3 201 A1
Twickenham TW2 152 C1
Wellesley Gr CR0 221 B6
Wellesley Ho NW1 232 C1
Wellesley Park Mews EN2 4 D3
Wellesley Pl NW1 232 C1
Wellesley Rd E17 53 C3
NW5 71 A3
W4 110 D1
Croydon CR0 205 A1
Harrow HA1 42 C4
Ilford IG1 57 A1
Sutton SM2 218 A2
Twickenham TW2 152 C1
Wanstead E11 55 A4
Wood Green N22 32 C1
Wellesley Road Sta CR0 221 B6
Wellesley St E1 96 D2
Wellesley Terr N1 95 A4 235 B2
Wellfield Ave N10 49 B6
Wellfield Rd SW16 182 B6
Wellfit St 6 SE24 138 D2
Wellgarth UB6 65 B2
Wellgarth Rd NW11 47 D1
Well Gr N20 14 B3
Well Hall Par SE9 144 B1
Well Hall Pleasaunce★ SE9 144 A1
Well Hall Rd SE9 144 B1
Well Ho 11 N9 18 A1
Wellhouse Rd BR3 207 C5
Wellingfield Ct 1 DA16 146 A2
Welling High St DA16 146 B2
Welling Sch DA16 146 B4
Wellings Ho UB3 106 B5
Welling Sta DA16 146 A3
Wellington N8 50 A5
1 NW9 27 D3
Wellington Arch★ SW1 248 B2
Wellington Ave DA15 168 A5
N15 52 A3
SE18 123 A3
Chingford E4 19 D2
Edmonton N9 18 B1
Hounslow TW3,TW4 151 C6
North Cheam KT4 216 C5
Pinner HA5 23 B2
Wellington Bldgs 14 E3 97 C4
SW1 258 B1
Wellington Cl SE14 140 D4
W11 91 C1
Walton-on-T KT12 193 D1
Wellington Cres KT3 199 A6
Wellington Ct NW8 229 D3
SW1 247 C1
SW18 158 C6
SW6 265 D1
WC2 250 A6
Ashford TW15 170 A6
Stanwell TW19 148 A4
5 Surbiton KT6 198 A3
Teddington TW12 174 B5
Wellington Gdns SE7 121 C1
Teddington TW12,TW2 174 B6
Wellington Gr SE10 142 B5
Wellington Ho 18 NW3 70 D2
4 Ealing W5 88 A4
Northolt UB5 63 C1
Stanmore HA7 9 A1
Wellington Hospl (North) NW8 92 B5 229 D3
Wellington Hospl (South) NW8 92 B5 229 D3
Wellington Mans 1 E10 53 C1
N16 73 D4
Wellington Mews SE22 140 A1
Streatham SW16 159 D1
Wellington Mus (Apsley Ho)★ SW1 115 A4 248 B2
Wellington Par DA15 168 A6
Wellington Park Est NW2 68 A6
Wellington Pl N2 48 C4
NW8 92 B4 229 D2
Wellington Prim Sch E3 97 C4
Chingford E4 19 D2
Hounslow TW3 129 B3
Wellington Rd E17 53 A5
E6 100 B5
E7 76 D4
NW10 90 D4

374 Wel – Wes

Wellington Rd continued
NW8 ....92 B5 229 D3
W5 ....109 C3
Ashford TW15 ....170 A5
Bexley DA5 ....168 D6
Bromley BR2 ....209 C5
Enfield EN1 ....17 C5
Erith DA17 ....125 B1
Harrow HA3 ....42 C6
Hatton TW14 ....149 C6
Pinner HA5 ....23 B2
Teddington TW12,TW2 ....174 B6
Thornton Heath CR0 ....204 D2
Walthamstow E10 ....53 A1
Wanstead E11 ....55 A4
Wimbledon SW19 ....157 C2
Wellington Rd N TW4 ....129 B2
Wellington Rd S TW4 ....151 B6
Wellington Row E2 ....96 A4
Wellington Sq
SW3 ....114 D1 257 C2
Wellington St SE18 ....122 C2
WC2 ....116 B6 250 C6
1 Barking IG11 ....101 A6
Wellington Terr 2 E1 ....118 B5
Harrow HA1 ....42 B1
Wellington Way E3 ....97 C4
Welling Way DA16 ....145 B2
Well La SW14 ....155 A6
Wellmead IG3 ....58 A2
Wellmeadow Rd W7 ....109 A2
Catford SE13,SE6 ....164 C3
Wellow Wlk SM5 ....202 B1
Well Rd NW3 ....70 B5
Barnet EN5 ....12 C6
Wells Cl 2 Northolt UB5 ....84 C4
South Croydon CR2 ....221 C3
Wells Ct N1 ....73 C3
16 NW3 ....70 A4
1 NW6 ....91 C5
Wells Dr NW9 ....45 B1
Wells Gdns
Dagenham RM10 ....81 D3
Redbridge IG1 ....56 A2
Wells Ho BR1 ....187 B5
EC1 ....234 C2
9 SE16 ....118 C3
12 W10 ....91 A3
4 Barking IG11 ....80 A1
Ealing W5 ....109 D6
Wells Ho The NW3 ....70 B4
Wells House Rd NW10 ....89 C2
Wellside Gdns SW14 ....155 A6
Wells Mews W1 ....239 B2
Wellsmoor Gdns BR1 ....210 C6
Wells Park Ct SE26 ....184 B6
Wells Park Rd SE26 ....184 B6
Wells Pl SW18 ....158 A4
Wells Prim Sch IG8 ....37 A6
Wells Rd BR1 ....188 B1
W12 ....112 C4
Wells Rise NW8 ....92 D6 230 C5
Wells Sq WC1 ....233 D1
Wells St W1 ....93 C1 239 B2
Well St E15 ....76 C2
E9 ....74 C1
Wellstead Ave N9 ....18 D4
Wellstead Rd E6 ....100 C5
Wells Terr N4 ....72 C6
Wells The N14 ....15 D4
Wells Way SE5 ....139 C6
SW7 ....114 B3 256 C6
Wells Yd 2 N7 ....72 C3
Well Wlk NW3 ....70 B5
Wellwood Ct SW15 ....134 C1
Wellwood Rd IG3 ....58 A2
Welsby Ct W5 ....87 C2
Welsford St SE1 ....118 A2
Welsh Cl E13 ....99 A4
Welsh Harp Field Centre
NW9 ....45 B1
Welsh Ho 14 E1 ....118 B5
Welshpool Ho 22 E8 ....96 A6
Welshpool St 1 E8 ....96 B6
Welshside NW9 ....45 C3
Welshside Wlk NW9 ....45 C3
Welstead Ho 5 E1 ....96 B1
Welstead Way W4 ....111 D2
Weltje Rd W6 ....112 A1
Welton Ho E1 ....96 D2
SE5 ....139 C4
Welton Rd SE18 ....145 C5
Welwyn Ave TW14 ....149 D5
Welwyn St E2 ....96 C4
Welwyn Way UB4 ....83 C3
Wembley HA0 ....65 D2
Wembley Arena HA9 ....66 C4
Wembley Bsns Ctr HA9 ....66 D5
Wembley Central Sta
HA9 ....66 A3
Wembley Commercial Ctr
HA9 ....65 D6
Wembley Conference Ctr
HA9 ....66 C4
Wembley Exhibition Halls
HA9 ....66 C4
Wembley High Sch HA0 ....65 C5
Wembley Hill Rd HA9 ....66 B4
Wembley Hospl HA0 ....65 D2
Wembley Manor Jun & Inf
Schs HA9 ....66 A5
Wembley Park Dr HA9 ....66 B5
Wembley Park Sta HA9 ....66 C5
Wembley Rd TW12 ....173 C2
Wembley Stadium HA9 ....66 C3
Wembley Stadium Ind Est
Wembley HA9 ....66 C5
Wembley Stadium Ind Est
continued
Wembley HA9 ....66 D4
Wembley Stadium Sta
HA9 ....66 B3
Wembley Way HA9 ....66 D2
Wemborough Rd HA7 ....25 C3
Wembury Rd N6 ....49 B2
Wemyss Rd SE3 ....142 D3
Wendela Ct HA1 ....64 C6
Wendell Park Prim Sch
W12 ....111 D4
Wendell Rd W12 ....111 D4
Wenderholme CR2 ....221 B3
Wendle Ct SW8 ....270 A5
Wendling NW5 ....70 D3
Wendling Rd SM1,SM5 ....218 B6
Wendon St E3 ....97 B6
Wendover NW9 ....45 D3
SE17 ....117 C1 263 A1
Wendover Cl UB4 ....85 A3
Wendover Ct 4 NW2 ....69 C5
W1 ....238 A3
W3 ....89 A3
Bromley BR2 ....209 B6
Wendover Dr KT3 ....199 D3
Wendover Ho W1 ....238 A3
Wendover Rd BR1,BR2 ....209 B6
NW10 ....89 D5
SE9 ....143 D2
Wendover Way
Bexley DA16 ....146 A1
Bushey WD23 ....8 A5
Wendy Cl EN1 ....17 D5
Wendy Ho N12 ....30 B5
Wendy Way HA0 ....88 A6
Wengham Ho W12 ....112 A6
Wenham Ho SW8 ....269 A3
Wenlake Ho EC1 ....242 A6
Wenlock Ct N1 ....235 D3
Wenlock Gdns 13 NW4 ....46 A5
Wenlock Rd HA8 ....27 A4
N1 ....95 A5 235 B3
Wenlock St N1 ....95 B5 235 C3
Wennington Rd E3 ....96 D5
Wensdale Ho E5 ....74 A6
Wensley Ave IG8 ....37 A3
Wensley Cl SE9 ....166 B5
Barnet N11 ....31 A4
Wensleydale Gdns
TW12 ....173 D3
Wensleydale Ho 8 N4 ....51 A2
Wensleydale Rd TW12 ....173 D3
Wensley Rd N18 ....34 B4
Wentland Cl SE6 ....164 B2
Wentland Rd SE6 ....164 B2
Wentway Ct W13 ....87 A3
Wentwood Ho 1 E5 ....74 B6
Wentworth Ave N3 ....29 C3
Borehamwood WD6 ....10 B6
Wentworth Cl BR2 ....225 A6
N3 ....29 D3
SE28 ....102 D1
Ashford TW15 ....170 D6
Long Ditton KT6 ....213 D6
Morden SM4 ....201 C2
Orpington BR6 ....227 C3
Wentworth Cres SE15 ....140 A5
Hayes UB3 ....105 B3
Wentworth Ct W6 ....264 A5
Barnet EN5 ....1 A2
20 Kingston KT6 ....198 A4
Southall UB2 ....106 C2
2 Surbiton KT6 ....214 A6
Twickenham TW2 ....152 C1
Wandsworth SW18 ....157 D5
Wentworth Dr HA5 ....40 A4
Wentworth Dwellings
E1 ....243 C2
Wentworth Gdns N13 ....16 D1
Wentworth Hall NW7 ....28 C5
Wentworth Hill HA9 ....44 B1
Wentworth Lo N3 ....29 D3
Wentworth Mews E3 ....97 B4
Wentworth Pk N3 ....29 D3
Wentworth Pl HA7 ....25 B4
Wentworth Rd E12 ....77 D4
NW11 ....47 B3
Southall UB2 ....106 D2
Thornton Heath CR0 ....204 C2
Wentworth St E1 ....95 D2 243 D3
Wentworth Way HA5 ....41 A5
Wenvoe Ave DA7 ....147 D3
Wepham Cl UB4 ....84 D2
Wernbrook St SE18 ....145 A6
Werndee Rd SE25 ....206 A5
Werneth Hall Rd IG5 ....56 C6
Werrington St
NW1 ....93 C5 232 B3
Werter Rd SW15 ....135 A1
Wesleyan Pl NW5 ....71 B4
Wesley Ave E16 ....121 B5
NW10 ....89 B4
Hounslow TW3 ....129 B3
Wesley Cl N7 ....72 B6
SE17 ....261 D3
Harrow HA2 ....64 A6
Wesley Ho SE24 ....161 B5
Wesley Rd E10 ....54 A2
N10 ....30 C2
NW10 ....89 A6
Hayes UB3 ....84 A1
Wesley Sq W11 ....91 A1
Wesley St W1 ....238 B3
Wessex Ave SW19 ....201 C6
Wessex Cl
Hinchley Wood KT10, KT7 ....212 D6
Ilford IG3 ....57 C3
Kingston KT1,KT2 ....176 D2
Wessex Ct Putney SW15 ....156 D6
Wessex Ct continued
5 Stanwell TW19 ....148 A5
Wessex Dr HA5 ....23 A3
Wessex Gardens Prim Sch
NW11 ....47 A1
Wessex Gdns NW11 ....47 A1
Wessex Ho 4 N19 ....71 D5
SE1 ....263 D1
Wessex La UB6 ....86 B5
Wessex Rd TW6 ....126 A2
Wessex St E2 ....96 C4
Wessex Way NW11 ....47 A1
Wesson Ho 3 CR0 ....206 A1
Westacott UB4 ....83 C2
Westacott Cl N19 ....49 D1
West Acton Prim Sch
W3 ....88 D1
West Acton Sta W3 ....88 C1
West App BR5 ....211 A4
West Arbour St E1 ....96 D1
West Ave E17 ....53 D4
N2 ....47 D6
N3 ....29 C4
NW4 ....46 D4
Hayes UB3 ....105 D6
Pinner HA5 ....41 B2
Southall UB1 ....107 B6
Wallington SM6 ....220 A3
West Avenue Rd E17 ....53 D5
West Bank N16 ....51 C2
Barking IG11 ....100 D6
Enfield EN2 ....5 A3
Westbank Rd TW12 ....174 A4
West Barnes La KT3,
SW20 ....200 B5
Westbeech Rd N22 ....50 C6
Westbere Dr HA7 ....25 D5
Westbere Rd NW2 ....69 A3
West Block 17 E1 ....118 C6
Westbourne Ave W3 ....89 B1
Cheam SM3 ....217 A6
Westbourne Cl UB4 ....84 C3
Westbourne Cres W2 ....246 C6
Westbourne Ct W2 ....236 A2
Westbourne Dr SE23 ....162 D2
Westbourne Gdns W2 ....91 D1
Westbourne Gr
W11 ....113 B6 244 D6
W2,W11 ....91 C1
Westbourne Gr Mews 7
W11 ....91 C1
Westbourne Gr Terr W2 ....91 D1
Westbourne Ho SW1 ....258 C2
Heston TW5 ....129 C6
8 Twickenham TW1 ....153 B4
Westbourne Par 4 UB10 ....82 D3
Westbourne Park Rd
W11 ....91 B1
W2 ....91 C1
Westbourne Park Sta
W11 ....91 B2
Westbourne Park Villas
W2 ....91 C2
Westbourne Pl N9 ....18 B1
Westbourne Prim Sch
SM1 ....217 C5
Westbourne Rd DA7 ....147 A5
N7 ....72 B2
Croydon CR0 ....205 D3
Feltham TW13 ....149 D1
Hillingdon UB8 ....82 D3
Penge SE26 ....184 D4
Westbourne St
W2 ....114 B6 246 C6
Westbourne Terr
W2 ....92 A1 236 B2
Westbourne Terr Mews
W2 ....236 A2
Westbourne Terr Rd
W2 ....92 A2 236 A3
Westbridge Cl W12 ....112 A5
Westbridge Prim Sch
SW11 ....267 B2
Westbridge Rd
SW11 ....136 C4 267 A2
West Brompton Sta
SW5 ....113 C1 255 B1
Westbrook Ave TW12 ....173 B3
Westbrook Cl EN4 ....2 B2
Westbrook Cres EN4 ....2 B2
Westbrook Ct SE3 ....143 B4
Westbrooke Cres DA16 ....146 C2
Westbrooke Rd DA15 ....167 B2
Bexley DA16 ....146 C2
Westbrooke Sch DA16 ....146 D2
Westbrook Ho 5 E2 ....96 C4
5 SW4 ....159 C6
Westbrook Rd SE3 ....143 B4
Heston TW5 ....129 B5
South Norwood CR7 ....183 B1
Westbrook Sq EN4 ....2 B2
West Brow BR7 ....188 D5
Westbury Ave
Claygate KT10 ....212 D2
Southall UB1 ....85 C3
Tottenham N22 ....32 D1
Wembley HA0 ....66 A1
Westbury Cl Ruislip HA4 ....40 A2
Shepperton TW17 ....192 D3
Westbury Ct SW4 ....159 B5
3 Barking IG11 ....101 B6
Beckenham BR3 ....185 D2
1 Buckhurst Hill IG9 ....21 C2
Tottenham N22 ....33 A1
Westbury Gr N12 ....29 C4
Westbury Ho 1 E17 ....53 C5
Westbury House Sch The
KT3 ....199 B4
Westbury La IG9 ....21 C2
Westbury Lodge Cl HA5 ....40 D6
Westbury Pl 2 TW8 ....131 D6
Westbury Rd E17 ....53 C5
E7 ....77 B2
N12 ....29 D5
Barking IG11 ....101 B6
Beckenham BR3 ....207 A6
Bowes Park N11 ....32 A4
Bromley BR1 ....187 D2
Buckhurst Hill IG9 ....21 C3
Ealing W5 ....88 A1
Feltham TW13 ....150 D3
Ilford IG1 ....78 C6
New Malden KT3 ....199 B4
Penge SE20 ....184 D2
Thornton Heath CR0 ....205 B3
Wembley HA0 ....66 A1
Westbury Terr E7 ....77 B2
Westbush Ct 1 W12 ....112 B4
West Carriage Dr
W2 ....114 C5 247 A4
West Central Ave NW10 ....90 B4
West Central St WC1 ....240 A2
West Chantry HA3 ....23 D2
Westchester Ct NW4 ....46 D6
Westchester Dr NW4 ....46 D6
Westchester Ho W2 ....237 C1
West Cl Ashford TW15 ....170 A6
Barnet EN5 ....12 B6
Cockfosters EN4 ....3 A1
Edmonton N9 ....17 D1
Greenford UB6 ....86 A5
Wembley HA9 ....44 B1
Westcliff Ho 18 N1 ....73 B2
Westcombe Ave CR0 ....204 B2
Westcombe Ct 1 SE3 ....142 D5
Westcombe Dr EN5 ....13 C6
Westcombe Hill SE3,
SE10 ....143 A6
Westcombe Park Lo UB4 ....83 B2
Westcombe Park Rd
SE3 ....142 D5
Westcombe Park Sta
SE3 ....121 A1
West Common Rd BR2 ....225 B5
Westcoombe Ave SW20 ....177 D2
Westcote Rd SW16 ....181 C5
Westcote Rise HA4 ....39 A2
Westcott Cl BR1 ....210 A4
2 N15 ....51 D3
Westcott Cres W7 ....86 C2
Westcott Ho 1 E14 ....119 D6
Westcott Rd SE17 ....138 D6
West Cotts NW6 ....69 C3
Westcroft Cl NW2 ....69 A4
Enfield EN3 ....6 C5
Westcroft Ct NW9 ....44 D4
3 W6 ....112 A2
Westcroft Gdns SM4 ....201 B5
Westcroft Rd SM5,SM6 ....219 A4
Westcroft Sq W6 ....112 A2
Westcroft Way NW2 ....69 A4
West Cromwell Rd
W14 ....113 B1 254 D2
West Cross Ctr TW8 ....131 B6
West Cross Route W10,
W11 ....112 D6
West Cross Way TW8 ....131 B6
West Croydon Sta CR9 ....205 A1
West Ct E17 ....53 D5
Hounslow TW7 ....130 A5
Wembley HA0 ....65 C6
Westdale Rd SE18 ....144 D6
Westdean Ave SE12 ....165 C3
Westdean Cl SW18 ....157 D5
Westdown Rd E15 ....76 A4
Catford SE6 ....163 C4
West Dr Stanmore HA3 ....24 B4
Streatham SW16 ....181 C6
West Drayton Park Ave
UB7 ....104 A3
West Drayton Prim Sch
UB7 ....104 A4
West Drayton Rd UB8 ....82 D1
West Drayton Sta UB7 ....104 A5
West Drive Gdns HA3 ....24 B4
West Dulwich Sta SE21 ....161 B3
West Ealing Bsns Ctr
W13 ....109 A6
West Ealing Sta W13 ....109 B6
West Eaton Pl SW1 ....258 A4
West Eaton Pl Mews
SW1 ....258 A4
West Ella Rd NW10 ....67 C1
West End Ave E10 ....54 B4
Pinner HA5 ....40 D5
West End Cl NW10 ....67 A1
West End Ct NW6 ....69 D1
Pinner HA5 ....40 D5
West End Gdns UB5 ....84 C5
West End La NW6 ....69 D2
Harlington UB7 ....127 A5
Pinner HA5 ....40 D5
West End Rd
Ruislip HA4,UB5 ....62 A4
Ruislip UB5 ....62 C1
Southall UB1 ....107 A5
Westerdale Ct N5 ....72 D4
Westerdale Rd 2 SE10 ....121 A1
Westerfield Rd 1 N15 ....51 D4
Westergate W5 ....88 A2
Westergate Rd SE2 ....147 A6
Westerham NW1 ....232 A5
13 Kingston KT6 ....198 A4
Westerham Ave N9 ....17 C1
Westerham Dr DA15 ....168 B5
Westerham Ho SE1 ....262 D6
Westerham Lo 10 BR3 ....185 C3
Westerham Rd E10 ....53 D2
Keston BR2 ....225 D2
Westerland BR7 ....189 A4
Westerley Cres SE26 ....185 B5
Western Ave NW11 ....46 D3
W3 ....89 B1
Hillingdon HA4,UB4,UB5,
UB10 ....61 C1
Northolt UB5 ....85 C6
Northolt UB5,UB6 ....85 B6
Ruislip UB8,UB9,UB10 ....60 B3
Wembley UB6 ....87 C4
Western Avenue Bsns Pk
W3 ....88 D3
Western Ct N3 ....29 C4
4 W3 ....89 B1
3 W9 ....91 B5
Southall UB2 ....107 A3
Western Dr TW17 ....193 B3
Western Eye Hospl The
NW1 ....92 D2 237 C4
Western Gdns W5 ....110 C6
Western Ho 1 W9 ....91 B3
Western International Market
UB2 ....106 B2
Western La SW12 ....159 A4
Western Mews W9 ....91 B3
Western Par EN5 ....13 D6
Western Pl 18 SE16 ....118 C4
Western Rd E13 ....99 C5
E17 ....54 A4
N2 ....48 D5
NW10 ....89 A3
SW9 ....138 C2
Ealing W5 ....109 D6
Mitcham CR4,SW19 ....180 C1
Southall UB2 ....106 D2
Sutton SM1 ....217 C3
Wood Green N22 ....32 B1
Western Terr W6 ....112 A1
Western View UB3 ....105 D4
Westernville Gdns IG2 ....57 A2
Western Way SE28 ....123 C4
New Barnet EN5 ....13 D5
Western Wharf 2 SE15 ....140 A6
West Ewell Inf Sch
KT19 ....215 B3
Westferry Cir E14 ....119 C5
Westferry Rd E14 ....119 C3
Westferry Sta E14 ....119 C6
Westfield 1 BR6 ....227 A3
NW3 ....69 C4
Loughton IG10 ....21 C6
Westfield Cl NW9 ....45 A6
SW10 ....266 A3
Cheam SM1 ....217 B4
Enfield EN3 ....7 A2
Westfield Ct 1 W10 ....90 D4
Kingston KT6 ....197 D4
Westfield Dr HA3 ....43 D5
Westfield Gdns HA3 ....43 D5
Westfield Ho 6 SE16 ....118 D2
Westfield La HA3 ....43 D5
Westfield Pk HA5 ....23 B3
Westfield Rd NW7 ....11 C1
Beckenham BR3 ....185 B1
Cheam SM1 ....217 B4
Croydon CR0 ....220 D6
Dagenham RM9 ....81 B4
Ealing W13 ....109 A5
Kingston KT6 ....197 D4
Mitcham CR4 ....180 D1
Walton-on-T KT12 ....195 A2
Westfields SW13 ....133 D2
Westfields Ave SW13 ....133 C2
Westfields Gdns RM6 ....58 C3
Westfields Rd W3 ....88 D2
Westfields Sch SW13 ....133 D2
Westfield St SE18 ....121 D3
Westfield Way E1 ....97 A3
Ruislip HA4 ....61 D5
West Finchley Sta N3 ....29 D4
West Garden Pl W2 ....237 B1
West Gate W5 ....88 A4
Westgate Bsns Ctr W10 ....90 D3
2 W10 ....91 A3
Westgate Ct 16 SW9 ....138 C2
6 Beckenham BR3 ....186 A2
Lewisham SE12 ....165 A3
Westgate Est TW14 ....148 D3
Westgate Rd
Beckenham BR3 ....186 A2
Croydon SE25 ....206 B5
Westgate St E8 ....96 B6
Westgate Terr
SW10 ....135 D6 265 D6
West Gdns
Mitcham SW19 ....180 C4
Stepney E1 ....118 B6
Westglade Ct HA3 ....43 D4
West Gr SE10 ....142 B4
Woodford IG8 ....37 C5
West Green Pl UB6 ....86 B6
West Green Prim Sch
N15 ....51 A5
West Green Rd N15 ....51 B5
Westgrove La SE10 ....142 A4
West Grove Prim Sch
N14 ....15 D4
West Halkin St
SW1 ....115 A3 258 A6
West Hallowes SE9 ....166 A3
West Hall Rd TW9 ....132 D4
West Ham Church Prim Sch
E15 ....98 D6
West Ham La E15 ....76 C1
West Hampstead Mews
NW6 ....69 D2
West Hampstead Sta
NW6 ....69 C2
West Hampstead Thameslink
Sta NW6 ....69 C2
West Ham Sta E15 ....98 C4
West Harding St EC4 ....241 B2
West Harrow Sta HA1 ....42 A3
West Hatch Manor HA4 ....39 D2
Westhay Gdns SW14 ....154 D6
West Heath Ave NW11 ....47 C1
West Heath Cl NW3 ....69 C5
West Heath Ct NW11 ....47 C1
West Heath Dr NW11 ....47 C1
West Heath Gdns NW3 ....69 C5
West Heath Rd NW3 ....69 D5
SE2 ....146 D6
West Hill N6 ....49 A1
Harrow HA2 ....64 C6
Putney SW15 ....157 A5
South Croydon CR2 ....221 C1
Wembley HA9 ....44 B1
Westhill Ct W11 ....244 D6
West Hill Ct N6 ....71 A5
West Hill Hall HA2 ....64 C6
Westhill Pk N6 ....70 D6
N6 ....71 A6
West Hill Prim Sch
SW18 ....157 C6
West Hill Rd SW18 ....157 B5
West Hill Way N20 ....13 D3
West Ho Barking IG11 ....78 D2
4 Penge SE20 ....184 D3
9 Streatham SW12 ....159 C4
Westholm NW11 ....47 D5
Westholme BR6 ....211 D2
Westholme Gdns HA4 ....40 A1
Westhope Ho 18 E2 ....96 A4
Westhorne Ave SE9,
SE12 ....165 C5
Westhorpe Gdns NW4 ....46 C6
Westhorpe Rd SW15 ....134 C2
West House Cl SW19 ....157 A3
Westhurst Dr BR7 ....188 D5
West India Ave E14 ....119 C5
West India Dock Rd
E14 ....119 C6
West India Ho 1 E14 ....119 C6
West India Quay Sta
E14 ....119 C6
West Kensington Ct
W14 ....254 C2
West Kensington Mans
W14 ....254 C1
West Kensington Sta
W14 ....113 B1 254 C2
West La SE16 ....118 B4
Westlake 10 SE16 ....118 C2
Westlake Cl Hayes UB4 ....85 A3
Palmers Green N13 ....16 C1
Westlake Rd HA9 ....65 D6
Westland Cl TW19 ....148 A5
Westland Ct 9 UB5 ....84 D4
Westland Dr BR2,BR4 ....224 D6
Westland Ho 1 E16 ....122 C5
Westland Lo 1 BR1 ....187 C1
Westland Pl N1 ....235 C2
Westlands Cl UB3 ....106 A2
Westlands Ct KT8 ....196 C5
Westlands Terr 3
SW12 ....159 C5
Westlea Rd W7 ....109 A3
West Lea Sch N9 ....17 C1
Westleigh Ave SW15 ....156 C6
Westleigh Ct N12 ....29 D4
12 Wanstead E11 ....55 A4
Westleigh Dr BR1 ....188 A2
Westleigh Gdns HA8 ....26 C1
West Links HA0 ....87 D4
Westlinton Cl NW7 ....29 A4
West Lodge Ave W3 ....110 C5
West Lodge Ct W3 ....110 C5
West Lodge Fst & Mid Schs
HA5 ....40 D5
West Lodge Sch DA15 ....168 A1
West London Shooting
Grounds UB5 ....84 B5
West London Stad The
W12 ....90 B2
Westly Ct NW2 ....68 D2
Westmacott Dr TW14 ....149 D3
Westmacott Ho NW8 ....236 D5
West Mall W11 ....245 B4
Westmark Point 13
SW15 ....156 B3
Westmead SW15 ....156 B5
West Mead Ruislip HA4 ....62 C4
West Ewell KT19 ....215 C2
Westmead Cnr SM5 ....218 C4
Westmead Rd SM1 ....218 B4
Westmeath Ho NW2 ....68 A5
Westmere Dr NW7 ....11 B1
West Mersea Cl 9 E16 ....121 B5
West Mews SW1 ....259 A3
West Middlesex Univ Hosp
TW7 ....131 A3
Westmill Ct N4 ....73 A6
Westminster Abbey★
SW1 ....116 A3 260 A6
Westminster Abbey Choir
Sch SW1 ....115 D3 259 D6
Westminster Ave CR7 ....182 D1
Westminster Boating Base
SW1 ....269 C6
Westminster Bridge
SE1,SW1 ....116 A4 250 B1
Westminster Bridge Rd
SE1 ....116 B4 250 C1
Westminster Cath★
SW1 ....115 C3 259 A5
Westminster Cath Choir Sch
SW1 ....115 C2 259 B4
Westminster Cath RC Prim
Sch SW1 ....115 D1 259 D2
Westminster City Hall
SW1 ....259 B6

Westminster City Sch
SW1 ... 259 B6
Westminster Cl
East Bedfont TW14 ... 150 A3
Teddington TW11 ... 175 A5
Westminster Coll of Bsns & Computing HA9 ... 66 A3
Westminster Ct
22 SE16 ... 118 D5
5 SW18 ... 157 C6
South Norwood CR7 ... 183 A1
Wanstead E11 ... 55 B3
Westminster Dr N13 ... 32 A5
Westminster Gdns SW1 ... 260 A4
Barking IG11 ... 101 C5
Chingford, Chingford Green E4 ... 20 C3
Westminster Ind Est E16 ... 121 D3
Westminster Kingsway Coll SW11 ... 137 A4 268 B2
WC1 ... 94 B4 233 C1
Westminster Pier SW1 ... 250 B1
Westminster Rd
Carshalton SM1,SM5 ... 218 B6
Ealing W7 ... 108 C5
Edmonton N9 ... 18 B3
Westminster Sch SW1 ... 116 A3 260 A6
Westminster Sta SW1 ... 116 A4 250 B1
Westmoat Cl BR3 ... 186 A3
Westmont Rd KT10 ... 212 C6
Westmoor Gdns EN3 ... 6 D3
Westmoor Rd EN3 ... 6 D3
Westmoor St SE7 ... 121 D3
Westmore Ct SW15 ... 157 A6
Westmoreland Ave DA16 ... 145 C1
Westmoreland Ho NW10 ... 90 A4
Westmoreland Pl
5 BR1 ... 209 A6
SW1 ... 258 D1
Ealing W5 ... 87 D2
Westmoreland Rd BR2 ... 209 A5
HA3,NW9 ... 44 B5
SE17 ... 139 B6
Barnes SW13 ... 134 A4
Beckenham BR2,BR3 ... 208 D5
Westmoreland St W1 ... 238 B3
Westmoreland Terr SW1 ... 115 B1 258 D1
Penge SE20 ... 184 B3
Westmorland Cl
3 Twickenham TW1 ... 153 B5
Wanstead E12 ... 77 D6
Westmorland Ct 12 KT6 ... 197 D2
Westmorland Dr SM2 ... 217 D1
Westmorland Rd BR2 ... 209 A5
E17 ... 53 C3
Harrow HA1 ... 41 D4
Westmorland Sq CR4 ... 204 A4
Westmorland Way CR4 ... 203 D4
Westmount Ct W5 ... 88 B2
Westmount Rd SE9 ... 144 C1
West Norwood Sta SE27 ... 160 D1
West Oak BR3 ... 186 B2
Westoe Rd N9 ... 18 B2
Weston Ave
East Molesey KT8 ... 195 B5
Thames Ditton KT10,KT7 ... 196 C2
Westonbirt Ct 6 SE15 ... 139 D6
Weston Ct N20 ... 14 A4
N4 ... 73 A5
3 Kingston KT1 ... 198 A6
Weston Dr HA7 ... 25 B2
Weston Ed Ctr The SE5 ... 139 A3
West One Ho W1 ... 239 A3
Westone Mans 5 IG11 ... 79 D1
Weston Gdns TW7 ... 130 C4
Weston Gn
Dagenham RM9 ... 81 B4
Thames Ditton KT7 ... 196 C1
Weston Gr 1 BR1 ... 186 D2
Weston Green Prep Sch KT7 ... 196 C1
Weston Green Rd KT7 ... 196 C2
Weston Ho 9 E9 ... 96 C6
4 NW6 ... 69 A1
Weston Park Cl KT7 ... 196 C1
Weston Park Prim Sch N8 ... 50 B4
Weston Pk N8 ... 50 B3
Kingston KT1 ... 176 A1
Thames Ditton KT10,KT7 ... 196 C1
Weston Rd W4 ... 111 A3
Bromley BR1 ... 186 D3
Dagenham RM9 ... 81 A4
Enfield EN2 ... 5 B3
Ruislip HA4 ... 61 D1
Thames Ditton KT7 ... 196 C1
Weston Rise N1, WC1 ... 94 B4 233 D2
Weston St SE1 ... 117 B4 252 D2
Weston Wlk 3 E8,E9 ... 74 B1
Westover Hill NW3 ... 69 C6
Westover Rd SW18 ... 158 A5
Westow Hill SE19 ... 183 D4
Westow St SE19 ... 183 C4
Westpark W5 ... 87 D1
West Park Ave TW9 ... 132 D4
West Park Cl
Heston TW5 ... 129 B6
Ilford RM6 ... 58 D4
West Park Rd
Richmond TW9 ... 132 C4
Southall UB2 ... 108 B5
West Parkside SE10 ... 121 A2
Greenwich SE10 ... 120 D3
West Pk SE9 ... 166 A3
West Pl SW19 ... 178 C5
West Point 2 SE1 ... 118 A1
Westpoint
Beckenham BR2 ... 208 B6
Putney SW15 ... 156 D5
Westpoint Trad Est W3 ... 88 D2
Westpole Ave EN4 ... 3 B1
Westport Ct UB4 ... 84 C3
Westport Rd E13 ... 99 B3
Westport St E1 ... 96 D1
West Poultry Ave EC1 ... 241 C3
West Quarters W12 ... 90 A1
West Quay Dr UB4 ... 85 A2
West Ramp TW6 ... 126 C4
West Rd E15 ... 98 D6
N2 ... 30 B2
SW3 ... 136 D6 267 D6
SW4 ... 159 D6
Dagenham RM6 ... 59 A3
Ealing W5 ... 88 A2
East Barnet EN4 ... 15 A3
East Bedfont TW14 ... 149 B4
Kingston KT2,KT3 ... 177 A2
Tottenham N17 ... 34 B4
West Drayton UB7 ... 104 B3
West Ridge Gdns UB6 ... 86 A5
West Row W10 ... 91 A3
Westrow SW15 ... 156 C5
Westrow Dr IG11 ... 80 A2
Westrow Gdns IG3 ... 79 D5
West Ruislip Elementary Sch UB10 ... 61 A5
West Ruislip Sta HA4 ... 61 A6
West Sheen Vale TW9 ... 132 B1
Westside N2 ... 48 D6
NW4 ... 28 B1
West Side Comm SW19 ... 178 C5
Westside Ct 1 W9 ... 91 C3
West Smithfield EC1 ... 94 D2 241 D3
West Sq SE11 ... 116 D3 261 C5
West St BR1 ... 187 A1
DA7 ... 147 B2
E11 ... 76 C5
E17 ... 53 D4
26 E2 ... 96 B5
WC2 ... 93 D1 239 D1
Carshalton SM5 ... 218 D4
Croydon CR0 ... 221 A4
Harrow HA1 ... 42 C1
Sutton SM1 ... 217 D3
West Street La SM5 ... 218 D4
West Street Pl 1 CR0 ... 221 A4
West Surrey Ests TW15 ... 171 A2
West Sutton Sta SM1 ... 217 C4
West Temple Sheen SW14 ... 154 D6
West Tenter St E1 ... 95 D1 243 D1
West Terr DA15 ... 167 C3
West Thames Coll TW7 ... 130 C4
West Thamesmead Bsns Pk SE28 ... 123 D3
West Thornton Prim Sch CR0 ... 204 B3
West Towers HA5 ... 40 D3
West Twyford Prim Sch NW10 ... 88 C5
Westvale Mews W3 ... 111 C4
Westview W7 ... 86 C1
West View Dagenham RM6 ... 58 C4
East Bedfont TW14 ... 149 A4
Westview Cl NW10 ... 67 D3
W10 ... 90 C1
Westview Cres N9 ... 17 C4
Westview Ct 3 WD6 ... 9 D5
Westview Dr IG8 ... 37 D1
West View Gdns WD6 ... 9 D5
Westville Rd W12 ... 112 A4
Thames Ditton KT7 ... 197 A2
Westward Rd E4 ... 35 B5
Westward Way HA3 ... 44 A3
West Warwick Pl SW1 ... 259 A3
Westway W10,W12 ... 112 A6
West Way BR5 ... 211 B4
HA8 ... 27 A4
NW10 ... 67 B5
Westway SW20 ... 200 C5
West Way Croydon CR0 ... 223 A5
Edmonton N18 ... 33 B6
Hounslow TW5 ... 129 B4
Pinner HA5 ... 40 D5
Ruislip HA4 ... 39 D1
Shepperton TW17 ... 193 B3
West Wickham BR4 ... 208 C3
Westway Cl SW20 ... 200 B6
Westway Cross Sh Pk UB6 ... 86 C6
Westway Ct UB5 ... 85 C6
Westway (Elevated Rd) W10 ... 91 B2
West Way Gdns CR0 ... 222 D6
Westway Lo 35 W2 ... 91 C2
Westways KT19 ... 215 D4
West Ways HA6 ... 22 A1
Westwell 4 NW5 ... 71 A2
Westwell Rd SW16 ... 182 A4
Westwell Road App SW16 ... 182 A4
Westwick 7 KT1 ... 176 C1
Westwick Gdns W14 ... 112 D4
Cranford TW4,TW5 ... 128 B3
West Wickham Sta BR3 ... 208 A2
West Wlk East Barnet EN4 ... 15 A3
Hayes UB3 ... 106 A5
Westwood Ave
Harrow HA2 ... 63 D4
South Norwood SE19 ... 183 A2
Westwood Cl BR1 ... 209 D6
Westwood Cl *continued*
Esher KT10 ... 212 A5
Ruislip HA4 ... 38 D3
Westwood Ct Enfield EN1 ... 17 C5
3 Forest Hill SE23 ... 162 C3
7 Wimbledon SW19 ... 179 B5
Westwood Gdns SW13 ... 133 D2
Westwood Hill SE26 ... 184 B6
Westwood Ho 5 N4 ... 51 B2
W12 ... 112 C5
Westwood La DA16 ... 145 D1
Westwood Language College for Girls SE19 ... 183 B3
Westwood Pk SE23 ... 162 B4
Westwood Pl SE26 ... 184 A6
Westwood Prim Sch DA16 ... 145 C1
Westwood Rd 12 E16 ... 121 B5
Barnes SW13 ... 133 D2
Ilford IG3 ... 58 A2
Westwood Sch WD23 ... 8 B2
Westwood Tech Coll DA16 ... 145 C1
Wetheral Ct SW17 ... 180 B6
Wetheral Dr HA7 ... 25 C1
Wetherby Cl UB5 ... 63 D2
Wetherby Ct SE25 ... 183 C1
Wetherby Gdns SW5 ... 114 A2 256 A3
Wetherby Mans SW5 ... 255 C2
Wetherby Mews SW5 ... 255 D2
Wetherby Pl SW7 ... 114 A2 256 B3
Wetherby Rd EN2 ... 5 A4
Wetherby Way KT9 ... 214 A1
Wetherden St E17 ... 53 B2
Wetherell Rd E9 ... 96 D6
Wetherill Rd N10 ... 31 A2
Wetland Centre The★ SW13 ... 134 B5
Wevco Wharf SE15 ... 140 B6
Wexford Ho 9 E1 ... 96 C2
Wexford Rd SW12 ... 158 D4
Weybourne St SW18 ... 158 A2
Weybridge Ct 19 SE16 ... 118 B1
Weybridge Ho N4 ... 51 A2
Weybridge Point 11 SW11 ... 136 D3
Weybridge Rd CR7 ... 204 C5
Wey Ct KT19 ... 215 A4
Weydown Cl SW19 ... 157 A3
Weyhill Ho 27 SE5 ... 139 A3
Weyhill Rd 6 E1 ... 96 A1
Wey Ho NW8 ... 236 D5
Weylands Cl KT12 ... 195 B1
Weylond Rd RM8 ... 81 B5
Weyman Rd SE3 ... 143 C4
Weymarks The N17 ... 33 B4
Weymouth Ave NW7 ... 27 C5
W5 ... 109 C3
Weymouth Cl 1 E6 ... 100 D1
Weymouth Ct 5 E2 ... 95 D5
Belmont SM2 ... 217 C1
15 Streatham SW2 ... 160 B4
Weymouth Ho SW8 ... 270 C3
Bromley BR2 ... 186 D1
Weymouth Mews W1 ... 93 B2 238 C4
Weymouth Rd UB4 ... 83 C4
Weymouth St W1 ... 93 B2 238 C4
Weymouth Terr E2 ... 95 D5
Weymouth Wlk HA7 ... 25 A4
Whadcoat St N4 ... 72 C6
Whadden Ho 10 SE5 ... 139 C2
Whaddon Ho SW1 ... 247 D1
Whalebone Ave RM6 ... 59 B3
Whalebone Gr RM6 ... 59 B3
Whalebone La E15 ... 76 C1
Whalebone La N RM6 ... 59 A6
Whalebone La S RM6, RM8 ... 59 B2
Whales Yd E15 ... 76 C1
Wharfdale Cl N11 ... 31 A4
Wharfdale Rd N1 ... 94 A5 233 B4
Wharfedale Ct 5 E5 ... 74 D4
Wharfedale Gdns CR7, SW16 ... 204 B6
Wharfedale St SW10 ... 255 C1
Wharf La TW1 ... 153 A3
Wharf Pl E2 ... 96 B6
Wharf Rd E15 ... 98 B6
N1 ... 95 A5 235 A3
NW1 ... 93 D6 232 D5
Enfield EN3 ... 19 A5
Wharfside HA0 ... 88 A6
Wharfside Rd E16 ... 98 C2
Wharf St E16 ... 98 C2
Wharncliffe Dr UB1 ... 108 B5
Wharncliffe Gdns SE25 ... 183 C1
Wharncliffe Rd SE25 ... 183 C1
Wharton Cl NW10 ... 67 C2
Wharton Ho SE1 ... 263 C6
Wharton Rd BR1 ... 187 B2
Wharton St WC1 ... 94 B4 233 D1
Whateley Rd SE22 ... 161 D6
Penge SE20 ... 184 D3
Whatley Ave SW20 ... 201 A6
Whatman Rd SE23 ... 162 D4
Wheatfields E6 ... 100 D1
Enfield EN3 ... 7 A3
Wheatfield Way KT1 ... 176 A1
Wheathill Ho SE20 ... 184 B1
Wheathill Rd SE20 ... 206 B6
Wheatland Ho 7 SE22 ... 139 C2
Wheatlands TW5 ... 129 C6
Wheatlands Rd SW17 ... 159 A1
Wheatley Cl NW4 ... 28 A1
Wheatley Gdns N9 ... 17 C2
Wheatley Ho NW5 ... 71 B4
Wheatley Ho *continued*
3 Putney SW15 ... 156 A4
Wheatley Mans 8 IG11 ... 80 A1
Wheatley Rd TW7 ... 130 D2
Wheatley's Ait TW16 ... 194 A4
Wheatley St W1 ... 238 B3
Wheatly Cres UB3 ... 106 A6
Wheat Sheaf Cl E14 ... 119 D2
Wheatsheaf Cl UB5 ... 63 A3
Wheatsheaf La SW6 ... 134 C5
SW8 ... 270 B4
Wheatsheaf Par 6 BR4 ... 207 D1
Wheatsheaf Terr SW6 ... 264 D3
Wheatstone Cl SW19 ... 180 C2
Wheatstone Ho 7 W10 ... 91 A2
Wheatstone Rd W10 ... 91 A2
Wheeler 2 NW9 ... 27 D3
Wheeler Ct 5 SW11 ... 136 B2
Wheeler Gdns N1 ... 233 B6
Wheelers Cross IG11 ... 101 B5
Wheelers Dr HA4 ... 39 A3
Wheeler's St SM1 ... 217 C5
Wheelock Cl DA8 ... 147 D5
Wheelwright St N7 ... 72 B1
Whelan Way SM6 ... 219 D5
Wheldon Ct SE1 ... 253 C2
Wheler Ho E1 ... 243 C5
Wheler St E1 ... 95 D3 243 C5
Whellock Rd W4 ... 111 C3
Whernside Cl SE28 ... 124 C6
Whetstone Cl N20 ... 14 B2
Whetstone Park WC2 ... 94 B1 240 C2
Whetstone Rd SE3 ... 143 D4
Whewell Rd N19 ... 72 A6
Whichcote St SE1 ... 251 A3
Whidborne Bldgs WC1 ... 233 A1
Whidborne Cl SE8 ... 141 C3
Whidborne St WC1 ... 233 B1
Whimbrel Cl SE28 ... 124 C6
Whimbrel Way UB4 ... 84 D2
Whinchat Rd SE18,SE28 ... 123 B3
Whinfell Cl SW16 ... 181 D5
Whinyates Rd SE9 ... 144 A2
Whippendell Cl BR5 ... 190 B2
Whippendell Way BR5 ... 190 B1
Whippingham Ho 17 E3 ... 97 B4
Whipps Cross E17 ... 54 B4
Whipps Cross Ho E17 ... 54 B4
Whipps Cross Hospl E10, E11 ... 54 B3
Whipps Cross Rd E11 ... 54 C3
Whiskin St EC1 ... 94 D4 234 C1
Whisperwood Cl HA3 ... 24 C3
Whistler Gdns HA8 ... 26 B1
Whistler Mews 2 SE15 ... 139 D5
Dagenham RM8 ... 80 B3
Whistlers Ave SW11 ... 136 B5 266 D3
Whistler St N5 ... 72 D3
Whistler Twr SW10 ... 266 A3
Whistler Wlk SW10 ... 266 B4
Whiston Ho 18 N1 ... 72 D1
Whiston Rd E2 ... 96 A6
Whitakers Lo EN2 ... 5 B4
Whitbread Cl N17 ... 34 A2
Whitbread Ctr EC1 ... 242 C5
Whitbread Rd SE4 ... 141 B1
Whitburn Rd SE13 ... 142 A1
Whitby Ave NW10 ... 88 D4
Whitby Ct N7 ... 72 A4
Whitby Gdns NW9 ... 44 C6
Carshalton SM1,SM5 ... 218 B6
Whitby Ho NW8 ... 229 A5
Whitby Rd SE18 ... 122 B2
Carshalton SM1,SM5 ... 218 B6
Harrow HA2 ... 64 A5
Ruislip HA4 ... 62 C6
Whitby St E1 ... 243 C6
Whitcher Cl SE14 ... 141 A6
Whitcher Pl NW1 ... 71 C2
Whitchurch Ave HA8 ... 26 B3
Whitchurch Cl HA8 ... 26 B4
Whitchurch Ct SW17 ... 180 B6
Whitchurch Fst & Mid Schs HA7 ... 25 D3
Whitchurch Gdns HA8 ... 26 B4
Whitchurch Ho 16 W10 ... 90 D1
Catford SE6 ... 164 A1
Whitchurch La HA8 ... 26 B3
Whitchurch Rd W11 ... 112 D6
Whitcomb Ct W1 ... 249 D5
Whitcombe Mews TW9 ... 132 D4
Whitcomb St WC2 ... 115 D6 249 D5
Whiteadder Way E14 ... 119 D2
Whitear Wlk E15 ... 76 B2
Whitebarn La RM10 ... 103 C6
Whitebeam Ave BR2 ... 210 C3
Whitebeam Cl SW9 ... 270 D3
Whitebeam Ho 3 NW3 ... 70 B2
White Bear Pl NW3 ... 70 B4
White Bear Yd EC1 ... 241 A5
White Bridge Ave CR4 ... 202 B6
White Bridge Cl TW14 ... 149 D5
White Butts Rd HA4 ... 62 D5
Whitechapel High St E1 ... 95 D1 243 D2
Whitechapel Rd E1 ... 96 B2
Whitechapel Sta E1 ... 96 B2
Whitechurch La 2 E1 ... 96 A1
White City W10 ... 90 C1
White City Cl W12 ... 112 C6
White City Est 21 W12 ... 112 B6
White City Rd W12 ... 112 C6
White City Sta W12 ... 112 C6
Whitecliff Ho SW18 ... 157 D5
White Conduit St N1 ... 234 B4
Whitecote Rd UB1 ... 86 A1
White Craig Cl HA5 ... 23 C5
Whitecroft Cl BR3 ... 208 B5
Whitecroft Way BR3 ... 208 B5
Whitecross Pl EC2 ... 242 D4
Whitecross St EC1 ... 95 A3 242 B5
White Cube art gallery★ N1 ... 95 C4
Whitefield Ave NW2 ... 46 C1
Whitefield Cl SW15 ... 157 A5
Whitefield Sch NW11 ... 46 D2
Chingford E17 ... 36 A1
Whitefoot La BR1 ... 164 B1
Whitefoot Terr BR1 ... 164 D1
Whitefriars Ave HA3 ... 24 C1
Whitefriars Centre Coll HA3 ... 42 C6
Whitefriars Ct N12 ... 30 B5
Whitefriars Dr HA3 ... 24 C1
Whitefriars Fst & Mid Sch HA3 ... 24 C1
Whitefriars St EC4 ... 94 C1 241 B1
Whitefriars Trad Est HA3 ... 24 B1
White Gate Gdns HA3 ... 24 D3
Whitegates 4 EN5 ... 13 D6
White Gdns RM10 ... 81 C2
Whitehall SW1 ... 250 A2
Whitehall Cres KT9 ... 213 D3
Whitehall Ct SW1 ... 116 A5 250 B3
Whitehall Gdns SW1 ... 250 A3
Acton W3 ... 110 C5
Chingford, Chingford Green E4 ... 20 C3
Chiswick W4 ... 132 D6
Whitehall La IG9 ... 21 A2
Whitehall Lo N10 ... 49 A6
Woodford IG8 ... 21 A1
Whitehall Mans 3 N19 ... 49 C1
Whitehall Park Rd W4 ... 132 D6
Whitehall Pk N19 ... 49 C1
Whitehall Pl WC2,SW1 ... 116 A5 250 A3
Wallington SM5 ... 219 B4
Whitehall Prim Sch E4 ... 20 C2
Whitehall Rd W7 ... 109 A4
Bromley BR2 ... 209 D5
Chingford E4 ... 20 C2
Harrow HA1 ... 42 C2
Thornton Heath CR7 ... 204 C4
Woodford IG8 ... 21 A1
Whitehall St N17 ... 33 D3
White Hart Ct EC2 ... 243 A3
White Hart La N10 ... 67 D2
Mortlake SW13 ... 133 C2
White Hart Lane Sch N22 ... 32 D3
White Hart Lane Sta N17 ... 33 D3
White Hart Lane (Tottenham Hotspur FC) N17 ... 34 A3
White Hart Rd SE18 ... 123 C2
White Hart Rdbt UB5 ... 84 D5
White Hart St EC4 ... 241 D2
SE11 ... 116 C1 261 B2
White Hart Terr N17 ... 33 D3
White Hart Yd SE1 ... 252 C3
Whitehaven Cl BR2 ... 209 A5
Whitehaven St NW8 ... 237 A5
Whitehead Cl
Edmonton N18 ... 33 B5
Wandsworth SW18 ... 158 A4
Whitehead Ct N10 ... 31 A1
Whitehead Ho 8 SW15 ... 156 D6
Whitehead's Gr SW3 ... 114 C2 257 B3
White Heart Ave UB8 ... 83 A2
Whiteheath Ave HA4 ... 39 A2
Whiteheath Inf Sch HA4 ... 39 A3
Whiteheath Jun Sch HA4 ... 39 A2
White Heron Mews TW11 ... 174 D4
White Ho N9 ... 18 C2
2 SW11 ... 136 B3
3 Streatham SW4 ... 159 D4
Whitehorn Ho 6 E1 ... 118 C5
White Horse Hill BR7, SE9 ... 188 C6
White Horse La E1 ... 96 D2
Whitehorse La SE25 ... 205 C5
Whitehorse Manor Inf Sch CR7 ... 205 B5
Whitehorse Manor Jun Sch CR7 ... 205 B5
Whitehorse Mews SE1 ... 261 C6
Whitehorse Rd E1 ... 97 A2
White Horse Rd E1 ... 97 A1
E6 ... 100 B4
Whitehorse Rd CR0,CR7 ... 205 B3
White Horse St W1 ... 115 B5 248 D3
White Horse Yd EC2 ... 242 C2
White Ho The N17 ... 51 C6
NW1 ... 238 D6
White House Ct N14 ... 15 D2
1 Beckenham BR3 ... 186 A2
White House Dr HA7 ... 25 C6
Whitehouse Est E10 ... 54 A3
White House La EN2 ... 5 A4
Whitehouse Way N14 ... 15 B1
White Kennett St E1 ... 243 B2
Whitelands Coll, Roehampton, Univ of Surrey SW18 ... 157 A4
Whitelands Ho SW3 ... 257 D2
Whiteledges W13 ... 87 C1
Whitelegg Rd E13 ... 98 D5
Whiteley Ho 8 SW4 ... 159 D4
Whiteley Rd SE19 ... 183 B5
Whiteleys Ctr W2 ... 91 D1
Whiteleys Ho TW13 ... 151 C1
Whiteleys Par 5 UB10 ... 82 D3
Whiteleys Way TW13 ... 151 C1
White Lion Ct EC3 ... 243 A1
White Lion Hill EC4 ... 116 D6 251 D6
White Lion St N1 ... 94 C5 234 B3
White Lion Yd W1 ... 248 C6
White Lo 7 Ealing W5 ... 87 C2
South Norwood SE19 ... 183 D3
Whitelock Ho 21 E9 ... 74 D2
White Lodge Cl N2 ... 48 B3
Sutton SM2 ... 218 A1
White Lodge The Royal Ballet Sch TW10 ... 155 B3
Whitely Ct TW13 ... 151 B1
Whiteness Ho 18 SW9 ... 138 C4
White Oak Dr BR3 ... 186 A1
White Oak Gdns DA15 ... 167 D4
Whiteoak Ho SE19 ... 183 A3
Whiteoaks La UB6 ... 86 B5
White Orchards
Barnet N20 ... 13 B3
Stanmore HA7 ... 25 A5
White Post La E9 ... 75 C2
White Post St SE14,SE15 ... 140 C5
White Rd E15 ... 76 C1
Whites Ave IG2 ... 57 C3
Whites Dr BR2 ... 208 D2
White's Grounds SE1 ... 117 C4 253 B2
White's Grounds Est SE1 ... 253 B2
White's Mdw BR1 ... 210 C5
White's Row E1 ... 95 D2 243 C3
White's Sq SW4 ... 137 D1
White St UB2 ... 106 D4
Whitestile Rd TW8 ... 109 D1
Whitestone La NW3 ... 70 A5
Whitestone Wlk NW3 ... 70 A5
Whitethorn Ave UB7 ... 104 B6
Whitethorn Gdns
Croydon CR0 ... 222 B6
Enfield EN2 ... 17 B6
Whitethorn Pl UB7 ... 104 B5
Whitethorn St E3 ... 97 C2
Whiteways NW4 ... 46 D5
Whitewebbs Way BR5 ... 189 D2
Whitfield Ct SW4 ... 270 A1
3 Dulwich SE21 ... 183 C6
Redbridge IG1 ... 56 B2
Whitfield Gdns W1 ... 239 B4
Whitfield Ho NW8 ... 237 A5
Whitfield Pl W1 ... 239 B5
Whitfield Rd DA7 ... 147 B5
E6 ... 77 C1
SE10,SE13 ... 142 B4
Whitfield St W1 ... 93 C2 239 B4
Whitford Gdns CR4 ... 202 D6
Whitgift Ave CR2 ... 221 A3
Whitgift Ct CR2 ... 221 A3
Whitgift Ctr CR0 ... 221 A6
Whitgift Ho SE11 ... 260 C4
SW11 ... 267 A2
Croydon CR2 ... 221 A3
Whitgift Sch CR2 ... 221 A3
Whitgift St SE11 ... 116 B2 260 C4
Croydon CR0 ... 221 A5
Whiting Ave IG11 ... 78 D1
Whitings Hill Prim Sch EN5 ... 12 C6
Whitings Rd EN5 ... 12 C6
Whitings The IG2 ... 57 C4
Whitings Way E6 ... 100 C2
Whitington Ave EC3 ... 243 A1
Whitland Rd SM5 ... 202 B1
Whitley Cl TW19 ... 148 A5
Whitley Ho SW1 ... 269 B6
Whitley Rd N17 ... 33 C1
Whitlock Dr SW19 ... 157 A3
Whitman Ho 20 E2 ... 96 C4
Whitman Rd E3 ... 97 A3
Whitmead Cl CR2 ... 221 C2
Whitmore Cl N11 ... 31 B5
Whitmore Comm Sch N1 ... 235 C6
Whitmore Gdns NW10 ... 90 C5
Whitmore High Sch HA1, HA2 ... 42 A1
Whitmore Ho 20 E1 ... 95 C6
N11 ... 30 D6
Whitmore Rd N1 ... 95 C6
Beckenham BR3 ... 207 B6
Harrow HA1 ... 42 A2
Whitnell Ct 7 SW15 ... 156 D6
Whitnell Way SW15 ... 156 D6
Whitney Ave IG4 ... 55 D5
Whitney Ho 6 SE22 ... 139 C2
Whitney Rd E10 ... 53 D2
Whitney Wlk DA14 ... 191 A4
Whitstable Cl
Beckenham BR3 ... 185 B2
Ruislip HA4 ... 61 C6
Whitstable Ho 11 W10 ... 90 D1
Whitstable Pl 9 CR0 ... 221 A4
Whitsters Ho SE1 ... 253 C2
Whittaker 3 NW9 ... 27 D3
Whittaker Ave TW10, TW9 ... 153 D6
Whittaker Ct SW4 ... 270 B1
Whittaker Pl 24 TW10 ... 153 D6
Whittaker Rd E6 ... 77 D1
Cheam SM3 ... 217 B5
Whittaker St SW1 ... 258 A3
Whittaker Way 17 SE1 ... 118 A2
Whittam Ho SE27 ... 183 A5
Whitta Rd E12 ... 77 D4
Whittell Gdns SE26 ... 162 C1

Whitten Lo N12 30 C6
Whittingham 6 N17 34 B3
Whittingham Ct W4 133 C5
Whittingstall Mans
SW6 264 D1
Whittingstall Rd
SW6 135 B4 264 D1
Whittington Ave UB4 83 D2
Whittington Ct N2 48 D4
Penge SE20 184 B1
Whittington Hospl The
N19 71 C6
Whittington Mews N12 30 A6
Whittington Rd N22 32 A3
Whittington Way HA5 41 A4
Whittle 4 NW9 27 D3
Whittlebury Cl SM5 218 D1
Whittlebury Ho N4 51 A2
Whittle Cl E17 53 A2
Southall UB1 85 D1
Whittle Rd Heston TW5 128 C5
Southall UB2 107 D4
Whittlesea Cl HA3 24 A3
Whittlesea Path HA3 24 A2
Whittlesea Rd HA3 24 A2
Whittlesea Sch HA3 24 A3
Whittlesey St
SE1 116 C5 251 B3
Whitton NW3 70 D1
Whitton Ave E UB6 65 A2
Whitton Ave W UB5,UB6 64 B3
Whitton Cl UB6 65 B2
Whitton Dene
Isleworth TW3,TW7 152 B5
Isleworth TW3,TW7 152 B6
Whitton Dr UB6 65 A2
Whitton Manor Rd TW7 152 A5
Whitton Rd
Hounslow TW3 151 D6
Twickenham TW1 153 A4
Whitton Road Rdbt
TW1 152 D5
Whitton Sch TW2 151 D2
Whitton Sta TW2 152 A4
Whitton Waye TW2,TW3 151 C5
Whitton Wlk E3 97 C4
Whitwell Ho 11 E5 74 B6
Whitwell Rd E13 99 A4
Whitworth Cres EN3 7 C6
Whitworth Ho SE1 262 B5
Whitworth Rd SE18 144 C5
South Norwood SE25 205 D5
Whitworth St SE10 120 C1
Whorlton Rd SE15 140 B2
Whychcote Point NW2 46 C2
Whymark Ave N22 50 D6
Whytecroft TW5 128 D5
Whyteville Ho E7 77 B2
Whyteville Rd E7 77 B2
Whytlaw Ho 11 E3 97 B2
Wickers Oake SE19 183 D6
Wicker St 2 E1 96 B1
Wicket Rd UB6 87 A4
Wickets The TW15 170 A6
Wicket The CR0 223 C3
Wickfield Ho 29 SE16 118 A4
Wickford Ho 4 E1 96 C3
Wickford St E1 96 C3
Wickford Way E17 52 D5
Wickham Ave
Cheam KT4,SM3 216 C3
Croydon CR0 207 A1
Wickham Chase BR4 208 C2
Wickham Cl E1 96 C2
Enfield EN3 6 C2
New Malden KT3 199 D4
Wickham Common Prim Sch
BR4 225 A4
Wickham Court Rd BR4 224 A6
Wickham Cres BR4 224 A6
Wickham Ct DA16 145 C3
Wickham Gdns SE4 141 B2
Wickham Ho SW15 156 D5
Wickham La SE2,SE18 146 A6
Wickham Mews SE4 141 B3
Wickham Rd SE4 141 B2
Beckenham BR3 207 D6
Chingford E4 36 A3
Croydon CR0 207 B1
Harrow HA3 24 B1
Wickham St DA16 146 A4
SE11 116 B1 260 C2
Bexley DA16 145 C3
Wickham Way BR3 208 A4
Wick Ho 1 KT1 175 D2
Wick La E3 75 B1
E3 97 C6
Wickliffe Ave N3 29 A1
Wickliffe Gdns HA9 66 D6
Wicklow Ct SE26 184 C5
Wicklow Ho N16 51 D1
Wicklow St WC1 94 B4 233 C2
Wick Mews 1 E9 75 A2
Wick Rd E9 75 A2
Hackney E9 75 A2
Teddington TW11 175 C3
Wicks Cl SE12 187 D6
Wick Sq E9 75 B2
Wickstead Ho TW8 110 B1
Wicksteed Ho SE1 262 B5
Wickway Ct 7 SE15 139 D6
Wickwood St SE5 138 D3
Widdenham Rd N7 72 B4
Widdicombe Ave HA2 63 B6
Widdin St E15 76 C1
Widecombe Ct N2 48 B4
Widecombe Gdns IG4 56 A5
Widecombe Ho 33 SE5 139 A3
Widecombe Rd SE9 166 A1
Widecombe Way N2 48 B5
Widegate St E1 243 B3
Widenham Cl HA5 40 C4
Wide Way CR4 203 D6
Widewing Cl TW11 175 B3
Widford 8 NW1 71 B2
Widford Ho N1 234 C3
Widgeon Cl E16 99 B1
Widgeon Path SE28 123 B3
Widley Rd W9 91 C3
Widmer Ct TW5 129 A3
Widmore Lodge Rd
BR1 187 D1
Widmore Rd BR1 187 C1
Hillingdon UB8 82 D3
Widnes Ho 6 N7 72 C3
Wieland Rd HA6 22 A3
Wigan Ho E5 52 B1
Wigeon Way UB4 84 D1
Wiggins La TW10 153 C2
Wiggins Mead NW9 27 D3
Wigginton Ave HA9 66 D2
Wightman Rd N4,N8 50 C4
Wighton Mews TW7 130 C3
Wigley Rd TW13 150 D3
Wigmore Ct 4 W13 109 A5
Wigmore Hall W1 238 C2
Wigmore Pl W1 93 B1 238 C2
Wigmore Rd SM5 202 C1
Wigmore St W1 93 A1 238 B2
Wigmore Wlk SM5 218 B6
Wigram Ct SW11 267 A2
Wigram Ho 6 E14 119 D6
Wigram Rd E11 55 C3
Wigram Sq E17 54 A6
Wigston Cl N18 33 C5
Wigston Rd E13 99 B3
Wigton Gdns HA7 26 A2
Wigton Pl SE11 261 B1
Wigton Rd E17 35 B2
Wilberforce Ct 2 SE28 124 C5
Edgware HA8 26 B6
Wilberforce Ho 4
SW11 136 B2
Wilberforce Prim Sch
W10 91 A4
Wilberforce Rd N4 72 D6
N4,N5 73 A5
NW9 46 A3
Wilberforce Way SW19 178 D4
Wilbraham Ho SW8 270 A3
Wilbraham Pl SW1 258 A4
Wilbury Prim Sch N18 33 B5
Wilbury Way N18 33 B5
Wilby Mews
W11 113 B5 244 D4
Wilcox Cl SW8 270 B4
Wilcox Gdns TW17 192 B6
Wilcox Ho 6 E3 97 B2
Wilcox Pl SW1 259 B5
Wilcox Rd SW8 138 A5 270 A4
Sutton SM1 217 D4
Teddington TW11 174 B6
Wildcroft Gdns HA8 25 D4
Wildcroft Manor SW15 156 C4
Wildcroft Rd SW15 156 C4
Wild Ct WC2 94 B1 240 C2
Wilde Cl E8 96 A6
Wilde Pl Edmonton N13 32 D4
Wandsworth SW18 158 B4
Wilder Cl HA4 40 B1
Wilde Rd DA8 147 D5
Wilderness Mews SW4 137 B1
Wilderness Rd BR7 188 D3
Wilderness The
East Molesey KT8 196 A4
Hampton TW12 173 D6
Wilderton Rd N16 51 C2
Wildfell Rd SE6 163 D4
Wild Goose Dr SE14 140 C4
Wild Hatch NW11 47 C3
Wilding Ho 17 E9 74 D2
Wild March Ct EN3 7 A6
Wild's Rents
SE1 117 C3 263 A6
Wild St WC2 94 B1 240 C1
Wildwood Cl SE12 164 D4
Wildwood Gr NW3 48 A1
Wildwood Rd NW11 48 A2
Wildwood Rise NW11 48 A1
Wildwood Terr NW3 48 A1
Wilford Cl EN2 5 B2
Wilford Ho 3 SE18 122 D1
Wilford Rd CR0 205 A2
Wilfred Fienburgh Ho
N7 71 D4
Wilfred Owen Cl SW19 180 A4
Wilfred St SW1 115 C3 259 A6
Wilfrid Gdns W3 89 A2
Wilkes Rd 3 TW8 132 A6
Wilkes St E1 95 D2 243 D4
Wilkie Ho SW1 259 D2
Wilkins Cl Hayes UB3 105 D1
Mitcham CR4 180 C2
Wilkins Ho SW1 269 A6
Wilkinson Cl UB10 83 A6
Wilkinson Ct SW17 180 B6
Wilkinson Ho N1 235 D3
Isleworth TW7 130 D2
Wilkinson Rd E16 99 C1
Wilkinson St
SW8 138 B5 270 C3
Wilkinson Way W4 111 B4
Wilkin St NW5 71 B2
Wilks Gdns CR0 207 A1
Wilks Pl N1 95 C5
Willan Rd N17 33 C1
Willan Wall E16 120 D6
Willard St SW8 137 B2
Willbury Ho 4 N7 71 D3
Willcocks Cl KT9 214 A5
Willcott Rd W3 110 D5
Will Crooks Gdns SE9 143 D1
Willenfield Rd NW10 89 A5
Willenhall Ave EN5 14 A5
Willenhall Ct EN5 14 A5
Willenhall Dr UB3 105 C6
Willenhall Rd SE18 122 D1
Willersley Ave BR6 227 B5
DA15 167 D4
Willersley Cl DA15 167 D3
Willesden Community Hospl
The NW10 68 A1
Willesden Green Sta
NW2 68 C2
Willesden High Sch
NW10 90 B6
Willesden Junction Sta
NW10 89 D4
Willesden La NW2,NW6 68 D2
Willes Rd NW5 71 B2
Willet Cl 3 UB5 84 C4
Willett Cl BR5 211 C3
Willett Ho 7 E13 99 A5
SW9 138 A2
Willett Pl CR7 204 C4
Willett Rd CR7 204 C4
Willett Way BR5,BR6 211 C3
William Allen Ho HA8 26 B3
William Atkinson Ho
N17 33 C3
William Banfield Ho 10
SW6 135 B3
William Barefoot Dr
SE9 166 C1
William Bellamy Inf Sch
RM10 81 C6
William Bellamy Jun Sch
RM10 81 C6
William Booth Meml Training
Coll SE5 139 B3
William Booth Rd SE20 184 A2
William Brown Ct SE27 160 D2
William Byrd Sch UB3 127 A6
William Carey Way HA1 42 C3
William Caslon Ho 28 E2 96 B5
William Channing Ho 6
E2 96 B4
William C Harvey Sch
N17 33 B1
William Cl SE13 142 A2
Finchley N2 30 B1
Southall UB2 108 A4
William Covell Cl EN2 4 B5
William Ct 4 Ealing W5 87 C2
Ilford IG6 57 B5
William Davies Prim Sch
E7 77 D2
William Davis Prim Sch
E2 96 A3
William Dromey Ct NW6 69 B1
William Dunbar Ho NW6 91 B5
William Dyce Mews 1
SW16 181 D6
William Ellis Sch NW5 71 A5
William Ellis Way 16
SE16 118 A3
William Evans Ho 9
SE8 118 D2
William Ford CE Jun Sch
RM10 81 C1
William Gdns SW15 156 B6
William Guy Gdns 47 E3 97 D4
William Harvey Ho 1
SW19 157 A3
William Ho NW2 68 C5
Edmonton N13 32 D4
William Hunt Mans
SW13 134 C6
William IV St
WC2 116 A6 250 A5
William Margrie Cl 1
SE15 140 A3
William Mews
SW1 114 D4 247 D1
William Morley Cl E6 99 D6
William Morris Acad
W6 112 D1
William Morris Cl E17 53 B6
William Morris Ho W6 134 D6
William Morris Mid Sch
CR4 203 D6
William Morris Sch E17 35 A2
William Morris Way
SW6 136 A3
William Patten Prim Sch
N16 73 D6
William Pl 31 E3 97 B5
William Rainbird Ho 8
N17 33 D3
William Rathbone Ho 3
E2 96 B4
William Rd NW1 93 C4 232 A1
Sutton SM1 218 A3
Wimbledon SW19 179 A3
William Rushbrooke Ho 4
SE16 118 A2
Williams Ave E17 35 B2
William Saville Ho 2
NW6 91 B5
William's Bldgs 1 E2 96 C3
Williams Cl SW6 ....
Williams Dr TW3 129 C1
Williams Gr
Kingston KT6 197 C3
Wood Green N22 32 C2
Williams Ho 9 E3 97 C4
9 E9 96 B6
Williams Ho continued
14 Streatham SW2 160 C3
Williams La Morden SM4 202 A4
Mortlake SW14 133 A3
William Smith Ho 10
DA17 125 C3
Williamson Cl SE10 120 D1
Williamson Ct SE17 262 A1
Williamson Rd N4 50 D3
Williamson St N7 72 A4
Williamson Way NW7 29 A4
William Sq 15 SE16 119 A6
Williams Rd UB2 107 A2
William's Rd W13 109 A5
William St E10 53 D3
SW1 114 D4 247 D1
Barking IG11 79 A1
Carshalton SM5 218 D5
Tottenham N17 33 D3
Williams Terr CR0 220 C2
William Torbitt Prim Sch
IG2 57 D4
William Tyndale Prim Sch
N1 72 D1
William Winter Ct 29
SW2 160 C4
William Wood Ho 3
SE26 162 C1
Willifield Way NW11 47 C4
Willingale Cl IG8 37 C4
Willingdon Rd N22 32 D1
Willingham Cl 4 NW5 71 C3
Willingham Terr NW5 71 C3
Willingham Way KT1 176 C1
Willington Ct E5 75 A5
Willington Prep Sch
SW19 179 B5
Willington Rd SW9 138 A2
Willis Ave SM2 218 C2
Willis Ho 7 E14 119 D6
2 Ilford E12 78 C5
Willis Rd E15 98 D5
Thornton Heath CR0 205 A2
Willis St E14 97 D1
Willows The CR0 223 A6
Will Miles Ct 6 SW19 180 A3
Willmore End SW19 179 D1
Willoughby Ave CR0 220 B4
Willoughby Gr N17 34 B3
Willoughby Hall Dyslexia Ctr
NW3 70 B4
Willoughby Ho 34 E1 118 B5
EC2 242 C3
Willoughby La N17 34 B3
Willoughby Mews N17 34 B3
Willoughby Park Rd N17 34 B3
Willoughby Rd N8 50 C5
NW3 70 B4
Kingston KT2 176 B2
Twickenham TW1 153 D6
Willoughby St WC1 240 A3
Willoughbys The SW14 133 C1
Willoughby Way SE7 121 B2
Willow Ave DA15 168 A5
Barnes SW13 133 D3
Yiewsley UB7 104 B6
Willowbank SW6 135 A2
Willow Bank TW10 153 B1
Willowbank Rd SE15 139 D6
Willow Bridge Rd N1 73 A2
Willowbrook Rd
Southall UB2 107 C3
Stanwell TW19 148 A2
Willow Bsns Pk SE26 162 C1
Willow Cl BR2 210 B4
Brentford TW8 131 C6
Buckhurst Hill IG9 21 D1
12 Catford SE6 164 D3
Sidcup DA5 169 B5
Willow Cotts
Carshalton CR4 202 D2
Feltham TW13 151 A1
Richmond TW9 132 C6
Willowcourt Ave HA3 43 B4
Willow Ct EC2 243 A6
N7 72 B3
SW9 138 C4
40 W2 91 C2
7 E11 76 C6
Ashford TW16 171 C3
Beckenham BR3 185 C2
Chiswick W4 133 C5
8 Dagenham RM8 58 D2
Edgware HA8 26 A6
Harrow HA3 24 D2
Ilford IG1 79 A3
Kingston KT3 198 D6
3 Streatham SW16 160 B1
Thornton Heath CR7 205 B4
Willow Ctr The CR4 202 D3
Willow Dean HA5 22 D1
Willowdene N6 48 D2
1 SE15 140 B4
5 SE15 140 B5
Willow Dene WD23 8 C4
Willowdene Cl TW2 152 A4
Willowdene Ct N20 14 A4
Willow Dene Sch SE18 145 C4
Willow Dr EN5 1 A1
Willow End N20 13 C2
Northwood HA6 22 A4
Surbiton KT6 198 A1
Willow Farm La SW15 134 B2
Willowfields Cl SE18 123 C1
Willowfield Sec Sch E17 52 D6
Willow Gdns
Heston TW5 129 C4
Ruislip HA4 61 D6
Willow Gn NW9 27 C2
Borehamwood WD6 11 B6
Willow Gr BR7 188 D4
E13 99 A5
Ruislip HA4 39 D1
Willow Hall NW3 70 B4
Willowhayne Dr KT12 194 B2
Willowhayne Gdns KT4 216 C4
Willow Ho 14 N2 30 B1
9 NW3 70 D2
W10 90 D3
Feltham TW14 150 B6
Willow La SE18 122 C2
Mitcham CR4 202 D3
Willow Lo
6 Ashford TW16 171 D3
Fulham SW6 134 D4
New Barnet EN5 14 A6
Putney SW15 134 B2
Willow Lodge 10 SW8 137 B2
Willow Manor SM1 217 B4
Willowmead Cl W5 87 D2
Willowmere KT10 212 A4
Willow Mount CR0 221 C5
Willow Pl SW1 115 C2 259 B4
Willow Rd NW3 70 B4
W5 110 A4
Dagenham RM6 59 A3
Enfield EN1 5 C3
New Malden KT3 199 A5
Wallington SM6 219 B1
Willows Ave SM4 201 D4
Willows Cl HA5 22 C1
Willows Sch The UB4 84 D3
Willow St EC2 95 C3 243 A6
Chingford E4 20 B4
Willows Terr NW10 89 D5
Willows The N20 14 A1
Beckenham BR3 185 C2
Claygate KT10 212 C2
Wallend E12 78 C1
Loughton IG10 21 D6
Willow Tree Cl E3 97 B6
Willowtree Cl UB10 61 A5
Willow Tree Cl
Hayes UB4 84 C3
Wandsworth SW18 157 D3
Willow Tree Ct DA14 189 D5
5 Wembley HA0 65 D3
Willow Tree La UB4 84 C3
Willow Tree Prim Sch
UB5 63 A2
Willowtree Way SW16 182 C2
Willow Tree Wlk BR1 187 B2
Willow Vale BR7 188 D4
W12 112 A5
Willow View SW19 180 B2
Willow Way N3 29 D3
9 W11 112 D6
Forest Hill SE26 162 C1
Sunbury TW16 194 A5
Twickenham TW2 151 D2
Wembley HA0 65 A5
West Ewell KT19 215 B2
Willow Wlk BR6 226 D5
E17 53 B4
N15 50 D5
12 N2 30 B1
SE1 117 D2 263 C4
Cheam SM1,SM3 217 B5
Southgate N21 16 B5
Willow Wood Cres
SE25 205 C3
Willrose Cres SE2 124 B1
Willsbridge Ct 1 SE15 139 D6
Wills Cres TW3 151 D5
Wills Gr NW7 28 B5
Willshaw St SE14 141 C4
Will Thorne Pav The
E16 100 A1
Wilman Gr E8 74 A1
Wilmar Cl UB4 83 B3
Wilmar Gdns BR4 207 D1
Wilmcote Ho W2 91 D2
Wilmer Cl TW10 176 B5
Wilmer Cres KT2,TW10 176 B5
Wilmer Gdns N1 95 C6
Wilmer Ho 5 E3 97 A5
Wilmer Lea Cl E15 76 B1
Wilmer Pl N16 73 D6
Wilmers Ct 5 NW10 89 B6
Wilmer Way N14 31 D5
Wilmington Ave W4 133 B5
Wilmington Ct SW16 182 A3
Wilmington Gdns IG11 79 C1
Wilmington Sq
WC1 94 C4 234 A1
Wilmington St WC1 234 A1
Wilmot Cl N2 30 A1
SE15 140 A5
Wilmot Pl NW1 71 C1
Ealing W7 108 C5
Wilmot Rd E10 75 D6
N17 51 B6
Wallington SM5 218 D3
Wilmot St E2 96 B3
Wilmount St SE18 122 D2
Wilna Rd SW18 158 A4
Wilnett Ct 4 RM6 58 B2
Wilnett Villas 5 RM6 58 B2
Wilsham St
W11 113 A5 244 A4
Wilshaw Ho 10 SE8 141 C5
Wilsmere Dr HA3 24 C3
Wilson Ave CR4 180 C2
Wilson Cl Croydon CR2 221 B3
Wembley HA9 44 B2
Wilson Dr HA9 44 B2
Wilson Gdns HA1 42 A2
Wilson Gr SE16 118 B4
Wilson Ho NW6 70 A1
2 SE7 143 C6
Wilson Ho continued
39 SW8 137 D3
Wilson Rd E6 99 D4
SE5 139 C4
Chessington KT9 214 B2
Redbridge IG1 56 B2
Wilson's Ave 2 N17 33 D1
Wilson's Pl E14 97 B1
Wilson's Rd W6 112 D1
Wilson's Sch SM6 220 A2
Wilson St E17 54 A4
EC2 95 B2 242 D4
Southgate N21 16 C4
Wilstone Cl UB4 85 A3
Wiltern Ct NW2 69 A2
Wilthorne Gdns RM10 81 D1
Wilton Ave W4 111 C1
Wilton Cres
SW1 115 A4 248 A1
Merton SW19 179 B2
Wilton Ct 16 E1 96 B1
N10 31 A1
4 Richmond TW10 154 A6
7 Woodford IG8 37 A4
Wilton Est E8 74 A2
Wilton Gdns
East Molesey KT8 195 C6
Walton-on-T KT12 194 D1
Wilton Gr Merton SW19 179 B2
New Malden KT3 199 D3
Wilton Ho 8 SE22 139 C2
Wilton Mews
SW1 115 B3 258 B6
Wilton Par TW13 150 B2
Wilton Pl SW1 115 A4 248 A1
2 Beckenham BR3 208 A6
4 Harrow HA1 42 D3
Wilton Rd N10 31 A1
SE2 124 C2
SW1 115 C2 259 A4
Cockfosters EN4 2 D1
Hounslow TW4 128 D2
Mitcham SW19 180 C3
Wilton Row SW1 248 A1
Wilton Sq N1 95 B6 235 C6
Wilton St SW1 115 B3 258 C6
Wilton Terr SW1 258 A6
Wilton Villas N1 235 C5
Wilton Way E8 74 A2
Wilton Wlk TW13 150 B3
Wiltshire Cl NW7 27 D5
SW3 257 C3
Wiltshire Ct 2 N4 50 B1
Barking IG11 79 A2
Wiltshire Gdns N4 51 A3
Twickenham TW2 152 A3
Wiltshire La HA5 40 A5
Wiltshire Rd SW9 138 C2
Thornton Heath CR7 204 C6
Wiltshire Row
N1 95 B6 235 D5
Wilverley Cres KT3 199 C3
Wimbart Rd SW2 160 B4
Wimbledon Bridge
SW19 179 B4
Wimbledon Central
SW19 179 B4
Wimbledon Chase Prim Sch
SW20 179 A2
Wimbledon Chase Sta
SW20 179 A1
Wimbledon Cl 2 SW20 178 D3
Wimbledon Coll SW19 178 D3
Wimbledon Common*
SW19 178 B6
Wimbledon Common Prep
Sch SW19 178 D3
Wimbledon High Sch
SW19 179 A4
Wimbledon Hill Rd
SW19 179 B4
Wimbledon House Sch
SW19 179 C2
Wimbledon Lawn Tennis
Mus* SW19 157 A1
Wimbledon Park Ct
SW19 157 B3
Wimbledon Park First Sch
SW19 157 D2
Wimbledon Park Rd
SW18,SW19 157 B3
Wimbledon Park Side
SW19 156 D3
Wimbledon Park Sta
SW19 157 C1
Wimbledon Rd SW17 180 A6
Wimbledon Sch of Art
SW19 179 A2
Wimbledon Sch of Art
Annexe SW19 179 C3
Wimbledon Sta SW19 179 B4
Wimbledon Stadium
SW17 180 A6
Wimbledon Stadium Bsns Ctr
SW17 157 D1
Wimbledon Windmill Mus*
SW19 156 C1
Wimbolt St E2 96 A4
Wimborne 2 DA14 190 B6
Wimborne Ave Hayes UB4 84 B1
Southall UB2 107 C2
Wimborne Cl SE12 164 D6
Buckhurst Hill IG9 21 C2
North Cheam KT4 200 C1
Wimborne Ct 1 UB5 63 C2
Wimborne Dr HA8,NW9 44 C6
Pinner HA5 41 A5
Wimborne Gdns W13 87 B2
Wimborne Ho E16 120 D6
NW1 237 B5

Wimborne Ho *continued*
SW8 270 D3
Croydon CR0 206 C4
Upper Tooting SW12 159 C1
Wimborne Rd
Edmonton N9 18 A2
Tottenham N17 33 C1
Wimborne Way BR3 207 A5
Wimbourne Ct N1 235 C4
Mitcham SW19 180 B3
South Croydon CR2 221 C2
Wimbourne St
N1 95 B5 235 C4
Wimpole Cl Bromley BR2 209 C5
1 Kingston KT1 176 C1
Wimpole Mews
W1 93 B2 238 C3
Wimpole St W1 93 B1 238 C2
Wimshurst Cl CR0 204 A1
Winans Wlk SW9 138 C3
Winant Ho 17 E14 119 D6
Wincanton Cres UB5 63 C3
Wincanton Gdns IG6 56 D6
Wincanton Rd SW18 157 B4
Winchcombe Rd SM5 202 C1
Winchcomb Gdns SE9 143 D2
Winchelsea Ave DA7 147 B5
Winchelsea Cl SW15 156 D6
Winchelsea Ho 11 SE16 118 C4
Winchelsea Rd E7 77 A4
N17 51 C6
NW10 89 B6
Winchelsey Rise CR2 221 D2
Winchendon Rd
Fulham SW6 135 B4 264 D2
Teddington TW11,TW12 174 B6
Winchester Ave NW6 69 A1
NW9 44 C6
Heston TW5 129 B6
Winchester Cl SE17 261 D3
Beckenham BR2 208 D6
Enfield EN1 17 C6
Kingston KT2 176 D3
11 Newham E6 100 B1
Winchester Ct W8 245 C2
Belvedere DA17 125 C1
Winchester Dr HA5 40 D4
Winchester Ho 18 E3 97 B4
1 SE18 143 D5
SW3 266 D5
W2 236 A1
5 Barking IG11 80 A1
Winchester Pk BR2 208 D6
Winchester Pl 6 E8 73 D3
N6 49 B1
Winchester Rd N6 49 B1
NW3 70 B1
Beckenham BR2 208 D6
Bexley DA16 146 D3
Chingford E4 36 A3
Edmonton N9 18 A3
Harlington UB3 127 C5
Harrow HA3 44 A5
Ilford IG1 79 B5
Northwood HA6 40 A6
Twickenham TW1 153 B5
Twickenham TW13 151 B1
Walton-on-T KT12 194 A1
Winchester Sq SE1 252 C4
Winchester St
SW1 115 B1 258 D2
Acton W3 111 A4
Winchester Wlk SE1 252 C4
Winchet Wlk CR0 206 C3
Winchfield Cl HA3 43 C3
Winchfield Ho SW15 155 D5
Winchfield Rd SE26 185 A5
Winch Ho SW10 266 B4
Winchilsea Cres KT8 174 A1
Winchilsea Ho NW8 229 D1
Winchmore Hill Rd N14,
N21 16 A4
Winchmore Hill Sta N21 16 D4
Winchmore Sch N21 17 A2
Winchmore Villas N21 16 B4
Winchstone Cl TW17 192 B5
Winckley Cl HA3 44 B4
Wincott St SE11 116 C2 261 B3
Wincrofts Dr SE9 145 B1
Windall Cl SE20 184 A2
Windborough Rd SM5 219 A1
Windcott Ct HA3 43 C2
Windermere NW1 231 D2
12 Putney SW15 156 D5
Windermere Ave N3 47 C6
NW6 91 A6
Merton SW19 201 D6
Ruislip HA4 40 D2
Wembley HA9 43 C1
Windermere Cl BR6 226 D5
East Bedfont TW14 149 D3
Stanwell TW19 148 A2
Windermere Ct
Barnes SW13 133 D6
Barnet EN5 1 D1
Carshalton SM5 219 A5
Wembley HA9 43 C2
Windermere Gdns IG4 56 A4
Windermere Gr HA9 43 C1
Windermere Hall HA8 26 B5
Windermere Ho E3 97 B3
Isleworth TW1 152 D6
Windermere Point 3
SE15 140 C5
Windermere Rd N10 31 B2
N19 71 C6
W5 109 C3
Croydon CR0 205 D1
Kingston SW15 177 C5
Mitcham SW16 181 D1
Windermere Rd *continued*
Southall UB1 85 B2
West Wickham BR4 224 C6
Windermere Way UB7 104 B5
Winders Rd SW11 136 C3
Windfield Cl SE26 184 D6
Windham Rd TW9 132 B2
Winding Way RM8 80 C5
Windlass Pl SE8 119 A2
Windlesham Gr SW19 156 D3
Windley Cl SE23 162 C2
Windmill WC1 240 C4
Windmill Alley 7 W4 111 C2
Windmill Ave UB2 108 A4
Windmill Bridge Ho 1
CR0 205 C1
Windmill Bsns Ctr UB2 108 A5
Windmill Bsns Village
TW16 171 C2
Windmill Cl NW2 69 A5
11 SE1 118 A2
3 SE13 142 A3
Ashford TW16 171 C3
Kingston KT6 197 C2
Windmill Ct NW2 69 A2
W5 109 C2
Windmill Dr BR2 225 C4
SW4 159 B6
Windmill Gdns EN2 4 C2
Windmill Gr CR0 205 A3
Windmill Hill NW3 70 A5
1 NW3 70 A4
Enfield EN2 5 A2
Ruislip HA4 39 D1
Windmill Ho SE1 251 B3
Windmill La E15 76 B2
Bushey WD23 8 C3
Edgware EN5 11 D5
Isleworth TW7,UB2,W7 108 C2
Southall UB2 108 A4
Southall UB6 86 A2
Thames Ditton KT7 197 B2
Windmill Lo TW16 171 C2
Windmill Pas 10 W4 111 C2
Windmill Rd SW18 158 B5
W4 111 C2
Brentford TW8,W5 109 C1
Charlton TW16 171 C2
Edmonton N18 33 B6
Hampton TW12 174 A5
Mitcham CR4 203 C5
Roehampton SW19 156 B1
Thornton Heath CR0 205 A2
Windmill Rd W TW16 171 C1
Windmill Rise KT2 176 D3
Windmill Row SE11 261 A1
Windmill St W1 93 D2 239 C3
Bushey WD23 8 C3
Windmill Terr TW17 193 C2
Windmill Trad Est
TW16 171 C2
Windmill Way HA4 39 D1
Windmill Wlk SE1 251 B2
Windmore Cl HA0 65 A3
Windrose Cl SE16 118 D4
Windrush KT3 199 A5
Windrush Cl SW11 136 B1
Chiswick W4 133 A5
Ickenham UB10 60 B4
Windrush Ho NW8 236 D4
Windrush La SE23 162 D1
Windrush Prim Sch
SE28 124 B5
Windrush Rd NW10 89 B6
Windsock Cl 1 SE16 119 B2
Windsor Ave E17 35 A1
Cheam SM3 217 A5
East Molesey KT8 195 C6
Edgware HA8 10 D1
Hillingdon UB10 60 D1
Merton SW19 180 A2
New Malden KT3 199 A4
Windsor Cl N3 29 A1
Brentford TW8 131 B6
Chislehurst BR7 188 D5
Harrow HA2 63 C5
Pinner HA6 22 A1
West Norwood SE27 183 A6
Windsor Cres Harrow HA2 63 C5
Wembley HA9 66 D5
Windsor Ct BR1 210 A6
E17 53 B6
N11 30 D5
N14 15 C4
NW11 47 A3
NW3 69 C4
20 SE16 118 D5
SW11 136 B3
4 SW18 157 C6
SW3 257 B2
2 SW4 137 C1
W2 245 C6
Bushey WD23 8 A4
Fulham SW6 135 A2
South Norwood SE19 183 C2
Sunbury TW16 172 A3
Windsor Ctr The SE27 183 A6
Windsor Dr EN4 14 D5
Windsor Gdns W9 91 C3
Hayes UB3 105 B3
Wallington CR0 220 A5
Windsor Gr SE27 183 A6
Windsor Ho 4 E2 96 D4
N1 235 B4
N4 51 A1
NW1 231 D2
NW2 69 A2
2 NW4 28 D1
4 W4 111 A1
7 Northolt UB5 63 C2
Windsor Mews
Catford SE6 164 A3
Forest Hill SE23 163 A3
Windsor Park Rd UB3 127 D5
Windsor Pk SW19 180 A2
Windsor Pl SW1 259 B4
Windsor Rd DA6 147 A1
E10 75 D6
E7 77 C3
N3 29 A1
N7 72 A5
NW2 68 B2
Ashford TW16 172 A4
Barnet EN5 12 D5
Chingford E4 35 D6
Cranford TW4,TW5 128 C3
Dagenham RM8 81 A5
Ealing W5 110 A6
Harrow HA3 24 B2
Ilford IG1 79 A4
Kingston KT2 176 A3
Palmers Green N13 16 C1
Richmond TW9 132 B3
Southall UB2 107 B3
South Norwood CR7 182 D1
Teddington TW11 174 B5
Tottenham N17 34 A1
Wanstead E11 77 A6
Worcester Park KT4 216 A6
Windsor St N1 94 D6 234 D6
Windsor Terr N1 95 A4 235 B2
Windsor Way
W14 113 A2 254 A4
Windsor Wharf E9 75 B3
Windsor Wlk SE5 139 B3
Walton-on-T KT12 194 D1
Windspoint Dr SE15 140 B6
Windus Rd N16 51 D1
Windus Wlk N16 51 D1
Windy Ridge BR1 188 A2
Windy Ridge Cl SW19 178 D5
Wine Cl E1 118 C6
Wine Office Ct EC4 241 B2
Winery La KT1 198 B6
Winey Cl KT9 213 C1
Winfield Ho SW11 136 B3
Winford Ct 15 SE15 140 A4
Winford Ho E3 75 B1
Winford Par 9 UB1 85 D1
Winforton St SE10 142 A4
Winfrith Rd SW18 158 A3
Wingate Cres CR0 204 A3
Wingate Ho 26 E3 97 D4
8 N16 73 B4
Wingate Rd W6 112 B3
Ilford IG1 78 D3
Sidcup DA14 190 C4
Wingate Trad Est N17 33 D3
Wingfield Ct 10 E14 120 B6
Wingfield Ho 16 E2 95 D4
NW6 91 D5
Wingfield Mews SE15 140 A2
Wingfield Prim Sch
SE3 143 B2
Wingfield Rd E15 76 C4
E17 53 D4
Kingston KT2 176 C4
Wingfield St SE15 140 A2
Wingfield Way HA4 62 B2
Wingford Rd SW2 160 A5
Wingham 3 NW5 71 A2
Wingham Ho 3 SE26 184 B5
Wingmore Rd SE24 139 A2
Wingrad Ho 14 E1 96 C2
Wingrave SE17 262 C3
Wingrave Rd W6 134 C6
Wingreen 13 NW8 91 D6
Wingrove Rd SE6 164 C2
Wings Cl SM1 217 C4
Winicotte Ho W2 236 D4
Winifred Cl EN5 11 D5
Winifrede Paul Ho 7
NW5 71 B4
Winifred Pl N12 30 A5
Winifred Rd
Dagenham RM8 59 A1
Hampton TW12 173 C6
Merton SW19 179 C2
Winifred St E16 122 B5
Winifred Terr EN1 17 D4
Winkfield Rd E13 99 B5
Wood Green N22 32 C2
Winkley Ct N10 49 B5
Harrow HA2 63 C5
Winkley St 6 E2 96 B5
Winkworth Cotts 18 E1 96 C3
Winlaton Rd BR1 186 B6
Winmill Rd RM8 81 B5
Winn Common Rd SE18 145 C6
Winnett St W1 249 C6
Winningales Ct IG5 56 A6
Winnings Wlk UB5 63 A2
Winnington Cl N2 48 B3
Winnington Ho 8 SE5 139 A5
19 W10 91 A3
Winnington Rd N2 48 B3
Enfield EN3 6 C6
Winnipeg Dr 3 BR6 227 D2
Winnipeg Ho UB4 84 B3
Winn Rd SE12 165 B3
Winns Ave E17 53 B6
Winns Mews N15 51 C5
Winns Prim Sch E17 35 B1
Winns Terr E17 53 C6
Winsbeach E17 36 B1
Winscombe Cres W5 87 D3
Winscombe Ct W5 87 D3
Winscombe St N19 71 B6
Winscombe Way HA7 25 A5
Winsford Rd SE6 163 B1
Winsford Terr N18 33 B5
Winsham Gr SW11 159 A6
Winsham Ho NW1 232 D2
Winslade Ho 4 E5 74 B6
Winslade Rd SW2 160 A6
Winslade Way SE6 163 D4
Winsland Mews W2 236 C2
Winsland St W2 92 B1 236 C2
Winsley St W1 239 B2
Winslow SE17 263 A1
Winslow Cl 2 NW10 67 C5
Pinner HA5 40 B3
Winslow Gr E4 20 C2
Winslow Rd W6 134 C6
Winslow Way TW13 151 A1
Winsmoor Ct EN2 4 D2
Winsor Prim Sch E6 100 C1
Winsor Terr E6 100 C2
Winstanley Rd SW11 136 B2
Winston Ave NW9 45 C2
Winston Cl Harrow HA3 24 D4
Romford RM7 59 D5
Winston Ct 7 BR1 187 B2
Harrow HA3 23 D3
Winston Ho WC1 239 D6
Winston Rd N16 73 B4
Winston Way IG1 79 A5
Winston Wlk W4 111 B2
Winter Ave E6 100 A6
Winterborne Ave BR6 227 B5
Winterbourne Ho W11 244 A5
Winterbourne Jun & Inf Schs
CR7 204 C5
Winterbourne Rd
Dagenham RM8 80 C6
Forest Hill SE6 163 B3
Thornton Heath CR7 204 C5
Winter Box Wlk TW10 154 B6
Winterbrook Rd SE24 161 A5
Winterburn Cl N11 31 A4
Winterfold Cl SW19 157 A2
Wintergreen Cl 7 E6 100 A2
Winterleys 7 NW6 91 B5
Winter Lo 19 SE16 118 A1
Winter's Ct E4 19 D1
Winterslow Ho 20 SE5 139 A3
Winters Rd KT7 197 B2
Winterstoke Gdns NW7 28 A5
Winterstoke Rd SE6 163 B3
Winterton Ct KT1 175 D2
Winterton Ho 15 E1 96 C1
Winterton Pl SW10 266 B6
Winterwell Rd SW2 160 A6
Winthorpe Rd SW15 135 A1
Winthrop Ho 10 W12 112 B6
Winthrop St E1 96 B2
Winthrop Wlk HA9 66 A5
Winton Ave N11 31 C3
Winton Cl N9 18 D4
Winton Ct 15 KT6 197 D2
Winton Gdns HA8 26 B3
Winton Prim Sch
N1 94 B5 233 C3
Winton Rd BR6 226 D4
Winton Way SW16 182 C5
Wintour Ho HA9 65 D6
Wirrall Ho 15 SE26 162 A1
Wirral Wood Cl BR7 188 C4
Wisbeach Rd CR0 205 B4
Wisden Ho SW8 270 D5
Wisdom Ct 5 TW7 131 A2
Wisdons Cl RM7,RM9 59 D1
Wise La NW7 28 A4
Wiseman Ct 12 SE19 183 C5
Wiseman Rd E10 75 C6
Wise Rd E15 98 B6
Wiseton Rd SW17 158 D3
Wishart Rd SE3 143 D3
Wishaw Wlk N13 32 A4
Wisley Ho SW1 259 C2
Wisley Rd SW11 159 A6
St Paul's Cray BR5 190 B3
Wistaria Cl BR6 226 D6
Wisteria Cl NW7 27 D4
Ilford IG1 78 D3
Wisteria Rd SE13 142 B1
Wistow Ho 14 E2 96 A6
Witanhurst La N6 49 A1
Witan St E2 96 B4
Witchwood Ho 11 SW9 138 C2
Witcombe Point 13
SE15 140 A4
Witham Ct E10 75 D5
Upper Tooting SW17 158 D1
Witham Ho 35 SE5 139 A3
Witham Rd
Dagenham RM10 81 C3
Ealing W13 109 B5
Hounslow TW7 130 B4
Penge SE20 206 C6
Witherby Cl CR0 221 C4
Witherington Rd N5 72 C3
Withers Cl KT9 213 C2
Withers Mead NW9 27 D2
Withers Pl EC1 242 B6
Witherston Way SE9 166 C1
Withington Rd N2 30 C2
Withycombe Rd SW19 156 D4
Withy Ho 4 E1 96 D3
Withy La HA4 39 A4
Withy Mead E4 20 B1
Witley Cres CR0 224 A2
Witley Ct UB2 107 B2
Witley Gdns UB2 107 B2
Witley Ho 2 SW2 160 B4
Witley Ind Est UB2 107 B2
Witley Point 8 SW15 156 B3
Witley Rd N19 71 C6
Witney Cl Ickenham UB10 60 B4
Pinner HA5 23 B4
Witney Path SE23 162 D1
Wittenham Way E4 20 B1
Witten Ho KT3 199 B1
Wittering Cl KT2 175 D5
Wittering Ho 9 SW11 136 D3
Wittersham Rd BR1 186 D5
Wittingham Com Prim Sch
E17 35 A2
Witts Ho KT2 198 B6
Wivenhoe Cl SE15 140 B2
Wivenhoe Ct TW4 129 B1
Wivenhoe Rd IG11 102 B5
Wiverton Rd SE26 184 C5
Wixom Ho SE9 143 C1
Wix Prim Sch SW4 137 B1
Wix Rd RM9 102 D6
Wix's La SW4 137 B1
Woburn W13 87 B2
Woburn Cl SE28 102 D1
Bushey WD23 8 A5
Wimbledon SW19 180 A4
Woburn Ct 32 SE16 118 B1
1 DA6 147 A1
Croydon CR0 205 A1
Richmond TW9 132 B2
4 Woodford E18 37 A1
Woburn Pl WC1 94 A3 240 A5
Woburn Rd
Carshalton SM5 202 C1
Croydon CR0 205 A1
Woburn Sq WC1 93 D3 239 D5
Woburn Twr 14 UB5 84 D4
Woburn Wlk WC1 232 D1
Wodehouse Ave SE15 139 D4
Wodehouse Ct 10 W3 111 A3
Woffington Cl KT1,KT8 175 C2
Woking Cl SW15 133 D1
Wolcot Ho NW1 232 B3
Woldham Pl BR2 209 C5
Woldham Rd BR2 209 C5
Wolds Dr BR6 226 C4
Wolfe Cl Hayes BR2 209 A3
Hayes UB4 84 B4
Wolfe Cres 33 SE16 118 D4
SE7 121 D1
Wolfe Ho 19 W12 112 B6
Wolferton Rd E12 78 B4
Wolf Fields Prim Sch
UB2 107 B2
Wolfington Rd SE27 182 D6
Wolfram Cl SE13 164 C6
Wolfson Ct NW11 47 A2
SE1 253 D2
Wolfson Hillel Prim Sch
N14 15 D5
Wolftencroft Cl SW11 136 B2
Wollaston Cl SE1 262 A4
Wolmer Cl HA8 26 D6
Wolmer Gdns HA8 10 C1
Wolmer Rd HA8 26 D6
Wolseley Ave SW18,
SW19 157 C2
Wolseley Gdns W4 132 D6
Wolseley Rd E7 77 B1
N8 49 D4
Acton W4 111 A2
Carshalton CR4 203 A2
Harrow HA3 42 C6
Wood Green N22 32 B2
Wolseley St SE1 117 D4 253 D1
Wolsey Ave E17 53 B6
Wallend E6 100 C4
Wolsey Cl Isleworth TW3 130 A1
Kingston KT2 176 D2
Southall UB2 108 A3
Wimbledon SW20 178 B3
Worcester Park KT19,KT4 216 A4
Wolsey Cres SM4 201 B2
Wolsey Ct NW6 70 A1
SE9 166 B5
Bromley BR1 186 D3
Wolsey Dr Kingston KT2 176 A4
Walton-on-T KT12 194 D1
Wolsey Gr HA8 27 B3
Wolsey Ho 2 TW12 173 D4
Wolsey Inf Sch CR0 224 A1
Wolsey Jun Sch CR0 224 A1
Wolsey Mews NW5 71 C2
Orpington BR6 227 D3
Wolsey Rd N1 73 B3
Ashford TW15 170 B6
Ashford TW16 171 D4
East Molesey KT8 196 B5
Enfield EN1 6 B3
Hampton TW12 174 A4
Wolsey St E1 96 C2
Wolsey Way KT9 214 C3
Wolstenholme HA7 25 B5
Wolstonbury N12 29 C5
Wolvercote Rd SE2 124 D4
Wolverley St E2 96 B4
Wolverton SE17 263 A2
Wolverton Ave KT2 176 C2
Wolverton Gdns W6 112 D2
Ealing W5 110 B6
Wolverton Mans W5 110 B5
Wolverton Rd HA7 25 B3
Wolverton Way N14 15 C6
Wolves La N22 32 C4
Womersley Rd N4,N8 50 B3
Wonford Cl KT2,KT3 177 C2
Wontner Cl 5 N1 73 A1
Wontner Rd SW12,SW17 158 D2
Wooburn Cl UB8 82 D3
Woodall Cl 24 E14 119 D6
Chessington KT9 213 D2
Woodall Ho TW7 130 D2
Woodall Rd EN3 18 D5
Woodbank Rd BR1 164 D1
Woodbastwick Rd SE26 185 A5
Woodberry Ave
Edmonton N21 16 D2
Harrow HA2 42 A5
Woodberry Cl NW7 28 D3
Ashford TW16 172 A4
Woodberry Cres N10 49 B6
Woodberry Down N4 51 A2
Woodberry Down Com Prim
Sch N4 51 A2
Woodberry Gdns N12 30 A4
Woodberry Gr N12 30 A4
N4 51 A2
Woodberry Way N12 30 A4
Chingford E4 20 A4
Woodbine Cl TW2 152 B2
Woodbine Gr Enfield EN2 5 B5
Penge SE20 184 B3
Woodbine La KT4 216 C5
Woodbine Pl E11 55 A3
Woodbine Rd DA15 167 C3
Woodbines Ave KT1 197 D6
Woodbine Terr E9 74 C2
Woodborough Rd SW15 134 B1
Woodbourne Ave SW16 159 D1
Woodbourne Cl SW16 160 A1
Woodbourne Dr KT10 212 D2
Woodbourne Gdns SM6 219 B1
Woodbridge Cl 10 N7 72 B6
4 NW2 68 A5
Woodbridge Ct N16 73 B5
Woodbridge High Sch
IG8 37 B3
Woodbridge Ho E11 54 D1
Woodbridge Rd IG11 79 D3
Woodbridge St
EC1 94 D3 241 C6
Woodbrook Rd SE2 146 B6
Woodbrook Sch BR3 185 B2
Woodburn Cl NW4 46 D4
Woodbury Cl
Croydon CR0 221 D6
Wanstead E11 55 B5
Woodbury Ct 1 W13 87 B3
Woodbury Ho 4 SE26 162 B1
Woodbury Park Rd W13 87 B3
Woodbury Rd E17 53 D5
Woodbury St SW17 180 C5
Woodchester Sq W2 91 D2
Woodchurch Cl DA14 167 B1
Woodchurch Dr BR1 187 D3
Woodchurch Ho 15
SW9 138 C4
Woodchurch Rd NW6 69 D1
Wood Cl E2 96 A3
NW9 45 B2
Harrow HA1 42 B2
Woodclyffe Dr BR7 188 C1
Woodcock Ct HA3 44 A2
Woodcock Dell Ave HA3 43 D2
Woodcock Hill HA3 43 C3
Woodcock Ho 4 E14 97 C2
Woodcocks E16 99 D2
Woodcombe Cres SE23 162 C3
Woodcote Ave NW7 28 C4
Thornton Heath CR7 204 D5
Wallington SM6 219 B1
Woodcote Cl Enfield N9 18 C5
Kingston KT2 176 B5
Woodcote Dr BR6 211 B2
Woodcote Ho 4 SE8 141 B6
Woodcote Mews
Loughton IG10 21 D4
Wallington SM6 219 B2
Woodcote Pl 1 SE27 182 D5
Woodcote Rd
Wallington SM6 219 C1
Wanstead E11 55 A2
Woodcott Ho 1 SW15 156 A4
Woodcroft SE9 166 B1
South Croydon CR0 221 C5
Southgate N21 16 C3
Wembley UB6 65 A2
Woodcroft Ave NW7 27 C4
Stanmore HA7 25 A2
Woodcroft Cres UB10 82 D6
Woodcroft Jun & Inf Schs
HA8 27 C3
Woodcroft Mews SE8 119 A2
Woodcroft Rd CR7 204 D3
Wood Dene 6 SE15 140 B4
Wood Dr BR7 188 A4
Woodedge Cl E4 20 D3
Woodend
South Norwood SE19 183 A4
Sutton SM1 218 A6
Thames Ditton KT10 212 A6
Wood End UB3 83 C1
Wood End Ave HA2 64 A4
Wood End Cl UB5 64 B3
Woodend Gdns EN2 4 A1
Wood End Gdns UB5 64 A3
Wood End Green Rd UB3 83 C1
Wood End Inf Sch UB5 64 B3
Wood End Jun Sch UB6 64 B3
Wood End La UB5 63 D3
Wood End Park Jun & Inf Sch
UB3 105 A6
Woodend Rd E17 36 A1
Wood End Rd HA1,UB5 64 B4
Wood End Way UB5 64 A3
Wooder Gdns E7 77 A4
Wooderson Cl SE25 205 C5
Woodfall Ave EN5 13 B6
Woodfall Rd N4 72 C6
Woodfall St SW3 257 C1
Woodfarrs SE5 139 B1
Wood Field NW3 70 D3

Woodfield Ave NW9 ......45 C5
Ealing W5 ......87 C3
Streatham SW16 ......159 D1
Wallington SM5 ......219 A1
Wembley HA0 ......65 C5
Woodfield Cl
1 Enfield EN1 ......5 C1
South Norwood SE19 ......183 A3
Woodfield Cres W5 ......87 D3
Woodfield Ct SW16 ......159 D1
Woodfield Ctr The
SW16 ......159 D2
Woodfield Dr EN4 ......15 A3
Woodfield Gdns KT3 ......199 D4
Woodfield Gr SW16 ......159 D1
Woodfield Ho 6 E5 ......74 B6
11 Forest Hill SE23 ......162 D1
New Malden KT3 ......199 D4
Woodfield Pl W9 ......91 B3
Woodfield Rd W9 ......91 B2
Cranford TW4,TW5 ......128 B3
Ealing W5 ......87 C3
Hinchley Wood KT10,KT7 ..212 D6
Woodfield Rise WD23 ......8 B4
Woodfield Sch NW9 ......45 C1
Woodfields Ct SM1 ......218 A5
Woodfield Way N11 ......31 D3
Woodford Ave IG2,IG4,
IG5,IG8 ......56 B5
Woodford Bridge Rd IG4 .56 A5
Woodford Cres HA5 ......22 B1
Woodford Cty High Sch
IG8 ......36 D4
Woodforde Ct UB3 ......105 B1
Woodford Green Prep Sch
IG8 ......37 A4
Woodford Ho 13 SE18 ...144 D6
5 Wanstead E18 ......55 A5
Woodford New Rd E17 ...54 C6
Woodford E18 ......36 D3
Woodford Pl HA9 ......44 A1
Woodford Rd E7 ......77 B4
Wanstead E18 ......55 A6
Woodford Sta IG8 ......37 B4
Woodford Trad Est IG8 ...37 D1
Woodgate Ave KT9 ......213 D3
Woodgate Cres HA6 ......22 A4
Woodgate Dr SW16 ......181 D3
Woodger Rd W12 ......112 C4
Woodget Cl E6 ......100 A1
Woodgrange Ave N12 ......30 B4
Ealing W5 ......110 C5
Enfield EN1 ......18 A5
Harrow HA3 ......43 D4
Woodgrange Cl HA3 ......43 D4
Woodgrange Ct 1 BR2 .208 D1
Woodgrange Gdns EN1 ...18 A5
Woodgrange Inf Sch E7 ..77 B4
Woodgrange Mans HA3 ..43 C4
Woodgrange Park Sta
E12 ......77 D3
Woodgrange Rd E7 ......77 A3
Woodgrange Terr EN1 ......18 A5
Wood Green Sta N22 ......32 C1
Woodhall NW1 ......232 A1
Woodhall Ave
Dulwich SE21 ......161 D1
Pinner HA5 ......23 A2
Woodhall Dr
Dulwich SE21 ......161 D1
Pinner HA5 ......23 A2
Woodhall Gate HA5 ......22 D3
Woodhall Ho SW18 ......158 B5
Woodhall La WD19 ......23 A6
Woodhall Sch WD19 ......23 A6
Woodham Ct E11 ......54 D5
Woodham Rd SE6 ......164 A1
Woodhatch Cl 10 E6 ......100 A2
Woodhaven Gdns IG6 ....57 A5
Woodhayes BR7 ......188 D4
Woodhayes Rd SW19,
SW20 ......178 C4
Woodhead Dr BR6 ......227 C6
Woodheyes Rd NW10 ......67 C3
Woodhill SE7,SE18 ......122 A2
Woodhill Cres HA3 ......43 D3
Woodhill Prim Sch
SE18 ......122 A2
Wood Ho 6 NW6 ......91 B5
4 SW4 ......137 D3
Woodhouse Ave UB6 ......86 D5
Woodhouse Cl
Hayes UB3 ......105 C3
Wembley UB6 ......86 D5
Woodhouse Eaves HA6 ...22 A5
Woodhouse Gr E12 ......78 A2
Woodhouse Rd E11 ......76 D5
N12 ......30 C4
Woodhouse Sixth Form Coll
N12 ......30 B4
Woodhurst Ave BR5 ......211 A3
Woodhurst Rd SE2 ......124 A2
W3 ......111 A6
Woodington Cl SE9 ......166 C5
Woodison St E3 ......97 A3
Woodknoll Dr BR7 ......188 B2
Wood La N6 ......49 B3
NW9 ......45 B2
W12 ......112 C6
Dagenham RM10 ......81 A5
Hounslow TW7 ......130 D5
Ruislip HA4 ......61 C6
Stanmore HA7 ......9 B2
Woodford IG8 ......36 D5
Woodland App UB6 ......65 A2
Woodland Cl NW9 ......45 A3
Uxbridge UB10 ......60 D6
Woodland Cl *continued*
West Ewell KT19 ......215 C2
West Norwood SE19 ......183 C4
Woodford IG8 ......21 B1
Woodland Cres SE10 ......142 C6
18 SE16 ......118 D4
Woodland Ct NW4 ......47 A4
Cheam SM1 ......217 C2
10 Wanstead E11 ......55 A4
Woodland Gdns E17 ......54 C5
N10 ......49 B4
Isleworth TW7 ......130 C2
Woodland Gr SE10 ......120 C1
Woodland Hill SE19 ......183 C4
Woodland Rd N11 ......31 B5
Chingford E4 ......20 A3
Penge SE19 ......183 D4
Thornton Heath CR7 ......204 C5
Woodland Rise N10 ......49 B5
Wembley UB6 ......65 A2
Woodlands N12 ......30 A4
NW11 ......47 A4
SW4 ......137 B1
Beckenham BR3 ......185 D3
Harrow HA2 ......41 C5
West Barnes SW20 ......200 D5
Woodlands Ave DA15 ......167 C3
N3 ......30 A2
Acton W3 ......110 D5
Dagenham RM6 ......59 A2
Kingston KT3 ......177 B2
Ruislip HA4 ......40 D2
Wanstead E11 ......55 B1
Worcester Park KT4 ......216 A6
Woodlands Cl BR1 ......188 B1
NW11 ......47 A4
Claygate KT10 ......212 D1
Woodlands Ct NW10 ......90 D6
9 Bromley BR1 ......186 D2
Dulwich SE22 ......162 B4
Southall UB1 ......107 C6
Woodlands Dr
Harrow HA7 ......24 D4
Sunbury TW16 ......172 C1
Woodlands Gr TW7 ......130 C3
Woodlands Gt SW15 ......157 B6
Woodlands Inf Sch IG1 ..79 B3
Woodlands Jun Sch IG1 ..79 B3
Woodlands Par TW15 ......171 A4
Woodlands Park Jun & Inf
Schs N15 ......51 A4
Woodlands Park Rd N15 .51 A4
SE10 ......142 C6
Woodlands Rd BR1 ......188 B1
DA7 ......147 A2
E11 ......76 C6
E17 ......54 A6
N9 ......18 C3
Barnes SW13 ......133 D2
Enfield EN2 ......5 B4
Harrow HA1 ......42 D4
Ilford IG1 ......79 A5
Isleworth TW7 ......130 C3
Southall UB1 ......106 D5
Surbiton KT6 ......197 D2
Woodlands St SE13 ......164 B4
Woodland St 2 E8 ......73 D2
Woodlands The N14 ......15 B3
N5 ......73 A4
Isleworth TW7 ......130 D3
Lewisham SE13 ......164 B4
Mitcham CR4 ......203 A6
South Norwood SE19 ......183 A3
Stanmore HA7 ......25 B5
Thames Ditton KT10 ......212 A6
Woodlands Way SW15 ...157 B6
Woodland Terr SE7 ......122 A2
Woodland Way BR5 ......211 A4
NW7 ......27 D4
SE2 ......124 D2
Croydon CR0 ......207 A1
Merton SM4 ......201 B5
Mitcham CR4 ......181 A3
Southgate N21 ......16 C2
Tolworth KT5 ......214 D6
West Wickham BR4 ......224 A5
Woodford IG8 ......21 B1
Woodland Wlk NW3 ......70 C3
9 SE10 ......120 C1
Chessington KT19 ......214 C2
Woodlane High Sch W12 .90 B1
Woodlawn Cl SW15 ......157 B6
Woodlawn Cres TW2 ......151 D2
Woodlawn Dr TW13 ......150 D2
Woodlawn Rd SW6 ......134 D4
Woodlea Dr BR2 ......208 C4
Woodlea Lo EN1 ......17 C5
Woodlea Rd N16 ......73 C5
Woodleigh
1 Kingston KT5 ......198 B4
3 Woodford E18 ......37 A2
Woodleigh Ave N12 ......30 C4
Woodleigh Ct N22 ......32 B2
Woodleigh Gdns SW16 ..160 A1
Woodley Cl SW17 ......180 D3
Woodley La SM1,SM5 ....218 C5
Woodlodge 4 SW19 ......179 B5
Wood Lodge Gdns BR1 ..188 A3
Wood Lodge La BR4 ......224 A5
Woodman La E4 ......20 C6
Woodman Par 4 E16 ......122 C5
Woodmans Gr NW10 ......67 D3
Woodmans Mews W12 ...90 B2
Woodman St E16 ......122 C5
E16 ......122 D5
Woodmansterne Prim Sch
SW16 ......181 D2
Woodmansterne Rd
Mitcham SW16 ......181 D2
Sutton SM5 ......218 C1
Wood Mead N17 ......34 A4
Woodmere SE9 ......166 B3
Woodmere Ave CR0 ......206 D2
Woodmere Cl 10 SW11 ..137 A2
Croydon CR0 ......206 D2
Woodmere Ct N14 ......15 B4
Woodmere Gdns CR0 ...206 D2
Woodmere Way BR3 ....208 B4
Woodnook Rd SW16 ......181 B5
Woodpecker Cl
Bushey WD23 ......8 A3
Enfield N9 ......18 B5
Harrow HA3 ......24 D2
Woodpecker Mews
SE13 ......142 B1
Woodpecker Rd
6 SE14 ......141 A6
Woolwich SE28 ......124 C6
Wood Point 8 E16 ......99 A2
Woodquest Ave SE24 ....161 A6
Wood Rd TW17 ......192 C5
Wood Ride Barnet EN4 ......2 B4
Orpington BR5 ......211 C5
Woodridge Cl EN2 ......4 C4
Woodridge Prim Sch
N12 ......13 C1
Woodridings Ave HA5 ....23 B2
Woodridings Cl HA5 ......23 B3
Woodridings Ct N22 ......31 D2
Woodriffe Rd E11 ......54 B2
Wood Rise HA5 ......40 A4
Woodrow SE18 ......122 B2
Woodrow Ave UB4 ......83 D3
Woodrow Cl UB6 ......65 B1
Woodrow Ct 3 N17 ......34 B3
Woodruff Ho SW2 ......160 C5
Woodrush Cl 4 SE14 ......141 A5
Woodrush Way RM6 ......58 D5
Woodseer St E1 ..95 D2 243 D4
Woodsford SE17 ......262 C1
Woodsford Sq
W14 ......113 A4 244 B2
Woodshire Rd RM10 ......81 D5
Woods Ho SW8 ......269 A2
Woodside N10 ......49 A6
NW11 ......47 C4
Buckhurst Hill IG9 ......21 C2
Palmers Green N13 ......16 C1
Walton-on-T KT12 ......194 A1
Wimbledon SW19 ......179 B5
Woodside Ave N12 ......30 A6
N6 ......48 D5
Chislehurst BR7 ......189 A5
Croydon SE25 ......206 B4
Thames Ditton KT10 ......196 C2
Wembley HA0 ......88 A6
Woodside Cl Ruislip HA4 ...39 B3
Stanmore HA7 ......25 B5
Tolworth KT5 ......199 A2
Wembley HA0 ......88 A6
Woodside Court Rd
CR0 ......206 A2
Woodside Cres DA15 ......167 C1
Woodside Ct 8 N12 ......29 D6
Ealing W5 ......110 A5
Enfield EN2 ......4 D4
Woodside End HA0 ......88 A6
Woodside Gdns
Chingford E4 ......35 D4
Tottenham N17 ......33 D1
Woodside Gn SE25 ......206 A3
Woodside Gr N12 ......14 A1
Woodside Grange Rd
N12 ......29 D6
Woodside Ho SW19 ......179 B4
Woodside Jun & Inf Sch
CR0 ......206 A2
Woodside Jun & Inf Schs
E17 ......54 A6
Woodside La DA5 ......168 D5
N12 ......14 A1
Woodside Park Ave E17 ..54 B5
Woodside Park Rd N12 ...30 A6
Woodside Pk SE25 ......206 B3
Woodside Pl HA0 ......88 A6
Woodside Rd BR1 ......210 A4
E13 ......99 C3
Croydon SE25 ......206 B3
Kingston KT2 ......176 A3
Kingston KT3 ......177 C1
Northwood HA6 ......22 A3
Sidcup DA15 ......167 C1
Sutton SM1 ......218 A5
Woodford IG8 ......37 A6
Wood Green N22 ......32 C3
Woodside Sch DA17 ......125 D2
Woodside Sta SE25 ......206 B3
Woodside Way
Croydon CR0 ......206 C3
Streatham CR4 ......181 C2
Wood's Mews
W1 ......115 A6 248 A6
Woodsome Rd NW5 ......71 B5
Wood's Pl SE1 ......263 B5
Woodspring Rd SW19 ...157 A2
Wood's Rd SE15 ......140 B4
Wood St E16 ......121 B6
E17 ......54 B5
EC2 ......95 A1 242 B2
W4 ......111 C1
Barnet EN5 ......1 A1
Carshalton CR4 ......203 A2
Kingston KT1 ......175 D1
Kingston KT2 ......176 A2
Woodstar Ho 3 SE15 ......140 A5
Woodstead Gr HA8 ......26 A4
Woods The
Moor Park HA6 ......22 A5
Uxbridge UB10 ......60 D4
Woodstock Ave NW11 ....47 A2
Woodstock Ave *continued*
W13 ......109 A3
Cheam SM3 ......201 B2
Isleworth TW7 ......153 A6
Southall UB1 ......85 B4
Woodstock Cl DA5 ......169 B3
Stanmore HA7 ......26 A1
Woodstock Cres N9 ......18 B5
Woodstock Ct SE11 ......260 D2
SE12 ......165 A5
Kingston KT2 ......176 D1
Woodstock Dr UB10 ......60 B4
Woodstock Gdns
Beckenham BR3 ......185 D3
Hayes UB4 ......83 D2
Ilford IG3 ......80 A6
Woodstock Gr W12 ......112 D4
Woodstock Ho 2 N5 ......73 A4
Hayes UB3 ......83 B2
Woodstock La N KT6 ......213 C6
Woodstock La S KT10,
KT6 ......213 C4
Woodstock Mews W1 ...238 B3
Woodstock Rd E7 ......77 C1
N4 ......50 C1
NW11 ......47 B1
W4 ......111 C3
Bushey WD23 ......8 D4
Chingford E17 ......36 B1
South Croydon CR0 ......221 B5
Wallington SM5,SM6 ......219 A3
Wembley HA0 ......66 B1
Woodstock Rise SM3 ......201 B2
Woodstock St W1 ......238 C1
Woodstock Terr E14 ......119 D6
Woodstock The SM3 ......201 B2
Woodstock Way CR4 ......181 C1
Woodstone Ave KT17,
KT4 ......216 A3
Wood Street Sta E17 ......54 B5
Woodsyre SE26 ......183 D6
Woodthorpe Rd
Ashford TW15 ......170 A6
Putney SW15 ......134 B1
Woodtree Cl NW4 ......28 C1
Wood Vale N10 ......49 C4
Dulwich SE22 ......162 B4
Woodvale Ave SE25 ......183 D1
Woodvale Ct BR1 ......187 B1
South Norwood SE25 ......205 D6
Woodvale Way NW11 ......68 D5
Woodvale Wlk SE27 ......183 A5
Woodview Ave E4 ......36 A6
Woodview Cl N4 ......50 D2
Kingston SW15 ......177 B6
Orpington BR6 ......227 A6
Woodville SE3 ......143 B4
Woodville Cl SE12 ......165 A6
Teddington TW11 ......175 A6
Woodville Ct 3 SE10 ......142 A4
Woodville Gdns NW11 ......46 D2
Ealing W5 ......88 A1
Ilford IG6 ......56 D5
Ruislip HA4 ......39 A2
Surbiton KT6 ......197 D2
Woodville Gr 2 DA16 ......146 A2
Woodville Ho SE1 ......263 C6
Woodville Rd E11 ......54 D1
E17 ......53 B5
N16 ......73 C3
NW11 ......47 A2
NW6 ......91 B5
Barnet EN5 ......1 D2
Ealing W5 ......87 D1
Morden SM4 ......201 C5
Richmond TW10 ......153 C1
South Norwood CR7 ......205 B6
Woodford E18 ......37 B1
Woodville St 16 SE7 ......122 A2
Woodville The W5 ......87 D1
Woodward Ave NW4 ......46 A4
Woodward Cl KT10 ......212 D2
Woodwarde Rd SE22 ......161 C5
Woodward Gdns
Dagenham RM9 ......80 C1
Harrow HA7 ......24 D3
Woodward Rd RM9 ......80 C1
Wood Way BR6 ......226 C6
Woodway Cres HA1 ......43 A3
Woodwell St SW18 ......158 A6
Wood Wharf SE10 ......142 A6
Woodyard Cl NW5 ......71 A3
Woodyard La SE21 ......161 C4
Woodyates Rd SE12 ......165 B4
Woolacombe Rd SE3 ......143 C3
Woolacombe Way UB3 ...105 C2
Woolcombes Ct 4
SE16 ......118 D5
Woolden Ho 2 E4 ......20 C4
Wooler St SE17 ..117 B1 262 D2
Woolf Cl SE28 ......124 B5
Woolf Ct 4 W3 ......111 A3
Woolf Mews WC1 ......240 A6
Woollaston Rd N4 ......50 D3
Woolley Ho SW9 ......138 D2
Woollon Ho 1 E1 ......96 C1
Woolmead Ave NW9 ......46 A2
Woolmer Gdns N18 ......34 A5
Woolmer Ho 2 E5 ......74 B6
Woolmer Rd N18 ......34 A5
Woolmore Prim Sch
E14 ......120 A6
Woolmore St E14 ......120 A6
Woolneigh St SW6 ......135 D3
Woolpack Ho 1 E9 ......74 C2
Wool Rd SW20 ......178 B4
Woolridge Way E9 ......74 C1
Woolstaplers Way SE16 .118 A2
Woolston Cl E17 ......34 D1
Woolstone Ho 7 E2 ......96 A6
Woolstone Rd SE23 ......163 A2
Woolven Ho SE3 ......142 D6
Woolwich Arsenal Sta
SE18 ......122 D2
Woolwich Church St
SE7,SE18 ......122 A3
Woolwich SE18 ......122 C3
Woolwich Comm SE18 ..144 C6
Woolwich Dockyard Ind Est
SE18 ......122 A3
Woolwich Dockyard Sta
SE18 ......122 B2
Woolwich & Greenwich Com
Coll SE18 ......123 A2
Woolwich High St SE18 .122 C3
Woolwich Manorway
E16 ......122 D4
Woolwich Manor Way
E16 ......122 D5
E6 ......100 C1
Woolwich New Rd
SE18 ......122 D2
Woolwich Poly Sch for Boys
SE28 ......124 A5
Woolwich Rd DA7 ......147 C2
Belvedere DA17 ......125 C1
Erith SE2 ......125 B1
Greenwich SE7,SE10 ......121 C2
Wooster Gdns E14 ......98 B1
Wootton KT10 ......212 A4
Wootton Gr N3 ......29 C2
Wootton Ho SE9 ......167 B5
Wootton St SE1 ..116 C5 251 B3
Worbeck Rd SE20 ......184 C1
Worcester Ave N17 ......34 A3
Worcester Cl NW2 ......68 B5
Croydon CR0 ......223 C6
Mitcham CR4 ......181 A1
Worcester Cres NW7 ......11 C1
Woodford IG8 ......37 C6
Worcester Ct N12 ......29 D5
44 W2 ......91 C2
Ashford TW15 ......170 D5
Ealing W7 ......86 D1
Harrow HA1 ......42 C6
Walton-on-T KT12 ......194 C1
Worcester Park KT4 ......215 C5
Worcester Dr W4 ......111 C4
Ashford TW15 ......170 D5
Worcester Gdns SW11 ..158 D6
Northolt UB6 ......64 B2
Redbridge IG1 ......56 A2
Worcester Park KT4 ......215 C5
Worcester Ho SE11 ......261 A5
W2 ......236 A1
9 Putney SW15 ......156 C4
Worcester Mews 2
NW6 ......69 D2
Worcester Park Rd KT4 .215 B5
Worcester Park Sta
KT4 ......200 A1
Worcester Rd E17 ......34 D1
Belmont SM2 ......217 C1
Ilford E12 ......78 B4
11 Wimbledon SW19 ......179 B5
Worcesters Ave EN1 ......6 A5
Worcesters Prim Sch EN1 .5 D5
Wordsworth N8 ......50 C5
Wordsworth Ave E12 ......78 A1
E18 ......54 D6
Greenford UB6 ......86 B5
Wordsworth Ct HA1 ......42 B2
Wordsworth Dr KT4,
SM3 ......216 C4
Wordsworth Ho NW6 ......91 C4
15 SE18 ......144 C6
Wordsworth Par 1 N15 ..50 D5
Wordsworth Pl 11 NW5 ...70 D3
Wordsworth Rd DA16 ......145 C4
N16 ......73 C4
SE1 ......263 D3
Hampton TW12,TW13 ......173 B6
Penge SE20 ......184 D3
Wallington SM6 ......219 D2
Wordsworth Way UB7 ...104 B2
Wordsworth Wlk NW11 ...47 C5
Worfield St
SW11 ......136 C5 267 B3
Worgan St SE11 .116 B1 260 C2
SE16 ......118 D2
Working Men's Coll The
NW1 ......93 C5 232 A4
Worland Rd E15 ......76 C1
World Bsns Ctr TW6 ......127 A4
Worlds End La BR6 ......227 D1
World's End La EN2 ......4 B1
World's End Pas SW10 ...266 C4
World's End Pl SW10 ...266 B4
Worley Ct NW2 ......68 D5
Worlidge St W6 ......112 C1
Worlingham Rd SE22 ...139 D1
Wormholt Park Prim Sch
W12 ......112 A6
Wormholt Rd W12 ......112 A5
Wormwood St EC2 ......243 A2
Wornington Rd W10 ......91 A2
Wornum Ho 3 NW6 ......91 A5
Woronzow Rd
NW8 ......92 C6 230 A5
Worple Ave
Isleworth TW7 ......153 A6
Wimbledon SW19 ......178 D3
Worple Cl HA2 ......41 B1
Worple Ct SW19 ......179 A4
Worple Prim Sch TW7 ...131 A1
Worple Rd
Isleworth TW7 ......131 A1
Wimbledon SW19,SW20 ..178 D2
Worple Road Mews
SW19 ......179 B4
Worple St SW14 ......133 B2
Worple Way Harrow HA2 ..41 B1
Richmond TW10 ......132 A1
Worship St EC2 ...95 C3 243 A5
Worslade Rd SW17 ......180 B6
Worsley Bridge Jun Sch
BR3 ......185 C3
Worsley Bridge Rd BR3,
SE6 ......185 C5
Worsley Ct N3 ......29 D4
Worsley Gr E5 ......74 A4
Worsley Ho 25 SE23 ......162 B2
Worsley Rd E11 ......76 C4
Worsopp Dr SW4 ......159 C6
Worth Cl BR6 ......227 C4
Worthfield Cl KT19 ......215 B1
Worth Gr SE17 ......262 C1
Worthing Cl 5 E15 ......98 C6
Worthing Rd TW5 ......129 B6
Worthington Cl CR4 ......203 B6
Worthington Ho EC1 ....234 B2
16 Streatham SW2 ......160 C4
Worthington Rd KT6 ......198 B1
Wortley Rd E6 ......77 D1
Thornton Heath CR0 ......204 C2
Worton Ct TW7 ......130 C1
Worton Gdns TW7 ......130 B3
Worton Hall Ind Est
TW7 ......130 C1
Worton Rd TW7 ......130 C2
Worton Way TW3,TW7 ...130 B3
Wotton Ct 8 E14 ......120 B6
Wotton Rd NW2 ......68 C5
18 SE8 ......141 B6
Wouldham Rd E16 ......98 D1
Wragby Rd E11 ......76 C5
Wrampling Pl N9 ......18 A3
Wrangthorne Wlk CR0 ..220 C4
Wray Ave IG5 ......56 C6
Wrayburn Ho 25 SE16 ...118 A4
Wray Cres N4 ......72 B6
Wray Ct N4 ......72 B6
Wrayfield Rd SM3 ......216 D5
Wray Ho 11 SW2 ......160 A3
Wraysbury Cl TW4 ......151 A6
Wrays Way UB4 ......83 C3
Wrekin Rd SE18 ......145 A5
Wren Ave NW2 ......68 C4
Southall UB2 ......107 B2
Wren Cl E16 ......98 D1
N9 ......18 D3
Wren Cres WD23 ......8 A3
Wren Ct CR0 ......221 B4
Wren Gdns RM9 ......80 D3
Wren Ho 27 E3 ......97 A5
SW1 ......259 C1
4 Hampton TW12 ......173 D4
Wren Landing E14 ......119 C5
Wrenn Ho SW13 ......134 C6
Wren Path SE28 ......123 B4
Wren Rd SE5 ......139 B4
Dagenham RM9 ......80 D3
Sidcup DA14 ......168 C1
Wrens Ave TW15 ......171 A6
Wren's Park Ho E5 ......74 B6
Wren St WC1 ......94 B3 240 D6
Wrentham Ave NW10 ......90 D5
Wrenthorpe Rd BR1 ......186 C6
Wren View N6 ......49 C1
Wrenwood Way HA5 ......40 B5
Wrestlers Ct EC3 ......243 A2
Wrexham Rd E3 ......97 C5
Wricklemarsh Rd SE3 ...143 D4
Wrigglesworth St SE14 .140 D5
Wright Cl SE13 ......142 B1
Wright Gdns TW17 ......192 C4
Wright Ho SW15 ......156 B6
Wrighton Ct SM1 ......217 B2
Wright Rd TW5 ......128 C5
Wrights Cl RM10 ......81 D4
Wright's Gn SW4 ......137 D1
Wright's La W8 ..113 D3 255 C6
Wrights Pl NW10 ......67 A2
Wright's Rd E3 ......97 B5
Wrights Rd SE25 ......205 C6
Wright's Row SM5 ......219 B4
Wrights Wlk SW14 ......133 B2
Writtle Ho 38 NW9 ......27 D1
Wrotham Ho SE1 ......262 D6
Beckenham BR3 ......185 B3
Wrotham Rd DA16 ......146 C4
11 NW1 ......71 C1
Barnet EN5 ......1 A3
Ealing W13 ......109 C5
Wrottesley Rd NW10 ......90 A5
SE18 ......145 A6
Wroughton Rd SW11 ......158 D5
Wroughton Terr NW4 ......46 B5
Wroxall Rd RM9 ......80 C2
Wroxham Gdns N11 ......31 D3
Wroxham Rd SE28 ......124 D6
Wroxton Rd SE15 ......140 C3
Wrythe Gn SM5 ......218 D5
Wrythe Green Rd SM5 ..218 D5
Wrythe La SM1,SM5,SM4 .218 C5
Wulfstan St W12 ......89 D1
Wyatt Cl SE16 ......119 B4
Bushey WD23 ......8 C4
Feltham TW13 ......150 D3
Hayes UB4 ......84 A2
Wyatt Ct HA0 ......66 A1
Wyatt Dr SW13 ......134 B5
Wyatt Ho NW8 ......236 D5
SE3 ......142 D3
Wyatt Park Mans 1
SW2 ......160 A2
Wyatt Park Rd SW2 ......160 B2
Wyatt Rd E7 ......77 A2
N5 ......73 A5
Wyatt's La E17 ......54 A6

Wybert St NW1 ....239 A6
Wyborne Ho NW10 ....67 A1
Wyborne Prim Sch SE9 .166 D3
Wyborne Way NW10 ....1 B2
Wyburn Ave EN5 ....1 B2
Wyche Gr CR2 ....221 A1
Wycherley Cl SE3 ....142 D5
Wycherley Cres EN5 ....13 C1
Wychwood Ave
 Edgware HA8 ....25 D4
 South Norwood CR7 ....205 A4
Wychwood Cl
 Ashford TW16 ....172 A4
 Edgware HA8 ....25 D4
Wychwood End N6 ....49 C2
Wychwood Gdns IG5 ....56 C5
Wychwood Ho N4 ....51 A2
Wychwood Way SE19 ..183 B4
Wyclif Ct EC1 ....234 C1
Wycliffe Cl DA16 ....145 D4
Wycliffe Ho 13 N16 ......73 C4
Wycliffe Rd SW19 ....179 D4
Wyclif St EC1 ....234 C1
Wycombe Ct SE3 ....143 A5
Wycombe Gdns NW11 ....69 C6
Wycombe Ho NW8 ......237 A6
Wycombe Pl SW18 ......158 A5
Wycombe Rd
 Redbridge IG2 ....56 B4
 Tottenham N17 ....34 A2
 Wembley HA0 ....88 C6
Wydell Cl SM4 ....200 D3
Wydenhurst Rd CR0 ...206 B2
Wydeville Manor Rd
 SE12 ....187 B6
Wye Cl BR6 ....211 D2
 Ashford TW15 ....170 D6
 Ruislip HA4 ....39 A3
Wye Ct W13 ....87 B2
Wyemead Cres E4 ....20 C2
Wyersdale Ho N4 ....51 A2
Wye St SW11 ....136 B3
Wyevale Cl HA5 ....40 A6
Wyfold Ho 10 SE2 ....124 D4
Wyfold Rd SW6 ..135 A5 264 A3
Wyke Cl TW7 ....130 D6
Wyke Gdns W7 ....109 A3
Wykeham Ave RM9 ......80 C2
Wykeham Cl UB7 ....126 C6
Wykeham Ct NW4 ....46 C4
Wykeham Gn RM9 ....80 C2
Wykeham Hill HA9 ....44 B1
Wykeham Ho SW19 .....179 C3
Wykeham Prim Sch NW9 .67 C5
Wykeham Rd NW4 ....46 C4
 Harrow HA3 ....43 B5
Wykeham Rise N20 ......13 A3
Wykehurst Ho SW17 ...180 B5
Wyke Rd E3 ....75 C1
 Merton SW20 ....178 C1
Wylchin Cl HA5 ....39 D6
Wyldes Cl NW11 ....48 A1
Wyldfield Gdns N9 ....17 D2
Wyld Way HA9 ....66 D2
Wyleu St SE23 ....163 A4
Wylie Rd UB2 ....107 C3
Wyllen Cl E1 ....96 C3

Wylo Dr EN5 ....12 A5
Wymering Mans 6 W9 ..91 C4
Wymering Rd W9 ....91 C4
Wymondham Ct NW8 ..229 D6
Wymond St SW15 ....134 C2
Wynan Rd E14 ....119 D1
Wynard Terr SE11 ......260 D2
Wynash Gdns SM5 ......218 C3
Wynaud Ct N22 ....32 B4
Wynbourne Ct SE20 ...184 B1
Wyncham Ave DA15 ....167 C3
Wynchgate Harrow HA3 ...24 C3
 Southgate N14 ....16 A4
Wyncroft Cl BR1 ....210 B6
Wyndale Ave NW9 ....44 C3
Wyndcliff Rd SE7 ....143 B6
Wyndcroft Cl EN2 ....4 D2
Wyndham Cl
 Belmont SM2 ....217 C1
 Orpington BR6 ....211 A1
Wyndham Cres N19 .....71 C5
 Hounslow TW4 ....151 C5
Wyndham Ct W7 ....109 A2
Wyndham Deedes Ho 27
 E2 ....96 A5
Wyndham Ho SW1 .....258 A3
Wyndham Mews W1 ...237 C3
Wyndham Pl W1 ....237 C3
Wyndham Rd E6 ....77 D1
 SE5 ....139 A5
 W13 ....109 B3
 Barnet, London EN4 ....14 D3
 Kingston KT2 ....176 B3
Wyndham St W1 ..92 D2 237 C4
Wyndham Yd W1 ....237 C3
Wyneham Rd SE24 .....161 B6
Wynell Rd SE23 ....162 D1
Wynford Pl DA17 ....147 C6
Wynford Rd N1 ..94 B5 233 D4
Wynford Way SE9 ......166 B1
Wynlie Gdns HA5 ....22 B1
Wynndale Rd E18 ....37 B2
Wynne Ct 4 TW7 ......131 A2
Wynne Rd SE14 ....140 D4
Wynne Rd SW9 ....138 C3
Wynn's Ave DA15 ......168 A6
Wynnstay Gdns
 W8 ....113 C3 255 B6
Wynter Ho 20 SW9 .....138 B3
Wynter St SW11 ....136 A1
Wynton Gdns SE25 ....205 D4
Wynton Pl W3 ....88 D1
Wynyard Ho SE11 ......260 D2
Wynyatt St EC1 ....94 D4 234 C2
Wyre Gr Edgware HA8 ....10 D1
 Hayes UB3 ....106 A2
Wyresdale Cres UB6 ....86 D4
Wyteleaf Cl HA4 ....39 A3
Wytham Ho NW8 ......236 D5
Wythburn Ct W1 ......237 C2
Wythburn Pl W1 ......237 C2
Wythenshawe Rd RM10 ..81 C3
Wythens Wlk SE9 .....166 D5
Wythes Cl BR1 ....188 B1
Wythes Rd E16 ....122 A5
Wythfield Rd SE9 .....166 B5

Wyvenhoe Rd HA2 ....64 A5
Wyvern Est The KT3 ...200 A5
Wyvil Prim Sch
 SW8 ....138 A5 270 B4
Wyvil Rd SW8 ..138 A5 270 A4
Wyvis St E14 ....97 D2

X

Xavier Ho E17 ....35 B1

Y

Yabsley St E14 ....120 A5
Yaldam Ho SE1 ....263 A3
Yalding Ho 20 E5 ....74 B3
Yalding Rd SE16 ....118 A2
Yale Cl TW4 ....151 B6
Yale Ct NW6 ....69 D3
Yarborough Rd SW19 ..180 B2
Yardley Cl E4 ....19 D6
Yardley Ct SM3 ....216 D4
Yardley La E4 ....19 D6
Yardley Prim Sch E4 ....20 A5
Yardley St WC1 ....234 A1
Yarmouth Cres N17 .....52 B4
Yarmouth Pl W1 ....248 C3
Yarnfield Sq 14 SE15 ..140 A4
Yarnton Way DA17,DA18 .125 B3
Yarrow Cres E6 ....100 A2
Yarrow Ho 10 E14 ......120 A3
 W10 ....90 C2
Yateley St SE18 ....121 D1
Yatesbury Ct E5 ....75 A3
Yates Ct NW2 ....68 D2
Yates Ho 15 E2 ....96 A4
Yatton Ho W10 ....90 C2
Yeading Ave HA2 ....41 A1
Yeading Ct UB4 ....84 C3
Yeading Fork UB4 ....84 C3
Yeading Gdns UB4 ......84 B2
Yeading Ho UB4 ....84 D2
Yeading Jun & Inf Schs
 UB4 ....84 C2
Yeading La Hayes UB4 ..84 B2
 Hayes, Northolt UB4,UB5 ..84 C4
Yeadon Ho W10 ....90 C2
Yeames Cl W13 ....87 A1
Yearby Ho W10 ....90 C3
Yeate St N1 ....73 B1
Yeatman Rd N6 ....48 D3
Yeats Cl NW10 ....67 C2
Yeend Cl KT8 ....195 C5
Yeldham Ho W6 ....112 D1
Yeldham Rd W6 ....112 D1
Yellowhammer Ct NW9 ..27 C1
Yelverton Lo TW1 .....153 C4
Yelverton Rd SW11 ....136 B3
Ye Market CR0 ....221 B3
Yenston Cl SM4 ....201 C3
Yeoman Cl E16 ....122 D6
 West Norwood SE27 ..160 D1
Yeoman Ct TW5 ....129 B5
Yeoman Ho SE1 ....263 D2
Yeoman Rd UB5 ....63 A1

Yeomans Acre HA4 ......40 A3
Yeomans Mews TW7 ...152 B6
Yeoman's Row
 SW3 ....114 C3 257 B5
Yeoman St SE8 ....119 A2
Yeomans Way EN3 ....6 C3
Yeo St E3 ....97 D2
Yeovil Cl BR6 ....227 C6
Yeovil Ho N7 ....72 B6
 W10 ....90 C3
Yeovilton Pl KT2 ....175 C5
Yerbury Prim Sch N19 ...71 D5
Yerbury Rd N19 ....71 D5
Yesodey Hatorah Sch
 N16 ....51 D2
Yester Dr BR7 ....188 A3
Yester Pk BR7 ....188 B4
Yester Rd BR7 ....188 B3
Yew Ave UB7 ....104 A6
Yew Cl IG9 ....21 C2
Yewdale Cl BR1 ....186 C4
Yewfield Rd NW10 ......67 D2
Yew Gr NW2 ....68 D4
Yew Ho SE14 ....141 B3
Yews The TW15 ....170 D6
Yew Tree Ave N2 ....47 D6
Yew Tree Cl DA16 ......146 A4
Yewtree Cl Harrow HA2 ..41 D5
 Wood Green N22 ....31 C2
Yew Tree Cl
 New Malden KT4 ......199 C1
 Southgate N21 ....16 C4
Yew Tree Cotts KT10 ..212 B6
Yew Tree Ct 4 NW11 ...47 B4
 Elstree WD6 ....9 D5
 8 Sutton SM2 ....218 A1
Yew Tree Gdns RM6 ....59 A4
Yew Tree Grange 2
 W5 ....109 C6
Yew Tree Ho KT4 ......199 C1
Yew Tree Rd W12 ......111 D6
Yewtree Rd BR3 ....207 B6
Yew Tree Rd UB10 ......82 B6
Yew Trees TW17 ....192 B5
Yew Tree Wlk TW4 ....151 B6
Yew Wlk HA1 ....42 C1
Yiewsley CE Sch UB7 ..104 A5
Yoakley Rd N16 ....73 C6
Yoke Cl N7 ....72 A2
Yolande Gdns SE9 .....166 A6
Yonge Pk N4,N7 ....72 C5
York Ave DA15 ....167 D2
 SE17 ....262 B2
 Ealing W7 ....108 C5
 Hayes UB3 ....83 A1
 Mortlake SW14 ....155 A6
 Stanmore HA7 ....25 B1
York Ct Beckenham BR3 .186 B2
 Kingston KT2 ....175 D4
 Wallington SM6 ....219 C3

York Gate NW1 ....238 B5
 Southgate N14 ....16 A4
York Gr SE15 ....140 C4
York Hill SE27,SW16 ...160 D1
York Ho N1 ....233 C3
 N5 ....72 C3
 3 N7 ....71 D2
 NW4 ....28 D1
 SE1 ....116 B3 260 D5
 SW3 ....257 C2
 W1 ....237 C4
 W3 ....111 A6
 W8 ....245 C2
 10 Acton W3 ....88 C1
 Chingford E4 ....35 C6
 Enfield EN2 ....5 B4
 Forest Hill SE26 ......184 C5
 1 Ilford IG1 ....78 D6
 4 Kingston KT2 ......176 B3
 Richmond TW10 ......154 C6
 Richmond TW9 ....132 C4
 South Norwood SE25 ..205 C5
York House Pl
 W8 ....113 D4 245 C2
Yorkland Ave DA16 .....145 D1
Yorkley Ho W10 ....90 C3
York Mans 1 NW9 ......46 A3
 SW11 ....268 B2
 W1 ....238 A4
York Mews NW5 ....71 B3
 Ilford IG1 ....78 C5
York Par NW9 ....46 A3
 Brentford TW8 ....109 D1
York Pl SW11 ....136 B2
 WC2 ....250 B5
 Ilford IG1 ....78 C6
York Place Mans NW1 .237 D4
York Rd E10 ....76 A5
 E17 ....52 D4
 E7 ....77 A2
 N11 ....31 D4
 SE1 ....116 B4 250 D2
 SW11,SW18 ....136 B2
 W3 ....89 B1
 W5 ....109 C3
 Belmont SM1,SM2 ....217 C1
 Brentford TW8 ....109 D1
 Chingford E4 ....35 C5
 Edmonton N18 ....34 B5
 Hounslow TW3 ....129 D2
 Ilford IG1 ....78 C6
 Kingston KT2 ....176 B3
 New Barnet EN5 ....14 B6
 Pinner HA6 ....22 A1
 4 Richmond TW10 ...154 B6
 Southgate N21 ....17 B4
 Teddington TW11 .....174 C6
 Thornton Heath CR0 ..204 C2
 Wimbledon SW19 .....180 A4
York Rise BR6 ....227 C6
 NW5 ....71 B5
York Road Bsns Ctr
 SW11 ....136 B3
Yorkshire Cl N16 ....73 C6
Yorkshire Gdns N18 ....34 B5
Yorkshire Grey SE9 ...165 D6
Yorkshire Grey Yd WC1 ..240 C3

Wyb – Zof   379

Yorkshire Rd E14 ....97 A1
 Mitcham CR4 ....204 A5
York Sq 14 E14 ....97 A1
York St W1 ..92 D2 237 D4
 Barking IG11 ....101 A6
 Carshalton CR4 ......203 A2
 Twickenham TW1 .....153 A3
York St Chambers W1 ..237 C4
York Terr EN2 ....5 A5
York Terr E NW1 ..93 A3 238 B5
York Terr W
 NW1 ....93 A3 238 A5
Yorkton St E2 ....96 A5
York Way N1 ....233 B5
 N1,N7,NW1 ....72 A1
 N20 ....14 D1
 Chessington KT9 .....214 A1
 Twickenham TW13 ...151 B1
York Way Ct N1 ....233 B5
Youngmans Cl EN2 ......5 A4
Young Rd E16 ....99 C1
Young's Bldgs EC1 ....242 B6
Youngs Ct SW11 ......268 B1
Youngs Rd IG2 ....57 B4
Young St W8 ..113 D4 245 C1
Yoxall Ho W10 ....90 C3
Yoxley App IG2 ....57 A3
Yoxley Dr IG2 ....57 A3
Yukon Rd SW12 ....159 B4
Yuletide Cl NW10 ....67 C2
Yunus Khan Cl E17 .....53 C4

Z

Zampa Rd SE16 ....118 C1
Zander Ct E2 ....96 A4
Zangwill Ho NW6 ....91 B5
Zangwill Rd SE18,SE3 ..143 D4
Zealand Ave UB7 ....126 A6
Zealand Ho 11 SE5 ....139 A3
 4 SE7 ....122 A2
Zealand Rd E3 ....97 A5
Zennor Rd SW12 ....159 C3
Zenoria St SE22 ....139 D1
Zermatt Rd CR7 ....205 A5
Zetland Ho W8 ....255 C6
Zetland St E14 ....98 A2
Zion Ho 6 E1 ....96 C1
Zion Pl CR7 ....205 B5
Zion Rd CR7 ....205 B5
Zoar St SE1 .....117 A5 252 A4
Zodiac Ct CR0 ....204 D1
Zodiac Ho 3 E3 ....97 C3
Zoffany St N19 ....71 D6

List of numbered locations

This atlas shows thousands more place names than any other London street atlas. In some busy areas it is impossible to fit the name of every place.

Where not all names will fit, some smaller places are shown by a number. If you wish to find out the name associated with a number, use this listing.

The places in this list are also listed normally in the Index.

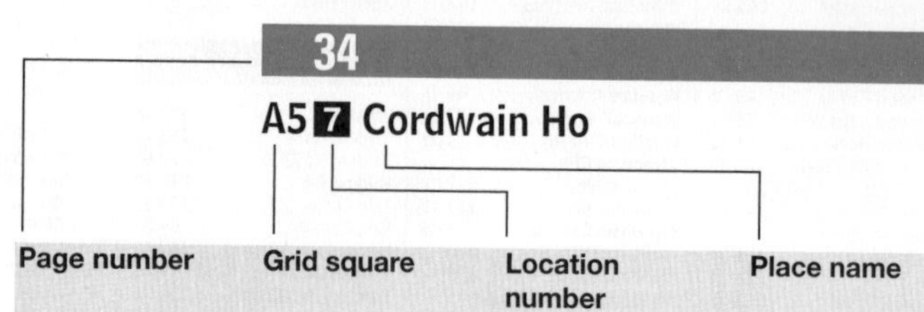

Page number	Grid square	Location number	Place name

A5 7 Cordwain Ho

1

A1 **1** Hertswood Ct
2 Sunbury Ct
3 Meriden Ho
4 Norfolk Ct
5 Morrison Ct
6 Kingshill Ct
7 Baronsmere Ct
8 Chartwell Ct

2

C1 **1** Braeburn Ct
2 Bramley Ct
3 Cox Ct
4 Golden Ct
5 Pippin Ct
6 Russet Ct
7 High Birch Ct
8 Joystone Ct
9 Mark Lo
10 Edgeworth Ct

5

1 Woodfield Cl
2 Fielders Cl

9

D5 **1** Watling Ct
2 Stuart Ct
3 Westview Ct
4 Potters Mews

13

D6 **1** Rowan Wlk
2 Ford Ho
3 Glenwood Ho
4 Whitegates
5 Lisa Lo
6 South Lo
7 Hockington Ct
8 Eysham Ct
9 Springfields
10 Bure Ct
11 Coleridge Ct
12 Chaucer Ct

14

B6 **1** Redrose
Trad Ctr
2 Lancaster Road
Ind Est
C5 **1** Feline Ct
2 Brookhill Ct
3 Littlegrove Ct
4 Desmond Ho

15

C6 **1** Tregenna Cl
2 Catherine Ct
3 Conisbee Ct
4 Ashmead
D3 **1** Dennis Par
2 Broadway The
3 Southgate Cir
4 Station Par
5 Bourneside
6 Bourneside
Cres

17

C6 **1** Wade Ho
2 Newport Lo
3 Halcyon
4 Lerwick Ct
5 Anchor Ct
6 Grassmere Ct
7 Datchworth Ct
8 Trentham Lo
9 Austin Ct
10 Cedar Grange
11 Brookview Ct
12 Chestbrook Ct

13 Paddock Lo
14 Hamlet Ct
15 Haven Lo

18

A1 **1** Plevna Ho
2 Lea Ho
3 Brook Ho
4 Valley Ho
5 Chiltern Ho
6 Blenheim Ho
7 Penn Ho
8 Romany Ho
9 Gilpin Ho
10 Anvil Ho
11 Well Ho
12 Passmore Ho
13 Durbin Ho
A2 **1** Market Par
2 Beechwood Mews
3 Keats Par
4 Cedars Rd
5 Cross Keys Cl
6 Dorman Pl
7 Concourse The

20

1 Lea Ct
2 Park Ct
3 Conference Cl
4 Berrybank Cl
5 Russell Lo
6 Brunswick Lo
7 Kenilworth Ct
8 Trinity Ct
9 Kingsmead Lo
10 Fairlawns
A3 **1** Grant Ct
2 Chantry The
3 Bowyer Ct
4 Pineview Ct
5 Ellen Ct
6 Leaview Ct
7 Chelsea Ct
8 Bramley Ct
9 Garenne Ct
10 Kendal Ct
B2 **1** Temple Hall Ct
2 Larkshall Bsns Ctr
3 Endlebury Ct
4 James Ct
5 Holmes Ct
B3 **1** Maddox Ct
2 Village Arc The
3 Cambridge Rd
4 Crown Bldgs
5 Pentney Rd
6 Scholars Ho
7 Cranworth Cres
C4 **1** Connaught Ct
2 Woolden Ho
3 Fairmead Ct
4 Lockhart Lo
5 Cavendish Ct
6 Oakwood Ct
7 Plains The
8 Hadleigh Ct
9 Forest Ho
10 Mathieson Ho

21

C2 **1** Westbury Ct
2 Palmerston Ct
3 Ibrox Ct
4 Richard Burton Ct
5 Queens Ct
6 Gunnels Ct &
Hastingwood Ct
7 Marlborough Ct
8 Avenue The
9 Tara Ct
D2 **1** Regency Lo
2 Kings Ct
3 Beech Ct
4 Sycamore Ho

22

C1 **1** Northcote
2 Edwin Ware Ct
3 Chalfont Wlk
4 Maple Ct
5 Montesole Ct

23

B3 **1** St Cuthberts Gdns
2 Cherry Croft Gdns
3 Cornwall Cl
4 Dunsford Ct

25

C5 **1** Belgrave Gdns
2 Heywood Ct
3 Norfolk Ho
4 Garden Ct
5 Chatsworth Ct
6 Chartridge Ct
7 Hardwick Ct
8 Cheltenham Ct
9 Cargrey Ho
10 Holbein Ho
11 Goodwood Cl
C6 **1** Bickley Ct
2 Kelmscott Ct
3 Elstree Ho
4 Brompton Ct
5 Kenmare Ct

27

A1 **1** Colesworth Ho
2 Crokesley Ho
3 Curtlington Ho
4 Clare Ho
5 Kedyngton Ho
A3 **1** Tadbourne Ct
2 Truman Cl
3 Lords Ct
4 Hutton Row
5 Compton Cl
6 Botham Cl
7 Bradman Row
A6 **1** Iris Wlk
2 Sycamore Cl
B5 **1** Monarchs Ct
2 Kensington Ct
C2 **1** Rufforth Ct
2 Riccal Ct
3 Lindholme Ct
4 Driffield Ct
5 Jack Ashley Ct
6 Folkingham La
7 Leander Ct
8 Daniel Ct
9 Nimrod
10 Nisbet
11 Pixton
12 Rapide
13 Ratier
D1 **1** Gauntlet
2 Guilfoyle
3 Grebe
4 Gates
5 Galy
6 Folland
7 Firefly
8 Halifax
9 Debussy
10 Crosbie
11 Grant Ct
12 Ham Ct
13 Deal Ct
14 Ember Ct
15 Canterbury Ct
16 Beaumont Ct
17 Cirrus
18 Defiant
19 Dessouter
20 Douglas
21 Cobham
22 Clayton
23 Camm
24 Bradon
25 Boarhound

26 Bodmin
27 Bleriot
28 Blackburn
29 Audax
30 Anson
31 Albatross
32 Arran Ct
33 Mavis Ct
34 Goosander Ct
35 Platt Halls (a)
36 Writtle Ho
37 Platt Halls (b)
38 Platt Halls (c)
D2 **1** Slatter
2 Sopwith
3 Saimet
4 Sassoon
5 Roe
6 Orde
7 Osprey
8 Prodger
9 Randall
10 Porte
11 Norris
12 Nardini
13 Noel
14 Nicolson
15 Napier
16 Nighthawk
17 Moorhouse
18 Moineau
19 Mitchell
20 Lysander
21 Lillywhite
22 Martynside
23 March
24 Kemp
25 Mercury
26 Merlin
27 Hudson
28 Hawker
29 Hawfinch
30 Heracles
31 Hector
D3 **1** Wellington
2 Wheeler
3 Whittaker
4 Whittle
5 Tedder
6 Cranwell Ct
7 Tait
8 Spooner

28

D1 **1** York Ho
2 Windsor Ho
3 Regency Cres
4 Normandy Ho
5 Allerton Ct

29

C2 **1** Sherringham Ct
2 St Ronan's
3 Crescent Rise
4 Elm Ct
D6 **1** Brookfield Ct
2 Magnolia Ct
3 Dunbar Ct
4 Haughmond
5 Nansen Village
6 Beechcroft
7 Speedwell Ct
8 Woodside Ct
9 Speedwell Ho
10 Rebecca Ho
11 Ashbourne Ct
12 Forest Ct
13 Beecholme
14 Greville Lo
15 St Johnstone Ho

30

B1 **1** New Trinity Rd
2 Garden Ho
3 Todd Ho
4 Sayers Ho
5 Mowbray Ho

6 Bouchier Ho
7 Cleveland Ho
8 Goodyear Ho
9 Lochleven Ho
10 Berwick Ho
11 Oak Ho
12 Willow Wlk
13 Craven Ho
14 Willow Ho
15 Vane Ho
16 Foskett Ho
17 Elmfield Ho
18 Sycamore Ho
19 Netherwood
D5 **1** Halliwick Ct
2 Halliwick Court
Par
3 Queen's Par
4 St John's Village
5 Hartland Ct
6 Kennard Mans
7 Bensley Cl

31

A3 **1** Campe Ho
2 Betstyle Ho
3 Pymmes Brook
Ho
4 Mosswell Ho
5 Hampden Ct
6 Crown Ct
B1 **1** Cedar Ct
2 Carisbrook
3 St Ivian Ct
4 Barrington Ct
5 Essex Lo
B5 **1** Caradoc Evans Ct
2 Roberts Ho
3 Lorne Ho
B6 **1** Grovefield
2 Lapworth
3 Stewards Holte
Wlk
4 Sarnes Ct
5 Stanhope Ho
6 Holmsdale Ho
C5 **1** Barbara Martin
Ho
2 Jerome Ct
3 Limes Cl
4 Arnos Grove Ct
5 Cedar Ct
6 Betspath Ho
7 Curtis Ho
8 Mason Ho
9 Danford Ho
10 New Southgate
Ind Est
11 Palmer's Ct

32

A4 **1** Brownlow Ct
2 Latham Ct
3 Fairlawns
4 Beaumaris
C1 **1** Penwortham Ct
2 Tarleton Ct
3 Holmeswood Ct
4 Kwesi Johnson Ct
5 Sandlings The

33

D1 **1** Honeysett Rd
2 Wilson's Ave
3 Palm Tree Ct
4 Stoneleigh Ct
5 Brook St
D3 **1** Charles Ho
2 Moselle Ho
3 Ermine Ho
4 Kathleen Ferrier
Ct
5 Concord Ho
6 Rees Ho
7 Nursery Ct
8 William Rainbird
Ho

D4 **1** Regan Ho
2 Isis Ho
3 Boundary Ct
4 Stellar Ho
5 Cooperage Cl

34

A5 **1** Angel Pl
2 Cross St
3 Scott Ho
4 Beck Ho
5 Booker Rd
6 Bridport Ho
7 Cordwain Ho
8 St James's Ct
9 Highmead
A6 **1** Walton Ho
2 Alma Ho
3 Brompton Ho
4 Field Ho
5 Bradwell Mews
6 Angel Corner Par
7 Paul Ct
8 Cuthbert Rd
9 Brockenhurst
Mews
B3 **1** Kenneth Robbins
Ho
2 Charles Brad-
laugh Ho
3 Woodrow Ct
4 Cheviot
5 Corbridge
6 Whittingham
7 Eastwood Cl
8 Alnwick
9 Bamburgh
10 Bellingham
11 Briaris Cl

36

B5 **1** Hedgemoor Ct
2 Hewitt Ho
3 Castle Ho
4 Bailey Ct
5 Harcourt Ho
6 Gerboa Ct
D1 **1** Chatham Rd
2 Washington Rd
3 Cherry Tree Ct
4 Grosvenor Lo
5 Torfell
D2 **1** Hillboro Ct
2 Dorchester Ct

37

A1 **1** Chiltons The
2 Ullswater Ct
3 Leigh Ct
4 Woburn St
A2 **1** Lindal Ct
2 Hockley Ct
3 Woodleigh
4 Milne Ct
5 Cedar Ct
6 Elizabeth Ct
7 Silvermead
8 Laurel Mead Ct
9 Mitre Ct
10 Pevensey Ct
11 Lyndhurst Ct
A3 **1** New Jubilee Ct
2 Chartwell Ct
3 Greenwood
4 Solway Lo
A4 **1** Terrace The
2 Broomhill Ct
3 Clifton Ct
4 Fairstead Lo
5 Hadleigh Lo
6 Broadmead Ct
7 Wilton Ct
8 Fairfield Ct
9 Higham Ct
A6 **1** Tree Tops
2 Cranfield Ct
B1 **1** Station Est

2 Station App
3 James Ct
C3 **1** Liston Way
2 Elizabeth Ct
3 Coopersale Cl
4 Sunset Ct
5 Lambourne Ct
C4 **1** Hope Cl
2 Rex Par
3 Shalford
4 Rodings The

40

C1 **1** Salisbury Ho
2 Rodwell Cl
3 Pretoria Ho
4 Ottawa Ho
5 Swallow Ct

42

D3 **1** Nightingale Ct
2 St John's Ct
3 Gayton Ct
4 Wilton Pl
5 Murray Ct
6 Cymbeline Ct
7 Knowles Ct
8 Charville Ct
9 Lime Ct
10 Petherton Ct
11 Chalfont Ct
D4 **1** Crystal Ctr The
2 Blue Point Ct
3 Ryan Ho
4 Bruce Ho
5 Ingram Ho
6 Arless Ho
7 Leaf Ho

46

A2 **1** Milton Rd
2 Stanley Rd
A3 **1** York Mans
2 Telford Rd
A5 **1** Pilkington Ct
2 Cousins Ct
3 Seton Ct
4 Frensham Ct
5 Chatton Ct
6 Geraldine Ct
7 Swynford Gdns
8 Miller Ct
9 Roffey Ct
10 Peace Ct
11 Rambler Ct
12 Lion Ct
13 Wenlock Gdns
14 Dogrose Ct
15 Harry Ct
16 Tribune Ct
17 Bonville Gdns
18 Pearl Ct
B4 **1** Vivian Mans
2 Parade Mans
3 Georgian Ct
4 Florence Mans
5 Park Mans
6 Cheyne Ct
7 Queens Par
8 Central Mans
C5 **1** Courtney Ho
2 Golderton
3 Thornbury
4 Brampton La
5 Ashwood Ho
6 Longford Ct
7 Short St
D5 **1** Midford Ho
2 Rockfield Ho
3 Lisselton Ho
4 Acrefield Ho

47

B2 **1** Berkeley Ct
2 Exchange Mans
3 Beechcroft

4 Nedahall Ct
B3 1 Charlton Lo
2 Clifton Gdns
B4 1 Hallswelle Par
2 Belmont Par
3 Temple Fortune Ho
4 Yew Tree Ct
5 Temple Fortune Par
6 Courtleigh
7 Arcade Ho
8 Queens Ct
9 Temple Fortune Ct
B5 1 Monkville Par
2 Ashbourne Par

48
A6 1 St Mary's Gn
2 Dunstan Cl
3 Paul Byrne Ho
4 Longfield Ct
5 Warwick Ct
6 Branksome Ct
7 Sherwood Hall

49
B6 1 Dorchester Ct
2 Old Chapel Pl
3 Athenaeum Pl
4 Risborough Ct
C1 1 Calvert Ct
2 Academy The
3 Whitehall Mans
4 Pauntley St
5 Archway Hts
6 Pauntley Ho
D1 1 Louise White Ho
2 Levison Way
3 Sanders Way
D2 1 Eleanor Rathbone Ho
2 Christopher Lo
3 Monkridge
4 Marbleford Ct
5 High London
6 Garton Ho
7 Hilltop Ho
8 Caroline Martyn Ho
9 Arthur Henderson Ho
10 Margaret Mcmillan Ho
11 Enid Stacy Ho
12 Mary McArthur Ho
13 Bruce Glasier Ho
14 John Wheatley Ho
15 Keir Hardie Ho
16 Monroe Ho
17 Iberia Ho
18 Lygoe Ho
19 Lambert Ho
20 Shelbourne Ho
21 Arkansas Ho
22 Lafitte Ct
23 Shreveport Ho
24 Packenham Ho
25 Orpheus Ho
26 Fayetville Ho
27 Bayon Ho
D4 1 Kelland Cl
2 Veryan Ct
3 Coulsdon Ct

50
A1 1 Beeches The
2 Lambton Ct
A2 1 Marie Lloyd Gdns
2 Jessie Blythe La
3 Leyden Mans
4 Brambledown
5 Lochbie
6 Edith Cavell Cl
A5 1 Mackenzie Ct
2 Stowell Ho
3 Campsbourne Ho
B1 1 Lawson Ct
2 Wiltshire Ct
3 Hutton Ct
D5 1 Wordsworth Par

51
A2 1 Finmere Ho
2 Keynsham Ho
3 Kilpeck Ho
4 Knaresborough Ho
5 Leighfield Ho
6 Lonsdale Ho
7 Groveley Ho
8 Wensleydale Ho
9 Badminton Ct
B2 1 Selwood Ho
2 Mendip Ho
3 Ennerdale Ho
4 Delamere Ho
5 Westwood Ho
6 Bernwood Ho
7 Allerdale Ho
8 Chattenden Ho
9 Farningham Ho
10 Oakend Ho

C1 1 Godstone Ct
2 Farnham Ct
3 Milford Ct
4 Cranleigh Ct
5 Haslemere Ct
6 Belmont Ct
7 Hockworth Ho
8 Garratt Ho
9 Fairburn Ho
C3 1 Oatfield Ho
2 Perry Ct
3 Henrietta Ho
4 Bournes Ho
5 Chisley Rd
6 Twyford Ho
7 Langford Cl
8 Hatchfield Ho
D1 1 Stamford Hill Mans
2 Montefiore Ct
3 Berwyn Ho
4 Clent Ho
5 Chiltern Ho
6 Laindon Ho
7 Pentland Ho
D2 1 Regent Ct
2 Stamford Lo
3 Holmwood Ct
D3 1 Sherboro Rd
2 Westcott Cl
3 Cadoxton Ave
4 Slater Ho
D4 1 Westerfield Rd
2 Suffield Rd
D5 1 Greenway Cl
2 Tottenham Gn E
3 Tottenham Gn E South Side
4 Deaconess Ct
5 Elliot Ct
6 Bushmead Ct
7 Beaufort Ho
8 Tynemouth Terr
D6 1 Holcombe Rd
2 Chaplin Rd
3 Reynardson's Ct
4 Protheroe Ho

52
A1 1 Stamford Grove E
2 Stamford Mans
3 Grove Mans
4 Stamford Grove W
B1 1 Hawkwood Mount
2 Holmbury View
3 High Hill Ferry
4 Leaside Ho
5 Courtlands
6 Ivy Ho
7 Shelford Ct

53
A4 1 Hammond Ct
2 St James Apartments
3 Grange The
A5 1 Bristol Park Rd
2 Stoneydown Ho
3 Callonfield
4 Hardyng Ho
C1 1 Wellington Mans
2 Clewer Ct
3 Cochrane Ct
C5 1 Westbury Ho
2 Hatherley Ho
3 Vintry Mews
4 Tylers Ct
5 Merchants Lo
6 Gillards Mews
7 Blacksmiths Ho
8 Central Par
D1 1 Fitzgerald Ct
2 Bechervaise Ct
3 Underwood Ct
D2 1 Station Ct
2 Howell Ct
3 Atkinson Ct
4 Russell Ct
5 St Luke Ct
6 St Matthews Ct
7 St Mark's Ct
8 St Elizabeth Ct
9 Emmanuel Ct
10 St Thomas Ct
11 Beaumont Ho
12 Shelley Ct
13 St Paul's Twr
14 Flack Ct
15 King Ct
16 Osborne Ct
17 Muriel Ct
18 All Saints Twr
19 St Josephs Ct
20 Mitchell Ct
21 Cornwell Ct
D5 1 Nash Ho
2 St Columbas Ho
3 Attlee Terr
4 Astins Ho
5 Lindens The
6 Kevan Ct
7 Squire's Almshouses
8 Berry Field Cl
9 Holmcroft Ho
10 Connaught Ct

D6 1 Hollingbury Ct
2 Mace Ho
3 Gaitskell Ho
4 Hancocke Ho
5 Trinity Ct
6 Fanshaw Ho
7 Hilltop
8 Batten Ho
9 Bradwell Ho
10 Walton Ho
11 Temple Ho
12 Gower Ho
13 Maple Ho
14 Poplars Ho
15 Cedars Ho
16 Kimm Ho
17 O'Grady Ho
18 Latham Ho
19 Powell Ct
20 Crosbie Ho

54
A2 1 Ayerst Ct
2 Dare Ct
3 St Edwards Ct
A4 1 Jane Sabina Colard's Almshouses
2 Ellen Miller Ho
3 Tom Smith Ho
A5 1 Northwood Twr
2 Walnut Ct
3 Albert Whicher Ho
4 Pelly Ct
5 Ravenswood Road Ind Est
6 Holland Ct
7 Emberson Ho
8 St Mark's Ho
9 Alfred Villas
A6 1 St David's Ct
2 Golden Par
3 Chestnuts Ct
4 Matthew Ct
5 Gilbert Ho
6 Manning Ho
7 Southgate Ho
8 Boyden Ho
9 Prospect Ho
10 Newton Ho

55
A3 1 Aldham Hall
2 Parkside Ct
3 Mapperley Cl
4 Weavers Ho
5 Cyns Ct
6 Reed Mans
7 Thornton Ho
8 Hardwick Ct
A4 1 Kingsley Grange
2 Station Par
3 Gwynne Ho
4 Staveley Ho
5 Devon Ho
6 Thurlow Ct
7 Hollies The
8 Little Holt
9 Dudley Ct
10 Woodland Ct
11 Struan Ho
12 Westleigh Ct
A5 1 Sherwood Ho
2 Orwell Lo
3 Hermitage Ct
4 Gowan Lea
5 Woodford Ho
6 Eagle Ct
7 Newbury Ct
8 Shelley Ct
9 Hardy Ct
10 Dickens Ct
11 Byron Ct
A6 1 Millbrook
2 Elmbrook
3 Grange The
4 Glenavon Lo
5 Glenwood Ct
6 Ferndown
7 Embassy Ct
8 Orestes Ct
9 Walbrook
10 Helmsley
11 Snaresbrook Hall
B4 1 Nightingale Ct
2 Chelston Ct
3 Grosvenor Ct
4 Louise Ct
5 St Davids Ct
6 Cedar Ct
7 Shrubbery The
B6 1 Victoria Ct
2 Kenwood Gdns
3 Thaxted Lo
4 Albert Rd
5 Albert Ho
6 Falcon Ct
7 Deborah Ct
8 Swift Ho
9 Pulteney Gdns
10 Spring Ct
11 Trinity Gdns

56
B4 1 High View Par

2 Spurway Par

57
A3 1 Catherine Ct
2 Lincoln Ct
3 Ivy Terr
4 Newbury Cotts

58
B1 1 Caledonian Cl
2 Talisman Ct
3 Norseman Cl
4 Frank Slater Ho
5 Brook's Mans
6 Brook's Par
B2 1 Mitre Ct
2 Coppins The
3 Stanetto Ct
4 Wilnett Ct
5 Wilnett Villas
D2 1 Pavement Mews
2 Chadview Ct
3 Granary Ct
4 Bedwell Ct
5 Chapel La
6 Faulkner Cl
7 Maple Ct
8 Willow Ct
9 Cedar Terr

63
C2 1 Wimborne Ct
2 Haydock Green Flats
3 Brighton Dr
4 Blaydon Ct
5 Fakenham Cl
6 Rutland Ho
7 Windsor Ho

65
D3 1 Oaklands Ct
2 Lowry Lo
3 Morritt Ho
4 Lancelot Par
5 Willow Tree La
6 Snow Ct

66
A2 1 Montrose Cres
2 Peggy Quirke Ct
3 Copland Mews
4 Coronet Par
5 Charlotte Ct
A3 1 Market Way
2 Lodge Ct
3 Central Sq
4 Manor Ct
5 Rupert Ave

67
A5 1 Curie Ho
2 Darwin Ho
3 Priestley Ho
4 Rutherford Ho
5 Fleming Ho
6 Lister Ho
7 Edison Ho
B1 1 Kingthorpe Terr
2 Scott Ho
3 Peary Ho
4 Shackleton Ho
5 Amundsen Ho
6 Brentfield Ho
7 Nansen Ho
8 Stonebridge Ct
9 Magellan Ct
10 Leadbetter Ct
11 Viant Ho
12 Jefferies Ho
13 Diamond St
C1 1 Beveridge Rd
C5 1 Hazelwood Ct
2 Winslow Cl

68
A2 1 Regency Mews
2 Tudor Mews
A5 1 Bourne Ho
2 Carton Ho
3 Woodbridge Cl
4 Mackenzie Ho
5 Banting Ho

69
A1 1 Fountain Ho
2 Kingston Ho
3 Waverley Ct
4 Weston Ho
5 Mapes Ho
6 Athelstan Gdns
7 Leff Ho
B1 1 Alma Birk Ho
2 Brooklands Ct
3 Brooklands Court Apartments
4 Cleveland Mans
5 Buckley Ct
6 Webheath
B5 1 Mortimer Cl
2 Sunnyside Ho

3 Sunnyside
4 Prospect Pl
C1 1 Linstead St
2 Embassy Ho
3 Acol Ct
4 Kings Wood Ct
5 Douglas Ct
6 King's Gdns
7 Carlton Mans
8 Smyrna Mans
9 New Priory Ct
10 Queensgate Pl
11 Brondesbury Mews
C2 1 Dene Mans
2 Sandwell Cres
3 Sandwell Mans
4 Hampstead West
5 Redcroft
C3 1 Orestes Mews
2 Walter Northcott Ho
3 Polperro Mans
4 Lyncroft Mans
5 Marlborough Mans
6 Alexandra Mans
7 Cumberland Mans
8 Cavendish Mans
9 Ambassador Ct
10 Welbeck Mans
11 Inglewood Mans
C5 1 Portman Hts
2 Hermitage Ct
3 Moreland Ct
4 Wendover Ct
D2 1 Beswick Mews
2 Worcester Mews
3 Minton Mews
4 Doulton Mews
5 Laurel Ho
6 Sandalwood Ho
7 Iroko Ho
8 Banyan Ho
9 Ebony Ho
10 Rosemont Mans

70
A1 1 Harrold Ho
2 Glover Ho
3 Byron Ct
4 Nalton Ho
A2 1 Petros Gdns
2 Heath Ct
3 Imperial Twrs
4 Fairhurst
5 St John's Ct
6 New College Ct
7 Chalford
8 Sutherland Ho
A4 1 Windmill Hill
2 Highgrove Point
3 Gainsborough Ho
4 Heath Mans
5 Pavilion Ct
6 Holly Berry La
7 New Campden Ct
8 Benham's Pl
9 Holly Bush Vale
10 Gardnor Mans
11 Mansfield Pl
12 Streatley Pl
13 New Ct
14 Bird In Hand Yd
15 Spencer Wlk
16 Wells Ct
17 Perrin's Ct
18 Village Mount
19 Prince Arthur Ct
20 Prince Arthur Mews
21 Monro Ho
22 Ellerdale Ct
23 Holly Bush Hill
24 Prospect Pl
A5 1 Stamford Cl
B1 1 New College Par
2 Northways Par
3 Noel Ho
4 Campden Ho
5 Centre Hts
6 Hickes Ho
7 Swiss Terr
8 Leitch Ho
9 Jevons Ho
10 Langhorne Ct
11 Park Lo
12 Avenue Lo
B2 1 Belsize Park Mews
2 Baynes Mews
3 McCrone Mews
B3 1 Belsize Court Garages
2 Roscommon Ho
3 Akenside Ct
C2 1 Linstead Ho
2 Glenloch Ct
3 Havercourt
4 Holmfield Ho
5 Gilling Ct
6 Howitt Cl
7 Manor Mans
8 Straffan Lo
9 Romney Ct
10 Lancaster Stables
11 Eton Garages
D1 1 Hancock Nunn Ho

3 Higginson Ho
4 Duncan Ho
5 Mary Wharrie Ho
6 Rockstraw Ho
7 Cleaver Ho
8 Chamberlain St
9 Sharples Hall St
10 Primrose Mews
11 St Georges Mews
D2 1 Alder Ho
2 Hornbeam Ho
3 Whitebeam Ho
4 Aspen Ho
5 Rowan Ho
6 Beech Ho
7 Chestnut Ho
8 Oak Ho
9 Willow Ho
10 Sycamore Ho
11 Maple Ho
12 Hazel Ho
13 Elaine Ct
14 Faircourt
15 Walham Ho
16 Stanbury Ct
17 Priory Mans
18 Wellington Ho
19 Grange The
D3 1 Cayford Ho
2 Du Maurier Ct
3 Isokon Flats
4 Palgrave Ho
5 Garnett Ho
6 Stephenson Ho
7 Park Dwellings
8 Siddons Ct
9 Mall Studios
10 Park Hill Wlk
11 Wordsworth Pl
12 Fraser Regnart Ct
13 St Pancras Almshouses

71
A1 1 Bridge Ho
2 Hardington
3 Mead Cl
4 Rugmere
5 Tottenhall
6 Beauvale
7 Broomfield
A2 1 Silverbirch Wlk
2 Penshurst
3 Wingham
4 Westwell
5 Chislet
6 Burmarsh
7 Shipton Ho
8 Stone Gate
9 Leysdown
10 Headcorn
11 Lenham
12 Halstow
13 Fordcombe
14 Cannington
15 Langridge
16 Athlone Ho
17 Pentland Ho
18 Beckington
19 Hawkridge
20 Edington
B1 1 Ferdinand Ho
2 Harmood Ho
3 Hawley Rd
4 Hawley Mews
5 Leybourne St
6 Barling
7 Tiptree
8 Havering
9 Candida Ct
10 Lorraine Ct
11 Donnington Ct
12 Welford Ct
13 Torbay Ct
14 Bradfield Ct
15 Torbay St
16 Leybourne Rd
17 Haven St
18 Stucley Pl
B2 1 Ashington
2 Priestley Ho
3 Leonard Day Ho
4 Old Dairy Mews
5 Monmouth Ho
6 Alpha Ct
7 Una Ho
8 Widford
9 Hey Bridge
10 Roxwell
B4 1 Denyer Ho
2 Stephenson Ho
3 Trevithick Ho
4 Brunel Ho
5 Newcomen Ho
6 Faraday Ho
7 Winifrede Paul Ho
8 Wardlow
9 Fletcher Ct
10 Tideswell
11 Grangemill
12 Hambrook Ct
C1 1 Durdans Ho
2 Philia Ho
3 Bernard Shaw Ct
4 Foster Ct

5 Bessemer Ct
6 Hogarth Ct
7 Rochester Ct
8 Soane Ct
9 Wallett Ct
10 Inwood Ct
11 Wrotham Rd
12 Caulfield Ct
13 Bruges Pl
14 Reachview Cl
15 Lawfords Wharf
C3 1 Eleanor Ho
2 Falkland Pl
3 Kensington Ho
4 Willingham Cl
5 Kenbrook Ho
6 Aborfield
7 Great Field
8 Appleford
9 Forties The
C4 1 Benson Ct
2 Tait Ho
3 Manorfield Cl
4 Greatfield Cl
5 Longley Ho
6 Lampson Ho
7 Davidson Ho
8 Palmer Ho
9 Lambourn Cl
10 Morris Ho
11 Owen Ho
C5 1 Hunter Ho
2 Fisher Ho
3 Lang Ho
4 Temple Ho
5 Palmer Ho
C6 1 Flowers Mews
2 Sandridge St
3 Bovingdon Cl
4 Laurel Cl
5 Forest Way
6 Larch Cl
7 Pine Cl
8 Alder Mews
9 Aspen Cl
D1 1 Hillier Ho
2 Gairloch Ho
3 Cobham Mews
4 Bergholt Mews
5 Blakeney Cl
6 Weavers Way
7 Allensbury Pl
D2 1 Rowstock
2 Carters Cl
3 York Ho
4 Hungerford Rd
5 Cliff Ct
6 Camelot Ho
D3 1 Blake Ho
2 Quelch Ho
3 Lee Ho
4 Willbury Ho
5 Howell Ho
6 Holmsbury Ho
7 Leith Ho
8 Betchworth Ho
9 Rushmore Ho
10 Dugdale Ho
11 Horsendon Ho
12 Colley Ho
13 Coombe Ho
14 Ivinghoe Ho
15 Buckhurst Ho
16 Saxonbury Ct
17 Charlton Ct
18 Apollo Studios
19 Barn Cl
20 Long Meadow
21 Landleys Field
22 Margaret Bondfield Ho
23 Haywood Lo
D4 1 Fairlie Ct
2 London Metropolitan Univ (Carleton Grange Hall)
3 Trecastle Way
4 Hilldrop Est
5 Hyndman Ho
6 Carpenter Ho
7 Graham Ho
D5 1 Melchester Ho
2 Norcombe Ho
3 Weatherbury Ho
4 Wessex Ct
5 Archway Bsns Ctr
D6 1 Bowerman Ct
2 Hargrave Mans
3 Church Garth
4 John King Ct

72
A3 1 Kimble Ho
2 Saxonbury Ct
3 Poynder Ct
4 Pangbourne Ho
5 Moulsford Ho
A4 1 Arcade The
2 Bovingdon Ct
A5 1 Northview
2 Tufnell Park Mans
A6 1 Christie Ct
2 Ringmer Gdns
3 Kingsdown Rd

4 Cottenham Ho
5 St Paul's Ct
6 Rickthorne Rd
7 Stanley Terr
B1 1 Kerwick Cl
2 Rydston Cl
3 Skegness Ho
4 Frederica St
5 Ponder St
6 Kings Ct
7 Freeling St
B4 1 Buckmaster Ho
2 Loreburn Ho
3 Cairns Ho
4 Halsbury Ho
5 Chelmsford Ho
6 Cranworth Ho
B6 1 Berkeley Wlk
2 Lazar Wlk
3 Thistlewood Cl
4 Tomlins Wlk
5 Andover Ho
6 Barmouth Ho
7 Chard Ho
8 Methley Ho
9 Rainford Ho
10 Woodbridge Cl
11 Allerton Wlk
12 Falconer Wlk
C1 1 Mountfort Terr
2 Davey Lo
3 Carfree Cl
4 New College Mews
C3 1 Slaney Pl
2 Wells Yd
3 Milton Pl
4 Hartnoll Ho
5 St James School Flats
6 Widnes Ho
7 Tranmere Ho
8 Victoria Mans
9 Formby Ct
10 Mersey Ho
11 Birkenhead Ho
C6 1 Brookfield
2 Churnfield
D1 1 Islington Park Mews
2 Evelyn Denington Ct
3 Bassingbourn Ho
4 Cadmore Ho
5 Adstock Ho
6 Garston Ho
7 Flitton Ho
8 Datchworth Ho
9 Battishill St
10 Almeida St
11 Edward's Cotts
12 Hyde's Pl
13 Tyndale Terr
14 Spriggs Ho
15 Barratt Ho
16 Spencer Pl
17 Chadston Ho
18 Whiston Ho
19 Wakelin Ho
20 Tressel Cl
21 Canonbury St
22 Shillingford St
23 Halton Ho
D4 1 Chestnuts The
2 Bowen Ct
3 Peckett Sq

73

A1 1 Haslam Ho
2 Horsfield Ho
3 Astey's Row
4 Melville Pl
5 Wontner Cl
6 Hedingham Ct
7 Eric Fletcher Ct
8 Ashby Ho
9 Annette Cres
10 Bentham Ct
11 New Bentham Ct
12 Cardigan Wlk
13 Lindsey Mews
14 Walkinshaw Ct
15 Laundry La
A2 1 Crowline Wlk
2 Bardsey Wlk
3 Handa Wlk
4 Lismore Wlk
5 Sark Ho
6 Clephane Rd
7 Sybil Thorndike Ho
8 Guernsey Rd
9 Guernsey Ho
10 Herm Ho
11 Florence Nightingale Ho
12 Jersey Ho
13 Jethou Ho
14 Upper Caldy Wlk
15 Caldy Wlk
16 Alderney Ho
17 Marquess Rd S
18 Oronsay Rd

19 Upper Gulland Wlk
20 Gulland Wlk
21 Church Rd
A3 1 Pearfield Ho
2 Larchfield Ho
3 Beresford Terr
4 Pondfield Ho
5 Ashfield Ho
6 Elmfield Ho
A4 1 Fountain Mews
2 Woodstock Ho
3 Henson Ct
4 Taverner Sq
B2 1 John Kennedy Ct
2 John Kennedy Lo
3 Ball's Pond Pl
4 Haliday Wlk
5 Rona Wlk
6 Threadgold Ho
7 Wakeham St
8 Saffron Ct
9 Callaby Terr
10 Tilney Gdns
11 Westcliff Ho
12 Ilford Ho
13 Ongar Ho
14 Greenhills Terr
15 Romford Ho
B4 1 Ledo Ho
2 Salween Ho
3 Prome Ho
4 Arakan Ho
5 Rangoon Ho
6 Mandalay Ho
7 Karen Ho
8 Wingate Ho
9 Jubet Ho
10 Orde Ho
11 Chindit Ho
12 Mabel Thornton Ho
13 Crawshay Ho
14 Avon Ho
15 Connaught Mans
16 Jonson Ho
17 Herrick Ho
18 Donne Ho
19 Grasmere Ho
20 Thirlmere Ho
B6 1 Chestnut Cl
2 Sycamore Ho
3 Lordship Ho
4 Clissold Ho
5 Beech Ho
6 Laburnum Ho
7 Ormond Ho
C1 1 Dorchester Ct
2 Wareham Ct
3 Dorset Ct
4 Stratton Ct
5 Swanage Ct
6 Blandford Ct
7 Portland Ct
8 Oscar Faber Pl
9 Lancaster Ct
C2 1 Kingsland Gn
2 Kingsland Pas
3 Metropolitan Benefit Societies Almshs
4 Nimrod Pas
5 De Beauvoir Pl
6 Warburton Cl
7 Buckingham Mews
C3 1 Hewling Ho
2 Matthias Ho
3 Port Royal Pl
4 Cressington Cl
5 King Henry's Yd
6 Bronte Ho
7 Sewell Ho
8 Lydgate Ho
9 Patmore Ho
10 Congreve Ho
11 Elton St
12 Conrad Ho
13 Southwell Ho
14 Neptune Ho
15 Campion Ho
16 Webster Ho
17 Meredith Ho
18 Beckford Ho
19 Ashley Ct
20 Hayling Cl
21 Millard Cl
22 Lydford Cl
23 Salcombe Rd
24 Truman's Rd
25 Templeton Cl
26 John Campbell Rd
27 Gillett Pl
28 Bradbury St
C4 1 Londesborough Ho
2 Knebworth Ho
3 Knebworth Rd
4 Bransby Ct
5 Imperial Ave
6 Leonard Pl
7 Shakspeare Mews
8 Binyon Ho
9 Shelley Ho
10 Browning Ho
11 Burns Ho
12 Andrew Marvell Ho

13 Wycliffe Ho
14 Blake Ho
15 Marlowe Ho
16 Fletcher Ho
17 Chaucer Ct
C5 1 Gujarat Ho
2 Marton Rd
3 Painsthorpe Rd
4 Selkirk Ho
5 Defoe Ho
6 Edward Friend Ho
7 Sheridan Ho
8 Barrie Ho
9 Arnold Ho
10 Macaulay Ho
11 Stowe Ho
12 Carlyle Ho
13 Shaftesbury Ho
14 Lillian Cl
15 Swift Ho
16 Dryden Ho
17 Scott Ct
18 Kingsfield Ho
19 Uhura Sq
D1 1 Hilborough Rd
2 Shoreditch Ct
3 Evergreen Sq
D2 1 Prospect Ho
2 Woodland St
3 Crosby Wlk
4 Kirkland Wlk
5 Bowness Ho
6 Carlisle Wlk
7 Skelton Cl
8 Camerton Cl
9 Buttermere Wlk
10 Houghton Cl
11 Hayton Cl
D3 1 Miller's Terr
2 Chow Sq
3 Drysdale Flats
4 Gateway Mews
5 Birkbeck Mews
6 Winchester Pl
D4 1 Coronation Ave
2 Morris Blitz Ct
3 Shacklewell Ho
4 Alexandra Ct
D5 1 Lawrence's Bldgs
2 Cottage Wlk
3 Batley Pl
D6 1 Garnham St
2 Garnham Cl
3 Sanford La
4 Sandford Wlk
5 Abney Gdns
6 Fleet Wood

74

A1 1 Aldington Ct
2 Bayton Ct
3 Rochford Wlk
A3 1 Kingsdown Ho
2 Glendown Ho
3 Moredown Ho
4 Blakeney Cl
5 Beeston Cl
6 Benabo Ct
7 David Devine Ho
8 Kreedman Wlk
9 Hermitage Row
10 Grafton Ct
11 Lushington Terr
A5 1 Ravenscourt
2 Mellington Ct
3 Rendlesham Ho
4 Florence Ct
5 Burnaston Ho
A6 1 Cazenove Mans
2 Chedworth Ho
3 Aldergrove Ho
4 Abbotstone Ho
5 Briggeford Cl
6 Inglethorpe Ho
7 Ashdown Ho
B1 1 Fortescue Ave
2 Pemberton Pl
3 Weston Wlk
4 Bayford St Ind Ctr
5 Bayford St
6 Sidworth St
7 Helmsley St
B2 1 Bohemia Pl
2 Graham Mans
3 Marvin St
4 Boscobel Ho
5 Royal Oak Rd
6 Colonnades The
7 Sylvester Ho
8 Sylvester Path
9 Doctor Spurstowe Almshos
10 Great Eastern Bldgs
11 Sojourner-Truth Cl
B3 1 Birchington Ho
2 Bicknor Ho
3 Boxley Ho
4 Adisham Ho
5 Cranbrook Ho
6 Marden Ho
7 Broome Ho
8 Crandale Ho
9 Cheriton Ho
10 Ditton Ho
11 Langley Ho
12 Dymchurch Ho

13 Elham Ho
14 Bodney Mans
15 Pembury Pl
16 Downs Ct
17 Perrywood Ho
18 Stapelhurst Ho
19 Pegwell Ho
20 Yalding Ho
21 Northbourne Ho
22 Monkton Ho
23 Milsted Ho
24 Athlone Cl
25 Clarence Pl
26 Gould Terr
27 Quested Ct
28 Brett Pas
29 Marcon Ct
B4 1 Sutherland Point
2 Embley Point
3 Downs La
4 Gaviller Pl
5 Robert Owen Lo
6 Apprentice Way
7 Arrowe Ct
8 Gilwell Ct
9 Sutton Ct
10 Kinnoull Mans
11 Rowhill Mans
12 Sladen Pl
13 Mothers Sq The
14 Richborough Ho
15 Sandgate Ho
16 Sheppey Ho
B6 1 Wentwood Ho
2 Woolmer Ho
3 Warwick Ct
4 Winslade Ho
5 Moriss Ho
6 Woodfield Ho
7 Rossendale Ho
8 Ettrick Ho
9 Charnwood Ho
10 Boyne Ho
11 Whitwell Ho
12 Scardale Ho
13 Hendale Ho
14 Brampton Cl
15 Aveley Ct
16 Aldeburgh Cl
C1 1 Dennington Cl
2 Pitcairn Ho
3 Lyme Grove Ho
4 Shakespeare Ho
5 Upcott Ho
6 Loddiges Ho
7 Parkinson Ho
8 Sloane Ho
9 Vanbrugh Ho
10 Cambridge Pas
11 Lyttleton Ho
12 Victoria Park Ct
13 Fairchild Ho
14 Forsyth Ho
15 Tradescant Ho
16 Mason Ho
17 Capel Ho
18 Cordwainers Ct
19 Bridgeman Ho
20 St Thomas's Pl
21 Barclay Ho
22 Clayton Ho
23 Danby Ho
24 Sherard Ho
25 Catesby Ho
26 Petiver Ct
27 Leander Ct
28 Philip Turner Est
29 Grendon Ho
30 Shore Mews
31 Shore Bsns Ctr
32 Kendal Ho
33 Classic Mans
34 Tudor Ho
35 Park Ho
36 Alpine Gr
37 Clarendon Cl
C2 1 Woolpack Ho
2 Elvin Ho
3 Thomas Ho
4 Hockley Ho
5 Retreat Ho
6 Butfield Ho
7 Brooksbank Ho
8 Cresset Ho
9 Brooksbank St
10 Lennox Ho
11 Milborne Ho
12 Collent Ho
13 Middlesex Pl
14 Devonshire Hall
15 Brent Ho
C6 1 Haybridge Ho
2 Framlingham Cl
3 Halesworth Cl
4 Harleston Cl
5 Lowestoft Cl
6 Cecil Ho
7 Clapton Ho
8 Howard Ho
9 Templar Ho
10 Warwick Ho
11 Audley Ho
D1 1 Stuart Ho
2 Gascoyne Ho
3 Chelsfield Point
4 Sundridge Ho
5 Banbury Ho
D2 1 Musgrove Ho

2 Cheyney Ho
3 Haynes Ho
4 Warner Ho
5 Gilby Ho
6 Gadsden Ho
7 Risley Ho
8 Baycliffe Ho
9 Sheldon Ho
10 Offley Ho
11 Latimer Ho
12 Ribstone Ho
13 Salem Ho
14 Fieldwick Ho
15 Lever Ct
16 Matson Ho
17 Wilding Ho
18 Rennell Ho
19 Dycer Ho
20 Granard Ho
21 Whitelock Ho
22 Harrowgate Ho
23 Cass Ho
24 Lofts on the Park
D4 1 Cromford Path
2 Longford Ct
3 Overbury Ho
4 Heanor Ct
5 Wharfedale Ct
6 Ladybower Ct
7 Ilkeston Ct
8 Derby Ct
9 Rushmore Cres
10 Blackwell Cl

75

A2 1 Wick Mews
2 Wellday Ho
3 Selman Ho
4 Vaine Ho
5 Trower Ho
B2 1 Merriam Ave
D6 1 Hammond Ct
2 Sorenson Ct
3 Hinton Ct

76

B4 1 Mulberry Ct
2 Rosewood Ct
3 Gean Ct
4 Blackthorn Ct
5 Cypress Ct
C1 1 Stratford Office Village The
2 Mandrake Way
3 Brimstone Ho
C5 1 Acacia Bsns Ctr
2 Brook Ct
3 Doreen Capstan Ho
4 Peppermint Pl
5 Denmark St
6 Mills Ct
7 Paramount Ho
C6 1 Nansen Ct
2 Mallinson Ct
3 Barbara Ward Ct
4 Noel Baker Ct
5 Corigan Ct
6 Norman Ho
7 Willow Ct
8 Lime Ct

77

A4 1 Bronte Cl
2 Anna Neagle Cl
3 Brownlow Rd
4 Carrington Gdns
5 Vera Lynn Cl

78

C3 1 Stewart Rainbird Ho
2 Rede Ho
3 George Comberton Wlk
C4 1 Annie Taylor Ho
2 Richard Fell Ho
3 Susan Lawrence Ho
4 Walter Hurford Par
5 John Cornwell VC Ho
6 Alfred Prior Ho
C5 1 Charlbury Ho
2 Willis Ho
3 Arthur Walls Ho
4 Blakesley Ho
5 Twelve Acre Ho
6 Beech Ct
7 Golding Ct
D1 1 Aveley Mans
2 Harlow Mans
3 Danbury Mans
4 Mayland Mans
5 Bowers Ho
6 Webber Ho
7 Paulson Ho
8 Collins Ho
9 Jack Cook Ho
D3 1 St Luke's Path
2 Springfield Ct
D5 1 Postway Mews
2 Oakfield Ho

3 Janice Mews
4 Kenneth Moor Rd
5 Clements Ct
6 Handforth Rd
7 Churchill Ho
8 Oakfield Lo
9 Langdale Ct
D6 1 York Ho
2 Opal Mews
3 Florentine Ho
4 Hainault Bridge Par

79

D1 1 Gibbards Cott
2 Edgefield Ct
3 Manor Ct
4 Lambourne Gdns
5 Westone Mans
6 Loveland Mans
7 Edward Mans
8 Clarke Mans
9 Dawson Gdns
10 Sebastian Ct

80

A1 1 Bristol Ho
2 Canterbury Ho
3 Durham Ho
4 Wells Ho
5 Winchester Ho
6 Rosalind Ct
7 Exeter Ho
8 Wheatley Mans
9 Greenwood Mans
10 Plymouth Ho
11 Graham Mans
12 Portia Ct

81

C5 1 Markham Ho
2 Webb Ho
3 Preston Ho
4 Steadman Ho
5 Hyndman Ho
6 Clynes Ho
7 Henderson Ho
8 Blatchford Ho
9 Rogers Ho
10 Sylvia Pankhurst Ho
11 Mary Macarthur Ho
12 Ellen Wilkinson Ho
D2 1 Picador Ho
2 Centurion Ho
3 Louis Ct
4 Watsons Lo
5 Carpenters Ct
6 Bell Ho
7 Rounders Ct
8 Oldmead Ho
9 Jervis Ct
10 Bartletts Ho
11 Royal Par
12 Richardson Gdns

82

D3 1 Marlborough Par
2 Blenheim Par
3 Lea Ct
4 Westbourne Par
5 Whiteleys Par
6 Hillingdon Par
7 New Broadway

84

C4 1 Dilston Cl
2 Wells Ct
3 Willet Cl
4 Merlin Cl
5 Glyndebourne Ct
6 Albury Ct
7 Osterley Ct
8 Hatfield Ct
9 Gayhurst Ct
D4 1 Caravelle Gdns
2 Forman Gr
3 Viscount Gr
4 Tomahawk Gdns
5 Martlet Gr
6 Trident Gdns
7 Latham Ct
8 Jupiter Ct
9 Westland Ct
10 Seasprite Cl
11 Convair Wlk
12 Mayfly Gdns
13 Valiant Ct
14 Woburn Twr
15 Brett Cl
16 Friars Ct
D5 1 Medlar Cl
2 Cranberry Cl
3 Lely Ho
4 Kneller Ho
5 Girtin Ho
6 Cotman Ho
7 Raeburn Ho
8 Gainsborough Twr
9 Stanfield Ho
10 Millais Ct
11 Hunt Ct

85

D1 1 Thurlestone Ct
2 Disley Ct
3 Burgess Ct
4 Selsdon Ct
5 Lytham Ct
6 Abbeydale Ct
7 Cromer Ct
8 Brunel Pl
9 Winford Par
10 Rutherford Twr

86

A1 1 Farnham Ct
2 Gleneagles Twr
3 Birkdale Ct
4 Verulam Ct
5 Hartsbourne Ct
6 Ferndown Ct
7 Deal Ct
8 St David's Ct
9 Portrush Ct
10 Alnmouth Ct
11 Panmure Ct
12 Peterhead Ct
13 Sunningdale Ct
D2 1 Denbigh Ct
2 Devon Ct
3 Dorset Ct
4 Glamorgan Ct
5 Gloucester Ct
6 Hereford Ct
7 Merioneth Ct
8 Oxford Ct
9 Monmouth Ct
10 Paddington Ct
11 Pembroke Ct
12 Chadwick Cl
13 Cotts Cl
D3 1 Berkshire Ct
2 Buckingham Ct
3 Cardigan Ct
4 Carmarthen Ct
5 Cornwall Ct
6 Merlin Ct
7 Osprey Ct
8 Pelham Pl
D5 1 Medway Par
2 Brabstone Ho
3 Cotswold Ct

87

B3 1 Woodbury Ct
2 Edward Ct
3 Park Lo
C1 1 Hurley Ct
2 Amherst Gdns
3 Tudor Ct
4 Hilton Ho
C2 1 Hutton Ct
2 Cain Ct
3 Langdale Ct
4 William Ct
5 Castlebar Ct
6 Warren Ct
7 White Lo
8 Queen's Ct
9 King's Ct
10 Cheriton Cl
11 Stanley Ct
12 Juniper Ct
C3 1 Holtoake Ct
2 Pitshanger Ct
3 Holtoake Ho

88

A4 1 Nelson Ho
2 Gordon Ho
3 Frobisher Ho
4 Wellington Ho
5 Fairfax Ho
A5 1 Carlyon Mans
2 Ainslie Ct
3 Millers Ct
4 Priory Ct
5 Tylers Ct
6 Twyford Ct
7 Rose Ct
8 Laurel Ct
9 Sundew Ct
10 Campion Ct
11 Foxglove Ct
C1 1 Buckingham Ho
2 Chester Ct
3 Devon Ct
4 Essex Ho
5 Fife Ct
6 Gloucester Ct
7 Hereford Ho
8 Inverness Ct
9 Warwick Ho
10 York Ho
11 Suffolk Ho
12 Perth Ct
13 Norfolk Ct
14 Thanet Ct
15 Rutland Ct
16 Oxford Ct

12 Poynter Ct
13 Hogarth Ho
14 Constable Ho
15 Bonnington Ct
16 Romney Ct
17 Landseer Ho

89

A1 1 Avon Ct
2 Bromley Lo
3 Walter Ct
4 Lynton Terr
5 Acton Ct
6 Fells Haugh
7 Springfield Ct
8 Tamarind Ct
9 Lynton Ct
B1 1 Rosebank Gdns
2 Rosebank
3 Edinburgh Ho
4 Western Ct
5 Kilronan
B6 1 Fitzsimmons Ct
2 Bernard Shaw Ho
3 Longlents Ho
4 Mordaunt Ho
5 Wilmers Ct
6 Stonebridge Sh Ctr
D5 1 New Crescent Yd
2 Harlesden Plaza
3 St Josephs Ct

90

D1 1 Kelfield Ct
2 Downing Ho
3 Crosfield Ct
4 Robinson Ho
5 Scampston Mews
6 Girton Villas
7 Ray Ho
8 Walmer Ho
9 Goodrich Ct
10 Arthur Ct
11 Whitstable Ho
12 Kingsnorth Ho
13 Bridge Cl
14 Prospect Ho
15 Whitchurch Ho
16 Blechynden Ho
17 Waynflete Sq
18 Bramley Ho
D4 1 Westfield Ct
2 Tropical Ct
3 Chamberlayne Mans
4 Quadrant The
5 Queens Park Ct
6 Warfield Yd
7 Cherrytree Ho

91

A1 1 Malton Mews
2 Lancaster Lo
3 Manning Ho
4 Galsworthy Ho
5 Hudson Ho
6 Cambourne Mews
7 Camelford Ho
8 Camelford Wlk
9 Talbot Grove Ho
10 Clarendon Wlk
11 Kingsdown Cl
12 Lower Clarendon Wlk
13 Upper Clarendon Wlk
A2 1 Murchison Ho
2 Macaulay Ho
3 Chesterton Ho
4 Chiltern Ho
5 Lionel Ho
6 Watts Ho
7 Wheatstone Ho
8 Telford Ho
9 Golborne Mews
10 Millwood Ho
11 St Columb's Ho
12 Norfolk Mews
A3 1 Sycamore Wlk
2 Westgate Bsns Ctr
3 Buspace Studios
4 Bosworth Ho
5 Golborne Gdns
6 Appleford Ho
7 Adair Twr
8 Gadsden Ho
9 Southam Ho
10 Norman Butler Ho
11 Thompson Ho
12 Wells Ho
13 Paul Ho
14 Olive Blythe Ho
15 Katherine Ho
16 Breakwell Ct
17 Pepler Ho
18 Edward Kennedy Ho
19 Winnington Ho
A4 1 Slomon Ho
2 Stansbury Ho
3 Tilleard Ho
4 Selby Ho
5 Mundy Ho
6 Macfarren Ho
7 Courtville Ho
8 Croft Ho
9 Batten Ho
10 Bantock Ho
11 Banister Ho
12 Symphony Mews
13 Bliss Mews

A5 1 Lancefield Ct
2 Verdi Ho
3 Wornum Ho
B1 1 Tavistock Mews
2 Silvester Ho
3 Melchester
4 Clydesdale Ho
5 Pinehurst Ct
6 Colville Sq Mews
7 Denbigh Ho
8 Golden Cross Mews
B2 1 Blagrove Rd
2 Tavistock Ho
3 Leamington Ho
B3 1 Western Ho
2 Russell's Wharf
B4 1 Boyce Ho
2 Farnaby Ho
3 Danby Ho
4 Purday Ho
5 Naylor Ho
6 St Judes Ho
7 Leeve Ho
8 Longhurst Ho
9 Harrington Ct
10 Mulberry Ct
11 Quilter Ho
12 Romer Ho
13 Kilburn Ho
B5 1 Claremont Ct
2 William Saville Ho
3 Western Ct
4 Bond Ho
5 Crone Ct
6 Wood Ho
7 Winterleys
8 Carlton Ho
9 Fiona Ct
C1 1 Shottsford
2 Tolchurch
3 Casterbridge
4 Sandbourne
5 Anglebury
6 Weatherbury
7 Westbourne Gr Mews
8 Rosehart Mews
9 Viscount Ct
10 Hereford Mans
11 Hereford Mews
C2 1 Ascot Ct
2 Ashgrove Ct
3 Lockbridge Ct
4 Swallow Ct
5 Nightingale Lo
6 Hammond Lo
7 Penfield Lo
8 Harvey Lo
9 Hunter Lo
10 Barnard Lo
11 Falcon Lo
12 Johnson Lo
13 Livingstone Lo
14 Nuffield Lo
15 Finch Lo
16 Polesworth Ho
17 Oversley Ho
18 Derrycombe Ho
19 Buckshead Ho
20 Combe Ho
21 Culham Ho
22 Dainton Ho
23 Devonport Ho
24 Hanwell Ho
25 Truro Ho
26 Sunderland Ho
27 Stonehouse Ho
28 Riverford Ho
29 Portishead Ho
30 Mickleton Ho
31 Keyham Ho
32 Moulsford Ho
33 Shrewsbury Mews
34 St Stephen's Mews
35 Westway Lo
36 Langley Ho
37 Brindley Ho
38 Radway Ho
39 Astley Ho
40 Willow Ct
41 Larch Ct
42 Elm Ct
43 Beech Ct
44 Worcester Ct
45 Union Ct
46 Leicester Ct
47 Kennet Ct
48 Oxford Ct
49 Fazerley Ct
C3 1 Westside Ct
2 Sutherland Ct
3 Fleming Cl
4 Hermes Cl
C4 1 Masefield Ho
2 Austen Ho
3 Fielding Ho
4 Park Bsns Ctr
5 John Ratcliffe Ho
6 Wymering Mans
7 Pavilion Ct
8 Nelson Cl
C5 1 Wells Ct
2 Cambridge Ct
3 Durham Ct
C6 1 Ryde Ho
2 Glengall Pass
3 Leith Yd

4 Daynor Ho
5 Varley Ho
6 Sandby Ho
7 Colas Mews
8 Bishopsdale Ho
9 Lorton Ho
10 Marshwood Ho
11 Ribblesdale Ho
12 Holmesdale Ho
13 Kilburn Vale Est
14 Kilburn Bridge
D1 1 Vera Ct
2 Alexander Mews
3 Gurney Ho
4 Burdett Mews
5 Greville Lo
6 Hatherley Ct
7 Bridge Field Ho
8 Ralph Ct
9 Peters Ct
10 Riven Ct
11 Cervantes Ct
12 Bishops Ct
13 Newbury Ho
14 Marlow Ho
15 Lynton Ho
16 Pembroke Ho
17 Pickering Ho
D3 1 Ellwood Ct
D5 1 Tollgate Ho
2 Regents Plaza
3 Royal Langford
D6 1 Farndale Ho
2 Birchington Ct
3 Greville Mews
4 Goldsmith's Pl
5 Remsted Ho
6 Bradwell Ho
7 Cheshunt Ho
8 Haliwell Ho
9 Braddock Ho
10 Philip Ho
11 Hillsborough Ct
12 Sandbourne
13 Wingreen
14 Toneborough
15 Silverthorn
16 Kington Ho
17 Marrick Ho
18 Broadoak Ho
19 Boadoak Ho

95

C4 1 Pimlico Wlk
2 Aske Ho
3 Hathaway Ho
4 Haberdasher Pl
5 Fairchild Ho
6 Burtt Ho
7 Enfield Cloisters
8 McGregor Ct
9 Royal Oak Ct
10 Hoxton Mkt
11 Bath Pl
12 Chapel Ct
13 Chapel Pl
14 Standard Pl
15 Cleeve Ho
16 Printing House Yd
17 Perseverance Works
18 Crooked Billet Yd
19 Drysdale Ho
20 Castlefrank Ho
21 School App
22 Basing House Yd
23 Mail Coach Yd
C5 1 Bracer Ho
2 Scorton Ho
3 Fern Cl
4 Macbeth Ho
5 Oberon Ho
6 Buckland Ct
7 Crondall Ct
8 Osric Path
9 Caliban Twr
10 Celia Ho
11 Juliet Ho
12 Bacchus Wlk
13 Malcolm Ho
14 Homefield St
15 Crondall Pl
16 Blanca Ho
17 Miranda Ho
18 Falstaff Ho
19 Charmian Ho
20 Myrtle Wlk
21 Arden Ho
22 Sebastian Ho
23 Stanway Ct
24 Jerrold St
25 Rosalind Ho
26 Cordelia Ho
27 Monteagle Ct
28 John Parry Ct
29 James Anderson Ct
30 Ben Jonson Ct
31 Sara Lane Ct
32 Walbrook Ct
C6 1 Portelet Ct
2 Trinity Ct
3 Rozel Ct
4 St Helier Ct
5 Corbiere Ho
6 Kenning Ho
7 Higgins Ho
8 Cavell Ho

9 Girling Ho
10 Fulcher Ho
11 Francis Ho
12 Norris Ho
13 Kempton Ho
14 Nesham Ho
15 Crossbow Ho
16 Catherine Ho
17 Strale Ho
18 Horner Hos
19 Stringer Hos
20 Whitmore Ho
21 Nightingale Ho
22 Fletcher Ho
24 Arrow Ho
25 Archer Ho
26 Meriden Ho
27 Rover Ho
28 Bowyer Ho
29 Longbow Ho
30 Tiller Ho
31 Canalside Studios
32 Bishopgate
33 Holburn
34 Fenchurch
D4 1 Gorsuch Pl
2 Strout's Pl
3 Vaughan Est
4 George Loveless Ho
5 Baroness Rd
6 James Brine Ho
7 Arthur Wade Ho
8 Robert Owen Ho
9 Sivill Ho
10 Georgina Gdns
11 Old Market Sq
12 Cuff Point
13 Bakers Rents
14 Leopold Bldgs
15 Dunmore Point
16 Wingfield Ho
17 Gascoigne Pl
18 Mandela Ho
19 Virginia Rd
20 Briggs Ho
21 Packenham Ho
22 Gowan Ho
23 Chambord Ho
24 Ducal St
25 Strickland Ho
26 Alliston Ho
27 Gibraltar Wlk
28 Equity Sq
29 Shacklewell St
30 Rochelle St
31 Sonning Ho
32 Culham Ho
33 Hurley Ho
34 Palissy St
35 Taplow Ho
36 Chertsey Ho
37 Sunbury Ho
38 Sunbury Workshops
39 Datchett Ho
40 Hocker Ho
41 Coll Sharp Ct
42 Marlow Studio Workshops
43 Marlow Ho
44 Shiplake Ho
45 Wargrave Ho
46 Iffley Ho
D5 1 Queensbridge Ct
2 Godwin Ho
3 Kent Ct
4 Brunswick Ho
5 Weymouth Ct
6 Sovereign Mews
7 Dunloe Ct
8 Cremer Bsns Ctr
9 James Hammett Ho
10 Allgood St
11 Horatio St
12 Cadell Ho
13 Horatio Ho
14 Shipton Ho
D6 1 Hilborough Ct
2 Scriven Ct
3 Livermere Ct
4 Angrave Ct
5 Angrave Pas
6 Benfleet Ct
7 Belford Ho
8 Orme Ho
9 Clemson Ho
10 Longman Ho
11 Lowther Ho
12 Lovelace Ho
13 Harlowe Ho
14 Pamela Ho
15 Samuel Ho
16 Acton Ho
17 Loanda Cl
18 Phoenix Cl
19 Richardson Cl
20 Thrasher Cl
21 Mary Secole Cl
22 Canal Path
23 Pear Tree Cl
24 Hebden Ct
25 Charlton Ct
26 Laburnum Ct
27 Mansfield Ct
28 Garden Pl
29 Amber Wharf

96

A1 1 Manningtree St
2 Whitechurch La
3 Morrison Bldgs
4 Mountford St
5 Mulberry St
6 Weyhill Rd
7 Fordham St
8 Myrdle St
9 Buckle St
10 Plough St
11 Goodman's Stile
12 Mitali Pas
13 Basil Ho
14 Hogarth Ct
15 Ropewalk Gdns
16 Golding Terr
17 Delafield Ho
18 Drewett Ho
19 Harkness Ho
20 Batson Ho
21 Danvers Ho
22 Bicknell Ho
23 Everard Ho
24 Philchurch Pl
25 Hadfield Ho
26 Kindersley Ho
27 Langmore Ho
28 Halliday Ho
29 Berner Terr
30 Victoria Yd
31
A2 1 Arthur Deakin Ho
2 Albert Cotts
3 Victoria Cotts
4 Boden Ho
5 Vollasky Ho
6 Daplyn St
7 Hobsons Pl
8 Hanbury Ho
9 Links Yd
10 Casson Ho
11 Ramar Ho
12 Greatorex Ho
13 Chicksand Ho
14 Spelman Ho
15 Tailworth St
16 Monthorpe Rd
17 Bloomfield Ho
18 Davenant Ho
19 Pauline Ho
20 Tannery Ho
21 Green Dragon Yd
22 King's Arms Ct
23 Fieldgate Mans
24 Mosque Tower
A3 1 Brentworth Ct
2 Kerbela St
3 Fuller Cl
4 Kinsham Ho
5 Menotti St
6 Barwell Ho
7 Grimsby St
8 Eckersley St
9 Stuttle Ho
10 McGlashon Ho
11 Fleet Street Hill
12 Bratley St
13 Weaver Ho
14 John Pritchard Ho
A4 1 Lygon Ho
2 Brabner Ho
3 Delta St
4 Tillet Way
5 Mullet Gdns
6 Elver Gdns
7 Cobden Ho
8 Lampern Sq
9 Jeremy Bentham Ho
10 Waring Ho
11 St James Ct
12 Hague St
13 Westhope Ho
14 Johnson Ho
15 Yates Ho
16 Simmons Ho
17 Swinton Ho
18 Eversley Ho
19 Rapley Ho
20 Dence Ho
21 Dickinson Ho
22 Hutton Ho
23 McKinnon Wood Ho
24 Satchwell Rd
25 Lorden Wlk
A5 1 London Terr
2 Sturdee Ho
3 Maude Ho
4 Haig Ho
5 Jellicoe Ho
6 Ropley St
7 Guinness Trust Bldgs
8 Ion Ct
9 Moye Ct
10 Morrel Ct
11 Courtauld Ho
12 Drummond Ho
13 Atkinson Ho
14 Gurney Ho
15 Halley Ho
16 Goldsmith's Sq
17 Ken Wilson Ho
18 Shahjalal Ho
19 Crofts Ho
20 April Ct

21 Sebright Ho
22 Beechwood Ho
23 Gillman Ho
24 Cheverell Ho
25 Besford Ho
26 Dinmont Ho
27 Wyndham Deedes Ho
28 Sheppard Ho
29 Mary James Ho
30 Hadrian Est
31 Blythendale Ho
32 George Vale Ho
33 Lion Mills
34 Pritchard Ho
A6 1 Broke Wlk
2 Rochemont Wlk
3 Marlborough Ave
4 Rivington Wlk
5 Magnin Cl
6 Gloucester Sq
7 Woolstone Ho
8 Marsworth Ho
9 Cheddington Ho
10 Linslade Ho
11 Cosgrove Ho
12 Blisworth Ho
13 Eleanor Ct
14 Wistow Ho
15 Muscott Ho
16 Boxmoor Ho
17 Linford Ho
18 Pendley Ho
19 North Church Ho
20 Debdale Ho
21 Broadway Market Mews
22 Welshpool Ho
23 Ada Ho
B1 1 Jacob Mans
2 Wicker St
3 Langdale St
4 Walford Ho
5 Welstead Ho
6 Peter Best Ho
7 Sly St
8 Barnett St
9 Kinder St
10 Richard St
11 Sarah Ho
12 Mellish Ho
13 Dickson Ho
14 Joscoyne Ho
15 Bridgen Ho
16 Wilton Ct
17 Silvester Ho
18 Greenwich Ct
19 Tylney Ho
20 Damien Ct
21 Siege Ho
22 Melwood Ho
23 Colstead Ho
24 Hungerford St
25 Burwell Cl
26 Chapman Ho
27 Tarling Ho
28 Sheridan St
29 Brinsley St
30 Dunch St
31 Luke Ho
32 Turnour Ho
33 Norton Ho
B3 1 Rochester Ct
2 Weaver Ct
3 Greenheath Bsns Ctr
4 Glass St
5 Herald St
6 Northesk Ho
7 Codrington Ho
8 Heathpool Ct
9 Mocatta Ho
10 Harvey Ho
11 Blackwood Ho
12 Rutherford Ho
13 Bullen Ho
14 Fremantle Ho
15 Pellew Ho
16 Ashington Ho
17 Dinnington Ho
18 Bartholomew Sq
19 Steeple Ct
20 Orion Ho
21 Fellbrigg St
22 Eagle Ho
23 Sovereign Ho
24 Redmill Ho
25 Berry Ho
26 Grindall Ho
27 Collingwood Ho
B4 1 Charles Dickens Ho
2 Adrian Bolt Ho
3 William Rathbone Ho
4 Southwood Smith Ho
5 Rushmead
6 William Channing Ho
7 John Cartwright Ho
8 Charles Darwin Ho
9 Thomas Burt Ho
10 John Fielden Ho
11 Gwilym Maries Ho
12 Joseph Priestley Ho

96 C2 383

13 Wear Pl
14 John Nettleford Ho
15 Thornaby Ho
16 Stockton Ho
17 Barnard Ho
18 Gainford Ho
19 Stapleton Ho
20 James Middleton Ho
21 Kedleston Wlk
22 Queen Margaret Flats
23 Hollybush Ho
24 Horwood Ho
25 Norden Ho
26 Newcourt St
27 Seabright St
28 Viaduct Pl
29 Sunlight Sq
B5 1 Dinmont St
2 Marian St
3 Claredale Ho
4 Bradley Ho
5 Connett Ho
6 Winkley St
7 Temple Dwellings
8 Argos Ho
9 Helen Ho
10 Lysander Ho
11 Antenor Ho
12 Paris Ho
13 Nestor Ho
14 Hector Ho
15 Ajax Ho
16 Achilles Ho
17 Priam Ho
18 Peabody Est
19 Felix St
20 Cambridge Cres
21 Peterley Bsns Ctr
22 Beckwith Ho
23 Parminter Ind Est
24 Ted Roberts Ho
25 Cambridge Ct
26 West St
27 Millennium Pl
28 William Caslon Ho
29 Hugh Platt Ho
30 Mayfield Ho
31 Apollo Ho
32 Tanners Yd
33 Teesdale Yd
B6 1 Welshpool St
2 Broadway Ho
3 Regents Wharf
4 London Wharf
5 Warburton Ho
6 Warburton St
7 Triangle Rd
8 Warburton Rd
9 Williams Ho
10 Booth Cl
11 Albert Cl
12 King Edward Mans
13 Victoria Bldgs
C1 1 Woollon Ho
2 Dundalk Ho
3 Anne Goodman Ho
4 Newbold Cotts
5 Kerry Ho
6 Zion Ho
7 Longford Ho
8 Bromehead St
9 Athlone Ho
10 Jubilee Mans
11 Harriott Ho
12 Brayford Sq
13 Clearbrook Way
14 Rochelle Ct
15 Winterton Ho
16 Sheridan Ho
17 Brinsley Ho
18 Dean Ho
19 Foley Ho
20 Robert Sutton Ho
21 Montpelier Pl
22 Masters Lo
23 Steel's La
24 Swift Ho
25 Glastonbury Pl
C2 1 Fulneck
2 Gracehill
3 Ockbrook
4 Fairfield
5 Dunstan Hos
6 Cressy Ct
7 Cressy Hos
8 Callahan Cotts
9 Wexford Ho
10 Sandhurst Ho
11 Colverson Ho
12 Beckett Ho
13 Jarman Ho
14 Wingrad Ho
15 Armsby Ho
16 Miranda Cl
17 Drake Ho
18 Louise De Marillac Ho
19 Sambrook Ho
20 St Vincent De Paul Ho

21 Jean Pardies Ho
22 Clichy Ho
23 Le Moal Ho
24 Odette Duval Ho
25 Dagobert Ho
26 Charles Auffray Ho
27 Boisseau Ho
28 Paymal Ho
C3 1 William's Bldgs
2 Donegal Ho
3 Frederick Charrington Ho
4 Wickford Ho
5 Braintree Ho
6 Doveton Ho
7 Doveton St
8 Cephas Ho
9 Sceptre Ho
10 Bancroft Ho
11 Stothard St
12 Redclyf Ho
13 Winkworth Cotts
14 Ryder Ho
15 Hadleigh Ho
16 Hadleigh Cl
17 Amiel St
18 Stathard Ho
19 Barbanel Ho
20 Colebert Ho
21 Kenton Ho
22 Ibbott St
23 Stannard Cotts
24 Rennie Cotts
25 Rickman St
26 Rickman Ho
27 Pemell Cl
28 Pemell Ho
29 Leatherdale St
30 Gouldman Ho
31 Lamplighter Cl
32 Hamilton Lo
33 Cleveland Gr
34 Montgomery Lo
35 Bardsey Pl
36 Cromwell Lo
37 Colin Winter Ho
38 Allport Mews
C4 1 Mulberry Ho
2 Gretton Ho
3 Merceron Ho
4 Montfort Ho
5 Westbrook Ho
6 Sugar Loaf Wlk
7 Museum Ho
8 Burnham Est
9 Globe Terr
10 Moravian St
11 Shepton Hos
12 Mendip Hos
13 Academy Ct
14 Pepys Ho
15 Swinburne Ho
16 Moore Ho
17 Morris Ho
18 Burns Ho
19 Milton Ho
20 Whitman Ho
21 Shelley Ho
22 Keats Ho
23 Dawson Ho
24 Bradbeer Ho
25 Forber Ho
26 Hughes Ho
27 Silvester Ho
28 Rogers Est
29 Pavan Ct
30 Stafford Cripps Ho
31 Sidney Godley (VC) Ho
32 Butler Ho
33 Butler St
34 Thorne Ho
35 Bevin Ho
36 Tuscan Ho
C5 1 Evesham Ho
2 James Campbell Ho
3 Thomas Hollywood Ho
4 James Docherty Ho
5 Ebenezer Mussel Ho
6 Jameson Ct
7 Edinburgh Cl
8 Roger Dowley Ct
9 Sherbrooke Ho
10 Calcraft Ho
11 Burrard Ho
12 Dundas Ho
14 Barnes Ho
15 Paget Ho
17 Maitland Ho
18 Chesil Ct
19 Reynolds Ho
20 Cleland Ho
21 Goodrich Ho
22 Rosebery Ho
23 Sankey Ho
24 Cyprus Pl
25 Royston St
26 Stainsbury St
27 Hunslett St
28 Baildon
29 Brockweir
30 Tytherton
31 Malmesbury
32 Kingswood
33 Colville Ho
C6 1 Halkett Ho
4 Christ Church Sq
5 Swingfield Ho
6 Greenham Ho
7 Dinmore Ho
8 Anstey Ho
9 Weston Ho
10 Carbroke Ho
16 Bluebell Cl
17 Cherry Tree Cl
19 Georgian Ct
20 Park Cl
21 Regency Ct
22 Norris Ho
D1 1 Pattison Ho
2 St Thomas Ho
3 Arbour Ho
4 Bladen Ho
5 Antill Terr
6 Billing Ho
7 Dowson Ho
8 Lipton Rd
9 Chalkwell Ho
10 Corringham Ho
11 Ogilvie Ho
12 Edward Mann Cl
13 Lighterman Mews
D2 1 Roland Mews
2 Morecambe Cl
3 Stepney Green Ct
4 Milrood Ho
5 Panama Ho
6 Galway Ho
7 Caspian Ho
8 Darien Ho
9 Rigo Ho
10 Flores Ho
11 Taranto Ho
12 Aden Ho
13 Frances Grey Ho
14 Master's St
16 Diggon St
D3 1 Raynham Ho
2 Pat Shaw Ho
3 Colmar Cl
4 Withy Ho
5 Stocks Ct
6 Downey Ho
7 Bay Ct
8 Sligo Ho
9 Pegasus Ho
10 Barents Ho
11 Biscay Ho
12 Solway Ho
13 Bantry Ho
14 Aral Ho
15 Pacific Ho
16 Magellan Ho
17 Levant Ho
18 Adriatic Ho
19 Genoa Ho
20 Hawke Ho
21 Palliser Ho
22 Ionian Ho
23 Weddell Ho
D4 1 Stubbs Ho
2 Holman Ho
3 Clynes Ho
4 Windsor Ho
5 Gilbert Ho
6 Chater Ho
7 Ellen Wilkinson Ho
8 George Belt Ho
9 Ayrton Gould Ho
10 O'Brian Ho
11 Sulkin Ho
12 Jenkinson Ho
13 Bullards Pl
14 Sylvia Pankhurst Ho
15 Mary Macarthur Ho
16 Trevelyan Ho
17 Wedgwood Ho
18 Pemberton Ct
20 Walter Besant Ho
21 Barber Beaumont Ho
22 Brancaster Ho
23 Litcham Ho
D5 1 Kemp Ho
2 Piggott Ho
3 Mark Ho
4 Sidney Ho
5 Pomeroy Ho
6 Puteaux Ho
7 Doric Ho
8 Modling Ho
9 Longman Ho
10 Ames Ho
11 Alzette Ho
12 Offenbach Ho
13 Tate Ho
14 Norton Ho
15 St Gilles Ho
16 Harold Ho
17 Velletri Ho
18 Bridge Wharf
19 Gathorne St
20 Bow Brook The
22 Palmerston Ct
23 Peach Walk Mews
24 Lakeview
25 Caesar Ct

97

A1 1 Coltman Ho
2 Repton Ho
3 Causton Cotts
9 Darnley Ho
10 Mercer's Cotts
11 Troon Ho
12 Ratcliffe Ho
13 Wakeling St
14 York Sq
15 Anglia Ho
16 Cambria Ho
17 Caledonia Ho
18 Ratcliffe La
19 Bekesbourne St
20 John Scurr Ho
21 Regents Canal Ho
22 Basin App
23 Powlesland Ct
A2 1 Waley St
2 Edith Ramsay Ho
3 Andaman Ho
4 Atlantic Ho
5 Pevensey Ho
6 Solent Ho
7 Lorne Ho
8 Cromarty Ho
12 Greaves Cotts
13 Donaghue Cotts
14 Ames Cotts
A3 1 Formosa Ho
2 Galveston Ho
3 Arabian Ho
4 Greenland Ho
5 Coral Ho
6 Anson Ho
7 Lindop Ho
8 Moray Ho
9 Azov Ho
10 Sandalwood Cl
11 Broadford Ho
A5 1 Bunsen Ho
2 Bunsen St
3 Beatrice Webb Ho
4 Margaret Bondfield Ho
5 Wilmer Ho
6 Sandall Ho
7 Butley Ct
8 Josseline Ct
9 Dalton Ho
10 Brine Ho
11 Ford Cl
12 Viking Cl
13 Stanfield Rd
14 Ruth Ct
15 School Bell Cloisters
16 Schoolbell Mews
17 Medhurst Cl
18 Olga St
19 Conyer St
20 Diamond Ho
21 Daring Ho
22 Crane Ho
23 Exmoor Ho
24 Grenville Ho
25 Hyperion Ho
26 Sturdy Ho
27 Wren Ho
28 Ardent Ho
29 Senators Lo
30 Hooke Ho
31 Mohawk Ho
32 Ivanhoe Ho
33 Medway Mews
B1 1 Dora Ho
2 Flansham Ho
3 Gatwick Ho
4 Ashpark Ho
5 Newdigate Ho
6 Salmon St
7 Midhurst Ho
8 Redbourne Ho
8 Southwater Cl
9 Aithan Ho
10 Britley Ho
11 Cheadle Ho
12 Elland Ho
13 Butler Ho
14 Fitzroy Ho
15 Leybourne Ho
B2 1 Wearmouth Ho
2 Elmslie Point
3 Grindley Ho
4 Stileman Ho
5 Baythorne St
6 Wilcox Ho
7 Robeson St
8 Couzens Ho
10 Perley Ho
11 Whytlaw Ho
12 Printon Ho
13 Printons Ho
14 Bowry Ho
15 Booker Cl
16 Tunley Gn
17 Callingham Cl
18 Tasker Ho
B4 1 Trellis Sq
2 Sheffield Sq
3 Howcroft Ho
4 Astra Ho
6 Byas Ho
7 George Lansbury Ho
8 Regal Pl
9 Coborn Mews
10 Cavendish Terr
11 Buttermere Ho
12 Tracy Ho
12 Hanover Pl
13 Coniston Ho
14 St Clair Ho
15 Verity Ho
16 Icarus Ho
17 Whippingham Ho
18 Winchester Ho
19 Hamilton Ho
20 Longthorne Ho
B5 1 Roman Square Mkt
2 John Bond Ho
3 McKenna Ho
4 Dennis Ho
5 McBride Ho
6 Libra Rd
7 Dave Adams Ho
8 Tay Ho
9 Sleat Ho
10 Ewart Pl
11 Brodick Ho
12 Lunan Ho
13 Mull Ho
14 Sinclairs Ho
15 Driftway Ho
16 Clayhall Ct
17 Berebinder Ho
18 Stavers Ho
19 Barford Ho
20 Partridge Ho
21 Gosford Ho
22 Gullane Ho
23 Cruden Ho
24 Anglo Rd
25 Dornoch Ho
26 Dunnet Ho
27 Enard Ho
28 Fraserburgh Ho
29 Forth Ho
30 Ordell Ct
31 William Pl
B6 1 Hampstead Wlk
2 Waverton Ho
3 Elton Ho
4 Locton Gn
5 Birtwhistle Ho
6 Clare Ho
7 Magpie Ho
8 Atkins Ct
9 Tait Ct
10 Ranwell Ho
11 Ranwell Cl
12 Tufnell Ct
13 Pulteney Cl
14 Vic Johnson Ho
C1 1 Landin Ho
2 Charlesworth Ho
3 Gurdon Ho
4 Trendell Ho
5 Menteath Ho
6 Minchin Ho
7 Donne Ho
8 Denison Ho
9 Anglesey Ho
10 Gough Wlk
11 Baring Ho
12 Hopkins Ho
13 Granville Ho
14 Gladstone Ho
15 Russell Ho
16 Pusey Ho
17 Overstone Ho
18 Stanley Ho
19 Old School Sq
C2 1 Bredel Ho
2 Linton Ho
3 Matthews Ho
4 Woodcock Ho
5 Limborough Ho
6 Maydwell Ho
7 Underhill Ho
8 Meyrick Ho
9 Ambrose Ho
10 Carpenter Ho
11 Robinson Ho
12 Bramble Ho
13 Bilberry Ho
14 Bracken Ho
15 Berberis Ho
16 Busbridge Ho
17 Metropolitan Cl
18 Invicta Cl
19 Bellmaker Ct
C3 1 Fairmont Ho
2 Healy Ho
3 Zodiac Ho
4 Buick Ho
5 Consul Ho
6 Bentley Ho
7 Cresta Ho
8 Daimler Ho
9 Riley Ho
10 Jensen Ho
11 Lagonda Ho
12 Ireton St
13 Navenby Wlk
14 Burwell Wlk
15 Leadenham Ct
16 Sleaford Ho
C4 1 Jarret Ho
2 Marsalis Ho
3 Lovette Ho
4 Drapers Almhouses
5 Mallard Point
6 Creswick Wlk
7 Bevin Ho
8 Huggins Ho
9 Williams Ho
10 Harris Ho
11 Marina Ct
12 Electric Ho
13 Matching Ct
14 Wellington Bldgs
15 Grafton Ho
16 Columbia Ho
17 Berkeley Ho
D1 1 Colebrook Ho
2 Essex Ho
3 Salisbury Ho
4 Maidstone Ho
5 Osterley Ho
6 Norwich Ho
7 Clarissa Ho
8 Elgin Ho
9 Shaftesbury Lo
10 Shepherd Ho
11 Jeremiah St
12 Elizabeth Cl
13 Chilcot Cl
14 Fitzgerald Ho
15 Vesey Path
16 Ennis Ho
17 Kilmore Ho
D2 1 Sumner Ho
2 Irvine Ho
3 David Ho
4 Brushwood Ho
5 Limehouse Cut
6 Colmans Wharf
7 Foundary Ho
8 Radford Ho
D3 1 Broxbourne Ho
2 Roxford Ho
3 Biscott Ho
4 Stanborough Ho
5 Hillstone Ct
D4 1 Bradley Ho
2 Prioress Ho
3 Alton Ho
4 Foxley Ho
5 Munden Ho
6 Canterbury Ho
7 Corbin Ho
8 Barton Ho
9 Jolles Ho
10 Rudstone Ho
11 Baxter Ho
12 Baker Ho
13 Insley Ho
14 Hardwicke Ho
15 Glebe Terr
16 Priory St
17 Sadler Ho
18 Ballinger Point
19 Henshall Point
20 Dorrington Point
21 Warren Ho
22 Fairlie Ct
23 Regent Sq
24 Hackworth Point
25 Priestman Point
26 Wingate Ho
27 Nethercott Ho
28 Thelbridge Ho
29 Bowden Ho
30 Kerscott Ho
31 Southcott Ho
32 Birchdown Ho
33 Upcott Ho
34 Langmead Ho
35 Limscott Ho
36 Northleigh Ho
37 Huntshaw Ho
38 Chagford Ho
39 Ashcombe Ho
40 Shillingford Ho
41 Patrick Connolly Gdns
42 Lester Ct
43 Franklin St
44 Taft Way
45 Washington Cl
46 Elizabeth Ho
47 William Guy Gdns
48 Denbury Ho
49 Holsworthy Ho

98

A1 1 Langdon Ho
2 Balfron Twr
3 Tabard Ct
4 Delta Bldg
5 Kilbrennan Ho
6 Thistle Ho
7 Heather Ho
8 Tartan Ho
9 Trident Ho
A2 1 Mills Gr
3 Duncan Ct
B1 1 Lansbury Gdns
2 Thesus Ho
2 Theseus Ho
3 Adams Ho
4 Jones Ho
5 Sam March Ho
6 Arapiles Ho
7 Athenia Ho
8 Jervis Bay Ho
9 Helen Mackay Ho
10 Gaze Ho
11 Ritchie Ho
12 Circle Ho
13 Dunkeld Ho
14 Braithwaite Ho
15 Rosemary Dr
16 Sorrel La
17 East India Dock Road Tunnel
C6 1 Barnby Sq
2 Barnby St
3 Brassett Point
4 David Lee Point
5 Worthing Cl
6 Bexhill Wlk
7 Old Borrowfield
8 Elmgreen Cl
9 Stafford Morris Ho
10 Nina Mackay Cl
11 Lime Wlk
D1 1 Newton Point
2 Sparke Terr
3 Montesquieu Terr
4 Crawford Point
5 Rathbone Ho
6 George St
7 Emily St
8 Fendt Cl
9 Sabbarton St
D2 1 Radley Terr
2 Rathbone Mkt
3 Thomas North Terr
4 Bernard Cassidy St
5 Mary St
6 Hughes Terr
7 Swanscombe Point
8 Rawlinson Point
9 Kennedy Cox Ho
10 Cooper St
D6 1 Harris Cotts
2 Moorey Cl
3 Euro Bsns Ctr
4 Ladywell St
5 Caistor Ho
6 Redfern Ho

99

A2 1 Odeon Ct
2 Edward Ct
3 Newhaven La
4 Ravenscroft Cl
5 Douglas Rd
6 Ferrier Point
7 Harvey Point
8 Wood Point
9 Trinity St
10 Pattinson Point
11 Clinch Ct
12 Mint Bsns Pk
A3 1 Webb Gdns
2 Eric Shipman Terr
3 Warmington St
4 Jellicoe Rd
5 Frank St
6 Seaton Cl
7 Tabernacle Ave
8 Upland Rd
9 Clove St
10 Edward St
A4 1 Bob Anker Cl
2 Lea Ct
3 Third Ave
4 Suffolk Rd
A5 1 Lettsom Wlk
2 Ashburton Terr
3 Grasmere Rd
4 Dimsdale Wlk
5 Rawstone Wlk
6 Scott Ho
7 Willett Ho
8 James Cl
9 Cordwainers Wlk
10 Victoria Point
11 Settle Point
12 Middle Rd
A6 1 Royston Ct
B4 1 Barbers Alley
2 Grengate Lo
3 Augurs La
4 Surrey St
5 Dongola Rd W
6 Bemersyde Point
7 Rowntree Clifford Cl
C5 1 Wellby Ct
2 Bishop Wilfred Wood Ct
3 Castle Point
4 Moat Dr
C6 1 Queen's Mkt
2 Tolpuddle Ave
3 Crown Mews
4 Lilac Ct
5 Hamara Ghar
6 Greenleaf Rd
7 Massey Ct
8 Florence Rd
9 Sissulu Ct
10 Austin Ct
D2 1 Partridge Cl
2 Vanbrugh Cl
3 Meadowsweet Cl
4 St Michaels Cl
5 Long Mark Rd
6 Congreve Wlk
D5 1 Foxcombe Cl
2 Rochford Cl
3 Kylemore Cl
4 Stondon Wlk
5 Imperial Mews
6 Dominica Cl
D6 1 Oldegate Ho
2 Gaitskell Ho
3 Cabot Way

100

A1 1 Hadleigh Wlk
2 Hawksmoor Cl
3 Fraser Cl
4 Moncrieff Cl
5 Burlington Cl
6 Dundonald Cl
7 Oakley Cl
8 Ashwell Cl
A2 1 Orchid Cl
2 Bellflower Cl
3 Partridge Sq
4 Larkspur Cl
5 Lobelia Cl
6 Stonechat Sq
7 Wintergreen Cl
8 Garnet Wlk
9 Mavis Wlk
10 Beacons Cl
11 Abbess Cl
12 Elmley Cl
13 Chetwood Wlk
14 Selby Cl
15 Denny Cl
16 Woodhatch Cl
A6 1 Oakwood Ct
2 Harrow Rd
3 Ray Massey Way
4 Madge Gill Way
5 Pilgrims Way
B1 1 Bowers Wlk
2 Barton Cl
3 Clayton Cl
4 Dixon Cl
5 Gautrey Sq
6 Wakerly Cl
7 Canterbury Cl
8 Goose Sq
9 Coventry Cl
10 Butterfield Sq
11 Winchester Cl
B2 1 Fleetwood Ct
2 Lymington Cl
3 Holyhead Cl
4 Bondfield Rd
5 Tulip Cl
6 Ambrose Cl
7 Sage Cl
8 Lindwood Cl
D1 1 Weymouth Ct
2 Founder Cl
3 Admirals Ct

101

A6 1 Wellington St
2 St Ann's Rd
3 Bamber Ho
B6 1 Jarvis Cl
2 Mayflower Ho
3 Westbury Ct
4 Millicent Preston Ho
5 Louise Graham Ho
6 Grange Ho
7 Basing Ho
8 Barnes Ho
9 Lexham Ho
10 Ripple Ct
11 Waldegrave Ct
12 Howard Ct

104

A6 1 Milburn Dr
2 Cousins Cl
3 Leacroft Cl

108

C5 1 Marlow Ct
2 Andrews Ct
3 Vine Cotts
4 Benjamin Ct
5 Broadway Bldgs
D5 1 Silverdale Cl
2 Burdett Cl
3 Hopefield
4 Maunder Rd

109

A5 1 Glastonbury Ct
2 Evesham Ct
3 Lacock Ct
4 Wigmore Ct
5 Melrose Ct
6 Brownlow Rd
7 Chignell Pl
8 Shirley Ct
9 Trojan Ct
10 Hatfield Rd
C6 1 Abbey Lo
2 Yew Tree Grange
3 Abinger Ct

110

A1 **1** Burford Ho
2 Hope Cl
3 Centaur Ct
4 Phoenix Ct
A6 **1** Watermans Mews
2 Hills Mews
3 Grosvenor Ct
4 Elton Lo
5 Hambledon Ct
C1 **1** Surrey Cres
2 Forbes Ho
3 Haining Cl
4 Melville Ct
5 London Stile
6 Stile Hall Par
7 Priory Lo
8 Kew Bridge Ct
9 Meadowcroft
10 St James Ct
11 Rivers Ho
C5 **1** Grosvenor Par
2 Oakfield Ct
3 Hart Grove Ct
4 Grosvenor Ct
D1 **1** Churchdale Ct
2 Cromwell Cl
3 Cambridge Rd S
4 Oxbridge Ct
5 Tomlinson Cl
6 Gunnersbury Mews
7 Grange The
8 Gunnersbury Cl
D4 **1** Cheltenham Pl
2 Beaumaris Twr
3 Arundel Ho
4 Pevensey Ct
5 Jerome Twr
6 Anstey Ct
7 Bennett Ct
8 Gunnersbury Ct
D5 **1** Lantry Ct
2 Rosemount Ct
3 Moreton Twr
4 Acton Central Ind Est
5 Rufford Twr
6 Narrow St
7 Mount Pl
8 Sidney Miller Ct
9 Mill Hill Terr
10 Mill Hill Gr

111

A1 **1** Arlington Park Mans
2 Sandown Ho
3 Goodwood Ho
4 Windsor Ho
5 Lingfield Ho
6 Ascot Ho
7 Watchfield Ct
8 Belgrave Ct
9 Beverley Ct
10 Beaumont Ct
11 Harvard Rd
12 Troubridge Ct
A2 **1** Chiswick Green Studios
2 Bell Ind Est
3 Fairlawn Ct
4 Dukes Gate
5 Dewsbury Ct
6 Chiswick Terr
A3 **1** Blackmore Twr
2 Bollo Ct
3 Kipling Twr
4 Lawrence Ct
5 Maugham Ct
6 Reade Ct
7 Woolf Ct
8 Shaw Ct
9 Verne Ct
10 Wodehouse Ct
11 Greenock Rd
12 Garden Ct
13 Barons Gate
14 Cleveland Rd
15 Chapter Cl
16 Carver Cl
17 Beauchamp Cl
18 Holmes Ct
A4 **1** Belgrave Cl
2 Buckland Wlk
3 Frampton Ct
4 Telfer Cl
5 Harlech Twr
6 Corfe Twr
7 Barwick Ho
8 Charles Hocking Ho
9 Sunninghill Ct
10 Salisbury St
11 Jameson Pl
A5 **1** Rectory Rd
2 Derwentwater Mans
3 Market Pl
4 Hooper's Mews
5 Cromwell Pl
6 Locarno Rd
7 Edgecote Cl
8 Harleyford Manor
9 Coopers Lo
B1 **1** Chatsworth Lo
2 Prospect Pl

---

3 Townhall Ave
4 Devonhurst Pl
5 Heathfield Ct
6 Horticultural Pl
7 Merlin Ho
8 Garth Rd
C1 **1** Glebe Cl
2 Devonshire Mews
3 Binns Terr
4 Ingress St
5 Swanscombe Rd
6 Brackley Terr
7 Stephen Fox Ho
8 Manor Gdns
9 Coram Ho
10 Flaxman Ho
11 Thorneycroft Ho
12 Thornhill Ho
13 Kent Ho
14 Oldfield Ho
C2 **1** Chestnut Ho
2 Bedford Ho
3 Bedford Cnr
4 Sydney Ho
5 Bedford Park Cnr
6 Priory Gdns
7 Windmill Alley
8 Castle Pl
9 Jonathan Ct
10 Windmill Pas
11 Chardin Rd
12 Gable Ho
C3 **1** Fleet Ct
2 Ember Ct
3 Emlyn Gdns
4 Clone Ct
5 Brent Ct
6 Abbey Ct
7 Ormsby Lo
8 St Catherine's Ct
C4 **1** Longford Ct
2 Mole Ct
3 Lea Ct
4 Wandle Ct
5 Beverley Ct
6 Roding Ct
7 Crane Ct
D1 **1** Miller's Ct
2 British Grove Pas
3 British Grove S
4 Beresford Rd
5 North Eyot Gdns
D2 **1** Flanders Mans
2 Stamford Brook Mans
3 Linkenholt Mans
4 Prebend Mans
5 Middlesex Ct
D3 **1** Stamford Brook Gdns
2 Hauteville Court Gdns
3 Ranelagh Gdns

112

A2 **1** Hamlet Ct
2 Derwent Ct
3 Westcroft Ct
4 Black Lion Mews
5 St Peter's Villas
6 Standish Ho
7 Chambon Pl
8 Court Mans
A4 **1** Victoria Ho
2 Lycett Pl
3 Kylemore Ct
4 Alexandra Ct
5 Lytten Ct
6 Becklow Mews
7 Northcroft Ct
8 Bailey Ct
9 Spring Cott
10 Landor Wlk
11 Laurence Mews
12 Hadyn Park Ct
13 Askew Mans
B2 **1** Albion Gdns
2 Flora Gdns
3 Lamington St
4 Felgate Mews
5 Galena Ho
6 Albion Mews
7 Albion Ct
8 King Street Cloisters
9 Dimes Pl
10 Clarence Ct
11 Hampshire Hog La
12 Marryat Ct
B4 **1** Westbush Ct
2 Goldhawk Mews
3 Sycamore Ho
4 Shackleton Ct
5 Drake Ct
6 Scotts Ct
B6 **1** Abercrombie Ho
2 Bathurst Ho
3 Brisbane Ho
4 Bentinck Ho
5 Ellenborough Ho
6 Lawrence Cl
7 Mackenzie Cl
8 Carteret Ho
9 Calvert Ho
10 Winthrop Ho
11 Auckland Ho
12 Blaxland Ho

---

13 Havelock Cl
14 Hargraves Ho
15 Hudson Ct
16 Phipps Ho
17 Lawson Ho
18 Hastings Ho
19 Wolfe Ho
20 Malabar Ct
21 White City Est
22 Commonwealth Ave
23 Charnock Ho
24 Canning Ho
25 Cornwallis Ho
26 Champlain Ho
27 Grey Ho
28 Durban Ho
29 Baird Ho
30 Campbell Ho
31 Mitchell Ho
32 Denham Ho
33 Mackay Ho
34 Evans Ho
35 Daws Ho
36 Mandela Cl
C1 **1** Bridge Avenue Mans
2 Bridgeview
3 College Ct
4 Beatrice Ho
5 Amelia Ho
6 Edith Ho
7 Joanna Ho
8 Mary Ho
9 Adela Ho
10 Sophia Ho
11 Henrietta Ho
12 Charlotte Ho
13 Alexandra Ho
14 Bath Pl
15 Elizabeth Ho
16 Margaret Ho
17 Peabody Est
18 Eleanor Ho
19 Isabella Ho
20 Caroline Ho
21 Chancellors Wharf
22 Sussex Pl
C2 **1** Phoenix Lodge Mans
2 Samuel's Cl
3 Broadway Arc
4 Brook Ho
5 Hammersmith Broadway
C4 **1** Verulam Ho
2 Grove Mans
3 Frobisher Ct
4 Library Mans
5 Pennard Mans
6 Lanark Mans
7 Kerrington Ct
8 Granville Mans
9 Romney Ct
10 Rayner Ct
11 Sulgrave Gdns
12 Bamborough Gdns
D3 **1** Grosvenor Residences
2 Blythe Mews
3 Burnand Ho
4 Bradford Ho
5 Springvale Terr
6 Ceylon Rd
7 Walpole Ct
8 Bronte Ct
9 Boswell Ct
10 Souldern Rd
11 Brook Green Flats
12 Haarlem Rd
13 Stafford Mans
14 Lionel Mans
D4 **1** Vanderbilt Villas
2 Bodington Ct
3 Kingham Cl
4 Clearwater Terr
5 Lorne Gdns
6 Cameret Ct
7 Bush Ct
8 Shepherds Ct
9 Rockley Ct
10 Grampians The
11 Charcroft Ct
12 Addison Park Mans
13 Sinclair Mans
D5 **1** St Katherine's Wlk
2 Dorrit Ho
3 Pickwick Ho
4 Dombey Ho
5 Caranday Villas
6 Mortimer Ho
7 Nickleby Ho
8 Stebbing Ho
9 Boxmoor Ho
10 Poynter Ho
11 Swanscombe Ho
12 Darnley Terr
13 Norland Ho
14 Hume Ho
D6 **1** Frinstead Ho
2 Hurstway Wlk
3 Testerton Wlk
4 Grenfell Wlk
5 Grenfell Twr
6 Barandon Wlk

---

7 Treadgold Ho
8 St Clements Ho
9 Willow Way
10 Florence Ho
11 Dora Ho
12 Carton Ho
13 Agnes Ho
14 Marley Ho
15 Waynflete Sq

118

A1 **1** Alison Ct
2 West Point
3 Centre Point
4 East Point
5 Proctor Ho
6 Tovy Ho
7 Brettinghurst
8 Colechurch Ho
9 Harman Cl
10 Avondale Ho
11 Lanark Ho
12 George Elliston Ho
13 Eric Wilkins Ho
14 Archers Lo
15 Culloden Cl
16 Fallow Ct
17 Fern Wlk
18 Ivy Ct
19 Winter Lo
A2 **1** Cadbury Way
2 Robert Bell Ho
3 Robert Jones Ho
4 William Rushbrooke Ho
5 Helen Taylor Ho
6 Peter Hills Ho
7 Charles Mackenzie Ho
8 Drappers Way
9 Abbey Gdns
10 Maria Cl
11 Windmill Cl
12 Townsend Ho
13 Mason Ho
14 Langdon Way
15 Hannah Mary Way
16 Kotree Way
17 Whittaker Way
A3 **1** Rudge Ho
2 Spenlow Ho
3 Darnay Ho
4 Carton Ho
5 Giles Ho
6 Bowley Ho
7 Casby Ho
8 Sun Pas
9 Ness St
10 Voyager Bsns Est
11 Dockley Road Ind Est
12 Spa Ct
13 Discovery Bsns Pk
14 Priter Road Hostel
15 Salisbury Ct
16 William Ellis Way
17 John McKenna Wlk
18 Toussaint Wlk
19 Gillison Wlk
20 Bromfield Ct
21 Ben Smith Way
22 Major Rd
23 Old Jamaica Bsns Est
A4 **1** Providence Twr
2 Springalls Wharf
3 St Saviours Ho
4 Providence Sq
5 Farthing Alley
6 Peter Butler Ho
7 Brownlow Ho
8 Fleming Ho
9 Dombey Ho
10 Copperfield Ho
11 Tapley Ho
12 Parkers Row
13 Wade Ho
14 Bardell Ho
15 Nickleby Ho
16 John Felton Rd
17 Pickwick Ho
18 Oliver Ho
19 Weller Ho
20 Tupman Ho
21 Haredale Ho
22 Havisham Ho
23 Micawber Ho
24 Wrayburn Ho
25 Dartle Ct
26 Burnaby Ct
27 Waterside Cl
28 Wickfield Ho
29 Fountain Ho
30 Fountain Green Sq
A5 **1** Trade Winds Ct
2 Spice Ct
3 Leeward Ct
4 Bridgeport Pl
5 Tamarind Yd
6 Cope Yd
7 Nightingale Ho
8 St Anthony's Cl
9 Stockholm Way
10 Miah Terr

---

11 Seville Ho
12 Douthwaite Sq
13 Codling Cl
14 Hermitage Ct
15 Capital Wharf
16 Cinnabar Wharf East
17 Cinnabar Wharf Central
18 Cinnabar Wharf West
19 Halcyon Wharf
A6 **1** Conant Mews
2 Hanson Ho
3 Victoria Ct
4 Swan Pas
5 Royal Mint Pl
6 Flank St
7 Ensign Ct
8 Sapphire Ct
9 George Leybourne Ho
10 Fletcher St
11 Wellclose St
12 Noble Ho
13 Hatton Ho
14 Shearsmith Ho
15 Breezer's Ct
16 Pennington Ct
17 Onedin Point
18 Liberty Pl
B1 **1** Newton Ho
2 Toulouse Ct
3 Lowry Ct
4 Barry Ho
5 Lewis Ct
6 Gainsborough Ct
7 Renoir Ct
8 Blake Ct
9 Raphael Ct
10 Rembrandt Ct
11 Constable Ct
12 Da Vinci Ct
13 Gaugin Ct
14 Michelangelo Ct
15 Monet Ct
16 Weald Cl
17 Jasmin Lo
18 Birchmere Lo
19 Weybridge Ct
20 Florence Ho
21 Gleneagles Cl
22 Sunningdale Cl
23 Muirfield Cl
24 Turnberry Cl
25 St Andrews Cl
26 Kingsdown Cl
27 St Davids Cl
28 Galway Cl
29 Edenbridge Cl
30 Birkdale Cl
31 Tralee Ct
32 Woburn Ct
33 Belfry Cl
34 Troon Ct
35 Holywell Cl
B2 **1** Market Pl
2 Trappes Ho
3 Thurland Ho
4 Ramsfort Ho
5 Hambley Ho
6 Holford Ho
7 Pope Ho
8 Southwell Ho
9 Mortain Ho
10 Radcliffe Ho
11 Southwark Park Est
12 Galleywall Road Trad Est
13 Trevithick Ho
14 Barlow Ho
15 Donkin Ho
16 Landmann Ho
17 Fitzmaurice Ho
18 Dodd Ho
B3 **1** Perryn Rd
2 Chalfont Ho
3 Prestwood Ho
4 Farmer Ho
5 Gataker Ho
6 Gataker St
7 Cornick Ho
8 Glebe Ho
9 Matson Ho
10 Hickling Ho
11 St Andrews Ho
B4 **1** Butterfield Cl
2 Janeway Pl
3 Trotwood Ho
4 Cranbourn Ho
5 Cherry Garden Ho
6 Burton Ho
7 Morriss Ho
8 King Edward The Third Mews
9 Cathay St
10 Rotherhithe St
B5 **1** China Ct
2 Wellington Terr
3 Stevedore St
4 Portland Sq
5 Reardon Ho
6 Lowder Ho
7 Meeting House Alley
8 Farthing Fields
9 Oswell Ho
10 Park Lo

---

11 Doughty Ct
12 Inglefield Sq
13 Chopin's Ct
14 Welsh Ho
15 Hilliard Ho
16 Clegg St
17 Tasman Ho
18 Ross Ho
19 Wapping Dock St
20 Bridewell Pl
21 New Tower Bldgs
22 Tower Bldgs
23 Chimney Ct
24 Jackman Ho
25 Fenner Ho
26 Franklin Ho
27 Frobisher Ho
28 Flinders Ho
29 Chancellor Ho
30 Beechey Ho
31 Reardon Path
32 Parry Ho
33 Vancover Ho
34 Willoughby Ho
35 Sanctuary The
36 Dundee Ct
37 Pierhead Wharf
38 Scandrett St
39 St Johns Ct
B6 **1** Richard Neale Ho
2 Maddocks Ho
3 Cornwall St
4 Brockmer Ho
5 Dellow Ho
6 Bewley Ho
7 Artichoke Hill
C2 **1** Damory Ho
2 Antony Ho
3 Roderick Ho
4 Pedworth Gdns
5 Beamish Ho
6 Gillam Ho
7 George Walter Ho
8 Richard Ho
9 Adron Ho
10 Westlake
11 McIntosh Ho
C3 **1** Blick Ho
2 Neptune Ho
3 Scotia Ct
4 Murdoch Ho
5 Edmonton Ct
6 Niagara Ct
7 Columbia Point
8 Ritchie Ho
9 Wells Ho
10 Helen Peele Cotts
11 Orchard Ho
12 Dock Offices
13 Landale Ho
14 Courthope Ho
C4 **1** Mayflower St
2 St Mary's Est
3 Rupack St
4 Frank Whymark Ho
5 Adams Gardens Est
6 Hatteraick St
7 Hythe Ho
8 Seaford Ho
9 Sandwich Ho
10 Winchelsea Ho
11 Western Pl
12 Kenning St
13 Ainsty St
14 Pine Ho
15 Beech Ho
16 Larch Ho
17 Seth St
18 Turner Ct
19 Risdon Ho
20 Risdon St
21 Aylton Est
22 Manitoba Ct
23 Calgary Ct
24 Irwell Est
25 City Bsns Ctr
26 St Olav's Sq
C5 **1** John Rennie Wlk
2 Malay Ho
3 Wainwright Ho
4 Riverside Mans
5 Shackleton Ho
6 Whitehorn Ho
7 Wavel Ct
8 Prusom's Island
C6 **1** Gosling Ho
2 Vogler Ho
3 Donovan Ho
4 Knowlden Ho
5 Chamberlain Ho
6 Moore Ho
7 Thornewill Ho
8 Fisher Ho
9 All Saints Ct
10 Coburg Dwellings
11 Lowood Ho
12 Solander Gdns
13 Chancery Bldgs
14 Ring Ho
15 Juniper St
16 Gordon Ho
17 West Block
18 North Block
19 South Block
D2 **1** John Kennedy Ho
2 Brydale Ho

---

3 Balman Ho
4 Tissington Ct
5 Harbord Ho
6 Westfield Ho
7 Albert Starr Ho
8 John Brent Ho
9 William Evans Ho
10 Raven Ho
11 Egret Ho
12 Fulmar Ho
13 Dunlin Ho
14 Siskin Ho
15 Sheldrake Ho
16 Buchanan Ct
17 Burrage Ct
18 Biddenham Ho
19 Ayston Ho
20 Empingham Ho
21 Deanshanger Ho
22 Codicote Ho
D4 **1** Schooner Cl
2 Dolphin Cl
3 Clipper Cl
4 Deauville Ct
5 Colette Ct
6 Coniston Ct
7 Virginia Ct
8 Derwent Ct
9 Grantham Ct
10 Serpentine Ct
11 Career Ct
12 Lacine Ct
13 Fairway Ct
14 Harold Ct
15 Spruce Ho
16 Cedar Ho
17 Sycamore Ho
18 Woodland Cres
19 Poplar Ho
20 Adelphi Ct
21 Basque Ct
22 Aberdale Ct
23 Quilting Ct
24 Chargrove Cl
25 Radley Ct
26 Greenacre Sq
27 Maple Leaf Sq
28 Stanhope Cl
29 Hawke Pl
30 Drake Cl
31 Brass Talley Alley
32 Monkton Ho
33 James Ho
34 Wolfe Cres
D5 **1** Clarence Mews
2 Raleigh Ct
3 Katherine Ct
4 Woolcombes Ct
5 Tudor Ct
6 Quayside Ct
7 Princes Riverside Rd
8 Surrey Ho
9 Tideway Ct
10 Edinburgh Ct
11 Falkirk Ct
12 Byelands Cl
13 Gwent Ct
14 Lavender Ho
15 Abbotshade Rd
16 Bellamy's Ct
17 Blenheim Ct
18 Sandringham Ct
19 Hampton Ct
20 Windsor Ct
21 Balmoral Ct
22 Westminster Ct
D6 **1** Barnardo Gdns
2 Roslin Ho
3 Glamis Ct
4 Peabody Est
5 East Block
6 Highway Trad Ctr The
7 Highway Bsns Pk The
8 Cranford Cotts
9 Ratcliffe Orch
10 Scotia Bldg
11 Mauretania Bldg
12 Compania Bldg
13 Sirius Bldg
14 Unicorn Bldg
15 Keepier Wharf

119

A2 **1** Trafalgar Cl
2 Hornblower Cl
3 Cunard Wlk
4 Caronia Ct
5 Carinthia Ct
6 Freswick Ho
7 Graveley Ho
8 Husbourne Ho
9 Crofters Ct
10 Pomona Ho
11 Hazelwood Ho
12 Cannon Wharf Bsns Ctr
13 Bence Ho
14 Clement Ho
15 Pendennis Ho
16 Lighter Cl
17 Mast Ct
18 Rushcutters Ct

4 Sycamore Mews
5 Maritime Ho
7 Floris Pl
C3 1 Seymour Ho
2 Lucas Ho
3 Durrington Twr
4 Amesbury Twr
5 Fovant Ct
6 Allington Ct
7 Welford Ct
8 Ilsley Ct
D1 1 Kendoa Rd
2 Felmersham Cl
3 Abbeville Mews
4 Saxon Ho
5 Gifford Ho
6 Teignmouth Cl
7 Holwood Pl
8 Oaklands Pl
D2 1 Chelsham Ho
2 Lynde Ho
3 Greener Ho
4 Towns Ho
5 Hugh Morgan Ho
6 Roy Ridley Ho
7 Lendal Terr
8 Slievemore Cl
9 Cadmus Cl
D3 1 Haltone Ho
2 Surcot Ho
3 Kingsley Ho
4 Wood Ho
5 Dalemain Ho
6 Fallodon Ho
7 Dartington Ho
8 Esher Ho
9 Kneller Ho
10 Lostock Ho
11 Croxteth Ho
12 Donnington Ho
13 Farnley Ho
14 Hardwick Ho
15 Bradfield Ho
16 Brocket Ho
17 Colchester Ho
18 Clive Ho
19 Chessington Ho
20 Rushbrook Ho
21 Stanmore Ho
22 Newton Ho
23 Netherby Ho
24 Oakwell Ho
25 Rydal Ho
26 Rushton Ho
27 Harcourt Ho
28 Metcalfe Ho
29 Lydwell Ho
30 Raleigh Ho
31 Spencer Ho
32 Shipley Ho
33 Naylor Ho
34 Mordaunt Ho
35 Stanley Ho
36 Alderley Ho
37 Effingham Ho
38 Grant Ho
39 Wilson Ho
40 Fraser Ho

138

A1 1 Morris Ho
2 Gye Ho
3 Clowes Ho
4 Thomas Ho
5 Stuart Ho
6 Storace Ho
7 Bedford Ho
8 Ascot Ct
9 Ascot Par
10 Ashmere Ho
11 Ashmere Gr
12 Vickery Ho
13 Stafford Mans
14 Beresford Ho
A2 1 Callingham Ho
2 Russell Pickering Ho
3 Lopez Ho
4 Coachmaker Mews
A3 1 Barling Ho
2 Jeffrey's Ct
3 Brooks Ct
4 Dalmeny Ct
5 Fender Ho
6 Fishlock Ct
7 Bedser Ct
8 Gover Ct
9 Clarence Wlk
10 Barton Ct
11 Allom Ct
12 Garden Ho
13 Otha Ho
14 Hayward Ct
15 Surridge Ct
16 Knox Ct
17 Jephson Ct
18 Holmes Ct
19 McIntyre Ct
20 Richardson Ct
21 Cassell Ho
22 Packington Ho
23 Bain Ho
24 Enfield Ho
25 Fawcett Ho
26 Sidgwick Ho
27 Jowett Ho
28 Beckett Ho

29 Arden Ho
30 Pinter Ho
31 Barrington Ct
B1 1 Freemens Hos
2 Roger's Almshouses
3 Gresham Almshouses
4 Exbury Ho
5 Glasbury Ho
6 Dalbury Ho
7 Fosbury Ho
8 Chalbury Ho
9 Neilson-Terry Ct
10 Pavilion Mans
11 Daisy Dormer Ct
12 George Lashwood Ct
13 Marie Lloyd Ct
14 Trinity Homes
15 Lethaby Ho
16 Edmundsbury Ct Est
17 Regis Pl
18 Belvedere Pl
19 Alpha Ho
20 Beta Pl
21 Cedars Ho
B2 1 Turberville Ho
2 Thrayle Ho
3 Percheron Ct
4 Draymans Ct
B3 1 Maurice Ho
2 Thring Ho
3 Paton Ho
4 Huxley Ho
5 Morell Ho
6 Mary Ho
7 Beale Ho
8 Rosa Parks Ho
9 Birrell Ho
10 Waltham Ho
11 Burford Ho
12 Thornicroft Ho
13 Addington Ho
14 Goffton Ho
15 Redmayne Ho
16 Norton Ho
17 Aytoun Ho
18 Colwall Ho
19 Burrow Ho
20 Wynter Ho
21 Crowhurst Ho
22 Lidcote Gdns
23 Cumnor Cl
24 Park View Mews
C1 1 Electric Mans
2 Electric La
3 Connaught Mans
4 Clifton Mans
5 Hereford Ho
6 Chaplin Ho
7 Brixton Oval
8 Lord David Pitt Ho
9 Marcus Garvey Way
10 Montgo Cl
11 Bob Marley Way
12 Leeson Rd
C2 1 Buckmaster Cl
2 Albermarle Ho
3 Goodwood Mans
4 Angell Park Gdns
5 Fyfield Rd
6 Howard Ho
7 Harris Ho
8 Broadoak Ct
9 Burgate Ct
10 Witchwood Ho
11 Blacktree Mews
12 Chartham Ct
13 Chilham Ct
14 Northgate Ct
15 Westgate Ct
16 Dover Mans
C3 1 Norval Gn
2 Hilda Terr
3 Church Gn
4 Lord Holland La
5 Sorrell Cl
6 Burton Rd
7 Holles Ho
8 Leys Ct
9 Warwick Ho
10 Fairfax Ho
11 Wayland Ho
12 Dudley Ho
13 Denchworth Ho
14 Fitzgerald Ho
15 Lambert Ho
16 Chute Ho
17 Bedwell Ho
18 Ferrey Mews
19 Serenaders Rd
C4 1 Hector Ct
2 Jason Ct
3 Creon Ct
4 Hermes Ct
5 Argos Ct
6 Cadmus Ct
7 Appollo Ct
8 Mercury Ct
9 County Ho
10 Seasalter Ho
11 Downbarton Ho
12 Garlinge Ho
13 Maria Ho
14 Alvanley Ho

15 Woodchurch Ho
16 Durlock Ho
17 Hallam Ho
18 Whiteness Ho
19 Bromstone Ho
20 Penelope Ho
21 Melbourne Sq
22 Cloisters The
23 Cliffsend Ho
24 Sacketts Ho
25 Hanway Ho
26 Brickworth Ho
27 Redlynch Ho
28 Stodmarsh Ho
29 Kingsgate Ho
30 Chardin Ho
31 Annesley Ho
32 Knowlton Ho
33 Russell Gr
34 Eamann Casey Ho
C5 1 Swift Ho
2 Listowel Cl
3 Deal Wlk
4 Plover Ho
5 Aigburth Mans
6 Glencoe Mans
7 Glenshaw Mans
8 Cleveland Mans
9 Leda Ct
10 Jupiter Ct
11 Juno Ct
12 Healy Ho
13 Ashton Ho
14 Ramsey Ho
15 Annesley Ho
16 Cowley Rd
C6 1 Sherwin Ho
2 Kilner Ho
3 Read Ho
4 Lohmann Ho
5 Hornby Ho
6 Abel Ho
7 Blythe Ho
8 Key Ho
9 Lockwood Ho
10 Alverstone Ho
11 Blades Ho
12 Rothesay Ct
D1 1 Mahatma Ganhi Ind Est
2 Dylan Rd
3 Bessemer Park Ind Est
4 Pablo Neruda Cl
5 Langston Hughes Cl
6 Walt Whitman Cl
7 James Joyes Wlk
8 Alice Walker Cl
9 Louise Bennett Cl
10 Chadacre Ho
11 Burwood Ho
12 Pyrford Ho
13 Wangford Ho
14 Ashford Ho
15 Kenwood Ho
16 Moyne Ho
17 Elveden Ho
18 Carrara Wlk
19 Broughton Dr
20 Tilia Wlk
21 Angela Davis Ind Est
D2 1 Mallams Mews
2 Amberley Ct
3 Harper Ho
4 Leicester Ho
5 Station Ave
6 Wellfit St
7 Loughborough Ct
8 Belinda Rd
9 Higgs Ind Est
D3 1 Langport Ho
2 Iveagh Ho
3 Newark Ho
4 Edgehill Ho
5 Hopton Ho
6 Ashby Ho
7 Nevil Ho
D4 1 Fairbairn Gn
2 Hammelton Gn
3 Foxley Sq
4 Silverburn Ho
5 Butler Ho
6 Dalkeith Ho
7 Turner Cl
8 Bathgate Ho
9 Black Roof Ho
D6 1 Faunce Ho
2 Garbett Ho
3 Harvard Ho
4 Doddington Pl
5 Kean Ho
6 Jephson Ho
7 Cornish Ho
8 Bateman Ho
9 Molesworth Ho
10 Walters Ho
11 Cruden Ho
12 Brawne Ho
13 Prescott Ho
14 Chalmer's Wlk
15 Copley Cl

139

A3 1 Bergen Ho
2 Oslo Ho
3 Viking Ho

4 Jutland Ho
5 Norvic Ho
6 Odin Ho
7 Baltic Ho
8 Nobel Ho
9 Mercia Ho
10 Kenbury Gdns
11 Zealand Ho
12 Elsinore Ho
13 Norse Ho
14 Denmark Mans
15 Dane Ho
16 Canterbury Cl
17 York Cl
18 Kenbury Mans
19 Parade Mans
20 Winterslow Ho
21 Lilford Ho
22 Cutcombe Mans
23 Bartholomew Ho
24 Guildford Ho
25 Boston Ho
26 Hereford Ho
27 Weyhill Ho
28 Lichfield Ho
29 Lansdown Ho
30 Honiton Ho
31 Pinner Ho
32 Baldock Ho
33 Widecombe Ho
34 Nottingham Ho
35 Witham Ho
36 Barnet Ho
37 Empress Mews
A4 1 Bertha Neubergh Ho
2 Mornington Mews
3 Badsworth Rd
4 Sycamore Ho
5 Elm Tree Ct
6 Samuel Lewis Trust Dwellings
7 Valmar Trad Est
8 Keswick Ho
9 Mitcham Ho
A5 1 Boundary Ho
2 Day Ho
3 Burgess Ho
4 Carlyle Ho
5 Myers Ho
6 Thompson's Ave
7 Palgrave Ho
8 Winnington Ho
9 Brantwood Ho
10 Lowell Ho
11 Jessie Duffett Ho
12 Otterburn Ho
13 Crossmount Ho
14 Venice Ct
15 Bowyer St
16 Livingstone Ho
17 Gothic Ct
18 Coniston Ho
19 Harlynwood
20 Carey Ct
21 Finley Ct
22 Grainger Ct
23 Hayes Ct
24 Moffat Ho
25 Marinel Ho
26 Hodister Cl
27 Arnot Ho
28 Lamb Ho
29 Kipling Ho
30 Keats Ho
31 Kenyon Ho
32 New Church Rd
33 Sir John Kirk Cl
B1 1 Shaftesbury Ct
2 Mayhew Ct
3 Morris Ct
4 Swinburne Ct
5 Perth Ct
6 Tayside Ct
7 Matlock Ct
8 Hunter Ct
9 Turner Ct
B3 1 Selborne Rd
2 Hascombe Terr
B4 1 Joiners Arms Yd
2 Butterfly Wlk
3 Cuthill Wlk
4 Colonades The
5 Artichoke Mews
6 Peabody Bldgs
7 Brighton Ho
8 Park Ho
9 Peabody Ct
10 Lomond Ho
11 Lamb Ho
12 Kimpton Ct
13 Belham Wlk
14 Datchelor Pl
15 Harvey Rd
B5 1 Masterman Ho
2 Milton Ho
3 Pope Ho
4 Chester Ct
5 Marvel Ho
6 Flecker Ho
7 Landor Ho
8 Evelina Mans
9 Habington Ho
10 Langland Ho
11 Drinkwater Ho
12 Procter Ho
13 Shirley Ho
14 Drayton Ho
15 Bridges Ho

16 Cunningham Ho
17 Hood Ho
18 Herrick Ho
19 Dekker Ho
20 Sansom St
21 Houseman Way
22 Coleby Path
23 Jago Wlk
B6 1 Queens Ho
2 Arnside Ho
3 Horsley St
4 St Peter's Ho
5 St Johns Ho
6 St Marks Ho
7 St Stephens Ho
8 St Matthew's Ho
9 Red Lion Cl
10 Boyson Rd
11 Bradenham
C2 1 Harfield Gdns
2 Karen Ct
3 Seavington Ho
4 Appleshaw Ho
5 Birdsall Ho
6 Whitney Ho
7 Wheatland Ho
8 Wilton Ho
9 Walcot Ho
10 Whadden Ho
11 Melbrook Ho
12 Ledbury Ho
13 Tidworth Ho
14 Riseholme Ho
15 Ringmer Ho
16 Petworth Ho
17 Stagshaw Ho
18 Ivybridge Ho
19 Inwood Ho
20 Gatcombe Ho
21 Gatebeck Ho
22 Felbridge Ho
23 Cowdray Ho
C3 1 Springfield Ho
2 Craston Ho
3 Walters Ho
4 Edgecombe Ho
5 Fowler Ho
6 Rignold Ho
7 Chatham Ho
C4 1 Barnwell Ho
2 Brunswick Villas
3 St Giles Twr
4 Bentley Ho
5 Dawson Ho
6 Dryden Ho
7 Mayward Ho
8 Longleigh Ho
9 Fairwall Ho
10 Bodeney Ho
11 Sandby Ho
12 Vestry Mews
13 Netley
14 Lakanal
15 Racine
C5 1 Tower Mill Rd
2 Tilson Cl
3 Dorton Cl
4 Granville Sq
5 Farnborough Way
6 Hordle Prom W
7 Samuel Jones Ind Est
8 Dibden Ho
9 Marchwood Cl
10 Pilgrims Cloisters
11 Beacon Ho
12 Teather St
13 Stacy Path
14 Rumball Ho
15 Ballow Cl
16 Rill Ho
C6 1 Pearse St
2 Watling St
3 Gandolfi st
4 Andoversford Ct
5 Downend Ct
D1 1 Dulwich Mews
2 St James's Cloisters
D4 1 Colbert
2 Voltaire
3 Finch Mews
4 Charles Coveney Rd
5 Crane St
6 Curlew Ho
7 Mallard Ho
8 Tern Ho
9 Crane Ho
10 Falcon Ho
11 Bryanston Ho
12 Basing Ct
13 Marcus Ho
14 Sheffield Ho
D5 1 Whistler Mews
2 Painswick Ct
3 Sharpness Ct
4 Hordle Prom N
5 Mattingly Way
6 Calypso Cres
7 Samuel St
8 Hordle Prom S
9 Cinnamon Cl
10 Savannah Cl
11 Thames Ct
12 Danube Ct
13 Tilbury Cl
14 Hordle Prom E

15 Indus Ct
16 Oakcourt
17 Palm Ct
18 Rowan Ct
19 Blackthorn Ct
20 Pear Ct
21 Lidgate Rd
D6 1 Willsbridge Ct
2 Cam Ct
3 Quedgeley Ct
4 Saul Ct
5 Quenington Ct
6 Westonbirt Ct
7 Wickway Ct

140

A3 1 William Margrie Cl
2 Choumert Sq
3 Parkstone Rd
4 Atwell Rd
A4 2 Angelina Ho
3 Jarvis Ho
4 Richland Ho
5 Honeywood Ho
6 Wakefield Ho
7 Primrose Ho
8 Hardcastle Ho
9 Dunstall Ho
10 Purdon Ho
11 Flamborough Ho
12 Lambrook Ho
13 Witcombe Point
14 Yarnfield Sq
15 Winford Ct
16 Portbury Cl
17 Robert Keen Cl
A5 1 Thornbill Ho
2 Vervain Ho
3 Woodstar Ho
4 Tamarind Ho
5 Hereford Retreat
6 Haymerle Ho
7 Furley Ho
8 Applegarth Ho
9 Freda Corbett Cl
10 Rudbeck Ho
11 Henslow Ho
12 Lindley Ho
13 Collinson Ho
14 Sister Mabel's Way
15 Timberland Cl
16 Hastings Cl
17 Neville Cl
18 Sidmouth Ho
19 Budleigh Ho
20 Stanesgate Ho
21 Braemore Ho
22 Ely Ho
A6 1 Bowles Rd
2 Western Wharf
3 Northfield Ho
4 Millbrook Ho
5 Denstone Ho
6 Deerhurst Ho
7 Caversham Ho
8 Battle Ho
9 Cardiff Ho
10 Bridgnorth Ho
11 Exeter Ho
12 Grantham Ho
13 Aylesbury Ho
14 Royston Ho
B2 1 Tilling Ho
2 Goodwin Ho
3 Citron Terr
4 Cheam St
B3 1 Walkynscroft
2 Ryegates
3 Hathorne Cl
4 Pilkington Rd
5 Russell Ct
6 Heaton Ho
7 Magdalene Cl
B4 1 Willowdene
2 Pinedene
3 Oakdene
4 Beechdene
5 Hollydene
6 Wood Dene
7 Staveley Cl
8 Carnicot Ho
9 Martock Ct
10 Kendrick Ct
B5 1 Tortington Ho
2 Credenhill Ho
3 Bromyard Ho
4 Hoyland Cl
5 Willowdene
6 Ashdene
7 Acorn Par
8 Carlton Gr
9 Springall St
10 Harry Lambourn Ho
C3 1 Honiton Gdns
2 Selden Ho
3 Hathway Ho
4 Hathway St
5 Station Ct
C5 1 Ambleside Point
2 Grasmere Point
3 Windermere Point
4 Roman Way
5 Laburnham Cl
6 Romney Cl

8 Hammersley Ho
9 Hutchinson Ho
10 Hammond Ho
11 Fir Tree Ho
12 Glastonbury Ct
13 Highbridge Ct
14 Filton Ct
15 Chiltern Ct
16 Cheviot Ct
C6 2 Penshurst Ho
3 Reculver Ho
4 Mereworth Ho
5 Camber Ho
6 Chilam Ho
7 Otford Ho
8 Olive Tree Ho
9 Lewis Silkin Ho
10 Richborough Ho
11 Dover Ho
12 Eynsford Ho
13 Horton Ho
14 Lamberhurst Ho
15 Canterbury Ind Pk
16 Upnall Ho
17 Sissinghurst Ho
18 Rochester Ho
19 Leybourne Ho
20 Lullingstone Ho
D1 1 Laxton Path
2 Barlings Ho
3 Bayfield Ho
4 Coston Wlk
5 Coverham Ho
6 Gateley Ho
7 Dereham Ho
8 Greenwood Ho
9 Hilton Ho
10 Goodall Ho
11 Horsley Ho
12 Jordan Ho
D5 1 Richard Anderson Ct
2 Palm Tree Ho
3 Edward Robinson Ho
4 Antony Ho
5 Gerrard Ho
6 Palmer Ho
7 Pankhurst Cl
D6 1 Harrisons Ct
2 Grantley Ho
3 Sunbury Ct
4 Tilbury Ho
5 Graham Ct
6 Connell Ct
7 St Clements Ct
8 Henderson Ct
9 Jemotts Ct
10 Verona Ct
11 Heywood Ho
12 Francis Ct
13 Hind Ho
14 Donne Ho
15 Carew Ct
16 Burbage Ho
17 Newland Ho
18 Dobson Ho
19 Dalton Ho
20 Greene Ct
21 Redrup Ho
22 Tarplett Ho
23 Stunnell Ho
24 Gasson Ho
25 Bryce Ho
26 Barnes Ho
27 Barkwith Ho
28 Bannister Ho
29 Apollo Ind Bsns Ctr

141

A5 1 Batavia Ho
2 Marlowe Bsns Ctr
3 Batavia Mews
4 Woodrush Cl
5 Alexandra St
6 Primrose Wlk
7 Vansittart St
8 Granville Ct
9 Cottesbrook St
A6 1 Portland Ct
2 Phoenix Ct
3 Rainbow Ct
4 Hawke Twr
6 Woodpecker Rd
B5 1 Austin Ho
2 Exeter Way
3 Crossleigh Ct
4 Mornington Pl
5 Maple Ho
B6 1 Chester Ho
2 Lynch Wlk
3 Arlington Ho
4 Woodcote Ho
5 Cornbury Ho
6 Prospect Pl
7 Akintaro Ho
8 Mulberry Ho
9 Laurel Ho
10 Linden Ho
11 Ashford Ho
12 Wardalls Ho
13 Magnolia Ho
14 Howard Ho

15 Larch Cl
16 Ibis Ct
17 Merganser Ct
18 Wotton Rd
19 Kingfisher Sq
20 Sanderling Ct
21 Dolphin Twr
22 Mermaid Twr
23 Scoter Ct
24 Shearwater Ct
25 Brambling Ct
26 Kittiwake Ct
28 Guillemot Ct
29 Marine Twr
30 Teal Ct
31 Lapwing Twr
34 Cormorant Ct
36 Shelduck Ct
39 Eider Ct
40 Pintail Ct
41 Tristan Ct
42 Skua Ct
43 Rosemary Ct
44 Violet Cl
45 Diana Cl
C4 1 Admiralty Cl
2 Harton Lo
3 Sylvia Cotts
4 Pitman Ho
5 Heston Ho
C5 1 Sandpiper Ct
2 Flamingo Ct
3 Titan Bsns Est
4 Rochdale Way
5 Speedwell St
6 Reginald Pl
7 Fletcher Path
8 Frankham Ho
9 Cremer Ho
10 Wilshaw Ho
11 Castell Ho
12 Holden Ho
13 Browne Ho
14 Lady Florence
Ctyd
15 Covell Ct
C6 1 Dryfield Wlk
2 Blake Ho
3 Hawkins Ho
4 Grenville Ho
5 Langford Ho
6 Mandarin Ct
8 Bittern Ct
9 Lamerton St
10 Armada St
11 Armada Ct
12 Benbow Ho
13 Oxenham Ho
14 Caravel Mews
15 Hughes Ho
16 Stretton Mans
D5 1 Finch Ho
2 Jubilee The
3 Gordon Ho
4 Haddington Ct
5 Maitland Cl
6 Ashburnham
Retreat

142

A3 1 Ellison Ho
2 Pitmaston Ho
3 Windmill Cl
4 Hertmitage The
5 Burnett Ho
6 Lacey Ho
A4 1 Penn Almshouse
2 Jarvis Ct
3 Woodville Ct
4 Darnell Ho
5 Renbold Ho
6 Lindsell St
7 Plumbridge St
8 Trinity Gr
9 Hollymount Cl
10 Cade Tyler Ho
11 Robertson Ho
A5 1 Temair Ho
2 Glaisher St
3 Prince of Orange
La
4 Lombard Ho
5 St Marks Cl
6 Ada Kennedy Ct
7 Arlington Ct
8 Topham Ho
9 Darnell Ho
10 Hawks Mews
11 Royal Pl
12 Swanne Ho
13 Maribor
14 Serica Ct
15 Queen Elizabeth
College
A6 1 Greenwich Mkt
2 Turnpin La
3 Durnford St
4 Sexton's Ho
5 Bardsley Ho
6 Wardell Ho
7 Clavell St
8 Stanton Ho
9 Macey Ho
10 Boreman Ho
B6 1 Frobisher Ct

2 Hardy Cotts
3 Palliser Ho
4 Bernard Angell
Ho
5 Corvette Sq
6 Travers Ho
7 Reade Ho
8 Maze Hill Lo
D5 1 Westcombe Ct
2 Kleffens Ct
3 Ferndale Ct
4 Combe Mews
5 Mandeville Cl
6 Heathway
7 Pinelands Cl

143

A5 1 Mary Lawrenson
Pl
2 Bradbury Ct
3 Dunstable Ct
A6 1 Nethercombe Ho
2 Holywell Cl
C6 1 Warren Wlk
2 Wilson Ho
3 Priory Ho
4 Mar Ho
5 Langhorne Ho
6 Games Ho
7 Erskine Ho
8 Ducie Ho
9 Downe Ho
10 Bayeux Ho
11 Elliscombe Mount
12 Harold Gibbons
Ct
13 Mascalls Ct
14 Leila Parnell Pl
15 East Mascalls
16 Birch Tree Ho
17 Cherry Tree Ct
18 Elm Tree Ct
19 Cedar Ct
D5 1 Winchester Ho
2 Brentwood Ho
3 Shenfield Ho
4 Chesterford Ho

144

A4 1 Master Gunner's
Pl
2 Nicholson Ho
3 Borgard Ho
4 Macleod Ho
5 Brome Ho
6 Ross Ho
7 Horne Ho
8 Pendlebury Gn
9 Dickson Ho
10 Roberts Ho
A5 1 Leyburn Ho
2 Greenwich Hts
3 Gardiner Ho
B4 1 Galton Ho
2 Florence Ho
3 Sidney Ho
4 Robertson Ho
5 Mennie Ho
6 Godwin Ho
7 Panbro Ho
8 Sutherland Ho
C6 1 Lawson Ho
2 Mabbett Ho
3 Petrie Ho
4 Memess Path
5 Ruegg Ho
6 Nile Path
7 Leslie Smith Sq
8 Spearman St
9 Siedle Ho
10 Watling Ho
11 O'Neill Path
12 Old Clem Sq
13 Jefferson Wlk
14 Millward Wlk
15 Wordsworth Ho
16 Fenwick Cl
D6 1 Acworth Ho
2 Griffiths Ho
3 Squires Ho
4 Cowen Ho
5 Turton Ho
6 Alford Ho
7 Boxshall Ho
8 Macallister Ho
9 Marvin Ho
10 Kelham Ho
11 Kimber Ho
12 Maxwell Ho
13 Woodford Ho
14 Penfold Ho

146

A2 1 Wellingfield Ct
2 Woodville Gr
3 Midwinter Ct
4 St Leonards Cl

147

A1 1 Woburn Ct
2 Arundel Ct
3 Longleat Villas
4 Upton Villas
B6 1 Bevercote Wlk
2 Boevey Path

3 Lullingstone Rd
4 Benjamin Ct
5 Charton Cl
6 Terence Ct
7 Renshaw Ct
8 Grove Rd
C1 1 Friswell Pl
2 Market Pl
3 Geddes Pl
4 Janet Ct
5 Broadway Sh Ctr
6 Mall The
7 Norwich Pl
8 Pincott Rd

148

A5 1 Stranraer Way
2 Deri Dene Cl
3 Lord Knyvetts Ct
4 Tudor Ct
5 Wessex Ct
6 Vanguard Ho
7 Shackleton Ct
8 Fleetwood Ct
9 Clifton Ct
10 Vickers Ct
11 Bristol Ct
12 Sunderland Ct

153

A3 1 Katharine Rd
2 Garfield Rd
3 Flood La
4 John Wesley Ct
5 King Street Par
6 Thames Eyot
A4 1 Perryn Ct
2 Ivybridge Cl
3 Brook Ho
4 Latham Cl
5 March Rd
6 Berkley Ct
7 Cole Court Lo
8 Cheltenham Ave
9 Railway App
A5 1 Greenways The
2 Cole Park View
B4 1 Melton Ct
2 Amyand Park
Gdns
3 Crown Ct
4 Burrell Ho
5 Owen Ho
6 Brentford Ho
7 Leeson Ho
8 Westbourne Ho
9 Orleans Ct
10 Lebanon Ct
B5 1 Grove The
2 Cumberland Cl
3 Westmorland Cl
4 Sussex Ct
5 Norfolk Cl
6 Nicol Cl
7 Old Lodge Pl
8 Kelvin Ct
9 St Margaret's Ct
10 Park Cotts
11 St Margarets Bsns
Ctr
12 Amyand Cotts
C5 1 Howmic Ct
2 Sefton Lo
3 Ravensbourne
4 Arlington Ct
5 Georgina Ct
6 Trevelyan Ho
7 Caradon Ct
8 Green Hedges
9 Old House Gdns
10 Queens Keep
11 Beresford Ct
12 Langham Ct
13 Poplar Ct
D5 1 Richmond Bridge
Mans
2 Heatherdene
Mans
3 Kenton Ct
4 Arosa Rd
5 Darling Ho
6 Turner Ho
7 Blanchard Ho
8 Ashe Ho
9 Bevan Ct
10 Lawley Ho
11 Leicester Ct
12 Roseleigh Cl
13 Beaulieu Cl
14 Richmond Mans
15 Mallard Ct
D6 1 Garrick Cl
2 Old Palace Yd
3 Wardrobe The
4 Maids of Honour
Row
5 Hunters Ct
6 Queensberry Ho
7 Green The
8 Old Palace Terr
9 Paved Ct
10 Golden Ct
11 Brewers La
12 Square The
13 Lower George St
14 St James's Cotts
15 Church Wlk

16 Victoria Pl
17 Castle Yd
18 Lewis Rd
19 Wakefield Rd
20 Church Terr
21 Warrington Rd
22 Ormond Ave
23 St Helena Terr
24 Whittaker Pl
25 Heron Sq
26 Northumberland
Pl
27 Church Ct
28 Holbrooke Pl

154

A5 1 Lancaster Cotts
2 Lancaster Mews
3 Bromwich Ho
4 Priors Lo
5 Richmond Hill Ct
6 Glenmore Ho
7 Hillbrow
8 Heathshot
9 Friars Stile Pl
10 Spire Ct
11 Ridgeway
12 Matthias Ct
A6 1 Lichfield Terr
2 Union Ct
3 Carrington Lo
4 Wilton Ct
5 Egerton Ct
6 Beverley Lo
7 Bishop Duppa's
Almshouses
8 Regency Wlk
9 Clearwater Ho
10 Onslow Avenue
Mans
11 Michels
Almshouses
12 Albany Pas
13 Salcombe Villas
B5 1 Chester Cl
2 Evesham Ct
3 Queen's Ct
4 Russell Wlk
5 Charlotte Sq
6 Jones Wlk
7 Hilditch Ho
8 Isabella Ct
9 Damer Ho
10 Eliot Ho
11 Fitzherbert Ho
12 Reynolds Pl
13 Chisholm Rd
B6 1 Alberta Ct
2 Beatrice Rd
3 Lorne Rd
4 York Rd
5 Connaught Rd
6 Albany Terr
7 Kingswood Ct
8 Selwyn Ct
9 Broadhurst Ho

155

D5 1 Allenford Ho
2 Swaythling Ho
3 Tatchbury Ho
4 Penwood Ho
5 Bramley Ho
6 Shalden Ho
7 Dunbridge Ho
8 Denmead Ho
9 Charcot Ho
10 Portswood Pl
11 Brockbridge Ho
12 Hurstbourne Ho

156

A3 1 Farnborough Ho
2 Rushmere Ho
3 Horndean Cl
4 Highcross Way
5 Timsbury Wlk
6 Foxcombe Rd
7 Ryefield Path
8 Greatham Wlk
9 Gosport Ho
10 Stoatley Ho
11 Milland Ho
12 Clanfield Ho
13 Fareham Ho
A4 1 Woodcott Ho
2 Lyndhurst Ho
3 Wheatley Ho
4 Allbrook Ho
5 Bordon Wlk
6 Chilcombe Ho
7 Vicarage Ct
8 Shawford Ct
9 Eastleigh Wlk
10 Kings Ct
A6 1 Theodore Ho
2 Nicholas Ho
3 Bonner Ho
4 Downing Ho
5 Johsen Ho
6 Fairfax Ho
7 Devereux Ho
8 David Ho
9 Leigh Ho
10 Clipstone Ho

11 Mallet Ho
12 Arton Wilson Ho
B3 1 Ramsdean Ho
2 Purbrook Ho
3 Portsea Ho
4 Blendworth Point
5 Eashing Point
6 Hindhead Point
7 Hilsea Point
8 Witley Point
9 Buriton Ho
10 Grately Ho
11 Hascombe Ho
12 Dunhill Point
13 Westmark Point
14 Longmoor Point
15 Cadnam Point
C4 1 Cumberland Ho
2 Devonshire Ho
3 Cornwall Ho
4 Norfolk Ho
5 Leicester Ho
6 Warwick Ho
7 Sutherland Ho
8 Carmarthen Ho
9 Worcester Ho
10 Rutland Ho
C6 1 Inglis Ho
2 Ducie Ho
3 Warncliffe Ho
4 Stanhope Ho
5 Waldegrave Ho
6 Mildmay Ho
7 Mullens Ho
D3 1 Sandringham Cl
2 Eastwick Ct
3 Oatlands Ct
4 Banning Ho
5 Grantley Ho
6 Caryl Ho
7 Duncombe Ho
8 Chilworth Ct
9 Kent Lo
10 Turner Lo
11 Marlborough
12 Parkland Gdns
13 Lewesdon Cl
14 Pines Ct
15 Ashtead Ct
16 Mynterne Ct
17 Arden
18 Stephen Ct
19 Marsham Ct
20 Doradus Ct
21 Acorns The
22 Heritage Ho
23 Conifer Ct
24 Spencer Ho
25 Chartwell
26 Blenheim
27 Chivelston
28 Greenfield Ho
29 Oakman Ho
30 Radley Lo
31 Simon Lo
32 Admirals Ct
D4 1 Brett Ho
2 Brett House Cl
3 Sylva Ct
4 Ross Ct
5 Potterne Cl
6 Stourhead Cl
7 Fleur Gates
8 Greenwood
D5 1 Balmoral Ho
2 Glenalmond Ho
3 Selwyn Ho
4 Keble Ho
5 Bede Ho
6 Gonville Ho
7 Magdalene Ho
8 Armstrong Ho
9 Newnham Ho
10 Somerville Ho
11 Balliol Ho
12 Windermere
13 Little Combe Cl
14 Classinghall Ho
15 Chalford Ct
16 Garden Royal
17 South Ct
18 Anne Kerr Ct
19 Ewhurst
D6 1 Geneva Ct
2 Laurel Ct
3 Cambalt Ho
4 Langham Ct
5 Lower Pk
6 King's Keep
7 Whitnell Ct
8 Whitehead Ho
9 Halford Ho
10 Humphry Ho
11 Jellicoe Ho

157

A3 1 William Harvey
Ho
2 Highview Ho
3 Cameron Ct
4 Galgate Cl
5 Green Ho The
6 King Charles Wlk
7 Florys Ct
8 Augustus Ct
9 Albert Ct
10 Hertford Lo
11 Mortimer Lo

12 Allenswood
13 Ambleside
A6 1 Claremont
2 Downside
3 Cavendish Cl
4 Ashcombe Ct
5 Carltons The
6 Draldo Ho
7 Millbrooke Ct
8 Coysh Ct
9 Keswick Hts
10 Lincoln Ho
11 Avon Ct
B6 1 Burlington Mews
2 Cumbria Ho
3 St Stephen's Gdns
4 Atlantic Ct
5 Burton Lo
6 Manfred Ct
7 Meadow Bank
8 Hooper Ho
C6 1 Pembridge Pl
2 Adelaide Rd
3 London Ct
4 Windsor Ct
5 Westminster Ct
6 Fullers Ho
7 Bridge Pk
8 Lambeth Ct
9 Milton Ct
10 Norfolk Mans
11 Francis Snary Lo
12 Bush Cotts
13 Downbury Mews
14 Newton's Yd
D6 1 Fairfield Ct
2 Blackmore Ho
3 Lancaster Mews
4 Cricketers Mews

159

A2 1 Upper Tooting
Park Mans
2 Cecil Mans
3 Marius Mans
4 Boulevard The
5 Elmfield Mans
6 Holdernesse Rd
A3 1 Heslop Ct
2 St James's Terr
3 Boundaries Mans
4 Station Par
5 Old Dairy Mews
A4 1 Hollies Way
2 Endlesham Ct
A5 1 Rayne Ho
2 St Anthony's Ct
3 Earlsthorpe Mews
B3 1 Holbeach Mews
2 Hildreth Street
Mews
3 Coalbrook Mans
4 Hub Buildings The
B4 1 Meyer Ho
2 Faraday Ho
3 Hales Ho
4 Frankland Ho
5 Graham Ho
6 Gibbs Ho
7 Anslie Wlk
8 Rokeby Ho
9 Caister Ho
10 Ivanhoe Ho
11 Catherine Baird
Ct
12 Marmion Ho
13 Devonshire Ho
C4 1 Limerick Ct
2 Homewoods
3 Jewell Ho
4 Glanville Ho
5 Dan Bryant Ho
6 Olding Ho
7 Quennel Ho
8 Weir Ho
9 West Ho
10 Neville Ct
C5 1 Joseph Powell Cl
2 Cavendish Mans
3 Westlands Terr
4 Cubitt Ho
5 Hawkesworth Ho
6 Normanton Ho
7 Eastman Ho
8 Couchman Ho
9 Poynders Ct
10 Selby Ho
11 Valentine Ho
12 Gorham Ho
13 Deauville Mans
14 Deauville Ct
C6 1 Timothy Cl
2 Shaftesbury Mews
3 Brook Ho
4 Grover Ho
5 Westbrook Ho
6 Hewer Ho
7 Batten Ho
8 Mandeville Ho
9 George Beare Lo
D3 1 Sinclair Ho
2 MacGregor Ho
3 Ingle Ho
4 St Andrews Mews
D4 1 Riley Ho
2 Bennett Ho
3 White Ho
4 Rodgers Ho

5 Dumphreys Ho
6 Homan Ho
7 Prendergast Ho
8 Hutchins Ho
9 Whiteley Ho
10 Tresidder Ho
11 Primrose Ct
12 Angus Ho
13 Currie Ho
D5 1 Parrington Ho
2 Savill Ho
3 Blackwell Ho
4 Bruce Ho
5 Victoria Ct
6 Victoria Ho
7 Belvedere Ct
8 Ingram Lo
9 Viney Ct
10 Bloomsbury Ho
11 Belgravia Ho
12 Barnsbury Ho

160

A1 1 De Montfort Par
2 Leigham Hall Par
3 Leigham Hall
4 Endsleigh Mans
5 John Kirk Ho
6 Raebarn Ct
7 Wavel Ct
8 Homeleigh Ct
9 Howland Ho
10 Beauclerk Ho
11 Bertrand Ho
12 Drew Ho
13 Dowes Ho
14 Dunton Ho
15 Raynald Ho
16 Sackville Ho
17 Thurlow Ho
18 Astoria Mans
A2 1 Wyatt Park Mans
2 Broadlands Mans
3 Stonehill's Mans
4 Streatleigh Par
5 Dorchester Ct
A3 1 Beaumont Ho
2 Christchurch Ho
3 Staplefield Cl
4 Chipstead Ho
5 Coulsdon Ho
6 Conway Ho
7 Telford Avenue
Mans
8 Telford Parade
Mans
9 Wavertree Ct
10 Hartswood Ho
11 Wray Ho
A4 1 Picton Ho
2 Rigg Ho
3 Watson Ho
4 MacArthur Ho
5 Sandon Ho
6 Thorold Ho
7 Pearce Ho
8 Mudie Ho
9 Miller Ho
10 Lycett Ho
11 Lafone Ho
12 Lucraft Ho
13 Freeman Ho
14 New Park Par
15 Argyll Ct
16 Dumbarton Ct
17 Kintyre Ct
18 Cotton Ho
19 Crossman Hos
20 Cameford Ct
21 Parsons Ho
22 Brindley Ho
23 Arkwright Ho
24 Perry Ho
25 Brunel Ho
26 New Park Ct
27 Tanhurst Ho
A6 1 King's Mews
2 Clapham Court
Terr
3 Clapham Ct
4 Clapham Park
Terr
5 Queenswood Ct
6 Oak Tree Ct
7 Park Lofts
B1 1 Carisbrook Ct
2 Pembrook Lo
3 Willow Ct
4 Poplar Ct
5 Mountview
6 Spa View
B3 1 Charlwood Ho
2 Earlswood Ho
3 Balcombe Ho
4 Claremont Cl
5 Holbrook Ho
6 Gwynne Ho
7 Kynaston Ho
8 Tillman Ho
9 Regent Lo
10 Hazelmere Ct
11 Dykes Ct
B4 1 Archbishop's Pl
2 Witley Ho
3 Outwood Ho
4 Dunsfold Ho
5 Deepdene Lo
6 Warnham Ho

7 Albury Lo
8 Tilford Ho
9 Elstead Ho
10 Thursley Ho
11 Brockham Ho
12 Capel Ho
13 Leith Ho
14 Fairview Ho
15 Weymouth Ho
16 Ascalon Ct
17 China Mews
18 Rush Common Mews
B6 1 Beatrice Ho
2 Florence Ho
3 Evelyn Ho
4 Diana Ho
5 Brixton Hill Ct
6 Austin Ho
7 Manor Ct
8 Camsey Ho
9 Romer Ho
10 Gale Ho
11 Byrne Ho
12 Farnfield Ho
13 Marchant Ho
14 Rainsford Ho
15 Springett Ho
16 Mannering Ho
17 Waldron Ho
C3 1 Valens Ho
2 Loveday Ho
3 Strode Ho
4 Ethelworth Ct
5 Harbin Ho
6 Brooks Ho
7 Godolphin Ho
8 Sheppard Ho
9 McCormick Ho
10 Taylor Ho
11 Saunders Ho
12 Talcott Path
13 Derrick Ho
14 Williams Ho
15 Baldwin Ho
16 Berkeley Ct
17 Churston Cl
18 Neil Wates Cres
19 Burnell Ho
20 Portland Ho
C4 1 Ellacombe Ho
2 Booth Ho
3 Hathersley Ho
4 Brereton Ho
5 Holdsworth Ho
6 Dearmer Ho
7 Cherry Cl
8 Greenleaf Cl
9 Longford Wlk
10 Scarlette Manor Wlk
11 Chandlers Way
12 Upgrove Manor Way
13 Ropers Wlk
14 Tebbs Ho
15 Bell Ho
16 Worthington Ho
17 Courier Ho
18 Mackie Rd
19 Hamers Ho
20 Kelyway Ho
21 Harriet Tubman Cl
22 Estoria Cl
23 Leckhampton Pl
24 Scotia Rd
25 Charles Haller St
26 Sidmouth Ho
27 Hunter Ct
28 Onslow Lo
29 William Winter Ct
30 Langthorne Lo
C5 1 Eccleston Ho
2 Scarsbrook Ho
3 Purser Ho
4 Rudhall Ho
5 Hardham Ho
6 Heywood Ho
7 Haworth Ho
8 Birch Ho
9 Lonsdell Ho
10 Lomley Ho
11 Laughton Ho
12 Bascome St
13 Dudley Mews
14 Herbert Mews
15 Blades Lo
16 Dick Shepherd Ct
17 Charman Ho
18 Morden Ho
19 Bishop Ct
20 Blackburn Ct
21 Leigh Ct
22 John Conwey Ho
C6 1 Crownstone Ct
2 Brockwell Ct
3 Nevena Ct
4 St George's Residences
5 Hanover Mans
6 Fleet Ho
7 Langbourne Ho
8 Turnmill Ho
9 Cossar Mews
10 Carter Ho
D1 1 Thanet Ho
2 Chapman Ho
3 Beaufoy Ho
4 Easton Ho

5 Roberts Ho
6 Lloyd Ct
7 Kershaw Ho
8 Wakeling Ho
9 Edridge Ho
10 Jeston Ho
11 Lansdowne Wood Cl

161
B2 1 Coppedhall
2 Shackleton Ct
3 Bullfinch Ct
4 Gannet Ct
5 Fulmar Ct
6 Heron Ct
7 Petrel Ct
8 Falcon Ct
9 Eagle Ct
10 Dunnock Ct
11 Dunlin Ct
12 Cormorant Ct
C6 1 Velde Way
2 Delft Way
3 Arnhem Way
4 Isel Way
5 Kempis Way
6 Terborah Way
7 Steen Way
8 Deventer Cres
9 Nimegen Way
10 Hilversum Cres
11 St Barnabas Cl

162
A1 1 Tunbridge Ct
2 Harrogate Ct
3 Bath Ct
4 Leamington Ct
5 Porlock Ho
6 Cissbury Ho
7 Eddisbury Ho
8 Dundry Ho
9 Silbury Ho
10 Homildon Ho
11 Highgate Ho
12 Richmond Ho
13 Pendle Ho
14 Tynwald Ho
15 Wirrall Ho
16 Greyfriars
A6 1 Dorothy Charrington Ho
2 Keswick Ct
3 Kendall Ct
4 Halliwell Ct
B1 1 River Ho
2 Fordington Ho
3 Arbury Terr
4 Woodbury Ho
5 Gainsborough Mews
6 Forest Hill Ct
B2 1 Bromleigh Ct
2 Parfew Ct
3 Thetford Ct
4 Attleborough Ct
5 Dunton Ct
6 Frobisher Ct
7 Julian Taylor Path
8 Grizedale Terr
9 Worsley Ho
C1 1 Forest Lo
2 Sydenham Park Mans
3 William Wood Ho
C2 1 Fitzwilliam Hts
2 Taymount Grange
3 McLeod Ho
4 Featherstone Ave
5 Kingswear Ho
6 Salcombe Ho
C3 1 Harlech Ct
2 Angela Ct
3 Westwood Ct
4 New Belmont Ho
5 Pearcefield Ave
6 Waldram Pl
7 Horniman Grange
8 South View Ct
9 Heron Ct
10 Katherine Ct
D1 1 Standlake Point
2 Radcot Point
3 Newbridge Point
4 Northmoor
5 Kelmscott
6 Radnor Ct
7 Heathwood Point
8 Ashleigh Point
9 Deepdene Point
10 Rosemount Point
11 Woodfield Ho
12 Clairville Point
13 Trevenna Ho
14 Hyndewood
D2 4 Soper Cl

164
C4 1 Beaumont Terr
2 Littlebourne
3 Verdant Ct
D2 1 Kinross Ct
2 Montrose Ct
3 Rattray Ct
4 Rothesay Ct

D3 1 Edinburgh Ct
2 McMillan Ct
3 Rowallan Ct
4 Meridian Ct
5 Braemar Ct
6 Barrow Ct
7 Blair Ct
8 Darlington Ct
9 Hamilton Ct
10 Inverness Ct
11 Oak Cottage Cl
12 Willow Ct
13 Keswick Ct

165
A4 1 Swallow Ct
2 Honeysuckle Ct
3 Venture Ct
4 Cheriton Ct
5 Askham Lo
6 Syon Lo

166
A2 1 Portland Cres
2 Bourdillon Ct
3 Hillary Ct
4 Tenzing Ct
5 John Hunt Ct
6 Everest Ct
A6 1 Horsfeld Gdns
2 Foxhole Rd
C5 1 Roper St
2 Arcade The
3 Elm Terr
4 Imber Ct
5 Ashcroft Ct
6 Fairlands Ct
7 Brecon Ct
8 Newlands Ct
9 Harvard Ct
10 Garden Ct
11 Chiltern Ct
12 Fairway Ct

167
A2 1 Mervyn Stockwood Ho
2 Michael Marshall Ho
3 Keith Sutton Ho

168
A1 1 Ham Shades Cl
2 Aspen Ho
3 Medlar Ho
4 Cornel Ho
5 Stanton Ct
6 Hornbeam Ho
7 Beech Ho
8 Spindle Ho
9 Moat Ho
10 Hunters Lo
11 Edam Ct
12 Monica James Ho
13 Oak Ho
14 Crescent Ct
B5 1 Rochester Ct
2 Cobham Cl
3 Shorne Cl
4 Warne Pl

169
C4 1 Close The
2 Parkhurst Gdns
3 Chichester Ct
4 Pound Green Ct

171
D3 1 Bishops Ct
2 Ash Lo
3 Lime Lo
4 Oak Lo
5 Elm Ct
6 Willow Lo
7 Sycamore Lo
8 Priscilla Ho
9 Sunbury Cross Ctr
10 Isobel Ho

173
A6 1 Gabriel Cl
2 Metcalfe Wlk
3 Dunmow Cl
4 Burgess Cl
5 Chamberlain Wlk
C2 1 Sherbourne Ct
2 Somerset Ct
3 Jubilee Ho
4 Rushbury Ct
5 Hemming Cl
6 Ryedale Ho
7 Norman Ct
C4 1 Begonia Pl
2 Snowdrop Cl
3 Hyacinth Cl
4 Cyclamen Cl
5 Jonquil Gdns
6 Gladioli Cl
7 Daffodil Pl
8 Partridge Rd
D4 1 Acorn Cl
2 Wolsey Ho

1 Lytton Ho
4 Wren Ho
5 Faraday Ho

174
C5 1 Knaggs Ho
2 Keeling Ho
3 Elizabeth Ct
4 Oakhurst Cl
D5 1 Waldegrave Ct
2 Gresham Ho
3 Traherne Lo
4 Fishers Ct
5 Waterhouse Cl
6 Walpole Pl
7 Walpole Cres
8 Alice Mews
9 Bychurch End

175
A5 1 Cherrywood Ct
2 Cambridge Ho
3 Gleneagles Ct
4 Christchurch Ave
5 Hales Ct
6 Springfield Rd
D2 1 Wick Ho
2 Spinnaker Ct
3 Osiers Ct
4 Trent Ho
5 Arun Ho
6 Medway Ho
7 Avon Ho
8 Tyne Ho
9 Clyde Ho
10 Mersey Ct
11 Severn Ct
12 John Williams Cl
D6 1 Byron Ct
2 Coleridge Ct
3 Tennyson Ct
4 Herrick Ct
5 Spenser Ct
6 Marlowe Ct
7 Brooke Ct
8 Gray Ct
9 Shelley Ct
10 Pope Ct
11 Dryden Ct

176
A1 1 Cleave's Almshos
2 Parade The
3 Drovers Ct
4 Gough Ho
5 Eden Wlk
6 Alderman Judge Mall
7 Lady Booth Rd
8 Caversham Ho
9 Littlefield Cl
10 Bentall Sh Ctr The
11 Adams Wlk
12 Kingfisher Sports Ctr The
13 Greencoat Ho
A2 1 Regents Ct
2 Walter St
3 Canbury 2000 Bsns Pk
4 Sigrist Sq
5 Ashway Ctr
6 Warwick Ho
B1 1 Vicarage Ho
2 Rayleigh Ct
3 School Pas
4 Chippenham
5 Camm Gdns
B2 1 Onslow Ho
2 Dowler Ct
B3 1 McDonald Ho
2 Elm Ho
3 Dale Ct
4 York Ho
5 Florence Ho
6 Florence Rd
7 Roupell Ho
8 Delft Ho
C1 1 Wimpole Cl
2 Burwell
3 Caldecote
4 Fordham
5 Connington
6 Chesterton Terr
7 Westwick
8 Eureka Rd
9 Fulbourn
10 Comberton
11 Madingley
12 Grantchester
13 Cambridge Grove Rd
14 Oakington
15 Harston
16 Graveley
17 Croxton
18 Brinkley
19 Impington
20 Shelford
21 Duxford
C2 1 Farthings The
2 Brae Ct
3 Princeton Mews
4 Station App
C3 1 Queen's Ct
2 St George's Rd

3 Park Road Ho
4 Dagmar Rd
5 Tapping Cl
6 Arthur Rd
7 Borough Rd
8 Belvedere Ct
9 Braywick Ho
10 Dean Ct
11 Rowan Ct
12 Richmond Ct
13 Sunningdale Ct
14 Hawker Ct
15 Cromwell Ct
16 Kings Ct
D2 1 Trevallyn Lo
2 Chichester Ct
3 Beechcroft
4 Cedars The
5 Liddlesdale Ho W
6 Liddlesdale Ho E
7 Deerhurst
8 Brockworth
9 Alderton
D3 1 Bramley Ho
2 Abinger Ho
3 Thursley Ho
4 Ridge Ho
5 Clone The
6 Mount Ct
7 Hillside Ct
8 Hill Ct
9 Royal Ct
10 Lakeside
11 High Ashton
D4 1 Godstone Ho
2 Hambledon Ho
3 Kingswood Ho
4 Leigh Ho
5 Milton Ho
6 Newdigate Ho
7 Farleigh Ho
8 Ockley Ho
9 Effingham Ho
10 Dunsfold Ho
11 Pirbright Ho
12 Clandon Ho
13 Ripley Ho

178
C3 1 Roskeen Ct
2 Chimneys Ct
3 Rosemary Cotts
4 Victoria Lo
D2 1 Beaufort Ho
2 Kinnear Ct
3 Ranmore Ct
4 Lantern Ct
5 Crescent Ho
D3 1 Kings View Ct
2 Kingsdown
3 Wimbledon Ct
4 Beryl Harding Ho
5 Upton Ct
6 Terraces The
7 Lanherne Ho
8 Cumberland Cl
9 Thaxted Pl
10 Rathbone Ho
11 Princess Ct
12 Downs Ct
13 Ravenscar Lo
14 Haverley
15 Savona Cl
16 Beaumont Ct
17 Gordon Ct
D5 1 Lancaster Ho
2 Haygarth Pl
3 Allington Cl
4 Homefield Pl

179
A3 1 Mayfair Ct
2 Brunswick Ct
3 Pavilion Ct
A4 1 Walham Rise
2 Grosvenor Ct
3 Sovereign Ho
4 Holly Lo
5 Florence Ct
6 Linden Cotts
7 Sheep Walk Mews
B5 1 Lawns The
2 Prentice Ct
3 Catherine Ct
4 Woodlodge
5 Queen Alexandra's Ct
6 Lake Cl
7 Westwood Ct
8 Brambles The
9 Lismore
10 Rose Ct
11 Worcester Rd
C3 1 Ashbourne Terr
2 Sir Cyril Black Way
3 Downing Ho
4 Palmerston Gr
5 Gladstone Ct
6 Harefield Ct
7 Viscount Point
D2 1 Gilbert Ct
2 Becket Cl
3 Priory Cl
4 Hudson Ct
5 Ryder Ho

3 Eleanor Ho
7 Ramsey Ho
D3 1 Hamilton Road Mews
2 Dowman Cl

180
A2 1 Tanner Ho
2 May Ct
3 Marsh Ct
4 Lovell Ho
A3 1 Fiske Ct
2 Mellor Ct
3 Olive Rd
4 Allerton Ho
5 Victory Road Mews
6 Will Miles Ct
7 Vanguard Ho
8 Mychell Ho
9 Merton Pl
10 De Burgh Ho
11 Norfolk Ho
12 Hotham Road Mews
B1 1 Ripley Ct
2 Brooklands Ct
3 Horner La
C2 1 Linford Ct
2 Searle Ct
3 Gunnell Ct
C5 1 Robertson Ho
2 Dewar Ho
3 Jean Ho
4 Marion Ct
5 Gravenel Gdns
D1 1 Elms Cotts
2 Sibthorp Rd
3 Armfield Cotts

181
A1 1 Kennedy Cl
2 Pearce Cl
3 Mainwaring Ct
4 Coningsby Ct
5 Laburnum Ct
6 Beaumont Ct
7 Penfold Ct
8 Fitch Ct
A5 1 Osbourne Terr
2 Limetree Wlk
C5 1 Tyers Ho
2 Boothby Ho
3 Adams Ho
4 Burney Ho
5 Boswell Ho
6 Chesterfield Ho
7 Garrick Ho
8 Levett Ho
9 Shelburne Ho
10 Marchmont Ho
11 Ryland Ho
C6 1 Walmsley Ho
2 Chambers Ho
3 Fordyce Ho
4 Percy Ho
5 Langton Ho
6 Moorfields Ho
7 Hidaburn Ct
8 Salter Ho
D6 1 William Dyce Mews

182
C5 1 Belltrees Gr
2 Ash Ct
3 Alder Ct
4 Beech Ct
5 Acacia Ct
6 Blackthorn Ct
7 Cypress Ct
8 Hawthorn Ct
9 Hazel Ct
10 Sycamore Ct
11 Maple Ct
12 Laburnum Ct
13 Fern Lo
C6 1 James Boswell Cl
2 St Albans Ho
3 Suffolk Ct
4 Rockhampton Cl
5 Delphian Ct
D5 1 Woodcote Pl
2 Joe Hunte Ct
3 Cork Tree Ho
4 Lake Ho
5 Cedars Ho
6 Portobello Ho
7 Cooper Ho
8 Farnsworth Ho
9 Hook Ho
10 Crest The
11 Renshaw Ho
12 Ruscoe Ho
13 Sardeson Ho

183
A6 1 Moore Ho
2 Chaucer Ho
3 Bushell Ho
4 Bligh Ho
5 Hobbs Rd
6 Hogarth Ho
7 Goodbehere Ho
8 Astley Ho

184 C3 389
9 Elder Gdns
10 Elderberry Gr
11 Pavement The
12 Dunkirk St
B6 1 Josef Perrin Ho
2 Jean Humbert Ho
3 Charles Staunton Ho
4 Violette Szabo Ho
5 Lilian Rolfe Ho
6 Odette Ho
7 Robert Gerard Ho
8 St Bernards Cl
9 Champness Cl
10 Pennington Cl
11 Queenswood Ct
C4 1 Northwood Way
2 High Limes
3 Valley Prospect
4 Plane Tree Wlk
5 City Prospect
6 Bankside Way
7 Ridge Way
8 Rochdale
9 Barrington Wlk
10 Gatestone Ct
11 Childs La
12 Carberry Rd
13 Norwood Heights Sh Ctr
C5 1 Oakdene
2 Thorsden Way
3 Oakfield Gdns
4 Georgetown Cl
5 Bridgetown Cl
6 Mountbatten Cl
7 Brabourne Cl
8 Alexandra Wlk
9 Compton Ct
10 Battenberg Wlk
11 Burma Terr
12 Wiseman Ct
C6 1 Linley Ct
2 Mellor Ho
3 Whitfield Ct
4 Michaelson Ho
5 Holberry Ho
6 Hovenden Ho
7 Huntley Ho
8 Telfer Ho
9 Markham Ho
10 Oldham Ho
11 Parnall Ho
12 Pierson Ho
13 Roper Ho
14 Roundell Ho
15 Sawyer Ho
16 Ransford Ho
17 Carmichael Ho
18 Bonne Marche Terr Mews
D3 1 Hetley Gdns
2 Claybourne Mews
3 Highland La
4 Mason Ct
5 Kendall Ct
6 High View

184
A3 1 Hanover Ct
2 Brunswick Ct
3 New Church Ct
4 Regency Ct
5 Owen Wlk
6 Bargrove Ct
7 Beaver Ct
B2 1 Dorset Ho
2 Collingwood Cl
3 Chartwell Way
4 Essex Twr
5 Appletree Cl
6 Ditton Pl
7 Kelvin Ct
8 Readman Ct
9 Glen Ct
10 Kingsbridge Ho
11 Carlton Ct
12 Benhurst Ct
13 Carole Ho
14 Dover Ho
15 Bettswood Ct
B5 1 Ragwort Ct
2 Firs The
3 Wingham Ho
4 Seath Ho
5 Ripley Ho
6 Lathwood Ho
7 Hurst Ho
8 George Ho
9 Browne Ho
10 Beacon Ho
11 Bailey Ho
12 Agate Ho
C2 1 Challin St
2 Rutland Ho
3 Pine Ct
C3 1 Watermen's Sq
2 St John's Cotts
3 Gladstone Ho
4 Middlesex Ho
5 Bethesda Ct
6 Ospringe Ho
7 Goudhurst Ho
8 Walmer Ho
9 Strood Ho

390 184 C3

13 Greatstone Ho
14 John Baird Ho
D3 1 Groombridge Ho
2 Provincial Terr
3 Smithers Ho
4 West Ho
5 Swallows Ct

185

A1 1 Clock House Ct
2 Blandford Ave
3 Old School Cl
4 Lynsted Ct
5 Florence Rd
A6 1 Paxton Ct
2 Kenton Ct
3 Grove Ct
4 Shirley Lo
B2 1 Ashton Ct
2 Coombe Ct
3 Fontaine Ct
4 Richfield Ct
5 Sheridan Way
C1 1 Christ Church Rd
2 Lea Rd
3 Stanmore Terr
C2 1 Erindale Ct
2 Bearsted Terr
3 Beck River Pk
4 Waterside
5 Station App
C3 1 Gardenia Ct
2 Brackendale Ct
3 Daniel Ct
4 Moliner Ct
5 Chartwell Lo
6 Randmore Ct
7 Dover Ho
8 Lucerne Ct
9 Malling Ho
10 Westerham Lo
11 Brasted Lo
12 Milton Ho
13 Bradsole Ho
14 Sandgate Ho
15 Adelaide Ct
16 Nettlestead Cl
17 Warren Ct
18 Alton Ct
19 Rockingham Ct
20 Camellia Ct
21 Sinclair Ct
22 Regents Ct
23 Minshull Pl
24 South Park Ct
D1 1 Parkside
2 Tudors The
3 Oakbrook
4 Tara Ct
5 Redlands The
6 Cambria
7 Hillworth
8 Kelsey Gate
9 Burrells
10 Lincoln Lo
11 Courtlands
12 Fairleas
13 Ashdown Cl
D2 1 Mayfair Ct
2 Clifton Ct
3 Fire Station Mews
D4 1 Warner Ho
2 Clifford Ho
3 Lloyd Ho
4 Thurston Ho
5 Byron Ho
6 Blake Ho
7 Keats Ho

186

A2 1 White House Ct
2 Hunters The
3 Sandringham Ct
4 Glenhurst
5 Copperfields
6 Westgate Ct
A6 1 Dedham Ho
2 Flatford Ho
3 Radley Ct
4 Langthorne Ct
5 Hoover Ho
6 Brunner Ho
7 Waterer Ho
8 Marriott Ho
9 Bourbon Ho
B5 1 Longford Ho
2 Ingrebourne Ho
3 Brent Ho
4 Darent Ho
5 Beverley Ho
6 Wandle Ho
7 Rythe Ho
8 Ember Ho
9 Crane Ho
10 Ravensbourne Ho
C1 1 Warwick Ct
2 Maplehurst
3 Mount Arlington
4 Arundel Ct
D2 1 Weston Gr
2 Gibbs Ho
3 Longfield
4 Hammelton Ct
5 Bracken Hill Cl
6 Townend Ct
7 Treversh Ct
8 Cameron Ho
9 Woodlands Ct
10 Blythwood Pk
11 Bromley Pk
D3 1 Homecoppice Ho
2 Kimberley Gate
3 Inglewood Ct
4 Mavery Ct
5 Glen Ct
6 Cawston Ct
7 Blendon Path

187

B2 1 Hansom Terr
2 Dainton Cl
3 St Timothy's
Mews
4 Andringham Lo
5 Kendall Lo
6 Summerfield
7 Winston Ct
8 Laurels The
C1 1 Westland Lo
2 Dairsie Ct
3 Beechfield Cotts
4 Oasis The
5 Cromarty Ct
6 Silverstone Ct

188

A6 1 Beaconsfield Par
2 Cranley Par
3 Kimmeridge Gdns
4 King & Queen Cl
C1 1 Merewood Cl
2 Alpine Copse
C2 1 Ivybridge Ct
2 Greenbank Lo

190

A6 1 Minshaw Ct
2 Cyril Lo
3 Milton Lo
4 Glenwood Ct

5 Culverton Ct
6 Holmbury Manor
B1 1 Swanscombe Ho
2 Haverstock Ct
3 Arrandene Ho
4 Broomfield Ho
5 Headley Ho
6 Kenley Ho
7 Ladywell Ho
B6 1 Chudleigh
2 Wimborne
3 St John's Par
4 Holly Ct
5 Rectory Bsns Ctr

197

A2 1 Raleigh Ho
2 Leicester Ho
3 Gresham Ho
D2 1 Napier Ct
2 Darlington Ho
3 Charminster Ct
4 Mulberry Ct
5 Leander Ct
6 Clinton Ho
7 Hollingworth Ct
8 Gloucester Ct
9 Palmerston Ct
10 Redwood Ct
11 Hursley Ct
12 Westmorland Ct
13 Lawson Ct
14 Alexander Ct
15 Winton Ct
16 Sydenham Ho
17 Caroline Ct
18 Ellswood Ct
19 Masefield Ct

198

A1 1 Ash Tree Cl
2 Shrubbery The
3 Malvern Ct
4 Gate Ho
A3 1 Station App
2 South Bank Lo
3 Bramshott Ct
4 Pandora Ct
5 Wellington Ct
6 Glenbuck Ct
7 Leighton Ho
8 Oakhill Ct
9 Downs View Lo
10 Osborne Ct
A4 1 Effingham Lo
2 Maple Ho
3 Channon Ct
4 Falconhurst
5 Ferndown
6 Viceroy Lo
7 Frensham Ho
8 Kingsley Ho
9 Rannoch Ct
10 Stratton Ct
11 Moray Ho
12 Dulverton Ct
13 Westerham
14 Hill Ct
15 Assheton-Bennett
Ho
16 Hatfield Ho
17 Oxford Ct
18 Pennington Lo
19 Austin Ho
20 Wentworth Ct
21 Priory The
22 Sheraton The
A5 1 Marquis Ct
A6 1 College Rdbt
2 Edinburgh Ct
3 Weston Ct
4 Grebe Terr

5 Heron Ct
6 Agar Ho
7 St James' Ct
8 Grove Ct
9 Springfield Ct
10 College Wlk
B3 1 Percy Ct
2 Holmwood
3 Middle Green Cl
B4 1 Woodleigh
2 Highcroft
3 Caernarvon Ct
4 Regency Ct
D1 1 Oakleigh Way
2 Chandler Ct

199

C2 1 Goodland Ho
2 Furzeland Ho
3 Oakcroft Ho
4 Meadcroft Ho
5 Newhouse
C4 1 Merryweather Ct
2 Roebuck Ct
3 Sable Ct
C5 1 Acacia Ho
2 Kingston Lo
3 Fairholme Ho
4 Marshall Ho
5 Norton Ho
6 Martin Ho

200

A1 1 Brookside Cres
2 Beverley Gdns
3 Purdey Ct
4 Avenue The
5 Briarwood Ct
6 Station App

202

D6 1 Fair Green Ct
2 Regal Ct
3 Lewes Ct
4 Esher Mews
5 Sibford Ct

205

B1 1 Tavistock Ct
2 Chartwell Cl
3 Speaker's Ct
4 Cumberland Ct
5 Viceroy Ct
6 Oriel Ct
7 Cherry Orchard
Gdns
C1 1 Windmill Bridge
Ho
2 Squire Ct
3 Houston Ct
4 St James's Lo
5 Kendal Ho
6 Warren Ct
7 Kendal Ct
D1 1 Hastings Pl
2 Grant Pl
3 Clive Ho
4 Havelock Ho
5 Bellmore Ho
6 Hereford Ct
7 Chequers Ct
8 Havelock Hall

206

A1 1 Farleycroft
2 Edgecumbe Ct
3 Wesson Ho
4 Sullivan Ct
5 Kenley Ho
6 Christopher Ct

7 Jayson Ct
D1 1 Cottongrass Cl
2 Oxlip Cl
3 Eyebright Cl

207

1 North Rd
2 Sussex Rd
3 Riverside Wlk
4 Christie Ho
5 Sherwood Ct
6 Wheatsheaf Par
D6 1 Linden Ct
2 Park Ct
3 Chilchester Ct
4 Iveagh Ct

208

A6 1 Overbury Ct
2 Wilton Pl
D1 1 Woodgrange Ct
2 Maycroft
3 Farnborough Cres
D4 1 Knowlton Gn
2 Speldhurst Cl
3 Bidborough Ct
4 Penshurst Wlk
D5 1 Wedgewood Ct
2 Birches The
3 Eccleshill
4 Tavistock Rd
5 Montpelier Ct

209

A5 1 Montague Terr
2 Chatsworth Ho
A6 1 Marina Cl
2 Cheveney Wlk
3 Bromley Manor
Mans
4 Mall The
5 Westmoreland Pl

211

B1 1 Gleneagles Gn
2 Tandridge Pl
3 Springfield Wlk
4 Pinehurst Wlk
5 Cromer Pl
6 Oakmont Pl

214

A6 1 St Bernards Ho
2 Wentworth Ct
3 Sunningdale Cl
4 Arklow Mews
5 Edward Pinner Ct

215

D6 1 Kingsley Dr
2 Kingsley Ct
3 Mowat Ct
4 Squirrels Ct

216

A6 1 Lansdowne Copse
2 Lansdowne Ct

217

A2 1 Cheam Court
Flats
2 Farnham Ct
3 Tabor Ct
C1 1 Lancaster Ct
2 Redclyffe Terr
3 Kenilworth Terr
4 Lincoln Terr

5 Garden Ct
6 Ashwood Pk
7 Lyndhurst Ct
8 Banbury Ct
9 Holly Ct
10 Castle Ho
11 Balmoral Ct
12 Hereford Ct
13 Lorac Ct
14 Camilla Ct
15 Midsummer
Apmts
D1 1 Hadrian Ct
2 Magnolia Ct
4 Larchvale Ct
5 Alford Ct
6 Brockham Ct
7 Berrylands Ct
8 Camberley Ct
9 Dunsfold Ct
10 Courtlands
11 Leith Towers
12 Kingslee Ct

218

A1 1 Beauclere Ho
2 Melford Ct
3 Elmhurst Lo
4 Mansard Manor
5 Tranmere Ct
6 Beechcroft Lo
7 Savin Lo
8 Yew Tree Ct
9 Avondale Ct
10 Devonshire Ho
11 Hidcote Ho
12 Munstead Ct
13 Lodden Lo
14 Steetley Ct
15 Grampian Cl
A2 1 Grosvenor Ct
2 Forest Dene Ct
3 Cedar Ct
4 Vanborough Ct
A3 1 Goossens Ct
2 Cliffe Wlk
3 Marlins Cl
4 Clowser Ct
5 Montana Gdns

219

B2 1 Runnymede Ct
2 Dolphin Ct
3 Kings Ct
4 Cheyne Ct
5 Hendfield Ct
6 Ellerslie Ct
7 Embassy Ct
8 Chandler Ct
9 Hambledon Ct
10 Wallington Ct
11 Jasmine Ct
B4 1 Loraine Ho
2 Harcourt Lo
3 Coniston Ct
4 Alcester Ct
5 Friars Ct
6 Campbell Ho
7 Brodie Ho
8 Lesley Ct
9 Birch Ct
10 Airborne Ho
C2 1 Rossendon Ct
2 Mulberry Mews
3 Nairn Ct
4 Wallington Sq
5 Rosemount Tow-
ers
6 Connell Ho
7 Ashby Grange

221

A4 1 West Street Pl
2 Maple Ct
3 St Andrew's Rd
4 Albury Ct
5 Chestnut Ct
6 Elgin Ct
7 Beechfield Ct
8 Barham Ct
9 Whitstable Pl
10 Ledbury Pl
A5 1 Mann Cl
2 Halstead Ct
3 Fellmongers Yd
A6 1 Otterbourne Rd
2 Charrington Rd
3 Tamworth Pl
4 Priddy's Yd
5 Hospital of the
Holy Trinity
(Almshouses)
6 Bellhill
B4 1 Holmlea Ct
2 Garlands Ct
3 Coombe Ct
4 Deepdale Ct
5 Galloway Path
B6 1 Wellesley Court
Rd
2 Norfolk Ho
3 Station App
4 Suffolk Ho
5 Cherry Orchard
Gdns
6 Harrington Ct
D6 1 Cheyne Ct
2 Fourways
3 Princess Ct
4 Tierney Ct
5 Sinclair Ct
6 Guinness Ct
7 Mayfair Ct
8 Bishopscourt
9 Gloucester Lo
10 Beverley Hyrst
11 Melton Ct
12 Cecil Ct
13 Napier Ct

227

A3 1 Westfield
2 Farnborough Ct
3 Fern Hill Pl
4 Churchill Ct
5 Spencer Ct
6 Ladycroft Gdns
7 Crabbs Croft Cl
8 Clifton Ct
D2 1 Brittenden Ct
2 Wardens Field Cl
3 Winnipeg Dr
4 Superior Dr
5 Huron Ct
6 Manitoba Gdns
7 Lynne Cl
8 Flint Cl
9 Bakers Mews
D3 1 Osgood Gdns
2 Amberley Ct
3 Rawlings Ct
4 Beblets Cl
5 Fir Tree Cl
6 Raleigh Mews
7 King Henry Mews
D4 1 Healy Dr
2 Marsden Way
3 Taylor Cl
4 Strickland Way
5 Dryland Ave
6 Adcot Wlk
7 Lichlade Cl

🏥 Hospitals with accident and emergency departments are highlighted in green

A

Acton Hospital W3 .....**110** C4
🏥 **Ashford Hospital,**
Stanmore Road, Ashford,
Middlesex TW15 3AA **148** A2
📞 **01784 884488**
Athlone House (The
Middlesex Hospital) N6 .**48** D1
Atkinson Morley Hospital
SW20 ....**178** B3

B

Barking Hospital IG11 .....**79** D1
Barnes Hospital SW14 ...**133** C2
Beckenham Hospital
BR3 ....**185** B1
Bethlem Royal Hospital The
BR3 ....**207** C2
Blackheath Hospital
SE3 ....**142** C2
Bolingbroke Hospital The
SW11 ....**158** C6
Bowden House Hospital
(Private) HA1 ....**64** C6
British Home and Hospital for
Incurables SW16 ....**182** D5
🏥 **Bromley Hospital**
Cromwell Avenue, Bromley,
Kent BR2 9AJ **209** B5
📞 **020 8289 7000**
Brompton Hospital
SW3 ....**114** B1 **256** D2
BUPA Bushey Hospital
WD2 ....**8** D3

C

Carshalton, War Memorial
Hospital SM5 ....**218** D2
Cassel Hospital TW10 ...**175** D6
Castlewood Day Hospital
SE18 ....**144** C4
🏥 **Central Middlesex
Hospital**
Acton Lane, Park Royal, London,
NW10 7NS **89** A4
📞 **020 8965 5733**
Central Public Health
Laboratory NW9 ....**45** C6
Chadwell Heath Hospital
RM6 ....**58** B4
🏥 **Charing Cross Hospital**
Fulham Palace Road, London
W6 8RF (A&E entrance off
St Dunstan's Road) **112** D1
📞 **020 8846 1234**
🏥 **Charter Nightingale Hospital
The** NW1 ....**92** C2 **237** B4
🏥 **Chase Farm Hospital**
The Ridgeway, Enfield,
Middlesex, EN2 8JL **4** C5
📞 **020 8366 6600**
Chelsea Hospital for Women
SW3 ....**114** C1 **257** A2
🏥 **Chelsea and
Westminster Hospital**
369 Fulham Road, London
SW10 9NH **136** A6 **266** B5
📞 **020 8746 8000**
Chingford Hospital E4 ....**20** A1
Chiswick Maternity
Hospital W4 ....**111** D1
Clayponds Hospital and Day
Treatment Ctr TW8 ....**110**A2
Clementine Churchill
Hospital The HA1 ....**64** D5

Colindale Hospital NW9 .**45** C6
Connaught Day
Hospital E11 ....**54** C3
Coppetts Wood Hospital
N10 ....**30** D2
Cromwell Hospital
SW5 ....**113** D2 **255** C4

D

Devonshire Hospital
W1 ....**93** A2 **238** B4
Dulwich Hospital SE22 ..**139** C1

E

🏥 **Ealing Hospital**
Uxbridge Road, Southall,
Middlesex UB1 3HW **108** B4
📞 **020 8574 2444**
East Ham Meml
Hospital E7 ....**77** D1
Eastman Dental
Hospital WC1 ....**94** B4 **240** C6
Edgware General
Hospital HA8 ....**26** D3
Elizabeth Garrett
Anderson and Obstetric
Hospital WC1 ....**93** C3 **235** B5

F

Farnborough Hospital
BR6 ....**226** C4
Finchley Memorial Hospital
N12 ....**30** A3
Fitzroy Nuffield
Hospital W1 .....**92** D1 **237** C2

G

Garden Hospital The
NW4 ....**46** C6
Goldie Leigh Hospital
SE2 ....**146** C2
Goodmayes Hospital
IG3 ....**58** A4
Gordon Hospital The
SW1 ....**115** D2 **259** C3
Great Ormond St Hospital
for Children WC1 **94** B3 **240** C5
🏥 **Greenwich District
Hospital**
Vanbrugh Hill, Greenwich,
London, SE10 9DH **120** D1
📞 **020 8858 8141**
Grovelands Priory
N14 ....**16** A3
Guy's Hospital
SE1 ....**117** B5 **252** D2

H

Hackney Hospital E9 ....**75** A3
Hamlet (Day) Hospital
The NW1 ....**132** A2
🏥 **Hammersmith Hospital**
Du Cane Road, London
W12 0HS **90** B1
📞 **020 8383 1111**
Harrow Hospital HA2 .....**64** C6
The Heart
Hospital, W1 ...**93** B2 **238** C3
🏥 **Hillingdon Hospital**
Pield Heath Road, Uxbridge,
Middlesex UB8 3NN **82** B2
📞 **01895 238282**
🏥 **Homerton University
Hospital**
Homerton Row, E9 6SR ..**74** D3
📞 **020 8510 5555**

Hornsey Central
Hospital N8 ....**49** D4
Hospital for Tropical
Diseases WC1 ....**232** C5
Hospital of St John
and St Elizabeth
NW8 ....**92** B5 **229** C3

I

Inverforth House Hospital
NW3 ....**70** A6

J

Jewish Home and Hospital
at Tottenham The N15 ...**51** D5

K

🏥 **King George Hospital**
Barley Lane, Goodmayes, Ilford,
Essex IG3 8YB **58** A4
📞 **020 8983 8000**
🏥 **King's College Hospital**
Denmark Hill, (A&E in
Ruskin Wing) SE5 9RS ..**139** B3
📞 **020 7737 4000**
Kings Oak Hospital
(Private) The EN2 ....**4** C5
Kingsbury Hospital
NW9 ....**44** C5
🏥 **Kingston Hospital**
Galsworthy Road, Kingston-
upon-Thames, Surrey
KT2 7QB **176** D2
📞 **020 8546 7711**

L

Langthorne Hospital
E11 ....**76** B5
🏥 **Lewisham Hospital**
High Street, Lewisham,
London SE13 6JH **163** D6
📞 **020 8333 3000**
Lister Hospital
SW1 ....**115** B1 **258** C6
London Bridge Hospital
SE1 ....**117** B5 **252** D4
London Chest Hospital
E2 ....**96** C5
London Clinic
NW1 ....**93** A3 **238** B5
London Foot
Hospital W1 ....**93** C3 **239** A6
London Hospital
(Mile End) The E2 .....**96** D4
London Hospital
(St Clements) The E3 ...**97** B4
London Independent
Hospital The E1 ....**96** D2

M

Maida Vale Psychiatric
Hospital W9 ...**92** A3 **236** B6
Manor House Hospital
NW11 ....**47** D1
Marlborough Day Hospital
NW8 ....**92** A5 **229** A4
Maudsley Hospital The
SE5 ....**139** B3
🏥 **Mayday University
Hospital**
Mayday Road, Thornton
Heath CR7 7YE **204** D3
📞 **020 8401 3000**
Memorial Hospital SE18
.........................**144** C3
Middlesex Hospital
W1 ....**93** C2 **239** B3

Mildmay Mission Hospital
E2 ....**95** D4
Molesey Hospital KT8 ...**195** C4
Moorfields Eye Hospital
EC1 ....**95** B4 **235** C1
Morland Road Day Hospital
RM10 ....**103** C6

N

National Hospital for
Neurology and Neurosurgery
N2 ....**48** C3
National Hospital The
WC1 ....**94** A3 **240** B5
National Physical
Laboratory TW11 ......**174** A4
Nelson Hospital SW20 ...**179** B1
New Cross Hospital
SE14 ....**140** C5
New Victoria Hospital
KT3 ....**177** C2
🏥 **Newham General
Hospital**
Glen Road, Plaistow,
London E13 8SL **99** C3
📞 **020 7476 4000**
Normansfield Hospital
EN2 ....**175** C3
North London Nuffield
Hospital EN2 ....**4** C3
🏥 **North Middlesex
Hospital**
Sterling Way, Edmonton, London,
N18 1QX **33** C5
📞 **020 8887 2000**
🏥 **Northwick Park
Hospital**
Watford Road, Harrow, Middlesex
HA1 3UJ **43** A2
📞 **020 8864 3232**
Northwood Pinner and
District Cottage Hospital
HA6 ....**22** A2
Norwood Hospital
SE19 ....**183** B4

O

Orpington Hospital
BR6 ....**227** D4

P

Paddington Com Hospital
W9 ....**91** C2
Penny Sangam Day Hospital
UB2 ....**107** B3
Plaistow Hospital E13 ...**99** C5
Portland Hospital for
Women and Children
The W1 ....**93** B3 **238** D5
Princess Grace
Hospital The W1 .**93** A3 **238** A5
Princess Louise
Hospital W10 ....**90** C2
Priory Hospital
The SW15 ....**133** D1
Putney Hospital SW15 ..**134** C2

Q

Queen Charlotte's Hospital
W12 ....**90** B1
Queen Elizabeth Hospital
for Children The E2 ....**96** A5
Queen Elizabeth Hospital
SE18 ....**144** A5
🏥 **Queen Mary's Hospital**
Frognal Avenue, Sidcup,
Kent DA14 6LT **190** A4
📞 **020 8302 2678**

Queen Mary's Hospital
NW3 ....**70** A5
Queen Mary's Univ Hospital
SW15 ....**156** A5
Queen's Hospital CR0 ...**205** A3

R

Roding Hospital IG4 .....**55** D6
Royal Brompton and Nat
Heart Hospital The
SW3 ....**114** C1 **257** A6
Royal Ear Hospital
WC1 ....**93** C3 **239** B5
🏥 **Royal Free Hospital**
Pond Street, London
NW3 2QG **70** C3
📞 **020 7794 0500**
Royal Hospital SW15 ...**157** A5
Royal London Homeopathic
Hospital The
WC1 ....**94** A2 **240** B4
🏥 **Royal London
Hospital (Whitechapel)**
Whitechapel Road,
London E1 1BB **96** B2
📞 **020 7377 7000**
Royal Marsden Hospital
SW3 ....**114** B1 **256** D2
Royal Masonic Hospital
W6 ....**112** A2
Royal National
Orthopaedic Hospital
HA7 ....**9** C2
W1 ....**93** B3 **238** D5
Royal Nat TN&E Hospital
The W5 ....**87** C2
WC1 ....**94** B4 **233** C2

S

St Andrew's Hospital
E3 ....**97** D3
St Ann's General Hospital
N4,N15 ....**51** A4
St Anthony's Hospital
KT4 ....**200** D1
St Bartholomew's Hospital
EC1 ....**94** D2 **241** D3
St Charles' Hospital
W10 ....**90** D2
St Christopher's Hospice
SE26 ....**184** C5
🏥 **St George's Hospital**
Blackshaw Road,
London SW17 ....**180** B5
📞 **020 8672 1255**
St Giles Hospital SE5 ....**139** C4
🏥 **St Helier Hospital**
Wrythe Lane, Carshalton,
Surrey SM5 1AA **202** A1
📞 **020 8296 2000**
St Joseph's Hospice
E9,E8 ....**96** B6
St Leonard's Hospital
N1 ....**95** C5
St Luke's Hospital
W1 ....**93** C3 **239** A5
St Luke's Woodside Hospital
N10 ....**49** A5
St Mark's Hospital
EC1 ....**94** D4 **234** D2
St Mark's Hospital
HA1 ....**43** A2
St Mary's Cottage Hospital
TW12 ....**173** B2
🏥 **St Mary's Hospital**
Praed Street, Paddington
W2 1NY **92** B1 **236** D2
📞 **020 7886 6666**
St Michael's Hospital
EN2 ....**5** B4
St Pancras Hospital
NW1 ....**93** D6 **232** C5

🏥 **St Thomas's Hospital**
Lambeth Palace Road, London
SE1 7EH **116** B3 **260** C6
📞 **020 7928 9292**
St Vincent's Hospital
HA5 ....**39** D6
Samaritan Hospital for
Women NW1 ....**237** C4
Shirley Oaks Hospital
CR0 ....**206** C2
Sloane Hospital BR3 ....**186** B2
South Western
Hospital SW9 ....**138** B2
Southwood Hospital
(Geriatric) N6 ....**49** A2
Springfield Hospital
SW17 ....**158** C1
Stepney Day Hospital
E1 ....**96** C1
Surbiton Hospital KT6 ..**198** A3

T

Teddington Memorial
Hospital TW11 ....**174** C4
Thorpe Coombe
Hospital E17 ....**54** A6
Tolworth Hospital
KT6 ....**214** C6
Travel Clinic, Hospital for
Tropical Diseases
WC1 ....**93** C3 **239** B5

U

🏥 **University College
Hospital**
A&E at Cecil Fleming House,
Grafton Way, London,
WC1E 3BG **93** C3 **239** B5
📞 **020 7387 9300**
Upton Day Hospital
DA6 ....**147** A1

W

Wanstead Hospital E11 ...**55** B5
Wellington Hospital
(North) NW8 ...**92** B5 **229** D3
Wellington Hospital
(South) NW8 ...**92** B5 **229** D3
Wembley Hospital HA0 ...**65** D2
🏥 **West Middlesex
University Hospital**
Twickenham Road, Isleworth,
Middlesex TW7 6AF **131** A3
📞 **020 8560 2121**
Western Hospital
The NW1 ....**92** D2 **237** C4
🏥 **Whipps Cross Hospital**
Whipps Cross Road, Leytonstone,
London, E11 1NR **54** B3
📞 **020 85395522**
🏥 **Whittington Hospital**
Highgate Hill, London,
N19 5NF **71** C6
📞 **020 7272 3070**
Willesden Community
Hospital The NW10 .....**68** A1
Winifred House Hospital
EN5 ....**11** D5

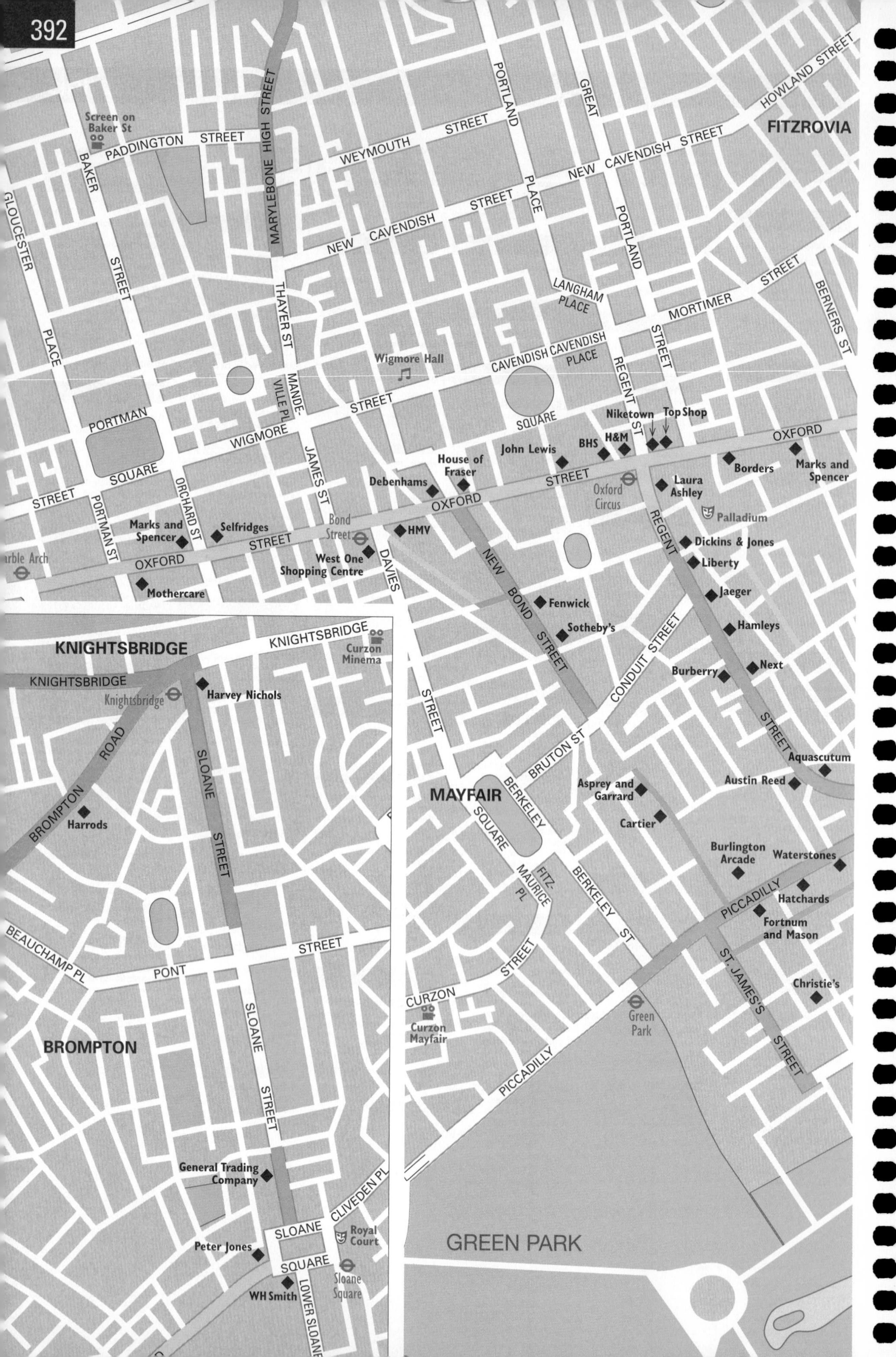

Screen on Baker St

BAKER STREET
PADDINGTON STREET
GLOUCESTER PLACE
STREET
MARYLEBONE HIGH STREET
THAYER ST
MANDE-VILLE PL
JAMES ST
WEYMOUTH STREET
NEW CAVENDISH STREET
PORTLAND STREET
PORTLAND PLACE
MORTIMER STREET
GREAT
NEW CAVENDISH STREET
HOWLAND STREET
BERNERS ST

FITZROVIA

Wigmore Hall

CAVENDISH PLACE
CAVENDISH PLACE
LANGHAM PLACE
REGENT STREET

PORTMAN SQUARE
WIGMORE STREET
STREET
SQUARE

Niketown Top Shop
John Lewis
BHS
H&M
OXFORD

House of Fraser
Debenhams

Laura Ashley
Borders
Marks and Spencer

STREET
OXFORD
Oxford Circus
Palladium

PORTMAN SQUARE
PORTMAN ST
ORCHARD ST
STREET
OXFORD

Marks and Spencer
Selfridges
Bond Street
HMV
Dickins & Jones
Liberty

REGENT STREET

Marble Arch
Mothercare
West One Shopping Centre
DAVIES STREET

Jaeger

NEW BOND STREET

Hamleys

Fenwick
Sotheby's

CONDUIT STREET

Next
Burberry

KNIGHTSBRIDGE
KNIGHTSBRIDGE
Curzon Minema

KNIGHTSBRIDGE
Knightsbridge
Harvey Nichols

BROMPTON ROAD
SLOANE STREET

BERKELEY SQUARE
BRUTON ST

MAYFAIR
Asprey and Garrard
Cartier

Aquascutum
Austin Reed

Burlington Arcade
Waterstones

Harrods

BERKELEY ST
FITZ-MAURICE PL

PICCADILLY
Hatchards
Fortnum and Mason

BEAUCHAMP PL
PONT STREET
SLOANE STREET

ST. JAMES'S STREET

Christie's

CURZON STREET
Curzon Mayfair

Green Park

BROMPTON

SLOANE STREET

PICCADILLY

General Trading Company

CLIVEDEN PL
Royal Court

SLOANE SQUARE

GREEN PARK

Peter Jones
Sloane Square
LOWER SLOANE

WH Smith

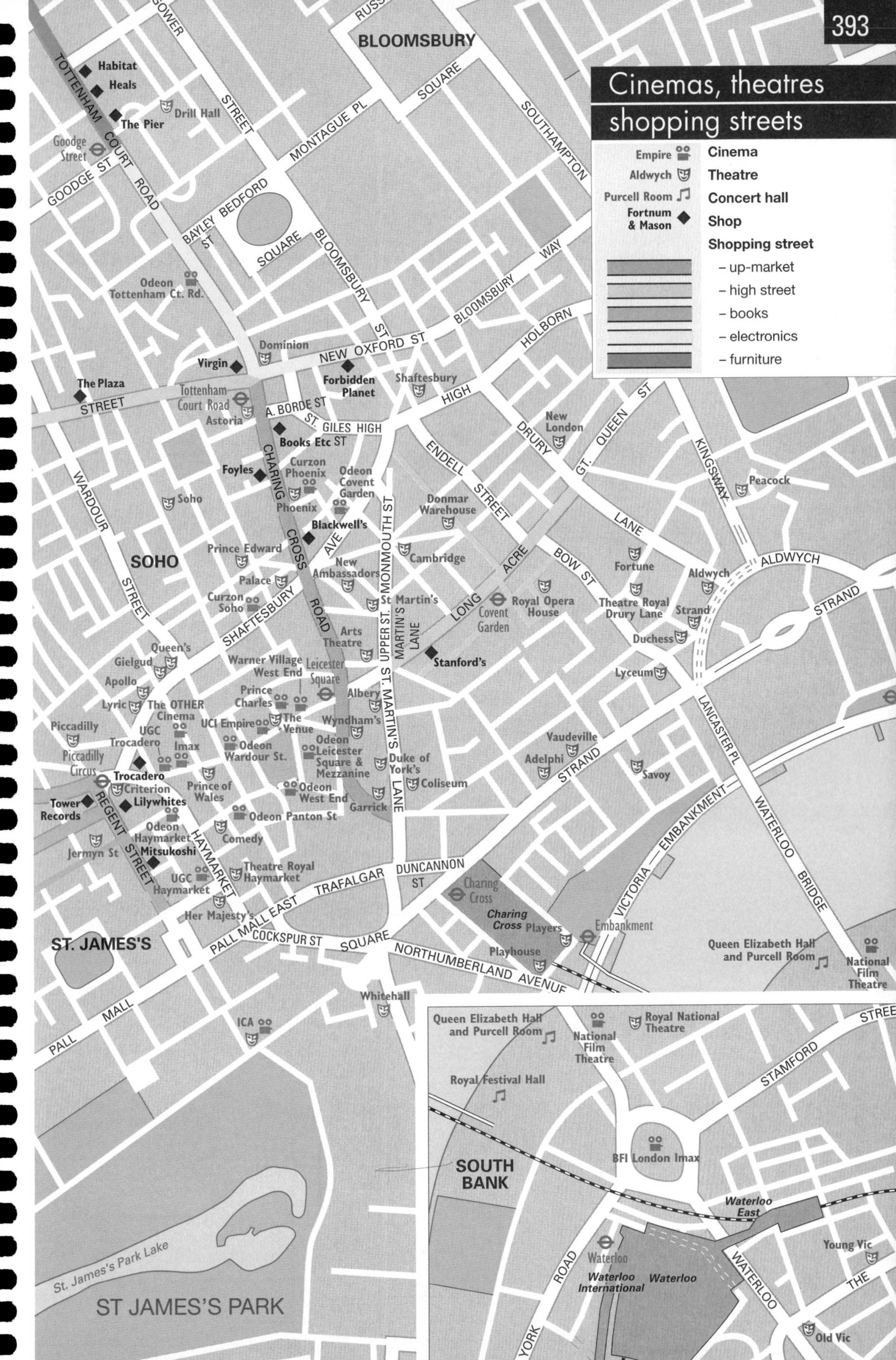

Cinemas, theatres shopping streets

Empire 🎥		Cinema
Aldwych 🎭		Theatre
Purcell Room ♫		Concert hall
Fortnum & Mason ◆		Shop
		Shopping street
		– up-market
		– high street
		– books
		– electronics
		– furniture

BLOOMSBURY

Habitat
Heals
The Pier
Drill Hall
Goodge Street
GOODGE ST.
Odeon Tottenham Ct. Rd.
TOTTENHAM COURT ROAD
GOWER STREET
MONTAGUE PL.
BEDFORD SQUARE
BAYLEY ST
BLOOMSBURY SQUARE
SOUTHAMPTON
BLOOMSBURY WAY
HOLBORN
RUSSELL SQUARE

Dominion
NEW OXFORD ST.
Virgin
Forbidden Planet
Shaftesbury
HIGH
DRURY
New London
GT. QUEEN ST.
KINGSWAY
Peacock

The Plaza
STREET
Tottenham Court Road
Astoria
A. BORDE ST
St. GILES HIGH ST.
Books Etc
ST. GILES HIGH
ENDELL STREET
LANE

WARDOUR
SOHO
Foyles
CHARING CROSS ROAD
Curzon Phoenix
Odeon Covent Garden
Donmar Warehouse
ALDWYCH
STRAND

Soho
Phoenix
Blackwell's
UPPER ST. MONMOUTH ST.
Cambridge
BOW ST.
Fortune
Aldwych
Strand

Prince Edward
New Ambassadors
St Martin's
LONG ACRE
Royal Opera House
Theatre Royal Drury Lane
Duchess
Lyceum

Palace
ST. MARTIN'S LANE
Covent Garden
LANCASTER PL.
WATERLOO BRIDGE

SOHO
SHAFTESBURY AVE
Curzon Soho
Arts Theatre
Stanford's

Queen's
Gielgud
Warner Village West End
Leicester Square
Albery
Vaudeville
Adelphi
STRAND
Savoy

Apollo
Prince Charles
Wyndham's
Duke of York's
Coliseum

Lyric
The OTHER Cinema
UCI Empire
The Venue
Odeon Leicester Square & Mezzanine

Piccadilly
UGC Trocadero
Imax
Odeon Wardour St.

Piccadilly Circus
Trocadero
Prince of Wales
Odeon West End
Garrick

Tower Records
Criterion
Lilywhites
Odeon Panton St
Comedy

REGENT STREET
Odeon Haymarket
Mitsukoshi
UGC Haymarket

Jermyn St
HAYMARKET
Theatre Royal Haymarket

ST. JAMES'S
PALL MALL
Her Majesty's
PALL MALL EAST
COCKSPUR ST.
TRAFALGAR SQUARE
DUNCANNON ST
Charing Cross
VICTORIA EMBANKMENT

NORTHUMBERLAND AVENUE
Charing Cross Players
Embankment
Queen Elizabeth Hall and Purcell Room ♫
National Film Theatre

Whitehall
Playhouse

ICA

PALL MALL

St. James's Park Lake

ST JAMES'S PARK

Queen Elizabeth Hall and Purcell Room ♫
National Film Theatre
Royal National Theatre
STAMFORD STREET

Royal Festival Hall ♫

SOUTH BANK
BFI London Imax

Waterloo East

WATERLOO ROAD
Young Vic

Waterloo
Waterloo International
Waterloo
YORK ROAD
THE
Old Vic

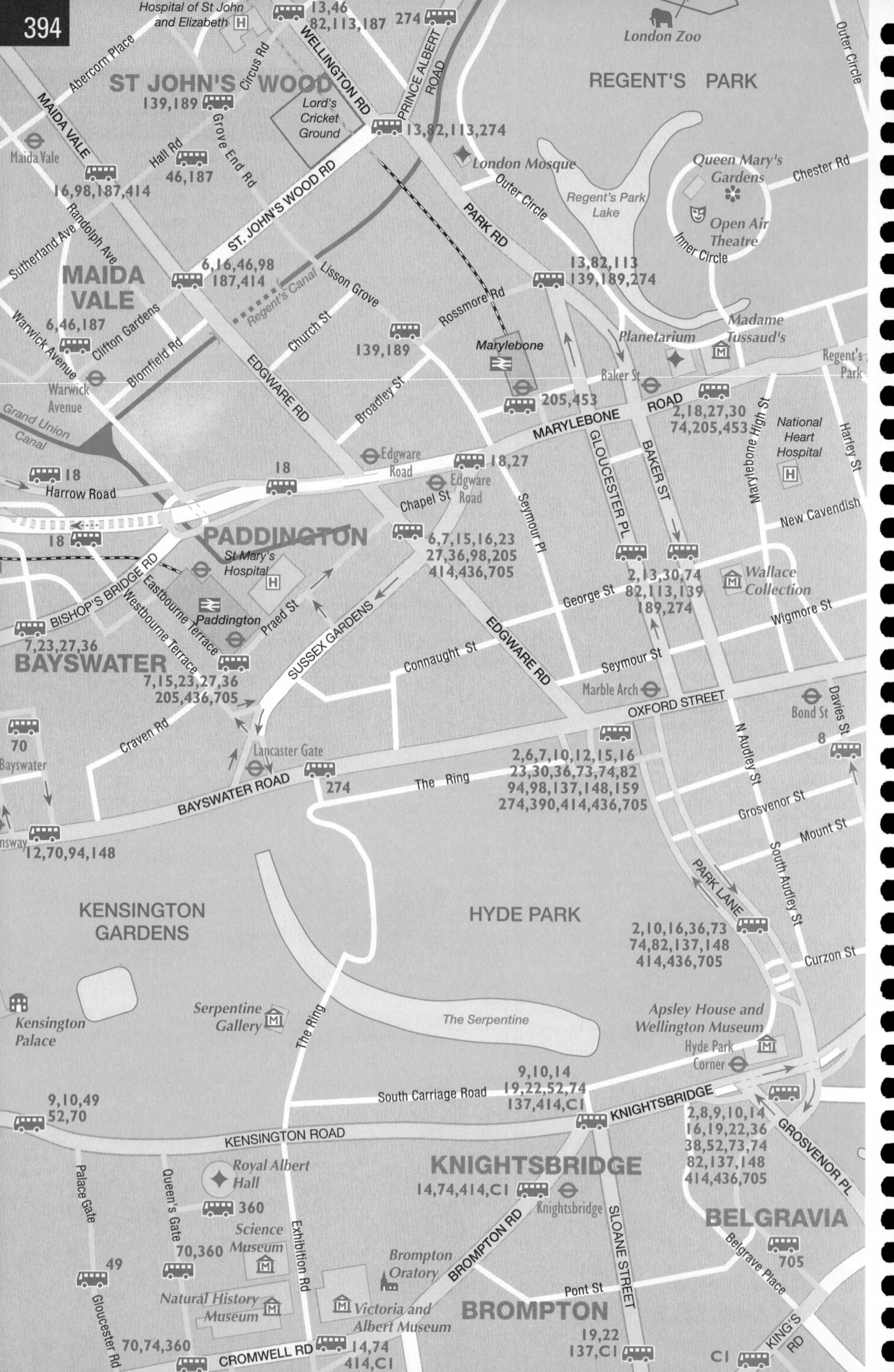

ST JOHN'S WOOD
REGENT'S PARK
London Zoo
MAIDA VALE
PADDINGTON
BAYSWATER
KENSINGTON GARDENS
HYDE PARK
KNIGHTSBRIDGE
BELGRAVIA
BROMPTON
Hospital of St John and Elizabeth
Lord's Cricket Ground
London Mosque
Regent's Park Lake
Queen Mary's Gardens
Open Air Theatre
Planetarium
Madame Tussaud's
Marylebone
National Heart Hospital
Wallace Collection
St Mary's Hospital
Paddington
Serpentine Gallery
The Serpentine
Kensington Palace
Apsley House and Wellington Museum
Royal Albert Hall
Science Museum
Natural History Museum
Brompton Oratory
Victoria and Albert Museum
Maida Vale
Warwick Avenue
Edgware Road
Baker St
Marble Arch
Bond St
Lancaster Gate
Bayswater
Hyde Park Corner
Knightsbridge
Regent's Park
Abercorn Place
Circus Rd
WELLINGTON RD
PRINCE ALBERT ROAD
Outer Circle
Inner Circle
Chester Rd
MAIDA VALE
Hall Rd
Grove End Rd
ST. JOHN'S WOOD RD
PARK RD
Sutherland Ave
Randolph Ave
Regent's Canal
Lisson Grove
Rossmore Rd
Church St
Clifton Gardens
Warwick Avenue
Blomfield Rd
EDGWARE RD
Broadley St
Grand Union Canal
MARYLEBONE ROAD
GLOUCESTER PL
BAKER ST
Marylebone High St
Harley St
Harrow Road
Chapel St
Seymour Pl
New Cavendish
BISHOP'S BRIDGE RD
Eastbourne Terrace
Westbourne Terrace
Praed St
SUSSEX GARDENS
George St
Wigmore St
Connaught St
Seymour St
OXFORD STREET
Davies St
Craven Rd
N Audley St
BAYSWATER ROAD
The Ring
Grosvenor St
Mount St
PARK LANE
South Audley St
Curzon St
South Carriage Road
KNIGHTSBRIDGE
KENSINGTON ROAD
GROSVENOR PL
Palace Gate
Queen's Gate
Exhibition Rd
BROMPTON RD
SLOANE STREET
Belgrave Place
Pont St
Gloucester Rd
CROMWELL RD
KING'S RD
13,46
82,113,187
274
139,189
13,82,113,274
46,187
16,98,187,414
6,16,46,98
187,414
13,82,113
139,189,274
6,46,187
139,189
205,453
2,18,27,30
74,205,453
18
18,27
18
6,7,15,16,23
27,36,98,205
414,436,705
2,13,30,74
82,113,139
189,274
7,23,27,36
7,15,23,27,36
205,436,705
70
8
274
2,6,7,10,12,15,16
23,30,36,73,74,82
94,98,137,148,159
274,390,414,436,705
12,70,94,148
2,10,16,36,73
74,82,137,148
414,436,705
9,10,14
19,22,52,74
137,414,C1
9,10,49
52,70
2,8,9,10,14
16,19,22,36
38,52,73,74
82,137,148
414,436,705
14,74,414,C1
360
70,360
49
705
70,74,360
14,74
414,C1
19,22
137,C1
C1

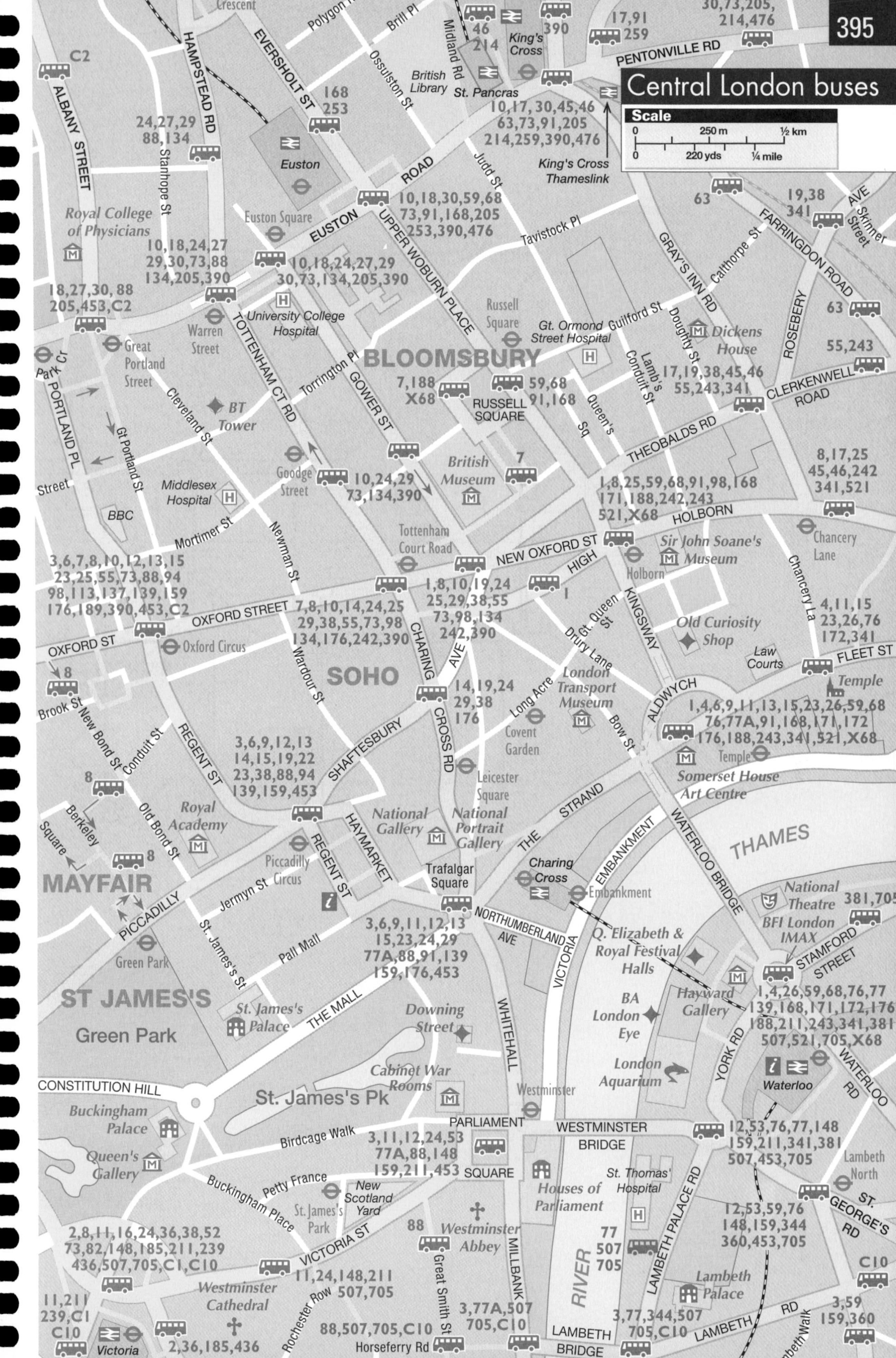
Central London buses
Scale
0
250 m
½ km
0
220 yds
¼ mile
King's Cross Thameslink
King's Cross
St. Pancras
British Library
Euston
Euston Square
Warren Street
Great Portland Street
Goodge Street
Tottenham Court Road
Russell Square
Holborn
Chancery Lane
Oxford Circus
Covent Garden
Leicester Square
Piccadilly Circus
Green Park
Charing Cross
Embankment
Temple
Westminster
St. James's Park
Victoria
Waterloo
Lambeth North
BLOOMSBURY
SOHO
MAYFAIR
ST JAMES'S
Green Park
St. James's Pk
THAMES
RIVER
EUSTON ROAD
PENTONVILLE RD
HAMPSTEAD RD
EVERSHOLT ST
ALBANY STREET
Polygon Rd
Brill Pl
Ossulston St
Midland Rd
Judd St
Stanhope St
UPPER WOBURN PLACE
Tavistock Pl
GRAY'S INN RD
Calthorpe St
FARRINGDON ROAD
ROSEBERY AVE
Skinner Street
Guilford St
Doughty St
Lamb's Conduit St
Queen's Sq
CLERKENWELL ROAD
THEOBALDS RD
TOTTENHAM CT RD
GOWER ST
Torrington Pl
Cleveland St
Gt Portland St
PORTLAND PL
Park Cr
Mortimer St
Newman St
HOLBORN
NEW OXFORD ST
HIGH
KINGSWAY
Gt. Queen St
Drury Lane
Chancery La
FLEET ST
OXFORD STREET
OXFORD ST
Wardour St
CHARING CROSS RD
SHAFTESBURY AVE
Long Acre
Bow St
ALDWYCH
THE STRAND
WATERLOO BRIDGE
EMBANKMENT
VICTORIA
REGENT ST
HAYMARKET
Brook St
New Bond St
Conduit St
Old Bond St
Berkeley Square
PICCADILLY
Jermyn St
St. James's St
Pall Mall
THE MALL
NORTHUMBERLAND AVE
WHITEHALL
CONSTITUTION HILL
Birdcage Walk
Petty France
Buckingham Place
VICTORIA ST
Rochester Row
Great Smith St
Horseferry Rd
MILLBANK
PARLIAMENT SQUARE
WESTMINSTER BRIDGE
LAMBETH BRIDGE
LAMBETH PALACE RD
LAMBETH RD
Lambeth Walk
YORK RD
STAMFORD STREET
WATERLOO RD
ST. GEORGE'S RD
Royal College of Physicians
University College Hospital
Gt. Ormond Street Hospital
Dickens House
BT Tower
Middlesex Hospital
BBC
British Museum
Sir John Soane's Museum
Old Curiosity Shop
Law Courts
Temple
London Transport Museum
Somerset House Art Centre
National Gallery
National Portrait Gallery
Royal Academy
Trafalgar Square
National Theatre
BFI London IMAX
Q. Elizabeth & Royal Festival Halls
Hayward Gallery
BA London Eye
London Aquarium
St. James's Palace
Downing Street
Cabinet War Rooms
Buckingham Palace
Queen's Gallery
Houses of Parliament
St. Thomas' Hospital
New Scotland Yard
Westminster Abbey
Westminster Cathedral
Lambeth Palace
RUSSELL SQUARE
Crescent
C2
46
214
390
17,91
259
30,73,205,
214,476
168
253
24,27,29
88,134
10,17,30,45,46
63,73,91,205
214,259,390,476
10,18,30,59,68
73,91,168,205
253,390,476
63
19,38
341
10,18,24,27
29,30,73,88
134,205,390
10,18,24,27,29
30,73,134,205,390
18,27,30,88
205,453,C2
63
55,243
17,19,38,45,46
55,243,341
7,188
X68
59,68
91,168
7
10,24,29
73,134,390
1,8,25,59,68,91,98,168
171,188,242,243
521,X68
8,17,25
45,46,242
341,521
3,6,7,8,10,12,13,15
23,25,55,73,88,94
98,113,137,139,159
176,189,390,453,C2
7,8,10,14,24,25
29,38,55,73,98
134,176,242,390
1,8,10,19,24
25,29,38,55
73,98,134
242,390
1
4,11,15
23,26,76
172,341
8
14,19,24
29,38
176
1,4,6,9,11,13,15,23,26,59,68
76,77A,91,168,171,172
176,188,243,341,521,X68
3,6,9,12,13
14,15,19,22
23,38,88,94
139,159,453
8
8
3,6,9,11,12,13
15,23,24,29
77A,88,91,139
159,176,453
381,705
1,4,26,59,68,76,77
139,168,171,172,176
188,211,243,341,381
507,521,705,X68
12,53,76,77,148
159,211,341,381
507,453,705
3,11,12,24,53
77A,88,148
159,211,453
12,53,59,76
148,159,344
360,453,705
2,8,11,16,24,36,38,52
73,82,148,185,211,239
436,507,705,C1,C10
88
77
507
705
11,24,148,211
507,705
C10
11,211
239,C1
C10
2,36,185,436
88,507,705,C10
3,77A,507
705,C10
3,77,344,507
705,C10
3,59
159,360

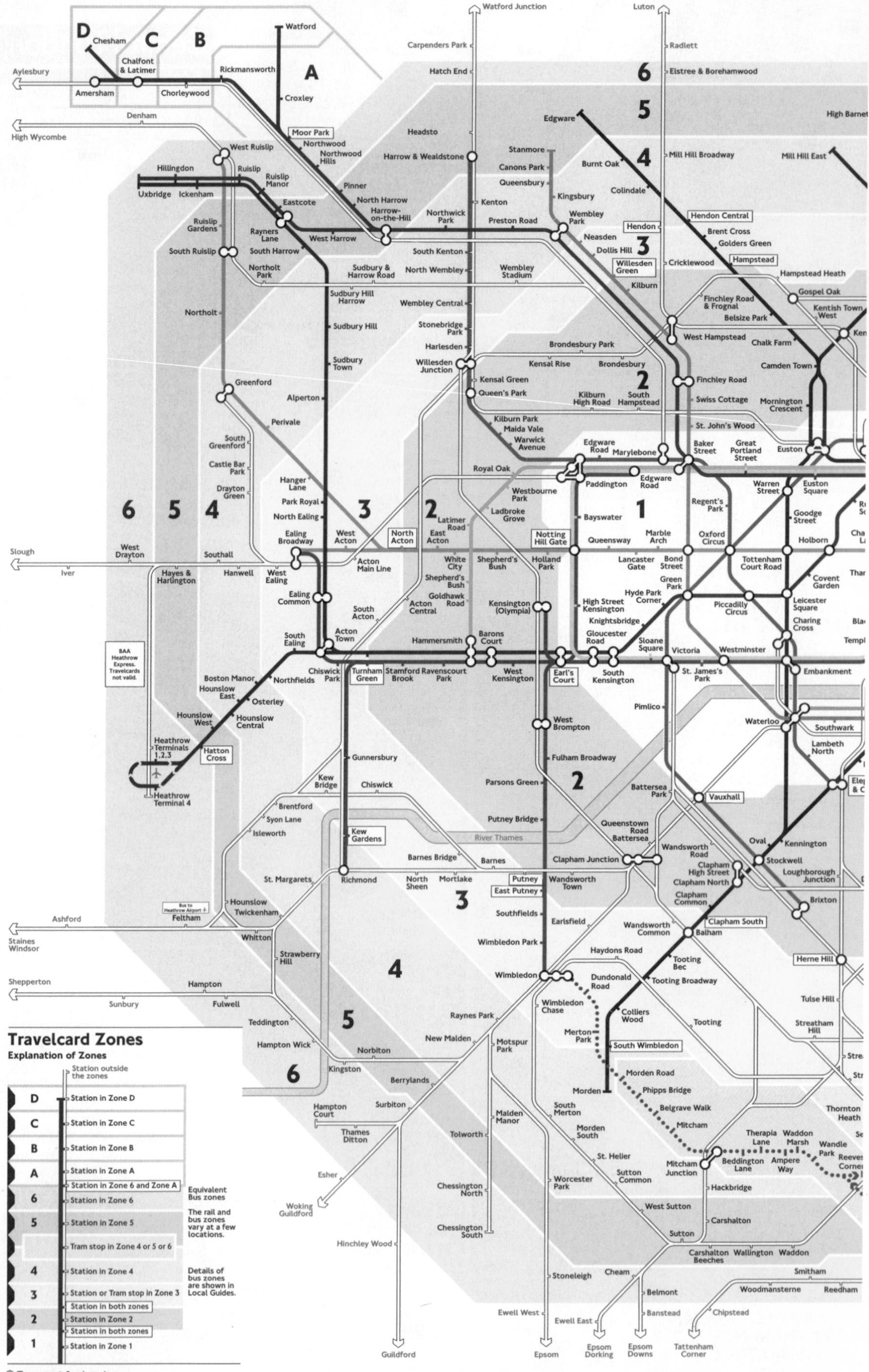

Travelcard Zones
Explanation of Zones

	Station outside the zones
D	Station in Zone D
C	Station in Zone C
B	Station in Zone B
A	Station in Zone A
	Station in Zone 6 and Zone A
6	Station in Zone 6
5	Station in Zone 5
	Tram stop in Zone 4 or 5 or 6
4	Station in Zone 4
3	Station or Tram stop in Zone 3
2	Station in both zones
2	Station in Zone 2
1	Station in both zones
1	Station in Zone 1

Equivalent Bus zones

The rail and bus zones vary at a few locations.

Details of bus zones are shown in Local Guides.

© Transport for London

Key to lines

	Station	Interchange Station
Bakerloo		
Central		
Circle		
District		
East London *Peak hours and Sunday mornings*		
Hammersmith & City		
Jubilee		
Metropolitan		
Northern		
Piccadilly		
Victoria		
Waterloo & City		
Docklands Light Railway		
Tramlink		
National Rail		

A Travelcard or LT Card valid in Zone 4 or 5 or 6 (or combination of these Zones) is available on Tramlink services throughout the grey area. If travelling on Tramlink services outside the grey area a Travelcard or LT Card which includes Zone 3 availability must be held

Some stations and lines have restricted opening times.

London Travel Information
020 7222 1234 24 hours

The national rail routes shown on this map are a guide to weekday, off-peak services but do not guarantee direct trains between the stations shown.

National Rail Enquiries
08457 48 49 50 24 hours
(all calls charged at local rate)

Reg. user No. 03/3952

Places of interest

Central

West End

Admiralty Arch SW1 ...249 D4
Apple Market WC2 ...250 B6
Banqueting House SW1 ...250 A3
Big Ben SW1 ...250 B1
British Library WC1 ...93 D4 232 D2
British Museum WC1 ...94 A2 240 A3
BT Tower W1 ...93 C2 239 A4
Buckingham Palace SW1 ...115 C4 249 A1
Cabinet War Rooms SW1 ...115 D4 249 D2
Carnaby Street W1 ...93 C1 239 A1
Cenotaph SW1 ...250 A2
Changing of the Guard (site of) SW1 ...249 A1
Chinatown W1 ...115 D6 249 D6
Clarence House SW1 ...115 C5 249 B3
Cleopatra's Needle WC2 ...116 B5 250 C5
Courtauld Galleries WC2 ...250 C6
Covent Garden WC2 ...116 A6 250 B6
Dickens House Museum WC1 ...94 B3 240 D5
Downing Street SW1 ...116 A4 250 A2
Eros W1 ...115 D6 249 C5
Green Park SW1,W1 ...115 B4 248 D2
Guards Museum SW1 ...115 C4 249 B1
Holocaust Memorial Garden W2 ...114 D4 247 D2
Horse Guards Parade SW1 ...115 D5 249 D3
Houses of Parliament SW1 ...116 A3 260 B6
Hyde Park W2 ...114 D5 247 C3
Leicester Square WC2 ...115 D6 249 D5
London's Transport Museum WC2 ...250 B6
Marble Arch W1 ...114 D6 247 D6
Methodist Central Hall SW1 ...115 D4 249 D1
National Gallery W1 ...115 D6 249 D5
National Portrait Gallery W1 ...115 D6 249 D5
Nelson's Monument WC2 ...250 A4
New Scotland Yard SW1 ...115 D3 259 C6
Parliament Square SW1 ...116 A4 250 A1
Pepsi Trocadero W1 ...249 C5
Piccadilly Circus W1 ...115 D6 249 C5
Queen Victoria Memorial SW1 ...249 A2
Queen's Gallery SW1 ...115 B4 248 D1
Rotten Row SW1 ...114 D4 247 C2
Royal Academy of Arts W1 ...115 C6 249 A5
Royal Mews SW1 ...115 B3 258 D6
Royal United Services Museum SW1 ...250 A3
St James's Palace SW1 ...115 C5 249 B3
St James's Park SW1 ...249 C2
Serpentine Gallery W2 ...114 B4 246 D2
Soho W1 ...93 D1 239 C2
Somerset House WC2 ...116 B6 250 D6
Speakers' Corner W1 ...114 D6 247 D6
Tate Britain SW1 ...116 A2 260 A3
Theatre Museum WC2 ...250 B6
Trafalgar Square SW1 ...115 D5 249 D4
Tyburn Tree (site of) W2 ...247 C6
Wallace Collection W1 238 A2
Wellington Arch SW1 ...248 B2
Wellington Museum (Apsley House) SW1 ...115 A4 248 B2
Westminster Abbey SW1 ...116 A3 260 A6
Westminster Cathedral SW1 ...115 C3 259 A5

City

Bank of England EC2 ...242 C1
Barbican Arts & Conference Centre EC2 ...95 A2 242 B4
Central Criminal Court (Old Bailey) EC4 ...94 D1 241 D2
Custom House EC3 ...117 C6 253 A5
Dr Johnson's House EC4 ...241 B1
Gray's Inn WC1 ...94 B2 240 D4
Guildhall EC2 ...95 A1 242 B2
Inner Temple EC4 ...251 A6
John Wesley's House & Museum EC1 ...242 D6
Lincoln's Inn WC2 94 B1 240 D2
Lloyd's Building EC3 ...95 C1 243 A1
Mansion House EC4 ...242 C1
Merchant Taylors Hall EC3 ...242 D1
Middle Temple EC4 ...116 C6 251 A6
Monument, The EC3 ...252 D6
Museum of London EC2 ...95 A2 242 A3
Nat West Tower EC2 ...243 A2
National Postal Museum EC1 ...95 A1 242 A2
Petticoat Lane Market EC2 ...95 D2 243 C3
Public Record Office Museum EC4,WC2 ...241 A2
Royal Exchange EC3 ...242 D1
St Katharine Dock E1 ...117 D5 253 D4
St Mary le Bow Church EC2 ...242 B1
St Paul's Cathedral EC4 ...95 A1 242 A1
Sir John Soane's Museum WC2 ...94 B1 240 C2
Spitalfields Market E1 ...95 D2 243 C4
Stock Exchange EC2 ...242 D1
Tower Bridge E1,EC3,SE1 ...117 D5 253 C4
Tower of London EC3 ...117 D6 253 C5
Traitors Gate EC3 ...117 D5 253 C4
Ye Olde Cheshire Cheese EC4 ...241 B2

Northern

Business Design Centre N1 ...94 C6 234 B5
Camden Market NW1 ...93 B6 231 D6
London Canal Museum N1 ...94 A5 233 B4
London Central Mosque NW8 ...92 C4 230 B1
London Zoo NW1 ...93 A5 231 A4
Lord's Cricket Ground NW8 ...92 B4 229 D2
Madame Tussaud's NW1 ...93 A3 238 A5
Open Air Theatre, Regent's Park NW1 ...231 A1
Planetarium NW1 ...93 A3 238 A5
Primrose Hill NW1 ...92 D6 230 C6
Queen Mary's Gardens NW1 ...231 A1
Regent's Park NW1 ...93 A4 231 A3
St George's Cathedral NW1 ...231 D2
Sherlock Holmes Museum NW1 ...92 D3 237 D5

Southern

Battersea Park SW11 ...137 A5 268 A3
Battersea Power Station SW8 ...137 B6 268 D6
Brompton Oratory SW7 ...114 C3 257 A5
Bear Gardens Museum SE1 ...117 A5 252 A4
Bermondsey Market SE1 ...117 C3 263 B8
Borough Market SE1 ...252 C3
Design Museum SE1 ...117 D4 253 D2
Florence Nightingale Museum SE1 ...250 D1
Gabriel's Wharf SE1 ...251 A4
George Inn SE1 ...252 C3
Globe Theatre SE1 ...252 A5
Hayward Gallery SE1 ...116 B5 250 D4
HMS Belfast SE1 ...253 B4
Imperial War Museum SE1 ...116 C3 261 B5
Lambeth Palace SE1 ...116 B3 260 C5
London Aquarium SE1 ...250 C1
London Dungeon SE1 ...117 B5 252 D4
London Eye SE1 ...116 B4 250 C2
London Peace Pagoda SW11 ...267 D4
Millennium Bridge SE1,EC4 ...252 A5
Museum of Garden History SE1 ...260 C5
National Film Theatre SE1 ...250 D4
National Theatre SE1 ...116 B5 250 D4
Old County Hall SE1 ...250 C2
Operating Theatre Museum & Herb Garret SE1 ...117 B5 252 D3
Oxo Tower SE1 ...251 B5
Royal Festival Hall SE1 ...116 B5 250 D3
Saatchi Gallery SE1 ...250 C2
St George's RC Cathedral SE1 ...116 C3 261 B6
Shakespeare's Globe Theatre (site of) SE1 ...252 B4
Southwark Cathedral SE1 ...117 B5 252 C4
Tate Modern SE1 ...116 D6 251 D4
Vinopolis SE1 ...117 B5 252 C4

Western

Albert Memorial SW7 ...114 B4 246 C1
Carlyle's House SW3 ...267 A5
Chelsea Barracks SW1 ...115 A1 258 B1
Chelsea Physic Garden SW1 ...115 A1 267 C6
Commonwealth Institute W8 ...113 C3 255 A6
Geological Museum SW7 ...114 B3 256 D5
Kensington Gardens W2 ...114 A5 246 B3
Kensington Palace W8 ...113 D5 245 D3
Leighton House W14 ...254 D6
Lindsey House SW10 ...266 D4
Little Venice W9 ...92 A2 236 A4
London Toy & Model Museum W2 ...114 A6 246 A6
National Army Museum SW3 ...136 D6 267 D6
Natural History Museum SW7 ...114 B3 256 C5
Ranelagh Gardens SW1 ...115 A1 258 B1
Royal Albert Hall SW7 ...114 B4 246 C1
Royal Hospital (Army Pensioners) SW1 ...115 A1 258 A1
Science Museum SW7 ...114 B3 256 C5
Victoria & Albert Museum SW7 ...114 B3 256 D5

East

Bethnal Green Museum of Childhood E2 ...96 C4
Canary Wharf E14 ...119 D5
Docklands Museum E14 ...119 D6
Epping Forest IG10 ...21 B6
Geffrye Museum E2 ...95 D5
London Docklands Visitor Centre E14 ...120 A4
London Gas Museum E16 ...98 B3
Museum of the Great Eastern Railway E16 ...122 C4
Queen Elizabeth's Hunting Lodge Museum E4 ...20 D4
Ragged School Museum E3 ...97 A2
Vestry House (Museum) E17 ...53 D5
Whitechapel Art Gallery E1 ...95 D1

North

Alexandra Palace N22 ...31 D1
Barnet Museum EN5 ...1 A1
Battle of Britain Museum NW9 ...27 D1
Bruce Castle Museum N17 ...33 C2
Church Farm House Museum NW4 ...46 B6
Coppetts Centre N12 ...30 D3
Forty Hall EN2 ...5 D6
Freud Museum NW3 ...70 A2
Grange Museum of Community History NW10 ...67 D4
Hampstead Heath NW3 ...70 B6
Harrow Museum & Heritage Centre HA2 ...42 A6
Highgate Cemetery N19 ...71 B6
Kensal Green Cemetery (All Souls) NW10 ...90 C4
Kenwood House NW3 ...48 C1
Old Court (Museum & Library) HA0 ...65 C3
RAF Museum NW9 ...28 A1
Ruislip Lido HA4,HA5 ...39 B5
Ruislip Lido Railway HA4 ...39 B5
White Cube N1 ...95 C4

South east

Blackheath SE3 ...142 C4
Brockwell Park SE24 ...160 D5
Cutty Sark SE10 ...142 A6
Docklands Heritage Museum SE16 ...119 B5
Dulwich Picture Gallery SE21 ...161 C4
Eltham Palace SE9 ...166 A4
Flamsteed House SE10 ...142 B5
Gipsy Moth IV SE10 ...142 A6
Greenwich Park SE10 ...142 C5
Horniman Museum & Gardens SE23 ...162 B3
Livesey Museum SE15 ...140 B6
Meridian Building SE10 ...142 B5
Millennium Dome SE10 ...120 C5
National Maritime Museum SE10 ...142 B6
Old Royal Observatory Greenwich SE10 ...142 B5
Queen's House SE10 ...142 B6
Rotunda Museum SE18 122 B1
Scadbury Park Nature Reserve BR7 ...189 D4
South Norwood Country Park SE25 ...206 C5
Thames Barrier Visitor Centre SE18 ...121 D3
Well Hall Pleasaunce SE9 ...144 A1

South west

Barnes Common SW13 134 A2
Clapham Common SW4 ...137 C1
Fulham Palace SW6 ...135 A3
Hampton Court Palace KT8 ...196 D6
Kingston Museum KT1 ...176 A1
Wandsworth Museum SW15 ...135 A1
Wetland Centre SW13 ...134 B5
Wimbledon Common SW19 ...178 B6
Wimbledon Lawn Tennis Museum SW19 ...157 A1
Wimbledon Windmill Museum SW19 ...156 C1

West

Chiswick House W4 ...133 B6
Eel Pie Island TW1 ...153 A3
Gunnersbury Park Museum W3 ...110 C3
Ham House TW10 ...153 C2
Kew Bridge Steam Museum TW8 ...110 B1
Kew Gardens (Royal Botanic Gardens) TW9 ...132 A4
Kew Observatory TW9 ...131 C2
Kew Palace TW9 ...132 A5
London Butterfly House TW8 ...131 B4
Marble Hill TW1 ...153 C4
Museum of Richmond TW10 ...153 D6
Musical Museum TW8 ...132 A6
Osterley Park TW7 ...108 B1
Pitshanger Manor Museum & Art Gallery W5 ...109 D5
Portobello Road Market W10 ...91 A2
Richmond Park TW10 ...155 A3
Syon House TW8 ...131 C4
Walled Garden TW16 ...194 B6